Abbreviations Dictionary

Augmented International Seventh Edition

Abbreviations Dictionary

Augmented International Seventh Edition

Ralph De Sola

★ Abbreviations ★ Acronyms ★ Airlines ★ Appellations
★ Astronomical Terminology ★ Battlegab Divulged
(euphemisms explained) ★ Birthstones ★ British and Irish
County Abbreviations ★ Canadian Provinces ★ Chemical Elements
★ Citizens-Band Call Signs ★ Computer Jargon ★ Contractions
★ Criminalistic Terms ★ Data Processing ★ Diacritical Marks
★ Dysphemistic Place-Names ★ Earthquake Data ★ Eponyms
★ Fishing Ports ★ Geographical Equivalents ★ Government
Agencies ★ Greek Alphabet ★ Historical, Musical and
Mythological Data ★ International Conversions ★ International
Vehicle License Letters ★ Medical Terms ★ Nations ★ Nicknames
★ Numbered Abbreviations ★ Numeration ★ Ports of the
World ★ Prisons of the World ★ Railroads ★ Roman Numerals
★ Russian Alphabet ★ Short Forms ★ Short Cuts ★ Signs &
Symbols ★ Slang ★ Steamship Lines ★ Superlatives ★ Weather
Symbols (Beaufort Scale) ★ Wedding Anniversaries
★ Winds of the World ★ Zip Coding ★ Zodiac

Elsevier
New York • Amsterdam • Oxford

Elsevier Science Publishing Co., Inc.
52 Vanderbilt Avenue, New York, New York 10017

Sole Distributors Outside the United States and Canada:
Elsevier Science Publishers B.V.
P.O. Box 211, 1000 AE Amsterdam, The Netherlands

Library of Congress Cataloging in Publication Data

De Sola, Ralph, 1908–
    Abbreviations dictionary: augmented international
    Seventh edition.

    Subtitle: Abbreviations, acronyms, airlines, appellations, astronomical
    terminology, bafflegab divulged (euphemisms explained), birthstones, Canadian
    Provinces, chemical elements, computer jargon, contractions, criminalistic
    terms, data processing, diacritical marks, earthquake data, eponyms, fishing
    ports, geographical equivalents, government agencies, Greek alphabet,
    historical, musical, and mythological data, international conversions, medical
    terms, nations nicknames, numbered abbreviations, numeration, ports of the
    world, prisons of the world, railroads, Roman numerals, Russian alphabet,
    short forms, shortcuts, signs & symbols, slang, steamship lines, superlatives,
    weather symbols (Beaufort scale), wedding anniversaries, winds of the world,
    zip coding, zodiac.

    Includes index.
    1. Abbreviations, English—Dictionaries. 2. Acronyms—Dictionaries.
    3. Signs and symbols—Dictionaries.   I. Title
PE1693.D4   1986   423'.1   85-1595
ISBN 0-444-00807-1

Current printing (last digit)
10 9 8 7 6 5 4 3 2 1

Manufactured in the United States of America

This is the short and the long of it.

—*Shakespeare*

Contents

Preface

Contemporary conversation and printed communication continue to be filled with undefined abbreviations, acronyms, appellations, contractions, geographical equivalents, initialisms, nicknames, and a host of specialized terms occupying more than 25 percent of the mass of words we hear or see in print. And anyone from another discipline, industry, profession, or occupation is almost completely baffled by such talk and writing.

This augmented and revised seventh edition of the *Abbreviations Dictionary* contains many items not found in other reference works: bell-code signals, Canadian provinces, Mexican states, nations of the world, ports of the world, railroad signals, superlatives, winds of the world, zip-coded automatic-processing abbreviations plus a host of criminal, medical, and military terms.

New items of interest have been collected from newspapers and other periodicals published in many parts of the world. The author's summer-time trips aboard freighters produced entries from all parts of the world. Some appear in his *Worldwide What & Where*, a geographical glossary and traveler's guide, while others are duplicated, in part, in his *Crime Dictionary*. The underground and the underworld have not been overlooked. The Law Enforcement Assistance Administration was most helpful. The compiler's ongoing effort to create order out of abbreviatorial acronymical chaos continues. Extensive and intensive listening, looking, and reading reveal new short forms emerging daily. And the publisher's staff is forever plagued by the author's steady flow of so-called last-minute entries deserving of inclusion. Every effort is made to keep this reference up to date. Readers and reference librarians are again solicited to direct new or revised findings to the author.

Bureaucratically buttressed government creates a host of new short forms. Only old timers seem to recall the attempts of President Hoover to consolidate and streamline government although at least eight presidents since then have pledged themselves and their administrations to stop creating more agencies, more bureaus, more commissions, more committees, and more governmental adornments laden with special abbreviations and acronyms. The end is not in sight. This augmented international seventh edition contains more abbreviations, acronyms, and other short forms than ever before.

RALPH DE SOLA

Acknowledgments

Arthur EE Ivory of Christchurch, New Zealand traded much material found in previous editions of our *Abbreviated Dictionary* for new items in his *Pacific Index of Abbreviations and Acronyms in Common Use in the Pacific Basin*. His splendid compendium was published in 1982 by Whitcoulls.

William A Reid of Union Postal Universel in Bern, Switzerland provided excellent up-to-date information about touring club abbreviations the world over.

MA Brossard, Secretary General of Interpol in Saint-Cloud, France, was most helpful and sent very useful material about prisons.

Dr Irmaisabel Lovera De-Sola of Caracas, Venezuela furnished most of the Venezuelan entries and others from other Latin American lands. She also put us in touch with Venezuela's best-known criminologist—Dr Helio Gómez Grillo and he also gave us entries.

Book lover and journalist Dean A Stahl of San Diego submitted more than two-hundred-and-fifty new entries plus some more from Karen Kerchelich a well-known San Diego researcher-writer. Someday one or the other might prove eligible to take on the task of continuing editions of this *Abbreviations Dictionary*.

Expatriate New Yorkers John and Fay Silverstein continued to supply vital information as did ex-New Yorker Lorraine Sherkin of Toronto, Ontario and her daughter Kari.

Another Canadian source was David Allen of Halifax, Nova Scotia.

The largest contribution in the field of education came from James C Palmer who compiled and edited the *ERIC Dictionary of Educational Acronyms, Abbreviations and Initialisms* published by the ERIC Clearinghouse for Junior Colleges in 1981.

Lots of liturgical abbreviations were sent by Brother John-Charles of the Society of Saint Francis American Province in Mount Sinai, New York. Another contributor was Mary Bucher the senior writer of the Battelle Columbus Laboratories in Columbus, Ohio.

Maritime contributors include Chief Officer Aage I Helde of the *Salvador* of the Ivaran Lines, Chief Officer Andrew Milligan of the Blue Star Line's *California Star*, and Chief Petty Officer Martin Parr of the United States Navy.

Very recently deceased contributors include my pen pal of some 40 years standing: Julius B. Kaiser of New York and Hollywood, and Harold Q Driscoll of San Diego. Often they would contribute ideas and items on an almost weekly basis.

San Diegans who helped include a former student: Anthony Marquez; Harold Cary and his son Dr David Cary; Dr Ira Levine; Dr Warren Kessler; Dr Rodrigo Muñoz.

The *List of Acronyms* compiled by Linda Blocki, technical editor and optics librarian of the University of Daton Research Institute at Kirtland Air Force Base in New Mexico, was most welcome. Another contributor was Professor PA Doyle of Williston Park, New York.

San Diego's many reference librarians were most helpful and include the names of Keith Anderson, Alyce and Michael Archuleta, Marianne Avila, Eileen Boyle, Elizabeth Byrne, Christina Clifford, Lucy van Donck and her cousin Laura Gulotta, Debbie Gray, Sally Hamburg, Susanna Hardy, Jean Hughes, Matt Katka, Evelyn Roy Kooperman, Curt Lang, Jean Lowerison, Anna M Martinez, Sharon Nelson, Jeanne C Newhouse, Angela Patterson, Margaret Queen, Margo Sasse, Jim Shaff, Don Silva, Lyn Slomowitz, Barbara Tuthill, John Vanderby, Vere Wolf, and many others whose names appear in previous editions of the *Abbreviations Dictionary*.

Dr Ronda De Sola Chervin's enthusiasm for the task of selecting and defining euphemisms was contagious and help flesh out the Bafflegab Divulged addendum suggested by Lucy van Donck. We thank both of them and all the foregoing including those mentioned in previous editions, and that indefatigable booster, Dan Pezze of Lakewood, New Jersey.

The entire staff at Elsevier continued to aid in the editing, marketing, and production of this and previous editions. Special thanks go to Caryl P Dreiblatt, Edmée Froment, Louise Calabro Gruendel, Marion Hess, Ethel G Langlois, Linda Leopold, Dr AW Kenneth Metzner, Phyllis Oehler, and Toni Ann Scaramuzzo of Elsevier, and to freelancers Charles Beaulein, Paul Duchesne, Chris Schreiber, and Maria Schreiber.

Maura Grant, working with Unitron Graphics, also deserves special thanks as this augmented international seventh edition of the *Abbreviations Dictionary* goes to press.

Introduction

Definitions of Terms

abbreviations   abridged contractions such as acdt: accident; AEC: Atomic Energy Commission; NASA: National Aeronautics and Space Administration.

acronyms   words formed from letters in a series of related words such as ABLE: Activity Balance Line Evaluation; AGREE: Advisory Group on Reliability of Electronic Equipment; DYNAMO: Dynamic Action Management Operations.

anonyms   attempts of authors to enjoy anonymity while maintaining their identity by such devices as the capitalized diphthong AE standing for Aeon, pen name of George William Russell.

contractions   words shortened by dropping nonpronounced letters; omitted letter(s) which are indicated by apostrophes as in can't: can not; li'l: little; doesn't: does not; let's: let us.

eponyms   designations derived from family names, nicknames or names of places or persons; e.g., Hapsburg dynasty, *Eroica* symphony, Paris of America (Montreal), Raynaud's disease.

exonyms   foreign-language equivalents of place names.

geographical equivalents   entries such as Far East: countries and islands of East Asia or in the Pacific—eastern Siberia, China, Japan, Taiwan, Korea, Indochina, the Philippines, the Malay Peninsula.

initials   FDR: Franklin Delano Roosevelt; HST: Harry S Truman; JFK: John Fitzgerald Kennedy; LBJ: Lyndon Baines Johnson; initials of all American Presidents are included as well as initials of other noted personalities.

nicknames   Al: Alfred; Bea: Beatrice; Hal: Harold; Ike: Dwight David Eisenhower; Issac.

place name pseudonyms   see *Cannery Row, Main Street, Middletown, Red Gap, Spoon River, Tortilla Flat, Winesburg, Yoknapatawpha, Zenith* entries.

short forms   amps: amperes; Olds: Oldsmobile; pots.: potentiometers.

signs $ & ¢—dollars and cents.

slang shortcuts B-girl: bar girl; C-note: $100 bill; 1-G: $1000.

symbols AL: aluminum; Pt: platinum; Rx: prescription; recipe.

toponyms place names convicts use when telling you where they were imprisoned.

Editors—Teachers—Writers

Editors, teachers, and writers will perform a splendid service for readers if they insist that abbreviations and acronyms be defined the first time they are used. The old argument, "everyone knows what that stands for," no longer is true. Many abbreviations stand for at least ten different things. Many acronyms, also, stand for several different things.

The style of writing abbreviations and acronyms requires the attention of editors, teachers, and writers. They should be unwilling to let things get out of hand to the point that a paragraph comes cluttered with unexplained capital-letter combinations. Technical literature will become almost impossible to read if the permissive trend continues wherein all abbreviations and acronyms appear in solid capital letters and without benefit of preliminary definition.

Throughout this *Abbreviations Dictionary* an attempt is made to follow the rules of English grammar. Capital letters are reserved for proper nouns. Lowercase letters are used for common nouns. However, when custom has become so strong that correctly written short forms are not recognized quickly, their more common equivalents are added parenthetically; icbm (ICBM): intercontinental ballistic missile.

Explanations

If readers and researchers did not continue to find themselves engulfed and ensnared in the modern abracadabra of abbreviations and acronyms, in the bewildering bafflegab and gobbledygook of computerese, corporationese, initialese, officialese, pentagonese, politicalese, and technicalese, there would be no need to provide this new international seventh edition of the *Abbreviations Dictionary*.

Because so many creators of abbreviations and coiners of acronyms fail to define their shortcuts the first time they use them, and because so many who use them also fail to define these things, it becomes increasingly difficult to understand what people are saying or writing when their sayings and writings are filled with abbreviations, acronyms, and anonyms, contractions, initials, nicknames, pseudonyms, short forms, signs, slang shortcuts, and symbols created for their own convenience, without regard for their ability to create communicative and easily understood statements.

Daily speech, newspapers, magazines, books, and signs along the airways, highways, railways, and waterways reveal the universality of these shortcuts to communication and the growing tendency to use and devise more and more of them. This appears to be done in response to the rapid development of technological civilization. But witness the confusion compounded when someone without a knowledge of Spanish turns on the C tap in a shower bath in Acapulco, Buenos Aires, or Madrid. Hot water streams out instead of cold. North is N in most languages of western civilization, but west can be W or O or even V.

Abbreviations of every sort cover contemporary civilization like a deep and ever-deepening snowdrift, concealing the main features of the landscape, leaving the beholder mystified and perplexed by the overwhelming obscurity imposed by these letter and number combinations. Usually these shortcuts to communication are created without reference to the niceties of typography, the requirements of official and logical regulations, or even the rules of grammar. Most appear without definitions. More and more appear each year. And more and more duplicate already existing abbreviations standing for other things. The letter a, for example, stands for more than 25 different things. Capital A stand for more than 30 different things. and so it goes through the alphabet, with many varied combinations of letters and numbers, sign, and symbols.

Arrangement

Everything in this book is arranged in alphabetical and numerical order. For entries containing the same letter, lowercase precedes capital (aa, AA); roman precedes italics (AWA, AWA); unpunctuated precedes punctuated (BAE, B.A.E.). An Arabic numeral precedes its Roman equivalent (3, III).

The following connectives are ignored in the alphabetical arrangement: & (ampersand), and, by, in, of, or, + (plus), the, to. All other·articles, particles, prepositions, and the like (between, de, del, di) are treated alphabetically. For example, U of P is alphabetized as UP; U de ST appears as if it were UdeST.

A dollar sign ($) is treated as it if were a lowercase "d," the pound sign (£) like a lowercase "P," and a mu (μ) like a lowercase "m."

In the case of a parenthetical plural ending, the parenthesis will be ignored [e.g., paren(s) is treated as parens].

Golden Rule

"When in doubt, spell it out," insisted Ralph Bayless when he was chief engineer of all General Dynamics engineering organizations of Convair. He urged all to define abbreviations the first time they were used.

If, for example, the Gulf Missile Range is being described, and the term GMR will be used again and again, the text should begin something like this:

The Gulf Missile Range (GMR) affords facilities for national defense and space exploration. GMR personnel are active in all phases of aerospace research, development, and engineering. GMR headquarters are in Mobile

Common sense rules about abbreviations are most often ignored. Therefore it is necessary to repeat that short words like Maine, Ohio, Samoa, etc., should not be abbreviated, although their unofficial abbreviations exist and are shown in this book. Similarly it is best to avoid the truncation of words spelling other words when abbreviated: cat.: catalog; king.: kingdom; man.: management.

Because this is a reference dictionary there are many duplications. Many items are included so it will not be necessary for readers to try to guess what the abbreviations are intended to mean. Many unauthorized abbreviations are included for the same reason—to help readers find their way through the alphabet soup.

Capitalization

Capitalization of abbreviations, according to Department of Defense Military Standard 12-B (Mil-Std 12-B), must follow the rules of English grammar. All proper nouns are capitalized. All common nouns are written in lowercase letters. Units of weight, measure, and velocity, such as lb, kg, in., cc, mm, rpm, and the like, appear in lowercase to avoid confusion with other letter combinations they resemble.

Many military establishments and officers use full capitals for everything because message machines are provided only with capital letters. That is why many engineering drawings supplied the armed forces contain all abbreviations in capital letters. It is also true many draftsmen are afraid small letters will fill up, especially a's, b's, e's, g's, o's, and the like Therefore they also like to use capital letters. In text, however, 1500 RPM presents a typographical blob, as compared to the more sophisticated 1500 rpm.

At first loran was LORAN. As people became more used to it, it became Loran. Today it is loran. The same is true of other combinations. The trend is to capitalize only those letters standing for proper nouns, running all common nouns in lowercase. Nevertheless, for the sake of readers and researchers, some incorrectly rendered abbreviations appear in this book. Many people have a marked tendency to capitalize everything they think is important. If this tendency is unchecked, confusion follows. All abbreviations and acronyms look alike. So follow the commonsense rules of good grammar and correct usage.

Chemical element symbols, however, have the first letter capitalized: Au (gold), Zn (zinc), etc. The second letter of a chemical symbol always appears in lowercase.

Exceptions

The singular, plural, and tense of the words abbreviated do not alter abbreviations except in a few instances, such as fig.: figure; figs.: figures; lb: pound; lbs: pounds; no.: number; nos: numbers; p: page; pp: pages; S: Saint; SS: Saints.

However, readers should be aware the International (*SI*) System of Measurements calls for the abolition of all pluralized abbreviations. Hence in. stands for inch or inches, lb for pound or pounds, oz for ounce or ounces. This system will probably gain widespread approval.

Documentary abbreviations are rendered as follows: FARs (Failure Analysis Reports), or IRs (Inspector's Reports) or RARs (Reliability Action Reports). In the singular they appear as FAR, IR, RAR.

Italics

Items from Latin and other non-English languages, as well as titles of books and periodicals, are usually set in italic type. Many physical symbols are also set in italics to differentiate them from other letter combinations they resemble.

Punctuation

Short forms are devised to save time and space and to overcome the necessity of repeating long words and phrases. All punctuation is avoided in modern practice unless the form is taken from Latin or there is some conventional use demanding punctuation, as in the case of academic degrees and a few governmental designations. U.S.A. is the country; USA is the army. D.C. is the District of Columbia; DC is direct current when used as a noun. Cash on delivery is not cod but c.o.d. Similarly, fig., figs. and no. require periods to keep readers from thinking they may be words instead of abbreviations for figure, figures, and number. Again, when in doubt, spell it out.

Capitalization and Punctuation Trends

American as well as British and Canadian publishers appear to be following the sensible trend to capitalize only those letters normally capitalized: proper nouns and important words in titles. They reserve lowercase letters for abbreviations consisting of adjectives and common nouns. This obviates the chaos brought about by those who capitalized all the letters in every abbreviation and then compounded their error by placing unnecessary full stops or periods after every letter as was the custom in bygone times.

Most periods are dropped because it is generally realized the purpose of all abbreviation is the thoroughgoing promotion of brevity. More than a decade ago, when Rudolf Flesch compiled one of his many useful books, *How To Be Brief—An Index to Simple Writing*, he stated:

> To save even more space, leave out abbreviation periods whenever you can. the British omit them regularly . . . *Mr, Mrs, Dr, St* (Saint), *Thos, Chas, jr.* Periods are often left out after standard abbreviations like *US, UN, FCC, PTA* . . . following the pattern of most telephone books (e.g., *plmbg & heatg supls, atty, flrst, acctnts, svce, rl est*).

Chemists, dentists, doctors, medical reference librarians, nurses, and psychiatrists used to write as if they were completely unaware of the rules of correct and effective English communication, confounding many chemical symbols with abbreviations and then capitalizing everything. They seemed to be in a world of their own and quite unaware that what they capitalized also stood for one or more other things in other and even everyday fields. Thus it sometimes becomes necessary to show abbreviations in both styles, correct and incorrect, so people may find out what they mean one way or another. Hence gmp (GMP?): guanosine monophosphate. It preceds GMP: Green Mansion Properties.

The reason for following the rules becomes apparent if we examine another entry: hpl: high(est) point level; human partoid lysozyme (HPL); human placental lactogen (HPL). It is followed by HPL: Halifax Public Library; Hamilton Public Library; Hartford Public Library; Houston Pipe Line; Houston Public Library.

Signs and Symbols

Frequently used signs and symbols are in the back of this dictionary. Many are found on typewriters (&: ampersand—the *and* sign; *: asterisk; ¢: cent; $: dollar; %: percent).

Symbols include the chemical elements (Al: aluminum; Au: gold—from the Latin *aurum*; C: carbon; Sn: tin—from the Latin *stannum*). All are listed in the alphabetical section without special definition to indicate they are not abbreviations but symbols. The chemical elements are also grouped together in the back of this dictionary.

Airlines use two-letter symbols for convenience in baggage handling, ticketing, and scheduling operations. Thus American Airlines is AA, Delta Air Lines is DL. National Airlines is NA, Pan American World Airways is PA. United Air Lines is UA. These two-letter designations are listed in a separate section at the back of the book as well as alphabetically along with other multiletter airline abbreviations.

Railroads and steamship lines are included both in the alphabetical section and in their own sections at the end of the book. Naval craft are designated by many arbitrary symbols. All available are given in the alphabetical section.

Abbreviations Dictionary

Augmented International Seventh Edition

A

a abbreviation; absent; absolute; acceleration in feet per second; account; acre; adjective; adult; aerial; afternoon; altitude; intercept; amateur; ampere; annealing; anthracite; arc; are (unit of metric land measure); area; argent; at; atmosphere; audit; auditor; automatic; available; aviation; aviator; axis; azure; distance from leading edge to aerodynamic center (symbol)

a' all (contraction); a minute (angle); a prime

a'' second (angle); a double-prime

a am, an, an der (German—on the, at the); angle of attack; *annus* (Latin—year), *arteria* (Latin—artery), attenuation constant (symbol); autonomous consumption (macroeconomics symbol); (Italian—and)—not an abbreviation

A absolute; absolute temperature; academy; accumulator (computerese); acid; acoustic source; actual weight of an aircraft; address (computer symbol); adulterer; adulteress (capital letter A branded on the foreheads of all who were convicted of this crime in the early days of New England)—also known as the scarlet letter because branding caused bleeding; aircraft; airman; Alaska Steamship Company; Alcoa Steamship Company; Alfa code for A; ambassador; America; American; Americanization; Americanize; A-mos, The Book of; ampere; amphibian; Anchor Line;

anode; anterior; April; argon; Army; artillery; aspect ratio; astragal; Atlantic; atomic weight; attack; August; Austria (auto plaque); chemical activity; first van der Waals constant; Fraunhofer line due to oxygen; linear acceleration; mean sound absorption coefficient; total acidity

Å angstrom unit

A abajo (Spanish—down); *abasso* (Italian—down); *absolvo* (Latin—I absolve, I acquit); *alas* (Finnish—down); *albus* (Latin—white); *Alp(en)* (German—Alp, The Alps); *Alpe(s)* (French—Alp, Alps Mountains); *Alpi* (Italian—The Alps); *Alt* (German old)—as in Alt Heidelberg; *Alteza* (Spanish—Highness); *aprobado* (Spanish—approved)—passed in an examination; arrival; *arrivare* (Italian—arrival); arrive; *arrivé* (French—arrival); *auf* (German—up); *Aulus* (Latin—Aulus Gellius) —2nd-century author noted for his *Noctes Atticae* about languages and literature as well as natural history; *aus* (German—out); *avbeta* (Swedish—departure); mountain meadow(s)

Å *aas* (Dano-Norwegian—hills)

A-1 air personnel officer; excellent; first class; first rate; *Lloyd's Register* symbol indicating a vessel's equipment is first rate; personnel section of an air force staff; skyraider single-engine general-purpose attack aircraft flown from aircraft carriers; top quality; tops;

very best

A-I (motion pictures) for general patronage

A1c Airman, first class

A/1C Airman First Class

A-1 **Skyraider** Douglas single-engine attack aircraft (formerly AD)

A-2 air intelligence officer; almost A-1 in quality; intelligence section of an air force staff; just short of being the best

A-II (motion pictures) for adults and adolescents only

A₂ aortic second sound; Asian influenza virus

A/2C Airman Second Class

A²C² *see* AACC

A-3 air operations and training officer; operations and training section of an air force staff; Skywarrior twin-engine turbojet tactical all-weather attack aircraft operating from aircraft carriers; training and operations

A-III (motion pictures) for adults only

A/3C Airman Third Class

A-3 **Skywarrior** Douglas carrier-based twin-engine jet reconnaissance and light bombing plane (formerly A3D)—USAF B-66 Destroyer

A-4 air material and supply officer; material and supply section of an air force staff; Skyhawk single-engine turbojet attack aircraft operating from aircraft carriers; supply and materiel

A-IV (motion pictures) for adults with reservations

A-5 planning; supersonic twin-engine turbojet all-weather attack aircraft operating from aircraft carriers

A-6 communications

A-6A Intruder twin-engine turbojet long-range carrier-based low-altitude attack aircraft

A-6 Intruder Grumman carrier-based twin-engine jet low-level attack bomber (formerly A2F)

A-7 Corsair II Ling-Temco-Vought carrier-based single-engine jet light-attack bomber

A-32 Lansen (Swedish—A-32 Lance)—Saab single-seat single-engine jet fighter-interceptor

A-37 radar-homing or television-guided air-to-surface missile made by Hawker-Siddeley in Britain and Matra in France —Martel

A-60 Saab twin-engine two-place jet trainer-utility aircraft also called the Saab 105

A-106 Agusta antisubmarine-warfare single-engine single-seat helicopter

A-109 Agusta high-performance eight-seat twin-engine helicopter

aa acetic acid; achievement age; acting appointment; adjectives; alveolar-arterial; always afloat; aminoacetone; approximate absolute; armature accelerator; arteries; ascending aorta; atomic absorption; author's alteration; equal parts

aa (AA) achievement age; antiaircraft; ascorbic acid

a-a air-to-air

a/a antiaircraft

a & a abbreviations and acronyms; additions and amendments; aid and attendance

aa *arterias* (Latin—arteries); (Hawaiian—block lava)—pronounced *ah-ah*

AA absolute alcohol; absolute altitude; achievement age; Addicts Anonymous; Administrative Assistant; Aerolineas Argentinas (Argentine Airlines); Affirmative Action; Airman Apprentice; Alcoholics Anonymous; Aluminum (Company of) America; American Airlines; American Association; Ann Arbor (railroad); Ansett Airways; antiaircraft; Appropriate Authority; arithmetic average; Arlington Annex; Asian-African; Athletic Association; author's altera-

tion(s); Automobile Association; Aviation Annex; *Aviatsionnaya Armiya* (Russian—Air Army)

A.A. Associate in Accounting; Associate in Arts

AA *Air Almanac; Astronautica Acta* (Journal of the International Astronautical Federation)

aaa abdominal aortic aneurism; acquired aplastic anemia; acute anxiety attack; amalgam; androgenic anabolic agent

aa & a armor, armament, and ammunition

Aaa Alaska (government style is to spell it out); unofficial abbreviation

AAA Agricultural Adjustment Administration; Agricultural Aircraft Association; Alaska (unofficial abbreviation—government style is to spell it out); All American Aviation; Allegheny Airlines (3-letter coding); Allied Artists of America; American Academy of Advertising; American Academy of Allergy; American Accordionists Association; American Accounting Association; American Airship Association; American Antartic Association; American Anthropological Association; American Arbitration Association; American Association of Anatomists; American Astronomers Association; American Australian Association; American Automobile Association; antiaircraft artillery; Antique Airplane Association; Appraisers Association of America; Archives of American Art; Area Agency on Aging; Army Audit Agency; Associated Agents of America; Association of Attenders and Alumni (Hague Academy of International Law); Association of Average Adjusters

AAA (AFL-CIO) Actors and Artistes of America

A.A.A. Amateur Athletic Association (British)

AAAA American Association for the Advancement of Atheism; American Association of Advertising Agencies; Army Aviation Association of America; Associated Actors and Artists of America; Association of Accredited Adver-

tising Agencies (Singapore); Australian Advertising Advisory Authority; Australian Association of Advertising Agencies

AAAANZ Association of Accredited Advertising Agencies of New Zealand

AAAB American Association of Architectural Bibliographers

AAAC American Association for the Advancement of Criminology; Antiaircraft Artillery Command; Australian Army Aviation Corps

AAACE American Association of Agricultural College Editors

AAACE *Alianza Apostolica y Anti-Comunista de España* (Spanish—Apostolic and Anti-Communist Alliance of Spain)—also known as the Triple-A

AAAD American Athletic Association for the Deaf

AAAE American Association of Airport Executives; Australian Association of Adult Education

AAAEE American Afro-Asian Educational Exchange

A.A. Ag. Associate of Arts in Agriculture

AAAH American Association for the Advancement of the Humanities

AAAI Affiliated Advertising Agencies International

AAAID Arab Authority for Agricultural Investment and Development

AAAIMH American Association for the Abolition of Involuntary Mental Hospitalization

AAAIP Advanced Army Aircraft Instrumentation Program

AAAIS Antiaircraft Artillery Information Service; Antiaircraft Artillery Intelligence Service

AAAIWA Automobile, Aerospace, and Agricultural Implement Workers of America

aaal abolish all abortion laws

AAAL American Academy of Arts and Letters

AAALAC American Association for Accreditation of Laboratory Animal Care

AAAM American Association of Aircraft Manufacturers; American Association for Automotive Medicine

AAAN American Academy of Applied Nutrition

AAAOC Antiaircraft Artillery Operation Center

AAAR American Association for Aerosol Research; Association for the Advancement of Aging Research

AAARC Antiaircraft Artillery Reception Center

AAARG American Atheist Addiction Recovery Groups

AAAS American Academy of Arts and Sciences; American Academy of Asian Studies; American Association for the Advancement of Science; Australian Association for the Advancement of Science

A.A.A.S. Associate in Arts and Science

AAASA Association for the Advancement of Agricultural Sciences in Africa; Australian and Allied All Services Association

AAASS American Association for the Advancement of Slavic Studies

AAASUSS Association of Administrative Assistants and Secretaries to United States Senators

AAAUS Association of Average Adjusters of the United States

AAB Aircraft Accident Board; American Association of Bioanalysts; Army Air Base; Army Artillery Board; Association of Applied Biologists

AABB American Association of Blood Banks

AABC American Amateur Baseball Congress; American Association of Bible Colleges; Association for the Advancement of Blind Children

AABD Aid to the Aged, Blind, or Disabled

AABEVM Association of American Boards of Examiners in Veterinary Medicine

AABGA American Association of Botanical Gardens and Arboretums

AABH Australian Association for Better Hearing

AABI American Association of Bicycle Importers; Antilles Air Boats Incorporated

AABL Associated Australian Banks of London; Australian Associated Banks in London

aaBm analytical anatomy by the Braille method

AABM Association of American Battery Manufacturers; Australian Association of British Manufacturers

AABNCP Advanced Airborne Command Post

AABP Australian Association of Business Publications

AABPDF Allied Association of Bleachers, Printers, Dyers, and Finishers

aabshil aircraft anti-collision-beacon-system high-intensity light(ing)

AABT Association for the Advancement of Behavior Therapy

AABTM American Association of Baggage Traffic Managers

aaby as amended by

aac automatic aperture control; average annual cost

AAC Aeronautical Advisory Council; Aeronautical Approach Chart; Aircraft Armament Change; Alaskan Air Command; All-American Canal (serving California and Baja California); Alumnae Advisory Center; American Academy of Criminalistics; American Alpine Club; American Alumni Council; American Archery Council; American Association of Criminology; American Atheist Center; American Cement Corporation (stock exchange symbol); Antiaircraft Command; Army Air Corps; Association of American Choruses; Association of American Colleges; Australian Agricultural Company; Australian Air Corps; Australian Association of Chiropractors; Automotive Advertisers Council

AAC *Associação Academica de Coimbra* (Portuguese—Coimbra Academic Association)

A.A.C. *anno ante Christum* (Latin—year before Christ)—same as before Christ

AACA Antique Automobile Club of America; Automotive Air Conditioning Association

AACAP Association of American Colleges Arts Program

AACB Aeronautics and Astronautics Coordination Board; Australian Association of Clinical Biochemists

AACBC American Association of College Baseball Coaches

AACBP American Academy of Crown and Bridge Prosthodontics

aacc all-attitude control capability; automatic approach control complex

AACC American Association of Cereal Chemists; American Association of Clinical Chemists; American Association for Contamination Control; American Association of Credit Counselors; American Automatic Control Council; Association for the Aid of Crippled Children

A.A.C.C.A. Associate of the Association of Certified and Corporate Accountants

AACCLA Association of American Chambers of Commerce in Latin America

AACCP American Association of Colleges for Chiropody-Podiatry

AACDP American Association of Chairmen of Departments of Psychiatry

AACE Airborne Alternate Command Echelon (NATO); American Association of Cost Engineers

AACFO American Association of Correctional Facility Officers

AACFT Army Aircraft

Aachen German geographical place-name equivalent of Aix-la-Chapelle on the Belgian-Dutch borders of West Germany

AACHS Afro-American Cultural and Historical Society

AACI American Association for Conservation Information; Association of Americans and Canadians in Israel

AACJC American Association of Community and Junior Colleges

AACM American Academy of Compensation Medicine

AACO Advanced and Applied Concepts Office (USA); American Association of Certified Orthoptists; Assault Airlift Control Office(r)

AACOBS Australian Advisory Council on Bibliographical Services

AACOMS Army Area Communications System

AACP American Academy for Cerebral Palsy; American Academy for Child Psychiatry; American Academy of Clinical Psychiatrists; American Association of Colleges of

Podiatry; American Association of Commercial Publications; American Association of Convention Planners; American Association of Correctional Psychologists

AACPP Association of Asbestos Cement Pipe Producers

AACPR American Association for Cleft Palate Rehabilitation

AACR American Association for Cancer Research

AACR Anglo-American Cataloguing Rules

AACRAO American Association of Collegiate Registrars and Admissions Officers

AACS Airborne Astrographic Camera System; Airways and Air Communications Service; Army Airways Communications System; Australian Amateur Cine Society

AACSA Anglo-American Corporation of South Africa

AACSB American Association of Collegiate Schools of Business

AACSL American Association for the Comparative Study of Law

AACSM Airways and Air Communications Service Manual

AACT American Association of Commodity Traders; Armenian Assembly Charitable Trust

AACTE American Association of Colleges for Teacher Education

AACTP American Association of Correctional Training Personnel

AACUBO American Association of College and University Business Officers

aad active acoustic(al) device

aad (AAD) alloxazine adenine dinucleotide

AAD Aircraft Assignment Directive; American Academy of Dentists; American Academy of Dermatology; Army Air Defense

AADA Advanced Air Depot Area; American Academy of Dramatic Arts; American Association of Deaf Athletes; Army Air Defense Area; Australian Automobile Dealers Association

AADC Army Air Defense Command(er)

AADCCS Army Air Defense Control and Coordination System

AADCP Army Air Defense Command Post

AADE American Association of Dental Editors; American Association of Dental Examiners

AA de L Academia Argentina de Letras (Spanish—Argentine Academy of Letters)

AADGB American Association of District Governing Boards

AA Dip Architectural Association Diploma

AADIS Army Air Defense Information Service

AADLA Art and Antique Dealers League of America

AADM American Academy of Dental Medicine

AADMS Advanced Academic Degree Management System

AADN American Association of Doctors' Nurses

AADOO Army Air Defense Operations Office(r)

AADP American Academy of Denture Prosthetics

AADPA American Academy of Dental Practice Administration

AADS Advanced Army Defense System; American Association of Dental Schools; American Association of Dermatology and Syphilology; Army Air Defense System

aae (AAE) above airport elevation; acute allergic encephalitis; average annual earnings

AAE American Association of Endodontists; American Association of Engineers; Army Aviation Engineers; Asia Australia Express

AAEA American Agricultural Editors Association

AAEC Association of American Editorial Cartoonists; Australian-American Engineering Corporation; Australian Army Educational Corps; Australian Atomic Energy Commission

AAEDC American Agricultural Economics Documentation Center (USDA)

A.Ae.E. Associate in Aeronautical Engineering

AAEE American Academy of Environmental Engineers; American Association of Economic Entomologists; American Association of Electromyography and Electrodiagnosis

AAEF Australian-American

Education Foundation

AAEFA Army Aviation Engineering Flight Activity

AAEH Association to Advance Ethical Hypnosis

AAEKNE American Association of Elementary-Kindergarten-Nursery Educators

AAELSS Active-Arm External-Load Stabilization System

AAEOCJ American Association of Ex-Offenders in Criminal Justice

AAEP American Association of Equine Practitioners

AAES Advanced Aircraft Electrical System; Australian Agricultural Economics Society; Australian Army Education Service

AAESA Alabama Association of Elementary School Administrators

AAESDA Association of Architects, Engineers, Surveyors, and Draughtsmen of Australia

AAESPH American Association for the Education of the Severely/Profoundly Handicapped

AAEW Atlantic Airborne Early Warning

aaf (AAF) acetylaminofluorine; ascorbic acid factor

a-a-f acetic-alcohol-formalin (fixing fluid)

AAF American Advertising Federation; American Air Filter (company); American Architectural Foundation; American Astronautical Federation; Army Air Field; Army and Air Force; Army Air Forces

AAFA Architectural Aluminium Fabricators Association; Australian Amateur Fencing Association

A.A.F.A. Associate in Arts in Fine Arts

A.A. Fair Erle Stanley Gardner

AAFB Auxiliary Air Force Base

aafc (AAFC) antiaircraft fire control

AAFC Air Accounting and Finance Center; Army Air Forces Center; Army Air Force Classification Center; Association of Advertising Film Companies

AAFCE Allied Air Force, Central Europe

AAFCO Association of American Feed Control Officials; Association of American Fertilizer Control Officials

AAFCWF Army and Air Force Central Welfare Fund; Army and Air Force Civilian Welfare Fund

AAFE Advanced Applications Flight Experiment; American Association of Feed Exporters

AAFEA Australian Airline Flight Engineers Association

AAFEC Army Air Forces Engineering Command

AAFEMPS Army and Air Force Exchange and Motion Picture Service

AAFES Army and Air Force Exchange Service

AAFFA Australian Air Freight Forwarding Association

AAFH Academy of American Franciscan History

AAFIS Army Air Forces Intelligence School

AAFM American Association of Feed Microscopists

AAFMC Army Air Forces Materiel Center

AAFMPS Army and Air Force Motion Picture Service

AAFNE Allied Air Force, Northern Europe

AAFNS Army Air Forces Navigation School

AAFOIC Army Air Forces Officer in Charge

AAFP American Academy of Family Physicians

AAFPS Army and Air Force Pilot School; Army and Air Force Postal Service

AAFRS American Academy of Facial, Plastic, and Reconstructive Surgery

AAFS American Association of Foot Specialists; American Academy of Forensic Sciences

AAFSE Allied Air Force, Southern Europe

AAFSS Advanced Aerial Fire Support System

AAFSW Association of American Foreign Service Women

AAFTS Army Air Forces Technical School

AAFU All-African Farmers' Union

AAFWB Army and Air Force Wage Board

AAG Air Adjutant General; Association of American Geographers; Australian Association of Gerontology

AAGC American Association of Gifted Children

AAGFO American Academy of Gold Foil Operators

AAGL American Association of Gynecological Laparoscopists

AAGp Aeromedical Airlift Group (USAF)

AAGP American Academy of General Practice

A. Agr. Associate in Agriculture

AAGR Air-to-Air Gunnery Range

A.Agri. Associate in Agriculture

AAGS All-American Gladiolus Selections

AAGUS American Association of Genito-Urinary Surgeons

aagw (AAGW) air-to-air guided weapon(s)

aah (AAH) anti-armor helicopter

AAH Alcoholism Awareness Hour (tv); American Academy of Homiletics; Australian Auxiliary Hospital

aaha awaiting action of higher authority

AAHA American Animal Hospital Association; American Association of Handwriting Analysts; American Association of Homes for the Aging; American Association of Hospital Accountants

AAHC American Academy of Humor Columnists; American Association of Hospital Consultants

AAHD American Academy of the History of Dentistry

AAHDC American Association of Hospital Dental Chiefs

AAHE American Association for Higher Education; American Association of Housing Educators

A.A.H.E. Associate in Arts in Home Economics

AAHM American Association for the History of Medicine; Association of Architectural Hardware Manufacturers

Aahp Army artificial heart pump

AAHP American Association for Hospital Planning; American Association of Hospital Podiatrists; American Association for Humanistic Psychology

AAHPA American Association of Hospital Purchasing Agents

AAHPER American Association for Health, Physical Education, and Recreation

AAHPERD American Alliance for Health, Physical Education, Recreation, and Dance

AAHPhA American Animal Health Pharmaceutical Association

AAHPS Australian Association for the History and Philosophy of Science

AAHQ Allied Air Headquarters

AAHRA Asia and Australia Hotel and Restaurant Association

AAHS American Aviation Historical Society

AAHSLD Association of Academic Health Sciences Library Directors

aai air-to-air identification; angle-of-approach indicator; azimuth angle increment

AAI African-American Institute; Afro-American Institute; Agricultural Ammonia Institute; Akron Art Institute; Alfred Adler Institute; Allied Armies in Italy (World War II); American Association of Immunologists

A.A.I. Associate of the Chartered Auctioneers' and Estate Agents' Institute

AAIA Association of American Indian Affairs

A.A.I.A. Associate of the Association of International Accountants

AAIAL American Academy and Institute of Arts and Letters

AAIAN Association for the Advancement of Instruction about Alcohol and Narcotics

AAIB American Association of Instructors of the Blind

AAIC Allied Air Intelligence Center; Australian Advertising Industry Council

AAICD American Association of Imported Car Dealers

AAICU Alabama Association of Independent Colleges and Universities

AAID American Academy of Implant Dentistry; American Academy of Implant Dentures; American Association of Industrial Dentists

AAIE American Association of Industrial Editors; American Association of Industrial Engineers

AAII American Association of Individual Investors; Association for the Advancement of

Invention and Innovation

AAIM American Association of Industrial Management

AAIMS An Analytical Information Management System

AAIN American Association of Industrial Nurses

AAIP Academic Administration Internship Program

AAIPS American Association of Industrial Physicians and Surgeons

AAIS Associate of the Australian Institute of Secretaries

AAIT American Association of Inhalation Therapists; Associate of the Australian Institute of Travel

AAJ American Association for Justice; Arab Airways, Jerusalem; Axel Axelson Johnson (Johnson Line)

AAJ Australian Anthropological Journal

AAJA Afro-Asian Journalists' Association

aajc automatic antijam circuit

AAJC American Association of Junior Colleges

AAJE American Association for Jewish Education

AAJR American Academy for Jewish Research

AAJS American Association for Jesuit Scientists

AAJSA American Association of Journalism School Administrators

AAK Alfred A Knopf

aal above aerodrome level; anterior axillary line

AAL American Airlines; Ames Aeronautical Laboratory; Arctic Aeromedical Laboratory; Association of Assistant Librarians; Australian Air League

AALA Afro-American Liberation Army; American Auto Laundry Association; American Automotive Leasing Association; Asian-American Librarians Association

AALAPSO Afro-Asian-Latin-American People's Solidarity Organization (Cuban overseas subversives)

AALAS American Association of Laboratory Animal Science

AALASO Afro-Asian Latin-American Students' Organization

AALC African-American Labor Center (AFL-CIO)

AALD Australian Army Legal Department

AALE Associate of Arts in Law Enforcement

AALL American Association of Law Libraries

aalmg (AALMG) antiaircraft light machine gun

AALPA Association of Auctioneers and Landed Property Agents

AALPP American Association for Legal and Political Philosophy

AALR American Association for Leisure and Recreation

AALS American Association of Language Specialists; Association of American Law Schools; Association of American Library Schools

AALT American Association of Library Trustees

AALU Association for Advanced Life Underwriting

aam (AAM) air-to-air missile

AAM Academy of Ancient Music; Acoustics Analysis Memo; American Association of Microbiology; American Association of Museums; Australian Air Mission

AAMA American Academy of Medical Administrators; American Apparel Manufacturers Association; American Association of Medical Assistants; Architectural Aluminum Manufacturers Association

AAMBP Association of American Medical Book Publishers

AAMC American Association of Marriage Counselors; American Association of Medical Clinics; Army Air Materiel Command; Association of American Medical Colleges; Australian Army Medical Corps

AAMCA Army Advanced Materiel Concepts Agency (USA)

AAMCH American Association for Maternal and Child Health

AAMD American Association on Mental Deficiency; Association of Art Museum Directors

aame (AAME) acetylarginine methyl ester

AAMES American Association for Middle East Studies

AAMF American Association of Music Festivals

AAMFT American Association for Marriage and Family Therapy

aamg (AAMG) antiaircraft machine gun

AAMGA American Association of Managing General Agents

AAMHPC American Association of Mental Health Professionals in Corrections

AAMI American Association of Machinery Importers; American Athletic Motivation Institute; Association for the Advancement of Medical Instrumentation; Association of Allergists for Mycological Investigation

AAMIH American Association for Maternal and Infant Health

AAML Arctic Aeromedical Laboratory

AAMMC American Association of Medical Milk Commissioners

AAMOA Afro-American Music Opportunities Association

AAMP American Academy of Maxillofacial Prosthetics

AAMR American Academy on Mental Retardation

AAMRL American Association of Medical Record Librarians

AAMS American Air Mail Society

AAMSW American Association of Medical Social Workers

AAMU Army Advanced Marksmanship Unit

A.A. Mus. Associate in Arts in Music

AAMVA American Association of Motor Vehicle Administrators

AAMW Association of Advertising Men and Women

AAMWS Australian Army Medical Women's Service

aan (AAN) aminoacetonitrile; assignment action number(s)

AAN Advance Acquisition Notification; American Academy of Neurology; American Academy of Nutrition; American Association of Neuropathologists; American Association of Nurserymen

A.A.N. Associate in Arts in Nursing

AANA American Association of Nurse Anesthetists; Australian Association of National Advertisers

AANNT American Association of Nephrology Nurses and Technicians

AANR American Association of Newspaper Representatives

AANS American Academy of

Neurological Surgery; American Association of Neurological Surgery; Australian Army Nursing Service

AANSW Archives Authority of New South Wales

aao amino-acid oxidase

aaO *am angeführten Ort* (German—in the place cited); *an anderen Orten* (German—elsewhere, in the place cited)

AAO Academy of Applied Osteopathy; American Academy of Ophthalmology; American Academy of Optometry; American Association of Orthodontists; Anglo-Australian Observatory

AAO *Abastumanskaya Astrofizicheskaya Observatoriya* (Russian—Abastumani Astrophysical Observatory)

AAOA Ambulance Association of America

AAOC American Association of Osteopathic Colleges; Antiaircraft Operations Center; Australian Army Ordnance Corps

AAOD Army Aviation Operating Detachment

AAODC American Association of Oilwell Drilling Contractors

AAOG American Association of Obstetricians and Gynecologists

AAOGAS American Association of Obstetricians, Gynecologists, and Abdominal Surgeons

AAOM American Academy of Occupational Medicine; American Academy of Oral Medicine

AAOME American Association of Osteopathic Medical Examiners

AAOMS American Association of Oral and Maxillofacial Surgeons

AAONMS Ancient Arabic Order of Nobles of the Mystic Shrine

AAO & O American Academy of Ophthalmology and Otolaryngology

AAOP American Academy of Oral Pathology; Antiaircraft Observation Post

AAOPB American Association of Pathologists and Bacteriologists

AAOPS American Association of Oral and Plastic Surgeons

AAOR American Academy of Oral Roentgenology

AAOS American Academy of Orthopaedic Surgery

aap advise if able to proceed; air at atmosphere pressure

AAP Academy of American Poets; Advance Acquisition Plan(ning); Affirmative Action Program; Allied Administrative Publication; American Academy of Pediatrics; American Academy of Periodontology; American Atheist Press; Association for the Advancement of Psychoanalysis; Association for the Advancement of Psychology; Association for the Advancement of Psychotherapy; Association of American Physicians; Association of American Publishers; Association of Applied Psychoanalysis; Australian Associated Press

A-A P Afro-American Police

AAP *Allied Army Procedures* (or *Publications*)

AAPA American Amateur Press Association; American Association of Physical Anthropologists; American Association of Port Authorities

A-A PA Anglo-American Press Association

AAPB American Association of Pathologists and Bacteriologists

AAPBS Australian Association of Permanent Building Societies

AAPC Advertising Agency Production Club; All-African Peoples' Conference; Australian Aluminium Production Commission

AAPCC American Association of Poison Control Centers; American Association of Psychiatric Clinics for Children

AAPCM Association of American Playing Card Manufacturers

AAPCO Association of American Pesticide Control Officials

AAPD American Academy of Physiologic Dentistry

AAPE American Academy of Physical Education

AAPF Academy of American Poets Fellowship

AAPG American Association of Petroleum Geologists

AAPH American Association of Professional Hypnologists

AAPHD American Association of Public Health Dentists

AAPHI Associate of the Association of Public Health Inspectors

AAPHP American Association of Public Health Physicians

AAPHR American Association of Physicians for Human Rights

AAPICU American Association of Presidents of Independent Colleges and Universities

AAPIU Allied Aerial Photographic Interpretation Unit

AAPL Afro-American Policemen's League; American Artists Professional League; American Association of Petroleum Landmen

AAPLE American Academy for Professional Law Enforcement; American Association for Professional Law Enforcement

aapm amphiapomict

AAPMR American Academy of Physical Medicine and Rehabilitation

AAPO All-African Peoples' Organization

AAPOR American Association for Public Opinion Research

AAPP American Association of Police Polygraphists; Association of Amusement Park Proprietors; Australian Association of Psychology and Philosophy

AAPPP American Association of Planned Parenthood Physicians

AAP/PSP Association of American Publishers—Professional and Scholarly Publishing Division

AAPRA All-African People's Revolutionary Army

AAPRM American Association of Passenger Rate Men

AAPRP All-African People's Revolutionary Party

AAPS American Association of Phonetic Sciences; American Association of Plastic Surgeons; American Association for the Promotion of Science; Association for Ambulatory Pediatric Services; Association of American Physicians and Surgeons

AAPSC American Association of Psychiatric Services for Children

AAPSD Alternative Automotive Power System Division (EPA)

AAPSE American Association

of Professors in Sanitary Engineering

AAPSS American Academy of Political and Social Sciences

AAPSW Associate of the Association of Psychiatric Social Workers

AAPT American Association of Physics Teachers; Association of Asphalt Paving Technologists

AAPTO American Association of Passenger Traffic Officers

AAPTSR Australian Association for Predetermined Time Standards and Research

AAPY American Association of Professors of Yiddish

AA & QMG Assistant Adjutant and Quartermaster General

aar after action report; against all risks; average annual rainfall

aar (AAR) antigen-antiglobulin reaction

Aar Aarhus; Australia antigen radioimmunoassay

AAR Aircraft Accident Record; Aircraft Accident Report; American Academy in Rome; Army Area Representative; Association of American Railroads; Australian Associated Resources; Automotive Affiliated Representatives

AARA Australian Association of Reprographic Arts

aa rating average-audience rating (percentage of tv-equipped homes viewing the average minute of a national telecast)

AARB Australian Road Research Board

AARC Ann Arbor Railroad Company; Association for the Advancement of Released Convicts; Australian Aeronautical Research Committee; Australian Applied Research Centre; Australian Automobile Racing Club

AARCO Afro-Asian Rural Construction Organisation

AARD American Academy of Restorative Dentistry

AARDCO Association of American Railroad Dining Car Officers

AARDS Australian Advertising Rate and Data Service

AARE Australian Association for Research in Education

AARF Australian Accounting Research Foundation

aarg *aargang* (Dano-Norwegian or Swedish—yearbook)

Aargau canton in northern Switzerland where its French name is Argovie

Aarh Aarhus

Aarhusium (Latin—Aarhus)— Danish port city also appearing as Arhisium, Arhusen, and Aarhusi

AARL Advanced Applications and Research Laboratory; Australian Academic and Research Libraries

aarp annual advance retainer pay

AARP American Association of Retired Persons

AARPS Air-Augmented Rocket-Propulsion System

AARR Ann Arbor Railroad

AARRC Army Aircraft Requirements Review Committee

AARRO Afro-Asian Rural Reconstruction Organization

AARS All-America Rose Selections (award); American Association of Railroad Superintendents; American Association of Railway Surgeons; Army Aircraft Repair Ship; Army Amateur Radio System

AART American Association for Rehabilitation Therapy; American Association of Retired Teachers

AARTA American Association of Railroad Ticket Agents

aarv aerial armored reconnaissance vehicle

AARWBA American Auto Racing Writers and Broadcasters Association

aas adjusted air speed; advanced antenna system; aortic arch syndrome

AAs Alcoholics Anonymous members; American Atheists; author's alterations

AAS Aberdeen Art Society; Academy of Applied Science; Aircraft Airworthiness Section; All-America Selections; American Amaryllis Society; American Antiquarian Society; American Astronautical Society; American Astronomical Society; Army Air Service; Army Attache System; Arnold Air Society; Association for Asian Studies; Australian Academy of Science; Australian Acoustic Society; Australian Air Services; Australian Art Society; Australian Association of Surgeons

A.A.S. Academiae Americanae Socius (Latin—Fellow of the

American Academy of Arts and Sciences)

AASA American Association of School Administrators; Associate of the Australian Society of Accountants

AASB Alabama Association of School Boards; American Association of Small Business

AASC Acupuncture Association of Southern California; Aerospace Applications Studies Committee (NATO); Allied Air Support Command; American Association of Specialized Colleges; Australian Accounting Standards Committee; Australian Army Service Corps

aascm awaiting action summary court martial

AASCO Association of American Seed Control Officials

AASCU American Association of State Colleges and Universities

aasd antiaircraft self-destroying

AASD American Association of Social Directories

AASDJ American Association of Schools and Departments of Journalism

AASE American Academy of Sanitary Engineers; American Association of Special Educators; Associated Australian Stock Exchanges; Association for Applied Solar Energy

AASEC American Association of Sex Educators and Counselors

AASECT American Association of Sex Educators, Counselors, and Therapists

AASF Advanced Air Striking Force

AASFE American Association of Sunday and Feature Editors

AASG Association of American State Geologists

AAS & GP American Association of Soap and Glycerin Producers

AASH American Association for the Study of the Headache

AASHO American Association of State Highway Officials

AASHTO American Association of State Highway and Transportation Officials

AASI Advertising Agency Service Interchange; American Academy for Scientific Interrogation; American Association for Scientific Interrogation

A'asia(n) Australasia(n)

aasir advanced atmospheric sounder and imaging radiometer

aasl antiaircraft searchlight

AASL American Antiquarian Society Library; American Association of School Librarians; American Association of State Librarians

A & ASL American & Australian Steamship Line

AASLH American Association for State and Local History

AASM Association of American Steel Manufacturers

AASMB Australian Association of Stud Merino Breeders

AASND American Association for the Study of Neoplastic Diseases

AASO Association of American Ship Owners

AASP American Association for Social Psychiatry

AASPA American Association of School Personnel Administrators

AASPB American Association of State Psychology Boards

AASPRC American Association of Sheriff's Posses and Riding Clubs

aasr airport and airways surveillance radar

AASR Abhazian Autonomous Soviet Socialist Republic; Adjarian Autonomous Soviet Socialist Republic

AASRC American Association of Small Research Companies

AASRI Arctic and Antarctic Scientific Research Institute

AASRM Ancient and Accepted Scottish Rite Masons

AASS Afro-American Students Society; American Association for Social Security

AASSP Arkansas Association of Secondary School Principals

AAST American Association for the Surgery of Trauma

AASTA Antiaircraft Station

AASTC Associate in Architecture—Sydney Technical College

AASTD Association for the Advancement of the Science and Technology of Documentation

AASU Afro-American Student Union

AASW Australian Association of Scientific Workers; Austra-

lian Association of Social Workers

AASWA American Association for the Study of World Affairs

AASWI American Aid Society for the West Indies

aat acute abdominal tympany; after acid treatment; auditory attending task

aat (AAT) alpha-1 antitrypsin

AAT Achievement Anxiety Test; Anglo-Australian Telescope (in NSW); Auditory Apperception Test; Australian Antarctic Territory

A-AT Anglo-Australian Telescope

AATA American Association of Teachers of Arabic; Anglo-American Tourist Association

AATB Advanced Amphibious Training Base

AATC Anti-Aircraft Training Center; Army Aviation Test Command

AATCC American Association of Textile Chemists and Colorists

AATCLC American Association of Teachers of Chinese Language and Culture

AATCO Army Air Traffic Coordinating Office

AATD Australian Association of Teachers of the Deaf

AATE American Association of Teachers of Esperanto; Association of Australian Teachers of English

AATEA American Association of Teacher Educators in Agriculture

AATEFL Australian Association for the Teaching of English as a Foreign Language

AATF American Association of Teachers of French

AATG American Association of Teachers of German

AATI American Association of Teachers of Italian

AATM American Academy of Tropical Medicine

AATOE American Association of Theatre Organ Enthusiasts

AATP American Academy of Tuberculosis Physicians

AATPA American Association of Traveling Passenger Agents

AATPS Australian Association of Temporary Personnel Services

AATRACEN Anti-Aircraft Training Center

AATRIS Army Air Traffic Reg-

ulation and Identification System

AATS American Academy of Teachers of Singing; American Association of Theological Schools; American Association for Thoracic Surgery

AATSEEL American Association of Teachers of Slavic and Eastern European Languages

AATT American Association for Textile Technology

AATTA Arab Association of Tourism and Travel Agents

AAT & TC Anti-Aircraft Training and Test Center

AATU Association of Air Transport Unions

AATUF All-African Trade Union Federation

AAU Administrative Area Unit; Al-Azhar University; Amateur Athletic Union; Associated Aviation Underwriters; Association of American Universities; Association of Atlantic Universities (Canada); Australian Athletics Union

AAUA Amateur Athletics Union of Australia; American Association of University Administrators

AAUBO Association of Atlantic University Business Officers (Canada)

AAUCG Americans Against Union Control of Government

AAUCS Australian-Asian Universities Cooperation Scheme

AAUN American Association for the United Nations; Australian Association for the United Nations

AAUP American Association of University Presses; American Association of University Professors

AAUQ Associate in Accountancy—University of Queensland

AAUTA Australian Association of University Teachers of Accounting

AAUTI American Association of University Teachers of Insurance

AAUUS Amateur Athletic Union of the U.S.

AAUW American Association of University Women

aav airborne assault vehicle

AAV Antiaircraft Volunteer

AAVA American Association of Veterinary Anatomists; Australian Automatic Vending

Association
AAVB American Association of Veterinary Bacteriologists
AAVC Australian Army Veterinary Corps
AAVCS Automatic Aircraft Vectoring Control System
aavd automatic alternate voice/ data
AAVIM American Associations for Vocational Instructional Materials
AAVMC Association of American Veterinary Medical Colleges
Aavn Army aviation
AAVN American Association of Veterinary Nutritionists
AAVP American Association of Veterinary Pathologists
AAVRO American Association of Vital Records and Organizations
AAVS American Anti-Vivisection Society
AAVSO American Association of Variable Star Observers
AAW Advertising Association of the West; American Atheist Women; Anti-Air Warfare
AAWA American Automatic Weapons Association
AAWB American Association of Workers for the Blind
AAWC Australian Advisory War Council
AAWD Association of American Women Dentists
AAWEXINPT Antiair Warfare Exercises in Port
AAWg Aeromedical Airlift Wing (USAF)
AAWM American Association of Waterbed Manufacturers
AAWO Afro-Asian Workers' Organization
AAWPI Association of American Wood Pulp Importers
AAWS American Association of Wardens and Superintendents
AAWU Amateur Athletic Western Union
AAXICO American Air Export and Import Company
AAYM American Association of Youth Museums
AAZK American Association of Zoo Keepers
AAZM Aqueducto y Alcantarillados de la Zona Metropolitana (Spanish—Aqueducts and Watercourses of the Metropolitan Area)
AAZPA American Association of Zoological Parks and Aquariums

ab abnormal; abortion; about; abscess; adapter booster; afterburner; airbrake; alcian blue; ambient brine; anchor bolt; antibody; asbestos body; asthmatic bronchitis; axiobuccal
a/b acid-base (ratio)
a/b (A/B) airborne
a & b applejack and benedictine; assault and battery
ab abril (Spanish—April); (Latin prefix—away from, off)
aB auf Bestellung (German—on order)
Ab abnormal; Abraham; alabamine
Ab Abade (Portuguese—Abbot) —also means fat man
AB able-bodied seaman; Accessories Bulletin; Aid to the Blind; Air Base; Arnold Bernstein (steamship line); Assembly Bill; Atlantic Beach
A-B Allen-Bradley; Ambrose Bierce; Anton Bruckner
A.B. *artium baccalureus* (Latin —Bachelor of Arts)
A/B Aid to the Blind; Airman Basic
AB Analecta Biblica
A/B Aktiebolag (Swedish—limited company)
AB-47 Agusta-Bell three-place utility helicopter.
AB-204 Agusta-Bell gunship twin-engine helicopter
AB-205 Agusta-Bell ten-place troop-transport helicopter
AB-206 Agusta Bell five-seat turbine-powered helicopter
aba antibacterial activity
ab-a abampere
ABA Aaron Burr Association; American Badminton Association; American Bakers Association; American Bandmasters Association; American Bankers Association; American Bar Association; American Bell Association; American Berkshire Association; American Booksellers Association; American Bowhunters Association; American Brazilian Association; American Buddhist Association; Annual Budget Authorization; Australian Badminton Association; Australian Bankers Association; Australian Booksellers Association; Australian Boomerang Association; Australian Bowhunters Association; Australian Bridge Association; Ayrshire Breeders Association

ABAA Antiquarian Booksellers Association of America
ab ab. ab absurdo (Latin—to the absurd)
abac a basic coursewriter
ABAC Abraham Baldwin Agricultural College
A Bachelor of Arts Phyllis Bentley's pseudonym
Abaco Great and Little Abaco islands in the Bahamas north of New Providence Island
abact abacterial
ABACUS Air Battle Analysis Center Utility System; Autonetics Business and Control United Systems
ABAD Air Battle Analysis Division
ab aet. ab aeterno (Latin—until eternity)
ABAG Association of Bay Area Governments (San Francisco)
A-bahn Autobahn (German—superhighway)
ABAI American Boiler and Affiliated Industries
ABAJ Antiquarian Booksellers Association of Japan
ABAJ American Bar Association Journal
ABAK Asociation di Biblioteka i Archivo di Korsow (Papiamento—Association of Libraries and Archives of Curaçao)
abamp absolute ampere (10 amperes)
aband abandoned
abandoned woman euphemistic nickname for a prostitute or whore
abandt abandonment
ABAO Asociación Bilbaina de Amigos de la Opera (Spanish —Bilbaoan Association of Friends of the Opera)
abap antibody against panel
ABAS American Board of Abdominal Surgeons; Australian Buying Advisory Service
abat abattoir
a batt a battuta (Italian—by the beat)—musical term
ABATU Advance Base Air Task Unit; Advance Base Aviation Training Unit
ABAUSA Amateur Basketball Association of the United States of America
abb ablating blunt body
abb abbassamento (Italian—abatement, decline, diminution, fall of temperature, lowering, subsiding); *abbonamento* (Italian—subscription); *abbuono* (Italian—allowance,

Abb   13   ABCM

bonus, discount)
Abb Abbess; Abbey; Abbot
Abb Abbildung (German—illustration)
Abb. abbas (Latin—abbot)
Ab of B Archbishop(ric) of Bremen
ABB Akron & Barberton Belt (railroad); Australian Barley Board
ABBA American Blind Bowling Association; American Board of Bio-Analysis; American Brahman Breeders Association; Australian Brahma Breeders Association
Abbamico Villa (Latin—Abbeville)—French town also appearing as Abbatis Villa
ABBB Association of Better Business Bureaus
Abbᵉ Abbaye (French—Abbey) —monastery
Abbé Sieyès Emmanuel Joseph Sieyès
ABBF Association of Bronze and Brass Founders
Abbild Abbildungen (German—illustrations)
ABBIM Association of Brass and Bronze Ingot Manufacturers
ABBMM Association of British Brush Machinery Manufacturers
A.B.B.O. Associate of the British Ballet Organisation
Abbot Vickers self-propelled fortress including 105mm gun, turret-mounted howitzer, and 7.62 machinegun
Abbotsford British Columbia's Matsqui Institution (for narcotic addicts) at Abbotsford; a town west of Wausau, Wisconsin
Abbotsford Sir Walter Scott's mansion on the Tweed near Melrose, Scotland
abbott nembutal sleeping tablet (nicknamed for its producer, Abbott Laboratories)
Abbot(t) Abbotson
Abbott and Costello Bud Abbott and Lou Costello
abbr abbreviate; abbreviated; abbreviation
ABBRA American Boat Builders and Repairers Association
abbrev abbreviatura (Italian—abbreviation)
abbrevia abbreviations
abbreviaz abbreviazione (Italian — abbreviation)
abbrevio abbreviomania(c) (al) (ly)

abbrev(s) abbreviation(s)
ABBS Australian Bibliography and Bibliographical Services
Abby Abigail
abc abecedarium (alphabet primer); advanced biomedical capsule (ABC); acid-balance control; aconite, belladonna, chloroform; alphabet; atomic, biological, chemical (ABC); alum, blood, charcoal; automatic bass compensation; automatic brightness control; axiobuccocervical
abc (ABC) advance-booking charter; alarms by carrier (panic-button device alerting fire and police stations)
AbC American-born Chinese
Ab of C Archbishop(ric) of Cologne
ABC Aberrant Behavior Center; A Better Chance (scholarship program for the poor); Abridged Building Classification; Advanced Booking Charters; Aerated Bread Company; Air Bridge to Canada; Alcohol Beverage Control; American Book (prices) Current; American Bowling Congress; American Brass Company; American, British, Canadian; American Broadcasting Company; American Business Conference; Animal Birth Control; Argentina, Brazil, Chile; Asahi Broadcasting Company; Asian Banking Council; Assisi Bird Campaign; Associated Bottlers Company; Atanasoff-Berry Computer; atomic, biological, chemical (warfare); Audit Bureau of Circulation; Australian Band Council; Australian Bankruptcy Cases; Australian Baseball Council; Australian Bowling Council; Australian Bridge Council; Australian Broadcasting Commission; Australian Broadcasting Corporation; automatic bandwidth control (computerese); automation of bibliography through computerization (computerese); Automotive Boosters Clubs
AB & C Atlanta, Birmingham and Coast (railroad)
ABC Academia Brasileira de Ciencias (Portuguese—Brazilian Academy of Sciences); Spain's most prestigious daily newspaper
ABC³ Airborne Battlefield Command and Control Center

ABCA American Business Communications Association; American-British-Canadian-Australian; Antique Bottle Collectors Association; Army Bureau of Current Affairs; Australian Bushmen's Carnival Association
ABCAL Associated British Cables (NZ)
ABC-ASP American-British-Canadian—Army Standardization Program
abcb air-blast circuit breaker
ABCB American Bottlers of Carbonated Beverages; Australian Broadcasting Control Board
ABCC Association of British Chambers of Commerce; Atomic Bomb Casualty Commission
ABCCC Airborne Battlefield Command and Control Center
ABC—Clio American Bibliographical Center—Clio Press (Santa Barbara, California)
ABCCTC Advanced Base Combat Communication Training Center
abcd above and beyond the call of duty; airway (opened), breathing (restored), circulation (restored), definitive (therapy); atomic, biological, chemical, and damage (control); awaiting bad conduct discharge
ABCD Accelerated Business Collection and Delivery (of mail); Action for Boston Community Development; Advanced Base Construction Depot; America, Britain, China, Dutch East Indies (ABCD Powers during World War II); American Society of Bookplate Collectors and Designers
ABCDCAL Alcoholic Beverage Control Department—California
ABCE Adult Basic and Continuing Education
ABC-fm Australian Broadcasting Commission—frequency modulation (system)
ABCI Australian Bureau of Criminal Intelligence
ABCL American Birth Control League
ABC Line Antwerp Bulk Carriers (container line)
ABCM Association for the Bedouin Culture Museum

ABCs of Opera *Aida, Boheme, Carmen*

ABC-tv Australian Broadcasting Commission—television

abd all but dissertation

Abe nickname for a $5-bill bearing Lincoln's portrait

ABECOR Associated Banks of Europe Corporation

abel air-breathing electric laser

Abel Abelard

ABES Association for Broadcast Engineering Standards

ABEU Australian Bank Employees Union

abf absolute bloody final (beverage)

ABF Australian Bridge Federation

ABFP American Board of Forensic Psychology

ABGC Australian Banana Growers Council

abi abstracted business information

ABIC Adaptive Behavior Inventory for Children

Abigail Van Buren Pauline Esther (Popo) Phillips, better known as Dear Abby

abi/inform abstracted business information/information needs

ABINZ Australian Banking Institute of New Zealand

ABIP Australian Books in Print

ABISA Association of Burglary Insurance Surveyors—Australia

ABJ Association of Broadcasting Journalists

able (Latin suffix—capable of)

ABLE Advocates for Border Law Enforcement

ABM Adventist Board of Missions; Australian Board of Missions (Anglican)

ABM *Asociación de Banqueros de México* (Spanish—Mexican Bankers Association)

ABMJ American Board of Missions to the Jews

ABMR Australian Board of Mineral Resources

ABM Treaty Anti-Ballistic Missile Treaty

ABO Admiralty Berthing Officer (UK)

ABOA Australian Bank Officials Association

Abolitionist Quaker Elias Hicks

abortus aborted fetus

abp absolute boiling point

ABPP American Board of Professional Psychology

ABQ Annapolis Brass Quintet

ABR Army Ballistic Research

ABRS Australian Biological Resources Study

ABS Association of Banks in Singapore; Australian Ballet Society; Australian Book Society; Australian Bureau of Statistics

ABSEL Association for Business Stimulation and Experiential Learning

ABSO Auxiliary Business Service Organization

ABS-PS Adaptive Behavior Scale—Public School (version)

ABSTI Advisory Board on Scientific and Technical Information (Canadian)

ABT American Board of Trade; Australian Broadcasting Tribunal

ABTA Australian-British Trade Association

ABU American Board of Urology

ABWA American Business Women's Association

ABWUA Amateur Boxing and Wrestling Union of Australia

ABY A.B. Byers (stock-exchange symbol)

ac absolute ceiling; accelerator; acetyl; acetyl-choline; acoustical(ly); adrenal cortex; aerodynamic center; air condition(ed); air conditioning; air conduction; air cool; air-cooled; alternating current; anodal closure; anticorrosive; antiphlogistic corticoid; arithmetic computation; asbestos cement; atriocarotid; auriculocarotid; auxiliary console; axiocervical; azimuth comparator

ac (AC) average cost

a-c alternating-current

a/c account; account current; air conditioning; aircraft

a & c addenda and corrigenda

ac (Latin prefix—to, toward)

a.c. *ante cibos* (Latin—before meals)

a/c *ao cuidado de* (Portuguese—in care of)

a C *avanti Cristo* (Italian—before Christ)

Ac actinium; altocumulus

AC Adelbert College; Adelphi College; Aden Colony; Administration of Correction (Puerto Rico); Adrian College; aerodynamic center (symbol); Air Canada; Alabama College; Al-

bion College; Albright College; Allegheny College; Alliance College; Alma College; alternating current; Alverno College; Amarillo College; Ambulance Corps; Amherst College; Anderson College; Andrew College; Annhurst College; anodal contraction or closure; Antioch College; Aquinas College; Arcadia College; Arithmetic Computation (test); Arkansas College; Armstrong College; Asbury College; Ashland College; Assumption College; Athens College; Athletic Club; Augusta College; Augustana College; Aurora College; Austin College; Australia Council; Australian Companion (Companion of the Order of Australia); Australian Corps; Averett College; Azusa College

A-C Allis-Chalmers

A/C Air Commodore; aircraft; Aviation Cadet

AC *Açāo Catolica* (Portuguese), *Acción Católica* (Spanish), *Action Catholique* (French), *Azione Cattolica* (Italian)—Catholic Action; *Atlanta Constitution*

A.C. *année courante* (French—current year); *Año Cristo* (Spanish—Year of Our Lord)—A.D.

A & C *Antony and Cleopatra*

AC-47 DC-3 Douglas 21-passenger transport also called C-47 Dakota or Skytrain

AC-119 Fairchild-Hiller armed gunship complete with Vulcan cannons and 7.2mm miniguns (C-119 Flying Boxcar conversion)

AC-130 Lockheed armed gunship similar to AC-119 but with more guns

aca adenocarcinoma; anterior cerebral artery; azimuth control amplifier

ac a acetic acid

Aca Acapulco (inhabitants—Acapulqueños)

ACA Acapulco, Mexico (airport); Aero Club of America; Aircraft Castings Association; Alberta College of Art; American Camping Association; American Canoe Association; American Carnivals Association; American Casting Association; American Cat Association; American Cemetery Association; American Chiropractic Association; American Civic Association; American College of Allergists; American College of Anesthesiologists; American College of Apothecaries; American Communications Association; American Composers Alliance; American Congregational Association; American Correctional Association; American Cryptogram Association; American Crystallographic Association; Americans for Constitutional Action; Anti-Corruption Agency (Singapore); Arms Control Association; Arts Council of America; Arts Council of Australia; Assembly Constitutional Amendment; Assocated Chiropodists of America; Association of Correctional Administrators

A.C.A. Associate of the Institute of Chartered Accountants (of England and Wales)

ACAA Agricultural Conservation and Adjustment Administration

ACAAE Australian Council on Awards in Advanced Education

ACAAI Air Cargo Agents Association of India

ACAB Air-Conditioning Advisory Bureau; Army Contract Adjustment Board

ACAC Allied Container Advisory Committee; Association of College Admission Counsellors; Australian Conciliation and Arbitration Commission; Australian Corporate Affairs Commission

ACACA Army Command and Administration Communication Agency

acad academic; academician; academy

Acad Acadia; Academy

ACAD American Conference of Academic Deans

Acad aper Academy of Motion Picture Arts and Sciences aperture (of sound films)

Acad B-A Académie des Beaux Arts (French—Academy of Fine Arts)

Academic Academic Press

Acad Fran Académie Française (French Academy)

Acadia Acadia National Park occupying Mount Desert Island, half of Isle au Haut, and Schoodic Point on the Maine

coast; old name for French-speaking Canada and Nova Scotia in the days of Longfellow's *Evangeline*

Acadia(n) Novia Scotia(n); native Louisianians of French origin are also called Acadians or Cajuns

Acad Ins B-L Académie des Inscriptions et Belles-Lettres (French—Academy of Inscriptions and Literature)

Acad mask Academy of Motion Picture Arts and Sciences mask (enclosing the aperture area of sound films)

Acad Med Academy of Medicine

Acad Mgmt Academy of Management

Acad Mus Academy of Music

Acad Pr Academic Press

Acad Pr Ark Academic Press of Arkansas

Acad Sci Académie des Sciences (French—Academy of Science); Academy of Science

Acad Sin Academia Sinica (Chinese Academy of Science)

Acad St Cec Academia di Santa Cecilia, Rome

Acad Therapy Academic Therapy Publications

Acad U Acadia University

ACAE American Council for the Arts in Education; Australian Commission on Advanced Education

AC & AE Association of Chemical and Allied Employees

acaf automatic circuit assurance feature

ACAF Amphibious Corps, Atlantic Fleet; Australian Citizen Air Force

ACAM Asian Centre for Agricultural Machinery; Australian Confederation of Apparel Manufacturers

ACAN Action Committee Against Narcotics; Army Command and Administrative Network

ACAnes American College of Anesthetists

a. cant. after cant frames

Acanth Acanthocephala

acanthite silver sulfide

Acap Acapulco

ACAP American Council on Alcohol Problems; Army Contract Appeals Panel

ACAPA American Concrete Agricultural Pipe Association

Acap gold Acapulco gold (high-grade golden-brown marijuana

of the type grown around the Mexican seaside resort of Acapulco)

a capp a cappella (Italian—in chapel style, without musical accompaniment)

Acapulco short form for Acapulco de Juárez (Mexico's leading seaside resort)

ACAR Australian Coal Association Research

ACARD Advisory Council for Applied Research and Development

ACAs Arms Control Associations

ACAS Aboriginal Children's Advancement Society; Advisory, Conciliation, and Arbitration Service; Airborne Collision Avoidance System; Association of Casualty Accounts and Statisticians

AC/AS Assistant Chief of Air Staff

ACAS Asociación Civil Amigos de la Salud (Spanish—Friends of Health Civil Association)

ACASP Australian Commonwealth Association of Simplified Practice

ACAST Advisory Committee on Applications of Science and Technology (UNESCO)

acata acatalectic(al)

acb air circuit breaker; asbestos cement board

acb (ACB) aortocoronary saphenous vein bypass; arterialized capillary blood

ACB Advertising Checking Bureau; Airman Classification Battery; Army Classification Battery; Association Canadienne des Bibliothèques (Canadian Library Association); Association of Customers' Brokers; Association of the Customs Bar; Australian Cricket Board

ACB Association Canadienne des Bibliothèques (French—Canadian Library Association)

ACBA Academy of Comic Book Artists

ACB of A Associated Credit Bureaus of America

ACBB American Council for Better Broadcasts

ACBCC Australia-China Business Cooperation Committee

ACBFC Academy of Comic-Book Fans and Collectors

ACBL American Commercial Barge Line; American Contract Bridge League; Australian Contract Bridge League

acbm atomic cesium beam maser

ACBM Associated Corset and Brassiere Manufacturers; Aviation Chief Boatswain's Mate

ACBNZ Associated Credit Bureau of New Zealand

ACBO Association of Chief Business Officials

ACBs Associated Credit Bureaus

ACBS Accrediting Commission for Business Schools

ACBWS Automatic Chemical Biological Warning System

acc accept (computerese); accident(al) (ly); accommodate(d); accommodation; according; account(ed); accounting; accusative; altocumulus castellatus (clouds); alveolar cell carcinoma; anodal closing contraction; astronomical great circle course (ACC); automatic chroma circuit (tv)

acc (ACC) accumulator

Acc Lucius Accius (Roman poet)

ACC Abilene Christian College; Academy of Canadian Cinema; Accra, Ghana (airport); accumulator [flow chart (computerese)]; Adirondack Community College; Administrative Committee on Coordination; Air Center Commander; Air Control Center; Air Coordinating Committee; Allied Control Commission; Allied Control Council; American College of Cardiology; American Concert Choir; American Conference of Cantors; American-Chilean Council; American Craftsmen's Council; Anglican Consultative Council; Army Chemical Center; Army Cooperation Command; Association of Choral Conductors; Auburn Community College; Australian Chamber of Commerce; Australian Chiropody Council; Australian Computer Conference; Australian Croquet Council

A-C-C Appleton-Century-Crofts

ACCA Aeronautical Chamber of Commerce of America; American Clinical and Climatological Association; American College of Clinic Administrators; American Correctional Chaplains Association;

American Cotton Cooperative Association; Art Collectors Club of America; Associated Chambers of Commerce of Australia

ACCAP Autocoder-to-Cobol Conversion Aid Program

ACCAs American Correctional Chaplains Association members

acc & aud accountant and auditor

ACCC Ad Hoc Committee for Competitive Communications; Advisory Council on College Chemistry; Alternate Command and Control Center; Association of Canadian Community Colleges; Association of Community Cancer Centers

ACCCA Association of California Community College Administrators

ACCCE Association of Consulting Chemists and Chemical Engineers

ACCCF American Concert Choir and Choral Foundation

Acc Chem Res Accounts of Chemical Research

ACCCI Associated Chinese Chambers of Commerce and Industry (Singapore); Australia-China Chamber of Commerce and Industry

AC & CCI American Coke and Coal Chemicals Institute

accd accelerated construction completion date

acc dec acceptable deception(s) —half truth(s) acceptable only by people willing to accept half truths

acce acceptance

ACCE American Chamber of Commerce Executives; American Council for Construction Education

accel accelerate; accelerate(d); accelerating; acceleration

accel accelerando (Italian—accelerating)

ACCELS Automated-Circuit Card-Etching Layout System

accepon acceptation (French—acceptance)

access accessory

ACCESS American College of Cardiology Extended Study Services; Architects Central Constructional Engineering Surveying Service; Association of Community Colleges for Excellence in Systems and Services; Automated Catalog

of Computer Equipment and Software Systems (USA); Automatic Computer-Controlled Electronic Scanning System

A.C.C.E.S.S. A Cooperative Community Educational School System

ACCF American Committee for Cultural Freedom; American Council for Capital Formation; Association of Community College Facilities

ACCFA Agricultural Credit Cooperative Finance Administration

AcCh acetylcholine

ACCH Association for the Care of Children in Hospitals

ACCHAN Allied Command Channel (NATO)

acci accidental injury

ACCI American Cottage Cheese Institute

accid accident(al)

ACCION Americans for Community Cooperation in Other Nations

accis accismus

accl anodal closure clonus

ACCL American Council of Commercial Laboratories

ACCM American College of Clinic Managers

ACCM P-H Appleton-Century-Crofts Medical (imprint of) Prentice-Hall

ACCN Associated Court and Commercial Newspapers

acco accompagnamento (Italian —accompaniment)

ACCO Associate of the Canadian College of Organists; Association of Child Care Officers

AcCoA acetyl coenzyme A

accom accommodation

accommodation houses euphemistic British nickname for whorehouses

accomp accomplish

ACCOMP Academic Computer Group

ACCOR Australian Coal Corporation

ACCORD Action Coalition to Create Opportunities for Retirement with Dignity

ACCORDS Acoustic Correlation and Detection System

ACCP American College of Chest Physicians

ACCP Asociación de Camaras de Comercio del Perú (Spanish —Association of Chambers of Commerce of Peru)

ACCR American Council on Chiropractic Roentgenogra-

phy
ACCRA Abortion and Contraception Counselling and Research Association; American Chamber of Commerce Researchers Association; Australian Chart and Code for Rural Accounting; Australian Committee for Coding Rural Accounts
accrd int accrued interest
accred accredited
ACCS Automated Calibration Control System
A.C.C.S. Associate of the Chartered Corporation of Secretaries
acct account; accountant; accounting
ACCT Association of Community College Trustees
acctd accented
ACCTU All-Union Central Council of Trade Unions (USSR)
accu automatic combustion-control unmanned
a-c cu alternating-current control unit
accum accumulate
accur accuratissime (Latin—most accurately)
accus accusative
accv (ACCV) armored cavalry cannon vehicle
accw alternating current continuous wave
accy accessory
acd absolute cardiac dullness; accord; accordion; acid-citrate-dextrose; active duty commitment; adopted child; advance delivery of correspondence; advice of duration and charges; anodal duration contraction; average daily census; axiodistocervical
acd (ACD) acid citrate dextrose
ACD Administrative Commitment Document, Allied Chemical Corporation (stock exchange symbol); American Choral Directors; American College of Dentists; Australian College of Dentistry; Australian College of Dermatologists
ACD American College Dictionary
ACDA American Choral Directors Association; Arms Control and Disarmament Agency; Asian Centre for Development Administration; Aviation Combat Development Agency

a-c/d-c alternating current/direct current; underground slang—bisexual
ACDC Australian Counter-Disaster College
ACDCM Archbishop of Canterbury's Diploma in Church Music
a-c/d-c's bisexuals
ACDE American Council for Drug Education
ACDFA American College Dance Festival Association
acdl asynchronous circuit-design language
ACDM Association of Chairmen of Departments of Mechanics
ACDMS Automated Control of Document Management System
A Cdre Air Commodore
ACDS Advanced Combat Direction System; Australian College of Dental Surgeons
acdt accident
A Cdt Air Commandant
acdu active duty
acdutra active duty for training
ACDUTRA Active Duty Reserve Army
ace. acceptance checkout equipment; acetic; adrenal cortical extract; aerospace control environment; air crash equipment; alcohol-chloroform-ether (anesthetic mixture); attitude control electronics; automatic checkout equipment; automatic circuit exchange
ace. (ACE) angiotensin converting enzyme
ACE African Container Express; Allied Command, Europe; American Cinema Editors; American Conservatory Theatre; American Council on Education; American Hard Rubber Company (trademark); Army Corps of Engineers; Association for Community Education; Australian College of Education; Aviation Construction Engineers
ACEA Air Line Communication Employees Association; Association of Consulting Engineers—Australia
ACEAA Advisory Committee on Electrical Appliances and Accessories
acearts airborne countermeasures environment and radar target simulator
ACEB Association Canadienne des Ecoles Bibliothecaires

(French—Canadian Association of Library Schools)
Ace Bks Ace Books
ACEC Alcoholism Counseling and Education Center; American Consulting Engineers Council; Army Communications and Electronic Command; Army Communications and Electronic Command (USA)
ACEC Ateliers de Constructions Electriques de Charleroi (French—Electrical Construction Workshops of Charleroi) —in Belgium
A.C.Ed. Associate in Commercial Education
ACED Advanced Communications Equipment Depot
ACEF Aboriginal Child Education Fund(ing); Aboriginal Children's Education Fund; Asian Cultural Exchange Foundation; Association of Commodity Exchange Firms; Australian Council of Employers Federations
a-c-e-g (musical mnemonic all cows eat grass)—bass clef note names of the four spaces (a-c-c-g)
ACEI Association of Consulting Engineers of Ireland; Association for Childhood Education International
ACEID Asian Centre of Educational Innovation for Development
ACEJ American Council on Education for Journalism
ACEL Air Crew Equipment Laboratory
ACELF Association Canadienne des Educateurs de Langue Française (Canadian Association of French Language Teachers)
ACEM Aviation Chief Electrician's Mate
a cemb a cembalo (Italian—by the harpsichord)
ACEN Assembly of Captive European Nations
ACENET Allied Command Europe Communications Network (NATO)
ACENZ Association of Consultant Engineers of New Zealand
ACEORP Automotive and Construction Equipment Overhaul and Repair Plant
ACEP American College of Emergency Physicians; American Council for Emigrés in the

Professions

ACEPD Automotive and Construction Equipment Parts Depot

ACEQ Association of Consulting Engineers of Québec

ACER Australian Council for Educational Research

Acerbic American Critic *American Mercury's* HL Mencken in the 1920s and 1930s; *American Spectator's* R Emmett Tyrell, Jr in the 1970s and 1980s

ACERP Advanced Communications-Electronics Requirements Plan

aces automatic control evaluation simulator

ACES Alternative Consumer Energy Society; Americans for the Competitive Enterprise System; Area Cooperative Educational Service; Association for Counselor Education and Supervision; Australian Council for Educational Standards

ACESA Arizona Council of Engineering and Scientific Associations; Australian Commonwealth Engineering Standards Association; Australian Computer Equipment Suppliers Association

ace-s/c acceptance checkout equipment—spacecraft

ACESIA American Council for Elementary School Industrial Arts

acet acetone

ACET Advisory Committee on Electronics and Telecommunications; Australian Council for Education through Technology

ACETA Australian Commercial and Economics Teachers Association

ACE Test American Council on Education Test

acetl acetylene

acetyl-co A acetyl-coenzyme A

ACEUR Allied Command, Europe

ACEWR American Committee for European Worker's Relief

acf accessory clinical findings

acf (ACF) air-combat fighter (aircraft)

ACF Alternate Communications Facility; American Car & Foundry; American Checker Federation; American Chess Foundation; American Choral Foundation; American Culinary Federation; Anglican Charismatic Fellowship; Anti-Crime Foundation; Association of Consulting Foresters; Australian Canoe Federation; Australian Chess Federation; Australian Conservation Federation

ACF *Académie Canadienne Française* (French-Canadian Academy); *Automobile-Club de France* (Automobile Club of France)

ACFA American Cat Fanciers Association; Association of Commercial Finance Attorneys

ACFAS *Association Canadienne-Française pour l'Avancement des Sciences* (French—Canadian Association for the Advancement of Science)

ACFB Australian Canned Fruits Board

ACFC Aviation Chief Fire Controlman

ACFEA Air Carrier Flight Engineers Association

ACFEL Arctic Construction and Frost Effects Laboratory (Greenland)

ACFES Association of Canadian Faculties of Environmental Studies

acfg automatic continuous function operation

ACFHE Association of Colleges for Further and Higher Education

ACFL Atlantic Coast Football League

ACFM Association of Canadian Fire Marshals

ACFN American Committee for Flags of Necessity

ACFO American College of Foot Orthopedics

ACFOD Asian Cultural Forum for Development (Thailand)

ACFP Advisory Commission on Federal Pay

ACFR Advisory Committee of the Federal Register; Advisory Council on Federal Reports; American College of Foot Roentgenologists

ACFS American College of Foot Surgeons

ACFSA American Correctional Food Service Association

acft aircraft

ac ft acre feet; acre foot

ACFT Aircraft Flying Training

acftc aircraft carrier

ACFTU All China Federation of Trade Unions (PRC)

acg automatic caution guard; automatic control gear

acg (ACG) apex cardiogram

ac-g accelerator globulin

ACG Airborne Coordinating Group; Air Cargo Express (symbol); Airline Carriers of Goods; American College of Gastroenterology; American Council on Germany; Association for Corporate Growth

ACG *An Comunn Gaidhealach* (The Gaelic Society)—also called the Highland Society

ACGA American Cranberry Growers' Association; Australian Cane Growers Association; Australian Citrus Growers Association

ACGB Arts Council of Great Britain

ACGBI Automobile Club of Great Britain and Ireland

ACGC Australian Cane Growers Council

ACGD Association for Corporate Growth and Diversification

ACGF American Child Guidance Foundation

ACGFC Associate of the City and Guilds Finsbury College

ACGI Associate of the City and Guilds Institute

ACGIH American Conference of Governmental Industrial Hygienists

ACGLA Alcoholism Council of Greater Los Angeles

ACGM Aircraft Carriers General Memorandum

ACGP Army Career Group; Australian College of General Practitioners

ACGPOMS American College of General Practitioners in Osteopathic Medicine and Surgery

ACGS Aerial Cartographic and Geodetic Squadron; American Council on German Studies

ACGSq Aerial Cartographic and Geodetic Squadron (USAF)

ach acetylcholine (Ach); actual obtained achievement; arm, chest, height

ach (Ach) (ACH) acetylcholine; adrenal cortical hormone

ach (ACH) automated clearing house

ACh acetylcholine

ACH Association for Computers and the Humanities; Australian Camp Hospital

ACHA American Catholic Historical Association; American

College Health Association; American College of Hospital Administrators

AC & HBR Algoma Central and Hudson Bay Railway

ache. acetylcholinesterase

ACHE Alabama Commission on Higher Education

achiev achievement

ach index arm (girth), chest (depth), hip (width) index (of nutrition)

Achmed Abdullah Alexander Nicholaievitch Romanov

ACHNHP Appomattox Court House National Historical Park

ACHPER Australian Council for Health, Physical Education, and Recreation

achr acetylcholine receptor

ACHR American Council of Human Rights

achrom achromatism

A Ch S Associate of the Society of Chiropodists

ACHS Association of College Honor Societies

ACHSA American Correctional Health Services Association

ACHTR Advisory Committee for Humid Tropics Research (UNESCO)

achvit achievement

aci airborne-controlled interception; automatic car identification

aci (ACI) adult correctional institution; anticlonus index

aci *assure contre l'incendie* (French—insured against fire)

ACI Air Cargo Incorporated; Air Combat Information; Air Combat Intelligence; Alliance Coopérative Internationale (International Cooperative Alliance); Alloy Casting Institute; American Carpet Institute; American Concrete Institute; American Cryogenics Incorporated; Associated Colleges of Indiana; Australian Consolidated Industries

ACI *Association Cartographique Internationale* (French—International Cartographic Association); *Azione Cattolica Italiana* (Italian Catholic Action)

acia asynchronous communications interface adapter

ACIA Associate of the Catering Institute of Australia; Associated Cooperage Industries of America

ACIAA Australian Commercial and Industrial Artists' Asso-

ciation

ACIAS American Council of Industrial Arts Supervisors

ACIASAO American Council of Industrial Arts State Association Officers

ACIATE American Council of Industrial Arts Teacher Education

ACIB Associate of the Corporation of Insurance Brokers

acic acicular

ACIC Aeronautical Chart and Information Center; Allied Captured Intelligence Center; Australian Chemical Industry Council; Auxiliary Combat Information Center

ACICU Arkansas Council of Independent Colleges and Universities

acid acidosis; acidulated drop; hallucinogenic drug such as LSD-25

acid phos acid phosphatase

acid p'tase acid phosphatase

ACIF All Canada Insurance Federation

ACIGS Assistant Chief of the Imperial General Staff

ACII Associate of the Chartered Insurance Institute

ACIID A Critical Insight Into Israel's Dilemmas

ACIL American Council of Independent Laboratories

acim axis crossing interval meter

ACIM American Committee on Italian Migration

ACIMS Aircraft Component Management System

ACIO Air Combat Intelligence Office(r)

acip aviation career incentive pay

ACIP Advisory Committee on Immunization Practices

ACIPCO American Cast Iron Pipe Company

ACIR Advisory Committee on Intergovernmental Relations; Automotive Crash Injury Research

AC/IREF American Chapter—International Real Estate Federation

ACIRL Australian Coal Industries Research Laboratories

ACIS American Committee for Irish Studies

A.C.I.S. Associate of the Chartered Institute of Secretaries

acit air-cannon impact tester

ACIV Associate of the Commonwealth Institute of Val-

uers

ACIWLP American Committee for International Wild Life Protection

ACJ American Council for Judaism

A.C.J. Associate in Criminal Justice

ACJA American Criminal Justice Association

ACJC Assembly Criminal Justice Committee

ACJHSIS Arkansas Criminal Justice Highway Safety Information System; Arkansas Criminal Justice/Highway Safety Information System

ACJP Airways Corporations Joint Pensions

ACJS Academy of Criminal Justice Sciences

ack acknowledge; acknowledgment

ACK accidentally killed; acknowledge [character (computerese)]; Armstrong Cork (stock exchange symbol)

ack-ack antiaircraft

Ack-Ack Aluminum Company of America (stock exchange nickname)

ackt acknowledgment

acl air-cushion landing; allowable cabin load

aCl aspiryl chloride

ACL Adjective Check List; Aeronautical Computers Laboratory (USN); American Classical League; Association of Cinema Laboratories; Association for Computational Linguistics; Atlantic Coast Line (railroad); Atlantic Container Line; Audit Command Language; Aviation Circular Letter

ACL *Automobile Club de Luxembourg* (Automobile Club of the Grand Duchy of Luxembourg)

ACLA American Comparative Literature Association; American Cotton Linter Association; Anti-Communist League of America; Australasian Communications Law Association

ACLAM American College of Laboratory Animal Medicine

AClant Allied Command, Atlantic

ACLC Air Cadet League of Canada; Assessment of Children's Language Comprehension

acld aircooled

ACLD Association for Children

with Learning Disabilities
aclg air-cushion landing gear
ACLI American Council of Life Insurance
ACLICS Airborne Communications Location, Identification, and Collection System
ACLM American College of Legal Medicine
ACLO Association of Cooperative Library Organizations
ACLP Association of Contact Lens Practitioners
ACLR American Criminal Law Review
acls automatic carrier landing system
ACLS American Council of Learned Societies; Automatic Carrier Landing System
ACLU American Civil Liberties Union; American College of Life Underwriters; Atlantic Container Line Unit
aclv accrued leave
acm active countermeasure(s); anatomy-covering material; anatomy-covering memo; asbestos-covered metal
acm (ACM) advanced cruise missile
a-c-m albumin-calcium-magnesium
ACM Air Chief Marshal; Air Commerce Manual; Air Court-Martial; American Campaign Medal; American College of Musicians; Associated Colleges of the Midwest; Association for Computing Machinery; Australian Carpet Manufacturers; Australian Consolidated Minerals; auxiliary mine layer (3-letter symbol); Aviation Chief Metalsmith
ACM Automobile Club de Monaco (French—Automobile Club of Monaco)
ACMA Acidproof Cement Manufacturers Association; Air Carrier Mechanics Association; Alumina Ceramic Manufacturers Association; American Certified Morticians Associations; American Circus Memorial Association; American Comedy Museum Association; American Cutlery Manufacturers Association; Associated Chambers of Manufacturers of Australia
acme. attitude control and maneuvering electronics
ACME Adult Community Movement for Equality; Advi-

sory Council on Medical Education; Association of Consulting Management Engineers; Australian Contemporary Music Ensemble
ACMET Advisory Council on Middle East Trade
ACMF Air Corps Medical Forces; Allied Central Mediterranean Forces; American Corn Millers' Federation; Australian Commonwealth Military Forces
ACMI American Cotton Manufacturers Institute; American Cystoscope Makers, Incorporated
ACML Association of Canadian Map Libraries
ACMM Aviation Chief Machinist's Mate
A.C.M.M. Associate of the Conservatorium of Music—Melbourne
acmp accompany
ACMP Amateur Chamber Music Players; Assistant Commissioner of the Metropolitan Police
ACMRR Advisory Committee on Marine Resources Research (FAO)
acmru audio commercial-message repeating unit
ACMS Advanced Configuration Management System; Army Command Management System; Australian Clay Minerals Society
ACMT American College of Medical Technologists
ACMWA Amon Carter Museum of Western Art (Fort Worth)
acn activities control number; acute conditioned necrosis (ACN); all concerned notified (ACN); assignment control number (ACN); automatic celestial navigation (ACN)
ACN American Chain & Cable (stock exchange symbol); American College of Neuropsychiatrists; American Council on NATO; Authorized Code Number
A.C.N. Ante Christum Natum (Latin—before the birth of Christ)
ACNA Advisory Council on Naval Affairs; Arctic Institute of North America
ACNB Australian Commonwealth Naval Board
acne acne vulgaris (medical term for pimples)

ACNE Action Committee for Narcotics Education; Alaskans Concerned for Neglected Environments
ACNHA American College of Nursing Home Administrators
ACNIL Azienda Comunale Navigazione Interna (Italian —City and Lagoon Rapid Transit Shipping Company)
ACNM American College of Nurse Midwifery
ACNO Assistant Chief of Naval Operations
ACNOT Assistant Chief of Naval Operations—Transportation
ACNS American Council for Nationalities Service; Associated Correspondents News Service
ACNY Advertising Club of New York
ACNYC Art Commission of New York City
aco anodal closing odor
a co a cargo (Spanish—against)
Aco Michel Accault (La Salle's lieutenant)
ACO Administrative Contracting Officer; Air Cargo (Leopoldville—Republic of the Congo); American Academy of Optometry; Australian College of Ophthalmologists; Australian College of Organists
ACOA Administrative and Clerical Officers Association
ACOC Air Command Operations Center (NATO)
ACOCA Army Communication Operations Center Agency
acodac acoustic data capsule
ACODS Army Container-Oriented Distribution System (USA)
ACOFO American College of Foot Orthopedists
ACOFS Australian Council of Film Societies
acog (ACOG) aircraft on ground
ACOG American College of Obstetricians and Gynecologists
ACOHA American College of Osteopathic Hospital Administrators
ACOI American College of Osteopathic Internists
acom automatic coding machine
ACOM Aviation Chief Ordnanceman
A.Comm. Associate in Commerce

A.Comm.A. Associate of the Society of Commercial Accountants

ACOMPLIS A Computerized London Information Service (GLC)

ACOMR Advisory Committee on Oceanic Meteorological Research (UN)

Acon Aconcagua (South America's highest mountain in the Andes where it rises in Argentina and towers over Valparaiso, Chile)

ACOOG American College of Osteopathic Obstetricians and Gynecologists

ACOP American College of Osteopathic Pediatricians; Association of Chief Officers of Police (England and Wales)

ACOPS Advisory Committee on Oil Pollution of the Sea

ACOR Auditory Cognition of Relationships

ACORD Advisory Council on Research and Development

ACORDE A Consortium on Restorative Dentistry Education

Açores (Portuguese—Azores)

acorn. acronym-oriented nut

ACORN Association of Community Organizations for Reform Now; Associative Content Retrieval Network

ACOS American College of Osteopathic Surgeons

ACOSH Appalachian Center for Occupational Safety and Health; Australian Council on Smoking and Health

acou (Latin prefix—hear)

acous acoustics

acous coup acoustic coupler (device allowing other electronic devices to listen to or make other sounds transmitted by an ordinary telephone)

acousid acoustic seismic intrusion detector

acoustint acoustical intelligence

acp acetyl-carrier protein (ACP); acid phosphatase; anodal closing picture; aspirin, caffeine, phenacetin; auxiliary control panel; azimuth change pulse

a-c-p aspirin-caffein-phenacetin

a & cp anchors and chains proved

aCp (ACP) automatic Colt pistol

ACP Academy for Contemporary (Criminal) Problems; Agricultural Conservation Program; Air Control Point; Airline Carriers of Passengers;

Allied Communications Publications; American College of Pharmacists; American College of Physicians; Anti-Comintern Pact; Area Characteristic Plan(ning); Associated Collegiate Press; Association of Clinical Pathologists; Association of Correctional Psychologists; Australian Conservative Party; Australian Consolidated Press

ACP Automóvel Clube de Portugal (Automobile Club of Portugal)

ACPA Affiliated Chiropodists-Podiatrists of America; American Capon Producers Association; American Cleft Palate Association; American College Personnel Association; American Concrete Paving Association; American Concrete Pipe Association; Association of Computer Professionals Australia; Association of Computer Programmers and Analysts; Australasian Corporation of Public Accountants; Australian Clay Products Association

A-CPA Asbestos-Cement Products Association

ACPAE Association of Certified Public Accounts Examiners

a/c pay accounts payable

ACPC American College of Probate Counsel; American Council of Parent Cooperatives

ACPCACP Atlantic, Caribbean, and Pacific Countries Association of Canadian Publishers

ACPD Anti-trust and Consumer Protection Division; Army Control Program Directive

ACPE American Council on Pharmaceutical Education; Association for Continuing Professional Education; Australian College of Physical Education

ACPF Amphibious Corps, Pacific Fleet

ACPFB American Committee for Protection of Foreign Born

ACPIC American Council for Private International Communications

acpm attitude-control propulsion motor(s)

ACPM American College of Preventive Medicine; American Congress for Preventive Medicine

ACPMR American Congress of Physical Medicine and Rehabilitation

acpp (ACPP) adrenocorticopolypeptide

acpr acoustical paper

ACPRA American College Public Relations Association

ACPs Area Concept Papers

ACPS American Coalition of Patriotic Societies; Arab Company for Petroleum Services (OPEC)

ACPSAHMWA American Commission for the Protection and Salvage of Artistic and Historical Monuments in War Areas

acpt accept

ACPT Arizona Congress of Parents and Teachers

ACPTA Australian Commonwealth Post and Telegraph Association

acpu auxiliary computer power unit

acq acquire; acquittal

ACQ Australian Church Quarterly

Acq Libr Acquisition(s) Librarian

ACQT Aviation Cadet Qualifying Test

acquis acquisition(s)

acr abandon call and retry; acrylic; advanced capabilities radar; aerial combat reconnaissance; airfield-controlled radar; anti-constipation regimen

ACR Abstracts of Classified Reports; Advisory Commission on the Realm; Aircraft Control Room; Allied Commission on Reparations; American Academy in Rome; American College of Radiology; Area Characterization Report

AC & R American Cable and Radio (Corp)

ACR American Criminal Review

ACRA American Collegiate Retailing Association; Association of Company Registration Agents

ACRB Aero-Club Royal de Belgique (Royal Belgian Aero Club); Army Council of Review Boards

ACRC Air Compressor Research Council

acrd accrued

ACRD Australian Council for Rehabilitation of the Disabled

ACRDC Australian Code of Residential Design and Construction

ACRE Automatic Call-Recording Equipment; Automatic Checkout and Readiness Equipment

a/c rec accounts receivable

ACREC American College of Real Estate Consultants

acre ft acre foot

ACRES Airborne Communication Relay Station

ACRFAET Aircraft Crash Rescue Field Assistance and Evaluation Team (USAF)

acrg acreage

ACRI Air Conditioning and Refrigeration Institute; American Cocoa Research Institute

ACRiLIS Australian Centre for Research in Library and Information Science (Riverina College of Advanced Education)

ACRIM Association for Correctional Research and Information Management

ACRL Association of College and Research Libraries

ACRM Aviation Chief Radioman

acro acrobat(ic); acrophobe; acrophobia

acrol acrolect(ic) (al) (ly)

acron acronym

acronym a contrived reduction of names yielding mnemonics (jocular interpretation of the term defined on page xi)

ACRONYM Allied Citizens Representing Other New York Minorities

Acronym Islands Indonesia, where politicians appear to delight in creating acronyms covering almost every occasion, organization, and situation

acronymiz acronymization; acronymizing; acronymizor(s)

ACRONYMS Acceptable Contractions of Randomly Organized Names Yielding Meritorious Spontaniety

Acropolis Acropolis Hill (topmost Athens where it contains the Erectheum with its caryatid-supported porch, the Parthenon, the Temple of Nike, the Acropolis Museum)

Acropolis of America New York City's Morningside Heights—site of Columbia University

across acrostic

ACRR American Council on Race Relations

ACRS Advisory Committee on Reactor Safeguards

ACRT Aviation Chief Radio Technician

acrw aircrew

ACRW American Council of Railroad Women

ACRY Australian Council of Rural Youth

acs alternating current synchronous; anodal closing sound; autograph card signed

acs (ACS) antireticular cytotoxic serum; attitude-control system

a-c s (ACS) alternating-current synthesizer

Ac of S Academy of Sciences (USSR); Assistant Chief of Staff

ACS Advanced Communications System; Airline Charter Service; Alaskan Communications System; American Camellia Society; American Cancer Society; American Carnation Society; American Ceramic Society; American Chemical Society; American College of Surgeons; American Colonization Society; American Crystal Sugar (company); Armament Control System; Assistant Chief of Staff; Associated Counseling Services; Association of Clinical Scientists; Australian Cancer Society; Australian Ceramic Society; Australian Chamber of Shipping; Australian Cinematographers Society; Australian Computer Society; Automatic Control System

AC/S Assistant Chief of Staff

A.C.S. Associate in Commercial Science

ACS Automobile Club de Suisse (French—Automobile Club of Switzerland)

ACSA Allied Communications Security Agency (NATO); American Cotton Shippers Association; Association of California School Administrators; Association of Collegiate Schools of Architecture; Australian Corps of Signals Association

ACSB Australian Commonwealth Shipping Board

acsc automated contingency support capability

ACSC Air Carrier Service Corporation; Air Command and Staff College; American Council on Schools and Colleges; Association of Casualty and Surety Companies; Australian Coastal Shipping Commission

A-C Scale Anti-Caucasian Scale (measuring negative attitudes towards white persons)

ACSCP Association of California State College Professors

ACS/DCI American Chemical Society/Division of Chemical Information

ACSDO Air Carrier Safety District Office(r)

ACSE Association of Consulting Structural Engineers

ACSEA Air Command—Southeast Asia; Allied Command South-East Asia

ACSEF Australian Coal and Shale Employees Federation

acsf artificial cerebrospinal fluid

ACSF Attack Carrier Striking Force

a-c sg alternating-current signal generator

ACSI Assistant Chief of Staff for Intelligence

ACSIL Admiralty Centre for Scientific Information and Liaison (United Kingdom)

ACSI-MATIC Assistant Chief of Staff—Intelligence (automatic processing system for large scale intelligence information)

ACSL Assistant Cub Scout Leader

acsm acoustic (warfare) support measure(s)

ACSM American Congress of Surveying and Mapping

ACSMA American Cloak and Suit Manufacturers Association

ACSN Association of Collegiate Schools of Nursing

ACSO Australian Council of School Organisations

ACSOC Acoustical Society of America

ACSP Advisory Council on Scientific Policy (United Kingdom); Association of Collegiate Schools of Planning

ACSPA Australian Council of Salaried and Professional Associations

A/cs Pay Accounts Payable

acsr aluminum cable, steel reinforced

A/cs Rec Accounts Receivable

acss (ACSS) analog computer subsystem; automated color-separation system (ACSS)

ACSS Air Command and Staff School; American Cheviot Sheep Society; Army Chief of Support Services

ACSSAVO Association of Chief State School Audio-Visual Officers

ACSSN Association of Colleges and Secondary Schools for Negroes

ACSSO Australian Council of State School Organisations

ACSSRB Administrative Center of Social Security for Rhine Boatmen

acst acoustic; acoustical; acoustics

ACST Army Clerical Speed Test; Australian College of Speech Therapists

acst plas acoustical plaster

acst t acoustical tile

ACSW Academy of Certified Social Workers

acsyn aircraft synthesis

acsys accounting computer system software

act acting; action; activated coagulation time; active; actor; actress; actual; actuarial; actuary; actuate; actuating; anticoagulant therapy; atropine coma therapy; azimuth control torquer

act. (ACT) advanced coronary treatment

ACT Access to Careers in Technology; Action for Childrens Television; actual [flow chart (computerese)]; Advanced Computer Techniques; Air Control Team; algebraic compiler and translator (computerese); American College Testing (program); American Conservatory Theatre; Anglican Theological College (British Columbia); Associated Community Theaters; Associated Container Transportation; Association of Classroom Teachers; Australian Capital Territory; Australian College of Theology; Australian Commonwealth Territory; automatic code translation (computerese); Aviation Classification Test

acta (Latin—gazette, journal, report, review)

a cta *a cuenta* (Spanish—on account)

ACTA Aircoach Transport Association; American Community Theatre Association; Associated Container Transpor-

tation Australia

Acta Chem Scand *Acta Chemica Scandinavia*

Acta Crystallog *Acta Crystallographica*

Acta Math Acad Sci Hung *Acta Mathematica Academiae Scientiarum Hungaricae*

Acta Metall *Acta Metallurgica*

Acta Oto-Laryngol *Acta Oto-Laryngologica*

Acta Phys *Acta Physica*

Acta Phys Austriaca *Acta Physica Austriaca* (Latin—Austrian Review of Physics)

Acta Phys Pol *Acta Physica Polonica* (Latin—Polish Review of Physics)

Acta Phys Sin *Acta Physica Sinica* (Latin—Chinese Journal of Physics)

ACTAR Asian Centre for Tax Administration and Research

ACTB Aircrew Classification Test Battery

ACTC Air Commerce Type Certificate; Australian Ceramic Tile Council

A.C.T.C. Art Class Teacher's Certificate

act. ct actual count

acte anodal closure tetanus

ACTFL American Council on the Teaching of Foreign Languages

actg acting

ACTG Advance Carrier Training Group

acth (ACTH) adrenocorticotrophic hormone

ACTI Advisory Committee on Technology Innovation

act/ic active—in commission

ACTIL Australian Cotton Textile Industries Ltd

actinolite (*see* asbestos)

ACTION American Council To Improve Our Neighborhoods; (not an acronym but the current fusion of U.S. government youth agencies such as the Peace Corps and VISTA)

act/is active—in service

ACTIS Auckland Commercial and Technical Information Service

activ activity

ACTIV Army Concept Team in Vietnam

ACTL American College of Trial Lawyers

ACTM Association of Cotton Textile Merchants of New York

ACTMC Army Clothing, Textile and Material Center

actn (ACTN) adrenocorticotrophin

actnt accountant

ACTNZ Associated Container Transportation New Zealand

acto automatic computing transfer oscillator

ACTO Action Office(r)—USA; Advisory Council on the Treatment of Offenders

act/oc active—out of commission

actol air-cushion takeoff and landing

Acton Bell pseudonym of Anne Brontë

ACTOR Askania cine-theodolite optical-tracking range

act/os active—out of service

actp (ACTP) adrenocorticotrophic polypeptide

ACTR Air Corps Technical Report

ACTREP Activities Report

actrl acoustic trial(s)

ACTRSWD Asian Centre for Training and Research in Social Welfare and Development

Acts The Acts of the Apostles

ACTS Acoustic Control and Telemetry System; Air Corps Tactical School; Airline Computer Tracing System (for identifying and returning lost luggage or other objects); American Catholic Theological Society; American Christian Television System; Association of Career Training Schools; Automatic Cage Transmission System; Automatic Computer Telex System

ACTSU Association of Computer Time-Sharing Users

ACTT Association of Cinematograph and Television Technicians; America's Christmas Train and Trucks

ACTU Association of Catholic Trade Unionists; Australian Council of Trade Unions

actv activate

actv (ACTV) armored cavalry towing vehicle

act. val actual value

act. wt actual weight

ACTWU Amalgamated Clothing and Textile Workers Union

ACTWUA Amalgamated Clothing and Textile Workers Union of America (formerly ACWA and TWUA)

acu address control unit; arithmetic computer; assault craft unit; automatic calling unit

ACU Abilene Christian University; Abused Child Unit (Los Angeles Police Department); American Church Union; American Congregational Union; American Conservation Union; American Conservative Union; American Cycling Union; Association of College Unions; Association of Commonwealth Universities; Australian Church Union; Autocycle Union

ACUA Association of Cambridge University Assistants; Association of College and University Auditors

ACUCAA Association of College, University, and Community Arts Administrators

ACUCM Association of College and University Concert Managers

ACUE American Committee of United Europe

ACUERI American Conservative Union Education and Research Institute

ACUG Association of Computer User Groups

ACUHO Association of College and University Housing Officers

ACUI Association of College Unions International

ACUIIS Association of Colleges and Universities for International Intercultural Studies

Acuña Ciudad Acuña (Mexican border town across the Rio Grande from Del Rio, Texas)

ACUNY Associated Colleges of Upper New York

ACUP Association of Canadian University Presses; Association of College and University Printers

ACURA Association for the Coordination of University Religious Affairs

ACURL Association of Caribbean University and Research Libraries

ACUs Asian Currency Units

ACUS Administrative Conference of the United States; Atlantic Council of the United States

ACU-SACC American Conservative Union—Save Our Canal Committee

ACUSNY Association of Colleges and Universities of the State of New York

ACUTE Accountants Computer Users for Technical Exchange

acv actual cash value; air-cushion vehicle; alarm check valve

ACV air-cushion vehicle; auxiliary aircraft carrier or tender (3-letter symbol)

ACVAFS American Council of Voluntary Agencies for Foreign Service

ACVC American Council of Venture Clubs; Arms Control Verification Committee

acvd acute cardiovascular disease

ACVO American College of Veterinary Ophthalmologists

ACVP American College of Veterinary Pathologists

ACVS Australian College of Veterinary Scientists

ACVSF Air-Cooled Vault Storage Facility

acw aircraft control and warning; alternating continuous waves; automatic car wash

ac/w acetone/water

ACW Air Control and Warning (system); Aircraftwoman; Alcoholism Center for Women; American Chain of Warehouses

AC & W Air Communications and Weather (naval group)

ACWA Amalgamated Clothing Workers of America; Australian Chinese Women's Association

A.C.W.A. Associate of the Institute of Cost and Work Accountants

ACWAI Automatic Car Wash Association International

ACWB Australian Council of Wool Buyers

acwbcn action will be cancelled

ACWC Advisory Committee on Weather Control

ACWF All-China Women's Federation; American Council for World Freedom; Army Central Welfare Fund

ACWL Army Chemical Warfare Laboratory

ACWM Americans for Customary Weights and Measures

ACWO Aircraft Control and Warning Officer

ACWRON Aircraft Control and Warning Squadron

ACWRRE American Cargo War Risk Reinsurance Exchange

ACWS Aircraft Control and Warning System

AC & WS Aircraft Control and Warning Station(s)

ACWW Associated Country Women of the World

acy average crop yield

ACY Akron, Canton & Youngstown (railroad); American Cyanamid Company (stock exchange symbol); Atlantic City, New Jersey (airport)

AC & Y Akron, Canton & Youngstown (railroad)

ACYF Administration for Children, Youth, and Families; Australian Council of Young Farmers

acyl-co A coenzyme A ester (general symbol for an organic compound)

acyro acyrologia; acyrologic(al); acyrology

ad a drink; a drug (addict); active duty; addict; advertisement; advertising; aerodynamic decelerator; after drain; air dried; airdrome; area drain; average deviation

ad (AD) aggregate demand; athletic director

a/d altitude/depth; analog-to-digital

a & d ascending and descending

a & d (A & D) accounting and disbursing

'ad had

ad (Latin prefix—to, toward) — as in adhesion, admixture, adopt, adoring, etc.

a d *a droit* (French—to the right)

a.d. *auris dexter* (Latin—right ear)

a D *ausser Dienst* (German—retired)

Ad Ada; Adah; Adalbert; Adam; Adams; Adán; Addington; Addis; Addison; Adela; Adelaide; Adelard; Adelardo; Adelbert; Adele; Adelina; Adeline; Adelle; Adelsteen; Adeodato; Adlai; Adna; Adolf; Adolfine; Adolfo; Adolph; Adolphe; Adolpho; Adolphus; Adriaan; Adriaen; Adrian; Adriano; Adrianus; Adrien; Adrienne; Aedh; Alzheimer's disease

AD Accession Document; Aden Airways; Air Defense; Air Depot; Air Division; Airdrome; Airframe Design (division); Airworthiness Directive; Appellate Division; Assembly District; Astia Document; Atlantic & Danville (railroad); Australian Dame (Dame of the Order of Australia); Australian Democrats; Australian dollar (telex); *Aviatsionnaya Diviziya* (Russian—Aviation Division); destroyer tender (naval symbol)

A-D Albrecht Dürer; Antonin Dvořák

A/D Air Depot; analog-to-digital

A & D Atlantic & Danville (railroad)

AD Acción Democratica (Spanish—Democratic Action Party)—Venezuela's democratic movement begun by Romulo Betancourt

A.D. Anno Domini (Latin—in the Year of our Lord)

ad 2 vic. ad duas vices (Latin—for two doses, for two times)

ada action data automation; actuarial data assembly; average daily attendance; average deviation adjustment

ada (ADA) adenosine deaminase

ada adalah (Arabic—equity, justice); American Dental Association (logotype)

Ada Adelaida; Adelaide

Ada (ADA) universal computer programming language promoted by the Department of Defense and named for Augusta Ada Byron, Lord Byron's daughter, who designed a set of instructions for a 19th-century mechanical analytical machine

Ad of A Archduchy of Austria; Archduke of Austria

ADA Air Defense Area; American Dairy Association; American Dehydrators Association; American Dental Association; American Dermatological Association; American Diabetes Association; American Diabetes Association diet number; American Dietetic Association; Americans for Democratic Action; Assistant District Attorney; Atomic Development Authority; Australian Dental Association; Australian Department of Agriculture; Australian Design Award; Australian Draughts Association; Automatic Data Acquisition (computerese); Automobile Dealers Association

ADA# American Diabetes Association diet number

ADAA American Dental Assistants Association; Art Dealers

Association of America; Australian Development Assistance Agency

ADABAS Adaptable Data Base System

adac automatic direct analog computer

ADAC Acoustic Data Analysis Center

ADAC Allgemeiner Deutscher Automobilclub (The German Automobile Club)

adacx automatic data acquisition and computer complex

adad air defense artillery director

Adag adagio (Italian—slowly and expressively)

ADAIS Aerodynamic Data Analysis and Integration System

adal action data automation language

adaline adaptive linear neuron

adam adamantine; adaptive arithmetical method; advanced data management; air deflection and modulation; area denial artillery munition; automatic distance and angle measurement

A'dam Amsterdam

ADAM Agriculture Department Automated Manpower; Alzheimer's Disease Association of Maryland; Automatic Document Abstracting Method

ADAMHA Alcohol, Drug Abuse, and Mental Health Administration

Adam Hall Elleston Trevor's pseudonym

adamite basic zinc arsenate

adaml advise by airmail

adamm (ADAMM) area defense anti-missile missile

Adam's Adam's Bridge (30-mile-long island chain linking Ceylon and India); Adam's Peak (7000-foot-high mountain in central Ceylon where it is called Samanaliya or Sri Padastanaya)

ADAMS Advanced Design Aluminum Metal Shelter (prefabricated ADAMS hut)

Adam's Bridge (*see* Rama's Bridge)

Adams Mans Adams Mansion (birthplace and home of John Adams and his son John Quincy Adams in Quincy, Massachusetts across the Neponsit River from Boston)

adandac administrative and accounting purposes

ADAOD Air Defense Artillery Operations Detachment

ADAOO Air Defense Artillery Operations Office(r)

adap adapted

ADAP Airport Development Aid Program (FAA)

ADAPCP Alcohol and Drug Abuse Prevention and Control Program

ADAPS Automatic Display and Plotting System

ADAPSO Association of Data Processing Service Organizations

adapt. adaption of automatically-programmed tools

adapticom adaptive communication

ADAPTS Air-Deliverable Anti-Pollution Transfer System (USCG)

adar advanced development array radar; analog-to-digital-to-analog recording

ADAR Air Defense Area

adare advise date of receipt

ADARF Alcoholism and Drug Addiction Research Foundation (Ontario, Canada)

ADAS Action Data Automation System; Agricultural Development Advisory Service; Airborne Dynamic Alignment System

ADASC Auto Dismantlers Association of Southern California (often called ADA)

adash advise date of shipment

ada(si) (Turkish—island)

ad ast. ad astra (Latin—to the stars)

adat automatic data accumulation and transfer

adaval advise availability

ADAWS Action Data Automation and Weapons System

A-day assault day

adb accidental death benefit

adb automatisk databehandling (Dano-Norwegian—automatic data handling)

adB acceleration decibel(s)

ADB Apollo Data Bank (NASA); Asian Development Bank; Atlantic Development Board (Canada)

A.D.B. Bachelor of Domestic Arts

ADB Australian Dictionary of Biography

ADBA American Dog Breeders Association

ADBC American Defenders of Bataan and Corregidor

ADBM Association of Dry Battery Manufacturers

ADBPA *Association pour le Développement des Bibliothèques Publiques en Afrique* (French—Association for the Development of Public Libraries in Africa)

adc active-duty commitment; adopted child; advance delivery of correspondence; albumin, dextrose, catalase; all damn confusion; anodal duration contraction; axiodistocervical

ADC Aerophysics Development Corporation; Aerospace Defense Command; Agricultural Development Council; Aid to Dependent Children; Aide-de-Camp; Air Defense Command; Air Development Center; Air Diffusion Council; Alaska Defense Command; American Distilling Company; American Dock Company; analog-to-digital converter (computerese); Area Dissemination Coordinator; Asian Development Centre; Australian Dairy Corporation; Australian Development Corporation; Australian Diabetic Council; Aviation Development Council

adca advanced-design composite aircraft

ADCA Australian Department of Civil Aviation

adcad airways data collection and distribution

ad cap. *ad captandum* (Latin—for pleasing, made attractive)

ADCC Air Defense Control Center

ADCG Australian Defence Co-operation Group

ADC Gen Aide-de-Camp General

ADCI American Die Casting Institute

ADCIS Association for the Development of Computer-based Instruction Systems

ADC/NORAD Air Defense Command/North American Air Defense (Command)

ADCO Alcohol and Drug Control Office(r); American Dredging Company

ADCOC Area Damage Control Center

ADCOM Administrative Command; Aerospace Defense Command

adcon advance concepts; advise or issue instructions to all concerned; analog-to-digital computer

ADCONSEN (with the) advice of consent of the Senate (of the United States)

a & d control alcohol and drug control (maintained by pimps who find prostitutes are much easier to control if their intake of alcohol and drugs is regulated)

ADCOP Area Damage Control Party

adc's analog-to-digital converters

ADCSP Advanced Defense Communications Satellite Program

adct assisted-draft crossflow tower

ADCT Art Director's Club—Toronto; Association of District Council Treasurers

ad curtain advertisement curtain (theater)

add. addenda; addendum; address; airborne digital decoder; attention deficit disorder; automatic drawing device; average daily dose

ad & d accidental death and dismemberment (insurance)

add. *addendum* (Latin—addition)

ADD Abstracts of Declassified Documents; Addis Ababa, Ethiopia (airport); Aerospace Defense Division; Aviastiia Dalnego Deistviia (Russian—Long-Range Bombing Force)

ADDA Air Defense Defended Area

addar automatic digital data acquisition and recording

ADDAS Automatic Digital Data Assembly System

ADDC Air Defense Direction Center; Australian Dairy Development Council

Add-Can Addicts-Canada

ADDDS Automatic Direct Distance Dialing System

addee addressee

ad. def. an. *ad defectionem animi* (Latin—to the point of fainting)

ad. deliq. *ad deliquium* (Latin—to fainting)

adder. automatic-digital data-error recorder

ADDF Abu Dhabi Defense Force

ad diag admitting diagnosis

ADDIC Alcoholic and Dependency Intervention Council

addict. addiction

Addie Ada; Adela; Adelaide; Adelina; Adeline

Addis Addis Ababa, Ethiopia

Addison's disease adrenal cortical deficiency

addit additional

ADDL Anti-Digit Dialing League

addm automated drafting and digitizing machine

addn addition

Addo Addo Elephant Park near Port Elizabeth, South Africa

ADDP Air Defense Defended Point

ADDR address [flow chart (computerese)]

ADDS Alcohol and Drug Dependence Service; American Digestive Diseases Society; Apollo Document Descriptions Standards (NASA); Automatic Data Digitizing System; Automatic Direct Distance Dialing System

addsd addressed

addu additional duty

Addy Ada; Adela; Adelaide; Adelina; Adeline

ade automated drafting equipment; automatic data entry; average daily enrollment

ADE Animal Disease Eradication (Department of Agriculture division); Association of Departments of English; Association for Documentary Editing; Australian Driver Education

ADEA American Driver Education Association

ADECOS *Acción Democrática* (Spanish—Democratic Action)—Venezuelan political party

adeda advise effective date

ADEDS Advanced Electronic Display System

adee addressee

Adee Adelaide, Australia

Adeen Aberdeen(shire)

ad effect. *ad effectum* (Latin—until effective)

A de JC *Antes de Jesucristo* (Spanish—before Jesus Christ)

Adel Adelaide; Adelar(d); Adelbern; Adelbert; Adelbold; Adelfred; Adelfrid; Adelgar; Adelhart; Adelmo; Adelochorda; Adelpho; Adelquist; Adelric; Adelrik; Adelwin

ADELA Atlantic Community Development Group for Latin America

Adélie Adélie Land (French

Antarctica)

adem acute disseminated encephalomyelitis

ADEMS Advanced Diagnostic Engine Monitoring System

aden augmented deflector exhaust nozzle

Aden former name of the Yemen People's Democratic Republic

ADEP Air Depot

ADEPO Automatic Dynamic Evaluation by Programmed Organizations

adept. a definitely empirical power of theorems; automatic data extractor and plotting table

ADEPT Agricultural and Dairy Educational Political Trust

a des *a destra* [Italian—at (to) the right]

A de S Académie des Sciences

ADES Automatic Digital Encoding System

A de T S Alex de Tocqueville Society

adex advanced antisubmarine warfare exercise

adf after deducting freight; air direction finder

adf (ADF) automatic direction finder

Adf Adolf

ADF Air Defense Force; Air Development Force; Arab Deterrent Forces; Army Distaff Foundation; Asian Development Fund

ADFA Australian Defence Force Academy; Australian Department of Foreign Affairs; Australian Dried Fruits Association

adfc adiabatic film cooling

ADFC Air Defense Filter Center

ADFF Australian Dairy Farmers Federation

ADFI American Dog Feed Institute

ADFIAP Association of Development Finance Institutions of Asia and the Pacific

ad fin. *ad finem* (Latin—to the end)

ADFL Association of Departments of Foreign Languages

ADFOR Adriatic Force

ADFS American Dentists for Foreign Service; Australian Documentary Facsimile Society

ADFSC Automatic Data Field Systems Command

ADFW Assistant Director of Fortifications and Works

adg axiodistogingival

ADG degaussing vessel (3-letter symbol)

ADGA American Dairy Goat Association

ADGB Air Defence of Great Britain

A & D G C Alliance and Dublin Consumers Gas Company

adge air-defense ground environment

adgo adagio

ad grat. acid. *ad gratam acidatem* (Latin—to a pleasing acidity)

ad grat. gust. *ad gratum gustum* (Latin—to an agreeable taste)

ADGRU Advisory Group

adh (ADH) alcohol dehydrogenase; antidiuretic hormone (vasopressin)

ADH Academy of Dentistry for the Handicapped; Association of Dental Hospitals

ADHA American Dental Hygienists Association

ADHC Air Defense Hardware Committee (NATO); Australian Department of Housing and Construction

adhca advise this headquarters of complete action

adhib *adhibeatur* (Latin ad minister)

ad h. l. *ad hunc locum* (Latin—at this place)

ad hoc (Latin—for this special purpose)

ad hom. *ad hominem* (Latin—to the man)

adi acceptable daily intake; adiabat(ic); air defense intercept; air defense interceptor; alien declared intention; antidetonation injection; attitude direction indicator; automatic direction indicator

adi (ADI) area of dominant (radio or tv station) influence

ADI Acoustical Door Institute; Air Defense Interceptor; Air Distribution Institute; American Documentation Institute; Assistance Doss International

ADI *Agencia para el Desarrolo Internacional* (Spanish—Agency for International Development)—AID

ADIC American Dental Interfraternity Council

ad id. *ad idem* (Latin—both are the same, likewise)

Adieu Chopin's Polonaise in B-flat minor

ad ig. *ad ignorantiam* (Latin—to ignorance)

adil (ADIL) air defense identification line

ADIL *Annual Digest of International Law*

adimd advise immediately by dispatch

ad inf *ad infinitum* (Latin—to infinity)

ad init. *ad initium* (Latin—at the beginning)

adinsp administrative inspection

ad int. *ad interim* (Latin—in the interim, meanwhile)

Ad Intel Cen Advanced Intelligence Center

ADIOS Automatic Digital Input-Output System

ADIP Advanced Developing Institutions Program

adipu advise whether individual may be properly used in your installation

Adirondacks Adirondack Mountains of northeastern New York

ADIS Air Defense Integrated System; Association for the Development of Instructional Systems; Automatic Data Interchange System

adit analog digital integrating translator

ADIT Alien Documentation, Identification, and Telecommunications

ADiv Air Division

ADIZ Air Defense Identification Zone

adj adjacent; adjective; adjoint; adjust

Adj Adjutant

ADJ adjust [flow chart (computerese)]

Adj. A. Adjunct in Arts

ADJAG Assistant Deputy Judge Advocate General

Adj Gen Adjutant General

Adjt Adjutant

adl activities of daily living; armament data line; automatic data link(ing); average decreasing line

Adl Adelaide

ADL Adelaide, Australia (airport); Admiral Corporation (stock exchange symbol); Anti-Defamation League (B'nai B'rith); Arthur D Little (corporation); Authorized Data List; Automatic Data Link(ing); Automotive Discount Leasing

ADLA Art Directors' (club) Los Angeles

Adlai Adlai Stevenson II

Adler Adler Planetarium (Chicago)

ad lib. *ad libitum* (Latin—at one's pleasure)

ADLIPS Automatic Data-Link Plotting System

adlm (ADLM) aerial-delivered land mine

ADLO Air Defense Liaison Office(r)

ad loc. *ad locum* (Latin—at this passage or place)

ADLOG Advance Logistical Command

ADLP Australian Democratic Labour Party

ADLS Air Dispatch Letter Service

ADLT Activities of Daily Living Test

ADLTDE Association of Dark Leaf Tobacco Dealers and Exporters

adm administration; administrative; administrator; admission; admit; air defense missile; atomic demolition munition; average daily membership

adm (ADM) air-launched decoy missile

Adm Admiral; Admiralty

ADM Action Description Memorandum; Affiliated Dress Manufacturers; Air Defense Missile; American Drug Manufacturers (association)

ADM *American Demographics Magazine*

adma automatic drafting machine

ADMA Aircraft Distributors and Manufacturers Association; American Drug Manufacturers Association; Australian Direct Marketing Association; Australian Display Manufacturers Association; Aviation Distributors and Manufacturers Association

admad advise method and date of shipment

Ad Man Advertising Manager

admap advise by mail as soon as possible

admass advertising & mass media effect on gullible readers and viewers

Adm Cen Administration Center; Administrative Center; Admiralty Center

Adm Co Admiralty Court

ADMI American Dry Milk Institute

ADMIG Australian Drug and Medical Information Group

admin administration; administrative; administrator

AdminInstr Administrative Instructions

AdminO Administrative Order(s)

adminord administrative order

adminplan administrative plan

Admirable Doctor English author-philosopher Francis Bacon—*Doctor mirabilis*

ADMIRAL Automatic and Dynamic Monitor with Immediate Relocation, Allocation, and Loading (system)

Admiral of the Atlantic Kaiser Wilhelm II created this sobriquet for himself and called his peace-loving cousin Czar Nicholas II the Admiral of the Pacific

Admiral of the Ocean Sea Christopher Columbus

Admiralties Admiralty Islands

admire. automatic diagnostic maintenance information retrieval

ADMIRES Automatic Diagnostic Maintenance Information Retrieval System

admix administratrix

adml average daily member load

Adml Admiral; Admiralty

admn administration

admon *administración* (Spanish —administration)

Admor *Administrador* (Spanish —Administrator)

admos automatic device for mechanical order selection

ad mov. *ad moveatur* (Latin—let it be moved)

admr administrator

adms administrator

ADMS American Donkey and Mule Society; Assistant Director of Medical Services

ADMSC Automatic Digital Message Switching Centers (DoD)

ADMSLBN Air Defense Missile Battalion (USA)

admsn admission

ADMT Association of Dental Manufacturers and Traders

Adm Ter Administered Territories (Gaza Strip, Golan Heights, much of the Sinai, and the West Bank of the Jordan as well as all of Jerusalem annexed by the Israelis in 1967)

Admty Admiralty

admx administratrix

adn (ADN) *ácido desoxirribonucleico* (Spanish—desoxyribonucleic acid)—dna (DNA)

Adn Aden

ADN Accession Designation Number; Allgemeiner Deutscher Nachrichtendienst (General German News Service); Ashley, Drew & Northern (railroad)

A.D.N. Associate Degree in Nursing

ADNA Assistant Director of Naval Accounts

ADNAC Air Defense of the North American Continent

ad naus. *ad nauseam* (Latin— boring to the point of nausea)

ADNC Air Defense National Center; Air Defense Notification Center; Assistant Director of Naval Construction

ad neut. *ad neutralizandum* (Latin—until neutral)

ADNI Assistant Director of Naval Intelligence

ADNOC Abu Dhabi National Oil Company

adnok advise if not correct

'ad n't had not

ado advanced development objective; axiodistoclusal

Ado *adagio* (Italian—slowly and expressively)

ADO Administration Duty Officer; Air Defense Officer; Air Defense Operations

ADOBE Atmospheric Dispersion of Beryllium (program)

Adobe State New Mexico

ADOC Air Defense Operations Center

ADOF Assistant Director of Ordnance Factories

ADOGA American Dehydrated Onion and Garlic Association

adoit automatically-directed out-going intertoll trunk (Bell)

Adolph Adolphus

ADONIS Automatic Digital On-Line Instruments System

Adonis of Fifty nickname of George IV

adop adoption

ADOPT Approach to Distributed Processing Transactions

ADOS Assistant Director of Ordnance Services

adot automatically-directed outbound trunk (Bell)

adoxograph adoxographer; adoxographic(al)(ly); adoxography

adp adenosine diphosphate; advanced data processing; airborne data processor; ammonium dihydrogen phosphate; automatic data processing

ADP Academy of Denture Prosthetics; Air Defense Position; Airport Development Program; Animal Disease and Parasite (Research Division—Department of Agriculture); Automatic Data Processing

ADPA American Defense Preparedness Association

ADPB Australian Dairy Produce Board

ADPC Abu Dhabi Petroleum Company; Automatic Data Processing Center

adpcm adaptive-differential pulse-code modulation

adpe automatic data processing equipment

ADPEA Australian Data Processing Employees Association

ADPESO Automatic Data Processing Equipment Selection Office (USN)

adpl average daily patient load

adplan advancement planning; advertising planning

adpo aircraft depot

ADPO Automatic Data Processing Operations

ad pond. om. ad pondus omnium (Latin—to the whole weight)

ADPR Assistant Director of Public Relations

ADPRIN Automatic Data-Processing Intelligence Network (U.S. Bureau of Customs)

ADPs Allied Defense Publications; Artillery Destruction Programs

ADPS Automatic Data Processing System(s)

ADPSD Automatic Data Processing Systems Development

ADPSO Association of Data Processing Service Organizations

adpt adapter

adr address; asset depreciation range

a-d r analog-to-digit recorder

adr addresse (Dano-Norwegian —address); address (Swedish —address)

Adr Adrian; Adriatic

Adr Adresse (German—address)

ADR Accepted Dental Remedies; adder (computerese); Aircraft Direction Room; Australian Defence Representative; Australian Design Rules (automotive)

ADR Accepted Dental Remedies; Association pour le Développement de la Recherche (French —Association for the Development of Research)

ADR 27-a Australian Design Rule 27-a (vehicle emission control)

ADRA Animal Diseases Research Association; Australian Drag Racing Association

adrac automatic digital recording and control

ADRB Army Disability Review Board; Army Discharge Review Board

ADRDA Alzheimer's Disease and Related Disorders Association

adrde advise reason for delay

ADRDE Air Defense Research and Development Establishment

adren adrenal; adrenalin

adrenals adrenal glands

ADRES Army Data Retrieval System

ADRI Angkatan Darat Republik Indonesia (Indonesian Army)

Adria Milton's abbreviation for the Adriatic Sea

Adria die Adria (German—the Adriatic)—das Adriatische Meer (The Adriatic Sea)

Adrian Hadrian

Adrian Girls (delinquent) Girls Training School at Adrian, Michigan

Adrianople former name of Eridne

Adriatic Adriatic Sea (arm of the Mediterranean between Italy on the west and Albania plus Yugoslavia on the east)

Adriatico (Italian or Spanish Adriatic)

Adriático (Portuguese—Adriatic)

Adriatique (French—Adriatic)

ADRIS Automatic Dead Reckoning Instrument Systems

adrm airdrome

Adro Alejandro

ADROBN Airdrome Battalion

adrp airdrop

ADRS Analog-to-Digital Data Recording System; Automatic Document Request Service

adrt analog data recording transcriber

adr tel adresse telegraphique (French—telegraphic address)

ads advertisements; antibody deficiency syndrome; antidiuretic substance; area, date, subject; autograph document

signed; automatic door seal

ADS Aerial Delivery System; Air Defense Sector; Alzheimer's Disease Society; American Daffodil Society; American Dahlia Society; American Dental Service; American Dental Society; American Denture Society; American Dialect Society; Analog & Digital Systems; Association of Diesel Specialists

ADS Académie des Sciences (French Academy of Science)

ADSA American Dairy Science Association; American Dental Society of Anesthesiology; Atomic Defense Support Agency

ad. saec. ad saeculum (Latin—to the century)

adsap advise as soon as possible

ADSAS Air-Derived Separation Assurance System

ad sat. ad saturandum (Latin— to saturation)

ADSATIS Australian Defence Science and Technology Information System

adsc average daily service charge (in hospitals)

ADSC Advanced Section Communication Zone; Automatic Data Service Center

ADSCAT Association of Distributors to the Self-service and Coin-operated Laundries and Allied Trades

adscom advanced shipboard communications

adsda advise earliest date

ad sec. ad sectam (Latin—at suit of (legal)

AdSec Advanced Section

adshpdat advise shipping data

adsid air-delivered acoustic-implant seismic-intrusion detector

ADSID Air Defense Systems Integration Division

ADSL Assembly Department Shortage List

adsm (ADSM) air defense suppression missile

ADSM American Defense Service Medal

ADSMO Air Defense Systems Management Office

ADSN Accounting and Disbursing Station Number

ADSOC Administrative Support Operations Center

ADSOT Automatic Daily System Operability Test

adss analysis of digitized seismic

signals

ADSS Aircraft Damage Sensing System; Australian Defense Scientific Service

ADST Atlantic Daylight Saving Time

adstadis advise status and/or disposition

adst.feb. *adstante febre* (Latin—when fever is present)

adstkoh advise stock on hand

adsu advanced direct support unit

ADSUP Automatic Data Systems Uniform Practice(s)

adsym automobile defog-defrost system model

adt aided tracking; any damn thing (abbreviation for a placebo); automatic damage template; automatic debit transfer; average daily dose

adT *an demselben Tage* (German—the same day)

ADT American District Telegraph; Applied Drilling Technology; Atlantic Daylight Time

ADTA American Dental Trade Association

adtam air-delivered target-activated munitions

ADTC Air Defense Technical Center; Air Defense Test Center; Armament Development Test Center (USAF)

adtech advanced decoy technology

ad tert. vic. *ad tertium vicem* (Latin—three times)

ADTF At-Depth Test Facility

ADTI American Dinner Theatre Institute

ADTIC Arctic, Desert, Tropic Information Center

ADTR Australian Department of Tourism and Recreation

ADTS Automatic Data and Telecommunications Service

ADTSEA American Driver Traffic Safety Education Association

adtu automatic digital test unit; auxiliary data translator unit

adu acceleration-deceleration unit; accumulation-distribution unit

ADU Aircraft Delivery Unit

adult. adulterant; adulterate; adulteration

ad us. *ad usum* (Latin—according to custom)

ad us. ext. *ad usum externum* (Latin—for external use)

adv advance; advantage; adverb(ial); advertising

a/dv arterio/deep venous (injection)

adv *advokat* (Dano-Norwegian—attorney)

adv. *adversum* (Latin—adversely, against)

Adv. Adventist; Adviser

ADV advance [flow chart (computerese)]

advac advise acceptance

ad val. *ad valorem* (Latin—according to value)

Advance Agent of Emancipation Lucretia Mott

Adv Appl Mech *Advances in Applied Mechanics*

Adv At Mol Phys *Advances in Atomic and Molecular Physics*

advb adverb; adverbial

Adv Bse Advanced Base

Adv Chem Phys *Advances in Chemical Physics*

adv chgs advance charges

advdisc advance discontinuance of allotment

advec advection

advect advection(al)(ly); advective

adven adventure; adventurer

adversat adversative

advert advertising

advertique advertising antique (old coffee can, old tobacco tin, old decanter bottle, old trade-marked tray, etc.)

advert(s) advertisement(s)

adv frt advance freight

Adv Intel Cen Advanced Intelligence Center

ad virus adenovirus

ADVISE Area Denial Visual Identification Security Equipment

advl adverbial

advm adaptive delta voice modulation

Adv Magn Reson *Advances in Magnetic Resonance*

adv mtr advertising matter

Advoc Advocate

advof advise this office

advon advanced echelon; advanced operations unit

Adv Phys *Advances in Physics*

adv pmt advance payment

adv poss adverse possession

Adv Quantum Chem *Advances in Quantum Chemistry*

advr advisor

ADVS Assistant Director of Veterinary Services

advst advance stoppage

advt advertise; advertisement; advertiser; advertising

advul air-defense vulnerability

adw assault (with) deadly weapon

ADW Air Defense Warning

ADWA Atlantic Deeper Waterways Association

ADWC Air Defense Weapons Center (USAF)

ADWKP Air Defense Warning Key Point

adx automatic data exchange

ADX Adams Express Company (stock exchange symbol); Air Defence Exercise (Australian)

Adyg Adygey

adz advise

ADZ Air Defense Zone

Adzh Adzhar

ae above the elbow; account executive; aircraft equipment; air escape; almost everywhere

a/e absorptivity-emissivity

a & e aerospace and electronic; armaments and electronics; azimuth and elevation

ae *aetatis* (Latin—aged, at the age of)

AE Agricultural Engineering (Department of Agriculture research division); Air Explorer; Airborne Equipment (naval division); American English; ammunition ship (naval symbol); Automatic Electric

A-E Adam and Eve; Architect-Engineer; Astro-Eugenics

A.E. Aeronautical Engineer; Agricultural Engineer; Architectural Engineer; Associate in Education; Associate in Engineering

A & E Agricultural and Engineering; Architectural and Engineering

AE *Aeon* (pen name of George William Russell); *Aktiebolaget Atomenergi* (Swedish—Atomic Energy Corporation); *American Ephemeris*; *Atomnaya Energiya* (Russian—Atomic Energy); *Australian Encyclopaedia*

A & E *Adolphus and Ellis*

aea actual expenses allowable; assignment eligibility and availability

AEA Actors' Equity Association; Adult Education Association; American Economic Association; American Education Association; American Enterprise Association; American Entrepreneurs Association; American Export Airlines; Arizona Education Association; Arkansas Education Association; Artists Equity Association; Arts, Education, and Americans; Atomic Energy Authority; Automotive Electric Association

AEAA Asociación de Escritores y Artistas Americanos (Spanish—Association of American Writers and Artists)

AEAF Allied Expeditionary Air Force

AEAO Airborne Emergency Actions Officer

AEARC Army Equipment Authorizations Review Center

AEAs American Entertainers Abroad

aea sol alcohol-ether-acetone solution

AEAUSA Adult Education Association of the United States of America

AEB Adult Education Board (Singapore); Area Electricity Board; Atomic Energy Bureau; Australian Egg Board

AEBIG Aslib Economics and Business Information Group

aec additional extended coverage; altitude engine control; at earliest convenience; attitude engine control

AEC Aeronautical Research Council; Agricultural Economics (division of Department of Agriculture); Aircraft Radio Corporation; Airworthiness Examination Committee; Alaska Engineering Commission (Alaska Railroad); Aluminum Extruders Council; American Engineering Council; Anglican Episcopal Church; Army Education Center; Army Educational Center; Army Educational Corps; Army Electronics Command (formerly Signal Corps); Atlantic & East Carolina (railroad); Atlas Educational Center; Atomic Energy Commission; Australian Environment Council

A & EC Atlantic & East Carolina (railroad)

AEC-A Atomic Energy Commission—Albuquerque Operations Office

AEC-AI Atomic Energy Commission—Argonne, Illinois

AEC-ANM Atomic Energy Commission—Albuquerque, New Mexico

AEC-ASC Atomic Energy Commission—Aiken, South Carolina

AECB Atomic Energy Control

Board (Canada)

AEC-BC Atomic Energy Commission—Berkeley, California

AECC Aeromedical Evacuation Control Center

AEC-CC Atomic Energy Commission—Canoga Park, California

AECE Asociación Española de Cooperación Europea (Spanish—Association for European Cooperation)

AEC-FOA Atomic Energy Commission—Fernal Office Area, Cincinnati, Ohio

AEC-HW Atomic Energy Commission—Hanford, Washington

AECI African Explosives and Chemical Industries

AECIA Australian Electronics Consumer Industry Association

AEC-II Atomic Energy Commission—Idaho Falls, Idaho

AECL Anglo-European Container Line; Atomic Energy of Canada, Limited

AEC-LN Atomic Energy Commission—Las Vegas, Nevada

AEC-LOC Atomic Energy Commission—Lockland Aircraft Reactors Operations, Cincinnati, Ohio

AECM Albert Einstein College of Medicine

AEC-NY Atomic Energy Commission—New York Operations Office

AECOM Army Electronic Command

AEC-OR Atomic Energy Commission—Oak Ridge Operations Office

AEC OT Atomic Energy Commission—Oak Ridge, Tennessee

aecp altitude engine control panel

AECP Airman Education and Commissioning Program

AEC-PP Atomic Energy Commission—Pittsburgh, Pennsylvania

AEC-PR Atomic Energy Commission—Pittsburgh Naval Reactors Operations Office

AEC-RW Atomic Energy Commission—Richland, Washington

AECS Australia-Europe Container Service

AECT Association for Educational Communications and Technology

AEC-UN Atomic Energy Com-

mission—Upton, LI, NY

aed (AED) automatic engineering design

A.Ed. Associate in Education

AED Academy for Educational Development; Associated Equipment Distributors; Association of Electronic Distributors

A.E.D. Artium Elegantium Doctor (Latin—Doctor of Fine Arts)

AEDB Apollo Engineering Development Board

AEDC Arnold Engineering Development Center

aedcm (AEDCM) advanced electrochemical depolarized concentrator module

AEDD Air Engineering Development Division

AEDE Association Européenne des Enseignants (French—European Teachers' Association)

AEDF Australian Executive Development Foundation

AEDO Aircraft Engineering District Office

AED-RCA Astro-Electronics Division-RCA

AEDS Association of Educational Data Systems; Association of Electronic Data Systems; Atomic Energy Detection System

AEDU Admiralty Experimental Diving Unit

aee absolute essential equipment; absolutely essential equipment

Ae.E. Aeronautical Engineer

AEE Alliance for Environmental Education; Association for Experimental Education; Atomic Energy Establishment

AE.E. Associate in Engineering

AEEB Association Européenne de l'Equipement de Bureau (French—European Office Equipment Association)

AEEC Airlines Electronic Engineering Committee

AEEI Arthur E E Ivory

AEEL Aeronautical Electronic and Electrical Laboratory

AEEN Agence Européenne pour l'Energie Nucléaire (European Agency for Atomic Energy)

AEEP Association of Environmental Engineering Professors

AEET Atomic Energy Establishment, Trombay (India)

AEEW Atomic Energy Establishment—Winfrith

AEF Advertising Educational

Foundation; Aerospace Education Foundation; Aircraft Engineering Foundation; Allied Expeditionary Force; American Economic Foundation; American European Foundation; American Expeditionary Force; Americans for Economic Freedom; Armenian Educational Foundation; Artists Equity Fund; Australian Expeditionary Force(s); Aviation Engineer(ing) Force

AEFC Australian-European Finance Corporation

A-effect alienation effect

AEFM Association Européenne des Festivals de Musique (French—European Association of Music Festivals)

AEFORT American-European Friends of ORT (Organization for Rehabilitation through Training)

AEFR Aurora, Elgin & Fox River (railroad)

aeg active element group(ing); air encephalogram(s)

aeg. aeger (Latin—sick)

Aeg Aegean

AEG Association of Engineering Geologists

AEG Allgemeine Elektrizitats Geseläschaft (German—General Electric Company)

Aegean Aegean Sea (arm of the Mediterranean between Greece and Turkey)

Aegean Ethicist Aristotle

Aegeans Aegean Islands (Cyclades, Dodecanese, Sporades, etc.)

AEGIMRDA Army Engineer Geodesy, Intelligence and Mapping Research and Development Agency

AEGIS Active Electronic Gimballess Inertial System; Aid for the Elderly in Government Institutions; Assessment of Effectiveness of Geologic Isolation Systems

AEGp Aeromedical Evacuation Group (USAF)

AEH A(lfred) E(dward) Housman

AEH Archives of Environmental Health

AEHA Army Environmental Health Agency

AEHA Anuario Español e Hispano-Americano (Spanish and Hispanic-American Annual)

AEHL Army Environmental Health Laboratory

aei azimuth error indicator

AEI Air Express International; American Enterprise Institute; American Express Institute; American Express International; Annual Efficiency Index; Associated Electrical Industries

AEI Association des Ecoles Internationales (French—Association of International Schools)

AEIB Association for Education in International Business

AEIBC American Express International Banking Corporation

AEIC Association of Edison Illuminating Companies

AEIDC American Express International Development Company

AEIL American Export Isbrandtsen Lines

AEIMS Administrative Engineering Information Management System

A.E.I.O.U. *Austria Erit In Orbe Ultima* (Latin—Austria will be the world's last survivor)—ancient acrostic of House of Hapsburg

AEIP Allied Electrical Industry Publications

AEIPPR American Enterprise Institute for Public Policy Research

AEIS Association of Electronic Industries in Singapore

AEJ Association for Education in Journalism

AEJI Association of European Jute Industries

aek all-electric kitchen

ael audit error list

AEL Admiralty Engineering Laboratory (UK); Aeronautical Engineering Laboratory; Aircraft Engine Laboratory; American Electronic Laboratories; American Emigrants League; American Express Line; Americanism Education League; Animal Education League; Automation Engineering Laboratory

AELC American Evangelical Lutheran Church; Association of Evangelical Lutheran Churches

AELE Americans for Effective Law Enforcement

AELE Association Européenne de Libre-Echange (French—European Free Trade Association)

AEL-Rx Appalachian Educational Laboratory—Regional

Exchange

AELTC All England Lawn Tennis Club

aem atomic emission monitoring

AEM Advance Engineering Memorandum; Aircraft and Engine Mechanic; American Meter Company (stock exchange symbol); Applications Explorer Mission; Association of Electronic Manufacturers; Aviation Electrician's Mate

AEMA Australian Electrical Manufacturers Association

AEMIS Aerospace and Environmental Medicine Information System

AEMP Association of European Management Publishers

AE & MP Ambassador Extraordinary and Minister Plenipotentiary

AEMS American Engineering Model Society

AEMSA Army Electronics Material Support Agency

aen advance evaluation note

aen. aeneus (Latin—made of bronze or copper)

Aen. Aeneid (Virgil's epic poem)

A.En. Associate in English

AEN Asahi Evening News (Japan)

AENA All-England Netball Association

A.Eng. Associate in Engineering

AEO Air Engineer(ing) Office(r); Appeal Examining Office(r); Australian Electoral Office

AEOB Advanced Engine Overhaul Base

AEODPs Allied Explosive Ordnance Disposal Publications

AEOE Association for Environmental and Outdoor Education

Aeol Aeolian; Aeolic

Aeolians Aeolian Islands off Sicily's north coast where they are called Isole Eolie and include Lipari, Stromboli, and Vulcano

AEOO Aeromedical Evacuation Operations Officer

aeop amend existing orders pertaining to

AEOS Ancient Egyptian Order of Sciots; Astronomical, Earth, and Ocean Sciences

aep accrued expenditure paid; average evoked potential

AEP Addo Elephant Park

(South Africa); Adult Education Program; American Electric Power

AE & P Ambassador Extraordinary and Plenipotentiary

AEP Agencè Européenne de Productivite (French—European Production Agency)

AEPC Appalachian Electric Power Company

AEPCO American Elsevier Publishing Company

AEPEM Association of Electronic Parts and Equipment Manufacturers

AEPG Army Electronic Proving Ground

AEPI American Educational Publishers Institute

aep(s) auditory-evoked potential(s)

AEPs Allied Engineering Publications; Allied Equipment Publications

AEPS Aircrew Escape Propulsion System; American Electroplaters Society

aeq age equivalent

aeq. aequales [Latin—equal(s)]

AEQA Alabama Environmental Quality Association

AEqPs Allied Equipment Publications

aer aldosterone excretion rate; alteration equivalent to a repair; auditory-evoked response; average evoked response

AER Abbreviated Effectiveness Report; Aeronautical Engineering Report; After Engine Room; Airman Effectiveness Report; Army Emergency Relief; Association for Education by Radio; Association Européenne pour l'Etude du Probleme des Réfugies (European Association for the Study of the Refugee Problem)

aera aeration

AERA American Educational Research Association; American Engine Rebuilders Association; Australian Endurance Riders Association

AERB Army Education Requirements Board

AERC Association of Executive Recruiting Consultants

aercab advanced escape/rescue capability; advanced aircrew escape/rescue capability

AERDL Army Electronics Research and Development Laboratory

Aer.E. Aeronautical Engineer

AERE Atomic Energy Research Establishment

AERI Agricultural Economics Research Institution; Automotive Exhaust Research Institute

aerl aerial

AERL Aero-Elastic Research Laboratory (M.I.T.)

Aer Méx Aero México (formerly Aeronaves de México)

AERNO Aeronautical Equipment Reference Number

aero aerographer; aeronautical; aeronautics

AERO Association of Electronic Reserve Officers

aerobatics aeronautical acrobatics

aerobee aerojet/bumblebee (naval missile)

aerob(s) aerobic exercise(s)

aerocade aerial parade; aviation parade (massed formations, stunts aloft)

Aero Commander U-4 transport aircraft

aerodyn aerodynamics

Aero E Aeronautical Engineer

Aer Of Aerological Officer

AEROFLOT Aero Flotilla (Soviet Air Lines)

aerol aerological

aeromed acromedical

aeromod aerodynamic modelling

aeromus aeronautical museum

aeron aeronautical

Aeron Aeronaut; Aeronautics

AERONAVES Aeronaves de México

AERONORTE Empresa de Transportes Aereos Norte do Brasil (North Brazil Airways)

Aero O/Y Finnair (Finnish Airlines)

Aerop Aeropuerto (Spanish—airport)

aeropost aerodynamic post-processing

AEROS Aerometric and Emissions Reporting System; Artificial Earth Research and Orbiting Satellite

AEROSAT Aeronautical Communications Satellite System

aerosp aerospace

aerospace aeronautics + space

aerospacecom aerospace communication(s)

AEROTAL Aerolineas Territoriales de Colombia (Spanish—Territorial Airlines of Colombia)

aerotel airplane hotel (hangar)

Aerovias "Q" Aerovias Cubana (Cuban Airlines)

AERS Atlantic Estuarine Research Society

AERT Association for Education by Radio-Television

AERU Agricultural Economics Research Unit (NZ)

aes annual expectation of sales; auger electron spectroscopy

Aes Aesop (Greek fabulist); (Latin—bronze or copper)—used by numismatists to denote bronze or copper coins or coins of such colors

AES Aerospace Electrical Society; Agricultural Estimates (division of Department of Agriculture); Agricultural Experiment Station; Aircraft Electrical Society; Airways Engineering Society; American Electrochemical Society; American Electroencephalographic Society; American Electroplaters Society; American Entomological Society; American Epidemiological Society; American Epilepsy Society; American Equilibration Society; American Ethnological Society; American Eugenics Society; Apollo Extension System; Army Exchange Service; Atlantic Estuarine Society; Audio Engineering Society; Australian Educational Secretariat; Australian Entomological Society

A&ES Arson and Explosion Squad

AESBOW Association of Engineers and Scientists of the Bureau of Weapons (USN)

AESC American Engineering Standards Committee

Aescul Aesculapius (Greek god of medicine killed by Jupiter who cast a bolt of lightning at him because he had restored life to several persons)

AESD Acoustic Environment Support Detachment (USN Office of Naval Research)

AESE Association of Earth Science Editors

AESHS Alfred E Smith High School

AESO Aircraft Environmental Support Office (USN)

AESOP Artificial Earth Satellite Observation Program; Automated Engineering and Scientific Optimization Program (NASA)

AESq Aeromedical Evacuation Squadron (USAF)

AESQ Air Explorer Squadron
AESRS Army Equipment Status Reporting System
AESS American Ethnic Science Society
AEST Aeromedical Evacuation Support Team
AESTE Association for the Exchange of Students for Technical Experience
aesth aesthete; aesthetic; aesthetician; aesthetics
Aesthetic Post-Impressionist Vasili Kandinski
AESU Aerospace Environmental Support Unit
aet absorption-equivalent thickness
aet. aetatis (Latin—at or of the age of)
AET Australian Eastern Time
A.E.T. Associate in Electrical Technology; Associate in Electronic Technology
AET Aerlinte Eireann Teoranta (Irish Airlines)
AETA American Educational Theatre Association
AETD Aero-Electronic Technology Department (USN)
AETE Aerospace Engineering Test Establishment (Canada)
AETFAT Association pour l'Etude Taxonomique de la Flore d'Afrique Tropicale (Association for the Taxonomic Study of African Tropical Flora)
AETM Aviation Electronic Technician's Mate
AETN American Educational Television Network
AEtPs Allied Electronic Publications
AETR Advanced Engineering Test Reactor
AETS Association for the Education of Teachers in Science
AETT Australian Elizabethan Theatre Trust
aeu accrued expenditure unpaid
AEU Amalgamated Engineering Union; American Ethical Union; Asia Electronics Union
aeuia alleluia (Italian—hallelujuh)
aev (AEV) aerothermodynamic elastic vehicle
AEV Asociación de Escritores Venezolanos (Spanish—Association of Venezuelan Writers)
AEVA Australian Equine Veterinary Association
aevac air evacuation

AEW Airborne Early Warning
AEWB Army Electronic Warfare Board (USA)
AEW & C Airborne Early Warning and Control
AEWCAP Airborne Early Warning Combat Air Patrol
AEWES Army Engineers Waterways Experiment Station
AEWHA All-England Women's Hockey Association
AEWIS Army Electronic Warfare Information System (USA)
AEWL Association of Employers of Waterside Labour (Australian)
AEWLA All-England Women's Lacrosse Association
AEWRON Airborne Early Warning Squadron
AEWS Advanced Earth Satellite Weapon System (USAF); Aircraft Early Warning System (DoD)
AEWSPS Aircraft Electronic Warfare Self-Protection System
aex automatic electronic exchange (facilitating telephony)
AExO Assistant Experimental Officer
af audiofrequency
af (AF) ale firkin; audio fidelity; autofocus
a-f anti-foam; audio-frequency
a/f *a favor* (Spanish—a favor)
af afgang (Danish—departure); *anno futuro* (Italian—next year); (Latin prefix—movement toward a central point)
a.f. ad finem (Latin—to the end)
aF attofarad(s)
Af Africa; Afrikaans; African(s); Académie française (French Academy)
AF Africa(n); Air Force; air freight; Anglo-French; Armored Force; Arthritis Foundation; Aviation Photographer's Mate; provision stores ship (2-letter symbol)
A-F Anglo-French
A.F. Admiral of the Fleet (Louis Mountbatten, the Earl Mountbatten of Burma, KG, signed himself Mountbatten of Burma, A.F.)
A/F Air Field
A & F Agriculture and Forestry (Senate Committee)
A of F Admiral of the Fleet
AF35m auto-focus 35mm (camera)
afa azimuth follow-up amplifier

AFA Actors Fund of America; Advertising Federation of America; Advertising Federation of Australia; Aerophilatelic Federation of the Americas; Air Force Association; Alien Firearms Act; American Finance Association; American Forensic Association; American Forestry Association; American Foundrymens Association; American Freedom Association; Association of Federal Appraisers; Australian Field Artillery; Australian Foundation for Alcoholism
AF of A. Advertising Federation of America
A.F.A. Associate in Fine Arts
AFAA Adult Film Association of America; Air Force Audit Agency; Automatic Fire Alarm Association
AFAAEC Air Force Academy and Aircrew Examining Center
afac (AFAC) airborne forward air controller
AFAC Air Force Armament Center; American Fisheries Advisory Committee; Arkansas Foundation of Associated Colleges
afactplan affirmative action plan(ning)
AFADD Australian Foundation for Alcoholism and Drug Dependence
AFADO Association of Food and Drug Officials
AFAFC Air Force Accounting and Finance Center
AFAG Airforce Advisory Group
AFAIM Associate Fellow of the Australian Institute of Management
AFAITC Armed Forces Air Intelligence Training Center
AFAL Air Force Avionics Laboratory
afam airfield attack ammunition; automatic frequency-assignment model
AF & AM Ancient Free and Accepted Masons
Af-Am(s) Afro-American(s)
AFAP Australian Federation of Airline Pilots
AFAPL Air Force Aero-Propulsion Laboratory
afar airborne fixed-array radar
AFAR Azores Fixed Acoustic Range (NATO)
AFAR Australian Foreign Affairs Record

Afars and Issas formerly French Somaliland now the Republic of Djibouti and still a port shipping many minerals as well as salt crystals

AFAS Air Force Aid Society; Automated Frequency-Assignment System

AFASE Association for Applied Solar Energy

AFA-SEF Air Force Association —Space Education Foundation

AFASIC Association For All Speech-Impaired Children

AFAUD Air Force Auditor General

afb acid-fast bacillus; antifriction bearing

afb afbeelding (Dutch—illustration)

AFB Air Force Base; American Farm Bureau; American Foundation for the Blind

AFBF American Farm Bureau Federation

AFBI Australian Fibre Box Industry

AFBMA Antifriction Bearing Manufacturers Association

AFBMD Air Force Ballistic Missile Division

AFBNM Agate Fossil Beds National Monument (Nebraska)

AFBS American and Foreign Bible Society; Ansett Flying Boat Services

AFBSD Air Force Ballistic Systems Division

afc antibody forming cells; automatic frequency control

afc (AFC) average fixed cost

AFC Air Force Cross; American Football Conference; Apollo Flight Control (NASA); Area Forecast Center; Australian Film Commission; Australian Flying Corps

AFCAI Associate Fellow of the Canadian Aeronautical Institute

AFCAL Association Française de Calcul

AFCBS Australian Federation of Commercial Broadcasting Stations

AFCC Air Force Communications Center; Australian Federal Cycling Council; Australian Federation of Construction Contractors

AFCCB Air Force Configuration Control Board

AFCCDD Air Force Command and Control Development Division

AFCCP Air Force Component Command Post

AFCD Air Force Cryptologic Depot

afce automatic flight-control equipment

AFCE Associate in Fuel Technology and Chemical Engineering

AFCEA Armed Forces Communications and Electronics Association

AFCEC Australian Federation of Civil Engineering Contractors

AFCent Allied Forces, Central Europe

afcfs advanced fighter-control-flight simulator

AFCI American Foot Care Institute

AFCL Africa Container Lines

AFCM Air Force Commendation Medal

AFCMA Aluminum Foil Container Manufacturers Association; Australian Fibreboard Container Manufacturers Association

AFCMC Air Force Contract Maintenance Center

AFCMD Air Force Contract Management Division

AFCMO Air Force Contract Management Office

AFCN American Friends of the Captive Nations

afco automatic fuel cutoff

AFCO Admiralty Fleet Confidential Order; Air Force Contracting Office(r); Australian Federation of Consumer Organisations

AF Compt Air Force Comptroller

AFCOMSECCEN Air Force Communications Security Center

AFCON Air Force Controlled (units)

AFCOS Armed Forces Courier Service

AFCR American Federation for Clinical Research

AFCRC Air Force Cambridge Research Center

AFCRL Air Force Cambridge Research Laboratories

AFCs Air Force Circulars

AFCS Active Federal Commissioned Service; Adaptive Flight Control System; Air Force Communications Service; Automatic Flight Control System

AFCS E&I Air Force Communications Service—Engineering and Installation

AFCSL Air Force Communications Security Letter

AFCSM Air Force Communications Security Manual

AFCSP Air Force Communications Security Pamphlet

AFCUL Australian Federation of Credit Union Leagues

AFCW Association of Family Case Workers

AFCWF Air Force Civilian Welfare Fund

afd accelerated freeze drying; alternate full day

afd afdeling (Dano-Norwegian —department, division, section); *afdeling* (Dutch—part)

AFD Air Force Depot; Association of Food Distributors; Association of Footwear Distributors; mobile floating drydock (naval symbol)

AFDA American Flag Day Association; Australian Defence Force Academy

AFDAA Air Force Data Automation Agency

AFDAP Air Force Directorate of Advanced Technology

AFDATACOM Air Force Data Communications System

AFDATASTA Air Force Data Station

AFDB African Development Bank; Air Force Decorations Board; large auxiliary floating drydock (naval symbol)

AFDC Aid for Dependent Children; Aid for Families with Dependent Children; Australian Film Development Corporation

AFDCB Armed Forces Disciplinary Control Board

AFDCMI Air Force Policy on Disclosure of Classified Military Information

AFDCUF Aid to Families with Dependent Children of Unemployed Fathers

AFDC-UP Aid to Families of Dependent Children—for Unemployed Parents

AFDE American Fund for Dental Education

AFDEA American Funeral Directors and Embalmers Association

AFDH American Fund for Dental Health

AFDL small auxiliary floating drydock (naval symbol)

AFDM medium auxiliary floating drydock (naval symbol)

AFDO Air Force Duty Officer; Association of Food and Drug Officials

AFDOA Armed Forces Dental Officers Association

AFDOUS Association of Food and Drug Officials of the United States

AFDP Air Force Development Plan

AFDRB Air Force Disability Review Board; Air Force Discharge Review Board

AFDRD Air Force Director of Research and Development

AFDRQ Air Force Director of Requirements

AFDS Air Fighting Development Squadron

AFDSC Air Force Data Services Center

AFE Administración de Ferrocarriles del Estado (State Railway Administration of Uruguay)

AFEA American Farm Economic Association; American Film Export Association

AFEB Armed Forces Epidemiological Board

AFEE Airborne Forces Experimental Establishment

AFELIS Air Force Engineering and Logistics Information System

AFEM Armed Forces Expeditionary Medal

AFEMS Air Force Equipment Management System

AFEOC Air Force Emergency Operations Center

AFEOS Air Force Electro-Optical Site

AFER Air Force Engineering Responsibility

AFERB Air Force Educational Requirements Board

AFERO Asia and the Far East Regional Office (FAO)

AFES Air Force Exchange Service; American Far Eastern Society; Armed Forces Examining Stations

AFESA Air Force Engineering and Services Agency

AFETR Air Force Eastern Test Range (see ETR)

AFEX Air Forces Europe Exchange

aff affairs

AFF affinity (computerese); Army Field Forces

AFFA Air Freight Forwarders Association; Angels Forever, Forever Angels (slogan of Hell's Angels motorcycle gang)

Affable Archangel Raphael

affaire *affaire de coeur* (French —affair of the heart)—love affair

AFFC Air Force Finance Center

affd affixed; afford(able); affordability

AFFDL Air Force Flight Dynamics Laboratory

AFFE Air Force Far East; Allied Forces Far East; Army Forces Far East

affec affectation; affection; affective

affet *affettuoso* (Italian—tenderly, with pathos)

afff aqueous film-forming foam

AFFFA American Forged Fitting and Flange Association

AFFI American Frozen Food Institute

Affie Alfred

affil affiliated

affirm affirmative

AFFJ American Fund for Free Jurists

AFFL Agricultural Finance Federation, Limited

afflat afflatus

AFFLC Air Force Film Library Center

AFFOR Air Force Forces (joint task force element)

affores afforestation

affret *affrettando* (Italian—speeding the tempo)

AFFS American Federation of Film Societies

afft affidavit

AFFTC Air Force Flight Test Center; Air Force Flying Training Command

afg analog function generator

afg *afgang* (Dano-Norwegian—departure)

Afg Afghan; afghani (currency); Afghanistan; Afghans

AFG Allied Freighter Guard

AFGC American Forage and Grassland Council

AFGCM Air Force Good Conduct Medal

AFGE American Federation of Government Employees

afghan afghan blanket (geometric pattern imposed on a crocheted or woven woolen background); afghan hound (originally from Afghanistan and noted for its long silklike coat and narrow head)

Afghan Afghanistan

Afghanistan Republic of Afghanistan (landlocked Asian nation famed for its carpets, textiles, and sheepskin coats, Afghans speak Pushtu and other oriental languages) *Doulat i Jumhouri ye Afghanistān*

AFGIS Aerial Free Gunnery Instruction School

AFGL Air Force Geophysics Laboratory

AFGM American Federation of Grain Millers

AFGU Aerial Free Gunnery Unit

AFGW American Flint Glass Workers

AFGWC Air Force Global Weather Central

AFH Air Force Hospital; American Foundation for Homeopathy; Associated Federated Hotels; Australian Field Hospital

AFHC Air Force Headquarters Command

AFHF Air Force Historical Foundation; American Foot Health Foundation

AFHQ Air Force Headquarters; Allied Forces Headquarters; Armed Forces Headquarters

AFHW American Federation of Hosiery Workers

afi amaurotic familial idiocy

AFI Air Filter Institute; Air Force Intelligence; American Film Institute; American Filter Institute; American Forest Institute; American Friends of Israel; Armed Forces Institute; Association of Federal Investigators; Atlantic Refining Company (stock exchange symbol); Australian Film Institute; Australian Foundry Institute; Australian Frontier Incorporated

AFIA American Footwear Industries Association; American Foreign Insurance Association

AFIAS Associate Fellow of the Institute of the Aerospace Sciences

afib atrial fibrillation

afic *aficionado* (Spanish—admirer, devotee, fan)

AFIC Air Force Intelligence Center; Australian Fishing Industry Council

AFICCS Air Force Interim Command and Control System

AFICE Air Forces—Iceland

AFIED Armed Forces Information and Education Division

AFII American Federation of

International Institutes

AFIIM Associate Fellow of the Institute of Industrial Managers

AFINE Association Française pour l'Industrie Nucleaire d'Equipement (French Association for the Nuclear Equipment Industry)

AFINS Airways Flight Inspector

AFIO Association of Former Intelligence Officers

AFIP Air Force Intelligence Publication; Armed Forces Information Program; Armed Forces Institute of Pathology

AFIPS American Federation of Information Processing Societies

AFIR Air Force Installation Representative

AFIRAN Africa-Indian Ocean Region Air Navigation

AFIRO Air Force Installations Representative Officer

AFIS Air Force Intelligence Services, Armed Forces Information School; Armed Forces Information System; Automated Field Interview System

AFISC Air Force Inspection and Safety Center

afism aluminum-free inorganic suspended material

AFISR Air Force Industrial Security Regulations

afit airblast fuel-injection tube

AFIT Air Force Institute of Technology

AFITAE Association Francçaise d'Ingénieurs et Techniciens de l'Espace (French Association of Aeronautical and Aerospace Engineers and Technicians)

AFJAG Air Force Judge Advocate General

AFJKT Air Force Job-Knowledge Test

afk afkorting (Dutch—abbreviation)

afl abstract family of languages; anti-fatty liver; atrial flutter

afl aflevering (Dutch—part)

AFL Aeroflot (Soviet Air Lines); Air Force Letter; American Federation of Labor; American Football League; Applied Fisheries Laboratory (University of Washington); Association for Family Living; Australasian Federation League; Australian Fertilizers Limited

AFLA Amateur Fencers League

of America; American Foreign Law Association; Asian Federation of Library Associations

AFLAT Air Force Language Aptitude Test

aflatox aflatoxin

AFLC Air Force Logistics Command

AFL–CIO American Federation of Labor and Congress of Industrial Organizations

AFLCPs Air Force Logistics Command Pamphlets

afld airfield

aflir advanced forward-looking infrared

AFLP American Farmer Labor Party; Armed Forces Language Program

AFLRL Army Fuels and Lubricants Research Laboratory

AFLS Air Force Library Service

AFLSA Air Force Longevity Service Award

aflt afloat

afm antifriction metal

AFM Air Force Manual; Air Force Medal; Air Force Museum; American Federation of Musicians; Associated Fur Manufacturers

AFMA American Footwear Manufacturers Association; Armed Forces Management Association

AFMA Air Force Manual of Abbreviations

AFMBE Australian Federation for Medical and Biological Engineering

AFMBT Artificial Flower Manufacturers Board of Trade

AFMDC Air Force Missile Development Center

AFME American Friends of the Middle East

AFMEA Air Force Management Engineering Agency

AFMEC African Methodist Episcopal Church

AFMed Allied Forces, Mediterranean

AFMF Air Fleet Marine Force

AFMH American Foundation for Mental Hygiene

AFMIC Air Force Materials Information Center

AFML Air Force Materials Laboratory; Armed Forces Medical Library

AFMMFO Air Force Medical Materiel Field Office

afmo afectísimo (Spanish—most affectionate)

AFMPA Armed Forces Medical

Publication Agency

AFMPC Air Force Military Personnel Center

afmr antiferromagnetic resonance

AFMR American Foundation for Management Research; Armed Forces Master Records

AFMS Air Force Medical Service; American Federation of Minerological Societies; Australian Farm Management Society

AFMSC Air Force Medical Specialist Corps

AFMTC Air Force Missile Test Center

AFMVOP Air Force Motor Vehicle Operator Test

AFMW Australian Federation of Medical Women

afn active filter network

AFN Afrique du Nord (French North Africa); Air Force Finance Center; Alaska Federation of Natives; American Forces Network; Armed Forces Network

AF of N Alaska Federation of Natives

AFNA Accordion Federation of North America; Air Force with Navy; American Foundation for Negro Affairs

AFNB Armed Forces News Bureau

AFNC Air Force Nurse Corps

AFNE Allied Forces, Northern Europe; Americans For Nuclear Energy

AFNIL Agence Francophone pour la Numérotation Internationale du Livre (French Agency for the International Numbering of Books)

AFNOR Association Française de Normalisation (French Standards Association)

AFNorth Allied Forces, Northern Europe

AFO Accounting and Finance Office(r); Admiralty Fleet Order; Airports Field Office; Atlantic Fleet Organization

AFOAR Air Force Office for Aerospace Research

AFOAS Air Force Office of Aerospace Sciences

AFOAT Air Force Office for Atomic Energy

AFOB American Foundation for Overseas Blind

AFOC Air Force Operations Center

AFOECP Air Force Officer

Education and Commissioning Program

AFOG Asian Federation of Obstetrics and Gynaecology

AFOIC Air Force Officer in Charge

AFOQT Air Force Officer Qualifying Test

AFORG Air Force Overseas Replacement Group

a fort a fortiori (Italian—with greater force)

AFOS Advanced Field Operations System; Automation of Field Operations and Services (NWS)

AFOSI Air Force Office of Special Investigations

AFOSP Air Force Office of Security Police

AFOSR Air Force Office of Scientific Research

AFOUA Air Force Outstanding Unit Award

afp anterior faucial pillar

afp (AFP) alphafetroprotein

AFP Agence France-Presse (successor to Havas); Air Force Pamphlet; Air Force Police; Alternate Flight Plan; American Family Publishers; American Federation of Police; Anglican Fellowship of Prayer; Annual Funding Program; Armed Forces Police; Authority for Purchase

AF of P American Federation of Police

afpa automatic flow process analysis

AFPA Aquarama and Fairmount Park Aquarium; Australian Fire Protection Association

AFPAO Air Force Property Accountable Office(r)

AFPAV Air Force Pavement

AFPB Air Force Personnel Board

AFPC Air Force Personnel Council; Air Force Procurement Circular; American Food for Peace Council; Armed Forces Policy Council

AFPCB Armed Forces Pest Control Board

AFPD Armed Forces Police Detachment

AFPE American Foundation for Pharmaceutical Education; American Foundation for Political Education

AFPH American Federation of the Physically Handicapped

AFPI Air Force Procurement Instructions; American Forest

Products Industries

AFPP Air Force Procurement Procedures

AFPPA American Federation of Poultry Producers Associations

AFPR Air Force Plant Representative

AFPRO Action for Food Production; Air Force Plant Representative's Office

AFPs American Freeway Patrol cars (American Oil Company's free service to motorists in trouble on freeways)

AFPS Armed Forces Press Service

AFPT Air Force Personnel Test

AFPTRC Air Force Personnel and Training Research Center

AFPU Air Force Postal Unit; Australian Federation of Police Unions

AFQ Association Forestière Québeçoise (Quebec Forestry Service)

AFQA Air Force Quality Assurance

AFQC Air Force Quality Control

AFQT Armed Forces Qualification Test

afr acceptable failure rate; airframe; air-fuel ratio; automatic field/format recognition; away from reactor

afr afrikansk (Dano-Norwegian —African)

Afr Africa; African; Africans; Afrikaans (South African Dutch)

A Fr Algerian franc

A-Fr Anglo-French

AFR Air Force Regulation(s); Air Force Reserve

AFR Australian Financial Review

afra average freight rate assessment

AFRA American Farm research Association; American Federation of Television and Radio Artists

AFRAeS Associate Fellow of the Royal Aeronautical Society

AFRAM Afro-American

A-frame capital-A-shaped support frame

Aframerican African + American

AFRASEC Afro-Asian Organization for Economic Cooperation

Afrasia Africa + Asia

AFRB Air Force Retiring Board

AFRBA Armed Forces Relief and Benefit Association

AFRBSG Air Force Reserve Base Support Group

AFRC Air Force Records Center; Air Force Regional Civil Engineer

AFRCC Air Force Rescue Coordination Center; Air Force Reserve Coordination Center

AFRCSTC Air Force Reserve Combat Support Training Center

afrd acute febrile respiratory disease (AFRD)

AFRD Air Force Research Division; Air Force Reserve Division; Association of Fund-Raising Directors

A-freak lsd (LSD) acid freak (addict)

AFRes Air Force Reserve

AFRESM Armed Forces Reserve Medal

AFRESNAVSQ Air Force Reserve Navigation Squadron

AFRFI American Friends of Religious Freedom in Israel

afri acute febrile respiratory illness (AFRI)

AFRI Applied Forest Research Institute

Afric Africa; African

Africa in Miniature Cameroon

African languages Hausa is the tongue of Central and West Africa and is used by at least 18 million people; Swahili prevails in many parts of East Africa, and some 18 million speak it; Yoruba is spoken by about 12 million in West Africa and is followed by Ibo used by about nine million; other African tongues include Rwanda used by some six million in southern Central Africa, Somali by some four million in East Africa, Xhosa and Zulu by some four million each in South Africa

African Queen Mrs Ian Smith of Salisbury, Rhodesia

Africa's big five Cape buffalo, elephant, leopard, lion, rhinoceros

Africs Africans

afrik afrikansk (Dano-Norwegian—African)

Afrik Afrikaans

Afrik Afrikaans (Dutch dialect spoken by about five million people in South Africa, this is the language of the Boers)

Afrique (French—Africa)

afrm airframe

Afr Nat Cnl African National Council

Afro prefix meaning African or Black

AFRO African Regional Office (FAO)

Afro-Am Afro-American(ese)

Afro-American African-American

Afro-America's First Great Poet Paul Laurence Dunbar

Afro-Bras Afro-Brasiliero (Afro-Brazilian)

Afro-Carib Afro-Caribbean; Afro-Caribeño

Afro(s) Afro-American(s)— Black(s), Negro(es)

AFROTC Air Force Reserve Officers Training Corps

AFRPL Air Force Rocket Propulsion Laboratory

AFRR Air Force Reserve Region

AFRRG Air Force Reserve Recovery Group

AFRRI Armed Forces Radiobiology Research Institute

afr's auditor freight receipts

AFRS Air Force Reserve Sector; Armed Forces Radio Service

AFRTS Armed Forces Radio-Television Service

AFRTVS Armed Forces Radio and Television Services

AFRVN Air Force of the Republic of Viet Nam

afs aerial fire support; aforesaid; atomic fluorescence spectroscopy

afs afsender (Danish—sender)

AFS Active Fusing System; Air Force Specialty; Air Force Station; Air Force Supply; Airline Feed System; Airways Facilities Shop; Alaska Ferry Service; American Feline Society; American Fern Society; American Field Service; American Fisheries Society; American Folklore Society; American Foundrymen's Society; American Fuchsia Society; Aviation Facilities Service; Azimuth Follow-up System

AFSA Air Force Sergeants Association; American Federation of School Administrators; American Flight Strips Association; American Foreign Service Association; Armed Forces Security Agency

AFSAB Air Force Science Advisory Board

AFSAS American Federation of

School Administrators and Supervisors

AFSATCOMS Air Force Satellite Communications System

AFSAW Air Force Special Activities Wing

Af-Sax Afro-Saxon (black person of part Anglo-Saxon parentage, white-oriented person of African origin)

AFSB American Federation of Small Business

AFSBO American Federation of Small Business Organizations

AFSC Air Force Service Command; Air Force Specialty Code; Air Force Supply Catalog; Air Force Systems Command; American Federation of Soroptimist Clubs; American Friends Service Committee; Armed Forces Staff College

AFSCC Air Force Special Communications Center; Armed Forces Supply Control Center

AFSCF Air Force Satellite Control Facility

AFSCM Air Force Systems Command Manual

AFSCME American Federation of State, County, and Municipal Employees

afsd aforesaid

AFSE Allied Forces Southern Europe (NATO)

AFSec Air Force Section

AFSF Air Force Stock Fund

AFSIL Accommodations for Students in London

AFSM Association for Food Service Management

AFSMAAG Air Force Section —Military Advisory Group

AFSN Air Force Serial Number; Air Force Service Number; Air Force Stock Number

AFSNCOA Air Force Senior Noncommissioned Officers' Academy

AFSouth Allied Forces, Southern Europe

AFSRS Australian Flying Saucer Research Society

AFSS Air Force Security Service; Air Force Service Statement

AFSSD Air Force Space Systems Division

AFSSO Air Force Special Security Office

AFSTC Air Force Space Test Center

AFSUB Army Air Forces Anti-Submarine Command

AFSWA Armed Forces Special

Weapons Agency

AFSWC Air Force Special Weapons Center

AFSWP Armed Forces Special Weapons Project

aft after; afternoon; at, near, or toward the rear; automatic fine tuning

aft. (AFT) automatic fund transfer

Aft Aftenposten (Evening Post— Oslo)

AFT Air Freight Terminal; American Federation of Teachers; Annual Field Training (USA)

AFT (AFL-CIO) American Federation of Teachers

AFTA Atlantic Free Trade Area; Australian Federation of Travel Agents

AFTAC Air Force Technical Applications Center

AFTAU American Friends of Tel Aviv University

aftb afterburner

AFTB Air Force Test Base

AFTC Airborne Flight Training Command; American Fair Trade Council; American Fox Terrier Club; American Free Trade Clubs

AFTE American Federation of Technical Engineers

AFTEC Air Force Test and Evaluation Center

AFTF Air Force Task Force

AFTI Advanced Fighter Technology Integration (USAF)

AFTIA Armed Forces Technical Information Agency

AFTLI Association of Feeling Truth and Living It

AFTM American Foundation for Tropical Medicine

AFTMA American Fishing Tackle Manufacturers Association

aftn afternoon

AFTN Aeronautical Fixed Telecommunications Network

afto afecto (Spanish—affectionate, fond)

AFTO Air Force Technical Order

AFTOSB Air Force Technical Order Standardization Board

aftp additional flight-training period

AFTR American Federal Tax Reports

AFTRA American Federation of Television and Radio Artists

AFTRC Air Force Technical Training Command

afts automatic frequency tone shift

AFTS Aeronautical Fixed Telecommunications Service; Aseptic Fluid Transfer System; Australian Film and Television School

AFTTH Air Force Technical Training Headquarters

AFTU Arizona Federation of Teacher Unions

afu all fucked up

AFU Advanced Flying Units; American Fraternal Union; Assault Fire Unit (U.S. Army)

AFU Association Fonciere Urbaine (French—Urban Land Association)

AFULE Australian Federated Union of Locomotive Enginemen

A-funk lsd (LSD) acid funk (drug depression)

AFUS Air Force of the United States; Armed Forces of the United States

AFUW Australian Federation of University Women

afv armored fighting vehicle; armored force vehicle

AFVA Air Force Visual Aid

AFvg Anglo-French variable geometry

AFVN Armed Forces Vietnam Network

AFVOA Aberdeen Fishing Vessel Owners Association

AFW Association for Family Welfare

AFWA Air Force with Army

AFWAL Air Force Wright Aeronautical Laboratories

AFWE Air Forces Western Europe (NATO)

AFWETS Air Force Weapons Effectiveness Testing System

AFWL Air Force Weapons Laboratory; Armed Forces Writers League

AFWN Air Force with Navy

AFWOFS Air Force Weather Observing and Forecasting System

AFWR Atlantic Fleet Weapons Range

AFWST Armed Forces Women's Selection Test

AFWTR Air Force Western Test Range (see WTR)

Afyon Afyonkarahisar (Turkish —Black Castle of Opium)— town in western central Turkey where much of the world's opium is grown

AFZ Australian Fishing Zone

ag against; agar-agar; agency; agent; aggie; aggressive; agribusiness; agricultural; agriculture; agrobiology; agroindustrial; agrology; agronomy; alternate geologies; armor grating; atrial gallop; axiogingival

a-g air-to-ground; anti-gas

a/g air-to-ground; albumin-globulin ratio

a g à gauche (French—to the left)

Ag Agostino

Ag argentum (Latin—silver)

AG Adjutant General; Aeronautical Standards Group; Air Group; Aktiengesellschaft (German—joint stock company); Allegheny Ludlum Steel (stock exchange symbol); Artists Guild; Attorney General; Auditor General; escort research vessel (naval symbol); miscellaneous auxiliary vessels (naval symbol); sonar research ship (naval symbol); technical research ship (naval symbol)

AG Aktien Gesellschaft (German —company, joint stock company); *Alberghi per la Gioventu* (Italian—Youth Hostels); *Arkansas Gazette; Astronomische Gesellschaft*

aga accelerated growth area; appropriate for gestational age

a/g/a air-to-ground-to-air

AGA Abrasive Grain Association; Adjutants General Association; Alabama Gas (symbol); American Gas Association; American Gastroenterological Association; American Gastroscopic Association; American Genetic Association; American Glassware Association; American Goiter Association; American Gold Association; Australian Garrison Artillery; Australian Gas Association

AGAA Art Galleries Association of Australia

AGAAC Acuerdo General sobre Aranceles Aduaneros y Comercio (Spanish—General Accord concerning Custom's Duties and Commerce)

AGAC American Guild of Authors and Composers

Aga cooker Aktiebolaget gas-accumulative cooker

agacs automatic ground-air-communication system

AGAFBO Atlantic and Gulf American Flag Berth Operators

AGAL Australian Government Analytical Laboratory

agalmatolite talc

Agaña Guam's capital

AGARD Advisory Group for Aeronautical Research and Development (NATO)

AGAS Australian Government Advertising Service

agate chalcedony

Agate Capital Prineville, Oregon's place-name nickname

Agatha Christie Agatha Mary Clarissa Miller before her first marriage when she became Agatha Christie and after her second marriage Agatha Mallowan

Agathon Agathon Press

agave. automatic gimballed antenna vectoring equipment

agb accessory gear box; any good brand

AGB Audits of Great Britain (television survey); icebreaker (3-letter symbol)

AGBAD Alexander Graham Bell Association for the Deaf

AGBI Artists' General Benevolent Institution

agbio agrobiology

AGBUC Association of Governing Boards of Universities and Colleges

agbus agribusiness; analog ground bus

agc air-ground communications; automatic gain control

AGC Adjutant General's Corps; Aerojet-General Corporation; American Grassland Council; amphibious force flagship (naval symbol); Armed Guard Center; Associated General Contractors; astronomical great circle (course); Australian Government Centre; Australian Guarantee Corporation

AGC Amgueddea Genedlaethol Cymru (Welsh—National Museum of Wales)

agca automatic ground control approach

AGCA Associated General Contractors of America

AGCan Auditor General of Canada

agcl automatic ground-controlled landing

AGCM Army Good Conduct Medal

AGCMWA Amon G Carter Museum of Western Art

agcol agricultural college

AGCRSP Army Gas-Cooled Reactor Systems Program

AGCSB Atlantic-Gulf Coastwise Steamship Freight Bureau

AGCSD Attorney General's Consumer Services Department

AGCT Army General Classification Test

AGCTS Armed Guard Center Training School

Ag-Cu al silver-copper alloy (new U.S. coin facing)

agcy agency

agd agreed; axial gear differential

AGD Academy of General Dentistry; Adjutant General's Department; American Gage Design; Auditor General's Department

AGD Australian Government Digest

AGDA American Gasoline Dealers Association; American Gun Dealers Association

AGDC Assistant Grand Director of Ceremonies

AGDE escort research ship (naval symbol)

Ag. Dei Agnus Dei (Latin—Lamb of God)

Ag Dept Agriculture Department

AGDS American Gage Design Standard

age. (AGE) aerospace ground equipment; automatic guidance electronics

Age The Age (Melbourne)

Ag.E. Agricultural Engineer

AGE AG Edwards; Amarillo Grain Exchange; Asian Geotechnical Engineering (Thailand)

A.G.E. Associate in General Education

Age of Anxiety Bernstein's Symphony No. 2

AGEC Army General Equipment Command

A.G.Ed. Associate in General Education

AGED Advisory Group on Electronic Devices

AGEH hydrofoil research ship (naval symbol)

AGEHR American Guild of English Handbell Ringers

agents provocs agents provocateurs (French—secret agents) —persons hired to provoke others to commit crimes so arrest and conviction can follow

ageocp aerospace ground equipment out of commission for parts

AGEP Advisory Group on Electronic Parts

AGER environmental research ship (naval symbol)

agerd aerospace ground-equipment requirements data

AGERS Auxiliary General Electronics Research Ship(s)

AG & ES American Gas & Electric System

AGET Advisory Group on Electronic Tubes

Age of Uncertainty John Kenneth Galbraith's name for our era

Age of Voltaire the Enlightenment

AGF Army Ground Forces; miscellaneous command ship (naval symbol)

AGFA Aktiengesellschaft für Anilinfabrikation (Corporation for Aniline Manufacture)

ag.feb. aggrediente febre (Latin —when fever increases)

Ag and Fish Ministry of Agriculture and Fisheries

AGFRTS Air and Ground Forces Resources and Technical Staff (U.S. Army)

AGFSRS Aircraft Ground Fire Suppression and Rescue System (DoD)

agg agammaglobulinaemia(c); agglutination(ed); aggravate(ed); aggregate(d); aggregation

aggie agriculture

Aggie Agatha; Agnes

aggies agate playing marbles; students of agricultural colleges or schools

agglut agglutination (ed)

aggr aggregate

AGGR Air-to-Ground Gunnery Range

aggred. feb. aggrediente febre (Latin—while fever is developing)

aggro aggression; aggressiveness

aggs anti-gas gangrene serum

AGGS American Good Government Society

Aggy Agatha; Agnes

AGH Australian General Hospital

AGHE Association for Gerontology in Higher Education

agi adjusted gross income

AGI American Geographical Institute; American Geological Institute; Annual General Inspection

AGI Agenzia Giornalistica Italiana (Italian News Agency); *Associazione Guide Italiane* (Italian Girl Guides' Association)

AGIC Air-Ground Information Center

AGIFORS Airlines Group of International Federation of Operations Research Societies

agil airborne general illumination light

agile. airborne general illumination light; analytic geometry interpretative language

AGILE Autonetics General Information Learning Equipment

ag imps hnd agricultural implements hand

ag imps ot hand agricultural implements other than hand

ag'in' against

agind agroindustrial

AGIO Australian Government Insurance Office

AGIP Azienda Generale Italiana Petroli (National Italian Oil Company)

agipa adaptive ground-implemented-phased array

agit agitate(d); agitation; agitato; agitator

agit. agitatum (Latin—shaken)

agit. ante sum *agita ante sumendum* (Latin—shake before using)

agit. a. us. agita ante usum (Latin—shake before using)

agit. bene agita bene (Latin—shake well)

agit-prop agitation and propaganda

agit. vas. agitato vase (Latin—shaking the vessel)

agl above ground level; acute granulocytic leukemia; airborne gun laying, aminoglutethimide

AGL Australian Gas Light (company); lighthouse tender (3-letter symbol)

agland(s) agricultural land(s)

AGLC Air-to-Ground Liaison Code

AGLINET Agricultural Libraries Information Network (UN)

aglm agglomerate

AGLS Association of General and Liberal Studies

AGLSP Association of Graduate Liberal Studies Programs

A-glue airplane glue

agm (AGM) air-to-ground mis-

sile
AGM American Guild of Music; Annual General Meeting (of shareholders); Australian Glass Manufacturers; missile range instrumentation ship (naval symbol)
AGM-53A North American-Rockwell Condor air-to-surface missile
AGMA American Gear Manufacturers Association; Athletic Goods Manufacturers Association
AGMA (AFL-CIO) American Guild of Musical Artists
AGMIS Adjutant General Management Information System
Agmk African green monkey kidney
AGMR major communications relay ship (naval symbol)
agn acute glomerulonephritis; again; agnomen
Agn Augustín
Agñ Agaña, Guam
AGN Aerojet-General Nucleonics
Agncy Agency (postal place-name abbreviation)
Agnes Lee Mrs Otto Freer
agnos agnostic; agnosticism
AGNS Allied General Nuclear Services
ago. atmospheric gas oil
ago *agitato* (Italian—agitated); *agosto* (Spanish—August)
AGO Adjutant General's Office; Air Gunnery Officer; American Guild of Organists; Attorney General's Office; Attorney General's Opinion
AGOR Auxiliary General Oceanographic Research (vessel)
agp above-ground pool; automatic guidance programming
AGP Academy of General Practice; Achievement Goals Program (to improve test scores in minority schools); Achievement Guidance Program; Adjutant General's Pool; Army Ground Pool; motor torpedo boat tender (naval symbol)
AGPA American Group Psychotherapy Association
AGPC Adjutant General Publications Center
agpe angle plate
agpi automatic ground position indicator
AGPL *Administraçāo-Geral do Porto de Lisboa* (Portuguese—Port of Lisbon Authority)
ag prov agent provocateur

AGPS Australian Government Publishing Service
agr agree(ment); agricultural; agriculture
agr (AGR) advanced gas-cooled graphite-moderated reactor
AGRA Australian Garrison Royal Artillery
Agram (German—Zagreb)—Croatia's capital city
agrar agrarian; agrarianism; agrarians
a/g ratio albumin-globulin ratio
Agra U Agra University
agrbl agreeable
agrd agreed
AGRE Atlantic Gas Research Exchange
AGREE Advisory Group on Reliability of Electronic Equipment
agrep agricultural research project(s)
AGRF American Geriatric Research Foundation
agri agricultural; agriculturalist; agriculture; agriculturist
agribusiness agricultural business (large-scale farming)
agric agriculture
Agric E Agricultural Engineer
Agricola George Bauer
agricrime agricultural crime (theft of crops and/or equipment)
Agricultural Wizard of Tuskegee George Washington Carver
Agri Dagi (*see* Ararat)
agridollars agricultural (market) dollars
agri-indus agricultural-industrial (complex)
agrimech agriculture mechanized
agripower agricultural power
AGRIS Agricultural Information System
AGRM Adjutant General—Royal Marines
agrmt agreement
agro aggravation; agrobiological; agrobiologist; agrobiology; agrologic; agrological; agronomical; agronomics; agronomist; agronomy; etc.
agro *agronomiae* (Dano-Norwegian—agronomy)
agrobio agrobiologic(al)(ly); agrobiologist; agrobiology
agrogeol agrogeology
agroind agroindustrial(ly); agroindustrialization; agroindustrialize(r); agroindustry
agron agronomy
agros agrostology
ags adrenogenital syndrome;

agencies
ags (Ags) antigens
ags (AGS) alternation gradient synchrotron
Ags Aguascalientes (inhabitants —Hidrocalidos)
AGS Abort Guidance System; Academic Guidance Service; Aircraft General Standards; Alabama Great Southern (railroad); Allied Geographic Section; American Gem Society; American Geographical Society; American Geriatrics Society; American Goat Society; American Gynecological Society; Army General Staff; Army Guard School; Association of Graduate Schools; Australian Geomechanics Society; surveying ship (naval symbol)
A.G.S. Associate in General Studies
AGSA Art Gallery of South Australia
AGSI Automatic Government Source Inspection
AGSM American Gold Star Mothers; Associate of the Guildhall School of Music; Australian Graduate School of Management
AGSRO Association of Government Supervisors and Radio Officers
AGSS American Geographical and Statistical Society
agst against
agt agent; agreement
agt (AGT) antiglobulin test
AGT Art Gallery of Toronto, Association of Geology Teachers
AGTA Australian Geography Teachers Association
AGTC Airport Ground Traffic Control
AGTE Association of Group Travel Executives
AGTELIS Automated Ground Transportable Emitter Location and Identification System
AGTELS Automated Ground Tactical Emitter Location System
AGTF Alternate Geology Test Facility
agto *agosto* (Portuguese and Spanish—August)
agtt (AGTT) abnormal glucose tolerance test
agtv advanced ground transportation vehicle
AGU American Geophysical Union

Aguacates Aguacate Mountains (avocado-colored hills and mountains of Costa Rica)

Agu Cur Agulhas Current

Aguecheek Charles B Fairbanks

Agunalaksh (Aleut—Unalaska) —the shores where the sea breaks its back on the Aleutian Islands

agv aniline gentian violet

AGVA American Guild of Variety Artists

AGvga Anglo-German variable-geometry aircraft

agw actual gross weight; allowable gross takeoff weight

AGWA Australian Government Workers Association

AGWAC Australian Guided Weapons and Analog Computer

AGWD Australian Government Weekly Digest

AGWI American Gulf and West Indies (steamship line)

agy agency

agz actual ground zero

ah abdominal hysterectomy; acetohexamide, after hatch, alter heading; amenorrhea and hirsutism; aminohippurate; antihalation; antihyaluronidase; arterial hypertension; astigmatism hypermetropic

a-h ampere-hour

a/h at home

a & h accident and health; alive and healthy

Ah ampere-hour; hyperopic astigmatism

AH Airfield Heliport; Alfred Holt's Blue Funnel Line (house flag and funnel mark); Allis Chalmers (stock exchange symbol); Animal Husbandry (division of Department of Agriculture); Army Hospital; hospital ship (naval symbol)

A-H American-Hawaiian Line; Arrow-Hart & Hegeman Electric Company

A & H Arm and Hammer (trade mark)

AH Akademiya Nauk (Russian —Academy of Sciences)

A.H. Anno Hebraico (Latin—in the Hebrew Year); *Anno Hegirae* (Latin—Year of Hegira)— Moslem

AH-1 Huey Cobra gunship military aircraft carrying machine-gun pods on its stub wings, a 7.62mm minigun in its nose plus a grenade launcher

AH-64 attack helicopter

aha acquired hemolytic anemia; all have automobiles; autoimmune hemolytic anemia

AHA Adirondack Historical Association; American Hardboard Association; American Heart Association; American Hereford Association; American Historical Association; American Hospital Association; American Hotel Association; American Humane Association; American Humanist Association; American Hypnotherapy Association; Association of Handicapped Artists; Association for Humane Abortion; Australian Hospital Association; Australian Housewives Association

ahab attacking hardened air bases

AHAM Association of Home Appliance Manufacturers

ahas (AHAS) acetohydroxy acid synthase

AHAUS Amateur Hockey Association of the U.S.

ahc acute haemorrhagic conjunctivitis

AHC Academy of Hospital Counselors; American Hardware Corporation; American Hockey Coaches; American Horticultural Council; American Hospital Corps; Army Hospital Corps; Australian Heritage Commission

ahca (AHCA) American Health Care Association

AHCA American Health Care Association

AHCEI American Histadrut Cultural Exchange Institute

AHCo Assault Helicopter Company (USAF)

ahd ahead; airhead; aired head; arteriosclerotic heart disease; atherosclerotic heart disease; auto-immune haemolytic disease

AHD American Heritage Dictionary

A-H DT Alaska-Hawaii Daylight Time

ahe acute hemorrhagic encephalomyelitis

AHE Association for Higher Education

A.H.E. Associate in Home Economics

AHEA American Home Economics Association; American Hungarian Educators Association

A-head acid head (underground slang—LSD addict); amphetamine addict

AHEAD Army Help for Education and Development

AHEL Army Human Engineering Laboratory (USA)

AHEM Association of Hydraulic Equipment Manufacturers

AHEPA American Hellenic Educational Progressive Association

AHES American Humane Education Society

ahf anti-hemophilic factor

Ahf Argentinian hemorrhagic fever

AHF American Health Foundation; American Heritage Foundation; American Hobby Federation; American Hungarian Foundation; Associated Health Foundation

AHF American Hospital Formulary; *Azod Hind Fouj* (Indian National Army)

AHFCR Anderson Hospital for Cancer Research

AHFS American Hospital Formulary Service

ahg antihemolytic globulin; antihuman globulin

ahg (AHG) antihemophilic globulin

AHG American Housing Guild

ahh alpha-hydrazine analog of histidine; arylhydrocarbon hydroxylase

AHHA Allied Home Health Association

AHHS Alexander Hamilton High School

AHI American Health Institute; American Honey Institute; American Hospital Institute; Animal Health Insurance

AHIL Association of Hospital and Institution Libraries

AHIP Australian Health Insurance Program

AHIRS Australian Health Information and Research Service

AHIS American Hull Insurance Syndicate

ahl alcohol-induced hyperlipidemia

a.h.l. ad hunc locum (Latin—at this place)

AHL Alaska Historical Library; American Hockey League; Associated Humber Lines; Association for Holistic Living

ahle acute hemorrhagic leukoencephalitis

AHLMA American Home Laundry Manufacturers Association

ahls antihuman-lymphocyte serum

ahm ampere-hour meter

Ahm Ahmadabad; Arnhem

ahma advanced hypersonic manned aircraft

AHMA American Hardware Manufacturers Association; American Hemisphere Marine Agencies; American Hotel and Motel Association

AHMC Association of Hospital Management Committees

Ahmed Mohammed Ahmed ibn-Seyyid Abdullah—the Mahdi

AHMI Appalachian Hardwood Manufacturers Incorporated

AHMPS Association of Headmistresses of Preparatory Schools

ahm(s) asiatic homosexual male(s)

AHMS American Home Missionary Society

AHMSA Altos Hornos de México (Spanish—Great Ovens of Mexico)—steel mills

AHN Assistant Head Nurse

AHNA Accredited Home Newspapers of America

a-hole ass hole (anus)

AHOP Assisted Home Ownership Plan

ahp acute hemorrhagic pancreatitis; air at high pressure; air horsepower; aviation horsepower

AHP American Home Products; Assistant House Physician; Association for Humanistic Psychology

AHPA American Horse Protection Association

AHPC American Heritage Publishing Company

AHPR Academy of Hospital Public Relations

ahps auxiliary hydraulic power supply

AHQ Air Headquarters; Allied Headquarters; Army Headquarters

ahr acceptable hazard rate

AHR Academy of Human Rights; Association for Health Records

AHRC Association for the Help of Retarded Children; Australian Housing Research Council; Australian Humanities Research Council

AHRGB Association of Hotels and Restaurants of Great Britain

ahs ablative heat shield

AHS Aerospace High School; American Harp Society; American Hearing Society; American Helicopter Society; American Hibiscus Society; American Home Security; American Horticultural Society; American Hospital Supply (stock exchange symbol); American Humane Society; American Hypnodontic Society; Assistant House Surgeon; Association for Humanistic Studies; Aviation High School; Aviation Historical Society

AHSA American Hampshire Sheep Association; American Horse Shows Association; Art, Historical, and Scientific Association; Aviation Historical Society of Australia

AHSB Authority Health and Safety Branch

AHSC American Hospital Supply Company

A-H Scale Anti-Hispanic Scale (measuring negative attitudes towards persons of Latin American origin such as Cubans, Mexicans, Puerto Ricans, etc.)

AHSCo Assault Helicopter Support Company (USAF)

ahse assembly, handling, and shipping equipment

AHSNZ Aviation Historical Society of New Zealand

ahsr air height-surveillance radar

AHSRC American High-Speed Railway Corporation (promotes bullet trains)

AHSS Association of Home Study Schools

AHSSPPE Association of Handicapped Student Service Programs in Postsecondary Education

A-H ST Alaska-Hawaii Standard Time

aht antihyaluronidase titer

AHT Animal Health Trust; Augmented Histamine Test

ahtm(s) asiatic heterosexual male(s)

AHTN Association of Hospital Television Networks

ahv (AHV) alternative fuel vehicle

a.h.v. ad hunc vocem (Latin—at this word)

AHV Altos Hornos de Vizcaya

Ahvenanmaa (Finnish—Ahvenanmaa Islands)—called Åland by the Swedes

AHWA Association of Hospital and Welfare Administrators

AHWG Ad Hoc Working Group (USA)

ai accidentally incurred; achievement via independence; airborne intercept; anti-icing; aortic incompetence; aortic insufficiency; apical impulse; articulation index; artificial insemination; artificial intelligence; axioincisal; azimuth indicator

a&i accident and indemnity

a & i abstracting and indexing

a. i. ad interim (Latin—in the interim)

AI Aaland Islands; Admiralty Islands; Adult Institutions (New Hampshire); Air India; Air Inspector; Air Installation(s); Airways Inspector; Alianza Interamericana (Inter-American Alliance); Allegheny International; American Institute; Amnesty International; Arctic Institute; Army Intelligence; Aspen Institute (Aspen, Colorado); Astrologers International; Avery Island

A/I Aptitude Index

A & I Afars and Issas (formerly French Somaliland); agricultural and industrial (college or school or subjects); Arts and Industries

aia advise if able; anti-icing additive

AIA Aerospace Industries Association; Allergy Information Association; Allred Interaction Analysis; American Institute of Accountants; American Institute of Aeronautics; American Institute of Architects; Archeological Institute of America; Arctic Institute of America; Association Internationale d'Allergologie; Australian Insurance Association; Australian Italian Association

A.I.A. Associate of the Institute of Actuaries

AIAA Aerospace Industries Association of America; American Industrial Arts Association; American Institute of Aeronautics and Astronautics

AIAC Air Industries Association of Canada

AIAD Acronymys, Initialisms, & Abbreviations Dictionary

AIADA American Imported Automobile Dealers Association

AIAE Association of Institutes

of Automobile Engineers

AIAESD American International Association for Economic and Social Development (AIA)

AIAL Associate of the Institute of Arts and Letters

AIAOS Academic Instructor and Allied Officer School

AIAP Ardmore Industrial Air Park

AIArb Associate of the Institute of Arbitrators

AIAS Australian Institute of Aboriginal Studies; Australian Institute of Agriculture and Science

AIAT Attitude-Interest Analysis Test

AIAW Association for Intercollegiate Athletics for Women

aib aminoisobutyric acid

AIB Academy for International Business; Accident Investigative Branch; Accident Investigative Bureau; American Institute of Baking; American Institute of Banking; Anti-Inflation Board; Assassination Information Bureau; Australian Infantry Battalion; Australian Institute of Building

A.I.B. Associate of the Institute of Bankers

AIB Association des Industries de Belgique (Association of Belgian Industries); *Associazione Italiana Biblioteche* (Italian Library Association)

aiba amino-isobutyric acid

AIBA American Industrial Bankers Association

AIBA Association Internationale de Boxe Amateur (French —International Amateur Boxing Association)

AIBC Architectural Institute of British Columbia

AIBCS American Intersociety Board of Certification of Sanitarians

AIBD Associate of the Institute of British Decorators and Interior Designers

aibf advanced internally blown jet flap

aibm (AIBM) anti-intercontinental ballistic missile

AIBM Association Internationale des Bibliothèques Musicales (French—International Association of Music Libraries)

AIBP Associate of the Institute of British Photographers

AIBS American Institute of Bio-

logical Sciences

aic aminoimidazole carboxamide

aic (AIC) aircraft in commission

AIC Accelerator Information Center; Advanced Intelligence Center; Agricultural Institute of Canada; Aircraft Industries Center; Allied Intelligence Center; Allied Intelligence Committee; American Indian Center; American Institute of Chemists; American Institution of Cooperation; Ammunition Identification Code; Arab Information Center; Arab Investment Company; Army Industrial College; Army Intelligence Center; Art Information Center; Art Institute of Chicago; Artificial Illumination Centre; Australian Institute of Cartographers; Australian Institute of Criminology

AICA Australasian Institute of Cost Accountants

AICA Association Internationale des Critiques d'Art (French —International Association of Art Critics); *Associazione Italiana per il Calco Automatico* (Italian Association for Automatic Data Processing)

aicar amino-imidazolecarboxamide ribonucleotide

AICB Association Internationale Contre le Bruit (French— International Association Against Noise)

aicbm (AICBM) anti-intercontinental ballistic missile

aicc antibody-induced cell-mediated cytoxicity

AICC All-India Congress Committee

AICCC American Institute of Child Care Centers

AICCU Association of Independent California Colleges and Universities

AICE Agency for Information and Cultural Exchange (formerly the USIA); American Institute of Chemical Engineers; American Institute of Consulting Engineers

AI-CE Atomic International— Combustion Engineering

aicf auto-immune complement fixation

AICF America-Israel Cultural Foundation

aich automatic integrated container handling

AIChE American Institute of

Chemical Engineers (preferred abbreviation)

AICK Associated Independent Colleges of Kansas

AICM Association of Independent Conservators of Music; Australian Institute of Credit Management

AICMA Association Internationale des Constructeurs de Matériel Aéronautique

AICMDM Association of Independent Copy Machine Dealers and Manufacturers

AICO Action Information Control Office(r)—USN; American Insulator Corporation

AICPA American Institute of Certified Public Accountants

AICQ Associazione Italiana per il Controllo della Qualità (Italian Association for Quality Control)

AICR American Institute for Cancer Research

AICRO Association of Independent Contract Research Organizations

AICS Air Induction Control System; American Institute of Ceylonese Studies; Association of Independent Colleges and Schools

A.I.C.S. Associate of the Institute of Chartered Shipbrokers

AICS Association Internationale du Cinéma Scientifique (French—International Scientific Film Association)

AICTA Associate of the Imperial College of Tropical Agriculture

AICU Association of International Colleges and Universities

AICUM Association of Independent Colleges and Universities in Massachusetts; Association of Independent Colleges and Universities of Michigan

AICUN Association of Independent Colleges and Universities of Nebraska

AICUO Association of Independent Colleges and Universities of Ohio

aicv armored infantry combat vehicle (AICV)

aid. acute infectious disease; artifical insemination donor; avalanche injection diode

Aid Aideen

AID Agency for International Development; Airline Interline Development; American

Institute of Decorators; American Instructors of the Deaf; Arkansas Information Dissemination; Army Information Digest; Army Intelligence Department; Artificial Insemination Donor; Association for International Development

A & ID Acquisition and Improvement District

AID Acronyms and Initialisms Dictionary; Association Internationale des Documentalists et Techniciens de l'Information (French—International Association of Documentalists and Information Technicians)

aida attention-interest-desire-action (marketing formula); automatic instrumented diving assembly; automobile information data advertising

aida (AIDA) automatic intruder-detector alarm

AIDA American Indian Development Association; Associated Independent Dairies of America; Australian Industries Development Association

AIDATS Army In-flight Data Transmission System

AIDC American Industrial Development Council; Arkansas Industrial Development Commission; Asian Industrial Development Council; Association of Information and Dissemination Centers; Australian Industries Development Corporation

AIDD American Institute of Design and Drafting

aide. airborne insertion display equipment; aircraft installation diagnostic equipment

AIDE American Institute of Driver Education; Arizona Information Dissemination for Educators

AIDE Association Internationale des Distributions d'Eau (French—International Water Supply Association)

aidecs automatic inspection device for explosive charge shell

AIDI Associazione Italiana per la Documentazione e l'Informazione (Italian Association for Documentation and Information)

AIDIA Associate of the Industrial Design Institute of Australia

AIDIS Asociación Interamericana de Ingeneria Sanitaria

(Inter-American Association of Sanitary Engineering)

AIDL Auckland Industrial Development Laboratory; Australian Industrial Development Laboratories

AIDP Advanced Institutional Development Program; Associate of the Institute of Data Processing

AIDP Association Internationale de Droit Pénal (French—International Association of Penal Law)

AIDRB Army Investigational Drug Review Board

aids. (AIDS) acquired immune deficiency snydrome (suffered primarily by hemophiliacs, homosexual males, and intravenous drug users)

AIDS Abstracts Information Dissemination System; Account Identification and Description Services; Action Information Display System; Activity Information Data System; Administrative Information Data System; Advanced Integrated Data System; Aerospace Intelligence Data System; Aircraft Intrusion Detection System; Alabama Information Development System; American Institute for Decision Services; Automated Identification Division System; Automatic Inventory Dispatching System

AI & DSC Army Information and Data System Command

AIDUS Automated Information Directory Update System; Automated Imput and Document Updating System

AIE American Institute of Esthetics; Australian Institute of Export

AIEA Agence Internationale de l'Energie Atomique (International Atomic Energy Agency)

AIEAL Australian Institute of Engineering Associates Ltd

AIEC Association of Iron Exporting Countries

AIECF American Indian and Eskimo Cultural Foundation

A.I.Ed. Associate in Industrial Education

AIEE American Institute of Electrical Engineers

AIEF Association Internationale des Etudes Françaises (International Association for French Studies)

AIEI Association of Indian Engineering Industry

aiep amount of insulin extracted from the pancreas

AIER American Institute for Economic Research

AIERI Association Internationale des Etudes et Recherches sur l'Information (French—International Association for Mass Communication Research)

AIES Accreditation and Institutional Eligibility Staff

AIESEC Association Internationale des Etudiants en Sciences Economiques et Commerciales (French—International Association of Students in Economics and Commerce)

AIEST Association Internationale d'Experts Scientifiques du Tourisme (International Association of Scientific Experts in Tourism)

AIF Air Intelligence Force; American Institute of France; Amphibian Imperial Forces; Army Industrial Fund; Atomic Industrial Forum; Atomic International Forum; Australian Imperial Forces; Australian Institute of Fuel

AIF Agencia Internacional de Fomento (Spanish—International Development Agency); *Agenzia Internazionale Fides* (Italian—International Faith Agency—Vatican State news service); *Alliance Internationale des Femmes* (French—Women's International Alliance); *Asociación Internacional de Fomento* (Spanish—International Development Association)—IDA

AIFA Associate of the International Faculty of Arts

AIFCS Airborne Interception Fire-Control System

AIFD Alaska Institute for Fisheries Development

AIFE Associate of the Institution of Fire Engineers

AIFLD American Institute for Free Labor Development

AIFM Association Internationale des Femmes Médecins (International Association of Women Doctors)

AIFR American Institute of Family Relations

AIFS American Institute for Foreign Study

AIFST Australian Institute of

Food Science and Technology

AIFT American Institute for Foreign Trade; Americans for Indian Future and Traditions

AIFTA Anglo-Irish Free Trade Area

aifv (AIFV) armored infantry fighting vehicle

aig all inertial guidance; angle of inner gimbal

Aig Aiguille (French—needle, peak)

AIG Address Indicating Group; Adjutant Inspector General

AIG Association Internationale de Geodesia (French—International Geodesy Association)

AIGA American Institute of Graphic Arts

AIGAM Australian Institute of Graphic Art Management

AIGCM Associate of the Incorporated Guild of Church Musicians

AIGS Agricultural Investment Grant Scheme

AIGT Association for the Improvement of Geometrical Teaching

aih artificial insemination by husband

AIH American Institute of Homeopathy; Aspen Institute of the Humanities; Australian Institute of Horticulture

AIH Association Internationale de l'Hôtellerie (French—International Hotel Association)

aiha autoimmune hemolytic anemias

AIHA American Industrial Hygiene Association

AIHC American Industrial Health Conference

AIHE Association for Innovation in Higher Education

AIHEC American Indian Higher Education Consortium

AIHED American Institute for Human Engineering and Development

AIHR Australian Institute of Human Relations

AIHS American Indian Historical Society; American Irish Historical Society; Aspen Institute of Human Studies; Association Internationale d'Hydrologie Scientifique (International Association of Scientific Hydrology); Australian Institute of Health Surveyors

AIHSC Auto Industry Highway Safety Committee

AII Air India International;

Australian Insurance Institute

AIIA Association of International Insurance Agents; Australian Institute of Incorporated Accountants; Australian Institute of International Affairs

AIIC Army Imagery Intelligence Corps; Associate of the Insurance Institute of Canada

AIID American Institute of Interior Designers

AIIDC Authorized Item Identification Data Collaborator

AIIDR Authorized Item Identification Data Receiver

AIIDS Authorized Item Identification Data Submitter

AIIE American Institute of Industrial Engineers

AIIMS All-India Institute of Medical Sciences

AIInfSc Associate of the Institute of Information Scientists

AIIP Australian Institute of Industrial Psychology

AIIS American Institute of Indian Studies

AIK Assistance-in-Kind (funds)

AIKD American Institute of Kitchen Dealers

ail aileron

Ail Aileen

AIL Aeronautical Instruments Laboratory; Air Intelligence Liaison; Airborne Instruments Laboratory; American Institute of Laundering; American Israeli Lighthouse; Art Institute of Light; Association of International Libraries; Australian Institute of Librarians; Aviation Instrument Laboratory

A.I.L. Associate of the Institute of Linguistics

AILA American Institute of Landscape Architects; Australian Institute of Landscape Architects

A.I.L.A. Associate of the Institute of Landscape Architects

AILA Association Internationale de Linguistique Appliquée (French—International Association of Applied Linguistics)

AILAS Automatic Instrument Landing Approach System

Aileen (Anglo-Irish—Helen)

Ailie Aileen; Alice; Alicia; Alison; Helen; Helena

AILO Air Intelligence Liaison Office(r)

AILS Advanced Integrated Landing System

AILSA American Indian Law Students Association

aim active inert missile; aerotriangulation (by observation of) independent models; air intercept missile; air-isolated monolithic (circuit)

AiM Anglicans in Mission

A i M Accuracy in Media; Adventures in Movement

AIM Abstracts of Instructional Materials; Academy Introduction Mission (USCG); Accuracy In Media; Aide Inter-Monasteries; American Indian Movement; American Institute of Management; American Institute of Musicology; Army Installation Management; Association for the Integration of Management; Australian Institute of Management; Australian Institute of Metals

AIM Abstracts of Instructional Material; Airman's Information Manual

AIM-9 Sidewinder air-to-air missile

AIM-47A Hughes air-to-air missile

aima as interest may appear

AIMA All-India Management Association

AIMACC Air Material Command Compiling (system)

AIMACO Air Materiel Command Compiler (language)

AIM Bankers Asian International Merchant Bankers (Singapore)

AIMBW American Institute of Men's and Boy's Wear

AIMC American Indian Medical Clinic; Association of Interstate Motor Carriers

aime (AIME) average indexed monthly earnings

AIME American Institute of Mechanical Engineers

AIMES Association of Interns and Medical Students

AIMF American International Music Fund; Australian Institute of Metal Finishing

AIMH Academy of International Military History

AIMILO Army/Industrial Material Information Liaison Office(s)

AIMIT Associate of the Institute of Musical Instrument Technicians

AIML All-India Muslim League

AIMLT Australian Institute of

Medical Laboratory Technology

AIMM Australasian Institute of Mining and Metallurgy

AIMME American Institute of Mining and Metallurgical Engineers

AIMMPE American Institute of Mining, Metallurgical, and Petroleum Engineers

aimo air mold; audibly-instructed manufacturing operations

AIMO Audibly Instructed Manufacturing Operation

aimp air intercept missile package

AIMPE Australian Institute of Marine and Power Engineers

AIMS Advanced Intercontinental Missile System; Air Traffic Control Radar Beacon/Identification Friend or Foe/Mark XII/System; American Institute for Marxist Studies; American Institute for Mathematical Statistics; American Institute for Mental Studies; American Institute of Merchant Shipping; Association of Independent Maryland Schools; Association for International Medical Study; Australian Institute of Marine Science; Australian Institute of Marine Studies; Automated Instructional Materials Services; Automatic Industrial Management System

AIMT Australian Institute of Medical Technologists

A.I.M.T.A. Associate of the Institute of Municipal Treasurers and Accountants

AIMU American Institute of Marine Underwriters

ain approved item name

AIN American Institute of Nutrition; Association of Interpretive Naturalists; Australian Institute of Navigation

aina automated immunoephelometric assay

AINA American Indian Nurses Association; American Institute of Nautical Archeology; American Israel Numismatic Association; Arctic Institute of North America

A-Ind Anglo-Indian

AINDT Australian Institute for Non-Destructive Testing

AINEC All-India Newspaper Editors' Conference

AINS Assateague Island National Seashore (Maryland and Virginia)

AINSE Australian Institute of Nuclear Science and Engineering

ainsuf aortic insufficiency

ain't ungrammatical contraction —am not, are not, has not, have not, is not

AINWR Aleutian Islands National Wildlife Refuge (Alaska)

AINZ Advertising Institute of New Zealand

aio activity, interest, opinion (marketing factors); activity-interest-option (marketing factor scores)

Aio Aioi

AIO Action Information Organization; Air Installation Office; Air Intelligence Organization; Americans for Indian Opportunity; Anglican Information Office; Arecibo Ionospheric Observatory; Artillery Intelligence Officer

AIOB American Institute of Oral Biology

AIOEC Association of Iron Ore Exporting Countries

AIOPI Association of Information Officers in the Pharmaceutical Industry

aip ablative insulative plastic; accident insurance policy; acute intermittent porphyria; average intravascular pressure

aip (AIP) aldosterone-induced protein; automated imagery processing

AIP Aeronautical Information Publication; Aerovias Panama (Panamanian airline); American Independent Party; American Institute of Physics; American Institute of Planners; American Institute for Psychoanalysis; Australian Institute of Petroleum; Australian Institute of Physics

A-I-P Afghanistan-Iran-Pakistan (heroin source derived from poppies grown in those countries)

AIP Association Internationale de Papyrologues (French—International Association of Papyrologists); *Association Internationale de Pediatrie* (French—International Pediatric Association)

AIPA American Indian Press Association

AIPA Association Internationale de la Psychologie Adlerienne (French—International Association of Adlerian Psychology)

AIPAC American Israel Public Affairs Committee

AIPC All Indian Pueblo Council; *Association Internationale de Prophylaxie de la Cécité* (French—International Association for the Prevention of Blindness); Association Internationale des Ponts et Charpentes (International Association of Bridges and Scaffolds); Australian Institute of Pest Control

AIPCEE Association des Industries du Poisson de la Communauté Economique Européenne (Association of Fishing Industries of the European Economic Community)

AIPCN Association Internationale Permanente des Congrès Navigation (French—International Association of the Permanent Congress of Navigation)

AIPCR Association Internationale Permanente des Congrès de la Route (French—International Association of the Permanent Congress of Routes)

AIPE American Institute of Park Executives; American Institute of Plant Engineers; American Institute for Professional Education

AIPG American Institute of Professional Geologists

AIPHE Associate of the Institution of Public Health Engineers

AIPLU American Institute for Property and Liability Underwriters

AIPO American Institute of Public Opinion; Asian Inter-Parliamentary Organisation

AIPR American Institute of Pacific Relations; Australian Institute of Parks and Recreation

AIPs Allied Intelligence Publications; Association of Irish Priests

AIPS Australian Institute of Political Science; Automatic Indexing and Proofreading System

AIPS Association Internationale pour la Prevention du Suicide (French—International Association for the Prevention of Suicide)

AIQ Associate of the Institute of Quarrying

AI & Q Animal Inspection and Quarantine

AIQS Australian Institute of Quantity Surveyors

A.I.Q.S. Associate of the Institute of Quantity Surveyors

air. average injection rate

a-i-r artist-in-residence

AIR Action for Industrial Recycling; Air Control Products; All-India Radio; American Institute of Refrigeration; American Institute of Research; Arkansas Intermediate Reformatory; Army Institute of Research; Army Intelligence Reserve; Association for Immigration Reform; Association for Institutional Research; Australian Industrial Refractories; Australian Institute of Radiography

AIR *Asociación Interamericana de Radiodifusión* (Spanish—Interamerican Broadcasters Association)

AIR-2A Douglas air-to-air rocket fitted with a nuclear warhead and called Genie

AIRA Air Attaché

airac (AIRAC) aeronautical information regulation and control

AIRAH Australian Institute of Refrigeration, Air Conditioning, and Heating

AIRB Alabama Inspection and Rating Bureau; Arkansas Inspection and Rating Bureau; Australian Industrial Relations Bureau

AIRBALTAP Allied Air Forces Baltic Approach (NATO)

airbm (AIRBM) anti-intermediate-range ballistic missile

AIRCAL Air California

Air Can Air Canada (formerly Trans-Canada Air Lines)

Air Capital of America Wichita, Kansas

Air Capital of the World Montreal, Québec—headquarters of the International Civil Aviation Organization and the International Air Transport Association

aircat automated integrated radar control for air traffic

Air Cav Airmobile Cavalry

Air Cdr Air Commander

AIRCENT Allied Air Forces, Central Europe

AIRCEY Air Ceylon

Air Cmdre Air Commodore

AIRCO Air Reduction Chemical Company

Air Coal Airport Coalition (*see* AIRPORT COALITION)

AIRCOM Air Force Communication Complex

AIRCOMNET Air Communications Network

AIRCOMS Airways Communications System

aircond air condition(ed); air conditioning

Air-Conditioned City Duluth, Minnesota

AIRDEF Air Defense (NATO division)

AIRDEP Air Deputy (NATO)

AIREA American Institute of Real Estate Appraisers

AIREASTLANT (Naval) Air Forces Eastern Atlantic (NATO)

AiRepDn Aircraft Repair Division

airew airborne infrared early warning

airfil air filter(s)

Air Force I Air Force One (aircraft reserved for or used by the President of the U.S.)

AIRH Association Internationale des Recherches Hydrauliques (International Association of Hydraulic Research)

air hp air horsepower

AIRI Atomic Industry Research Institute

AIRIMP ATC/IATA (*q.q.v.*) reservations interline message procedures

Air Jam Air Jamaica

AIRL Aeronautical Icing Research Laboratory

AIRLEX Air Landing Exercise

Air LO Air Liaison Officer

AIRLORDS Airlines Load Optimization Recording and Display System

Air Mad Air Madagascar

airmada airplane armada

airmap air monitoring, analysis, and prediction

AIRMIC Association of Insurance and Risk Managers in Industry and Commerce

Air Mike Air Micronesia's nickname

airmiss aircraft-in-flight collision barely missed

air/mmh acoustic intercept receiver/multimode hydrophone

AIRMOVEX Air Movement Exercise

Air NG Air National Guard

Air Niu Air Niugini (national airline of Papua, New Guinea)

AIRNON Allied Air Forces in Northern Norway (NATO)

AirNorth Allied Air Forces, Northern Europe

Air NZ Air New Zealand

AIROPNET Air Operational Network

AIRPAC Air Pacific

AIRPASS Aircraft Interception Radar and Pilots Attack Sight System

airpl airplane(s)

AIRPORT COALITION acronym covering fifteen San Diego organizations united to control air and noise pollution by relocating Lindbergh Field away from endangered homes, offices, and schools in its flight path

airpt art airport art (spurious souvenirs of the *Greetings from* variety)

Air Res Squad Air Reserve Squadron

airs. (AIRS) advanced inertial reference sphere

AIRS Aircraft Inventory Reporting System; Airline Interline Reservations System; Automatic Image Retrieval System

AIRSONOR Allied Air Forces in Southern Norway (NATO)

AIRSouth Allied Air Forces, Southern Europe

Air-Std Air Force International Standard

airsurance air insurance

Air Svc Air Service

airtel air + hotel (airport hotel)

Airtourer single-engine trainer plane built by Aero Engine Services of New Zealand

airvan airmobile van

AIRWORK Airwork Atlantic Limited

AIRX American Industrial Radium and X-Ray Society

ais ablating inner surface; agreed industry standard; answer in sentence; average insurance set

ais (AIS or Lunik III) automatic interplanetary station

AIS Abbreviated Injury Scale; Academic Instructors School (USAF); Administrative and Information Services; Advanced Information System; Aeronautical Information Service; Air Intelligence Service; Alexander I Solzhenitsyn; American Indian Scholarships; American Indian Studies; American Israeli Shipping (Zim Lines); Army Intelligence School; *Association Internationale de la Savonnerie et de la Detergence* (French—International Association of Soaps and Detergents); *Association Internationale de Sociologie* (French—International Sociology Association); Association of Iron and Steel; Australian Information Service; Australian Institute of Sport; Australian Iron and Steel

AI & S Army Intelligence and Security

aisa analytical isoelectrofocusing scanning apparatus

AISA Associate of the Incorporated Secretaries Association; Australian Institute of Systems Analysis

AISA *Association Internationale pour la Securite Aerienne* (French—International Air Security Association)

AISB Artificial Intelligence and Simulation of Behavior (group in the BCS)

AISC American Institute of Steel Construction; Association of Independent Softwear Companies; Australian Institute of Steel Construction

AISE Association of Iron and Steel Engineers

AISI American Iron and Steel Institute

AISM *Association Internationale des Societes de Microbiologie* (French— International Association of Microbiology Societies)

AISS *Association Internationale de la Science du Sol* (French— International Solar Science Association)

AIST Australian Institute of Science Technology

ait auto-ignition temperature

AiT Anjuman-i-Tarikh (Historical Society of Afghanistan)

AIT Agency for Instructional Television; American Institute in Taiwan; American Institute of Technology; Army Intelligence Translator; Australian Institute of Travel; Automatic Information Test

AIT *Academie Internationale du Tourisme* (French—International Academy of Tourism)

AITA Act Inside the Army (antiwar society); Air Industries and Transport Association;

Australian Industrial Truck Association

AITC Action Information Training Center; American Institute of Timber Construction

AITC *Association Internationale des Traducteurs de Conference* (French—International Association of Conference Translators)

aitd all-inclusive trust deed

AITD Australian Institute of Training and Development

AITI Aero Industries Technical Institute

AITO Association of Independent Tour Operators

AITVS Association of Independent Television Stations

aiu abort interface unit; absolute iodine uptake; advanced instrumentation unit

AIU Action for Interracial Understanding; Aero Insurance Underwriters; American International Underwriters

AIU *Alliance Israelite Universelle* (French—Universal Israelite Alliance)

AIUM American Institute of Ultrasound in Medicine

AIUS Australian Institute of Urban Studies

AIUSA Amnesty International in the United States of America

aiv accelerated inverse voltage

AIV *Association Internationale de Volcanologie* (French—International Association of Vulcanology)

AIVAF American-Israeli Vocal Arts Foundation

aiw auroral intrasonic wave

AIW Atlantic Intracoastal Waterway (Cape Cod to Florida Bay)

AIWM American Institute of Weights and Measures

Aix Aix-en-Provence

Aix-la-Chapelle French placename for Aachen on West Germany's Belgian-Dutch borders

AIYW Association for International Youth Work

aj ankle jerk; antijamming; apple juice

aj *a jini* (Czech—and others)

AJ Air Jordan; Alma & Jonquieres (railroad); Americans for Justice; Andrew Jackson (7th U.S. President); Andrew Johnson (17th U.S. President); Associate Justice

A.J. Associate in Journalism

AJ *American Jurisprudence; Architects Journal; l'Armee Juife* (French—Jewish Army)—anti-Nazi resistance group

AJ-37 Swedish Thunderbolt multimission combat aircraft also called Viggen

AJA American Jail Association; American Jewish Archives; American Judges Association; Australian Journalists Association

A-JA Anglo-Jewish Association

AJA *American Journal of Anatomy*

AJADD *Australian Journal of Alcoholism and Drug Dependence*

AJAG Assistant Judge Advocate General

ajai antijamming anti-interference

AJAs Americans of Japanese Ancestry

AJAS *Australian Journal of Applied Science*

AJASS African Jazz Art Society Studios

Ajax Douglas Nike-Ajax surface-to-air missile; mythological Greek hero of the Trojan Wars and title of a play by Sophocles

AJAZ American Jewish Alternatives to Zionism

AJB Arthur J(ames) Balfour

AJB *Association des Juifs de Belgique* (French—Association of the Jews of Belgium); *Australian Journal of Botany*

AJBC American Junior Bowling Congress

AJBP Association of Jewish Book Publishers

aJc *antes de Jesucristo* (Spanish—before Jesus Christ)

AJC Altus Junior College; American Jewish Committee; American Jewish Congress; Anderson Junior College; Australian Jockey Club

AJCA Association of Juvenile Compact Administrators

AJCC Alternate Joint Communications Center

AJCL Australia-Japan Container Line

AJC-RC American Jewish Committee—Records Center

AJCSA All-Japan Cotton Spinners Association

AJCU Association of Jesuit Colleges and Universities

AJCW Association of Jewish Center Workers

AJDC American Joint Distribution Committee; Asian-Japan Development Corporation
AJE Adult Jewish Education
AJEI Australia-Japan Economic Institute
AJF Asian-Japan Forum; Australia-Japan Foundation
AJHS American Jewish Historical Society; Andrew Jackson High School
AJI American Justice Institute
AJIF Australia-Japan International Finance
AJIL American Journal of International Law
AJIS Automated Jail Information System
AJJUST Automated Juvenile Justice System Technique
AJL Association of Jewish Libraries; Association of Junior Leagues
AJLAC American Jewish League Against Communism
AJNHS Andrew Johnson National Historic Site (Greeneville, Tennessee)
ajo antijam operator
ajp alarm and jettison panel
AJP Additional-Jobs Programme (New Zealand)
AJPA American Jewish Press Association
AJR Association of Jewish Refugees
AJR Australian Jurist Reports
AJRC American Junior Red Cross
AJRJ Association of Japanese Residing in Japan
AJS American Judicature Society; Australia-Japan Society
AJS American Journal of Sociology
AJSJ American Justinian Society of Jurists
AJSR Australian Journal of Scientific Research
ajvd abrupt junction varactor doubler
AJY Association for Jewish Youth
AJYB American Jewish Year Book
ak above the knee (amputation); ass kisser (underground slang)
a k alter kocker (Yiddish colloquialism—old man)
Ak Auckland, New Zealand
AK Alaska Coastal—Ellis Airlines; Australian Knight (Knight of the Order of Australia); cargo ship (2-letter naval designation)
AK Avtomat Kalasnikov (Rus-

sian—submachine gun)
AK 47 automatic rifle developed by the communists for use in Vietnam
aka above-the-knee amputation; also known as
Aka Akasaka (Tokyo nightlife district)
AKA American Kiteflyers Association; Associated Klans of America; Australian Karate Association; Australian Kidney Association; cargo vessel, attack (3-letter coding)
Akad Akademie (German—Academy)
Akad Akademi (Dano-Norwegian—Academy)
Akad Nauk Akademiya Nauk (USSR Academy of Sciences)
AKAG Albright-Knox Art Gallery
ak amp above-the-knee amputation
Akan Akan National Park on Hokkaido Island, Japan
AKBS Advanced Kinematic Bombing System
AKC American Kennel Club; Associate King's College
AKCF Arthur Kill Correctional Facility
Aken (Dutch—Aix-la-Chapelle)
AKG Astronomischen Gesellschaft Katalog (German—Astronomical Society Catalog)
Akhiar formerly Sevastopol
AKI Alfred Kinsey Institute; American Kynol Incorporated
akk akkusativ (Dano-Norwegian—accusative)
Akk Akkadian
AKL Algemene Kunstzijde Unie (Artist's Union); Auckland, New Zealand (airport)
AKLD Auckland (telex)
AKM Soviet standard military weapon capable of firing up to 600 rounds per minute
Akmechet formerly Simferopol
AKN King Salmon, Alaska (airport)
Akr Akron
Akr Akrotirion (Modern Greek—Cape)
AKR vehicle cargo ship (naval symbol)
Akropolis (Greek—Upper City) —Acropolis Hill section of Athens
AKS general stores issue ship (3-letter symbol)
Akt Aktiebolag (Swedish—limited company)
AKT Akita Television (Japan)

Akt Ges Aktiengesellschaft (German—corporation or joint stock company)
Aktieb Aktiebolag (Swedish—limited company)
Akties Aktieselskab (Swedish—joint stock company)
Akust Zh Akusticheskii Zhurnal (Russian—Acoustics Journal)
AKV cargo ships and aircraft ferries (3-letter symbol)
akwic author and key word in context
al absolute limen; accommodation ladder; air lock; albumin; alcohol; alias; all lengths; annual leave; autograph letter; axiolingual
a l apres livraison (French—after delivery)
aL assumed latitude
Al accommodation ladder; air lock; Alan; Albert; Albin; alcohol; Alden; Alex(ander); Alf; Alfred; alias; Allan; Allen; Alley; Allied; all lengths; Alton; aluminum; Alva; Alvah; Alvin; Alvina; Alyn; annual leave; autograph letter
Al. Book of Alma
AL Abraham Lincoln (16th President U.S.); Accession List(s); Acoustics Laboratory; Aeronautical Laboratory; Air Liaison; Aircraft Laboratory; Aircraft Logistics; Allegheny Airlines; Aluminum Limited; aluminum (machine shop symbol); América Latina (Portuguese or Spanish—Latin America); American League; American League (of Professional Baseball Clubs); American Legion; Angkatan Laut (Indonesian—Naval Forces); Anglo-Latin; Annual Lease; Annual Leave; Architectural League; Assumed Latitude; Astronomical League; Aviation Electronicsman
A-L Allegheny-Ludlum; Anglo-Latin
A/L airlift
A.L. Anno Lucis (Latin—in the Year of Light)
AL-60 Lockheed Associates Conestoga—six-seat piston-powered transport aircraft
ala alanine; alternate living arrangement; axiolabial
ala (ALA) alighting area
Ala Alabama; Alabamian; Alameda(n)
ALA Amalgamated Lithographers of America; American Landrace Association; Ameri-

can Landscape Architects; American Laryngological Association; American Latvian Association; American Legion Auxiliary; American Liberal Association; American Library Association; American Livestock Association; American Lung Association; Arkansas Library Association; Army Launching Area; Assembly of the Librarians of the Americas; Australian Lebanese Association; Australian Legal Aid; Authors League of America

ALA (I) Amalgamated Lithographers of America (Independent)

A.L.A. Associate in Liberal Arts; Associate of the (British) Library Association

ALAA Associate of the Library Association of Australia

alaar air-launched air-recoverable rocket

A-lab lsd (LSD) acid laboratory (illegal laboratory)

Alabama Port Mobile

Alabama's Only Port Mobile's place-name nickname

alabaster calcite (onyx marble); variety of gypsum

ALABEL American Library Association Board of Education for Librarianship

alabol algorithmic and business-oriented language

ALAC Alcoholic Liquor Advisory Council (New Zealand); Australian Labor Advisory Council

ALACP American League to Abolish Capital Punishment

alacranes (Spanish—scorpions) —nickname for persons from the Mexican state of Durango where scorpions abound

alad abnormal left axis deviation; aminolevulinic acid dehydrase; automatic liquid agent detector

aladdin atmospheric layer and density distribution of ions and neutrons

ALAEA Australian Licensed Aircraft Engineers Association

alag axiolabiogingival

Al Ahr Al Ahram (Arabic—The Pyramids)—Cairo's daily paper

alairs advance low-altitude infrared-reconnaissance sensor

ALA—ISAD American Library Association—Information

Science and Automation Division

alal axiolabiolingual

ALAL Association of Legal Aid Lawyers

ALALC Asociación Latinoamericana de Libre Comercio (Latin American Free Trade Association)

ALAM Associate of the London Academy of Music

Alameda Bernardo O'Higgins formerly Las Delicias

Alamo City San Antonio, Texas

Alan Alain; Allan; Allen

Alan Alda Alphonso d'Abruzzo

Åland (Swedish—Aland Islands)—between the Gulf of Bothnia and the Baltic Sea separating Sweden from Finland where they are called Ahvenanmaa

Alanders Aland islanders

Alands Aland Islands

Alan King Irving Kniberg

alanon alcoholics' anonymous (rehabilitation program)

ALAO Australian Legal Aid Office

alara as low as reasonably achievable

Alaric Cottin Voltaire's nickname for Frederick the Great, inferring his majesty was a poor poet but a splendid soldier

alarm. automatic light aircraft readiness monitor

ALARM Assessment of Language and Reading Maturity (test)

Alas. Alaska; Alaskan; (unauthorized abbreviation)

ALAS Army Library Automated Systems; Automated Literature Alerting System

A.L.A.S. Associate in Letters, Arts, and Sciences

Alas Cur Alaska Current

Alas DST Alaskan Daylight Saving Time

Alasia Australasia

Alaska (Aleut—Great Land)— Pacific Northwest state inhabited by Alaskans

Alaskan Ports (south to north) Ketchikan, Wrangell, Petersburg, Sitka, Juneau, Cordova, Seward, Anchorage, Kodiak, Dutch Harbor, Adak Naval Station, Nome

Alaska's Scenic Capital Juneau

Alaska turkey Alaska salmon

Al-Ass Al-Assifa (Syrian terrorist group)

Alas ST Alaskan Standard Time

(150th meridian west of Greenwich, however, Alaskans use four time zones— 120, 135, 150, and 165 degrees west of Greenwich)

Alastair Alexander

alateen program for aiding teenagers affected by someone else's drinking (*see* prealateen)

a la v a la vista (Spanish—at sight, payable upon presentation)

alb albumin; aluminum-bronze

alb (ALB) air-land battle

Alb Albania; Albanian; Albany; Albert; Alberta; Albertan; Albion; Albalasserdam

ALB American League Baseball

alba (Latin prefix—pale, white)

ALBA Aluminium Bahrain; American Lawn Bowling Association; American Leather Belting Association

Albac Albacete

Alban Albania; Albanian

Alban *Albanensis* (Latin—of St. Albans)

Albania People's Republic of Albania (smallest of the Balkan nations and once called Illyria by the Romans, Albanians speak Albanian and export oil, ores, textiles, and woodenware), *Republika Popullore Socialiste e Shqipipërīse*

Albanian Ports (north to south) Shengjin, Durres, San Nicolo, Vlore

Albanië (Dutch—Albania)

Albanien (German—Albania)

albany adjustment of large blocks with *any* number of photos, points, or images, using *any* photogrammetric-measuring instrument on *any* computer

Albany capital of New York State

Albany beef Hudson River sturgeon

Albatross Grumman amphibian transport aircraft; name of a series of oceanographic survey ships flying the American flag (the author travelled on the *Albatross II* to the Galápagos and back); Piaggo P-166M coastal patrol aircraft built in Italy

Albaturkey Albuquerque, New Mexico's nickname

ALBE Air League of the British Empire

Albemarle Island, Galápagos Isabela

Alber Alberic; Albern; Albert(ino)

Albers-Schonberg disease abnormal bone calcification resulting in spontaneous fracturing

Albert Albert Canal connecting Antwerp and Liege by linking the Scheldt and the Meuse rivers; Albert National Park in the Congo (Zaire); Albert Nyasa (Albert Lake, Africa's third largest); Halbert; Halbertus

Alberta Girls Alberta Institution for Girls

Albert the Good Prince Albert Francis Charles Augustus Emmanuel of Saxe-Coburg-Gotha, Prince Consort of Queen Victoria

Alberto Moravia (pseudonym—Alberto Pincherle)

Alberto Savinio (pseudonym—Andrea de Chirico)

Albert's disease inflammation of the bursae over the Achilles tendon

Albertville former name of Kalima, Zaire

albi air-launched booster intercept

Albion Britain's ancient name

Albion Correctional Albion State Institution and Western Correctional Facility (at Albion, NY)

ALBIS Australian Library-Based Information System

albm (ALBM) air-launched ballistic missile

Alb Mus Albany Museum (Grahamstown, South Africa)

Albn Albanian

Albq Albuquerque

Albr Albrecht

Albt Albert

Albturist Albanian Tourism

Albuquerque Girls New Mexico Girls Welfare Home at Albuquerque

albus all bureaus (naval coding)

Albuturkey Albuquerque, NM

alc alcohol; approximate lethal concentration; avian leukosis complex; axiolinguocervical

a l c *a la carte* (French—on the menu)

ALC Air Logistics Center (USAF); Alabama Central (railroad); American Life Convention; American Lutheran Church; Area Logistics Center; Area Logistics Command; Armament Logistics Center; Armament Logistics Command;

Asian Law Collective; Associated Lutheran Charities

ALCA American Leather Chemists Association; Associated Landscape Contractors of America

ALCAC Airlines Communications Administrative Council

AlCan Alaska-Canada (as in Al-Can Highway)

ALCAN Aluminium Company of Canada

alcapp automatic list classification and profile production

Al Capp Alfred Gerald Caplin

ALCC Airborne Launch-Control Center

ALCC *Asociación de Libre Comercio del Caribe* (Spanish—Caribbean Free Trade Association)

Alc^{de} *Alcalde* (Spanish—justice of the peace, mayor)

alch approach-light contact height

alchem alchemy

Alcibiades Alfred Lord Tennyson's pseudonym used in *Punch*

alcid alcohol + acid

alcism alcoholism (addiction to alcohol)

ALCL Association of London Chief Librarians

alcm (ALCM) air-launched cruise missile

ALCM Associate of the London College of Music

ALCO American Lava Corporation

ALCOA Aluminum Company of America

Alcofribas Nasier anagrammatic pseudonym of François Rabelais

alcoh alcohol

alcohol ethyl alcohol (C_2H_5OH)

alcolic alcoholic

alcom algebraic compiler; algebraic computer

alcon all concerned

ALCOP Alternate Command Post

alcotrician alcohol + nutrition (adverse effects of alcohol on good nutrition)

alcr aluminum crown (dental)

ALCTP Academic Library Consultant Training Program

ald a later date; acceptable limit for dispersion; aldolase

Ald Aldabra; Alderman; Aldermanic

ALDA Air Line Dispatchers Association; American Land Development Association; Aus-

tralian Land Development Association

ALDCS Active Lift Distribution Control Center

aldehyde al(cohol) dehy(drogenated)—dehydrogenated (oxidized) alcohol

aldep automated layout design program

Alder Alderic; Alderley

Alderson minimum-security Federal Reformatory for Women at Alderson, West Virginia

ALDEV African Land Development

Aldm Alderman

aldo aldosterone

Aldo Teobaldo; Teobaldo Manuzio the 16th-century Venetian printer and typographer whose classic italic type bears his name—Aldine

aldp automatic language-data processing

ALDS Apollo Launch-Data System

ALE Association for Liberal Education

ALEA Airline Employees Association

alec algebraic components and coefficients

ALEC American Lutheran Evangelical Churches

Alec(k) Alexander

ALECS Automated Law-Enforcement Communications System

ALECSO Arab League Educational, Cultural, and Scientific Organization

Alec Waugh Alexander Raban Waugh

alegar ale + vinegar (vinegar derived from ale)

Alejandría (Spanish—Alexandria)

Ale^{jo} Alejandro

Aleksei Maksimovich Peshkov Maxim Gorki

Alemanha (Portuguese—Germany)

Alemania (Spanish—Germany)

ALEOA American Law Enforcement Officers Association

Alep (Turkish—Aleppo)—Syrian city

Ale RD *República Democrática Alemana* (Spanish—German Democratic Republic)—communist East Germany

Ale RF *República Federal Alemana* (Spanish—Federal German Republic)—West Germa-

ny

alerfa alert phase

ALERT Automatic Linguistic Extraction and Retrieval Technique

ALERT II Automatic Law Enforcement Response Time (computerized criminal file in Kansas City, Missouri)

ale(s) additional living expense(s)

Ales Alessandro

ALESCO American Library and Educational Service Company

Aleut Aleutian; Aleutian Islands

Aleut Cur Aleutian Current

Aleutians Aleutian Mountains; Aleutian islanders; Aleutian Islands

Aleut Is Aleutian Islands

A-levels advanced levels (of educational tests)

alex alexandrine (verse)

alex (ALEX) alert exercise

Alex Alexander; Alexandra; Alexandria

Alexa Alexandra

Alexander Girls Arkansas Training School for (delinquent) Girls at Alexander

Alexander of the North Charles XII of Sweden

Alexanders Alexander Archipelago; Alexander cocktails; Alexander islanders; Alexander Islands of southeastern Alaska

Alexander Serafimovich Alexander Serafimovich Popov

Alexandretta English placename equivalent of Iskenderun

Alexandria English place-name equivalent for the Egyptian port city of El Iskandariya

Alexandrian Century the 4th century before the Christian era when Alexander of Macedonia conquered Egypt, Persia, and India as well as encouraging Greek philosophers and poets—the 300s

Alex City Alexander City, Alabama

Alexes ten-dollar bills bearing the portrait of America's first Secretary of the Treasury—Alexander Hamilton

alf automatic letter facer

alf (Swedish—river)

Alf Alfa; Alfhild; Alfonso; Alford; Alfred; Alfred(o)

ALF American Life Federation; American Life Foundation; Animal Liberation Front;

Arab Liberation Front; Association of Libertarian Feminists; Australasian Labour Federation; Australian Labor Federation

Alfa letter A radio code

ALFA Anonima Lombarda Fabbrica Automobili

Alfalfa Bill Governor William Henry Murray of Oklahoma

ALFC Aboriginal Land Fund Commission (Australia)

ALFCE Allied Land Forces in Central Europe (NATO)

Alfie Alfred

Alfo Alfonso

Alfonso XIII León Fernando María Isidro Pascual António

ALFORD Appalachian Laboratory for Occupational Respiratory Diseases

Alfred, Lord Tennyson Alfred Tennyson (1st Baron Tennyson—poet laureate of England from 1850 until 1892 when he died of old age—a favorite of Queen Victoria but detested by critics because of his utterly unimaginative conservatism)

ALFSEA Allied Land Forces—South-East Asia

ALFSH Allied Land Forces in Schleswig-Holstein (NATO)

alft airlift

alg algae; algal; algebra; algebraic; allergic; allergical; allergy; along; alongside; antilymphocyte globulin (ALG) (Latin suffix—pain)—as in neuralgia

alg *algemeen* (Dutch—generally or universally)

Alg Algeria; Algiers

ALG Air Algérie; Algiers, Algeria (airport)

ALGC Association of Local Government Clerks

Alge Algeciras

Alger Algernon

Alger (French—Algiers)

Algeri (Italian—Algiers)

Algeria Democratic and Popular Republic of Algeria (North African Arab nation whose Algerians speak Arabic and French, best known for its exports of natural gas and oil as well as Marxist-oriented guerrillas), *El Djemhouria El Djazairia Demokratia Echaabia* (Arabic name for Algeria); *République Algérienne Démocratique et Populaire* (French name)

Algerian onyx stalagmitic calcite

Algerian Ports (large, medium,

and small from east to west) Annaba (Bone), Skikda, Bejaia, Alger (Algiers), Mostaganem, Arzew, Oran, Mers el Kebir

Algérie (French—Algeria)

Algerien (German—Algeria)

Algie Algernon

algins algae derivatives

alglyn aluminum glycinate

algol algebraically oriented language (algorithmic international language)

Algonquin Algonquin Peak in the Adirondacks; Algonquin Provincial Park in Ontario between Georgian Bay and the Ottawa River

Algonquin Circle F(ranklin) P(ierce) A(dams), Robert Benchley, Heywood Broun, Irvin S Cobb, Edna Ferber, George S Kaufman, Ring Lardner, Harpo Marx, Dorothy Parker, Harold Ross, Robert E Sherwood, Alexander Woolcott, and others who joked with one or more of the foregoing who met informally around the bar of the Algonquin Hotel in midtown Manhattan or in the offices of the *New Yorker*

ALGU Association of Land Grant Colleges and Universities

ALGWA Australian Local Government Women's Association

Algy Algernon

alh anterior lobe hormone; anterior lobe of the hypophysis

Alh Alhambra

ALH Australian Light Horse

Alhambra (Arabic—Red House) —ancient Moorish castle in Granada whence the Moors ruled most of Spain from 711 to 1492

ALHS Abraham Lincoln High School

Alht Apollo lunar hand tool

Alhtc Apollo lunar hand tool carrier

ali. alibi (Latin—elsewhere)

'ali (Arabic—high)

Ali Alicante

ALI American Law Institute; American Library Institute

ALIA Royal Jordanian Airlines

Alianza *La Alianza Federal de las Mercedes* (Spanish—Federal Alliance of Mercedes)— New Mexican organization founded by Reies Lopez Tijerina to reclaim Mexican land acquired by the United States

Alic Alicante

ALIC Association of Life Insurance Counsel

alice (ALICE) automatic laundering instrument control equipment

Alice The Alice—Alice Springs, Northern Territory, Australia; Allis-Chalmers Manufacturing Company (stock exchange slang)

ALICE Artillery Line Communications Equipment

Alice Faye Alice Leppert

Alice Markova Alice Marks

Alick Alexander

ALICS Advanced Logistics Information and Control System (USAF)

alien alienist

'Alifax (Cockney contraction—Halifax)

align. alignment

alim (ALIM) air-launched interceptor missile

ALIMD Association of Life Insurance Medical Directors

ALIMDA Association of Life Insurance Medical Directors of America

Al Imp Reps Alert Implementation Reports

Aline Adeline

alirt (ALIRT) adaptive long-range infrared tracker

ALIS Advanced Life Information System; Automated Library Information Service; Automated Library Information System

Al Iskandariyah (Arabic—Alexandria)

Al Ismailiyah (Arabic—Ismailia)

alit automatic line insulation tester

Alitalia Italian national airlines (AZ)

ALITALIA Italian International Airline

A.Litt. Associate in Letters

Alize Breguet carrier-based three-place antisubmarine-warfare aircraft

ALJ *Australian Law Journal*; *Australian Library Journal*

aljak aluminum-jacketed coaxial cable

Al Jazair (Arabic—Algeria)

ALJC Alice Lloyd Junior College

Aljezair (Arabic—Algiers)

ALJH Association of Libraries of Judaica and Hebraica (in Europe)

Al Jolson Asa Yoelson's stage-and-screen name

ALJR *Australian Law Journal Reports*

alk alkali

Alkali NATO codename for a Soviet air-to-air radar-guided homing missile

alki alcohol; homeless alcoholic

alk phos alkaline phosphatase

alkums air-launched cruise missiles (ALCMs)

Alkyd Winsor & Newton's trade name for alkyd-base watercolors

all. above lower limit; acute lymphocytic leukemia; allergy

al.l. *alia lectio* (Latin—a different reading)

All Alley; Alloa; Aloha

Al-L Alsace-Lorraine

ALL Admiralty Lines Limited; Airborne Laser Laboratory

ALL *Admiralty List of Lights*

All 8va all'ottava (Italian—in the octave)

ALLA Allied Long Lines Agency (NATO)

Allagash Allagash River and Allagash Wilderness Waterway in northern Maine

all.(ALL) airborne laser laboratory

All-American Mirror Upton Sinclair

All Bunny Albany, New York

allcat all critical atmospheric turbulence (programs)

alld allowed

Alld Allahabad

alleg allegation; allegoric; allegorical; allegory

Alleghenies Allegheny Mountains of Pennsylvania, Maryland, Virginia, and West Virginia

Allem Allemagne (French—Germany)

Allenwood Camp Federal Prison Camp at Allenwood, Pennsylvania

allergol allergologic(al)

allg *allgemein* (German—general)

All H All Hallows (Halloween)

all hands all hands on deck (everyone needed for fire drill, lifeboat drill, or some task requiring all hands)

Allie Alice; Alison

Alligator Alley trans-Florida highway between Fort Lauderdale on the Atlantic coast and Naples on the Gulf of Mexico

Alligators Alligator Rivers of Australia's Northern Territory

(East, South, and West Alligator)

Alligator State sobriquet shared by Alabama, Florida, Louisiana, Mississippi, and Texas

all'ingr *all'ingrosso* (Italian—wholesale)

Allison Allison Division, General Motors

allit alliteration; alliterative

ALLNAVSTAS All Naval Stations

allo allonym

allo (Greek prefix—other)—allele, allopathic, allopatric, allophone, alloplasm, allotetrapoid

Allo allegro (Italian—lively, quickly)

alloc allocate; allocation

allop allophone

all'ott *all'ottava* (Italian—an octave higher)

allow. allowance

allp audiolingual language programming

All S All Souls College, Oxford

ALLS Apollo Lunar Logistic Support

All Saint's All Saint's Day (November 1)

allstat all-purpose statistical (package)

All-the-Talents Administration of Prime Minister William Wyndham Grenville

Alltto allegretto (Italian—lively but less so than *allegro*)

allu allude; allusion; allusively

allus allusion

alluv alluvial; alluvium

Ally Pally Alexandra Palace in North London

alm. alarm

alm *almindelig* (Dano-Norwegian—common, frequent, plain, simple)

Alm Almería

Alm Almirante (Spanish—Admiral); (German—mountain pasture)

ALM American Leprosy Missions

A & LM Arkansas & Louisiana-Missouri (railroad)

ALM *Antilliaanse Luchtvaart Maatschappij* (Dutch—Antillean Airline Company)

A.L.M. *Artium Liberalium Magister* (Latin—Master of Liberal Arts)

ALMA Aircraft Locknut Manufacturers Association; Association of Literary Magazines of America

ALMAC Association of Labor-

Management Administrators and Consultants

Alma Gluck Reba Fierson

ALMAJCOM All Major Commands

ALMC Army Logistic Management Center

alme acetyl-lysine methyl ester

Almer Almeric

almi anterior lateral myocardial infarct

ALMIDS Army Logistics Management Integrated Data System

ALMs Amindivi, Laccadive, and Minicoy Islands off India's Malabar Coast

ALMS Analytic Language Manipulation System

ALMT Association of London Tailors

Almte Almirante (Spanish—Admiral)

aln anterior lymph node

aln (ALN) accounting line number

alnico aluminum, nickel, copper (magnet alloy also containing iron and cobalt)

alnmt alignment

ALNP Abraham Lincoln National Park

ALNZ Air League of New Zealand

alo axiolinguoclusal

alo' alow

Alo Alonso

ALO Air Liaison Office(r); Allied Liaison Office(r); Aloha Airlines; Amalgamated Lace Operatives; American Liaison Office(r); Army Liaison Office(r)

ALOA Amalgamated Lace Operatives of America; Amalgamated Lithographers of America; Assembly of Librarians of the Americas; Associated Locksmiths of America

aloc air lines of communication; allocation

ALOC Air Line of Communication

ALOE A Lady Of England—pseudonym of Charlotte Maria Tucker

alof' aloft

aloft. airborne light optical fiber technology

ALOHA Aboriginal Lands of Hawaiian Ancestry; Aloha Airlines

Aloha State Hawaii's official nickname

ALON Air Liaison Officer Net

alo'-'n'-alof' alow and aloft

(everywhere aboard ship—in the lower rigging and in the upper rigging)

ALOO Albuquerque Operations Office

alor advanced lunar orbital rendezvous

alot allotment

aloteen alcoholic teenagers (rehabilitation program)

alotm allotment

ALOTS Airborne Lightweight Optical Tracking System

Alouette Aerospatiale armed helicopter made in 4-passenger and 6-passenger versions of this military skylark

Aloys Aloysius

Aloysha (Russian nickname—Aleksei)—Alex; Alexander

alp. anterior lobe (of) pituitary; assembly language program (data processing); autocode list processing; automated language processing

Alp Alphen; Alpine

ALP Air Liaison Party; Allied Liaison and Protocol; Ambulance Loading Post; American Labor Party; Australian Labor [most recent official spelling] Party; Australian Labour Party; Australian Liberal Party; Automated Learning Process; Automated Library Program

ALP Agence Lao Press (French —Lao Press Agency)

ALPA Air Line Pilot's Association

ALPAC Automatic Language Processing Advisory Committee (National Research Council)

alpak algebra package

ALPB American Lutheran Publicity Bureau

ALPC Army Logistics Policy Council; Australian Library Promotion Council

ALPCA Auto License Plate Collectors Association

Alpen (Dutch or German—Alps)—short form for Richard Strauss's *Alpine Symphony*

Alpes (Spanish—Alps)—*Los Alpes*—The Alps

ALPGA Australian Liquefied Petroleum Gas Association

Alph Alphonse

alpha alphabetical

Alpha letter A radio code

ALPHA Action League for Physically Handicapped Advancement

alphameric alphanumeric and alphabetic-numeric

alphametic alphabet arithmetic

alphanumeric alphabetical-numerical

alpha order alphabetical order

ALPHAS Automatic Literature Processing, Handling, and Analysis System

Alpine Alpine Symphony (symphonic poem by Richard Strauss—*Eine Alpensinfonie*)

Alpine Principality Liechtenstein (in the Alps between Austria and Switzerland)

Alpine Republic Switzerland

ALPL Advanced Lunar Projects Laboratory

alpo (ALPO) Apollo lunar polar orbiter

ALPO Allen Products; Amalgamation of Left Political Organizations; Association of Lunar and Planetary Observers

ALPOWAD Alaska Power Administration

Alps Alpine Mountains extending from Franco-Italian border at Mediterranean to Yugoslavia; mountain system of south central Europe; passing through France, Italy, Switzerland, Germany, Austria, and Czechoslovakia

ALPS Advanced Linear Programming System; Automated Library Processing Services; Automatic Landing Positioning System

ALPSP Association of Learned and Professional Society Publishers

Alpujarras Alpujarras Mountains of Almería and Granada in Spain

ALPURCOMS All-Purpose Communications System

ALQAS Aircraft-Landing Quality-Assessment Scheme

alr. *aliter* (Latin—otherwise)

ALR Australian League of Rights

ALR American Law Reports

ALRA Abortion Law Reform Association; Agricultural Labor Relations Act

ALRANZ Abortion Law Reform Association of New Zealand

ALRB Agriculture Labor Relations Board; Agriculture Labor Relations Bureau

ALRC Anti-Locust Research Center; Australian Law Reform Commission

alri airborne long-range input

ALRI Angkatan Laut Republik Indonesia (Indonesian Navy)

ALRM Aboriginal Legal Rights Movement (Australia)

ALROS American Laryngological, Rhinological, and Otological Society

a l r p de V M *a los reales pies de Vuestra Majestad* (Spanish—at the royal feet of Your Majesty)

ALRS *Admiralty List of Radio Signals*

ALRTF Army Long-Range Technological Forecast

als amyotrophic lateral sclerosis; antilymphocytic serum; autograph letter signed

als (ALS) automatic line supervision

ALS Aborginal Legal Service; Advanced Laser System; Alton & Southern (railroad); American Littoral Society; Approach Light System; Area Licensing Scheme (Singapore); Australian Literary Society; Australian Literary Studies

A.L.S. Associate of the Linnean Society

ALSA American Land Sailing Association; American Law Student Association

ALSAA Americans of Lebanese-Syrian Ancestry for America

Alsace-Lorraine (French—Elsass-Lothringen)

Alsacia y Lorena (Spanish—Alsace-Lorraine)

alsam (ALSAM) air-launched surface-attack missile

Alsat Alsatian

ALSC American Lumber Standards Committee; Association for Library Service to Children

ALSCP Appalachian Land Stabilization and Conservation Program

alse aviation life-support equipment

Al seg *al segno* (Italian—return to the sign: S: and play to end or finale)

alsep (ALSEP) apollo lunar surface experiments package

Also *Also Sprach Zarathustra* (German—Thus Spake Zarathustra)—symphonic poem by Richard Strauss

ALSO Alex Lindsay String Orchestra (New Zealand)

alsor air-launch sounding rocket

alss airline system simulator

ALSS Advanced Location Strike System; Airborne Location and Strike System; Apollo Logistics Support System

ALST Alaska Standard Time

alt academic learning time; alter(ation); altered; altering; alternative; alternator; altimeter; altitude

alt *altitud*; *altura* (Spanish—altitude, height)

Alt alternating (light)

Alt Altesse (French—Highness)

ALT Aboriginal Lands Trust; Aer Lingus (Irish Air Lines); alteration (computerese)

ALT *Australian Law Times*

Alta Alberta

ALTA Agricultural Landlords and Tenants Act; American Land Title Association; American Library Trustee Association; Association of Local Transport Airlines

altac algebraic translator and compiler

Alta California (Spanish—Upper California), used in contradistinction to *Baja California* in Mexico (Lower California)

altair (ALTAIR) ARPA (q.v.) long-range tracking and instrumentation radar

Altais Altai Mountains

Altamont, Catawba Thomas Wolfe's fictitious name for Asheville, North Carolina

altan alternate alerting network

altare automatic logic testing and recording equipment

Altay high mountains rising above northern edge of Gobi Desert in Central Asian portion of Russia

ALTCOMIND Alternate Commander, Indian (USN)

ALTCOMLANT Alternate Commander, Atlantic (USN)

ALTCOMPAC Alternate Commander, Pacific (USN)

altd altered

alt. dleb. *alternis diebus* (Latin—alternate days)

Alte Fritz (German—Old Fritz)—Frederick the Great of Prussia

alter. alteration; alternate

Alter Steffl (German—Old Stevie)—St Stephen's Cathedral in Vienna

Alt F Fl alternating fixed and flashing (light)

Alt F Gp Fl alternating fixed and group flashing (light)

Alt Fl alternating flashing (light)

Alt Got Alternate Gothic

Alt Gp Occ alternating group occulting (light)

Alt Gr Fl alternating group flashing (light)

altho although

alt. hor. *alternis horis* (Latin—at alternate hours)

Altiplano de México (Spanish—Mexican Plateau), extends from the American Border to Tehuantepec on the Guatemalan Border

altm altimeter

alt. noc. *alternis noctibus* (Latin—on alternate nights)

altnr alternator

Alt Occ alternating occulting (light)

Alto Perú (Spanish—High Peru)—Bolivia

ALTPR Association of London Theatre Press Representatives

altran algebraic translator

altrec automatic life testing and recording of electronic components

altru altruism; altruist; altruistic

ALTS Advanced Lunar Transportation System; Airborne Laser Tracker System

alt set. altimeter setting

ALTUC All-India Trade Union Congress

alt udk *alt udkomne* (Dano-Norwegian—all published)

alu (ALU) arithmetic and logic unit

Alucon Aluminium Conductors (New Zealand)

alue admissible linear unbiased estimator

alum. alumna; alumnae; alumni; alumnus; hydrated potassium aluminum sulfate

alv alveolar

alv (ALV) avian leukemia virus(es)

älv (Swedish—river)

alv. adstrict. *alvo adstricto* (Latin—bowels being constipated)

ALVAO *Association des Langues Vivantes pour l'Afrique Occidentale* (French—West African Modern Languages Association)

alv. deject. *alvi dejectiones* (Latin—intestinal discharges)

Alver Alvern(on)

Alvⁿ Alvaro

alvx alveolectomy

alw allowance; arch-loop whorl

Alweg Axel Lennert Wenner-Gren (Swedish industrialist's name applied to monorailroad systems)

alwin algorithmic wiswesser notation

ALWL Army Limited War Laboratory

alwt advanced lightweight torpedo

Alx Alexandria

aly alloy

Aly Alley

Alyce Girls Alyce D. McPherson School for (delinquent) Girls at Ocala, Florida

ALYESKA Alaska Pipeline Service

Alzheimer's disease degenerative pre-senile brain disease

am. aircooled motor; ammeter; amplitude modulation; auditory (sequential) memory

am. (AM) air-locked module

a.m. *ante meridiem* (Latin—before noon)

a/m auto/manual

a & m agricultural and mechanical; ancient and modern; architectural and mechanical; archy and mehitabel

am amerikansk (Dano-Norwegian—American)

Am Amazonas; America; American; americium; myopic astigmatism (symbol)

Am. Amós (Spanish—The Book of Amos)

AM Academy of Management; Aeronaves de México (Mexican Airlines); Air Marshal; Air Medal; Air Ministry; Alexander Mackenzie (Canada's Prime Minister); Almacenes Maritimos; Alpes Maritimes (Maritime Alps); amplitude modulation; angular momentum; Arthur Meighen (Canada's tenth and twelfth Prime Minister); Australian Member (Member of the Order of Australia); Aviation Medicine; Aviation Structural Mechanic; large minesweeper (naval symbol); metric angle (symbol)

A-M Addressograph-Multigraph; Alpes-Maritimes

A.M. Air Mail

A/M Aviation Medicine

A & M Agricultural and Mechanical; Agricultural and Mechanical College of Texas; Ancient and Modern (hymns)

A of M Academy of Music

AM Almanaque Mundial (Spanish—World Almanac)

A.M. artium magister (Latin—Master of Arts); *Ave Maria* (Latin—Hail Mary)

a/m¹ amperes per square meter

AM-3C Aeritalia-Aermacchi single-engine three-place armed-trainer aircraft

ama actual mechanical advantage; against medical advice

amª amiga (Spanish—female friend)

AMA Academy of Model Aeronautics; Acoustical Materials Association; Aerospace Medical Association; Agricultural Marketing Administration; Air Matriel Area; Aircraft Manufacturers Association; Amarillo, Texas (airport); Amateur Trapshooting Association; Ambulance Manufacturers Association; American Machinery Association; American Management Association; American Maritime Association; American Marketing Association; American Matthay Association; American Medical Association; American Ministerial Association; American Monument Association; American Motel Association; American Motorcycle Association; American Municipal Association; Arena Managers Association; Australian Medical Association; Australian Meteorological Association; Automobile Manufacturers Association

A & MA Advertising and Marketing Association

AMAA Adhesives Manufacturers Association of America; Army Mutual Aid Association; Association of Medical Advertising Agencies

AMAB Army Medical Advisory Board

Am Acad Pol Soc Sci American Academy of Political and Social Science

Am Acad Rel American Academy of Religion

AMACUS Automated Microfilm Aperture Card Updating System

amad aircraft-mounted accessory drive

Amad Amadeus

AMA-DE American Medical Association—Drug Evaluation(s)

AMAE American Museum of Atomic Energy; Association of Mexican-American Educators

AMAERF American Medical Association Education and Research Foundation

Amahl Amahl and the Night Vis-

itors (Menotti one-act chamber opera popular at Christmas time)

amal amalgam; amalgamate; amalgamation

AMAL Aero-Medical Acceleration Laboratory; American Medical Acceleration Laboratory

amalg amalgamated

amalgam mercury and silver mixture

a M (a/M) am Main (German—on the Main River)

Aman Agaf Modiin (Hebrew—Military Information Bureau)—Israel

amap advanced multiprogramming analysis

AMAR Annual Major Additions Rate

AMARC Army Materiel Acquisition Review Committee

AMARS Air Mobile Aircraft Refueling System; Automatic Message Address Routing System

AMAS American Military Assistance Staff; Automatic Message Accounting System

Am Assn Blood American Association of Blood Banks

Am Assn Coll Pharm American Association of Colleges of Pharmacy

Am Assn Comm Jr Coll American Association of Community and Junior Colleges

amat amateur

AMATC Air Materiel Armament Test Center

amatol ammonia & toluene (explosive)

A-matter advance matter (written in advance of a newspaper story)

AMATYC American Mathematical Association of Two-Year Colleges

AMAUS Aero Medical Association of the United States

AMAWA American Medical Association Women's Auxiliary

AMAX American Metal Climax

Amazon South America's greatest river flows more than 3900 miles from headwaters in eastern Peru across northern Brazil and into Atlantic off river port of Belém do Pará near Majaró Island on the Equator

Amazonas (Portuguese or Spanish—Amazon)

Amazon of the Keyboard Teresa Carreño

amb amber; ambient; ambulance

Amb Ambassador

AMB Airways Modernization Board; Associação Médica Brasileira (Brazilian Medical Association); Australian Meat Board

AMB Asociación Mundial de Boxeo (Spanish—World Boxing Association); *Association Maritime Belge* (French—Belgian Maritime Association)

amba andelsselskab med begraenset ansvar (Dano-Norwegian—limited liability cooperative)

AMBAC American Bosch Arma Corporation; American Municipal Bond Assurance Corporation

Am Bankr Reps American Bankruptcy Reports

Am Baptist American Baptist Historical Society

Ambassador of the Air Charles A Lindbergh

Ambassador of Good Will Will Rogers

AMBBA Associated Master Barbers and Beauticians of America

Amb Brdg Ambassador Bridge (Detroit—Windsor)

Amb Col Ambassador College

ambel ambiguity eliminator

Amber Amberes (Spanish—Antwerp)

Amberes (Spanish—Antwerp)

A.M. Bernard Louisa M Alcott's pseudonym she used for popular novels

Amb Ex Ambassador Extraordinary

Amb Ex/Plen Ambassador Extraordinary and Plenipotentiary

ambi (Latin prefix—both)—ambidextrous

Am Bibl American Bibliographic Center—Clio Press

ambidex ambidextrous

ambig ambiguity; ambiguous

ambisex ambisextrous (bisexual)

ambish ambition

ambit algebraic manipulation by identity translation

ambiv ambivalence; ambivalent

Am Bk American Book Company

Am Bk Prices American Book Prices Current

ambl ambulatory

amblads advise method, bill of lading, and date shipped

Amb Lib Ambrosian Library (Milan)

Ambo Ambrose

Ambon Amboina, Indonesia

Am Booksellers American Booksellers Association

Amboys collective short form for New Jersey's Amboys, Perth Amboy and South Amboy, plus other Amboys ranging from California to Indonesia where the name is Amboina

Ambrianum (Latin—Amiens)—French city and ancient capital of Picardy

Ambridge American Bridge (company)

AMBRL Army Medical Biomechanical Research Laboratory

ambros ambrosia

Ambroslan Ambrosian Library (Milan)

ambt ambulant

ambul ambulation; ambulatory

Amburgo (Italian—Hamburg)

amc arthrogryposis multiplex congentia (AMC); automatic mixture control; axiomesiodistal

amc (AMC) armed merchant cruiser

AMc coastal minesweeper (3-letter naval symbol)

AMC Aerospace Manufacturers Council; Air Mail Center; Air Materiel Command; Aircraft Manufacturers Council; Albany Medical Center; Albany Medical College; Alternate Media Center; American Maritime Cases; American Mining Congress; American Mission to the Chinese; American Motors Corporation; Animal Medical Center; Appalachian Mountain Club; Army Materiel Command; Army Medical Center; Army Medical Corps; Army Missile Command; Army Mobility Command; Army Munitions Command; Association of Management Consultants; automatic message counting (computerese)

AMCA Air Moving and Conditioning Association; American Medical College Association; American Mosquito Control Association; Australian Management Consultants Association

AMCALMSA Army Materiel Command Automated Logistics Management Systems Agency

Am Camping American Camping Association

Am Can American Can

AMCAS American Medical College Application Service

AMC-ASC Air Materiel Command—Aeronautical Systems Center

AMCAWS Advanced Medium-Caliber Aircraft Weapon System

amcbh auxiliary machine casing bulkhead

AMC & BW Amalgamated Meat Cutters and Butcher Workmen

AMCD American Medical Center at Denver

AMCEA Advertising Media Credit Executives Association

AMCFSA Army Materiel Command Field Safety Agency

Am Chem American Chemical Society

AMCI&SA Army Materiel Command Installations and Service Agency

amcl amended clearance

AMCL African Metals Corporation Limited; Association of Metropolitan Chief Librarians

AMCLDC Army Materiel Command Logistic Data Center

AMCLSSA Army Materiel Command Logistics Systems Support Agency

amcm airborne mine countermeasures

AMCM Air Materiel Command Manual; Army Materiel Command Memorandum

AMCMFO Air Materiel Command Missile Field Office

AMCO American Manufacturing Company

AMCOA AiResearch Manufacturing Company of Arizona

AMCOM American Stock Exchange Communications

Am Con American Consul(ate)

AMCOS Aldermaston Mechanized Cataloguing and Ordering System; Australian Mechanical Copyright Owners Society

AMCPI Army Materiel Command Procurement Instruction(s)

AMCR Air Materiel Command Regulation(s); Army Materiel Command Regulation(s)

AMCRD Air Materiel Command Research and Development; Army Materiel Command Research and Development

AMCS Airborne Missile Control System; Association of Military Colleges and Schools

AMCSA Army Materiel Command Support Activity

AMCSOF Army Combat Surveillance Office

AMCST Associate of the Manchester College of Science and Technology

AMCTB Associated Motor Carriers Tariff Bureau

AMCU Australian Malaria Control Unit

am. cur. *amicus curiae* (Latin—a friend at court)

amd air movement designator; alpha-methyldopa; axiomesiodistal

AMD Accident Model Document; Aero-Mechanics Department (USN); Aerospace Medical Division; Air Movement Data; Army Medical Department; Atomic and Molecular Data

AMD Aerospace Material Document

AMDA Advanced for Mutual Defense Assistance; Advances for Mutual Defense Assistance; Airlines Medical Directors Association

AMDB Agricultural Machinery Development Board

AMDEA Associated Manufacturers of Domestic Electrical Appliances

AMDEC Associated Manufacturers of Domestic Electric Cookers

Amdel Australian Mineral Development Laboratories

Am Dent American Dental Association

a.m. D.g. *ad majorem Dei gloriam* (Latin—to the greater glory of God)—also A.M.D.G.

AMDI Associazione Medici Dentisti Italiani (Association of Italian Medical Dentists)

AmdlEvac aeromedical evacuation

Amdoc American Doctors (organization)

Am Doc Inst American Documentation Institute

AMDS Advanced Missions Docking Subsystem (NASA); Association of Military Dental Surgeons; Automatic Message Distribution System

amdsbsc amplitude-modulation double-sideband suppressed carrier

amdt amendment

ame angle-measuring equipment; automatic microfiche editor

AME Admiralty Mining Establishment (UK); Aero-Medical Evacuation; African Methodist Episcopal; Aviation Medical Examiners

A.M.E. Advanced Master of Education

AMEB Australian Music Examinations Board

amec aft master-events controller

AMEC Airframe Manufacturing Equipment Committee; Australian Minerals and Energy Council

amecd antimechanized

amech account mechanical (failure or malfunction)

ameda automatic-microscope electronic-data accumulator

AMedD Army Medical Department

AMEDDPAS Army Medical Department Property Accounting System

AMedP Army Medical Publication(s)

AMedS Army Medical Service

AMEE Admiralty Marine Engineering Establishment

Ameer Baraka Lee Roy Jones

AMEG Association for Measurement and Evaluation in Guidance

AMEIC Associate Member of the Engineering Institute of Canada

AMEL Aero Medical Equipment Laboratory

Amelia Amelia Goes to the Ball (Menotti one-act comic opera)

amelior amelioration

Am Elsevier American Elsevier Publishing Company

AMEM African Methodist Episcopal Mission

Am Emb American Ambassador; American Embassy

AMEME Association of Mining, Electrical, and Mechanical Engineers

AMEMIC Association of Mill and Elevator Mutual Insurance Companies

amend. amendment(s)

Am Engr American Engineer

Amenia Girls Amenia Center for (delinquent) Girls at Amenia,

New York

amer amerikansk (Dano-Norwegian—American)

Amer America; American

AMERADC Army Mobility Equipment Research and Development Center

Amerasians American Asians (offspring of Americans and Asians)

Amer-Eng American-English

América Central (Spanish—Central America)

América del Norte (Spanish—North America)

América del Sur (Spanish—South America)

América Española Spanish America

AMERICAL Americans in New Caledonia (Army division)

América Meridional (Spanish—South America)—more properly Southern America

american american aloe (century plant); american beauty (crimson rose); american buffalo (bison); american cheese (cheddar); american cloth (oilcloth); american cotton (upland cotton); american leopard (jaguar); american plan (hotel or motel including food with the room and bath); american rig (oil rig using a chisel bit dropped from on high); american sable (pine marten); american twist (tennis term describing a service wherein the ball is spun so it bounces high and to the receiver's left); all other eponymic american items of interest such as the foregoing lowercase derivatives

American Century the 20th century

American Nine America's nine best-known classical composers arranged chronologically: MacDowell, Ives, Piston, Hanson, Gershwin, Copland, Barber, Hovhaness, Bernstein

American Ports (large, medium, and small) *see entries under states and territories such as* Alabama Port, American Samoan Port, California Ports, etc.

American Samoa Pacific Island possession of the United States; inhabitants called American Samoans

American Samoan Port Pago Pago

Americans United Americans

United for Separation of Church and State

American Virgin Islands St Thomas, St John, St Croix, and other Virgin Islands belonging to United States since purchase from Denmark in 1917

American West Indies American Virgin Islands such as St Thomas, St John, St Croix, and other Virgin Islands belonging to United States; Commonwealth of Puerto Rico and nearby islands such as Culebra, Vieques, and Mona; smaller islands used for navigational purposes—Navassa between Haiti and Jamaica, Swan Islands off Honduras, Corn Islands leased from Nicaragua, certain coral reefs in Caribbean between Central America and Cuba

Americas Western Hemisphere; including North, Central, and South America

América Septentrional (Spanish —North America)—more properly Northern America

America's Finest Television Hour 60 Minutes

America's Largest State Alaska

America's Premier City New York

America's Principal Port New York

America's Second City Chicago (according to many New Yorkers)

America's Silent Disease smotherlove also known as momism

America's Tropical Islands Hawaiian Islands and the Virgin Islands

Ameridish American Yiddish

Amerika (Afrikaans, Dutch, Flemish, German—America)

Amerikaan (Dutch—American)

Amerind American & Indian (American Indian or Eskimo)

Amer Ind American Indian

Amerindians American Indians

Ameringlish American English

Amérique (French—America)

Ameritech American Information Technologies

Amer Men Sci American Men of Science

AmerSp American Spanish

Amer Spec American Spectator

Amer Std American Standard

Amer Trauma Soc American Trauma Society

AMeS American Meteorological Society

AMES Association of Marine Engineering Schools

Ameslan American sign language

Amesterdão (Portuguese—Amsterdam)

AMETA Army Management Engineering Training Agency

AMETS Artillery Meteorological System

AMEWA Associated Manufacturers of Electric Wiring Accessories

Amex American Stock Exchange

AMEX Agencia Mexicana de Noticias (Mexican News Agency)

Amexco American Express Company

AMEZ African Methodist Episcopal Zion

AMEZC African Methodist Episcopal Zionist Church

amf (AMF) airmail facility

AMF AIDS Medical Foundation; Air Material Force; American Machine and Foundry; Arab Monetary Fund; Arctic Marine Freighters; Australian Marine Force; Australian Military Forces

AMF(A) Allied Mobile Force (Air)—NATO

Am Feed American Feed Manufacturers Association

AMFGC Association of Midwest Fish and Game Commissioners

AMFIC Automatic Microfilm Information System

AMFIE Association of Mutual Fire Insurance Engineers

AMFIS American Microfilm Information Society; Automatic Microfilm Information System

AMF(L) Allied Mobile Force (Land)—NATO

am/fm amplitude modulation/frequency modulation

Am Friends American Friends Service Committee

amg automatic magnetic guidance; axiomesiogingival

AMG Aircraft Machine Gunner; Albertus Magnus Guild; Allied Military Government; Australian Map Grid

Am Geol American Geological Institute

Am Geophysical American Geophysical Union

AMGNY Associated Musicians of Greater New York

AMGOLD Anglo-American Gold Investment Trust

AMGOT Allied Military Government

AMGS Acceleration Monitoring Guidance System

Am Guidance American Guidance Service

amh astigmatism with myopia predominating; automated medical history

Amh Amharic

AMH Australian Military Hospital

AMHA American Motor Hotel Association

AMHCI Associate Member of the Hotel and Catering Institute

Am Heart American Heart Association

Am Heritage American Heritage Publishing Co

AMHIS American Marine Hull Insurance Syndicate

Am Hist Res American History Research Associates

Am Home Prod American Home Products

AMHS Alaska Marine Highway Authority; American Material Handling Society; Australian Maritime Historical Society

AMHT Automated Multiphasic Health Testing

ami acute myocardial infarction; advanced manned interceptor; air mileage indicator; amitriptyline; axiomesioincisal

AMI Advanced Manned Interceptor; American Marine Institutes; American Meat Institute; American Medical International, Inc.; American Military Institute; American Museum of Immigration; American Mushroom Institute; Association of Medical Illustrators; Association for Multi-Image; Australian Marketing Institute; Australian Motor Industries

AMI Aeronautica Militare Italiana (Italian Air Force)

AMIA American Metal Importers Association; American Mutual Insurance Alliance

AMIADB Army Member—Inter-American Defense Board

AMIAE Associate Member of the Institute of Automobile Engineers

AMIAMA Associate Member of the Incorporated Advertising Managers Association

AMIAP Associate Member of

the Institution of Analysts & Programmers

AMIC Aerospace Materials Information Center; Air Movement Information Center (NATO); Australian Mining Industry Council

AMICA Automobile Mutual Insurance Company of America

AMICE Associate Member of the Institution of Civil Engineers

AMICI Association Mondiale des Interprètes de Conférences International

AMICO American Measuring Instrument Company

AMICOM Army Missile Command

Ami des Hommes (French—Friend of Mankind)—Marquis de Mirabeau's nickname

AMIDS Advanced Multispectral Image Descriptor System; Area Manpower Instructional Development System

Ami du Peuple (French—Friend of the People)—nickname of Jean Paul Marat; title of the revolutionary journal he edited

amigo ants, mice, gophers (electromagnetic device affecting the neurological system of such pests and causing them to die or flee from areas they infest)

AMIGOS Americans Interested In Giving Others a Start

AMII Association of Musical Instrument Industries

AMILO Army-Industry Materiel Information Liaison Office

AMIN Advertising and Marketing International Network

AMINA Association Mondiale des Inventeurs (French—World Association of Inventors)

Am Ind American Indian

Am Indus Arts American Industrial Arts Association

AMINOIL American Independent Oil (company)

Am Inst American Institute

Am Inst Disc American Institute of Discussion

AM International Addressograph-Multigraph International

AMIO Arab Military Industrialization Organization

AMIOP Associate Member of the Institute of Printing

AMIPA Associate Member of the Institute of Practitioners in Advertising

Amirantes Amirante Islands

AMIRS Alternative Mortgage Instruments Study

AMIS Aircraft Movement Information Section; Automated Mask Inspection System

Amistad Amistad National Recreation Area surrounding the Amistad Reservoir near Del Rio, Texas and close to Ciudad Acuña in Coahuila, Mexico

AMJ Assemblée Mondiale de la Jeunesse (French—World Assembly of Youth)

Am Jour Sci American Journal of Science

Am J Phys American Journal of Physics

Am J Psy American Journal of Psychiatry

aml acute monocytic leukemia; acute myelocytic leukemia; acute myoblastic leukemia

aml (AML) adjustable-mortgage loan; amplitude-modulated link

Aml Amlwch

Am L American Lawyer

AML Aberdeen Marine Laboratory; Admiralty Materials Laboratory; Aeromedical Laboratory; American Mail Line; Applied Mathematics Laboratory

AML-60 French four-wheeled armored car with 7.5mm machineguns and a 60mm mortar

AML-90 French four-wheeled armored car with 7.5mm machineguns and a 90mm mortar

AMLC Aerospace Medical Laboratory (USAF)

Am Lib Dir American Library Directory

Am Librarians American Librarians' Agency

Am-Lib(s) Americo-Liberian(s)

amls antimouse lymphocyte serum

AMLS American Medico-Legal Society; Master of Arts in Library Science

amm agnogenic myeloid metaplasia; ammonia; ammunition; anti-missile missile (AMM)

AMM Air Mining Mission; Amman, Jordan (airport); Anti-Missile Missile; Associated Millinery Men; Association Medicale Mondiale (World Medical Association); Avia-

tion Machinist's Mate

AM & M Applied Mathematics and Mechanics

AMMA Adult Movies and Magazines Association (of pornographers); American Museum of Marine Archeology

Am Mach American Machinist

Am Malacologists American Malacologists

Am Management American Management Association

Am Map American Map Company

Am Math Soc American Mathematical Society

AMMC Aviation Materiel Management Center

Am Media American Media

Am Metal Mkt American Metal Market/Metalworking News

Am Meteorite American Meteorite Laboratory (Denver)

ammeter amperemeter (current-measuring instrument)

AMMI American Merchant Marine Institute

AMMINET Automated Mortgage Management Information Network

AMMIS Aircraft Maintenance Manpower Information System (USAF)

amml acute myelomonocytic leukemia

AMMLA American Merchant Marine Library Association

ammo ammunition

Ammo American Motors (stock exchange slang)

ammobr ammunition bearer

ammon ammonia

Ammon Ammonite

Ammonia King Edward Mallinckrodt

ammonia water ammonium hydroxide (NH_4OH)

Am Motors American Motors

AMMPE American Mining, Metallurgical, and Petroleum Engineers

ammrpv advanced multimission remotely-piloted vehicle

Am Mus Mag American Museum of Magic

amn airman

amnes amnesia(c)(al)(ly)

AMNH American Museum of Natural History

amnip adaptive man-machine nonarithmetic information processing

AmnM Airman's Medal

AMN & PA Australian Monthly Newspapers and Periodicals Association

amnswp acoustic minesweeping

AMNZIE Associate Member of the New Zealand Institution of Engineers

amo (AMO) air mail only; alternant molecular orbit

amo amigo (Spanish—male friend); axiomesio-occlusal

AMO Advance Material Order; Aircraft Material Officer; Air Ministry Order; American Motors (stock exchange symbol)

amob automatic meterological oceanographic buoy

AMOCO American Oil Company

amol acute monocytic leukemia

Amon Carter Amon Carter Museum of Western Art

AMOP Association of Mail Order Publishers

amor amorphous

AMORC Ancient Mystic Order Rosae Crusis (Rosicrucian Order)

amorph amorphous

amos antireflection-coated metal-oxide semiconductor

AMOS Acoustic, Meteorological, and Oceanographic Survey; Associated Migrant Opportunity Services; Automatic Meterological Observation Station

Amos and Andy Freeman F Gosden and Charles J Correll

Amoy English equivalent of Hsia-men Island off the coast of mainland China but belonging to Taiwan

amp acid mucopolysaccharide; adenosine monophosphate (hormonal chemical); amperage; ampere; amphetamine; ampicillin; amplification; amplifier; amplitude; ampule; amputation; average mean pressure

AMP Air Mail Pioneers; American Museum of Photography; Army Mine Planter; Association of Media Producers; Aurora Memorial Park (Philippines); Automated Mathematics Program; Aviation Modernization Program

AMPA American Medical Publishers Association; Associate of the Master Photographers Association; Australian Magazine Publishers Association

AMPAC American Medical Political Action Committee

AMPAS Academy of Motion Picture Arts and Sciences

AMPC Automatic Message Processing Center

AMPCO Associated Missile Products Corporation; Association of Major Power Consumers of Ontario

Am Peace American Peace Society

ampersand and per se and

Ampersand Ampersand Press (Princeton)

Ampersand NYC Ampersand Press (New York City)

AMPFTA American Military Precision Flying Teams Association

amph amphibian; amphibious; amphimict; amphoric

Amph Amphibia

AMPH Association of Management in Public Health

amphet amphetamine (stimulant)

amphetamine alphamethylpenethylamine

amphets amphetamines

amphi (Greek prefix—both, both sides of, two) amphibian, amphibolite, amphibological

amphib amphibia(n); amphibious

amphibex amphibious exercise

amphig amphigoric; amphigorical; amphigorist; amphigory

Am Philatelic American Philatelic Society

Am Philos Soc American Philosophical Society

Amphoto American Photographic Book Publishing Co

amp hr ampere hour

AMPI Associated Milk Producers, Incorporated; Associated Music Publishers, Incorporated

Ampico American Piano Company

ampl a macroprogramming language; amplifier; amplitude

ampl ampliata (Italian—enlarged); *amplus* (Latin—large)

AMPOL American Petroleum

ampp advanced microprogrammable processor

ampr advanced multipurpose radar; automatic manifold pressure regulator

AMPR Aeronautical Manufactures Planning Report; Airframe Manufacturers Planning Report; Area Manpower Planning Report; Area Manpower Planning Review

amps amperes; ampules; atmospheric, magnetospheric, and plasmas in space

AMPS Accrued Military Pay System; American Metered Postage Society; Army Mine Planter Service; Army Motion Picture Service; Associated Music Publishers; Association for Media Psychology; Automatic Message Processing System

AMPSS Advanced Manned Precision Strike System

AMPTC Arab Maritime Petroleum Transport Company

AMPTP Association of Motion Picture and Television Producers

amp-turns ampere-turns

Am Public Health American Public Health Association

ampul. ampulla (Latin—ampule)

ampus (s) amputee (s)

AMQ American Medical Qualification

AMQUA American Quaternary Association

amr (AMR) automatic message routing

AMR Abnormal Mission Routine; Advanced Material Request; Airman Military Record; American Airlines (stock exchange symbol); Atlantic Missile Range; Auxiliary Machinery Room (USN)

A.M.R. Master of Arts in Research

AMRA American Medical Records Association; Army Materials Research Agency; Australian Model Railways Association

AMRAC Anti-Missile Research Advisory Council

Am Radio American Radio Relay League

AMRC Advanced Metals Research Corporation; Army Mathematics Research Center; Automotive Market Research Council

AMRCA American Miniature Racing Car Association

AMRCUS Alternative Marriage and Relationship Council of the United States

AMR & DL Air Mobility Research and Development Laboratory (USA)

Am Record American Record Collectors Exchange

Am Red American Red Cross

Am Res American Research Council

AMREX American Real Estate

Exchange
AM & RF African Medical and Research Foundation
AMRINA Associate Member of the Royal Institution of Naval Architects
AMRIP Avionics Module Repair Improvement Program
Amrit Amritsar
AMRL Aerospace Medical Research Laboratories; Army Medical Research Laboratory
AMRNL Army Medical Research and Nutrition Laboratory
AMRO Amsterdam-Rotterdam (bank); Association of Medical Record Officers
amrpd applied manufacturing research and process development
AMRS Air Ministry Radio Station; American Moral Reform Society; Australian Media Research Services
ams aggravated in military service; auditory memory span; automated multiphasic screening
Ams Amsterdam
AMs auxiliary motor minesweeper
AMS Administration and Management Services; Administration Management Society; Aeronautical Material Specification; Agricultural Marketing Service; American Mathematical Society; American Meteor Society; American Meteorological Society; American Microscopical Society; American Mineral Spirits; American Montessori Society; American Museum of Safety; American Musicological Society; Anglican Men's Society; Army Map Service; Army Medical Service; Association of Messenger Services; Association of Museum Stores; Australian Medical Services; Aviation Marketing Services (Australia)
AM & S Australian Mining and Smelting
AMS Acta Medica Scandinavica
amsa (AMSA) advanced manned strategic aircraft
AMSA American Metal Stamping Association; American Museum of Social Anthropology; Association of Metropolitan Sewerage Agencies; Australian Marine Sciences Association; Australian Medical

Students Association
AMSACP Advanced Multistage Axialflow Compressor Program (NASA)
amsam anti-missile surface-to-air-missile
Am Sam American Samoa
AMSANZ Aviation Medicine Society of Australia and New Zealand
amsat amateur satellite
AMSAT Amateur Satellite
AMSC Army Medical Specialist Corps
Am Sch Athens American School of Classical Studies at Athens
Am School American Scholar
Am Sci & Eng American Science and Engineering, Inc
AMSCO American Mineral Spirits Company; American Sterilizer Company
AMSE Associate Member of the Society of Engineers
amsef anti-mine-sweeping explosive float
AMSGA Association of Manufacturers and Suppliers for the Graphic Arts
AMSH Association for Moral and Social Hygiene
AMSIR Agriculture, Marine, Scientific, and Industrial Research Ministry
amsl above mean sea level
AMSMH Association of Medical Superintendents of Mental Hospitals
AMSO Air Member for Supply and Organisation (RAF)
AMSOC American Miscellaneous Society
Am Soc Afr Cult American Society of African Culture
Am Soc HRAC Eng American Society of Heating, Refrigerating, and Air-Conditioning Engineers
Am Society Pr American Society Press
Am Soc Indxrs American Society of Indexers
Am Soc Metals American Society for Metals
Am Soc Not American Society of Notaries
Am Soc Soc American Sociological Society
Am Soc Tool and Mfg Eng American Society of Tool and Manufacturing Engineers
Am Sp American Spanish (Latin American)
AMSP Army Master Study Program

AMSq Avionics Maintenance Squadron (USAF)
ams s autographed manuscript signed
AMSS Advanced Meterological Sounding System; Automatic Music Select System
AMSSEE Area Museum Service for South-Eastern England
AMSSFG Association of Manufacturers of Small Switch and Fuse Gear
a mss s autographed manuscripts signed
Amst Amsterdam
AMSTAT News American Statistical Association News
Amstelodamun (Latin—Amsterdam)
Amstelredamun (Latin—Amsterdam)
AMSUS Association of Military Surgeons of the United States
amt alpha-methyltryrosine; amethopterin; amount; amphetamine
AMT Academy of Medicine, Toronto, Canada; Aerial Mail Terminal; American Medical Technologists; Astrograph Mean Time
A.M.T. Associate in Mechanical Technology; Associate in Medical Technology; Master of Arts—Teaching
amta airborne moving target attack
AMTA American Massage and Therapy Association
amtank amphibious tank
AMTC Airframe Manufacturing Tooling Committee
A.M.T.C. Art Master's Teaching Certificate
AMTCL Association for Machine Translation and Computational Linguistics
AMTD Automatic Magnetic Tape Dissemination (Service)
AMTDA Agricultural Machinery and Tractor Dealers Association
Am Technical American Technical Society
Am Tech Soc American Technical Society
AMTEG Australian Metal Trades Export Group
Am Tel & Tel American Telephone and Telegraph
amtex air mass-transportation experiment
Am Theatre Assoc American Theatre Association
amti airborne moving target in-

dicator

Amtorg Amerikanskaya Torgovlya (Russian-American Trading Company)

AMTPI Associate Member of the Town Planning Institute (UK)

amtrac amphibious tractor

Amtrak (American railroad tracks)—the National Railway Passenger Corporation

amtran automatic mathematical translator

amt(s) amphetamine(s)

AMTS Associate Member of the Television Society

amu air mileage unit; air mission unit; astronaut maneuvering unit; atomic mass unit

AMU Alaska Methodist University; American Malacological Union; American Marksmanship Unit; Army Marksmanship Unit; Associated Midwestern Universities; Association of Marine Underwriters

AMUA Associate in Music—University of Adelaide

AMUBC Association of Marine Underwriters of British Columbia

Am U Field American Universities Field Staff

Am Univ Artforms American Universal Artforms

Amur 2700-mile river entering Sea of Japan at Tatar Strait

AMURT Anada Marga Universal Relief Team (India)

A.Mus. Associate in Music

A.Mus.A. Associate in Music—Australia

A.Mus.C. Associate in Music—Canada

A.Mus.L.C.M. Associate in Music—London College of Music

A.Mus.N.Z. Associate in Music—New Zealand

A.Mus.S.A. Associate in Music—South Africa

A.Mus.T.C.L. Associate in Music—Trinity College of Music—London

amv alfalca-mosaic virus; avian myeloblastitis virus

AMV Association Mondiale Vétérinaire (Franch—World Veterinary Association)

AMVAP Associate Manufacturers of Veterinary and Agricultural Products

AMVER Atlantic Merchant Vessel Report; Automated Mutual Assistance Vessel Res-

cue (USCG)

AMVERS Automated Merchant Vessel Reporting System

AMVETS American Veterans (World War II, Korea, Vietnam)

AMVM Administrative Motor Vehicle Management

amw actual measurement weight

AMW Antimissile Warfare; Association of Married Women

AMWA American Medical Women's Association; American Medical Writers' Association

AMWC Association of Workers for Maladjusted Children

Am West American West Publishing Company

AMWG Academy of Master Wine Growers

AMWM Association of Manufacturers of Woodworking Machinery

AMWSU Amalgamated Metalworkers and Shipwrights Union (Australia)

AMX-13 French light tank carrying SS-11 antitank guided missiles and a 75mm gun

AMX-30 French medium tank carrying a 105mm gun plus machineguns (antiaircraft and ground)

AMX-105 French self-propelled 105mm howitzer

AMX-155 French self-propelled 155mm howitzer

Am Xiamen (Pinyin Chinese—Amoy)

AMX-VTT French armored personnel carrier (crew of 2 plus 12 troops)

amy amytal (barbituate depressant and sedative)

Amy Amelia; Amoy, China

amyl amyl nitrate

amys amyl nitrate

an. above named; airman; annual; anode

an' and

a/n acidic and neutral

an (Greek—lacking, not, without)—anaerobic, anemic, anonymous, anorexia

an. *anno* (Latin—year); *ante* (Latin—before)

An Annam; Annamese

A$_n$ normal atmosphere

AN Acid Number; Aerodynamic Note; Air Force-Navy; Airmail Notice; Air Navigation; Air Navigator; Air Reduction (stock exchange sym-

bol); alphanumeric (computerese); Anglo-Norman; Apalachicola Northern (railroad); Army-Navy; net laying vessel (naval symbol)

A.N. Associate in Nursing

A & N Army and Navy

AN-2 Soviet Antonov 14-passenger biplane nicknamed Colt by NATO forces

AN-12 Soviet Antonov 100-passenger cargo plane nicknamed Cub by NATO

AN-14 Soviet Antonov 6-seat transport aircraft nicknamed Clod by NATO

AN-14M Soviet Antonov 15-passenger turboprop plane

AN-22 Soviet Antonov 22 (super transport plane)

AN-26 Soviet Antonov 50-passenger transport plane nicknamed Coke by NATO

ana anesthesia; anesthesiac

ana (ANA) antinuclear antibodies

ana (Greek prefix—up or up against) analogy, analysis, anatomy

Ana Anaheim; Anita; Anna; Annabel(la)

'Aña Agaña, Guam

ANA Air Force-Navy Aeronautical; All Nippon Airways; American Nature Association; American Neurological Association; American Newspaper Association; American Numismatic Association; American Nurses' Association; Army-Navy Aeronautical; Asociación Nacional Automovilista (National Automobile Association); Association of National Advertisers; Australian National Airways; Australian Natives Association

ANA Automotive News Almanac

ANAAS Australian and New Zealand Association for the Advancement of Science

anab anabasis

anac anachronism; anachronistic

ANACHEM Association of Analytical Chemists

anacol anacoluthon

anacom analog computer

anacreon anacreontic(s); anacreontist

anacru anacrusis

ANADIS Australian National Animal Disease Information System

anaesth anaesthesia; anaesthet-

ic(s); anaesthesiologist; anaesthesiology
ANAF Army, Navy, Air Force
anag anagram; anagrammatic-
(al) (ly); anagramist; ana-
grams
ANA/HEW Administration for
Native Americans—HEW
ANAHL Australian National
Animal Health Laboratory
*ANAI Asociacion Nacional de
Administradores de Inmuebles*
(Spanish—National Association of Real Estate Administrators)
anal analogy; analysis; analytical
*Anal Chem Analytical Chemis-
try*
analg analgesic
anal psychol analytical psychology
analyst psychoanalyst
analyt analytical
Anambas Anambas Islands (in
the South China Sea where
governing Indonesians permitted Vietnamese boat-
people refugees to land and
live while awaiting international aid)
anap agglutination negative, absorption positive
*ANAP Asociación Nacional de
los Agricultores Pequeños*
(Spanish—National Association of Small Farmers)
*ANAPO Alianza Nacional Po-
pular* (Spanish—Popular National Alliance)—fusion of
Colombia's conservative and
liberal political forces
ANARC Association of North
American Radio Clubs
anarch anarchist; anarchism;
anarchy
Anarchist Geographer Prince
Peter Kropotkin and Elisée
Reclus share this title
Anarchist Protagonist Michael
Bakunin
ANARE Australian National
Antarctic Research Expedi-
tions
ANAS Australian National Air-
lines Commission
anat anatomical; anatomist;
anatomy
Anat Anatomy
anath anathema; anathematize
Anatole France Jacques Anatole
François Thibault
Anatolia Asia Minor
Anatomist of Humanity Jean
Baptiste Poquelin Molière
anatran analog translator

anav area navigation
ANB Army-Navy-British Stan-
dard
*ANB Australian National Bibli-
ography*
anbs (ANBS) armed nuclear
bombardment satellite
ANB & TC American National
Bank and Trust Company
anc all numbers calling; ancient
Anc Ancona
ANC African National Con-
gress; African National Coun-
cil; Air Force-Navy-Civil;
American News Company;
Anchorage, Alaska (airport);
Arlington National Cemetery;
Army and Navy Civil Com-
mittee on Aircraft; Army
Nurse Corps; Australian
Newspaper Council
ANCA Allied Naval Communi-
cations Agency; American Na-
tional Cattlemen's Associa-
tion
ANCAP Administratión Nacio-
nal de Combustibles Alcohol y
Portland
ANCAR Australian National
Committee for Antarctic Re-
search
ancc anodal closure contraction
ANCC Australian National Cat-
tlemen's Council
ANCCAC Australian National
Committee on Computation
and Automatic Control
anch anchorage
anchor. alphanumeric character
generator
Anchorage Youth McLaughlin
Youth Center at Anchorage,
Alaska
Anchor Your Age Anchor Your
Age in Anchorage founded in
1915—Alaska's capital and
largest city
Ancient Capital of England
Winchester
ANCIRS Automated News
Clipping, Indexing, and Re-
trieval System
ANCLD Australian National
Committee on Large Dams
Anco Ancohuma
ANCO Andersen-Collingwood
(tanker service)
ANCOA Aerial Nurse Corps of
America
ANCOM Andean Common
Market
ancova analysis of covariance
ancr aircraft not combat ready
ANCs African National Con-
gress members
ANCS American Numerical

Control Society
ANCSA Alaska Native Claims
Settlement Act
ANCUN Australian National
Committee for the United Na-
tions
ANCW Australian National
Council of Women
ANCXF Allied Naval Com-
mander Expeditionary Force
and andante (Italian—of moder-
ate speed)
And Andalucía; Andaman Is-
lands; Andromeda
AND Army-Navy Design
AND Australian News Digest
ANDA Australian National
Dance Association
andalusite aluminum silicate
Andamans Andaman islanders;
Andaman Islands
Andamans and Nicobars Anda-
man and Nicobar Islands off
Burma in the Bay of Bengal
ANDB Air Navigation Develop-
ment Board
ANDC Australian National
Dairy Committee
Andean America (north to
south) Venezuela, Colombia,
Ecuador, Peru, Bolivia, Argen-
tina, Chile
Andean Common Market Bo-
livia, Colombia, Ecuador,
Peru, Venezuela (Andean Pact
Nations)
Andean Group Bolivia, Colom-
bia, Ecuador, Peru, Venezuela
Andean Lands Argentina, Bo-
livia, Chile, Colombia, Ecuad-
or, Peru, Venezuela
Andes Cordillera de los Andes;
Los Andes; main mountain
chain of South America, extends from Venezuela to Panama and southward to Patagonia and Tierra del Fuego with
highest peaks and ranges along
west coast
And I Andaman Islands
Andie Andrew
Andno andantino (Italian—
slower than andante)
Ando Andorra; Andorran
*An Donau An der schönen
blauen Donau* (German—On
the beautiful blue Danube)—
waltz by Johann Strauss Jr
Andorra Valleys of Andorra
(Pyrenees principality only
half the area of New York
City, Andorrans speak Catalan, French, and Spanish, philatelists prize its stamps and
skiers its slopes)
Andover Hawker-Siddeley troop

transport designated HS-748 and holding 40 paratroopers or 58 regular soldiers
Andr Andromeda
ANDRA *Agence National pour la Gestion des Dechets Radioactifs* (French—National Radioactive Management Agency)
Andre Andrea
Andrea del Sarto Andrea Domenico d'Agnolo di Francesco
Andreaofs Andreaof Islands
Andreapolis (Latin—St Andrews)—Scottish place known to all golfers
Andrei Sinyavsky Abram Tertz
Andre Maurois Emile Salomon Wilhelm Herzog
Andrew Furuseth Anders Andreassen
Andrew Garve pseudonym of Paul Winterton
Andrews twenty-dollar bills bearing the portrait of President Andrew Jackson
Andrew York Christopher Nicole's pseudonym
andro androsterone
andro (Greek prefix—old)—androgen(ic)(al)(ly)
androg androgyn (girlish male)
Andryusha (Russian nickname —Andrei)—Andrew; Andy
Ands Andreas
ANDSA *Almacenes Nacionales de Deposito SA* (Spanish—National Depository Warehouse Company)
andte anodal duration tetanus
Andte *andante* (Italian—of moderate speed)
Andy Andrew
andz anodize
ane acoustic noise environment
ANEAC Australian National Energy Advisory Committee
anec anecdotal; anecdote(s)
Aneda (Latin—Edinburgh)
ANEDA *Association Nationale d'Etudes pour la Documentation Automatique* (National Association for Automatic Documentation Studies)
ANEF American Nepal Education Foundation
ANEQ *Association Nationale des Estudiants du Québec* (French—National Association of Students of Québec)
anes anesthesia; anesthesiologist; anesthesiology; anesthetician; anesthetic(s)
anesth anesthetic
anesthesiol anesthesiology
an. ex anode excitation

anf anchored filament; antinuclear factor(s)
ANF American Nurses Foundation; Atlantic Nuclear Force (NATO); Atomic Nuclear Forum; Australian Nursing Federation
anfe (ANFE) aircraft not fully equipped
anfi automatic noise-figure indicator
ANFIA *Associazione Nazionale fra le Industrie Automobilistiche* (Italian—National Association of Automobile Industries)
anfo ammonium nitrate fuel oil (explosive)
ang angiogram; angle; angular
ang *angaende* (Danish, Norwegian, Swedish—concerning)
Ang Anchorage; Angel (phonograph records); Anglo-; Angola
ANG Air Force-Navy-Army Guided Missile; Air National Guard; American Newspaper Guild; Australian National Gallery; Australian New Guinea
ANGAU Australian New Guinea Administrative Unit
Angela Angelica
Angel of the Battlefield Clara Barton
angel dust phencyclidine (PCP) nickname
Angelenos natives of Los Angeles, California
Angeles Port Angeles, Washington opposite Victoria, British Columbia
Angelic Doctor Thomas Aquinas
Ångfart *Ångfartygas* (Swedish—steamship company)
Angie Angela, Angelina, Angeline
angiol angiology
angkor (Khmer—city)
Angkor Angkor Thom (Walled City of Angkor) or Angkor Vat (Temple City of Angkor)—both part of the ancient Cambodian capital of the Khmers
Angkor Thom (Khmer—Great City)
Angkor Vat (Khmer—Temple City)
Angl Anglican
Angl *Angleterre* (French—England)
Angleterre (French—England)
Anglia (Latin—England)
Anglic Anglican; Anglicism
ANGLICO Air and Naval Gun-

fire Liaison Company
Anglo-Afg Anglo-Afghan
Anglo-Afr Anglo-African
Anglo-Amer Anglo-American
Anglo-Ant Anglo-Antarctic(an); Anglo-Antillean
Anglo-Arab Anglo-Arabian
Anglo-Arg Anglo-Argentine
Anglo-Art Anglo-Arctic
Anglo-Aus Anglo-Australian; Anglo-Austrian
Anglo-Bah Anglo-Bahaman
Anglo-Barb Anglo-Barbadian
Anglo-Bas Anglo-Basque
Anglo-Bel Anglo-Belizian
Anglo-Belg Anglo-Belgian
Anglo-Bhu Anglo-Bhutanese
Anglo-Bol Anglo-Bolivian
Anglo-Bots Anglo-Botswana
Anglo-Braz Anglo-Brazilian
Anglo-Bul Anglo-Bulgarian
Anglo-Bur Anglo-Burman; Anglo-Burundian
Anglo-CA Anglo-Central American
Anglo-Cam Anglo-Cameroonian
Anglo-Can(ad) Anglo-Canadian
Anglo-Cat Anglo-Catalan
Anglo-Cath Anglo-Catholic
Anglo-Cey Anglo-Ceylonese
Anglo-Chi Anglo-Chinese
Anglo-Chil Anglo-Chilean
Anglo-Col Anglo-Colombian
Anglo-Cub Anglo-Cuban
Anglo-Cyp Anglo-Cypriot
Anglo-Czech Anglo-Czechoslovak(ian)
Anglo-Dah Anglo-Dahomean
Anglo-Dan Anglo-Danish
Anglo-Du Anglo-Dutch
Anglo-Ecu Anglo-Ecuadorean
Anglo-Egypt Anglo-Egyptian
Anglo-Epis Anglo-Episcopal(ian)
Anglo-Ethio Anglo-Ethiopian
Anglo-Fin Anglo-Finnish
Anglo-Fr Anglo-French
Anglo-Gam Anglo-Gambian
Anglo-Ger Anglo-German
Anglo-Gr Anglo-Greek
Anglo-Guy Anglo-Guyanese
Anglo-Hond Anglo-Honduran
Anglo-Hung Anglo-Hungarian
Anglo-Ice Anglo-Icelandic
Anglo-Ind Anglo-Indian
Anglo-Indo Anglo-Indonesian
Anglo-Ir Anglo-Iranian; Anglo-Iraqi; Anglo-Irish
Anglo-Isr Anglo-Israeli
Anglo-Ital Anglo-Italian
Anglo-Jam Anglo-Jamaican
Anglo-Jap Anglo-Japanese
Anglo-Jew Anglo-Jewish
Anglo-Jor Anglo-Jordanian
Anglo-Ken Anglo-Kenyan

Anglo-Kuw Anglo-Kuwaiti
Anglo-Lat Anglo-Latin
Anglo-Mal Anglo-Malawian; Anglo-Malaysian; Anglo-Maltese
Anglo-Mald Anglo-Maldivian
Anglo-Mex Anglo-Mexican
Anglo-N Anglo-Norse
Anglo-Nep Anglo-Nepalese
Anglo-Nig Anglo-Nigerian
Anglo-Nor Anglo-Norwegian
Anglo-Norm Anglo-Norman
Anglo-NZ Anglo-New Zealand
Anglo-Pak Anglo-Pakistani
Anglo-Para Anglo-Paraguayan
Anglo-Per Anglo-Persian; Anglo-Peruvian
Anglo-Pol Anglo-Polish
Anglo-Port Anglo-Portuguese
Anglo-Rho Anglo-Rhodesian
Anglo-Rom Anglo-Romanian
Anglo-Rus(s) Anglo-Russian
Anglo(s) Anglo-Saxon(s)
Anglo-SA Anglo-South African; Anglo-South American
Anglo-Sam Anglo-Samoan
Anglo-Scot Anglo-Scottish
Anglo-SL Anglo-Sierra Leonean
Anglo-Som Anglo-Somali
Anglo-Sov Anglo-Soviet
Anglo-Span Anglo-Spanish
Anglo-Sud Anglo-Sudanese
Anglo-Swi Anglo-Swiss
Anglo-Tanz Anglo-Tanzanian
Anglo-Tob Anglo-Tobagan
Anglo-Togo Anglo-Togolese
Anglo-Ton Anglo-Tongan
Anglo-Trin Anglo-Trinidadian
Anglo-Turk Anglo-Turkish
Anglo-Ugan Anglo-Ugandan
Anglo-Uru Anglo-Uruguayan
Anglo-Ven Anglo-Venezuelan
Anglo-W Anglo-Welsh
Anglo-Yem Anglo-Yemini
Anglo-Yugo Anglo-Yugoslav(ian)
Anglo-Zamb Anglo-Zambian
Angl-Swe Anglo-Swedish
Angola People's Republic of Angola (formerly Portuguese West Africa; Angolans speak Portuguese and tribal tongues; coffee, diamonds, and oil exported)
Angolan Ports (north to south) Ambriz, Luanda, Porto Amboim, Novo Redondo, Lobito, Benguela, Mocamedes, Porto Alexandre
angora eponym or lowercase derivative for a breed of longhair cat originally from Angora (Ankara), Turkey; or for long hair goats or rabbits originally from Angora or the long

and fluffy strands of wool called angora
Angora Goat Capital Rocksprings, Texas
Ang Pam Akla Ang Pambansang Aklatan (Pilipino—The National Library)—in Manila
ang pec angina pectoris (Latin—strangling of the chest)—heart attack
Angry Eagle of Aviation General William (Billy) Mitchell
Ang-Sax Anglo-Saxon
ANGTS Alaska Natural Gas Transportation System
Angus Aeneas
ANGUS Air National Guard of the United States
anh anhydrite; anhydrous
Anh Anhang (German—appendix)
ANH Australian National Highway; Australian National Hotels
ANHA American Nursing Home Association
ANHAL Australian National Humanities and Arts Library
anhed anhedral
ANHF Australian National Heart Foundation
anhic anhydritic
ANHS Adams National Historic Site
Anhui (Pinyin Chinese—Anhwei)
anhyd anhydrous
ani automatic number identification
ani atmosphère normale internationale (French—international normal atmosphere)
ANI Agencia Nacional de Informaciones (Uruguayan press service); Army-Navy-Industry; Australian National Industries
A & NI Andaman and Nicobar Islands
ANI Agência Nacional de Informaçao (Portuguese—National Information Agency); *Agencia Nacional de Informaciones* (Spanish—National Information Agency)
ANIB Australian News and Information Bureau
ANICA Associazione Nazionale Industrie Cinematografiche e Affini (Italian—National Association of Cinematographic and Related Industries)
ANICO American National Insurance Company
anil aniline
aniline phenyl amine

anim animal; animate; animism
anim animato (Italian—animated)
ANIM Association of Nuclear Instrument Manufacturers
animad animadversion
Animist Nation Dahomey
ANIP Army-Navy Instrumentation Program
ank ankle
ank ankomen (Dutch—arrival); *ankomst* (Danish—arrival); *ankunft* (German—arrival)
Ank Ankara
ANK Ankara, Turkey (airport)
Ankara place-name formerly called Ancyra or Angora
Ankerplatz Ankerplatz der Freude (German—Anchorage of Joy)—St Pauli's Reeperbahn section of Hamburg featuring naughty nightlife
anl anneal; annoyance level (aircraft noise); automatic noise limiter
ANL Argonne National Laboratory; Australian National Library; Australian National Line; net-laying ship (naval symbol)
A-N L Anti-Nazi League
ANLCA Alaska Native Land Claims Act
anld annealed
ANLINE Australian National Line
an. lt anchor light
anlys analysis
anm anmaerkning (Danish, Norwegian, Swedish—footnote, note, remark, observation)
Anm Anmerkung (German—footnote, note)
ANM Anacostia Neighborhood Museum; Australian Newsprint Mills
ANM Admiralty Notices to Mariners
ANMC American National Metric Council
ANMCC Alternate National Military Command Center
ANMEF Australian Naval and Military Expeditionary Force
anmi air navigation multiple indicator
ANMI Allied Naval Maneuvering Instructions (NATO)
ANMPE Asociacion Nacional de Municipalidades del Perú (Spanish—National Association of Municipalities of Peru)
ANMRC Australian Numerical Meteorology Research Centre

ANMS Automated Notice to Mariners System

ann announce(ment); announcer; annual(ly); annuity; annunciator

ann annonce (Dano-Norwegian —advertisement, announcement)

ann. anni (Latin—years); *anno* (Latin—year)

Ann Anastasia; Angela; Angelina; Angeline; Anita; Anna; Annabelle; Anne; Annelida; Annetta; Annette; Annie; Antoinette

Ann Annalen (German—annals); *Annales* (French—annals); *Annali* (Italian—annals)

ANN All Nippon News (network)

Anna Annabella; Annapolis, Maryland; Annette

ANNA Army, Navy, NASA, Air Force

Anna Akhmatova Anna Andreyevna Gorenko

Annaba Algerian place-name equivalent of Bone

Annabella Suzanne Georgette Carpentier

ANNAF Army/Navy/NASA/Air Force

Anna O Bertha Pappenheim— feminist crusader against white slavery and first person to be psychoanalyzed

Annapolis Maryland's capital and site of the U.S. Naval Academy whose short form is *Annapolis*

Annapolis of the Air Pensacola, Florida

Ann Arbor Pub Ann Arbor Publishers

Anna Seghers (pseudonym— Netty Radvanyi)

Ann Chim Phys Annales de Chimie et de Physique (French —Annals of Chemistry and Physics)

Anne Campbell Mrs George W Stark (contemporary American poet who described her child as: *You are the trip I did not take, You are the pearls I cannot buy, You are my blue Italian lake, You are my piece of foreign sky.*)

ANNECS Automated Nikkei News Editing

Anne Morrow Mrs Charles Lindbergh

Ann Fluid Dyn Annals of Fluid Dynamics

Ann Geophys Annales de Geo-

physique (French—Annals of Geophysics)

Ann Harding Dorothy Gatley's motion-picture-reel name

Annie Oakley Phoebe Anne Oakley Mozee

Annie's Town Anniston, Alabama

Ann Inst Henri Poincaré Annales de l'Institut Henri Poincaré

anniv. anniversarium (Latin— anniversary)

Ann Landers Esther Pauline (Eppie) Lederer

Ann Math Annals of Mathematics

Ann Miller Lucille Ann Collier

Annng Annapolis graduate

annot. annotated; annotation

Ann Oto Rhino Laryngol Annals of Otology, Rhinology, and Laryngology

Ann Phys Annalen der Physik (German—Annals of Physics); *Annales de Physique* (French —Annals of Physics); *Annals of Physics* (New York)

Ann Rept Annual Report

Ann Rev Nucl Sci Annual Review of Nuclear Science

Ann Sothern Hariette Lake

annu annual; annuale; annuario

annuit annuitant

annul. annulment

Annunc Annunciation

ano above-named officer

ANO Air Navigation Office; Anti-Narcotics Office

anoc anodal opening contraction

ANOC Authorized Notice of Change

anod. anodize

anom anomia; anomiac, anomiacal

Anon. anonymous (Latin— nameless)

anop assembly no operation

ANOP Australian Nationwide Opinion Polls

ANOPP Aircraft Noise Prediction Program

anorex anorexia nervosa

anorm aircraft not operationally ready—maintenance

anors aircraft not operationally ready—supplies

ANOS Australian Native Orchid Society

anot annotate

A.N. Other another (person)

anov analysis of variance

anova analysis of variance

anp aircraft nuclear propulsion

A-np A-norprogesterone

ANP Aberdare National Park (Kenya); Acadia National Park (Maine); Aircraft Nuclear-propulsion Program; Akan National Park (Japan); Albert National Park (Zaire); American Nazi Party; Angkor National Park (Cambodia); Arusha National Park (Tanzania); Associated Negro Press; Australian Nationalist Party; Awash National Park (Ethiopia)

ANP Administración Nacional de Puertos (Colombia's National Administration of Ports); *Algemeen Nederlandsch Persbureau* (Netherlands Press Bureau)

ANPA American Newspaper Publishers Association; Australian National Publicity Association; Australian Newspaper Proprietors Association

ANPAT American Newspaper Publishers Abstracting Technique

ANPI Associazione Nazionale Partigiani d'Italia (National Association of Italian Partisans)

ANPO Aircraft Nuclear Propulsion Office

anpod antenna-positioning device

ANPP Aircraft Nuclear Propulsion Program

ANPPF Aircraft Nuclear Power Plant Facility

ANPPIA Associazione Nazionale Perseguitati Politici Italiani Antifascisti(National Association of Italian Antifascist Political Victims)

ANPRM Advanced Notices of Proposed Rule Making (FAA)

ANPs Allied Navigation Publications

ANPS American Nail Producers Society

anpt aeronautical national taper pipe threads

ANPWS Australian National Parks and Wildlife Service

ANQUE Asociación Nacional de Quimicos de España (National Chemical Association of Spain)

anr another

ANR American Natural Resources (formerly American Natural Gas); American Newspaper Representatives; Antwerp, Belgium (airport); Australian National Railways

ANR Asociación Nacional Re-

publicana (Spanish—National Republican Association)—Paraguay's Colorado Party

ANRA Amistad National Recreation Area (Texas); Arbuckle National Recreation Area (Oklahoma)

anrac aids navigation radio control

ANRAO Australian National Radio Astronomy Observatory

ANRC American National Red Cross; Animal Nutrition Research Council; Australian National Railways Commission; Australian National Research Council

ANRF Australian Nomads Research Foundation

ANRPC Association of Natural Rubber Producing Countries

ANRT Association Nationale de la Recherche Technique (National Association of Technical Research)

ans answer; answered; answering; autograph note signed; autonomic nervous system

Ans Anselm; Anselmo

ANS Agencia Noticiosa Saporiti (Argentine press service); American Name Society; American Nuclear Society; American Numismatic Society; American Nutrition Society; Army Newspaper Service; Army News Service; Army Nursing Service; Astronomical Netherlands Satellite (first joint United States-Netherlands satellite)

ansa aminonapthosulfonic acid; automatic new structure alert

ANSA Australian National Sportfishing Association

A(N)SA American (National) Standards Association

ANSA Agenzia Nazionale Stampa Associata (Italian—National Press Association Agency)

ansam (ANSAM) antimissile surface-to-air missile

ANSC American National Standards Committee

A-N Scale Anti-Negro Scale (measuring negative attitudes toward persons of Negroid origin)

ANSCO Anthony and Scovill (New York camera and film manufacturer who merged with AGFA to become Agfa-Ansco and more recently GAF

—General Aniline and Film Corporation)

ANSETT Ansett Airways

ANSETT-ANA Ansett Australian National Airways

ANSI American National Standards Institute; Australian National Standards Institute

ANSIC Aerospace Nuclear Safety Information Center

ANSL Australian National Standards Laboratory

ANSP Academy of Natural Sciences of Philadelphia; Australian National Socialist Party

ANSS American Nature Study Society

ANSSL Australian National Social Sciences Library

ANSSMFE Australian National Society of Soil Mechanics and Foundation Engineering

ANST Appalachian Nature Scenic Trail (Maine to Georgia)

ANSTEL Australian National Scientific and Technological Library

answ (ANSW) antinuclear submarine warfare

ant. antenna(s); anterior; anticipated; antilog; antilogarithm; antiquarian; antique; antiquities; antiquity; antonym

ant antología (Spanish—anthology)

ant. antico (Italian—antique); *antiporta* (Italian—half-title)

Ant Antigua; Antillean; Antillea—West Indian Federation; Antilles; Antlia (constellation); Antwerp

ANT AN Tupolev (Soviet aircraft designer's initials and designation of planes he designed); Australian Northern Territory

ANT Australian National Times

ANTA American National Theater and Academy; Australian National Travel Association

antag antagonistic

Antananarivo English name for Tananarive, the capital of the Malagasy Republic (Madagascar)

Antar Rimsky-Korsakov's Symphony No. 2

Antarc Antarctic; Antarctica

Antarc O Antarctic Ocean

Antarctica's Only Known Active Volcano Mount Erebus on Ross Island in the New Zealand sector of Antarctica

Antarctic Circle 66 degrees 17

minutes South latitude; imaginary line encircling southern part of earth to delimit south frigid zone

Antarctico (Italian—Antarctic)—Antarctic Ocean

Antárctico (Portuguese or Spanish—Antarctic)—Antarctic Ocean

Antarctique (French—Antarctic)—Antarctic Ocean

Antarktisch (German—Antarctic)—Antarctic Ocean

ant. ax line anterior axillary line

Ant & Bar Antigua and Barbuda (emerging island nation in the eastern Caribbean and formerly British)

ANTC Australian National Television Council

Ant & Cl Antony and Cleopatra

Ant Cur Antilles Current

ant. d anterior diameter

ante (Latin prefix—before, in front of); (Latin—before)

antec annual technical conference

ANTELCO Administración Nacional de Telecomunicaciones (Paraguayan National Telecommunication Administration)

Antelope State Nebraska

antennafier antenna + radiofrequency amplifier

antennamitter antenna + transmitter

antennaverter antenna + converter

Antf Antofagasta

Ant f Antillean florin (guilder)

anthol anthological(ly); anthologist, anthologize, anthology

Anthony Abbot Charles Fulton Oursler's pseudonym

Anthony Armstrong George Anthony Armstrong Willis

Anthony Berkeley Anthony Berkeley Cox's pseudonym

Anthony Boucher William Anthony Parker White

Anthony Hope nom de plume of Sir Anthony Hope Hawkins

Anthracite City Scranton, Pennsylvania

anthro anthropogeography; anthropological; anthropologist; anthropology; anthropometry; anthropomorphism; anthropophagy

anthroco anthrocosis (sickness due to coal-dust inhalation)

anthrop anthropology

anthropom anthropometry

Anthroposophic Anthroposo-

phic Press
Anthy Anthony
anti (Latin prefix—against)—
anticommunist
antibio(s) antibiotic(s)
antichlor anti + chlorine; an-
tichloristic
anticli anticlimactic(al)(ly); anti-
climax; anticlinal; anticline;
anticlinorium
antidis antidisestablishmentar-
ianism
Antid Oto Trotsky's pseudonym
used in his writings covering
the arts, politics, and science
antid(s) antidote(s)
antifreeze grain or methyl alcohol (CH_3OH) mixture
Antig Antigua
antikv antikvarisk (Dano-Norwegian—antiques)
Antilles West India Islands excluding Bahamas
antilog antilogarithm
antimag antimagnetic
antinuke anti nuclear (energy,
power, or war)
Antioch Antioch Press
antip antiparasitic; antiparticle;
antipasti; antipasto; antipa-
thetic; antipathy; antiperiodic;
antipersonnel; antiperspirant;
antipodal; antipode; antipoet-
ic; antipollution; antipoverty;
antiproton; antipsychotic; an-
tipyretic; antipyrine
antiphon antiphonal(ly)
Antipodes Australia and New
Zealand; rocky islands off
Dunedin, New Zealand—al-
most exactly on the other side
of the world from London,
England—hence the expres-
sion *Antipodes*
antipol antipollutant; antipollu
tion
antiporn antipornographic; anti-
pornography
antiq antiquarian, antique; antiquities; antiquity
antiquar antiquarian
Antiques Antiques Publications
antisem antisemite; antisemitic;
antisemitism (pseudoscientific
term for Jew hatred)
antisex antisexual
Anti-Trinitarian Author Faustus
Socinus, originally Fausto
Sozzini
Anti-Trinitarian Martyr Michael Servetus, originally Miguel Serveto
antivox antivoice-operated
transmission
ant. jentac. *ante jentaculum*
(Latin—before breakfast)

Antl Antlia
Ant Lat Antique Latin
ant. ld antique laid
Anto Antofagasta
Antº Antonio
anton antonym
Anton Antonio; Antony
Ant Ops Antarctic Operations
ant. pit. anterior pituitary
ant. prand. *ante prandium* (Lat-
in—before dinner)
antr apparent net transfer rate
Antr Antrim
Antrims Antrim Mountains of
Northern Ireland
ant(s). antonym(s)
Antsirane Diégo-Suarez
ant. sup. spine anterior superior
spine
antu alpha-naphthyl-thiourea
(rat poison)
ANTU Atlantic (Line container)
Unit
Antuer Antuérpia (Portuguese—
Antwerp)
Antuerpa (Portuguese—Ant-
werp)
Antverpia (Latin—Antwerp)
Antw Antwerpen (Dutch, Flem-
ish, German—Antwerp)
Antwerpen Antwerp province's
capital in Belgium
Antwerpen (Dutch, Flemish,
German—Antwerp)
ant. wo antique wove
ANU Australian National Uni-
versity (Canberra); St John's,
Antigua (3-letter code)
ANUP Australian National
University Press
Anuradhapura site of Bo tree in
Ceylon where Gautama Budd-
ha is reputed to have attained
supreme enlightenment
anv anvendelse (Dano-Norwe-
gian—application, use)
Anver Anversa (Italian—Ant-
werp)
Anvers (French—Antwerp)
anvo accept no verbal orders
ANWA *Abstracts of New World
Archeology*
ANWG Apollo Navigation
Working Group (NASA)
ANWR Agassiz National Wildlife Refuge (Minnesota); Aran-
sas NWR (Texas); Arrowhead
NWR (North Dakota); Audu-
bon NWR (North Dakota)
anx. annex
Anx Annex (postal place-name
abbreviation)
ANX Anixter Brothers (stock-
exchange symbol)
anytimeteller anytime bank teller

Anz Anzania (African name for
South Africa)
ANZ Air New Zealand; Austra-
lia and New Zealand (bank)
ANZA Association of New Zea-
land Advertisers
ANZAAS Australian and New
Zealand Association for the
Advancement of Science
ANZAC Australia and New
Zealand Army Corps
Anzac Day April 25 (in Austra-
lia, New Zealand, and asso-
ciated territories)
ANZAM Australia, New Zea-
land, and Malaysia (defense
pact)
ANZAMRS Australia and New
Zealand Association for Medi-
eval and Renaissance Studies
Anzania (black African—South
Africa)
ANZAR Australian and New
Zealand Association of Radi-
ology
ANZASA Australian and New
Zealand American Studies As-
sociation
ANZ Bank Australia and New
Zealand Bank
ANZCAN Australia-New Zea-
land-Canada (submarine cable
system)
ANZCP Australian and New
Zealand College of Psychia-
trists
ANZDEC Asian-New Zealand
Development Consultants
ANZECO Australia and New
Zealand Exploration Compa-
ny
ANZECS Australia-New Zea-
land-Europe Container Ser-
vice
ANZESC Australian and New
Zealand Eastern Shipping
Conference
ANZGAM Australian and New
Zealand Graduates Associa-
tion of Malaysia (Singapore)
ANZHES Australian and New
Zealand History of Education
Society
ANZIA Associate of the New
Zealand Institute of Archi-
tects
ANZIC Associate of the New
Zealand Institute of Chemists
ANZJS *Australian and New
Zealand Journal of Sociology*
ANZLA Associate of the New
Zealand Library Association
ANZPC Australia and New Zea-
land Passenger Conference
ANZPPA Australia and New
Zealand Professional Pho-

tographers Association

ANZQR *Australia and New Zealand Bank Quarterly Review*

ANZS Africa New Zealand Service

ANZSNM Australian and New Zealand Society of Nuclear Medicine

ANZSOM Australian and New Zealand Society of Occupational Medicine

ANZSOS Australian and New Zealand Society of Oral Surgeons

ANZSTS Australia and New Zealand Society for Theological Study

ANZUK Australia, New Zealand, United Kingdom (cultural, military, and trading alliance)

ANZUS Australia, New Zealand, United States (mutual security pact)

ao access opening; anodal opening; anterior oblique; anti-oxidant; aorta; aortic opening; area of operation(s); axio-occlusal

ao (AO) accuracy only; account of; arresting officer

a/o (A/O) account of

A⁰ anno (Latin—year)

AO Administration Office; Airdrome Office(r); American Optical (company); Arkansas & Ozarks (railroad); Australian Officer (Officer of the Order of Australia); Autonomous Oblast; Aviation Ordnanceman; fleet tanker (2-letter naval designation)

A/O Administrator's Office (EPA)

AO Ahonim Ortalik (Turkish — Anonymous Company)— joint stock company; *Avtonómnaya Oblast* (Russian—Autonomous Region)—province

A-O Auslands-Organisation (German—Overseas Organization)—Hitler's overseas public relations agency spreading sympathy for Germany and the Nazi ideology

aoa abort once around; at or above

AoA Administration on Aging (HEW)

AOA American Oceanology Association; American Optometric Association; American Ordnance Association; American Orthopedic Association;

American Orthopsychiatric Association; American Osteopathic Association; American Overseas Airlines; American Overseas Association; Australian Optometrical Association; Australian Orthopaedic Association

AOAC Association of Official Agricultural Chemists; Association of Official Analytical Chemists

AOAD Army Ordnance Arsenal District

a O (a/O) an der Oder (German —on the Oder River)

AOATC Atlantic Ocean Air Traffic Control

aob alcohol on breath; angle on the bow; any other business; at or below

aob (AOB) annual operating budget

AOB Advanced Operational Base

AO-BIRMDis Army Ordnance —Birmingham District

AOBMO Army Ordnance Ballistic Missile Office (USA)

AO-BOSTDis Army Ordnance —Boston District

AOBs Antediluvian Order of Buffaloes

AOBSR Air Observer

aoc anodal opening contraction

AoC Architect of the Capitol (D.C.)

A o C Academy on Computers

AOC Air Officer Commanding; Air Operations Center; Airport Operators Council; American Optical Company (stock exchange symbol); American Orthoptic Council; Arabian Oil Company; Army Ordnance Corps; automatic output control (computerese); Aviation Officer Candidate

AOCA American Osteopathic College of Anesthesiologists

AOCCOS Australian Organisations Coordinating Committee for Overseas Students

AO-CHIDis Army Ordnance—Chicago District

AOCI Airport Operators Council International

AO C-in-C Air Officer Commander-in-Chief

aocl anodal opening clonus

AO-CLEVDis Army Ordnance —Cleveland District

aocm advanced optical countermeasures

aocm (AOCM) aircraft out of commission for maintenance

AOCO Atomic Ordnance Cataloging Office

aocp (AOCP) aircraft out of commission for parts

AOCs American Olympic Committee members; Association of Old Crows

AOCS American Oil Chemists' Society; Atlantic Outer Continental Shelf

aod arterial occlusive disease; as of date

A o D Airport of Departure

AOD Academy of Oral Dynamics; Air Officer of the Day

ao diag acridine-orange diagnosis (cancer)

AODs Ancient Order of Druids

AODS All Ordnance Destruct System

aoe airborne operational equipment; auditing order error

AoE Aerodrome of Entry

A o E Airport of Entry

AOE Association of Overseas Educators

AOEHI American Organization for the Education of the Hearing Impaired

AOEM Automotive Original Equipment Manufacturers

AOER Amry Officers' Emergency Reserve

AOF Afrique Occidentale Française (French West Africa); Ancient Order of Foresters; Australian Olympic Federation

AOFS Active Optical Fuzing System

aog (AOG) aircraft on ground

AOG Atlantic Oceanographic Group; Australian Oil and Gas; gasoline tanker (3-letter symbol)

AOGM Army of Occupation of Germany Medal

AOH Ancient Order of Hibernians

aoi accent on information; angle of incidence; area of interest

A o I Aims of Industry

AOIB Anglo-Oriental International Bank

AOIPS Atmospheric and Oceanic Information Processing System

aoiv automatically-operated inlet valve

AOJDD Anglican Orthodox Joint Doctrinal Discussions

aok all okay; everything in good order

aol absent over leave

AOL American-Oriental Lines; Atlantic Oceanography Laboratories

AO-LADis Army Ordnance—Los Angeles District

aolo advanced orbit laboratory operations

AOLP Action Organization for the Liberation of Palestine

AOM Army of Occupation Medal

A.O.M. Master of Obstetric Art

AOMA American Occupational Medical Association

AOMAA Apartment Owners and Managers Association of America

AOMC Army Ordnance Missile Command

AOMSA Army Ordnance Missile Support Agency

AOMSC Army Ordnance Missile Support Center

aonb area of outstanding natural beauty

AO-NYDis Army Ordnance—New York District

aoo anodal opening odor

AOO American Oceanic Organization

aop anodal opening picture; aortic-pressure pulse

AOP Apprenticeship Outreach Program; Association of Optical Practitioners; Association of Osteopathic Publications

AOPA Aircraft Owners and Pilots Association

AOPC Australian Overseas Projects Corporation

AOPE Associated Organization for Professionals in Education

AOPEC Arab Organization of Petroleum Exporting Countries

AO-PHILDis Army Ordnance—Philadelphia District

aoProf *auszerordentlicher Professor* (German—associate professor or special lecturer)

A Ops Air Operations

AOPs Allied Ordnance Publications

AOPU Asian Oceanic Postal Union (China, Korea, Philippines, Thailand)

aoq average outgoing quality

AOQC Australian Organisation for Quality Control

aoql average outgoing quality limit

aor angle of reflection; aorist; area of responsibility

a/or and/or

AOR Army Operational Research; Australian Oil Refining; auxiliary oil replenish-

ment (USN)

Aorangi (Maori—Cloud Piercer)—Mount Cook, New Zealand's tallest towering to 3764 meters or 12,349 feet

AORB Aviation Operational Research Branch

AORG Army Operational Research Group (United Kingdom)

AORL Apollo Orbital Research Laboratory

AORN Association of Operating Room Nurses

AOrPA American Orthopsychiatric Association

AORS Army Operations Research Symposium

AORT Association of Operating Room Techniques

AORTF American Organization for Rehabilitation through Training Federation

aort regurg aortic regurgitation

aort sten aortic stenosis

aos acquisition of signal; add or subtract; angle of sight; anodal opening sound

AOS American Opera Society; American Ophthalmological Society; American Orchid Society; American Oriental Society; American Otological Society; Australian Overseas Smelting; Azimuth Orientation System

AOSC Association of Oilwell Servicing Contractors

A-O Scale Anti-Oriental Scale (measuring negative attitudes towards persons of Oriental origin)

AOSE American Order of Stationary Engineers

AOSO Advanced Orbiting Solar Observatory

aosp automatic operating and scheduling program

AOSPS American Otorhinologic Society for Plastic Surgery

AOSs Ancient Order of Shepherds

AO-STLDis Army Ordnance—St Louis District

AOSTRA Alberta Oil Sands Technology and Research Authority

AOSW Association of Official Shorthand Writers

aot active on target; anodal opening tetanus

Aot Askania optical tracker

AOT Alameda-Oakland Tunnel; Association of Occupational Therapists

AOTA American Occupational Therapy Association; Australian Overseas Transport Association

AOTC Australian Overseas Trading Corporation

Aotearoa (Maori—Long White Cloud)—New Zealand

ao technique acridine-orange technique (two-color fluorescent test for cancer)

AOTOI American Organization of Tour Operators to Israel

AotOS Admiral of the Ocean Sea (U.S. Merchant Marine award recalling title of Christopher Columbus)

AOtS American Otological Society

aou apparent oxygen utilization; azimuth orientation unit

AOU American Ornithologists' Union; Australian Ornithologists Union

AOUSC Administrative Office of the United States Courts

AOUW Ancient Order of United Workmen

AOVP Australian Ordnance Vehicle Park

AOW Articles of War

ap above proof; access panel; acid phosphatase; acid proof; action potential; acute proliferation; aerial port; aiming point; airplane; alkaline phosphatase; alum precipitated; aminopeptidase; angina pectoris; antepartum; anterior pituitary; anteroposterior; aortic pressure; appendectomy; appendices; appendix; arithmetic progression; armor piercing; arterial pressure; artificial pneumothorax; as prescribed; association period; attached processor; author's proof; axiopulpal; (Welsh prefix—son of)

ap (AP) advanced placement; average product

a/p after perpendicular; air port (porthole); angle point; authority to pay; authority to purchase; autopilot

a&p agricultural and pastoral; anterior and posterior; apogee and perigee (apex and antapex); auscultation and percussion

a$_p$ geomagnetic index

ap *anno passato* (Italian—last year)

ap. *apud* (Latin—according to)

a.p. *ante prandium* (Latin—before a meal)

Ap Apothecary

Ap. Apostolus (Latin—Apostle)

AP Acquisition Plan; Air Police; Air Publication; Airport; American Party (third largest in the United States); American President Lines; Associated Press; Australia Party; Aviation Pilot; personnel transport (naval symbol)

A-P American Plan (includes meals)

A/P allied papers; authority to pay

A & P Agricultural and Pastoral Society of New Zealand; Atlantic & Pacific Travel International; Great Atlantic & Pacific Tea Company

AP Acción Popular (Spanish—Popular Action); *Administration Pénitentiare* (French—Penitentiary Administration); *Arbeiderpartiet* (Norwegian—*Det Norske Arbeiderpartiet*—The Norwegian Labor Party); *Atlanska Plovidba* (Russian—Atlantic Press); *Australia Post*; *Aviapolk* (Russian—Air Regiment)

A.P. a protester (French—to be protested later)

apa aldosterone-producing adenoma; aminopenicillanic acid; antipernicious anemia factor; axial pressure angle

APA Adult Parole Authority; Aerovias Panamá Airways; Agricultural Publishers Association; Airline Passenger Association; American Patients Association; American Pharmaceutical Association; American Philological Association; American Philosophical Association; American Photoengravers Association; American Physiotherapy Association; American Pilots Association; American Planning Association; American Podiatry Association; American Polygraph Association; American Poultry Association; American Press Association; American Protective Association; American Psychiatric Association; American Psychoanalytical Association; American Psychological Association; American Psychosomatic Association; American Psychotherapy Association; American Pulpwood Association; Animation Producers Association; Anthracite Producers As-

sociation; Anti-Papal Association; Apache Railway; Associated Press of Australia; Association of Paroling Authorities; Association of Physicians of Australasia; Association for the Prevention of Addiction (London); Australian Provincial Insurance; transport attack vessel (naval symbol)

APA Austria Presse Agentur (German—Austrian Press Agency)

APAA Australian Port Authorities Association

APAAC Asian-Pacific-American Advocates of California (representing California's Asian Americans)

APAC Aerial Photographic Analysis Center

apache analog programming and checking

APACHE Accelerator for Physics and Chemistry of Heavy Metals; Application Package for Chemical Engineers

Apache State Arizona—land of the Apache Indians

APACI Associación Peruana para el Avance de la Ciencia (Spanish—Peruvian Association for the Advancement of Science)

APACL Asian People's Anti-Communist League

apacs adaptive planning and control sequence (marketing)

APADA Australian Petroleum Agents and Distributors Association

APADS Automatic Programmer and Data System

APAE Association of Public Address Engineers

apaf antipernicious anemia factor

APAFA ASEAN Professional Association on Food and Agriculture

APAG Atlantic Political Advisory Group (NATO)

APAIS Australian Public Affairs Information Service

APAL American Puerto-Rican Action League

AP & AM Adler Planetarium and Astronomical Museum

APANZ Associate of the Public Accountants of New Zealand

APAP American People for American Prisoners

APAP Asociación Peruana de Agencias de Publicidad (Spanish—Peruvian Association of Publicity Agents)

apar apparatus

APAR Automatic Programming and Recording

apart. apartment

a-part alpha particle(s)

apart apartheid (Afrikaans—apartness, racial segregation) — South African government policy pronounced *apart-hate* and resulting in much misunderstanding as well as violence on a wide scale

APAs American Polygraph Association members and polygraphers; Anti-Papal Association members and sympathizers (as immortalized in a poem displayed in Steve Broadie's Museum and Saloon on the lower Bowery of New York where beneath a red brick atop a mound of green velvet the display legend announced— *Here is the brick that hit the Mick, he'll never throw another, for calling me an APA he now lies undercover.*)

APAS Automatic Performance Analysis System

APASCO Australian Planning and Systems Company

APATS Antenna Pattern Test System (USA)

APAVIT Asociación Peruana de Agencias de Viajes y Turismo (Spanish—Peruvian Association of Travel Agencies and Tourism)

apb atrial premature beat; auricular premature beat

apb (APB) all-points bulletin (police radio-car call)

APB barracks ship, self-propelled (3-letter symbol)

APB All-Points Bulletin

APBA American Power Boat Association; Association Press Broadcasters Association

APBPA Association of Professional Ball Players of America

APBS Accredited Poultry Breeding Scheme; Australian Permanent Building Society

APBSD Advanced Post Boost System Development

APBSQ Association of Permanent Building Societies of Queensland

apc acoustical plaster ceiling; all-purpose capsule (aspirin, phenacetin, caffeine); antiphlogistic corticoid; aperture current; armor-piercing capped (ammunition); aspirin-phenacetin-caffeine (mixture);

atrial premature contractions; automatic performance control; automatic phase control

apc (APC) average propensity to consume

a/p c autopilot capsule

APc coastal transport (3-letter symbol)

APC Aeronautical Planning Chart; Aerospace Primus Club; Agricultural Productivity Commission; American Parents Committee; American Philatelic Congress; Area Positive Control; Arkansas Polytechnic College; Armored Personnel Carrier; Army Petroleum Center; Army Policy Council; Association of Private Camps; Association of Pulp Consumers; Australian Police College; Australian Postal Commision; Avian Propagation Center

APCA Air Pollution Control Association; American Petroleum Credit Association; American Planning and Civic Association; Anglo-Polish Catholic Association; Australian Physical Culture Association

APCB Air Pollution Control Board

apcbc armor-piercing carbide ballistic cap

apc-c aspirin, phenacetin, caffeine with codeine

APCC Asian and Pacific Coconut Community

APCD Air Pollution Control District

APCG Association of Pacific Coast Geographers

apche automatic programmed checkout equipment

apci armor-piercing capped with incendiary

apcit armor-piercing capped incendiary with tracer

APCK Association for Promoting Christian Knowledge

apcm authorized protective connecting module

APCM Asiatic-Pacific Campaign Medal

APCO Air Pollution Control Office; Alabama Power Company

apcr armor-piercing-composite rigid

APCS Air Photographic and Charting Service; Associative Processor Computer System

apct armor-piercing capped with tracer

a/p ctl autopilot control

apc virus adenoidal, pharyngeal, conjuctival virus

APCYA A Presidential Classroom for Young Americans

apd action potential duration; aiming point determination; anteroposterior diameter

APD Air Pollution Division (U.S. Dept Agriculture); Air Procurement District; high-speed troop transport (3-letter naval symbol)

APDA American Parkinson's Disease Association

APDC Agricultural Pest Destruction Council; Albany Port District Commission

Ap Del Apostolic Delegate

APDF Asian-Pacific Dental Federation

apdl algorithmic processor description language

Apdo Apartado (Spanish—post-office box)

apds armor-piercing discarding sabot

APdS American Pediatric Society

APDSMS Advanced Point Defense Surface Missile System

APDU Association of Public Data Users

APDUSA African People's Democratic Union of Southern Africa

apdy appropriate duty

ape. adapted physical educator; aerial port of embarkation (APE), aminophylline, phenobarbital, ephedrine; anterior pituitary extract; apparent effect; automatic photomapping equipment

APE aerial port of embarkation; Amalgamated Power Engineering

A.P.E. Air Pollution Engineer

APEA Association of Professional Engineers (Australia); Australian Petroleum Exploration Association

Apeco American Photocopy Equipment Company

Apennines Apennine Mountains running the length of the Italian Peninsula

aper aperture

APER Air Pollutant Emissions Report

apers antipersonnel

APETS Australia-Papua New Guinea Education and Training Scheme

apex. advance-purchase excursion (airline fare); air-pollu-

tion exercise; assembler and process executive

APEX Advance-Purchase Excursion (Plan)—pay 90 days ahead of excursion flight; Association of Professional Executive and Management Staff

apf acidproof floor; animal protein factor

APF American Progress Foundation; Anglican Pacifist Fellowship; Asia Pacific Forum; Asian Packaging Federation; Association of Pacific Fisheries; Association of Protestant Faiths; Australian Parachute Federation

APF Australian Pharmaceutical Formulary

APFA American Pipe Fittings Association; Associated Poultry Farmers of Australia

APFA Association des Professeurs Franco-Americains (French—Association of Franco-American Professors)

APFC Asia-Pacific Forestry Commission

APFF American Police and Fire Foundation

APFM Australian Postgraduate Federation in Medicine

APFO Association on Programs for Female Offenders

APFRI American Physical Fitness Research Institute

apfsds armor-piercing fin-stabilized discarding sabot

Apg Appingedam

APG Aberdeen Proving Ground; Air Proving Ground; American Pewter Guild; Army Planning Group; Army Proving Ground; Australian Proving Ground

APG Autoridad Portuaria de Guayaquil (Spanish—Port Authority of Guayaquil)

APGA Alabama Personnel and Guidance Association; American Personnel and Guidance Association; Apple and Pear Growers Association; Arizona Personnel and Guidance Association; Arkansas Personnel and Guidance Association

APG-BRL Aberdeen Proving Ground—Ballistics Research Laboratory

APGC Air Proving Ground Center

apgcu autopilot ground control unit

APG/HEL Aberdeen Proving Ground—Human Engineering Laboratory

APG/OBDC Aberdeen Proving Ground—Ordnance Bomb Disposal Center

APGOEF Air Proving Ground —Eglin, Florida

APGp Aerial Port Group

aph antepartum hemorrhage; anterior pituitary hormone (APH); aphelion

APH Access Permit Holder; transport fitted for evacuation of wounded (3-letter symbol)

A.P.H. A(lan) P(atrick) Herbert

APhA American Pharmaceutical Association

APHA American Printing History Association; American Protestant Hospital Association; American Public Health Association; Australian Pneumatic and Hydraulic Association

APHB American Printing House for the Blind; Army Pearl Harbor Board

APHCA Animal Production and Health Commission for Asia, Far East and South West Pacific

aphet aphetic

APHI Association of Public Health Inspectors

APHIA Association for the Promotion of Humor in International Affairs

A & PHIS Animal and Plant Health Inspection Service

Aph of Lath Aphorism of Lathem ("There is nothing edible or potable failing to find someone to take it as a sovereign remedy for some disease and upon the earnest recommendation of some eminent physician.")

aphor aphorism; aphorist(ic)(ally); aphorize

aphp antipseudomonas human plasma

Aphrodite (Greek—Venus)— goddess of beauty and love

aphro(s) aphrodisiac(s)

APHS Arizona Pioneer Historical Society; Australian Psychology and Hypnotherapy Association

api acceptable periodic inspection; air position indicator; armor-piercing incendiary tracer

API Academic Press, Inc; Alabama Polytechnic Institute; American Paper Institute; American Petroleum Institute; American Pipe Institute; American Potash Institute;

American Press Institute; Animal Protection Institute; armor-piercing incendiary; Australian Pharmaceutical Industries; Australian Planning Institute

API *Association Phonetique Internationale* (French—International Phonetic Association); *Associazione Pionieri Italiani* (Italian Boy Scouts Association)

APIA Animal Protection Institute of America

APIC Apollo Parts Information Center; Army Photo Interpretation Center; Association for Practitioners in Infection Control

APICORP Arab Petroleum Investments Corporation

APICP Association for the Promotion of the International Circulation of the Press

APICS American Production and Inventory Control Society

APICSC Atlantic-Pacific Interoceanic Canal Study Commission

apicult apiculture

APID Army Photo Interpretation Detachment

APIDC Andhra Pradesh Industrial Development Corporation

APIF Automated Process Information File

APIJ *Australian Planning Institute Journal*

A-pill abortion pill

APIM Association Professionelle Internationale des Médecins (International Professional Association of Physicians)

APIN Atlas Propulsion Information Notice

apipocc appropriating property in possession of (a) common carrier

APIS Army Photographic Intelligence Service; Australian Professional Interpreting Society

APIU Army Photo Interpretation Unit

apivr artificial pacemaker ventricular rhythm

APJ American Power Jet (company)

APJE Association of Philosophical Journals Editors

apl a programming language; adult performance level; aluminum-polythene laminate; automatic premium loan

apl (APL) anterior pituitary-like hormone

a/pl armorplate

Apl Appledore

APL Air Pacific Limited; Air Provost Marshal; Akron Public Library; Albany Public Library; Albuquerque Public Library; American Pioneer Line; American President Lines; Applied Physics Laboratory; Assembly Parts List; Augusta Public Library; Australian Pensioners League; barracks ship (naval symbol)

A-PL All-Purpose Linotype

APLA American Patent Law Association; Armenian Progressive League of America; Atlantic Provinces Library Association

ap/lat anteroposterior and lateral

APLC Automated Parking Lot Control

Aplcrs Applecross

apld (APLD) automatic program locate device

APLE Association of Public Lighting Engineers

APLIC Association of Parliamentary Librarians in Canada

apll analog phased-locked loop(s)

aplns applications

APLQ *Agence de Presse Libre du Québec* (French—Free Press Agency of Québec)— left-wing Canadian news agency

APLS American Plant Life Society

AP-LS American Psychology-Law Society

APLU American President Line (container) Unit

apm apomict; associative principle for multiplication

apm (APM) antipersonnel missile

APM Academy of Physical Medicine; Academy of Psychosomatic Medicine; Air Power Museum; Association for Psychoanalytic Medicine; Australian Paper Manufacturers; Australian Paper Mills

apma advance payment of mileage authorized

APMA Absorbent Paper Manufacturers Association; Automatic Phonograph Manufacturers Association

APMAC A.P. Moller Associated Concerns

APMC Academy of Physchologists in Marital Counseling; Andhra Pradesh Mining Corporation; Asia and Pacific Maritime Cooperation Centre

a/p mcu autopilot monitor and control unit

APME Associated Press Managing Editors (Association)

APMF Australian Paper Manufacturers Federation

APMG Assistant Postmaster General

APMHC Association of Professional Material Handling Consultants

apmi area precipitation measurement indicator

APMIS Automated Project Management Information System

APMR Association for Physical and Mental Rehabilitation

APMT Antenna Pattern Measuring Test (USA)

apn artificial pneumothorax; average peak noise

APN American Practical Navigator

APNA Asia-Pacific News Agencies

APNP Arthur's Pass National Park (South Island, New Zealand)

apo apogee

APO Accountable Property Office(r), Advanced Post Office, Air Force (Army) Post Office; American Potash & Chemical (stock exchange symbol); Animal Procurement Office(r); Area Patrol Office(r); Area Petroleum Office(r); Association of Physical Oceanographers; Australian Post Office

apob airplane observation

Apoc Apocalypse; Apocrypha; Apocryphal

APOC Army Point of Contact

APOD Aerial Port of Debarkation

APOE Aerial Port of Embarkation

apol apologete; apologetic(al); apologetics; apologia; apologise; apologist(s); apologize; apology

Apollinaire Guillaume Apollinaire (Wilhelm Apollinaris Kostrowitski's pen name)

Apollo (Latin—Apollon)—the Sun

APOLLO Article Procurement and On-Line Local Ordering

Apollon (Greek—Apollo)—the Sun

Apollyon The Devil

APON Association of Pediatric Oncology Nurses

APOP Australian Public Opinion Polls

apos apostrophe

APOS Advanced Polar Orbiting Satellite

apost apostacy; apostate

Apostle of Absolute Beauty Jean Sibelius

Apostle of the Anglo-Saxons Saint Augustine (first Archbishop of Canterbury)

Apostle of Caledonia Irish-born Saint Columba

Apostle of Common Sense Voltaire

Apostle of Culture Matthew Arnold

Apostle of Dissent William Penn

Apostle of Free Trade Richard Cobden

Apostle of the French Saint Denys (beheaded in Paris in the year 272 of the Christian era)

Apostle of the Gentiles Saint Paul (formerly Saul of Tarsus)

Apostle of Humanity Thomas Paine

Apostle of the Hungarians Saint Anastasius

Apostle of the Indians Bartolomé de Las Casas

Apostle of the Indies Saint Francis Xavier

Apostle of Ireland Saint Patrick

Apostle of Liberty Benjamin Franklin

Apostle of Mexican Rebellion Francisco I Madero

Apostle of New Zealand Reverend Samuel Marsden

Apostle Rebel Dorothy Day

Apostles short form for the Apostle Islands in Lake Superior off northern Wisconsin unless the context indicates New Testament characters such as the twelve apostles of Christ

Apostle of the Scottish Reformation John Knox

Apostles of Freedom Sam Adams and Thomas Paine

Apostle of the Slavs St Cyril (alleged designer of the Cyrillic alphabet used in the USSR and many of its satellites)

Apostle of the Sword Mohammed (who enforced the religion of Islam at the point of a sword)

Apostle of Temperance Theo-

bold Mathew (Irish priest who crusaded for temperance during the last century when he preached in the big cities of the British Isles)

apota automatic positioning of telemetering antenna

apotek   *apoteket* (Danish—apothecary)—drugstore

apoth apothecaries' (weight); apothecary

Apotheosis of the Dance Beethoven's Symphony No. 7

A-powered atomic-powered

app apparatus; apparel; apparent; appeal; appelate; appendage; appended; appendix; apperception; appetite; appetizer; applause; applied; appointed; apprehended; apprentice; approach; appropriate; appropriation; approval; approve; approximate

App Appellate; Lucius Appuleius

App   *Apparat* (German—apparatus); Lucius Appuleius (Roman philosopher)

App. Apostoli (Latin—Apostles)

APP Advanced Placement Program; Air Parcel Post; Algonquin Provincial Park (Ontario); *Alianza Para Progreso* (Spanish—Alliance for Progress); Army Procurement Procedure; Association of Professional Photogrammetrists; automatic priority processing (computerese)

appa advise present position and altitude

APPA American Penal Press Association; American Probation and Parole Association; American Pulp and Paper Association

APPAG All Party Penal Affairs Group (Britain)

Appalachia poverty-stricken areas of eastern Kentucky, southeastern Ohio, eastern Tennessee, and western West Virginia; region in the Appalachian Mountains extending from Québec to northern Alabama

Appalachians Appalachian Mountains, major mountain system of eastern North America extending from Alabama to Québec

Appalachian Trail 2000-mile hikers' trail through Appalachian Mountains from Mount Katahdin in Maine to Mount Oglethorpe in Georgia

appar apparatus

Appassionata Beethoven's Piano Sonata No. 23 in F minor (opus 57); nicknamed for its impassioned mood

APPAUC Association of Physical Plant Administrators of Universities and Colleges

APPC Advance Procurement Planning Council

appd approved

Appeasement Premier Neville Chamberlain

APPECS Adaptive Pattern-Perceiving Electronic Computer System

appellat appellative

appi advanced planning procurement information

APPITA Australian Pulp and Paper Industries Technical Association

appl applicable; application; applied

APPL Advance Procurement Planning List(s)

applan. applanatus (Latin—flattened)

APPLE Advanced Propulsion Payload Effects (NASA); Association of Public and Private Labor Employees

Apple Blossom state flower of Arkansas and Michigan

Apple Capital of the World Wenatchee, Washington

Apple Island Tasmania's nickname

Apple Islanders Tasmanians

Apple Isle Tasmania

Appleton Appleton-Century-Crofts

applican. applicandus (Latin—applied, to be applied)

appln application

Appl Opt Applied Optics

Appl Phys Lett Applied Physics Letters

Appl Spectrosc Applied Spectroscopy

APPM Association of Publication Production Managers

appmt appointment

appn appropriation

App^{no} Appennino (Italian—Appenines)

a/p poi autopilot positioning indicator

appr approval; approve; approved

APPR Army power package reactor

appren apprentice

appro approval

approp appropriation

approx approximate(ly)

apps appendices; appendixes

APPS Australian Physiological and Pharmacological Society; Australian Plant Pathology Society

appt appoint; appointment

apptd appointed

App Thorn Appleton Thorn prison in Lanchashire, England

APPU Australian Primary Producers Union

appx appendix

appy appendectomy

apr amoebic prevalence rate; annual percentage rate; anterior pituitary reaction; apprentice

apr (APR) aerial photographic reconnaissance

apr aprile (Italian—April)

Apr April

Apr Aprel (Russian—April)

APR Air Pictorial Service; Air Priority Raging; Airman Performance Report; Annual Progress Reports; Association of Petroleum Re-Refiners; Association for Promoting Retreats; Association of Publishers' Representatives

Apra San Luis de Apra (Guam's principal port)

APRA Aircraft Resources Production Agency; Australian Performing Rights Association; Australian Plastics Research Association

APRA Alianza Popular Revolucionaria Americana (Spanish—Popular American Revolutionary Alliance)—Peru's Aprista Party of Haya de la Torre

aprax apraxia(1)

APRC Army Physical Review Council

APRDC Army Polar Research and Development Center

APRE Air Procurement Region—Europe

APREF Asia Pacific Real Estate Federation

après-40 after 40 years of age

après JC après Jesus Christ (French—after the birth of Jesus Christ)

APRF Army Pulse Radiation Facility

APRFE Air Procurement Region—Far East

APri air priority

april automatically programmed remote indication logged

April Fool's April Fool's Day (April 1)

A/Prin Assistant Principal

APRL American Prosthetic Research Laboratory

Aprmay April and May

aprmd appointment recommended

APRO Aerial Phenomena Research Organization; Army Personnel Research Office

apróx apróximadamente (Spanish—approximately)

AprS American Proctologic Society

APRS Association of Professional Recording Studios

aprt airport

APRTA Associated Press Radio and Television Association

aprthd Apartheid (Afrikaans—apartness)

APRU Asia Pacific Research Unit

aprx approximately

aps accessory power supply; adenosine phosphosulfate; autograph postcard signed; auxiliary power supply; auxiliary propulsion system

aps (APS) average propensity to save

Aps Apus

ApS AnpartsSelskab (Dano-Norwegian-limited company)

APS Aboriginal Protection Society; Academy of Political Science; Adenosine Phosphosulfate; Alternative Press Syndicate; American Metal Products (stock exchange symbol); American Pediatric Society; American Pheasant Society; American Philatelic Society; American Philosophical Society; American Physical Society; American Physiological Society; American Phytopathological Society; American Plant Selections; American Poinsettia Society; American Polar Society; American Proctologic Society; American Prosthodontic Society; American Psychosomatic Society; Army Pilot School; Army Postal Service; Association of Photo Sensitizers; Atmospheric Protection System; Australian Pig Society; Australian Psychological Society; Australian Public Service; submarine transport (naval symbol)

APS Algerie Presse Service (French—Algerian Press Service); *Associated Press Stylebook and Libel Manual*

APSA Aerolíneas Peruanas, South America; American Political Science Association; Associate of the Photographic Society of America; Association of Professional Scientists of Australia; Australian Pharmaceutical Sciences Association; Australian Political Studies Association; Australian Pre-School Association

A & PSA Aden and Protectorate of South Arabia

APSA Aerolineas Peruanas SA (Spanish—Peruvian Airlines Corporation); *Azufrera Panamericana SA* (Spanish—Panamerican Sulfur Corporation)

APsaA American Psychoanalytic Association

APSB Aid to the Potentially Self-supporting Blind; Australian Public Service Board

APSE Abstracts of Photographic Science and Engineering

APSF Alfred P Sloan Foundation; Australian Public Service Federation

APS/HEW Administration for Public Services—HEW

APSq Aerial Port Squadron

APSS Association for the Psychophysiological Study of Sleep

A.P.S.T. Associate in Public Service Technology

APsychoA American Psychoanalytic Association

APsychosomS American Psychosomatic Society

APsychpthA American Psychopathological Association

apt. airborne pointer-tracker; alum-precipitated toxoid; apartment; armor-piercing with tracer; automatic picture transmission; automatically-programmed tool(s)

apt. (APT) afterpeak tank

apt apartadero (Spanish—platform)

APT Advanced Passenger Train; Airman Proficiency Test; Applied Performance Test(s); Automatic Picture Transmission; Automotive Professional Training

APTA American Physical Therapy Association; American Pioneer Trails Association; American Platform Tennis Association; American Public Transit Association

APTC Allied Printing Trades Council

APTD Aid to the Permanently and Totally Disabled

Aptdo apartado (Spanish—post office box)

apte advance passenger train express (149 mph British turbine-powered train)—APTE

apth apthong (a silent letter like the *p* in pneumatic)

apti actions per time interval

APTI Association of Principals of Technical Institutions

APTIC Air Pollution Technical Information Center

apto aluminum plastic tearoff (container cover)

apt(s) apartment(s)

APTs Advanced Passenger Trains

APTS Automatic Picture Transmission System

APTU African Postal and Telecommunications Union; Australian Postal and Telecommunications Union

apu auxiliary power unit

APU Army Postal Unit; Asian Parliamentary Union

apu-hs automatic program unit —high speed

apu-ls automatic program unit —low speed

apv automatic-patching verification

APV Avenida Presidente Vargas, Rio de Janeiro, Brazil

apw architectural projected window

APW Accelerated Public Works; American Prisoner of War; Apia, Western Samoa (airport)

APWA American Public Welfare Association; American Public Works Association

APWP Accelerated Public Works Program

APWSS Asian-Pacific Weed Science Society

APWU American Postal Workers Union

apx appendix; approximate(ly)

APZ Assiniboine Park Zoo

aq accomplishment quotient; achievement quotient; any quantity; aqueous

a-q aircraft quality

aq. aqua (Latin—water)

AQ achievement quotient; aviation fire-control technician (USAF symbol); Schreiner Aerocontractors (Hague)

AQ Australian Quarterly

AQA Australian Quadriplegic Association

AQAB Air Quality Advisory Board

AQAPs Allied Quality Assurance Publications

Aqar Aquarius

aq. astr. aqua adstricta (Latin—ice)

aq. bull. aqua bulliens (Latin—boiling water)

aq. cal. aqua calida (Latin—warm water)

AQCL Analytical Quality Control Laboratory

aq. com. aqua communis (Latin—ordinary water)

AQCR Air Quality Control Region (EPA)

aq. dest. aqua destillata (Latin—distilled water)

aqdm air quality display model

AQE Airman Qualifying Examination

aq. ferv. aqua fervens (Latin—hot water)

aq. fluv. aqua fluvii (Latin—river water)

aq. font. aqua fontana (Latin—spring water)

aqgv azimuth-quantized gated video

AQHA Australian Quarter Horse Association

Aqil Aquila

aql acceptable qualifying levels; acceptable quality level; approved quality level

Aql Aquila

aq. mar. aqua marina (Latin—sea water)

aq. ment. pip. aqua menthae piperitae (Latin—peppermint water)

AQMG Assistant Quartermaster General

AQMP Air Quality Master Plan

aqn azimuthal quantum number

aq. niv. aqua nivalis (Latin—snow water)

aq. pluv. aqua pluvialis (Latin—rain water)

aq. pur. aqua pura (Latin—pure water)

Aqr Aquarius

AQREC Army Quartermaster Research and Engineering Command

aq. regia (Latin—royal water) hydrochloric and nitric acid

aqs additional qualifying symptoms

AQT Applicant Qualification Test

aq. tep. aqua tepida (Latin—tepid water)

aqu aqueous

aqua. aquaria; aquarium; aquatic

aquacade aquatic parade (or exhibition of diving, swimming, water sports)

aquacult aquaculture

Aquae Bonae (Latin—Bonn)—Beethoven's birthplace and capital of West Germany

Aquae Grani (Latin—Aachen or Aix-la-Chapelle)—depending on whether it belongs to Germany or France and also called Aquisgranum

Aquae Sextiae (Latin—Aix-en-Provence)—spa north of Marseille

aqua fortis (Latin—strong water) nitric acid

aquamarine gemstone beryl

aquar aquarium

Aquar Aquarius

aqua regia (Latin—royal water) hydrochloric and nitric acid

aque aqueduct

Aqued Aqueduct

Aqueduct Aqueduct Books

Aquisgranum (Latin—Aachen or Aix-la-Chapelle)

Aquitania Roman name for a province in Gaul extending from the Loire River to the Pyrenees with Bordeaux as its capital; Aquitaine

ar achievement ratio; acid resisting; active resistance; alarm reaction; all rail; all risks; allocated reserve; analytical reagent; antireflection; aromatic; arrival; artificial respiration; aspect ratio; auditory reception

ar (AR) address register; armed robbery; average revenue

a/r all risks; armed robbery; at the rate of

a & r approved and removed; artists and repertory; assault and robbery; assembly and repair

ar avis de reception (French—return receipt)

a/R am Rhein (German—on the Rhine River)

Ar Arab; Arabia; Arabian; Arabic; Aragon; argon; Aries; aryl

Ar Arabic (principal language of the Middle East and North Africa, spoken by no fewer than 121 million people); *Arroyo* (Spanish—brook, creek, or rivulet)

AR Aberdeen & Rockfish (railroad); Administrative Ruling; Aerodynamic Report; Aerolineas Argentinas (Argentine Airlines); Aeronautical Radionavigation; Airman Recruit; Airship Rigger; Amend-ment Request; American Smelting & Refining (stock exchange symbol); Annual Report; Army Regulation(s); Army Reserve; repair ship (naval symbol)

A/R Antwerp-Rotterdam (range of ports)

A & R Angus and Robertson; assembly and repair

AR Aller et Retour (French—roundtrip); *American Rationalist; Andata-Ritorno* (Italian—roundtrip)

A.R. Anno Regni (Latin—In the Year of the Reign of)

A/R Aksjerederi (Norwegian—shipping company)

ara assigned responsible agency (DoD)

ara (ARA) aerial rocket artillery

Ara Ara (a three-letter constellation without an abbreviation); Argentina

ARA Academy of Rehabilitative Audiology; Aerospace Research Association; American Radio Association; American Railway Association; American Rationalist Association; American Relief Association; American Rental Association; American Republics Area; American Rheumatism Association; Applied Research of Australia; Arcade & Attica (railroad); Area Redevelopment Administration; Armada República Argentina (Argentine Navy); Artists' Representatives Association; Association of Radiologists of Australasia; Auckland Regional Authority; Australian Regular Army; Australian Retailers Association; Automatic Retailers of America

ARA (AFL-CIO) American Radio Association

A.R.A. Associate of the Royal Academy

A/R/A Antwerp-Rotterdam-Amsterdam (range of ports)

ARA Acçao Revolucionaria Armada (Portuguese—Armed Revolutionary Action)

Arab. Arabia; Arabian; Arabic

ARAB Australian Radio Advertising Bureau

Arab Africa northern Africa from Egypt to Morocco and from Mauretania to the Sudan

Arab Emirates United Arab Emirates including the seven Tru-cial Sheikdoms along the southern shore of the Persian Gulf with Abu Dhabi its capital

Arabia Deserta Desert Arabia in the northern sector of the Arabian Peninsula

Arabia Felix Fertile Arabia in the southern section of the Arabian Peninsula also known as Aden, the Hadhramaut, or Yemenite section

arabian arabian baboon (hamadryas baboon worshipped by the ancient Egyptians); arabian camel (one-hump dromedary of northern Africa and western Asia); arabian coffee (East African cultivated by the Arabians); arabian horse (usually a white breed cultivated by the Arabs for its grace, intelligence, and speed); plus all other arabian eponyms readers may know

Arabian Arabian Desert occupying most of Saudi Arabia; Arabian Peninsula of southwestern Asia; Arabian Sea section of the Indian Ocean between Arabia and India; inhabitant of Saudi Arabia also called Saudi (plural or singular)

Arabian Gulf Persian Gulf

Arabia Petraea Rocky Arabia in the northwestern section of the Arabian Peninsula

arabic arabic numbers (1, 2, 3, 4, 5, etc., as distinct from roman numbers—I, II, III, IV, V, etc.)

Arabiya as-Sa'udiya (Arabic—Saudi Arabia)

Arab League League of Arab States (Algeria, Bahrain, Egypt, Iraq, Jordan, Kuwait, Lebanon, Libya, Morocco, Oman, Qatar, Somalia, Southern Yemen, Sudan, Syria, Tunisia, United Arab Emirates, Yemen)

ARABS Australian Racing and Breeding Stables

ARAC Aerospace Research Applications Center; Associate of the Royal Agricultural College; Australian Refugee Advisory Council

arach arachnology

Arach Arachnida

ARACI Associate of the Royal Australian Chemical Institute

arad airborne radar and doppler

ARAD Associate of the Royal Academy of Dancing

ARADCOM Army Defense Command

ARAeS Associate of the Royal Aeronautical Society

Arafat Yasir Arafat (Palestinian terrorist leader)

Arafura Arafura Sea between Australia and New Guinea

ARAgS Associate of the Royal Agricultural Society

ARAIA Associate of the Royal Australian Institute of Architects

aral automatic record analysis language

Aral Aral Sea (landlocked body of water in Soviet Kazakhatan, called Aralskoye More by the Russians)

Aralskoye More (Russian—Aral Sea)

Aram Aramaic

ARAM Association of Railroad Advertising Managers

A.R.A.M. Associate of the Royal Academy of Music

Aramco Arabian-American Oil Company

Arans Aran Islands off County Clare, Ireland

Aransas Aransas National Wildlife Refuge near Rockport, Texas

ARAPCS Association for Research, Administration, Professional Councils, and Societies

Ararat Mount Ararat (Turkey's highest mountain and place where Noah's Ark supposedly beached after the flood subsided and then debarked the most improbable zoological collection ever assembled; Ararat is the Armenian name of the mountain the Turks call Agri Dagi although on the border of Soviet Armenia); assuming the account of the deluge is accurate, and using the most conservative lumpings of known species, and remembering Captain Noah assembled, transported for a 40-day voyage, and then debarked no less than 8000 mammals, 20,000 birds, 10,000 reptiles, 3600 amphibians, plus unknown numbers of fishes, and invertebrates such as insects, spiders, centipedes, crustaceans, molluscs, worms, starfishes, corals, sponges, and protozoans, the importance of this landing place cannot be denied

aras ascending reticular activating system

ARAS Accept (each person you encounter), Respect (each person however they look and whatever their position), Affect (each person with the warmth of your heart), Support (each person in the place they are now); Ascending Reticular Activating System; Associate of the Royal Astronomical Society

Araucania region of central Chile south of Bío-Bío River; home of Araucanian Indians

araucanos (Latin American nickname—Chileans or *chilenos*)—sobriquet recalls the liberty-loving Araucanian Indians who were never conquered by the Spaniards

Arava Israeli IAI-201 light transport plane

arb arbitrary; arbitration

arb *arbeid(er)* [Dano-Norwegian—work(s)]; *arbejde* (Dano-Norwegian—job, labor, work)

Arb Arbroath

ARB Accident Records Bureau (NYC Police Dept.); Air Registration Board; Air Research Bureau; Air Resources Board; Armored Rifle Battalion; Army Rearming Base; Army Retiring Board; Asian Reserve Bank; ASTIA Report Bibliography; battle damage repair ship (naval symbol)

ARBA American Railway Bridge and Building Association; American Road Builders Association; Associated Retail Bakers of America

ARBA *American Reference Books Annual*

arb & aw arbitration and award

ARBED Aciéries Réunies de Burbach-Eich-Dudelange

ARBM Association of Radio Battery Manufacturers

arbo arthropod-borne (viral diseases)

arbor. arboriculture

arbor. virus arthropod-borne virus

ARBP Associated Reinforcing Bar Producers

ARBs Air Resources Boards (pollution-control agencies)

ARBS Angular-Rate Bombing System; Associate of the Royal Society of British Sculptors

arbtrn arbitration

arbtror arbitrator

Arbuckle Arbuckle National

Recreation Area near Sulphur, Oklahoma

arc Association for Retarded Citizens

arc. arcade; auto-refrigerated cascade

arc arco (Italian—bow, indicating end of *pizzicato* passages)

Arc Arachon; Arcade; Archaic; Arctic

ARC Aboriginal Research Club; Addicts Rehabilitation Center; Agricultural Relations Council; Agricultural Research Council; Air Rescue Center; Air Reserve Center; Aircraft Radio Corporation; Airworthiness Requirements Committee; Alcoholic Rehabilitation Center; American Red Cross; Ames Research Center (NASA); Appalachian Regional Commission; Armada República de Colombia (Colombian Navy); Asian Research Center (Harvard); Association of Rehabilitation Centers; Association of Retail Confectioners; Association for Retarded Citizens; Atlantic Research Corporation; Atomedic Research Center; automatic radio control (computerese); cable laying or repair ship (naval symbol)

ARCA Associate of the Royal College of Art

ARCAA Associate of the Royal Canadian Academy of Arts

arcade. automatic radar-control and data equipment

Arc Arch Arctic Archipelago (Canadian Arctic)

ARCAS Automatic Radar Chain Acquisition System

ARCB Air Resources Control Board

arccos arccosine

arccot arccotangent

arccsc arccoscecant

Arc Cur Arctic Current

arce amphibious river-crossing equipment

ARCE American Record Collectors Exchange

ARCen Air Reserve Center

arch. archaic; archipelago; architect(s); architectural; architecture

Arch Archway

ARCH Articulated Computing Hierarchy

Archam Archambault; prison in Archambault, Québec

Arch-Bish Archbishop

Arch City St Louis dominated

by the monumental Jefferson National Expansion Memorial arch commemorating the Louisiana Purchase making St Louis the Gateway to the West

archcrit arch critic; architechtural critic(ism)

Archd Archdeacon; Archduke

Arch de Cln Archipelago de Colón

Archdn Archdeacon

Archduke Beethoven's Trio in B minor (opus 97) for violin, cello, and piano; dedicated to his patron the Archduke Rudolph

Arch E Architectural Engineer

archeo archeological; archeologist; archeology

archeo (Latin prefix—beginning)—archaic, archeologist, archeology

archeol archeology

Archeol Archeology

Archeological Capital of Africa Cairo, Eqypt

Archeological Capital of North America Chichen Itza, Mexico

Archeological Capital of South America Cuzco, Peru

Archeoz Archeozoic

Arches Arches National Monument in eastern Utah; features wind-sculptured stone arches

archi archival; archive; archivist

ARCHI Asociación de Radiofusoras de Chile (Association of Chilean Broadcasters)

Archie Archibald

Archie Archie Bunker (archetype of the average white American bigot, role created by actor Carroll O'Connor in the television serial entitled *All In The Family*)

archip archipelago

archit architecture

Archit Architecture

Architect of the Atomic Bomb J Robert Oppenheimer

Architect in Chief of St Peters Raphael (Raffaello Santi)

Architect of Mexican Independence Padre Miguel Hidalgo

Architect-Naturalist-Philosopher-Statesman President Thomas Jefferson

Architect of the New Deal Franklin Delano Roosevelt

Architect of Non-Alignment Josip Broz Tito

Archive Archive Press

Archives Soc Hist Archives of

Social History

Arch Rec Bks Architectural Record Books

archv archive

Archy Archibald

ARCI Addiction Research Center Inventory; American Railway Car Institute

ARCIC Anglican-Roman Catholic International Commission

Arclos Army Close support

ARCM Associate of the Royal College of Music

ARCNS American Red Cross Nursing Services

Arco Arco Publishing Company

Arc O Arctic Ocean Command

ARCO Associate of the Royal College of Organists; Atlantic Richfield Company

ARCom Army Research

ARCOMET Area Commander's Meeting (NATO)

ARCON Advanced Research Consultants

ARCOPS Arctic Operations

arcos arc cosine

ARCOS Anglo-Russian Cooperative Society

ARCOV Army Combat Operations Vietnam

arcp air refueling control point

ARCR Arthritis and Rheumatism Council for Research

ARCRL Agricultural Research Council Radiobiological Laboratory

ARCs Alcoholic Rehabilitation Centers

ARCS Air Resupply and Communication Service; Australian Red Cross Society

A.R.C.S. Associate of the Royal College of Science; Associate of the Royal College of Surgeons

ARCSA Aviation Requirements for the Combat Structure of the Army

arcsec arcsecant

arcsin arcsine

ARCST Associate of the Royal College of Science and Technology

arct air refueling control time

arctan arctangent

Arctic Arctic Current flowing south from Baffin Bay and Greenland to cool the coasts of Labrador, Newfoundland, and most of New England; Arctic Ocean washing the north coast of Asia, Europe, and North America including Alaska and Canada

Arctic Vassilenko's Fourth Symphony

Arctic big three muskox, polar bear, walrus

Arctic Canada Northwest Territories and the Yukon

Arctic Circle 66 degrees 17 minutes North latitude; imaginary line encircling northern part of the earth to delimit north frigid zone

Arctic Territories Canadian Northwest Territories

Arctique (French—Arctic)—Arctic Ocean

ARCUK Architects' Registration Council of the United Kingdom

ARCUP Atlantic Region Canadian University Press (news cooperative)

ARCVS Associate of the Royal College of Veterinary Surgeons

arc/w arcweld

ard acute respiratory disease

ar & d aeronautical research and development; air research and development

Ard Ardrossan

ARD Accelerated Rehabilitated Disposition; Accelerated Rural Development; Air Reserve District; American Research and Development (corporation); Appalachian Regional Development; Arbeitsgemeinschaft Rundfunkanstalten Deutschland (German National Broadcasting); Army Renegotiation Division; Association of Research Directors; auxiliary floating dock (naval)

AR & D air research and development

arda analog recording dynamic analyzers

ARDA Advanced Reactor Development Associates; American Railway Development Association

ARDB Australian Resources Development Ban

ARDC Aberdeen Research and Development Center; Action Resource Development Center; Agricultural Refinance and Development Corporation; Air Research and Development Command; American Racing Drivers Club

ARDCM Air Research and Development Command Manual

ARDCO Applied Research and

Development Company

ardddie analysis, requirements determination, design, development, implementation, and evaluation

ARDE Armament Research and Development Establishment (Ministry of Supply)

Ardennes Ardennes Forest of Belgium, France, and Luxembourg

Ardent City Liège, Belgium

Ardent Conservationist Rachel Carson

ARDG Army Research and Development Group (USA)

ARDG(E) Army Research and Development Group (Europe)

ARDG(FE) Army Research and Development Group (Far East)

ARDIS Army Research and Development Information System

ARDM medium auxiliary repair drydock (naval symbol)

Ardnamurchan Point Ardnamurchan—Scottish headland in northwestern Argyll and westernmost mainland of all Great Britain

ard's analog recording dynamic analyzers

ARDS Aviation Research and Development Service

ARDU Analytical Research and Development Unit

ARDXC Australian Radio DX Club

are. (ARE) air reactor experiment

ARE Arab Republic of Egypt; Association for Research and Enlightenment

A.R.E. Associate in Religious Education

AREA Aerovias Ecuatorianas (Ecuadorian Airways); American Railway Engineering Association; American Recreational Equipment Association; Army Reactor Experimental Area; Association of Records Executives & Administrators; Australian Remedial Education Association

AREC Amateur Radio Emergency Corps

AREFS Air Refueling Squadron

AREI Associate of the Real Estate and Stock Institute (Australia)

Arelate (Latin—Arles)

Arelatum (Latin—Arles)—

French town also called Arelas or Arelate

ARENA Adoption Resource Exchange of North America

ARENA *Aliança Renovadora Nacional* (Portuguese—National Renovating Alliance)—political party in Brazil

aren't are not

ARENTS ARPA Environmental Test Satellite

Areop Areopagite; *Areopagitica* (Milton's pamphlet advocating freedom of the press); Areopagus

Ares (Greek—Mars)—god of war

arestem a recording stray energy monitor

ARETO Arab Republic of Egypt Telecommunications Organization

AREUEA American Real Estate and Urban Economics Association

arf acute respiratory failure; (cartoonist's symbol—dog's bark)—*arf-arf*

ARF Addiction Research Foundation; Advertising Research Foundation; African Research Foundation; Air Reserve Force(s); American Radio Forum; American Rationalist Federation; American Rehabilitation Foundation; American Retail Foundation; American Rose Foundation; Armour Research Foundation; Arthritis and Rheumatism Foundation; Australian Road Federation

ARFA Allied Radio Frequency Agency

ARFC Air Reserve Flying Center

ARFCOS Armed Forces Courier Service

ARFDC Atomic Reactor and Fuel Development Corporation

ARFL Australian Rugby Football League; Australian Rules Football League

arfo after receipt firm order

arfor area forecast

ARFPC Air Reserve Forces Policy Committee

ARFU Australian Rugby Football Union

arfx automatic riveting fixture

arg argent; argot; argument; argumentation; argumentative; argumentator (a controversialist); argus; arresting; arresting gear

arg (Arg) arginine

arg argang (Dano-Norwegian—yearbook); *argol* (Mongolian—dried camel or cattle dung fuel)

Arg Argentina; Argentinian; Argyll

ARG Aerolineas Argentinas; repair ship, internal combustion engine

ARG American Record Guide

arga appliance, range, adjust (data processing)

ARGCA American Rice Growers Cooperative Association

Argel Argelia (Spanish—Algeria); *Argelía* (Portuguese—Algeria)

Argelia (Spanish—Algeria)

Argen Argentine; Argentinian

Argentina Argentine Republic (second largest South American nation whose Spanish-speaking Argentinos export cotton, frozen meat, and many valuable minerals), *República Argentina*

Argentina Day Argentina's Independence Day (July 9)

Argentina's Principal Port Buenos Aires

Argentinian First Argentina's best known classical composer—Alberto Ginastera

Argentinian Ports (large, medium, and small from north to south) Santa Fé, Rosario, Zárate, Campana, Buenos Aires, La Plata, Mar del Plata, Puerto Belgrano, Ingeniero White, Puerto Madryn, Ushuaia

Argentoratum (Latin—Strasbourg)—on the Franco-German border

Argie(s) Argentino(s)

argmt arrangement

Argosy Argosy-Antiquarian Limited; Hawker-Siddeley four-engine turboprop transporting 54 paratroopers or 69 regular troops

argus advanced research on groups under stress

Argus Canadair long-range reconnaissance plane designated CL-38

ARGUS Automatic Routine Generating and Updating System

Argyll Argyllshire

Argyrol King Dr Albert C Barnes

arh (ARH) advanced reconnaissance helicopter

a Rh am Rhein (German—on the Rhine)

ARH heavy-hull repair ship (3-letter symbol)

ARHA Associate of the Royal Hibernian Academy

arh/ir anti-radiation homing/infrared

ARHS Associate of the Royal Horticultural Society; Australian Railway Historical Society

Ari Aries (constellation); Aristotle

ARI Acne Research Institute (Newport Beach, California); Air-Conditioning and Refrigeration Institute; Alcoholic Rehabilitation, Inc; Aluminum Research Institute; American Reciprocal Insurers; American Refractories Institute; American Russian Institute; Automatic Radio Information

ARIA Accounting Research International Association; Adult Reading Improvement Association; American Risk and Insurance Association

ARIANA Ariana Afghan Airlines

ARIB Asphalt Roofing Industry Bureau

ARIBA Associate of the Royal Institute of British Architects

Aribistan (Turkish—Arabia)

ARIC Associate of the Royal Institute of Chemistry

ARICRSU American Russian Institute for Cultural Relations with the Soviet Union

ARICS Associate of the Royal Institution of Chartered Surveyors

ARIEL Automated Real-Time Investments Exchange Limited

ARIEM Army Research Institute of Environmental Medicine

aries astronomical radio interferometric earth surveying

ARIES Advanced Radar Information Evaluation System

Ariha (Arabic—Jericho)

arima autoregressive integrated moving average

ARINA Associate of the Royal Institution of Naval Architects

ARINC Aeronautical Radio Incorporated

ARIO Association of Retired Intelligence Officers

arip automatic rocket impact predictor

aris (ARIS) advanced range instrumentation ships

ARIS Activity-Reporting Information System; Advanced Research Instrument System; Aerial Radio Instrument System; Aircraft Research Instrumentation System

Arist Aristotle

ARIST *Annual Review of Information Science and Technology*

Arista high-school honor society

Aristo Aristocles; Aristol; Aristotle

aristocat(s) aristocratic cat(s)

Aristocrat of Orchestras The Boston Symphony Orchestra

Aristocrat of Sports billiards

Aristoph Aristophanes

aristo(s) aristocrat(s)

ARISTOTLE Annual Review and Information Symposium on the Technology of Training, Learning, and Education (DoD)

arit *aritmética* (Portuguese or Spanish—arithmetic)

A.R.I.T. American Registered Inhalation Therapist

arith arithmetic(al)(ly); arithmetician

Arith Arithmetic

Ariz Arizona; Arizonian

Ariz Hist Found Arizona Historical Foundation

Arizona Girls Arizona Girls School at Phoenix (correctional facility for juvenile delinquents)

ARJIS Automated Regional Justice Information System

Ark Arkansas; Arkansan

Arkansawyer Arkansan nickname for a native of Arkansas also called Arkie

Ark City Arkansas City, Arkansas

Ark f Fys *Arkiv for Fysik* (Danish—Physics Archives)

ARKIA Israel Inland Airlines

Arkie Arkansas (or person from there); migratory farm worker or sharecropper from Arkansas

Arkopolis Little Rock, Arkansas

Arktisch (German—Arctic)—Arctic Ocean

arl acceptable reliability level; air run landing; average remaining lifetime

ARL Admiralty Research Laboratory (UK); Aeromedical Research Laboratory; Aeronautical Research Laboratory;

Aerospace Research Laboratory; American Reefer Line; American Republics Line; American Roque League; Anesthesia Research Laboratories; Applied Research Laboratory (Johns Hopkins University); Association of Research Libraries; Australian Rugby League; landing craft repair ship (3-letter naval symbol)

ARLA Arab Latin American Bank

Arlanda Stockholm, Sweden's airport

ARLD Army Logistics Research and Development

Arletty Arlette-Léonie Bathiat (French actress)

ARLHS Australian Railway and Locomotive Historical Society

Arlington Arlington Books (Louisville, Ky); Arlington House (New Rochelle, NY); Arlington National Cemetery in Arlington, Virginia overlooking Washington, DC

Arlington House Robert E Lee's home in Arlington, Virginia overlooking the Potomac and Washington, D.C.

Arlington Hse Arlington House

ARLIS Arctic Research Laboratory Island (USN)

ARLIS/NA Art Libraries Society/North America

ArLO Army Liaison Officer

ARLO Art Reference Libraries of Ohio

Arlon Luxembourg, Belgium's provincial capital

ARLSEA Active-Retired Lighthouse Service Employees Association

arm. anti-radar missile (ARM); anti-radiation missile; area radiation monitor(s); armature; arming; armor(ed)

arm. (ARM) adjustable-rate mortgage; anti-radar missile; anti-radiation missile

Arm Armagh; Armenia(n)

Ar.M. Architecturae Magister (Master of Architecture)

ARM Auditory Rehabilitation Mobile; Australian Reform Movement

A.R.M. Allergy Relief Medicine

arma armature

ARMA American Bosch Arma Corporation; American Records Management Association; Anglican Renewal Ministries Australia; Association of

Records Managers and Administrators; Australian Rubber Manufacturers Association

Armageddon English name for Meggido in Palestine where the British defeated the Turks in 1918 and liberated the country for all its people—Arabs and Jews

a&r man artist and repertory man (supervising phonograph record production)

Armand Armando

ARMCM Associate of the Royal Manchester College of Music

ARMCOM Armament Command (USA)

ARMCOMSAT Arab Communications Satellite System

armd armored

Armen Armenia(n)

armet area forecast (given in metric system)

armgrd armed guard

ARMH Academy of Religion and Mental Health

ARMI American Rack Merchandisers Institute; American Research Merchandising Institute; Army Resources Management Institute

Armin Armindo

Arminius Jacobus Arminius (originally Jacob Harmensen)

ARMIS Agricultural Research Management Information System

ARMIT Associate of the Royal Melbourne Institute of Technology

arml airmail

armm analysis and research methods for management

ARMM Association of Reproduction Materials Manufacturers

ARMMA American Railway Master Mechanics' Association

ARMMS Automated Reliability and Maintainability Measurement System

AR/MONP Ayers Rock/Mount Olga National Park (Northern Territory, Australia)

ARMOP Army Mortar Program

Armor Armoric

armpl armorplate

armr armorer

ARMS Advanced Receiver Model System; Aerial Radiological Measuring Survey; Amateur Radio Mobile Society; Automated Records Management System

arm-saf arm-safe (switch)

armt armament

ARMU Associated Rocky Mountain Universities

army disease drug addiction

Army NG Army National Guard

Army ROTC Army Reserve Officers' Training Corps

arn (ARN) ácido ribonucleico (Spanish—ribonucleic acid)—rna (RNA)

a Rn am Rhein (German—on the Rhine)

Arn Arnold

ARN Stockholm, Sweden (Arlanda Airport)

ArNa Army with Navy

ARNAT Asia Research News Analysis Team

arng arrange

ARNG Army National Guard

Arnhem provincial capital of Gelderland in the Netherlands

Arnhem Land northern end of Australia's Northern Territory

A Rn I Association of Rhodesian Industries

Arnie Arnold

ARNM Aztec Ruins National Monument

ARNMD Association for Research in Nervous and Mental Disease

Arno Arnold; Arnon; Arnot

Arnold Bennett Enoch Arnold Bennett

aro after receipt of order; airborne range only

ARO Air Radio Office(r); Applied Research Objective; Army Research Office; Army Routine Order; Asian Regional Organization; Association for Research in Ophthalmology; Association of Roentgenological Organizations

AROCC Association for Research of Childhood Cancer

arod airborne range and orbit determination

ARO-FE Army Research Office—Far East

arom aromatic; artificial rupture of membranes

AR-ONP Ayers Rock-Olgas National Park (Australia)

arp airborne radar platform; airport reference point; alternator research package; (cartoonist's symbol—dog's bark)

ARP Advanced Research Project(s); Aeronautical Recommended Practice(s); Air Raid Precautions; American Registry of Pathologists; Ammunition Refilling Point; Area Redevelopment Program; Association for Realistic Philosophy; Australian Reptile Park (New South Wales); Australian Republican Party

ARP Anti-Revolutionaire Partij (Dutch—Anti-Revolutionary Party)

ARPA Advanced Research Projects Agency

ARPANET Advanced Research Projects Agency (computer) Network

ARPAS Air Reserve Pay and Allowance System

ARPAT Advanced Research Projects Agency Terminal (defense system)

ARPC Air Reserve Personnel Center

arpd (ARPD) applied research planning document

arpege air-pollution episode game

ARPEL Asistencia Recíproca Petrolera Estatal Latinoamericana (Spanish—Latin American State Petroleum Reciprocal Assistance)—international agency

arpl a retrieval process language

Arpo arpeggio (Italian—producing the tones in a chord successively rather than simultaneously)

ARPO Association of Resort Publicity Officers

ARPOA Association of Railway Professional Officers of Australia

Arprt Airport (postal placename abbreviation)

ARPS Advanced Radar Processing System; Arab Physical Society; Associate of the Royal Photographic Society; Australian Radiation Protection Society; Australian Royal Photographic Society

ARPSA Army Postal Service Agency

Arpt Airport

ARPT American Registry of Physical Therapists

a-r pulse apical-radial pulse

arq arquitecto (Spanish—architect); arquitectura (Spanish—architecture); arquiteto (Portuguese—architect); arquitetura (Portuguese—architecture)

ARQ automatic error correction

(computerese); automatic request for repetition (computerese)

Arq^to *Arquitecto* (Portuguese or Spanish—Architect)

arquo *arquipélago* (Portuguese —archipelago)

arr airborne radio receiver; arrange(ment); arrestor; arrival; arrive; arriving

arr (ARR) arrest(ed)

Arr arrondissement (French—district)

ARR Air Regional Representative; Air Reserve Record(s); American Right to Read; Army Retail Requirements

ARRA Amateur Radio Retailers Association; Australian Rough Riders Association

ARRB Australian Road Research Board

ARRC Air Reserve Records Center; Associate of the Royal Red Cross

ARRCS Air-Raid Reporting Control Ship

ARRDO Australian Railway Research and Development Organisation

arre arrecife (Spanish—reef, roadbed, rocky road)

ARRES Automatic Radar-Reconnaissance Exploitation System

arrex arriving ex . . .

ARRF Australian Reading Research Federation; Automatic Recording and Reduction Facility

ARRGp Aerospace Rescue and Recovery Group (USAF)

Arri Arnold and Richter (reflex motion-picture camera)

ARRL American Radio Relay League

arr n arrival notice

arro arroyo (Spanish—creek, brook, stream)—as in Arroyo de las Vacas (Cow Creek)

arro seco arroyo seco (Spanish—dry creek, brook bed, streambed, or riverbed)—many such seasonally dry watercourses exist in Spanish-speaking countries

arrowhead symbol used to indicate direction

Arrowhead Herman Melville's home in Pittsfield, Massachusetts

Arroyo del Ajo (Spanish—Garlic Gulch)—John Steinbeck's name for his home near Los Gatos, California

ARRS Aerospace Rescue and Recovery Service; Aircraft Refueling and Rearming System; American Roentgen Ray Society; American-Russian Research Society

ARRSq Aerospace Rescue and Recovery Squadron (USAF)

ARRT American Registry of Radiologic Technologists

ARRTC Aerospace Rescue and Recovery Training Center (USAF)

ARRWg Aerospace Rescue and Recovery Wing (USAF)

arry arrythmia

ars active repeater satellite; aerospace research satellite; arsenal; asbestos roof shingles

Ars Arsenal

ARs Action Requests

ARS Aerospace Research Satellite; Agricultural Research Service; Airail Service (monorail); Air Rescue Service; American Records Society; American Recreation Society; American Repair Society; American Rescue Service; American Rhododendron Society; American Rocket Society; American Rose Society; Army Relief Society; salvage ship (naval symbol)

ARS Annual Report to Shareholders

ARSA Associate of the Royal School of Art

arsab arsonist sabotage; arsonist saboteur

arsabs arsonist saboteurs

ARSC Association of Recorded Sound Collections

ARSD Advanced Reentry System Deployment; salvage lifting ship (naval symbol)

ARSDEP Asian Regional Skills Development Programme

arsen arsenal

Arsenal of the Nation Connecticut

Arsetralia waterfront slang for Australia

arsg arising

ARSH Associate of the Royal Society for the Promotion of Health

ARSI Associate of the Royal Sanitary Institute

arsin arc sine

Arsl Arsenal (postal place-name abbreviation)

ARSL Associate of the Royal Society of Literature

ARSM Associate of the Royal School of Mines

Arson Capital of the World New York City

ARSP Aerospace Research Support Program

arspa aerial reconnaissance and surveillance penetration analysis

ARSPH Associate of the Royal Society for the Promotion of Health

arsr air route surveillance radar

ARST Aerial Reconnaissance and Security Troop; salvage craft tender (naval symbol)

ARSTAF Army Staff

ARSTRAC Army Strike Command

ARSU Alcohol Rehabilitation Services Unit (Navy Regional Medical Center in Long Beach, California)

ARSV armored reconnaissance scout vehicle (USA)

art. advanced research and technology; airborne radiation thermometer; art assembly; arterial; artery; article; articulate; articulation; artifact; artificial; artillery; artisan; artist; artistic; artistry; automatic reporting telephone

'art heart

art artikel (Dano-Norwegian—article)

Art Arthur; Arturo

Art Artikel (German—article)

ART Accredited Record Technician; Air Reserve Technician; Arithmetic Reading Test; Arithmetic Reasoning Test; Aviation Radio Technician

ARTA American River Touring Association; Association of Retail Travel Agents

artac advanced reconnaissance and target acquisition capabilities

ARTADS Army Tactical Data Systems

artb (ARTB) automatic return to base

ARTC Addiction Research and Treatment Center; Addiction Research and Treatment Corporation; Air Route Traffic Control

ARTCC Air Route Traffic Control Center

Art Center of Rhode Island Wickford

Art Center of the Southwest Taos, New Mexico

Art C-Part articles of co-partnership

artcrit art critic(ism)

art deco arts décoratifs (French —decorative arts)—decorative style of the 1920s and 1930s emphasizing bold outlines, geometric forms, streamlining, and strong colors

art. dir artistic director

ARTDO Asian Regional Trade Development Organisation

ARTE Admiralty Reactor Test Establishment

Artemis (Greek—Diana)—goddess of the hunt and the Moon; protectress of women

ARTEMIS Automatic Retrieval of Text through European Multipurpose Information Systems

Artemus Ward Charles Farrar Browne (19th-century American humorist who confessed: *I can't sing. As a singist I am not a success. I am saddest when I sing. So are those who hear me. They are sadder even than I am.*)

ARTEP Army Training and Evaluation Program; Asian Regional Team for Employment Promotion

artesian artesian well (of the type originating in Artois, France)

ARTF Advanced Radiation Technology Facility; Asian Rice Trade Fund; Australian Road Transport Federation

Arth Arthropoda; Arthur; Arthurian

arthro *arthron* (Greek—joint)—arthritis, arthropod

artlc articulate(d), articulation

Artichoke Capital Castroville, California

Articles Articles of Agreement between a ship's crew and its master

Artico (Italian—Arctic)—Arctic Ocean

Ártico (Portuguese or Spanish—Arctic)—Arctic Ocean

Artie Artemas; Artemisia; Artemus; Arthur; Artur; Arturo; Artus

Artie Shaw Arthur Arshawsky

artif artificer(s); artificial(ly)

Artigas José Gervasio Artigas—defender of Uruguayan independence after leading Gaucho revolt against Spanish misrule

ARTINS Army Terrain Information System

art. insem artificial insemination

Artist of the French Revolution Jacques Louis David

Art Kill Arthur Kill waterway between New Jersey and Staten Island, New York

art nr *artikelnummer* (Dano-Norwegian—article number)

arto air run takeoff

art⁰ *articulo* (Italian—article); *artículo* (Spanish—article); *artigo* (Portuguese—article)

art⁰ *artículo* (Spanish—article)

ARTO Advanced Radiation Technology Office

ARTOC Army Tactical Operational Control; Army Tactical Operations Central

ARTP Army Rocket Transportation System

art. pf artist's proof

artrac advanced range testing, reporting, and control

artron(s) artificial neuron(s)

arts. articles

ARTS Advanced Radar Traffic Control System; Automatic Radar Traffic Control System

ArtSci Arts and Sciences (students or studies)

artsem artificial insemination

ARTSM Association of Road Sign Makers

ARTS & P Australian Radio Technical Services and Patents

artt automatic rubber tensile tester

ARTT Annual Review Travelling Team (NATO)

artu automatic range tracking unit

Arturo de Cordova Arturo Garcia

arty artillery

aru analog remote unit; audio response unit

Aru Aruba

ARU Air Reserve Unit; American Railway Union; Australian Railway Union

Aruba's Ports Sint Nicolaas (Lago Refinery), Paardenbaai (Oranjestad), Druif

arv (ARV) advanced reentry vehicle; aeroballistic reentry vehicle

Arv *Arvoisa* (Finnish—esteemed)

ARV aircraft engine overhaul and structural repair ship; American Revised Version

ARVA aircraft repair ship for aircraft (4-letter designation)

ARVE aircraft repair ship for engines (4-letter designation)

ARVH aircraft repair ship for helicopter (naval symbol)

ARVIA Associate of the Royal

Victorian Institute of Architects

ARVN Army of the Republic of Vietnam

ARVO Association for Research in Vision and Ophthalmology

ARVSG Air Reserve Volunteer Support Group

arw attitude reaction wheel

ARW Air Raid Warden; Air Raid Warning; Air Reserve Wing (Canada)

ARW 493 Stig Sverker Foghammar's pseudonym

ARWC Army War College

ARWH Air Reserve Wing Headquarters

ARWS Antiradiation Weapon System; Associate of the Royal Society of Painters in Water Colours

Aryabhata Indian spacecraft named for the fifth-century astronomer

Arz *Arzobispo* (Spanish—Archbishop)

ARZ Active Reconnaissance Zone

Arzbpo *Arzobispo* (Spanish—Archbishop)

as. airscoop; air-to-surface missile; alloy steel; antiseptic; aortic stenosis; asymmetric

a-s ascendance-submission

a/s airspeed; antisubmarine

a & s accident and sickness (insurance)

a.s. *auris sinistra* (Latin—left ear)

a/s. *aux soins de* (French—in care of)

As altostratus; arsenic; Asia; Asian; Asiatic; astigmatism; aunicles; Australia(n)

A_8 atmosphere standard

AS Abilene & Southern (railroad); Academy of Science(s); Aeronautical Standard(s); Air Service; Air Speed; Air Staff; Air Station; Air Surveillance; Airports Service; air-to-surface missile; Alaska Airlines; Ambulatory Surgi-Center; Anglo-Saxon; antisubmarine; Apprentice Seaman; Army Security; Army Staff; Associated Steamships; Australian Standard(s); Auto Squad (police); submarine tender (naval symbol)

A.S. Antonius Stradivarius (initials usually accompanied by a Maltese cross, both enclosed in a double circle)

A/S alongside (barge, cargo carrier, lighter)

A & S Alton & Southern (railroad); Arts and Sciences
A of S Academy of Science
AS *Anonim Sirket* (Turkish—joint stock company); *Aviaeskadra* (Russian—air squadron)
A/S *Aksjeselskap* (Norwegian—limited company); *Aktieselkab* (Danish—joint stock company)
AS-11 Nord air-launched antitank missile
AS-12 Nord automatic-telecommand antitank missile
AS-20 Nord air-to-surface radio-controlled missile
AS-30 improved version of AS-20 with longer range and heavier warhead
AS-33 Nord air-launched inertial-guidance missile
asa acetylsalicylic acid (aspirin); antistatic additive; azimuth servo assembly
asa (Norwegian or Swedish—hill)
aSa anti-Soviet agitation
A-S a Adams-Stokes attack
ASA Acoustical Society of America; Actuarial Society of America; Aerovias Sud Americana (South American Airways); African Studies Association; Alaska Airlines; Aluminum Siding Association; Amateur Softball Association; Amateur Swimming Association; American Scientific Affiliation; American Shorthorn Association; American Sightseeing Association; American Society for Abrasives; American Society for Aesthetics; American Society of Agronomy; American Society of Anesthesiologists; American Society of Appraisers; American Society of Auctioneers; American Sociological Association; American Sociometric Association; American Softball Association; American South African Line; American Soybean Association; American Standards Association; American Statistical Association; American Stockyards Association; American Studies Association; American Sunbathing Association; American Surgical Association; Anthroposophical Society of America; Army Seal of Approval; Army Security Agency; Assistant Secretary of the Army; Asso-

ciated Stenotypists of America; Association of Secretaries in Asia; Association of Southeast Asia; Atomic Security Agency; Australian Shareholders Association; Australian Sheepbreeders Association; Australian Society of Anaesthetists; Australian Society of Authors; Aviation Supply Annex
A of SA (ASA) Association of Southeast Asia
ASAA Amateur Softball Association of America; American Society for the Abandonment of Acronyms; Armenian Students Association of America; Asian Studies Association of Australia
ASAALH Association for the Study of Afro-American Life and History
ASAB Association for the Study of Animal Behavior
ASAC American Society for African Culture; American Society of Agricultural Consultants; Army Study Advisory Committee; Assistant Special Agent in Charge
ASAE American Society of Agricultural Engineers; American Society of Association Executives; American Society of Automotive Engineers
AS of AF Assistant Secretary of the Air Force
ASAH American Society of Association Historians
Asahi *Asahi Shimbun* (Japanese—Rising Sun Newspaper)
ASAIHL Association of Southeast Asian Institutions of Higher Learning
ASAIO American Society for Artificial Internal Organs
ASALA Armenian Secret Army for the Liberation of Armenia; Associate of the South African Library Association
asalm (ASALM) advanced strategic air-launched multimission missile
ASAM American Society for Abrasive Methods
ASAN Adriatica Società per Azioni di Navigazione
ASAnes American Society of Anesthesiologists
ASAO Association for Social Anthropology in Oceania
asap analog system assembly pack; as soon as possible
asap (ASAP) antisubmarine attack plotter

ASAP Aircraft Synthesis Analysis Program; Airlines of South Australia Pty; Airlines of South Australia Pty; Antenna-Scatterer Analysis Program; antisubmarine attack plotter; Australian Society of Animal Production
ASAPs Alcohol Safety Action Projects
ASAPS American Society for Aesthetic Plastic Surgery; Anti-Slavery and Aborigines Protection Society
asar (ASAR) advanced surface-to-air ramjet
ASARCO American Smelting and Refining Company
ASAS Advertising Standards Authority of Singapore; American Society of Abdominal Surgery; American Society of Animal Science; Army Security Agency School; Australian Staffing Assistance Scheme
ASATs antisatellite weapons
asatt advanced small-axial-turbine technology
ASAWS Advanced Surface-to-Air Weapon System
asb aircraft safety beacon; asbestos
asb (ASB) anxiety scale for the blind
as & b aloin, strychnine, and belladona (pills)
ASB Administration and Storage Building; Air Safety Beacon; Air Safety Board; Air Staff Board; Aircraft Safety Beacon; American Society of Bacteriologists; Associated Student Body; Australian Savings Bonds; Australian Shipping Board
A.S.B. Associate in Science in Business; Associate in Specialized Business
ASBA Australian Sheep Breeders Association
ASBAH Association for Spina Bifida and Hydrocephalus
asb c asbestos covered
ASBC American Society of Biological Chemists
ASBC *American Standard Building Code*
ASBCA Armed Services Board of Contract Appeals
ASBCO American Ship Building Company
ASBD Advanced Sea-Based Deterrent Program
ASBDA American School Band Directors Association
ASBE American Society of Ba-

kery Engineers

A.S.B.E. Associate in Science in Basic Engineering

asbestos actinolite (calcium magnesium silicate varying to calcium magnesium iron silicate)

asb & i aloin, strychnine, belladona, and ipecac

asbl assemble

ASBO Association of School Business Officials

ASBPA American Shore and Beach Preservation Association

ASBPE American Society of Business Press Editors

asc altered state of consciousness; arteriosclerosis; arteriosclerosistic; ascarid; ascaridian; ascend; ascender; ascending; ascension; ascent; ascertain; ascertainable; automatic sequence control, automatic switching center; auxiliary switch closed

as & c aerospace surveillance and control

Asc Ascidian

A.Sc. Associate in Science

ASC Adelaide Steamship Company; Aeronautical Systems Center; Air Service Command; Air Support Command; Air Support Control; Air Systems Command; Alabama State College; Alaska Steamship Company; Albany State College; All Souls College; American Samoa Commission; American Security Council; American Silk Council; American Society of Cinematographers; American Society of Criminology; American Society for Cybernetics; American Society of Cytology; Area/Site Characterizations; Arizona State College; Arkansas State College; Army Service Corps; Army Subsistence Center; Asian Socialist Conference; Associated Sandblasting Contractors; Associated Schools of Construction; Australian Schools Commission; Australian Shippers Council

A & SC Adhesive and Sealant Council

asca automatic science citation alerting; automatic subject citation alert

ASCA American School Counselor Association; American Senior Citizens Association; American Speech Correction

Association; Association for Science Cooperation in Asia; Association of State Correctional Administrators

ASCAA Automobile Seat Cover Association of America

ASCAC Antisubmarine Contact Analysis Center

ASC/AIA Association of Student Chapters/American School of Architects

ascap at-sea calibration procedure

ASCAP American Society of Composers, Authors, and Publishers

ASCAT Antisubmarine Contact Analysis Team

ASCATS Apollo Simulation Checkout and Training System

ASCB American Society of Cell Biology

ASCC Adams State College of Colorado; Air Standardization Coordinating Committee; American Society for the Control of Cancer; Army Strategic Communications Command; Association of Senior Citizens Clubs; Australian Society of Cosmetic Chemists

ASCD Association for Supervision and Curriculum Development

ASCE American Society of Civil Engineers

ASCEA American Society of Civil Engineers and Architects

ASCEF American Security Council Education Foundation

ASCEP Australian Society of Clinical and Experimental Pharmacologists

ASCET American Society of Certified Engineering Technicians

ASCHAL American Society of Corporate Historians, Archivists, and Librarians

ASCHE American Society of Chemical Engineers

ASCI American Society for Clinical Investigation

ASCIE American Standard Code for Information Exchange (computers and telecommunications)

ASCII American Standard Code for Information Interchange (pronounced *asky*)

ASCL Australia Straits Container Line

ASCLA Association of Special-

ized and Cooperative Library Agencies

ASCLD American Society of Crime Laboratory Directors

ASCLU American Society of Chartered Life Underwriters

ascm (ASCM) antiship capable missile

ASCM Association of Steel Conduit Manufacturers

ASCMA American Sprocket Chain Manufacturers Association

ASCN American Society of Clinical Nutrition

asco automatic sustainer cutoff

Asco Automatic Switch Company

ASCO American Society of Contemporary Ophthalmology

ASCom Army Service Command

ASCOPE ASEAN Council on Petroleum

ascore automatic shipboard checkout and readiness equipment

A Scot type-A Scottish influenza virus

ASCP American Society of Clinical Pathologists; American Society of Consulting Pharmacists; American Society of Consulting Planners

ASCPC American Society of Clinical Pharmacology and Chemotherapy

ASCPT American Society for Clinical Pharmacology and Therapeutics

ascr. *ascriptum* (Latin—ascribed to)

ASCRO Active Service Career for Reserve Officers

asc's (ASCs) altered states of consciousness

ASCs All Savers Certificates

ASCS Agricultural Stabilization and Conservation Service; American School of Classical Studies (Athens); Automatic Stabilization and Control System

ASCU Association of State Colleges and Universities

ascvd arteriosclerotic cardiovascular disease; atherosclerotic cardiovascular disease

A Sc W Association of Scientific Workers

asd aldosterone secretion defect; atrial septal defect

ASD Aeronautical Systems Division; Army Shipping Document; Artillery Spotting Division; Assistant Secretary of Defense; Association of Steel Distributors; Aviation Supply Depot

ASD (PA & E) Assistant Secretary of Defense (Program Analysis and Evaluation)

ASD Association Suisse de Documentation (Swiss Association of Documentation)

ASDA American Safe Deposit Association; American Seafood Distributors Association; American Stamp Dealers Association; Asbestos and Danville (railroad); Association of Structural Draftsmen of America; Atomic and Space Development Authority; Australasian Stamp Dealers Association

ASDAE Association of Seventh-Day Adventists Educators

ASD–ALA Adult Services Division—American Library Association

AsDB Asian Development Bank

ASDC Aeronomy and Space Data Center (NOAA); Automobile Safe Driving Center

asde aircraft surface detection equipment

a/s de aux soins de (French—in care of)

asder airfield surface-detection radar

ASDF Air Self-Defense Force (Japanese Air Force)

ASDG Aircraft Storage and Disposition Group

asdi automatic selective dissemination of information

ASDIC Anti-Submarine Detection Investigation Committee (British sonar, named for this wartime committee); Armed Services Documents Intelligence Center

ASDIRS Army Study Documentation and Information Retrieval System

ASDM Apollo-Soyuz Docking Module

asdng ascending (flow chart)

asdr airport surface-detection radar

ASDR American Society of Dental Radiographers

ASDS American Society of Dental Surgeons

A/S D/S Akties Dampskibsselskab (Danish—steamship company, limited)

ASDT Australian Society of Dairy Technology

ASD(T) Assistant Secretary of Defense (Telecommunications)

ase airborne search equipment

ASE Amalgamated Society of Engineers; American Society of Enologists; American Steel Equipment; American Stock Exchange; Association of Science Education; Australian Society of Engineers; Australian Stock Exchange(s)

AS & E American Science and Engineering

ASEA Allmänna Svenska Elektriska Aktiebolaget; American Society of Engineers and Architects; Association of South-East Asia

ASEAN Association of Southeast Asian Nations (Indonesia, Malaysia, the Philippines, Singapore, Thailand)

ASEANTA ASEAN Travel Association

ASEB Aeronautics and Space Engineering Board; Assam State Electricity Board

ASEC All Saints' Episcopal College; American Standard Elevator Code

ASECA Association for Education and Cultural Advancement (South Africa)

ASECS American Society for Eighteenth-Century Studies

ASED Aviation and Surface Effects Department

ASEE American Society for Ecological Education; American Society of Electrical Engineers; American Society for Engineering Education; American Society for Environmental Education

ASEET Associate in Science in Electronic Engineering Technology

ASEI American Sports Education Institute

ASEM Anti-Ship Euro-Missile

ASEP American Society for Experimental Pathology; ASEAN Environment Program(s)

aseptics aseptically packaged liquids

ASESA Armed Services Electro-Standards Agency

ASESB Armed Services Explosive Safety Board

ASESS Aerospace Environment Simulation System

aset aeronautical satellite earth terminal

ASET Assistant Secretary for Energy Technology; Author

System for Education and Training

ASETC Armed Services Electron Tube Committee

asew airborne and surface early warning

ASEWS Airborne and Surface Early Warning System

asf additional selection factor; amperes per square foot

a-s-f aniline-formaldehyde-sulfur

AsF America's Future

ASF Advisory Support Force; Aircraft Services Facility; Alaskan Sea Frontier; American Scandinavian Foundation; American Schizophrenia Foundation; Ammunition Storage Facility; Army Service Forces; Army Stock Fund; Association of State Foresters; Australian Soccer Federation; Australian Speleological Federation; Automotive Safety Foundation

ASFA American Steel Foundrymen's Association; Association of Superannuation Funds of Australia

ASFC All Sports Federation of China; Atlantic Salt Fish Commission (Canada)

ASFCO American Soda Fountain Company

asfe accelerometer scale factor error

ASFE American Society For Aesthetics; Association of Specialized Film Exhibitors

ASFEC Arab States Fundamental Education Center

ASFFHF Association of Science Fiction, Fantasy, and Horror Films

ASFH Albert Schweitzer Friendship House

asfip accelerometer scale factor input panel

asfir active swept-frequency interferometer radar

ASFIS Aquatic Science and Fisheries Information Service (FAO)

ASFM American Sexual Freedom Movement

ASFMRA American Society of Farm Managers and Rural Appraisers

ASFP Association of Specialized Film Producers

ASFS Australia-Soviet Friendship Society

ASFSA American School Food Service Association

asfts airborne systems function-

al test stand
asfx assembly fixture
asg assignment
ASG Aeronautical Standards Group (Air Force and Navy); American Saint Gobain (glass); American Society of Genetics
ASGA Advertising Specialty Guild of America
ASGB Aeronautical Society of Great Britain
ASGBI Association of Surgeons of Great Britain and Ireland
asgd assigned
ASGE American Society of Gastrointestinal Endoscopy
asgmt assignment
asgn assign; assignment
ASGp Aeronautical Standards Group (USAF)
ASGP Australian Society of General Practitioners
ASGS American Scientific Glassblowers Society
ash. airship; armature shunt
ash. (ASH) aerial scout helicopter
Ash Ashbel; Ashburton; Ashbury; Ashdown; Asher; Asheto; Ashley; Ashman; Ashton; Ashur; Ashville; Ashvillian; NATO nickname for Soviet infrared and radar-homing missile
Ash *Asahi Shimbun* (leading Japanese newspaper)
AsH hyperopic astigmatism
ASH Action on Smoking and Health; American Society of Hematology; Ashland Oil and Refining (stock exchange symbol); Australian Society of Herpetologists; Australian Stationary Hospital
A–S–H Allen-Sherman-Hoff
A & SH Argyll and Southerland Highlanders
ASHA American School Health Association; American Social Health Association; American Social Hygiene Association; American Speech and Hearing Association
ASHACE American Society of Heating and Air-Conditioning Engineers
ASHBM Associate Scottish Hospital Bureau of Management
ASHC All-States Hobby Club
Ashcan Artist John Sloan
Ashcan School *see* Eight
ashd arteriosclerotic heart disease
ASHE American Society of

Hospital Engineers; Association for the Study of Higher Education
Ashenden W. Somerset Maugham
Ashfo'd Ashford remand prison center in the London area
ASHG American Society of Human Genetics
ASHH American Society for the Hard of Hearing
ASHI Association for the Study of Human Infertility
Ashken *Ashkenazim* (Hebrew—Jews of central and northern Europe)
Ashland Henry Clay's home in Lexington, Kentucky
Ashland Youth Federal Youth Center (for delinquents) at Ashland, Kentucky
Ash Mus Ashmolean Museum
ashp airship
ASHP American Society of Hospital Pharmacists
ASHRAE American Society of Heating, Refrigerating, and Air-Conditioning Engineers
ASHS Advanced Study of Human Sexuality; American Society for Horticultural Science
ASHU Airline Stewards and Hostesses Union (New Zealand)
asi airspeed indicator; azimuthal speed indicator
ASI Advanced Scientific Instruments; Aero-Space Institute; Aerospace Studies Institute; Africa Service Institute; Air Society International; Amended Shipping Instruction(s); American Society of Indexers; American Specifications Institute; American Statistics Index; American Statistics Institute; American Swedish Institute; Asian Statistical Institute (Japan); Audience Studies, Incorporated; Australian Shipbuilding Industries; Aviation Simulations International
ASIA Airlines Staff International Association; Army Signal Intelligence Agency; Australian Scientific Industry Association; Australian Stevedoring Industry Authority
ASIAC Aerospace Structures Information and Analysis Center; Asian International Acceptances and Capital
ASIAL Australian Security Industry Association Ltd
Asian Subcontinent Bangladesh,

Bhutan, India, Nepal, Sikkim, and Sri Lanka; Indian Peninsula
Asia's big five elephant, leopard, rhinoceros, tiger, water buffalo
Asia's Largest Country the USSR
ASIC Air Service Information Circular; Australian Standard Industry Classification
ASID American Society of Interior Designers; Australian Society of Implant Dentistry
ASIDIC Association of Scientific Information Dissemination Centers
ASIF Airlift Service Industrial Fund
ASI & H American Society of Ichthyologists and Herpetologists
ASII American Science Information Institute
ASIL American Society of International Law
ASIM American Society of Insurance Management; American Society of Internal Medicine
ASIMET *Asociación de Industrias Metalurgicas* (Spanish—Association of Metallurgical Industries)—Chile
a sin *a sinistra* [Italian—at (to) the left]
ASI/NATO Advanced Study Institute/NATO
ASIO Australian Security Intelligence Organisation
ASIP Army Stationing and Installation Plan
ASIRC Aquatic Sciences Information Retrieval Center (U of RI)
asis anterior superior iliac spine
ASIs American Society of Indexers
ASIS Abort-Sensing Implementation System; American Society of Industrial Security; American Society for Information Science; American Society for Information Science; ammunition stores issue ship (naval designator); Association of Small Island States; Australian Security Intelligence Service
asist advanced scientific instruments symbolic translator
ASIST Alzheimer Support, Information, and Service Team
ASIWPCA Association of State and Interstate Water Pollution

Control Administrators

ASJ Asiatic Society of Japan

ASJA American Society of Journalists and Authors

ASJJA Association of State Juvenile Justice Administrators

ASJSA American Society of Journalism School Administrators

ask. amplitude shift keying

Ask American standard keyboard (typewriter)

ASK Associated Students of Kansas; Association for Social Knowledge

ASKA Automatic System for Kinematic Analysis

askg asking

Askham G Askham Grange (female offender's prison in Yorkshire, England)

ASKS Automatic Station-Keeping System

ASKT American Society of Knitting Technologists

asky *see* ASCII

asl abandon ship ladder; above sea level

Asl American sign language

ASL American Association of State Libraries; American Scantic Line; American Shuffleboard Leagues; Anti-Saloon League; Australian Society for Limnology

A-SL Abelard-Schuman Limited

ASLA American Savings and Loan Association; American Society of Landscape Architects; Arizona State Library Association; Australian School Library Association

ASLAB Atomic Safety and Licensing Appeal Board

ASLB Atomic Safety and Licensing Board (AEC)

AS & LB American Savings and Loan Bank

ASLBP Atomic Safety and Licensing Board Panel (NRC)

ASLE American Society of Lubrication Engineers

ASLEC Association of Street Lighting Erection Contractors

ASLEF Associated Society of Locomotive Engineers and Firemen

ASLEP Apollo Surface Lunar Experiments Package

ASLH American Society for Legal History

ASLHA American Speech-Language-Hearing Association

ASLIB Association of Special Libraries and Information Bureaus

reaus

ASLIS Association of Special Libraries and Information Services

ASLNY Art Students League of New York

aslo assembly layout

ASLO American Society of Limnology and Oceanography; Australian Scientific Liaison Office (London)

ASLP Association of Special Libraries in the Philippines

ASLR American Short Line Railroads

ASLRA American Short Line Railroad Association

aslt advanced solid logic technology; assault(ing)

aslv *assurance sur la vie* (French —life insurance)

ASLW Amalgamated Society of Leather Workers

asm air-to-surface missile; assembly

AsM myopic astigmatism

ASM Air-to-Surface Missile; American Society of Mammalogists; American Society for Metals; American Society for Microbiology; Antarctic Service Medal

ASMA Aerospace Medical Association; American Society of Music Arrangers; American Student Media Association

ASMAR *Astilleros Maritimos* (Spanish—Maritime Shipyards)—Chile

asmbl assemble (flow chart)

asmblr assembler

ASMC Army Supply and Maintenance Command (formerly Quartermaster Corps)

asmd (ASMD) anti-ship missile defense

asmd/ew antiship-missile defense/electronic warfare

ASME American Society of Magazine Editors; American Society of Mechanical Engineers; Association for the Study of Medical Education; Australian Society for Music Education

As Mem Associate Member

ASMFC Atlantic States Marine Fisheries Commission

ASMFS American Society of Maxillo-Facial Surgeons

ASMH Association for Social and Moral Hygiene

asmi airfield surface movement indication

ASMM American Supply and Machinery Manufacturers

ASMP American Society of Magazine Photographers

ASMPA Armed Services Medical Procurement Agency

ASMPE American Society of Motion Picture Engineers

asmr (ASMR) advanced short-to-median-range (twin-engine aircraft)

ASMR Australian Society for Medical Research

ASMRO Armed Services Medical Regulating Office

ASMS Advanced Surface Missile System

asmt assortment

ASMT American Society of Medical Technologists

Asmus Rasmus nickname of the Rasmus Meyer Museum in Bergen, Norway and of JT Miller

asn average sample number

asn (ASN) asparagine (amino acid)

Asn Association

As of N Assistant Secretary of the Navy

ASN Allotment Serial Number; American Society of Naturalists; Army Serial Number; Army Service Number; Asiatic Steam Navigation; Assistant Secretary of the Navy

ASN (R & D) Assistant Secretary of the Navy (Research and Development)

ASNA Advertising Specialty National Association

asnap automatic-steerable null-antenna processor

ASNC Atlantic Steam Navigation Company

ASNDE Associate of the Society of Non-Destructive Examination

ASNE American Society of Naval Engineers; American Society of Newspaper Editors; Assistant Secretary for Nuclear Energy (DoE)

ASNLH Association for the Study of Negro Life and History

As & Ns Andamans and Nicobars (Andaman and Nicobar Islands)

ASNSW Anthropological Society of New South Wales; Art Society of New South Wales; Astronomical Society of New South Wales

ASNT American Society for Nondestructive Testing

aso arteriosclerosis obliterans; auxiliary switch open

ASO Aeronautica Supply Office(r); Air Signal Officer; Air Staff Officer; Air Staff Orientation; Air Surveillance Officer; Akron Symphony Orchestra; Albany Symphony Orchestra; Albuquerque Symphony Orchestra; American School of Orthodontists; American Sokol Organization; American Symphony Orchestra; Area Supply Office(r); Assistant Secretary's Office; Athens Symphony Orchestra; Atlanta Symphony Orchestra; Australian Security Organisation; Australian Society of Orthodontists; Aviation Supply Office(r)

ASOA Australian Shipping Officers Association

ASOC Air Support Operations Center

ASOK Ängfartygas Svenska Ostasiatiska Kompaniet (Swedish East Asiatic Steamship Line)

ASOL American Symphony Orchestra League

ASOP Atomic Standing Operating Procedures

ASOPA Australian School of Pacific Administration

ASOR American Schools of Oriental Research

ASOS American Society of Oral Surgeons

aso titer antistreptolysin titer

asp (ASP) aspartic acid

asp. affirmative self protection; ammunition supply point; aspartic acid; aspen; automatic servo plotter; automatic switching panel; automatic system procedure

a s p accepté sous protêt (French—accepted under protest)

Asp American selling price

ASP Amalgamated Society of Printers; American Schutzhund Products; American Society of Parasitologists; American Society of Pharmacognosy; American Society of Photogrammetry; Ammunition Supply Point; Antisubmarine Patrol; Archival Security Program; Arizona State Prison; Assistant Superintendent of Police; Association of Seattle Prostitutes; Astronomical Society of the Pacific; atmosphere-sounding projectile; Atomic Strike Plan; Australian Socialist Party; Australian Society for Parasitology; Austra-

lian Society of Prosthodontists; Automatic Schedule Procedure

A-S P Anglo-Saxon Protestant

A/S/P Aleksander Sergeevich Pushkin—apostle of freedom and father of Russian literature

A.S.P. accepté sans protêt (French—accepted without protest)

ASPA Alloy Steel Producers Association; American Society for Personnel Administrators; American Society for Public Administration; Australian Sugar Producers Association

ASPAC Asia and South Pacific Area Council; Asian and Pacific Council

A-span anticipation span (eye-voice span); capital-A-shaped span

ASPAP Australian South Pacific Aid Programme

Asparagus Capital Isleton, California

ASPB Armed Services Petroleum Board

aspc accepté sous protêt pour acompte (French—accepted under protest for account)

ASPC American Sheep Producers Council

ASPCA American Society for the Prevention of Cruelty to Animals

ASPCC American Society for the Prevention of Cruelty to Children

ASPD American Society of Professional Draftsmen

aspect. acoustic short-pulse echo-classification techniques

ASPER Assembly System for Peripheral Processors; Assistant Secretary (of Labor) for Police Evaluation and Research

ASPERS Armed Services Procurement Regulations

ASPET American Society for Pharmacology and Experimental Therapeutics

ASPF Association of Specialized Film Producers; Association of Superannuation and Pension Funds

ASPFA Association of Superannuation and Provident Funds of Australia

asph asphalt; asphaltic

ASPH Australian Society of Professional Hypnotherapists

asphalt solid bitumen pitch

Asphaltic Lake the Dead Sea's

sobriquet

asphaltum mineral pitch

asphic asphaltic

asph mac asphalt macadam

asphy asphyxia

ASPI American Society for Performance Improvement

ASPIRE Associated Students Promoting Individual Rights for Everyone

aspirin acetylsalicylic acid

ASPIRIN Automatic System for Passenger Reservation by Notation

ASPL Associated Steamships Proprietary Limited

ASPM American Society of Paramedics

ASPM Armed Services Procurement Manual

aspn asparagine

ASPO American Society of Planning Officials; Avionics System Project Officer

aspp alloy-steel protective plating

ASPP American Society for the Perfection of Punctuation; American Society of Picture Professionals; American Society of Plant Physiologists; American Society of Polar Philatelists; Australian Society of Plant Physiologists

ASPPA Armed Service Petroleum Purchasing Agency

ASPPO Armed Services Procurement Planning Office

ASPQ Association Suisse pour la Promotion de la Qualité (Swiss Association for Quality Improvement)

ASPR American Society of Psychical Research; Armed Services Procurement Regulations; Association of South Polar Research

ASPRL Armament Systems Personnel Research Laboratory (USAF)

aspro ass prostitute (male homosexual)

ASPRS American Society of Plastic and Reconstructive Surgery

ASPs Anglo-Saxon Protestants; Assistant Superintendents of Police

ASPS Acoustic Ship-Positioning System

ASPSPOM American Society for the Preservation of Sacred, Patriotic, and Operatic Music

ASPT American Society of Plant Taxonomists

ASPTC Army Support Center

ASQ Anthropological Society of Queensland; Anxiety-Scale Questionnaire

ASQ Administrative Science Quarterly

ASQC American Society for Quality Control

ASQDE American Society of Questioned Document Examiners

asr airport surveillance radar; air-sea rescue; answer and receive; automatic send-receive; available supply rate

ASR American Society of Rocketry; American Sugar Company (stock exchange symbol); Association of Southeastern Railroads; Aviation Safety Regulation(s); submarine rescue vessel (naval symbol)

asra athwartships reference axis

asradi adaptive surface-signal recognition-and-direction indicator

ASRAPS Acoustic Sonar Range Prediction System

ASRB Australian Sales Research Bureau

asrc (ASRC) air-sea rescue craft

ASRC Air-Sea Rescue Craft; Alabama Space and Rocket Center; Atmospheric Sciences Research Center

asrd aircraft shipment readiness date

ASRE Admiralty Signal and Radar Establishment (UK); American Society of Refrigeration Engineers

ASRI Aluminum Smelters Research Institute

ASRL Aero-elastic and Structures Research Laboratory (M.I.T.)

ASRM American Society of Range Movement

asro (ASRO) astronomical roentgen observatory (satellite)

asroc (ASROC) antisubmarine rocket

ASRP American Society for the Republic of Panama

ASRPP American Society for Research in Psychosomatic Problems

a-s rs air-sea rescue service

ASRT Air Support Radar Team; American Society of Radiologic Technologists

asrv angle-stop radiator valve

ASRY Arab Shipbuilding and Repair Yard (Bahrain)

ass. anterior superior spine; as-

surance

Ass Assyrian

ASS Accordion Symphony Society; Anglo-Swedish Society; Army Special Staff; Associated Scholastic Society; Associated Sociologists Society; Australian Security Service

A-SS Anti-Slavery Society

A.S.S. Associate in Secretarial Science; Associate in Secretarial Studies

ASSA American Society for the Study of Allergy; Army Signal Supply Agency; Astronomical Society of South Australia; Australian Society of Security Analysts

ASSArthr American Society for the Study of Arthritis

ASSASSIN Agricultural System for Storage and Subsequent Selection of Information

assassrep assassination report

A-S Scale Anti-Semitism Scale (measuring negative attitudes toward persons of Judaic origin)

assce assurance

ASSCO American Steam Ship Company

Ass Com Gen Assistant Commissary General

assd assigned

ASSE American Society of Safety Engineers; American Society of Sanitary Engineers

assem assemble

Assemblyman from the Bowery Al Smith (Alfred E. Smith)

Assem God Assemblies of God

Assen Drenthe's provincial capital in the Netherlands

assess. analytical studies of surface effects of submerged submarines

ASSESS Airborne Science-Spacelab Experiments-Simulation System

ASSET Aerothermodynamic Elastic Structural System Environmental Tests

ASSGB Association of Ski Schools in Great Britain

ASSH American Society for Surgery of the Hand

ASSIFONTE Association de l'Industrie de la Fonte de Fromage (French—Association of the Processed Cheese Industry)

assigt assignment

assim assimilated

assist. assistant

assmt assessment

Assn Association

Assn Brain Injured New York Association for Brain Injured Children

Assn Brit Zool Association of British Zoologists

assnce assurance

Assn Clin Biochem Association of Clinical Biochemists

Assn Consumer Res Association for Consumer Research

assnd assigned

Assn Ed Comm Tech Association for Educational Communications and Technology

Assn Pr Association Press

Assn Sch Busn Association of School Business Officials of the United States and Canada

Assn Study Anim Behav Association for the Study of Animal Behaviour

Assn Supervision Association for Supervision and Curriculum Development

Assn Tchr Ed Association of Teacher Educators

Assn Under Man Association for the Understanding of Man

ASSOBANCA Associazione Bancaria Italiana (Italian Bankers' Association)

assoc associate; associated; association

Assoc Associate; Associated; Association

Assoc Bk Associated Booksellers

Assoc Coun Arts Associated Councils of the Arts

Assoc Eng Associate in Engineering

ASSOCHAM Associated Chambers of Commerce

Associated States Caribbean island states (Antigua-St Kitts-Nevis, Dominica, Grenada, St Lucia, St Vincent

Assoc IEE Associate of the Institution of Electrical (Electronic) Engineers

Assoc I Min E Associate of the Institute of Mining Engineers

Assoc INA Associate of the Institute of Naval Architects

Assoc ISI Associate of the Iron and Steel Institute

Assoc Met Associate of Metallurgy

Assoc Pr Associated Press

Assoc Sci Associate in Science

assoc w associated with

asson assonance

ASSP All Saints Sisters of the Poor

ASSPHR Anti-Slavery Society

for the Protection of Human Rights

ASSR American Society for the Study of Religion; Armenian Soviet Socialist Republic; Autonomous Soviet Socialist Republic; Azerbaijan Soviet Socialist Republic

ASSS American Society for the Study of Sterility; Australian Society of Soil Science

asst assist; assistance; assistant

ASST American Society for Steel Treating

ASST *Aziendo de Stato per i Servizi Telefonici* (Italian—State Telephone Service)

Asst Chf Engr Assistant Chief Engineer

asstd assented; assorted

Asst Engr Assistant Engineer

Asst Pur Assistant Purser

Asst Stwd Assistant Steward

assu (ASSU) air support signal unit

ASSU American Sunday School Union

As Suways (Arabic—Suez)

assw antistrategic submarine warfare

assy assembly

Assyr Assyria(n)

Assyr-Babyl Assyro-Babylonian

Assyrian Century the 7th century before the Christian era when Assyria ruled the Middle East and conquered Egypt—the 600s

ast absolute space-time

ast (AST) advanced supersonic transport; average spring tides

Ast astigmatism; Astoria(n); Asturian; Asturias

AST Academic Salaries Tribunal; Aerial Survey Team; Air Service Training; Air Surveillance Technician; Alaska State Troopers; Alaskan Standard Time; American Radiator and Standard Sanitary (stock exchange symbol); Army Satellite Tracking; Army Specialized Training; Arts Society of Tasmania; Association for Student Training; Astronomical Society of Tasmania; Atlantic Standard Time

ASTA Aerial Surveillance and Target Acquisition; American Seed Trade Association; American Society of Travel Agents; American String Teachers Association; Army Strategy and Tactics Analysis; Australian Science Teachers Association

ASTA *Allgemeiner Studentenausschuss* (German—General Students Committee)

ASTAC Australian Shipping, Trading, and Chartering

ASTANO *Astilleros y Talleres del Noroeste* (Spanish—Dockyards and Workshops of the Northwest)

ASTAP Advanced Statistical Analysis Program

ASTAS Antiradar Surveillance and Target Acquisition System

astc (ASTC) airport surface traffic control

ASTC Appalachian State Teachers College; Arkansas State Teachers College; Aroostook State Teachers College

A.S.T.C. Associate of the Sydney Technical College

ASTD American Society of Teachers of Dancing; American Society for Training and Development; American Society of Training Directors

ASTE American Society of Tool Engineers

astec advanced solar turboelectric concept; advanced solar turboelectric conversion

ASTEC Antisubmarine Technical Evaluation Center; Australian Science and Technology Council

ASTECNAVAIR Assistant Secretary of the Navy for Air

a sten aortic stenosis

ASTEO *Association Scientifique et Technique pour l'Exploration des Océans* (French Scientific and Technical Association for the Exploration of the Oceans)

ASTF Acropropulsion System Test Facility; Aerospace Structures Test Facility

asth asthenopia

asti antispasticity index

asti (ASTI) antisubmarine training indicator

ASTI American School of Technical Intelligence

ASTI Applied Science and Technology Index

ASTIA Armed Services Technical Information Agency

astig astigmatic; astigmatism; astigmatizer; astigmatoscope; astigmatoscopy; astigmia; astigmometer; astigmoscope; etc.

'astinator procrastinator

ASTIP Army Scientific and Technical Information Program

ASTM American Society for Testing and Materials; American Society of Tropical Medicine

ASTME American Society of Tool and Manufacturing Engineers

ASTMH American Society of Tropical Medicine and Hygiene

ASTMS Association of Scientific, Technical, and Managerial Staffs

asto antistreptolysin

as tol as tolerated (by the patient)

astor (ASTOR) antisubmarine torpedo

ASTP Apollo-Soyuz Test Project; Army Specialized Training Program

astr astronomy

ASTR American Society of Therapeutic Radiologists

astra advanced structure analyzer; advanced system for radiological assessment; automatic scheduling with time-integrated resource allocation

ASTRAC Arizona Statistical Repetitive Analog Computer

astrakhan astrakhan cloth or astrakhan wool of the type originally clipped from sheep native to Astrakhan on the Caspian in the delta of the Volga

ASTREA Air Support to Regional Enforcement Agencies (helicopter surveillance)

astrion astrionic(al)(ly); astrionics

astro astrograph(ic); astrolabe; astrology; astrometry; astronautics; astronomer; astronomical; astronomy; astrophysics

Astro Astronautics

ASTRO Air-Space Travel Research Organization

astro-ad-anon astrological adventures anonymous

astrobio astrobiological; astrobiologist; astrobiology

astrochem astrochemical(ly); astrochemist(ry)

astrochronies astrochronological relatives

astrodyn astrodynamic(al)(ly); astrodynamic(ist)

astrog astrogeological; astrogeologist; astrogeology

astrogen astrogenealogy

astrol astrology

Astrol Astrology

astromonk astronautical monkey (specimen used in biological tests)

astron astronomy

Astron Astronomy

Astron *Astrophys* *Astronomy and Astrophysics*

Astron J *Astronomical Journal*

Astron *Nachr* *Astronomische Nachrichten* (German—Astronomical News)

Astron *Zh* *Astronomicheskii Zhurnal* (Russian—Astronomical Journal)

Astro Obsv Astrophysical Observatory

astrophys astrophysics

Astrophys J *Astrophysical Journal*

Astrophys *Lett* *Astrophysical Letters*

ASTS Alabama State Training School (for female delinquents at East Lake near Birmingham)

ASTSECNAV Assistant Secretary of the Navy

astt (ASTT) action-speed tactical trainer

ast t astronomical time

ASTT American Society of Traffic and Transportation

A.S.T.T. Associate in Science Teacher Training

asu all screwed up

asu (ASU) administrative systems unit; aeromedical staging unit

ASU American Secular Union; American Student Union; Arab Socialist Union; Arizona State University; Asunción, Paraguay (airport); Atheist Student Union; Australian Swimming Union

ASU-57 Soviet self-propelled 57mm gun on tracked chassis

ASUA Amateur Swimming Union of the Americas

ASUC American Society of University Composers; Associated Students of the University of California

ASU Lat Am St Arizona State University Center for Latin American Studies

asupt advanced simulator for undergraduate pilot training

ASUSSR Acadamy of Sciences of the USSR

ASUTS American Society of Ultrasound Technical Specialists

ASUUS Amateur Skating Union of the U.S.

asv acceleration switching valve; airborne radar for detecting surface vessels; aircraft-to-surface vessel; angle stop valve

asv (ASV) automatic self-verification

a-s v anti-snake venom; arterio-superficial venous

a/sv arterio/superficial venous

ASV American Standard Version; Anthropological Society of Victoria; Astronomical Society of Victoria

ASVA Associate of the Society of Valuers and Auctioneers

ASVAB Armed Services Vocational Aptitude Battery

asveo advance space vehicle engineering operation

ASVT Applications Systems Verification Test

ASVU Army Security Vetting Unit

asw antisubmarine warfare

ASW Anti-Submarine Warfare; Association of Scientific Writers; Association of Social Workers; Australian Standard White (wheat)

ASW (LR) Antisubmarine Warning (long-range)

ASW (SR) Antisubmarine Warning (short-range)

AS & W American Steel and Wire (gage)

ASWA Anthropological Society of Western Australia

A/S WA Aviation/Space Writers Association

asw/aaw antisubmarine warfare/ anti-air warfare

ASWC Antisubmarine Warfare Center (NATO)

ASWE Admiralty Surface Weapons Establishment

ASWEPS Anti-Submarine Warfare Environmental Prediction System

aswf arithmetic-series weight function(s)

ASWG American Standard Wire Gage; American Steel and Wire Gage

ASWI Antisubmarine Warfare Installations (NATO)

ASWIPT Antisubmarine Warfare In-Port Training (NATO)

ASWRC Antisubmarine Warfare Research Center (NATO)

ASWS Audubon Shrine and Wildlife Sanctuary

ASWSS Antisubmarine Warfare Schoolship (USN)

ASWTDS Antisubmarine Warfare Tactical Data System

asy asylum

Asylum for Talent Jacques Copeau's *Theatre du Vieux Colombier*

asym asymmetrical

async asynchronous

ASZ American Society of Zoologists

ASZD American Society for Zero Defects

at. accounting tabulating (card); airtight; asphalt; asphaltic; asphalt tile; atmosphere (technical); atomic

at. (AT) alternative technology; appropriate technology

at.% atomic percent

a/t action/time; antitank; antitorpedo

a & t acceptance and transfer; assemble and test

At ampere-turn; astatine

AT Adirondack Trail; Advanced Trainer; Air Travel; antitank; Appalachian Trail; Atherton Tablelands (Queensland parks)

A/T American terms

A T *Antico Testamento* (Italian —Old Testament)

A-T *'Alef-Tav* (Hebrew—from the first to the last letter of the alphabet)—similar to the English expression from A to Z

AT$_1$9 dihydrotachysterol

AT$_7$ hexachlorophene (disinfectant)

AT-26 Aermacchi jet-trainer ground-attack aircraft also known as Xavante

ata academic travel abroad; actual time of arrival; air-to-air; azimuthal torque amplifier

ATA Advertising Typographers Association; Air Transport Association; Amateur Trapshooting Association; American Taxicab Association; American Taxpayers Association; American Teachers Association; American Theatre Association; American Thyroid Association; American Title Association; American Topical Association; American Transit Association; American Translators Association; American Tree Association; American Trucking Association; American Tunaboat Association; Applied Technology Associates; Area Transportation Authority; Army Transportation Association; Asia Teachers Association; Atlantic Treaty Association; Australian Taxpayers Association; Australian Toolmakers Association; Australian Translators Association; auxiliary ocean tug (naval symbol)

A.T.A. Associate Technical Aide

ATA Agence Telegraphique Albanaise (French—Albanian News Service)

ATAA Advertising Typographers Association of America; Air Transport Association of America; Amateur Trapshooting Association of America

ATAC Air Transport Association of Canada; Allied Tactical Air Force; Army Tank Automotive Center; Army Tank and Automotive Command

Atacama 600-mile-long 2000-foot-high Chilean desert devoid of vegetation but rich in copper and nitrate deposits

atacamite basic copper chloride

ATACS Army Tactical Communications System

atad absent on temporary additional duty

ATAD Air Transport and Delivery (service)

ATAE Association of Tutors in Adult Education

ATAF Allied Tactical Air Force

ATAFCS Airborne Target-Acquisition and Fire-Control System

ATAG Air Training Advisory Group

ATAI Air Transport Association International

ATAJ Association of Transport Advisers of Japan

ATALA Association pour l'Etude et de la Linguistique Appliquée (Association for the Study of Applied Linguistics)

ATAM Association for Teaching Aids in Mathematics

atan arc tangent

atar above transmitted and received

atar (ATAR) antitank aircraft rocket

ATAR Automated Travel Agents Reservation

ATARS Anti-Terrain-Avoidance Radar System

ATAs American Tinnitus Association members

ATAS Academy of Television Arts and Sciences; Air Transport Auxiliary Service

at.(AT) appropriate technology

Ataturk (Turkish—Chief Turk) —sobriquet of General-Presi-

dent Mustafa Kemal—first president of Turkey

atav atavism; atavist; atavistic(al) (ly)

atb asphalt tile base; at the time of bombing

ATB Air Transportation Board

A & TBCB Architectural and Transportation Barriers Compliance Board

ATBI Allied Trades of the Banking Industry

atbm average time between maintenance

atbm (ATBM) advanced technology ballistic missile; antitactical ballistic missile

atbt acoustic telemetry bathythermometer

atbyropt at buyer's option

atc ablative thrust chamber; acoustic test(ing) chamber; acoustical tile ceiling; aerial tuning condenser; allergic to combat; approved type certificate; automatic temperature control; automatic tint control(tv)

atc (ATC) automatic train control; average variable cost

atc Amsterdam Towing Company's italicized logotype abbreviation

ATC Advertising Training Center; Air Traffic Conference; Air Traffic Control; Air Training Command, Air Transport Command; Air Transportation Corps; Aircraft Technical Committee; Airport Traffic Control; Airway Traffic Control; Alcohol Treatment Center; Alpine Tourist Commission; Appalachian Trail Conference; Armament Test Center; Army Training Center; Army Transportation Corps; Associated Traffic Clubs; Associated Travel Clubs; Athletic Training Council; Australian Tariff Council; Australian Tourist Commission

atca (ATCA) advanced tanker-cargo aircraft

ATCA Air Traffic Conference of America; Air Traffic Control Association; American Theater Critics Association

ATCAS Air-Traffic-Control Automated System

atcase aspartate transcarbamylase

ATCB Air Traffic Control Board

ATCC Air Traffic Control Center; American Type Culture

Collections; Automatic Train Control Center

ATCDE Association of Teachers in Colleges and Departments of Education

atce ablative thrust chamber engine

atceu air traffic control evaluation unit

ATCF Automobile and Touring Club of Finland

atch attach; attaching; attachment

atchd attached

ATCL Associate of Trinity College of Music—London

ATCMD Atlanta Contract Management District

ATCMS Advanced Technology Cruise Missile Study

ATCMU Associated Third-Class Mail Users

ATCO Air Traffic Coordinating Office(r)

ATCOM Atoll Commander

ATCOS Atmospheric Composition Satellite

ATCRBS Air Traffic Control Radar Beacon System

atc's airtight containers; any-terrain motorcycles

ATCU Association of Texas Colleges and Universities

atd absent (on) temporary duty; actual time of departure; anthropomorphic test dummy

atd a tak dale (Czech—et cetera)

ATD Actual Time of Departure; Aid to the Totally Disabled; Armament Test Division; Art Teachers Diploma

atda augmented target docking adapter

ATDA American Train Dispatchers Association; Army Training Device Agency; Australian Telecommunications Development Association

atdc after top dead center (valve setting)

atdp attitudes toward disabled persons

ATDS Airborne Tactical Data System; Association of Teachers of Domestic Science; Automated Data and Telecommunications Service

ate altitude transmitting equipment; automatic test equipment

Ate Almirante (Spanish—admiral)

ATE Associated Telephone Exchanges; Association of Teacher Educators; Automatic Telephone and Electric (New Zealand company)

ATEA American Technical Education Association; American Toy Export Association; Australian Telecommunications Employees Association

ATEC Air Transport Electronics Council; Aviation Technician Education Council

A.Tech. Associate in Technology

ATEM Aircraft Test Equipment Modification

ATEMIS Automated Traffic Engineering and Management Information System

A *temp* *a tempo* (Italian—in the speed written)

Aten Atenas (Portuguese or Spanish—Athens); *Atene* (Italian—Athens); *Athenes* (French—Athens)

ATEN Association Technique pour la production et l'utilisation de l'Energie Nucleaire (Technical Association for the Production and Use of Nuclear Energy)

Atenas (Spanish—Athens)

Atene (Italian—Athens)

At Energ Atomnaya Energiya (Russian—Atomic Energy)—journal

ATEP Aboriginal Teacher Education Programme

ATerm Air Terminal

ATESL Association of Teachers of English as a Second Language

ATEWS Advanced Tactical Electronic Warfare System

Atex Atlantic tradewind experiment

atf accounting tabulating form; actual time of fall

ATF Acceptance Test(ing) Facility; Air Task Force; Alcohol, Tobacco, and Firearms (bureau); Alternative Test Facility; American Type Founders; Australian Teachers Federation; ocean tug (3-letter symbol)

ATFAC American Turpentine Farmers Association Cooperative

ATFCNN Allied Task Force Commander—Northern Norway (NATO)

atfi attitudes toward feminist issues scales

atfr automatic terrain-following radar

ATFS Association of Track and Field Statisticians

atg air-to-ground

ATG Accordion Teachers Guild; Army Technical Group

atgar (ATGAR) anti-tank guided air rocket

ATGSB Admission Test for Graduate Study in Business

atgw (ATGW) antitank guided weapon(s)

ath above the horizon; atheism; atheist(ic); athletic

Ath Athens

ATH Athens, Greece (airport)

AT-H August Thyssen-Hütte

Athab Athabasca(n)

athc allotetrahydrocortisol

ath dfld atheism defiled (by atheists who misuse their philosophy to mask anti-semitism, promote racism, and engage in many self-serving ventures they find profitable although at the expense of other unbelievers such as agnostics and skeptics)

Atheist Penologist Jeremy Bentham

Atheist Poetess Ellen Prouse Mardan

Atheist's Bible Thomas Paine's *The Age of Reason*

Athel Athel Line

Athen Athenian

Athenai (Greek—Athens)

Athene (Greek—Minerva)—goddess of wisdom

Athenes (French—Athens)

Athenian Century the 5th century before the Christian era when the Athenians destroyed the Persian fleet at Salamis and completed the Parthenon in Athens—the 400s

Athens English place-name equivalent for Athinai, the capital of Greece

Athens of America Boston

atheol atheological; atheologist; atheology

Athinai (Modern Greek—Athens)

athodyd aerothermodynamic duct (ramjet engine)

athsc atherosclerosis

athw athwartship

ati actual time of interception; aerial tuning inductance; aptitude-treatment interaction; average total inspection

ATI Air Technical Intelligence; American Technology Institute; American Television Institute; Ansett Transport Industries; Asbestos Technical Institute; Asbestos Textile Institute; Australian Textile Institute

A & TI Agricultural and Technical Institute

ATI Aero Transporti Italiani (Italian Air Freight Line); Air Technical Index; *Azienda Tabacchi Italiani* (Italian State Tobacco Board)

ATIC Aerospace Technical Intelligence Center; Air Technical Intelligence Center; Antigua Tourist Information Center; Australian Tin Information Centre

ATIGS Advanced Tactical Inertial Guidance System

ATII Associate of the Taxation Institute Incorporated

ATIL Air Target Intelligence Liaison Program (USAF)

atiob as this is our best

ATIP Alaskan Talent, Information, and Practices

atis automatic terminal information service

ATIS Adirondack Trail Improvement Society; Air Technical Intelligence Study

ATISC Air Technical Intelligence Services Command (USAF)

ATJ Association of Teachers of Japanese

ATJS Advanced Tactical Jamming System

atk attack

a-tk anti-tank

atl analog threshold logic

Atl Atlanta; Atlantic

Atl Atlantico (Italian or Spanish—Atlantic); *Atlantico* (Portuguese—Atlantic); *Atlantique* (French—Atlantic); *Australia* (Spanish—Australia)

ATL Acoustic Test(ing) Laboratory; Alexander Turnbull Library (Wellington, NZ); Associated Truck Lines; Atlanta, Georgia (airport); Atlantic Tankers Limited; Automatic Totalisators Limited

ATLA Air Transport Licensing Authority; American Theological Library Association; American Trial Lawyers Association

Atlanta capital of Georgia; U.S. Penitentiary at Atlanta, Georgia

Atlanta Youth Atlanta Youth Development Center (for female juvenile delinquents) in Atlanta, Georgia but not to be confused with the U.S. Penitentiary there

ATLANTIC Atlantic Refining Company

Atlantic Bitch Atlantic Beach

Atlantic Canada Labrador and Newfoundland, New Brunswick, Nova Scotia, Prince Edward Island, Québec

Atlantic Community NATO nations

Atlantic Highlands Highlands of the Navesink or Navesink Highlands around Sandy Hook, New Jersey

Atlantic Narrows relatively restricted area uniting North and South Atlantic between bulge of Africa and bulge of Brazil, Freetown and Natal, respectively

Atlantico (Italian, Portuguese, Spanish—Atlantic)—Atlantic Ocean

Atlantic Provinces New Brunswick, Newfoundland, Nova Scotia, Prince Edward Island

Atlantic Scandinavia Denmark, Iceland, Norway

Atlantique (French—Atlantic Ocean)—also name of the Breguet maritime-patrol aircraft BR-1150

Atlantischer Ozean (German—Atlantic Ocean)

Atlantol Atlantologic(al)(ly); Atlantolgist(ic)(al)(ly); Atlantology

Atlas Atlas Mountains of Algeria and Morocco

ATLAS Abbreviated Test Language for Avionic Systems; Automated Tape Label Assignment System; Automatic, Tabulating, Listing, and Sorting System

Atlas-Agena two stage launch vehicle

Atlas-Centaur first American high-energy launch vehicle for space exploration—D-Series Atlas boosts Centaur space vehicle

Atlas-E intercontinental ballistic missile designed to place a thermonuclear warhead on a 9000-mile-distant target

atlas fol atlas folio—a book about 25 inches high

Atlas icbm first American intercontinental ballistic missile

ATLB Air Transport Licensing Board (UK)

Atl C Atlantic City

ATLD Air-Transportable Loading Dock

ATLIS Army Technical Library Improvement Studies; Automatic-Tracking Laser-Illumination System

Atl O Atlantic Ocean

Atl Pil Aut Atlantic Pilotage Authority

atm atmosphere (normal)

atm (ATM) automatic teller machine

at. m atomic mass

at/m ampere turns per meter

At/m ampere turns per meter

ATM Apollo Telescope Mount; Association of Teaching Aids in Mathematics; Associated Tobacco Manufacturers

ATM Amateur Telescope Making; *Azienda Tranviaria Municipale* (Italian—Municipal Rapid Transit Board)

ATMA Adhesive Tape Manufacturers' Association

ATMAC Air Traffic Management Automated Center

ATMC Army Transportation Materiel Command

ATMI American Textile Manufacturers Institute

atmos atmosphere; atmospheric(al)(ly)

atm press atmospheric pressure

ATMS Air Traffic Management System; Automatic Transmission Measuring System

ATMX code name of special railcar used by the Department of Energy for shipping defense waste from DoE sites around the United States

atn actual test number; acute tubular necrosis

ATN Alabama, Tennessee and Northern (railroad)

ATNA Australian Trained Nurses' Association

atnav acoustic-transponder navigation

atndt attendant

at. no. atomic number

ATNP Atherton Tablelands National Parks (Queensland)

ato according to others; assisted takeoff; automatic train operation

ATO Academy of Teachers of Occupations; Australian Taxation Office; ocean tug, old (3-letter symbol)

ATOA Australian Transport Officers Association

atoll. acceptance, test, or launch language

Atoll NATO nickname for Soviet Sidewinder-type missile

Atoll Nation Nauru

atomdef atomic defense

atomdev atomic device

Atomic Age Capital Los Alamos, New Mexico

Atomic Cities Los Alamos, New Mexico; Oak Ridge, Tennessee; Richland, Washington—created during World War II for generation of atomic bombs as well as nuclear energy sources

Atomic City place-name nickname shared by Los Alamos, New Mexico and Oak Ridge, Tennessee

Atomic Energy City Oak Ridge, Tennessee

atoms. automated technical order maintenance sequence(s)

ATOMSTATREP Atomic Status Report

aton at once

atorp antitorpedo; atomic torpedo

ATOS American Theatre Organ Society; Association of Temporary Office Services

atot actual time over target

atp actual time of penetration; array transform processor

atp (ATP) adenosine triphosphate, material found in almost all terrestrial life

atp a tout prix (French—at any price)

ATP Acceptance Test(ing) Procedure; Admissions Testing Program; Allied Technical Publication; Army Training Program; Association of Tennis Professionals

atpa auxiliary turbopump assembly

ATPAS Association of Teachers of Printing and Allied Subjects

ATPase adenosine triphosphate

atpcc attitudes toward parental control of children

atpd ambient temperature and pressure—dry

ATPE Association of Teachers in Penal Establishments

ATPI American Textbook Publishers Institute

ATPM Association of Toilet Paper Manufacturers

at pres at present

atps ambient temperature and pressure—saturated with water vapor

atpu air transport pressurizing unit

atr advanced test reactor; anti-transmit-receive; transmitter-receiver

Atr Achilles tendon reflex

ATR Advanced Test Reactor;

Association of Teachers of Russian; ocean tug, rescue (3-letter naval symbol)

ATR Anglican Theological Review

ATRA American Television and Radio Artists

atran automatic terrain recognition and navigation

atrax air-transportable communications complex

atrc anti-tracking control

ATRC Air Traffic Regulation Center

atr fib atrial fibrillation

atrid automatic target recognition, identification, and detection

atrima as their respective interests may appear

ATRIS Air Traffic Regulation Identification System (USA)

atrl atrial

atrls actual time of release

atrm after torpedo room

ATRM American Tax Reduction Movement

atro actual time of return to operation

atrop atrophy

A Tr Ps Allied Training Publications (NATO)

atrr advanced threat-reactive receiver

ATRS Australian Tape Recording Society

atrso accepts transfer as offered

atrt anti-transmit-receive tube

ats absolute temperature scale; advanced technological satellite; air-to-ship; anxiety-tension state; astronomical time switch

ATs Achievement Tests

ATS Acoustic Transmission System; Acquisition and Tracking System; Administrative Terminal System; Advanced Technological Satellite; Aeronautical Training Society; Air Tactical School; Air Traffic Services; American Theological Society; American Therapeutic Society; American Travel Service; American Trudeau Society; Anglican Truth Society; Application Technology Satellite; Army Transport Service; Association of Theological Schools; Automatic Transfer Service (bank accounts); salvage tug (naval symbol)

ATSA Aero Transportes

ATSBNZ Associated Trustee Savings Banks of New Zea-

land

ATSC American Traffic Safety Council

ATSE Alliance of Theatrical Stage Employees

AT & SF Atchison, Topeka and Santa Fe (railway)

ATSFSD Air Traffic Service Flight Services Division (FAA)

atsit automatic techniques for the selection and identification of targets

ats/jea automated test system/jet engine accessories

ATSOCC Applications Technology Satellite Operations Control Center (NASA)

ATS's Advanced Technological Satellites

AtST Atlantic Standard Time

ATSU Association of Time-Sharing Users

att attach; attempt; attorney

a t & t all tacos and tamales (American Southwestern roadside-stand short form); always talking and talking

Att Attic(a)

ATT Army Training Test

AT & T American Telephone & Telegraph

A & TT Alcohol and Tobacco Tax

atta atenta (Spanish—attentively)

ATTA Association of Travel and Tourist Agents (Singapore)

ATTC American Towing Tank Conference

atten attenuation, attenuator

Atterdag (Danish—Another Day)—nickname of King Valdemar IV

ATT & F Alcohol, Tobacco Tax, and Firearms (Division of U.S. Treasury Dept)

Att Gen Attorney General

ATTI Association of Teachers in Technical Institutions

Attica Facility Attica Correctional Facility (for males) at Attica, New York

Attic Muse the Athenian historian Xenophon

attn attention

atto attorney

atto atento (Spanish—attentively); 10-18

Attorney for the Damned Clarence Darrow

attr attractive

attrd attributed

attrest(s) attitude arrest(s)—made by law-enforcement offi-

cers who dislike the attitude(s) of the person(s) arrested

attrib attributive

attrit attrition

ATTS Automatic Telemetry Tracking System

Attunusia (Arabic—Tunisia)

atty attorney

atty & c attorney and client

Atty Gen Attorney General

AT type adenine and thymine type

atu alien tax unit; atomic time unit

Atu Atmosphärenüberdruck (German—atmospheric excess pressure)

ATU Alliance of Telephone Unions; Amalgamated Transit Union; Anchorage Telephone Utility; Anglo-Turkish Union; Anti-Terrorist Union; Anti-Terrorist Unit; Arab Telecommunications Union

atum antitank nonmetallic

ATURM Amphibious Training Unit—Royal Marines

atv (ATV) all-terrain vehicle

ATV Associated Tele Vision

ATV Akademiet for de Tekniske Videnskaber (Danish—Academy of Technical Sciences)

atvm attenuator thermo-element voltmeter

at. vol atomic volume

atw (ATW) antitank weapon

at/w atomic hydrogen weld

ATW American Theater Wing; Atlantic & Western (railroad)

at/wb ampere turns per weber

ATWE Association of Technical Writers and Editors

ATWg Air Transport Wing (USAF)

atws adjustable thermal wire stripper; automatic track while scanning

at. wt atomic weight

ATWU Australian Textile Workers Union

atx air taxi

at. xpl atomic explosion

ATYP Australian Theatre for Young People

A Typ I Association Typographique Internationale (French—International Typographic Association)

atyropt at your option

ATZ Air Traffic Zone

au activity unit; angstrom unit; antitotxin unit; arbitrary unit(s); author; azauridine

au aurum (Latin—gold)

a.u. *aures unitas* (Latin—both ears); *au usum* (Latin—ac-

cording to custom)
Au angstrom unit; astronomical unit; gold (symbol)
AU Aarhus Universitet (University of Aarhus); Air University; Alfred University; Allen University; American University; Andrews University; Army Unit; Assumption University; astronomical unit; Atheists United; Atlanta University; Auburn University
AÜ Ankara Üniversitesi (University of Ankara)
A/U advanced undersea weapons
A & U Allen & Unwin
Au¹⁹⁸ radioactive gold (symbol)
Au₂H₂O political campaign nickname of Arizona's Senator Barry Goldwater
AU-23A Fairchild piston-powered stol aircraft
AUA American Unitarian Association; American Urological Association; Aruba, Netherlands West Indies (airport); Associated Unions of America; Austrian Airlines
A.U.A. Associate of the University of Adelaide
AUAF Association of University Affiliated Facilities
AUAS Academy of Underwater Arts and Sciences
Aub Aubrey
AUB American University of Beirut
AUBC Association of Universities of the British Commonwealth
AUBER Association for University Business and Economic Research
AUBTW Amalgamated Union of Building Trade Workers
Auburn Facility Auburn Correctional Facility (for males) at Auburn, New York
auc average unit cost
a.u.c. ab urbe condita (Latin—from the founding of the city, usually refers to Rome)
AUC Aberystwyth University College; American University of the Caribbean; American University Club; Australian United Corporation; Australian Universities Commission
AU of C American University of Cairo
AUCA American Unitarian Christian Association
AUCANNZUKUS Australia, Canada, New Zealand, United

Kingdom, United States
AUCANUKUS Australia, Canada, United Kingdom, United States
AUCAS Association of University Clinical Academic Staff
AUCC Association of Universities and Colleges of Canada
Auck Auckland
Aucklands Auckland Islands
AUCOA Association of United Contractors of America
AUCSRLFRVWAM All-Union Central Scientific Research Laboratory for the Restoration of Valuable Works of Art in Museums
auct auction(eer)
auct auctorum (Latin—of authors)
AUCTU All-Union Council of Trade Unions
aud audible; audit; audition; auditor; auditorium
Aud (AUD) Australian dollar(s)
Aud audiencia (Spanish—court of justice, hearing)
AUDACIOUS Automatic Direct Access to Information with On-Line UDC System
audar autodyne detection and ranging
aud disb auditor disbursements
AUDDITS Automated Dynamic Digital Test System
Audel Theodore Audel
Aud Gen Auditor General
Aud Gen Nav Auditor General of the Navy
Audie Audry
auding auditory hearing, listening, and understanding
audio audiofrequency; audiogenic; audiogram; audiology; audiometer; audiometry; audiophile; audiovisual; audiovisual aids; etc
audiol audiologist; audiology
audiom audiometer; audiometric(al)(ly); audiometrist
audiovis audiovisual; audiovisual aids
audre audio response; automatic digit recognizer
Audrey Hepburn Edda van Heemstra
AUEC Association of University Evening Colleges
AUEW Amalgamated Union of Engineering Workers
AUF Australian Underwriters Federation
Aufdr Aufdrucke (German—imprint)
Aufl Auflage (German—edition)

AUFL Americans United For Life
AUFS American Universities Field Staff
AUFUSAF Army Unit for United States Air Force
aug augment; augmentation; augmentative
Aug Augsburg; August; Augusta; Augustan
Augember August and September
Augie August; Augusta, Georgia; Augustine; Augustus
augm augmente (French—augmented)
augra authority granted
August Augustine; Augustus
Augusta Maine's capital and popular place-name in ancient and modern times
Augustan Age Latin literature's golden era when Horace, Livy, Ovid, and Virgil flourished during the reign of the Emperor Augustus (27 B.C. to A.D. 14)
Augusta Tiberii (Latin—Ratisbon) known to the Germans as Regensburg
Augusta Trevirorum (Latin—Treves)—called Trier by the Germans
Augusta Trimobantum (Latin—London)
Augusta Vanglonum (Latin—Worms)
Augusta Vindelicorum (Latin—Augsburg)
Augustina de Aragon Augustina Domenech Zaragoza
Augustoritum Lemavicensium (Latin—Limoges)
AUI Associated Universities Incorporated
auj aujourd'hui (French—today)
Auk Auckland
aul above upper limit
AUL Aberdeen University Library; Air University Library; American United Life (insurance)
AULC American University Language Center
Auld Ane (Scottish Gaelic—Old One)—the devil
Auld Brig o' Don Dundee, Scotland's Brig o' Balgownie (brig = bridge)
Auld Clootie (Scottish Gaelic—Old Cloven)—cloven-footed devil
Auld Reekie (Scottish Gaelic—Old Smelly)—smogbound Edinburgh's nickname

Auld Sod (Scottish Gaelic—Old Land)—Scotland

AULLA Australasian Universities Language and Literature Association

aum (AUM) air-to-underwater missile

aum aumentado (Spanish—augmented)

AUMLA Australian Universities Modern Language Association

a. u. n. abesque ulla nota (Latin —without annotation)

AUNT Alliance for Undesirable but Necessary Tasks

auntie. automatic unit for national taxation and insurance (UK)

Aunty Vicky Queen Victoria

AUO African Unity Organization; Atlantic Union Oil

AUP Andrews University Press; Australian United Press

au pair (French—room and board in exchange for services such as housekeeping)—neither an abbreviation nor an acronym

AUPE Amalgamated Union of Public Employees (Singapore)

AUPELF Association of Wholly or Partially French Language Universities

AUPF Australian Uranium Producers Forum

AUPG American University Publishers Group

AUPHA Association of University Programs in Hospital Administration

AUPO Association of University Professors of Ophthalmology

AUPOSTCOM Australian Postal Commission

aur auricle; auricular; auricularis; aurum

Aur Auriga

AUR Association of University Radiologists

AURA Association of Universities for Research in Astronomy; Automated Reasoning Assistant

Aurelia (Latin—Orleans)—also known as Aureliacum, Aureliani, and Aurelianum

Aurelia Allobrogum (Latin—Geneva)

Aurelian Century the 100s—reign of Roman emperor-philosopher Marcus Aurelius—the 2nd century

aureq authority is requested

aur fib auricular fibrillation

Auri Auriga

AURI Angkatan Udara Republik Indonesia (Indonesian Air Force)

auric auricular

AURISA Australian Urban and Regional Information Systems Association

aurist. auristillae (Latin—ear drops)

aurora australis (Latin—southern lights)

aurora borealis (Latin—northern lights)

Aus Austin; Austria; Austrian

AUs Area Units (New Zealand)

AUS Army of the United States; Austin, Texas (airport); Australian Union of Students

AUSA Assistant United States Attorney; Association of the United States Army; Australian Universities Sports Association

ausc auscultation

Auschwitz (German—Oswiecim)—World War II concentration camp city in Poland

AUSCS Americans United for Separation of Church and State

Ausg Ausgabe (German—edition)

Au sh Australian serum hepatitis

AUSHC Australian High Commission

AUSIMM Australian Institute of Mining and Metallurgy

Aus Ital Aus Italien (German—From Italy)—symphonic poem by Richard Strauss

AUSLFL All-Union State Library of Foreign Literature (Moscow)

Aus meinem Aus meinem Leben (German—From My Life)—Smetana's autobiographical String Quartet No. 1 in E minor (George Szell transcribed it for orchestra)

AUSS Association of University Summer Sessions

AUSSAT Australian Satellite

Aussieland Australia

Aussie(s) Australian(s)

Aust Australia; Australian

Aust Alps Australian Alps of New South Wales and Victoria

Aust Cur Australian Current

Aust$ Australian dollar

austen austenitic

Austen Australian sten gen

Auster Auster-Beagle light liaison aircraft

Austerlitz Slavkov, Czechoslovakia

Austin Augustina; Augustine; capital of Texas

AUSTIRAN Australian-Iran Shipping Company

Aust J Phys Australian Journal of Physics

AUSTRAFORD Ford Motors of Australia

Austrail Railways of Australia

austral (Spanish—southern)

Austral Australian

Australas Australasian

Australasian Australian-Asian region including Australia, Tasmania, New Zealand, and islands of Melanesia

Australia Commonwealth of Australia (Down-Under English-speaking continental nation exporting crude oil, frozen meat, and many valuable minerals as well as fine wines)

Australia Day first Monday after January 26

Australia Felix (Latin—Happy Australia)—fertile central Victoria in southeastern Australia

Australian Alps mountains of New South Wales and Victoria in Australia

Australian Commonwealth Australia and its territories

Australian Desert 1,300,000-square-mile area (530,000 hectares) in central and western Australia

Australian Dominion Australia and its territories

Australian Duo Australia's two best-known classical composers ranked chronologically—Percy Grainger and Arthur Benjamin

Australian Ports (large, medium, and small in clockwise order) Port Kennedy, Cairns Harbour, Townsville, Port of Bowen, Port of Mackay, Rockhampton, Gladstone, Maryborough, Brisbane, Clarence River, Port Waratah, Newcastle, Sydney, Port Kembla, Melbourne, Williamstown, Geelong, Portland, Port Adelaide, Port Vincent, Port Pirie, Port Augusta, Whyalla, Port Lincoln, Albany, Busselton, Bunbury, Freemantle, Perth, Geraldton, Carnarvon, Broome, Wyndham, Darwin, Gove, Hobart (*in Tasmania along with* Burnie, Devonport,

Beauty Point, Launceton)

Australian States New South Wales, Queensland, South Australia, Tasmania, Victoria, Western Australia

Australian Territories Australian Antarctic; Australian Capital Territory (Canberra), Northern Territory, Papua New Guinea (Admiralty Islands, Heard and McDonald Islands, New Britain, New Guinea, New Ireland, the Solomons)

Australia's Largest Port Sydney

Australia's Largest State Western Australia

Australia's Little England Tasmania

Australie (French—Australia)

Australië (Dutch—Australia)

Australs Austral Islands of Polynesia where they are also called the Tubuais

Austria Republic of Austria (former seat of the Austro-Hungarian Empire but now a small landlocked central European country populated by Austrians who call it *Österreich*), *Republik Österreich*

Austria-Hungary dual monarchy ruling Austria, Hungary, Czechoslovakia, and parts of northern Italy, Yugoslavia, Romania, and Polish Galicia from 1867 to the end of World War I in 1918

Austrian Quintet Austria's five best-known classical composers arranged chronologically— Haydn, Mozart, Schubert, Bruckner, Mahler

Austrian Waltz Kings Joseph Lanner, Johann Strauss, and his son Johann Strauss Jr

AUSTRIATOM Austrian Atomic Energy Group

Austriche (French—Austria)

Austronesia islands of South Pacific from Madagascar in Indian Ocean to Hawaiian Islands in the Pacific

AUSUDIAP Association of U.S. University Directors of International Agricultural Programs

aut autore (Italian—author)

Aut Autriche (French—Austria)

AUT American Union Transport; Association of University Teachers

AUTA Association of University Teachers of Accounting

AUTE Association of Universi-

ty Teachers of Economics

AUTEC Atlantic Underwater Test Evaluation Center

AUTELCOM Australian Telecommunications Commission

auth authentic; authenticate; authenticity; author; authority; authorization; authorize(d)

Auth Authority

authab authorized abbreviation (USAF)

Author of the Declaration of Independence Thomas Jefferson

Author of the First Amendment James Madison

Author of the first draft of the Declaration of Independence Thomas Paine

Auth Ver Authorized Version

AUT(I) Association of University Teachers (Ireland)

autiobio autobiograph; autobiographer; autobiographic(al); autobiography

autmwtr ck automatic water check

auto. automobile; automatic; automotive

auto (Latin prefix—self)—automobile (self-moving vehicle)

autocade automobile parade

AUTOCAP Automobile Consumer Action Programs(s)

autocolor automatic color (tv)

autocom automated combustor (design code)

Autocrat of all the Russias Czar Nicholas II (last of the czars and last of the Romanov rulers)

Autocrat of Austria Prince Clemens Wenzel Lothar von Metternich

Autocrat of the Breakfast Table Dr Oliver Wendell Holmes

autodidac autodidact(ic)(al) (ly)

autodin automatic digital network

autodoc automatic documentation

autog autograph

autogrom autoprompter (tape)

auto. lean automatic lean

autom automobile; automotive

autom automobile (Italian—automobile); *automóvel* (Portuguese—automobile); *automóvil* (Spanish—automobile)

automag automatic-loading magnum (handgun)

automap automatic machining program

automast automatic mathematical analysis and symbolic

translation

automát automática; automático (Spanish—automatic)

automatic automatic revolver

automation automation action; automatic operation

Automobile City Detroit, Michigan

Automobile State Michigan

Automobile Wizard Henry Ford

automtn automation

auton autonomous; autonomy

autonet automatic network

autonym a writer's real name

autop automatic pistol; autopsy

AUTOPIC Automatic Personal Identification Code

autopilot automatic pilot

autopistol automatic pistol

autoprompt automatic programming of machine tools

AUTOPROS Automated Process Planning System

AUTOPSY Automatic Operating System (IBM)

auto pts automobile parts

autoqest automatic generation of requests

auto. recl automatic reclosing

auto. rich automatic rich

autorotic(s) automobile neurotic(s)

autos automobiles; automatics

autosate automatic data systems analysis technique

autoscript automated system for composing, revising, illustrating, and typesetting

auto s & cv automatic stop-and-check valve

AUTOSERVCEN Automated Service Center

autosevocom automatic secure voice communication(s)

autospec automated specification(s)

autospot automatic system for positioning tolls

auto s & sv automatic stop and check valve

Auto State Michigan

autostatis automatic statewide auto theft inquiry

AUTOSTATIS Automatic Statewide Theft Inquiry System (California)

autostrad automated system for transportation data

autosyn automatically synchronous

autotr autotransformer

autotran automatic translation

autovon automatic voice network

au tr aural training

autran automatic target-recognition analysis

AUTRANAVS Automated Transponder Navigation System

AUT(S) Association of University Teachers (Scotland)

AUT(W) Association of University Teachers (Wales)

AUU Association of Urban Universities

auv administrative use vehicle; armored utility vehicle

Au virus Australian antigen

AUVMIS Administrative Use Vehicle Management Information System (USA)

auw airframe unit weight

auw (AUW) advanced underwater weapon(s)

AUWE Admiralty Underwater Weapons Establishment

aux auxiliary

aux (Greek—grow, increase)—auxiliary, auximones, auxocardia

Aux Cayes former name of Les Cayes, Haiti

aux m auxiliary machinery

AUXOPS Auxiliary Operational Members (USCG)

auxrc auxiliary recording control

av acid value; anteversion; aortic valve; arteriovenous; assessed valuation; atrioventricular; auriculoventricular; average; average; aviator; avoirdupois

a-v atriventricular; audio-visual

av avril (French—April)

a v a vista (Italian—at sight)

a/v (A/V) ad valorem (Latin—as valued)

Av Avenue; Aves; Avestan; Avian; Avila(n)

Av avenida (Portuguese or Spanish—avenue)

AV *alta voltagem* (Portuguese—high voltage); *alto voltaggio* (Italian—high voltage); *alto voltaje* (Spanish—high voltage); American viewpoint; Antonio Vivaldi; arteriovenous; audiovisual; Authorized Version; large seaplane tender (naval symbol)

AV Avtomat Kalashnikov (Russian—Kalashnikov automatic)—Soviet assault rifle

A.V. Anno Vixit (Latin—he (she) lived (a given number of) years)

AV-8B U.S. Marine Corps fighter-bomber jump-jet (capable of taking off and landing vertically)

ava arteriovenous anastomosis; azimuth versus amplitude

ava (AVA) automatic voice alarm

AVA Aerodynamische Versuchsanstalt; American Vocational Association; Asbestos Victims of America; Audio-Visual Aids; Australian Veterinary Association; Australian Volunteers Abroad; Award(s) in the Visual Arts

A-V A All-Volunteer Army

AVAC Asociación Venezolana para la Avance de la Ciencia (Spanish—Venezuelan Association for the Advancement of Science)

AVADS Autotrack Vulcan Air Defense System

av/af anteverted/anteflexed

Ava Gardner Lucy Johnson

avail. available; availability

aval availability; available

Avalon Somerset region of southwestern England believed to be Avalon of Arthurian legend; resort port of Catalina Island off Los Angeles, California

'Avana Cockney contraction for La Habana de Cuba—Havana

avasi abbreviated visual-approach slope indicator

AVASIS Abbreviated Visual Approach Slope Indicator System

avb avbeta (Swedish—departure)

AVB advanced aviation base ship (naval symbol)

avbl armored vehicle bridge launcher

avc acceleration vector control; allantoid vaginal cream; automatic volume control; average variable cost

avc (AVC) average variable cost

av C avanti Cristo (Italian—Before Christ)

AVC American Veterans Committee; Antelope Valley College; Association of Virginia Colleges; Association of Vitamin Chemists; Audio-Visual Center

AVCA Australian Volunteer Coastguard Association

AvCad Aviation Cadet

avcat aviation high-flash turbine fuel

Av Cert Aviation Certificate

avcs atrioventricular conduction system

AVCS Advanced Videocon Camera Systems; Assistant Vice Chief of Staff

avd automatic voice data; automatic voltage digitizer

avd avdeling (Dano-Norwegian—part, section)

AvD Automobil Club von Deutschland (German Automobile Club)

AVD Army Veterinary Department; high-speed seaplane tender (3-letter naval symbol)

Avda Avenida (Spanish—Avenue)

AVDA American Venereal Disease Association

a-v **difference** arteriovenous concentration difference

AVDO Aerospace Vehicle Distribution Office(r)

avdp avoirdupois

avdth average depth

ave automatic volume expansion

'ave have

Ave Avenue

AVE Asociación Venezolana de Ejecutivos (Spanish—Venezuelan Association of Executives)

avec amplitude vibration exciter control

AVEM Association of Vacuum Equipment Manufacturers

Avenio (Latin—Avignon)

AVENSA Aerovias Venezolanas (Venezuelan Airlines)

Avenue of the Americas modern name of New York City's Sixth Avenue

AVERA American Vocational Education Research Association

Averroes Abul-ibn-Roshd

Aves Los Aves—Bird Islands off coast of Venezuela, a group of guano-encrusted rocks to the west of Curaçao in the Caribbean

avf arteriovenous fistula; azimuthally varying field

AVF All-Volunteer Force

avfr available for reassignment

avfuel aviation fuel

avg average

Avg Avgust (Russian—August)

Av Gar Avant Garde

avgas aviation gasoline

avge average

avh acute viral hepatitis

Avh Avhandlinger (Swedish—transactions)

avi airborne vehicle identification; air velocity index; aviation

AVI American Virgin Islands; Association Universelle d'Aviculture Scientifique (Universal Association of Scientific Aviculture); Audio-Visual Institute; Automatic Vehicle Identification

Aviaco Aviación y Comercio (Spanish airline)

AVIANCA Aerovias Nacionales de Colombia (National Airlines of Colombia)

AVIATECA Empresa Guatemalteca de Aviacion (Guatemalan Aviation Enterprise)

Avicenna Arabian astronomer-mathematician-physician Abu ibn Sina (980-1037)

AVID Audio-Visual Instruction Department

avigation aircraft navigation

aviob aviation observation

Aviocar Spanish transport aircraft designated C-212

avionics aviation and astronautics electronics

AVIP Association of View-data Information Providers

AVIS Active Vibration Isolation System

AVISCO American Viscose Corporation

AVISPA Aerovias Interamericanas de Panamá (Interamerican Airways of Panama)

avit(AVIT) audiovisual instruction(al) technology

av JC avant Jésus Christ (French—before Jesus Christ, B.C.)

avl average versus length

av l average length

AVL Asheville, North Carolina (airport)

AVLA Audio-Visual Language Association

Av Labs Aviation Laboratories (USA)

AVLINE Audiovisuals On-Line (computer retrieval system)

avlm anti-vehicle land mine

avloc airborne visible-laser optical communication

AVLS Automatic Vehicle Location System

avlub aviation lubricant

avm automatic voting machine

avm (AVM) arteriovenous malformation

AVM guided-missile ship (naval symbol)

AVMA American Veterinary Medical Association

AVMF Aviatsiya Voenno Morskikh Flota (Russian—Soviet Naval Aviation)

avn atrioventricular node; aviation

Avn Avonmouth

AVN Air Vietnam

AVNA Australian Visiting Nurses Association

AVNMED Aviation Medicine (DoD)

av node arterioventricular node

avo ampere-volt-ohm; avocado

AVO Állam Védelmi-Osztály (Hungarian—Hungarian-Secret Soviet Police); avoid verbal orders

Avocado County San Diego County, California

Avog Avogadro

avoid. airfield vehicle obstacle indication device

avoil aviation oil

avoir avoirdupois

avolo automatic voice link observation

Avon Avon Books; Avonmouth (Port of Bristol); Avon Water (flowing from Ayrshire to Lanark); Avonwick (Devonshire); plus all other Avon place-name combinations

avos avocados

avozvots average Australian voters

avp arginine vasopressin

AVP seaplane tender, small (3-letter symbol); Wilkes-Barre, Pennsylvania (airport)

AVP Aruba Volkspartie (Dutch —Aruba People's Party)

avr aortic valve replacement

AVR Army Volunteer Reserve

AVRA Audio-Visual Rsearch Association

AVRI Animal Virus Research Institute

AVRO A.V. Roe (Ltd)

AVRO Algemeene Vereeniging Radio Omroep (Dutch—General Broadcasting Association)

AVROS Algemeene Vereeniging van Rubberplanters ter Oostkust van Sumatra (Dutch—General Association of Rubber Plantations of the East Coast of Sumatra

avrp atrioventricular refractory period; audiovisual recording and presentation

AVRS Audiovisual Recording System

avs aerospace vehicle simulation; area vocation school(s)

AVS American Vacuum Society; Association for Voluntary Sterilization; aviation supply ship (naval symbol)

A-V S Anti-Vivisection Society

AVSA African Violet Society of America

AVSC Audio-Visual Support Center (USA)

AVSL Assistant Venture Scout Leader; Association of Visual Science Librarians

avst automated visual-sensitivity test(er)

AVSYCOM Aviation Systems Command (USA)

avt audiovisual tutorial

Avt Allen vision test

AVT Adult Vocational Training; auxiliary aircraft transport (naval symbol); Aviation Medicine Technician

avta automatic vocal transaction analyzer

avtag aviation wide-cut turbine fuel

av tmp average temperature

AVTP Adult Vocational Training Program

AVTRW Association of Veterinary Teachers and Research Workers

avtur aviation turbine fuel

AVUS Automobile Versuchs und Untersuchungs Strecke (German—Automobile Test Track)

avv avvocato (Italian—advocate)—lawyer

av vales atrioventricular (heart) valves

av w average width

AVWV Antilliaans Verbond van Werknemers Vereenigingen (Dutch—Antillean Confederation of Workers' Unions)

AVX Avalon Bay, Catalina Island, California (airport)

aw abandoned woman (euphemistic nickname for whore although the phrase suggests a deserted, forsaken, and lost adult of the feminine sex); above water; acid waste; actual weight; air-to-water; anterior wall; antiwear; atomic warfare

Aw Antwerpen (Dutch–Antwerp)

a/w actual weight; all-water; all-weather

a & w alive and well

AW air warning; Air Work, Ltd; American Welding; Articles of War; atomic warfare; atomic weight; automatic weapons(s); distilling ship (naval symbol)

A-W Addison-Wesley

A & W Atlantic & Western (railroad)

awa absent without authority;

advise when able
AWA Air Warfare Analysis; All-Weather Attack; Aluminum Wares Association; American Warehousemen's Association; American Watch Association; American Waterfowl Association; American Wine Association; American Woman's Association; Association of Women in Architecture; Aviation/Space Writers Association
AWA *All the World's Aircraft*
awac airborne warning and control
AWACS Airborne Warning and Control System
AWADS All-Weather Aerial Delivery System
AWAIK Abused Women's Aid in Crisis
Awakener of Bulgaria George Venelin
AWAL American-West African Line
AWAM Association of West African Merchants
AWANS Aviation Weather and Notice to Airmen System
awar area-weighted average resolution
aware. advance warning equipment
AWARE Addiction Workers Alerted to Rehabilitation and Education (NYC); Association for Women's Active Return to Education
AWARS Airborne Weather and Reconnaissance System
AWAS Acoustic Wave Analysis System; Australian Women's Army Service
AWASA Australian Women's Army Service Association
AWASM Associate of the Western Australia School of Mines
awb air waybill
AWB Agricultural Wages Board (UK); Australian Wheat Board; Australian Wine Board; Australian Wool Board; Australian Wool Bureau
AWBA American World Boxing Association
AWB/CN Air Waybill or Consignment Note
AWC Air War College; American Watershed Council; American Wool Council; Anaconda Wire & Cable (stock exchange symbol); Area Wage & Classification (office); Arizona Western College; Army War

College; Army Weapons Command; Australian Whaling Commission; Australian Wool Corporation
AWC Amgueddfa Werin Cymru (Welsh Folk Museum)
AWCC Australian Wine Consumer's Cooperative
AWCO Area Wage and Classification Office
awcs agency-wide coding structure
AWCS Air Weapons Control System
AWCU Association of World Colleges and Universities
awd awards
AWD Action for World Development; Air Worthiness Division
AWDA Automotive Warehouse Distributors Association
AWDCS Alternate Waste Disposal Concepts Study
awdr advanced weapon-delivery radar
awe accepted weight estimate; advise when established; average weekly earnings
AWEA Australian Wind Energy Association
AWEASVC Air Weather Service
AWED American Woman's Economic Development
A Weld I Associate of the Welding Institute
AWES Army Waterways Experiment Station; Association of Western European Shipbuilders
awf awful(ly)
a wf acceptable work-load factor; adrenal weight factor
AWF American Wildlife Foundation; Australian Wheatgrowers Federation
AWFS All-Weather Fighter Squadron
AWG American Wire Gage; Art Workers Guild; Australian Writers Guild
AWH Association of Western Hospitals; Australian Women's Hospital
AWHA Australian Women's Home Army
A Whitman Albert Whitman Company
AWHPS Association of White House Press Secretaries
awi anterior wall infarction
AWI All-Weather Interceptor; Animal Welfare Institute; Australian Welding Institute; Australian Wire Industry;

Australian Wool Industries
AWIA American Wood Inspection Agency
AWIRA American Wax Importers and Refiners Association
AWIS Association of Women in Science
AWIU Allied Workers International Union; Aluminum Workers International Union
awiy as we informed you
awk awkward
AWK Wake Island (airport)
awkm a wonderfully knowledgeable man
awl. absent with leave; administrative weight limitation; all-weather landing; artesian well lease
Awl NATO nickname of Soviet infrared or radar-guidance system
AWL Animal Welfare League
AWLC Association of Women Launderers and Cleaners
AWLF African Wildlife Leadership Foundation
AWLNET Area Wide Library Network
AWLOGS Army Wholesale Logistic System
AWLS All-Weather Landing System
awm automatic washing machine; awaiting maintenance
AWM American War Mothers; Association of Women Mathematicians; Australian Wallcovering Manufacturers; Australian War Memorial
AWMF Andrew W Mellon Foundation
awmi anterior wall myocardial infarction
AWMPF Australian Wool and Meat Producers Federation
awn awning
AWN Activation Work Notice; Automated Weather Network
AWngSvc Air Warning Service
AWNL Australian Women's National League
AWNY Advertising Women of New York
AWO Accounting Work Order; American Waterways Operators
awol a wolf on the loose; absent without leave; absent without official leave
AWOP All-Weather Operations Panel
awp amusements with prizes
A & WP Atlanta and West Point (railroad)
AWPA Academy of Wind and

Percussion Arts; American Wood Preservers Association; Australian Women Pilots Association

AWPB American Wood Preservers Bureau

A-WPC Addison-Wesley Publishing Company

AWPL Australia-West Pacific Line

AWPs *Allied Weather Publications*

awr adaptive waveform recognition

AWR Arctic Wildlife Refuge (Alaska); Association of Western Railways; Australian Wire Rope

AWRA American Water Resources Association; Australian Welding Research Association; Australian Wool Realization Agency

AWRC Australian Water Resources Council

AWRE Atomic Weapons Research Establishment

AWRIS Army War Room Information System

AWRNCO Aircraft Warning Company (Marines)

AWRO Atomic Weapon Retrofit Order

AWRT American Women in Radio and Television

aws adjustable wire stripper

AWS Air Warning Service; Air Warning Squadron; Air Warning System(s); Air Weapon System(s); Air Weather Service; Aircraft Warning Service; Aircraft Warning System; Alston Wilkes Society; American War Standards; American Water-color Society; American Weather Service; American Welding Society; Atlas Weapon System; Attack Warning System; Automatic Warning System; Automatic Weather Station; Aviation Weather Service

AWSA American Water Ski Association; Association of Wisconsin School Administrators

AWSF Australian Wholesale Softgoods Federation

AWSG Army Work Study Group

AWSP Association of Washington School Principals

AW & ST *Aviation Week & Space Technology*

awt advanced waste treatment

AWT Aero-elastic Wind Tunnel; Associate in Wildlife Technology

AWTA Australian Wool Testing Authority

AWTE Association for World Travel Exchange

AWTI Air Weapons Training Installation

awu atomic weight unit

AWU Aluminum Workers Union; Australian Workers Union

AWWA American Water Works Association; Asian Women's Welfare Association; Australian Water and Wastewater Association

awwf all-weather wood foundation(s)

AWWU American Watch Workers Union

awx (AWX) all-weather aircraft

awy airway

ax. axiom(atic); axes; axis

AX American Air Export & Import Company (stock exchange symbol)

axbt aircraft-expendable bathythermograph

axd auxiliary drum

axe. (AXE) automatic electronic exchange

AXF Advanced X ray Facility

axfl axial flow

axgrad axial gradient

axio axiological(ly); axiologist; axiology; axiom; axiomatic (al)(ly)

Axis Sally Mildred E. Gillars, American traitor convicted of treason for broadcasting Nazi propaganda during World War II

axmin(s) axminster(s)

axminster eponymic name for good grade carpets and rugs originally made in the English town of Axminster in Devonshire; modern axminsters often copy well-known oriental designs

AXO Assistant Experimental Officer

Axon *Axelson* (Swedish—son of Axel)

Ay Ayala

Ay *Ayios* (Modern Greek—Holy)

AY Allied Youth

AYA American Yachtsmen's Association

Ayat *Ayatullah* (Persian—Sign of God)—fanatical religious leader capable of declaring and masterminding holy wars

AYC Albany Yacht Club; American Yacht Club; American

Youth Congress; Arthur Young & Company; Atlantic Yacht Club; Audubon Yacht Club

AYD American Youth for Democracy

ayer (Malay—water); (Spanish—yesterday)

Ayer NW Ayer and Son

Ayers Ayers Rock National Park, in Australia's Northern Territory, features a colossal red sandstone rock—the world's largest monolith

ayf anti-yeast factor

AYF Australian Yachting Federation

AYH American Youth Hostels

AYHA Australian Youth Hostels Association

AYI Academic Year Institute (NSF)

Ayla Aylett; Aylmar; Aylmer; Aylsworth; Aylward; Aylwin

AYLC Association of Young Launderers and Cleaners

Aym Aymara

AYM Ancient York Mason; Ancient York Masonry

AYM-YWHAs Association of Young Men-Young Women's Hebrew Associations of Greater New York

AYP Alaska-Yukon Pioneers

ayr all-year 'round

Ayr Ayrshire

Ayrshire Poet Robert Burns born in Alloway, Ayrshire, Scotland

AYSA American Yarn Spinners Association

AYSO American Youth Soccer Organization

aytng anything

az azure

a Z aan Zee (Dutch—on sea); *auf Zeit* (German—on account, on credit)

Az azimuth; Azores; Aztec; Aztecan; azure

Az *Azote* (Greek—nitrogen)

AZ Active Zone; Alitalia (Linee Aeree Italiane); Alzheimer's disease

A-Z Ascheim-Zondek (pregnancy test)

A to Z from A to Z; from the beginning to the end; thoroughly covered

AZ *Akademisch Ziekenhuis* (Dutch—Academic Hospital)

AZA American Zionist Association

Azalea Trail City Lafayette, Louisiana

Azania South Africa's name ac-

cording to African nationalists

AZAPO Azania People's Organization (militant South African blacks)

azas adjustable-zero adjustable-
span

Azb Azerbaijan; Azerbaijani;
Azerbaijanian

AZC American Zionist Counicl

azel azimuth elevation

AZF American Zionist Federation

azg azaguanine

AZGS Azusa Ground Station

azi azimuth

Az I Azores Islands

AZI American Zinc Institute

Azië (Dutch—Asia)

az ld azure laid (paper)

azm azimuth

azon azimuth only

Azores Azores Islands; Azores
Islands in the North Atlantic

far to the west of Portugal

Azorín José Martínez Ruiz

Azov Sea of Azov (landlocked
body of water within the Crimean section of the USSR
where it is called Azovskoye
More)

Azovskoye More (Russian—Sea
of Azov)

Azr Azores

azran azimuth and range

AZRI Arid Zone Research Institute

azrock asbestos rock

Azru Aztec Ruins National
Monument

azs automatic zero set

azt azusa transponder

Azt Aztec; Aztecan

AZT Ascheim-Zondek Test

aztc azusa transponder coherent

Aztecan and Incan Century the
1000s—great stone structures

still standing in the highlands
of Mexico and Peru are mute
witnesses to these indigenous
American cultures—the 11th
century

Aztec Ruins Aztec Ruins National Monument in north-
western New Mexico

Aztec two-step another name for
loose bowels acquired in Mexico, the land of the Aztecs

Aztec type microcephalic idiocy

A–Z Test Ascheim-Zondek Test
(for pregnancy)

aztran azimuth from transit

azur azauridine

Azure Coast Côte d'Azur on the
French Riviera

Azure Sea Lake Rudolf in northern Kenya

azusa azimuth, speed, altitude

az wo azure wove (paper)

azy azyme (matzos, unleavened
bread)

B

b baby; base; bicuspid; bituminous; black; blue; book; born; brass; breadth; bridge; bulb (camera exposure device); wing span (symbol)
b. *bis* (Latin—twice)
b span
B Bacillus; bad; *bajar* (Spanish—to descend); balboa (Panamanian currency); Baltic; bandwidth; Barber Lines; *bas* (French—down); bastard; Baume; Baume scale; bay; *Bay* (Turkish—Mister); Beatrice (Beatrice Foods); Beech; Belgium (auto plaque); belted; Bendix; Benoist scale; unit of marijuana measurement consisting of just enough to fill a small matchbox; benzene; body; Boeing; boils at; bolivar (Venezuelan currency); boliviano (Bolivian currency); bomber; bonded; borderline; boron; Boston; bowels; Bravo —code for letter B; British; brightness (symbol); Brother; Bruning; Buddhist; Bull Lines; buoyancy; Burroughs; flux density (symbol); Fraunhofer line caused by terrestrial oxygen
B/ balboa (Panamanian currency unit 9 $1.00 U.S.)
°B degrees Baumé
B Baai (Afrikaans or Dutch—bay); *Bad* (German—bay); *Bahía* (Spanish—bay); *Bata* (Portuguese—bay); *Baie* (French—bay); *Baja* (Spanish—lower); *bajar* (Spanish—to descend) as on an elevator; *Ban* (Indo-Chinese—bay); *bas* (French—down); *Bay* (Turkish—Mister); *Bir* (Arabic—

cistern, well); *Bucht* (German—bay); *bueno* (Spanish—good)—examination grade; *Bukhta* (Russian—bay)
B' Ben (Hebrew—son, son of)
b 1 booster 1
B-1 North American-Rockwell strategic supersonic bomber equivalent to the Soviet Backfire
B_1 thiamine vitamin
b 1 p booster 1 pitch
b 1 y booster 1 yaw
b 2 booster 2
B_2 riboflavin vitamin
B2F Boeing 320 fan jet airplane; Boeing 720 fan jet airplane
b 2 p booster 2 pitch
b 2 y booster 2 yaw
B3F Boeing 320 aircraft
b4 before
b7d buyer (has) seven days (to pay)
B7D buyer has seven days to pay (for whatever was bought —usually securities)
B7F Boeing 707 fan jet airplane
B8H Boosey and Hawkes
B-25 World War II light bomber called the Mitchell
B-26 modernized Douglas B-26 Invader renamed Counter Invader
B-47 Stratojet all-weather strategic medium bomber
B-52 Stratofortress all-weather intercontinental strategic heavy bomber
B-57 Canberra two-place twin-engine turbojet all-weather tactical bomber
B-58 Hustler strategic all-weather supersonic bomber
B-66 Destroyer twin-engine turbo-jet tactical all-weather

light-bombardment aircraft
B 77 Bratislava 77 (viral) strain
B-707 one of a Boeing aircraft series containing other popular transport planes such as the 727, 737, 747, etc.
B-747 Boeing jumbo jet aircraft
ba base line; bath(room); blind approach
b-a bare ass(ed); naked; unclothed
b/a backache; billed at; boric acid; budget authority; budget authorization; budget authorized
b a balneum arenae (Latin—sand bath)
Ba Baia (Portuguese—Bahia); barium (symbol)
BA Bank of America; Basic Airman; Bellas Artes (Fine Arts); Berkshire Athenium; Boeing (stock exchange symbol); Boston & Albany (railroad); British Academy; British Admiralty; British Army; British Association (for the Advancement of Science); Buenos Aires; Bureau of Accounts; Bureau of Apprenticeship; Busted Aristocrat (an officer reduced to the ranks)
B-A Basses-Alpes
B.A. *Baccalaureus Artium* (Latin—Bachelor of Arts)
B/A Bank of America; British American (oil company)
B & A Bangor & Aroostook (railroad); Boston & Albany (railroad)
BA Bayerische Landesbank (German—Bavarian National Bank); *Biological Abstracts*; *Bonne Action* (French—Good Deed); *Bowker Annual*; *Busi-*

ness Automation

baa benzoyl arginine amide; bleat of a sheep

Baa Baal; Baalam

BAA Brewers Association of America; British Acetylene Association; British Airports Authority; British Archeological Association; British Astronomical Association; Bureau of African Affairs

B.A.A. Bachelor of Applied Arts

BAAA British Association of Accountants and Auditors

BAAB British Amateur Athletic Board

BAAC Bank of Agriculture and Agricultural Cooperatives (Thailand)

BAADS Bangor Air Defense Sector

BAAF Brigade Airborne Alert Force

baai (Dutch—bay)

Baal Baalbek

BAAL Black Academy of Arts and Letters; British Association for Applied Linguistics

Baal Shem-Tov (Hebrew—Kind Master of the Holy Name)—Israel Ben Eliezer's pseudonym

BAAP Bilateral Aid to Asia and Pacific (program)

BAAR Board of Aviation Accident Research

BAAS British Association for the Advancement of Science

bab (Arabic—gate, strait)

Bab Barbara; Babylon; Babylonia; Babylonian; WS Gilbert's nickname

BAB British Airways Board; BT Babbitt (Babo cleanser)

BABA British Antiquarian Bookseller's Association

Babar Jean de Brunhoff's little elephant of storybook fame; Zahir ud-Din Muhammad (founder of India's Mogul dynasty)

Babars Babar Islands of Indonesia

babb babbit metal

Babbie Barbara

babbitt babbitt metal (named for its inventor, Isaac Babbitt of Taunton, Massachusetts)

Babb's computer Babbage's computer (the first computer)

Bab-el-Mandeb (Arabic—Gate of Tears)—strait linking the Indian Ocean's Gulf of Aden with the Red Sea; scene of many shipwrecks and hence

its name

Babenburga (Latin—Bamberg)—also known as Bamberga

Babe Ruth George Herman Ruth the Sultan of Swat

Babette Elizabeth

Babeuf François Noël

BABI Brooke Army Burn Institute (San Antonio, Texas)

Babines short form for the Babine Mountains of British Columbia

Babi Yar Symphony No. 13 of Shostakovich inspired by poems of Yevtushenko protesting Soviet anti-semitism

bab met babbitt metal

Babo Boolean approach for bivalent optimization; BT Babbitt detergent scouring powder

Babs blind approach beacon system

Bab(s) Barbara

BABS Babbage Society; Blind-Approach Beacon System

BABT Brotherhood of Associated Book Travelers

Babushka (Russian—grandmother)—nickname of Ekaterina Breshkovskaya, the turn-of-the-century revolutionary leader

Baby Babylon(ia); Babylonian

Baby Langdon Harry Langdon

bac bacilli; bacillus; bacteria; bacterial; bacterial antigen complex; bacteriologist; bacteriology; blood-alcohol concentration; buccoaxiocervical

bac (BAC) binary asymmetric channel

bac bachot (French abbreviations for baccalaureat)—bachot also means ferryboat

Bac. Baccalaureus (Latin—Bachelor)

BAC Bendix Aviation Corporation; Black Action Committee; Blair Athol Coal; Boeing Airplane Company; British Aircraft Corporation; British Association of Chemists; Bureau of Air Commerce; Business Advisory Council (U.S. Department of Commerce); Business Archives Council of Australia

BAC Baile Atha Cliath (Gaelic—Dublin)

BAC-145 British Jet Provost trainer aircraft

BACA Business and Consumer Affairs

BACAH British Association of Consultants in Agriculture

and Horticulture

BACAIC Boeing Airplane Company Algebraic Interpretive Computing

BACAICS Boeing Airplane Company Algebraic Interpreter Coding System

BACAL Butter and Cheese Association Limited

BACAN British Association for the Control of Aircraft Noise

bacat barge aboard catamaran

bac bag bactine bag (underground slang—plastic bag containing bactine antiseptic sniffed by some school children in imitation of drug-addicted elders)—results often fatal due to suffocation

B.Acc. Bachelor of Accountancy

BACC British-American Collectors' Club

BA & CC Billiards Association and Control Council

Bacchus (Latin—Dionysos)—god of revelry and wine

BACCHUS British Aircraft Corporation Commercial Habitat Under the Sea

BACD Boeing Airplane Company Design

bace basic automatic checkout equipment

BACE British Association of Consulting Engineers; Bureau of Agricultural Chemistry and Engineering

BACGA British-Australian Cotton Growing Association

bach bachelor

Bach (German—brook, stream)

Bachelor Painter Sir Joshua Reynolds

Bachelor President James Buchanan—fifteenth President of the United States

B.A. Chem. Bachelor of Arts in Chemistry

bach girl(s) bachelor girl(s)

bachot (French—baccalaureat, ferryboat)—an abbreviation and a definition

Bach Soc Bach Society

BACIE British Association for Commercial and Industrial Education

back. backwardation

Back Bay Boston's old residential section built on mud flats reclaimed from Boston Bay more than a century ago

Backbone of Asia the Himalayas

Backbone of the Confederacy the Mississippi River

Backbone of England Pennine Ridge extending from the Cheviots to the south Midlands

Backbone of Europe the Alps

Backbone of North America the Rockies

Backbone of South America the Andes

Backfire Soviet strategic supersonic bomber equivalent to the North American-Rockwell B-1 proposed for the USAF

Back-of-Beyond Australia's sparsely inhabited interior

'backs wetbacks (illegal immigrants from Mexico)

BACM British Association of Colliery Management

BACMA British Aromatic and Compound Manufacturers Association

BACNATO British Atlantic Committee of NATO

BACO British Aluminium Company

BACP Blair Athol Coal Pty

BACS Ben Asia Container Service

bact bacteria; bacteriological; bacteriologist; bacteriology; bacterium

BACT Best Available Control Technology

bacter bacteriologist

Bacteria Beach nickname of your favorite beach once its sands and waters become afflicted with the pollution of human and industrial wastes

bacteriol bacteriologic(al)(ly); bacteriologist; bacteriology

bactrian bactrian camel (two-hump camel of Asia)

Bactrian Sage Zoroaster (founder of the Magian religion and native of Bactria)

BACU Battle Area Control Unit

Bad Badajoz

Bad (German—Bath)—short form for more than a hundred Austro-German hydrotherapeutic resorts ranging from Bad Abbach and Bad Aussee to such as Bad Gastein, Bad Homburg, Bad Kissingen, and Bad Reichenhall to Bad Zwischenahn where it is possible to watch sausages being stuffed while drinking the waters guaranteed to eliminate the waste products of even the most constipating cooking; many Bads provide classical and popular music for their patrons

BAD Bantu Administration and Development; Base Air Depot; Berlin Airlift Device; Black, Active, and Determined; British Association of Dermatology

BADA Base Air Depot Area; British Antique Dealers' Association

BADAS Binary Automatic Data Annotation System

Bad Boy of Music George Antheil's self-imposed nickname

badc binary asymmetric dependent channel

baddies bad ones

baddie(s) bad guy(s)—incorrigible criminal(s)

Baden Baden-Baden

Baden (German—Baths)—short form for Baden bei Wien (Baden near Vienna) an Austrian resort just south-southwest of the city and for Baden-Baden near Karlsruhe, Germany; other places named Baden are in Canada, Maryland, northwestern Germany, and Switzerland

BADGE Basic Air Defense Ground Environment

Badger NATO nickname for Soviet Tupolev medium bomber (Tu-16)

Badger(s) Wisconsinite(s)

Badger State Wisconsin's official nickname

BADGES Base Air Defense Ground Environment System

badhouse bawdyhouse

Badian(s) Barbadian(s)

Badlands arid and eroded areas of Nebraska and South Dakota as well as other places

B.Admin. Bachelor of Administration

BADS British Association of Dermatology and Syphilology

bae Deacon antenna equipment

Ba e barium enema

BAE Bureau of Agricultural Economics; Bureau of American Ethnology

BA of E Badminton Association of England

B.A.E. Bachelor of Aeronautical Engineering; Bachelor of Agricultural Engineering; Bachelor of Architectural Engineering; Bachelor of Art Education; Bachelor of Arts in Education

BAE Buque Armada Ecuatoriana (Ecuadorian Naval Ship)

BAEA British Actors' Equity Association

BAEC British Agricultural Export Council

B.A.Econ. Bachelor of Arts in Economics

B.A.Ed. Bachelor of Arts in Education

BAED British Airways European Division

B.Ae.E. Bachelor of Aeronautical Engineering

BAEF British-American Educational Foundation

Ba enem barium enema

BAEng. Bureau of Agricultural Engineering

baf baffle; bunker adjustment factor

ba & f budget, accounting, and finance

BAF British Air Force; Burma Air Force; Burundi Air Force

BAFCom Basic Armed Forces Communication Plan

Baffin Basin deeper parts of Arctic Ocean between Baffin Island and Greenland

batflegab ambiguous, somewhat incomprehensible, and often verbose expressions also known as cover-up, euphemistic expression, mellowspeak, nice-nellyisms, and officialese (*see* Bafflegab addendum)

bafgab bafflegab (euphemisms, gobbledygook, jet-age jargon, nice-nellyisms, officialese, pentagonese, Watergate English, etc.)—*see* Bafflegab addendum

DAFM British Association of Forensic Medicine; British Association of Friends of Museums

BAFMA British and Foreign Maritime Agencies

BAFO British Air Forces of Occupation; British Army Forces Overseas

BAFS British Academy of Forensic Science

BAFSC British Association of Field and Sports Contractors

BAFSV British Armed Forces Special Vouchers

BAFTA British Academy of Film and Television Arts

BAFTM British Association of Fishing Tackle Makers

bag. bagasse; baggage; ballistic attack game; buccoaxiogingival

Bag Baghdad

B.Ag. Bachelor of Agriculture

BAG Beaverbrook Art Gallery

BAGA British Amateur Gymnastics Association

BAGBI Booksellers Association of Great Britain and Ireland

BAGDA British Advertising Gift Distributors Association

Bagdad by the Bay San Francisco

Bagdad-on-Hudson New York

Bagdad on the Subway one of O Henry's nicknames for New York City. He also called it the City of Razzle Dazzle

B.Ag.E. Bachelor of Agricultural Engineering

bagg buffered azide glucose glycerol

B. Agr. Bachelor of Agriculture

BAGR Bureau of Aeronautics General Representative

B.Agr.Eco. Bachelor of Agricultural Economics

B.Agric. Bachelor of Agriculture

B.Ag.Sc. Bachelor of Agricultural Science

Bag Town San Diego, California, where so many sailors tote their seabags as they go afloat or ashore

Bah Bahamas; Bahia; Bahrain

BAH Bahrain Island, Persian Gulf (airport); British Airways Helicopters

B-A H British-American Hospital

Baha'i (Abdul) Baha Bahai

Bahamas Commonwealth of the Bahamas (subtropical island nation off coast of Cuba as well as Florida, discovered by Columbus on October 12, 1492 and now inhabited by Bahamians)

Bahamian Ports (north to south) Freeport (Grand Bahama), Bimini (Bimini Islands), Nassau (New Providence), Matthew Town (Great Inagua)

Bahams Bahamas

Bahia Sao Salvador de Bahia

Bahía de Campeche (Spanish—Campeche Bay)—southern sector of the Gulf of Mexico

Bahía de Cochinos (Spanish—Bay of Pigs)

Bah Ind Bahasa Indonesian (national language)

BAHOH British Association of the Hard of Hearing

BAHPA British Agricultural and Horticultural Plastics Association

Bahrain Bahrain Island sheikdom in the Persian Gulf where Bahrains fish for pearls, refine oil, and smelt aluminum; its Arabic name, *Bahrain*, means

water all around

Bahraini Ports (north to south) Al Manamah Harbour, Mina Sulman, Sitra

Bahrains Bahrain Islands in the Persian Gulf between Qatar and Saudi Arabia

Bahr en Nil (Egyptian Arabic—Nile River)

BAHS British Agricultural History Association

Ba I Bahama Islands

BAI Bank Administration Institute; Bank of America International; Barrier Industrial Council; British Airports International; Bureau of Animal Industry

B.A.I. *Baccalaureus in Arte Ingeniaria* (Latin—Bachelor of Engineering)

Baía de Guanabara (Portuguese—Guanabara Bay)—Rio de Janeiro's inner harbor

baib beta-amino-isobutyric (acid)

BAIC Bureau of Agricultural and Industrial Chemistry

baid boolean array identifier

BAIE British Association of Industrial Editors

Baile Atha Cliath (Gaelic—Dublin)

BAINS Basic Advanced Integrated Navigation System

Baird Leonard Mrs Harry S Clair Zogbaum

bait. bacterial automated identification technique

B.A.J. Bachelor of Arts in Journalism

baja (Spanish—lower)

Baja Baja California (Spanish—Lower California)

Baja California (Spanish—Lower California)—used in contradistinction to *Alta California*, Upper California, north of the Mexican border

Bajan Barbadan (inhabitant of Barbados)

Baja Norte Baja California Norte (Spanish—Northern Baja California)—Mexican state including Ensenada, Mexicali, Tecate, and Tijuana next to Caliente

Baja Sur Baja California Sur (Spanish—Southern Baja California)—Mexican territory including Cabo San Lucas, La Paz, and Loreto

B.A.Jour. Bachelor of Arts in Journalism

Bajuns Barbadans

bak bakery

bakelite bormaldehyde formaldehyde plus phenol resin

Bakery Workers Bakery and Confectionery Workers International Union of America

baking soda sodium bicarbonate ($NaHCO_3$)

bakke (Danish—hill)

Bakst Leon Bakst (originally Rozenberg)

bal balance; balcony; baloney; blood-alcohol level

bal (BAL) basic assembly language (computer programming)

Bal Baleares; Ballarat; Balthasar; Baltimore; British anti-lewisite

BAL Baltimore, Maryland (Friendship Airport); Barclays Australia Ltd; Belgian African Line; Bonanza Airlines (3-letter coding); Borneo Airways Ltd.

balance. basic and logically applied norms—civil engineering

Balanchine Georgi Balanchivadze

bal. arenae balneum arenae (Latin—sandbath)

balast balloon astronomy

Balaton Lake Balaton, central Europe's largest lake, nicknamed the Hungarian Ocean

Balb Balboa

balc balconette; balconied; balcony

Bald Baldwin

Baldie Archibald; Baldassare; Baldomero; Balduin; Baldur; Baldwin; Baldwina

baldie(s) bald person(s)

Baldy Baldemar; Baldram; Baldred; Baldrey; Baldric; Baldur; Baldwin

Baleares (Spanish—Balearic Islands)

Balearic Islands (ranked by area) large islands of Majorca, Minorca, Ibiza, and Formentera; smaller islands of Aire, Aucanada, Botafoch, Cabrera, Dragonera, Pinto, and El Rey

Balearics Balearic Islands of Spain in the Mediterranean off the Gulf of Valencia where they include Ibiza, Mallorca, and Menorca

Baleful Prophet Cassandra

Balgol Burroughs algebraic compiler

balid ballistics identification

balkan (Turkish—mountain range)

Balkans Balkan mountains,

peoples, and states in south-eastern Europe (Albania, Bulgaria, Greece, Romania, Turkey, Yugoslavia)

ball. ballast

Ball Ballerup; Balliol College, Oxford

Ball Coll Balliol College—Oxford

Ballenys Balleny Islands

Ballo Un Ballo in Maschera (Italian—A Masked Ball), three-act opera by Verdi

ballots. bibliographic automation of large library operations

ballute balloon parachute

bally ballyhoo

Ballyhouras Ballyhoura Hills of southern Ireland

bal. mar. balneum maris (Latin—salt-water bath, sea-water bath)

Bal-Mol Ballester-Molina (45-caliber Argentine semi-automatic pistol)

balop balopticon (projector)

B Alp Basses-Alpes

balpa balance of payments; ballpark

BALPA British Airline Pilot's Association

B-alpes Basses-Alpes

bals balsam

bals. balsamum (Latin—balsam)

B.A.L.S. Bachelor of Arts in Library Science

Balt Balthasar; Baltic; Baltimore

balth balthazar (16 bottle capacity)

balthum balloon temperature and humidity

Balti Baltimore (slang)

Baltic Baltic and Mercantile Shipping Exchange (in London); Baltic Sea

Báltico (Spanish—Baltic)

Baltic Republics Estonia, Latvia, Lithuania

Baltic Scandinavia Finland and Sweden (Denmark sometimes included although much of its coast is on the Atlantic)

Baltic States Estonia, Latvia, Lithuania (secret protocol of the Hitler-Stalin Pact of 1939 assigned all three to the Soviet sphere)

Baltimore beefsteak broiled liver's military nickname in the U.S.

Baltimore Oracle HL Mencken

Balto Baltimore

Balts Baltic peoples; Balto-Slavs

(East Prussians, Estonians, Latvians, Lithuanians); Balto - Slavic - speaking peoples

Balt Sym Baltimore Symphony

Baluch Baluchistan

balun balance-to-balance (network)

balute balloon parachute

bal. vap. balneum vapour (Latin—steambath, vapor bath)

Balzac Honoré de Balssa

bam broadcasting am

Bam Bamberger

BAM Baikal-Amur-Magistral (railroad); BankAmerica Corporation (stock-exchange symbol); Basic Access Method; broadcasting AM; Brooklyn Academy of Music

B-A-M Baikal-Amur-Magistral (mainline railway of eastern Siberia)

'Bama Alabama

BAMA British Amsterdam Maritime Agencies

bambi (BAMBI) ballistic missile bombardment interceptor

Bambino George Herman (Babe) Ruth

Bamboo Curtain old nickname for the barrier between anti-communist and communist countries of Southeast Asia

bame benzoylarginine methyl ester

BAMIRAC Ballistic Missile Radiation Analysis Center

BAMM Black Afro Militant Movement

BAMO BuAer Material Officer

bamp basic analysis and mapping program

BAMR DuAer Maintenance Representative

B.A.M.S. Bachelor of Ayurvedic Medicine and Surgery

BAMTM British Association of Machine Tool Merchants

B.A.Mus. Bachelor of Arts in Music

BAMW British Association of Meat Wholesalers

ban. best asymptotically normal

Ban Bantu; Byron Bancroft Johnson

BAN Base Activation Notice; British Association of Neurologists

BAN Biblioteka Akademii Nauk (Russian—Library of the Academy of Sciences)—in Leningrad

Banaba Ocean Island near the Gilberts in the equatorial mid-Pacific Ocean

Banaca Banco Nacional de Credito Agricola (Spanish—National Agricultural Credit Bank)—Mexico

Banace Banco Nacional de Credito Ejidal (Spanish—Public Land Credit National Bank)—Mexico

Banacoex Banco Nacional de Comercio Exterior (Spanish—National Bank of Foreign Commerce)

Banafoco Banco Nacional de Fomento Cooperativo (Spanish—National Bank for Cooperative Promotion)

Banamex Banco Nacional de México (Spanish—National Bank of Mexico)

Banana Benders Queensland Australians

banana boat cargo vessel built to carry bananas

Banana City Brisbane—a big banana export port

Bananagate Honduran-style Watergate-type scandal involving some of the banana republic's highest officials bribed to lower export taxes on bananas

Bananaland Queensland, Australia

Bananalanders people of banana-growing Queensland, Australia

Banana Republics countries of Central and northern South America where bananas are the principal export; Jamaica often included

Banape Banco Nacional de la Pequeña Empresa (Spanish—National Small Business Bank)—Mexico

BANC British Association of National Coaches

Banco El Banco (Spanish—The Bank)—World Bank for Reconstruction and Development

Bancomer Banco de Comercio (Spanish—Bank of Commerce)

Bancoop Banco Nacional de las Cooperativas del Peru (Spanish—National Bank of Peruvian Cooperatives)

Banc.Sup. Bancus Superior (Latin—Upper Bench)—King's or Queen's Bench

band (Persian—mountain range)

Band Bandung

Banda Oriental (Spanish—Eastern Ribbon)—former name

and present-day nickname of Uruguay

Bandaranaike Colombo, Sri Lanka's airport named for the island's first native prime minister

Bandas Banda Islands of Indonesia

Band City Elkhart, Indiana, where so many band instruments are made

banded agate chalcedony

Bandeirante Brazilian 12-passenger transport honoring frontier pioneers, Bandeirantes

Bandelier Bandelier National Monument and cliff-dweller Indian reservation in New Mexico west of Santa Fe

Bandit Queen of the Old West Belle Starr

Bane of the Bureaucrats Parkinson's Law

banewort *Atropa belladonna*'s nickname (also called beautiful lady, deadly nightshade, or death's herb)

Banffs Banffshire

Bang Bangalore

bangkok bangkok hat (straw hat of a type first woven in Bangkok); bangkok straw (Siamese straw used in making baskets and hats)

Bangla Bangladesh (formerly East Pakistan)

Bangladesh People's Republic of Bangladesh (Asian country whose name in Bengali means Bengal Nation, world's largest grower and manufacturer of jute)—formerly East Pakistan

Bangladesh Ports (north to south) Chalna Anchorage, Chittagong, Cox's Bazar

bang(s) bombing(s); explosion(s)

banir bombing and navigation inertial reference

Banjul formerly Bathurst, The Gambia

bank. banking

Bank Bangkok

BANK International Bank for Reconstruction and Development

BankCal Bank of California

bankcy bankruptcy

Bankers Bankers Publishing (Boston); Bankers Trust (New York)

Bankhead Bankhead National Forest in northwest Alabama

BANKPAC Bankers Political Action Committee

Bank Robbery Capital of the World Los Angeles

banks. bank holidays (West Indian English)

Banks the Banks (short form for the shallow fishing banks offshore Canada—the Grand or Newfoundland Banks, or the Georges Banks off New England)

banks clgs bank clearings

bankster(s) banker gangster(s) who deprive(s) you of your deposits under the cloak of bank management

Bann Bannockburn

Banobras *Banco Nacional de Obras y Servicios Publicos* (Spanish—National Bank of Public Works and Services)—Mexico

Banpeco *Banco Peruano de los Constructores* (Spanish—Peruvian Constructor's Bank)

Banrural *Banco Nacional de Credito Rural* (Spanish—National Rural Credit Bank)—Mexico

ban's bond anticipation notes

BANS Bright Alphanumeric Subsystem; British Association of Numismatic Societies

BANSA *Banco del Ahorro Nacional* (Spanish—National Savings Bank)—Mexico

BANSW Band Association of New South Wales

Bantam Bantam Books; Swedish antitank guided missile

BANTSA Bank of American National Trust and Savings Association

B.A. Nurs. Bachelor of Arts in Nursing

BANWR Bosque Apache National Wildlife Refuge (New Mexico)

BANZ Bahrain-New Zealand Trading and Storage Company

BANZARE British, Australian, New Zealand Antarctic Research Expedition

bao basal acid output

BAO Bankruptcy Annulment Order; British Association of Otolaryngologists; British-American Oil

B.A.O. Bachelor of the Art of Obstetrics; Bachelor of Arts in Oratory

BAOD British Airways Overseas Division

bao-mao basal acid output to maximal acid output (ratio)

BAOP British Atlantic Ocean

Possessions (Ascension, St Helena, and Tristan da Cunha islands)

BAOR British Army on Rhine

Baotou (Pinyin Chinese—Paotou)

bap baptism; baptized; base auxiliary power; beginning at a point; blood-agar plate; brachial artery pressure

bap *billets a payer* (French—bills payable)

Bap Baptist; Baptista; Baptiste

BAP Bankers Association of the Philippines; Booksellers Association of Philadelphia

B A & P Butte, Anaconda & Pacific (railroad)

BAP *Barco de la Armada Peruana* (Spanish—Ship of the Peruvian Navy)

BAPA British Airline Pilots' Association

BAP & C British Association of Print & Copyshops

BAPCO Bahrain Petroleum Company

bape baseplate

B.A.P.E. Bachelor of Arts in Physical Education

BA Phys Med British Association of Physical Medicine

BAPL Bettis Atomic Power Laboratory (AEC)

BAPM British Association of Physical Medicine

B.App.Arts Bachelor of Applied Arts

B.App.Sci. Bachelor of Applied Science

BAPS British Association of Pediatric Surgeons; British Association of Plastic Surgeons; Bureau of Air Pollution Sciences

BAPSA Broadcast Advertising Producers Society of America

Bapt Baptist

BAPT British Association of Physical Training

Bapu (Gujerati—father)—Gandi's title affectionately bestowed by his many followers in India and elsewhere

baq basic allowance for quarters

BAQ Barranquilla, Colombia (airport)

BAQC Bureau of Air Quality Control

bar. barometer; barometric

bar. (BAR) buffer address register

bar *billets à recevoir* (French—bills receivable)

Bar Baroque; Baruch, Book of

Bar Barone (Italian—Baron)

B.Ar. Bachelor of Architecture

BAR Base Address Register (computer); Board of Airline Representatives (Singapore); Board of Anthropological Research; Broadcast Advertisers' Reports; Browning automatic rifle; Bureau of Aeronautics Representative; Bureau of Automotive Repair

BARA Bureau d'Analyse et de Recherche Appliquêes (French —Bureau of Analysis and Applied Research)

Barajas Madrid, Spain's airport

Barak Israeli version of the French Mirage military aircraft

Barão de Rio Branco (Baron Rio Branco) José María de Silva Paranhos

barb. barbarian; barbecue; barber; barbiturate

Barb Barbados Islands; Barbara; Barbary

Barbadian Ports (north to south) Speightstown, Bridgetown

Barbados English-speaking West Indian island nation about a seventh the size of Rhode Island but vastly overpopulated; tourism promoted by its beautiful beaches and friendly people

Barbara Bel Geddes Barbara Geddes Lewis

Barbara Stanwyck Ruby Stevens

Barbara Ward Lady Jackson (wife of Sir Robert Jackson)

Barbarossa nickname of red-bearded Frederick I of the Holy Roman Empire, whereas Barbarossa I (Koruk) and Barbarossa II (Khaireddin) were Greek-born Algerian pirates

Barbary Coast North African coast once infested by pirates; San Francisco's gambling, red-light, and waterfront district a century ago

Barbary States Algeria, Libya (Tripolitania), Morocco, Tunisia

Barbellion WNP Barbellion (pseudonym of Frederick Cummings)

Barber Barber of Seville (Rossini's most popular comic opera)

Barber Poet Provençal poet Jacques Jasmin—a barber by profession and also called the Last of the Troubadors as he died in 1864

barbi baseband radar bag initiator

Barbie Barbara

Barbiere Il Barbiere di Siviglia (Italian—The Barber of Seville), two-act comic opera by Rossini

bar-b-q barbecue

Barbra Barbara

barbs. barbiturates

barbus barbudos (Spanish—bearded ones)

Barc Barcelona; Barclay

BARC Bay Area Reference Center; Bay Area Research Collective; British Aeronautical Research Committee

Barca Barcelona

Barca the Carthaginian Maharbal

B.Arch. Bachelor of Architecture

B.Arch.E. Bachelor of Architectural Engineering

Barchino (Latin—Barcelona)—also called Barcino or Barxino

B.Arch. & T.P. Bachelor of Architecture and Town Planning

Barcino (Latin—Barcelona)

BARCS Battlefield Area Reconnaissance System

Bard of Avon William Shakespeare

Bard of Ayrshire Robert Burns

Bard of Olney William Cowper

Bard of Prose Boccaccio

Bard of Sheffield James Montgomery

Bard of the Stumblebum Nelson Algren

Bard of Twickenham Alexander Pope

Barefoot King of Cocos John Clunies Ross (owner of the Cocos or Keeling Islands in the South Indian Ocean)

Barents Barents Sea in the Arctic between Norway and Russia

Barentsovo More (Russian—Barents Sea)

barg(s) bargain(s)

bari baritone; baritone saxophone

Bari Bari delle Puglie, Italy

Bariloche San Carlos de Bariloche, Argentina

Barisans Barisan Mountains of Sumatra

barite barium sulfate

Baritone-Conductor Dietrich Fischer-Dieskau

Bark Barker; Barkham

Barlinnie Glasgow, Scotland's great prison

Barme Bartolome

bar mitz bar mitzvah (Hebrew—one who is responsible for the Commandments)—religious ritual marking a boy's 13th birthday; similar ceremony for girls called *bas mitzvah* or *bat mitzvah*

barn. bombing and reconnaissance navigation

Barn Barnard

Barna Barcelona

Barndütsch Bernese dialect of Schwyzerdütsch

Barney Barnabas; Barnett; Bernard; Bernardino; silver cigarette box engraved with drawings of Barney Google and Snuffy Smith (awarded to the year's best cartoonist)

Barney Barnato Barnett Barnato (Barnett Isaacs)

BARNS Bombing and Reconnaissance Navigation System

Barnum P(hineas) T(aylor) Barnum; 19th-century American impresario and showman who brought his circus to all parts of the United States; presented the Swedish soprano Jenny Lind, the midget General Tom Thumb, Jumbo the enormous elephant, the first hippopotamus ever shown in America; also established model industrial and workers community in Bridgeport, Connecticut

Baron Burnham Edward Levy-Lawson

Baron Corvo Frederick William Rolfe

Baron Cuvier Georges Léopold Chrétien Frédéric Dagobert

Baron de Reuter Israel Beer Josaphat (founder of Reuter's news agency)

Baroness Orczy Mrs Montagu Barstow—author of *The Scarlet Pimpernel*

Baronet Peel Robert Peel (former Prime Minister of Great Britain)

Baron Grenville William Wyndham Grenville (former Prime Minister of Great Britain)

Baron Lugard Frederick John Dealtry Lugard

Baron Munchausen Rudolf Erich Raspe who told many tall tales under his own name as well as under the pseudonym of Baron Munchausen—an aristocrat of Gottingen

Baron Passfield Sidney Webb

BARONS Business-Accounts Reporting Operating Network System

Baron Stiegel ironmaster Henry William Stiegel

Baron Tweedsmuir John Buchan

b & arp bare and acid resisting paint

barq barquentine

Barq Barranquilla

barr barrister

barra (Spanish—reef)

Barrens Barren Grounds of northern Canada west of Hudson Bay in treeless tundra; Pine Barrens of New Jersey

Barrington Island, Galápagos Santa Fé

Barrio Chino (Spanish—Chinese Quarter)—Barcelona's brothel area close to the waterfront

Barrow Point Barrow (Alaska's most northerly point of land and settlement)

Barry Barrymore

Barry Cornwall Bryan Waller Procter

Barry Fitzgerald William Shields

Barrymore family containing some of America's best beloved actors (Lionel, Ethel, John—children of Maurice and Georgiana Barrymore)—actual surname was Blythe

Barry Perowne pseudonym of Philip Atkey

Barry Sullivan Patrick Barry

BARS Backup Attitude-Reference System; Ballistic Analysis Research System; British Association of Residential Settlements

BARSR *Biblioteca Academiei Republicii Socialiste Romania* (Academic Library of the Socialist Republic of Romania) —in Bucharest

BARSTUR Barding Sands Underwater Test Range

bart bartender; barter

Bart Baronet; Bartel; Barth(el); Barthold; Bartholomew; Bartimeus; Bartlet(t); Bartley; Bartolo; Bartolomeo; Barton; Bartram

BART Bay Area Rapid Transit (San Francisco); Brooklyn Army Terminal (New York)

BARTD Bay Area Rapid Transit District

Bartenders Union Hotel and Restaurant Employees and Bartenders International

Union

Barton Cannon Barton Danzilio

Barts Saint-Barthelemy in the French West Indies; Saint Bartholomew's Hospital in London

Barty Bartholomew

barv beach armored recovery vehicle

Barxino (Latin—Barcelona)— also called Barchino or Barcino

bas basenji; basic airspeed; basic allowance for subsistence; basilica; basophil(s); basset; beam-alignment sensor; benzyl analog of serotonin

Bas Basel; Basil; Basilica; Basilicata; Bass Strait; Bastogne; Bastrop; Basuto; Basutoland

BAs Business Agents (of unions)

B.As Buenos Aires (according to *Lloyd's Register of Shipping* although usual abbreviation is BA)

BAS Basic Allowance for Subsistence; Behavioral Approach Scale; Brazilian-American Society; British Acoustical Society; British Antarctic Survey; British Arachnological Society

B.A.S. Bachelor of Agricultural Science; Bachelor of Applied Science

Basa *Baronessa* (Italian—Baroness)

BASA British Architectural Students' Association; Buckeye Association of School Administrators

BASAF British and South Africa Forum

basalt gabbro-type igneous rock

BASAM British Association of Grain, Seed Feed, and Agricultural Merchants

B. A. Sc. Bachelor of Applied Science

BASC Booth American Shipping Corporation

basc b bascule bridge

basd basic active service date

base. (BASE) basic semantic element

BASE Bank-Americard Service Exchange; Business Assessment Study and Evaluation

Base 2 binary

Base 8 octal

Base 10 decimal

Base 16 hexadecimal

BASEC British Approvals Service for Electric Cables

BASEEFA British Approvals Service for Electrical Equipment in Flammable Atmospheres

Basel formerly spelled Basle; called Bâle by the French

BASF Badische Anilin und Soda Fabrik

bash. body acceleration given synchronously with the heartbeat

BASH Bulimia Anorexia Self Help

BASI British Association of Ski Instructors

basic. (BASIC) battle-area surveillance and integrated communications; beginner's all-purpose symbolic instruction code (computer language)

BASIC British-American Scientific International Commercial (English)

BASIC *Biological Abstracts Subjects in Context*

BASICO Behavior Science Corporation

basicpac basic processor and computer

basictng basic training

BASIE British Association for Commercial and Industrial Education

basil. basilect(ic)(al)(ly)

BASIL Barclays Advanced Staff Information Language

Basilea (Spanish—Basel)

Basilia (Latin—Basle)

Basil Rathbone Lawrence Northrup

basis. (BASIS) bibliographic author of subject interactive researches

BASIS-H BASIS history

BASIS-P BASIS political science, public administration, urban studies, and international relations

BASIS-S BASIS sociology

Bask Baskir(ia)

Bask(er) Baskerville

Basket of Eggs egg-shaped hills of Downs in Northern Ireland

Baslerdütsch Basle dialect of Schwyzerdütsch

BASMA Boot and Shoe Manufacturers' Association

bas mitz see *bar mitz*

BASO Base Accountable Supply Officer; Bureau of Aeronautics Shipping Order

basops base operations

baso(s) basophile(s)

baspm basic planning memorandum

Basque Provinces Álava, Guipúzcoa, and Viscaya in northeastern Spain where Basque is spoken

BASR Bureau of Applied Social Research (Columbia University)

BASRA British Amateur Scientific Research Association

bass. bassoon

BASS Basic Analog Simulation System; Bass Anglers Sportsman Society

B.A.S.S. Bachelor of Arts in Social Science

bass con basso continuo (Italian —continuous bass)—figured bass background

Bassie Sebastian

BASSR Bashkirian Autonomous Soviet Socialist Republic; Buriat Autonomous Soviet Socialist Republic

bast. bastard; bastardization; bastardize; bastardly; bastard title; bastardy

Bast Sebastian

Bastille great prison of Paris destroyed on July 14, 1789 at the outset of the French Revolution and since then celebrated by freedom-loving Frenchmen and others every Bastille Day, July 14

Bastille by the Bay inmates' nickname for San Quentin prison on a peninsula in San Francisco Bay

Bastion of the Caribbean Puerto Rico

bas tit. bastard title (half title)

Basto Sebastiano

Basutoland former name of Lesotho

ba sw bell alarm switch

basys basic system

bat. battery; battle; best available technology

Bat Bartholomew; Battista

BAT Beaux Arts Trio; Blind Approach Training; Body Adjustment Test; Boeing Air Transport; Bureau of Apprenticeship and Training

BA & T Bureau of Apprenticeship and Training

B-AT British-American Tobacco

BATAB Baker and Taylor Automated Bookordering

Batavia former name of Djakarta, Indonesia on Java's northwest coast

Batavian Republic name for the Netherlands during the French Revolutionary wars (1795 to 1806)

BATC British Amateur Television Club

bat. chg battery charger; battery charging

BATDIV battleship division

bate base activation test equipment

batea best available technology economically available

b-a test blood-alcohol test (used to determine if an automobile driver is under the influence of an intoxicating beverage)

BATF Bureau of Alcohol, Tobacco, and Firearms (U.S. Treasury)

BATFOR battle force

bath. bathroom; best available true heading

Batham Bantam Books

Bath City Mt Clemens, Michigan

hath mitz bath mitzvah

batho bathometer

bathy bathymeter; bathysphere; bathyscaphe

BATM British Admiralty Technical Mission

Bat Masterson William Barclay Masterson

bat mitz see bar mitz

bato baloon-assisted takeoff

Baton Rouge Louisiana's capital

B.A.T.P. Bachelor of Arts in Town Planning

batreadcompl battle readiness and competition instructions

BATRON battleship squadron

batrop baratropic

Bat Rou Baton Rouge

Bats British-American Tobacco (stock-exchange sobriquet)

BATS Business Air Transport Service

batt batter; batteries; battery

Battenberg Mountbatten

Battery old seawall containing gun emplacements in Charleston, South Carolina, at tip of Manhattan Island in New York, at other places similarly fortified and situated

Battle-Born State Nevada—admitted as territory in 1848 following the Mexican War

Battlefield City Gettysburg, Pennsylvania

Battlefield of the Nations Leipzig in Germany in 1813; Plain of Esdraelen in Israel between Megiddo (where Armageddon is supposed to occur) and Nazareth (where Jesus is reported to have lived as a boy);

Waterloo in Belgium (where Napoleon was finally defeated two years after his defeat at Leipzig)

Battling Bob Robert M La Follette, Sr

Batumskaya formerly Batum

bau basic assembly unit; British absolute unit (BTU, Btu)

Bau Bauer; Bauhaus

BAU Bangladesh Agricultural University; British Association Unit

BAUA Business Aircraft Users' Association

Baubie (Scottish—Barbara)

baud telecommunication unit measuring speed of signalling and equal to one code element or pulse per second—named for its French inventor, JME Baudot (1845-1903)

BAUS British Association of Urological Surgeons

bauxite hydrated aluminum-oxide mixture (source of aluminum)

bav bon à vue (French—good at sight); *bon à vue* (French—good at sight)—sight draft

Bav Bavaria; Bavarian

BAV Biblioteca Apostolica Vaticana (Latin—Apostolic Vatican Library), in Rome's Vatican City

BAVA Bureau of Audio-Visual Aids (NY)

BAVE Bureau of Audio-Visual Education (Calif)

Baviera (Portuguese or Spanish —Bavaria)

BAVIP British Association of Viewdata Information Providers

BAVTE Bureau of Adult, Vocational, and Technical Education (HEW)

baw bare aluminum wire

BAWA British Amateur Wrestling Association

BAWHA Bide-A-Wee Home Association

BAWRA British Australian Wool Realization Association

Bay Bay of(Bengal, Biscay, Fundy, Islands, Naples, Panama, Pigs, Whales, etc.); The Bay— Algoa Bay or Port Elizabeth Bay in South Africa

Bay of Biscuits (naval nickname —Bay of Biscay)

bay cand dc bayonet candelabra double contact

Bay Cities cities surrounding San Francisco Bay

Bay City San Francisco

Bayer *Bayerisch* (German—bavarian)

Bayern (German—Bavaria)

Bay of Gold San Francisco Bay's nickname before wide-scale pollution threatened its destruction

Bayou City Houston, Texas

Bayou State Louisiana and Mississippi vie for this nickname

Bay of Pigs Cuba's south coastal Bahía de Cochinos where an unsuccessful attempt was made to liberate Cubans from Castro's rule supported by Soviet armament

Bayreuth Wagnerian festival held in the Franconian city of Bayreuth in Germany

BAYS British Association of Young Scientists

Bay State official nickname of Massachusetts known in colonial times as the Colony of Massachusetts Bay

Bay Stater(s) Massachusettan(s)

Bay Street financial center of the Bahamas in Nassau on New Providence Island; financial center of Canada in Toronto, Ontario (for whom the former was named)

Bazel (Dutch—Basel)

bb ball bearing; bank burglar(y); bayonet base (lamp or socket); below bridges; bill book; blood bank; blood buffer (base); blue bloaters; both bones (fractured); both to blame; breakthrough bleeding; breast biopsy; buffer base; bungling bureaucrat; double black; pellet fired from or made for a bb gun

bb (BB) billboard (television script)

b-b black bordered; bogie-bogie (single-unit locomotive)

b/b bail bond; bottled in bond

b & b bed and board; bed and breakfast; benedictine and brandy

b or b brass or bronze (cargo)

b to b back to back

bb *babord* (Swedish—port side)

BB Banco do Brasil (Bank of Brazil); battleship; Before Bach; B'nai B'rith; Brigitte Bardot; Bureau of the Budget

BB (DCO) Barclays Bank (Dominion, Colonial and Overseas)

B-B Bora-Bora

B.B. Bernard Berensen; Bjørnstjerne Bjørnson; Boys' Brigade

B & B Brown and Bigelow

B of B Bureau of the Budget

BB *Banco do Brasil* (Portuguese—Bank of Brazil)

BB 62 USS *New Jersey*

bba born before arrival

BBA Big Brothers of America; British Bankers' Association

B.B.A. Bachelor of Business Administration

bbac bus-to-bus access circuit(ry)

b/bar bull bar (fender)

bbb banker's blanket bond; basic boxed base; bed, breakfast, and bath; blood brain barrier; triple black

BBB Best Berlin Broadcast; Best British Briar (pipes); Better Business Bureau

BBBC British Boxing Board of Control

BBBS Boat Builder's Benefit Society

BB & BU Bagel Boilers and Bakers Union

bbc barrels, boxes, and crates (cargo); bromobenzylcyanide (gas)

BBC Bank of British Columbia; Beautiful British Columbia; Biwako Broadcasting Corporation (Japan); British Broadcasting Corporation; Brown Boveri Corporation; Buchanan Borehole Colleries

BBCC Big Bend Community College

BBCCS B'nai B'rith Career and Counseling Services

BBC dissociation Braid-Berheim-Charcot dissociation

BBC English cultured way of speaking English

BBCF British Bacon Curers' Federation

BBCL Bermuda Broadcasting Company Limited

BBCM Bandmaster—Bandsmen's College of Music

BBCMA British Baby Carriage Manufacturers' Association

BBCS Browne Book-Charging System

BBCSO British Broadcasting Corporation Symphony Orchestra

bbcw bare beryllium copper wire

bbd baby born dead; beta-binomial distribution; bucket-brigade device; bulletin board

bbdc before bottom dead center

BB(DCO) Barclays Bank (Dominion, Colonial, Overseas)

BBEA Brewery and Bottling Engineers Association

bb & em bed, breakfast, and evening meal

bbf boron-based fuel

BBF Biblioteca Benjamin Franklin (Mexico City); Boilermakers, Blacksmiths, Forgers (union)

BBFC British Board of Film Censors

B-b f's Buddah-befuddled fanatics (who set themselves afire to protest man's inhumanity to man)

bbg bundle branch block

BBG Bermuda Botanical Gardens; Brooklyn Botanic Garden

BBGA British Broiler Growers' Association

bb-gun airgun shooting bb's (ball bearings)

BBHC Buffalo Bill Historical Center (Cody, Wyoming)

BBHF B'nai B'rith Hillel Foundations

BBI Barbecue Briquet Institute; Brandeis-Bardin Institute

B Bibl Bachelier en Bibliothèconomie (French—Bachelor in Library Science)

BBINA Bed and Breakfast Inns of North America

BBiP *British Books in Print*

BBIRA British Baking Industries Research Association

B Bisc Bay of Biscay

bbj ball-bearing joint

bbk breadboard kit

bbl barrel

BBL Bahia Blanca; Bangkok Bank Ltd; Barclay's Bank Limited; Big Brothers League

bbl roll barrel roller

bbls/day barrels per day

bbm break-before-make

b & b magazine periodical featuring breasts and buttocks

BBMRA British Brush Manufacturers Research Association

BBNNR Braunton Burrows National Nature Reserve (England)

BBNP Big Bend National Park (Texas)

BBNR Back Bay National Refuge (Virginia)

Bbo Bilbao

B-Bomb benzedrine bomb (underground slang—benzedrine inhaler)

B-boy busboy; mess sergeant

bbp boxes, barrels, packages, (cargo); building block principle

BBP Beech Bottom Power Company

BBP *Boletim de Bibliografia Portuguesa (Bulletin of Portuguese Bibliography)*

b&b pericarditis bread-and-butter pericarditis

BBPR Bianfi, Barbiano, Peresutti, and Rogers (avant-garde Italian architects)

bbq barbecue

BBQ Brooklyn, Bronx, Queens

bbr balloon-borne radio

BBRR Brookhaven Beam Research Reactor (AEC)

BBRS Balloon-Borne Radio System

bbs ball bearings; barrels of basic sediment; box bark strips

Bbs British biscuits

BBS Barber Blue Sea (steamship line); Bermuda Biological Station; Brunei Broadcasting Service

B.B.S. Bachelor of Business Science

BBSATRA British Boot, Shoe and Allied Trades Research Association

BBSI British Boot and Shoe Institution

bbsj ball-bearing swivel joint

B & B SNC British and Burmese Steam Navigation Company

BBSR Bermuda Biological Station for Research

bbsu bid bond service undertaking

bbs & w barrels of basic sediment and water

bbt basal body temperature; bombardment

BBT Brotherhood of Book Travelers

BBTA British Bureau of Television Advertising

BB & TC Bahamas Broadcasting and Television Commission

BBU Bagel Boilers Union

bbw bare brass wire

BBWAA Baseball Writers' Association of America

BBX Bluebird (stock-exchange symbol)

BBYO B'nai B'rith Youth Organization

bbz bearing bronze

bc back course; bad check; ballistic camera; base (shield) connection; between centers; bills for collection; binary code; binary counter; birth control; bogus check; bolometric correction; bolt circle; bone connection; born in colony;

bottom (dead) center; broadcast control; budgeted cost; building center; burden center

bc (BC) bio-conversion; bulk carrier

b/c bales of cotton; bills for collection; birth control; broadcast

b & c building and contents

B^c *Banc* (French—bank, sandbank)

BC Bacone College; Baja California, Mexico; Bakersfield College; Balliol College (Oxford); Bank Clearing; Bankruptcy Court; Bard College; Barnard College; Barrington College; Barry College; Bates College; Battery Commander; Battle Cruiser; Beaver College; Beckley College; Before Christ; Belgian Congo; Belhaven College; Bellarmine College; Belmont College; Beloit College; Benedict College; Bennett College; Bennington College; Berea College; Berry College; Bethany College; Bethel College; Bishop College; Blackburn College; Blinn College; Bliss Classification; Bliss College; Bloomfield College; Bluefield College; Bluffton College; Bomber Command; Borough Council; Boston College; Bourget College; Bowdoin College; Brandon College; Brasenose College (pronounced *Brazenose* at Oxford); Brenau College; Brentwood College; Brescia College; Brevard College; Briarcliff College; Bridgewater College; British Columbia; British Commonwealth; British Council; Brooklyn College; Bruyere College; Bryant College; Burdett College; Butler College

B-C Barber-Colman

B.C. Bachelor of Chemistry; Bachelor of Commerce; Baja California; Before Christ; British Columbia

B & C Banking and Currency (Senate Committee)

B of C Bank of Canada; Bureau of the Census

BC *Baja California* (Spanish—Lower California), northern section is a state whose capital is Mexicali while the southern part is a territory whose capital is La Paz; *Banco Central* (Spanish—Central Bank), Spain's largest; *Biological*

Conservation

B C *basso continuo* (Italian—continuous bass background)

bca best cruise altitude; blood color analyzer

bca *barrica* (Spanish—cask, keg); *biblioteca* (Portuguese or Spanish—library)

B^ca *Boca* (Portuguese or Spanish—mouth, river mouth)

BCA Battery Control Area; Billiard Congress of America; Blue Cross Association; Boys' Clubs of America; British Caledonian Airways; British Colonial Airlines; Bureau of Consular Affairs; Bureau of Consumer Affairs

B/C of A British College of Aeronautics

BCAA British Columbia Automobile Association

BCAB Birth Control Advisory Bureau; British Computer Association for the Blind

bcac biology classroom activity checklist

BCAC British Conference on Automation and Computation

BCA/DoS Bureau of Consular Affairs—Department of State

BCAir British Commonwealth Air Force

BCAL British Caledonian Airways

BCALA Black (librarians) Caucus (of the) American Library Association

BCAP Beacon Collision-Avoidance Program

BCAPT Braverman-Chevigny Auditory Projective Test

BCAR British Civil Airworthiness Requirements; British Council for Aid to Refugees

BCAS British Compressed Air Society

b'cast(ing) broadcast(ing)

BCAT Birmingham College of Advanced Technology

bcb binary code box; broadcast band; button-cell battery

BCBC British Cattle Breeders' Club

bcbh boiler casing bulkhead

BC/BS Blue Cross/Blue Shield

bcc beam-coupling coefficient; body-centered cubic

BCC Battery Control Central; Berkshire Community College; Board of Crime Control (Montana); British Communications Corporation; British Council of Churches; British Crown Colony; Broadcasting

Corporation of China; Bronx Community College; Bureau Central de Compensation; Bureau of Charities and Corrections (South Dakota); Burlington Community College

BCCA Beer Can Collectors of America; British Cyclo-Cross Association

BCCBP *Biblioteca de Cataluña y Central de Bibliotecas Populares* (Spanish—Library of Catalonia and Central Public Library)—Calle Carmen, Barcelona

BCCCUS British Commonwealth Chamber of Commerce in the United States

bccd buried-channel charge-coupled device

BCCF British Cast Concrete Federation

BCCG British Cooperative Clinical Group

BCCI Bank of Credit and Commerce International

BCCO Base Consolidation Control Office(r)

BCCR Banco Central de Costa Rica

BCCS British Columbia Coastal Service

bcd barrels per calendar day; binary-coded data

BCD Battelle's Columbus Division

bcdc binary coded decimal counter

BCDIC Binary-Coded Decimal Interchange Code

BCESL British Commonwealth Ex-Services League

BCF Battle Cruiser Fleet; Battle Cruiser Flotilla; Battle Cruiser Force

Bch Beach

bchcmbr(s) beachcomber(s)

BCHP *Banco Central Hipotecario del Peru* (Spanish—Central Mortgage Bank of Peru)

BCI Bureau of Correctional Institutions (Iowa); Bureau of Criminal Identification

BCL Battelle's Columbus Laboratories; Bermuda Container Line; Bougainville Copper Limited

BCLA Birth Control League of America

bcm basic control monitor

BCM *Banco Comercial Mexicano* (Spanish—Mexican Commercial Bank)

bcmg becoming

BCNZ Broadcasting Corporation of New Zealand

BCP *Banco de Credito del Peru* (Spanish—Credit Bank of Peru)

BCPA British Copyright Protection Association

BCPs Black College Presidents

BCRP *Banco Central de Reserva del Peru* (Spanish—Central Reserve Bank of Peru)

bcs because

BCS Battle Cruiser Squadron; British Conchological Society; Budget Control System

B-C-S Bardeen-Cooper-Schriefer

B.C.S. Bachelor of Criminal Science

BCT Bell Canyon Test

bcwp budgeted cost of work performed

bcws budgeted cost for work schedule

bcz because

bd behavior(ally) disorder(ed); boat deck; bridge deck

b & d bondage and discipline (sado-masochism)

bd *bind* (Dano-Norwegian—volume)

bdi both days included

bdl baseline demonstration laser

BDMS Bulk Direct Mail Service

bds brands

B-D Squad Bomb-Disposal Squad

bdt *bundt* (Dano-Norwegian—bundle)

bdt's back-door trots (diarrhea)

be. beam expander; bilingual education

b & e breaking and entering

BE Black English; Borough Engineer; British Embassy; British English

BE *Buque Escuela* (Spanish—Schoolship)

be4 before

BEA Broadcast Education Association

BEAR HUG *Basic Extended Acronym Human Users Guide*

Beau Beauford; Beaufort; Beaumont; Beauregard

Beautiful Kingdom translation of China's name for the United States of America

beautility beauty + utility

BECC Boeing Engineering & Construction Company

bedoc beds occupied

Bee Beatrice

BEE Basic Economic Education

B.E.E. Bachelor of Electrical En-

gineering

BEE *Bulletin of Environmental Education*

Beeb BBC (British Broadcasting Corporation)

beec binary error-erasure channel

Beech 99 Beechcraft seventeen-seat aircraft

Beecham Beauchamp

Beech F-33C five-place Bonanza training airplane

Beech Queen Air Beechcraft Seminole transport aircraft

Beedle General Walter Bedell Smith

beef. business-and-engineering-enriched fortran

beefalo beef cattle + buffalo (hybrid)

Beef Barons Armour, Cudahy, Morris, Swift, and their ilk

Beefeaters Her (His) Majesty's Honourable Corps of Gentlemen at Arms

Beef State Nebraska's nickname

Bee Gee British Guiana (now called Guyana)

Beehive of Industry Providence, Rhode Island

Beehive State Utah whose great seal displays a beehive symbolic of the energy of its settlers

Beelzebub The Devil

Beer City Milwaukee

Beethoven 1st, 2nd, 3rd, 4th, 5th, 6th, 7th, 8th, 9th First, Second, Third (*Eroica*), Fourth, Fifth, Sixth (*Pastoral*), Seventh, Eighth, Ninth (*Choral*) —symphonies composed by Beethoven

Beethoven Town Bonn, Germany—birthplace of Ludwig van Beethoven

Beetle Juice (American navalese —Betelgeuse)—variable giant red star serving navigators as it is of the first magnitude and belongs to the constellation of Orion

beet sugar sucrose

Bee Wee nickname for a British West Indian

bef before; blunt end first; buffered emitter follower

Bef *Befehl* (German—command, order)

BEF Bonus Expeditionary Force; British Expeditionary Force

BEFA British Emigrant Families Association

befm bending form

befo' before (as in *befo' de wo'*—before the War of the Secession when a few Southerners owned plantations allegedly extending from the coast of Georgia and South Carolina to the banks of the Mississippi—*befo' de wo'*)

beg. begin; beginning

beg begynde(lse) [Dano-Norwegian—begin(ning)]

BEG Belgrade, Yugoslavia (airport); Bureau of Economic Geology

BEG Bank Europaeischer Genossenschafsbanken (German—European Cooperative Bank)

Beggar's The Beggar's Opera (three-act ballad opera by John Christopher Pepusch)

Beggars of the Sea Dutch pirates and privateers

begr begrundet (German—established)

BEH Bureau of Education for the Handicapped

BEIIA British Export Houses Association

behav behavior; behavioral; behaviorist(ic)

Behavioral Res Behavioral Research Laboratories

BEHC Bio-Environmental Health Center

bei butanol-extractable iodine

BEI Bridgeport Engineering Institute

BEI British Education Index

BEIA Board of Education Inspectors' Association

Beibl Beiblatt (German—supplement)

beif beifolgend (German—sent herewith)

Beih *beihft* (German—supplement)

Beijing (official Chinese name for Peking)—pronounced *Bay Jing*

beil beiliegend (German—enclosed)

Beil Beilage (German—appendix, supplement)

BEIS British Egg Information Service

Beit Lahm (Arabic—Bethlehem)

Beitr Beitrag (German—contribution)

bek bekendgørelse (Dano-Norwegian—announcement)

BEK AS Beck Shoe Corp (symbol)

bel below; 10 decibels

bel (Turkish—pass)

Bel Bela; Belcher; Belden; Belem; Belen; Belfast; Belford; Belham; Belize; Bellamy; Bellanca; Belmont; Belorussia; Belos; Beltram

Bel Bacharel (Portuguese—Bachelor)—academic degree

BEL Belém do Pára, Brazil (airport)

BELAIR Belgian Air Staff (NATO)

Bela Lugosi Bela Paul Blasko

Bel Anglais (French—Handsome Englishman)—nickname of John Churchill—Duke of Marlborough

Belau Republic of Belau (formerly Palau)

Belchers Belcher Islands in Hudson Bay just north of James Bay

belcrk bellcrank

Bel & Dr Bel and the Dragon

B.Elec. & Tel. Eng. Bachelor of Electronics and Telecommunication Engineering

Belém (Portuguese—Bethlehem)—also the Amazon River port of Belém do Pará; Lisbon suburb

Belén (Spanish—Bethlehem)

bel ex bel example (French—fine example)—fine copy of a book, engraving, map, etc.

Belf Belfast; Belfastian(s)

Belfast British turboprop transport aircraft; Northern Ireland's capital city

belg belgisk (Dano-Norwegian—Belgian)

Belg Belgian; Belgium

Belg Belgica (Portuguese or Spanish—Belgium); *Belgio* (Italian—Belgium)

Belgek(s) Belgian(s) so called by American, British, and Canadian armed forces during World War II

belgian belgian griffon (small black or reddish-black terrier); belgian horse (draft horse first raised in Belgium); belgian hare (rabbit originally bred in Belgium); belgian sheepdog (used for herding sheep and protecting property, a police dog)

Belgian Congo colonial possession of Belgium occupying the greater part of central Africa from 1884 to 1963 and now called Zaire

Belgian East Africa former name of Ruanda

Belgian Ports (east to west) Antwerpen (Anvers), Bruxelles

(Brussel), Gente (Gand), Brugge (Bruges), Zeebrugge, Blankenberge, Oostende (Ostend), Nieuwpoort (Nieuport)

Belgian Quartet Belgium's best-known classical composers, ranked chronologically, include Gretry, Vieuxtemps, Franck, and Ysaÿe

Belgica (Latin—Belgium)—plus northern France

Bélgica (Portuguese or Spanish—Belgium)

België (Dutch or Flemish—Belgium)

Belgien (German—Belgium)

Belgio (Italian—Belgium)

Belgíque (French—Belgium)

Belgium Kingdom of Belgium (Flemish and French spoken in this lowland nation on the North Sea, Belgians noted for their hospitality and their excellent products); *Royaume de Belgique* (its French name); *Koninkrijk België* (its Flemish name)

Belgium Film Pioneer Jacques Feyder

Belgium's Largest Port Antwerp

Belglais Belgian-English

Belgolux Belgium and Luxembourg

Belgrade English equivalent of Beograd

Belgrado (Spanish—Belgrade)

Belial The Devil

Belice (Spanish—Belize)

Believing Unbeliever Supreme Court Justice Felix Frankfurter who described himself as a reverent agnostic as well as a believing unbeliever

Belize formerly called British Honduras and still the name of its principal seaport city

Bell Bell Aircraft; Bell System (American Telephone and Telegraph and associated companies collectively called Ma Bell or Mother Bell)

Bell 47 Sioux utility helicopter built by Bell Aircraft

Bell 204 gunship helicopter nicknamed Huey as it is designated UH-1

Bell 206 five-seat turbopowered helicopter also called Jet Ranger or Sea Ranger

bella belladonna (drug stimulant whose overdose results in delirium and death)

Bella Arabella; Isabella

Bellas Artes Instituto Nacional de Bellas Artes (Spanish—National Institute of Fine Arts)—in Mexico City

Belle Bella; Arabella; Isabella

Belle of Amherst Emily Dickinson

Belleau Wood Bois de Belleau

Belle City of the Lakes Racine, Wisconsin

Belle Riviere (see *La Belle Riviere)*

Belle Starr Myra Bell Shirley

BELLMATIC Bell Laboratories Machine-Aided Technical Information Center

Bell Rock Inchcape Rock off the Forfarshire coast of Scotland and the subject of Robert Southey's *Ballad of Inchcape Rock*

bells. bell-bottom pants

Bells (see *The Bells)*

Bell Sys Tech J Bell System Technical Journal

Bells of Zlonice Dvořák's Symphony No. 1

Bell Town East Hampton, Connecticut

Belmo Belmopan

BELNAV Belgian Naval Staff (NATO)

Belomorsko-Baltiyskiy Kanal (Russian—Belomorsk-Baltic Canal)—the waterway linking Belomorsk on the White Sea with Leningrad on the Baltic via lakes Onega and Ladoga

Belostok (Russian—Bialystok)

Beloved Butler Angus Hudson of Scotland within the Bellamy household in London depicted in *Upstairs Downstairs*

Beloved Friend Nadejda von Meck (Tchaikovsky's patroness and lifetime friend he never met)

Beloved Infidel Colonel Robert Ingersoll

Below Sea-Level Cities Brawley and El Centro in the Imperial Valley of southern California

Beloye More (Russian—White Sea)—north of Leningrad in the Arctic

Belsen Bergen-Belsen (World War II concentration camp town in northwest Germany)

Belvac Societe Belge de Vacuologie et de Vacuotechnique (Belgian Society for Vacuum Science and Technology)

bem (BEM) behavior engineering model

Bem Bemerkung (German—comment, note, observation)

BEM British Empire Medal

B.E.M. Bachelor of Engineering of Mines

BEMA Business Equipment Manufacturers Association

BEMB British Egg Marketing Board

BEMO Base Equipment Management Office

bems bug-eyed monsters (science-fiction jargon)

BEMS Bakery Equipment Manufacturers Society

BEMSA British Eastern Merchant Shippers Association

ben (Gaelic—mountain, summit); (Hebrew—son)

ben. bene (Latin—good, well); *benedictio* (Latin—blessing)

Ben Benard; Benedict; Beniah; Benito; Benjamin; Bennet(t); Benno; Beno; Benoni; Bentley; Benvenuto

BEN Bureau d'Études nucleaires (Belgian Bureau of Nuclear Studies)

Ben Block nickname for a British sailor

Ben Cur Benguela Current

Bend Bendigo

benday benday (photoengraving) process (named for a 19th-century American printer, Benjamin Day)

BENDEX Beneficial Data Exchange (linking Social Security Administration with state welfare agencies)

B en Dr Bachelier en Droit (French—Bachelor of Law)

bene benzine

BENECHAN Benelux Subarea Channel (NATO)

Bened Benedict; Benedictine

Benedictines monastic order founded by St Benedict

benef beneficiary

Benef Benefice

Ben Eil Benedenwindse Eilanden (Dutch—Leeward Islands)

Benelux economic union of Belgium, Netherlands, and Luxembourg

Benemérito de las Américas (Spanish—Meritorious Man of the Americas)—the Mexican Indian Benito Juárez

Bene't Benedict

benev benevolent

Beng Bengal; Bengali

B.Eng. Bachelor of Engineering

bengals bengal tigers; thick cigars

Bengis Bengalis

Bengs Bengalis

B.Eng. Sci. Bachelor of Engineering Science

B.Eng.Tech. Bachelor of Engineering Technology

Ben-Gurion Israeli modification of Centurion tanks made to carry 105mm guns; Tel-Aviv's airport also named in honor of Israel's first prime minister, David Ben-Gurion

Ben-Gurion (Hebrew—Son of a Lion)—name adopted by David Green

Beni Israel (Hebrew—Sons of Israel)—Jewish community of Bombay, India

Benin People's Republic of Benin (West African nation formerly called Dahomey and whose people still call themselves Dahomeans and converse in French as well as many tribal languages)

Benin Ports (Formerly Dahomey) (north to south) Cotonou, Kpeme

Benito Juárez Mexico City's principal airport named for its greatest president who ousted the French and Maximilian from Mexico

Benj Benjamin

Benja Benjamin

Benjies hundred-dollar bills bearing the portrait of America's libertarian-patriot philosopher-scientist Benjamin Franklin

Benjn Benjamin

Benjy Benjamin

Bennie Benjamin

bennies benzedrine stimulants

benny (underground slang—benzedrine)

Benny Benjamin

Benny Goodman Benjamin David Goodman

ben sug beneficial suggestion

bent-nail syndrome medical nickname for Peyronie's disease (malady wherein the penis is bent out of shape)

Bento Baruch; Benito

b & ent & pl breaking and entering and petty larceny

Benvenuto Benvenuto Cellini, Berlioz opera nicknamed *Malvenuto* by carping critics of his era

benz benzedrine; benzine

Benziger Benziger, Bruce, and Glencoe

BEO Borough Education Officer(r)

beoc battery echelon operating control

BEOG Basic Educational Opportunity Grant

Beograd (Serbo-Croatian—Bel-

grade)
BE & P Bureau of Engraving and Printing
B.E.P. Bachelor of Engineering Physics
BEP *Brevet d'Études Professionnelles* (French—Professional Studies Diploma)
B EpA British Epilepsy Association
BEPC Beijins Electron Positron Collider
BEPI Budget Estimates Presentation Instructions
BEPO British Experimental Pile Operation
bepoc Burrough's electrographic printer-plotter for ordnance computing
BEPQ Bureau of Entomology and Plant Quarantine
bepti bionomics, environment, plasmodium, treatment, immunity (factors in malaria epidemiology)
BEPZ Bataan Export Processing Zone (Philippines)
beq bequeath
BEQ Background and Experience Questionnaire
beqd bequeathed
beqt bequest
ber buffer (flow chart)
ber *berechnet* (German—computed)
Ber Berlin, Berwickshire
Rer *Bericht* (German—report)
BER Berlin, West Germany (Tempelhof airport); Bureau of Economic Regulation
BERA Business Education Research Associated
Berb Berber
Berbería (Spanish—Barbary)—North Africa
Ber Bunsenge Phys Chem *Berichte der Bunsengesellschaft für Physikalische Chemie* (German—Report of the Bunsen Society for Physical Chemistry)
BERC Biomedical Engineering Research Corporation; Black Economic Research Center
BERCO British Electric Resistance Company
BERCON Berlin Contingency (NATO)
Berdoo San Bernardino, California
berg iceberg (sometimes written 'berg)
Berg Berger; Bergin
Bergen Bergen-Belsen (site of Nazi German concentration camp); Norway (seaport city

and birthplace of Grieg); Bergen op Zoom (Dutch port on Zoom River near Scheldt estuary); county in northern New Jersey; former name of Mons, Belgium; etc.
Bergomum (Latin—Bergamo)
BERH Board of Engineers for Rivers and Harbors
Bering Bering Sea linking the Arctic Ocean with the North Pacific between Alaska and the USSR; Bering Strait (56-mile-wide ocean passage connecting the Arctic Ocean with the North Pacific)
Beringia Bering and Chukchi Seas area
Berk Berkeley
Berks Berkshire
Berks the Beautiful Pennsylvania's Berks County settled by Pennsylvania Germans who are noted for their neatness
Berkshires Berkshire Hills of western Connecticut and Massachusetts
Berl Berlin
Berlim (Portuguese—Berlin)
Berlin Bach Karl Philipp Emanuel Bach—also nicknamed Hamburg Bach
Berlin Wall barricading wall erected by Soviet authorities to separate free zone of West Berlin from Communist-controlled zone of East Berlin; many who choose freedom scale this wall despite risk of being killed for seeking liberty
Berlioz symphonies *Symphonie Fantastique* and *Symphonie Funèbre et Triomphale*
Berl Tid *Berlingske Tidende* (Danish—Berling's Times)—a leading daily newspaper
Berm Bermuda Islands
Berma (Latin—Bremen)
Bermuda formerly called Somers Islands
Bermudas Bermuda Islands
Bermuda Triangle area between Bermuda, Cape Hatteras, and Key West in the western North Atlantic—also called the Devil's Triangle or the Limbo of the Lost because of the many planes and ships lost in the area; area is also said to be between Bermuda, Florida, and Puerto Rico
bermudite gabbro-type igenous rock plus biotite crystals and iron ores
Bern Berna; Bernal(do); Bernan;

Bernard(o); Bernarr; Berner; Bernhard; Bernold
Berna (Latin—Berne)
Bernese Oberland Bernese Alps
Bernh Bernhard
Bernhardt Sarah Bernhardt—stage name of Rosine Bernard
Bernie Bernard
Berno Bernardo
Berolinum (Latin—Berlin)
Berona (Latin—Münster)
Berry City Woodburn, Oregon
Berserkeley Berkeley, California's nickname
Bert Albert; Alberta; Albertina; Bertel; Bertha; Berthel; Bertillon (system); Bertin; Bertol; Berton; Bertram; Bertrand; Bertwin; Cuthbert; Delbert; Elbert; Elberta; Filbert; Gilbert; Herbert; Hilbert; Ibert; Lambert; Norbert; Philbert; Roberta; Wilbert; Zilbert
Bertie (affectionate nickname—Bertrand Russell—colossus of twentieth-century philosophy)
Bert Lahr Irving Lahreim
bertm berth term
Ber Tri Bermuda Triangle (North Atlantic Ocean shipwreck area within a triangle extending from Bermuda to Cape Hatteras to Key West and back to Bermuda)
Berts Bertillon Measurements
BERU Building Economics Research Unit
Berw Berwick
beryl beryllium aluminum silicate
bes balanced electrolyte solution
bes *besonders* (German—especially)
Bes Bessel's functions
BES Biological Engineering Society; Bureau of Employment Security
B.E.S. Bachelor of Engineering Science
B es A *Bachelier des Arts* (French—Bachelor of Arts)
BESA British Engineering Standards Association
BESE Bureau of Elementary and Secondary Education
BeShT Baal Shem-Tov (Israel Ben Eliezer)
besi bus electronic-scanning indicator
B es L *Bachelier des Lettres* (French—Bachelor of Letters)
BESL British Empire Service League
BESN British Empire Steam

Navigation (company)

BESRL Behavioral Science Research Laboratory (USA)

bess binary electromagnetic signature

Bess Bessemer; Mrs Harry S. Truman

B es S Bachelier es Sciences (French—Bachelor of Science)

BESS Bank of England Statistical Summary

bessel bessel equation, bessel function, or bessel method (named for the German 19th-century astronomer Friedrich Wilhelm Bessel)

bessemer bessemer converter or bessemer steel (named for its English inventor, Sir Henry Bessemer)

Bessie Bethlehem Steel (Wall Street slang); Elizabeth

Bessie Love Juanita Horton's stage name

Bessy Elizabeth

BESSY Bestell System (German teleordering)

best Bestellung (German—order); *bestyrelse* (Dano-Norwegian—board, direction)

BEST Basic Essential Skills Training; Black Efforts for Soul in Television

bet. best estimate of trajectory; between

Bet Beirut; Betsy; Elizabeth

BET Biker Enforcement Team (of law-enforcement officers investigating militant motorcycle gangs); British Electric Traction

Beta Betamax (video-cassette system)

BETA Business Equipment Trade Association

Betel Nut Island Penang, Malaysia

Beth Bethlehem; Elizabeth

Beth Israel (Hebrew—House of Israel)—many synagogues bear this name

Bethlehem Bethlehem Steel Corporation

Bethlehem (Hebrew—House of Bread)

Bethnel Bethnel Green, London

Beth Steel Bethlehem Steel

betr better

betr betrefend (German—concerning)

Betsy Elizabeth

Betsytown Elizabeth, New Jersey

BETTS Bolt Extrusion Thrust

Termination System

Betty Elizabeth

Betty Grable Elizabeth Grasle

betw between

BEU British Empire Union

BEUC Bureau Européen des Unions Consommateurs (Bureau of European Consumer Unions)

bev bevel; beverage; billion electron volts

bev (BeV) billion electron volts

Bev Beva; Bevan; Beveridge; Beverley; Beverly; Bevis

BEV Black English Vernacular; Blake E Vance

Beverly Sills Belle Silverman

BEW Board of Economic Warfare

BEWT Bureau of East-West Trade

bex broadband exchange

bexec budget execution

BEY Beirut, Lebanon (airport)

bez bezahlt (German—paid); *bezuglich* (German—referring to)

Bez Bezirk (German—district)

bezw bezichungsweise, beziehungsweise (German—respectively)

bf back feed; beer firkin; before; bloody fool; boiler feed; bold face; both faces; boy friend; buffered; butter fat

b-f beat-frequency

b/f black female; brought forward; brown female

b & f bell and flange

bf bassa frequenza (Italian—bass frequency); *bestemt form* (Dano-Norwegian—definite shape); *bouillon filtrate* (French—filtered bouillon)

b.f. bona fide (Latin—genuine, sincere)—in good faith; without deception; without fraud

BF Banque de France (Bank of France); Battle Fleet; Battle Force

B.F. Bachelor of Forestry

BF Beogradska Filharmonica (Serbo-Croat—Belgrade Philharmonic)

bfa basal forebrain area

BFA Black Faculty Association; British Fellmongers' Association; British Film Academy; Broadcasting Foundation of America; Bureau of Financial Assistance

B.F.A. Bachelor of Fine Arts

bfaln buffer boundary alignment

BFAP British Forces—Arabian Peninsula

BFB Bureau of Forensic Ballistics

BFBC British Forces Broadcasting Service

BFBPW British Federation of Business and Professional Women

BFBS British Forces Broadcasting Service; British and Foreign Bible Society

bfc benign febrile convulsion

BFCA British Federation of Commodity Associations

BFCC Brothers for Christian Community

BFCF Bremerton Freight Car Ferry

BFCS British Friesian Cattle Society

BFCSD Brewery, Flour, Cereal, Soft Drink and Distillery (Workers of America)

bfct boiler feed compound tank

bfcy beneficiary

BFDC Bureau of Foreign and Domestic Commerce

bfe beam-forming electrode

BFEA Bureau of Far Eastern Affairs (U.S. Department of State)

BFEBS British Far Eastern Broadcasting Society

BFFA British Film Fund Agency

BFFC British Federation of Folk Clubs

bfg brute-force gyro

Bfg Bank für Gemeinwirtschaft (German—Bank for Municipal Management)

BFG BF Goodrich

BFHMF British Felt Hat Manufacturers' Federation

BFHS Benjamin Franklin High School

bfi beam-forming interfact

BFI British Film Institute; Business Forms Institute; Seattle, Washington (Boeing Field)

BFIA British Flour Industry Association

BFICC British Facsimile Industry Compatability Committee

bfl back focal length

BFL Barber Fern Line; Belgian Fruit Line; Blue Funnel Line (Holt's); Books For Libraries

BFLF Biblioteca della Facoltà di Lettere e Filosofia (Italian—Library of the Faculty of Letters and Philosophy)—in Florence

BFM Ballet Folklorico de Mexico (Spanish—Folklore Ballet of Mexico)

BFMA Business Forms Management Association

BFMF British Federation of Music Festivals; British Footwear Manufacturers' Federation

BFMIRA British Food Manufacturing Industries Research Association

BFMO Base Fuels Management Officer (USAF)

BFMP British Federation of Master Printers

Bfn Bloemfontein

BFN British Forces Network

bfo beat-frequency oscillator; blood-forming organs

Bfo Buffalo

BFO Bureau of Field Operations

bfoq bona-fide occupational qualification

B.For. Bachelor of Forestry

bform budget formulation

B.For.Sci. Bachelor of Forestry Science

bfozp best-fit optic Z-plane

bfp biological false-positive (reactions); boiler feedpump

BFP British Fishing Port (registration symbols appearing on the bows of British fishing vessels and indicating their home ports)—(*see* British Fishing Port appendix)

BFPA British Film Producers Association

BFPC British Farm Produce Council

bfpdda binary floating-point digital-differential analyzer

BFPO British Field Post Office

BFPPS Bureau of Foods, Pesticides, and Product Safety (FDA)

bfpv bona fide purchaser for value

bfr biologic false reactor; blood flow rate; bone formation rate; buffer

Bfr *Belgische frank* (Dutch—Belgian franc)

B Fr Belgian franc

bfr(s) *belgisk(e) franc(s)* [Dano-Norwegian—Belgian franc(s)]

BFRS Bio-Feedback Research Society

bfR sol buffered Ringer's solution

Bf's Buddhist fanatics (who'll set themselves afire as a token of their faith)

BFS Belfast, Northern Ireland (airport); Board of Foreign Scholarships; Bureau of Family Services; Bureau of Federal Supply

B.F.S. Bachelor of Foreign Service

BFS *Bundesanstalt für Flugsicherung* (German—Air-Traffic Control Authority)

BFSA Black Faculty and Staff Association; British Fire Services Association

BFSS British and Foreign Sailors' Society

bft bio-feedback training

BFT Bentonite Flocculation Test

B.F.T. Bachelor of Foreign Trade

BFTA British Fur Trade Alliance

BFTC Boeing Flight Test Center

BFTS British and Foreign Temperance Society

BFUP Board of Fire Underwriters of the Pacific

BFUSA Basketball Federation of the United States of America

BFUW British Federation of University Women

BfV *Bundesamt für Verfassungsschutz* (German—Federal Office for the Protection of the Constitution)—West German FBI roughly equivalent to the Special Branch in Britain

bfw boiler feedwater

bg back gear; before girls (entered the armed forces); bluish-green; buccogingival; business girl

bg (BG) background (behind tv performers); block grant

b/g bonded goods

bG bluish green

Bg Bengal; Bengalese; Bengali

Bg *Berg* (German—mountain); *Bogen* (German—bow)—musical term

BG Benny Goodman; Birmingham Gage; British Guiana

B-G *Bach Gesellschaft*; David Ben-Gurion

B & G Barton and Guestier; Bing and Grondahl; buildings and grounds

BG *Bibliothèque publique et universitaire de Genève* (French—Public and University Library of Geneva)

bga blue-green algae (virus)

BGA Better Government Association; British Gliding Association

BGAS Boys and Girls Aid Society

B-G b Bordet-Gengou bacillus

BGB Booksellers of Great Britain

bgc blood group class

BGC British Gas Corporation

BGCC Bowling Green College of Commerce

BGCCC Board of Governors of the California Community Colleges

BG & E Baltimore Gas and Electric

B.G.E. Bachelor of Geological Engineering

B.Gen.Ed. Bachelor of General Education

BGF Banana Growers' Federation; Black Guerrilla Family

BGFE Boston Grain and Flour Exchange

BGFO Bureau of Government Financial Operations

bgg booster gas generator; bovine gamma globulin

BGGRA British Gelatine and Glue Research Association

bgh bovine growth hormone

bght bought

BGI Bechtel Group Inc; Bridgetown, Barbados (airport)

BGIRA British Glass Industry Research Association

B-girl bar girl

Bgk Bangkok

bgl below ground level

B.G.L. Bachelor of General Laws

BGLA Business Group for Latin America

bglb brilliant-green lactose broth

bglr burglar

bgl(s) bagel(s); beagle(s); bugle(s)

bgm background music

BGM Bethnal Green Museum; Binghamton, New York (airport)

BGMA British Gear Manufacturers' Association

bgmn baggageman

Bgn Bergen

BGN Board on Geographic Names

BGNR Barren Grounds Nature Reserve (New South Wales)

BGNY Bookbinders' Guild of New York

Bgo Bugo

bgp below-ground pool

bgr bombing and gunnery range

bgrv (BGRV) boost-glide reentry vehicle

bgs bags

bg(s) back gear(s); bag(s)

Bgs Brightlingsea

BGS British Geriatrics Society;

Brotherhood of the Good Shepherd

BGS Bundesgrenz Schutz (German-Frontier Troops)—West German NATO forces

bgsa blood-granulocyte specific activity

BGSC Belfer Graduate School of Science (Yeshiva University); Boise-Griffin Steamship Company

BGSM Bowman Gray School of Medicine

BGSU Bowling Green State University

bgt bought

Bgt Bight

Bgt Bugt (Danish—Bay)

BGT Bender Gestalt Test; British Guiana Time

BGTA Birmingham Group Training Association

BGTT Borderline Glucose Tolerance Test

B Gu British Guiana

BGU Ben Gurion University (Beersheba); Bowling Green University

BGU Biblioteca General da Universidade (Portuguese—University General Library)—in Coimbra

BgUL Bibliothèque générale de l'Université de Liège (French—General Library of the University of Liege)

bgw (BGW) battlefield guided weapon

BGW Baghdad, Iraq (airport)

bh bloody hell (British expletive); boiler house; breast height (4 feet in U.S.); brinell hardness

bh bougie-heure (French—candlehour); *brysholder* or *busteholder* (Dano-Norwegian—bra or brassiere)

Bh Brinell hardness

BH Base Hospital; Bath & Hammondsport (railroad); Benjamin Harrison (23rd President U.S.); Bill of Health; Brigade Headquarters; Brinell hardness; British Honduras; Broken Hill; magnetization curve (symbol)

B/H Bill of Health; Bordeaux-Hamburg (range of ports)

B&H Bell and Howell; Breitkopf and Härtel

B of H Board of Health

BH Bonne Humeur (French—Good Humor); *Boston Herald; Thai bhat(s)*—monetary unit(s)

bha base helix angle

bha (BHA) butylated hydroxyanisole

BHA British Homeopathic Association; British Honduras Airways

bh ad broach adapter

B.H.Adm. Bachelor of Hospital Administration

BHAFRA British Hat and Allied Feltmakers' Research Association

B'ham Birmingham

Bharat Republic of India

Bharat (Hindi-India)

BHB British Hockey Board

BHBNM Big Hole Battlefield National Monument

B Hbr boat harbor

BHBS British Honduras Broadcasting Service

bhc beaching cradle; benzene hexachloride (BHC)

BHC Barbers, Hairdressers, Cosmetologists (and Proprietors' Union); Black Hawk College; British High Commissioner; British Hovercraft Corporation; Brotherhood of the Holy Cross

BHCIUS Barbers, Hairdressers, and Cosmetologists International Union of America

BHCSA British Hospitals Contributory Scheme Association

bhd beachhead; bulkhead

BH$ British Honduras dollar

BHD Bronx House of Detention

B.H.E. Bachelor of Home Economics

B of HE Board of Higher Education

B'head Birkenhead

BHEW Benton Harbor Engineering Works

Bhf Bahnhof (German—station)

BHF Berliner Handels und Frankfurter (bank)

bhf(s) black homosexual female(s)

bhfx broach fixture

B H & G Better Homes and Gardens

BHGMF British Hang Glider Manufacturers Federation

bhi brain-heart infusion

BHI British Horological Institute; Bureau Hydrographique Internationale (International Hydrographic Bureau)

BHI British Humanities Index

bhib beef-heart infusion broth

BHIS Burroughs Hospital Information System

BHISSA Bureau of Health Insurance, Social Security Administration

BHK type-B Hong Kong influenza virus

bhl biological half-life

BHL Borax Holdings Limited

Bhm Birmingham, England

BHM Birmingham, Alabama (airport); Bureau of Health Manpower

BHMA Bald-Headed Men of America; British Hard Metal Association

BHMC Bell & Howell/Mamiya Company

BHMH Benjamin Harrison Memorial Home (Indianapolis, Indiana)

BHMRA British Hydromechanics Research Association

bhm(s) black homosexual male(s)

BHMS Bishop's Home Mission Society

bhn bephenium hydroynaphthoate

Bhn Bremerhaven; Brinell hardness number

BHNWR Bombay Hook National Wildlife Refuge (Delaware)

B Hond British Honduras

B.Hort. Bachelor of Horticulture

B.Hort.Sci. Bachelor of Horticultural Science

bhp biological hazard potential; boiler horsepower; brake horsepower

BHP Borehole Plugging Program; Broken Hill Proprietary

bhp hr brake horsepower hour

BHPRD Bureau of Health Planning and Resource Development (HEW)

Bhpric Bishopric

BHQ Brigade Headquarters

bhr basal heart rate; biotechnology and human research

BHRA British Hotels and Restaurants Association; British Hydromechanics Research Association

B & HRO Biotechnology and Human Research Office (NASA)

bhs betahemolytic streptococcus

Bhs Bohus

BHS Balboa High School; Boys High School; British Home Stores; British Horse Society; Bureau of Health Services; Burlesque Historical Society; Bushwick High School

B&HS Bonhomie and Hattiesburg Southern (railroad)

B.H.Sci. Bachelor of Household Science

BHSS Bronx High School of Science

bhst bottom-hole static temperature

bht baht tical (Thai monetary unit)

bht (BHT) butylated hydroxytoluene

BHTA British Herring Trade Association

bhtm(s) black heterosexual male(s)

Bhu Bhutan

Bhutan Kingdom of Bhutan (Asian Himalayan nation famed for its lac, its spices, waxes, and yak butter, Bhutanese speak Nepali and Tibetan); *Druk-yul* (its name in the official language called Dzonkha Bhután)

Bhv Bhavnagar

bh/vh body hematocrit/venous hemocrat (ratio)

Bhvn Bremerhaven

bhw boiling heavy water

BHW Boston Hospital for Women

BHYC Boothbay Harbor Yacht Club

B.Hyg. Bachelor of Hygiene

bi background investigation; bacteriological index; base ignition; base of prism in; burn index; bodily injury; buffer index

bi (BI) binary

b/i battery inverter

b & i bankruptcy and insolvency; base and increment

b or i brass or iron (cargo)

Bi biot; bismuth (symbol)

B^i Bani or Beni (Arabic—sons of)

BI Babson Institute; background investigation; Bahama Islands; Bermuda Islands; Braniff International; British India; Brookings Institution; Bureau of Investigation; National Biscuits (stock exchange symbol)

B of I Bureau of Investigation

BI Banca d'Italia (Bank of Italy)

BIA Bicycle Institute of America; Binding and Industries of America; Braille Institute of America; Brazilian International Airlines; Building Industry Association; Bureau of Indian Affairs; Bureau of Insular Affairs; Bureau of Inter-

American Affairs

BI & A Bureau of Intelligence and Research (US Department of State)

BIAA Bureau of Inter-American Affairs (US Department of State)

BIAC Business and Industry Advisory Committee (NATO)

BIAE British Institute of Adult Education

BIALL British and Irish Association of Law Librarians

bialy bialystok roll (holeless onion-flaked bagel)

Bialystok (Polish-Belostok)—town best known for its onion-flavored rolls whose recipe has been duplicated in many American cities

Biandrata Giorgio Blandrata

BIAS Brooklyn Institute of Arts and Sciences

BIATA British Independent Air Transport Association

bib. bibliography; biographical inventory blank; bottled in bond

bib. (BIB) baby incendiary bomb

bib *biblioteca* (Italian, Latin, Portuguese, Romanian, Spanish—library); *biblioteka* (Albanian, Bulgarian, Macedonian, Polish, Russian, Serbo-Croatian, Slovene, Ukrainian); *bibliotek* (Dano-Norwegian or Swedish); *biblioteket* (Dano-Norwegian or Swedish); *bibliotheek* (Dutch or Flemish); *bibliotheka* (Latin); *bibliotheke* (Greek); *Bibliothek* (German); *bibliotheque* (French)

bib. *bibe* (Latin—drink)

Bib Bible; Biblical

Bib *Biblica* (Latin—Bible)

BIB Biennale of Illustrations Bratislava (international exhibition of children's book illustrations); Bureau of International Broadcasting

BIB *Berliner Institut für Betriebsführung* (German—Berlin Business Management Institute)

BIBA Babson Institute of Business Administration

Bib Amb *Biblioteca Ambrosiana* (Italian-Ambrosian Library)—in Milan

Bib Apo Vat Biblioteca Apostolica Vaticana (Vatican Library)

bib b *biblioteksbind* (Dano-Nor-

wegian—library binding)

Bib Bod *Bibliotheca Bodmeriana* (Latin—Bodmer Library)—in Cologny/Geneva where it treasures first editions of Cervantes, Dante, Goethe, Homer, and Shakespeare as well as a Gutenberg Bible and one if the three recorded copies of Luther's *Disputio pro Declaratione Indulgentiarum* dating from 1517

BIBC British Isles Bowling Council

Bib Cen *Biblioteca Central* (Spanish—Central Library)—in Mexico City's Ciudad Universitaria

Bib Ecu *Biblioteca Ecuatoriana* (Spanish—Ecuadorian Library)—in Quito where it also bears the name of its founder —Padre Aurelio Espinosa Pólit

Bib Esc *Biblioteca de San Lorenzo el Real de El Escorial* (Spanish—Library of Royal San Lorenzo of the Escorial Palace)—monastic library within the Escorial Palace in the Guadarramas near Madrid

BIBF British and Irish Basketball Federation

bi or bin (Latin *bini*—two by two, Latin *bis*—twice)—binary, binoculars, binomial, bipolar

bibl bibliotec-; bibliotek-; bibliothec-; bibliothek; bibliothèque

Bible Belt rural areas of the southern United States where incredible biblical statements are taken literally

biblio bibliographical imprint or note; biblioclasm (book destruction); biblioclast (book destroyer); bibliogenesis (book production); bibliognost (bibliographic expert or book expert); bibliogony (book production); bibliograph (bibliographer); bibliographee (the person the bibliography is concerned with); bibliographer (describer of books or a preparer of bibliographies); bibliographic(al); bibliography

biblioc biblioclasm; biblioclast

bibliog bibliographer; bibliographic(al); bibliography

bibliograph bibliographer; bibliographee; bibliography

biblioklept bibliokleptomania(c)

bibliol bibliolater (person with

excessive admiration or reverence for books); bibliolatrous (characterized by bibliolatry); bibliolatry (book worship); bibliological; bibliologist; bibliology (scientific description and study of books)

bibliom bibliomancy (divination by books such as the *Bible*); bibliomane (avid collector of books); bibliomania (mania for collecting books); bibliomaniac (person affected with the mania for book collecting); bibliomanist (synonym for bibliomaniac)

bibliop bibliopegic (relating to book binding); bibliopegist (bookbinder); bibliopegy (bookbinder's art); bibliophagist (devourer of books); bibliophile (book lover); bibliophilia (love of books); bibliophobe (book hater); bibliophobia (aversion, dislike, or dread of books); bibliopole (bookdealer)

bibliopsy bibliopsychology (study of authors, books, and readers as well as their interrelationships)

bibliothec bibliotheca (bibliographer's catalog or a library); bibliothecal (belonging to the library); bibliothecar (librarian); bibliothecary (librarian or library)

bibliother bibliotherapeutic; bibliotherapist; bibliotherapy

bibliothetic(al) arrangement or placement of books

bibliotrain railroad car converted into a mobile library

bibl mun *bibliothèque municipale* (French—city library, public library)

Bib Mus *Biblioteca Musicale* (Italian—Musical Library)— in Rome's Via dei Greci

Bib Nac *Biblioteca Nacional* (Spanish—National Library) —the original in Madrid and others throughout Latin America

Bib Nar *Biblioteka Narodowa* (Polish—National Library)— in Warsaw

Bib Nat *Bibliothèque Nationale* (National Library—Paris)

Bib Naz Bra *Biblioteca Nazionale Braidense* (Italian—Braidense National Library)—in Milan

Bib Naz Cen Biblioteca Nazionale Centrale (Italian National Central Library—Florence,

Naples, Rome, etc. International Business Operations)

Bib Pal *Biblioteca de Palacio* (Spanish—Palace Library)— Madrid

BIBRA British Industrial Biological Research Association

bibs. bibliographies

Bib Soc Am Bibliographical Society of America

Bib Soc Can Bibliographical Society of Canada

Bib Sor *Bibliothèque de la Sorbonne* (French—Sorbonne Library)

Bib Uni *Biblioteca Universitaria* (Spanish—University Library)—the one in Salamanca, Spain and all others so named in Latin America

Bic Societe Bic (ballpoint pen factory founded by Baron Marcel Bich)

BIC Barrier Industrial Council; Bronx Irish Catholic; Bureau of International Commerce; Bureau International des Containers (International Bureau of Containers)

bicarb sodium bicarbonate

bicarbonate (of soda) baking soda; sodium bicarbonate

BICC British Insulated Callenders Cables

BICEMA British Internal Combustion Engine Manufacturers Association

bicept book indexing with context and entry points from text

BICERA British Internal Combustion Engine Research Association

BICERI British Internal Combustion Engine Research Institute

bichloride of mercury mercuric chloride

bichrome sodium bichromate

Bi-City Port Gdansk-Gdynia, Poland

BICS British Institute of Cleaning Science

BICTA British Investment Casters' Technical Association

bicv biconcave

bicx biconvex

bicyea best ice cream you ever ate

bicyplane bicycle-powered airplane (first cross-Channel flight between Folkestone, England and Cap Gris-Nez, France achieved June 12, 1979 in 2 hours and 49 minutes by the *Gossamer Albatross* de-

signed by Paul MacCready of Pasadena, California who had it pedalled and piloted by Bakersfield bicyclist Bryan Allen)

bid. (BID) brought in dead

b.i.d. *bis in die* (Latin—twice daily)

Bid Bideford

BId Bureau of Identification

BID Banco Interamericano de Desarrollo (Interamerican Development Bank)

B.I.D. Bachelor of Industrial Design

B. of I.D. Bachelor of Interior Design

bidap bibliographic data processing program

Biddy Bridget; Briged; Brigid

bidec binary-to-decimal converter

BIDP Basic Institutional Development Program

BIE Bureau of Industrial Economics (DoC); Bureau International d'Education (International Bureau of Education); Bureau International des Expositions (International Bureau of Expositions)

B.I.E. Bachelor of Industrial Engineering

Bieder Biedermeier

BIEE British Institute of Electrical Engineers

Bielorrussia White Russia (lowlands around Minsk)

bien biennial

Bien Aime (French—Well Beloved)—sobriquet of Louis XV

BIEPR Bureau of International Economic Policy and Research

BIET British Institute of Engineering Technology

BIETA *Biblioteca Interamericana de Estadistica Teórica y Aplicada* (Spanish—Interamerican Library of Theoretical and Applied Statistics)

bif buyer-induced failure

BIF Bombardier's Information File; British Industries Federation

BIFN *Banque Internationale pour le Financement de l'Énergie Nucléaire* (French—International Bank for the Financing of Nuclear Energy)

bif O opium

BIFUS Britain, Italy, France, United States

big. best in group; bigamist; bigamy; biological isolation gar-

ment

BIG Bartoni International Gallery (Melbourne); Basic Industries Group; Beneficial Insurance Group; Better Independent Grocers

BIG Bazak Israel Guide

Big A underworld nickname of the Federal Penitentiary in Atlanta, Georgia

Big Apple New York City's nickname

Big Belts Big Belt Mountains of Montana

Big Ben aircraft carrier USS *Franklin*; battleship USS *Franklin*; huge bell attached to clock in Parliament tower, Westminster district of London, named after Sir Benjamin Hall, commissioner of works in 1859 when bell was hung

Big Bend big bend of the Rio Grande—bounding southern section of the Big Bend National Park on the Texas border of Mexico

Big Bertha World War I howitzer capable of hurling a one-ton projectile nine miles, named for a member of the Krupp family—*Die dicke Bertha*—fat Bertha

Big Bill Haywood William Dudley Haywood (founder of IWW)

Big Board New York City's Stock Exchange

Big Brother big government's watchful eye as described in George Orwell's *1984*

Big Burg New York City

big C cancer; cocaine

Big Charlie Charles de Gaulle

big D (underground slang—hallucinogen such as diethyltryptamine, dimethyltryptamine, dipropylphyptamine, etc.)

Big-D Dallas, Texas

Big Dan Daniel Joseph Tobin

Big Ditch Panama Canal's nickname

Big Drink Atlantic or Pacific Ocean

Big-D of the West Denver, Colorado

Big-E aircraft carrier USS *Enterprise*

Big Eddy Portland, Maine's skid-row area

Big Finger Australia's Cape York Peninsula

Big Five (British banks) Barclays, Lloyds, Midland, National Provincial, Westminster

Big Four at the Johns Hopkins Medical School—William Howard Welch, William Osler, Howard Atwood Kelly, William Stewart Halsted; California railroad builders Charles Crocker, Mark Hopkins, Collis P Huntington, and Leland Stanford; Cleveland, Cincinnati, Chicago, and St Louis; Great Britain, France, Italy, and the United States at the end of World War I or their representatives at the Peace Conference—Lloyd George, Georges Clemenceau, Vittorio Orlando, and Woodrow Wilson, respectively

Big Four Automakers General Motors, Ford, Chrysler, American Motors

Big Four Opera Houses Covent Garden in London, La Scala in Milan, Staatsoper in Vienna, The Met in New York

Biggest Little City Reno, Nevada's nickname

biggies big ones

big H big house (underground slang—penitentiary such as San Quentin or Sing Sing); hernia; heroin

Big Heart of Texas Austin

Big Horns Big Horn Mountains of Wyoming

Big Inch 24-inch pipeline carrying petroleum products from east Texas to the New York-Philadelphia area

Big Island Hawaii (largest of the Hawaiians)

big J big John (underground slang—policeman or other law-enforcement officer)

Big-J battleship USS *New Jersey*

Big Jim Postmaster General James Aloysius Farley

Big-M battleship USS *Missouri*

Big Mac Mac Donald hamburger; New York's Municipal Assistance Corporation (MAC) —Big Mac

Big Mamie battleship USS *Massachusetts*

Big Minny Minnesota

Big Miss Mississippi River

Big Momma HMS *Ark Royal*

Big Muddy Missouri River

Big N Vladimir Nabokov

Big Nail translation of the Eskimo nickname for the North Pole

big O opium

Big-O attack aircraft carrier USS *Oriskany*

Big Orange Los Angeles

Big P golden-voice outsize-tenor Luciano Pavarotti

bigr bigger

Big Red racehorse Man-o'-War's nickname

bigs biological isolation garments

Big Seven America's leading symphony orchestras—Boston, Chicago, Cleveland, Los Angeles, New York, Philadelphia, Pittsburgh

Big Six New York City's Typographical Union Number Six

Big Sky Country Montana

Big Smoke old nickname of London, England as well as Sydney, New South Wales

bigst biggest

Big Sur mountainous coastal resort area of California's Monterey County

Big Three The Big Three (music publishers Robbins, Feist, Miller)—Robbins Music Corp; World-War-I peacemakers Georges Clemenceau, Lloyd George, and Woodrow Wilson; World-War-II peacemakers Winston Churchill, Franklin Roosevelt, and Joseph Stalin

Big Three Automakers General Motors, Ford, Chrysler

Big Town Chicago

Big Two Soviet Russia, United States of America

big. unlwfl—trig awf bigamy is unlawful—trigamy is awful, explained Ogden Nash

Big Windy Chicago, Illinois

bih benign intracranial hypertension

BIH Beth Israel Hospital

BIHA British Ice Hockey Association

bihor. *bihorium* (Latin—two hours)

BII Beckman Instruments Incorporated; Biosophical Institute Incorporated

BIIA British Institute of Industrial Art

BIICL British Institute of International and Comparative Law

Bij Benjamin

bijb *bijbelse term* (Dutch—biblical term)

bijv *bijvoorbeeld* (Dutch—for example)

bi k bilge keel

bike bicycle

bikers motorcycle gangs(ters)

biki bikini

Bikini State Florida
bil bilateral; billet; billion; block input length
b-i-l brother-in-law
Bil Bilbao
BIL Billings, Montana (airport); Braille Institute Library; Brierly Investments Limited; British India Line; Bulk Items List
BILA Bureau of International Labor Affairs
Bilad al-Sudan (Arabic—Land of the Blacks)—nickname applied to Guinea as well as the Sudan
bilat bilateral
Bilders Bilderbergers (now called Tri-Laterals)
bildg bill of lading
bildl bildeich (German—figuratively)
bile. balanced-inductor logical element
BILG Building Industry Libraries Group
bili bilirubin
Bilibid Manila's great prison and reformatory noted for its inmate-produced handicrafts
biling bilingual(ism); bilingualist(ic)(al)(ly)
bilj biljarttern (Dutch—billiards)
bil k bilge keel
bill billede (Dano-Norwegian—illustrations)
Bill Billie; Billy; William; William F Buckley, Jr and all other distinguished Williams nicknamed Bill
bill. acad billiard academy
Bill Arp Charles Henry Smith
Billie William
Billie Holiday Eleanora Fagan
billion (American—a thousand million, 10^9); (British—a million million, 10^{12})
Bill Mauldin William H Mauldin (contemporary American cartoonist who suggested: *Look at an infantryman's eyes and you can tell how much war he has seen.*)
Bill Nye Edgar Wilson Nye
Bill of Rights first ten amendments to the *Constitution of the United States*
Billtown Williamstown, Kansas
Billy William
Billy the Kid William Bonney alias William Wright
Billy Mitchell General William Mitchell
Billy Sanders (pseudonym—Joel Chandler Harris)

bil(s) billion(s)
BILS British International Law Society; Butterworth Industrial Laws Service
bilt built
bim beginning of information marker
bi-m bi-monthly
bim bimensile (Italian—semi-monthly); *bimestrale* (Italian—bimonthly); *bimestre* (Italian—two-month period)
Bim Barbadan
BIM British Institute of Management
B.I.M. Bachelor of Indian Medicine
BIM Bord Iascaigh Mhara (Gaelic—Sea Fisheries Board) —an Irish organization
bimac bi-stable magnetic core
BIMCAM British Industrial Measuring and Control Apparatus Manufacturers Association
BIMS Business Information Management System
Bimshire Barbados
BIMT Bahama Islands Ministry of Tourism
bin. binary
BINA Bureau International des Normes de l'Automobile (International Bureau of Automobile Standards)
binac high-speed electronic digital computer
b-in-B banned in Boston (and therefore a best-seller)
BINCOS Binder Control System
bind. binding
B.Ind. Bachelor of Industry
B.Ind.Ed. Bachelor of Industrial Education
Bindloe Island, Galápagos Marchena
BINDT British Institute of Non-Destructive Testing
Bing Crosby Harry Crosby
Binj Benjamin
BINL Basic Inventory of Natural Language
BINM Buck Island National Monument, St Croix, Virgin Islands
binocam binocular and camera (combination instrument)
binocs binoculars
bins (Cockney contraction—binoculars)
BINS Barclays Integrated Network System
binsum brief intelligence summary
BINWR Blackbeard Island Na-

tional Wildlife Refuge (Georgia)
BINZ Bankers Institute of New Zealand
bio biographical; biography; biological; biology
bio (Latin prefix—life)—biology, the study of life and living things
Bio Biology
BIO Base Installation Officer; Bedford Institute of Oceanography; Biological Information-Processing Organization; Broadcasting Information Office
BIOA Bureau of International Organization Affairs (US Department of State)
bioact bioactive; bioactivity
bioastro bioastronaut(ic)(al)(ly)
bioauto bioautograph(ic)(al)(ly)
biocam binocular camera
biochem biochemical; biochemist; biochemistry
Biochem Biochemistry
biochron biochronometry
biocid biocidal; biocide
bioclean biologically clean
biocon biocontamination
biocyb biocybernetics
biodef biological defense
biodeg biodegradability; biodegradable; biodegradation; biodegrade; biodegraders; biodegrading
biodeg(s) biodegradable(s)
biodes biodestructible
biodet biodeterioration
bioelectrog bioelectrogenesis
bioelectron bioelectron(ic)(al)(ly); bioelectronics
bioeng bioengineer(ing); biological engineer(ing)
bioenv bioenvironment(al)(ly); bioenvironmentalist
bioex bioexperiment(ation)
biog biographer; biographical; biography
biogeo biogeology
biogeog biogeographer; biogeographic(al); biogeography
bioinstru bioinstrument(al)(ly); bioinstrumentation
biol biological; biologist; biology
biol biologi or *biologisk* (Dano-Norwegian—biology or biologist)
Biol Biology
Biol Abstr Biological Abstracts
Biologist of the Mind Sigmund Freud
BIOLWPNSYS Biological Weapon System (USA)
biomass mass of biological ma-

terial

bio-mass biological mass source of ethanol and methanol from crops and trees

BIOMASS Biological Investigations of Marine Antarctic Systems and Stocks

biomath biomathematician; biomathematics

biomed biomedical; biomedicine

bionics biology + electronics

bio-org bio-organic(al)(ly)

biophys biophysical; biophysicist; biophysics

biopol(s) biopolymer(s)

bior business input-output rerun

biore bioresearch(er)

BIOREP Biological Attack Report

bios (BIOS) biological satellite

BIOS Basic Input Output System; Biological Investigations of Space

biosat biosatellite

biosci bioscience; bioscientific; bioscientist

biosen(s) biosensor(s)

BIOSIS Biosciences Information Service of *Biological Abstracts*

biospel biospeleologist(ic)(al)(ly); biospeliology

biostat biostatistic(s)

biostitutes biologist prostitutes (biologists who prostitute themselves to the specious claims of ammunition and gun makers who with so-called sportsmen insist hunting and killing are essential in controlling wildlife on our planet although man has always been its principal predator)

biot biotron(ic)(al)(ly)

BIOT British Indian Ocean Territories

biotec biotechnical(ly); biotechnological(ly); biotechnologist; biotechnology

biotel biotelemetric; biotelemetry

biotrans biotransformation; biotransformer

biowar biological warfare

bip background interference procedure(s); bacterial intravenous protein; balanced in plane; bismuth iodoform paraffin; books in print; borough-interborough problem(s)

Bip Marcel Marceau

BiP *Books in Print*

BIP Board for International Broadcasting; Border Indus-

trial Program; British Industrial Plastics; British Institute of Physics

BIP *Banco Industrial del Peru* (Spanish—Industrial Bank of Peru)

BIPAD Bureau of Independent Publishers and Distributors

bipco built-in-place components

bipd biparting doors

biphet biphetamine (drug stimulant)

BIPL Burmah Industrial Products Limited

BIPM Bureau International des Poids et Mesures (International Bureau of Weights and Measures)

BIPO British Institute of Public Opinion

bipp bismuth, iodoform, paraffin paste

BIPP British Institute of Practical Psychology

BIPS British Integrated Programme Suite

bipyr bipyramidal

blquln biquinary

bir basic incidence rate; built-in robes (closets)

Bir Birmania (Italian or Spanish —Burma); *Birmânia* (Portuguese—Burma)

BIR Board of Inland Revenue; Board of Internal Revenue; British Institute of Radiology; Bureau of Intelligence and Research; Bureau of Internal Revenue

Bird Haydn's String Quartet in C (opus 33, no. 3)

BIRD Banque Internationale pour la Reconstruction et le Développement (International Bank for Reconstruction and Development)

Bird Dog Cessna L-19 liaison aircraft

BIRDDOG Basic Investigation of Remotely Detectable Deposits of Oil and Gas

Bird of Happiness the Japanese crane

birdie battery integration and radar display equipment

Bird-of-Paradise Island Little Tobago (whose bird sanctuary is the only one outside New Guinea where birds of paradise may be seen in their wild state)

Birdofredum Sawin (pseudonym —James Russell Lowell)

Birds *The Birds* (Respighi's symphonic poem—*Gli Uccel-*

li)

Bird Woman Sacajawea

BIRE British Institution of Radio Engineers

B.Ir.Eng. Bachelor of Irrigation Engineering

BIRF Brewing Industry Research Foundation

BIRF *Banco Internacional de Reconstrucción y Fomento* (Spanish—International Bank for Reconstruction and Development)

Birken'ead drill maritime tradition dating from 1852 with the sinking of HMS *Birkenhead* when women and children were given first place in the lifeboats and all others carried on with exemplary order even though it meant drowning for many

birl girlish boy (transvestite)

Birm Birmingham

Birmania (Spanish—Burma)

Birmingham notation (*see* GKD-notation)

BIRMO British Infra-Red Manufacturers' Association

BIRMPDis Birmingham Procurement District (U.S. Army)

BIRMS Battelle Interactive Resources Management System (computerized)

BIRP Beverage Industry Recycling Program

BIRS Basic Indexing and Retrieval System; British Institute of Recorded Sound

birt bolt installation and removal tool

Birthplace of the American Industrial Revolution Pennsylvania's Lehigh Valley

Birthplace of American Jazz New Orleans (where it was imported from Europe)

Birthplace of American Liberty Faneuil Hall, Boston

Birthplace of American Presidents Massachusetts (3); New York (4); Ohio (7); Virginia (8)

Birthplace of Aphrodite or Venus Cyprus

Birthplace of Aviation Dayton, Ohio where the Wright Brothers were born and where they built their flying machine in their own bicycle shop

Birthplace of Bach, Beethoven, and Brahms Germany (Eisenach, Bonn, and Hamburg, respectively)

Birthplace of Baseball Cooperstown, New York

Birthplace of Berlioz Côte-Saint-André, Isère, France

Birthplace of Bolívar Caracas, Venezuela

Birthplace of Brahms and Mendelssohn Hamburg, Germany

Birthplace of the British Industrial Revolution Severn Valley in England and Wales

Birthplace of Burns Alloway, Scotland

Birthplace of Camões (Camoëns) Lisbon, Portugal

Birthplace of Cervantes Alcalá de Heneres, Spain

Birthplace of Colombia Tunja, Boyacá

Birthplace of Dante Florence, Italy

Birthplace of Democracy ancient Greece where in the fourth century before the Christian era an assembly of aristocrats and artisans ruled all Athens

Birthplace of the Gods Greece

Birthplace of Handel Halle, Germany

Birthplace of Hans Christian Andersen Odense, Denmark

Birthplace of Hindemith Hanau, Germany

Birthplace of Kant Kaliningrad (formerly Königsberg, East Prussia)

Birthplace of Liszt Raiding, Hungary

Birthplace of Melodramatic Opera Italy

Birthplace of Mozart Salzburg, Austria

Birthplace of Paganini Genoa

Birthplace of Purcell London, England

Birthplace of Richard Strauss Munich, Germany

Birthplace of Saint-Saëns Paris, France

Birthplace of Schubert Vienna, Austria

Birthplace of Schumann Zwickau, Germany

Birthplace of Shakespeare Stratford-upon-Avon, England

Birthplace of Sibelius Tavastehus, Finland

Birthplace of Skiing Morgedal in the Telemark region of Norway

Birthplace of Spinoza Amsterdam, Netherlands

Birthplace of the Tuna Fishing Industry San Diego

Birthplace of the United States of America Philadelphia, Pennsylvania where the *Decla-*

ration of Independence was signed July 4, 1776

Birthplace of Vaudeville Sainte-Mère-Église (near Norman coast of France behind Utah Beach)

Birthplace of Villa-Lobos Rio de Janeiro, Brazil

Birthplace of Vivaldi Venice, Italy

Birthplace of Wagner Leipzig, Germany

Birthplace of Wilde, Shaw, Joyce, and Behan Dublin, Ireland

birthquake population explosion

bis best in show; bissextile

Bis Bismarck; Bissau

BIS Bank for International Settlements; Bismarck, North Dakota (airport); Board of Inspection Survey (USN); British Imperial System; British Information Service; British Interplanetary Society; Business Information System

bis in 7d. *bis in septem diebus* (Latin—twice in seven days, twice weekly)

bisad business information systems analysis and design

BISAKTA British Iron, Steel, and Kindred Trades Association

BISAM Basic-Indexed Sequential-Access Method

BisArch Bismarck Archipelago

Bisc Biscayan

BISCA Building Industry Subcontractors Association

Biscay English place-name equivalent for Biscaye or Vizcaya

Biscaye (French—Biscay)

BISCO British Iron and Steel Corporation

bis in d. *bis in dies* (Latin—twice daily)

bisett *bisettimanale* (Italian—bi-weekly)

bisex bisexual

BISF British Iron and Steel Federation

BISFA British Industrial and Scientific Film Association

BISG Book Industry Study Group

Bish Bishop

bishaw bicycle rickshaw

Bish Mus Bishop Museum

Bishop Bishop Museum; Bishop Museum Press

Bishop of Rome the Pope

BISITS British Iron and Steel Industry Translation Service

(BISRA)

BISL British Information Service Library

Bismarck North Dakota's capital named for the celebrated German chancellor; Prince Otto Eduard Leopold von Bismarck-Schönhausen—the Iron Chancellor

Bismarck Pen North Dakota Penitentiary at Bismarck

Bismarcks Bismarck Islands

BISN British India Steam Navigation (company)

Bison NATO nickname for Soviet Mya-4 four-engine jet heavy bomber

Bison City Buffalo, New York

bisp between ischial spines; bispinous (interspinous diameter)

BISPA British Independent Steel Producers Association

BISRA British Iron and Steel Research Associates

BISS Battlefield Identification System Study (NATO)

BISTA Bureau of International Scientific and Technological Affairs (U.S. Department of State)

Bister Bicester

Bisuntia (Latin—Besanson)—French place also called Bisuntium, Vesontio, or Vesuntio

bisw *bisweilen* (German—sometimes)

bisync binary synchronous computer

bit. binary digit; bituminous

BIT Bradford Institute of Technology; British Independent Television; Bureau International du Travail (International Labor Organisation)

BITA British Industrial Truck Association

BITB Building Industry Training Board

BITC Bahamas International Trust Company

BITCH Black Intelligence Test of Cultural Homogeneity

bite. base installation test equipment; built-in test equipment

BITE Base Installation Test Equipment

bitm bituminous

BITM Birla Industrial and Technological Museum

bitn bilateral iterative network

bito burnishing tool

BITO British Institution of Training Officers

bit(s). binary digit(s)

BITTC Building Industry Tech-

nicians Training Council
Bitter Bierce Ambrose Bierce
Bitterroot Montana state flower
bitu benzyl-thiourea
BITU Bustamante Industrial Trade Union
bitum bituminous
bitumd bituminized
bituminous soft coal
Bituminous City Connellsville, Pennsylvania
biu basic income unit
B-I U Bar-Ilan University
BIU *Bureau International des Universités* (French—International University Bureau)
biv bivouac
BIV *Banco Industrial de Venezuela* (Spanish—Industrial Bank of Venezuela)
bivar bivariant (function generator)
bi-w bi-weekly
BIW Bath Iron Works; Boston Insulated Wire (and Cable Company)
BIWF British Israel World Federation
BIWS Bureau of International Whaling Statistics
bix binary information exchange
Bix Leon Bismarck Beiderbecke
biz bizarre, business
BIZ Bank für Internationalen Zahlungsausgleich (Bank for International Settlements)
bizad business administration
Bizancio (Spanish—Byzantium)
bizjet business-type jet airplane
bizmac business machine computer
bizman business man
BIZNET American Business Network (data base of Chamber of Commerce)
bj back judge (football); biceps jerk; blow job (fellatio)
b & j bone and joint
Bʲ *Burj*(Arabic—bluff, cliff, fort, tower)
BJ Benito Juarez; Byron Jackson (Borg-Warner)
B.J. Bachelor of Journalism
B & J Burke & James
B of J Bank of Japan
BJA Burlap and Jute Association
b/Jan binding expected in January (for example)
Bjarmaland (Norse—Russia)
BJC Baltimore Junior College; Bismarck Junior College; Boise Junior College; Brevard Junior College; Bureau of Ju-

venile Correction (Delaware)
BJCEB British Joint Communications-Electronics Board
BJCO British Joint Communications Office
bjf batch-job format
BJIP Better Jobs and Incomes Program
B Jon Ben Jonson
Bjønyøa (Norwegian—Bear Island)
Björko (Swedish—Birch Island)
Bjørn   **Bjørn**   Bjørnstjerne Bjørnson
Björneborg (Swedish—Pori)—Finnish port
BJOS *British Journal of Occupational Safety*
BJp Bence Jones protein
BJS Bureau of Justice Statistics
BJSM British Joint Services Mission
bjt bipolar junction transistor
BJTRA British Jute Trade Research Association
BJU Bob Jones University
B.Juris. Bachelor of Jurisprudence
bk bank; below the knee; black; book; brake
Bk berkelium; Brook
Bᵏ Bank
Bk *Buku* (Indonesian or Malay—hill, mountain)
B-K Blaw-Knox
BK *Biblioteka Kombëtare* (Albanian—National Library)—Tirana
bka below-knee amputation
BKA *Bundeskriminalamt* (German—Federal Criminal Ministry)
bkble bookable; bookmobile
bkbndg bookbinding
bkbndr bookbinder
bkc benzalkonium chloride (BKC)
bkcy bankruptcy
bkd blackboard
bk di brake die
bkfst breakfast
bkg banking; bookkeeping
bkgd background
bkhs blockhouse
BKII *Vsesoyuenaya Kommunisticheskaya Partiya* (Russian—All-Union Communist Party)
BKK Bangkok, Thailand (airport)
bklr black letter
bklt booklet
Bklyn Brooklyn
Bklyn Brdg Brooklyn Bridge
Bklyn HTF Brooklyn Homicide Task Force
Bklyn Mus Brooklyn Museum

bkm buckram
BKM Moscow, USSR (Bykovo Airport)
bkn broken
Bkn Birkenhead
B Kovner Jacob Adler
bkpg bookkeeping
bkpr bookkeeper
bkpt bankrupt
bkr baker; beaker; breaker
bks bunks; barracks; books; brakes
Bk's Black killers (Negro terrorist gangs)
BKS British Kinematograph Society
bk sh bookshelves
Bks for Libs Books for Libraries
bksp backspace (flow chart)
bkt basket; bracket
Bkt *Bukit* (Malay—Hill, Hilly Street)
bkt(s) basket(s)
bktt below knee to toe
bkw breakwater
bkwp below-knee walking plaster (cast)
bl bank larceny; baseline; billet; bleed(ing); blood; blood loss; blue; bomb line; buccolingual; butt line; buttock line
b/l basic letter; bill of lading (B/L); blueline; blueprint
b & l ball and lever; business and loan
bl *blad, blank* (Dano-Norwegian—leaf, sheet, blank)
Bl Burkitt's lymphoma (BL)
Bl *Blatt(er)* [German—leaf; leaves, page(s)], *Bölük* (Turkish—company)
BL Barrister-at-Law; Basutoland; Blessed Lady; Bonanza Airlines; British Leyland; British Library (formerly British Museum Reading Room now open only to accredited visitors)
B-L Belgium-Luxembourg
B.L. Bachelor of Letters
B & L Bausch & Lomb; Building and Loan (association or bank)
bl a *blandt andet*; (Dano-Norwegian—among other things); *blandt andre* (Danish—among other things)
Bla Belawan; Brasilia
BLA Bangladesh Library Association; Black Liberation Army; Bombay Library Association; British Library Association
B.L.A. Bachelor of Landscape Architecture; Bachelor of Lib-

eral Arts

BL-AA *Biblioteca Luis-Angel Arango* (Spanish—Luis-Angel Arango Library)—Bogotá, Colombia's library showplace named for a former bank president

BLAC British Light Aviation Center

BLACC British and Latin American Chamber of Commerce

black. blackmail

Black Abolitionist-Author-Editor-Orator Frederick Douglass

Black Africa equatorial Africa from Ethiopia, Somalia, and Kenya to Gabon, the Congo, and Zaire

Black Astronomer-Inventor-Mathematician Benjamin Banneker

Blackbeard Edward Teach—privateer-pirate also known as Edward Thatch

black beauties biphetamine

Black Belt black-soil growing area extending from South Carolina and Georgia to Alabama and Mississippi

Blackberry Capital McCloud, California

Blackbird Lockheed SR-71 jet reconnaissance aircraft

Black Botanist-Chemurgist-Educator George Washington Carver

Black Canyon Black Canyon of the Gunnison National Monument (in Colorado)

Black Castle of Opium translation of Afyonkarahisar or Afyon in western Turkey where much of the world's opium is grown

Black Charley Sir Charles Napier

Black Country Midlands of England around smoke-blackened Birmingham

Black Dan swarthy-complected Daniel Webster

Black Death bubonic plague devastating Asia, Africa, and Europe during the fourteenth century

black diamond black or gray industrial diamond also called framesite bort; nickname for anthracite or hard coal

Black Diamond City Wilkes-Barre, Pennsylvania

black diamonds coal

black disease anthrax of sheep; braxy

Black Douglas Sir James de Douglas

Black Eagle Hubert F Julian

Black Educator Booker T Washington (founder and first president of the Tuskegee Institute)

Black Explorer Matt(hew) A Henson who pushed Peary to the North Pole and placed the American flag there after assisting Peary in making navigational fixes; modern sobriquet given Matthew Henson who in his day was called the Negro Explorer because he had accompanied Peary on all his Arctic expeditions and even pushed him to the North Pole as well as helping him survey the Nicaraguan canal route

Black-eyed Susan Maryland state flower

Blackfeet Blackfoot Indians (but not black bears who reputedly have black feet because they walk around in their bare feet)

black fever kala-azar (leishmaniasis)

black flag symbol of death or emblem of piracy

Black Flower of Society Nathaniel Hawthorne's nickname for any jail, penitentiary, or prison

Black Forest Schwarzwald (dense fir forest in mountainous south-central and southwestern Germany)

Black Friday September 24, 1869 (financial panic occurred when speculators tried to corner the gold market in the U.S.)

black gold petroleum

black gold of the Amazon and Malaya rubber

black gold of the Caspian caviar

Black Hand secret terrorist society linked with the Camorra and the Mafia

Black Heart of Montana Butte

Black Historian Carter G Woodson

Black Islands *see* Melanesia

blackjack nickname for a card game, the bubonic plague, the black flag of pirates, blackjack chewing gum, hand-held leather-covered flexible club; zinc blende or zinc sulfide

Black Jack General John J Pershing, USA who advocated

the enlistment and promotion of black troops and led their crack regiment, the 10th Cavalry, in 1916 when they fought along the Mexican Border. During World War I he was commander in chief of the American Expeditionary Force fighting in France

Black Key Chopin's Piano Etude No. 5 in G-flat major

black lead cerrusite (lead carbonate)

Black Messiah Booker T Washington

Black Monk Grigori Efimovich Rasputin—the Holy Man Gregory who served as intermediary between the czarina and the German secret service during World War I

Black Moses Harriet Tubman (underground railroad conductor before the Civil War)

Black Muslims religious-oriented group composed of black nationalists and some militant extremists

Black Nationalist Marcus M(oziah) Garvey

Black Novelist Richard Wright

Black Panthers militant black party active in the United States and overseas

Black Pope traditionally the head of the Jesuit Order—the Jesuit General

Black Prince Edward—Prince of Wales—son of Edward III; so nicknamed as he always wore black armor

Black Republic Haiti originally and more recently applied to many emerging African nations

Black Rock nickname of the Columbia Broadcasting System (CBS) situated in the black granite building at 51 West 52nd Street in New York City

Black Saturday Commander's Internal Management Review (held on Saturdays)

Black Sea English equivalent of the Russian's *Chernoye More* and the Turk's *Kara Deniz*

Black Sheep of Canadian Liquors 100-proof Yukon Jack, according to the label on bottles of this blended whisky

Black Shirts Mussolini's black-shirted followers and legions of bullies

blacksploitation black exploitation (exploitation of black people by advertisers, film makers, and others)—also written blaxsploitation

black spots black settlements in white-owned South African land

Blackstairs Blackstairs Mountains of Ireland

Blackstone Sir William Blackstone's *Commentaries on the Laws of England*

Black Stream Japan Current

Black Tom Black Tom Island off the Jersey City shore of New York's Upper Bay where munitions awaiting shipment overseas where detonated by German saboteurs in July 1916

Black Tuesday October 29, 1929 (the day the stock market crashed and some ruined financiers leaped out of Wall Street skyscrapers)

Black Watch Royal Highland Regiment whose tartans display dark colors

blackwater fever malaria

Blackwater State Nebraska

Blackwell's Island former name of Welfare Island in New York City's East River where it has long contained public correctional and medical institutions

black widow nickname of the poisonous spider *Lactrodectus mactans*

blad blotting pad

blade. basic level automation of data through electronics

BLADES Bell Laboratories Automatic Design System

BLAISE British Library Automated Information Service

Blake Blakely; Blakeman; Blakeslee

Blan Blanca; Blanchard; Blanco; Bland(on)

Blanca Blanche

B.Land.Arch. Bachelor of Landscape Architecture

Blarney Stone Port Cork or Corcaigh in Ireland (Eire) close to Blarney Castle containing the Blarney Stone reputed to bestow the gift of gab to all who kiss it

Blaskets Blasket Islands on Ireland's Atlantic coast

blast *blastos* (Greek—sprout)— blastoderm, blastodisc, blastopore, osteoblast

Blast Blastoidea

BLAST Black Legal Action for Soul in Television

Bla Sta Blackfriars Station

BLAT British Life Assurance Trust

BLB Boothby-Lovelace-Bulbulian (oxygen mask)

blc balance; boundary-layer control

BLC British Lighting Council

blchd bleached

blchg bleaching

bl cult. blood culture

bld blood; blood and lymphatic system; bloody; bold; boldface

BLD Burglary Larceny Division (NYPD)

bldg building

Bldg Engr Building Engineer

bldi blank die

bldr builder

BLE Brotherhood of Locomotive Engineers

B & LE Bessemer and Lake Erie (railroad)

bleaching powder calcium hypochlorite

bleap bought ledger and expenditure analysis package

BLEDCO Brooklyn Local Economic Development Corporation

Blemish Belgian & Flemish

blems blemishes (acne, blackheads, pimples)

blenno blennorrhea

BLESMA British Limbless Ex-Service Men's Association

bless. bath, laxative, enema, shampoo, and shower

Blessed Isles *see* Fortunate Isles

bleu blind landing experimental unit

BLEU Belgium-Luxembourg Economic Union

bleve boiling-liquid expanding-vapor explosion

Blf Bluff

BLF & E Brotherhood of Locomotive Firemen and Enginemen

blg betalactoglobulin

BLG *Burke's Landed Gentry*

BLH Baldwin-Lima-Hamilton

BLHA British Linen Hire Association

BLHS Ballistic Laser Holographic System

BLI Bliss & Laughlin Industries; Buyers Laboratory Incorporated

B.L.I. Bachelor of Literary Interpretation

BLI *Bank Leumi le-Israel* (Bank Association of Israel)

B.Lib.S. Bachelor of Library Science

B.Lib.Sci. Bachelor of Library Science

Blick Blickensderfer (portable typewriter popular before World War I)

Bligh's Islands Fiji Islands (once named after Captain William Bligh who soon after the mutiny on the *Bounty* was the first European to sail through these islands from east to west on his way to Timor in an overloaded open boat)

Blighty (British slang—England)

Blind Bards Homer and Milton

Blinder NATO code name for Soviet Tu-22 bomber

Blindheim (German—Blenheim)—near Augsburg, Bavaria

Blind Poet John Milton

Blind Publisher Joseph Pulitzer

Blind Tom Thomas Bethune

blip. background-limited infrared photography

BLIP Big Look Improvement Program

BLIS Bell Laboratories Interpretive System

B-lite baton-flashlight combination

B.Litt. *Baccalaureus Literarum* (Latin—Bachelor of Literature)

Blitz *Blitzkreig* (German—lightning war)

bliz blizzard; blizzardly; blizzardous

blk black; block; blocking

Blk Block

blkcnt block count (flow chart)

blkd bulkhead

blk lt black light

blksh blackish

blksmith blacksmith

blkstp blackstrap (molasses)

bll below lower limit

BLL Butyrka, Lefortovo, and Lubyanka (Moscow's most dreaded prisons, the last of the three is closest to the Kremlin)

BLLD British Library Lending Division (Boston Spa)

BLLRCS Bureau of Library and Learning Resources and Community Services (Office of Education)

blm bilayer lipid membrane

blm *besa la mano* (Spanish—a kiss to your hand)

BLM British Leather Manufacturers; British Leland Motor

(corporation merging Austin, British Motor Moldings, Jaguar, Morris, Riley, Rover, Triumph, Wolseley); Bureau of Land Management (General Land Office and Grazing Service)

B.L.M. Bachelor of Land Management

BLM Bonniers Literaray Magasin (Bonnier's Literary Magazine)

BLMA British Lead Manufacturers' Association

BLMC British Leyland Motor Corporation

BLMRA British Leather Manufacturers' Research Association

BLMS Book-Library-Management System

bln balloon; bronchial lymph nodes

Bln Berlin

blnk blank (flow chart)

blnkt blanket

BLNR Benton Lake National Refuge (Montana)

BLNWR Big Lake National Wildlife Refuge (Arkansas); Bitter Lake NWR (New Mexico); Buffalo Lake NWR (Texas)

BLNY Book League of New York; Booksellers League of New York

blo blower

Bloater(s) inhabitant(s) of Yarmouth on the North Sea coast of England where herrings are salted and smoked

BLOB Ban Large Office Buildings (in residential communities)

Bloch Pub Bloch Publishing Company

block. blockade

Blockhousers America's oldest Negro regiment whose gallant assault of a well-defended blockhouse won them this nickname during the Spanish-American War

blodi block diagram (compiler)

blokops blockade operations

Blondin Charles Emile Gravele —the tightrope walker who crossed Niagara Falls in the mid-nineteenth century

Blood and Guts General George S Patton, USA

Bloodhound British surface-to-air missile

bloodstone heliotrope plasma with red jasper inclusions

bloody (Early English—By Our

Lady)

Bloody Ground Kentucky

Bloody Mary Mary I of England (Mary Tudor)

Bloomsbury Bloomsbury Group of writers whose center of activities was London's Bloomsbury Square in the early 1900s; members included Clive Bell, EM Forster, Roger Fry, John Maynard Keynes, Lytton Strachey, V Sackville-West, Leonard and Virginia Woolf; synonym for snobbish aestheticism

blooper blunder and error

Blos Blossom

BLOT British Library of Tape Recordings

blou blouse

B-love being love (unselfish accepting love of another person, according to Maslow)

blp besa los pies (Spanish—a kiss to your feet)

BLP British Labor Party

BLPES British Library of Political and Economic Science (London)

bl pr blood pressure

blr boiler; breech-loading rifle

BLR Ballistic Research Laboratories (USA)

BLRA British Launderers' Research Association

BLRD British Library Reference Division (British Museum Library)

blrmkr boilermaker

BLROA British Laryngological, Rhinological, and Otological Association

blrp boilerplate

bls bales; barrels; binary light switch; blood sugar

BLS Brooklyn Law School; Bureau of Labor Statistics

B.L.S. Bachelor of Library Science; Bachelor of Library Service

B.L.S. Benevolenti Lectori Salutem (Latin—Salutations to the Kind Reader)

BL & SA Bank of London and South America

BLSGMA British Lampblown Scientific Glassware Manufacturers' Association

blsh bluish

blsn blowing snow

blstg pwd blasting powder

blstl billet steel

blsw barrels of load salt water

blswd barrels of load salt water per day

blt blood type; built

blt (BLT) bottom-loading transporter

b-l-t bacon, lettuce, and tomato (sandwich)

BLT Battalion Landing Team

Bltc Baltic

bltg belting

bltn(s) built-in(s)

blu blue

B-L u Bessey-Lowry units

Blubo Blut und Boden (German —blood and soil)

BLUCB Bancroft Library of the University of California at Berkeley

blue amytal (barbiturate)

blue acid pale-blue liquid LSD-25

blue angels amytal (barbiturate)

blue asbestos crocidolite

Blue-backed Speller nickname for *The American Spelling Book* by Noah Webster of dictionary fame

Bluebeard nickname of any wife killer such as the Chevalier Raoul whose seventh wife discovered the bodies of his six previous wives

Bluebeard's Duke Bluebeard's Castle (Bartók's one-act opera)

Bluebird state bird of Nevada

bluebirds capsules of sodium amytal

Bluebonnet Texas state flower

Bluebonnet Bowl athletic stadium in Houston, Texas

blue bullet blue-tipped bullet color-coded to indicate its incendiary purpose

blue devils amobarbital capsules

Blue Grass Capital Lexington, Kentucky

Blue Grass Country Kentucky

Blue Grass State Kentucky's official nickname

Blue Grotto marine cavern on shore of Capri island in Bay of Naples

Blue Hen Chickens nickname given Delawareans as their state bird is the Blue Hen Chicken

Bluehen(s) Delawarean(s)

Blue Hen State Delaware (whose gamecocks were born of blue hens)

Blue Law State Connecticut nickname

Bluenose fisherman or sailor from Canada's Maritime Provinces

Bluenose Province Nova Scotia

Bluenose(s) native(s) of Canada's Maritime Provinces, especially Nova Scotia; puritan(s)

blue ointment mercurial ointment

blue peter blue signal flag with a white rectangle in its center; flown when a ship is ready to sail; letter P or Papa in the international code

Blue Ridge Blue Ridge Mountains of the Appalachian range extending from Georgia to Maryland and Pennsylvania where one near Macungie bears the name South Mountain; prominent in the Carolinas and Virginia

Blues Blue Mountains

Blue Steel Hawker-Siddeley air-to-surface missile

bluestone blue vitriol (copper sulfate)

blue vitriol bluestone (copper sulfate)

Bluff City place-name nickname shared by Hannibal, Missouri; Memphis, Tennessee; and Natchez, Mississippi—all on bluffs above the Mississippi River

Bluff King Hal nickname of Henry VIII

BLV British Legion Village

Blvd Boulevard

BLW Baldwin-Lima-Hamilton

BLWA British Laboratory Ware Association

Bly Blyth

BLYMSA *Banco de Londres y México SA* (Spanish—Bank of London and Mexico Corporation)

Blz Belize (formerly British Honduras); Belizian

blz(n) *bladzijde(n)* [Dutch—page(s)]

bm basal metabolism; basement membrane; beam; board measure; body mass; bone marrow; book of the month; bowel movement; buccomesial

bm (BM) buffer mark (flow chart); buffer modules

b/m (B/M) bill of material; black male; brown male

bm *bez mista* (Czech—no place of publication)

b.m. *balneum maris* (Latin—bath in sea water)

Bm beam; birthmark; board measure; bowel movement; Burma; Burmese

BM Banco de México (Bank of Mexico); bench mark; Boat-

swain's Mate; Boston & Maine (railroad); Brian Mulroney—Canada's 18th prime minister if counted by name and 23rd if counted by terms in office; Brigade Major; British Museum; Brooklyn Museum; Bureau of Medicine; Bureau of Mines; Bureau of the Mint; Business Manager

B-M Bolinder-Munktell; Bristol-Myers

B.M. Bachelor of Medicine; Bachelor of Music

B & M Beaufort & Morehead (railroad); Boston & Maine (railroad)

B of M Bank of Montreal; Bishop(ric) of Münster; Bureau of Mines

BM *Banca Mondiale* (Italian—World Bank); *Banco de México* (Spanish—Bank of Mexico); *Banco Mundial* (Portuguese or Spanish—World Bank), *Banque du Monde* (French—World Bank); *Beata Maria* (Latin—Blessed Mary)

BMA Baltimore Museum of Art; Bank Marketing Association; Bible Memory Association; Bicycle Manufacturers' Association; British Medical Association; British Military Authority; Stockholm, Sweden, airport (3-letter code)

B.Mar.E. Bachelor of Marine Engineering

B.Mar.Eng. Bachelor of Marine Engineering

BMASR Bureau of Military Application of Scientific Research

bmat beginning of morning astronomical twilight

B.Math. Bachelor of Mathematics

BMB Ballistic Missile Branch (USA); British Medical Board; British Metrication Board

BMB *British Medical Bulletin*

B-M B *Baader-Meinhof Bande* (German—Baader-Meinhof Gang)—terrorist Red Army Group's nickname reflecting its West German leadership

BMBW *Bundesministerium für Bildung und Wissenschaft*—West German Ministry for Education and Science

bmc blockhouse monitor console

BMC Ballistic Missile(s) Center; Ballistic Missiles Committee; British Mountaineering Council; Bryn Mawr College; Busi-

ness Microcomputer (Technology Group)

BMCC Blue Mountain Community College

BMCS Ballistic Missile Cost Study; Bureau of Motor Carrier Safety

bmd births, marriages, deaths; bone marrow depression

BMD Ballistic Missile Defense; Bureau of Medical Devices

B-M-D Blow-Me-Down, Nova Scotia

BMDATC Ballistic Missile Defense Advanced Technology Center (USA)

BMDCA Ballistic Missile Defense Communications Agency

BMDEAR Ballistic Missile Defense Emergency Action Report

BMDITP Ballistic Missile Defense Integrated Training Plan

BMDM British Museum Department of Manuscripts

BMDMB Ballistic Missile Defense Missile Battalion (USA)

BMDMP Ballistic Missile Defense Master Plan

bmdns basic mission, design number, and series (aircraft)

BMDO Ballistic Missile Defense Operations

BMDOA Ballistic Missile Defense Operations Activity

BMDPM Ballistic Missile Defense Program Manager

BMDPO Ballistic Missile Defense Program Office(r)

bmdr bombardier

BMDSCOM Ballistic Missile Defense System Command (USA)

BMD System Ballistic Missile Defense System

bme biomedical engineering

BME Blue Mountains Expeditions; Brotherhood of Marine Engineers

B.M.E. Bachelor of Mechanical Engineering; Bachelor of Mining Engineering; Bachelor of Music Education

BMEC British Marine Equipment Council

B. Med. Bachelor of Medicine

B.M.Ed. Bachelor of Music Education

B.Med.Biol. Bachelor of Medical Biology

B.Med.Sc. Bachelor of Medical Science

BMEF British Mechanical Engineering Federation

BMEG Building Materials Export Group
BMEL Barber Middle East Line
bmep brake mean effective pressure
BM & ESA Building Materials and Equipment Southeast Asia (Singapore)
B.Met. Bachelor of Metallurgy
B.Met.E. Bachelor of Metallurgical Engineering
BMEWS Ballistic Missile Early Warning System
BMFA Boston Museum of Fine Arts
bmg business management game
B.Mgt.Eng. Bachelor of Management Engineering
BMH British Military Hospital
bmi ballistic missile interceptor (BMI)
BMI Barley and Malt Institute; Battelle Memorial Institute; Book Manufacturers Institute; Broadcast Music Incorporated; Broadway Memorial Institute
B.Mic. Bachelor of Microbiology
BMIC British Music Information Centre (London); Broadcast Music Incorporated (Canada)
BMIC Bureau of Mines Information Circular
B.Min.E. Bachelor of Mining Engineering
BMIP Basic Medical Insurance Plan
BMIS Business Management Information System
BMJ British Medical Journal
bmk birthmark; bookmark(er)
bmkr boilermaker
BML Belfast & Moosehead Lake (railroad); Bodega Marine Laboratory (University of California); Bougainville Mining Limited; British Maritime League; British Museum Library (London)
B.M.L. Bachelor of Modern Languages
B & M L Belfast & Moosehead Lake (railroad)
BMLA British Maritime Law Association
BMLG Branch and Mobile Libraries Group
BMM Belfast, Mersey and Manchester Steamships
BMMA British Mantle Manufacturers' Association
BMMA Biblioteca Municipal

Mário de Andrade (Portuguese —Mario de Andrade Municipal Library)—named in honor of Brazil's musician-poet promoter of modernism
BMMFF British Man-Made Fibres Federation
BMMO Birmingham and Midland Motor Omnibus
bmn bone marrow necrosis
Bmn Bremen
BMN British Merchant Navy
BMNH British Museum (Natural History)
BMNP Bale Mountains National Park (Ethiopia); Blue Mountains National Park (New South Wales)
BMNT beginning morning nautical twilight
bmo business machine operator
BMO Ballistic Missile Office
bmoc big man on campus
bmom base maintenance and operations model
B'mouth Bournemouth
bmp brake mean power; buttermilk powder
BMP Bricklayers, Masons and Plasterers' (Union)
BMP Banco Minero del Peru (Spanish—Mining Bank of Peru)
BMP-76PB Soviet amphibious armored-infantry combat vehicle also designated BTRM
BMPA British Metalworking Plantmakers' Association
BMPIUA Bricklayers, Masons, and Plasterers International Union of America
bmpp benign mucous-membrane pemphigus
BMPS British Medical Protection Society; British Musicians Pension Society
BMQA Board of Medical Quality Assurance
bmr basal metabolic rate; bomber
BMR Basal Metabolism Rate; Bureau of Mineral Resources
BMRA British Manufacturers' Representatives' Association
BMRB British Market Research Bureau
BMRL Building Materials Research Laboratories
BMRR British Museum Reading Room
BMRS Ballistic Missile Recovery System
bms balanced magnetic switch
BMs Black Muslims; Boatswain's Mates
BMS Boston Museum of

Science; British Malachological Society; British Ministry of Supply; Buffalo Museum of Science; Bureau of Medical Services; Bureau of Medicine and Surgery
B.M.S. Bachelor of Marine Science; Bachelor of Medical Science
BMSA British Medical Students' Association
BMSE Baltic Mercantile and Shipping Exchange
BMSG British Merchant Service Guild
BMSS British and Midlands Scientific Society
BMT Basic Military Training; Boston & Maine Transportation (railroad); Brooklyn-Manhattan Transit (subway system)
B.M.T. Bachelor of Medical Technology
BMTA Boston Metropolitan Transit Authority
BMTFA British Malleable Tube Fittings Association
BMTP Bureau of Mines Technical Paper
BMTS Ballistic Missile Target System
BMTV Ballistic Missile Test Vessel
BMU British Medical Union
B. Mus. Bachelor of Music
bmv bromegrass-mosaic virus
BMVM British Military Volunteer Service
BMW Bayerische Motoren Werke (Bavarian Motor Works)
BMWE Brotherhood of Maintenance of Way Employees
BMWS Ballistic Missile Weapon System
bmx (BMX) bicycle motorcross
BMYC Baltimore Motor Yacht Club
bmz basement membrane zone
bn battalion; between; billion; bloody nuisance; branchial neuritis
bn (BN) binary number (system)
bn bijvoeglijk naamwoord (Dutch—adjective)
Bn beacon (daybeacon); bearing (as distinguished from bearing angle); Benjamin
Bn Bayan (Turkish—Miss, Mrs.)
Bⁿ Bassin (French—basin, pond)
BN Braniff; Bureau of Narcotics; Burlington Northern

(merger of Chicago, Burlington, and Quincy, Frisco—St Louis and San Francisco, Great Northern, Northern Pacific, Spokane, Portland, and Seattle railroads)

B-N Bloomington-Normal, Illinois

B.N. Bachelor of Nursing

B & N Barnes & Noble; Bauxite & Northern

B of N Bureau of Narcotics

BN Biblioteca Nacional (Portuguese or Spanish—National Library); *Biblioteca Nazionale* (Italian—National Library); *Bibliothèque National* (French —National Library)

bna (BNA) beta-naphthylamine

BNA Brazil Nut Association; British Naturalists' Association; British North America; British North Atlantic; Bureau of National Affairs; Nashville, Tennessee (airport)

BNA Basle Nomina Anatomica (Basel Anatomical Nomenclature)

BNAF British North Africa Force

B'nai B'rith Benai Berith (Hebrew—Sons of the Covenant)

BNAs British Naval Attaches

BNAU Bulgarian National Agrarian Union

B.Nav. Bachelor of Navigation

BNB British National Bibliography; British North Borneo (Sabah)

BNB British National Bibliography

BNBC British National Book Centre

BNC Biblioteca Nacional de Chile, Biblioteca Nacional de Colombia

B.N.C. Brasenose College (Oxford)

BNCC Bay de Noc Community College

BNCF Biblioteca Nazionale Centrale Firenze (Italian— National Central Library— Florence)

bnchbd benchboard

BNCM Bibliothèque Nationale du Conservatorie de Musique (National Library of the Conservatory of Music—Paris)

BNCOR British National Committee for Oceanographic Research

BNCS British Numerical Control Society

BNCSR British National Committee for Space Research

(Royal Society)

BNCVE Biblioteca Nazionale Centrale Vittorio Emanuele II (Italian—Victor Emanuel IInd Central Library)—in Rome

b/nd binding—no date available

Bnd Bend

BND Bundesnachrichtendienst (German—Federal Intelligence Service)

BNDD Bureau of Narcotics and Dangerous Drugs

Bndr Bandmaster

Bndr S-L Bandmaster—Sub-Lieutenant

bndy bindery; boundary

bne but not exceeding

BNE Board of National Estimates (CIA); Brisbane, Australia (airport); Buffalo Niagara Electric Corporation

BNEC British National Export Council; British Nuclear Energy Conference

BNES British Nuclear Energy Society

BNE & SAA Bureau of Near Eastern and South Asian Affairs (US Department of State)

bnf bomb nose fuse

Bnf Banff

BNF Brand Name Foundation; Braniff International Airways

BNF British National Formulary

BNFC British National Film Catalogue

BNFEX Battalion Field Exercise

BNFL British Nuclear Fuels Limited

BNFMF British Non-Ferrous Metals Federation

BNFMRA British Non-Ferrous Metals Research Association

BNFMTC British Non-Ferrous Metals Technology Centre

BNFP Barnwell Nuclear Fuel Plant

BNFSA British Non-Ferrous Smelters' Association

Bng Bangor

BNGA British Nursery Goods Association

BnG-DL Bibliothèque nationale du Grand-Duche de Luxembourg (French—National Library of the Grand Duchy of Luxembourg)—on FD Roosevelt boulevard in Luxembourg

BNGM British Naval Gunnery Mission

BNGS Bomb Navigation Guid-

ance System

bnh burnish

BNHA Badlands Natural History Society

BNHQ Battalion Headquarters

BNHS British National Health Service

BNI Bechtel National Inc; Black Nation of Islam

BNIB British National Insurance Board

BNJ Bonn, Germany (Cologne-Bonn airport)

BNJM Biblioteca Nacional José Martí (Spanish—José Martí National Library)—Havana's great library named for Cuba's apostle of independence active in the late nineteenth century

bnkg banking

BNL Brookhaven National Laboratory

BNL Banco Nazionale del Lavoro (Italian—National Bank of Labor); *Biblioteca Nacional de Lisboa* (Portuguese—National Library of Lisbon); *Bibliothèque Nationale du Liban* (French—National Library of Lebanon)—in Beirut

BNM Badlands National Monument (South Dakota); Biblioteca Nacional de México (National Library of Mexico— Mexico City)

BNM Banco Nacional de México (Spanish—National Bank of Mexico); *Biblioteca Nacional de México* (Spanish —National Library of Mexico) —in Mexico City; *Biblioteca Nazionale Marciana* (Italian —Marcian National Library) —in Venice

bno barrels of new oil; bladder neck obstruction; but not over

BNO Bank of New Orleans

BNOC British National Oil Corporation; British National Opera Company

bnp (BNP) bruttonationalprodukt (Dano-Norwegian—gross national product)

BNP Bahamas NP (West Indies); Bako National Park (Sarawak); Banco Nacional de Panama; Banff NP (Alberta); Belair NP (South Australia); Bontebok NP (South Africa)

BNP Banque Nationale de Paris (French—National Bank of Paris)

bnpa binasal pharyngeal airway

bnr burner

BNRDC British National Research Development Corporation

BNS Bathymetric Navigation System; British Nylon Spinners

B.N.S. Bachelor of Natural Science; Bachelor of Naval Science

B of NS Bank of Nova Scotia

B.N.Sc. Bachelor of Nursing Science

BNSM British National Socialist Movement

bnst bassoonist

Bnt Burntisland

BNTL British National Temperance League

BNU *Banco Nacional Ultramarino* (Portuguese—Overseas National Bank)

B-nut B-shaped nut

BNV *Biblioteca Nacional de Venezuela* (Spanish—National Library of Venezuela)—in Caracas

BNVE *Biblioteca Nazionale Vittorio Emanuele III* (Italian—Victor Emanuel III Library)—in Naples

BNW Battelle-Northwest; Bureau of Naval Weapons

BNWR Blackwater National Wildlife Refuge (Maryland); Bowdoin National Wildlife Refuge (Montana); Brigantine National Wildlife Refuge (New Jersey)

Bnx Bronx

BNX British Nuclear Export Executive

BNZ Bank of New Zealand

bnzn benzoin

bo base (of prism) out; blackout; body odor; bowel obstruction; bowels open; bucco-occlusal

bo' bore; brother

b/o back order; boiloff; brought over; budget outlay

b & o belladonna and opium

'bo hobo (vagrant)

Bo Bolivia; Bolivian

BO Baltimore & Ohio (stock exchange symbol); Base Order; black oil (bunker oil fuel); Board of Ordnance; body odor; box office; branch office; broker's order; Bureau of Ordnance

B.O. Bachelor of Oratory

B & O Baltimore & Ohio Railroad; Bang & Olufsen

BO *Boletín Oficial* (Spanish—Official Bulletin)

BO-5 Messerschmidt-Bolkow-Blohm five-seat helicopter

boa. born on arrival; breakoff

altitude

Boa Balboa, Panama

BOA Basic Ordering Agreement; Boat Owners Association; British Optical Association; British Orthopedic Association; British Osteopathic Association; British Overseas Airways (BOAC)

BOA (Disp) British Optical Association (Dispensing Certificate)

BOAC British Overseas Airways Corporation

Boadbil nickname of Abu Abdallah—last Moorish king of Granada

BOAdicea British Overseas Airways digital information computer for electronic automation

BOADS Boston Air Defense Sector

BOAE Bureau of Occupational and Adult Education (Office of Education)

BOAFG British Order of Ancient Free Gardeners

'board aboard; all aboard; on board; starboard

BOAS British Orphans Adoption Society

boat short form for advice boat, agent's boat, airboat, albacore boat, assault boat, bait boat, banana boat, bass boat, bum boat, bunder boat, canal boat, cargo boat, catboat, cattle boat, clam boat, cockboat, cockleboat, cockleshell boat, crab boat, crash boat, custom's boat, diesel boat, dispatch boat, eagle boat, eight-oar boat, electric boat, excursion boat, faltboat, ferryboat, fireboat, fishing boat, flyboat, flying boat, foldboat, four-oar boat, freight boat, garbage boat, gas(oline) boat, gliding boat, grain boat, guardboat, gunboat, hag boat, harborpatrol boat, herring boat, houseboat, iceboat, immigration boat, jigboat, johnboat, jollyboat, junk boat, kelpboat, liberty boat, lifeboat, line boat, lobster boat, longboat, love boat (a tv invention), mail boat, market boat, menhaden boat, mosquito boat, motorboat, nefboat, oil boat, ore boat, outboard motorboat, oyster boat, packet boat, paddleboat, paddlewheel boat, passenger boat, patrol boat, patrol torpedo boat, picket

boat, pilot boat, pogey boat, police boat, powerboat, public-health boat, Q-boat, railroad-car ferryboat, river boat, river gunboat, rocketboat, rowboat, sailboat, sailing boat, sardine boat, seine boat, showboat, shrimp boat, slow boat (to China), small boat, snagboat, speedboat, sponge boat, swan boat (a Wagnerian invention disclosed in *Lohengrin* and sometimes seen in public parks), tow boat, toy boat, trawl boat, troll boat, tugboat, tunaboat, U-boat, viking boat, waterboat, welder's boat, whaleboat, work boat, xebec boat, yawlboat, zenana boat, etc. (seafarers usually reserve the term *boat* for a lifeboat, a small craft, or a submarine but never say *boat* when referring to a bulk carrier, a freighter, a large motor vessel, a lightship, a naval vessel other than small craft, a nuclear-powered ship, an ocean liner, a passenger ship other than a ferry, a steamship, or a tanker)

BOAT Business Operational and Administrative Training (program)

boat dk boat deck (lifeboat-boarding deck)

boatel boat + hotel (waterside hotel or motel)

boats. boatswain (bo'sun)

BOAT/US Boat Owners Association of the United States

bob best of breed

Bob Robert

B o B Bookbuilders of Boston

BOB Bureau of the Budget

BOBA British Overseas Banks Association

Bobbie Robert

Bobbs Bobbs-Merrill

Bobby Robert(a); nickname for a London policeman and so named after Sir Robert Peel who organized the London police force

Bobby Jones Robert Tyre Jones

b-o-b cult ban-on-bathing cult (hippie subculture)

Bob Dylan Robert Zimmerman; Robert Zimmerman

Bob Hope Leslie Townes Hope

BOBMA British Oil Burner Manufacturers Association

bo-bo bo-bo-type locomotive

bobr boring bar

boc back outlet central; blowout

coil; body on chassis

Boc Boccaccio

B o C Bureau of Correction (Pennsylvania); Bureau of Corrections (Virgin Islands)

BOC Bank of China; Brooklyn Opera Company; Burmah Oil Company

BOCA Building Officials Conference of America

boca(s) [Spanish—gulf(s); inlet(s); mouth(s)]

BOCCI Bureau of Organized Crime and Criminal Intelligence (California)

B.Occu.Ther. Bachelor of Occupational Therapy

bocd barrels of oil per calendar day

BOCE Board of Customs and Excise

BOCES Board of Cooperative Educational Services

Boche (French—German person)

BoCHS Bureau of Community Health Services

DOCM British Oil and Cake Mills

B & O—C & O Baltimore and Ohio—Chesapeake and Ohio (merged railroad)

BOCS Board of Cooperative Services

bod beneficial occupancy date; biochemical oxygen demand; biological oxygen demand; blackout door

bod bodega (Spanish—wineshop); bodoniana (Italian—Bodoni-style type)

Bod Bodaway; Bodel; Boden; Bodil; Bodleian; Bodnar; Bodo; Bodoni

BoD Board of Directors, Bureau of Drugs

Bodensee Austro-German name for Lake Constance washing the borders of Austria, Germany, and Switzerland

Bodl Bodleian Library

bod lang body language (communication via body movements or postures)

Bodleian Oxford University's superb library established in 1445

Bodley Bodley Head

b-o d(s) box-office disaster(s)—frequently called artistic success(es)

Bod units Bodansky units

boe back outlet eccentric

BOE Board of Osteopathic Examiners

BOE Boletín Oficial del Estado

(Spanish—Official State Bulletin)

Boeing 707 four-engine long-range jet transport

Boer (Afrikaans or Dutch—farmer)—South African of Dutch descent whose language is called Afrikaans

BOES Branch Ordinary Enquiry System

bof basic oxygen furnace; binary oxide film

bof beurre, oeufs, fromages (French—butter, eggs, cheeses)—slang for a big butter-and-egg man

BoF Bureau of Foods

B-o-F Books-on-File

Bog Bogotá

BoG Board of Governors

B o G Board of Governors

BOG Bogotá, Colombia (airport); Boston Opera Group

boggan toboggan

bogh boghandel (Dano-Norwegian— bookstore, booktrade)

bogie unidentified aircraft

Bogie Maxwell Bodenheim; Humphrey Bogart

Bogland Ireland

Boglander Irishman

Bogor (Indonesian—Buitenzorg)

bogsaat bunch of guys sitting around a table

Bogside Catholic workingclass district of Derry (Londonderry)

boh breakoff height

Boh Bohemia(n)

BoH Bank of Hawaii

B O'H Bernardo O'Higgins

Bohem Bohemia; Bohemian

Bohemia Austro-Hungarian Empire and German name for what is now Czechoslovakia; habitat of the gypsies and other unconventional people who call themselves Bohemians

Bohemian Forest English name for the Böhmerwald

bohica bend over—here it comes again

BoHM Bureau of Health Manpower

Böhmen (German—Bohemia—Czechoslovakia)

Böhmerwald (German—Bohemian Forest)—extending from Bohemia in Czechoslovakia to Bavaria in Germany

BoHP&RD Bureau of Health Planning and Resources Development

BOHS British Occupational Hygiene Society

boi basis of issue; break of inspection

boi (BOI) branch output interrupt

Boi Boise

BoI Board of Investment

BOI Boise, Idaho (airport)

B & OI Bank and Office Interiors

BoIA Board of Immigration Appeals

BOIC Boarding Officer in Charge

BOIESA Bureau of Oceans and International Environmental and Scientific Affairs (US Department of State)

boil. boiling

boil.pt. boiling point

Bois (French—woods)—short form for the Bois de Boulogne park, racetrack, and recreation area of Paris

Bois de Belleau (French—Belleau Wood)—village northwest of Chateau-Thierry

Boise Idaho's capital

Boise St Univ Boise State University

boj booster jettison

BoJ Bank of Japan

Bojangles Bill (Bojangles) Luther Robinson

bo juice body-odor deodorant

BOK Book-of-the-Month Club

Boko Bohner & Kohle

'boks springboks

bol bill(s) of lading; bollard(s)

bol (BOL) block output length

bol. bolus (Latin—large pill)

Bol Bolivia; Bolivian; boliviano

Bol Bol'shaya or Bol'shoy(e) (Russian—big)

bol-148 (also BOL-148) d-2-bromolysergic acid tartrate (lsd-type hallucinogen)

Bol cols Bolivarian colors (yellow, blue, and red as in the flags of Colombia, Ecuador, and Venezuela)

BOLD Bibliographic On-Line Display (document retrieval system); Blind Outdoor Leisure Development

BOLDS Burroughs Optical Lens Docking System

Bolerium (Latin—Seat of Storms)—Land's End

bolf barge off loading facility

Bolingbroke Henry IV of England

Bolívar Simón Bolívar (Guayaquil, Ecuador's airport named for the great South American liberator)

Bolivarian Block Colombia,

Ecuador, Peru, Bolivia
Bolivarian Republics Bolivia, Columbia, Ecuador, Peru, Venezuela
Bolivia Republic of Bolivia (landlocked Andean nation named for Simón Bolívar who liberated it from Spain, Bolivians mine its tin and other precious metals) *República Boliviana*
Bolivia Day Bolivian Independence Day (August 5 and 6)
Bolonia (Spanish–Bologna)
bolo(s) bolshevik(s)
Bolo(s) Bolshevik(s)
bolovac bolometric voltage and current (voltage measurement)
bols bolster
BOLSA Bank of London and South America
Bol'shaya (Russian—Big)—old Russian name for Mt McKinley
Bolshevik Feminist Aleksandra Kollontai
bolshie(s) bolshevik(s)
Bolshoi Kavkaz (Russian—Great Caucasus)—Caucasus Mountains
bolt. beam-of-light transistor
BOLT Basic Occupational Language Training; Basic Occupational Literacy Test
boltop better on lips than on paper (a kiss)
Bolv Bolivia; Bolivian
bom business office must
Bom Bombay
BoM Bureau of Mines; Bureau of the Mint
BOM Bombay, India (airport)
BOMA Building Owners and Managers Association
BOMAP Barbados Oceanographic and Meteorological Analysis Project
Bomarc Boeing long-range surface-to-air missile bearing nuclear warhead
BOMARC Boeing-Michigan Research Center
BOMAS Business Opportunity and Management Advisory Service
bomb. bombardment
Bomb Bombardier
Bomba (Italian—Bass Drum) — nickname of Ferdinand II—King of the Two Sicilies
bombay bombay duck (Asiatic lizardfish, dried and salted lizardfish served with curry, also called bummalo)
Bombay Hook Bombay Hook

National Wildlife Refuge near Dover, Delaware
bombex bombing exercise
BOMC Book of the Month Club
Bom Com Bomber Command
BoMD Bureau of Medical Devices
BOMEX Barbados Oceanographic and Meteorological Experiment
bomfog brotherhood of man under the fatherhood of god (shortform cherished by many political-speech reporters)
Bompo Bompensiero (Frank Bompensiero—San Diego, California's mob boss for many years until slain by the Mafia in 1977 when it was revealed he had provided the FBI with information about organized crime for more than a decade during his retirement)
bomrep bombing report
BoMS Bureau of Medical Services
bomst bombsight
Bon Bonin Islands
BON Bonaire, Netherlands West Indies (airport)
Bona (Spanish—Bonn)
Bonaire's Port Kralendijk
Bon Air Girls Bon Air School (for delinquent) Girls at Bon Air, Virginia
Bonanza Beech U-22 trainer aircraft
Bonanza Land Fort Smith, Arkansas area's nickname
Bonanza State Montana
bond. bonding
Bond Street London's street of fashionable shops
Bone Algerian port city now called Annaba
boneblack animal charcoal
bone(s) trombone(s)
Bo'ness Borrowstounness
Boney Napoleon Bonaparte
Bon Homme Richard (French—Good Man Richard)—Benjamin Franklin
Boni Boniface
Boniato Santiago de Cuba's prison noted for its inhuman treatment of common as well as political prisoners held by Castro's communist regime
Bonins Bonin Islands (Ogasawaras)
Bonna (Latin—Bonn)—West German capital
Bonnie Prince Charles Charles Edward Stuart—the Young

Pretender
Bonny Johnny John Adams—second President of the United States
Bononia (Latin—Bologna)
Boo Bootes
boobtube television's nickname
Book Bookman
bookie(s) bookmaker(s)
bookmobile book + automobile (mobile branch library within a truck fitted with book-filled shelves and a book-issuing desk)
Bookstax Bookstax of Britain
Boolist Booklist and Subscription Books Bulletin
Boonie Daniel W. Russell
boonies boondocks
BOOST Broadened Opportunities for Officer Selection and Training (USN)
Boot Bootes
Boothia Boothia Peninsula in the Canadian Arctic where it is the northernmost extension of North America
Booze Bourse Brooklyn, New York nickname
bop balance of payments; basic oxygen process(ing); bebop (loud jazz accompanied by nonsensical lyrics); best operating procedure; buy our product(s)
b-o-p balance of payments
Bop Buffalo orphan prototype (virus)
BoP Bay of Pigs (invasion); Bay of Plenty
B o P Bureau of Prisons (United States Department of Justice)
BoPa Borgelige Partisaner (Danish—Middleclass Partisans)— underground resistance against occupying German forces during World War II
BoPat Border Patrol
bopd barrels of oil per day
bops blowout preventer stack(s)
bopt broken orange pekoe tea
B.Opt. Bachelor of Optometry
BOQ Bachelor Officers' Quarters; Base Officers' Quarters
boquerón(es) malagueño(s)—person(s) of Málaga
bor boring; bowels open regularly
Bor Boris; Borough
BOR Board of Review; Borg-Warner (stock exchange symbol); Bureau of Outdoor Recreation
boracic acid boric acid
BORAD British Oxygen Re-

search and Development
Borains people of Belgium's Borinage mining district
boram block-oriented random-access memories
borax sodium tetraborate
Borax King Francis Marion Smith of Death Valley, California
borazon boron nitrogen compound harder than diamond; boron nitride heated and pressed with a catalyst
Borba (Serbo-Croat—Struggle) —Yugoslavia's leading newspaper although under control of the Yugoslav Communist Party
Border Country The Border (locally the U.S.–Mexican border extending for 1952 miles or 3141 kilometers from Brownsville, Texas opposite Matamoros, Tamaulipas to San Diego, California opposite Tijuana, Baja California Norte)
Border Minstrel Sir Walter Scott
Border States former slave-holding states of Delaware, Maryland, Virginia, Kentucky, and Missouri; before the Civil War they divided the North from the South
Bore Ro-Ro Bore Roll-on Roll-off Line
Borgogna (Italian—Burgundy)
Borgoña (Spanish—Burgundy)
boric acid H_3BO_3
boricua(s) [Spanish-American slang—Puerto Rican(s)]—slang truncation of *borinqueño(s)*
borino(s) *borinqueño(s)* [Spanish-American slang derived from native name—Puerto Rican(s)]
Boris Boris Godunov (Mussorgsky's four-act opera)
Boris Karloff William Henry Pratt
Boris Pilnyak Boris Andreyevich Vogau
Boris Savinkov (pseudonym—Vladimir Ropshin)
Borneo old name for Kalimantan
BORN FREE Build Options, Reassess Norms, Free Roles through Educational Equity
boro borough
Boro Borough
Boro' Borough
Borodin party name of Mikhail Markovich Grusenberg the Soviet's political advisor of

the Kuomintang and later editor of the *Moscow Daily News*
Borromeans Borromean Islands in Lake Maggiore
Borscht Belt Catskill Mountain resort area in New York State
bos basic oxygen steel
Bos Bosphorus; Boston
Bos Bosanski (Serbo-Croatian—Bosnian)
BoS Bureau of Ships
BOS Boston, Massachusetts (airport); British Oil Shipping
Boschaps Boston Symphony Chamber Players
Bösend Bösendorfer
Bósforo (Spanish—Bosphorus)
bo's'n boatswain
Bo'sn Boatswain
Bosna (Yugoslav—Bosnia-Herzegovina)
Bosnia Bosnia-Herzegovina (once a kingdom, once part of the Austro-Hungarian Empire, now a federated republic within Yugoslavia)
Bosox Boston Red Socks (baseball team)
Bosphorus 20-mile-long Bosphorus Strait between Asiatic and European Turkey and connecting the Black Sea with the Sea of Marmora leading via the Dardanelles to the Mediterranean; strait separates Galata and Üsküdar (Scutari) sections of Istanbul once called Constantinople
BosPops Boston Pops Orchestra
BOSS Bioastronautic Orbital Space System; Boeing Operational Supervisory System; Bureau of State Security (South Africa's Secret Service)
Boss of Bosses Lucky Luciano (Salvatore Lucania)
Boss Kett Charles F(ranklin) Kettering
Boss Tweed William Marcy Tweed
Bost Boston
Boston capital of Massachusetts, named for a Boston in England formerly St Botolph's Town
Boston Brahmin Historian William Hickling Prescott
Boston Spa place-name nickname of the British Library Lending Division in Boston Spa, Wetherby, West Yorkshire
Boston Strong Boy John L Sulli-

van
Boston Tech Boston Technical Publishers
BOSTPDis Boston Procurement District (U.S. Army)
bo'sun boatswain (pronounced as contracted)
Boswash Boston-to-Washington (city complex)
bot balance of time (to be served by a convict); botanic; botanical; botanist; botany; bottle; bottled; bottom; bottomed; bottoming
bot (BOT) beginning of tape
bot *botanik* or *botanisk* (Dano-Norwegian—botany or botanist)
Bot Botany
BoT Bank of Tokyo
B o T Board of Trade (British); Board of Transport (NATO)
BOT Board of Trade; Board of Trade unit; Books On Tape
B.O.T. Bachelor of Occupational Therapy
BOTAC Board of Trade Advisory Committee
botan botanic(al)(ly), botanist, botany
BOTB British Overseas Trade Board
bot & can bottle and can
botel boat hotel
BOTEX British Office for Training Exchange
both. bombing over the horizon
botmg bottoming
BOT-ohm Board of Trade ohm
bot(s) bottle(s)
Botswana Republic of Botswana (landlocked South African country inhabited by Bantus and Bushmen adept in raising cattle as well as corn, peanuts, and sorghum)—formerly Bechuanaland
Botticelli Sandro di Botticelli—palette name of Alessandro Filipepi
bottle baby alcoholic addict
botu botulism
BOTU Board of Trade Unit
boty bike of the year
Bou Boulogne-sur-Mer
BOU Bank Officers Union; Boat Operating Unit; British Ornithologists' Union
boul boulevard
Boul' Mich' (contraction—Boulevard St Michel)—in the student quarter of Paris
Boulogne Boulogne-sur-Mer (French—Boulogne by the Sea)—English Channel port not to be confused with the

commune of Boulogne—Billancourt on the Seine southwest of Paris

bound. boundaries; boundary

Bourbon Street New Orleans nightlife center

Bourgogne (French—Burgundy)

'**bout** about

Bouvetøya (Norwegian—Bouvet Island)—Antarctic dependency of Norway

bov best of variety; bovine; bovril; brown oil of vitriol

Bov Eil Bovenwindse Eilanden (Dutch—Windward Islands, Aruba, Bonaire, Curaçao)

bovinol bovinologic(al)(ly); bovinologist; bovinology

bow. bag of water (amniotic sac); blackout window; born out of wedlock

bo & w barrels of oil and water

bowdler bowdlerize

Bowery north-south thoroughfare on Lower East Side of Manhattan, New York City; notorious for the number of its shabby hotels and saloons catering to derelict habitues and itinerant tramps

Bowie State Arkansas

Bowker RR Bowker Company

bowla bowlathon

BOWO Brigade Ordnance Warrant Officer

boxitos nickname for people from Yucatan, Mexico where in Mayan the word means dark people

boyc boycott (named for C C Boycott, a British army officer, and allegedly the first victim of this system of coercion and intimidation brought on by not having any dealings—commercial or social—with a company, a country, a person, or their products or services)

Boyhood Home of Mark Twain Hannibal, Missouri

Boy Orator of the Platte William Jennings Bryan

Boy's Town Omaha, Nebraska; redlight sections of many Mexican border towns also bear this place-name nickname

Boz Charles Dickens

Bozzy James Boswell—biographer and friend of Dr Samuel Johnson

bp back pressure; bandpass; baptized; bathroom privileges; beautiful people; bedpan; before present; behavior pattern; below proof; benzypyrene; be-

tween perpendiculars; bills payable; biotic potential; biparietal; birthplace; black pimp; blood pressure; blueprint; boiling point; bronchoplural; buccopulpal

bp (BP) back projection (tv slide-or-film background projection)

b/p baking powder; bills payable; blood pressure; blueprint

b & p bare and painted

b of p balance of payments

bp Bergstrom Paper Company; *buono per* (Italian—good for)

b.p. bonum publicum (Latin—the public good)

Bp Bishop

Bp Boerenpartij (Dutch—Farmers' Party)

BP Beach Party (amphibious military operation); Beschleunigter Personenzug (German—express train); Board of Parole; British Petroleum; British Pharmacopoeia; British Public; Bureau of Power; Bureau of Prisons (United States Department of Justice); Burns Philp Lines

B-P Basses-Pyrénées; Bermuda Plan (breakfast only); Lord Robert S Baden-Powell—founder of the Boy Scout movement

B.P. Bachelor of Pharmacy; Bachelor of Philosophy

B of P Bishop(ric) of Passau; Bureau of Prisons

BP Biblioteca Publica (Italian—Public Library); *Biblioteca Pública* (Portuguese or Spanish—Public Library); *British Pharmacopoeia*

bp 120/80 lar blood pressure 120 (systolic)/80 (diastolic) left arm reclining

bpa broadband power amplifier

Bpa Bahnpostampt (German—railway post office)

BPA Beach Protection Authority; Bedding Plants Australia; Biological Photographers Association; Blanket Purchasing Agreement; Bonneville Power Administration; Book Publishers Association; British Pediatric Association; British Ports Association; Broadcasters Promotion Association; Brunswick Port Authority; Bureau of Public Assistance; Bush Pilots Association (Australia); Business Press Association; Business Publications

Audit (of circulation)

B.P.A. Bachelor of Professional Arts

BPA Banco Português do Atlántico (Portuguese Bank of the Atlantic)

BPAA Bowling Proprietors' Association of America

BPAC Budget Program Activity Code; Business Publications Audit of Circulation

BP-ACT Blueport Associated Container Transporation

BPA/DoS Bureau of Public Affairs—Department of State

B.Paed. Bachelor of Paediatrics

BPAGB Bicycle Polo Association of Great Britain

bpam basic partitioned access method

BPANZ Book Publishers Association of New Zealand

BPAO Branch Public Affairs Office(r)

BPAS British Pregnancy Advisory Service

BPASC Book Publishers Association of Southern California

bpay bill(s) payable

bpb bank post bills; blanket position bond; bromophenol blue

BPBD Bill Posters, Billers and Distributors (Union)

BPBF British Paper Box Federation

BPBI British Plaster Board Industries

BPBIF British Paper and Board Industry Federation

BPBIRA British Paper and Board Industry Research Association

BPBM Bernice P. Bishop Museum (Honolulu)

BPBMA British Paper and Board Makers Association

bpc back-pressure control; book prices current; book and periodical circulation

BPC British Pharmaceutical Codex; British Phosphate Commission; British Printing Corporation; British Purchasing Commission; Business and Professional Code

b-p cartridge barricade-penetrating cartridge

BPCC British Printing and Communication Corporation

bpcd barrels per calendar day

BPCF British Precast Concrete Federation

BPCI Bulk Packaging and Containerization Institute

BPCR Brakes on Pedal Cycle

Regulations

BPCRA British Professional Cycle Racing Association

bpctca best practicable control technology currently available

bpd barrels per day; boxes per day

B. Pd. Bachelor of Pedagogy

BPD Bureau of the Public Debt

bpd & a basic planning data and assumption

BPDC Berkeley Particle Data Center; Books and Periodical Development Council (Canadian)

BPDMS Basic Point-Defense Missile System

BPDP Brotherhood of Painters, Decorators, and Paperhangers

bpe bit-plane encoding; black powder express (cartridge)

BPE Bureau of Postsecondary Education (Office of Education)

B.P.E. Bachelor of Physical Education

BPE-LCA Board of Parish Education—Lutheran Church in America

B.Pet.E. Bachelor of Petroleum Engineering

bpf bottom pressure fluctuation

bpf bon pour francs (French—good for francs)

BPF British Polio Fellowship

bpg break pulse generator

BPGC Building Performance Guarantee Corporation

Bpge bearing per gyro compass

bph barrels per hour; benign prostatic hypertrophy

B.Ph. Bachelor of Philosophy

BPh British Pharmacopoeia

B.P.H. Bachelor of Public Health

B.Pharm. Bachelor of Pharmacy

B.P.H.E. Bachelor of Physical and Health Education

B.Phil. Bachelor of Philosophy

BP & HL Brown Picton and Hornby Libraries (Liverpool)

B.Phys. Bachelor of Physics

B.Phys.Ed. Bachelor of Physical Education

B.Phys.Thy. Bachelor of Physical Therapy

bpi bits per inch; bytes per inch

BPI Bernreuter Personality Inventory; British Pacific Islands; Brooklyn Polytechnic Institute; Bureau of Public Information

BPICA Bureau Permanent Internationale des Constructeurs d'Automobiles (Permanent

International Bureau of Automobile Manufacturers)

B picture moving picture designed as a second or supporting feature in a cinema program

b-pid book-physical inventory difference

BPIF British Printing Industries Federation

BPISAE Bureau of Plant Industry, Soils, and Agricultural Engineering

BP & JC FL Birmingham Public and Jefferson County Free Library

BPKT Basic Programming Knowledge Test

bpl birthplace

Bpl Barnstaple

BPL Belfast Public Library; Binghamton Public Library; Birmingham Public Library; Boston Public Library; Brass Pounders League; Bridgeport Public Library; Brooklyn Public Library; Buffalo Public Library

BP Lib Broadcast Pioneers Library

bpm barrels per minute; beats per minute

BPMA British Photographic Manufacturers Association; British Printing Machinery Association; British Pump Manufacturers Association

BPMA/DoS Bureau of Politico-Military Affairs—Department of State

BPMD Battelle Project Management Division (publishes *Preferred Usage Guide* of NWTS-related words and abbreviations)

BPMF British Postgraduate Medical Federation; British Pottery Manufacturers' Federation

BPMS Blood Pressure Measuring System

bpn bloody public nuisance

Bpn Balikpapan

BPNHM Banff Park Natural History Museum

BPNMA British Plain Net Manufacturers' Association

BPO Base Post Office; Base Procurement Office; Berlin Philharmonic Orchestra; Boston Pops Orchestra; British Post Office; British Postal Order; Brooklyn Philharmonia Orchestra; Brooklyn Post Office

BPO Berliner Philharmonisches Orchester (German—Berlin

Philharmonic Orchestra)

BPOE Benevolent and Protective Order of Elks

BPOEW Benevolent and Protective Order of Elks of the World (Black, Chinese, and some White)

BPP Black Panther Party; Botswana People's Party

BPP Banco Popular del Peru (Spanish—Popular Bank of Peru); *British Parliamentary Papers*

BPPMA British Power Press Manufacturers Association

BPR Bureau of Public Roads

BPR Bloque Popular Revolucionario (Spanish—Popular Revolutionary Block)—leftist terrorists active in El Salvador since 1975; *Book Publishing Record* (periodical)

BPRA Book Publishers' Representatives' Association

bprf bulletproof

bprs brief psychiatric rating scale

bps bits per second; bytes per second

bp(s) black pimp(s)

bp's beautiful people

BPs Book Publishers (sales reports); Burns Philp steamships

B.Ps Bachelor in Psychology

BPS Balanced-Pressure System; Basic Programming System; Benchmark Portability System; Border Patrol Sector; Border Patrol Station; Bureau of Product Safety

B_{psc} bearing per standard compass

bpsd barrels per steam day

bpsm bulk pre-sorted mail

BPsS British Psychological Society

$B_{p\,stg\,c}$ bearing per steering compass

B.Psych. Bachelor of Psychology

bpt boiling point

bpt (BPT) bound plasma tryptophan

BPT Board of Prison Terms; British Petroleum Tanker; Bureau of Prison Terms

B.P.T. Bachelor of Physiotherapy

bpti bovine pancreatic trypsin inhibitor

bptv battleship propulsion test vehicle

bpu base production unit

BPU British Powerboating Union

BPUNP *Biblioteca Pública de la Universidad de la Plata* (Spanish—Public Library of the University of La Plata)

bpv bovine papilloma virus; bullet-proof vest

BPWA Business and Professional Women's Association

bpwr burnable poison water reactor

B-Pyr Basses-Pyrénées

bq beauty quotient; boiler quality

Bq Becquerel

BQ Bachelor's Quarters; Basic Qualification; Basically Qualified (member of USCG Aux)

B Q *Bibliothèque nationale du Québec* (French—National Library of Quebec)—Montreal

Bqa Barranquilla

BQL Bank of Queensland

BQLI Brooklyn, Queens, Long Island

BQMS Battery Quartermaster Sergeant

BQSF British Quarrying and Slag Federation

b quark bottom quark

bque barque

Bquilla Barranquilla

br bank rate; bank robber(y); berth; bill of rights; branch; bread (underground slang—money); breath; breeder reactor; brown; builder's risk; butadiene rubber

br (BR) bedroom; bedroom steward; branch (flow chart); break (request signal)

b/r bills receivable

b & r budget and reporting

b or r bales or rolls (freight)

br *bez roku* (Czech—no date, no year)

Br Branch; Bridge; Britain; British

Br *Bachiller* (Spanish—Bachelor)—academic degree; *Bratsche* (German—viola); *Bredning* (Danish—Bay); *Brücke* (German—Bridge); *Burun* (Turkish—nose, Point)

BR Baton Rouge; bearing; branch; Brazil (auto plaque); Breeder Reactor; bridge; British; British Railways; British Resident (commissioner); British United Airways; bromine; brown (buoy); Bureau of Reclamation

B-R Bas-Rhin; Business Route

B/R Bordeaux or Rouen

B of R Bureau of Reclamation; Bureau of Rehabilitation

BR *Banco di Roma* (Italian—Bank of Rome)

B.R. *Bancus Reginae* (Latin—Queen's Bench); *Bancus Rex* (Latin—King's Bench)

BR-1150 Breguet maritime-patrol aircraft also called Atlantique

bra brassiere

Bra Beira

Bra *Brasil* (Portuguese or Spanish—Brazil)

BrA *Bibliothèque royale Albert I* (French—Albert Ist Royal Library)—Brussels library called *Koninklijke Bibliotheek Albert I* in Flemish

BRA Bankruptcy Reform Act; Bee Research Association; Boston Redevelopment Authority; British Records Association; Building Renovating Association

bra burner brassiere burner (militant-feminist nickname)

BRAC Brotherhood of Railway and Airline Clerks

bracelets slang for handcuffs

brachi *brachion* (Greek—arm)—brachiation, brachiopod, brachium

brachycephs brachycephalics (short-skulled people)

Braclara (Latin—Braga)—Portuguese place also known as Brachara

Bra Cur Brazil Current

Brad Bradburn; Bradbury; Braden; Bradfield; Bradford; Bradley; Bradner; Bradshaw; Bradstreet; Brady

Bradshaw's *Bradshaw's Railway Guide*

brady bradycardia

Brady Bradenton, Florida; Brady Glacier, Alaska; Brady Lake, Ohio; Brady Mountains, Texas; Dr Brady C Hartman

Bragança (Portuguese—Braganza)—commune near the Spanish border of northwestern Portugal

Bragman's Bluff British pirate's name for what is now Puerto Cabezas, Nicaragua sometimes called El Bluff

Brahmaputra 1800-mile Indian river flowing from Himalayas into Bay of Bengal

Brahmsburg Hamburg, Germany—birthplace of Johannes Brahms

Brahms's 4 Brahms's four symphonies

braid. bidirectional reference array internally deprived

BRAINS Behavior Replication by Analog Instruction of Nervous System

Bram Abraham

Br.Am. British America safety lock invented by Joseph Bramah

Brambach Radiumbad Brambach in Saxony

Brampton Women Vanier Centre for (criminal) Women at Brampton, Ontario

Bram Stoker Abraham Stoker

BRANCHHYDRO Branch Hydrographic Office

Brandenburg Bach's Brandenburg Concertos he dedicated to Duke Christian Ludwig of Brandenburg, Germany

Brandy Nan Queen Anne so nicknamed because of her fondness for brandy

brane bombing radar navigation equipment

Brangonia (Latin—Worcester)

Brangus ⅜ Brahman + ⅝ —Angus cattle

Brann the Iconoclast William Cowper Brann, editor and publisher of *The Iconoclast*

BRANZ Basketball Referees Association of New Zealand; Building Research Association of New Zealand

bras ballistic rocket air suppression

bra(s) brassiere(s)

Bras Brasenose (pronounced *Brazenose*) College, Oxford; Brasil; Brasileiro

Bras *Brasil* (Portuguese or Spanish—Brazil); *Brasile* (Italian—Brazil)

BRAs Bosom-Rehabilitation Associates

BRASCFHESE Brotherhood of Railway, Airline, and Steamship Clerks, Freight Handlers, Express, and Station Employees

Bras Coll Brasenose College—Oxford

b-r-a-s-s breathe, relax, aim, squeeze, shoot (the marksman's acronym)

Brass Butte, Montana

BRASS Bottom Reflecting Active Sonar System

Brassai Gyula Halàsz

Brass City Waterbury, Connecticut

brass knucks brass knuckles

BRASTACS Bradford Scientific, Technical, and Commercial Service

Brat bi-drive recreational all-terrain transporter

Bratislava (Slovak—Pressburg) —Slovakia's principal metropolis called Pozsony by the Hungarians

Brattle Island, Galápagos Tortuga

Bratwurst Capital Sheboygan, Wisconsin

Braunschweig (German—Brunswick)

Bravo letter B radio code

braz Brazil; Brazilian

Braz Brazil(ian)

Brazil Federative Republic of Brazil (South America's largest country whose language is Portuguese and whose exports include coffee, cotton, and many minerals) *Republica Federativa do Brasil*

Brazil Day Brazilian Independence Day (September 7)

Brazilian Comedian Chico Anisio

Brazilian Composer-Conductor Heitor Villa-Lobos (in this century or Carlos Gomes in the last)

Brazilian emerald green variety of tourmaline

Brazilian Film Pioneer Alberto Cavalcanti

Brazilian National Composer Heitor Villa-Lobos

Brazilian Pianist Guiomar Novais

Brazilian Ports (large, medium, and small from north to south) Manaus (up the Amazon), Belém do Pará, São Luis, Enseada de Mucuripe, Natal, Recife, Maccio, Salvador de Bahia, Ilheus, Vitoria, Rio de Janeiro, Niteroi, Angra dos Reis, Santos, Paranagua, São Francisco, Itajai, Florianopolis, Laguna, Rio Grande, Porto Alegre

Brazilian ruby topaz altered by heating so when cooling it turns purple-red to salmon-pink and hence passes for a ruby

Brazilian sapphire blue tourmaline

Brazilian Trio Brazil's three best-known classical composers ranked chronologically—Antonio Carlos Gomes, Alberto Nepomuceno, and Heitor Villa-Lobos

Brazilië (Dutch—Brazil)

Braziller George Braziller

Brazil's Largest Port Rio de Janeiro

Brazil water slang nickname for

coffee

Brazza Brazzaville

Brb Borba (Yugoslavia—Struggle)—leading newspaper in Communist-controlled Yugoslavia

BRB Benefits Review Board; British Railways Board; Builders' Registration Board

brbc bovine red blood cells

BRBMA Ball and Roller Bearing Manufacturers Association

brbzc brass, bronze, or copper (cargo)

brc business reply card

Br.C. British Columbia

BRC Balcones Research Center (University of Texas); Base Residence Course; Bolivia Railway Company; British Research Council; Broadcast Rating Council; Brotherhood of Railway Carmen

BRCA Brotherhood of Railway Carmen of America

BRCCP British Royal Commission on Capital Punishment

Brch Branch

BRCMA British Radio Cabinet Manufacturers' Association

Br Col British Columbia

BRCS British Rail Catering Service; British Red Cross Society

BRCUSC Brotherhood of Railway Carmen of the United States and Canada

Br Cwlth British Commonwealth

brd basic retirement date; board; bomb-release distance; broad

BRD Bundesrepublik Deutschland (Federal Republic of Germany)—West Germany

BRDC British Racing Drivers' Club

brdcst broadcast

brdf bidirectional reflectance distribution function

BRDM Soviet amphibious reconnaissance vehicle carrying three men and antitank missiles

Brdw Broadwood

Bre Bremen; Bremerhaven

BRE Bureau of Readjustment Education

B.R.E. Bachelor of Religious Education

Bread Basket Fargo, North Dakota's nickname

Breadbasket of Canada Saskatchewan with its tremendous wheat fields

Breadbasket of Russia the

Ukraine

Breadbasket of Sweden southernmost province of Skåne given over to large-scale agriculture

Breadbasket of the World central North America (Canada and the U.S.)

Breakfast Food City Battle Creek, Michigan

brec bills receivable

breccia pyroclastic volcanic rock

Breck Breckinridge; Brecknockshire

Brecon Breconshire (Brecknockshire)

Breguet 765 Sahara flying transport for 145 troops

Breguet 1150 Atlantique maritime-patrol aircraft

brek breakfast

BREL British Rail Engineering Limited

'brella umbrella

Brem Bremen; Bremerhafen; Bremerhaven; Bremerton

BREMA British Radio Equipment Manufacturers Association

Brenner Brenner Pass in the Alps where it connects Bolzano, Italy with Innsbruck, Austria

Brennero Brenner Pass

Brent Brentford and Chiswick

Br'er Brother

Bres Breslau

Breslau German equivalent of Wroclaw, Poland (formerly a German port city)

Bret Brittany; Breton

Bretagne (French—Brittany)—but *Gran Bretagne* means Great Britain

Bretaña (Spanish—Brittany)—but *Gran Bretaña* means Great Britain

Bret Harte Francis Brett Harte

Brett Halliday Davis Dresser's pseudonym

brev brevet; breviary; breviate; brevier

brev breveté (French—patent); *brevetto* (Italian—patent)

brev. breviarium (Latin—abridgement or breviary)

brew. brewer; brewery; brewing

Brew Brewer; Brewster

brew'd brewed

Brewer NATO nickname for Soviet Yakovlev Yak-28 tactical bomber aircraft

Brewer's Brewer's Dictionary of Phrase and Fable

Brewery Capital Milwaukee

brf brief; briefing
BRF Bass Research Foundation; Bible Reading Fellowship; British Road Federation
BRFC British Record Fish Committee (of rod anglers)
brg bearing; brewing; bridge; brigantine
Brg Bridge
BrG British Guiana
BRG *Bibliotheek van de Rijksuniversiteit te Gent* (Flemish— Royal University Library of Ghent)—founded by King William I of the Netherlands
brghd bridgehead
brghm brougham (pronounced *broom*)
Brgo Spgs Borrego Springs
Br Gu British Guiana
BrH British Honduras
BRH Brussels, Belgium (airport); Bureau of Radiological Health
BRHL British Rail Hovercraft Limited
BrHon British Honduras
BRHS Bay Ridge High School; Betsy Ross High School
Bri Bridge; British(er)(s); Briton(s)
Br I British Isles
BRI Babson's Reports Incorporated; Banque des Réglements Internationaux (Bank of International Settlements); Biological Research Institute; Brain Research Institute; Building Research Institute; Bureau of Rehabilitation Inc; Burlington-Rock Island (railroad)
BRI *Banque des Règlements Internationaux* (French—Bank for International Settlements); *Brand Rating Index*
BRIA Biological Research Institute of America; Bread Research Institute of Australia
BRIC British Columbian Resource Investment Corporation
Brick Lane London, England's East End ghetto populated by poor Bengalis and Pakistanis
Bricklayers Union Bricklayers, Masons, and Plasterers International Union of America
BRICS British Rail Inter-City Service
BRICSHST British Rail Inter-City Service High-Speed Train
Bride of the Adriatic Venice
Bride of the Sea nearly inundated Venice on the Adriatic
Bridewell London's old house of

correction and long a nickname or synonym for such a place or prison
Bridge Bum Alan Sontag
Bridge House Wilmington, Delaware's detention home for juvenile delinquents
Bridge of Sighs 16th-century Venetian bridge arching a canal and connecting a prison with a ducal palace where prisoners were tried; nickname of any similar structure connecting a courthouse with a prison
BRIDGEX Bridge Construction Exercise
brig brigantine; slang for ship's prison
Brig Brigade; Brigadier
Brigette Bardot Camille Jarval
Brig Gen Brigadier General
Bright's disease kidney disease named for its diagnostician Dr Richard Bright of London
Brigitte Bridget
BRIGLEX Brigade Landing Exercise
Brigton Glasgow's Bridgetown
Brilab bribery-labor (FBI investigation's code name)
brill *brillante* (Italian—brilliant)
Brilliant Madman nickname of Charles XII of Sweden
Brill's disease epidemic typhus disease recurring years after the original infection and named for its American diagnostician Dr Nathan E Brill
BRIMEC British Mechanical Engineering Federation
brimstone sulfur
BRINCO British Newfoundland Corporation
BRINDEX British Independent Oil Exploration (Companies Association)
Bringer of Freedom's Light John Huss
Bris Brisbane
Brisb Brisbane
Brissie Brisbane
Brist Bristol
brit *britisk* (Dano-Norwegian— British)
Brit Britain; Britannia; British
Brit *Encyclopaedia Britannica*
Britain Great Britain (England, Scotland, and Wales)
Britain's First Woman Prime Minister Margaret Thatcher
Britain's Most Exclusive Club the House of Commons
Britain of the South New Zealand (halfway between the

Equator and the South Pole but very British)
Britain's Playground Blackpool (seaside resort on Irish Sea near Liverpool)
Britain's Premier Passenger Port Southampton
britannia britannia metal (alloy of antimony, copper, and zinc used as antifriction material and for dinnerware)
Britannia Bristol-built military transport aircraft; Britannia metal; Britannia prima (England); Britannia secunda (Wales)—symbol of Great Britain including Scotland with England and Wales; British Empire; Commonwealth of Nations once constituting most of the British Empire; Great Britain and Northern Ireland—the United Kingdom; Roman name for the island of Great Britain
Britannien (German—Britain)
Brit Book Centr British Book Centre
Britic Briticism
Brit Info British Information Services
British pertaining to the British Commonwealth, the British Empire, or the British people (English, Scottish, and Welsh)
British Am Bks British American Books
British America British possessions in or adjacent to the Americas
British Anatomist Extraordinary Henry Gray
British Bk Ctr British Book Center
British Century the 19th century
British Comedian Peter Ustinov
British Commonwealth British Commonwealth of Nations: Great Britain and Northern Ireland; British dominions, republics, and dependencies
British Guiana formerly Demerara and now called Guyana
British Hardware Centre Birmingham
British Honduras former name of Belize
British Isle Ports (large, medium, and small from the east coast of England, plus Scotland, Ireland, Wales, as well as England's west and south coasts) Whitstable, Port Victoria, Chatham, Tilbury Docks,

Gravesend, Woolwich, Greenwich, London, Wivenhoe, Harwich, Parkeston, Ipswich, Felixstowe, Lowestoft, Great Yarmouth, King's Lynn, Boston, Grimsby, Immingham, Kingston-upon-Hull, Goole, Whitby, Middlesbrough, Hartlepool, Seaham, Sunderland, North Shields, Newcastle, Gateshead, Blyth, Leith, Granton, Rosyth Dock Yard, Boness, Grangemouth, Alloa, Burntisland, Kirkcaldy, Methil, Perth, Abroath, Montrose, Aberdeen, Peterhead, Fraserburgh, Hopeman, Inverness, Cromarty, Invergordon, Port Mahomack, Helmsdale, Wick, Thurso, Scrabster, Stornoway, Oban, Campbeltown, Greenock, Finnart, Rothesay Dock, Glasgow, Ardrossan, Irvine, Troon, Cairnryan, Douglas, Bangor, Belfast, Larne Lough, Londonderry, Sligo, Westport, Galway, Kilrush, Limerick, Foynes, Cobh, Cork Harbour, Rosslare, Dublin, Silloth, Mayrport, Whitehaven, Barrow-in-Furness, Fleetwood, Preston, Liverpool, Manchester, Port Dinorwic, Holyhead, Caernarvon, Milford Haven, Llanelly, Swansea, Port Talbot, Barry, Cardiff, Newport, Sharpness, Gloucester, Avonmouth, Bristol, Portishead, Bideford, St Ives, Penzance, Falmouth, Fowey, Plymouth, Dartmouth, Portland, Weymouth, Poole, Cowes, Yarmouth, Southampton, Gosport, Portsmouth, Folkestone, Dover

British Isles Great Britain and Ireland

British Laugh Master Benny Hill

British Librettist Italian nickname for Shakespeare (*Librettista Brittanico*) because many of his dramatic plots inspired Italian composers ranging from Rossini to Verdi

British lion symbol of the British Commonwealth as well as of Great Britain

British North Borneo now known as Sabah

British Riviera England's south coast from Land's End to Margate

British Rock Gibraltar

British West Indies island possessions or former possessions

of Great Britain in or near the Caribbean: Bahamas; British Leeward, Virgin, and Windward islands; Jamaica, Tobago, Trinidad, etc.

Brit J Psychiat British Journal of Psychiatry

Brit J Surg British Journal of Surgery

brit met britannia metal (tin, copper, antimony alloy—sometimes bismuth, lead, and zinc)

Brit Mus British Museum

Britons English, Scottish, and Welsh people

Brit Pat British Patent

Brit Phos Comm British Phosphate Commission

BritRail British Railways

Brit—Rail Hover British Railways Hovercraft

Brits British; Britons

Brit(s) British(ers); Briton(s)

Brits (Dutch—British)

Brit Sam British Samoa

BRITSHIPS British Shipbuilding Integrated Production System

Britt. *Britannorum* (Latin—of the Britons)

Brittanje (Dutch—Britain)

Brittannië (Dutch—Britain)

Brittiska Üarna (Swedish—British Isles)

Brix Brixham; Brixton

Brixton Brixton Prison southeast of Plymouth, England; London, England's backwater of black Jamaicans and other West Indians in this slum; one of London's largest prisons is also in Brixton

Br J App Phys British Journal of Applied Physics

brk brick

Brk Brook

brkf breakfast

brklyr bricklayer

brkmn breakman

brks breakers

brkt bracket

brkwtr breakwater

brl bomb-release line

br/l brown line positive

BRL Babe Ruth League; Ballistic Research Laboratories; Beecham Research Laboratories; Bible Research Library; *Bibliotheek der Rijksuniversiteit te Leiden* (Dutch—Library of the Royal University in Leyden); British Research Library

BRL 1241 Beecham Research Laboratories formula 1241

(methicillan)

BRL 1341 Beecham Research Laboratories formula 1341 (penbritin)

brlg bomb radio longitudinal generator-powered

brlp burlap

brl sys barrier ready light system

brm bedroom

BRM British Racing Motors

BRMA Board of Registration of Medical Auxiliaries; British Rubber Manufacturers' Association

BRMBR Bear River Migratory Bird Refuge (Utah)

BRMC Business Research Management Center (USAF)

BRMCA British Ready-Mixed Concrete Association

BRMF British Rainwear Manufacturers' Federation

brn brown

Brn Bahrain; Brunei

BRNC Britannia Royal Naval College (Dartmouth)

brng bearing; browning; burning

Brno (Czechoslovakian—Brunn)

BRNP Blue Ridge National Parkway

brnsh brownish; burnish

Brnx Bronx

brnz bronze; bronzing

bro broach, bronchoscopy, brother

brO brownish orange

Bro Brother

BRO Brigade Routine Order(s)

Broad-bottomed Administration of Prime Minister Henry Pelham during the reign of George II

Broads The Broads (Norfolk Broads)—England's east coast holiday resort area

Broadway main north-south 13-mile-long arterial avenue of New York City; extends from Spuyten Duyvil and Harlem River to Bowling Green Park at the Battery facing Statue of Liberty in New York Harbor; Broadway crosses many principal avenues as it meanders in its march through Manhattan's residential, institutional, theatrical, commercial, financial, and shipping districts; originally was a cow path used by Dutch and English farmers taking their produce to market; often main street of other cities such as San Diego

broast(ed) broil(ed) + roast(ed)

broc brocaded

Brod Broderick; Brodie; Brody

broficon broadcast fighter control

BROILER Biopedagogical Research Organization on Intensive Learning Environment Reactions

brok broker; brokerage

Broken Hill former name of Kabwe, Zambia

brom bromide; bromidic; bromo; bromo-seltzer

bromat bromatology (treatise on foods)

Bromberg (German—Bydgoszcz)—city in central Poland

bromidrosis bromohydrosis

bromo bromidrosis; bromoform; bromo-seltzer

bromo-seltzer (bromide + seltzer)

bromot bromotology [study of smell(s)]

bronc bronco (Spanish—small half-wild horse)

bronch bronchial; bronchitis; bronchoscopic; bronchoscopist; bronchoscopy

broncho bronchus (Greek—windpipe)—bronchi(tis)

Bronco North American-Rockwell OV-10 counterinsurgency aircraft

Brontes family of English writers including the sisters Charlotte, Emily, and Anne

Bronx HTF Bronx Homicide Task Force (NYPD)

Bronx Zoo New York Zoological Gardens (Bronx Park)

bronze 92% copper, 6% tin, 2% zinc

Bronze Age era of mankind when implements and weapons were forged from bronze; period marked by wars and widespread violence

Bronzino Agnolo di Cosimo

Brook Farm utopian community dedicated to combine plain living with high thinking; founded by leading American transcendentalists in 1841 but disbanded by 1847 because it proved impractical; near West Roxbury, now within Boston, Massachusetts; nickname of similar socialistic ventures

Brook Farmers Albert Brisbane, Orestes Brownson, Charles A Dana, John S Dwight, Ralph Waldo Emerson, Margaret Fuller, Horace Greeley, Na-

thaniel Hawthorn, Isaac Hecker, George Ripley (Unitarian minister who founded Brook Farm in West Roxbury, Massachusetts near Boston), Henry David Thoreau, and others who lived in or visited the experimental farm based on cooperative living; it was active from 1841 to 1847 and rapidly declined when its central building burned down in 1846

Brookings Brookings Institution

Brooklyn HTF Brooklyn Homicide Task Force (NYPD)

Brookolino (Italian—Brooklyn)

Brookwood Girls Brookwood Center for (delinquent) Girls at Claverack, New York

Bros brothers

brosch broschiert (German—stitched)

Brose Ambrose

brot brought

brotel brothel + hotel

Brother John nickname for John Bull—long the personification of the British Empire as well as of Great Britain and its people

Brother Jonathan British nickname for the United States and its citizens

Brothers Goncourt Edmund and Jules de Goncourt—literary collaborators

BROU Banco de la República Oriental del Uruguay (Bank of the Oriental Republic of Uruguay)

Brown Bomber Joe Lewis

brown coal lignite

browners brown nosers

brown lung byssinosis or cotton-dust disease

Brown Shirts Hitler's brown-shirted followers and storm-trooper bullies

brownulated granulated brown sugar

Brown U Pr Brown University Press

Brownwood Girls State Home, Reception Center, and School for Delinquent Girls at Brownwood, Texas

brp bathroom privileges

BRP Breeder Reactor Program

BRPF Bertrand Russell Peace Foundation

brph bronchophony

brPk brownish pink

BRPL Baton Rouge Public Library

brpp basic radio propagation prediction(s)

Br Rys British Railways

brs brass

brs (BRS) break request signal

Brs Bristol

Br S Bedroom Steward

BRS Bertrand Russell Society; Bibliographic Retrieval Services (data base); Bomber Recorder System; British Road Services; British Roentgen Society; Brotherhood of Railway Signalmen; Bureau of Railroad Safety; Business Radio Service; Buyers' Research Syndicate

BRSA British Railway Staff Association

BR & SC Brotherhood of Railway and Steamship Clerks

BRSCC British Racing and Sports Car Club

br snds breath sounds

br sounds breath sounds

brst burst

Br std British standard

brstr burster

brt bright

brt (BRT) *bruttoregisterton* (Dano-Norwegian—registered gross tonnage)

Brt Brest

BRT Brotherhood of Railroad Trainmen

B.R.T. Before Recorded Time

BRT Belgische Radio en Televisie (Belgian Radio and Television); *Brutto-Register-Tonnen* (German—registered gross tons)

BRTA British Regional Television Association; British Road Tar Association

BRTC British Rail Travel Centre

BR & TC Bermuda Radio and Television Company

brt fwd brought forward

brtg bartering

Bru Bruce; Brunei; Bruno; Brutus

BRU Brussels, Belgium (National Airport)

BRU Bibliotheek der Rijksuniversiteit te Utrecht (Dutch—Library of the Royal University in Utrecht)

Bruce Graeme pseudonym of Graham Montague Jeffries

Bruckner's 10 Bruckner's ten symphonies comprising *Die Nullte* (The Zero) and 1 through 9 including *Romantische* (Romantic, No. 4)

B.Ru.Eng. Bachelor of Rural En-

gineering
BRUFMA British Rigid Urethane Foam Manufacturers Association
Bruges (French—Brugge)
Brugge West Flanders's provincial capital in Belgium
Brugge (Flemish—Bruges)
Brum Brummagen (Birmingham, England's nickname)
Brum Brumaire (French—Foggy Month)—beginning October 22—second month of the French Revolutionary Calendar
Brummagen Birmingham (colloquial)
Brun Brunei
brunch(eon) breakfast-lunch (eon)
Brundisium (Latin—Brindisi)
Brünn (German—Brno)—chief city of Moravia in Czechoslovakia
Brunna (Latin—Brno)—Czechoslovakian place called Brünn by the Germans
Bruno Walter Bruno Walter Schlesinger
Bruns Brunswick
Brunsviga (Latin—Brunswick)
Brunsw Brunswick
Brun U Brunel University
B.Rur.Sci. Bachelor of Rural Science
Brus Bruselas (Spanish—Brussels); *Bruselle* (Italian—Brussels); *Brussel* (Dutch or Flemish); *Brüssel* (German—Brussels)
Bruselas (Spanish—Brussels)
Brussel (Dutch or Flemish—Brussels)
Brüssel (German—Brussels)
brussels brussels carpet (woven with a raised pattern by a method first used in Brussels); brussels griffon (toy dog first bred in Brussels); brussels lace (high-quality floral-pattern lace); brussels sprouts (small cabbage-like vegetable)
Brussels English place-name equivalent of Belgium's capital—Brussel in Dutch or Flemish, Brüssel in German, Bruxelles in French
Brussels system universal decimal classification
brut (French—unadulterated) almost completely tart champagne or wine
BRUTE British Universal Trolley Equipment
brux bruxism; bruxitic
Brux Brussels

Brux Bruxelas (Portuguese—Brussels); *Bruxelles* (French—Brussels)
Bruxellae (Latin—Brussels)
Bruxelles Brabant's provincial capital in Belgium
Bruxelles (French—Brussels)
brv (BRV) ballistic reentry vehicle
BRVMA (BVA) British Radio Valve Manufacturers' Association
Brw Barrow
BRW British Relay Wireless
Brx Bronx
bry bryology
Bry Barry; Bryant
Bryce Bryce Canyon National Park in Utah; Mount Bryce in British Columbia
bryol bryology
Bryth Brythonic
brz bronze
brzg brazing
bs beam splitter; blood sugar; bluestone; bomb service; bonded single-silk (insulation); both sides; bowel sound; breath sound; bullshit
bs (BS) backspace (data-processing character); binary subtract(ion)
b's boomerangs
b/s (B/S) bill of sale
b & s beams and stringers; bell and spigot; boosters and sustainers, brandy and soda
Bs bolivares (Venezuelan currency); bolivianos (Bolivian currency)
BS Battle Squadron; Battle Star; Bethlehem Steel, Berlin Sector, Birmingham Southern (railroad); British Standard; Bureau of Ships; Bureau of Standards
B S Bedford-Stuyvesant
B.S. Bachelor of Science
B & S Bank and Savill (steamship line); Brown and Sharpe; Butterfield and Swire
BS Bayerische Staatsbibliothek (German—Bavarian State Library)—München's treasure despite the ravages of war
bsa bismuth-sulphite agar; body surface area; bovine serum albumin; brown strain apparent
BSA Bank Stationers Association; Bibliographical Society of America; Birmingham Small Arms; Blind Service Association; Blinded Soldiers Association (Australia); Botanical Society of America; Boy Scouts of America; Boy Scouts

Association; British School of Athens; British South Africa; Brotherhood of St Andrew; Bruckner Society of America; Bureau of Supplies and Accounts
B.S.A. Bachelor of Agricultural Science
BSAA British South American Airways
BSA(A) British School of Archeology (Athens)
B.S.A.A. Bachelor of Science in Applied Arts
BSAC British South Africa Company; Brotherhood of Shoe and Allied Craftsmen
B.S.Adv. Bachelor of Science in Advertising
B.S.A.E. Bachelor of Science in Aeronautical Engineering; Bachelor of Science in Architectural Engineering
BSAF British Sulphate of Ammonia Federation
BSAG Bristol Social Adjustment Guides
B.S.Agr. Bachelor of Science in Agriculture
BSAM Basic Sequential Access Method
B.S.A.M. Bachelor of Suddha Ayurvedic Medicine
BSAOT Bell System American Orchestras on Tour
BSAP British South Africa Police
B.S.Arch. Bachelor of Science in Architecture
B.S.Arch. Eng. Bachelor of Science in Architectural Engineering
B.S.Art Ed. Bachelor of Science in Art Education
Bs As Buenos Aires
BSAS British Ship Adoption Society
BSAVA British Small Animals Veterinary Association
bsb body surface burned
bsb (BSB) backspace block
Bsb Brisbane
BSB Brasilia, Brazil (airport); Brotherhood of St. Barnabas
BSBA British Starter Battery Association
B.S.B.A. Bachelor of Science in Business Administration
BSBC British Social Biology Council
bsbg burst and synchronous bit generator
BSBI Botanical Society of the British Isles
BSBSPA British Sugar Beet Seed Producers' Association

B.S.Bus. Bachelor of Science in Business

bsc basic; basic-message switching center; binary synchronous communication

Bsc British standard channel (steel)

B.Sc. Bachelor of Science

BSC Bank Street College; Beltsville Space Center; Bemidji State College; Bethlehem Steel Corporation; Bibliographical Society of Canada; Biological Stain Commission; Biomedical Sciences Corporation; Bloomsburg State College; Bluefield State College; Booth Steamship Company; British Society of Cinematographers; British Steel Corporation; British Supply Council

B.S.C. Bachelor of Science in Commerce

BSCA Bureau of Security and Consular Affairs (US Department of State)

B.Sc.Acc. Bachelor of Science in Accounting

B.Sc.Ag. & A.H. Bachelor of Science in Agriculture and Animal Husbandry

B.Sc.Agr.Bio. Bachelor of Science in Agricultural Biology

B.Sc.Agr.Eco. Bachelor of Science in Agricultural Economics

B.Sc.Agr.Eng. Bachelor of Science in Agricultural Engineering

B.Sc.Ag(ri)(c). Bachelor of Science in Agriculture

B.Sc.Arch. Bachelor of Science in Architecture

B.Sc.B.A. Bachelor of Science in Business Administration

BSCC British Society for Clinical Cytology

B.Sc.C.E. Bachelor of Science in Civil Engineering

B.Sc.Chem.E. Bachelor of Science in Chemical Engineering

B.Sc.Dent. Bachelor of Science in Dentistry

B.Sc.Dom.Sc. Bachelor of Science in Domestic Science

BSCE Bank Street College of Education

B.S.C.E. Bachelor of Science in Civil Engineering

B.S.Ch. Bachelor of Science in Chemistry

B.S.Chm. Bachelor of Science in Chemistry

B-school(s) business school(s)

bscn bit scan

B.Sc.Nurs. Bachelor of Science

in Nursing

BSCO British Security Coordination Office

B.S.Comm. Bachelor of Science in Commerce

BSCorp British Steel Corporation

BSCP Brotherhood of Sleeping Car Porters; Business Service Centers Program

BSCP *British Standard Code of Practice*

BSCRA British Steel Castings Research Association

BSCS Biological Sciences Curriculum Study

B.Sc.S.S. Bachelor of Science in Secretarial Studies

BSCU Blue Star (Line) Container Unit

B.Sc.Vet.Sc. Bachelor of Science in Veterinary Science

bsd beam-steering device; bit storage density; blast-suppression device; burst-slug detection

BSD Ballistic Systems Division (USAF); Bank of San Diego; British Space Development

B.S.D. Bachelor of Science in Design

BSDA British Spinners and Doublers Association

BSD Bancorp Bank of San Diego Bank Corporation

bsdc binary symmetric dependent channel

BSDC British Space Development Company; British Standard Data Code

B.S.Dent. Bachelor of Science in Dentistry

bsdg *breveté sans garantie du gouvernement* (French—patented without government guarantee)

B.S.D.H. Bachelor of Science in Dental Hygiene

bsdl boresight datum line

bse base support equipment; breast self-examination (cancer control)

BSE Base Support Equipment; Birmingham & Southeastern (railroad); Broadcast Satellite Experiment; Broadcasting Satellite for Experimental Purposes; Building Service Employees (Union); Bureau of Steam Engineering

B.S.E. Bachelor of Sanitary Engineering; Bachelor of Science Education; Bachelor of Science Engineering

B & SE Birmingham & Southeastern (railroad)

B.S.Ec. Bachelor of Science in Economics

B.S.Ed. Bachelor of Science in Education

B.S.E.E. Bachelor of Science in Electrical Engineering

B.S.El.E. Bachelor of Science in Electronic Engineering

B.S.Eng. Bachelor of Science in Engineering

b's'er bullshiter

BSES British Schools Exploring Society

bsf back scatter factor; bulk shielding facilities

bsf (BSF) beta-s-fetoprotein

BSF Basic Skill Films; British Shipping Federation

B.S.F. Bachelor of Science in Forestry

BSFA British Sanitary Fireclay Association; British Steel Founders' Association; Brotherhood of St Francis of Assisi; Building Science Forum of Australia

bsfc brake specific fuel consumption

BSFC Baltic States Freedom Council

BSFF Buffer Stock Financing Facility

B.S.Fin. Bachelor of Science in Finance

BSFL British Shipping Federation Limited

B.S.For. Bachelor of Science in Forestry

B.S.F.S. Bachelor of Science in Foreign Service

BSFT Basalt Spent Fuel Test(ing)

BSF & W Bureau of Sport Fisheries and Wildlife

BSG British standard gage

B.S.G.E. Bachelor of Science in General Engineering; Bachelor of Science in Geological Engineering

B.S.Gen. Nur. Bachelor of Science in General Nursing

B.S.Geog. Bachelor of Science in Geography

B.S.Geol. Bachelor of Science in Geology

B.S.Geol.Eng. Bachelor of Science in Geological Engineering

B & S glands Bartholin and Skene's glands

bsh bushel

BSH British Society of Hypnotherapists; British Standard of Hardness

B.S.H.A. Bachelor of Science in Hospital Administration

B.S.H.E. Bachelor of Science in Home Economics

B.S.H.Eco. Bachelor of Science in Home Economics

B.S.H.Ed. Bachelor of Science in Health Education

BSHS British Society for the History of Science

bsi basic shipping instructions; bound serum iron

BSI Baker Street Irregulars; British Sailors' Institute; British Standards Institution

BSI Business Survey Index

BSIA Better Speech Institute of America

BSIB Boy Scouts International Bureau; British Society for International Bibliography

bsic binary-symmetric independent channel

BSIC British Ski Instruction Council

B.S.I.E. Bachelor of Science in Industrial Engineering

BSIHE British Society for International Health Education

B.S.Ind.Art Bachelor of Science in Industrial Art

B.S.Ind.Chem. Bachelor of Science in Industrial Chemistry

B.S.Ind.Ed. Bachelor of Science in Industrial Education

B.S.Ind.Eng. Bachelor of Science in Industrial Engineering

BSIP British Solomon Islands Protectorate

B.S.I.R. Bachelor of Science in Industrial Relations

BSIRA British Scientific Instrument Research Association

BSIs Baker Street Irregulars

BSIS BioScience Information Services

BSIU British Society for International Understanding

bsj balanced swivel joint; ball-and-socket joint

B.S.J. Bachelor of Science in Journalism

BSJA British Show Jumping Association

B.S.Jr. Bachelor of Science in Journalism

bsk basket(s)

Bskrvlle Baskerville

bskt basket

bsl billet split lens

bs/l bills of lading

Bsl Bislig Bay

BSL Barber Steamship Lines; Behavioral Sciences Laboratory; Black Star Line; Blue Sea Line; Blue Star Line; Building Service League; Bull Steam-

ship Lines

BSLA Bus Services Licensing Authority (Singapore)

B.S.Lab.Rel. Bachelor of Science in Labor Relations

bslb ball-and-socket lower bearing

bsln ball-and-socket lower bearing

bsl(s) bushel(s)

B.S.L.S. Bachelor of Science in Library Science; Bachelor of Science in Library Service

bsm bi-stable multivibrator; bottom sonar marker

BSM Battery Sergeant Major; Birmingham School of Music; Branch Sales Manager; Bronze Star Medal

BSM beso sus manos (Spanish —I kiss your hands)—respectfully yours

BSMA British Skate Makers' Association

B.S.Mar.Eng. Bachelor of Science in Marine Engineering

BSMD Business System Marketing Division

B.S.M.E. Bachelor of Science in Mechanical Engineering; Bachelor of Science in Mining Engineering; Bachelor of Science in Music Education

B.S.Med. Bachelor of Science in Medicine

B.S.Med.Rec. Bachelor of Science in Medical Records

B.S.Med.Rec.Lib. Bachelor of Science in Medical Records Librarianship

B.S.Med.Tech. Bachelor of Science in Medical Technology

B.S.Met. Bachelor of Science in Metallurgy

B.S.Met.Eng. Bachelor of Science in Metallurgical Engineering

B.S.Mgt.Sci. Bachelor of Science in Management Science

B.S.Min Bachelor of Science in Minerology; Bachelor of Science in Mining

B.S.Min.Eng. Bachelor of Science in Mining Engineering

BSMMA British Sugar Machinery Manufacturers Association

bsmt basement

B.S.Mus.Ed. Bachelor of Science in Music Education

bsmv barley-stripe-mosaic virus

bsn bowel sounds normal

BSN Baker School of Navigation; Broadcasting System of Niigata (Japanese)

B.S.N. Bachelor of Science in Nursing

BSN Bayerische Staatsoper— Nationaltheater (German— National Theater—in Munich)

bsna bowel sounds normal and active

B.S.N.A. Bachelor of Science in Nursing Administration

B.S.Nat.Hist. Bachelor of Science in Natural History

BSNDT British Society for Non-Destructive Testing

BSNH Boston Society of Natural History; Buffalo Society of Natural History

B.S.N.I.T. Bachelor of Science in Nautical Industrial Technology

B.S.Nurs. Bachelor of Science in Nursing

B.S.Nurs.Ed. Bachelor of Science in Nursing Education

bso blue stellar objects

BSO Baltimore Symphony Orchestra; Bamberg Symphony Orchestra; Birmingham Symphony Orchestra; Bombay Symphony Orchestra; Boston Symphony Orchestra; Bournemouth Symphony Orchestra; Budapest Symphony Orchestra

BSOA British Sexual Offenses Act

B.S.Occ.Ther. Bachelor of Science in Occupational Therapy

B.Soc.Sci. Bachelor of Social Science

B.Soc.St. Bachelor of Social Studies

B.Soc.Wk. Bachelor of Social Work

BSOIW Bridge, Structural and Ornamental Iron Workers

B.S.Opt. Bachelor of Science in Optometry

B.S.O.T. Bachelor of Science in Occupational Therapy

bsp bromosulphalein

Bsp British Standard pipe

BSP Bering Sea Patrol; Border Security Police (NATO); Boy Scouts of the Philippines; British Society for Parasitology; Brotherhood of St Paul; Brunei Shell Petroleum

B-S-P Bartlett-Snow-Pacific (foundry division)

B.S.P. Bachelor of Science in Pharmacy

BSP Bureau de Sécurité Publique (French—Bureau of Public Security)

BSPA Basic Slag Producers' Association; Black Students Psychological Association

B.S.P.A. Bachelor of Science in Public Administration

B.S.P.E. Bachelor of Science in Physical Education

B-Specials Belfast's special soldiers (attached to the Ulster Special Constabulary)—Protestant organization

B.S.Per. & Pub.Rel. Bachelor of Science in Personnel and Public Relations

B.S.Pet. Bachelor of Science in Petroleum

B.S.Pet.Eng. Bachelor of Science in Petroleum Engineering

B.S.P.H. Bachelor of Science in Public Health

B.S.Phar. Bachelor of Science in Pharmacy

B.S.Pharm. Bachelor of Science in Pharmacy

B.S.P.H.N. Bachelor of Science in Public Health Nursing

B.S.Phys.Ed. Bachelor of Science in Physical Education

B.S.Phys.Edu. Bachelor of Science in Physical Education

B.S.Phys.Ther. Bachelor of Science in Physical Therapy

bspl behavioral science programming language

BSPL Blue Star Port Lines

BSPM Battlefield Systems Project Management

BSPMA British Sewage Plant Manufacturers Association

B.S.P.T. Bachelor of Science in Physical Therapy

bsp test bromsulphalein test

B.Sp.Thy. Bachelor of Speech Therapy

bspw bare silver-plated wire

Bsq Basque

BSQ Bachelor Sergeant Quarters

bsr backspace recorder; balloon-supported rockets (rockoons); basal skin resistance; basic service rate; battle short relay; blood sedimentation rate; blue-streak request; bore sight restricted

Bsr Basra (Busreh)

BSR British Society of Rheology

B.S.R. Bachelor of Science in Rehabilitation

BSRA British Ship Research Association

BSRC Battelle Seattle Research Center; Biological Serial Record Center

BSRD Behavioral Sciences Research Division

B.S.Rec. Bachelor of Science in Recreation

B.S.Ret. Bachelor of Science in Retailing

bsrf brain stem reticular formation

BSRI Bem Sex Role Inventory

BSRIA Building Services Research and Information Association

BSRL Boeing Scientific Research Laboratories

B.S.R.T. Bachelor of Science in Radiological Technology

bss balanced salt solution; basic shaft system; beam-steering system; black-silk suture; buffered saline solution

BSS Bibliothèque Saint-Sulpice (Montreal); Biological and Social Sciences (NSF); British Sailors Society; British Standard Specification; Bronze Service Star; Bureau of School Systems; Bureau of State Services

B.S.S. Bachelor of Sanitary Science; Bachelor of Science in Science; Bachelor of Secretarial Science; Bachelor of Social Science(s)

Bssa Baronessa (Italian—Baroness)

B.S.S.A. Bachelor of Science in Secretarial Administration

B.S.Sc. Bachelor of Sanitary Science

B.S.Sc.Eng. Bachelor of Science in Science Engineering

B.S.Sec.Ed. Bachelor of Science in Secondary Education

B.S.Sec.Sci. Bachelor of Science in Secretarial Science

BSSG Biomedical Sciences Support Grant

BSSM Blue Star Ship Management

BSSML Blue Star Ship Management Limited

BSSO British Society for the Study of Orthodontics

B.S.Soc.Serv. Bachelor of Science in Social Service

B.S.Soc.St. Bachelor of Science in Social Studies

B.S.Soc.Wk. Bachelor of Science in Social Work

bssp broadband solid-state pre-amplifier

BSSP Battelle Seminars and Studies Program

BSSR Bureau of Social Science Research; Byelorussia Soviet Socialist Republic

BSSS British Society of Soil Science

B.S.S.S. Bachelor of Science in Secretarial Studies; Bachelor of Science in Social Science

B.S.S.Sc. Bachelor of Science in Social Science

B.S.Struc.Eng. Bachelor of Science in Structural Engineering

bssw bare stainless-steel wire

bst beam-steering transducer; blood serological test(ing); brief stimulus therapy

b s & t blood, sweat, and tears

b/st bill of sight

BST Bering Standard Time; Blood Serological Test; British Summer Time

BSTA British Surgical Trades Association

BSTC Ball State Teachers College

bstd bastard

B.S.Text. Bachelor of Science in Textiles

bst lt blue stern light

bstm biaxial shock-test machine

bstr booster

B.S.Trans. Bachelor of Science in Transportation

bstrk bomb service truck

bstr rkt booster rocket

BSU Black Students Union; Boat Support Unit; British Standard Unit(s)

bsub ball-and-socket upper bearing

B.Sur. Bachelor of Surgery

B.Surv. Bachelor of Surveying

bsut beam-steering ultrasonic transducer

bsv Boolean simple variable

BSV Batten-Spielmyer-Vogt (syndrome)

B.S.Voc.Ag. Bachelor of Science in Vocational Education

bsw barrels of salt water

bs & w basic sediment and water

BSW Boot and Shoe Workers (union); Botanical Society of Washington; British Standard Whitworth

B.S.W. Bachelor of Social Work

BSWB Boy Scouts World Bureau

bswd barrels of salt water per day

BSWE Boy Scouts in Western Europe

BSWG British Standard Wire Gage

BSWIA British Steel Wire Industries Association

bt baby talk; *Bacillus thuringiensis* (biological pesticide); bathtub; bathythermograph; bedtime; bent; bitemporal; blue tetrazolium (stain); boat; boattail; body temperature; bombing table; bought; brain tumor; broader term; brought; bulk transport

bt (BT) basic typing

b & t bacon and tomato sandwich; (cabin or room with) bath and toilet

b of t balance of trade

Bt baronet

Bt Bukit (Indonesian or Malay —Height, Hill)

B-t Bacillus thuringiensis (biological pesticide fatal to gypsy moth caterpillars)

BT basic trainer; Burgtheater (Vienna)

B & T Baker & Taylor

B of T Bank of Tokyo; Board of Trade

BT Berlingske Tidende (Berling's Times—Copenhagen); *Brevet Technique* (French—Technical Diploma)

BT-13 Vultee two-place basic-trainer aircraft used during World War II

bta better than average

bta (BTA) best time available (for tv broadcast)

BTA Blood Transfusion Association; Board of Tax Appeals; Boston Transportation Authority; Brazilian Travel Agency; Brith Trumpeldor of America; British Tourist Authority; British Travel Association

BTAM Basic Telecommunications Access Method; Basic Terminal Access Method

BTANZ British Trade Association of New Zealand

BTAO Bureau of Technical Assistance Operations (UN)

BTAP Bond Trade Analysis Program

BTASA Book Trade Association of South Africa

btb braided tube bundle; bus tie breaker

BTB Barbados Tourist Board; Belgian Tourist Bureau

BTBA Blood Transfusion Betterment Association

BTBL Braille and Talking Book Library

BTBS Book Trade Benevolent Society

btc below threshold change; be-

ryllium thrust chamber

BTC Bankers Trust Company; Basic Training Center; Bethlehem Transportation Company; Board of Transport Commissioners; British Textile Confederation; Building Trades Council

B.T.C. Bachelor of Textile Chemistry

btca biblioteca (Spanish—library)

BTCC Bloom Township Community College; Board of Transportation Commissioners for Canada; Broome Technical Community College

B.T.C.P. Bachelor of Town and Country Planning

BTCV British Trust for Conservation Volunteers

btd bomb testing device

BTDB Bermuda Trade Development Board

btdc before top dead center

btdl basic-transient diode logic

bte battery terminal equipment; blunt trailing edge; Boltzmann transport equation; bourdon tube element; Brayton turbo-electric engine; bulk tape eraser

bte breveté (French—patent)

BTE Board of Teacher Education; Board of Transport Economics

B.T.E. Bachelor of Textile Engineering

BTEA British Textile Employers Association

B.Tech. Bachelor in Technology

Btee Brayton turboelectric engine

BTEF Book Trade Employers' Federation

B.Tel.E. Bachelor in Telecommunications Engineering

BTEMA British Tanning Extract Manufacturers' Association

BTES Beginning-Teacher Evaluation Study

B.Text. Bachelor of Textiles

btf balance to follow; barrels of total fluid; bomb tail fuse

b/tf balance transferred

BTF British Trawlers Federation

btg ball-tooth gear; battery timing group; beacon trigger generator; burst transmission group

BTG Building Trades Group

btgj ball-tooth gear joint

bth bath; bathroom; berth;

beyond the horizon

B.Th. Bachelor of Theology

BT-H British Thompson-Houston

BTHS Brooklyn Technical High School

B th u British thermal unit (btu, Btu, BTU)

bti bank-and-turn indicator; bridgetape isolator

bti (BTI) bacillus thuringiensis israelensis (developed for mosquito abatement)

Bti Bacillus thuringiensis israelensis (mosquito-control substance)

BTI Bandung Technical Institute

BTI British Technology Index

BTIA British Tar Industries Association

BTIPR Boyce Thompson Institute for Plant Research

btj ball-tooth joint

BTJ Board of Trade Journals

btk buttock

btk l buttock line

btl beginning tape label; behind the lens (camera); bottle

BTL Bell Telephone Laboratories

BTLS Bell Telephone Laboratories System

btlv biological threshold limit value

btm bottom

btm (BTM) bromotrifluoro methane (fire extinguisher)

Btm Bottom (postal abbreviation)

BTMA British Typewriter Manufacturers Association

BTME Babcock Test of Mental Efficiency

btn button

Btn Batangas

BTN Brussels Tariff Nomenclature

bto big-time operator; bombing through overcast

bto bruto (Spanish—gross weight); *brutto* (Dano-Norwegian—bulk or gross weight); *bulto* (Spanish—bulk)

BTO Branch Transportation Office(r); British Trust for Ornithology

bto(s) big time operator(s)

BTOW Boiler Technician of the Watch (USN)

B-town Bean Town (Boston—sailor's sobriquet)

btp body temperature and pressure

BTP Bailment Test Program; British Transport Police; Bush

Terminal Piers

B.T.P. Bachelor of Town Planning

btps body temperature and pressure—saturated

btr bus transfer

BTR Baton Rouge, Louisiana (airport); Bureau of Trade Regulation

BTR *British Tax Review*

BTR-40 Soviet armored personnel carrier and scout car for 10 troops including the driver

BTR-50 Soviet amphibious personnel carrier for 15 troops including the driver

BTR-60P Soviet amphibious armored personnel carrier including 12.7mm machinegun

B.T.R.A. Bachelor of Town and Regional Planning

B. Traven nom de plume of Berick Traven Torscan Croves

BTRM Soviet armored-infantry combat vehicle armed with 76.2 gun and antitank missile

btrmlk buttermilk

btry battery

bts back to school; base of terminal service (USAF); Boolean time sequence

BTS Blood Transfusion Service; British Tanzania Society; British Textile Society

BTSA British Tensional Strapping Association

BTSB Bound-to-Stay-Bound Books

BTSC British Transport Staff College

BTSS Basic Time-Sharing System

bttns battens

btu (BTU, Btu) British thermal unit

BTU Board of Trade Unit

btv basic transportation vehicle

btw between

BTWHS Booker T. Washington High School

btwn between

btx benzene, toluene, xylene

BTX *Bildschirmtext* (German— viewdata interactive videotext system)

bty battery

B-type Basedow type

bu base (of prism) up; base unit; base up; biological urge; brick unprotected; bromouracil; builder; burglary; bushel

Bu Bulgaria; Bulgarian; Bureau (United States Navy); butyl

Bü *Büyük* (Turkish—big)

BU Baker University; Baylor University; Bishop's Universi-

ty; Board of Underwriters; Boston University; Bradley University; Brandeis University; Brown University; Brunel University; Bucknell University; Burma (symbol); Butler University

B & U Beechey and Underwood

BU *Bollettino Ufficiale* (Italian —Official Gazette)

BUA Belfast Urban Area; British United Airways

BuAer Bureau of Aeronautics (USN)

BUAF British United Air Ferries

BUAV British Union for the Abolition of Vivisection

bubbly champagne

Bubs Bubbles

buc buccal; buccaneer; buccinator

BUC Bangor University College

bucc buccal

Buccaneer Hawker-Sidddeley jet aircraft for military applications

BUCCS Bath University Comparative Catalogue Study

Buchar Bucharest

Bucharest English name for Bucuresti (Romania's capital)

buck buckram

Buckeye North American-Rockwell trainer aircraft designated T-2

Buckeye(s) Ohioan(s)

Buckeye State Ohio's official nickname

Buck House Buckingham House (Buckingham Palace—London residence of British royalty)

Buckie R(ichard) Buckminster Fuller

Buck Island Buck Island Reef National Park off the north shore of St Croix in the American Virgin Islands

Bucknell U Pr Bucknell University Press

Buck Pal Buckingham Palace

Bucks Buckinghamshire

Bucks Co Hist Bucks County Historical Society

BUCOP *British Union Catalogue of Periodicals*

bucu burring cutter

Bucuresti (Romanian—Bucharest)

bud. budget

Bud Buddha; Buddhism; Buddhist; Buddy; Budweiser

BUD Budapest, Hungary (air-

port)

Buda Budapest

Buddha's Buddha's Birthday (April 8)

Bud(dy) Brother

Buddy Rogers Charles Rogers

Budejovice (Czech—Budweis)— home of fine beer and quality pencils

BUDFIN Budget and Finance Division (NATO)

budgie(s) budgerigar(s)

BuDocks Bureau of Yards and Docks (USN)

Budpst Budapest

budr bromodeoxyuridine

Budweis (German—Budejovice)

bue built-up edge

BUE Buenos Aires, Argentina (Ezeiza airport)

Buen Buenaventura

Buerger's disease chronic inflammation of the blood vessels in a limb or limbs

BUET Bangladesh University of Engineering and Technology

buf buffer(ed)

Buf Buffalo (city and port)

BUF British Union of Fascists; Buffalo, New York (airport)

BUFF Big Ugly Fat Fellow (Air Force nickname for the eight-engine B-52 bomber)

Buffalo De Haviland military transport aircraft

Buffalo Acad Buffalo Fine Arts Academy

Buffalo Bill Colonel William F Cody

Buffalonians people of Buffalo, New York

bufg buffing

bufno buffers, number of

Bug Bugatti; standard-model Volkswagen (also called the Beetle)

BUG Brooklyn Union Gas (company)

Bugd Nyramdakh Mongol Ard Uls (Mongolian People's Republic)—Outer Mongolia

Bughouse Square square where cafeteria theoreticians and street people congregate to argue and to loaf—Pershing Square in Los Angeles, Union Square in New York, Washington Square in Chicago

Bugs Baer Arthur Baer

BUH Bucharest, Rumania (airport)

Buhl's disease fatty degeneration associated with hemoglobinuria

BUIA British United Island Air-

ways
buic (BUIC) backup interceptor control
BUIC Bureau (of Naval Personnel) Unit Identification Code (USN)
build. building
Built on Oil, Soil, and Toil Ponca City, Oklahoma
buisys barrier-up indicating system
Buitenzorg (Dutch—Bogor)—famed for its botanic gardens on the Indonesian island of Java
Buk Bukit (Malay—Hill, Hilly Street)
Bukavu Costermansville's present name
Bukh Bukhta (Russian—Bay)
bul below upper limit; bulletin
Bul Bulgaria(n)
BUL Bombay University Library
BUL Bibliothèque de l'Université Laval (French—Laval University Library)—Québec
Bulg Bulgaria; Bulgarian
Bulgaria (People's Republic of Bulgaria) (behind-the-Iron-Curtain Balkan nation whose Bulgarians speak Bulgarian plus some Greek and Turkish, exports to other Comecon countries) *Narodna Republika Bulgaria*
Bulgarian Ports (north to south) Michurin, Akhtopol, Bukhta Tsiganski, Burgas, Varna, Evksinograd, Kavarna
Bulgarian Quadrilateral fortress towns of Rustchuk, Schumla, Silistria, and Varna
Bulgaria's Largest Seaport Varna (formerly called Stalin)
Bulgarien (German—Bulgaria)
Bulge The Bulge of Brazil consisting of South America's easternmost coast between João Pessoa and Recife
bull. bulla (Latin—leaden seal, nickname for a papal pronouncement bearing such a seal)
Bull bulletin
BULL Bank Users Legislative Lookout
Bull Acad Sci Bulletin of the Academy of Sciences
Bull Am Astron Soc Bulletin of the American Astronomical Society
Bull Am Phys Soc Bulletin of the American Physical Society
Bull Astron Inst Neth Bulletin of the Astronomical Institutes of

the Netherlands
Bull Chem Soc Jp Bulletin of the Chemical Society of Japan
Bulldog Scottish Aviation single-engine two-place trainer
bullet(s) bullet train(s)
bulli. bulliat (Latin—let it boil)
Bullion State Missouri (long in favor of gold- and silver-backed currency)
bull market stock market short form indicating an upward trend in securities as if a bull were charging forward with uplifted horns; (*see* bear market)
Bull Moose Theodore Roosevelt—twenty-sixth President of the United States
Bull NYZS Bulletin of the New York Zoological Society
Bullpup Maxson air-to-surface missile
Bullring of Basra white-slave market close to Iraq's Persian Gulf coast
Bull Run Manassas (called First or Second Bull Run by Union troops who fought there in July 1861 or August 1862, respectively, and First Manassas or Second Manassas by Confederate soldiers, Northerners named battles after the Bull Run creek, Southerners after Manassas Courthouse near the creek)
bull(s) bulletin(s)
Bull Seismol Soc Am Bulletin of the Seismological Society of America
bullsh Australian contraction of bullshit
Bullwood Hall borstal in Essex, England
buloga business logistics game
BULVA Belfast and Ulster Licensed Vintner's Association
BuMed Bureau of Medicine and Surgery
bump-and-run bump-and-run mugger-team technique (wherein two muggers run alongside the intended victim and as one knocks the victim to the sidewalk the other snatches the victim's handbag or purse and then the muggers run away in opposite directions)
Bu M & S Bureau of Medicine and Surgery (USN)
B.U.M.S. Bachelor of Urani Medicine and Surgery
Bun Bunbury, Western Australia

BUN blood urea nitrogen
buna butadiene + natrium (synthetic rubber)
BUNAC British Universities North America Club
Bund German-American Volksbund (pre-World War II alliance of Hitler's supporters in the U.S. now supplanted by the American Nazi Party); secret cells of Jewish Social Democrats in Russian Lithuania and Poland in 1897 who organized the General Union of Jewish Workers known as the Bund
Bundesrepublik Deutschland (German—Federal Republic of Germany—West Germany)
Bung Karno (Malay—Brother Karno)—nickname for Indonesian dictator Sukarno
bunsen bunsen burner (named for the German chemist Robert Wilhelm Bunsen)
bunsenite nickel oxide
Buntline Ned Buntline—nom de plume of Edward ZC Judson
Bunty Barbara
bunwich bun + sandwich (sandwich made in a bun)
BuOrd Bureau of Ordnance (USN)
bup backup plate; bull pup
BUP Boston University Press; British United Press
BUPA British United Provident Association
bup-bup-bup-bum Beethovenian kettledrumming
Bupers Bureau of Personnel (USN)
BuPers Bureau of Personnel (USN)
bupp backup plate perforated
BuPubAff Bureau of Public Affairs
bur built-up roof(ing); bureau
Bur Burma; Burmese
BUR Burbank, California (Lockheed Airport)
Buranello Baldassare Galuppi
BURCEN Bureau of the Census
burd biplane ultralight research device
Burdeos (Spanish—Bordeaux)
Burd suc Burdick suction
BuRec Bureau of Reclamation
Bur Eco Aff Bureau of Economic Affairs (US Department of State)
Bur Eur Aff Bureau of European Affairs (US Department of State)

Bur Fu'ad (Egyptian Arabic—Port Fuad)

burg burgess; burgomaster

Burg Burgess; Burgo; Burgos; Burgwald

burger(s) hamburger(s)

Burgi (Latin—Burgos)—Spanish place also called Bravum Burgi

Burgis Street Singapore's street of sin

burgle(d) burglarize(d)

burgrep burglary report

Bur Intl Aff Bureau of International Affairs

Burk Burke; Burkhardt

Burke's Burke's Peerage

Burkina Faso (More—Ancestral Home of the Dignified)—new and official name since mid-1984 of Upper Volta on the southern edge of the Sahara

burl. burlesque

Burl Burleigh; Burley; Burlingame

Burlington Route Chicago, Burlington and Quincy (railroad)

Burl Ives Icle Ivanhoe Ives

Burl N Burlington Northern and St Louis San Francisco (railway merger)

Burm Burmese (oriental tongue of more than 22 million people living in Burma)

Burma Socialist Republic of the Union of Burma (Burmese-speaking Burmans inhabit this mountainous Asian country between India and Malaysia, precious minerals, oil, rubber, and teak are exported)

Burma's Principal Port Rangoon

burmese burmese cat (orange-eye cat originating in Burma); burmese lacquer (grayish varnish); burmese ruby (peony)

Burmese Ports (north to south) Sittwe, Kyaukpyu, Bassein, Rangoon, Moulmein

Burn Burnell; Burnett; Burney

Burnaby Lower Mainland Regional Correctional Centre in British Columbia's Burnaby

buro bureau

burocrap bureaucratic crap (excess personnel, special studies, unnecessary forms, etc.)

burp. backup rate of pitch

Bur Pub Aff Bureau of Public Affairs (US Department of State)

Burs Bursar

Bur Sa'id (Egyptian Arabic—Port Said)

Bursting Bursting Day (Febru-

ary 18 when the sea ice bursts apart and crumbles in Iceland's icy waters)

Burt L Standish pseudonym of Gilbert Patten—creator of the American boy hero—Frank Merriwell

Burun Burundi; Burundian

Burundi Republic of Burundi (Central African land once controlled by Germany and later by Belgium, French and many tribal tongues used by Burundians who export precious minerals)

bus. business; omnibus

Bus autobus; Busan; business

BuSanda Bureau of Supplies and Accounts (USN)

BUSARB British-United States Amateur Rocket Bureau

busbar omnibus bar

buscrit business critic(ism)

BUSF British Universities' Sports Federation

BuS glands Bartholin's, urethral, Skene's glands

bush. bushing(s)

BuShips Bureau of Ships (USN)

bus hrs business hours

busk(s) busker(s)

BUSM Boston University School of Medicine

Bus Mgr Business Manager

Busn Intl Business International

Busta Sir Alexander Bustamante

bust(ed) arrest(ed)—slang

Bustees Calcutta's celebrated slum (filled with depravity, filth, and misery)

Buster Keaton Joseph Francis Keaton

Bus W Business Week

buswrec ban unsafe schoolbuses which regularly endanger children

but. butter; button

but. butyrum (Latin—butter)

BUT British United Traction

Butch Fiorello H La Guardia

Butcher of Budapest Soviet Prime Minister Nikita Krushchev so named because of his brutal suppression of the Hungarian freedom fighters

Butcher of the Caribbean Rafael Trujillo

Butcher of Prague Reinhard Heydrich—Hitler's Reichsprotektor of Bohemia

bute butazolidin (phenylbutazone)

Buten Mus Buten Museum of

Wedgewood

Butter Capital Owatonna, Minnesota

Butterfly Chopin's Piano Etude No. 9 in G flat; Puccini's opera *Madame Butterfly*—a Japanese tragedy in two acts

Butterick Butterick Publishing

Bu-Tyur Butyrskaya Tyurma (Russian—Butyrki Prison)—one of Moscow's major prisons

buv backscatter ultraviolet

buvs backscatter ultraviolet spectrometer

BUW Biblioteka Uniwersytecka w Warszawie (Polish—Warsaw University Library)

BuWeps Bureau of Weapons (USN)

buy. buyer; buying

buz buzzer

Buzzard State Georgia

bv balanced voltage; bellows valve; biologic(al) value; blow valve; blood vessel; blood volume; bonnet valve; breviary; bronchovesicular

bv (BV) breakdown voltage

b/v brick veneer

bv bijvoorbeeld (Dutch—for example)

b.v. balneum vaporis (Latin—steambath, vapor bath)

Bv Benvenuto

B/v book value

BV Bureau Veritas (French ship-classification bureau)

B + V Blohm und Voss (shipbuilders)

BV Bayerische Vereinsbank (German—Bavarian Union Bank); Besloten Vennootschap (Dutch—closed corporation, private partnership)

BV. Beata Virgo (Latin—Blessed Virgin); bene vale (Latin—a good farewell); bene vixit (Latin—he lived a good life)

BV-202 Norwegian Army armored personnel carrier

BVA British Veterinary Association

B.V.A. Bachelor of Vocational Adjustment; Bachelor of Vocational Agriculture

BVAL Blackman's Volunteer Army of Liberation

bvbrf blood vessel of bronchial filament

BVC Buena Vista College

bvd beacon video digitizer

BVD Bradley, Vorhees & Day

BVD Binnenlandse Veiligheids-dienst (Dutch—Internal

Security Service)—FBI-type organization in the Netherlands

BVDs suits of underwear (derived from BVD)

BVDT Brief Vestibular Disorientation Test

Bve Buenaventura

B.V.E. Bachelor of Vocational Education

Bventura Buenaventura

B/ventura Buenaventura, Colombia

b ver back verandah

BVES British Voluntary Euthanasia Society

B.Vet.Med. Bachelor of Veterinary Medicine

B.Vet.Sci. Bachelor of Veterinary Science

B.Vet.Sur. Bachelor of Veterinary Surgery

BVG *Berliner Verkehrs-Betriebe* (German—Berlin Traffic Carrier)—Berlin's transit system

bvh biventricular hypertrophy

BVH British Van Heusen

bvi blood vessel invasion

BVI Better Vision Institute; British Virgin Islands

Bville Bougainville (Papua New Guinea)

BVJ *British Veterinary Journal*

bvm broncho-vascular markings

B.V.M. Bachelor of Veterinary Medicine

B.V.M. *Beata Virgo Maria* (Latin—Blessed Virgin Mary)

BVMA British Valve Manufacturers Association

BVMGT Bender Visual-Motor Gestalt Test

B.V.M.S. Bachelor of Veterinary Medicine and Surgery

BVN Bund der Verfolgten des Nazi Regimes (League of Persons Persecuted by the Nazi Regime)

BVNP Bolusan Volcano National Park (Luzon, Philippines)

bvo brominated vegetable oil

bvp beacon video processor; booster vacuum pump; boundary value problem

BVP British Volunteer Programme

BVPS Beacon Video Processing System; Booster Vacuum Pump System

bvr balanced valve regulator; black void reactor

BVR British Vehicle Registration (symbols appearing on automotive vehicle license plates)—*see* British Vehicle

Registration Symbols *in appendix*; Bureau of Vocational Rehabilitation

BVRO Base Vehicle Reporting Officer

BVRR Bureau of Veterans Reemployment Rights

BVRS Breadboard Visual Reference System

BVS Best Vested Socialists; Bevier & Southern (railroad)

B-V S Brisch-Vistem System (Visican punched-cards)

B.V.S. Bachelor of Veterinary Science; Bachelor of Veterinary Surgery

B.V.Sc. Bachelor of Veterinary Science

B.V.Sc. & A.H. Bachelor of Veterinary Science and Animal Husbandry

bvt brevet; brevetted

bvv bovine vaginitis virus

bvw binary voltage weigher

bw best of winners; biological warfare (BW); birth weight; body water; body weight; both ways; braided wire (armor)

b/w black-and-white

b & w black and white; bread and water

bw bijwoord (Dutch—adverb); *bitte wenden* (German—please turn over)

bW blood Wassermann

BW Bendix-Westinghouse; Biological Warfare; Black Watch; Borg-Warner; Business Week

B-W Bendix Westinghouse Automotive Air Brake; Borg-Warner

B & W Babcock and Wilcox; Barker and Williamson; Burmeister and Wain

B of W Bishop(ric) of Würzburg

BW *Bitte Wenden* (German—please turn over); *Business Week*

bwa backward-wave amplifier; bent-wire antenna

BWA Baptist World Alliance; Baseball Writers Association; British West Africa; Building Waterproofers Association

BWAL Barber West African Line

Bway Broadway

BWB British Waterways Board

BWB *Bundestampt für Wehrtechnik und Beschaffung* (German—Federal Office for Military Technology and Procurement)

bwc basic weight calculator; broadband waveguide oscilla-

tor

BWC Battered Women's Coalition; British War Cabinet

BWCC British Weed Control Conference

bwcdi best we can do is

BWCI Beauty Without Cruelty, Incorporated

bwcp bench welder control panel

bw-cw biological warfare—chemical warfare

bwd bacillary white diarrhea; backward; barrels of water per day

BWD Baldwin Wallace College; British War Cabinet

B & WE Bristol and West of England

BWF Baha'i World Faith

Bwg Bowling

BWG Birmingham Wire Gage

bwh barrels of water per hour

BWH Book Week Headquarters

BWI Baltimore Washington International (airport); British West Indies

bwia better walk if able

BWIA British West Indian Airways

BWI$ British West Indian dollar

BWIP Basalt Waste Isolation Project

BWIPO Basalt Waste Isolation Project Office

BWIR British West India Regiment

BWISA British West Indies Sugar Association

BWIU Building Workers Industrial Union

bwk brickwork; bulwark

bwl belt work line

BWL Biological War Laboratory

bwlt bow light

bwm barrels of water per minute

BWM British War Medal; Broom and Whisk Makers (union)

BWMA British Woodwork Manufacturers Association

BWMB British Wool Marketing Board

BWN Brown Company (stock-exchange symbol)

bwo backward-wave oscillator

bwoc big woman on campus

B'worth Butterworth

bwos backward-wave oscillator synchronizer

bwot backward-wave oscillator tube

bwp ballistic wind plotter

BWP Basic War Plan

bwpa backward-wave parametric amplifier

BWPA British Wood Preserving Association; British Wood Pulp Association

bwpd barrels of water per day

bwph barrels of water per hour

bwr (BWR) boiling-water reactor

BWRA British Water Research Association; British Welding Research Association

BWRC Biological Warfare Research Center

BWRWS Biological Warfare Rapid Warning System (USA)

bws beveled wood siding

BWS Bandipur Wildlife Sanctuary (India); Bank of Western Samoa; Batch Weighing System; Battlefield Weapons System; Beaufort Wind Scale; Biological Weapons System; British Watercolour Society

BW & S Boyd, Weir & Sewell

BWSF British Water Ski Federation

BWSL Battlefield Weapons Systems Laboratory

bwso backward wave sweep oscillator

BWSR Bruno Walter Society Recording(s)

bwt both-way trunk

BWT Boeing Wind Tunnel

BWTA British Women's Temperance Association

BWTP Bureau of Work-Training Programs

bw-tv black-and-white television

bwv back-water valve

BWVA British War Veterans of America

bwvs black-and-white vertical stripes

BWW Bad Weather Watch (Coast Guard)

BWWA British Water Works Association

bx biopsy; box; electrical cable contained in flexible tubing (bx cable)

Bx Beatrix; Box (post-office box); Brix; Bronx

BX Base Exchange (USAF); Bellingham-Seattle Airways (2-letter code)

bx cable insulated wires within flexible tubing

bxd boxed

bxk broadband X-band klystron

bx k box keel

BXL Bakelite Xylonite Limited

Bxm Brixham

Bx Pk Bronx Park

bxs boxes

by. billion years; brilliant yellow (litmus paper for testing alkalinity)

b-y bloody

By Buryat(ic); Byron(ic)

BY blowing spray

BYC Baltimore Yacht Club; Bayside Yacht Club; Bensonhurst Yacht Club; Beverley Yacht Club; Boston Yacht Club; Brewers Yeast Council; Bridgeport Yacht Club; Bronx Yacht Club; Buffalo Yacht Club

bydv barley yellow dwarf virus

Bye Byelorussia; Byelorussian

Byelorussia White Russia bordering on Latvia, Lithuania, and Poland

byfml by first mail

byg buying

byo bring your own

Byo Bulawayo

byob bring your own beer

byod bring your own drinks

byog bring your own girl

byp bypass

Byp Bypass

bypro(s) by-products(s)

Byron pen name of George Gordon who used the family title of Lord Byron

Byron Janis Byron Yanks

byr(s) billion year(s)

byssin byssinosis

byt bright young things (British younger set)

byte digital word with a string of eight bits of 0 and 1

Bytown original name of Ottawa, Canada

Byu Bayou (postal place-name abbreviation)

BYU Brigham Young University

Byz Byzantine

Byzantium (Latin—Istanbul)—formerly called Constantinople

bz blank when zero; buzzer; (cartoonist's symbol—buzzing, sawing, snoring)

Bz benzene; benzoyl; Brazil; Brazilian

Bz *Beobachtungszimmer* (German—examining room)—hospital observation room

BZ Air Congo (Brazzaville, Congo Republic); B'nai Zion

B/Z British Zone

BZ *Bild Zeitung* (German—Picture Newspaper)

Bza Bizerta

BZA Board of Zoning Adjustment

bz brigade (Danish—*besaet brigade*)—occupiers claiming squatter's rights on vacant property such as apartments or houses

bzbx brazing box

Bze Belize

bzfm brazing form

bzfx brazing fixture

Bzi Benghazi

bzw *beziehungsweise* (German—respectively)

bzz cartoonist's symbol—buzzing; sawing; snoring

bzzz same as bzz

C

c calorie (large); candle; canine; capacity; carbon; cathode; caudal; cent; centavo; center; centi (prefix); centime; centimeter; central; certified; cervical; cervix; charm; chest; child; chord length (symbol); cirrus; clearance; clonus; closure; coarse; cocaine; coefficient; colón; colones (currency in Costa Rica and El Salvador); color; colored; complement; conductor; contact; contraction; control; cortex; cranial; crystal(line); cube; cubic; cubical; cycle(s); cylinder(s); cytidine; cytochrome; cytosine; heat capacity per mole (symbol); see; speed of light (symbol)

c (C) convict

c. cibus (Latin—meal); circa (Latin—about); congius (Latin gallon); cum (Latin with)

c/ cargo (Spanish—total, weight); contra (Spanish—against, versus)

C calculated weight (symbol); candle; capacitance; capacitor; Cape; carat; carbon; Cardinal; cargo or transport airplane; cargo vessel; carton; case; cathode; cavalry; celestial; Celsius; Celtic; Centigrade; century; cervical; chairman; Charlie—code for letter C; Chief; Christ(ian); coast; cocaine (drug user's abbreviation); cold; college; colored; combat aircraft; commander; compliance; concentration; Conservative; consul; control; Convair; copyright; Cosmopolitan Shipping; coulomb; council; course; Curie's constant; Fraunhofer line characteristic of hydrogen (symbol); hundredweight (symbol); molecular heat (symbol); see (popular phonetic spelling)

C. carbohydrates (dietary symbol); cocaine; Conservative (political party)

"C" Costa Line

°C degree Celsius; degree centigrade

C Cabo (Spanish—cape); Cap (French—cape); centum (Latin—one hundred); Col (French or Italian—high pass, pass), (Latin—Gaius)

C^0 Comisario (Spanish—Commisariat)

C_1 first class

C^1 bacteriologic complement

C^11, C^12, C^13, etc. complements of complements

C 1, C 2, C 3, etc. cervical nerves or vertebrae 1, 2, 3, etc.

C I, C II, C III, etc. cranial nerves I, II, III, etc.

C_1, C_2, C_3, etc. cytochromes 1, 2, 3, etc.

C_2 second class

C^2D^2 (ARDC) Command and Control Development Division

C-3 mentally or physically defective (British equivalent of American 4-F)

C_3 command, control, communications; third class

C^3I Command, Control, Communications, and Intelligence

C.3.3. cell 3, 3rd landing, gallery C (occupied by Oscar Wilde while in Reading Gaol and the nom de plume he used there)

C3S College Chemistry Consultants Service

C4 Convair 440 airplane; crown quarto (7-1/2 x 10 inches)

C5 Convair 580 turboprop airplane

C-5A Lockheed military cargo transport airplane

C-6 hexamethonium

C8 crown octavo (5 x 7-1/2 inches)

$c8^{va}$ coll'ottava (Italian—in octaves)

C-9 McDonnell-Douglas twin-engine jetliner designed for medical evacuation and named Nightingale to honor nurse-philanthropist Florence Nightingale of Crimean War fame

C-10 decamethonium

$C_{12}H_{22}O_{11}$ cane sugar

C^{14} radioactive carbon (used in determining age of objects by radioactivity measurement)

$C_{17}H_{21}NO_4$ cocaine (also known as blow, coke, flake, freeze, happy dust, nose candy, lady, Peruvian, white girl)—derived from the leaves of the coca plant (Erythroxylon coca)

C 19 ster steroids containing 19 carbon atoms

C 21 ster steroids containing 21 carbon atoms

C 33 Oscar Wilde's identification number while incarcerated in Reading Gaol

C-42 Brazilian Neiva four-seat utility aircraft called Regente

C-45 Beechcraft four-passenger transport plane

C-46 Curtiss-Wright World War II Commando 36-passenger transport

C-47 Douglas DC-3 Dakota or Skytrain 21-passenger air

transport

C-54 Douglas DC-4 44-passenger transport called Skymaster

C-95 Brazilian 12-passenger transport aircraft named Bandeirante honoring frontier pioneers

C-118 Douglas DC-6 92-passenger transport also called Liftmaster

C-119 Fairchild-Hiller Flying Boxcar carrying 62 paratroopers or an equal weight of cargo

C-121 Lockheed Constellation or Super-Constellation transport carrying 63 or 99 passengers, respectively

C-123 Provider twin-engine assault transport

C-124 Globemaster heavy cargo four-engine transport airplane

C-130 Hercules medium-range cargo and troop transport airplane powered by four turboprop engines; Lockheed four-engine transport aircraft for military use

C-131 Convair 48-passenger military transport adapted from 24/440 commercial airliners

C-133 Cargomaster heavy four-engine turboprop cargo transport airplane

C-135 Boeing Stratofreighter military transport carrying 126 troops or equivalent cargo

C-140 Jet Star support-type transport aircraft powered by four turbojet engines

C-141 Starlifter large cargo transport airplane powered by four turbojet engines

C-212 Casa 15-seat aeromedical or paratrooper transport plane made in Spain and called Aviocar

ca cable; calibrated altitude; cancer; capital asset; carbonic anhydrase; carcinoma; cardiac arrest; cathode; caudal; centare; cervoaxial; chronological age; civil affairs; civil authorities; clerical aptitude; cold agglutinin; common antigen; convening authority; coronary artery; council accepted; covert action; croup associated; current assets

ca (CA) cancer; carcinoma

ca' calf; call (Scottish contraction)

c/a capital account; center angle; coated abrasive; current account

c&a (C&A) command and administration

c & a classification and audit

ca *circa* (Latin—about); *corrente alternada* (Portuguese—alternating current); *corriente alterna* (Spanish—alternating current)

cᵃ *compañia* (Spanish—company)

Ca calcium; Canada; Canadian

Ca *Compagnia* (Italian—company)

Ca' *Casa* (Venetian—house)

Cᵃ *Cabeça* (Portuguese—head, headland); *Companhia* (Portuguese—company); *Compañia* (Spanish—company)

CA Canadian Army; Capital Airlines; Central America; Certificate of Airworthiness; Charge d'Affaires; Chartered Accountant; Chemical Abstracts; Chief Accountant; Church Army; Civil Affairs; Coast Artillery; Combat Aircrew; Combat Aircrewman; Commercial Agent; Companhia de Navegação Carregadores Açoreanos (Azore Line); Compensation Act; Comptroller of the Army; Confederate Army; Construction Authority; Construction Authorization; Consular Agent; Convening Authority; Coordinating Agency; County Attorney; Court of Appeals; Cranial Academy; heavy cruiser (naval symbol)

CA (Aust) Institute of Chartered Accountants in Australia

C.A. Chartered Accountant

C & A Clemens and August Breeninkmeyer's international house of fashion

C of A College of Aeronautics; Commonwealth of Australia

CA *Centre Agricole* (French—Agricultural Center)—prison farm; *Chemical Abstracts*; *corriente alterna* (Spanish—alternating current)

caa caging amplifier assembly; circular aperture antenna; computer amplifier alarm; crime aboard aircraft

CAA Canadian Authors' Association; Canadian Automobile Association; Cantors Assembly of America; Caribbean Atlantic Airlines; Central African Airways; Chester Alan Arthur (21st President U.S.); Chief of Army Aviation; Civil Aeronautics Administration; Civil Aeronautics Authority; Clean Air Act; Collectors of American Art; College Art Association; Commercial Apiarists Association; Community Action Agencies; Community Aid Abroad; Correctional Administrators Association; Cremation Association of America; Custom Agents Association

C.A.A. Civil Aviation Authority (United Kingdom)

CAA *Clean Air Act*; *Congressional Assassination Act*

CAAA Canadian Association of Advertising Agencies; College Art Association of America; Composers, Authors, and Artists of America

CAAB California Avocado Advisory Board

CAABU Council for the Advancement of Arab-British Understanding

CAAC Civil Aviation Administration of China

CAADRP Civil Aircraft Airworthiness Data Recording Program (UK)

CAAE Canadian Association for Adult Education

CAAFS Chinese Academy of Agricultural and Forestry Sciences

CAAIS Computer-Assisted Action Information System(s)

caar compressed-air-accumulator rocket

CAAR Committee Against Academic Repression

CAARC Commonwealth Advisory Aeronautical Research Council

CAAs Community Action Agencies

CAAS Ceylon Association for the Advancement of Science; Computer-Assisted Acquisition System; Connecticut Academy of Arts and Sciences

CAASE Computer-Assisted Area Source Emissions

CAAT Campaign Against Arms Trade; Canadian Academic Aptitude Test; Colleges of Applied Arts and Technology

CA Att Civil Air Attaché

CAAV Central Association of Agricultural Valuers

cab cabal; cabbage; cabin; cabinet; cable; cabochon; cabriolet; calibration; captured air bubble; cellulose acetate butyrate;

taxicab

cab (CAB) cellulose acetate butyrate; coronary artery bypass

Cab Cabell; Cabot; NATO nickname for Soviet Lisunov transport plane designated Li-2

CAB Canadian Association of Broadcasters; Charles A(ustin) Beard; Circulation Audit Board; Citizens Advice Bureau; Civil Aeronautics Board; Civil Aeronautics Bulletin; Commonwealth Agricultural Bureau; Consumer Affairs Bureau; Contract Appeals Board (Veterans Administration)

CABA Charge Account Bankers Association

cabaf currency and bunker adjustment factor

cabal *cabbala* (Hebrew—something secret)—(*see also* CABAL)

CABAL Clifford of Chudleigh, Ashley (Lord Shaftesbury), Buckingham (George Villiers), Arlington (Henry Bennet), Lauderdale (John Maitland)—members of the cabal or secret cabinet of Charles II of England; by coincidence their initials spelled cabal

CABAS City and Borough Architects Society

CABB Captured Air-Bubble Boat (naval)

Cabbage Patch Victoria, Australia

Cabbage Town Toronto, Ontario slum

CABE California Association of Bilingual Education

CABEI Central American Bank for Economic Integration

Cabelia (Latin—Chablis)—French town also called Cabelium by the Romans

CABIC Copper and Brass Information Centre (Australia)

CABIN Campaign Against Building Industry Nationalization

CABLE Computer-Assisted Bay Area Law Enforcement (San Francisco)

cablecast broadcast by cable tv; cablecaster; cablecasting

cablecast(ing) cable television telecast(ing)

cablese cablegram language (abbreviated, telegraphic, truncated style)

cable tv community-antenna television

cablevision cable television

CABM Commonwealth of Australia Bureau of Meteorology

CABMA Canadian Association of British Manufacturers and Agencies

CABMS Chinese-oriented Anti-ballistic Missile System

cabo (Portuguese or Spanish—cape)

Cabo Cabo San Lucas, Baja California

Cabo da Boa Esperança (Portuguese—Cape of Good Hope)

Cabo da Roca (Portuguese—Cape Roca)—Europe's westernmost point

Cabo de Buena Esperanza (Spanish—Cape of Good Hope)

Cabo de Hornos (Spanish—Cape of the Ovens)—Cape Horn

Cabo de São Vicente (Portuguese—Cape Saint Vincent)

cabot cabotage (coastal navigation)

Cabo Tormentoso (Portuguese—Cape of Storms)—realistic name for the Cape of Good Hope

Ca bp Calcium-binding protein

CABRA Copper and Brass Research Association

cabs. cabbages

cab(s) cabochon(s)

CABS Children's Adaptive Behavior Scale; Computer-Augmented Block System; Computerized Annotated Bibliographic System

cabtmkr cabinetmaker

CABWA Copper and Brass Warehouse Association

cac cardiac-accelerator center

Cac Caceres

CAC California Administration Code; California Advisory Council (on Vocational Education); California Aeronautics Commission; California Arts Commission; California Arts Council; Canadian Armoured Corps; Chief of Air Corps; City Administration Center; Civic Administration Center; Civil Administration Commission; Coast Artillery Corps; College Admissions Center; Colonial Ammunition Company; Combat Air Crew; Commander Air Center; Commission of Accreditation for Corrections; Community Administration Council; Commuter Aircraft Corporation; Consumer Advisory Council; Consumer Affairs Council; Consumer Association of Canada; Continental Air Command; Corrective Action Commission; Corrective Action Committee; Cosmetology Accrediting Commission; County Administration Center

CAC *Comité de Acción Cultural* (Spanish—Cultural Action Committee)

CACA Canadian Agricultural Chemicals Association; Central After-Care Association

cacb compressed-air circuit breaker

CACB Council Against Cigarette Bootlegging

cacc cathodal closure contraction

CACC Civil Aviation Communications Center; Corrective Action Control Section

CA-CC Christian Anti-Communist Crusade

CACCE Council of American Chambers of Commerce in Europe

CACCI Confederation of Asian Chambers of Commerce and Industry

CACDA Combined Arms Combat Development Activity

CACE California Association for Childhood Education; Chicago Association of Consulting Engineers

CACEX *Carteira do Comercio Exterior* (Portuguese—Foreign Commerce Department)—Bank of Brazil

CACF Colombian-American Culture Foundation

Cach *Cachoeira* (Portuguese—rapids, waterfall)

cache. computer-controlled automated cargo-handling envelope

CACHE Computer Aids for Chemical Engineering Education

cachi *cachivache* (Spanish—broken crockery, foolish or worthless person, poor quality, pots and pans, utensils)—dialect heard around Buenos Aires where it has many Italian, Portuguese, and Yugoslavian terms mixed with Spanish; dialect also called *porteño*

CACJ California Attorneys for Criminal Justice

CACL Canadian Association of Children's Librarians

CACM Central American Common Market

Caco *Cacoliche* (pidgin Argentine-Spanish including many Italian words)

CACO Casualty Assistance Call Office(r)

CaCO₃ calcium carbonate (limestone)

cacoph cacaphonic; cacophony

Cacos (Spanish—Pickpockets, Poltroons)—nickname of a Guatemalan political party successful in the removal of Spanish authority from this Central American nation

cacp cartridge-actuated compaction press

CACS California Aqueduct Control System

CACSW Citizens' Advisory Council on the Status of Women

Cactus code name for French Mach 1.2 surface-to-air missile

CACTUS *Capteur Accelerometrique Capacitif Triaxial Ultra-Sensible* (French—Ultra-Sensitive Triaxial Capacitive Accelerometric Detector)

Cactus Blossom Capital Phoenix, Arizona

Cactus Jack Vice President John Nance Garner also called the Sage of Uvalde

Cactus State New Mexico

CACUL Canadian Association of College and University Libraries

CACVE California Advisory Council on Vocational Education

CAC & W Continental Aircraft Control and Warning

cad. cadastral; cadaver; caddie; cadenza; cadet; cadmium; cartridge-actuated device; cartridge-actuated device; cash against disbursements; cash against documents; computer-aided design; contract award date

cad. (CAD) computer-aided design

c.a.d. cash against disbursements

cad *cadenza* (Italian—solo passage near end of a concerto movement)

c-a-d *c'est-à-dire* (French—that is to say)

Cad Cadell; Cadiz; Cadmar; Cadmus; Cadogan; Cadwalader or Cadwallader (often pronounced *Calder*)

CAD California Association of

the Deaf; Civil Air Defense; Claude Archille Debussy; Combat Air Division; Commission Against Discrimination; Crown Agents Department

cada clean air dot angle

CADA Centre d'Analyse Documentaire pour l'Archéologie (Document Analysis Center—Archaeology)

CADAFE *Compañía Anónima de Administración y Fomento Electrico* (Spanish—Corporation for Electrical Administration and Development)

CADAM Computer-graphic Augmented Design and Manufacturing

CADAN Centre d'Analyse Documentaire pour Afrique Noir (Document Analysis Center—Africa)

cadav cadaver(ous)

cadc central air data computer

CADC Continental Air Defense Command; Corrective Action Data Center

cad/cam computer-aided design/computer-aided manufacturing

cadco core and drum corrector

cadd computer-aided design drafting

Caddie Charlotte

Cad(dy) Cadillac

cade computer-aided design engineering; computer-aided design evaluation; computer assisted data engineering; computer-assisted data evaluation

cadet. computer-aided design experimental translator

Cadet old Russian acronym for Constitutional Democratic Party or one of its members

Cadets Constitutional Democrats (in czarist Russia)

cadf commutated antenna direction finder

CADF Central Air Defense Force; Contract Administrative Data File

cadfiss computation and data flow integrated subsystems

'Cadian(s) Acadian(s)

CADIG Coventry and District Information Group

CADIN Continental Air Defense Integration North

cadis coronary artery disease

CADIZ Canadian Air Defense Identification Zone

CADL Christian Anti-Defamation League

CADM CONUS (Continental

United States) Air Defense Modernization

CADO Central Air Documents Office (USAF); Central American Development Organization; Current Actions Duty Office(r)

Cadomum (Latin—Caen)

Ca'd'Oro Casa de Oro (Italian—House of Gold)

'cado(s) avocado(s)

CADPIN Customs Automatic Data Processing Intelligence Network (U.S. Bureau of Customs)

CADPOS Communications and Data Processing Operation System

cadre. current awareness and document retrieval for engineers

cads. cellular-absorbed-dose spectrometer

CADS Central Air Data System (USAF); Containerized Ammunition Distribution System (USA)

cadss combined analog-digital systems simulator

CADSYS Computer-Aided Design System

cadte cathodal duration tetanus

Cadwal Cadwallader

cae carrier aircraft equipment; computer-assisted electrocardiography; computer-assisted enrollment

Cae Caelum

CAE Canadian Aviation Electronics; Columbia, South Carolina (airport); Council on Anthropology and Education

CA&E Council on Anthropology and Education

CAE *Cóbrese al Entregar* (Spanish—cash on delivery)

CAEA California Aviation Education Association; Chartered Auctioneers and Estate Agents

CAEAI Chartered Auctioneers and Estate Agents Institute

CAED Canadian Association of Equipment Dealers

Ca edta calcium disodium ethylene diamine tetra-acetate

Cael Caelum

CAEL Council for the Advancement of Experimental Learning

CAEM *Conseil d'Assistance Economique Mutuelle* (French—Council for Mutual Economic Assistance)

Caer (Cornish or Welsh—fortress)—short form for places

such as Caermarthen, Caernarvon, Caerphilly, Caerwent, and Caerwys—the Caers

CAER Centre for Applied Economic Research (New South Wales)

Caern Caernarvonshire

caerul. caeruleus (Latin—cerulian)—sky blue

caes compressed-air energy storage

Caes Caius Julius Ceasar

CAES Canadian Agricultural Economics Society; Connecticut Agricultural Experiment Station

caesar computerized automation by electronic system with automated reservations

Caesar Augusta (Latin—Zaragoza)—called Saragossa by the British

Caesarodonum Turonum (Latin—Tours)

CAET Corrective Action Evaluation Team

CAEU Council of Arab Economic Unity

CAEWW Carrier Airborne Early Warning Wing (USN)

caf cafeteria; caffeine; clerical, administrative, and fiscal; cost and freight; cost, assurance, and freight

caf coût assurance, fret (French—cost, assurance, freight)

CAF Canadian Armed Forces; Central African Federation; Ceylon Air Force; Citizen Air Force

CAF Corporación Andina de Fomento (Spanish—Andean Promotion Corporation)

CAFA Chicago Academy of Fine Arts

CAFB Clark Air Force Base

CAFCINZ Campaign Against Foreign Control in New Zealand

cafd contact analog flight display

cafe (CAFE) corporate average fuel economy

cafe. computer-aided film editor; corporate average fuel economy

CAFEA-ICC Commission on Asian and Far Eastern Affairs—International Chamber of Commerce

CAFEI Central American Fund for Economic Integration

cafetorium cafeteria-auditorium

caff caffeine

Caffarelli Gaetano Majorano

cafga computer applications for

the graphic arts

CAFI Commercial Advisory Foundation in Indonesia

CAFIC Combined Allied Forces Information Center

CAFIT Computer-Assisted Fault Isolation Test(ing)

cafm commercial air freight movement

CAFMS Continental Association of Funeral and Memorial Societies

CAFO Command Accounting and Finance Office

CAFR Comparative Annual Financial Report

C Afr Fed Central African Federation

CAFS Cartridge-Actuated Flame System

CAFSC Control Air Force Specialty Code

CAFTA Council of Australian Food Technology Associations

CAFU Civil Aviation Flying Unit

cag chronic atrophic gastritis; constant aerial glide; constant altitude glide

Cag Cagliari; Cagliostro

CAG Carrier Air Group; Civil Air Guard; Composers-Authors Guild; Computer Analysis Group; Concert Artist Guild; Corrective Action Group; heavy guided-missile cruiser (naval symbol)

CAGA California Asparagus Growers Association; Commercial and General Acceptance

CAGE Convicts' Association for a Good Environment

cagel consolidated aerospace ground equipment list

CAGEO Council of Australian Government Employee Organisations

CAGI Compressed Air and Gas Institute

Cagliostro Giuseppe Balsamo

CAGS Canadian Arctic Gas Study

cah congenital adrenal hyperplasia

CAH Community of All Hallows; Conzinc Asia Holdings

cahd coronary atherosclerotic heart disease

CAHOF Canadian Aviation Hall of Fame

CAHS Comprehensive Automation of the Hydrometeorological Service

CAHT Canadian Association

for Humane Trapping

cai computer-aided instruction; computer-assisted instruction; confused artificial insemination

Cai Cairo; Gonville and Caius College, Cambridge

C-a I Computer-assisted Instruction

CAI Canadian Aeronautical Institute; Career Assessment Inventory; Computer Applications Incorporated; Confederation of Australian Industry; Configuration Audit Inspection (USA); Container Aid International; Cruelty to Animals Inspectorate; Culinary Arts Institute

CAI Club Alpino Italiano (Italian Alpine Club)

CAIA Customs Agents Institute of Australia

CAIB Certified Associate of the Institute of Bankers

caic computer-assisted indexing and classification

CAIC Civil Aviation Information Circular

Cai Col Gonville and Caius College—Cambridge

Caicos Caicos and Turks Islands (in British West Indies southeast of the Bahamas and north of Hispaniola)

CAIG Canadian Aircraft Insurance Group

CAIL Coal and Allied Industries Limited

CAIMAW Canadian Association of Industrial, Mechanical, and Allied Workers

CAIN CAtaloging-INdexing (National Agricultural Library data base)

CAINS Carrier Aircraft Inertial System

caint counter-air and interdiction

caiop computer analog input-output

CAIP Computer-Assisted Indexing Program (UN)

CAIQ Chamber of Automotive Industries of Queensland

CAIRA Central Automated Inventory and Referral Activity (USAF)

CAirC Caribbean Air Command

CAIRS Central Automated Inventory and Referral System (USAF); Computer-Assisted Information Retrieval System; Computer-Assisted Interactive Resources Scheduling

System
CAIS Canadian Association for Information Science; Center for Advanced International Studies (Univ of Miami); Central Abstracting and Indexing Service; Connecticut Association of Independent Schools
Caith Caithness
CAITS Chemical Agent Identification Training Set
caj calked joint
CAJ Center for Administrative Justice; Confederation of ASEAN Journalists
caje consolidated antijam equipment
Cajetan Tommaso de Vio—Italian cardinal who failed to persuade Martin Luther to remain within the Catholic Church and carry on reforms from within
'cajun Acadian (native of Louisiana)
cak conical alignment kit; cube alignment kit
CAK Akron, Ohio (airport)
CAK-C Concept Assessment Kit —Conservation
cal caliber; calorie (small); computer-aided learning; computer-assisted learning; conversational algebraic language
cal calando (Italian—calming); carbine automatique légère (French—light automatic carbine)—CAL
Cal Calabar; Calabozo; Calabria; Calafat; Calahan; Calais; Calamar; Calbert; Calcutta; Caldecott; Calder; Caldwell; Cale; Caleb; Caledonia(n); Calgary; Calhoun; Caliente; California; Calixto; Calkins; Call; Callaghan; Callahan; Callao; Callcott; Callyhan; Calorie (large); Calpurnius; Calumet; Calvagh; Calvary; Calven; Calvert; Calvin; Calvus
CAL Center for Applied Linguistics; China Airlines; Citizens Action League; Commonwealth Acoustic Laboratories; Computer Accounting Limited; Computer-Assisted Learning; Conference-Approved Literature (Australia); Continental Airlines; Conversational Algebraic Language; Cornell Aeronautical Laboratory; Cyprus Airways; Point Arguello (California) tracking station
CAL Comandos Armados por Liberación (Spanish—Armed Commandos for Liberation)— Puerto Rican underground militants fighting for decolonialization
cala calabozo (Spanish—cell, dungeon, jail)
CALA Chinese-American Librarians Association; Civil Aviation Licensing Act
Calabrie (Italian—Calabria)— Italy's toe
calaham California ham (picnic ham)
calamine smithsonite (zinc carbonate)
Calamity Jane Martha Jane Burke also known as Canary Jane whose activities resulted in the death of eleven of her twelve husbands
CALANS Caribbean and Latin American News Service
CalArts California Institute of the Arts
CALAS Computer-Assisted Language Analysis System
calavo California-grown avocado
calb computer-assisted line balancing
C_{alb} albumin clearance
calbr calibration
calc calculate(d); calculation; calculus
calc (CALC) calculate; calculator (flow chart)
calc (Latin prefix—stone or stony)—as in the stony calculus your dentist scrapes off your teeth
Calc Calcutta
Calc Calçada (Portuguese— Street)
Calcasieu Calcasieu Lake or Calcasieu Pass in southwestern Louisiana where the lake waters flow into the Gulf of Mexico
calcd calculated
CALCOFI California Cooperative Oceanic Fishery Investigation
Calcomp California Computer Products
Calc Univ Calcutta University
cald calculated; caldera
CALDA Canadian Air Line Dispatchers Association
CALDAC California Debt Advisory Commission
CALDEA California Driver Education Association
Calder Cadwalader; Cadwallader
Cale (Latin—Oporto)
CALE Canadian Army Liaison Executive
CALEA Canadian Air Line Employees Association
Caled Caledonia
Caled Can Caledonian Canal
Caledonia (Latin—Scotland)
Caledonian Caledonian Canal bisecting northern Scotland and connecting the Atlantic Ocean with the North Sea; pertaining to Scotland and things Scottish
calef. calefactus (Latin— warmed)
calen calendar; calender
calendar (see JFMAMJJA-SOND and French Revolutionary Calendar)
Caletum (Latin—Calais)
CALEV Compañía Anónima Luz Electrica de Venezuela (Spanish—Electric Light of Venezuela Corporation)
Calex Calexico (California border city)
Cal Expo California Exposition (permanent show at Sacramento)
CALFAA Canadian Air Line Flight Attendants Association
calfin calendered finish
Calg Calgary
Calhan Calahan
Calhoun Calquahoun; originally Colquhoun
Calhoun Gulch Charleston, South Carolina sporting-house district
calib calibrate; calibration
calibn calibration
caliche calcium carbonate crust (or) dust—$CaCO_3$
Caliente Agua Caliente, Mexico; Nevada (delinquent) Girls Training Center at Caliente, Nevada; racetrack town adjacent to Tijuana, in Baja California
Calif California; Californian
CALIF California
Calif Cur California Current
Calife Le Calife de Bagdad (French—The Caliph of Bagdad)—one-act opera by Boieldieu
Calif Hist California Historical Society
California Ports (south to north) San Diego, Long Beach, Los Angeles, San Pedro, Monterey, San Francisco, Alameda, Oakland, Port Richmond, Mare Island, Port Chicago, Stockton, Sacremento, Eureka
California Riviera oceanside resorts ranging from San Diego

to Santa Barbara

California's Cornerstone San Diego

Californicators California fornicators

Calif Rev Pr California Review Press

Caligula Gaius Caesar

Calipuerto Cali Aeropuerto (Cali, Colombia)

cal$_{It}$ calorie (International Table calorie)

CALIT California Institute of Technology (also Caltech or CIT)

CALL Canadian Association of Law Libraries; Community Access Library Line; Community Action for Limited Learners; Composite Aeronautical Load List(ing); Counselling at the Local Level (SBA)

callas calla lillies

Calle de la Ballesta (Spanish—Street of the Crossbow)—Madrid's naughty nightclub neighborhood

Calle Florida (Spanish—Florida Street)—celebrated shopping center of Buenos Aires

Calli Callimachus of Alexandria (bibliographer-poet-scholar)

callig calligrapher; calligraphic; calligraphy

call-in call-in radio or television program soliciting audience participation; call in telephone call advising of an anticipated absence due to illness, etc.

calm. collected algorithms for learning machines

CALM Citizens Against Legalized Murder; Computer-Assisted Library Mechanization

CALMA California Marine Associates

Cal Maritime California Maritime Academy

Calmex California-Mexico

CALMS Computer Automatic Line Monitoring System

caln calculation

calo *calando* (Italian—softer and slower, bit by bit)

calogsim computer-assisted logistics simulation

calomel mercurous chloride (Hg$_2$Cl$_2$)

CAL/OSHA California Occupational Safety and Health Administration

CALPA Canadian Air Line Pilots Association

Calpe (Phoenician—Rock of Gibraltar)—one of the Pillars of Hercules flanking Straits of

Gibraltar

CALPIRG California Public Interest Research Group

Cal Poly California Polytechnic

CALRI Central Artificial Leather Research Institute

CALS Canadian Association of Library Schools

CALSO California Transport

CalSpace California Space Institute

CalTec California Institute of Technology

CALTEX California-Texas Petroleum; Overseas Tankship Corporation

cal$_{th}$ calorie (thermochemical calorie)

CALTIP Californians Turn In Poachers (who fish with two poles or hunt out of season)

CALTRAC California Track

Caltrans California Department of Transportation

CALURA Corporation and Labour Unions Returns Act

Calv Calvin; Calvinism; Calvinist

Calvary Calvary Hill outside Jerusalem where its Aramaic name is Golgotha—Place of the Skull

Cal-VDAC California Venereal Disease Advisory Council

Calve Emma Calvé—operahouse name of the soprano Emma de Roquer

Calvin John Calvin (originally Jean Chauvin)

Calypso Capital Port-of-Spain, Trinidad

Calz *Calzada* (Spanish—boulevard, highway)

cam. camber; camouflage; circular area method; cockpit area microphone; commercial air movement; comprehensive achievement monitoring; computer-addressed memory

cam. (CAM) central address memory; checkout and automatic monitoring; computer-aided manufacturing

ca'm calm

Cam Camaguey; Cambodia; Cambodian; Camden; Camelopardalis (constellation); Cameron; Cameroons; Campbell (often pronounced *Camel*); Campechanos; Campeche

C$_{am}$ amylase clearance

CAM Certified Administration Manager; Civil Aeronautics Manual; Civil Aviation Medicine; Composite Army-Marine; Computer-Aided Man-

agement; Consumers Action Movement; Contract Air Mail; Contract Audit Manual; Co-operative Autoworks Malaysia; Cost-Account Manager; Course-A-Month

cama centralized automatic message accounting

CAMA Children's Aid Movement of Australia; Civil Aerospace Medical Association

camal (CAMAL) continuous air borne missle alert

C'Amalie Charlotte Amalie

CAMALS Cambridge Algebra System

Camb Cambrian; Cambridge

Cambod Cambodia; Cambodian

Cambodia formerly Preah Reach Ana Chak Kampuchea or simply Kampuchea, the Khmer Republic, or Democratic Kampuchea; an Asiatic Indo-Chinese country inhabited by Cambodians and occupying Vietnamese troops

Cambodian Ports (north to south) Kampong Saom, Kampot, Phumi Phsar Ream

Cambria (Latin—Wales)

Cambrian Cambrian Airways

Cambrians short form for the Cambrian Mountains of Wales

Cambridge Group Ralph Waldo Emerson, Oliver Wendell Holmes, Henry Wadsworth Longfellow, James Russell Lowell, John Greenleaf Whittier

Cambridge UP Cambridge University Press

Cambs Cambridgeshire

CAMC Canadian Army Medical Corps

CAMDA Car and Motorcycle Drivers Association

camel. common automatic manifest language; computer-assisted machine loading

Camel NATO name for Soviet Tu-104 transport aircraft

Camel-driver of Mecca the Prophet Mohammed's nickname

Camellia Alabama state flower

Camellia Capital Sacramento, California

Camellia City Greenville, Alabama

CAMEO Capitol Area Motion Pictures Education Organization (D.C.)

camera. cooperating agency method for event reporting

and analysis

Cameroon United Republic of Cameroon (equatorial African nation whose Cameroonians speak some English and French plus tribal languages, mineral exports predominate); *République Unie du Cameroun*

Cameroon Ports (north to south) Tiko, Douala, Victoria, Kribi

CAMESA Canadian Military Electronics Standards Agency

Cam High Camden High School; Cameron Highlanders

CAMI Civil Aeromedical Institute; Columbia Artists Management, Incorporated

Camille Erlanger Fréderic Regnal

Camille Pissarro Jacob Pizarro

CAMIS Computer-Assisted Makeup and Imaging System

camisole(s) straitjacket(s)—institutional euphemism

Caml Camelopardus

CAML Canadian Association of Music Libraries

CAMM Canadian Association of Medical Microbiologists

CAMMIS Command Aircraft Maintenance Manpower Information System

camof camouflage

camol computer-assisted management of learning

camp. computer-assisted menu planning; cosmopolitan art—modern and personalized; cyclic adenosine monophosphate

cAMP cyclic adenosine 3', 5'-monophosphate

Camp Campeche (inhabitants—Campechanos); Campion Hall, Oxford

CAMP Campaign Against Marijuana Planting; Campaign Against Moral Persecution; College-Assistance Migrant Program; Computer Applications of Military Problems; Continuous Air Monitoring Program; Course-A-Month Program; Craft Attitude Monitoring Package

Campagna di Roma (Italian—Roman Campagna)—undulating lowlands around Rome

campan campanological; campanologist; campanology

Campanella Tommaso Campanello (originally Giovanni Somenico)

Campanello *Il Campanello di Notte* (Italian—The Night Bell)—one-act Donizetti opera

Camp Hall Campion Hall—Oxford

Campo Alegre (Papiamento or Spanish—Happy Country)—Curaçao's controlled brothel above the hills of Willemstad

Campoformido Campo Formio

campos (Portuguese or Spanish—plains)

campo santo (Italian, Portuguese, Spanish—sacred ground)—name of the superb cemetery in Pisa as well as many other burial places throughout the Latin world

CAMPS Cooperative Area Manpower Planning Systems

CAMPSA Compañia Arrendataria del Monopolio de Petroleos

CAMP Test Christie-Atkins-Munch-Peterson Test

CAMPUS Comprehensive Analytical Methods for Planning in University Systems

CAMQAB Consumer Affairs Medical Quality Assurance Board (California)

CAMRA Campaign for Real Ale

CAMRC Child Abuse and Maltreatment Reporting Center

cams. cybernetic anthropomorphous machines

CAMS Chinese Academy of Medical Sciences; Coastal Anti-Missile System; Communication, Advertising, and Marketing Studies (System); Confederation of Australian Motor Sports; Continuous Air-Monitoring System

CAMSI Canadian Association of Medical Students and Interns

Cam Soc Camden Society

Camulodonum (Latin—Colchester)

can. canal; canalization; canalize; cancel; canceled; cancellation; canister; cannon; canon; canopy; canto; canvasback (duck)

can. (CAN) cancel character (data processing)

can *canto* (Italian—melody, song)

Can Caen; Canada; Canadian; Canal; Canberra; Cancer (constellation); Canfield; Cano; Canyon

Can *Canal* (French, Portuguese, Spanish—canal); *Canale* (Italian—canal); *Cañon* (Spanish—canyon)

Can. *Cantoris* (Latin—cantor's or preceptor's side of the choir)

CAN Canberra, Australia (airport); Citizens Against Noise; Compagne Auxiliare de Navigation; Corporate Angel Network; Customs Assignment Number

CANA Canadian Army; Clergy Against Nuclear Arms

CANABRIT Canadian Navy Joint Staff in Great Britain

CANACIN Camara Nacional de la Industria (Spanish—National Chamber of Industries)—Mexico

CANACO Camara Nacional de Comercio (Spanish—National Chamber of Commerce)

CANACOR Canadian Agro-Industrial Corporation

Canad Canadian

Canada formerly the Dominion of Canada (largest nation in the western hemisphere and second largest in the world, its English-speaking Canadians have maintained close cultural and economic ties with the United States for more than two hundred years)

Canada Day Dominion Day (July 1)

Canada's Breadbasket Saskatchewan

Canada's Doorstep Nova Scotia

Canada's Heartland The Province of Manitoba

Canada's Largest Province Québec

Canada's Ocean Playground Nova Scotia

Canada's Principal Ports Halifax and Montreal on the Atlantic, Vancouver on the Pacific

Canada's Storied Province Québec

Canada's Wonder City Toronto—financial center and industrial headquarters

Canad Fr Canadian French (French Canadian)

Canadian Canadian bacon (boned pork loin strips); Canadian cheddar (usually smoother and spicier than American cheddar cheese); Canadian football (rouge); Canadian-French (Canadian-style French spoken by French Canadians); Canadian humorist (Stephen Leacock); Canadian whiskey (rye); etc.

Canadian black Canadian-grown marijuana

Canadian Comedians Lou Jacobi; Rich Little; and any other favorite in this rare field of achievement

Canadian Commonwealth Canada and its territories

Canadian Dominion Canada and its territories

Canadian Gateway to the Pacific British Columbia

Canadian Humorist Stephen B(utler) Leacock

Canadian Kaleidoscope The Province of Ontario

Canadian Ports (east coast and Great Lakes large, medium, and small from north to south to west) Churchill, Cartwright, Saint Anthony, Roddickton, Springdale, Baie Verte, Fortune Harbour, Botwood, Catalina, Clarenville, Harbour Grace, Wabana, St John's, Argentia, Burin, St Pierre, Grand Bank, St George's, Corner Brook, Humbermouth, Sept-Iles, Baie-Comeau, Rimouski, Tadoussac, Port Alfred, Chicoutimi, Riviere du Loup, Québec, Trois Rivieres, Sorel, Varennes, Montreal, Ottawa, Lower Lakes Terminal, Prescott, Belleville, Trenton, Cobourg, Port Hope, Oshawa, Port Whitby, Toronto, Hamilton, Port Weller, Welland, Port Colborne, Port Maitland, Rondeau Harbor, Amhertsburg, Windsor, Sarnia, Port Edward, Goderich, Owen Sound, Collingwood, Midland, Parry Sound, Little Current, Sault Ste Marie, Thunder Bay—(*and back to the east coast*) Gaspé, Chandler, Paspébiac, Dalhousie, Bathurst, Caraquet, Chatham, Newcastle, Souris, Georgetown, Charlottetown, Summerside, Pictou, North Sydney, Sydney, Halifax, Lunenburg, Liverpool Shelburne Yarmouth, Digby, Parrsboro, Moncton, St John, Letang Harbor; (west coast large, medium, and small from south to north) New Westminster, Vancouver, Horseshoe Bay, Powell River, Comox, Nanaimo, Victoria, Esquimalt, Port Alice, Ocean Falls, Prince Rupert

canadian potato slang nickname for artichoke

Canadian Twin Cities Fort William and Port Arthur—three miles apart in southwestern Ontario on northwest shore of Lake Superior and now united and named Thunder Bay

Ca Na F Campaña Nacional Fronterizo (National Frontier Campaign)

CANAIRDEF Canadian Air Force Defense Command

CANAIRDIV Canadian Air Force Division

CANAIRHED Canadian Air Force Headquarters

CANAIRLIFT Canadian Air Force Transport

CANAIRLON Canadian Air Force Joint Staff—London, England

CANAIRMAT Canadian Air Force Material Command

CANAIRNEW Canadian Air Force—Newfoundland

CANAIRNORWEST Canadian Air Force—Northwest, Edmonton

CANAIRPEG Canadian Air Force—Winnipeg

CANAIRTAC Canadian Air Force Tactical Command

CANAIRTRAIN Canadian Air Force Training Command

CANAIRVAN Canadian Air Force—Vancouver

CANAIRWASH Canadian Air Force Joint Staff—Washington, D.C.

Canakkale Bogazi (Turkish—Dardanelles Strait)

Canal Concessionaire Vicomte Ferdinand Marie de Lesseps—original promoter of the Suez and the Panama Canal

Canal de la Mancha (Spanish—English Channel)

Canal de Panamá (Spanish—Panama Canal)

Canal de Suez (Spanish—Suez Canal)

Canaletto Antonio Canale

Canal of Fire Suez Canal's nickname as it was hot to dig, is hot to live along, and is hot to transit

canalimony so-called $25-million-dollar alimony United States paid Colombia in 1922 for alienating and separating its province of Panama in 1903 so it could proceed unhindered in the task of controlling tropical disease and constructing the Panama Canal linking the Atlantic and the Pacific

Canal Zone Panama Canal Zone

Canal Zone Capital Balboa Heights

Can-Am Canadian-American

Canar Cur Canaries Current

Canarias (Spanish—Canaries) —Canary Islands

Canaries Canary Islands in the Atlantic off southern Morocco and what was formerly the Spanish Sahara

CANAS Canadian Naval Air Station

Canavaral Cape Canaveral also called Cape Kennedy

CANAVAT Canadian Naval Attaché

CANAVCHARGE Canadian Naval Officer in Charge

CANAVHED Canadian Naval Headquarters

CANAVSTORES Canadian Naval Stores

CANAVUS Canadian Naval Joint Staff in United States

Canb Canberra

Canberra British twin-jet light bomber built by BAC

canc cancel; canceled; cancellation; cancelling

Canc Cancer (constellation)

Canc. Cancellarius (Latin—Chancellor)

CANCARAIRGRP Canadian Carrier Air Group

CANCEE Canadian National Committee for Earthquake Engineering

CANCIRCO Cancer International Research Cooperative

CANCOMARLANT Canadian Maritime Commander, Atlantic

CANCOMARPAC Canadian Maritime Commander, Pacific

Can Cus Canadian Customs

cand candelabra; candidate

Can$ Canadian dollar

cande command and edit (computer program)

CANDEP Canadian Naval Depot

candf cost and freight

candi cost and insurance

Candia Erakleion

Candn Canadian

CANDOC Canadian Electronic Document Ordering Service

cand sc candelabra screw

Candu Canadian deuterium uranium

CANDU Chelsea Against Nuclear Destruction United

CANDUR Canadian Deuterium-Uranium Reactor

Candy Candice
CANDY Cigarette Advertising Normally Directed to Youth
Canea Khania
Canecutters sugar-cane-cutting Queensland, Australians
CANEL Connecticut Advanced Nuclear Engineering Laboratory
Can-End Canton and Enderbury Islands
cane sugar saccharose or sucrose
Cane Sugar State Florida, Hawaii, and Louisiana share this nickname
CANF Combined Allied Naval Forces
CANFARMS Canadian Farm Management Data System
CANFORCEHED Canadian Forces Headquarters
Can Fr Canadian French
Can I Canary Islands
CANI Committee on Non-discrimination and Integrity
Can Imm Cen Canada Immigration Centre
canis canister
Can J Chem Canadian Journal of Chemistry
Can J Phys Canadian Journal of Physics
Can J Res Canadian Journal of Research
Can-Jud Canadian-Judeo (Canadian Jewish)
CANLANT Canadian Atlantic
Can Ltd Canadair Limited (operating unit of General Dynamics Corporation)
Can. maj. Canis Major (Latin—Greater Dog)—astronomical constellation
Can Man Cen Canadian Manpower Centre(s)
Can Met Ser Canadian Meteorological Service (EAES)
Can. min. Canis minor (Latin—Lesser Dog)—astronomical constellation
canned cow slang nickname for condensed milk
Canned Salmon Capital Ketchikan, Alaska
Cannery City Seattle, Washington
Cannery Row Monterey, California's fishery foreshore described by John Steinbeck in his novel
Cannon City Kannapolis, North Carolina where Cannon towels are made
Cannon King Alfred Krupp—German armament manufac-

turer (1812–1887)
Cannon Kings of Germany the Krupp family
Canoe City Old Town, Maine
Can/ole Canadian on-line enquiry
Canon City Colorado State Penitentiary at Canon City
CANP Campaign Against Nuclear Power; Civil Air Notification Procedure
Can Pac Canadian Pacific
Can Pen Ser Canadian Penitentiary Service; Canadian Pension Commission
cans. canvasbacks (ducks); custom-assigned numbers
CANSAV Canadian Save the Children Fund
Can/sdi (CAN/SDI) Canadian selective dissemination of information
CANSG Civil Aviation Navigational Services Group
Can St Cannon Street (rail terminal)
Can Sym Canadian Symphony
cant. cannot; cantaloupe
can't can not; cannot
cant. canticum (Latin—canticle or hymn of praise)
Cant Canterbury; Canton; Cantonese
cantab cantabile (Italian—singable or songlike)
Cantab. Cantabrigiensis (Latin—of Cambridge)
Cantabrians Cantabrian Mountains of northern Spain
Cantabrian Surge Bay of Biscay
Cantabrigia (Latin—Cambridge)—also called Camboricum or Capitabrigia
CANTAP Canadian Technical Awareness Programme
CANTAT Canadian Transatlantic Telephones
cant b cantilever bridge
Cant Chin Cantonese Chinese (*see Chin*)
Can Telsat Canadian Telecommunications Satellite System
Cantinflas Mario Moreno
Canton English place-name equivalent of China's Kuangchou
cantran cancel(led) in transmission
Can Tran Comm Canadian Transport Commission
cants cantaloupes
CANTT Cantonment Telegraph
CANTU Compañía Anónima Nacional Telefonos de Venezuela (Spanish—National

Telephone Corporation of Venezuela)
Cantuar. Cantuaria or Cantuariensis (Latin—of Canterbury)
can't win mnemonic abbreviation for community property states—California, Arizona, Nevada, Texas, Wyoming, Idaho, New Mexico
canu can you
CANU Constabulary Anti-Narcotics Unit (Philippines)
Canuck French-Canadian; two-place jet interceptor built in Canada by Avro and designated CF-100
Canuckland Canada
CANUKUS Canada—United Kingdom—United States
CANUS Canada—United States
CANUSE Canadian-United States Eastern (electric power interconnection)
CANUSPA Canada, Australia, New Zealand, and United States Parents Association
canv canvas
CANY Correctional Association of New York
Canyon de Chelly Canyon de Chelly National Monument (cliff-dweller ruins in northern Arizona)
Canyonlands Canyonlands National Park surrounding the junction of the Colorado and Green rivers in southeastern Utah
CANYPS Canadian Yellow Pages Service
canz canzone; canzonetta
CANZ Composers Association of New Zealand
cao chronic airway obstruction
CAO Canadian Association of Optometrists; Central Accounting Office(r); Chief Accounting Office(r); Civil Affairs Office(r); Crimean Astrophysical Observatory (USSR); Cultural Affairs Office(r)
caoc cathodal opening contraction
CAOC Consumers' Association of Canada
CAOGA Crown Agents for Oversea Governments and Administrations
CAOOAA Civil Air Operations Officers Association of Australia
CAORB Civil Aviation Operational Research Branch
CAORE Canadian Army Operational Research Establish-

ment
CAOS Completely Automatic Operational System
CAOSOP Coordination of Atomic Operations—Standard Operating Procedures
CAOT Canadian Association of Occupational Therapy
Cao Tú Phan Van Khoai's pseudonym
cap. capacity; capital letter; capsule; caput; client assessment package
cap. (CAP) computer-aided production
'cap handicap
cap capitolo (Italian—chapter); capitulo (Portuguese or Spanish—chapter); (French—cape)
cap. capiat (Latin—take); *capsula* (Latin—capsule)
c/a/p codice di avviamento postale (Italian—mailing code)—zip coding
Cap capitol; Capricornus (constellation); captain; Captain; Caspar; Charles A. Pearce
Cap. Chapter—Number of Act of Parliament
CAP Canadian Association of Pathologists; Certificat d'Aptitude Professionnelle (Certificate of Professional Aptitude); Citizens Against Pornography; Civil Air Patrol; College of American Pathologists; Combat Air Patrol; Common Agricultural Policy; Commonwealth Association of Planners; Community Action Program; Community Advancement Program; Computer Address Panel; Consumer Action Panel; Cooperating Accountability Project
CAPA California Association of Port Authorities; Canadian Association of Purchasing Agents; Commission on Asian and Pacific Affairs; Confederation of Asian and Pacific Accountants; Council of Australian Postgraduate Associations
capac capacity; cathodic protection
CAPAC Canadian Association of Primary Air Carriers; Composers, Authors, and Publishers Association of Canada
capal computer-and-photographic-assisted learning
CAPAR Cost-Account Problem Analysis Report
CAPC Civil Aviation Planning Committee

capche component automatic programmed checkout equipment
cap com capsule communicator
capcon(s) captured conversation(s)—electronically recorded tape of speech between two or more persons; recorded conversation
capd (CAPD) continuous ambulatory peritoneal dialysis
Cape The Cape—short form for the Cape of Good Hope, Cape Hatteras, Cape Horn, Cape Verde, or other well-known headlands such as Cape Aguilhas, Cape Ann, Cape Blanc, Cape Blanco, Cape Breton, Cape Camorin, Cape Canaveral (Cape Kennedy), Cape Charles, Cape Clear, Cape Cod, Cape Columbia, Cape Cornwall, Cape Cruz, Cape Disappointment, Cape Fear, Cape Finisterre, Cape Flattery, Cape Guardafue, Cape Law, Cape Leeuwin, Cape Maisi, Cape May, Cape Mendocino, Cape Muhammad, Cape Palliser, Cape Race, Cape Sable, Cape San Antonio, Cape San Lucas, Cape Spear, Cape St Vincent, Cape Wrangell, Cape Wrath, Cape York, etc.
CAPE California Association of Polygraph Examiners; Classification and Placement Examination; Confederation of American Public Employees; Council for American Private Education; Course and Professor Evaluation
Cape Breton Highlands Cape Breton Highlands National Park near north end of Cape Breton Island
Cape-Cairo Cape Town-to-Cairo Highway; Cape Town-to-Cairo Railway
Cape of the Californias Cabo San Lucas (at the lower tip of Baja California)
Cape Cod National Cape Cod National Seashore conservation and recreation reservation on Cape Cod, Massachusetts famed for its shore birds and sand dunes
Cape Cod turkey codfish
Cape Colony Cape of Good Hope Colony (South Africa)
CAPED California Association of Postsecondary Educators of the Disabled
Cape Horner(s) deep-sea sailing vessel(s) rounding Cape Horn

in southernmost South America
Cape Horn fever imaginary malady of maritime malingerers who complain they are ill whenever the sea is rough or there is too much work
Cape Kennedy Cape Canaveral, Florida
Cape Province Cape of Good Hope Province
Cape Roca Cabo da Roca, Portugal (Europe's westernmost point)
capertsim computer-assisted program evaluation review technique simulation
CAPES College Association for Public Events and Services
Cape Stiff Cape Horn
Cape of Storms Cape of Good Hope
Cape Verde Island Ports (north to south) Mindelo, Santa Maria, Pregulça, Praia
Cape Verde Islands Republic of Cape Verde (small island nation off Africa's westernmost tip, Cape Verdeans speak Portuguese and export some minerals and salt) *República de Cabo Verde*
Cape Verdes Cape Verde Islands off the Senegal coast of West Africa and called Ilhas do Cabo Verde by the Portuguese who discovered them
CAPEXIL Chemicals and Allied Products Export Promotion Council
CAPH California Association of Physically Handicapped
Capirucha Mexican-Americanism for Mexico City
capit (Latin prefix—head)—as in capitation tax or head tax
Capital of the Cotswolds Cirencester
Capital of Hope Brasilia
Capital of the Incan Empire Cuzco, Peru
capitalinos (Spanish—capital people)—in Mexico this means the people of Mexico City, capital of Mexico
Capital Island Oahu, Hawaii
Capital of the Pirate Coast Ras Al-Khaimak (northernmost sheikdom of Trucial Oman at the Strait of Ormuz connecting the Gulf of Oman and the Persian Gulf)
Capital Province Ontario containing Canada's capital—Ottawa
Capital of the Rhineland Co-

logne (Köln), Germany

Capital of the World New York City—capital of the United Nations

Capitol Reef Capitol Reef National Park in Utah

CAPL Canadian Association of Public Libraries; Controlled Assembly Parts List

CAPLOT Canadians Against PLO Terrorism

CAPM Computer-Aided Patient Management

cap. moll. capsula mollis (Latin —soft capsule)

CAPMS Central Agency for Public Mobilization and Statistics

Cap'n Captain

Cap^n Capitán (Spanish—captain)

capo [Italian—boss or Cosa Nostra syndicate chief; cape (geog); *capobanda*—bandmaster; *capo cameriere*—chief steward; *capo fabbrica*—factory foreman or overseer; *caporione*—ringleader; *capo stazione*—station master]

CAPO Canadian Army Post Office

Caporetto Italian name for Kobarid, Yugoslavia

CAPOSS Capacity · Planning and Operation Sequencing System

C App Chartered Appraiser

CAPPA Crusher and Portable Plant Association

capp^n capellán (Spanish—chaplain)

CAPPS Council for the Advancement of the Psychological Professions and Sciences

cap & puncless capitalization and punctuationless American author e e cummings of *enormous room* fame written without any capital letters or punctuation

cap. quant. vult capiat quantum vult (Latin—allow the patient to take as much as he will)

Capr Capricornus

capri computerized advance personnel requirements and inventory

Capric Capricorn (constellation)

capris capri pants

Cap-Rouge Maison Notre-Dame de la Garde facility for juvenile delinquents at Cape-Rouge, Québec

caps. capital letters

caps. (CAPS) computer-assisted problem solving

caps. capsule (Latin—capsule)

CAPs Community Action Programs; Consumer Action Panels

CAPS Casette Programming System; Cashiers Automatic Processing System; Clearinghouse on Counselling and Personnel Services; Coastal Aerial Photolaser Survey; Collins Adaptive Processing System; Combat Air Patrol Support; Computer-Aided Pipe Sketching System; Computer-Aided Project Study; Computer-based Aid-to-Aircraft Project Studies; Creative Artists Public Service

capsep capsule separation

caps and lower case capital letters and lower case letters

CAPSS Computer-Assisted Public Safety System

caps and small caps upper case capital letters and small capital letters

Capstone of Negro Education Howard University

capt caption

Capt(.) Captain

CAPT Clearinghouse for Applied Performance Testing

Captain Kidd William Kidd—privateer-pirate

CAPTAINS Character and Pattern Telephone Access Information Network System

Captive of History Northern Ireland

Captn old-style English abbreviation—Captain

Capucine Germaine Lefebvre

Capulin Capulin Peak, Capulin Mountain National Monument, Mount Capulin—all in New Mexico

capun capital punishment

capy capacity; capybara

CAQ Craft Association of Queensland

caqa (CAQA) computer-aided quality assurance

car baggage car, boxcar, buffet car, cattle car, club car, coal car, dining car, electric car, elevated car, freight car, mail car, motor car, observation car, parlor car, passenger car, prison car, pullman car, railroad car, refrigerator car, sleeping car, steam car, street car, subway car, surface car, tourist car, trolley car

car. carat; carton; cloudtop altitude radiometer

car. (CAR) channel address register

Car Caradoc; Carberry; Carbury; Carel; Carew(e); Carey; Carina (constellation); Carleton; Carlow; Caroline Islands; Carter; Carvel; Carver

Car. Carolus (Latin—Charles)

CAR California Association of Realtors; Canadian Association of Radiologists; Central African Republic; Chief Airship Rigger; Civil Air Regulation(s); Civil Air Reserve; Comité Agricole Régional (Regional Agricultural Committee); Commonwealth Arbitration Reports; Contract Authorization Request; Corrective Action Request; US Army, Caribbean (area)

CAR Cadena Azul de Radiodifusión (Spanish—Blue Broadcast Chain)

cara combat air rescue aircraft

CARA Center for Applied Research in the Apostolate; Chinese-American Restaurant Association

CARAC Civil Aviation Radio Advisory Committee

CARAL California Abortion Rights Action League

Caran d'Ache Emmanuel Poiré

Carat City diamond-mining Kimberly, South Africa

Carav Caravelle

Caravaggio, Michelangelo da Michelangelo Merisio

Caravaggio, Polidoro da Polidoro Caldara

carb carbon; carbonacious; carbonate; carburetor; carburize

CARB California Air Resources Board

carbecue car + barbecue (device for melting waste out of junked automobiles)

carbo carbohydrate

carbolic acid phenol

carboloy carbon-cobalt-tungsten alloy

carbonado black or grayish-black industrial diamond; meat scored before grilling over charcoal

carbon dioxide carbonic acid gas

Carbonif Carboniferous

carbon monoxide CO

carbontet carbon tetrachloride

carbopol carboxpolymethylene

carborundum silicon carbide (SiC)

carb(s) carburetor(s)

CARBS Computer-Assisted Ra-

tionalized Building System
carcin (Latin prefix—cancer)—
carcinogenic
Carcross Caribou Crossing
card. cardamom; cardinal
card. (CARD) compact automatic retrieval device; compact automatic retrieval display
Card Cardiganshire; Cardinal
CARD Campaign Against Racial Discrimination; Civil Aeronautics Research and Development; Compact Automatic Retrieval Device (or Display)
CARDA Continental Airborne Reconnaissance for Dammage Assessment (USAF)
cardamap cardiovascular data analysis by machine processing
CARDE Canadian Armament Research and Development Establishment
cardi (Latin prefix—heart)—cardiac arrest (heart failure)
Cardinal state bird of Illinois, Indiana, Kentucky, North Carolina, Ohio, Virginia, and West Virginia
cardioac cardioacceleration; cardioaccelerator(y); cardioactive; cardioactivity
cardiog cardiogenesis; cardiogenetic, cardiograph(ic); cardiography
cardiol cardiolith(ic); cardiologist(ic)(al)(ly); cardiology; cardiolysin
cardiomeg cardiomegaly
cardiomyo cardiomyopathy
cardiopul cardiopulmonary
cardiov cardiovascular
cardiover cardioversion (electric-shock therapy)
CARDIV Carrier Division (naval)
Cardl Cardenal (Spanish—Cardinal)
CARDPACS Card Packet System
card(s). (CARDs) computer-aided research device(s)
Cards Cardinals
CARDS Combat Aircraft Recording and Data System; Computer-Assisted Recording of Distribution Systems
care. continuous aircraft reliability evaluation
Care Caretaker
CARE Citizens Association for Racial Equality; Consumer Awareness Retailer Effort; Cooperative for American Relief

Everywhere; Cooperative for American Remittances to Everywhere
CAREL Central Atlantic Regional Educational Laboratory
CARES Computer-Assisted Regional Evaluation System
CARF Canadian Amateur Radio Federation; Canadian Arthritis and Rheumatism Society; Central Altitude Reservation Facility
CARG Caribbean Ready Group (USN); Corporate Accountability Research Group (Nader's)
Cargomaster Douglas 200-passenger military transport designated C-133
Cargo Port of the Pacific Vancouver, British Columbia
cargotainer cargo container
Cari Carina
CARI Civil Aeromedical Research Institute
Carib. Caribbean
CARIBAIR Caribbean Atlantic Airlines
CARIBANK Caribbean Development Bank
Caribbean Caribbean Area (islands and lands in or washed by the Caribbean Sea); Caribbean Sea; correct pronunciation used by local Latin Americans and West Indians is *Ca-ribb-ean*
CARIBCOM Caribbean Command
Carib Cur Caribbean Current
Caribe (Spanish—Carib language, Caribbean Sea)
Caribisch (Dutch—Caribbean)
Caribou De Havilland twin-engine stol transport designated DHC-4 in Canada and C-7A in the United States where it is also called CV-2A
Caribous Caribou Mountains of British Columbia
CARIBSEAFRON Caribbean Sea Frontier
caric caricature; caricaturist
CARIC Contractor All-Risk Incentive Contract (USAF)
Caricom Caribbean Community Anguilla, Antigua, Barbados, Belize, Dominica, Grenada, Guyana, Jamaica, Montserrat, St Kitts-Nevis, St Lucia, St Vincent, Trinidad and Tobago
CARIFESTA Caribbean Festival of the Arts
CARIFTA Caribbean Free

Trade Association
CARIH Children's Asthma Research Institute and Hospital (Denver)
Carioca(s) native(s) of Rio de Janeiro
CARIPLO Cassa di Risparmio delle Provincie Lombarde (Italian—Saving's Bank of the Province of Lombardy)
CARIS Computerized Agricultural Research Information System; Current Agricultural Research Information System (FAO)
carl computer-assisted reference locator
Carl Carla; Carle; Carleton; Carlisle; Carlo(s); Carlton; Carlyle
CARL Canadian Academic Research Libraries; Chatfield Applied Research Laboratories; Computer Audio Research Laboratory
Carla Carlotta; Caroline
Carl Brandes Edvard Cohen
Carleton Kendrake Erle Stanley Gardner
Carl Gustaf 9mm Swedish submachine gun firing parabellum bullets; recoilless 84mm antitank weapon whose name also honors this military monarch of Sweden
Carl Milles Vilhelm Carl Emil Anderson
Carlo Collodi Carlo Lorenzini (under pseudonym of Collodi wrote *Pinocchio: the Story of a Puppet*)
Carlo Maria Carlo Maria Giulini
Carlos Arruza Carlos Ruiz Camino
Carlsbad English name for Karolvy Vary or Karlsbad
Carm Carmarthenshire; Carmichael; Carmo; Carmody
Carmella Ponselle Carmella Ponzillo
Carmen Miranda Maria de Cormo Cunha
Carmen Silva (pseudonym—Elisabeth Queen of Romania)
CARML County and Regional Municipality Librarians (Ontario)
carmrand civilian application of the results of military research and development
Carn Caernarvonshire
Carnegie Inst Carnegie Institution of Washington
Carnegie Tech Carnegie Institute of Technology

carni carnival
Carnics Carnic Alps
carnie(s) carnival(s); carnival workers
Carnutum (Latin—Chartres)
Caro Carolina; Caroline
Carol Carola; Carole; Carolina; Caroline; Carolyn
CAROL Caribbean Overseas Lines
Carol Carnac Edith Caroline Rivett's pseudonym
Carolina Art Carolina Art Association
Carolina del Norte (Spanish—North Carolina)
Carolina del Sur (Spanish—South Carolina)
Carolina Game Cock Thomas Sumter
Carolina Pop Ctr Carolina Population Center
Carolinas North and South Carolina
Carolines Caroline Islands (Kusaie, Palau, Ponape, Truk, Yap) in the Western Pacific
Carol Lombard Jane Peters
Carolus Magnus Charlemagne
Caronia La Coruña (northwestern Spain in Roman times)
carot centralized automatic recording on trunks (Bell)
carp. carpenter; carpentry; carpet(ing); computed air-release point; construction of aircraft and related procurement
Carp Carpathian; Carpentaria
CARP Campaigns Against Rising Prices; computed air-release point
CARPAS Comisión Asesora Regional de Pesca el Atlantico Sud-Occidental (Spanish—Regional Fisheries Advisory Commission for the Southwest Atlantic)
Carpathians Carpathian Mountains between Czechoslovakia and Poland
Carpaths Carpathian Mountains
Carpet City Amsterdam, New York
carpilf cargo pilferage
carp(s) stage carpenter(s)
Carps Carpathian Mountains
carr carriage (flow chart); carrier
Carrasco Montevideo, Uruguay's airport
Carrie Carolina; Caroline
Carrie Mac California Association of Realtors Mortgage Assistance Corporation
Carrion's disease Peruvian-

sandfly anemia
CARRIS Companhia Carris de Ferro de Lisboa (Portuguese—Lisbon Street Railway)
Carroll of Carrollton Charles Carroll of Carrollton, Maryland—self-identified signer of the *Declaration of Independence*
Carry Nation Carry Amelia Moore Nation's nickname
cars. community antenna relay service
CARS Canadian Arthritis and Rheumatism Society; Central American Research Station (for disease control); Community Antenna Relay Station; Community on Alcohol and Road Safety; Computer-Aided Routing System; Computer-Assisted Reliability Statistics
Carson Carson City; Nevada State Penitentiary in Carson City
Carson City Nevada's capital
Carson City Women's Women's Prison at Carson City, Nevada
CARSTRIKFOR Carrier Striking Force
cart. cartage; carton; collision-avoidance radar trainer
Cart Carter; Cartwright
CART Cargo Automation Research Team; Central Automated Replenishment Techniques; Championship Auto Racing Teams; Complete Automatic Rating Technique; Complete Automatic Reliable Testing
Cartagena de Indias (Spanish—Cartagena of the Indies)—Colombia's walled seaport city of Cartagena on the Caribbean leading to the West Indies
Cartago (Latin or Spanish—Carthage)
CARTB Canadian Association of Radio and Television Broadcasters
Carter Curtain Chicano and leftist nickname for the Tortilla Curtain
Carth Carthage; Carthaginian; Carthusian
cartobib cartobibliographer; cartobibliography
cartog cartographer; cartographic; cartography
Cartoonist Humorist Al Capp
cartoonitorial cartoon editorial
CARTS Computer-Automated Reserved Track System
Cary Grant Archibald Leach

Car Z Caribische Zee (Dutch—Caribbean Sea)
cas calibrated airspeed; casual; casualty; close air support
cas (CAS) cooperative applications satellite
ca's combat actions; covert actions
Cas Caracas; Casimir; Caslon; Cassiopeia (constellation); Castle
CAs Consumers Associations; Cooperative Associations
CAS California Academy of Sciences; Cambrian Airways (symbol); Capital Assistance Scheme; Casualty Actuarial Society; Center for Administrative Studies; Center for Auto(mobile) Safety; Change Analysis Section; Chemical Abstracts Service; Chicago Academy of Sciences; Chief of Air Staff; Children's Aid Society; Chinese Academy of Sciences; Civil Affairs Section; Civil Air Surgeon; Clean(er) Air System(s); Collision Avoidance System (aircraft); Commercial Air Service; Computer Acquisition System; Contemporary Art Society; Contract Administration Services; Cost Accounting Standards; Courier Air Services; Current Australian Serials; Current Awareness Service; Customs Agency Service
C.A.S. Certificate of Advanced Studies
ca.sa. capias ad satisfaciendum (Latin—writ of execution)
CASA Campaign Against Psychiatric Abuse (in the USSR); Canadian Association of School Administrators; Canadian Automatic Sprinkler Association; Catgut Acoustical Society of America; Citizens Against Sneakin' Aroun'; Contemporary Art Society of Australia; Crafts Association of South Australia
CASA Construcciones Aeronauticas, SA (Spain)
Casa Grande Casa Grande National Monument near Phoenix, Arizona
Casanova Giacomo Girolamo
CASANZ Clean Air Society of Australia and New Zealand
CASAO Chartered Accountants Students Association of Ontario
Casa Pacifica former President Nixon's Spanish-colonial sea-

side home at San Clemente, California

Casa Rosada (Spanish—Pink House)—Argentine president's office building in Buenos Aires

CASB Cost-Accounting Standards Board

Casbah Algiers, Algeria's hillside redlight and underworld district

CASBS Center for Advanced Study in the Behavioral Sciences (Stanford)

casc computer-assisted cartography

CASC Council for the Advancement of Small Colleges

CASCADE Citizens and Scientists Concerned About Dangers to the Environment

Cascades Cascade Mountains extending from British Columbia to California via Washington and Oregon

cascan casualty cancelled

CASCOMP Comprehensive Airship Sizing and Performance Computer Program

cascor casualty corrected

CASCU Cooperative Association of Suez Canal Users

CASD Center for Applied Studies in Development

casdac computer-aided ship design and construction

CASDO Computer Applications Support and Development Office (USN)

casdos computer-assisted detailing of ships

case. common-access switching equipment; computer-automated support equipment

Case Casey

CASE Coalition of Agencies Serving the Elderly; Coalition for Safe Energy; Colorado Association of School Executives, Commission on the Accreditation of Service Experiences; Committee on Academic Science and Engineering; Committee on the Atlantic Salmon Emergency; Coordinated Aerospace Supplier Evaluation; Council of Administrators of Special Education; Council for the Advancement of Secondary Education; Council for Advancement and Support of Education; Counselling Assistance to Small Enterprises

CASEA Center for the Advanced Study of Educational Administration

CASETT Cases of Settlements and Removals

CASEX Close Air Support Exercise; Combined Aircraft Submarine Exercise

Casey Jones John Luther Jones

Casey Stengel Charles Dillon Stengel

CASF Combat Alert Strike Force; Composite Air Strike Forces

cash. cashier

Cash Cashlin; Cassius

CASH Catalog of Available and Standard Hardware; Citizen Action for Safer Harlems; Commission for Administrative Services in Hospitals

Casi Casimir

CASI Canadian Aeronautics and Space Institute

CASIA Chemical Abstracts Subject Index Alert

CASIG Careers Advisory Service in Industry for Girls

Casino City Monte Carlo, Monaco

Casl Caslon

Ca S-L Catering Sub-Lieutenant

CASLE Commonwealth Association of Surveying and Land Economy

CASLIS Canadian Association of Special Libraries and Information Services

casm cycling air sampling monitor

CASMT Central Association of Science and Mathematics Teachers

CASNP Canadian Association in Support of Native Peoples

CASO Civil Aviation Safety Order

CASOE Computer Accounting System for Office Expenditures

casoff control and surveillance of friendly forces

CASOS Center for Advanced Study in Organization Science (U of Wisconsin)

Casp Caspar(d)

CASP Capability Support Plan; Cape Arago State Park (Oregon); Country Analysis and Strategy Paper (U.S. State Department)

Caspar Cambridge analog simulator for predicting atomic reactions

CASPER Contact Area Summary Position Estimate Report

CASPERS Computer-Automat-

ed Speech-Perception System

Caspian Caspian Sea (landlocked body of water between Iran and the USSR where it is called Kaspiskoye More)

Caspio (Spanish—Caspian)

Cas Reps Casualty Reports

CASRO Council of American Survey Research Organizations

cass cassowary

Cass Casimir; Cassander; Cassandra; Casseus; Cassidy; Cassius; Casso

CASS Command Active Sonobuoy System; Connecticut Association of Secondary Schools

CASSA Continental Army Command Automated System Support Agency (USA)

Cassi Cassiopeia

CASSI Chemical Abstracts Service Source Index

CASSIS Communication and Social Science Information Service (Canada)

CASSR Chuvash Autonomous Soviet Socialist Republic

cast. computer applications and systems technic; computer-augmented scanning technics

Cast Castel; Castile; Castilian; Castillon; Castimir; Castislav; Castle; Castor

CAST Center for Application of Sciences and Technology; Contemporary Artists Serving the Theater; Council for Agricultural Science and Technology

CAST Clearinghouse Announcements in Science and Technology

CASTE Collision-Avoidance System Technical Evaluation

castile castile soap (mild cleaning agent originally made in Castile, Spain from olive oil and sodium hydroxide)

Castilla (Spanish—Castile)

Castilla la Nueva (Spanish—New Castile)—province to the south of the Guadarrama Mountains where its capital is Toledo

Castilla la Vieja (Spanish—Old Castile)—province to the north of the Guadarrama Mountains where its capital is Burgos

Cast-Iron Commodore Matthew Calbraith Perry

CASTLE Computer-Assisted System for Theater-Level Engineering

CASTOR College Applicant Status Report

CASTS Canal Safe Transit System

Casurgis (Latin—Prague)

CASW Council for the Advancement of Science Writing

cat. carburetor air temperature; catalog; catamaran; catapult; catboat; category; caterpillar tractor; clear air turbulence; compressed air tunnel; computer-assisted transcription; computerized axial tomography

cat. (CAT) choline acetyltranferase; computer-aided typesetting; computer-assisted test(ing); computerized adaptive test(ing); computerized axial test(ing)

Cat Catalán; Catalina; Catalonia; Catalonian; Cataluña; Catalunya; Catamarca; Catania; Cataño; Catarina; Caterino; Catasauqua; Catawba; Caterpillar Tractor; Catesby; Catlett

Cat Cat Duet (Rossini's comic work for two voices imitating a domestic-cat conversation); Catalan (Romance language spoken in the Spanish province of Catalonia as well as in nearby France and Andorra, more than five million people speak Catalan)

CAT California Achievement Test; California Advocacy for Trollops; Child's Apperception Test; Civil Air Transport; Civilian Actress Technician; Clerical Aptitude Test; Cognitive Abilities Test; College Ability Test; Colleges of Advanced Technology; Commercial Airlift Contract; Computer-Aided Training; Computer-Aided Translation; Computer-Aided Typesetting; Computer-Assisted Teaching; Consolidated Atomic Time; Container Associates Transport; Control and Assessment Team; Corrective Action Team

CAT Comisaría de Abastecimientos y Transportes (Spanish—Commisariat of Supply and Transport)

CATA Canadian Air Transport Association; Canadian Air Transportation Administration

catal catalog; catalogue

Catal Catalan; Catalonia; Cataluña

Catalina Catalina de Güines southeast of Havana, Cuba; Santa Catalina Island off Long Beach, California

Cataluña (Spanish—Catalonia)

Catana (Latin—Catania)—Sicilian province at the foot of Mount Etna

catawump catawumpus (catamount, mountain lion)

cat. burglar(s) caterpillar-tractor-type earthmoving automotive-equipment burglar(s)

catc computer-assisted test construction

CATC Commonwealth Air Transport Council; Continental (Oil), Atlantic (Refining), Tidewater (Oil), and Cities (Service) (combined in mutual drilling)

CATCALL Completely Automated Technique for Cataloging and Acquisition of Literature for Libraries

CATCC Canadian Association of Textile Colorists and Chemists; Carrier Air Traffic Control Center

CATCH Citizens Against The Concorde Here

Catch-Me-Who-Can nickname of Richard Trevithick's railway engine tested in 1808

CATCO Catalytic Construction Company

cate comprehensive automatic test equipment

CATE Current ARDC (Air Research and Development Command) Technical Efforts (program)

catec catechism; catechist(ic)(al)(ly)

Cater Trac Caterpillar Tractor

Ca Test Calcium Test (dental)

CATF Canadian Achievement Test in French

cat gold mica; yellowish mica

cath cathartic; cathedral; catheter; catheterize

Cath Cathedral; Catherine; Catholic; St Catharine's College, Cambridge; St Catherine's College, Oxford

Cathay China

CATHAY Cathay Pacific Airways

Cathedral of Learning University of Pittsburgh's 52-story building

Cathedrals Cathedral Caverns near Grant, Alabama

cath fol cathode follower

Cathie Catherine

Cath Lib Assn Catholic Library Association

cathol catholic; catholically; catholicly; catholicalness; catholicness; catholicate; catholice; catholicity

Cath U Pr Catholic University of America Press

Cathy Catherine

Catia Venezuelan house of detention in the Caracas suburb of Catia where many await trial

CATIB Civil Air Transport Industry Training Board

CATIE Centro Agronómico Tropical de Investigación y Enseñanza (Spanish—Tropical Agriculture Center of Investigation and Teaching)—Turrialba, Costa Rica

catk counterattack

catlg catalog(ue)

CATM Canadian Achievement Test in Mathematics

CATNIP Computer-Assisted Technique for Numerical Index Preparation

Catoctins Catoctin Mountains of Maryland and Virginia

CATOR Combined Air Transport and Operations Room

CATP Computer-Assisted Typesetting Process

catproc catalog(ue) procedure

CATRA Cutlery and Allied Trades Research Association

Catracho(s) Honduran(s)

CATRALA Car and Truck Renting and Leasing Association

CATs Civic Action Teams

CATS Certificates of Accrual on Treasury Certificates; Civil Affairs Training School (USN); Comprehensive Analytical Test System; Compute Air-Trans Systems; Computer-Assisted Test Shop; Computer-Automated Test System (AT & T)

CATSA Cooperative Air Transport System for Antarctica

cat's eye chrysoberyl

catsie cat's-eye playing marble; polished agate resembling a cat's eye

Catskills Catskill Mountains of southeastern New York (scene of Washington Irving's *Rip Van Winkle* and other humorous tales)

CATSS Cataloguing Support System

catt conveyorized automatic tube tester

cattalo cattle + buffalo—hy-

brid
Cattaro (Italian—Kotor)
CATTCM Canadian Achievement Test in Technical and Commercial Mathematics
CAT test Computerized Axial Tomography Test
Cattle Capital Willcox, Arizona
CATTS California and Texas Telecommunications System
Catty Catherine
catv cabin air temperature valve; cable television; community antenna television
catva computer-augmented total-value assessment
cau command arithmetic units
Cau Caucasian
CAU Child Abuse Unit (police department); Congress of American Unions; Consumer Affairs Union; Consumer Affairs Unit
Caucasus between Iran and Russia with some in each country; Caucasus Mountains between the Black Sea and the Caspian Sea
Cauc(s) Caucasian(s)
caud caudal; caudate
caud (Latin prefix—tail)—caudal appendage
Caudillo de la Independencia de Uruguay (Spanish—Chief of the Independence of Uruguay) —José Gervasio Artigas
CAUL Committee of Australian University Librarians
cauli cauliflower
caus causation; causative
CAUS Color Association of the United States
CAUSA Compania Aeronautica Uruguay SA; Confederation of Associations for the Unity of the Societies of the Americas (*causa* is Spanish for cause)
causat causative
'cause because
CAUSE College and University Systems Exchange; Comprehensive Assistance to Undergraduate Science Education (National Science Foundation); Counselor Advisor University Summer Education
caust caustic
caustic potash potassium hydroxide (KOH)
caustic soda sodium hydroxide (NaOH)
caut caution
CAUT Canadian Association of University Teachers
CAUTION Citizens Against Unnecessary Tax Increases

and Other Nonsense (St Louis citizens)
cav cavalier; cavalry; cavitation; cavity; congenital absence of vagina; congenital adrenal virilism; continuous airworthiness visit
cav (CAV) class attendance verification; construction assistance vehicle
cav. caveat (Latin—warning, writ of suspension)
c.a.v. curia advisare vult (Latin —the court cares to consider)
Cav Cavanagh; Cavanaugh; Cavell; Cavendish
Cav Cavaliere (Italian—Knight)
Cavalier State Virginia
Cavalleria Cavelleria Rusticana (Mascagni one-act opera concerning Sicilian-style rustic chivalry)
Cavalleria espanola nickname of Massenet's verismo opera *La Navarraise* also called *Calvelleria espanola* after the creatrix of its title role— Emma Calvé
cav brk cavity brick
cavd completion, arithmetic, vocabulary, directions (test)
CAVE California Association of Vocational Educators; Catholic Audio-Visual Educators Association; Consolidated Aquanauts Vital Equipment
CAVEA Connecticut Audio-Visual Education Association
caveat code and visual entry authorization technic
cav. emp. caveat emptor (Latin —let the buyer beware)—also appears as *c.e.*
Cavendish Cavendish Laboratory (Cambridge University)
CAVI Centre Audio-Visuel International (French—International Audio-Visual Center)
caviar of drugs cocaine
caviol caviology
ca virus croup-associated virus
CAVN Compañía Anonima Venezolana de Navegación (Venezuelan Steamship Line)
Cav-Pag Cavalleria Rusticana and *I Pagliacci* (Italian operas frequently performed in succession)
cavu ceiling and visibility unlimited
caw cam-action wheel; channel address word
c-a w conflict-alert warning
CAW Cables and Wireless (company); Californians Against Waste

CAWA Canadian-American Women's Association
CAWC Committee on Air and Water Conservation (American Petroleum Institute)
CAWD Canadian-American Wolf Defenders
CAWE California Association of Work Experience Educators
cawg coaxial adapter waveguide
CAWM College of African Wildlife Management
CAWP Center for the American Woman and Politics
CAWS Central Aural Warning System; Conflict Alert Warning System; Conservation and Wildlife Studies
CAWSPS Computer-Aided Weapon Stowage Planning System (USN)
CAWU Clerical and Administrative Workers' Union
cax community automatic ex change (telephone)
Caxton Caxton Printers, Ltd
Cay Cayenne; Cayman
Cayenne French Guiana's popu lar name and the name of its fever-infested capital
Cayes Haitian seaport also called Aux Cayes or Les Cayes
Caymans Cayman Islands (Grand Cayman, Little Cayman, Cayman Brac)
cayo (Spanish—cay, key, shoal)
Cayo Hueso (Spanish—Bone Key)—Key West
Cayos de la Florida (Spanish— Florida Keys)
Cayuse Hughes OH-6 observation helicopter
cb cast brass; catch basin; cement base; center of buoyancy; chemical and biological; circuit breaker; collective bargaining; common battery; continuous breakdown
cb (CB) container base
c-b circuit breaker
c/b caught and bowled
c & b collating and binding
c of b confirmation of balance
Cb columbium (symbol); cumulo-nimbus
CB Cape Breton (island); Caribair (airline); Caribbean-Atlantic Airlines; Carte Blanche; Cavalry Brigade; Census Bureau; Chairman of the Board (of directors); Chief Boilermaker; Children's Bureau; citizen's band (radiofrequency band for short-range two-way

communication); Companion of the Bath; compass bearing; confidential book; confidential bulletin; confinement to barracks; Construction Battalions (hence the nickname "seabees"); Consultants Bureau; Control Branch; Counter Battery; Cumulative Bulletin; Currency Bond; large cruiser (naval symbol); William Cullen Bryant

C-B (Sir Henry) Campbell-Bannerman

C.B. *Chirurgiae Baccalaureus* (Latin—Bachelor of Surgery); Companion of the Bath

C & B Clemens and Brenninkmeyer; Cleveland and Buffalo (steamship line)—*Seeandbee*

C of B Commonwealth of the Bahamas

CB *Carte Blanche* (French—white card indicating its holder can order as he or she pleases)

C-B *Creditanstalt-Bankverein* (German—Credit Institution and Bank Association)—Austria's largest banking institution

cba chemical bond approach; chronic bronchitis with asthma; cost-benefit analysis

cba (CBA) colliding beam accelerator

CBA California Benefit Association; Canadian Booksellers Association; Caribbean Atlantic Airlines; Christian Booksellers Association; Clydesdale Breeders Association; College of Business Administration; Community Broadcasters Association; Consumer Bankers Association

CBA *Chemical-Biological Activities*

CBAA Canadian Business Aircraft Association

CBAC *Chemical-Biological Activities*

cbaf cobalt-base alloy foil

CBAICP Chemical and Biological Accident and Incident Control Plan (USA)

c/bale cents per bale

cbam concerns-based adoption model

cbar counterbore arbor

CBARC California Border Area Resource Center

CBAT Central Bureau of Astronomical Telegrams

cbb commercial blanket bond

CBB Chesapeake Bay Bridge (Maryland)

CBB *Centre Belge du Bois* (French—Belgian Forestry Research Center)

CBBA Christian Brothers Boys Association

CBBB Council of Better Business Bureaus

CBBI Cast Bronze Bearing Institute

CBBII Council of the Brass and Bronze Ingot Industry

CBBT Chesapeake Bay Bridge-Tunnel (Maryland to Virginia)

cbc (CBC) combined blood count; complete blood count

CBC Canadian Broadcasting Corporation; Caribbean Broadcasting Company; Central Bank of China; Ceylon Broadcasting Corporation; Children's Book Council; Columbia Basin Council; Commendation for Brave Conduct; Commercial Banking Company; Commonwealth Banking Corporation; Contraband Control; Corset and Brassiere Council; Cyprus Broadcasting Corporation; large tactical-command ship (naval symbol)

CBCA California Black Commission on Alcoholism

cbcc common bias—common control

CBCII California Bureau of Criminal Identification and Investigation

CB circuit common-base amplifier for junction transistors

CB Club Citizen's-Band (radio) Club

cbcm cheque book-charging method

CBCMA Carbonated Beverage Container Manufacturers Association

CBCS Commonwealth Bureau of Census and Statistics

cbct circuit board card tester

CBCT Customer-Bank Communication Terminal

cbcu counterbore cutter

cbd cash before delivery; closed bladder drainage; common bile duct

CBD Central Business District; Construction Battalion Detachment

CBD *Commerce Business Daily*

cbdn can be done

CBDNA College Band Directors National Association

CBDS Carcinogenesis Bioassay Data System

cbe cesium bombardment engine; chemical binding effect; circuit board extractor; competency-based education; compression bonding encapsulation

CBE Cheese Bureau of England; Community-Based Education; Competency-Based Education; Computer-Based Education; Conference of Biological Editors; Council for Basic Education; Council of Basic Education; Council of Biology Editors

C.B.E. Commander of the Order of the British Empire; Companion of the Order of the British Empire

CBEL *Cambridge Bibliography of English Literature*

CBEMA Canadian Business Equipment Manufacturers Association; Computer and Business Equipment Manufacturers Association

CBer operator or owner of a Citizen's-Band radio

CB-er(s) citizen's radio-frequency band (short-wave two-way) broadcaster(s)

cbf cerebral blood flow; coronary blood flow

CBF Children's Blood Foundation

CBFC Commonwealth Bank Finance Company

CBFCA Commander, British Forces, Caribbean

cbfm constant bandwidth frequency modulation

cbft cubic feet

cbg (CBG) corticosteroid-binding globulin; transcortin

CBG Compagnie des Bauxites de Guinée

CBH Cooperative Bulk Holding

C B & H Continent between Bordeaux and Hamburg

CBHE Connecticut Board of Higher Education

cbi complete background investigation; compound batch identification; computer-based information

CBI Cape Breton Island; Carbonated Beverage Institute; Caribbean Basin Initiative; Central Bureau of Investigation; Chesapeake Bay Institute; Chicago Bridge and Iron (company); China-Burma-India (theater of war); Coffee Brewing Institute; Confederation of British Industries; Confederation of British Industry; Council of the Building Industry; Council of Burma Industries

CB & I Chicago Bridge and Iron (company)

CBI Cumulative Book Index

CBIA California Building Industry Association

cbid counter bid

CBIS Campus-Based Information System (NSF); Communist Bloc Intelligence Service; Computer-Based Instruction(al) System

cbit (CBIT) contract bulk inclusive tour (travel plan)

cbj common bulkhead joint

CBJO Coordinating Board of Jewish Organizations

cbk checkbook

cbl cable; cement-bond log; commercial bill of lading

cb/l commercial bill of lading

c bl carte blanche (French— white card)—full power to act

CBL Configuration Breakdown List; Chesapeake Biological Laboratories

CB of L Chartered Bank of London

cbm chemical biological munitions; conventional buoy mooring; cubic meter(s)

cbm Kubikmeter (German— cubic meter)

CBM Christian Blind Mission

CBMA Carbonated Beverage Manufacturers Association

CBMC Corregidor-Bataan Memorial Commission

CBM-I Common Bahasa Malay-Indonesian

CBMIS Computer-Based Management Information System

CBMM Council of Building Materials Manufacturers

CBMPE Council of British Manufacturers of Petroleum Equipment

CBMQA California Board of Medical Quality Assurance

CBMS Conference Board of Mathematical Sciences

cbmu current bit monitor unit

CBMU Canadian Board of Marine Underwriters

CBMUA Canadian Boiler and Machinery Underwriters Association

cbn chemical, bacteriological, nuclear; courses by newspaper

CBN Columbia Carbon Company (stock-exchange symbol);

Commonwealth Broadcasting Network

CBNE California Bureau of Narcotics Enforcement

CBNM Custer Battlefield National Monument

CBNS Commander, British Naval Staff

CBNY Chemical Bank, New York

cbo compensation by objectives

Cbo Colombo

CBO Community-Based Organizations; Conference of Baltic Oceanographers; Congressional Budget Office (U.S.A.)

CBOA Commonwealth Bank Officers Association

cboc completion bed occupancy care

CBOE Chicago Board Options Exchange

C-bomb cobalt bomb

cbore counterbore

CBOT Chicago Board of Trade

cbp ceramic beam pentode; constant boiling point

CBP Centro de Biologia Piscatória (Piscatorial Biological Center—Lisbon)

CBPA Connecticut Book Publishers Association

CBPBG Commonwealth Bureau of Plant Breeding and Genetics

CBPC Canadian Book Publishers' Council

CBPDC Canadian Book and Periodical Development Council

CB & PGNCS Circuit Breaker and Primary Guidance Navigation Control System

CBPI Canadian Business Periodicals Index

CBPO Consolidated Base Personnel Office

CBQ Children's Behavior Questionnaire; Civilian Bachelor Quarters

C B & Q Chicago, Burlington & Quincy (railroad)

CBQ Catholic Biblical Quarterly

cbr change board register; chemical, biological, radiological; crude birth rate

Cbr Calabar

CBR Canberra, Australia (airport); Center for Brain Research (University of Rochester)

CBRA Chemical, Biological, Radiological Agency

CB radio citizen's band radio (26.965 to 27.405 MHz)

CBRC Crichton Behavioral Rating Scale

CBRE Chemical, Biological, and Radiological Element

CBRI Central Building Research Institute

CBRL Chemical, Biological, and Radiation Laboratories (Ottawa)

cbrn chemical, biological, radiological, and nuclear

CBRO Chemical, Biological, Radiological Officer

CBRS Canadian Bond Rating Service (Montreal); Child Behavior Rating Scale; Citizen's Band Radio Service

CBRTGW Canadian Brotherhood of Railway, Transport, and General Workers

cbrw chemical, biological, radiological warfare

cbs chronic brain syndrome; concrete-block stucco

cb's citizen's-band transceivers

cBs concerned Black students

CBs cost-of-living benefits

CBS Central Bureau of Statistics (Jerusalem); Columbia Broadcasting System; Common Beliefs Survey; Commonwealth Bureau of Soils; Confraternity of the Blessed Sacrament; Currumbin Bird Sanctuary (Queensland); Custom Bucket Service

cbse caboose

CBSO City of Birmingham Symphony Orchestra; City of Bournemouth Symphony Orchestra; Czechoslovak Broadcasting Symphony Orchestra

cbt cesium beam tube; criminal breach of trust

CBT Chicago Board of Trade; Computer-Based Testing; Connecticut Bank and Trust (company)

CBT Centre Belge de Traductions (French—Belgian Translations Center)

CB & TC Connecticut Bank & Trust Company

CBTE Competency-Based Teacher Education

cbts cesium beam time standard

cbu cluster bomb unit

CBU Chicago Board of Underwriters

c/bush cents per bushel

cbv central blood volume; circulating blood volume; corrected blood volume

CB-VD citizen's-band radio-contracted venereal disease

(resulting from sexual pickups made along byways and highways)

CBVHS Clara Barton Vocational High School

cbw chemical-biological warfare

cbx's (CBXs) computerized business exchanges (telephone service)

cby carboy

cc camp chair; carbon copy (or copies); centuries; chapters; close control; closed cup; closing coil; cognitive complexity; color code; combustion chamber; command and control; complex conjugate; condemned cell; contrasting color; cubic centimeter(s)

cc (CC) chief complaint

c/c center to center

c & c carpets and curtains; consultation and concurrence

c of c cost of construction

c-to-c center-to-center

c.c. corpora cardiaca (Latin—cardiac body)—heart

c/c compte courant (French); *conta corrente* (Portuguese); *conto corrente* (Italian); *cuenta corriente* (Spanish)—current account

Cc cirrocumulus

Cc. Confessores (Latin—Confessors)

CC Calvin Coolidge (30th President U.S.); Clare College (Cambridge); Community College

C-C Coca-Cola

C & C Columbia & Cowlitz (railroad); Command and Control; Computer and Communications

C-by-C Come-by-Chance, Newfoundland

C of C Conclave of Cardinals; Count(y) of Cleves

CC corriente continua (Spanish—direct current)

CC-106 Canadair version of the Britannia called Yukon

CC-109 Canadian-built medium-range transport designed by General Dynamics and known as the Cosmopolitan

CC-115 Canadian twin-engine turboprop transport called the Buffalo

cca carrier-controlled approach; cellular cellulose acetate (plastic)

CCA Cacchetti Council of America; California Central Airlines; California Correctional Association; Camp and

Cabin Association; Canadian Construction Association; Chief of Civil Affairs; Circuit Court of Appeals; Citizens for Clean Air; Citizens' Councils of America; Cleaning Contractors Association; Colorado Correctional Association; Comics Code Authority; Committee for Conventional Armaments; Commonwealth Correspondents Association; Community Concerts Association; Community Corrections Act; Conquest of Cancer Act; Conservative Clubs of America; Consumers Cooperative Association; Container Corporation of America; Continental Control Area; Coordinating Committee on Alcoholism; Corduroy Council of America; Crafts Council of Australia; Cruising Club of America; Current Cost Accounting

C & CA Consumer and Corporate Affairs (Canada)

CCAA Cement and Concrete Association of Australia

CCAB Canadian Circulation Audit Board

CCAC California College of Arts and Crafts

CCAD Commerce and Consumer Affairs Department

CCAE California Council for Adult Education

CCAF Commander-in-Chief—Atlantic Fleet; Community College of the Air Force

CCAHC Central Council for Agricultural and Horticultural Cooperation; Central Council for Agricultural and Horticultural Cooperatives

CCAIA California Council of the American Institute of Architects

CCAIT Community College Association for Instruction and Technology

CCAM Colby College Art Museum

ccap communication capability application program

CCAP Citizens Crusade Against Poverty

CCAQ Consultative Committee on Administrative Questions (UN)

CCAR Central Conference of American Rabbis

CCAs California Correctional Association members; Cruising Club of America members

CCAS Council of Colleges of Arts and Sciences

ccat conglutinating complement absorption test

CCATS Communications, Command, and Telemetry Systems

cca unit chicken-cell agglutination unit

ccb command control block; convertible circuit breaker; cubic capacity of bunkers

CCB California Canadian Bank; command-and-control boat (naval symbol); Configuration Control Board; Criminal Courts Building

CCBD Council for Children with Behavioral Disorders

cc black conductive channel black

CCBM Copper Cylinder and Boiler Manufacturers

CCBO Cape Clear Bird Observatory (Ireland)

CCBS California Canadian Banks

ccbv central circulating blood volume

CCBW Commission on Chemical and Biological Warfare

ccc central computer complex; command control console; computer-command control

CCC California Conservation Corps; Canadian Chamber of Commerce; Car Care Council; Central Community Center; Central Control Commission; Central Criminal Court; Chopin Cultural Center; Christ Church College; Civil Construction Corps; Civilian Conservation Corps; Columbian Carbon Company; Commercial Credit Corporation; Commissioner's Coordination Council; Commodity Credit Corporation; Commodity Credit Corporation; Commonwealth Credit Corporation; Community Care Center; Consumer Credit Counselors; Copyright Clearance Center; Corning Community College; Corpus Christi College; Crime and Correction Commission; Crime and Correction Committee; Customs Cooperation Council; Cuyahoga Community College

CC & C Command Control and Communications (USAF)

CCC Consejo de Cooperación Cultural (Spanish—Council of Cultural Cooperation)—of the

Council of Europe

C.C.C. Constitutio Criminalis Carolina (Latin—Carolingian Criminal Code)

CCCA Classic Car Clubs of America; Conservative Christian Churches of America

CCCB Component Change Control Board (DoD)

CCCC Cape Cod Community College; Conference on College Composition and Communication

CCCCO Chicago Coordinating Council of Community Organizations

CCCCSA California Community College Community Service Association

CCCD California Commission of College Districts

CCC-FID Central Classification Committee—Fédération Internationale de Documentation

CCC Highway Cleveland-Columbus-Cincinnati Highway

CCCI Computer Control Company, Inc

CC circuit common-collector amplifier for junction transistors

CCCJ California Council on Criminal Justice

cccl cathodal closure clonus

CCCN Customs Cooperation Council Nomenclature

CC Co Commercial Cables Company

CCCP California Coalition for Capital Punishment; Citizens Crime Commission of Philadelphia; Council on Cooperative College Projects

CCCP (Russian transliteration —USSR)—*Soyuz Sovetchikh Sotsialisticheckikh Respublik* (Union of Soviet Socialist Republics)

CCCPS Chicago College of Chiropody and Pedic Surgery

CCCR Communications and Command Control Requirements

CCCS Concerned Citizens for Community Standards; Consumer Credit Counseling Services

CCCT California Community College Trustees

ccd charge-coupled device; computer-controlled display

ccd (CCD) charge-coupled device

CCD Center for Curriculum Development; Confraternity of

Christian Doctrine; Cost Center Determination; Criminal Conspiracy Division

CCDA Commercial Chemical Development Association

CCDB Canadian Car Demurrage Bureau

CCDC Central Citizens' Defence Committee; Centre City Development Corporation; Commission on Crime, Delinquency, and Corrections (Nevada)

CCDN Central Council for District Nursing

cce carbon-chloroform extract

CCE California Cooperative Extension; Casa de la Cultura Ecuatoriana (House of Ecuadorian Culture); Council for a Competitive Economy

CCEBS Committee for the Collegiate Education of Black Students

CCED County Council Electoral Division

ccei composite cost-effectiveness index

CCEM Comprehensive Career Education Model

CCES Catholic Church Extension Society

CCET Carnegie Commission on Educational Television

CCETT Centre Commun d'Etudes de Télévision et de Télécommunication (French —Public Center for the Study of Television and Telecommunication)

ccf cephalin-cholesterol flocculation; compound comminuted fracture; congestive cardiac failure; chronic cardiac failure; concentrated complete fertilizer

CCF Canadian Commonwealth Federation; Citizens Council Forum; Combined Cadet Force; Common Cold Foundation; Congressional Clearinghouse on the Future; Cooperative Commonwealth Federation; Credit Commercial de France

CCFA Combined Cadet Force Association

CCFC Citizens Committee for a Free Cuba

ccfe commercial customer-furnished equipment

CCFG California Contemporary Fashion Guild

ccfm cryogenic continuous-film memory

ccfr constant current flux reset

CCG Canadian Coast Guard; Choral Conductors Guild; Control Commission of Germany

CCGB Cycling Council of Great Britain

CCGE California Council for Geographic Education

CCGEA Community College General Education Association

CCGNY Community Council of Greater New York

CCGS Canadian Coast Guard Service; Canadian Coast Guard Ship

ccgt closed-cycle gas turbine

cch cubic capacity of holds

Cch Christchurch, New Zealand

CCH Chaminade College of Honolulu; Commercial Clearing House; Computerized Criminal Histories

C of CH Chief of Chaplains

CCHE California Coordinating Council for Higher Education; Central Council for Health Education; Coordinating Council for Higher Education

CC-HEW Clinical Center— HEW

CCHF Children's Country Holidays Fund

CCHK Crown Colony of Hong Kong

CCHPP California Council for the Humanities in Public Policy

cc/hr cubic centimeters per hour

CCHS Christopher Columbus High School; Computerized Criminal Histories System (FBI)

cci chronic coronary insufficiency; circuit condition indicator; concentric coordinate incident; corrugated, cupped, or indented (cargo)

CCI Community Concerts, Incorporated; Computer Consoles Inc; Connecticut Correctional Institution; Conservative Caucus, Inc

CCI Central Campesina Independiente (Spanish—Independent Peasant Central)—political party in Mexico

CCIA Consumer Credit Insurance Association

CCIAP Cooperative Committee on Interstate Air Pollution (New Jersey-New York)

ccib computerized central information bank

CCIB Chinese Commodities Inspection Bureau; Computerized Central Information Bank; Cook County Inspection Bureau

ccig cold cathode ion gage

CCIL Commander's Critical Item List (USA)

CCINC Cabinet Committee for International Narcotic Control

ccip continuously computed impact point (USAF)

CCIR Comité Consultatif International de la Radiodiffusion (French—International Consultative Committee on Broadcasting)

CCIs Citizens Committee of Investigation members (investigating assassination of President Kennedy)

CCIS Command Control Information System

CCIT California Council for International Trade

CCITT Consultative Committee in International Telephone and Telegraph

CCIW Canada Centre for Inland Waters

CCJ Center for Correctional Justice (Harvard Law School); Center for Criminal Justice (Washington, D.C.); Circuit Court Judge; Cook County Jail (Chicago); County Court Judge

CCJC Canadian Centre for Justice Statistics; Chicago City Junior College; Cook County Junior College; Custer County Junior College

CCJCA California Community and Junior College Association

CCJO Consultative Council of Jewish Organizations

cck (CCK) cholecystokinin

CCK Centre College of Kentucky

cck-pz (CCK-PZ) cholecystokinin-pancreozymin

cckw counterclockwise

CCL Canadian Congress of Labour; Caribbean Cruise Lines; Commissioner for Crown Lands; Commodity Control List; Council for Civil Liberties

CCl$_4$ carbon tetrachloride

C-clamp C-shaped clamp

C-class Soviet C-class nuclear-powered submarines nicknamed Charlies by NATO; undersea boats capable of under-water missile launchings against other submarines and surface ships

CCLC Cooperative College Library Center

c clef alto clef (on the third line); soprano clef (on the first line); tenor clef (on the fourth line)

CC List Critical Condition List

cclkws counterclockwise

CCLM Coordinating Council of Literary Magazines

CCLN Council for Computerized Library Networks

CCLP Cabinet Council on Legal Policy

ccl's criminal criminal lawyers

CCLs Court of Claims

CCLS Canadian Council of Library Schools

ccm cubic centimeter(s); counter-countermeasure(s)

ccm *Kubikzentimeter* (German—cubic centimeter)

CCM California College of Medicine; Canadian Cycle Manufacturers; Caribbean Common Market

CCMA Canadian Council of Management Association; Community College Media Association

ccmc coincident-current magnetic core

CCMC College-Conservatory of Music of Cincinnati; Cross-Country Motor Club

ccmd continuous-current monitoring device

CCMD Chicago Contract Management District

cc/min cubic centimeters per minute

CCMP Coalition of Concerned Medical Professionals

CCMR Central Contract Management Region

CCMS California College of Mortuary Science; Chicago Chamber Music Society; Committee on the Challenges of Modern Society (NATO)

ccmt catechol-O-methyl transferase

CCMTC Crown Cork Manufacturers' Technical Council

ccmv (CCMV) cowpea chlorotic-mottle virus

ccn coronary care nurse; coronary care nursing

CCN Command Control Number; Community of the Cross of Nails; Companhia Colonial de Navegação (Colonial Navigation Company); Contract Change Notice; Contract Change Notification

CCNA Canadian Community Newspapers Association

CCNDT Canadian Council for Non-Destructive Testing

CCNI Cía Chilena de Navegación Interoceanica (Spanish—Chilean Interoceanic Navigation Company)

CCNM Chaco Canyon National Monument

CCNP Callao Cave National Park (Luzon, Philippines); Carlsbad Caverns National Park (New Mexico)

CCNR Citizens Committee on Natural Resources; Consultative Committee for Nuclear Research

CCNS Cape Cod National Seashore (Massachusetts)

CCNSC Cancer Chemotherapy National Service Center

CCNV Community for Creative Non-Violence

CCNWR Cross Creeks National Wildlife Refuge (Tennessee)

CCNY Carnegie Corporation of New York; City College of the City University of New York

cco current-controlled oscillator

Cco Curaçao

CCO Chicago College of Osteopathy; Clandestine Communist Organization; Commonwealth Communications Organization; Comprehensive Certificate of Origin

CCOA California Correctional Officers Association; County Court Officers' Association; Crafts Council of Australia

CCOC Command Control Operations Center (USA)

CCOFI California Cooperative Oceanic Fisheries Investigations

c conc cast concrete

CCOS Cabinet Committee on Opportunity for the Spanish Speaking

CCOU Construction Central Operations Unit

ccp control change proposal; credit card purchase

ccp conto corrente postale (Italian—current postal account)

CCP Caribbean Conservation Program; Central Cataloging Project; Chinese Communist Party; Code of Civil Procedure; Code of Criminal Procedure; Commonwealth Centre Party; Consolidated Cryptologic Program; Cultural Center of the Philippines

ccpa cloud chamber photographic analysis

CCPC Community Crime-Prevention Centers

CCPE Canadian Council of Professional Engineers

CCPF Commander-in-Chief—Pacific Fleet

CCPG Chemical Corps Proving Ground

CCPI California Consumer Price Index

cc-pill compound-cathartic pill

CCPIT China Commission for the Promotion of International Trade

CCPL Corpus Christi Public Library

CCPO Central Civilian Personnel Office

CCPO *Comité Central Permanent de l'Opium* (French—Permanent Central Opium Committee)

CCPOA California Correctional Peace Officers Association

CCPOST California Commission on Peace Officer Standards and Training

CCPP Citizen Commission on Pension Policy

ccpr coherent cloud physics radar

CCPR Central Council of Physical Recreation

CCPS Consultative Committee for Postal Studies, Council of Commonwealth Public Service

CCPSHE Carnegie Council on Policy Studies in Higher Education

CCPSO Council of Commonwealth Public Service Organisations

ccr closed-cycle refrigerator; combat crew; command control receiver; complex chemical reaction; computer character recognition; consumable case rocket; control circuit resistance; credit card reader; cross-channel rejection; crystal can relay; cube corner reflector

C_{cr} creatinine clearance

CCR Central Commission for the Navigation of the Rhine; Commission on Civil Rights; Contract Change Request

CCRB Civilian Complaint Review Board

CCRB *Cooperatief Centraal Raiffeisen-Boerenleenbank* (Dutch—Raiffeisen's Central Cooperative Farmer's Loan

Bank)—largest bank in the Netherlands

CCRDC Chemical Corps Research and Development Command

CCRE Canadian Council for Research in Education

CCRESPAC Current Cancer Research Project Analysis Center

CCRF City College Research Foundation

CCRKBA Citizens Committee for the Right to Keep and Bear Arms

CCRMA Center for Computer Research in Music and Acoustics (Stanford University)

ccros card-capacitor read-only storage

C Cr P Code of Criminal Procedure

CCR & R covenants, conditions, restrictions, and reservations

CCRs Covenants, Conditions, and Restrictions (affecting apartment, condominium, and town-house dwellers)

CCRS Canadian Centre for Remote Sensing

ccrt cathodochromic cathode-ray tube

CCRT Check Collectors Round Table

ccru complete crew

CCRU Common Cold Research Unit

ccs central computer and sequencer; collective call sign; column code suppression; command, control, support (military function), computer control station(s); custom contract service(s)

cc's carcasses

cc & s central computer and sequencer

Ccs Caracas (inhabitants called Caraqueños)

CCs Community Centers; Community Colleges

CCS Cape Cod System; Caracas, Venezuela (Maiquetia Airport); Casualty Clearing Station; Catholic Community Service; Center for Chinese Studies (University of California); Center for Cuban Studies; Chemical Corporation of Singapore; Chief Commissary Steward; Church of Christ, Scientist; Civil Communications Section; Combined Chiefs of Staff; Controller of Communication Services; Council of Communication

Societies; Customer Conversion Statistics

CCSA Canadian Committee on Sugar Analysis; Community College Service Association; Community College Student Association

CCSB Credit Card Service Bureau

CCSC Central Connecticut State College; Central Coordinating Staff, Canada

CCSEA Council of the Church of Southeast Asia

cc/sec cubic centimeters per second

ccsem computer-controlled-scanning electron microscope

ccsep cement-coated single epoxy

CCSF City College of San Francisco

CCSL Communications and Control Systems Laboratory

CCSN Center City Shelter Network

CCSO Corpus Christi Symphony Orchestra

ccsr cash-to-common-stock ratio

CCSS Charles Camille Saint-Saëns; Cleveland-Cliffs Steamship (company)

CCSSO Council of Chief State School Officers

CCST Chelsea College of Science and Technology

cct cathodal closing tetanus; chocolate-coated tablet; controlled cord traction

CCT Clarkson College of Technology; Combat Control Team; Cumberland College of Tennessee

C & CT Chemistry and Chemical Technology

CCTA Central Computer and Telecommunications Agency; Community College Trustees Association

CCTC Chinese Cultural and Trade Center; Columbia County Teachers College

ccte cathodal closure tetanus

CCTE Canadian Council of Teachers of English

cctep cement-coated triple epoxy

CCTF California Correctional Training Facility

CC & TI Community College and Technical Institute

cctks cubic capacity of tanks

CCTP Center City Transportation Program; Coronary Care Training Project

CCTS Canaveral Council of Technical Societies; Combat Crew Training School

CCTT Cornell Critical Thinking Test

cctv closed-circuit television

CCTWg Combat Crew Training Wing (USAF)

ccu chart comparison unit; color-control unit; coronary care unit

ccu (CCU) cardiac care unit; coronary care unit; correctional custody unit (U.S. naval vessel's brig or jail)

Ccu Calcutta

C-C u Cherry-Crandall units

CCU Calcutta, India (airport); California Conservative Union; Community College Unit; Cooperative Care Unit; Council for Canadian Unity

CCUDA Community College Urban District Association

CCUL California Credit Union League

CCUN Collegiate Council for the United Nations

CCURR Canadian Council on Urban and Regional Research

CCUS Chamber of Commerce of the United States

c/cut crosscut

ccv closed-circuit voltage; coolant control valve

ccv (CCV) control-configured vehicle

ccw carrying a concealed weapon; channel command word; counterclockwise

CCW Caldwell College for Women; Circulation Control Wing; Citizens Crime Watch; Combat Crew Wing

CCWA Consultative Commission on Workers Affairs

cc wr hdr canvas-covered wire-rope handrail

ccws counterclockwise

ccxd computer-controlled X-ray diffractometer

ccy currency

cd caesarean delivery; candela; canine distemper; cash discount; center door; certificate of deposit; civil defense; coin dimpler; cold drawn; communicable disease; confidential document; conjugate diameter (pelvic inlet); contagious disease; convulsive disorder; convulsive dose; cord; countdown; curative dose

cd (CD) compact disc; compact-disc player; compact-disc re-

cord(ing); companion dog

c-d countdown

c/d cash against documents; cigarettes per day; cigars per day

c/d (C/D) carried down (bookkeeping); certificate of deposit

c & d carpets and drapes; censorship and documents; collection and delivery

cd *cadde* (Turkish—street); *corriente directa* (Spanish—direct current)

c.d. *conjugata diagonalis* (Latin—diagonal conjugate)—pelvic inlet diameter

Cd cadmium; caudal; coefficient of drag

C $ cordoba (Nicaraguan monetary unit)

Cd *ciudad* (Spanish—city)

CD Canadair turboprop airplane; Civil Defense; coastal defense radar (for surface-vessel detection); communicable disease; Community Development; confidential document; *Corps Diplomatique* (French—Diplomatic Corps); Corrections Department (New Mexico); Corrections Division (Hawaii, Oregon); countdown

C.D. Chancery Division

C/D Consular Declaration; Customs Declaration

C & D Chemist and Druggist; collection and delivery

CD *Centre de Détention* (French—Detention Center); *Centre Démocrate* (French—Democratic Center); *Computer Design*

C & D *Crime and Delinquency*

cd₅₀ median curative dose (abolishing symptoms in 50 percent of all test cases)

Cd₁₁₅ radioactive cadmium

cda chain data address; command and data acquisition

cda (CDA) chenodeoxycholic acid

CDA California Dietetic Association; Canadian Dental Association; Canadian Dietetic Association; Catholic Daughters of America; Child Development Association; Compañía Dominicana de Aviación (Dominican Aviation Company); Control Data Australia; Copper Development Association

CD Act(s) Contagious Diseases Act(s)

CDAE Civil Defense Adult Education

Cd A Eng Commissioned Air Engineer

CD Aim Commissioned Airman

Cd Airn Commissioned Airman

Cdale Carriedale

CDAP Civil Defense Auxiliary Police

CDARC Chelsea Drug Addiction and Research Centre

CDAS Civil Defense Ambulance Service

C Day Lewis Nicholas Blake

cdb caliper disk brake; capacitance decode box; cast double base; central data bank; could be; current data bit

Cd B Commissioned Boatswain

CDB Caribbean Development Bank; Combat Development Branch

cdba clearance divers breathing apparatus

CDBA California Dining and Beverage Association

cdbd cardboard

CDBG Community Development Block Grant

CD/BMI Columbus Division/Battelle Memorial Institute

Cd Bndr Commissioned Bandmaster

cdc calculated date of confinement; call direction code; career development course; command and data-handling console

CDC Cadaver Disposal Center; California Debris Commission; California Democratic Council; Canada Development Corporation; Caribbean Defense Command(er); Center for Disease Control; Certificate of Disposition of Classified Documents; Cesspool Detergent Chemistry; Citizens' Defense Corps; Civil Defense Coordinator; Civil Defense Council; Combat Development Command; Command Destruct Control; Commissioners of the District of Columbia; Commonwealth Development Corporation; Communicable Disease Center; Configuration Data Control; Control Data Corporation; Control Distribution Center; Criminal Diagnostics and Counseling

C.D.C. Commonwealth Development Corporation (formerly Colonial Development Corporation)

CDC Centro de Documentação Científica (Portuguese—Scientific Documentation Center)

CDCA chenodeoxycholic acid

cdce central data-conversion equipment

CD circuit common-drain circuit for field-effect transistors

cdcm carbon-dioxide concentration module

Cd Cmy O Commissioned Commissary Officer

Cd C O Commissioned Communications Officer

Cd Con Commissioned Constructor

CDCP Construction and Development Corporation of the Philippines

CDCR Center for Documentation and Communication Research; Control Drawing Change Request

CDCs Community Development Corporations

CDCS Civil Defense Countermeasures System; Construction Dollar Control System

CDCT Centro de Documentación Científica y Técnica (Spanish—Center of Scientific and Technical Documentation)—Mexico City

cdd central data display; chart distribution data; coded decimal digit; color data display; command-destruct decoder; computer-directed drawing; cosmic dust detector; cratering demolition device

CDD Certificate of Disability for Discharge

cddd comprehensive dishonesty, disappearance, and destruction (insurance policy)

cddi computer-directed drawing instrument

CDDP Canadian Department of Defense Production

cde carbon dioxide economizer; contamination - decontamination experiment

cde (CDE) canine distemper encephalitis

CDE Central Document Exchange; Cornell-Dubilier Electronics

C.D.E. Certificate in Data Education

C de C (CDC) Canyon de Chelly

CDEE Chemical Defense Experimental Establishment

C de F Collège de France (College of France)

C de G Croix de Guerre (French—War Cross)

CDEG Chicago District Electric Generating Corporation

CDEI Control Data Education Institutes

C de J Compañía de Jesus (Spanish—Company of Jesus)—Society of Jesuits

cdek computer data entry keyboard

Cd El O Commissioned Electrical (Electronic) Officer

C del S Corriere della Sera (Evening Courier—Milan)

C-de-N Côtes-de-Nord

Cd Eng Commissioned Engineer

CDEOS Civil Defense Emergency Operations System

CDER Center for Death Education and Research

cdf command decoder film; command decoder filter; confined detonating fuse; constant current fringes; continuous desk file

CDF California Department of Forestry; Canadian Department of Forestry; Children's Defense Fund; Civil Defence Force; Colorado Department of Forestry; Community Development Foundation; Connecticut Department of Forestry

CDFA California Dried Fruit Association

CDFC Commonwealth Development Finance Company

CDFGI Charles Darwin Foundation for the Galápagos Islands

CD film camouflage detection film

cdfr (CDFR) commercial demonstration fast reactor

CDFRS Charles Darwin Foundation Research Station (Academy Bay, Santa Cruz, Galápagos)

CDFS Chief of Defence Force Staff

CDFSB Canadian Dairy Foods Service Bureau

cd/ft² candela per square foot

cd fwd carried forward

Cdg Cardigan; Cardiganshire

CDG Coder-Decoder Group (USA)

CDGA California Date Growers Association

CD & GB TC Chicago, Duluth and Georgian Bay Transit Company

Cd Gr Commissioned Gunner

Cd Gr O Commissioned Gunnery Officer

cdh constant differential height

CDH College Diploma in Horticulture

CDHS Comprehensive Data-Handling System

cdhv could have

cdi course deviation indicator

cdi (CDI) capacitor discharge ignition

CDI Center for Defense Information; Children's Depression Inventory; Classified Defense Information; Comprehensive Dissertation Index; Contractor Demonstration Inspection

CDIC Canada Deposit Insurance Corporation

Cd In O Commissioned Instructor Officer

C Dip F & A Certified Diploma in Finance and Accounting

c div cum dividend

Cd J Ciudad Juárez (inhabitants —Juaristas)

CDJ California Department of Justice

CDJ Comité de Défense des Juifs (French—Committee of the Defense of Jews)

cdk containers (carried on) deck

c$k consumer's survival kit (consumer-oriented educational tv program)

cdl common display logic

Cdl Cardinal

CDL Central Dockyard Laboratory (UK); Citizens for Decency through Law; Citizens for Decent Literature; Country and Democratic League

CDLC Canadian Dental Laboratory Conference

cdm contributing to the delinquency of a minor

CDM Consolidated Diamond Mines (South Africa)

cd/m² candela per square meter

cdma code division multiple access

Cd M-a-A Commissioned Master-at-Arms

CDMB Civil Defense Mobilization Board

CDMMA Canadian Direct Mail Marketing Association

CDMSWA Consolidated Diamond Mines of South-West Africa

CDN Chicago Daily News

CDNAC Canadian Daily Newspaper Advisory Council

CDNPA Canadian Daily Newspaper Publishers Association

CDNRA Coulee Dam National Recreation Area (Washington)

CDNS Chicago Daily News Service

cdnt could not

cdo (CDO) chronic drunkenness offender

Cd O Commissioned Officer

C-d'O Côte-d'Or

CDO California Disaster Office; Civil Defense Organization; Community Development Office(r)

Cd Ob Commissioned Observer

Cd O E Commissioned Ordnance Engineer

CDOGS Council for the Defence of Government Schools

Cd O O Commissioned Ordnance Officer

cdos controlled date of separation

cdo(s) commando(s)

cdp checkout data processor; communications data processor; contract definition phase

CDP Centralized Data Processing; Certified Data Plan; Critical Decision Point

C.D.P. Certificate in Data Processing

CDPA Civil Defense Preparedness Agency

cdpc central data-processing computer

CDPC California Delinquency Prevention Commission

CDPE Continental Daily Parcels Express

cd pl cadmium plate

cdp's comprehensive dwelling policies

cdr command-destruct receiver; composite damage risk (audiometry)

Cdr Commander

C d R Casa di Risparmio (Italian—Savings Bank)

CDR Change Design Request; Conceptual Design Report; Countdown Deviation Request; Critical Design Review(s)

CDR Comité Defensa Revolucionario (Spanish—Revolutionary Defense Committee)—Cuba's basic communist neighborhood organization

CDRA Canadian Drilling Research Association; Committee of Directors of Research Associations

CDRB Canadian Defense Research Board

CDRBTE Canadian Defense Research Board Telecommunication Establishment

CDRC Civil Defense Regional Commission(er)

Cdre Commodore

CDRF Canadian Dental Research Foundation

CDRI Central Drug Research Institute

cdrill center drill

Cdrngtn C Codrington College

Cd R O Commissioned Radio Officer

CDRS Charles Darwin Research Station

CDRSC Children's Depression Rating Scale for Classrooms

cds cards; cold-drawn steel; single cotton double silk (insulation)

cd's (CDs) certificates of deposit; compact-disc players; compact-disc record(ing)s—played by a laser beam

C d S Circolo della Stampa (Italian—Press Club); *Codice della Strada* (Italian—Highway Traffic Code); *Consiglio di Sicurezza* (Italian—Security Council)

CDs Catholic Documents

CDS California Dental Service; Center for Degree Studies; Civil Defence Services; Civil Defense Staff; Climatological Data Sheet; Commander, Destroyer Squadron

Cd S B Commissioned Signals Boatswain

cdse computer-driven simulation environment

CdSh Commissioned Shipwright

CDSHA Country Day School Headmasters Association

Cd S O Commissioned Supply Officer

CDSO Commonwealth Defense Service Organization

CDSP Church Divinity School of the Pacific

CDSP Current Digest of the Soviet Press

CDSs Civil Disobedience Squads

CDSS British Post Office trade mark covering telecommunications and telephonic apparatus, instruments, and installations; Compressed Data Storage System; Customers' Digital Switching System

CDST Central Daylight Saving Time

cdt command-destruct transmit-

ter; conduct; conductor

Cdt Cadet; Commandant

CDT Canadian Department of Transport; Central Daylight Time

CDT (ADA) Council on Dental Therapeutics (American Dental Association)

C.D.T. Certified Dental Technician

Cdte Comandante (Spanish—Commander)

CDTE Council for Distributive Teacher Education

Cdt Mid Cadet Midshipman

cdts constant-depth temperature sensor

cdu cable distribution unit; central display unit

CDU Cable Distribution Unit; Civil Disobedience Unit; coastal defense (radar) unit; Computer Display Unit

CDU Christlich-Demokratische Union (German—Christian Democratic Union)—political party

CDUEP Civil Defense University Extension Program

cdv cadaver; *carte de visite* (visiting card, sometimes with photograph); computed dollar value; current domestic value

Cdv Commonwealth dollar value

CDV Civil Defense Volunteer(s)

cdvr cadaver

cdw charge density wave; chilled drinking water

CDW Civil Defense Warning; Collision Damage Waiver

CD & W Colonial Development and Welfare

Cd Wdr Commissioned Wardmaster

cdwe could we

Cd W O Commissioned Writer Officer

c dwr chest of drawers; chilled drinking water return

CDWS Civil Defense Wardens Service

cdwt cordwelt

cdx control differential transmitter

cdz concordant zone

Cdz Cádiz

ce carbon equivalent; career education; center of effort (naval architecture); center entrance; circular error; compression engine; constant error; consumption entry; counterespionage; critical examination; cum entitlement

ce (CE) counterespionage

c-e communications-electronics

c/e custom entry

c & e commission and exchange; customs and excise

c of e coefficient of elasticity

c.e. caveat emptor (Latin—let the buyer beware); *curvêe extra* (French—special sort)—special quality

Ce Ceará; cerium; Ceylon

CE Canada East; Chief Engineer; Chief Executive; Christian Endeavor; Church of England; circular error; Common Era; compass error; Corps of Engineers; cost effectiveness; Counselor of Embassy; Customer Engineer

C-E communications electronics

C.E. Chemical Engineer; Civil Engineer

C/E Chancellor of the Exchequer; Chief Engineer

C of E Church of England; Corps of Engineers

CE Chemical Engineering

C.E. Christian Era; Civil Engineer

cea circular error average

cea (CEA) carcinoembryonic antigen

CEA Canadian Education Association; Canadian Electrical Association; Canadian Export Association; Captain's Endowment Association (police); Childbirth Education Association; Classified Employees Association; College English Association; Combined Educational Associations; Combustion Equipment Associates; Commodity Exchange Authority; Connecticut Educational Association; Conservation Education Association; Cooperative Education Association; Correctional Education Association; Council of Economic Advisers; Council of Engineering Associations; County Employees Association

CEA Commissariat à l'Energie Atomique (French—Atomic Energy Commission)

CEAA Center for Editions of American Authors; Council of European-American Associations

CEAC Commission for European Airspace Coordination; Consulting Engineers Association of California

CEAC Commission Europêenne de l'Aviation Civile (French—European Civil Aviation Commission)

CEAFU Concerned Educators Against Forced Unionism

CEAN Community Energy Action Network

CEANAR Commission on Education in Agriculture and National Resources

CEAPD Central Air Procurement District

CEARC Computer Education and Applied Research Center

CEAT Canadian English Achievement Test

ceb cryogenic expulsive bladder

Ceb Cebu

CEB Central Electricity Board; Continuing Education Books

CEB Comitê Electrotechnique Belge (Belgian Electrotechnical Committee)

cebar chemical, biological, radiological warfare

CEBS Certified Employee Benefit Specialist; Church of England Boys' Society; Commonwealth Experimental Building Station

Ceb-Vis Cebu-Visayan

CEC California Energy Commission; Canadian Electrical Code; Central Economic Committee; Ceramic Educational Council; Chief Executive Commissioner; Civil Engineer Corps; Coal Experts Committee; Commission of the European Communities; Commodity Exchange Commission; Commonwealth Economic Committee; Commonwealth Edison Company; Communications and Electronics Command; Consolidated Edison Company; Consolidated Electrodynamics Corporation; Consulting Engineers Council; Continental Entry Chart(s); Correctional Economics Center; Council for Exceptional Children

CECA Communautê Europêenne du Charbon et de l'Acier (French—European Coal and Steel Community); *Comunidad Europea del Carbon y del Acero* (Spanish—European Coal and Steel Community)

CECC California Educational Computer Consortium

Cece Cecil

CECEW Catholic Education

Council for England and Wales (often truncated to CEC —Catholic Education Council)

CECH Citizenship Education Clearinghouse

Cechy (Czechoslovakian—Bohemia)

CECIL Compact Electronic Components Inspection Laboratory

CE circuit common-emitter amplifier for junction transistors

CECLA Comisiôn Especial de Coordinaciôn Latinoamericana (Special Commission for Latin American Coordination)

Cecoslovacchia (Italian—Czechoslovakia)

CECR Center for Environmental Conflict Resolution; Central European Communication Region (USAF)

CECs California Ecology Corpsmen

CECS Church of England Children's Society; Communications Electronics Coordinating Section

CECS Comisiôn Especial de Consulta sobre Seguridad (Spanish—Special Commission for Security Consultation)

ced capacitance electronic disc; communications - electronics doctrine; computer entry device

c-e-d carbon-equivalent-difference

c & ed clothing and equipment development

Ced Ceda; Cedomil; Cedric; Cedron

CED Committee for Economic Development; Communautê Europêenne de Defense (European Defense Community); Communications - Electronics Doctrine (USAF manuals)

CED Centro Elletronnico di Documentazione (Italian—Electronic Documentation Center)—in Rome

CEDA California Economic Development Agency; Canadian Electrical Distributors Association

CEDA Confederaciôn Española de Derechas Autonomas (Spanish—Spanish Confederation of Autonomous Rights) —right-wing Catholic-fascist party

cedac central differential analyzer control; cooling effect detection and control

CEDAL Centro de Estudios Democráticos de America Latina (Latin American Center of Democratic Studies)

CEDAM Conservation, Exploration, Diving, Archeology, Museums (organization)

CEDAR Council for Educational Development and Research

Cedar Breaks Cedar Breaks National Monument in Utah's Wasatch Mountains

Cedar Crest executive mansion of the governor of Kansas and eponym for executive government throughout the state

CEDDA Center for Experimental Design and Data Analysis

CEDI Centre Européen de Documentation et d'Information (French—European Documentation and Information Center); *Centro Europeo de Documentación e Información* (Spanish—European Documentation and Information Center)

CEDIC Church Estates Development and Improvement Company

CEDO Centre for Educational Development Overseas (UK)

CEDPA California Educational Data Processing Association

ced's captured enemy documents

cee computer-enhanced education

CEE Center for Environmental Education; Central Engineering Establishment; Certificate of Extended Education; Common Entrance Examination; Cultural Environment Emergency

CEE Comunidad Económica Europea (Spanish—European Economic Community)

CEEA Communauté Européenne de l'Energi Atomique (European Atomic Energy Community)

CEEB College Entrance Examination Board

CEEC Council for European Economic Cooperation

CEECC Consolidated-Edison Energy Control Center

Ceece Cecil

Cee Cee Claudia Cardinale

CEEED Council on Environment, Employment, Economy, and Development

ceefax see the facsimile; see the facts

CEEP Centre Européen d'Etudes de Population (French—European Center for Population Studies)

CEev Central European encephalitis virus

cef cellular-expansion factor; chicken-embryo fibroblasts

CEF Canadian Expeditionary Force; Children's Emergency Fund(ing); Citizens for Educational Freedom; Citizens for Energy and Freedom

C of EF Count(y) of East Friesland Country

CEFA Council for Educational Freedom in America

ceff controlled energy flow forming

CEFP Council of Educational Facility Planners

CEFT Children's Embedded Fissures Test(ing)

CEFTRI Central Food Technological Research Institute

CEG Coalition for Economic Growth

CEGB Central Electricity Generating Board

CEGGS Church of England Girls' Grammar School

CEGJA Coalition to End Grand Jury Abuse

CEGS Church of England Grammar School

CEHHS Charles Evans Hughes High School

CEHS Civilian Employee Health Service

cei contract end item

CEI Claremont Economics Institute; Cleveland Electric Illuminating Company; Commission Electrotechnique Internationale (International Electrotechnical Commission); Communications-Electronics Instruction; Cost Effectiveness Index; Council of Engineering Institutions

C & EI Chicago & Eastern Illinois (railroad)

CEI Chemical Engineering Index; *Commision Electrotechnique Internationale* (French—International Electrotechnical Commission)

CEIC Commission on Excellence in Education (U.S)

CEIF Community Employment Initiatives Fund; Council of European Industrial Federations

Ceilán (Spanish—Ceylon)

cein contract end-item number

CEIP Carnegie Endowment for International Peace; Communications-Electronics Implementation Plan

C-E-I-R Corporation for Economic and Industrial Research

CEIS California Education Information System; Cost and Economic Information System

ceisd customer engineering instruction system diagram

CEIWT Central Europe Inland Waterways Transport (NATO)

cej cement-enamel junction

CEJEDP Central Europe Joint Emergency Defense Plan (NATO)

CEJNSA Council of European and Japanese National Shipowners Associations

cel celluloid; cellulose

c-e-l carbon-equivalent-liquid

Cel Celeban; Celebes; Celsius

CEL Constitutional Educational League; Cryogenics Engineering Laboratory

cel acet cellulose acetate

CELADE Centro Latinoamericano de Demografía (Latin American Demographic Center)

CELDS Computerized Environmental Legislative Data System

celeb celebrate; celebration; celebrity

Celebes (see *Sulawesi*)

celebs celebrities

Celery Capital Kalamazoo, Michigan; Sanford, Florida; San Ysidro, California

Celery City Kalamazoo, Michigan

Celestial City John Bunyan's name for Heaven described in his *Pilgrim's Progress*; old traveller's name for China's capital city—Peking

Celestial Empire Chinese Empire

Celia Cecilia

Celine Louis-Ferdinand Destouches

celintrep accelerated intelligence report

cell celluloid

CELL Case Existological Laboratories Limited; Continuing Education Learning Laboratory

celli cellos (violoncellos)

Cellini Benvenuto Cellini (three-act opera by Berlioz but nicknamed *Malvenuto* by its critics)

Cellist - Conductor - Composer Pablo Casals

Cellist-Conductors Barbirolli, Casals, Herbert, Kindler, Rostropovitch, Toscanini, Wallenstein (to mention seven within the author's memory)

'cellist(s) violoncellist(s)

cello violoncello

cellulose $(C_6H_{10}O_5)$

celnav celestial navigation

cel nitr cellulose nitrate

celo chicken embryo lethal orphan (virus)

CELOS Centrum voor Landbouwkundig Onderzoek in Suriname (Dutch—Center for Agricultural Research in Surinam)

cels (Cels) celsius

CELS Continuing Education for Library Staffs

cel sheet cellulose (plastic) sheet

CELSS Closed Ecological Life Support System

celt classified entries in lateral transposition

Celt Celtic

CELT Comprehensive English Language Test(ing)

Celtic Fringe Celtic peoples of Cornwall, Ireland, Scotland, and Wales on the fringe of England

Celts Celtic peoples (Bretons, Cornish, Gaels, Irish Gaelics, Manx, Scots Gaelics, etc.)

celtuce celery-lettuce (lettuce-derived vegetable whose stalks taste like celery)

cem cement; cement asbestos; cemetery; communication-electronics and meteorological

CEM Council of European Municipalities

CEM Confederación Evangelical Mundial (Spanish—World Evangelical Confederation)

CEMA Canadian Electrical Manufacturers Association; Connecticut Educational Media Association; Conveyor Equipment Manufacturers Association; Council for Economic Mutual Assistance; Council for the Encouragement of Music and the Arts

CEMAA Council for Egg Marketing Authorities of Australia

cem ab cement asbestos board

cemad coherent echo modulation and detection

cemb cembalo (Italian—harpsichord)

CEMB Communications-Electronic-Meteorological Board (USAF)

CEMCO Continental Electronics Manufacturing Company

Cement City Allentown, Pennsylvania

cemf counter-electromotive force

cem fl cement floor

c-e mix chloroform-ether mixture

CEMLA Centro de Estudios Monetarios Latinoamericanos (Center of Latin American Monetary Studies)

CEMO Command Equipment Management Office

cemon customer engineering monitor(ing)

cem p cement paint

CEMPIMS Communications Electronics Meteorological Program Implementation Management System (USAF)

cem plas cement plaster

CEMR Canadian Energy, Mines, and Resources

CEMREL Central Midwestern Regional Educational Laboratory

CEMS Church of England Mens' Society

CEMT Conferencia Europea de Ministros de Trasporte (Spanish—European Conference of Ministers of Transport)

cen center; central; centralization; centralize

Cen Cenozoic; Centaurus (constellation)

CEN Captive European Nations; Central Airlines

CEN Comité Européen de Coordination des Normes (European Committee of the Coordination of Standards)

CENA Coalition of Eastern Native Americans

CENACO Centro Nacional de Computación (Spanish—National Computation Center)

Cenacolo Il Cenacolo (Italian—Refectory, Supper Room)—another name for the tempera masterpiece of Leonardo da Vinci—*L'Ultima Cena*—The Last Supper

CENAMEC Centro Nacional para el Mejoramiento de la Enseñanza de la Ciencia (Spanish—National Center for

the Betterment of the Teaching of Science)—Venezuelan society

CENCOMMURGN Central Communications Region

CENCOMS Center for Communication Sciences (USA)

CENDES Centro de Enseñanza para el Desarollo (Spanish—Center of Learning for Development)

CENDHRRA Center for the Development of Human Resources in Rural Asia

CENDIT Centre for Development of Instructional Technology

CENEUR Compañía Española de Navegación Marítima

CENFAM Centro Nazionale di Fisica dell'Atmospera e Meteorologia (Italian—National Center of Physics of the Atmosphere and Meteorology)

C Eng Chartered Engineer; Chief Engineer

CENIM Centro Nacional de Investigaciones Metalúrgicas (Spanish—National Center for Metallurgical Research)

cenog computerized electro-neuro-ophthalmograph

cens censor; censorship

CENS China Economic News Service

censor. centrifugal solids recovery

Censor of the Age Thomas Carlyle

cent. centrifugal; century

cent. centum (Latin—hundred)

Cent Centaurus; Century

CENTA Committee for Establishing a National Testing Authority

centac(s) central tactical report(s)

CENTACS Center for Tactical Computer Sciences (USA)

CENTAG Central European Army Group

centen centennial

Centennial(s) Coloradan(s)

Centennial State Colorado's official nickname recalling the state was admitted a century after the *Declaration of Independence* was signed.

Center of Austria Salzburg

Center of the Copper Circle Tucson, Arizona

Center of the Nation Topeka, Kansas

Center of Scenic America Utah

Center of the Sunshine State Pierre, South Dakota

centi 10⁻²

CENTO Central Treaty Organization (Great Britain, Iran, Pakistan, Turkey)

central (French—middle)

Central African Empire formerly the Central African Republic created from the Ubangi Shari territory of French Equatorial Africa; its Banda and Baya tribes speak some French and mine diamonds

Central America land between Colombia and Mexico (Belize, Costa Rica, El Salvador, Guatemala, Honduras, Nicaragua, and Panamá)

Central America Day Central American Independence Day (September 15) in Costa Rica, El Salvador, Guatemala, Honduras, and Nicaragua

Central American States (seven republics—north to south) Belize, Guatemala, Honduras, El Salvador, Nicaragua, Costa Rica, Panamá

Central Bureau Amsterdam's old section (taken over by junkies, porn club owners, prostitutes, and criminals from Surinam) for illegal & illicit activities

centrale (Italian—middle)

Central Powers Austria-Hungary; Bulgaria; Germany, and Turkey (in World War I)

Central Prairie Province Saskatchewan

Central Provinces Ontario and Québec

Central State Kansas

centrex central exchange

cents. centuries

cent(s) céntimo(s); one-hundredth of a peseta

Centurion British tank carrying a crew of 4 and guns up to 105mm

Century of Confusion the 9th century when the Carolingian empire of Charlemagne disintegrated; European unity dismembered and divided—the 800s

Century of the Exodus the 13th century before the Christian era when Moses lead the Israelites out of Egypt and across the Red Sea—the 1200s

ceo chick embryo origin

ceo (CEO) chief executive officer

CeO Chairman ex-Oficio

CEO Chief Education Office(r); Chief Engineer's Office; Chief

Executive Officer

CEOA Central European Operating Agency

CEOAS Corps of Engineers Office of Appalachian Studies (USA)

CEOED Compact Edition of the Oxford English Dictionary

CEOs Chief Executive Officers (conglomerate and multinational corporations)

CEOSL Confederación Centroamericana de Organizaciones Sindicales Libres (Spanish—Central American Confederation of Free Trade Unions)

cep circle of equal probability; circle of error probability

'cep' except

Cep Cepheus

CEP Capability Evaluation Plan; Chicano Education Project; Civil Emergency Planning (NATO); Color Evaluation Program; Concentrated Employment Program; Continuing Education Program; Council on Economic Priorities

CEPA Chicago Educational Publishers Association; Civil Engineering Program Applications; Consumers Education and Protective Association

CEPACS Customs Entry Processing and Cargo System

CEPAL Comisión Económica Para América Latina (Spanish—Economic Commission for Latin America)—UNs ECLA

CEPB Civil Emergency Planning Bureau (NATO)

CEPC City of Erie Port Commission

CEPC Comité Européen pour les Problèmes Criminels (French—European Committee on Crime Problems)

CEPD Career Education Planning District; Council for Economic Planning and Development

CEPDs Communications Electronics Policy Directives (NATO)

CEPE Central Experimental and Proving Establishment; Corporación Estatal Petrolera Ecuatoriana (Ecuadorian State Petroleum Corporation)

CEPEX Controlled Ecosystem Pollution Experiment

CEPG Cambridge Economic Policy Group

Ceph Cepheus

cephal (Latin prefix—head)—cephalic

ceph floc cephalin flocculation (test)

CEPM Center for Educational Policy and Management

CEPO Central Engineering Projects Office (NATO); Corps of Engineers—Portland, Oregon

CEPR Center for Educational Policy Research

ceps civil engineering problems

CEPS Central Europe Pipeline System (NATO); Commonwealth-Edison Public Service; Cornish Engines Preservation Society

Cepsa Compañía Española de Petróleos (Spanish Petroleum Company)

'cept accept; except

CEPT Conférence Européenne des Administrations des Postes et des Télécommunications (French—European Conference of Posts and Communications)

CEPTA Committee to End Pay Toilets in America

'cepted accepted; excepted

'cepting accepting; excepting

'ception deception; exception; perception; reception

cept(s) concept(s); precept(s)

CEQ Council on Environmental Quality (appointed by the President of the United States)

CEQA California Environmental Quality Act

ceqom combined electron quench and optical masker

cer ceramic; conditioned emotional response

c & er combustion and explosives research

CER Center for Educational Reform; Certification Evaluation Review; Combat Effectiveness Report; Community Educational Resource

CERA/ACCE Canadian Educational Researchers Association/Association Canadienne des Chercheurs en Education

ceram ceramic; ceramicist; ceramics

ceramal ceramic + alloy

Ceramic City East Liverpool, Ohio

CERB Coastal Engineering Research Board (USA)

cerc centralized engine-room control

CERC Coastal Engineering Research Center; Coastal Engineering Research Council

CERCA Commonwealth and Empire Radio for Civil Aviation

Cerdeña (Spanish—Sardinia)

CERDS Charter on the Economic Rights and Duties of States

Cer.E. Ceramic Engineer

Cereal City Battle Creek, Michigan, and Cedar Rapids, Iowa, claim this title

cerebro (Latin prefix—brain)—cerebral, cerebrospinal fluid

CERES Center for Research and Education in Sexuality

CERI Center for Educational Research and Innovation; Clean Energy Research Institute (University of Miami)

CERIC Central ERIC

CERL Central Electricity Research Laboratories; Coastal Engineering Research Laboratory; Cooperative Educational Research Laboratory

CERLAL, Centro Regional para el fomento del Libro en America Latina (Spanish—Regional Center for the Development of Books in Latin America)

cermet ceramic-metallic (powders fused to form solid nuclear fuel elements)

CERN Center for Nuclear Research

CERN Commission Européenne pour la Recherche Nucléaire (French—European Commission for Nuclear Research)

CEROILFOOD China National Cereals, Oils, and Foodstuffs Import and Export Corporation

CERP Current Economic Reporting Program

CERP Centre Européen des Relations Publiques (French—European Center of Public Relations)

CERR Commonwealth Employees Redeployment and Retrenchment

cerro(s) [Spanish—hill(s); mountain(s)]

CE/RRT Central Europe Railroad Transport (NATO)

cert certificate; certify

CERT Communications Effectiveness Response Test; Cost-Effective Rapid Transit; Council of Energy Resources Tribes

CE/RT Central Europe Road Transport (NATO)

certif certificate(d)

cert inv certified invoice

certs certificates

cerv cervical

ces central excitatory state; compressor end seal; constant elasticity of substitution; constructive error source

Ces (German—C-flat)

CEs Council of Europe members

CES California Employment Security; Closed Ecological System; Commercial Earth Station; Commonwealth Education Scheme; Commonwealth Employment Service; Comprehensive Export Schedule; Conference on European Security; Consolidated Electronic Services; Cost Effectiveness Study; Cost-Effectiveness Study; Council for European Studies; Crew Escape System

CES Certificat d'Etudes Supérieures (French—Advanced Studies Certificate)

CESA Canadian Engineering Standards Association; Commercial Education Society of Australia; Cooperative Educational Service Agency

CESAALA Charles E. Stevens American Atheist Library and Archives (Austin, Texas)

CESAME Commonwealth Employment Service Animated Memory

CESAR Capsule Escape and Survival Applied Research

CESAR Compagnie d'Etudes des Stations Air-Route (French—Company for the Study of Airfields)

CESC Calcutta Electric Supply Corporation

cescmi computer evaluation of scanning electron microscopic image

cesi closed-entry socket insulator

CESI Council for Elementary Science International

cesk cable end-sealing kit

Ceskoslovensko (Czechoslovakian—Czechoslovakia)

CESMM Civil Engineering Standard Method of Measurement

CESO Canadian Executive Service Overseas; Civil Engineer Support Office (USN)

CESO-W Council of Engineers and Scientists Organizations—West

c esp con espressione (Italian—

with expression)

CESP Centrais Electricas de São Paulo

cesr conduction electron spin resonance

CESR Canadian Electronic Sales Representatives

cess assess; assessment; cessation; cession(aire); cessionary; cessment; cesspipe; cesspit; cesspool; success

cess. cesspit; cesspool; excrement

Cess Cecil

CESS Council of Engineering Society Secretaries; Crew Escape Subsystem

CESSAC Church of England Soldiers, Sailors, and Airmens Clubs

Cessna 180 6-passenger utility aircraft

Cessna 185 6-passenger utility aircraft called the Cessna 185 E Skywagon

Cessna 310 6-passenger aircraft designated U-3

Cessna FR-172 French four-place rocket launcher aircraft built for counterinsurgency operations

Cesspool of Crime London or Paris around the turn of the century; New York today

Cesspool of Latin America Cayenne, French Guiana (or any other place in Latin America where the venality of the politicians operates to the detriment of human health and public welfare)

Cesspool of Pirates nickname of the John F Kennedy International Airport in New York where cargo thefts are the highest in the nation

CEST Career Education Study Trip(s)

Cestr Chester

Cestr. Cestrensis (Latin—of Chester)

cet capsule-elapsed time; controlled environmental test(ing); corrected effective temperature; cumulative elapsed time

Cet Centus; Cetus (constellation)

CET Center for Employment Training; Central European Time; Certified Electrical Technician; Certified Electronics Technician; Common External Tariff (European Communities); Council for Educational Technology

CET *Collèges d'Enseignement Technique* (French—Technical Education Colleges)

CETA Chinese-English Translation Assistance; Comprehensive Employment and Training Act

CETA *Centre d'Études pour la Traduction* (French—Center for the Study of Automatic Translation)

CETAG *Centre d'Études pour la Traduction, Grenoble* (French —Center for the Study of Translation, Grenoble)

CETAP *Centre d'Études pour la Traduction, Paris* (French — Center for the Study of Translation, Paris)

CETC Community and Education Center

CETC *Centro de Estudios Tecnicos* (Spanish—Center for Technical Studies)

CETDC China External Trade Development Council

CETEC Consolidated Engineering Technology Corporation

CETEDOC *Centre de Traitement Electronique des Ducments* (French—Center of Electronic Treatment of Documents)

CETEKA *Ceskoslovenskà Tiskovà Kancelàr* (Czechoslovakian Press Bureau)

CETEM Comprehensive Elementary Teacher Education Models

CETEX Committee on Contamination of Extra-Terrestrial Exploration (NASA)

CETF Clothing and Equipment Test Facility (USA)

ceti communications with extra-terrestrial intelligence

CETIS Centre de Traitement de l'Information Scientifique (Center for Processing Scientific Information)

CETME *Centro de Estudios Tecnicos de Materiales Especiales* (Spanish—Center of Technical Studies of Special Materials)

CETO Center for Educational Television Overseas

cet. par. *ceteris paribus* (Latin—other things being equal)

CETS Church of England Temperance Society; Commission on the Education of Teachers of Science; Contractor Engineering and Technical Services

ceu continuing education unit

CEU Christian Endeavor Union; Constructional Engineering Union

CEUCA Customs and Economic Union of Central Africa

CEUs Continuing Education Units

CEUSA Committee for Exports to the U.S.A.

Ceuta Spanish name for the Moorish city of Sebta

cev cryogenic explosive valve

cevat combined environmental, vibration, acceleration, temperature

cevi contract exhibit vendor item

cew circular electric wire

CEW Church-Employed Women

cewrm communications-electronics war-readiness materiel

cex charge exchange; civil effects exercise

CEX Corn Exchange Bank (stock-exchange symbol)

Cey Ceylon; Singhalese

CEY Century Electric (stock-exchange symbol)

CEYC Church of England Youth Council

Ceyl Ceylon

Ceylon Sri Lanka in Sinhala, the official language of the Ceylonese or Sinhalese inhabiting this Indian Ocean country off the southern tip of India

Cey Rs Ceylon rupees

cf calf binding; carried forward; carrier frequency; carry forward; cement floor; center of flotation; center forward; central files; central filing; centrifugal force; communication factor; complement fixation; conception formulation; conditional freedom; continuous focusing; contract formulation; corrugated furnaces; cost and freight; counterfire; counting fingers; cystic fibrosis

c/f carried forward

c & f clearing and forwarding; cost and freight

c-to-f center-to-face

cf. *confer* (Latin—compare)

c.f. *cantus firmus* (Latin—fixed song)

Cf californium

Cf. *Confessor* (Latin—Confessor)

CF Cape Fear (railroad); Chaplain to the Forces; Chief of Finance; Coastal Frontier; Colorado Fuel & Iron (stock-exchange symbol); Common-

wealth Fund(ing); Conservation Foundation; Consolidated Freightways; Corresponding Fellow

C/F Contract Formulation

C of F Chief of Finance

CF *Chemin de Fer* (French—Railroad); *Club de Fútbol* (Spanish—Football Club)

CF-5 Canadian version of the F-5 jet fighter

CF-86 Australian-built Canadian version of the F-86 jet fighter called Sabre

CF-100 Avro two-seat jet interceptor called the Canuck

CF-101 Canadian-built version of the F-101 jet interceptor named Voodoo

CF-104 Canadian version of the F-104 interceptor called Starfighter

cfa complement-fixing antibody; configural frequency analysis; cowl flap angle; crossed-field amplifier

cFa complete Freund's adjunct

CFA Canadian Federation of Agriculture; Canadian Football Association; Canadian Forestry Association; Canadian Freight Association; Chartered Financial Analyst; Clearing and Forwarding Agents; Colonies Française d'Afrique; Commission on Fine Arts; Commonwealth Firemen's Association; Community Facilities Administration; Consumer Federation of America; Correctional Facilities Association; Council for Foreign Affairs; Country Fire Authority

CF & A Chief of Finance and Accounting (USA)

C & FA Cookery and Foods Association

CFA *Colonies Française d'Afrique* (French Colonies of Africa)

CFAA Circus Fans Association of America

c factor cleverness factor

CFAD Commander, Fleet Air Defense

CFADC Canadian Forces Air Defence Command; Controlled Fusion Atomic Data Center

cfae contractor-furnished aerospace equipment

CFAE Council for Financial Aid to Education

CFAE *Centre de Formation en Aérodynamique Expérimentale* (French—Training Center for Experimental Aerodynamics)

CFAF California Financial Aid Form

CFAL Current Food Additives Legislation

CFAP Canadian Foundation for the Advancement of Pharmacy

cfar constant false alarm rate

CFAT Carnegie Foundation for the Advancement of Teaching

CFAW Canadian Food and Allied Workers

CFB California Farm Bureau; Canadian Forces Base; Commonwealth Forestry Bureau; Consumer Fraud Bureau; Council of Foreign Bondholders

cf black conductive furnace black

CFBS Canadian Federation of Biological Societies

CFBT Canadian Forces Base Toronto

cfc campus-free college; capillary filtration coefficient; colony-forming cells; complex facility console

cfc (CFC) chlorofluorocarbon

cf & c cost, freight & commission

CFC Citizens for a Free Cuba, Combined Federal Campaign (USA); Committee for a Free China; Consolidated Freight Classification

CFCA Canterbury Farmers Cooperative Association

cfcb card feed circuit breaker

CFCC Canadian Forces Communications Command

CFCF Central Flow Control Facility

cfd control functional diagram; cubic feet per day

CFD Consumer Fraud Division

CFDA Catalog of Federal Domestic Assistance

CFDC Canadian Film Development Corporation

CFDT Confederation Française et Democratique du Travail (French Democractic Confederation of Labor)

CFDTS Cold-Flow Development Test System (AEC)

cfe contractor-furnished equipment

CFE Canadian Forces Europe; Central Fighter Establishment; College of Further Education

CFE Comisión Federal de Elec-

tricidad (Spanish—Federal Electricity Commission)

CFEME Canadian Forces Environmental Medicine Establishment

cff computer forms feeder; counter flip-flop; critical flicker frequency

Cff Cardiff

CFF Commission for the Future; Compensatory Financing Facility

CFF Chemin de Fer Fédéraux (Swiss Federal Railroad)

cffc counterflow film cooling

CFFC Catholics For a Free Choice

cfg cubic feet of gas

CFG Camp Fire Girls

cfgd cubic feet of gas per day

cfgh cubic feet of gas per hour

cfgm cubic feet of gas per minute

cfh cubic feet per hour

CFH Council on Family Health

CFHO Canada-France-Hawaii Observatory

CFHQ Canadian Forces Headquarters

CFHS Canadian Federation of Humane Societies

cfi cost, freight, and insurance

CFI Canadian Film Institute; Canadian Forest Inventory; Chief Flying Instructor; Committee on Foreign Intelligence (CIA); Corporate Financial Instruction; Counselor Function Inventory; Court of First Instance

CF & I Colorado Fuel and Iron

CFI Corporación Financiera Internacional (Spanish—International Finance Corporation) —IFC

CFIA Cavity Foam Insulation Association; Center for Independent Action; Component Failure Impact Analysis

CFIAB Canadian Federation of Insurance Agents and Brokers

CFIP Chamber of Furniture Industries of the Philippines

CFIT Culture Fair Intelligence Test(ing)

cfl context-free language

CFL Canadian Football League; Carnegie Free Library; Chemins de Fer Luxembourgeois (Luxembourg State Railways); Consolidated Fertilizers Limited; Container Fleets Limited

cflg counter flashing

cfm chlorofluoromethane; con-

firm; confirmation; confirmed; cubic feet per minute; cubic feet per month

CFM Canterbury Frozen Meat (New Zealand); Council of Foreign Ministers

CFMA Central Financial Management Activities

CFMC Consumer-Farmer Milk Cooperative

CFMUA Cotton Fire and Marine Underwriters Association

CFN Compagnie France-Navigation

CFNI Caribbean Food and Nutrition Institute

CFNP Community Food and Nutrition Programs

cfo calling for orders; coast for orders

Cfo Channel for orders; Coast for orders

CFO Chief Fire Officer; Commonwealth Fisheries Offices; Complex Facility Operator

CFOA Chief Fire Officers Association

cfp cold frontal passage; computer forms printer; contractor-furnished property; cystic fibrosis of the pancreas

CFP Common Fisheries Policy; Consumer Fraud Protection

CFP Colonies Française du Pacifique; Compagnie Française des Pétroles; Cours du Franc Pacifique (French Pacific francs)

CFPC College of Family Physicians of Canada

CFPF Central Food Preparation Facility (USA)

CFPO Compagnie Française des Phosphates de l'Océanie

CFPS Central Food Preparation System (USA)

CFPTS Coalition For Peace Through Strength

cfr catastrophic failure rate; chauffeur; crash fire rescue

CFR Center for Future Research; Code of Federal Regulations; Contact Flight Rules; Coorong Fauna Reserve (South Australia); Council on Foreign Relations

CFRC Canadian Forces Recruiting Centre

CFR engine Cooperative Fuel Research (Council) engine (for measuring quality of fuels)

cfrg carbon-fiber-reinforced glass

cfrgc carbon-fiber-reinforced glass ceramic

cfrp carbon fiber reinforced

plastic
CFRPA California Fire Rescue and Paramedic Association
CFRS Central Fisheries Research Station
cfs completely-finished sets; cubic feet per second
cf's confessions of fornication (colonial-style abbreviation originating in Massachusetts and used before the American Revolution)
C f's Christian fanatics (who murdered their fellow men during the Crusades of the 11th, 12th, and 13th centuries; during the Sicilian Vespers in 1282; in the Religious Wars in the late 1500s; in the Saint Bartholomew's Day Massacre in 1572; during the Spanish Inquisition lasting from 1487 to 1834; during the Puritan Revolution in England in the 1640s; the Polish, Romanian, and Russian pogroms from the 1880s to the early 1900s; Hitler's holocaust in the 1930s and 1940s; the present-day; troubles in Northern Ireland where Christian fanatics continue to kill one another in the name of Christ, etc.)
CFS Canadian Forestry Service; Central Federal Savings; Central Flying School; Container Freight Station; Contract Field Service
CFS *Chemins de Fer Fédéraux Suisses* (French—Swiss Federal Railways)
CFSA College Food Service Association
CFSC Canadian Forces Staff College
CFSR Commission on Financial Structure and Regulation (White House); Contract Funds Status Report
CFSTI Clearinghouse for Federal Scientific and Technical Information
cft clinical full time; complement fixation test; craft; craftsman; cubic feet; cubic foot
CFT California Federation of Teachers; Colorado Federation of Teachers; Concept Formation Test; Cooperative Field Test(ing)
CFT *Compagnie Française de Télévision* (French Television Company)
CFTA Cattle Food Trade Association
CFTAU Canadian Friends of

Tel Aviv University
cftb controlled-flight test bed
CFTB Commonwealth Forestry and Timber Bureau
CFTC Commodity Failures Trading Commission; Commodity Futures Trading Commission; Commonwealth Fund for Technical Cooperation
c-f tests complement-fixation tests
CFTH Compagnie Française Thomson-Houston
cftmn craftsman
CFTR Citizens For The Republic (Reagan-type conservative Democrats and Republicans)
cfts captive firing test set(s)
CFTSD Canadian Forces Technical Services Detachment
cfu colony-forming units
CFU Central Functional Unit; Commonwealth Film Unit; Consumer Fraud Unit
cfv conventional friend virus
cfvd constant-frequency variable dot
CFWA Canadian Fruit Wholesalers Association
CFWI County Federation of Women's Institutes
CFWIS Central Fighter Weapons Instructor School
cfy clarify
CFZ Contiguous Fisheries Zone
cg cardiogreen; center of gravity; centigram; choking gas (phosgene); chorionic gonadotropin; chronic glomerulonephritis; colloidal gold
c/g coincidence guidance
c of g center of gravity
cg *Zentigram* (German—centigram)
CG Captain General; cargo glider aircraft (DoD symbol); Central of Georgia (railroad); Chaplain General; Coast Guard; Commanding General; Commissary General; Connecticut General (Life Insurance Company); Consul General; Covent Garden; guided-missile cruiser (naval symbol)
CG (ROH) Covent Garden (Royal Opera House)
C of G Central of Georgia (railway); College of Guam (Agaña)
CG *Consumer Guide; Croix de Guerre* (French—War Cross)
C G *cassa grande* (Italian—bass drum)
cga cargo (proportion of) general

average
CGA Canadian Gas Association; Coast Guard Auxiliary; Coat Guard Academy; Commonwealth General Assurance; Compressed Gas Association; Corcoran Gallery of Art
CGADC Commanding General, Air Defense Command
CGAIRFMLANT Commanding General, Air Fleet Marine Force, Atlantic
CGAS Coast Guard Air Station; Cornell Guggenheim Aviation Safety Center
CGB Canadian Geographic Board
cgc ceramic gold coating; critical grid current
CGC Coast Guard Cutter; Continental Grain Company
CGCARC Commanding General, Continental Army Command
CG circuit common-gate amplifier for field-effect transistors
cgd chronic granulomatous disease
cgd (CGD) cow grazing day (13.5 kg pasture matter or feed in average bale of hay)
cge carriage
CG & E Cincinnati Gas and Electric Company
CGE *Compagnie Générale d'Electricité* (General Electric Company)
cge fwd carriage forward
CGEL & PB Consolidated Gas, Electric Light and Power Company of Baltimore
C Gen Consul General
cge pd carriage paid; charge paid
cgf center of gravity factor; chemotaxis-generating factor; coarse-glass frit
CGF College of Great Falls
CGFA Columbus Gallery of Fine Arts; Consolidated Gold Fields of Australia
CGFMLANT Commanding General, Fleet Marine Force, Atlantic
cgfp calcined gross fission product
CGFSA Consolidated Gold Fields of South Africa
cgg continuous grinding gage
cgh computer-generated hologram
cgh (CGH) chorionic gonadotrophic hormone
CGH São Paulo, Brazil (Congonhas Airport)

C of GH Cape of Good Hope
CGHB Cape of Good Hope Bank
CGHSB Cape of Good Hope Savings Bank
cgi computer-generated imagery; corrugated galvanized iron; cruise guide indicator
CGI Chief Ground Instructor; Chief Gunnery Instructor; City and Guilds of London Institute
CGIAR Consultative Group on International Agricultural Research
CGIC Comisaria General de Investigación Criminal (Spanish —Commissariat General of Criminal Investigation)— Spain's Interpol office
CGIL Confederazione Generale Italiana del Lavoro (Italian General Confederation of Labor)—communist inspired
C.-girl call girl (prostitute); hundred-dollar girl
cgit compressed-gas-insulated tube
C G Jung Foun C G Jung Foundation for Analytical Psychology
cgk grid cathode capacitance
cgl center-of-gravity locator; continuous-gas laser; controlled ground landing, corrected geomagnetic latitude (CGL)
cgl (CGL) chronic granulocytic leukemia
CGL Canadian Gulf Line; Central Gulf Lines
CGL Confederazione Generale del Lavoro (Italian—General Confederation of Labor)
CGLAT Cassel Group Level of Aspiration Test
CGLI City and Guilds of London Institute
cg lkr cleaning gear locker
cgm centigram(s); ciliated groove to mouth
cgm (CGM) central gray matter
CGM Compagnie Genéral Maritime; Conspicuous Gallantry Medal
CGMA Covent Garden Market Authority
CGMIS Commanding General's Management Information System
cGMP cyclic GMP
CGMW Commission for the Geological Map of the World
cgn chronic glomerulonephritis
Cgn Cartagena, Colombia (British maritime abbreviation)

(*see* Ctg)
CGN Cologne, Germany (airport); nuclear-powered guided-missile cruiser (naval symbol)
CGNM Casa Grande National Monument
cgo cargo
Cgo Chicago
CGO Committee on Government Operations
Cgo Chkr Cargo Checker
cg/oq cerebral glucose oxygen quotient
CGOT Canadian Government Office of Tourism
CGOU Coast Guard Oceanographic Unit
cgp choline glycerophosphatide; chorionic growth hormone prolactin; circulating granulocyte pool; grid plate capacitance
CGP College of General Practitioners; Comparative Guidance and Placement Program
CGP Current Geographical Publications
CGPM Conférence Générale des Poids et Mesures (General Conference of Weights and Measures)
CGPP Comparative Guidance Placement Program
CGPU Canadian Government Purchasing System
CGPSq Cartographic and Geodetic Processing Squadron (USAF)
cgr captured gamma ray; crime on government reservation
CGRA Canadian Good Roads Association; Chinese Government Radio Administration (Taiwan)
CGRDO Coast Guard Radio
CGRLS Coast Guard Radio Liaison Station
CGRM Commandant General —Royal Marines
cgs centimeter gram second
CGS Canadian Geographical Society; Central Gulf Steamship (corporation); Chief of General Staff; Coast and Geodetic Survey; Council of Graduate Schools (in the U.S.)
C & GS Coast and Geodetic Survey
CGSA Carriage of Goods by Sea Act; Computer Graphics Structural Analysis
CGSAC Commanding General, Strategic Air Command
CGSB Canadian Government

Specifications Board
C & GSC Command and General Staff College
cgse centimeter-gram-second electrostatic
cgsfu ceramic glazed structural facing units
cgsm centimeter-gram-second-electromagnetic
CGSS Cryogenic Gas Storage System
CGSSC Columbia Gas Service Corporation
CGSTC Centro Giovanile Scambi Turistici e Culturali (Italian —Youth Center for Tourism and Culture)
cgsub ceramic glazed structural unit base
CGSUS Council of Graduate Schools in the United States
cgt capital gains tax(ation); chorionic gonadotropin; combustible gas tracer; gains tax(ation)
cgt (CGT) corrected geomagnetic time
CGT Compagnie Générale Transatlantique (French Line); *Confederación General del Trabajo* (Spanish—General Confederation of Labor); *Confederation du Travail* (French—General Confederation of Labor)
CGTA Companie Générale de Transports Aériens (Air Algeria)
CGTAC Commanding General, Tactical Air Command
CGTB Canadian Government Travel Bureau
CGTEL Coast Guard Teletype
CGTSF Compagnie de Télégraphie San Fils (French wireless company)
cgtt cortisone glucose tolerance test (CGTT)
cgtv (CGTV) command guidance test vehicle
cgu ceramic glazed units
CGU Canadian Geophysical Union
CGUSACOMZEUR Commanding General, United States Army, Communications Zone, Europe
CGUSARMC Commanding General, United States Army Materiel Command
CGUSCONARC Commanding General, United States Continental Army Command
CGUSFET Commanding General, United States Forces— European Theater

cgv critical grid voltage
cgvs ciliated groove to ventral sac
CGW Chicago Great Western Railway; Coast Guard Women
Cgy Cagayan de Oro
ch case harden; chain; change; chapter; chest; chief; child; choke; choline; church; coat hook
ch (CH) critical hours (when broadcast signals can cause interference)
c/h cards per hour
c & h cocaine and heroin; cold and hot
ch chambre (French—room); *cheque* (French, Portuguese or Spanish—check)
ch. chori (Latin—choruses)
Ch Channel; Chile; Chilean; China; Chinese; choreographer; Christchurch (New Zealand or Oxford or other); church; Clearinghouse
Ch. Chirurgiae (Latin—Surgery)
CH Camp Hospital; Carnegie Hall; Chicago Helicopter (airways); compass heading; concentration of hydrogen ions in moles per liter (symbol); Court House; Custom House; Switzerland (autoplaque)
C-H Crouse-Hinds; Cutler-Hammer
C.H. Companion of Honour
C and H California and Hawaiian Sugar Company
CH Confederatio Helvetico (Latin—Swiss Confederation)
CH₃COOH acetic acid
CH-46 Boeing-Vertol twin-rotor helicopter called Sea Knight
CH-47 Boeing-Vertol helicopter called Chinook
CH-53 Sikorsky heavy-assault helicopter called Sea Stallion
CH-54 Sikorsky crane helicopter called Sky Crane or S-64
CH-113 Canadian version of Boeing-Vertol helicopter designated CH-46 and called Labrador
cha cable-harness analyzer; congenital hypoplastic anemia; cyclohexylamine
cha (CHA) cyclohexylamine
Cha Chamaeleon (constellation); Charles
CHA California Hospital Association; Catholic Hospital Association; Chattanooga, Tennessee (airport); Chicago Helicopter Airways; Child Health

Association; Community Health Association
CHABA Committee on Hearing and Bio-Acoustics (US Army)
chabak chabakano (Philippine Spanish dialect)
C-habit cocaine habit
Chaco Canyon Chaco Canyon National Monument near Bloomfield, New Mexico
chacom chain of command
Chaconne Bach's Partita No. 2 in D minor for solo violin; or its transcription for the guitar of Segovia by Marc Pincherle; or for piano by either Brahms, Busoni, Mendelssohn, Raff, or Schumann; or for orchestra by Hubay, Stokowski, or Wilhelmj
chad code to handle angular data
Chad Chadburn; Republic of Chad (landlocked North African country formerly ruled by France but now by Sudanese Arabs who speak Arabic and some French, tribesmen produce cattle, cotton, and some fish taken from Lake Chad) *République du Tchad*
CHAD Combined Health Agency Drive
CHADS Chicago Air Defense Sector
Chafarinas Chafarinas or Zafarinas Islands (in the Spanish Mediterranean off Morocco and southeast of Melilla)
CHAFB Chanute Air Force Base
chaffroc (CHAFFROC) chaff rocket
Chagas-Cruz disease South American sleeping sickness
Chagos Chagos Archipelago
CHAIN California Housing, Action, and Information Network
Chair Chairman
Chairman Mao Mao Tse-Tung
Chairp Chairperson
chal challenge
chal chaleur (French—heat, warmth)
Chald Chaldean
CHALFA Charlottesville/Albemarle Foundation for the Encouragement of Artists
chalicos chalicosis (sickness caused by metallic-dust inhalation)
chalk calcium carbonate (CaCO₃)
Chalybon (Latin—Aleppo)
cham chamfer; champagne;

champion; combustion, heat, mass
Cham Chamaeleon
chamb chamber
Chamb Chamberlain
Chamb Ency Chamber's Encyclopaedia
Chambly Girls Girls' Cottage School (for delinquents) at Chambly, Québec
chammy (English slang—champagne)
champ champion(ship)
Champ Beauchamp
CHAMP Character Manipulation Procedure(s); Civilian Health and Medical Program; Community Health Air Monitoring Program
Champagne of Drugs cocaine (derived from the leaves of the coca shrub—*Erythroxylon coca*)—found in the highland valleys of Africa, Australia, and India as well as in South American lands such as Bolivia, Colombia, Ecuador, and Peru
Champ Intl Champion International
champion. compatible hardware and milestone program for integrating organizational needs
Champion of Darwin Thomas Henry Huxley
Champion of Education Horace Mann
Champion of Freethought President John F Kennedy who believed in an America where the separation of church and state is absolute and who renounced the appointment of an American ambassador to the Vatican and tax support of parochial schools
Champion of the Old South President John Tyler
Champions of Individualism John Stuart Mill and Herbert Spencer
Champion of States Rights John C. Calhoun—U.S. Senator from South Carolina
Champion of the Underdog Clarence Darrow
Champs Champs Elysées (French—Elysian Fields)—main boulevard of Paris
CHAMPUS Civilian Health and Medical Program of the Uniformed Services
CHAMPVA Civilian Health and Medical Program of the Veterans Administration
chan channel

Chan Channel

Chanc Chancellor; Chancery

CHANCE Complete Help and Assistance Necessary for College Education

Chance Personified Fortuna (Roman); Tyche (Greek)

CHANCOM Channel Command (NATO)

CHANCOMTEE Channel Committee (NATO)

Chandeleurs Chandeleur Islands of Louisiana

'change exchange; produce exchange; stock exchange

'Change Royal Stock Exchange in London

Chang Jiang (Pinyin Chinese—Yangtse River)

Channel The Channel (Beagle, Bristol, English, Old Bahama, Saint George's, Santa Barbara, Ten Degree, etc.)

Channel City Santa Barbara, California (on the Santa Barbara Channel)

Channel fever not a true fever but the name given the sense of excitement evident aboard ships approaching their home port or one well known for its recreational facilities

Channel Islands (ranked by area) Jersey, Guernsey, Alderney, Brechau, Great Sark, Little Sark, Herm, Jethou, Lihou

Channels Channel Islanders; Channel Islands

chans chunson (French—song)

CHANSEC Channel Committee Secretary (NATO)

Chans Jiang (Pinyin Chinese—Yangtse River)

Chanukka Hebrew Feast of Lights

CHAOS Committee for Halting Acronymic Obliteration of Sense; Consortium for the Hastening of the Annihilation of Organized Society

CHAOTIC Computer-and-Human-Assisted Organization of a Technical Information Center (NBS)

chap. chapter

Chap Chaplain

CHAP Certified Hospital Admissions Program; Charring Ablation Program (NASA); Child Health Assistance Program

Chapino(s) Guatemalan(s)

Chap(pie) Chapin; Chapman; Chappell

Chappiequack Chappaqua, New York's nickname

chaps. chaparajos (Spanish—open backed leather overall pants worn by cowboys and charros when riding through thorny country)

CHAPS Children Have A Potential Society; contractor-held Air Force property

Chapter 7 liquidation

Chapter 11, etc. (legal euphemism—bankruptcy)—Chapter 11, etc., of the Bankruptcy Act of the U.S.

char character; characteristic; charcoal; charwoman

char (CHAR) character (data processing)

Char Charter

Char Amal Charlotte Amalie

Charbray Charolais-Brahman cattle

charc charcoal

Charcot-Marie-Tooth disease muscular atrophy

Charger Convair multipurpose short takeoff-and-landing airplane

Charlotte British World War II medium tank armed with an 83.4mm gun

Charl Charlottenburg

Charlemagne (French—Charles the Great)

Charles Atlas Angelo Siciliano

Charles the Bald Charles I of France

Charles B. Child C Vernon Frost's nickname

Charles Blondin Jean François Gravelet (French acrobat who walked tightrope above Niagara River near Niagara Falls in 1855, 1859, 1860)

Charles Bronson Charles Buchinski

Charles Dalmorès Henry Alphonse Boin

Charles the Fat Charles II of France

Charles Island, Galápagos Floreana or Santa Maria

Charles J Kenney Erle Stanley Gardner

Charles the Simple Charles III of France

Charleston South Carolina's seaport city and name of West Virginia's capital

Charles University University of Prague

Charley Charles

Charley Car St Charles Avenue trolleycar; one of America's oldest and the last in New Orleans where there was a streetcar named Desire

Charley South Charleston, South Carolina

Charley West Charleston, West Virginia

Charlie Charles; letter C radio code; NATO name for Soviet C-class submarines built to launch missiles underwater against other submarines and surface ships

Charlie Chaplin Charles Spencer Chaplin

Charlot (Spanish—Charlie)—Charlie Chaplin

Charlotte Amalie capital of the American Virgin Islands on St Thomas; (pronounced *Charlotte Amal-e-uh*)—capital of the American Virgin Islands—for a short time was known as St Thomas

Charm Charmian

Charm Spot of the Deep South Mobile, Alabama

char reac character reaction (sometimes simply cr)

chars characters

char(s) charwoman; charwomen

chart. charta (Latin—paper)

chart. bib. charta bibula (Latin—blotting paper)

chart. cerat. charta cerata (Latin—waxed paper)

Charter Oak City Hartford, Connecticut, where the original charter was hidden in an oak tree to insure the liberty of the first settlers

Charter Oak State Connecticut

chartul. chartula (Latin—small paper)

Char X Charing Cross (rail terminal)

chas chassis

Chas Charles

CHAS Catholic Housing Aid Society

chase. cut holes and sink 'em (navalese acronym for sinking old ammunition cases or obsolescent barges or boats)

Chase Chase Manhattan Bank

Chasn Charlestown

Chat Choo-Choo Chattanooga Choo-Choo (restaurant)

Chatham Island, Galápagos San Cristóbal

chat mtg chattel mortgage

Chat(ty) Charlotte

Chau Chateau (French—castle, country mansion)

Chauc Geoffrey Chaucer

chaud chemical audit

chauf chauffeur

Chávez Jorge Chávez International Airport of Lima, Peru (named for the Peruvian aviator who was the first to fly over the Alps)

chb complete heart block

Chb Cherbourg; Chiba

Ch B Chief of Bureau

Ch.B. *Chirurgiae Baccalaureus* (Latin—Bachelor of Surgery)

chbd chalkboard

ChBuAer Chief of the Bureau of Aeronautics

ChBuDocks Chief of the Bureau of Yards and Docks

ChBuMed Chief of the Bureau of Medicine and Surgery

ChBuOrd Chief of the Bureau of Ordnance

ChBuPers Chief of the Bureau of Naval Personnel

ChBuSanda Chief of the Bureau of Supplies and Accounts

ChBuShips Chief of the Bureau of Ships

ChBuWeps Chief of the Bureau of Weapons

chc choke coil

CHC Chicago House of Correction; Christchurch, New Zealand (airport); Community Health Council; Comprehensive Health Center

ch cab china cabinet

CHCF Component Handling and Cleaning Facility

Chch Christchurch

Ch Ch Christ Church College, Oxford

CHCl₃ chloroform

CHCMD Chicago Contract Management District

chd chaldron; childhood disease(s); congestive heart disease; coronary heart disease

Ch D Charles Darwin

Ch.D. Chirurgiae Doctor (Latin —Doctor of Surgery)

C-H d Chediak-Higashi disease

CHD Charles Halliwell Duell

Ch d'A Chargé d'Affaires

CHDF Civilian Home Defense Force

chdl computer hardware description language

chdm cyclohexanedimethanol

che cholinesterase

che (CHE) channel end(ing)

c & he consumer and homemaking education

Che *Chetverg* (Russian—Thursday); Ernesto (Che) Guevara (from Argentina where *Che* is a popular nickname)

Cheᵉ *Chapelle* (French—Chapel)

Cʰᵉ *Chaine* (French—chain)

Ch E Chief Engineer

Ch.E. Chemical Engineer

CHE Chete Game Reserve; Chewore Game Reserve; Chizarira Game Reserve—(all in Rhodesia)

C-head coke head (underground slang—cocaine addict)

Cheaha Cheaha Mountain or Cheaha State Park south of Anniston, Alabama

CHEAP Computerized Health Education Assessment Program

cheapies cheap goods; cheap merchandise; cheap stocks

CHEAR Council on Higher Education in the American Republics

chec checked; checkered

CHEC Citizens Helping Eliminate Crime; Commonwealth Human Ecology Council

Checkpoint Charlie international frontier between East and West Berlin

Checo *Checoslovaquia* (Spanish —Czechoslovakia)

Checoslovaquia (Spanish— Czechoslovakia)

Cheesebox convict's nickname for the Illinois penitentiary at Statesville

cheesesan cheese sandwich

cheesewich cheese sandwich

Cheka *Chrezvychainaya Kommissiya po Borbe s Kontrrevolutisiei i Sabotazhem* (Russian —Extraordinary Commission for Combating Counterrevolution and Sabotage)—original Soviet Secret Police founded December 20, 1917, at Lubianka Prison in Moscow (*q.v.* —VOT)

CHEL *Cambridge History of English Literature*

Chelm (ancient Jewish town in Poland known in folklore as the Town of Fools); short form for Cheltenham

Chelmer native of Chelm (ancient Jewish town in Poland known in folklore as the Town of Fools)

Chelon Chelonia

cheloniol cheloniologic(al)(ly); cheloniologist; cheloniology

chelons chelonians (tortoises, terrapins, turtles)

Chelsea Gang John Dos Passos, Suzanne La Follette, Sinclair Lewis, Mary McCarthy, Ben Stolberg, and some of their friends who were among the first to expose the totalitarian nature of the USSR and the

tyranny of Stalin; many lived in the Chelsea Hotel in New York City and hence they were called the Chelsea Gang

Chelt Cheltenham

chem chemical; chemist; chemistry

Chem Chemistry

chemanal chemical analysis

Chem E Chemical Engineer(ing)

Chem.E. Chemical Engineer

Chem Econ Chemical Economic Services

Chem Ed Chemical Education Publishing Company

Chem Educ Chemical Education Publishing Co

Chem Elements Pub Chemical Elements Publishing Co

chem etch chemically etched; chemical etching

CHEMI Chemical Engineering Modular Instruction

chemly chemically

Chem & Met Eng *Chemical and Metallurgical Engineering*

chem mill chemically milled; chemical milling

Chemnitz Karl-Marx-Stadt

chemonuc chemonuclear

chemos chemosphere; chemospheric(al)(ly)

chemosens chemosensory

chemoster chemosterilant; chemosterilization; chemosterilize(d)

chemosurg chemosurgical(ly); chemosurgery

chemotax chemotaxonomic(al)(ly); chemotaxonomist; chemotaxonomy

chemoth chemotherapy

Chem Phys *Chemical Physics*

Chem Phys Lett *Chemical Physics Letters*

Chem Pub Chemical Publishing Company

Chem Rev *Chemical Reviews*

Chem Rubber Chemical Rubber Company

CHEMS Chemical Education Materials Study

chemsearch chemicals selected for equal, analogous, or related characters

chemsol chemical solution (for decontamination)

CHEMTREC Chemical Transportation Emergency Center

chem war. chemical warfare

CHEN *Chail Nashim* (Hebrew-Women's Force of the Israeli Army); *chen* is the Hebrew word for grace

Chengdu (Pinyin Chinese—

Chengtu)
Chenyang (Chinese—Mukden)
CHEOPS Chemical Operations System
CHEP Commonwealth Handling and Equipment Pool
Chequers British prime minister's country home
Cher Cherilyn; Cherilyn Sarkisian
Chernoye More (Russian—Black Sea)
Cherokee Rose Georgia state flower
Chero(s) Salvadoran(s)—person or people of El Salvador, Central America
chert ironstone sedimentary rock
Cherv Cherville; Chervin
Ches Cheshire
Cheskey(s) Czechoslovakian(s)
chesky cherry-flavored whiskey
Chester Conklin Jules Cowles
chester(s) (Early English—city, old fortification, town)—short form for such places as Manchester, Winchester, and even Tadcaster and Worcester
Chet Chester
chev chevron
Chev Chevalier (French—Knight)
Cheviots Cheviot Hills between England and Scotland
Chevron Standard Oil of California
Chev(y) Chevrolet
Chewko Chewing Tobacco Company
Chey Cheyenne
Cheyenne Wyoming's capital
chf congestive heart failure; critical heart flux
Chf Chief; Crimean hemorrhagic fever
Ch F Chaplain of the Fleet
CHF Carnegie Hero Fund; Coalition for Health Funding
CHFA California Housing Finance Agency
ch-factor chutzpah factor (degree of guts or nerve)
Chf Bkr Chief Baker; Chief Bookkeeper
CHFC Carnegie Hero Fund Commission
Chf Engr Chief Engineer
Chf Libr Chief Librarian
Chf M Sgt Chief Master Sergeant
Chf Off Chief Officer
Chf Pur Chief Purser
Chf Stwd Chief Steward
Chf Surg Chief Surgeon
Chf Wt Ofcr Chief Warrant Officer

chg change; charge
Chg Chittagong
CHGC Committee for Hand Gun Control
chgd charged
Chgo Chicago
chgph choreographer; choreographic; choreography
chg pl change plane
chgs charges
chh cartilage-hair hypoplasia
CH&H Continent between Havre and Hamburg
chi specific magnetic susceptibility
Chi Chicago; Chichester; China; Chinese
CHI Catastrophic Health Insurance; Chicago; Crouse-Hinds (stock-exchange symbol)
CHIA Canadian Health Insurance Association
CHIAA Crop-Hail Insurance Actuarial Association
chic cermet hybrid integrated circuit
Chic Chicago
Chicago Group poets and writers born in the Chicago area around 1900—Sherwood Anderson, Willa Cather, Floyd Dell, John Dos Passos, Theodore Dreiser, Finley Peter Dunne, James T Farrell, Francis Hackett, Harry Hansen, Ernest Hemingway, Vachel Lindsay, Archibald MacLeish, Edgar Lee Masters, Harriett Monroe, Frank Norris, Burton Rascoe, Carl Sandburg, and others if relatively nearby places are added to admit Kay Boyle, TS Eliot, Scott Fitzgerald, Sinclair, Lewis, Carl and Mark Van Doren (although Frank Norris was born in 1870, Sherwood Anderson and Willa Cather in 1876, and Carl Sandburg in 1878, they are included in the Chicago Group although somewhat older than the others named)
Chicagorican Chicago Puerto Rican
Chicano (diminutive nickname for *Mexicano* used by some Mexican-Americans in Arizona, California, Nevada, New Mexico, and Texas—formerly Mexican territory)
Chich Chichester
Chi-chi naval nickname for Christchurch, South Island, New Zealand
Chick Chickering

Chickadee state bird of Maine and Massachusetts
Chickasaw Sikorsky transport helicopter designated H-19 or UH-19
chickensand chicken sandwich
chickenwich chicken sandwich
chick(s) chicken(s)
Chico Francisco
Chicom Chinese communist
Chico Marx Leonard Marx
Chicos Chinese communists
Chi$ Chilean peso
Chidic Chinese dictionary
Chief Chief Engineer
CHIEF Controlled Handling of Internal Executive Functions
Chieftain British main battle tank armed with a 120mm gun
Chih Chihuahua (inhabitants—Chihuahuenses, chihuahua dogs characteristic of this area —chihuahueños)
chil children('s)
CHI-LAX Chicago—Los Angeles
Chil Cur Chilean Current
child. computer having intelligent learning and development
child. (CHILD) children having individual learning difficulties
Children of Joseph Israelites
Children of Pharoah Egyptians
Children's Children's Crusade (in 1212 when some 90,000 children from France and Germany set out to free the Holy Land from the Infidels, many thousands died enroute or were sold into slavery); Children's Opera [Hansel and Gretel *Hänsel und Gretel* by Engelbert Humperdinck (1854-1921)]
Chile Republic of Chile (Spanish-speaking South American nation of industrious people producing many export items such as precious metals and minerals as well as textiles and wines) *República de Chile*
Chilean First Chile's outstanding classical composer—Pedro Umberto Allende
Chilean Ports (large, medium, and small from north to south) San Juan Bautista, Arica, Iquique, Tocopilla, Antofagasta, Taltal, Valparaiso, San Antonio, Talcahuano, Coronel, Lota, Valdivia, Puerto Montt, Puerto Quellon, Punta Arenas

Chile Day Chilean Independence Day (September 18 and 19)

Chile's Principal Port Valparaiso

chilidog chile-con-carne sauced hotdog (frankfurter)

chili(es) chili pepper(s)

Chillicothe Institute Chillicothe Correctional Institute at Chillicothe, Ohio

Chillicothe School Training School for Girls at Chillicothe, Missouri

Chilterns Chiltern Hills of England

Chilton Chilton Book Company

chim chimica (Italian—chemistry)

Chimbo Chimborazo, Ecuador; Chimbote, Peru

Chi Met Chicago Metropolitan Correctional Center

CHI-MIA Chicago—Miami

Chimneyville Jackson, Mississippi

chimponaut chimpanzee astronaut (primate used in space travel experiments)

chimp(s) chimpanzee(s)

chin. chinchilla

Chin China; Chinese

Chin Chinese (world's leading language in terms of numbers as more than 788 million people speak either Mandarin Chinese in communist-controlled mainland China or Cantonese Chinese or Wu, Min, or Hakka Chinese, in nationalist offshore China—Taiwan—and in most overseas places—the language most often heard is Cantonese Chinese)

China People's Republic of China (communist-controlled mainland China whose Chinese speak Mandarin or official Chinese plus local dialects vast country larger than the United States but smaller than the USSR); Republic of China (nationalist offshore China on the island of Taiwan once known as Formosa plus islands such as Matsu, Quemoy, and the Penghus or Pescadores between Taiwan and the mainland, its people are among the most industrious and almost everyone works and produces)

china clay kaolin (hydrous aluminum silicate)

CHINALIGHT China National Light-Industry Products Import and Export Corporation (mainland China)

China Nac China Nacionalista (Spanish—Nationalist China) —offshore China also known as Formosa or Taiwan

China Sea(s) East China Sea and South China Sea

China's Largest Port Shanghai

China's Main Street *Yangtze Kiang* (Chinese—Yangtze River)

Chinat Chinese nationalist

CHINATEX China National Textiles Import and Export Corporation (mainland China)

CHINATIVE China National Native Produce (mainland China)

Chinatown Chinese quarter of any city outside mainland or offshore China

Chi Nats Chinese Nationalists

CHINATUHSU China National Trading Corporation (mainland produce and animal by-products)

china white synthetic heroin (often deadly)

Chine (French—China)

chinese eponymic prefix found in such things as chinese banana (dwarf banana), chinese cabbage (*pe-tsai*), chinese checkers (played with marbles on a star-shaped board), chinese gelatin (agar or isinglass), chinese glue (alcohol + shellac), chinese greens (chinese vegetables), chinese ink (india ink), chinese puzzle (any complicated or perplexing puzzle), chinese red (chrome red), chinese watermelon (wax gourd), chinese white (barium sulfate), chinese wood oil (tung oil)

chinese anesthesia acupuncture

Chinese Gordon British general Charles George Gordon who suppressed the Taiping rebels; later named Gordon Pasha for similar services in the Sudan where he lost his life during the storming of Khartoum by the Mahdi

Chinese Mainland Ports (large, medium, and small from south to north) Macao, (nominally Portuguese), Huang-Pu, Kuang-Chou, Hong Kong (British Crown Colony), Shant-T Ou, Hsia-Men, Lo-Hsing-Ta, Mao-Ti, Ning-Po, Shanghai, Chen Chiang, Nan-Ching, Wu-Hu, Chiu-Chiang, Hang-kou, Chang-Sha, Ching-Tao, Wei-Hai, Yen-Tai, Ta-Ku, Tieng-Ching, Chin-Huang-Tao, Hu-Lu-Tao, Ying-K-Ou, Lu-Shun, Luta (Dairen)

Chinese Offshore Ports on Formosa or Taiwan Chilung (Keelung), Kaohsiung, *plus smaller ports of* Su-Ao, Hua-Lien, Tso-Ying, An-Ping, Tan-Shui

chinese white zinc oxide (ZnO)

Ch'ing-hua ta hsueh t'u shu kuan (Chinese—Tsinghua University Library)—Peking where reportedly there is no short form for this center of culture

Chin J Phys Chinese Journal of Physics *(Acta Physica Sinica— Wuli Xuebao)*

CHINKUNG China National Trading Corporation for Light Industrial Products (mainland China)

Chin-men (Chinese—Quemoy) —island off the coast of mainland China but belonging to Taiwan

Chino Men California (correctional) Institution for Men at Chino

Chinook Boeing-Vertol twin-rotor helicopter designated CH-47

Chinook State Washington where the warm Chinook wind blows from the Pacific to the Rockies

chins. children in need of supervision

Chinsyn Chinese-English synthesis-oriented machine translation system

CHI-NY Chicago—New York

Chios English equivalent of Khios island in the Aegean

Chip Chipre (Portuguese or Spanish—Cyprus)

CHIP Community Housing Improvement Programme (New Zealand)

CHIPDis Chicago Procurement District (US Army)

Chipitt Chicago-to-Pittsburgh (complex of cities)

Chipmunk Hawker-Siddeley trainer aircraft

Chippy Chipping Norton, England

Chipre (Spanish—Cyprus)

chips. coherent high-intensity photon source

Chips ship's carpenter

CHiPs California Highway Patrol cops

CHIPS Chemical Engineering Information Processing System

chir chiropody

chir chirurgia (Italian—surgery)

Chir. Doc. *Chirurgiae Doctor* (Latin—Doctor of Surgery)

Chiricahua Chiricahua National Monument in southeastern Arizona

Chiricahuas Chiricahua Mountains of Arizona

Chiricano(s) Panamanian(s)

chiro chirography; chiropractic; chiropractor

CHIRP Community Housing Improvement and Revitalization Program

Chis Chiapas (inhabitants—Chiapanecos)

CIII-SAN Chicago—San Diego

CHI-SEA Chicago—Seattle

CHI—SFO Chicago—San Francisco

Chish Chisholm

Chisox Chicago White Sox (baseball team)

Chi Sym Chicago Symphony

chit chitty (Hindustani—voucher signed to cover small debts for drinks, food, tobacco, etc.)

Chita Conchita

Chitlin Capital of the World Salley, South Carolina

Chi-Trib Chicago Tribune

chiv chivalry

chix chickens

Ch J Chief Justice

CHJM Carnegie Hall—Jeunesses Musicales

CHJMKIIK Chung-Hua Jen-Min Kung-Ho Kuo (People's Republic of China—communist mainland China whose capital is Peking)

chk check

chkpt checkpoint

chkr checker

chl chloroform; confinement at hard labor

Chl Chalna

CHL Central Hockey League

Chla Vsta Chula Vista

chlb chlorobutanol

Ch Lbr Chief Librarian

ch-lkr chiffonier-locker

Ch^lle Chapelle (French—Chapel)

chlor chloride; chlorination; chlorine

chloride of lime bleaching powder

chloro chloroform; chlorophyll;

chloroprene

chloro chlorus (Greek—green)—chlorine, chlorophyll

chloroform trichloromethane $(CHCl_3)$

chloroprene synthetic rubber (C_4H_5Cl)

chlw commercial high-level waste

chm chamber; checkmate

Chm Chairman; Chairwoman; Choirmaster; Choirmistress

Ch.M. *Chirurgiae Magister* (Latin—Master of Surgery)

CHM Cleveland Health Museum

CHMC Children's Hospital Medical Center (Boston)

CHMDDA Cooper-Hewitt Museum of Design and Decorative Arts

ch-mir chiffonier-mirror

CHMK Chung-Hua Min-Kuo (Republic of China—offshore nationalist China whose capital is Taipei on the island of Formosa or Taiwan)

chmn chairman

ChMNH Chicago Museum of Natural History

chmp chairperson

Chn Cochin

CHN College of the Holy Name; Community of the Holy Name

C-H-N carbon, hydrogen, nitrogen, oxygen, phosphorus, sulfur (compounds)

CHNAVPERS Chief, Naval Personnel

CHNAVSECMAAG Chief, Navy Section, Military Assistance Advisory Group

Chne Chaîne (French—Chain)—mountain range

chns chains

CHNS Cape Hatteras National Seashore (Buxton, North Carolina)

CHNSRA Cape Hatteras National Seashore Recreational Area

CHNSY Charleston Naval Shipyard (South Carolina)

ChNZAgCo China New Zealand Agricultural Consultants

cho (Cho) containers carried in hold

Cho Chosen (Korea)

CHO carbohydrate (generalized formula); Community Health Organization

CHOBS Chief Observer (USN)

choc chocolate

chocbar(s) chocolate bar(s)

chocmalt chocolate malted milk

choco chocolate

Chocolate City Hershey, Pennsylvania

Chocolate Coast Ghana

chocs chocolate candies; chocolate drops; chocolates

Choctaw Sikorsky troop-transport helicopter designated H-34

CHOD Chief of Defense

choke choke hold (bar hold or carotid hold)

CHOKE Care How Others Keep the Environment

chol cholesterol

chol (Latin prefix—bile)—cholecyst, cholera, cholesterol(ic), cholic

Cholera Capital Calcutta

chol est cholesterol esters

Cholly Knickerbocker Igor Cassini

Chomolungma (Tibetan—Mount Everest)

CHOMPS Canine Home Protection System

Chongqing (Pinyin Chinese—Chungking)

Chonos Chonos Islands

CHOP Change of Operational Control

CHOPS Chief of Operations

chor choral; choreographer; choreographist; choreography; chorus; choruses

Choral Beethoven's Symphony No. 9 in D minor whose last movement contains Schiller's *Ode to Joy* sung by chorus and soloists with full orchestral support

Chord Chordata

Choreographic Symphony Ravel's name for his *Daphnis et Chloé* ballet

C Horn Cur Cape Horn Current

chortle chuckle and snort

Chosen (Japanese—Korea)

Choson (Korean—Korea)

Chotzie Samuel Chotzinoff

Chou Chou (pronounced *Joe*) En-lai

cho/vac cholera vaccine

chovr changeover

chow (Chinese—small town)

chp child psychiatry; comprehensive health plan(ning)

Chp Chepstow

CHP California Highway Patrol; Chihuahua Pacific (railroad—Ferrocarril de Chihuahua al Pacifico)

CHPA California Highway Patrol Academy

chpae critical human performance and evaluation

Chpn Chairperson

CHPP Cypress Hills Provincial Park (Saskatchewan)

ch ppd charges prepaid

chpx chickenpox

chq cheque

CHq Corps Headquarters

chr character; chrome; chromium; chromobacterium; chronic

c hr candle-hour

Chr Choir; Christ; Christ College, Cambridge; Christian; Church

Chr *Chronicles*

CHR Commission on Human Rights; Connecticut Hard Rubber (company)

CHRB California Horse Racing Board

Chr Coll Christ College—Cambridge

chrg charge

CHRG Citizens Health Research Group

CHRIE Council on Hotel, Restaurant, and Institutional Education

Chris Christian(a); Christopher

CHRIS Cancer Hazards Ranking and Information System

Chrissie Christina; Christine

Christ. Christian; Christianity; Christmas

Christiania Oslo's medieval name

Christianna Brand Mary Christianna Milne Lewis

christie Christiania turn

Christmas Christmas Day (December 25)

Christmas sobriquet of Corelli's Concerto Grosso Opus 6 Number 8, Rimsky-Korsakov's *Christmas Eve* opera, Bach's *Christmas Oratorio*, Haydn's *Christmas Symphony* in D minor—No. 26 also called *Lamentation* because it uses a chant recalling the Lamentations of Jeremiah

Christmas Cove South Bristol, Maine

Christopher Columbus Cristóbal Colón (Spanish); Cristoforo Colombo (Italian)

Chrlstn Charleston

Chrlstn SC Charleston, South Carolina (where one old inhabitant declared the Ashley and Cooper rivers joined to form the Atlantic Ocean)

Chrm Chairman; Chairwoman

chrom (Latin prefix—color)—chromatic, chromoplast, chro-

mosome, chromosphere

chromite iron chromate

chromolith chromolithograph(y)

chromo(s) chromolithograph(s); chromosome(s)

chron chronogram; chronograph; chronology; chronometer; chronometry

Chron *Chronicle(s)*—First Book of Chronicles; Second Book of Chronicles

chrono chronologic(al)(ly); chronology; chronometer; chronometric(al)(ly)

chrono order chronological order

chro pltd chrome plated

Chrp Chairperson

Chrs Chambers; Christians; Churches

Chrys Chrysler

chrysanthemum nationalist symbol of China and Japan; symbol of the Orient Overseas Line

chrysoberyl beryllium aluminate

chrysocolla hydrous copper silicate

chrysoprase chalcedony gemstone

chs chapters; crime on the high seas

Chs Chambers; Charles; Chester

Ch of S Chamber of Shipping

C-H s Chediak-Higashi syndrome

CHS Canadian Hydrographic Service; Charleston, South Carolina (airport); Chicago Historical Society; Childrens Home Society; Citizens for Highway Safety; Community Health Service (HEW); Community of the Holy Spirit; Cristobal High School; Curtis High School

ch'ship championship

Ch Skr Chief Skipper

CHSL Cleveland Health Sciences Library

CHSM China Service Medal

CHSS Children's Hypnotic Susceptibility Scale; Cooperative Health Statistics System

cht cylinder head temperature

Cht Chittagong

chtg charting

CHTNP Chittagong Hill Tracts National Park (Bangladesh)

cht tanks collect, hold, transfer (raw sewage) tanks (used by naval vessels to overcome harbor pollution when in port)

Chu Centigrade heat unit

CHU *Christelijk-Historische Unie* (Dutch-Christian Historical Union)—political party

CHUA Canadian Hail Underwriters Association

Chubu Nippon Shimbun (Japanese—Central Japan Newspaper)

Chuck Charles

Chuco Mexican-Americanism for El Paso, Texas

Chudskoe (Russian—Peipus)—lake also called Peipsi by the Estonians in its area

Chuey (Spanish-American nickname—Jesus)

Chugach Chugach National Forest in Alaska

Chugaches Chugach Mountains of Alaska

Chukchi Chukchi Peninsula and the Chukchi Sea in the Arctic between Alaska and Siberia where the peninsula is located

Chukotskoe (Russian—Chukchi Sea)

Chulajuana Chula Vista-Tijuana area of southwesternmost California and northwesternmost Tijuana—border area largely inhabited by Mexicans

CHUM *Computing and the Humanities*

Chumley (British contraction—Chalmondeley)

CHUMS Cancer Hopefuls United for Mutual Support; Care and Help for Unmarried Mothers

Chung Chungking

Chung-Hua Jen-Min Kung-Ho Kuo People's Republic of China (Red China)

Chung-Hua Min-Kuo Republic of China (Nationalist China)

Chung-kuo k'o hsueh yuan t'u shu kuan (Chinese—Central Library of the China Academy of Sciences)—Peking

Chunnel Channel Tunnel (under the English Channel where it will link England and France)

Chuqui Chuquicamata

Chur Churchill College, Cambridge

Churchill Sir Winston Churchill—First Lord of the Admiralty during World War I and just before World War II when he became Great Britain's Prime Minister

chut cable households using tv (audience survey)

'chute parachute

ch v check valve
chw chilled water; cladding hull waste; cold-and-hot water; constant hot water
CHW Charleston, West Virginia (airport)
CH & W Canadian Health and Welfare
CHWA California Health and Welfare Agency
Chwdn Churchwarden(ess)
chx chiro-xylographic
chy chimney
C Hy Commission for Hydrology
chyd churchyard
Chy Div Chancery Division
ci cardiac index; cardiac insufficiency; cast iron; cerebral infarction; chemotherapeutic index; clinical investigator (CI); clonus index; coefficient of intelligence; colloidal iron; color index; compression ignition; contamination index; contrast index; coronary insufficiency; cost and insurance; counterintelligence; criminal informant; crystalline insulin
ci (CI) consular invoice; cooperative individual (informant)
c-i criminal-investigation
c.i. (C.I.) consular invoice
c/i carriage-to-interference (ratio); configuration interface
c/i (C/I) certificate of insurance
c & i cost and insurance; cowboys and indians
Ci cirrus; curie (unit of activity in radiation dosimetry)
Ci cerveau isolè (French—isolated intellect, intellectual)
CI Carnegie Institute; Cayman Islands; Channel Islands; Color Index; Combustion Institute; Communist International; Consumers Institute; Cranberry Institute; Curtis Institute
C.I. Lady of the Imperial Order of the Crown of India
C & I Currier and Ives
CI Colour Index
cia captured in action; cash in advance; child(ren) in arms; computer interface adaptor
Cia Compagnia (Italian—Company); Companhia (Portuguese—Company); Compañia (Spanish—Company)
CIA Caribbean International Airways; Catering Institute of Australia; Central Intelligence Agency; Commerce and Industry Association; Cook Island Airways; Correctional In-

dustries Association; Cotton Insurance Association; Culinary Institute of America
CIA Comitè International d'Auschwitz (French—International Auschwitz Committee); Conseil International des Archives (French—International Council on Archives)
CIAA College Inventory of Academic Adjustment; Coordinator Inter-American Affairs
CIAB Canadian Immigration Appeal Board
Ciac Compania (Spanish—company)
CIAC Canadian Independent Adjusters Conference; Career Information and Counseling (USAF)
CIAL Communautè Internationale des Associations de la Librairie (French—International Community of Booksellers' Associations)
CIAM Congreso Internacional de Arquitectura Moderna (Spanish—International Congress of Modern Architecture)
CIANY Commerce and Industry Association of New York
CIAO Congress of Italian-American Organizations
CIAP Comite Interamericano de la Alianza para el Progreso (Spanish—Inter-American Committee of the Alliance for Progress)—ICAP
CIAPS Customer-Integrated Automated Procurement System
CIAS California Institute of Asian Studies; Council for Inter-American Security
CIASSR Cecheno-Ingush Autonomous Soviet Socialist Republic
CIAT Centro Interamericano de Administradores Tributarios (Inter-American Center of Revenue Administrators)
CIAU Canadian Interuniversity Athletic Union
CIAW Commission on Intercollegiate Athletics for Women
cib. cibus (Latin—food)
CIB California Industries for the Blind; Canadian International Bank; Central Intelligence Board; Commonwealth Investment Bank; Criminal Intelligence Bureau; Criminal Investigation Bureau
CIB COBOL Information Bulletin (USAF)
CIBA Corporation of Insurance

Brokers of Australia
CIBC Canadian Imperial Bank of Commerce; Council on Interracial Books for Children
CIBG Canadian Infantry Brigade Group
cibha congenital inclusion body hemolytic anemia
cibhp closed-in-bottom hole pressure
CIBNC Cook Islands Broadcasting and Newspaper Corporation
CIBNZ Corporation of Insurance Brokers of New Zealand
CIBS Chartered Institution of Building Services
cic cardio-inhibitor center; cloud in cell; command input coupler; critical item code
Cic Marcus Tullius Cicero
CIC Caribbean Investment Corporation; Cedar Rapids & Iowa City (railroad); Center for Instructional Communications (Syracuse University); Central Inspection Commission; Central Intelligence Center; Change Identification Control; Chemical Institute of Canada; Combat Information Center; Combat Intelligence Center; Combined Intelligence Committee; Comité International de la Conserve (International Canning Committee); Command Information Center; Commander-in-Chief; Committee on Institutional Cooperation; Commonwealth Industrial Court; Commonwealth Information Centre; Community Information Centre(s); Conseil International des Compositeurs (International Council of Composers); Consumer Information Center (Pueblo, Colorado 81009); Continental Insurance Companies; Cooperative Insurance Corporation; Counter-Intelligence Corps; Crime Intelligence Center; Criminal Investigation Command; Critical Issues Council; Curaçao Information Center; Customer Identification Code
CIC Consejo Interamericano Cultural (Spanish—Interamerican Cultural Council); Cymdeithas yr Iath Cymraeg (Welsh Language Society)
CICA Canadian Institute of Chartered Accountants; Council of International Civil Aviation

CICA *Centro de Investigaciones Ciencias Agronómicas* (Spanish—Agronomic Sciences Investigation Center)

CICAR Cooperative Investigations of the Caribbean and Adjacent Regions (UNESCO)

CICAS Computer-Integrated Command-and-Attack Systems

CICB Criminal Injuries Compensation Board

CICC California Institute of Color Consulting; Criminal Injuries Compensation Commission (Hawaii)

CICCU Cambridge Inter-Collegiate Christian Union

Cicero Marcus Tullius

Cicestr. *Cicestrensis* (Latin—of Chichester)

CICI Composite Index of Coincident Indicators

CICJ *Comité International pour la Coopération des Journalistes* (French—International Committee for the Cooperation of Journalists)

CICMA Canadian Insurance Claims Managers Association

CICO Combat Information Center Office(r)

CICOM *Centro de Comercialización Nacional e Internacional* (Spanish—Center of National and International Marketing)

CICP Capital Investment Computer Program; Center Program(ming); Committee to Investigate Copyright Problems

CICRIS Cooperative Industrial and Commercial Reference and Information Service

CICs Community Improvement Corpsmen; Community Improvement Corpswomen

CIC's Change Information Control (numbers)

CICS Committee for Index Cards for Standards; Customer Information and Control System

CICSB Coalition of Indian-Controlled School Boards

CICS/VS Customer Information Control System/Virtual Storage

CICT Commission on International Commodity Trade

CICT *Conseil International du Cinéma et de la Télévision* (French—International Council of Cinema and Television)

cicu cardiology intensive care unit (CICU); computer-integrated converter unit; coronary intensive care unit (CICU)

CICU Commission for Independent Colleges and Universities

CICUNM Council of Independent Colleges and Universities of New Mexico

CICUP Commission for Independent Colleges and Universities of Pennsylvania

CICV Council of Independent Colleges in Virginia

CICYP *Consejo Interamericano de Comercio y Producción* (Spanish—Interamerican Council of Commerce and Production)

cid cash in drawer; chick infective dose; cubic-inch displacement

cid (CID) cytomegalic inclusion disease

CID Center for Industrial Development; Central Institute for the Deaf; Centre d'Information et de Documentation (Center for Information and Documentation—Belgium); Change in Design; Classification of Instructional Disciplines; Commission for International Development; Council for Independent Distribution; Criminal Investigation Department (Scotland Yard); Criminal Investigation Division

CID *Colegio Interamericano de Defensa* (Spanish—Inter-American Defense College)

CIDA Canadian International Development Agency

CIDA *Comite Interamericano de Desarollo Agricola* (Inter-American Committee of Agricultural Development)

CIDALC *Comité International du Cinéma d'Enseignement et de la Culture* (French—International Committee of Film Education and Culture)

CIDC Cryogenic Information and Data Section; Curriculum and Instructional Development Center

cide (Latin suffix—destroy)—germicide, insecticide

CIDEM *Consejo Interamericano de Música* (Spanish—Inter-American Music Council)

CIDG Civil Indigenous Defense Group (Vietnam)

CIDH *Comisión Interamericana de Derechos Humanos* (Inter-American Commission of Human Rights)

cidi crimping die

cidnp chemically induced dynamic nuclear polarization

CIDOC *Centro Intercultural de Documentación* (Intercultural Documentation Center)

cids cellular immunity deficiency syndrome

CIDS Chemical Information and Data System

cidstat civil disturbance status (USA reporting activity)

cie coherent infrared energy

Cie *Compagnie* (French—company)

CIE Center for Independent Education; Chrysler Institute of Engineering; Cleveland Institute of Electronics; Commonwealth Institute of Entomology

C.I.E. Companion of the Order of the Indian Empire

CIE *Centro de Informações do Exército* (Portuguese—Military Intelligence Center)—Brazil; *Comite Interamericano de Educación* (Inter-American Committee of Education)

CIEA California Indian Education Association

CIEA *Centro Internacional de Estudios Agricolas* (Spanish—International Center of Agricultural Studies)

CIEBM Committee on the Interplay of Engineering with Biology and Medicine

CIEC *Centre International d'Études Criminologiques* (French—International Center of Criminological Studies)

CIECC *Consejo Interamericano para la Educación, la Ciencia, y la Cultura* (Inter-American Council for Education, Science, and Culture)

CIEE Companion of the Institution of Electrical Engineers; Council on International Educational Exchanges

Cie Gle Transatlantique Compagnie Générale Transatlantique (French Line)

CIEM Conseil International pour l'Exploration de la Mer (International Commission for the Exploration of the Sea)

CIEN Comision Interamericana de Energia Nuclear (Inter-American Commission for Nuclear Energy)

cienaga (Spanish — swamp, marsh)

CIENES Centro Interamericano de Enseñaza de Estadística (Inter-American Center for the Study of Statistics)

CIENT Cambridge and Isle of Ely Naturalist Trust (England)

CIEO Catholic International Education Office

ciep counterimmunoelectrophoresis

CIEP Council on International Economic Policy

CIER Centro Interamericano de Educación Rural (Inter-American Center of Rural Education)

CIES Comparative and International Education Society; Council for International Exchange of Scholars

CIES Consejo Interamericano Economico y Social (Inter-American Economic and So cial Council)

CIESMM Commission Interna tional pour l'Exploration Scientifique de la Mer Méditerranee (French—International Commission for the Scientific Exploration of the Mediterranean Sea)

CIESPAL Centro Internacional de Estudios Superiores de Periodismo para America Latina (International Center for Advanced Studies of Journalism in Latin America)

CIET Centro Interamericano de Estudios Tributarios (Inter-American Center of Revenue Studies)

CIETA Calcutta Import and Export Trade Association

CIETA Centre International d'Etude des Textiles Anciens (French—International Center for the Study of Ancient Textiles)

cif central index(ing) file; central integration facility; cost, insurance, and freight

CIF California Interscholastic Federation; Canadian Institute of Forestry; Construction Industry Foundation

CIF Commission Interaméricaine des Femmes (French—Interamerican Commission of Women; *Conseil International des Femmes* (French—International Council of Women)

CIFA Courtauld Institute of Fine Arts

CIFAR Central Institute of For-

eign Affairs Research

CIFAS Consortium Industriel Franco-Allemand pour Symphonie (French—Franco-German Industrial Consortium for Symphonie)—communication satellite linking systems between points in Africa, the Americas, Europe, and the Middle East

cif&c cost, insurance, freight, and commission

CIFC Council for the Investigation of Fertility Control

cifc & e cost, insurance, freight, and exchange

cifci (CIF and C & I) cost, insurance freight (plus) commission and interest

CIFE Central Index File—Europe

CIFEJ Centre International du Film pour l'Enfance et la Jeunesse (French—International Center of Films for Children and Young People)

CIFF Cannes International Film Festival; Comprehensive International Freight Forwarders

cif&i cost, insurance, freight, and interest

cifLt cost, insurance, and freight, London terms

cig cigarette

CIG Comité International de Geophysique; Commonwealth Industrial Gases

CIGA Compagnia Italiana dei Grandi Alberghi (Italian Great Hotels Company)

CIGAR Common Interactive Graphics Application Routine (USA)

Cigar Capital Key West, Florida; Tampa, Florida

Cigar City Tampa, Florida

Cigarette Josiah Flynt Willard

CIGGT Canadian Institute of Guided Ground Transportation

CIGNA Connecticut General Corporation combined with the Insurance Company of North America

CI Gov Cook Islands Government

CIGS Chief of the Imperial General Staff (Great Britain)

cigsmug cigarette smuggler

CIGTF Central Inertial Guidance Test Facility

cih carbohydrate-induced hyperglyceridemia

CIHR Clinical Institute for Human Relations

CII Chartered Insurance Institute; Coffee Information Institute; Combat Information Intelligence

CIIA Canadian Institute of International Affairs

CIIB Consumers Insurance Information Bureau

CIIC Chemical Industry Institute of Toxicology; Counter Intelligence Interrogation Center

CIIIA Soedinennye Shtaty Ameriki (Russian—United States of America)—U.S.A.

c-i info criminal-investigation information

CIIR Central Institute for Industrial Research

CIIS California Institute of International Studies

CIIT Chemical Industry Institute of Toxicology

cij control joint

CIJ Consejo Interamericano de Jurisconsultos (Inter-American Council of Legal Consultants)

CIJE Current Index to Journals in Education

CIKCU Council of Independent Kentucky Colleges and Universities

cil control interpreter language; core-image library; current-inhibit logic

CII Cilicap

CIL Canadian Industries Limited; Center for Independent Living; Commissioner of Irish Lights; Council for Interinstitutional Leadership

C/I/L Computer/Information/Library Sciences

cila casualty insurance logistics automated

CILA Centro Interamericano de Libros Académicos

CILES Central Information Library and Editorial Section (CSIRO)

Cilla Priscilla

CILSA Chief Inspector of Land Service Ammunition

CILT Center for Information on Language and Teaching

cim capital investment model; communication-interface module(s); computer-input microfilm(ing); conductance-increase mechanism; continuous-image microfilm(ing)

CIM California Institution for Men; Canadian Institute of Management; Canadian Institute of Mining; Canadian Institute of Music; Commission for Industry and Manpower; Curtis Institute of Music

C & IM Chicago & Illinois Midland (railroad)

CIM Centro Italiano della Moda (Italian Fashion Center); *Conseil International de la Musique* (French—International Music Council); *Consejo Internacional de Mujeres* (Spanish—International Council of Women)

CIMA Construction Industry Manufacturers Association; Coordinated Investigation of Micronesian Anthropology

Cimabue Cenni di Pepo

CIMB Construction Industry Management Board

CIMBA Contractor Installation Make-or-Buy Authorization

CIMC Commander's Internal Management Conference

CIMC Colegio Interamericano Médicos y Cirujanos (Spanish—Interamerican College of Physicians and Surgeons)

cimco card image correction

CIMCO Congo International Management Corporation

CIME Council of Industry for Management Education

CI Mech E Companion of the Institution of Mechanical Engineers

CIMIC Civilian Military Cooperation

cimm constant-impedance mechanical modulation

CIMM Canadian Institute of Mining and Metallurgy

CIMMS Civilian Information Manpower Management System (USN)

CIMMYT Centro Internacional de Mejoramiento de Maíz y Trigo (Spanish—International Center for the Improvement of Corn and Wheat)

CIMP Conseil International de la Musique Populaire (French—International Folk Music Council)

CIMR Commander's Internal Management Review

cims chemical ionization mass spectrometry

CIMS Computer-Integrated Manufacturing System; Convair Integrated Management System

CIMTP Congrès International de Médecine Tropicale et de Paludisme (French—International Congress of Tropical

Medicine and Malaria)

cimu compatibility-integration mockup

cin cervical intra-epithelial neoplasia; code identification number; component identification number; cost item number

cin (CIN) communication identification navigation

c_{in} insulin clearance

Cin Cincinnati

CIN Change Incorporation Notice; Change Instrumentation Notice; Cooperative Information Network (linking libraries by twx)

CIN Chemical Industry Notes

Cina (Italian—China)

CINAT Cook Islands National Art Theatre

CINB&T Continental Illinois National Bank and Trust

Cinc Cincinnati

C-in-C Commander-in-Chief

CINC Commander-in-Chief

CINCAFE Commander-in-Chief, Air Forces Europe

CINCAFLANT Commander-in-Chief, Air Force Atlantic Command

CINCAFMED Commander-in-Chief, Allied Forces Mediterranean

CINCAFSTRIKE Commander-in-Chief, Air Force Strike Command

CINCAL Commander-in-Chief, Alaskan Command

CINC ATL FLT Commander-in-Chief, Atlantic Fleet

CINCEASTLANT Commander-in-Chief, Eastern Atlantic

CINCENT Commander-in-Chief, Central Europe

CINCEUR Commander-in-Chief, Europe

CINCHAN Commander-in-Chief—Channel (NATO)

CINCHF Commander-in-Chief, Home Fleet (British)

CINCHOMEFLT Commander-in-Chief, United Kingdom Home Fleet

Cinci Cincinnati

CINCIBERLANT Commander-in-Chief, Iberian Atlantic

Cincin Cincinnati

Cincinnati oysters pigs' feet

CINCLANT Commander-in-Chief, Atlantic

CINCLANTFLT Commander-in-Chief, Atlantic Fleet

CINCMEAFSA Commander-in-Chief, Middle East, Southeast Asia, Africa South of the

Sahara

CINCMED Commander-in-Chief, Mediterranean

CINCMELF Commander-in-Chief, Middle-East Land Forces

CINCNELM Commander-in-Chief, U.S. Naval Forces in Europe, the Eastern Atlantic, and the Mediterranean

CINCNORAD Commander-in-Chief, North American Defense Command

CINCNORTH Commander-in-Chief, Northern Europe

CINCONAD Commander-in-Chief, Continental Air Defense Command

CINCPAC Commander-in-Chief, Pacific

CINCPACFLT Commander-in-Chief, Pacific Fleet

CINCRDAF Commander-in-Chief, Royal Danish Air Force

CINCRDN Commander-in-Chief, Royal Danish Navy

CINCRNAF Commander-in-Chief, Royal Norwegian Air Force

CINCRNORN Commander-in-Chief, Royal Norwegian Navy

CINCSOUTH Commander-in-Chief, Southern Europe

CINCSTRIKE Commander-in-Chief, United States Strike Command

CINCUNC Commander-in-Chief, United Nations Command

CINCUSAFE Commander-in-Chief, United States Air Forces in Europe

CINCUSAFLANT Commander in Chief—United States Air Force Atlantic

CINCUSAFSTRIKE Commander-in-Chief—United States Air Force Strike

CINCWESTLANT Commander-in-Chief, Western Atlantic

Cincy Cincinnati

Cindy Cinderella; Cynthia

cine cinema; cinematography

CINECA Cooperative Investigation of the Eastern Central Atlantic

Cinecitta (Italian—Cinema City)—Italy's Hollywood on the Tiber on the periphery of Rome

cinemactor cinema actor

cinemactress cinema actress

cinerama cinematic panorama (three-dimensional film)

CINFAC Counterinsurgency Information Analysis Center

CINFO Chief of Information

CINM Channel Islands National Monument (Southern California)

cinn cinnabar

Cinn Cincinnati

cinna cinnamon

cinnabar mercuric sulfide (H_gS)

cinnamon stone hessonite

Cinn Sym Orch Cincinnati Symphony Orchestra

CINOA *Confédération International des Négociants en Oeuvres d'Art* (French—International Confederation of Art Dealers)

CINPDis Cincinnati Procurement District (US Army)

cins child(ren) in need of supervision

CINS CENTO Institute of Nuclear Science

Cin Sym Cincinnati Symphony

CINTA Compañia Nacional del Turismo (Chilean Airline)

Cinty Cincinnati

CINVA *Centro Interamericano de Vivienda y Planteamiento* (Inter-American Center of Housing and Planning)

cio central input/output (multiplexer)

CIO Church Information Office(r), Commission Internationale d'Optique (International Optical Commission); Congress of Industrial Organizations

Cio-Cio-San (Japanese— Madame Butterfly)

CIOCS Communications Input-Output Control System

CIOMS Council for the International Organization of Medical Sciences

ciopw *charcoal, ink, oil, pencil, and watercolor* (title of a book illustrated and written by e e cummings in 1931)

CIOSL *Confederación Internacional de Organizaciones Sindicales Libres* (Spanish—International Confederation of Free Trade Union Organizations)

cip cast-iron pipe; cataloging in publication; cipher (zip is derived from this and is a slang shortcut for a cipher or zero—zero)

cip (CIP) capital investment program; commercially important passenger

C i P Cataloging in Publication

(Library of Congress program)

CIP Canadian International Paper; Career Internship Program; Cataloging-in-Publication; Citizens Involvement Project; Civilian Institution Program; Composite Interface Program; Consolidated Intelligence Program; Cook Islands Party; Cost Improvement Proposal

CIP *Comisión Interamericana de Paz* (Inter-American Peace Commission)

CIPA Canadian Industrial Preparedness Association; Chartered Institute of Patent Agents; Committee for Independent Political Action

CIPAC Collaborative International Pesticides Analytical Council (UK)

Cipango Japan, as it was called by early European explorers

CIPASH Committee for an International Program in the Atmospheric Sciences and Hydrology

cipc cast-in-place concrete

CIPC Christmas Island Phosphate Commission

CIPCE *Centre d'Information et de Publicité des Chemins de Fer Européens* (French—Information and Publicity Center of the European Railways)

CIPE *Centro Interamericano para la Promoción de las Exportaciones* (Spanish—Inter-American Center for the Promotion of Exports); *Consejo Internacional de la Película de Enseñanza* (Spanish—International Council for Educational Films)

CIPEC *Conseil Intergouvernmental des Pays Exportateurs de Cuivre* (French—Intergovernmental Council of Copper Exporting Nations)

CIPFA Chartered Institute of Public Finance and Accountancy

ciph cipher

CIPHER Calculations of Patient and Hospital Education Resources

ciphony enciphered telephony

CIPL Canada India Pakistan Line; Commission of Inquiry into Public Libraries (Australian)

CIPL *Comité International Permanent de Linguistes* (French—Permanent International

Committee of Linguists)

CIPM Council for International Progress in Management

Cipo Cipriano

CIPO Conseil International pour la Préservation des Oiseaux (International Council for the Preservation of Birds)

CIPP Cataloging-in-Publication Program (Library of Congress); Comprehensive Income and Price Policy

CIPP *Conseil Indo-Pacifique des Pêches* (French—Indo-Pacific Fisheries Council)

CIPR *Commission Internationale de Protection Contre les Radiations* (French—International Commission on Radiological Protection)

CIPRA Cast-Iron Pipe Research Association

CIPRA *Commission Internationale pour la Protection des Régions Alpines* (French—International Commission for the Protection of Alpine Regions)

CIPREC Canadian Institute of Public Real Estate Companies

Cipro (Italian—Cyprus)

CIPs Commercially-Important Persons

CIPS Canadian Information Processing Society

CIQ Customs, Immigration, Quarantine

cir circle; circuit; circular

cir. circa (Latin—about)

cIR crime on Indian Reservation

Cir Circimus; Circinis (constellation); Circle; Circus

CIR Commission on Intergovernmental Relations; Commissioner of Internal Revenue; Consumer Information Report; Cost Information Report; Court of Industrial Relations; Current Industrial Reports

CIRA Committee on International Reference Atmosphere; Conference of Industrial Research Associations

CIRA *Centro Interamericano de Reforma Agraria* (Spanish—Inter-American Center of Agrarian Reform)

CIRADS Counter-Insurgency Research and Development System

cir ant. circular antenna

cir bkr circuit breaker

circ circle; circular; circulate; circulation; circumcision; circumference; circumferential(ly); circumstance; circus

Circ Circimus; Circle; Circus

CIRC Central Information Reference and Control

CIRC Centre International de Recherche sur le Cancer (French—International Center for Cancer Research)

CIRCA Computerized Information Retrieval and Current Awareness

circad circadic; circadian; circadianly

circal circuit analysis

CIRCALS Circle Analysis System

CIRCAS Contract Information Retrieval and Cost Accounting System

circle ancient symbol of annual, eternal, or female principle; Earth symbol if divided into four sectors by an erect cross or if bisected by a horizontal line; Full Moon (sometimes circle contains a cartoon face); Full Moon denoted by solid circle; rain represented by circle with vertical lines; solar corona if circle is divided by a vertical line; Sun if containing a central dot or if periphery contains radiating lines

circltr circular letter

circs circumstances

circum circumference

circum (Latin prefix—around) —circumnavigation

circum haema circumorbital haematoma (medical euphemism for a black eye)

Circumv Stz Circumvesuviana Stazione (Neapolitan railroad station serving Herculaneum, Mt Vesuvius, and Pompeii)

Circus circular intersection (Oxford Circus, Piccadilly Circus, St Giles Circus, etc.)

circuscade circus parade

Circus King John Ringling

Ciren Cirencester (Sisister)

CI Rep Communist International Representative

CIRES Cooperative Institute for Research in Environmental Studies

CIRF Corn Industries Research Foundation

CIRF Centre International d'Information et de Recherche sur la Formation Professionelle (French—Vocational Training and Research Center)

CIRIA Construction Industry Research and Information Association

CIRIEC Canadian International Centre of Research and Information on Public and Cooperative Economy

CIRIS Completely Integrated Range-Instrumentation System (NASA)

CIRJP Commission on International Rules of Judicial Procedure

CIRM Centro Internazionale Radio-Medico

CIRO Consolidated Industrial Relations Office

CIRP City Improvement and Restoration Program; Cooperative Institutional Research Program

CIRVIS Communication Instructions for Reporting Vital Intelligence Sightings (of ufo's from aircraft)

cis carcinoma in situ; cataloging in source; central inhibitory state

cis (CIS) cataloging in source

ci's conflict indicators

Cis Cecilia

Cis (German—C-sharp)

CIs Current Investigations

CIS Cancer Information Service; Career Information System; Catholic Information Society; Center for International Studies (MIT); Central Industrial Secretariat; Central Instructor School; Chartered Industries of Singapore; Chartered Institute of Secretaries; Congressional Indexing Service; Congressional Information Service; Cost Inspection Service; Cranbrook Institute of Science

CISA Canadian Industrial Safety Association; *Commission Internationale pour le Sauvetage Alpin* (French—International Commission for Alpine Rescue); Cook Islands Sports Association; Council for Independent School Aid

CISAC Confédération Internationale des Auteurs et Compositeurs (International Federation of Authors and Composers)

cisam compressed index sequential access method

Cisco San Francisco

CISCO Civil Service Catering Organization; Commercial and Industrial Security Corporation (Singapore)

Cisco Kid Duncan Reynaldo (Renault Renaldo Duncan)

CISE Colleges, Institutes, and Schools of Education (Library Association)

CISF Confédération Internationale des Sages-Femmes (French—International Confederation of Midwives)

CISHEC Chemical Industry Safety and Health Council

CISI Command Inspection System Inspection (USAF); Compagnie Internationale de Service et Information

CISIR Ceylon Institute of Scientific and Industrial Research

Cisister Cirencester, England

CISL Confederazione Italiana Sindacati Lavoratori (Italian Confederation of Labor Syndicates)—Catholic inspired

CISLE Centre International des Syndicalistes Libres en Exil (French—International Center of Free Trade Unionists in Exile)

cislun cislunar; cislunarian; cislunarite

CISR Center for International Systems Research; Commonwealth Inscribed Stock Registry

CISS Computerized Information Storage System

Cissie Cecilia

Cissie Patterson Eleanor Medill Patterson

Cissy Cecilia

Cissy Loftus Mary Cecilia M'Carthy

Cist Cistercian

CISTI Canada Institute of Scientific and Technical Education

CISV Children's International Summer Village

cit citation; cited; citizen(ship); citrate; compression in transit; computer interface terminal; configuration identification table(s); counterintelligence team

cit (CIT) call-in time

cit citat (Dano-Norwegian—quotation)

Cit Citadel

CIT Calcutta Improvement Trust; California Institute of Technology (Cal Tech); Carnegie Institute of Technology; Case Institute of Technology; Central Institute of Technology; Chartered Institute of Transport; Coal Industry Tribunal (Australian); Conference of Interpreter Trainers; Continental Inclusive Tour; Counterintelligence Team; Cranfield Institute of Technology

CIT (ARIA) Commission on Insurance Terminology (American Risk and Insurance Association)

CIT Compagnia Italiana di Turismo (Italian Travel Bureau)

cit a citric acid

CITA Commercial-Industrial-Type Activity; Cook Islands Tourist Authority

CITAB Computer Instruction and Training Assistance for the Blind

Citaltepetl (Aztec—Mount Orizaba: highest peak in Mexico)

CITARS Crop Identification Technology Assessment for Remote Sensing (NATO)

CITB Construction Industry Training Board

CITC Canadian Institute of Timber Construction; Cook Islands Trading Corporation

cite. compression ignition and turbine engine

CITE Consolidated Index of Translations into English; Coordinating Information for Texas Educators; Council of the Institute of Telecommunication Engineers; Current Information on Tapes for Engineers

CITEL Comisión Interamericana de Telecomunicaciones (Inter-American Telecommunication Commission)

CITEP Canadian Indian Teacher Education Projects

CITES Convention on International Trade in Endangered Species

CITGO Cities Service Gulf Oil

cithp closed-in tubing head pressure

Citi Citibank

Citians people of Minneapolis and St Paul also called Twin Citians

Citibank First National City Bank

CITIC China International Trust and Investment Corporation

Citicorp First National City Bank Corporation

Cities of the Plain Admah, Gomorrah, Sodom, and Zeboim on the Jordan River Plain of ancient Israel near the Dead Sea

CITIS Centralized Integrated Technical Information System

Citizen Capet Louis XVI (beheaded during French Revolution although Citizen Tom Paine pleaded with the General Assembly to abolish the position of king but not the man)

Citizen Composer Dmitri Shostakovich

Citizen of Geneva Jean-Jacques Rousseau

Citizen King Louis Philippe of France

Citizen Louis Capet Louis XVI

Citizen of the World Oliver Goldsmith and Thomas Paine share this name

CITL Canadian Industrial Traffic League

CITO Charter of the International Trade Organization

cito disp. cito dispensetur (Latin —dispense rapidly)

CITP Civilian Industrial Technology Program

CITRAIL Centre Inter-Regional de Transit Rail-Route (French Canadian)

citric acid $C_8H_6O_7$

citricult citriculture

citrine false topaz (quartz with ferric iron)

Citrus Metropolis Los Angeles

CITS China International Travel Service

CITT Canadian Institute of Traffic and Transportation

citta (Italian—city, town)

Città del Vaticano (Italian—Vatican City)

citu (CITU) coronary intensive-care unit

Cit U City University

City The City—business and financial section of the City of London within its historic bounds

City of 1000 Lakes Oklahoma City, Oklahoma

City of Abraham Hebron, Israel

City of a Hundred Hills San Francisco

City of a Hundred Spires Prague

City of a Hundred Towers Italy's Pavia with its many towers and turrets

City of Alexander the Great Alexandria, Egypt

City of Aluminum Arvida, Québec

City of Angels nickname shared by Bangkok and Los Angeles

City of the Apprentice Boys Londonderry, Northern Ireland

City of the Arctic Tromso, Norway

City of the Arts Minneapolis

City of Athena Athens

City of Baked Beans Boston, Massachusetts

City by the Bay San Francisco

City of Beaches Montevideo, Uruguay

City of Beautiful Spires Copenhagen

City of Bells Strasbourg, France

City of Berwald Stockholm, Sweden

City Beside the Broad Missouri Bismarck, North Dakota

City Between Bridges medieval Stockholm

City of Bicycles Copenhagen

City of Big Shoulders Carl Sandburg's sobriquet for Chicago

City of Birches Umeå, Sweden

City of Black Diamonds Scranton, Pennsylvania

City of the Blues Memphis, Tennessee (home of W.C. Handy)

City of Brotherly Love Philadelphia (derived from the Greek) *philos* (love) and *adelphos* (brother)

City of the Caliphs Cairo

City of the Camellias Pensacola, Florida

City of Canals and Bridges sobriquet shared by Amsterdam, Copenhagen, Leningrad, Stockholm, and Venice

City of the Carmel Haifa, Israel, on the slopes of Mount Carmel

City of Castles Copenhagen

City of Certainties Des Moines, Iowa

City of Cheese sobriquet shared by the Dutch cities of Alkmaar and Gouda

City of Cheese, Chairs, Children, and Churches Sheboygan, Wisconsin

City of Churches Brooklyn, New York

City College British euphemistic nickname for Newgate Gaol—the old London lockup; New Yorker nickname for the The Tombs prison in downtown Manhattan

City of Corsairs St Malo, France

City of Cypresses Rome

City of David Jerusalem

City of Death Kipling's name for Lahore, India

City of Destiny Tacoma, Washington

City of the Doges Venice

City of Dreadful Night Kipling's nickname for Calcutta

City of Dreaming Spires Oxford, England

City of the Dunes Dunkerque, France

City Ed City Editor

City of Elms New Haven's nickname before Dutch-elm disease attacked her trees

City of Eternal Spring Caracas

City of Fair Breezes Buenos Aires, Argentina

City of Five Seasons Cedar Rapids, Iowa

City of Flamboyants and Jacarandas Salisbury, Rhodesia

City of Fountains Aix-en-Provence in France and Bratislava in Czechoslovakia claim this sobriquet

City of Four Lakes Madison, Wisconsin

City of Fun and Frolic Atlantic City, New Jersey

City of Gardens Lahore, Pakistan; Victoria, British Columbia

City of Gardens and Beaches Adelaide, Australia

City of the Gods Teotihuacán—religious capital of Mexico in the fifth century before the Christian Era

City of Gold Dawson, Yukon Territory

City by the Golden Gate San Francisco

City of the Golden Horn Istanbul

City of Good Neighbors Arlington Heights, Illinois

City of Green Spires Copenhagen

City of Grieg Bergen, Norway

City Grown Too Big For Its Bridges San Francisco

City of Hans Christian Andersen Copenhagen, Denmark

City of Heat Thermopolis, Wyoming

City of Historical Charm Savannah

City of Illicit Love Paphos on Cyprus in the Greek Isles

City of the Immortals Amarapura, Burma

City of Jade Oaxaca, México

City of Jazz and Mardi Gras New Orleans, Louisiana

City of Kielland and Bjelland Stavanger, Norway

City of Lakes Dartmouth, Nova Scotia

City of Light Paris, France and Perth, Western Australia share this sobriquet

City of Lillies Florence, Italy

City by the Lion's Gate Vancouver, British Columbia

City of Lost Angels Los Angeles, California

City of Louis Paris

City of Magnificent Distances Washington, D.C.

City of Manifold Advantages Augusta, Maine

City of Mankind Jerusalem

City of Masts Port of London

City of Millionaires Colorado Springs

City of Minarets Miknès, Morocco

City of Money Zurich, Switzerland (home of the Swiss bank account)

City of Monuments Baltimore, Maryland and Florence, Italy, both claim this nickname

City of Mosques Istanbul, Turkey

City in Motion San Diego, California

City of Mozart Salzburg, Austria

City of Nielsen Copenhagen, Denmark

City of Nine Dragons Kowloon, Hong Kong

City of Notions Boston, Massachusetts

City of Oaks Raleigh, North Carolina

City on the Neva Leningrad (formerly called Petrograd or St Petersburg)

City on the Water sobriquet shared by Amsterdam, Copenhagen, Stockholm, and Venice

City of Palaces Rome, Italy, and its Vatican City replete with papal palaces

City of Palms Acajutla, El Salvador; Fort Myers, Florida; and Maracaibo, Venezuela, all claim this nickname

City of the Pampas Buenos Aires

City of Peace Brunei

City of Penn Philadelphia, Pennsylvania founded by William Penn

City of Personality Cincinnati, Ohio

City of Peter the Great Saint Petersburg (later called Petrograd and Leningrad)

City of the Plains Christchurch, New Zealand

City of Poets Jérémie, Haiti, birthplace of the father of Alexandre Dumas (*Dumas père*) and grandfather of Alexandre Dumas (*Dumas fils*)—he was Alexandre Pailleterie who abandoned his father's name to use his Negro mother's—Césette Dumas

City of Power Peking, People's Republic of China

City of Presidents Quincy, Massachusetts

City of the Prophet Medina, Saudi Arabia, where Mohammed was protected after fleeing from Mecca

City of Quays and Grieg Bergen, Norway

City of Razzle Dazzle one of O Henry's nicknames for New York City he also called Bagdad on the Subway

City of Receptions Washington, D.C.

City of Rocks Nashville, Tennessee

City of Roses Portland, Oregon

City of Ruins and Roses Visby on Sweden's Gotland Island

City of Rumors Washington, D.C.

City of Rum and Sugar Georgetown, Guyana

City of Saints Montreal where so many street names are saint names

City of Salt Salzburg, Austria, and Syracuse, New York—both in salt-producing regions

City of the Sea Venice

City of Seven Hills Rome, Italy, as it is built on seven hills—Aventine, Caelian, Capitoline, Esquiline, Palatine, Quirinal, and Viminal

City of Seventy Isles Venice

City of Shoes Brockton, Massachusetts

City of Sibelius Helsinki, Finland

City of Silver Taxco, México

City of the Silver Gate San Diego

City of Sinbad Basra, Iraq

City of Sinding Oslo, Norway

City in the Sky Macchu Picchu in the high Andes of Peru

City of Skyscrapers New York

City of the Slain Arlington National Cemetery in Arlington, Virginia

City of Smells Old Delhi, India

City of Smokestacks Everett, Washington

City of Soles Lynn, Massachusetts

City of Sorrow Buchenwald (concentration camp near Weimar, Germany)

City of Southern Charm Savannah, Georgia

City of Spies name often applied to Beirut, Berlin, Copenhagen, Hong Kong, London, New York, Paris, Singapore, Stockholm, Vienna, and Zurich as well as Washington, D.C.

City of Spires Copenhagen

City State Singapore (at the tip of the Malay Peninsula) and the Vatican City State (in the middle of Rome)

City of St Mark Venice

City of St Michael Dumfries, Scotland whose patron saint is St Michael

City of St Mungo Glasgow, Scotland whose patron saint is St Mungo

City of the Straits Detroit, Michigan, on the Straits of Belle Isle

City of Suds Milwaukee

City of the Sun sobriquet shared by ancient Baalbec, Heliopolis, and Rhodes; Campanella's utopian republic also bore this title

City of Sunshine Colorado Springs, Colorado; Los Angeles, California; Tucson, Arizona; and all other sun-drenched cities

City of Surprises Amsterdam

City of Symphonies London, England where the BBC, LP, LPO, New Philharmonia, RPO, and other orchestras receive public support

City of Tamales O Henry's sobriquet for San Antonio, Texas

City of Temples Benares

City of Ten Million Roosters Port-au-Prince, Hatti

City That Boeing Built Seattle

City That Care Forgot New Orleans

City That Knows How San Francisco

City That Swims on the Water Stockholm

City of the Thousand and One Nights Baghdad, Iraq

City of Three Capitols Little Rock, Arkansas

City of the Three Kings Cologne, Germany, where it is reputed the Magi or Three Kings are buried; Lima, Peru

City of Trees Christchurch, New Zealand; Saratoga Springs, New York

City of the Tribes Galway, Ireland—home of the thirteen families or tribes—Athy, Blake, Budkin, Browne, Burke, d'Arcy, Ffont, Joyce, Kirwan, Lynch, Martin, Morris, Skerrett

City under Vesuvius Naples

City of the Violet Crown Athens

City of Washington Washington, D.C.

City of Witches Salem, Massachusetts

City without Clocks Las Vegas, Nevada

CIU Coopers' International Union; Criminal Intelligence Unit (police)

Ciudad (Spanish—City)—abbreviated *C* or *Cd* as in C Juárez or Cd Juárez (Juárez opposite El Paso)

Ciudad Acuña formerly Villa Acuña (opposite Del Rio, Texas)

Ciudad Blanca (Spanish—White City)—Guayaquil, Ecuador's cemetery; (Spanish—White City)—Merida, Yucatan's nickname

Ciudad Bolívar (formerly Angostura)

Ciudad Darío formerly Metapa, Nicaragua but renamed to honor the poet Rubén Darío

Ciudad de El Cabo (Spanish—City of the Cape)—South Africa's Cape Town

Ciudad de las Casas San Cristóbal de las Casas

Ciudad de los Reyes (Spanish—City of the Kings)—Lima, Peru's sobriquet

Ciudad del Vaticano (Spanish—Vatican City)—religious capital of most Spanish-speaking people

Ciudad de México (Spanish—City of Mexico)—Mexico City

Ciudad Imperial y Coronado (Spanish—Imperial and Crowned City)—Toledo, Spain's official title

Ciudad Juárez Juárez (opposite El Paso, Texas)

Ciudad Loca (Spanish—Crazy City)—Barranquilla, Colombia's nickname during carnival

Ciudad Madero formerly Villa de Cecilia but renamed to honor Mexico's greatest democratic president (across the lagoon from Tampico)

Ciudad Trujillo (Spanish—Trujillo City)—Santo Domingo City's name during the dictatorial rule of Rafael Leonidas Trujillo

CIUL Council for International Urban Liaison

CIUS Conseil International des Unions Scientifiques (International Council of Scientific Unions)

civ civil; civilian; civilization; civilize

CIV City Imperial Volunteers (London); Commonwealth Institute of Valuers

CIV Commission Internationale du Verre (French—International Glass Commission)

CIVA Cook Islands Visitors Association

Civ Air NM Civil Aircraft National Marking(s)

civd cold-induced vasodilation

Civ E Civil Engineering

civ eng civil engineering

Civ Eng Civil Engineer

civies civilian clothes; civilians

civiling civilingeniør (Dano-Norwegian—civil engineer)

Civil War Photographer Mathew Brady

CIVIS Centro Italiano per i Viaggi d'Instruzione per Studenti (Italian Center for Students' Educational Travel)

civ svc civil service

civ svt civil servant

civvies civilian clothes; civilians

civvy civilian

eiw current instruction word

CIW California Institution for Women

CIWS Close-in Weapons System

cixa constant infusion excretory urogram

cj clip joint; conjectural; construction joint

CJ Chief Justice; Civil Jail; Court of Judiciary

C of J Collector of Junk

CJ Computer Journal

CJA Carpenters and Joiners of America

CJA Criminal Justice Abstracts

C-jam cocaine

CJB Constructors John Brown (British shipbuilders)

CJC Colby Junior College; Community Junior College

CJC Corpus Juris Canonici

(Latin—Code of Canon Law)

CJCA California Junior College Association

CJCiv Corpus Juris Civilis (Latin—Code of Civil Law)

CJCs Criminal Justice Councils

C-J disease Creutzfeldt-Jakob disease (afflicting all primates)

cje corretaje (Spanish—brokerage)

CJE Citizens for Jobs and Energy

CJF Carlos J. Finley

CJFWF Council of Jewish Federations and Welfare Funds

CJI Concrete Joint Institute

CJI Comite Juridico Interamericano (Inter-American Juridical Committee)

CJIS Criminal Justice Information System (Rhode Island)

CJLF Criminal Justice Legal Foundation

CJM Congregation of Jesus and Mary

C-joint cocaine joint · (place where cocaine is sold)

CJP Criminal Justice Publications

CJR Cecil John Rhodes

CJR Columbia Journalism Review

CJRL Criminal Justice Reference Library (Austin)

cjs cotton, jute, or sisal (cargo)

CJS Canadian Joint Staff; College of Jewish Studies

CJS Corpus Juris Secundum

CJTF Commander Joint Task Force

ck cask; certified kosher; check; coke; cork

ck ceekay (Spanish-American slang—cocaine)

Ck chalk; Creek

CK cyanogen chloride (poison gas)

C K Cape Kennedy

ckb cork base

ckbd cork board

CKC Canadian Kennel Club

CKCJP Center for Knowledge in Criminal Justice Planning

CKCL Chicago-Kent College of Law

ckd completely knocked down

CKD Certified Kitchen Designer

CKE Central Kingdom Express (*see* Ori Exp)

ckf cork floor

ckfm checking form

ckga checking gage

CKIC Chemical Kinetics Information Center (NBS)

ckm cents per kilometer

CKMTA Cape Kennedy Missile Test Area

cko checking operator

ck os countersink other side

ckout checkout

ckpt cockpit

cks casks; checks

ckt circuit

CKT Chung-Kuo Kung-ch'an Tang (Chinese Communist Party)

ckt bd circuit board

ckt bkr circuit breaker

ckt cl circuit closing

ck tp check template

ck ts countersink this side

ck vlv check valve

ckw clockwise

cl carload; center line; centiliter; chest and left arm (cardiology); chloride; class; clavicle; clear; clearance; climb; clinic; close; closure; conceptual level; confidence limits; corpus luteum; critical list

cl (CL) control leader (data processing)

c/l combat loss

c/l (C/L) carload lot; cash letter

cl. classis (Latin—class or collection)

Cl chlorine; chlorine gas; Cloister; Close

Cl Calle (Spanish—street)

CL Capital Airlines; chlorine; chlorine gas; Cooperative League; Critical List; light cruiser (2-letter naval symbol)

C-L Canadair Limited (Division of General Dynamics)

C/L craft loss (insurance)

C & L Canal and Lake; Coopers and Lybrand

C of L Count(y) of Lippe

CL. Clericus (Latin—cleric or clergyman)

CL-1 Computer Language One

CL-13 Canadair-built F-86 Sabre aircraft

CL-28 Canadair-built long-range reconnaissance version of the Britannia

CL-41 Canadair-built jet-trainer aircraft nicknamed Tutor

cla center line average; communication link analyzer

Cla Clare College, Cambridge

CLA California Library Association; Canadian Library Association; Canadian Lumbermen's Association; Catholic Library Association; Chinese Librarians Association; College Language Association; Commercial Law Association; Computer Law Association; Connecticut Library Association; Conservative Library Association; Copyright Licensing Agency

C.L.A. Certified Laboratory Assistant

CLAA anti-aircraft light cruiser (4-letter naval symbol)

CLA-ACB Canadian Library Association—l'Association Canadienne des Bibliothéques

Clack Clackmannan(shire)

cl ad collet adapter

CLAE Council of Library Associations Executives

CLAH Conference of Latin American History

CLAIMS Class Codes Assigned Index Method Search

CLAIRA Chalk Lime and Allied Industries Research Association

clam (CLAM) chemical low-altitude missile

clam. chemical low-altitude missile

clamato clam-and-tomato juice

Clamcatcher(s) New Jerseyite(s)

Clamgrabber(s) Washingtonian(s)

clamsan clam sandwich

Clam State New Jersey and Washington both have claimed this nickname

Clam Town Norwalk, Connecticut

clamwich clam sandwich

cland lit clandestine literature (underground)

cland press clandestine press

CLAO Contact Lens Association of Ophthalmologists

CLAP Citizens Lobbying Against Prostitution

clar clarification; clarify; clarinet

Clar Clarence

Clara Clarabelle; Clarissa; Clarita

Clara Covell North Clara E. Ellis

Clare Clara; Clarita

Clar(en) Clarendon

Claribel Charlotte Alington-Barnard

Clarin (pseudonym—Leopoldo Alas y Urena)

Clarita Clara Elena

clark combat launch and recovery kit

Clark William Andrews Clark Memorial Library of the University of California at Los Angeles

Clark Gable William Gable

CLARNICO Clark, Nichols, and Coombes (confectioners)

Clarrie Clarice; Clarissa

clas classification; classify; congenital localized absence of skin

c-l-a-s crowd-lift-actuate-swing (tractor backhoe control)

CLAS Chartered Land Agents Society; Computer Library Applications Service

CLASB Citizens League Against the Sonic Boom

CLASC Confederación Latinoamericana de Sindicalistas Cristianos (Spanish—Latin American Confederation of Christian Trade Unionists)

clasn classification

clasp. (CLASP) computer liftoff and staging program

CLASP Center for Law and Social Policy, Citizens Local Alliance for a Safer Philadelphia; Client's Lifetime Advisory Service Program; Computer Language for Aeronautics and Space Programming; Computer Launch and Separation Problem

CLASPS Coded Label Additional Security and Protection System

class. classification

Class Classical

CLASS California Library Authority for Systems and Services; Christian Leaders And Speakers Seminars; Class Action Study and Survey; Close Air-Support System; Closed-Loop Accounting for Store Sales; Computer-based Laboratory for Automated School Systems; Current Literature Alerting Search Service

class A's class-A narcotics (addictive drugs such as opium and its derivatives)

class B's class-B narcotics (almost non-addictive drugs such as codeine and nalline)

CLASSIC Classroom Interactive Computer

Classical Prokofiev's Symphony No. 1

Classic City Kyoto, Honshu Island, Japan—famed for Buddhist and Shinto shrines and temples

classif classification

Classifier and Compiler Extraordinary Dr Peter Mark Roget

CLASSMATE Computer Language to Aid and Stimulate Scientific, Mathematical, and Technical Education

class M's class-M narcotics (non-addictive drugs)

classn classification

class X's class-X narcotics (drugs containing small amounts of narcotics such as cough syrups with non-narcotic and almost non-addictive codeine)

clat communication line adapters for teletype

CLAT Confederation of Latin American Teachers

Claude Lorraine Claude Gellée of Lorraine

Claudette Colbert Lily Cauchoin

Claudio Lars Carmen Brannon de Samayoa

clav clavecin; clavichord; clavicle

clave autoclave; steamclave (sterilizer)

clavicemb clavicembalo (Italian —clavichord)

claw. clustered atomic warhead

CLAW Community Law Workshop (New Zealand)

clax claxon

clayie playing marble made of clay and often coated with enamel paint

Claymont Girls Woods Haven-Kruse School for (delinquent) Girls at Claymont, Delaware

Clb Caleb

CLB Church Lads' Brigade; Configuration Liaison Board

clbbb complete left bundle branch block

clbr calibration

CLBs Combat Lessons Bulletins

c & lc capital and lower case letters

CLC Canadian Labour Congress; Canners League of California; Chiriqui Land Company; Cost of Living Council; task-fleet command cruiser (naval symbol)

CLCB City of Liverpool College of Building; Committee of London Clearing Banks

CLCCS Cammel-Laird Cable-Control System

cl/cll counseling learning/community language learning

CLCMD Cleveland Contract Management District

CL & Co Cammell Laird and Company (shipbuilders)

clcs current-logic-current switching

clct collector

CLCT City of Liverpool College of Technology

cld cancelled; chronic liver disease; chronic lung disease; cleared; colored; cooled; cost laid down

cld (CLD) called (line)

CLD Central Library and Documentation

CLDAS Clinical Laboratory Data Acquisition System

cldwn cooldown

cldy cloudy

CLE Cleveland, Ohio (Hopkins Airport)

Clea Cleopatra

CLEA Canadian Library Exhibitor's Association

clean. comprehensive lake-ecosystem analyzer

CLEAN Committee for Leaving the Environment of America Natural; Commonwealth Law Enforcement Assistance Network (Pennsylvania)

Cleanest Port in the Orient Singapore

CLEAPSE Consortium of Local Education Authorities for the Provision of Science Equipment

CLEAR Center for Lake Erie Area Research; Civic Leaders for Ecological Action and Responsibility; Closed-Loop Evaluation and Reporting (system); Committee to Leach the Environment of Acid Rain; County Law Enforcement Applied Regionally

Clearwaters Clearwater Mountains of Idaho

Cleat NATO name for Soviet Tupolev Tu-124 long-range transport

clec closed-loop ecological cycle

CLEC Citizen/Labor Energy Coalition

Clem Clemens; Clement; Clementina; Clementine

CLEMARS California Law-Enforcement Mutual-Aid Radio System

Clemte Clemente

CLENE Continuing Library Education Network and Exchange

cleo clear language for expressing orders

Cleo Cleopatra

CLEO Council on Legal Education Opportunity

cleopatra comprehensive language for elegant operating system and translator design

CLEP College-Level Education Program; College-Level Examination Program

CLEPR Council on Legal Education for Professional Responsibility

cler clerical; controlled letter contract reduction

cleric. clerical(s); clerical error; clericalism; clericality; clerically

CLES Customs Law-Enforcement Service

CLETS California Law Enforcement Telecommunications System

CLEU Coordinated Law Enforcement Unit

Cleve Cleveland

Cleve Orch Cleveland Orchestra

CLEVPDis Cleveland Procurement District (US Army)

CLEW Chicago Law Enforcement Week

clf capacitive loss factor

CLF Chicano Liberation Front; Church of the Larger Fellowship (Unitarian Universalist); Commonwealth Literary Fund(ing)

CLFNE Conservational Law Foundation of New England

Clfs Cliffs

clg calling; ceiling; clearing

Clg College

CLG light guided-missile cruiser (3-letter symbol)

CLGA Composers and Lyricists Guild of America

CLGES California Life Goals Evaluation Schedules

clgp (CLGP) cannon-launched guided projectile

clgsfu clear glazed structural facing units

clgsub clear glazed structural unit base

cl gt cloth gilt

CLGW Cement, Lime and Gypsum Workers (union)

Cl H Clare Hall, Cambridge

CLH *Croix de la Légion d'Honneur* (French—Cross of the Legion of Honor)

CLHU Computation Laboratory of Harvard University

cli central life interests; coin-level indicator; cost-of-living index

CLI Cost-of-Living Index

CLIA Clinical Laboratory Improvement Act; Cruise Lines International Association

C-library circulating library

CLIC Corporate Library Information Centre (Canadian)

clics computer-linked information for container shipping

Cliff Clifford; Clifton

Clifford Ashdown pseudonym shared by R Austin Freeman and John James Pitcairn

Clifton Webb Webb Parmalee Hollenbeck

clim climatic

CLIMAPS Climate Long-range Investigation, Mapping, and Prediction Study

climat climatological; climatologist; climatology

Climatol Climatology

CLIMPO Contract Liaison and Master Planning Office

clin clinic; clinical; clinicial; clinometer

CLIN Contract Line Item Number

clin/d clinical death

clink (generic nickname—prison)—also the nickname for brothels and in London, where it originated in Clink Prison, also stands for the Southwark Fair depicted by Hogarth

clin path clinical pathology

clin proc clinical procedures

Clint Clinton

Clinton Men Clinton Correctional Facility at Dannemora, New York

Clinton's Big Ditch Erie Canal advocated by Governor De Witt Clinton of New York

Clinton Women Correctional Institution for Women at Clinton, New Jersey

Clio Joseph Addison's pseudonym; in Greek mythology the muse of history or of lyre playing

clip. compiler language for information processing; contused, lacerated, incised, and punctured (wounds)

CLIP Cancel Launch in Progress (USAF); Country Logistics Improvement Program (USAF)

clips. clippings; computer launch interference problems

CLIS Central Library and Information Services; Clearinghouse for Library Information Sciences

clit clitoral; clitoridectomy; clitoris

C. Litt. Companion of Literature

clj control joint

Clj *Callejon* (Spanish—alley, blind alley, cul-de-sac, lane)

CLJ *Cambridge Law Journal*

CLJC Copiah-Lincoln Junior College

clk clerk; clock

CLK hunter-killer cruiser (naval symbol)

clkg caulking

clks clockwise

clkws clockwise

cll cholesterol lowering lipid; chronic lymphatic leukemia; chronic lymphocytic leukemia; circuit load logic; community language learning

CLL Chief of Legislative Liaison

cllo *cuartillo* (Spanish—fourth of a real, pint)

Cllr Councillor

clm column; columnar

c-lm common-law marriage

Clm Culham

CLM Canadian Liberation Movement

CLMA Cigarette Lighter Manufacturers Association; Contact Lens Manufacturers Association

CLML *Current List of Medical Literature*

CLMS Clinical Laboratory Monitoring System; Company Lightweight Mortar System

cln colon; corrective lens

Cln Colón

clnc clearance

CLNP Crater Lake National Park (Oregon)

clnr cleaner

CLNS Cape Lookout National Seashore (North Carolina)

clnt coolant

CLNTS China Lake Naval Test Station

CLNWR Crescent Lake National Wildlife Refuge (Nebraska)

clo closet; cloth; clothing; cod liver oil

Clo Callao

CLO Cali, Colombia (Calipuerto airport); Chief Liaison Officer; Citizens for Law and Order; Civic Light Opera (Los Angeles); Cornell Laboratory of Ornithology

CLOB Composite Limit Order Book

CLOC Computerized Logging and Outage Control

CLOCE Contingency Lines of Communication Europe

Clock Haydn's Symphony No. 101 in D major

Clod NATO nickname for the

Soviet Antonov 6-seat piston-powered transport plane

CLODS Computerized Logic-Oriented Design System

clog. change log (for software); computer-logic graphics

clor container loaded at owner's risk

clora closed-form ray analysis

clos closure; command to line of sight

Cloud Piercer New Zealand's Mount Cook (12,349 feet or 3764 meters)

clousy cloudy—lousy (weather)

Clown Prince of Music Danny Kaye

Clowns of the Canine World dachshunds

clp control line platform; criminal law and procedure

clp (CLP) command language processor

Clp Cornell list processor (language)

CLP Cargo Loss Prevention; Carnegie Library of Pittsburgh; Country Liberal Party

CLPA Common Law Procedure Acts

cl pal cleft pallet

clpr caliper

clr center of lateral resistance; clear; clearing; cooler

clr (CLR) computer language recorder

CLR Central London Railway; Council on Library Research; Council on Library Resources

CL&R Canal, Lake, and Rail

CLR *Common Law Reports*; *Commonwealth Law Reports*

CLRA Consumer Law Reform Association

CLRB Canada Labour Relations Board

CLRI Council on Library Resources Incorporated

clrm classroom

clr test chloride test

CLRU Cambridge Language Research Unit

CLRV Canadian Light Rail Vehicle

cls coils

cls (CLS) close (flow chart)

CLS Certificate in Library Science; Country Library Service

CLSA Conservation Law Society of America; Contact Lens Society of Australia

CLSB California Library Services Board

CLSC Chautauqua Literary and Scientific Circle

CLSCS Cain-Levine Social Competency Scale

clsd closed

clsg closing

CLSG Contact Lens Study Group

CLSI Computer Library Services, Inc

clsl chronic lymphosarcoma leukemia

CLSP Cape Lookout State Park (Oregon)

clsr closure

clst clarinettist

clsx close-loop support extended

clt communications line terminals

CLT Charlotte, North Carolina (airport)

CLT *Canadian Law Times*

CLTA Canadian Library Trustees Association; Canterbury Lawn Tennis Association; Chinese Language Teachers Association

C Lt-Cdr Communication Lieutenant-Commander

cltgl climatological

cltgr climatographer

cltv closed-loop television

clu central logic unit; circuit lineup

CLU Chartered Life Underwriter

CLUB Central Library of the University of Baghdad

Clubland Pall Mall clubhouse section of London

Club Med Club Méditerranée

CLUC Central Library Union Catalog

CLUM Civil Liberties Union of Massachusetts

CLUMIS Cadastral and Land-Use Mapping Information System

clurt come let us reason together (mediator's motto)

CLUS continental limits United States

CLUSA Cooperative League of the USA

clv clevis

Clv Cleveland

clvd calved

clvs calves

Clw Collingwood

CLW Council for a Livable World

clwg clear wire glass

clws clockwise

Cly Clyde; Clydebank

Clydebank Scotland's shipyard city on the River Clyde northwest of Glasgow

clz copper, lead, or zinc (cargo)

cm center of mass; centimeter(s); circular mil; circular muscle; contrast media; costal margin; countermortar; mechanic (symbol)

cm (CM) command module; communications multiplexor

c'm' come

c/m color modulation (tv); communications multiplexer; control and monitoring; corrected manifest; current month

c&m cocaine and morphine

cm *carat métrique* (French—metric carat); *Zentimeter* (German—centimeter)

c.m. *causa mortis* (Latin—cause of death); *cras mane* (Latin—tomorrow morning)

Cm curium

Cm *Camino* (Spanish—highway)

CM absolute coefficient of pitching moments (symbol); Canadian Militia; Certificate of Merit; Certificated Master (or Mistress); Circulation Manager; Clyde-Mallory (steamship line); Command Module; Commercial Message; Common Market; Configuration Management; Corporate Member(ship); Corresponding Member; Court Martial; Cow Month (New Zealand); mine layer (naval symbol)

C-M Charente-Maritime

C.M. central meridian; *Chirurgiae Magister* (Latin—Master of Surgery)

C/M Curtis/Mathes

C of M Certificate of Merit; Count(y) of Mark

CM *Collegiate Microcomputer*; *Correo Maritimo* (Spanish—sea mail)—appears on flags of Spanish mail ships

cm² square centimeter

cm³ cubic centimeter

CM4 Comet 4 jet airplane

cma civil-military affairs

Cma Camilla

Cᵐᵃ *Cima* (French or Italian—summit)

C Ma Canis Major

CMA Cable Makers Australia; California Maritime Academy; California Medical Association; Canadian Manufacturers Association; Canadian Medical Association; Candle Manufacturers Association; Canterbury Manufacturers Association; Cash Management

Account(ing); Casket Manufacturers Association; Central Monetary Authority; Certified Medical Assistant; Chemical Manufacturers Association; Chinese Manufacturers Association; Chocolate Manufacturers Association; Cigar Manufacturers Association; Cleveland Metal Abrasive (company); Clothespin Manufacturers Association; Colleges of Mid-America; Colorado Mining Association; Commonwealth Medical Association; Confederate Memorial Association; Continental Marketing Association; Court of Military Appeals; Crucible Manufacturers Association

CMA (C.M.A.) Certified Management Accountant

CMA Compañia Mexicana de Aviación (Spanish—Mexican Aviation Company)

CMAA Cleveland Musical Arts Association; Comics Magazine Association of America; Crane Manufacturers Association of America

CMAAC Certified Medical Assistant Administrative and Clinical

CMAAO Confederation of Medical Associations in Asia and Oceania

cmab clothing maintenance allowance, basic

CMAC Capital Military Assistance Command; Catholic Marriage Advisory Council; Computer Management and Control

CMAD Computer Manufacture and Design

cmai clothing maintenance allowance, initial

C Maj Canis Major

CMAL Clothing Monetary Allowance List; Coal Mines Authority Limited

CMAR Can't Manage A Rifle

C/marca Cundinamarca, Colombia

CMAS Confédération Mondiale des Activités Subaquatiques (World Confederation of Subaquatic Activities); Council for Military Aircraft Standards

CMAT Canadian Mathematics Achievement Test

CMAV Coalition Mondiale pour l'Abolition de la Vivisection (French—World Coalition for the Abolition of Vivi-

section)

cmb carbolic methylene blue; chloromercuribenzoate

Cmb Colombo

CMB Chase Manhattan Bank; Cheese Marketing Board; Cina Motor Bus; coastal motor boat; Colombo, Ceylon (airport); Combat Maneuver Battalion(s); Compagnie Maritime Belge (Royal Belgian Lloyd Line)

CMB Consejo Mundial de Boxeo (Spanish—World Boxing Commission); *cuyas manos beso* (Spanish—whose hands I kiss)—very respectfully yours

CMBARMTNG Combined Arms Training

CMBI Caribbean Marine Biological Institute

CMBs Certified Mortgage Loan Brokers

cmbt combat

cmc code for magnetic characters; contact-making clock; coordinated manual control

cmc (CMC) carboxymethyl cellulose

CMc coastal mine layer (naval symbol)

CMC Canadian Marconi Company; Canadian Music Council; China Machinery Company; Commandant of the Marine Corps; Commercial Metals Company

CMCC Canadian Memorial Chiropractic College; Classified Matter Control Center

cm-cellulose carboxymethyl cellulose

cmcr continuous melting, casting, and rolling

CMCR Compagnie Maritime des Chargeurs Réunis

cmct communicate; communication

cmd command; common meter double

CMD California Moderate Democrats; Center for Management Development; Center for Moral Democracy (NYC); Central Marine Depot; Contract Management District

cmdg commanding

Cmdr Commander

CMDR Council for Microphotography and Documentary Reproduction

Cmdre Commodore

Cmdt Commandant

cmdty commodity

cme continuing medical education

CME California Motor Express; Center for Musical Experience; Central Medical Establishment; Chicago Mercantile Exchange (formerly Chicago Butter and Egg Board); Chicago Merchandise Exchange; Courtesy Motorboat Examination (U.S. Coast Guard)

CME Conférence Mondiale de l'Energie (French—World Power Conference)

CMEA Council for Mutual Economic Assistance (also called CEMA or COMECON or by its founder's Russian name *Soviet Ekonomicheskoi Vzaimopomoshchi–SEV*)

CMEC Council of Ministers of Education (Canadian)

CMERD Centre for Medical Education, Research, and Development (New South Wales)

c'mere come here

CMERI Central Mechanical Engineering Research Institute (India)

cmet coated metal

cmf calcium-and-magnesium-free; countermortar fire; cylindrical magnetic film

cmf (CMF) cyclophosphamide methotrexate 5-fluorouracil (anticarcinogen)

CMF Citizen Military Forces; Commonwealth Military Forces; Composite Medical Facility

CMFNZ Chamber Music Federation of New Zealand

CMFRI Central Marine Fisheries Research Institute

cmfsw calcium-and-magnesium-free seawater

cmg call me gov(ernor); control-moment gyroscope

CMG Computer Management Group; Corning Museum of Glass

C.M.G. Companion of the Order of St Michael and St George

CMGH Cleveland Metropolitan General Hospital

cmh countermeasures homing

CMH Columbus, Ohio (airport); Combined Military Hospital; Congressional Medal of Honor; Council for the Mentally Handicapped; County Mental Health

cmha confidential, modified handling authorized

CMHA Canadian Mental Health Association

CMHC Central Mortgage and Housing Corporation; Community Mental Health Center(s)

CMHCA Community Mental Health Centers Act

CMHPA Cloves Memorial Hall for the Performing Arts (Indianapolis)

cmi carbohydrate metabolism index; cellular-mediated immune (response); container master information; cumulative monthly issue

cmi (CMI) computer-managed instruction

C Mi Canis Minor

CMI Can Manufacturers Institute; Career Maturity Inventory; Christian Michelson Institute (for Science and Free Thought—Bergen, Norway); Church Management Institute (Episcopal); Comité Météorologique Internationale (International Meteorological Committee); Command Maintenance Inspection (US Army); Commission Mixte Internationale (International Mixed Commission for Experience Relative to the Protection of Telecommunication Lines and Underground Cables); Commonwealth Mining Investments; Commonwealth Mycological Institute; Consolidated Metal Industries; Cornell Medical Index

CMI *Cornell Medical Index*

CMIA Coal Mining Institute of America; Cultivated Mushroom Institute of America

cmid cytomegalic inclusion disease

cmif career-management individual file

CMIK *Choson Minjujuui In'min Konghwaguk* (North Korea)

cmil circular mil

c/min cycles per minute

C Min Canis Minor

CMIU Cigar Makers' International Union

CMJ Church Mission to the Jews; Church's Ministry among the Jews

CMJ *Computer Music Journal*

cml chemical; circuit micrologic; commercial; current mode logic

cml (CML) chronic myelocytic leukemia

CML Central Music Library; Colonial Mutual Life; Container Marine Lines

CML *Camara Municipal de Lisboa* (Portuguese—Lisbon Town Council)

CMLA Canadian Music Library Association; Central Medical Library Association; Chief Martial Law Administrator (Bangladesh); Civilian Maimed and Limbless Association

CmlC Chemical Corps

cml def chemical defense

CMLEA California Media and Library Educators Association

cmlops chemical operations

CMLS Cleveland-Marshall Law School

CM/LSCNP Cradle Mountain/Lake Saint Clair National Park (Tasmania)

CMLU Container Marine Lines (container) Unit

cmm cubic millimeter(s); cutaneous malignant melanoma

CMM Center for Male Medicine, Central Methodist Mission; Chief Machinist's Mate (USN); Commission for Maritime Meteorology (WMO)

cmma clothing monetary maintenance allowance

CMMA Concrete Mixer Manufacturers Association

CMMBE Comissão Militar Mista Brasil-Estados Unidos (Mixed Brazilian-American Military Commission)

cmmch combat Mach change

cmme carcinogenesis of chloromethyl-methyl ether

CMMM Chase Manhattan Money Museum (New York City)

cmmnd command(ing)

CMMP Commodity Management Master Plan

CMMS Columbia Mental Maturity Scale

cmn commission; cystic medial necrosis

CMN Common Market Nationals; Common Market Nations

CMN *Common Market News*; *Conselho Monetario Nacional* (Portuguese—National Monetary Council)—Brazil

cmn-aa cystic medial necrosis of the ascending aorta

cmnce commence

CMNH Cleveland Museum of Natural History

CMNM Capulin Mountain National Monument; Craters of the Moon National Monument

cmnr commissioner

cmo cardiac minute output; computer microfilm output

CMO Chief Medical Officer; Commonwealth Medical Officer; Configuration Management Office; Contract Management Office(r)

c'mon come on

cmos (CMOS) complementary metal-oxide semiconductor

cmp corrugated metal pipe; cost of maintaining product

cmp (CMP) compare (flow chart); computation(al)

CMP Catoctin Mountain Park (Maryland); Christian Movement for Peace; Church Music Publishers; Company of Mission Priests; Controlled Materials Plan; Cornell Maritime Press; Corps of Military Police

CMPC California Manpower Planning Council

CMPC *Compañia Manufacturera de Paneles y Cartones* (Spanish—Paper and Carton Manufacturing Company)

cmpd compound; compounded; compounding

cm pf cumulative preference; cumulatve preferred (shares)

cmpl complement (flow chart)

cmpld compiled

cmplx complex

Cmpn Companion

Cmpn IAP Companion of the Institution of Analysts & Programmers

cmpnt component

CMPO Calcutta Metropolitan Planning Organisation

cmps centimeters per second

cmpt component

cmptr computer

cmr cerebral metabolic rate; common-mode rejection

CMR Communications Monitoring Report; Consolidated Mail Room; Contract Management Region

cmrO$_2$ cerebral metabolic rate for oxygen

CMRA Chemical Marketing Research Association

CMRB Chemicals and Minerals Requirements Board

CMRE California Marriage-Readiness Evaluation

CMRF Childrens Medical Research Foundation

cmrg cerebral metabolic rate of glucose

CMRL Chamber of Mines and

Research Laboratories

CMRN Cooperative Meteorological Rocket Network

CMRNWR Charles M. Russell National Wildlife Range (Montana)

cmro cerebral metabolic rate of oxygen

CMRO County Milk Regulations Office(r)

cmrr common mode rejection ratio

cmrs computer-managed rotation schedules

CMRs Classified Material Receipts

CMRS Countermeasures Receiver System

cm/s centimeters per second

c.m.s. *cras mane sumendus* (Latin—to be taken tomorrow morning)

CMS California Museum of Science; Center for Measurement Science (George Washington University); Chicago Medical School; Chief Master Sergeant; Christian Medical Society; Church Missionary Society; College Music Society; Compagnie Maritime de la Seine; Computer Management System; Configuration Management System; Consumers and Marketing Service; Contemporary Music Society; Correctional Medical Systems

CM & SA Canning Machinery and Supplies Association

CMSC Central Missouri State College

CMSEP Contractor Management System Evaluation Program

CMSER Commission on Marine Science, Engineering, and Resources

CMSG Canadian Merchant Service Guild

CMSgt Chief Master Sergeant

CMSI California Museum of Science and Industry

CMS & I California Museum of Science and Industry

cm/sm command module/service module

CMSN China Merchants Steam Navigation (company)

CMSTP & P Chicago, Milwaukee, St Paul and Pacific (railroad)

cmt comment; confluence of major and tributary (rivers); cut, make, and trim (clothing)

CMT California Mastitis Test; California Motor Transport;

Camden Marine Terminals; Compulsory Military Training; Concert Memory Test; Current Medical Terminology; Current Mortuary Tables

CMT *Confederation Mondiale du Travail* (French—World Confederation of Labor)

CMTA Chinese Musical and Theatrical Association

CMTC Citizens Military Training Camp

cmt/conc cement or concrete

CMTCS Computer Management Transaction Control System

CMTCU Communications Message Traffic Control Unit

cmte committee

Cmto Caminito

Cmto *Caminito* (Spanish—small street)

cmu central markup unit; chlorophenyldimethylurea; concrete masonry unit

CMU Central Michigan University; Church Management Institute

C-M U Carnegie-Mellon University

CMUA Commercial Motor Users Association

cmv cytomegalovirus

cmv (CMV) cytomegalovirus (herpes)

cmvm contact-making (or breaking) voltmeter

CM von W Carl María von Weber

CMVPB California Motor Vehicles Pollution Board

cmw critical minimum weight

CMW Citizens for Migrant Workers

CMWA Country Meat Works Association

cmy civilian man-years

cmz concordant memory zone

CMZ Compagnie Maritime du Zaire

CMZS Corresponding Member of the Zoological Society

cn canal; cannon; coordination number

cn (CN) chloroacetophenone

c/n carbon-to-nitrogen ratio; carrier-to-noise ratio

c/n (C/N) credit note

c.n. *cras nocte* (Latin—tomorrow night)

Cn contract number; cumulonimbus

CN absolute coefficient of yawing moments (aerodynamic symbol); Carl Nielsen; Central Airlines; Chinese Nationalist;

Code Napoléon; Commonwealth Nations; compass north; Confederate Navy; cosine of the amplitude (mathematical symbol)

C & N communication and navigation

CN Canadian National-Grand Trunk Railways

cna code not allocated

CNA Canadian Nuclear Association; Canadian Numismatic Association; Canadian Nurses Association; Center for Naval Analyses (Franklin Institute); Central News Agency (Nationalist China); Central Northern Airways; Chemical Notation Association; Chief of Naval Air; Chief of Naval Aviation; Community Newspaper Association

CNA *Comisión Nacional del Azúcar* (Spanish—National Sugar Commission)—Mexico

CNAA Council for National Academic Awards

CNAC China National Aviation Corporation

CNADS Conference of National Armaments Directors

CNAEA California Narcotic Addict Evaluation Authority

CNAN Compagnie Navale Afrique du Nord

CNAS Chief of Naval Air Services; Civil Navigation Aids System

CNASA Council of North Atlantic Shipping Associations

CNATra Chief of Naval Air Training

CNAV Canadian Naval Auxiliary Vessel

CNAVSTA Charleston Naval Station (South Carolina)

CNB Central Narcotic Bureau (Singapore); Crocker National Bank

Cnbr Canberra

CNBS *Comisión Nacional Bancaria y Seguros* (Spanish—National Banking and Security Commission)—Mexico

cnc central navigation computer; computer numerical control; consecutive number control

Cnc Cancer

CNC Christopher Newport College

Cncl(r) Council(or)

CNCMH Canadian National Committee for Mental Hygiene

CNCO China Navigation Company

CNCP Canadian National/Canadian Pacific (telecommunications)

cncr concurrent

cnct connect(ion)

cnd condition(ed); conduit

CND Campaign for Nuclear Disarmament; Commission on Narcotic Drugs (UN)

CND Code Names Dictionary

cndi commercial nondevelopment items

cn di combination die

CNDP Communications Network Design Procedure(s)

cnds condensate

cne chronic nervous exhaustion

CNE Canadian National Exhibition

cnee consignee

Cnel Coronel (Spanish—Colonel)

CNEL community noise equivalent level

C'nella Cornelia

CNEN Comisión Nacional de Energía Nuclear (National Nuclear Energy Commission)

CNEngO Chief Naval Engineering Officer

CNEP Cable Network Engineering Program (Bell)

CNES Centre National d'Etudes Spatiales (National Center for Space Studies)

CNET Chief of Naval Education and Training

CNET Centre National d' Etude des Télécommunications (Telecommunication National Study Center)

CNEXO Centre pour d'Exploitationdes Océans (Center for the Exploitation of the Oceans)

cnf confine

CNF Caribbean National Forest (Puerto Rico); Cleveland National Forest (near San Diego, California)

cng compressed natural gas

CNG Connecticut Natural Gas

CNGA California Natural Gas Association

CN-gas cyanide gas (deadly poisonous and forbidden by the Geneva Convention)

CNGB Chief, National Guard Bureau

CNGO Committee on Non-Governmental Organizations (UN)

CNGT Commonwealth New Guinea Timbers

CN-GT Canadian National

Railways-Grand Trunk Western

CNH Community Nursing Home

cnhd congenital nonspherocytic hemolytic disease

CNHI Committee for National Health Insurance

CNHM Chicago Natural History Museum (Field Museum of Natural History)

CNI Chief of Naval Information; Communications—Navigation and Identification

CNI Centro de Información Nacional (Spanish—National Information Center)—Chilean security police; *Centro Nacional de Informaciones* (Spanish—National Information Center)—Chile's intelligence service

CNIB Canadian National Institute for the Blind

CNIE Comisión Nacional de Inversión Extranjiera (Spanish—National Commission for Foreign Investment)—Mexico

CNIF Conseil National des Ingénieurs Français (National Council of French Engineers)

CNIN California Narcotic Information Network

CNIPA Committee of National Institutes of Patent Agents

CNJ Central of New Jersey (railroad)

cnl cancel(lation); cardiolipin natural lecithin

cnl (CNL) circuit net loss

CNL Canadian National Library (Ottawa); Commonwealth National Library (Canberra)

CNLA Canadian National Library Association; Council of National Library Associations

CNLIA Council of National Library and Information Associations

CNM Cabrillo National Monument; Chief of Naval Material; Chiricahua National Monument; Colombo National Museum; Colorado National Monument

CN-M Certified Nurse-Midwife

CNN Cable News Network

CNN Compagnie de Navigation Nationale (French—National Navigation Company)

CNNR Caerlaverock National Nature Reserve (Scotland); Cairngorms National Nature Reserve (Scotland)

cno computer non-operational

C^{no} Corno (Italian—peak, summit)

CNO Chief of Naval Operations; Chief Nursing Officer

CNOA California Narcotics Officers Association

CNOAE Council of National Organizations of Adult Education

CNOBO Chief of Naval Operations Budget Office

cnop conditional no operation

cnor consignor

C-note $100 bill

CNP Canyonlands National Park (Utah); Caramoan NP (Philippines); Cleveland NP (South Australia); Colonial NP (Virginia); Compagnie Navale des Pétroles; Compagnie de Navigation Paquet; Corbett NP (India); Cyril Northcote Parkinson

CNP Compañía Navegación Peruana (Peruvian Navigation Company)

CNPA California Newspaper Publishers Association

CNPB Canadian National Parole Board

cn/pnl contractor's panel

CNPP Centre National de Prévention et de Protection

CNPS California Native Plant Society

cnr carrier-to-noise ratio; composite noise rating; corner

Cnr Corner

CNR Canadian National Railway; Civil Nursing Reserve; Coleford Nature Reserve (South Africa)

CNR Consiglio Nazionale delle Ricerche (Italian—National Research Council)

CNRA Curecanti National Recreation Area (Colorado)

CNRS Centre National de la Recherche Scientifique (National Center for Scientific Research)

cnrt concrete

cns central nervous system

cns (CNS) central nervous system

c.n.s. cras nocte sumendus (Latin—to be taken tomorrow night)

Cns Cairns

CNS Center for New Schools; Chief of the Naval Staff; Congress of Neurological Surgeons; Copley News Service

CNS Chubu Nippon Shimbun (Central Japan Newspaper)

CNSA Carl Nielsen Society of

America
cnsg consolidated nuclear steam generator
cnsl console (flow chart)
Cnst Pty Constitution Party
cnstr canister
CNSWTG Commander, Naval Special Warfare Task Group
cnt celestial navigation trainer (CNT); count(er)
cnt (CNT) celestial navigation trainer
CNT Canadian National Telegraphs; Composite Negotiating Text(s)
CNT *Compañia Nacional de Teléfonos* (Spanish—National Telephone Company); *Confederación Nacional de Trabajo*(Spanish—National Confederation of Labor)—anarchosyndicalist trades-union confederation; *Conselho Nacional de Telecomunicação* (Portuguese—National Telecommunications Council)—government-controlled radio and television for all Brazil
CNTB Colombia National Tourist Board
CNTCA Canadian National Railway—Transcanada Airlines
cntn contain
cntr container; contribute; contribution; counter
Cntr Centaur (space vehicle)
cntrfugl centrifugal
cntrl central; control(ler)
cntrs containers
CNTU Canadian National Trade Unions; Confederation of National Trade Unions
CNUCE *Centro Nazionale Universitario di Calcol Electronico* (Italian—National University Center of Electronic Calculation)
Cnut King Canute II of Denmark and England
cnv contingent negative variation
CNV Cape Canaveral, Florida (tracking station)
CNVA Committee for Non-Violent Action
cnvc conveyance
cnvr conveyor
cnvt convict
C & NW Chicago and North Western (railway)
CNWDI Critical Nuclear Weapons Design Information
CNWR Camas National Wildlife Refuge (Idaho); Chassahowitzka NWR (Florida); Cha-

tauqua NWR (Illinois); Chincoteague NWR (Virginia); Columbia NWR (Washington)
CNX Canadian National Exposition
CNYP Central New York Power (corporation)
co carbon monoxide; cardiac output; castor oil; cervicoaxial; cleanout; coenzyme; conscientious objector; convenience outlet; corneal opacity; criminal offense; crossover(s); cutoff; cutout
co (CO) close/open (to official correspondece)
c-o cutoff
c/o care of; carried over; cash order; complains of
co *compagno* (Italian—company); (Latin prefix—together) —copulation (sexual togetherness)
co. *compositus* [Latin—compound(ed)]
Co cobalt; Colombia; Colombian; Colombiano; Columbia; Columbian; Company; County
C/o complained of
C[v] *Cabeço* (Portuguese—hillock, knoll, mound)
CO carbon monoxide; Certificate of Origin; Cleveland Orchestra; Colonial Office; Commanding Officer; conscientious objector; Continental Airlines (2-letter code); Copyright Office; Correctional Officer; Criminal Office; Crown Office(r)
C/O cash order; Chief Officer
C & O Chesapeake & Ohio (railroad)
C of O Count(y) of Oldenburg
co *1mo canto primo* (Italian—first treble)
CO₂ carbon dioxide
Co⁶⁰ radioactive cobalt
coa condition on admission
coA coenzyme A
CoA Committee on Accreditation (ALA); Council of the Americas
C o A Committee on Accreditation (ALA)
COA Canadian Orthopedic Association; Change Order Account; Chattanooga Opera Association; Connecticut Opera Association; Cordova Airlines; Correctional Officers Association
CO(A) Change Order (Aircraft)
COA *Comunidad Oriental Africana* (Spanish—East African

Community)
coac clutter-operated anti-clutter receiver
Coach NATO nickname for Soviet Ilyushin transport plane Il-12
Coad Coadjutor
COADS Command and Administration System (USA)
coag coagulant; coagulate; coagulation
coag time coagulation time
Coah Coahuila (inhabitants—Coahuileños or Coahuilenses)
Coal. Coalition
Coal City Pottsville, Pennsylvania
Coaley Samuel Coleridge-Taylor
coalit govt coalition government
coam coaming; customer-owned-and-maintained equipment
coam equip customer-owned-and-maintained equipment (data processing)
CO-AMP Cost Optimization-Analysis of Maintenance Policy
coas crewman optical alignment sight
COAS Council of the Organization of American States
Coast The Coast (Pacific coast of Canada and the United States)
Coastal Eastern East-Coast-of-the-United-States English reflecting cultural influences
Coast Line Atlantic Coast Line Railroad
Coatzacoalcos formerly Puerto Mexico
coax coaxial
c-o-b close of business
CoB Chief of Base (CIA)
C o B Chief of Boat (submarine)
COB Change Order Board; Command Operating Budget
COBA Correction Officers Benevolent Association
COBAS Council of Black Architectural Schools
Cobbler Poet Hans Sachs of Nuremberg also known as Prince of the Meistersingers
cobble(s) cobblestone(s)
COBF Cobol-F (program)
cobh carboxyhemoglobin
Cobh Gaelic name for Queenstown
cobility cobol utility (program)
Coblenz Koblenz
coblib cobol library

C & O-B & O Chesapeake and Ohio-Baltimore & Ohio (merged railroads)

cobol common business-oriented language

cobra. (COBRA) coolant boiling in rod arrays

Cobra Bolkow wire-guided anti-tank missile made in West Germany

COBRA Computadores Brasileiros (Portuguese—Brazilian Computers)

COBRAY Cobra + Moray (anti-terrorist academy)

COBSI Committee on Biological Sciences Information

COBTU Combined Over-the-Beach Terminal Unit

coc cathodal opening clonus; cathodal opening contraction; cocaine; coccygeal; combination-type oral contraceptive

Coc Cleveland open cup

CoC Chamber of Commerce

COC Canadian Opera Company; Combat Operations Center

coca cocaina(Spanish—cocaine)

coca-colon coca-colonization; coca-colonize; coca-colonizer

Cocaine Capital Bogotá, Colombia (close to the source of coca leaves) and Jackson Heights, Queens, New York (where so many Colombian cocaine pushers reside)

C & O Canal Chesapeake and Ohio Canal

COCAST Council for Overseas Colleges of Art, Science, and Technology

cocb crossed olivochochlear bundles

cocc coccyx

coccy coccidioidomycosis

COCESS Contractor-Operated Civil Engineer Supply Store

coch coach(es)

coch. cochleare (Latin—spoonful)

Coch Cochin

coch. ampl. cochleare amplum (Latin—tablespoonful)

COCHASE Code for Coupled-Channel Schrödinger Equations

coch. infant. cochleare infantis (Latin—teaspoonful)

Cochise Beech T-42 transport aircraft

coch. mag. cochleare magnum (Latin—tablespoonful)

coch. med. cochleare medium (Latin—dessertspoonful)

coch. parv. cochleare parvum

(Latin—teaspoonful)

COCI Council on Consumer Information

cock. cockney (dialect of London's East End and waterfront residents who by their own definition are born within sound of the bells of the Church of Saint Mary-le-Bow —Bow bells)

Cock Cockburn; NATO nickname for the Soviet Antonov 350-passenger plane

Cockade City Petersburg, Virginia

cockapoo crocker spaniel-poodle mix-breed dog

cockaterr cocker-terrier mixed-breed dog

Cockpit of Europe Belgium

Cockpit of the Middle East Syria

cocl cathodal opening clonus

C & OC NM Chesapeake and Ohio Canal National Monument

co-co carried-on-carried-off (break-bulk cargo)

Coco (French—Little Pet)

Coco Chanel Gabrielle Bonheur Chanel

cocohol coconut-oil-extended ethanol (diesel fuel)

COCOM Coordinating Committee for Export to Communist Area(s)

COCOSEER Coordinating Committee on Slavic and East European Library Services

cocp closed olivocochlear potential

cocr cylinder overflow control record

COCS Container Operating Control System

coct. coctio (Latin—boiling)

Co Cts County Courts

COCU Churches of Christ Uniting; Consultation on Church Union (of Episcopalians, Methodists, Presbyterians, and others)

cod. cause of death; chemical oxygen demand; cleanout door; codeine

c-o-d cargo-on-deck

c.o.d. cash-on-delivery

Co D Costume Designer

COD coding

COD Concise Oxford Dictionary

CODA Came Out Decades Ago; Committee on Drugs and Alcohol

codac coordination of operating data by automatic computer

CODAC Community Organization for Drug Abuse Control

CODAF Commission on Border Development and Friendship (U.S.-Mexican)

codag combined diesel and gas (turbine machinery)

codan carrier-operated device anti-noise

Codania (Latin—Copenhagen)

CODAP Client-Oriented Data-Acquisition Process; Control Data Assembly Program

CODAS Customer-Oriented Data System

CODASYL Conference on Data Systems Languages

CODC Canadian Oceanographic Data Center

codd codices

Codder(s) Cape Codder(s)

CODE Commission on Declining Enrollments; Committee on Donor Enlistment

Code 2 urgent call (proceed immediately but without siren—red or blue lights optional)

Code 3 emergency call (proceed immediately using red or blue lights and siren)

Code 7 time out to eat

codec coder decorder

coded. computer-oriented design of electronic devices

CODEF Chairman of Defense Committee

CODELCO Corporación del Cobre (Spanish—Copper Corporation)—Chile

codel(s) congressional delegation(s)

CODELS Computer Development System

Code N Code Napoléon

CODES Computer-Oriented Data Entry System

Codfishland Newfoundland

codic computer-directed communication(s)

codiphase coherent digital-phased array system

codit computer direct to telegraph

cod. memb. codex membranacius (Latin—book printed or written on skin or vellum)

CoDoC Cooperation in Documentation and Communication

codog combined diesel or gas

CODOT Classification of Occupations and Directory of Occupational Titles (UK)

CODSIA Council of Defense Space Industries Association

coe cab over engine (truck);

close of escrow (realty); crude oil equivalent

coe (COE) crossover electrophoresis

CoE Corps of Engineers

COE Commonwealth Office of Education; Corps of Engineers; Council for Occupational Education; Council on Optometric Education

CO(E) Change Order (Electronic)

COE Conseil Aecuménique des Eglises (French—World Council of Churches)

coea cost and operational effectiveness analysis

COEA Consejo de la Organización de los Estados Americanos (Spanish—Council of the Organization of American States)

coed coeducation(al); girl or woman student

coed (COED) computer-operated electronic display

co-ed co-editor

COEDS Char Oil Energy Development Systems

COEES Central Office Equipment Engineering System (Bell)

coef coefficient

coel (Greek *koilos*—cavity, hollow)—coelenterate, coelomate, coelostat(ic)

Coel Coelenterata

COENCO Committee for Environmental Conservation

COEP Community Outreach Educational Program

COEPS Cortically-Originating Extra-Pyramidal System

COESA Committee on Extension of the Standard Atmosphere (United States)

coet (COET) crude oil equalization tax(ation)

cof cause of failure; coefficient of friction

CoF Chaplain of the Fleet; Chief of Finance

cofad computerized facilities design

cofc container on flat car

coff cofferdam

COFFEE Community Organization for Full-Employment Economy

c/offer counter offer

Coffs Coffs Harbour, Australia

COFHE Consortium on Financing Higher Education

COFI Committee on Fisheries (FAO)

COFIDE Corporación Finan-

ciera de Desarrollo (Spanish—Financial Development Corporation)

COFIPS Central Ohio Federation of Information Processing Societies

COFIS Canadian On-Line Financial Information Service

COFO Council of Federated Organizations (CORE, NAACP, SCLC, SNCC)

COFPHE Capital Outlay Fund for Public Higher Education

co/fr counter offer

COFRC Chevron Oil Field Research Company

cofron copper iron (patent medicine mixture)

COFSAF Chief of Staff, U.S. Air Force

cofx component fixture

cog. cognate

c-o-g coal to oil to gas

CoG Council of Governments

COG Change Our Gender; Change Our Goal; Council of Governments

cogag combined gas and gas

CoGARD Coast Guard

cogas coal-oil-gas

cogb certified official government business

cogent. compiler and generalized translator

cogita computerized general I.Q. test(ing)

cogn cognomen

cognit cognition(al)(ly); cognitive(ly)

cogn w cognate with

cogo coordinate geometry

cog/prsl cognizant personnel

cogs. combat-oriented general support

COGS Continuous Orbital Guidance System

COGSA Carriage of Goods by Sea Act

cogtt cortisone-primed oral glucose tolerance test

coh cash-on-hand; coefficient of haze

COH carbohydrate (generalized formula)

COHA Council on Hemispheric Affairs

COHATA Compagnie Haitienne des Transports Aériens

cohb carboxyhemaglobin

Co Hd coral head

COHD Copyright Office History Document

coher cohere(d); coherence; coherency; coherer; cohering; coherent(ly)

COHM Copyright Office His-

tory Monograph

coho coherent oscillator

COHO Council of Health Organization

Cohoun Colquhoun

COHSE Confederation of Health Service Employees

coi classroom observation instrument; crack-opening interferometry

COI Central Office of Information; Certificate of Origin and Interest; Coordinator of Information

COI Comite Olimpico Internacional (Spanish—International Olympic Committee); *Commission Oceanographique Intergouvernementale* (French—Intergovernmental Oceanographic Commission)

COIC Canadian Oceanographic Identification Center; Combined Operations Intelligence Center

CoID Council of Industrial Design

coif coiffure

COIMS Council for International Organizations of Medical Sciences

coin. coinage; counterinsurgency—anti-guerrilla warfare

coin. (COIN) complete operating information

COIN Counterinsurgency

Coin & Curr Coin and Currency Institute

coin gold 90% gold, 10% copper

coin-op coin-operated

COINS Computer and Information Sciences; Computerized Information System(s); Control in Information Systems; Cooperative Intelligence Network System

coin silver 50 to 92.5% silver with balance of copper or other metals

co-intel counterintelligence

COINTELPRO Counterintelligence Program (FBI)

Cointrin Geneva, Switzerland's airport

COIR Commission on Intergroup Relations (NYC)

Cois François

COIT Central Office of the Industrial Tribunal (UK)

COIU Congress of Independent Unions

COJ Court of Justice

COJO Conference of Jewish Organizations

Cok Cochin

coke coca drink; cocaine

Coke Coca Cola; NATO nickname for the Soviet Antonov AN-26 350-passenger transport plane

Coke City Uniontown, Pennsylvania

cokesmoke cocaine smoker; cocaine smoking (doctors consider it dangerous)

cokesmokes cocaine smokers

col colon; colonial; colonic; colonist; colonization; colonize; colony; color; coloring; colorist; colors; column

col (COL) computer-oriented language

c-o-l (COL) cost of living

col. colatus (Latin—strained, as through a filter); *collum* (Latin —collar); *colon* (Latin—large intestine)

co-L co-latitude

Col Colchester; Colima; College; Cologne; Colombia(no); Colón; Colonel; Colossians; Epistle to the; Columba (con stellation); Coronel

Col Lucius Iunius Moderatus Columella (Roman writer on agriculture)

COL Computer Oriented Language

cola (COLA) cost-of-living adjustment; cost-of-living allowance

cola. cost-of-living allowance

cola colonia (Spanish—colony)

COLA Committee on Latin America; Committee on Library Automation (ALA)

COLAC Central Organization of Liaison for Application of Circuit

Col Alb College of the Albermarle

COLAs Cost-of-Living Adjustments

colat. colatus (Latin—strained)

col bh collision bulkhead

col C col canto (Italian—follow the voice)

COLC Cost of Living Council

cold. chronic obstructive lung disease

Col$ Colombian peso

COLDEMAR Compañía Colombiana de Navegación Maritima

colen. colentur (Latin—let them be strained, strain them)

Col Ency Columbia Encyclopedia

Col Ent Exam College Entrance Examination

coleop coleoptera; coleopterist

colet. coleatur (Latin—let it be strained, strain it)

Colette Sidonie Gabrielle Claudine de Jouvenal

colidar coherent light detection and ranging

Colin Nicholas

colingo compile online and go (data processing)

coll collect(or); collection; colloid(al); colloquial(ism)

Coll College; Collegiate

collab collaboration; collaborator

collabo(s) collaborator(s)

coll agc collection agency

Collar City Troy, New York

collat collateral

collect. collection; collective; collectively

College of New Jersey Princeton University's original name

College of Rhode Island Brown University's original name

Coll Ency Colliers' Encyclopedia

Collier-Macmillan Collier-Macmillan Library Service

Collins Wm Collins Sons & Co

Collins Bay Canadian penitentiary on Collins Bay near Kingston, Ontario

Coll L Collection Letter

Collodi (pseudonym—Carlo Lorenzini)

colloq colloquial(ism); colloquium

coll'ott coll'ottava (Italian—play in octaves, with the octave)

collr collector

collun. collunarium (Latin— nose wash)

collut. collutorium (Latin— mouthwash)

coll vol collective volume

Coll Wooster College of Wooster

colly collicry

collyr. collyrium (Latin—eyewash)

colm column

Colm Columba

COLMIS Collection Management Information System

colo colophon (printer's or publisher's device, symbol, or trademark)

Colo Colorado; Coloradan

Colo Colossians

Colo Assoc Colorado Associated University Press

colog cologarithm

cologne cologne brown (vandyke brown); cologne spirits (highly-concentrated ethyl alcohol); cologneware (mottled brown and gray stoneware); cologne water (eau de cologne toilet water); cologne yellow (chrome-yellow and lead-sulfate pigment)

Cologne (French—Köln)

colograph color lithograph

Colom Colombia; Colombian

Colom Christovão Colom (Portuguese—Christopher Columbus)

Colombia Republic of Colombia (Spanish-speaking South American two-ocean nation rich in such exports as bananas, coffee, emeralds, oil, and rubber, formerly included the territory of Panamá) *República de Colombia*

Colombia Británica (Spanish— British Columbia)

Colombia Day Colombian Independence Day (July 20)

Colombian Colombian-grown marijuana; Colombian mountain-grown coffee

Colombian connection nickname for network of Colombian brokers, farmers, gangsters, politicians, and smugglers connected with the export of Colombian-grown cocaleaf narcotic products and marijuana to Canada and the United States

Colombian First Colombia's best-known classical composer —Guillermo Uribe Holguin

Colombian Ports (largo, medium, and small from east to west) Santa Marta, Barranquilla, Cartagena, Covenas, Buenaventura, and small but notorious ports such as Ríohacha

Colombia's Principal Port Barranquilla

Colombo Christoforo Colombo (Italian—Christopher Colombus)

Colón formerly Aspinwall

Colonels natives of Kentucky

Colonia (Italian, Latin, Portuguese, Spanish—Cologne)— also called Colonia Agrippina, Colonia Claudia, or Colonia Ubiorum by the Romans or Köln by the Germans

Colonia Allobrogum (Latin— Geneva)

Colonia Julia Romana (Latin— Seville)—the Sevilla of the Spaniards

Colonia Munatiana (Latin—Basle)

Colonia Viriata (Latin—Madrid)

coloph colophon

Colorado Springs U.S. Air Force Academy at Colorado Springs, Colorado

colorectal colon rectal (area or cancer)

coloreds colored persons (South Africans of mixed blood)

Colossus of the African Continent the Sudan

Colossus of the Eurasian Continent the USSR

Colossus of Independence John Adams

Colossus of the Indian and Pacific Oceans Australia

Colossus of the North Latin American anti-imperialist nickname for the United States of America

Colossus of the North American Continent Canada

Colossus of the South American Continent Brazil

Colo St U Comm Colorado State University Institute in Technical and Industrial Communications

col p color page

COLPA Commission on Law and Public Affairs

Colquhoun Calhoun

colrad collegiate research and development

COLREG Regulations Governing Collisions

COLS Communications for On-Line Systems

Col-Sgt Colour-Sergeant

colspd collapsed

Col Sym Columbia Symphony

colt computerized on-line test(ing)

Colt Colt revolver (invented by Samuel Colt of Hartford, Connecticut); NATO nickname for the Soviet Antonov 14-passenger biplane designated AN-2

COLT Council on Library Technology; Council on Library-Media Technical-Assistants

Colt .45 Colt .45 automatic pistol or revolver

Colu Columba

Columbia America; South Carolina's capital; the United States

Columbia world's first space shuttle launched from Kennedy Space Center at Cape Canaveral, Florida—after a 54-½-hour flight across the Atlantic and over Africa, Asia, and the Pacific, landed at Edwards Air Force Base in California on April 14, 1981

Columbia City Vancouver, Washington

Columbia the Gem of the Ocean United States of America

Columbia the Gem of the Ocean symphonic poem by Charles Ives

Columbia River 1200-mile-long river serving British Columbia, Oregon, and Washington on its way to the North Pacific Ocean

Columbia School Columbia Training School at Columbia, Mississippi

Columbine Colorado's state flower—the Rocky Mountain Columbine

Columbus Columbus Day (October 12); Cristóbal Colón (Spanish); Cristoforo Colombo (Italian); name of places in some twelve states in the United States; Ohio's capital

Columbus House Columbus Workhouse and Women's Correctional Institution at Columbus, Ohio

Columbus of the Subconscious Sigmund Freud

com comedy; comma; command; commercial; commission; committee; common; communication(s); complement; compliment

com (COM) computer output on microfilm; computer-output microfilm(ing)

com or *con* or *cor* (Latin *cum*—together, with)—compound, confine, correct

com. commemoratio (Latin—commemoration)

Com Coma Berenices (constellation); Comoro Islands

COM Chief Operations Manager; Council of Ministers

COMA Coke Oven Managers' Association

comac continuous multiple-access comparator

COMACH Confederación Marítima de Chile (Spanish—Maritime Confederation of Chile)

COMAEGEAN Commander, Aegean

COMAINT Command Maintenance

COMAIR Commercial Airways

COMAIRCENT Commander, Allied Air Forces, Central Europe

COMAIRCENTLANT Air Commander, Central Atlantic

COMAIRCHAN Maritime Air Commander, Channel

COMAIRESTLANT Air Commander, Eastern Atlantic

COMAIRLANT Commander, Air Force, Atlantic

COMAIRNON Commander, Allied Air Forces, Northern Norway

COMAIRNORLANT Air Commander, Northern Atlantic

COMAIRNORTH Commander, Allied Air Forces, Northern Europe

COMAIRSONOR Commander, Allied Air Forces, Southern Norway

COMAIRSOUTH Commander, Allied Air Forces, Southern Europe

Comalco Commonwealth Aluminum Company (Australia)

COMANSEC Computation and Analysis Section (Canadian Defense Research Board)

COMANTDEFCOM Commander, United States Antilles Defense Command

comar computer aerial reconnaissance

COMARC Cooperative Machine Readable Cataloging

COMARRHIN Commander, Maritime Rhine

COMART Commander, Marine Air Reserve Training

comat computer-assisted training

COMAT Committee on Materials

COMATS Commander Military Air Transport Service

comb. combat; combination; combine; combing; combustion

COMBALTAP Allied Command Baltic Approaches (NATO)

COMBARFORCLANT Commander, Barrier Forces, Atlantic

COMBATCRULANT Commander, Battleship-Cruiser, Atlantic Fleet

combi combination

combine. combined harvester

COMBISLANT Commander, Bay of Biscay, Atlantic

COMBLACKBASE Commander, Black Sea Defense Sector

combo combination (of musicians, or of a safe)

COMBO Combined Arts of San Diego

combo lock(s) combination

lock(s)

COMBOSFORT Commander, Bosphorus Fortifications

COMBQUARFOR Combined Quarantine Force

Com Brit Comunidad Británica (Spanish—British Commonwealth of Nations)—Great Britain and former colonies

COMBRITELBE Commander, British Naval Elbe Squadron

COMBRITRHIN Commander, British Naval Rhine Squadron

combs. combinations

combu combustion

COMCANLANT Commander, Canadian Atlantic

COMCARIBSEAFRON Commander, Caribbean Sea Frontier

COMCAT Computer Output Microfilm Catalog

COMCEN Communications Center

COMCENTLANT Commander, Central Atlantic

ComCm communications counter-measures and deception

COMCRUDESFLOT Commander Cruiser-Destroyer Flotilla

COMCRUDESPAC Commander Cruisers and Destroyers in the Pacific (USN)

COMCRULANT Commander, Cruisers, Atlantic

comd command

COMDARFORT Commander, Dardanelles Fortifications

COMDESFLOT Commander, Destroyer Flotilla

COMDEV Commonwealth Development

comdg commanding

Comdr Commander

Comdt Commandant

COME Chief Ordnance Mechanical Engineer

comeas countermeasures

COMEASTSEAFRON Commander, Eastern Sea Frontier

COMECON Council of Mutual Economic Assistance (of communist nations)

COMED Communications Editing Unit

COMEDBASE Commander, Mediterranean Defense Sector

Comedian Pianist Victor Borge

Comedian's Comedian Bert Williams

COMEDS Continental Meteorological Data System

COMEINDORS Composite

Mechanized and Document Retrieval System

Comenius John Amos Komensky

COMERMEX Comercial Mexicano (Banco) (Spanish—Commercial Bank of Mexico)

Com Err Comedy of Errors

comet. computer operated management evaluation technique

Comet British medium tank built during World War II; De Haviland four-engine jet transport aircraft

COMET Committee for Middle East Trade; Controllability, Observability, and Maintenance Engineering Technic

COMETS Computer-Operated Multifunction Electronic Test Station

COMEX Commodity Exchange (NY)

COMEXCO Committee for Exploitation of the Oceans

COMFAIRELM Commander, Air Fleet, Eastern Atlantic and Mediterranean

COMFAIRWINGLANT Commander, Fleet Air Wing, Atlantic

Com Fran Comunidad Francesa (Spanish—French Community of Nations)—France and former colonies

comfy comfortable

Com-Gen Commissary-General

COMGENEUCOM Commanding General, European Command

COMGENTHIRDAIR Commanding General, Third Air Division

COMGENUSAFE Commanding General, U.S. Air Forces, Europe

COMGENUSAREUR Commanding General, U.S. Army, Europe

COMGERNORSEA Commander, German North Sea Subarea

COMGIBLANT Commander, Atlantic Approaches Gibraltar

COMIBERLANT Commander, Iberian Atlantic Area

COMIBOL Corporación Minera de Bolivia (Bolivian Mining Corporation)

COMICEDEFOR Commander, United States Iceland Defense Force

COMICS Computer-Oriented Managed-Inventory Control System

COMIL Chairman of Military Committee

comin' coming

COMINCH Commander-in-Chief, United States Fleet

COMIND Commander, Indian (USN)

Cominform Communist Information Bureau (latter-day name for the Comintern)

comint communications intelligence

Comintern Communist International; Cominform

Com Int Sec Committee on Internal Security (formerly House Committee on Un-American Activities—HUAC)

Com Isl Comoro Islands

comis° comisario (Spanish—commissary, delegate, deputy, manager, police inspector)

comit computer operations management information training

COMJUWATF Commander, Joint Unconventional Warfare Task Force

comkd completely knocked down

coml commercial

COMLA Commonwealth Library Association

COMLANDCENT Commander, Allied Land Forces, Central Europe

COMLANDEAST Commander, Allied Land Forces, Southeastern Europe

COMLANDMARK Commander, Allied Land Forces, Denmark

COMLANDNON Commander, Allied Land Forces, Northern Norway

COMLANDNORWAY Commander, Allied Land Forces, Norway

COMLANDSOUTH Commander, Allied Land Forces, Southern Europe

COMLANT Commander, Atlantic (USN)

COMLOGNET Combat Logistics Network

comm commerce; commercial; commission; committee; commonwealth; commune; communication; commutator

comm. commune (Latin—all the people, the community)

Comm. Commodore

Comm Commendatore (Italian—Commander, commended individual given this title, knight)—equivalent to the

British Sir

COMMAIRGIBLANT Commander, Maritime Air, Gibraltar, Atlantic

Commanders Commander Islands in the Bering Sea where the Russians call them Komandorskie

Commando C-46 Curtiss-Wright 36-passenger transport built during World War II; Cadillac-Gage amphibious armed car and military personnel carrier (XM-706); Dodge-built military personnel carrier built during World War II

Com Mat Cen Communication Materials Center (Columbia University)

Comm Bio Pest Committee for Biological Pest Control (San Ysidro, California)

COMMCEN Communications Center

commd command(ing); commissioned

commdg commanding

Commdr Commander

Commdt Commandant

Commedia Divina (Italian—Divine Comedy)—Dante's epic poem describing hell, purgatory, and paradise

commem commemoration; commemorative

Comments Nucl Part Phys Comments on Nuclear and Particle Physics

Commerce Department of Commerce; High School of Commerce

COMMFEX Communications Field Exercise

commfu complete and utterly monumental foulup

commi communism; communist

commie commissary; communist

commies communists

COMMIR Commissioner of Inland Revenue

Commiss Commissary

commn commission

commo communications

Commo Office of Communications (CIA)

commod commodity

Commoner The Commoner—William Jennings Bryan

Commons House of Commons

Commonwealth free association of the United Kingdom, Australia, Bahamas, Bangladesh, Barbados, Botswana, Canada, Cyprus, Ghana, Grenada,

Guyana, Fiji, India, Jamaica, Kenya, Lesotho, Malawi, Malaysia, Malta, Mauritius, Nauru, New Zealand, Nigeria, Sierra Leone, Singapore, Sri Lanka, Swaziland, Tanzania, The Gambia, Tonga, Trinidad and Tobago, Uganda, Western Samoa, Zambia, and their dependent territories

Commonwealth of Australia Australia and its territories

Commonwealth Day third Monday in May and celebrated in many parts of the British Commonwealth of Nations once called the British Empire

Commr Commissioner

commstitch communications failure detecting and switching (equipment)

commun communication

Communauté française French Community

commun dis communicable disease

Communism Peak Garmo or Stalin Peak (highest in the USSR with name subject to change with the politicians)

Communist Capitalist Friedrich Engels—well-paid factory executive in England and Prussia who collaborated with Karl Marx

Communist East oriental countries dominated by Red China

Communist West occidental countries dominated by the Soviet Union

Community of True Inspiration Amana, Iowa

Commun Math Phys Communications in Mathematical Physics

Commun Pure Appl Math Communications on Pure and Applied Mathematics

commuterport(s) commuter-type airport(s)

commy commissariat; commissary; communist

commz communications zone

comn common

ComNAB Commander, Naval Air Bases

COMNAVBASE Commander, Naval Base

COMNAVBREM Commander, Bremerhaven Naval Group

COMNAVCAG Commander, Naval Forces, Central Army Group Area and Bremerhaven

COMNAVCENT Commander, Allied Naval Forces, Central Europe

COMNAVCRUITCOMINST Commander, Naval Recruiting Command Instructions

COMNAVFORCESMARIANAS Commander, Naval Forces, Marianas Islands

COMNAVFORJAPAN Commander, Naval Forces, Japan

COMNAVGERBALT Commander, German Naval Forces, Baltic

COMNAVNORCENT Commander, Northern Air Forces, Central Europe

COMNAVNORTH Commander, Allied Naval Forces, Northern Europe

COMNAVSONOR Commander, Allied Naval Forces, Southern Norway

COMNAVSOUTH Commander, Naval Forces, Southern Europe

COMNAVSUPPACT Commander, Naval Support Activity

comnd commissioned

COMNEATLANT Commander, Northeast Atlantic

COMNON Commander, Allied Forces, Northern Norway

COMNORASDEFLANT Commander, North American Anti-Submarine Defense Force, Atlantic

COMNORLANT Commander, Northern Atlantic

COMNORSEACENT Commander, North Sea Subarea, Central Europe

comnr commissioner

Como Commodore; Comodoro Rivadavia (Argentine naval hero and seaport name); Comoro

Comodoro Rivadavia (Spanish—Commodore Rivadavia) Argentine port often called Rivadavia

Comoro Island Ports Moroni, Patsy, Mutsamudu, Fomboni

Comoros Republic of the Comoros (island nation in the Indian Ocean northwest of Madagascar, people speak some French as well as Arabic and Swahili, copra, fruits, and vanilla are exported) *Etat Comorien*

comp accompaniment; accompany; comparative; comparator; compare; comparison; compass; compensate; compensation; compilation; compile(d); compiler; complimentary; compose(d); composition; compositor; compound(ed); comprehensive; comptroller; rhetorician's mark meaning false comparison

comp (COMP) complainant

comp. compositus (Latin—compounded of)

COMP Conceptually-Oriented Mathematics Program

comp a compressed air

compac computer-output microfilm package; computer program for automatic control

COMPAC Commander, Pacific (USN); Commonwealth Pacific Telephone Cable (linking Australia, New Zealand, and Pacific Ocean islands with the rest of the world)

COMPACS Computer-Output Microforms Program and Concept Study (USA)

compact. compatible algebraic compiler and translator; computer planning and control technique

COMPACT Computator Planning and Control Technique

compand compress to expand (radio communication term describing compression followed by expansion)

compar comparative

compare. computerized performance and analysis response evaluator; console for optical measurement and precise analysis of radiation from electronics

COMPASS Comprehensive Assembly System, Computerized Movement Planning and Status System

COMPATFOR Commander, Patrol Forces

COMPATFORNORLANT Commander, Patrol Forces, Northern Subarea, Atlantic

comp case compensation case

Comp Curr Comptroller of the Currency

compd compound

compdes compensator design; competitive design

COMPELS Computerized Evaluation and Logistics System (USA)

compen compensate; compensation; compensatory

compend compendious; compendium

Compendex Computerized Engi-

neering Index

compf composition floor

Comp Gen Comptroller General

compl complaint; complete; compilation; compiled

Compl A Lover's Complaint

complic complications

Compliment Beethoven's String Quartet in G major Opus 18 No. 2

complt complainant; complaint

Complutum (Latin—Alcalá de Henares)

comp mar companionate marriage

COMPMR Commander, Pacific Missile Range

compn composition

compo compensation; component; composer; composite; composition; compositor

compool common pool; communications pool(ing)

compos components; composers; composites; compositions; compositors

Composer-Bandmaster Edwin Franko Goldman; Ivan Ivanovici; John Philip Sousa

Composer-Chemist Alexander Borodin

Composer-Conductor Johan Sebastian Bach; Hector Berlioz; Leonard Bernstein; Carlos Chávez; Aaron Copland; Edward Elgar; Carlos Gomes, Morton Gould; George Frederick Handel; Ferde Grofé; Howard Hanson, Aram Khachaturian; Franz Liszt; Gustav Mahler; Felix Mendelssohn; Carl Nielson; Oscar Straus, Richard Strauss; Franz von Suppé; Peter Ilyich Tchaikovsky; Heitor Villa-Lobos; Carl Maria von Weber; Richard Wagner

Composer-Conductor-Cellist Pablo Casals; Victor Herbert

Composer-Conductor-Critic Hector Berlioz

Composer-Conductor-Musicologist Hector Berlioz; Nicholas Slonimsky; Richard Wagner

Composer-Conductor-Organist-Pianist Camille Saint-Saëns and Sir Charles Villiers Stanford as well as Sir Arthur S Sullivan

Composer-Conductor-Pianist title shared by many, including Beethoven, Bernstein, Britten, Damrosch, Dohnanyi, Foss, Gottschalk, Grainger, Liszt, Mendelssohn, Prokofiev,

Rachmaninoff, Stravinsky, and Villa-Lobos

Composer-Conductor-Pianist-Statesman Ignacy Jan Paderewski

Composer-Conductor-Pianist-Violinist Georges Enesco; Bedrich Smetana

Composer-Conductor-Violinist Hans Christian Lumbye; Juventino Rosas; Johann Strauss; Johann Strauss Jr; Josef Strauss; Eugéne Ysaye

Composer-Critic Joseph McCabe; Robert Schumann; Carl Shapiro; Virgil Thomson

Composer-Orchestrators Hector Berlioz; Maurice Ravel; Nikolai Rimsky-Korsakov; Richard Strauss; Richard Wagner

Composer-Organist Johann Sebastian Bach; Anton Bruckner; Dietrich Buxtehude; César Franck; Charles Gounod; George Friedrich Handel; Camille Saint-Saëns

Composer-Pianist Ludwig van Beethoven; Johannes Brahms; Frédéric Chopin; George Gershwin; Percy Grainger; Franz Liszt; Edward MacDowell; Wolfgang Amadeus Mozart; Sergei Prokofiev; Sergei Rachmaninoff; Robert Schumann

Composer-Pianist-Conductor Ludwig van Beethoven; Louis Moreau Gottschalk; Franz Liszt; Sergei Rachmaninoff; Camille Saint-Saëns

Composer-Violinist many deserve this title exemplified by Kreisler, Paganini, Sarasate, Vieuxtemps, Vivaldi, and Wieniawski

compound A 11-dehydrocorticosterone

compound B corticosterone

compound E cortisone

compound F cortisol

compound S 11-deoxycortisol

compr compressor

compreg compressed-impregnated (wood)

comprosl compound procedural scientific language

comp(s) complimentary ticket(s)

compt catecholomethyltransferase; compartment; comptroller

Compt Comptroller

Comptes Rend. Comptes rendus de l'Académie des Sciences (Proceedings of the Academy of Science)

Compton Mackenzie Edward Montagu Compton
COMPTUEX Composite Training Unit Exercise
compu computable; computability; computation(al); computer; computerization; computerize
CompuServ Computer Service (network)
Compu Sex Computer Sex (X-rated erotic messages conveyed to home-computer owners by telephone lines)
comput computer
computes. computers
computime computer-computed time
Comr Commissioner
COMRAC Combat Radius Capability (DoD)
com rcm command reconnaissance
comrel community relations
COMRNDN Commander, Riverine Division (USN)
COMRNFLOT Commander, Riverine Flotilla (USN)
COMRNRON Commander, Riverine Squadron (USN)
coms communications support
COMS College of Osteopathic Medicine and Surgery (Des Moines)
comsab communist sabotage; communist saboteur
comsabs communist saboteurs
COMSAMAR Commander, Straits and Marmara Defense Sector
Comsat Communications Satellite (corporation)
comsat(s) communications satellite(s)
ComSeaFron Commander Sea Frontier (USN)
comsec communications security
COMSECONDFLT Commander, Second Fleet (USN)
COMSENEX Combined Sensor Tracking Exercise
COMSER Commission on Marine Science and Engineering Research
COMSEVFLT Commander, Seventh Fleet (USN)
COMSIXFLT Commander, Sixth Fleet (USN)
comsn commission
comsoal computer method of sequencing operations for assembly lines
comstar communications satellite network
Comsteel Commonwealth Steel

comstock comstockery
COMSTRATRESCENT Commander, Strategic Reserve, Allied Land Forces, Central Europe
COMSTRIKFLTLANT Commander, Striking Fleet Atlantic (USN)
COMSTRIKFORSOUTH Commander, Naval Striking and Forces Support, Southern Europe
COMSTS Commander Military Sea Transport Service
COMSUBEASTLANT Commander, Submarine Force, Eastern Atlantic
COMSUBLEDNOREAST Commander, Submarines, Northeast Mediterranean
COMSUBPAC Commander, Submarines, Pacific
comsy commissary
comsymp communist sympathizer
comt comptroller
comt (COMT) catechol-O-methyltransferase
COMTAC Command Tactical (USN)
COMTAFDEN Commander, Tactical Air Force, Denmark
comte committee
COMTEC Computer Micrographics Technology (group)
com tech communications technician
COMTRAC Computer-aided Traffic Control
comtran commercial translation; computer translation
Comum (Latin—Como)
COMUSAFSO Commander, United States Air Forces, Southern Command
COMUSFORAZ Commander, U.S. Forces, Azores
COMUSJAPAN Commander, U.S. Forces, Japan
COMUSKOREA Commander, U.S. Forces, Korea
COMUSMACV Commander, United States Military Assistance Command Vietnam
COMUSRHIN Commander, U.S. Rhine River Patrol
COMUSTDC Commander, U.S. Taiwan Defense Command
Com Ver Common Version (of the Bible)
com wc command weapon carrier
Comy-Gen Commissary-General
Com Z Communications Zone

con confidence (game, man, men); conned; conning; consolidated; control; conversation; convict
con (CON) constant (flow chart)
con (Latin prefix—together or with)—confab, conference
con. contra (Latin—against)
Con Concord(e); Connie; Conservative; Constance; Consuela
CON Conservative; Conservative Party
con8va. con ottava (Italian—with octaves)
CONAC Continental Air Command
CONACS Contractor's Accounting System
CONACYT Consejo Nacional de Ciencia y Tecnologia (Spanish—National Council for Science and Technology)
CONAD Continental Air Defense Command
CONADE Consejo Nacional de Desarrollo (Spanish—National Development Council)
conaloc continuity and logic
ConArC Continental Army Command
CONASA Council of North Atlantic Shipping Associations
conc concentrate; concentration; concentric; concrete
Conca D'oro (Italian—Shell of Gold)—nickname of the hills encircling Palermo
concb concrete block
conc c concrete ceiling
conc clg concrete ceiling
concd concentrated; concerned
concentr concentrate(d)
CONCEPT Computation On-line of Networks of Chemical Engineering Processes
Concertg Concertgebouworkest (Dutch—Concertgebouw Orchestra)—Amsterdam's celebrated symphony orchestra
conc f concrete floor
conc fl concrete floor
concg concentrating
conch. conchology
Concha Maria de la Concepción
conchie conscientious objector
Conch(s) inhabitant(s) of Key West, Florida and nearby keys; pronounced *konk(s)*
Conchtown Key West, Florida
Conch Town Key West, Florida
Conciergerie (French—porter's lodge)—the great prison of Paris on the Ile de la Cité

where it was founded in 1392
concis. concisus (Latin—cut)
concn concentration
concomp conversational computation project
Con Con Constitutional Convention
Concord Massachusetts town northwest of Boston and site of the first battle of the American Revolution; New Hampshire's capital city northwest of Manchester
Concordance Cruden Alexander Cruden—compiler of the Complete Concordance of the Holy Scriptures published in 1737
Concorde Anglo-French supersonic airplane attaining normal cruising speeds of 1300 miles per hour
Concord Group Bronson Alcott, Ralph Waldo Emerson, Margaret Fuller, Nathaniel Hawthorn, Henry David Thoreau
Concordski nickname for the Soviet supersonic Tu-144 airplane (world's first civilian aircraft to break the sound barrier)
Con Cpt Constructor Captain
concr concrete
Concrete Jungle nickname applied to most modern metropolitan centers
cond condenser; condition; conductivity; conductor
condeep(s) concrete deepwater structure(s)
Condemned Rock Tasmanian nickname for Grummet Island in Macquarie Harbour where there is a penitentiary for desperate criminals
condit conditional
condiv continental divide
Condivincum Nannetum (Latin —Nantes)
Condor North American-Rockwell air-to-surface missile (AGM-53A)
condo(s) condominium(s)
condr conductor
cond ref conditioned reflex
cond resp conditioned response
condrill concrete drill(ing)
conductimetric conductance + metric
Conductor-Cellist Barbirolli, Casals, Rostropovich, Toscanini, and Wallenstein are remembered contenders for the title
Conductor-Chorus Master Frank Damrosch, Robert

Shaw, Roger Wagner, and others readers recall
Conductor-Composer George Barati; Pierre Boulez; Stanislaw Skrowaczewski
Conductor-Composer-Pianist Leonard Bernstein; Walter Damrosch; André Previn
Conductor-Double-Bass Henry Lewis, Zubin Mehta, Serge Koussevitsky
Conductor-Organist Edouard Nies-Berger; Leopold Stokowski; Walter Teutsch
Conductor-Organist-Pianist Eduard Nies-Berger, Leopold Stokowski, and Walter Teutsch come to mind but readers should feel free to supply names of other gifted musicians
Conductor-Pianist title includes many from Ashkenazy to Zinman plus Barenboim, Dello Joio, Foss, Ganz, Hendl, Iturbi, Mitropoulos, Previn, Solti, Szell, von Karajan, and Walter
Conductor-Violinist Boskovsky, Brusilow, Burgin, Giulini; Haitink, Katims; (Daniel) Lewis, Menuhin, Munch, Oistrakh (father and son), Ormandy, Paganini, Piastro, Schneider, Silverstein, Stern, and Zukerman share the title with others as other concertgoers may recall
CONE Chamber Orchestra of New England; Collectors of Numismatic Errors
CONEA Confederation of National Educational Associations
Con Ed Consolidated Edison (gas and electric light company)
CONEFO Conference of New Emerging Forces (Sukarno's planned rival to the United Nations)
conelrad control of electromagnetic radiation
CONESCAL Centro Regional de Construcciones Escolares para America Latina (Regional Center for Latin American Construction Students)
con esp con espressione (Italian —with expression)
co-netic high-permeability non-shock-sensitive (alloy developed for maximum attenuation at low flux density)
conex connection(s); container export

conex (CONEX) connection(s)
Coney Coney Island
Coney Island spectacular seaside amusement resort at south Brooklyn entrance to New York Harbor; famed for the diversity of its attractions including beach, boardwalk, and New York Aquarium
conf confer; conference; confidential
conf. confer (Latin—compare)
Conf Confucian; Confucius
CONF Conference Papers Index
confab confabulation; confabulate
CONFAD Concept of a Family of Army Divisions
confec. confectio (Latin—confection)
Conf Econ Prog Conference on Economic Progress
Confed Confederate
Confederacy Confederate States of America (Virginia, North and South Carolina, Georgia, Florida, Alabama, Mississippi, Louisiana, Texas, Arkansas, Tennessee)—and temporarily in Kentucky and Missouri
Confederate Raider Rear Admiral Raphael Semmes, CSN
Confederation Province Prince Edward Island
confer. conference
confi confidant(e); confidence; confidential
confid confidential
confid(l)(ly) confidence; confidential(ly)
confit(s) confiture(s)
confr confectioner
Confucius Kung Fu-tse
cong congress(ional)
cong. congius (Latin—gallon)
Cong Congress; Vietcong member
congal (cuarto) con gal [Mexican-American—(room) with girl]—house of prostitution
con game confidence game; confidence trick(ery)
Cong Christ Congregational Christians
Cong Digest Congressional Digest
congen common specification statements generator; congenial; congenital(ly)
Cong Fr Congolese franc
Congl Congregational
conglom(s) conglomerate(s); conglomerator(s)
Congo People's Republic of the Congo (formerly the French

Congo in western central Africa where the Congolese speak French and tribal languages, tropical crops and minerals are exported) *République Populaire du Congo*

Congo Ports (north to south) Loango, Pointe Noire, Malongo Oil Terminal

Cong Orat Congregation of the Oratory

Congrats congratulations

Cong Rec Congressional Record

Congreg Congregationalist

Cong Staff Congressional Staff Directory

Cong U Congregational Union (England and Wales)

CONGU Council of National Golf Unions

conics conic sections

Conimbrica (Latin—Coimbra) —also called Conimbria by the Romans

conj conjugal; conjugate; conjunction; conjunctivitis

CONLIS Committee on National Library and Information Systems

Con Lt Constructor Lieutenant

Con Lt-Cdr Constructor Lieutenant-Commander

con man confidence man; swindler

conn connection; connective; connector

Conn Connecticut; Connecticuter

CONN Connellan Airways

CONNECT Connecticut On-Line Enforcement Communication and Teleprocessing (computerized criminal file)

Connecticut Ports (east to west) New London, New Haven, Bridgeport

Connection City Amsterdam, Marseilles, Miami, Singapore, and other major airports where drugs are smuggled in or taken out

Connie Conrad; Constance; Consuela; Cornelia; Cornelius

Connie Mack Cornelius McGillicuddy

Conn Turn Connecticut Turnpike

Conny Constance

co/no current operator/next operator

conobjtr conscientious objector

CONOCO Continental Oil Company

con of consisting of

conopt constrained optimization

Conquering Lion of Judah and King of Kings Emperor Haile Selassie of Ethiopia

Conqueror of Mount Everest Sir Edmund Hillary

Conqueror of Suez Ferdinand de Lesseps of Suez Canal fame

Conquerors of Yellow Fever Walter Reed and his colleagues Aristides Agramonte, James Carroll, and Jesse Lazear

Conr Conrad

conrad contour radar data

Conrad Veidt Konrad Weidt

ConRail Consolidated Rail Corporation (government-sponsored railroads including the Ann Arbor, Central Railroad of New Jersey, Erie-Lackawanna, Lehigh and Hudson River, Lehigh Valley, Penn Central, Reading)

con rod connecting rod

cons consider; consist

con(s) confidence (games); conviction(s); convict(s)

cons. conserva (Latin—a preserve)

Cons Conservative

CONSAL Congress of Southeast Asian Librarians

CONSCIENCE Committee on National Student Citizenship in Every National Case of Emergency

Conscience of the American Theater Brooks Atkinson

Conscience of the Left George Orwell

Consc⁰ Consejo (Spanish—Council)

con sect conic section

Cons Eng Consulting Engineer

CONSER CONversion of SERials (Council on Library Resources project)

conserv conservation; conservationist; conservatoire; conservatory

Conserv Conservatoire; Conservatory

Conservatory Concerto for the Piano Mendelssohn's *Concerto No. 1 in G-minor* opus 25

Conservatory Concerto for the Violin Mendelssohn's *Concerto in E* opus 64

cons. et prud. consilio et prudentia (Latin—by counsel and prudence)

Cons Gen Consul General

consgt consignment

conshelf continental shelf

conship control by ship

conshore control from shore

consid consideration

consig consignee

Con S-Lt Constructor Sub-Lieutenant

consltnt consultant

consol consolidated

Consol Consolidated Coal

consolex consolidation exercise

consols consolidated annuities

CONSORT Conversation System with On-Line Remote Terminals

consperg. consperge (Latin—dust, sprinkle)

conspic conspicuous

const constant; constitution; constitutional; construction; constructor

Const Constable; Constitution; Constructor

Const Constitution (of the United States)

constab constabulary

Constable Country East Berghott in England's Sussex where James Constable's award-winning landscapes were painted

Constable of France Charles De Gaulle

Constan Constantine; Constantinople (Istanbul)

Constance Lake Constance called Bodensee by the Austrians and the Germans

Constantia Judith Sargent Murray

Constantinople Istanbul's former name

Constant Reader Dorothy Parker's pseudonym

Constellation Lockheed 63-passenger transport

constit constituent(s); constitution(al)

Constitution State Connecticut's official nickname honoring its charter oak constitution of 1639

constn constitution; construction

constocs contingency support stocks

constr construction; constructor

Const US Constitution of the United States

consub continental-shelf submersible

consult. consultant

consumcrit consumer critic(ism)

consv conservation; conserve

cont contact; content(s); continent(al); continue(d); contract(or); control(ler)

cont. *contra* (Latin—against); *contusus* (Latin—bruised, contused)

Cont Continent; Continental

contac (CONTAC) cold capsule's continuous action

Contadora Group Colombia, Mexico, Panama, Venezuela (involved in a peaceful settlement of Central American problems)

contag contagious

containerport container-ship seaport (equippped for handling and storing containers)

contam contaminant; contaminate; contamination

CONTAM Committee on Nationwide Television Audience Measurement

contax consumers and taxpayers

contbg contributing

cont. bon. mor. *contra bonos mores* (Latin—contrary to good manners)

contd contained; continued

contemp contemporary

contempo contemporary

Contemporary Cassandra Dorothy Thompson

conter. *contere* (Latin—rub together)

conter US conterminous United States (forty-eight states having common boundaries)

Cont Eur Continental Europe

Cont Eur & Br I Continental Europe and British Isles

contg containing

Cont HH continental range of ports from Havre to Hamburg

cont hp continental horsepower

Contl Constantine, Constantinople

contig US contiguous United States (fifty states having close proximity)

contin continental; continuous

contin *continuo* (Italian—continuous); *continuetur* (Latin—let it be continued)

Continent The Continent (Africa, Antarctica, Asia, Australia, Europe, North America, South America)

Continental Divide Rocky Mountain ridge separating rivers flowing eastward to the Atlantic Ocean and the Gulf of Mexico from those flowing westward to the Pacific

Continental Nation Australia

Continent of Hope South America

contin US continental United States (Alaska plus the forty-eight conterminous states occupying much of the North American continent)

contl continental

contr contracted; contraction; contractor

contra against; contra-indicated

contra (Latin prefix—against or opposite)—contradict, contraception

CONTRA Coalition of Non-Theist Religious Alternatives

contractio (Latin—abbreviation)

contrail condensation trail

contralat contralateral

contran control translator

contraprop contra + propeller

contra(s) contraceptive(s)

contr. bon. mor. *contra bonos mores* (Latin—contrary to good manners)

cont. rem. *continuetur remedia* (Latin—let the remedy be continued)

contrib contribution; contributor

contrit. *contritus* (Latin—broken, ground, macerated)

CONTU Commission on New Technological Uses of Copyrighted Works (Library of Congress)

contus. *contusus* (Latin—bruised, contused)

cont w continuous window

CONU Contrans (container) Unit

conurb(s) conurbation(s)

Con US (CONUS) Continental United States

CONUS Intel Continental United States Intelligence (USA)

conv convalescent; convention; conventional

convair conveyed by air

Convair 600 Convair-Liner powered by Rolls-Royce turboprop engines

convce conveyance

conv encl convector enclosure

convex convoy exercise

convg convergence

ConVis Convention and Visitors Bureau

Convis Bur Convention and Visitor's Bureau

convl conventional

convn convenient

convt convert(ible)

conv^{te} *conveniente* (Spanish—convenient)

CONWR Crab Orchard National Wildlife Refuge (Illinois)

Coo Coos Bay

Coo *Coo blimey* (Cockney contraction—God blind me)

CoO (COO) Chief of Outpost (CIA)

COO Chief Ordnance Officer

cooc contact with oil or other cargo

COOC Commission on Organized Crime

COOH (carboxyl group found in all organic acids)

cook. cookery

Cook Islands Danger, Manahiki, Penrhyn or Tongareva, Rakahanga and nearby islets in the South Pacific

Cookpot NATO name for Soviet Tupolev Tu-124 jet-transport aircraft

Cooks Cook Islanders; Cook Islands; Cook's Tours (Thomas Cook and Son, Ltd)

cool. coolant

Cool-Kal Coolgardie-Kalgoorlie

Coon Dog Capital Vienna (pronounced *Vi-enna*) Illinois

coon(s) coonhound(s)—contraction of racoon hounds

'coon(s) racoon(s)

coop. cooperation

co-op cooperative

Coop Cooper

COOP ED Cooperative Education

coopg cooperage

Co-op L Cooperative League

COOPLAN Continuity of Operations Plan (USN)

Co-op U Co-operative Union

coorauth coordinating authority

coord coordinate; coordination; coordinator

COORS Communications Outage Restoration Section

COOS Chemical Orbit-to-Orbit Shuttle (NASA)

Coot NATO nickname for Soviet Ilyushin transport designated Moskva or Il-18

cop capillary osmotic pressure; casing operating pressure; constable on patrol (origin of cop); copper; copyright; customer owned property; policeman (slang)

cop (COP) computer optimization package

cop. coefficient of performance; commencement of passage; custom of port

c-o-p change of plea

Cop Copernican; Coptic

Cop *Copenhague* (French, Portuguese, Spanish—Copenhagen)

COP Career Opportunity Program; Certificate of Proficiency; City of Prineville (railroad); Coalition on Police; Combat Outpost; Commissary Operating Program; Community-Oriented Policing; Continuity of Operations Plan; Cox's Orange Pippin; Custom of the Port

Copa Copacabana

COPA Compañía Panameña de Aviación; Council on Postsecondary Accreditation

copac continuous operation production allocation and control

Copa de Oro (Spanish—Cup of Gold)—pirate's nickname for Panama

COPAL Cocoa Producers' Alliance

COPANT Comisión Panamericana de Normas Tecnicas (Panamerican Commission for Technical Standards)

COPAO Council of Philippino-American Organizations

COPAR Corrective or Preventive Action Report

COPARS Contractor-Operated Automotive Parts Store (DoD)

copd chronic obstructive pulmonary disease; coppered

COPDAF Continuity of Operations Plan—Department of the Air Force

cope chronic obstructive pulmonary emphysema

COPE Champions of Private Enterprise; Committee on Political Education (AFL-CIO); Committee for Original People's Entitlement (Canadian Eskimo's claim to Canadian land); Concerned Organization of Parents to Educate; Congress on Optimum Population and Environment; Council on Population and Environment

COPEC Compañía Petrolera Chilena (Spanish—Chilean Petroleum Company)

COPEI Comité Organizador del Partido Electoral Independiente (Spanish—Organization Committee of the Independent Electoral Party)—Venezuela's Social Christian Party

Copeia not a short form but the periodical of the American Society of Ichthyologists and Herpetologists named for the

naturalist Edward Drinker Cope

Copen Copenhagen

Copenague (Spanish—Copenhagen)

copenhagen copenhagen blue (gray blue); copenhagen snuff (strong snuff characteristic of Copenhagen where it originated); copenhagen surprise (naval attack without warning of a fleet at anchor as in the manner of Nelson's sortie in 1801)

Copenhague (French—Copenhagen)

Copernicus Latinized name of the Polish astronomer Nikolaus Kopernicki

COPES College Occupational Programs Educational System; Conceptually-Oriented Program in Elementary Science

COPH Congress of Organizations of the Physically Handicapped

COPICS Copyright Office Publication and Interactive Cataloging System (Library of Congress)

COPL Council of Planning Librarians

copo copolymer

copp cobaltiprotoporphyrin

Copp Copperplate

COPP Conservation Organization Protesting Pollution

copperas ferrous sulfate; green vitriol

Copper City Butte, Montana

Copper John nickname of Auburn Prison near Syracuse, New York

Coppernose Henry the VIII whose portrait exhibited a copper-colored nose on the so-called silver coins minted during his reign

copper pyrites chalcopyrite (copper iron sulfide)

Copper State Arizona's old nickname

COPPS Committee on Power Plant Siting (Nat Acad Engineering)

COPR Center for Overseas Pest Research; Critical Officer Personnel Requirement (USAF)

cops coppers; policemen (slang)

COPs Coalition on Police members (radicals dedicated to hampering police work)

COPS California Organization of Police and Sheriffs; Chief of Operations (CIA); Committees Organized for Public Ser-

vice

Copt Coptic

coptec controller overload prediction technic

copter(s) helicopter(s)

co-ptr co-partner

copu copulate; copulation; copulatory

COPUL Council of Prairie University Libraries

copy. copyright

coq cost of quality

coq. coque (Latin—boil)

co Q coenzyme Q

coq. s.a. coque secundum artem (Latin—boil correctly)

coq. in s.a. coque in sufficiente aqua (Latin—boil in sufficient water)

coq. sim. coque simul (Latin—boil together)

cor contactor, running; corner; cornet; correction

cor corno (Italian—horn)

cor. corpus (Latin—body)

Cor Corinthians; Corona; Coronado; Coroner; Corsica; Coruña

Cor Corea (Portuguese or Spanish—Korea)

COR Commonwealth Oil Refineries

COR Comisión(es) de Orientación Revolucionaria [Spanish—Revolutionary Orientation Committee(s)]—Cuba

cora conditioned orientation reflex audiometry

Cor A Corona Australis

CORA Corporación de la Reforma Agraria (Spanish—Agrarian Reform Corporation)—Chile

coral. class-oriented ring-associated language

Coral Coral Sea; Coral Sea Island Territory beyond Australia's Barrier Reef

CORAL Coherent Optical Radar Laboratory (USAF)

Coral Atoll Country Nauru

Coral Coast Fiji's luxury-hotel complex between Sigatoka and Yanuca on Viti Levu

Cora Montgomery Jane McManus

Cor B Corona Borealis

cor bd corner bead

corbfus copy of reply to be furnished us

Corbu Le Corbusier (nickname of Edouard Jeanneret-Gris meaning the crow)

Corc Cornell computing (language)

Córcega (Spanish—Corsica)

Cor Chr Col Corpus Christi College—Cambridge

CORCO Commonwealth Oil Refining Company (Puerto Rico)

cord. computer on-line devices

cord. cordillera (Spanish—mountain range)

Cord Cordelia; Córdoba

C of Ord Chief of Ordnance

CORD Commissioned Officer(s) Residency Deferment; Congress on Research and Dance

cordat coordinate data set

cordic coordinate rotation digital computer

Cordilleras Cordillera Mountains of the Americas

CORDIPLAN Oficina Central de Coordinación y Planificación (Spanish—Central Office of Coordination and Planning)

Córdoba (Spanish—Cordova)

Cordova English place-name equivalent of Córdoba

cordovan cordovan leather (originally made in Córdoba, Spain of goatskin and noted for its lustrous smoothness)

cordpo correlated radar data printout

cords. corduroy pants; corduroy trousers

CORDS Civil Operations and Revolutionary Development Support

Corduba (Latin—Cordova)

core. computed oriented reporting efficiency

CORE Competitive Operational Readiness Evaluation (Air Force); Congress of Racial Equality

Corea (Spanish—Korea)

corex coordinated electronic countermeasures exercise

corf classroom observational rating form

corfam (computer-devised word — not an acronym—microporous artificial leather)

corflu correction fluid

CORFO Corporación de Fomento (Spanish—Development Corporation); Corporación de Fomento de la Producción (Spanish—Production Development Corporation)—Chile

CORG Combat Operations Research Group

CORGI Confederation for Registration of Gas Installers

corin corinthian

Corinto (Spanish—Corinth)

Coriol Coriolanus

CORL Canadian Operations Research Society

CORLS Central Ontario Regional Library System

CORM Council for Optical Radiation Measurements

CORMA Corporación de la Madera (Spanish—Wood Corporation)

cormant cormorant

CORMAR Coral Reef Management and Research

Cor Mem Corresponding Member

Corn Cornelius; Cornish; Cornwall

Corn Belt midwestern United States where bumper corn crops are produced in Illinois, Indiana, Iowa, and Nebraska

Corn City Toledo, Ohio

Corncob Capital Washington, Missouri (where so many corncob pipes are manufactured)

Corncracker(s) Kentuckian(s)

Corncracker State Kentucky

corned-beefsan corned-beef sandwich

corned-beefwich corned-beef sandwich

Cornell Maritime Cornell Maritime Press

Cornell U Pr Cornell University Press

Corner House Central Mining and Finance Corporation (South Africa)

Cornerstone of Western Music Beethoven's Ninth Symphony, according to Japanese-born conductor Seiji Ozawa

Corney Cornelia; Cornelius

Corn Geneticist Barbara McClintock

Cornhusker(s) Nebraskan(s)

Cornhusker State Nebraska's official nickname

Cornie Cornelia; Cornelio; Cornelis; Cornelisz; Corneliu; Cornelius; Cornewall; Cornwall; Cornwallis

Corning Mus Corning Museum of Glass

Cornish Riviera English Riviera extending from Falmouth to the Isles of Scilly

Corno di Bassetto (Italian—basset horn)—pen name used by George Bernard Shaw when he was a music critic

Cornopolis Chicago

Corns Corn Islands in the Caribbean

Cornubian Shore Cornwall, England

coroll corollary

coron coronary

Coron Convair 990 Coronado (aircraft)

Coronados Coronado Islands (Los Coronados) south-southwest of San Diego

Coronation Mozart's Mass in C or his Piano Concerto in D major (K 537)

corp (Latin prefix—body)—corporation, corpus delicti (the body of the crime)

Corp Corporation; Corpus Christi College, Cambridge or Oxford

Corp Coll Corpus Christi College—Oxford

Corpl Corporal

Corpn Corporation

CORPOANDES Corporación de los Andes (Spanish—Andes Corporation)

Corporal John early nickname of John Churchill who later became the first Duke of Marlborough; known to the Spaniards as Mambrú

CORPORIENTE Corporación de Oriente (Spanish—Corporation of the East)—active in eastern Venezuela's development

corppin corporeal pin (tuberculin testing)

Corpus Corpus Christi, Texas

CORPUS Corps of Reserve Priests United for Service

corr correction; correspondence; corrosion; corrugate

corr corregido (Spanish—corrected); corriage (French—corrected)

Corr Corriere della Sera (Italian—Daily Courier)—Milan's leading newspaper

CORRA Combined Overseas Rehabilitation Relief Appeal

corr case corrugated case

corregate correctable gate

Corregio Antonio Allegri

correl correlative

corres correspondence; correspondent; corresponding

corresp corresponding

Corridor of Six Continents sobriquet given the Panama Canal, Suez Canal, and projected interoceanic sea-level canals across Mexico and Nicaragua

Corridor State New Jersey—serving as a corridor between New York and Pennsylvania

Corrie Denison Eric Partridge

corrig corrigenda

Corr Memb Corresponding Member

corros corrosive

corrosive sublimate mercuric chloride

corr^te corriente (Spanish—current month)

corrupt. corruption

Cors Corners; Corsica; Corsican

CORS Canadian Operational Research Society

corsa (CORSA) cosmic-ray satellite

Corsair Chance-Vought single-engine fighter popular during World War II (F4U)

Corse (French—Corsica)

Cor Sec Corresponding Secretary

Corsican Ogre one of Napoleon's many nicknames

cort cortex; cortical

cort. cortex (Latin—bark)

CORT Council On Radio and Television

CORTEX Computer-based Optimization Routines and Techniques for Effective X

Cortissoz Aeropuerto Ernesto Cortissoz (Barranquilla, Colombia's airport named for the chemical engineer whose grandfather introduced paddlewheel steamers plying the Magdalena)

CORU Coordinación de Organizaciones Revolucionarias Unidas (Spanish—Coordination of United Revolutionary Organizations)—Cuban exiles

Coruña (Spanish—Corunna)

corundolite emery

corundum aluminum oxide

Corunna La Coruña in northwestern Spain

Corv Corvette; Corvus

CORVA California Off-Road Vehicle Association

Corvette antisubmarine-warfare convoy escort ship

Cory Cornelia

cos cash-on-shipment; contactor, starting; cosine; cosmic; cosmogany; cosmography; cosmology; cosmopolitan

co's career officers

Cos Consul; Counties

Cos Kosinus (German—cosine)

CoS Chief of Staff; Chief of Station

C-o-S Clacton-on-Sea

COS Canadian Ophthalmological Society; Central Opera Service; Chamber of Shipping; Chief of Section; Colorado

Springs, Colorado (airport); Czechoslovak Ocean Shipping

COS College Outline Series

cosa combat operational support aircraft

co sa come sopra (Italian—as above)

COSAD Classroom Observation System for Analyzing Depression

cosag combined steam and gas (turbine machinery)

COSAL Consolidated Shipboard Allowance List

COSAMREG Consolidation of Supply and Maintenance Regulations

cosa nostra (Italian—our thing)—nickname for international criminal syndicate network

COSA NOSTRA Computer-Oriented System And Newly Organized Storage-To-Retrieval Apparatus

cosar compression scanning-array radar

COSATI Committee on Scientific and Technical Information (Federal Council for Science and Technology)

COSBA Computer Services and Bureaus Association

COSBAL Coordinated Shore-based Allowance List

COSBO Council on Small Business Organizations

COSCO China Ocean Shipping Company

COSCOE Congress of Seniors and Coalition of Elders

COSD Council of Organizations Serving the Deaf

Cos de Mar Costa de Marfil (Spanish—Ivory Coast)

COSEBI Corporación de Servicios Bibliotecarios (Spanish—Librarian Services Corporation)—Puerto Rico

cosec cosecant

COSEC Coordinating Secretariat of National Unions of Students

cosecy company secretary

cosfad computerized safety and facility design

COSFPS Commons, Open Spaces, Footpaths Preservation Society

cosh hyperbolic cosine (symbol)

COSHTI Council for Science and Technological Information

Cosi Cosi Fan Tutti (Italian—Thus Do They All)—two-act

opera by Mozart whose title is often translated as Women Are Like That

COSI Center of Science and Industry (Columbus, Ohio); Committee on Scientific Information

Cosie Kathleen

Cosimo palette name of Piero di Lorenzo who took the given name of his teacher Cosimo Roselli

COSINE Committee on Computer Science in Electrical Engineering Education

COSIP College Science Improvement Program

COSIRA Council for Small Industries in Rural Areas

cosis care of supplies in storage

COSLA Chief Officers of State Library Agencies

cosm cosmetic; cosmetics; cosmetologist; cosmetology

cosma computerized service for motor freight activities

COSMD Combined Operations Signals Maintenance Department (Division)

COSMEP Committee of Small Magazine Editors and Publishers

cosmetol cosmetologist(ic); cosmetology

COSMIC Computer Programmes Information Center (Univ of Georgia); Computer Software Management and Information Center

COSMIS Computer System for Medical Information Services

cosmo cosmoline; cosmopolitan

cosmog cosmogony; cosmographical; cosmography

cosmograph(s) composite photograph(s)

Cosmological Popularizer Carl Sagan

cosmonaut. cosmonautic(al)(ly); cosmonautics

Cosmopolis of the Heartland Kansas City

Cosmopolitan Canadian-built medium-range transport designed by General Dynamics and designated CC-109

cosmor component open/short monitor

COSMOS Coast Survey Marine Observation Station

co so come sopra. (Italian—as above)

COSPAR Committee on Space Research (International Council of Scientific Unions)

COSPEC Christian Organizations for Social, Political, and Economic Change

COSPUP Committee on Science and Public Policy (National Academy of Sciences)

cosr cutoff shear

COSR Committee on Space Research

coss. consules (Latin—consuls)

cossac cooled spectral shared-aperture concept

COSSAC Chief of Staff to the Supreme Allied Commander

cost. contaminated oil settling tank; costume

COST Congresional Office of Science and Technology; Cost-Oriented Systems Technique

costa (Italian, Portuguese, Spanish—coast)

Costa Azul (Spanish—Blue Coast)—Uruguayan resort area near Montevideo

Costa Blanca (Spanish—White Coast)—from Alicante to Valencia

Costa Brava (Spanish—Wild Coast)—Catalonian coast from Barcelona to the French frontier

Costa Cantábrico (Spanish—Cantabrian Coast)—between San Sebastian and Santander

Costa d'Avorio (Italian—Ivory Coast)—West African nation

Costa de la Luz (Spanish—Coast of Light)—from Almería to Cartagena

Costa del Azahar (Spanish—Orange-Blossom Coast)—between Castellón and Valencia

Costa del Bálsamo (Spanish—Balsam Coast)—El Salvador's coast from Acajutla to La Libertad

Costa del Marfil (Spanish—Ivory Coast)

Costa del Oro (Spanish—Gold Coast)

Costa de los Mosquitos (Spanish—Mosquito Coast)—Nicaragua's Caribbean coast

Costa de los Piratos (Spanish—Pirate Coast)—Trucial Coast of Arabia

Costa del Sol (Spanish—Sun Coast)—from Almería to Gibraltar

Costa Dorada (Spanish—Gilt Coast)—Catalonian coast south of Barcelona

Costa d'Oro (Italian—Gold Coast)—Ghana

Costa do Sol (Portuguese—Sun Coast)—resort area extending from Cascais and Estoril to Lisbon's outskirts

Costa Firme (Spanish—Compact Coast)—name Columbus gave the Caribbean coast between Colombia and Nicaragua—the Panamanian coast

costar conversational on-line storage and retrieval

Costa Rica Republic of Costa Rica (Central American two-ocean nation whose Spanish-speaking Costa Ricans boast they have more schoolteachers than police or priests, bananas and coffee are exported) *República de Costa Rica*

Costa Rica Day Costa Rican Independence Day (September 15)

Costa Rican Ports (east coast Caribbean port) Limón; (west coast Pacific ports) Puntarenas and Golfito

Costa Smeralda (Italian—Emerald Coast)—resort area on Sardinia's north shore

Costa Verde (Spanish—Green Coast)—Oviedo's coastline along the Bay of Biscay

COSTEP Commissioned Officer Student Training and Extern Program

custer costermonger

Costermansville former name of Bukavu

COSTPRO Canadian Organization for the Simplification of Trade Procedures

COSTS Committee on Sane Telephone Service

COSW Citizen's Organization for a Sane World

coswap coaxial switch and alternator panel

COSY Checkout Operating System

COSYWOG Communications System Working Group

cot. card or tape reader; cathodal opening tetanus; cotangent; cotter; cotton

COT Consecutive Overseas Tour

COTA confirming telephone or message authority

COTAL Confederación de Organizaciones Turísticas de la América Latina (Confederation of Touristic Organizations of Latin America)

COTAM Commandement du Transport Aerien Militaire (French—Military Air Transport Command)—Air Force

cotan cotangent

cotar correction tracking and ranging

CotB Commonwealth of the Bahamas

COTC Canadian Officers' Training Corps; Canadian Overseas Telecommunications Corporation

cote cathodal opening tetanus

COT & E Contractor Operation Test and Evaluation

Côte d'Argent (French—Silver Coast)—along the Bay of Biscay around Biarritz

Côte d'Azur (French—Azure Coast)—on the Mediterranean between Menton and Toulon—the French Riviera

Côte-de-l'Or (French—Coast of Gold)—Ghana

Côte d'Ivoire (French—Ivory Coast)—West African nation

Côte d'Or (French—Gold Coast)—range of hills southwest of Dijon

Côte Française des Somalis French Somaliland

Côte-Saint-André birthplace of Hector Berlioz—foremost composer, conductor, and critic of the Romantic Era; near Grenoble, France

Côtes du Nord (French—North Coasts)—Brittany's coastline along the English Channel

Côte Vermeille (French—Vermillion Coast)—on the Mediterranean near the Spanish frontier

cotfin cotton finish(ed)

cotg component tooling gage

coth hyperbolic cotangent (symbol)

COTH Council on Teaching Hospitals

cotics narcotics

cotnsd cottonseed

Coto Cotopaxi

CotP Captain of the Port

COTPAL Comité Tecnico Permanente sobre Asuntos Laborales (Spanish—Permanent Technical Committee for Labor Matters)

COTR Contracting Officers' Technical Representative

COTRANS Coordinated Transfer Applications System

cots. checkout test set; cottages

cot's classical organizational theories

'cot(s) apricot(s)

C o t S College of the Sea

Cotswolds Cotswold Hills of south-central England

Cott Cottesloe

COTT Central Organization for

Technical Training

Cottians Cottian Alps between France and Italy

Cotton Belt cotton-growing areas of the southern United States; also known as the Cotton Kingdom

Cotton Bowl Dallas, Texas

cotton-dust disease brown lung or byssinosis

Cottonopolis Manchester, England

Cotton State Alabama's nickname

Cottonwood City Leavenworth, Kansas

cott(s) cottage(s)

coty car of the year

cou clip-on unit; coupon

couch couchant

Cougar Grumman carrier-based transonic fighter aircraft (F9F-6)

couldn't could not

Coun Council; Councillor; Counsellor; County

Coun Biology Eds Council of Biology Editors

Coun Exc Child Council for Exceptional Children

Count Basie William Basie

Country of a Thousand Hills Rwanda

COUP Congress of Unrepresented People

cour *courant* (French—current)

Courland Kurland

Court Courtenay; Courtland; Courtney

Courtrai (French—Kortrijk)

Court of St James British royal court

COUSA Confederation of Ontario University Staff Associations

Cousin Jack a Cornishman; a Cornish miner

Cousin Jenny Cornish girl or woman

cov concentrated oil of vitriol; cutout valve; cover

c-o v cross-over value

Cov Covell; Covenant; Coventry

COVE Citizens Opposed to the Violation of the Environment

Covent Garden The Royal Opera House in London where it is adjacent Covent Garden marketplace

covers. coversed sine

COVET Cooperative Venture in the Education of Teachers

covff coverings, facing, or floor (cargo)

COVINCA *Corporacón Venezo-*

lana de la Industria Naval (Spanish—Venezuelan Corporation of the Naval Industry)

cov pl coverplate

cow. chlorinated organics in wastewater; crude oil washing

Cowansville Québec penitentiary on the Yamaska River near Cowansville

COWAR Committee on Water Research

Coward Coward, McCann and Geohegan

Cowboy Artist Charles M Russell

Cowboy Capital Dodge City, Kansas

Cowboy Philosopher Will Rogers

cowboys of the sea porpoises

COWEAEX Cold-Weather Exercise (military)

cowl. cowling

Cowles Cowles Education Corporation

COWLEX Cold-Weather Landing Exercise (military)

COWPS Council on Wage and Price Stability

COWRR Committee on Water Resources Research

cow(s) cow juice; cowboy(s); cowchip(s); cowhand(s); cowpaper(s); cowpoke(s); cowpuncher(s); cowthief(s) or cowthieves; cowtown(s)

Cowtown Fort Worth, Texas and Omaha, Nebraska share this place-name nickname

Cox Coxwain

cox'n coxswain (pronounced as contracted)

coxsec coexsecant

Coy Company

coydog(s) coyote(s) + dog(s)—mixed-breed canine(s)

COYOTE Call Off Your Old Tired Ethics (underworld organization urging legalization of just about every evil)

Coyote Cowboy Pecos Bill

Coyote(s) South Dakotan(s)

Coyote State South Dakota's official nickname

Coyte Coyte Lines

coz cousin (colloquial contraction)

Coz Cozumel Island, Mexico

cozi communication zone [indicator(s)]

cp camp; candlepower; capillary pressure; center of pressure; centipoise; cerebral palsy; cesspool; chemically pure; chloropurine; chloroquinine and primaquine; chronic py-

elonephritis; claw plate; closing pressure; cochlear potential; code of practice; cold-punch(ed); combination product; combining power; command post (CP); compare; compound; compressed; concrete-piercing; constant pressure; cor pulmonale; creatine phosphate

cp (CP) carotid pulse; cerebral palsy; construction permit

c/p carport; change package; composition/printing; control panel

c/p (C/P) charter party

c & p carriage and packing; collated and perfect

cP centipoise; polar continental air

Cp Caucasian pimp; Chicano pimp; Chinese pimp; Compline

CP Caminhos de ferro Portuguese (Portuguese Railways); Canadian Pacific; Canadian Press (news agency); cerebral palsy; Characterization Plan; charter party; chemically pure; Communist Party; Conservative Party; Constitution Party; copilot; Country Party

C-P Colgate-Palmolive

C & P Compensation and Pension

C of P Captain of the Port

CP *Centre Pénitentiaire* (French—Penitentiary Center); Crescendo Publishers

cpa closest point of approach; cost planning and appraisal; critical path analysis

c-p a cattle-prod approach (electric-shock stimulation)

CPA Canadian Pacific Airlines; Canadian Psychological Association; Canaveral Port Authority; Cathay Pacific Airways; Certified Public Accountant; Chartered Patent Agent; Chicago Publishers Association; Civilian Production Administration; Cocoa Producers Alliance; Combat Pilots Association; Combined Pensioners Association; Commonwealth Parliamentary Association; Commonwealth Preference Area; Communist Party of Australia; Connecticut Prison Association; Consumer Protection Agency; Council of Professional Associations; Country Press Association; Creditors Protection Association

CPA Community Planning Act
CPAA Current Physics Advance Abstracts
CPAB California Prune Advisory Board
CPAC Center for Protection Against Corrosion; Conservative Political Action Conference; Corrosion Prevention Advisory Center
CPACS Coded Pulse Anticlutter System
CPAE Certified Public Accountant Examination
cpaf cost plus award fee
CPAG Collision Prevention Advisory Group
C_{pah} para-aminohippurate clearance
CPAI Canvas Products Association International
CP Air Canadian Pacific Air
C **Pal** Crystal Palace
cpam continental polar air mass
CPAM Committee of Purchasers of Aircraft Material
CPAO Country Public Affairs Office(r)
cpap continuous positive airway pressure
CPAP Committee on Pan-American Policy
CPAR Cooperative Pollution Abatement Research (Canadian)
CPARS Compact Programmed Airline Reservation System
CPAUS&C Catholic Press Association of the United States and Canada
cpaws computer-planning and aircraft-weighting scales
cpb cardiopulmonary bypass; casual payments book; cetyl pyridinium bromide; competitive protein-binding (clearance)
cpb (CPB) charged-particle beam(s)
cpb cuyos pies beso (Spanish—whose feet I kiss)
Cpb Campbelltown
CPB Casual Payments Book; Central Planning Bureau; Consumer Protection Bureau; Corporation for Public Broadcasting
CPB Centraal Plan Bureau (Dutch—Central Planning Bureau)
cpba competitive protein-binding analysis
cpbl capability; capable
CPBMP Committee on Purchases of Blind-Made Prod-

ucts
cpc card-programmed calculator; chronic passive congestion; clinicopathological conference (CPC); coated-paper copier; commerical property coverage; computer-production control
CPC California Polytechnic College; Canterbury Promotion Council; Cessna Pilots Center; China Petroleum Company; China Productivity Council; Church Periodical Club; City Planning Commission; City Police Commissioner; City Projects Council; Cogswell Polytechnical College; College Placement Council; Communist Party of China; Consumers Power Company; Creole Petroleum Corporation
CPCC Central Piedmont Community College
CPCG Comite Panamericano de Ciencias Geofícicas (Panamerican Committee of Geophysical Sciences)
CPCGN Canadian Permanent Committee on Geographical Names (Ottawa)
CPC(M-L) Communist Party of Canada (Marxist-Leninist)
CPCN Canadian Pacific—Canadian National (telecommunications)
CPCS Canadian Pacific Consulting Services
CPCU Chartered Property and Casualty Underwriter
c-p cycle constant-pressure cycle
cpd charter pays dues; compound, contact potential difference; contagious pustular dermatitis; container-padded delivery
cpd (CPD) charter (party) pays (port) dues
CPD Committee on the Present Danger (from Soviet penetration); Community Planning and Development; Consumer Protection Division; County Probation Department
CPD Catalog of the Public Documents
CPDA Council for Periodical Distributors Associations
cpdd command-post digital display
CPDL Canadian Patents and Developments Limited
C-P D L Christian-Patriots Defense League (see C f's)

cpds compounds
CPDS Computerized Preliminary Design System
cpe chronic pulmonary emphysema; circular probable error; compensation, pension, and education; customer-provided equipment; cytopathic effect; cytopathogenic effect
cpe (CPE) central programmer and evaluator
CPE Certificate for Proficiency in English; Certified Property Exchanger; Chief Polaris Executive (missiles); Clinical Pastoral Education; College of Physical Education; Contractor Performance Evaluation
CPEA Confederation of Professional and Executive Associations; Cooperative Program for Educational Administration
CPEC California Post-secondary Education Commission
CPEG Contractor Performance Evaluation Group
CPEHS Consumer Protection and Environmental Health Service
c pen code pénal (French—penal code)
CPEP Contractor Performance Evaluation Plan
CPEQ Corporation of Professional Engineers of Quebec
cpf conditional peak flow; cost per flight
CPF Central Provident Fund; Church Pension Fund; Commission on Federal Paperwork; Commonwealth Police Force
cpfa (CPFA) cyclopropenoid fatty acid
cpff (CPFF) cost plus fixed fee
CPFS Council for the Promotion of Field Studies
cpg controlled-pore glass; cotton piece goods
CPG College Publishers Group
CPGA California Personnel and Guidance Association; Colorado Personnel and Guidance Association; Connecticut Personnel and Guidance Association
CPGB Communist Party of Great Britain
Cpge course per gyro compass
cph cards per hour; cycles per hour
CPH Certificate of Public Health; Copenhagen, Denmark (airport); Corps of Public Health

C-PH Columbia-Presbyterian Hospital

CPHA Canadian Public Health Association

CP & HA Canadian Port and Harbour Association

CPHC Central Pacific Hurricane Center (Honolulu)

cpi characters per inch; commercial performance index; constitutional psychopathic inferior; consumer price index; crash position indicator

CPI California Personality Inventory; California Psychological Inventory; Canadian Pacific Investments; Chemical Processing Industries; Chief Pilot Instructor; Communist Party of India; Conference Papers Index; Consolidated Plastic Industries; Consumer Price Index

cpia close-pair interstitial atom

CPIA Chemical Propulsion Information Agency

cpiaf (CPIAF) cost-plus-incentive-award fee

cpib chlorophenoxyisobutyrate

CPIB Corrupt Practices Investigation Bureau

CPIC Canadian Police Information Centre

cpif character position in frame

cpif (CPIF) cost plus incentive fee

CPILS Correlation-Protected Integrated Landing System

CPIM Curaçaosche Petroleum Industrie Maatschappij

cpin crankpin

CPI-U Consumer Price Index-Urban

CPI-W Consumer Price Index-revised

CPJ Communist Party of Japan (also called JCP)

CPJI *Cour Permanente de Justice Internationale* (French—Permanent Court of International Justice)

cpk (CPK) creatinine phosphokinase

cpkg cents per kilogram

cpl cement plaster; characters per line; common program language; complete; completion

Cpl Corporal

CPL Calgary Public Library; Canadian Pacific Limited; Cats' Protection League; Central Public Library; Certified Parts List; Certified Products List; Charleston Public Library; Charlotte Public Library;

Chattanooga Public Library; Chicago Public Library; Cincinnati Public Library; Civilian Personnel Letter; Cleveland Public Library; Clio Press Limited (Oxford); Colonial Products Laboratory; Columbus Public Library; Commercial Pilot's License; Commonwealth Parliamentary Library; Commonwealth Public Library; Coronado Public Library; Council of Planning Librarians; Crew Procedures Laboratory

CPLA California Palace of the Legion of Honor

cpld coupled (flow chart)

cplg coupling

cplmt complement

cplr center of pillar; coupler

CPLS Canberra Public Library Service; Certified Professional Legal Secretary

cplt copilot

cpm cards per minute; commutative principle of multiplication; condensed particulate matter; counts per minute; critical path method; cycles per minute

cpm (CPM) cost per thousand

cp/m control program/microcomputers

CPM Center for Preventive Medicine; Central Pacific Minerals; Certified Property Manager; Certified Purchasing Manager; Chief Postmaster; Colonial Police Medal (British); Communist Party of Malaya

CPMA Computer Peripheral Manufacturers Association

CPMC Columbia-Presbyterian Medical Center

CPMS Civilian Personnel Management System; Computer Performance Monitoring System

cpn chronic pyelonephritis; coupon

Cpn Copenhagen

CPN *Communistische Partij van Nederland* (Dutch Netherlands Communist Party)

CPNP Cape Perth National Park (Western Australia)

CPNZ Communist Party of New Zealand

cpo cost proposal outline

CPO Calgary Philharmonic Orchestra; Chief Petty Officer; Chief Post Office; Civil Post Office; Civilian Personnel Office(r); Community Post Of-

fice; Community Producers Organization; Comprehensive Planning Organization; County Planning Office(r); Czech Philharmonic Orchestra

CPOA California Peace Officers Association; Chief Petty Officers Association

CPOG Canadian Pacific Oil and Gas

cpp critical path plan

CPP Caltech Population Program; Canada Pension Plan; Center for Policy Process; Chemical Processing Plant; Communist Party of the Philippines; Critical Path Planning

CPP *Civilian Personnel Pamphlet*

CPPA Canadian Pulp and Paper Association

cppb continuous positive-pressure breathing

CPPB Canada Pension Plan Benefits; Commonwealth Prickly Pear Board

CPPCA California Probation, Parole, and Correctional Association

cppd calcium pyrophosphate dihydrate

CPPD Collaborative Program for Professional Development

CPPL Canadian Pacific Princess Lines (Vancouver-Nanaimo run)

CPPR Cassel Psychotherapy Progress Record

cpps critical path planning and scheduling

CPPS *Comisión Permanente para la Explotación y Conservación de las Riquezas Maritimas del Pacífico Sur* (Spanish —Permanent Commission for the Exploitation and Conservation of the Maritime Riches of the South Pacific)

CPQ Children's Personality Questionnaire

cpr cardiopulmonary resuscitation; copper

cpr (CPR) chemical propulsion rocket

CPR Canadian Pacific Railway; Carlos Peña Romulo; Central Premonitions Registry; Cobourg Peninsula Reserve (Australian Northern Territory); Committee on Polar Research; Cost Performance Report; Council for Public Responsibility

CPRA Council for the Preservation of Rural America

CP Rail Canadian Pacific Rail

CPRE Council for the Preservation of Rural England

CPRF Cancer and Polio Research Fund

CPRG Computer Personnel Research Group

CPRI Council for the Protection of Rural Ireland

CPR-nummer Centrale Person Register nummer (Dano-Norwegian—Central Person Register number)

CPRS Council for the Protection of Rural Scotland

CPRSA Cape Peninsula Road Safety Association

CPRW Council for the Protection of Rural Wales

CPR-WBS Cost Performance Report—Work Breakdown Structure

cps characters per second; constitutional psychopathic state; coupons; creative problem solving; critical path scheduling, cycles per second

Cp(s) Caucasian pimp(s); Chicano pimp(s); Chinese pimp(s)

CP's Command Posts

CPS California Physician's Service; California Production Service; Canadian Pacific Steamships; Canadian Penitentiary Service; Catholic Pamphlet Society; Center for Population Studies (Harvard); Certified Professional Secretary; College Placement Service; College Press Service; Commission on Presidential Scholars; Commonwealth Public Service; Computer Processing Service(s); Condensate Polishing System; Congregational Publishing Society; Consumer Price Survey; Consumer Purchasing Service; Conversational Programming System; Current Population Survey

C.P.S. *Custos Privati Sigilli* (Latin—Keeper of the Privy Seal—Great Britain)

CPS Compendium of Pharmaceuticals and Specialities; Conseil Permanent de Sécurité (French—Permanent Security Council)

CPSA Canadian Political Science Association; Civil and Public Services Association (UK); Clay Pigeon Shooting Association; Commonwealth Public Service Association

CPSAA Commonwealth Public Service Artisans Associations

cpsac cycles-per-second alternating current

C_psc course per standard compass

CPSC Consumer Product Safety Commission

CPSCU College of Physicians and Surgeons—Columbia University

cpsd cross-power spectral density

cpse counterpoise

cpsi causing pressure shut in

CPSI Council of Profit-Sharing Industries

CPSL Canadian Pacific Steamship Line

CPSLCS Complete Power Signalling Local Control System

CPSM Colonial Prison Service Medal (British)

CPSP Cove Palisade State Park (Oregon)

CPSR Calibration Procedure Status Report (Polaris); Contractor Procurement Systems Review

CPSS Certificate in Public Service Studies; Common Program Support System

C_p stg c course per steering compass

CPSU California Polytechnic State University; Combined Public Service Unions; Communist Party of the Soviet Union

cpt carpet(ed); casement-projected transom; chest physiotherapy; cockpit procedure trainer; continuous performance task; counterpoint; critical path technique

cpt (CPT) California Public Television; critical path technic

Cpt Capitaine (French—Captain)

CPT Canadian Pacific Telegraphs; Cape Town, South Africa (Malan Airport); Civilian Pilot Training; Communist Party of Thailand; Continuing Performance Test(ing)

CPT Current Physics Titles

C.P.T. *Contador Público Titulado* (Spanish—Certified Public Accountant)

CPTB Clay Products Technical Bureau

CPTL Canadian Pacific Transport Limited

Cptn Captain

cptng mats rgs carpeting, mats, or rugs

cptr capture; carpenter; carpentry

CPTS California Public Television Stations; Council of Professional Technological Societies

CPTV Connecticut Public Television

cpu (CPU) central processing unit

CPU California Pacific University; Canadian Paperworkers Union; Central Processing Unit; Commonwealth Press Union; Crime Prevention Unit

CPUBINFO Chief of Public Information Division (NATO)

CPUC California Public Utilities Commission

CPUSA Communist Party USA

cpv (CPV) cytoplasmic polyhedrosis virus

CPV Combination Pump Valve; Communist Party of Vietnam; Compañía Peruana de Vapores (Peruvian Steamship Line)

cpvc critical pigment volume concentration

CPVPL Charles Patterson Van Pelt Library (University of Pennsylvania)

cpw commercial projected window

cPw polar continental air warmer than underlying surface

CPW California Press Women; Central Park West

CPWH Committee for the Preservation of the White House

CPX Command Post Exercise

cpy copy

CPY Communist Party of Yugoslavia

cpz chlorpromazine

CPZ Central Park Zoo

cq chloroquine quinine; circadian quotient; come quick; conceptual quotient; copy correct; copy (spelled) correctly

cq (CQ) class quotient (lowerclass, upperclass, etc.)

CQ call to quarters (radio signal meaning message following is intended for all receivers); Charge of Quarters; Conditionally Qualified

CQ Caribbean Quarterly; Congressional Quarterly

CQC Citizens for a Quiet City

CQCA Central Queensland Coal Associates

cqcm cryogenic quartz-crystal microbalance

CQD wireless distress signal
cqm chloroquine mustard
CQM Chief Quartermaster; Company Quartermaster
CQMS Company Quartermaster Sergeant
cqr secure anchor (British short form for a plowshare-shaped single-fluke anchor)
CQR Customer Quality Representative
CQR Church Quarterly Review
CQs Citizens for Quieter Cities
CQS California Q-Set
CQSW Certificate of Qualification in Social Work
cqt circuit; correct
CQT College Qualification Test
CQU College Qualification Test(s)
CQUCC Commission on Quantities and Units in Clinical Chemistry
cr calculus removal; calculus removed; cardiorespiratory; carriage return; cathode ray; center of resistance; chest and right arm; clinical research; clot reaction; coefficient (of fat) retention; cold roll; cold-rolled; colon resection; complete remission; complete round; compression ratio; conditioned reflex; conditioned response; cranial; creatinine; credit; creek; cresyl red; crew; critical; critical ratio; crown; crown-rump; cruise
cr (CR) carriage return (data processing); conditional release(parole); conditioned reflex; conditioned response; critical ratio
c-r cognitive restructuring
c/r company risk; correction requirement(s)
c & r cops and robbers
cr. crux (Latin—cross)
c/r cuenta y riesgo (Spanish—for account and risk of)
Cr chromium; Commander; creatinine; creditor
Cr Contador (Spanish—Bookkeeper, Cashier, Purser)
Cr. Credo (Latin—I believe, the creed); *Ceskoslovensky rozhlas* (Czechoslovak Radio)
CR Camping Reserve; Central Registry; Ceskoslovenska Republika (Czechoslovakian Republic); Change Recommendation; Characterization Report; Chief Ranger; Classified Register; Combat Ready; Commonwealth Railways

(Australia); Contract Requisition; cost reimbursement; Costa Rica; Costa Rican
C-R Crouse-Hinds; Cutler-Hammer
C/R Chicago Rawhide (manufacturing company)
C & R convoy and routing
C of R Count(y) of Ravensberg
CR Centre de Réadtation (French—Rehabilitation Center); *Computing Reviews; Consumer Reports*
C R comptes rendus (French—proceedings, report)
C.R. Carolina Regina (Latin—Queen Caroline); *Carolus Rex* (Latin—King Charles); *Civis Romanus* (Latin—Citizen of Rome); *Custos Rotulorum* (Latin—Roll Keeper)
cra central retinal artery
Cra Carretera (Spanish—highway); *Contadora* (Spanish—Bookkeeper, Cashier, Purser)
Cr A Commander at Arms; Corona Australis
CRA California Redwood Association; California Republican Assembly; Canadian Rheumatism Association; Cave Research Associates; Centres de la Recherche Appliqué (Applied Research Centers); Coal Research Association; College of Radiologists of Australia; Colorado River Aqueduct; Colorado River Authority; Community Redevelopment Agency; Concentrated Rehabilitation Area; Continuing Resolution Authority; Convair Recreation Association; Conzinc Riotinto of Australia
C.R.A. Conzinc Riotinto of Australia (their periods as shown)
CRAB Central Registry at Bethesda
CRABS Close-Range Analytical-Bundle System
crabsan crab sandwich
Crabtown nickname of Annapolis, Maryland
crabwich crab sandwich
CRAC Careers Research and Advisory Center; Community Research Action Center
CR Acad Sci Comptes Rendus Hebdomadaires des Seances de l'Academie des Sciences (French—Weekly Reports of Meetings of the Academy of Sciences)
Crackers rural Floridians and Georgians
Cracker State Georgia

Cracovia (Latin—Cracow)
CRAD Committee for Research into Apparatus for the Disabled; Contracted Research and Development
Cradle of American Independence Independence Hall, Philadelphia
Cradle of the American Revolution Faneuil Hall, Boston
Cradle of Aviation San Diego
Cradle of California San Diego (discovered 1542, first mission in California, San Diego de Alcalá, dedicated 1769)
Cradle of Civilization Armenia, China, Egypt, Greece, India, Iran, Iraq, Israel, Italy, Jordan, Lebanon, Mexico, Peru, Syria, and Turkey all claim this title
Cradle of Classical Civilization Greece
Cradle of the Confederacy capitol building—Montgomery, Alabama
Cradle of Electrical Engineering Berlin, Germany where the first electric railroad and first large-scale power station were built
Cradle of the French Revolution Marseille and Paris compete for the name
Cradle of Human Civilization Iraq's claim to fame
Cradle of Islam Saudi Arabia
Cradle of Japanese Art Nara, Honshu Island, Japan
Cradle of Japanese Civilization Kyoto, spiritual home of the people
Cradle of Liberty Carpenters' Hall, Philadelphia; Faneuil Hall, Boston; House of Burgesses, Williamsburg, Virginia; Holland during formation of the Dutch Republic; Switzerland in William Tell's time; any other place where liberty was valued more than life or security
Cradle of Nuclear Research Los Alamos, New Mexico
Cradle of Psychoanalysis Berlin and Vienna vie for this place-name nickname
Cradle of the Renaissance Florence, Italy
Cradle of the Russian Revolution Petrograd
Cradle of Secession Charleston, South Carolina
Cradle of Texas Liberty The Alamo in San Antonio
Cradle of the Union Albany, New York where in 1754 Ben-

jamin Franklin presented his Plan of Union to the Albany Congress

Cradle of Violent Crime the United States, according to Brazil where the crime rate is spiraling

CRAF Civil Reserve Air Fleet

CRAFT Commonwealth Rebate for Apprentice Full-time Training; Computerized Relative Allocation of Facilities Technic; Cycle Reporting and Fatigue Tracking

CRAG Combat Readiness Air Group

CRAGS Chemical Records and Grading System

cram. card random access memory

CRAM Contractual Requirements Recording, Analysis, and Management

cran cranial; craniology; cranium

cranapple cranberry-and-apple juice

cranio (Latin prefix—skull, from the Greek *kranios*)—cranial and cranium

craniol craniologic(al)(ly); craniologist; craniology

craniom craniometry

crank. underworld nickname for methamphetamine, a mind-altering drug

cran(s) cranberries; cranberry

Cranston Juvenile (delinquent) Diagnostic Center at Cranston, Rhode Island

crap crapola (cover-up phrases and words characterized by their ambiguity, insincerity, and mendacity)

CRAR Critical Reliability Action Request

cras coder and random access switch

CRASC Commander—Royal Army Service Corps

CRASH Citizens Rally and Appeal to Save Our Homes; Citizens to Reduce Airline Smoking Hazards; Community Resource and Self Help; Community Resources Against Street Hoodlums (Los Angeles Police Department detail)

crast. *crastinus* (Latin—of tomorrow)

'**crastinator(s)** procrastinator(s) —thief or thieves of time

Crat Crater

Crate NATO nickname for Soviet Ilyushin transport Il-14

Craters of the Moon Craters of

the Moon National Monument in southeastern Idaho

C-rat(s) C-ration(s)

CRAV Compañía Refineria de Azucar Viña del Mar (Spanish —Viña del Mar Sugar Refining Co)

CRAW Combat Readiness Air Wing (USN)

Crawfish Town New Orleans, Louisiana

Crawthumper(s) Marylander(s)

cray(s) crayfish(es)

Crazy Alley nickname of San Quentin Prison's insane asylum

crb central radio bureau; curb; curbing

crb (CRB) chemical, radiological, biological (warfare)

Cr B Corona Borealis

CRB Central Reproduction Bureau; Change Review Board; Civilian Review Board; Commission for Relief in Belgium; Cooper River Bridge (Charleston, South Carolina); County Roads Board

crbbb complete right bundle branch block

CRBC Chinese Road and Bridge Company

cr bl credit balance

cr & br crown and bridge (dental)

CRBRP Clinch River Breeder Reactor Plant

CRBS Customer Records and Billing System

crc cavity rim cap (contraceptive device); complete round chart; cyclic redundancy check

CrC control and reporting center; Crew Chief

CRC California Rehabilitation Center; Certified Recreation Counselor; Chemical Rubber Company; Civil Rights Commission; Commonwealth Reply Coupon; Consolidated Rail Corporation; Consolidated Railroads of Cuba; Control and Reporting Center; Coordinating Research Council; Corrosion Reaction Consultant

CRCA Canadian Rodeo Cowboys Association

CRCC Consolidated Record Communications Center (USA)

CRCE Centaur Reliability Control Engineering

crchf crew chief

CRCNJ Central Railroad Company of New Jersey

crcp continuously reinforced concrete paving

CRCP Certificate of the Royal College of Physicians

CRCR Center for Rate-Controlled Recordings

CRCRS Civil Rights Community Relations Service

CRCS Canadian Red Cross Society; Certificate of the Royal College of Surgeons

Crct Circuit

crd chronic renal disease; chronic respiratory disease; complete reaction of degeneration

Cr$ cruzeiro (Brazilian monetary unit)

CRD Community Relations Department; Crop Research Division (USDA)

CRDHE Center for Research and Development in Higher Education

crdl cradle

CRDL Chemical Research and Development Laboratories; Contractor Data Requirements List

crdm control-rod device mechanism

CR & DP Cooperative Research and Development Program

CRDS Clarence Ralph De Sola; Colgate-Rochester Divinity School

CRDSD Current Research and Development in Scientific Documentation

cre corrosion resistant

Cre Crescent

CRE Center for Radical Education; Commission for Racial Equality

CREA California Real Estate Association; Clearinghouse of Resources for Educators of Adults

C Real Ciudad Real

cream of tartar potassium acid tartrate ($KHC_4H_6O_6$)

creat creatine

CREAT Combined Resources for Editing Automated Teaching

CREATE Computational Requirements for Engineering, Simulation, Training, and Education (USAF time-sharing computer complex)

Creation Sci Creation Science Research Center

Creative Ed Creative Educational Society

Creator of French Existentialism Jean-Paul Sartre

Creator God *Viracocha* (Quechua—supreme god)—deity venerated in Incan and pre-Incan times

Creator of Modern Democracy Thomas Paine

Creator of Musical Laughter Rossini

Creatrix of the Female Language for Sexuality Anaïs Nin

Crébillon Prosper Jolyot

crectte creciente (Spanish—crescent, growing)

cred credit; creditor

credd customer requested earlier due date

CREDO Chaplain's Religious Education Development Organization

Creek The Creek—oilfields scattered along the creeks of western Pennsylvania

CREEP Committee to Re-elect the President (Nixon's Watergate Gang)

CREF College Retirement Equities Fund

CREFAL Centro Regional de Educación Fundamental para la America Latina (Regional Center of Fundamental Education for Latin America—United Nations organization)

CREG Cancer Research Emphasis Grants

CREI Capitol Radio Engineering Institute

crem cremation

cremains cremation remains

CREMI Credito Minero y Mercantil (Spanish—Mining and Mercantile Credit)

crem mus crematorium music (Beethoven's Marcia funebre from his *Eroica* Symphony, Berlioz's Death March from *Les Troyens*, Chopin's Funeral March, Handel's Death March from *Saul*, Mozart's Masonic Funeral Music, Rachmaninoff's *Isle of the Dead*, Richard Strauss's *Tod und Verklaerung*, Wagner's funeral music from *Siegfried*)

cremo crematorium

CREO Central Real Estate Office; Crystalline Regions Exploration Office (ONWI)

Creole Country southern counties of Alabama and Mississippi as well as coastal parishes of Louisiana where many people are of French or Spanish origin

Creole State Louisiana

crep. crepitus (Latin—crepita-

tion)

crepe(s) crepe(s) suzette

cres corrosion-resistant stainless steel; crescent; crescentic

cres crescendo (Italian—expanding, swelling)

Cres Crescent

CRES Center for Research in Engineering Science (University of Kansas); Corrosion Resistant Stainless Steel

cresc crescendo (Italian—increasing, swelling)

Crescendo Crescendo Publishing Company

Crescent City Appleton, Wisconsin; New Orleans, Louisiana

cress garden cress; watercress

CRESS Combined Reentry Effort in Small Systems; Computer Reader Enquiry Service System

crest. crew-escape and rescue techniques (USAF)

CREST Committee on Reactor Safety Technology

Crestwood Heights Toronto, Ontario's Forest Hill Village

Cret Cretaceous

Crete English place-name equivalent of Kriti

CrewTAF Crew Training Air Force

crf capital recovery factor; carrier frequency; continuous reinforcements; control relay forward; cross-reference file

crf (CRF) corticotropin-releasing factor

CRF Cancer Research Foundation; Citizens Research Foundation

CRFA Czechoslovak Rationalist Federation of America

CRFG California Rare Fruit Growers

crfs copper reverbatory furnace slag

crf's change request forms

crg carriage

CRG Cave Research Group; Cooperative Republic of Guyana (formerly British Guiana)

cri chemical rust inhibitor; cold running intelligibility; criminal; criterion-referenced instruction

CRI Caribbean Research Institute; Coconut Research Institute; Committee for Reciprocity Information; Communications Research Institute; Composers Recordings Incorporated

CR & I Chicago River and In-

diana (railroad)

CRI Croce Rossa Italiana (Italian Red Cross)

CRIB Computerized Resources Information Bank

CRIC Canon Regular of the Immaculate Conception

CRICAP Carpet and Rug Industry Consumer Action Panel

CRIEPI Central Research Institute of the Electrical Power Industry

CRIF Comité Representatif des Israélites de France (Representative Committee of the Jews of France)

CRILC Canadian Research Institute of Launderers and Cleaners

CRILI Center for Research in Learning and Instruction

crim criminal; criminalism; criminalist; criminologist; criminology

crim con criminal conversation (British euphemism—adultery)

Crimea Crimean Peninsula called Krym by the Russians and between the Sea of Azov and the Black Sea

criminol criminologist; criminology

criminotechnol criminological technology (using electronic and photographic devices and techniques to apprehend criminals and secure evidence needed for their conviction)

criminotic criminal neurotic

crip cripple

CRI & P Chicago, Rock Island and Pacific (railroad)

CRIPA Civil Rights of Institutionalized Persons Act

crips cripples

crip(s) crippler(s)—gangster(s) noted for crippling victims

CR & IR Chicago River and Indiana (railroad)

Cris Cristóbal

CRIS Command Retrieval Information System; Current Research Information System

crisco cream received in separating cottonseed oil

Crisopolis (Latin—Parma)

CRISP Computer Resources Integrated Support Plan; Cosmic Radiation Ionization Spectrographic Program (NASA)

Cristiania (Latin—Christiania) —Oslo's previous name used from 1624 to 1925 although Oslo was the original name

crit critic; critical; criticality;

criticism

criticalese language and style of professional critics who delight in using such terms as value judgement

CRITICOMM Critical Intelligence Communications System

crits critical reactor experiments

Crk Creek; Cork

crkc crankcase

CRL California Republican League; Cambridge Research Laboratory; Cardiac Research Laboratory; Center for Research Libraries; Chemical Research Laboratory; Civil Rights Law(s); County Rugby League; Crown Renewable Lease

C.R.L. Certified Record Librarian; Certified Reference Librarian

CRLA California Rural Legal Assistance; Canadian Railway Labor Association

CRLLB Center for Research on Language and Language Behavior (Univ Mich)

crls carelessness

crm confidence rulemaking; count rate meter; counter-radar missile; cross-reacting material; crucial reaction measure(ment)

cr/m crew member

CRM Certified Records Manager; Combat Readiness Medal; Communications/Research/ Machines (publisher); Counter-Radar Missile

CRM *Consumer Research Magazine*

CRMA Cotton and Rayon Merchants Association

crmch cruise Mach change

CRMD Children with Retarded Mental Development

CRME Council for Research in Music Education

Crml Carmel

crmn crewman

crmnls criminalism; criminalist; criminalistics; criminals

crmoly chrome molybdenum

CRMP Corps of Royal Military Police

crmr continuous-reading meter relay

CRMT Community Resources Management Team (parole and probation)

CRMWD Colorado River Municipal Water District

crn crane; crown

Crn (The) Crown (The Monarchy)

CRN Course Reference Number

CRNA Certified Registered Nurse Anesthetist

CRNL Chalk River Nuclear Laboratories (Canada)

CRNLE Center for Research in the New Literatures in English (Australian)

CRNM Capitol Reef National Monument

cr note(s) credit note(s)

CRNP Cape Range National Park (Western Australia)

CRNPTG Commission on the Review of the National Policy Toward Gambling

CRNSS Chief of the Royal Naval Scientific Service

CRNWR Cape Romain National Wildlife Refuge (South Carolina); Clarence Rhode National Wildlife Range (Alaska)

cro cathode-ray oscilloscope

Cr O chrome oxide (recording tape)

CRO Carnarvon, Australia (tracking station); Chief Recruiting Officer; Commonwealth Relations Office; Community Relations Office; Contractor's Resident Office; County Recorder's Office; Criminal Records Office

CrO$_2$ chromium dioxide (recording tape coating)

Croat. Croatia; Croatian

CROC Committee for the Rejection of Obnoxious (tv) Commercials

crock. crockery; crocks (English slang—broken-down animals or athletes)

Crockett Girls Crockett State School for (delinquent) Girls at Crockett, Texas

Croco Crocodilia

Crocodile Crocodile River of Mozambique and South Africa where it is also called Limpopo

crocodiliol crocodiliologic(al)(ly); crocodiliologist; crocodiliology

croc(s) crocodilian(s)—alligator(s), caiman(s) or cayman(s), crocodile(s), gavial(s)

Croix St Croix, American Virgin Islands

cro'jack crossjack

crom control read-only memory

Crom Cromwell

Cromwell's Curse Ireland (also

called the Curse of Cromwell)

Cronian Sea Arctic Ocean

Cronus Greek name for Saturn

CROP Christian Rural Overseas Program; Community Response in Opposition to Poverty

cross. crossing

Cross King's Cross (Sydney, Australia's nightlife section also called The Cross)

CROSS Committee to Retain Our Segregated Schools (Arkansas); Computerized Rearrangement of Special Subjects

CROSSBOW Computerized Retrieval of Organic Structures Based on Wiswesser

'crosse lacrosse; lacrosse stick

Cross of Geneva emblem of the Red Cross (red cross on a white field) used to show the neutrality of ambulances, hospitals, and hospital ships during wartime

Crossroads of Africa, Asia, and Europe Egypt

Crossroads of Africa and Europe Spain

Crossroads of Europe Belgium

Crossroads of the Pacific Oahu —the Aloha Islands, Hawaii

Crossroads of the Seven Seas Singapore

Crossroads of the South Pacific Fiji

Crossroads of the World Panama Canal (bisecting the Americas); Straits of Gibraltar (between Gibraltar in Europe and Tangier in Africa); Suez Canal (waterway linking Africa, Asia, and Europe); any place where there is intense international transport activity

Crotale Thompson surface-to-air guided missile made in France

Croves Hal Croves (pseudonym of D. Traven—nom de plume of Berick Traven Torsvan Croves)

Crow Eaters South Australians

Crowell Crowell Collier; Thomas Y. Crowell

Crown Crown Publishers

Crown City Coronado, California

Crown Prince of Keynesism John Kenneth Galbraith

Crozets Crozet Islands in the South Indian Ocean

crp cathode-ray tube/keyboard printer

Crp C-reactive protein

CrP creatinine phosphate

CRP Committee to Re-elect the President (Nixon's fund-raising organization also known as CREEP and run by a number of government officials who later went to jail for their part in the Watergate affair); Control and Reporting Post; Corpus Christi, Texas (airport); Cost Reduction Program; Crime Restitution Program

CRP Cruz Roja Peruana (Spanish—Peruvian Red Cross)

CRPD Chicago Regional Port District

cr pl chromium plate

CRPL Central Radio Propagation Laboratory

Cr Pr Criminal Procedure

CRPR Child-Rearing Practices Report

crr constant ratio roll

CrR Croix-Rouge (French—Red Cross)

CRR Cost Reduction Representative

CRRA Component Release Reliability Analysis

CRRB Centaur Reliability Review Board

CRRC Costa Rica Railway Company

crrd conceptual reference repository description

CRREL Cold Regions Research and Engineering Laboratory (USA)

CRRERIS Commonwealth Regional Renewable Energy Resources Information System

crrl contour roller

CRRS Combat-Readiness Rating System (USAF)

crs coast radio station(s); cold-rolled steel; colon-rectal surgery; creditors; credits; crew reserve status

cr's character reactions

Crs Cristóbal, CZ

CRs counter-revolutionaries (sometimes appears as KRs)

CRS Calibration Requirements Summaries; Career Service Status (USAF); Child Rearing Study; Coast Radio Service; Commonwealth Rehabilitation Service; Community Relations Service; Computing Research Station; Congressional Research Service; Corrective and Rehabilitation Squadron (USAF)

CRS Conseil de la Recherché Scientifique (French—Scientific Research Council)—Quebec; *Corps Républicain de la Securite* (French—Republican Security Corps)—anti-riot squads

CRSA Canadian Retail Shipment Association; Cold-Rolled Sections Association; Concrete Reinforcement Steel Association; Connecticut River Salmon Association

CRSC Center for Research in Scientific Communications (Johns Hopkins)

CRSG Classification Research Study Group

CRSI Concrete Reinforcing Steel Institute

crsp criminally receiving stolen property

CRSP Colorado River Storage Program

CRSR Center for Radiophysics and Space Research (Cornell University)

CRSS Collectors of Religion on Stamps Society; Community Refugee Settlement Scheme (Australia)

crst syndrome calcification and clinical signs of Raynaud's phenomenon, scleroderma, and telangiectasis

crt cargo-restraint transporter; cathode-ray tube; cold-rolled and tempered

Crt Court; Crater

CRT Certified Radiologic Technician; Combat Readiness Training; Criterion-Referenced Tests

cr tan lthr chrome-tanned leather

CRTC Canadian Radio-Television Commission; Cavalry Replacement Training Center

crtgc cartographer

crtkr caretaker

crtl criticality

crtn correction

crtog cartographer; cartographic; cartography

cr tp contour template

CRTPB Canadian Radio Technical Planning Board

crt's cathode-ray tubes

CRTS Commonwealth Reconstruction Training Scheme

crtu combined receiving and transmitting unit

cru clinical research unit; combined rotating unit; crucible; cruise

Cru Crux

CRU Cecil Rhodes University; Civil Resettlement Unit; Collective Reserve Union; Crime Reduction Unit

Cru Base Cruiser Base

CRUBATFOR cruisers, battle force

CRUD Chalk River Unidentified Deposit

CRUDESLANT Cruiser-Destroyer Forces, Atlantic

CRUDESPAC Cruiser-Destroyer Forces, Pacific

CRUDIV cruiser division

CRUEL Commission on Reform of Undergraduate Education and Living (Univ Ill)

crug corrugated

cruis cruiser; cruising

CRULANT Cruiser Forces, Atlantic

CRUPAC Cruiser Forces, Pacific

cru's collective reserve units (international banking currency)

CRUSK Center for Research on Utilization of Scientific Knowledge (Univ Mich)

Crust Crustacea

crustas ice-encrusted cocktails

cruz cruzeiro (Brazilian currency)—also appears as *C, Cr, Cruz, Crz*

Cruz(an) St Croix Island (or person from there)—American Virgin Islands

CRUZEIRO Servicos Aéreos Cruzeiro do Sul (Southern Cross Air Service—Brazil)

crv central retinal vein

Crv Corvus

CRV Corvette aircraft

crvan chrome vanadium

cr. vesp. cras vespere (Latin—tomorrow evening)

crvf congestive right ventricular failure

CRW Clean Radwaste (System); Commission on Rural Water

CRWG Computer Resources Working Group

CRWM Committee on Radioactive Waste Management (NAS-NRC)

CRWPC Canadian Radio Wave Propagation Committee

cry. crystal(s)

cryng carrying

cryobio cryobiological(ly); cryobiologist; cryobiology

cryochem cryochemical(ly); cryochemist(ry)

cryoelectro cryoelectronic(al)(ly); cryoelectronicist; cryoelectronics

cryogen cryogenic(al)(ly)

cryolite sodium aluminum fluoride

cryon cryonic(s)

cryosurg cryosurgeon; cryosur-

gic(al)(ly); cryosurgery
crypt. cryptography
crypt (Latin prefix—hidden)—
cryptogram, cryptographer,
cryptographic
crypta cryptanalysis; cryptanalyst
crypto cryptograph; cryptographer; cryptographic; cryptography
cryptocom cryptocommunism;
cryptocommunist
cryptofasc cryptofascism; cryptofascist
cryptonet crypto-communication network
crypton(s) cryptonym (s)
cryptos cryptocommunists;
cryptofascists; cryptograms
cryptozool cryptozoological(ly);
cryptozoologist(s); cryptozoology
crys crystal; crystalline; crystallization; crystallize; crystallography; crystalloids
crysnet crystallographic computing network
cryst crystal; crystalline; crystallography
Crystal City Corning, New York
Crystal Hills New Hampshire's White Mountains
crystd crystallized
crystn crystallization
cs caesarean section; capital stock; carbon steel; cast steel; cast stone; center section; cerebrospinal; cirrostratus; close support; cognitive style; color stabilizer; common steel (projectile); concentrated strength; conditioned stimulus; corticosteroid; crucible steel; cryptographic system; current series; current strength; cutting specification(s); cycloserine
cs (CS) central service; closeup shot (waist-up tv picture); conditioned stimulus
c/s cases; con safos (Spanish-American slang—impervious to attack, the same to you, you're stuck with it); cycles per second
c & s clean and sober
cs céntimos (Spanish—centimes, hundredths)—coins worth a hundredth part of any unit; come sopra (Italian—as above); cours (French—course, currency, current price); cuartos (Spanish—apartments, fourths)—coins worth a fourth part of any unit

cS centistoke(s)
Cs cesium; cirrostratus
CS Cadbury Schweppes; Call Sign; Casualty Station; Chemical Society; Chief Secretary; Chief of Staff; Civil Service; Colonial Secretary; Commonwealth Secretariat; Communications Station; Communications System; contract surgeon; Cooperative Society; Correspondence School; Credit Suisse (bank); Cryptographic System; Cultural Survival; current series; current strength; cutting specifications
C/S call signal; certificate of service
C&S Chicago and Southern (Delta Airlines); Citizens and Southern (bank); Colorado and Southern (railroad)
C of S Chief of Staff; Chief of Service
C.S. Custos Sigilli (Latin—Keeper of the Seal)
Cs137 radioactive cesium
CSA Canadian Standards Association; Canterbury Society of Arts; Central South Australia; Central Surgical Association; Ceskoslovenske Aerolinie (Czechoslovakian Airline); Chief of Staff, Army; College of Surgeons of Australasia; Commercial Service Authorization; Commonwealth Sugar Agreement; Communication Service Authorization; Community Services Administration; Community of St Andrew; Computer Sciences of Australia; Confederate States of America, Confederate States Army; Contractor Service Action; Controlled Substances Act
C & SA Counterinsurgency and Special Activities (Joint Chiefs of Staff)
CSAA California State Automobile Association; Child Study Association of America; Council of Specialized Accrediting Agencies
CSAC Cameron State Agricultural College; Conners State Agricultural College
CSADC Canadian—South African Diamond Corporation
CSAE Canadian Society of Agricultural Engineering
CSAF Chief of Staff, United States Air Force
CSAL Central Scientific Agri-

cultural Library (Moscow)
CSANZ Cardiac Society of Australia and New Zealand
CSAO Civil Service Association of Ontario
CSAP Canadian Society of Animal Production; Career Skills Assessment Program
csar communication satellite advanced research
CSAR Comité Secret de l'Action Révolutionnaire (French—Secret Committee of Revolutionary Action), the Cagoule and its hooded Cagoulard rightist terrorists active during World War II in aiding the invading Nazis
CSAV Compañía Sud America de Vapores (Chilean Line)
csb calcium silicate brick; chemical stimulation (of the brain); concrete splash block
Csb Casablanca
CSB Canterbury Savings Bank; Central Statistical Board; Christian Service Brigade; Committee for Safe Bicycling; Commonwealth Savings Bank; Copra Stabilization Board
C.S.B. Bachelor of Christian Science
CSB Centro Simón Bolívar (Spanish—Simón Bolívar Center), metropolitan management investment in Caracas, Venezuela
CSBA California School Board Association
CSBE California State Board of Education
CSBG Concerned Seniors for Better Government
CSBs Canada Savings Bonds
csc cartridge storage case; change schedule chart; cosecant
c & sc capital and small capital letters
CSC Canadian Shippers Council; Canadian Space Centre; Central Security Control; Central Security Council; Child Safety Council; Citizens Service Corps; Civil Service Commission; Civilian Screening Center; Colorado State College; Combat Support Company; Command and Staff College (USAF); Commonwealth Scientific Committee; Commonwealth Steel Company; Communications Satellite Corporation; Community Service Center; Com-

puter Science Corporation; Consolidated Coal Company (stock exchange symbol); Conspicuous Service Cross; Continuous Service Certificate

CSCA Central States Corrections Association; Civil Service Clerical Association

CSCAW Catholic Study Circle for Animal Welfare

CSCC Civil Service Commission of Canada

CSCCL Center for Studies in Criminology and Criminal Law (University of Pennsylvania)

CSCD Center for Studies of Crime and Delinquency; Community Service Center for the Disabled

CSCE Conference on Security and Cooperation in Europe

CSCFE Civil Service Council for Further Education (UK)

csch hyperbolic constant; hyperbolic cosecant

CS Ch E Canadian Society for Chemical Engineering

CS circuit common-source amplifier for field-effect transistors

CSCJ Center for Studies in Criminal Justice

CSCl Community of St Clare

cscn character scan(ning)

CScO Chief Scientific Officer

CSCP Christian Science Committee on Publications

CSCS Cost, Schedule, and Control System; Crusader S-wire Container Service

C/SCSC Cost-Schedule Control Systems Criteria

cscu countersink cutter

csd closed shelter deck(ing); constant-speed drive; controlled-slip differentials; convection suppression device(s); cortical spreading depression

CSD Civil Service(s) Department; Commonwealth Society for the Deaf; Consumer Correctional Services Department; Consumer Service(s) Division; Convair San Diego (Division of General Dynamics Corporation); Correctional Services Department; Corrective Services Department

CSD *Ceskoslovenske Statne Drahy* (Czechoslovak State Railway)

CSD-ALA Children's Services Division—American Library Association

csdc computer signal data con-

verter

CSDE California State Department of Education; Central Servicing Development Establishment

CSDI Center for the Study of Democratic Institutions

CSDP Coordinated Ship Development Plan (USN)

CSDPH California State Department of Public Health

CSDS Chicago Sewage Disposal System

csdv closed shelter-deck vessel

cse course

cs & e crew station and escape

Cse *Causse* (French—limestone plateau)

CSE Calcutta Stock Exchange; Cincinnati Stock Exchange; Certificate of Secondary Education

CSEA California State Electronics Association; California State Employees Association; Combat System Engineering Authorization

CSEAA Civil Service Employees Association of America

csect control section; cross section

c-sect cesarian section

csed coordinated ship electronics design

CSEE Canadian Society for Electrical Engineering

csei concentrated solar-energy imitator

CSEIP Center for the Study of the Evaluation of Instructional Programs

CSEL Consolidated Support Equipment List(ing)

CSEPA Central Station Electrical Protection Association

cseq/cseqt consequences/consequent

CSERB Computers, Systems, and Electronic Research Board

CSEU Confederation of Shipbuilding and Engineering Unions

csf cerebrospinal fluid

CSF Center for Southern Folklore; Community of St Francis; Correctional Service Federation

CSF *Compagnie Générale de Télégraphie Sans Fil*

CSFA Canadian Scientific Film Association; Citizens Scholarship Foundation of America

CSFAC Colorado Springs Fine Arts Center

CSFE Canadian Society of Forest Engineers

CSFPA Central Station Fire Protection Association

CSFS Commonwealth Scholarship and Fellowship Scheme

CSFT Climax/Granite-Spent Fuel Test(ing)

csf-Wr cerebrospinal fluid-Wassermann reaction

csg casing

CSG Capital Systems Group; Configuration Steering Group; Council of State Governments

CSG *Centre Spatial Guyanais* (French-Guiana Space Center)

CSGA Canadian Seed Growers Association; Central States Gas Corporation

CS-gas civil(ian)-security or cyanide-simulating gas also called Mace or tear gas as it causes temporary blindness, burning, tearing, and I-can't-breathe sensations including choking, coughing, stinging, and vomiting; used to control unruly mobs

CSGBI Cardiac Society of Great Britain and Ireland

csgn consign

csgnd consigned

c/sgnd countersigned

csgnee consignee

csgng consigning

csgnmt consignment

CSGUS Clinical Society of Genito-Urinary Surgeons

csh calcium silicate hydrate; cash

CSH Combat Support Hospital

cshaft crankshaft

CSHP Canadian Society of Hospital Pharmacists

csi contractor standard item

CSI Campus Studies Institute; Child Study Institute; Construction Specification Institute; Container Status Information

C.S.I. Companion of the Order of the Star of India

CSI *Cinematique Scientifique Internationale* (French—International Scientific Film Library)

CSIC *Consejo Superior de Investigaciones Cientificas* (Spanish—Superior Council of Scientific Investigations)

CSICC Canadian Steel Industries Construction Council

CSICOP Committee for the Scientific Investigation of

Claims of the Paranormal
csid consider
csidd considered
csidl considerable
csidn consideration
CSIE Center for the Study of Information and Education
CSigO Chief Signal Officer
csink countersink
CSIP Committee for the Scientific Investigation of the Paranormal
CSIR Council of Scientific and Industrial Research; Council for Scientific and Industrial Research (South Africa); Council of Scientific and Industrial Research (India)
CSIRA Council for Small Industries in Rural Areas
CSIRO Commonwealth Scientific and Industrial Research Organization (Australia)
CSIROLCA Commonwealth Scientific and Industrial Research Organization Laboratory Craftsmens Association
CSIRONET Commonwealth Scientific and Industrial Research Organization Computing Network
CSIROTA Commonwealth Scientific and Industrial Research Organization Technical Association
CSIS Canadian Security Intelligence Service, Center for Strategic and International Studies (Georgetown University)
CSISRS Cross-Section Information Storage and Retrieval System (AEC)
CSIT Chapin Social Insight Test
CSIVP California State Influenza Vaccine Program
CSJ Christian Science Journal
CSJB Community of St John Baptist
csk cask; countersink; countersunk
CSK Cooperative Study of the Kuroshio (UNESCO)
CSK Consumer Survival Kit (public tv program)
csk hd countersunk head
csko countersink other side
csl computer simulation language; computer-sensitive language; console
csl (CSL) crane stores lighter
CSL Canada Steamship Lines; Cedar Springs Library; Chicago Short Line (railroad); Cinderella Softball League; Circle of State Librarians; Colorado

State Library; Consumer Service Litigants
CSL Centre de Semi-Liberté (French—Semi-Liberty Center)—halfway house for criminals; *Conseil Supérieur du Livre* (French—Better Book Council)
CSLA Canadian School Library Association; Church and Synagogue Library Association
CSLATP Canadian Society of Landscape Architects and Town Planners
CSLEA Center for the Study of Liberal Education for Adults
CSLICC Counseling Service of the Long Island Council of Churches
CSLO Canadian Scientific Liaison Office; Combined Services Liaison Office(er)
CSLP Center for Short-Lived Phenomena (Smithsonian)
cslr consular
CSLS Civil Service Legal Society (UK)
CSLT Canadian Society of Laboratory Technologists
csm cerebrospinal meningitis; combustion space monitor; command service module (CSM); corn-soya-milk (mixture)
CSM Central States Motor Freight Bureau; Chief Stipendiary Magistrate; Christian Socialist Movement; Colorado School of Mines; Command and Service Module; Commission for Synoptic Meteorology; Company Sergeant-Major; Correctional Service of Minnesota; Cosmopolitan School of Music
CSM Christian Science Monitor
CSMA Chemical Specialities Manufacturers Association
CSMC Catholic Students' Mission Crusade; Council for the Single Mother and her Child
CSMFTA Central and Southern Motor Freight Tariff Association
csmith coppersmith
CSM-LM Command Service Module—Lunar Module (Apollo spacecraft)
CSMMG Chartered Society of Massage and Medical Gymnastics
CSMP Comprehensive School Mathematics Program; Continuous System Modeling Program

c/smp(s) counter sample(s)
CSMPS Computerized Scientific Management Planning System
CS/Ms Commander, Submarines
CSMSW Carver School of Missions and Social Work
csn colloidal suspension
CSN Canadian Switched Network; Community of the Sacred Name; Companhia Siderurgica Nacional (National Steel Company); Confederate States Navy; Contract Serial Number; Control Symbol Number
CSNAR Charles Sheldon National Antelope Refuge (Nevada)
CSNDA Center for the Studies of Narcotic and Drug Abuse (National Institute of Mental Health)
CSNH Cincinnati Society of Natural History
CSNI Committee for the Safety of Nuclear Installations
CSNMDU Center for the Study of Non-Medical Drug Use
CSNWR Carolina Sandhills National Wildlife Refuge (South Carolina)
cso central signoff; chained sequential operation
C^so Corso (Italian—Street)
CSO Cairo Symphony Orchestra; Cargo Security Office; Central Selling Organisation (diamonds sold in London); Central Statistical Office; Charlotte Symphony Orchestra; Chattanooga Symphony Orchestra; Chicago Symphony Orchestra; Chief Signal Officer; Chief Staff Officer; Chief Surgical Officer; Cincinnati Summer Opera; Cincinnati Symphony Orchestra; Clothing Supply Office(r); Columbia Symphony Orchestra; Columbus Symphony Orchestra; Command Signal Office(r); Commonwealth Scientific Office; Community Service Organization; Community Standards Organization; Montevideo, Uruguay (Carrasco airport)
csocr code-sort optical-character recognition
CSOP Commission to Study the Organization of Peace (UN)
csoro conical span on receive only
CSOs Community Service Offi-

cers; Community Service Organizations

csp central switching point; concurrent spare parts; constant-speed drive

Csp Caspar; Caspean

CSP Certified Safety Professional; Chartered Society of Physiotherapy; Connecticut State Police; Continuous Sampling Plan; Contractor Support Program; Corporation Standard Practice

C.S.P. Congregation of St Paul

CSPA California State Psychological Association; Civil Service Pensioners' Alliance; Columbia Scholastic Press Association

CSPAA Columbia Scholastic Press Advisers Association

CSPB California State Personnel Board

CSPC California State Polytechnic College

CSPCA Canadian Society for the Prevention of Cruelty to Animals

CSPCo Caledonian Steam Packet Company

C/SPCS Cost-Schedule Planning Control Specification

CSPE Columbia Storage Power Exchange

CSPI Center for Science in the Public Interest

CSPM Communications Security Publications Memorandum

cspp corrugated structural plate pipe

CSPP Community Shelter Planning Program

cspr chlorosulphonated polyethylene rubber

CSPR(s) Christian Science Practitioner(s)

CSPS Cable-Suspended Pumping Station; Christian Science Publishing Society

csqm climax stock quartz monsonite

CSQs College Student Questionnaires

csr circumsolar radiation; compulsive security ritual; corrected sedimentation rate; corrugated steel reinforcement

C-S r Cheyne-Stokes respiration

CSR Certified Shorthand Reporter; Chartered Stenographic Reporter; Civil Service Requirement; Colonial Sugar Refining; Commonwealth Strategic Reserve

CSRA Central Savannah River Area (Planning and Development Commission)

CSRC Communication Science Research Center (Batelle Memorial Institute—Columbus, Ohio)

CSRF Childrens Surgical Research Fund

CSRG Commonwealth Special Research Grant

CSRL Center for the Study of Responsive Law

CSRO Consolidated Standing Route Order (USA)

CSRP Canadian Sprinkler Risk Pool; Cognitive Systems Research Program

CSRS Cooperative State Research Service

CSRUIDR Chemical Society Research Unit in Information Dissemination and Retrieval

css center spar station; computer systems simulator; control-stick steering

CSS Calcutta School Society; Central Security Service (DoD); City Shuttle Service; Clandestine Services Staff (CIA); Coded Switch System (to arm nuclear weapons); College Scholarship Service; Combat Service Support (USA); Commit Sequence Summary; Community Service Society; Computerized Shipping Service; Confederate States Ship (C.S.S.); Contractor Storage Site

C.S.S. Charles Stuart Calverley (nineteenth-century satirist whose works appear under the initials shown)

Cssa *Contessa* (Italian—Countess)

CSSA Cactus and Succulent Society of America; Central States Speech Association; Central Supply Support Activity

cssb compatible single sideband

CSSB Civil Service Supply Board

CSSC California Seismic Safety Commission

CSSCG Container Systems Standardization-Coordination Group

C S-S Co Cunard Steam-Ship Company

CSSD Central Sterile Supply Department

CSSDA Council of Social Science Data Archives

CSSDC Canadian Society for the Study of Diseases in Children

CSSE Canadian Society for the Study of Education

cssl continuous system simulation language

CSSL Central Sierra Snow Laboratory (Norden, California)

CSSLRP Commonwealth Secondary School Libraries Research Project

cssm compatible single-side-band modulation

CSSM Council of State Supervisors of Music

CSSO Combined State Services Organization; Consolidated Surplus Sales Office

CSSP Center for Studies of Suicide Prevention; Customer Standard Settlement Program

CSSR Cost Schedule Status Report

CSSRC Canadian Social Science Research Council

CSSS Canadian Soil Science Society; Council of State Science Supervisors

csst computer system science training

CSSU Crime Scene Search Unit

cst cargo ships and tankers; centistokes; channel status indicator; combined station power; convulsive shock therapy

c's/t certificates of title

CST Celeban Standard Time; Central Standard Time; Council for Science and Technology

CSta consolidating station

CSTA Canadian Society of Technical Agriculturists; Canterbury Science Teachers Association; Correspondence School Teachers Association

cs & tae combat surveillance and target acquisition equipment (DoD)

CSTAL *Confederación Sindical de Trabajadores de América Latina* (Spanish—Trade Union Confederation of the Workers of Latin America)

CSTC Charleston Submarine Training Center (South Carolina); Coordinating Scientific and Technical Council (UN); Coppin State Teachers College

C'sted Christiansted, St Croix

cstg casting

CSTI California Specialized Training Institute (for coping with terrorism); Chattanooga

State Technical Institute

cstmr customer

cstol combined short takeoff and landing; controlled short takeoff and landing

cstr canister

CSTS Combined Systems Test Stand; Computer Science Time Sharing

cstv community-supported television

C/Stwd Chief Steward

csu catheter specimen of urine; central statistical unit; central statistical unit; circuit switching unit(s); constant-speed unit

CSU California State University; Casualty Staging Unit; Civil Service Union; Colorado State University; Combined State Unions; Connecticut State University; Crime-Suppression Unit

CSU Christlich-Soziale Union (German—Christian Social Union)—political party

CSUC California State Universities and Colleges; California State University at Chico

CSUCA Consejo Superior Universitaria Centroamericano (Superior Council of Central American Universities)

CSUF California State University at Fresno

CSUH California State University at Humboldt

csul consult

CSULA California State University at Los Angeles

CSULB California State University at Long Beach

csuld consulted

csulg consulting

CSUN California State University at Northridge

CSUS California State University at Sacramento

CSUSA Copyright Society of the U.S.A.

CSUSB California State University at San Bernardino

CSUSD California State University at San Diego

CSUSF California State University at San Francisco

CSUSJ California State University at San Jose

CSV Community Service Volunteer

csw channel status word(ing); continuous seismic wave

CSW Certified Social Worker; Commission on the Status of Women

CSWA Chinese Seamens Welfare Association

CSWAE Commission on the Status of Women in Adult Education

CSWE Council on Social Work Education

CSWI Commission for Synoptic Weather Information

csws crew-served weapon sight

Cswy Causeway

CSX Chessie and Seaboard (railroads consolidated)

csz copper, steel, or zinc (freight)

ct cable transfer; carat; caught; cellular therapy; cent; center; center tap; central timing; ceramic tile; circuit; coated tablet; coffee table; compressed tablet; compute topography; contrast threshold; control transformer; corrective therapist; corrective therapy; court; credit; current; current transformer

ct (CT) computed tomograph(y); corrective therapist; corrective therapy

c/t conference terms

c & t classification and testing

ct. centum (Latin—hundred)

Ct celtium; Court

CT Canadian Terms; Certificate of Title; Copy Typist; Credit Transfer; Sir Charles Tupper (Canada's seventh Prime Minister)

C/T California Terms

C of T Certificate of Title; Count(y) of Tyrol

CT Corrections Today

CT-4 New Zealand-built Airtrainer aircraft

cta call time adjustor; catamenia (menstruation); cystine trypticase agar

cta (CTA) cyano-trimethyl-androsterone

cta communiquer à toutes adresses (French—circulate to all addresses); *cuenta* (Spanish—account)

c.t.a. cum testamento annexo (Latin—with the will annexed)

Ct A Control Area

CTA California Taxpayers Association; California Teachers Association; Canadian Tuberculosis Association; Caribbean Tourist Association; Chemical Toilet Association; Chicago Transit Authority; Colorado Teachers Association; Commercial Travellers Associa-

tion; Container Truckers Association; Council for Technical Advancement; Covered Threads Association

cta corr^te cuenta corriente (Spanish—current account)

cta cte cuenta corriente (Spanish —current account)

CTAF Crew Training Air Force

cta/ir control area/instrument restricted

cta/iv control area/instrument visual

CTAL Container Terminals Australia Ltd

CTAL Confederacion de Trabajadores de America Latina (Spanish—Confederation of Latin American Workers)

ctam continental tropical air mass

CTAU Catholic Total Abstinence Union

cta/ve control area/visual excepted

ctb cement-treated base; ceramic-tile base

CTB Cable Television Bureau; California Test Bureau; Canadian Tourist Board; Commercial Traffic Bulletin; Commonwealth Telecommunications Board; Commonwealth Trading Bank; Comprehensive Test Ban; Corporation for Television Broadcasts

CTD Centre Technique do Bois (French—Wood Research Center)

CTBA California Toll Bridge Authority, Commonwealth Trading Bank of Australia

ctbid(s) counterbid(s)

ctbm cetyl-trimethyl-ammonium bromide

ctbore counterbore

CTBRD Commonwealth Taxation Board of Review Decisions

CTBS Comprehensive Tests of Basic Skills

CTBT Comprehensive Test Ban Treaty

ctc carbon tetrachloride; contact

ctc (CTC) central traffic control; central train control; chlortetracycline

CTC California Tankers Company; Canadian Tire Corporation; Canadian Transport Commission; Canberra Technical College; Catholic Teachers College; Central Test Control; Certified Travel Consultant; Charter Travel Company; Chicago Teachers College; Chicago Technical College; Citizens Training Camp; Citizens Training Corps; Concordia Teachers College; Corn Trade Clauses; Curaçao Trading Company; Cyclists Touring Club

CTC *Congrès du Travail du Canada* (French—Canadian Congress of Labour)

CTCA Canadian Telecommunications Carriers Association; Channel and Traffic Control Agency

CTCB Contract Technical Compliance Board

ctcd contacted

ctcg contacting

CTCL Community and Technical College Libraries

CTCOSBA Cape Town Computer Services and Bureaux Association

CTCP Contract Task Change Proposal

CTCs Community Treatment Centers (US Bureau of Prisons)

CTCSS Continuous-Tone Coded-Squelch System

ctd coated; crated

c-t-d conductivity-temperature-depth

CTD Central Training Depot; Classified Telephone Directory; Corrective Therapy Department

CTDAS Canadian Trade Document Alignment System

ctdc control track direction computer

CTDC Chemical Thermodynamics Data Center (NBS)

ctdh command and telemetry data handling

CT & DM *Canadian Transportation and Distribution Magazine*

CTDO Central Technical Documents Office (USN)

cte coefficient of thermal expansion

cte *corriente* (Spanish—current)

Cte *Comte* (French—Count)

Cte *Conte* (Italian—Count)— Earl

CTE Car Tours in Europe; Compañía Transatlántica Espanola (Spanish Line)

CTEB Council of Technical Examining Bodies

CTEC Chemical Transportation Emergency Center

Ctee Committee

Cten Ctenophora

Cteno Ctenocephalides (fleas)

CTES Computer Telex Exchange System (RCA)

Ctesse *Comtesse* (French— Countess)

CTETOC Council for Technical Education and Training for Overseas Countries

CT Exam Computed Tomography Examination

ctf certificate; correction to follow; cytotoxic factor

Ctf Colorado tick fever

CTF Canadian Teachers Federation; Cayman Turtle Farm; Commander Task Force

CTFA Cosmetics, Toiletry, and Fragrance Association

CTFC Commodity Futures Trading Commission

CTFE Colleges of Technology and Further Education (subsection of the University and Research Section of the Library Association)

ctfet counterfeit

ctfm continuous-transmission frequency-modulated (sonar)

CTFT *Centre Technique Forestier Tropical* (French—Tropical Forest Technical Center)

ctfy certify

ctg cartage; cartridge; cutting

Ctg Cartagena, Spain (*see* Cgn)

CTG Center Theatre Group; Commander Task Group; Commercial Travellers Guild; Components Technology Group

ctge cartage; cartridge; cottage

ctgf clean tanks, gas free

CTGI Canadian Test of General Information

Cth Commonwealth

CTH Chalmers Tekniska Högskola (Swedish—Chalmers Institute of Technology); Corporation of Trinity House

Cthse Courthouse

cti Container Transport International (trademark)

CTI Central Technical Institute; Container Transport International; Contract Technical Instructor; Cooling Tower Institute

CTI *Communication Technology Impact*

CTIA Caravan Trades and Industries Association; Committee to Investigate Assassinations

CTIAC Concrete Technology Information Analysis Center (USA)

CTIC Cable Television Information Center

CTIU Container Transport International (container) Unit

ctk capacity-ton kilometer

cTk tropical continental air colder than underlying surface

CTK *Ceskoslovenska Tiskova Kancelar* (Czechoslovak Press Bureau)

ctl castellate; cental; central; complementary transistor logic; constructive total loss; control

ctl (CTL) checkout test(ing) language

Ctl central

CTL Certified Tool List; Cincinnati Testing Laboratories; Container Terminals Limited

ctlg catalog

ctlo constructive total loss only

ctm capacity ton mile; centrifugal turning moment; communications terminal modules

CTM Contract Termination Manual; Contractor Technical Meeting

CTM *Confederación de Trabajadores de México* (Spanish— Confederation of Workers of Mexico)

CTMA Collapsible Tube Manufacturers Association; Commercial Truck Maintenance Association; Country Timber Merchants Association (Australia)

ctmc communications controller; communications terminal modules

ctmdr clamptop metal drum

CTMM California Test of Mental Maturity

ctn carton; cotangent

C Tn Cape Town (British maritime contraction)

CTN Canton Island (tracking station)

ctnd contained

CTNE Compañía Telefonica Nacional de España (National Telephone Company of Spain)

ctng containing

ctnrs containers

ctns cartons

ctn's confectioners, tobacconists, newsagents

CTNS Chicago Tribune News Service

cto cancelled to order; concerto

c^{to} *conto* (Italian—account); *cuarto* (Spanish—fourth)

CTO Central Telegraph Office;

Central Treaty Organization; Chief Technical Officer; City Ticket Office; Cognizant Transportation Office; Combined Transport Operator; Container Transport Operator; Courier Transfer Officer

CTOA Commonwealth Telephone Officers Association; Creative Tour Operators Association

ctocu central technical order control unit

ctofr counteroffer

ctol conventional takeoff and landing

ct ord court order

ctp central transfer point; close to profit

ctp (CTP) cytidine triphosphate

CTP Canterbury Timber Products; Columbia Television Pictures

CTP Centre de Tutelle Pénale (French—Penal Surveillance Center)—tor recidivists; *Confederación de Trabajadores del Peru* (Spanish—Confederation of Workers of Peru)

CTPL Commission for Teacher Preparation and Licensing

CTPOA Commonwealth Telephone and Phonogram Officers Association

ctprt counterpart

ctpt counterpoint

CTPTA Centro Tropical de Pesquisas y Tecnologías de Alimentos (Tropical Center of Food Research and Technology)

ctptal contrapuntal

ctptst contrapuntist

ctr center; contour; controlled thermonuclear reactor; counter; cutter

Ctr Center

CTR Controlled Thermonuclear Reactor

CTRA Coal Tar Research Association

Ctr Appl Ling Center for Applied Linguistics

Ctr Appl Res Center for Applied Research in Education (New York)

Ctr Byz Center for Byzantine Studies

CTRC Caribbean Tourism Research Center

Ctr Calif Pub Center for California Public Affairs (Claremont)

Ctr Chin Stud Center for Chi-

nese Studies (Berkeley, California)

Ctr Cont Celeb Center for Contemporary Celebration (Chicago)

Ctr Cont Poetry Center for Contemporary Poetry (La Crosse, Wisconsin)

Ctr Info Am Center for Information on America

ctr/iv control zone/instrument visual

ctrl control (flow chart)

Ctr Land Arch Center for Landscape Architecture

Ctr Marital Sexual Center for Marital and Sexual Studies (Long Beach, Calif)

Ctr Mig Center for Migration Studies (New York)

ctrofr counteroffer

ctrofrdcl counteroffer declined

CTRP Controlled Thermonuclear Research Program

Ctr Pol Process Center for Policy Process (DC)

Ctr Pre-Col Center for Pre-Columbian Studies (DC)

Ctr Sci Pub Center for Science in the Public Interest (DC)

Ctr Sci Study Rel Center for the Scientific Study of Religion (Chicago)

Ctr S&SE Asian Center for South and Southeast Asian Studies (Ann Arbor, Mich)

CTRU Colonial Termite Research Unit

Ctr Urb Pol Res Center for Urban Policy Research (New Brunswick, NJ)

ctr/ve control zone/visual exempted

ctry country

cts carats; cents; computer typesetting; contralateral threshold shift (audiometry); crates

cts (CTS) communications technology satellite(s)

cts centavos (Spanish—cents); *centimes* (French—cents); *centimos* (Spanish—cents)

Cts courts

CTS Canadian Thoracic Society; Captive Trajectory System; Card-to-Magnetic Conversion System; Catholic Truth Society; Central Transportation System; Centralized Title Service; China Travel Service; Commercial Teachers Society; Commonwealth Teaching Service; Commonwealth Time Service; Component Test(ing) Set; Computer Test(ing) Site;

Computerized Type System; Consolidated Translation Survey; Container Terminal Station; Contract Technical Services; Contractor Technical Service; Conversational Terminal System; Cosmic Top Secret; Courier Transfer Station; Custom Track Service

CTSA Crucible and Tool Steel Association

ctsp contract technical services personnel

CTSS Compatible Time-Shared System

ctt capital transfer tax(ation); compressed tablet triturate

CTT Columbia Technical Translations

CTT Correios e Telecommuniações de Portugal (Postal and Telegraph Services of Portugal)

ct ta control tape

CTTB Central Trade Test Board

CTTC Central Telegraph Test Center

Cttee Committee

CTTF California Turtle and Tortoise Club

CTTP Complementary Trade Training Program

ctu centigrade thermal unit; central terminal unit; components test unit

CTU Combat Training Unit; Commander Task Unit

CTU (AFL-CIO) Commercial Telegraphers' Union

C-tube C-shaped tube

CTUS Carnegie Trust for the Universities of Scotland

ctv (CTV) cable television; color television

CTV Canadian Television; Children's Television

CTV Confederación de Trabajadores de Venezuela (Spanish—Confederation of Venezuelan Workers)

ctvo centavo (Spanish—cent)

CTVW Children's Television Workshop

ctw counterweight

cTw tropical continental air warmer than underlying surface

CTW Children's Television Workshop

ctwt counterweight

ctx computer telex exchange (RCA system)

Ct X Court Exhibit

Cty City; County

ctz chlorothiazide

CTZ Corps Tactical Zone

ct zone chemoreceptor trigger zone

cu cleanup; clinical unit; close-up; container unit (CU); control unit; cube; cubic; cumulus

c-u see you

c/u *cada uno*(Spanish—each one)

Cu Cuba; Cuban; cumulus; cuprum (Latin—copper)

C$_u$ urea clearance

CU Cambridge University; Capital University; Carleton University; Church Union; City University; Clafkin University; Clark University; Colgate University; Columbia University; Commercial Union; Concordia University; Consumers Union; Cooper Union; Cooperative Union; Cornell University; Creighton University; Cumberland University; Customs Union

Cu$_2$SO$_4$ copper sulfate

Cu-7 copper-constructed 7-shaped intrauterine device

cua central unit assembly; computer unit assembly

CUA Canadian Underwriters Association; Catholic University of America; Council on Urban Affairs

CUAC Cambridge University Athletic Club

cuad *cuadrado* (Spanish—square)

CUAFC Cambridge University Association Football Club

CUAG Computer Users Associations Group

CUAS Cambridge University Agricultural Society; Cambridge University Air Squadron

cub. control unit busy; cubic

cúb *cúbico* (Spanish—cubic)

Cub NATO nickname for the Soviet Antonov 100-passenger cargo plane

Cu b copper band

CUB advanced unit base; Carlton and United Breweries; Citizens Utility Board; Consumers Utility Board

Cuba Republic of Cuba (largest West Indian island and formerly one of the world's largest producers of sugar, Soviet support has failed to increase or maintain former productivity or solve pressing social problems of these Spanish-speaking libertarians),

República de Cuba

cuban cuban heel (broad-based heel used on women's shoes)

CUBANA Compañía Cubana de Aviación

cubanite copper iron sulfide

Cuban Ports (north coast large, medium, and small ports from west to east) Bahia Honda, Cabañas, Mariel, La Habana (Havana), Matanzas, Cardenas, La Isabela, Caibarien, Nuevitas, Puerto Padre; (south coast large, medium, and small from east to west) Santiago de Cuba, Manzanillo, Cienfuegos

Cuba's Principal Port Havana

CUBC Cambridge University Boat Club; Cambridge University Boxing Club

cubo conduct unbecoming an officer

CUBS Congress for the Unity of Black Students

cuc chronic ulcerative colitis

CUC Canadian Unitarian Council; Canberra University College; Canterbury United Council

CUCA Carpet and Upholstery Cleaning Association

cu cap. cubic capacity

CUCC Cambridge University Cricket Club

Cuch *Cuchillas* (Spanish—mountain chain, range)

cu cm cubic centimeter

CUCNY Citizens Union of the City of New York

cud. congenital urinary (tract) deformities

'cuda(s) barracuda(s)

Cuddy Cuthbert

CUDN Common User Data Network

CUDS Cambridge University Dramatic Society

cue. coastal upwelling experiment; computer update equipment; configuration utilization efficiency; control unit end; correction update extension

CUE Center for Urban Education; Coastal Upwelling Experiment; Concentrated Urban Enforcement (of gun control)

CUEA Coastal Upwelling Ecosystem Analysis

CUEBS Commission on Undergraduate Education in the Biological Sciences

CUED Council for Urban Economic Development

Cuen Cuenca

CUEPACS Congress of Unions of Employees in the Public and Civil Services

CUERAC Computer-Controlled Random-Access Cartridge Libraries

CUERD Committee for Upgrading Environmental Radiation Data

CUES College and University Environment Scales

CUEW Congregational Union of England and Wales

CUF Canadian Universities Foundation

CUF *Companhia Uniao Fabril* (Portuguese—United Manufacturing Company)—Iberian conglomerate whose company street in Barreiro is named Rua do Acido Sulfúrico (Sulfuric Acid Street) and is a constant source of air pollution

CUFC Consortium of University Film Centers

'cuffs handcuffs

cu ft cubic feet; cubic foot

cu ft min cubic feet per minute

cu ft sec cubic feet per second

cug closed-user group; cystourethrogram

CUGC Cambridge University Golf Club

CUHC Cambridge University Hockey Club

CUHK Chinese University of Hong Kong

CUIC Canadian Unemployment Insurance Commission

CUIHC California Urban Indian Health Council

cu in cubic inch

cuis *cuisine* (French—cookery, kitchen)

cuj. *cujus* (Latin—of which)

cuj. lib. *cujus libet* (Latin—of any you wish)

CUK São Paolo, Brazil (Combica Airport)

cukes cucumbers

CUKT Carnegie United Kingdom Trust

cul culinary

c-u-l see you later

CUL Cambridge University Libraries; China Union Lines; Columbia University Library; Cooper Union Library; Cornell University Library

Culenburgum (Latin—Culemborg)

cull. cullage; cullboard; culling; cullion

CULP California Union List of Periodicals

cult. cultural; culture

CULT Chinese University Language Translation (system)

cult. anthro(s) cultural anthropologist(s); cultural anthropology

CULTC Cambridge University Lawn Tennis Club

Cultured Pearl of the Orient Hong Kong

culv culvert

cul vul(s) culture vulture(s)

cum central unit memory; cumulative

cu m cubic meter

CUM Centro Universitario México (Spanish—Mexico University Center)

CUMA Canadian Urethane Manufacturers Association

Cumb Cumberland

Cumberland River City Nashville, Tennessee

Cumberlands Cumberland Caverns in central Tennessee; Cumberland Islands off the east coast of Queensland, Australia; Cumberland Mountains extending from Alabama to Virginia via Tennessee, Kentucky, and West Virginia

cum/d cubic meters per day

cum d(iv) cum dividend (with dividend)

cumes cumulative audience survey (radio/tv)

cu mm cubic millimeter

Cummins Farm Cummins Prison Farm in Arkansas

CUMMM Council of Underground Mining Machinery Manufacturers

Cum Nursing Lit Cumulative Index to Nursing Literature

Cump Tecumseh

cum pref cumulative preference

CUMS Cambridge University Musical Society

cum/sec cubic meters per second

cumshaw (Chinese—grateful thanks)—quasi-legal barter supply system; under-the-table graft

cu mu cubic micron

CUMWA Consortium of Universities in the Metropolitan Washington Area

cun cuneiform

CUN Convent van Universiteitsbibliothecarissen in Nederland (Dutch—Association of University Librarians in the Netherlands)

CUNA Credit Union National Association

cuni cupro-nickel (coin alloy)

cu-nim cumulo-nimbus (clouds)

CUNSA Canadian University Nursing Students Association

CUNY City University of New York

CUOG Cambridge University Opera Group

cup. cupboard

CUP Cambridge University Press; Canadian University Press; Columbia University Press; Cornell University Press

CUPA College and University Personnel Association

CUPBEQ Canadian University Press Québec Region

CUPE Canadian Union of Public Employees

Cupid (Latin—Eros)—god of love and lust

cupper cup-tie-er (athletic matches played for a trophy cup)

CUPR Catholic University of Puerto Rico

cuprite cuprous oxide

cupronic copper-nickel alloy

CUPS Consolidated Unit Personnel Section

CUPW Canadian Union of Postal Workers

cur. curiosa; curiosity; currency; current

Cur Curaçao (maritime abbreviation)

CUR Council on Undergraduate Research; Curaçao, Netherlands West Indies (Plesman Airport)

CURA Center for Urban Research and Action; Comprehensive Urban Renewal Area

CURAC Coal Utilization Research Advisory Committee

Curaçao capital island of the Netherlands Antilles comprising Aruba, Bonaire, Curaçao, Saba, Sint Eustatius, and Sint Maarten; Willemstad is the capital city of the Dutch West Indies and is also the capital port-city of Curaçao

Curaçao Day July 26 (celebrated throughout the Netherlands Antilles)

Curaçao's Ports (medium, small, and very small on the oil-refinery island's south coast) Willemstad, Bullen Baai, Caracas Baai, New Port

curat curative

curat. curatio(Latin—dressing, wound dressing)

Curator of Culture Lord Kenneth M(ackenzie) Clark

Curazao (Spanish—Curaçao)

CURB Campaign on the Use and Restriction of Barbiturates

cure. (C-U-R-E) care, understanding, research (organization for the welfare of drug addicts)

CURE Citizens United for Racial Equality

C-U-R-E Care, Understanding, Research (organization for the welfare of drug addicts)

CURES Computer Utilization Reporting System

CURF Citizens Union Research Foundation

CURFC Cambridge University Rugby Football Club

curio curiosa; curiosity

CURLS College, University, and Research Libraries Section (California Library Association)

CURMCO City Urban Renewal Management Corporation (NYC)

Curmudgeon Philosopher Ambrose Bierce

curr currency; current

Current the current [usually refers to any of the many oceanic currents such as the Agulhas, Alaskan, Aleutian, Antarctic, Antilles, Arctic, Australian (East or West), Benguela, Black (Black Stream or Kuroshio), California, Canaries, Cape Horn, Caribbean, Chilean (or Peruvian), El Niño, Equatorial, Falkland, Florida, Greenland, Guinea, Gulf Drift (North Atlantic Drift), Gulf Stream, Humboldt (Chilean or Peruvian Current), Japan (Kurile or Kuroshio), Labrador, Monsoon, Mozambique (Indian or Natal Current), North Atlantic Drift or North Atlantic Current, North Equatorial, North Pacific (drift or current), Norwegian, Okhotsk or Oyashio, South Atlantic, South Equatorial, South Indian, South Pacific, Subarctic (Aleutian), Tsushima (Kuroshio), West Australian, West Greenland, West Wind Drift (Antarctic West Wind Drift); etc.]

Currer Bell pseudonym of Charlotte Brontë

curric curriculum

Curse of Balboa Panamanian-style dysentery marked by

acute nausea and much retching

Curse of Cortez tourist nickname for Mexican-acquired diarrhea or dysentery also called Montezuma's Revenge

Curse of Cromwell Ireland (also called Cromwell's Curse)

curt. current (Scottish—instant); curtain

Curt Curtis

Curt Quintus Curtius Rufus (Roman historian)

Curt Jurgens Curd Jurgens

CURTS Common-User Radio Transmission System

curv cable-operated unmanned recovery vehicle

CURV Cable-controlled Underwater Research Vehicle

cury currently

Curzio Malaparte pseudonym— Curzio Suckert

Curzon Lord Curzon (George Nathaniel Curzon)—Viceroy and Governor General of India

cus customer

Cus Customs

CUS Cambridge Union Society; Continental United States

CUSA Conservative United Synagogue of America; Council of Unions of South Africa

cusecs cubic feet per second

Cus Ho Custom House

CUSIP Committee on Uniform Security Identification Procedures (for computer user protection); Committee for Uniform Securities Information

CUSIP No. CUSIP Number (assigned to every issue of either a bond or stock to identify that particular issue)

cusm customs

CUSM Columbia University School of Medicine

cusmr customer

CUSO Canadian University Service Overseas

CUSP Central Unit for Scientific Photography

Cuspidor of Europe France's nickname given it by Alexander Herzen the Russian anarchist who spent most of his adult life in Paris

CUSR Canada/United States Region

CUSRPC Canada-United States Regional Planning Committee

CUSRPG Canada-United States Regional Planning Group

CUSS Continental, Union,

Shell, Superior (oil companies' deep-sea oil-drilling ship)

cust custard; custodian; custody; custom(s)

Cust Ct Customs Court

custod custodian

custs custards; customers

CUSW/NAS Committee on Undersea Warfare—National Academy of Sciences

CUT California United Terminal

CUTF Commonwealth Unit Trust Fund

cutg cutting

Cuth Cuthbert; Cuthwald; Cuthwold

cuti *cutis* (Latin—skin)—cutaneous, cuticle, cutin

'cutor prosecutor

CUTS Computer-Utilized Turning System

Cuu Chihuahua

CUUS Consumers Union of the United States

cuv current use value

Cuvier Georges Léopold Chrétien Frédéric Dagobert

CUW Committee on Undersea Warfare (DoD)

Cux Cuxhaven

cu yd cubic yard

cv caloric value; capital value; cardiovascular; carrier vehicle; check valve; chief valve; coefficient of variation; collection voucher; concave; contributing valve; convertible; culture vulture

cv *caballo de vapor* (Spanish), *cavallo vapore* (Italian), *cavalo vapor* (Portuguese), *cheval-vapeur* (French)—horsepower (also appears as *CV*); *curriculum vitae* (Latin—biographical résumé)

c.v. *conjugata vera* (Latin—true conjugate)—pelvic inlet diameter; *cras vespere* (Latin—tomorrow evening); *cursus vitae* (Latin—course of life)

Cv Cove; molecular heat (symbol); specific heat at constant volume (symbol)

CV aircraft carrier (2-letter naval symbol); Central Vermont (railroad); Chula Vista; collection voucher; combat vehicle; Community of the Visitation; Community Volunteers; Convair

C-V Convair (Division of General Dynamics)

CV *cheval-vapeur* (French—horsepower)

CV4 Convair 440 airliner

cva cerebrovascular accident (medical euphemism for a stroke); costovertebral angle

CVA attack aircraft carrier (naval symbol); Civilian Voluntary Agency; Columbia Valley Authority

CVA *Centro Venezolano América* (Spanish—Venezuelan-American Center), cultural display promoted by the U.S. Embassy

CVAA Centre de Vulgarisation Aéro-Astronautique

CVAC Consolidated Vultee Aircraft (now Convair)

cvae coordinated vocational academic education

CVALI Crime Victims Legal Advocacy Institute

CVAN nuclear-powered aircraft carrier (naval symbol)

CVAS Configuration Verification and Accounting System

cvb combined very-high-frequency band

CVB large aircraft carrier (naval symbol)

c-v-c consonant-vowel-consonant

CVC Clinch Valley College; Consolidated Vacuum Corporation

CVCB Crime Victims Compensation Board (New York)

cvcc compound vortex-controlled combustion (Japanese automotive engine designed by Honda to reduce air pollution by reducing pollutant emissions)

cvcm collected volatile condensable material

cvcr control van connecting room

cvd cardiovascular disease; cash versus documents; chemical vapor deposition; coordination of valve development; coupled vibration dissociation; current-voltage diagram

CVDE *Columbia-Viking Desk Encyclopedia*

cve (**CVE**) customer-vended equipment

CVE aircraft carrier, escort (naval symbol)

C Ven Canis Venatici

CVF Caravelle fan jet airplane

CVF *Corporación Venezolano de Fomento* (Spanish—Venezuelan Promotion Corporation)

CVG Cincinnati, Ohio (Greater Cincinnati Airport); Corporación Venezolana de Guayana

cvh combined ventricular hypertrophy

cvh (CVH) compound-valve hemispherical head (cam-in-head automotive powerplant)

CVHC coastal helicopter aircraft carrier (naval symbol)

CVHS Chelsea Vocational High School

cvi cerebrovascular insufficiency; common variable immunodeficiency

CVI Cape Verde Islands; College of the Virgin Islands

CVIA Commercial Vehicle Industry Association

C viruses Coxsackie viruses

CVIS Computerized Vocational Information System

cvk centerline vertical keel

CVL Caravelle jet airplane; small aircraft carrier (naval symbol)

CVLAI Crime Victims Legal Advocacy Institute

cvli cash value life insurance

CVM Company of Veteran Motorists

CVMA Canadian Veterinary Medical Association

cvn convene

C Vn Canis Venatici

CVN nuclear-powered aircraft carrier (naval symbol)

c.v.o. conjugata vera obstetrica (Latin—conjugate obstetric diameter)

CVO Chief Veterinary Office(r)

C.V.O. Commander of the Royal Victorian Order

c voc colla voce (Italian—with the voice)

cvou (CVOU) cardiovascular observation unit

cvp central venous pressure; climate, vegetation, productivity

CVP Corporación Venezolana de Petroleo (Spanish—Venezuelan Petroleum Corporation)

cvr cardiovascular renal; cardiovascular-respiratory; cerebrovascular resistance; continuous video recorder

cvr (CVR) cockpit voice recorder; crystal video receiver

cvrd cardiovascular renal disease

cvrd hpr covered hopper (freight car)

cvs cardiovascular surgery; cardiovascular system

CVS antisubmarine warfare support aircraft carrier (3-letter symbol); Change Verifica-

tion System

cvsd continuously variable slope-delta (modulation)

cvt chemical vapor transport; constant-voltage transformer; controlled variable time (fuze); convertible

CVT training aircraft carrier (naval symbol)

c/vta cuenta de venta (Spanish—bill of sale)

Cvt Gdn Covent Garden (Royal Opera House)

cvtr charcoal viral transport medium

CVV conventional oil-powered aircraft carrier (naval symbol)

CVW attack carrier air wing (naval symbol)

CVWS Combat Vehicle Weapon System

cw call(s) waiting; canistered waste(s); cardiac work; casework(er); chemical warfare (CW); chest wall(s); child welfare; children's ward; cladding waste(s); clockwise; continuous wave; copperweld (copper-covered steel); cubic weight

c-w chronometer time minus watch time

c/w chainwheel; counterweight

c & w country and western (music)

CW Canada West; Channel Airways; chemical warfare, continuous wave

C-W Curtiss-Wright

C&W Cable and Wireless

C of W College of Wooster (Ohio)

CW Computer World

CWA Civil Works Administration; Clean Water Act; Communication Workers of America; Concerned Women for America; Country Womens Association; County Water Authority; Crime Writers Association; Customer Work Authorization

CWA Clean Water Act

CWAA Cotton Warehouse Association of America

CWAC California Wildlife Advisory Committee; City-Wide Anti-Crime Unit (sometimes called Quacks)

CWAM Cliffs Western Australian Mining Company

cwar continuous-wave acquisition radar

cwas contractor-weighted average share

cwb clay-water-base (oil well)

mud

CWB Canadian Wheat Board; Central Wages Board; Child Welfare Board

CWBS Cost Work Breakdown Structure

cwbts capillary whole blood true sugar

cw-bw chemical warfare—biological warfare

CWC Canadian Welfare Council; Central Wesleyan College

CWCA California Women's Commission on Alcoholism

CWCC Civil War Centennial Commission

c & w ck caution and warning check

CWCO China Wire and Cable Company

CWCP Combat Wing Command Post

cwd civilian war dead; clerical work data

cwe current working estimate

CWE Commonwealth Edison

C'wealth Commonwealth

CWEP Community Work Experience Program

CWET Community Work Experience Training

CWETA California Worksite Education and Training Act

CWF California Wildlife Federation; Central Wool Facility; Christian Women's Fellowship; Cornell Word Form(ation)

cwfm continuous-wave frequency modulated

cwfp clean wool fibers present

CWFT Cornell Word Form Test

cwg corrugated wire glass

CWG California Writers Guild

CWGC Commonwealth War Graves Commission

cwgt counterweight

CWHSSA Contract Work Hours and Safety Standards Act

cwi cardiac work index; clear word identifier

CWI California Wine Institute; Colonial Williamsburg Incorporated; Country Women's Institute

cwik cutting with intent to kill

CWINC Central Waterways, Irrigation, and Navigation Commission

CWIS Chaim Weizmann Institute of Science

CWISS Child Welfare Information Services System

cwit concordance words in title

cwl calm waterline
CWL Catholic Women's League
CWLA Child Welfare League of America
C & W Ltd Cables and Wireless Limited
cwm (CWM) commercial waste management
CWMH Colonial War Memorial Hospital
CWMTU Cold Weather Materiel Test Unit
CWNA Canadian Weekly Newspapers Association
cwo cash with order; continuous-wave oscillator
CWO Chief Warrant Officer
CWOD California's War On Drugs
cwp childbirth with(out) pain; circulating water pump; communicating word processor; community work plan
CWP Communist Workers Party
CWPEA Childbirth Without Pain Education Association
CWPLs Childbirth Without Pain Leagues
CWPP Commercial Waste Packaging Program
CWPS Council on Wage and Price Stability
CWPU Central Water Planning Unit
cwr continuous welded rail
CWR California Western Railroad
CWRA California Water Resources Association
cwrb (CWRB) canistered waste-receiving building
CWRSM Case-Western Reserve School of Medicine
cws clockwise; cold-water soluble; countersunk wood screw
cw & s crushed, washed, and screened
Cws Cowes
CWS California Water Service; Canadian Welding Society; Canadian Wildlife Service; Chandraprabha Wildlife Sanctuary (India); Child Welfare Services; Church World Service; Clearinghouse on Women's Studies; College Work Study; Cooperative Wholesale Society; Cunard-White Star (steamship line)
C-WS Crop-Weather Service
CWSC Canterbury Winter Sports Club; Central Washington State College

cwsfp commercial waste spent-fuel packaging
cw sig gen continuous wave signal generator
CWSP College Work-Study Program
CWSS Center for Women's Studies and Services
Cwsy Causeway
cwt centum weight; counterweight; hundredweight
CWT Central War Time; Command Word Trap; Community Work Training; Container Warehousing and Transportation; Cooperative Wind Tunnel
CWTC California World Trade Center
cwtd continuous-wave target detector
cwtdc continuous-wave target detection console
cwu composite weighted work unit
CWU California Western University; Chemical Workers Union; Culinary Workers Union
cwv continuous-wave video
CWV Catholic War Veterans
cww cruciform wing weapon
CWWC Concerned Women in the War on Crime
cwy clearway
cx cervix; chest X-ray; complex; connection; control transmitter; convex; correct copy (instruction to the printer)
cx (CX) central exchange
Cx Caxton; Caxton Printers
Cx Caixa (Portuguese—Box)—post office box; also written cx
CX Cathay Pacific Airways; outsize cargo-transport aircraft
Cxo Calexico
cxr carrier
cXr chest X-ray
cxs consort parallax servo
CXT Common External Tariff
cy calendar year; capacity; copy; currency; current year; cyanide; cyanogen; cycle; cylinder(s)
Cy City; cyanogen; Cyprus; Cyrus
CY Container Yard
cya cover your ass (protect yourself)
CYA California Youth Authority; Canadian Yachting Associaton; Carded Yarn Association; Catholic Youth Adoration (Society); Chicano Youth Association; Covenant Youth

of America
cyan cyanamid; cyanic; cyanide; cyanogen; cyanotype
cyan (Latin prefix—blue)—cyanometer (the device for measuring the blue in the sky)
cyanide cyanide of potassium
cyath. cyathus (Latin—cup, ladle, glass)
cyath. vin. cyathus vinarius (Latin—wineglassful)
cyb cybernetic; cyberneticist; cybernetics
CYB Canada Year Book
cyber cybernetics
cybercult cybercultural(ly); cyberculture
cyberlog cybernetic logistics
cybernat cybernated; cybernation(al)(ly)
cyborg(s) cybernetic organism(s)
cyc curb your curiosity; cyclazogine (narcotic antagonist used in curing victims of addiction); cycle; cyclorama
CYC Capital Yacht Club; Chicago Yacht Club; Cleveland Yacht Club; Colorado Youth Center; Columbia Yacht Club; Company of Young Canadians; Corinthian Yacht Club
CYCA Clyde Yacht Clubs Association; Cruising Yacht Club of Australia
Cycl Cyclostomata
Cyclades Cyclades Islands
cyclams cyclamates
cyclaz cyclazocine
cycle bicycle; motorcycle
cycle (Latin—circle, ring)—bicycle, circle, cyclorama
cyclecade bicycle parade; motorcycle parade; tricycle parade
cyclo cyclopedia; cyclopedic; cyclophosphamide; cyclopropane; cyclorama
cyclon cyclonometer
Cyclone Coast Australia's northwest coast
Cyclone State Kansas
Cyclops of the Kremlin Josef Stalin
Cyclorama City Atlanta, Georgia with its cyclorama painting of the Battle of Atlanta
cyclos (Latin—circle, ring)—bicycle, circle, cyclorama
CY/CY Container Yard to Container Yard
c yd cubic yard(s)
CYEE Central Youth Employment Executive (UK)
CYFA Club for Young Friends of Animals
cyflo cylinder overflow

Cyg 257 czy

Cyg Cygnus
CYHA Canadian Youth Hostels Association
cyk consider yourself kissed
cyke cyclorama
cyl cylinder; cylindrical; cylindroid
CYL Chinese Youth league
cyl l cylinder lock
cyls cylinders
cym cymbal(s)
Cym Cymric
CYMA Catholic Young Men's Association
Cymb Cymbeline
Cymr Cymric (Welsh—Wales)
Cymru (Welsh—Wales)
CYMS Catholic Young Men's Society
cyn cyanide
Cyn Canyon; Cynthia
cynl cynical; cynicism
Cynic and Skeptic Par Excellence George Bernard Shaw
cynol cynologic(al)(ly); cynologist; cynology
CYO Catholic Youth Organization; Civic Youth Orchestra; Community Service Corps
Cyp Cyprian; Cypriote; Cyprus
CYP Commonwealth Youth Programme; Cyprus Airways
Cyprian Ports (counterclockwise north to south coast) Kyrenia, Xeros, Paphos, Limasol, Larnaca, Famagusta
Cypriot Apostle Barnabas—Cyprus-born companion of Paul and Mark, according to the New Testament
Cyprus Republic of Cyprus (Mediterranean island country split between Greek and Turkish settlers whose fighting is detrimental to farming and tourism) Kypriaki Dimokratia (Greek name for Cyprus); Kibris Cumhuriyeti (Turkish name)
CYRA Commission Yellowfin Regulatory Area
Cyrano Cyrano de Bergerac
cys cysteine; cystoscopy
cys (CYS) cystine (amino acid)
CYS Cheyenne, Wyoming (airport)
CYSA Combed Yarn Spinners Association

CYSS Community Youth Support Scheme (Australia)
cysti (Latin prefix—bladder or sac)—cystoscope (the device for examining the bladder)
cysto cystoscope; cystoscopic examination
CYSYS Center for Cybernetics System Synergism
cyt cytology
cytac control of tactical aircraft
cytd calendar year to date
cyto (Latin prefix—cell)—cytology
cytoeco cytoecologic(al)(ly); cytoecologist; cytoecology
cytol cytological; cytologist; cytology
Cytol Cytology
cytomorph cytomorphologic(al)(ly); cytomorphologist; cytomorphology
cytopatho cytopathogenic(al)(ly); cytopathogenicity
cytophoto cytophotometer; cytophotometric(al)(ly); cytophotometry
cytostat cytostatic(al)(ly)
cyto syst cytochrome system
cytotech cytotechnic(al)(ly); cytotechnician; cytotechnologist; cytotechnology
cz coryza
Cz Czech; Czechoslovakia; Czechoslovakian
CZ Canal Zone; combat zone; communications zone; Consolidated Zinc
C-Z Crown-Zellerbach
C.Z. Canal Zone
CZ Ceska Zbrojovka (Czechoslovak Arms Factory)
Cza Constanza
CZA Canal Zone Authority; Coastal Zone Authority
CZAG Committee for Zero Automobile Growth
CZBA Canal Zone Biological Area
CZC Canal Zone College
CZC Canal Zone Code(legal)
CZCA Coastal Zone Conservation Act
czcs coastal-zone color scanner
czd calculated zenith distance; combat zone distance
Czech Czechoslovakia, Czechoslovakian

Czech Czechoslovakian (Slavic language used by no less than 11 million Czechs who also speak some German as well as Russian)
Czech Duo Czechoslovakia's two best-known classical composers born in Bohemia when it was part of the Austro-Hungarian Empire, now called Czechoslovakia: Bedrich Smetana and Antonin Dvořák, in chronological order
Czech J Phys Czechoslovak Journal of Physics
Czechoslovakia Czechoslovak Socialist Republic (central European Iron-Curtain country valuable for its high industrial productivity and its uranium deposits), Ceskoslovenská Socialistická Republika
Czechoslovakian Capital Prague
Czechoslovakian National Composer Anton Dvořák
Czechoslovakian Operetta Composer Rudolf Friml
Czech Phil Czech Philharmonic
CZF Canadian Zionist Federation
CZG Canal Zone Government
czi (CZI) crystalline zinc insulin
CZI Canal Zone Institute
CZJC Canal Zone Junior College
Cz kr Czechoslovakian kronen (monetary unit)
CZL-M Canal Zone Library-Museum (Balboa Heights)
CZm compass azimuth
CZMA Coastal Zone Management Act
Czml Cozumel
C-Zone commercial zone
CZP Chicago Zoological Park (Brookfield Park); Consolidated Zinc Proprietary
CZ Pen Canal Zone Penitentiary
czr combat zone radius
CZRs Canal Zone Regulations
C-Z strain Carr-Zilber (viral) strain
c-Z-t chirp-Z-transform
czy crazy

D

d angular deformation (symbol); date; daughter; day; declination; degree; depth; dextrorotatory; died; differentiation; dime; dinar; diopter; divorced; dorsal; drizzling; dyne; grating space in calcite (symbol); liter (symbol); pence (symbol); penny (symbol)

d (D) demand

d' surname prefixes such as da, de, di, etc.— d'Acosta, d'Sola, d'Silva, etc.

'd (contraction—could, did, had, would)

d *decimus* (Latin—tenth); *der* (German—the); *denarii* (Latin —pennies); *denarius* (Latin— penny); *dexter* (Latin—right)

D December; degree of curve (symbol); Delta—code for letter D; democracy; Democrat (ic); density; Denver; department; derivation; Detroit; deuterium; diameter; dielectric flux density (symbol); Dietzgen; dioptric power (symbol); director aircraft; disaster; disaster broadcasting; dollar; dose; Douglas; down; drag (symbol); drone-control version (symbol); Dublin; Dutch; Fraunhofer lines caused by sodium (symbol); propeller diameter (symbol)

D' surname prefixes such as Da, De, Di, Do, Du, etc.—D'Acosta, D'Sola, D'Silva, etc.

D *Dagh* (Persian—*Daglar* (Turkish—mountain range); *Dagi* (Turkish—mountain range); *Dag* (Turkish—mountain); *Damas* (Portuguese or Spanish —ladies); *damas* (Spanish— ladies); *Damen* (German—la-

dies); *darin* (German—in); *Darreh* (Persian—valley); *Daryaceh* (Persian—lake); *Dauer* (German—bulb-type camera shutter stop); *dehors* (French —out); *départ* (French—departure); *derecha* (Spanish— right); *Deus* (Latin—God); *dexter* (Latin—right); *Don* (Spanish—Sir)—Mr in its most formal meaning; *dun* (Danish—down)

D. *Don* (Spanish—Sir)—Mr

d₁ diffusing capacity—lung

d 1/2 d dispatch money payable at one-half demurrage rate

D₁, D₂, D₃, etc. 1st dorsal vertebra, 2nd dorsal vertebra, 3rd dorsal vertebra, etc.

D₂O deuterium oxide (heavy water)

d2s & cm dressed two sides and center matched (lumber)

d2s & m dressed two sides and matched (lumber)

d2s & sm dressed two sides and standard matched (lumber)

D3 Douglas DC-3 airplane

D4 Douglas DC-4 airplane

D-5-HS dextrose 5 percent in Hartman's Solution

D-5-S dextrose 5 percent in saline (solution)

d₅w 5 percent dextrose in water

D6 Douglas DC-6 airplane

D7 Douglas DC-7 airplane

D8F Douglas D8F fan jet airplane

D8S Douglas super DC-8 fan jet airplane

D9S Douglas super DC-9 fan jet airplane

D-18 Beechcraft four-passenger transport also designated C-45

D 40 iopax (uroselectan)

D'66 Democrats 1966 (Dutch political party)

D of '98 Daughters of '98

D-150 Dimension 150 (150-degree field of vision achieved by deeply curved motion-picture screen)

da daughter; days after acceptance; defined adult; delayed action; delayed arming; density altitude; deposit account; direct action; discharge afloat; district attorney; do not answer; documents against acceptance; documents attached; doesn't answer (the telephone); double acting; double aged; drift angle

da (DA) diphenylchlorasine (deadly gas); directional antenna; dopamine

d-a direct-action (adjective)

d/a digital-to-analog

d/a (D/A) deposit account

d in a (found) dead in automobile (or) airplane

d-to-a digital-to-analog

da *dansk* (Dano-Norwegian— Danish); *dette år* (Dano-Norwegian—that year); *dette ar* (Norwegian—this year)

dA *der Altere* (German—senior); *dette Aar* (Danish—this year)

Da Danish; Danmark

Dᵃ *Doña* (Spanish—lady, woman of rank)

DA Daughters of America; Defense Aid; Dental Apprentice; Department of Agriculture; Department of the Army; direct action (DA as a noun, d-a as an adjective); District Attorney; Division Artillery;

does not affect; Dominion Atlantic (railroad); Dragon Airways; drift angle (symbol)

D-A Devin-Adair

D.A. Diploma in Aesthetics; Diploma in Anesthetics; Doctor of Arts

D/A ditigal-to-analog

D of A Defenders of Animals; Department of Agriculture

DA Dalniya Aviatsiya (Russian —Long-Range Aviation); *Dissertation Abstracts*

daa data access arrangement; direct access arrangement

DAA Danish Atlantic Association; Dental Assistants Association; Department of Aboriginal Affairs (Australian); Diploma of the Advertising Association; Direct Action Associates

DAACA Department of the Army Allocation Committee —Ammunition

DAAG Deputy Assistant Adjutant General

DAA & QMG Deputy Assistant Adjutant and Quartermaster General

dab. daily audience barometer; delayed-action bomb; dimethylaminoazobenzene

DAB Daytona Beach, Florida (airport)

DAB Deutsches Apothekerbuch (German Pharmacopoeia); *Dictionary of American Biography*

dabco diazabicyclooctane

DABPN Diplomate American Board of Psychiatry and Neurology

DABS Discrete Address Beacon System

DABSIPCS Discrete Address Beacon System with Intermittent Positive Control System

dac data acquisition and control; data assistance and control; deductible average clause; digital-to-analog converter; digital arithmetic center; direct air cycle; dynamic amplitude control

Dac Dacca

DAC Daughters of the American Colonists; Debt Advisory Commission; Defenders of the American Constitution; Department of Adult Corrections (Alaska); Douglas Aircraft Company; Durex Abrasives Corporation

daca (DACA) diphenylaminochloroarsine

DACA Drug Abuse Control Amendments

DACAN Douglas Aircraft Company of Canada

dacbu data acquisition and control buffer unit

D.Acc. Doctor of Accountancy

DACC Dangerous Air Cargoes Committee

DACCC Defense Area Communications Control Center

DACCEUR Defense Area Communications Control Center Europe (NATO)

dachs dachsbracke (Swedish basset); dachshund (underslung German hound)

dachsaterr dachshund-terrier mixed-breed dog

dacks slacks (sport pants) made of dacron

DACL Depression Adjective Check List(s)

DACO Douglas Aircraft Corporation Overseas

DACOM Datascope Computer Output Microfilmer

dacon digital to analog converter

d/a converter device converting digital input to analog input

dacor data correction

DACOS Deputy Assistant Chief of Staff

Da Costa's syndrome soldier's heart

DACOWITS Defense Advisory Committee on Women In the Services

dacr dacron (synthetic fiber)

DACRP Department of the Army Communication Resources Plan

DACs Department of the Army Civilians; Desegregation Assistance Centers

DACS Data Acquisition and Correction System

dact dactyl(ic); dactylology; dactylus; dissimilar air combat training

dacty dactylography; dactyloscopy

dactygram dactylogram (fingerprint)

dactyl dactylogic(al)(ly); dactylologist(ic); dactylology

dacum designing a curriculum

dad daddy (father)

dad. design-approval data; dispense as directed; double-acting door

Dad Daddy; Dadiangas

DAD Directorate of Armament Development; Double Atmospheric Density (rocket)

DADEE Dynamic-Analog Differential-Equation Equalizer

DADIT Daystrom Analog-to-Digital Integrating Translator

D.Adm. Doctor of Administration

dads (DADS) dual air density satellite

DADS Director Army Dental Service

dadsm direct-access device (for) space management

D.Ae. Doctor of Aeronautics

DAE Diploma in Advanced Engineering; Director of Army Education; Division of Adult Education

DAE Dictionary of American English

daea dimethyl aminoethyl acetate

DAEC Danish Atomic Energy Commission

DAEDARC Department of the Army Equipment Data Review Committee

D.Ae.Eng. Doctor of Aeronautical Engineering

daemon data-adaptive evaluator and monitor

DAEP Division of Atomic Energy Production

DAER Department of Aeronautical Engineering Research

D.Ae.Sc. Doctor of Aeronautical Science

daf delayed auditory feedback; described as follows; discharge afloat

DAF Danish Air Force; Department of the Air Force; Dutch Air Force

DAF Dansk Arbejdsgiverforening (Danish Employers Confederation); *van Doorne Auto Fabriek* (Dutch—van Doorne's Auto Factory), autos and trucks

dafa data accounting flow assessment

DAFA Data Accounting Flow Assessment

dafc digital automatic frequency control

DAFCCS Department of the Air Force Command and Control System

DAFFO Dansk Forening til Fremme af Opfindelser (Danish Society for Encouraging Inventions)

daffs daffodils

daff(y) daffodil

DAFIE Directorate for Armed Forces Information and Education

dafm discard-at-failure mainte-

nance
DAFM Department of the Army Field Manuals
DAFO Division Accounting and Finance Office
DAFS Department of Agriculture and Fisheries (Scotland); Duty Air Force Specialty
DAFSC Duty Air Force Specialty Code
DAFSO Department of the Air Force Special Order
daft. digital/analog function table
dag decagram; dysprosium aluminum garnet
Dag Dagestan(i); Dag Hammarskjöld; Dagmar; Dagna
Dag Dagbladet (Oslo's Daily Blade)
D.Ag. Doctor of Agriculture
DAG Deputy Adjutant General; Deputy Attorney General
DAG Deutsche Angestellten-Gewerkschaft (German Employees Union)
dagc delayed automatic gain control
dag(h) (Turkish—mountain)
dagl daglig (Dano-Norwegian—daily); *dagligdags* (Dano-Norwegian—ordinary)
daglari (Turkish—mountain range)
dagmar defining advertising goals for measured advertising results; drift-and-ground-speed-measuring radar
Dagmar Dagmar Godowsky
Dag Nyh Dagens Nyheter (Sweden's Daily News)
Dago (navalese for San Diego, California)
Dago Garcia navalese slang—Diego Garcia (Indian Ocean naval base)
D.Agr. Doctor of Agriculture
D.Agr.Eng. Doctor of Agricultural Engineering
D.Agr.Sc. Doctor of Agricultural Science
DAGS Department of Accounting and General Services
dah disordered action of the heart
Dah Dahomey
DAH disordered action of the heart
Dahlaks Dahlak Islands in the Red Sea off Eritrea, Ethiopia
dai (DAI) death from accidental injuries
Dai David
DAI Dayton Art Institute; Drug Abuse Information
DAI Dissertation Abstracts In-

ternational
DAIA Department of Aboriginal and Island Affairs (Australian)
daigc direct-aqueous-injection gas chromatography
DAIM Data Analysis Information Memo
DAIMC Defense Advanced Inventory Management Course (USA)
DAIMS Department of the Army Integrated Materiel Support (USA)
Dai Nippon (Japanese—Great Japan)
DAIR Driver Aid Information and Routing (System)
DAIRE Delaware Application of Information and Research in Education
DAIS Defense Automatic Integrated Switching System
DAISY Data Acquisition and Interpretation System; Decision-Aiding Information System; Displacement-Automated Integrated System
DAISY-201 Double-Precision Automatic Interpretive System
Daisy Ashford Margaret Mary Ashford
DAJAG Deputy Assistant Judge Advocate General
Dak Dakota; Dakotan
Dakoming Dakota + Wyoming
Dakota Douglas DC-3 21-passenger transport also called Skytrain
Dakota del Norte (Spanish—North Dakota)
Dakota del Sur (Spanish—South Dakota)
Dakotas North and South Dakota
Dak Ter Dakota Territory
Dak Zoo Dakota Zoo (Bismarck, North Dakota)
dal decaliter
d'AL d'Amico Line
Dal Dallas; Dalmatia; Dalmatian
DAL Dallas, Texas (Love Field); Delta Air Lines; Department of Agriculture Library; Deutsche Afrika Linien (German Africa Line)
dala delta-amino-levulinic acid
dalapon dialphapropionic acid (herbicide)
Dalarna Swedish truncation of Dalecarlia, the lake district of folklore
Dalarna (Swedish—Dalecarlia), derived from *Dalkarl*—Man

from Dalarna—Sweden's agricultural valley area
DALATS Data Logging and Transmission System
DALE Drug Abuse Law Enforcement
dalgt daylight
Dalh Dalhousie
Dali (Pinyin Chinese—Tali)
Dall Dallas' Reports—U.S. Supreme Court
Dalmatia western Yugoslavia
dalmatian dalmatian dog (black-spotted white coach dog believed to have been bred in Dalmatia although its natives declare it is unknown in this Adriatic coastal area of Yugoslavia); dalmatian cherry (marasca); dalmatian insect powder (pyrethrum dust)
Dalmatian First Yugoslavia's best-known operetta composer of the last century—Franz von Suppé—remembered for the overtures he composed when he lived in Vienna and Dalmatia was part of the Austro-Hungarian Empire
Dalmazia (Italian—Dalmatia)
Dalny (Russian—Dairen)
dalpo do all possible
dalr dry adiabatic lapse rate
DALRLV Department of the Army Logistics Readiness Liaison Visit(s)
DALRTF Department of the Army Long-Range Technological Forecast(ing)
dal s dal segno (Italian—from the sign)
DALS Distress Alerting and Locating System
dal seg dal segno (Italian—from the sign)
Dal Sym Orch Dallas Symphony Orchestra
dalvp delay enroute authorized chargeable as ordinary leave provided it does not interfere with reporting on date specified and provided individual has sufficient accrued leave
dam. damage; decameter; degraded amyloid; diacetyl monoxime; divided and mashed
dam. (DAM) direct-access method; down-range anti-missile (program)
Dam Damascus; Damman
DAM Damascus, Syria (airport); Dayton Art Museum; Denver Art Museum
DAM Dictionary of Abbreviations in Medicine
Damas (Turkish—Damascus)—

Syrian capital
Damás (French—Damascus)
Damasco (Spanish—Damascus)
Damascus English place-name equivalent of Damas or Es Sham
Damaspo (Latin—Damascus)
DAMCO Dampier Mining Company
dame. data acquisition and monitoring equipment; digital automatic-measuring equipment
Dame Cicely Dr Cicely Saunders
Dame Clara Dame Clara Butt
Dame Joan Dame Joan Sutherland
Dame Margot Fonteyn Margot Hookham
Dame Myra Dame Myra Hess
Dame Ngaio Dame Ngaio Marsh
DAMIS Department of the Army Management Information System
Damnable Place Hong Kong, according to GBS
Damnación de Fausto (Spanish—Damnation of Faust)—four-part dramatic legend composed by Berlioz
Damnation La Damnation de Faust (French—The Damnation of Faust)—four-part legend by Berlioz
Dam on the Amstel Amsterdam
DAMOS Data Moving System
DAMP Down-Range Anti-Missile Measurement Project
Damplers Dampier Islands in the Indian Ocean off northwestern Westralia
DAMPS Data Acquisition Multiprogramming System
damp Spain Atlantic coasts of Spain, especially along Bay of Biscay where rains are heaviest
DAMRIP Department of the Army Management Review and Improvement Program
DAMS Defense Against Missiles System; Deputy Assistant Military Secretary
DAMT Draw-A-Man Test
DAMWO Department of the Army Modification Work Order
dan dekanewton
Dan Daniel (name); Daniel, Book of; Danish; Danmark (Denmark)
Dan Daniel
DAN Dan-Air Service
DANA Diffraction Analysis

System
Dan Beard Daniel Carter Beard
DANBIF Danske Boghandleres Importrfrening (Danish Booksellers Importation Association)
dancin' dancing
DANCOM Danube Commission (Austria, Bulgaria, Czechoslovakia, Hungary, Romania, the USSR, Yugoslavia)
Dand(ie) Andrew
Dandy Andrew
Dandy King Joachim Murat—King of Naples
Danemark (French, German—Denmark)
Danglish Danish-English
dang mod dangling modifier
Dani Daniel
Daniel Nikolai Arzhak
Daniel Stern pseudonym of Liszt's paramour, the Countess Marie d'Agoult
danish danish pastry (light pastry often filled with stewed fruit, crushed nuts, cup custard, and raisins)
Danish Capital of the United States Racine, Wisconsin
Danish Caribees colonial name for what are now the U.S. Virgin Islands
Danish Ports (large, medium, and small from east to west) Ronne (*on Bornholm*), Køge, København (Copenhagen), Helsingor, Frederiksvaerk, Frederikssund, Roskilde, Holbaek, Nykøbing, Kalundborg, Korsor, Skaelskor, Naestved, Vordingvorg, Stubbekøbing, Stege, Masnedsund, Nykøbing, Falster, Sakskøbing, Naskov, Rudkøbing, Marstal, Svendborg, Nyborg, Kerteminde, Odense, Middelfart, Assens, Faborg, Grasten, Sonderborg, Augustenborg, Abenra, Haderslev, Kolding, Frederikcia, Horsens, Arhus, Grena, Randers, Alborg, Frederikshavn, Skagen, Esbjerg
Danish Quintet Denmark's five best-known classical composers named in chronological order—Buxtehude, Kuhlau, Lumbye, Gade, Nielsen
Danish Waltz King Hans Christian Lumbye
Danish West Indies former name of the American Virgin Islands when they belonged to Denmark
Danl Daniel

Danl W Daniel Webster
Danm Danmark (Denmark)
Danmark (Danish—Denmark)
Dannazione di Faust (Italian—Damnation of Faust)—four-part legend by Berlioz
Dannebrog (Danish—Danish cloth)—Denmark's flag reputed to be the oldest national symbol in western Europe
Dannemora Clinton Correctional Facility (for males) at Dannemora, New York
Dan-Nor Dano-Norwegian (lingua franca of some 5 million Danes and 4 million Norwegians, however, there are many exclusively Danish and Norwegian words and indeed several styles in each of these Scandinavian languages of Germanic origin)
d'Annunzio (Gabriel) Gaetano Rapagnetta
Danny Daniel
Danny Kaye Daniel Kominski
Danny O'Neill fictionalized name of James T Farrell (*Studs Lonigan*)
Danny Thomas Amos Jacobs
DANR Department of Agriculture and Natural Resources
dans dansyl chloride (fluorescent dye)
Dansker Dane; Danish sailor
Dante Dante (Durante) Alighieri
DANTES Defense Activity for Non-Traditional Education Support (USN)
Dantiscum (Latin—Danzig)
Danube 1700-mile river of southern Europe; flows southeast from southern Germany to the Black Sea; passes Vienna in Austria, Budapest in Hungary, Belgrade in Yugoslavia
Danube Delta Land Romania
Danube Empire Austro-Hungarian Empire
Danubian Monarchy Austro-Hungarian Empire
Danubio (Spanish—Danube)
DANZ Dyslexia Association of New Zealand
Danzig (German—Gdansk)
dao duly-authorized officer, paldao (Philippine wood)
DAO Dairy Advisory Office(r); District Accounting Office(r); District Aviation Office(r); Division Air Office(r); Division Ammunition Office(r); Dominion Astrophysical Observatory (Victoria, British Co-

lumbia)

DAOT Director of Air Organization and Training

dap data analysis package; data automation proposal; digital audio processor; direct-agglutination pregnancy (test); do anything possible; documents against payment

dap (DAP) diaminopimelic acid; diammonium phosphate; dihydroxyacetone phosphate

d-a-p draw-a-person (psychological test)

DAP Democratic Action Party; Development Academy of the Philippines; Director of Administrative Planning; Division of Air Pollution (US Public Health)

DAPA Drug Abuse Programs of America

DAPD Directorate of Aircraft Production Development

DAP & E Diploma in Applied Parasitology and Entomology

Daphnis Ravel's ballet *Daphnis et Chloe*

dapi (DAPI) diamidinophenylindole

DA Plan Deposit Administration Plan

DAPM Deputy Assistant Provost Marshal

DAPMC Defense Advanced Procurement Management Course (USA)

dapon diallyl phthalate resin

Da Ponte Lorenzo Da Ponte (Mozart's librettist, born Emanuèle Conegliano—an Italian Jew)

DAPP Data Acquisition and Processing Program

D.App.Sci. Doctor of Applied Science

dapr digital automatic pattern recognition

daps downed airman power source (USN)

DAPS Direct-Access Programming System

dapsone diaminodiphenyl sulfone

dapt daptazole; direct-agglutination pregnancy test (DAPT)

DAPT Direct Latex Agglutination Pregnancy Test; Draw-a-Person Test

Daqing Oilfield (Pinyin Chinese —Taching Oilfield)

DAQMG Deputy Assistant Quartermaster General

dar damned average raiser (good student whose high marks raise the grading scale);

dressed all 'round

dar (Arabic—land)

Dar Dar-es-Salaam

Dar *Dar-es-Salaam* (Arabic— There is the Peace)—capital and seaport of Tanzania; nickname for Dar-es-Salaam

DAR Daily Activity Report; Data Automation Request; Data Automation Requirements; Daughters of the American Revolution; Department of Animal Regulation; Directorate of Atomic Research; Dominion Atlantic Railway

Dar-al-Baida (Arabic—Casablanca)

DARAS Direction and Range Acquisition System

Darb Darby(shire)

D & ARC Drug and Alcohol Resource Center

DARCEE Demonstration and Research Center for Early Education (Peabody College)

D.Arch. Doctor of Architecture

D.Arch.E. Doctor of Architectural Engineering

DARCOM Development and Readiness Command (USA)

dard data acquisition requirements document

DARD Directorate of Aircraft Research and Development

Dardan Dardanelles

Dardanelles Dardanelle Straits called Hellespont by the Greeks and Canakkale Bogazi by the Turks; links the Aegean Sea at the eastern end of the Mediterranean with the Sea of Marmara, the Bosporus, and the Black Sea

dare. data automatic reduction equipment; data automation research and experimentation; destination arrival research engineering; documentation automated retrieval equipment; doppler automatic reduction equipment

DARE Drug Abuse Research and Education (UCLA's neuropsychiatric institute); Drug Assistance, Rehabilitation, and Education

DARE *Directory of American Regional English*

daren't dare not

DARES Data Analysis and Reduction System

DARF Defense Atomic Research Facility

Darién (Spanish—Isthmus of Panama)

Dark and Bloody Ground Kentucky

Dark Continent Africa

Darlings short form for the Darling Ranges of Westralia

darms digital alternate representation of music scores

Darmstadium (Latin—Darmstadt)

DARPA Defense Advanced Research Projects Agency

DARR Department of the Army Regional Representative; Drawing and Assembly Release Record

Darren Darwen, England

dars differential absorption remote sensing (laser)

DARs Design Assist Reports; Development Appraisal Reports

DARS Digital Adaptive Recording System

darss diode-array rapid-scan spectrometer

dart. datagraphic automated retrieval technique(s); deployable automatic relay terminal; detection, action, and response technique(s); development advanced rate techniques; disappearing automatic retaliation target

DART Dallas Area Rapid Transit; Direct Access to Regional Transit; Disaster Assisted Radio Teams; Dublin Area Rapid Transit

Dartmouth Darmouth College at Hanover, New Hampshire; Massachusetts fishing port near New Bedford; Nova Scotia port and rail terminus across Halifax harbor from Halifax; Royal Naval College at Dartmouth near Plymouth on the English Channel

DARTS DoE Audit Report Tracking System; Dynamically-Actuated Road Transit System

Dar-ul-Kutub (Arabic—National Library)—best known is the Egyptian National Library in Cairo

Darw Darwin College, Cambridge

Darwin formerly Port Darwin, Australia

darwin glass queenstownite (silica glass)

Darwin Island, Galápagos Culpepper

Darwin Pr Darwin Press

Darwin's Bulldog nickname of Professor Thomas Henry

Huxley, president of the Royal Society, whose defense of Darwin's *Origin of the Species* pulverized the arguments of the Bishop of Oxford, Samuel (Soapy Sam) Wilberforce, who had set out to demolish Darwin's theory of evolution

darya (Persian—salt lake)

das data analysis station; dekastere; delivered alongside ship; dial-assistance switchboard

das (DAS) dextroamphetamine sulfate (stimulant)

da's domestic afflictions (menses)

DAs Design Assist Reports

DAS Data Acquisition System; Data Analysis System; Dean A Stahl; Defense Atomic Support Agency; Defense Audit Service; Digital Analog Simulator; Digital Attenuator System; Director(ate) of Administrative Services; Director(ate) of Aerodrome Standards; Division of Apprenticeship Standards

DAS *Departamento Administrativo de Seguridad* (Spanish—Security Administration Department); *Dictionary of American Slang*

dasa dual aerospace servoamplifier

DASA Defense Atomic Support Agency

DASA-TP Defense Atomic Support Agency—Technical Publication(s)

DASC Defense Automotive Supply Center; Direct Air Support Center

D.A.Sci. Doctor of Agricultural Science

dasd direct access storage device

DASD Director of Army Staff Duties

DASDL Data and Structure Definition Language

dash. dashboard; drone antisubmarine helicopter

Dash Dashiell Hammett

DASH Delta Airlines Special Handling (of small packages); Drug Abuse Services of Hawaii

dasi diffusion of arsenic in silicon

dasm (DASM) delayed-action space missile

DASNET Data Switching Network

daso (DASO) development and shakedown operations

dasp discrimination among sound patterns; double-arm magnetic spectrometer

DASP Director(ate) of Advanced Systems Planning

dass defined antigen substrate sphere

DASS Direct Air Support Squadron (USAF)

DASSR Dagestan Autonomous Soviet Socialist Republic

DAST Division for Advanced Systems Technology

DAST *Detective-Agents-Science Fiction-Thriller* (acronymically titled magazine)

dastard. destroyer anti-submarine transportable array detector

DASTL Defense Atomic Support Agency Technical Letters

dat date after tomorrow; dative; datum; delayed-action tablet; differential agglutination titer

dat (DAT) differential aptitude test(ing)

d a t diet as tolerated

DAT Dental Aptitude Test; Development Acceptance Test (USA); Differential Aptitude Test; Docking Alignment Test (NASA)

DATA Data Acquisition and Technical Analysis; Defense Air Transportation Administration; Development and Technical Assistance (UN); Dial-a-Teacher Assistance (telephone-service program); Draughtsmen's and Allied Technicians' Association

datac digital automatic tester and classifier

DATAC Development Areas Treasury Advisory Committee

datacom data communications

datacor data correction; data correlator

datan data analysis

datanet data network

datap data transmission and processing

datar digital automatic tracking and ranging

DATC Developmental and Training Center

datda (DATDA) diallytartardiamide

DATDC Data Analysis and Technic Development Center

Date Capital Indio, California amidst date palms

datel data + telecommunication

datico digital automatic tape intelligence checkout

datin data inserter

dating street slang term meaning prostituting

DATM *Department of the Army Technical Manual*

DATO Disbursing and Transportation Office; Discover America Travel Organizations

datom data aids for training, operations, and maintenance

dator digital (data), auxiliary (storage), track (display), outputs (and) radar (display)

DATOR Data Operational Requirements Board (NATO)

datran data transmission

datrec data recording

datrix direct access to reference information

dats data accumulation/transmittal sheet

DATS Dynamic Accuracy Test System

DATSC Department of the Army Training and Support Committee

dau data adapter unit

D.Au.Eng. Doctor of Automobile Engineering

Daughter of the Baltic Helsinki

dau(s) daughter(s)

DAUS Despatch Agency of the United States

dav data above voice

dav *davaerende* (Dano-Norwegian—then)

Dav David

DAV Dayanana Anglo Veolic (Fiji school); Disabled American Veterans

davc delayed automatic-volume control

Dave David

Daventria (Latin—Deventer)

Davey David; General David C. Jones

DAVI Department of Audio-Visual Instruction (National Education Association)

David Frome Zenith Jones Brown

davidite uranium ferric ferrous iron titanate

David St John E. Howard Hunt

David Wayne Wayne McKeekan

Davie David

da Vinci Leonardo da Vinci (Rome, Italy's airport named for its most famous Florentine architect-engineer-painter-sculptor-scientist-author

Davis Mountains West Texas

range of Rocky Mountain system running south through Big Bend National Park into Mexico; named after Jefferson Davis

D.Av.Med. Diploma in Aviation Medicine

DAVNO Division Aviation Office(r)

DAVRS Director of Army Veterinary and Remount Services

Davy David

Davy Jones' Locker traditional resting place of all who are buried at sea or who are drowned in the depths of the ocean

DAW Directorate of Atomic Warfare

DAWE Daughters Already Well-Endowed

dawid device for automatic word identification and discrimination

DAWN Drug Abuse Warning Network

Dawn on the Mesabi Aurora, Minnesota

DAWS Director of Army Welfare Services

dax dachshund

Day Birthday; Dayton; Daytona; Natal Day; President's Birthday; President's Day (holiday)

DAY Dayton, Ohio (airport)

Day of Infamy Deember 7, 1941 (when Japanese aircraft carriers attacked Pearl Harbor, Hawaii while diplomatic negotiations were in progress in Washington, D.C.)

daysoap(s) daytime (tv) soap opera(s)

db damned bad; day book; dead body; decibel(s); dextran blue; diameter baudelocque (external pelvic conjugate diameter); diode block; disability; distobuccal; distribution board; distribution box; domestic boiler; double bayonet-base (lamp); double bed; double braid(ed); double breasted; double-biased (relay); down(ward) bound; draw bar; dry bulb; dynamic brake

db (DB) delayed broadcast

d/b documentary bill

d & b dead and buried

d in b (found) dead in bed

dB decibel

Db dubhium (ytterbium symbol)

DB Data Bank; David Brown (tractors); Daytona Beach; Detective Bureau; Disciplinary Barracks; Dispersal Base; Dodge Brothers; Dominion Breweries

D-B Daimler-Benz

D & B Dun & Bradstreet

D of B Daughters of Bilitis

DB *Danmarks Biblioteksforening* (Danish Library Association); *Danske Bank* (Danish Bank); *Deutsche Bank* (German Bank); *Deutsche Bundesbahn* (German State Railways); *Dresdner Bank* (German—Dresden Bank)

D.B. *Divinitatis Baccalaureus* (Latin—Bachelor of Divinity)

dba design-basis accident; doing business as/at

dba (DBA) Dibenzanthracene; dihydro-dimethyl-benzopyran butyric acid

d b a doing business as

dBa decibel A (unit of noise measurement)

Dba Dubai

DBA Data Base Administrator; Duke Bar Association

D.B.A. Doctor of Business Administration

dbacc debit account(ing)

dbam data-base-access method(ology)

DBAP Darien Book Aid Plan

d/bar draw bar

DBAS Development Bank of American Samoa

DBAT Dating Behavior Assessment Test

dbb detector back bias; dinner, bed, breakfast; distance between bends

db & b deals, boards, and battens

dbbal debit balance

dbbd (DBBD) dibromopolybutadiene

dbc diameter bolt circle; dry breast care; dye-binding capacity

DBC Demerara Bauxite Company; Detective Book Club; Drums and Bugle Corps

D.B.C. Doctor of Beauty Culture

DBCA Du Bois Clubs of America

dbcl dilute blood clot lysis

DBCM De Beers Consolidated Mines

DBCO Dairy Board Consulting Office(r)

dbcp (DBCP) dibromochloropropane

DBCSO DeBeers Central Selling Organisation

dbcu data bus control unit

dbd death by drugs (execution by lethal injection); double-base diode

D Bd Distribution Board; Drug Board

dbe design-basis earthquake; design-basis event; double-bell euphonium (marching band tuba)

dbe (DBE) dibasic ester

D.B.E. Dame Commander of the Order of the British Empire

dbeats despatch payable at both ends (for) all time saved

dbed (DBED) dibenzyl-ethylene-diamine (penicillin)

D.B.Ed. Doctor of Business Education

dbelts despatch payable both ends (for) all laytime saved

dbf design-basis fire; design-basis flood

DBG Division of Basic Grants

dbh diameter breast high

DBHNT Detective Bureau Hostage Negotiating Team (NYPD)

dbhp drawbar horsepower

dbi database index; development-at-birth index (DBI)

Dbi Dubai

DBib Douay Bible

D.Bi.Chem. Doctor of Biological Chemistry

D.Bi.Eng. Doctor of Biological Engineering

D.Bi.Phy. Doctor of Biological Physics

dbir double built-in (ward)robes

D.Bi.Sc. Doctor of Biological Sciences

DBIU Dominion Board of Insurance Underwriters

DBJC Daytona Beach Junior College

dbk debark; drawback

DBK Daiichi Bussan Kaisha (Japanese steamship line); Dobeckmun (company)

dbkn debarkation

dbl double; doubler

DBL Disability Benefit Law; Displaced Business Loan (SBA)

dbl act. double acting

dblb double room with bath

dbl cnt double contract

dbl eleph fol. double elephant folio—books about 50 inches high

dblr doubler

dbls double room with shower

dbm decibels per milliwatt; diabetic management

dBm decibel referred to one milliwatt

DBM Division of Biology and Medicine (Atomic Energy Commission)

D.B.M. Diploma in Business Management

DBM *Deutches Bundes Marine* (German Federal Navy)— West German

db meter decibel meter

DBMS Data Base Management System; Director of Base Medical Services

Dbn Durban

dbo dead blackout; distobucco-occlusal; dreadful body odor

DBOS Data-Based Operating System

D-box distribution box

dbp design-basis probability; diastolic blood pressure; distobuccopulpal; drawbar pull

DBP Development Bank of the Philippines; Division of Beaches and Parks

DBP *Dicionario Bibliografico Portugues* (Portuguese Bibliographic Dictionary)

db part double-beaded partition

DBPO Data Buoy Project Office

dbr double book rack

D Br Defendant's Brief

DBR Division of Building Research

dbrap decibels above reference acoustic power

dbre *diciembre* (Spanish—December)

DBRL DeBeers Research Laboratory

dbrn data bank release notice; decibels above reference noise

DBRS Dominion Bond Rating Service (Toronto)

db rts debenture rights

dbs damn bloody soon; despeciated bovine serum; double bottoms

dbs (DBS) direct broadcast satellite

db's dirty books; dune buggies

DBS Development Bank of Singapore; Distressed British Seaman (provided free passage home); Division of Biological Standards

dbsm decibels per square meter

dbsr double bed sitting room

dbst double bituminous surface treatment

DBST Double British Summer Time

dbt debit; design-basis tornado; dry-bulb temperature

DBT David Brown Tractors

dbtd debited

dbtfl doubtful

dbtg debiting

dbtl doubtful

dbtt ductile-brittle transmission temperature

dbtu (DBTU) dibutylthiourea

dbtw design-basis tornado and windstorm

dbuf dry-buffed (leather)

d-bug debug; debugged; debugging

dbur data bank update request

dbv decibel referred to 1 volt

DBV *Deutscher Bibliotheksverband* (German—Library Association); *Deutscher Bund für Vogelschutz* (German Birdshooters Bund)

dbw differential ballistic wind

dbx design-basis explosion

dc data collection; dead center; death cell; deck cargo; deposited carbon; deviation clause; device control; diagonal conjugate; diesel car; differential calculus; digital computer; direct credit; direct cycle; directional coupler; disorderly conduct; door closer; double cap; double certificated; double column; double contact; double crochet; double crown; down center; draft card; drawing change; drift correction; drill collar (oil well)

dc (DC) cancrizans of the duration series; diagonal conjugate

d-c direct-chill (casting); direct-current (adjective)

d/c deviation clause; double-column (bookkeeping)

d & c dilation and curettage

dc *da capo* (Italian—again); Dick Cavett

d/c *dinero contante* (Spanish—cash)

dC *dopo Cristo* (Italian—after the birth of Christ)

DC Dana College; Dartmouth College; Davidson College; Death Certificate; decimal classification; Defiance College; Dental Corporation; Dental Corps; Department of Commerce; Deputy Chief; Deputy Commissioner; Deputy Consul; Deviation Clause; Diagnostic Center; Dickinson College; Diners Club; Dining Car; direct current (when used

as a noun); District of Columbia (D.C.); District Commissioner; District Court(house); Doane College; Doctor of Chiropractic; Dominican College; Donnelly College; Dordt College; Douglas Commercial (aircraft); Downing College (Cambridge); Drury College; Duchesne College; Dumbarton College; Dyke College; D'Youville College

D-C Denver-Chicago (truck line); Dow-Corning (chemical products)

D/C drift correction

D & C Dean and Chapter; Detroit and Cleveland (steamship line); Doctrine and Covenants

D of C Daughters of the Confederacy; Department of Commerce; Department of Communications (DoC); Department of Correction(s); District of Columbia (D.C.); Duchy (Duke) of Carinthia, Duchy (Duke) of Carniola

DC *Democrazia Christiana* (Italian—Christian Democracy)— political party; *Distrito Capital* (Spanish—Capital District)

D C *da capo* (Italian—from the beginning)

DC-1 Defense Condition-1 (war)

DC1, DC2, DC3, etc. device-control characters (data processing)

DC-2 through DC-5 Defense Condition-2 through Defense Condition-5 (stages of military alert short of war)

DC-3 Douglas 21-passenger twin-engine transport aircraft also known as the C-47, Dakota, or Skytrain

DC-4 Douglas 44-passenger four engine transport aircraft also called C-54 or Skymaster

DC-6 Douglas 64 to 92-passenger transport also known as C-118 Liftmaster because of its cargo-carrying capacity

DC-8 Douglas DC8 jet airplane

DC-9 Douglas twin-jet short-range airplane

DC-9 Super 80 McDonnell-Douglas commercial jetliner billed as the world's quietest

DC-10 McDonnel-Douglas jumbo jetliner

dca deoxycholate citrate sugar

Dca Dacca

DCA Dachshund Club of America; Dalmatian Club of America; Damage Control Assistant; Defence Costs Agreement (Hong Kong); Defense Communications Agency; Department of Civil Aviation; Department of Consumer Affairs; desoxycorticosterone acetate; Diamond Council of America; Diapulse Corporation of America; Digital Computers Association; Director of Civil Aviation; Disassembly Compliance and Analysis; Disc Company of America; Distribution Contractors Association; District Court of Appeals; Division of Consumer Affairs; Drafting Contractors Association; Drawing Change Authority; Drug Control Agency; Dynamics Corporation of America; Washington, D.C. (national airport)

DCA Défense Contre Aéronefs (French—anti-aircraft defense)

DCAA Defense Contract Audit Agency

DCA/A Disassembly Compliance and Analysis/Abbreviated

DCADA District of Columbia Alley Dwelling Authority

D.C.Ae. Diploma of the College of Aeronautics

DCAEUR Defense Communications Agency, Europe

DCAF Design Corrective Action Form

DCAO Deputy County Advisory Officer

DCAOC Defense Communications Agency Operations Center

d cap double foolscap (paper)

DCAP Disadvantaged Country Areas Program

DCAR Design Corrective Action Report; Disassembly Compliance and Analysis Report

DCAS Data Collection and Analysis System; Defense Contract Administration Services; Defense Control Administration Services; Deputy Chief of Air Staff

DCASR Defense Contract Administrative Service Region

DC-AST McDonnell Douglas Advanced Supersonic Transport

DCATA Drug, Chemical, and Allied Trades Association

D Cath Documentation Catho-

lique (French—Catholic Documentation)

dcb data control block

DCB Decimal Currency Board (British)

D.C.B. Dame Commander of the Most Honourable Order of the Bath

DCBD Division for Children with Behavioral Disorders (Council for Exceptional Children)

DCBRE Defense Chemical, Biological, and Radiation Establishment

dcc dark curtain closed; double concave; double cotton covered

dcc (DCC) decade counter code

DCC Damage Control Center; Day Care Center; Defense Concessions Committee; Design Change Control; Disease Control Center; Dutchess Community College

DCCA Design Change Cost Analysis

DCCB Defense Center Control Building (USA)

DCCC Domestic Coal Consumers Council

DCCDCA Day Care and Child Development Council of America

d & c color drug and cosmetic color (synthetic dye)

DCCP Design Change Control Program; Directorate of Communication Components Production

DCCS Digital Command Communications System

dccu data communications control unit

dcd differential current density

DCD Daitch Crystal Dairies; Damage Control Diagram(s) (USN); Design Change Document; Directorate of Civil Disturbance

D.C.D. Diploma in Chest Diseases

DCD Dansk Central för Dukumentation (Danish Center for Documentation)

DCDMA Diamond Core Drill Manufacturers Association

DCDPO Directorate for Civil Disturbance Planning and Operations (USA)

dcdr decoder

dcds double cotton double silk

DCDS Digital-Control Design System

dcdt direct-current differential transformer

dce dairy cow equivalent; data conversion equipment; differential compound engine; domestic credit expansion

DCE Division of Career Education; Division of Compensatory Education

D.C.E. Doctor of Civil Engineering

DCEA Dictionary of Civil Engineering Abbreviations

dcel direct-current electroluminescence

D.C.E.P. Diploma of Child and Educational Psychology

dcf deal-cased frame; direct centrifugal flotation; discounted cash flow

DCF Deputy Chief

dcfem dynamic crossed-field electron multiplication

dcfp dynamic cross-field photomultiplier

dcg dancing; decigram; displacement cardiograph; dynamic cardiogram

dcg (DCG) deoxycorticosterone glucoside

dcgm decorticated groundnut meal

DCGS Deputy Chief of the General Staff

dch dicyclohexyl

D. Ch. Doctor Chirugiae (Latin—Doctor of Surgery)

DCH Diploma in Child Health

dcha derecha (Spanish—right)

DCHCL Dropsie College for Hebrew and Cognate Learning

D.Ch.E. Doctor of Chemical Engineering

dchn dicyclohexylamine nitrate

DChO Diploma in Ophthalmic Surgery

dci dichloroisoprenaline; dischloroisoproterenol; double-column inch; driving car intoxicated

DCI Department of Citizenship and Immigration; Des Moines and Central Iowa (railway); Director of Central Intelligence

DCIC Defense Ceramic Information Center

dcid decide

DCID Department of Commercial and Industrial Development

DCIGS Deputy Chief of the Imperial General Staff

DCII Defense Central Index of Information

dcisn decision

D.Civ.L. Doctor of Civil Law

DCJ Dade County Jail (Miami, Florida); Department of Criminal Justice; District Court Judge

dckng docking

dcl decaliter; declaration; declarative; decline

DCL Dartmouth College Library; Detroit College of Law; Deuterium of Canada, Limited; Distillers Company Limited

D.C.L. Doctor of Canon Law; Doctor of Civil Law

DCLA Deputy Chief of Staff, Logistics and Administration (NATO)

dcld declined

DCLE Department of Criminal Law Enforcement (Florida)

dclg declining

DCLI Duke of Cornwall's Light Infantry

dclrt decelerate

dcls deoxycholate citrate lactose saccharose (agar); disclose

D.Cl.Sci. Doctor of Clinical Science

dclsd disclosed

dclsg disclosing

dclsr disclosure

DCLTC Dry Cargo Loading Technical Committee (NATO)

dcltr declines transfer (offered)

DCLU Developing Countries Liaison Unit

dcm decameter; defense combat maneuvers

DCM Director of Civilian Marksmanship; Directorate of Classified Management; Distinguished Conduct Medal; District Court Martial; Dominican Campaign Medal

D.C.M. Doctor of Comparative Medicine

DCMA Defense Contract Management Association; District of Columbia Manpower Administration; Dry Color Manufacturers Association

DCMBA Dairy, Confectionery, and Mixed Business Association

D.C.M.G. Dame Commander of the Order of St Michael and St George

dcmi disclosure of classified military information

dcmps degaussing compass

dcmptr degaussing computer

DCMs Deputy Chiefs of Missions

DCMS Deputy Commissioner of Medical Services

dcmsn decommission

dcmt document

dcmu dichlorophenyldimethylurea

dcn delayed conditioned necrosis; double crown

DCN Data Change Notice; Defense Communication Network; Design Change Notice; Drawing Change Notice

DCNI Department of the Chief of Naval Information

D.Cn.L. Doctor of Canon Law

DCNO Deputy Chief of Naval Operations

DCNS Deputy Chief of Naval Staff

dco doppler cutoff; draft collection only

D$_{co}$ diffusing capacity—carbon monoxide

DCO Dallas Civic Opera; Data Change Order; Deputy Chief of Staff, Operations (NATO); Director of Combat Operations; District Control(ling) Office(r); Dominion, Colonial, and Overseas (Department of Barclays Bank)

DCOBE Dame Commander—Order of the British Empire

DCOG Diploma of the College of Obstetricians and Gynecologists

d & coh daughter and co-heiress

d col double column

D. Com. Doctor of Commerce

D.Com.L. Doctor of Commercial Law

D. Comp. L. Doctor of Comparative Law

dcop displays, controls, and operation procedures

DCOR Defense Committee on Research (USAF)

DCOS Deputy Chief of Staff

dcp dental continuation pay; depot condemnation percent; development cost plan; discrete component parts

dcp (DCP) dicalcium phosphate

DCP Department of Consumer Protection; Diploma in Clinical Pathology; Disaster Control Plan; Division of Consumer Protection

dcpa (DCPA) dicylcopentenyl acrylate

DCPA Defense (Department's) Civil Preparedness Agency

DCPANDP Deputy Chief of Staff, Plans and Policy (NATO)

DC Path Diploma of the College of Pathologists

dcpd (DCPD) dicyclopentadiene

DCPL District of Columbia Public Library

DCPO Deputy Chief of Staff, Personnel and Organization (NATO)

DCPR Defense Contractors Planning Report

dcp's development concept papers

dcpta (DCPTA) dichlorophenoxy triethylamine

dcr data conversion receiver; decrease; decreasing; direct cortical response; division credit rebate

DCR Design Change Request; Design Characteristic Review; District Chief Ranger; District Court Report(s); Division of Computing Research; Drawing Change Request

DCRB Design Change Review Board

DCRE Deputy Commandant—Royal Engineers

DCRLA District of Columbia Redevelopment Land Agency

DCRO Dyers and Cleaners Research Organization

DCRR Drawing Change Recorder Request

dcs dorsal column stimulator; double cotton silk

DCs Douglas Commercial-type airplanes

DCS Damage Control School (USN); Data Control System; Deaf Community Services; Defense Communications System; Department of Correctional Services (Nebraska, New York); Deputy Chief of Staff; Digital Command System; Direct Coupler System; Director of Community Services; Distillers Corporation—Seagrams; Domestic Contact Service (CIA)

DC of S Deputy Chief of Staff

D.C.S. Doctor of Christian Science; Doctor of Commercial Science

DCSAB Distinguished Civilian Service Awards Board

DCSADN Defense Communication System Automatic Digital Network

DCSC Defense Construction Supply Center

DCSCD Deputy Chief of Staff for Combat Developments (NATO)

DCSCOMPT Deputy Chief of

Staff, Comptroller (NATO)

DCSF Dry Caisson Storage Facility

DCSFOR Deputy Chief of Staff, Force Development (NATO)

DCSL Deputy Chief of Staff, Logistics (NATO); District Cub Scout Leader

DCSM Deputy Chief of Staff, Materiel (NATO)

DCSMIS Deputy Chief of Staff, Management Information System (NATO)

DCSO Deputy Chief Scientific Officer

DCSOI Deputy Chief of Staff for Operations and Intelligence (NATO)

dcsp digital control signal processor

DCS/P Deputy Chief of Staff for Personnel

DCSPA Deputy Chief of Staff, Personnel and Administration (NATO)

DCS/P&O Deputy Chief of Staff for Plans and Operations

DCS/P&R Deputy Chief of Staff for Programs and Resources

DCS/R&D Deputy Chief of Staff for Research and Development

DCSRDA Deputy Chief of Staff —Research, Development, and Acquisition (USA)

DCSRM Deputy Chief of Staff for Resource Management (NATO)

DCSROTC Deputy Chief of Staff for Reserve Officers' Training Corps

DCS/S&L Deputy Chief of Staff for Systems and Logistics

DCST Deputy Chief of Supplies and Transport

DCSTS Deputy Chief of Staff for Training and Schools

dct depth-charge thrower; depth-control tank; distal convuluted (kidney) tubule; document(ary); documentation

DCT Department of Commerce and Trade

DCTC District of Columbia Teachers College; Dodge County Teachers College

DCTD Diploma in Chest and Tuberculous Diseases

dctl direct-coupled transistor logic

DCTSC Defense Clothing and Textile Supply Center

dcu display and control unit; dynamic checkout unit

dcu (DCU) dichloral urea (herbi-cide)

dcutl direct-coupled unipolar transistor logic

dcv double cotton varnish

DCVO Dame Commander of the Royal Victorian Order; Deputy Chief Veterinary Officer

dcw dead carcass weight

DCW Detroit Chemical Works

dcwv direct-current working volts

dcx double convex

dd days after date; day's date; deadline date; decreased (sexual) desire (often due to depressing effects of hard drugs such as heroin); deep-drawn; deferred delivery; delayed delivery; delivered; development directive; developmentally disabled; differential diagnosis; digital display; discharged dead; double draft; drydock; due date; dutch door

d-d dumb-dumb; dum-dum

d'd deceased

d/d dated; delivered at dock(s); demand draft; detergent dispersant; domicile to domicile; due date

d & d deaf and dumb; death and decay; death and dying; defiled and deflowered; drinking and drugging; drunk and disorderly; dungeons and dragons (game)

d & d (D & D) decontamination and decommissioning; development and demonstration

d-to-d dawn-to-dusk (daylight patrol); dusk-to-dawn (night patrol)—"when in doubt—spell it out"

dd_ dags dato (Dano-Norwegian —days to date)

d.d. dono dedit (Latin—he gave as a gift)

d(D) dead; died

Dd David; Drydock

DD Deputy Director; destroyer (naval symbol); Detective District; Detective Division; Development Directive; Dishonorable Discharge; E.I. du Pont de Nemours & Company (stock exchange symbol)

D.D. Doctor of Divinity

D & D Dungeons and Dragons

DD Doctores (Spanish—Doctors); *Dottores* (Italian—Doctors); *Doutores* (Portuguese— Doctors)

DD-2 Second Development Decade (1971-1980)

DD-214 Department of Defense Honorable Discharge (form DD-214)

dda duty deposit account

dda (DDA) digital differential analyzer

DDA Dangerous Drug Act; Deputy Director of Administration (CIA); Diemakers and Diecutters Association; Disabled Drivers Association; Display and Decision Area

ddalv days delay enroute authorized chargeable as leave

DDAS Digital Data Acquisition System

DDAU Doctoral Dissertations Accepted by American Universities

ddavp (DDAVP) decamino-D arginine vasopressin

D-Day day of attack; Decimalisation Day (Feb 15, 1971 when British money was decimalized)

ddc data documentation costs; decision-difficulty checklist; direct digital control; double-deck car(s)

DDC corvette (naval symbol); Defense Documentation Center; Defensive Driving Course; Dewey Decimal Classification; Diamond Dealers Club; Digital Development Corporation

ddce digital data-conversion equipment

DDCI Deputy Director of Central Intelligence (CIA)

ddcmp digital-data communication-message protocol

ddc's deck decompression chambers

DDCs Desk and Derrick Club members (petroleum professionals)

ddd deadline delivery date; detail data display; digital data distributor; digital display driver; drink, drank, drunk (alcoholic's progress); dynamic dummy director

d.d. in d. de die in diem (Latin— from day to day)

DDD Department of Decentralization and Development; direct distance dialing

ddda decimal digital differential analyzer

dd/dc diamond differential direct current

DDDIC Department of Defense Disease and Injury Code

d & dd's depraved and deprived dropouts (street people characteristic of many great cities)

DDDS Deputy Director of Dental Services

dde direct data entry; dual-displacement engine

dde (DDE) dichlorodiphenyl-dichloroethylene

DDE dichlorodiphenyldichloroethylene (insecticide less toxic than DDT); Dwight David Eisenhower (34th President U.S.)

D De L Daniel De Leon

D de l'U Docteur de l'Université (French—Doctor of the University of Paris)—the Sorbonne

DDEM Dwight D. Eisenhower Museum

DDEP Defense Development Exchange Program

ddf design disclosure format; double defruit

DDF Dental Documentary Foundation

ddg (DDG) digital display generator

DDG guided missile destroyer (naval symbol)

DDGSE Deputy Director General—Signals Equipment

DDGSR Deputy Director General of Signals Equipment

ddh diamond drill hole

DDH Digital Data Handling (system); Diploma in Dental Health

DDHA Detective Division Homicide Assault Squad

ddi depth deviation indicator; digital data indicator; discrete digital input; document disposal indicator

DDI Deputy Director, Intelligence (CIA)

dd-ing double dipping (cheating, milking the government)

ddis data display

DD & J Deacons for Defense and Justice

ddl digital data link

ddl (DDL) data definition language

DDL Data Disclosure List; Det Danske Luftfartsselskab (The Danish Airways)

ddm data demand module; difference in depth of modulation; digital drawing monitoring

DDM Diploma in Dermatological Medicine

DDME Deputy Director of Mechanical Engineering

DDMI Deputy Director of Military Intelligence

DDMOI Deputy Director of Military Operations and Intelligence

DDMS Deputy Director of Medical Services

DDMT Deputy Director of Military Training

Ddn Dunedin, NZ

DDN nuclear-powered destroyer (naval symbol)

ddnc direct digital numerical controller

DDNI Deputy Director of Naval Intelligence

ddo despatch money payable (for) discharging only

DDO David Dunlap Observatory (Ontario); Deputy Director of Operations (CIA)

D.D.O. Diploma in Dental Orthopedics

D-dog detector dog (U.S. Customs)

DDOS Deputy Director of Ordnance Services

ddp digital data processor

ddp (DDP) distributed data processing

DDP Data Distribution Point (NATO); Declaration of Design Performance; Department of Defence Production (Canadian); Deputy Director, Plans (CIA); Design Development Plan; Devalued Dollar Planning

DDPH Diploma in Dental Public Health

DDPR Deputy Director of Public Relations

DDPS Discrimination Data Processing System

ddr direct debit

DDr Doktor, Doktor (Austrian-German—person with two doctor's degrees)

DDR Deutsche Demokratische Republik (German Democratic Republic); radar picket destroyer (3-letter naval symbol)

D.D.R. Diploma in Diagnostic Radiology

DDRA Deputy Director—Royal Artillery

DDRD Deputy Directorate of Research and Development

DD R & D Department of Defense Research and Development

DDRE Danish Defense Research Establishment

DDR&E Defense Development Research and Engineering

DDRM Deputy Director of Repair and Maintenance

ddrr directional discontinuity ring radiator

DDRS Declassified Documents Reference System

dds diaminodiphenysulfone; digital display scope; digital dynamics simulator

d/d's developer/demonstrators

DDS Deep-Diving System; Demos D-Scale; Department of Developmental Services; Deployable Defense System; Deputy Director of Support (CIA); Documentation Distribution System

D.D.S. Doctor of Dental Science; Doctor of Dental Surgery

D.D.Sc. Doctor of Dental Science

DDSD Deputy Director of Staff Duties

DDSG Donau-Dampfschif-fahrts-Gesellschaft (Danube Steamship Travel Service)

dd & shpg dock dues and shipping

ddso diamino-diphenyl sulphoxide

DDSR Deputy Director of Scientific Research

DDST Denver Developmental Screening Test; Deputy Director of Supplies and Transport; Double Daylight Saving Time (two hours ahead)

DDS & T Deputy Director of Science and Technology (CIA)

DDSTs Denver Developmental Screening Tests

ddt deduct; digital data transceiver; digital data transmitter; digital debugging tape(s); drop dead twice (epithet); ductus deferens tumor; dynamic debugging technique

ddt (DDT) direct-decision therapy

DDT dichlorodiphenyl-trichloro-ethane (insecticide)

ddt & e design, development, test, and evaluation

DDTE Deputy Director, Test and Evaluation (NASA)

DDTF Dynamic Docking Test Facility (NASA)

ddtl dreary desk-top lunch

DDTS Dynamic Docking Test System (NASA)

DDTV Dry Diver Transport Vehicle (naval)

ddu data diagnostic unit; data display unit; design diagnostic unit; display driver unit; distribution data unit

ddv deck drain valve

ddvp (DDVP) dimethyldichloro-vinylphosphate

DDVS Deputy Director of Veterinary Services

ddw displaying a deadly weapon

DDWE&M Deputy Director of Works, Electrical and Mechanical

DDx differential diagnosis

DDY *Devlet Demiryollari* (Turkish Railways)

de deckle edge; deckle edging; deflection error; development engineering; diatomaceous earth; diesel-electric; digestive energy; direct elimination; direct entry; double end; double entry; dream elements; duration of ejection

d/e date of establishment

d & e dilation and evacuation

de *det er* (Norwegian—that is); (Latin prefix—down, from)—descent, description

DE Deere (stock exchange symbol); Department of Education; Department of Employment; Department of the Environment; destroyer escort (naval symbol); District Engineer; Dynamite Engineer(ing)

D.E. Doctor of Economics

D of E Department of Energy; Department of the Environment; Department of the Environment (UK)

dea (DEA) dehydroepiandrosterone

Dea Deacon

DEA Dance Educators of America; Department of External Affairs; Detectives Endowment Association; Digital Equipment Australia; Drug Enforcement Administration

deac deacon; diethylaluminum chloride

DEACONS Direct English Access and Control System

dead. (DEAD) destruction-entrusted automatic devices

Deadeye Dick Nat Love, a black cowboy of the last century who was noted for his superior marksmanship

Dead Horses Dead Horse Mountains between Mexico and Texas in the Big Bend Area where it is also called Sierra del Caballo Muerto

deadly nightshade belladonna

Deadman's Cove geographic placename and nickname of the San Diego Police Department headquarters close to the

waterfront

dead President slang for American paper money bearing the portrait of a dead President or an eminent statesman—$1—Washington, $5—Lincoln, $10—Hamilton, $20—Jackson, $50—Grant, $100—Franklin

DEADS Detroit Air Defense Sector

Deadwood Dick Richard W Clarke—English-born South Dakota frontier pioneer

DEAE Division of Eligibility and Agency Evaluation (Office of Education)

DEAE-cellulose diethylaminoethyl cellulose

Deaf Smith Erastus (Deaf) Smith, Texan patriot-soldier

deal. decision evaluation and logic

dealer prep dealer preparation

DEAN Deputy Educators Against Narcotics

Dean of Classical Guitarists Andrés Segovia

Dean Martin Dino Crocetti

dear. diamonds, emeralds, amethysts, rubies

Dear Abby Abigail Van Buren

dearg. pil. *deargentur pilulae* (Latin—let the pills be silvered)

DEAS Delaware Educational Accountability System

Death and *Death and Transfiguration* (symphonic poem by Richard Strauss—*Tod und Verklärung*)

Death and the Maiden Schubert's Quartet No. 14 in D minor for two violins, viola, and cello

Death Ride Charge of the Light Brigade at Balaclava in Crimea

death's head nickname of the deadly mushroom *Amanita muscaria*

Death Valley Death Valley National Monument on the border of California and Nevada

Death Valley Scottie Walter Scott

DEAUA Diesel Engineers and Users Association

deaur. pil. *deaurentur pilulae* (Latin—let the pills be gilded)

deb debenture; debit; debut(ante); diethylbutanediol

DEB Dental Examining Board

Debbie Deborah

Deb(by) Deborah

de Bc Honoré de Balzac

debk debark; debarkation

Deborah Kerr Deborah Kerr-Trimmer

deb(s) debenture(s); debutante(s)

deb. spis. *debita spissitudine* (Latin—of the correct consistency)

deb stk debenture stock

dec decant; decanter; deceased; deciduous; decimal; decimeter; decision; declination; decompose(d); decorate; decoration; decorator; decrease(d)

dec. *décembre* (French—December); *décor* (French—decoration, stage scenery); *decubitus* (Latin—lying down)

Dec Decca; December

DEC Detroit Edison Company; Developmental Education Center; Digital Equipment Corporation; Dominion Executive Council

deca- 10

DECA Distributive Education Club of America

decad decadence; decadency; decadent(ly)

Decade of Disillusionment the 1970s

decaf decaffeinated

decal decalcomania

DECAL detection and classification of an acoustic lens

decap(ped) decapitation(ed), behead(ed)

decasyl decasyllable; decasyllabic

decb data event control block

Decca Decca Navigation System

Deccan Deccan Plain of southern India

DECCO Defense Commercial Communications Office

decd deceased

decd est deceased estate

decel deceleration

deci 10⁻¹

decid deciduous

DECIDE Decide the problem precisely, Enumerate two groups of decision factors, Collect relevant information, Identify the best alternatives, Develop and implement a detailed plan, Evaluate the decision (many acronyms follow this general pattern and without explanation are useless)

decim decimeter

decis decision

decit decimal digit

decl declension

DECL Direct Energy Conver-

sion Laboratory (NASA)
declon declaration
decm defensive electronic countermeasure
DECMD Detroit Contract Management District
decn decision; decontamination
deco direct energy conversion operation
deco (DECO) decreasing consumption of oxygen
decoct decoction
decomm decommissioning (date)
decomp decomposition
DECOMPS Decomposition Mathematical Programming System
decon decontaminate; decontamination
D. Econ. Doctor of Economics
decor decorate; decoration; decorative
decr decrease; decrement(al)(ly)
Decr Decreto (Italian, Portuguose, Spanish Docroo)
decres decrescendo (Italian—contracting, subsiding)
decrim decriminalization(al)(ly); decriminalize(r)
DECS Direct Evacuation Control System (air filtration)
decsn decision
DECTRA Decca Track and Range
decu data-exchange control unit
Decuary December and January
decub. decubitus (Latin—lying down)
DECUS Digital Equipment Computer Users Society
ded date expected delivery; dedendum; dedicate; dedicated; deduct; deducted; deduction; diesel engine driven
Ded Dedan; Dedham; Dedric(k)
D. Ed. Doctor of Education
DED Data Element Dictionary (USA)
de d. in d. de die in diem (Latin—from day to day)
dedic dedicate(d)(ly); dedicating; dedication; dedicative; dedicator(y)
dedl data element description list
dedn deduction
deduct. deduction
dee digital events recorder; discrete event evaluator
dee (DEE) diethoxyethylene
DEE Diploma in Electrical (Electronic) Engineering
Dee Cee Washington, D.C.

dee-dee deaf and dumb
Deedee Dorothy
Dee High Doctor of Hygiene
dee jay disc jockey
deeks duck decoys
DEEP Developmental Economic Education Program; Diffusion of Exemplary Educational Practices
deep 6 burial at sea; disposing of anything unwanted in at least six fathoms of water
deep-6'd deep-sixed (cast overboard in six or more fathoms of water, thrown into the trash basket)
Dee Pee Doctor of Pharmacy
Deep North Queensland, Australia
Deep South South Carolina, Georgia, Florida, Alabama, Mississippi, Louisiana, and Texas; the conservative south coast of England
Dee R doctor
dees dynamic electromagnetic environment simulator
Deeside River Dee valley around Aberdeen
deet diethyl toluamide (insecticide)
def defeated; defecate; defecation; defect; defection; defective; defector; defendant; defense; defensive; defer; deferred; deficiency; deficient; define; definite; definition; deflagrate; deflagrating; deflagration; deflect; deflecting; deflection; defoliate; defoliating; defoliation; defrost; defroster; defrosting; defunct; defunction; defunctive
def. defunctus (Latin—deceased)
Defaced City once elegant New York City where so many buildings, buses, and subways are defaced by so-called ghetto art and by graffitic initials
def art. definite article
defcon defense condition; defensive concentration
Def Con-1 Defense Condition-1 (war)
Def Con-2 through Def Con-5 stages of military alert short of war
Def Con(s) Defense Condition(s): Def Con I—war, Def Con II—attack imminent, Def Con III—highest state of readiness for war, Def Con IV—readiness alert, etc.
defec defective
Defender of the Damned nick-

name of Clarence Darrow the atheist attorney unafraid of defending even the most unpopular causes such as the teaching of evolution in Tennessee
Defender of Darwin Thomas Henry Huxley
Defender of Democratic Socialism John Dewey in the United States or Harold Laski in Great Britain
Defender of Freethought Thomas Jefferson, Thomas Paine, Robert Ingersoll, and Clarence Darrow come to mind for this eponym
Defender of Religious Freedom Supreme Court Justice Hugo Lafayette Black who insisted the First Amendment meant separation of church and state
Defense Department of Defense
defi deficiency
defib defibrillate
defic deficiency; deficit
defl deflate; deflation; deflect; deflection
deflor defloration
deform. deformity
DEFREPNAMA Defense Representative North Atlantic and Mediterranean
defs definitions
DEFSIP Defense Scientists Immigration Program
deft. defendant; dynamic error free transmission (DEFT)
DEFY Drug Education For Youth
deg degenerate; degeneration; degree(s)
deg (DEG) diethylene glycol
DEG guided-missile escort ship (naval symbol)
D & EG Development and Engineering Group
DEG Derechos Especiales de Giro (Spanish—Special Drawing Rights)
de ga depth gage
de Gaulle Charles de Gaulle (Paris, France's airport honoring General Charles de Gaulle of military and political fame)
degen degeneration
deglut. deglutiatur (Latin—let it be swallowed)
degrad(s) degradable(s)
De Graff John De Graff
degsvc degaussing service(s)
DE-H destroyer escort—hydrofoil

deha (DEHA) diethylhydroxylamine

DEHCD Department of Environment, Housing, and Community Development

DeHoCo Detroit House of Correction

DEHS Division of Emergency Health Services

dehyd dehydrate(d)

dei design engineering identification; development engineering inspection; double electrically isolated

DEI Digital Electronics Incorporated; Dutch East Indies

DEIC Diver Equipment Information Center; Dutch East India Company

Deich Bib Deichmanske Bibliotek (Norwegian—Deichman's Library)—Oslo

DEIR Department of Employment and Industrial Relations

deis design engineering inspection simulation; design engineering inspection simulator

DEIS Defense Energy Information System; Draft Environmental Impact Statement

dej dento-enamel junction

Dejerine's disease infants' interstitial neuritis

Dek Dekabr (Russian—December)

deka 10

dekag dekagram

dekal decaliter

dekam decameter

Deke Deacon; Donald

dekon economic declaration (Indonesian)

del delegate; delegation; delete; deletion; deliberate; deliberation; delineate; delineated; delineation; deliver(y)

del (DEL) delete character (data processing)

del. delineavit (Latin—he or she drew it)

Del Delaware; Delawarean; Delhi; Delphinus

del acct delinquent account

Delaware Port Wilmington

Delaware River serves New York, New Jersey, Pennsylvania, and Delaware before emptying into Delaware Bay and Atlantic Ocean; Wilmington, Philadelphia, and Trenton are on the Delaware

delcap delay capacity

DELCO Dayton Engineering Laboratory Company

deld delivered

dele delete

deleat. deleatur (Latin—delete)

deleg delegation

del ent delete entirely

Delfi (Latin—Delft)—Dutch city also spelled Delphi by the Romans and many scholars

Delfos (Spanish—Delphi)

delft delft blue (characteristic of a popular china developed in the Dutch city of Delft); delft china; delftware (latter two of the same origin)

delg delivering

Delhi belly traveller's diarrhea picked up in India

deli delicatessen

delib deliberate; deliberation

delic delicatamente (Italian—delicately)

deli-market delicatessen and market

DELIMCO German-Liberian Mining Company

delin delineate(d); delineating; delineation; delineative; delineator; delineatrix; delinquencies; delinquency; delinquent; delinquently; delinquents

delinq delinquent

deliq deliquescent

De L Isls De Long Islands

Dell Dell Publishing Company

Dells The Dells (the Dells of Wisconsin), short form alluding to the scenic gorge of the Wisconsin River in south-central Wisconsin

Del-Mar-Va Delaware-Maryland-Virginia (Eastern Shore peninsula)

Delmarvia another name for the Delaware-Maryland-Virginia peninsula called Del-Mar-Va

delmes delay message

Del Mus Nat Hist Delaware Museum of Natural History

D. Elo. Doctor of Elocution

De Longs De Long Islands in the Arctic where the Russians call them Ostrova De Longa

delphi declaiming eclectic liberalism possessively, hotly, instantaneously

delpho deliver(y) by telephone

dels deliveries

DELS Direct Electrical Linkage System

delt delete; deletion

de lt deck edge light(ing)

delt. delineavit (Latin—he or she drew it)

delta. detailed labor and time analysis

Delta letter D radio code

DELTA Daily Electronic Lane Toll Audit

Delta Dagger Convair F-102 single-engine turbojet interceptor aircraft

Delta Dart Convair F-106 supersonic-interceptor aircraft

deltic delay line time compression

delu delusion

delv deliver

Delv Delvalle

delvd delivered

dely delivery

dem demand; dementia; democracy; democrat; democratic; demodulate; demodulator; demolish; demolition; demonstrate; demonstration; demonstrative; demote; demotion; demur; demurrage; demy

dem (DEM) demerol

Dem Demerera (British Guiana); democracy; Democrat; democratic; Democratic Party

DEM Department of Environmental Management

DEM Developpement-Études-Marketing (French—Marketing Studies Development)

DEMA Diesel Engine Manufacturers Association

dem adj demonstrative adjective

Demba Demarara bauxite

Dembos (Dutch truncation—'s-Hertogenbosch)

de/me decoding memory

DEME Director of Electrical (Electronic) and Mechanical Engineering

dementia pugilistica (Latin—punch drunk)—dementia often evidenced by cauliflower ears and resulting from brain concussion due to prizefights

Demerera old name of British Guiana and name of a river in what is now Guyana

Demeter (Greek—Ceres)—goddess of agriculture

Demetia South Wales

demij demijohn

DEMKO Dansk Elektrische Materialkontrol (Danish Board for Approving Electrical Equipment)

demo demolition; demonstration (model)

Demo Democrat(ic)

demob demobilization; demobilize

demobed demobilized

democ democracy; democrat; democratic; democratization; democratize; democratizer

Democratic Kampuchea formerly Kampuchea, the Khmer Republic, or Cambodia

demod demodulator

demogr demographer; demographic(al); demography

demon. demonology; demonstrate; demonstration; demonstrator

Demon of Deception Beelzebub

Demon of Disease Black Death (bubonic plague); hunger plague; murine plague (carried by rats); pneumonic plague; septicemic plague; sylvatic plague (carried by many species of rodents)

Demon of Misfortune and Ruin the Sphinx

demonol demonologic(al)(ly); demonologist(ic)(al)(ly); demonology; [see maj dem(s)]

demonstr demonstrative

demos demonstrators

demo(s) demolition(s); demonstration(s); demonstrator(s)

Demos Democrats

DEMOS Director(ate) of Estate Management Overseas

dem pro demonstrative pronoun

dems defensively-equipped merchant ship

Dem(s) Democrat(s)

DEMS Development Engineering Management System

demur demurrage

den denotation; dental; dentist; dentistry

den Denier (German—denier)

Den Denbighshire; Deniz; Denmark; Denver

Den Denizi (Turkish—lake, sea)

D. En. Doctor of English

DEN Denver, Colorado (airport)

Denali old Russian name for Mt McKinley also called Bol'shaya

denat denatured

Denb Denbighshire

dend dendrology

D en D Docteur en Droit (French —Doctor of Law)

dendro dendrometer

dendrol dendrology

Denemarken (Dutch—Denmark)

D. Eng. Doctor of Engineering

D.Eng.Sc. Doctor of Engineering Science

Den Haag (Dutch—The Hague)

D èn L Docteur èn Leyes (French —Doctor of Law)

D en M Docteur en Médecine

(French—Doctor of Medicine)

Denmark Kingdom of Denmark (Scandinavian nation known for fine dairy, fish, and meat products as well as ships and teak furniture, Danes speak Danish and many speak an English-accented English) *Kongeriget Danmark*

Denmark Day Constitution Day (June 5)

Denmark's Principal Port Copenhagen

Denny Denis; Dennis

Dennys Dennys Lascelles

denom denomination

denot denotation; denotative (ly); denote(ment)

dens density

dent. dental; dentist; dentistry; denture

dent. dentur (Latin—give, let it be given)

Dent J.M. Dent & Sons Ltd

D. Ent. Doctor of Entomology

dentac dental accounting

Dental Capital of Europe Vaduz, Liechtenstein where artificial teeth are made

Dent Corps Dental Corps

Dent Hyg Dental Hygienist

Denticare Dental Care

Dentist-Novelist Zane Grey

dent. tal. dos. dentur tales doses (Latin—give of such doses)

Denver Colorado's capital

DEO District Engineering Office; District Engineers Office; Divisional Education Office(r), Divisional Entertainment Office(r)—British Army

DEOR Duke of Edinburgh's Own Rifles

dep depart; department; departure; dependency; dependent; depilate; depilatory; depose; deposit; depositor; depot; depotize; deputy; do everything possible

dep. depuratus (Latin—purify)

Dep Deputy

Dep Département (French—Department); Député (French—Deputy)

DEP Defense Electronic Products (RCA); Department of Employment and Production

depa diethylene phosphoramide

DEPA Defense Electric Power Administration

depart. department; departure

Dep CFO Deputy Chief Fire Officer

dep con departmental control

depcru dependent's (daylight)

cruise (USN)

dep ctf deposit certificate

Dep Dir Deputy Director

depend. dependent; dependency

depi differential equations pseudocode interpreter

dep inst depot installed

depl depilate(d); depilation; depilator(y); deplete; depletion(ary); deploy(ed); deployment

deplab depilatory laboratory

DEPMIS Depot Management Information System (USA)

depn dependency; dependent

DEPNAV Naval Deputy (NATO)

depo deposit

depod deposited

depog depositing

depon deponent

depor depositor

depos depositary

deposn deposition

depr depreciation; depreciative; depression

DEPRA Defense European and Pacific Redistribution Activity

Depression-born Cartoonist Al Capp—creator of Li'l Abner, Hairless Joe, Lonesome Polecat, Moonbeam McSwine, and Senator Jack S Phogbound

DEPS Diploma in Economics and Political Science

DEPSACLANT Deputy Supreme Allied Commander, Atlantic (NATO)

DepSO Departmental Standardization Office

dept depart; department; departure; deponent; depot; deputy

dep't (contraction—department)

Dept Ag Department of Agriculture

deptr departure

Dept State Bull Department of *State Bulletin*

DePU De Paul University; De Pauw University

deputn deputation

Depy Deputy

DEQ Department of Environmental Quality

der derivation; derivative; derived; dermatine; derrick(s)

der derecha (Spanish—right); dernier (French—last)

Der Derringer

DeR reaction of degeneration

DER Department of Environmental Resources; Development Engineering Review; Draft Environmental Report;

radar picket escort ship (naval symbol)

Der Alte *Der Alte Fritz* (German —Old Fritz)—Frederick the Great's nickname given him by his soldiers

Der alte Steffl Old Saint Stephen's Cathedral in Vienna; begun in the 12th century

DERAP Development Economics Research and Advisory Service

Derb(s) Derby; Derbyshire

Derby. Derbyshire

DERBY Derby Aviation

Derbys Derbyshire

Derbyville Louisville (home of the Kentucky Derby)

Dercum's disease subcutaneous connective-tissue dystrophy

DERE Dounreay Experimental Reactor Establishment

dereg deregulation [of drugs, marijuana, pornography, and prostitution advocated by such groups as COYOTE (Call Off Your Old Tired Ethics), NOW (National Organization for Women), and NTPF (National Task Force on Prostitution) recently merged with COYOTE]

Derek Theodoric

Der Führer (German—The Leader)—sobriquet of Adolf Hitler—dictator of Germany before and during World War II

deriv derivation; derivative

derm dermatitis; dermatology; dermatophyte

derm (Latin prefix—skin)—dermatology, epidermis

dermat dermatology

dermatol dermatologic(al)(ly); dermatologist; dermatology

Der Meister (German—The Master)—Johann Wolfgang von Goethe

dernier(e) (French—last)

Derniers Dernieres Islands

deros date eligible for return from overseas; date of estimated return from overseas service

DERR Duke of Edinburgh's Royal Regiment

Derrick Theodoric

Derrick City Oil City, Pennsylvania

Derry Londonderry

DERT *Division Électronique, Radioélectricité et Télécommunications* (French—Electronic, Radioelectric, and Telecommunications Divi-

sion)

derv diesel-engine road vehicle

des descend(ed); descending; desert; design; designate; designation; designator; designer; desire; dessert

des (Des) diethylstrlbesterol (morning-after contraceptive)

des *descubrimiento* (Spanish—discovery)

de S de Sola; de Solá

Des Des Moines; Desmond

Des *Desierto* (Spanish—desert); (German—D-flat)

De S De Sola

DES Data Exchange System; Department of Education and Science; destroyer (naval symbol); Director of Educational Services; Director of Engineering Stores; Dispersed Emergency Station; Draft Environmental Statement; Drug Education Specialist

DESAC Destroyer Sonar Analysis Center (USN)

desal desalinization; desalinize(r)

desat desaturated

DESAT Defense (Department) Small (Business) Advanced Technology (Program)

DESB Devereaux Elementary School Behavior Rating Scale

Des Base Destroyer Base

desc descend(ant)

DESC Defense Electronics Supply Center

Descendants of Eagles the founders of Algeria, according to tradition

descr description

descron description

descto *descuento* (Spanish—discount)

desdg descending (flow chart)

DESDIV Destroyer Division (naval)

Deseret Salt Lake City, Utah

Desert Arabia Arabia Deserta in the northern sector of the Arabian Peninsula

Desert Fox Field Marshal Erwin Rommel

Desert of Ice Antarctica

Desert and Prairie Painter Georgia O'Keefe

desert roses barytes or gypsum concretions whose shapes resemble roses

desfex desert field exercise

desfirex desert firing exercise

desg designate; designation

desi designated hitter

DESI Division for Economic and Social Information (UN)

desid desiderata; desideratum

desider desiderative

desig designate; designer

D es L *Docteur es Lettres* (French—Doctor of Literature)

DESLANT Destroyer Forces—Atlantic

Des Moines Iowa's capital

desp despatch

DESP Department of Elementary School Principals

DESPAC Destroyer Forces—Pacific

despd despatched

despg despatching

despot. design performance optimization

DesRCA Designer of the Royal College of Art

DESRON destroyer squadron

dess dessiatine

d ès S *Docteur ès Science* (French—Doctor of Science)

D ès S Dar ès Salaam

DESS destroyer schoolship (naval symbol)

dest destination; destroy; destroyer; destruction

dest. *destilla* (Latin—distilled)

DEST Diplôme de l'Ecole Supérieure Technique (Diploma of the Technical Institute)

destdist destructive distillation

destil. *destilla* (Latin—distill)

destination SPPK destination Singapore, Penang, and Port Klang (headed for far places, outward bound)

destn destination

destr desires to transfer; destructor

destr fir destructive firing

desubex destroyer/submarine antisubmarine warfare exercise

det detach; detachment; detail; detective; detector; determinant; determine; detonator; double end trimmed

det (DET) diethyltryptamine (quick-acting hallucinogen drug)

det. *detur* (Latin—let it be given)

Det. Detective; Detroit

DET Design Evaluation Testing; Detroit, Michigan (Detroit City Airport)

DETA Direcção de Exploração dos Transportes Aéreos (Mozambique airline)

detab decision table

detab/X decision table(s)/experimental

DETAPS Decision Table Processing System

detcom(s) detected communist(s)

Det Con Detective Constable

detd determined

det. in dup. *detur in duplo* (Latin —give twice as much); *detur in duplo* (Latin—let twice as much be given)

detectionary dictionary of detectives (mystery-fiction type)

determin determination

DETEST Demystify Established Standardized Tests

DETG Defense Energy Task Group

Det Insp Detective Inspector

detl detail

detm determine

DETMAHOG Deliver-the-Mail/Holy-Grail (dichotomous theory of problem protection practiced by adept bureaucracies worldwide)

detn detention

detox detoxification; detoxification center (for alcoholic and narcotic addicts)

detoxcen detoxification center (for alcoholics and others addicted to imbibing, inhaling, injecting, or otherwise putting poisons into their bodies)

detr detector

detrins detailed routing instructions

Detroit Inst Detroit Institute of Arts

d. et s. *detur et signatur* (Latin— let it be given and labelled); *detur et signatur* (Latin—let it be given and labelled)—dispense and label

Det Sgt Detective Sergeant

Det Sup Detective Superintendent

Det Sym Orch Detroit Symphony Orchestra

deu data exchange unit; digital evaluation unit; display electronics unit

DEU Data Exchange Union; Drug Epidemiology Unit

DEUA Diesel Engines and Users Association

deuce. digital electronic universal computing engine

Deut Deuteronomy

Deut *Deuteronomy*

Deutsche Bücherei (German Library)—Leipzig's largest

Deutsche Demokratische Republik German Democratic Republic (Soviet-controlled Germany)

Deutsches Meer German Ocean

(the North Sea)

Deutsche Staatsbibliothek (German State Library)—on East Berlin's Unter den Linden

Deutschland (German—Germany)

Deuxponts (French—Zweibrücken)—Two Bridges

dev develop; developer; development; deviate; deviation; deviator

dev (DEV) duck embryo vaccine

Dev Devon; Devonian; Devonshire; Eamon De Valera's nickname

De V De Vilbiss

DEV Development Well

deva development acceptance

Deva (Latin—Chester)

DEVCO Development Committee

devd device data set residence

devel developer; development

Dev-Genc *Devrimci-Gencler* (Turkish—Revolutionary Youth)—Maoist communists

devil. development of integrated logistics

Devil of Cultured Vice Mephistopheles

Devils *The Devils of Loudon* by Aldous Huxley

Devil's Chaplain Robert Taylor (1784–1844), English cleric born in Edmonton near London and imprisoned for blasphemy when he exposed the universality of all religious beliefs

Devil's Half Acre Augusta, Maine's old slum

Devil's Island generic nickname for the French Guiana penal colony in use up to 1950 and translated name of the Isle du Diable off its coast where Alfred Dreyfus was imprisoned from 1894 to 1899

Devils Postpile Devils Postpile National Monument in northern California southeast of Yosemite National Park

Devil's Rock Garden California's Death Valley also called Devil's Bathtub; Devil's Parade Ground; Devil's Pulpit; Devil's Speedway and Golf Course

devil's testicle mandrake's nickname (also called mandragora or satan's apple)

Devils Tower Devils Tower National Monument on Wyoming's Belle Fourche River

Devil's Triangle (*see* Bermuda

Triangle)

devil's trumpet nickname for jimson weed also called devil's apple or devil's weed

Devin Devin-Adair

devlp develop

devlpd developed

devlpg developing

devlpmt development

dev^{mo} *devotissimo* (Italian—devotedly yours)—yours truly

Devon Devonshire

devp develop

devpt development

devs developers; devotions

DEVSIS Development of Science Information Systems

dew. dewpoint

DEW Demineralization Water (decontamination subsystem); Distant Early Warning

dewat deactivated war trophy

dewd detailed elementary wiring diagram(s)

De Witt De Witt Clinton High School

De Witt Clinton's Ditch the Erie Canal

DEWIZ Distant Early Warning Identification Zone

DEW Line Distant Early Warning Line

DEWS Diagnostic Evaluation of Writing Skills

dex dextroamphetamine tablet

dex *dexter* (Latin—right)

Dex Dexter

D. Ex. Doctor of Expression

dexan digital experimental airborne navigator

dexe dexedrine

dexies dexedrine tablets (stimulant drugs)

d. ex m. *deus ex machina* (Latin —god from a machine)— introduction of a god-like device to resolve a play or problem

dext. *dexter* (Latin—right)

dextrose glucose $(C_6H_12O_6H_2O)$

dez diethyl zinc

dez *dezembro* (Portuguese—December)

Dez *Dezember* (German—December)

Dezhda Nadezhda

df damage free; dead freight; decontamination factor; defensive fire; defogging; degree(s) of freedom; dense film; derrick floor; diamond flap; direction finder; disposition form; double feeder; double foolscap; double fronted; draft; drinking fountain; drive fit; drop forge;

drop forging; dummy fuse; dummy fuze; dunnage free

d/f defogging; direct flow; double fleece; double fronted

d & f determination and finding

d/f días fecha (Spanish—days from date)

Df Douglas fir

DF Dean of the Faculty; Defender of the Faith; Destroyer Flotilla; deuterium fluoride

D-F Dansk-Franske; deflection factor (symbol)

D of F Department of Fisheries

DF Distrito Federal (Spanish—Federal District)

D.F. Defensor Fidei (Latin—Defender of the Faith)

dfa digital fault analysis

DFA Dairy Farmers Association; Department of Foreign Affairs; Division Freight Agent; Drop Forging Association

D.F.A. Doctor of Fine Arts

DFAC Dried Fruit Association of California

DFAR Daily Field Activity Report

dfb damage-free bulkheads; distributed feedback; distribution fuse board; dunnage-free bulkheads

dfc data format converter; discriminant function coefficient; dry-filled capsules

DFC Department Frequency Coordinator; Development Finance Corporation; Distinguished Flying Cross

dfclt difficult

dfcs digital flight-control software

DFCT Deputy Federal Commissioner of Taxation

dfcty difficulty

dfd data function diagram; defend(ed); deferred

DFD Dogs For Defense

dfdr digital flight-data record(er)

DFDS Det Forende Dampskibs-Selskab (United Steamship Company, Limited, Denmark)

DFDT difluoro-diphenyl trichloroethane (insecticide)

dfe derivative fighter engine; derrick floor elevation; double fish eye (buttons)

DFE Department of Further Education

dff dilutent-free formulation

dfg digital function generator; diode function generator

DFG Department of Fish and Game

dfga distributed floating-agate amplifier

DFGJPC Daniel and Florence Guggenheim Jet Propulsion Center

DFH Danmarks Fiskeri og Havundersogelser

dfi definite; direct-flame impingement

DFI Director(ate) of Food Investigation

DFIB Data Function Information Book

DFIC Dairy Foods Information Center

d/fing direction finding

DFISA Dairy and Food Industries Supply Association

dfiy definitely

D fl Dutch florins

DFL Daily Flight Log; Democrat Farmer-Labor; Deutsche Forschungsanstalt für Luft und Raumfahrt

dfld defiled; deflated

DFLP Democratic Front for the Liberation of Palestine (terrorists formerly called PFLP—Popular Front for the Liberation of Palestine)

DFLS Day Fighter Leaders' School

DFM Distinguished Flying Medal

DFMR Dazian Foundation for Medical Research

DFMS Domestic and Foreign Missionary Society

DFMSR Directorate of Flight and Missile Safety Research

dfn distance from nose

dfndt defendant

DFNWR Deer Flat National Wildlife Refuge (Idaho)

DFO District Field Office(r)

d forg drop forging

dfp (DFP) diisopropyl phosphofluoridate

DFP Detroit Free Press

DFPA Douglas Fir Plywood Association

dfq day frequency

dfr decreasing failure rate; defrost(ing); dropped from rolls

Dfr Dounreay fast reactor

D fr Djibouti franc

DFRA Drop Forging Research Association

DFRC Dryden Flight Research Center (NASA)

dfr(d) defer(red)

DFRDBA Defence Forces Retirement and Death Benefits Authority (Australian)

dfrn differential

dfrs differs

dfs distance finding station

DFs Duty Frees (tobacco products)

DFS Dirección Federal de Seguridad (Spanish—Federal Security Directorate)—Mexico's famed *Federales*, the Feds or Federals

D.F.Sc. Doctor of Financial Science

DFSC Defense Fuel Supply Center

DFSM Distinguished Fire Service Medal

dfsr diffuser

dft deaerating feed tank; defendant; draft

DFT Diagnostic Function Test

dfti distance from touchdown indicator

dftmn draftsman

dft(s) draft(s)

d-f tube double-flare tube

dfu data file utility; dead fetus in uterus; dummy flying unit

dfus diffuse

DFW Dallas-Fort Worth, Texas (airport); Director of Fortifications and Works

dg dark ground; decigram(s); degenerate(d); deoxyglucose; diagnosis; diastolic gallup; diglyceride; disk grind; distogingival; double glass; double groove; durable gum

d/g dangerous goods; decomposed granite; directional gyroscope; displacement gyroscope

DG Deutsche Grammophon; Diego Garcia; Director General

DG Déclaration de Guerre (French—Declaration of War)

D.G. Dei Gratia (Latin—By the Grace of God)

dga (DGA) diglycolamine

DGA Directors Guild of America

DGAA Distressed Gentlefolk's Aid Association

DGAMS Director General of Army Medical Services

DGAS Double-Glazing Advisory Service

DGB Deutscher Gewerkschaftsbund (German Federation of Trade Unions)

DG Bank Deutsche Genossenschaftsbank (German Cooperative Bank)

dgbus digital ground bus

DGC Dangerous Goods Classification; Data General Corporation; Duty Group Captain

D.G.C. Diploma in Guidance and Counseling

DGCA Director General of Civil Aviation

DGCE Director General of Communications Equipment

dgd double glass doors

DGD Director Gunnery Division

DGDC Deputy Grand Director of Ceremonies

DGD & M Director General Dockyards and Maintenance

DGE Directorate General of Equipment; Division of Geothermal Energy (DoE)

DGEIS Draft Generic Environmental Impact Statement

DGG Deutsche Grammophon Gesellschaft (German Gramophone Record Company)

dgi disseminated gonococcal infection

DGI Date Growers Institute; Director General of Information; Director General of Inspection; Directorate of General Intelligence

DGI *Directorio General de Inteligencia* (Spanish—Directorate General of Intelligence)—Cuban branch of the Soviet KGB

DGIP Division of Global and Interregional Projects (UN)

Dgls Douglas

Dglsh Daglish

dgm decigram

DGM Diploma in General Medicine; Director General of Manpower; Director(ate) of General Mobilization

DGMS Director General of Medical Services

DGMT Director General of Military Training

dgmw double-gimbal momentum wheel

DGMW Director General of Military Works

Dgn Dragoon(s)

dgnast (DGNAST) design assist

dgnl diagonal

Dgo Durango

DGO Diploma in Gynecology and Obstetrics

DGP Director General of Production

DGPS Director General of Personnel Services

dgr danger(ous)(ly); door gunner

d Gr der Grosse (German—the

Great)

DGR Director of Graves Registration

DGR Dirección General de Radiocomunicaciones (Spanish—General Administration of Radio Communications)—Bolivian broadcasting control

DGRR Deutsche Gesellschaft für Raketentechnik und Raumfahrt (German Society for Rocket Technique and Space Flight)

dgs double green silk

DGS Degaussing System; Diploma in General Surgery; Director General of Ships

DGSC Defense General Supply Center

DGSRD Director(ate) General of Scientific Research and Development

DGSS Director General Secret Service

Dgt Dumaguette

DGT Director General of Training

DGT Dirección General de Turismo (Spanish—Administration of Tourism)

DGTA Dry Goods Trade Association

DGTTT Dirección General de Transporte y Transito Terrestre (Spanish Ministry of Communications)

DGW Director General of Weapons

dgz designated ground zero

dh dead heat; deadhead; dehydrogenase (DH); delayed hypersensitivity; double hung; drill hole

dh (DH) designated hitter

d & h daughter and heiress; dressed and headed

dh das heisst (German—that is to say)

Dh Moroccan dirham(s)

DH Declaration of Homestead; De Havilland (aircraft); Department of Health

D.H. Doctor of Humanities

D & H Delaware & Hudson (railroad)

D of H Degree of Honor; Degree of Honour

dha dicha (Spanish—good luck, happiness)

DHA Dhahran, Saudi Arabia (airport); Drug Houses of Australia

D & HAA Dock and Harbour Authorities Association

DHAC De Havilland Aircraft of Canada Limited

d'Haiti Haiti

D-handle D-shaped handle

dhap (DHAP) dihydroxyacetone phosphate

dhard dehaired (skins)

Dharma Chakra blue wheel of the law symbol included on central white stripe of India's saffron, white, and green horizontal tricolor

dhas (DHAS) dehydroepiandrosterone sulfate

dhc (DHC) dihydrochalcone

DHC Department of Housing and Construction; Detroit House of Correction

DHC-3 Canadian version of De Haviland Otter utility aircraft

DHC-6 Canadian De Havilland Twin Otter transport aircraft

DH Canada De Havilland Aircraft of Canada Limited

dhcv down-hole control valve

dhd distillate hydrosulfurization

dhdd digital high-definition display

dh di drophammer die

dhe data-handling equipment

dhea (DHEA) dehydroepiandrosterone

DHEW Department of Health, Education, and Welfare

DHHF Dag Hammarskjöld Foundation

dhfr dihydrofolarte reductase

D. Hg. Doctor of Hygiene

DHHS Department of Health and Human Services

DHI Dental Health International

DHI Deutsches Hydrographisches Institut (German Hydrographic Institute)

dhia dehydro-isoandrosterol (DHIA)

dhic dihydro-isocodeine (DHIC)

DHL Dag Hammarskjold Library (UN in NYC)

D.H.L. Doctor of Hebrew Letters; Doctor of Hebrew Literature

dhllp direct high-level language processor

dhlw defense high-level waste(s)

DHM Detroit Historical Museum

dhma dehydroxymandelic acid (DHMA)

DHMPGTS Department of Her (His) Majesty's Procurator General and Treasury Solicitor

dhn dynamic hardness number

DHN Department of Hospital

Nursing
dho dicho (Spanish—said)
DHO deuterium hydrogen oxide; District Health Office(r); Downhill Only (ski club)
dhon dishonor(able)
D.Hor. Doctor of Horticulture
dhp developed horsepower
DHP Diplome en Hygiène Publique (French—Diploma in Public Health)
dhpg dehydroxyphenylglycol (DHPG)
dhq mean diurnal high water inequality
DHQ Division Headquarters
dhr delayed hypersensitivity reaction(s)
DHR Division of Housing Research
dhrr de herrer (Dano-Norwegian —the gentlemen)
dhs dry heat sterilization
dh's deadheads (freeloaders who never buy a ticket or pay their own way)
DHS Detroit High School; Diploma in Horticultural Science; District High School; Dublin High School
D.H.S. Doctor of Health Science(s)
DHSC Department of Health and Social Security
dhsm dihydrostreptomycin (DHSM)
DHSS Department of Health and Social Security
dht distillate hydrotreating
dht (DHT) dihydrotestosterone
dhtv downhole television
DHUD Department of Housing and Urban Development
D.Hum.L. Doctor of Humane Letters
dhw domestic hot water; double-hung windows
DHX Dependable Hawaiian Express
D. Hy. Doctor of Hygiene
di daily inspection; de-ice; diameter; diametral; diplomatic immunity; direction indicator; display indicators; document identifier; double imperial
di (DI) diabetes insipidus; double indemnity; inversion of the duration series
di (Latin prefix—two)—dipole antenna
d i das ist (German—that is)
Di Diana; Diane; didymium; Dinorah
DI Defense Intelligence; Denizyollari Isletmesi (Turkish Maritime Lines); Department

of the Interior; Departmental Instruction(s); Detective Inspector; Deterioration Index (annual rate for the deterioration of a mailing list to the point it ceases to be deliverable); Diffusion Index; Director of Intelligence; District Inspector; Division Instruction; Divisional Inspector; Drill Instructor
D-I Dai-Ichi
D of I Daughters of Isabella; Declaration of Independence; Department of Insurance; Department of the Interior; Division of Intelligence
DI-5 Defense Intelligence (British agency)
dia date of initial appointment; diagram; diameter; diaphone; diathermy; due in assets
dia (Greek prefix—passing through or through)—diabetes, diagnosis, dialysis, diaphragm
DIA Defense Intelligence Agency; Department of Institutions and Agencies (NJ); Design and Industries Association; Designated International Accounts; Dulles International Airport (Washington, D.C.)
diab diabetic
DIAB Defense Internal Audit Board
diac di-iodothyroacetic acid (DIAC)
DIAC Defense Industry Advisory Council
diacrit diacritic(al)(ly)
di ad die adapter
Día de la Raza (Spanish—Day of the Race)—Columbus Day, October 12
diag diagnose; diagnosis; diagnostic; diagnostician; diagonal; diagram
dial. dialect; dialectical; dialectician; dialectics
DIAL Disc Interrogation and Loading (system)
dial-a-mation dial-a-cremation (telephone service offering low-cost cadaver disposal)
dialec dialectic(al)(ly); dialectician(s); dialectics; dialectologist(s); dialectological(ly); dialectology
dialgol dialect of algol (*q.v.*)
diam diameter
DIAMANG Companhia de Diamantes de Angola (Portuguese —Angolan Diamond Company)
diamat dialectical materialism

diamond carbon
Diamond Head 760-foot-high extinct crater forming cape and marking entrance to Honolulu on Oahu, Hawaii
Diamond Jim James Buchanan (Diamond Jim) Brady
Diamond Lil Mae West
Diamond State diamond-shaped Delaware's official nickname
Diamond Street nickname of New York City's 47th Street between 5th and 6th avenues where so many diamond merchants maintain offices
dian digital analog
Diana (Latin—Artemis)—goddess of the hunt and the Moon; protectress of women
DIAND Department of Indian Affairs and Northern Development (Canada)
diane digital-integrated attack and navigation equipment (DIANE)
DIANE Direct Information Access Network for Europe
diap. diapason (Greek—consonant harmony, octave)
diaph diaphragm
diaphor diaphoresis
DIAR Defense Intelligence Agency Regulation
Diario de Caracas Venezuela's best tabloid
dias. defense-integrated automatic switch
DIAS Drug Information and Assistance Service; Dublin Institute for Advanced Studies; Dynamic Inventory Analysis System
diast diastolic
diat diathermy
DIAT Dundee Institute of Art and Technology
diath diathermy
Diazpotism despotism of Porfirio Diaz during his forty years as president of Mexico
dib dead in bed (not physically but sexually); diameter inside bark
DIB Department of Information and Broadcasting; Department Information Bulletin
DIB Dictionary of International Biography
DIBA Domestic and Internal Business Administration; Dominion Investment and Banking Association
dibah (DIBAH) diisobutylaluminum hydride
dibas dibasic
DIBR Dartnell Institute of Busi-

ness Research

dic data insertion converter; data item category; defense identification code; dependency and indemnity compensation; dictionary; digital integrated circuit; digital integrating computer; disseminated intravascular coagulopathy; drunk in charge; inverted cancrizans of the duration series

d & ic dependency and indemnity compensation

dic dicembre (Italian—December); *diciembre* (Spanish—December)

DiC diesel cargo vessel

DIC Dai Nippon Ink and Chemicals; Diplomate of the Imperial College (London); Direct Importing Company (New Zealand); Diving Information Center (USN)

DICAP Direct-Current Circuit-Analysis Program

DICASS Directional Command Active Sonobuoy System

dicautom automatic dictionary look-up

DICB Demolition Industry Conciliation Board

dice. digital intercontinental-conversion equipment; digital-interface countermeasure equipment; direct-installation coaxial equipment

DICEF Digital Communications Experimental Facility (USAF)

DIChem Diploma of Industrial Chemistry

dichlorvos dimethyldichlorovinyl phosphate (insecticide)

dicht dichterlijk (Dutch—poetic)

Dick Richard

Dick Donavan Joyce Emmerson Preston Muddock's pseudonym

dickel dime and nickel (unofficial unit of American currency sometimes worth as much as 7½ cents)

Dickie Dickman; Richard

Dickon Richard(son)

dick(s) detective(s)

Dicky Richard; Tricky Dicky

Dicky Sam(s) inhabitant(s) of Liverpool

DICNAVAB Dictionary of Naval Abbreviations

dicot(s) dicotyledon(s)

dict dictated; dictation; diction; dictionary

dicta dictaphone

DICTA Diploma of the Imperial College of Tropical Agriculture

Dict Amer Slang Dictionary of American Slang

Dictator of Nicaragua William Walker—American filibuster

Dictionary Johnson Dr Sam(uel) Johnson

dictsort dictionary sorter

did. data item description; dead of intercurrent disease; didactic; direct in dialing

did. (DID) drum information display

Did Didot

DID Department of Industrial Development; Division of Institutional Development; Drainage and Irrigation Department

DID Daily Intelligence Digest

dida differential in-depth analysis

didac didactic(al)(ly); didacticism; didactics

didad digital data display

DIDAS Dynamic Instrumentation Data Automobile (Automotive) System

DIDC Depository Institutions Deregulation Committee (aiding bank depositors)

dident distortion identity

DIDMCA Depository Institutions Deregulation and Monetary Control Act

didn't did not

di/do data input/data output

DIDS Digital Information Display System

die. died in emergency room (DIE)

DIE Diploma in Industrial Engineering; Diploma of the Institute of Engineering; Division of International Education

DIEA Dictionary of Industrial Engineering Abbreviations

dieb. alt. diebus alternus (Latin—on alternate days)

dieb. secund. diebus secundis (Latin—every second day)

dieb. tert. diebus tertius (Latin—every third day)

Dieciséis (Spanish—Sixteenth) —September 16 (Mexican Independence Day)

Diedrich Knickerbocker (pseudonym—Washington Irving)

Dief the Chief John George Diefenbaker

Die Frau Die Frau Ohne Schatten (German—The Woman Without a Shadow)—three-act opera by Richard Strauss

Diego (Mexican-American truncation—San Diego)—San Diego, California

die Kö Königsallee (main street of Dusseldorf)

diel dielectrics; diesel electric

di el diesel electric

DIEME Director(ate) of Inspection of Electrical (Electronic) and Mechanical Equipment

Die Nullte (German—The Zero) —Bruckner's Symphony No. 0 in D minor

DIEPO Dieterich-Post

diesel diesel engine, diesel fuel, diesel locomotive, diesel oil (all named for the German automotive engineer, Rudolf Diesel)

Dies Irae (Latin—Day of Wrath)—medieval mass for the dead theme used by romantic composers such as Berlioz, Liszt, and Rachmaninov

diet. dietary; dietetic(s); dietician

DIEX Dirección de Identificación y Extranjería (Spanish—Directorate of Identification and Immigration)

dif differ; difference; differential; diffuse(er)(s)

dif (DIF) discriminant function

DIF Defense Industrial Fund; Descriptive Item File; Discriminant Function (auditing system for income tax returns); District Inspector(ate) of Fisheries

dif-amps differential amplifiers

difar directional frequency analysis and recording

difce difference

diff difference; differential

diff calc differential calculus

diff diag differential diagnosis

diffr diffraction

diffu diffusion

DiFr diesel fruit vessel

dift different

diftl differential

dig. digest; digestion; digestive

dig. digeratur (Latin—let it be digested)

DIG Deputy Inspector General

DIGA Dynamics International Gardening Association

digas digastric

DIGEPOL Dirección General de Policías (Spanish—General Directorate of Police)—Venezuela

Digger Land Australia

digger(s) gold digger(s); gold miner(s); parasite(s) gifted at talking people out of their pos-

sessions
digi digital
Digi Digiform (business forms typesetter)
digicom digital communications (system)
digital IC digital integrated circuit
digres digression(al)(ly); digressionary; digressive(ly); digressiveness
digrm digit/record mark(ing)
dig r-o digital readout
digs. archeological excavation; diggings (apartment, dwelling place, flat)
DIGs Development Import Grants
DIGS Delta Inertial Guidance System
di-H hydrogen
DIH Diploma of Industrial Health; Division of Indian Health
DIHJHU Department of International Health—Johns Hopkins University
Dij Dijon
di ji drill rig
dik drug-identification kit
DIKB Dai-Ichi Kangyo Bank
dil dilute; dissolve
dil. dilue (Latin—dilute); *dilutus* (Latin—diluted)
DIL Deliverable Items List; Director of International Logistics; Division of Insured Loans
dilat dilatation; dilate; dilation (ed)
dild diluted
dilet dilettante
dilligaf do I look like I give a fuck?
dilligas do I look like I give a shit?
Dilmun (Persian—Bahrain)
diln dilution
diluc. diluculo (Latin—at daybreak)
dilut. dilutus (Latin—dilute)
dim. defense information memo; description, installation, and maintenance; digital dimmer memory; dimension; dimensional; dimension(al)(ly); diminutive
dim dimanche (French—Sunday); *dimidius* (Latin—one half); *diminuendo* (Italian—diminishing gradually)
DIM Dialogue Inter-Monasteries; Diploma in Industrial Management
DIMA Detroit Institute of Musical Art

dimate depot-installed maintenance automatic test equipment
DIMD Dorland's Illustrated Medical Dictionary
DIMDI Deutsches Institut für Medizinische Dokumentation und Information (German Institute for Medical Documentation and Information)
dime. dual independent map encoding
DIME Division of International Medical Education (Assn Amer Med Colleges)
DIMES Defense Integrated Management Engineering Systems
dimin diminish; diminution; diminutive
DIMIS Depot Installation Management Information System (USA)
dimn dimension
dimorph dimorphous
dimple deuterium-moderated pile low energy
DIMS Data Information and Manufacturing System; Director International Military Staff Memo (NATO)
din. dinar(s); dining room; dinner; do it now
din dinar (Yugoslavian monetary unit)
Din Dinsdag (Dutch—Tuesday)
DIN Data Identification Number
DIN Deutsche Industrie Norm (German Industry Standard) —film rating sometimes written *din* and said to mean *das ist norm* (this is standard); *Deutsches Institut für Normung* (German Standards Institute)
Dina Dinamarca (Portuguese or Spanish—Denmark)
DINA Dirección de Inteligencia Nacional (Spanish—Directorate of National Intelligence) —Chilean secret police
Dinamarca (Portuguese or Spanish—Denmark)
diner dining car
Ding J.N. Darling
D.Ing. Doctor Ingeniariae (Latin —Doctor of Engineering)
dinin' dining
dino dinosaur
Dino Dean (Crocetti) Martin
dinos dinosaurs
Dinosaur Dinosaur National Monument in northwestern Colorado and northeastern Utah

DINP Dunk Island National Park (Queensland)
DINS Dormant Inertial Navigation System
dio diode
DIO Director(ate) of Intelligence Operations; District Intelligence Office(r); Duty Intelligence Officer
diob digital input-output buffer
dioc dioceasan; diocese
diode. digital input-output display equipment
Dion Dionisio
Dionysus (Greek—Bacchus)— god of revelry and wine
diop di-iso-octyl phthalate (plasticizer); diopter; dioptrics
dior diorama
dios diver lockout submersible
DIOS Distributed Input-Output System
diox dioxygen
dip. digital inline pins; dipeptide; diphtheria; diphthong; diplex; diplococcus; diploma; diplomat; dipsomania(c); dissemination and improvement of practice; dual incline package; (slang for pickpocket)
DIP Document Improvement Program (DoD)
DIPA Diploma of the Institute of Park Administration
Dip AD Diploma in Art and Design
Dip Agr Diploma in Agriculture
Dip A Ling Diploma in Applied Linguistics
Dip AM Diploma in Applied Mechanics
Dip Amer Bd P & N Diplomate of the American Board of Psychiatry and Neurology
Dip AMS Diploma in Ayurvedic Medicine and Surgery
Dip Anth Diploma in Anthropology
Dip App Sci Diploma in Applied Science
Dip Arch Diploma in Architecture
Dip Ars Diploma in Arts
Dip Bac Diploma in Bacteriology
Dip BMS Diploma in Basic Medical Sciences
Dip CAM Diploma in Communications, Advertising, and Marketing
Dip Card Diploma in Cardiology
Dip Com Diploma in Commerce
dipcrit diplomatic critic(ism)

Dip DP Diploma in Drawing and Painting

Dip DS Diploma in Dental Surgery

DIPEC Defense Industrial Plant Equipment Center

Dip Eco Diploma in Economics

Dip Ed Diploma in Education

Dip Eng Diploma in Engineering

Dip FA Diploma in Fine Arts

Dip For Diploma in Forestry

Dip G & O Diploma in Gynaecology and Obstetrics

Dip GT Diploma in Glass Technology

diph diphtheria

Dip HA Diploma in Hospital Administration

Dip HE Diploma in Highway Engineering

diph tet diphtheria tetanus

diph tox diphtheria toxin

diph tox ap diphtheria toxin alum precipitated

Dip Hus Diploma in Husbandry

dipj distal interphalangeal joint

Dip J Diploma in Journalism

dipl diplomacy; diplomat; diplomatic

Dipl Diplom (German—Diploma)

Dip L Diploma in Languages

Dip Lib Diploma in Librarianship

Dip Lib Sci Diploma in Library Science

diplo diploma; diplomacy; diplomat; diplomatic; diplomatics; diplomatism; diplomatist

diplo diplomatico (Spanish—diplomat); diplotienda (Spanish—diplomat store)—special store catering only to diplomats and off limits to natives as in Cuba and other places where some animals are more equal, as Orwell explained in *Animal Farm*; (Greek *diploos* —two-fold)—diploid, diplomacy, diplomat(ic)

Diplomat pseudonym of John Franklin Carter

Dip ME Diploma in Mechanical Engineering

Dip MFOS Diploma in Maxial, Facial, and Oral Surgery

Dip Mgmnt Diploma of Management

Dip Micro Diploma in Microbiology

Dip Mus Edu Diploma in Musical Education

Dip NA & AC Diploma in Numerical Analysis and Automatic Computing

Dip NS Edu Diploma in Nursery School Education

Dip NZLS Diploma of the New Zealand Library Service

Dip OL Diploma in Oriental Learning

Dip Phar Diploma in Pharmacology

Dip Phys Edu Diploma in Physical Education

Dip P & OT Diploma in Physical and Occupational Therapy

Dip Pub Adm Diploma in Public Administration

Dip RADA Diploma of the Royal Academy of Dramatic Art

Dip RSAM Diploma of the Royal Scottish Academy of Music

diprt discharge printed

dips. dipeptides; diphtheria patients; diphthongs; diplexes; diplomas; diplomats; dipsomaniacs

DIPS Dendenkosha's Information Processing System; Development Information Processing System

dipsey deep-sea lead (line for measuring depths)

dipso dipsomania(c); drunkard

Dip SS Diploma in Social Studies

Dip SW Diploma in Social Work

Dip T Teachers Diploma

Dip T & CP Diploma in Town and Country Planning

Dip Tec Diploma in Technology

Dip TEFL Diploma in Teaching English as a Foreign Language

dipth diphthong (single sound as ae in aeolian)

Dip The Diploma in Theology

Dip TP Diploma in Town Planning

dipu diputado (Spanish—deputy)

Dip VFM Diploma in Valuation and Farm Management

dIQ deviation IQ

dir direct; direction; director

dir (DIR) digital instrumentation radar

dir. directione (Latin—directions); direxit (Latin—directed by)

Dir Director(ate); Dirham(s)— Moroccan money

DIR Detailed Inspection Report; Diesel Inspector's Report

Dirceu Tomaz Antonio Gonzaga

dir conn direct-connect

dir coup directional coupler

dircty directly

direct. directory

D.Ir.Eng. Doctor of Irrigation Engineering

Dir Gen Director General

Dir Gen Direttore Generale (Italian—General Manager)

Dirk Derek; Everett McKinley Dirksen

Dirk Bogarde Dirk van den Bogaerd

dir max directional maximum

dir min directional minimum

diron direction

dir. prop. directione propria (Latin—with proper directions)

DIRT Department of Industrial Relations and Technology (Australian)

dirty dishes evidence planted to incriminate another or others

dis delivered into store; disability; disable(d); disciple; discipline; disconnect(ed); discontinue(d); discount(ed); disease(d); distance; distant; distribute(d); distribution

dis (Latin prefix—apart, away from)—disable, disarticulate

Dis Disney (Walt Disney), Disneyland; Disraeli (Benjamin Disraeli); Pluto

Dis (German—D-sharp)

DIs Department(al) Instructions

DIS Dairy Industry Society; Defense Intelligence School; Defense Intelligence Service; Defense Investigative Service; Department of Industrial Services; Disney Productions (stock exchange symbol); Distribution Advisory Service; Distribution Information System; Dow Industrial Service; Drug Instruction Service; Ductile Iron Society

disab disable; disabled

disabl disability

disac digital simulator and computer

disap disapprove

disassy disassembly

disb disburse; disbursement

disbmt disbursement

disbt disbursement

disc. (DISC) direct-injection stratified charge (automobile engine)

disc. dimension of schooling questionnaire; discography; disconnect; discontinue; discophile; discount

DISC Defense Industrial Supply Center; Distribution Stock Control System; Domestic International Sales Corporation

discd discounted

discg discounting

disch discharge; discharging

dischd discharged

dischg discharging

disc jock(s) disc jockey(s)

disco disc jockey; discotheque; discotheque music

DISCO Defense Industrial Security Clearance Office

discol discolored

discom digital selective communication(s)

discomb discombobulate(d); discombobulation

discon disconnect; disorderly conduct

DISCON Defence-Integrated Secure Communications Network (Australian)

discontd discontinued

discos discotheques

discr discriminator

discron discretion

discrtn discretion

DISCs Domestic International Sales Corporations

disct discount

discum discumbobulate(d); discumgalligumfricate(d)

discus (*see* DSSCS)

Discuss Faraday Soc *Discussions of the Faraday Society*

DISD Data and Information System Division

DISE Digital Systems Education

disemb disembark

disg disagreeable

dishon dishonest; dishonesty; dishonorable; dishonorably

DISI Dairy Industries Society International

disid disposable seismic intrusion detector

disin disinfectant; disinfection

dis int discrete integrator

DISIP *Dirección de Seguridad e Inteligencia Policiales* (Spanish—Directorate of Police Security and Intelligence)

disk *diskonto* (Norwegian—discount)

disloc dislocation

dism dismiss; dismissal

Dismals Dismal Gardens near Phil Campbell, Alabama

dismal science Carlyle's nick-

name for economics

Dismal Swamp City (naval argot—Norfolk, Virginia)—less complimentary nicknames are usually used by sailors when referring to this port on the edge of the Dismal Swamp

dismd dismissed

dis/min disintegrations per minute

diso die shoe

disod disodium

disord disorder

disp dispatch; dispensary; dispensatory; dispenser; displacement; display; disposal; disposition

disp. *dispensa* (Latin—dispense)

dispen dispensatories; dispensatory

displ displacement

dispr dispatcher

disr disrated

diss disassembly; dissent; dissenter; dissertation

DISS Director(ate) of Information Systems and Settlement (stock exchange)

dissd dissolved

dissec dissection

dis/sec disintegrations per second

dissem disseminate; disseminated

dissert dissertation(s)

Dissident Publisher Henry Regnery

disson dissonance; dissonant(ly)

Dissonant Mozart's String Quartet in C (K 465)

disspla display integrated software system and plotting language

dissyl dissyllable

dist distance; distant; distribute; distribution; distributor; district

dist. *distilla* (Latin—distill)

Dist District

distab disestablish(ment)(tarian)(ism)

Dist Ad District Administrator

distads administrative districts

distar direct instruction

DISTAR Direct Instruction System for Teaching Arithmetic and Reading

Dist Atty District Attorney

distb distillable

distbtr distributor

Dist Ct District Court

distil distillation; distilled; distilling

Dist J District Judge

distn distillation

distng distinguish; distinguishing

Dis TP Distinction in Town Planning

distr distribute; distribution

DISTRAMS Digital Space Trajectory Measurement System

distran diagnostic fortran

distrib distribution; distributive; distributor

District of Columbia capital district of United States; Washington, D.C.

DISTRIPRESS *Fédération Internationale des Distributeurs de Presse* (French—International Federation of Wholesale Book, Newspaper, and Periodical Distributors)

Distrito Federal (Spanish—Federal District)—includes Mexico City

Dists Districts

DISUM Daily Intelligence Summary (USAF)

disy disyllabic

dit domestic independent tour; dual input transponder

dit (DIT) diiodotyrosine

DIT Defining Issues Test; Detroit Institute of Technology; Drexel Institute of Technology; Durham Institute of Technology

DIT *Deutscher Investment-Trust*

DiTa diesel tanker vessel

ditar digital telemetry analog recording

DITC Disability Insurance Training Council

Ditch The Ditch, 3100-mile-long (4989-kilometer-long) Intracoastal Waterway along the Atlantic coast from Boston, Massachusetts to Key West, Florida as well as from the St Marks, River in Florida to Brownsville, Texas across the Rio Grande from Matamoros, Mexico via a series of open-water extensions linking many sheltered passages used by barges as well as pleasure craft

ditchweed Mexican marijuana's nickname attesting to its low quality as compared to Caribbean and Colombian varieties

dithy dithyramb(ic)(al)(ly); dithyrambs

ditmco data information test material checkout

Dito Ernesto

diu data interface unit; digital

interface unit
DIU Diversion Investigation Unit
div data in voice; digits in voice; divergence; diverse; divide; divided; dividend; divisibility; division; divisor; divorce; divorced
Div Divide (postal abbreviation); Divine; Divinity; Division
divab digital input/voice answer back
Div Arty Division Artillery
divd dividend
divde dividende (French—dividend)
Div E Division Engineer
divear diving instrumentation vehicle for environmental and acoustic research
div. en p. aeq. divide in partes aequales (Latin—divide into equal parts)
divi divide; dividend
Divine Poet John Donne
divine Sarah the divine Sarah—Oscar Wilde's nickname for Sarah Bernhardt who began life as Rosine Bernard
Divio (Latin—Dijon)
divi(s) dividend(s)
Division No. 1 Chicago's Cook County Jail
Division No. 2 Chicago's House of Correction
divn division
divnl divisional
Divodurum (Latin—Metz)
Divorce Capital of America Reno, Nevada
div. in par. aeq. dividatur in partes aequales (Latin—divide into equal parts)
divs dividends
divvy divide; dividend
diw dead in the water
DIW Deutsches Institut für Wirtschaftforschung (German Institute for Economic Research)
Dix Dixie; Fort Dix, New Jersey
Dixie southern United States; the South
Dixiecrat Southern Democrat
diy do it yourself
diz dizionario (Italian—dictionary)
Dizzy Benjamin Disraeli—British Prime Minister
Dizzy Dean Jay Hanner (Dizzy) Dean
Dizzy Gillespie John Birks (Dizzy) Gillespie
dj disc jockey; dust jacket

d J der Jüngere (German—junior); *dieses Jahres* (German—of this year)
Dj Djawa (Indonesian—Java); *Djebel* (Arabic—mount, mountain)
DJ David Jones (Australian department store chain); Department of Justice; District Judge; Divorce Judge; Don Jail (Toronto)
D-J Dow-Jones (average)
D of J Department of Justice; Dominion of Jamaica
DJ Divehi Jumhuriyya (Divehi Arabic—Republic of Maldives)—Maldive Islands
D.J. Doctor Juris (Latin—Doctor of Law)
Dja Djakarta
DJAD Department of Justice Antitrust Division
DJAG Deputy Judge Advocate General
Djailolo (Indonesian—Halmahera Island)—in the Moluccas
Djajapura another name for Kotabaru formerly called Hollandia by the Dutch when they controlled western New Guinea
Djakarta Indonesian city on the northwest coast of Java where it was once called Batavia
Django Jean (Django) Reinhardt
Djawa (Indonesian—Java)
DJCD Department of Justice Civil Division; Department of Justice Criminal Division
DJCP Division of Justice and Crime Prevention (Virginia)
DJCRD Department of Justice Civil Rights Division
djd degenerative joint disease
djeziret (Arabic or Turkish—island)
Dji Djibouti
DJI Dow-Jones Industrials (average)
DJIA Dow-Jones Industrial Average
Djib Djibouti (formerly Afars and Issas Territory also known as French Somaliland)
Djibouti Republic of Djibouti (formerly French Somaliland, Djiboutis speak Somali, Afar, French, and Arabic, livestock and salt are principal exports)
Djibouti Ports (north to south) Obock, Djibouti
Djinn Sud-Aviation two-seat helicopter built in France
Djkta Djakarta (Batavia), Java

Djl Djalan (Malay—road or street)
DJLNRD Department of Justice Land and Natural Resources Division
DJNR Dow Jones News Retrieval
Djokja Djokjakarta, Java, Indonesia
Djokjakarta (Indonesian—Jogjakarta)
D.Journ. Doctor of Journalism
dj's (DJs) disc jockeys
DJs Department of Justice investigators
D.J.S. Doctor of Juridical Science
DJTD Department of Justice Tax Division
D.Jur. Doctor of Jurisprudence
dk dark; decay; deck; diseased kidney(s); dock; dog kidney; don't know; drop kick; duck; duct keel; dusky
d & k dining and kitchen
DK Danny Kaye
D & K Dalhott and King
DK Danmark (Danish—Denmark)
DKB Dai-ichi Kangyo Bank; *Det Kongelige Bibliotek* (Danish—The Royal Library)—Copenhagen
DKC De Kalb College
dk di dinking die
dkftcol dark fast color
dkg dooking; dokogram(s)
dkga (DKGA) diketogulonic acid
dkgrcol dark-ground color
dkhse deckhouse
dk hse deck house
DKI Det Kriminalistiriske Institute (Danish—The Criminalistic Institute)—Copenhagen
DKK Danmark Kroner (Danish crowns)
dkl dekaliter
dkm dekameter
dkm² square dekameter
dkm³ cubic dekameter
dkp deck passenger(s)
DKP Democratic Korea Party
DKP Danmarks Kommunistiske Parti (Danish Communist Party); *Deutsche Kommunistische Partei* (German Communist Party)
Dkr Dakar
DKr Danish krone(r)
DKR Dakar, Senegal (airport)
dks dekastere
DKS Deputy Keeper of the Signet; Direct Keying System
dkt docket
DKTC Door-Kewaunee Teach-

ers College

DKW Deutsche Kraftfahrt Werks (German—German Power-drive Works)

DKW Dampf Kraft Wagen (German—steam power vehicle); *Das Kleine Wunder* (German—The Little Wonder—automobile)

dkyd dockyard

dl data link; day letter; dead load; deadlight; deciliter; delay line; demand loan; difference limen (threshold); dog license; dollar; double acetate; drawing list; driver's license

d-l -dextro-levo

d/l data link; demand loan

Dl Daniel

DL Danger List; Delta Air Lines (2-letter symbol); Department of Labor; difference of latitude; Djakarta Lloyd; Drawing List; frigate (naval symbol)

D-L Deputy-Lieutenant

D/L De Luxe

D of L Department of Labor; Department of Labour; Department of Law; Duchy (Duke) of Lancaster; Duchy (Duke) of Lorraine; Duchy (Duke) of Luneburg

DL Danske Lov (Danish Law)

dla distolabial

Dla Douala

DLA Defense Logistics Agency; District Licensing Authority; Divisional Land Agent (UK); Documentation, Libraries, and Archives Director(ate)

dlab disc label

dlai distolabioincisal

D.Lang. Doctor of Languages

D-L antibody Donath-Landsteiner antibody

DLAS Defence of Literature and the Arts Society

d lat difference in latitude

DLAT Defense Language Aptitude Test (USA)

dlb's dead-letter boxes

dlc direct lift control; down left center

DLC Disaster Loan Corporation; Duquesne Light Company

DLCO Desert Locust Control Office

DLCO–EA Desert Locust Control Organization—East Africa

dld deadline date; delivered

dle data link escape; disseminated lupus erythematosus (DLE)

dlea double leg elbow amplifier

D.L.E.S. Doctor of Letters in Economic Studies

dlet delete

dletd deleted

dletg deleting

D Lett Docteur en Lettres (French—Doctor of Letters)

DLF Development Loan Fund(ing)

DLG David Lloyd George; guided-missile frigate (naval symbol)

DLG Deutsche Landwirtschafts Gesellschaft (German Agricultural Society)

DLGA Decorative Lighting Guild of America

DLGCD Department of Local Government and Community Development

DLGN nuclear-powered guided missile frigate (naval symbol)

DLH Deutsche Lufthansa (German airline)

DLI Defense Language Institute; Department of Labour and Industry (Australian)

DLIA Dental Laboratories Institute of America

D-library duplicating library

dlimp descriptive language for implementing macroprocessors

dlir depot-level inspection and repair

DLIS Desert Locust Information Service

D. Litt. Doctor Litterarum (Latin—Doctor of Letters, Doctor of Literature)

dll dial long line

DLL Deutsche Levante-Linie (Levant Line); Donaldson Line Limited

dllf design limit load factor

dlli dulcitol lysine lactose iron (DLLI)

dlM des laufenden Monats (German—this month)

DLM Daily List of Mails; Depot-Level Maintenance

DLMA Decorative Lighting Manufacturers Association; Downtown Lower Manhattan Association

DLNS Department of Labour and National Service (Australian)

DLNWR Des Lacs National Wildlife Refuge (North Dakota)

dlo difference in longitude; dispatch loading only; distolinguo-occlusal

D'Lo The Lord (town in Mississippi)

DLO Dead Letter Office; Difference of Longitude; District Legal Office(r)

D.L.O. Diploma in Laryngology and Otology

DLOC Division Logistical Operation Center

DLOCA Department of Law Office Consumer Affairs

d lock dial-lock

d long difference in longitude

D-love deficiency love (exploitative and possessive love of another person)

DLOY Duke of Lancaster's Own Yeomanry

dlp date of last payment; distolinguopulpal; double-large post; mean diurnal low-water inequality

DLP Democratic Labor Party; Director of Laboratory Programs (USN)

DLPS Department of Law and Public Safety (New Jersey)

dlq deliquescent; mean diurnal low water inequality

dlr dealers; discharge, land, and reload; discharged, landed, and reshipped; dollar; double lift restow; double-lens reflex (camera)

d-l-r discharge-load-reposition (containers)

DLR District Land Registrar; Driving Licences Regulations

DLR Distrito de la Luz Roja (Spanish—Red Light District)

dlra door lock rotary actuator

DLRA Divorce Law Reform Association

DLRO District Labor Relations Office(r)

dlrs dollars

DLRs Dominion Law Reports

dls debt liquidation schedule; dollars

dls dólares (Spanish—dollars)

DLs Defence Lists

DLS Debt Liquidation Schedule; District Law Society

D.L.S. Doctor of Library Science; Doctor of Library Service

D.L.Sc. Doctor of Library Science

DLSC Defense Logistics Service Center

DLSEF Division of Library Services and Educational Facilities (U.S. Office of Education)

dls/shr dollars per share

dlt deck landing training; dry long tons

dlt (DLT) data-loop transceiver

(data processing)

dlt dans le texte (French—in the text)

DLT Development Land Tax(ation); Discrimination Learning Test

D-L T Donath-Landsteiner Test

dlts deep-level transient spectroscopy

DLTS Deck Landing Training School

dlu digitizer logic unit

dlvd delivered

dlvr deliver; delivery

dlvry delivery

DLW Diesel Locomotive Works

DL & W Delaware, Lackawanna and Western (railroad)

dlwg daily weight gain

dlx deluxe

dly daily; delay; dolly

dlyd delayed

dm data management; decimeter(s); delta modulation; demand meter; development milestone; diabetes mellitus (DM), diabetic mother; diagnostic monitor; diastolic murmur; diesel-mechanical; diphenylaminearsine chloride (Adamsite war gas); direct monitoring; double medium; draftsman; dry matter

d/m date and month; day and month; density/moisture

d & m dressed and matched

d M dieses Monats (German— this month)

DM Deputy Master; Des Moines; Design Manual; Deutsche Mark (German mark—currency unit); Drafting Manual; Du Mont (television network); Dungeon Master; Dungeon Module; light minelayer, high-speed (naval symbol)

D.M. Doctor of Mathematics; Doctor of Medicine; Doctor of Music; Doctor of Musicology

D & M Detroit and Mackinac (railroad)

D of M Duchy (Duke) of Milan

DM Daily Mail; Deutsche Mark (German mark)

dm² square decimeter

dm³ cubic decimeter

dma direct memory access; direct memory asset

DMA Dance Masters of America; Defence Manufacturers Association (Australian); Defense Mapping Agency; Delicatessen Managers Associa-

tion; Direct Mail Association; Division of Military Application; Dominion Marine Association

DMAA Direct Mail Advertising Association

DMAAC Defense Mapping Agency Aerospace Center

dmac dimethylacetamide (DMAC)

DMAC Des Moines Art Center

D.Ma.Eng. Doctor of Marine Engineering

DMAHC Defense Mapping Agency Hydrographic Center

D-man drug-enforcement officer

D Mark Deutsche Mark (German mark)—currency unit

DMATC Defense Mapping Agency Topographic Center

D.Math. Doctor of Mathematics

d-max density maximum

dmb dual-mode bus

Dmb Dumbarton

dmba dimethylbenzanthracene (DMBA)

dmbc direct material balance control

DMBC Detroit Motor Boat Club

dmbl demobilization; demobilize; demobilized

dmc digital microcircuit(ry); dimethylcarbinol (DMC)—insecticide; direct manufacturing cost(s); dough moulding compound

DMC Del Mar College; Democratic Movement for Change; Developing Member Country; District Materials Center

dmcl (DMCL) device media control language

dmctc dimethylchlortetracycline (DMCTC)

DM & CW Diploma in Maternity and Child Welfare

dmd demand; diamond; disc memory drive

Dmd Duchenne's muscular dystrophy

D.M.D. *Dentariae Medicinae Doctor* (Latin—Doctor of Dental Medicine)

dmdd demanded

dmdg demanding

dme distance measuring equipment

DME Designated Medical Examiner; Director of Mechanical Engineering; Director of Medical Education

DMEA Defense Minerals Exploration Administration

DMEA Dictionary of Mechanical Engineering Abbreviations

D.Mec.E. Doctor of Mechanical Engineering

D.Mech. Doctor of Mechanics

dmed digital message entry device

D.Med. Doctor of Medicine

D.M.Ed. Doctor of Musical Education

D-men drug-enforcement officers; narcotics officers

dmet distance-measuring equipment and tacan

D.Met. Doctor of Metallurgy

DMET Director(ate) of Marine Engineering Training

D.Met.Eng. Doctor of Metallurgical Engineering

D. Meteor. Doctor of Meteorology

dmetu (DMETU) dimethylethylthiourea

dmf decayed, missing, or filled (teeth)

DMF Decorative Marble Federation

DMFA Direct Mail Fundraisers Association

DMFOS Diploma in Maxillo-Facial and Oral Surgery

dmg damage; damaged; damaging

DMG Defense Marketing Group

D of M G Duchy (Duke) of Mecklenburg-Güstrow

DMGO Division(al) Machine-Gun Officer

dmh drop manhole

DMH Director of Mental Hygiene; Division of Mental Hygiene

dm/ha dry matter per hectare

DMHS Director of Medical and Health Services; Dolley Madison High School

dml defense mechanisms inventory

DMI Data Machines Incorporated; Data Management Inquiry; Department of Manufacturing Industry; Director(ate) of Military Intelligence

DMIAAI Diamond Manufacturers and Importers Association of America, Incorporated

DMIC Defense Metals Information Center (Batelle Memorial Institute)

D.Mi.Eng. Doctor of Mining Engineering

D.Mil.S. Doctor of Military Science

d-min density minimum

DMIR Duluth Mesabi and Iron Range (railroad)

DMJ Diploma in Medical Jurisprudence

dml demolish; demolition

dml (DML) data manipulation language; dimyristoyl lecithin

D.M.L. Doctor of Modern Languages

d mld depth moulded

DMLT Diploma in Medical Laboratory Technology

dmm digital multimeter

DMM Defense Market Measures; Directorate of Materiel Management

dmma Direct Mail/Marketing Association (abbreviated trade mark)

DMMA Direct Mail/Marketing Association (dmma)

dmmf dry mineral matter free

dmmp (DMMP) dimethyl-methyl phosphonate

dmn dimension; dimensional

Dmn Drammen

dmna (DMNA) dimethylnitrosamine

Dmn Fst *Damnation of Faust*

DMNH Delaware Museum of Natural History; Denver Museum of Natural History

dmnstr demonstrator

dmo demetallized oil

DMO Deputy Medical Officer; Director of Military Operations; District Medical Officer

dmod displacement-measuring optical device

DMO & I Director of Military Operations and Intelligence

dmp difference of meridional parts; dimethylphthalate (insect repellent also abbreviated DMP)

DMP Developing Mathematical Processes; Director of Manpower Planning; Dublin Metropolitan Police

dmpa depomedroxyprogesterone (DMPA)

DMPA Dublin Master Printers' Association

DMPB Diploma in Medical Pathology and Bacteriology

dmpea (DMPEA) dimethoxyphenylethylamine

dmpi desired mean point of impact

DMPL Des Moines Public Library

DMPP Duck Mountain Provincial Park (Manitoba and Saskatchewan)

dmpr damper

DMPS Deepwater Motion Picture System

DMR Data Management Routines; Defective Material Report; Department of Main Roads; Diploma in Medical Radiology; Director of Materials Research

DMRC Deering Milliken Research Corporation

DMRD Diploma in Medical Radio-Diagnosis

DMRE Diploma in Medical Radiology and Electrology

DMRT Diploma in Medical Radio-Therapy

dms dermatomyositis; diacritical marking system (DMS); digital multiplex switching; drums

DMS Data Management System; Decision Making System; Director of Medical Services; Disk Monitoring System; Display Management System; Division of Medical Standards; Dominion Mutual Securities

D.M.S. Doctor of Medical Science

D of M-S Duchy (Duke) of Mecklenburg-Schwerin

D.M.Sc. Doctor of Medical Science

DMSC Defense Medical Supply Center

DMSDS Direct Mail Shelter Development System

DMSE Developing Models for Special Education

DMSGR Dowd's Morass State Game Reserve (Victoria, Australia)

dmsh diminish

DMSI Directorate of Management and Support of Intelligence

dmso (DMSO) dimethyl sulfoxide

DMSP Defense Meteorological Satellite Program

DMSS Data Multiplex Subsystem; Director of Medical and Sanitary Services

dmst demonstrate; demonstration

dmstn demonstration

dmstr demonstrator

dmt demountable; dimethyltryptamine—DMT (dangerous hallucinogen)

DMT Department of Motor Transport(ation); Director(ate) of Military Training

DM & TS Department of Mines and Technical Surveys

dmu dual maneuvering unit

DMU Des Moines Union (railway)

D.Mus. Doctor of Music

D.Mus.A. Doctor of Musical Arts

D.Mus.Ed. Doctor of Musical Education

DMV Department of Motor Vehicles

D.M.V. Doctor of Veterinary Medicine

dmy dummy

DmZ demilitarized zone

dn debit note; decinem; dekanem; delta amplitude (symbol); dibucaine number; dicrotic notch; died near; down; downward

d'n damn

d/n (D/N) debit note

d & n dumb and numb (insensitivity factor)

d/N dextrose/nitrogen (ratio)

Dn Dale; Daniel; Dragoon(s)

Dⁿ *Don* (Spanish—title equivalent to "Sir")

DN Department of the Navy; Division Notice

D.N. Diploma in Nursing; Diploma in Nutrition

D of N Daughters of the Nile

D.N. *Dominus Noster* (Latin—Our Lord)

dna did not attend; does not answer

Dna *Doña* (Spanish—Lady)—Mrs

DNA Defense Nuclear Agency; desoxyribonucleic acid (chromosome and gene component)

DNA *Deutscher Normenausschusz* (German Committee on Standards)

DNAD Director of Naval Air Division

DNAN Department Number Assignment Notice

DNANR Department of Northern Affairs and National Resources

D.N.Arch. Doctor of Naval Architecture

dna(s) *docena(s)* [Spanish—dozen(s)]

DNase deoxyribonuclease

dnb departure from nucleate boiling; dinitrobenzene

DNB Distribution Number Bank

D.N.B. Diplomate of the National Board of Medical Examiners

DNB *Dictionary of National Biography*

dnc direct numerical control

DnC *Det Norske Creditbank* (The Norwegian Credit Bank) —also shown as *DNC*

DNC Democratic National Committee; Domestic National Committee; Director of Naval Construction

dncb dinitrochlorobenzene (DNCB)

DNCCC Defense National Communications Control Center

DNCMD Dayton Contract Management Office

dn ctl down control

dnd died a natural death

Dnd Dunedin

DND Department of National Defense; Department of National Development; Director of Navigation and Direction; Division of Narcotic Drugs (UN)

DN & D Director of Navigation and Direction

dne *douane* (French—customs)

DNE Director of Naval Equipment; Director of Nursing Education

D.N.Ed. Doctor of Nursing Education

D.N.Eng. Doctor of Naval Engineering

Dnepr (Russian—Dnieper)

DNES Director of Naval Education Service

dnf did not finish

dnfb dintrofluorobenzene

DNHW Department of National Health and Welfare (United Kingdom)

DNI Director of Naval Intelligence

DNI *Dana Normalisasi Indonesia* (Indonesian Institute of Standards)

DNIC Data Network Identification Code

DNII *Dirección Nacional de Información e Inteligencia* (Spanish—National Direction of Information and Intelligence)—Uruguay

dnj drone noise jammer

DNJ *Det Norske Justervesen* (Norwegian Bureau of Weights and Measures)

D.N.J.C. *Dominus Noster Jesus Christus* (Latin—Our Lord Jesus Christ)

Dnk Dunkirk

dnka did not keep appointment

dnl do not load; dynamic noise limiter

DNL Det Norske Luftfartselkap (Norwegian Airlines)

dnm data name

DNM Dinosaur National Monument

DNMS Director(ate) of Naval Medical Services; Division of Nuclear Materials Safeguards

DNO Director of Naval Ordnance; District Naval Office(r)

DNO *Den Norske Opera* (The Norwegian Opera)—Oslo

dnoc dinitro-orthocresol (DNOC)

d/note debit note

D-Note $500 bill

D-Notices Defense Notices

D-notice system British defense-notice system for protecting state secrets with the cooperation of the press

dnp do not publish

DNP 2, 4-dinitrophenol; Dinder National Park (Sudan)

dnpm dinitrophenyl morphine (DNPM)

D.N.P.P. *Dominus Noster Papa Pontifex* (Latin—Our Lord the Pope)

dnpt (DNPT) dinitrosopentamethylene tetramine

dnr does not run; do not renew

D/N r dextrose-to-nitrogen ratio

DNR Department of National Revenue; Department of Natural Resources; Director(ate) of Naval Recruiting

d/n ratio ratio of dextrose (glucose) to nitrogen in the urine

dns dinoyl sebacate (DNS)

Dns Downs

DNS Decimal Number System; Department of National Savings (British)

DNSA Diploma in Nursing Administration; Director of National Security Affairs

D.N.Sc. Doctor of Nursing Science

dnslp downslope

DNSS Defense Navigation Satellite System

dnt dinitrotoluene

DNT Director(ate) of Naval Training

DNTO Danish National Travel Office

dntp diethyl-nitrophenyl thiophosphate (DNTP)—insecticide

Dnus. *Dominus* (Latin—Lord)

DNV Det Norske Veritas (Norwegian ship classifier)

dnwind downwind

DNWR Darling National Wildlife Refuge (Florida); Delta NWR (Louisiana); Desert NWR (Nevada)

DNWS Director(ate) of Naval Weather Service(s)

do first tone in diatonic scale; *C* in fixed-do system

do. day(s) off; defense optics; delivery order; diamine oxidase (DO); diesel oil; direct order; dissolved oxygen; ditto; dropout; dual ownership

do' door

d-o dropout

d/o delivery order

do (Korean—island)

do. *dictum* (Latin—as before, the same); *ditto* (Italian—the same)

d:o: dito (Swedish—ditto)

d O *der (die, das) Obige* (German—the aforementioned)

Do Dominican; Dominican Republic; Dominican or Santo Domingan; Dornier

DO Defense Order; Department of Oceanography; Design Office; Director of Operations; Disbursing Office(r); District Office(r); Division(al) Office(r); Dominion Observatory; Dominion Office(r); Duty Officer

D.O. Doctor of Optometry; Doctor of Osteopathy

D/O Disbursing Officer

DO-27 Dornier 6-passenger utility aircraft built in West Germany and also called Skyservant

doa date of arrival; date of availability; dead on arrival; direction of approach; disposal of assets; dissolved oxygen analysis

DoA Department of Agriculture; Department of the Army (DOA)

DOA Dead on Arrival; Draft on Arrival

Doac Dubois oleic albumin complex

DOAE Defence Operational Analysis Establishment (UK)

DOAL *Deutsche Ost Afrika Linie* (German East Africa Line)

DOARS Donnelley Official Airline Reservations System

dob date of birth; degree of bend(ing); diameter overbark; disbursed operating base; doctor's order book

dob (DOB) 2.5-dimethoxy-4-bromoamphetamine (hallucinogen causing blood-vessel constriction leading to possible loss of limbs)

DoB Daughters of Bilitis

DOB Date of Birth; doctor's order book

DOB *Deutsche Oper Berlin* (German Opera of Berlin)

Dob(bin) Robert

Dobbs School for Girls State Training School for (delinquent) Girls at Kinston, North Carolina

'dobe adobe

dobe(s) doberman dog(s)

doc data optimizing computer; desoxycorticosterone (DOC); died of other causes; diesel oil cement; direct operating cost; doctor; doctoral; document; documentary; documentation; drive(s) other cars

doc (DOC) desoxycorticosterone

Doc doctor

DoC Department of Commerce

D o C Department of Correction (Arkansas, Connecticut, Delaware, Indiana, Masssachusetts, North Carolina, Tennessee); Department of Corrections (Arizona, California, District of Columbia, Florida, Guam, Idaho, Illinois, Kansas, Kentucky, Louisiana, Maine, Michigan, Minnesota, Mississippi, Missouri, New Jersey, Rhode Island, South Carolina, Texas, Vermont, Washington, West Virginia); Division of Corrections (Utah, Wisconsin)

D-o-C Doctors-on-Call

DOC Department of Commerce; Department of Communications; District Officer in Command; District Officer Commanding

doca data of current appointment; deoxycorticosterone acetate

DOCA Deoxycorticosterone Acetate

doce date of current enlistment

Doc.Eng. Doctor of Engineering

docg desoxycorticosterone glucoside (DOCG)

DOCIT Directors of Central Institutes of Technology (Australian)

DOCLINE Document Delivery On-Line (computer service)

docn documentation

Doc.Pol.Sci. Doctor of Political Science

DOCS Department of Correctional Services (NY)

Doct. Doctor (Latin—Doctor)

Doctª *Doctora* (Spanish—Doctor)—feminine

Doctor Angelicus (Latin—Angelic Doctor)—Italian scholastic philosopher Thomas Aquinas also known as the *Princeps Scholasticorum* (Prince of Scholastics)

Doctor Charlie Dr Charles Horace Mayo—co-founder of the Mayo Clinic (*see* Doctor Will)

Doctor Donne John Donne

Doctor Evangelicus (Latin—Evangelical Doctor)—religious reformer John Wickliffe

Doctor Holmes John Haynes Holmes (contemporary American Universalist minister who observed: *If Christians were Christians, there would be no anti-Semitism. Jesus was a Jew. There is nothing that the ordinary Christian so dislikes to remember as this awkward historical fact.*)

Doctor of the Industrial Revolution Dr Erasmus Darwin

Doctor Irrefragabilis Alexander of Hales

Doctor Jameson Sir Leander Starr Jameson

Doctor Johnson Doctor Samuel Johnson—critic, conversationalist, lexicographer

Doctor Livingston David Livingstone

Doctor Mirabilis (Latin—Admirable Doctor)—English savant Roger Bacon

Doctor of Revolution Erasmus Darwin

Doctor Rizal José Rizal (intellectual leader of Philippine insurrection against Spanish misrule)

Doctor Seuss author-cartoonist Theodore S. Geisel

Doctor Singularis (Latin—Singular Doctor)—William Occam

Doctor Subtilis (Latin—Subtle Doctor)—Duns Scotus

Doctor Universalis Albertus Magnus

Doctor Watson Dr John B Watson, M.D. of London; companion of the world-famous consulting detective Sherlock Holmes of 221-B Baker Street who with "My dear Watson" entered the mythology of almost modern times as literary creations of Sir Arthur Conan-Doyle

Doctor Will Dr William James

Mayo—co-founder with his brother Charles of the Mayo Foundation for Medical Education and Research at Rochester, Minnesota

docu document(ary)

docubio documentary biographee; documentary biographer; documentary biography

docudrama(s) documentary drama(s) (radio or tv)

docum document; documentary; documentation; documented

Documentary Photographer Alfred Stieglitz

documᵗᵒ *documento* (Spanish—document)

DOCUS Display-Oriented Computer Usage System

dod date of death; died of disease; dust of desuetude (usually unrelated to the grime of crime)

Dod Dodecanese

DoD Department of Defense

DOD date of death; Department of Defense; died of disease; Domestic Operations Division (CIA)

DODAS Digital Oceanographic Data Acquisition System

DoDCI Department of Defense Computer Institute

Dodd Dodd, Mead

DODD Department of Defense Directive

DoDDAC Department of Defense Damage Assessment Center

DoDDS Department of Defense Dependent Schools

Dod(dy) Dorothy

Dodec Dodecanese

Dodecanese Dodecanese Islanders; Dodecanese Islands

DODI Department of Defense Instruction

Dodo Islands Mascarene Islands of Mauritius, Réunion, and Rodrigues formerly inhabited by dodo birds

dodprt date of departure

doe. date of enlistment; dyspnea on exercise; dyspnea on exertion

DoE Department of Education (DoEd is better); Department of Energy (DoEn is better); Department of the Environment; Director(ate) of Education

DOE Department of Education (DoEd is better); Department of Energy (DoEn is better)

DoEd Department of Education

DoEn Department of Energy

DOES Disk-Oriented Engineering System

doesn't does not

dof degrees of freedom; delivery on field

DOF Defense Optics Facility; Developmental Optics Facility

dofab damned old fool about books

dofic domain-originated functional integrated circuit

DOFL Diamond Ordnance Fuze Laboratories

dog. disgruntled old graduate

Dogger Dogger Bank in the North Sea off England's east coast

dogm dogmatic; dogmatism; dogmatist

DOGMAD Dissatisfied Owners of General Motors Automotive Diesels

Dogwood state flower of North Carolina and Virginia

doh direct operating hours

Doh Doha

dohc double overhead cam; dual overhead cam

doi dead of injuries; descent orbit insertion

doi (Thai—mountain)

DoI Department of Industry; Department of the Interior (DoInt is better); Director(ate) of Information

D o I Department of Institutions (Montana); Department of the Interior; Director of Institutions (North Dakota); Division of Institutions (Oklahoma)

doin' doing

DoInt Department of the Interior

do/it digital output/input translator

DoJ Department of Justice

D Ø K Det Østasiatiske Kompagni (Royal Danish East Asiatic Company)

Dok Akad Nauk Doklady Akademii Nauk (Russian—Proceedings of the Academy of Science)—USSR

dol dear old lady; display-oriented language; dollar

dol (DOL) dioleoyl lecithin

dol dolce (Italian—sweet); *dolor* (Latin or Spanish—pain)—the *dol* is the unit of pain; *dolore* (Italian—pain)

Dol Dolph (Adolf); dolphin; Dorothea; Dorothy

DoL Department of Labor (Do Lab is better)

D o L Department of Labor; Department of Labour

D.o.L. Doctor of Oriental Learning

Do Lab Department of Labor

DOLARS Dynamic Preferential Runway System

dolciss dolcissimo (Italian—very sweetly)

Dolf Adolph; Adolphus; Rudolph

dolichocephs dolichocephalics (long-skulled people)

Doll Dorothy

Dollar Mark Mark Hanna

Dolley (Dolly) Mrs Dorothea (Dolley) Payne Madison (wife of President James Madison); Dorothea; Dorothy

dollies dolophine pills

dolo dolophine (methadone hydrochloride used as a morphine substitute in withdrawing addicts from heroin)

Dolomites Dolomite Alps of northeastern Italy

Dolores Dolores Hidalgo, Guanajuato, Mexico

Dolores del Rio Lolita Dolores Asunsolo de Martinez

DOLPHIN Dump Obsolete Laws—Prove Hypocrisy Isn't Necessary (Honolulu prostitutes' slogan)

dols dollars

dom date of marriage; digestible organic matter; dirty old man; division-owned material(s); domestic; domicile; dominant; dominion; drawn over man

drel

dom domenica (Italian—Sunday); *domingo* (Portuguese or Spanish—Sunday)

Dom Domain, Domenico; Dominic; Dominican; Dominican Republic; Dominion

Dom. Dominicus (Latin—of the Lord, as in *Dies Dominica*—the Lord's Day)

DOM Date of Marriage; dimethoxyalpha methyl phenethylmine (dangerous psychedelic drug also called STP)

D.O.M. Deo Optimo Maximo (Latin—to God the Best and the Greatest)—inscription found on some cemetery cornerstones and on labels of some benedictine bottles

DOMAINS Deep-Ocean Manned Instrument Station(s)

Dom Bk Domesday Book

Dom Can Dominion of Canada

Dom Day Dominion Day (celebrated in Canada July 1)

dom econ domestic economy (home economics)

DOMES Deep-Ocean Mining Experimental Study

dom ex domestic exchange

Dom Getulio President Getulio Dornelles Vargas of Brazil

domi domicile

domina distribution-oriented management information analyzer

Dominica Commonwealth of Dominica (formerly a British Windward Island and the most northern of the Windwards in the Caribbean)

Dominican Day Dominican Independence Day (February 27)

Dominican Ports (clockwise north to south) Pepillo Salcedo, Montecristi, Puerto Plata, Sosua, Santa Barbara de Samana, Sanchez, La Romana, San Pedro de Macoris, Andres, Santo Domingo (formerly Trujillo), Rio Jaina, Bahia de las Calderas, Azua, Barahona

Dominican Republic Spanish-speaking eastern half of Hispaniola in the West Indies where Santo Domingans produce tropical crops and valuable mineral exports, *República Dominicana*

Dominie Hawker Siddeley HS-125 jet transport

Dominion Dominion Day or Canada Day (July 1)

dom° domingo (Spanish—Sunday)

Dom° Domingo (man's name)

DOMO Dispensing Opticians Manufacturing Organization

Dom Pedro II Dom Pedro de Alcantara, emperor and president of Brazil

Dom.Proc. Domus Procerum (Latin—House of Lords)

Dom Rep Dominican Republic

DOMS Diploma in Ophthalmic Medicine and Surgery

domsat domestic communication satellite; domestic satellite carrier

dom sci domestic science

don' don't (do not)

don. donec (Latin—until)

Don Donald; Donegal

Don Donderdag (Dutch—Thursday); *Donnerstag* (German—Thursday); (Spanish—Lord and Master, from the Latin—dominus); *Don Quixote* (fantastic variations for cello and orchestra by Richard Strauss); The Don—Mozart's two-act comic opera—*Don Giovanni*

DoN Department of the Navy

Doña Fela Felisa Rincón (female mayor of San Juan, Puerto Rico for twenty-two years)

Donalbane Donald Bane

Doña Marina Malinche (Indian interpreter-mistress of Hernán Cortés—Spanish conqueror of Mexico)

Donatello Donato di Betto Bardi

Donau (German—Danube)

Donbas Donets Basin in the Ukraine

donec alv. sol. fuerit donec alvus soluta fuerit (Latin—until the bowels move)

Doneg Donegal (sometimes Don)

Don Emilio General Emilio Aguinaldo (fighter for Philippine independence)

Donets Donets Basin or Donbas of the Ukraine

Donets River City Kharkov in the Ukraine

Donetzk formerly Stalino in Stalin's time but originally Yuzovka

Don Francisco Francisco I Madero—Mexican president

Dong Phan Van Dong

Don Giovanni Don Juan

Don Juan Don Juan Tenorio of Seville (Mozart's *Don Giovanni*)

donk donkey; donkeyback; donkeyboiler; donkey boy; donkey breakfast (sailor's straw-stuffed mattress); donkeycart; donkey crosshead; donkey engine(man); donkey house; donkeyman; donkey pump; donkey puncher; donkey sled; donkey stack; donkeywork(man)

Don Marquis Donald Robert Perry Marquis

Don Muang Bangkok, Thailand's airport

Donnie Donald

Don Pepe José (Don Pepe) Figueres Ferrer—democratic leader of Costa Rica

Don Porfirio Don Porfirio Diaz —Mexican dictator-president

Don Q Don Quixote

Don Quixote pseudonym Alonso Quixano gave himself in *The Adventures of Don Quixote—Man of La Mancha*, by Cervantes

Don Romulo Romulo Betancourt—democratic leader and recent president of Venezuela

DONS Department of National Security (South Africa)

don't do not

Don't Give Up The Ship nickname of Captain James Lawrence, USN

do-nut doughnut

Don Venus Don Venustiano Carranza—Mexican general-president

Don Venustiano Don Venustiano Carranza—former president of Mexico

doo diesel oil odor

DOO Director—Office of Oceanography

doom. deep ocean optical measurement

Doornik Flemish place-name equivalent for Tournai

Doorstep to Canada Nova Scotia

dop dermo-optical perception; designated overhaul point; developing-out paper; dressing-out percentage

dop (DOP) diocytl phthalate

D o P Department of Prisons (Nevada)

dopa dynamic output printer analyzer

dopa (DOPA) dihydroxyphenylalanine

dopase dopa oxidase

Dope Capital of Canada Vancouver

D. Oph. Doctor of Ophthalmology

D.Ophth. Doctor of Ophthalmology

dopl doplene (Czech—enlarged)

dopp ped doppio pedale (Italian —double pedal)—musical term

d-o psychiatrists directive-organic psychiatrists

D.Opt. Doctor of Optometry

dor date of rank; dental operating room; digital optical recording; doric; dormitory

Dor Dorado; Doric; Dorothy

DoR Department of Rehabilitation

D. Or. Doctor of Oratory

DOR Department of Offender Rehabilitation (Georgia); Director(ate) of Operational Research

dora dynamic operators research apparatus; dynamic operators response apparatus

Dora Deborah; Dorothea; Dorothy; Eudora; Theodora

DORA Defence of the Realm Act

doran Doppler range and navigation

Dord Dordogne

DORDEC Domestic Refrigerator Development Council

Dordracum (Latin—Dordrecht) —Dutch city also called Dordrechtum or Dorteracum

Doric(k) Theodoric(k)

Dorie Doris; Theodora; Theodore

Doris Doreen; Dorothea; Dorothy; Eudora; Theodora

DORIS Direct Order Recording and Invoicing System

Doris Day Doris Kappelhoff

DORL Developmental Orbital Research Laboratory

dorm(s) dormitory; dormitories

dorna desoxyribose nucleic acid

Dornford Yates Cecil William Mercer's pseudonym

Dorothy Dix Elizabeth M Gilmer

Dorothy Gish Dorothy de Guiche

Dorothy Lamour Dorothy Kaumeyer

Dorothy Malone Dorothy Maloney

Dorothy Parker Dorothy Rothchild

dorp (Dutch—village)

Dors Dorset; Dorsetshire

Dorset Dorsethshire

Dort Dordrecht

DORT Detroit Objective Reference Test

D Orth Diploma in Orthodontics; Diploma in Orthoptics

dos date of sale; date of separation; dosage; dose; dosimetric; dosimetry; dosiology

dos. dosis (Latin—dose)

Dos John Dos Passos

DoS Department of State

DOS Date of Separation; Department of State; Digital Operation System; Disk Operating System

D.O.S. Doctor of Ocular Science; Doctor of Optical Science; Doctor of Optometric Science

Dosc Dubois oleic serum complex

DOSCO Dominion Steel and Coal Corporation

Dosh Univ Doshira University

dosim dosimetry (measurement of radiation doses)

DOSS Deep-Ocean Search System

Dosso Dossi palette name of

Giovanni de Lutero

DOST *Dictionary of the Older Scottish Tongue*

dosv deep ocean survey vehicle

dot. deep ocean transponder; deep-ocean technology; deep-oceanic turbulence; dotation(al); draft(s) on treasury

Dot Dorothy; Dotty

DoT Defense of the Territory; Department of Telecommunications; Department of Tourism; Department of Trade (United Kingdom); Department of Transport (Canada); Department of Transport(ation); Department of Transportation (US); Department of the Treasury

D o T Defense of the Territory; Department of Trade; Department of Transport; Department of Transportation

DOT Deep Oil Technology (company); Department of Overseas Trade; Diploma in Occupational Therapy

DOT *Dictionary of Occupational Titles*

DOTIPOS Deep Ocean Test-in-Place and Observation System

DOTM Department of Ordnance, Torpedoes, and Mines

Dott *Dottore* (Italian—Doctor)

D o T & T Dominion of Trinidad and Tobago

Dotty Doreen; Dorothea; Dorothy; Eudora

dou (DOU) definitive observation unit

Douanier (*see Le Douanier*)

Douay *Douay Version of the Bible* (published at Douai, France in 1609)

double-B double-backed; double-banked; double-barreled; double-bass; double-bedded; double-benched; double-bonded; double-bottomed; double-breasted; double-brooded

Double D Doubleday

Double-Vay Sir Henry Wilson's nickname among the French general staff of World War I

double-X doublecross; double quality; double quantity; double thickness; doubleweight; two-X; XX

doubt. doubtful

Doug Douglas(s)

Doug fir Douglas fir

Douglas Fairbanks Douglas Ulman

Douvres (French—Dover)

dov data over voice; double oil of vitriol (sulphuric acid)

Dov Dover; Dovid

dovap Doppler velocity and position

Dove Hawker-Siddeley twin-engine light transport carrying up to 11 passengers

Dover Delaware's capital named after an English Channel port; Dover Publications

Dover Strait narrow section of the English Channel called Pas de Calais by the French

dow died of wounds; dowager; dowel; dowelled

Dow Dowager

DOW Died of Wounds; Dow Chemical Company; Dow Chemicals

DoWaPO *Dictionary of Word and Phrase Origins*

dowb deep ocean work boat

Down Downing College, Cambridge

Down East Atlantic coast area extending from New York to Nova Scotia and particularly the coastal New England states

Down Easter person from eastern coast of New England or from Nova Scotia

downers nickname for sedative drugs also called sleeping pills or tranquilizers

Downing Street London street containing colonial and foreign offices as well as residence of the prime minister at number 10

Down South nickname shared by the federal penitentiary at Atlanta, Georgia and the southern United States

Down's syndrome mongolism resulting from mental retardation due to extra chromosome-21 material

Down Under Australia and New Zealand—both down under the Equator

Down Yonder coastal North Carolina's nickname

dows dowsing; dowsers

Doyen of European Diplomacy Prince Klemens Wenzel Nepomuk Lothar von Metternich

doz dozen

dozer bulldozer

dp damp proof(ing); dash pot (relay); data processing; deck piercing; deep penetration; deep pulse; deflection plate; departure point; dewpoint; diametral pitch; diastolic pres-

sure; diffusion pressure; digestible protein; diphosgene (deadly gas); diproprionate; disability pension; discriminatory power; disphosphate; displaced person; distopulpal; distribution point; donar's plasma; double paper; double pole; drip-proof; drop point; dump; durable press; potential difference (symbol)

dp (DP) data processing; dementia praecox

d/p delivery papers; documents against payment; door-to-port/port-to-door (delivery)

d & p developing and printing; development and printing; drain and purge

d.p. *directione propria* (Latin—with proper direction)

d/p *días plazo* (Spanish—pay days)

d. in p. *divide in partes* (Latin—divide)

DP by direction of the President; Democratic Party; Department of the Pacific; Detrucking Point; Director of the Port; Displaced Person

D-P Data-Phone

D.P. dementia praecox; Doctor of Pharmacy; Doctor of Podiatry

D & P Deberny and Peignot

D of P Daughters of Pennsylvania; Daughters of Pocahontas; Director of Planning; Director of Plans; Duchy (Duke) of Prussia

DP *Denver Post*

D.P. *Domus Procerum* (Latin—House of Lords)

dpa deferred payment account; diagnostic prescriptive arithmetic

dpa (DPA) diphenylamine; dipicolinic acid

dPA di Pietro Aretino

Dpa *Diputada* (Spanish—Deputy)—feminine

DPA Data Processing Agency; Data Protection Authority; Diabetes Press of America; Discharged Prisoners Association; Division of Performing Arts; Division of Public Affairs

D.P.A. Doctor of Public Administration

DPA *Deutsche Press Agentur* (German news agency); *Doulat i Padshahi ye Afghanistan* (Kingdom of Afghanistan)

d. in p. aeq. *divide in partes aequales* (Latin—divide into equal parts)

dpars data processing automatic record standardization

DPAS Discharged Prisoners' Aid Society

dpb deposit passbook

DPB Department of Printed Books (British Museum Library); Domestic Purposes Benefit

dpbc double pole both connected

dpc damp-proofing course; data processing computer; data processing control; double paper single cotton

DPC Daniel Payne College; Data Processing Center; Defense Plant Corporation; Defense Procurement Center; Defense Procurement Circular; Defense Production Chief; Deputy Police Commissioner; Desert Protective Council; Displaced Persons Commission; Dissemination Policy Council; District Police Commissioner; Division Planning Corporation; Duke Power Company

DPCE Data Processing Customer Engineering

dpcm differential pulse-code modulation

DPCP Department of Prices and Consumer Protection (British)

dpd data project directive; diffuse pulmonary disease

DPD Data Products Division (Stromberg-Carlson); Department of Public Dispensary; Diploma in Public Dentistry

DPD *Data Processing Digest*

dpdc double paper double cotton

dp di dimple die

DPDS Defense Property Disposal Service

dp dt double pole, double throw

dpe data processing equipment; digital processing effects; digital production effects; direct plate exposure

d-p-e development-printing-enlargement

Dpe Dieppe

DPE Diploma in Physical Education; Director of Primary Education; Director of Public Education

D.P.E. Doctor of Physical Education

D.Ped. Doctor of Pedagogy

DPED Department of Planning and Economic Development

DP/ED *Data Processing for Education*

dpe service developing-printing-enlarging service

DPEWS Designed-to-Price Electronic Warfare System

dpf deferred pay fund

DPf Deutsche Pfennig (German —pfennig)

dpfc double pole front connected

dpft double-pedestal flat-top (desk)

dpg data processing group; deck plate girder; digital pattern generator

dpg (DPG) diphosphoglyceric acid

DPG Dugway Proving Ground

DPGA Delaware Personnel and Guidance Association

DPGs Development Planning Groups

dph diamond pyramid hardness; diphenylhydantoin (DPH)

D. Ph. *Doctor Philosophiae* (Latin—Doctor of Philosophy)

DPH Department of Public Health; Department of Public Highways; Diploma in Public Health; Domestic Packing House

D.P.H. Doctor of Public Health

D.Pharm. Doctor of Pharmacy

DPHD Diploma in Public Health Dentistry

D.Phil. Doctor of Philosophy

DPHN Diploma in Public Health Nursing

d'phone dictaphone

D.Ph.Sc. Doctor of Physical Science

D Phys Med Diploma in Physical Medicine

dpi data processing installation

DPI Department of Primary Industries; Department of Public Information; Department of Public Instruction; Disorderly Persons Investigation; Distillation Products Industries; Division of Plant Industry

DPIF *Drug Product Information File*

DPII Dairy Products Improvement Institute

dp-ing data processing; durable pressing

dpir data processing and information retrieval

dpl deferred pastoral lease; deferred payment license; diploma; diplomat; dual propellant loading; duplex

dpl (DPL) dipalmitoyl lecithin

DPL Dallas Public Library; Dayton Power and Light; Dayton Public Library; Delhi Public Library; Denver Public Library; Detroit Public Library; diplomatic corps (license plate)

DP & L Dallas Power and Light

DPL *Den Polytekniske Laeranstalt* (Danish—The Polytechnic Institute)—Copenhagen

DP & LC Dundee, Perth & London (shipping) Company

dplx duplex

dpm data processing machine; disintegrations per minute; documents per minute

DPM Data Processing Manager; Deputy Prime Minister; Deputy Provost Marshal; Development Program Manual; Diploma in Psychological Medicine

D.P.M. Doctor of Pediatric Medicine

DPMA Data Processing Management Association

dpn diamond pyramid number

dpn (DPN) diphosphopyridine nucleotide

dpng deepening

dpnh (DPNH) reduced diphosphopyridine (same as nadh or NADH)

d pnl distribution panel

DPNM Devil's Postpile National Monument

dpo development planning objective

Dpo Depot (postal abbreviation)

Dpo *Diputado* (Spanish—Deputy)—masculine

DPO Dayton Philharmonic Orchestra; Distributing Post Office; District Pay Office(r)

dpob date and place of birth

D.Pol. Eco. Doctor of Political Economy

D.Pol.Sci. Doctor of Political Science

dpp deferred payment plan

DPP Director of Public Prosecutions; Disease Prevention Program

DPPS Department of Public Printing and Stationery

dpr day press rates; double lapping of pure rubber

DPR Democratic Peoples' Republic; Director(ate) of Public Relations

DPRGR *Dewan Perwakilan Ratjat-Gotong Rojong* (Indonesian—Mutual Cooperation House of Representatives)

DPRI Disaster Prevention Research Institute

DPRK Democratic People's Republic of Korea (North Korea)

DPRS Dynamic Preferential Runway System

dps double-pole snap switch

dp's (DPs) displaced persons

dp&s data processing and software

dPs displaced Palestinians

DPs Detention Pens

DP's displaced persons

DPS Data Processing Service; Data Processing Station; Data Processing System; Defense Printing Service; Department of Public Safety; Department of Public Safety (American Samoa); Division of Primary Standards; Domestic Policy Staff

DPSA Data Processing Supplies Association

DPSB Defense Production Supply Board (NATO)

DPSC Defense Personnel Support Center; Defense Petroleum Supply Center

DPSCS Department of Public Safety and Correctional Services (Maryland)

DPSS Data Processing Subsystem, Department of Public Social Services

dpst deposit

dp st double pole, single throw

DPsy Diploma in Psychiatry, Diploma in Psychology

D. Psch. Doctor of Psychology

D.Psy.Sci. Doctor of Psychological Science

dpt deeper-pool (pay) test (oil well); department; deponent; deposition; depth

dpt (DPT) dipropylphytamine

DPT Design Proof Test(ing)

Dpto *Departamento* (Spanish—Department)

dpt vaccines diphtheria, pertussis, tetanus vaccines

dptw double-pedestal typewriter (desk)

dpty deputy

dpu data processing unit

D.Pub.Adm. Doctor of Public Administration

dpv dry pipe valve; duty-paying value

dp/w drawbar pull/weight (ratio)

DPW Department of Public

Works

DPWA Data Processing Work Assignment

DPWG Defense Planning Working Group (NATO)

DPWO District of Public Works Office

dpx duplex

dq definite quantity; deterioration quotient; direct question(s)

dqd digital quadrature detection

dqm data quality monitors

DQMG Deputy Quartermaster General

DQMS Deputy Quartermaster Sergeant

DQU Deganawidah-Quetzalcoatl University (University of California at Davis)

dr debit; differential rate; door; double-reduction; drachma; dram; draw; drawn; drill; drive; drum

dr (DR) data register; dead reckoning; delivery room

d/r deposit receipt

Dr debtor; doctor; Drive; drachma (Greek monetary unit)

DR Data Report; Date of Rank; Dead Reckoning; Deficiency Report; Dental Recruit; Design Requirements; Despatch Rider; Detailed Report; Development Report; Document Report; National Distillers and Chemical Corporation (stock exchange symbol); reaction of degeneration (symbol)

D/R date of rank; dead reckoning

DR *Deutsche Reichsbahn* (German State Railway)

dra dead-reckoning analyzer

dr & a data reporting and accounting

dra *derecha* (Spanish—right)

Dra Draco (constellation)

Dra *Doctora* (Spanish—woman doctor)

Dra *Doctora* (Spanish—doctor) —feminine form; *Doutora* (Portuguese—doctor)— feminine form

Drac Draco

DRAC Director of the Royal Armoured Corps

dr ad drill adaptor

Dra Dna *Doctora Doña* (Spanish—Madam Doctor)

Dr.Ae.Sc. Doctor of Aeronautical Science

dragon symbol of China and the Chinese

Dragonfly Cessna T-37 jet-train-

er aircraft

Dragon Nation Bhutan

Dragon's Mouth Port-of-Spain, Trinidad's harbor entrance

Dr. Agr. Doctor of Agriculture

drai dead-reckoning analog indicator

drain. drainage

Draken (Swedish—Dragon)— Saab double-delta-wing supersonic fighter or fighter-bomber designated J-35 or S-35

Drakensberg (Afrikaans—Dragon Mountain)—range running from South Africa to Lesotho where it is called Quathlamba

dram. drama; dramatic; dramatist

dram. (DRAM) detection radar automatic monitoring

dram. pers. *dramatis personae* (Latin—cast of characters)

dr ap dram, apothecaries'

Draper Utah State Prison at Draper

drapes draperies

Drapier Jonathan Swift

Dr Arne Thomas Arne

dras *derechas* (Spanish—duties, fees, tariffs)

Dr Atl Gerardo Murillo

dr av dram avoirdupois

Drav Dravidian

draw. direct read after write; drawing

drb design requirements baseline

Drb Durban

DRB Defense Research Board (Canada); Discharge Review Board; Druggists' Research Bureau

DRBC Delaware River Basin Commission

dr bg drill bushing

Dr.Bi.Chem. Doctor of Biological Chemistry

DRBU Dharma Realm Buddhist University

Dr.Bus.Adm. Doctor of Business Administration

drc damage-risk criteria (noise-exposure limits); down right center (driving, lighting, or seating)

DRC Department of Rehabilitation and Correction (Ohio); District Recruiting Command(er); Driver Re-education Course; Drug Referral Center; Drug Rehabilitation Center; Dutch Reformed Church; Dynamics Research Corporation

drch drachma

Dr. Chem. Doctor of Chemistry

dr ck drill chuck

DRCOG Diploma of the Royal College of Obstetricians and Gynaecologists

Dr.Com. Doctor of Commerce

Dr D Doctor Don (Spanish—Sir Doctor)

DR & D Defense Research and Development

DRDO Defense Research and Development Organization

drdp detection radar data processing

DRDT Division of Reactor Development and Technology (AEC)

drdto detection-radar data take-off

dre dead reckoning equipment

DRE Defense Research Establishment (Canada); Department of Real Estate (California); Director of Religious Education

DR & E Defense Research and Engineering

D.R.E. Doctor of Religious Education

DREA Defense Research Establishment, Atlantic

Dream Capital of the Western World Hollywood, California

Dream King Ludwig II of Bavaria

drec detection-radar electronic component

Dr.Ec. Doctor of Economics

dred. dredging

DREE Department of Regional Economic Expansion (Canada)

Dreigroschen Die Dreigroschenoper (German—The Threepenny Opera)—Kurt Weill's modern reworking of the Beggar's Opera

drek dead reckoning

Dr.Eng. Doctor of Engineering

Dr.Ent. Doctor of Entomology

DREO Defense Research Establishment, Ottawa

DREP Defense Research Establishment, Pacific

Dres Doctores (Spanish—Doctors)

DRES Defense Research Establishment, Suffield

Dresda (Latin—Dresden)

Dresde (Spanish—Dresden)

Dr. es L. Docteur ès Lettres (French—Doctor of Letters)

Dr. es S. Docteur es Sciences (French—Doctor of Sciences)

Dress-Rehearsal Revolution Russian Revolution of 1905

DRET Defense Research Establishment, Toronto

DREV Defense Research Establishment, Valcartier

Drew Andrew; Charles E. Drew Postgraduate Medical School

drews (DREWS) direct readout equatorial satellite

drf differential reinforcement; dose reduction factor

DRF Deafness Relief Foundation; Direct Relief Foundation

drftmn draftsman

dr fx drill fixture

drg dorsal root ganglion; drawing(s); drogue; during

DRG Detroit Rubber Group; Dickinson Robinson Group

DRGM Deutsches Reichgebrauchsmuster (German registered design)

DRGs diagnosis-related groups

D & RGW Denver and Rio Grande Western (railroad)

DRH Division of Radiological Health

Dr. h.c. Doctor honoris causa (Latin—honorary doctor)

dr hd drill head

Dr.Hor. Doctor of Horticulture

Dr.Hy. Doctor of Hygiene

dri data rate indicator; data reduction interpreter; direct reduced iron; drive

DRI Dairy Research Institute; Data Resources Incorporated; Defense Research Institute; Denver Research Institute; Direct Relief International

drib deoxyribose

DRIC Dental Research Information Center

drid direct-readout image dissector

DRIFT Diagnostic Retrieval Information For Teachers

drill. drilling

DRINC Dairy Research Incorporated

D-ring capital-D-shaped ring

Dr. Ing. *Doktor-Ingenieur* (German—Doctor of Engineering)

drinkin' drinking

drip. digital ray and intensity projector

drir direct readout infrared

DRIS Department of Defense Retail Interservice Support Program

Drisheen City Cork, Ireland

DRIVE Developing Resources for Instructors of Vocational Education

driving under the influence short form meaning driving under the influence of alcohol and or

another drug

dr jg drill jig

Dr Drenthe (Dutch province)

Dr Jinnah Mohammed 'Ali Jinnah—president of All-India Moslem League and first governor-general of Pakistan

Dr.J.Sc. Doctor of Judicial Science

Dr. Jur. *Doctor Juris* (Latin—Doctor of Law)

drk dark; display request keyboard

DRK Deutsches Rotes Kreuz (German Red Cross)

Dr Karl Dr Karl Augustus Menninger

drl data retrieval language

DRL Design Report Letter; Diamond Research Laboratory

Dr.Lit. Doctor of Literature

DRLS Dispatch Rider Letter Service

drm direction of relative movement

DRM Drafting Room Manual

Dr Med *Doktor der Medizin* (German—Doctor of Medicine)

Dr. Med. *Doctor Medicinae* (Latin—Doctor of Medicine)

Dr.Mus. Doctor of Music

drn drawn

Drn Dairen; Darien

DRN Daily Reports Notice; Detroit River Navigation

drna (DRNA) desoxyribose nucleic acid

Dr.Nat.Sci. Doctor of Natural Science

drnt diagnostic roentgenology

dro destructive readout

dro (DRO) differential reinforcement of other behavior

dro derecho (Spanish—custom duty, right)

DRO Disablement Resettlement Office(r)

Droch Robert Bridges

drod delayed readout detector

DRO-LA Defense Research Office—Latin America (USA)

Droll Breughel Pieter Breughel the Elder

dromdi direct readout miss-distance indicator

'drome aerodrome; airdrome

'Drome Hippodrome

dron data reduction

Dronning Maud Land (Norwegian—Queen Maud Land)—Antarctic dependency of Norway

dros date returned from overseas

dros derechos (Spanish—duties,

fees, tariffs)

Drottningholm (Swedish—Queen's Island)—Sweden's royal summer castle

drp dead reckoning position

DRP Democratic Republican Party (Korean); Deutsches Reichspatent (German—patent); Diebold Research Program

DRP Deutsche Reichspartei (German Reich Party)

DRPA Delaware River Port Authority

DRPC Defense Research Policy Committee

Dr.P.H. Doctor of Public Health

Dr. Phil. *Doktor der Philosophie* (German—Doctor of Philosophy)

DRPL Del Rio Public Library

Dr.Pol.Sc. Doctor of Political Science(s)

DRPP Director(ate) of Research Programs and Planning

drps digital random program selector; drapes

drq discomfort relief quotient

DRR Drawing Release Record

Dr.Ra.Eng. Doctor of Radio Engineering

DRRB Data Requirements Review Board (DoD)

Dr.Rec. Doctor of Recreation

Dr.Re.Eng. Doctor of Refrigeration Engineering

DRRI Defense Race Relations Institute (DoD)

d-r-r-r-r-r-r-um snaredrum roll

drs data-reduction situation; data reduction system; digital range safety; drawers; drowsiness

DRs Development Rights; Discrepancy Reports

DRS Dairy Research Station; Data Reduction System; Data Relay Station; Debtor Reporting System; Development Reference Service; Diagnostic Research System; Diagnostic Rework Sheet(s); Document Retrieval System

Dr Salazar Antonio de Oliveira Salazar—dictator and prime minister of Portugal from 1932 to 1969

DRSAM Diploma of the Royal Scottish Academy of Music

drsc direct radarscope camera

Dr.Sc. Doctor of Science

Dr.Sci. Doctor of Science

DRSCS Digital Range-Safety Command System

Dr Seuss Theodor Seuss Geisel

dr sh drill shell

drsmkr dressmaker

drsn drifting snow

DRSO Danish Radio Symphony Orchestra

drsr dresser

DRSS Discrepancy Report Squawk Sheet

drt data review technique; dead reckoning tracer; dead reckoning trainer

dr t dram troy

Drt Dartmouth

DRT Diagnostic Rhyme Test

DRTC Documentation Research and Training Center

DRTE Defense Research Telecommunications Establishment (Canada)

Dr.Tech. Doctor of Technology

Dr.Theol. Doctor of Theology

Dr. Theol. *Doktor der Theologie* (German—Doctor of Theology)

dr tp drill template

dru digital register unit; digital remote unit

Dru Drusila

drub digital remote unit buffer

D.Ru.Eng. Doctor of Rural Engineering

Drug Abuse Drug Abuse Council

Drug-Addict Prostitute Center nickname applied to most metropolitan places

Drug Capital of America southeast Florida around the Miami area

drugola bribes given venal law-enforcement officers by narcotics dealers in exchange for protection from discovery and prosecution

Druk Yul Bhutan

Druk Yul (Tibetan—Realm of the Dragon)—Bhutan

Drum Roll Haydn's Symphony No. 103 in E-flat major

Dr und Vrl Druck und Verlag (German—printed and published by)

Dr.Uni.Par. Doctor of the University of Paris

D.Rur.Sci. Doctor of Rural Science

drv data-recovery vehicle

Drv Drive

DRV Democratic Republic of Vietnam (North Vietnam)

DRVN Democratic Republic of Vietnam

drvr driver

dr vs drill vise

drw defensive radio(logical) warfare; drawing

DRW Darwin, Australia (airport)

drwg drawing

DRWS Dirty Radwaste System

DRWW Distillery, Rectifying, Wine Workers (union)

drx drachma (Greek monetary unit)

Dr X Alan E Nourse

dry. drying

dry disco alcohol-free, drug-free, tobacco-free discotheque

dry ice solidified carbon dioxide

dry Spain Mediterranean coast of Spain

drzl drizzle

ds days after sight; day's sight; dead-air space; debenture stock; decanning scuttle; decimal selector; density standard; detached service; dilute strength; dioptric strength; direct support; discarding sabot; document signed; domestic service; donar's serum; double silk; double stout; double strength; double-screened; doublestitch(ed); downspout; draft stop

ds (DS) data set (data processing); duration series

d-s dead slow (ship's engine signal)

d.s. document signed

d/s dextrose in saline

d & s demand and supply; dermatology and syphilology; distribution and supply

ds destro (Italian—right)

Ds Down's syndrome; dysprosium (symbol)

Ds. Deus (Latin—God)

DS Date of Service; Delphian Society; Delta Society; Dental Surgeon; Department of Sanitation; Department of State; Design Standard(s); Detached Service; Direct Support; Directing Staff; Director of Services; Drill Ship; Drug Store; Durham & Southern (railroad)

D-S Deux-Sèvres; Ditlev-Simonsen Lines

D & S Durham & Southern Railway

D of S Daughters of Scotia; Department of State; Duchy (Duke) of Savoy; Duchy (Duke) of Silesia; Duchy (Duke) of Styria

DS Danske Standardiseringsraad (Danish Standards Institute)

D S dal segno (Italian—return

to the sign:*S:)*

D/S Dampskip (Norwegian—steamer, steamship)

dsa data set adapter; dial service assistance; dimensionally-stabilized anode; discrete sample analyzer

DSA Danish Sisterhood of America; Dante Society of America; Defense Shipping Authority; Defense Supply Agency; Defense Supply Association; Department of Substance Abuse; Deputy Sheriff's Association; Design Schedule Analysis; Division Service Area; Drum Seiners Association; Duluth, South Shore and Atlantic (railroad); Duodecimal Society of America

DSAA Defense Security Assistance Agency

DSAB Dictionary of South African Biography

dsabl disable; disability

DSACEUR Deputy Supreme Allied Command, Europe

DSAHBK Defense Supply Agency Handbook

DSAM Defense Supply Agency Manual

DSANZ Direct Selling Association of New Zealand

DSAO Diplomatic Service Administration Office(r)

DSAP Data Systems Automatic Program; Data Systems Automation Program; Defense Systems Application Program

DSARC Defense Systems Acquisition Review Council

dsas dial-service-assistance switchboard

D/S A/S Dampskipaksjeselskap (Norwegian—joint stock steamship company, limited)

dsasbl disassemble

DSASO Deputy Senior Air Staff Officer

dsb double sideband

DSB Danske Stats Baner (Danish State Railways); De Sola Brothers; Defense Science Board; Drug Supervisory Body (UN)

DSBA Delaware School Boards Association

dsbg disbursing

dsbn disband

dsc downstage center; dynamic standby computer

D.Sc. Doctor of Science

DSC Defense Supply Corporation; Delaware State College; Depot Supply Center; Die Casters' Conference; Distin-

guished Service Cross; Document Service Center

DSC (I) Die Sinkers' Conference (International)

D.S.C. Doctor of Christian Science; Doctor of Commercial Science; Doctor of Surgical Chiropody

D & SC Defense and Space Center (Westinghouse)

DSCA Douglas Social Credit Association

dscb data set control block

DSCC Deep Space Communications Complex

D.Sc.Com. Doctor of Science in Commerce

DSCDP Delaware State Central Data Processing

D.Sc.Eco. Doctor of Science in Economics

D.Sc.Eng. Doctor of Science in Engineering

D Sch Dmitri Shostakovich (in his *Tenth Symphony* uses his initials to form a four-note theme, applying German letters D, S for Es—E-flat, C, and H—German for B natural)

D.Sch.Mus. Doctor of School Music

D.Sc.Hyg. Doctor of Science in Hygiene

D.Sc.I. Doctor of Science in Industry

D.Sc.Jur. Doctor of the Science of Jurisprudence

D.Sc.L. Doctor of the Science of Law

DSCM Diploma of the Sydney Conservatorium of Music

DSCMD Dallas Contract Management District

D.Scn. Doctor of Scientology

D. Sc. Os. Doctor of the Science of Osteopathy

DSCP Detailed Site Characterization Plan

D.Sc.Pol. Doctor of Political Science(s)

DSCR Detailed Site Characterization Report

dscs direct-set cheese starter

DSCS Defense Satellite Communication System(s)

dsd dry surgical dressing

DSD Daily Staff Digest; Defence Signals Directorate (Australian); Director of Signals Division

DSDP Deep Sea Diving Project; Deep Sea Drilling Program; Deep Sea Drilling Project

DSDS Deep Sea Diving School (USN)

dse data-storage equipment; de-

pot support equipment; development support equipment

D.S.E. Doctor of Science in Economics

DSE Departamento de Seguridad del Estado (Spanish—Department of State Security)—Cuba

DSEA Davis Submerged Escape Apparatus; Delaware State Education Association

dsf day-second-feet (or foot)

Dsf Dusseldorf

DSF Dainippon Silk Foundation; Daughters of St Francis of Assisi; Division of Sea Fisheries

dsfc direct side force control

dsg designate; designation

DSG Deutsche Schlaf- und Speisewagen Gesellschaft (German Sleeping-and-Dining-Car Company)

dsgl desgleichen (German—ditto)

dsgn design; designed; designer

dsgnd designated

DSHC Defence Service Homes Corporation

dshe downstream heat exchanger

d s'horn dairy shorthorn

dsi data systems inquiry; digital speech interpolation

DSI Dairy Society International; Dalcroze Society Incorporated; Distilled Spirits Institute; Drinking Straw Institute

DSIA Diaper Service Institute of America

DSIATP Defense Sensor Interpretation and Application Training Program

DSIF Deep-Space Instrumentation Facility

dsipt dissipate

DSIR Department of Scientific and Industrial Research

DSIs Directorate of Service Intelligence members or operatives

DSIS Directorate of Scientific Information Services

D-site decoy site

dsj differential space justifier

Dsk Dvorak simplified keyboard

dsl deep scattering layer; diesel; doppler speed log

DSL Dampier Salt Ltd; Deep Scattering Layer; Defence Standards Laboratory; Delta Steamship Lines; Dickinson School of Law; Dominican Steamship Line

D & SL Denver and Salt Lake

(railroad)

DSL Directory of Special Libraries and Information Centers

DSLC Defense Logistics Services Center

D-sleep desynchronized sleep; rem sleep

dsl elec diesel electric

ds lt deck surface light

dsltd dry-salted (hides)

dsm dense-staining material; dried skim milk

d & sm dressed and standard matched (lumber)

DSM Des Moines, Iowa (airport); Development Shop Memorandum; Distinguished Service Medal; District Sales Manager

DSM Diagnostic and Statistical Manual (of mental disorders)

DSMC Defense Systems Management College

dsmd dismissed

D.S.Met.Eng. Doctor of Science in Metallurgical Engineering

DSMG Designated Systems Management Group

DSM Project Development of Substitute Materials (Manhattan Engineer District secret project from 1942 to 1947, responsible for development of A-bomb)

dsn design

DSN Deep Space Network; Department of School Nurses (NEA)

DSNA Dictionary Society of North America

dsnd descend

dsndi descend immediately

dsnrv double-swivel-nose reentry vehicle

DSNWR De Soto National Wildlife Refuge (Iowa)

dso data set optimizer; deck stowage only; direct shipment order; direct shipping ore

D.So. Doctor of Sociology

DSO Dallas Symphony Orchestra; Defence Systems Operator; Denver Symphony Orchestra; Detroit Symphony Orchestra; Distinguished Service Order; District Security Office(r); District Service Officer(r); District Staff Office(r); District Supply Office(r); Division Signal Officer; Duluth Symphony Orchestra

D.S.O. Doctor of the Science of Oratory

DSOC Democratic Socialist Organizing Committee

D.Soc.Sci. Doctor of Social

Science

dsorg data set organization

D.So.Se Doctor of Social Service

dsp (DSP) digital signal processing

d.s.p. decessit sine prole (Latin—died without issue)

DSP Defense Standardization Program; Democratic Socialist Party; Detroit Steel Products; Director of Selection and Personnel; Division Standard Practice

DS & P Duell, Sloan & Pearce

dspch dispatch; dispatcher

d spec(s) design specification(s)

dsph diopter spherical

dspl disposal

d.s.p.l. decessit sine prole legitima (Latin—died without legitimate issue)

dspln disciplinary; discipline

d.s.p.m. decessit sine prole mascula (Latin—died without male issue)

d.s.p.m.s. decessit sine prole mascula superstite (Latin—died without surviving male issue)

dspn disposition

dspo disposal; dispose; disposition

dsprsl dispersal

d.s.p.s. decessit sine prole superstite (Latin—died without surviving issue)

DSPS Dynamic Ship-Positioning System

d.s.p.v. decessit sine prole virile (Latin—died without male issue)

dsq discharged to sick quarters

D-squad death squad (composed of vigilantes)

dsr depolymerized scrap rubber; digit storage relay; digital stepping recorder

dsr (DSR) dynamic spatial reconstructor

ds&r data storage and retrieval; document search and retrieval

ds & r document search and retrieval

DSR Danmarks Radio (Danish radio and tv); Detroit Street Railways; Director of Scientific Research; District Sales Representative

DSRC David Sarnoff Research Center (RCA)

DSRD Director(ate) of Signals Research and Development

DSRK Deutsche Schiffs Revision und Klassifikation (German

Ship Revision and Classification)—society

dsRNA double-stranded ribonucleic acid

d's & r's dailies and rushes (motion-picture film editing)

DSRS Data Storage and Retrieval System

dsrv (DSRV) deep-submergence rescue vehicle

dss developmental sentence scoring; documents signed; dry surface storage

Dss Deaconess

DSS Data Systems Services; David S(olomon) Schwab; Deaf Supportive Services; Decision Support System; Defense Supply Service; Department of Supply and Services; Director(ate) of Statistical Services

DS & S Data Systems and Statistics

D.S.S. Doctor of Sacred Scripture; Doctor of Social Science

D S S & A Duluth, South Shore & Atlantic (railroad)

DSSc Diploma in Sanitary Science

DSSC Defense Subsistence Supply Center

DSSCS Defense Special Security Communications System (spoken of as *discus*)

DSSD Dry Surface Storage Demonstration

DSSH Department of Social Services and Housing

DSSL Delta Steamship Lines

DSSN Disbursing Station Symbol Number

DSSO Defense Surplus Sales Office; Duty Space Surveillance Officer

dssp deep sea submergence project

DSSRG Deep Submergence System Review Group

DSSS Division of Special Schools and Services

DSSSP Division of Student Support and Special Programs (Office of Education)

DSSV Deep Submergence Search Vehicle

dst door stop; drop survival time

DST Daylight Saving Time; Defense et Sécurité du Territoire (French equivalent of FBI); Dermatology and Syphilology Technician; Desensitization Test (for allergies); Director of Supplies and Transport; Double Summer Time

DS & T Directorate of Science

and Technology (CIA)

D.S.T. Doctor of Sacred Theology

d-std vehicle driver-seated vehicle

D.St.Eng. Doctor of Structural Engineering

d-stg vehicle driver-standing vehicle

dstl distill

dstn destination

DSTO Defence Sciences and Technology Organization (Australian); Divisional Sea Transport Office(r)

DSTP Director, Strategic Target Planning

dstpn dessert spoon

dstr distribution; distributor

dsu dissemination services unit; drum storage unit

DSUE Dictionary of Slang and Unconventional English

dsuh direct suggestion under hypnosis

dsuphtr desuperheater

D.Sur. Doctor of Surgery

D.Surg. Dental Surgeon

dsv double silk varnish

dsw door switch

DSW Department of Social Welfare

D.S.W. Doctor of Social Welfare

dsz decrement and skip on zero (calculator)

D Sz Diego Suarez

dt dead time; delirum tremens; dinette; diphtheria tetanus; double throw; double time; drain tile; dual tires

dt (DT) deep tank(s)

d-t deuterium-tritium; double-throw

d/t deaths (total ratio); dictaphone typist

d of t deed of trust

dt doit (French—debit)

Dt duration tetanus

DT Daylight Time; Dental Technician; Department of Tourism; Department of Transportation; Department of the Treasury; Detroit Terminal (railroad); Director of Transport(ation); Directorate of Tests; Distance Test; Distance Test(ing); Dylan Thomas

D.T. Dental Technician; Doctor of Theology

DT Daily Telegraph (London); *Danmarks Turistrad* (Danish Tourist Board)

dta daily travel allowance; development test article; differ-

ential thermal analysis; distributing terminal assembly; double tape armored cable

DTA Defense Transportation Administration; Development Test Article; Differential Thermal Analysis; Diploma in Tropical Agriculture; Divisão de Exploração dos Transportes Aéreos

D.T.A. Democratic-Turnhalle Alliance (of South-African oriented Namibians)

dtas diffuse thalamic activating system

DTASW Department of Torpedo and Anti-Submarine Warfare

dtbc disturbance

dtc deposit-taking company; design to cost; direct-to-consumer

DTC Department of Trade and Commerce

DTC Deutscher Touring Club (German Touring Club)

DTCD Diploma in Tuberculosis and Chest Diseases

D.T.Chem. Doctor of Technical Chemistry

DTCN Direction Technique des Constructions Navales (French —Technical Direction of Naval Construction)

DTCS Digital Test Command System

dt c sk don't countersink

dtcw data transfer command word

dtd dated; direct to disc (recording system)

d.t.d. detur talis dosis (Latin— let such a dose be given)

DTD Diploma in Tuberculosis; Director(ate) of Technical Development

DTD Dekoratie voor Trouwe Dienst (Dutch—Decoration for Loyal Service)

DTDRS Direct-to-Disc Recording System

dte data terminal equipment; development, test(ing), and evaluation; diagnostic test equipment; digital television equipment; diploma test of empathy (DTE)

D.Tech. Doctor of Technology

DTEE Division of Technology and Environmental Education

D.T.Eng. Doctor of Textile Engineering

dtf daily transaction file

DTF Deep Test(ing) Facilities; Dental Traders' Federation;

Division of Training and Facilities; Domestic Tariff Federation; Domestic Textiles Federation

dtfc differential temperature-flow controller

dtfcd define the file for card

dtfcn define the file for console

dtfda define the file for direct access

dtfdi define the file for device independence

dtfdr define the file data recorder

DT & FE Department of Technical and Further Education (Australian)

dtfis define the file for indexed sequential (files)

dtfmr define the file for magnetic reader

dtfmt define the file for magnetic tape

dtfor define the file for optical reader

dtfph define the file for physical input-output multiplexer

dtfpr define the file for printer

dtfpt define the file for paper tape

dtfsd define the file for sequential direct-access storage device

dtfsr define the file for serial device file

dtg data time group; date time group(ing); display transmission generator

Dtg Dienstag (German—Tuesday)

dth delayed-type hypersensitivity

D.Th. Doctor of Theology

DTH Diploma in Tropical Hygiene

D.Theol. Doctor of Theology

D ThPT Diploma in Theory and Practice of Teaching

dti dial test indicator

DTI Department of Trade and Industry (UK)

DT & I Detroit, Toledo and Ironton (railroad)

DTIC Defense Technical Information Center

d-time dream time

dt-ist drunkard

dtl detail; detailed; diode transistor logic

dtl (DTL) diode-transistor logic

DTL Detroit Testing Laboratory

dtm duration time modulation

Dtm Dortmund

DTM Diocesan Travelling Mission; Diploma in Tropical

Medicine

D.T.M. Doctor of Tropical Medicine

DTMB David Taylor Model Basin

DTMBAL David Taylor Model Basin Aerodynamics Laboratory

dtmf dual-tone multifrequency (telephone)

DTMH Diplomate of Tropical Medicine and Hygiene

DTMI Dairy Training and Merchandising Institute

dt mld draft moulded

DTMO Design Test and Mission Operations; Development Test and Mission Operations

DTMS Defense Traffic Management Service

dtn detain

dtn (DTN) diphtheria toxin, normal

DTN Defense Teleprinter Network

DTN Drug Trade News

DTNM Devil's Tower National Monument

DTNSRDC David Taylor Naval Ship Research and Development Center (USN)

dto detailed test objective; dollar tradeoff; due to

dto descuento (Spanish—discount)

dtº direito (Portuguese—right)

DTO Dental Therapists of Ontario; Director(ate) of Trade and Operations; Disbursing and Transport(ation) Office(r)

DTO Dansk Teknisk Oplysningstjeneste (Danish Technical Information Service)

dtol digital test-oriented language

dtp data tape punch; diphtheria, tetanus, pertussis (whooping cough)—combined vaccination

dtp (DTP) directory tape processor

DTP distal tingling on pressure

dtpb divider time pulse distributor

DTPEWS Design-to-Price Electronic Warfare System

dtps diffuse thalamic projection system

dtr data tape recorder; deep tendon reflexes; demand totalizing relay; double tax(ation) relief

dtr (DTR) distribution tape reel (data processing)

d/tr documents against trust re-

ceipt

DTR Diploma in Therapeutic Radiology

DTRA Defense Technical Review Agency (USA)

dtrm determine

DTRP Diploma in Town and Regional Planning

dtrt deteriorate; do the right thing

Dtrt Detroit

dts dense tar surfacing

dt's deep tanks; delerium tremens; dementia tremors

DTS Data Transmission System; Defense Telephone Service; Defense Transportation System; Dynamic Test Station

D & TS Detroit and Toledo Short Line (railroad)

Dtsch Deutsch (German—German)

DTSG Data Transmission Study Group

DTSS Dartmouth Time-Sharing System

dtt diphtheria tetanus toxin; duplicate title transferred

D of TT Dominion of Trinidad and Tobago

dt/tm delayed-time/telemetry

dtu data transfer unit; data transformation unit

DTU Delft Technical University

dtur departure

dtv diver transport vehicle

DTV Deutsche Taschenbuch Verlag (German Pocketbook Publisher)

DTVM Diploma in Tropical Veterinary Medicine

DTVP Developmental Test of Visual Perception

DTW Dance Theater Workshop; Detroit, Michigan (Detroit Metropolitan Airport)

dtx detoxification

Dtz Dutzend (German—dozen)

DTZ Division Tactical Zone (USA)

Dtzd Dutzend (German—dozen)

du density unknown; diagnosis undetermined; died unmarried; digital unit; distribution unit; dog unit; duodenal ulcer

Du Ducal; Duchy; Duke; Dutch

Du Dutch (Germanic language spoken by some 20 million people in the Netherlands and in its former overseas colonies in the East Indies, South America, and the West Indies); Dutch is akin to Flemish

and is understood by the Flemings of Belgium and Flanders

DU Dalhousie University; Deakin University; Denison University; diagnosis undetermined; Dillard University; Drake University; Drew University; Duke University; Duquesne University

du 26 ct du 26 mois courant (French—the 26th of this month)

dua digital uplink assembly

DUA Digitronics Users Association

Duacum (Latin—Douai)

DUADS Duluth Air Defense Sector

DUAH Department of Urban Affairs and Housing

dual. dynamic universal assembly language

DUAL Data Use and Access Laboratories

Dual Cities Minneapolis and Saint Paul, Minnesota

Dual Protectorate Andorra under the protection of France and Spain

dub. diameter underbark; double; dubber; dubbing; dubious

dub. dubius (Latin—dubious)

Dub Dublin

DUB Dublin, Eire (airport)

DUBC Durham University Boat Club

Dubini's disease rapid and rhythmic muscular contraction

Dubl Dublin; Dubliner

Dublin Ireland's capital officially named Baile Atha Cliath in Gaelic

Dublinum (Latin—Dublin); (Latin — Dublin) — also known as Eblana

Dubrovnik Yugoslavian port city formerly called Ragusa

DUBS Durham University Business School

duc demonstration unity capsule

DUC Datatron Users Organization; Distinguished Unit Citation; Durban University College

D.U.C. Doctor of the University of Calgary

Duca Minimo Gabriele D'Annunzio

Duce (Italian—Leader)—Dictator Benito Mussolini

Duchenne de Boulogne Guillaume-Benjamin-Amand Duchenne—father of modern neurology

Duchess of Dupont Circle Alice Roosevelt Longworth

Duchess of Windsor Bessie Wallis Warfield

Duck Mountain Duck Mountain Provincial Park in western Manitoba and adjacent Saskatchewan

Ducky Joe Medwick

DUCS Deep Underground Communications System

duct. ductile

duct (Latin prefix—conduct or lead)—conductor, ductless

Dud Dudley

dudat due date

Dude Ranch Capital Wickenburg, Arizona

DUF Democratic Unification Party (Korean)

Duff Duffield; Duffle; Mc Duff

DUFFEL Dutch Far East Lines

Du Fl Dutch Flemish

DUH Duke University Hospital

dui driving under the influence (of alcohol and/or drugs)

Duitsland (Dutch—Germany)

Duke Marmaduke; The Duke, actor John Wayne

Duke of the Abruzzi Italian alpinist and arctic explorer Prince Luigi Amadeo Giuseppe Maria Ferdinando Francesco

Duke of Alba Fernando Alvarez de Toledo

Duke of Buckingham George Villiers

Duke City Albuquerque, New Mexico (named for El Duque de Alburquerque, a Spanish nobleman who wrote his surname with two r's)

Duke of Devonshire William Cavendish (former Prime Minister of Great Britain like so many of the following dukes)

Duke Ellington Edward Kennedy Ellington

Duke of Grafton Augustus Henry Fitzroy

Duke of Newcastle Thomas Pelham-Holles

Duke of Portland William Henry Cavendish Bentinck

Duke of Shrewsbury Charles Talbot

Duke of Vicenza Marquis Louis de Caulaincourt

Duke of Wellington Arthur Wellesley

Duke of Windsor (formerly King Edward VIII, formerly Prince

of Wales when his father, George V, was king of England)

dukw (DUKW) code letters, pronounced *duck*, for an amphibious automotive vehicle

DUKW amphibious truck

Dul Duluth

DUL Duke University Library; Durham University Library

Dulag Durchgangslager (German—prisoner-of-war transit camp)

dulc. dulcis (Latin—sweet)

Dulles John Foster Dulles International Airport named for a former secretary of state and serving Washington, D.C. along with the Baltimore-Washington and National airports

Dullsville nickname of any dull place anywhere

du'log duolog (conversation wherein the conversants talk without listening to one another)

Duluthians people of Duluth

DUM Dublin University Mission(aries)

Dumas fils Dumas the son, Alexandre Dumas (1824–1895) playright-creator of Camille (Verdi's *La Traviata*), son of the novelist

Dumas père Dumas the father, Alexandre Dumas (1802–1870), author of *The Count of Monte Cristo, The Three Musketeers,* etc., father of the playright

Du Maurier George Louis Palmella Busson

Dumb Dumbarton

DUMB Deep Underground Missile Basing

Dumb Girl Dumb Girl of Portici (Auber's five-act opera—*La Muette de Portici*)

DUMBO seaplane used for rescue work (naval symbol) Duke University Medical Center

Dumf Dumfries

Dumf & Gall Dumfries and Galloway

Dumky Dvořák's Trio (opus 90) for violin, piano, and cello; name comes from a Czechoslovakian term meaning a musical lament

dums deep unmanned submersibles

dun. dunnage

Dun Dun Laoghaire (Dunleary); Dunbar; Duncan; Dundalk; Dundas; Dundee; Dundren-

nan; Dunedin; Dunellen; Dunelm; Dunfermline; Dungarvan; Dungeness; Dunglas; Dunglison; Dunlap; Dunlop; Dunmore; Dunn; Dunnachie; Dunning; Dunnsville; Dunoon; Dunscore; Dunsmuir; Dunstable; Dunstan; Dunvegan; Dunwood; Dunwoody

Dunb Dunbarton

dunc deep underwater nuclear counter

Dunc Duncan

Duncan Island, Galápagos Pinzón

Dunedin nickname for Edinburgh, Scotland and placename for a South Island, New Zealand port as well as a Florida resort near St Petersburg

Dun Edin (Celtic—Edwin's burgh)—Edinburgh

Dunelm Dunelmensis (Latin—of Durham)

Dunelmia (Latin—Durham)

Dungeness Crab Capital Newport, Oregon

D.Univ. Doctor of the University

Dunk Dunkerque (Dunkirk)

Dunkerque (French—Dunkirk)

Dun Laoghaire (Gaelic—Dunleary)—modern name for Kingstown on Dublin Bay

Dunleary Dun Laoghaire or Kingstown

Dunleary (Gaelic Irish—Dun Laoghaire)

Dunnet Head northernmost point on Scotland's mainland although John o'Groats to the east is popularly believed to be the northernmost point

Dunquerque (Spanish—Dunkirk)

DUNS Data Universal Numbering System

Dunsany Edward John Moreton Drax Plunkett, Lord Dunsany

duo. duodecimo

duod duodenum

duodec duodecimo

dup duplicate; duplicating; duplication

DUP Diplomate of the University of Paris; Duquesne University Press

D.U.P. Docteur de l'Université de Paris (French—Doctor of the University of Paris)—the Sorbonne

du pa duplicating pattern

DUPA Drug Users Parent Aid

dup^do duplicado (Spanish—duplicate)

dupe. duplicate; duplicate copy

dupe. neg duplicate negative
dupes. duplicates; duplicate copies
dupl duplicate; duplication
dupli duplicate; duplicated; duplication
DUPONT EI du Pont de Nemours & Company
Dupontonia Wilmington, Delaware
Dupont Town Wilmington, Delaware (home of EI du Pont de Nemours & Co)
dur duration
dur (Latin prefix—hard)—durable
dur. duris (Latin—hard)
Dur Durango (natives nicknamed alacranes—Spanish term for scorpions as they abound in this Mexican state); Durban; Durham
Dur (German—major musical key)
Duraks Durak Ranges of northernmost Western Australia
duralumin durable aluminum-copper-magnesium-manganese alloy
Durazzo English and Italian place-name equivalent for the Albanian port of Durrës
Durban formerly Port Natal, South Africa
DURD Department of Urban and Regional Development
dur. dolor. durante dolore (Latin—as long as the pain lasts)
Durf Durfee's Reports
durg during
durgc during climb
durgd during descent
Durh Durham
Dur Mus Durban Museum
Durobrivae (Latin—Rochester)
Durocortorum (Latin—Rheims)
Duroverum (Latin—Canterbury)
Durrës (Albanian—Durazzo)
DUS Düsseldorf, Germany (airport)
DUSA Defense Union of South Africa
DUSA Dispensatory of the United States of America
dusam dummy surface-to-air missile
DUSC Deep Underground Support Center (USAF)
dus/testing distinctness, uniformity, and stability testing
DUSW Director(ate) of the Undersurface Warfare Division
dut device under test(ing); dunnage untreated
Dut Dutch; Dutch Harbor

dutch dutch belted (black dairy cattle with a broad body-encircling white belt of hair as originally bred in the Netherlands); dutch door (horizontally divided so either the top or bottom section may be closed or opened); dutch courage (inspired by alcohol); Dutch Harbor (U.S. naval base on Alaska's Unalaska Island); dutch lunch (cold cuts); dutch treat (where all pay their own way for drinks, entertainment, or food); all other dutch connections or items
dutch act suicide
Dutch Caribees colonial name for the Netherlands Antilles
Dutch City Holland, Michigan
Dutch Cradle of U.S. Presidents the Netherlands—ancestral home of both Presidents named Roosevelt and President Van Buren
Dutch Delight Delft's nickname
Dutch East Indies unofficial name for the Netherlands East Indies now known as Indonesia
Dutch Guiana Netherlands Guiana or Surinam
Dutch Islands Dutch West Indies Islands [Aruba, Bonaire, Curaçao, Saba, Sint Eustatius (Statia), Sint Maarten]
Dutchman The Flying Dutchman (Wagner three-act opera whose German title is *Der Fliegende Holländer*)
Dutch Masterpiece in the Caribbean Curaçao
Dutch Microscopists Zacharias Janssen credited with the invention of the compound microscope plus two compatriots who improved upon his design, Anton van Leeuwenhoek and Jan Swammerdam
Dutch New Guinea West Irian, Indonesia formerly Netherlands New Guinea
Dutch Ports (northeast to southwest) Delfzigl, Harlingen, Den Helder, Ijmuiden, Zaandam, Amsterdam, Scheveningen, Hoek van Holland, Europoort, Maasluis, Vandelingenplaat, Vlaardingen, Schiedam, Rotterdam, Dordrecht, Middelharnis, Willemstad, Middelburg, Vlissingen, Terneuzen, Hansweert, Haven Catzand
Dutch Quartet the Netherlands contained many of the earliest composers of classical music

including Wagenaar, Pijper, Badings, and Otterloo (arranged in chronological order)
Dutch Reformed Dutch Reformed Church of North America where it has been called the Reformed Church since 1867
Dutch Republic the Netherlands sometimes called Holland although Holland is but one of its eleven provinces
Dutch-speaking Places Flemish sections of Belgium; the Netherlands; colonies and former colonies of the Netherlands such as Aruba, Bonaire, Curaçao, Saba, Sint Eustatius, Sint Maarten—the Netherlands Antilles; Netherlands New Guinea now part of Indonesia formerly the Netherlands East Indies; Netherlands Guiana or Surinam and the Dutch-speaking community in and around Holland, Michigan
Dutch Ultramodernist Pieter Cornelis Mondriaan
Dutch West Indies the Netherlands Antilles
Dutch William William III of Orange—Dutch-born British king
Dutton EP Dutton & Co
Dutz Dutzend (German—dozen)
duv data under voice
duvd direct ultrasonic visualization of defects
Duvres (Spanish—Dover)
dv dependent variable; device; dilute volume; direct vision; distemper virus, distinguished visitor; dive; double vibrations; double vision
d.v. dorsiventral
d/v declared value
d & v diarrhea and vomiting
d/v días vista (Spanish—days at sight)
DV Diploma in Venereology; Douay Version
D/V Discovery Vessel
D.V. Deo volente (Latin—God willing)
dva dynamic visual acuity
DVA Department of Veterans Affairs; Distribuidora Venezolana de Azucareros (Venezuelan Sugar Growers Distributing Organization)
D.V.A. Doctor of Visual Aids
D-value death value (minutes needed for a lethal agent or

environment to kill the population)

dvars doppler velocity altimeter radar set

dva test duration of voluntary apnoea test

DVC Diablo Valley College; Deputy Vice-Chancellor

DVCSA Delaware Valley College of Science and Agriculture

dvd direct-view device

DV & D Diploma in Venereology and Dermatology

DVDP Dry Valley Drilling Project

dve device end

Dve Drive

DVECC Disease Vector Ecology and Control Center

d Verf der Verfasser (German— the author)

DVES Defense Value Engineering Services

dvfr defense visual flight rules

dvg digital video generator

DVH Diploma in Veterinary Hygiene; Division for the Visually Handicapped

dvin deviation

dvl direct voice line

dvlp development

dvm digital voltmeter

d.v.m. *decessit vita matris* (Latin —he died during his mother's lifetime)

D.V.M. Doctor of Veterinary Medicine

D.V.M.S. Doctor of Veterinary Medicine and Surgery

DvN D. Van Nostrand

DVNM Death Valley National Monument

Dvnport Devonport

Dvo Davao

DVO Divisional Veterinary Office(r)

dvom digital volt ohmmeter

Dvořák's 9 Dvořák's nine symphonies including *Bells of Zlonice* (No. 1) and *From the New World* (No. 9)

dvp differential value profile; direct vision panel

d.v.p. *decessit vita patris* (Latin —he died during his father's lifetime)

DVPH Diploma in Veterinary Public Health

dvppi daylight-view plan-position indicator

dvr driver

DVR Division of Vocational Rehabilitation

D.V.R. Doctor of Veterinary Radiology

dvrg diverge

dvrsn diversion

dvs *det vill säga* (Swedish—that is); *det vil si* (Norwegian—that is); *det vil sige* (Danish—that is)

DVS Division of Vital Statistics

D.V.S. Doctor of Veterinary Surgery

D.V.Sc. Doctor of Veterinary Science

DVSL District Venture Scout Leader

DVSM Diploma of Veterinary State Medicine

dvst direct-view storage tube

dvt deep venous thrombosis

DVTE Division of Vocational and Technical Education

DVTI De Vry Technical Institute

dvtl dovetail

Dvwp Deo volente, weather permitting (God willing, weather permitting)

dw data word(ing); deadweight; delivered weight; developed width; diameter width; dishwasher; distilled water; double weight; dry wine; dumbwaiter; dust wrapper

d/w dextrose in water; dock warrant

DW Defenders of Wildlife; Department of Waters

dwa double wire armor(ed)

DWA Deadly Weapons Act; Distributive Workers of America

DWAA Dog Writers' Association of America

dwb double with bath

dwba direct-wire burglar alarm

dwc deadweight capacity

dwcc deadweight cargo capacity

DWCHS De Witt Clinton High School

DWCP Detroit-Wayne County Port

dwd died while drinking; driving while drunk; dumbwaiter door

dw di draw die

DWDL Donald W Douglas Laboratory

dwel dwelling

Dwellers of the Field the Poles

dwf divorced white female

dw fm draw form

dwg drawing; dwelling

DWG Diamond Walnut Growers

dwg-ho dwelling house

DWGNRA Delaware Water Gap National Recreation Area

(New Jersey and Pennsylvania)

dwi driving while intoxicated

DWI Descriptive Word Index; Durable Woods Institute; Durham Wheat Institute; Dutch West Indies (Netherlands Antilles)

DWIC Disaster Welfare Inquiry Center

Dwig Dwiggins

dwim do what I mean

DWK *Deutsche Gesellschaft für Wiederraufarbeitung von Kernbrennstoffen* (German— Society for Reprocessing Nuclear Waste); *Die Wit Kommando* (Afrikaans—The White Commando)—underground white vigilantes claiming credit for many bombings and death threats to black religious leaders in South Africa

dwl derived working level; designed waterline; displacement waterline; dowel

dwm dangerous waste material; deadweight machine(ry); divorced white male

DWM Deutsche Waffen und Munitionsfabriken

dwn down

dwndfts downdrafts

dwo delta-wing orbiter

DWOP Denver War On Poverty

dwp deepwater port

DWP Department of Water and Power

D W & P Duluth, Winnipeg & Pacific (railroad)

DWPF Defense Waste Processing Facility (Savannah River)

dwpnt dewpoint

dwr drawer

DWR Duke of Wellington's Regiment

dws drop wood siding; double white silk

DWS Department of Water Supply

DWSG & E Department of Water Supply, Gas, and Electricity

DWSO Drainage and Water Supply Office(r)

dwt deadweight ton(nage)(s); denarius weight; double weight; pennyweight

DWT *Deutsche Gesellschaft für Wehrtechnik* (German Society for Defense Technology)

dw tk drinking water tank

dwuld dewooled (skins)

dwv drain, waste, and vent (pipe)

dww downward

dwz *dat wil zeggen* (Dutch—that is to say)

dx de luxe; dextran; diagnosis; distance (radio); double cash ruled; duplex; static (symbol)

dx (DX) defense exhibit

Dx diagnosis (medical)

DX Aerotaxi (Colombia); distance radio reception or transmission; Sun Ray Mid-Continent Oil (stock exchange symbol)

dxc data exchange control

DXC Penn-Dixie Cement (stock exchange symbol)

dxd discontinued

dxda-mc ductile metals experimental diamond abrasive—metal clad

dxer (DX-er) long-distance radio receptionist

dx-ing long-distance (radio) communicating

dxm dexamethasone

dxr deep X-ray

dxrt deep X-ray therapy

dXt deep X-ray therapy

dy delivery; demy (paper); dockyard; duty; penny (nails)

Dy Dylan; dysprosium

Dy *Douay Bible* (Roman-Catholic English translation of the Latin Vulgate made at Douay and Rheims in 1610)

D-y *Druk-yul* (Bhutanese—Bhutan)

DY De Young Memorial Museum; Druk-Yul (Kingdom of Bhutan)

DYA Department of Youth Authority (California)

dyana dynamics analyzer

dyb do your best; dynamic braking

dy bf hl day before holiday

DYC Detroit Yacht Club; Dominion Yeast Company

dyd dockyard

dydff dyed and fully finished (leather)

dye. dyeing

dyf damned young fool

DYF Democratic Youth Front

dy fl hl day following holiday

DYFS Division of Youth and Family Services

dyk (Dutch—dam, dike)

dyke bulldike

dykes diagonal wire cutters

dymaxion dynamic maximum

DYMM M.H. De Young Memorial Museum

DYMM (Malay—His Highness the Ruler or Her Highness the Ruler)

dyn dynamic; dynamics; dynamo; dynamometer; dyne

dyna dynamite

dynam dynamic; dynamics; dynamite; dynamo

dynamit dynamic allocation of manufacturing inventory and time

dynamo. dynamic model

DYNAMO Dynamic Action Management Operation

dynasoar dynamic soaring (space flight)

dynatac dynamic adaptive total area coverage

dyncm dyne centimeter

dynmt dynamite

dyno dynamite, undiluted drugs; dynamometer

dypao dypsomania(c)

dy r dynamic response

dys (Latin prefix—bad, difficult; painful)—dysentery, dyspepsia

DYS Department of Youth Services; Department of Youth Services (Alabama); Division of Youth Services; Division of Youth Services (Arkansas)

dysac digitally simulated analog computer

dysen dysentery

dyslex dyslexia; dyslexic

dysm dysmenorrhea

dysp dyspepsia

dysphem dysphemistic(al)(ly); dysphemism(s)—antonym(s) for euphemism(s)

dystac dynamic storage analog computer

dystal dynamic storage allocation language

dysto dystopia(n)

dystope(s) dystopian(s)—slum dweller(s) leading a fear-filled and wretched existence

dyu do your utmost

DYW Dynamic Youth Workers

dz dizygotic; dizziness; dizzy; dozen; drizzle

dz *deppelzentner* (German—100 kilograms); *distance zénithale* (French—zenith distance)

d Z der Zeit (German—of the time)

Dz Deniz (Turkish—sea)

DZ Department of Zoology; Drop Zone

D.Z. Doctor of Zoology

DZA Drop Zone Area

Dzerzhinsky Academy KGB School (in Moscow where it bears the name of the first head of the Soviet secret service)

DZF *Deutsche Zentrale für Fremdenverhkehr* (German National Tourist Association)

dzg dizygotic

Dzl Delfzijl (Dutch port)

dzne *douzaine* (French—dozen)

D.Zool. Doctor of Zoology

dzt digit zero trigger

D-Zug *Durchgangszug* (German—express train, through train)

Dzun Dzungaria

Dzungaria Sungaria or Zungaria region between Mongolia and Russia

E

e base for natural logarithms 2.7182818; coefficient of impact (symbol); electron; emulsifier; emulsion; error; errors; exa(E)—10^{18} (one quintillion); longitudinal strain per unit length (symbol); numerical value of electron charge in an electron or proton (symbol)

'e he

e angle of downwash (symbol); natural logarithmic (Napierian) base; (Portuguese—and)—not an abbreviation; (Spanish—and)—not an abbreviation but used when the following word begins with *i* or *hi* as in *Juana e Ignacio* or *padre e hijo*

e/ *envío* (Spanish—sent)

E American Export-Isbrandtsen Lines; Eagle Airways; Earth; east; eccentricity of a curve (symbol); Echo—code for letter E; Edinburgh; efficiency; einsteinium; emmetropia; engineer; engineering; England; English; Equator; equatorial; erbium; estimated weight (symbol); excellent; exempt; eye; Fraunhofer line caused by iron (symbol); instantaneous value alternating current (symbol); modulus of elasticity (symbol)

E east; Einstein unit of energy (symbol); electromotive force (symbol); (Latin—*Egregius*); *en* (Dutch, Portuguese, Spanish—in); Envoy Extraordinary and Minister Plenipotentiary; *est* (French or Italian—east); *este* (Portuguese or Spanish—east); *etelä* (Finnish—south); experiment (symbol); voltage (symbol)

E^1 Lhotse I (27,890-ft adjoining peak of Mount Everest, world's highest mountain—29,028 ft)

E1, E2, etc. East One, East Two, etc. (London postal zones)

E-2 Hawkeye airborne early-warning and fighter-control aircraft

E^2 Lhotse II (27,560-ft adjoining peak of Mount Everest)

E-14 Hispano Saeta twin-engine jet trainer, also designated HA-200

E 107 tribromoethanol (anesthetic)

E 605 parathion (deadly insecticide)

ea each; ends annealed; enemy aircraft; enlistment allowance

ea (EA) educational age

e/a (E/A) experimental aircraft

EA East Africa(n); Eastern Air Lines; Economic Adviser; educational age; Egyptian Army; Electrical Artificer; Electronic Artificer; Electronic Associates; Environmental Agency; Environmental Assessment; expectancy age; experimental aircraft

E/A Ecology Action; enemy aircraft

EA *Ente Autonomo* (Italian—Autonomous Corporation)

EA-6B Grumman electronic-intelligence-gathering aircraft named Intruder

eaa essential amino acid (EAA); ethylene acrylic acid (EAA)

EAA Education Amendment Act; Electrical Appliance Association; Electronics Association of Australia; Employment Agents Association; Engineer in Aeronautics and Astronautics; Engineers and Architects Association; Equipment Approval Authority; Experimental Aircraft Association; Export Advertising Association

E.A.A. Engineer in Aeronautics and Astronautics

EAA *Encyclopedia of American Associations*

EAAA European Association of Advertising Agencies

EAAC East African Airways Corporation

EAAFRO East African Agriculture and Forestry Research Organization

EAAM European Association for Aquatic Mammals

EAAP European Association for Animal Production

EAB Ethnic Affairs Bureau; European American Bank; European Asian Bank

EABn Engineer Aviation Battalion

eabrd electrically-actuated band-release device

eac end around carry; erythrocyte antibody complement; estimate at completion

EAC East African Community (Kenya, Tanzania, Uganda); East Asiatic (Line) Container; East Asiatic Company; Eastern Air Command; Estate Agents Cooperative; European Atomic Commission

eaca (EACA) epsilon-aminocaproic acid

eacd eczematous allergic contact dermatitis

E & A Co Eastern and Australian Steamship Company

ea content effective-agent content

EACR Environmental Area Characterization Report

EACSO East African Common Services Organization

EACU East Asiatic (Line) Container Unit

ead equipment allowance document; error adjusted; estimated availability date; extended active duty

ead. eadem (Latin—the same)

EAD Employer Association of Detroit

EADB East African Development Bank

EADF Eastern Air Defense Force

eadi electronic attitude and direction indicator

eae experimental allergic encephalomyelitis

EAEBP European Association of Editors of Biological Periodicals

EAEC East African Economic Community; European Atomic Energy Community

EAEG European Association of Exploration Geophysicists

EAEI Ecology Action Educational Institute

EAES Environment-Atmospheric Environment Service (Canada); European Atomic Energy Society

eaf emergency action file

EAFB Eglin Air Force Base (near Pensacola, Florida)

EAFC Eastern Area Frequency Coordinator; Eastern Association of Fire Chiefs

EAFFRO East African Freshwater Fishery Research Organization

EAG Edmonton Art Gallery

EAGGF European Agricultural Guidance and Guarantee Fund

Eagle (see Columbia)

Eagle Forgotten Governor Peter Altgeld of Illinois

Eagle of the North Swedish statesman Count Axel Oxenstierna

Eagle Pass formerly El Paso del Aguila when Texas was Tejas

Eagle and Serpent *Aguila y Serpiente* (Mexican coat of arms contains pictorialization of Aztec legend stating their people could not settle until they found an island on a lake and on that island a cactus

plant surmounted by an eagle grasping a serpent—the lacustrine island representing Mexico City, capital of Mexico—and the two creatures the struggle between celestial and earthly elements)

Eagle Springs Girls Samarkand Manor for female misdemeanants and juvenile delinquents at Eagle Springs, North Carolina

Eagle State Mississippi

EAHC East African Harbours Corporation; East African High Commission

eahf eczema, asthma, and hay fever

EAI East Asian Institute (Columbia University); Education Audit Institute

EAIC East African Industrial Council

EAID Equipment Authorization Inventory Data

EAJC Eastern Arizona Junior College

eal electromagnetic amplifying lens; estimated average life

Eal English as an additional language

EAL East Asiatic Line; Eastern Air Lines; Ethiopian Airlines

EALA East African Library Association

eam electronic accounting methods

eam (EAM) electrical accounting machine; electronic accounting machine; electronic automatic machine(ry)

EAM Eastern Atlantic and Mediterranean

EAM Ethniko Apelevtherotiko Metopo (Greek—National Liberation Front)

EAME European, African, Middle Eastern

EAMECM European-African Middle Eastern Campaign Medal

eamedpm (EAMEDPM) electric accounting machine and electronic data processing machine

EAMF European Association of Music Festivals

EAMFRO East African Marine Fisheries Research Organization

EAMPA East Anglian Master Printers' Alliance

EAMS Empire Air Mail Scheme

EAmst Elsevier Amsterdam

EAMTC European Association

of Management Training Centers

EAN Emergency Action Notification

EANA Esperanto Association of North America

EANDC Edgewood Arsenal Nuclear Defense Center; European American Nuclear Data Center

EANS Emergency Action Notification System (radio broadcasting)

EANSW Electricity Authority of New South Wales

eaon except as otherwise noted

eaos expiration of active obligated service

eap engines, armament, and pyrotechnics; equivalent air pressure; eye artifact potential

eap (EAP) erythrocyte acid phosphatase

EAP Edgar Allan Poe; Emergency Action Procedure; Employee Assistance Program; Environmental Analysis and Planning

EAP École d'Administration Pénitentiaire (French—Penitentiary Administration School)

EAPA Employment Aptitude Placement Association

EAPD Eastern Air Procurement District

EAPG Eastern Atlantic Planning Guidance (NATO)

EAPR European Association for Potato Research

'eap(s) heap(s)

EAPTC East African Posts and Telecommunications Corporation

ear electronic array radar; electronically agile radar; estimate after release

ear. electronic analog resolver

Ea-R Entartungs-Reaktion (German—degeneration reaction)

EAR East African Railways; Edwin Arlington Robinson

EARB Engineering Associates Registration Board

EARC East African Railways Corporation; Eastern Air Rescue Center

EARDHE European Association for Research and Development in Higher Education

EAR & H East African Railways and Harbours

EARI Equipment Acceptance Requirements and Inspection

Earl of Aberdeen George Hamilton Gordon (former Prime Minister of Great Britain like the following earls except Carnarvon, Lytton, the Second and Third Russells)

Earl Baldwin of Bewdley Stanley Baldwin

Earl Balfour Arthur James Balfour

Earl of Beaconsfield Benjamin Disraeli (19-century British prime minister who declared: *A conservative government is an organized hypocrisy.)*

Earl of Bute John Stuart

Earl of Carlisle Charles Howard

Earl of Carnarvon George ESM Herbert, the Egyptologist

Earl of Chatham William Pitt

Earl of Derby Edward Stanley

Earl of Godolphin Sidney Godolphin

Earl Grey Charles Grey

Earl of Guilford Frederick North

Earl of Halifax Charles Montagu

Earl of Liverpool Robert Banks Jenkinson

Earl of Lytton Edward Robert Bulwer Lytton, diplomat and poet whose pseudonym was Owen Meredith

Earl of Orford Robert Walpole

Earl of Oxford Robert Harley

Earl of Oxford and Asquith Herbert Henry Asquith

Earl of Ripon Frederick John Robinson

Earl of Rosebery Archibald Philip Primrose

Earl Russell Prime Minister John Russell, first earl; John Stanley Russell, second earl; Bertrand (Arthur William) Russell, third earl

Earl of Shelburne William Petty

Earl of Stanhope James Stanhope

Earl of Sunderland Charles Spencer

Earl of Wilmington Spencer Compton

Earnie Ernest; Ernestine; Ernesto

earom electrically alterable read-only memory

earp equipment anti-riot projector

EARS Electronic Airborne Reaction System; Electronically Agile Radar System; Emergency Airborne Reaction System

earssn early season

Earth Planet Sci Lett *Earth and Planetary Science Letters*

eas equivalent airspeed; estimated air speed

EAs East African shilling

EAS Early American Society; Executive Assignment Service; Extended Area Service

EASA Electrical Apparatus Service Association; Engineers Association of South Africa

EASE Emigrant's Assured Savings Estate; European Association of Science Editors

easmt easement

EASEP Early Apollo Scientific Experiments Payload

EA sh East African shilling

easl engineering analysis and simulation language

EASS Engine Automatic Stop-and-Start System

east. easterly; eastern

EAST Eastern Australian Standard Time

EASTAF Eastern Transport Air Force

East African Community Kenya, Tanzania, Uganda

East Berlin Soviet sector of Berlin occupied by Russian troops and communist-controlled Germans

Eastcommrgn Eastern Communications Region

East End congested and depressed eastern section of London

easter storm from the east

Easter Easter Island (see *Isla de Pascua*); Easter lily; Easter Monday; Easter Sunday; Easter vacation

Easter Island English place-name equivalent of Isla de Pascua whose Chilean settlers are called Pascuenses

Eastern Desert Arabian Desert

Eastern Empire Byzantine Empire

Eastern Europe Czechoslovakia, Hungary, Poland, the Soviet Union

Eastern Hemisphere half of the world containing Africa, Asia, Australia, Europe, and associated islands

Eastern Malaysia Sabah and Sarawak

Eastern Samoa American Samoa

Eastern Sea East China Sea

Eastern Shore eastern shore of Delaware, Maryland, and Virginia comprising the Del-Mar-

Va Peninsula

Eastern States states east of the Mississippi

East German Ports (east to west) Warnemunde, Rostock, Wismar

East Germany Soviet-dominated eastern Germany behind the Iron Curtain—the so-called German Democratic Republic

East Indies Malay Archipelago formerly called the Dutch East Indies or the Netherlands East Indies and now known as Indonesia

Eastinghouse international nickname for Soviet nuclear power plants built in Finland

East L East Lothian

East Lake Girls Alabama State Training School (for female juvenile delinquents) at East Lake near Birmingham

EASTLANT Eastern Atlantic Area

East London formerly Port Rex, South Africa

East Los East Los Angeles, California

East Lothian Haddington

East Malaysia Bandar Seri, Brunei, Sabah, and Sarawak comprising North Borneo and on the island of Borneo now known as Kalimantan

East North Central States Indiana, Illinois, Michigan, Ohio, and Wisconsin

East Phil Eastman Philharmonia

East Prussia old name for what is now western Poland along the Baltic

EASTROLANT Eastern Tropical Atlantic

EASTROPAC Eastern Tropical Pacific

East Siberian East Siberian Sea in the Arctic off East Siberia

East South Central States Alabama, Kentucky, Mississippi, and Tennessee

East Sutton Park borstal for delinquent girls in Kent, England

Eastview Canadian city now called Vanier

East Village modern euphemism for New York City's Lower East Side

easy. efficient assembly system; expense-account spending money

EASY Early Acquisition System (USA); Engine Analyzer System

eat. earliest arrival time (EAT); earnings after taxes; estimated arrival time (EAT); expected approach time (EAT)

e/at. electrons per atom

EAT earliest arriving time; Experiments in Art and Technology

EATA East Asia Travel Association

EATC Ecology and Analysis of Trace Contaminants

EATCS European Association for Theoretical Computer Science

EATRO East African Trypanosomiasis Research Organization

EATS Equipment Accuracy Test Station; Extended Area Tracking System (USN)

EATTA East Africa Tourist Travel Association

eau extended arithmetic unit

EAVRO East African Veterinary Research Organization

eaw Electrical Association for Women; equivalent average words

EAW Electrical Association for Women

EAWP Eastern Atlantic War Plan (NATO)

EAWS East African Wildlife Society

eax electronic automatic exchange

eb electron beam; elementary body; emergency brake; engine burn; environmental buoy

e-b estate-bottled

e/b eastbound

eb *point d'ébullition* (French—boiling point)

Eb Ebba; Ebed; Eben; Ebenezer; erbium (symbol); erbium (symbol)

EB Avitour Airlines; Eesti Vabariik (Estonian Republic); Electricity Board

E-B Electric Boat (Division of General Dynamics)

E & B Ellerman and Bucknall (Ellerman Lines)

EB *Encyclopaedia Britannica; Engineering Bulletin*

eb 1 s edge bead one side (lumber)

eb 2 s edge bead two sides (lumber)

EBA Education Boards Association; English Bowling Association

EBAA Eye-Bank Association of America

EBAILL European Bureau for the Allocation of International Long Lines

ebam electron-beam-addressed memory

EBAM Electron-Beam Addressed Memory

ebar edited beyond all recognition

EBAR E.B. Aabys Rederi (Norwegian freight line)

EBB Elias Baseball Bureau; Elizabeth Barrett Browning

ebc enamel bonded single cotton

EBC Educational Broadcasting Corporation; European Bibliographical Center (Oxford, England)

ebcdic extended binary-coded decimal interchange code

EBCDIC Extended Binary Coded Decimal Interchange Code (pronounced *ebsidick*)

ebce experience-based career education

ebd education by discussion; effective biological dose

ebd *ebenda* (German—in the same place)

ebds enamel bonded double silk

EBEC Encyclopedia Britannica Educational Corporation

Eben Ebenezer

Eber Eberard; Eberhard; Eberhart; Ebert

EBES Electron-Beam Exposure System

ebf electronically blown flap; erythroblastosis foetalis; externally blown flap

EBF Encyclopedia Britannica Films

ebfa electron-beam fusion accelerator

ebi (EBI) emetine bismuth iodide

EBI Emerson Books, Incorporated

EBIC European Banks International Corporation (lowercase logotype appears as *ebic*)

ebicon electron-bombardment-induced conductivity

ebit earnings before interest and taxes

ebiv electron-beam-induced voltage

ebk embryonic bovine kidney

EBL Eastern Basketball League

Eblana (Latin—Dublin)

ebm electronic bearing marker; expressed breast milk

EBM *Empresa Bacaladera Mexicana* (Mexican Codfish-

ing Enterprise)

EBMC English Butter Marketing Company

EBMUD East Bay Municipal Utility District

EBNI Electricity Board for Northern Ireland

Ebnr Ebenezer

EBNY Edition Bookbinders of New York

E-boat enemy boat

Ebor. *Eboracensis* (Latin—of York); *Eboracum* (Latin—York)

ebp enamel single paper bonded

ebpa electron-beam parametric amplifier

ebr electron-beam recorder; experimental breeder reactor

EBR Emu Bay Railway; Engineering Business Report

EBR-75 Panhard armored car carrying a 75mm gun

EBR-90 Panhard armored car carrying a 90mm gun

EBRA Engineer Buyers' and Representatives' Association

EBRD Export Business Division (U.S. Department of Commerce)

Ebreo (Italian—Jew)—nickname of Salomone Rossi the composer-violinist of Mantua in the late 1500s and early 1600s

EBRI Employee Benefit Research Institute

'Ebrides (Cockney contraction —Hebrides)

ebs enamel single cotton

eb(s) eager beaver(s)

EBS Emergency Bed Service; Emergency Broadcast System; English Bookplate Society; Ethiopian Broadcasting Service

ebsidick *see* EBCDIC

EBSR Eye-Bank for Sight Restoration

ebt earth-based tug (NASA); electron-beam technique

EBU European Broadcasting Union

ebul ebullition

EBv Epstein–Barr virus

ebw exploding bridge wire

E.B.White Elwyn Brooks White

ebwr (EBWR) experimental boiling-water reactor

EBYC European Bureau for Youth and Childhood

ec earth closet; economics; electric(al) coding; electrolytic corrosion; electronic calculator; electronic computer; emergency capability; emulsifiable concentrate; enamel coated; enteric coated; entering complaint; error correcting; expansive classification; expiratory center; extended coverage; extension and conversion; extension course; exterior closet; extra choice (wool)

e-c ether-chloroform (mixture)

e/c estrogen-to-creatinine (ratio)

ec en cuento (Spanish—on account)

e.c. exempli causa (Latin—for example)

Ec Ecclesiastic; Ecuador; Ecuadorian

EC Earlham College; East African Airways; East Carolina (railroad); East Central; East Coast; Eastern College; Eastern Command; Edgewood College; Electricity Council; Elizabethtown College; Elmhurst College; Elmira College; Elon College; Emergency Commission(er); Emergency Coordinator; Emerson College; Emmanuel College; Engineer Captain; Engineering Change; Engineering Construction; Environmental Control; Episcopal Church; Erskine College; Essex College; Established Church; Eureka College; European Communities; European Community; Evangel College; Evansville College; Executive Committee; Executive Council; Exeter College; Explorers Club

EC (followed by numbers) Enzyme Commission (numbers indicate enzyme classification)

E-C Erckmann-Chatrian (combined name for two friendly collaborators: Emile Erckmann and Alexandre Chatrian)

E & C Engineering and Construction

EC Encyclopedia Canadiana; *Era Cristiana* (Spanish—Christian Era); *Étoile du Courage* (French—Star of Courage)

EC1, EC2, etc. East Central One, East Central 2, etc. (London postal zones)

eca electronic control amplifier; electronics control assembly

ECA Earthmovers and Contractors Association; Economic Commission for Africa (UN);

Economic Control Agency; Economic Cooperation Administration; Educational Communication Association; Electrical Contractors Association; Engineering Change Analysis; European Confederation of Agriculture; Exchange Control Act

ECA Empresa de Comercio Agricola (Spanish—Agricultural Commerce Enterprise)

ECAB Early Case Assessment Bureau; Employees' Compensation Appeals Board

ECAC Eastern College Athletic Conference; Electromagnetic Compatibility Analysis Center; Extra-Curricular Activities Center

ecad error check analysis diagram

ECAFE Economic Commission for Asia and the Far East (UN)

ecal equipment calibration

ecam extended communications access method

ecan excitation, calibration, and normalization

ECAP Electronic Circuit Analysis Program; Environmental Compatability Assurance Program (USN)

ECARS Electronic Coordinatograph Readout System

ECAS Electrical Contractors Association of Scotland

ecat emission computerized axial tomography

ECB E(benezer) Cobham Brewer; Energy Conservation Board (US)

e & cb 1 s edge and center bead one side (lumber)

e & cb 2 s edge and center bead two sides (lumber)

ecbo enteric cytopathogenic bovine orphan (virus)

ecc eccentric; electrically-continuous cloth; electrodeposited composite coat(ing); emergency combat capability; equipment classification control; equipment configuration control; equipment control classification; error correction code; execute control cycle

ecc (ECC) electrocorticogram; exchange control copy

ecc eccetera (Italian—et cetera)

Ecc Eccellenze (Italian—Excellency)

ECC Economic Council of Canada; Educational Cultural Complex; Educational Cultur-

al Complex; Elderly Citizens Club(s); Electronics Capital Corporation; Emergency Conservation Committee; Employees Compensation Commission; Ethnic Communities Council; European Coordinating Committee; European Coordinating Council; European Cultural Center; European Cultural Commission

ECCA East Caribbean Currency Authority

ECCA Empresa Consolidada Cubana de Aviación (Spanish—Consolidated Cuban Aviation Enterprise)

ECCAA Executive Chefs de Cuisine Association of America

ECCC English Country Cheese Council

ECCCS Emergency Command Control Communications System

ECCDA Eastern Connecticut Clam Diggers Association

eccen eccentric; eccentrics

Eccentric Naturalist Constantine Rafinesque

ECCET Engineering Casualty Control Evaluation Team (USN)

Ecc. Hom Ecce Homo (Latin—Behold the Man)

ECCI Executive Committee Communist International

eccl ecclesiatic(al)

Eccl Ecclesiastes

eccles ecclesiastic; ecclesiastical

Ecclus. Ecclesiasticus

eccm electronic counter-counter-measures

eccmo electronic counter-countermeasures operation(s); electronic counter-countermeasures operator(s)

ec^{co} eclesiástico (Spanish—clergyman, ecclesiastic, ecclesiastical, priest)

ECCP East Coast Coal Port; Engineering Concepts Curriculum Project; European Commission on Crime Problems

ECCR Engineering Calibration Cycle Request

ECCs Emitter-Coupled Circuits

ECCS Emergency Core Cooling Systems (AEC)

eccsl emitter-coupled-current steered logic

ECCT Eddy Current Conductivity Test(ing)

ECCTYC English Council of the California Two-Year Colleges

ECCU English Cross-Country

Union
ecd early closing day; endocardial cushion defect; estimated completion date
ec&d electronic cover and deception
ec & d electronic components and devices
ECD Energy Conversion Devices
EC & D Electronic Components and Devices
ecdc electrochemical diffused-collector transistor
ECDC Economic Cooperation among Developing Countries
ecdi electronic course deviation indicator
ECDIN European Chemical Data and Information Network
ecdn electrical cables down
ECDP Estimating Controlled Data Package
ECDU European Christian Democratic Union
ece eligible capital expenditure; extended coverage endorsement
ECE Early Childhood Education; Economic Commission for Europe (UN)
ECEO Economic Crime Enforcement Office (U.S. Dept. of Justice) [Economic Crime Units established nationwide to combat white-collar crimes such as corporate embezzlement, fraud, or theft of securities]
ECES Educational and Career Exploration System
ecf extracellular fluid
ECF Edgar Cayce Foundation; Electrical Contractors Federation; Episcopal Charismatic Fellowship; European Cultural Foundation; Ex-Communist Forces
ECFI Eastern Caribbean Farm Institute
ECFMG Educational Council for Foreign Medical Graduates
ECFMS Educational Council for Foreign Medical Students
ecg export credit guarantee(s)
ecg (ECG) electrocardiogram; electrocardiograph(y)
ECG electrocardiogram
ECGB East Coast of Great Britain
ECGC Empire Cotton Growing Corporation
ECGD Export Credit Guarantee Department

ech echelon; engine compartment heater
echo. enteric cytopathogenic human orphan (virus)
echo. (ECHO) electronic computing, hospital oriented
Echo letter E radio code; NATO nickname for Soviet missile-carrying nuclear-powered submarine designated E-class
ECHO Efficient Car-Handling Operations (railroad); European Commission Host Organization; Evidence for Community Health Organization; Experimental Contract Highlight Operation
ECHS Evander Childs High School
eci extracorporeal irradiation
ECI Electronic Communications Incorporated; Extension Course Institute (Air University)
ECIAL *Enseñanza de las Ciencias y de la Ingeniería en la América Latina* (Spanish—Teaching of Science and Engineering in Latin America)
ECIC Export Credits Insurance Corporation (Canada)
ECICS Export Credit Insurance Corporation of Singapore
ECIS Error-Correction Information System (NASA)
ECITO European Central Inland Transport Organization
ECIUSAF Extension Course Institute, USAF
ECJ Erie County Jail (Buffalo)
eck embryonic chicken kidney
Eck(ie) Alexander; Alexandra; Alexis; Hector; Hecuba
Eckma Jan de Hartog's pseudonym
ecl eclipse; electrocardiograph log; electronic crash locator (aircraft); extended center line
ecl (ECL) emitter-coupled logic
ecl *eclairage* (French—lighting)
ECL Electronic Components Laboratory; Engineering Computing Laboratory; Equipment Component List; Europe-Canada Line
ECL *Encyclopedia of Comparative Letterforms*
ECLA Economic Commission for Latin America (UN)
E-class NATO designation for a Soviet class of missile-carrying nuclear-powered submarines also known as Echo
eclec eclectic; eclecticism
ecli eclipse; ecliptic
eclo emitter-coupled logic opera-

tor
ecm electric coding machine; electrochemical machining; electronic countermeasure(s); ends matched, center (lumber); extended core memory
ECM Engineering Change Management; European Common Market
EC & M Electric Controller and Manufacturing (company)
e/cm³ electrons per cubic centimeter
ECMA Engineering College Magazines Associated; European Computer Manufacturers Association
Ecmalgol European Computer Manufacturers Association Algorithmic Language
ECMCA Eastern-Central Motor Carriers Association
ecmd electronic countermeasures display
ecme electronic countermeasures equipment
ECME Economic Commission for the Middle East (UN)
ecmex electronic countermeasures exercise
ECMF Electric Cable Makers' Federation
ECM & FS East Coast Marine and Ferry Service
ECMHP East Coast Migrant Health Project
e-c mix. ether-chloroform mixture
ecmo (ECMO) enteric cytopathogenic monkey organ (virus)
ECMR Eastern Contract Management Region
ECMRA European Chemical Market Research Association
ECMS Engine Condition Monitoring System
ECMSA Electronics Command Meteorological Support Agency (USA)
ecmtng electronic countermeasures training
ECN Engineering Change Notice
ECNA East Coast of North America
ECNOS Eastern Atlantic, Channel, and North Sea (orders for ships given by NATO)
eco ecological; ecologist; ecology; economic; economist; economics; electron-coupled oscillator; exempted by commanding officer
eco (Latin prefix—home or house)—ecology, economy, ecosphere, ecosystem

ECO East Coast Overseas; Economic Corporation Organization; Effective Citizens Organization; Engineering Change Order; Environment and Conservation Organizations; Environmental Control Organization; European Coal Organization

ECOA Equal Credit Opportunity Act; Equipment Company of America

ECOCEN Economic Cooperation Center

ecocrit economic critic(ism)

ecodoom large-scale ecological destruction

ecodoomster(s) predictor(s) of large-scale ecological destruction

ecofuel ecology fuel (made from garbage and other wastes generated by man and his domestic animals)

ecog electrocorticogram

ecogeo ecogeographer; ecogeographic(al)(ly); ecogeography

ecol ecology

Ecol Ecology

ecolcrit ecological criticism; ecology critic

E coli *Escherichia coli* (intestinal bacillus)

Ecol Soc Am Ecological Society of America

ecom (ECOM) electronic computer-originated mail

ECOM Electronic Computer-Originated Mail; Electronics Command (USA)

ECOMINAS *Empresa Colombiana de Minas* (Spanish—Colombian Mining Enterprise)

econ economic; economics; economist; economy

e con. *e contrario* (Latin—on the contrary)

Econ Economics

Econ Jrnl *Economic Journal*

economan effective control of manpower

economet econometric

Econ Rev *Economic Review*

ECOP Extension Committee on Organization and Policy

ECOPETROL *Empresa Colombiana de Petróleos* (Spanish—Colombian Petroleum Enterprise)

ecophys ecophysiologic(al)(ly): ecophysiologist; ecophysiology

ecopow(s) economic superpower(s)—U.S.A., USSR, Japan, West Germany

ECOR Engineering Committee on Ocean Resources

ECORS Eastern Counties Operational Research Society

EcoSoc Economic and Social (Council)

Écosse (French—Scotland)

ecosupow(s) economic superpower(s)—U.S.A., USSR, Japan, West Germany

eco system ecological system; economic system

ecotopia(n) ecologically ideal utopia(n)

ecou electric clip-on unit; electronic clip-on unit

ECP Engineering Change Proposal; Examiner of Commercial Practices; Executive Control Program

ECPA Evangelical Christian Publishers Association

ECPAC East County Performing Arts Center

ECPD Engineers Council for Professional Development

ecpiu electronic circuit plug-in unit

ecpnl equivalent continuous preceived noise level

ecpo enteric cytopathogenic porcine orphan (virus)

ECPO Environmental Characterization Projects Office

ecpog electrochemical potential gradient

ECPR European Consortium for Political Research

ecp(s) external casing packer(s)

ECPS European Center for Population Studies

ecpt egress cockpit procedure trainer

ECPTA European Conference of Postal and Telecommunication Administrations

ECQAC Electronic Components Quality Assurance Committee

ecr electronic cash register; energy consumption rate; error cause removal; external channels ratio

ECR Engineering Change Request; Environmental Characterization Report

ECRB Export Control Review Board

ECRC Earth Colonization Research Center; Electronic Component Reliability Center; Engineering College Research Council

ECRL Eastern Caribbean Regional Library

ECR Lorac Edith Caroline Riv-

ett's pseudonym

ecro erection counter readout

ECRO European Chemoreception Research Organization

ECRs Enemy Contact Reports

ECRS Empty Car Routing System

ecs electroconvulsive shock; emperor's clothes syndrome; ends cut square; error correction servomechanism; error correction signals; extended core storage

ECS Education Commission of the States; Electrochemical Society; Electronic Composing System; Employment Counseling Service; Engineering Change Schedule; Engineering Change Sheet; Environmental Control Systems; Episcopal Community Services; Equipment Concentration Sites; Equipment Configuration Study; Etched Circuit Society; European Communications Satellite; Experimental Communications Satellite (NASA)

ECSA East Coast of South America; European Communication Security Agency; Expanded Clay and Shale Association

ECSC European Coal and Steel Community

ECSCF Eastern Connecticut State College Foundation

ECS/HCS Education Career Services/Health Career Service

ECSIL Experimental Cross-Section Information Library (University of California—Livermore)

ecss extendable computer system simulator

ECST European Convention on the Suppression of Terrorism

ECSTC Elizabeth City State Teachers College

ECSU Educational Cooperative Service Unit

ect electroconvulsive therapy; engine cutoff time; enteric coated tablet

ect (ECT) electroconvulsive treatment

ECT Environmental Control Technology (DoE division); Equivalence Conversion Training; European Container Terminus

ECTA Economics and Commercial Teachers Association; Electrical Contractors' Trading Association; Electronic

Components Test(ing) Area

ectl emitter-coupled transistor logic

ecto (Latin prefix—external, outer, outside)—ectoderm

ectohorm ectohormonal; ectohormone

ectomy (Latin suffix—surgical removal)—tonsillectomy

ecu ecumania(c); ecumenism; electronic computing unit; engine compatability unit; environmental control unit; extra closeup; extreme closeup

ecu (ECU) extra closeup; extreme closeup

Ecu Ecuador; Ecuadorean

Ecu (ECU) European currency unit

ECU East Carolina University; Economic Crime Unit; English Church Union; European Customs Union

Ecua Ecuador; Ecuadorean

Ecuador Republic of Ecuador (Spanish-speaking South American country including the Galápagos Islands. Ecuadoreans export bananas, minerals, and many tropical products), *Republica del Ecuador*

Ecuador Day Ecuadorean Independence Day (August 10)

Ecuadorean Ports [north to south and west to the Galápagos (last port listed)] Puerto de San Lorenzo, Esmeraldas, Bahia de Caraquez, Bahia de Manta, Puerto de Cayo, La Libertad, Salinas, Guayaquil, Puna, Puerto Bolívar, Bahia Baquerizo Moreno (on Chatham or San Cristóbal)

Ecuador's Principal Port Guayaquil

ecube energy conservation using better engineering

Ecu Con Ecumenical Conference; Ecumenical Council

ecufuel eucalyptus-tree fuel

ECUK East Coast of United Kingdom

ecumen ecumenical(ism)(ist); ecumenicist; ecumenicity; ecumenics; ecumenism

ECUSA Episcopal Church of the U.S.A.

ecusat ecumenical satellite

ECUSATCOM Ecumenical Satellite Commission

ecv extracellular virus

ecv (ECV) energy conservation vehicle

e & cV 1 s edge and center-V one side (lumber)

e & cV 2 s edge and center-V two

sides (lumber)

ecw extracellular water

ECW Episcopal Church Women

ECWA Economic Commission for Western Asia (UN)

ECY European Conservation Year

ECYO European Community Youth Orchestra

ecz eczema(tic)

ed edge distance; edit; edited; edition; editor; editorial; educate; educated; education; educational; educator; effective dose; emotionally disturbed; enemy dead; error detecting; erythema dose; excused from duty; ex-dividend; existence doubtful; extra dividend; extra duty

e & d (E & D) exploration and development

ed *edición* (Spanish—edition); *édition* (French—edition); *edizione* (Italian—edition)

e_d price elasticity of demand

Ed Edgar; Editor; Edmond; Edmund; Edson; Edvard; Edvardson; Edward; Edwin

Ed. Editor

E$ Eurodollar (American dollar deposited in Europe)

ED Consolidated Edison Company (stock exchange symbol); Eastern District; Economics Division; Education Department; Efficiency Decoration; Elder Dempster Line; Electric Dynamo; Engineering Data; Engineering Depot; Engineering Design; Engineering Draftsman; Export Declaration

E-D Electro-Dynamics (division of General Dynamics); Elsevier-Dutton

E.D. Doctor of Engineering

ed₅0 median effective dose

eda early departure authorized; equipment design agent; equivalent design axles; erection digital assembly

E d A *Ejercito del Aire* (Spanish—Air Force)

EDA Economic Development Administration (Puerto Rico); Electrical Development Association; Employment Development Act; Environmental Development Administration; Environmental Development Agency

edac error detection and correction

EDAC Engineering Decision

Analysis Company; Evaluation, Dissemination, Assessment Centers

E da M Escuatrão da Morte (Portuguese—Death Squad)— Brazilian right-wing terrorists

EDANA European Disposables and Non-Wovens Association

EDAQ Electrical Development Association of Queensland

EDARR Engineering Drawing and Assembly Release Record

edb emergency dispersal base(s); end of data block(s); ethene dibromide (EDB); extended double base

edb (EDB) ethylene dibromide (deadly pesticide)

edb *elektronisk databehandling* (Dano-Norwegian—electronic data handling)

Edb Edinburgh

Ed.B. Bachelor of Education

EDB Economic Development Board; Energy Development Board

edbiz educational business

EDBP Epidemiology, Demography, and Biometry Program

edc electronic digital computer; emergency digital computer; energy distribution curve; engine-driven compressor; error detection and correction; estimated date of completion; estimated date of confinement; extra dark color

EDC Eastern Defense Command; Economic Development Corporation; Educational Development Centers; Educational Development Corporation; Educational Development Council; Engineering Data Consultants; European Defense Community; Export Development Corporation

EDCC Environmental Dispute Coordination Commission

edcl electric discharge coaxial laser

edcn education

edcom editor-compiler

E/DCP Equipment/Document Change Proposal

EDCPF Environmental Data Collection and Processing Facility (USA)

EDCs Economic Development Committees

edcsa effective date of change of strength accountability

edcv enamel double cotton varnish

edcw external-device control

word(ing)

edd electronic data display; estimated delivery date; expected date of delivery

edd ediderunt (Latin—published by)

edd. editiones (Latin—editions)

Ed. D. Doctor of Education

EDD Eastman Dental Dispensary; Economic Development Division (Singapore); Employment Development Department; Engineering Data Depository; Engineering Development Department; Engineering Development and Design; Engineering and Development Directorate (NASA)

EDD English Dialect Dictionary

eddf error detection and decision feedback

Eddie Edgar; Edmund; Edoardo; Edouard; Edsel; Eduard; Eduardo; Edvard; Edward; Edwin; Edwina

Eddie Albert Eddie Albert Heimberger's motion-picture-reel name

Eddie Cantor Izzie Itskowitz

EDDS Electronic Devices Data Service

E-D DS Elsevier-Dutton Distribution Services

Eddy Edgar; Edmund; Edward; Edwin; Edwina

ede electronic defense evaluator; emitter dip effect

ede (Latin prefix—swelling)—edema

EDE Electrical Design Engineering; Electronic Design Engineering; Elevator Design Engineering; Engineering Design Establishment

Eden of the Orient Thailand

edent edentate; edentulous

EDEO Episcopal Division Ecumenical Officers

edexs education of exceptional students

EDF Environmental Defense Fund; European Development Fund; Everyman Defense Fund

Edg Edgar

EDG Export Development Group(ing)

Edgar The Edgar (bust of Edgar Allan Poe given for the best mystery novel)

Edgar Box Gore Vidal

EDGB Export Development Grants Board

edge. electronic data-gathering equipment

edh efficient deck hand

edhe experimental data-handling equipment

edi electron-diffraction instrument

EDI Economic Development Institute; Edinburgh; Scotland (airport); Engineering Department Instruction

EDIA Engineering Department Instruction Amendment

edic electric diesel injection control

edict. engineering document information collection technique

Edie Edith

Edim Edimburgo (Portuguese or Spanish—Edinburgh)

Edin Edinburgh

Edin(a) Edinburgh's poetical name

Edinburghshire Midlothian

Edinburgum (Latin—Edinburgh)— also known as Edinbruchium or Edinum

Ed-in-Ch Editor-in-Chief

edinet education instruction network

Edinglassie Edinburgh + Glasgow (early name of the Moreton Bay Settlement now called Brisbane)

EDIP European Defence Improvement Program (NATO)

EDIS Engineering Data Information Service; Engineering Data Information System

edit. editing; edition; editor; editorial

EDIT Estate Duties Investment Trust

editar electronic digital tracking and ranging unit

Editor of Genius Max(well) E Perkins

EDITS Electronic Data Information Technical Service; Experimental Digital Television System

edl edition de luxe; electric(al) discharge laser

EDL Elder Dempster Lines; Every-Day Life (psychological test); Executive Data Link

Ed Lacy Len Zinberg's pseudonym

EDLD Employee Daily Labor Distribution

EDLNA Exotique Dancers League of North America

edm early diastolic murmur; electrical-discharge machining; electromagnetic discharge measuring; electrostatic discharge machining

Edm Edmund; St Edmund's House, Cambridge

Ed. M. Master of Education

EDM Engineering Development Model

EDM Engineering Drafting Manual (USAF)

Ed McBain Salvatore A. Lombino

EDMICS Engineering Data Management Information Control System

Edm & Ips St Edmundsbury and Ipswich

Edmn Edmonton

Edmo Edmonton (inhabitants—Edmontonians)

Edmond Adam French author-editor Juliette Lamber

EDMS Engineering Data Microreproduction System

Edmund Crispin Robert Bruce Montgomery's pseudonym

edn electrodesiccation

Edn Edwin

EDN Engineering Department Notice

EDNA Emergency Department Nurses Association

Edna St Vincent Millay Mrs Eugen Jan Boissevain

edo effective diameter of objective; error demodulator output; error detector output

Edo old name for Tokyo also written Yedo

EDO Employee Development Officer; Engineering Duty Officer; Engineering Duty Only

edoc effective date of change

Edogawa Rampo Hirai Taro (Japan's Edgar Allan Poe)

Edoo (EDU) Lady Elgar's nickname for her husband Sir Edward Elgar (EDU is the title of the fourteenth section or finale of his *Enigma Variations on an Original Theme* scored for full orchestra)

EDOPAC Enlisted Personnel Distribution Office Pacific Fleet

Edouard Colonne Judas Colonne (a conductor unblamed for this Christian name he changed)

edp engineering data processing

edp (EDP) electronic data processing

EDP Educational Data Processing; Engineering Design Proposal

EDPAA Electronic Data-Processing Auditors Association

edpac electronic data processing air conditioning

EDPC Electronic Data-Processing Center

edp crimes electronic data-processing crimes

edpe electronic data processing equipment

ed-ped-psych-soc education-pedagogy-psychology-sociology

edpm electronic data processing machine(s)

EDPRESS Educational Press Association of America

EDPS Electronic Data Processing System

EDPT Electronic Data Processing Test

Ed & Pub *Editor and Publisher*

edr electrical distance recorder; electrodermal response; electronic decoy rocket; equivalent direct radiation

EDR Engineering Data Requirements; Engineering Division Regulation(s); Equipment Damage Report

EDRA Environmental Design Research Association

EDRI Electronic Distributors Research Institute

edrl effective damage risk level

EDRs European Depository Receipts

EDRS Education Document Reproductive Service; Engineering Data Retrieval System

edrt effective date of release from training

eds editors; enamel double silk; estimated date of separation

ed's endangered species (for an account of the number of such during the time of Noah it is suggested readers refer to the Ararat entry)

EDs Explosive Disposal specialists

E-Ds Ehlers-Danlos syndrome

EDS Electronic Data Systems; Electronic Devices Society; Engineering Data Sheet; English Dialect Society; Environmental Data Service; Episcopal Divinity School

edsac electronic delayed-storage automatic computer

edsat educational television satellite (EDSAT)

EDSC Engineering Data Support Center (USAF)

Ed. Spec. Educational Specialist

edst elastic diaphragm switch technology

EDST Eastern Daylight Saving Time

edsv enamel double silk varnish

edt effective date of training

EDT Eastern Daylight Time

edta ethylene diamine tetraacetic (acid)

edtr experimental, developmental, test, and research

edtsr electronic dial tone speed register

edu electronic display unit; experimental diving unit

Edu Sir Edward Elgar

EDU European Democratic Union

Eduardo E Howard Hunt

educ education; educational

Educ Education

Educational Film Educational Film Library Association

Educator-Freethinker Horace Mann

Educ Digest *Educational Digest*

educom education communication(s)

Educ Pr Educational Press; Educational Press Association of America

Educ Pub Educational Publications Services; Educational Publishers

educrat educational bureaucrat

educrit educational critic(ism)

educ(s) eductor(s)

EDUPLAN *Oficina de Planeamiento Integral de Educación* (Spanish—Office of Integral Planning in Education)

edutainment educational entertainment (via tv)

edutele educational television

edutherap educational therapist; educational therapy

edv end-diastolic volume

edvac electronic discrete variable automatic computer

edw energy dump window

Edw Edward

Edward G Edward G Robinson (Emmanuel Goldberg)

Edwardian Radical Hilaire Belloc

Edward I Prime Stevenson Xavier Mayne's pseudonym

Edward Longshanks Edward I of England

Edward O Wilson Frank J Baird, Jr

Edward the Peacemaker Edward VII, eldest son of Queen Victoria

Edward the Rake Edward VII (whose rakish reputation dated from when he was Prince of Wales)

Ed Wynn Isaiah Edwin Leopold

eDx electrodiagnosis

ee eased edges (lumber); electric eye (camera); embryo extract; environmental education; equine encephalitis; errors excepted; exoelectron(ic)(al) emission; expiration of enlistment; eye and ear

ee (EE) errors excepted

e/e electrical/electronic

e & e evacuation and evasion; evasion and escape; eye and ear

e-to-e end-to-end

'ee thee

EE Early English; Electrical Engineer(ing); Electronics Engineer(ing); Envoy Extraordinary; Estado Español (The Spanish State)

E.E. Electrical Engineer

EE *Euer Ehrwürden* (German— Your Reverence)

eea engineering evaluation article

EEA Electronic Engineering Association; Emergency Employment Act; Environmental Education Act; Ethical Education Association

EEA *Electrical and Electronic Abstracts*

EEAC Energy and Education Action Center

EEAIE Electrical, Electronic, and Allied Industries of Europe

eeat end-of-evening astronomical twilight

EEB Eastern Electricity Board; Educational Employees Board

EEB *Enosis Ellenon Bibliotekarion* (Modern Greek— Greek Library Association)

eec electronic engine control

EEC East Erie Commercial (railroad); Education Exploration Center; English Electronic Computers; European Economic Community (Belgium, Denmark, France, Italy, Luxembourg, the Netherlands, the Republic of Ireland, West Germany, the United Kingdom)

EECA Engineering Economic Cost Analysis

eecom electrical, environmental, and communications

e.e. cummings Edward Estlin Cummings' lowercase way of writing his name

eed elastic energy density; electrical explosive device

eee eastern equine encephalitis

EEE Environmental-Ecological Education (program)

EEF Egyptian Expeditionary Force

eefi essential elements of friendly information

eeg (EEG) electroencephalogram; electroencephalograph

EEG Environmental Education Group

ee/ha ewe equivalents per hectare

EEI Edison Electric Institute; Environmental Equipment Institute; Essential Elements of Information

EEIA Electrical and Electronic Insulation Association

EEIBA Electrical and Electronic Industries Benevolent Association

EEIS Evanston Early Identification Scale

EEL Ecology and Epidemiology Laboratory; Engineering Electronic Laboratory; English Electric Limited; Evans Electroselenium Limited

eem Electronic Engineers Master (catalog)

EE & MP Envoy Extraordinary and Minister Plenipotentiary

een exceptional educational needs

e'en even; evening

E Eng Early English

E-engine(s) electric engine(s)

EENT end, evening nautical twilight; eye, ear, nose, and throat

EENWR Exe Estuary National Wildlife Refuge (England)

eeo equal employment opportunity

EEOC Economic Employment Opportunity Committee; Equal Employment Opportunity Commission

eep electronic evaluation and procurement; electronic event programmer(s); emergency essential personnel

EEP Energy Emergency Plan(ning)

eepnl estimated effective-perceived noise level

eeprom electrically erasable programmable read-only memory

eer energy efficiency ratio; explosive echo ranging

e'er ever

EER Engineering (Equipment) Evaluation Report; Experimental Ecological Reserves

EERC Earthquake Engineering

Research Center (NSF)

EERI Earthquake Engineering Research Institute

EERL Electrical Engineering Research Laboratory (University of Texas)

eerom electrically erasable read-only memory

ees electronic environment simulator

EES Engineering Experiment Station; Enlisted Evaluation System; European Exchange System

EESS Encyclopedia of Engineering Signs and Symbols

Eesti (Estonian—Estonia)

eet estimated elapsed time

EET Eames Eye Test; Eastern European Time; Education Equivalency Test; Engineering Evaluation Test(ing)

E-et-L Eure-et-Loire

EETS Early English Text Society

EETU Electrical Electronic Telecommunication Union

EEUA Engineering Equipment Users Association

EEUU Estados Unidos (Spanish—United States)

EEV English Electric Valve (company)

EEVC English Electric Valve Company

eex electronic egg exchange (computer program)

eez (EEZ) eastern economic zone; exclusive economic zone

ef each face; electroflotation; elevation finder; equivalent focal length; expectant father; experimental flight; extra fine; extremely fine

EF Educational Foundation; Emergency Fleet; Engineering Foundation; Expeditionary Force

E & F Elders and Fyffes (steamship line)

EF Europaiske Faellesskaber (Danish—European Common Market)

efa essential fatty acids

EFA Environmental Financing Authority; Epilepsy Foundation of America; European Free Associations; Evangelical Friends Alliance

EFA Empresa Ferrocarriles Argentinos (Spanish—Argentine Railway Enterprise)

EFAS Enroute Flight Advisory Service

efc earth fixed coordinate; elec-

tronic feedback carburetor; engineered for color (tv); Evergreen Fir Corporation (initials)

e & fc examined and found correct

EFC Educational Facilities Center; Electronic Fabrication Center; European Forestry Commission

EFCB Emergency Financial Control Board

EFCX Evergreen Freight Car Express

efd electro fluid dynamics; excused from duty

EFDSS English Folk Dance and Song Society

efe early fuel evaporation; endocrinal fibro-elastosic; expected field emergence

EFEA Empresa Ferrocarriles del Estado Argentino (Argentine State Railways); European Free Exchange Area

EFEA Empresa Ferrocarriles del Estado Argentino (Spanish—Argentine State Railways)

EFEC Efforts From Ex-Convicts (Washington, D.C.'s parole project)

eff effect; effective; efficiency

eff effeto (Italian—bill, promissory note)

EFF Educational Freedom Foundation; European Furniture Federation

effcy efficiency

effect. effective; effectivity

effer efferent

Effie award for effective advertising; Euphemia

Effigy Mounds Effigy Mounds National Monument on the Mississippi in northeastern Iowa

effl efflorescent

eff wd effective wind

EFG Educational Fee Grant(s); Edward FitzGerald

EFH Eileen F Hodges

efi electronic flight instruments; electronic fuel injection

ef & i engineer, furnish, and install

EFI Educational Forces Inventory; Electronic Fuel Injection (system)

EFIB European Freight Inspection Bureau

EFIC Export Finance and Insurance Corporation

eficon electronic financial control

EFINS Enrico Fermi Institute for Nuclear Studies (Univ of

Chicago)

efl effective focal length; emitter-follower logic

Efl (EFL) English as a foreign language

EFL Educational Facilities Laboratories; English as a Foreign Language

EFLA Educational Film Library Association

EFLC Engineers Foreign Language Circle

efm electronic fuel management; electronic fuel metering

efm (EFM) electronic fetal monitor(ing)

EFM European Federalist Movement

EFMCNTA Elastic Fabric Manufacturers Council of the Northern Textile Association

EFMG Electric Fuse Manufacturers Guild

EFMM Education for Mission and Ministry

EFNIR Exhibition/Festival for New Instrumental Resources

EFNS Educational Foundation for Nuclear Science

efp effective filtration pressure; electric(al) fuel propulsion; end of flight plan

efp (EFP) electronic field production (on-location videotape production); emergency firing panel

EFPA Educational Film Producers Association

EFPW European Federation for the Protection of Waters

efr effective filtration rate, engine firing rate

EFR Electronic Failure Report(ing)

EFRC Edwards Flight Research Center

E Fris East Frisian

efs economic farm surplus; equivalent standard fillet

EFS Edinburgh Festival Society; Emergency Feeding Service; Emergency Fire Service(s)

EFSA European Federation of Sea Anglers

EFSC European Federation of Soroptimist Clubs

EFSS Emergency Food Supply Scheme

eft earliest finish time

eft (EFT) electronic funds transfer

EFT Embedded Figures Test; Engineering Flight Test

EFTA European Free Trade Association

EFTC Electrical Fair Trading

Council

eftf *efterfölger* (Dano-Norwegian —successor)

Eftf(lg) *Efterfölgere* (Dano—Norwegian—successor)

EFTI Engineering Flight Test Instrumentation

eftm *eftermiddag* (Norwegian—after noon)—p.m.

efto encrypt for transmission only

EFTS Electronic Funds-Transfer System; Elementary Flying Training School

efu energetic feed unit; environmental force unit

EFU European Football Union

EFU *Europäische Frauenunion* (German—European Women's Union)

efv equilibrium flash vaporization

EFVA Education Foundation for Visual Aids

EFWA Eastern Farmworkers Association

eg electrogalvanized; electronic guidance

e.g. *exempli gratia* (Latin—for example)

Eg Egypt; Egyptian

EG Electrographic (copier); Engineers Guild; Equatorial Guinea (formerly Spanish Guinea); Evaluation Group(ing); grid voltage (symbol)

EGA Elizabeth Garrett Anderson (hospital); European Golf Association

egabrag neither an abbreviation nor an acronym but garbage spelled backwards and sometimes used as a euphemism for garbage boat or garbage scow

egad. electronegative gas detector

egads electronic ground automatic destruct sequencer (system for destroying malfunctioning missiles)

egal egalitarian(ism)

EGAT Electricity Generating Authority of Thailand

Egb Egbert

e-g-b-d-f (musical menemonic —every good boy does fine)—treble clef note names of the five lines (e-g-b-d-f)

egc electrogalvanized coated

egcr experimental gas-cooled reactor

EGCRNR Eilat Gulf Coral Reef Nature Reserve (Israel)

EGCS English Guernsey Cattle Society

egd electrogasdynamics

egdg electrogasdynamic generator

EGDS Equipment Group Design Specifications

ege expected grade equivalent

ege *eau, gaz, electricite* (French —water, gas, electricity)

Egeo (Spanish—Aegean)

E Ger East Germany

egg. electrogastrogram

EG & G Edgerton, Germeshausen & Grier

Egg Basket of California Petaluma

eggler egg + dealer (an egg dealer)

eggsan egg sandwich

eggwich egg sandwich

EGIFO Edward Grey Institute of Field Ornithology

Egip *Egipto* (Portuguese or Spanish—Egypt)

Egipto (Portuguese or Spanish—Egypt)

Egit *Egitto* (Italian—Egypt)

Egitto (Italian—Egypt)

egl *egentlig* (Dano-Norwegian—actual, proper, real)

EGL Eglin, Florida (tracking station); European Guarantee Loan(s)

egm extraordinary general meeting

EGM Extraordinary General Meeting (of shareholders)

EGmc East Germanic

EGMEX Eastern Gulf of Mexico

Egmonts Egmont Islands in the Chagos Archipelago northwest of Diego Garcia

EGMRSA Edible Gelatin Manufacturers Research Society of America

EGNR Ein Gedi Nature Reserve (Israel's Dead Sea oasis)

EGO Ankara Elektrik, Havagazi ve Ötobüs Isletme Müessesesi (Ankara Electricity, City-Gas, and Bus Traffic Department); Eccentric-Orbiting Geophysical Observatory; Educational Growth Opportunities

egomac effect of gravity on methane-air combustion

egp embezzlement of government property; exhaust gas pressure

EGPA Egyptian General Petroleum Authority

EGPC Egyptian General Petroleum Corporation

EGPS Electric Ground Power System

egr egress; exhaust gas recirculation

egr (EGR) erythrocyte gluta-thione reductase

EGRET Explorer Gamma-Ray-Experiment Telescope (NASA)

egrs extragalactic radio source

EGS Electronic Guidance Section; Employment Guarantee Scheme

egt exhaust gas temperature

Egyp Egypt; Egyptian; egyptology

Egypt Arab Republic of Egypt (North African nation teeming with Egyptians speaking an Arabic dialect, cotton, minerals, and oil among leading exports from the Land of the Pharoahs)

Egypt. Egyptian

Egyptian Piano Concerto No. 5 by Saint-Saëns

Egyptian Badlands Assiut area about 175 miles (282 kilometers) south of Cairo and notorious for narcotic raids, religious clashes, and village vendettas

Egyptian Ports (on the Mediterranean) El Iskandariya (Alexandria); Bur Said (Port Said); (on the Red Sea) El Suweis (Suez)

egyptol egyptology

Egypt's Principal Port Alexandria

eh educationally handicapped

e/h exercise-head

e & h environment and heredity

eH oxidation-reduction potential (symbol)

EH Ernest Hemingway; extra hazardous

EH Enciclopedia Hoepli (Italian —Hoepli's Encyclopedia)

eha enroute high altitude

EHA Economic History Association; Education of the Handicapped Act; Environmental Health Association; Equipment Handover Agreement

EHB Environmental Hearing Board

ehbf extrahepatic blood flow

ehc enterohepatic circulation; enterohepatic clearance

E & HC Emory and Henry College

EHCD Environment, Housing, and Community Development (Australian Department of)

ehd electrohydrodynamics

ehd (EHD) epizootic hemor-rhagic disease

ehec (EHEC) ethylhydroxyeth-ylcellulose

EHES Environmental Health Engineering Services (USA)

ehf extreme high-frequency— 30,000-300,000 mc

ehf (EHF) epidemic hemorrhag-ic fever

EHF Experimental Husbandry Farm

EHG Edvard Hagerup Grieg

EHH Ernst Heinrich Haeckel

EHHS Erasmus Hall High School

EHI Emergency Homes, Incorporated

EHIS Emission History Information System

ehl effective half life

Ehl English as a home language

EHL Eastern Hockey League; Environmental Health Laboratory (USAF)

e/h/m eggs per hen per month

EHMA Electric Hoist Manufacturers Association

EHMS Engine Health Monitoring System

EHN Exploring Human Nature

EHOG European Host Operators Group

ehp effective horsepower; electric horsepower; extra-high potency

EHP Eric Honeywood Partridge (British lexicographer)

EHPT Eddy Hot-Plate Test

ehr enhanced reflector

EHS Emergency Health Service; Environmental Health Services; Experimental Horticultural Station (UK)

ehsi electronic horizontal-situation indicator

EHSP Environment Health Safety Program

eht extra-high tension

EHTRC Emergency Highway Traffic Regulation Center

ehv extra-high voltage

EHV Empresa Hondureña de Vapores (Honduran Steamship Line)

EHVIST Ethical and Human Value Implications of Science and Technology

ehw extreme high water

ehws electric hot water service; extreme-high-water-level spring tides

e/h/yr eggs per hen per year

ei electrical insulation; end item; engineering installation; exposure index

ei (EI) environment(al) illness

e-i electromagnetic interference; electronic interface; electronic interference; extraversion-introversion

e/i endorsement irregular

e by i execution by injection (of air or poison)

e^i income elasticity of demand

Ei Eire (Irish Free State)

Ei encéphale isolé (French—isolated intellectual)

EI East Indies; Electro Institute; Embrittlement Index; Essex Institute; Eunice Institute

EI Engineering Index

eia enzyme immunoassay

EIA East Indian Association; Electronic Industries Association; Empire Industries Association; Energy Information Administration; Engineering Institute of America; Environmental Impact Assessment

EIA Environmental Information Abstracts

EIAC Environmental Information Analysis Center

EIAJ Electronics Industry Association of Japan

EIAR Environmental Impact Analysis Report

EIB Ernst Ingmar Bergman; European Investments Bank; Export-Import Bank

EIB Economisch Instituut voor de Bouwnijverheid (Dutch—Economics Institute of the Building Industry); *Elsevier International Bulletins*

EIBA Electrical Industries Benevolent Association

EIBUS Export-Import Bank of the United States

EIBW Export-Import Bank of Washington

eic emotional inertia concept; equipment installation and checkout

EIC Ecology International Corporation; Education Information Center; Energy Information Center; Engineering Institute of Canada; European Investment Center

EICBL Eastern Independent Collegiate Basketball League

EICF European Investment Casters' Federation

e-i children emotionally-impaired children

eicm employer's inventory of critical manpower

EICR Eppley Institute for Cancer Research (Omaha)

EICS East India Company's Service

eid electron impact desorption; end item description

EID End Item Delivery; End Item Description; Engineering Item Description

EIDA Engineering Industries Development Agency

EIDC East Indian Defense Commission; East Indian Defense Committee (Canada)

EIDEBOEWABEW Economic Intelligence Division of the Enemy Branch of the Office of Economic Warfare Analysis of the Board of Economic Warfare

Eidg Eidgenössisch (Swiss—federal)

eid lt emergency identification light

EIDs East India Docks (London)

eie end-item equipment

EIES Electronic Information Exchange System (called *eyes*)

EIF Elderly Invalids Fund; Executive Inventory File

EIFAC European Inland Fisheries Advisory Committee (FAO)

eiff enemy identification—friend or foe

eig eigenlijk (Dutch—proper)

EIG Exchange Information Group

Eight The Eight (Ashcan School of American Art comprising Arthur B Davies, William Glackens, Robert Henri, Ernest Lawson, George Luks, Maurice Prendergast, Everett Shinn, and John Sloan)

Eighteenth State Louisiana

Eight Great Eight Great Islands of Japan (largest islands of the Japanese archipelago)

Eighth State South Carolina (*see* First State)

Eighth Wonder of the World compound interest, according to Baron de Rothschild, who would have agreed the man who invented interest was no slouch; the Panama Canal

EII East Intercourse Island (Australia)

eiii Electrical Industry Information Institute

eil electron injection laser

Eil Eileen; English as an international language

Eil Eiland(en) [Afrikaans or Dutch—island(s)]

EIL Electronic Instruments Limited; Experiment in International Living

Eimac Eitel-McCullough

EIMO Electronic Interface Management Office

EIMS Engineering Installation Management System

EIN Equipment Installation Notice

EIN Empresa Insulana de Navegação (Island Navigation Line)

E-in-C Engineer-in-Chief

E Ind East Indian; East Indies

Eine Kleine Nachtmusik (German—A Little Night Music) —Mozart's Serenade for String Orchestra (K 525)

Ein Heldenleben (German—A Hero's Life)—autobiographical symphonic poem by Richard Strauss

EINP Elk Island National Park (Alberta)

einschl einschliesslich (German —including)

Einw Einwohner (German—inhabitants, population)

EINZ Export Institute of New Zealand

EIO Emergency Information Office(r)

EIP Environmental Improvement Program; Experiment Implementation Plan

EIPC European Institute of Printed Circuits

eir earned income relief (tax)

EIR East Indian Railway; Emergency Information Readiness; Engineering Information Request; Environmental Impact Report; Equipment Interchange Receipt

Eire (Gaelic—Ireland)

EIRMA European Industrial Research Management Association

eirnv extra incidence rate in non-vaccinated groups

eiro evaluation of infra-red optics

EIRs Environmental Impact Reports

EIRS Education Information Resources Service

eirv extra incidence rate in vaccinated groups

eis electrical intersection splice; electron impact spectroscopy; end interruption sequence; extended instruction set

Eis (German—E-sharp)

EIS Early Implementation System; Economic Information Systems; Education Information Services; Electronic Ignition System; Electronic Inqui-

ry System; End Item Specification; Environmental Impact Statement; Epidemic Intelligence Service (HEW); Exxon Information System

Eisted (Welsh—Eisteddfod—annual meeting of Welsh bards)

e-i student(s) emotionally-impaired student(s)

eit engineer in training

ei & t emplacement, installation, and test(ing)

EIT Electrical Information Test

EITA Electric Industrial Truck Association

EITB Engineering Industry Training Board

Either/Or Soren Kierkegaard's nickname

eitp environmental interaction theory of personality

EITS Educational and Industrial Testing Service

eiu economist intelligence unit

EIVT European Institute for Vocational Training

EIWS Engineering Installation Workload Schedule

ej elbow-jerk

ej ejemplo (Spanish—example)

EJ ERIC Journal

EJA Executive Jet Aviation

EJC Edison Junior College; Engineers Joint Council; Engineers Junior College; Everett Junior College

EJCC Eastern Joint Computer Conference

eject, ejector

EJ & E R Y Elgin, Joliet & Eastern Railway

EJMA Educational Jewelry Manufacturers Association; Expansion Joint Manufacturers Association

EJN Edicott Johnson (stock exchange symbol)

ejp excitatory junction potential

EJS Engineering Job Sheet

EJT Engineering Job Ticket

EJTA Emergency Jobs Training Act

ejusd. ejusdem (Latin—of the same)

ek even keel; single enamel single cellophane (insulation symbol)

eK etter Kristi (Norwegian—after Christ)

EK Eastman Kodak

EK Eisernes Kreuz (German—Iron Cross)—military decoration

Ekaterinburg czarist name for

Sverdlovsk

ekc epidemic keratoconjunctivitis

EKCO E.K. Cole (Limited)

EKD *Evangelische Kirche in Deutschland* (Protestant Church in Germany)

Eken (Swedish slang—Stockholm)

ekg electrokardiogram (electrocardiogram); electrocardiography

EKG electrokardiogram

eKr *efter Kristus* (Dano-Norwegian—after Christ)

eks *eksempel* (Dano-Norwegian—example)

EKSC Eastern Kentucky State College

ekskl *eksklusive* (Dano-Norwegian—exclusive)

eksp *expederet* or *ekspedition* (Dano-Norwegian—expedite or expedition)

ekspl *eksemplar* (Dano-Norwegian—example or sample)

ekv electron kilovolt

ekw electrical kilowatt(s)

el each layer; educational level; elastic level; elect(ed); electric(ity); electroluminescence; element(ary); elevated; elevation; elongation; extra line

el *eller* (Dano-Norwegian—or)

El Elbert; Elevated Railroad; Elias; Elvie; Elvira

EL Eastern League; Electrical Laboratory; Electronics Laboratory; Empresa do Limpopo (Limpopo Line); Engineer Lieutenant; English Leicester (sheep); Epworth League; Erie-Lackawanna (railroad); Everyman's Library; Export Licence

E-L Erie-Lackawanna (railroad)

el2 elongation in 2 inches

elab elaborate(d); elaborately; elaborating; elaboration; elaborative

ELAC East Los Angeles College

e lacte. *e lact* (Latin—with milk)

EL AL El Al Israel Airlines

El Alto (Spanish—The Tall One)—La Paz, Bolivia's airport serving the world's highest capital city

ELAM *Escuela Latinoamericana de Matemáticas* (Latin American School of Mathematics)

ELAP Emergency Legal Assistance Project

ELAPR *Estado Libre Asociado de Puerto Rico* (Spanish—Associated Free State of Puerto Rico)—the Commonwealth of Puerto Rico's official name

elas elastic; elasticity; emergency logistical air support

ELAS *Ethnikos Laikos Apeleptherotikos Stratos* (Greek—Hellenic Peoples' Army of Liberation)

Elasm Elasmobranchia

elasmobranchs elasmobranch fishes (cartilaginous fishes such as chimaeras, dogfishes, rays, and sharks)

El-ay Los Angeles, California

elb electronic lean burn; emergency locator beacon

Elb Egyptian pound

El of B Elector(ate) of Bavaria; Elector(ate) of Brandenburg

ELB English Language Battery

E.L.B. Bachelor of English Literature

elba emergency location beacon aircraft

Elba (Portuguese or Spanish—Elbe)

El Banco (Spanish—The Bank)—World Bank for Reconstruction and Development

El Bosco Spanish nickname for Hieronymus Bosch

El'brus Mount El'brus (Europe's highest mountain in the Caucasus of the USSR)

ELBS English Language Book Society

elc extra-low carbon (electrodes)

El C El Centro

ELC Electronic Location Center

El Caballo (Spanish—The Horse)—nickname of Cuba's Communist dictator Fidel Castro Ruz

El Cabrón (Spanish—The Goat)—nickname of dissolute Dominican dictator Generalissimo Rafael Leonidas Trujillo Molino

El Caj El Cajon

El Cajohn El Cajon, California

El Cap El Capitan Dam; El Capitan Reservoir

elcar electric car

El Caudillo (Spanish—The Chief)—sobriquet of General Francisco Franco-Bahamonde

El Cen El Centro

El Cid *El Cid Campeador* (Spanish—The Lord Champion)—Rodrigo Díaz de Bivar

ELCID Enforcement of Law Through Court Intervention and Diversion

El Coco (Spanish—Coconut Palm)—San José, Costa Rica's airport

elct electronics

elct rm electronics room

eld edge-lighted display; elder; eldest; electric load dispatcher; extra-long distance

Eldercare plan providing medical care for the elderly

Elder Pitt William Pitt the Earl of Chatham also called the Great Commoner

Eldest Daughter of the Church France (where more than 20% of its population admit to being unbelievers)

el-dl electric locomotive-diesel locomotive

ELDO European Launcher Development Organization

El Dorado the mythical land of gold sought by the Spaniards and others in the jungles and mountains of the Americas

El Dorado State California

ELDS Editorial Layout Display System

Elean Eleanor

Eleanor Mrs Anna Eleanor Roosevelt—wife of President Franklin Delano Roosevelt

elec electric; electrical; electrician; electricity; electro-; electuary

Elec Elector; Electorate; Electra; Electricity

ELEC Election Law Enforcement Commission; European League for Economic Cooperation

Elec Engr Electrical Engineer; Electronic Engineer

elec pt electric(al) point

elecpub electronic publishing (dissemination of information via any electronic distribution means)

elect. election; elector; electoral; electrolyte; electrolytic

elect. *electuarium* (Latin—electuary)—confectioned drug; lollipop

elec tech electrical technician; electronic technician

electn electrician

ELECTRA Electrical, Electronics, and Communications Trades Association; trademark of the London Electricity Board

electraac electronic auto analysis clinic

Electric Motor City Detroit

electro electrocute; electrocu-

tion; electrotype
electrochem electrochemistry
electrocortico electrocorticograph(ic)(al)(ly); electrocorticography
electroderm electrodermal(ly)
electroenceph electroencephalography
electrogas electrogasdynamic(s)
electrogen electrogenic(al)(ly); electrogenesis
electrohyd electrohydraulic(s)
electrohydraul electrohydraulic(al)(ly)
electrol electrolysis
electrolev electronic levitation; electronically levitated
electromusic electronic music
electron. electronic(s)
Electron Lett Electronics Letters
electro-ocu electro-oculogram
electrophys electrophysics
electroret electroretinograph(ic)(al)(ly); electroretinography
electro(s) electrotype(s)
electrosen electrosensitive; electrosensitivity
electrostat electrostatic copy; electrostatic printing
Electrovette electric-battery-powered Chevette
electrum 50% gold, 50% silver
electy electricity
elek electric(al); electronic
Elekt Elektrizität (German—electricity)
elektr elektriciteit (Dutch—electricity)
elem element; elementary
elephantocade elephant parade
eleph fol elephant folio—books about 23 inches high
El Español (Spanish—The Spaniard)—Giuseppe Maria Crespi—Italian painter's nickname
El Españoleto Spanish painter José Ribera
e-less e-less novel written by British author Ernest Vincent Wright in 1939 with more than 50,000 words without the letter e; Georges Perec's *La Disparition,* published in French in 1969, is also e-less and deals with disappearance
elev elevated; elevation; elevator
Eleventh State New York (*see* First State)
elex electronics; electronics exercise
elf. early lunar flare; electric-light fitting; extra low frequen-

cy; extremely low frequency
elf (Swedish—river)
El F El Ferrol
ELF Early Lunar Flare; Eritrean Liberation Front
ELFA Electric Light Fittings Association
El Fatah disease virulent antisemitism
elfc electroluminescent ferroelectric cell
El Fénix de España The Phoenix of Spain—Lope de Vega
ELF-HELP Educators, Librarians, and Families—Helping Loving Prescholars
El Fondo (Spanish—The Fund)—International Monetary Fund—IMF
Elg Elgar; Elgin
El G El Paso Natural Gas Company
ELG European Liaison Group (USA)
elgas electricity and gas
ELGB Emergency Loan Guarantee Board
El Gran Libertador (Spanish—The Great Liberator)—Simón Bolívar—liberated Venezuela, Colombia, Ecuador, Peru, and Bolivia from Spanish rule
El Gran Supremo (see *El Supremo*)
El Greco (Spanish—The Greek)—Kryiakos Theotokopoulos (Domingo Theotocopuli)
El Havre (Spanish—Le Havre)
elhi elementary and high school (textbooks)
El Hombre (Spanish—The Man)—nickname of Dr Arnulfo Arias de Madrid of Panama who is remembered for appointing the first woman consul general; his sister, Zita Arias, served in that capacity in New York City in the 1930s
Eli Elias; Elihu; Elijah; nickname for a student or alumnus of Yale University
ELI English Language Institute; Environmental Law Institute
Elia Charles Lamb
ELIA English Language Institute of America
ELIC Electric Lamp Industry Council
Eli Edwards Claude McKay
Elien. Eliensis (Latin—of Ely)
elig eligible
Elij Elijah
Elijah Muhammad Robert Poole
El Ilustre Americano (Spanish—

The Illustrious American)—self-title of Venezuelan dictator Antonio Guzman Blanco
elim eliminate; eliminated; elimination
ELIM Evangelical Lutherans in Mission
elin exhibit line item number
El Inca (Spanish—The Inca)—Garcilaso de la Vega
elint electronic intelligence
elints electronic intelligence-gathering vessels
elip electrostatic latent image photography
Elis Elisabeth
elisa enzyme-linked immunosorbent assay
Elisabethville former name of Lubumbashi, Zaire
Elise Elizabeth
Elisir L'Elisir d'Amore (Italian—The Elixir of Love)—two-act opera by Donizetti
El Iskandariya (Egyptian Arabic—Alexandria)
elix elixir
Eliz Elizabeth(an)
Eliza Elizabeth
Elizabeth II Elizabeth Alexandra Mary of Windsor (Queen of United Kingdom of Great Britain and Northern Ireland and Her Other Realms and Territories)
Elizabeth Arden Florence N Graham
Elizabeths Elizabeth Islands; queens named Elizabeth
Elk Hills U.S. Navy's petroleum reserve at Elk Hills, California
Elk Island Elk Island National Park east of Edmonton, Alberta
ell. elbow; ellipsoid(al); elliptic(al)
ell eller (Spanish—or)
Ell English language learning
Ella Eleanor; Eleanora; Eleanore; Isabella
ELLA European Long Lines Agency
Ellas (Modern Greek-Greece)
Ellen Eleanor(a)(e)
Ellen Glasgow Ellen Anderson Gholson
Ellerman Ellerman Lines Ltd
Ellery Queen Frederic Dannay and Manfred B Lee
El Libertador (Spanish—The Liberator)—Simón Bolívar
El Licenciado Tomé de Burguillos (Spanish—Attorney Tomé de Burguillos)—a pseudonym of Lope de Vega

Ellices Ellice Islands now called Tuvalu

Ellie Alice

el lign *eller lignende* (Dano-Norwegian—or similar)

ellip elliptic; elliptical; elliptically

ELLIS Ellis Air Lines

Ellis Bell pseudonym of Emily Brontë

el lt electric light; electric lighting

Elly Eleanor

elm. element; energy-loss meter

ELM Eastern Atlantic and Mediterranean; Edgar Lee Masters

elma electromechanical aid

Elma Elizabeth Mary; Wilhelmina

ELMA Empresa Lineas Maritimas Argentinas (Argentine Lines)

El Manco de Lepanto (Spanish—The One-handed Man of Lepanto)—Cervantes whose left hand was maimed at the Battle of Lepanto

El Mar Del Norte (Spanish—The North Sea)

El Mar del Sur (Spanish—The South Sea)—Balboa's name for the Pacific Ocean he sighted in 1513 from a peak in Darien, the Isthmus of Panama

Elm City New Haven, Connecticut

Elmer R Rice Elmer Reizenstein

ELMG Engine Life Management Group (USN)

elmint electromagnetic intelligence

Elmira Men's Reception Center (for male prisoners) at Elmira, New York

ELMO Engineering and Logistics Management Office (USA)

elmobile electric automobile

Elmo Lincoln Otto Elmo Linkenhelt

ELMS Earth Limb Measurement Satellite; Experimental Library Management System

El Mus East London Museum

Elmwood James Russell Lowell's home in Cambridge, Massachusetts

E Ln East London

ELN Ejército de Liberación Nacional (Spanish—Army of National Liberation)—Bolivian and Colombian underground group

ELNA Esperanto League of North America

El Ng Ela Nguema (formerly San Fernando)

elngn elongation

El Niño El Niño Current (warm ocean current sweeping northward from the west coast of South America to the west coast of North America)

ELNM Edison Laboratory National Monument (West Orange, New Jersey)

elo elocution; eloquence

Elo Eloheimo

ELO Electric Light Orchestra; English Language Office(r)

eloc elocution(ary); elocutionist(ic)(al)(ly)

ELOI Emergency Letter of Instruction

Eloise European large-orbiting instrumentation for solar experimentation

elong elongate; elongation

E long east longitude

eloq eloquence; eloquent(ly)

E Loth East Lothian

elox electrical spark erosion

ELP El Paso, Texas (airport)

El Pais (Spanish—The Country) —daily morning newpaper published in Madrid

El Paso del Aguila (Spanish—Eagle Pass)—Texas border town across Rio Grande from Piedras Negras in Coahuila, Mexico

elpc electroluminescence photo conductor

El Pisshole trucker's nickname for El Paso, Texas

El Pisso trucker's nickname for El Paso, Texas

El Precursor (Spanish—the Precursor)—Francisco Miranda —fighter for Venezuelan freedom from Spanish rule; Antonio Nariño—fighter for Colombian freedom from Spanish rule

El Qahira (Egyptian Arabic—Cairo)

ELR Engineering Laboratory Report

elra electronic radar

ELRACS Electronic Reconnaissance Accessory System

elrat electrical ram air turbine

El Reno Federal Reformatory at El Reno, Oklahoma

ELRO Electronics Logistics Research Office (USA)

Elroy American country-boy name derived from the French for king—*Le Roi* or the Span-

ish equivalent—*El Rey*—or their combination

Els Elsinore (Helsingör); Elspeth

El of S Elector(ate) of Saxony

ELS Escabana and Lake Superior (railroad)

Elsa Elizabeth

Elsa Lanchester Elizabeth Sullivan

El Salv *El Salvador* (Spanish—Republic of El Salvador)

El Salvador Republic of El Salvador (Central America's smallest nation but most productive of coffee and people, Spanish-speaking Salvadorans, *Salvadoreños*) *República de El Salvador*

El Salvador Day Salvadorean Independence Day (September 15)

El Salvador's Ports (east to west) La Unión, Puerto El Triunfo, La Libertad, Acajutla

Elsass-Lothringen (German-Alsace-Lorraine)

elsbm exposed location single buoy mooring

ELSE European Life Science Editors

elsec electronic security

ELSEGIS Elementary and Secondary General Information System

Elsev Elsevier (family of Dutch printers and publishers dating from the 16th century)—also spelled Elzevir like the typeface named for this family

Elsevier Sci Elsevier Scientific Publishing Co

El Sgndo El Segundo

Elshender (Scottish—Alexander)

elsie electronic location of status-indicating equipment; electronic signalling and indicating equipment; emergency life-saving instant exit

Elsie Elizabeth

El Silencio (Spanish—The Silence)—downtown Caracas where bus routes start and automotive traffic is at its noisiest

El Smoggo trucker's nickname for any smog-smitten city in the Southwest from El Paso to Los Angeles

Elspet(h) (Scottish—Elizabeth)

ELSS Emplaced Lunar Scientific Station

elsse electronic sky screen equipment

El Stinko *see* El Smoggo

El Supremo (Spanish—The Supreme)—Juan Vicente Gómez, Venezuelan dictator commander-in-chief and president dominating his country for 27 years from 1908 to 1935 when he died; also known as *El Gran Supremo* so as not to confuse him with another dictator, Paraguayan strong man José Gaspar Rodriguez de Francia—also known as *El Supremo*

El Suweis (Egyptian Arabic—Suez)—terminal port of the Suez Canal

elt electrometer; emergency locator transmitter

Elt European letter telegram

E Lt Engineer Lieutenant

ELT *English Language Teaching*

E Lt-Cdr Engineer Lieutenant-Commander

ELTDA English Language Teaching Development Aid

eltec electrical technician; electronic technician

ELTI English Language Teaching Institute

ELTJ *English Language Teaching Journal*

ELU English Lacrosse Union

El Uqsor (Egyptian Arabic—Luxor)

elv extra-low voltage

elv (Dano-Norwegian—river)

Elvira Madigan motion picture and nickname of Mozart's Piano Concerto No. 21 in C major (K 467) used as the musical theme of the film

elw extreme low water

elwh elsewhere

El Wld *Electrical World*

elws extreme-low-water-level spring tides

Ely easterly

Elysian Fields mythological place thought by the Portuguese to be the Madeira Islands or by the Spaniards to be the Canary Islands—also known as Isles of the Blest

Elz (*see* Elsev)

ELZ Environmental Living Zone

Elzas (Dutch—Alsace)

em electromagnetic(al)(ly); emanation; embargo; emergency maintenance; emergency mobilization; enlisted man; expanded metal

em (EM) electron microscope; electron microscopy; end of

medium character (data processing)

e/m specific electronic mass

e & m endocrine and metabolism; erection and maintenance

e of m error of measurement

'em them

em *eftermiddag* (Dano-Norwegian—after midday)

Em Emily; Emma; Emmanuel; Emy

EM Earl Marshal; Education Manual; Electrician's Mate; electromagnetic (symbol); Engineer Manager; Engineering Memorandum; Enlisted Man (Men); Etna & Montrose (railroad); European Movement; External Memorandum

E-M Electric Machinery (company); Electro-Motive (corporation); Embden-Meyerhof (glycolitic path)

E.M. Engineering of Mines; Engineer of Mining

EM *Estado-Maior* (Portuguese—general staff, headquarters); *Estado Mayor* (Spanish—general staff, headquarters); *Excerpta Medica* (Elsevier logotype)

E-M *Etat-Major* (French—Headquarters)

E.M. *Equitum Magister* (Latin—Master of Horse)

EM 1 C Electrician's Mate First Class (USN)

EM 2 C Electrician's Mate Second Class (USN)

EM 3 C Electrician's Mate Third Class (USN)

EMA Electronics Manufacturers Association; Employment Management Association; Envelope Manufacturers Association; European Marketing Association; European Monetary Agreement; Evaporated Milk Association; Exposition Management Association; Extended Mission Apollo

E MacD Edward MacDowell

EMAD Engine Maintenance Assembly and Disassembly

EMAIA Electrical Meter and Allied Industries Association

Emancipator of the Serfs Czar Alexander II of Russia

Emancipator of the Slaves William Wilberforce

Emanuel Swedenborg Emanuel Svedberg

Em Ar Un *Emiratos Arabes Unidos* (Spanish—United Arab Emirates)

EMAS Emergency Medical Advisory Service; Emergency Message Authentication System; Employment Medical Advisory Service; Employment Medical Advisory Service (UK)

EMATS Emergency Message Automatic Transmission System

emb embankment; embargo; embark; embarkation; embassy; embroidered; embroidery; embryo; embryology

Emb Embankment; Embassy

EMB Egg Marketing Board; Energy Mobilization Board (US)

Embakasi Nairobi, Kenya's airport

emball *emballasje* (Norwegian—packing)

EMBERS Emergency Bed Request System

embgo embargo

embk embark

Embkmt Embankment

embkn embarkation

EMBL Eniwetok Marine Biological Laboratory

embo emboss(ed); embossing

EMBO European Molecular Biology Organization

embr embroider(y)

embry embryology

embryol embryology

EMBS Energy Management Bumper System

embsy embassy

emc electromagnetic capability; engineered military circuit; equilibrium moisture content

emc (EMC) electromagnetic control; encephalomyocarditis

EMC Education Media Council; Einstein Medical Center; Electronic Material Change; End Mollycoddling in America; Engineering Maintenance Center; Engineer(ing) Maintenance Control; Engineering Manpower Commission; Evergreen Marine Corporation

E = mc² Einstein's equation where energy *(E)* equals the atomic mass *(m)* and the speed of light *(c)* squared; the speed of light being 186,000 miles per second

EMCC European Municipal Credit Community

EMCCC European Military Communications Coordinating Committee

EMCE Eastern Montana College of Education

emcee master of ceremonies

emcees masters of ceremony

EMCF European Monetary Co-operation Fund

EMCMF Embarked Mine Countermeasures Force

emcon emission control

EMCU Evergreen Maritime Container Unit

emcv encephalomyocarditis virus

emd electric-motor-driven

Emd Emden

EMD Energy Management Display

E-MD Electro-Motive Division (General Motors)

EMDI Export Market Development Incentive

emdp electromotive difference of potential

EMDP Export Market Development Programme

EME Electrical and Mechanical Engineering; Electrical and Mechanical Engineer(s)

EMEA Electrical Manufacturers Export Association

EMEB East Midlands Electricity Board

EMEC Electronics Maintenance Engineering Center

EMELEC trademark of East Midlands Electricity Board

emend. emendate(d); emendating; emendation(s); emendator(s); emendatory; emender(s)

emend. *emendatis* (Latin—corrected, edited, emended)

emer emergency

Emer Emeritus

emerald beryllium chromium aluminum silicate (gemstone variety of beryl)

Emerald of the Caribbean Guadeloupe Island, French West Indies

Emerald City Seattle, Washington

Emerald Empire Idaho's panhandle

Emerald Isle Ireland

Emerald Necklace 18,000 acres of parks surrounding Cleveland

emerald nickel zaratite (basic hydrated nickel carbonate)

Emerald of the Spanish Main Colombia

emerg emergency

emergcons emergency conditions

emerit. *emeritus* (Latin—retired with honor)

emery aluminum oxide (Al_2O_3)

E.Met. Engineer of Metallurgy

E-meter electrical-resistance galvanometer

EMETF Electromagnetic Environment Test Facility (USA)

EMEU East Midlands Educational Union

emf electromotive force; erythrocyte maturing factor; every morning fix (your old automobile)

EMF European Motel Federation; Excerpta Medica Foundation

E.M.F. E(dward) M(organ) Foster

emg electromyogram; electromyography

EMG Economic Monitoring Group

EMG *Estado-Maior General* (Portuguese—Staff General); *Estado Mayor General* (Spanish—Staff General)

emgcy emergency

emh electrical, mechanical, and hydraulic

emi electromagnetic interference

EMI Electrical and Musical Industries; Equipment Manufacturing Incorporated; Experiences in Mathematical Ideas

EMI *Edizioni Musicali Italiane* (Italian Music Publications)

emia (Latin suffix—a condition of the blood)—anemia

emic emergency maternity and infant care

emid electromagnetic intrusion detector

E Midl East Midland

EMIETF Ethnic Materials Information Exchange Task Force

emig emigrant; emigration

Emil Jannings Theodore Friderich Emil Janez

Emil Ludwig Emil Cohn

Emin Eminence

Eminent Humanist Julian Huxley

emip equivalent means investment period

Emirates United Arab Emirates (on the Trucial Coast of the Persian Gulf)

emis emission

EMIS Electromagnetic Intelligence System; Electronic Materials Information Services; Engineering Maintenance Information System

EMIT Engineering Management Information Technique

EMJC East Mississippi Junior College

Emjo Emmanuel Jobe

emK *elektromotorische Kraft* (German—electromotive force)

eml electromagnetic levitation; equal matrix languages

Eml Emily

EML Earthquake Mechanisms Laboratory; Equipment Modification List

EML *Everyman's Library*

em log electromagnetic log

EMLTS Electromagnetic Levitation Transportation System (wheelless railway)

emm electromagnetic measurement

Emm Emmanuel; Emmanuel College, Cambridge

emma electron microscopy and microanalysis

Emma Calve Rosa Calvet

Emma Lathen pseudonym shared by Mary J Latsis and Martha Hennissart

Emm Coll Emmanuel College—Cambridge

Emmet Street Brendan Behan's pen name

Emmie Emma; Emy; Emmy

Emml Emmanuel

EM^MO *Eminentísimo* (Spanish—Most Eminent)—masculine ecclesiastical title applied to cardinals

EMMS Electronic Mail and Message System

EMMSA Envelope Makers and Manufacturing Stationers Association

Emmy award given for outstanding television performances in the United States; statuette named after tv entertainer Faye Emerson

Emmy Destinn Ema Kittl

EMNM El Morro National Monument

EMO Emergency Measures Organization; Emergency Services Organization; Engineering Maintainability Organization; Equipment Move Order

emol *emolumentos* (Portuguese or Spanish—emoluments, official fees)

EMOL Excerpta Medica On-Line

Emos Earth's mean orbital speed

emot emotion(al)

E-motor(s) electric motor(s)—submarine

EMOW Electrician's Mate of the Watch (USN)

emp electromagnetic pulses; em-

pennage
emp. *emplastrum* (Latin—adhesive, a plaster)
e.m.p. *ex modo prescripto* (Latin —in the manner prescribed)
Emp Emperor; Empire; Empress
EMPAC Engineering Management Planning and Control
emp agcy employment agency
empath empathetic; empathy
EMPC Educational Media Producers Council
empd employed
Emperor Beethoven's Piano Concerto No. 5 in E flat; Haydn's String Quartet in C (opus 76, no. 3)
Emperor of Europe Napoleon Bonaparte's self-imposed but short-lived title
Emperor Franz-Joseph of the Austro-Hungarian Empire rolls down the Prater in the imperial coach drum-roll and trumpet-punctuated finale of the *Emperor Waltz* by Johann Strauss Jr
Emperor Philosopher Marcus Aurelius
emph emphasis
emphy emphysema; emphysematous; emphyteusis; emphyteuta; emphyteutic
EMPI European Motor Products Incorporated
EMPIRE Early Manned Planetary Interplanetary Round-Trip Experiment
Empire City New York; Wellington, New Zealand
Empire Day nearest Monday to May 24 and celebrated in many parts of what was once the British Empire and now called the British Commonwealth of Nations
Empire State New York's official nickname
Empire State of the South Georgia's official nickname
empl emplace; emplacement; employ; employee; employer; employment
empld employed
EMPOCOL Empresa Puertos de Colombia (Colombian Port Works)
EMPORCHI Empresa Portuaria de Chile (Spanish—Chilean Port Enterprise)
Emporium of the West Indies Charlotte Amalie, St Thomas, Virgin Islands; Willemstad, Curaçao (or any other West Indian port city catering to the

tourist trade with an array of specialty shops)
EMPPO European and Mediterranean Plant Protection Organization
Empress of the Blues Bessie Smith
Empress Carlota Marie Charlotte Amélie Augustine Victoire Clémentine Léopoldine —empress of Mexico under Maximilian
Empress Eugenie Eugénie Marie de Montijo de Guzman—empress of the French under Napoleon III
Empress of Hollywood Bette Davis
Empress of India Queen Victoria
Empress of Vice Mary Jeffries (who in the 1800s controlled London's most elegant brothels)
empro emergency proposal
empsked employment schedule
empsz emphasize
emp. vesic. *emplastrum vesicatorium* (Latin—a blistering plaster)
emq electromagnetic quiet
emr educable mentally retarded; electromagnetic resonance; electromagnetic riveting
EMR Emerson Electric (stock exchange symbol); Engineering Master Report; Engineering Model Report; Enlisted Manning Report
EM & R Equipment Maintenance and Readiness
em-related emission-related (smog)
EMRIC Educational Media Research Information Center
EMRODA Electronic Maintenance Repair Operation Distributors Association
EMRS East Malling Research Station
ems emergency medical services; expected mean squares
Ems Bad Ems
EMS Econometric Society; Electronic Message System; Emergency Medical Service; Engineering Material Specification; European Monetary System; Export Marketing Service
EMSA Electron Microscope Society of America
EMSC Educational Media Selection Center
EMSO European Mobility Service Office (USA)

EMSS Electromechanical Subsystem
EMSU Environmental Meteorological Support Unit
emt electrical metallic tubing; emergency medical technique; equivalent megatonnage
EMT Emergency Medical Technician; Evaluation Modality Test
EMTA Electro-Mechanical Trade Association
EMT-A Emergency Medical Technician—Ambulance
EMTN European Meteorological Telecommunications Network
EMT-P Emergency Medical Technician—Paramedic
emtr emitter
emu. electromagnetic unit
Emu European monetary unit
EMU Eastern Michigan University; Economic and Monetary Union
EMU *Europese Monetaire et Economische Unie* (Dutch— European Monetary and Economic Union)
emul emulsion
emuls. *emulsio* (Latin—emulsion)
emut electric multiple-unit train
emux electronic multiplexer
emv electromagnetic vulnerability; electron megavolt
Emy Emilia; Emily
en enema; enemy; exceptions noted
en (Greek—in, into)—encephalitis, energy, entropy, environment
En Engineer; English
EN Esquimalt and Nanaimo (railway)
EN *Emissora Nacional* (Portuguese—National Broadcast); *Estrada Nacional* (Portuguese or Spanish—National Highway); *Evening News*
En 1 c Engineman first class
ENA English Newspaper Association
ENA *Escuela Nacional de Agricultura* (Spanish—National School of Agriculture); *L'Ecole Nationale d'Administration* (French—National Administration School)— France's civil-service academy
ENAB Evening Newspaper Advertising Bureau
ENAF *Empresa Nacional de Fundiciones* (Spanish—National Smelters Enterprise)

ENAFRI *Empresa Nacional de Frigorificos* (Spanish—National Freezer Enterprise)

enam enamel; enameled; enamels

ENAMI *Empresa Nacional de Mineria* (Spanish—National Mining Enterprise)—Chile

ENAP Empresa Nacional del Petroleo (Chile)

ENAP *Empresa Nacional del Petróleo* (Spanish—National Petroleum Enterprise)

ENAPUPERU *Empresa Nacional de Puertos del Peru* (Spanish—National Enterprise of the Ports of Peru)

ENASA *Empresa Nacional de Autocamiones* (Spanish—National Trucking Enterprise)

ENATA *Empresa Nacional de Tabaco* (Spanish—National Tobacco Enterprise)

ENATEL *Empresa Nacional de Telecomunicaciones* (Spanish—National Telecommunication Enterprise)

ENB East New Britain

ENBPS *Ente Nazionale per le Biblioteche Populari e Scolastiche* (Italian—National Organization of Popular and Scholastic Libraries)

enc enclosed

ENC *Empresa Nacional de Carbon* (Spanish—National Coal Enterprise)

ENCA European Naval Communications Agency

encap encapsulate(d); encapsulation

Enc Can *Encyclopedia Canadiana*

Enchanted Isles the Galápagos or Tortoise Islands originally called *Las Islas Encantadas* by early Spanish explorers

ENCI *Empresa Nacional de Comercializacion de Insumos* (Spanish—National Enterprise for the Commercialization of Raw Materials)

Enc Jud *Encyclopedia Judaica*

encl enclose; enclosed; enclosure

encld enclosed

enclg enclosing

enclit enclitic

enclo enclosure

ENCO Energy Company (Humble Oil & Refining)

encom encomiast(ic); encomium(s)

ENCORE Encouragement, Normalcy, Counseling, Opportunity, Reaching out, Energies

revived (YWCA program for women who have undergone breast surgery)

ENCOTEL *Empresa Nacional de Correos y Telegrafos* (Spanish—Post and Telegraph National Enterprise)

ENCP European Naval Communications Plan (NATO)

enct encounter

ency encyclopedia

Ency Assn *Encyclopedia of Associations*

Ency Brit *Encyclopaedia Britannica*

end. endorsement

end (Latin prefix—within)—endoderm

ENDE *Empresa Nacional de Electricidad* (Spanish—National Electricity Enterprise)

ENDESA *Empresa Nacional de Electricidad SA* (Spanish—National Electricity Enterprise Corporation)

ENDEX Environmental Data Index

endis endispiece (smart-alek's antonynm for frontispiece, whereas the correct term is tailpiece)

end mth end of month

endo endocrine; endocrinology

endo *endon* (Greek—within)—endocrine, endodermic, endoskeletal

endocrin endocrinological; endocrinologist; endocrinology

endocrino endocrinologic(al)(ly); endocrinologist; endocrinology; endocrinopath(ic)(al)(ly); endocrinopathy; endocrinosis; endocrinotherapy; endocrinous

EndocSoc Endocrine Society

endor electron nuclear double resonance

endor(s) endorsement(s)

endow. endowment

endp endpaper(s)

ends. endpapers

ENDS Euratom Nuclear Documentation System

ENDS *Empresa Nacional de Semillas* (Spanish—National Seed Enterprise)

end tel *endereço telegráfico* (Portuguese—cable address)

endv *endvidere* (Dano-Norwegian—furthermore)

endvr endeavor

endvrg endeavoring

end wk end of week

end yr end of year

ene *enero* (Spanish—January)

ENE east northeast

ENE *Escuela Nacional de Economica* (Spanish—National School of Economics)

ENEA European Nuclear Energy Association

ENEL Ente Nazionale per l'Energia Elettrica (National Electric-Power Company of Italy)

enem. *enema* (Greek—injection)

ener energize

ENERGAS *Empresa Nacional de Gas* (Spanish—National Gas Enterprise)

energe *energicamente* (Italian—energetically)

Energy City Houston, Texas

ENEWS Effectiveness of Navy Electronic Warfare System

ENEX Engineering Export Association

ENF European Nuclear Force

en fav de *en faveur de* (French—in favor of)

enf(d) enforce(d)

enft enforcement

eng electronic news gathering; electronystagmogram; engine

eng (ENG) electronic news gathering (tv news reports)

eng *engelsk* (Dano-Norwegian—English)

Eng England; English

Eng *Engineering* (British periodical)

Engañol English-Spanish

ENGBCA Engineers Board of Contract Appeals (USA)

Eng. D. Doctor of Engineering

eng dvr engine driver

Engel (Dutch—England)

eng err engineering error

eng fnd engine foundation

enggmt engagement

Eng hrn English horn (a low oboe and neither English nor horn)

engin engineering

Eng Index *Engineering Index*

Engineer of the Animal World the busy beaver

Engineer of Fantasy Walt Disney

Engineer-Humanitarian-Statesman Herbert Hoover

Engineers' Town Coulee City, Washington

engitist engineer + scientist

Engl England; English

Engl English (most popular language of our time and third only to Chinese and Indian tongues in the number who speak it: 352 million people, English is followed by Russian, Spanish, Hindi, Arabic,

Bengali, German, Portuguese, Japanese, Malay, French, Italian, and Urdu, and in that order); English has the largest vocabulary of any West European language as well as a great many others; its slanguage is some of the most colorful and expressive as readers know or will discover

England section of Great Britain inhabited by Englishmen and Englishwomen, the English

England's Wooden Walls the Royal Navy during the Napoleonic wars

Englebert Humperdinck Jerry Dorsey (who took the name of Wagner's protégé)

Englewood Federal (delinquent) Youth Center at Englewood, Colorado

english english horn (*cor anglais* or bass oboe); english laurel (cherry laurel); english muffin (griddle-baked yeast dough made in a muffin shape); english saddle (hornless well-padded saddle with full side flaps placed forward); english setter (black-and-white or tan-and-white setter originally bred in England); all other eponymic terms prefixed with *english*, a lowercase derivative

English Alexander nickname of King Henry V

English Bach Johann Christian Bach (who lived in London from 1759 to 1852)

English Caribees colonial name for the British West Indies

English Channel La Manche

English Cradle of U.S. Presidents England—ancestral home of both Presidents named Adams; Presidents Carter, Cleveland, Coolidge, Fillmore, Ford, Garfield, Grant, Harding; both Presidents named Harrison; both Presidents named Johnson; Presidents Lincoln, Madison, Pierce, Taft, Taylor, Tyler, and Washington

English Lit English literature

English Nonet England's nine best-known classical composers listed chronologically—Tallis, Byrd, Purcell, Sullivan, Elgar, Delius, Vaughan-Williams, Walton, Britten

English Nonsense Poet Edward Lear

English Operetta Composer Sir Arthur S Sullivan

English Opium Eater Thomas De Quincey

English penicillin a nice cuppa' tea

English Polynesia jocular nickname for the Seychelles Islands in the Indian Ocean far from Polynesia in the South Pacific

English Ports (*see* British Ports)

English Riviera (*see* Cornish Riviera)

English Symphonist Ralph Vaughan Williams

Eng Lit English Literature

Eng News-Rec Engineering News-Record

eng° engenheiro (Portuguese—engineer)

engr engineer

eng rm engine room

engrv engraver; engraving

Eng. Sc. D. Doctor of Engineering Science

ENGSS Engineering Schoolship (USN)

EN-H Elsevier North-Holland

ENI Ente Nazionale Idrocarburi (National Fuel Agency)

ENI Escuela Nacional de Ingeniería (Spanish—National School of Engineering)

eniac electronic numerical integrator and computer

ENIC Ente Nazionale Industrie Cinematografiche (Italian—National Association of Film Producers); *Ente Nazionale della Cinofilia Italiana* (National Organization of Italian Dog Lovers)

ENICO Exxon Nuclear Idaho Company

ENIDS Ethnic Name Identification System

Enigma Elgar's *Enigma* Variations for Orchestra with an enigmatic program wherein the composer dedicates its movements to his friends described by their initials

ENIM Ente Nazionale dell'Istruzione Media (Italian—National Organization for Intermediate Instruction)

ENIT Ente Nazionale Industrie Turistiche (Italian—National Tourist Industry)

Eniwetok Kili Atoll

enk enkelvoud (Dutch—singular)

enl enlist

E n l English as a national language

enlgd enlarged

Enlightened Philanthropist Andrew Carnegie

Enlightenment (*see* The Enlightenment)

Enlightenment Centuries the 17th and 18th centuries (1600s and 1700s) when in America and Europe human reason prevailed in educational, political, and religious doctrine

en ml end mill

ENMU Eastern New Mexico University

Enn Quintus Ennius (Roman poet)

En Nasira (Arabic—Nazareth)

ENNWR Eastern Neck National Wildlife Refuge (Maryland)

eno enero (Spanish—January)

en° enero (Spanish—January)

E/no estacionamiento no (Spanish—no parking)

ENO English National Opera

Enoch Pratt Enoch Pratt Free Library

enol enology

Enos Book of Enos

Enu's Enu's Fruit Salts

ENP Egmont National Park (North Island, New Zealand); Etosha NP (South-West Africa); Everglades NP (Florida)

ENPA Ente Nazionale Protezione Animali (National Society for the Protection of Animals—Italy)

ENPI Ente Nazionale Prevenzione Infortuni (Italian—National Institution for the Prevention of Accidents)

ENPMA Eastern National Park and Monument Association

enq enquire; enquiry

enr en route; equivalent noise resistance

enr (ENR) extrathyroidal neck radioactivity

ENR Emissora Nacional de Radiodifusão (Radio Portugal)

E & NR Esquimalt and Nanaimo Railway

ENRI Electronic Navigation Research Institute

enrpae enroute (to/from) public affairs event

enrt enroute

Ens Ensign

Ens Ensenadas (Spanish—inlets, small bays)

ENS Empresa Naviera Santa; European Nuclear Society; experimental navigation ship

ENSA Entertainments National Service Association

Ensen Ensenada

ensi equivalent—noise sideband input

ENSIDESA *Empresa Nacional Siderurgica SA* (Spanish—National Steel Works)

ENSIP Engine Structural Integrity Program (USAF)

en-skids National Security Intelligence Directives

ent ear, nose, and throat; enter; entrance

ent *ental* (Dano-Norwegian—singular)

ENT Aerolineas Argentinas (Argentine Airlines); Ear, Nose, and Throat (clinic or hospital department)

ENTA Environmental Test Area

Entac Nord wire-guided antitank missile made in France

entd entered

ENTE Ente Nazionale per l'Energia Elettrica (National Electric Energy Enterprise)

ENTEL *Empresa Nacional de Telecomunicaciones* (Spanish—National Telecommunications Enterprise)

Entendard Dassault single-engine jet attack aircraft made in France

entero (Latin prefix—intestine) —enteritis

enterobact enterobacterial(ly); enterobacteriologist; enterobacterium

enteropath enteropathogenic(al)(ly)

enterov enterovioform

ent hall entrance hall

entl entitle

entn entertain

entom entomology

entomol entomologic(al)(ly); entomologist; entomology

entr entrance

entspr *entsprechend* (German—corresponding)

Ent Sta Hall Entered at Stationers' Hall

ENTURPERU *Empresa Nacional de Tourismo del Peru* (Spanish—National Tourist Enterprise of Peru)

ent-vio entero-vioform (anti-diarrhetic)

enur enuresis

enus end user

enutech enuresis technology (controlling bedwetting)

env envelop; envelope; environ; envoy

Env Envoy

Env Ext Envoy Extraordinary

ENVI Envirosphere Company

environ. environment; environmental; environmentalism; environmentalist

ENWR Erie National Wildlife Refuge (Pennsylvania); Eufaula National Wildlife Refuge (Alabama)

ENY Elsevier New York

enz *enzovoort(s)* (Dutch—and so on)

enza influenza

En Zed(er)(s) New Zealand (er)(s)

eo end of operation; engine oil

e-o electro-optical; even-odd

e & o errors and omissions

e.o. *ex officio* (Latin—by virtue of office)

Eo Ecuadorian escudo(s); escudo(s) (Portuguese currency)

E₀ electric affinity (symbol)

EO Eastern Orthodox; Education Officer; Employers Organization; Engineering Order; Entertainments Office(r); Examining Office(r); Executive Office(r); Executive Order

E & O Eastern and Oriental

eoa effective on or about; end of address; examination, opinion, advice (medical)

EOA Economic Oil Association; Education Officers Association; Essential Oil Association

EOARDC European Office of the Air Research and Development Command (USAF)

eob end of block (character); expense operating budget

EOB Executive Office Building

eoc electric overhead crane; emotional-organic combination; end of card

Eoc Eocene

EOC Economic Opportunity Commission; Educational Opportunity Center; Electronic Operations Center; Enemy Oil Committee; Equal Opportunities Commission; Executive Officers Council

EOCC Engineering Operational Casualty Control (USN)

EOCI Electric Overhead Crane Institute

eocp engine out of commission for parts

eod entry on duty; every other day; explosive ordnance disposal

eod (EOD) explosive ordnance device

eodad end-of-data-set address

EODAP Earth and Ocean Dynamic Applications Program

(NASA)

EODG Explosive Ordnance Disposal Group

EODP Engineering Order Delayed for Parts

EODU Explosive Ordnance Disposal Unit

eoe earth orbit ejection; equal opportunity employer

e & oe errors and omissions excepted

e and oe errors and omissions excepted

EOE Enemy-Occupied Europe

eof end of flight

eof (EOF) end of file

EOF Earth Orbital Flight

eog effect on guarantees; electro-oculogram

EOG English Opera Group

eogb (EOGB) electro-optical glide bomb(ing); electro-optical guided bomb(ing)

EOGs Educational Opportunity Grants

eoh end of overhaul; equipment on hand

EOH Emergency Operation Headquarters

eohp except otherwise herein provided

eoj (EOJ) end of job

eol effective operational length; end of life; expression-oriented language

Eol Eolic

EOL Ex Oriente Lux (The Light of the Orient—The Oriental Society)

eolb end-of-line block

eolm electro-optical light modulator

eom end of month; every other month; extra-ocular movements

eom (EOM) end of message (data processing)

EOM Employment Office Manager(s)

EOMB Explanation of Medicare Benefits

eomi end of message incomplete

eoms end-of-message sequence

EONR European Organization for Nuclear Research

eooe error or omission excepted

EOOW Engineering Officer of the Watch (USN)

eop earth orbit plane; end of part; end of passage

EOP Educational Opportunity Programs; Engineering Operational Procedure; Equal Opportunity Program; Equipment Operations Procedure;

Executive Office of the President

EOPs Extended Opportunity Programs

EOPS Equal Opportunity Programs and Services; Extended Opportunity Program and Services

eoq economical ordering quantity; end of quarter

EOQC European Organization for Quality Control

eor earth orbital rendezvous; end of reel; explosive ordnance reconnaissance

eor (EOR) end of record; end of run

EOR Earth Orbit Rendezvous

EORSA Episcopalians and Others for Responsible Social Action

EORTC European Organization for Research on the Treatment of Cancer

eos eligible for overseas service; end operation suppress; end of segment

EOS Engineering Orders

EOS Earth Observation Satellite; Earth Orbiting Satellite; Earth Orbiting Shuttle (NASA); Electro-Optical System; Engine Overhaul Shop; European Orthodontic Society

eosins eosinophils

eosp economic order and stocking procedure

EOSS Earth Orbital Space Station; Engineering Operational Sequencing System

eot end of tape; end of transmission; enemy-occupied territory; engine order telegraph

EOT Eagle Ocean Transport

EOTP European Organization for Trade Promotion

eou electro-optical unit

EOU Epidemic Observation Unit

eov economic order van; end of volume

eow engine(s) over wing(s); every other week

EOx Elsevier Oxford

ep easy projection; electric primer; electrically polarized; electroplate; electroplated; electroplating; electropneumatic; endpaper(s); entrucking point; estimated position; exit pupil; experienced playgoer; explosion-proof; extended play (records); external publication; extreme pressure

ep (EP) extended play (45 rpm phonograph disc)

e/p endpaper

e & p exploration and production (area)

e p en passant (French—in passing)

e.p. editio princeps (Latin—first edition)

Ep. Episcopus (Latin—Bishop or overseer)

EP Eagle-Picher; Ecole Polytechnique (Polytechnic School); Engineering Personnel; Engineering Publications; entrucking point; estimated position; exceptions passed

E-P European Plan (no meals)

E & P Extraordinary and Plenipotentiary

EP Environmental Pollution

E & P Editor & Publisher

epa economic price adjustment; electron probe analyzer; estimated profile analysis

EPA Eastern Psychological Association; Economic Planning Agency; Emergency Powers Act; Empire Parliamentary Association; Empire Press Agency; Engineering Practice Amendment; Environmental Planning Authority; Environmental Protection Agency; European Productivity Agency; Evangelical Press Association; Executive Protective Agency

EPAA Educational Press Association of America; Emergency Petroleum Allocation Act; Employing Printers Association of America

EPAC Electronic Parts Advisory Committee

EPACCI Economic Planning and Advisory Council for the Construction Industries

epam (EPAM) elementary perceiver and memorizer

epaq electronic parts of assessed quality

EPAT Every Pupil Achievement Test

epb equivalent pension benefit

EPB Electronic Planning Board; Environmental Periodicals Bibliography

epbm electroplated base metal

EPBX Electronic Private Branch Exchange

epc easy processing channel; edge-punched card; electronic program control; electroplate on copper; engine performance computer; every poor cluck

EPC Economic and Planning Council; Economic Policy Committee; Education Products Center; Educational Publishers' Council; Environmental Policy Center; Esso Petroleum Company; European Planning Council

epca external-pressure circulatory assist

EPCA Energy Policy and Conservation Act; European Petro-Chemical Association

EPCAF El Paso Coalition Against the Fence (*see* Tortilla Curtain)

epc black easy-processing channel black

ep cells epithelial cells

epcg endoscopic pancreaticholangiography (EPCG)

EPCOT Experimental Prototype Community of Tomorrow

epcp electric plant control panel

epcrbs emergency-position communication radio beacons

EPCS Equitable Pioneers Cooperative Society

epd earliest practicable date; excess profits duty

ep & d electric power and distribution

epd en paz descanse (Spanish—may he rest in peace)

EPD Excellent Policy Duty (citation)

EPDA Education Professions Development Administration; Exhibit Producers and Designers Association

epdc economic power dispatch computer

EPDC Electric Power Development Corporation

ep disc extended-play (45 rpm) disc

epdm epidemiological; epidemiologist; epidemiology

epe electrical parts and equipment; electronic parts and equipment

EPE Editorial Projects for Education

EPEA Electrical Power Engineers Association

epedemiol epedemiology

EPEM Electric Parts and Equipment Manufacturers

epf exopthalmos-producing factor

EPF Employees Provident Fund; European Packaging Federation

EPF Empresa Petrolera Fiscal (Spanish—State Petroleum

Enterprise)—Peru

EPFL Enoch Pratt Free Library (Baltimore)

ÉPFL *École Polytechnique Fédérale de Lausanne* (French —Federal Polytechnic School of Lausanne)

epg eggs per gram (parasitology); electropneumogram

EPG Economic Policy Group; Electronic Proving Ground (US Army)

EPGA Emergency Petroleum and Gas Administration

EPGS Export Programme Grants Scheme (New Zealand)

Eph Ephraim

Eph *Ephesians*

EPHC Eastern Pacific Hurricane Center

ephmer ephemeral; ephemerides; ephemeris

epi electronic position indicator; emotional-physiologic illness

epi (Latin prefix—after, in addition, upon)—epicardial, epidemic, epidermis, epilogue, epithelium

EPI Edwards Personality Inventory; Emergency Public Information; Environmental Policy Institute; Eysenck Personality Inventory

epic. electronic printer image construction; electron-positron intersecting complex

EPIC Early Purchase Individual Contract; Education Professional for Indian Children; El Paso Intelligence Center; Electronic Properties Information Center; Elyria Project for Innovative Curriculum; End Poverty in California; Exchange Price Indicators; Exports Payments Insurance Corporation

epicen epicenter; epicentral(ly)

Epict Epictetus

epid epidemic

EPIE Educational Products Information Exchange

EPIEI Educational Products Information Exchange Institute

epig epigastric; epigeal; epigeous; epigenesis; epigenetic; epigenic; epiglottal; epiglottic; epiglottis; epigone; epigonic; epigonism(s); epigonus; epigram; epigrammatic(al)(ly); epigrammatism; epigrammatist(s); epigrammatize; epigrammatized; epigrammatizing; epigraph(er); epigraphic(al)(ly); epigraphist(s); epi-

graphy; epigynous; epigyny

epil epilogue

epineph epinephrine

epingrad equal participation in the great American dream

Epiph Epiphania; Epiphany

Epiphany Epiphany Day (January 6, Feast of the Three Kings)

epirb emergency position-indicating radio beacon

epirb (EPIRB) emergency position-indicating radio beacon

epis episiotomy

Epis Episcopal(ian)

Epist. *Epistola* (Latin—epistle or letter)

epistem epistemic(al)(ly); epistemological (ly); epistemologist(s)

epistom. *epistomium* (Latin—stopper)

epit epitaph; epitome

EPIT Equipment Procurement and Installation Team

epith epithelial; epithelium

epithal epithalamic; epithalamion

epivag epivaginitis

epl early programming language; extreme pressure lubricant

EPL Engineering Parts List; Erie Public Library; Evansville Public Library

EPL *Ecole Polytechnique de Lausanne* (French— Polytechnic School of Lausanne)

EPLF Eritrean People's Liberation Front

epm electric pedestrian mover; explosions per minute

epm *en propia mano* (Spanish— in good hands, the right way)

EPM Easy Pickin's Mine (Imperial County, California); Environmental Program Manager

epma electron-probe micro analysis

EPMS Engine Performance Monitoring System; Engineering Project Management System

epn effective-perceived noise

epn (EPN) ethyl paranitrophenyl

epnd effective-perceived noise decibels

epndbl effective-perceived noise decibel level

EPNG El Paso Natural Gas

epnl effective perceived noise level(s)

epns electroplated nickel silver

EPNS English Place-Name Society

epo experimental processing op-

eration

EPO Emergency Planning Office(r); Energy Policy Office; European Patent Office

EPOC Earthquake Prediction Observation Center; Eastern Pacific Ocean Conference

EPOCS Effectual Planning for Operation of Container Systems

epon eponym(s) [(designation(s) derived from proper names of families, places, or persons such as Hapsburg dynasty, Paris of America (Montreal), or Raynaud's disease)]

EPOSS Environmental Protection Oil Sands System

epp end plate potential; excess personal property

epp *edellä puolenpäiven* (Finnish—before noon)

Epp. *Episcopi* (Latin—Bishops or overseers)

EPP Earth Physics Program; European Pallet Pool

EPPL El Paso Public Library

EPPO European and Mediterranean Plant Protection Organization

EPPR Engineering Procurement Proposal Request

EPPS Edwards Personal Preference Schedule; Engineering Procurement Planning Sheet

EPQ Eysenck Personality Questionnaire

epr electronic paramagnetic resonance; engine pressure ratio

epr (EPR) electric propulsion rocket

EPR Engineering Power Reactor; Engineering Purchase Request; Essential Performance Requirements; External Planning Regent(s)

EPRA Early Planning for Retirement (Australia); Eastern Psychiatric Research Association

EPRC Educational Policy Research Center (Syracuse University)

EPRI Electric Power Research Institute

EPRL Electric Power Research Laboratory

eprom erasable-programmable read-only memory

EPRS Engineering Proposal Requirement Specification

eps earnings per share; electric power supply; electron proton spectrometer; emergency power supply

eps (EPS) energetic particle(s)

satellite(s); extrapyramidal side effect(s)

ep's epithelial cells

EPS El Paso Southern (railroad); Emergency Power System; Emergency Pressurizing System; Emergency Procurement Service; Engineering Purchase Specification; Escape Propulsion System

EPSA Energy Products and Services Administration

EPSA Empresa Publica de Servicios Agropecuarios (Spanish—Public Enterprise Agricultural Services)

epsdt early and periodic screening, diagnosis, and treatment

EPSEP Empresa Publica de Servicios Pesqueros (Spanish—Public Enterprise Fishing Services)

EPSIS Education Program and Studies Information Services

epsom epsom salt(s) named for the English racetrack town of Epsom Downs

epsom salt magnesium sulfate (MgSO⁴ • 7H²O)

epsp excitatory postsynaptic potential

Eps Vle Epsom Vale

ept egress procedures trainer; ethylene-propylene terpolymer; excess profits tax; external pipe thread

EPT Early Pregnancy Test(ing); Excess Profits Tax(ing)

EPTA Expanded Program of Technical Assistance (UN)

epte existed prior to entry

EPTG Electronic Publication Technology Group

EPTI Export Performance Taxation Incentive

epts existed prior to service

epu electrical power unit; electronic power unit; emergency power unit; entry processing unit

EPU Empire Press Union; European Payment Union

EPUL Ecole Polytechnique de l'Université de Lausanne (Polytechnic School of the University of Lausanne)

Epus Episcopus (Latin—Bishop)

eput events-per-unit-time

EPUY Education Program for Unemployed Youth

EPVT English Picture Vocabulary Test

epw enemy prisoner of war

epwm electroplated white metal

EPZ Ecole Polytechnique de

Zürich (Polytechnic School of Zurich); Export Processing Zone

eq encephalization quotient; equal; equalization quotient; equation; equivalent; (*also see* EQ)

Eq Equator

EQ educational quotient; enthusiasm quotient; ethnic quotient

EQA Environmental Quality Act (California)

EQAA Environmental Quality Advisory Agency

EQAD Electrical (Electronic) Quality-Assurance Directorate

EQB Environmental Quality Board

EQC Environmental Quality Council

eqcc entry-query-control console

Eq Guin Equatorial Guinea

eqi environmental quality index

eqiv equivalent

eqm equal-flow manifold

eqn equation; equine

eqn prdx equine paradox (the fact there are more horses asses than horses)

eqp equip; equipment

eqpmt equipment

eqpt equipment

eqq electric quadripole-quadripole

eqs equations

eqs (EQS) equivalents (20-foot containers)

EQSC Environmental Quality Study Council

eqt equivalent training

Eq T equation of time

eq tr equipment trust

equ equate; equation

Equ Equerry; Equuleus

Equa Equator; Equatorial

Equa C Cur Equatorial Countercurrent

Equality State Wyoming's official nickname reminding all it was the first state to guarantee women's suffrage (1869) and the first state to have a woman governor (1924)

EQUAP Engineering Qualification Approval Program

Equa Pac Equatorial Pacific

equat equator; equatorial

Equator imaginary line encircling widest part of the earth; designated as zero degrees latitude; divided into 360 degrees of longitude—180 East and

180 West of a prime meridian —usually the Greenwich Observatory outside of London

Equatorial Guinea Republic of Equatorial Guinea (West African island and mainland country formerly a Spanish possession, tropical crops and some lumber are exported) *República de Guinea Ecuatorial*

Equatorial Guinea's Main Port Bata

Equatorials short form for the Equatorial Islands close to the Equator in the central and South Pacific Ocean where they are also called the Line Islands

equil equilibrium

equin equinox

equinol equinologic(al)(ly); equinologist; equinology

equip. equipment

equipt equipment

Equity Actors' Equity Association

equiv equivalent

eq & wd earthquake and war damage (insurance)

er echo ranging; electronic reconnaissance; emergency rescue; enhanced recovery (oil well); established reliability; external resistance

e/r editing/reviewing; en route

'er her

Er erbium; Eritrea, Eritrean

ER East Riding; East River; Edwardus Rex (King Edward); Effectiveness Report; Eliz abeth Regina (Queen Elizabeth); Emergency Request; Emergency Rescue, Emergency Reserve; Emergency Room; Engine Room, Engineering Release; Engineering Report; Environmental Report; Equipment Requirement; Evaluation Report; Expense Report; Expert Rifleman; Explosives Report; Express Route; External Report

E by R English by Radio

E.R. Elizabeth Regina (Queen Elizabeth)

ER-200 high-speed train between Leningrad and Moscow

era. electronic reading automation; electronic ring accelerator

era. (ERA) earned run average

ERA Earthquake Risk Analysis; Economic Regulatory Administration; Economic Regulatory Agency; Electrical Research

Association; Electronic Representatives Association; Energy Resources of Australia; Engine Room Artificer; Engineering Research Associates; Engineering Research Association; Equal Rights Amendment; Equitable Reserve Association; Evaporative Rate Analysis

ERA *Equal Rights Amendment*

ERAA Equipment Review and Authorization Activity

Era of Good Feeling (administration of James Monroe—fifth President of the United States)

ERAI Embry-Riddle Aeronautical Institute

Era of Mediocrity post-World-War-II era

ERAP Economic Research and Action Project

ERAP *Entreprise de Recherches et d'Activités Petroliènes* (Petroleum Research Development Enterprise—French)

Era of Renewal (administration of Ronald Reagan, fortieth President of the United States)

Eras Erasmus

erase. electromagnetic radiation source elimination

eraser. (**ERASER**) elevated radiation seeker rocket

Erasmus Desiderius Erasmus (originally Geert Geerts or Gerard Gerardzoon)

erb economic requirement batching; electron beam recording; emergency radio beacon; enlisted record brief; epigram record bureau

'Erb Herbert

Erb *Erbitten* (German—ask for, beg for, request)

ERB Educational Records Bureau; Electricians Registration Board; Engineering Review Board; Engineers Registration Board; Environmental Review Board; Equipment Review Board

er bh engine room bulkhead

erbm (**ERBM**) extended-range ballistic missile

erc earnings-related compensation; en-route chart; equatorial ring current; equipment record card; expendability repair classification

ERC Economic Research Council; Economic Resources Corporation; Educational Resources Center; Electronics

Research Center (NASA); Elmira Reception Center (for male prisoners in Elmira, NY); Enlisted Reserve Corps

ERCA Educational Research Council of America

ERC & I Economic Reform Club and Institute

Erckmann-Chatrian pseudonym of literary collaborators Emile Erickmann and Alexandre Chatrian

ERCO Electric Reduction Company

Ercoli Palmiro Togliatti

ercp endoscopic retrograde cholangiopancreatography

ercr electronic retina-computing reader

ERCS Emergency Rocket Communications System

erd emergency return device; equivalent residual dose

ERD Earth Resources Data; Emergency Reserve Decoration; Equipment Requirements Data

ERDA Electrical and Radio Development Association; Electronics Research and Development Agency; Energy Research and Development Administration

ERDC Earth Resources Data Center; Electronic Research and Development Command (USA)

ERDE Explosives Research and Development Establishment

ERDIP Experimental Research and Development Incentives Program

ERDL Engineering Research and Development Laboratory

ere before (contraction found in the palindromic sentence—Able was I ere I saw Elba); expected repository environment(s)

'ere here

ERE Edison Responsive Environment

erect. erection

'Ereford(shire) [Cockney contraction—Hereford(shire)]

EREP Earth Resources Experiment Package (NASA)

Eretz Israel (Hebrew—Land of Israel)

Erewhon Samuel Butler's novel about a utopia and if spelled backwards it is almost "nowhere"

erf error function

ERF Education and Research Foundation; Eye Research

Foundation

ERFA European Radio-Frequency Agency

ERFAA European Radio-Frequency Allocation Agency

erfc error function complement

Erfurtum (Latin—Erfurt)—also called Erfordia

erg electrical resistance gage; unit of mechanical energy or work (derived from the word *energy*)

erg (**ERG**) erase gap

erg. electroretinogram

ERG Energy Research for the Governors; Energy Research Group

ERGOM European Research Group on Management

ergon ergonomic; ergonomical; ergonomics

ergp emergency removal gate pass

ergs (**ERGS**) earth geodetic satellite (USAF)

ERGS Electronic Route Guidance System

Erh Erhard

E & R: Hist Soc Evangelical and Reformed Historical Society

Eri Eridamus; Eridanus (constellation)

ERI Earthquake Research Institute (Tokyo University); Economic Research Institute; Environmental Research Institute; Erie, Pennsylvania (airport)

E.R.I. *Edwardus Rex et Imperator* (Latin—Edward, King and Emperor)

eric electronic remote and independent control; energy rate input controller

ERIC Educational Resources Information Center (US Office of Education)

ERIC/AE Educational Resources Information Center/Adult Education

ERIC/CAPS Educational Resources Information Center/Clearinghouse on Counseling and Personnel Services

ERIC/CE Educational Resources Information Center/Clearinghouse in Career Education

ERIC/CEA Educational Resources Information Center/Clearinghouse on Educational Administration

ERIC/CEC ERIC Clearinghouse for Educational Change

ERIC/CEM ERIC Clearinghouse on Educational Management

ERIC/CHE Educational Resources Information Center/ Clearinghouse on Higher Education

ERIC/CHESS Educational Resources Information Center/ Clearinghouse for Social Studies and Social Science

ERIC/CIR Educational Resources Information Center/ Clearinghouse on Information Resources

ERIC/CLL ERIC Clearinghouse on Languages and Linguistics

ERIC/CLS Educational Resources Information Center/ Clearinghouse for Library and Information Sciences

ERIC/CRESS Educational Resources Information Center/ Clearinghouse on Rural Education and Small Schools

ERIC/CRIER Educational Resources Information Center / Clearinghouse on Retrieval Information and Evaluation on Reading

ERIC/CUE ERIC Clearinghouse on Urban Education

ERIC/ECE Educational Resources Information Center/ Clearinghouse on Early Childhood Education

Eric Evergood King Eric I of Denmark

ERIC/HE Educational Resources Information Center/ Clearinghouse on Higher Education

Erich Maria Remarque Erich Maria Kramer

Erich von Stroheim Hans Maria Nordenwell

ERIC/IR Educational Resources Information Center/ Clearinghouse for Information Resources

ERIC/IRCD Educational Resources Information Center/ Information Retrieval Center on the Disadvantaged

Eric the Lamb King Eric III of Denmark

Eric the Memorable King Eric II of Denmark

Ericofon Ericsson telephone

ERIC/RCS ERIC Clearinghouse on Reading and Communicaton Skills

Eric the Red Eric Thorvaldsson

Eric Rohmer Maurice Scherer

ERIC/SMEAC Educational Resources Information Center/ Clearinghouse for Science,

Mathematics, and Environmental Education

ERIC/TME Educational Resources Information Center/ Clearinghouse on Tests, Measurement, and Evaluation

Eric von Stroheim Eric Oswald Stroheim

Erid Eridamus

Eridanium (Latin—Milan)

Eridne (Turkish—Adrianople)

Erie Erie-Lackawanna (railroad)

ERIE Eastern Regional Institute for Education

Erie Canal New York State Barge Canal

ERiEI Eastern Regional Institute for Education

Eriha (Arabic—Jericho)

erild earth rotation in lunar distances

ERIM Environmental Research Institute of Michigan

Erin Ireland

Erinyes (Greek—Furies)

ERISA Employee Retirement Income Security Act

Erit Eritrea

ERJA E R Johnson Association

erk enroute kit

erl emergency reference level

Erl Erläuterung (German—explanatory note)

ERL Environmental Research Laboratories

erm elastic reservoir moulding; ermine

Erm European red mite

erma electronic recording machine accounting

ERMS Educational Resource Management System

Ern Ernest, Ernst

Ernest Bramah Ernest Bramah Smith's pseudonym

ernic earnings-related national insurance contribution

ernie electronic random-numbering-and-indicating equipment

Ernie Ernest

ERNIE Electronic Random Number Indicator Equipment

Ernie Pyle Ernest Taylor Pyle

Ernst von Dohnányi Ernö Dohnányi

ERO Eastman-Rochester Orchestra

eroa economic rehabilitation in occupied area(s)

eroduction(s) erotic production(s)

Eroica Beethoven's Symphony No. 3 in E-flat major *(Sinfonia*

eroica)

erom erasable read-only memory

E-room engine room

EROPA Eastern Regional Organization for Public Administration

eropt error option(s)

Eros (Greek—Cupid)—god of love and lust

EROS Earth Resources Observation Satellite; Eliminate Zero Range System (for collision avoidance); Experimental Reflector Orbital Shot (space probe)

Eros Center sex supermarket nickname applied to the original one in Hamburg and its capital-city branch in Bonn, West Germany

EROSP Earth Resources Observation Systems Program

erot erotic; erotica; erotical(ly); eroticism; eroticist; eroticization; eroticize; eroticizing; erotism(s); erotogenic(s); erotologic(al)(ly); erotologist; erotology

erotol erotologist; erotology

erp effective radiated power; electro rustproofing

ERP Easy Revolving Plan; Emerson Radio & Phonograph (stock exchange symbol); European Recovery Program

ERP Ejército Revolucionario Popular (Spanish—Popular Revolutionary Armed Force) —Trotskyite terrorists active in Argentina; *Ejército Revolucionario del Pueblo* (Spanish— People's Revolutionary Army) — Argentine Trotskyist combat wing

ERPC Eastern Railroads Presidents Conference

erpf effective renal plasma flow

ERPFI Extended-Range Floating-Point Interpretive System

ERPSL Essential Repair Stock List

err. error; erroneous

ERR Engineering Release Record; Engineering Research Report

err & app error and appeals (legal)

errc expandability, recoverability, repairability cost

ERRDF Earth Resources Research Data Facility (NASA)

erron erroneous(ly)

ERRS Environmental Response and Referral Service

ers (ERS) environmental research satellite

ERS Economic Research Service; Educational Research Service; Edwards Rocket Site; Emergency Relocation Site; Experimental Research Society

ER & S Eletrolytic Refinery and Smelting (company)

ERSA Economic Research and Statistics Service

ersir earth-resources shuttle-imaging radar

E-R S O Eastman-Rochester Symphony Orchestra

ersos (ERSOS) earth-resources-survey operational satellite

ERSP Earth Resources Survey Program (NASA)

ERSR Equipment Reliability Status Report

ert electrical resistance temperature; electrical resistance thermometer; extended research telescope

ert (ERT) estrogen replacement therapy

ERTA Economic Recovery Tax Act; Energy Research and Technology Administration

ERTC European Regional Test Center (NATO)

ERTS Earth Resources Technology Satellite; European Rapid Train System

eru emergency reaction unit

ERU English Rugby Union

Erudite Americans Will and Ariel Durant

erv expiratory reserve volume

ERV English Revised Version

ERVAD Engineering Release for Vendor Article Data

erw electro-resistance welding

erw (ERW) enhanced radiation weapon (neutron bomb)

erw erweiterte (German—enlarged, extended)

ERWS Engineering Release Work Sheet

erx electronic remote switching

ery erysipelothrixia

ER Yorks East Riding, Yorkshire

erythro (Latin prefix—red)—erythrocyte

es echo sounding; effect size; eldest son; electric starting; electrical sounding; electrostatic; enamel single silk (insulation); engine speed; engine-sized (paper); equal section; exploratory shaft

es (ES) ejection sound

e/s early shorn (sheep); en suite

es esempio (Italian—example)

e_s price elasticity of supply

Es einsteinium; Essen

ES East Sussex; Eastern States; Econometric Society; Educational Specialist; El Salvador; Electrochemical Society; Ellis Air Lines; Employee Suggestion; Endocrine Society; Engineering Study; Entomological Society; Environmental Studies; Espirito Santo; Ethnological Society; Etymological Society; Experiment(al) Station; Extension Service

ESA Ecological Society of America; Economic Stabilization Agency; Economic and Statistical Analysis; Electric(al) Supplies Authority; Electrical Supply Authorities; Electrolysis Society of America; Employment Standards Administration; Engineers and Scientists of America; Entomological Society of America; Epiphyllum Society of America; European Space Agency; Euthanasia Society of America; Exceptional Service Award; Export Screw Association

ES & A English, Scottish, and Australian (Bank)

ESA Endangered Species Act

ESAA Electrical Supply Authorities Association; Electricity Supply Association of Australia; Emergency School Aid Act

ESAAB Energy Systems Acquisition Advisory Board

ESAB Energy Supplies Allocation Board (Canada)

ESAC Environmental Systems Applications Center

ESAEI Electric Supply Authority Engineers Institute

ESA-IRS European Space Agency—Information Retrieval Service

E Sam Eastern Samoa (American Samoa)

ESANZ Economic Society of Australia and New Zealand; Electrical Supply Authorities of New Zealand; Ergonomics Society of Australia and New Zealand

ESAP Emergency School Assistance Program

ESAPP Energy System Acquisition Project Plan

esar electronically-steered array radar

ESARS Employment Service

Automated Reporting System

ESAs Eastern Socially Attractives (Ivy League graduates)

ESA System Easy, Speedy Accounting System

eSat except Saturday

ESAWC Evaluation Staff, Air War College

esb electrical stimulation (of the) brain; electric storage battery

ESB Economic Stabilization Board; Electricity Supply Board; Electric Storage Battery (company); Empire State Building

ESBA English Schools' Badminton Association

ESBBA English Schools' Basket Ball Association

esc electronic service change; electronic spark control; elongation-sensitive cell; escadrille; escalator; escape; escape character; escort; escrow; escutcheon; evanescent space charge; extended core storage

esc (ESC) escape character (data processing)

esc escompte (French—discount)

Esc escudo (Portuguese currency)

ESC Economic and Social Council (UN); Education Service Center; Electronic Systems Command (USN); Electronics Systems Center; Energy Security Corporation (US); Executive Service Corps

esca electron spectroscopy for chemical analysis

ESCA English Schools' Cricket Association; English Schools' Cycling Association

Escandinavia (Portuguese or Spanish—Scandinavia)

escap escapologist; escapology

ESCAP Economic and Social Commission for Asia and the Pacific (UN)

Escape King Harry Houdini

Escarp Escarpment

ESCAT Emergency Security Control of Air Traffic

Escaut (French—Scheldt)

eschat eschatology

ES/CIP Employee Suggestion/ Cost Improvement Proposal

escl esclamazione (Italian—exclamation); esclamativo (Italian—exclamative); esclusivo (Italian—exclusive)

ESCL Elias Sourasky Central Library (Tel Aviv); Evans Signal Corps Laboratory

ESCMA Electric Steel Conduit Manufacturers' Association

escn electrolyte-and-steroid-produced cardiopathy characterized by necrosis

esc⁰ escudo (Portuguese or Spanish—coat of arms, Portuguese monetary unit, shield)

Esco Escocia (Spanish—Scotland); *Escócia* (Portuguese—Scotland)

ESCO Educational, Scientific, and Cultural Organization (UN)

Escocia (Spanish—Scotland)

Escom Electrical Supply Commission

Escondildo dysphemistic nickname for California town of Escondido and meaning *is with a dildo* instead of *hidden*

ESCORTDIV escort division

ESCOW Engineering and Scientific Committee on Water (New Zealand)

escp expendable surface-current probe

ESCP Earth Science Curriculum Project

ESCP École Supérieure de Commerce de Paris (French—Paris College of Commerce)

escr escrow

escrit⁴ escritura (Portuguese or Spanish—assignment, contract, deed, writ)

escrnia escribania (Spanish—notary's office)

escrno escribano (Spanish—notary)

escrⁿ⁰ escribano (Spanish—court clerk, notary, scribe)

escs escudos (Portuguese or Spanish—coats of arms, Portuguese monetary units, shields)

ESCS Economics, Statistics, and Cooperatives Service

esd echo-sounding device; electronic smoke detector; estimated shipping date; estimated standard deviation; extended school day

esd (ESD) echo-sounding device; external symbol dictionary (data processing)

Esd (ESD) English as a second dialect

ESD Electronic Systems Division (USAF); Emergency Service Division (NYPD)

ESDA Earth-Science Data Acquisition

ESDAC European Space Data Analysis Center (Darmstdat)

ESDAG Earth-Science Data Acquisition Guidelines

esdp external stores data package

Esdr Esdras (The Book of Esdras)

esE electrostatische Einheit (German—electrostatic unit)

Ese Ensenada

ESE east southeast

ESEA Electrical Supply Engineers Association; Elementary and Secondary Education Act

ESECA Energy Supply and Environmental Coordination Act

ESEF Electrotyping and Stereotyping Employers Federation

esf electrostatic focusing; erythropoietic stimulating factor

ESF Eastern Sea Frontier; Engineering Specification Files; Extended Spooling Facility

esfc extended specific fuel consumption

esfp environment-sensitive fracture process(es)

esfswr extra-special flexible-steel wire rope

esg electrically suspended gyro(scope); electronic-sweep generator; extended-sweep generator

e sg e seguente (Italian—and the following one)

Esg English standard gage

esgm electrostatically supported gyro monitor

esh equivalent solar hour(s)

ESH European Society of Haematology

eshp equivalent shaft horsepower; established standard horsepower

Esh Sham (Arabic—Damascus)

esi emergency stop indicator; equivalent spherical illumination; externally specified indexing

ESIL European Standard Inventory List (NATO)

ESIS Executive Selection Inventory System

Esk Eskimo

Eskie(s) Eskimo(s)

Eskimo Opera Hakon Axel Einar Børresen's opera about Greenland Eskimos (produced in Copenhagen in 1921 under the title of *Kaddara*)

Eskimo Village Kotzebue, Alaska

esl expected significance level

Esl English as a second language

Esl (ESL) English as a second language

ESL Eagle Shipping Ltd; Earth Sciences Laboratory; Eastern Steamship Lines; Engineering Societies Library

E S-L Engineer Sub-Lieutenant

ESL Endangered Species List

ESLAB European Space Laboratory (Delft)

esle engineering special laboratory equipment

ES/LES Equipment Section/Loaded Equipment Section

ESLO European Satellite Launching Organization

esm electronic support measures; electrostatic memory; ends standard matched (lumber)

ESM Eastman School of Music; Engineering Services Memo; Engineering Shop Memo

ESMA Electronic Sales-Marketing Association; Engraved Stationery Manufacturers Association; Episcopal Society for Ministry on Aging

Esmirna (Spanish—Smyrna)—Izmir

ESMRI Engraved Stationery Manufacturers Research Institute

esm's electronic-support measures

esn essential

esn (ESN) educationally subnormal

ESN Elastic Stop Nut (corporation); Engineering Shipping Notice; English-Speaking Nations (NATO)

esna electrical survey net adjuster

ESNA Elastic Stop Nut Corporation of America; Empire State Numismatic Association

ESNE Engineering Societies of New England

ESN-H Elsevier North-Holland

esntl essential

ESNZ Entomological Society of New Zealand

ESO Educational Services Office(r); Electronic Supply Office(r); Embarkation Staff Office(r); Emergency Services Organization; Engineering Service Order; Engineering Stop Order

ESOC European Space Operations Center

Esol English for speakers of other languages

ESOMAR European Society for Opinion Surveys and Market Research

ESOP Employees Stock Ownership Plan
esoph esophageal; esophagus
esor electronically scanned optical receiver
esot esoteric; esoterica; esoterical(ly); esotericism(s)
ESOT Employee Stock Ownership Trust
esp easy solution possible; echeloned series processor; electromagnetic surface profiler; electro-sensitive paper; electrosensory panel; engine sequence panel; especially; extrasensory perception
esp (ESP) electrosensitive programming
e & sp equipment and spare parts
Esp Esperanto; Esplanade
Esp (ESP) English for special purposes
Esp Espagne (French—Spain); *España* (Span—Spain); *Español* (Spanish—Spanish)
ESP East Sepik Province; Eastern State Penitentiary (Philadelphia, Pennsylvania); Elsevier Science Publishing; English for Special Purpose(s); Equipment Status Panel; Extrasensory Perception
ESP Ecole des Sciences Politiques (French—School of Political Science)
espa electronically steered phased array
ESPA Elementary School Principal's Association; Evening Student Personnel Association
ESPAC Elementary School Principal's Association of Connecticut
Espagne (French—Spain)
España (Spanish—Spain)
Espanha (Portuguese—Spain)
Española (Spanish—Hispaniola)—West Indian island shared by the Dominican Republic (Santo Domingo) and Haiti
Espantuguese Spanish-Portuguese
Esparta (Spanish—Sparta)
ESPAW Elementary School Principal's Association of Washington
ESPC Elsevier Scientific Publishing Company (Amsterdam)
espec especial(ly)
Esper Esperanto
Esperanto pseudonym of Dr L.L. Zemenhoff—inventor of

Esperanto—his artificially-contrived universal language
espg espionage
espi electronic speckle-pattern interferometer
Esplish Spanish-English
ESPN Entertainment and Sports Programming Network
ESPOA Electricity Supply Professional Officers Association
ESP Pioneer Dr JB Rhine who coined the term extrasensory perception, ESP
ESPQ Early School Personality Questionnaire
espress espressivo (Italian—expressive)
ESPRI Education Service of the Plastics and Rubber Institute
esq extra-special quality
esq esquerdo (Portuguese—left)
Esq Esquire
ESQ Entomological Society of Queensland
ESQA English Slate Quarries Association
esqᵒ esquerdo (Portuguese—left)
Esqrr Esquire
ESQST Ego-Strength Q-Sort Test
esr effective signal radiated; electrical skin resistance; electron skin resonance; electronic slide rule; electronically-scanned radar; electroslag resmelting; equivalent series resistance; erythrocyte sedimentation rate
ESR Engineering Societies Library; Engineering Stop Release; Engineering Summary Report
ESRANGE European Space Research (northern rocket range)—Kiruna
esrc electronics recovery control; engine surge recovery control
ESRC European Science Research Council
ESRD End-Stage Renal Disease
ESRG Earth Sciences Review Group
ESRIN European Space Research Institute
ESRO European Space Research Organization
ESRP Environmental Standard Review Plans
ESRU Environmental Sciences Research Unit
ess empty solution set; essence; essences; essential; expendable sound source

eSS except Saturday and Sunday
Ess Essex
ESS Eastern Searoad Service; Educational Services Section; Electrical Standards System; Electronic Switching System; Elementary School Science; Elementary Science Study; Emplaced Scientific Station; Employment Security System; English Speaking Society; Evaluation SAGE Sector; Experimental SAGE Sector
ESS Encyclopedia of the Social Sciences
essa environmental survey satellite (weather satellite)
ESSA Environmental Science Services Administration—Central Radio Propagation Laboratory, Coast and Geodetic Survey, Weather Bureau (Department of Commerce); environmental survey satellite
Essandess Simon and Schuster
Essaouira (Arabic—Mogador)
Essequibos Essequibo Islands (in the Essequibo River estuary off Guyana)
ESSEX Effects of Sub-Surface Explosions (USA)
Es Sham (Arabic—Damascus)
Essie Esther
ess neg essentially negative
ESSO Esso Shipping; Standard Oil
ESSPO Electronic Support System Project Office
ess pos essentially positive
ESSR Estonian Soviet Socialist Republic
ESSS Electronic Security Surveillance System
essu electronic selective switching unit
Es Sur (Arabic—Tyre or Zor)
ESSWACS Electronic Solid-State Wide-Angle Camera System
est earliest start time; elastic surface transformation; electrolytic sewage treatment; establish; established; establishment; estimate; estimated; estimation; estimator; estuary; external static pressure
est (EST) electroshock therapy
est estación (Spanish—station); *estimado* (Spanish—estimated)
Est The Book of Esther; Estates (postal abbreviation); Estonia(n); Estuary
Est Estado (Spanish—State);

(French—east)

EST Eastern Standard Time; Eastern Summer Time; English in Science and Technology; Enlistment Screening Test; Enroute Support Team; Epidemiology and Sanitation Technician; Erhard Seminars Training

estab established

Estab Establishment

Established Church Established Church of England

estab tip *establecimiento tipografico* (Spanish—publishing company)

Estados Unidos (Portuguese or Spanish—United States)

Estambul (Spanish—Istanbul)

estar estimated arrival

estb establish

estbl establishment

este (Italian, Portuguese, Spanish—east)

ESTEC European Space Technology Center

estero (Spanish—estuary)

ESTF Exploratory Shaft Task Force; Exploratory Shaft Test Facility

estg estimating

esth esthetics

Esth Esthonia; Esthonian

Esth *Esther*

Esther Hester

Esthr Apocryphal Book of Esther

ESTI European Space Technology Institute

estm estimate

estmd estimated

estmg estimating

estmn estimation

estn estimation

Estoc *Estocolmo* (Portuguese or Spanish—Stockholm)

Estocolmo (Portuguese or Spanish—Stockholm)

Estonia Baltic country formerly inhabited by Estonians before resettlement by Soviet captors

ESTP Earth Science Technical Plan

ESTPP Earth Science Teacher Preparation Project

ESTRACK European Space Satellite Tracking and Telemetry Network

Estrasburgo (Spanish—Strasbourg)

Estr B Estero Bay

estrecho (Spanish—strait)

Estrecho de Gibraltar (Spanish—Strait of Gibraltar)

Estrecho de Magallanes (Span-

ish—Strait of Magellan)

Estremadura province of west central Portugal containing Lisbon; not to be confused with Extremadura, old southwestern province of Spain bordering Portugal and including present provinces of Badajoz and Cáceres

estriff encryptic-secure tracking-radar identification friend or foe

Ests Estates

est wt estimated weight

esu educational service unit(s); electrostatic unit

ESU English-Speaking Union

E-SU English-Speaking Union

e sub excitor substance

E Suffolk East Suffolk

eSun except Sunday

ESUNA Ethiopian Students Union of North America

E Sussex East Sussex

E-SUUS English-Speaking Union of the United States

esv earth satellite vehicle; enamel single varnish (insulation code)

ESV Earth Satellite Vehicle; Experimental Safety Vehicle

ESW Ethical Society of Washington

eswl equivalent single-wheel loading

Esx Essex

esy extended school year

et edge thickness; educational therapy; educational training; effective temperature, electric telegraph; electric telegraphy; electric typewriter; electrical time; electrical transcription; electronic tests; engineering test; engineering testing; equation of time

et (ET) elapsed time; electronic timing; external tank; extra terrestrial

e/t (E/T) ergotamine tartrate; ergotin tartrate

e t en titre (French—in the title)

Et Ethyl; Etienne

ET East Texas (Pulp & Paper Company); Eastern Time; Educational Therapy; Electronics Technician; English Text; English translation; Entertainment Tax; Ethiopian Airlines; European Theater (of war); Exchange Telegraph

ET *Extra Terrestrial* (symphonic suite by John Williams)

eta estimated time of arrival; ex-

pect to arrive

ETA Educational Telecommunications for Alaska; Employment Training Administration; English Teachers Association; European Teachers Association; Exception Time Accounting; Express Transport Association

ETA *Euzkadi ta Azkatasuna* (Basque Nation and Liberty)

Etab *Etablissement* (French—business establishment or factory)

ETAB Environmental Testing Advisory Board (Dow)

ETAC Environmental Technical Applications Center

et al. *et alibi* (Latin—and elsewhere); *et alia* (Latin—and others)

etang (French—lake, pond)

ETAP Expanded Technical Assistance Program

ETAQ English Teachers Association of Queensland

ETAS Escort-Towed Array System

ETASS Escort-Towed-Array Sonar System

etat (French—state)

États-Unis (French—United States)

etb early to bed; end of transmission block; estimated time of berthing

etb (ETB) end of transmission block character (data processing)

ETD Engineering Test Basis

ETBO Engineering Test Base Office

etc earth terrain camera; effluent treatment cell; electronic travel computer; electronic typing calculator; employee timecard; estimated time of completion; extraterrestrial civilization

etc. *et cetera* (Latin—and so forth)

e t c en tout cas (French—in any case)

ETC Electrical Technician Certificate; Electro Tech Corporation; Electronic Technician Certificate; Emergency Training Center; Engine Technical Committee; Environmental Testing Corporation; Episcopal Travel Club; European Translations Center; European Travel Commission

ETC. A Review of General Semantics (Official Organ of the International Society for General Semantics)

ETCC Eastern Tank Carrier Conference

ETCE Empresa Transportes Colectivos del Estado (Spanish—State Collective Enterprise Transport)

etcg elapsed-time code generator

Etcher of Disaster Francisco de Goya y Lucientes

Etcher of Prisons Giambattista Piranesi

etcrrm electronic teleprinter cryptographic regenerative repeater mixer

etd estimated time of departure; extension trunk dialing

ETD English Teaching Division

ETDS Electronic Theft Detection System

ete estimated time enroute

ete este (Spanish—east)

ETE Experimental Tunnelling Establishment

ETE Escuela Technica del Ejercito (Spanish—Technical School of the Army)

ETEMA Engineering Teaching Equipment Manufacturers Association

eter estimated time enroute

Eternal City Rome

etf electron-transferring flavorprotein; enhanced tactical fighter

Étg Étang (French—lagoon, pond)

etgm estimate to get money

eth ether; ethical; ethics; ethmoid; ethmoidal; ethnic; extraterrestial hypotheses (explaining close encounters of the third kind such as ufo's); extraterrestrial hypothesis

Eth Ethiopia; Ethiopian; Ethiopic

Eth. Book of Ether

ETH Eidgenössiche Technische Hochschule (Swiss Federal Institute of Technology)

ethanol ethyl alcohol or grain alcohol (C_2H_5OH)

Eth$ Ethiopian dollar

eth dat ethic dative

Ethel Ethelberg; Ethelberta; Ethelburg; Ethelda; Etheldrid; Ethelind; Etheljean; Ethelrede; Ethelsa; Ethelwyn

Ethel Barrymore Ethel Blythe

Ethel Leginska Ethel Liggins

Ethel Merman Ethel Zimmerman

Ethelred the Unready Ethelred II of England

ether ethyl ether ($CH_2H_5)_2O$

Ethical Culturist Felix Adler

Ethiop Ethiopia; Ethiopian

Ethiopia East African nation as ancient as Egypt (Ethiopians speak Amharic, Hamatic, and Semitic tongues as well as Arabic, exports include coffee and many valuable minerals)

Ethiopian Ports (north to south) Massawa, Port Smyth, Assab

ethno ethnology

ethnoc ethnocide (systematic killing of countries and peoples by destruction of their educational system, language, and national, racial, or religious identity)

ethnog ethnography

ethnograph ethnograph(er); ethnographic(al)(ly); ethnography

ethnol ethnology

ethnomus ethnomusicologist; ethnomusicology

ethnomusi ethnomusic(al)(ly); ethnomusicologist; ethnomusicology

ethnophaul ethnophaulism (study of international slurs); ethnophaulist(ic)(al)(ly)

ethnophaulisms disparaging allusions sometimes descriptive and often humorous although seldom in good taste (e.g. Bananalander—tropical Australian from Queensland whose bananas are grown, taco bender—Mexican-American whose diet includes tacos made from tortillas)

ethnosci ethnoscience; ethnoscientific(al)(ly); ethnoscientist(s)

etho ethylene oxide

ethog ethogram; ethographer; ethographic; ethography

ethol ethologic(al)(ly); ethologist(ic)(al)(ly); ethology

Ethopië (Dutch—Ethiopia)

eti elapsed-time indicator; estimated time of interception

Eti Etiopia (Italian, Spanish—Ethiopia); *Etíopia* (Portuguese—Ethiopia)

ETI Electric Tool Institute; Electronic Technical Institute; Equipment and Tool Institute

ETIA European Tape Industry Association

ETIC English Training Information Centre (London)

etio etiocholandone

etiol etiology

ETIS-MARFO European and Technical Information Service in Machine-Readable Form

etk (ETK) erythrocyte transketolase

etkm every test known to man

etl emergency tolerance limit; ending tape label; etching by transmitted light

ETL Electrical Testing Laboratory; Electro-Technical Laboratory; Engineering Test Laboratory; Essex Terminal (railroad)

ETM Electronic Technician's Mate

ETMA English Timber Merchants Association

ETMA-A Engineering Tooling and Manufacturing Aide

ETMWG Electronic Trajectory Measurements Working Group

etn equipment table nomenclature

ETN Eastern Technical Net (USAF)

eto electric truck operator; estimated takeoff; estimated time off; ethylene oxide

ETO Energy Technology Office; European Theater of Operations; European Transport Organization; Executive Training Office(r)

etoc expected total operating cost

Et OH ethyl alcohol

Etona (Latin—Eton)

etp estimated turnaround point; estimated turning point

etp (ETP) electron transfer particle

ETP Education and Training Program; Effluent Treatment Plant; Engineering Test Plan; Evaluation Test Plan

ETPI Eastern Telecommunications Philippines Inc

et-pnl engine test panel

ETPS Empire Test Pilots School

etr effective thyroid ratio; estimated time of return; export traffic release

etr (ETR) engineering test reactor

Etr Etruscan

Etr entrada (Spanish—entrance)

ETR Eastern Test Range; Electric Target Range; Engineering Test Reactor; Export Traffic Release; External Technical Report

etra estimated time to reach altitude

ETRC Educational Television and Radio Center; Engineering Test Reactor Critical Facility

etro estimated time of return to operation

ETRs Encrypted Traffic Reports

etry entirely

ets electronic telegraph system; estimated time of sailing; expiration term of service; expiration of time of service

Ets *Etablissements* (French—establishments)

ETS Educational Television Stations; Educational Testing Service; Electronic Telegraphic System; Engine Test Stand; Engineering Task Summary; Engineering Test Satellite

ETSA Electricity Trust of South Australia

ETSC East Tennessee State College; East Texas State College

et seq. *et sequens* (Latin—and following)

etsp entitled to severance pay

etsq electrical time superquick

ETSS Engineering Time-Sharing System; Entry Time Sharing System; Experimental Time-Sharing System

ett early thrust termination; electromagnetic thickness tool; exercise tolerance test(ing)

ett (ETT) evasive target tank

ETT Elizabethan Theatre Trust; Explosion Tear Test(ing)

etta electronic temperature trip and alarm

Etta Henrietta

ETTA English Table Tennis Association

ETTDC Electronics Trade and Technology Development Corporation

et to extractor tool

et tp etch template

ETTU English Table Tennis Union

etu electron tube

ETU Electrical Trades Union; Emergency Treatment Unit

ETUC European Trade Union Confederation

et ux. *et uxor* (Latin—and wife)

etv educational television; engine test vehicle

etv (ETV) educational television

ETV Educational Television; Electrotechnischer Verein (Electrotechnical Society); Engine Test Vehicle

etvm electrostatic transistorized voltmeter

etw empty tank weight; end-of-tape warning

etw *etwas* (German—something)

ETWN East Tennessee & Western North Carolina (railroad)

etx (ETX) end of text character (data processing)

etym etymologic(al)(ly); etymologist(ic)(al)(ly); etymology

eu electron unit; emergency unit; external upset (oil well)

eu (Greek—good or well)—eubacterium, eucalyptus, euphoria

Eu entropy unit (symbol); Euler unit; Europe; European; europium; Eustace; Eustatia

EU Emory University; Estados Unidos (Spanish—United States); Evacuation Unit; Everyman's University (Tel Aviv); Experimental Unit

E-U Etats-Unis (French—United States)

EU *Estados Unidos* (Spanish—United States); *Europa Unie* (French—United Europe)

eua examination under anesthetic

Eua European unit of account

EUA Eastern Underwriters Association; Estados Unidos de America (Spanish—United States of America); Etats-Unis Amérique (French—United States of America)

EUB Estados Unidos do Brasil (Brazil)

euc end-use check(ing)

EUC Euclid (railroad)

eucd emotionally unstable character disorder

Eucl Euclid

EUCLID Experimental Use Computer—London Integrated Display

EUCOM European Command

euc(s) eucalyptus tree(s)

EUDISED European Documentation and Information System for Education

euf *eufemismo* (Italian, Portuguese, Spanish—euphemism)

EUF European Union of Federalists

eufe *eufemismo* (Italian, Portuguese, Spanish—euphemism)

EUFTT European Union of Film and Television Technicians

Eug Eugene; Eugenia

eugen eugenics

Eugenie Marlitt Eugenie John's pseudonym

Eugº Eugenio

EUI *Enciclopedia Universal*

Ilustrada (Spanish—Universal Illustrated Encyclopedia)

EUL Edinburgh University Library

EUL *Everyman's University Library*

Eulenberg's disease congenital muscular spasms

EUM European Mediterranean

EUM *Entr'aide Universitaire Mondiale* (French—World University Service); *Estados Unidos Mexicanos* (Spanish—United States of Mexico)

EUM-AFTN European-Mediterranean Aeronautical Fixed Telecommunications Network

Eumenides the Furies

EUMOTIV European Association for the Study of Economic, Commercial, and Industrial Motivation

EUMR Emergency Unsatisfactory Material Report

Euni Eunice

EUP Edinburgh University Press; English Universities Press

euph euphemism(s); euphemistic(al)(ly); euphemize(d); euphemizer(s); euphemizing

euphé *euphémisme* (French—euphemism)

Euphe *der Euphemismus* (German—euphemism)

euphem euphemism, euphemistic(al)

euphem *euphémique* (French—euphemistic); *euphémisme* (French—euphemism)

Euphie Euphemia

euphon euphonic, euphonically; euphony

eur *europæisk* (Dano-Norwegian—European)

Eur Europe; European

EUR *Erasmus Universiteit Rotterdam* (Dutch—Erasmus University of Rotterdam)

Eurafrica Europe and Africa

Eurailpass European tourist railroad pass

EURAS European Anodisers Association

Eurasafrica Europe, Asia, and Africa

EURASBANK European Asian Bank

Eurasia Europe and Asia; (where Europe and Asia meet from the Caspian Sea and the Caucasus Mountains to the Ural Mountains)

Eurasian(s) person(s) of European and Asian parents such as Euro-Chinese, Euro-Indian, Euro-Japanese, etc.

Euratom six-nation atomic energy pool consisting of France, Germany, Italy, and the three Benelux countries: Belgium, Netherlands, and Luxembourg

EURATOM European Atomic Energy Community

eurex enriched uranium extraction

EURIMA European Insulation Manufacturers Association

Eurip Euripides

EURIPA European Information Providers Association

EURO European Regional Office (FAO)

Eurobonds European bonds

EUROCAE European Organization of Civil Aviation Electronics

Euro-Can(s) European-Canadian(s)

EUROCEAN European Oceanographic Association

Eurochemic European chemical processing of irradiated fuels

EUROCOM European Coal Merchants Union

Eurocom(s) European communism; European communist(s)

EUROCOOP European Community of Cooperative Societies

EUROCORD European Cord, Rope, and Twine Industries

eurocrat European bureaucrat

EURODICAUTOM European Automated Dictionary

EURODIDAC European Association of Manufacturers and Distributors of Educational Materials

Eurodol(s) European dollar(s)

Eurofima European Company for the Financing of Rolling Stock

Eurofinance Union International d'Analyse Economique et Financière

EUROFINAS European Financial Houses

Eurolex full-text electronic legal-research network

Euromart European Common Market

Europ European railway car pool

Europa (Italian, Latin, Portuguese, Spanish—Europe)

Europe Eastern Hemisphere continent joined to Asia; this western half of the Eurasian

land mass is called The Continent

European Community Belgium, Britain, Denmark, France, Greece, Ireland, Italy, Luxembourg

Europe's Largest Country the USSR

Europhot European professional photographers

Eurosac European paper sack manufacturers

Eurosat European application satellite systems

EUROSPACE European Space Study Group

eurotainer European-owned container

Euroterro European terrorism; European terrorist

EUROTEST European Association of Testing Institutions

Eurotories European tories (conservative parties such as Britain's Conservatives and West Germany's Christian Democratic Union)

Eurotox European Committee on Toxicity Hazards

Eurovision European Television

EUS Eastern United States; Engineering Undergraduates Society

EUSA Eighth United States Army

EUSAFEC Eastern United States Agricultural and Food Export Council

Euseb Eusebius Pamphili

Eusebius *see* Florestan and Eusebius

EUSIDIC European Association of Scientific Information Dissemination Centers

Eus Sta Euston Station

eutec eutectic; eutectoid

euv energetic ultraviolet; equivalent ultraviolet; expected utility value; extreme ultraviolet

euvsh equivalent ultraviolet solar hour

euw engine(s) under wing(s)

EUW European Union of Woman

Eux Euxine

Euxine Sea Black Sea

Euzkadi (Basque—Basque Provinces)

ev earned value; efficient vulcanization; electric vehicle; electron volt; enclosed and ventilated; escort vessel; evangelical; exposure value

ev *electrón-voltio* (Spanish—

electron volt)—also appears as *eV; en ville* (French—local); *evangelisch* (German—Protestant)

eV electronvolt

eV *eingetragener Verein* (German—registered society)

Ev Evenkian; Everett

Ev *Eingang vorbehalten* (German—rights reserved)

Ev. *Evangelium* (Latin—the Gospel)

EV Elivie (Italian Heliways); English Version; Erne Valley; Everett (railroad)

eV 1 s edge-V one side (lumber)

eV 2s edge-V two sides

eva electronic velocity analyzer; ethyl-vinyl acetate; extra-vehicular activity

EVA Educational Voucher Authority; Electrical Vehicle Association; Engineer Vice Admiral

evac evacuate; evacuation

evacship evacuation ship

eval evaluate; evaluation

Evan Evangelical; Evangelist

Evangel of Liberty Thomas Paine

evap evaporate; evaporation; evaporator; evaporize

evapd evaporated

evaptr evaporator

evata electronic visual auditory training aid

EVC Educational Video Corporation; Electric Vehicle Council

evce evidence

evco electron vibration cutoff

EVCP Engineering Value Control Proposal

EVCS Extravehicular Communications System

EVDF Eugene V. Debs Foundation

eve evening

Eve Eveleen; Evelina; Eveline; Evelyn; Everarda; Everett; Everette; Everina; Everline

evea extravehicular engineering activities

Eve Arden Eunice Quedons

evenin' evening (anytime after noontime in many parts of the American Southwest)

event. *eventuell* (German— possibly)

Ever Everest—world's highest mountain towering over the Himalayas of Nepal and Tibet

Everglades Everglades National Park in Florida

Everglade State Florida

Evergreen State Washington's official nickname

Every Good Boy Does Fine (mnemonic for remembering the line notes of the treble clef —E, G, B, D, F)

Eve Trib *Evening Tribune*

evg evening

EVG Europäische Verteidigungsgemeinschaft (European Defense Community)

evi evidence

EVI Extreme Value Index

evict. evaluation of intelligence-collection tasks

evid evidence

Evil Florist Charles Pierre Baudelaire—famous for his *Les Fleurs du Mal* (Flowers of Evil)—drug-addicted leader of French decadents

e viv. disc. e vivis discessit (Latin —departed from life)

EVL E(dward) V(errall) Lucas

evln evolution

ev-luth *evangelisch-luterisch* (German Evangelical Lutheran)

evm extraneous vegetable matter

evm (EVM) earth-viewing module

evminfin everglazed minicare finish

evmu extra-vehicular material unit

evng evening

evol evolution; evolutionary; evolutionist

evop evolutionary operation

EVP Executive Vice President

evr electronic video recording

evrep event recording potential

EVRS Electronic Video Recording System

evs expected value saved

evs (EVS) extravehicular system

EvS Environmental Science

EVS Electronic Voice Switching (system); Electronic-optical Viewing System

evsd energy-variant sequential detection

evss extravehicular space suit

evstc (EVSTC) extravehicular suit telemetry and communications

evt educational and vocational training; effective visual transmission; equiviscous temperature; eventually; extra-value trimmed (meat)

evt *eventuel* (Dano-Norwegian —possible)

E v T E van Tongeren

EVT Engineering Verification-Test(ing)

EVT *Europäische Vereinigung für Tierzucht* (German—European Association for Animal Production)

evtl *eventuell* (German—eventually, perhaps, possibly)

EVV Evansville, Indiana (airport)

EVW European Voluntary Workers

evythg everything

ew earthenware; effective warmth; electrically welded; electronic warfare; extensive wound

ew (EW) earth watch

e/w equipped with

Ew Ewart; Ewbanke; Ewell; Ewen; Ewing

Ew *Euere* or *Eure* or *Eurer* (German—your)—abbreviation used in titles

EW early warning, electronic warfare; enlisted woman; enlisted women

E & W England and Wales

EWA East and West Association; East-West Airlines; Education Writers Association; Electrical Wholesalers Association

ewac electronic warfare anechoic chamber

EWACS Electronic Wide-Angle Camera System

EWAD Early Warning Air Defense

EWAS Economic Warfare Analysis Section

ewb estrogen withdrawal bleeding

ewc electric water cooler

ewc (EWC) electronic warfare coordinator

EWC East-West Center (University of Hawaii)

EWCB Electrical Workers and Contractors Board

EWCRP Early Warning Control and Reporting Post

ewd elementary wiring diagram

EWD Economic Warfare Division

ewdt early warning data transmission

ewe. electronic warfare element

ewec electromagnetic wave energy conversion

ewes electronic warfare evaluation simulator

EWES Engineering Waterways Experiment Station

ewex electronic warfare exercise

ewexipt electronic warfare exercise in port

ewf equivalent weight factor

EWF Earth, Wind, and Fire (music group); Electrical Wholesalers Federation

EWG Executive Working Group (NATO)

EWG *Europäische Wirtschaftsgemeinschaft* (German—European Common Market)

ewgcir early-warning ground-control-intercept radar

EWHS Eli Whitney School

ewi education with industry; entered without inspection

Ewi English winter index

ewicb electronic-warfare interface-connection box

ewl evaporative water loss

EWL Ellerman's Wilson Line

EWLD Engineering Weekly Labor Distribution

ewma exponentially weighted moving average

EWMC Eli Whitney Metrology Center

EWO Electrical and Wireless Operators; Electronic Warfare Officer; Emergency War Order; Engineering Work Order; Essential Work Order

EWO-DS Engineering Work Order—Drawing Summary

ewops electronic warfare operations

EWOS Electronic Warfare Operational System (USAF)

EWP Emergency War Plan

EWPI Eysenck-Withers Personality Inventory

EWPs Electronic Warfare Plans

ewr early-warning radar

EWR Electrical Wiring Regulations; Engineering Work Request; Newark, New Jersey (airport)

EWRC European Weed Research Council

ews experienced workers standard

ew's edge weapons (sharp-bladed daggers, cutlasses, knives, machetes, swords, etc.)

EWS Emergency Water Supply; Emergency Welfare Service; European Wars Survey

EWSC Eastern Washington State College; Electric Water Systems Council

EWSF European Work Study Federation

ewsl equivalent single-wheel load(ing)

ewsm electronic-warfare support measures

EWT Eastern War Time (advanced time)

eww extended work week

EWWS Electronic Warfare Warning System

ex etc.; exact(ed); exacting; exactitude; exactly; examination; examine(d); examiner; examining; example; excess(ive); exclusive; exclusively; exclusivity; execute(ed); executing; exercise; exercising; experiment(al's); extra(neous)

ex (Latin prefix—out of)—excision; (Latin—from)

Ex Excelsior; Exchange; Exchequer; Exeter; Exmoor; Exmouth; Extremadura; Exuma

Ex Exodo (Spanish—The Book of Exodus); *Exodus*

EX experimental broadcasting

exacct expense account

ex af. *ex affinis* (Latin—of affinity)

exafs extended X-ray-absorption final structure

exag exaggerate; exaggerated; exaggeration

Ex Agt Executive Agent

exam examination; examine; examiner

examd examined

exametnet experimental meteorological sounding rocket network

examg examining

examn examination

examr examiner

exams examinations

ex aq. *ex aqua* (Latin—out of water)

exbedcap expanded bed capacity

Ex B/L exchange bill of lading

exc excavate; excellent; exciter

exc. *excudit* (Latin—he engraved it)

Exc Excelencia (Spanish—Excellency); Excellency

Exc Excélsior (Mexico City); *Exelencia* (Spanish—Excellency)

exca excavate; excavation

Excᵃ Excelencia (Spanish—Excellency)

ex cath. *ex cathedra* (Latin—from the seat of authority)

Excel Excelsior

EXCEL Corporation for Excellence in Public Education; Ex-offender Coordinated Employment Lifeline (Indiana's parole project)

Excelsior State New York

whose motto is Excelsior

exch exchange

ex champ ex-champion; former champion

Excheq exchequer

exch oper exchange operator

exchq exchequer

exchr extra charge

excl exclude; exclusion; exclusive; exclusivity

exclam exclamation; exclamatory

exclt excellent

exclu exclusive(ly); exclusivity

Excᵐᵃ Excelentísima (Spanish—Most Excellent)—feminine

Excmo Excelentísimo (Spanish—Most Excellent)

Excᵐᵒ Excelentísimo (Spanish—Most Excellent)—masculine

Ex Cncl Executive Council

Ex Co Executive Council

Ex Com Executive Committee

ex-con(s) ex convict(s); former convict(s)

ex cont from contract

excp except(ion)(al)(ly); execute channel program

ex cp ex coupon

excpt except(ion)(al)(ly)

excs excess

exct execution

excv exclusive

exd examined

EXDAMS Extendable Debugging and Monitoring System

ex det explosives detector

ex div ex dividend

Ex Div Experimental Division

Ex Doc Executive Document

Exe Exeter

exec execute(d); execution; executive; executive officer; executor

exec (EXEC) execute statement (data processing)

Exec Dir Executive Director

Exec Off Executive Officer

execs executives

Exec Sec Executive Secretary

Executive City Washington, D.C.

Exemplar of Feminine Fascination Cleopatra

exeod expects to enter on duty

exer exercise

exes expenses

Exet Coll Exeter College—Oxford

Exeter Exeter College (Oxford or elsewhere)

exf external function

ex f extremely fine

ex fac ex factory

ex fy extra fancy

exg existing

ex ga external gage

EXGO Export Guarantee Office(r)

ex gr. *exempli gratia* (Latin—for example)

exh exhaust

exhib exhibit; exhibition; exhibitor

exhib. *exhibeatur* (Latin—let it be shown)

exhn exhibition

exh t exhaust turbine

exh v exhaust vent

ex hy extra heavy

EXIAC Explosives Information and Analysis Center (USA)

Ex-Im Export-Import Bank

EXIMBANK Export-Import Bank

ex int ex interest

exis existential; existentialism; existentialist

exist. existing

Existenial Dane Søren Kierkegaard

Existentialist-Leftist Jean-Paul Sartre

EXIT Ex-offenders In Transit (Maine's parole project)

exkl *exklusiv* (German—excepted, not included)

ex lib. *ex libris* (Latin—from the library of)

ExᵐᵃSrᵃD Excelentissima Senhora Dona [Portuguese—Mrs (precedes full name in formal style)]

ex-mer ex-meridian

ExᵐᵒSr Excelentissimo Senhor [Portuguese—Mr (precedes full name in formal style of address)]

exmr examiner

ex n(ew) excluding new shares

ex-nupt(s) ex-nuptial(s)—person(s) born out of wedlock

ExO executive officer; executive order

Ex O Experimental Office(r)

EXO European X-ray Observatory

exobio exobiologic(al)(ly); exobiologist; exobiology

Exocet Aerospatiale surface-to-surface missile for use aboard warships

exocrin exocrinologic(al)(ly); exocrinologist; exocrinology

Exod Exodus

ex off. *ex officio* (Latin—by authority of his office)

Exon. Exonia (Latin—Exeter)

exonum exonumia(l)(ly); exonumic(al)(ly); exonumist(s)

exonym foreign-language place-name equivalent such as

Londres (Spanish for London), Florence (English for Firenzi), Hongrie (French for Hungary)—exonym derived from *exo*, the Latin prefix for outside, and *toponym*, the Latin for place-name

Ex O P Executive Office of the President

exopac exoatmospheric jettisonable control wafer

exor executor

exord exercise order

exos (EXOS) exospheric satellite

exosat (EXOSAT) European X-ray observatory satellite

exot exotic

exotheo exotheologic(al); exotheologist(s); exotheology

exp expansion; expenditure; expense; experience; experiment(al); exponential; export; Exposition; express; expulsion

exp expreso (Spanish—express)

ex p. ex parte (Latin—on one side only)

EXP Exchange of Persons (UNESCO office)

expate(s) expatriate(s)

expdivun experimental diving unit

expdn expedition

expdt expiration date

exped expedite; expedition

exper experiment; experimental

Expert Expanded Pert (program evaluation and review technique)

expi export performance taxation incentive

exp-imp export-import

expir expiratory; expiration

expl explain; explanation; explanatory; explosimeter; explosimetric; explosion; explosive(s)

expl exemple (French—example)

explan exercise plan

EXPLIC Export Licence

explo explosion; explosive

exploit. exploitation

explor exploration

Explora Exploratorium

explos explosive

expn exposition

expnd expenditure

expo expose; exposition

exp o experimental order(s)

expo expreso (Spanish—express)

Expo 67 1967 exposition in Montreal

Expo 70 1970 exposition at Tokyo

expol expanded polysterene (light-weight packing moulding)

export exportaciones (Spanish—exports)

Expounders of Utilitarianism Jeremy Bentham, James Mill, and John Stuart Mill were foremost

expr expiration; expire

ex-Pres ex-President

EXPRESO Expreso Aéreo Interamericano

expressway express highway

exps expenses

expt experiment

exptl experimental

expto expedite travel order

exptr exporter

expul expulsion

expur expurgate(d)

Expwy Expressway

Expy Expressway

ex-quay free on quay

exr executor

ex r ex rights

exrav expendible relay

exrx executrix

exs expenses; expropriations

ex's expenses

exsec exsecant

exshi expedite shipment

ex ship delivered out of the ship

exspec exercise specification(s)

exst exempt sales tax

Ex Sta Experimental Station

ext extend; extension; exterior; external; extinguish; extinguisher; extra

ext (EXT) extraction (dental)

ext. extend (Latin—spread); *extractum* (Latin—extract)

Ext Extended; Extension

extal extra time allowance

extd extracted

ext d & cc external drug and cosmetic color

Extel Exchange Telegraph (press agency)

EXTEL Exchange Telegraph (British news agency)

extemp extemporaneous(ly)

exten extension

extend. *extensus* (Latin—spread)

extern external; externally

EXTERRA Extraterrestrial Research Agency (USA)

ext fl extract fluid (fluid extract)

extg extinguish(er)

extgh extinguish

exting extinguished

ext. liq. extractum liquidum (Latin—liquid extract)

extm extended telecommunications module

ex tm. ex testamento (Latin—in accord with the testament)

extn extraction

extr extract; extrude; extruded; extrusion

Extr Extremadura

extra extraordinary

extra (Latin prefix—beyond, in addition, outside)—extracurricular

extrad extradition

extradop extended range doppler

extradovap extended-range doppler velocity and position

extrap extrapolate; extrapolated; extrapolating; extrapolation; extrapolative; extrapolator

extra sess extra session (legislature)

extrd extruded

extrem extremity

extro extroversion; extrovert

extrx executrix

extsn extension(al)

exurb exurban; exurbanite; exurbia; exurbian

ex works out of the factory (factory price exclusive of delivery charge)

exx examples; executrix

Exxon (formerly ESSO)—Standard Oil

e_{xy} cross-elasticity of demand

Exy Expressway

Exz Exzellenz (German—Excellency)

eyawtkas everything you always wanted to know about sex

EYC Eastern Yacht Club; Encinal Yacht Club; European Youth Campaign

eyco estimated yearly cost of operation

EYD Ejaan Yang Disempurnakan (Indonesian—Improved Spelling System)

"Eye" I Street in Washington, D.C. and other places

Eye of the Baltic Gotland

Eye of England London

Eye of Greece Athens

Eye into Europe St Petersburg more recently known as Petersburg, Petrograd, or Leningrad

Eye of Italy Rome

Eyetie(s) British slang for Italian(s)

Eyetie(s) [Cockney—Italian(s)]

Eyety (Cockney—Italian)

Eyety Navy (Cockney—Italian Navy)

EYOA Economic and Youth Opportunities Agency
EYR East Yorkshire Regiment
EYS Ecumenical Youth Service
EYW Key West, Florida (airport)
ez easy; eczema; electrical zero
e-z easy
e/z equal zero
Ez Ezekiel; Ezra; The Book of Ezra

EZ Eastern Zone; Emile Zola; Extraction Zone
EZ *Einelige Zwillinge* (German —monozygotic twins)
EZ Duzit Easy Does It
Ezeiza Ezeiza International Airport (Buenos Aires, Argentina)
Ezek The Book of Ezekiel
Ezek *Ezekiel*
Ezi Ezias; Eziel; Eziongaber

EZI Electrolytic Zinc Industries
EZPERT Easy Programme Evaluation and Review Technic
Ezr *Ezra*
EZU Emiliano Zapata Unit (Chicano terrorists); Europäische Zahlungsunion (European Payment Union)

F

f fair; family; farthing; fast; father (capitalized in religious orders); fathom, feet; female; feminine; filment; final target; fine; first class (travel), flat, focal length; fog; folio; following; following page; force; forecastle; founded; franc(s); frequency; freshwater; fuel; fugacity; full; function; latitude factor (symbol); relative humidity (symbol)

f/ relative aperture of a lens (also shown as f:)

f fecit (Latin—he did); filius (Latin—son); forte (Italian—loud); fundada; fundado (Spanish—founded); für (German—for)

f/ fardo(s) [Spanish—bale(s); bundle(s); package(s)]

F Fahrenheit; Fairchild; farad; Faraday; Faraday constant (symbol); Farrell Lines, fathom(s); February; Fellow; field of vision (symbol); fighter; fire; fixed; fixed broadcast; fixed broadcasting; flagship; florin; fluorine; formal(ity); formula; Foxtrot —code for letter F; France; franc(s); Fraunhofer line (caused by hydrogen); freedom; freedom, degree of (symbol); free energy (symbol); French; Friday; fuel; furlong(s); Furness Lines; Grumman; longitude factor

F. fats (dietary symbol)

°F degree Fahrenheit

F feria (Latin, Portuguese, Spanish—fair or market); fora (Portuguese—out); framkomst (Swedish—arrival); Frauen (German—women); freddo

(Italian—cold); frio (Portuguese, Spanish—cold); froid (French—cold); fuera (Spanish—out); fuori (Italian—out); (Latin—Filius)

F 1 Formula One (automobile sport)

F-1 Fury single-engine jet fighter-bomber flown from aircraft carriers

F_1 F_1 layer [lower of two atmospheric layers wherein the F region of the ionosphere splits during the day at heights varying from 90 to 150 miles (145 to 241 kilometers) above the earth's surface]; first filial generation

$F_1$0 decimetric solar flux (symbol)

F 1C Fireman 1st Class (USN)

F1S finish one side

F 2 Formula Two (automobile sport)

F_2 F_2 layer [upper of two atmospheric layers wherein the F region of the ionosphere splits during the day at heights varying from 150 to 250 miles (241 to 402 kilometers) above the earth's surface; second filial generation

F^2 prostaglandin alpha (abortion-producing hormone)

F2S finish two sides

F-3 Demon single-engine supersonic all-weather jet fighter

F-4 Phantom II twin-engine all-weather supersonic jet fighter-bomber

f4p fortran 4 plus

F-4U Chance-Vought single-engine fighter popular during World War II and called the Corsair

F-5 Northrup Freedom Fighter twin-jet aircraft

F-6 Skyray single-engine supersonic all-weather jet fighter

F6F Grumman single-seat piston-powered fighter aircraft named Hellcat

F-8 Crusader single-engine all-weather supersonic jet fighter

f/8 @ 1/50th camera lens aperture ratio 8 at an exposure of 1/50th of a second

F-9 Shen Yang single-engine single-seat jet fighter aircraft made by the Shen Yang Aircraft Production Complex of the People's Republic of China (mainland communist China)

F9F-2 Grumman Panther single-engine single-seat naval fighting aircraft

F9F-6 Grumman carrier-based transonic fighter aircraft called Cougar

F 11 fluorocarbon (concentrations and emissions)

F-11 Tiger single-engine supersonic jet fighter

f-12 freon (refrigerant)

F-13 dope; drugs; narcotics

F-14 swing-wing jet fighter aircraft nicknamed Tomcat and carried on some U.S. naval vessels

F-15 Eagle supersonic-jet fighter aircraft

F-16 high-performance low-cost air-combat fighter aircraft produced by Convair's Fort Worth Division for the U.S. Air Force and the air forces of Belgium, Denmark, the Netherlands, and Norway—NATO allies

F-16B two-place fighter/trainer

aircraft

F-18 all-weather fighter and attack airplane

F-18A McDonnell-Douglas Hornet strike fighter aircraft

F-18L McDonnell-Douglas-Northrup multirole fighter aircraft

F-27 Fokker Friendship (aircraft)

F-27M Fokker Troopship built in the Netherlands

F-28 Fokker turbojet aircraft

F-47 Republic fighting aircraft developed during World War II and called Thunderbolt

F-51 North American fighter aircraft developed during World War II and called Mustang

f/64 Group f/64 (photographers Ansel Adams, Imogen Cunningham, Edward Weston, Willard Van Dyke, and their followers)

F-80 Lockheed Shooting Star jet fighter-bomber

F-84 Republic Thunderjet fighter-bomber

F-86 North American Sabre single-engine jet fighter aircraft

F-89 Scorpion all-weather interceptor with twin turbojet engines

F-100 Super Sabre supersonic turbojet fighter

F-101 Voodoo supersonic twin-engine turbojet aircraft

F-102 Delta Dagger single-engine supersonic turbojet interceptor

F-104 Starfighter supersonic single-engine turbojet fighter

F-105 Thunderchief supersonic single-engine turbojet tactical fighter

F-106 Delta Dart supersonic single-engine turbojet interceptor aircraft

F-111 twin-engine turbojet tactical fighter-bomber all-weather interceptor aircraft (TFX)

F-111A variable-geometry supersonic fighter-bomber (TFX)

F-404 General Electric turbofan jet engine

fa family allowance; fatty acid; field activities; filterable agent; fire alarm; first aid; first attack; fluorescent antibody; folic acid; fortified aqueous; free acid; free aperture; frequency agility; friendly aircraft; fuel-air (ratio)

fa (FA) fatty acid; fluvic acid

f/a friendly aircraft; fuel-air ratio; further advances

f & a fire and allied (insurance); fore and aft

fa *firma* (Dano-Norwegian—company or firm); *foregående (forrige) år* (Dano-Norwegian—previous year); (Italian—fourth tone, *D* in diatonic scale, *F* in fixed-do system)

få *forrige år* (Dano-Norwegian—last year)

fᵃ *factura* (Spanish—invoice)

fA *forrige Aar* (Danish—last year)

Fa Faeroes

Fa *Firma* (German—firm, business)

FA Factory Act; Failure Analysis; Farm Advisor; Field Allowance; Field Ambulance; Field Artillery; Final Acceptance; Financial Adviser; Fine Art(s); Fireman Apprentice; Flota Argentina (de Navegación Fluvial)—Argentine River Navigation Line; Football Association; Forecast Area; Foreign Affairs; Frankford Arsenal

F-A fighter-attack (aircraft)

F/A friendly aircraft

F & A Finance and Accounting; Financing and Accounting

F of A Foresters of America; Freethinkers of America

FA *Forze Armate* (Italian—Armed Forces); *Frontoviya Aviatsiya* (Russian—Frontal Aviation)—Soviet air force

F-A-18 McDonnell-Douglas fighter-attack aircraft named Hornet

faa field artillery airborne; formalin, acetic acid, alcohol (mixture); free of all average

FAA Federal Aviation Administration; Federal Aviation Agency; Fifth Avenue Association; Film Artists' Association; Finska Angpartygs (Finnish Steamship Line); Fleet Air Arm; Foreman's Association of America; Foundation for Aboriginal Affairs; Foundation for American Agriculture; Fraternal Actuarial Association

Faaa Papeete, Tahiti's airport

FAAA Fellow of the American Academy of Allergy

FAAAS Fellow of the American Academy of Arts and Sciences; Fellow of the American Association for the Advancement of Science

FAABMS Forward Army Anti-Ballistic Missile System

FAAG First Advertising Agency Group

FAAI Filipinos for Affirmative Action, Inc.

FAAN First Advertising Agency Network

FAAO Federation of American Arab Organizations; Finance and Accounts Office (US Army)

FAAOS Fellow of the American Academy of Orthopaedic Surgeons

FAAP Federal Aid to Airports Program

FAAPS Fine Art, Antique, and Philatelic Squad (Scotland Yard)

faar forward area alerting radar

FAAR Feminist Alliance Against Rape

fab fable; fabric; fabricate; fabrication; fabulist; fabulous; first-aid box

fab *fabrique* (French—factory); *franco à bord* (French—free on board); *frei an bord* (German—free on board)

Fab Fabio; Fabius; Fabre; Fabrian; Fabrice; Fabrizio

FAB Facilities Advisory Board; Fijian Affairs Board; Fleet Air Base; Força Aérea Brasileira (Brazilian Air Force); Fourth Avenue Booksellers (NYC); Frédéric Auguste Bartholdi

FAB *Força Aérea Brasileira* (Portuguese—Brazilian Air Force)

FABAS Farm Amalgamations and Boundary Adjustment Schemes

fabbr *fabbrica* (Italian—factory)

FABI Fédération Royale des Associations Belges d'Ingénieurs (Royal Federation of Belgian Engineering Associations)

Fabien Sevitzky Fabien Koussevitzky

fabl fire alarm bell

FABMDS Field Army Ballistic Missile Defense System

FABMIDS Field Army Ballistic Missile Defense System

fabr fabricate; fabrication

Fab Soc Fabian Society

FABSS Fellow of the Architectural and Building Surveyors' Society

FABU Fleet Air Base Unit

Fabulous Philadelphians the Philadelphia Orchestra

fabx fire alarm box

fac façade; facial; facility; facsimile; factor; factory; faculty; fast as can; field accelerator; forward air cargo

fac. *factum similie* (Latin—facsimile)

Fac Faculty

FAC Factor (Max, stock exchange symbol); Federal Advisory Council; Federal Aviation Commission; Financial Administrative Control; Financial Affairs Commission; Fleet Air Control; Forward Air Controller; Frequency Allocation Committee; Friday Afternoon Club (collegiate drinking group)

FACA Fellow of the American College of Anaesthetists; Fellow of the American College of Angiology; Fellow of the Association of Chartered Accountants

FAC(A) Forward Air Controller (Airborne)

FACA *Federación Argentina Cooperative Agrarias* (Spanish—Argentine Agrarian Cooperative Federation)

FACAl Fellow of the American College of Allergists

FACAn Fellow of the American College of Anesthesiologists

FACB Federation of Australian Commercial Broadcasters

FACC Fellow of the American College of Cardiology; Florida Association of Community Colleges; Ford Aerospace and Communications Corporation

FACCA Fellow of the Association of Certified and Corporate Accountants

FACCC Faculty Association of the California Community Colleges

faccm fast-access charge-coupled memory

facd foreign area consumer dialing

FACD Fellow of the American College of Dentistry

FACDS Fellow of the Australian College of Dental Surgeons

face. field artillery computer equipment; forced-air-cooled electronics

FACE Facilities and Communications Evaluation (USA); (mnemonic for remembering the space notes of the treble clef—F, A, C, E)

FACEM Federation of Associations of Colliery Equipment Manufacturers

FACES Fortran Automatic-Code-Evaluation System

facet facetious(ly)

FACFI Federal Advisory Committee on False Identification

FACFO Fellow of the American College of Foot Orthopedics

FACFP Fellow of the American College of Family Physicians

facg fast attack-craft gun

FACG Fellow of the American College of Gastroenterology

FACHA Fellow of the American College of Health Administrators; Fellow of the American College of Hospital Administrators

FACI First Article Configuration Inspection

facil facility

facile. fire and casualty insurance library edition

facl facilitate

facm fast attack-craft missile

FACMTA Federal Advisory Council on Medical Training Aids

FACO Fellow of the American College of Otolaryngology

FACOG Fellow of the American College of Obstetricians and Gynecologists

facp fast attack-craft patrol; forward air control point

FACP Fellow of the American College of Physicians

FACPM Fellow of the American College of Preventive Medicine

fac pwr ctl facility power control

fac pwr mon facility power monitor

fac pwr pnl facility power panel

FACR Fellow of the American College of Radiology

facs facsimile(s)

FACS Family and Community Services; Faxon's Automatic Claim System; Federation of American-Controlled Shipping; Fellow of the American College of Surgeons; Financial Accounting and Control System; Floating-Decimal Abstract Coding System

FACSAF Fleet Air Control and Surveillance Facility (USN)

FACSFAC Fleet Air Control and Surveillance Facility

facsim facsimile(s)

facsim(s) facsimile(s)

fact. factory; fast attack-craft torpedo; flexible automatic circuit tester; fully-automatic compiler translator

fact *factura* (Spanish—bill of lading, invoice)

FACT Facilitation and Coordination Therapy; Family Action Council of Texas; Fast Access Current Text Bank; Financial Accounting Control Technique; Flanagan Aptitude Classification Test; Flight Acceptance Composite Test(ing); Fully-Automatic Compiler Translator; Fully-Automatic Compiling Technique

fact\u00aa *factura* (Spanish—invoice)

FACTS Facilities Administration Control and Time Schedule; Federation of Australian Commercial Television Stations; Financial Accounting and Control Techniques for Supply

facty fact filled; factory

fad. force activity designator; fracture analysis diagram; free air delivered; free air delivery

fad. (FAD) flavine adenine dinucleotide; funding authorization document

FAD Fleet Air Defense

fadac field artillery digital automatic computer

FADD Fight Against Dictating Designers

F Adm Fleet Admiral

FADM Functional Area Documentation Manager (USAF)

FADO Fellow of the Association of Dispensing Opticians

fadsid fighter-aircraft-delivered seismic intrusion detector

FADT First Article Demonstration Test(ing)

fae fine-alignment equipment; forward air express; fuel air explosive

FAE Federation of Arab Engineers; Fund for the Advancement of Education

FAE *Federación de Amigos de Enseñanza* (Spanish—Federation of the Friends of Teaching); *Fuerza Aérea Ecuatoriana* (Spanish—Ecuadorian Air Force)

FAEA Federation of ASEAN Economic Associations

FAECC Fellow of the Accountants and Executives Corporation of Canada

faer *faerøsk* (Dano-Norwegian —Faeroese)

Faer Faeroe Islands

Faer Eyjaer (Norse—Faeroe Islands)

Faerøerne (Danish—Faeroe Islands)—north of Scotland in the North Atlantic

Faeroes Faeroe Islands in the North Atlantic

fae's fuel air explosives

faeshed fuel-air-explosive-system helicopter delivered

FAETUA Fleet Airborne Electronic Training Unit, Atlantic

FAETUP Fleet Airborne Electronic Training Unit, Pacific

faf final approach fix; financial-aid form; first article flow; flyaway factory; forage acre factor; forward air freight; free at field; fuzing, arming, and firing

FAF Fafnir Bearings (stock exchange symbol); Financial Analysts Federation; Fine Arts Foundation

FAFT First Article Factory Test(s)

fag fagotto (Italian—basson)

FAG Failure Analysis Group; Finance and Accounting Group (USAF); Fine Arts Gallery; Finished Americans Group; Fiscal Activities Guide

Faga Fagatoa (American Samoa's seat of government facing Pago Pago harbor)

Fagatogo American Samoa's capital on Tutuila Island adjacent to Pago Pago (pronounced *Pango Pango*)

fagms (FAGMS) field artillery guided missiles

FAGO Fellow of the American Guild of Organists

fag(s) faggot(s)

fags fagottos (Italian—bassoons)

FAGS Federation of Astronomical and Geophysical Permanent Services; Fellow of the American Geographical Society

fagt first available government transportation

fagtrans first available government transportation

FAGU Fleet Air Gunnery Unit

fah failed to attend hearing

FAHA Finnish-American Historical Archives

fahqmt fully automatic high-quality machine translation

Fahr Fahrenheit

fai final acceptance inspection; first article inspection; frequency-azimuth intensity; fresh air intake

FAI Fairbanks Alaska (airport); Fédération Aéronautique In-

ternationale

FAI Fédération Abolitionniste Internationale (French—International Abolitionist Federation); *Federación Anarquista Iberica* (Spanish—Iberian Anarchist Federation)

FAIA Fellow of the American Institute of Architects

FAIAS Fellow of the Australian Institute of Agricultural Science

FAIB Federation des Associations Internationales Establies en Belgique (French—Federation of International Associations Established in Belgium)

FAIC Federation of Australian Investment Clubs; Fellow of the American Institute of Chemists

FAIEx Fellow of the Australian Institute of Export

FAIHA Fellow of the Australian Institute of Hospital Administration

FAII Fellow of the Australian Insurance Institute

FAIM Fellow of the Australian Institute of Management

FAIME Foreign Affairs Information Management Effort (Dept State)

fain. functional air index number

FAIO Field Army Issuing Office(r)

FAIP Fellow of the Australian Institute of Physics

FAIPM Fellow of the Australian Institute of Personnel Management

fair. fairing; fast-access information retrieval

FAir fleet air

FAIR Fair Access to Insurance Requirements; Federation for American Immigration Reform; Financial Assistance for Independent Rehabilitation (of disabled, handicapped, impaired, retarded, and wheelchair people); Fleet Air (Wing); Friends in America for Independence of Rhodesia

FAIRA Foundation for Aboriginal and Island Reserve Action (Australia)

Fairbanks Institute Northern Region Correction Institute at Fairbanks, Alaska

Fair City Perth, Scotland

Fair Deal (administration of Harry S Truman—thirty-third President of the United

States)

FAIRELM Fleet Air Eastern Atlantic and Mediterranean

FAIRS Fair and Impartial Random Selection System (military draft); Federal Aviation Information Retrieval System

fairships fleet airships

Fairy of Dreams Queen Mab

Fairytale Land Denmark—home of Hans Christian Andersen

FAIS Fellow of the Amalgamated Institute of Secretaries

FAITH Fending Alone In The Home (Girl Scout program)

Faithful City Worcester, Massachusetts whose motto is *Floreat Semper Civitas Fidelis*

fak fly-away kit; freights all kinds

Fak Faktura (German—invoice)

FAK Federasie van Afrikaanse Kultuurvereniginge (Afrikaans —Federation of Afrikaans Cultural Societies)

fak-pak freight all kinds (in a box on wheels)

faks faksimile (Dano-Norwegian—facsimile)

Fakt Faktura (German—invoice)

fal fusil automatique légère (French—light automatic rifle)—*FAL*

Fal Falmouth

F a L Fathers-at-Large

FAL Frequency Allocation List; Frontier Airlines

FAL Frente Argentino de Liberación (Spanish—Argentine Liberation Front)—pro-Cuban

FALA Federation of Asian Library Associations; Federation of Australian Literature and Art

Falcon Dassault twin-engine executive transport made in France and called Mystere 20

falcons of the sea clipper ships

'falfa alfalfa

Falk Cur Falkland Current

Falk Isl Falkland Islands (Islas Maldivas)

Falklands Falkland Islands and Dependencies (South Georgia, South Sandwich Islands, South Shetlands)

fallex fall exercises

fall(s) waterfall(s)

Falls The Falls (short form for any waterfall place-name such as Angel Falls, Niagara Falls, Victoria Falls, Yosemite Falls, etc.)

Falls City Louisville, Kentucky

Falls of the Rhine Rheinfall or Schaffhausen

fallwarn fallout warning

FALN Fuerzas Armadas de Liberación Nacional (Armed Forces of National Liberation —Communist paramilitary organization)

FALNP Fuerzas Armadas de Liberación Nacional Puertoriqueña (Spanish—Armed Forces for Puerto Rican National Liberation)—sometimes called FALN and often taking credit for assassinations and bombings

FALS Ford Authorized Leasing System

false topaz citrine (quartz with ferric iron)

fam familiar; familiarization (of flights); family; foreign air mail; free at mill

Fam Famagusta; Family

FAM Football Association of Malaysia; foreign airmail; forward air mail; Free and Accepted Masons

F & AM Free and Accepted Masons

FAMA Federal Agriculture Marketing Authority; Fellow of the American Medical Association; Fire Apparatus Manufacturers Association

FAMAS Flutter and Matrix Algebra System

FAMC Fitzsimons Army Medical Center

fame. fatty-acid methyl ester(s); financial accounting made easy

FAME Farmers Allied Meat Enterprises Cooperative; Future American Magical Entertainers

FAMEM Federation of Associations of Mining Equipment Manufacturers

FAMEME Fellow of the Association of Mining, Electrical, and Mechanical Engineers

famex familiarization exercise

FAMHEM Federation of Associations of Materials Handling Equipment Manufacturers

FAMIS Financial and Management Information System

F-am-M Frankfurt-am-Main (Frankfurt-on-Main)

FAMOS Fleet Applications of Meteorological Observations from Satellites

FAMOUS French-American Mid-Ocean Undersea Study (of an Atlantic reef off the Azores on the line of an undersea rift extending from the Arctic to Antarctica)

fam per para familial periodic paralysis

fam phys family physician

fam rm family room

FAMS Fellow of the Ancient Monuments Society

FAMSF Fine Arts Museum of San Francisco

FAMU Florida A & M University

fan. fanatic (usually in sense of enthusiast); fantasia; fantasy

FANA Federation of Australian Nurserymens Associations

FANAC Fabrica Nacional de Aceite (Spanish—National Oil Factory)

FANALOZA Fabrica Nacional de Loza (Spanish—National Porcelain Factory)

Fanciulla La Fanciulla del West (Italian—The Girl of the Golden West)—Puccini three-act opera whose libretto recalls David Belasco's play

Faneuil Faneuil Hall meeting house in Boston's Dock Square where colonial Americans met to plot their revolution against British tyrants

Fanguito (Spanish—Little Muddy)—San Juan, Puerto Rico's most notorious slum

FANK Forces Armées Nationales Khmères (French—Khmer National Armed Forces)—Cambodian armed forces

Fannie Mae Federal National Mortgage Association

Fan(ny) Frances; Francisca; Frasquita

Fanny Brice Fanny Borach

FANPT Freeman Anxiety and Psychosomatic Test

FANS Food and Nutritional System

Fanshaw Featherstonehaugh

fant fantasia; fantasy

fantabulous fantastic + fabulous

fantac fighter analysis tactical air combat

Fantastique Symphonie Fantastique (French—Fantastique Symphony)—composed by Berlioz who subtitled it *Épisode de la Vie d'un Artiste* (Episode in the Life of an Artist)

FANU Flota Argentina de Navegación de Ultramar (Argentine High Seas Navigation Line)

FANY First-Aid Nursing Yeomanry

FANZAAS Fellow of the Australian and New Zealand Association for the Advancement of Science

fanzines fan + magazines

fao finish all over

FAO Farm Advisory Office(r); Field Audit Office(r); Finance and Accounts Office(r); Fleet Accountant Officer; Fleet Administration Office(r); Food and Agriculture Organization (UN); Free Albania Organization

F & AO Finance and Accounts Office (US Army)

faop full away on passage

fap final approach; fixed action pattern; floating arithmetic package

fap (FAP) fixed action pattern

fAp full American plan

FAP Failure Analysis Program; Family Assistance Plan; Family Assistance Program(ming); First Aid Post; Foreign Assistance Program; Frequency Allocation Panel

FAP Forca Aérea Portuguesa (Portuguese Air Force); *Fuerza Aerea del Peru* (Spanish—Peruvian Air Force), *Fuerzas Armadas Peronistas* (Spanish —Peronist Armed Forces)— right-wing Argentine guerrilla group

FAPA Filipino-American Political Association

FAPC Food and Agriculture Planning Committee (NATO)

FAPHA Fellow of the American Public Health Association

FAPHI Fellow of the Association of Public Health Inspectors

FAPI First Article Production Inspection

FAPIG First Atomic Power Industry Group

FAPP Federation of Associations of Periodical Publishers

FAPR Federal Aviation Procurement Regulations

FAPREC Federación de Asociaciones de Padres, Representantes, y Educadores Católicos (Spanish—Federation of Associations of Fathers, Representatives, and Catholic Educators)

FAPRS Federal Assistance Programs Retrieval System

FAPS Fellow of the American Physical Society

FAPT Fellow of the Association of Photographic Technicians

faq fair average quality; free at quay

FAQ Free at Quay

faqs fair average quality of season

far. false alarm rate; farad; Faraday; faradic; farriery; farthing; finned air rocket; floor/area ratio; forward-acquisition radar

Far Faraday

FAR Failure Analysis Report; Federal Aviation Regulations; Financial Accounts Receivable; Foundation for Australian Resources; finned air rocket; flight aptitude rating

FAR *Fuerzas Armadas Rebeldes* (Spanish—Rebel Armed Forces)—Guatemala; *Fuerzas Armadas Revolucionarias* (Spanish—Revolutionary Armed Forces)—Cuba

FARA Foreign Agents Registration Act

FARACS Faculty of Anaesthetists of the Royal Australian College of Surgeons

FARADA Failure Rate Data (BuWeps Program)

Farallones Farollon Islands off San Francisco

Farasans short form for the Farasan Islands of the Red Sea off Saudi Arabia

FARB Federation of Australian Radio Broadcasters

FARC Federal Addiction Research Center

FARC *Fuerzas Armadas Revolucionarias de Colombia* (Spanish—Armed Revolutionary Forces of Colombia)—pro-Soviet communists

Far East countries and islands of East Asia or in the Pacific—eastern Siberia, China, Japan, Taiwan, Korea, Indochina, the Philippines, the Malay Peninsula

FARELF Far East Land Forces

faret fast reactor test

Farewell Beethoven's Piano Sonata No. 32 in C minor (opus 111); Haydn's Symphony No. 45 in F-sharp minor

FARI Foreign Affairs Research Institute

Farinelli Carlo Broschi

Farl Farley

FARL Frick Art Reference Li-

brary

farm *farmacia* (Spanish—pharmacy)—drugstore

Farmer President sobriquet shared by William Henry Harrison and George Washington

farmobile farm automobile

FARN *Fuerzas Armadas de Resistencia Nacional* (Spanish—Armed Forces of National Resistance)—El Salvador's underground guerrillas

Farnes Farne Islands off England's Northumberland coast

faro. flow(ed, ing) at rate of

FARO Flare-Activated Radiobiological Observatory

Fär Öer (Dutch—Far East)

Faroes Faerøerne (Faroe Islands)

FARP *Fronte Antifascista e di Rinascita Populare* (Italian—Antifascist Front and Popular Revival)—left-wing group

Far Pom Farther Pomerania (coastal Poland)

Farrar Farrar, Straus and Giroux

Fars Faristan

Farther India Indochina; Indochinese Peninsula

Far West the Rocky Mountain States

fas fetal alcohol syndrome; first and seconds; free alongside ship

FAS Facility Activity Schedule; Farm Advisory Service; Federal Agricultural Service; Federal Air Surgeon; Federation of American Scientists; Fellow of the Society of Arts; Food Advice Service; Foreign Agricultural Service; Free Alongside Ship; Frequency Assignment Subcommittee

FASA Federation of ASEAN Shipowners Associations; Fellow of the Acoustical Society of America; First Audit(or) of Sheriff's Accounts; Florida Association of School Administrators

FASAP Fellow of the Australian Society of Animal Production

FASB Financial Accounting Standards Board

FASBA Florida Association of School Business Administrators

fasc *fascicule* (French—part); *fasciculus* (Latin—little bundle)

FASC Federation of ASEAN Shippers Councils; Free-

Standing Ambulatory Surgical Center

FASCE Fellow of the American Society of Civil Engineers

fasci (Latin prefix—band)—fascia board

FASCO Forward Area Support Coordination Office(r)

fase fundamentally-analyzable simplified English

FASE Fellow of the Antiquarian Society—Edinburgh

FASEB Federation of American Societies of Experimental Biology

fasgrolia fast-growing language of initialisms and acronyms

fash (FASH) forward area support helicopter

FASH Fraternal Association of Steel Haulers

Fashoda former name of Kodok, Sudan

FASII Federation of Associations of Small Industries in India

FASL Florida Association of School Librarians

FASOC Forward Air Support Operations Center

FASPAC Ford Asia Pacific

faspl fair average sample

FASPM Flotte Administrative des Iles Saint Pierre et Miquelon

FASS Fine Alignment Sub-System

fast. fuel and sensor tanks; fully automatic switching teletype

fast. (FAST) facial affect scoring technique; facility for automatic sorting and testing; failure analysis by statistical technics; field data applications, systems, and technics; file analysis and selection technics; fleet-sizing analysis and sensitivity technic; flexible algebraic scientific translator; forecasting and scheduling technic; formula and statement translator; free and single tourist

FAST First Atomic Ship Transport; flexible algebraic scientific translator; freight accounting system tracing

FASTM Freight Automated System for Traffic Management

fastnr fastener

fat. fatigue; final assembly test(ing); fixed asset transfer; free alongside terminal; free at terminal; full annual toll

FAT Family Adjustment Test;

Flight Test Station; Folk Arts Theater; Fresno, California (airport)

fata fatigue test(ing) article

Fatah Harakat-Tahrir Falastin (Arabic—Palestinian terrorist underground organization)— Arabic acronyms such as this have inverted initials

fatdog fatty hotdog (fat-filled frankfurter)

Fate American nickname for Lafayette and one adorning many country boys

Fate Beethoven's Symphony No. 5 in C minor (see *Victory*)

fa technique fluorescent antibody technique

fatfurters fat-filled frankfurters

fath fathom

Father of Abolition Samuel Hopkins

Father of the A-bomb J Robert Oppenheimer

Father Abraham Abraham Lincoln

Father of Air Conditioning WH Carrier

Father of Algebra Diophantus of Alexandria

Father of All Yankees Benjamin Franklin

Father of America Sam(uel) Adams

Father of American Anarchy Josiah Warren of Cincinnati, Ohio who in 1827 advocated government activities be transferred to private citizens

Father of American Anthropology Lewis Henry Morgan

Father of the American Ballet George Balanchine

Father of American Baptists John Clarke

Father of American Botany John Bartram

Father of American Boxing William Muldoon

Father of American Conchology Thomas Say

Father of American Conservatism John Jay

Father of American Dance Ted Shawn

Father of American Egyptology James Henry Breasted

Father of American Football Walter Camp

Father of American Freethought Thomas Paine

Father of American Geography Jedidiah Morse

Father of American Geology William Maclure

Father of American History George Bancroft and William Bradford—both have backers for this title

Father of American Horticulture Peter Henderson

Father of American Independence John Adams

Father of American Lexicography Noah Webster

Father of American Literature Washington Irving

Father of the American Medical Association Dr Nathan Smith Davis

Father of American Medical Botany Jacob Bigelow

Father of American Mineralogy Parker Cleaveland

Father of American Naval Architecture William A Webb

Father of American Navigation Nathaniel Bowditch

Father of American Nutrition W(ilbur) O(lin) Atwater

Father of American Oceanography Matthew Fontaine Maury

Father of American Orchestral Music Johann Christian Gottlieb Graupner

Father of American Ornithology appellation shared by John James Audubon and Alexander Wilson

Father of American Paleontology O(thniel) C(harles) Marsh

Father of American Photography S(amuel) F(inley) B(reese) Morse

Father of American Photo-Journalism Matthew Brady

Father of American Poetry Philip Freneau

Father of American Poets William Cullen Bryant

Father of American Pragmatism Charles Sanders Peirce

Father of American Prison Reform George O Osborne

Father of American Psychiatry Dr Benjamin Rush

Father of American Psychobiology Adolf Meyer

Father of American Psychology William James

Father of American Railroads Peter Cooper

Father of the American Revolution Sam(uel) Adams

Father of American Rocketry Robert H. Goddard

Father of American Surgery Dr William Halsted or Dr Philip Syng Physick, depending on whose doing the nicknaming

Father of American Technology Eli Whitney

Father of the American Turf Leonard Jerome

Father of American Universalism nickname shared by Hosea Ballou and John Murray

Father of American Zoology Thomas Say

Father of Anatomical Dissection Andreas Vesalius

Father of Andean Archeology Max Uhle

Father of Angling Izaak Walton

Father of Annapolis George Bancroft

Father of Antarctic Whaling Captain Carl A Larsen

Father of Antiseptic Obstetrics Ignaz Semmelweis

Father of Antiseptic Surgery Sir Joseph Lister

Father of Argentina's School System Domingo Faustino Sarmiento

Father of Argentine Education Faustino Sarmiento

Father of Argentine Independence General José de San Martín

Father of the Atomic Age Enrico Fermi

Father of the Atomic Submarine Admiral Hyman Rickover, USN

Father of the Automobile Gottlieb Daimler

Father of Baseball Henry Chadwick, Alexander Cartwright, and Abner Doubleday share this sobriquet

Father of Basic Flying John Joseph Montgomery

Father of Basketball James Naismith

Father of Belgian Opera Andre Ernest Modeste Gretry

Father of Believers Mohammed

Father of the Bill of Rights James Madison

Father of Black History Chester G Woodson

Father of Blood Banks and Blood Plasma Charles R Rich

Father of the Blues W(illiam) C(hristopher) Handy

Father of Botany Aristotle

Father of Brazilian Opera Antonio Carlos Gomes

Father of British Boxing Jack Broughton

Father of British Musicology Sir Charles Grove

Father of the British Navy Alfred the Great

Father of British Printing William Caxton

Father of British Unitarianism John Biddle

Father of Buffalo Joseph Ellicot

Father of Chemistry Robert Boyle

Father of Chemurgy George Washington Carver

Father of Child Psychology Leo Kanner

Father of the Chinese Revolution Dr Sun Yat-sen

Father Christmas Santa Claus; Snow King

Father of Church History Eusebius

Father of Civilian Atomic Power Admiral Hyman Rickover

Father of the Civil Rights Movement Martin Luther King, Jr

Father of Civil Service Reform George Hunt Pendleton

Father of Comedy Aristophanes

Father of Confederation John A Macdonald—Canada's first prime minister

Father of the Constitution James Madison—fourth President of the United States

Father of the Continental Congress Benjamin Franklin

Father of the Copyright William Hogarth

Father of the Cotton Gin Eli Whitney

Father of Courtesy Richard Beauchamp—Earl of Warwick

Father of the Cowboys Charles Goodnight

Father of Cuban Independence José Martí

Father of Czechoslovakian Music Bedrich Smetana

Father Damien Joseph Damien de Veuster

Father of Danish Opera Friedrich Kuhlau

Father of Dano-Norwegian Literature Ludvig Holberg

Father of the Declaration of Independence title many historians agree must be shared by Thomas Paine who wrote the first rough draft and Thomas Jefferson who wrote the final draft with John Adams and Benjamin Franklin lending support

Father of the Detective Story Edgar Allan Poe

Father Divine Morgan J Divine born George Baker

Father of Dominican Independence Juan Pablo Duarte

Father of the Dominican Republic José Nuñez de Cáceres

Father of Dutch Poetry Jakob van Maerlant

Father of the Dutch Reformed Church in America John Henry Livingston

Father of Ecclesiastical History Eusebius Pamphili

Father of Egyptian Archeology Sir Flinders Petrie

Father of Embryology Carl Ernst von Baer

Father of the Encyclopedia Diderot

Father of English Cathedral Music Thomas Tallis

Father of English Empiricism John Locke

Father of English Lexicography Dr Samuel Johnson also celebrated as the leading conversationalist of his era, according to his biographer James Boswell called Bozzy

Father of the English Novel Henry Fielding

Father of English Poetry Geoffrey Chaucer

Father of English Printing William Caxton

Father of English Song Caedmon

Father of English Unitarianism John Biddle

Father of Epic Poetry Homer

Father of the Erie Canal De Witt Clinton

Father of Ethical Culture Felix Adler

Father of Ethology Konrad Lorenz

Father of Euphuism John Lyly

Father of Experimental Physiology Galen

Father of the Faithful Abraham

Father of Fascism Italian bullyboy tyrant Benito Mussolini

Father of the Federal Reserve System George Carter Glass

Father of the Film Industry D(avid) W(ark) Griffith

Father of Fingerprinting Alphonse Bertillon

Father of the Flivver Henry Ford

Father of the Free School System Governor James Edward English of Connecticut

Father of Free Trade Adam Smith

Father of French-Canadian Poetry Octave Cremazie

Father of French Lyric Poetry Pierre de Ronsard

Father of French Opera Jean-Baptiste Lully

Father of the French School of Neurology Jean-Martin Charcot

Father of French Surgery Ambroise Paré

Father of French Tragedy Pierre Corneille

Father of Frozen Foods Clarence Birdseye

Father of Geography Strabo the Greek Stoic who wrote seventeen books about Asia, Egypt, Libya, and Europe

Father of Geometry Pythagorus

Father of German Literature Gotthold Ephraim Lessing

Father of German Opera Christoph Willibald von Gluck

Father of the German Reformation Martin Luther

Father of German Unification Prince Otto von Bismarck

Father of Gods and Men Odin or Wotan, according to the Norse; Jove or Jupiter, according to the Romans; Zeus, according to the Greeks; etc.

Father of the Gramophone Emile Berliner

Father of Greater Philadelphia John Christian Bullitt

Father of Greek Didactic Poetry Hesiod whose poem *Theogony* describes the beginning of the world, its gods, and the five Ages of Mankind (*see entry*)

Father of Greek Music Terpander of Lesbos

Father of Greek Sculpture Phidias

Father of Greek Tragedy Aeschylus

Father of Greenbacks Salmon Portland Chase

Father of the H-bomb Edward Teller

Father of His Country Cicero and several Roman caesars; George Washington—Commander-in-Chief of the Continental Army and first President of the United States

Father of History Herodotus

Father of Homeopathy in America Dr Constantine Hering

Father of the Household Heater Benjamin Franklin

Father of Humanism in America John Dietrich

Father of the Hydrogen Bomb Edward Teller

Father of Hypnotism Friedrich Anton Mesmer

Father of Individual Psychology Alfred Adler

Father of Inductive Philosophy Francis Bacon

Father of Israel Chaim Weizmann

Father of Italian Landscape Painting Andrea del Verrocchio (Andrea di Michele Cione)

Father of Italian Opera Claudio Monteverdi

Father of Japanese Caricature Toba Sojo

Father of Japanese Shipbuilding Thomas Glover known to the Japanese as Kuraba

Father of Jests Joseph Miller

Father of the Juvenile Court Judge Benjamin Barr Lindsey

Father of the Kindergarten Friedrich Froebel

Father of Latin Song Ennius (239–169 BCE)

Father of the Legal Code David Dudley Field

Father of Lies Satan

Father of the Locomotive Richard Trevethick

Father of Massachusetts Governor John Winthrop

Father of Medicine Hippocrates

Father of Mexican Independence Miguel Hidalgo y Costilla

Father of Mexican Muralism Dr Atl (born Gerardo Murillo)

Father of Military Strategy Hannibal

Father of Mineralogy Agricola

Father of Modern Architecture Frank Lloyd Wright

Father of Modern Art Masaccio (Tommaso Guidi)

Father of Modern Astronomy Copernicus (Nikolaus Kopernicki)

Father of Modern Baseball Alexander Joy Cartwright

Father of Modern Brazil Getulio Vargas

Father of Modern Conservative Thought Edmund Burke

Father of Modern Criminology Alphonse Bertillon and Cesare Lombroso vie for this title

Father of Modern Democratic Philosophy John Locke

Father of Modern Drama Henrik Ibsen

Father of Modern Economics Adam Smith

Father of Modern English Poetry Walt Whitman (although many Englishmen might prefer Walter Pater, Thomas Hardy, Robert Bridges, or Oscar Wilde)

Father of Modern Fingerprinting Sir Edward Richard Henry

Father of Modern French Poetry Charles Baudelaire

Father of Modern Genetics Gregor Mendel

Father of Modern Geology Sir Charles Lyell

Father of Modern German Poetry Heinrich Heine

Father of Modern Guitar Music Francisco Tárrega

Father of Modern Gynecology Dr J Marion Sims

Father of Modern Italian Poetry Gabriele D'Annunzio

Father of Modern Magnetism John Van Vleck

Father of Modern Medicine Canadian-born Sir William Osler

Father of Modern Music Franz Liszt; Mozart

Father of Modern Navies Captain Alfred T Mahan author of *The Influence of Sea Power upon History* published in 1890

Father of Modern Neurology Guillaume-Benjamin-Amand Duchenne

Father of the Modern Novel Lion Feuchtwanger

Father of the Modern Orchestra Hector Berlioz

Father of Modern Painters Giovanni Cimabue (Cenni di Pepo)

Father of Modern Pedagogy Heinrich Pestalozzi

Father of Modern Philosophy René Descartes

Father of Modern Photography William Henry Fox Talbot

Father of Modern Physics Albert Einstein

Father of Modern Physiology William Harvey

Father of Modern Prose Fiction Daniel Defoe

Father of Modern Russian Poetry Nikolai Alekseevich Nekrasov

Father of Modern Spanish Poetry Rubén Darío

Father of Modern Surgery of the Brain Paul Broca

Father of the Modern Zoo Carl Hagenbeck

Father of Moral Philosophy Thomas Aquinas

Father of the Mormons Joseph Smith

Father of Muckrakers Upton Sinclair, Lincoln Steffens, and Joseph Flynt Williard share

this unattractive sobriquet attesting to their success as reporters revealing corruption and graft

Father of Music Festivals Edinburgh

Father of Natural History Aristotle

Father of Negro History Carter G(odwin) Woodson

Father of the Neighborhood Settlement House Jacob August Riis

Father of Neurosurgery American-born Canadian Doctor Wilder Penfield

Father of New England John Endicott—its first governor

Father of the New Left Herbert Marcuse

Father of Niagara Power William Birch Rankine

Father of the Nuclear Submarine Admiral Hyman Rickover

Father of Oceanography Matthew Fontaine Maury

Father of Ontario Hydro Sir Adam Beck

Father of Organic Architecture Frank Lloyd Wright

Father of Organized Labor Samuel Gompers

Father of Osteopathy Dr Andrew T Still

Father of Paleontology Georges Cuvier

Father of Parole Captain Alexander Maconochie the governor of the Norfolk Island penal colony from 1840 to 1844

Father of the Patent Office John Ruggles

Father of Penitentiary Science Jean Jacques Vilain

Father of Pennsylvania William Penn—its founder

Father of Philippine Independence Emilio Aguinaldo

Father of Philosophy Thales

Father of the Phonograph Thomas A Edison

Father of Photojournalism Alfred Eisenstaedt

Father of Physiography William Morris Davis

Father of Pianoforte Playing Muzio Clementi

Father of Pittsburgh George Washington who proposed the location and the name during the French and Indian War

Father of Poetry Orpheus

Father of the Potteries Josiah Wedgwood

Father of Psychoanalysis Sigmund Freud

Father of Radio Lee De Forest

Father of Radio Broadcasting Harry P(hillips) Davis

Father of Railways George Stephenson

Father of Reform John Cartwright

Father of the Reformed Church John Henry Livingston

Father of the Republic of China Sun Yat Sen

Father of Ridicule Rabelais

Father of the Robot Joseph Engelberger

Father of Roman Philosophy Cicero

Father of the Royal Navy King Alfred

Father of Rural Free Delivery Marion Butler of North Carolina

Father of Russian Art and Music Criticism V(ladimir) V(asilievich) Stasov

Father of Russian Literature Alexander Pushkin

Father of Russian Marxism Georgi Valentinovich Plekhanov

Father of the Russian Navy Peter the Great

Father of Russian Opera Michael Glinka

Fathers of Canadian Confederation Sir John A Macdonald and George Brown of Ontario, Sir George S Etienne Cartier and Sir Alexander Galt of Quebec, Sir Charles Tupper of Nova Scotia, Sir Samuel Leonard Tilley of New Brunswick

Father of the Science of Eugenics Sir Francis Galton

Father of Science Fiction Jules Verne *(see entry)*

Fathers of the Enlightenment Diderot, Rousseau, Voltaire

Father of the Sewing Machine Elias Howe

Fathers of Italian Unification Camillo Cavour, Giuseppe Garibaldi, Giuseppe Mazzini

Fathers of Kodachrome Leopold Godowsky and Leopold Mannes

Father of the Skyscraper Cass Gilbert

Father of South African Poetry Thomas Pringle

Father of the Soviet Hydrogen Bomb Nobel-Peace-Prize-winner Andrei D Sakharov

Father of Spanish Drama Lope de Vega

Father of Spanish Satire Miguel Cervantes de Saavedra

Fathers of the Religion of Reason (Unitarianism) James Martineau in England plus Ralph Waldo Emerson and Theodore Parker in the United States

Father of States' Rights John Caldwell Calhoun

Father of State Universities Manasseh Cutler

Father of Steam Navigation Robert Fulton

Father of the Steam Navy Commodore Matthew C Perry—also known as Old Bruin

Father of the String Quartet and the Symphony Franz Joseph Haydn—his 85 string quartets and 104 symphonies set the style for such works up to the end of the 19th century

Father of the Submarine John Philip Holland

Father of Supersonic Flight Theodor von Karman

Father of Swedish Music Johan Helmich Roman

Father of Swedish Opera Ivar Hallström

Father of Swiss Reformation Huldreich Zwingli

Father of the Symphony Franz Josef Haydn

Father of the Tablet Triturate Dr Robert Mason Fuller

Father of the Tariff Secretary of the Treasury Alexander Hamilton

Father of Taxonomy Linnaeus

Father of the Telegraph S(amuel) F(inley) B(reese) Morse

Father of the Telephone Alexander Graham Bell usually given credit although he stated he had only improved the work of a German named Philipp Reis who was the inventor

Father of Television John Logie Baird

Father of Texas sobriquet shared by Stephen F Austin and Sam(uel) Houston

Father of Theoretical Chemistry Antoine Laurent Lavoisier

Father of The Pill Dr Gregory Pincus of Shrewsbury, Massachusetts—formulator of the contraceptive pill

Father Time time personified and symbolized by a bearded elder wielding a scythe

Father of Traffic Safety William Phelps Eno

Father of Tragedy Aeschylus

Father of Tropical Medicine Sir Patrick Manson

Father of the Typewriter Christopher Latham Sholes

Father of the United States Lighthouse Service President John Quincy Adams

Father of the United States Military Academy Brigadier General Sylvanus Thayer, USA

Father of the United States National Museum John Quincy Adams who when President advocated the founding of what became the Smithsonian Institution

Father of the United States Naval Academy Secretary of the Navy George Bancroft

Father of the United States Naval War College Rear Admiral Stephen Bleecker Luce

Father of the United States Navy nickname shared by President John Adams and Commodore John Barry

Father of Universalism in the United States Hosea Ballou

Father of the University of Virginia Thomas Jefferson—third President of the United States

Father of Uruguay José Gervasio Artigas

Father of Uruguay's School System José Pedro Varela

Father of the U.S. Post Office Benjamin Franklin—author, inventor, patriot, printer, philosopher, scientist, statesman

Father of Vaccination Edward Jenner

Father of Vasectomy Sir Astley Paston Cooper

Father of Venezuelan Democracy Rómulo Betancourt

Father of Verismo Giovanni Verga (whose realism is realized in operas by Mascagni, Leoncavallo, and Puccini)

Father of the Viennese Operetta Franz von Suppé

Father of Virginia Captain John Smith

Father of the Waltz Johann Strauss Sr

Father of the Waters sobriquet shared by great rivers such as the Amazon, Amur, Congo, Euphrates, Huang, Irrawaddy, Lena, Mackenzie, Mekong, Mississippi, Niger, Nile, Ob, Volga, Yangtze, Yenisei

Father of the Western Story Zane Grey

Father of West Point Sylvanus Thayer

Father of Yellowstone National Park Nathaniel Langford

Father of Zionism Theodor Herzl

Father of Zoology Aristotle

FATIS Food and Agriculture Technical Information Service

Fats Thomas (Fats) Waller

FATS Factory Acceptance Test Specification; Fast Analysis of Tape Surfaces; Fiji Air Travel Service

Fats Waller Thomas Waller

fatt fattura (Italian—invoice)

fau faucet; field action units; fixed asset utilization; forced air unit

fau (FAU) fine-alignment unit

FAU Florida Atlantic University; Friends' Ambulance Unit

F & AUA Fire and Accident Underwriters Association

FAUI Federation of Australian Underwater Instructors

FAUL Five Associated University Libraries (Binghamton, Buffalo, Cornell, Rochester, Syracuse)

Faulkner's County Yoknapatawpha (an invention of novelist William Faulkner)

Faultless Painter Andrea del Sarto

Faunty Fauntleroy

FAUSA Federation of Australian University Staff Associations

FAUSST French-Anglo-U.S. Supersonic Transport

faustite basic hydrated zinc aluminum phosphate (zinc-rich form of turquoise)

Fausts Verdammnis (German—Damnation of Faust) four-part dramatic legend composed by Berlioz

Faustus Socinus Fausto Sozzini

Fauvist Painter Raoul Dufy

fav favor; favorable; favorite

FAVA Fixed Asset Valuation Assignment

Favelas Rio de Janeiro's hillside slums

FAVO Fleet Aviation Officer

Favorite Island of Columbus Jamaica

FAW Fellowship of Australian Writers

FAWA Factory Assist Work Authorization; Federation of Asian Women's Associations

Fawcett Fawcett World Library

FAWCO Federation of American Women's Clubs Overseas

fawg free at wharf gate

Fawkes Fawkes Day (November 5 in Great Britain)

FAWS Flight Advisory Weather Service

FAWU Fishermen and Allied Workers Union

fax facilities (tv technical equipment such as cameras, lights, microphones); facsimile transmission; facsimile(s); facts; fuel air explosion; photo facsimile transmission

Fax Faxon

FAX fixed aeronautical station

Faxon Fetherstoneaugh

Fay Fagele; Faith; Fanny

FAZ Frankfurter Allgemeine Zeitung (Frankfurt's Universal Newspaper)

fb film bulletin; flat bar; flat bottom (rails); fog bell; foreign body; freight bill; fringe benefits; full American breakfast; full board; fullback; fully bleached

f-b full-bore (greater than 22 caliber)

f/b feedback; flock book; front to back (ratio)

f & b fire and bilge; fumigation and bath

f/B female Black

FB Fenian Brotherhood; Fernandina Beach; fighter bomber; Film Bulletin; Fire Brigade; Fisheries Board; Flying Boat; Forth Bridge; Free Baptist

FB-111 Convair strategic-bomber version of the F-111 with variable-geometry wings

fba fighter-bomber aircraft; fighter-bomber attack; fluorescent brightening agent

FBA Federal Bar Association; Fellow of the British Academy; Fibre Box Association; Freshwater Biological Association; Fur Brokers Association

FBAA Fellow of the British Association of Accountants and Auditors

f'ball football

FBBO Fellow of the British Ballet Organisation

fbc fallen building clause; fluidized bed combustion; fully-buffered channel; fully-buxomed charmer

FBC Family Benefit Capitalization; Federal Broadcasting Corporation; Fiji Broadcasting Commission; First Boston Corporation; Fukui Broadcasting Company (Japan)

FBCM Federation of British Carpet Manufacturers; Federation of British Cutlery Manufacturers

FBCP Fellow of the British College of Physiotherapists

FBCS Fellow of the British Computer Society; Foreground-Background Operating System

fbcw fallen building clause waiver

fbd freeboard

FB & D Ford, Bacon and Davis

FBEA Fellow of the British Esperanto Association

FBF Federal Buildings Fund; Frankfurt Book Fair

fbfm frequency feedback frequency modulation

FBFM Federation of British Film Makers

FBG Federation of British Growers

fbh fire-brigade hydrant

FBIII Fellow of the British Horological Institute

fbhp flowing bottom hole pressure (oil well)

FBHTM Federation of British Hand Tool Manufacturers

FBI Federal Bureau of Investigation; Federation of British Industries; Food Business Institute

FBIA Fellow of the Bankers' Institute of Australasia

FBIM Fellow of the British Institute of Management

FBIRA Federal Bureau of Investigation Recreation Association

FBIRE Fellow of the British Institution of Radio Engineers

FBIs Forgotten Boys of Iceland (American armed forces personnel stationed in Iceland)

FBIS Fellow of the British Interplanetary Society; Foreign Broadcast Information Service (CIA)

fbk flat back (lumber); fast buck

FBKS Fellow of the British Kinematograph Society

fbl forged billet; form block line

FBL Federal Barge Lines; Furness Bermuda Line

FBLA Future Business Leaders of America

fbm feet board measure; fleet ballistic missile; forward branch mail

FBM Fleet Ballistic Missile

FBMP Fleet Ballistic Missile Project (Polaris-Poseidon)

FBMWS Fleet Ballistic Missile Weapon System

FBN Federal Bureau of Narcotics

fbnrv fixed bent-nose reentry vehicle

fbo fixed-base operation; foreign building office

FBOA Fellow of the British Optical Association

fboe frequency band of emission

FBOU Fellow of the British Ornithologists' Union

fbp final boiling point

FBP Federal Bureau of Prisons; Federation of Podiatry Boards

FBPI Franklin Book Programs, Incorporated

FBPS Fellow of the British Psychological Society; Forest and Bird Protection Society

fbr fast burst reactor; fiber

fbr (FBR) fast breeder reactor; fast burst reactor

FBR Full Bibliographic Record(ing)

FBRAM Federation of British Rubber and Allied Manufacturers

fbrk firebrick

fbrl final bomb release line

fbro *febrero* (Spanish—February)

FBRS Farm Business Recording Scheme

fbs fasting blood sugar; fighter-bomber strike

fbs (FBS) frontal bovine serum

fb's fullbacks

FBS Fellow of the Botanic(al) Society; Fighter Bomber Squadron; Forward-Base System(s); Franco-Belgian Services; Fukuoka Broadcasting System

FBSC Fellow of the British Society of Commerce

FBSE Fellow of the Botanical Society—Edinburgh

FBSM Fellow of the Birmingham School of Music

FBTT Federal Board of Tea Tasters

f/bu flowing/buildup (oil well)

FBu Burundi Franc(s)

FBU Oslo, Norway (Fornebu Airport)

FBUI Federation of British Umbrella Industries

fbw full bandwidth

FBW Fighter-Bomber Wing

FBW System Fly-by-Wire System

fby future budget year

fbyracc for buyer's account

fc facilities control; file cabinet; filter center; fire clay; fire-control; first cross(ing); follow copy; foot-candle; franc; front-connected; functional code; fund code

fc (FC) field champion; fixed cost

f/c for cash; fill and check; fixed contract; flight control; foolscap; free and clear

f & c fire and casualty (insurance); full and change (tides)

fc *ferrocarril* (Spanish—railroad, railway)

Fc fractocumulus

FC Fairbury College; Federal Cabinet; Federal Conference; Federal Convention; Fencing Club; Fenn College; Fighter Command; Finch College; Findlay College; fire control; Fisheries Convention; Fitzwilliam College; Fontbonne College; Foothill College; Franconia College; Frederic Chopin; Frederick College; Free Church (Scotland)

F-C Franche-Comté

FC *Ferrocarril(es)* [Spanish railroad(s)]

fca frequency control and analysis; functional configuration audit

FCA Facility Change Authorization; Farm Credit Administration; Federated Confectioners Association; Federation of Canadian Artists; Federation of College Academics; Fellow (of the Institute) of Chartered Accountants; Fiji College of Agriculture; Finance Corporation of Australia; Financial Corporation of America; Fishermen's Cooperative Association; Foster Care Association; Freight Claim Agent; Freight Claim Association

FCAA Federal Clean Air Act; Florence Crittenton Association of America

FCAAA Federal Council of Australian Apiarists Association

FCAATSI Federal Council for the Advancement of Aborigines and Torres Strait Islanders

FCACS Federal Civil Agencies Communications System

FCAI Federal Chamber of Automotive Industries

f cant. forward cant frames

fcap foolscap

f/cap foolscap

FCAP Fellow of the College of American Pathologists

F-car(s) French car(s)

FCAS Federal Council of Agricultural Societies; Fellow of the Casualty Actuarial Society

FCASA Foreign Correspondent's Association of South Africa

FCASI Fellow of the Canadian Aeronautics and Space Institute

fcb free-cutting brass

FCB Facility Clearance Board; Flight Certification Board; Foundation for Commercial Banks; Freight Container Bureau

FCBA Federal Communications Bar Association

fcbu foreign currency banking unit

fcc face-centered cubic; facilities control console; fire-control computer; fire-control console; flat conductor cable; flight-control console; fluid catalytic cracking; fluid convection cathode; freight control computer

fcc (FCC) first-class certificate

FCC Fairbanks Correctional Center (Alaska); Farm Credit Corporation (Canada); Federal Communications Commission; Federal Council of Churches; Federal Court of Canada; First-Class Certificate; Flight Coordination Center; Florida Citrus Commission; Foreign Correspondents Club

FC of C Foundation Company of Canada

FCC *Food Chemicals Codex*

FCCA Federal Court Clerks Association; Four Cylinder Club of America

fccc fire-control control console

FCCCA Federal Council of Churches of Christ in America

FCCD Florida Council on Crime and Delinquency

fcci fuel-cladding chemical interaction

fcck fire-control check

FCCO Fellow of the Canadian College of Organists

fccp (FCCP) carbonylcyanide p-trifluoromethoxyphenylhydrazone

FCCP Fellow of the College of Chest Physicians

FCCS Federal Cost-Control

Survey; Fellow of the Corporation of Certified Secretaries

FCCSS Fire-Control Control Subsystem

fccu fluid catalytic cracking unit

fcd failure-correction coding; function circuit diagram

FCDA Federal Civil Defense Administration

F & CD—IR Failure and Consumption Data—Inspector's Report

FCDNA Field-Command Defense Nuclear Agency (DoD)

FCDR Failure Cause Data Report

FCDU Foreign Currency Deposit Unit

fce food conversion efficiency

FCE Florida Citrus Exchange; Foreign Currency Exchange; French-Canadian Enterprises

FCE Fondo de Cultura Económica (Spanish—Foundation of Economic Culture)

FCECA Fishery Committee for the Eastern Central Atlantic

fcepc fire-control electrical package container; flight-control electrical package container

FCEX Fruit Growers Express

fcf front-end communications facility; functional check flight

fcg facing

FCG Foreign Clearance Guide

fcga facility gage

FCGB Forestry Committee of Great Britain

FCGI Fellow of the City and Guilds of London Institute

FCGP Fellow of the College of General Practitioners

fcgpc flight-control gyro-package container

fcgr fatigue crack growth rate

FCGS Freight Classification Guide System

FChS Fellow of the Society of Chiropodists

fci fuel-coolant interaction

FCI Federal Correctional Institution; *Federazione Calcistica Italiana* (Italian Football Association); *Federazione Ciclista Italiana* (Italian Cycling Association); *Federazione Colombotila Italiana* (Italian Carrier-pigeon Fanciers' Association); Fellow of the Clothing Institute; Fluid Controls Institute; Franklin College of Indiana

FCI Federación Cynological Internacional (Spanish—International Cynological Federation)

FCIA Fellow of the Canadian Institute of Actuaries; Fellow of the Corporation of Insurance Agents; Foreign Credit Insurance Association; Friends of Cast-Iron Architecture

FCIB Fellow of the Corporation of Insurance Brokers

FCIC Fairchild Camera and Instrument Corporation; Farm Crop Insurance Corporation; Fellow of the Chemical Institute of Canada

FCIF Flight Crew Information File

FCII Fellow of the Chartered Insurance Institute

fcim farm, construction, and industrial machinery

FCIP Federal Crime Insurance Program; Fire Company Inspection Program

FCIPA Fellow of the Chartered Institute of Patent Agents

FCIs Federal Correctional Institutions

FCIS Fellow of the Chartered Institute of Secretaries; Florida Council of Independent Schools; Foreign Counterintelligence System (FBI)

FCIT Fellow of the Chartered Institute of Transport

FCIV Fellow of the Commonwealth Institute of Valuers

FCJ Foreign Criminal Jurisdiction

FCJC Flit Community Junior College

FCJS Federal Criminal Justice System

fcl freon coolant loop; front connecting loop; full container load

FCL Foundation for Christian Living

F-class NATO designation for a Soviet class of attack submarines also known as Foxtrot

f clef bass clef

f-c los fire-control line of sight

FCLS Family Colonization Loan Society

fclty facility

fcly face lying

fcm fat-corrected milk

FCM Ferrocarril Mexicano (Mexican Railway); Firestone Conservatory of Music (Akron)

FCMA Finch College Museum of Art; Fishery Conservation and Management Act

FCMI Federation of Coated Macadam Industries

FCMIE Fellow of the Colleges of Management and Industrial Engineering

FCMS Fellow of the College of Medicine and Surgery

FCMSBR Federal Coal Mine Safety Board of Review

FCN Federal Catalog Number; Friendship, Commerce, and Navigation

FCNA Fellow of the College of Nursing—Australia

FCNM Ferrocarriles Nacionales de México (Spanish—National Railroads of Mexico)

fco cleanout flush with finished floor; fair copy; franking privilege; free postage

fco franco (Italian—free)

Fco Francisco (Spanish—Francis)

FCO Facility Change Order; Fire Control Officer; Fleet Construction Officer; Fleet Constructor Officer; Rome, Italy (Leonardo da Vinci airport, formerly Fiumicino—hence FCO)

F & CO Foreign and Commonwealth Office

fcos francos (Spanish—francs)

fcp final common pathway; foolscap

FCP Family Circle Publications; Fellow of the College of Preceptors; Ferrocarril de Chihuahua al Pacifico (Chihuahua Pacific Railroad)

FCPA Fellow of the Canadian Psychological Association; Foreign Corrupt Practices Act (designed to prevent American businessmen from bribing foreign officials)

FC Path Fellow of the College of Pathology

FCPC Federal Committee on Pest Control

fc pl face plate

FCPO Fleet Chief Petty Officer

FCPS Fellow of the College of Physicians and Surgeons

fcr forward contactor; full cold rolled (steel sheeting)

FCR Facility Capability Report; Facility Change Request; Field Contact Report; Fire Control Room; First City Regiment; Flight Configuration Release; Flinders Chase Reserve (South Australia); Forwarders Certificate of Release

FCR Free China Review

FCRA Fellow of the College of

Radiologists of Australia; Fellow of the Corporation of Registered Accountants

FCRLS Flight-Control Ready Light System

fcs forged carbon steel; francs

fc & s free of capture and seizure (insurance)

FCS Facsimile Control System; Farmer Cooperative Service; Fellow of the Chemical Society; Financial Control System; Fire Control School; Fire Control Station; Fire Control System

F/CS Flight-Control System

fcsad free of capture, seizure, arrest or detainment (shipping insurance)

fcsb fire-control switchboard

FCSBC Ferrocarril Sonora-Baja California (Sonora-Baja California Railroad)

FCSC Foreign Claims Settlement Commission

FCSCUS Federal Claims Settlement Commission of the United States

fcsle forecastle

fcsm fire-control system module

fc sm functional simulation

fcsrcc free of capture, seizure, riots and civil commotion (shipping insurance)

fc & s and r & cc free of capture, seizure, riots, and civil commotion

fcst forecast

FCST Federal Council for Science and Technology (Executive Office of the President)

fcsu fire-control simulator unit

fcswbd fire-control switchboard

fct factory; filament center tap; fraction thereof; function

FCT Federal Capital Territory; Federal Commission(er) of Taxation

FCTB Fellow of the College of Teachers of the Blind

FCTC Fleet Combat Training Center (USN)

fcte fire-control test equipment

fctry factory

fcts fire-control test set; firing-circuit test set; flight-control test stand

FCTU Fiji Council of Trades Unions

fcty factory

fcu fare calculation unit; fare construction unit; fire-control unit; fuel-control unit

FCU Federal Credit Union(s);

Federated Clerks Union

FCUS Federal Credit Union System

FCUSAA Federated Council of University Staff Associations of Australia

fcv fill-and-check valve

FCW Fire-Control Workshop

FCWA Fellow of the Chartered Institute of Cost and Works Accountants

fcy fancy

fcy pks fancy packs

FCZ Ferrocarril de Coahuila y Zacatecas (Coahuila and Zacatecas Railroad); Fishery Conservation Zone; Forward Combat Zone

fd face of drawing; faculty development; fan douche; fatal dose; field; field dependence; field discharge; finite difference; fiord; flame detector; flight deck; floor drain; focal dispatch; focal distance; forced draft; framed; free delivery; free discharge; free dispatch; freeze-dried; front of dash; full duplex; functional description; fund

fd (Fd) ferredoxin

f/d father and daughter; free dock

f & d faced and drilled; fill and drain; findings and determination; fire and flushing; freight and demurrage

Fd Ferdinand; Fiord (Fjord)

F$ Fiji dollar

FD field drum; Finance Department; Fire Department; Fleet Duties; Flight Director; Flying Dutchman (yacht); Foundation for the Disabled; Free Democrat

F.D. *Fidei Defensor* (Latin—Defender of the Faith)

fd₅₀ median fatal dose

fda flight-direction attitude; fronto-dextra anterior; fully drawn account; functional demonstration and acceptance

FDA Fisheries Development Authority; Food and Drug Administration

FDAA Federal Disaster Assistance Administration

FDATC Flying Division, Air Training Command

fdau flight-data acquisition unit

FDAWU Food, Drinks, and Allied Workers Union

fdb field dynamic braking; forced-draft blower

FDB Fiji Development Bank

fdc fire-direction center (FDC); first-day cover (postage stamp); flight-director computer; formation density content (oil well log)

fdc *fleur de coin* (French—mint condition)

FDC Facility Design Criteria; Fire-Detection Center; Flight Data Center; Forsyth Dental Center (Harvard); Friends of Democratic Cuba

FD & C Food, Drug, and Cosmetic (Act)

FDCC Fort Dodge Community College

F D & C-color Food, Drug, and Cosmetic (Act) color

FDCD Facility Design Criteria Document

FDCs Federal Detention Centers (Florence, Arizona and El Paso, Texas)

FDCT Franck Drawing Completion Test

fdd *franc de droits* (French—free of charge)

FDD Fondation Documentaire Dentaire (Dental Documentation Foundation)

fddc (FDDC) ferric dimethyl dithiocarbonate

fddl frequency division data link

fddlp. frequency division data link printout

fde field decelerator

FDEA Federal Drug Enforcement Administration

f/deck flat deck (truck)

F del P Ferrocarril del Pacífico (formerly Southern Pacific of Mexico); Ferrocarril del Pacífico (Pacific Railroad)

F del S Ferrocarril del Sureste (Southeast Railway—Tabasco, Campeche, Veracruz, Yucatan)

F de P *Ferrocarril de Panamá* (Spanish—Panama Railroad)

F de PS General Francisco de Paula Santander—South American liberator assisting Bolívar

F de S Ferrovie dello Stato (Italian State Railways)

F de T *Fulano de Tal* (Spanish—So-and-So)

Fdez Fernández

FDF Footwear Distributors' Federation

FDFU Federation of Documentary Film Units

fdg funding

FDH Federal Detention Headquarters

FDHO Factory Department—Home Office

fdi fat depth indicator; field discharge

FDI Farm Dairy Instructor; Federal Department of Information (Malaysia); Federation Dentaire Internationale (International Dental Federation); Fir Door Institute

FDIC Federal Deposit Insurance Corporation; Fire Department Instructor's Conference

FDIF *Fédération Démocratique Internationale des Femmes* (French—International Democratic Federation of Women)

FDIM *Federación Democrática Internacional de Mujeres* (Spanish—International Democratic Federation of Women)

FDIT Federal Daily Income Trust

FDJ *Freie Deutsche Jugend* (Free German Youth)—communist youth organization in East Germany

FDL Fast Deployment Logistic(s)—naval logistic(s)—naval cargo carrier(s); fleet deployment logistic ship (naval symbol); Flight Dynamics Laboratory; Foremost Defended Localities

F & DL Food and Drug Laboratory

fd ldg forced landing

FDLE Florida Department of Law Enforcement

FDLI Food and Drug Law Institute

FDLS Fast Deployment Logistics Ship

fdm frequency division multiplexing

FDM *Forenede Dansk Motorejere* (Federation of Danish Motorists)

FDMA Fibre Drum Manufacturers Association

FDMBB Ferruccio Dante Michelangelo Benvenuto Busoni (Ferruccio Busoni—for short)

FDMHA Frederick Douglass Memorial and Historical Association

FDMS Flight Data Management System (USAF)

fdn foundation

FDN Field Designator Number

fdnb (FDNB) fluorodinitrobenzene

Fdo Ferdinando

FDO Fighter Duty Officer; Fleet Dental Officer

F do I *Foz do Iguaçu* (Portuguese—Mouth of the Iguazu)—three miles above the gigantic Iguazu Waterfalls shared by Argentina, Brazil, and Paraguay at their juncture

fdor four door (vehicle)

FDOS Floppy Disc Operating System

fdp field-developed program; foreign duty pay; forward defense post; funded delivery period

fdp (FDP) fructose 1,6-diphosphate

f/dp field despatch

FDP foreign duty pay; fronto-dextra posterior

FDP *Freie Demokratische Partei* (German—Free Democratic Party)

FDPA Fogg Dam Protected Area (Australian Northern Territory)

FDPC Federal Data Processing Center(s)

Fd PO Field Post Office

fdr feeder; field data recorder; functional demonstration requirement

fdr (FDR) flight data recorder

f dr fire door

Fdr Founder

FDR Franklin Delano Roosevelt—thirty-second President of the United States

FDRHS Franklin Delano Roosevelt High School

FDRL Franklin D Roosevelt Library (Hyde Park, New York)

FDRMC Franklin Delano Roosevelt Memorial Commission

FDRS Fire Department Rescue Squad; Flight Data Recording System; Flight Display Research System

fdry foundry

fds fixed disc store

FDS Fellow in Dental Surgery; fighter-director ship

FDSRCPS Glas Fellow in Dental Surgery of the Royal College of Physicians and Surgeons of Glasgow

FDSRCS Fellow in Dental Surgery of the Royal College of Surgeons

FDSRCS Edin Fellow in Dental Surgery of the Royal College of Surgeons of Edinburgh

FDSRCS Eng Fellow in Dental Surgery of the Royal College of Surgeons of England

fdt first destination transporta-

tion; fronto-dextra transverse

FDT Failure Diagnostic Team

fdte force development testing and experimentation

FDTL'O François Dominique Toussaint L'Ouverture (Haitian patriot who freed his country from Napoleon's control)

fdtn foundation

FDU Fairleigh Dickinson University

f/d vlv fill-and-drain valve

fdw feed water

fdx (FDX) full duplex (data processing)

FD-Zug *Fernschnellzug* (German—long-distance express train)

fe feather-edged (lumber); female employee; fighter escort; finite element; fire extinguisher; first edition; fish-eye (buttons), flanged ends, for example; format effector; front end; further education

fe (FE) format effective character (data processing)

f/e fortnight ending

f & e facilities and equipment

Fe *ferrum* (Latin—iron)

FE Far East; Fighter Escort; Flight Engineer; Foreign Editor

F & E Fearnley & Eger [Fernville (steamship) Lines]

F of E Friends of the Earth

FE *Fonetic English* (for spelling words as they sound)

Fe₂O₃ • H₂O rust

$Fe_2O_3 \cdot H_2O$ rust

fe3dgw finite-element three-dimensional ground water (model)

Fe⁵²/³ radioactive iron

$Fe^{52/3}$ radioactive iron

fea front end analysis

FEA Failure Modes and Effects Analysis; Federal Energy Administration; Federation of Employment Agencies; Fiji Electricity Authority; French Equatorial Africa

FEAA Federal Employees Appeal Authority

FEAD *Fondo Especial de Asistencia para el Desarrollo* (Spanish—Special Assistance Fund for Development)

FEAF Far East Air Force

Fe-Ag iron-silver blend

FEA(I) Federal Employees Association (Independent)

FE al P Ferrocarril Eléctrico al Pacífico (Costa Rican electric railway)

FEAMIS Foreign Exchange Accounting and Management In-

formation System
FEANI Fédération Européenne d'Associations Nationales d'Ingénieurs (Federation of European National Associations of Engineers)
Fearkar Farquhar
feat. frequency of every allowable term
feath feather(ed)(ing)
Feathers Featherstone
Featherstone Featherstone Prison near Wolverhampton northwest of Birmingham, England
FEAU Florida Education Association United
feb functional electronic block
feb febrero (Spanish—February)
feb. febris (Latin—fever)
Feb February
FEB Field Engineering Bulletin; Financial and Economic Board; Flying Evaluation Board
feba (FEBA) forward edge of battle area
Febarch February and March
febb febbraio (Italian—February)
FEBC Far Eastern Broadcasting Company
feb.dur. febre durante (Latin—as long as fever lasts)
FEBF Far East Bridge Federation
febº febrero (Spanish—February)
febr (Latin prefix—fever)—febrile
FEBs Federal Executive Boards
FEBS Federation of European Biochemical Societies
FEBTC Far East Bank and Trust Company
fec feckless; forward error correction; forward exchange control
fec foi, espérance, charité (French—faith, hope, charity)
fec. fecit (Latin—he made)
FEC Facilities Engineering Command; Faculty Exchange Center; Far East Command; Federal Election Commission; Federal Election Council; Federal Electoral Council; Federal Electric Corporation; First Edition Club; Florida East Coast (railway); Free Europe Committee
FECA Facilities Engineering and Construction Agency; Fiji Employers Consultative Association
FECB Foreign Exchange Con-

trol Board
FECIT Federación Española de Centros de Iniciativas y Turismo (Spanish Federation of Centers of Initiative and Tourism)
feck (Scottish abbreviation—effect, efficacy, value)
FECL Fleet Electronics Calibration Laboratory
fecm ferret electronic countermeasures
FECM Fellowship of the Elder Conservatorium of Music
feco fringes of equal chromatic order
FECONS Field Engineer Control System
fe cr ferrichrome (recording tape)
FECU Far Eastern Container Unit
FECUA Farmers Educational and Cooperative Union of America
fed. federal; federal law-enforcement officer; federal narcotics agent; federated; federation
Fed Federal; Federalist (Party); Federation; The Fed—The Federal Reserve Board
Fed Federación (Spanish—Federation)
FED Facilities Engineering Department; Field Experience Data; Fuel Element Design
FEDC Federation of Engineering Design Consultants
FEDECAM Federación de Cameras de Comercio (Spanish—Federation of Chambers of Commerce)
FEDECAMARAS Federación (Venezolana de Cameras y Asociaciones de Comercio y Producción) (Spanish—Venezuelan Federation of Chambers of Commerce and Manufacturers)
FEDECAME Federación Cafetalera de America (Spanish—Coffee-Growers' Federation of America)
Federal Capital Territory now called Australian Capital Territory (around and in Canberra)
Federal City Washington, D.C.
federalese the jargon of bureaucrats on the federal payroll (*see* Watergab)
Federal Hill Providence, Rhode Island's slum section
Federal Republic of Germany Bundesrepublik Deutschland
Federation of Malaysia Malay-

sia (formerly Brunei, Federation of Malaya, Sabah, Sarawak, and Singapore)
Federation of South Arabia Ittihad al Janub al 'Arabi—formerly Aden Colony and Aden Protectorate
FEDFU Federated Engine Drivers and Firemens Union
fedja (Arabic—pass)
FEDLINK Federal Library and Information Network
Fed Mal Federation of Malaya; Federation of Malay States; Malaysia
Fed Mal Sta Federated Malay States
fedn federation
fed narc federal narcotics agent
Fed Ref Federal Reformatory
Fed Reg Federal Register
Fed Rep Federal Reporter
Feds federal excise tax collectors; federal law-enforcement officers
Feds Federales (Spanish—federal police, federal troops)
FEDS Fixed Exchangeable Disc Store; Foreign Economic Development Service
FEDSIM Federal Computer Performance Evaluation and Simulation Center (GSA)
Fed-Spec Federal Specification(s)
Fed-Std Federal Standard
Fedya Fyodor
FEE Foundation for Economic Education; Foundation for Environmental Education
feeb feeble; feebleminded
FEEB Fleet Electronic Effectiveness Branch (USN)
Feebie (American slang—member of the Federal Bureau of Investigation)
Feeney Leonard Feeney
FEER Far Eastern Economic Review
fef fast-extrusion furnace
FEF Foundry Educational Foundation
FEFC Far Eastern Freight Conference
FE & FO Francis E and Freeland O Stanley of Stanley Steamer fame
FEGA Film Editors Guild of Australia
FEGLI Federal Employees Group Life Insurance
FEHB Federal Employees Health Benefit
FEHD Far Eastern Hotel Development
fei for engineering information;

for engineer's information; fluidic explosive initiator

FEI Farm Equipment Institute; Financial Executives Institute; Flight Engineers International; Free Enterprise Institute

FEIA Flight Engineers International Association

FEICRO Federation of European Industrial Cooperative Research Organizations

FEIS Fellow of the Educational Institution of Scotland; Final Environmental Impact Statement; Florida Educators Information Service

fekg fetal electrocardiogram

feks for eksempel (Dano-Norwegian—for example)

f eks for eksempel (Dano-Norwegian—for example)

fel fellow; front-end loader; front-end loading

Fel Felicita; Felix

FEL Financial Enterprises Limited; Food Engineering Laboratory (USA)

FELABAN Federación Latinoamericana del Caribe de Asociaciones de Exportadores (Spanish—Latin American Federation of Caribbean Exporters Associations)

FELCRA Federal Land Consolidation and Rehabilitation Authority (Malaysian)

FELDA Federal Land Development Authority

feldspar barium, calcium, potassium, or sodium silicates (mineral mixtures such as orthoclase)

felinol felinologic(al)(ly); felinologist; felinology

Felix Felixstowe

Felixstowe (Old English—St Felix's Holy Place)

Fell Fellow

FELL Finland, Estonia, Latvia, and Lithuania (the first country—Finland—fell under Soviet domination whereas the others named were absorbed into the Soviet Union during World War II)

fella fellaheen (Arabic—tillers) —peasant farmers of Egypt, Syria, and nearby lands

FELO Far Eastern Liaison Office

f/e loader front-end loader; front-end loading

Fels (German—rock)

Felsina (Latin—Bologna)

Felsto Felixstowe

felv feline complex leukemia virus(es)

fem female; feminine; femur; femoral; field-effect mode; fuel efficiency monitor

fem femininum (Dano-Norwegian—feminine)

fem. feminea (Latin—female); *femoris* (Latin—femur, thigh)

f.e.m. (fem or FEM) fuerza electromotriz (Spanish—electromotive force)

FEMA Farm Equipment Manufacturers Association; Federal Emergency Management Administration; Fire Equipment Manufacturers Association; Foundry Equipment Manufacturers Association

Female Seminary Mount Holyoke College

femboy(s) feminine boy(s)

fem. ext. femur externum (Latin —external thigh)

FEMIC Fire Equipment Manufacturers Institute of Canada

Feminist Reformer Lucy Stone

Feminist Revolutionist Mary Wollstonecraft also known as Mary Godwin

fem.int. femur internum (Latin —inner thigh)

femlib feminine liberation (women's liberation); feminine liberationist

femm femminile (Italian—feminine)

femo femoral

FEMSA Fire Equipment Manufacturers and Suppliers Association

FEMSACO Fabrica Electromecanica SA (Spanish—Electromechanical Factory)

fem-sem feminine seminary (woman's college)

femto 10^{-15}

FEMUSI Federación Mundial de Sindicatos de Industrias (Spanish—World Federation of Industrial Unions)

Fen Fenner; Fenwick; Fenwood

fenc fencing

fender bender fender-bending automotive vehicle accident

F/Eng Flight Engineer

Fenno-Scandinavia Finland, Greenland, Iceland, Norway, Sweden, Denmark

FENSA Film Entertainment National Service Association

FENSA Fabrica Nacional de Electrodomesticos SA (Spanish —National Factory for Domestic Electric Appliances Incorporated)

Fen-Scan Fenno-Scandia; Fen-

no-Scandinavian

Fen St Fenchurch Street (rail terminal)

FEO Federal Energy Office; Federal Executive Office; Federation of Economic Organizations; Fleet Engineer(ing) Office(r)

FeO_2 ferric oxide (recording tape coating)

feov force end of volume

fep fore edges painted; front-end processing

FEP Federal Employees Program; Financial Evaluation Program

FEP Federación de Estudiantes del Peru (Spanish—Peruvian Students Federation)

FEPC Fair Employment Practices Commission; Federation of Electric Power Companies

FEPE Fédération Européenne pour la Protection des Eaux (European Federation for the Protection of Waters)

FEpow Far East prisoner of war

fer forward engine room

fer ferre (Latin—to bear)—fertile, fertilization, fertilize

fer. ferrum (Latin—iron)

Fer Ferdinand; Fermanagh; Ferris

FERA Federal Emergency Relief Administration; Foreign Exchange Regulation Act

Fer. Aet. Ferrea Aetas (Latin— Iron Age)—last of the four ages of the human race the Plutonian period marked by avarice, crime, and cunning in the absence of honor, justice, or truth

FERC Federal Energy Regulatory Commission; Franco-Ethiopian Railway Company

fer con ferrule-contact

Ferd Ferdinand

Ferdie Ferdinand

FERF Financial Executives Research Foundation

Ferg Fergus(on)

Fergie Fergus

FERIC Florida Educational Resources Information Center

Ferihegy Budapest, Hungary's airport

FERIT Far East Regional Investigation Team

Ferm Fermanagh

fermentol fermentology

Fernán Caballero Cecilia Francisca Josefa de Arrom

Fernandel Fernand Contandin

Fernando de Magallanes (*Span-*

ish—Ferdinand Magellan)—originally Fernão de Magalhães

Fern^{do} Fernando (Spanish—Ferdinand)

Fernspr *Fernsprecher* (German —telephone)

ferp family educational rights and privacy

FERPC Far Eastern Research and Publications Center

ferr ferrovia (Italian—railroad)

Ferraria (Latin—Ferrara)

Ferret Daimler armored scout car made in Great Britain

Ferryville old name for Menzei-Bourguiba in Tunisia

fert fertility; fertilization; fertilizer

fertd fertilized

Fertile Arabia Arabia Felix in the southern sector of the Arabian Peninsula and particularly in the Yemenite lands once called Aden or the Hadhramaut

Fertile Crescent Australia's well-watered coastal plain extending from southern New South Wales to southern Queensland

FERTIPERU *Fertilizantes del Peru* (Spanish—Fertilizers of Peru)

fertz fertilizer

ferv. fervens (Latin—boiling)

Ferv Fervidor (French—Glowing Month)—synonym sometimes used for *Messidor* (see *Mess*)

fes festival(s); fundamental electrical standards

Fes (German—F-flat)

FES Farm Employment Scheme; Fellow of the Entomological Society; Fellow of the Ethnological Society; Final Environmental Statement; Fisheries Experiment Station; Florida Engineering Society

FESA Fonetic English Spelling Association

FESCO Far Eastern Shipping Company

FESE Far East Stock Exchange (Hong Kong)

FESIP Fifth Estate Security Information Project

FESO Federal Employment Stabilization Office

FESPAC Far East and South Pacific

'fess confession

FESS Flywheel-Energy Storage System

'fession confession

'fessor professor

fest festival; festive; festivities; festivity

fest. festivus (Latin—festive or gay)

FEST Federation of Engineering and Shipbuilding Trades (British)

fesv feline sarcoma virus

fet field-effect transistor

FET Federal Estate Tax; Federal Excise Tax

FET Falange Española Tradicionalista (Spanish Traditional Falange)—fascist organization

FETF Flight Engine Test Facility (National Reactor Test Station, Idaho)

fetol fetological; fetologist; fetology

fets field-effect transistors

FETS Far East Trade Service

FETU Federation of Entertainment Trade Unions

feu forty-foot equivalent container unit

FEU Federated Engineering Union

FEU Federación de Estudiantes Universitarios (Spanish—Federation of University Students)

feud. feudal; feudalism; feudalistic

fev fever(ish); forced expiratory volume

fev fevereiro (Portuguese—February); *février* (French—February)

fev 1 forced expiatory volume in 1 second

FEVA Federal Employees Veterans Association

Fevr Fevral' (Russian—February)

FEW Federally-Employed Women

fex fleet exercise

fext far-end crosstalk

fey forever yours

ff far field; fat-free; file finish; fixed focus; flip-flop; folded flat; following folios; form factor; form feed; fortissimo; french fried; front focal (length); front focus; fuel flow; full fashioned; full field

ff (FF) form feed character (data processing); folios

f/f face to face; fat and forward (sheep); flip-flop; full force

f & f fat and forward (stock); fire and flushing; fire-and-forget missile; fittings and fixtures; furniture and fixtures

f to f face to face; foe to foe; friend to friend

ff følgende (Dano-Norwegian—following or next); *folgende Seiten* (German—following pages); *fortissimo* (Italian—very loud)

Ff French franc(s)

Ff Fortsetzung folgt (German—to be continued)

FF Federated Farmers; Field Force(s); Field Foundation; fleet flagship (naval symbol); Ford Foundation; Foreign Friend (tourist to the People's Republic of China); Formula Ford; Freight Forwarder; Frontier Force(s)

F & F Faber & Faber

F of F field of fire; Firth of Forth

FF Faith and Freedom; Fianna Fail (Irish—Republican Party); *fratres* (Latin—brothers); *frères* (French—brothers)

ffa foreign freight agent; free for all; free of fatty acid; free foreign agency; free from alongside; for further assignment

FfA Fund for Animals

FFA Fellow of the Faculty of Actuaries; Fire Fighters Association; Foreign Freight Agent; Forum Fisheries Agency; Foundation for Foreign Affairs; Future Farmers of America; Future Fuels of America (hydrogen, methanol, etc.)

FFAC Freshwater Fisheries Advisory Council

ffar folding-fin aircraft rocket; forward-fighting aircraft rocket

FFARACS Fellow of the Faculty of Anaesthetists of the Royal Australasian College of Surgeons

FFARCS Fellow of the Faculty of Anaesthetists of the Royal College of Surgeons

FFAS Fellow of the Faculty of Architects and Surveyors

ffb fat-free body

FFB Federal Financing Bank; Fellow of the Faculty of Building

ff black fine furnace black

ffbp free-fall bomb pod

ffc first flight cover; free from chlorine

ffC foreign friend of China

FFC Farmers Federation Co-operative; Federal Facilities Corporation; Federal Fire Council

FFCB Federal Farm Credit

Board

ff cc ferrocarriles (Spanish—railroads)

FFCC Nales Ferrocarriles Nacionales (Colombian National Railways)

FFCDPA Federal Field Committee for Development Planning in Alaska

FFCM Fellow of the Faculty of Community Medicine

FFCSA Florida Fresh Citrus Shippers Association

ffd focus film distance; forward floating depot; fuel failure detection; functional flow diagram

ffda fiber fineness distribution analyzer

FFDA Flying Funeral Directors of America

FFDRCS Fellow of the Faculty of Dental Surgery of the Royal College of Surgeons

FFE Fight for Free Enterprise; Fire Fighting Equipment (company)

ffex field firing exercise

fff fat, forty, and female

f,ff following folios (following pages)

fff forte fortissimo (Italian—very, very loud)

FFF Fellowship of First Fleeters; Frozen Food Foundation

ffff forte forte fortissimo (Italian—very, very, very loud)

ffft (not an abbreviation but the symbol for the sound of a pump spray)—see *ssst*

ffg friendly foreign government

FFG-7 guided-missile frigate

ffgt firefighter; firefighting

ffh formerly-fat housewife; formerly-fat husband

FFHC Freedom from Hunger Campaign

FFHMA Full-Fashioned Hosiery Manufacturers of America

FFHom Fellow of the Faculty of Homeopathy

ffi free from infection

FFI Fiji Forest Industry; Finance for Industry (Bank of England); Flanders Filters Incorporated; Freight Forwarders Institute; Frozen Food Institute; Frozen Foods Industries

FFI Forces Françaises de l'Intérieur (French Forces of the Interior)—underground soldiers fighting against the Germans in occupied France during World War II

ffim far-field image maximizer

ff ind fact-finding index

ffl field failure; fixed and flashing

F Fl fixed and flashing (light)

FFL Feminists for Life; Forces Françaises Libres (Free French Forces)

FFLA Federal Farm Loan Association

FFLI Frozen Food Locker Institute

ffly faithfully

FFM Fulton Fish Market (Governor Alfred Emanuel Smith claimed it was his only alma mater)

FFMC Federal Farm Mortgage Corporation

FFML Franklin Ferguson Memorial Library

ffn free-floating nozzle

FFN nuclear-powered frigate (naval symbol)

FFNM Fort Frederica National Monument (Georgia)

ffo furnace fuel oil

ffp ferromagnetic fine particles; firm fixed price; fuel fabrication plant

f & fp fraud and false pretenses

FFP Forest Fires Prevention; Free Flight Plan

F & FP Force and Financial Program

ffpa free from prussic acid

FFPB Flora and Fauna Protection Board

FFPS Fellow of the Faculty of Physicians and Surgeons

FFPSG Fellow of the Faculty of Physicians and Surgeons

ffr foreign force reduction; free-flight rocket; frequency following response

FFR Fellow of the Faculty of Radiologists; Fleay's Fauna Reserve (Queensland)

FFRF Freedom From Religion Foundation

ffrr full frequency range recording

ffr(s) fransk(e) franc(s) [Dano-Norwegian—French franc(s)]

ffs fat-free solids

FFs first families

FFS Family Financial Statement; Ferrovie Federali Svizzere (Swiss Federal Railways); Financial Forecasting System; Fruit Frost Service

ffss full-frequency stereophonic sound

FFSS Ferrovie dello Stato (Italian—State Railways)

fft fast fourier transform; for further transfer

FFT Formation Flight Trainer (USAF); Functional Field Test(er)

FFTA Foundation of the Flexographic Technical Association

FFTB Freight Forwarders Tariff Bureau

FFTC Food and Fertilizer Technology Center

FFTF Fast Flux Test Facility

ff/tot fuel-flow totalizer

fftr firefighter

FFU Feminist Free University; Fire Fighters Union

ffv foreign fishing vessel

FFV First Families of Virginia

FFVMA Fire-Fighting Vehicle Manufacturers Association

ffw fast flood watch

FFW Failure-Free Warranty

ffwd fast forward; full-speed forward

ffwm free-floating wave meter

Ffy Faithfully

FFY Fife and Forfar Yeomanry

FFZ Free Fire Zone (USA)

fg fencing; filter gate; fine grain(ed); fire glaze(d); fiscal guidance; flashgun; flat grain(ed); fog; friction glaze(d); frog(ged); fuel gas; full gilt; fully good

fg faubourg (French—suburb)

FG Federal Government; Fire Guard(s); Fitzroy Gardens

F & G Farmers and Graziers

FG Fine Gael (Irish—United Ireland Party)

fga foreign general average; free of general average

FGA Fellow of the Gemological Association; Fighter, Ground Attack; Freer Gallery of Art

FGAA Federal Government Accountants Association

FGAJ Fellow of the Guild of Agricultural Journalists

fgc facility group control; fine-grained concrete

f & gc failure and guilt complex

FGC Fish and Game Code; Friends General Conference

FGCM Field General Court Martial

fgcr (FGCR) fast gas-cooled reactor

FGCSO Florida Gulf Coast Symphony Orchestra

FGCSSWA Federation of Glass, Ceramic, and Silica Sand Workers of America

fgd flue-gas desulfurization

FGDS Fédération de la Gauche Démocrate et Socialiste (French—Federation of the

Democratic and Socialist Left)

FGEX Fruit Growers Express

fgf fully good, fair

FGG-1 First-Generation Fuel-cell System

FGGE First GARP Global Experiment

fgim figures or images

FGIS Federal Grain Inspection Service

FGJS Farm Groups Joint Secretariat

FGL Federico García Lorca

f/glass fiberglass

fgm (FGM) field guided missile

FGMC Federal Government Micrographics Council

FGMD Fairchild Guided Missile Division

fgn foreign; foreigner

FGN Family Group Number(s)

FGNRA Flaming Gorge National Recreation Area (Utah and Wyoming)

FGO Fellow of the Guild of Organists; Fleet Gunnery Officer

Fg Off Flying Officer

FGP Foster Grandparent Program

FGR Franklin Game Reserve

f & g's folded-and-gathered signatures

FGS Fellow of the Geological Society

FGSA Fellow of the Geological Society of America

FGSM Fellow of the Guildhall School of Music

fgt freight

FGT Federal Gift Tax

FGTO French Government Tourist Office

FGU Fuel Geoscience Unit

fh firehose; flathead; foghorn; forehatch; full hole (oil well)

f/h freehold(er)

f.h. fiat haustus (Latin—make a draft)

FH Fair Haven; Family History; Far Hills; Fashion Hills; Field Hospital

FH₂ dihydrofolic acid

FH₄ tetrahydrofolic acid

FH₅ Firehouse Five

FH-1100 Fairchild-Hiller observation helicopter

fha filterable hemolytic anemia

fha fecha (Spanish—date)

FHA Farmers Home Administration; Federal Highway Administration; Federal Housing Administration; Finance Houses Association; Fine Hardwoods Association;

Friends Historical Association; Future Homemakers of America

FHAA Field Hockey Association of America

FHAI Federal Housing Authority Insurance

FHAS Fellow of the Highland and Agricultural Society (Scotland)

FHASA Forces Hydroelectriques de l'Andorre (Andorra Hydroelectric Power)

fhb family hold back

FHBC Federation of Historical Bottle Clubs

FH/B USA Freedom House/Books USA

fhc firehose cabinet

FHC Freed-Hardeman College

FHCI Fellow of the Hotel and Catering Institute

fhd first-hand distribution; fixed-head disc

fhdo fechado (Spanish—dated)

F & HE Fridays and Holidays Excepted (Moslem)

fhf (FHF) fulminant hepatic failure

fhh fetal heart heard

FHI Fraser-Hickson Institute; Fuji-Hakone-Izu (national park on Honshu, Japan)

FHI Federation Halterophile Internationale (French—International Weightlifting Federation)

FHIP Family Health Insurance Plan

FHKSC Fort Hays Kansas State College

FHL Friends Historical Library (Swarthmore)

FHLB Federal Home Loan Bank

FHLBB Federal Home Loan Bank Board

FHLBs Federal Home Loan Banks

FHLBS Federal Home Loan Bank System

FHLC Forest Hill Learning Centre (Toronto)

fhld freehold

FHNWR Flint Hills National Wildlife Refuge (Kansas)

f-holes f-shaped sound holes in tops of stringed instruments such as violins, violas, cellos, double basses

fhp fractional horsepower

FHP Family Health Program

FHPRP Family Housing Program Review Panel

fhr fetal heart rate; firehose rack

FHR Federal House of Representatives (Australian)

fhs fetal heart sounds

FHS Fellow of the Heraldry Society; Forest History Society

fhsg family housing

fht fetal heart tone

FHT Fellowship Houses Trust

FHTA Federated Home Timber Association

fhtl first-class hotel

FHU Foundation for Human Understanding

fhv forhenvaerende (Dano-Norwegian—former)

FHVMA Flowers and Hughes Values for Marriage Analysis

FHWA Federal Highway Administration

fhws flat-headed wood screw

FHWU Federated Hotel Workers Union

fhy fire-hydrant

fi fade in; failed item; female impersonator; field independence; field ionization; fire insurance; fixed interval; free in; fuel injection; fuel inspection; for instance

fi (FI) foreign intelligence

fi finsk (Dano-Norwegian—Finnish)

Fi Fidel; Finland; Finnie; Finnish

FI Faeroe Islands; Falkland Islands; Field Interview; Fiji Islands; Fog Index; Fourth International; Franco-Iberian; Franklin Institute

F of I Fruit of Islam (Black Muslim storm-troop disciplinary corps)

fia financial inventory accounting; full interest admitted

FIA Factory Insurance Association; Faculty Insurance Association; Fashion Industries of Australia; Federal Insurance Administration; Federal Intelligence Agency; Federated Ironworkers Association; Fellow of the Institute of Actuaries; Flatware Importers Association; Flight Information Area

FIA Fédération Internationale de l'Automobile (French—International Automobile Federation); *Federazione Internazionale Automabilistica* (Italian—International Automobile Association); *Freedom of Information Act*

FIAB Foreign Intelligence Advisory Board

FIAB Fédération Internationale

des Associations de Bibliothécaires (French—International Federation of Librarian Associations)

FIABCI *Federation Internationale des Administrateurs de Biens Conseils Immobiliers* (French—International Federation of Real Estate Administrators)

FIAC Federation of International Amateur Cycling; Flanders Interaction Analysis Categories

FIAJY Fellowship in Israel for Arab-Jewish Youth

FIAL Fellow of the Institute of Arts and Letters

FIAM Fellow of the International Academy of Management

FIAMA Fellow of the Incorporated Advertising Managers' Association

FIAMS Fellow of the Indian Academy of Medical Sciences

Fiandre (Italian—Flanders)

FIANZ Fellow of the Institute of Actuaries of New Zealand

FIAP Fédération Internationale de l'Art Photographique (International Federation of the Photographic Art); Fellow of the Institution of Analysts & Programmers

FIAR Fabbrica Italiana Apparecchi Radio (Italian Radio Apparatus Factory)

FIArb Fellow of the Institute of Arbitrators

fias free in and stowed

FIAS Flanders Interaction Analysis System

fiaT fix it again Tony (angry Fiat owners' acronym for un satisfactory automobiles)

FIAT Fabrica Italiana Automobili, Torino (Italian Automobile Factory—Turin)

FIAV Fédération Internationale des Agences de Voyage (International Federation of Travel Agencies)

fiawol fandom is a way of life

fib. fibro cement; fibula; free into barge; free into bond; free into bunkers

FIB Fellow of the Institute of Bankers; First Interstate Bank (formerly UCB); Fishing Industry Board; Franklin Institute of Boston

FIB *Fédération des Industries Belge* (French—Federation of Belgian Industries); *Félag Islenzkra Bifreidaeigenda* (Ice-

landic Automobile Association)

FIBA *Federation Internationale de Basketball Amateur* (French)

FIBEX First International Biomass Experiment

FI Bio Fellow of the Institute of Biology

FIBM Fellow of the British Institute of Management

FIBP Fellow of the Institute of British Photographers

fibrd fiberboard

fibril fibrillation

FIBST Fellow of the Institute of British Surgical Technicians

fic fiction; freight, insurance, carriage; frequency interference control

FIC Farm Improvement Club(s); Federal Information Center(s); Federal Insurance Corporation; Fellow of the Institute of Chemistry; Flight Information Center; Forest Industries Council; Foundation for International Cooperation; Freedom of Information Committee

FIC *Federación Internacional de Carreteras* (Spanish—International Highway Federation)

FICA Federal Insurance Contributions Act; Ferrocarriles Internacionales de Centro America (International Railways of Central America); Food Industries Credit Association

FICA *Foreign Intelligence Surveillance Act*

FICAP Furniture Industry Consumer Advisory Panel

FICB Federation of International Commercial Broadcasters

FICBs Federal Intermediate Credit Banks

FICCI Federation of Indian Chambers of Commerce and Industry

FICD Fellow of the International College of Dentists

FICE Fellow of the Institute of Civil Engineers

FICeram Fellow of the Institute of Ceramics

FIC/HEW Fogarty International Center—HEW

fi/ci foreign intelligence/counterintelligence

FICO Ford Instrument Company

FICOA Film Instruction Company of America

FICP Federal Information Centers Program

fic(s) *aficionado(s)* [Spanish—devotee(s)]

FICS Fellow of the International College of Surgeons; Fellow of the Institute of Chartered Shipbrokers

FICSA Federation of International Civil Servants Associations

fict fiction; fictitious

fict. *fictilis* (Latin—made of pottery)

FICWA Fellow of the Institute of Cost and Works Accountants

fid fiduciary; force identification; free induction decay

Fid *Fidji: (Spanish—Fiji)*

FID Falkland Island Dependencies; Federation of International Documentation; Fellow of the Institute of Directors; Field Intelligence Department

FIDA Federal Industrial Development Authority

fidac film input to digital automatic computer

fidal fixed-wing insecticide-dispersal apparatus, liquid (USNs defoliant spraying system)

FIDCR Federal Interagency Day Care Requirements

Fiddler NATO nickname for Soviet long-range interceptor aircraft (Tu-28) designed by Tupolev

Fiddler's Green traditional haven of drowned sailors as it is supposedly filled with friendly girls, lots of grog, and unlimited amounts of fine food and tobacco; some life-after-death believers opine it is a suburb of Davy Jones' Locker while others insist it is a synonym for Fiddler's Grotto

Fiddler's Grotto music-filled tropical marine cavern inhabited by lovely young women of all races; roast turkeys fly about slowly; fine beer, whiskey, and wine cascade down its marble walls; only seafarers with more than fifty years of maritime experience are admitted; its location, according to Captain Ed Hassel, is exactly two miles this side of Hell

Fiddlers Three Isaac Stern, Itzhak Perlman, Pinchas Zukerman

FIDE Fédération Internationale des Echecs (International Chess Federation)

Fidel Fidel Castro

FIDEL *Frente Izquierda de Li-*

beración (Spanish—Leftist Liberation Front)

FIDER Foundation for Interior Design Education Research

fidivan fiber-diameter video analyzer

fido fog investigation dispersal operation; freaks, irregulars, defects, oddities (created by minting errors); fugitive information data organizer

FIDO Facility for Integrated Data Organization; Federal Island Development Organization; Fire Incident Data Organization; Flight Dynamics Officer

FIDOR Fibre Building Board Development Organisation

fidos freaks, imperfections, defects, and oddities

FIDP Fellow of the Institute of Data Processing

FIDS Falkland Islands Dependencies Survey; Foolproof Identification System

FIED Fellow of the Institution of Engineering Designers

FIEE Fellow of the Institution of Electrical Engineers

FIEL *Fundación de Investigaciones Económicas Latinoamericanas* (Spanish—Foundation for Latin American Economic Investigations)

FIEN *Forum Italiano dell'Energia Nucleare* (Italian Nuclear Energy Forum)

FIER Foundation for Instrumentation Education and Research

FIERE Fellow of the Institute of Electronic and Radio Engineers

FIES Fellow of the Illuminating Engineering Society

Fiesta Bowl Phoenix, Arizona

fif ferric ion free

FIF First Investment Fund; Friends of Irish Freedom

fi. fa. *fieri facias* (Latin—see it done)

FIFA *Federation Internationale de Football Associations* (French—International Federation of Football Associations)

Fife Fifeshire

FIFE Fellow of the Institution of Fire Engineers

fifo first in, first out (inventory)

FIFO Flight Inspection Field Office(r)

FIFRA Federal Insecticide, Fungicide, and Rodenticide Act

Fifteenth State Kentucky

Fifteen-Year War (*see* Pacific War)

Fifth Avenue important north-south thoroughfare of Manhattan Island, New York City; leading from Washington Square in Greenwich Village northward through commercial, shopping, institutional, and residential districts; ending at the Harlem River

Fifth Estate The Underworld of Organized Crime—international conglomerates and syndicates aided by corrupt public officials, unlawful labor leaders, and bribable politicians

Fifth State Connecticut (*see* First State)

Fiftieth State Hawaii

fig. figuratively; figure

Fig. *Figur(en)* [German—figure(s)]; *Le Figaro* (Paris' oldest daily newspaper)

FIG Farmers Insurance Group

FIG *Federazione Italiana Golf* (Italian Golf Association)

FIGA Fretted Instrument Guild of America

Figaro Mariano José de Larra's pseudonym

FIGB *Federazione Italiana Gioco Bocce* (Italian Bocce Ball Association)

FIGCM Fellow of the Incorporated Guild of Church Musicians

Fighting Bob Rear Admiral Robley Evans; English prizefighter Robert P Fitzsimmons; Senator Robert M La Follette, Sr

Fighting Lady USS *Lexington*

Fighting Quaker General Nathanael Greene

FIGM Fellow of the Institute of General Managers

figs (FIGS) figures shift (data processing)

fig(s). figure(s); finger-sized banana(s)

Fig(s) figure(s)

figt fully inclusive group tour

fih fat-induced hyperglycemia; free in harbor

FIH Fédération Internationale des Hôpitaux (International Federation of Hospitals)

FIHVE Fellow of the Institution of Heating and Ventilating Engineers

FII Fellow of the Imperial Institute; Foreign Investment Institute

FIIA Fellow of the Institute of

Industrial Administration

FIIAL Fellow of the International Institute of Arts and Letters

FIIC Fellow of the Insurance Institute of Canada

FIICU Federation of Independent Illinois Colleges and Universities

fiigmo forget it, I've got my orders

FIIGS Federal Item Identification Guide System

FIIM Fellow of the Institute of Industrial Management

FIIN Federal Item Identification Number

FI Inf Sc Fellow of the Institute of Information Scientists

FIIP Fellow of the Institute of Incorporated Photographers

FIIT Federal Individual Income Tax

FIJ Fellow of the Institute of Journalists

FIJ *Fédération Internationale des Journalistes* (French—International Federation of Journalists)

Fiji Dominion of Fiji (island nation in the western South Pacific where its people speak English, Fiji, and some Hindi, molasses, sugar, and other tropical products compete with tourism)

Fijian Ports Suva (on Viti Levu) and Levuka (on Ovalau plus several very small ports on other islands)

Fijis Fiji islanders; Fiji Islands

FIJL *Federation Internationale des Journalistes Libres* (French—International Federation of Free Journalists)

fil filament; fillet; fillister; filter; filtrate

f-i-l father-in-law

Fil Filbert; Filemón; Filiberto; Filinto; Filipevna; Filipp; Filippino; Filippo; Filley; Fillmore; Filmore; Filpot; Filpotts

FIL Fellow of the Institute of Linguists

FILA Fellow of the Institute of Landscape Architects

Filadelfia (Italian, Portuguese, Spanish—Philadelphia)

Fil-Am Filipino-American

Filatov's disease scarlatina-like exanthematous affection

Filbert Center Hillsboro, Oregon

fild federal item logistics data

fildr federal item logistics data

record

File *Filemón* (Spanish—The Book of Philemon)—The Epistle of St Paul to the Philippians

FILE Fellow of the Institute of Legal Executives

file 13 trashcan; wastebasket

fil h fillister head

Fili *Filipinas* (Portuguese or Spanish—Philippines)

FILIM *Fédération Internationale des Langues et Litteratures Moderne* (French—International Federation of Modern Languages and Literature)

Filipinas (Italian, Portuguese, Spanish—Philippines)

Filipino Libertarian Emilio Aguinaldo

Filippijnen (Dutch—Philippines)

fill. filling

Film Capital Hollywood, California

filo first in, last out

filos *filosofia* (Italian or Portuguese—philosophy); *filosofia* (Spanish—philosophy)

filt filter; filtrate; filtration

filt. *filtra* (Latin—filter)

Filthydelphia Philadelphia

fim field ion microscope

Fim Finnish mark(s)

FIM Fellow of the Institute of Metallurgists; Flight Information Manual

FIM *Fédération Internationale Motocycliste* (French—International Motorcycle Federation)

FIMA Fellow of the Institute of Municipal Administration; Food Industries of Malaysia; Forging Ingot Makers' Association; Friendly International Males' Association

FIMC Fellow of the Institute of Management Consultants

FIME Fellow of the Institute of Mechanical Engineers

FIMI Fellow of the Institute of the Motor Industry

FIMIT Fellow of the Institute of Musical Instrument Technology

FIMLT Fellow of the Institute of Medical Laboratory Technology

FIMT Fellow of the Institute of the Motor Trade

FIMTA Fellow of the Institute of Municipal Treasurers and Accountants

fin. finance; financial; financier; finish

fin. *finis* (Latin—the end)

Fin Finistère; Finland; Finnic; Finnish

Fin Finnish (Uralic language close to Estonian and remote to Hungarian and Turkish, more than four million people speak Finnish and some 5% of the people in Finland also speak Swedish)

FIN Fellow of the Institute of Navigation

fina following items not available

FINAC Fast Interline Non-Active Automatic Control (automatic teletype service)

Finality John Lord John Russell

final solution final solution of the Jewish problem (Hitlerian truncation covering the extermination of all the Jews)—phrase frequently used by the Nazis, their collaborators and their sympathizers

Financial Center of the Rockies Denver, Colorado

Financial Genius of the Underworld Meyer Lansky

Financier of the Revolution Robert Morris

FINAST First National Stores

FINCANTIERI *Società Finanziaria Cantieri Navali* (Italian—Dockyards Finance Company)

fincl financial

FIND Friendless, Isolated, Needy, Disabled (older people)

FIND *Federal Item Name Directory*

fin dec final decree

Findel Luxembourg's principal airport

FINEBEL France, Italy, Netherlands, Belgium, and Luxembourg (economic agreement)

fined finished

FINELETTRICA *Società Finanziaria Elettrica* (Italian—Electric Power Finance Company)

fines. fine particulates

fin fl finished floor

FINFO Flight Inspection National Field Office (FAA)

fing finishing

F-ing fucking (slang—copulating)

Fingal Finn Mac Cumhail (semimythical Irish fighter whose Hebrides hideaway is described in Mendelssohn's *Fingal's Cave* overture)

finif field-induced negative ion formation

Finisterre (Cape Finisterre—northern Spain's westernmost cape)

Finlan *Finlândia* (Italian or Spanish—Finland); *Finlandia* (Portuguese—Finland)

Finland Republic of Finland (north European land whose Finns speak Finnish and produce food, mineral, and timber exports as well as textiles and woodenware of superior quality), *Suomen Tasavalta* (Finnish name); *Republiken Finland* (Swedish name)

Finlande (French—Finland)

Finlandia (Italian, Portuguese, Spanish—Finland)

Finland's Principal Port Helsinki

FINMARE *Società Finanziaria Marittima* (Italian—Maritime Shipping Finance Company)

Finn Finnish

FINNAIR Aero O/Y (*q.v.*, Finnish Airlines)

Finnglish Finnish + English

Finnish First Finland's best known classical composer—Jean Sibelius

Finnish National Composer Jan Sibelius

Finnish Ports (large, medium, and small from north to south) Tornio, Roytta, Kemi, Koivoluoto, Oulu, Raahe, Kokkola, Ykspihlaja, Jakobstad, Nykarleby, Vaasa, Vasklot, Kasko, Kristinestad, Pori, Mantyluoto, Reposaari, Kaunissaari, Rauma, Uusikaupunki, Turku, Storby, Mariehamn, Hango, Lappvik, Ekenas, Helsinki, Kotka, Hamina

Finnland (German—Finland)

Fi-No-Tro Finmark-Nord-Troms (fish processing)

FINS Fire Island National Sea shore

Fin Sec Financial Secretary

FINSINDER Società Finanziaria Siderurgica (Stell Financing Society)

F Inst Fellow of the Institute; Fellow of the Institution

F Inst F Fellow of the Institute of Fuel

F Inst P Fellow of the Institute of Physics

F Inst Pet Fellow of the Institute of Petroleum

F Inst SP Fellow of the Institute of Sewage Purification

f insulin fibrous insulin

FINTEL Financial Times Publishing Group

Fin-Ug Finno-Ugric

fio for information only; free in and out

FIO Fleet Information Office; Flight Information Office(r)

Fiona Macleod William Sharp's pseudonym

Fiordland Fiordland National Park (southwest corner of New Zealand's South Island); Norway's nickname

fios free into owner's store; free in and out stowed

fiot free in and out trimmed

fip fair in place; fi'pence (fivepence); fi'penny (fivepenny); fire insurance policy

FIP Fleet Introduction Program; Flight Instruction Program; Forestry Incentives Program

FIP Fédération Internationale des Phonothèque (International Federation of Record Libraries); *Fuerze Interamericana de Paz* (Spanish—Interamerican Peace Force)

FIPA Fellow of the Institute of Practitioners in Advertising

FIPAGO Fédération Internationale des Fabricants de Papiers Gommes (French—International Federation of Manufacturers of Gummed Paper)

FIPD Fellow of the Institute of Professional Designers

FIPLV Fédération Internationale de Professeurs des Langues Vivante (French—International Federation of Professors of Living Languages)

FiPo Fire and Police (Research Association)

FIPS Federal Information Processing Standards

FIPSE Fund for the Improvement of Postsecondary Education

FIPTP Federation Internationale de la Presse Technique et Periodique (French—International Federation of the Technical and Periodical Press)

FIQ Fédération Internationale des Quilleurs (French—International Bowling Federation)

FIQS Fellow of the Institute of Quantity Surveyors

fir(.) financial inventory report; firkin; flight information requirement; floating-in rate(s); fuel indicator reading; future issue requirement(s)

fir. flight information region

FIR Fabrication Information Report; Field Interrogation Record; Flight Information Report

FIRA Federal Investment Review Agency; Foreign Investments Review Agency; Furniture Industry Research Association

FIRAA Fire Insurance Research and Actuarial Association

FIRB Fire Insurance Rating Bureau; Florida Inspection and Rating Bureau; Foreign Investment Review Board

FIRCE Fiscalização e Registro de Capitais Estrangeiros Banco Central do Brasil (Portuguese—Central Bank of Brazil's Foreign Capital Regulations)

FIRE Fellow of the Institution of Radio Engineers

Firebar NATO name for Soviet Yakovlev all-weather fighter interceptor aircraft Yak-28P

Firebrand of the Navy Lieutenant Stephen Decatur, USN

Firebrand of the World Tamerlane (Timur Lenk or Timur the Lame)

FIREBRICK Federal Inter-Agency River Basin Committee

fireclay sedimentary rock containing chlorite-kaolinite with illite

Fireclay Capital Mexico, Missouri

firecracker factory missile manufacturing plant

fire damp methane

Firenze (Italian or Latin—Florence)

fires. firearms

FIRES Fire Inspection Reporting and Evaluation System

Firestreak Hawker-Siddeley air-to-air missile

fir. ex fire extinguisher

FIRFLT First Fleet

FIRI Fellow of the Institute of the Rubber Industry; Fishing Industry Research Institute

FIRME Fondo de Inversiones Rentables Mexicanas (Spanish—Mexican Rental Investments Fund)

FIRST Fast Interactive Retrieval System Technology; Financial Information Reporting System; Foster Initial Reading Skills in Time

First All-American Poet Walt Whitman

First American Advertiser William Penn

First American Penitentiary Walnut Street Jail in Philadelphia where it was built in 1790

First American Poet Philip Frenau

First American Republic Iceland

First American Woman Novelist Charlotte Lennox

First Astrophysicist Johannes Kepler

First Black American Conductor Dean Dixon

First Citizen of Ghana Dr WEB Du Bois

First City of the First State Wilmington, Delaware

First City of the South Savannah, Georgia

First Concentration Camp Made in Germany Dachau (erected in March 1933 in a Bavarian town near Munich)

First Estate The Clergy

First Execution by Electrocution August 6, 1890 in New York State's Auburn Prison

First Family family of the President of the United States; usually the President and the immediate members of his family

First Fleeters Australians tracing their lineage to their ancestors' arrival in 1788

First Foreign Enclave Macao, Portuguese China

first-generation money cash; currency

First Gentleman of the Land charming President Chester A Arthur

First Gospel Gospel according to Saint Matthew

First Great Cheerful Giver George Peabody

First Great Operatic Composer of the New World Carlos Gomes

First Halfway House Isaac T Hooper Home opened in New York City in 1845 by the Society of Friends (Quakers)

First International First International Workingmen's Association (of anarchists, communists, and socialists convening in Paris in 1864)

First Internationally Prominent Albanian Poet Naim Erashëri

First Internationally Prominent American Humorist Mark Twain

First Internationally Prominent

American Novelist James Fenimore Cooper

First Internationally Prominent Argentinian Author Domingo Faustino Sarmiento

First Internationally Prominent Australian Novelist Nevil Shute

First Internationally Prominent Austrian Dramatist Hugo von Hofmannsthal

First Internationally Prominent Barbadan Novelist George Lamming

First Internationally Prominent Belgian Author Maurice Maeterlinck

First Internationally Prominent Bolivian Author Ricardo Jaimes Freyre

First Internationally Prominent Brazilian Novelist Joaquim María Machado de Assis

First Internationally Prominent Bulgarian Novelist Dimiter Dimov

First Internationally Prominent Canadian Author Robert W. Service

First Internationally Prominent Canadian Humorist Stephen Leacock

First Internationally Prominent Canadian Novelist Chandler Haliburton

First Internationally Prominent Chilean Poet Gabriela Mistral

First Internationally Prominent Chinese Novelist Ts'ao Msüeh-Ch'in

First Internationally Prominent Colombian Author Germán Arciniegas

First Internationally Prominent Costa Rican Writer Ricardo Fernández Guardia

First Internationally Prominent Cuban Author José Martí

First Internationally Prominent Curaçaon Political Polemicist Daniel De León

First Internationally Prominent Czech Novelist Franz Kafka

First Internationally Prominent Danish Essayist George Morris Cohen Brandes

First Internationally Prominent Danish Novelist Hans Christian Andersen

First Internationally Prominent Dutch Author Jan de Hartog

First Internationally Prominent Ecuadorean Author Juan Montalvo

First Internationally Prominent

English Dramatist William Shakespeare

First Internationally Prominent English Novelist Charles Dickens

First Internationally Prominent English Poet Geoffrey Chaucer

First Internationally Prominent Finnish Novelist Mika Waltari

First Internationally Prominent French Dramatist Molière

First Internationally Prominent French Novelist Honoré de Balzac

First Internationally Prominent German Dramatist Johann Wolfgang von Goethe

First Internationally Prominent German Poet Friedrich von Schiller

First Internationally Prominent Greek Novelist Nikos Kazantzakis

First Internationally Prominent Guatemalan Essayist Enrique Gómez Carillo

First Internationally Prominent Guatemalan Novelist Miguel Angel Asturias

First Internationally Prominent Guyanese Poet Jan Carew

First Internationally Prominent Haitian Novelist Oswald Durand

First Internationally Prominent Honduran Novelist Argentina Díaz Lozano

First Internationally Prominent Hungarian Dramatist Ferenc Molnar

First Internationally Prominent Icelandic Author Jon Sigurdsson

First Internationally Prominent Indian Poet Rabindranath Tagore

First Internationally Prominent Indian Political Polemicist Mahatma Gandhi

First Internationally Prominent Irish Dramatist Oscar Wilde

First Internationally Prominent Irish Novelist James Joyce

First Internationally Prominent Irish Poet William Butler Yeats

First Internationally Prominent Italian Author Dante Alighieri

First Internationally Prominent Jamaican Poet Claude McKay

First Internationally Prominent Japanese Author Yasunari

Kawabata

First Internationally Prominent Mexican Author José Vasconcelos

First Internationally Prominent New Zealand Author Katherine Mansfield

First Internationally Prominent Nicaraguan Author Rubén Darío

First Internationally Prominent Norwegian Dramatist Henrik Ibsen

First Internationally Prominent Norwegian Novelist Knut Hamsun

First Internationally Prominent Panamanian Author Justo Arosemena

First Internationally Prominent Paraguayan Author Juan Silvano Godoy

First Internationally Prominent Peruvian Author Manuel González Prada

First Internationally Prominent Polish Novelist Henryk Sienkiewicz

First Internationally Prominent Portuguese Poet Luís de Camões

First Internationally Prominent Puerto Rican Author Eugenio María de Hostos

First Internationally Prominent Romanian Novelist Mihail Sandoveanu

First Internationally Prominent Russian Dramatist Aleksander Sergeevich Pushkin

First Internationally Prominent Russian Novelist Fëdor Dostoevski

First Internationally Prominent Salvadoran Poet Juan José Cañas

First Internationally Prominent Scottish Poet Robert Burns

First Internationally Prominent South African Novelist Olive Schreiner

First Internationally Prominent Spanish Author Miguel de Cervantes Saavedra

First Internationally Prominent Spanish Dramatic Poet Lope de Vega

First Internationally Prominent Spanish Dramatist Pedro Calderon de la Barca

First Internationally Prominent Spanish Essayist José Ortega y Gasset

First Internationally Prominent Swedish Dramatist August Strindberg

First Internationally Prominent Swedish Novelist Pär Lagerkvist

First Internationally Prominent Swiss Novelist Johanna Spyri

First Internationally Prominent Trinidadian Novelist Vidiadhur Surayprasad Naipaul

First Internationally Prominent Uruguayan Author José Enrique Rodó

First Internationally Prominent Uruguayan Poet Juana de Ibarbourou

First Internationally Prominent Venezuelan Author Rómulo Gallegos

First Internationally Prominent Venezuelan Poet Irma De Sola de Lovera

First Internationally Prominent Welsh Author Daniel Owens

First Internationally Prominent Yugoslav Author Milovan Djilas

First Lady First Lady of the Land (the wife of any American President)

First Lady of the Air Amelia M(ary) Earhart

First Lady of America Pocahontas

First Lady of the American Revolution Mercy Otis Warren also known as Philomela

First Lady of Computers Lady Augusta Ada Byron Lovelace (the poet Lord Byron's daughter)

First Lady of Crime Agatha Christie

First Lady of Liberty sobriquet of Abigail Adams—wife of President John Adams

First Lady of the Library President Millard Fillmore's wife Abigail—founder of the first library in the White House

First Lady of the Skies Amelia Earhart

First Lady of Song Ella Fitzgerald

First Lady of the World sobriquet of Anna Eleanor Roosevelt—wife of President Franklin D Roosevelt

First Lawyer of the Land U.S. Attorney General

First Mayor of Chicago William Butler Ogden

First Person to Announce His Discovery of Photography William Henry Fox Talbot on January 31, 1839

First Perspective Painter Paolo Uccello (Paolo di Dono)—known for his studies in foreshortening and linear perspective

First Picaresque Novel Lazarillo de Tormes (author unknown)

First Poet Laureate Ben Jonson

First Prison Newspaper The Summary published by the inmates of the New York State Reformatory at Elmira on November 22, 1883—Thanksgiving Day

First Quaker George Fox, founder of the Society of Friends

First Romantic Artist Giambattista Piranesi

First State Delaware's official nickname recalling it was first of the original thirteen states to ratify the Constitution

First Street in Europe Disraeli's nickname for London's Strand

First University Plato's Academy

First White House of the Confederacy temporary home of Jefferson Davis in Montgomery, Alabama in 1861

First Woman Physician Dr Elizabeth Blackwell

First Woman Reporter Anne Royale of Virginia (publisher of Paul Pry) and Nellie Bly of Pennsylvania (reporter for the New York World) share this nickname

First World highly industrialized countries such as Japan, the United States, the USSR, and most Western European nations

First and Yessler First Avenue and Yessler (Seattle's waterfront redlight district)

First Zen First Zen Institute of America

firta far infrared technical area

Firth of Clyde sea entrance to Clydebank and Glasgow on west coast of Scotland off North Channel leading to Atlantic Ocean or Irish Sea

Firth of Forth estuary of North Sea leading to Edinburgh

Firth of Lorne Atlantic Ocean and Scottish Sea entrance to Caledonian Canal crossing northern Scotland

FIRTO Fire Insurers Research and Testing Organization

Firton Girton College, Cambridge

fis family income supplement; foam in salvage; free in store; freight, insurance, and shipping (charges)

fis fisica (Italian—physics)

fís físíca (Portuguese or Spanish —physics)

Fis (German—F-sharp)

FIS Facial Identification Systems; Field Instruction System; Fighter Interceptor Squadron; Financial Information System (DoE); Flight Information Service

FISA Fellow of the Incorporated Secretaries Association

FISAR Federal Institute for Snow and Avalanche Research

FISARS Fleet Information Storage and Retrieval System (USN)

FISC Federation of Infant School Clubs; Financial Industries Service Corporation

fisc irre fiscal irresponsibility

FIS countries France, Ivory Coast, Senegal

FISD Fédération Internationale de Sténographie et de Dactylographie (French—International Federation of Stenography and Typewriting)

FISE Fédération Internationale Syndicale de l'Enseignement (French—International Federation of Teachers' Unions)

fish. fishery; fishes; fishing

FISH Friends in Service Here

Fish-Canning Capital of the World Stavanger, Norway

Fishpot NATO name for Soviet SU-9 all-weather jet fighter aircraft

fishsan fish sandwich

fishwich fish sandwich

FISIPE Fibras Sintéticas de Portugal (Portuguese—Synthetic Fibers of Portugal)

FISL Federally Insured Student Loan(s)

fiss (Latin prefix—split)—fissure

FIST Federation of Interstate Truckers; Field Intelligence Simulation Test; Fugitive Investigative Strike Team (for catching criminals at large)

fisteg fiscal integrity

fit. fabrication in transit; foreign inclusive tour; foreign independent traveler; foreign independent trip; formation interval tester (oil well); free of income tax; free in truck; freely independent traveller; fully inclusive tour

fit. (FIT) foreign independent travel (tour)

FIT Fashion Institute of Technology; Federal Income Tax; Fédération Internationale des Traducteurs (International Federation of Translators); Fellow of the Institute of Transport; Fiji Institute of Technology; Footscray Institute of Technology; Foreign Independent Tours

fits. foreign individual travellers

Fitter NATO name for Soviet SU-7 jet ground-attack aircraft

fitw federal income tax withholding

fitwh federal income tax withholding

Fitz Fitzedward; Fitzgerald; Fitzgreen(e); Fitzhugh; Fitzjames; Fitzjohn; Fitzmaurice; Fitzrandolph; Fitzroy; Fitzsim(m)ons; Fitzwilliam(s)

Fitzbill Fitzwilliam

Fitzw Fitzwilliam College, Cambridge; Fitzwilliam Library (Cambridge)

Fitzw Coll Fitzwilliam College —Cambridge

FIU Federation of Information Users; Florida International University; Forward Interpretation Unit (US Army)

Fiume Italian name for Rijeka, Yugoslavia formerly belonging to Italy

FIV Fellow of the Institute of Valuers

FIV Fondo de Inversiones de Venezuela (Spanish—Investments Fund of Venezuela)

fiva fluid inject valve actuator

Five The Five (*see Kutchka*)

Five Ages of Mankind according to classical mythology mankind evolved to the Golden Age after passing through the Silver, Bronze, Iron, and Stone ages (*see entries for each age*)

Five Nations Cayugas, Oneidas, Onondagas, Mohawks, and Senecas (American Indian tribes on the English side in the French and Indian Wars)

fiw free in wagon

FIWC Fiji Industrial Workers Congress

fix. fixture

Fiz Fizika (Russian—physics)

Fiz Elem Chastits At Yadra Fizika Elementarnykh Chastits i Atomnogo Yadra (Russian—Journal of Particles and Nuclei)—USSR

Fiz Met Fizika Metallov i Metal-

lovedenie (Russian—Physics of Metals and Metallography) —USSR

Fiz Nizk Temp Fizika Nizkikh Temperatur (Russian—Journal of Low-Temperature Physics)—USSR

Fiz Plazmy Fizika Plazmy (Russian—Plasma Physics)— USSR

Fiz Tekh Poluprovodn Fizika i Tekhnika Poluprovodnikov (Russian—Semiconductor Physics and Technology)— USSR

Fiz Tverd Tela Fizika Tverdogo Tela (Russian—Solid-State Physics)—USSR

fj flush joint

Fj Fjord

FJ Fiji Airways; Flying Junior

F-J Fisher-John

FJA Future Journalists of America

FJC Federal Judicial Center; Fullerton Junior College

Fjd Fjord

Fjd(s) Fiji dollar(s)

FJH Franz Josef Haydn

Fji Fiji

FJI Fellow of the Institute of Journalists

FJIC Federal Job Information Center

FJNM Fort Jefferson National Monument

Fjord Land Norway with its more than 365 arms of the sea indenting its shoreline

fjp first job program

FJS Fulton J Sheen

fk flat keel; fork

Fk Frank

FK Fluid Kinetics; Franz Kafka; Fujita Airways

FK Frankfurt Kassenverein (German—Frankfurt Clearinghouse)

FKBD Fort Knox Bullion Depository

FKBI Fourdrinier Kraft Board Institute

FKC Fellow of King's College

Fkd Frankford

FKI Federation of Korean Industries

FKJC Florida Keys Junior College

FKL Frauen Konzentrations-Lager (German—Women's Concentration Camp)

Fkn Franklin; Frederikshavn

fkr før Kristus (Dano-Norwegian —Before Christ)

Fks Fredrikstad

FKSNS Fort Kent State Normal

School

FKTU Federation of Korean Trade Unions

FKWR Florida Keys Wildlife Refuges

fl flash(ing); flash(ing) light; flight level; flood(ing); floor(ing); flourish; flow line; flow(ing); fluid loss; fluid(s); fluorescent level; flush(ing); focal length; follow(ing); footlambert; foreign language; forklift

f&l fuel and lubricants

fl flaske (Dano-Norwegian— bottle, flask); *flauti* (Italian— flute, flutes); *flauto*; *flores* (Latin—flowers; *florin* (Dano-Norwegian or Dutch—florin); *floruit* (Latin—he flourished)

f.l. falsa lectio (Latin—false reading)

fL foot-lambert

Fl Fall (postal abbreviation); Flemish; fluorine

Fl Fleuve (French—large river)

FL Ferdinand Laeisz; First Lady; Flag Lieutenant; Flight Lieutenant; focal length; Football League; foreign language; Frontier Airlines (2-letter code)

F.L. Franz Liszt

F for L Feminists for Life

Fl Fürstentum Liechtenstein (Principality of Liechtenstein)

fla fronto-laeva anterior

f.l.a. fiat lege artis (Latin— according to the rules of art)

Fla Florida; Floridian

FLA Federal Loan Administration; Federal Loan Agency; Fellow of the Library Association; Florida; Florida East Coast Railway (symbol); Foam Laminators Association

FLA Frente de Libertação Açoriana (Portuguese—Azorian Liberation Front)

FLAA Fellow of the Library Association of Australia

Flabussce (Italian-American— Flatbush section of Brooklyn, NY)

fl abwth flush armor balanced watertight hatch

FLAC Florida Automatic Computer (USAF)

FLACCS Florida Climate and Control System

Fla Cur Florida Current

flag. flageolet

Flag of Alfonso yellow-and-red emblem of Spain dating from fifteenth century when it was

carried by Alfonso el Mag-
nánimo

Flag Day June 14 in the United
States

Flagellum Dei (Latin—Scourge
of God)—Attila the king of the
Huns

Flagon-A NATO code name for
Soviet SU-11 delta-wing
fighter aircraft

FLAI Fellow of the Library Association of Ireland

FLAIR Floating Airport

FLAIRS Fleet Locating and Information Reporting System
(for police-patrol vehicles)

flak fondest love and kisses

flak *Fliegerabwehrkanone* (German—anti-aircraft cannon,
anti-aircraft shrapnel)

FLAME Facility Laboratory for
Ablative Materials Evaluation

flam(s) flamenco (songs); flam-
ing(s); flammable(s)

Flandern (German—Flanders)

Flandes (Spanish—Flanders)

Flandre (French—Flanders)

Flandres (Portuguese—Flanders)

flang flowchart language

FLAP Flores Assembly Program

FLAPS Flexibility Analysis of
Piping Systems

flar florward-looking airborne
radar

FLAS Fellow of the Land
Agents Society

FLASH Foreign Fishing Vessels
Licensing and Surveillance
Hierarchical Information Sys-
tem (Canadian)

Flashlight NATO name for Soviet Yakovlev Yak-25 two-
place interceptor fighter aircraft

Flats Durango, Colorado's
slums

flav flavor(ing)

flav. *flavus* (Latin—yellow)

flb flight-line bunker

FLB Federal Land Bank

FLBAs Federal Land Bank Associations

flbin floating-point binary

flbm (FLBM) fleet-launched
ballistic missile

fl bp filter, band-pass

fl bs filter, band-suppression

FLC Federal Library Committee; Foundation Library Center

flcc flight-control computer

FLCM Fellow of the London
College of Music

FLCO Fellow of the London

College of Osteopathy

fl crs flat cars

fld failed; field; flowered; fluid

Fld Field (postal abbreviation)

FLD Friends of the Lake District

Fld Com DNA Field Command,
Defense Nuclear Agency

fldec floating-point decimal

fldg folding

fldg chr folding chair(s)

fl di flare die

FL & DI Food Law and Drug
Institute

fldl field length (flow chart)

fldo final limit, down

fldop field operations

fl dr fluid dram

Flds Fields

fldxt fluid extract

Fl e Flemish ell (unit of measure)

flea. flux logic element array

fleact fleet activities

Fledermaus *Die Fledermaus*
(German—The Bat)—operet-
ta by Johann Strauss, Jr

flee. fast-linkage editor

FLEEC Federal Libraries' Experiment in Cooperative Cataloging

fleetex fleet exercise

Fleet Street London's street of
periodical publishers

Flem Flemish

fleming(s) fleming-gear hand-
propelled lifeboat(s)

Flemish Colorist Peter Paul Ru-
bens

Flemish Primitive Painter
Gheeraert David long accorded this title

Flem(s) British slang for Bel-
gian(s)

Flensbørg (Danish—Flensburg)

fles foreign language in elementary school

FLES Foreign Languages in Elementary Schools (linguistic
teaching program)

FLETC Federal Law Enforcement Training Center

FLETRABASE Fleet Training
Base (USN)

fleur-de-lis symbol of France
and the French

FLEWEACEN Fleet Weather
Center

FLEWEAFAC Fleet Weather
Facility

flex. flexible

FLEX Federal Licensing Examination

flexo flexographic

flf final limit, forward; flip flop

FLF Freedom Leadership Foun-

dation

flg failing; flagging; flange; flashing; flooring; flying

FLG Flagship (USN)

FLGA Fellow of the Local Government Association

FLGB Federal Loan Guarantee
Board

flgd flanged

flgstn flagstone

flh familial lefthandedness; final
limit, hoist

fl hd flathead

flhls flashless

fl hp filter, high-pass

flia *familia* (Spanish—family)

flib friggin little itinerant bas-
tard(s)

FLIC Film Library Information
Council

Flickertail(s) North Dakotan(s)

Flickertail State North Dakota

flick(s) flicker(s), [motion pic-
ture(s)]

flicon flight control

flicr fluid-logic industrial control relay

fliden flight data entry

Flight 182 ill-fated PSA Flight
182 (one of the worst passen-
ger-plane disasters in American aviation history when, on
September 25, 1978, Flight
182 collided in midair with a
private plane in the perilous
approach area of San Diego's
Lindbergh Field surrounded
by many hills, private homes,
and schools)—144 lives lost

FLIM Flight Mechanics Internal Memorandum

Flinders Flinders Ranges of
South Australia

flint variety of chalcedony

flint. (FLINT) floating interpretive language

Flint Flintshire

Flints Flintshire

flip. film library instantaneous
presentation

FLIP Flexible Loan Insurance
Program; Flight Information
Publication; Floated Light-
weight Inertial Platform;
Floating Instrument Platform;
Free-form Language for Image
Processing

Flip(s) Filipino(s)

flir forward-look infrared

FLIRT Federal Librarians
Round Table

flit functional literacy

fliv flivver

Flivver King Henry Ford

FLIWR Functional Listing and
Interconnection Wiring Rec-

ord
flkprt flock printed
Flks Falkland Islands
fll final limit, lower
FLL Finanglia Line Ltd; Fort Lauderdale, Florida (airport); Friends Library, London
fllar forward-looking light attack radar
fl ld floor load
Flli *fratelli* (Italian—brothers)
fl lp filter, low-pass
flm functional-level manager
FLM Free Library Movement
FLM *Fédération Luthérienne Mondiale* (French—Lutheran World Federation)
FLMI Fellow of the Life Management Institute
fl/mtr flow meter
fln fallen; following landing numbers
Fln Flensburg
FLN *Frente de Liberación Nacional* (Spanish—National Liberation Front); *Front de Libération Nationale* (French—National Liberation Front)—official Algerian party
FLNC *Frente de Liberacion Nacional de Cuba* (Spanish—National Liberation Front of Cuba)
flng falling
FLNM Fort Laramie National Monument
flo floodlight(s)
Flo Flobert; Florence; Florentz; Florian; Floris
Fl O Flight Officer
FLO Foreign Liaison Office(r)
float. floating offshore attended terminal
floatel floating motel
floc floccule; flocculent; floccus
FLOC For Love of Children
flod (Danish or Swedish—river)
flodac fluid-operated digital-automatic computer
Fl Offr Flying Officer
FLOG Fleet Logistics Air Wing
FLOOD Fleet Observation of Oceanographic Data (USN)
Flood City Johnstown, Pennsylvania
flop. floating octal point
flor floriculture
flor *flores* (Latin—flowers); *floruit* (Latin—he flourished)
Flor *Floréal* (French—Flowery Month)—beginning April 20—eighth month of the French Revolutionary Calendar
Flor(a) Florence
Floral Watercolorist William

Demuth
Floreana Island, Galápagos Santa María
Florença (Portuguese—Florence)
Florence English place-name equivalent of Firenze; Federal Detention Headquarters at Florence, Arizona
Florence Austral Florence Wilson
Florencia (Spanish—Florence)
Florentia (Latin—Florence)
Florestan Robert Schumann
Florestan and Eusebius pseudonyms invented by Robert Schumann to represent the two sides of his character shown in his compositions and in his music criticisms—he claimed Florestan was impetuous and passionate whereas Eusebius was the dreamer
Floribbean Floridian-Caribbean (resort area)
Florida Keys chain of small islands extending from the southernmost tip of mainland Florida to Key West
Florida Ports (east to west) Jacksonville, Port Everglades, Miami, Key West, Tampa, St Petersburg, Port St Joe, Panama City, Pensacola
Florrie Flora; Florence
florsent fluorescent
floss. flossing (dental care)
Floss(ie) Florence
flot flotation; flotilla; flotsam
Flota *Flota Oceanica Brasileira* (Portuguese—Brazilian Oceanic Fleet)
Flour City nickname shared by Buffalo or Rochester as both New York State cities are proud of their flour mills
fl ovth flush oiltight ventilation hole
Flower Capital Encinitas, California or other places specializing in the cultivation of flowering plants
Flower City Rochester, New York
Flower Garden of England The Sorlings or Isles of Scilly off Land's End
Flower King Carl von Linné (Linnaeus)
Flower of the Levant Zante in the Ionian Islands
Flower of Quakerism abolitionist Lucretia Mott
Flower Seed Capital of the West Santa Maria, California
Flower Town Brampton, Ontar-

io
Flowertown in the Pines Summerville, South Carolina
Flower of the Transvaal Pretoria
Flowery Kingdom China
flox fluorine + liquid oxygen
Floy Florence
fl oz fluid ounce
flp fault location panel; fronto-laeva posterior
FLP Free Library of Philadelphia
flpl fortran-compiled list-processing language
fl pl. *flore pleno* (Latin—in full bloom)
FLPMA Federal Land Policy and Management Act
fl prf flameproof
FLPS First Log Procurement Status
fl pt flashpoint; fluid pint
FLQ *Front de Libération Quebecois* (French—Front for the Liberation of the people of Quebec)—radical terrorist separatists
flr failure; final limit, reverse; flame resistant; flare(s); floor; florin; flow rate; forward-looking radar
FLR Florence, Italy (Firenze Airport)
FLR *Federal Law Reports*
FLRA Federal Labor Relations Authority
flrg flooring
flrng flash ranging
llrs flares; flowers; forward-looking radar set
fl/rt flow rate
fls forward-looking sonar
Fls Falls (postal abbreviation); Flushing
FLS Fellow of the Linnaean Society; Flashing Light System
FLSA Fair Labor Standards Act
flsc flexible linear-shaped charge; flight shape charge
FLSEP Family Life and Sex Education Program
flsh flesh (side) leather
flshd fleshed (skins)
FLSO Fort Lauderdale Symphony Orchestra
FLSP Fort Lincoln State Park (North Dakota)
flst flautist; flutist
flt filter; fleet; flight; float; flotation; fork-lift truck; fronto-laeva transverse
flt *flertal* (Dano-Norwegian—majority or plural)
Flt Flats (postal abbreviation);

Fleetwood
Flt Adm Fleet Admiral
fltbcst fleet broadcast (USN)
Fltcher C Fletcher College
fltck flight check
Flt Cmdr Flight Commander
fltg floating
flt ld sim flight-load simulator
Flt Lt Flight Lieutenant
Flt No. Flight Number
fltp flight template
flt/pg flight programmer
flt pln flight plan
fltr floater
flts flights
FLTSATCOM Fleet Satellite Communications (DoD)
Flt Sgt Flight Sergeant
Flt Sgt Nav Flight Sergeant Navigator
fltstrikex full general-emergency striking force (USN)
flu fault location unit; final limit, up; first line unit; influenza
fluc fluctuant; fluctuate; fluctuating; fluctuation
FLUG Flugfelag Islands (Iceland Airways)
flummery foolish humbuggery (named after British custard made of flour or oatmeal boiled with water until almost too thick to swallow)
fluor fluor-apatite; fluorescence; fluorescent; fluorite; fluorspar; fluotaramite—generally fluor is the synonym of fluorite although the abbreviation for the foregoing so when in doubt —spell it out
fluorspar calcium fluoride (CaF2)
flur fluorescent
fluss flüssig(German—fluid)
flv foreign leave
flw follow(s)
FLW Frank Lloyd Wright
flwd followed
flwg following
flwop forced landing without power
flx flexible
fly. flinty; flying; flyweight
FLY Flying Tiger Line
Flying Boxcar C-119 Fairchild-Hiller transport carrying 62 paratroopers or an equal weight of cargo
Flying Dutchman mythical character immortalized in Richard Wagner's opera *Der Fliegende Holländer*; nickname of the baseball batting champion of the early 1900s—Honus Wagner

Flying Finn Paavo Nurmi
FlyTAF Flying Training Air Force
FLZO Farband-Labor Zionist Order
fm face measurement; facial measurement; fan marker; farm; farmer; fathom; fathometer; femtometer(s); fermi; fine measurement; form; frequency modulation; from; fumigation
f-m frequency modulation
f/m feet per minute
f & m foot-and-mouth disease
fm formiddag (Dano-Norwegian—before noon)—a.m.; *formiddagen* (Swedish— before noon)—a.m.
f.m. fiat mistura(Latin—make a mixture)
f/M female Mexican
Fm fermium
F/m unit of permittivity
FM Fed Mart; Ferrocarril Mexicano (Mexican Railroad); Field Manual; Field Marshal; Flight Mechanic; Foreign Minister; frequency modulation
F & M Franklin and Marshall College
fma forward maintenance area
FMA Federal Maritime Administration; Felt Manufacturers Association; File Manufacturers Association; Financial Management Association; Fish Marketing Authority; Flour Mills of America; Ford Motor Argentina; Forging Manufacturers Association; Fulfillment Management Association
FMACC Foreign Military Assistance Coordinating Committee
FMAI Financial Management for Administrators Institute
fman foreman
FMANA Fire Marshals Association of North America
FMAO Farm Machinery Advisory Office(r)
FMAS Foreign Marriage Advisory Service
fmb (FMB) fast missile boat
FMB Federal Maritime Board; Felix Mendelssohn Bartholdi
fmbid firm bid
FMBRA Flour Milling and Baking Research Association
FMBSA Farmers and Manufacturers Beet Sugar Association
FMC Failure Mode Center (Reliability Laboratory); Federal

Maritime Commission; Federated Motor(ing) Clubs; Federated Mountain Clubs; Federation of Mothers Clubs; Felt Manufacturers Council; Food Machinery Corporation; Ford Motor Company
FMC *Federación de Mujeres Cubanas* (Spanish—Federation of Cuban Women)
fmca forming cam
FMCA Family Motor Coach Association; Fire Mark Circle of the Americas
FM Can Ford Motor of Canada
FMCC Fulton-Montgomery Community College
F McH NM Fort McHenry National Monument
FMCL Fleet Mechanical Calibration Laboratory
FMCS Federal Mediation and Conciliation Service
fm cu form cutter
fmcw frequency-modulated continuous wave
fmd foot-and-mouth disease
FMD Federated Metals Division—American Smelting and Refining; Fisheries Management Division; Fixtures Manufacturers and Dealers; Flota Mercante Dominicana (Dominican Steamship Line); Forward Metro Denver
fmdf fixed mirror-distributed focus
fm di form die
fme frequency-measuring equipment
FMEA (FEA) Failure Modes and Effects Analysis
FMECA Failure Mode, Effects, and Criticality Analysis
fmer factory mutual engineering and research
fmeva floating-point means and variance
fmf fetal movement felt; field maintenance factor
fMf (FMF) familial Mediterranean fever
FMF Fleet Marine Force
FMF-A Fleet Marine Force— Atlantic
fmfb frequency-modulation feedback
FMFIC Federation of Mutual Fire Insurance Companies
FMFLANT Fleet Marine Force, Atlantic
FMF-P Fleet Marine Force— Pacific
FMFPAC Fleet Marine Forces — Pacific

fmfs fat in the moisture-free substance

fmg foreign medical graduate

FMG Flota Mercante Grancolombiana (Colombian national steamship lines); franc(s) Malagasy

FMGJ Federation of Master Goldsmiths and Jewelers

fmh (FMH) fat-mobilizing hormone

FMH Friends Meeting House

FmHA Farmers Home Administration

FMHCSS Federal Mobile Home Construction and Safety Standard

FMHHS Fort McHenry Historic Shrine (Baltimore)

FMI Farmers Mutual Insurance; Fiber Materials Inc; FM Intercity (relay broadcasting); Fonds Monétaires Internationals (International Monetary Fund); Food Marketing Institute; Freight Management International

FMI Fondo Monetario Internacional (Spanish—International Monetary Fund)

fmicw frequency-modulated intermittent-continuous-wave (radar)

FMIG Farmers Mutual Insurance Group; Food Manufacturers' Industrial Group

FMIS Functional Management Inspection System

fmk full-mouth radiograph

Fmk Finnmark; Finnish markka (currency unit)

FML Factory Mutual Laboratories; Fermi National Laboratory (Batavia, Illinois)

FMLNF Farabundo Marti National Liberation Front (Salvadoran Marxist guerrillas)

fmly formerly

fmly k a formerly known as

FMM Federation of Malay Manufacturers; French Military Mission

FMMA Floor Machinery Manufacturers Association

fmmd form mandrel

FMME Fund for Multinational Management Education

fmn formation

fmn (FMN) flavin mononucleotide

FMN Ferrocarril Mexicano del Norte (Northern Mexican Railroad)

FMNH Field Museum of Natural History

FMNM Fort Matanzas National Monument

FMO Fleet Mail Office; Fleet Medical Officer; Flight Medical Officer

FMOF First Manned Orbital Flight (NASA)

fmofr firm offer

fmp first menstrual period; functional maintenance procedure; funny-man prop

FMP Fairbanks Morse Pump; Family Medicine Program; Final Management Plan; Fourth Malaysia Plan; Frontier Mounted Police; Fuel Management Panel

FMPA Fellow of the Master Photographers' Association

FMPE Federation of Master Process Engravers

FMPEC Financial Management Plan for Emergency Conditions (USA)

fm/pm phase-modulated telemetering system

fm prot fine-mesh (cover) protected

FMPS Fairbanks Morse Power Systems

fmr fair market rent; farmer; fast metabolic rate; ferromagnetic resonance; former; former(ly)

FMR Field Maintenance Reliability; Field Materials Request; Franco Maria Ricci (or his magazine *FMR*)

F-M-R Friend Moloney Rauscher (virus)

FMRA Fertilizer Manufacturers Research Association

FMRC Financial Management Research Center

fm rl form roll

fmrly formerly

FMRS Federal Mediation and Reconciliation Service

fms fathoms; fat-mobilizing substance; flush metal saddle; foreign military sales; free-machining steel; frequency-multiplexed subcarrier

fm's formerly-married persons

FMS Federal Mining and Smelting (company); Federated Malay States; Field Music School; Financial Management System; Flexible Manufacturing System; Floating Machine Shop; Fort Myers Southern (railroad); Frequency Monitoring System; Friends Mission Society

fmsa frequency measuring spectrum analyzer

FMSA Fellow of the Mineralogical Society of America

FMSI Friction Materials Standards Institute

FMSL Fort Monmouth Signal Laboratory

FMSM Fédération Mondiale pour la Santé Mentale (World Mental Health Federation)

fmswr flexible mild-steel wire rope

fmt flush metal threshold

fmt (FMT) format (flow chart)

FMT Factory Marriage Test; Flight Management Team (NASA)

fm to. form tool

FMTS Field Maintenance Test Station

F & MTVHS Food and Maritime Trades Vocational High School

fmu force measurement unit; freight multiple unit

FMVSS Federal Motor Vehicle Safety Standard

FMWC Federation of Medical Women of Canada

FMWS Fairbanks Morse Weighing Systems

fmx full-mouth radiography

fn fence; flatnose (projectile); footnote; fusion

f/n freight note

fn fête nationale (French—national holiday)

Fn Factonimbus

F_n Fibonacci number(s)

FN Flight Nurse; Fridtjof Nansen

FN Fabrique Nationale (French — National Factory)—Belgian arms firm's initials appearing on all its products, *Forenede Nationer* (Danish—United Nations)

FN4RM/62FAB Belgian four-wheeled armored vehicle armed with a 60mm mortar and two machineguns or a 90mm cannon

fna for necessary action

FNA following named airmen; French North Africa

FNAA Fellow of the National Association of Auctioneers

FNAF Federal Nigerian Air Force

FNAL Fermi National Accelerator Laboratory

FNB First National Bank; Food and Nutrition Board

FNBC First National Bank of Chicago

FNBP Far North Bicentennial Park (Anchorage)

fnc finance

FNC Federación Nacional de

Cafeteros (National Federation of Coffee Growers—Colombia); Ferrocarriles Nacionales de Colombia (National Railroads of Colombia)

FNCB First National City Bank

fncg financing

fncl financial

FNCR Ferrocarril del Norte de Costa Rica (Northern Railway of Costa Rica)

fnd found; foundation; foundered

FND Flinders Naval Depot (Australia)

fndd founded

fndg founding

fndn foundation

fndr founder

fndrs fenders

fndry foundry

FNDTS Fellow of the Non-Destructive Testing Society

fne fine

fnf flying needle frame

fng fuckin' new guy

fnh flashless nonhygroscopic (gunpowder)

FNH Ferrocarril Nacional de Honduras (National Railway of Honduras)

FNIC Food and Nutrition Information and Educational Materials Center

FNIF Florence Nightingale International Foundation

FNIMC Florida Normal and Industrial Memorial College

fnl final

FNL Friends of the National Libraries

FNLA *Frente Nacional de Libertação de Angola* (Portuguese—Angolan National Liberation Front)

FNLO French Naval Liaison Office(r)

fnl qtr final quarter

fnly finally

fnlz finalize

FNM Ferrocarriles Nacionales de México (National Railroads of Mexico); Financial Network Manager

FNMA Federal National Mortgage Association

FNN Fiji News Network

FNNWR Fort Niobrara National Wildlife Refuge (Nebraska)

FNO following-named officers

FNOA following-named officers and airmen

fnp fusion point

fnp (FNP) floating nuclear-power plant

FNP Fiordland National Park (South Island, New Zealand); Fundy National Park (New Brunswick, Canada)

FNPF Fiji National Provident Fund

FNRC Federal Nuclear Regulatory Commission

FNRJ Federationa Narodna Republika Jugoslavija (Yugoslavia)

fns flask-nitrogen supply

FNS Food and Nutrition Service; Frontier Nursing Service

FNSAE Fellow of the National Society of Art Education

fnsh finish

fnshd finished

fnshg finishing

fnshr finisher

FNTO Finnish National Travel Office

fnu first name unknown

FNU Forces des Nations Unies (United Nations Forces)

f number focal length of a lens

f-number diameter of a lens aperture in relation to its focal length

FNV *Financiera Nacional de la Vivienda* (Spanish—National Housing Finance)

FNWA Foreign National Weather Agency

FNWF Fleet Numerical Weather Facility

FNZDT Federation of New Zealand Dancing Teachers

FNZLA Fellow of the New Zealand Library Association

FNZSA Fellow of the New Zealand Society of Accountants

FNZSID Fellow of the New Zealand Society of Industrial Designers

fo faced only; fade out; fast operating; filter output; firm offer; firm order; flat oval; folio; formal offer; free out; free overside; freight on; fuel oil; full out terms; for orders

fo' for; four

f/o for credit of; firm offer; free overside; for orders

f⁰ folio

f⁰ *firmato* (Italian—signed)

f/O female Oriental

Fo Fornax

F₀ pure parental type

FO Federal Office(r); Federal Official(dom); Field Office(r); Field Operations; Field Order; Finance Office(r); Finance Officer; Fisheries Office(r); Flag Officer; Flying Officer; Foreign Office; Forward Observer

F.O. Foreign Office

F/O Flight Officer; Flying Officer

FOA Farmers Organization Authority; Football Officials Association; Foreign Operations Administration; Foresters of America; Friends of Animals

FOAC Flag Officer, Aircraft Carrier(s)

Foam City Milwaukee, Wisconsin famous for its beers

fob feet out of bed

fob. feet out of bed; fresh off the boat (immigrant or refugee); front of body (hoist); fuel on board; full of baloney

fo & b fuel oil and ballast

f.o.b. free on board; fuel on board

FoB Friends of the Bureau (FBI)

F o B Faculty of Building

FOB Federal Office Building; Forward Operating Base; Free on Board

fobcnlf free on board cars, named point, lighterage free

fobcnp free on board cars, named point

fobot free on board, owners trim

FOBS Fractional-Orbit Bombardment System

fobse free on board, sacks extra

fobsi free on board, sacks included

foc final operation capability; flag of convenience; focal; focus(ing); free of charge; free on car(s); free on container(s); full operational capability

f.o.c. free of charge; free on car(s); free on container(s)

FoC Father of the Chapel (printer's union)

FOC Ferrocarriles Occidentales de Cuba (Western Railroads of Cuba); Flight Operations Center

FOCA Federation of Citizens Associations; Formula-One Constructors Association

FOCAS Ford Operating Cost Analysis System

fochr free of charge

FOCI Farrand Optical Company, Incorporated

FOCIS Financial On-Line Central Information System

FOCLA Federation of Country Local Associations

focmg forthcoming

FOCOL Federation of Coin-

Operated Launderettes
FOCS Freight Operation Control System
FOCSL Fleet-Oriented Consolidated Stock List
fo'c's'le forecastle
FOCT Flag Officer Carrier Training
FOCUS Federation of Community United Services
fod fodder; foreign object damage; free of damage
f.o.d. free of damage
FOD Flag Officer, Denmark; follow-on destroyer
fo/do fuel oil/diesel oil (consumed daily)
foe fuel oil equivalent
FOE Fraternal Order of Eagles; Friends of the Earth
fof free on field (airmail)
FOF Facts-On-File
fofr firm offer
fog. flow of gold
FoG Friends of Gill
FOG Flag Officer, Germany; Florida Orange Growers
FOGA Fashion Originators Guild of America
FOGAIN Fondo de Garantia y Fomento a la Industria Mediana y Pequeña (Spanish—Fund for the Guarantee and Promotion of Medium and Small Industry)—Mexico
Fogfoundland fog-bound Newfoundland's east coast
Foggy Bottom nickname of the U.S. State Department
Fog Sig fog signal (station)
foh front of house
foi freedom of information
foi (FOI) fighter officer interceptor; follow-on interceptor
F o I Freedom of Information
FOI (station) Operations Intelligence; Fighter Officer Interceptors; Fruit of Islam (Black Nationalists)
FoIA Freedom of Information Act
FOIC Flag Officer in Charge
foil. file-oriented interpretive language
FOIR Field-of-Interest Register
f.o.k. free of knots
fol folio; folios; follow; following; follows; free-on-lorry oil and lubricants
fol. folium (Latin—leaf); folia (Latin—leaves)
FOL Federation of Labor; Federation of Labour (New Zealand); Foreign Office Library; Friends of the Land
fold. folding

folg folgend (German—following)
Folkes Folkestone
foll followed by
folnoaval following (items) not available
fols folios; follows
Folsom California State Prison at Folsom
fom fat off mothers (sheep); fault of management; figure of merit
fomaj force majeure
FOMC Federal Open Market Committee
FOMCA Federation of Malaysian Consumers Association
FOMEX Fondo Nacional de las Exportaciones (Spanish—National Fund for the Promotion of Exports); Fondo para el Fomento de las Exportaciones de Productos Manufacturados (Spanish—Fund for the Promotion of Export of Manufactured Products)
FOMIN Fondo Nacional de Fomento Industrial (Spanish—National Fund for Industrial Promotion)
fomm functionally-oriented maintenance manual(s)
FoMoCo Ford Motor Company
fomth for one month
FONADE Fondo Nacional de Desarrollo (Spanish—National Development Fund)
FONASBA Federation of National Associations of Shipbrokers and Agents
FONATUR Fondo Nacional de Fomento al Turismo (Spanish—National Fund for Tourist Promotion)
Fondo El Fondo (Spanish—The Fund)—International Monetary Fund—IMF
fonecon telephone conversation
FONEI Fondo Nacional de Equipamiento Industrial (Spanish—National Fund for Industrial Equipment)
fonet fonetica (Portuguese or Spanish—phonetics)
fonét fonética (Italian—phonetics)
F on F Facts-on-File
fono photograph
fonoff foreign office
Fons Alphonse; Fonseca
Fontanka Fontanka Canal linking Leninport with the main section of Leningrad and the Neva River
FONZ Friends of the National Zoo

fo° folio (Spanish—folio)
FOO Forward Observation Officer
foob (FOOB) firing out of the battery (artillery project)
fool's gold pyrites (copper, iron, tin, etc.)
Football Capital of the South Birmingham and New Orleans vie for this title as each supports a tremendous stadium
foot(s) footnote(s)
fop. forward observation post
f/op firing/observation port
FOP Fraternal Order of Police
fopt fiber-optics photon transfer
f.o.q. free on quay
for. foreign; foreigner; forensic; forest; forester; forestry; forint (Hungarian monetary unit); free on rail; free on road
f.o.r. free on rail
for (Latin prefix—opening)—foramen
For Formosa(n); Fornax
FOR Fellowship of Reconciliation; Final Outturn Report; Foundation for Ocean Research
forac for action
FORACS Fleet Operational Readiness Accuracy Check Site
forast formula assembler translator
FORATOM Forum Atomique Européen (French—European Atomic Forum)
for. bal forensic ballistics
FORBID Federatie van Organisaties op het gebied van Bibliotheek—Informatieen Dokumentatiewezen (Dutch—Federation of Organizations on Libraries, Information, and Documentation Services)
Forbidden City Lhasa, Tibet
Forbidden Kingdom Bhutan
forbloc fortran-compiled block-oriented (simulation programme)
for. bod foreign body
forcap forward combat air patrol
for & cc free of riots and civil commotion
for'd forward
FORD Families Opposed to Revolutionary Destruction; Fix Or Repair Daily; Found On the Road Dead
Fordham Flash Frank Frisch
Ford Madox Ford Ford Madox Hueffer
FORDS Floating Ocean Research and Development Sta-

tion

Fordtown Detroit, Michigan

'fore before

FORE Foundation of Record Education

fore 1/4s fore-quarters (meat cuts)

Forellen Quintet (see *Trout*)

foren forensic(ally); forensic medicine

Forensic Psychiatrist Richard von Krafft-Ebing

Forerunner of the Reformation John Huss who denounced the abuses of the Roman Catholic hierarchy and was burned at the stake

Forerunner of Spanish-American Independence Francisco Miranda

fores'l foresail

FOREST Freedom Organisation for the Right to Enjoy Smoking Tobacco

Forest Cantons Swiss cantons of Lucerne, Schwyz, Unterwalden, and Uri

Forest City Cleveland, Ohio and London, Ontario compete for this sobriquet

Forest of Forests forested belt stretching from northern Norway to eastern Siberia

FOREWAS Force and Weapon Analysis System

forf forfeit; forfeiture

forf *forfattare, författarinna* (Swedish—author, authoress)

förf *forfatter* (Dano-Norwegian —author)

forg forger; forgery; forging

Forget-Me-Not Alaska's state flower

Forgotten Philosopher Giordano Bruno (burned at the stake by the Holy Inquisition in 1600)

fork *forkortelse* (Dano-Norwegian—abbreviation); *forkortning* (Swedish—abbreviation)

fork. *forkortelse* (Danish—abbreviation)

for. lang foreign language(s)

form. format; formation; former(ly)

form *formiddag* (Dano-Norwegian—morning, before midday)

forma fortran matrix analysis

formac formula manipulation compiler

formal. formaldehyde; formalin

formalin HCHO

format. fortran matrix abstraction technique(s)

Former Naval Person code name of Prime Minister Churchill formerly First Lord of the Admiralty

For Min Foreign Minister; Minister of Foreign Affairs

formn foreman

Formosa Portuguese name for Taiwan

FORMS Federation of Rocky Mountain States

for'm'st foremast

formul formulary

Fornebu Oslo, Norway's airport

forpac forecasting passengers and cargo

For Pol *Foreign Policy*

forr *forretning* (Dano-Norwegian—business or store)

for'rd forward

for. rts foreign rights

Forsch *Forschung* (German—research)

FORSIC Forces Intelligence Center

forsk *forskellig* (Dano-Norwegian—different, distinct, unlike)

for's'l foresail

FORSTAT Force Status and Identity Report (USAF)

fort. fortification; fortify; fortnight(ly); fortress; full-out rye terms (grain trade)

fort. *fortis* (Latin—strong)

Fortaleza formerly Caerá

Fort Dimanche Haiti's infamous prison close to Pétionville

fortel formatted teletypewriter

Fort Frederica Fort Frederica National Monument on Saint Simon's Island off Brunswick, Georgia

Fort Hill John C Calhoun's country seat in the Pendleton district of South Carolina near Anderson

Fortieth State South Dakota

Fort Jeff Fort Jefferson National Monument on the Dry Tortugas in the Gulf of Mexico west-northwest of Key West

Fort Laramie Fort Laramie National Monument on the Oregon Trail in southeastern Wyoming

Fort Leavenworth U.S. Disciplinary Barracks at Fort Leavenworth, Kansas

Fort Liquordale Fort Lauderdale, Florida (when college students make their Easter vacation visit)

fortly fortnightly

Fort Matanzas Fort Matanzas National Monument near St

Augustine, Florida where it was built by the Spaniards in 1736

Fort McHenry Fort McHenry National Monument in Baltimore Harbor where the *Star Spangled Banner* was written

for. tox forensic toxicology

Fort Pulaski Fort Pulaski National Monument at the mouth of the Savannah River

fortran formula translation

For-Trans Ford Foundation Transfer Student Project

FORTRANS Formula Translating System

fortransit formula translator internal translator

Fort Riley U.S. Army Correctional Training Facility at Fort Riley, Kansas

forts *fortsaettelse* (Dano-Norwegian—continuation or sequel)

Forts *Fortsetzung* (German—continuation)

Fort Savage New York City's East Harlem police precinct

Fortschr Phys *Fortschritte der Physik* (German—Advances in Physics)

fortsim fortran simulation

Fort Sumter national monument in Charleston Harbor (South Carolina)—first shot of Civil War fell on this fort

fort. twn fortified town

Fortunate Island Monhegan, Maine

Fortunate Islands Canary Islands

Fortunate Isles Madeira Islands, according to the Portuguese but believed by the Spaniards to be the Canaries—also called Isles of the Blest in classical mythology;

Fortune **Five Hundred** *Fortune Magazine's* annual listing of the 500 leading corporations

Fort Union Fort Union National Monument near Santa Fe, New Mexico

Fort Worth Federal Correctional Institution at Fort Worth, Texas

Forty-eighth State Arizona

Forty-fifth State Utah

Forty-first State Montana

Forty-fourth State Wyoming

Forty Immortals collective nickname of the forty members of the French Academy

Forty-ninth State Alaska

Forty-second State Washington

Forty-seventh State New Mexico

Forty-sixth State Oklahoma

Forty-third State Idaho

forum. formula for optimizing through realtime utilization of multiprogramming

forwn forewoman

'forz sforzando (Italian—emphasized forcefully)

Forza La Forza del Destino (Italian—The Force of Destiny)—Verdi four-act opera

fos fossil; free on station; free on steamer; fuel-oxygen scrap; full of shit

fos (FOS) full operational status

f.o.s. free on station; free on steamer

fos (Dano-Norwegian—waterfall)

F-o-S Frinton-on-Sea

FOS File Organization System; Fisheries Organization Society; Fuel Oil Supply (company)

FOSATU Federation of South African Trade Unions

tosdic film optical sensing device for input to computers

fos fls fossil fuels (coal, natural gas, oil, etc.)

FOSG Factory Outlet Shopping Guide

FOSH Foshing (airlines)

FOSI Florida Ocean Sciences Institute

fosplan formal space-planning language

Foster Mother of the Sciences Medicine

fot free of tax(ation); free on truck; frequency optimum traffic; fuel-oil transfer

f.o.t. free on truck

fot fotographie (Dutch—photography)—plus all derivatives

FOT Fraternal Order of Police

fot & e follow-on test(ing) and evaluation

F o t L Friends of the Library

FOTM Friends of Old-Time Music

foto photograph(ic)

foto fotografia (Italian or Portuguese—photography); *fotografía* (Spanish—photography)—plus all derivatives in all three languages

Foto (Jewtongo—Fort)—native nickname for Paramaribo, Surinam

fotog fotografia (Italian or Portuguese—photography); *fotografía* (Spanish—photography)

fo'ty forty

found foundation; foundling; foundling; foundry

Found Econ Educ Foundation for Economic Education

Founder of Agnosticism Thomas Henry Huxley

Founder of Agricultural Chemistry Justus von Liebig

Founder of the American Federation of Labor Sam(uel) Gompers

Founder of American Military Intelligence General Ralph H Van Deman

Founder of the American Navy John Paul Jones

Founder of the Aniline Dye Industry Sir William Perkin

Founder of Antiseptic Surgery Lord Lister (Joseph Lister—first Baron Lister of Lyme Regis

Founder of Art History and Criticism Giorgio Vasari

Founder of Bacteriology Ferdinand Cohn

Founder of Behaviorism John Watson

Founder of the Birth Control Movement Margaret Sanger

Founder of Brazil Pedro Alvares Cabral

Founder of British Imperial India Robert Clive

Founder of Buddhism Prince Siddhartha (Gautama Buddah)

Founder of Buenos Aires Pedro de Mendoza

Founder of Cellular Pathology Rudolf Virchow

Founder of Chemistry Robert Boyle

Founder of Chicago Jean de Sable whose pioneer trading post at the portage between the Chicago and Des Plaines rivers became the site of present-day Chicago in 1775

Founder of Cleveland, Ohio Moses Cleaveland

Founder of the Columbia University School of Journalism Joseph Pulitzer

Founder of Comparative Anatomy Baron Georges Cuvier

Founder of Confucianism King Futzu (Confucius)

Founder of Conservative Surgery Sir William Fergusson

Founder of Continental Rationalism René Descartes

Founder of Cubism George Braque, Pablo Picasso, and others claim this title

Founder of Cybernetics Norbert Wiener

Founder of Electromagnetism Michael Faraday

Founder of Electrophysiology Emil du Bois Reymond

Founder of English Empiricism Sir Francis Bacon

Founder of Episcopalianism Henry VIII

Founder of Experimental Hygiene Max von Pettenkofer

Founder of the Faculty of Physicians and Surgeons of Glasgow Peter Lowe

Founder of Fauvism Henri Emile Benoit Matisse

Founder of French Grand Opera Daniel François Esprit Auber

Founder of French Opera Jean-Baptiste Lully

Founder of French Socialism Compte Claude Henri de Rouvroy de Saint-Simon

Founder of the Friends George Fox of Quaker fame

Founder of Functionalism Louis Sullivan

Founder of Georgia James Oglethorpe

Founder of Gestalt Therapy Fritz Perls

Founder of Histology Marcello Malpighi

Founder of Homeopathy Christian Friedrich Samuel Hahnemann

Founder of Humanistic Psychology Abraham Maslow

Founder of Hungary Arpad

Founder of Iconography and Physiologic Anatomy Leonardo da Vinci

Founder of Impressionism Claude Monet

Founder of Islam Mohammed

Founder of Jainism Mahavira also known as Vardhamana

Founder of Japanese Color-Print Making Iwasa Matabei

Founder of Judaism Moses

Founder of the Kelmscott Press William Morris

Founder of the Lutheran Church Martin Luther

Founder of Medical Statistics Pierre-Charles Alexander Louis

Founder of the Methodist Church John Wesley

Founder of Modern Astronomy Nicolaus Copernicus (Nikolaus Kopernicki)

Founder of Modern Chemistry Antoine Lauret Lavoisier

Founder of Modern Existentialism Sören Kierkegaard

Founder of Modern German Sculpture Johann Gottfried Schadow

Founder of Modern Military Medicine Sir John Pringle

Founder of Modern Philosophy René Descartes

Founder of Modern Sculpture Donatello (Donato di Niccolo di Betto Bardi)

Founder of Mormanism Joseph Smith who founded the Church of Jesus Christ of the Latter-Day Saints

Founder of Oklahoma Jean Pierre Chouteau

Founder of Optics Giovanni Battista della Porta

Founder of Pennsylvania William Penn

Founder of Phenomenology Edmund Husserl

Founder of Philosophic Radicalism James Mill

Founder of Positivism Auguste Compte

Founder of Postimpressionism Paul Cézanne

Founder of Pragmatism C(harles) S(anders) Peirce

Founder President of Zambia Kenneth Kaunda

Founder of Providence, Rhode Island Roger Williams

Founder of Psychoanalysis Sigmund Freud

Founder of Psychology Wilhelm Wundt

Founder of Québec Samuel de Champlain

Founder of the Religious Society of Friends Quaker leader George Fox

Founder of Rhode Island Roger Williams

Founder of Rome Romulus, according to legend

Founder of the Royal Navy Samuel Pepys

Founder of Russian Literature Alexander Pushkin

Founder of Salt Lake City Brigham Young

Founders of Christianity disciples of Jesus Christ regarded by many as a mythological character of doubtful historicity

Founder of the Science of Eugenics Sir Francis Galton

Founder of Scientific History Thucydides

Founder of Scottish Presbyterianism John Knox

Founders of Cubism Georges Braque and Pablo Picasso

Founder of Secularism George Holyoake who in 1846 gave it its name as an ethical system based on natural morality

Founders of Flemish Painting the van Eyck brothers— Hubrecht and Jan

Founders of French Romantic Painting Delacroix, Géricault, and Gros

Founders of the Hudson River School (of painting) Thomas Cole and Asher Brown Durand

Founder of Singapore Sir Thomas Stamford Raffles

Founders of Neo-Impressionism Georges Seurat and Paul Signac

Founder of Social Psychology Gustave Le Bon

Founder of Sociology Auguste Compte

Founders of Scientific Socialism Karl Marx and Friedrich Engels

Founder of State Socialism Louis Blanc

Founder of Taoism Lao-tse

Founder of Transcendentalism Ralph Waldo Emerson who believed in the mystical unity of nature

Founder of Troy Tros, according to Greek mythology, who was the father of Assaracus, Cleopatra, Ganymede, and Ilus

Founder of Unitarianism John Biddle

Founder of the University of Pennsylvania Benjamin Franklin

Founder of the University of Virginia Thomas Jefferson

Founder of Uruguay José Gervasio Artigas

Founder of the U.S. Navy Captain John Paul Jones

Founder of the Venetian School of Painting Giovanni Bellini

Founder of Vermont Ira Allen

Founder of Victimology Hans von Hentig or Benjamin Mendelsohn

Founder of Zoroastrianism Zoroaster also known as Zarathustra

Founding Father City Austin, Texas named in honor of Stephen F Austin

Founding Father of Israel David Ben-Gurion

Founding Fathers of Economics Adam Smith and David Ricardo

Founding Father of the Smith-sonian Joseph Henry

Founding Philosopher of Modern Capitalism Adam Smith

Found Phys Foundations of Physics

Foundress of Swarthmore College Martha Ellicott Tyson and a few concerned Friends

Foun Mot Dent Foundation for Motivation in Dentistry

fount fountain

Fountains The Fountains of Rome (Respighi's symphonic poem—*Fontane di Roma*)

Fountain of Youth St Augustine, Florida

Foun Than Foundation of Thanatology

FOUO For Official Use Only

Four-C City El Paso, Texas (famous for its cattle, climate, copper, and cotton)

Four Corners any highway or street intersection bearing this name; boundary-line junction of Arizona, Colorado, New Mexico, and Utah

Four Cs Community-Coordinated Child Care

four-dimensional science geology involving the application of biology, chemistry, mathematics, and physics

Four Forest Cantons Lucerne, Schwyz, Unterwalden, and Uri—all in Switzerland

Four H Four H (hand, head, heart, and health) Club (of boys and girls training in agriculture, development of rural leadership, and home economics)

Four Horsemen Four Horsemen of the Apocalypse (each mounted, respectively, on a white horse symbolizing pestilence, a red horse—war, a black horse—famine, a pale horse—death); title of a novel by Vicente Blasco Ibañez— *Los cuatro jinetes del Apocalipsis*

Four Lakes City Madison, Wisconsin

Four Mountains Islands of the Four Mountains

Four Seasons Antonio Vivaldi's concerto Le Quattro Staggioni

Four Seasons Crossroad of New England Manchester, New Hampshire

Fourteenth State Vermont

Four Temperaments Nielsen's Symphony No. 2

Fourth Bureau Red Army bureau in charge of overseas intelligence-gathering activities of the Soviet Union

Fourth Estate The Media—press, radio, television

Fourth Gospel Gospel according to Saint John

Fourth International Trotsky-oriented organization rejecting the Second and Third Internationals in the direction of the class struggle

Fourth State Georgia (*see* First State)

Fourth World very poorest of the Third World nations

Four Winds Boreas (north), Eurus (east), Notus (south), Zephyrus (west)

FOUSA Finance Office(r), United States Army

fov field of view

fov (FOV) flyable orbital vehicle

fow first open water; free on wagon; free on warehouse; free on wharf

f.o.w. first open water (shipping term); free on wagon

Foxardo (naval argot—Fajardo, Puerto Rico)

Foxes Fox Islands off southwestern tip of Alaska

Fox Populi Charles James Fox

Foxtrot letter F radio code

Foy Fowey

fp factory pass; family plan(ning); fast peak; field punishment; film pack; fine paper; fire plug; fire policy; fireplace; first performance; first performed; first proof; fix point; fixed price; flameproof(ed); flash point; flat pad(ded); flat pattern; flat point(ed); flight pay; flight plan; floating (open) policy; flower people; focal plane; food poisoning; foot path; foot pound(s); forward perpendicular; free piston; freezing point; fresh paragraph; frontispiece; full page; full point; full price; fully paid

fp (FP) family practitioner; flavoprotein

f/p flat pattern

f.p. *fiat potio* (Latin—make a potion)

FP Federal Parliament; Ferrocarril del Pacífico (Pacific Railroad); former pupil; Franklin Pierce (14th President U.S.)

F/P Fire Policy (insurance)

FP *Freiheitliche Partei* (German

—Freedom Party)—Austrian party with neo-Nazi orientation

fp4c full page four colors

fpa fluorescent pen aerosol; free of particular average

FPA Family Planning Association; Federal Preparedness Agency; Federation of Motion Picture Producers in Asia; Flexible Packaging Association; Flying Physicians Association; Foreign Policy Association; Forest Products Association; Franklin Pierce Adams; Free Pacific Association; Freemantle Port Authority; Freethought Press Association

fpaa free from particular average, absolutely

FPAA Family Planning Association of Australia

fpaAc free of particular average, American conditions

FPAD Fund for Peaceful Atomic Development

fpaEc free of particular average, English conditions

fpaf fixed-price award fee

FPAS Federal Property and Administrative Services; Fellow of the Pakistan Academy of Sciences

FPASA Federal Property and Administrative Services Act

FPAT Family Planning Association of Tasmania

fpaucb free from particular average unless caused by (stranding, etc.)

FPB fast patrol boat (USN)

FPBA Folding Paper Box Association

FPBAI Fellow of the Publishers' and Booksellers' Associations in India

FPBG fast patrol boat, guided-missile (USN)

FPBRS Fels Parent Behavior Rating Scale(s)

fpc fish protein concentrate; fixed price contract; fixed-price call; flat plate (solar) collector(s); flight progress chart; full-page color (ad); for private circulation

FPC Facility Power Control; Family Planning Center; fast patrol craft; Federal Pacific Electric (stock exchange symbol); Federal Power Commission; Federal Prison Camp; Fiji Pine Commission; Food Packaging Council; Friends Peace Committee; Frozen Pea

Council

FPCA Federal Post Card Application (for absentee ballot)

fpcc flight propulsion-control coupling

FPCC Fair Play for Cuba Committee

FPCE Fission Products Conversion and Encapsulation (AEC plant)

FPCI Federal Penal and Correctional Institutions

FPCS Fire Power Control Subsystem; Full-Page Composition System

FPD Federal Public Defender

FPD *Fundación Panamericana de Desarrollo* (Pan-American Development Foundation)

FPDA Finnish Plywood Development Association; Five-Power Defence Arrangement (Malaysian)

fpdi flight path deviation indicator

FPDO Federal Public Defender Organization(s)

fne fixed price with escalation

FPE Foundation for Personality Expression; Full Personality Expression

FPEB Family Planning Evaluation Branch (USPHS)

FPEBT Fire Prevention and Engineering Bureau of Texas

fpec four-pile-extended cantilever (platform)

FPED Farm Production Economics Division (USDA)

FPF French Protestant Federation

fph feet per hour (oil well drilling)

FPH Federal Pacific Hotels (Australian)

FPHA Federal Public Housing Authority

F Pharm S Fellow of the Pharmaceutical Society

fphs fallout protection in homes

F Ph S Fellow of the Philosophical Society

F Phy S Fellow of the Physical Society

fpi faded prior to interception; family pitch in; fixed price incentive

FPI Federal Prison Industries; Fellow of the Plastics Institute

FPI *Fédération Prohibitionniste Internationale* (French—International Prohibitionist Federation)

fpif fixed-price-incentive firm

fpil full premium if lost

f. pil. *fiat pilulae* (Latin—make pills)

fpis fixed-price incentive successive; forward propagation ionosphere scatter

FPJMC Four-Power Joint Military Commission

fpl final protective line; fire plug; fireplace

FPL Family Protection Law; Florida Power and Light; Forest Products Laboratory

FPL *Fuerzas Populares de Liberación* (Spanish—Popular Forces of Liberation)—El Salvador

FPLA Fair Packaging and Labelling Act

fplce fireplace

fpm facility power monitor; feet per minute; fissions per minute; frequency pulse modulation

FPML Forest Products Marketing Laboratory

FPMR Federal Property Management Regulation(s)

FPMSA Food Processing Machinery and Supplies Association

FPMT Filter Paper Microscopic Test

FPNM Fort Pulaski National Monument

fpo fixed price open

FPO Field Post Office; Field Project Office; Fleet Post Office; Fleet Postal Organization

FPOA Federal Probation Officers Association

fpoe first port of entry

fpoh food prepared outside the home

FPOP Family Planning Organization of the Philippines

fpp facility power panel; fixed-pitch propeller; floating-point processor; forward(ing) parcel(s) post

FPP Family Planning Program; Foster Parents Plan; Foster Parents Program; Friendly Peoples Proviso

FPPB Family Planning and Population Board (Singapore)

FPPC Fair Political Practices Commission

fppe fluorescent pen-post emulsified

FPPS Flight Plan Processing System; Full-Page Phototypesetting System

fpr feet per revolution; fixed price redeterminable; flat-

plate radiometer; forward parcels rail

FPR Factory Problem Report; Field Personnel Record

FPRC Fair Play for Rhodesia Committee

fprf fireproof

FPRI Foreign Policy Research Institute (University of Pennsylvania)

FPRL Forest Products Research Laboratory

FPRS Forest Products Research Society

fps feet per second; focus projection and scanning; foot per second; foot-pound-second; frames per second

f'ps former priests

FPs Flying Physicians; Flying Psychologists

FPS Farm Placement Service; Fauna Preservation Society; Federal Protection Service; Fellow of the Pharmaceutical Society; Fellow of the Philharmonic Society; Fellow of Philological Society; Fellow of the Philosophical Society; Fence Protection System; Financial Planning System; Fire Protection System; Fluid Power Society

FPSA Fellow of the Photographic Society of America

FPSAA Federated Public Service Assistants Association

FPSE Federation of Public Service Employees

FPSL Fellow of the Physical Society of London

FPSO Fleet Publication Supply Office

fpsps feet per second per second

fpt female pipe thread; fixed price tenders; forepeak tank; full power trial

FPT Flight Proof Test(ing); Four Picture Test

fptm fluorescent pen-tank method

fpts forward propagation tropospheric scatter

FPTU Federation of Progressive Trade Unions

fpu field pickup unit

FPU Food Preservers Union

fpv fixed-price vendor

FPWA Federation of Professional Writers of America

fq fiscal quarter

FQ French Quarter (New Orleans)

fqawt flush quick-acting watertight

fqcy frequency

FQL Food Quality Laboratory

FQO Federation of Quarry Owners

FQS Federal Quarantine Service

fr family room; fast release (relay); father; field relay; fire retardant; fixed response; flight request; flow rate; frame; franc; frequent; from; front; fruit

f/r fixed response; flat rack; freight release; front to rear

f & r feed and return (plumbing); force and rhythm (pulse)

fr *franco* (Spanish—franc); *franc(s)* or *fransk* [Dano-Norwegian—franc(s) or French]

fr. *folio recto* (Latin—front of the sheet)

Fr France; francium; Franco-; Franklin; Frau (German—Missus); French; Friday; Friesian(s); Frisian(s); Froude number

F/r restricted first-class (travel)

Fr *Frau* (German—Misses); *Fray* (Spanish—Friar); *Fredag* (Danish—Friday); French (Romance language spoken by 87 million people in France and its former or present overseas colonies scattered around the world, including French-speaking Canada, mainly Québec)

FR Facilities Request; Feather River (railroad); Federal Reformatory; Federal Register; Federal Reserve; Field Report; fighter reconnaissance (aircraft); Final Report; Fireman Recruit; flash red—enemy aircraft nearby; Fleet Reserve; Freight Release; Friden (stock exchange symbol)

F of R Fellowship of Reconciliation

FR *Federal Register*

F.R. *Forum Romanum* (Latin—Roman Forum)

FR-172 French-built four-place rocket-launching counterinsurgency aircraft

fra forward refueling area; functional residual air

fra *factura* (Spanish—invoice)

Fra Francis

Fra *Francia* (Spanish—France)

Fra. *frater* (Latin—brother, monk)

FRA Federal Railroad Administration; Fleet Reserve Association; Food Retailers Association; Footwear Research Association; Frankfurt-am-Main (airport)

Fra Angelico Giovanni da Fiesole

Fra Bartolommeo Baccio della Porta

frac frationator reflux analog computer

FRAC Food Research and Action Center

FRACA Failure Reporting, Analysis, and Corrective Action

FRAC Arts Foundation for Research in the Afro-American Creative Arts

FRACHE Federation of Regional Accrediting Commissions of Higher Education

FRACI Fellow of the Royal Australian Chemical Institute

FRACP Fellow of the Royal Australian College of Physicians

FRACS Fellow of the Royal Australian College of Surgeons

fract fraction; fracture

fract. dos. *fracta dosi* (Latin—in divided doses)

FRAD Fellow of the Royal Academy of Dancing

Fra Diavolo Michele Pezza (an Italian brigand formerly Fra Angelo)—leading character in Auber's opera *Fra Diavolo*

Fra Elbertus Elbert Hubbard

FRAeS Fellow of the Royal Aeronautical Society

frag fragile; fragment; fragmentary; fragmentation; fragmented

frago fragmentary order; fragmented order

Fragrant Harbor Hong Kong

FRAgS Fellow of the Royal Agricultural Societies

FRAHS Fellow of the Royal Australian Historical Society

FRAI Fellow of the Royal Anthropological Institute

FRAIA Fellow of the Royal Australian Institute of Architects

FRAIC Fellow of the Royal Architectural Institute of Canada

'fraid afraid

FRAM Fellow of the Royal Academy of Music; Fleet Rehabilitation and Maintenance (USN)

FRAME Fund for the Replacement of Animals in Medical Research

Framer of the *Declaration of In-*

dependence Thomas Jefferson who rewrote Thomas Paine's first rough draft with the aid of John Adams and Benjamin Franklin

Framingham Massachusetts Correctional Institution (for female felons) at Framingham, Massachusetts

fran framed-structure analysis; franchise

Fran Frances; Francis; Franciscan

França (Portuguese—France)

France French Republic (French-speaking western European nation exerting tremendous cultural and economic impact on its neighbors as well as overseas dominions and former colonies), *République Française*

Frances Alda Frances Davis

Francesca Francesca da Rimini (Tchaikowsky symphonic fantasia, Zandonai four act opera)

France's Largest Port Marseille

Franche-Compté Burgundy

Francia (Italian or Spanish—France)

Francine Frances

Francis Beeding John Leslie Palmer's pseudonym

Franciscan Wine Capital Würzburg, Germany

Franck symphony Cesar Franck's Symphony in D

Franco Francisco Paulino Hermenegildo Teodulo Franco-Bahamonde—Spanish dictator

Franco Francisco (Spanish—Francis)

Francofurtum ad Moenum (Lat in—Frankfurt-am-Main)—German printing and publishing center on the Main River about 250 miles or 400 kilometers southwest of Berlin

Francofurtum ad Oderam (Latin —Frankfurt-an-der-Oder)—German city on the Oder River about 50 miles or 80 kilometers southeast of Berlin

Franco-Hispanic Co-Principality Andorra (in the Pyrenees between France and Spain)

Francoise Sagan (pseudonym—Françoise Quoirez)

François Villon François de Montcorbier

Francophone Africa Afars and Issas, Algeria, Burundi, Cameroon, Central African Republic, Chad, Congo, Dahomey,

Gabon, Guinea, Ivory Coast, Madagascar, Mali, Mauritania, Mauritius, Niger, Reunion, Rwanda, Senegal, Seychelles, Togo, Tunisia, Upper Volta, Zaire

Francophone America French Guiana; Guadeloupe; Haiti; coastal parishes of Louisiana; Martinique; some places in northern New York, Vermont, New Hampshire, Maine, and New Brunswick close to Québec; Québec; St Pierre and Miquelon; Asia: Cambodia, Laos, Vietnam

Francophone Europe Andorra; French-speaking parts of Belgium, France, Luxembourg, Monaco; French-speaking cantons of Switzerland

Francophone Pacific French Polynesia, New Caldonia, New Hebrides, Wallis and Fatuna Islands

Francophone Province Québec

frangi(s) frangipani(s)

Franglais *francais* + *anglais* (French + English)—English-filled French heard around airports, travel agencies, and many French resorts visited by American and British travelers

Fran-Jud Franco-Judeo (French Jewish)

Frank Frank; Frankford; Frankfort; Frankfurt; Frankish; Franklin

Frankfort Kentucky's capital

Frankfurt-am-Main (Dutch or German—Frankfurt-on-Main)—airline, printing, and publishing center on the River Main about 250 miles or 400 kilometers southwest of Berlin

Frankfurt-an-der-Oder German city on the Oder River about 50 miles or 80 kilometers southeast of Berlin

Frank Leslie business name of Henry Carter

franklinite ferric iron and zinc crystalline compound

Frankreich (German—France)

Frank Richards Charles Hamilton's pen name

Frankrijk (Dutch—France)

Frankrike (Dano-Norwegian or Swedish—France)

frank(s) frankfurter(s)

Frans Francis

Frans (Dutch—French)

Franz Josef Land Arctic islands called Zemlya Frantsa Iosifa by the Russians

FRAP Fellow of the Royal Academy of Physicians

FRAP Frente Revolucionario de Acción Popular (Spanish—Revolutionary Popular Action Front)—Chile

FRAPS Farm Record Analysis Pilot Scheme

Fras Francis

FRAS Fellow of the Royal Asiatic Society; Fellow of the Royal Astronomical Society

Frasca Francesca

Frasco Francisco

frat fraternity

frat fratello (Italian—brother)

FRAT Free Radical Assay Technique (heroin-morphine test)

FRATADD Foundation for Research and Treatment of Alcoholism and Drug Dependence (Australian)

frate formula for routes and technical equipment

frater fraternity brother

fratting fraternizing

fraud. fraudulent

frav first available

Fraxi Pisanus Fraxi (Herbert Specer Ashbee)

FRB Federal Reserve Bank; Federal Reserve Board; Fisheries Research Board

frbb fracture of both bones; free room, board, and beverages

FRBC Fisheries Research Board of Canada

fr bel from below

FRBk Federal Reserve Bank

FRBNY Federal Reserve Bank of New York

FRBs Federal Reserve Banks

FRBS Fellow of the Royal Botanic Society; Fellow of the Royal Society of British Sculptors

frc fiber-reinforced concrete; functional residual capacity

FRC Facility Review Committee; Fasteners Research Council; Federal Radiation Council; Federal Radio Commission; Federal Records Center; Federal Republic of Cameroon; Filipino Rehabilitation Commission; Flight Research Center; Foreign Relations Committee; Foreign Relations Council; Forwarder's Receipt Certificate; Fuels Research Council

FRCA Fellow of the Royal College of Art

FRC—AAP Freedom-to-Read Committee—Association of American Publishers

Fr-Can French-Canadian

FRCAT Fellow of the Royal College of Advanced Technology

fr & cc free of riots and civil commotion

FRCD Fellow of the Royal College of Dentists

frcd's floating-rate certificates of deposit

FRCGP Fellow of the Royal College of General Practitioners

FRCI Fellow of the Royal Colonial Institute

FRCM Fellow of the Royal College of Music

FRCO Fellow of the Royal College of Organists

FRCOG Fellow of the Royal College of Obstetricians and Gynaecologists

FRCP Federal Rules of Civil Procedure; Fellow of the Royal College of Physicians

FRCPath Fellow of the Royal College of Pathologists

FRCP(C) Fellow of the Royal College of Physicians of Canada

FRCPE Fellow of the Royal College of Physicians of Edinburgh

FRCPGlas Fellow of the Royal College of Physicians of Glasgow

FRCPI Fellow of the Royal College of Physicians of Ireland

FRCP Lond Fellow of the Royal College of Physicians of London

FRCPSG Fellow of the Royal College of Physicians and Surgeons of Glasgow

FRC Psych Fellow of the Royal College of Psychiatrists

FRCR Fellow of the Royal College of Radiologists

FRCrP Federal Rules of Criminal Procedure

FRCs Federal Regional Councils

FRCS Fellow of the Royal College of Surgeons

FRCSc Fellow of the Royal College of Science

FRCS(C) Fellow of the Royal College of Surgeons of Canada

FRCSE Fellow of the Royal College of Surgeons of Edinbrugh

FRCSGlas Fellow of the Royal College of Surgeons of Glas-gow

FRCSI Fellow of the Royal College of Surgeons of Ireland

FRCSL Fellow of the Royal College of Surgeons of London

FRCTS Fast Reactor Core Test Facility

FRCVS Fellow of the Royal College of Veterinary Surgeons

frd formerly restricted data; friend; friendly

Frd Ford (postal abbreviation)

FRD Federal Rules Decisions

FR Dist Federal Reserve District

Frdn Friedenau

fre free energy region

fre fracture (French—invoice)

Fre Freemantle; French

Fre Freitag (German—Friday)

FRE Federal Rules of Evidence

FREB Federal Real Estate Bord

FR Econ S Fellow of the Royal Economic Society

FR Econ Soc Fellow of the Royal Economic Society

fred figure-reader electronic device

Fred Alfred; Alfredo; Freddie; Frederic; Frederick; Fredric; Fredrick; Wilfred

Freda Winifred

Fred Alan John Sullivan

Fred Astaire Frederick Austerlitz

Fred(die) Frederica; Fredrica

Freddie Mac Federal Home Loan Mortgage Corporation

Fred(dy) Alfred; Frederick; Wilfred

Frederick Douglass Frederick Augustus Washington Bailey

Frederick the Great Frederick II of Prussia

Frederic March Frederich McIntyre Bickel

Fredk Frederick

Fredk D Frederick Douglass

Fred Niblo Frederico Nobile

Fredo Alfredo

Free Freeway

FREE Florida Resources in Education Exchange

freebd freeboard

freebies free services; free things; free tickets

Freedman's Bureau Bureau of Refugees, Freedmen, and Abandoned Lands (set up after the Civil War in the United States)

Freedom Defender U.S. Supreme Court Justice William

O. Douglas

Freedom Fighter former name of the Northrup Tiger II or F-5 tactical fighter plane

Free and Hanseatic City Hamburg

Free Lib Phila Free Library of Philadelphia

Freep *Free Press* (Los Angeles underground newspaper)

Free State Maryland whose constitution guarantees religious freedom—the right to believe or to disbelieve, to worship or not to worship

Freestone State Connecticut with its many freestone quarries

Freethinker American President sobriquet shared by George Washington, John Adams, Thomas Jefferson, James Madison, John Quincy Adams, Abraham Lincoln, Andrew Johnson, Ulysses Simpson Grant, James Abram Garfield, Theodore Roosevelt, William Howard Taft

Freethinker American Statesman eponym shared by Benjamin Franklin and Henry Clay

Freethinker Anthropologist Franz Boas, Earnest Albert Hooten, Ales Hrdlicka, and Margaret Mead are the first of many who come to mind

Freethinker Astronomer Simon Newcomb and Carl Sagan follow in the footsteps of Tycho Brahe, Nicolaus Copernicus, and Galileo Galilei

Freethinker Author-Editor-Translator Max Forrester Eastman

Freethinker Bacteriologist Hans Zinsser

Freethinker Biochemist Isaac Asimov

Freethinker Biographer Joseph Lewis

Freethinker Botanist Luther Burbank and George Washington Carver are but two of many freethinker botanists of distinction

Freethinker of Canada Marshall Jerome Gauvin

Freethinker Composer Charles Ives, Maurice Ravel, and Dmitri Shostakovich are outstanding but readers will think of others

Freethinker Conservationist John Burroughs, William

Temple Hornaday, John Muir, Henry David Thoreau and many others will come to the reader's mind

Freethinker Dramatist-Critic George Bernard Shaw

Freethinker Economist and Novelist Harriet Martineau

Freethinker Editor, Printer, and Writer Elbert G(reen) Hubbard

Freethinker Editor, Satirist, and Scholar H(enry) L(ouis) Mencken

Freethinker Educator title shared by Mortimer Adler, Nicholas Murray Butler, John Dewey, and many other educators

Freethinker Educator-Historian-Sociologist Harry Elmer Barnes

Freethinker Electrical Engineer Charles Proteus Steinmetz and Nikola Tesla were among the most outstanding

Freethinker Encyclopedists in France Jean le Rond d'Alembert, Denis Diderot, Charles Montesquieu, Francois Quesnay, Jean Jacques Rousseau, Anne Robert Jacques Turgot, and Voltaire are outstanding

Freethinker Essayist-Physician-Poet-Novelist Oliver Wendell Holmes

Freethinker Essayist-Poet Philosopher Ralph Waldo Emerson

Freethinker Evolutionist Julian Huxley and his grandfather Thomas Henry Huxley

Freethinker Explorer William Beebe, Jacques Costeau, Alexander von Humboldt, and many others share this title

Freethinker Fabians Beatrice and Sidney Webb

Freethinker Family Planner Margaret Sanger—founder of the American Birth Control League

Freethinker Geologist Sir Charles Lyell

Freethinker Herpetologist-Mammalogist Raymond L(ee) Ditmars

Freethinker Historian David Hume and many more such as Will and Ariel Durant, Harry Allen Overstreet, John Eleazer Remsburg, James Harvey Robinson, Hendrik Willem van Loon

Freethinker Horticulturalist

Luther Burbank

Freethinker-Humorist-Philosopher-Television Teacher Steve Allen

Freethinker Ichthyologist Eugene Willis Gudger and David Starr Jordan were well regarded for their outspoken views and their scholarship

Freethinker Inventor Thomas Edison

Freethinker Inventor-Printer-Philosopher-Scientist Benjamin Franklin

Freethinker Lawyer Clarence Darrow, Josiah Quincy, and Samuel Untermeyer come to mind but there are certainly others here and abroad

Freethinker Libertarian Patriot names such as Ethan Allen, Patrick Henry, and John Paul Jones come to mind

Freethinker Libertarian-Patriot-Pamphleteer Thomas Paine

Freethinker Literary Critic Georg Morris Cohen Brandes and Edmund Wilson are but two of many who could deserve the title

Freethinker Mathematician-Philosopher Bertrand Russell

Freethinker Naturalist-Philosopher Henry David Thoreau

Freethinker Novelist Ambrose Bierce, Aldous Huxley, George Orwell, Edgar Allan Poe, Upton Sinclair, Mark Twain, H(enry) G(eorge) Wells, Thornton Wilder, Émile Zolá, and many more readers will recall

Freethinker Novelist-Journalist James T(homas) Farrell

Freethinker Orator Robert Green Ingersoll

Freethinker Orator-Reformer Frances (Fanny) Wright

Freethinker Paleontologist William King Gregory

Freethinker Pathologist Simon Flexner and Hideyo Noguchi could compete for the title and readers will be sure to think of others

Freethinker Philanthropist Andrew Carnegie, Peter Cooper, Stephen Girard, and James Lick are foremost among Americans in this rank

Freethinker Philosopher title shared by Socrates, Epicurus, Lucretius, John Stuart Mill, Thomas Hobbes, John Locke, Benjamin Franklin, Thomas

Paine, Ralph Waldo Emerson, Karl Marx, Robert Green Ingersoll, Friedrich Nietzsche, William James, George Santayana, John Dewey, Bertrand Russell, Will and Ariel Durant, Mortimer Jerome Adler, and other eminent thinkers better known to other readers

Freethinker Philosopher-Poet many would nominate Ralph Waldo Emerson and Friedrich Wilhelm Nietzsche

Freethinker Physician Jonas E(dward) Salk and Benjamin M(cLane) Spock are outstanding contemporary contenders for this title

Freethinker Physicist Albert Einstein

Freethinker Physicist-Chemist Marie Sklodowska Curie

Freethinker Physiologist Anton Julius Carlson

Freethinker Poet title shared by many such as George Gordon Byron, Leigh Hunt, Rudyard Kipling, Edgar Lee Masters, Edgar Allan Poe, Percy Bysshe Shelley, Walt Whitman

Freethinker Political Reformer Charles Bradlaugh who championed a bill now law permitting Members of the House of Commons to affirm rather than swear on the Bible

Freethinker Psychologist Havelock Ellis (*Studies in the Psychology of Sex*) is the most outstanding in the author's opinion but readers will recall many others

Freethinker Publisher and Writer Emanuel Haldeman-Julius

Freethinker Quaker Minister Lucretia Mott

Freethinker Rationalist Philosopher Joseph McCabe

Freethinker Researcher Walter Reed

Freethinker Sanitarian William Crawford Gorgas

Freethinker Satirist Voltaire

Freethinker Senator Henry Clay

Freethinker Suffragette Susan Brownell Anthony and Elizabeth Cady Stanton share this title dating from 1848 when they organized the first women's rights convention

Freethinker Zoologist many come to mind including Charles Darwin, Ernst Heinrich Haeckel, Willard Gibbs Van Name, Alfred Russel Wallace

Freethought Author and Publisher E(manuel) Haldeman-Julius whose *Little Blue Books* sold for 5¢ a copy

freeture freedom, the wave of the future

freeway toll-free express highway

Freeway City Los Angeles bisected and surrounded by automotive freeways also known as smogways

freeworld countries living in freedom and not under communist, fascist, military, or other totalitarian domination

FREI Fellow of the Real Estate Institute

Freib Freiburg (Germany)

Freiburg (German—Fribourg)

FRELIMO *Frente de Libertação de Moçambique* (Portuguese—Mozambique Liberation Front)

FRELP Flexible Real Estate Loan Plan

Frem Fremantle

Fremantle Perth, Australia's port

frem. voc. fremitus vocalis (Latin —vocal fremitus)

french french bread (usually baked in long and heavily-crusted loaves); french bull (small breed of bulldog); french chalk (tailor's talc); french cuff (wide cuff made of folded cloth held by a cufflink); french curve (drafting instrument); french door (largely glass casement door); french dressing (salad oil, spice, and vinegar mixture); french endive (blanched chicory); french fries (french-fried potatoes); french harp (harmonica); french heel (high curved heel); french horn (brass instrument); french ice cream (made with cream and eggs); french kiss (tongue kiss also called soul kiss); french pancake (thin and sweet); french pastry (whipped cream or fruit-filled pastry); french polish (alcohol + shellac); french pox (syphilis); french roll (women's coiffure); french roof (mansard-style roof); french seam (completely covered seam); french system (spinning system); french tamarisk (salt cedar); french telephone (handle unites receiver and speaker); french toast

(bread dipped in egg batter and well toasted before serving with syrup)

French Antilles French West Indies

French Canada French-speaking Canada but mainly the Province of Québec

French-Canadian Conductor Sir Wilfred Pelletier

French-Canadian Freethinker Marshall Jerome Gauvin (1881-1978)

French Caribees colonial name for the French West Indies

French Century the 18th century–the 1700s

French Community metropolitan France together with its overseas departments, territories, and former territories (*Communauté française*)

French disease pejorative nickname for syphilis also known as the Italian disease or the Spanish disease as well as *morbus gallicus* (Latin—Gallic disease)—the French disease

French Dozen France's twelve best-known classical composers arranged chronologically— Lully, Couperin, Rameau, Berlioz, Gounod, Offenbach, Saint-Saëns, Bizet, Massenet, Debussy, Ravel, Milhaud

French Equatorial Africa former colonies of France such as Benin or Dahomey, Cameroon, the Central African Empire, the French Congo, Gabon, and Guinea

french fries french fried potatoes

French Guiana South America's only French-speaking country known officially as *Guyane française* and also referred to by the name of its capital— Cayenne

French India former French possessions in India (Chandernagore, Pondicherry, etc.)

French Indo-China former name of area comprising Annam, Cambodia, Chochin China, Laos, Tonkin, and Vietnam

French Morocco eastern Morocco closest to Algeria and the Sahara when under French control

French Polynesia French island possessions in the South Seas where the official name is Polynésie Française

French Ports (large, medium, and small from the north to the south) Dunkerque, Calais, Boulogne-sur-Mer; Le Treport, Dieppe, Fecamp, Le Havre, Rouen, Cherbourg, Granville, St Malo, Brest, Douarnenez, Aupierne, Port Louis, Lorient, Le Palais, Le Croisic, Saint Nazaire, Donges, Paimboeuf, Basse-Indre, Les Asables Dolonne, La Pallice, La Rochelle, Rochefort, Tonnay-Charente, Le Verdon, Mortagne, Trompeloup, Paulillac, Blaye, Ambes, Le Marquis, Bordeaux, Arcachon, Boucau, Bayonne, Biarritz, (*and on the south coast from west to east*) Port Vendres, Port La Nouvelle, Sete, Port St Louis du Rho, Port de Bouc, Berre Letang, Marseille, La Ciotat, Toulon, Cannes, Nice, Villefranche, Bastia and Ajaccio (on Corsica), Menton

French Quarter Vieux Carré in New Orleans

French Revolutionary Calendar (see *Vend, Brum, Frim, Niv, Pluv, Vent, Germ, Flor, Prair, Mess, Therm, Fruc.* entries)

French Riviera resort areas along the Mediterranean from Marseilles to Menton, including Cannes, Monaco, and Nice

French Sahara former colonial areas such as the desert portions of Algeria, French Morocco, Mauritania, and Niger

French Shore Newfoundland's northern and western coasts where the French have certain fishing rights

French Somaliland *Côte Française des Somalis* (French Coast of the Somalis)—now known as Djibouti

French-speaking Places (*see entries under* Francophone)

French Sudan former name of Mali when it was a colony of France later known as the Sudanese Republic

French Switzerland French-speaking areas of Switzerland

French Togoland former name of Togo after World War I when it was ceded by Germany

French Union France plus its overseas colonies and departments as well as all its former possessions

French West Africa former colonies of France such as Alger-

ia, Chad, French Morocco, Mali, Mauritania, Niger, Senegal, and Upper Volta

French West Indies Desirade, Guadeloupe, Les Saintes, Marie Galante, Martinique, Petite Terre, Saint Bartholomew (Barthelemy), Saint Martin (French half of that island)

Frenglish frenchified English

FREntS Fellow of the Royal Entomological Society

freon tf trifluorotrichloroethane (solvent)

FREP Fleet Return Evaluation Program

freq frequency; frequent; frequentative; frequently

FrEqAfr French Equatorial Africa

freq m frequency meter

fres fire-resistant

fres frères (French brothers)

FRES Fellow of the Royal Entomological Society

frescanar frequency scan radar

fresh. freshman; freshmen

Freud. Freudian

frev fast reverse

frf flight-readiness firing; frequency response function

fr-f french-fried (potatoes)

FRF Fringe Reduction Facility

FRFPS Fellow of the Royal Faculty of Physicians and Surgeons

Frf(s) French franc(s)

FRFS Fast Reaction Fighting System

Frg Forge (postal abbreviation)

FrG Federal Republic of Germany (West Germany)

FRG Facility Review Group; Federal Republic of Germany (West Germany)

FRGS Fellow of the Royal Geographical Society

frgt freight

FRHB Federation of Registered House Builders

frhgt free height

FR Hist S Fellow of the Royal Historical Society

FR Hort S Fellow of the Royal Horticultural Society

Fr hr French horn

Frhr Freiherr (German—Baron)

Fr hrn French horn

FRHS Fellow of the Royal Horticultural Society

fri feeling rough inside

Fri Friday

FRI Fellow of the Royal Institution; Fels Research Institute;

Forest Research Institute; Friends of Rhodesian Independence

FRIA Fellow of the Royal Irish Academy

FRIAI Fellow of the Royal Institution of Architects of Ireland

Friar Antonio Agapida pseudonym of Washington Irving

FRIAS Fellow of the Royal Incorporation or Architects of Scotland

Frib Fribourgh (Switzerland)

FRIBA Fellow of the Royal Institute of British Architects

fric frication; fricative; fricatruce; fricatrix; friction; frictional

FRIC Fellow of the Royal Institute of Chemistry

Frick Frick Collection (New York City)

FRICS Fellow of the Royal Institution of Chartered Surveyors

frict friction

fridg frigidaire (refrigerator)

fridge(s) refrigerator(s)

Fridjof Nansen Land formerly Franz Josef Land (Arctic island group in Queen Victoria Sea north of Barents Sea sector of Arctic Ocean)

Friedrh Friedrichshafen

Fried Test Friedman Test (for pregnancy)

Friend of the American Revolution Caron de Beaumarchais

Friend of Helpless Children Herbert Clark Hoover—thirty-first President of the United States

Friendliest Town in the West Geraldton, Western Australia

Friendly Island Molokai, Hawaii in the North Pacific; St Maarten, Netherlands Antilles

Friendly Islands Tonga Islands in the South Pacific

Friendly Kingdom Tonga Islands

Friends Society of Friends (Quakers)

Friends Meet Friends Meeting

Fries Friesic

Friesn Friesian (cattle, language, or people)

frig refrigerator

frig. frigidus (Latin—cold)

FRIGS Fellow of the Royal Imperial Geographical Society

FRIIA Fellow of the Royal Institution of International Affairs

Frim Frimaire (French—Sleety Month)—beginning November 21st—third month of the French Revolutionary Calendar

FRINA Fellow of the Royal Institution of Naval Architects

fringe. file-and-report information-processing generator

Fringlish French + English (English interlarded with French expressions and words)

fring(s) french onion ring(s)

f'r instance for instance

FRIPA Fellow of the Royal Institution of Public Administration

FRIPHH Fellow of the Royal Institute of Public Health and Hygiene

Fris Friesland; Frisia; Frisian

frisco fast-reaction integrated submarine control

Frisco (navalese—San Francisco)—but no San Franciscan will use this nickname

FRISCO St. Louis-San Francisco Railway

Frisco Bay (sailor's slang—San Francisco Bay)

Frisia (Latin—Friesland)—in the Netherlands

Frisians Frisian islanders or the Frisian Islands in the North Sea where they are under Dutch, German, or Danish control as some belong to the Netherlands, to Germany, and to Denmark

Fritalux France, Italy, and Benelux nations

frits fritters

Fritz Friedrich

frjm full-range joint movement

frk fröken (Swedish—Miss)

Frk Fork (postal abbreviation); Frankfort

Frk Froken (Dano-Norwegian—Miss)

Frks Forks (postal abbreviation)

frl fractional; fuselage reference line

Frl El Ferrol

Frl Fräulein (German—Miss)

FRL Fuel Research Laboratory

FRLL Farrell Lines (container unit)

frm fiberglass-reinforced metal; fireroom; framing; frequency meter

FRM Federal Reformatory for Men

FRMA Floor Rug Manufacturers Association

FRMCM Fellow of the Royal Manchester College of Music

FR Met Soc Fellow of the Royal Meteorological Society

FRMIT Fellow of the Royal Melbourne Institute of Technology

frmn formation

frmr former

Frms Farms (postal abbreviation)

FRMS Federation of Rocky Mountain States; Fellow of the Royal Microscopical Society

FRN Federal Republic of Nigeria; Federal Reserve Note

frna foreign rations not available

FRNHS Fort Raleigh National Historic Site

FRNM Foundation for Research on the Nature of Man

FRNS Fellow of the Royal Numismatic Society

FRNSA Fellow of the Royal Navy School of Architects

Frnz Fernandez

FRNZIH Fellow of the Royal New Zealand Institute of Horticulture

'fro Afro

FRO Fellow of the Register of Osteopaths; Fire Research Organization; Friends Religious Order

FROC Federated Russian Orthodox Clubs

frof fire risk on freight

frog. free rocket over ground

Frog Haydn's String Quartet in D (opus 50, no. 6)

FROGIE Fellowship to Resist Organized Groups Involved in Exploitation (by clicking cricket-shaped or frog-shaped toys in the presence of panhandlers such as members of the Hare Krishna sect)

Frogner Park Oslo's public park filled with the surpassing nude statuary of Vigeland

Frog(s) Anglo-American slang for French (people)

from full range of movement

from. full range of movement

From My Life Smetana's String Quartet No. 1 in E minor (transcribed for orchestra by George Szell)

From the New World Dvořák's Symphony No. 9 (formerly No. 5)

fron frontal; frontalis

FRONAPE Frota Naccional de Petroleiros (National Petroleum Fleet—Brazil)

front. frontispiece

FRONT BC Frontera (Fronteriza) Baja California (Spanish

—Baja California Frontier)—appears on Mexican border city and town license plates

Frontera Girls California Institution for Women at Frontera

Frontier Fighter Davy Crockett

Frontier States last states to be admitted to the United States; the 49th and the 50th were Alaska and Hawaii

frosh freshman; freshmen

Frostbite nickname of Fairbanks, Alaska

frp fiberglass reinforced plastic; forward refueling area

FRP Fuel Reprocessing Plant; Fundamental Research Press

frpf fireproof

frpng fireproofing

FRPS Fellow of the Royal Photographic Society

FRPSL Fellow of the Royal Philatelic Society of London

frq frequent(ly)

FRR Facilities and Rearrangement Request

FRRA Facilities and Rearrangement Request and Authorization

frs flight reference selector; francs

frs (FRS) first readiness state

Frs Fresno; Frisian

Fr S French Somaliland (French Territory of the Afars and the Issas)

FRS Federal Reserve System; Fellow of the Royal Society; Financial Relations Society; Fisheries Research Society; Foundation Research Service; Frequency Response Survey; Fuel Research Station

FRSA Fellow of the Royal Society of Arts

FRSAI Fellow of the Royal Society of Antiquaries of Ireland

frsc full range source code

FRSC Fellow of the Royal Society of Canada

FRSCM Fellow of the Royal School of Church Music

FRSE Fellow of the Royal Society of Edinburgh

FRSGS Fellow of the Royal Scottish Geographical Society

FRSH Fellow of the Royal Society of Health

FRSI Fellow of the Royal Sanitary Institute

FRSL Fellow of the Royal Society of Literature; Fellow of the Royal Society—London

FRSM Fellow of the Royal Society of Medicine

FRSNA Fellow of the Royal School of Naval Architecture

FRSNZ Fellow of the Royal Society of New Zealand

Fr Som French Somaliland

FRSPS Fellow of the Royal Society of Physicians and Surgeons

FRSS Fellow of the Royal Statistical Society

FRSSA Fellow of the Royal Scottish Society of Arts

FRS(SA) Fellow of the Royal Society of South Africa

FRSSI Fellow of the Royal Statistical Society of Ireland

FRSSS Fellow of the Royal Statistical Society of Scotland

Frst Forest (postal abbreviation)

FRSTAT Fringe Software System

FRSTM & H Fellow of the Royal Society of Tropical Medicine and Hygiene

frt free return trajectory; freight; fruit

frt *før vor tidregning* (Dano-Norwegian—before time was reckoned)

FRT Family Relations Test

FRTC Fast-Reactor Training Center

frt/fwd freight forward

frtiso floating-point root isolation

frto flight radio telephone operator

Fr To French Togoland

FRTO Federated Road Transport Organization(s)

frt ppd freight prepaid

frtr freighter

fru *fructose; fruit sugar*

FRU Federal Reserve Unit; Fiji Rugby Union

fruat. *frustrillatum* (Latin—in small bits)

fruc. *fructus* (Latin—fruit)— sometimes abbreviated *fr.*

Fruc *Fructidor* (French—Fruitful Month)—beginning August 18th and extending through September 16th— twelfth month of the French Revolutionary Calendar whose remaining five days— September 17th through the 21st—were called Sansculottides and named respectively for the Virtues, Genius, Labor, Reason, and Rewards

frugal. fortran rules used as a general applications language

Fruit Bowl of the Nation Yakima, Washington

Frunze modern name of Pishpek in Kirgizia

FRUS *Foreign Relations of the United States*

frust. *frustillatim* (Latin—in small portions)

fru veg fruits and/or vegetables

frv (FRV) flight-readiness vehicle

FRVIA Fellow of the Royal Victorian Institute of Architects

FRW Federal Reformatory for Women (Alderson, West Virginia)

FRWI Framingham Relative Weight Index

frwis frost warnings issued

frwk framework

Frwy Freeway

frx firex

Fry Ferry (postal abbreviation); Freeway (highway abbreviation)

FRYC Fall River Yacht Club

fr yr gdnce for your guidance

FRZS Fellow of the Royal Zoological Society

FRZS (NSW) Fellow of the Royal Zoological Society of New South Wales

FRZS(Scot) Fellow of the Royal Zoological Society of Scotland

fs facsimile; factor of safety; far side; film strip; fin stabilized; fire station; flight service; flying status; foot second; foreign service; foresight; freight supply; front scalloped; front spar; sulfur trioxide chlorsulfonic acid (commercial short form or symbol)

fs (FS) file separator character (data processing)

f/s feet per second; first-stage

f *francos* (Spanish—francs)

fs *faites suivre* (French—please forward)

Fs fractostratus

FS Faraday Society; Feasibility Study; Federal Specification(s); Field Security; Field Service; Fighter Squadron; Financial Statement; Fire Station; Flight Sergeant; Fog Signal (Station); Foreign Service; Forest Service; Franciscan Studies; Franz Shubert; Free State; Freedom School; freight supply (vessel); Friendly Society; Friends Society; Friendship Store(s); small freighter (naval symbol)

F-S Fenno-Shipping

F.S. Father of Sion

F/S Financial Statement

FS *Filharmonisk Selskap* (Norwegian—Philharmonic Orchestra); *Forente Staterna* (Swedish—United States)

fsa family separation allowance; fuel storage area

fsa (FSA) fetal sulfoglycoprotein

f.s.a. *fiat secundum artem* (Latin —let it be done skillfully)

FSA Farm Security Administration; Federal Security Administration; Federal Security Agency; Federal Supply Classification; Federation of South Arabia; Fellow of the Society of Antiquaries; Fellow of the Society of Arts; Field Survey Association; Finance Service —Army; Fire Support Area; Flax Spinners Association; Florida Student Association; Fraternal Scholastic Association; Free Selectors Association, Free Society Association, Freethinkers Society of America; Friendly Societies Act; Future Scientists of America

F & SA Farmers and Settlers Association (Australian)

FSAA Family Service Agency of America; Family Service Association of America; Flight Stewards Association of Australia

FSAC Freight Station Accounting Code

FSAG Fellow of the Society of Australian Genealogists

fsaga first sortie after ground alert

FSAICU Federation of State Associations of Independent Colleges and Universities

FSAL Fellow of the Society of Antiquaries of London

FSALA Fellow of the South African Library Association

f.s.a.r. *fiat secundum artem regulas* (Latin—let it be prepared according to the rules of the art)

FSAR Final Safety Analysis Report

FSAS Fellow of the Society of Antiquaries of Scotland

FSAScot Fellow of the Society of Arts of Scotland

FSASM Fellow of the South African School of Mines

fsb forward space block

FSB Federal Specifications Board; Field Selection Board; Final Staging Base; Floating Supply Base

FSBA Florida School Boards Association
FSBC Ferrocarril Sonora—Baja California (Sonora—Baja California Railway)
fsbl feasible
fsbly feasibility
fsbo for sale by owner
fsc foreign service credit
fsc (FSC) fast strike craft
FSC Family Services Bureau; Federal Safety Council; Federal Stock Catalog; Federal Stock Code; Federal Supply Classification; Federal Supply Code; Federal Supreme Court; Fiji Sugar Corporation; Five Star Corporation; Flight Service Center; Flying Status Code; Food Standards Committee; Foreign Service Credits; Foundation for Student Communication; Foundation for the Study of Cycles
FSC Federal Supply Catalog
f/scap foolscap
FSCC Federal Surplus Commodities Corporation; Fire Support Coordination Center; Food Surplus Commodities Corporation
fsce fire-support coordination element
FS Cen Flight Service Center
fscl fire-support coordination line
FSCM Federal Supply Code for Manufacturers
fscp foolscap
FSCS Fire Support Coordination Section; Flight Service Communications System
fsd flying spot digitizer; foreign sea duty; full-scale deflection; full-scale development; functional sequence diagram
fsd (FSD) focus skin distance
FSD Federal Systems Division; Flight Service Director; Fuel Supply Depot; Sioux Falls, South Dakota (airport)
FSDC Fellow of the Society of Dyers and Colourists
fse field-support equipment; forward support element
FSE Federation of Stock Exchanges; Fellow of the Society of Engineers; Field Service Engineer
FSEA Food Service Executives Association
FSER Field Service Engineering Report
FSERI Federal Solar Energy Research Institute
FSES Federal-State Employ-

ment Service
fsf forward space file
FSF Fleet Servicing Facility; Flight Safety Foundation; Forensic Sciences Foundation
FSFA Federation of Specialized Film Associations
fsg first-stage graphitization
FSG Federal Supply Group; Fellow of the Society of Genealogists; Friends School Group
FS&G Farrar, Straus & Giroux
FSGB Foreign Service Grievance Board
FSgt Flight Sergeant
FSGT Fellow of the Society of Glass Technology
fsh (FSH) follicle-stimulating hormone
FSHM Fellow of the Society of Housing Managers
fshrf (FSHRF) follicle-stimulating hormone releasing factor
fshrh (FSHRH) follicle-stimulating hormone releasing hormone
FSHS Friendly Societies Health Services
fsh stk fish steak
FSI Federal Stock Item; Fellow of the Sanitary Institute; Fellow of the Surveyors' Institution; Foreign Service Institute; Foundation Sciences Inc; Free Sons of Israel
FSIA Fellow of the Society of Industrial Artists
FSIC Federal Savings Insurance Corporation; Foreign Service Inspection Corps (US Department of State)
FSIO Foreign Service Information Office(r)
FSIS Food Safety and Inspection Service (USDA)
FSJC Fort Smith Junior College
fsk frequency shift keying
FSK Fatigue Scales Kit
fsklf frequency shift keying low frequency
fskof for the sake of
fsl fire services levy; formal semantic language; frequency-selective limiter
FSL First Sea Lord; Folger Shakespeare Library; Food Science Laboratory (USA)
FSLA Federal Savings and Loan Association
FSLAC Federal Savings and Loan Advisory Council
FSLAs Federal Savings and Loan Associations
FSLIC Federal Savings and Loan Insurance Corporation

FSLN Frente Sandinista de Liberación Nacional (Spanish—Sandinista National Liberation Front)—Castro-supported
fslracc for seller's account
fsm flying-spot microscope
FSM Federated States of Micronesia; Federation Syndicale Mondiale (World Federation of Trade Unions); Fiji School of Medicine; Fort Smith, Arkansas (airport); Free Speech Movement
FSMA Friendly Societies Medical Association; Full Service Maintenance Agreement
FSMB Federation of State Medical Boards
FSMC Flora Stone Mather College
FS Method Federal Standard Method
fsmtc full-size moving target carrier
FSMWO Field Service Modification Work Order
FSN Federal Stock Number
FSNA Fellow of the Society of Naval Architects
FSNC Federal Steam Navigation Company
FSNM Fort Sumter National Monument
FSNP Fuyot Spring National Park (Philippines)
FSNWR Fish Springs National Wildlife Refuge (Utah)
FSNY Free Synagogue of New York
fso field service operation(s)
FSO Field Security Office(r); Fleet Signals Officer; Flint Symphony Orchestra; Florida Symphony Orchestra; Flying Safety Officer; Foreign Safety Officer; Foreign Service Office(r); Fuel Supply Office(r)
FSOs Foreign Service Officers
FSOTS Foreign Service Officers Training School
fsp fiber saturation point; flat salary payroll; foreign service pay
FSP Family Survival Project; Field Security Police; Food Stamp Program
FSPB Field Service Pocket Book; Forward Support Patrol Base
FSPT Federation of Societies for Paint Technology
fs&q functions, standards, and qualifications
F Sq Flying Squadron
FSQS Food Safety and Quality

Service

fsr flight safety research; free of strikes and riots; full-scale repository

FSR Fellow of the Society of Radiographers; Field Service Report; Field Service Representative; Foreign Service Reserve

FSRA Federal Sewage Research Association

FSRJ Federativna Socijalisticka Republika Jugoslavija (Republic of Yugoslavia)

FSRS Frequency Selective Receiver System

fss finite solution set (mathematics)

FSS Federal Supply Schedule; Federal Supply Service; Fellow of the Statistical Society; Field Support System; Fire Support Station; Flight Service Station; Flight Standard Service; Forward Scatter System; Friday(s), Saturday(s), Sunday(s)

FSSC Federal Standard Stock Catalog; Foreign Student Service Council

FSSCT Forer Structured Sentence Completion Test

fssd foreign service selection date

fssp fuel system supply point

FSSP Friendly Sons of Saint Patrick

FSSS Fuel Set Subsystem

fsst flying spot-scanner tube

FSSU Federated Superannuation Scheme of Universities

fsswt full-scale subsonic wind tunnel

fst forged steel; full-scale tunnel

Fst *Funkstation* (German—radio station)

FSTA Food Science and Technology Abstracts

fstacoe fleet special test and checkout equipment

FSTC Farmington State Teachers College; Fayetteville State Teachers College

FS & TC Foreign Science and Technology Center (US Army)

FSTD Fellow of the Society of Typographic Designers

F'sted Frederiksted, St Croix

FSTL Future Strategic Target List

FSTMB *Federación Sindical de Trabajadores Mineros de Bolivia* (Spanish—Syndicalist Federation of Working Miners of Bolivia)

f-stop camera diaphragm setting of an f-number stop

FSTPP Foreign Service Team Preceptorship Program

fsts fuze set test set

FSTWP Fellow of the Society of Technical Writers and Publishers

fsty firstly

fsu freak student union

FSU Family Service Unit; Florida State University; Friends of the Soviet Union

FSuH Fridays, Sundays, Holidays

fsv final-stage vehicle

fsv *for så vidt* (Dano-Norwegian —as far as)

FSVA Fellow of the Society of Valuers and Auctioneers

fsw final status word(ing); flexible steel wire (cable)

FSWA Federation of Sewage Works Associations

F & SWMA Fine and Specialty Wire Manufacturers Association

fswr flexible steel wire rope

fswt free-surface water tunnel

ft feet; firing table; fixed tannin; flat; flush threshold; foot; formal training; free of tax(ation); free trade; frequent traveller; full terms; fume-tight

f-t follow through

f/t freight ton

f & t fire and theft

ft. *fiat* (Latin—let it be made)

Ft Fort; forint (Hungarian currency unit)

Ft *Folyoirat* (Hungarian—journal, review)

FT Field Test; Flying Test; Flying Tiger Lines (2-letter coding); Functional Test(ing)

FT *Financial Times* (London); *Freethought Today*

ft² square feet; square foot

ft³ cubic feet; cubic foot

ft³/min cubic feet per minute

ft³/s cubic feet per second

fta failure to appear (in court); fatigue test(ing) article; film training aid; fluorescent treponemal antibody; full-throttle altitude

ftA fuck the Army (to hell with the rules)

FTA Finnish Travel Association; Free Trade Area; Free Trade Association; Future Teachers of America

fta-abs fluorescent treponemal antibody absorption (test for syphilis)

FTAC Foreign Trade Arbitration Commission

FTAF Flying Training Air Force

FTAT Fluorescent Treponemal Antibody Test

ftb fails to break

FTB fleet torpedo bomber; Forestry and Timber Bureau; Franchise Tax Board; Fukui Television Broadcasting (Japan)

ftbd fit to be detained; full-term born dead

ft black fine thermal black

ftbm foot board measure

ftbrg footbridge

FTBS Free Throwers Boomerang Society

ftc fast time constant; final turn collision

ft c foot-candle

FTC Fair Trade Commission; Farmers Trading Company; Federal Telecommunications Laboratories; Federal Trade Commission; Fleet Training Center, Flight Test Center, Flying Training Command

FTCA Federal Tort Claims Act

ft. cata. *fiat cataplasma* (Latin—make a poultice)

FTCC Flight Test Coordinating Committee; French Telegraph Cable Company

ft cd foot candela

FTCD Fellow of Trinity College —Dublin

ft. cerat. *fiat ceratum* (Latin—make a cerate)

ft. chart. *fiat chartulae* (Latin—let powders be made)

FTCL Fellow of Trinity College of Music—London

ft col fast color

ft. colly. *fiat collyrium* (Latin—make an eyewash)

ftcolovprt fast color overprint

ftd fails to drain; flight test(ing) direction

FTD Field Training Detachment; Florists' Telegraph Delivery; Foreign Technology Division; Fuel Testing Department

FTDA Fellow of the Theatrical Designers and Craftsmens Association

FTDC Fellow of the Society of Typographic Designers of Canada

ft di flattening die

ftdr friction-top drum

fte fracture transition elastic; full-time equivalence; full-time equivalent

ftee full-time equivalency enrollment

ft. emuls. *fiat emulsio* (Latin—make an emulsion)

ft. enem. *fiat enema* (Latin—make an enema)

FTESA Foundry Trades Equipment and Supplies Association

F test Fisher Test (forestry)

ftet full-time equivalent terminals

ftf face to face

FTF Flygtekniska Forsoksantalten (Aeronautical Research Institute of Sweden)

ftfet four-terminal field-effect transistor

ftg fitting; footing

FTG Fleet Training Group (USN); Fuji Texaco Gas

ft. garg. *fiat gargarisma* (Latin—make a gargle)

FTGSVC Fleet Training Group Services

ft hd flathead

fth(m) fathom

fthp flowing tubing head pressure (oil well)

ft/hr feet per hour

fti federal tax included; fixed time indicator; fixed time interval; frequency time indicator; frequency time intensity

FTI Facing Tile Institute; Federal Tax Included; Fellow of the Textile Institute; Functional Test(ing) Instruction(s)

FTIG Fort Indiantown Gap (USA)

FTII Fellow of the Taxation Institute Incorporated

FTIMA Federal Tobacco Inspectors Mutual Association

FT Index *Financial Times Index*

ft. infus. *fiat infusum* (Latin—make an infusion)

ft. injec. *fiat infectio* (Latin—make an injection)

ftir functional terminal innervation ratio

ftit fan turbine inlet temperature

FTIT Fellow of the Institute of Taxation

ftk forward track kill

ftka failed to keep appointment

ftl faster than light

ft l foot -lambert

FTL Federal Telecommunications Laboratory; Flight Test Letter; Flying Tiger Line

ft lb foot pound

ft-lbf foot-pound force

Ftle Fremantle

ft. linim. *fiat linimentum* (Latin—make a liniment)

ftm fractional test meal; functional testing machine(ry)

FTM Flight Test(ing) Manual; Flight Test(ing) Model; Flying Training Manual

FTM *Federación de Trabajadores de México* (Spanish—Federation of Mexican Workers)

FTMA Federation of Textile Manufacturers Associations

ft. mas. *fiat massa* (Latin—make a mass)

ft. mas. div. in pil. *fiat massa dividenda in pilulas* (Latin—make a mass and divide into pills)

ft md flattening mandrel

ft/min feet (foot) per minute

ft. mist. *fiat mistura* (Latin—make a mixture)

ftn fortification

Ftn Fountain (postal abbreviation); Freetown (maritime abbreviation)

FTN Facsimile Transmissión Network

ftnd full-term normal delivery

f° *firmato* (Italian—signed)

FTO Field Test(ing) Operations; Field Training Officer (police); Fleet Torpedo Officer; Fleet Training Officer (naval); Franciscan Third Order

ftp field terminal platform (oil well); final-turn pursuit (aircraft); folded, trimmed, and packed (books); full-time personnel (civil service)

FTP Field Test Plan; Fleet Training Publication; Flight Test Program; Functional Test(ing) Procedure

FTP *Francs Tireurs Partisans* (French—Partisan Sharpshooters)—communists active in the anti-Nazi underground of France during World War II

FTPAA Film and Television Production Association of Australia

ft-pdl foot poundal

ft/pf foot-pound force

ft. pil. *fiat pilulae* (Latin—make pills)

ft/pnl fuel-tanking panel

FTPR *Federacion del Trabajo de Puerto Rico* (Spanish—Federation of Labor of Puerto Rico)

FTPS Fellow of the Technical Publishing Society

ft. pulv. *fiat pulvis* (Latin—make a powder)

ftr fighter; fixed-transom; flattile roof; fusion test reactor

F Tr flag tower

FTR Final Technical Report; flag tower (chart and map designation); Flight Test Report; Fruehauf (stock exchange symbol); Functional Test Report; Functional Test Request

ftrac full-tracked (vehicle)

FTRF Freedom-to-Read Foundation

ftro fighter operations

FTRO Flight Test Release Order

ftrp fighter plans

ft/s feet (foot) per second

FTS Federal Telecommunications System; Federal Telephone System; Field Test Support; Flying Traffic Specialist; Flying Training School; Forged Tool Society; Funeral Telegraph Service; Furnishing Trades Society

ft/s² foot per second squared

ft sec foot second

ft. so. *fiat solutio* (Latin—make a solution)

ft. suppos. *fiat suppositorium* (Latin—make a suppository)

ftt field test telescope; formation tester tool (oil well); framed timber trestle; full-time temporary (civil-service employee); functional test tool

FTT Fever Therapy Technician; Five Task Test

fttp full-time temporary personnel

fttr fitter

ft & tw combination flat top and typewriter (desk)

ftu field transfer unit; fuel tanking unit

Ftu Freeman time unit

FTU Federation of Trade Unions; Field Torpedo Unit; First Training Unit

FTUC Fiji Trades Union Congress

ft. ung. *fiat unguentum* (Latin—make an ointment)

FTUR Flight Test Unsatisfactory Report

FTV Flight Test Vehicle; Fukushima Television; Functional Test Verification

ftw free-trade wharf

Ft W Fort Worth

Fty Factory

FTZ Foreign Trade Zone; Free Trade Zone

FTZB Foreign Trade Zones Board

fu Farmers Union; feed(ing)

unit; frame unprotected (insurance classification)

f/u fine used (postage stamps)

Fu Finsen unit

F-u fuck you (underground slang —very insulting epithet)

FU Fairfield University; Farmers Union; Fisk University; Fordham University; Franklin University; Freie Universität (Berlin Free University); Friends University; Furman University

FUA Farm Underwriters Association

FUB Freie Universität Berlin (Free University, Berlin)

fubar fouled up beyond all recognition

fubb fouled up beyond belief

fuc full usable capacity

FUC Ferrocarriles Unidos de Yucatan (United Railroads of Yucatan)

fuchsite chrome mica

fucm (FUCM) full-utility cruise missile

FUDR Failure and Usage Data Report

FUE Federated Union of Employers

FUEL Fuel-Users Emergency Line

fuel of the future solar power

FUEN Federal Union of European Nationalities

Fuente (Spanish—Fountain, Source, Spring)—short form for such Spanish places as Fuente-Alamo, Fuente de Cantos, Fuente-Palmera, Fuente Vaqueros, etc.

fuetap (concrete) formed under elevated temperature and pressure

fufo fly under, fly out

FUG-1966 Hungarian-built armored vehicle based on Soviet model

Fuhlsbuttel Hamburg, Germany's airport

Fuhrer (German—Leader)— Hitler's title

FUIB Fire Underwriters Inspection Bureau

Fuji Fujinoyama, Fujisan, or Mount Fuji (Japan's highest peak, the long dormant volcano towering over Tokyo and Yokohama)

Fujian (Pinyin Chinese—Fukien)

Fujinoyama (Japanese—The Mountains of Fuji)—Mount Fuji rendered poetically

Fujisan (Japanese—Mount Fuji)

Fujita Leonardo Fujita

Fujiyama Europeanized form similar to Fusiyama and also standing for Fujisan or Mount Fuji—Japan's highest peak— 3775 meters or 12,388 feet above sea level

Ful Fulcran; Fulgence; Fulgencio; Fulke; Fuller; Fullerton; Fulton; Fulvia; Fulvius

FULICO Fidelity Union Life Insurance Company

fulnm full name

Fulton's Folly inventor Robert Fulton's steamship *Clermont* which ascended the Hudson River in 1809

fum fuming

FUM Friends United Meeting

Fum the Fourth nickname of George IV

fumi fumigant; fumigate; fumigation

fumtu fouled up more than usual

fun. funeral; funerary

FUNAI Fundação Nacional do Indio (Portuguese—National Foundation of the Indian)

funamb funambulation; funambulist (tightrope or tightwire walker)

func function(al)

Fun Capital of Scandinavia Copenhagen, Denmark

Fun City New York

funct function; functional; functionally

fund. fundamental; fundamentalism; fundamentalist

fund. fundador (Spanish—founder)

FUND International Monetary Fund

Fundador de la Republica (Spanish—Founder of the Republic) —José Nuñez Cáceres—founder and first president of the Dominican Republic (Spanish Haiti)

Fundador de Nueva Granada (Spanish—Founder of New Granada)—Francisco de Paula Santander—founder of Colombia (Nueva Granada)

Fundy Bay of Fundy; Fundy National Park on the north shore of the Bay of Fundy in New Brunswick, Canada

Fünen (German—Fyn)

Funeral March Sonata Piano Sonata in B-flat minor by Chopin (contains his celebrated funeral march)

funeral order maritime tradition of older persons standing back to give younger people first chance when boarding lifeboats or using other life-saving equipment; *(see* Birken'ead drill)

fungi. fungicide

Fungus Corners (naval argot— Bremerton, Washington)—a rainy port

Funk Funk & Wagnalls

FUNK Front Uni National du Kampuchea (French—Khmer National United Front)— Cambodia and Khmer forces

Funk&W Funk & Wagnalls

Fun-Loving Philosopher Mark Russell

FUNM Fort Union National Monument

FUNNs For Your Nieces and Nephews

Fun and Sun Cities Acuña, México across the Rio Grande from Del Rio, Texas

FUNU Force d'Urgence de Nations Unies (French—United Nations Emergency Force)

fuo fever (of) unknown origin

fup fusion point

f/up follow up

FUP Friends United Press; Furman University Press

FUP Frente Unido del Pueblo (Spanish—People's United Front)—Cuban-oriented Colombian terrorists

fuposat follow-up on supply action taken

fur. furlong; further

FUR Follow-up Report

furl. furlough

furlong furrow long (one eighth mile or 220 yards—201.17 meters), originally the average length of a plowman's furrow

furmr furthermore

furn furnace; furnish(es, ed, ing, ings); furniture

Furn Furnace (postal abbreviation)

furngs furnishings

furnit furniture

furn pts furniture parts

Fur Seals Fur Seal Islands (Alaska's Pribilofs)

furt (German—ford)

fus far ultraviolet spectrometer; firing unit simulator; fuselage; fusing

FUSA Flinders University of South Australia

FUSE Federation for United Science Education

FuSf Fortsetzung und Schluss folgen (German—to be concluded in the next issue)

Fuss and Feathers General Winfield Scott, USA

fut future

Fut Futura

FUTC Fidelity Union Trust Company

futs firing unit test set

FUW Farmers' Union of Wales; Federation of University Women

Fuzhou (Pinyin Chinese—Foochow)

fv fire vent; flats vacant; flush valve; forward visibility; fuel valve; future value

fv. *folio verso* (Latin—back of the sheet)

FV Falck's Flyvetjeneste (Copenhagen); fishing vessel; Fruit and Vegetable (US Department of Agriculture)

FV-432 British armored personnel carrier called Trojan

FV-1609 advanced model of the preceding armored personnel carrier designated FV-432

FVA Fellow of the Valuers Association

FVB Fiji Visitors Bureau

fvc forced vital capacity

FVCQFRA Fruit and Vegetable Canning and Quick Freezing Research Association

FVDE Fighting Vehicles Design Establishment

f vd & w firearms, venereal disease, and whiskey (attributed by many historians and sociologists as being the main factors in the corruption and destruction of entire societies such as the American Indians, the Australian aborigines, the peoples of Polynesia, etc.)

FVI Fellow of the Valuers' Institution

FVMMA Floor and Vaccum Machinery Manufacturers Association

FVNM Fort Vancouver National Monument

FVPA Flat Veneer Products Association

FVPRA Fruit and Vegetable Preservation Research Association

fvq full variable quality

fvrbl favorable

FVRDE Fighting Vehicles Research and Development Establishment

fv's fashion victims

f. vs. *fiat venaesectio* (Latin—perform a venesection)

FVS Forer Vocational Survey

FVSC Fort Valley State College

fvt family vewing time

fw fire wall; fixed wing; flash welding; formula weight; fresh water; fresh weight; front wiring

f & w feed and water; feeding and watering

fw Funk & Wagnalls

f/W female White

FW Fairbanks Whitney (stock exchange symbol); FockeWulf; Fog Whistle; Fort Worth; Foster Wheeler

F & W Funk and Wagnalls

fwa financial working arrangement; first word address; fluorescent whitening agent

FWA Family Welfare Association; Farm Workers Association; Federal Works Agency; French West Africa; Future Weapons Agency

FWAA Football Writers Association of America

FWAS Fort Wayne Art School

FWAT Fish and Wildlife Advisory Team (Alaskan)

fwb four-wheel brake; four-wheel braking; free-wheel bicycle; front-wheel bicycle; furnished with bed

FWB Fort Worth Belt (railroad); Free-Will Baptists

fw ball. freshwater ballast

fwc full weight contents

FWC Federal Warning Center; Foster Wheeler Corporation

FW & C Furness, Withy & Company

FWCC Friends' World Committee for Consultation

fwd forward(ing); four-wheel drive; freshwater damage; freshwater draught; front-wheel drive

F W & D Fort Worth & Denver (railroad)

FwdBL forward bomb line

fwdct fresh water drain collecting tank

fwdg forwarding

fwdr forwarder

fwe finished with engines

f-w-e finished with engine(s)

FWeldI Fellow of the Welding Institute

fwg following

FWGE Fort Worth Grain Exchange

fwh flexible working hours; free-wheeling hubs

FWHC Feminist Women's Health Center

FWHF Federation of World Health Foundations

FWI Federation of West Indies; French West Indies

FWID Federation of Wholesale and Industrial Distributors

fwl foilborne waterline

FWL Foundation for World Literacy

FWLERD Far West Laboratory for Educational Research and Development

FWO Facilities Work Order; Fleet Wireless Officer

FWOA Fort Worth Opera Association

FWONA Free World Outside North America

fwop furloughed without pay

fwp filament-wound plastic(s)

FWP Federal Writers' Project

FWPCA Federal Water Pollution Control Administration

FWPO Federal Wildlife Permit Office; Fort Wayne Philharmonic Orchestra

FWQA Federal Water Quality Administration; Federal Water Quality Association

fwr full-wave rectifier; full-wave reflector

F-W r Felix-Weil reaction

FWRC Federal Water Resources Council

FWRM Federation of Wire Rope Manufacturers

fws filter wedge spectrometer

FWS Fighter Weapons School

F & WS Fish and Wildlife Service

FWSG Farm Water Supply Grant

FWSO Fort Worth Symphony Orchestra

FWSSUSA Federation of Worker's Singing Societies of the U.S.A.

fwt fair wear and tear; featherweight

FWT Free World Trade

fwth flush watertight hatch

FWU Food Workers Union

FWWS Fire-Weather Warning Service

Fwy Freeway

fx extraneous (television) effects; fixed; foreign exchange; foxed; fractured; fractures; frozen section

fx *for eksempel* (Dano-Norwegian—for example)

Fx fracture (bone)

FX Foreign Exchange

F.X. Francis Xavier

fxd fixed; foxed

fxg fixing

fxle forecastle

fy (FY) fiscal year

Fy Ferry
FY fiscal year; Ferdinand(e) Ysabella
FY2 fuck you too (graffitic defacement)
fya first-year algebra
FYC Federal Youth Center; Florida Yacht Club
FYDP First-Year Development Program
fyg for your guidance
fyi for your information
fyig for your information and guidance
fym farmyard manure
FYP Five-Year Plan; Four-Year Plan; etc.
FYPB Five-Year Planning Base (USA)

fypi for your personal information
FYPP Five-Year Procurement Program (USA)
fyr for your reference
fyracc for your account
fys *fysik* or *fysisk* (Dano-Norwegian—physics, physical)
fytd fiscal year to date
FYTP Five-Year Test Program
Fyz Fyzabad
fz freeze; freezing; fuze (ordnance explosive device)
fz *forzando* (Italian—accented strongly)
Fz Fernández; Franz
FZ Franc Zone; Free Zone; French Zone
FZA Fellow of the Zoological

Academy; Fellow of the Zoological Association
fzdz freezing drizzle
fzfg freezing fog
FZGBI Fellow of the Zoological Gardens of Great Britain and Ireland
FZIA First Zen Institute of America
fzr freezer
fzra freezing rain
FZS Fellow of the Zoological Society
FZSL Fellow of the Zoological Society, London
FZSScot Fellow of the Zoological Society of Scotland

G

g gage; garage; gelding; gender; generator; gilbert; glucose; gold; good; grain; gram; gravitational acceleration (symbol); gravity; grease; great; green; grey; gross; ground; guide; gun; gyromagnetic ratio (symbol); Lande factor (symbol)

g (G) glucose

g acceleration of gravity (symbol); gloom (gloomy weather symbol)

g/ *giro* (Spanish—bank check)

G conductance (symbol); control grid (symbol); Fraunhofer line caused by iron (symbol); gap; gauss; gear; German(ic); Germany; Gibbs function (free energy symbol); glider; go; God (on Masonic emblems); Golf—code for letter G; good; Goodyear; gourde (Haitian unit of currency); government (broadcasting); Grace (steamship line); Green Line; Greene Line; Greenwich; Greyhound (bus line); guineas; gulden (Netherlands guilder); gulf; Gulf Oil (stock exchange symbol); Newtonian gravitational constant (symbol); specific gravity (symbol); thousand-dollar bill

G (G) government spending

G *Gade* (Danish—Street); *Gallica* (Latin—Gaul or Germania); *Gasse* (German—Street); *Gata* (Swedish—Street); *Gate* (Norwegian—Street); *gawa* (Japanese—river, stream)— also shown as *kawa*; *Gebel* (Arabic—mountain); *Göl* (Turkish—lake); *Golfe* (French—gulf); *Golfo* (Italian or Spanish—gulf); *Gôlfo* (Por-

tuguese—gulf); *Gora* (Russian —hill, mountain); *Góra* (Polish—hill, mountain); *Guba* (Russian—bay); *Gunung* (Indonesian or Malay—mountain)

G-1 Army or Marine Corps personnel section; personnel officer

G-2 military intelligence section of Army or Marine Corps; military intelligence officer

G-3 operations and training section of Army or Marine Corps; operations and training officer

G3P glyceraldehyde 3-phosphate

G-4 logistics officer or section of U.S. Army or Marine Corps; undercover anti-terrorist group within the Royal Canadian Mounted Police

G$_4$ dichlorophen (bactericide and fungicide)

G-5 civil affairs section of Army; civil affairs officer

G6P glucose 6-phosphate

G6PD glucose-6-phosphate dehydrogenase

G-6-pdd glucose-6-phosphate dehydrogenase deficiency

G$_{11}$ hexachlorophene (antibacterial agent)

G-91 Fiat-built single-engine jet fighter-bomber

ga gage; gas amplification; gastric analysis; gauge; general average; general aviation; glide angle; go ahead; greenhouse annual; ground to air; ground alert; ground attack

g/a general average; ground-to-air

g & a general and administra-

tive

Ga gallium; Georgia; Georgian; Ghana (tribe)

G^a García

GA Gage Man; Gamblers Anonymous; Garrison Adjutant; Garrison Artillery; Gemmological Association; General Accounting; General Agent; General Assembly (UN); General Assignment; Geographical Association; Geologists Association; Georgia (railroad); Glen Alden (stock exchange symbol); Government Actuary; Government Agency; Grant Award; Graphic Arts; Gypsum Association

G-A General Atomic (Division of General Dynamics)

gaa ground-aided acquisition

GAA Gaelic Athletic Association; Gay Activists Alliance; Gemmological Association of Australia; General Aviation Association

GAA *Glossary of Aeronautical Abbreviations*

GAAC Graphics Arts Advisers Council

gaafr governmental accounting, auditing, and financial reporting

gáambatjih (Cantonese Chinese —abbreviation)

GAAP Generally Accepted Accounting Principles

GAATV Gemini-Atlas-Agena Target Vehicle

gab gabardine; gabbing; gabble; gable; girth above buttress

Gab Gabon Republic (République Gabonaise); Gabriel

GAB Games and Amusement Board; General Adjustment

Bureau; General Arrangements to Borrow

GABA gamma-aminobutyric acid

Gabba Wollongabba, Brisbane

Gabby Gabriel; Gabriella; Gabrielle

Gabe Gabriel

Gabl Gabriel

Gabon Gabonese Republic (West African country whose Gabonese speak some French as well as Bantu and Fang, minerals and tropical food products are its chief exports)

Gabon Ports (north to south) Cocobeach, Libreville, Port Gentil, Sette Cama, Gamba Oil Terminal

Gabr Gabriel; Gabriella; Gabrielle

Gabriel Israeli surface-to-surface missile

Gabriela Mistral Lucila Godoy de Alcayaga

Gabriel d'Annunzio Gaetano Rapagnetta

Gabriel Padecopeo Lope de Vega

Gaby Gabrielle Dupont

gac granular-activated carbon; grilled american cheese (sandwich)

GAC General Acceptance Corporation; General Advisory Committee; General Apprenticeship Committee; General Atomic Company; Geological Association of Canada; Georgia Association of Colleges; Goodyear Aircraft Corporation; Gustavus Adolphus College

GACHAL Gush Herut Liberalim (Hebrew—Herut-Liberal Bloc)—right-wing party

g/a con general average contribution

GAD Gases Applications Development; Great American Desert

g/a dep general average deposit

Gadis Gaditanas (dancing girls of Cadiz who perfected abdominal dancing to a fine art representing fertility rites and child bearing)

GADNA Gdud Noar (Hebrew—Youth Corps)

GADO General Aviation District Office

gadpet graphic data presentation and edit(ing)

GADS Goose Air Defense Sector

Gae Gaelic

GAE General American English; Georgia Association of Educators

GAEC Goodyear Aircraft and Engineering Corporation; Grumman Aircraft Engineering Corporation

Gael Gaelic

Gaelic Gaelic Symphony by Mrs HHA Beach (first symphonic work by an American woman)

GAER Gay Alliance for Equal Rights

Gaet Gaetano

gaf General Aniline & Film Corporation (trademark)

GAF General Aniline & Film; Government Aircraft Factories

GAFB Goodfellow Air Force Base

GAFD Guild of American Funeral Directors

gaffer (motion-picture and tv slang—chief electrician)

gaffer and gammer grandfather and grandmother

GAFLAC General Accident Fire and Life Assurance Corporation

gag. gaging

g/a/g ground-air-ground

GAG Graphic Artists Guild

gag mm gage thickness (in millimeters)

GAHH Good American Help ing Hands

gai guaranteed annual income

GAI Government Affairs Institute

GAIA Graphic Arts Information Association

GAIF General Assembly of International Federations

Gail Abigail

Gail Hamilton Mary Abigail Dodge

Gaillard Cut formerly called Culebra Cut (in the Panama Canal where a U.S. Army engineer's name replaced the Spanish word for snake)

Gainful NATO name for a Soviet surface-to-air missile also designated SA-6

GAIS Georgia Association of Independent Schools

GAIU Graphic Arts International Union

GAJ Guild of Agricultural Journalists

GAJC Georgia Association of Junior Colleges

GAK Garlock (stock-exchange symbol)

Gaku Univ Gakushuin University

gal galileo (unit of acceleration); gallon (unit of capacity)

Gal Epistle to the Galatians; Galacia; Galatians; Galveston; Galway

Gal Galatians; *Général* (French —General)

GAL Gdynia America Line; General Assembly Library (Wellington, NZ); Guggenheim Aeronautical Laboratory; Guinea Airways

G A & L General Aircraft and Leasing (Division of General Dynamics Corporation)

GALA Gay Atheist League of America

galacto [Latin—milk(y)]—from the Greek *galakt* as in galactic (the Milky Way)

Galap Galápagos Islands

Galápagos short form for Galápagos Islands or Galápagos tortoise(s)

galaxy. general automatic luminosity and x y (measuring machine)

gal cap gallon capacity

GALCIT Guggenheim Aeronautical Laboratory, California Institute of Technology

Gal Col Gallaudet College

Gale Gale Research Company

Galeão (Portuguese—Galleon) Rio de Janeiro, Brazil's air port

Galeb Yugoslav two-place single-engine jet aircraft also known as the Seagull

Galen (sometimes Galin) Vasily Konstantinovich Blücher

galena lead sulfide (Germans call it Bleischweif)

Gales (Portuguese or Spanish— Wales)

Galich (Russian—Galicia)

Galileo Galileo Galilei

gall. gallery

Gall Galleria (Italian—gallery or tunnel)

Galla (Portuguese or Spanish— Gaul)

Galleria glass-topped rainproof arcade of specialty shops and restaurants linking Duomo— Milan Cathedral—and La Scala—Teatro alla Scala—the opera house of Milan; lesser gallerias serve other Italian cities

Galles (French or Italian— Wales)

Gallia (Italian or Latin—Gaul)

Gallië (Dutch—Gaul)

Gallien (German—Gaul)

Gallo-Rom Gallo-Romance

Gallup Dr George Horace Gallup of Gallup Poll fame

GALOP Gay London Police Monitoring Group

gal per min gallons per minute

gals gallons

gals (GALS) generalized assembly-line simulator; geographic adjustment by least squares

gal(s) girl(s)

galt gut-associated lymphoid tissue

Galtees southern Ireland's Galty Mountains

galumphing galloping and triumphing

galv galvanic; galvanism; galvanize(d); galvanometer

Galv Galveston

galv i galvanized iron

galvnd galvannealed

galvo(s) galvanometer(s)

Galvy Galveston

Galw Galway

gam gammon (sailor's gossip, seamen's talkfest); gamut; guided-aircraft missile

gam (GAM) ground-to-air missile

gam gamos (Greek—marriage) —gamete(s)

Gam Gamaliel; Gambia

GAM Guest Aerovías Mexico; Guided-Aircraft Missile

GAMA Gas Appliance Manufacturers Association; General Aviation Manufacturers Association

GAMAA Guitar and Accessories Manufacturers Association of America

Gambia Republic of The Gambia (West African coastal country whose Gambians speak English and some tribal languages, cattle raising, peanut and rice cultivation, as well as tourism are principal occupations)

Gambia's Port Georgetown

Gambiers Gambier Islands in the South Pacific

Gamblers Anon Gamblers Anonymous

gamblin' gambling

Gambling Capital of the Far East Macao, Portuguese China

Gambling Capital of the Far West Las Vegas, Nevada

Gamboa Penitentiary (close to the midsection of the Panama Canal)

GAMC General Agents and Managers Conference

Gamerco (acronymic placename—Gallup American Coal Company)—coal-mining town near Gallup in northwestern New Mexico

GAMET Gyro Accelerometer Misalignment Erection Test

GAMIS Graphic Arts Marketing Information Service

Gamla Stan (Swedish—Old Town)—old Stockholm

Gamle Bergen (Norwegian— Old Bergen)

gamm gimbal angle matching monitor

GAMM Gesellschaft für Angewante Mathematik und Mechanik

GAMMA Guns and Magnetic Material Alarm (anti-hijacking device)

GAMTA General Aviation Manufacturers and Traders Association

gan generating and analyzing networks

gan (GAN) gyrocompass automatic navigation

gan ganado (Spanish—cattle; livestock)

GAN Generalized Activity Network

Gand (French or Italian— Ghent)

Ganda (Latin—Ghent)—also known as Gandavum in Roman times

Gandhi *Mahatma* (Hindustani —Great Souled)—Mohandas Karamchand Gandhi

Gandhi's Mahatma Gandhi's Birthday (October 2)

Ganef NATO nickname for the Soviet SA-4-type mobile surface-to-air missile

ganefo games of new emerging forces

gang. ganglia; ganglion

Ganga (Hindi or Sanskrit— Ganges)

Ganges great river of India flowing from Himalayas to central Bengal where it unites with Brahmaputra and descends into Bay of Bengal below Calcutta; Ganges is more than 1500 miles long

Gangland Chicago

Gannet Westland three-place early-warning aircraft developed in Britain

Gansu (Pinyin Chinese—Kansu)

Gante (Spanish—Ghent)

GANZ Gas Association of New Zealand

ganzl gänzlich (German—complete, entire)

gao general alert order

GAO General Accounting Office; General Administrative Order; General American Oil (company); General American Overseas (corporation); General Auditing Office; Government Accounting Office

GAO Glavnaya Astronomicheskaya Observatoriya (Russian —Main Astronomical Observatory)

gaof gummed all over flap

gap. guidance autopilot

gap. (GAP) gross agricultural product

Gap The Gap—Delaware Water Gap between New Jersey and Pennsylvania on the upper reaches of the Delaware River or Semangko Gap just north of Kuala Lumpur in Malaysia; Pennington Gap

GAP Government Aircraft Plant; Great American Public; Great Atlantic & Pacific (Tea Company); Group for the Advancement of Psychiatry

GAP Grupo de Amigos Personales (Spanish—Group of Personal Friends)—President Allende's bodyguard; *Gruppo d'Azione Partigiana* (Italian— Partisan Action Group)

gapa ground-to-air pilotless aircraft

Ga-Pac Georgia-Pacific

GAPAN Guild of Air Pilots and Air Navigators

GAPCE General Assembly of the Presbyterian Church of England

GAPEFA Graphic Arts Platemaking Employers Federation of Australia

GAPL Group Assembly Parts List

gapo giant armpit odor; gorilla armpit odor

gapp growth and profit plan(ning)

GAPR Grant Application Request

GAPs Geographic Applications Programs

gapsfas graduate and professional students financial statement

gapt graphical automatically programmed tools

gaq general average quality; good average quality

gar. garage; garrison; ground

avoidance radar; guided aircraft rocket

gar. (GAR) gross annual return; growth analysis and review; guided air(craft) rocket

GAR Gioacchino Antonio Rossini; Grand Army of the Republic; Guided Aircraft Rocket; Gustavus Adolphus Rex (King Gustav II of Sweden)

Gara Garamond

garade gathers, alarms, reports, displays, and evaluates

garb. garbage; green, amber, red, blue (airway priority color code)

GARB Garment and Allied Industries Requirements Board

Garbage Dump California's San Quentin Prison holding some of the most hardened and troublesome inmates; Green Meadow Correctional Facility at Comstock, NY

garbd garboard

garbol garbologic(al)(ly); garbologist(ic)(al)(ly); garbology (archeological study of man's discards such as garbage and trash)

garbologist garbage collector

garbz *garbanzos* (Spanish—chickpeas)

GARC Graphic Arts Research Center

G.Arch. Graduate in Architecture

Garcia Diego Garcia (Anglo-American naval base in the Chagos Archipelago or Oil Islands of the Indian Ocean)

gard gamma atomic radiation detector; garden; gardener; gardening; general address reading device; guard

GARD Gamma Atomic Radiation Detector

Garden of the Andes Mendoza, Argentina

Garden of the Antilles St Croix, Virgin Islands (or any Caribbean island whose inhabitants make the effort to give nature a helping hand)

Garden of Argentina Tucuman

Garden of Canada Ontario

Garden of the Caribbean Puerto Rico

Garden City of Georgia Augusta

Garden City of India Mysore

Garden City of New Zealand Christchurch

Garden of Denmark Fyn or Funen—home of Hans Christian Andersen

Garden of the East Burma, Malaysia, and Sri Lanka use this eponym

Garden of England Kent and Worcester share this sobriquet

Garden of France Amboise and Touraine share this nickname

Garden of God ancient eponym of Lebanon just north of the Holy Land

Garden of the Gods multicolored rock formations adorn this park near Colorado Springs, Colorado

Garden of the Gulf rural Prince Edward Island in the Gulf of St Lawrence

Garden of Ireland Carlow

Garden Island Kauai, Hawaii

Garden Isle of Micronesia Ponape

Garden of Italy Sicily

Garden of Love Shalimar waterside garden on Kashmir's Dal Lake

Garden of Maine Aroostook County

Garden of the Morning Breeze Naseem Bagh on Kashmir's Dal Lake

Garden of Paradise in the Sea Madeira

Garden Province Canada's Prince Edward Island

Garden of Spain fields of Andalucía and Valencia

Garden State New Jersey's official nickname

Garden of the Sun Indonesia

Garden of Sweden Blekinge

Garden of Switzerland Thurgau

Garden of Wales southern Glamorganshire

Garden of the West California, Kansas, or other western places devoted to gardening

Garden of the World Mississippi River Valley

gards gardenias

garg. *gargarisma* (Latin—gargle)

Gargantua François I of France (or) Henri d'Albret—King of Navarre

garioa government and relief in occupied areas

Garmo Garmo Peak (formerly Stalin Peak and the highest in the USSR)—also called Communism Peak

GARP Global Atmospheric Research Program

Garry Moore Thomas Garrison Morfit

G.A.R.S. Gustavus Adolphus Rex Sueciae (Gustavus Adolphus King of Sweden)

gar str garboard strake

Gart Garrett

GARUDA Garuda Indonesia Airways

Gary Gareth; Garvey

Gary Cooper Frank J Cooper

gas gasoline

ga & s general average and salvage

g-a s general-adaptation syndrome

GAs Gamblers Anonymous

GAS Georgia Academy of Science; Ghana Academy of Sciences; Government of American Samoa; Grant's Acronymical Shorthand (*see* JERK); Great American Smokeout (Smokeless Thursday campaign to get smokers to kick the habit); Guild of All Souls

GASAA Graphic Arts Services Association of Australia

gasahol nine parts gasoline and one part alcohol (fuel extender mixture)

GASBO Georgia Association of School Business Officials

GASC German-American Securities Corporation

GASCO General Aviation Safety Commission; General Aviation Safety Committee

Gascogne (French—Gascony)

Gascuña (Spanish—Gascony)

gasdyn gas dynamic; gas dynamicist; gas dynamics

gaser gamma ray laser

Gas House of the Nation Washington, D.C.

gasid gas-acid (indigestion)

Gaskin NATO nickname for Soviet SA-9 air-defense missile system contained in an amphibious armored vehicle

GASL General Applied Science Laboratories

GA S&L Great American Savings & Loan

gaso gasoline

gasoff gasoline ripoff

gasohol gasoline + alcohol (fuel-extender fluid)

Gasopolis Los Angeles (on smog-filled days); a term also applied to places with similar conditions of polluted air

gasp. gravity-assisted space probe

Gasp Gaspar(o)

GASP Global Air Sampling Program; Greater (Washington, D.C.) Alliance to Stop Pollu-

tion (air and water); Group Against Smog and Pollution; Group Against Smokers' Pollution; Group Against Smoking Pollution
Gaspar Jasper
Gasparilla (Spanish—Little Gaspar)—nickname of José Gaspar—pirate active along west coast of Florida around 1750
gasphyxiation gas + asphyxiation (death by gas)
GASS Gimbal Assembly Storage System
GASSAR General Atomic Standard Safety Analysis Report
gast gastric
Gast Gaston
Gastown waterfront area of Vancouver, BC
gastro gastronomy
gastro (Latin prefix—relating to the stomach)—gastrointestinal
gastroc gastrocnemius
gastroenterol gastroenterology
gastrol gastrolithiasis; gastrolith(ic)(al); gastrolithograph(y); gastrologist; gastrology
gat gatling gun; ground air transmitter; gun; revolver
gat (GAT) generalized algebraic translator
g-at. gram-atom
gat gata (Swedish—Street); (Dano-Norwegian—channel)
GAT Georgetown Automatic Translation; Greenwich Apparent Time
GATA Graphic Arts Technical Association
gatac general assessment tridimensional analog computer
GATAP Generally Accepted Tax-Accounting Principles
GATB General Aptitude Test Battery
GATCO Guild of Air Traffic Control Officers
Gate The Gate (harbor entrance such as the Golden Gate at San Francisco, the Lion's Gate at Vancouver, the Silver Gate at San Diego)
GATE Group to Advance Total Energy (American Gas Association)
Gate City Keokuk, Iowa; Laredo, Texas; St Louis, Missouri; other places acting as gateways to a country or region
Gate City of the South Atlanta, Georgia
Gates of Hell old nickname for

the entrance to Macquarie Harbour on the Indian Ocean coast of Tasmania when it was a penal settlement in Van Diemen's Land
Gate of Tears Bab-el-Mandeb Strait linking Gulf of Aden and Indian Ocean with the Red Sea; Arabic name means Gate of Tears although many sailors call it Gate of Hell because of its desert-heated hot winds
Gateway to Alaska Seattle, Washington
Gateway to the Alps Zurich
Gateway to America New York City
Gateway Arch City St Louis, Missouri
Gateway to the Arctic Fairbanks, Alaska
Gateway to the Bahamas Bimini Island—nearest Florida—off Miami
Gateway to the Big Bend National Park Marfa, Texas
Gateway to the Caribbean Tampa, Florida
Gateway City old nickname of Pittsburgh, Pennsylvania, after the Revolutionary War
Gateway to the Dakotas Sioux Falls, South Dakota
Gateway of the Day Fiji Islands in the South Pacific close to the International Date Line
Gateway to the East Port Said, Egypt
Gateway to Eastern India Calcutta
Gateway to the Golden Isles Brunswick, Georgia
Gateway to the Great Seaway Green Bay, Wisconsin
Gateway to India Bombay
Gateway to Israel Haifa
Gateway to Japan Yokohama
Gateway to Lapland Rovaniemi, Finland
Gateway to Latin America Miami, Florida
Gateway to Moroland Zamboanga, Mindinao
Gateway to Mount Rainier Tacoma, Washington
Gateway to the Negev Beersheba, Israel
Gateway to the North North Bay, Ontario
Gateway to Northern Europe Göteborg (Gothenburg), Sweden
Gateway to the NY-NJ Market Bayonne, New Jersey
Gateway to Parris Island Beau-

fort, South Carolina
Gateway to the Rhine Valley Bonn, Germany
Gateway to the Smokies Knoxville, Tennessee
Gateway to South America Colombia (with ports on the Atlantic and the Pacific)
Gateway to Southwest Japan Kobe
Gateway States California, Louisiana, New Jersey, New York
Gateway to the West sobriquet shared by Pittsburgh, Pennsylvania, and St Louis, Missouri
Gateway to Western India Bombay
GATF Graphic Arts Technical Foundation
Gator Bowl Jacksonville, Florida
'gator(s) alligator(s)
'Gator State Alligator State (Florida)
gatri gamma technology research irradiator
GATS Guidance Acceptance Test Set
GATT General Agreement on Tariffs and Trade
Gatti Guilio Gatti-Casazza
Gatun Girls Gatun Prison for Women and Juveniles at Gatun, Panamá
g at. wt gram atomic weight
GATX General American Transportation Corporation (tank car marking)
GAU Gay Academic Union
Gaucho Land Uruguay (although Argentina and Brazil also have many gauchos)
Gauda (Latin—Gouda)—cheese center in the Netherlands
GAUFCC General Assembly of Unitarian and Free Christian churches
Gaul. Gaulish
Gáu-luhng (Cantonese Chinese —Nine Dragons)—Kowloon —the mainline side of Hong Kong
Gautama Buddah Prince Siddhartha
gav gavage(r); gavel; gavelkind; gavial; gavotte; gross annual value
g/av general average
Gavin Ogilvy Hames M Barrie
gav(s) gavial(s); gavotte(s)
gaw guaranteed annual wage
gawam great American wife and mother
gawr gross axle weight rating
Gay Gaylord

Gay City San Francisco

Gay Gateway to Europe Copenhagen (København)

Gay Lib Gay Liberation Movement

gayola homosexual payola (forced payments made by homosexual establishments to crime syndicates offering them protection)

Gay Paree Paris, France

Gay White Way New York City's Broadway in the 42nd Street and Times Square area

gaz gazette; gazetteer

GAZ (Russian—*Gorki Avtomobilnii Zavod*)—Gorki Automobile Factory producing the Volga sedan-type auto

Gazelle Embraer of Brazil's version of the Aerospatiale SA-341 observation helicopter

gb gall bladder; generator breaker; glide bomb; goodbye; grid bearing; gun bed

gb (GB) code name for sarin (high-toxicity warfare chemical)—$C_4H_{10}FO_2P$

g-b goof-ball (barbiturate pill)

g/b ground based

gB greenish blue

Gb gilbert

GB Gas Board; General Board; General Bronze (corporation); Georges Bizet; Girls' Brigade; Great Books; Great Britain; gunboat (naval symbol)

GB *Gran Bretaña* (Spanish—Great Britain)

gba give better address

GBAD Great Britain Allied and Dominion

gbb glossopharyngeal breathing

GBBA Glass Bottle Blowers Association

GBBCS Ground Base Beam Control System

GBC General Binding Corporation; Gibraltar Broadcasting Company; Greenland Base Command

GB & C General Battery and Ceramic (corporation)

GB COLL George Brown College

gbd grain boundary dislocation

gb'd goofballed (underground slang—drugged)

GBDC Grand Bahama Development Company

g-b-d-f-a (musical mnemonic—good boys do fine always)—bass clef note names of the five lines (g-b-d-f-a)

GBDO Guild of British Dispensing Opticians

gbe gilt bevelled edge

G.B.E. Dame or Knight of the Grand Cross of the British Empire

GBF Gakujitsu Bunken Fukyukai (Japanese Society of Scientific Documentation and Information); Great Books Foundation

GBG General Baking (Stock exchange symbol); Golden Bay Group

gb gas US Army symbol for a colorless and odorless nerve gas of extreme lethality as a one-milligram dose can kill in a few minutes; as a token of its lethality it is also referred to as general biological gas, goodbye gas, or gruesome business gas

GBGB Gaming Board for Great Britain

gbh girth breast height; grievous bodily harm

gbh (GBH) gamma benzene hydrochloride

GBHC Governor Bacon Health Center

gbi great bodily injury

GBI Georgia Bureau of Investigation; Grand Bahama Island (tracking station)

GB & I Great Britain and Ireland

gblu geoballistic input unit

g/bl government bill of lading

GBL Georgian Bay Line; government bill of lading

gbm glomerular basement membrane

GBMA Golf Ball Manufacturers Association

GBMC Greater Baltimore Medical Center

GBMD Global Ballistic Missile Defense

GBNE Guild of British Newspaper Editors

GBNM Glacier Bay National Monument

gbo goods in bad order

G-bomb gravitational bomb

GBOTA Greyhound Breeders, Owners, and Trainers Association

g/box gearbox

GBp Great Britain pound

GBPA Grand Bahama Port Authority

gbr give better reference; gun, bomb, rocket

gbr *gebräuchlich* (German—usual)

GBR *Guinness Book of Records*

GBRMP Great Barrier Reef Marine Park

GBRMPA Great Barrier Reef Marine Park Authority

gbs gall-bladder series

gb's goofballs (barbiturates)

G-B s Guillain-Barré syndrome

GBS George Bernard Shaw; Gifu Broadcasting System (Japanese); Guyana Broadcasting Service

GBSM Guild of Better Shoe Manufacturers

GBST Grass Block Substitution Test

GBSTC General Beadle State Teachers College

gbu (GBU) guided bomb unit

GBV Gustahlwerk Bochumer Verein (Krupp Steel)

GBW Guild of Book Workers

GB & W Green Bay & Western (railroad)

g'bye goodbye

gc gas check; general cargo; general contract(or); geographical coordinates; gigacycle; glucocorticoid; going concern; gonorrhea case; good condition; good conduct; great circle; grid course; ground clearance; ground control(led); guidance control; gun carriage; gun control

Gc great tropic range; gyrocompass

GC Gallaudet College; Gannon College; Gas Council; Gaston College; General Command; Geneva College; Georgetown College; Gettysburg College; Girton College; Glendale College; Gliding Club; glucocorticoid; Goddard College; Golf Club; Gordon College; Goshen College; Goucher College; Government Chemist; Graceland College; Grambling College; Greensboro College; Greenville College; grid course (symbol); Grinnell College; Grover Cleveland (22nd and 24th President U.S.); Guilford College; Gustave Charpentier

G.C. George Cross; gonorrhea case

G & C Gonville and Caius (Cambridge)

GC *Guardia Civil* (Spanish—Civil Guard); *Guardia Costa* (Spanish—Coast Guard)

gca group capacity assessment

gca (GCA) ground-controlled approach

GCA Girls' Clubs of America; Green Coffee Association; Greeting Card Association; Government Contract Committee; Ground Control Center

GCAA Government Corporations Athletic Association

GCAHS Guggenheim Center for Aviation Health and Safety

g cal gram calorie

G-car(s) German car(s)

G-Cass Gomes-Cáceres; Gomez-Cásseres

GCB Glen Canyon Bridge

G.C.B. Knight of the Grand Cross, Order of the Bath

GCBA Golf Course Builders of America

GCBS General Council of British Shipping

GCC Grand Canyon College; Ground Control Center; Gulf Coast College; Gulf Cooperation Council (Persian Gulf countries including Bahrain, Kuwait, Oman, Qatar, Saudi Arabia, United Arab Emirates)

G & CC Gonville and Caius College—Cambridge

GCCA Graduate Careers Council of Australia

GCCC Goshen County Community College

GCCS Government Code and Cypher School (nicknamed Government Golf, Cheese, and Chess Society)

gcd general and complete disarmament; great circle distance; greatest common divisor

GCD Grand Coulee Dam

gce ground cooperational equipment

GCE Gas City Empire; General Certificate of Education; General College Entrance (diploma or examination)

GCEC Greater Colombo Economic Community

gcf greatest common factor

GCFI Gulf and Caribbean Fisheries Institute

gcfr gas-cooled fast reactor

GCFT Gonorrhea Complement Fixation Test

gcg gas-chamber green (institutional paint color)

GCGR Giant's Castle Game Reserve (South Africa)

GCHQ Government Communications Headquarters

gci gray cast iron; ground-controlled interception

gci (GCI) gas chromatograph intoximeter (test for drunk drivers)

GCI General Cognitive Index; Grand Canary Island (tracking station); ground-controlled interception

GCIA Granite Cutters' International Association

G. C. I. E. Knight Grand Commander of the Order of the Indian Empire

gcip guidance correction input panel

GCIS Ground Control Interception Squadron

gcitng ground-control intercept training

GCJC Gulf Coast Junior College

gcl general control language

gcl (GCL) ground-controlled landing

GCL Gulf Caribbean Lines

GCL *Guide to Catholic Literature*

G-class Soviet diesel-powered submarines fitted for launching missiles and nicknamed Golf by NATO

G clef treble clef

GCLH Grand Cross of the Legion of Honour

gcm gas-cut mud (oil well); greatest common measure; greatest common multiple

GCM General Court-Martial; Gian Carlo Menotti; Good Conduct Medal; Grand Cayman, Cayman Islands (airport)

GCMA Government Contract Management Association

GcmG God calls me God

G.C.M.G. Knight Grand Cross of the Order of Saint Michael and Saint George

GCMI Glass Container Manufacturers Institute

GCMO General Court-Martial Order

gcmps gyro(scope) compass

GCMRU General Control of Mosquitoes Research Unit (India)

gcms gas chromatograph mass spectrometer

GCN Greenwich Civil Noon

GCNA Guild of Carillonneurs in North America

GCNM Grand Canyon National Monument

GCNP Grand Canyon National Park (Arizona)

GCNRA Glen Canyon National Recreation Area (Arizona and Utah)

GCO Greater Coin Operators; Guidance Control Officer; Gun Control Officer

gcos general comprehensive operating supervisor

GCOS Great Canadian Oil Sands

GCPL Glasgow Corporation Public Libraries

gcr great circle route

gcr (GCR) gas-cooled graphite-moderated reactor; ground-controlled radar

GCR Geological Characterization Report; Great Central Railway

g crg gun carriage

GCRI Gilette Company Research Institute; Glasshouse Crops Research Institute

GCRO Grand Council and Register of Osteopaths

gcs gate-controlled switch; gram-centimeter-second

gc's genetic girls (real girls)

gc/s gigacycles per second

Gc/s gigacycle per second

GCS Game Conservation Society; General Computer Systems; Georgia Consumer Services; Grant and Contract Service; Group Computer Service(s)

GCSCO Göta Canal Steamship Company

Gc/sec gigacycles per second

G.C.S.G. Knight Grand Commander of the Order of Saint Gregory the Great

G.C.S.I. Dame or Knight Grand Commander of the Star of India

gct ground-control unit

GCT General Classification Test; Glamorgan College of Technology; Greenwich Civil Time

GCTC Green County Teachers College

gcte guidance computer test equipment

GCTS Ground Communication Tracking System

gcu generator control unit; ground control unit

GCU Glasgow Choral Union

G.C.V.O. Dame or Knight of the Grand Cross of the Victorian Order

gcw gross combination weight (of tractor and loaded trailer)

gd general duties; good; good delivery; grade; grading; granddaughter; gravimetric density; ground; ground detector; guard; guardian

g-d god-damned

g/d gallons per day

g & d galvanized and dipped
gd gade (Danish—street)
Gd gadolinium
G-d God (Hebraic contraction)
G^d Grand (French—big, large, principal)
GD Gaol Delivery; General Discharge; General Dispensary; General Dynamics (corporation); Geologic(al) Depository (for spent fuel); George Dewey; Grand Duchy; Gudermannian or hyperbolic amplitude (symbol); Gunnery Division
G-D General Dynamics Corporation
G & D Garcia & Diaz (steamship line); Grosset & Dunlap (publisher)
GD Globe-Democrat
gda gun-damage assessment; gun-defended area; gunned accelerator
GDA General Dynamics Ardmore
GD/A General Dynamics/Astronautics
Gdansk (Polish—Danzig)
GDBA Guide Dogs for the Blind Association
GDBMS Generalized Data Base Management System
gdc geocentric dust cloud
GDC General Dynamics Convair; Gesellschaft Deutscher Chemiker (Society of German Chemists)
Gd Ch Grand Choeur (French—full choir, full organ)
GDCL General Dynamics Canadair Limited
GD/Convair General Dynamics/Convair
GD/D General Dynamics/Daingerfield
GDDQ Group Dimensions Descriptions Questionnaire
gde gilt deckle edging; gross domestic expenditure
Gde gourde (Haitian monetary unit)
G^de Grande (Italian, Portuguese, Spanish—big, large, principal)
GDE General Dynamics Electronics; Graduate Diploma in Extension
GD/EB General Dynamics/Electric Boat
GDED General Dynamics Electro Dynamic
G de F Gaz de France (Gas of France)
g del's golden-delicious apples
GDEUT Guidance Digital Evaluation Test

GDFB Guide Dog Foundation for the Blind
GD Fort Worth General Dynamics Fort Worth
GDFW General Dynamics Fort Worth
GDGA General Dynamics General Atomic
gdh growth and development hormone
gdh (GDH) glutamate dehydrogenase
GDHS Ground Data Handling System
gdi god-damned independent (college student failing to join a fraternity or a sorority)
GDI General Dynamics International
GDIFS Gray and Ductile Iron Founders' Society
GDIS General Dynamics International Service
Gdk Gdansk (Danzig)
gdl ground dynamic laser
Gdl Guadalajara; Guadalajareños (inhabitants)
GDL Grand-Duche de Luxembourg (Grand Duchy of Luxemburg); Guadalajara, Mexico (airport)
GDLC General Dynamics Liquid Carbonic
gdling good looking
GDLST General Dynamics Low-Speed Tunnel
GDM General Dynamics Manufacturing
gdml gas dynamic mixing laser
GDMO General Duty Medical Officer
GDMS General Dynamics Material Service
gdn garden
Gdn Gardener; Godown; Guardian
GDNA Gesellschaft Deutscher Naturforscher und Arzte (Society of German Naturalists and Physicians)
gdnce guidance
Gdnk Gdansk (Danzig)
gdnr gardener
Gdns Gardens
gdo gun direction officer
GDO Guild of Dispensing Opticians
gdop geometric dilution of precision
gdp graphic display processor; gross domestic product; guanosine diphosphate; gun director pointer
gdp (GDP) gross domestic product; guanosine diphosphate
GDP General Defense Plan;

General Dynamics Pomona; Guanosine diphosphate
GDP(D) General Dynamics Pomona (Daingerfield)
GDPS Global Data Processing System (WMO); Government Document Publishing Service
gdr guard rail
GDR German Democratic Republic
gds goods
GDS Gradual Dosage Schedule; Graphic Data System; Graphic(al) Display System; Greater Danube Society
Gdsk Gdansk (Danzig)
Gdsm Guardsman; Guardsmen
gdsob god-damned son of a bitch
gdt graphic display terminal
gd&t guidance dimensioning and tolerancing
GDTP Geologic(al) Disposal Technology Program
gdu graphic display unit
GDU Guide Dog Users
gdwnd gradient wind
Gdy Gdynia
ge gas ejection; gastroenterology; gilt edge(s); good evening; gross energy; gyroscope error
Ge German; Germanic; germanium; Germany
GE Garrison Engineer; General Election; General Electric; Great Exuma; Group Engineer
GEA Gravure Engravers Association; Greater East Asia
GEACS Great East Asia Co-prosperity Sphere
GE-ANPD General Electric Aircraft Nuclear Propulsion Development
gear, gearing
geb *geboren* (German—born); *gebunden* (German—bound)
Geb *Gebergte* (Afrikaans or Dutch—mountain range); *Gebirge* (German—mountains)
GEB General Education Board; Gerber Products (stock exchange symbol); Grain Elevators Board; Guiding Eyes for the Blind
gebco general bathymetric chart of the oceans
GEBECOMA Groupement Belge des Constructeurs de Matériel Aérospatial
Gebr *Gebroeders* (Dutch—brothers); *Gebrüder* (German—brothers)
gec *gecartonneerd* (Dutch—bound in boards)
GEC General Electric Compa-

ny
GECAM Gerência de Operações de Cambio (Portuguese—Exchange Operations Agency)
Gecko NATO nickname for Soviet SA-8 missile system
gecom general(ized) compiler
GECOMIN General Congolese Ore Company
gecref geographic reference (worldwide geographic reference system, also appears as GECREF)
ged gedampft (German—muted)
GED General Education Diploma; General Educational Development (testing service); Geologic(al) Exploration Department; Ground Environmental Development
Geda Goodyear electronic differential analyzer
GEDP General Educational Development Program (USA)
gedr gedrukt (Dutch—printed)
GEDT General Educational Development Test
GEE Generic Environmental Evaluation
GEEC General Egyptian Electricity Corporation
GEEIA Ground Electronics Engineering Installation Agency
geek geomagnetic electrokinetograph
Ge. Eng. Geological Engineer
geep goat + sheep (hybrid)
GEEP General Electric Electronic Evaluator
gef gonadotrophin enhancing factor
GEG Spokane, Washington (airport)
GEGAS General Electric Gas (process)
gegr gegründet (German—founded)
GEHP George Eastman House of Photography (Rochester)
Geh Rat Geheimrat (German—Privy Councillor)
GEI Giovani Esploratori Italiani (Italian Boy Scouts)
GEIA Generic Environmental Impact Assessment; Ground Equipment Electronics Installations Agency
GEIC Gilbert and Ellice Islands Colony
GEICO Government Employees Insurance Company
GEIS Generic Environmental Impact Statement
geistl geistlich (German—spiritual)

gek geomagnetic electrokinetograph
gek gekürzt (German—abbreviated)
GEKTUSA Grand Encampment of the Knights Templar of the United States of America
gel gelatine; gelatinous; gelding
GEL General Electric Laboratory; Great Eastern Line
gelat gelatinous
Gelibolu (Turkish—Gallipoli)
GELISH Ground Emitter Location Identification System—High
Gell Aulus Gellius (Roman grammarian)
gel. quav. gelatina quavis (Latin—in some jelly)
gem. ground-effect machine; guidance evaluation missile
gem. (GEM) growing equity mortgage
Gem Gemini
GEM Gas Equipment Manufacturers; General Education Model
GEMA Gymnastic Equipment Manufacturers Association
GEMAC General Electric Measurement and Control
Gem Beside the Amstel Amsterdam on the Amstel River
GEMCO Grazing Export Meat Company; Groot Eylandt Mining Company
GEMCOS Generalized Message Control System
gemi grating efficiency measurement instrument
Gemini two-man spacecraft
Gem of the Mountains Idaho
gemms geophysical exploration manned mobile submersible
GEMMWU General, Electrical, Mechanical, and Municipal Workers' Union
gems. growth, economy, management, and customer satisfaction (mnemonic for setting up management goals)
gem's ground-effect machines
GEMS Geostationary European Meteorological Satellite; Global Environmental Monitoring System; Goodyear Electronic Mapping System
Gem of the South Pacific New Zealand
Gem State Idaho's official nickname
Gemy General Motors Corporation
gen gender; genealogy; genera; general; generating; generator;

generic; genetic(s); genital; genitive; gentian; genus
Gen General; Gennadi; Genoa; Genoese
Gen Genesis
GEN Oslo, Norway (Gardermoen Airport)
gen av general average
Gend Gendarme (French—Policeman)
genda general data analysis and simulation
Gene Eugene; Eugenia
geneal genealogy
Genebra (Portuguese—Geneva)
gen eng genetic engineer(ing)
General (Portuguese or Spanish—General)—short form for many Latin American places ranging from General Acha in Argentina to General Zuazua in Mexico
General Booth Salvation Army founder William Booth
General Bor Tadeusz Komorowski—cavalry leader of 63-day uprising of Polish underground against Germans occupying Warsaw in 1944 when Russian troops stood by only 10 miles away to watch slaughter of the Polish patriots by the Nazis
General Douglas pseudonym of Soviet corps commander Yakov Smuskevich while leading the Spanish Republican air force in 1936–37
General John nickname of the first Duke of Marlborough—John Churchill
General Kleber pseudonym of Soviet general Grigory Shtern while serving as chief advisor to the Spanish Republican army in 1936–37
General's Lady Martha Washington—wife of General George Washington
General Tom Thumb Charles S Stratton
General Tubman Harriet Ross Tubman of Underground Railroad fame
genet genetic; geneticist; genetics
Genet Janet Flanner's pen name
gen. et sp. nov. genus et species nova (Latin—new genus and species)
Geneva Cross (*see* Cross of Geneva)
Geneva Girls Illinois State Training School for (delinquent) girls at Geneva; a simi-

lar girls training school at Geneva, Nebraska
Genève (French—Geneva)
Genf (German—Geneva)
Genghiz Khan (Mongolian—Perfect Warrior)—his empire stretched from the China Sea to the Dnieper and his subjects called him Ruler of the World
Gen Hosp General Hospital
genic (Latin suffix—produced from, producing)—carcinogenic (cancer producing)
Genie Douglas air-to-air rocket fitted with a nuclear warhead and designated AIR-2A
GENIRAS Generalized Information Retrieval System
genit genitive
Genius of the Renaissance Leonardo da Vinci
genl general
Gen¹ General (Spanish—General)
Gen Mgr General Manager
genn *gennaio* (Italian—January)
gen. nov. *genus novum* (Latin—new genus)
Genoa English place-name equivalent of Genova (Italy's most important port city)
genoc genocide (destruction of people through man-imposed arrests, deportations, executions, famines, harassments, and tortures)
Genova (Italian—Genoa)
Génova (Spanish—Genoa)
gen prac general practice
gen proc general procedure
gen pub general public
genr generate; generation; generator
Gen Rel Gravit General Relativity and Gravitation
genrl general
Gensek *Generalnyi Sekretar* (Russian—Secretary General)—leader of the secretariat of the Central Committee of the Communist Party—post held by Stalin
Gen Supt General Superintendent
gent gentleman
Gent East Flanders' provincial capital in Belgium
Gen Tel & El General Telephone and Electric
Gentleman Boss Chester Alan Arthur
Gentleman Explorer Giovanni da Verrazano
Gentleman Jim prizefighter

James John Corbett
Gentleman Johnny General John Burgoyne, also a noted British playwright
Gentle Peasant-Prince—the loving Cotter-King Robert Burns, according to Robert G. Ingersoll in his poem *The Birthplace of Burns*
Gentle Rebel of Psychoanalysis Karen Horney
gents gentlemen; gentlemen's
Genua (Latin—Genoa)
genvst general visiting (aboard ships of the USN inviting the public)
GENZL Geothermal Energy New Zealand Limited
geo geocentric; geochemistry; geodesy; geodetic; geodynamics; geognosy; geography; geology; geometry; geophysics; geopolitics; geostatic; geothermal (and all their derivatives)
Geo George
GEO Georgetown, Guyana (Atkinson Field)
GEOC General Estate and Orphan Chamber (trust company)
Geochim Cosmochim Acta *Geochimica et Cosmochimica Acta* (Latin—Geochemical and Cosmochemical Review)
geod geodesic; geodesist; geodesy; geodetic; geodynamic(s)
Geo Dat Pt Geodetic Datum Point (North America's geodetic datum point is the National Ocean Survey's triangulation station at Meades Ranch in Osborne County, Kansas)
Geod. E. Geodetic Engineer
geodss ground electro-optical deep-space surveillance
Geof Geoffrey; Geoffroy
Geoffrey Jeffrey
Geoffrey Crayon Washington Irving
Geoffrey Homes Daniel Mainwaring's pseudonym
geog geographer; geographical; geography
Geog Geographic(al); Geography
geogr *geografi* or *geografisk* (Dano-Norwegian — geography or geographer)
Geographical Center of North America Rugby, North Dakota
geohy geohygiene
GEOIS Geographic Information System
geol geologic; geological; geolo-

gist
geol *geologi* or *geologisk* (Dano-Norwegian—geology or geologist)
Geol Geology
Geol.E. Geological Engineer
Geol Surv Geological Survey
geom geometry
Geom Geometry
geomed geometric editor
geomorph geomorphologic(al); geomorphologist; geomorphology
geon (GEON) gyro-erected optical navigation
geoph geophysics
geophy geophysical; geophysics
geopol geopolitical; geopolitics
geor Georgian
Geordie George; Newcastle-on-Tyne, England
Geordieland Newcastle-on-Tyne area of northeastern England
Geordies people from the coalmining and industrial area of Newcastle-on-Tyne and its satellite cities
Geordie(s) Newcastle (persons)
Georef World Geographic Reference System
Georg Brandes Morris Cohen
George George Jefferson (black counterpart of white bigot Archie Bunker and central character of the television serial called *The Jeffersons*)
George Bellairs Harold Blundell's pseudonym
George Brent George Nolan
George Burns Nathan Birnbaum
George Eliot Mary Ann Evans Cross
George Gissing J Storer Clouston
George London George Burnstein
George Orwell Eric Blair
George Raft Georg Ranft
Georges one-dollar bills bearing the portrait of President George Washington
George Sand Amandine Aurore Lucie Dupin (Baroness Dudevant)
Georges Banks submerged fishing grounds off Cape Cod, Massachusetts
Georges Duhamel Denis Thevenin
George Spelvin John Chapman
Georges Simenon (pen name—Georges Sim)
Georgia Ports (north to south) Savannah, Brunswick, Fernandina Beach

Georgia's Oldest City Savannah

Georgie George

Georgies one-dollar bills bearing the portrait of President George Washington

Georgi Vladimov Georgi Volosevich

Georgy George

geos generator, earth orbital scene; geodetic earth-orbiting satellite; geodetic orbiting satellite

GEOS Geodetic Orbiting Satellite; Geodynamics Experimental Ocean Satellite

GEOSECS Geochemical Ocean Sections Study

gep gross energy product

GEPAC General Electric Programmable Automatic Comparator

Geph Gephyra

GEPI *Gestioni e Partecipazioni Industriali* (Italian—Industrial Management and Participation)

GEPURS General Electric General Purpose (Computer)

ger gerund; gerundial; gerundival; gerundive

Ger German; Germanic; Germany

Ger German (language spoken by 120 million people in Austria, Germany, and Switzerland and understood by many people whose language is of Germanic origin such as the Dutch, German Jews, and Scandinavians)

GER Great Eastern Railway

gera geratic(al)(ly); geratologic(al)(ly); geratologist; geratology

Gerard de Nerval (pseudonym —Gerard Labrunie)

ger grndng gerund grinding (pedagogic pedantry)

geriat geriatrics

germ. ground-effect research machine

Germ *Germinal* (French—Seedy Month)—beginning March 21st—seventh month of the French Revolutionary Calendar and also title of a novel by Zola

german german camomile (tea); german ivy (South African ivy); german knot (figure-8 knot); german lapis (imitation lapis lazuli); german measles (virus disease also called rubella); german shepherd (german police dog); german silver

(copper-nickel-zinc alloy resembling silver)

German Africa former German colonies (Cameroons, German East Africa, German Southwest Africa, Togoland)

German Cradle of U.S. Presidents Germany—ancestral home of Presidents Eisenhower and Hoover

German East Africa colonial possession of Germany from 1885 to 1916; included most of Tanganyika but not British Zanzibar later merged with Tanganyika to form Tanzania in 1964

German Fourteen Germany's fourteen best-known classical composers arranged chronologically: Telemann, Handel, Glück, Beethoven, von Weber, Mendelssohn, Schumann, Wagner, Brahms, Bruch, Strauss, Schoenberg, Hindemith, Weill

German Hanseatic Seaport Cities Bremen, Danzig, Hamburg, Lübeck

Germania (Latin—Germany)

German Ocean North Sea; old German name for the North Sea

Germanophone Countries Austria, Germany, Liechtenstein, Luxembourg, German-speaking cantons of Switzerland, and many places in the United States where German or German dialects such as Pennsylvania German (Pennsylvania Dutch) are spoken

German Ports (*see* East German Ports *and* West German Ports)

Germans the Germans [Former President Nixon's Chief of Staff—HR (Bob) Haldeman and Domestic Adviser John Erlichman]

german silver 50% copper, 30% nickel, 20% zinc

German South-West Africa colonial possession of Germany from 1884 to 1915 when it was surrendered to South Africa; the UN calls the area Namibia

German-speaking Places (*see* Germanophone Countries)

Germany Federal Republic of Germany (West Germany) and German Democratic Republic (East Germany) make up central Europe's most industrious sector; in both coun-

tries German is the main tongue; *Bundesrepublik Deutschland* (West); *Deutsche Demokratische Republik* (East)

Germany's Largest Port Hamburg

germi germicide

GERNORSEA German Naval Forces in the North Sea

Geron Geronimo

gerontol gerontology

Gerry Gerald; Gerard; Gerhard

Gersis General Electric range safety instrumentation system

gert graphical evaluation and review technique

Gert Gertie; Gertrude

Gertie Lawrence Gertrude Lawrence (Gertrud Alexandra Dagmar Lawrence Klasen)

Geru *Gerusalemme* (Italian—Jerusalem)

Gerunda (Latin—Gerona)

ges *gesetzlich* (German—registered)

Ges (German—G-flat); *Gesellschaft* (German—association, company, society)

GES General Engineering Service; Government Economic Service; Great Eastern Shipping

GE-S Gold Exchange—Singapore

GESAMP Group of Experts on the Scientific Aspects of Marine Pollution

gesch *geschützt* (German—registered)

Gesch *Geschichte* (German—history)

GESCO General Electric Supply Corporation

gespeg (Micmac Indian—end of the earth)—Quebec's Gaspé Peninsula

gest gas-explosive simulation technique

gest *gestorben* (German—dead, deceased)

Gestapo Geheime Staatspolizei (German—State Secret Police)

get. ground-elapsed time; ground-engaging tool(s)

GET Getty Oil (stock exchange symbol); Great Eastern Television (Australian); Gross Error Test(ing)

get 1/2 gastric emptying half-time

GETIS Ground Environment Technical Information System

getlo get locally

getma get from local manufacturer; purchase for local manufacturer

getol ground-effect takeoff and landing

Getty The Getty (J Paul Getty Museum in Santa Monica, California)

Gettysburg Battlefield Painter Henri Emmanuel Félix Philippoteaux

GEU Genetic Evaluation and Utilization

gev giga electron volt (10^9 electron volts)

gev (GEV) ground-effect vehicle

GeV giga electron volt

GEVIC General Electric Variable Increment Computer

gew gram equivalent weight

gew *gewoonlijk* (Dutch—as a rule, generally, usually)

Gew *Gewehr* (German—rifle)

gez *gezeichnet* (German—signed)

Gez *Gezira* (Arabic—island)

GEZ Gosudarstvennoe knigoisdatelstvo (Russian—State Publishing House)

gf gap filler; generator field; girl friend; globular fibrous; glomerular filtrate; goldfield; government form; green feed; ground fog; growth fraction; guiltfree

g-f globular-fibrous

Gf Gottfried

GF General Fireproofing; General Foods; Georgia & Florida (railroad); Guggenheim Foundation

G & F Georgia & Florida (railroad)

gfa good fair average; good freight agent; gunfire area

GFA Game Fishing Association; Gardens For All; Glider Flying Area; Gliding Federation of Australia

GFA *Générale Française (de Construction) Automobile*

GFAA Game Fishing Association of Australia

g factor general factor

gfae government-furnished aerospace equipment

gfam graphics flutter analysis methods

gfci ground fault circuit interrupter

GFCM General Fisheries Council for the Mediterranean (FAO)

gfd general functional description

GFD General Freight Department

GFDL Geophysical Fluid Dynamics Laboratory

gfe government-furnished equipment

gff granolithic finish floor

GFG *Good Food Guide*

GFH George Frideric Handel

gfi gas-flow indicator; ground-fault interrupter

GFI General Felt Industries

GFIC Georgia Foundation for Independent Colleges

Gfk Gustafsvik

Gfl Genfle (Gävle)

GFL Glossary Function List

gfm government-furnished materiel; government-furnished missile

gfme government-furnished missile equipment

GFMVT General Foods Moisture Vapor Test

GFO General Freight Office

μ-force(s) gravity force(s)

G forces acceleration forces

gfp government-furnished parts; government-furnished property

gfr gap-filled radar; glomerular filtration rate

GFR German Federal Republic; Government Facilities Request

gfrc glass-fiber reinforced cement; glass-fiber reinforced concrete

gfrp glass-fiber reinforced plastic

GFS Girls Friendly Society

gfst ground fuel start tank

gft graphical firing table

GFTU General Federation of Trade Unions

gfu glazed facing units

gfut ground fuel ullage tank

GFWC General Federation of Women's Clubs

gg gamma globulin; gas generator; great gross

g-g ground-to-ground

gg *gange* (Dano-Norwegian—multiply)

Gg Georgian

GG Government Gazette; Governor General

G-G Goodrich-Gulf (chemicals)

G & G Gordon and Gotch

GGA Girl Guides Association; Gulf General Atomic

GGAC Gulf General Atomic Company (formerly General Atomic division of General Dynamics)

Ggb *Gorilla gorilla beringei* (the mountain gorilla)

GGB Golden Gate Bridge

GGB & HD Golden Gate Bridge and Highway District

ggc ground guidance computer

GGC Golden Gate College

GGCST Gleb-Goldstein Color Sorting Test

ggd great granddaughter

gge garage; generalized glandular enlargement

ggf ground gained forward

g.g.g. *gummi guttae gambiae* (Latin—gamboge)—cathartic

Ggg *Gorilla gorilla gorilla* (the lowland gorilla)

GGHNP Golden Gate Highlands National Park (South Africa)

GGI Guided Group Interaction

g gl ground-glass

ggm (GGM) ground-to-ground missile

GGNRA Golden Gate National Recreation Area (San Francisco)

Ggo Gallego

GGOC Goldovsky Grand Opera Company

g gr great gross

GGR Gambill Goose Refuge (Texas); Ground Gunnery Range

ggs great grandson; ground gained sideways

g-g's go-go girls

GGS Ground Guidance System

GGSM Graduate of the Guildhall School of Music

ggts gravity-gradient test satellite

gh grid heading; growth hormone; guardhouse

gh (GH) growth hormone

Gh Ghana, Commonwealth of

GH General Hospital; Grosvenor House

GH *Good Housekeeping*

GHA Greenwich Hour Angle

GHAA Group Health Association of America

GhAF Ghanian Air Force

GHAMS Greenwich Hour Angle of the Mean Sun

Ghan Afghan Express

Ghana Republic of Ghana (West African nation whose English-speaking Ghanians farm for cocoa and other tropical crops as well as mining for bauxite, industrial diamonds, gold, and manganese), formerly the Gold Coast and British Togoland

GHANA Ghana Airways

Ghana Ports (west to east) Takoradi and Tema plus six very small ports

GHATS Greenwich Hour Angle of the True Sun

Ghazze (Arabic—Gaza)

GHB Good Housekeeping Bureau

ghc guidance heater control

GHC Gray Harbor College; Group Health Cooperative

GHDVHS Grace H Dodge Vocational High School

ghe ground handling equipment

G H & H Galveston, Houston & Henderson (railroad)

GHI Good Housekeeping Institute

Ghirlandaio Domenico di Tomaso Bigordi

GHMC Good Harvest Marine Company

GHMS Graduate in Homeopathic Medicine and Surgery

GhN Ghana Navy

ghost. global horizontal sounding technique

g/hphr gallons per horsepower hour

GHQ General Headquarters

g/hr gallons per hour

ghrf growth hormone-releasing factor

ghrh growth hormone releasing hormone

GHS Galileo High School; Girls High School

Ght Ghent

Ghub Ghubba (Arabic—bay, cove)

ghx ground heat exchanger

GHz gigahertz (gigacycle per second)

gi galvanized iron; gastrointestinal; general issue; generation interval; gill; globulin insulin; government issue; gross income; gross inventory

g-i granuloma inguinale

Gi Giles; Guy

GI Air Guinée; American Soldier (from *gi*—general issue or government issue); Garden Island; General Intelligence; Gideons International; Gimbel Brothers (stock exchange symbol); Government of India; Gunner Instructor

GI Gessellschaft für Informatik (German—Society for Data Processing)

gia grant-in-aid (diplomatese—handout)

GIA Garuda Indonesian Airways; Gemological Institute of America; Goodwill Industries

of America; Gregorian Institute of America; Gummed Industries Association

Giacomo Meyerbeer Jakob Liebmann Beer

GIAHA Gilcrease Institute of American History and Art (Tulsa)

Giamaica (Italian—Jamaica)

Giant of Danish Literature Hans Christian Andersen

Giant of Freethought Charles Bradlaugh

Giant of Mexican Music Carlos Chavez

Giant in the Nursery Jean Piaget

Giappone (Italian—Japan)

giardiasis diarrhea due to contaminated food or water and common in many places around the globe

gib guy in the back

Gib Gibraltar; Gibraltarian

GIB Gibraltar, British Crown Colony (airport); Gulf International Bank

GIBAIR Gibraltar Airways

Gib(bie) Gilbert

gibb(s) gibbon(s)

Gibfo Gibraltar for orders

Gibilterra (Italian—Gibraltar)

GIBMED Gibraltar Mediterranean Command (NATO)

gibs guy in the back seat

gib(s) gibbon(s)—smallest of the anthropoid apes and found in the forests of southeast Asia where the largest is the siamang

Gibs Gibraltarians

Gibson Gibson Desert of east-central Western Australia

Gib-tv Gibraltar television

gic ground intercept control

GIC General Investment Corporation; Government Information Center

GICA Green Island Coral Atoll (Queensland)

gi'd prepared for military-type inspection

Gid Gideon

GID General Intelligence Division

GIDAP Guidance Inertial Data Analysis Program

GIDC Georgia Information Dissemination Center

GIDEP Government-Industry Data Exchange Program

gi distress gastro-intestinal distress

gidp grounded into double plays

GIEE Graduate of the Institu-

tion of Electrical Engineers

gif (GIF) growth hormone-inhibiting factor

GIF Rio de Janeiro, Brazil (Galeo Airport)

GIFAS Groupement des Industries Françaises Aéronautiques et Spatiales (French Aeronautical and Aerospace Industry Association)

giga 10^9

Gig Harbor Purdy Treatment Center for Women at Gig Harbor, Washington

gigo garbage in, garbage out (acronym describing a computer whose operation is suspect because input is suspect)

GIIS Graduate Institute of International Studies (Geneva)

GIJ Guild of Irish Journalists

Gil Gilbert; Gilchrist; Gilder; Gildo; Gilead; Giles; Gilford; Gilland; Gillespie; Gillian; Gilman; Gilmore; Gilroy

Gilberts Gilbert and Ellice Islands in the Pacific close to the Equator and including the Line Islands plus the Phoenix Islands

Gilded Age opulent post-Civil War period in the United States

Gill(y) Gillian

Gilo Gilberto

Gilois French-built scissors bridge mounted on a tank and useful in spanning canals, ditches, and small streams

gim general information management; gimmick

GI Mech Eng Graduate of the Institution of Mechanical Engineers

gimic guard-ring-implanted monolithic integrated circuit

GIMLCS Generalized Information Management Language and Computer System

gimp. gimbal position(ing)

GIMPEX Guyana Import-Export

GIMRADA Geodesy, Intelligence and Mapping Research and Development Agency (US Army)

gin giugno (Italian—June)

Gin Ginebra (Spanish—Geneva)

Gina Genevieve; Virginia

Ginebra (Spanish—Geneva)

Ginevra (talian—Geneva)

ging gingival; gingivitis

ging. gingiva (Latin—gum)

Ginger Rogers Virginia McMath

gink ginkitis; ginkitological(ly); ginkitology (science and study of elderly ginks); ginkoid(al)

Ginnie Mae nickname of the Government National Mortgage Association

Ginny Virginia

gins aborigine girls

G Inst T Graduate of the Institute of Transport

GI Nuc Eng Graduate of the Institution of Nuclear Engineers

Ginza center of downtown Tokyo

gio giovedi (Italian—Thursday)

GIO Government Information Organization; Government Insurance Office; Guild of Insurance Officials

g ion gram ion

Giorgione Giorgio Barbarelli

giorn giornaliero (Italian—daily); *giornalist* (Italian—journalist)

Giov Giovanna; Giovanni

gip gas in place (oil well); get(ting) into publication(s); get(ting) into publishing

GIP Great Indian Peninsular (railway)

Gippesvicum (Latin—Ipswich)

Gipps Gippsland, Victoria, Australia

Gippsland not a country but Victoria—Australia's best-endowed province and holiday paradise for surfers and others

GIPR Great Indian Peninsula Railway

GIPSY General Information Processing System

giq giant imperial quart (of beer)

gir girder

GIR Gulf Interior Region

giraffe. graphic interface for finite elements

GIRB Georgia Inspection and Rating Bureau

gird ground-installed recording data

GIRDHS Ground Installation Reconnaissance Data Handling System

girl. generalized information retrieval language

GIRLS Generalized Information Retrieval and Listing System

Girls' Cottage Girls' Cottage School (for delinquents) at Chambly, Québec

Girls' Town correctional facility for misdemeanants at Tecum-

seh, Oklahoma

giro autogiro

Gironde river on west coast of France connecting Bordeaux with Bay of Biscay and Atlantic Ocean

GIRU General Intelligence and Reconnaissance Unit (Israel's anti-terrorist commando force is GIRU 269)

gis galvanized iron sheet(ing); gastrointestinal series

gi's gastrointestinal troubles (diarrhea)

Gis (German—G-sharp)

GI's enlisted men; enlisted soldiers in the US Army

GIS General Mills (stock exchange symbol); Generalized Information System; Geographic Information Systems; Geoscience Information Society; Global Information System; Government Information Service(s)

Gisep Giuseppe

GISP Greenland Ice Sheet Program; Guided Independent Study Program

gi spasm gastrointestinal spasm

GISS Goddard Institute of Space Studies (NASA)

git guitar

git (GIT) group inclusive tour; group insurance tour (travel plan)

GIT General Information Test; Georgia Institute of Technology

Gita Bhagavad-Gita

Gitmo Guantánamo Naval Base (Guantánamo Bay, Cuba)

giu geoballistic input unit

GIUK Greenland, Iceland, United Kingdom

Gius Giuseppe

Givhans Ferry Givhans Ferry State Park (near Charleston, South Carolina)

GIW Gulf Intracoastal Waterway

gj gigajoule (1000-million joules); grapefruit juice

GJB George Jackson Brigade (underground black extremists)

GJC Galdhöppigen Jotunheimen Climbers; Gibbs Junior College; Grand Junction Canal

GJD Grand Junior Deacon

Gjn Gijon

GJO Grand Junction Office

Gk Greek

GK Gaol Keeper

GKC Gilbert Keith Chesterton

GKD-notation Gordon-Kendall-Davison notation for chemical formulas (sometimes called Birmingham notation)

Gk I Greek Isles

GKIAE *Gossurdarstveinny Komitet po Ispolzovaniyu Atomnoi Energi* (Russian— State Committee for the Use of Atomic Energy)

GKN Guest, Keen, and Nettlefold

GK & N Guest, Keen & Nettleworth

gkw god knows what

gl gas lifting (oil well); general ledger; glass; glazed; gloss; gold lease; gothic letter; ground level; gun layer; gun license

gl (GL) general liability

g/l grams per liter

Gl Glagolitic; glucinium

Gl. Gloria in excelsis Deo (Latin Glory be to God in the highest)

GL Germanischer Lloyd's (German ship classifier); Goldstar Liner; Government Laboratory; Great Lakes (load line mark); Greek line

G.L. Graduate in Law

GL Gamle (Swedish—old); *Glacier* (French—glacier; ice field)

gla gingivolinguo—axial

GLA General Laboratory Associates; Georgia Library Association; Glasgow, Scotland (airport)

glab glabrous

glac glacial

GLAC Greek Library Association of Cyprus

Glacier place-name in British Columbia or Montana; short form for Glacier Bay National Monument, Glacier Highway, or Glacier Island in Alaska, Glacier Mountain in Colorado, Glacier National Park in British Columbia and Montana, Glacier Peak in Washington

glaciol glaciologist(ic)(al)(ly); glaciolographic(al)(ly); glaciolography; glaciology

Glad Gladstone; Gladwin; Gladys

GLAD Gay and Lesbian Advocates and Defenders

'Glades Florida's Everglades

glads gladiolas

Glam Glamorganshire

GLAMO Great Lakes Association of Marine Operators

Glamorgan Glamorganshire

gland. glandular
gland. glandula (Latin—gland)
Glas Glasgow; Glaswegian
Glascovia (Latin—Glasgow)—also known as Glascua
GLASLA Great Lakes—St Lawrence Association
glasphalt glass + asphalt (paving)
glass silicon dioxide—SiO_2
glass. glassware
Glass Capital of Massachusetts Boston
Glass Capital of New York Corning
Glass Capital of Ohio Toledo
Glass Capital of Pennsylvania Pittsburgh
Glass Center Toledo, Ohio
Glass House the glassed-in Los Angeles County Jail in California
glassie glass playing marble
Glass Menagerie on the East River United Nations headquarters facing New York City's East River
glassteel glass + steel (skyscrapers)
Glaswegian(s) Glasgow person(s)
glau glaucous
glauberite calcium sodium sulfate
glauber's salt sodium sulfate
glauc glaucoma
Glav Red Glavnyi Redaktor (Russian—Editor-in-Chief)
Glazunov 6 Alexander Glazunov's six symphonies
glb glass block
GLB Greater London Borough (City of London)
GLBA Great Lakes Booksellers' Association
glbs globes
GLBSA Greater London Building Surveyors Association
glc gas-liquid-chromatographic; global loran (navigation) chart(s)
GLC Greater London Council; Great Lakes Carbon; Great Lakes Colleges; Great Lakes Commission
GLCA Great Lakes College Association
glcm (GLCM) ground-launched surface-to-surface cruise missile
GLCM Graduate of the London College of Music
GLCSC Gay and Lesbian Community Service Center
gld gilded; glider; gold; guilder
Gld Cst Gold Coast

GLDP Greater London Development Plan
gld pltd gold plated
gldr guilder
GLE Grand Larousse Encyclopedie (French—Great Larousse Encyclopedia)
gleep graphite low-energy experimental pile
GLEF Gay and Lesbian Emergency Fund
Gleiwitz (German—Gliwice)
Glenard's disease prolapse of one or more internal organs
Glen Ford Gwyllyn Ford
GLERL Great Lakes Environmental Research Laboratory
Glesca Glasgow
GLF Gay Liberation Front
GLFB Greater London Fund for the Blind
GLFC Great Lakes Fisheries Commission
Glf Mex Gulf of Mexico
Glf Str Gulf Stream
GLHA Great Lakes Harbor Association
gli glider
gli (GLI) glucagon-like immunoreactive factor from gastrointestinal mucosa
GLI General Time (stock exchange symbol); Great Lakes Institute (University of Toronto)
glickums ground-launched cruise missiles (GLCMs)
Glimmerglass James Fenimore Cooper's nickname for Lake Otsego in New York State; Lake Otsego at Cooperstown, New York
GLIS Greater London Information Service
glit glittering
glitch unexpected transient
Glitter Gulch Reno, Nevada's nickname
Glitz Galitzianer (Yiddish—Galician)—person of Judaic origin from Austrian or Polish Galicia
Gliwice (Polish—Gleiwitz)
glld ground laser locator designator
GLLO Great Lakes Licensed Officer's Organization
glm graduated learning method; graduated length method
glm grand livre du mois (French—great book of the month)—best-seller
GLM Gay Liberation Movement
GLMI Great Lakes Maritime Institute

gln (GLN) glutamine (amino acid)
Gln Glen (postal abbreviation)
GLNTC Great Lakes Naval Training Center
GLO General Land Office; Goddard Launch Operations (NASA); Ground Liaison Office(r); Gunnery Liaison Office(r)
g LO₂ t ground liquid-oxygen tank
glob globular; globule
globecomm global communications
Globemaster Douglas transport designated C-124 and built for cargo carrying or flying 200 troops
glock glockenspiel
GLOE Gay and Lesbian Outreach to Elders
glomb glide bomb
glomex global oceanographic and meteorological experiment (GLOMEX)—1975–1980
Gloria Gloria Swanson
Glorious Fifty glorious fifty states comprising the United States of America
Glorious Fourth July 4 (Independence Day in the U.S.A.)
Glorious Gloria Gloria Swanson
Glos Gloucestershire
gloss. glossary
gloss (Latin prefix—tongue)—glossary, glossopharyngeal
glossies slick-paper magazines
Gloster Gloucester
Glostr Glostrup
glotrac global tracking
Glou Gloucester(shire)
Gloucestr Gloucester
glow. gross liftoff weight
GLOW Gay and Lesbian—an Older Way
glp general layout plan(ning); general letter packet
GLP Good Laboratory Practice(s); Greater London Plan
GLP Great Lakes Pilot
GLPA Great Lakes Pilotage Administration
glq greater than lot quantities
glr gas liquid ratio (oil well)
Glr Gloucester
Gls Glasgow
GLS Georgetown Law School; Graduate Library School; Greene Line Steamers (Mississippi); Gypsy Lore Society
GLSOA Great Lakes Ship Owners Association
glt gilt; greetings letter telegram;

guide light
glu glutamic acid
Glubb Pasha John Bagot Glubb
gluco* or *glyco (Greek *glykys*—sweet)—glucose, glycerol, glycogen, glycoprotein
glulam(s) glue-laminated wooden beam(s)
glv globe valve
GLV Gemini Launch Vehicle
GLW Corning Glass Works (stock exchange symbol)
glwb glazed wallboard
GLWQB Great Lakes Water Quality Board (Canada-U.S.)
gly glycerine; glycerol glycogen
gly (GLY) glycine (amino acid)
Gly Gulley; Gully
glycerol glycerine—$C_3H_5(OH)_3$
glyc-pos glycerine suppositories
glyp glyphography; glyptics; glyptography
glyph hieroglyph
glyph(s) hieroglyph(s)
GLZ General Bronze Corporation (stock exchange symbol)
gm general medicine; general mortgage; good morning; gram; gross margin; guard mail; guided missile; mutual conductance (symbol)
gm (GM) group mark (data processing); group mark(ing)
g/m gallons per minute
GM General Manager; General Medicine; General Motors; Grand Master; Guided Missile; Gunner's Mate; Gustav Mahler
G-M Geiger-Muller (detector)
G.M. George Medal; Gold Medal
GM metacentric height (symbol)
G & M Globe and Mail (Toronto)
gm² grams per square meter (paper weight)
GMA Gallery of Modern Art; Glass Manufacturers Association; Government Modification Authorization; Grocery Manufacturers of America; Grocery Manufacturers of Australia
GMAA Gold Mining Association of America
gmac gaining major air command
GMAC General Motors Acceptance Corporation
GMAD General Motors Assembly Division
GMAIC Guided Missile and Aerospace Intelligence Committee

G-man FBI law-enforcement officer also known as a special agent
GMAS Ground Munitions Analysis Study
GMAT Graduate Management Admissions Test; Greenwich Mean Astronomical Time
GMATS General Motors Air Transport Section
gm-aw gram atomic weight
gmb good merchandise brand
GMB Georg Morris Brandes (originally Cohen)
GMBE Grand Master (of the Order of the) British Empire
GmbH Gesellschaft mit beschränkter Haftung (German—incorporated, limited liability company)
gmbl gimbal
gmc gun motor carriage
Gmc Germanic
GMC General Medical Council; General Motors Corporation; George Mason College; Global Marine Corporation; Guggenheim Memorial Concerts; Guided Missile Command; Guided Missile Committee; Gulf Maritime Company
GMCC Geophysical Monitoring for Climatic Change
GMCO General Mathematics Computing Option
g-m counter Geiger-Muller counter for measuring cosmic rays and radioactivity
GMCS Group Medicare Cooperative Society
gmd (GMD) green-monkey disease
GMDRL General Motors Defense Research Laboratories
G men FBI law-enforcement officers
g met gun-metal
GMF Glass Manufacturers Federation
GMFC General Mining and Finance Corporation
gmfp guided-missile firing panel
Gmh Grangemouth
GM-H General Motors-Holden (Australia)
GMI General Motors Institute
GMIA Gelatin Manufacturers Institute of America
gmidg garnish moulding
gmk grand master keyed; green monkey kidney
GMK Gold Mines of Kalgoorlie
GMK Gomei Kaisha (Japanese—Mercantile Partnership)

gm/l grams per liter
GML Gold Mining Lease
gmldg garnish molding
GMMC Godden Memorial Medical Centre (Fiji)
GMNNR Glasson Moss National Nature Reserve (England)
GMNP Guadalupe Mountains National Park (Texas)
GMNZ General Motors New Zealand
Gmo Guillermo (Spanish—William)
GMO Government Medical Office(r); Guided Missile Office(r)
GM & O Gulf, Mobile & Ohio (railroad)
g mol g molecule
GMOO Guided Missile Operations Office(r)
gmp guaranteed minimum price
gmp (GMP) guanosine monophosphate
GMP General Medical Practice; Green Mansion Properties
gmpa gas-metal-plasma arc
gmpg ground nautical miles per gallon
GMPI Guilford-Martin Personnel Inventory
gmq good merchantable quality
gmr ground mapping radar
GMRD Guided Missiles Range Division (Pan American World Airways)
gm rm games room
gms guidance monitor set
gms (GMS) geostationary meteorological satellite
gm & s general, medical, and surgical
Gms Grimsby
GMS General Maintenance System; General Medical Services
GMSB Guided Missile System Branch
GMSC Guangdong Manpower Service Corporation
GMSL Group Management Service Limited
GMST General Military Subjects Test
GMT General American Transportation (stock exchange symbol); Greenwich Mean Time; Greenwich Meridian Time
GMT Geo Marine Technology*; *Geriatric Medicine Today
GMTC General Motors Technical Center; Glutamate Manufacturers Technical Committee

GMTL Goudy Memorial Typographic Laboratory (Newhouse Communications Center—Syracuse University)

gmts guided missile test set

g-m tube geiger-müller tube

gmv gram molecular volume

GMV Government Motor Vehicle; Government Motor Vessel

gmw gram molecular weight

GMWU General and Municipal Workers Union

gn general; glen; golden number; good night; green; guide number; guinea (21 shillings); gun

g:n glucose-nitrogen (ratio)

GN Great Northern (railroad); great novel (in sense of great American novel as discussed in World-War-I days by e.e. cummings, John Dos Passos, Gilbert Seldes, and their generation of writers)

G.N. Graduate Nurse

G & N Gippsland and Northern

GN *Gas Natural* (Spanish—natural gas); *Guardia Nacional* (Spanish—National Guard)

GN₂ gaseous nitrogen

GN₂ s/a gaseous nitrogen storage area

g N₂ stor gaseous nitrogen storage

GNAL Georgia Nuclear Aircraft Laboratory

GNAS Grand National Archery Society

GNB *Good News Bible*

gnc general nuclear war

gn & c guidance, navigation, and control

GNC General Nursing Council; Good Neighbor Council(s)

gnd gross national demand; ground

gndck ground check

gnd ht xgr ground heat exchanger

gne gross national effluent

gne (GNE) gross national expenditure

gni (GNI) gross national income

gnl general

GNL Georgia Nuclear Laboratory

GNM Ghana National Museum

GNMA Government National Mortgage Association

GNN Great Northern Nekoosa

Gnomes of Zürich Swiss bankers

g noz grease nozzle

gnp (GNP) gross national product

g np gas, nonpersistent

GNP Glacier National Park (one in British Columbia and another in Montana); Gombe National Park (Tanzania); Gorongoza National Park (Mozambique); gross national product

GNP & BL Great Northern Pacific & Burlington Lines (merger of Chicago, Burlington & Quincy, Great Northern, Northern Pacific, Pacific Coast Railroad, Spokane, Portland & Seattle Railway)

GNPC Great Northern Paper Company

gnr goods not received; gunner; gunnery

gnr (GNR) gaseous nuclear rocket

GNR Great Northern Railway

GNRA Gateway National Recreation Area (New York City's designation by the Department of the Interior)

g/n ratio glucose-nitrogen ratio

gnrh (GnRH) gonadotropin-releasing hormone

gnrl general

gnry gunnery

gns guineas

Gns Guernsey

GNS General Naval Staff

GNSRA Great North of Scotland Railway Association

GNT *Gesellschaft für Nukleartransporte* (German—Nuclear Transport Society)

GNTC Girls' Nautical Training Corps

gnte *gerente* (Spanish—manager)

GNTO Greek National Tourist Organization

GNTP Georgia Narcotics Treatment Project

gnw (GNW) gross national welfare

Gny Sgt Gunnery Sergeant

go. gas operated; gear oil; growth opportunities

go' gore

g/o gear box oil

Go gadolinium; Gothic

G⁰ Gonzalo (Spanish)

GO General Office; general order(s); George Orwell (Eric Blair); Group Officer; Gulf Oil (stock exchange symbol)

GO₂ gaseous oxygen

goa gone on arrival; gyro(scope) output amplifier

Goa NATO nickname for Soviet SA-3 air-defense missile system

GOA Gun Owners of America

GOAL Gay Organized Alliance for Liberation

goar ground-observer aircraft recognition

GOAT Give Our Animals Time (acronymically named organization devoted to saving the many endangered goats on California's offshore islands such as San Clemente)

gob. gobbledygook; good ordinary brand

gob *gobierno* (Spanish—government)

Gob *Gobernador* (Spanish—Governor)

G o B Government of Belize (formerly British Honduras)

GObC Ground Observers Corps (Canada)

Gobi great desert of Central Asia in Mongolia

gobᵒ *gobierno* (Spanish—government)

Gobr *Gobernador* (Spanish—Governor)

goc gas-oil content (oil well)

GOC General Officer Commanding; Ground Observer Corps; Gulf Oil Company

GOC in C General Officer Commanding in Chief

GO City Greater Omaha, Nebraska

goco government-owned contractor-operated

god. (GOD) government observing device (acronym suggesting big brother is watching)

g.o.d. good old days

God of Animals, Crops, Fertility, Prophecy, and Rural Life Faunus (Roman); Pan (Greek)

GODAS Graphically Oriented Design and Analysis System

God of Battle, Inspiration, and Death Odin (Norse)

God of Blacksmithing and Forges Hephaistos (Greek); Vulcan (Roman)

God of Blame and Ridicule Momus (Roman)

God of Bloodshed and War the Greek god Ares; the Roman god Mars

God of Boundaries Terminus (Roman) whose name in Latin means boundary

God of the Christians and Jews Jehovah

God of Corn and Grain Robigus (Roman)

God of Creation and Destruction

Siva (Hindu)

God of Cunning Dexterity Hermes (Greek); Mercury (Roman)

God of the Dead and the Underworld Dis (Roman); Hades or Hiades (Greek); Mantus (Etruscan); Pluto (Roman)

God of Death Mors (Roman); Thanatos (Greek)

Goddess of Agriculture Ceres or Vacuna (Roman); Demeter (Greek)

Goddess of Animals, Crops, Fertility, Prophecy, and Rural Life Bona Dea or Bona Mater or Fauna (Roman)

Goddess of Arts, Crafts, and Sciences Athena (Greek); Minerva (Roman)

Goddess of Athens Athena

Goddess of Avenging Justice Nemesis (Greek)

Goddess of Beauty and Love Aphrodite (Greek); Venus (Roman)

Goddess of Birth the Roman goddess Carmenta also known as Carmentis

Goddess of the Breeze Aura (Greek)

Goddess of Bridesmaids Juno Pronuba (Roman)

Goddess of Burials, Corpses, and Funerals Libitina (Roman)

Goddess of Cattle and Pastures Pales (Roman)

Goddess of Chance Fortuna (Roman)

Goddess of Chaos, Sickness, and Death Kali (Hindu)

Goddess of Childbirth and Prophecy Roman names include those of Carmenta, Juno Lucina, and Postverta

Goddess of the Crops the Greek goddesses Auxesia and Demeter share this appellation

Goddess of the Dead Mania (Roman)

Goddess of Death Hel (Norse folklore)

Goddess of Destiny or Fate Necessitas (Roman)

Goddess of Discord and Strife Discordia (Roman) or Eris (Greek); each credited with throwing the apple of discord and strife in revenge for not being invited to a wedding

Goddess of Domestic Animals Bubona (Roman)

Goddess of Earth Gaea or Rhea (Greek); Cybele, Tellus, or Terra (Roman)

Goddess of Fair Speech and

Good Report Eufemia (Greek)

Goddess of Faith, Honesty, and Oaths Fides (Roman)

Goddess of Fame Fama (Roman); Pheme (Greek)

Goddess of Family Harmony Verplaca (Roman) also spelled Virplaca

Goddess of Famine Fames (Roman goddess whose Latin name means famine or hunger)

Goddess of the Fertile Earth Opalia or Ops (Roman)

Goddess of Fertility Frigga (Queen of Asgard and wife of Odin in Nordic mythology)

Goddess of Fertility, Love, Lust, and War Ishtar (Assyrian and Babylonian)

Goddess of Fertility and Procreation Aphrodite (Greek); Isis (Egyptian), Mylitta (Assyrian); Venus (Roman)

Goddess of Fertility and Purity Bona Dea (Roman)

Goddess of Fire Hestia (Greek); Vesta (Roman)

Goddess of Flowers, Gardens, and Love Flora (Roman)

Goddess of Freedom Libertas (Roman)

Goddess of Fruit Trees Pomona (Roman)

Goddess of Funerals Naenia (Roman)

Goddess of the Future Antevorta (Roman)

Goddess of Gardens and Fruit Trees Pomona (Roman)

Goddess of Good Faith Fides (Roman goddess whose Latin name means faith)

Goddess of Groves, Orchards, and Woods Feronia (Roman)

Goddess of Harmony Concordia (Roman)

Goddess of Healing Iaso (Greek)

Goddess of Health Hygeia (Roman); Hygieia (Greek)

Goddess of the Hearth Hestia (Greek); Vesta (Roman)

Goddess of Heaven Hera (Greek); Juno (Roman)

Goddess of the Home Hera (Greek); Juno (Roman)

Goddess of Home Security the Roman goddess Cardea or Carna who guarded the door hinges and locks

Goddess of Horses Epona (Gallic); Hippona (Roman)

Goddess of Hunting and the Moon Artemis (Greek); Diana

(Roman)

Goddess of Imposters and Thieves Laverna (Roman)

Goddess of Law and Order Eunomia or Themis (Greek); Justitia (Roman)

Goddess of Leisure and Repose Vacuna (Roman)

Goddess of Lightning Fulgora (Roman)

Goddess of Love and Lust Aphrodite (Greek); Venus (Roman)

Goddess of Magic, Sorcery, and the Underworld Hecate or Hekate (Greek—working afar); Trivia (Latin—of the three ways) and hence the Romans placed her wherever three roads met

Goddess of Married Women Juno Matronalis (Roman)

Goddess of Memory Mnemosyne (Greek)—mother of the muses; her name gives rise to mnemonic—an aid to memory such as the lines beginning *Thirty days hath September, April, June, and November*

Goddess of Menstruation Mena (Roman)

Goddess of Midwives Deverra (Roman); Eileitia (Greek)

Goddess of Mirth Thalia

Goddess of the Moon Luna (Roman); Selene (Greek)

Goddess Mother of the World Mount Everest

Goddess of Nature Cybele (Roman) or Kubele (Greek)—sometimes called Mistress of the Animals

Goddess of Newborn Babes Levana (Roman)

Goddess of Night Nux (Greek) sometimes spelled Nyx

Goddess of Nursing Mothers Rumina (Roman)

Goddess of Passion Stimula (Roman)—her name, translated from Latin, means she who excites

Goddess of the Past Postvorta (Roman)

Goddess of Peace known to the Romans as Concordia, Irene, or Pax, and to the Greeks as Eirene

Goddess of Profit Laverna (Roman)

Goddess of Public Welfare Salus (Roman) whose Latin name means health

Goddess of the Rainbow Iris (Roman)

Goddess of Robbers Furina (Roman)

Goddess of Rome Roma

Goddess of the Sea and Seaports Matuta (Roman)—originally goddess of the dawn

Goddess of Sensual Pleasure Voluptas (Roman)

Goddess of Shepherds Pales (Roman)

Goddess of Silence Muta (Roman)

Goddess of Storms and Winds Tempestes (Roman)

Goddess of Suckling Infants Rumina (Roman)

Goddess of Treachery Fraus (Roman)

Goddess of Truth Alethia (Greek); Veritas (Roman)

Goddess of the Underworld Persephone (Greek); Proserpina (Roman)

Goddess of Vice Kakia (Greek)

Goddess of Victory Nike (Greek)

Goddess of Virgins Juno Virginalis (Roman)

Goddess of War Bellona (Roman); Enyo (Greek)

Goddess of Wisdom Athena (Greek); Minerva (Roman)

Goddess of Youth Hebe (Greek); Juventus (Roman)

God of Dreams Morpheus—Greek god of dreams and sleep

God of Drinking Comus (Roman)

GODE Gulf Organization for the Development of Egypt (funded by Kuwait and Saudi Arabia)

God of Earth Tellumo (Roman) —his name is derived from the Latin *tellus* meaning earth

God of Eloquence and Oratory Hermes (Greek); Mercury (Roman)

Godfather of American Invention Thomas Jefferson

Godfather of American Liberty Thomas Paine

Godfather of Organized Crime in the U.S. Meyer Lansky

God of Fertility Frey (Norse); Priapos (Greek); Priapus (Roman)

God of Fields, Pastures, Shepherds, and Woods Faunus (Roman); Pan (Greek)

God of Fire Agni, according to the Hindus

God of Fire and Forges Hephaestus (Greek); Vulcan (Roman)

God of Forests, Herds, Plants,

and Trees Silvanus (Roman) from whose name is derived *silva*—Latin for wood

God of Gods and Ruler of Heaven and Earth Zeus (Greek); Jove or Jupiter (Roman)

God of Gold Mammon the Materialist

God of Good Harvests and Successful Undertakings *Eventus Bonus* (Latin—Good Results) —a Roman god

God of the Greeks Panhellenius or Zeus

God of Healing and Medicine Asclepius (Greek); Aesculapius (Roman)

God of Heaven Uranus (Greek); Coleus (Roman)

God of Heaven, Lightning, Rain, Storm, and Thunder Indra, according to the Hindus

God of Inanimate Dreams Phantastus (Greek)

God of the Infernal Regions Dis (Greek); Pluto (Roman); Yama (Hindu); etc.

God-Intoxicated Man Benedictus de Spinoza

God of Landmarks Terminus (Roman)

God of Light Mithra (Aryan, Indian, Persian)

God of Love Cupid (Roman); Eros (Greek); Krishna (Hindu)

God of Marriage Hymen, according to Greek mythology, also leader of the nuptial chorus and personification of the wedding feast

God of the Mohammedans Allah

God of Music Johann Sebastian Bach, according to Catalan cellist-composer-conductor, Pablo Casals

God of Music, Poetry, and the Sun Apollo (Roman) or Apollon (Greek)

God of the Nile and Vegetation Osiris (Egyptian)

God of Purification Februus (Roman)

God of Revelry and Wine Dionysus (Greek); Bacchus (Roman)

God of the Romans Jupiter—supreme god

godsd godsdienst (Dutch—religion)

God of the Sea Neptune (Roman); Poseidon (Greek)

God of Ships and the Sea Nyörd (Norse)

God of Skill Hermes (Greek);

Mercury (Roman)—the winged cap-and-shoes messenger of Jove or Jupiter (Zeus) presided over anything requiring dexterity and skill—commerce, gymnastics, medicine, thieving, wrestling, et cetera; in one hand he bore a rod entwined by two serpents (the caduceus)—symbol of the medical profession

God of Sleep Hypnos (Greek); Somnus (Roman)

God of Soil Fertilization Saturn or Stercutus (Roman)—*stercus* is Latin for dung

God of Springs Fons (Roman)

God of the Sun Adonis (Syrian); Apollo (Roman); Apollon (Greek); Baal (Chaldean); Helios Hyperion (Greek in Homer's time); Horus (symbolized in Upper Egypt by a hawk); Mithras (Persian); Moloch (Canaanite); Osiris (Egyptian); Ra or Re (symbolized in Egypt's Old Kingdom by an obelisk); Sol Invictus (Latin—Sun Invincible)—Romans shortened this to Sol and to this day Old Sol is the sun's nickname; Surya (Hindu)

Godthaab (Danish—Good Hope)—Greenland's capital called Nuk by the Eskimos

God of Thunder Thor (Norse)

God of Time Cronus (Greek); Saturn (Roman)

God of Trade and Travelers Hermes (Greek); Mercury (Roman)

God of the Underworld (Dis (Roman); Hades or Haides (Greek); Mantus (Etruscan); Pluto (Roman)

God of Vineyards and Wine Bacchus (Roman); Dionysus (Greek)

God of War Ares (Greek); Mars (Roman)

God of Wine Bacchus (Roman); Dionysus (Greek)

Godzone God's own country (New Zealanders insist this is New Zealand)

goe gas, oxygen, ether (mixture); ground operating equipment

GOE General Ordination Examination

GOES Geostationary Operational Environmental Satellite

gof good old Friday; government-owned facilities

G o F Gang of Five

GOFAR Global Ocean Floor

Analysis and Research

gogo government-operated government-owned

Gogol Nikolai Vasilyevich Gogol-Yanovsky

gogs goggles

goi gross operating income

Goi Goidelic

GoI Government of Indonesia

GOI Gallup Organization Incorporated

goin' going

GOIN Gossudarstvienny Okeanograficheskiy Institut (Russian—State Oceanography Institute)

gol general operating language

GOLB Gosudarstvennaya Ordena Lenina Biblioteka (Russian—Lenin State Library)—Moscow's largest library and the one best known in the USSR it serves

gold. geometric on-line definition

Golda Golda Meir (Israel's first woman prime minister)

Goldberg Bach's *Goldberg Variations*; composed for a keyboard pupil named Johann Gottlieb Goldberg; black slang for a person of Judaic origin

Gold Coast Africa's Ghana—formerly the Gold Coast; Australia's beach-fronted resort area extending from Coolangatta to Southport near Brisbane, Florida's resort coast extending from Key West to Palm Beach

Golden Age era of mankind, according to classical mythology, when people lived in contentment and peace with arts and crafts superior to those of the preceding Silver, Bronze, Iron, and Stone ages; mankind's age of innocence where there was springtime all the time and happiness, right, and truth prevailed; there were no bodily ailments and nobody had to work as the earth gave men all they needed, according to Greek and Roman mythology —(see *Siglo de Oro*)

Golden Age of Greece 5th and 4th centuries before the Christian era when Aristotle, Euripides, Plato, and Sophocles were contemporaries or near contemporaries

Golden Age of Opera late 1800s and early 1900s

Golden Age of Rome the reign of Augustus from 27 B.C.E. to 14 A.D.

golden beryl heliodor

Golden Century Nineteenth Century

Golden City Johannesburg

Golden City of a Hundred Spires Prague

Golden Flutist Georges Barrère

Golden Gate entrance to San Francisco Bay

Golden Gate City San Francisco

Golden Gate to South America Cartagena, Colombia (last of the fortified walled cities)

Golden Horn Istanbul's harbor formed by the curved arm of the Bosporus

Golden Horseshoe Hamilton-Toronto-Oshawa industrial complex along Lake Ontario

Golden Hyphen Winston-Salem, North Carolina

Golden Isles Jekyll, Saint Simons, and Sea Island off Brunswick, Georgia

Golden Key to the Fjords Stavanger, Norway

Golden Peninsula Malay Peninsula

Golden Poppy California's state flower

Golden Prison of Paris the Louvre (whose subterranean vaults once held hunting dogs and political prisoners)

Golden Province Canada's Ontario

Golden Rock of the Caribbean Sint Eustatius (Statia), Netherlands Antilles

Goldenrod state flower of Kentucky and Nebraska

Golden Rule *What is hateful to thee do not do unto thy neighbor.*—Hillel (30 B.C.-10 A.D.) stated in explaining essence of the Torah

Golden State California's official nickname

Golden Triangle point of downtown Pittsburgh where the three rivers meet: the Allegheny, Monongehela, and Ohio rivers; industrialized northern Europe where the three points are Birmingham, Paris, and the Ruhr; opium-productive fields where Burma, Laos, and Thailand meet near southern Yunnan, China

Golden Trombone of Abolition Frederick A Douglass

Golden-voiced Crooner Jack (Bing) Crosby

Golden-voiced Tenor Enrico Caruso and Luciano Pavarotti fans would be about equally divided in awarding this title

Goldhunter(s) Californian(s)

Goldie Gold; Golden; Goldilocks; Goldsborough; Goldsmith; Goldsworthy; Goldwin; Goldwyn

Gold Rush Town Nome, Alaska

gold(s) gold bond(s); gold coin(s); gold medal(s)

Goldy Oliver Goldsmith's nickname bestowed him by Dr Samuel Johnson

Golf letter G radio code; NATO nickname for Soviet G-class submarines with missile-launching capability

Golfe de Gascogne (French—Gulf of Gascony)—inner corner of the Bay of Biscay

Golfe du Lion (French—Gulf of Lyons)—on France's Mediterranean coast

Golfo de Cádiz (Spanish—Gulf of Cadiz)—where the Atlantic washes the southwest coast of Portugal and Spain

Golfo de California (Spanish—Gulf of California)—arm of the Pacific between Lower California's peninsula and the Mexican mainland; also called *Mar Bermejo* or *Mar de Cortés* (the Vermillion Sea or the Sea of Cortez)

Golfo de Chiriquí (Spanish—Gulf of Chiriquí)—where the Pacific washes the coast of western Panama

Golfo de Fonseca (Spanish—Gulf of Fonseca)—arm of the Pacific between El Salvador, Honduras, and Nicaragua

Golfo de Honduras (Spanish—Gulf of Honduras)—leading from the Caribbean to Belize, Guatemala, and Honduras

Golfo de México (Spanish—Gulf of Mexico)—arm of the Atlantic washing southern Cuba as well as the Gulf Coast of Mexico and the United States

Golfo de Nicoya (Spanish—Gulf of Nicoya)—on Costa Rica's Pacific coast

Golfo de Panamá (Spanish—Gulf of Panama)—leading from the Pacific to the Panama Canal

Golfo de Tehuantepec (Spanish —Gulf of Tehuantepec)—arm of the Pacific near the Guatemalan border of Mexico and the seat of many tropical storms

Golfo de Valencia (Spanish—Gulf of Valencia)—where the western Mediterranean washes the east coast of Spain

Golfo de Venezuela (Spanish—Gulf of Venezuela)—connecting the Caribbean Sea with Lake Maracaibo

Golfo Pérsico (Spanish—Persian Gulf)

Golftown Pinehurst, North Carolina

Golgotha (Aramaic—Place of the Skull)—supposed site of the Roman crucifixion of Jesus Christ in a place also called Calvary and within the walls of Jerusalem

Gollancz Victor Gollancz Ltd

gom (GOM) government-owned material

Gom God's own medicine (opiates)

G.O.M. Grand Old Man (sobriquet for William Ewart Gladstone)

goma general officer money allowance

GOMA Good Outdoor Manners Association

go'n' going

gon *goniff* (Yiddish—thief)

gond(s) gondola(s); railroad car(s); car(s)

GONP Gal Oya National Park (Ceylon)

Gonz Gonzàles

Goo Goole

GOO Get Oil Out (of Santa Barbara, California)

Goober(s) nickname for peanut (goober) grower(s) and particularly natives of Alabama, Georgia, and North Carolina where so many goobers are grown

goobs going out of business sale(s)

Goochland State Industrial Farm for Women (convicts) at Goochland, Virginia

goodbye god be with you (contracted)

Good Friday Friday before Easter Sunday and the day commemorating the crucifixion of Christ

Good Gray Poet Walt Whitman

Good H *Good Housekeeping*

goodies good ones

Good Queen Bess Queen Elizabeth I of England (1558 to 1603)

Good Richard (pseudonym—Benjamin Franklin)

Good Samaritan City of the Mississippi Memphis

Goodwill Ambassador of México Henryk Szering (Polish-born violinist)

Goodwins Goodwin Sands off Kent near the North Sea entrance to the English Channel

goof. general on-line oriented function

googol 10 raised to the 100th power (10^{100})

goon *goonda* (Hindi—hired killer)

GOP Grand Old Party (Republican)

GO & P Griffith Observatory and Planetarium

Gopher Prairie see *Main Street*

Gopher(s) Minnesotan(s)

Gopher State Minnesota

gor gas/oil ratio; general operational requirement(s); gorilla

Gor Gordon; Gorham; Gorki; Gorman

GOR General Operating Room; General Operational Requirements

GORA Government Oil Refineries Administration

Gordie Gordon

Gordon Holmes pseudonym shared jointly by Louis Tracy and MP Shiel

Gordon Pasha Charles George Gordon

Goree Unit Women's Prison at Huntsville, Texas

GORF Goddard's Optical Research Facility

g org great organ

goric paregoric (an opiate narcotic)

gorill(s) gorilla(s)

Gorki Soviet name for Nizhni Novgorod renamed to honor the writer

Gorki (Russian—Bitter One)—pen name of Aleksei Maxsimovich Peskov

gorm gormandize(r)

gos *gosudarstvo* (Russian—state)—as in *gosplan*—state plan

Gos *Gosudarstvo* (Russian—State)

GOS General Operating Specification(s); Global (weather) Observing Systems

Gos Alb *Gossamer Albatross* (see bicyplane)

GOSS Ground Operational Support System

gost government-owned special tooling

GOST Goddard Satellite Track-

ing

Gösta Björling Karl Gustaf Björling

got. (GOT) glutamic oxaloacetic transaminase

Got Gothenburg (Göteborg)

Goteborg (Swedish—Gothenburg)—pronounced *Gyot-eh-bor*

Goten (German naval contraction—Gotenhafen)—Gdynia's name during World-War-II Nazi occupation

goth. gothic type

Goth. Gothic

Göt(h) Göteborg (Gothenburg)

Gotham New York City

Gothamite(s) native(s) of New York City; nickname derived from *The Three Wise Men of Gotham* by Washington Irving

gothic gothic script or gothic type (without hairlines or serifs and square cut)

Gothoburgum (Latin—Göteborg)— Gothenburg; the Swedish seaport city of Gothenburg

Gotland (Swedish—Gothland) —Baltic island

Gotorum (Latin—Lund)

gotran go fortran

got-roy *gotong-royong* (Indonesian—cooperation, mutual aid)

Gott Gottingen

Götterdämmerung (German—Twilight of the Gods)—sometimes called the God Damnation of the Gods by anti-Wagnerites

Goturum (Latin—Lund)—Swedish university town

gou *gourde* (Haitian currency)

Gou Goudy

Gouv Gouverneur

gov government

Gov Governor

goveclop government closest to the people

govg governing

Gov Gen Governor General

Gov Is Governor's Island

govt government

govtalk government talk

Govt Print Government Printer

GOW Grand Old Woman (Queen Victoria)

GOWA Guild of Watchmen of Australia

gox gaseous oxygen

goya & kod get off your ass and knock on doors (detective's mnemonic initialism meaning an investigation needs more work in interviewing people and less sitting around)

Goyo Gregorio

gp galley proofs; gas, persistent; general paralysis; general practice; general practitioner; general public; general purpose; geographic position; glide path; government property; grateful patient; gratitude patient; greenhouse perennial; ground pneumatic; group; guinea pig; gun pointer

g-p general purpose; graduated-payment

gp *grand prix* (French—grand prize)

g/p *giro postal* (Spanish—money order)

Gp Group

GP Gallup Poll; Gaspesian Park (Quebec); general public; Georgia-Pacific (stock exchange symbol); Giacomo Puccini; Gulf Province

G P Georgia Pacific (forest products); Gunier-Preston zone

GP *Generalpause* (German—general pause)—musical term

gpa grade-point average

GPA Gas Processors Association; Genealogical Publications of Australia; General Practitioners' Association; General Public Accounting

gpac grade point average category

gpad gallons per acre per day

gpae general-purpose aerospace equipment

GPAEVD Greater Philadelphia Alliance for the Eradication of Venereal Disease

GPAL Gold Producers Association Limited

gpate general-purpose automatic test equipment

GPATS General-Purpose Automatic Test System

gpb glossopharyngeal breathing

GPB *Gosudarstvennaya Publichnaya Biblioteka* (Russian —State Public Library)—in Leningrad

gpc gallons per capita; general purpose computer; gypsum-plaster ceiling

gpc (GPC) general physical condition

GPC Georgia Power Company; Gulf Park College

Gp Capt Group Captain

gpcd gallons per capita per day

Gp Cmdr Group Commander

Gp Comdr Group Commander

GPCR Great Proletarian Cultural Revolution (in mainland China)

GPCT George Peabody College for Teachers

gpd gallons per day

GPDA Gypsum Plasterboard Development Association

gpdc general-purpose digital computer

GPDS General-Purpose Display System

GPDST Girls' Public Day School Trust

gpdw gypsum-plaster dry wall(ing)

gpe good phonetic equivalents

GPE General Precision Equipment; Global Perspectives in Education

Gp. Eng. Geophysical Engineer

gperf ground passive electronic reconnaissance facility

GPES Ground Proximity Extraction System

gpete general purpose electronic test equipment

gpf gasproof

GPF Generic Packaging Facility

Gp Fl group flashing (light)

GPFS General-Purpose Financial Statement

gpg grains per gallon

gph gallons per hour; graphite

G.Ph. Graduate in Pharmacy

GPH Game Packing House; Grand Pacific Hotel (Suva)

GPHI Guild of Public Health Inspectors

gpi general paralysis of the insane (symptom of tertiary syphilis); ground-position indicator (aviation)

gpi (CPI) general price index; glucosephosphate isomerase

GPI General Printing Ink; Gordon Personal Inventory; Government Property Inventory

gpid guidance package installation dolly

GPII Geist Picture Interest Inventory

gp int qk fl group interrupted quick flashing

gpl generalized programming language; geographic position locator; grams per liter; gypsum lath

GPL General Precision Laboratory

GPLC Guild of Professional Launderers and Cleaners

gply gingivoplasty

gpm gallons per minute; gross profit margin

gpm (GPM) graduated payment mortgage

GPM General Preventive Medicine; Grand Past Master

gpmg general-purpose machine-gun

g-p mortgage graduated-payment mortgage

GPMS Gross Performance Measuring System (USAF)

GPN Graduate Practical Nurse

GPNITL Great Plains National Instructional Television Library

gpo gun position officer

GPO General Post Office; Government Printing Office

Gp Occ group occulting (light)

gpp galley page proofs; graphic part programmer

gpp (GPP) graduated property payment(s)

GPP Gordon Personal Profile

gppl gypsum plaster

GPPT Group Personality Projective Test

GPR Glider Pilot Regiment

GPRA General Practice Reform Association

gps gage pressure switch; gallons per second; general-purpose solver; ground plane simulator; guidance power supply

gp's galley proofs; guinea pigs

g-p's general practitioners (GPs)

Gps general-parents motion pictures (for youngsters only with parent's consent)

GPs Great Performances

GPS General Practitioners Society; Gibbs-Poole-Stockmeyer (algorithm); Global Positioning System; Graduated Pension Scheme; Great Persons Society; Greater Public Schools

GPSA General Practitioners Society of Australia

gpsdw general-purpose scientific document writer

gpse general-purpose simulation environment

gpss general-purpose systems simulator

GPSS General Process Simulation Studies

gpt gas power transfer; guidance position tracking; gypsum tile

gpt (GPT) glutamic pyruvic transaminase

GPT Grayson Perceptualization Test; Guild of Professional Toastmasters; Guild of Professional Translators

gpte general-purpose test(ing)

equipment
gp th group therapy
gptr guidance power temperature regulator
gpu ground power unit
GPU General Postal Union
GPU *Gosudarstvennoe Politicheskoe Upravlenie* (Russian —State Political Administration)—secret police—*Gay-Pay-Ooo*
GPV *Gereformeerd Politiek Verbond* (Dutch—Reformed Political Union)—Calvinist party
gpw gross plated weight; gypsum-plaster wall
GPW Geneva (Convention Relative to Treatment of) Prisoners of War
GPWS Ground Proximity Warning System
gpx generalized programming extended
GPX Greyhound Package Express
GPY Government Property Yard
GQ general quarters
gqa give quick answer; government quality assurance; grain quality analyzer
GQG *Grand Quartier Général* (French—General Headquarters)
GQNM Gran Quivira National Monument
GQR Gauss Quadrature Rule
GQS General Quarter Sessions
Gquil Guayaquil
gr gear; grab rod; grade; grain; gram; grammar; grand; grass runway; gravity; great(er); grind(er); gross; ground; group; gunner
g-r gamma ray
gr *gravida* (Latin—gravid)—pregnant
Gr Grashof number; Great (postal abbreviation); Grecian; Greece; Greek; Grove
Gr *Graben* (German—ditch, trench); Greek (classical language of Grecian antiquity, some 10 million people speak Modern Greek and many of them are found in Canada, England, Latin America, and the United States); *Groot* (Afrikaans—big, great); *Gross(e)* (German—big, great, vast)
GR B.F. Goodrich (stock exchange symbol); General Radio; General Reconnaissance; General Reserve; Georgius

Rex (King George); Government Report; Grand Recorder; Grasse River (railroad); Graves Registration; Group Report; Gunnery Range
GR *Guardia Republicana* (Spanish—Republican Guard)
GRA Girls Rodeo Association; Government Reports Announcements; Governmental Research Association; Grass Roots Association; WR Grace & Company (stock exchange symbol)
gr ab grade ability
GRAB Group Rooms Availability Bank (hotel-motel convention service)
Grã-Bretanha (Portuguese—Great Britain)
GRACE Grace Agencies; Grace Chemicals; Grace Line; WR Grace and Company (stock exchange symbol); graphic arts composing equipment; group routing and exchange equipment (telephone)
Grace Greenwood Sara Jane Clarke Lippincott's pseudonym
Gracie Fields Grace Stansfield
grad gradient; grading; graduate
grad (GRAD) graduate résumé accumulation and distribution
grad. *graditim* (Latin—by degrees)
Grad IAE Graduate of the Institution of Automobile Engineers
Grad IM Graduate of the Institution of Metallurgists
Grad Inst BE Graduate of the Institution of British Engineers
Grad Inst P(hys) Graduate of the Institute of Physics
Grad Inst R(frg) Graduate of the Institute of Refrigeration
Grad IRI Graduate of the Institution of the Rubber Industry
Grad NDTS Graduate (member) of the Non-Destructive Testing Society
Grad RIC Graduate (member) of the Royal Institute of Chemistry
grad(s) gradient(s); graduate(s)
GRADS Great Falls Air Defense Sector
Grad SE Graduate of the Society of Engineers
Grad Soc Eng Graduate of the Society of Engineers
gradu gradual(ly); graduate(d); graduating

Graduate of Oxford John Ruskin's pseudonym
graf graphic additions to fortran
Graffiti Capital defaced buildings, buses, streets, and subways of New York City
Graffitic City New York City (or any other graffitically defiled place)
graf(s) graphic addition(s); paragraph(s)
Grahams Grahamstad or Grahamstown in South Africa
Grail NATO name for a Soviet shoulder-fired surface-to-air missile called SA-7
Grain Coast West African coastal area of Sierra Leone and Liberia
gral *general* (Spanish—general)
Gral General (Spanish—General)
gram. grammar; gramophone
'gram cablegram; radiogram; telegram
gram (Latin suffix—record)—radiogram
Gram Grammar; Grandfather; Grandpa(pa)
Gram *Gramaphone*
Grampians Grampian Hills of Scotland or the Grampian Mountains of Australia
gramp(s) grandfather
GRAMS Ground Recording and Monitoring System
gran granite; granular; granulated sugar
gran. *granulatus* (Latin—granulated)
Gran Granada; Granjon
GRAN Global Rescue Alarm Net
Granary of Canada Saskatchewan
Granary of Portugal the fertile province of Alemtejo
Granary of Russia Ukraine's vast wheat fields
Granary of Spain lower valley of the Guadalquivir
Granary of Sweden Skåne
Granata (Latin—Granada)
Gran Bretagna (Italian—Great Britain)
Gran Bretaña (Spanish—Great Britain)
Gran Canaria (Spanish—Grand Canary Island)
Gran Chaco lowlands of Bolivia, Paraguay, and Argentina
Gran Colombia (Spanish—Great Colombia)—post-colonial consolidation of Colombia, Ecuador, and Venezuela

Grand Banks cod fishery on a submerged plateau washed by the Labrador Current off Newfoundland

Grand Canal principal waterway thoroughfare of Venice

Grand Canyon short form for the Grand Canyon of the Colorado in the Grand Canyon National Park in Arizona, the Grand Canyon of the Arkansas in Colorado where it is also called the Royal Gorge, the Grand Canyon of Santa Elena in the Big Bend National Park in Texas, the Grand Canyon of the Snake River in Idaho, the Grand Canyon of the Tuolumne in California, the Grand Canyon of the Yellowstone in the Yellowstone National Park in Wyoming

Grand Canyon Grand Canyon Suite—symphonic work by Ferdé Grofé

Grand Canyon State Arizona's official nickname

Grand Cham of Literature Dr Samuel Johnson

Grand Commanders Cayman Islanders

Grand Coulee Grand Coulee Dam; Grand Coulee Valley in eastern Washington

Grand Dame of the Piano Alicia de Larrocha

Grand Divide Continental Divide

Grand Duke Duke of Wellington

Grande Banco (Portuguese—Grand Banks)

Grande-Bretagne (French—Great Britain)

Grand Hotel nickname of French Polynesia's prison in Tahiti where it is called *Le Grand Hotel* as if to display the acerbic quality of Gallic wit

Grand Inquisitor Tomás de Torquemada

Grandma Moses Anne Mary Moses

Grand Master of Humorous Verse Ogden Nash

Grandmother of Boston preacher-reformer-teacher Elizabeth Palmer Peabody

Grandmother of the Russian Revolution Katherine Breshkovska

Grandmother of Shopping Streets Calle Florída in Buenos Aires

Grandmother of the Women's Movement Margaret Mead

grando grandioso (Italian—grandiose)

Grand Old Lady of Fifty-seventh Street Carnegie Hall

Grand Old Lady of Opera Ernestine Schumann-Heink

Grand Old Man William Ewart Gladstone—four times Prime Minister of Great Britain

Grand Old Man of American Labor Samuel Gompers

Grand Old Party Republican Party of the United States—the GOP

Grandsire of American Painting Benjamin West

Grand Teton Grand Teton Mountain; Grand Teton National Monument in northwestern Wyoming

Grand Zohra General Charles de Gaulle

Granger States farm-filled Illinois, Iowa, Minnesota, and Wisconsin

Granite boy(s) New Hampshirite(s)

Granite Center Barre, Vermont

Granite City Aberdeen, Scotland

Granite Island Corsica

Granite State New Hampshire's official nickname

Gran Libertador (Spanish—Great Liberator—Simón Bolívar)

Granny Grandmother

Gran Quivira Gran Quivira National Monument in central New Mexico

grapden graphic data entry

grape sugar glucose ($C_6H_{12}O_6$)

graph. graphology

graph (Latin suffix record, recording)—radiograph

grapheme written language symbol representing an oral language code

graphite carbon

graph rec graphic record(ing)

GRAPO Grupos Antifascista Para Octubre (Spanish—October 1st Antifascist Groups)—leftist terrorists active in Spain

gr ar grinding arbor

GRAR Government(al) Report Authorization and Record

gras generally recognized as safe (beverage or food additives)

graser gamma-ray laser

grasp. graphics-augmented structural-post processing

grass marijuana's nickname along with pot and weed

grat graticule

Gratianopolis (Latin—Grenoble)

grats congratulations

Graubünden (German—Grisons)

Graudenz (German—Grudziadz)

grav gravimetric; gravitation; gravity

Graveyard of the Atlantic nickname shared by Cape Hatteras, North Carolina and Sable Island off Nova Scotia

gravi (Latin prefix—heavy)—gravid with unborn offspring

grazo grazioso (Italian—gracious)

grb gamma-ray burst; granolithic base

GRB Gerakan Rakjat Baru (Indonesian—New People's Movement); *Guide to Reference Books*

GRBI Gardeners' Royal Benevolent Institution

grbm (GRBM) global-range ballistic missile

Gr Br Grande Bretagne (French—Great Britain); Great Britain

Gr Brit Great Britain

GRBS Gardeners' Royal Benevolent Society

grc glass-reinforced cement

GRC Gale Research Company; Gerontology Research Center; Government Research Corporation; Gulf Research Corporation

GRC Gendarmarie Royale du Canada (French—Royal Gendarmarie of Canada)—Royal Canadian Mounted Police

GRCB Greyhound Racing Control Board

GRCM Graduate of the Royal College of Music

grcol ground color

Gr Cpt Group Captain

grd grind; ground; ground detector; guard

Grd Ground (postal abbreviation)

Gr d Greek drachmae

Gr D Grand Duchy

GRD Geophysics Research Directorate

GRDC Gulf Research and Development Company

grdl gradual(ly)

Grdn The Guardian (London and Manchester)

grd tot grand total

gre ground reconstruction equipment

Gre Grecia (Spanish—Greece)

GRE Graduate Record Examination; Guardian Royal Exchange

Great The Great Symphony No. 9 in C major by Schubert (formerly No. 7)

Great Agnostic Colonel Robert G. Ingersoll

Great American Desert great basin of western United States; includes Death Valley and Imperial Valley in California; Mojave Desert in California and Nevada; Sonoran Desert of northwestern Mexico, including adjacent sections of Arizona and California

Great American Pastime baseball, basketball, and football vie for this nickname

Great Assassin Abdul-Hamid II (notorious for his participation in the Armenian atrocities)

Great Britain England, Scotland, and Wales—GB

Great Canal waterway between Australia and the Great Barrier Reef

Great Cham of Literature Dr Samuel Johnson

Great Charter Magna Charta

Great C-major Schubert's Symphony No. 9

Great Commoner Henry Clay, William Ewart Gladstone, William Pitt (the Elder Pitt also known as the Earl of Chatham), and Thomas Paine have all borne this nickname

Great Compromiser Henry Clay —U.S. Senator from Kentucky

Great Debunker H(enry) L(ouis) Mencken—editor of *The American Mercury*

Great Destroyer syphilis

Great Disappointment October 22, 1844, when many thousands of Christians expected the second coming of Jesus Christ to occur

Great Dissenter Supreme Court Justice Oliver Wendell Holmes, Jr

Great Divide continental divide formed by Rocky Mountains; waters on western slopes flow to the Pacific, on eastern slopes flow to Gulf of Mexico

Great Dividing Great Dividing Range of Australia's New South Wales and Queensland

Great Duke Duke of Wellington

Great Emancipator Abraham Lincoln—sixteenth President of the United States and author of the *Emancipation Proclamation*

Great Engineer Herbert Hoover —thirty-first President of the United States

Greater Antilles Cuba, Hispaniola (Dominican Republic and Haiti), Jamaica, Puerto Rico

Greater Sunda Islands Borneo, Celebes, Java, Sumatra, and nearby Indonesian islands

Greatest American Jurist John Marshall—Chief Justice of the Supreme Court from 1801 to 1835

Greatest Artist of the South Seas Paul Gauguin

Greatest Composer Haydn's name for Mozart

Greatest Heavyweight Boxer Jack Johnson

Greatest Show on Earth Barnum and Bailey—Ringling Brothers Circus

Great Fatherland War Soviet name for World War II

Great Jailer of the Caribbean Comrade Fidel Castro

Great Lakes (east to west) Ontario, Erie, Huron, Michigan, Superior; (ranked by area) Superior, Huron, Michigan, Ontario, Erie

Great Lakes Canada Ontario (on the northern shores of Superior, Huron, Erie, and Ontario)

Great Lakes Province Ontario on lakes Ontario, Erie, Huron, and Superior

Great Lakes States New York, Pennsylvania, Ohio, Michigan, Indiana, Illinois, Wisconsin, Minnesota

Great Lake State Michigan

Great Land The Great Land— Alaska

Great Lon Greater London

Great Moralist Dr Samuel Johnson

Great Outsider B Traven (expatriate American author maintaining almost full anonymity during more than 40 years in Mexico where he chose exile, silence, and cunning to conceal his humble origin in Chicago's slums and his early career as an anarchist while writing for a worldwide corps of readers enthralled by his tales about bandits, cowboys, miners, peasants, and sailors)

Great Pacificator Henry Clay

Great Patriotic Struggle official Soviet name for Russia's participation in World War II—a war begun by Hitler who got the green light from Stalin to invade Poland

Great Plains plains and prairies of Canada and the United States east of the Rockies

Great Poet of Democracy Walt Whitman

Great River Road 3700-mile-long Mississippi-Missouri-Red Rock river system serving central United States from Canadian border to Gulf of Mexico where their waters run into the sea

Great Sandy Great Sandy Desert of South and Western Australia

Great Sea Biblical name for the Mediterranean

Great Separationist Paul Blanshard (*Religion and the Schools, Some of My Best Friends Are Christians,* etc.)

Great Smoke London's unenviable nickname before air-pollution control was enforced

Great Smokies Great Smoky Mountains of North Carolina and Tennessee

Great Smoky Great Smoky Mountains; Great Smoky Mountains National Park in North Carolina and Tennessee

Great Society (administration of Lyndon Baines Johnson— thirty-sixth President of the United States)

Great Stink nickname of the Thames River before English conservationists set out to clean up its pollution

Great Stone Face Daniel Webster; Old Man of the Mountain also known as Profile Mountain in New Hampshire's White Mountains

Great Street State Street that Great Street in Chicago

Great Thirst Land South Africa

Great Vic Great Victoria Desert of Western Australia

Great Wall of China built to separate China and Mongolia

Great Wet Ditch British nickname for the English Channel

Great White Father (American Indian term—the President of the United States)

Great White Fleet white-hulled flotilla of United States Navy displayed in principal ports of the world during circumnavigation ordered by President Theodore Roosevelt; white-painted ships of the United Fruit Company—also called *La Gran Flota Blanca*

Great White Strip brilliantly illuminated main street of Las Vegas, Nevada

Great White Way New York City's brightly illuminated theatrical section of midtown Broadway

Great White Wizard Dr Albert Schweitzer

GREB Graduate Records Examination Boards

Grec Grécia (Italian or Spanish —Greece); *Grecia* (Portuguese —Greece)

GRECC Geriatric Research, Education, and Clinical Center (Seattle)

Grèce (French—Greece)

Grecia (Italian—Greece)

Grécia (Portuguese or Spanish Greece)

Greece Hellenic Republic (Balkan nation whose history antedates classical antiquity, Greeks speak Modern Greek and engage in farming and industry as well as shipbuilding and textiles), *Elliniki Dimokratia*

Greece's Principal Port Piraeus

Greek Century 5th century before the Christian era—the 400s BCE

Greek First Yannis Xenakis— best-known classical composer of modern Greece

Greek Isles Cyclades, Dodecanese, Ionian, Sporades

Greek Muses (*see* Nine Muses)

Greek Ports (large, medium, and small from west to east) Argostolion (*on Kefallinia*), (*on Peloponnisos*—Patrai, Kalámai, Póros), Piraievs (Piraeus), Vólos, Thessaloniki, Mililini (*on Lesbos*), Khíos (*on Khíos*), Iraklion (*or Candia on Crete*), Ródhos (*or Rhodes on Rhodes*)

Greeks Greek Islands; Greek people

Green Green College (Oxford or elsewhere)

Green. Greenland

green flag all-clear signal; express; go-ahead

Green Goddess Gro Harlem Brundtland (Norway's former environment minister and its

first female and youngest prime minister)

Green Hell Paraguayan Chaco

Green Isle Ireland

Greenland Sea sector of Arctic Ocean between Greenland and Spitsbergen Islands

green light all-clear signal; go-ahead signal; safety signal; starboard side of aircraft, ships, or other vessels

Green Line division between Christian East Beirut and Muslim West Beirut

Green Mountain boy(s) Vermonter(s)

Green Mountain City Montpelier, Vermont

Green Mountain State Vermont's official nickname

Green Mts Green Mountains of Vermont

Greenock Girls prison for female offenders in Greenock, Scotland

green vitriol copperas, ferrous sulfate ($FeSO_4 • 7H_2O$)

Greenwood Brooklyn's historic cemetery and eponym standing for similar burial places

Grefco General Refractories

Greg Gregorian; Gregory

Greg⁰ Gregorio (Spanish— Gregory)

Greichenland (German— Greece)

gr el greatest elongation

Gren Grenada

Grenada State of Grenada (West Indian island nation whose Grenadans speak English and a Franco-African patois, livestock, rum, and tropical crops are exported)

Grenada's Port St George

Grenadines Bequia, Cannouan, Carriacou, and Mustique islands in British Windward Islands of West Indies—south of St Vincent and north of Grenada; (*see* Saint Vincent and the Grenadines)

Grendr Grenadier

Grepo Grenzpolizei (German— border-control police)

Greta Greta Garbo; Margaret

Greta Garbo Greta Gustafson

Gretchen Marguerite

Greyf Greyfriars College, Oxford

Greyhound M-8 6-wheeled armored car carrying a 37mm gun and made in the U.S.A. just like the popular buses of the same name

Grey Owl George S Belaney

Greytown San Juan del Norte

grf (GRF) growth hormone-releasing factor

gr f grass firm (on runway)

GRF Gerald Rudolph Ford— thirty-eighth President of the United States; Grassland Research Foundation; Gravity Research Foundation

gr Fl grosse Flöte (German— full-size flute)

GRFMA Grand Rapids Furniture Market Association

grfrp graphite fiberglass-reinforced plastic

gr fx grinding fixture

grg generalized reduced gradient; gravimetric rain gage

grh (GRH) gonadotrophin-releasing hormone

GRI Geothermal Resources International; Government Reports Index; Government of the Ryukyu Islands

G.R.I. Georgius Rex et Imperator (Latin—George, King and Emperor)

Griechenland (German Greece)

Griekenland (Dutch—Greece)

grif (GRIF) growth hormone-inhibiting factor

Grif Griffin; Griffith; Griffiths

griff griffin

Griffon NATO name for Soviet SA-5-type surface-to-air missile

Grimes Peter Grimes (three-act opera by Britten)

grip (motion-picture and tv slang—stage hand delegated to move camera and sound equipment)

GRIP Grass Roots Improvement Program

griphos general retrieval and information processor humanities-oriented studies

Gris Griswold

Grishka (Russian—Gregory)

Grisons (French—Graubünden)

grit. gradual reduction in temperature; gradual reduction in tensions

grits boiled grits; hominy grits; rockahominie in Algonquian Indian

GRITS Goddard Range Instrumentation Tracking System (NASA)

griz grizzly

grizz grizzly bear

GRJC Grand Rapids Junior College

Grk Greenock

Gr-L Graeco-Latin

gr lp ground lamp
Gr Lt Gunner Lieutenant
grm gaseous radiation monitor; gram; gross rent multiplier; guidance rate measuring
grmp generalized report module program
grn green
g/r/n goods received note
Gr.N. Graduate Nurse
grnd ground
Grnd Grand (postal abbreviation)
grndr grinder(s)
grnl giornalista (Italian—newspaperman)
GRNL Gay Rights National Lobby
Grnld Greenland
grns green skins
grnsh greenish
grnt guarantee
gro gross
Gro Grocer(y); Groningen; Grove; Guerrero
GRO Greenwich Royal Observatory
GROBDM General Register Office of Births, Deaths, and Marriages
groc grocer(y)
Groen Groenlandia (Italian or Spanish—Greenland); *Groenlandia* (Portuguese—Greenland)
Gröfaz Grösster Feldherr aller Zeiten (German—greatest general of all time)—Hitler's acronymic nickname bestowed by WW-II Berliners
GROIN Garbage Removal Or Income Now
Grolier Grolier Society
grom grommet
Gron Groningen
Gronaicum (Latin—Greenwich)—also known as Gronvicum
Groningen provincial capital of Groningen in the Netherlands
Grønland (Dano-Norwegian—Greenland)
groot (Dutch—great)
Groot Brittanje (Dutch—Great Britain)
Groot-Brittannië (Dutch—Great Britain)
Groperland Western Australia
gros. grossus (Latin—coarse, gross)
Gross Britannien (German—Great Britain)
Grosse Freiheit Strasse (German—Great Freedom Street)—Hamburg's street of bars and brothels
Grosse Ozean (German—Great

Ocean)—the Pacific
Grosset Grosset & Dunlap
Grotius Hugo de Groot
Groucho Marx Julius Henry Marx
Groundhog Groundhog Day (February 2)
Group W Westinghouse Broadcasting
Grove's Sir George Grove's *Dictionary of Music and Musicians*
GROW Gay Rights for Older Women; Group Recovery Organizations of the World
Growlers Growler Mountains of southwestern Arizona
growsy grumpy and drowsy
grp glass-reinforced plastic (fiberglass); graphite-reinforced plastic; ground relay panel; group repetition panel
Grp Group
grp(s) group(s)
grp's gross rating points
grr growler
GRR Grand Rapids, Michigan (airport); Graphic Reproduction Request
grreg graves registration
GrReg graves registration
grs grains; grass; greens
gr s grass soft (on runway)
gr-s government rubber plus styrene (buna-S synthetic rubber)
GRs Government Regulations; Granitic Regions
GRS General Railway Signal; Graves Registration Service
GRSE Guild of Radio Service Engineers
Gr S-Lt Gunner Sub-Lieutenant
GRSM Graduate of the Royal Schools of Music (Royal Academy of Music and the Royal College of Music)
GRSP General Revenue Sharing Program
grst gross ton(s)
grsy greasy
grt gross register(ed) tonnage (tons)
grtee guarantee
grtg grating
grtm gross-ton mile
gr tons gross tons
grtr greater
gr tr graphite treatment
gr Tr grosse Trommel (German—bass drum)
Gru Grus; Gruyère
GRU Glavnoye Razvedyvatelnoye Upravlenie (Russian—Intelligence Directorate of the

Red Army)—*(q.v. VOT)*
grub. grubby; grubstreet (Grubstreet, according to Dr Johnson—"Originally the name of a street in Moorfield in London, much inhabited by writers of small histories, dictionaries, and temporary poems, whence any mean production is called *grubstreet*."
grub. (GRUB) grocery update and billing
Grudziadz (Polish—Graudenz)
GRULA Grupo Latino Americano (Spanish—Latin American Group)—UN power bloc
gr'ups grownups
Grv Grove
grvl gravel(ly)
Grwd Grunewald
gr wt gross weight
gry grocery; gross redemption yield
gs galvanized steel; gauss; german silver; glide slope; grand slalom; grandson; ground speed; guardship; guineas
gs (GS) gold standard; group separator character (data processing)
g/s gallons per second
Gs force of gravity; general motion pictures (for the general public); Gomes
GS General Schedule (civil service classification system); General Secretary; General Service; General Sessions; General Staff; General Studies; General Support; Geochemical Society; Geological Survey; Gerontological Society; Gillette (stock exchange symbol); Girl Scouts; Glow Start (tractor); Government Servant; Grand Secretary; Ground Staff; Ground Station; Guidance Station; Gunnery School; Gunnery Sergeant
G-S Gallard-Schlesinger
G & S Gilbert and Sullivan
GS Garda Siochana (Gaelic—Police Force)—Ireland's police force
gsa gross soluble antigen
gsa (GSA) general (travel) sales agency; general (travel) sales agent
GSA Garden Seed Association; General Services Administration; Genetics Society of America; Geological Society of America; Girl Scouts of America; Gourd Society of America
G & SA Gulf and South Ameri-

can (steamship line)

GSABCA General Services Administration Board of Contract Appeals

GSAI General Services Administration Institute

gsap gunsight aiming point

GSAPBS General Services Administration Public Building(s) Service(s)

gsb gypsum sheathing board

gsb (GSB) go subroutine

GSB Government Savings Bank

GSBA Georgia School Boards Association

GSBAA General Service Board of Alcoholics Anonymous

gs bot glass-stoppered bottle

gsbr gravel-surface built-up roof

gsc gas-solid chromatography; geodetic spacecraft; ground speed continue; guidance systems console

GSC General Staff Corps; Genetics Society of Canada; Geological Survey of Canada; Gold Star Cable (Korean); Group Study Course; Group Switching Center

GSCBA Georgia State College of Business Administration

GSCP Generic Site Characterization Plan

GSCT Goldstein-Scheerer Cube Test

GSCW General Society of Colonial Wars

gsd general system description; genetically significant dosage; grid sphere drag

GSD General Supervisor's Directive; General Supply Depot

GSDFJ Ground Self-Defense Force Japan

GSDNM Great Sand Dunes National Monument

gse (GSE) government-supplied equipment; ground-service equipment; ground-support equipment

GSE Graduate School of Education (Harvard University)

GSED Ground Support Equipment Division (USN)

GSEL Ground-Support Equipment List

GSERD Ground-Support Equipment Recommendation Data

GSES Geocentric Solar Ecliptic System (NASA)

GSE/TD General Systems Engineering/Technical Direction

gsf general scientific framework

GSF General Support Force (USAF); Government Superannuation Fund

GSFC Goddard Space Flight Center

GSFG Group of Soviet Forces in Germany

GSFLT Graduate School Foreign Language Test

GSFSR Ground Safety and Flight Safety Requirements

gsfu glazed structural facing units

GSG *Grenzschutzgruppe* (German—Border Protection Group)—anti-terrorist commando force used by West Germany to combat terrorism

GSGB Geological Survey of Great Britain

GSGS Geographical Section—General Staff

GSGS maps General Staff, Geographical Section (British War Office) maps covering Africa, Asia, the East Indies, and Europe

gsh good study habits

GSH glutathione

gshr grand-slam home run(s)

gshv globe stop hose valve

gsi glide scope indicator; graphic structure input; gross scheduled income; ground speed indicator

GSI General Safety Inspection; General Safety Inspector; General Service Infantry; General Steel Industries; Geological Survey of Israel; Geophysical Services International; Government Source Inspection

G & SI Gulf and Ship Island (railroad)

gsid ground-emplaced seismic intrusion detector

g sil german silver

GSIS Government Service Insurance System; Group for the Standardization of Information Services

gskt gasket

gsl guaranteed student loan

GSL Geological Society of London; Guaranteed Student League

GS & LA Guam Savings and Loan Association

GSLP Guaranteed Student Loan Program

gsm good sound merchantable; grams per square meter; gross

sales monthly; ground-supplied material

GSM General Sales Manager; Gibson Spiral Maze; Guildhall School of Music

GSMD General Society of Mayflower Descendants; Guildhall School of Music and Drama

GSML General Stores Material List

GSMNP Great Smoky Mountains National Park (Tennessee and North Carolina)

GSMOL Golden State Mobilehome Owners League

GSMS Geocentric Solar Magnetospheric System (NASA); Graduate Student of the Management Society

GSNC General Steam Navigation Company

GSNWR Great Swamp National Wildlife Refuge (New Jersey)

gso ground speed outbound

GSO General Staff Officer; Girls Service Organization; Greensboro, North Carolina (airport); Ground Safety Officer

GSOST Goldstein-Scheerer Object Sorting Test

GSP Generalized System of Preferences

GSPA Gulfport State Port Authority

G-spot Grafenberg spot—erotic vaginal area present in some women

GSPOT Geometric Spot Analysis System

gsps guidance spare power supply

gsr galvanic skin reflex; galvanic skin response; general service reinforcement(s); ground speed return; ground surveillance radar

GSRI Gulf South Research Institute

GSRS General Support Rocket System (surface-to-surface missile planned for NATO)

gsrv globe stop radiator valve

gss guidance system simulator

GSS General Service School; General Social Services; General Supply Schedule; Geo-Stationary Satellite; Gilbert and Sullivan Society; Global Surveillance System; Grumman Standard Specification

GSSF General Supply Stock Fund

GSSH Grand Street Settlement House

GSSL Genoa, Savona, Spezia,

and Leghorn (ports)
GSSLNCV Genoa, Savona, Spezia, Leghorn, Naples, Civetta, and Vecchia (ports)
GSSR Georgian Soviet Socialist Republic; Ground Support System Review
GSSS Ground Support System Specification(s)
GSST Goldstein-Scheerer Stick Test
gst garter stitch (knitting); ground special tools
GST General Service Test; General Staff Target; Greenwich Sidereal Time; Guamanian Standard Time
GSTC Gorham State Teachers College
gste guidance system test equipment
GSTP Generalized System of Tariff Preferences
G-string capital-G-shaped string-like genital covering worn by exotic entertainers
gsts guidance system test set
gstu guidance system test unit
gsu glazed structural units; ground-support unit
GSU General Service Unit; Gulf States Utilities
gsub glazed structural unit base
gsuc ground stub-up connection
g-suit antigravity suit worn during supersonic flight
GSUSA Girl Scouts of the USA
GSUSDA Graduate School, United States Department of Agriculture
gsv globe stop valve
GSV Grumman Submersible Vehicle; Guided Space Vehicle
gsvr ground-to-surface vessel radar
gsw gunshot wound
GSW Fort Worth, Texas (Greater Southwest International Airport)
GSW 1812 General Society of the War of 1812
gt gas turbine; gastight; gilt; gilt top; glass tube; grand total; grease trap; great; greater than; greetings telegram; gross tonnage; gross ton(s); ground transmit(ter); group technology; gun target; gut tripe
g/t gooseneck tunnel; grams per ton; granulation time; granulation tissue
gt gate (Norwegian—street)
gt. gutta (Latin—drop)

Gt Great; Greenwich time
Gt Groot (Afrikaans—big, large, vast)
GT General Tariff; Good Templar; Goodyear Tire & Rubber (stock exchange symbol); Gran Turismo; Grand Tiler; Grupo de Transportes (Transport Group)
G/T Gas Turbine (vessel)
GT Gamle Testamente (Dano-Norwegian—Old Testament); *Gran Turismo* (automobile)
gta gas-tungsten arc; graphic training aid
GTA Gatt Textiles Arrangement; Geography Teachers Association; Gospel Truth Association; Government Telecommunications Agency; Graduate Teaching Assistant; Gravure Technical Association; Gun Trade Association
GTAP General Technical Assistance Program
gtaw gas turbine arc welding
Gtb Godthab
GTB Government Tourist Bureau
GTBC Guild of Teachers of Backward Children
Gt Br Great Britain
Gt Brit Great Britain
gtc gain time control; gas turbine compressor; good till cancelled
GTC Girls Training Corps; Government Training Center; Government Travel Center; Guam Territorial College; Guild of Television Cameramen; Gulf Transport Company (railroad)
GTCs Government Training Centres (UK)
gtd geometrical theory of diffraction; guaranteed
GTDS Goddard Trajectory Determination System (NASA)
gte general total energy; gilt top edge; ground test(ing) equipment; guidance test(ing) equipment; gunner tracking evaluator
gt-e gas turbo-electric ,
gte gerente (Spanish—manager)
GT & E General Telephone and Electronics (Corporation)
GT & EA Georgia Teachers and Education Association
GTEC Georgia Institute of Technology
gtee goatee; guarantee
gtee od guaranteed overdraft
GTEIS General Telephone and Electronics Information System

GT & EL General Telephone and Electronics Laboratories
GTEP Guaranteed Training Equipment Program
gtev (GTEV) gas-turbine electric vessel
gtf glucose tolerance factor
GTF Gang Task Force (police function); General Trust Fund; Government Test(ing) Facilities; Government Test(ing) Facility; Granite Test Facility; Great Falls, Montana (airport)
gtg gas to gasoline
GTG Sappho's daddy
gth go to hell
gth (GTH) gonadotrophic hormone
gthtgr (GTHTGR) gas-turbine high-temperature gas-cooled reactor
gti general transportation importance
GTI Grand Turk Island (tracking station)
GTIL Government Technical Institute Library
GTIO German Tourist Information Office
GTL Glass Technology Laboratories
Gt Ldn Greater London
gtm good this month; gross ton(nage) mile(s)
GTM General Traffic Manager
GTMA Gauge and Tool Makers Association
Gt Man Greater Manchester
Gtmo Guantanamo Bay
GTMS Graphic Text Management System
gtn glomerulo-tubulo nephritis
GTN Government Training News
GTNP Grand Teton National Park (Wyoming)
gto gate turnoff
g to go to (calculator)
Gto Gunajuato
GTO Government Team of Officials
GTO Gran Turismo Omologato [hard-top type of high-performance auto certified (*omologato*) to enter Gran Turismo automobile race]
gtol graphic takeoff language; ground takeoff and landing
gtow gross takeoff weight
gtp ground test(ing) plotter
gtp (GTP) guanosine triphosphate
GTP General Test Plan
gtr gantry test rack; greater;

ground test(ing) reactor

GTR Grand Trunk Railway; Gurkha Transport Regiment(als)

GT-R Grand Touring-Racing (version)

Gtr Ant Greater Antilles

gtrp general transpose

gts guidance test(ing) set

gts (GTS) geostationary technology satellite

gt's grand touring cars

g/t/s gas-turbine ship

Gts Gateshead

GTS gas turbine vessel (3-letter code); General Telephone System; General Theological Seminary; Global Telecommunications System (WMO); Greenwich Time Signal; Ground Transport System; Guinean Trawling Survey

GTSC German Territorial Southern Command (NATO)

gtss gas turbine self-contained starter

GTSTD Grid Test of Schizophrenic Thought Disorder

gtt glass transition temperature

gtt (GTT) gelatin-tellurite-taurocholate

gtt. guttae (Latin—drops)

gtT gone to Texas (one jump ahead of the sheriff)

GTT Glucose Tolerance Test

gtu guidance test unit

GTU Graduate Theological Union

gtv gate valve; gravity vacuum transit

gtv (GTV) gas turbine vessel

GTV Gumma Television (Japan)

gtw good this week; gross ton(nage) weight

GTW Grand Trunk Western (railroad)

Gtwy Gateway (postal abbreviation)

gty gritty

Gtz Galatz

gu gastric ulcer; genitourinary; geographically unsuitable; glycogenic unit

Gu Gujarat; Gujarati

Gu Göteborgs Universitetsbiblioteket (Swedish—Gothenburg's University Library)

GU genito-urinary; Georgetown University; Gonzaga University; Griffith University

GUA Guatemala City, Guatemala (airport)

Guad Guadeloupe

Guadal Guadalajara

Guadalupes Guadalupe Mountains of New Mexico and Texas

Guadalupe Victoria Manuel Felíx Fernández

Guadarramas Guadarrama Mountains of central Spain (*Sierra de Guadarrama*)

Guahan (Chamorro—We Have) —Guam

Guaján (Spanish—Guam)

Guam Pacific Island possession of United States; inhabited by Guamanians

Guamanian Port Apra

Guam ST Guamanian Standard Time

'Guana Iguana Island, British Virgin Islands

Guanacastes Guanacaste Mountains of northwestern Costa Rica (*Cordillera de Guanacaste*)

Guanaco Central American nickname for a farmer or other rustic and Andean name for a member of the camel family resembling a llama

Guanahani (Lucayan—San Salvador or Watling Island)— first land discovered by Columbus in the New World

Guanajay Cuban prison in Guanajay southwest of Havana in Pinar del Rio province

'guana(s) iguana(s)

Guangdong (Pinyin Chinese— Kwangtung)

Guangxi Zhuang (Pinyin Chinese—Kwangsi Chuang)—autonomous province of mainland China

Guangzhou (Pinyin Chinese— Canton)

GUANOMEX Guanos y Fertilizantes de México (Spanish— Guanos and Fertilizers of Mexico)

guar guarantee

Guar Guarani (Brazil)

guard. guaranteed

GUARD Government Employees United Against Discrimination

Guardian The Guardian (a leading British newspaper published simultaneously in London and Manchester)

Guardian Angel of Israel Michael

Guardian of the Gulf Oman (guarding the Gulf of Oman flowing between the Arabian Sea and the Persian Gulf)

guarg guaranteeing

Guarnerius Giuseppi Antonio Guarneri

Guat Guatemala(n)

GUATEL Empresa Guatemalteca de Telecomunicaciones (Spanish—Guatemalan Telecommunications Enterprise)

Guatemala Republic of Guatemala (Central American Spanish-speaking country whose Guatemalans produce coffee and other crops as well as mining for minerals and creating excellent textiles), *República de Guatemala*

Guatemala Day Guatemalan Independence Day (September 15)

Guatemalan Ports (east coast) Livingston, Puerto Barrios, Santo Tomas de Castillo; (west coast) San José, Iztapa, Champerico

Guay Guayaquil

Guaya Guayaquil

Guayana (Spanish—Guiana)

gub generalized upper boundary

guba (Russian—bay, gulf)

GUBC Guyana United Broadcasting Company (Radio Demerara)

gubernalection gubernatorial election

GUGK Glavnoje Upravlenije Geodesii i Kartografii (Russian—Administrative Agency for Geodesy and Cartography)

GUGMS Glavnoje Upravlenije Gidrometeorologicheskoi Sluzhby (Russian—Administrative Agency of the Hydrometeorological Service)

Gug Mus Guggenheim Museum

Gui Guinea

GUI Golfing Union of Ireland

Gui-Bis Guinea-Bissau (formerly Portuguese Guinea)

Gui Cur Guinea Current

guid guidance

guide. guidance for users of integrated data equipment

Guideline NATO nickname for Soviet SA-2 missile system

guidn guidance

guil guilder(s)

Guil Guillaume

Guild The Newspaper Guild (in American periodical circles)

Guildhall Lib Guildhall Library (London)

Guild Prof Trans Guild of Professional Translators

Guilin (Pinyin Chinese—Kweilin)

Guillaume Appolinaire Guillaume Appolinaire de Kostro-witsky

Guill° Guillermo (Spanish—William)

guin guinea(s)

Guinea Republic of Guinea (West African nation whose French-speaking Guineans herd cattle, produce tropical crops, and mine for precious minerals), *République de Guinée*

Guinea-Bissau Republic of Guinea-Bissau (former West African colony of Portugal whose people speak Portuguese and tribal languages, exports include bauxite, oil, palm oil, and peanuts)

Guinea-Bissau Ports Casheu, Bissau, Bolama

Guinea Ecuatorial (Spanish—Equatorial Guinea)—formerly Spanish Guinea

Guinea Port Conakry

Guinee (French—Guinea)

Guip Guipuzcoa

guit *guitarra* (Spanish—guitar); *guitarrazo* (Spanish—blow struck with a guitar); *guitarrear* (Spanish—strumming the guitar); *guitarrista* (Spanish—guitar player)—masculine or feminine; *guiterrera* or *guiterrero* (Spanish—guitar maker or guitar player)

Guiyang (Pinyin Chinese—Kweiyang)

Guizhou (Pinyin Chinese—Kweichow)

Guj Gujarat; Gujarati

GULAG Chief Administration of Corrective Labor Camps, Prisons, Labor, and Special Settlements of the Soviet Secret Police (*q.v. VOT*)

Gulag Archipelago Solzhenitsyn's title for the thousands of prisons found from the Bering Strait almost to the Bosporus and all within his former country, the USSR

gulag gas natural gas pipeline built by Soviet forced labor and extending from Siberia to the border of West Germany

GULC Georgetown University Law Center

Gulf Gulf of (Adalia, Aden, Alaska, Alexandretta, Aqaba, Boothia, Bothnia, Cadiz, California, Cambay, Campeche, Canada, Carpentaria, Cattaro, Chihli, Chiriqui, Cutch, Darien, Eilat, Finland, Fonseca, Gabes, Genoa, Guayaquil,

Guinea, Honduras, Izmir, Kotor, Kutch, Lepanto, Lions, Maine, Manaar, Maracaibo, Martaban, Mexico, Nicoya, Oman, Panama, Paria, Quarnero, Santa Catalina, Siam, Sidra, Smyrna, St Lawrence, Suez, Taranto, Tehuantepec, Tonkin, Venice); Gulf Oil; Spencer Gulf

GULF Gays United for Liberty and Freedom (street-people subculture society)

Gulf City Mobile, Alabama

Gulf of Mexico's Principal Port New Orleans

Gulf States Florida, Alabama, Mississippi, Louisiana, and Texas along the Gulf of Mexico; Iran, Iraq, Kuwait, Saudi Arabia, Bahrain, Qatar, United Arab Emirates, and Oman along the Persian Gulf

Gulf Stream northward-flowing warm ocean current originating in Gulf of Mexico; going through Florida Straits, and making itself felt in British Isles and northern Europe's waters including Scandinavian peninsula

Guli Gulielma

Gull's disease myxedema resulting from atrophy of the thyroid gland

gulp (data-processing slang—a succession of bytes)

gulp. **(GULP)** general utility language processor

GULP General Utility Library Program

gum. **(GUM)** genito-urinary malignancy

Gum Guam (container port)

GUM Gosudarstvennoe Universalny Magasin (Russian—State Universal Store); Guam (airport)

GUM *Gosurdarstvennoe Universalny Magasin* (Russian—State Universal Store)—facing Moscow's Red Square across from Lenin's Tomb

gun. guncotton; guncrete; gunnery; gunpowder

gun *gunung* (Malay—mountain)

gun dip gunboat diplomacy

Gunflint(s) Rhode Islander(s)

gunk nickname for aerosols, glues, and solvents inhaled by would-be addicts of the younger set

gun'l gunwale

Gun Sgt Gunnery Sergeant

GUNSS Gunnery Schoolship

(USN)

guo government use only

GUO Greater Union Organization

GUOOF Grand United Order of Odd Fellows

gup guppy

GUPCO Gulf Petroleum Corporation; Gulf of Suez Petroleum Company

guppie(s) gay urban professional(s)

guppy. greater underwater propulsive-powered (guppy-shaped) submarine

gups guppies

gup(s) gay urban professional(s)

GURC Gulf Universities Research Corporation

Gus August; Augustus; Gustaf; Gustave; Gustavus

GUs Guns Unlimited

GUS Globe Universal Services; Great Universal Stores; Grocers United Stores

Gussie Augusta; Augustina; Augustine

Gussies Great Universal Stores

Gustus Augustus

gut. gutter

Gut Gutenberg; The Gut (Valetta's redlight street on the island of Malta in the Mediterranean)

Gutenberg Johannes Gensfleisch (German—John Gooseflesh)—the inventor of movable type

GUTS Georgians Unwilling to Surrender

gutt. *gutta* (Latin—drop)

guttat. *guttatim* (Latin—drop by drop)

gutt. quibus. *guttis quibusdam* (Latin—a few drops)

guv governor

GuV *Gerecht und Volkommen* (German—correct and complete)

guv'nor governor

Guy Guayaquil; Guido; Guyana; Guyon

Guyana Cooperative Republic of Guyana (formerly called British Guiana or Demerara, South America's only English-speaking nation whose Guyanans mine for bauxite, gold, and diamonds as well as raising many tropical crops)

Guyana's Ports (west to east) Bartica, Georgetown, McKenzie, New Amsterdam

Guyane française French Guiana

Guybau Guyana Bauxite

Guy d'Hardelot Mrs WI Rhodes (Helen Guy)

Guy Esse Guyana Essequibo (between Guyana's Essequibo River and Venezuela's eastern border)—area claimed by Venezuela for more than a century although it occupies about five-eighths of Guyana (formerly British Guiana)

Guy's Guy's Hospital

Guys Marsh borstal in Dorset, England

gv gate valve; gentian violet; government valuation; gravimetric volume; grid variation; ground visibility

gv (GV) granulosis virus

gv *grande vitesse* (French—fast-freight train); *gran velocidad* (Spanish—high velocity)

Gv Gustav

GV gigavolt; Giuseppe Verdi; Göta Verken (steel company); grid variation

gva general visceral afferent

GVA Geneva, Switzerland (airport); Grants by Voluntary Agencies

gvb gelatine veronal buffer

GVB Guam Visitors Bureau

GVC Grand View College

gve general visceral efferent

Gve Grove (postal abbreviation); Gustave

GVF *Grazhdanskii Vozdushnyi Flot* (Russian—Civil Air Fleet)

gvh graft-versus-host (disease)

gvhd graft versus host disease(s)

gvhr graft versus host reaction(s)

gvhrr geosynchronous very-high-resolution radiometer

GVI Gas Vent Institute

gvl gravel

GVL Global Van Lines

gvm generating voltmeter; gross vehicle mass

GVMDS Ground-Vehicle Mine-Dispensing System

gvo gross value of output

GVP General Vice President

GVP *Gereformeerd Politiek Verbond* (Dutch—Reformed Political Union)

GVRD Greater Vancouver Regional District

GVS Government Vehicle Service

gvt government; gravity vacuum transit; gravity vacuum tube

GVT Ground Vibration Test(ing)

gvty gingivectomy

gvw gross vehicle weight

gvwr gross vehicle weight rating

gw gigawatt(s); green weight; ground wave(s); guerrilla warfare

g/w gross weight(s)

GW George Washington—first President of the United States; Great Western (savings)

G-W Globe-Wernicke

G & W Gulf and Western

G + W Gulf and Western

GWA Girl Watchers of America; Golden West Airlines

GWA *Goode's World Atlas*

GWB George Washington Bridge

gwc gas-water contact (oil well)

GWCHS George Washington Carver High School

GWCM George Washington Carver Museum

gwcswbd gunnery weapon-control switchboard

gwe gigawatts electrical

Gwen Gwendolyn

Gwenda Gwendolen

Gwennie Gwendolen

GWG George Washington Geist

gwh gigawatt hour

gwh/day gigawatt hours per day

GWHNWR Great White Heron National Wildlife Refuge (Florida)

GWHS George Washington High School; George Wenting house High School

GWI Grinding Wheel Institute; Ground Water Institute

G'wich Village Greenwich Village

Gwin Gwinett

GWK Grenswisselk-Kantoren

GWMNP George Washington Memorial National Parkway

GWO General Wage Order

GWOA Guerrilla Warfare Operational Area

gwp (GWP) gross world product

GWP *Government White Paper*

GWPA *Grote Winkler Prins Atlas* (Dutch—Great Winkler Prins Atlas)—Elsevier publication printed in Amsterdam

GWR General War Reserves; Great Western Railway

GWRI Ground Water Resources Institute

gws grid-wire sensor

GWS Geneva (Convention for the Amelioration of the) Wounded and Sick (in Armed Forces in the Field); George Washington School; Gir Wild-

life Sanctuary (India)

gwt glazed wall tile

GWTA Gift Wrappings and Tyings Association

GWU George Washington University

GWVA Great War Veterans Association

GWWD Greater Winnipeg Water District (Railway)

Gwyn Gwynedd; Gwynne

gx (GX) government exhibit

gxmtr guidance transmitter

gxt graded exercise test(ing)

gy gray; gunnery; gyro; gyrocar; gyrocompass; gyrodyne; gyroscope

gY greenish yellow

Gy gray

gya got yuh again (slang for caught you again)

GYE Guayaquil, Ecuador (airport)

gym gymnasium; gymnastics

Gym Gymnastics

GYM General Yard Master; Guyamas, Mexico (tracking station)

gymstic gymnastic(s)

gyn gynecology

gyn *gyne* (Greek—woman)—gynecologist, gynecology, misogyny, polygyny

G.Y.N. gynecologist

gynae(col) gynaecological; gynaecologist; gynaecology

gynecol gynecologic(al)(ly); gynecologist; gynecology

gyp gypsum; gypsy; cheat or swindle (slang)

Gyp Gypsy; Gyp the Blood; Marie Antoinette de Riquetti de Mirabeau, Countess de Martel de Janville's pseudonym

GYP Guild of Young Printers

Gyppy (British slang—Egyptian)

gypsiol gypsiologic(al)(ly); gypsiologist(s); gypsiology

gypsum calcium sulfate ($CaSO_4 \cdot 2H_2O$)

Gypsum City Fort Dodge, Iowa

Gypsy Rose Lee Rose Hovick

'gyptian(s) Egyptian(s)

gyro gyrocompass; gyroplane; gyroscope

gyrocop gyrocopter

gyrocopter autogyro helicopter (rotary-wing aircraft driven forward by a conventional propeller)

gyrodyn gyrodynamic(al)(ly); gyrodynamicist; gyrodynamics

GYS Co Great Yarmouth Shipping Company

gywp gee you're wonderful, professor

gz ground zero

Gz Gomez

GZ Girozentrale Vienna

G-Z Guilford-Zimmerman

test(ing)

GZ *Girozentrale Vienna* (German—Vienna Central Exchange)—Austrian international bank

GZG *Gutegemeinschaft Zinn-*

gerat (German—Pewter Quality Society)

GZn grid azimuth

GZT Greenwich Zone Time

H

h hail; hard; hardening; hardness; hazy; hectare; hecto; height; high(er); hit(s); home; horse; hour(s); house; hundred(s); husband; hydrant; hydraulic(s); hydrodynamic head (symbol); hydrolysis; Planck's constant (symbol); Planck's element of action (symbol)

(h) per hypodermic

h altitude (symbol); atmospheric head (symbol)

H amateur broadcasting (symbol); ceiling (symbol); Fraunhofer line produced by calcium (symbol); Hamiltonian function (symbol); Hangarage; Harbor; hard; hard (pencil); hardness; hatch; headlines; heat; heater; helicopter; henry; heroin (drug-user's abbreviation); Hill (postal abbreviation); Hindu; Hinduism; horizontal component of the earth's magnetism (symbol); hot; Hotel—code for letter H; humidity; hydrogen; hyperopia; intensity of magnetic field (symbol); latent hypermetropia (symbol); maximum altitude (symbol); McDonnel Aviation; Minneapolis-Honeywell (trademark); very hazy (symbol)

H hacienda (Spanish—customs service, treasury); *haut* (French—up); *heet* (Dutch—hot); *Herren* (German or Swedish—gentlemen); *herrer* (Norwegian—gentlemen); *het* (Norwegian—hot); *hinaus* (German—out); *hombres* (Spanish—men); *Hoyre* (Norwegian—Right)— Conservative Party

H- Hauptstimme (German—principal voice)—12-tone term

H¹ protium

H¹+ proton

H-2 Australian macadamia

H² deuterium (heavy hydrogen symbol)

H_2O water

H_2O_2 hydrogen peroxide

H_2SO_4 sulfuric acid

H_3 procaine hydrochloride (symbol)

H³ tritium

H_3BO_3 boric acid

H-13 Bell three-place helicopter named Sioux and made in Britain, Italy, and Japan

H-19 Sikorsky transport helicopter called Chickasaw or UH-19

H-23 Hiller utility helicopter used by USA and called Raven

H24 hard rolled and partially annealed (half hard)

H-34 Sikorsky troop-transport helicopter called Choctaw

H-37 Sikorsky heavy helicopter called Mojave

H-43 Kaman utility helicopter called Huskie

H-53 Sikorsky CH-53 Stallion assault helicopter

ha hardy annual; hatch(way); hectare; heir apparent; high altitude; high angle; home address; hostile aircraft; hour angle; hour aspect

ha (HA) humic acid

ha' half

h.a. hoc anno (Latin—in this year)

Ha hahnium (element 105); Haiti(an); Hawaii(an)

Ha (German pronunciation for B sharp)

HA Hatch Act; Hawaiian Airlines; Headquarters Administration; Heavy Artillery; Horse Artillery; Hospital Apprentice; House of Assembly; Housing Authority

H-A Hautes-Alpes

H/A Havre–Antwerp (range of ports)

HA Hardware Age

HA-200 Hispano Saeta jet trainer

HA-220 Hispano Saeta ground-attack jet fighter

haa heavy anti-aircraft; heavy antiaircraft artillery; height above airport

haa (HAA) hepatitis-associated antigen

HAA Helicopter Association of America; Hospital Activity Analysis; Hotel Accountants Association; Humanist Association of America

haaat height of (transmission) antenna above average terrain

HAAC Harper Adams Agricultural College

HAAFE Hawaiian Army and Air Force Exchange

Haag (Afrikaans, Dutch, Flemish, German—Hague)

Haakon the Good King Haakon I of Norway

Haakon Jarl (Norwegian–Earl Haakon)

Haakon the Old King Haakon IV of Norway

haandb haandbog (Dano-Norwegian—handbook)

Ha'aretz (Hebrew—The Land)

— Israel's leading daily newspaper both independent and non-partisan

Haar *Haarlem* (Dutch—Harlem) provincial capital of North Holland in the Netherlands

haat height (of tv transmission antenna) above average terrain

haatc high altitude air traffic control

haaw heavy anti-tank assault weapon

hab high-altitude bombing; habitat; habitation

hab habitantes (Spanish–inhabitants)—often seen on road signs

Hab Habana (Spanish—Havana); The Book of Habakkuk

Hab Habakkuk

HAB Hazards Analysis Board (USAF)

HAB Handels Aktie Bolag (Swedish—Limited Trading Company)

HABA Hardwood Agents and Brokers Association

Habana (Spanish—Havana)— *La Habana*

Hab(bie) Albert; Alberta; Halbert

hab. corp. habeas corpus (Latin —may you have the body)— prisoner's right to be brought before the court so its judge may decide on the legality of the detention

habe habeas corpus

Habeas Corpus Howe William Frederick Howe also nicknamed Criminal Bar Howe

habit. habitat (Latin—it inhabits)

Habitants (French—Inhabitants)—Canadian farmers and fishermen of French descent

habs high-altitutde bombsight

HABS Historic American Buildings Survey

habt. habeat (Latin—let him have)

hac high acceleration cockpit; high alumina cement

HAc acetic acid

HAC Hawkesbury Agricultural College; Helicopter Aircraft Command(er); Hines Administrative Center; Honourable Artillery Company; Hughes Aircraft Company

hacc high alumina cement concrete

HACC Harrisburg Area Community College

hack hackney coach; hackney horse; taxicab

hack. hacking (illegally breaking into computerized electronic byways and tapping into a system or systems)

hacls (HACLS) harpoon-type aircraft command and launch subsystem missile

HACTL Hong Kong Air Cargo Terminal Limited

HACU Hansa (Line) Container Unit

had. head acceleration device; heat-actuated device (thermostat); hereinafter described

Had Hadley

H/A or D Havre-Antwerp or Dieppe (grain trade)

H^{ada} Hacienda (Spanish—Estate, Farm, Ranch)

HADA Hawaiian Defense Area

hadbn had been

HADC Holloman Air Development Center

Haddadland Christian-controlled buffer zone between Israel and Lebanon

Hades (Greek—invisible)— equivalent to the Roman god Pluto who was god of the dead and the invisible underworld

HADES Hypersonic Air Data Entry System

HADIS Huddersfield and District Information Service

HADIZ Hawaiian Air Defense Identification Zone

hadn't had not

Hadrianapolis (Latin—Adrianople)

hads hypersonic air data sensor

hads. hypersonic air data sensor

ha'e (Gaelic contraction—have)

Haeck Ernst Heinrich Haeckel; Haeckelian; Haeckelism

HAECO Hong Kong Aircraft Engineering Company

HAER Historic American Engineering Record

haes high-altitude-effects simulation

haf high-abrasion furnace; high-altitude fluorescence

HAF Hebrew Arts Foundation; Helicopter Assault Force; Hellenic Armed Forces; Helms Athletic Foundation; Helvetia-America Federation

HAFB Homestead Air Force Base (Florida)

haf black high-abrasive furnace black

Haffner Mozart's Serenade Suite in D or his Symphony

No. 35 in D major; both honor the Burgomeister of Salzburg —Sigmund Haffner

HAFMED Headquarters—Allied Forces Mediterranean

Hafnia (Latin—Copenhagen)

HAFO Home Accounting and Finance Office (USAF)

HAFRA Hat and Allied Feltmakers Research Association

HAFSE Headquarters, Armed Forces, Southern Europe

HAFTB Holloman Air Force Test Base

Hafun formerly Dante when Somalia was Italian Somaliland

Hag The Book of Haggai; The Hague

Hag Haggai

HAG Hardware Analysis Group

Haga (Latin—The Hague)— also known as Haga Comitis or Hage Comitum

HAGB Helicopter Association of Great Britain

Haggisland Scotland

hagiol hagiology

Hague The Hague (English name for s'Gravenhage)

HAI Hospital Audiences Incorporated

HAIA Hearing Aid Industry Association

haic hetero-atom in context

haid hand-emplaced acoustic intrusion detector

Haight-Ashbury section of San Francisco taken over by junkies, porn clubs, prostitutes, and criminal-type street people

HAIL Hague Academy of International Law

H&A Ins Health and Accident Insurance

hair. high-accuracy instrumentation radar

hairdrsr hairdresser

hairies long-haired hippies

HAISS High-Altitude Infrared Sensor System

Haiti Republic of Haiti (French-speaking West Indian nation occupying western half of Hispaniola, Haitian rum, tropical crops, and tourism rank high in the economy of the Black Republic founded by an ex-slave—Toussaint l'Ouverture), *République d'Haiti*

Haiti's Principal Port Port-au-Prince

HAJ Hanover, Germany (airport)

Hak Hakka; Hakodate

HAKASH *Hayl Kashish* (Hebrew—Army of Elders)—Israel's senior-citizen corps

Hak Soc Hakluyt Society

hal halogen(ic); handicapped assistance loan; helmet audio link(age)

Hal Halawa; Halbert; Halcott; Halden; Halensee; Halex; Halford; Halfrid; Haliburton; Hallam; Halleck; Hallett; Halogen; Halsey; Halsom; Halstead; Halvar; Halworth; Harold

HAL Hamburg-Amerika Linie (Hamburg-America Line); Hamburg-Atlantic Line; Hardboards Australia Limited; Hawaiian Airlines; Holland America Line

Hala (Latin—Halle)

Halawa Halawa Jail at Aiea on Oahu, Hawaii

Hal Croves another pseudonym of B Traven whose full name was Berick Traven Torsvan and whose mother's maiden name was Croves; during his lifetime his full name was concealed by his publisher as he was a fugitive from justice best known for *The Treasure of the Sierra Madre* and *Ghost Ship*

HALDIS Halifax and District Information Service

Haleakala Haleakala National Park and Haleakala Volcano on the Hawaiian island of Maui

Halebum (Latin—Aleppo)

Halévy Jacques Fromental Elie Lévy

half-g half-gallon(s)

Hali Halifax

Halicz (Polish—Galicia)

Halifax (named for the second Earl of Halifax)

Halim Jakarta, Indonesia's airport

halite rock salt (sodium chloride)

Halka (Polish—Helen)—Moniuszko's most popular opera and the most popular Polish one

Halle a/S Halle an der Saale (German—Halle on the Salle River)

Halloween All-Hallow's Eve (October 31)

Hallowell Girls Stevens School for female juvenile delinquents at Hallowell, Louisiana

hallu hallucinant; hallucinate; hallucination; hallucinogen;

hallucinogenic

halluc hallucination

hallus hallucinations; hallucinogens

Hal Meredith Harry Blyth's pseudonym

halo. high-altitude large optics; high-altitude low opening

Hal Orch Hallé Orchestra

HALS Harwell Automated Loans System

Halstern's disease endemic syphilis

HALT Help Abolish Legal Tyranny; Houston Anti-Litter Team

haltata high-and-low-temperature-accuracy testing apparatus

Halterm Halifax Container Terminal

halv hamster leukemia virus

Halv Halvøy (Dano-Norwegian—peninsula)

ham. hardware-associated memory

Ham Hamal; Haman; Hamblin; Hamburg; Hamed; Hamilton; Hamitic; Hamlet; Hamlin; Hamlyn; Hammerfest; Hamnet; Hamon

HAM Hamburg, Germany (airport)

HA & M Hymns Ancient and Modern

ham and ham and eggs

Hamb Hamburg

Hambourg (French—Hamburg)

hamburg hamburg brandy (beet or potato alcohol flavored to imitate grape brandy); hamburger (grilled ground-meat patty often extended with cereals); hamburg steak (a hamburger)

Hamburg Bach Karl Philipp Emanuel Bach—also nicknamed Berlin Bach

Hamburgo (Spanish—Hamburg)

Haml Hamlet, Prince of Denmark

hamlet ham omelet

Hamlet funeral march by Berlioz; fantasy overture by Tchaikovsky; five-act opera by Thomas—all based on Shakespeare's character in his play of the same name

hamletom ham, lettuce and tomato (sandwich)

Hamlet's Town Helsingør, Denmark (called Elsinore by the English)

Hamm Hammerfest, Norway

hamma' hammer

Hammerfestinger native of Hammerfest, Norway

Hammering Hank Henry Aaron

Hammerklavier Beethoven's Piano Sonata No. 29 in B flat (opus 106)

Hammerman John Henry

Hammer of Scotland Edward I

hammer and sickle communist symbol appearing wherever communists are found; the crossing of the proletarian hammer and the agrarian sickle also appears on the flags of the Congo and the USSR

Hammersleys short form for the Hammersley Mountains of Western Australia

Hammond Innes pseudonym of Ralph Hammond-Innes

Ham 'n' Eggs musician's nickname for *Cavalleria Rusticana* and *Pagliacci* as these two operas seem to go well together and are usually billed together

ham 'n' eggsan ham-and-egg sandwich

ham 'n' eggwich ham-and-egg sandwich

Hamona (Latin—Hamburg)

Hamp Hampton Roads; Lionel Hampton

Hampton Roads Ports Newport News, Norfolk, Portsmouth

Hamptons collective short form for all Hamptons such as Bridgehampton, East Hampton, Hampton Bays, Southampton, West Hampton, and West Hampton Beach—all at the eastern end of Long Island, New York plus the original English estates and homestead place-names such as Hampton, Hampton Bishop, Hampton Court Palace, Hampton Heath, Hampton in Arden, Hampton Lovett, Hampton Lucy, Hampton Poyle, Hampton Wick, and Northampton as well as the great port of Southampton, nearby Southampton Airport, and adjacent Southampton Water plus all other Hamptons wherever they may be from Maine, Maryland, Massachusetts, New Brunswick, and New Hampshire to Virginia's roadstead—Hampton Roads

hams. hour angle of the mean sun

hamsan ham sandwich

hamt human-aided machine

translation
HAMTC Hanford Atomic Metal Trades Council
hamwich ham sandwich
han' hand
Han Handel Society
hand. handling
HAND Hawaii Association for National Defence
Handb Phys Handbuch der Physik (German—Handbook of Physics)
Handcuff King Harry Houdini
hande hydrofoil analysis and design
Hand of Fatima five-fingered heraldic symbol topping the emblem of Algeria
Handl Handlingar (Swedish—transactions)
HANDS High-Altitude Nuclear-Detection Studies
hane high-altitude nuclear effects; high-altitude nuclear explosion
Haneda Tokyo, Japan's old airport (*see* Narita)
HANES Health and Nutrition Examination Survey
HANG Hawaii Air National Guard
Hanging Judge Judge Roy Bean of Langtry, Texas—Law West of the Pecos, and many other judges who earned this nickname from the number of criminals they eliminated by hanging
Hangman's Day Friday (customary day for hangings)
Hangö (Swedish—Hanko)
Hangtown El Dorado, California's nickname recalling when so many bandits were hanged during the Gold Rush
Hangzhou (Pinyin Chinese—Hangchow)
Hank Henry
hanki handkerchief
Hanko (Finnish——Hangö)
Han Kook Republic of Korea
Hanot's disease cirrhosis of the liver accompanied by jaundice
Hanover Girls Jane Porter Barrett School for (delinquent) Girls at Hanover, Virginia
Hanover Street Kingston, Jamaica's bar-and-brothel center
Hanovre (French—Hannover)
Hans Johann(es)
HANS High-Altitude Navigation System
Hansa Ports Hanseatic League ports—Bremen and Hamburg

on the North Sea, Danzig and Lübeck on the Baltic, Visby on Gotland Island in the Baltic
Hansard official verbatim reports of debates of both Houses of Parliament
Hänsel Hänsel und Gretel (Humperdinck's Christmastime entertainment and opera about a brother, sister, parents, and an old witch in a gingerbread house)
Hansen's disease leprosy
Hans Fallada (pseudonym—Rudolf Ditzen)
han't has not; have not (British contraction)
Hants Hampshire
Hanuk Chanukkah (Hebrew—Feast of Lights)
HANZ Hotel Association of New Zealand
hao hardware action officer; high-altitude observation
HAO High Altitude Observatory; Horticultural Advisory Office(r)
haoa hight angle of attack
hap happening; heading axis perturbation
HAP Home Attendant Program
HAPAG Hamburg-American Line
HAPAG Hamburg-Amerikanische Packetfahrt Aktien Gesellschaft (German—Hamburg-American Packet Company)—packet steamship service carrying cargo, mail, and passengers on a regular schedule
Hap Arnold General Henry Harley Arnold, USA and USAF
hapd happened
hapdar hardpoint demonstration array radar
hapdec hard point decoy
ha'penny halfpenny
ha'p'orth half-pennyworth (*heypennyworth*)
happ high air pollution potential
Happy Chandler High Commissioner of Baseball Albert Benjamin Chandler
Happy Home of the Bulldozer Los Angeles or any other fast-growing metropolis
Happy Land Burma's sobriquet
Happy Valley The Vale of Kashmir in the Himalayas
Happy Warrior Franklin D Roosevelt's nickname for Al Smith (New York State's Governor Alfred E Smith); Hubert

Horatio Humphrey shares this nickname with Al Smith
haps happenings
hap's housing assistance payments
har harbor; harmonic
Har Harbin; Harbor; Harbour; Harold; Harwich
HAR Harrisburg, Pennsylvania (airport)
Harald Hårdråde (Norwegian—Harold Hardruler)—viking king and founder of Oslo
HARAO Hartford Aircraft Reactor Area Office
harb harbor
Harbin Russian name for Pinkiang, Manchuria
Harbison Girls Harbison Correctional Institution for Women at Irmo, South Carolina
Harbor City Erie, Pennsylvania
Harbor of the Sun San Diego, California
Harbrace Harcourt Brace Jovanovich
HarBraceJ Harcourt Brace Jovanovich
HARC Human Affairs Research Center
harcft harbor craft
Harcourt Harcourt Brace Jovanovich
hard. hardware
Hard Hardangerfelen (Norwegian—Hardanger fiddle)
Harden (British contraction—Harwarden)
Hard Heart of Hickland Cleveland, Ohio, according to authors Jack Lait and Lee Mortimer—*U.S.A. Confidential*
hard porn hard-core pornography
Hard Rock nickname of the American Broadcasting Company (ABC)
hardtack ship's biscuits
hardware computerese for computer and peripheral apparatus; data-processing electromechanical equipment (computerese) (*see* software)
Hardware City New Britain, Connecticut
Hardwick Girls Georgia Rehabilitation Center for Women at Hardwick
hare. high-altitude ramjet engine
Hare Soviet Mi-1 utility helicopter
HAREP Harbour Repairs
HARES High-Altitude Radiation Environment Study
Har Hakarmel (Hebrew—

Mount Carmel)

har-har not a hyphenated abbreviation but a cartoonist's symbol for loud laughter

HARIS High-Altitude Radiation Instrument System

Harke Soviet Mi-10 heavy-transport helicopter

Harlem section of Upper East Side of Manhattan Island, New York City, contains world's largest Negro community—a city within a city—and sections populated by other Americans; mainly of Italian and Latin-American origin, Puerto Ricans predominating

Harlemum (Latin—Haarlem)

harm. harmonic; harmony

harm. (HARM) high-speed anti-radiation missile; hyper-velocity anti-radiation missile

HARM Humans Against Rape and Molestation

Harmony former place-name of Ambridge, Pennsylvania (named for the American Bridge Company's factory here) where it contained the communistic settlement of Economy belonging to the Harmony Society founded by George Rapp whose celibate ● system caused its demise

harn harness

harn ldhr harness leather

Harold *Harold en Italie* (Italian —Harold in Italy)—Berlioz symphony with viola solo

Harold Bluetooth King Harold of Denmark

Harold Harefoot Harold I of Denmark and England

Haroun al Raschid (Arabic— Aaron the Upright)—Caliph of Arabia who befriended Charlemagne, thereby becoming an idealized character in *The Arabian Nights*

harp symbol of Ireland and the Irish

harp. harpoon; harpsichord; harpsichordist; heater above reheat point; heating, air conditioning, refrigeration, plumbing; high-altitude relay point; high-altitude research probe

Harp Halpern's anti-radar point

Harp Beethoven's String Quartet in E-flat major (opus 74) for two violins, viola, and cello with harplike arpeggio passages for all the instruments;

Chopin's Piano Etude in A flat (opus 25, no. 1)

HARP Helmlich-Armstrong-Rieveschi-Patrick (aerospace heart pump); Honeywell Acoustic Research Program

Harp Baz *Harper's Bazaar*

Harper Harper & Row

Harp/Hormone Soviet Ka-20 or Ka-25k helicopter for military or commercial use (Harp is military and Hormome is commercial version)

Harpo Marx Adolph Arthur Marx

Harpoon harpoon-type aircraft command and launch subsystem missle; Lockheed maritime reconnaissance bomber

harps. harpsichord

Harrier Hawker-Siddeley fixed-wing fighter aircraft; McDonnell-Douglas AV-8B jump-jet bomber

Harrisburg Pennsylvania's capital

Har-Row Harper and Row

Harry Harold; Henry

Harry Golden Herschel Goldhirsch

Harry Houdini Ehrich Weiss

hart. (HART) hyper-velocity anti-aircraft rocket tactical

Hart Hartford

HART Halt All Racist Tours; Highway Advisory Radio Tactical; Honolulu Area Rapid Transit

Hartford Connecticut's capital

Hartford Wits Joel Barlow, Timothy Dwight, Jonathan Trumbull

Hartran Hartwell Atlas fortran

Hart Sym Orch Hartford Symphony Orchestra

HARU Harrison Line (container) Unit

harv (HARV) high-altitude research vehicle

Harv Harvard; Harvey

Harvard's Heroic Historian John Lothrop Motley

Harw Harwarden (*Harden*)

HARYOU Harlem Youth Opportunities Unlimited

has. high-altitude sample

Has Haselhorst

HAs Housing Assistants

HAS Helicopter Air Service; Hellenic Affiliation Scale; Hospital Adjustment Scale; Hospital Administrative Services

HASAWA Health and Safety at Work Act

HASC House (of Representa-

tives) Armed Services Committee

HASCO Haitian-American Sugar Company

HASD Humanist Association of San Diego

hash. hashish

Hashbury Haight-Ashbury (district of San Francisco)

Hashemite Kingdom Jordan

Hashemite Kingdom of Jordan Jordan; Transjordania

Hashish Hasan-ibn-al-Sabbah (11th-century Persian founder of the Assassins)

Hashish Trail extends from the Balkans to India; trail filled with narcotic addicts searching for something cheaper but stronger; many go but few return to tell the tale of the Hashish Trail

Hasid Hasidim (Hebrew—godly pious people)

HASL Health and Safety Laboratory (Atomic Energy Commission)

hasn't has not

hasp. hardware-assisted software polling; high-altitude sampling program; high-altitude space platform

HASP Hawaiian Armed Services Police; Houston Automatic Simulator of Peripherals

haspa high-altitude superpressure-powered aerostat

hasr high-altitude sounding rocket

Hasselt Limburg's provincial capital in Belgium

hast high-altitude supersonic target

Hastings Hastings House; Hastings-on-Hudson

Ha strain Harris (viral) strain

hasvr high-altitude space-velocity radar

hat. height above touchdown; high-altitude temperature

HATA Hong Kong Association of Travel Agents

hato handling tool

hatoff highest astronomical tide of the foreseeable future

hatom highest astronomical tide of the month

hatoy highest astronomical tide of the year

HATRA Hosiery and Allied Trades Research Association

hatrack. hurricane and typhoon tracking

HATREMS Hazardous and Trace Emissions System

HATRICS Hampshire Technical Research Industrial and Commercial Service

hats. hour angle of the true sun

HATS Helicopter Advanced Tactical System

Hatteras short form for Cape Hatteras, the Cape Hatteras National Seashore Recreational Area, Hatteras Inlet, Hatteras Island, the village of Hatteras—all part of North Carolina's Outer Banks area

Hattie Harriet

Hau Hausa

Hauai (Spanish—Hawaii)

Haunt of Yachtsmen British Virgin Islands

Hauptw Hauptwerk (German—great or chief work)

haust. haustus (Latin—a draught)

haut hautboy (oboe)

Hautes Alpes (French—Upper Alps)

Haute-Volta (French—Upper Volta)

hav haversine

hAv hepatitis A virus

Hav Havre

HAV Havana, Cuba (airport)

Havana High Miami High School's nickname reflecting the overwhelming number of Cuban students

HAVEN Help Addicts Voluntarily End Narcotics

Haven for Arthritics Jacumba, California

haven't have not

Havercake(s) native(s) of Lancashire

Havnia (Latin—Copenhagen)

havoc. histogram average ogive calculator

Havre Havre de Grace, Maryland; Le Havre (de Grace), France (seaport city)

haw highly active waste (radioactive); hour angle west

haw. (HAW) heavy anti-tank assault weapon

Haw Hawaii; Hawaiian (unauthorized abbreviations)

HAW Kauai, Hawaii (tracking station)

HAWA Hammond Ambassador World Atlas

Hawaiian Island Ports Hilo, Hawaii; Kahului, Maui; Honolulu, Oahu; Port Allen, Kauai; Nawiliwili Bay; Kauai;

Hawaiian Pineapple King James Drummond Dole

Hawaiians Hawaiian Islanders; Hawaiian Islands

hawb house air waybill

HAWE Honorary Association for Women in Education

HAWEIT Hamburg-Wechsler Intelligence Test

hawk. (HAWK) homing-all-the-way kill (missile)

Hawkeye airborne early-warning and fighter-control aircraft —the E-2

Hawkeye(s) Iowan(s)

Hawkeye State Iowa's official nickname

Hawks Nest Hawks Nest State Park, West Virginia

Haw'n Hawaiian

Hawna Hawaiiana

Hawn Isl Hawaiian Islands

Haw Tel Hawaii Telephone (company)

Hawthorn Hawthorn Books; Missouri state flower

hax hrir/apt interface (high-resolution infrared radiometer/automatic picture transmission)

Hay Hayle

Haya (Spanish—Hague)—*La Haya* (The Hague)

Haydn's 104 Franz Joseph Haydn's 104 symphonies with many named ones such as No. 6—*Le Matin*, 7—*Le Midi*, 8—*Le Soir*, 22—*Der Philosoph*, 26—*Lamentatione*, 31—*Horn Signal*, 43—*Mercury*, 44—*Trauer*, 45—*Farewell*, 48—*Maria Theresia*, 49—*La Passione*, 55—*Der Schulmeister*, 59—*Fire*, 60—*Il Distratto*, 63—*La Roxolane*, 73—*Hunt*, 82 —*l'Ours*, 83—*Poule*, 85—*La Reine*, 92—*Oxford*, 94—*Surprise*, 96—*Miracle*, 100—*Military*, 101—*Clock*, 103—*Drum Roll*, 104—*London*

haystaq have you stored answers to questions?

haz hazard; hazardous

hb half breadth; halfback; halfbound; handbook; hard black; hardback (book); hardy biennial; heavy barrel; heavy bombardment; heavy bombing; hemoglobin; herringbone; high band; hollow bar; homing beacon; horizontal bands; horizontal bombing; hose bib; human being

h/b handbook

Hb hemoglobin; Herbarium

Hb deuterium (heavy hydrogen symbol)

Hb Hoboe (German—oboe)

HB Hawke's Bay; Hawthorn Books; Hector Berlioz; High Bridge; House (of Representatives) Bill

H-B Huebner-Bleistein (process)

H & B Humboldt and Bonpland

HB Hindi Bharat (Hindustani —Republic of India)

Hba Habana (Spanish—Havana)

HBA Hoist Builders Association; Hollywood Bowl Association; Home Builders Account; Honest Ballot Association; Hospital Benefit Association; Housing Builders Association

h'back hatchback

h/back hardback

h B ag hepatitis B antigen

H-bar capital-H-shaped bar

HBAVS Human Betterment Association for Voluntary Sterilization

hbb hollow-bored bar

hbc high breaking capacity

HBC Hokkaido Broadcasting Company; Hudson's Bay Company

HbCO carbon monoxide hemoglobin

hbd hardboard; has been drinking; headboard; herein-before described

hbd (HBD) hydroxybutyrate dehydrogenase

HBD Harbor Board; Harbour Board

hbe hard-boiled egg(s)

H-beam capital H-shaped beam

hbf hepatic blood flow

Hbf fetal hemoglobin

Hbf Hauptbahnhof (German—depot, main station)

HBF Hospital Benefit Fund

Hbg Hamburg; Harrisburg; Helsingborg (Hälsingborg)

HBG Henry B(arbosa) Gonzalez; Hongkong Bank Group; Huntington Botanical Gardens

HBJ Harcourt Brace Jovanovich

hbk halfback; hardback (book); hatchback; hollow back (lumber); hollowback

Hbk Hoboken

HB & K Humboldt, Bonpland, and Kunth (botanists)

HBM His (Her) Britannic Majesty

hbn hazard beacon

HBNNR Hickling Broad National Nature Reserve (England)

HBNWR Holla Bend National

Wildlife Refuge (Arkansas)
Hbo Hoboken
HBO Home Box Office (pay tv)
h/board hardboard; headboard
HBOG Hudson's Bay Oil and Gas
H-bomb hydrogen bomb
HBO S oxyhemoglobin
hbp high blood pressure; hit by pitcher (baseball)
HBPS Home Building Plan Service
hbr has been reviewed
Hbr Harbor
HBR Hudson Bay Railway
***HBR** Harvard Business Review*
hbr acw has been reviewed and concurred with
hb's halfbacks
Hbs sickle-cell hemoglobin
HBS Harvard Business School; Hawaiian Botanical Society; Hope Botanic Gardens
Hbt Hobart
HB & T Houston Belt and Terminal (railroad)
hbt's human-breast tumors
hBv hepatitis B virus
H&BV Houston and Brazos Valley (railroad)
hbw highspeed black-and-white (photography)
Hbwr Halden boiling heavy water reactor
hby hereby
hc habitual criminal; hand control; hard copy; heating cabinet; hexachlorethane; high carbon; high-capacity; highly commended; hydrocarbons
hc (HC) hard copy
h/c held covered
h & c heroin + cocaine; hot and cold; (running water)
***h.c.** hac nocte* (Latin—tonight); *honoris causa* (Latin—out of respect for); *hors commerce* (French—not for sale, privately printed)
Hc computed altitude; Hermitian conjugate; Huntington's chorea
HC Hagerstown College; Hague Convention; Hamilton College; Hamline College; Hanover College; Harding College; Harpur College; Hartford College; Hartnell College; Hartwick College; Hastings College; Haverford College; Health Certificate; Heidelberg College; Helicopter Council; Hendrix College; Hershey College; Hertford College; Hesston College; High Commis-

sion(er); Higher Certificate; Highway Code; Hillsdale College; Hiram College; Hood College; Hope College; Hospital Consult(ation); Hospital Corps; House of Commons; House of Correction(s); Housing Commission; Housing Corporation; Howard College; Humphreys College; Hunter College; Huntingdon College; Huntington College; Huron College; Hussan College; Hutchinson College
H C Holy Communion
H-C Harbison-Carborundum
H.C. High Commission
H of C House of Commons; House of Correction
***HC** Hartford Courant*
HC-54 Douglas C-54 modified for search-and-rescue missions
hca held by civil authorities
HCA High Conductivity Association; Hobby Clubs of America; Hospital Corporation of America; Hotel Corporation of America; Hunting-Clan Air Transport
HC(A) Helicopter Coordinator (Airborne)
HCAAS Homeless Children's Aid and Adoption Society
hcap handicap
H-caps heroin capsules
hcb hard-core base; hard-covered book; heating and cooling of buildings; hollow concrete block(s)
HCB House of Commons Bill
hcc hydraulic cement concrete
hcc (HCC) 25-hydroxycholecalciferol (vitamin D^3 metabolite)
HCC Hebrew Culture Council; Holyoke Community College
HCCA Health Care Consumers Association
HCCJ Harvard Center for Criminal Justice
hcd high current density
hcd (HCD) human chorionic gonadotropin
HCDCS Harmonized Commodity Description and Coding System
***HC Deb** House of Commons Debates*
hce human-caused error
HCEEP Handicapped Children's Early Education Project
hcef henceforth
HC & ES Hull Chemical and Engineering Society

hcex high-speed color exterior
hcf haemolytic complement fixation; hardened compacted fibers; height-correction factor; high carbohydrate fiber (diet); high cycle fatigue; highest common factor; hundred cubic feet
hcf (HCF) high-carbon ferrochrome
HCF Health Care Financing; Honorary Chaplain to the Forces; Hospital Contribution Fund(ing); Hungarian Cultural Foundation
HCFA Health Care Financing Administration
hcg horizontal location of center of gravity; human chorionic gonadotropin pregnancy test
hch (HCH) hexachlorocyclohexane (insecticide)
HCH Herbert Clark Hoover (31st President U.S.)
HCHI Hand Chain Hoist Institute
HCHP Harvard Community Health Plan
HCI Hotel and Catering Institute
HCIL Hague Conference on International Law
HCIS House Committee on Internal Security
HCITB Hotel and Catering Industry Training Board
HCJ High Court of Justice
HCJC Howard County Junior College
hcl high cost of living; horizontal center line
h cl hanging closet
HCl hydrochloric acid (muriatic acid)
HCL Hod Carriers, Building and Common Laborers
H-class Soviet missile-launching nuclear-powered submarines called Hotel by NATO
HCM Her (His) Catholic Majesty
***HCM** Ho Chi Minh* (Chinese—He Who Shines)
HCMC Ho Chi Minh City (Saigon's new name imposed upon its surrender to Vietcong communist guerrillas wishing to honor the founder of their forces—Ho Chi Minh)
hcmm heat-capacity map mission (NASA)
hcmr heat-capacity mapping radiometer
HCMT Ho Chi Minh Trail
HCMW Hatters, Cap and Millinery Workers (union)

hcn hydrocyanic acid

HCn hydrocyanic acid

HCN House (of Representatives) Committee on Narcotics

HCNZ Housing Corporation of New Zealand

hco hydrogenated coconut oil

HCO Harvard College Observatory; Headquarters Catalog Office

HCO₃ bicarbonate ion

hcp handicap; hexachlorophene; hexagonal close-packed; humidity control(ler's) panel

HCP Honors Cooperative Program

HCP House of Commons Proceedings

HCPNI Hardware Cloth and Poultry Netting Institute

HCPT Historic Churches Preservation Trust

hcptr helicopter

HCR High Chief Ranger

HCRAO Hat Creek Radio Astronomy Observatory (University of California)

HCRC Honeywell Corporation Research Center

hcrit hematocrit

HCRS Heritage Conservation and Recreation Service

hcrw hot and cold running water

hcs high-carbon steel

hcs (HCS) human chorionic somatomammotropin; hydrological communications satellite

hc's hard cover books

HCS Hallé Concerts Society; Harvey Cushing Society; Home Civil Service; Hydromechanical Control System

HC & S Hawaiian Commercial and Sugar (company)

HCSA House (of Representatives) Committee on Space and Astronautics

hcsht high-carbon steel heat treated

HCSI Health Correspondence Schools International

hct hematocrit

HCT Huddersfield College of Technology

HCTBA Hotel and Catering Trades Benevolent Association

hcu homing comparator unit; hydraulic cycling unit

HCUA Honeywell Computer Users Association

HCV Housing Commission of Victoria

HCVA Historic Commercial Vehicle Association

HCVC Historic Commercial Vehicle Club

hcvd hypertensive cardiovascular disease

hd half day; hand; hard-drawn; head; hearing distance; heavy duty; high density; hogshead; horse-drawn; hourly difference; hundred; hurricane deck

hd (HD) half duplex (data processing)

h-d heavy-duty; high-density

h/d holddown

h.d. hora decubitus (Latin—at bedtime)

Hd Head

Hd Hochdruck (German—high pressure)

HD Hansen's Disease (leprosy); Harbor Defense; Harbor Drive; Historical Division; Home Defense; Honorable Discharge; Hoover Dam

H.D. Hilda Doolittle

H/D Havre-Dunkirk (range of ports)

H & D Hurter & Driffield (photo emulsion speed)

hda high-duty alloy(s); horizontal danger angle; hydroxydopamine

HDA High Duty Alloys

hdatz high-density air traffic zone

HDB Housing Development Board

hdbk handbook

hdbn had been

hdc half double crochet; high-density cotton; holder in due course

HDC Housing Development Corporation

HD Clinic Hansen's Disease Clinic (for lepers)

hd cr hard chromium

hdd head-down display; heavy-duty detergent

HDD Higher Dental Diploma

hddr high-density digital recording

HDDS High-Density Data System

HDE Higher Diploma in Education

h de c hidratos de carbono (Spanish—carbohydrates)

hded heavy-duty enzyme detergent

H de S Herbert de Sola

hdg heading

HDGA Hot Dip Galvanizers Association

HDH Hawker de Haviland

hdhc high-density hydrocarbon(s)

HDHD Hawaiian District Harbors Division

hdhl high-density helicopter landing (USA)

HDHQ Hostility and Direction of Hostility Questionnaire

HDI Humane Development Institute

hdip hazardous-duty incentive pay

H Dip E Higher Diploma in Education

H disease Hart's disease

hdk husbands don't know

h dk hurricane deck

hdkf handkerchief

hdl handle; hardware description language

hdl (HDL) high-density lipoproteins

HDL Harry Diamond Laboratory (US Army Diamond Ordnance Fuze Laboratory); Hydrologic Data Laboratory (USDA)

hdlg handling

hdlr handler

hdls headless

hdlw hearing distance, watch at left ear

hdm high-duty metal

HDML Harbor Defense Motor Launch

hdmr high-density moderated reactor

hdn harden

hdn (HDN) hemolytic disease of the newborn

H Doc House Document

hdp (HDP) hexose diphosphate

hdpe high-density polyethylene

hdpg half deck plate girder

hdqrs headquarters

hdr handrail; header

hd & r human development and relationships

HDRA Heavy-Duty Representatives Association

HDRI Hannah Dairy Research Institute

HDRSS High-Data-Rate Storage System(s)

hdrw hearing distance, watch at right ear

hds heat detectors; holidays; hundreds; hydrodesulfurization

Hds Holidays (of Obligation)

HDS Hospital Discharge Survey; Human Development Services

Hd Schm Head Schoolmaster

hdsp hardship

hdst high-density shock tube
HDST Hawaiian Daylight Saving Time
HDT Henry David Thoreau
hdta high-density-traffic airport
HDTI Human Development Training Institute
hdtm heavy-duty target mechanism
HDTMA Heavy-Duty Truck Manufacturers Association
HDTS Harbor Drive Test Site (Convair Ramp)
hdu hemodialysis unit
h/duty heavy duty
hdv heavy-duty vehicle; high dollar value
hdw hardware
Hdwbch Handwörterbuch (German—pocket dictionary)
hdw c hardware cloth (wire screen)
hdwd hardwood
hdwe hardware
hd whl hand wheel
hdx (HDX) half duplex (data processing)
he. hammerless ejector; heat engine; heavy enamel; height of eye; high explosive; horizontal equivalent; hub end; human enteric; hydrogen embrittlement
h&e hemotoxylin and eosin; heredity and environment
h.e. hic est (Latin—this is)
He Hebraic; Hebrew; helium; Hertz
He. Book of Helaman
HE Her Eminence; Her Excellency; high explosive; His Eminence; His Excellency; Hollis & Eastern (railroad); Human Engineering; Hydraulics Engineer(ing)
H.E. His Eminence; His Excellency
HE Human Events
HEA Higher Education Act; Home Economics Association; Horticultural Education Association
heaa high-explosive anti-aircraft (shell)
HEAA Home Economics Association of Australia
Head of the Adriatic Trieste
Head of the Commonwealth Her (His) Most Excellent Majesty the Queen (King) of the United Kingdom of Great Britain and Northern Ireland and of Her (His) other Realms and Territories Queen (King)
head(s). headache(s)
HEADS-UP Health Care De-

livery Simulator for Urban Populations
heaf heavy end aviation fuel
heafs high-explosive antitank fin-stabilized
HEAL Health Education Assistance Loans; Home Environment Aid for Living
HEALT Helicopter Employment and Assault Landing Table
Health City Battle Creek, Michigan
HEAO High-Energy Astronomical Observatory
heap. high-explosive armor-piercing (shell)
HEAR Hospital Emergency Administrative Radio
HEARS Higher Education Administration Referral Services
Hearst's Castle (see *La Casa Grande*)
Heart of America Kansas City
Heart of California Sacramento
Heart of Canada Ontario
Heart of Central Alaska Fairbanks
Heart of Darkness Zaire (formerly called the Congo)
Heart of Dixie Alabama's official nickname
Heart of England Warwickshire
Heart of Historic Virginia Charlottesville
Heart of Kentucky Frankfort
Heartland of America the Midwest
Heartland City Kansas City
Heartland of Monarchy Grand Duchy of Luxembourg
Heart of Midlothian Tolbooth Prison in Edinburgh—an old jail commemorated in Scott's novel of the same title
Heart of Polynesia Western Samoa
Heart of Portugal Mondego Valley
Heart of the Roman Empire Italy
Heart of the South Atlanta, Georgia
Heart of South America Bolivia
Heart of Sweden Dalarna Province formerly called Dalecarlia
HEARU Higher Education Advisory and Research Unit
heat. heating; high-explosive anti-tank (projectile)
HEATH Higher Education and the Handicapped
Heathrow London, England's principal airport
Heb Epistle of Paul the Apostle

to the Hebrews: Hebraic; Hebrew
Heb Hebrew (classical language of the Old Testament and modern language of Israel where it is spoken by some 3-million Israelis); Hebrews
HEBA Home Extension Building Association
hebc heavy enamel bonded single cotton
hebd hebdomadal (weekly)
hebdom. hebdomas (Latin—week)
hebdp heavy enamel bonded double paper
hebds heavy enamel bonded double silk
Hebei (Pinyin Chinese—Hopei)
Hebr Hebrides
Hebrew Opera-Oratorio *Samson et Delila* by Saint-Saëns
Hebrides Hebrides Islands off Scotland's west coast
hec heavy-enamel single-cotton (insulation)
Hec Hasselblad electric camera; Hector; Hecuba; Hollerith electronic computer
HEC Hydro-Electric Commission
HECC Higher Education Coordinating Council (St Louis library network)
he cls b heating coils in bunkers
he cls ct heating coils in cargo tanks
HECO Hawaiian Electric Company; Hydro-Electric Commission of Ontario
he comp helium compressor
hect hectare; hectoliter
Hect Hector
HECT Hydro-Electricity Commission of Tasmania
hecticity hectic activity
hecto 10^2
hectog hectogram
hectol hectoliter
hectom hectometer
hector. heated experimental carbon thermal oscillator reactor (HECTOR)
hed horizontal electric dipole
hed (HED) high-energy detector
he'd he had; he would
HED Haupt-Einheits Dosis (German—unit skin dose)—X—rays
HEDCO Hawaii Economic Development Corporation
HEDCOM Headquarters Command
Hedda Hopper Elda Furry

HEDL Hanford Engineering Development Laboratory

hed('s) hearing-ear dog(s)

HEDS Hall-Effect Distribution System

hed sked headline schedule

hedsv heavy-enamel double-silk varnish (insulation)

Hedy Hedvig; Hedwig

Hedy Lamarr Hedwig Kiesler

HEEA Home Economics Education Association

HEED Health and Education (department or ministry)

heei high-energy electronic ignition

Heel of Italy Salentine Peninsula

heent head, ears, eyes, nose, throat

HEEP Highway Engineering Exchange Program

HEERA Higher Education Employer-Employee Relations Act

hef heifer; high-energy fuel

HEF High-Energy Fuel; Hospital Employees Federation

HEFA Higher Education Facilities Act

HEFC Higher Education Facilities Commission

heg heavy-enamel single-glass (insulation)

HEGIS Higher Education General Information Survey; Higher Education General Information System

HEH Her (His) Exalted Highness

HEHF Hanford Environmental Health Foundation (AEC)

HEHL Henry E Huntington Library

hei high-explosive incendiary; holographic exposure index

HEI Heat Exchange Institute; Hotel Enterprises Incorporated

HEI H/F Eimiskipafelag Islands (Icelandic Steamship Company)

HEIAC Hydraulic Engineering Information Analysis Center (USA)

HEIAS Human Engineering Information and Analysis Service (Tufts U)

HEIC Honourable East India Company

HEICN Honourable East India Company Navy

HEICS Honourable East India Company Service

Heiddelburga (Latin—Heidelberg)—also called Heidelberga

by many scholars

Heide Adelaide

Heidel Heidelberg

Heidelberg short form of the Ruprecht-Karl-Universität pouplarly called the University of Heidelberg

Hein Heinersdorf

Heine-Medin disease muscular atrophy sometimes followed by permanent deformity

heip high-explosive incendiary plug

heir app heir apparent

heir pres heir presumptive

heisd high-explosive incendiary self-destroying

heit high-explosive incendiary with tracer

heitdisd high-explosive incendiary tracer dark ignition self-destroying

heitsd high-explosive incendiary tracer self-destroying

hek heavy-enamel single-cellophane (insulation)

hek (HEK) human embryo kidney

hel helicopter

hel (HEL) hen's egg-white lysozyme; high-energy laser (beams); human embryonic lung

Hel Helen; Helena; Helsinki (Helsingfors); Helvetia (Switzerland)

HEL Hartford Electric Light; Helsinki, Finland (airport); Human Engineering Laboratories (USA); Hydraulic Engineering Laboratory

HeLa Helen Lake (tumor cells)

HELCIS Helicopter Command Instrumentation System

HELCO Hilo Electric Company

Helena Montana's capital

Helena Modjeska Helena Modrejewska

Helena, Montana founded as Last Chance Gulch

Helen Hayes Helen Hayes Brown

Helen Twelvetrees Helen Jurgens

Helgoland (German—Heligoland)

heli helicopter; heliport

helio heliochrome; heliodon; heliodor; helioelectric; helioengraving; heliogram; heliograph; heliogravure; heliology; heliostat; heliotherapy; heliotrope; heliotype

helipad helicopter landing pad

he'll he will

Hell Hellerup

HELL Higher Education Learning Laboratory

Hellas (Classical Greek—Greece)

Hell Breughel Pieter Breughel the Younger who painted hellish scenes

Hellcat Grumman F6F single-seat fighter aircraft; U.S.-made 76mm gun mounted in a fully traversing turret on a tracked chasis (M-18)

Hellen Hellenic; Hellenism; Hellenistic

Hellenic Republic Greece

Hellespont (Greek—Dardanelles)—strait connecting the Aegean Sea with the Sea of Marmara leading to the Black Sea

hellfire. (HELLFIRE) helicopter-launched fire-and-forget missile

Hell in the Hills Pittsburgh, Pennsylvania

Hellinikon airport of Athens, Greece

Hell of Java Trinil (where Dr Eugene Dubois discovered *Pithecanthropus erectus*)

Hell of Macquarie Harbour Station nickname of an old penal colony on the Indian Ocean coast of Tasmania

Hell and Maria Charles G Dawes

Hellongjiang (Pinyin Chinese—Hellungkiang)

Hell on Wheels Cheyenne, Wyoming

Hell's Forty Acres San Carlos, Arizona

Hell's Gates Macquarie Harbour, Tasmania's first convict settlement

Hell's Kitchen New York City's lower west side including San Juan Hill

Hell's Parlor Zanzibar (in the opinion of many foreign officers stationed there)

Helluland (Norse—Labrador)

helminthol helminthology

helo helicopter; heliport

Heloise Heloise Fulbert (abbess-scholar best remembered for her love of Abelard—a monk living in a nearby monastery he founded in 1112)

helosid helicopter-delivered seismic intrusion detector

help. high-energy-level pneumatic automobile bumpers

HELP Helicopter Electronic Landing Path; Help Elderly

Locate Positions; Help Establish Lasting Peace; High School Education Law Project; Highway Emergency Locating Plan; Home Environment and Living Program; Home Equity Living Plan

HELPR Handbook of Electronic Parts Reliability

hel rec health record

Hel San Helsingin Sanomat (Helsinki's News)

Helsingfors (Swedish—Helsinki)

Helsingør (Danish—Elsinore)

Helsinki (Finnish—Helsingfors)

Helv Helvetia; Helvetica

Helv Chim Acta Helvetica Chimica Acta (Latin—Swiss Review of Chemistry)

Helvetia (Latin—Switzerland)

Helv Phys Acta Helvetica Physica Acta (Latin—Swiss Review of Physics)

hem. hemoglobin; hemorrhage; hemorrhoid

hem. (HEM) hybrid electromagnetic wave

HEM Ernest Hemingway

hema (Latin prefix—blood)—hematology

HEMA Heavy Engineering Manufacturers Association

hematol hematolith(ic)(al)(ly); hematologist; hematology; hematolymphangioma; hematolysis; hematolytic

HEMF Handling Equipment Maintenance Facility (USN)

hemi (Latin prefix—half)—hemisphere

hemi engine hemispherical combustion chamber engine

he. missile high-energy missile

hemlaw (HEMLAW) helicopter-mounted laser weapon

hemloc heliborne-emitter-location countermeasures

hemo (Latin—blood)—hemoglobin, hemophilia, hemorrhage, hemostat

hemolysis hemocytolysis

Hem Soc Hemlock Society

Hen Henrietta; Henry; Soviet Ka-15 light-utility helicopter

Hen V King Henry V

Hen VIII King Henry VIII

HENA Home Economics and Needlework Association

Henan (Pinyin Chinese—Honan)

Hence Henderson

H'english Limey English

HENILAS Helicopter Night Landing System

Henk Hendrik

Hennie Henrietta

Henriqz Henriquez

Henry Henry Ford Commercial College; Patrick Henry Commercial College; Patrick Henry High School; Patrick Henry State Junior College

Henry B Henry B Gonzalez of San Antonio, Texas

Henry Bolingbroke Henry IV of England

Henry Cecil Henry Cecil Leon

Henry Green Henry Vincent Yorke (*Living, Loving, Nothing, Doting*, other novels)

Henry the K Henry Kissinger

Henry the Navigator Dom Henrique o Navegador (Prince of Portugal and patron of explorers and voyagers)

Henry Wade Henry Lancelot Aubrey-Fletcher

HEOC Honeywell Electro-Optics Center

HEOP Higher Education Opportunity Program

heos (HEOS) high eccentric orbiting satellite

hep high-energy phosphate; high-explosive plastic

Hep Hepburn; Hepple; Hepworth

HEP Have Error-free Product; High School Equivalency Program(s); Higher Education Panel

HEPAC High-Energy Physics Advisory Council

hepaf high-efficiency particulate air filter

HEPALIS Higher Education Policy and Administration Library and Information Service

hepat high-explosive plastic antitank

hepat (Latin prefix—liver)—hepatitis

HEPC Hydro-Electric Power Commission

HEPCAT Helicopter Pilot Control and Training (educational program)

HEPCC Heavy Electrical Plant Consultative Council

hepdnp high-explosive point-detonating nose plug

Hephaestus (Greek—Vulcan)

hepl high-energy pulse laser

HEPL High Energy Physics Laboratory

HEPP Hoffman Evaluation Program and Procedure

her. heraldry

her. (HER) high-energy rotor

(helicopter)

her. heres (Latin—heir)

Her Hercules (constellation); Hereford; Hereford(shire)

HER Harvard Educational Review

hera high explosive rocket assisted

Hera (Greek—Juno)—goddess of the heavens

HERA Heavy Engineering Research Association; Housewives for ERA

Herakles (Greek—Hercules)

Heraklion (Greek—Candia or Crete)

Herald Handley-Page turboprop transport plane

HERALD Highly-Enriched Reactor—Aldermaston

herb. herbarium

Herb Herbert

Herbert Strasse (German—Herbert Street)—one of Hamburg's redlight districts

Herblock Herbert Lawrence Block

Herc Hercules (constellation)

HERC Humber Estuarial Research Committee

Hercules Lockheed KC-130 tanker aircraft

Hercules of Music Christoph Willibald Gluck

Herdez (Spanish contraction—Hernandez)

herd'o herdeiro (Portuguese—heir)

herdr herdruk(ken) [Dutch—reprint(s)]

HERE Hotel Employees and Restaurant Employees (union)

hered heredity

hereds herederos (Spanish—heirs)

Heref Herefordshire

Herefs Herefordshire

here's here is

Here & Worcs Hereford and Worcester

herf high-energy rate forging

herfs high-energy-rate forging systems

HERI Higher Education Research Institute

herj high explosive ramjet

Herkimer diamond gem-quality quartz from New York State's Herkimer County

herm hermetically

Her Majesty the Queen

Hermanus Vanderdonk Washington Irving

hermes heavy element and radioactive material electromagnetic separator (HERMES)

Hermes (Greek—Mercury)—the messenger

HERMES Helicopter Energy and Rotor Management System

Hermitage Andrew Jackson's home in Nashville, Tennessee

Hermit Kingdom Korea

Hermit of Slabsides John Burroughs

Hernandarias Hernando Arias de Saavedra (first American-born governor of Rio de la Plata Province)

hero nickname for heroin

hero. hazards of electromagnetic radiation to ordnance; hot experimental reactor of 0 (zero power)—also appears as HERO

hero heroína (Spanish—heroin)

HERO Heath Educational Robot; Historical Evaluation and Research Organization; Home Economics Research Organization

Hero of a Hundred Battles the Duke of Wellington

Hero of a Hundred Fights Admiral Horatio Nelson

Hero of Antiquity Heracles or Herakles (Greek); Hercules (Roman)

Hero of Appomattox General Ulysses Simpson Grant, USA

Hero of the Cities Alfred E(manuel) Smith—usually called Al Smith

Herod. Herodotus

Hero of Fort Sumter Confederate General Pierre Gustave Toutant Beauregard (known to his soldiers as Old Alphabet or Old Bore)

Hero of the Frontier George Rogers Clark

Heroic City Cartagena, Colombia (*Ciudad Heroica*)

Heroin Capital of America New York City's Harlem

Hero of Lake Erie Commodore Oliver Hazard Perry, USN

Hero of Manila Bay Commodore George Dewey, USN

Hero of Mobile Bay Admiral David Glasgow Farragut

Hero of Modern Italy Guiseppe Garibaldi

Heron Hawker-Siddeley 17-passenger transport plane

Hero of Nacozari Jesús Garcia

Hero of New England Captain Miles Standish

Hero of New Orleans General Andrew Jackson

Hero of the Nile Lord Horatio Nelson

Hero of the Plain People Andrew Jackson

Hero of San Juan Hill Lt Col Theodore Roosevelt, USV

Hero of the Spanish-American War Admiral George Dewey, USN

Hero of Tampico General Antonio López de Santa Anna

Hero and Traitor Benedict Arnold

Hero of Upper Canada Sir Isaac Brock

herp herpetologist; herpetology

herpetol herpetologic(al)(ly); herpetologist; herpetology

HERPOCO Hercules Powder Company

herps herpetologists

Herring Chokers Newfoundlanders

Herring Pond Atlantic Ocean

Herr Kaleun Herr Kapitänleutnant (German—Mr Captain Lieutenant)—U-boat commander

HERS Higher Education Resource Services; Home Economics Reading Service

Hersch Herschel

herst herstellung (German—manufacture)

Hertf Hertford College, Oxford

HERTIS Hertfordshire County Council Technical Information Service

Herts Hertfordshire

HERU Higher Education Research Unit

Hervey Allen William Hervey Allen

hes heavy enamel single silk (insulation)

he's he has; he is

Hes Hesba; Hesione, Hesper(ian)(s); Hesketh; Hesperides; Hesperus; Hessels; Hessian(s); Hessin; Hester; Hesther

HES Hawaiian Entomological Society; Health Economic Service; Health Examination Survey; History of Economics Society

HESCA Health Sciences Communication Association

hesd high-explosive self-destroying

hesh high-explosive squash head

HESIS Hazard Evaluation System and Information Service

Hesperides Canary and Madeira Islands

Hesperus the evening star—Venus, son of Aurora and Cephalus (see *Lucifer*)

hess human-engineering systems simulator

hessian hessian boots (kneehigh and tasseled); hessian fly (insect feeding on grass and wheat stems)

hest heavy-end aviation fuel emergency service tanks

h'est highest

HEST High-Explosive Simulation Test

Hestia (Greek—Vesta)—goddess of hearth and home

he. stor helium storage

hesv heavy-enamel single-silk varnish (insulation)

het heavy equipment transporter

Hetch Hetchy Hetch Hetchy Dam; Hetch Hetchy Lake (both in Yosemite National Park)

hetdi high-explosive tracer dark ignition

hetero (Latin prefix—different, other)—heterosexual

heterocl heteroclite

heterog heterogeneous

heterosex heterosexual(ity); heterosexuals

HETS High-Energy Telescope System; Hyper-Environmental Test System

Hetty Hester

heu highly enriched uranium; hydroelectric units

Hèung-góng (Cantonese—Hong Kong)—insular section of the Crown Colony of Hong Kong on the south coast of mainland China

Heung Kong (Chinese—Fragrant Harbor)—Aberdeen Anchorage's original name now applied to all Hong Kong

Heungshan (Chinese—Macao)

heur heuristic (problem solution by trial and error)

hev health and environment; heavy

HEVAC Heating, Ventilating, and Air Conditioning Manufacturers Association

hevr heavier

Hew Heward; Hewett; Hewitt; Hewlett; Hewson; Hugh; Hugo

HEW Health, Education, and Welfare (US department); Housing, Education, and Welfare (Philippines)

HEWPR Health, Education, and Welfare (department) Procurement Regulations

hex hexagon(al); uranium hexafluoride

hex (HEX) hexadecimal

hexa hexamethylene tetramine

hexag hexagon(al)

hex hd hexagonal head

Hez Hezekiah

hf hageman factor; half; hard finish(ed); hard firm; height finding; high frequency (3000 to 30,000 kc); hold fire; home freezer; hook fast; horse and foot (cavalry and infantry); hot finished; hyper filtration; hyperfocal

h/f held for

Hf hafnium

HF Handwriting Foundation; Home Fleet; Home Forces; hydrofluoric acid; hydrogen fluoride

H of F Hall of Fame

H/F Hlutafjelagid (Icelandic—limited company)

Hfa Haifa

HFA Headquarters Field Army; Hollywood Film Archive

HFAA Holstein-Friesian Association of America

HFARA Honorary Foreign Associate of the Royal Academy

hf bd half–bound

hf bd cf half bound in calfskin (calf leather back and corners)

hf bd cl half bound in cloth (cloth back and corners or cloth sides)

hf bd mor half bound in morocco (morocco leather back and corners)

HFBLB Hokkaido Farmland Bride Liaison Bureau

hfbr high flux beam reactor

hfc hard-filled capsules; high-frequency current

HFC Household Finance Corporation; Human Freedom Center

HFCC Henry Ford Community College

hf cf half-calf

hf cl half-cloth (binding)

hfcs high-fructose corn sweetener; high-fructose corn syrup

HFCT Hawaii Federation of College Teachers

Hfd Hereford

hf-df high-frequency direction finder

hfe human factors (in) electronics; human factors engineering

hff horizontal falling film

HFFF Hungarian Freedom

Fighters Federation

hfg heavy free gas

HFGA Hall of Fame for Great Americans

hfh half-hard (steel)

HfH Habitats for Humanity

hfi hydraulic fluid index

HFIA Heat and Frost Insulators and Asbestos Workers Union

hfim high-frequency instruments and measurements

hfir high flux isotope reactor

HFL Human Factors Laboratory (NBS)

hfm hold for money

HFM Henry Ford Museum

hfmd hand-foot-and-mouth disease

hfmf home-furnish monolithic floor

hf mor half-morocco

hfmr high-fat milk replacer

hfo heavy fuel oil; high-frequency oscillator; hole full of oil

Hford Hereford

HFORL Human Factors Operations Research Laboratory

Hfors Helsingfors

hfp hostile fire pay

h&f pool heated and filtered (swimming) pool

HFPS Home Fallout Protection Survey

hfr heifer; held for release; high-frequency range; high frequency recombination; hold for release

HFR (Sir Edward) Hallstrom Faunal Reserve (New South Wales)

HFRA Honorary Fellow of the Royal Academy

h-f radar height-finder radar

HFRB Hawaii Fire Rating Bureau

Hfrz Halbfranzband (German—halfbound in calf)

hfs high-fructose syrup(s); hot-finished seamless; hyperfine structure

Hfs Helsinki (Helsingfors)

HFS Human Factors Society

HFSSA Historical Firearms Society of South Africa

hfssb high-frequency single sideband

hft hot flow test(ing)

hft hefte (Dano-Norwegian—part, issue)

Hft Heft (German—part)

HFT Hawaii Federation of Teachers; Heavy Fire Team; Human Factors Team

HFTS Human Factors Trade Studies (USU)

hfupr hourly fetal urine produc-

tion rate

hfw hole full of water

Hfx Halifax

hg hand generator; hectogram; heliogram; high grade; hydrostatic gage

h & g harden and grind

Hg *hydrargyrum* (Latin—mercury)

Hg Hegység (Hungarian—mountain, mountainous)

HG Haute-Garonne; Her (His) Grace; H(erbert) G(eorge) (Wells); High German; Home Guard; Horse Guards

H-G Haute-Garonne

hga high gain antenna

HGA Heptagonal Games Association, Hobby Guild of America; Holological Guild of Australia; Hop Growers of America; Hotel Greeters of America; Hungarian Gypsy Association

h-galv hot-galvanize

hgb hemoglobin

HGCA Home-Grown Cereals Authority

HgCl₂ bichloride of mercury; mercuric chloride

HGD Hourglass Device

HGDH Her (His) Grand Ducal Highness

hge heavy gold electroplate; hogshead

HGEA Hawaii Government Employees Association

hgf (HGF) hyperglycemic-glucogenolytic factor

HGF Human Growth Foundation

HGFA Hang Gliding Federation of Australia

hg ga height gage

HGH human growth hormone

HGHCA Hotels, Guest Houses, and Caterers' Association

HGJP Henry George Justice Party

Hglds Highlands

HGMM Hereditary Grand Master Mason

hgo hepatic glucose output

Hgo Hidalgo

HGOA Houston Grand Opera Association

HGOAA Hobby Greenhouse Owners Association of America

hgor high gas-oil ratio

HGP Humbug Gulch Press

hgps high-grade plow steel

hg pt hard-gloss paint

hgr hangar; hanger

HGR Hluhluwe *(shloosh-looway)* Game Reserve (northern

Zululand)
hgs hangars; hangers
Hgs Haugesund
HGS Hydrological Growing Season
hgsw horn gap switch
hgt height; hogget
HGTAC Home Grown Timber Advisory Committee
HGTB Haiti Government Tourist Bureau
hgts heights; hoggets
Hgts Heights
hgv heavy goods vehicle
Hgw Hanford (basalt) ground water
HGW Herbert George Wells
Hgy Highway
Hgz Hoogezand
hh half-hard; handhole; hands high (horse's height); heavy hydrogen
h/h half height; hard of hearing; house-to-house (search or transport)
h to h heel-to-heel
hh *hojas* (Spanish—leaves)
hH heavy hydrogen
HH double-hard (pencils); Harry Hansen; Helen Hunt Jackson; Her (His) Highness; His Holiness; Howard Hanson; Huntington Hartford
H/H Havre-Hamburg (range of ports)
H & H Handy & Harman; Holland & Holland
HH *Herren* (German—Gentlemen)
HH-52 Sikorsky 12-passenger helicopter
HH-53 Sikorsky Sea Stallion CH-53 assault helicopter
hha half-hardy annual
hhb half-hardy biennial
HHBS Hereford Herd Book Society
hhcc higher-harmonic circulation control
hhd hogshead
HH. D. *Humanitatis Doctor* (Latin—Doctor of Humanities)
hhdws heavy handy deadweight scrap
hhf household furniture
HHFA Housing and Home Finance Agency
HHFTH Happy Horsemanship for the Handicapped (foundation)
hhg household goods
hhh triple hard
HHH Hubert Horatio Humphrey; triple-hard (pencils)
HHHC Hunt the Hunters Hunt

Club (Amory Foundation funded)
Hhhs Hincherton hayfever helmets
HHI Hellenic Hydrobiological Institute
H-hinge capital-H-shaped hinge
HHKA Husband's Housemaid's Knee Association
hhld household
HHMS His Hellenic Majesty's Ship
hhmu hand-held maneuvering unit
HHNSR Hudson Highlands National Scenic Riverway
H-hour hostile operations commencement hour
hhp half-hardy perennial; hydraulic horsepower
HHPL Herbert Hoover Presidential Library
HHRA Heartland Human Relations Association
HHRC Health and Human Resource Center
HHS Haaren High School; Health and Human Services; Hunter High School
hhsd holographic horizontal situation display
HHSP Highland Hammock State Park (Florida)
hht (HHT) high-temperature helium turbine
HHT Horn-Hellersberg Test
hhtg house(hold) heating
hhtv hand-held thermal viewer
HHUMC Hadassah-Hebrew University Medical Center
HHW higher high water
HHWI higher high water interval
hi contracted form of "hail"; high; high intensity; horizontal interval; humidity index
hi (HI) hyperglycemic index
h & i harassing and interdictory (artillery fire)
h.i. *hic iacet* (Latin—here lies)— also appears on tombstones as H.I.
Hi Hering illusion; High (postal abbreviation); Hindi; Hiram
H^i *Hasi* (Arabic—waterhole)— also appears as *Hasy*
HI Hammersley Iron; Hampton Institute; Handwriting Institute; Harris Intertype; Hat Institute; Heat Index; Henrik Ibsen; Holiday Inns; Humidity Index; Hydraulic Institute
hia hold in abeyance
HIA Handkerchief Industry Association; Hobby Industry As-

sociation; Homeopathic Institute of Australia; Horological Institute of America; Hospital Industries Association; Housing Improvement Association; Housing Industry Association; Hungarian Imperial Association
HIAA Health Insurance Association of America; Health Insurance Association of Australia
HIAB *Hydrauliska Industri AB* (Swedish—Hydraulic Industry Company)
hiac high acuity
hi-ac high accuracy
HIAD *Handbook of Instructions for Airplane Designers*
HIAG *Hilfsorganisation auf Gengenseitigkeit* (German— Mutual Aid Organization)
HIAGSED *Handbook of Instruction for Aircraft Ground Support Equipment Designers*
HIAS Hebrew Sheltering and Immigrant Aid Society
HIAVED *Handbook of Instructions for Aerospace Vehicle Equipment Design*
Hib Hibernia (Ireland); Hibernian (Irish)
HIB Herring Industry Board
Hibbd *Halbband* (German— half binding)
Hibernia (Latin—Ireland)
hibex high-acceleration booster experiment
Hibiscus Hawaii state flower; Hawaiian girl's nickname
Hibiscus Coast bordering Hauraki Gulf north of Auckland, New Zealand
HIBR Huxley Institute for Biosocial Research
HIBT Howard Ink-Blot Test
hic hearing-impaired children; hot isostatic compaction; hybrid integrated circuit; hydrologist in charge
HIC Heart Information Center; Herring Industries Council
hicapcom high-capacity communications
hicat high-altitude clear-air turbulence
hic jac *hic jacet* (Latin—here lies)
hiclass hierarchical classification
Hi Com High Command; High Commission; High Commissioner
HICS Hardened Intersite Cable System
hid. hallucinations, illusions,

and delusions; headache, insomnia, depression (syndrome); high-intensity discharge (lamps)

Hid Hidalgo

hidal helicopter insecticide-dispersal apparatus, liquid

hidalgo *hijo de algo* (Spanish—son of someone)

Hidalgo Miguel Hidalgo y Costilla (Padre Hidalgo)

HIDB Highlands and Islands Development Board (Scotland)

Hidden Empire Ethiopia

hidvl high-intensity-discharge vapor lamp

HIE Hibernation Information Exchange; Histrionic Instruction Education

hier hieroglyphics

Hier. *Hierosolma* (Latin—Jerusalem)

Hicronymus Bosch palette name of Hicronymus van Aeken

HIES Hadassah Israel Education Services

HIF Health Information Foundation

hifar high-flux Australian reactor (HIFAR)

hifc hog intrinsic factor concentrate

hi-fi high-fidelity

Hi Fi High Fidelity and Musical America

hiflex high flexibility

HIFNY Hospitality Industry Foundation of New York

hifo highest in, first out

hifor high-level forecast

hig hermetically sealed integrating gyroscope; higgler

Hig Higgins; Higginson

HIG Hartford Insurance Group; Hawaii Institute of Geophysics

higashi (Japanese—east)

HIGED *Handbook of Instruction for Ground Equipment Designers*

higher 3-Rs remedial reading, remedial writing, remedial arithmetic

Highlands Highlands of the Hudson; Highlands of the Navesink close to where Henry Hudson first landed in 1609 before entering New York Bay and sailing up the Hudson River; Highlands of Scotland —hills and mountains of northern Scotland

High Lonesome southwestern Colorado's nickname

High Plains States Arkansas, Kansas, Missouri, New Mexico, Oklahoma, Texas

High Priestess of Transcendentalism Margaret Fuller

highpro high protein (diet)

high-Q high quality

High Sierras higher Sierra Nevada Mountains of California

High Tatras high Tatra Mountains of Czechoslovakia's Carpathians

high tech high technology

High-Tide Province Canada's New Brunswick

HIH Her (His) Imperial Highness

HII Health Industries Institute; Health Insurance Institute

hijack hijacked; hijacker; hijacking

hik hiking

Hikari (Japanese—Sunbeam)—nickname of the world's fastest train linking Tokyo with other coastal cities of Honshu

hil high intensity lighting; high lift

Hil Hilary

hila health insurance logistics automated

hilac heavy-ion linear accelerator

Hilaire Belloc Joseph Hilary Pierre Belloc

HILC Hampshire Inter-Library Center (Amherst, Mount Holyoke, and Smith colleges)

Hilda Hildegarde

Hildegarde Neff stage name of Hildegard Knef

Hill The Hill (Capitol Hill in Washington, D.C. where the Congress meets within the Capitol)

Hillbilly Country mountainous parts of the Carolinas, Georgia, Tennessee, Kentucky, and West Virginia

Hill City Portland, Maine

Hill District Pittsburgh's worst slum recently redeveloped into a low-rent housing area

Hill of Spring Tel Aviv

hi-lo high-low

Hil-Vis Hiligaynon-Visayan

him. high impact; horizontal impulse

HIM Her (His) Imperial Majesty

Himalaya (Sanskrit—Abode of Snow)—mountains between China and India including some of the world's highest in Tibet; often called Roof of the World because of their superior elevations

Himalayas Himalaya Mountains between India and Tibet

himat high-maneuverable advanced-fighter technology

hi mi high mileage

HIMM Hallberg Index of Male Menopause

HIMS Heavy Interdiction Missile System

Hinck Hinckley

Hind Hindi; Hindu; Hindustani

Hindenburg General Paul Ludwig Hans Anton von Benackendorf und von Hindenburg

Hindu Monarchy Nepal

'hinga(s) anhinga(s)

Hinglish Hindi + English (English interlarded with Hindi expressions and words)

hinil high noise-immunity logic

hinny nickname of the offspring of a jennet or female donkey sired by a stallion or male horse whereas a mule is the offspring of a jackass and a mare

Hi-no-maru (Japanese—Sun Flag)—emblem of Japan

HINP Hundred Islands National Park (Philippines)

Hint Hinton; Hinton Test (for syphilis)

HINWR Hawaiian Islands National Wildlife Refuge

hio hypoiodite

hiomt (HIOMT) hydroxyindole-O-methyltransferase

H-ion hydrogen ion

HI-OVIS Highly Interactive Optical Video Information System

hip. hierarchical information processor; high-impact pressure; hot isostatic pressure; humanizing, individualizing, and personalizing

Hip Hippolyte; Soviet Mi-8 transport helicopter used by Afghanistan, Cuba, Czechoslovakia, East Germany, Poland, and the United Arab Republic (Egypt)

HIP Health Insurance Plan; Hoover Institution Press; Houston's Informed Parents

hipar high-power acquisition radar

HIPCO Hunt International Petroleum Company

hipdom hippiedom

HIPERNAS High-Performance Navigation System

hipi high-performance intercept(ion)

hipo hierarchy plus input pro-

cess output
hipoe high-pressure oceanographic equipment
hipot high potential
Hipp Hippocrates
Hippiedam hippie-infested Dutch city such as Amsterdam or Rotterdam
Hippocrates of Pennsylvania Benjamin Rush
hippo(s) hippopotamus(es)
hi pres high pressure
hips. hippies
hiptoc high-power testing of optical components
hi-q high iq (IQ)
hir hydrostatic impact rocket
HIR Harbour Improvement Rate; Heron Island Resort (Queensland); Honiara (Solomon Islands airport)
hiran high-precision shoran
HIRB Health Insurance Registration Board
HIRC Housing Industry Research Committee
HIRE Help Through Industry Retraining and Employment
hirel high reliability
HIRI Hawaiian Independent Refinery Incorporated
hirl high-intensity runway lights
Hirohito Emperor Hirohito Showa (Japan's 124th emperor in direct lineage)
Hiroshige Ando Hiroshige (19th-century Japanese landscape painter)
HIRS High-Impulse Retrorocket System; Holographic Information Retrieval System
Hirschsprung's disease congenital colonic dilatation
HIRS/smrd High-Impulse Retrorocket System/spin-motor rotation detector
Hirt Aulus Hirtius (Roman historian)
his. (HIS) histidine (amino acid); history
h.i.s. *hic iacet sepultus* (Latin— here lies buried)—also appears as h.i.s.
Hi-S Hi-Standard (firearms)
HIS Health Interview Survey; Horticultural Improvement Scheme; Hospital Information System; Human Intrusion Studies
HISA Hawaii International Services Agency; Headquarters and Installation Support Activity (USA)
HISAM Hierarchical Indexed Sequential Access Method

HISC House Internal Security Committee (formerly House Un-American Activities Committee—HUAC)
His Holiness the Pope
His Majesty the King
his'n his own
Hisp Hispaniola
HISPA History of Sport and Physical Education (association)
Hispan Hispanic
Hispania (Latin—Iberian Peninsula)—land now divided between Portugal and Spain; poetic name for Spain
Hispanic America Portuguese-and-Spanish-speaking countries of Latin America (Portuguese is spoken in Brazil and Spanish in most other countries)
Hispanic American City Los Angeles, California; San Antonio, Texas; San Diego, California
Hispanic Places Andorra, Argentina, Azores, Balearic Islands, Bolivia, Brazil, Canary Islands, Cape Verde Islands, Ceuta and Melilla, Chile, Colombia, Costa Rica, Cuba, Dominican Republic, Ecuador, El Salvador, Equatorial Guinea, Guam, Guatemala, Honduras, Macao, Madeira, Mexico, Morocco, Nicaragua, Panama, Paraguay, Peru, Philippines, Portugal, Puerto Rico, Spain, Spanish Sahara, Uruguay, Venezuela
Hispanics people of Portuguese or Spanish descent or a study of their culture and language
Hispaniola West Indian island containing the French-speaking Republic of Haiti and the Spanish-speaking Dominican Republic also known as Santo Domingo
Hispano Hispanoamericano (Spanish American); Hispano-Suiza (automobile)
Hispanoamérica (Spanish—Hispanic America)
HISSG Hospital Information Systems Sharing Group
hist historical; history
hist historie or *historisk* (Dano-Norwegian—history or historian)
Hist historic(al); History
Hist Abs *Historical Abstracts*
Histadrut (Hebrew—General Federation of Labor)
Hi Stan 22 plus High Standard

.22-caliber automatic plus silencer (assassin's special)
histn historian
histo histoplasmosis
histo (Latin prefix—tissue or web)—histology
histocrit historical critic(ism)
histol histologic(al)(ly); histologist; histology
Historian of the American Forest Francis Parkman
Historian of Liberty Lord Acton
Historian With A Camera Mathew B Brady
Historic Center of North Carolina New Bern
hit. high-intensity tutoring; homing intercept(ion) technology
hi-T high torque
Hit Holtzman inkblot technique
HIT Health Indication Test; Hitachi Innovative Technology; Hong Kong International Terminals
Hitac Hitachi computer
Hitch Hitchborn(e); Hitchcock
hi-tec(h) high technology
Hi-Tech Capital of the World Massachusetts
hi-temp high temperature
Hitler Adole Schickphlgruber
Hit Pom Hither Pomerania (coastal East Germany)
Hitt Hittite
HIU Hypnosis Investigation Unit (Los Angeles Police Department)
HIUS Hispanic Institute of the United States
HIUS Historisches Institut der Universität Salzburg (German —Historical Institute of the University of Salzburg)
HIUV Historisches Institute der Universität Vienna (German —Historical Institute of the University of Vienna)
hiv hiver (French—winter)
hivos high-vacuum orbital simulator
hi wat high water
Hiwi Hilfsfreiwilliger (German —auxiliary volunteer); *Hilfswillige* (German—volunteers)
HIWRP The Hoover Institution on War, Revolution and Peace
h & j hyphenation and justification
HJ Hitler Jugend (German— Hitler Youth); Honest John (short-range unguided missile); Howard Johnson (stock

exchange symbol)

H. J. *hic jacet* (Latin—here lies)

HJBS Hashemite Jordan Broadcasting Service

HJC Hershey Junior College

HJPA Holmes Junge Protected Area (Australian Northern Territory)

H J Res House Joint Resolution

H.J.S. *hic jacet sepultus* (Latin —here lies buried)

h-k hand to knee

HK Heckler and Kock (firearms); Hong Kong

HK *Helsingin Kaupunginorkesteri* (Finnish—Helsinki City Symphony Orchestra)

HKA Hong Kong Airways

HKCEC Hong Kong Catholic Education Council

hk cells human kidney cells

HKCL Hong Kong Container Line

Hkd Hakodate

HK$ Hong Kong dollar

HKDR Hong Kong Depository Receipt

HKECIC Hong Kong Export Credit Insurance Corporation

HKEL Hong Kong Export Lines

hkf handkerchief

H Kg Hong Kong

HKG Hong Kong, British Crown Colony (airport)

HKGMA Hosiery and Knit Goods Manufacturers Association

HKH *Hans (Hendes) Kongelige Højhed* [Dano-Norwegian— His (Her) Royal Highness]

HKI Helen Keller International

HKIL Hong Kong Islands Line

HKJ Hashemite Kingdom of Jordan

HKL Halldor Kilyan Laxness

HKLA Hong Kong Library Association

hkm high-velocity kill mechanism

h-k m (H-K M) hunter-killer missile

HKMA Hong Kong Management Association

H'Kong Hong Kong

HKP Hong Kong Polytechnic

HKPO Hong Kong Philharmonic Orchestra

HK & S Hong Kong and Shanghai Bank

HKTA Hong Kong Tourist Association

HKTC Hong Kong Training Council

HKTDC Hong Kong Trade Development Council

HKU Hong Kong University

HK virus Hong-Kong type of influenza virus

HKX Hong Kong Express (container service)

hky hand knitting yarn(s)

hl hand lantern; heavy lift; hectoliter; high level; high lift; hinge line; holiday

h-l highest and lowest (quotations)

h/l heading line; high or low

h&l door hinge resembling ligature of capital H and capital L

h.l. *hoc loco* (Latin—in this place)

HL Haute-Loire; Herpetologists League; Home Lines; Homestead Lease; Honours List; House of Lords; Hygienic Laboratories; Hygienic Laboratory

H-L Haute Loire

H & L Harbour and Light Department

H of L House of Lords

hla (HLA) homologous leucocytic antibodies; human leucocytic antigen

HLA Hawaii Library Association

HL&AG Henry E Huntington Library and Art Gallery

HLAHWG High-Level Ad-Hoc Working Group (NATO)

H-land Headland

hlb hydrophile-lipophile balance

HLB Hotel Licensing Board

HLBB Home Loan Bank Board

hlc health locus of control

HLC Hapag-Lloyd Container (steamship line); Hospital Library Council (Dublin)

HLCAS House of Lords Cases

HLCU Hapag-Lloyd Container Unit

hld held; hold; holder

HLD Harold Handley Page (aircraft)

hldg holding

hl di hole die

HLDI Highway Loss Data Institute

hlds holdings

hldw high-level defense waste(s)

hlem horizontal-loop electromagnetic method

HLF Human Life Foundation

hlg halogen

hlge handling equipment

hlgp heavy-lift general purpose

HLH Haroldson Lafayette Hunt

HLHS Heavy-Lift Helicopter System

HLI Highland Light Infantry

HLIC Housing Loans Insurance Corporation

hll high-level language

HLL Hellenic Lines Limited

hllw high-level liquid waste(s)

hl lX high-level language X

HLM HL Mencken

HLMR Hunter-Leggitt Military Reservation

HLNP Hattah Lakes National Park (Victoria, Australia)

h/l number hydrophile/lipophile number

hlnw high-level nuclear waste(s)

HLNWR Havasu Lake National Wildlife Refuge (California); Hutton Lake National Wildlife Refuge (Wyoming)

hlo horizontal lockout

hlp (HLP) hyperlipidemia

hlpr helper

HLPR Howard League for Penal Reform

hlr heart-lung resuscitation

HLRS Homosexual Law Reform Society

hls heavy liquid separation; heavy logistics support; hills; holes

hl S *heilige Schrift* (German— holy scripture)

Hls Hills (postal abbreviation)

HLS Harvard Law School; Heavy Logistics Support; High-Level Scheduler

hl sa hole saw

hlse high-level single-ended

HLSS Harry Lundeberg School of Seamanship

HLSUA Honeywell Large Systems Users Association

hlsw high-level solidified waste(s)

hlt halt; halter

HLT Holborn Law Tutors

hlth prof health professions

hlttl high-level transistor-translator logic

hltw high-level transuranic waste(s)

Hlu Honolulu

hlv herpes-like virus

HLVA Hospital Lady Visitors Association

hlw higher low water; high-level waste

Hlw *Halbleinwand* (German— half-bound cloth)

HLW higher low water

HLWI higher low water interval

HLW-ICB High-Level Waste-Interface Control Board

HLWIP High-Level Waste Immobilizaton Program

hlwn highest low-water neap tides

HLWRP Hoover Library on War, Revolution, and Peace (Stanford University)

Hlzbl *Holzbläser* (German—woodwinds)

hm hallmark; harmonic mean; heavy metal; hectometer; hollow metal

h & m hit and miss; hull and machinery

h.m. *hoc mense* (Latin—in this month)

Hm manifest hypermetropia

HM Harbour Master; Haute-Marne; Head Master; Head Mistress; Her (His) Majesty; Herman Melville; Home Missions; Houghton Mifflin

H-M Haute-Marne

hm² square hectometer

hm³ cubic hectometer

Hma Hiroshima

HMA Head Masters Association; Her (His) Majesty's Airship; Hoist Manufacturers Association; Home Manufacturers Association

H & MA Hotel and Motel Association

HMAA Horse and Mule Association of America

HMAC Her (His) Majesty's Aircraft Carrier

HMARC Houston Metropolitan Archives and Research Center

HMAS Her (His) Majesty's Australian Ship

hmb homatropine methyl bromide (HMB)

HMB Home Mission Board; Hops Marketing Board

HMBDV Her (His) Majesty's Boom Defence Vessel

HMBI Her (His) Majesty's Borstal Institution

HMBP Heavy Machine Building Plant

hmc heavy media cyclone; heroin-morphine-cocaine (mixture); howitzer motor carriage

hmc **(HMC)** hydroxymethyl cystosine

HMC Harvey Mudd College; Her (His) Majesty's Customs; Hospital Management Committee

hmcc housewife/mother career concept

HMCG Her (His) Majesty's Coastguard

HMC & H Hahnemann Medical College and Hospital

HMCIF Her (His) Majesty's Chief Inspector of Factories

HMCN Her (His) Majesty's Canadian Navy

HM Comm Historical Manuscripts Commission

HMCS Her (His) Majesty's Canadian Ship

HMCSC Her (His) Majesty's Civil Service Commissioners

HMCyS Her (His) Majesty's Ceylonese Ship

hmd hollow metal door; humid; hydraulic mean depth

hmd **(HMD)** hyaline membrane disease

HMD Her (His) Majesty's Destroyer

HMDBA Hollow Metal Door and Buck Association

hmde hanging-mercury-drop electrode

hmdf hollow metal door and frame

hmdi **(HMDI)** hexamethylene diisocyanate

HMDS Hazardous Material Data System

hmf hollow metal frame

HMF Her (His) Majesty's Forces

hmf black high-modulus furnace black

HMFI Her (His) Majesty's Factory Inspectorate

hmg heavy machine gun; high modulous graphite

hmg **(HMG)** human menopausal gonadotrophin

HMG heavy machine gun; Her (His) Majesty's Government

HMHS Horace Mann High School

hmi heavy maintenance interval

HMI Hahn-Meitner Institut; Her (His) Majesty's Inspector; Hughes Medical Institute

HMI *Himpunan Mahasiswa Islam* (Indonesian—Islamic Students Society)

HMIC Her (His) Majesty's Inspectorate of Constabulary

HMIS Her (His) Majesty's Indian Ship; Her (His) Majesty's Inspector of Schools

HMIT Her (His) Majesty's Inspector of Taxes

HMK His Majesty the King

HML Harper Memorial Library (University of Chicago); Horace Mann—Lincoln Institute

HMLR Her (His) Majesty's Land Registry

hmlt hamlet

HMM Her (His) Majesty's Minister; Hyundai Merchant Marine

hmma **(HMMA)** 4-hydroxy-3-methodxy-mandelic acid

HMML Her (His) Majesty's Motor Launch

HMMS Her (His) Majesty's Motor Mine Sweeper

HMNAO Her (His) Majesty's Nautical Almanac Office

HMNAR Hart Mountain National Antelope Refuge (Oregon)

HMNZS Her (His) Majesty's New Zealand Ship

hmo heart minute output

HMO Health Maintenance Organization; Hospital Medical Office(r)

HMOCS Her (His) Majesty's Overseas Civil Service

H moll (German—B minor)

hmo's (HMOs) health maintenance organizations

HMOW Her (His) Majesty's Office of Works

hmp handmade paper

hmp **(HMP)** hexose monophosphate

HMP Her (His) Majesty's Penitentiary; Her (His) Majesty's Prison

H.M.P. *hoc monumentum posuit* (Latin—he erected this monument)

HMPMA Historical Motion Picture Milestones Association

HMQ Her Majesty the Queen

HMRC Heineman Medical Research Center

HMRCS Her (His) Majesty's Royal Canadian Ship

HMRT Her (His) Majesty's Rescue Tug

hms hours, minutes, seconds

HMS Harvard Medical School; Her (His) Majesty's Service, Ship, or Steamer; Home Mission Society

H & MS Headquarters and Maintenance Squadron

HMS *Hotel and Motel Systems*

HMSA Hawaii Medical Service Association

HMSG Hirshhorn Museum and Sculpture Garden

HMSO Her (His) Majesty's Stationery Office

HMSS Hospital Management Systems Society

hmstd homestead

HMT Her (His) Majesty's

Transport; Her (His) Majesty's Trawler; Her (His) Majesty's Treasury; Her (His) Majesty's Tug

HMTA Hotel-Motel Association

hmu (HMU) hydroxymethyl uracil

HMV His Master's Voice (phonograph records)

hmw high molecular weight

hmwp high molecular weight polyethylene

hmy too little

h.n. *hac nocte* (Latin—tonight)

Hn Herman(n); Horn

Hⁿ Horn

HN Head Nurse; Hoff und Nationaltheater (Munich)

Hna Habana

HNBI Hellenic National Broadcasting Institute

hnc hypothalamic-neurohypophysical complex

HNC Harbors and Navigation Code; High National Council; Higher National Certificate; Human Nature Cooperative; Human Nature Council; Human Nutrition Center; Human Nutrition Council

Hnd *The Hindu* (Madras)

HND Haneda-Tokyo (airport); Higher National Diploma

hndbk handbook

hnddiprt hand-discharge printed

hndflshd hand-fleshed (skins)

hndlr handler

hndovprt hand overprint(ed)

hndprt hand print(ed)

HNEI Hawaii Natural Energy Institute

HNF Home Nursing Foundation

hn fm hand form

HNG Hawaii National Guard; Houston Natural Gas

Hnl Honolulu

HNL Honolulu, Hawaii (airport)

hnml hindumeal

HNMS High NATO Military Structure

HNNNR Herma Ness National Nature Reserve (Scotland)

Hno Hanover

HNO₃ nitric acid

Hnos *Hermanos* (Spanish—brothers)

hnp high needle position

HNP Haleakala National Park (Maui, Hawaii)

HNP *Herstigte Nasionale Partij* (Afrikaans—Reformed National Party)—South African

segregationists

hnr handwritten numerical recognition; hiss noise reduction

hnrna (HNRNA) heterogeneous nuclear ribonucleic acid

hnrs honors

hn(s) horn(s)

HNTLA Hiskey-Nebraska Test of Learning Aptitude

HNWR Hagerman National Wildlife Refuge (Texas); Horicon National Wildlife Refuge (Wisconsin)

ho held over; hoist; hold over; holds; hostilities only; house

h & o hook and oil (damage to cargo)

'ho' whore

ho (Chinese—river)

Ho Ho Chi Minh; holmium; Honduran; Honduras; Hondureño; House (of Representatives)

HO Head Office; Health Office(r); Home Office (British); Hydrographic Office (USN)

HO *Handelsorganisation* (German—trade organization)

hoa hands off—automatic

HOA Homeowners A (insurance policy); Home Owners Association

Hoa Lo Hanoi's prison nicknamed Hanoi-Hilton

hoax (Contraction—hocus pocus)

hob. height of burst; horizontal oscillating barrel; human observation(al) blunder

Hob Anthony van Hoboken (Dutch chronologist-enumerator of Haydn's music); Hobart, Tasmania; Hoboken (Belgian seaport near Antwerp, place near Waycross, Georgia, port city in New Jersey opposite lower Manhattan)

HOB Homeowners B (insurance policy); House Office Building

Hoban Holborn

Hob(bie) Albert

hobe honeycomb before expansion

hobgob(s) hobgoblin(s)

Hob-Job Hobson-Jobson (similar-sounding words to those of other languages with some or complete loss of meaning, e.g., Hobson-Jobson supposedly equivalent to Arabic cry of mourning for grandsons of Mohammed—*ya Hasan!—o Husain!*, Key West believed same as *Cayo Hueso* (Spanish

—Bone Key), Leghorn invented by British sailors who thought it equivalent to *Livorno*, Coromuel—beach in Baja California—named after English pirate—*Cromwell*, white rhino really the Dutch *weid rhino*—a wide-mouthed rhinoceros and really not white)

hobo. (HOBO) homing bomb

Hobo Hoboken

Hobo Composer Harry Partch (inventor of the forty-three microtone to the octave scale and composer of *And On the Seventh Day Petals Fell on Petaluma*)

Hobohemia Hobo bohemia (skid-row areas such as Manhattan's Bowery or its East Village, name but two New York Hobohemias)

HOBOS Homing Bombing System

Hobt Hobart

hoc heavy organic chemical(s); held on charge

hoc (HOC) hydrofoil ocean combatant

HoC House of Commons

HOC Homeowners C (insurance policy); Hydrology Overview Committee

hoch (German—high)

Ho Chi Minh (Vietnamese—He Who Enlightens)—Nguyen Ai Quac whose patronym was Nguyen Van Coong but is also known as Nguyen That Thanh with Nguyen pronounced like *wee-un*

Ho Chi Minh City formerly Saigon—new name imposed upon its surrender to Vietcong communist guerrillas wishing to honor the founder of their forces liberating French Indo-China—Ho Chi Minh

hock. Hockheimer (Rhine wine)

H.O.C.S. *Hostem Occidit, Civem Servavit* (Latin—A foe he slew, a citizen he saved)—inscription found on Roman civic crowns

hocus one of morphine's many nicknames

hoc vesp. *hoc vespere* (Latin—this evening)

hod. hyperbaric oxygen drenching

HoD Head of Department

HOD Hoffer-Osmond Diagnostic Test

Hodara's disease hair splitting

Hodge nickname for the typical

English farmer or for Roger
Hodgkin's disease progressive enlargement of the lymph nodes
HOD Test Hoffer, Osmond, and Desmond Test (for schizophrenia)
hoe. holographic optical element
Hoeck van Holland (Dutch—Hook of Holland)—Channel-crossing port
HoF Hall of Fame
Hoff Hoffman; Hoffmann; Hofman reflex
hofin hostile fire indicator
HOFSL Home Office Forensic Science Laboratory (London)
Hog NATO nickname for Soviet Ka-18 utility-transport helicopter
HOG heavy-ordnance gunship
HO-gage $5/8$-inch track gauge (model railroads)
Hogarth's Act Act of Parliament passed in 1735 "for the Encouragement of the Arts of Designing, Engraving, Etching, etc."—William Hogarth campaigned for this act granting copyright protection and hence it bears his name
Hog Butcher for the World Chicago's nickname in the early 1900s
ho & gem heavy oil and gas-cut mud
hogen-mogen Hobson-Jobson for *hoog mogendheden* (Dutch—lord high mightinesses)
Hog and Hominy State Tennessee
Hog Lane Hoxton
Hogopolis Chicago
hoh hard of hearing
Hohhot (Pinyin Chinese—Huhetot)
HOHI Home Ownership and Home Improvement (loan program)
HOI Headquarters Operating Instruction
HOI Handbook of Operating Instructions
hoj home on jamming
HoJo Howard Johnson (roadside restaurants)
H o K House of Keys
hoke hokum
hoku (Japanese—north)
Hokusai Katsushika Hokusai (19th-century Japanese engraver-illustrator-teacher)
hol holiday; hollow; holly
Hol Holland; Hollander
Hol Holanda (Portuguese or

Spanish—Holland)
HoL House of Lords
Holanda (Portuguese or Spanish—Holland)—the Netherlands
HOLC Home Owners Loan Corporation
hold. holding
holidaze alcohol-or-drug-induced daze characterized by incidence of over-the-holidays accidents and fatalities
holl hollandais (French—Dutch); *hollandsk* (Dano-Norwegian—Dutch)
Holl Holland; Hollander
Holland popular name for the Netherlands containing the province of Holland
Holland in the Caribbean Netherlands Antilles (Aruba, Bonaire, Curaçao, Saba, Sint Eustatius, Sint Maarten)
Hollande (French—Holland)—the Netherlands
Holländer Die Fliegende Holländer (German—The Flying Dutchman)—three-act opera by Wagner
Hollandia Dutch capital of western New Guinea or West Irian where it is now known as Djajapura or Kotabaru
hollands hollands gin (juniper flavored)—also called dutch gin as it originated in the Netherlands
Holland's Holland & Holland (British gunmakers)
Hollie Holiday; Holladay; Hollingsworth; Hollis; Hollister; Hollway
Holloway women's prison in London, England
Hollyw'd Hollywood
Holmes Sherlock Holmes (or any great detective)
Holmia (Latin—Stockholm)
holo holograph
holo (Latin prefix—entire or whole)—holocaust
Holocaust Hitler's extermination, humiliation, and torture of the Jews and others he and his Nazi minions persecuted
holog hologram; holograph(ic)al(ly); holography
hol-ry whole rye
hols holidays
Holstein Capital Northfield, Minnesota
holsum wholesome
Holt Holt, Rinehart & Winston
HOLUA Home Office Life Underwriters Association
holupk holiday upkeep
Hol Via Holborn Viaduct (rail

terminal)
Holw Hollow (postal abbreviation)
Holy Alliance Austria, Prussia, Russia (in 1815)
Holy Cities Mecca and Medina in Saudi Arabia; Mohammed was born in Mecca and died in Medina
Holy City fond place-name nickname given Charleston, South Carolina by its charming inhabitants
Holy Devil Rasputin
Holy Horatio Horatio Alger, Jr
Holy Land Israel
Holy Land of Three Religions Israel (where so-called Christians, Jews, and Moslems murder in the name of all they consider holy)
Holy Rabble Rouser Ayatullah Ruhollah Khomeini
Holy Three of Criminology Enrico Ferri, Raffaele Garofalo, Cesare Lombroso
hom homonym
hom homing; hominy
Hom Homer
Hom Homerton College, Cambridge
Hom. Homilia (Latin—homily, sermon)
HOMA Houston Oil and Minerals
Home Home Office (England and Wales)
HOME Home Opportunities Made Equal; Home Ownership Made Easy; Homemakers Organized for More Employment
Home of Abraham Lincoln Springfield, Illinois
Home of the Alamo San Antonio, Texas
Home of Baseball Cooperstown, New York
Home of the Bean and the Cod Boston, Massachusetts or the Commonwealth of Massachusetts
Home of the Blizzard Adelie Land, Antarctica
Home of the Blues Memphis, Tennessee
Home of the Casbah Algiers
Home of Casey Jones Jackson, Tennessee
Home of the Comstock Lode Virginia City, Nevada
Home of Contented Cows Carnation, Washington
Home of the Cotton Carnival Memphis, Tennessee
Home of Diamond Walnuts

Stockton, California

Home of the Dinosaurs Glen Rose, Texas where petrified footprints of 30-foot-long dinosaurs are displayed

home ec home economics

Home of Franklin Delano Roosevelt Hyde Park, New York

Home of George Washington Mount Vernon, Virginia

Home of the Giants Jotunheimen Mountains in Norway

Home of Goethe Heidelberg, Germany

Home of Holbein Augsburg, Germany

Home of Jesse James St Joseph, Missouri

Home of the Kentucky Derby Louisville

Homeland of the Bengalis Bangladesh

Homeland of Yogurt Bulgaria

homeo homeopath; homeopathic; homeopathy

homeo (Latin—same or similar) —homeostasis, homogeneous, homogenized, homologous

Home of Old Miss Oxford, Mississippi—the home of Ole Miss—The University of Mississippi

Homer NATO name for Soviet heavy helicopter designated Mi 12

Homer. Homeric

Homer Wilbur (pseudonym— James Russell Lowell)

HOMES mnemonic for remembering the five Great Lakes— Huron, Ontario, Michigan, Erie, Superior

Home of the Snow Himalaya Mountains

Home of Storms Gulf of Alaska

Home of Theodore Roosevelt Oyster Bay, Long Island, New York

Home of Thomas Jefferson Monticello, Virginia

Hometown Hamilton, Ohio as defined by author Peter Davis in his contemporary American chronicle of the same name

Home of the Waltz Vienna

Homicide City New York City's sobriquet dating from 1972 when 1691 killings were reported (a vital statistic since topped)

Hominoid Hominoidea [primate superfamily including the great apes (chimpanzees, gorillas, orangutans), the gibbons, and humans]

homo homeopath; homeopathic;

homeopathy; homosexual; homosexuality

homo (Latin prefix—alike or same)—homosexual

homoeo homoeopath(ic); homoeopathy

homolat homolateral

homomilk homogenized milk

homop homophobia (anti-homosexual hysteria)

homosex homosexual; homosexuality

homrep homicide report

homungus not an acronym as some suggest, while others insist it means human fungus, but a slang term meaning colossal, outsize, or tremendous

hon honey; honor; honorable; honorarium; honorary; honored

Hon Honduran; Honduras; Hondureño; Honolulu; Honorable

Hon'ble Honourable

Hon Consul Honorary Consul

hond honored

Hond Honduran; Honduras

Honduran Ports (east coast, west to east) Puerto Cortés, Tela, Puerto Este, La Ceiba, Trujillo, Puerto Castilla, Roatán (*on* Roatán *island*); (west coast) Amapala, San Lorenzo

Honduras, Republic of Honduras (Spanish-speaking Central American nation whose chief exports include bananas, coffee, cotton, and sugar shipped by Hondurans on both coasts) *República de Honduras*

Honduras Británica (Spanish— British Honduras)—now known as Belize or *Belice*

Honduras Day Honduran Independence Day (September 15)

Honest Abe Abraham Lincoln

Honest Harold Secretary of the Interior Harold Le Claire Ickes also called the Old Curmudgeon

Honest John solid-sustainer motor surface-to-surface ballistic missile produced by Douglas Aircraft

Honey Capital Uvalde, Texas

Honey Fitz John F. (Honey Fitz) Fitzgerald

Honey Lulu Honolulu, Hawaii

Honeymoon City Niagara Falls, New York

Honey State Western Australia

Hong (Chinese—trading wharf)

Hong Kong British-controlled Chinese port city comprising Hong Kong Island, peninsula

of Kowloon, and New Territories adjoining Chinese communist border—subtropical trading center of international renown—inhabited by Hong Kongese and many refugees from communist China

Hong Kong (Chinese—Fragrant Harbor)

Hongrie (French—Hungary)

Hono Honolulu

Honolulu Hawaii's capital

Honorary Citizen of the United States Winston Churchill (first and only foreigner to bear this title)

hons honors

Hon Sec Honorary Secretary

HOO House Officer Observer

hood. hoodlum

'hood neighborhood

Hood Island, Galápagos Española

Hook Hook Point, Ireland; Hooker; The Hook—Hook of Holland *(Hoek van Holland)*, Hooky Nail; Sandy Hook, New Jersey

Hooker Boulevard El Cajon Boulevard

Hoosier Capital Indianapolis, Indiana

Hoosier City Indianapolis, Indiana

Hoosier Poet James Whitcomb Riley

Hoosier(s) name believed to be a frontier-era contraction of *Who's there?*—pronounced *hoosier*; native(s) of Indiana

Hoosier State Indiana's official nickname

Hoover Hoover Dam southeast of Las Vegas, Nevada; Hoover Institution (Stanford University)

hop. high oxygen pressure; holding procedures

Hop Hopkin; Hopkins; Hopkinson; Hopwood

HOP Hong Kong Outline Plan; Hydrographic Office Publication(s)

HOPE Harbingers of Productive English; Health Opportunity for People Everywhere

HOPE Help Organize Peace Everywhere

HOPEG Hotel and Public Building Equipment Group

HOPES High-Oxygen-Pulping Enclosed System

hoppers grasshoppers

HOQ Hysteroid-Obsessoid Questionnaire

hor home of record; horizon;

horizontal; horology
Hor Horace; Horatio
Hor Horologium (constellation)
HoR House of Representatives
H-O-R Hoover-Owens-Rentschler (engines)
Horace Quintus Horatius Flaccus
hora decub. hora decubitus (Latin—at bedtime)
hora interm. hora intermedius (Latin—at the intermediate hours)
hora som. hora somni (Latin—at bedtime)
HO & RC Humble Oil and Refining Company
HoReCa Hotel, Restaurant, and Cafe Keepers
horen horizontal enlarger
horiz horizontal
Hormone NATO nickname for Soviet armed helicopter in naval service (KA-25)
Horn The Horn (Cape Horn—southernmost South America); Hornblower (Midshipman, Lieutenant, Captain, Commodore, Lord, or Admiral—indomitable naval character created by C.S. Forester)
Horn (German—peak)
Horn of Africa Djibouti, Ethiopia, Somalia, Sudan but particularly northeasternmost Somalia terminating in Cape Guardafui the Arabs call the Ras Asir
Hornet F-A-18 McDonnell Douglas fighter-attack aircraft
horo horoscope
Horo Horologium (constellation)
horol horology
Hor Q Horatius Quintus Flaccus (Roman poet)
HORSA Hut Operation Raising School-leaving Age
horse. (HORSE) hydrofoil-operated rocket submarine
Horse Latitudes belts of calms about 30 or 35 degrees north or south of Equator; horses were cast overboard in these places when sailing vessels were becalmed and drinking water became scarce
Horseman Haydn's String Quartet in G minor (opus 74, no. 3)
Horsemonger Horsemonger Lane Gaol (notorious London prison in the early 1800's when it held Robert Taylor who was convicted of blasphe-

my because he preached the universality of all religious beliefs and cast doubt on the historical authenticity of Jesus Christ, he bore the nickname of Devil's Chaplain)
Horseshoe Curve Altoona, Pennsylvania's nickname as it is a railroad town close to the celebrated Horseshoe Curve built by the Pennsylvania Railroad to cross the Alleghenies and traverse the valley of the Juniata River
Horse Thief Hollow Oak Lawn, Michigan's original name and now a nickname
hort horticulture
Hort Horticulture
horti horticultural; horticulturalist; horticulture
hortic horticultural; horticulture; horticulturist
HORU Home Office Research Unit
hor. un. spatio horae unius spatio (Latin—at the end of an hour)
hos human operator simulator
'ho's whores
Hos The Book of Hosea
Hos Hosea
H-o-S Holland-on-Sea
HOS Hawaiian Orchid Society
HOSC History of Science Cases
hose. hosiery
Hosea Biglow (pseudonym—James Russell Lowell)
Hosp Hospital (postal abbreviation)
hosp ins hospital insurance
Hostess to the Nation Dolley Madison—wife of President James Madison
Hostos Eugenio María Hostos Birthday (January 11) celebrated in Puerto Rico
hot. human old tuberculin
Hot high-subsonic optically-guided tube-launched Franco-German antitank missile
HOT Hamilton-Oshawa-Toronto (industrial complex); Hot Springs, Arkansas (airport)
ho/ta hold tank(s)
HOTAC Hotel Accommodation (London hotel service)
hot arts hot art dealers (trafficking in stolen works of art)
Hotbed of Secession Charleston, South Carolina
HOT Car Hands Off This Car (antitheft program)
Hotel letter H radio code; NATO nickname for H-class

Soviet missile-launching nuclear-powered submarines
Hotlanta Atlanta, Georgia
HOTLIPS Honorary Order of Trumpeters Living in Possible Sin
Hot Potato Luke Hamlin
Hot Springs Country southwest Arkansas
Hotspur Sir Henry Percy
Hottest Town in Arizona Quartzite (where noon temperatures of 108°F are not unusual)
Hottest Town in Texas Presidio —on the Rio Grande opposite Ojinaga in Mexico
Hot Water State Arkansas
Hotz Hotzenplatz (also known as Osoblaha by its Czechoslovakian citizens)
Hou Houston
HOU Houston, Texas (airport)
Houdini Harry Houdini (real name Ehrich Weiss)—America's foremost escapologist-magician
Houghton Houghton Mifflin
Hound Dog North American-Rockwell air-to-surface missile
Hounds Houndsditch
Hous Houston
House House of Representatives in the United States; The House—House of Commons in England; London's Stock Exchange; Oxford University's Christ College
house apes other people's unhousebroken children
House of the Book (see *LCL*)
House of D (Women's) House of Detention (NYC)
household coal bituminous coal; soft coal
House Ruth Built New York City's Yankee Stadium in the Bronx where Babe Ruth hit so many home runs
Houston haze smog of the petrochemical variety sometimes called Los Angeles haze or metropolitan mist mixed with automotive exhausts
Hou Sym Orch Houston Symphony Orchestra
houv houvere (Finnish—charity)
Hovaness 39 Alan Hovaness's thirty-nine symphonies including *Mysterious Mountain* (No. 2), *Celestial Gate* (No. 6), *Saint Vartan* (No. 9), *All Men are Brothers* (No. 11), *Silver Pilgrimage* (No. 15), *Vishnu* (No. 19), *Etchmiadzin* (No.

21)
hoved (Dano-Norwegian—cape)
Hovensweep Hovensweep National Monument in southwestern Colorado and southeastern Utah
how. howitzer
How Howard (U.S. Supreme Court Reports)
HoW Happiness of Womanhood
HOW Home-Owners' Warranty
Howard Rhode Island town containing most of the state's correctional facilities
Howard U Pr Howard University Press
Howie Howard; Howarth; Howe; Howell; Howland
howtar howitzer-mortar
HOW-TO Housing Operation with Training Opportunity (OEO)
Hox Hoxie
Huxford(shire) [(Cockney—Oxford (shire)]
hp halt pay; hardy perennial; high pass; high performance; high potency; high potential; high power; high pressure; hire purchase; holiday pay; hollowpoint; horizontal parallax; horizontally polarized; horsepower; hot pressed; hybrid perpetual; hyperbolic; hypoid(al)
h/p house to pier
h & p history and physical (examination); hydraulic and pneumatic
HP Haute-Pyrénées; House Physician; Houses of Parliament
H-P Handley-Page; Haute-Pyrénées; Hewlett-Packard
HP Homeopathic Pharmacopoeia
hpa high power amplifier; horn-parabola antenna; hydraulic pneumatic area
HPA Hospital Physicists Association
HPAAS High-Performance Aerial Attack System
hpac hydropress accessor
HPAC Hawaii Performing Arts Company
HPAL Holland Pan-American Line
hpb hinged plotting board
HPBA Housing Patrolmen's Benevolent Association
HPC Hercules Powder Company; Highland Park College
hpc black hard-processing channel black

HPCC High-Performance Control Center
hpchd harpsichord
hpchdst harpsichordist
HPCL Hindustan Petroleum Corporation Limited
HP Club Homing Pigeon Club
hp cyl high-pressure cylinder
hpd high-performance diesel; hydraulic pump discharge
H-P d Hough-Powell digitizer
HPD Hawaii Police Department; Housing Preservation and Development
HPDC High-Pressure Data Center (NBS)
HPDF High-Performance Demonstration Facility
hpdo high-performance diesel oil
hpe high-power effect(s)
hper health, physical education, and recreation
HPERB Hawaii Public Employment Relations Board
hpew high-power(ed) early warning
hpf highest possible frequency; high-powered field; hydropress form
HPF Horace Plunkett Foundation
hpfm hydropress form
hpg (HPG) human pituitary gonadotrophin
HPGA Hawaii Personnel and Guidance Association
hp Ge high-purity Germanium
H$_{pgc}$ heading per gyro compass
hp hd high-pressure high-density
hp hr horsepower hour
hpi high-power illuminator; history of present illness; homing-position indicator
HPI Handicap Problems Inventory; Hydrocarbon Processing Industry
hpl high(est) point level; human parotid lysozyme; human placental lactogen
Hpl Hartlepool
HPL Halifax Public Library; Hamilton Public Library; Hartford Public Library; Houston Pipe Line; Houston Public Library
hplc high-pressure-liquid chromatography
hpll hybrid phase-locked loop
hplr hinge pillar
hpls hopeless
hpm high polymer molecular; human potential movement
H-P m Harding-Passey melano-

ma
HPM Human Potential Movement
HPMA Hardwood Plywood Manufacturers Association
hpmv high-pressure mercury vapor
hpn home parental nutrition; horsepower nominal
hpns high-pressure nervous syndrome
hpo high-pressure oxygenation
HPO Hamilton Philharmonic Orchestra; Highway Post Office
HPOL High-Power Optical Laboratory
H-pole H-shaped telegraph or telephone pole
hpox high-pressure oxygen
hpp hydraulic pneumatic panel
HPP Harvard Project Physics; Hawker Pacific Proprietary
HPPA Horses and Ponies Protection Association
HPPB Historic Pensacola Preservation Board
h-p plan hire purchase plan (British equivalent of American installment-plan purchasing)
HPPP High-Priority Production Program
hpr high penetration resistant; high-power(ed) radar homer; hot particle rolling
HPR House of Pacific Relations
HPRF Hypersonic Propulsion Research Facility
HPRP High-Performance Reporting Post; High-Power(ed) Radar Post
hps high primary sequence; high protein supplement; high-pressure sodium; high-pressure steam; hot-pressed sheet
HPS Harlem Preparatory School; Health Physics Society; High Protestant Society
H$_{psc}$ heading per standard compass
hpsn hot-pressed silicon nitride
hpst harpist
H$_{pstgc}$ heading per steering compass
hpt high point; high-pressure test
HPTA High-Power Test Area; Hire Purchase Trade Association
hptn hypertension
Hptw Hauptwerk (German—great work)
hpu hot-plate unit; hydraulic pumping unit

hpv high-passage virus; human-powered vehicle

hpv-de high-passage virus (grown in) duck embryo

hpv-dk high-passage virus (grown in) dog kidney

hpw high-power window

hq headquarters

h.q. hoc quaere (Latin—see this)

Hq Headquarters

H-Q Hydro-Quebec

HQASC Headquarters Air-Support Command (NATO)

HQBA Headquarters Base Area

hqc hydroxyquinoline citrate

HQCC Headquarters Coastal Command (UK)

HQ Comdt Headquarters Commandant

HQ COMD USAF Headquarters Command, USAF

HQD Harold Q(uinten) Driscoll

HQDA Headquarters, Department of the Army

hqdt handling qualities during tracking

HQDTMS Headquarters, Defense Traffic Management Service

HQEARC Headquarters, Equipment Authorization Review Center (USA)

HQFC Headquarters, Fighter Command (NATO)

HQFT Humanist Quest For Truth

HQMC Headquarters—Marine Corps

hq's (Hq's) headquarters

HQSC Headquarters, Signal Command (UK)

HQSTC Headquarters, Strike Command (UK)

HQTC Headquarters, Transport Command (UK)

Hqtrs Headquarters

HQ USAF Headquarters, USAF

hr hairspace; handling room; heat resisting; height range; high resilient; home run; homing relay; hook rail; hoserack; hospital recruit; hot rolled; hour; human relations; relative humidity (symbol)

h(r) hail and rain (meteorological symbol)

h/r heart rate

hr herr (Swedish—Sir)—Mr

Hr Herr (Danish or German—Mr, Sir)

HR Hospital Recruit; House of Representatives; House Reso-

lution; International Harvester (stock exchange symbol)

H-R Haut-Rhin

H & R Harper & Row; Harrington & Richardson; Herweg & Romine

HR Hauptrhythmus (German—outstanding rhythm)—12-tone term; Hellenic Register (Greek ship-classification book); House (of Representatives) Resolution

hra housing review account

hra (HRA) hypersonic research airplane

hRA hardness Rockwell A (scale)

Hra Herra (Finnish—Mister)

HRA Hardware Retailers Association; Health Resources Administration; Historical Records of Australia; Human Resources Administration; Hunters' Rights Association; Hypnotic Research Association

HRA Historical Records of Australia

HRAA Hypnotic Research Association of Australia

Hradec Kralove (Czechoslovakian—Königgrätz)

HRAF Human Relations Area File

HRAG Helena Rubinstein Art Gallery

hRB hardness Rockwell B (scale)

HRB Highway Research Board; Highway Research Bureau; Housing and Redevelopment Board

hrc high rupturing capacity

hRC hardness Rockwell C (scale)

HRC Herpes Resource Center; Humacao Regional College; Human Relations Commission; Human Resources Center; Human Rights Commission (OAS); Humanities Research Council

HRCC Humanities Research Council of Canada

HRCF Human Rights Campaign Fund(ing)

hrd hard; high roughage diet

HRD Hertzsprung-Russell Diagram; Human Resources Development

HRDA Human Resources Development Agency

HRDF Human Resource Development Foundation

HRDI Hospital Reserve Disaster Inventory

HRDL Hudson River Day

Line

hrdly hardly

hrdwd hardwood

hrdwr hardware

hre hypersonic research engine

hre (HRE) high-resolution electrocardiography

HRE Holy Roman Empire

HREBU Hotel and Restaurant Employees and Bartenders Union

H reflex Hoffmann reflex (of the tibial nerve)

H Rept House Report

HRes House Resolution (US House of Representatives)

HRET Hospital Research and Educational Trust

HREU Hotel and Restaurant Employees Union

hrf high rate of fire

Hrf Harfe (German—harp)

HRF Hat Research Foundation

HRFA Hudson River Fishermen's Association

hrf's health-related facilities

HRG Halford, Robins, and Godfrey

HRGs Health Research Groups

hrh high resistance hold

HRH His (Her) Royal Highness

hri height-range indicator

HRI Hotel Reservations International; Human Relations Inventory

HRIP Highway Research in Progress

H.R.I.P. hic requiescit in pace (Latin—here rests in peace)

hrir high-resolution infrared radiometer

hrirs high-resolution infrared-radiation sounder

HRIS Highway Research Information Service; Human Resource Information System

hrl horizontal reference line

Hrl Harlingen

HRL Hughes Research Laboratories; Human Resources Laboratory

Hrm Herman

HRMA Hampton Roads Maritime Association

Hr Ms Haar Majesteits Schip (Dutch—Her Majesty's Ship)

Hrn Herren (German—gentlemen)

HRNTWT High-Reynolds-Number Transonic Wind Tunnel

HRO Housing Referral Office (USAF)

hrp horizontal radiation pattern

HRP Hampton Roads Ports; Human Reliability Program; Huntsville Research Park

HRPA Hudson River Pilots Association

HRPP Human Rights Protection Party (Samoa)

hrr higher reduced rate (taxation)

HRRA Human Resources Research Organization

HRRC Human Resources Research Center

HRRL Human Resources Research Laboratory

HRRO Human Resources Research Office

hrs high-resolution spectrometer; hot-rolled steel; hours

HRS Hamilton Rating Scale; Health Resources Statistics; Human Resource System; Hydraulics Research Station; Hydrostatic Research System

HRSA Honorary Member of the Royal Scottish Academy

hrsg herausgegeben (German—edited or published)

Hrsg Herausgeber (German—editor)

hrsi high-temperature reusable-surface insulation

HRSRS Hartbeestehoek Radio Space Research Station

hrt high-resolution track(er)

HRT Honolulu Rapid Transit

hrts high risk test site

hrtwd heartwood

Hrtz Ha'aretz (Hebrew—The Land)—Israel's leading newspaper

HRU Hydrological Research Unit

hrv hypersonic research vehicle

HRVC Hudson River Valley Commission

HR & W Holt, Rinehart & Winston

HRWMC House of Representatives Ways and Means Committee

Hry Henry

HRYC Halifax River Yacht Club; Hampton Roads Yacht Club

HRZ Hertz Corporation (stock exchange symbol)

hs half strength; hardstand; head suppression; heating surface; hide substance; high-speed; hinged seat; horizontal shear; horizontal stripe(s); hot stuff; hypersonic

hs (HS) hardened site

h.s. hic situs (Latin—laid here); *hoc sensu* (Latin—in this sense)

Hs Henriques

Hs Handschrift (German—manuscript)

HS Hakluyt Society; Haute-Saône; Haute-Savoie; Hawker Siddeley; High School; Home Secretary; Home Service; Hospital Ship; House Surgeon; Hunterian Society; hydrofoil ship (naval symbol)

H-S Haute-Saône; Haute-Savoie

H & S Health and Safety (Code); Home & School

H.S. hic sepultus or *hic situs* (Latin—here lies buried)

HS-30 West German armored-personnel carrier

HS-125 Hawker-Siddeley Dominie jet transport

HS-748 Hawker Siddeley support aircraft; Hawker-Siddeley troop transport carrying 40 paratroopers or 50 regular soldiers

hsa human serum albumin; hypersonic aircraft (HSA)

HSA Hawker Siddeley Aviation; Health Service Area; Health Services Administration; Health Systems Agency; Herb Society of America; Hispanic Society of America; Holly Society of America; Home Servicemens Association; Hospital Savings Association; Hunt Saboteurs Association

HSAA Health Sciences Advancement Award

HSAC House (of Representatives) Science and Astronautics Committee

HSA & D High School of Art and Design

HSAL Hispanic Society of America Library (NYC)

hsb human sexual behavior

HSBC Hongkong and Shanghai Banking Corporation

hsbr high-speed bombing radar

hsc (HSC) engine high-swirl combustion engine

HSC Health and Safety Code

H-S-C Hand-Schüller-Christian (disease)

HSCA Health Sciences Communication Association

HSCC Historical Society of Southern California

H Sch High School

Hschonhsn Hohenschonhausen

HS-Co A reduced coenzyme A

hscp high-speed card punch

hscr high-speed card reader

hsct high-speed compound terminal

HSCTB Heavy and Specialized Carriers Tariff Bureau

hsctt high-speed-card teletypewriter terminal

hsd hard-site defense; high-speed diesel (oil)

HSD Hawker Siddeley Dynamics

hsda high-speed data acquisition

HSDE High-School Driver Education

HSDG Hamburg-Sudamerika Dampfschiffahrts Gesellschaft (Columbus Line)

HSDM Harvard School of Dental Medicine

hse house

hse (HSE) syndrome hemorrhagic shock and encephalopathy syndrome

Hse House (postal abbreviation)

HSE Health and Safety Executive

H.S.E. hic sepultus est or *hic situs est* (Latin—here lies buried)

HSERF High-Score Educational Research Foundation

HSFI High School of Fashion Industries

hsg housing

Hsg Helsingör (Elsinore)

HSG Hawker Siddeley Group

hsgt high-speed ground transport

HSGTC High-Speed Ground Test Center

HSGTP High-Speed Ground Transportation Program

HSH Her (His) Serene Highness

h & s hole hellhole and smell-hole (epithet applied to many African, Asian, Latin American, and Levantine places)

hsi heat-stress index; horizontal situation indicator

HSI Health Services Inc; Home and School Institute

Hsia-men (Chinese—Amoy)

Hsiang-Kiang (Chinese—Hong Kong)

hsien (Chinese—district, district capital)

Hsinhua New China News Agency

HSIS Highway Safety Information Service

hsk housekeeper; housekeeping (flow chart); housekept

HSK Honorary Surgeon to the King

hskpg housekeeping

hskpr housekeeper
hsl herpes simplex labialis (HSL); hytran simulation language
HSL Hawaii State Library; Huguenot Society of London
hsla high-strength low-alloy (steel)
HSLA Home and School Library Association
HS Lab Health Service Laboratory (USA)
hslkfin high silky finish
hsltd hand salted
HSLWI Helical Spring Lock Washer Institute
hsm high-speed memory
hsm (HSM) holosystolic murmur
HSM Her (His) Serene Majesty; Historical Society of Montana
HSMA Hotel Sales Management Association
HSMB Hydronautics Ship Model Basin
HSMHA Health Services and Mental Health Association
HSNP Hot Springs National Park
HSNR Huleh Swamp Nature Reserve (Israel)
HSNY Handel Society of New York
HSO Haifa Symphony Orchestra; Hamburg Symphony Orchestra; Hartford Symphony Orchestra; Hitachi Symphony Orchestra; Honolulu Symphony Orchestra; Houston Symphony Orchestra
HSORS High-Seas Oil-Recovery System
hsp high-speed printer
h of sp hybrid of species
H-S p Henoch-Schönlein purpura
HSP Historical Society of Pennsylvania; Hospital Surgical Plan
HSP Haute Société Protestant (French—High Protestant Society)
HSPA Hawaiian Sugar Planters' Association; High School of the Performing Arts
h-span hydrolized starch-polyacrylonitrile copolymer graft(ing)
HSPG Hansard Society of Parliamentary Government
HSPH Harvard School of Public Health
HSPQ High-School Personality Questionnaire
hsptp high-speed paper-tape

punch
hsptr high-speed paper-tape reader
HSQ Historical Society of Queensland; Honorary Surgeon to the Queen
hsr high-speed reader; high-speed rewind
hsr (HSR) high-speed rail(road); high-speed railway
HSR Health Service Region (USA)
hsrc high-speed rail concept
HSRC Health Sciences Resource Center (Canadian)
HSRI Health Systems Research Institute; Highway Safety Research Institute
hsro high-speed repetitive operation
hss high-speed steel
hss (HSS) hydrological-sensing satellite
H-S s Hallervorden-Spatz syndrome
HSS History of Science Society; Hungarian State Symphony
HSSA History of Science Society of America
HSSO Hungarian State Symphony Orchestra
hsss high-speed stainless steel; high-strength stainless steel
hsst (HSST) high-speed surface transport (vehicle floats above its track on a magnetic cushion)
hst highest spring tide; high-speed train; hoist; hypersonic transport
H St Hugo Stinnes (steamship line)
HST Harry S Truman—thirty-third President of the United States; Hawaiian Standard Time; hypersonic transport
HSTA Hawaii State Teachers Association
HSTC Henderson State Teachers College
h/stead homestead(er)(s)
HSTI Hartford State Technical Institute
HSTL Harry S Truman Library
Hstn Houston
HSTRU Hydraulic System Test and Repair Unit
hsts horizontal stabilizer trim setting(s)
HSTS House Subcommittee on Traffic Safety
HSU Hardin-Simmons University
H substance histamine-like capillary vasodilator

H-substance histamine-like substance
HSUL Haile Selassie University Libraries (Addis Ababa, Ethiopia)
HSUNA Humanist Student Union of North America
HSUS Humane Society of the United States
hsv heat-suppression valve
hsv (HSV) herpes simplex virus
HSV Huntsville, Alabama (airport)
hswf housewife
HSWT High-Speed Wind Tunnel
hszd hermetically-sealed zener diode
ht half title; halftime; halftone; hard top; heat; heat treat; heat treatment; heat-treated; heavy formex; heavy tank; heavy traffic; height; height telling; high temperature; high tensile; high tension; high tide; high treason; hired transport; hollow tile; hybrid tea (rose); hydrotherapy; hypertropia; hypodermic tablet
ht (HT) horizontal tabulation (data processing)
h & t harden(ed) and temper(ed); hospitalization and treatment; hospitalize and treat
h.t. hoc tempore (Latin—at this time); *hoc titulo* (Latin—under this title)
Ht total hypermetropia
Hᵗ Haut (French—high, upper)
HT Hawaiian Telephone; Hawaiian Territory; Hawaiian Theater; Hawaiian Time; Height Technician; Horsed Transport; Hospital Train
HT-2 trichothecense toxin used in biochemical warfare waged by the Soviets in Afghanistan and Laos
hta heavier than air
HTA Hardcourt Tennis Association; Horticultural Trades Association
Htal Hospital (Spanish—hospital)
htb high-tension battery
HTB Highway Tariff Bureau; Horserace Totalisator Board
htc head(ing) to come; headline to come; heat transfer coefficient; hydraulic temperature control
htd heated
HTD Hospital for Tropical Diseases

htd pl heated pool
htd rm heated room
H^{te} *Haute* (French—high, upper)
Hte-Gar Haute-Garonne
Hte-L Haute-Loire
Hte-M Haute-Marne
H^{ter} *Hinter* (German—behind, rear)
Hte-Sao Haute-Saône
Hte-Sav Haute-Savoie
Htes-Pyr Hautes-Pyrénées
htfc high-temperature fuel cell
ht fx heat treat fixture
htg heating
htgr (HTGR) high-temperature gas-cooled reactor
Htg & Vent Heating & Ventilating
hth (HTH) holiday travel hostility
hthp high temperature high pressure
hti high-temperature isotope
HTI Hand Tools Institute; High Twelve International
htk headline to come
htl hearing threshold level, heavy-traffic licence; high threshold logic
Htl Hotel
htls high torque low speed
htlv human T-cell leukemia virus
htm heat transfer medium; high-temperature metallography
HTMC High Temperature Materials Corporation
Htn Hamilton, Bermuda
hto high-temperature oxidation; horizontal takeoff
htofore heretofore
htol (HTOL) horizontal-takeoff-and-landing
h top hardtop
HTOT High-Temperature Operating Test
htp high-test peroxide
h-t p half-title page
h-t-p house-tree-person (psychological drawing test)
HTP House-Tree-Person (test); Humor Test of Personality
htr heater
htr (HTR) high-temperature reactor
HTR Highway Traffic Regulations(s)
HTR Harvard Theological Review
htrac half-track
htrb high-temperature reverse bias
HTRDA High-Temperature Reactor Development Associates

htres heat resistant
H Trin Holy Trinity
hts half-time survey; heights; high-tensile steel
Hts Heights
HTS Huntington, West Virginia (airport)
HTSA Highway Traffic Safety Administration
htst high-temperature short-time (pasteurization)
htt (HTT) heavy tactical transport
ht tr heat treat
htu heat transfer unit
htv (HTV) hypersonic test vehicle
HTV Hiroshima Television
htvt heating and ventilating
htw high-temperature water
HT&W Hoosac Tunnel & Wilmington (railroad)
ht wkt hit wicket
htxgr heat exchanger
hu hyperemia unit
Hu Hungarian; Hungary
HU Haifa University; Harvard University, Hebrew University; Howard University
HUA Highway Users Association; Housing and Urban Affairs
HUAC House Un-American Activities Committee
Hua Guofeng Hua Kuo-feng (in official and phonetic Pinyen spelling used since January 1, 1979 throughout the People's Republic of China)
Huang Ho (Cantonese Chinese —Yellow River)—also written Hwang Ho
Huangpu Whampoa, China's new name
Huaris He (Pinyin Chinese— Yellow River)
Huascán Huascarán (Peru's highest mountain)
Huáscar's revenge loose bowels contracted in Peru where one of the last Inca emperors, Huáscar, was betrayed by his brother, Atahualpa, and then was executed by the Spaniards under Pizarro
Hub The Hub—Boston, Massachusetts also called Hub of American Culture, Hub of New England, and even Hub of the Universe
HUB Humboldt Universität zu Berlin (German—Humboldt University of Berlin)—library on East Berlin's Clara-Zetkin Strasse
hubby husband

Hub of the Castilian Wheel Madrid (capital of Spain and equidistant from all her boundaries)
Hub of Christianity Jerusalem
Hubei (Pinyin Chinese—Hupeh)
Hub of Empire London
Hubey Hubert
Hub of the Golden Mile Kalgoorlie in Western Australia where gold and nickel are found
Hub of Hinduism Benares
Hubie Hubert
Hub of Islam Mecca
Hub of Islamic Culture Cairo
Hub of Judaism Jerusalem
Hub of New England Boston
Hub of New York City Columbus Circle
Hub of the Pacific Guam
Hub of the South Pacific Fiji
Hub of the Universe nickname given by Oliver Wendell Holmes to the statehouse in Boston and later by others to the entire city
HUC Hebrew Union College
Hu Chwan (Chinese—Little Tiger)—mainland Chinese hydrofoil patrol boat
HUCIA Harvard University Center for International Affairs
HUCJIR Hebrew Union College Jewish Institute of Religion
hucks huckleberries
Huck(y) Huckleberry Finn
hucr highest useful compression ratio
hud head-up display
Hud Huddleston; Hudson
HUD Hong Kong United Dockyard; Housing and Urban Development
HUDC Housing and Urban Development Corporation
hud-eu head-up display electronic unit
Hud Inst Hudson Institute
HUDPR Housing and Urban Development Procurement Regulations
hudson hudson seal (imitation seal made of dyed muskrat fur)
Hudson Bay inland sea in northern Canada; southern end called James Bay; entrance to Atlantic Ocean through Hudson Strait
Hudson Girls New York School for (delinquent) Girls at Hudson

Hudson River extends some 300 miles from lower Adirondacks to New York Bay; serves cities along its banks such as Troy, Albany, New York, and Jersey City

hudwac head-up-display weapon-aiming computer

Huel Huelva

Hueneme Port Hueneme, California

Hues Huesca

Huey Cobra AH-1 gunship aircraft

huff-duff high-frequency direction finder

HUFSM Highway Users Federation for Safety and Mobility

Huggin Hugh; Hugo

Hugh Hugh the Drover (two-act opera by Ralph Vaughan Williams)

HUGHES Hughes Aircraft Company

Hughie Hugh

hugo highly unusual geophysical operations

Hugo Wast Gustavo Martínez Zuviria

Hugues Capet Hugh Capet

Hu H Hughes Hall, Cambridge

HUJ Hebrew University of Jerusalem

huk (HUK) hunter-killer

HUKFORLANT Hunter-Killer Forces—Atlantic (USN)

HUKFORPAC Hunter-Killer Forces—Pacific (USN)

huks (HUKS) hunter-killer submarine(s)—USN

Huks Hukbong Mapgapalayang Bayan (Philippine Communist Armed Forces)

Hul Hulbert; Huldreich; Hulton

HUL Harvard University Library; Helsinki University Library; Hokkaido University Library

Hull if in England it's Kingston-upon-Hull

Hully Hulbert

HULTIS Hull Technical Interloan Scheme

hum human; humane; humanism; humanities

hum. humaniora (Latin—humanities)—also appears as H.U.M.

Hum Humbert; Hummel; Humphrey; Humphreys; Humphry

Huma L'Humanité (French—communist daily paper)

human eng human engineering

Humanist Historian Harry El-

mer Barnes

Humanitarian Scientist Louis Pasteur

HUMARIS Human Materials Resources Information System

Humb humberside

HUMBLE Humble Oil (Company)

Humboldt Current cold Antarctic current flowing northward along West Coast of South America and veering west at the Galápagos

humer humerus

humi humidity

humint human intelligence

Humist Philosopher philosophical skeptic David Hume

hummer. high-mobility multipurpose wheeled vehicle

hummer(s) humming bird(s)

Hummon Herman

Humorist-Pianist Steve Allen, Victor Borge, and Mark Russell appear to vie for the title

Humorists of Europe the Danes —also probably the happiest people despite the tradition of Hamlet, Shakespeare's Prince of Doom and Gloom

humpday Wednesday (usually the middle-of-the-week day)

Humph Humphrey

HUMRRO Human Resources Research Office

hums humanitarian reasons

humungus human fungus (*see* homungus)

hun hundred

Hun Hungarian; Hungary

Hun Hungria (Portuguese—Hungary); *Hungría* (Spanish —Hungary)

hund hundred

Hung Hungaria; Hungarian; Hungarica; Hungary

Hung Hungarian (Uralic language used by 13 million Magyars in addition to some German-speaking Hungarians)

Hungaria (Latin—Hungary)

hungarian hungarian goulash (stew characteristic of Hungary or in Hungarian style); hungarian paprika (red paprika—permeability vitamin or vitamin P)

Hungarian Ocean Lake Balaton —largest lake in central Europe

Hungarian Quartet Hungary's four best-known classical composers in chronological order —Liszt, Dohnanyi, Bartók, Kodaly

Hungary Hungarian People's Republic (Hungarian-speaking central European nation behind the Iron Curtain but once the largest part of the Austro-Hungarian Empire and still noted for its productivity) *Magyar Népköztársaság*

Hungria (Portuguese—Hungary)

Hungría (Spanish—Hungary)

Hunkyland Hungary

Hunt Hunter; Huntington; Huntley; Huntly

Hunter Hawker jet fighter-bomber

Hunter's Point San Francisco slum section

hunth hundred thousand

Hunting Mozart's String Quartet in B flat (K 458)

Huntington Huntington Library, Art Gallery, and Botanical Gardens at San Marino, California

Huntington's chorea hereditary disease marked by choreic movements and mental deterioration

Hunts Huntingdonshire

Huntsville Girls Goree Unit Women's Prison at Huntsville, Texas

HUP Harvard University Press

HUPAS Hofstra University Pro Arte Symphony

hur hurricane

hur (HUR) homes using radio (HUS)

hurcn hurricane

hurevac hurricane evacuation

HURRAH Help Us Reach and Rehabilitate America's Handicapped (HEW program)

hus hemolytic uremic syndrome (HUS)

HUSAT Human Sciences and Advanced Technology

husb husbandry

Huskie Kaman H-43 utility helicopter

Husky Territory the Yukon

Huss Jan Huss known in German as Johannes von Husinetz although born near Budweis in Bohemia where the Czech family name was Husinec—his death by being burned at the stake for heresy caused widespread indignation and led to the Hussite War lasting from 1419 to 1434

hustle. helium-underwater speech-translating equipment

Hustleton on the Canal Houston, Texas on its own ship

canal linking it with the Gulf of Mexico, the Caribbean Sea, and the oceans of the world

hut. (HUT) homes using television

hutch. humidity-temperature charts

Hutch Hutcheson; Hutchings; Hutchins; Hutchinson; Hutchison

hutv home(s) using television

Hux Huxley

hv heavy; high velocity; high voltage

h-v high-voltage

h & v heating and ventilating

h.v. *hoc verbum* (Latin—this word)

HV Hardness Vickers (symbol); Health Visitor; Hospital Visit

H-V *Haute-Volta* (French—Upper Volta)

hva homovanillic

Hva Huelva

HVA Health Visitors' Association

hvac heating, ventilating, and air conditioning; high-voltage alternating current

hvap hyper-velocity armor-piercing

hvar (HVAR) high-velocity aircraft rocket

HVB Hawaii Visitors Bureau

hvbn have been

hvc hardened voice circuit

hv & c heating, ventilating, and cooling

HVCA Heating and Ventilating Contractors' Association

HVCC Hudson Valley Community College

hvd high-velocity detonation; hypertensive vascular disease

hvdc high-voltage direct current

hvdn have done

hve home video entertainment

HVEC High Voltage Engineering Corporation

hvem high voltage transmission electron microscopy

hvf high viscosity fuel

hvg having

hvgo heavy-vacuum gas oil

hvh herpesvirus hominis

hvh (HVH) herpesvirus hominis (type 1 transmitted by mouth and marked by cold sores and fever blisters; type 2 transmitted venereally and characterized by genital lesions)

Hvh *Herpesvirus hominus* (Latin—herpes simplex virus)

H v H *Hoek van Holland* (Dutch—Hook of Holland)

hvhmd holographic visor-helmet

mounted display

hvi high viscosity index

HVI Hartman Value Inventory; Home Ventilating Institute

H'ville Huntsville, Alabama

hvJ hemagluttinating virus of Japan

H v K Herbert von Karajan

hvl half-value layer

HVL Hanseatic Vaasa Line; Heitor Villa-Lobos

Hvn Haven

HVNP Hawaii Volcanoes National Park

HVO Hawaiian Volcano Observatory

HVOT Hooper Visual Organization Test

hvp high-value package

HVP Hudson Vitamin Products

HVPO Hudson Valley Philharmonic Orchestra

hvps high-voltage power supply

hvpve high-voltage photovoltaic effect

hvr high-vacuum rectifier

HVRA Hawaiian Volcano Research Association

hvrap (HVRAP) hyper-velocity rocket-assisted projectile

hvsa high-voltage slow activity

hvss horizontal volute spring suspension

hvtp high-velocity target-practice

HVWS Hebrew Veterans of the War with Spain

hvy heavy

hw headwaiter; headwind; herewith; high water; hot water

h/w husband and wife

Hw *Hauptwerk* (German—great work)

HW high water

H-W Harbison-Walker (refractories)

H & W Harland and Wolff (Belfast shipbuilders); Hereford and Worcester

hwang (Chinese—yellow, as in Hwang Ho)

Hwang Hai (Chinese—Yellow Sea)

Hwang Ho (Chinese—Yellow River)

Hwang Pu (Chinese—Whangpoo)

Hway Highway

Hwb *Handwörterbuch* (German—pocket dictionary)

hwc hot-water circulating

HWC Heriot-Watt College

hwctr heavy-water components test reactor

hwd hardwood

H'w'd Hollywood

HWDYKY How Well Do You Know Yourself? (psychological test)

hwf & c high water full and change

hwgcr (HWGCR) heavy-water-moderated gas-cooled reactor

hwi high water interval

HWI Helical Washer Institute

hwl high-water line

HWL Henry Wadsworth Longfellow; Hutchison Whampoa Limited

hwLB high water London Bridge

hwlwr (HWLWR) heavy-water-moderated boiling light-water-cooled reactor

hwm high-water mark; high-wet modulus

HWM Hiram Walker Museum (Windsor, Ontario)

HWMC House Ways and Means Committee

HWMD Hazardous Waste Management Division (EPA)

hwmnt high-water mark neap tide

hwmont high-water mark ordinary neap tide

hwmost high-water mark ordinary spring tide

hwmst high-water mark spring tide

hwnt high-water neap tide

HWO Homosexual World Organization

hwocr (HWOCR) heavy-water (moderated) organic-cooled reactor

hwont high-water ordinary neap tide

Hwood Hollywood

hwos high-water ordinary springs

hwost high-water ordinary spring tides

hwq high-water quadrature; tropic high-water inequality

hwr (HWR) heavy water reactor (AEC)

hws hot-water soluble; hot-water system

HWS Hazardous Waste Service; Hurricane Warning Service

H & WSC Hobart and William Smith Colleges

HWSS Hot Water Service System

hwst high-water spring tide

HWT *Herald and Weekly Times*

H-W U Heriot-Watt University

hwwr however

HWW Hochschule für Welt-

handel, Wien (School for World Trade—Vienna)
hwwc hand wash with care
Hwy Highway
hx hexode; history
Hx history (medical case)
Hxd Hardinxveld
hy heavy; henry; high yield; hundred yards; hydrant
Hy Highway; Hiram; Hyman
Hy Highway
*H*y *Hasy* (Arabic—waterhole)— also appears as *Hasi*
HY Helsingin Yliopisto (University of Helsinki)
Hya Hydra (constellation)
hyb hybrid
hyball hydraulic ball
HYC Harlem Yacht Club; Hartford Yacht Club; Haverhill Yacht Club
hycol hybrid computer link
hycon hydraulic control
hycotran hybrid computer translator
hyd hydrate; hydraulic(s); hydrostatics
Hyd Hyderabad; Hydrus (sometimes abbreviated Hyi for the genitive Hydri)
hydac hybrid digital-analog computer
hydapt hybrid digital-analog pulse time
h-y dash hundred-yard dash
hydel hydroelectric(al)
Hyde Park Franklin Delano Roosevelt's home and library on the banks of the Hudson at Hyde Park, New York
hyd/pnu hydraulic/pneumatic
hydr hydrographer
hydrarg. *hydrargyrum* (Latin—mercury)
HYDRAS Hydrographic Digital Positioning and Depth Recording System
hydraul hydraulic(s)
hydraweld hydraulic-drawn welded (steel tubing)
hydro hydrodynamic group of hydrodynamics (slang); hydroelectric; hydroelectrical; hydrographic; hydrology; hydrostatic
hydro (Latin prefix—water)— hydrodynamics
HYDRO Hydrographic Office

hydrodyn hydrodynamics
hydroelec hydroelectric
hydrog hydrography
HYDROIND Hydrography of the Indian Ocean
hydrol hydrology
HYDROLANT Hydrography of the Atlantic Ocean
hydrom hydromechanics
hydromag hydromagnetic(s)
hydromagnetics magnetohydrodynamics
HYDROPAC Hydrography of the Pacific Ocean
hydros hydrostatics
hydrot hydrotherapy
hydrox hydroxyline
HYDRSS High Data Rate Storage System (NASA)
hydt hydrant
hydx hydroxide(s)
hyf (HYF) hydrofoil
HYF Hong Kong and Yaumati Ferry
hyfes hypersonic flight environmental simulator
hyg hygiene; hygienic; hygroscopic
hygas hydrogen gasification
hygst hygienist
Hyk Helsingin yliopiston kirjasto (Finnish—Helsinki University Library)
hyl (Hyl) hydroxylysine
hyla hybrid language assembler
HYMA Hebrew Young Men's Association
hymnol hymnologist; hymnology
Hymn of Praise Mendelssohn's Symphony No. 2 in B-flat major (also known as *Lobgesang*)
hynmm have you not made a mistake
hyp hyperbola; hyperbolic; hyphen; hyphenate; hyphenation; hypochondria(c); hypothesis; hypothetical
hyp (Hyp) 4-hydroxyproline
Hyp Hypolite
HYP Harvard, Yale, and Princeton
hype high performance (bullet); hyperbole; hypertension; hypodermic (underground slang —person who injects drugs with a hypodermic syringe)

hyper hypercritical
hyper (Latin prefix—above, beyond, excessive)—hypercritical
hyperb hyperbole; hyperbolic
hyperdip hyperdiploid(al); hyperdiploidy
hyperdop hyperbolic doppler
hypersex hypersexual(ity)
hypert hypertape (flow chart); hypertension
hypn hypertension
hypno hypnotism
hypnot hypnotic; hypnotism; hypnotist
hypo hypochondria; hypochondriac; hypochondriacal; hypodermic (injection or needle); hyposulfite of soda (sodium thiosulfate—NaS_2O_3 $5H_2O$)
hypo (Latin prefix—below or under)—hypodermic
hypodip hypodiploid(al); hypodiploidy
hypoth hypothesis
hypro hydroxyproline
Hyrcanian Caspian
hys hysteria; hysteric; hysterical; hysterics
HYSAS Hydrofluidic Stability Augmentation System
hyst hysteresis; hysteria
hystad hydrofoil stabilizing device
hyster hysterectomy
hysterec hysterectomic (sterilization); hysterectomy (removal of the uterus)
HYSTU Hydrofoil Special Trials Unit (USN)
HYSURCH Hydrographic Survey and Charting System
hytemco high-temperature coefficient nickel-iron alloy
hy tr heat treat
hyv's high-yielding varieties (of grain)
hz haze; heritability zone; herpes zoster
hz (Hz) hertz (one cycle per second); hertzian
Hz Henriquez; hertz (cycles per second)
Hzk Hezekiah
hzy hazy

I

i angle of incidence (symbol); incisor; indigo; infant(icide); instantaneous current (symbol); interceptor; interest; intransitive; isotopic fine structure (symbol); moment of photographic plate (symbol); optically inactive (symbol); rate of interest (symbol); Van't Hoff factor (symbol); vapor pressure constant (symbol)

i (I) inversion (12-tone matrix)

i' in

i Imperial Savings

i. id (Latin—that)

I acoustic intensity (symbol); candlepower or intensity of luminosity (symbol); conduction current (symbol); convection current (symbol); Ido (artificial language); in; inclination; Independent; India—code for letter I; Indian; industrial broadcasting; inertia; infantry; Inspector; Institute; Institution; Instructor; Intelligence; iodine; ionic strength (symbol); Ireland; Irish; Island; Isthmian Line; Italian Line; Italy—auto plaque; izzard

I (*I*) investment (macroeconomics symbol)

I Ile (French—Island, Isle); *in* (German or Italian—in); *inde* (Danish—in); *Isle* (French—island); *itä* (Finnish—east); *izquierda* (Spanish—left)

I^{128} radioactive iodine

I^{130} radioactive iodine

I^{131} radioactive iodine

I^{2}L integrated-injection logic

ia immediately available; impedance angle; indicated altitude; infra-audible; initial allowance; initial appearance; international angstrom; intra-arterial; intra-articular

i & a indexing and abstracting; integration and assembly

i.a. in absentia (Latin—in the absence of)

i A im Auftrage (German—by order, for, under instruction)

Ia Ingegerda

IA Incorporated Accountant; Indian Army; Industrial Arts; Infected Area; Inspection Administration; Institute of Actuaries; Instructional Aide; Internal Affairs; International Angstrom; Iraqi Airways; Irrigation Area

I/A Insurance Auditor; Isle of Anglesey

I of A Inspector of Anatomy; Institute of Accountants; Institute of Acoustics; Instructor of Artillery

IA International Atlas (Rand McNally)

IAA Independent Airlines Association; Indian Association of America; Inspector Army Aircraft; Insurance Accountants Association; Interment Association of America; International Academy of Astronautics; International Acetylene Association; International Advertising Association; International Apple Association; International Association of Allergology; Intimate Apparel Associates; Inventors Association of Australia

IAA Instituto do Acuar e do Alcool (Portuguese—Sugar and Alcohol Institute); *International Aerospace Abstracts*

IAAA Institute of Air Age Activities; International Airforwarders and Agents Association

IAAAA Intercollegiate Association of Amateur Athletes of America

IAAB Inter-American Association of Broadcasters

IAABA International Association of Aircraft Brokers and Agents

IAAC International Agriculture Aviation Center; International Antarctic Analysis Center

IAACC Inter-Allied Aeronautical Control Commission

IAAE Institution of Automotive and Aeronautical Engineers

IAAER International Association for the Advancement of Educational Research

IAAF International Amateur Athletic Federation

IAAFA Inter-American Air Force Academy

IAAHU International Association of Accident and Health Underwriters

IAAI International Airports Authority of India; International Association of Arson Investigators

IAALD International Association of Agricultural Librarians and Documentalists

IAAM International Association of Auditorium Managers; International Association of Automotive Modelers

IAANZ Institute of Actuaries of Australia and New Zealand

IAAO Interlochen Arts Academy Orchestra; International Association of Assessing Officers

IAAOPA International Association of Aircraft Owners and Pilots Associations

IAAP International Association of Applied Psychology

IAAPEA International Associations Against Painful Experiments on Animals

IAAS Institute of Advanced Arab Studies; International Association of Agricultural Students

IAASE Inter-American Association of Sanitary Engineering

IAASS International Association of Applied Social Science

iab increasing assurance benefits

IAB Industry Advisory Board; Inter-American Bank; International Air Bahama; International Association of Bureaucrats

IABA Inter-American Bar Association

IABBE International Association for Better Basic Education

IABC International Association of Business Communicators

IABG International Association of Botanic Gardens

IAB-ICSU International Abstracting Board—International Council of Scientific Unions

IABLA Inter-American Bank for Latin America; Inter-American Bibliographical and Library Association

IABO International Association of Biological Oceanography

IABPAI International Association of Blue Print & Allied Industries

IABPC International Association of Book Publishing Consultants

IABSE International Association for Bridge and Structural Engineering

IABSIW International Association of Bridge and Structural Iron Workers

IABTI International Association of Bomb Technicians and Investigators

iac integrating assembly contractor; integration, assembly, checkout; interview after combat

IAC Ibrahim Ali Commission (Malaysia); Indian Airlines Corporation; Industrial Arbitration Court; Industry Advisory Commission; Industry Assistance Commission; Information Analysis Center; Insurance Advertising Conference; Intelligence Advisory Committee (CIA); Intermediate Air Command; Interview After Combat; Irish Air Corps

IACA Independent Air Carriers Association; Inter-American College Association

IACB Indian Arts and Crafts Board; International Advisory Committee on Bibliography (UNESCO); International Association of Convention Bureaus

IACC International Anti-Counterfeiting Coalition; Italy-America Chamber of Commerce

IACC *Instituto Argentino de Control de la Calidad* (Spanish —Argentine Institute for Quality Control)

IACCI International Association of Credit Card Investigators

IACCP Inter-American Council of Commerce and Production

IACD International Association of Clothing Designers

IACDLA International Advisory Committee on Documentation, Libraries, and Archives (UNESCO)

IACE International Air Cadet Exchange

IACES International Air Cushion Engineering Society

IACHR Inter-American Commission on Human Rights

IACI Inter-American Childrens Institute; Irish-American Cultural Institute

IACID Inter-American Center for Integral Development

IACM International Association of Circulation Managers; International Association of Concert Managers

IACOMS International Advisory Committee on Marine Sciences (FAO)

IACP International Association of Chiefs of Police

IACP & AP International Association for Child Psychiatry and Allied Professions

IACRL Italian-American Civil Rights League

IACS International Annealed Copper Standard; International Association of Cooking Schools; International Asso-

ciation of Counseling Services; Irish-Australian Cultural Society

IACT Illinois Association of Classroom Teachers; Indiana Association of Cities and Towns

IACTE Iowa Association of Colleges for Teacher Education

IACUSD International Association of College and University Security Directors

IACVB International Association of Convention and Visitor Bureaus

IACW Inter-American Commission for Women

iad initiation area discriminator; installation, assembly, or detail; intergrated automatic documentation

IAD Dulles International Airport (Washington, DC); Integrated Area Development; Internal Affairs Department; Internal Affairs Division (LAPD and NYPD); International Agricultural Distribution; International Astrophysical Decade—1965–1975

IADB Inter-American Defense Board; Inter-American Development Bank

IADC Inter-American Defense College; International Association of Dredging Companies

IADF Inter-American Association for Democracy and Freedom

IADIS Irish Association for Documentation and Information Services

iadl (IADL) instrumental activities of daily living

IADL International Association of Democratic Lawyers; Italian-American Defense League

IADO Iranian Agriculture Development Organization

IADPC Inter-Agency Data Processing Committee

IADR International Association for Dental Research

IADS Integrated Air Defense System; International Association of Dental Students; International Association of Department Stores

iadt initial active duty training

iae in any event; integral absolute error

IAE Institute of Army Education; Institute of Automobile Engineers; Institution of Automobile Engineers; International Animal Exchange

IAE Institut Atomnoi Energii (Russian—Atomic Energy Institute)

IAeA Institution of Aeronautical Engineers

IAEA Inter-American Education Association; International Association for Educational Assessment; International Atomic Energy Agency

IAEC Israel Atomic Energy Commission

IAECOSOC Inter-American Economic and Social Council

IAEE International Association of Earthquake Engineers

IAEI International Association of Electrical Inspectors

IAEL International Association of Electrical Leagues

IAES International Association of Electrotypers and Stereotypers

IAESP Indiana Association of Elementary School Principals; Iowa Association of Elementary School Principals

IAESTE International Association for the Exchange of Students for Technical Experience

IAET In-Flight Aeromedical Evacuation Team

IAEVG International Association for Educational and Vocational Guidance

IAEWP International Association of Educators for World Peace

iaf immobilizing accelerating factor; interview after flight

IAF Industrial Areas Foundation; Inter-American Foundation; International Abolitionist Federation (for abolition of prostitution); International Association of Firefighters; International Astronautical Federation; Israeli Air Force

I-AF Inter-American Foundation

IAFAE Inter-American Federation for Adult Education

IAFC International Association of Fire Chiefs

iafd intentionally administered fatal dose(s)

IAFD International Association of Food Distribution

IAFE International Association of Fairs and Expositions

IAFF Institute of Australian Flora and Fauna; International Association of Fire Fighters

iafi infantile amaurotic family idiocy

IAFMM International Association of Fish Meal Manufacturers

IAFV Infantry Armed Fighting Vehicle

IAFWNO Inter-American Federation of Working Newspapermen's Organizations

IAG Institute of Australian Geographers; Interagency Advisory Group; International Association of Geodesy; International Association of Gerontology

IAGA International Association of Geomagnetism and Aeronomy

IAGB & I Ileostomy Association of Great Britain and Ireland

iagc instantaneous automatic gain control

IAGC International Association for Geochemistry and Cosmochemistry

IAGFCC International Association of Game, Fish, and Conservation Commissioners

IAGLP International Association of Great Lakes Ports

IAGM International Association of Garment Manufacturers

I Agr E Institution of Agricultural Engineers

IAGS Inter-American Geodetic Survey

IAH Houston International Airport (Texas); Inter-American Highway; International Asian Highways; International Association of Hydrology

IAHA Inter-American Hotel Association

IAHF International Aerospace Hall of Fame

IAHIC International Association of Home Improvement Councils

IAHM International Association of Head Masters

IAHP Institutes for the Achievement of Human Potential; International Association of Horticultural Producers

IAHR International Association for Hydraulic Research

IAHS International Association of Hydrological Sciences

IAI Icelandic Airlines Incorporated; International African Institute; International Association for Identification

IAI-201 Israeli Arava light transport plane

IAIA Institute of American Indian Arts

IAIAS Inter-American Institute of Agricultural Sciences

IAICM International Association of Ice Cream Manufacturers

IAIE Inter-American Institute of Ecology

IAII Inter-American Indian Institute

IAIs Israeli Aircraft Industries

IAIS Industrial Aerodynamics Information Service (UK)

ial initial; initial appearance; initialism; instrument approach and landing; interlaminar adhesive layer; international algebraic language

IAL Icelandic Airlines; Imperial Airways Limited; International Aeradio Limited; International Algebraic Language; International Arbitration League; International Association of Limnology; Irish Academy of Letters

IAL Icelandic Airlines-Loftleider

IALA International Association of Lighthouse Authorities

IALC International Association of Lions Clubs; International Association of Lyceum Clubs

IALL International Association of Law Libraries

i allg im allgemeinen(German—generally, in general)

IALS International Association of Legal Science

iam interactive algebraic manipulation

IAM Institute of Appliance Manufacturers; Institute of Aviation Medicine; International Academy of Medicine; International Association of Machinists; International Association of Meteorology

IAMA International Abstaining Motorists Association

IAMAM International Association of Museums of Arms and Military History

IAMAP International Association of Meteorology and Atmospheric Physics

IAMAT International Association for Medical Assistance to Travelers

IAMAW International Association of Machinists and Aerospace Workers

IAMB International Association of Microbiologists

IAMC Institute for Advancement of Medical Communication; Inter-American Music Council

IAMCA International Association of Milk Control Agencies

IAMCL International Association of Metropolitan City Libraries

IAMCR International Association for Mass Communication Research

IAMFE International Association on Mechanization of Field Experiments

IAMFS International Association of Milk and Food Sanitarians

IAML International Association of Music Libraries

IAMLT International Association of Medical Laboratory Technologists

IAMM International Association of Master Mariners; International Association of Medical Museums

IAMO Inter-American Municipal Organization

IAMP Inter-Agency Motor Pool

IAMPTH International Association of Master Penmen and Teachers of Handwriting

IAMR Institute of Arctic Mineral Resources

IAMS International Association of Microbiological Societies; International Association of Municipal Statisticians

IAMSO Inter-African and Malagasy States Organization

IAMTCT Institute of Advanced Machine Tool and Control Technology

IAMTF Inter-Agency Maritime Task Force

IAMWF Inter-American Mine Workers Federation

Ian (Gaelic—John)

IAN *Instituto Agrario Nacional* (Spanish—National Agrarian Institute)

IANA Inter-African News Agency

IANAP Interagency Noise Abatement Program

IANC International Airline Navigators Council

IA & ND Indian Affairs and Northern Development (Canada)

IANEC Inter-American Nuclear Energy Commission

Ian F Ian Fleming

IANSA *Industria Azucarera Nacional SA* (Spanish—National Sugar Industry Corporation)

IANSW Institute of Architects of New South Wales

iao intermittent aortic occlusion

IAO Incorporated Association of Organists

IAOC Indian Army Ordnance Corps

IAOL International Association of Orientalist Libraries

IAOR *International Abstracts in Operations Research*

IAOS International Association of Oral Surgeons; Irish Agricultural Organization Society

IAOT International Association of Organ Teachers

iap interceptor aim point(s)

IAP Institute of Agricultural Parasitology; Institute of Australian Photographers; Institute of Australian Photography; Institution of Analysts & Programmers; International Academy of Pathology; International Academy of Proctology

IAPA Inter-American Parliamentary Association; Inter-American Parliamentary Organization; Inter-American Police Academy; Inter-American Press Association; International Association of Police Artists

IAPB International Association for the Prevention of Blindness

IAPC Institute for the Advancement of Philosophy for Children; International Association of Political Consultants; International Association for Public Cleansing

IAPCO International Association of Professional Congress Organizers

IAPCU Iowa Association of Private Colleges and Universities

IAPESGW International Association of Physical Education and Sports for Girls and Women

IAPG Interagency Advanced Power Group; International Association of Physical Geography

IAPH International Association of Paper Historians; International Association of Ports and Harbors

IAPHA International Associa-

tion of Port and Harbor Authorities

IAPHC International Association of Printing House Craftsmen

IAPI Institute of American Poultry Industries; Instituto Argentino de Producción Industrial (Argentine Industrial Production Institute)

IAPIP International Association for the Protection of Industrial Property

IAPL International Association of Penal Law

IAPM International Academy of Preventive Medicine; International Association of Progressive Montessorians

IAPN International Association of Professional Numismatists

IAPO International Association of Physical Oceanography

IAPP International Association of Police Professors

IAPPW International Association of Pupil Personnel Workers

IAPR Indian Air Patrol Reserve

iaps inductosyn angle position simulator

IAPs Industry Application Programs

IAPS Incorporated Association of Preparatory Schools; International Affiliation of Planning Societies; International Association for the Properties of Steam

IAPSC Inter-African Phytosanitary Commission

IAPSO International Association of Physical Sciences of the Oceans

IAPT International Association for Plant Taxonomy

IAPTA International Allied Printing Trades Association

IAPW International Association of Personnel Women

IAQ Independent Activities Questionnaire

IAQR Indian Association for Quality and Reliability

iar intersection of air routes

IAR Institute for Air Research

IARA Inter-Allied Reparations Agency

I Arb Institute of Arbitrators

IARC International Agency for Research on Cancer

IARD Information Analysis and Retrieval Division (American Institute of Physics)

IARF International Association

for Liberal Christianity and Religious Freedom

IARI Industrial Advertising Research Institute

IARIGAI International Association of Research Institutes for the Graphic Arts Industry

IARIW International Association for Research into Income and Wealth

IARP Indian Association for Radiation Protection; Inflation Accounting Research Project

IARQ Intellectual Achievement Responsibility Questionnaire

IARS International Anesthesia Research Society

IARSS Illinois Association of Regional Superintendents of Schools

IARU International Amateur Radio Union

ias immediate access storage; indicated airspeed; instrument approach system

IAS Industrial Arbitration Service; Institute for Advanced Study; Institute of the Aeronautical Sciences; Institute of Aerospace Sciences; Institute of American Strategy; Institute of Andean Studies; Instrument Approach System; Intelligent Authoring Systems; International Accountants Society; International Association of Siderographers; International Aviation Service

IASA Idaho Association of School Administrators, Illinois Association of School Administrators, Insurance Accounting and Statistical Association; International Air Safety Association; International Association of Sound Archives; Iowa Association of School Administrators

IASB Iowa Association of School Boards

IASBO Indiana Association of School Business Officials; Iowa Association of School Business Officials

IASC Inter-American Safety Council; International Association of Seed Crushers

IASCH Institute for Advanced Studies in Contemporary History (formerly Wiener Library)

iasd interatrial septal defect

IASDI Inter-American Social Development Institute

IASG Inflation Accounting

Steering Group

IASH International Association of Scientific Hydrology

IASI Inter-American Statistical Institute

IASL Illinois Association of School Librarians; International Association for the Study of the Liver; International Association of School Librarians; Irish Association of School Librarians

IASLIC Indian Association of Special Libraries and Information Centers

iasor ice and snow on runway

IASP International Association for Social Progress; International Association for Suicide Prevention; International Association of Scholarly Publishers

IASPEI International Association of Seismology and Physics of the Earth's Interior

IASPO International Association of Senior Police Officers

IASPS International Association for Statistics in Physical Sciences

IASS Insurance Accounting and Statistical Society; International Association for Shell Structures

IASSS International Association for Shell and Spatial Structures

IASSW International Association of Schools of Social Work

iasy international active sun years

iat inside air temperature

IAT Individual Acceptance Test(ing); Institute for Applied Technology; Institute of Atomic Physics (Peking); International Academy of Tourism

IATA International Air Transport Association

iatc inlet air temperature control

IATC International Association of Tool Craftsmen

iatd is amended to delete

IATE Illinois Association of Teachers of English; International Association for Television Editors; International Association for Temperance Education

IATL International Association of Theological Libraries

IATM International Association for Testing Materials

IATME International Association of Terrestrial Magnetism and Electricity

IATP Individual Aircraft Tracking Program

iatr is amended to read

IATSE International Alliance of Theatrical Stage Employees

IATTC Inter-American Tropical Tuna Commission

IATUL International Association of Technical University Libraries

iau intrusion alarm unit

IAU International Association of Universities; International Astronomical Union

IAUPE International Association of University Professors of English

IAUPL International Association of University Professors and Lecturers

IAUPPR Inter-American University Press of Puerto Rico

IAUPR Inter-American University of Puerto Rico

IAV International Association of Volcanology

IAVA Industrial Audio-Visual Association

iavc instantaneous automatic volume control

IAVCEI International Association of Volcanology and Chemistry of the Earth's Interior

IAVE Interaction Analysis for Vocational Educators

IAVFH International Association of Veterinary Food Hygienists

IAVG International Association for Vocational Guidance

IAVRS International Audiovisual Resource Service (UNESCO)

IAVTC International Audio-Visual Technical Center

iaw in accordance with

IAW International Alliance of Women

IAWA International Association of Wood Anatomists

IAWL International Association for Water Law

IAWMC International Association of Workers for Maladjusted Children

IAWP International Association of Women Police

IAWPR International Association on Water Pollution Research

IAWS Intercollegiate Association for Women Students;

Irish Agricultural Wholesale Society

IA WWW International Authors and Writers Who's Who

IAZ Inner Artillery Zone

ib in bond; illegal behavior; inbound; incendiary bomb; inclusion body; index of body build; infectious bronchitis; inner bottom; instruction book; instructional brochure; invoice book(let); inward bound

i & b improvements and betterments

ib. ibidem (Latin—in the same place)

i b im besonderen (German—in particular)

Ib Ibadan

IB Iberia Líneas Aéreas de España (Iberian Airlines of Spain); Imperial Bank; incendiary bomb; Infantry Battalion; Information Bulletin; Information Bureau; Intelligence Branch; International Bank(ing); international broadcast(ing)

I of B Institute of Bankers; Institute of Biology

IB Istanbul Bankasi (Turkish—Istanbul Bank)

IBA Independent Bankers Association; Independent Bar Association; Independent Broadcasting Association; Independent Broadcasting Authority (United Kingdom); Institute for Bioenergetic Analysis; Institute of British Architects; International Bar Association; International Briqueting Association; Investing Builders Association; Investment Bankers Association

IBAA Investment Bankers Association of America; Italian Baptist Association of America

Ibadan (Hausa—Between Forest and Savannah)—Nigeria's capital and world's largest black city

IBAE Institution of British Agricultural Engineers

IBAHP Inter-African Bureau for Animal Health and Protection

IBAM Institute of Business Administration and Management

IBAP Intervention Board for Agricultural Produce

I-bar capital-I-shaped metal bar

IBAR Inter-African Bureau of

Animal Resources

IBAS Indonesian Business Association of Singapore

IBAU Institute of British-American Understanding

ibb intentional bases on balls (baseball)

IBB Illinois Inspection Bureau; International Bowling Board; International Brotherhood of Bookbinders

IBBD Instituto Brasileiro de Bibliografía e Documentação (Brazilian Institute of Bibliography and Documentation)

IBBISBBFH International Brotherhood of Boilermakers, Iron Ship Builders, Blacksmiths, Forgers, and Helpers

ibbm iron body bronze (or brass) mounted

IBBY International Board on Books for Young People

ibc (IBC) intermediate bulk carrier; intermediate bulk container

IBC Insurance Bureau of Canada; International Biographical Centre; International Broadcasting Corporation; Iwate Broadcasting Company (Japan)

IBC Instituto Brasileiro do Café (Portuguese—Brazilian Coffee Institute)

IBCs Institutional Biosafety Committees

IBCS Integrated Battlefield Control System (USA)

IBCUSCAN International Boundary Commission, United States and Canada

ibd interest-bearing debentures; interest-bearing deposit

IBD Institute of British Decorators; International Bank of Detroit

ibda indirect bomb damage assessment

ibe integrity basis earthquake; inventory by exception

IBE Institute of British Engineers; International Bureau of Education

I-beam capital-I-shaped metal beam

IBEC International Bank for Economic Cooperation; International Basic Economy Corporation

IBECC Instituto Brasileiro de Educação Ciencia e Cultura

IBEG International Book Export Group

iben incendiary bomb with explosive nose

Iber Iberia(n); Iberic(a)(n); Iberville

Iberia (Greek—Spain); peninsula containing Portugal and Spain; romantic name for Spain

IBERIA Líneas Aéreas de España (Iberian Airlines of Spain)

IBERLANT Iberian Atlantic

ibes integrated building and equipment scheduling

IBES Illinois Bureau of Employment Security

IBEW International Brotherhood of Electrical Workers

ibf internally blown flap

IBF Institute of Banking and Finance; Institute of British Foundrymen

IBFD International Bureau of Fiscal Documentation

IBFI International Business Forms Industries

IBFMP International Bureau of the Federations of Master Printers

IBFO International Brotherhood of Firemen and Oilers

IBFs International Banking Facilities

ibg inter-block gap

IBG Institute of British Geographers

IBHA Insulation, Building, and Hardwood Association

IBhd initial beachhead

IBHE Illinois Board of Higher Education

ibi invoice book, inward

IBI Illinois Bureau of Investigation; Indiana Bureau of Investigation; Insulation Board Institute

IBI Instituto Bancario Italiano (Italian Banking Institute)

ibid. international bibliographical description

ibid. ibidem (Latin—in the same place)

IBiol Institute of Biology

IBIS International Book Information Service

Ibiza (Spanish—Ibiza)—in the Balearic Islands

IBJ Industrial Bank of Japan

IBK Institute of Bookkeepers

IBK Institut für Bauen mit Kunststoffen (German—Institute for Building with Plastics)

ibkr icebreaker

IBL Institute of British Launderers; Irish Biscuits Limited

ibm (IBM) intercontinental ballistic missile

IBM Institute for Burn Medicine; International Business Machines

IBM Industrias Biologicas Mexicana (Spanish—Mexican Biological Industries)

IBMA Independent Battery Manufacturers Association

IBM JRD IBM Journal of Research and Development

IBMR International Bureau for Mechanical Reproduction

ibn identification beacon

IBN Institut Belge de Normalisation (French—Belgian Standards Institute)

ibnr incurred but not reported

ibo invoice book, outward

IBO International Baccalaureate Office

I-boats Japanese transport submarines used in World War II to carry small scouting airplanes

IBOB International Brotherhood of Old Bastards

ibol integrated business-oriented language

Ibop (IBOP) international balance of payments

IBOP International Brotherhood of Operative Potters; International Business Opportunity Program

ibp initial boiling point

IBP Institute of British Photographers; International Biological Program; Iowa Beef Processors

IBPAT International Brotherhood of Painters and Allied Trades (U.S. and Canada)

IBPI International Bureau for Protection and Investigation

IBPOEW Improved Benevolent and Protective Order of Elks of the World

ibp's imperial belch pills (nonfattening diet-reduction capsules produced in five favorite flavors—bacon and eggs, chocolate soda with vanilla ice cream, seafood dinner, steak-'n'-potatoes, strawberry shortcake)—users enjoy flavored belch while avoiding preparation and cleanup costs as well as weight-increasing after effects detrimental to the full life

ibr information-bearing radiation; integral boiling reactor

ibr (IBR) infectious bovine rhinotracheitis

IBR Institute of Behavioral Research; Institute of Biosocial Research

IBRA International Bible Reading Association

IBRD International Bank for Reconstruction and Development (World Bank)

ibrl initial bomb-release line

IBRM Institute of Boiler and Radiator Manufacturers

IBRMR Institute for Basic Research on Mental Retardation

IBRO International Bank Research Organization; International Brain Research Organization; International Brewers' Research Organization

ibs inflatable boat, small; international belt skimmer (for cleaning oil slicks)

ibs (IBS) ionospheric beacon satellite; irritable bowel syndrome

IBS Ibaraki Broadcasting System; Indian Boy Scouts; Institute of Basic Standards; Institute of Biblical Studies; Intercollegiate Broadcasting System; International Bach Society; International Bank of Singapore; Israel Broadcasting Service

IBSA International Barber Schools Association; International Bible Student Association

IBSC Iranian-British Shipping Company

IB Scot Institute of Bankers in Scotland

IBSGR Isiolo Buffalo Spring Game Reserve (Kenya)

ibsr individual base stock requirements; individual battle shooting range

IBSS Imperial Bureau of Soil Science

IBST Institute of British Surgical Technicians

IBSTP International Bureau for the Suppression of Traffic in Persons

ibt in-barrel time; initial boiling-point temperature

IBT Industrial Bio-Test (laboratories); International Brotherhood of Teamsters

IBTA International Baton Twirlers Association

IBTCWH International Brotherhood of Teamsters, Chauffeurs, Warehousemen, and Helpers

IBTCWHA International Brotherhood of Teamsters, Chauffeurs, Warehousemen, and Helpers of America

ib test inkblot test (Rorschach test)

IBTS International Bicycle Touring Society

IBTTA International Bridge, Tunnel, and Turnpike Association

ibu imperial bushel

IBU Inland Boatmen's Union; International Broadcasting Union

ibv infectious bronchitis vaccine

IBVL Instituut voor Bewaring van Landbowprodukten (Dutch—Institute for Storing and Processing Agricultural Products)

ibw information bandwidth

IBW International Boiler Works

IBWCUSMEX International Boundary and Water Commission, United States and Mexico

IBWM International Bureau of Weights and Measures

IBWS International Bureau of Whaling Statistics

ibx (IBX) intermediate branch exchange

IBY International Book Year (1972)

Ibz Ibiza

ic in calf; in charge of; in command; ice crystals; index correction; informal communication; inspected and condemned; inspiratory capacity; inspiratory center; instruction counter; instrument correction; integrated circuit; interference control; interior communication; intermediate language; internal classification; internal combustion; internal communication; internal connection; international control; interstitial cells; intracerebral; intracutaneous

ic. *icon* (Latin—figure, woodcut)

i-c integrated circuit

i/c in charge; in command; ice cream; intercom (intercommunication via interphone)

i&c inspected and condemned

i & c installation and checkout; installation and construction; instrumentation and control

i.c. inter cibos (Latin—between meals)

Ic Iceland; Icelander; Icelandic

IC Idaho College; Identity Card; Ignatius College; Illinois Central (railroad); Illinois College;

Immaculata College; Industrial Court; Information Center; Information Circular; integrated circuit; Integrating Contractor; Intelligence Corps; Interchemical Corporation; Intercity; International Control; International Control; Iola College; Iona College; Itaska College; Itawamba College; Item Code; Ithaca College

I-C Indo-China; Indo-Chine; Indo-Chinese

I.C. *Iesus Christus* (Latin—Jesus Christ); Institute of Charity (Rosminian)

I & C Ictinus and Callicrates (designers of the Parthenon)

IC 4-A Intercollegiate Amateur Athletic Association of America

ica ignition control additive; Imperial Corporation of America; Institute of Contemporary Arts; instrument compressed air

ICA Illinois Correctional Association; Imperial Corporation of America; Indiana Correctional Association; Industrial Communication Association; Industrial Coordination Act; Institute of Chartered Accountants; Institute of Contemporary Arts; Institute of Criminal Anthropology; Insurance Council of Australia; Intermuseum Conservation Association; International Chefs' Association; International Chiropractors Association; International Claims Association; International Coffee Agreement; International Commodity Agreement; International Communication Agency; International Communication Association; International Communications Agency; International Cooperative Administration; International Cooperative Alliance; International Cooperative Association; International Council on Archives; Iowa Corrections Association

I of CA Institute of Chartered Accountants

ICA *Ingenieros Civiles Asociados* (Spanish—Civil Engineers Associated)

icaa integrated cost-accounting application(s)

ICAA Institute of Chartered Accountants of Australia; Inter-

national Council on Alcohol and Addictions; Invalid Children's Aid Association; Investment Counsel Association of America

ICAAAA Intercollegiate Association of Amateur Athletes of America

ICAB International Council Against Bullfighting

ICAC Independent Commission Against Corruption (in Hong Kong)

icad integrated control and display

icade interactive computer-aided design evaluation

icadg interactive computer-aided design and graphics

ICADS Integrated Control and Display System

ICAE International Commission on Agricultural Engineering; International Council for Adult Education

ICAESD International Center for African Economic and Social Documentation

ICAEW Institute of Chartered Accountants in England and Wales

ICAF Industrial College of the Armed Forces; International Committee on Aeronautical Fatigue

ICAFI International Commission on Agriculture and Food Industries

ICAI Institute of Chartered Accountants in Ireland; International Commission of Agricultural Industries

ICAITI *Instituto Centroamericano de Investigacion y Tecnologia Industrial* (Spanish—Central American Institute of Industrial Investigation and Technology)

ICAM Institute of Corn and Agricultural Merchants

I Can Information Canada

ICAN International Commission for Air Navigation

ICAO International Civil Aviation Organization

ICAP Institute of Certified Ambulance Personnel; Integrated Criminal Apprehension Program (computerized system seeking out criminals by the types of crimes they commit); Inter-American Committee of the Alliance for Progress; International Civil Aviation Policy

ICAP *Instituto Cubano de Amis-*

tad con los Pueblos (Spanish—Cuban Institute for Friendship with Peoples)—Castro-controlled

ICAPR Interdepartmental Committee on Air Pollution Research (UK)

ICAPS Integrated Carrier Acoustic Prediction System (for aircraft carriers)

ICAR International Committee Against Racism

ICARMO International Council of the Architects of Historical Monuments

I-car(s) Italian car(s)

Icarus *International Journal of the Solar System*

icas intermittent commercial and amateur service

ICAS Institute for Chartered Accountants in Scotland; Interdepartmental Committee for Atmospheric Sciences; Intermittent Commercial and Amateur Service; International Council of the Aeronautical Sciences; International Council of Aerospace Sciences

ICASALS International Center for Arid and Semi-Arid Land Studies

ICASB Iowa Council of Area School Boards

ICATS Intermediate-Capacity Automated Telecommunications System (USAF)

icav intracavity

icb interlocking concrete block; international competitive bid; international competitive bidding

ICB Indian Coffee Board; Industrial and Commercial Bank(ing); Institute of Collective Bargaining; Institute of Comparative Biology; Interface Control Board; International City Bank; International Container Bureau

ICBA International Community of Booksellers Associations

ICBC Insurance Corporation of British Columbia; International Commercial Bank of China

ICBIF Inner-City Business Improvement Forum

icbm (ICBM) intercontinental ballistic missile

ICBO Interracial Council for Business Opportunities

icbp intracellular binding proteins

ICBP International Council for Bird Preservation

ICBR Institute for Child Behavior Research

ICBS Interconnected Business System; International Call-Boy Service (for women)

icbt intercontinental ballistic transport

icc improved contemporary comparison; integrated circuit computer; international catalog card (3 x 5 inches or 7.5 x 12.5 centimeters); intra-company correspondence

ic & c invoice cost and charges

ICC Indian Claims Commission; Instrumentation Control Center; International Chamber of Commerce; International Control Commission; International Correspondence Course(s); Interstate Commerce Commission

I.C.C. Isthmian Canal Commission

icca initial cash clothing allowance

ICCA Infants' and Children's Coat Association; International Congress and Convention Association; International Consumer Credit Association; International Corrugated Case Association

ICCAD International Center for Computer-Aided Design

ICCAT International Commission for the Conservation of Atlantic Tunas

ICCB Illinois Community College Board

ICCC International Center for Comparative Criminology

iccd internal coordination control drawing

ICCD Information Center on Crime and Delinquency

ICCF International Correspondence Chess Federation

ICCI Inter-Continental Computing Incorporated

ICCO International Carpet Classification Organization

ICCP International Conference on Cataloguing Principles

ICCR Indian Council for Cultural Relations; International Charge Card Registry

ICCS International Center of Criminological Studies

ICCSL International Commission of the Cape Spartel Light

ICCTA Illinois Community College Trustees Association

IC & CY Inns of Court and City Yeomanry

icd immune complex disease; interface control document; interface control drawing; investment certificate of deposit (ICD)

ic & d installation, checkout, and demonstration

ICD Industrial Cooperation Division; Industry Cooperation Division; Inland Clearance Depot; Inland Container Depot; Institute for the Crippled and Disabled; International College of Dentists; International Cooperative Distributors

ICD International Classification of Diseases

ICDA International Classification of Diseases, Adapted for Use in the United States

icdh (ICDH) isocitric dehydrogenase

ICDO International Civil Defense Organization

ICDRG International Contact Dermatitis Research Group

icd's investment certificates of deposit

ICDS Information Collection Dissemination System

ice. in-car entertainment; increased combat effectiveness; input-checking equipment; instruction-curriculum environment; internal combustion engine; inventory control effectiveness

Ice Iceland; Icelander; Icelandic

ICE Institution of Chemical Engineers; Institution of Civil Engineers; Instituto Costarricense de Electricidad (Costa Rican Electric Institute); Instruction-Course Evaluation; Instructor Course Evaluation; International Cultural Exchange

Iceberg Alley North Atlantic Ocean between Greenland and Labrador where icebergs float down from the Arctic and endanger ships

ICEC Illinois Citizens Education Council

ICECAP Infrared Chemistry Experiments—Coordinated Auroral Program (DoD)

ICED International Council for Educational Development

ICEED International Center for Energy and Economic Development

ICEF International Children's Emergency Fund; International Council for Educational Films

ICEG Insulated Conductors'

Export Group

ICEI International Combustion Engine Institute

Icel Icelandic

ICEL International Committee on English in the Liturgy; International Council of Environmental Law

Iceland Republic of Iceland (Icelandic-speaking island nation in the North Atlantic where it is noted for its fishery and its parliament—the Althing or Old Thing begun in 930 A.D.) *Lydveldio Island*

Icelandic Ports (small ports from west to north to east to south) Reykjavik, Seydhisfjordhur, Heimaey, Eyrarbakki

Iceland spar calcite (calcium carbonate)

ICEM International Commission for European Migration

Ice Mine City Coudersport, Pennsylvania

icepack. individual career exploration pack(age)

ICEPS International Center for Economic Policy Studies

ICER Information Centre of the European Railways

I Ceram Institute of Ceramics

ICEs International Customs Examinations

ICES Instructor and Course Evaluation System; Integrated Civil Engineering Systems; International Council for the Exploration of the Sea

ICESC Industry Crew Escape Systems Committee

ICET Institute for the Certification of Engineering Technicians; International Center of Economy and Technology; International Council on Education for Teaching

ICETEX Instituto Colombiano de Especialización Tecnica en el Exterior (Spanish—Colombian Institute of Technical Specialization Abroad)

ICETT Industrial Council for Educational and Training Technology

ICEWATER Inter-Agency Committee on Water Resources

icf inertial confinement fusion; intermediate care facilities; intracellular fluid

ICF Ingénieur Civil de France (Civil Engineer of France); Inter-bureau Citation of Funds; International Canoe Federation; International Cynological Federation; Iowa College Foundation

ICFA Independent College Funds of America; International Chicken Flying Association; International Cystic Fibrosis Association

ICFC Industrial and Commercial Finance Corporation

icff intercommunication flip-flop

ICFNC Independent College Fund of North Carolina

ICFNJ Independent College Fund of New Jersey

ICFPW International Confederation of Former Prisoners of War

ICFR Intercollegiate Conference of Faculty Representatives (Big Ten)

ICFTU International Confederation of Free Trade Unions

ICFU International Council on the Future of the University

icg icing

ICG Industries Consultative Group; Interface Coordination Group; International Commission on Glass; International Congress of Genetics; Interviewers Classification Guide; Iowa Corn Growers

ICGB International Cargo Gear Bureau

ICGE International Center of Genetic Epistemology

ICGS Icelandic Coast Guard Service; International Call-Girl Service (Amsterdam)

ich ichthyology; in-calf heifer

ich (ICH) infectious canine hepatitis

Ich Ichabod

ICHAM Institute of Cooking and Heating Appliance Manufacturers

ICHCA International Cargo Handling Coordination Association

IChemE Institute of Chemical Engineers

ICHEO Inter-University Council for Higher Education Overseas

ichnol ichnolite; ichnologist; ichnology

ICHPER International Council for Health, Physical Education, and Recreation

ichs ichthyologists

ICHS International Committee of Historical Sciences

ichth ichthyology

ichthyol ichthyologic(al)(ly); ichthyologist; ichthyology

ICI Imperial Chemical Industries; Institution of Chemistry in Ireland; International Commission on Illumination; Interpersonal Communication Inventory; Investment Casting Institute; Investment Company Institute; Investment Costing Institute

ICIA Interagency Committee on International Athletics; International Credit Insurance Association; International Crop Improvement Association

ICIANZ Imperial Chemical Industries of Australia and New Zealand

ICIAP Interagency Committee on International Aviation Policy

ICIC International Copyrights Information Center

ICID International Commission on Irrigation and Drainage

ICIE International Council of Industrial Editors

ICIECA Interagency Council on International Educational and Cultural Affairs

ICIMP Interagency Committee for International Meteorological Programs

ICIP International Conference on Information Processing

ICIPE International Center for Insect Physiology and Ecology

ICIREPAT International Cooperation in Information Retrieval among Examining Patent Offices

ICIS International Cargo Information System

ICITA International Cooperative Investigation of the Tropical Atlantic

ICITO Interim Commission for the International Trade Organization

ICJ Institute of Creative Judaism; Institute of Criminal Justice; International Commission of Jurists; International Court of Justice

ICJP Irish Commission for Justice and Peace

ICJW International Council of Jewish Women

icky sticky

icl incoming correspondence log(ging); input capacitor-less (circuitry or hi-fidelity)

ICL Institut de Chimie de Lyon; International Computers Limited; International Confedera-

tion of Labor; International Containers Limited

ICLA International Committee on Laboratory Animals

Iclnd Iceland

ICLP Institute of Criminal Law and Procedure (Georgetown University)

ICLS Irish Central Library for Students

icm increased capability missile; intercostal margin; interference control monitor

icm (ICM) increased capability missile

ICM Increased Capability Missile; Indian Campaign Medal; Industrial and Construction Machines; Institute of Computer Management

ICMA International City Manager's Association

ICMF Indian Cotton Mills Federation

ICMPH International Center of Medical and Psychological Hypnosis

icmps induction compass

ICMR Indian Council of Medical Research

ICMREF Interagency Committee on Marine Science, Research, Engineering, and Facilities

ICMs Instructional Curriculum Maps

ICMS International Commission on Mushroom Science

ICMUA International Commission on the Meteorology of the Upper Atmosphere

ICN Instrumentation and Calibration Network; International Chemical and Nuclear (corporation); International Council of Nurses

ICNAF International Commission for the Northwest Atlantic Fisheries

ICND International Commission on Narcotic Drugs

ICNV International Committee on Nomenclature of Viruses

ico in case of; iconology

ICO Immediate Commanding Officer; Immediate Controlling Office(r); Instrumentation Control Office(r); Interagency Committee on Oceanography; International Coffee Organization; International Commission for Optics; International Congress of Ophthalmology; Israel Chamber Orchestra

ICOA International Castor Oil Association

ICOGRADA International Council of Graphic Design Associations

ICOM International Council of Museums

ICOMIA International Council of Marine Industries Associations

icon. iconic; iconoclasm; iconoclast; iconography

Iconoclast English freethought author-lecturer-publisher Charles Bradlaugh who lectured under that pseudonym to escape imprisonment for alleged heresy

Iconoclast Poet Percy Bysshe Shelley

Iconoclasts dramatist-authors Becque, d'Annunzio, Duse, Gorki, Hauptmann, Herpieu, Huneker, Ibsen, Maeterlinck, Shaw, Strindberg, Sudermann

ICONS Information Center on Nuclear Standards; Isotopes of Carbon, Oxygen, Nitrogen, and Sulfur (AEC)

ICOO Iraqi Company for Oil Operations

icop imported crude oil processing

ICOPA International Conference of Police Associations

icor incremental capital-output ratio

ICOR Intergovernmental Conference on Oceanic Research (UNESCO)

I Corr Tech Institution of Corrosion Technology

ICOT Institute of Coastal Oceanography and Tides; Institute for New Generation Computer Technology

icp inventory control point

ICP Industry Cooperative Program; Institut de Chimie de Paris (Chemical Institute of Paris); International Center of Photography; International Commerce Promoters; International Council of Psychologists

ICPA International Commission for the Prevention of Alcoholism; International Conference of Police Associations

ICPC International Criminal Police Commission (Interpol)

ICPCCP Illinois Council of Public Community College Presidents

ICPHS International Council for Philosophical and Humanistic Studies

ICPI Insurance Crime Prevention Institute

i/c/pm/m incisors, canines, premolars, molars (dentition formula, *e.g.*, . i 4/4 means 4 upper and 4 lower incisors, c 2/2 means 2 upper and 2 lower canines, etc.)

icpo intercompany payment orders

ICPO International Criminal Police Organization (Interpol)

ICPP Idaho Chemical Processing Plant (AEC)

ICPS International Congress of Photographic Science; International Credit Protection Services

ICPSR Inter-university Consortium for Political and Social Research

ICQ Invested Capital Questionnaire

icr increase; increment; instrumentation control rack; ion cyclotron resonance

icr (ICR) iron-core reactor

ICR Independent Congo Republic; Institute of Cancer Research; Institute for Cooperative Research; International Council for Reprography

ICRA International Copper Research Association

ICRC International Committee of the Red Cross

ICRDB International Cancer Research Data Bank

ICRF Imperial Cancer Research Fund

ICRH Institute for Computer Research in the Humanities (NYU)

icrm intercontinental reconnaissance missile (ICRM)

ICRM Institute of Certified Records Managers

ICRO International Cell Research Organization

ICRP International Commission on Radiation Protection; International Commission on Radiological Protection

ICRSC International Council for Research in the Sociology of Cooperation

ICRT Individualized Criterion-Referenced Test(ing)

ICRU International Commission on Radiological Units and Measurements

ICRUM International Commission on Radiological Units and Measurements

ics installment credit selling; intercostal space; interim contractor support

ic's immediate constituents; integrated circuits

ic's (ICs) integrated circuits

ICS Indian Civil Service; Information Centers Service; Inner Continental Shelf; Institute of Chartered Shipbuilders; Institution of Computer Sciences; Integrated Command System; Integrated Container Service; Intelligence Community Staff; Interagency Communications System; Inter-Communications System; International Cardiovascular Society; International Chamber of Shipping; International Chamber of Shipping; International Clarinet Society; International College of Surgeons; International Container Service; International Contract Specialists; International Correspondence Schools; International Telephone and Telegraph Communications System; Interway Container Service

ICSA Institute of Chartered Secretaries and Administrators, International Council of Shopping Centers

ICSAC International Confederation of Societies of Authors and Composers

ICSB International Center of School Building

ICSC Independent Colleges of Southern California, Interoceanic Canal Study Commission

ICSDW International Council of Social Democratic Women

icse intermediate current stability experiment

ICSE International Committee for Sexual Equality

ICSEAF International Commission for the Southeast Atlantic Fisheries

ICSEM International Center of Studies on Early Music

ICSEMS International Commission for the Scientific Exploration of the Mediterranean Sea

icsh (ICSH) interstitial cell-stimulating hormone

ICSH International Committee for Standarization in Haematology

ICSI International Conference on Scientific Information

ICSID International Center for the Settlement of Investment Disputes; International Council of Societies of Industrial

Design
ICSLS International Convention for Safety of Life at Sea
icsm instant corn-soya milk
ICSOM International Conference of Symphony and Opera Musicians
ICSP International Council of Societies of Pathology
ICSPE International Council of Sport and Physical Recreation
ICSPRO International Calcium Silicate Products Research Organization
icss intracranial self stimulation
ICSS International Council for the Social Studies
ICSSD International Committee for Social Sciences Documentation
ICSST Institute of Child Study Security Test
ICST Institute for Computer Sciences and Technology
ICS & T Imperial College of Science and Technology
ICSTA International Cooperative Study of the Tropical Atlantic
ICSTS Intermediate Combined System Test Stand
ICSU Integrated Container Services Unit; International Council of Scientific Unions; Interway Container Service (container) Unit
ICSW Interdepartmental Committee on the Status of Women
icswbd interior communications switchboard
ict icterus; identity conversion training; inflammation of connective tissue; insulin coma therapy (ICT)
ic/t integrated computer/telemetry
ICT Inter-City Train; International Computers and Tabulators; Wichita, Kansas (airport)
ICT International Critical Tables
ICTA Imperial College of Tropical Agriculture; International Center for the Typographic Arts
ICTB International Customs Tariffs Bureau
icte integration and calibration test(ing) equipment
ICTF International Cocoa Trade Federation
ICTMM International Con-

gresses of Tropical Medicine and Malaria
ICTN Industry Center for Trade Negotiations
ICTP International Center for Theoretical Physics
ICTR International Center of Theatre Research
ICTS Intermediate-Capacity Transit System
Ictus. Iurisconsultus (Latin—attorney, counsellor-at-law)
ic tv integrated-circuit television
icu indicator console unit; intensive care unit (medical)
icu (ICU) intensive care unit
Icu I see you
ICU International Code Use
ICUA Institute for College and University Administrators
ICUF Independent Colleges and Universities of Florida
ICUI Independent Colleges and Universities of Indiana
ICUM Independent Colleges and Universities of Missouri
ICUMSA International Commission for Uniform Methods of Sugar Analysis
ICUS inside continental United States
ICUT Independent Colleges and Universities of Texas
icv improved capital value; intracellular virus
ICVA International Council of Voluntary Agencies
icw in connection with; interrupted continuous wave; intracellular water
ICW India-China Wing (World War II); Institute of Child Welfare; Inter-American Commission of Women; International Chemical Workers; International Commission on Whaling; International Council of Women
ICWA Institute of Current World Affairs; International Coil Winding Association
ICWG International Cooperative Women's Guild
ICWL International Creative Writers League
ICWM International Committee on Weights and Measures
ICWP International Council of Women Psychologists
ICWU International Chemical Workers Union
ICX International Cultural Exchange
ICY International Cooperation Year (1965)

ICZ Intertropical Convergence Zone
ICZN International Commission on Zoological Nomenclature
id idea; identification; immediate delivery; independent development; independent distributor; induced draft; industrial design; infectious disease; infective dose; inside diameter; instructional development; intercept director; interest deductible; intradermal; island; islander; item description
id (ID) import duty; instruction decoder
i & d incision and drainage
id. idem (Latin—the same)
Id Iraqi dinar (monetary unit of Iraq)
I'd I could; I had; I should; I would
ID Import Declaration; Institute of Distribution; Intelligence Department; Interior (US department); Interior Department; Iraqi dinar (currency unit)
id$_{50}$ median infective dose
ida integrated digital avionics
ida (IDA) iminodiacetic acid
Ida Idah; Idaho; Idalah; Idalia; Idalina; Idaline
IDA Industrial Development Agency; Industrial Development Authority; Industrial Diamond Association; Institute for Defense Analyses; Institute for Design Analysis; Institute of Directors in Australia; Intercollegiate Dramatic Association; International Development Assistance; International Development Association; International Discotheque Association; International Dredging Association
IDA Import Duty Act
IDAA Industrial Diamond Association of America; International Doctors in Alcoholics Anonymous
idac interim digital-analog converter
id. ac idem ac (Latin—the same as)
IDAC Import Duties Advisory Committee
Idaho Lion Senator William E. Borah
IDAI Industrial Development Authority of Ireland
IDA Ireland Industrial Development Authority of Ireland

IDAS Information Display Automatic System

idast interpolated data and speech transmission

idb illicit diamond buyer; illicit diamond buying; integrated data base; intercept during burning

IDB Industrial Development Board; Inter-American Development Bank; Islamic Development Bank(ing); Israel Diamond Building (Ramat Gan)

IDBT Industrial Development Bank of Turkey

idc interest during construction

IDC Imperial Defense College; Industrial Development Commission; Industrial Development Corporation; Industry Development Commission; Intelligence Documentation Center; Intercontinental Dynamics Corporation; Interdepartmental Committee; Interdepartmental Communication; Inter-Departmental Correspondence; International Danube Commission; Iowa Development Commission

IDC *Internationale Dokumentationgesellschaft für Chemie* (German—International Chemical Documentation Society)

IDCA Industrial Design Council of Australia

id card identification card

ID-card identification card

IDCAS Industrial Development Center for Arab States

idcf indirect command file

IDCF Industrial Development Completion Form

IDC(orp) International Disposal Corporation

IDCSP Initial Defense Communications Satellite Program

IDCSS Initial Defense Communications Satellite System

i-d curve intensity-duration curve

idd identified; industrial diamond drill; interface designation drawing

idd (IDD) insulin-dependent diabetes

i/d/d illicit diamond dealer

IDD International Direct Dialing; Island Development Department

IDD *Industrielle Designere Danmark* (Danish—Denmark Industrial Design)

IDDD International Direct Distance Dialing

IDDD *International Demographic Data Directory*

IDDS International Dairy Development Scheme; International Digital Data Service

ide industry-developed equipment

IDE Industrial Development Executive; Institute of Diesel Engineers; Israel Desalination Engineering

IDEA Illinois Drug Education Alliance; Institute for the Development of Educational Activities; Institute of Diesel Engineers of Australia; Instructional Development and Effectiveness Assessment; International Downtown Executives Association; International Drug Enforcement Association

IDEAS Integrated Design and Analysis System

I de C *Islas del Cisne* (Spanish—Swan Islands)

IDEC Industrial and Domestic Equipment Corporation; Interior Design Educators Council

IDECC Interstate Distributive Education Curriculum Consortium

ideea information and data exchange experimental activities

Idef intercept during exo-atmospheric fall

I de F Institut de France (Institute of France)

iden identification; identify; identity

ident identification; identify; identity

IDEP Interagency Data Exchange Program; Interservice Data Exchange Program

Ides Ides of January, February, March, etc.—usually the 13th or the 15th of the month

idex initial defense experiment

idf intermediate distribution frame; international distress frequency

idf (IDF) integrated data file; interceptor day fighter

IDF International Dairy Federation; International Democratic Fellowship; International Diabetes Federation; Israeli Defense Force (Israeli Secret Service or Zahal)

IDFC Indo-Pacific Fisheries Council

IDFF *Internationale Demokratische Frauenfederation* (German—Women's International Democratic Federation)

idfm induced directional fm

idg integrated-drive generator

idgprt indigo print

ID grinding internal grinding

idh (IDH) isocitrate dehydrogenase

id he. index head

IDHEC *Institut des Hautes Etudes Cinématographiques, Paris* (Paris Institute of Higher Cinematographic Studies)

IDHS Intelligence Data Handling System

idi improved data interchange; inter-division invoice

IDI Industrial Designers' Institute

IDI *Institut de Droit International* (French—International Law Institute); *Instituto Venezolano de Derecho Imobiliario* (Spanish—Venezuelan Institute of Withholding Law)

IDIA Industrial Design Institute of Australia

IDIB Industrial Diamond Information Bureau

IDIL Institute for the Development of Indiana Law

IDIMS Interactive Digital Image Manipulation System

idio (Latin prefix—distinct, self, separate)—idiograph, idiomatic, idiot

Idiot. instrumentation digital online transcriber

idiot pills barbiturates

IDIU Interdivisional Information Unit; Interdivisional Intelligence Unit

IDL International Date Line; Ira D Levine; New York, New York (Kennedy International Airport—Idlewild)

IDLE Idaho Department of Law Enforcement

IDLIS International Desert Locust Information Service

id lt identification light

idm illicit diamond mining; integrated direct metering

IDM Institute of Defence Management (Indian)

IDMA Indian Drug Manufacturers Association; Isaac Delgado Museum of Art

IDMS Integrated Database Management System

idne inertial-doppler navigation equipment

IDNL Indiana Dunes National Lakeshore (Indiana)

ido industrial diesel oil

IDO Intelligence Division Office; Interim Development Order; International Disarmament Organization

idoc inner diameter of outer conductor

IDOC Illinois Department of Corrections

IDOE International Decade of Ocean Exploration—1970–1980

idon. vehic. idoneo vehiculo (Latin—in a suitable vehicle)

idp information data processing; input data processing; input data processor; integrated data processing

idp (IDP) inosine diphosphate

IDP Independent Development Project; Industrial Development Bank; Integrated Data Processing; International Driving Permit

IDPE Incorporated Data Processing Executives

IDPS Incremental Differential Pressure System

idr intercept during reentry

idr idraulica (Italian—hydraulics)

IDR Incremental Design Review; Infantry Drill Regulations; Institute for Desert Research; Institute for Dream Research

IDRC International Development Research Centre; International Drycleaning Research Committee

IDRDS International Directory of Research and Development Scientists

ids illicit diamond smuggling; inadvertent destruct; input data strobe; integrated data store; interdiction and strike; intermediate drum storage

IDS Inertial Doppler System; Instructional Dimensions Study; Interior Design Society; Interior Designers Society; International Development Services; International Development Strategy; International Documents Service; Investigative Dermatological Society; Investors Diversified Services

IDSA Industrial Designers Society of America

IDSC Information Dissemination Service Center

IDSCS Initial Defense Satellite Communication System

IDSO International Diamond Security Organization

idt identification disposition

tag(ging); inter-division transfer

idt in de text (Dutch—in the text)

IDT Industrial Detergents Trade; Instrument Definition Team

IDTA International Dance Teachers Association

IDTS Instrumentation Data Transmission System

idu interactive data-base utilities; intermittent drive unit; iododeoxyuridine

IDU idoxuridine; International Dendrology Union

idur intercept during unpowered rise

i Durchshn im Durchschnitt (German—on an average)

IDV International Distillers and Vinters

IDX Index to Dental Literature

IDZ Internationales Design Zentrum (German—International Design Center)

ie index error; initial equipment; inside edge; ion exchange

i-e internal-external

i/e ingress/egress

i & e identification and exposition (lines)

i.e. id est (Latin—that is); *inside english* (journal of the English Council of California Two-Year Colleges)

IE Indo-European; Industrial Engineering; Industrial Espionage; Information and Education; Institute of Education; Institute of Electronics; Institute of Engineers; Institution of Electronics; Institution of Engineers

I-E Indo-European; Internal-External Scale

I.E. Industrial Engineer

I & E Information and Education; Inspection and Enforcement

I of E Institute of Export

IE Immunitäts Einheit (German—immunizing unit)

iea intravascular erythrocyte aggregation

IEA Idaho Education Association; Illinois Education Association; Index of Economic Activity; Institute of Economic Affairs; Institute of Engineers—Australia; International Association for the Evaluation of Educational Achievement; International Economic Association; International Energy Agency; International En-

trepreneurs Association; International Epidemiological Association; International Study of Educational Achievement

IEA Indian Education Act (1972)

IEAF Imperial Ethiopian Air Force

IEB International Energy Bank; International Environmental Bureau (of the Non-Ferrous Metals Industry)

iec injection electrode catheter; integrated electronic control; intra-epithelial carcinoma

iec (IEC) inherent explosion clause

IEC Industry-Education Council; Institut d'Etudes Centrafricaines (Institute of Central African Studies); International Education Center; International Electrochemical Commission; International Electrotechnical Commission

IECE Institute of Electronic and Communication Engineers

IECEJ Institute of Electronic and Communication Engineers of Japan

IECI Institute for Esperanto in Commerce and Industry

iecm internal electronic countermeasures

IECO International Engineering Company

IECOK International Economic Consultative Organization for Korea

IECP Intermediate Engineering Change Proposal

iec's integrated electronic components

ied improvised explosive device; individual effective dose

IED Institute for Educational Development; Institution of Engineering Designers; Integrated Electronics Division (USA Electronics Command)

IEDC International Energy Development Corporation

ied's income equalization deposits

IEDs Intermediate Educational Districts

iee inner enamel epithelium

IEE Institute of Electrical Engineers; Institute of Electronic Engineering; Institute for Environmental Education; Institute of Environmental Engineers; Institution of Electrical Engineers

Ieee I expect everything eventually

IEEE Institute of Electrical and Electronics Engineers
IEEE J Quantum Electron IEEE Journal of Quantum Electronics
IEEE Trans Antennas Propag IEEE Transactions on Antennas and Propagation
IEEE Trans Electron Devices IEEE Transactions on Electronic Devices
IEEE Trans Inf Theory IEEE Transactions on Information Theory
IEEE Trans Instrum Meas IEEE Transactions on Instrumentation and Measurement
IEEE Trans Magn IEEE Transactions on Magnetics
IEEE Trans Microwave Theory Tech IEEE Transactions on Microwave Theory and Techniques
IEEE Trans Nucl Sci IEEE Transactions on Nuclear Science
IEEE Trans Sonics Ultrason IEEE Transactions on Sonics and Ultrasonics
ieef ion-integrated evaporation filter
IEEJ Institute of Electrical Engineers of Japan
IEES International Educational Exchange System
IEETE Institution of Electrical and Electronics Technician Engineers
ief integrated electronic flash(ing)
IEF International Ecumenical Fellowship; International Exhibitions Foundation; International Eye Foundation
IEG Information Exchange Group
IEHA International Economic History Association
iei indeterminate engineering items
IEI Industrial Education Institute; Industrial Engineering Institute; Institute of Electrical Inspectors; Institution of Engineering Inspection; Institution of Engineers of Ireland; Iran Electronics Industries
IEIC Iowa Educational Information Center
IEKV Internationale Eisenbahn-Kongress-Vereiningung (German—International Railway Congress Association)
IEL Industrial Engineering Limited; Industrial Equity Limited; Institute for Educational

Leadership
iem iemand (Dutch—a man, somebody, someone)
IEMA Iowa Educational Media Association
IEMCAP Intrasystem Electromagnetic Compatability Analysis Program (USAF)
IEME Inspectorate of Electrical and Mechanical Engineering
IEMS Institute of Experimental Medicine and Surgery
IEN Imperial Ethiopian Navy
IEO Instituto Español de Oceanografia (Spanish Oceanographic Institute)
IEOM Institute of Environment and Offshore Medicine
ieop immunoelectro-osmophoresis
iep iso-electric point
IEP Individual Education Plan; Individual Educational Program; Institut d'Etudes Politiques (Institute of Political Studies); Institute of Experimental Psychology
IEPA International Economic Policy Association
IEPs Individualized Education Programs
ieq index of environmental quality
ier installation enhancement release
Ier (Dutch—Irishman)
IER Industrial Equipment Reserve; Institute for Econometric Research; Institute of Educational Research; Institute of Engineering Research; Interim Engineering Report
IERC Indian Education Resources Center (Bureau of Indian Affairs); International Electronic Research Corporation
IERE Institution of Electronic and Radio Engineers
Ierl Ierland (Dutch—Ireland)
Ierland (Dutch—Ireland)
IERT Institute for Education by Radio-Television
IER Test Institute of Educational Research Test (intelligence)
ie & s institutional, environmental, and safety
IES Illuminating Engineering Society; Independent Educational Services; Indian Educational Service; Information Exchange Service; Institute of Environmental Sciences; Institute of European Studies; Institution of Engineers and Shipbuilders

IE–S Institution of Engineers—Singapore
IESA Illuminating Engineering Societies of Australia
IESC International Executive Service Corps
IESS Institution of Engineers and Shipbuilders in Scotland
iet interest equalization tax
IET Initial Engine Test; Institute of Educational Technology
IETG International Energy Technology Group
I-et-L Indre-et-Loire
I-et-V Ille-et-Vilaine
IEWS Integrated Electronic Warfare System
if. ice fog; immunofluorescence; information feedback; infrastructure; instrument flight; intermediate frequency; internal flush(ing); interstitial fluid; intrinsic factor
if. (IF) interferon
i-f inflight, intermediate frequency
i & f inverter and cathode fol lower
if iflge (Danish—according to)
i.f. ipse fecit (Latin—he did it himself)
If Ifni; Sidi Ifni (Spanish West Africa)
IF grid current (symbol)
I-F Isotta-Fraschini
ifa instrumental fuel assembly; integrated file adapter
I f A Institutt for Atomenergi (Norwegian—Atomic Energy Institute)
IFA Industrial Forestry Association; Industry Film Association; Institute of Foresters of Australia; Intercollegiate Fencing Association; International Federation of Actors; International Fertility Association; International Fiscal Association; International Footprints Association; International Franchise Association
IFA Institut Fiziki Atmosfery (Russian—Atmospheric Physics Institute)
IFABC International Federation of Audit Bureaus of Circulations
IFAC International Family Association of Canada; International Federation of Automatic Control
IFAD International Fund for Agricultural Development
IFALPA International Federa-

tion of Air-Line Pilots' Associations

Ifan (Welsh—John)

IFAN Institut Français d'Afrique Noire (Dakar, Ivory Coast)

IFAP Industrial Foundation for Accident Prevention; International Federation of Agricultural Producers

IFAPA International Federation of Airline Pilots Association

IFAR International Foundation for Art Research

IFAS Institute for American Strategy; International Federation of Aquarium Societies

IFATCA International Federation of Air Traffic Controllers Associations

IFATCC International Federation of Associations of Textile Chemists and Colourists

IFATE International Federation of Airworthiness Technology and Engineering

IFAW International Fund for Animal Welfare

IFAWPCA International Federation of Asian and Western Pacific Contractors Associations

ifb invitation for bid(s)

IFB International Federation of the Blind; Invitation for Bid(s)

IFBA International Fire Buff Association

IFBB International Federation of Bodybuilders

IFBPW International Federation of Business and Professional Women

IFBWW International Federation of Building and Woodworkers

ifc independent fire control; inflight collision; inner front cover; institute freight clause(s); integrated fire control

IFC Inland Fisheries Commission; International Finance Corporation; International Fisheries Commission; International Freighting Corporation

IFC-ALA Intellectual Freedom Committee—American Library Association

IFCATI International Federation of Cotton and Allied Textile Industries

IFCC International Federation of Camping and Caravanning;

International Federation of Clinical Chemistry

IFCCTE International Federation of Commercial, Clerical, and Technical Employees

IFCJ International Federation of Catholic Journalists

IFCL International Fixed Calendar League

IFCO Interreligious Foundation for Community Organization

ifcr interface control register

IFCS Improved Fire-Control System; International Federation of Computer Sciences

IFCU International Federation of Catholic Universities

i.f.d. *in flagrante delicto* (Latin —in the heat of the evil deed) —caught in the act

IFD International Federation of Documentation

IFDA Institutional Food Distributors of America

IFDP Institute for Food and Development Programs

IFE Industrial Foundation on Education; Institution of Fire Engineers

IFEBP International Foundation of Employee Benefit Plans

IFEBS Integrated Foreign Exchange and Banking System

IFEE Institute for Free Enterprise Education

IFEMS International Federation of Electron Microscope Societies

IFEP *Instituttet for Elektronikmateriels Palideliged* (Danish —Electronic Materials Reliability Institute)

IFEW Inter-American Federation of Entertainment Workers

iff invert fluid fill(ing)

iff (IFF) identification friend or foe

if & f intermediate flush and fill

IFF Institute of Freight Forwarders; Institute for the Future; Intermediate Financing Facility; International Flavors and Fragrances (corporation)

IFFA International Federation of Film Archives; International Frozen Food Association

IFFC Integrated Fire and Flight Control

IFFCO Indian Farmers Fertilizer Cooperative

IFFF *Internationale Frauenlige für Frieden und Freiheit* (German—International Women's

League for Peace and Freedom)

IFFJ Independent Federation of Free Journalists

IFFJP International Federation of Fruit Juice Producers

IFFNM *Internationale Ferienkurse für Neue Musik* (German—International Vacation Courses for New Music)— held in Darmstadt

IFFPA International Federation of Film Producers Associations

IFFS International Federation of Film Societies

IFFTU International Federation of Free Teachers' Unions

ifg instrument flight guide

IFGO International Federation of Gynecology and Obstetrics

ifh in-flight helium

IFHE International Federation of Home Economics

IFHP International Federation for Housing And Planning

IFHTM International Federation for the Heat Treatment of Materials

IFI Industrial Fasteners Institute; Institutional Functioning Inventory

IFI *Instituto de Fomento Industrial* (Spanish—Institute for Industrial Promotion)

IFIA International Federation of Ironmongers' and Iron Merchants' Associations; International Fence Industry Association

IFIAS International Federation of Institutes for Advanced Studies

IFIF International Foundation for Internal Freedom (hallucinogenic experimenter's society found by former Harvard professors Richard Alpert and Timothy Leary)

IFIP Iguazu Falls International Park (shared by Argentina, Brazil, and Paraguay)—Argentinians spell it Iguazu, Brazilians—Igauçu, Paraguayans— Iguassu; International Federation of Information Processing

IFIPS International Federation of Information Processing Societies

I Fire E Institution of Fire Engineers

IFIS Integrated Flight Instrument System

IFJ International Federation of Journalists

IfK *Institut für Kriminologie* (German—Institute of Criminology); *Institut for Kriminologi* (Norwegian—Institute of Criminology)

IFKM *Internationale Föderation für Kurzschrift und Maschinenschreiben* (German—International Federation of Shorthand and Typewriting)

IfL *Institut für Landeskunde* (German—Geographical Institute)—at Bad Godesberg

IFL Imperial Fascist League

IFLA International Federation of Landscape Architects; International Federation of Library Associations

iflet interim focal-length optical tracker

IFLWU International Fur and Leather Workers Union

ifm intermediate frame memory

IFM Industrial Facility Manager; Institute for Forensic Medicine

IFMA International Federation of Margarine Associations; International Foodservice Manufacturers Association

IFMBE International Federation for Medical and Biological Engineering

IFMC International Folk Music Council

IFME International Federation of Medical Electronics; International Federation of Municipal Engineers

IFMEO International Fish Meal Exporters Organization

if/mf intermediate frequency/medium frequency

IFMI Irish Federation of Marine Industries

IFMP International Federation of Medical Psychotherapy

IFMS Integrated Financial Management System

IFMSA International Federation of Medical Students Associations

ifn information

IFN *Institut Français de Navigation* (French Institute of Navigation)

IFNB Idaho First National Bank

IFNE International Federation for Narcotic Education

if nec if necessary

ifo in favor of; in front of; identified flying object; intermediate fuel oil

IFOFSAG International Fellowship of Former Scouts and Guides

IFOP *Institut Français d'Opinion Publique* (French Institute of Public Opinion)

Ifor (Welsh—Ivo, Ivor)

IFOR International Fellowship of Reconciliation

IFORS International Federation of Operational Research Societies

IFOSA International Federation of Stationers' Associations

ifov instantaneous field of view; instrument field of view

ifp in-flight performance; in-flight printer; international fixed public broadcast band

IFP Imperial and Foreign Post; Institute of Fluid Power; International Federation of Purchasing

IFP *Institut Français du Pétrole* (French Petroleum Institute)

IFPA Industrial Film Producers Association; Institute for Foreign Policy Analysis

IFPCW International Federation of Petroleum and Chemical Workers

IFPI International Federation of the Phonographic Industry

ifpm in-flight performance monitor

IFPM International Federation of Physical Medicine

IFPMA International Federation of Pharmaceutical Manufacturers Associations

IFPMM International Federation of Purchasing and Materials Management

IFPP Imperial and Foreign Parcel Post

IFPRA International Federation of Park and Recreation Administrators

IFPTO Internation Federation of Popular Travel Organizations

IFPTS Intertype Fototronic Photographic Typesetting System

IFPW International Federation of Petroleum Workers

ifr infrared; inflight refueling

ifr (IFR) internal function register

i-f-r image-to-frame ratio

IFr *Internationaler Frauenrat* (German—International Council of Women)

IFR Instrument Flight Rules

IFRA International Foundation for Research in the Field of Advertising

IFRB International Frequency Registration Board

IFRC International Fusion Research Council

IFRF International Flame Research Foundation

IFRT Institute for Fitness Research and Training

ifru interference rejection unit

IFS Instrument Flight System; International Federation of Surveyors; International Foundation for Science; International Freight Services; Irish Free State

IFS *International Financial Statistics*

IFSA International Federation of Sound Archives

IFSDP International Federation of the Socialist and Democratic Press

IFSEA International Federation of Scientific Editors Associations

IFSEM International Federation of Societies for Electron Microscopy

IFSF Independent Fuel Storage Facility; Irradiated-Fuels Storage Facility

IFSIT In-Flight Safety Inhibit Test

IFSMA International Federation of Ship Master Associations

IFSO In-Flight Safety Officer

IFSP International Federation of Societies of Philosophy

IFSPO International Federation of Senior Police Officers

IFSPS International Federation of Students in Political Sciences

ifss infinite solution set

IFSS Instrumentation Flight Safety System; International Fertilizer Supply Scheme; International Flight Service Station(s)

IFSSO Irish Free State Stationery Office

IFST International Federation of Shorthand and Typing

IFSTA International Fire Service Training Association

IFSW International Federation of Social Workers

ift inflight text

IFT Indiana Federation of Teachers; Institute of Food Technologists; International Federation of Translators; International Foundation for Telemetering; International

Frequency Tables

IFT *Institut für Tieflagerung* (German—Institute for Geologic Disposal)

IFTA International Federation of Travel Agencies

IFTC International Film and Television Council

iftcd in-flight thrust-calculation deck

IFTF Inter-Faith Task Force

IFTPP International Federation of the Technical and Periodical Press

iftr in-flight thrust reverser

IFTR International Federation for Theatre Research

IFUW International Federation of University Women

ifv (IFV) infantry fighting vehicle

IFVME Inspectorate of Fighting Vehicles and Mechanical Equipment

IFWL International Federation of Women Lawyers

IFZ Industrial Free Zone

ig ignition; immunoglobulin; inertial guidance

ig (Ig) (IG) immunoglobulin

i/g in ground

IG Illustrators Guild; Indo-Germanic; Inspector General

IG *Interessengemeinschaft* (German—pool, trust)

iga integrating gyro(scope) accelerometer

IGA Independent Grocers' Alliance; Integrated Grant Administration; International Geneva Association; International Geographical Association; International Golf Association; International Graduate Achievement

IGAEA International Graphic Arts Education Association

i gal imperial gallon

IGAM *Internationale Gesellschaft für Allgemeinmedizin* (German—International Society of General Medicine)

IGAS International General Aviation Society; International Graphic Arts Society

I Gas Eng Institution of Gas Engineers

IGB International Gravimetric Bureau

IGB *International Geophysics Bulletin*

igc intellectually gifted children

IGC Institute for Graphic Communication; Intergovernmental Copyright Committee; International Geophysical Coop-

eration

IGCA Industrial Gas Cleaning Association

IGCC Inter-Governmental Copyright Committee

igce independent government cost estimate

IGCI Industrial Gas Cleaning Institute

IGCM Incorporated Guild of Church Musicians

i/g/d illicit gold dealer

IGD Inspector General's Department

ig det ignition detector

IGDS Iodine Generating and Dispensing System

ige in ground effect; individually guided education; instrumentation ground equipment

IGE International General Electric

IGF International Grieg Festival

igf-1 (IGF-1) insulin-like growth factor 1

IGFA International Game Fish Association

I.G. Farben Interessengemeinschaft der Farbenindustrie (German Dye Trust)

ig. fat. *ignis fatuus*(Latin—foolish fire)—will-o'-the- wisp; marsh gas

igfet insulated gate field-effect transistor

IGH Incorporated Guild of Hairdressers

IGI Institutional Goals Inventory

IGI *I Grandi Interpreti* (Italian—The Great Interpreters)—of classical music

IGIA Interagency Group on International Aviation

IGIS International Guild for Infant Survival

igl information grouping logic

igl *iglesia* (Spanish—church)

igl^a *iglesia* (Spanish—church)

igla *iglesia* (Spanish—church)

ign ignite; ignition

ign. *ignotus* (Latin—unknown)

Ign Ignacio; Ignatius; Ignatz; Ignazio

IGN International Great Northern (railroad)

Ignatius Loyola Iñigo López de Recalde

Ignatz von Aschendorf pseudonym used by Joseph Conrad and Ford Madox Ford when they wrote *The Nature of a Crime*

Ignazio Silone (pseudonym—Secondo Tranquilli)

Ign^o *Ignacio*(Spanish—Ignatius)

IGO Independent Garage Owners; Intergovernmental Organization

igor injection gas-oil ratio; intercept ground optical recorder

Igor Prince Igor (four-act opera by Borodin)

igortt intercept ground optical recorder tracking telescope

IGOSS Integrated Global Ocean Station System

igp inside gravel pack (oil well)

IGP Industrial Government Party; Inspector General of Police

igpm imperial gallons per mile; imperial gallons per minute

igpp (IGPP) interactive graphics packaging program

IGPP Institute of Geophysics and Planetary Physics (UCLA)

igr. *igitur*(Latin—therefore)

igrf international geomagnetic reference field

IGROF *Internationale Rorschach Gesellschaft* (German—International Rorschach Society)

IGRS Irish Geneological Research Society

igs (IGS) interactive graphics system

IGS Imperial General Staff; Inert Gas System; Inertial Guidance System; Infogram Service; Institute of General Semantics; Institute of Geological Sciences; International Geranium Society

igse interim ground-support equipment

IGSEAP Inertial Guidance System Error Analysis Program

IGSESS International Graduate School for English-Speaking Students

IGSS *Instituto Guatemalteco de Seguridad* (Spanish—Guatemalan Social Security Institute)

IGST Intergovernmental Committee on Science and Technology

igt (IGT) interactive graphics terminal

IGT Institute of Gas Technology

IGTO India Government Tourist Office; Israel Government Tourist Office; Italian Government Tourist Office

IGU International Gas Union; International Geographical

Union
igv inlet guide vane
IGWF International Garment Workers Federation
IGWT In God We Trust
IGWUA International Glove Workers Union of America
IGY International Geophysical Year (July 1957 through December 1958)
ih inside height
ih (IH) infectious hepatitis
i.h. iacet hic (Latin—here lies)
IH International Harvester
I of H Institute of Hydrology
IH International Humanism
iha (IHA) idiopathic hyperaldosteronism
IHA International Hahnemannian Association; International Hotel Association; International House Association
IHAR Institute for Human-Animal Relationships
IHAS Integrated Helicopter Avionics System
IHB International Hydrographic Bureau (Monaco)
IHBR Indiana Harbor Belt Railroad
ihc interstate highway capability
IHC Intercontinental Hotels Corporation; International Help for Children
IHCA International Hebrew Christian Alliance
IHCC International Harvester Credit Company
IHCD International Holocaust Commemoration Day
ihd (IHD) ischemic heart disease
IHD Institute of High Fidelity; Institute of Human Development; International Health Division (Rockefeller Institute for Medical Research); International Hydrological Decade (1965–1974)
IHDS Interstate Highway and Defense System
IHE Institute of Highway Engineers; Institute of Home Economics; Institutions of Higher Education
I-head capital-I-shaped head (gasoline engine)
IHEU International Humanist and Ethical Union
ihf interesting historic figure
IHF Industrial Hygiene Foundation; Institute of High Fidelity; International Hockey Federation; International Hospital Federation

IHFA Industrial Hygiene Foundation of America
IHFAS Integrated High-Frequency Antenna System
ihff inhibit halt flip-flop
IHHA International Halfway House Association
IHI Ishikawajima-Harima Heavy Industries
IHK Internationale Handelskammer (German—International Chamber of Commerce)
IHL International Homeopathic League
IHM Institute of Hotel Marketing; Institute of Housing Managers
I.H.M. Immaculate Heart of Mary
iho in-house operation
IHOP International House of Pancakes
IHOU Institute of Home Office Underwriters
ihp indicated horsepower; ischemic heart disease
IHP Integrated Humanities Program
IHPA Imported Hardwood Plywood Association
ihph indicated horsepower hour
ihp/hr indicated horsepower hour
IHQ International Headquarters
IHR Institute of Historical Research; Institute of Human Relations
IHRA Independent Human Rights Association
IHRB International Hockey Rules Board
ihrd international rubber hardness degree(s)
ihs independent hemopathic syndrome; integrated heat sink; intellectually handicapped society
i.h.s. a variant of I.H.S. and also believed by some believers to mean *I have suffered*
IHS Immigration Historical Society; Indian Health Service; Infrared Homing System; Institute for Humane Studies; Institute of Hypertension Studies; International Horn Society; Interstate Highway System; Irish Hospitals Sweepstakes; Ivory Hunters Society
I.H.S. Iesus Hominum Salvator (Latin—Jesus Savior of Men); *In Hoc Signo* (Latin—In This

Sign)
ihsa iodinated human serum albumin
IHSA Italian Historical Society of America
ihsbr improved high-speed bombing radar
ihss idiopathic hypertrophic subaortic stenosis (IHSS)
IHSS Integrated Hydrographic Survey System
IHT Institute of Handicraft Teachers
IHT International Herald Tribune
IHU Interservice Hovercraft Unit
ihv intravenous hyperalimentation
IHVE Institute of Heating and Ventilating Engineers
ihx intermediate heat exchanger
IHY International Historical Year
IHYC Indian Harbor Yacht Club; Indian Harbour Yacht Club
ii illegal immigrant; individualized instruction; ingot iron; initial issue; injectivity index (oil well); interest included; inventory and inspection
i & i intercourse and intoxication (aspects of r & r); introduce and interview
II Ikebana International; Instituto Interamericano (Interamerican Institute); Irish Institute
I/I Inventory and Inspection (Report)
I & I instruction and inspection
II Instituto Interamericano (Spanish—Interamerican Institute)
iia if incorrect advise; inertial instrument assembly; inner-inch adjustment; integrated irradiance analyzer
IIA Aerlinte Eireann (3-letter symbol for Irish Airlines); Incinerator Institute of America; Information Industry Association; Institute of Industrial Arts; Institute of Internal Auditors; Insurance Institute of America; International Information Administration; Invention Industry Association
IIAA Independent Insurance Agents Association
IIAC Industrial Injuries Advisory Council
IIAF Imperial Iranian Air

Force
IIAG Interbureau Insurance Advisory Group
IIAL International Institute of Arts and Letters
IIAPCO Independent Indonesian-American Petroleum Company
IIAS International Institute of Administrative Services
IIASA International Institute of Applied Systems Analysis
IIB Institut International de Bibliographie; International Investment Bank; Internordic Investment Bank
IIB *Institut International de Bibliographie* (French—International Institute of Bibliography)
IIC Independent Insurance Conference; Insurance Institute of Canada; International Institute of Communications; International Institute for the Conservation of Historic and Artistic Works; International Inter-City (train)
IICA Indians Into Communications Association; Institute of Instrumentation and Control—Australia
IICA *Instituto Interamericano de Ciencias Agrícolas* (Inter-American Institute of Agricultural Sciences)
I-ICB Isolation-Interface Control Board
IICLRR International Institute for Children's Literature and Reading Research
iid impact ionization diode; infrared intrusion detection; interior intrusion device
IID Internal Investigation Division
IID *Institut International de Documentation* (French—International Documentation Institute)
IIDA Irish Industrial Development Authority
IIDS Interior Intruder Detection System
IIDS *Instituto Interamericano de Desarrolo Social* (Spanish—Interamerican Social Development Institute)
IIE Institute of Industrial Engineers; Institute for International Economics; Institute for International Education; International Institute of Embryology
IIE *Instituto Interamericano de Estadistica* (Inter-American

Institute of Statistics)
IIEA International Institute for Environmental Affairs
IIEC Inter-Industry Emission Control (program)
IIEG Interest Inventory for Elementary Grades
IIEP International Institute of Educational Planning
IIET Inspection Instructions for Electron Tubes
IIF Institute of International Finance; Institut International du Froid (International Institute of Refrigeration)
IIFA International Institute of Films on Art
IIFT Indian Institute of Foreign Trade
IIGF Imperial Iranian Ground Forces
IIHCEHV International Institute of Health Care, Ethics, and Human Values
IIHF International Ice Hockey Federation
IIHS Insurance Institute for Highway Safety
III Insurance Information Institute; International Institute of Interpreters (UN); International Isostatic Institute
III *Instituto Indigenista Interamericano* (Inter-American Indigenist Institute); *International Intertrade Index*
IIIC International Irrigation Information Center (Israeli)
IIIRI Illinois Institute of Technology Research Institute
IIJR Illinois Institute of Juvenile Research
iil integrated injection logic
IIL Intelligence International Limited
IILC International Instituut voor Landaanwinning en Cultuurtechniek (International Institute of Land Reclamation and Cultivation)
IILRI International Institute for Land Reclamation and Improvement
IILS International Institute for Labour Studies
IIM Indian Institute of Management
IIME Institute of International Medical Education
IIMS Intensive Item Management System
IIMSD International Institute for Music Studies and Documentation
IIMT International Institute for the Management of Technolo-

gy
IIN Item Identification Number
IIN *Instituto Interamericano del Niño* (Inter-American Children's Institute); *Instituto Italiano di Navigazione* (Italian Institute of Navigation)
IInfSc Institute of Information Scientists
IINZ Insurance Institute of New Zealand
IIOE International Indian Ocean Expedition
IIOOF International Independent Order of Odd Fellows
IIOS International Indian Ocean Survey
iip index of industrial production; individualized instructional planning
IIP Institute International de la Presse (International Institute of the Press); International Ice Patrol; International Institute of Peace; International Institute of Philosophy
IIP *Institute International de la Presse* (French—International Institute of the Press)
IIPER International Institution of Production Engineering Research
IIPs Individualized Instruction(al) Program(s)
iir imaging infra-red; isobutylene isoprene rubber
IIR International Institute of Refrigeration
IIRA International Industrial Relations Association
IIRE International Institute for Resource Economics
iirs instrumentation inertial reference set
IIRS Institute for Industrial Research and Standards (Erie)
ii's illegal immigrants
IIs Immigration Inspectors
IIS Industrial Inquiry Service; Institute of Information Science; Institute of Information Scientists; Insurance Institute of Singapore; Integrated Instrument System; Interactive Instructional System
IIS *Institut International de la Soudre* (French—International Institute of Welding); *Institut International de la Statistique* (French—International Institute of Statistics); *Internationales Institut der Sparkassen* (German—International Institute of Savings Banks)
IIS & EE International Institute

of Seismology and Earthquake Engineering

IISG *Internationaal Instituut voor Sociale Geschiedenis* (Dutch—International Institute of Social History)—in Amsterdam

IISL International Institute of Space Law

IISL *Istituto Internazionale di Studi Liguri* (Italian—International Institute for Ligurian Studies)

IISO Institution of Industrial Safety Officers

IISR International Institute for Submarine Research

IISRP International Institute of Synthetic Rubber Producers

IISS International Institute of Strategic Studies

IISWM International Institute of Iron and Steel Wire Manufacturers

iit independent inclusive tour; individual inclusive tour

IIT Illinois Institute of Technology; Israel Institute of Technology

IIT *Institut International du Théâtre* (French—International Institute of the Theater)

IITB Indian Institute of Technology—Bombay

IITM Indian Institute of Technology—Madras

IITRAN Illinois Institute of Technology Translators

IITYWYBAD? If I tell you will you buy a drink?

IIW International Institute of Welding

iiwfm if it weren't for me

iiwfy if it weren't for you

iJ *im Jahre* (German—in the year)

IJ IJssel; Institute of Journalists

I of J Institute of Jamaica

IJ *Internationale Jugendbibliothek* (German—International Youth Library)—a unique collection in München or Munich

IJA Institute of Jewish Affairs; Institute of Judicial Administration; International Judiciary Association

IJA *International Journal of the Addictions*

IJC International Joint Commission (Canada—U.S.); Itawamba Junior College

IJF International Judo Federation

I-J FC Iselin-Jefferson Financial Company

IJIAP International Juridical Institute for Animal Protection

IJISID Imperial Japanese Institute for the Study of Infectious Diseases

IJK *Internationale Juristen Kommission* (German—International Jurists Commission)

IJland (Dutch—Iceland)

IJMS *Israel Journal of Medical Sciences*

IJO International Juridical Organization (for developing countries of the third world)

IJOA International Juvenile Officers Association

ijp inhibitory junction potential

IJPPR Institute for Jewish Policy Planning and Research

IJR Institute for Juvenile Research

IJS Institute of Jazz Studies; Institute of Jewish Studies

IJslands (Dutch—Icelandic)

IJsselmeer lake bordered by lands reclaimed from the Zuider Zee in the Netherlands

IJVA International Journal of Verbal Aggression (*Maledicta*)

ik inner keel

ik *ikke* (Danish—not)

Ik Ichabod

IK *Immune Korper* (German—immune bodies)

IKAR *Internationale Kommission für Alpines Rettungswesen* (German—International Commission for Alpine Rescue)

Ikaría (Greek—Nikaria)

IKB Isambard Kingdom Brunel

ike iconoscope; ikebana; ikebanism; ikebanist(ic)

Ike Dwight David Eisenhower (nickname)—thirty-fourth President of the United States; Isaac

Ikey (*see* Ikie)

Ikie Isaac; Isaak; Isack; Izaak; Isaque

I-K-P In-Ko-Pah (Park or Mountains in California)

IKPK International Kriminal-Polizei-Kommission (International Criminal Police Commission)

I kr Icelandic krona (monetary unit)

ikrd inverse kinetics rod drop

ik unit infusoria killing unit

IKV-91 Hagglund and Soner tank destroyer made in Sweden

il illustrate; illustrated; illustration; illustrator; including loading; incoming letter; inside layer; inside left; inside length; instrument landing; interline; interlinear; interlinearly; interpretative language

Il illinium

Il *Illiad*

IL Identification List(ing); Import License; Incres Line; Independent Laboratory; Instruction Leaflet; International Logistics; Interocean Line; Israel (auto plaque)

I/L Import License

I & L Installations and Logistics

I of L Institute of Linguists

IL *Institut Littéraire*

Il-12 Soviet Ilyushin transport called Coach by NATO

Il-14 Soviet Ilyushin transport called Crate by NATO

Il 18 Soviet Ilyushin transport called Coot by NATO

Il-28 Soviet Ilyushin jet bomber called Beagle by NATO

Il-38 Soviet Ilyushin transport called May by NATO

IL-62 Ilyushin 62 aircraft

ila insurance logistics automated

ila (ILA) instrument landing approach

ILA Illinois Library Association; Indian(a) Library Association; Indonesian Library Association; Institute of Landscape Architects; International Laundry Association; International Law Association; Inter national Leprosy Association; International Linguistic Association; International Longshoremen's Association; Iowa Library Association; Iranian Library Association; Iraq Library Association; Israel Library Association (and all other library associations omitted unintentionally)

ILAA International Legal Aid Association

ILAAS Integrated Light Aircraft Avionics System; Integrated Light Attack Avionics System; International League Against Anti-Semitism

ILAB International League of Antiquarian Booksellers

ILAFA Instituto Latinamericano del Fierro y del Acero (Latin American Institute of Iron and Steel)

ILAMA International Lifesaving Appliance Manufacturers Association

ILAP Individualized Language Arts Program

ILAR Institute of Laboratory Animal Resources

ilas interrelated logic accumulating scanner

ILAS Institute of Latin American Studies; Instrument Low-Approach System

ilb inshore lifeboat

ilc irrevocable letter of credit

ilc (ILC) instruction length code

ILC Independent Learning Center; Individualized Learning Center; International Law Commission (UN)

ILCA International Livestock Centre for Africa

Il Cieco (Italian—The Blind One)—Italy's blind poet—Luigi Groto who lived and wrote in the mid-sixteenth century

ILCNY I Love a Clean New York

ILCOP International Liaison Committee of Organizations for Peace (UN)

ILCW Inter-Lutheran Commission on Worship

ild instructional logic diagram

Ildef⁰ Ildefonso (Spanish)

ildf integrated logistic data file

ildt item logistics data transmittal

Il Duca di Spoleto (Italian—The Duke of Spoleto)—composer-impresario Gian Carlo Menotti's nickname as he directs the Spoletto Festival

Il Duce (Italian—The Leader)—sobriquet of Benito Mussolini —dictator of Italy before and during World War II

ile individual learning expectations; isoleucine

ile (ILE) isoleucine (amino acid)

île (French—island)

Ileᵉ Illustre (Spanish—illustrious)

ILE Institution of Locomotive Engineers

ILEA Inner London Education Authority

Île d'Ouessant (French—Isle of Ushant)—off Brittany's coast

Île du Diable (French—Devil's Island)—small island off French Guiana where political

prisoners were isolated and which was so terrible it became the name of the entire penal colony

ILEI Internacia Ligo de Esperantistaj Instruistoj (International League of Esperanto Instructors)

ILERA International League of Esperantist Radio Amateurs

ILESA International Law Enforcement Stress Association

Îles Comores (French—Comoro Islands)

Îles de la Madeleine (French—Magdalen Islands)—in the Gulf of St Lawrence

Îles de la Société (French—Society Islands)—in the South Pacific

Îles du Vent (French—Windward Islands)—in the Lesser Antilles of the West Indies

Îles Normandes (French—Norman Islands)—the Channel Islands in the English Channel between England and France

Îles sous le Vent (French—Leeward Islands)—in the Lesser Antilles of the West Indies

ileu isoleucine

ilf inductive loss factor

Ilf Ilya Arnoldovich Feisliber

ILF International Landworkers Federation

ILFI International Labor Film Institute

ILFO International Logistics Field Office (USA)

Il Furioso (Italian—the Furious One)—nickname of Tintoretto who painted at a furious rate

ILGA Institute of Local Government Administration

ILGPNWU International Leather Goods, Plastics, and Novelty Workers Union

ILGWU International Ladies' Garment Workers' Union

ILH Imperial Light Horse; International League of Honolulu; Interscholastic League of Honolulu

Ilha Formosa (Portuguese—Beautiful Isle)—main island of the Republic of China-Taiwan

Ilhas da Madeira (Portuguese—Madeira Islands)

Ilhas do Cabo Verde (Portuguese—Cape Verde Islands)

Ilhas dos Açores (Portuguese—Islands of the Azores)

ILHR International League of Human Rights

ILI Indiana Limestone Institute; Institute of Life Insurance; International Language Institute

ILIA Indiana Limestone Institute of America

Ilia Mourometz Gliere's Symphony No. 3

ILIAS Inforonics Library Automation Services

ILIC International Library Information Center

Ilich Russian patronymic often used as the popular name for Lenin—the party name of Vladimir Ilich Ulyanov

ill. illusion; illusionary; illusionist; illustrate; illustrated; illustration; illustrator

ill. illustrissimus (Latin—most illustrious)

Ill Illinois; Illinoisan

I'll I shall; I will

ILL Institute of Languages and Linguistics; Institute of Lifetime Learning; Inter-Library Loan; Interstate Loan Library

ILLC Inner London Library Committee

illegals illegal aliens

illegit illegitimate

ILLIAC Illinois Automatic Computer

ILLINET Illinois Library Information Network

Illinois Ports (south to north) Chicago, Wilmette, Great Lakes, Waukegan

Illinois River City Peoria

ILLRI Industrial Lift and Loading Ramp Institute

Ill St Hist Lib Illinois State Historical Library

Ill St Hist Soc Illinois State Historical Society

illu illustrate

illud illustrated

illum illuminant; illuminate; illumination

illun illustration

illus illustrated; illustration; illustrator

Illusion Factory Hollywood

Illustrator of Early Twentieth-Century America Norman Rockwell

Illustrator of the Russian Underground Ilya Efimovich Repin

Illustrious Infidel Colonel Robert G Ingersoll

illw intermediate-level liquid waste

Illyria (Latin—Albania)

ilm insulin-like material

ILM International Literary Management

ILMA Incandescent Lamp

Manufacturers Association

Il Maestro (Italian—The Master)—honorific title usually accorded someone of the artistic stature of Arturo Toscanini

Ilmo *Illustrissimo* (Italian—Most Illustrious)

Il^mo Illustrísimo (Spanish—Most Illustrious)

Il Moro (Italian—The Moor)—Ludovico Sforza's nickame given him because of his dark Moorish appearance

ILMP International Literary Market Place

ILN Illustrated London News

ilo in lieu of

Ilo Iloilo

I lo iodine lotion

ILO International Labour Office (UN); International Labor Organization

ILOA Industrial Life Officers Association

I Loco E Institution of Locomotive Engineers

I Loco Eng Institution of Locomotive Engineers

Ilona Massey Ilona Hajmassy

Ilopango San Salvador, El Salvador's airport named for a nearby lake

iloue in lieu of until exhausted

ilp instant linear programming

ILP Independent Labour Party

ILPA Independent Labor Press Association

Il Perugino (Italian—The Perugian)—Pietro Santi Bartoli

ILPES Instituto Latinoamericano de Planificación Económica y Social (Latin American Institute for Economic and Social Planning)

ILPH International League for the Protection of Horses

ILQ International Law Quarterly

ILR Institute of Library Research; International Luggage Registry

ILR Instituut voor Landbowtechniek en Rationalisatie (Dutch—Institute for Agricultural and Planning Technics); International Law Reports

ILRA International Log Rolling Association

ILRAD International Laboratory for Research into Animal Diseases

ILRC Indian Law Resources Center

ILRI Indian Lac Research Institute

ILRM International League for the Rights of Man

ILS Incorporated Law Society; Instrument Landing System; Integrated Logistic Support; International Latitude Service; International Lunar Society

ILSA Insured Locksmiths and Safemen of America

ilsam international language for servicing and maintenance

ILSC International Learning Systems Corporation

ILSMT Integrated Logistic Support Management Team

ILSP Integrated Logistic Support Plan(ning)

ILSR Institute for Law and Social Research; Institute for Local Self-Reliance

ilsw interrupt-level status word

ilt interferometric landmark tracker; in lieu thereof

ILT Illinois Terminal (railroad)

ILTF International Lawn Tennis Federation

ILTS Institute of Low Temperature Science; Integration Level Test Series

iltw intermediate-level transuranic waste

ILU Institute of Life Insurance; Institute of London Underwriters

ilv induced leukemia virus(es)

iiw intermediate-level wastes

ILWU International Longshoremen's and Warehousemen's Union

Ilya Murometz Glière's Symphony No. 3

Ilyusha (Russian nickname—Ilya)

ILZ Illinois Zinc (company)

ILZRO International Lead Zinc Research Organization

im immature; imperial measure; impulse modulation; infectious mononucleosis; inner marker; installation maintenance; installment mortgage; intensity modulation; intermodulation; intramuscular

im (IM) inland marine (insurance); interceptor missile

i&m improvement and modernization

'im him

im in dem (German—in the); *imeni* (Russian—in the name of); (Latin—in)—imprint(ing)

Im Imperial

I'm I am

IM impulse modulation; Industrial Management; Institute of

Metallurgists; Institute of Metals; intermediate modulation; Inventory Manager

I of M Institute of Medicine

IM Index Medicus

ima ideal mechanical advantage

I^ma prima (Italian—first)

IMA Ignition Manufacturers Institute; Indian Military Academy; Indonesian Mining Association; Industrial Marketing Association; Industrial Medical Association; Institute for Mediterranean Affairs; Institute of Municipal Administration; Instituto Mobiliare Italiano; International Management Association; International Mineralogical Association; Islamic Mission of America

IMAA Indochinese Mutual Assistance Association

imac integrated microwave amplifier converter

IMAC International Metals and Commodities

imag imaginary

IMAGE Instruction in Motivation Achievement and General Education

Image Maker Thomas Nast

IMAGI Index Measuring Accurate Growth of Inflation

IMAJ International Management Association of Japan

Imamu Amiri Baraka Le Roi Jones

IMAR Inner Mongolia Autonomous Region (of the People's Republic of China)

IMarE Institute of Marine Engineers

IMARPE Instituto de Mar del Peru (Spanish—Sea Institute of Peru)

IMARS Institutional Management for Accountability and Renewal System

IMAS Integrated Management Accounting System

IMAU International Movement for Atlantic Union

IMAU Instituto Municipal de Aseo Urbano (Spanish—Municipal Institute of Urban Sanitation)

IMAWU International Molders and Allied Workers Union

imb interaction of man and the biosphere

IMB Institute of Marine Biochemistry; Institute of Marine Biology; International Maritime Bureau

IMBC Independent and Multi-

Cultural Broadcasting Corporation

IMBE Institute for Minority Business Education

IMBLMS Integrated Medical and Behavioral Laboratory Measurement System (NASA)

IMBO Institutt for Marin Biologi (Oslo)

imc image motion compensation; instrument meteorological condition

IMC Industrial Management Center; Instructional Materials Center; Instructional Media Center; International Maritime Committee; International Medical Corps; International Meteorological Committee; International Minerals & Chemical; International Mining Corporation; International Missionary Council; International Monetary Conference; International Music Council; Iran Meat Corporation

IMC Instituto Mexicano del Café (Spanish—Mexican Coffee Institute)

IMCA Institute of Management Consultants in Australia

imcc item management control code

IMCC Integrated Mission Control Center

IMCE Instituto Mexicano de Comercio Exterior (Spanish—Mexican Institute of Foreign Commerce)

IMCEA International Military Club Executives Association

IMCI Interracial Music Council, Incorporated

imco improved combustion

IMCO Inter-Governmental Maritime Consultative Organization

IMCOS International Meteorological Consultant Service

IMCOV Iron Mines Company of Venezuela

IMCS Interactive Manufacturing Control System

IMD Indian Medical Department; Inventory Management Division

IMDA Indirect Missile Damage Assessment

IMDC Internal Message Distribution Center

IMDGC International Maritime Dangerous Goods Code

IMDS International Microform Distribution Service

imdt immediate(ly)

imdtty it's my duty to tell you

ime (IME) international magnetospheric explorer

IME Indo-Malaysian Engineering; Institute of Makers of Explosives; Institute of Marine Engineers; Institution of Mechanical Engineers

I&ME Indiana and Michigan Electric Company

I of ME Institution of Mining Engineers

I Mech E Institution of Mechanical Engineers

IMEG International Management and Engineering Group

IMEO Interim Maintenance Engineering Order

imep indicated mean effective pressure

IMER Institute for Marine Environmental Research

I Met Institute of Metals

imf intermediate fuel

imf (IMF) integrated maintenance facility

IMF International Metalworkers Federation; International Monetary Fund; International Motorcycle Federation; Interstate Motor Freight (stock exchange symbol); Israel Music Foundation

IMFC Investment and Merchant Finance Corporation

IM FI International Mineral Fiber Institute

IMFJC International Metalworkers Federation Japan Council

im/fm intensity modulated/frequency modulated

imfrad integrated multiple-frequency radar

IMF/SDR International Monetary Fund—Special Drawing Rights

imfu immense military fuckup

img informational media guarantee

IMG International Marxist Group

IMH Institute of Materials Handling

imhe international management in higher education

IMHT Institute for Material Handling Teachers

imi improved manned interceptor

IMI Ignition Manufacturers Institute; International Masonry Institute; Irish Management Institute; Israel Military Industries; Israeli Military Intelligence

IMI Instituto Mobiliare Italiano (Italian Assets Institution)—credit bank

IMIA International Marketing Institute of Australia

IMIB Inland Marine Insurance Bureau

imid inadvertent missile ignition detection

imieo initial mass in earth orbit

IMIMI Industrial Mineral Insulation Manufacturers Institute

IMINCO Iran Marine International Oil Company

IMinE Institute of Mining Engineers

IMINOCO Iranian Marine International Oil Company

imit imitate; imitation

IMIT Institute of Musical Instrument Technicians

imitac image input to automatic computers

imit lea imitation leather

iml inside mold layer; inside mold line

Iml Imanuel

IML International Music League; Irradiated Materials Laboratory; Island Merchants Limited (Cook Islands)

IMLS Institute of Medical Laboratory Sciences

IMLT Institute of Medical Laboratory Technology

imm immediate; immune; immunization; immunologist; immunology; impairing a minor's morals; impairing the morals of a minor

Imm Immingham

IMM Institute of Mining and Metallurgy; Integrated Maintenance Management; International Mercantile Marine; International Monetary Market (Chicago)

immac inventory management and material control

immat immature; immaturity

immed immediate

immedly immediately

immie imitation marble; low-grade playing marble

immig immigrant; immigration

immob immobilization; immobilize

Immortal Beloved Nadejda von Meck (benefactress and friend of Tchaikovsky who dedicated his Fourth Symphony to this admirer he never met)

Immortal Dreamer John Bunyan

Immortal Four Italian poets Dante Alighieri, Ludovico

Ariosto, Francesco Petrarca (Petrarch), Bernardo Tasso
Immortal Infidel Col Robert G Ingersoll
Immortals the forty members of the French Academy
Immortal Sarah Sarah Bernhardt (originally Rosine Bernard)
Immortal Tinker author-tinker John Bunyan
Immortal Trio John Caldwell Calhoun, Henry Clay, Daniel Webster
IMMS International Material Management Society
IMMT Integrated Maintenance Management Team
IMMTS Indian Mercantile Marine Training Ship
immun immunity; immunization
immunol immunologist; immunology; imunologic(al)(ly)
immy immediately
imn indicated mach number
IMNS Imperial Military Nursing Service
imo imitation (slang short form); immobilized
IMO Integrated Marketing Organization; Inter-American Municipal Organization; International Meteorological Organization (World Meteorological Organization)
imos inadvertent modification of the stratosphere
imp. imperative; imperfect; imperial; implement; implementation; import; imprint; improve; improvement
imp. (IMP) indeterminate mass particle; inertial measuring platform; international match point
imp. impotentia (Latin—impotent); *imprenta* (Spanish—printing office, printing press); *imprimatur* [Latin—let it be printed (R.C. Church)]; *imprimé* (French—printed); *imprimis* (Latin—especially, particularly)
Imp. Imperator (Latin—Emperor); *Imperatrix* (Latin—Empress)
IMP Instrumented Mobile Platform (oceanographic drone boat); International Monitoring Probe (space instrument); Interplanetary Monitoring Platform (space vehicle)
IMP Instituto Mexicano del Petroleo (Spanish—Mexican Petroleum Institute)

imp. 8 imperial octavo (7½ × 11-inch or 19 × 28-cm book size)
IMPA International Master Printers Association; International Museum Photographers Association; International Myopia Prevention Association
impact. implementation planning and control technique
IMPACT Improving Public Awareness of Concepts of Telecommunications; Interdisciplinary Model Programs in the Arts for Children and Teachers
Impala South African version of Aermacchi MB-326 counterinsurgency aircraft
Imp B Imperial Beach
impce importance
imper imperative
imperf imperfect
Imperial Haydn's Symphony No. 99 in E flat
Imperial City Rome
Imperial Impersonation of Force and Murder Napoleon
Imperialist Composer Sir Edward Elgar (whose *Pomp and Circumstance March*—No. 1 in D major—contains the second national anthem of the British *Land of Hope and Glory*)
Imperialist Poet Rudyard Kipling (although it was the comic writer Hilaire Belloc who wrote: *Whatever happens we have got/The Maxim gun, and they have not.*)
Imperialist Poet-Writer Rudyard Kipling
Imperial President Franklin D Roosevelt
impers impersonal
imp-exp import-export
impf imperfect
impg importing; impregnate
imp. gal imperial gallon
IMPI International Microwave Power Institute
impig impignorate; impignorated; impignorating; impignoration
impl imperial; implement
implic import license
import importaciones (Spanish—imports)
imposs impossible
impr improvement
impr impresión; imprenta (Spanish—edition, printing office)
impracl impracticable
impreg impregnate(d); impreg-

nation
IMPRESS Inter-disciplinary Machine Processing for Research and Education in the Social Sciences
imprim. imprimatur (Latin—let it be printed)
Impr Nat Imprimerie Nationale (French—National Printing Office of France)
improp improper(ly)
Improper Bostonian Dr Oliver Wendell Holmes
improv improvement
imps. interplanetary measurement probes
Imps Imperial Tobacco Company
IMPS Inpatient Multidimensional Psychiatric Scale; Institute of Management Public Speaking
impt important
imptd imported
imptr importer
Imptypco Imperial Typewriter Company (also appears as ITC)
impv imperative
impvt improvement
impx impaction
imqc imported merchandise quantity control
IMR Individual Medical Report; Institute of Marine Resources; Institute of Masonry Research; Institute for Materials Research; Institute for Medical Research; Institute for Mortuary Research; Institute for Motivational Research; Institute for Muscle Research; International Medical Research
IMRA Industrial Marketing Research Association
IMRADS Information Management, Retrieval, and Dissemination System
imran international marine radio aids to navigation
IMRC International Marine Radio Company
IMRL Individual Material Readiness List(ing)
IMRO Inspection Minor Rework Order; Interior Macedonian Revolutionary Organization
IMRS Inpatient Multidimensional Rating Scale
ims industrial methylated spirit(s); inertial measurement set
im's intramuscular injections
IMS Index Management System; Indian Medical Service;

Individualized Mathematics System; Industrial Management Society; Industrial Mathematics Society; Information Management System; Institute of Management Sciences; Institute of Marine Science; Institute of Mathematical Statistics; Institute of Museum Services; Institute on Man and Science; International Magnetic System; International Magnetosphere Study; International Musicological Society; International Mythological Society

IMSA International Management Systems Association; International Municipal Signal Association

IMSC International Maritime Satellite Corporation; International Military Sports Council

IMSCOM International Military Staff Communication (NATO)

IMS/HEW Institute of Museum Services—HEW

IMSL Independent Measurement Standards Laboratory; International Mathematical and Statistical Library

IMSM Institute of Marketing and Sales Management

IMSO Institute of Municipal Safety Officers

IMSR Isle of Man Steam Railway

imss integrated manned-system simulator

IMSS Integrated Manned Systems Simulator; International Museum of Surgical Science

IMSS Instituto Mexicano del Seguro Social (Spanish—Mexican Social Security Institute)

imt independent model triangulation

IMT International Military Tribunal

IMTA Imported Meat Trade Association; Institute of Municipal Treasurers and Accountants

IMTC Instituto Municipal de Transporte Colectiva (Spanish—Municipal Institute of Collective Transport)—metropolitan bus system

IMTD Inspectors of the Military Training Directorate

IM Tech Institute of Metallurgists Technician

IMTFE International Military Tribunal for the Far East

IMTP Industrial Mobilization Training Program

imu inertial measurement unit

IMU International Mailers Union; International Maritime Union

IMUA Inland Marine Underwriters Association

I Mun E Institution of Municipal Engineers

imusc intramuscular

imv imperative; improve

IMVS Institute of Medical and Veterinary Science

imw international map of the world

IMW Institute of Masters of Wine

imwxprt imitation wax prints

IMX Inquiry Message Exchange

Im Yem Imamate of Yemen

IMZ Internationales Musikzentrum (German—International Music Center)

in. inch(es); interest

in. (In) inch(es)

i/n item number

in (Latin—in)—inbreed(ing), indirect, insulin

In India; Indian; indium; Indus; Instructor

In Indre (Norwegian—inner, interior, inside)

IN Institute of Neurobiology (Göteborg); Interested Negroes

I & N Immigration and Naturalization

I of N Institute of Navigation

in.² square inch(es)

in.³ cubic inch(es)

ina international normal atmosphere

INA Indian National Army; Inspector Naval Aircraft; Institute of National Affairs; Institution of Naval Architects; Insurance Company of North America; Iraqi News Agency; Israeli News Agency

inabi inability

inacdutra inactive duty training

INACESA Industria Nacional de Cemento SA (Spanish—National Cement Industry Company)

INACH Instituto Antártico Chileno (Spanish—Chilean Antarctic Institute)

inactv inactivate; inactivation; inactive

INAEA International Newspaper Advertising Executives Association

InAF Indian Air Force

inah (INAH) isonicotinic acid hydrazide

INAH Instituto Nacional de Antropología e Historia (National Institute of Anthropology and History)—Mexico

INALPRE Instituto Nacional de Preinversión (Spanish—National Investment Control Institute)—Bolivia

inanim inanimate; inanimative

INANTIC Instituto Nacional de Normas Tecnicas Industriales y Certificación (Spanish—National Institute of Technical Standards)

inappbl inapplicable

INAR Institute of Northern Agricultural Research

in'ards innards

INAS Inertial Navigation and Attack System(s)

inaud inaudible

inaug inaugurate; inaguration

inaug diss inaugural dissertation (thesis for doctor's degree)

Inauguration Inauguration Day (January 20 in the U.S.A.)

in bal. in ballast

inbd inboard

inbu internal navigation battery unit

INBUCON International Business Consultants

inc in cloud; inclosure; include; income; increase; incumbent

Inc Inchon; Incorporated

In C Instructor Captain

INC Indian National Congress; Industrial National Corporation; International Narcotics Control; Island Navigation Company (tankers)

INC Instituto Nacional de Cultura (Spanish—National Institute of Culture)—Lima, Peru's Library

inca inventory control and analysis

Inca Incahuasi

INCA Information Council of the Americas; International Newspaper Color Association; Inventory Control and Analysis

incair including air

incalz incalzando (Italian—increasing dynamics and tone)

incan incandescent

Incan and Aztecan Century the 1000s—great monuments standing in the highlands of Peru and Mexico attest to these astounding American cultures—the 11th century

incap incapacitant; incapacitating

INCAP *Instituto de Nutrición de Centroamerica y Panamá* (Spanish—Institute of Nutrition of Central America and Panama)

incaps incapacitating agents

Inca's curse diarrhea picked up in the Land of the Incas—Bolivia and Peru as well as neighboring countries such as Ecuador and Chile

incb inclusion body

INCB International Narcotics Control Board (Geneva, Switzerland)

incct incorrect

inccty incorrectly

incd incendiary; incident

incdt incident

ince insurance

INCE Institute of Noise Control Engineering

incfmy inconformity

inch. inchoative; integrated chopper

In-Ch Indo-China

Inchcape Rock (*see* Bell Rock)

inchoat inchoative

Inchon formerly Chemulpo or Jinsen

incid incidence; incident; incidental

incid mus incidental music

INCING International Copyright Information Center

INCIRS International Communication Information Retrieval System

incl inclose; inclosure; include; including; inclusive

incl *inclusivement* (French—inclusively)

incld included

inclu inclusion

inclr intercooler

inclsv inclusive

INCMD Indianapolis Contract Management District

INCO International Nickel Company

incog incognito

INCOLSA Indiana Cooperative Library Services Authority

INCOMAG International Communication Agency

INCOMEX International Computer Exhibition

INCOMEX *Instituto Colombiano de Comercio Exterior* (Spanish—Colombian Institute of Overseas Commerce)

incomp incomplete

Incomparable Infidel Voltaire

incompat incompatible; incompatibility

incompl incomplete

incor incorrect

INCORA *Instituto Colombiano de Reforma Agraria* (Spanish—Colombian Institute of Agrarian Reform)

Incorp Incorporated; Incorporation

incorr incorrect

Incorruptible The Incorruptible —sobriquet given Robespierre by his followers

inco(s) incorrigible(s)

incpt intercept

incr increase; increased; increasing; increasingly; increment; incremental

INCRA International Copper Research Association

INCREF International Children's Rescue Fund

incrim incriminate; incrimination; incriminatory

incumb incumbent

incun incunabula

incur. incurable

ind independent; index; indicate; indicative; indicator; indigo; indorse; indorsement; industrial; industry

ind (IND) investigational new drug

in d. *in diem*(Latin—daily)

Ind India; Indian; Indiana; Indianapolis; Indianian; Indo-; Indus (constellation); Industries; industry

Ind Indian (second only to Chinese in terms of the number of people who speak one or more of India's languages—205 million who speak Hindi, 12 million who speak Bengali, 57 million—Urdu, 53 million— Telugo, another 53 million— Punjabi, plus the million more communicating in Tamil, Marathi, Gujarati, Kannada, Oriya, Malayalam, Bihari, Rajasthani, the Pushtu of Pakistan, as well as the Assamese, Nepali, Sinhalese, Sindi, and lesser languages of the great subcontinent—India); *Indiano* (Italian—Indian, Indian Ocean); *Indico* (Portuguese or Spanish—Indian, Indian Ocean); *Indien* (French—Indian, Indian Ocean)

IND India (auto plaque); Indianapolis, Indiana (airport)

INDA International Non-wovens and Disposables Association

indac industrial data acquisition and control

INDALUM *Industria del Aluminio* (Spanish—Aluminum Industry)

INDASAT Indian Scientific Satellite

INDAX Interactive Data Exchange

Ind Day Independence Day (celebrated in the U.S. every July 4)

Ind Dem Independent Democrat

Ind. E. Industrial Engineer

indecl indeclinable

INDECO Industrial Development Corporation; International Development and Construction Corporation

indef indefinite

indef art. indefinite article

Indefatigable Island, Galápagos Chaves *or* Santa Cruz

Indefatigable Polemicist Alexander Solzhenitsyn

indefops indefinite operations

indem indemnify; indemnity

inden indenture; indentured; indenturing

Ind Eng Industrial Engineer(ing)

Ind Eng Chem *Industrial and Engineering Chemistry*

Ind & Eng Chem *Industrial and Engineering Chemistry*

indep independent

INDEP *Industria Nacional del Plomo* (Spanish—National Lead Institute)

Independence Day July 4 (commemorating the signing of the *Declaration of Independence* on July 4, 1776 in Philadelphia)—other independence days listed by countries, e.g, Bolivia Day, Chile Day, etc

Ind-et-L Indre-et-Loire

Index *Index Librorum Prohibitorum [Latin—Index of Forbidden Books (RC Church)]*; *Index on Censorship*

indi indicate; indication

india india chintz or india cotton (heavy figured fabric used by upholsterers); india ink (glue + lampblack) also called chinese ink

India letter I radio code; Republic of India (Asian nation with one of the world's oldest civilizations), Indians have fourteen official languages including English and Hindi, overpopulation imperils its people); *Bharat* (India's name in Hindi)

Indian MacDowell's Suite No. 2

for Orchestra introducing American Indian themes

Indiana Girls Indiana Girls School (for juvenile delinquents at Indianapolis)

Indianap Indianapolis

Indianapolis Indiana's capital

Indiana Ports (east to west) Michigan City, Gary, Buffington, Indiana Harbor

Indian Film Pioneer Satyajit Ray

Indian Girl Guide Sacajawea who guided Lewis and Clark; both Idaho and South Dakota claim her as a native daughter

Indiano (Italian—Indian)—Indian Ocean

Indian Ocean between Africa, India, and Indo-Australia area; southern reaches extend to Antarctica

Indian OPEC CERT (Council of Energy Resource Tribes) holding coal, geothermal, and oil-productive lands in many parts of the United States

Indian Ports (large, medium, and small from the west coast to the east coast) Mamdvi, Kandla, Okha, Porbandar, Bhaunagar, Bombay, Mangalor, Cochin, Alleppy, Quilon, Kolachel, Tuticorin, Negapatam, Madras, Kakinada, Vishakhapatnam, Paradip, Calcutta

Indian Princess Pocahontas

Indian's Friend Roger Williams

Indian Territory old name of Oklahoma

India's Day Indian Independence Day (August 15)

Indias Occidentales (Spanish—West Indies)

Indias Orientales (Spanish—East Indies)

India's Principal Ports Calcutta on the Bay of Bengal, Bombay on the Arabian Sea—both are Indian Ocean ports

indic indicative; indicator

indic indicateur (French—informer)

Índico (Portuguese or Spanish—Indian)—Indian Ocean

indicolite blue tourmaline

Indien (German—Indian)—Indian Ocean

Indie Occidentali (Italian—West Indies)

Indie Orientale (Italian—East Indies)

indies independents

Indies East Indies; West Indies

Ind. Imp. Indiae Imperator (Latin—Emperor of India)

Indira Indira Ghandi (India's first woman prime minister)

INDITECNOR Instituto Nacional de Investigaciones Tecnologicas y Normalización (Spanish—National Institute for Technical and Standardization Investigation)

indiv individual

indivl individual

indiv psychol individual psychology

Ind L Independent Liberal

Ind Lab Independent Labor (party)

indm indemnity

Ind Med Index Medicus

Ind Mgr Industrial Manager

indn indication (flow chart)

Indo Indonesia; Indonesian

Ind O Indian Ocean

Indo-Afr Indo-African

Indo-Austral Indo-Australasian

indoc indoctrinate; indoctrination

Indoc Indochina; Indochinese

Indo-Chi Indo-China; Indo-Chinese

Indochina southeast-Asian peninsula containing peoples of Burma, Kampuchea or Cambodia, Laos, Thailand or Siam, and Vietnam

indocin indomethacine

Indo-Eur Indo-European

Indo-Ger Indo-German(ic)

Indo-Mal Indo-Malayan

Indon Indonesia(n)

Indon Indonesian (modified Malay language used by more than 93 million Indonesians)

Indonesia Republic of Indonesia (Asian island nation occupying what was the Dutch East Indies consisting of some 13,000 islands strung along the Equator, Bahasa Indonesian, a form of Malay, is the official tongue) *Republik Indonesia*

Indonesian Ports (large and medium) Tandjungpriok (Djakarta or Jakarta on Java), Surabaya (on Java), Makassar (on Celebes or Sulawesi)

Indonesias Indonesian Islands

Indonesia's Largest Port Djakarta (Jakarta)—also called Tandjungpriok

Indo-Pak India-Pakistan; Indo-Pakistan(i)

Indostán (Spanish—Hindustan, India)

INDOSUEZ Banque de l'Indochine et de Suez (French—

Bank of Indochina and Suez)

indpol industrial pollutant; industrial pollution

indr indicator (flow chart)

indre indenture

ind reg induction regulator

Ind Rep Independent Republican

Ind Sym Indianapolis Symphony

indt indent

Ind Ter Indian Territory (now Oklahoma)

indtr indentor

induc inductance; induction

INDUGAS Industria de Gas (Spanish—Gas Industry)

Ind U Pr Indiana University Press

indus industrial; industry

Indus 1900 mile Indian river entering Arabian Sea near Karachi

indust industrial; industrialization; industrialize; industrialized; industry

Industrial Capital of Connecticut Bridgeport

indvl individual

Indy Indianapolis; Indianapolis Speedway

Indy-style Indianapolis-style

inec inverted emulsifiable concentrate

ined. ineditus (Latin—unpublished)

INED Institute for New Enterprise Development

ineffv ineffective

inefvy ineffectively

inel inelastic

INEL Idaho National Engineering Laboratory (ERDA)

INEOA International Narcotic Enforcement Officers Association

Iness Inverness-shire

in ex. in extenso (Latin—at length)

Inextinguishable Nielsen's Symphony No. 4

inf infant(ile); infantry; infect(ious); inferior; infinitive; infinity; influence; information

inf (INF) interceptor night fighter; intermediate-range nuclear force

inf. infra (Latin—below, beneath); *infunde* (Latin—pour into)

Inf Infirmary

Inf Inférieur (French—lower, nether)

INF Intermediate-Range Nuclear Forces; International

Naturist Federation; International Nudist Federation

INFA *Institut pour l' Etude du Fascisme* (French—Institute for the Study of Fascism)

INFAMA International Fair Promotion and Marketing

INFANTS Iroquois Night Fighter And Night Tracker System

infarc infarction

Inf Bat Infantry Battalion

infce international nuclear-fuel-cycle evaluation

infe inferior

infect. infection; infectious

infin infinitive

infirm. infirmary

infl inflammable; influence(d)

in-fl in-flight

influ influence; influential

infm information

infmry infirmary

INFN Istituto Nazionale di Fisica Nucleare (National Institute of Nuclear Physics)—Italy

info inform; information

INFO International Fortean Organization

Info Can Information Canada

infol **(INFOL)** information-oriented language

INFONAC *Instituto de Fomento Nacional* (Spanish—Institute for National Production)

inforem inventory forecasting and replenishment module(s)

INFORFILM International Information Film Service

Informbureau Communist Information Bureau (Cominform)

Informburo (Soviet) Information Bureau

Informex *Informaciones Mexicanas* (Mexican Information Service)

INFORS International Federation of Engineers

INFORSA *Industrias Forestal SA* (Spanish—Forest Industries Corporation)

INFOTERM International Information Center for Terminology (UNESCO)

info theory information theory

infr inferior

infra below

infra (Latin prefix—beneath)—infraspinal, infrastructure

infra dig. *infra dignitatem* (Latin —beneath one's dignity, undignified)

infral information retrieval atuomatic language

---

infraptum. *infrascriptum* (Latin —written below)

Infrared Phys Infrared Physics

infric. *infricetur* (Latin—let it be rubbed in)

infross information requirements of the social sciences

inft infant

infus infusible

infx inspection fixture

ing inguinal

ing *ingégnere* (Italian—engineer); *ingegneria* (Italian—engineering); *ingeniør* (Dano-Norwegian—engineer)

Ing Ingmar

Ing *Ingênieur* (French—engineer); *Ingenieur* (German—engineer)

inga inspection gage

INGA Interstate Natural Gas Association

INGAA Interstate Natural Gas Association of America

INGEOMINAS *Instituto de Investigaciones Geologica Mineras* (Spanish—Institute of Geological Sources Research)

Ingg *Inggeris* (Malay—English)

Inghilterra (Italian—England)

Ingl *Inghilterra* (Italian—England); *Inglaterra* (Portuguese or Spanish—England)

Inglaterra (Portuguese or Spanish—England)

Ingm Berg Ingmar Bergman

INGO International Non-Governmental Organization

Ingred(s) ingredient(s)

Ingria Ingermanland

Ingrid Ingrid Bergman

inh **(INH)** isonicotinic hydrazide

Inh *Inhaber* (German—proprietor)

INH *Instituto Nacional de Hipódromos* (Spanish—National Institute of Racetracks)

inhab inhabitant(s)

inhal inhalation

in. Hg inch of mercury

inhib inhibition; inhibitory

INHP Independence National Historical Park

INHS Indian Naval Hospital Ship

INI Indianapolis Newspapers Incorporated; Industrial Nurses Institute; Institut National De l'Industrie (National Institute of Industry)

INI *International Nursing Index*

INIA *Instituto Nacional de Investigaciones Agricolas* (Spanish—National Institute of

---

Agricultural Research)

INIBP Instituto Nacional de Investigaciones Biológico-Pesqueras

INIC *Instituto Nacional de Investigaciones Cientifica* (Spanish—National Institute for Scientific Investigation)

INIF *Instituto Nacional de Investigaciones Forestales* (Spanish—National Institute for Forestry Research)

in./in. inch per inch

in init. *in initio* (Latin—in the beginning)

INIP *Instituto Nacional de Investigaciones Pecuarias* (Spanish–National Institute for Cattle Research)

INIS International Nuclear Information System

init initial

initv initiative

inj inject; injection; injections; injure; injury

Inj. *Injectio* (Latin—inject, injection)

inj. enema *injiciatur enema* (Latin—inject an enema)

inj. hyp. *injectio hypodermica* (Latin—hypodermic injection)

inj mldg injection moulding

inkl *inklusiv* (German—inclusive)

inl initial

In L Instructor Lieutenant

INL Independent Newspapers Limited

INLA International Nuclear Law Association; Irish National Liberation Army

Inland Empire official nickname of Illinois

Inland Sea Pacific Ocean inlet between Honshu and Kyusho islands, Japan—about 250 miles

inlaw (INLAW) infantry laser weapon

in.-lb inch-pound

In L-Cdr Instructor Lieutenant-Commander

in lim. *in limine* (Latin—at the outset)

in litt. *in litteris* (Latin—in correspondence)

in loc. *in loco* (Latin—in the place)

in. loc. cit. *in loco citato* (Latin—in the place cited)

Inlt Inlet (postal abbreviation)

inly initially

INM Institute of Naval Medicine; Irish National Museum

inmarsat international marine

satellite
INMARSATORG International Maritime Satellite Organization
INMAS Intensifikasi Massnal (Indonesian—Mass Intensification)
INMED Indians into Medicine
in mem. in memoriam (Latin—in memory of)
i n mi international nautical mile(s)
INMM Institute of Nuclear Materials Management
inn. inning
Inn. Innoshima
INN Instituto Nacional de Normalización (Spanish—National Institute of Standards); *Instituto Nacional de Nutrición* (Spanish—National Institute of Nutrition)
inner cities euphemism for abandoned or poor downtown areas formerly called ghettos or slums
inner city economically deprived downtown residential area often called the ghetto and often including the slums; inner-core city
Inner City Peking's Forbidden or Tartar City containing the Palace Museum
Inner Libya the Sudan Desert extending from southern Egypt and the Sudan to Africa's west coast
Inner Mongolia northern China bordering on Mongolia
innerv innervated; innervation
Innis Inniskilling
Innisfail (Gaelic—Isle of Destiny)—Ireland
INNOTECH Institute for Educational Innovation and Technology
inns. innings
INO Inspectorate of Naval Ordnance
inoc inoculation; inoculate
INOC Iraq National Oil Company
INOCO Indonesian Nippon Oil Corporation
inop inoperative
inorg inorganic
Inorg Chem Inorganic Chemistry
INOS Instituto Nacional de Obras Sanitarias (National Institute of Sanitation—Venezuela)
in-out input-output
inp inert nitrogen protection
INP Inyanga National Park

(Rhodesia)
INPA International Newspaper Promotion Association
in partibus in partibus infidelium (Latin—in the region of the unbelievers)
INPFC International North Pacific Fisheries Commission
inph interphone
in p. inf. in partibus infidelium (Latin—in the region of the unbelievers)
INPO Institute of Nuclear Power Operations
INPOLSE International Police Services (CIA)
inpr in progress
in pr. in principio (Latin—in the first place)
Inprecorr International Press Correspondence
in prep in preparation
in pro in proportion
inprons information processing in the central nervous system
inps if not previously sold
in pulm. in pulmento (Latin—in gruel)
inq inquiry
Inq Inquisidor (Spanish—inquisitor, investigator)
INQUA International Association on Quaternary Research
inr impact noise rating; impact noise ratio; intelligence and research
in'r inner
i-n r interference-to-noise ratio
INR Institut National de la Radio (National Radio Institute); Institute of Natural Resources; Intelligence and Research
INRA Instituto Nacional de la Reforma Agraria (National Institute of Agrarian Reform)—exercises economic control of Cuba
in re (Latin—in the matter of)
in ref in reference (to)
in req information requested
In Res Indian Reservation
I.N.R.I. Iesus Nazarenus Rex Iudaeorum (Latin—Jesus of Nazareth, King of the Jews)
INRO International Natural Rubber Organization
ins inches; inscribe(d); inscription; inspector; insular; insulate(d); insulation; insurance; insure(d)
ins (INS) inertial navigation system
in's in his
in./s inch(s) per second
in s in situ (Latin—in the original place)

Ins Insecta
INS Immigration and Naturalization Service; Indian Naval Ship; Inertial Navigation System; Institute of Naval Studies; Institute of Nuclear Sciences; Institute of Nutritional Sciences; Integrated Navigation System; International News Service
I & NS Immigration and Naturalization Service
INSA International Shipowners Association
INSA Industria Nacional de Neumaticos SA (Spanish—National Tire Industry Corporation)
InsACS Interstate Airway Communication Station
Ins Agt Insurance Agent
INSAIR Inspector of Naval Aircraft
INSAT Indian National Satellite
insav interim shipyward availability
INSCAIRS Instrumentation Calibration Incident Repair Service
insce insurance
INSCO Intercontinental Shipping Corporation
inscr inscribed; inscription
INSDC Indian National Scientific Documentation Center
INSDOC Indian National Scientific Documentation Center
insd val insured value
INS & E Institute of Nuclear Science and Engineering
INSEA International Society for Education Through Art
in./sec inches per second
insecti insecticide(s)
INSEL International Nickel Southern Exploration Limited
INSENG Inspector of Naval Engineering Material
insep inseparable
Ins Gen Inspector General
insh inspection shell
Inside Passage protected inland passage between southern Alaska and northern Washington; also called Inner Passage
insig insignificant
insinuendo insinuate + innuendo
INSIS Inter-Institutional Integrated Services Information System
INSJ Institute for Nuclear Study—Japan

insl insulate; insulation
INSMACH Inspector of Naval Machinery
INSMAT Inspector of Naval Material
INSNAVMAT Inspector of Navigational Material (USN)
insol insoluble
insolv insolvent
insolv insolubility
***INSORA** Instituto de Organización y Administración de Empresas* (Spanish—Institute for the Organization and Administration of Enterprises)
INSORD Inspector of Naval Ordnance
insp inspect; inspected; inspection; inspector; inspiration; inspire; inspired
Insp Inspector
in-spec within specifications
INSPECC Information Services in Physics, Electrotechnology, Computers, and Control
INSPECT Infrared System for Printed-Circuit Testing; Inquiry into Pollution and Environmental Conservation; Integrated Nationwide System for Processing Entries from Customs Terminals
***INSPEL** International Journal of Special Libraries*
INSPETRES Inspector of Petroleum Resources
insp Gen Inspector General
***inspir.** inspiretur* (Latin—let it be inspired)
INSPIRE Institute for Public Interest Representation
Inspired Innovator Edgar Allan Poe
Inspr Inspector
INSRADMET Inspector of Radio Materials
INSRP Interagency Nuclear Safety Review Panel
inst install; installation; installment; instant; instantaneous; institution; instruct; instruction; instructor; instrument; instrumentation; instrumented; institute
Inst Institute; Institution
INSTAAR Institute of Arctic and Alpine Research
INSTAB Information Service on Toxicity and Biodegradability
insta-cam instant camera (tv)
Instant Asia polyglot Singapore with its Chinese, Indian, Malay, Pakistani, and Singhalese mixtures and tongues making this seaport nation a global crossroads

Instant Orient Singapore—crossroads of Asia
instar inertialess scanning, tracking, and ranging
INSTARS Information Storage and Retrieval System
Inst CE Institute of Civil Engineers
Inst Ceram Institution of Ceramics
inst ctl instrumentation control
instd instead
Inst Dirs Institute of Directors
Inst EE Institute of Electrical Engineers
Inst F Institute of Fuel
Inst Gas Eng Institute of Gas Engineers
Inst Gen Sem Institute of General Semantics
Inst HE Institute of Highway Engineers
Inst Int Educ Institute of International Education
instln installation
instm instrument; instrumentation; instrumented
Inst ME Institute of Mechanical Engineers
Inst Mediaeval Mus Institute of Mediaeval Music
Inst Met Institute of Metals
Inst Mod Lang Institute of Modern Languages
instn institution(al)
INSTN Institut National des Sciences et Techniques nucléaires (National Institute of Science and Nuclear Techniques)
instns instructions
Inst P Institute of Physics
Inst Pat Institute of Patentees
Inst Pckg Institute of Packing
Inst Pet Institute of Petroleum
Inst Plan & Res Institute for Planning and Research
instpn instrument panel
Inst P S Institute of Purchasing and Supply
instr instruct; instruction; instructor; instrument(s)
instru instrumentation
instruct. instruction; instructor
Instru Soc Am Instrument Society of America
Inst W Institute of Welding
Inst WE Institute of Water Engineers
insuf insufficient
insultant(s) nickname for overpaid consultant(s)
insur insurance
Insurance Capital Hartford, Connecticut and Omaha, Ne-

braska both claim this nickname
Insurance City place-name nickname shared by Atlanta, Georgia and Hartford, Connecticut
insurd insured
INSURV Board of Inspection and Survey
in sync in synchronization; perfectly synchronized
int intake; integer; integral; interest; interior; interjection; internal; international; intersection
int (INT) initial (flow chart)
Int International
INT Air Inter (Lignes Aériennes Intérieures); Interpool
INTA International New Thought Alliance
***INTA** Instituto Nacional de Tecnologia Agropecuaria* (Spanish—National Institute of Agricultural Technology)
INTACS Integrated Tactical Communications Systems
INTAF Internal Affairs (ministry)
***int. al.** inter alia* (Latin—among other things)
***INTAL** Industria Nacional de Tejidos de Alambre* (Spanish—National Wire Netting Industry)
INTAMEL International Association of Metropolitan City Libraries
INTASGRO Interallied Tactical Study Group (NATO)
***int. cib.** inter cibos* (Latin—between meals)
intcl intercoastal
intcol intelligence collecting; intelligence collection
int comb. internal combustion
Int Com Illum International Commission on Illumination
intcp intercept; interception; interceptor
int dec interior decorator
Int Doc Serv International Documents Service (Columbia University)
INTECOM International Council for Technical Communication
Integ Ed Assoc Integrated Education Associates
intel intelligence
Intellectual Emperor of Europe Voltaire
Intellectual Historian Sir Isaiah Berlin
Intellectual Seed Pod of the Nation Emerson's nickname for Concord, Massachusetts

where he lived with such neighbors as the Alcotts, Hawthorne, and Thoreau

intelpost (INTELPOST) international post (computerized postal service)

intelsat international telecommunications satellite

Intelsat International Telecommunications Satellite Organization

INTELSAT International Telecommunications Satellite Organization

inteltng intelligence training

INTEM *Instituto Interamericano de Educacion Musical* (Inter-American Institute of Musical Education)

Intend *Intendente* (Spanish—manager, police commissioner, provincial governor, superintendent, supervisor)

intens intensive

inter intercalation; interest; intermediate; interrogation

inter (Latin prefix—among or between)—interborough, international

Interarmco International Armament Corporation

INTERASMA Association Internationale d'Asthmologie (International Association for the Study of Asthma)

Interavia *World Review of Aviation and Astronautics*

Interchem Interchemical Corporation

intercom intercommunication system

interd interested

INTERDATA Interdata Computers

interdict. intelligence detection and interdiction countermeasures

interdisc interdisciplinary

INTER-EXPERT International Association of Experts

INTEREXPO International Expositions

interf interference

INTERFILM International Church Film Center

INTERFLORA International Florists (telegraphic service)

interg interesting

interi (Japanese short form—intellectual)

Interior US Department of the Interior

Interior Plains Canada's great plains

interj interjection

INTERMARC International

Machine-Readable Catalog

Intermex International Mexican Bank

InterMilPol International Military Police (NATO)

intern. internal

internat international; internationalism; internationalist

International Capital New York City—headquarters of the United Nations

International Functionalists Walter Gropius and Mies van der Rohe

International Prizegiver Alfred Nobel

INTERNOISE International Conference on Noise Control Engineering

interp interpolation

Interpace International Pipe and Ceramics

Interpen/IAB Intercontinental Penetration Force/International Anti-communist Brigade

Interpol International Criminal Police Commission

INTERPOL International Criminal Police Organization (Saint-Cloud, France)

Interpreter of the Sea Winslow Homer

Interpreter of the Wild West Frederic Remington

interr interrogative

interrog interrogation; interrogative

INTERSTENO International Federation of Short Hand and Typewriting Stenographers

INTERTANKO International Association of Independent Tanker Owners

Intertel International Television

INTERTELL International Intelligence Legion

intertwangled intertwined + wangled

inter/w intersection with

intest intestinal; intestine

INTEXT International Textbook Company

intfc interference

intg interrogate; interrogator

inth intrathecal

Int Harv International Harvester

intip integrated information processing

INTIPS Integrated Information Processing System

Int J Mag *International Journal of Magnetism*

Int J Quantum Chem *Interna-*

tional Jounral of Quantum Chemistry

Int J Theor Phys *International Journal of Theoretical Physics*

intl international

intl comb. internal combustion

Intl Ctr Envir International Center for Environmental Research

Intl Film Bur International Film Bureau

Intl Review International Review Service

Intl Univs Pr International Universities Press

intmed intermediate

int med (Int Med) internal medicine

intmt intermittent

int. noct. *inter noctem* (Latin—during the night)

intns intransit

INTO Irish National Teachers' Organization

intops interdiction operations

Intourist Soviet Tourist Office

intox intoxicant; intoxicate; intoxicated; intoxication

Int Pap International Paper

intpr interpret; interpretation; interpreter

int qk fl interrupted quick-flashing light

intr intransitive; intruder; intrusion

intra (Latin prefix—inside or within)—intracranial, intrastate

INTRACO International Trading Company

intran input translator

intrans intransitive

in trans in transit

in trans. *in transitu* (Latin—in transit)

intransit intransitive

Int Rep Intelligence Report

Int Rev Internal Revenue

intrex information transfer complex

intrmt interment

intro introduce; introduced; introducing; introduction; introductory; introversion; introvert

introd introduction

introd *introduzione* (Italian—introduction)

intropta. *introscripta* (Latin—written within)

intro(s) introduction(s)

intrp interrupt(ion)

intrpt interpret(ation); interrupt(ion)

Intruder Grumman electronic-intelligence-gathering aircraft

(EA-6B)
intrvlmtr intervalometer
intsf intensification; intensify
int sig interval signal
int std d international standard depth
Int Sum Intelligence Summary
INTU Interpool (container unit)
INTUC Indian National Trades Union Congress
intv independent television
intvlmtr intervalometer
intvw interview
Int Wildlife *International Wildlife*
inu internal navigation unit
INU Nauru Island (airport)
I Nuc E Institute of Nuclear Engineering
inurn inurnment
InUS inside the United States
in ut. *in utero* (Latin—within the uterus)
inv invent; inventor; inventory; invert; inverter; investment; invoice
inv. invenit (Latin—he devised it)
Inv Inverness
INV *Instituto Nacional de la Vivienda* (Spanish—National Housing Institute)
inval invalid(ate)
invc invoice
invcd invoiced
Inventor of Bifocals Benjamin Franklin
Inventor of Calculus Baron Gottfried Wilhelm von Leibniz and Sir Isaac Newton are both credited with this title
Inventor of the Detective Story Edgar Allan Poe
Inventor of the Stethoscope René-Théophile-Hyacinthe Laennec
Inventor of the Telephone a German named Philipp Reis although the Scottish-Canadian Alexander Graham Bell is usually given credit
invert. invertebrate
inves investigate; investigation; investigator
investig investigate; investigation; investigator
invest(s) investigation(s)
inv. et del. *invenit et delineavit* (Latin—devised and drawn)
invic. *invictus* (Latin—unconquerable)—title of a poem by William Ernest Henley—*Invictus*
invisible disease dyslexia
in vit. *in vitro* (Latin—within

glass, within a test tube or other laboratory glass vessel)
in viv. *in vivo* (Latin—within a living body)
invol involuntary
invt inventory
invtn invitation
invtrx inventrix
INWATS Inward Wide Area Telephone Service
INWR Imperial National Wildlife Refuge (Arizona); Iroquois National Wildlife Refuge (New York)
INX Inexco Oil (stock-exchange symbol)
INZP *Index to New Zealand Periodicals*
io ion engine; intraocular
io (IO) inverted original (12-tone)
i/o in and/or over; inboard-outboard (motorboat engine); input/output; instead of
i & o input and output
Io ionium
IO India Office; Information Officer; Inspecting Office(r); Inspection Office(r); Intelligence Office(r); Intercept Office(r); Irish Office; Issuing Office(r)
I/O Inspection Order; Investigating Officer
ioa instrument-operating assembly; instrumentation-operating area
IOA Intelligence Oversight Act; International Omega Association
IOAM Institute of Appliance Manufacturers
IOAT International Organization Against Trachoma
ioau input/output access unit
iob input/output buffer; internal operating budget
I o B Institute of Bakers; Institute of Bankers; Institute of Bookkeepers; Institute of Brewers; Institute of Builders
IOB Institute of Brewing; Intelligence Oversight Board (CIA)
IOBB Independent Order of B'nai B'rith
IOBC Indian Ocean Biological Center; International Organization for Biological Control of Noxious Animals and Plants
IOBI Institute of Bankers in Ireland
IOBS Institute of Bankers in Scotland
ioc initial operational capability;

in our culture
i-o c input-output channel(s)
I o C *Index on Censorship*
IOC Institute of Chemistry; Intergovernmental Oceanographic Commission; International Olympic Committee; Interstate Oil Compact
IOCA Interstate Oil Compounders Association
IOCC Interstate Oil Compact Commission
IOCI Interstate Organized Crime Index
ioco industry-owned contractor operator
iocs interoffice comment sheet
IOCS Input-Output Control System
IOCU International Office of Consumers Unions; International Organization of Consumer Unions
IOCV International Organization of Citrus Virologists
IOD Imperial Order of the Dragon
IODE Imperial Order of Daughters of the Empire
Iodine State South Carolina
I o E International Office of Education; Isle of Ely
IOE Institute of Education; International Office of Epizootics; International Organization of Employers
IOEC International Order for Ethics and Culture
ioem invert oil emulsion mud (oil well)
I o F Institute of Fuel
IOF Independent Order of Foresters; International Oceanographic Foundation; International Olympic Federation; International Olympic Foundation
iofb I only fire blanks (promised a sterile male); intraocular foreign body
IOFC Indian Ocean Fishery Commission
IOFI International Organization of the Flavor Industry
IOFSI Independent Order of the Free Sons of Israel
ioga industry-organized government-approved
IOGP Independent Oil and Gas Producers
IOGT International Order of Good Templars
ioh item(s) on hand
IOH Institute of Heraldry
ioi internal operating instruction

IOI Industrial Oxygen Incorporated; International Ocean Institute; Israel Office of Information

I o J Institute of Journalists

IOJ International Organization of Journalists

IOJD International Order of Job's Daughters

iol intraocular lens

I o L Institute of Librarians

IOL India Office Library (London); Interoffice Letter

Iola Ida B. Wells

Iolo Morgannwg bardic name of Edward Williams

iol('s) interocular lens(es)

IO Ltd Imperial Oil Limited

iom input/output multiplexer

IoM Isle of Man

IOM Institute for Organization Management; Institute of Medicine; Institute of Metallurgists; Institute of Metals

IOMC International Organization for Medical Cooperation

IOME Institute of Marine Engineers

IOMM & P International Organization of Masters, Mates and Pilots

IOMR International Offshore Multihull Rule

IOM SPC Isle of Man Steam Packet Company

IOMTR International Office for Motor Trades and Repairs

iomux input/output multiplexer

Ion Ionic

ION (pseudynymic initials—George Jacob Holyoake); Institute of Navigation

Ionians Ionian Islands

iont in order not to

IOO Inspecting Ordnance Officer

IOOC International Olive Oil Council; Iranian Oil Operating Companies; Irish Organization of Celts

IOOF Independent Order of Odd Fellows

IOOTS International Organization of Old Testament Scholars

iop input-output processor; intraocular power; irrespective of percentage

i & op in-and-out processing

IoP Institute of Poverty; Isle of Palms; Isle of Pines

IOP Institute of Petroleum; Integrated Obstacle Plan; International Organization of Paleobotany; Iranian Oil Participants; Irish Organization of Papists

IOPAB International Organization for Pure and Applied Biophysics

IOPC Interagency Oil Policy Committee

IOPK Independent Order of Panamanian Kangaroos

IOP & LOA Independent Oil Producers and Land Owners Association

IOPS Input/Output Processing System

IOQ Institute of Quarrying

ior input/output register; item on request

IOR Independent Order of Rechabites (Quaker abstainers); International Ocean Rule; International Offshore Rules

IORD International Organization for Rural Development

IORM Improved Order of Red Men

IORS International Orders' Research Society

IoS Isles of Scilly; Isles of Shoals; Isles of the Sea

IOS Inspection Operation Sheet; Institute of Oceanographic Science; Institute of Oceanographic Services; International Organization for Standardization; Investors Overseas Services

IOSA Incorporated Oil Seed Association; Irish Offshore Services Association

IOSHD International Organization for the Study of Human Development

IOSM Independent Order of the Sons of Malta

IOSOT International Organization for the Study of the Old Testament

IoT Institute of Transport; Isle of Thanet

iota. inbound-outbound traffic analysis; information overload testing aid

IOTA Institute of Traffic Administration

IOTC International Originating Toll Center

IOT & E Interim Operational Test and Evaluation

Iotthy I'm only trying to help you

IOTTSG *International Oil Tanker and Terminal Safety Guide*

iou immediate operation use; industrial operations unit; inevitability of the unpredictable

IOU I owe you

I.O.U. I owe you

IO UBC Institute of Oceanography—University of British Columbia

I.O.U.s (plural of I.O.U.)

IOUSP Instituto Oceanográfico da Universidade de São Paulo (Oceanographic Institute of the University of São Paulo)

IOV Instituto Oceanográfico de Valparaíso (Oceanographic Institute of Valparaíso)

IOVST International Organization for Vacuum Science and Technology

iow in other words

IoW Isle of Wight

I o W Isle of Wight

IOW Institute of Welding

iox instructional objectives exchange

IOY Iron Ore Year

ip identification point; impact predictor; improvement purchase; incentive pay; induced polarization; industrial photographer; industrial photography; information provider; initial phrase; initial point; injured person; input primary; installment plan(ning); integer programming; intermediate pressure; iron pipe; plate current (symbol)

ip (IP) insurance payment

i/p input

i & p indexed and paged

iP *in Preussen* (German—in Prussia)

Ip Ipanema

I£ Israeli pound

IP Institut Pasteur; Institute of Petroleum; Instructor Pilot; Insular Police; Interpool (container unit); Isla de Pinos (Isle of Pines); plate current (symbol)

I-P Indian-Pacific (transcontinental train linking Perth in Western Australia on the Indian Ocean with Sydney, New South Wales, on the Pacific)

I & P Island and Peninsular (development bank)

I & P *Izvestia* and *Pravda* (Russian—*News* and *Truth*)

ipa including particular average; initial perceptual alphabet; intermediate power amplifier; internal power amplifier; international phonetic alphabet (IPA)

IPA Illinois Principals Association; Independent Petroleum Association; Independent Publishers Association; Independent Publishers of Australia; Institute for Physics of the Atmosphere; Institute of Propaganda Analysis; Institute of Public Administration; Institute of Public Affairs; International Police Association; International Peace Academy; International Pediatric Association; International Phonetic Association; International Platform Association; International Police Academy; International Police Archives (Manchester Central Library); International Police Association; International Press Association; International Psychoanalytical Association; International Publishers Association; (*see* TALA)

IPA Information Please Almanac; International Pharmaceutical Abstracts

IPAA Independent Petroleum Association of America; Institute of Patent Attorneys of Australia; International Prisoners Aid Association

ipac isopropyl acetate

IPAC Independent Petroleum Association of Canada; Iranian Pan-American Oil Company

IPACK International Packaging Material Suppliers Association

IPACS Integrated-Power/Attitude-Control System

IPAD Integrated Program for Aerospace Vehicle Design

IPAI Information Processing Association of Israel; International Primary Aluminum Institute

IPAR Institute of Personality Assessment and Research

IPARA International Publishers Advertising Representatives Association

IPARS International Programmed Airline Reservation System

IPAT Institute for Personality and Ability Testing

ipb illustrated parts breakdown

IPB International Peace Bureau

ip & be initial program and budget estimate

ipbm (IPBM) interplanetary ballistic missile

IPBMM International Permanent Bureau of Motor Manufacturers

ipc industrial process control; isopropyl carbanilate

IPC Illinois Power Company; Industrial Process Control; Industrial Property Committee; Institute of Paper Chemistry; Institute of Pastoral Care; Institute of Printed Circuits; Integrated Programme for Commodities; Intelligence Priorities Committee (CIA); Inter-African Phytosanitary commission; International Pacific Corporation; International Packings Corporation; International Paper Chemists; International Petroleum Company; International Polar Commission; International Poplar Commission; Iraq Petroleum Company; Isopropyl Carbanilate

IPCA Industrial Pest Control Association

IPCAIL International Pacific Corporation Australian Investments Limited

ipce independent parametric cost estimate

IPCEA Insulated Power Cable Engineers Association

IPCI International Potato Chip Institute

IPCPA Institute of Private Clinical Psychologists of Australia

IPCR Institute of Physical and Chemical Research

IPCS Integrated Propulsion Control System; International Peace Corps Secretariat

IPCU Intensive Psychiatric Care Unit

ip cyl intermediate-pressure cylinder

ipd individual package delivery; insertion phase delay

IPD Institute for Professional Development; Institute of Professional Designers

IPDA International Periodical Distributor's Association

I pd cash I paid cash

ipe industrial plant equipment; interpret parity error

IPE Institution of Plant Engineers; Institute of Production Engineers

IPE Instituto de Providência do Estado (Portuguese—State Loan Institute); *International Petroleum Encyclopedia*

IPEC International Petroleum Exploration Company; Interstate Parcel Express Company

ipecac ipecacuanha

IPEU International Photo Engravers' Union

ipf initial production facilities

IPF Irish Printing Federation

IPFC Indo-Pacific Fisheries Council

ipfm impact form; integral pulse frequency modulation

ipg immediate participation guarantee (insurance plan)

IPG Independent Publishers' Group; Information Policy Group

IPGA Illinois Personnel and Guidance Association; Iowa Personnel and Guidance Association

IPGCU International Printing and Graphic Communications Union

IPGH Instituto Panamericano de Geografía e Historia (Spanish—Pan-American Institute of Geography and History)

iph impressions per hour; inches per hour; interphalangeal

IPHC International Pacific Halibut Commission

IPHE Institute of Public Health Engineers

ipi individually planned instruction; interior point intermodal

i.p.i. in partibus infidelium (Latin—in the region of unbelievers)

IPI Industrial Production Index; Institute of Poultry Industries; International Patent Institute; International Press Institute

IPI Intelligence Publications Index (DIA)

IPICS Initial Production and Information Control System

IPIECA International Petroleum Industry Environmental Conservation Association

IPIP Information Processing Improvement Program

IPIR Initial Photographic Interpretation Report (USAF); Institute for Public Interest Representation; Integrated Personnel Information Report(s)

Ipiranga Ypiranga

IPISD Interservice Procedures for Instructional Systems Development

ipl information program loading; initial program load(er)

ipl (IPL) information processing language

IPL Illustrated Parts List; Integrated Parts List; Italian Pacific Line

I Plant Eng Institution of Plant Engineers

IPLE Institute for Political/

Legal Education
IPLGY Institute for the Protection of Lesbian and Gay Youth
ip log(ging) induced polarization log(ging)
ipm impulses per minute; inches per minute; inches per month; incidental phase modulation; interruptions per minute; inventory policy model
ipm (IPM) integrated pest management
IPM Institute of Personnel Management; Institute of Police Management; Institute for Police Management; Integrated Post Management
IPMA International Personnel Management Association
ipmin inches per minute
IPMP Industrial Plant Modernization Program
ipms impact predictor monitor set
IPMS International Polar Motion Service
ipn inspection progress notification
ipo initial public offer(ing)(s)
ipo (IPO) input processing output
IPO Installation Production Order; International Projects Office (NATO); Israel Philharmonic Orchestra
IPO Instituut voor Perceptie Onderzoek (Dutch—Institute for Perception Research)
ipod initial phase of ocean drilling
IPOD Interstate Project on Dissemination
IPOEE Institution of Post Office Electrical Engineers
IPOH Instituto Panamericano de Geografía e Historia (Spanish—Panamerican Institute of Geography and History)
IPOT Imperial Philharmonic Orchestra of Tokyo
ipp imaging photopolarimeter; impact prediction point; india paper proof(s); intrapleural pressure
Ipp Ippolito
IPP Immediate Past President; Ivan Petrovich Pavlov
ippa inspection, palpitation, percussion, auscultation
IPPA International Planned Parenthood Association
IPPAU International Printing Pressmen and Assistants' Union
ippb intermittent positive-pres-

sure breathing
ippb/i intermittent positive pressure breathing/inspiratory
IPPF International Penal and Penitentiary Foundation
IPPJ Institute of Plasma Physics—Japan
IPPL International Primate Protection League
IPPNW International Physicians for the Prevention of Nuclear War
IPPP Industrial Property Policy Program
IPPPE Institute on Public Policy and Private Enterprise
ippr intermittent positive pressure respiration
IPPTA Indian Pulp and Paper Technical Association
IPPTT Internationale du Personnel des Postes, Télégraphes et Téléphones (French—International Postal, Telegraph, and Telephone personnel)
ippv intermittent positive pressure ventilation
ipq intimacy potential quotient
IPQ International Petroleum Quarterly
ipr inches per revolution; inflow performance relationship (oil well); interpersonal process recall
IPR Individual Pay Record; Industrial Public Relations; Institute of Pacific Relations; Institute of Philosophical Research; Institute for Public Representation
IPR International Public Relations
IPRA International Professional Rodeo Association; International Public Relations Association
IPRC Institute of Puerto Rican Culture
IPRE Incorporated Practitioners in Radio and Electronics
IPRO International Patent Research Office
I Prod Eng Institute of Production Engineers
IPRR Integrated Personnel Requirement Report
ips inches per second; interceptor pilot simulator; interruptions per second; iron pipe size
Ips Ipswich
IPS Incremental Purchasing System; Industrial Planning Specification; Industrial Promotion Service; Inertial Positioning System; Information

Processing Society; Institute of Pacific Studies; Institute for Policy Studies; Institute of Population Studies (Japan); Institute of Private Secretaries; Institute of Public Safety; Integrated Publishing System; International Phenomenological Society; International Pipe Standard; Interpretive Programming System; Introductory Physical Science; Ionospheric Prediction Service; Israel Prison Service
IPS Instituto Poligrafico dello Stato (Italian—State Printing and Stationery office)
IPSA Independent Passenger Steamship Association; Independent Postal System of America; International Political Science Association
IPSB Institute of Psycho-Structural Balancing
IPSC International Pacific Salmon Committee
IPSCE Inventory of Psychic and Somatic Complaints in the Elderly
IPSF International Pharmacy Students Federation; International Piano Symphony Foundation
IPSFC International Pacific Salmon Fisheries Commission
IPSJ Information Processing Society of Japan
IPSM Institute of Purchasing and Supply Management
ipsp inhibitory postsynaptic potential
IPSP Industrial Personnel Security Program
IPSS International Packet Switching Service
IPSSB International Processing Systems Standards Board
ipt indexed, paged, titled; internal pipe thread
IPT Initial Production Test (USA); Institute of Photographic Technology; International Planning Team (NATO)
IPT Instituto Panameño de Turismo (Spanish—Panamanian Institute of Tourism)
IPTCCS Integrated Pipeline Transportation and Coal-Cleaning System
ipth (IPTH) immunoreactive parathyroid hormone
ipto independent power takeoff
IPTPA International Professional Tennis Players' Asso-

ciation

ipts international practical temperature scale

IPTS Improved Programmer Test Section; International Practical Temperature Scale

ipu input preparation unit

IPU Institute for Public Understanding; International Paleontological Union; Inter-Parliamentary Union

ipv inactivated poliomyelitis vaccine; infectious pustular vaginitis; infectious pustular vulvovaginitis

ipv in plaats van (Dutch—in place of)

IPW interrogation prisoner of war

ipy inches penetration per year; inches per year

IPY International Polar Year

IPZ Investment Promotion Zone

IPZE Istituto Poligrafico dello Stato (Italian—State Polygraphic Institute)—issues paper money and stamps

i.q. idem quod (Latin—the same as)

Iq Iraq

IQ Import Quota; intelligence quotient

I.Q. I Quit (smoking)

I of Q Institute of Quarrying

IQA Institute of Quality Assurance

IQCA Irish Quality Control Association

IQCT Institute for Quality Control Training

i.q.e.d. id quod erat demonstrandum (Latin—that which was to be proved)

iqf instant quick frozen

IQHL Institute for Quality in Human Life

IQI Instructional Quality Inventory

I Qk interrupted quick flashing (light); interrupted quick (light)

iqmf image-quality merit function

iqrp interactive query and report processor

iq & s iron, quinine, and strychnine

IQS Institute of Quality Surveyors; Institute of Quantity Surveyors

IQSA Institute of Quantity Surveyors of Australia

IQSY International Quiet Sun Year (1964–1965)

Iqu Iquique

ir ice on runway; incidence rate; information retrieval; infrared; inland revenue; inside radius; inside right; instantaneous relay; instrument rating; instrument reading; insulation resistance; intelligence resource(s); internal resistance; interrogator-responder

ir (IR) inflation rate

i-r infra-red

i/r interchangeability and replaceability

i & r information and retrieval; intelligence and reconnaissance; interchangeability and replaceability

i R im Ruhestand (German—in retirement)

Ir Iran; Irania; Ireland; iridium; Irish

Ir Iers (Dutch)—Ireland, Irish(man) (woman)

IR Index Register; Industrial Relations; Informal Report; Information Request, Inspection Rejection; Inspector's Report; Institutional Research; Intelligence Report; Internal Revenue; Invention Report; Investigation Record

I-R Ingersoll-Rand

I & R Initiative and Referendum; Intelligence and Reconnaissance

ira independent retirement account (IRA)

ira (IRA) immunoregulatory alpha globulin

Ira Di Ira D Levine; Iraq

IRA Indian Rights Association; Individual Retirement Account; Institute of Registered Architects; Intercollegiate Rowing Association; International Racquetball Association; International Reading Association; International Recreation Association; Iranian Airways; Irish Republican Army; Israel Railway Administration

IRAA Independent Refiners Association of America

IRAB Institute for Research in Animal Behavior

irac mnemonic abbreviation helpful in making legal or logical presentations; letters stand for issue, rule, application, and conclusion

IRAC Indochina Refugee Assistance Program; Industrial Relations Advisory Committee; Intelligence Resources Advisory Committee; Interde-

partmental Radio Advisory Committee; Interfraternity Research and Administrative Council

iracq instrumentation radar acquisition

irad independent research and development

IRAD Institute for Research on Animal Diseases

iraf interferogram requirements and analysis funnel

iran inspect and repair as necessary

Iran formerly Persia; Imperial Government of Iran (Iranians speak Persian as well as Arabic, Kurdish, and Turkish, this ancient Asian nation, produces crude oil, oriental rugs, and many valuable minerals) *Keshvaré Shahanshahiyé Iran*

IRANAIR Iran National Airlines

Iran(ian) Persia(n)

Iranian Ports (west to east) Khorramshahr, Abadan, Bandar-e-Mahshahr, Bandar-e-Shapur, Kharg Island Terminal, Bandar Abbas

IRANOR Instituto Nacional de Racionalización y Normalización (Spanish—National Institute of Rationalization and Standards)

Iran's Principal Port Abadan

IRAP Indochinese Refugees Assistance Program

Iraq Republic of Iraq (oil-producing Persian-Gulf country formerly called Mesopotamia, Iraqis speak Arabic and Kurdish, farmers produce many edible crops as well as tobacco) *al Jumhouriya al 'Iraqia*

Iraq Ports Al Faw and Al Basrah

Iraq's Principal Port Basra

Iraquia Iraq (Mesopotamia)

IR/AR Inspector's Report/Action Request

iras (IRAS) infrared astronomical satellite; infrared-measuring astronomical satellite

IRAs Individual Retirement Accounts; Irish Republican Army members or supporters and sympathizers

IRASA International Radio Air Safety Association

IRASE Institute of Refrigeration and Air Conditioning Service Engineers

iraser infrared amplification by stimulated emission of radiation

irb (IRB) in-shore rescue boat

IRB Indiana Rating Bureau; Industrial Relations Bureau; Industrial Review Board; Insurance Rating Board; International Resources Bank; Irish Republican Brotherhood

IRBDC Insurance Rating Bureau of the District of Columbia

IRBEL *Indexed References to Biomedical Engineering Literature*

irbm (IRBM) intermediate range ballistic missile

irc infrared countermeasures; international reply coupon; item responsibility code

IRC Immigration Restriction Council; Indonesian Red Cross; Industrial Recreation Council; Industrial Relations Center; Industrial Relations Committee; Industrial Relations Council; Inebriate Reception Center; Information Resources Center; Institutional Research Council; Instructional Resources Center; Internal Revenue Code; International Railways of Central America (stock exchange symbol); International Rainwear Council; International Red Cross; International Relief Committee; International Rescue Committee; International Resistance Company; International Rice Commission

IRCA International Railways of Central America

IRCAM *Institut de Recherche et de Coordination Acoustique-Musique* (French—Institute of Research and Acoustic-Music Coordination)

IRCAR International Reference Center for Abroation Research

irccd infrared charge-coupled device

IRCD Information Retrieval Center on the Disadvantaged

i-r charts infrared correlation charts

ircm infrared countermeasures

IRCO Industrial Rustproof Company

IRCP International Commission on Radiological Protection

IRCs Inebriate Reception Centers (where nonviolent abusers of alcohol and other drugs accept coffee and counseling in lieu of being jailed)—pilot facility in San Diego, California

IRCS International Research Communications System

ird (IRD) internal research and development; international resource development

ir & d international research and development

IRD Institute on Religion and Democracy (anti-communist); Institute of Reading Development; Instituto Rubén Darío; International Resource Development

IR & D International Research and Development

IRDA Industrial Research and Development Authority

IRDC International Research Development Centre (Canadian)

ir & dg industrial research and development grants

IRDI Indian Resources Development and Internship

irdm illuminated runway distance marker

IRDN Illinois Resource and Dissemination Network

IRDOE Institute for Research and Development in Occupational Education

irdome infrared dome

irds idiopathic respiratory-distress syndrome

irdu infrared detection unit

Ire Ireland

IRE Institute of Radio Engineers; Institute for Responsive Education; Investigative Reporters and Editors

IREC International Real Estate Corporation (Singapore); Irrigation Research and Extension Commission

IREE Institute of Radio and Electronic Engineers

IREF International Real Estate Federation

Ireland Irish Republic (North Atlantic island nation whose people speak English and some Irish-Gaelic, farming, industry, and tourism contribute to the economy of this hospitable country not lacking in humor) *Eire*

Ireland the Great Newfoundland's name given it by Irish explorers who found it in Viking times

Ireland's Principal Port Dublin

IREM Institute of Real Estate Management

irene indicating random electronic numbering equipment

IREQ Institute of Research—Québec

irer infrared extra rapid

IREX International Research and Exchanges (New York-based board arranging scholarly interchanges between the United States and the USSR as well as other communist nations eager to learn American methods and advanced technologies)

irf instrument reliability factor; interrogation repetition frequency

IRF International Road Federation

IRFAA International Rescue and First Aid Association

IRFC Ingersoll-Rand Finance Corporation

IRFM *Industrias Reunidas Francisco Matarazzo* (Francisco Matarazzo's Reunited Industries)

IRFU Iriah Rugby Football Union

irg interrecord gap

IRG Interdepartmental Regional Group

Ir Gael Irish Gaelic

IRGDLP International Research Group on Drug Legislation and Programs (Geneva, Switzerland)

irgl immunoreactive glucagon

IRGRD International Research Group on Refuse Disposal

IRH *Internationalen Roten Hilfe* (German—International Red Aid)—Red Fighting Fund of international communists

irha injured as a result of hostile action

irhd international rubber hardness degrees

iri immunoreactive insulin

Iri Irina

IRI Industrial Reconstruction Institute; Industrial Research Institute; Institute of the Rubber Industry; Islamic Republic of Iran

IRIA Infrared Information and Analysis

Irian Barat (Indonesian—West Irian)—formerly Dutch or Netherlands New Guinea

IRIC Inter-Regional Insurance Conference

IRICA Industrial Research Institute for Central America

iricbm (IRICBM) intermediate-range intercontinental ballistic missile

irid iridescent

IRIG Inter-Range Instrumentation Group

IRIR Interchangeability Replaceability Information Report

iris. infrared interferometer spectrometer

Iris Tennessee state flower and sobriquet

IRIS Infrared Information Symposia; Integrated Reconaissance Intelligence System

irish eponymic preface to many terms such as irish boat (cutter-rigged fishing vessel), irish ford (paved ford), irish coffee (coffee spiked with irish whiskey and topped with whipped cream), irish moss (edible seaweed also called carrageen), irish pennant (unwhipped rope end flying in the breeze), irish potato (white potato), irish setter (red setter originally from Ireland), irish sweater (fisherman's knit sweaters), irish terrier (red-hair terrier originally bred in Ireland), irish tweed (heavy type of tweed originally from Ireland), irish whiskey (originally distilled in Ireland where it was made from barley), irish wolfhound (large breed of dog noted for its courage and originally bred in Ireland)

Irish *Irish Rhapsody* by Victor Herbert; *Irish Symphony* by Sir Charles Villiers Stanford; *Irish Symphony* by Sir Hamilton Harty

Irish Channel New Orleans waterfront slum

irish confetti bricks; thrown bricks used in street fighting

Irish Cradle of U.S. Presidents Ireland—ancestral home of Presidents Jackson, Kennedy, Nixon, and Reagan as well as Arthur, Buchanan, McKinley, Polk, Truman, and Wilson from Northern Island or Ulster

Irish First Ireland's best known cellist-composer-conductor was Victor Herbert, best remembered for his many operettas produced in the United States where he became a naturalized citizen

Irish FP Irish Fishing Port (registration symbols displayed on the bows of fishing vessels)

Irish Free State Republic of Ireland

Irish Navigator Saint Brendan (formerly spelled Brandon)

Irish Ports (large, medium, and small from north to south) Bangor, Belfast, Larne Lough, Londonderry, Sligo, Westport, Galway, Kilrush, Limerick, Foynes, Cobh, Cork Harbour, Rosslare, Dublin

irish turkey corned beef

Irish VR Irish Vehicle Registration (symbols on automotive vehicle licenses)

irish whist copulation

irish wine whiskey

IRJC Indian River Junior College

irl information retrieval language

Irl *Irlanda* (Italian, Portuguese, Spanish—Ireland)

Irl *Irlande* (French—Ireland)

IRL Illustrations Requirements List

IRLA Independent Research Library Association

Irland (German—Ireland)

Irlanda (Italian or Spanish—Ireland)

Irlandia (Portuguese—Ireland)

IRLC Illinois Regional Library Council

IRLCS International Red Locust Control Service

IRLS Interrogation Recording Location System

irm infrared measurement; inmate release mechanism; intermediate range monitor

IRM Improved Risk Mutuals; Islamic Republic of Mauritania

IRM (NYU) Institute of Rehabilitation Medicine (New York University)

irma information revision and manuscript assembly; integrated revenue and marketing applications

IRMMH Institute of Research into Mental and Multiple Handicaps

IRMP Intermountain Regional Medical Program

IRMPC Industrial Raw Materials Planning Committee (NATO)

IRMRA Indian Rubber Manufacturers Research Association

IRMS Information Retrieval and Management System

IRN Independent Radio News

IRNP Isle Royale National Park (Michigan)

iro in rear of

IRO Industrial Recycling Organization; Industrial Relations Office(r); Information Resource Office(r); Inland Revenue Office(r); Internal Revenue Office(r); International Refugee Organization; International Relief Organization

IRO-ALA International Relations Office—American Library Association

irod instantaneous readout detector

iron. ironic(al)

Iron Age era of mankind when implements and weapons were forged from iron; period of vast degeneracy, corruption, and toil following the Stone and Bronze ages

Iron Alley cosmic corridor littered with meteorites whose fall extends from Portland, Oregon to Mexico City in a lane about 250 miles or 400 kilometers wide

Iron Butterfly Imelda Romauldos Marcos

Iron Chancellor Prince Otto Eduard Leopold von Bismarck-Schönhausen—first chancellor of German Empire

Iron Charles Charlemagne (Carolus Magnus)

Iron City place-name nickname shared by Bessemer, Alabama and Pittsburgh, Pennsylvania

Iron Curtain barrier raised by Stalin at the end of World War II between eastern and western Europe—between communist-controlled Europe and free Europe

Iron Curtain Countries Albania, Bulgaria, Cuba, Czechoslovakia, Estonia, East Germany, Hungary, Latvia, Lithuania, North Korea, North Vietnam, Poland, Red China, Rumania, Soviet Union, Tibet, or other places dominated by Red Chinese or Soviet Russian communist parties—those dominated entirely by Chinese communists are called Bamboo Curtain Countries

Iron Duke Arthur Wellesley the Duke of Wellington

Iron Gate narrow rapids in the Danube below Orsova in Romania

Iron Horse baseball-fan nickname for Lou Gehrig; old nickname for a steam locomotive

Iron Lady Margaret Thatcher—Britain's first woman prime minister

iron pyrites sulfide of iron

Ironquill Eugene Fitch Ware

Iron Range nickname of the Mesabi Range

Ironsides Oliver Cromwell

Iron Triangle Cologne (Köln), Siegen, Solingen (all noted for their steel products including fine cutlery)

IROPCO Iranian Offshore Petroleum Company

Iroquois Bell turbo-power helicopter designated UH-1

iros ipsilateral routing of signal

IROS Increase Reliability of Operational Systems

irp initial receiving point

Ir£ Irish pound

IRP Individualized Reading Program; Information Resources Press

IRPA International Radiation Protection Association

irpm individual risk premium modification

IRPS Institute of Reconstructive Plastic Surgery (NYU); International Religious Press Service (Vatican City)

irr infrared rays; infrared reflectance; internal rate of return; irredeemable; irregular(ity)

irr (IRR) integral rocket ramjet

IRR Institute of Race Relations

IRRA Industrial Relations Research Association

Irrawaddy 1200-mile Indian river entering Bay of Bengal at Gulf of Martaban

irrd international road research documentation

IRRD International Road Research Documentation

IRRDB International Rubber Research and Development Board

irreg irregular

irres irrespective

irrev irrevocable

irrg irregular

irrgty irregularity

irrgy irregularly

IRRI International Rice Research Institute

irrig irrigation

IRRN Illinois Research and Reference Center (libraries)

IRRP Icefield Ranges Research Project

irr/ssm (IRR/SSM) integral rocket ramjet/surface-to-surface missile

irs incremental range summary; independent rear suspension

IRs Inspector's Reports

IRS Indian Register of Shipping; Industrial Rubber Sales; Ineligible Reserve Section; Infernal Revenue Service; Information Retrieval System; Internal Revenue Service; International Recruiting Service; International Referral System; International Rorschach Society; Irrigation Research Station

I & RS Information and Research Services

IRSA Industrial Relations Society of Australia

IRSE Institution of Railway Signal Engineers; International Reactor Safety Evaluation

IRSF Inland Revenue Staff Federation

IRSG International Rubber Study Group

IRSID Institut des Recherches de la Sidérurgie Française (French Steel Research Institute)

IRSNB Institut Royal des Sciences Naturelles de Belgique (Royal Belgian Institute of Natural Sciences)

IRSP Irish Republican Socialist Party

IRSS Instrumentation Range Safety System

irt infrared temperature; infrared tracker; intermediate range technology; interrogator responder transponder

IRT Institute for Rapid Transit; Institute of Reprographic Technology; Interborough Rapid Transit (subway system)

IRT *Industria Radio y Televisión* (Spanish—Radio and Television Industry)

IRTA Illinois Retired Teachers Association

IRTAC International Round Table for the Advancement of Counseling

IRTE Institute of Road Transport Engineers

IRTP Integrated Reliability Test Program

irts infrared target seeker

IRTS International Radio and Television Society

IRTU International Railway Temperance Union

IRTWG Inter-Range Telemetering Working Group

iru industrial rehabilitation unit; inertial reference unit; infrared unit; international radium unit; international rat unit

IRU International Road Transport Union

irupt interrupt

iruptd interrupted

iruptn interruption

iruptng interrupting

irv inspiratory reserve volume

Irv Irvin; Irvine; Irving; Irwin

Irve Irving

Irving Irving Trust Company; Sir Henry Irving; Washington Irving

Irving Berlin Irving Baline

Irving Stone Irving Tannenbaum

Irvington, New Jersey Newark suburb originally known as Camptown and celebrated in Stephen Foster's *Camptown Races*

Irw Irwin

IRW Iowa Reformatory for Women

IRWC International Registry of World Citizens

irwl interchangeability/replaceability working list

is his

is. ingot sheet; integrally stiffened; intercoastal space; interim storage; internal shield; international status; interval signal; island; isle

i&s installation and service; investigation and suspension; iron and steel

i & s inspection and security; inspection and survey; interchangeability and substitutability

Is Islam; Islamic; Island; Isle; Israel; Israeli

Is Israeli pound

Is *Isaías* (Spanish—Isiah)

Is *Îles* (French—islands); *Ilhas* (Portuguese—islands); *Islas* (Spanish—islands)

IS Identification Section (NYPD); Igor Stravinsky; Indian Summer (freeboard marking); Information Service; Instruction(s) to Ship; Irish Society

I of S Institute of Sound; Isle of Skye

IS 201 Intermediate School 201 (for example)

isa international standard atmosphere

Isa Isaiah, The Book of the Prophet

Isa *Indonesia* (Spanish—Indonesia); *Isaiah*

ISA Independent Showmen of America; Institute of Strategic

Affairs; Institution of Surveyors—Australia; Instrument Society of America; Insulating Siding Association; Intermediate Service Agency; Internal Security Act; International Schools Association; International Scientific Affairs; International Seabed Authority; International Security Affairs; International Security Assistance; International Sign Association; International Silk Association; International Society of Appraisers; International Sociological Association; International Standards Association; International Student Association; International Sugar Agreement

ISA Information Science Abstracts; Irregular Serials and Annuals

ISAA Institute of Shops Acts Administration

Isab Isabella

ISAB Institute for the Study of Animal Behavior

Isabela Spanish name for Albemarle Island in the Galápagos

ISABPS Integrated Submarine Automated Broadcast Processing System

ISAC International Security Affairs Committee

ISACP Italian Society of Authors, Composers, and Publishers

ISAD Information Science and Automation Division (ALA)

ISADPM International Society for the Abolition of Data-Processing Machines

ISAE Internacia Scienca Asocio Esperantista (International Esperantist Scientific Association)

IsAF Israeli Air Force

isaf black intermediate superabrasive furnace black

ISAFP Intelligence Service of the Philippine Armed Forces

ISAGA International Simulation and Gaming Association

ISAHM International Society for Animal and Human Mycology

Isak Dinesen Baroness Karen Blixen-Finecke

ISALPA Incorporated Society of Auctioneers and Landed Property Agents

ISAM Independent School Association of Massachusetts; Indexed Sequential Access Method; Institute for Studies

in American Music; Integrated Switching and Multiplexing

ISAP Institute for the Study of Animal Problems

ISAPC Incorporated Society of Authors, Playwrights, and Composers

ISAPM International Shipowners Association of Peninsular Malaysia

isar information storage and retrieval

ISAR International Society for Astrological Research

isarc installation shipping and receiving capability

ISAS Industrial Sales and Service; Institute of Social and Administrative Studies; Institute of Space and Aeronautical Science; Isotopic Source Assay System

ISAT International Society of Analytical Trilogy

ISAW International Society of Aviation Writers

isb independent sideband; intermediate sideband

ISB International Society of Biometeorology

ISBA Incorporated Society of British Advertisers; Indiana School Boards Association

ISBB International Society for Bioclimatology and Biometeorology

ISBD International Standard Book Description

ISBD(M) International Standard Bibliographic Description for Monographic Publications

ISBD(NBM) International Standard Bibliographic Description for Non-Book Materials

ISBD(S) International Standard Bibliographic Description for Serial Publications

ISBE International Society for Business Education

ISBN International Standard Book Number

ISBNA International Standard Book Numbering Agency

ISBOA Idaho School Business Officials Association

ISBP International Society for Biochemical Pharmacology

isbr interior salt basin region

ISBS Icelandic State Broadcasting Service; International Scholarly Book Services

isc intermediate slack compensation; interstate commerce; intrasite cabling; item status

code; item status coding; in such case

ISC Icelandic Steamship Company; Idaho State College; Imperial Service College; Imperial Staff College; Indian Staff Corps; Indiana State College; Indoor Sports Club; Industrial Security Commission; Institute for the Study of Conflict; Inter-American Society of Cardiology; International Salt Company; International Science Center; International Sericultural Commission; International Society of Cardiology; International Softball Congress; International Statistical Classification; International Sugar Council; International Supreme Council (World Masons); Interseas Shipping Corporation; Interservice Sports Council; Interstate Sanitation Commission

IS&C International Systems and Controls

Isca (Latin—Exeter)

ISCA International Senior Citizens Association

iscan inertialess steerable communication antenna

ISCB International Society for Cell Biology

ISCC Inter-Society Color Council

ISCDD International Scheme for the Coordination of Dairy Development

ISCE International Society for Christian Endeavor

ISCED International Standard Classification of Education

ISCEH International Society for Clinical and Experimental Hypnosis

ISCERG International Society for Clinical Electroretinography

ISCET International Society of Certified Electronics Technicians

ISCII International Standard Code for Information Interchange

ISCM International Society for Contemporary Music

ISCO International Standard Classification of Occupations

ISCOR Iron and Steel Industrial Corporation (South Africa)

ISCP International Society of Clinical Pathology

ISCPET Illinois Statewide Curriculum Study Center in the Preparation of Secondary

School English Teachers

ISCRP International Society of City and Regional Planners

ISCS Information Service Computer System; Intermediate Science Curriculum Study

ISCTP International Study Commission for Traffic Police

isd installation start date; instructional systems development; integrated symbolic debugger

isd (ISD) inhibited sexual desire (asexuality)

ISD Independent School District; Information Systems Design; Instructional Systems Design; Instructional Systems Development; Intermediate School District; Internal Security Department; Internal Security Division (U.S. Dept of Justice); International Subscriber Dialing

ISDAIC International Staff Disaster Assistance Information Coordinator (NATO)

ISDD Institute for the Study of Drug Dependence (London, England)

ISDI International Social Development Institute

ISDO International Staff Duty Officer (NATO)

ISDRA International Sled Dog Racing Association

ISDS Inadvertent Separation Destruct System; International Serials Data System

ISDSI Insulated Steel Door Systems Institute

ISDS/IC International Center of the International Series Data System (UNESCO)

ise integral square error

ISE Institute for Services to Education; Institute for Sex Education; Institute of Social Ethics; Institution of Structural Engineers; Irish School of Ecumenics

ISE *Instituto de Seguros del Estado* (Spanish—Institute of State Insurance)

ISEA Industrial Safety Equipment Association; Iowa State Education Association

ISEAS Institute of Southeast Asian Studies

ISEE International Sun-Earth Explorer (NASA/ESRO)

ISEEP Infrared-Sensitive Element Evaluation Program

ISEF International Science and Engineering Fair

ISELS Institute of Society, Ethics, and Life Sciences

ISEP Instructional Scientific Equipment Program; International Society for Educational Planners; Interservice Experiments Program

isepc installation specification; insulation specification

iseq input sequence check(ing)

ISES International Ship Electric Service Association; International Society of Explosives Specialists; International Solar Energy Society

ISETU International Secretariat of Entertainment Trade Unions

ISEU International Stereotypers' and Electrotypers' Union

isf intermittent storage flood(ing); interstitial fluid

ISF Intermediate-Scale Facilities; International Science Foundation; International Shipping Federation; International Society for Fat Research; International Softball Federation

ISFA Institute of Shipping and Forwarding Agents; Intercoastal Steamship Freight Association; International Scientific Film Association

ISFL International Scientific Film Library

ISFMS Indexed Sequential File Management System

ISFR Institute for the Study of Fatigue and Reliability

ISFSC International Society of Free Space Colonizers

isfsi independent spent-fuel storage installation

ISFSI International Society of Fire Service Instructors

isg imperial standard gallon

ISGE International Society of Gastroenterology

ISGM Isabella Stewart Gardner Museum

ISGS International Society for General Semantics

ISGW International Society of Girl Watchers

Ish Isham; Ishbel; Ishmael

ISH International Society of Hematology

ISHAM International Society for Human and Animal Mycology

Isherman Israeli version of Super Sherman tank

ISHI Institute for the Study of Human Issues

ISHL Illinois Social Hygiene

League

ISHR International Society for Human Rights

ISHS International Society for Horticultural Science

isi industrial standard item; internally specified index(ing); interstimulus interval

ISI Information Sciences Institute (USC); Institute for Scientific Information; Intercollegiate Society of Individualists; Intercollegiate Studies Institute; International Statistical Institute; Iron and Steel Institute

ISIB Inter-Services Ionospheric Bureau

isic (ISIC) immediate superior in command

ISIC International Standard Industrial Classification; International Student Identity Card

ISIM International Society of Internal Medicine

isinglass mica

isip inertial system indication position

ISIP Iron and Steel Industry Profile Service

ISIR International Society for Invertebrate Reproduction

isirta *I'm sorry, I'll read that again* (BBC comedy)

isis (ISIS) ionospheric studies

ISIS Individualized Science Instructional System; Instant Sales Indicator System; Institute of Scrap Iron and Steel; Integral Spar Inspection System; Integrated Scientific Information Service; Integrated Set of Information Systems; Integrated Ship Instrumentation System; Integrated Statistical Information Service; International Satellites for Ionospheric Studies; International Science Information Service; International Species Identification System; Investigative Support Information System (FBI)

ISIT Institute for Studies in International Terrorism (SUNY)

ISIYM International Society of Industrial Yarn Manufacturers

isk insert storage key

ISK Isambard Kingdom Brunel

ISK *Internationale Seidenbau Kommission* (German—International Sericulture Commission)

Iskandariyah (Arabic—Alexander)

Iskander Alexander Herzen (Aleksandr Ivanovich Yakoviev)

ISKC International Society for Krishna Consciousness

Iskenderun (Turkish—Alexandretta)—port in the easternmost Mediterranean

iskr identification, station keeping, and rendezvous

Iskra (Russian—Spark)—Polish single-engine jet aircraft designated TS-11

Isku Finnish guided-missile patrol boat

isl intermediate-stage letter; island

isl (ISL) intersatellite link

isl islandsk (Dano-Norwegian—Icelandic)

Isl Islanda (Italian—Iceland); *Islandia* (Spanish—Iceland); *Islândia* (Portuguese—Iceland)

ISL Iceland Steamship Company; Interseas Shipping Lines; Iranian Shipping Lines; Irish Shipping Limited

I S-L Instructor Sub-Lieutenant

isla (Spanish—island, as in Isla de Cuba)

ISLA International Survey Library Association

Isla de Juventud (Spanish—Isle of Youth)—Cuba's Isle of Pines also called *Isla de Pinos* until Castro's time

Isla de Pascua (Spanish—Easter Island)—Chilean island in the eastern South Pacific and noted for its huge stone monuments; Polynesians call it Rapa Nui

Isla de Pinos (Spanish—Isle of Pines)—island prison off Cuba's southwest coast where it was established during colonial times and held pirates since replaced by political prisoners

Islam (Arabic—Submission) submission to the will of God

Islamic Century the 600s—Mohammed flees from Mecca to Medina and dies in 632; Islam begins expanding throughout the Middle East and Africa—the 7th century

Island (Dano-Norwegian or Icelandic—Iceland)

Islanda (Italian—Iceland)

Island-and-Mainland Province Newfoundland

Island at the End of the World Madagascar as described by the Malagasy

Island of Bearded Figs Barbados

Island of Betelnut Palms Penang

Island of Birds Kusadasi

Island City Manhattan, Montreal, Singapore, and Stockholm hold this title as all are built on islands

Island of Cloves Zanzibar

Island Continent Australia

Island of Copper Cyprus

Island of Death Kahoolawe, Hawaii (used for target practice by Air Force and Navy)

Island of Dragons Komodo (home of the dragon lizards)

Island of Dreams Capri

Island of Flowers Taboga, Panama

Island Fortress Malta

Island of the Gods Bali

Island of Hell Norfolk Island in the South Pacific where it was the most dreaded of all Australian prison stations

Islandia (Portuguese or Spanish—Iceland)

Island of Knights Hospitaliers Malta

Island of Light New Caledonia

Island Ministate Nauru in the Central Pacific

Island of Monks and Pirates Lantau or Tai Yue Shan—largest island off Hong Kong

Island of the Moon Madagascar

Island Nation nickname shared by Australia, an island of continental magnitude, with the Bahamas, Bahrain, Barbados, the Cape Verde Islands, the Republic of China (offshore China or Taiwan), the Comoro Islands, Cuba, Cyprus, the Dominican Republic (sharing the island of Hispaniola with Haiti), Fiji, Grenada, Haiti, Iceland, Indonesia, Ireland, Jamaica, Japan, Madagascar, the Maldives, Malta, Mauritius, Nauru, New Zealand, Papua New Guinea, the Philippines, São Tomé and Principe, the Seychelles, Singapore, Sri Lanka (Ceylon), Tonga, Trinidad and Tobago, the United Kingdom consisting of Great Britain (England, Scotland, and Wales) plus Northern Ireland, Western Samoa

Island of Olives Cyprus

Island of Roses Rhodes in the Dodecanese

Island of Ruins and Roses Gotland, Sweden

Island of Sages and Saints Ireland

Islands of Eternal Spring the Balearics (Ibiza, Formentera, Mallorca, Menorca)

Islands of the Maoris New Zealand

Islands of Perpetual June Turks and Caicos Islands between the Bahamas and Hispaniola

Island State Tasmania, Australia

Island in the Sun Key West, Florida

Island of Venus Tahiti

Islas Baleares (Spanish—Balearic Islands)

Islas Británicas (Spanish—British Isles)

Islas Canarias (Spanish—Canary Islands)

Islas Encantadas (Spanish—Enchanted Islands)—Galápagos

Islas Filipinas (Spanish—Philippine Islands)

Islas Lucayas (Spanish—Lucayan Islands)—the Bahamas

Islas Malvinas (Spanish—Falkland Islands)—in the South Atlantic

Islas Vírgenes (Spanish—Virgin Islands)

Isla Verde (Spanish—Green Island)—San Juan, Puerto Rico's international airport

Isle (see *The Isle*)

Isle of Cloves Zanzibar

Isle of Destiny Ireland

Isle of Fragrant Waters Hong Kong

Isle of Roses Rhodes

Isle Royale short form for Isle Royale National Park in Michigan

Isle of Saints Iona Isle in the Inner Hebrides off Scotland's west coast; Ireland

Isle of Sappho Lesbos in the Aegean

Isles of the Blest the Canary Islands; (*see* Fortunate Isles)

Isle of Sleep Tasmania so nicknamed by other Australians

Isle of Springs Jamaica

ISLFD Incorporated Society of London Fashion Designers

ISLIC Israel Society of Special Libraries and Information Centers

isl of Lan islands of Langerhans

isln isolation

ISLRS Inactive Status List Reserve Section

isl's initial stock lists; islands

isls L islands of Langerhans

Islw Indian spring low water

ISLWF International Shoe and Leather Workers Federation

ism industrial, scientific, medical wave length; interpretive structural modeling; interstellar matter

ism (Latin suffix—condition or state)—capitalism, communism, rheumatism

ISM Industrial Sugar Mills; Institute of Sales and Marketing; Institute of Sports Medicine; International Society for Musicology

ISMA International Superphosphate Manufacturers Association

Ismailiyah (Arabic—Ismailia)

ISME International Society of Musical Education

ISMEC Information Service in Mechanical Engineering

ISMH International Society of Medical Hydrology

ISMI Institute for the Study of Mental Images

ISMLS Interim Standard Microwave Landing System

ism of the modern world racism (according to anthropologist Ruth Benedict)

ISMR Independent Snowmobile Medical Research (organization)

ISMRC Inter-Services Metallurgical Research Council

ISMS Inherently-Safe Mining System(s)

ISMUN International Student Movement for the United Nations

Is N (Sir) Isaac Newton

ISN International Society for Neurochemistry

ISNAC Inactive Ships Navy Custody

ISNP International Society of Naturopathic Physicians

isn't is not

iso isolate; isolation; isolator (Soviet penal colony specializing in solitary confinement of political prisoners); isotope; isotopic; in spite of

iso (ISO) infrared space observatory

iso (Latin suffix—equal or like) —isometric, isotonic

ISO Imperial Service Order; Indianapolis Symphony Orchestra; Individual System Operation; Information Service(s) Office(r); Information Sys-

tems Office (Library of Congress); Insurance Service(s) Office(r); International Science Organization; International Standardization Organization; International Standards Organization; International Sugar Organization; Irish Symphony Orchestra

ISO-4 international code for the abbreviation of periodical titles

ISO-833 international list of periodical title word abbreviations

isobu isobutyl

is/oc individual system/organization cost

ISOC Internal Security Operation Command

isochr isochronal

ISODOC International Center for Standards in Information and Documentation

Isol Isolation; Isolator

Isolator of Dysentery Kiyoshi Shiga

Isolator of Gangrene Shibasaburo Kitazato

Isolde Yseult

Isole Eolie (Italian—Aeolian Islands)—the Liparis in the Tyrrhenian Sea off Sicily

isoln isolate; isolated; isolation

isolr isolationer

isom isometric(s)

ISOMATA Idyllwild School of Music and Art

isomorph isomorphic(al)(ly); isomorphism

ison isolation network

ISONET International Standards Organization Network

ISOO Information Security Oversight Office

isordil isorbide dinitrate

ISORID International Information System on Research in Documentation

ISORT Interdisciplinary Student-Originated Research Training (NSF)

ISOS International Ship Operating Services

isot isotropic

iso wd isolation ward

isp intraspinal

Isp specific impulse (symbol)

ISP Idaho State Penitentiary; Index of Social Position; Indiana State Police; Industrial Security Program; Institute of Social Psychiatry; Institute of Store Planners; Integrated Support Plan(ning); Interamerican Society of Psycholo-

gy

ISPA International Screen Publicity Association; International Society for the Protection of Animals; International Sporting Press Association

Ispalis (Latin—Sevilla)—Seville

ISPC International Statistical Program Center (AID)

ISPHS International Society of Phonetic Sciences

ISPM International Staff Planners Message (NATO)

ISPMEMO International Staff Planners Memo (NATO)

ISPO Instrumentation Ships' Project Office; International Society for Prosthetics and Orthotics

ISPP Inter-Services Plastic Panel

isps international standard paper sizes

ISPS International Society of Phonetic Sciences

ISPT Initial Satisfactory Performance Test(ing)

isq in status quo

ISQA Israeli Society for Quality Assurance

isr information storage and retrieval

isr Israel (Portuguese or Spanish —Israel); *Israele* (Italian—Israel)

Isr Israel; Israeli

Isr Israel (Portuguese or Spanish —Israel); *Israele* (Italian—Israel)

ISR Indian State Railways; Institute for Sex Research; Institute for Social Research; Institute of Surgical Research; International Sanitary Regulations; International Society of Radiology

IS & R Information Storage and Retrieval (system)

I & SR Institutional and Staff Relations

ISRAD Institute for Social Research and Development

Israel State of Israel (most advanced Middle Eastern country despite unceasing hostility of Arab terrorists, Hebrew and Arabic are its official languages but English is widely spoken) *Medinat Israel* known as Judea Palestine before the Christian era

Israeli National Composer Ernst Bloch

Israeli Ports (north to south)

Akko (Acre), Hefa (Haifa), Netanya, Tel-Aviv-Yafo (Jaffa), Ashdod (Azotus), Ashquelon (Ascalon), Elat, Sharm el Sheik

Israel's Largest Port Tel-Aviv-Yafo (Jaffa or Joppa)

Israfel Edgar Allan Poe

ISRB Idaho Surveying and Rating Bureau; Inter-Services Research Bureau

ISRC International Synthetic Rubber Company

ISRD International Society for the Rehabilitation of the Disabled

ISRF International Squash Rackets Federation

ISRI Israeli Shipping Research Institute

ISRR Institute of Social and Religious Research

ISRRT International Society of Radiographers and Radiological Technicians

ISRSA International Synthetic Rubber Safety Association

isru information search and retrieval unit

ISRU International Scientific Radio Union

iss ideal solidus structures; ion-scattering spectroscopy; issue

iss (ISS) ionospheric sounding satellite

ISS Industry Standard Specifications; Inertial Sensor System; Information Service Specialist; Inspection Surveillance Sheet, Institute for Socioeconomic Studies; Institute of Space Sciences; Institute of Space Studies, Institutional Staff Services; Integrated Start System; International School Service; International Seismological Summary; International Shoe Company (Stock Exchange Symbol); International Social Service; International Students Society; International Sunshine Society; Israeli Secret Service

ISSA International Social Security Association

ISSAS Interactive Structural Sizing and Analysis System

ISSB Inter-Services Security Board

ISSC Institute for the Study of Social Conflict; International Social Science Council

ISSCA Institute of Steel Service Centres of Australia

ISSCAAP International Standard Statistical Classification

of Aquatic Animals and Plants

ISSCB International Society for Sandwich Construction and Bonding

ISSCO Integrated Software Systems Corporation

ISSCT International Society of Sugar Cane Technologists

ISSE Inter-Sun-Earth Explorer

issei (Japanese—first generation)—Japanese immigrant to the U.S. (see *kibei, nisei, sansei)*

ISSL Initial Spares Support List

ISSLIC Israel Societies of Special Libraries and Information Centers

ISSMFE International Society of Soil Mechanics and Foundation Engineering

ISSMIS Integrated Support Services Management Information System

ISSMS Integrated Support Services Management System (USA)

ISSN International Standard Serial Number

ISSOE Instructional Support System for Occupational Education

ISSOL International Society for the Study of the Origin of Life

issr information storage, selection, and retrieval

ISSS International Society for the Study of Symbols; International Society of Soil Science

ISST International Society of Skilled Trades

IS Standards International Safety Standards

ist insulin shock therapy; interstellar travel

is't is it

ist istituto (Italian—institute)

Ist Istanbul

IST Indian Standard Time; Industrial Steel and Tube (consolidated); In-Service Training; Institute on Strategic Trade (Washington, D.C.); Institute of Science and Technology (University of Michigan); International Society of Toxicology; Istanbul, Turkey (airport)

IST International Steam Table

IS & T International Science and Technology

ISTA Indiana State Teachers Association; Industrial Science and Technology Agen-

cy; International Seed Testing Association

Istan Istanbul

Istanbul formerly Byzantium or Constantinople

istar information storage translation and reproduction

ISTB Interstate Tariff Bureau

ISTC Interdepartmental Screw Thread Committee; International Shade Tree Conference

ISTD Institute for the Study and Treatment of Delinquency; International Society of Tropical Dermatology

ISTEA Iron and Steel Trades Employers' Association

ISTEM Inter-Seminary Theological Education for Ministry

isth isthmian; isthmus

Isth Isthmiam; Isthmus

Isthmian Nation Panama

Isthmian Waterway Panama Canal linking the Caribbean-Atlantic and the Pacific; Suez Canal linking the Mediterranean-Atlantic and the Red Sea leading to the Indian Ocean

Isthmus of Panama formerly Isthmus of Darien

ISTI Iowa State Technical Institute

istim interchange of scientific and technical information in machine language

ISTM International Society for Testing Materials

ISTO Italian State Tourist Office

istom interstate transportation of obscene matter

I Struct E Institute of Structural Engineers

istse integral square time square error

ISU Idaho State University; International Seamen's Union; International Shooting Union; International Skating Union; Iowa Southern Utilities; Iowa State University; Italian Service Unit; Southern Iowa Railway (railroad coding)

I-sub inhibitor substance

ISUM Intelligence Summary

ISUP Iowa State University Press

ISUST Iowa State University of Science and Technology

ISV Institute for the Study of Violence (Brandeis U); International Scientific Vocabulary

ISVA Incorporated Society of Valuers and Auctioneers

ISVR Institute of Sound and Vibration Research
ISVS International Secretariat for Volunteer Service
isw interstitial water
ISW Institute for Solid Wastes
ISWA International Science Writers Association; International Solid Wastes and Public Cleansing Association
ISWG Imperial Standard Wire Gauge
isy intrasynovial
isz increment and skip on zero
it Intermediate Technology; slang term for sex appeal
it. information theory; inspection tag; internal thread; international tolerance; inventory transfer; item; itemization(s); in transit
it. (IT) information technology; intertuberous; transposed inversion (12-tone)
i/t intensity duration
it italiensk (Dano-Norwegian—Italian); *item* (Spanish—item)
i.t. in transitu (Latin—in transit)
i/t in transitu (Latin—in transit)
It Italy
It Italia (Italian, Portuguese, Spanish—Italy); Italian (language spoken by more than 60 million people including those in Sicily who speak a Sicilian dialect often heard there and wherever Sicilians have emigrated)
IT Immunity Test; Imperial Territory; Imperial Typewriter; Income Tax; Indian Territory; Inner Temple; Institute of Technology; International Telephone and Telegraph (Wall Street slang)
ita initial teaching alphabet; inner transport area; interface test adapter(s); imperial teaching alphabet; international teaching alphabet; international telegraph alphabet
Ita Italia (Spanish—Italy)
ITA Independent Teachers Association; Independent Television Authority; Industrial Truck Association; Industry and Trade Administration; Institut du Transport Aerien (Air Transport Institute); International Tea Agreement; International Temperance Association; International Tin Agreement; International Touring Alliance; International Trade Administration; International Twins Association
ITAA International Transactional Analysis Association
ITAB Industry Technical Advisory Board
ITAC Interconnect Association of Canada
ITACS Integrated Tactical Air Control System
itae integrated time and absolute error
ITAI Institute of Technical Authors and Illustrators
ital italic; italicize; italics
ital italiensk (Dano-Norwegian—Italian)
Ital Italian
Italia Italia Società di Navigazione (Italian Line); (Italian, Latin, Spanish—Italy)
Itália (Portuguese—Italy)
italian italian grayhound (toy dog originally bred in Italy); italian hand (script originating in Italy in medieval times or a nickname for craftiness such as detecting one's *fine italian hand*); italian dressing (salad dressing composed of olive oil, wine vinegar, and spices such as garlic)
Italian Mendelssohn's Symphony No. 4 in A major
Italian Architect-Engraver-Painter Giambattista Piranesi
Italian Architect-Painter-Poet-Sculptor Michelangelo Buonarroti
Italian Architect-Painter-Sculptor Giovanni Lorenzo Bernini
Italian boot boot-shaped Italian peninsula
Italian Century the 14th century—the 1300s
Italian Classicist Sculptor Antonio Canova
Italian East Africa Mussolini's imperial plan forcibly uniting Eritrea, Ethiopia, and Italian Somaliland from 1936 to 1941
Italian Engraver Giambattista Piranesi
Italian Family of Sculptors the della Robbias
Italian Film Magician Frederico Fellini
Italian Fourteen Italy's fourteen best-known classical composers arranged chronologically—Palestrina, Monteverdi, Fescobaldi, Vivaldi, Scarlatti (2), Cherubini, Paganini, Rossini, Donizetti, Bellini, Verdi, Puccini, Respighi
Italian Goldsmith and Sculptor Benvenuto Cellini
Italian Illustrator-Painter Sandro di Botticelli
Italian Lakes Como, Garda, Isea, Lecco, Lugano, Maggiore, Orta
Italian National Composer Ottorino Respighi
Italian Naturalist Painter Michelangelo da Caravaggio
Italian North Africa Libya from 1912 to the end of World War II when it ceased being an Italian colony
Italian Ports (large, medium, and small from the west coast to the east coast) (*on Sardinia*—La Maddalena, Olbia, Cagliari, Alghero, Porto Torres), Savona, Genova (Genoa), La Spezia, Livorno (Leghorn), Portoferraio (*on Elba*), Civitavecchia, Gaeta, Forio, Ischia, Bagnoli, Napoli (Naples), Torre Annunziata, Castellamare di Stabia, Reggio di Calabria, (*on Sicily*—Messina, Palermo, Trapani, Marsala, Licata, Siracusa, Augusta, Catania), Crotone, Taranto, Gallipoli, Brindisi, Monopoli, Bari, Molfetta, Barletta, Manfredonia, Ancona, Ravenna, Chioggia, Porto di Lido (Venice), Monfalcone, Trieste
Italian Pre-Renaissance Painter Giotto (Giotto di Bondone)
Italian Riviera resort area between La Spezia and Ventimiglia
Italian Somaliland Indian Ocean coast of what is now southern Somalia
Italie (French—Italy)
Italië (Dutch—Italy)
Italien (German—Italy)
Italy Italian Republic (European nation whose civilization antedates the Roman Empire and is reflected in the industry of its Italian-speaking people of great artistic talent) *Repubblica Italiana*
Italy's Principal Port Genoa
ITAM Instituto Tecnologico Autonomo de México (Spanish—Technological Institute of Mexico)
ITAP Interim Track Analysis Program
itar interstate and foreign travel (or transportation) in aid of racketeering enterprises
ITAR International Traffic in

Arms Regulations; Interstate and Foreign Travel (or Transportation) in Aid of Racketeering Enterprises

ITASS Interim Towed-Array Surveillance System

Itavia Italian Aviation (domestic airline)

itax italics

itb (ITB) integrated tug barge

ITB Industrial Training Board; Integrated Tug Barge; International Theft Bureau; International Time Bureau; Invitation to Bid; Irish Tourist Board; Irish Tourist Bureau

ITB *Internationaler Turnerbund* (German—International Gymnastic Federation)

itbh internal broach

ITBL Integrated Transportation Bill of Lading

IT & BL Island Tug & Barge, Ltd.

ITBS Iowa Test of Basic Skills

itc installation time and cost

ITC Illinois Terminal Company (railroad); Imperial Tobacco Company; Inclusive Tour Charter; Industrial Training Council; Infantry Training Center; International Tea Council; International Tin Council; International Toastmistress Clubs; International Trade Commission; International Traders Clubs; International Training Center; Island Trading Company

IT & C Industry, Trade, and Commerce (Canada)

ITCA International Typographic Composition Association

ITCA *Instituto Tecnologico Centroamericano* (Spanish—Central American Technical Institute)

itcan inspect, test, and correct as necessary

ITCC International Technical Cooperation Center

itcm integrated tactical countermeasures

ITCP Integrated Test and Check-out Procedures

ITCRM Infantry Training Center—Royal Marines

ITCV Inter-Tropical Convergence Zone

it'd it had; it would

ITD *International Telephone Directory*

itda indirect target damage assessment

ITDC Indian Tourist Development Corporation

ITE Institute of Telecommunication Engineers; Institute of Terrestrial Ecology; Institute of Traffic Engineers

ITED Iowa Tests of Educational Development

ITEP Indian Teacher Education Project; Integrated Test-Evaluation Program

itf inland transit floater (insurance)

ITF Integration Task Force; International Television Federation; International Trade Federation

ITF *Institut Textile de France* (Textile Institute of France)

ITFCA International Track and Field Coaches Association

ITFCS Institute for Twenty-First Century Studies

itfs instructional television fixed service

ITFS Instructional Television Fixed Service; International Television Fixed Service

ITG International Trumpet Guild

itga internal gage

ITGWF International Textile and Garment Workers Federation

ithp increased take-home pay

iti intertial interval

ITI Inagua Transports Incorporated; Integrated Task Indices; International Technical Institute; International Theatre Institute; International Thrift Institute

ITIB Iceland Tourist Information Bureau

ITIC International Tsunami Information Center

ITIM Interchurch Trade and Industry Mission

itin itinerary

Itiopia Ethiopia (Abyssinia)

itis (Latin suffix—inflammation)—bronchitis, meningitis

Iti(s) Italian(s)

ITITA *Instituto Veterinario de Investigaciones Tropicales y de la Altura* (Spanish—Veterinarian Institute of Tropical and High-Altitude Research)

itk *intetkøn* (Dano-Norwegian —neuter)

itl integrate-transfer-launch

Itl Italian

it'll it will

itlx italics (used for items from Latin or other languages, titles of books and periodicals, physical symbols)

itm inch trim moment; information transfer module

ITM Institute of Travel Managers

ITMA Institute of Trade Mark Agents

ITMA *It's That Man Again* (Tommy Handley's most popular World-War-II BBC series)

ITMRC International Travel Market Research Council

ITN International Television Network

ITN *Independent Television News*

ITNA Independent Television News Association

ITNS Integrated Tactical Navigation System (USN)

ITO Interim Technical Order; International Terminal Operators; International Trade Organization (UN); Invitational Travel Orders

ITOA Independent Taxi Owners Association

ITOFCA Industrial Trailer-on-Flatcar Associates

ITOL International Thomson Organisation, Ltd

itom interstate transportation of obscene matter

itp (ITP) idiopathic thrombocytopenic purpura; immune thrombocytopenic purpura; inosine triphosphate

ITPA Illinois Test of Psycholinguistic Abilities

ITPP Institute of Technical Publicity and Publications

ITPS Income Tax Payers' Society

itq's in-text questions

itr incremental tape recorder; integrated test requirement(s)

ITR Indiana Toll Road

ITRA International Truck Restorers Association

ITRC International Terrorist Research Center (El Paso, Texas); International Tin Research Council

ITRP Institute of Transportation and Regional Planning

ITRU Industrial Training Research Unit

its (ITS) invitation to send (data processing)

it's it has; it is

Its Italians

ITS Idaho Test Station; Institute for Transportation Studies; Integrated Trajectory System; Interactive Training System; Intermarket Trading System; International Technogeographical Society; International Thespian Society; International Trade Secretariat; International Transportation Service

itsa interstate transportation of stolen aircraft

ITSA Institute for Telecommunication Sciences and Aeronomy

itsb interstate transportation of strikebreakers

itsc interstate transportation of stolen cattle

ITSC International Telecommunications Satellite Consortium

itse integral time square error

itsmv interstate transportation of a stolen motor vehicle

itsp interstate transportation of stolen property

ITSS Integrated Tactical Surveillance System

itt instant-touch tuning

ITT Institute of Textile Technology; Insulin Tolerance Test

IT & T International Telephone and Telegraph

ITTA International Table Tennis Association

ITTC International Television Trading Corporation

ITTCS International Telephone and Telegraph Communications System

ITTE Institute of Transportation and Traffic Engineering

ITTF International Table Tennis Federation

ITTP Indian Teacher Training Program

ITTTA International Technical Tropical Timber Association

ITU Income Tax Unit; International Telecommunications Union; International Typographical Union

ITUA Industrial Trades Union of America

ITURM International Typographical Union Ruling Machine

itv instructional television; internal television

ITV Independent Television

ITVA Instructional Television Authority

ITW Illinois Tool Works

ITWF International Transport Workers Federation

itx inclusive tour excursion(s)

Itz Itzik

***ITZEL** Irgun Tzvai Le'umi* (Hebrew—National Military Or-

ganization)

iu immunizing unit(s); indicator unit; internal upset (oil well); international unit(s)

i of u inevitability of the unpredictable

IU Indiana University; Indianapolis Union (railroad); international unit; International Utilities

IÜ Istanbul Üniversitesi (Universityo) (University of Istanbul)

IUA International Union of Architects

IUAA International Union of Alpine Associations

IUAES International Union of Anthropological and Ethnological Sciences

IUAI International Union of Aviation Insurers

IUAIWA International Union of Allied Industrial Workers of America

IUAJ International Union of Agricultural Journalists

IUAO International Union for Applied Ornithology

IUAPPA International Union of Air Pollution Prevention Associations

IUAT International Union Against Tuberculosis

IUB International Union of Biochemistry; Interstate Underwriters Board

IUBS International Union of Biological Sciences

IUC International Union of Chemistry; International Union for Conservation

IUCc International Union of Crystallography

iucd intrauterine contraceptive device

IUCL Istanbul University Central Library

IUCN International Union for Conservation of Nature and Natural Resources

IUCNNR International Union for Conservation of Nature and Natural Resources

IUCr International Union of Crystallography

IUCSTP Inter-Union Commission on Solar-Terrestrial Physics

IUCW International Union for Child Welfare

iud intrauterine device; intrauterine diaphragm

***Iud** Iudicum* (Spanish—Epistle of St Paul to the Hebrews)—Book of the Jews

IUD Institute for Urban Development

iudr idoxuridine

IUDTPNAPUSCAN International Union of Dolls, Toys, Playthings, Novelties, and Allied Products of the United States and Canada

IUDZG International Union of Directors of Zoological Gardens

IUE International Ultraviolet Explorer (space vehicle); International Union of Electrical Workers; International Union for Electroheat

IUEC International Union of Elevator Constructors

IUEF International University Exchange Fund

IUER & MW International Union of Electrical, Radio & Machine Workers

IUFA International Union of Family Organizations

IUFOST International Union of Food Science and Technology

IUFRO International Union of Forest Research Organizations

IUGG International Union of Geodesy and Geophysics

***Iugoslávia** (Portuguese—Yugoslavia)

IUGS International Union of Geological Sciences; International Union of Geological Services

IUHA Industrial Unit Heater Association

IUHE International Union for Health Education

IUHPS International Union of the History and Philosophy of Science

IUHS International Union of the History of Science

IUIS International Union of Immunological Societies

IUL (Bloomington); Ibadan University Library (Nigeria); Indiana University Library

IULA International Union of Local Authorities

IULIA International Union of Life Insurance Agents

iumbb if unworkable, make best bid

IUMC Indiana University Medical Center

IUMI International Union of Marine Insurance

***IUMK** Istanbul Üniversitesi Merkez Kütüphanesi* (Turkish—Istanbul University Central

Library)
IUMM & SW International Union of Mine, Mill and Smelter Workers
IUMP International Union of the Medical Press
IUMSA International Union for Moral and Social Action
IUMSWA Industrial Union of Marine and Shipbuilding Workers of America
IUNS International Union of Nutritional Sciences
IUOE International Union of Operating Engineers
IUOPA International Union of Practitioners in Advertising
IUOPAB International Union of Pure and Applied Biophysics
IUOT Indiana University Opera Theater
IUOTO International Union of Official Travel Organizations
IUOW Industrial Union of Workers
iup intrauterine pregnancy
IUP Indiana University Press; International University Press; Irish Universities Press; Israel Universities Press
IUPA International Union of Police Associations
IUPAC International Union of Pure and Applied Chemistry
IUPAP International Union of Pure and Applied Physics
IUPLAW International Union for the Protection of Literary and Artistic Works
IUPM International Union for Protecting Public Morality
IUPN International Union for the Protection of Nature
iups installed user programs
IUPS International Union of Physiological Sciences
IUPW International Union of Petroleum Workers
IUR International Union of Railways
I U Res Ctr Indiana University Research Center (for the Language Sciences)
ius inertial upperstage; interim upperstage
IUs international units
IUS Institute of Urban Studies; International Union of Students; International Urban Society; International Urban Studies
IUSA Institute of the U.S.A. (Soviet office charged with analyzing American news and political statements concern-

ing the USSR)—Russian counterpart of American kremlinologists
IUSP International Union of Scientific Psychology
IUSS Institute of United States Studies
IUSSI International Union for the Study of Social Insects
IUSSP International Union for the Scientific Study of Population
IUT Instituts Universitaires de Technologie (University Institutes of Technology)
IUTAM International Union of Theoretical and Applied Mechanics
iutip if unworkable, telegraph idea of price
IUUAAAIWA International Union of United Automobile, Aerospace, and Agricultural Implement Workers of America
IUUCLGW International Union, United Cement, Lime & Gypsum Workers
IUVD International Union Against Venereal Diseases
IUVDT International Union against the Venereal Diseases and the Treponematoses
IUVSTA International Union for Vacuum Science Techniques and Applications
IUW Industrial Union of Workers
IUWCC Inshore Undersea Warfare Control Center (USN)
IUWWML International Union of Wood, Wire, and Metal Lathers
iv increased value; initial velocity; intravenous(ly); intravertebral; inverted vertical (engine); invoice value; ivory
i/v increased value; instrument/visual
i.v. in verbo (Latin—under the word)
i V in Vertretung (German—as a substitute, by proxy)
IV Imperial Valley; Ivan; Ivy
IV Islas Virgenes (Spanish—Virgin Islands)
iva inspection visual aid
Iva Godiva
IVA Independent Voters Association; International Volleyball Association
IVAAP International Veterinary Association for Animal Production
ivala integrated visual approach and landing aids

Ivan (nickname for the typical Russian)
Ivan Ivanovich the typical Russian
Ivan-Kremlin disease endemic antisemitism
Ivan Lermolieff Giovanni Morelli (19-century Italian art expert, patriot, and senator)
Ivan the Terrible Czar Ivan IV Vasilievich—ruler of Russia
Ivaran Ivar Anton Christensen's steamship company
IVBF International Volley-Ball Federation
ivc inferior vena cava; intermittent vertical chambers
IVC Imperial Valley College
ivcd intraventricular conduction defect
ivc's inner van connectors
Iv Cst Ivory Coast
ivd interpolated voice data; intervertebral disk
IVDP Identification, Validation, and Dissemination Process
ivds independent variable depth sonar
Ive Ivan; Iven
I've I have
IVECO Industrial Vehicles Corporation
I've had it (popular American contraction—I have had enough of it)
Ives 4 four symphonies by Charles Ives
I-vets Iceland veterans
ivf in-vitro fertilization
IVF Innocent Victims Fund
IVFZ International Veterinary Federation of Zootechnics
IVGMMA International Violin, Guitar Makers, and Musicians Association
IVI Independent Voters of Illinois
IVIC Instituto Venezolano de Investigaciones Científicas (Venezuelan Institute of Scientific Investigations)
IVIS International Visitors Information Service
ivjc intervertebral joint complex
IVK Institutet för Vaxtforskning och Kyllagring (Institute for Foodstuff Research and Refrigeration—Sweden)
IVL Ivaran Lines
IVLA International Visual Literacy Association
IVLU Ivaran Lines (container) Unit
IVMB Internationale Vereini-

gung der Musikbibliotheken (German—International Association of Music Libraries)

ivmu inertial velocity measurement unit

ivo in view of

Ivory Coast Republic of the Ivory Coast (West African nation whose Ivoirians speak French and tribal languages, diamond and manganese mining as well as tropical agriculture contribute to the economy)

Ivory Coast Ports (west to east) Grand-Lahou, Jacqueville, Port-Bouet, Abidjan, Grand-Bassam

ivp initial vapor pressure; inspected variety purity (certified seeds); intravenous pyelogram

IVP Instituto Venezolano de la Petroquimica (Venezuelan Petrochemical Institute)

ivr instrumented visual range

IVR International Vehicle Registration (symbols displayed on automotive license plates)

IVR Internationale Vereinigung des Rheinschiffsregisters (German—International Association of Rhine Ships Registers)

ivs intraventricular septum

iv's intravenous feedings; intravenous injections

IVS Integrated Versaplot Software; International Voluntary Service

IVS Instituto Venezolano de los Seguros Sociales (Spanish—Venezuelan Institute of Social Security)

ivsd interventricular septal defect

ivsi instantaneous vertical speed indicator

IVSU International Veterinary Students Union

ivt intravehicular transfer; intravenous transfusion

ivu intravenous urography

IVU International Vegetarian Union

IVU Instituto de Vivienda Urbana (Spanish—Institute of Urban Housing)

ivvs instantaneous vertical-velocity sensor

Ivy League college athletic conference consisting of Brown, Columbia, Cornell, Dartmouth, Harvard, Pennsylvania, Princeton, and Yale; students and graduates of the abovementioned schools as well as their "characteristic"

style of dress, which was considered "quiet and neat." (The term was originally coined by Stanley Woodword, sports editor for *The Herald Tribune*.)

iw index word; indirect waste; individually wrapped; inside width; instruction word(ing); isotopic weight; ivory woodpecker

iw (IW) index word

i/w interchangeable with; in work

iW innere Weite (German—inside diameter)

IW Aero Trasporti Italiani (2-letter coding, Italian Air Transport)

IWA Institute of World Affairs; Insurance Workers of America; International Woodworkers of America

IWA International Wheat Agreement

IWAHMA Industrial Warm Air Heater Manufacturers Association

IWAIU Industrial Workers of America International Union

iwc in which case

IWC Inland Waterways Corporation; International Watch Company; International Whaling Commission; International Wheat Council

IWCA International World Calender Association

IWCC International Wrought Copper Council

IWCCA Inland Waterways Common Carriers Association

IWCI Industrial Wire Cloth Institute

IWCS Integrated Wideband Communications System

IWCT International War Crimes Tribunal

IWD International Waterways and Docks; International Women's Day (March 12)

IWE Institution of Water Engineers

IWG Imperial Wire Gauge; Interface Working Group; International Working Group (NATO)

IWGC Imperial War Graves Commission

IWGM Intergovernmental Working Group on Monitoring (or Surveillance)—UN

IWGMP Intergovernmental Working Group on Marine Pollution (UN)

iwistk issue while in stock

IWIU Insurance Workers International Union

iwl insensible water loss

IWL Institute of World Leadership

IWLA Izaak Walton League of America

IWM Imperial War Museum; Institute of Works Managers

IWMA International Working Men's Association

iwmi inferior wall myocardial infarction

IWML Imperial War Museum Library

Iwo Iwo Jima (Sulfur Island)

IWO Institute of World Order; International Wine Office; International Workers Order

IWP Indicative World Plan (FAO)

IWPA International Word Processing Association

IWPC Institute of Water Pollution Control

IWPO International Word Processing Organizations

IWPPA Independent Waste Paper Processers Association

IWPS Institute of War and Peace Studies (Columbia)

IWRI Informal Word Recognition Inventory; International Wildfowl Research Institute

IWRMA Independent Wire Rope Manufacturers Association

IWS Inland Waterway Service; Institute of Wood Science; International Wool Secretariat

IWSA International Water Supply Association

IWSB Insect Wire Screening Bureau

IWSc Institute of Wood Science

IWSC Irrigation and Water Supply Commission

IWSG International Wool Study Group

IWSP Institute of Work Study Practitioners

IWST Integrated Weapon System Training

IWT Indus Water Treaty; Inland Water Transport; Institute of Women Today; International Working Team (NATO)

IWT Industriewerke Transportsystem (cargo container system)

IWTA Inland Water Transport Authority

IWTD Inland Water Transport

Department
IWTO International Wool Textile Organization
iwu illegal wearing of uniform
IWU Illinois Wesleyan University; Insurance Workers Union
IWVA International War Veterans Alliance
iwvmts interim water velocity meter test set
iww inland waterway
IWW Industrial Workers of the World; Intracoastal Waterway
IWWP International Who's Who in Poetry
IWY International Women's Year (1975–1984)
IX unclassified vessel (2-letter naval code)
I.X. Iesous Christos (Greek—Jesus Christ)
ixc interexchange
ixey morphine
IXSS unclassified miscellaneous submarine (letter symbol)

Ixta Ixtaccihuatl
iy ionized yeast
IY Imperial Yeomanry; International Petroleum (stock exchange symbol)
IYB International Year Book
IYC Inland Yacht Club; International Year of the Child
IYDP International Year of Disabled Persons (1981)
IYEO Institute of Youth Employment Officers
IYF International Youth Federation
IYHF International Youth Hostel Federation
IYL International Youth Library
IYRU International Yacht Racing Union
iyswim if you see what I mean
i y v ida y vuelta (Spanish—round trip)
I y v ida y vuelta (Spanish—round trip)
iz izzard; zed

Iz Izar; Izar: Izmir (Smyrna)
IZ Institute of Zoology; Israel Zangwill
Izd izdatl' (Russian—publisher)
izdat izdatel (Russian—publisher)
IZL Irgun Z'vai Leumi (Hebrew—National Army Organization)
Izmir (Turkish—Smyrna)
izqᵃ izquierda (Spanish—left)
izqᵒ izquierdo (Spanish—left)
izs insulin zinc suspension
IZTO Interzonal Trade Office (NATO)
Izv Izvestia (Russian—news)—official newspaper of the Presidium of the Supreme Soviet —published in Moscow
Iz: Wa: Izaak Walton, *The Complete Angler*, used colons after his initials
Izzie Isador; Isadora; Isadore; Isidro; Isodoro; Ysidro
Izzy (*see* Izzie)

J

j inner quantum number (symbol); jack; joint (marijuana); joist(ing); junior; junk(ie)—narcotics (addict or vendor); square of minus 1 (symbol); unit vector in y direction (symbol)

j *journal*; *jour(nal)* (French—day, newspaper)

j. *juris* (Latin—of law); *jus* (Latin—law)

J action variable (symbol); advance ratio (symbol); electric current density (symbol); gram-equivalent weight (symbol); heat transfer factor (symbol); Jacob; Jacobean; Jacobian; Jaeger; Jaen; Jamaica; Jamaican; January; Japan; Japanese; jet; Jew; Jewish; joint; joule; Judaic; Judaism; Juliet—code for letter J; Julliard; July; Junction; junction devices; June; North American Aviation (symbol); polar movement of inertia (symbol); radiant intensity (symbol)

J *Jabal* (Arabic or Persian—mountain, mountain range); *Jebel* (Arabic—mountain, mountains); *Jejunium* (Latin—fast, hunger); *Jibal* (Arabic—mountain range); *Jogi* (Estonian—river); *Jøkel* (Norwegian—glacier); *Joki* (Finnish—river); *Jökull* (Icelandic—glacier); *Journal* (French—journal)

J-1 personnel section of joint military staff

J-2 intelligence section of joint military staff

J-3 operations and training section of joint military staff

J-4 logistics section of joint military staff

J-4 fuel jet-engine fuel (derived from coal oil or kerosene)

J-5 Plans and Policy (Joint Chiefs of Staff)

J-6 Communications, Electronics (Joint Chiefs of Staff)

J-32 Saab Lansen jet interceptor aircraft

J-35 Saab double-delta-wing supersonic fighter or fighter-bomber built in Sweden and named Draken (Dragon)

J-37 Swedish Thunderbolt or Viggen jet fighter aircraft

ja jack; jack adapter; jetavator assembly; job analysis; joke awful

ja (JA) jump address

j/a (J/A) joint account

j & a junk and abandon; junked and abandoned

Ja Jacob; Jacque(s); James; Japan; Japanese

JA Jamaica(n); Japan Association; Jewish Agency; John Adams (2nd President U.S.); Judge Advocate; Junior Achievement; Justice of Appeal

JAA Japan Aeronautic Association; Japan Asia Airways; Joint Airways Association

JAAA Japan Amateur Athletic Association

JAAB Joint Airlift Allocations Board

JAAF Joint Army-Air Force

JAAFU Joint Anglo-American Foulup; Joint Anglo-American Fuckup

JAALD Japanese Association of Agricultural Librarians and Documentalists

JAAOC Joint Anticraft Operation Center (NATO)

JAAR *Journal of the American Academy of Religion*

jaarg *jaargang* (Dutch—annual volume)

JAARS Jungle Aviation and Radio Service

JAAS Jewish Academy of Arts and Sciences

Jab Jabal; Jabalpur; Jabez; Jabneel

JAB Joint Amphibious Board; Junior Advisory Board

JABA Jefferson Area Board for Aging

Jabal Tariq (Arabic—Mountain of Tarik)—Moorish name for Gibraltar in honor of their chief Jabal Tariq who settled the Rock in the year 711

JABC Japan Audit Bureau of Circulations

jac jet aircraft coating

Jac Jacobean; Jacobite; Jacobus; Jacumba

Jac. Book of Jacob

Jac. *Jacobus* (Latin—James)

JAC Japan Advisory Committee; Joint Advisory Committee; Joint Apprenticeship Council

JAC *Journal of Applied Chemistry*

JACA Japan Air Cleaning Association

Jacaranda Capital jacaranda-tree-lined avenues and streets comprising South Africa's capital city—Pretoria

JACC Joint Admissions Centre for Colleges (Australia); Journalism Association of Community Colleges

JACCC Japnese-American Cultural and Community Center;

Joint Air Control and Coordination Center (USAF)

Jace Jason

jack jackass

Jack Jackson; Jacob; John

Jack Benny Benjamin Kubelsky

Jack Frost frosty weather personified

Jack Higgins Harry Patterson's pseudonym

Jackie Jack Roosevelt Robinson; Jacqueline Kennedy Onassis

Jack London John Griffith London

Jack Lord John Joseph Ryan

Jack Palance Walter Paluniuk

JACKPOT Joint Airborne Communications Center and Command Post

jack(s) jackass(es)—male donkey(s)—*see* hinny

Jackson Mississippi's capital

Jacksonopolis Jackson, Michigan

Jack Soo Jack Suzuki

Jacky Jaqueline

JACL Japanese-American Citizens League

JACM Journal of the Association for Computing Machinery

JACOB Junior Achievement Corporation of Business

Jacopo Jacopo Tatti

Jacq Jacques; Jacquin

Jacq's loom Jacquard's loom

Jacques Halevy Jacques Francois Fromental Elias Levi

Jacques Offenbach Jakob Eberst

Jacques Tati Jacques Tatischeff

JACS Journal of the American Chemical Society

JACT Joint Association of Classical Teachers

Jad Jadavpur, India

JAD Julian astronomical day

JADA Japan Automobile Dealers Association

JADA Journal of the American Dental Association

JADB Joint Air Defense Board

JADE Japanese Air Defense Environment

jadeite sodium aluminum silicate

JADF Japan Air Defense Force

jaditbhkycc just a drop in the basket helps keep your city clean (anti-litter-civic-responsibility campaign)

Jadotville former name for Likasi, Zaire

JADPU Joint Automatic Data Processing Unit (shared by the Home Office and the Metropolitan Police of London)

Jadroplov Jadranska Slobodna Plovida (Yugoslav Great Lakes Line)

J Adv Judge Advocate

J Adv Gen Judge Advocate General

JAE Joint Atomic Exercise (NATO)

JAEC Japan Atomic Energy Commission

JAEIA Japan Atomic Energy Industrial Association

JAEIC Joint Atomic Energy Intelligence Committee

JAEIP Japan Atomic Energy Insurance Pool

JAERI Japan Atomic Energy Research Institute

JAES Japan Atomic Energy Society

JAF Japan Automobile Federation; Jordanian Air Force; Judge Advocate of the Fleet

JAFC Japan Atomic Fuel Corporation

Jaffa Tel Aviv's seaport also known as Joppa or Yafo

Jaffna Jaffnapatam

JAFPUB Joint Armed Forces Publication

jag. jaguar; jaguarundi

Jag Jaguar

JAG James Abram Garfield (20th President U.S.); Judge Advocate General

JAG-A Judge Advocate General —Army

Jagananth Juggernaut or Puri on the Bay of Bengal

JAGC Judge Advocate General's Corps

JAGD Judge Advocate General's Department

JAG-N Judge Advocate General —Navy

jag(s) jaguarundi(s)

JAGS Judge Advocate General's School

JAH John Adams House

Jahrb Jahrbuch (German—yearbook)

Jahrg Jahrgang (German—annual publication, vintage of the year); year's growth

jai juvenile amaurotic idiocy

JAIEG Joint Atomic Information Exchange Group

JAIF Japan Atomic Industrial Forum

JAIL Justice Against Identification Laws

JAIMS Japan-America Institute of Management Science

JAIS Japan Aircraft Industry Society

Jak Jakarta (Batavia)

Jakarta formerly Batavia now Djakarta

Jake Jacob; Jacobus

Jaksch's disease infantile anemia

Jal Jalisco (inhabitants nicknamed tapatios as they excel in dancing the tapatio jarabe)

Jal Jalan (Malay—Lane, Road, Street)

JAL Japan Air Lines; Jet Approach and Landing Chart

JAL Journal of Academic Librarianship

JALMA Japan Leprosy Mission for Asia

JALTOS Japan Air Lines Computerized Air Cargo Terminal System

jam. jamming; job analysis memo

Jam Jamaica

JAM James A. Michener; Joint Action for Mission; Joslyn Art Museum; Sir John Alexander Macdonald (Canada's first and third Prime Minister)

JAMA Japan Automobile Manufacturers Association

JAMA Journal of the American Medical Association

JAMAG Joint American Military Advisory Group

jamaica jamaica ginger (originally from the island of Jamaica but found in many parts of the subtropical and tropical world); jamaica rum (heavy pungent rum originally distilled in Jamaica); jamaica shorts (mid-thigh short pants)

Jamaica English-speaking West Indian island nation whose Jamaicans produce many tropical crops as well as mining for bauxite, gypsum, marble, and silica

Jamaica ganga Jamaica-grown marijuana

Jamaican Ports (north coast to south coast clockwise) Lucea, Montego Bay, Falmouth, Rio Bueno, Dry Harbour, St Ann's Bay, Ocho Rios, Oracabessa Bay, Port Maria, Annotto Bay, Buff Bay, Port Antonio, Manchioneal, Port Morant, Morant Bay, Port Royal, Kingston, Long's Wharf, Little Pedro Point, Black River, Bluefields; Savanna la Mar

Jambalaya Capital Gonzales, Louisiana

JAMC Japan Aircraft Manufacturers Corporation

J Am Ceram Soc Journal of the American Ceramic Society

J Am Chem Soc Journal of the American Chemical Society

James Gardner James Baumgardner

James Hadley Chase René Raymond's pseudonym

James Herriot author-veterinarian James Alfred Wight's pseudonym

James Island, Galápagos Bartolomé, San Salvador, Santiago

James O'Brien James Bronterre

jamex jamming exercise

J Am Geriatrics Soc Journal of the American Geriatrics Society

JaMi Jacksonville-Miami (metropolitan area including Fort Lauderdale, Hollywood, Tampa, and St Petersburg)—also called Metro or Metro Area

Jamie James

J Am Inst Electr Eng Journal of the American Institute of Electrical Engineers

JAMMAT Joint Military Mission for Aid to Turkey

jammies pyjamas

jamocha java & mocha (prison argot—coffee)

jams pajamas

jamsan jam sandwich

Jamsat Japan radio amateur satellite

JAMSTEC Japan Marine Science and Technology Center

jamtrac jammers tracked by azimuth crossings

JAMTS Japan Association of Motor Trade and Service

jamwich jam sandwich

jan janitor; janitorial

Jan Janice; Jansen; Janson; January; John

JAN Jackson, Mississippi (airport); Joint Army-Navy

JANAF Joint Army-Navy Air Force

JANAIR Joint Army-Navy Aircraft Instrument Research

JANAP Joint Army-Navy-Air Force Publication

JANAST Joint Army-Navy-Air Force Sea Transport

JANBMC Joint Army-Navy Ballistic Missile Committee

Jane Doe name used on subpoenas and summonses if the name of the woman to be served is unknown; nickname

for the average American female

Janet Frame Janet Peterson Frame Clutha's pseudonym

Janet Gaynor Laura Gainor

Jane Welsh Mrs Thomas Carlyle

Jane Wyman Sarah Jane Fulks

Janey Canuck Judge Emily Murphy

JanFeb January and February

JANFU Joint Army-Navy Foulup; Joint Army-Navy Fuckup

Janie Jane; Jean

JANIS Joint Army-Navy Intelligence Surveys

jan mer jangan merokok (Malay —no smoking)

Jan Peerce Jacob Pincus Perelmuth

Jans Janson

JANS Jet Aircraft Noise Survey; Joint Army-Navy Specification

Jan Smuts Johannesburg, South Africa's airport named for its Boer War leader and statesman

JANSPEC Joint Army-Navy Specification

JANSRP Jet Aircraft Noise Survey Research Program

JANSTD Joint Army-Navy Standard

Jan Struther Joyce Anstruther

janv janvier (French—January)

Jan Valtin Richard J Krebs

jap japanned

jap japansk (Dano-Norwegian— Japanese)

Jap Japan; Japanese; Jasper

Jap Japanese (oriental language spoken by more than 109 million people in Japan and in its former colonies or occupied territories)

JA£ Jamaican pound

JAP Joint Acceptance Plan(ning); Joint Apprenticeship Program

J-AP Jewish-American Prince(ss)

JAPAC Japan Atomic Power Company; Joint Air Photo Center

japan japan lacquer or japan varnish; japan wax also called japan tallow or sumac wax as it is made from sumac flowers

Japan Asia's most productive country; Japanese is the language of the homogeneous Japanese people whose ingenuity and workmanlike attitudes have put them at the top

of the automotive, electronic, and optical industries—*Nippon* or *Nihon*

Japan Current Kuroshio (Japanese—Black Stream)—Pacific Ocean's equivalent to the Atlantic Ocean's warm Gulf Stream

japanese japanese gelatin (agar also called japanese isinglass); japanese paper (high rag content quality paper); japanese silk (high quality raw silk produced in Japan)

Japanese Drama Painter Torii Kyonobu—originator of this school of painting

Japanese Lacquer Artist Korin (Ogata Korin)—regarded as Japan's greatest artist in lacquer decoration

Japanese Landscape Artist Supreme Sesshu

Japanese Naturalist Artist Korin

Japanese New Year December 28 through January 3

Japanese Ports (large and medium from north to south clockwise) Moruran, Hakodate, Otaru (*on Hokkaido*); Tokyo, Yokosuka, Shimuzu, Nagoya, Yokkaichi, Senboku, Osaka, Kobe, Fukuyama, Kure, Shimminato, Shimonoseki, Maizuru, Niigata (*on Honshu*), Kita Kyushu, Kagoshima, Nagasaki, Sasebo, Karatsu, Fukuoka (*on Kyushu*)

Japanese Riviera Enoshima Island recreation area

Japan's Back Door Sasebo

Japan's Front Gate Yokohama

Japan's Largest Port Yokohama (including Kawasaki, Tokyo, and Yokosuka)

Japão (Portuguese—Japan)

JAPATIC Japan Patent Information Center

JAPC Joint Air Photo Center

JAPCO Japan Atomic Power Company

Jap Cur Japan Current

Japdic Japanese dictionary

Japex Japan Petroleum Exploitation Company

JAPEX Japan Express

JAPIA Japan Auto Parts Industries Association

Japlish Japanese & English

Japon (French—Japan)

Japón (Spanish—Japan)

J App Crystallogr Journal of Applied Crystallography

J Appl Phys Journal of Applied Physics

Jar. Book of Jarom
JARC Joint Air Reconnaissance Center (NATO)
Jardines' Jardine, Matheson & Company
JARE Japanese Antarctic Research Expedition
jarg jargon; jargonese; jargonist; jargonistic; jargonize
Jarg Soc Jargon Society
JARI Japan Automotive Research Institute
JARL Japan Amateur Radio League
JARO Johore Area Rehabilitation Organization
JARS Journalization and Recovery System
JARTS Japan Railway Technical Service
Jarvis Street Toronto, Ontario's skid row around Sherbourne Street
Jas James
JAS Jamaica Agricultural Society; Japan Agricultural Standards; Japan Association of Shipbuilders; Japan Astronautical Society; Jewish Agricultural Society; Jordanian Agricultural Society
J-A S Japan-Australia Society
JASA Journal of the Acoustical Society of America
JASC Japan-Asia Sea Cable
Jascha (Russian nickname—Iacob)—Jake
JASDF Japan Air Self-Defense Force
JASG Joint Advanced Study Group
JASI Joint Asian Surgical Industries
JASIN Joint Air-Sea Interaction (oceanographic experiment)
JASIS Journal of the American Society for Information Science
jasp jasper; jasperoid
Jasp Jasper
Jasper short form for Jasper National Park and place-name for many American and Canadian places
Jaspr Jasper
JASRAC Japanese Society of Rights of Authors and Composers
jastop jet-assisted stop
Jastreb Yugoslav jet trainer aircraft called Hawk
jasu jet aircraft starting unit
JAT Jugoslovenski Aero-Transport (Yugoslav Airlines)
JATC Joint Apprenticeship

Training Committee
JATCA Joinery and Timber Construction Association
JATCC Joint Aviation Telecommunications Coordination Committee
JATCRU Joint Air Traffic Control Radar Unit
JATMA Japan Automobile Tire Manufacturers Association
J Atmos Sci Journal of Atmospheric Sciences
J Atmos Terr Phys Journal of Atmospheric and Terrestrial Physics
jato jet-assisted takeoff
JATS Joint Air Transportation Service
J Audio Eng Soc Journal of the Audio Engineering Society
jaund jaundice
JAUNT Jefferson Area United Transporation
Jav Java; Javanese
Java Djawa
JAVA Jamaica Association of Villas and Apartments
Java Sea between Java and Borneo
Javelin Gloster delta-wing jet fighter aircraft
javelle water sodium hypochlorite solution (NaOCl)
JAVHS Jane Addams Vocational High School
JAWA June's All the World Aircraft
Jawbone Flats Clarkston, Washington
JAWS Japan Animal Welfare Society; Jet Advance Warning System
Jax Jacksonville, Florida
JAX Jacksonville, Florida (airport)
jaycee (JC) Junior Chamber of Commerce
Jayhawker(s) Kansan(s)
Jazz Ambassador Louis (Satchmo) Armstrong
Jazz Capital of the Americas New Orleans
Jazz Capital of Europe Copenhagen
jb jet black; jet bomb (JB); job blank (form); joint board; junction box
Jb Jacob
Jb Jahrbuch(German—annual, yearbook)
JB Jacksonville Beach; James Buchanan (15th President U.S.); Jodrell Bank; John Bull (British empire personified); Joint Board; Stetson hat (after its original maker—JB Stet-

son)
J-B Jacques Barzun; Jean-Baptiste; Johannes Brahms
J.B. *Jurum Baccalaureus* (Latin —Bachelor of Laws)
JB Jerusalem Bible
JBA Japan Binoculars Association; Junior Bluejackets of America
JBAA Journal of the British Archeological Association
JBAKC John Brown Anti-Klan Committee
J-bar capital-J-shaped bar (as used in ski tow lifts)
JBC Jamaica Broadcasting Corporation; Japan Broadcasting Corporation (*q.v.* NHK); Jewish Book Council
JB & C John Brown and Company (shipbuilders)
JBCA Jewish Book Council of America
JB & Co John Brown and Company (shipbuilders)
JBCSA Joint British Committee for Stress Analysis
jbd jet blast deflector
JBe Japanese B encephalitis
Jber Jahresbericht (German—annual report)
JBES Jodrell Bank Experimental Station (Cheshire, England)
JBG Jewish Board of Guardians
JBHS John Bartram High School
JBIA Jewish Braille Institute of America
J-bird jailbird (underground slang—convict)
JBL James B Lansing (sound eqipment)
JBL Journal of Biblical Literature; Journal of Business Law
JBMA John Burroughs Memorial Association
JBMMA Japanese Business Machine Makers Association
J-boat large yacht, often 76 feet or longer; small racing boat sailed by youngsters
J-bolt capital-J-shaped bolt
J-box J-shaped bleaching box; junction box
JBP Jewel Bearing Program
JBPA Japan Book Publishers Association
JBPI Japanese Bicycle Promotion Institute
JBPS Jamaica Banana Producers Steamship
JBS Japan British Society; John Birch Society
JBSW Joseph Bulova School of

Watchmaking
JBT Jewelers Board of Trade
JBUSDC Joint Brazil-United States Defense Commission
JBUSMC Joint Brazil-US Military Commission
JBYC Jamaica Bay Yacht Club
jc joint compound
Jc Junction
JC Brother John Charles SSF; Jackson College; Jacksonville College; Jamestown College; Jefferson City; Jefferson College; Jersey City; Jesus College (Cambridge); Jet Club; Job Corps; Jockey Club; Johnstown College; Joliet College; Judson College; Juniata College; Junior Chamber (of Commerce, members called *Jaycees*); Juvenile Corps; Juvenile Court
J.C. Jesus Christ; Julius Caesar
J-C Jésus-Christ (French—Jesus Christ)
J.C. Juris Consultus (Latin—Juris Consult)
JCA Jewelry Crafts Association; Johore Consumers Association; Joint Commission on Accreditation (of colleges and universities); Joint Communication Activity; Joint Communications Agency; Joint Construction Agency; Junior College of Albany
JCAA Japanese Civil Aviation Authority
JCAB Japan Civil Aviation Bureau
JCAE Joint Committee on Atomic Energy
JCAH Joint Committee on Accreditation of Hospitals
JCAM Joint Commission on Atomic Masses
JCAP Joint Conventional Ammunition Panel (DoD)
JCAR Joint Commission of Applied Radioactivity
J-car(s) Japanese car(s)
JCB Japan California Bank; Japan Credit Bank; Japan Credit Bureau; Joint Consultative Board (NATO)
JCB Journal of Crime and Delinquency
J.C.B. Juris Canoni Baccalaureus (Latin—Bachelor of Canon Law); *Juris Civilis Baccalaureus* (Latin—Bachelor of Civil Law)
JCBC Junior College of Broward County
JCBL John Carter Brown Library (of Americana)—Brown

University, Providence, Rhode Island
JCBSF Joint Commission for Black Sea Fisheries
JCC Jamestown Community College; Japan Cotton Center; Jefferson Community College; Jewish Community Center; Job Corps Center; John C Calhoun; Joint Communications Center; Joint Communications Committee; Junior Chamber of Commerce
JC of C Junior Chamber of Commerce
JCCA Joint Conex Control Agency
JCCI Japan Chamber of Commerce and Industry
JCCRG Joint Command Control Requirements Group
JCCSO Jewish Community Center Symphony Orchestra
JCD Journal of Crime and Delinquency
J.C.D. Juris Canonici Doctor (Latin—Doctor of Canon Law); *Juris Civilis Doctor* (Latin—Doctor of Civil Law)
JCE Johannesburg College of Education; Junior Certificate Examination
JCE Journal of Chemical Education
JCEC Joint Communication Electronics Committee
JCED Japan Committee for Economic Development
JCEE Joint Council on Economic Education
JCEG Joint Communications Electronics Group
JCENS Joint Communication Electronic Nomenclature System
JCET Joint Council on Educational Telecommunications
JCFA Japan Chemical Fibres Association
J Chem Phys Journal of Chemical Physics
J Chem Soc Journal of the Chemical Society
J Chim Phys Journal de Chimie Physique (French—Journal of Chemical Physics)
JCI Joint Communications Instruction; Junior Chamber International
JCIA Japan Camera Industry Association; Japan Chemical Industry Association
JCIC Johannesburg Consolidated Investment Company
JCIEABJ Joint Commission for the Investigation of the Ef-

fects of the Atomic Bomb in Japan
JCII Japan Camera Inspection Institute
JCJC Jasper County Junior College; Jefferson County Junior College
Jck Jacksonville
jcl job-control language
Jcl Johnny come lately
JCL Job Control Language; John Crerar Library
J.C.L. Juris Canonici Licentiatus (Latin—Licentiate in Canon Law)
JCLA Joint Council of Language Associations
J-class NATO name for Soviet diesel-powered missile-launching submarines nicknamed Juliet
JCLCPS Journal of Criminal Law, Criminology, and Police Science
JCLS Junior College Libraries Section
jcm jettison control module
JCM Joint Committee on Microcards
JCMC Joint Conference on Medical Conventions
JCN Job Change Notice
JCNAFF Joint Canadian Navy-Army-Air Force
JCNM Jewel Cave National Monument
JCO José Clemente Orozco
JCOA Jazz Composers Orchestra Association
JCOC Joint Combat Operations Center; Joint Command Operations Center
J Comput Phys Journal of Computational Physics
JCOSA Joint Chiefs of Staff in Australia
jcp jettison control panel; jungle canopy penetration
JCP Japan Communist Party; J.C. Penney; Joint Committee on Printing (Congress); Junior Collegiate Players; Justice of the Common Pleas
JCPCI Junior College of Packer Collegiate Institute
JCPI Japan Cotton Promotion Institute
JCR Junior Common Room
JCRFD Joint Commission for Regulation of Fishing on the Danube
JCRR Joint Commission on Rural Reconstruction
J Cryst Growth Journal of Crystal Growth
JCs Job Corpsmen

JCS Jewish Community Center(s); Joint Chiefs of Staff; Joint Commonwealth Societies

JCS-ACA Joint Chiefs of Staff —Automatic Conference Arranger

JCS-IDTN Joint Chiefs of Staff —Interim Data Transmission Network

JCSMR John Curtin School of Medical Research

JCS-PUBS Joint Chiefs of Staff —Publications

JCSRE Joint Chiefs of Staff Representative, Europe (NATO)

JCSUK Jersey Cattle Society of the United Kingdom

jct junction

Jct Junction (postal abbreviation)

JCT Joint Committee on Taxation

JCTC Japanese Cultural and Trade Center; Juneau County Teachers College

jctn junction

jct pt junction point

JCU James Cook University; John Carroll University

JCUDI Japan Computer Usage Development Institute

JCUNQ James Cook University of North Queensland

JCUS Joint Center for Urban Studies (MIT and Harvard); Judicial Conference of the United States

JCW JC Williamson

JCWA Japan Child Welfare Association

jd joined; joint dictionary; junior debutante; jury duty; juvenile delinquency; juvenile delinquent

jd jemand (German—someone, somebody)

Jd Jordanian dinar (monetary unit of Jordan)

JD Julian day; Junior Deacon; Junior Dean; Justice Department

J.D. Doctor of Jurisprudence; Juris or Jurum Doctor (Latin —Doctor of Law or Laws)

JDA Japan Defense Agency; Japan Domestic Airline; Jefferson Davis Association

J-day Judas Day (Wednesday before Good Friday when Judas is believed to have betrayed Jesus)

JDB Japan Development Bank

JDC Joint Distribution Committee; Juvenile Delinquency Control; Juvenile Detention Center

JDCC Juneau-Douglas Community College

J/deg joule per degree

JDHS Jefferson Davis High School

JDI Juvenile Delinquency Index

jdl job description language

JDL Jewish Defense League

JDP John Dos Passos

JDPA Japan Dairy Products Association

JDR Japanese Depository Receipts

jds job data sheet

jd's juvenile delinquents

JDS Job Diagnosis Survey; John Dewey Society; Joint Defense Staff (NATO)

J.D.S. Doctor of Juridical Science

JDSCS Joint Defence Space Communications Station (Nurrangar, Australia)

JDSFA Japan Self-Defense Forces Academy

JDSRF Jim Dandy's Still and Refreshment Factory (Australian definition for the Joint Defense Space Research Facility near Alice Springs)

je job estimate

jé jésus (French—paper of super royal size)

jea joint export agent

JEA Jesuit Educational Association; Joint Engineering Agency; Journalism Education Association

Jean Baptiste French-Canadian's sobriquet

Jean Baptiste Lully Giovanni Battista Lulli

Jean Crapaud (nickname for the typical Frenchman)

Jean Gabin Jean-Alexis Moncorgé

Jean Hagen Jean Verhagen

Jean Harlow Harlean Carpenter

Jean-Jacques Jean-Jacques Rousseau

Jean l'Oiseleur (French—Jean the bird tamer)—pseudonym of Jean Cocteau

Jean Meslier Voltaire's pseudonym concealing his authorship of an heretical tract whose title page reads—Superstition In All Ages by Jean Meslier, A Roman Catholic Priest, who after a pastoral service of thirty years at Entrepigny and But, in Champagne, France, wholly

abjured religious dogmas, and left as his last will and testament the following pages entitled Common Sense (Le Bon Sens); Voltaire was an assumed name for François-Marie Arouet who without this double-cover pseudonym might have been burned at the stake along with his books and his tracts, his plays and his poems.

Jean Moreas pseudonym—Jannis Papadiamantopolous

Jeanne d'Arc Joan of Arc's original French name

Jeannie Jane; Jean

Jean Paul Johann Paul Friedrich Richter's pseudonym

Jean-Pierre Aumont Jean-Pierre Salomons

Jean Stapleton Jeanne Murray

jebm jet engine base maintenance

Jeb Stuard Major General J(ames) E(well) B(rown) Stuart, CSA

JEC Jardine Engineering Corporation; Joint Economic Committee (Congress)

JECC Japan Eelctronic Computer Company

JECMA Japan Export Clothing Makers Association

JECMOS Joint Electronic Countermeasures Operation Section (NATO)

Jed Jedediah

J Ed Journal of Education

JED Japan Engineering Development

JEDEC Joint Electron Device Engineering Committee

JEDPE Joint Emergency Defense Plan, Europe (NATO)

JEDS Japanese Expeditions to the Deep Sea

JEE Japan Electronics Engineering

jeep (from GP meaning general purpose) 4-wheel-drive quarter-ton utility vehicle

JEEP Joint Emergency Evacuation Plan

jeepney jeep jitney (Filipino conversion of a jeep into a jitney bus)

Jef(f) Geoffrey; Geoffroy; Jefferson; Jeffery; Jeffry

Jeff City Jefferson City, Missiouri

Jeff D Jefferson Davis

Jefferson City Missouri's capital

Jefferson's Thomas Jefferson's Birthday (April 13)

Jefferson's Country Charlottesville, Virginia

Jefferson Territory old name of Colorado

jefm (JEFM) jet engine field maintenance

JEFR Japan Experimental Fast Reactor

JEG John Edward Gray; Joint Exploratory Group (NATO)

Jeho Jehosaphat

JEI Japan Electronics Industry

JEIA Japanese Electronic Industries Association

JEIDA Japan Electronic Industry Development Association

jeim jet engine intermediate maintenance

JEIPAC Japan Electronic Information Processing Automatic Computer

JEJ Japan Economic Journal

jejun jejunectomy; jejunitis; jejunostomy

J Electrochem Soc Journal of the Electrochemical Society

jello gelatin dessert

Jelly Roll Ferdinand Joseph Morton

jem jet engine modulation

Jem Jemima

JEMC Joint Engineering Management Conference

JEN Junta de la Energia Nuclear (Atomic Energy Board)

JEN Journal of Emergency Nursing

Jenghis Khan Genghis Kahn— Mongol conqueror and grandfather of Kublai Kahn

Jen Jih Jen-min Jih-pao (People's Daily)—published in Peking by Communist Party of China

Jennie Jane; Jean; Jennifer; Lady Randolph Churchill

Jennifer Jones Phyllis Isley

Jenny Jane; Jean; Jennifer

Jenny Lind Johanna Maria Lind —the Swedish Nightingale

jentac. jentaculum (Latin— breakfast)

JEOCN Joint European Operations Communications Network

JEOL Japan Electron Optics Laboratory

JEPI Junior Eysenck Personality Inventory

JEPIA Japan Electronic Parts Industry Association

JEPO Jet Engine Project Office

JEPOSS Javelin Experimental Protection Oil Sands System

JEPS Joint Exercise Planning Staff (NATO)

Jer Jersey

Jer. Jeremiah, The Book of the Prophet

Jer Jeremiah; *Jeroesjalaim* (Dutch—Jerusalem)

JER Japan Economic Review

JERC Japan Economic Research Center; Joint Electronic Research Committee

Jere Jeremiah; Jerry

Jeremiah Bernstein's Symphony No. 1 commemorating the prophet Jeremiah and his dire prophecies

Jeremiah Stukeley Percy Bysshe Shelley used this pseudonym on his pamphlet, *The Necessity of Atheism*

Jerez Jerez de la Frontera

JERI Japan Economic Research Institute; Joint Economic Research Institute

JERK Journalist's Easy Road to Knowledge (routed through an impasse of acronyms such as GAS—Grant's Acronymical Shorthand)

jerky beef jerky; buccan; charqui; jerked beef

jerob jeroboam (4-bottle capacity)

Jerome Hines Jerome Heinz

Jeron⁰ Jerónimo (Spanish—Jerome)

Jerrie(s) British slang for German(s)

Jerry Gerald(ine); Governor Edmund G Brown, Jr of California who shares this nickname with many others including President Gerald R Ford; Jeremiah; Jeremy; Jerome

Jerry Lewis Joseph Levitch

JERS Japanese Ergonomics Research Society

jersey jersey justice (reputedly efficient and speedy); jersey lightning (applejack)

Jersey Lily Lily Langtry—English actress born on the island of Jersey where her original name was Emily Charlotte Le Breton

Jersey Shore coastal New Jersey; former name of Waynesburg, Pennsylvania

Jerusalem of the West Amsterdam

Jerusalén (Spanish—Jerusalem)

Jervis Island, Galápagos Rábida

Jes Jessica; Jesus; Jesus College, Cambridge

JES James Ewing Society; Japan Electroplating Society; Japan Engineering Standards; John Ericsson Society

JES Journal of Ecumenical Studies

JESA Japanese Engineering Standards Association

Jes Coll Jesus College—Cambridge

Jessamine South Carolina's state flower

Jesselton former name of Kota Kinabalu, Sabah

Jessie James Cleveland (Jesse) Owens; Jess; Jessica

Jessup Maryland House of Corrections at Jessup

Jessup Girls Maryland Correctional Institution for Women at Jessup

Jesus Jesus College, Oxford

jet black lignite; jet-engine aircraft

jet. jetsam

JETDS Joint Electronics Type Designation System

JETEC Joint Electron Tube Engineering Council

jet fag jet flight fatigue

jetma jet mechanic

jet-p jet-propelled; jet propulsion

JETP Journal of Experimental and Theoretical Physics (Academy of Sciences, USSR)

Jet Provost British jet trainer aircraft designated BAC-145

Jet Ranger Bell turbine-powered helicopter also called Sea Ranger

JETRO Japan Exterior Trade Research Organization; Japan External Trade Organization

JETS Joint Enroute Terminal Systems (air traffic); Junior Engineers Technical Society

Jet Star C-140 Lockheed light transport plane

jett jettison

jeu jeudi (French—Thursday)

Jev Japanese encephalitis virus

JEVA Japan Electric Vehicle Association

Jew. Jewish

Jewel The Jewel (La Jolla, California); Jewel Cave National Monument near Custer in southwestern South Dakota

Jewel of Africa Lake Kivu

Jewel of the East Bali

Jewel of the Eastern Sea Sri Lanka

jewelers' putty stannous oxide

Jewel of German Cities Heidelberg

Jewel Island Ceylon

Jewell Manor Jewell Manor (delinquent) Girls Center at Louisville, Kentucky

Jewels of the Caribbean U.S. Virgin Islands

Jewish ampicillin cream of chicken soup

Jewish champagne celery tonic (carbonated celery-flavored water)

Jewish dristan horseradish (celebrated for its ability to bring about nasal decongestion)

Jewish penicillin chicken soup (believed by Jewish mothers to cure all ailments)

Jewtong Jewtongo (Surinam dialect spoken by former slaves who picked it up from their masters who spoke Dutch, English, Portuguese, or Spanish within their hearing in the belief they would not understand—African and Indian words were added to this multilingual language somewhat like Papiamento spoken in the Netherlands Antilles)

JEZ Johannes Enschede en Zonen

JEZ Journal of Experimental Zoology

jf distant fog (meterological symbol)

j/f jigs and fixtures; journal folio

JF Jewish Federation; Joint Force

JFACT Joint Flight-Acceptance Composite Test

JFAI Joint Formal Acceptance Inspection (NATO)

jfb jet flying belt

jfc Japan Food Company

JFC Japan Film Center

JFCC Japanese Federation of Culture Collections of Microorganisms

JFCS Jewish Family and Child Service

JFEA Japan Federation of Employer's Associations

jfet junction field-effect transistor

JFK John F Kennedy (airport); John Fitzgerald Kennedy—thirty-fifth President of the United States

JFKCAS John F Kennedy College of Arts and Sciences (Trinidad)

JFKCPA John F Kennedy Center for the Performing Arts

JFKMF John F Kennedy Memorial Forest (near Jerusalem, Israel)

JFKMH John F Kennedy

Memorial Highway (Baltimore, Maryland to Wilmington, Delaware)

JFKML John F Kennedy Memorial Library

JFKSC John F Kennedy Space Center

JFKYCC John F Kennedy Youth Correctional Center

jfl joint frequency list

J Fluid Mech Journal of Fluid Mechanics

JFMAMJJASOND January, February, March, April, May, June, July, August, September, October, November, December (as abbreviated to conserve space on charts and graphs)

JFMIP Joint Financial Management Improvement Program

JFNP John Forrest National Park (Western Australia)

JFO San Francisco, California (heliport)

jfp joint frequency panel

JFP Jobs For Progress

JFPS Japan Fire Prevention Society

jfr jevnfr (Dano-Norwegian—compare)

JFR Joint Fiction Reserve

JFRC James Forrestal Research Center

JFRCA Japanese Fisheries Resources Conservation Association

JFRO Joint Fire Research Organisation (UK)

jfs jet fuel starter

JFS Japan Fishery Society; Jewish Family Service

JFS Jane's Fighting Ships

JFSOC Junior Foreign Service Officers Club

JFTC Joint Fur Trade Committee

JFU Jersey Farmers' Union

JFV Jobs For Veterans

JG junior grade

jga juxtaglomerular apparatus

JGA Japan Golf Association

JGC Japan Gas Chemical; Japan Gasoline Company

JGD John George Diefenbaker (Canada's seventeenth Prime Minister)—also known as Dief the Chief

jg di joggle die

JGE Journal of General Education

J Geophys Res Journal of Geophysical Research

J-girl joy girl (prostitute)

jgn junction gate number

JGNP Japanese Gross National

Product

JGR Jaldapara Game Reserve (India)

JGS Joint General Staff (NATO)

JGSA John G Shedd Aquarium

JGSDF Japan Ground Self-Defense Force

jg sm joggle shims

JGTC Junior Girls Training Corps

JGW Junior Grand Warden

JGWTC Jungle and Guerrilla Warfare Training Center (USA)

jh juvenile hormone

Jh Jahresheft (German—yearly publication)

J & H Jack & Heintz

JH Jugendherberge (German—youth hostel)

jha job hazard analysis

JHA John Howard Association

JHAH John Howard Association of Hawaii

JHAI John Herron Art Institute

Jhb Johannesburg

JHC John Hancock Center

Jhd Japanese haakon dahl (log measure of 11.7 cubic feet being 100 Jhd)

JHDA Junior Hospital Doctors Association

Jhdf Japanese haakon-dahl feet

JHE Journal of Higher Education

JHH Johns Hopkins Hospital

JHI Jacob Hiatt Institute; Jesuit Historical Society; Jewish Historical Society

jhj jail-house juvenile (delinquent)

JHL John Harvard Library

JHMI Johns Hopkins Medical Institutions

JHMO Junior Hospital Medical Officer

JHO Jam Handy Organization; Japan Hydrographic Office

JHOS Johns Hopkins Oceanographic Studies

JHP Jackson Hole Preserve; Johns Hopkins Press

JHS John Howard Society; Judaic Heritage Society; Junior High School

J.H.S. Jesus Hominum Salvator (Latin—Jesus Savior of Men)

JHU Johns Hopkins University

JHUL Johns Hopkins University Library

JHUP Johns Hopkins University Press

JHUSHPH Johns Hopkins University School of Hygiene and Public Health
JHUSM Johns Hopkins University School of Medicine
JHVH Jehovah [transliteration of Hebrew tetragrammaton Yhwh, Yahwah, or Jahvah (he was, he is, he will be), used by Hebrew tribes in 3rd century BCE because they thought "Jehovah" was too sacred to pronounce]; perhaps the world's oldest abbreviation
ji jet interaction; junction isolation; junction isolator
JI Aerovias Sudamericanos (symbol)
JI Japan Interpreter
JIA Japanese Interchange Association
Jiangsu (Pinyin Chinese—Kiangsu)
Jiangxi (Pinyin Chinese—Kiangsi)
JIAS Jewish Immigration Aid Society
jib. job-information block
Jib Jibouti
JIB Jack-in-the-Box; Japan International Bank
JIBA Japan Institute of Business Administration
JIBC Japan International Biological Program
JIBICO Japan International Bank and Investment Company
jíb(s) jíbaro(s) [Spanish—peasant farmer(s)]—Puerto Rican(s)
Jibuti Djibouti
jic jet-induced circulation; jet-induced combustion
JIC Joint Industrial Council; Joint Industry Council; Joint Intelligence Center; Joint Intelligence Committee
JICA Japan International Cooperation Agency; Joint Intelligence Collecting Agency
JICST Japan Information Center of Science and Technology
JICTAR Joint Industry Committee for Television Advertising Research
JID Junta Interamericana de Defensa (Spanish—Inter-American Defense Board)
JIDA Japan Industrial Designers Association
JIDC Jamaica Industrial Development Corporation
JIDPO Japan Industrial Design Promotion Organization

JIE Junior Institution of Engineers
JIEA Japan Industrial Explosives Association
JIFA Japanese Institute of Foreign Affairs
JIFE Junta Internacional de Fiscalización de Estupefacientes (Spanish—International Council for the Investigation of Narcotics)
JIG Joint Intelligence Group
JIIST Japan Institute for International Studies and Training
JILA Joint Institute for Laboratory Astrophysics
Jilin (Pinyin Chinese—Kirin)
Jill Jillian
Jim James
JIM Japan Institute of Metals; Junior Index of Motivation
JIMA Japan Industrial Management Association
JIMA Journal of the Israel Medical Association
Jimmu Jimmu Tenno—first emperor of Japan who began his reign in 660 BCE
Jimmy James; James Earl Carter —thirty-ninth President of the United States
Jimmy Higgins Upton Sinclair's personification of the radical who does the work of running off the leaflets, setting up the speaker's platform, or sweeping out the meeting place of other comrades who feel themselves too superior for such menial tasks
jimson weed *Datura stramonium*
Jim Thorpe formerly Mauch Chunk, Pennsylvania
Jimtown Jamestown, North Dakota
Jinan (Pinyin Chinese—Tsinan)
J Inorg Nucl Chem Journal of Inorganic and Nuclear Chemistry
JINR Joint Institute for Nuclear Research
jins juveniles in need of supervision
Jinx Falkenburg Eugenia Falkenburg
JIO Joint Intelligence Organization
JIOA Joint Intelligence Objectives Agency
JIP Joint Installation Plan(ning)
JIPS Japanese Information Processing Service
JIR Jewish Institute of Religion;

Job Improvement Request
JIRA Japan Industrial Robot Association
JIRP Juneau Icefield Research Project
jirv jet-interaction reentry vehicle
JIS Jail Inspection Service; Japan Industrial Standard; Jewish Information Society; Joint Intelligence Staff
JISA Japan Industrial Safety Association
JISC Japanese Industrial Standards Committee
JISEA Japan Iron and Steel Exporters Association
JISF Japan Iron and Steel Federation
JISP Jack Island State Park (Florida)
jit jitney bus
JIT Job Instruction Training
Jiugiang (Pinyin Chinese—Chiuchiang)
jj jaw jerk
JJ Judges, Justices
J-J Jean-Jacques
J & J Johnson & Johnson
J-J Jen-min Jih-pao (Chinese—people's daily communist-controlled Peking newspaper)
JJA John James Audubon
JJC Juvenile Justice Center (Los Angeles)
JJCA Sir John Joseph Caldwell Abbott (Canada's fourth Prime Minister)
JJCCJ John Jay College of Criminal Justice
J.J. Connington Alfred Walter Stewart's pseudonym
JJHL John Jay Hopkins Laboratory for Pure and Applied Science (General Atomic Division of General Dynamics Corporation)
JJHS John Jay High School
jj's joyless jobs (pimping and prostituting)
JJS James Joyce Society
JJS Journal of Jewish Studies
JJSC Juvenile Justice Standards Committee
JJSS Jean-Jacques Servan-Schreiber
J-J S-S Jean-Jacques Servan-Schreiber
jk just kidding
JK Jack Kerouac
J/°K joule(s) per degree Kelvin (unit of entropy)
J & K Jammu and Kashmir (University)
Jka Jakarta
JKC Japan Kennel Club

jkg joules per kilogram

JKG John Kenneth Galbraith

J/kg°K joule(s) per kilogram degree Kelvin

JKP James Knox Polk (11th President U.S.)

JKS Julius Kayser (stock-exchange symbol)

jkt jacket

Jkt Jakarta

JKT Jakarta, Indonesia (airport); Job Knowledge Test

jl just looking (pseudo customer)

Jl Joel

JL J Lauritzen (steamship line); Japan Airlines (2-letter code); Johnson Line; Jones and Laughlin; Joseph Lewis

Jla Julia

JLA Jamaica Library Association; Japan Library Association; Jewish Librarians Association; Jordan Library Association

JLB Jewish Lads' Brigade; John Logie Baird (tv's inventor)

JLC Japan Logistical Command; Jewish Labor Committee; Joint Logistics Command(ers)

JLCU Johnson Line Container Unit

Jlem Jerusalem

JLMIC Japan Light Machinery Information Center

Jln Jalan (Malay—Lane, Road, Street)

JLOIC Joint Logistics, Operations, Intelligence Center (NATO)

J Low Temp Phys *Journal of Low Temperature Physics*

JLP Jamaica Labour Party

JLPPG Joint Logistics and Personnel Policy Guidance

jlr(s) jeweler(s)

JLRSS Joint Long-Range Strategic Study

jls jewels

JLS Jail Library Service (California State Library); Junior Literary Society

Jlt Juliet

J Lumin *Journal of Luminescence*

JM James Madison (4th President U.S.); James Monroe (5th President U.S.); Japan Mail; Jardine Matheson; Jewish Museum; José Martí

J-M Johns-Manville

J-M *Jiyu-Minshuto* (Japanese— Liberal Democratic Party)

J/m² joule per meter (impact strength) squared

JMA Japan Management Association; Japan Medical Association; Japan Meterological Agency; Jewish Music Alliance

J Macromol Sci *Journal of Macromolecular Science*

J Math Phys *Journal of Mathematical Physics* (published in New York City); *Journal of Mathematics and Physics* (published in Cambridge, Mass)

JMB J(ames) M(atthew) Barrie

JMBA *Journal of the Marine Biological Association*

JMC Japan Metals and Chemicals; Japan Monopoly Corporation; Jefferson Medical College; Jerusalem Music Centre; Joint Maritime Commission; Joint Maritime Congress

JMCC Joint Mobile Communications Center (NATO)

JMD M(alaby) Dent

JMDC Japan Machinery Design Center

J Mech Phys Solids *Journal of the Mechanics and Physics of Solids*

jmed jungle message encoder decoder

JMF Jewish Music Forum; Juilliard Musical Foundation

JMHS James Madison High School; James Monroe High School; John Muir High School

JMI Japan Machinery and Metal Inspection; John Muir Institute

JMIA Japan Mining Industry Association

JMIF Japan Motor Industrial Federation

JMJ Jesus, Mary, and Joseph

JMMA Japan Materials Management Association

JMMC James Madison Memorial Commission

JMMF James Monroe Memorial Foundation

JMMII Japan Machinery and Metal Inspection Institute

J Mol Spectro *Journal of Molecular Spectroscopy*

JMP *Jen Men Piao* (Chinese— People's Bank Dollar)

jmpr jumper

JMPTC Joint Military Packaging Training Center

JMRMA John and Mable Ringling Museum of Art

JMS Japan Medical Society; Johannesburg Musical Society

JMSA Japanese Maritime Safety Association

JMSDF Japanese Maritime Self-Defense Force

JMT Job Methods Training

JMTBA Japan Machine Tool Builders Association

JMTR Japan Material Testing Reactor

JMUSDC Joint Mexico-United States Defense Commission

jn join; junction

j-n jet navigation

Jn John

Jn *Juan* (Spanish—John)

JNA *Jena Nomina Anatomica*

JNB Johannesburg, South Africa (airport)

Jnc Junction

JNC Joint Negotiating Committee

JNCA Junior Naval Cadets of America

jnd joined; just noticeable difference

JND Juvenile Narcotics Division

JNDC Jamaica National Dance Company

JNDNWR JnN. (Ding) Darling National Wildlife Refuge (Florida)

jne *ja niin edespäin* (Finnish— and so on)

JNF Japan Nuclear Fuel (company), Jewish National Fund

JNI Journal of the Nautical Institute

Jnl Journal

JNL Japanese National Laboratory

jnls journals

jnlst journalist

JNM *Journal of Nuclear Medicine*

JNN Japan News Network

jnnd just not noticeable difference

Jno John

JNODC Japanese National Oceanographic Data Center

J Non-Cryst Solids *Journal of Non-Crystalline Solids*

JNP Jasper National Park (Alberta)

JNPGC Japan Nuclear Power Generation Corporation

jnr joiner; junior

Jnr Jesurun

JNR Japanese National Railways

jns just noticeable shift

Jns Johannes

JNS Japan Nuclear Society; Jet Noise Survey

JNSDA Japan Nuclear Ship Development Agency

jnt joint; junction; juncture

JNT John Napier Turner—Canada's 17th Prime Minister if counted by name and 22nd if counted by terms in office

JNTA Japan National Tourist Association

JNTO Japan National Tourist Office; Japan National Tourist Organization

jnt stk joint stock

JNU Juneau, Alaska (airport)

J Nucl Energy Journal of Nuclear Energy

J Nucl Mater Journal of Nuclear Materials

JNUL Jewish National and University Library (Jerusalem)

JNV Junta Nacional do Vinho (Portuguese—National Wine Board)

jnwpu joint numerical weather-prediction unit

JNZ Jewelers of New Zealand

jo journalist

Jo Joel; Joseph; Josephine

JO Job Order; Jupiter Orbiter

JO Justie Ombudsman (Swedish—representative of justice)

Joa Joachim

JOA Joint Operating Agreement

Joan Crawford Lucille le Sueur

João Pessoa formerly Parahiba, Brazil

Joaquin Miller Cincinnatus Heine Miller's pen name

Jo Bapt John the Baptist

joblib job library

jo block(s) johannson block(s)

jobman job management

JOBS Job Opportunities in the Business Sector

Jo'burg Johannesburg

joc jocose; jocular

JOC Japan Olympic Committee; Joint Operations Center; Joint Opposition Council

Jochanan John

jock jockey; jockstrap

Jock John

jocks athletically oriented teenage gangs named for the jockstraps they wear for identification and protection

jock(s) jock strap(s)—nickname for physical education student(s)

Jock(s) Scot(s)

joco jocose

JOCV Japan Overseas Cooperation Volunteers (Peace Corps)

jod joint occupancy date

JODC Japanese Oceanographic Data Center

Jo Div John the Divine

Joe Joel; Joseph; Josephine

JOE Juvenile Opportunities Extension

Joe Bananas nickname of New York Mafia chief Joe Bananos

Joe C Joe Clark (Canada's 16th or 20th Prime Minister, depending on how the count is made as several Prime Ministers served two or three times)

Joe Doakes nickname for the average American man

Joe Doe name used on subpoenas and summonses if the name of the man to be served is unknown; nickname for the average American male

Joe Louis Joseph Louis Barrow

JOERA Japan Optical Engineering Research Association

Jo Evang John the Evangelist

joey baby kangaroo

Joe Zilch the average American formerly called Joe Blow or Joe Doakes

J-off jack off (underground slang—masturbate)

jog. joggle

JOG Joint Operations Group; Junior Ocean Group (*jay-oh-gees*—smallest sailing cruisers); Junior Offshore Group

Jogja Jogjakarta

Jogjakarta Djokjakarta

Joh St John's College, Cambridge

Joh Johann(es) (German—Hans, John)

Johan Johannesburg

Johann Gutenberg Johann Ganzfleisch

John The Gospel According to John; St John, American Virgin Islands; St John, New Brunswick, Canada

John I John the First (John Adams—second President of the United States)

John II John the Second (John Quincy Adams—sixth President of the United States)

John XXIII Angelo Giuseppe Roncalli

John B John B Stetson (hat)

John Barleycorn personification of beer or malt liquor

John Barrymore John Blythe

John Bull Great Britain

John Bull's Other Island Ireland before its independence was declared in 1919

John Cabot Anglicized form of navigator Giovanni Caboto's

Italian name

John Calvin Jean Chauvin

John Company British East India Company's nickname

John D. John D Rockefeller, Sr.

John Danger Hough Baillie (colorful journalist who rose from reporter to head of the United Press)

John Doe fictitious name used when real name is withheld or unknown; if more than one name is needed Philip Poe may be used as well as Jane or Mary Doe; Richard or Susan Miles; Richard or Susan Roe, John, Jane, or Mary Stiles, or others selected by the court

John and Emery Bonett pseudonym shared by the husband-and-wife team—John Hubert Arthur Coulson and Felicity Winifred Carter

John Ford Sean O'Fienne

John Garfield Julius Garfinkle

John Gilbert John Pringle's stage name

John Hancock signature (nickname memorializing most prominent autograph on *Declaration of Independence*)

John Houseman Jacques Haussmann

John le Carré pseudonym of David John Moore Cornwell

JOHNNIAC John von Newman's Integrator and Automatic Compiler

Johnny John; John M Grant, Jr

Johnny Appleseed John (Johnny) Chapman

Johnny Crapaud nickname for a Frenchman or a New Orleans creole of French descent

Johnny Reb(s) Johnny Rebel(s)—Confederate soldier(s)

John o' Groat's in Caithness near northernmost point of Scotland's mainland—popularly believed to be the northernmost point of the mainland of Great Britain—also called John o' Groat's House (see Dunnet Head)

John Oxenham William Arthur Dunkerly

John Paul Charles Henry Webb

John Paul I Albino Luciani

John Paul II Karol Wojtyla

John Rhode Cecil John Charles Street's pseudonym

John's St John's

Johns of Geneva Jean Calvin

and Jean-Jacques Rousseau

Johns H Johns Hopkins University

John Sinjohn John Galsworthy

John Wayne Marion Michael Morrison

Joh Seb Bach Johann Sebastian Bach

JOI Joint Oceanographics Institution

JOIDES Joint Oceanographic Institutions for Deep Earth Sampling

JOIDESP Joint Oceanographic Institutions Deep Earth Sampling Program

join. joinery

JOIN Job Orientation in Neighborhoods; Jobs Or Income Now

Joint American Jewish Joint Distribution Committee

JOIS Japan On-Line Information System

JOK Oakland, California (heliport)

Joke Haydn's String Quartet in E flat (opus 33, no. 2)

jol job organization language

JOLA Journal of Library Automation

Jolly Roger black flag flown by pirates, sometimes emblazoned with a white hourglass or a white skull and crossbones

Jolo (Malay—Sulu)

JoLoPo José Lopez Portillo

Jolyon Joseph Lyons

JOM Job-Oriented Manual

JOM Johnson O'Malley Act

JOMO Junta of Militant Organizations (Black Nationalists)

Jon. The Book of Jonah

Jona Jonathan

Jonathan Jonathan David

Jonathan Fogarty Titulescu James T(homas) Farrell

Jonathan Oldstyle (pseudonym —Washington Irving)

JONS Juntas de Ofensiva Nacional Sindicalista (Spanish— United National Syndicalist Offensive)—fascist anti-syndicalists

JONSDAP Joint North Sea Data Acquisition Program

JONSIS Joint North Sea Information Systems

JONSWAP Joint North Sea Wave Project

JOOD Junior Officer of the Deck

JOOM Junior Observers Of Meteorology

JOP Joint Operating

Plan(ning); Joint Operations Procedure

JOPCN Job Order Program Control Number (USA)

JOPM Joint Occupancy Plan Memo; Joint Operation Procedure Memo

JOPR Joint Operation Procedure Report

JOPS Joint Operating Study

JOPS Journal of the Patent Office Society

J Opt Soc Am Journal of the Optical Society of America

JOR Jet Operations Requirements

Jord Jordan

Jord Jordânia (Portuguese— Jordan); *Jordania* (Spanish— Jordan)

Jordan Hashemite Kingdom of Jordan (Middle East country formerly called Transjordania, Arabic-speaking Jordanians produce edible crops, textiles, and many valuable chemicals from the Dead Sea) *Al Mamluka al Urduniya al Hashemiyah*

Jordan River 200-mile long watercourse capable of serving such Near East countries as Israel, Jordan, and Syria before what is left of it sinks into the Dead Sea

Jordan's Port Al Aqabah (opposite Israel's Elat)

Jordie Jordan(a)

Jordy Jordan

JORG Joint Oceanographic Research Group

Jos Joseph; Joshua; Josiah; Jossic

JOS Junior Ordinary Seaman

Josa Josepha; Josephine

José Ferrer José Vicente Ferrer y Cintron

José Greco Constanzo Greco

Joseph a Guarneri violin (short form of Giuseppe Guarneri)

Joseph Bentonelli Joseph Horace Benton

Joseph Conrad Teodor Josef Konrad Korzeniowski

Joseph Hansen James Colton's pseudonym

Josephine Josephine Baker

Josephine Bell Doris Bell Collier Ball's pseudonym

Josephus Flavius Josephus— apostate Jew and recorder of the Roman conquests

Joseph von Sternberg Josef Stern

Josh Joshua; (pseudonym— Samuel L Clemens)

Josh. The Book of Joshua

Josh Joshua

Josh Billings stage name of humorist Henry Wheeler Shaw

Joshua Tree Joshua Tree National Monument north of the Salton Sea in southern California

Josiah Flynt Josiah Flynt Willard's pseudonym

Josie Josephina; Josephine

JOSS JOHNNIAC Open-Shop System

Josy Joseph

jot. jump-oriented terminal; junction optimization technique

JOT Joint Observer Team

JOTS Job-Oriented Training Standards

Jotunheim mountain range between Norway and Sweden— the land of the giants or jotuns

Jotunheimen Home of the Giants—spectacular mountain range of Norway

JOUAM Junior Order of United American Mechanics

jour journal; journalese; journalism; journalist; journalistic; journey

journ journal; journalese; journalism; journalist; journalistic; journey

Jove Jupiter or Zeus

JOVE Job Placement on the Job Training Vocational Educational Assistance; Jupiter Orbiting Vehicle for Exploration

JOVIAL Jules' Own Version of IAL (International Algebraic Language)

jp jet penetration; jet pilot; jet power; jet propulsion, junior partner; precipitation in sight but not at weather station reporting (symbol)

j & p joists and planks

Jp Japan(ese)

JP Japan Press (news agency); Jaya Prakash Narayan, Prime Minister of India; Jet Pilot; Justice of the Peace

J.P. Jayaprakash Narayan; J Pierpont Morgan

JP-4 jet propellant 4

jpa jack panel assembly

JPA Japan Petroleum Association; Japan Procurement Agency; Joint Passover Association; Joint Powers Agreement

JPB Joint Planning Board; Joint Production Board; Joint Pur-

chasing Board
JPBHS Judah P Benjamin High School
jpbs jettison pushbutton switch
JPC Jan Pieterszoon Coen; Japan Productivity Center; Jet Propulsion Center; Joint Planning Center; Joint Planning Council; Joint Production Council; Joint Publishers Committee
JPCC Joint Petroleum Coordination Center (NATO)
JPCRSP John Pennekamp Coral Reef State Park (Florida)
JPDC Japan Petroleum Development Corporation
JPDR Japan Power Demonstration Reactor
JPF Jewish Peace Fellowship
j-p fuel jet-propulsion fuel
JPG Job Proficiency Guide; Joint Planning Group (NATO)
JPGA Japan Professional Golf Association
JPGM J Paul Getty Museum
J Phys Journal de Physique (French—*Journal of Physics*)
J Phys Chem Journal of Physical Chemistry
J Phys Chem Ref Data Journal of Physical and Chemical Reference Data
J Phys Radium Journal de Physique et le Radium (French—Journal of Physics and Radium)
J Phys Soc Jpn Journal of the Physical Society of Japan
JPI Joint Packaging Instruction
JPIA Japan Plastics Industry Association
JPJ John Paul Jones
JPL Jacksonville Public Library; Java Pacific Line; Jet Propulsion Laboratory (California Institute of Technology); Job Parts List
J Plasma Phys Journal of Plasma Physics
Jpn Japan(ese)
Jpn J Appl Phys Japanese Journal of Applied Physics
Jpn J Phys Japanese Journal of Physics
Jpns Japanese; Japan's
JPO Joint Petroleum Office; Joint Project Offices; Junior Police Officer
J Polymer Sci Journal of Polymer Science
jpp *jälkeen puolenpäiven* (Finnish—afternoon, P.M.)
JPPS Japan Pearl Promoting Society

JPPSOWA Joint Personal Property Shipping Office (Washington, D.C.)
JPR Joint Procurement Regulation(s)
J Prob Judge of Probate
JPRS Joint Publications Research Service
JPRST (guo) Joint Publications Research Service Translations (government use only)
JPS Jet Propulsion Systems; Jewish Publication Society; Johannesburg Philharmonic Society; Joint Planning Staff; Juvenile Probation Services
J-P S Jean-Paul Sartre
JPSA Jewish Publication Society of America
JPSA Journal of Police Science and Administration
JPSO Jamaica Philharmonic Symphony Orchestra
jpt jet pipe temperature
JPT Journal of Petroleum Technology
JPTDS Joint Photographic Type Designation System
jpto jet-propelled take-off
JPV Japan Peace Volunteers
jpw job processing word
JP-X jet-propellant rocket fuel
JPz4-5 West German tank-destroyer tracked vehicle
jq job questionnaire
JQ Japan Quarterly; Journalism Quarterly
JQA John Quincy Adams (6th President U.S.)
JQAH John Quincy Adams House
J Quant Spectros Radiat Transfer Journal of Quantitative Spectroscopy and Radiative Transfer
Jr Journal; Junior
JR Joint Resolution
JR Journal of Religion; Jugoslav Register (of shipping)
J.R. Jacobus Rex (Latin—King James)
jra junior rheumatoid arthritis
JRA Japan Racing Association; Japan Ryokan Association
JRAI Journal of the Royal Anthropological Institute
Jr Asst Pur Junior Assistant Purser
JRATA Joint Research and Test Activity
JRB New York, New York (Wall Street Heliport)
JRC Jamaica Railway Corporation; Japan Red Cross; Joint Rivers Commission; Junior Red Cross

JRCA Junior Ruritan Clubs of America
JRCD Journal of Research in Crime and Delinquency (published semi-annually by NCCD)
jrci jamming radar coverage indicator
JRCS Jet Reaction Control System
JRD Riverside, California (heliport, 3-letter code)
JRDB Joint Research and Development Board
JRDC Japan Research and Development Corporation
JREA Japanese Railway Engineering Association
J Res Nat Bur Stand Journal of Research of the National Bureau of Standards
JRF Job Request Form; Judicial Research Foundation
jrg jaargang (Dutch—year)
jr gr junior grade
Jr HS Junior High School
JRHS Julia Richman High School
jri jail release information
JRIA Japan Radioisotope Association; Japan Rocket Industry Association; Japan Rubber Industry Association
JRMO Junior Resident Medical Officer
JRN Japan Radio Network
Jro Jerome
JROTC Junior Reserve Officers' Training Corps
JRPG Joint Radar Planning Group
JRR Japan Research Reactor
JRRC Joint Regional Reconnaissance Center (NATO)
J.R.R. Tolkien John Ronald Reuel Tolkien
JRS Jerusalem, Jordan (airport)
JRSMA Japan Rolling Stock Manufacturers Association
JRSWG Joint Reentry System Working Group
JRT Jaguar Rover Triumph Inc; Job Relations Training
JRTUR Jugoslovenska Radio-Televisija Udruzenja Radiostancia (Yugoslav Association of Radio and Television Stations)
Jrw Jarrow-on-Tyne
j's joints (of marijuana)
j/s jamming-to-signal ration
Js Jesuits
JS Al-Jamhourya as-Souriya (Syria); Jan Sibelius; Japan Society; Jet Study; Johnson So-

ciety; Judeo-Spanish; Judgement Summons; Judicial Separation; Junior Sailor

J-S Judeo-Spanish

JS-2 Soviet heavy tank of World War II vintage

JS-3 Soviet post WW II heavy tank

JSA Jewelers Security Alliance; Journeymen Stone Cutters Association; Junior Statesmen of America

jsact jetstream anti-countermeasure trainer

JSACT Joint Strategic Air Control Team

JSAE Japan Society of Automotive Engineers

JSAP Japan Society of Applied Physics

JSB Jewish Society for the Blind; Jewish Statistical Bureau; Johann Sebastian Bach

JSBs Joint Stock Banks

JSC Jackson State College; Japan Science Council; Johnson Space Center (NASA); Joint Staff Council; Joint Standing Committee; Joint Stock Company

JS-C Jesus College—Cambridge (also appears as JCC, J.C.C., and Jes Coll or Jcs. Coll.)

JSCA Journeyman Stone Cutters Association

JSCC Japan Securities Clearing Corporation

J.Sc.D. Doctor of Juristic Science

J-school journalism school

J Sci Instrum *Journal of Scientific Instruments*

JSCM Joint Service Commendation Medal

JSCP Joint Strategic Capabilities Plan

JSCR Job Schedule Change Request

JS & CS Jewish Family and Child Services

J.S.D. *Jurum Scientiae Doctor* (Latin—Doctor of the Science of Laws)

JSDA Japan Self-Defense Agency

JSDFA Japan Self-Defense Forces Academy

JSDFs Japan Self-Defense Forces

JSDT Sir John Sparrow David Thompson (Canada's fifth Prime Minister)

JSDTI John S. Donaldson Technical Institute (Trinidad)

JSE Johannesburg Stock Exchange

JSEA Japan Ship Exporters Association

JSEE Japanese Society for Engineering Education

JSEM Japan Society of Electrical Discharge Machining; Japan Society for Electron Microscopy

JSESPO Joint Surface Effect Ships Program

Jsey Jersey

JSF Japan Scholarship Foundation; Jewish Student Federation; Junior Statesman Foundation

JSFC Japanese-Soviet Fisheries Commission

JSGMF John Simon Guggenheim Memorial Foundation

JSGMRAM Joint Study Group for Material Resource Allocation Methodology

jsi job satisfaction inventory

JSIA Japan Software Industry Association

JSIF Japan Spinners Inspecting Foundation

JSIIDS Joint-Services Interior-Intruder Detection System

JSL Jurong Shipyard Limited

JSLB Joint Stock Land Bank(s)

JSLE Japan Society of Lubrication Engineers

JSLS Joint Services Liaison Staff

JSM Joint Staff Mission; Juilliard School of Music

JSMA Joint Sealers Manufacturers Association

JSMB Joint Sealift Movements Board

JSMDA Japan Ship Machinery Development Association

JSME Japan Society of Mechanical Engineers

JSMEA Japan Ship Machinery Export Association

J-smoke (underground slang—marijuana cigarette)

JSNP Japan Satellite News Pool

JSO Jackson Symphony Orchestra; Jacksonville Symphony Orchestra; Joint Services Organization; Judgement Summons Order

JSOP Joint Strategic Objectives Plan

J Sound Vib *Journal of Sound and Vibration*

JSP Japan Socialist Party

JSP *Jadranska Slobodena Plovida* (Yugoslavian Shipping Line)

JSPA Japan Screen Printing Association

JSPB Joint Staff Pension Board (UN)

JSPC Joint Strategic Plans Committee

J Speech Hear Disorders *Journal of Speech and Hearing Disorders*

J Speech Hear Res *Journal of Speech and Hearing Research*

jspf jet shots per foot

JSPF Joint Staff Pension Fund (UN)

JSPG Joint Strategic Plans Group

JSPS Japan Society for the Promotion of Science; Japan Sword Preservation Society

JSQC Japan Society for Quality Control

JSQS Japan Shipbuilding Quality Standard

jsrt joint short range technology

JSS Johnson Scan Star (Johnson, East Asiatic, and Blue Star lines); Joint Services Standard

JSSA Japan Science Student Awards

JSSC Joint Services Staff College; Joint Strategic Service Committee

JST Japan Standard Time; Javanese Standard Time; Job Safety Training

J Stat Phys *Journal of Statistical Physics*

JSTC Japan-Singapore Training Center

J-stick joystick (underground slang—marijuana cigarette)

JSTPB Joint Strategic Target Planning Board

JSTPS Joint Strategic Target Planning Staff

JSU Jewish Student Union

JSU-122 Soviet 122mm assault-gun howitzer (SU-122)

JSU-152 Soviet assault-gun howitzer (SU-152)

J-S unit Junkerman-Schoeller unit (of thyrotrophin)

JSW Japan Steel Works

JSWPB Joint Special Weapons Publications Board

JSY Jersey Airlines

jt joint; joint tenancy; junction

JT Air Oregon (2-letter code); Jamaica Air Service (symbol); John Tyler (10th President U.S.); joint tenancy; Juvenile Templar

JT *Japan Times* (Japan's oldest English newspaper); *John Thomas* (British slang—penis)

JTA Jewish Telegraphic Agency (news service)

JTAC Joint Technical Advisory Committee

JTAD Joint Tactical Aids Detachment

jt agt joint agent

jt auth joint author

jtb joint bar

JTB Jamaica Tourist Board; Japan Travel Bureau; Jute Trade Board

JTBI Japan Travel Bureau International

JTC Japan Tobacco Corporation; Joint Technical Committee; Joint Telecommunications Committee; Junior Training Corps

JTCGALNNO Joint Technical Coordinating Group for Air-Launched Non-Nuclear Ordnance (DoD)

JTCGAS Joint Technical Coordinating Group for Aircraft Survivability (DoD)

jt comp joint compiler

jtda joint track data storage

jtde joint technology demonstration engine

J-teacher journalism teacher

Jt Ed Joint Editor

JTES Japan Techno-Economics Society

JTF Joint Task Forces

JTFOA Joint Task Force Operating Area

Jth. Apocryphal Book of Judith

jthh justice the helping hand

JTI *Jydsk Teknologisk Institut* (Danish—Jutland Technological Institute)

JTIDS Joint Tactical Information Distribution System (USAF and USN)

JTII Japan Telescopes Inspection Institute

jtly jointly

JTM&H *Journal of Tropical Medicine and Hygiene*

jtms jamb-template machine screws

JTNM Joshua Tree National Monument

jto jump takeoff

JTO Jordan Tourist Office

J-town Juarez

JTPA Job Training Partnership Act

JTPT Job Task Performance Test

jt r joint rate

JTR Joint Termination Regulation; Joint Travel Regulation; Jordan Travel Research

JTRC Joint Theater Reconnaissance Committee (NATO)

JTRE Joint Tsunami Research Effort

JTRU Joint-Services Tropical Research Unit

JTS Jewish Theological Seminary; Job Training Standards

JTS *Journal of Theological Studies*

JTSA Jewish Theological Seminary of America

JTSG Joint Trials Subgroup (NATO)

jtst jet stream

jt stk joint stock

JTTA Japan Table Tennis Association

jt ten. joint tenant(s)

JTWC Joint Typhoon Warning Center

ju jackup (oil well); joint use

Ju June; Junkers

JU Jacksonville University; Jadavpore University

JU *Jeunesse Universelle* (French —World Youth)

JU-52 German Junkers transport developed before World War II and used by many airlines

juana marijuana

Juana *Juana la Loca* (Spanish— Crazy Jane)—nickname of the demented and lisping daughter of Ferdinand and Isabella; when queen of Castile in 1504 her courtiers flattered her by lisping in the manner still called Castilian; title of an opera by Gian Carlo Menotti —*Juana la Loca*

Juan Bimba the typical Venezuelan

Juan Carlos Juan Carlos de Bourbon—chief of state and king of Spain succeeding Generalissimo Francisco Franco and supported by many democratic elements

Juan Gris José Victoriano Gonzalez

Juanita Juana (Jane, Joan)

Juan Pablo (Spanish—John Paul)—the Pope

Juárez Ciudad Juárez (formerly El Paso del Norte)

Juariles (Mexican-Americanism —Ciudad Juarez)

Jubilee Girls Jubilee Lodge for (delinquent) Girls at Brimfield, Illinois

juco junior college

jucund. *jucunde* (Latin—pleasantly)

jud judgment; judicial; judo

Jud Judah; Judaic; Judaism; Judean; Judson

J.U.D. *Juris Utriusque Doctor* (Latin—Doctor of Civil and Canon Law)

Jud-Alg Judeo-Algerian (Algerian Jewish)

Jud-Amer Judeo-American (American Jewish)

Jud-Arg Judeo-Argentinian (Argentine Jewish)

Jud-Ash Judeo-Ashkenazic (Ashkenazic Jewish) or the oriental branch of Yiddish-speaking Jews of eastern Europe (*see* Jud-Sep)

Judas Priest Jesus Christ (rendered as a palatable exclamation or oath)

Jud-Aus Judeo-Austrian (Austrian Jewish)

Jud-Aust Judeo-Australian (Australian Jewish)

Jud-Bel Judeo-Belgian (Belgian Jewish)

Jud-Bol Judeo-Bolivian (Bolivian Jewish)

Jud-Bra Judeo-Brazilian (Brazilian Jewish)

Jud-Bul Judeo-Bulgarian (Bulgarian Jewish)

Jud-Can Judeo-Canadian (Canadian Jewish)

Jud-Chi Judeo-Chilean (Chilean Jewish)

Jud-Chr Judeo-Christian (biblical and historic connection between Jews and Christians)

JUDCLA *Juventud Demócrata Cristiana Latino-Americana* (Spanish—Latin American Christian Democratic Youth)

Jud-Col Judeo-Colombian (Colombian Jewish)

Jud-CR Judeo-Costa Rican (Costa Rican Jewish)

judcrit judicial critic(ism)

Jud-Cub Judeo-Cuban (Cuban Jewish)

Jud-Cur Judeo-Curaçoan (Curaçoan Jewish)

Jud-Czech Judeo-Czechoslovakian (Czechoslovakian Jewish)

Jud-Dan Judeo-Danish (Danish Jewish)

Jud-Dut Judeo-Dutch (Dutch Jewish)

Jude The General Epistle of Jude

Jud-Ecu Judeo-Ecuadorean (Ecuadorean Jewish)

Jud-Egy Judeo-Egyptian (Egyptian Jewish)

Jud-Eng Judeo-English (English Jewish)

Judes Judesmo (Ladino)
Jud-Eth Judeo-Ethiopian (Ethiopian Jewish)
Jud-Fin Judeo-Finnish (Finnish Jewish)
Jud-Fre Judeo-French (French Jewish)
Judg. The Book of Judges
Judg Judges
Judge Adv Gen Judge Advocate General
Jud-Ger Judeo-German (German Jewish)—Yiddish dialect varying from country to country but retaining many German words although written in Hebrew
Jud-Gib Judeo-Gibraltarian (Gibraltarian Jewish)
Jud-Gre Judeo-Grecian (Grecian Jewish)
judgt judgment
Jud-Guat Judeo-Guatemalan (Guatemalan Jewish)
Jud-His Judeo-Hispanic (Hispanic Jewish)—Portuguese-Spanish Jewish as in the Hispanic Peninsula, Latin America, the United States, and other places where Portuguese-Spanish Jews have settled as in France, Germany, England, and the Netherlands as well as their colonies
Jud-HK Judeo-Hong Kongese (Hong Kongese Jewish)
Jud-Hung Judeo-Hungarian (Hungarian Jewish)
Jud-Ind Judeo-Indian (Indian Jewish)
Jud-Ire Judeo-Irish (Irish Jewish)
Jud-Irn Judeo-Iranian (Iranian Jewish)
Jud-Isr Judeo-Israeli (Israeli Jewish)
Jud-Itl Judeo-Italian (Italian Jewish)
Jud-Jam Judeo-Jamaican (Jamaican Jewish)
Jud-Jap Judeo-Japanese (Japanese Jewish)
Jud-Jor Judeo-Jordanian (Jordanian Jewish)
Jud-Lad Judeo-Ladino (Ladino Jewish)—Ladino-speaking Jews who settled in Muslim lands around the Mediterranean following the expulsion of the Jews from Portugal and Spain; Ladino combines medieval Castilian with Arabic, Hebrew, Turkish, and other elements local to places where they settled
Jud-Leb Judeo-Lebanese (Lebanese Jewish)
Jud-Mex Judeo-Mexican (Mexican Jewish)
Jud-Mor Judeo-Moresque (Moorish Jewish) also called Judeo-Moroccan (Moroccan Jewish)—Ladino-speaking Jews whose ancestors came to Morocco and other parts of northwest Africa when expelled from Spain by the Holy Inquisition
Jud-Nor Judeo-Norwegian (Norwegian Jewish)
Jud-NZ Judeo-New Zealand (New Zealand Jewish)
Jud-Pan Judeo-Panamanian (Panamanian Jewish)
Jud-Par Judeo-Paraguayan (Paraguayan Jewish)
Jud-Per Judeo-Peruvian (Peruvian Jewish)
Jud-Pol Judeo-Polish (Polish Jewish)
Jud-Port Judeo-Portuguese (Portuguese Jewish)
Jud-Rho Judeo-Rhodesian (Rhodesian Jewish)
Jud-Rom Judeo-Romanian (Romanian Jewish)
Jud-Rus Judeo-Russian (Russian Jewish)
Jud-SAf Judeo-South African (South African Jewish)
Jud-Scot Judeo-Scottish (Scottish Jewish)
Jud-Sep Judeo-Sephardic (Sephardic Jewish)—Portuguese-Spanish Jewish or the occidental branch of European Jews who settled in Portugal and Spain before expulsion by the Inquisition (*see* Jud-Ash)
Jud-Sin Judeo-Singaporan (Singaporan Jewish)
Jud-Slav Judeo-Slavic (Slavic Jewish)
Jud-Span Judeo-Spanish (Spanish Jewish)—also called Ladino or Spanish Yiddish as it is a dialect composed of medieval Spanish (current in the late 1400s when the Jews were expelled from Spain) plus Arabic, Hebrew, and Turkish terms acquired by the refugees; Ladino is still heard in various places around the Mediterranean from Morocco to the Balkans, Greece, and Turkey; Ladino is written in Hebrew characters as are better-known Yiddish dialects of German, Polish, and Russian sometimes called Jewish although Jewish is a religion and not a dialect or a language despite this most popular misconception

Jud-Sur Judeo-Surinamer (Surinamer Jewish)
Jud-Swe Judeo-Swedish (Swedish Jewish)
Jud-Swiss Judeo-Swiss (Swiss Jewish)
Jud-Syr Judeo-Syrian (Syrian Jewish)
Jud-Tun Judeo-Tunisian (Tunisian Jewish)
Jud-Tur Judeo-Turkish (Turkish Jewish)—Ladino-speaking Jews who settled in Turkey and other parts of the Turkish Empire after their expulsion from Spain and Portugal by the Holy Inquisition
Jud-Uru Judeo-Uruguayan (Uruguayan Jewish)
Jud-Ven Judeo-Venezuelan (Venezuelan Jewish)
Judy Judith
Jud-Yem Judeo-Yemenite (Yemenite Jewish)
Judy Garland motion-picture-reel name of Frances Gumm
Judy Holliday Judith Tuvim
Jud-Yug Judeo-Yugoslavian (Yugoslavian Jewish)
jue jueves (Spanish—Thursday)
Juec Jueces (Spanish—Judges)
Juev jueves (Spanish—Thursday)
JUG Joint Users Group
JUGC Jugolinija Container
Juggernaut Jagananth or port of Puri on the Bay of Bengal
Jugolinija Yugoslav Line
Jugoslav(ia)(n) Yugoslav(ia)(n)
Jugoslavien (German—Yugoslavia)
Jugoslavija Yugoslavia
Jugoslawien (German—Yugoslavia)
Jug(s) Jugoslavia(n)(s)
juil juillet (French—July)
jul julho (Portuguese—July); *julio* (Spanish—July)
Jul July
Jul Caes Julius Caesar
Jules Romains (pseudonym—Louis Farigoule)
Jules Verne father of science fiction and grandson of Juliusz Olchewitz who left Poland to escape its pogroms but still found antisemitism strong enough in France to change the family name to Verne
Julia Marlowe Sarah Frances Frost's stage name
Julians Julian Alps (northwestern Yugoslavia)

Julie Andrews Julia Wells

Juliet J-class Soviet submarines (diesel-powered and missile-launching) as named by NATO; letter J radio code

Julio Diniz Joaquim Guilherme Coelho

Jul^n Julián (Spanish—Julius)

Julust July and August

July Revolution French middle class revolt of 1830

Jumbo Barnum's famous 6-½-ton 11-foot-high trained elephant exhibited in the 'eighties

Jumbo Bill America's 27th President—300-pound William Howard Taft

JUMIP Juror Utilization and Management Incentive Program

Jump Jet nickname of U.S. Marine Corps AV-8B fighter-bomber capable of vertical takeoff and landing

JUMPS Joint Uniform Military Pay System

jun *juniore* (Italian—junior); *junio* (Spanish—June)

Jun June; Juneau

Ju^n *Julián* (Spanish—Julius)

Junc Junction

Junct Junction

June Allyson Ella Geisman

Juneau Alaska's capital

Jungle Novels collective name given to B Traven's books including *The Carreta, General from the Jungle, Government, March to the Monteria, Rebellion of the Hanged* (*see* Hal Croves)

Jung-wàh (Cantonese Chinese —China)

junk heroin's nickname, also called smack

Juno (Latin—Hera)—goddess of the heavens

jun part. junior partner

Junuly June and July

Jup Jupiter

Jupiter (Latin—Zeus)—god of the heavens also called Jove; Mozart's Symphony No. 41 in C major—his last

Jupiter of Wall Street JP Morgan

jur juridical

jur *juridisch* (Dutch—juridical); *juridisk* or *jurist* (Dano-Norwegian—legal or lawyer)

Jur Jurassic

Jur *Juridisch* (German—juridical)

Juras Jura Mountains between France and Switzerland

Jur.D. *Juris Doctor* Latin—Doctor of Law

jurimet(s) jurimetrician(s); jurimetric(s)

juris jurisdiction

JURIS Justice Retrieval and Inquiry System (U.S. Department of Justice); Juvenile Referral Information System

jurisd jurisdiction

jurisp jurisprudence

jus justice(s)

jus' just

jusc. *jusculum* (Latin—broth)

JUSCIMPC Joint United States-Canada Industrial Mobilization Planning Committee (NATO)

JUSE Japanese Union of Scientists and Engineers

Jusepe José de Ribera

J-U.S. FC Japan-United States Friendship Commission

JUSMAG Joint United States Military Advisory Group; Joint United States Military Aid Group to Greece

JUSMAP Joint United States Military Advisory and Planning Group

JUSMG Joint United States Military Group

JUSMMAT Joint United States Military Mission for Aid to Turkey

JUSPAO Joint United States Public Affairs Office

juss jussive

Juss Jussieu

Jussi Björling Johan Jonaton Björling

just. justification

Just Justinian

Justice Department of Justice; Hall of Justice; United States Department of Justice

Justice Personified Justitia (second goddess wife of the Roman god Jupiter or Themis who held the same post under the Greek god Zeus); she stands blindfolded, holding a balance in one hand and a palm frond in the other

Justin Justin cowboy boots (made by Joe Justin in Fort Worth, Texas)

JUSTIS Japan-United States Textile Information Service

Jute Port Dundee, Scotland

Jutland mainland of Denmark and Schleswig-Holstein

Jütland (German—Jutland)

Jutlandia (Portuguese or Spanish—Jutland)

juv juvenile

Juv Juvenal

juve juvenile

juve delinq juvenile delinquent

juve gang juvenile gang

juven juvenile; juvenilization; juvenilized; juvenilizing

Juvenal Decimus Junius Juvenalis

juvie juvenile delinquent; juvenile hall; juvenile law-enforcement officer

JUWTFA Joint Unconventional Warfare Task Force—Atlantic

JUWTFP Joint Unconventional Warfare Task Force—Pacific

jux juxtapose; juxtaposition

jv japanese vellum; joint venture; jugular vein; jugular venous

Jv Java; Javanese

JV Jules Verne; Junior Varsity

JVA Jordan Valley Authority

J Vac Sci Technol *Journal of Vacuum Science and Technology*

JVC Japan Victor Company

jvp japanese vellum proofs; jugular venous pulse

jvp (JPV) jugular venous pulse

JVS Jewish Vocational Service; Joint Vocational School

jw jacket water; jugwell (hydrocarbon storage well); junior wolf (a young philanderer)

JW Jehovah's Witnesses

JWA Japan Whaling Association

jwac jacket water aftercooled

J-walk jaywalk (cross streets against traffic lights, heedless of consequences, and at any part of the street except the pedestrian crossing)—some of the most expert jaywalkers may be found in hospital beds

J-walker jaywalker

JWB Jewish Welfare Board; Joint Wages Board; Joint Welfare Board

jwc junction wire connector

JWC Joint Working Committee

JWCA Japan Watch and Clock Association

JWDS Japan Work Design Society

JWEF Joinery and Woodwork Employers Federation

JWGA Joint War Games Agency

JWI Jack Winter (stock-exchange symbol)

JWJ James Weldon Johnson

JWJL JW Jagger Library (Cape Town)

jwl jewel; jeweler

JWL Johnston Warren Lines

jwlr jeweler

jwlry jewelry

j & wo jettison and washing overboard

JWO Jardine Waugh Organisation

JWPAC Joint Waste Paper Advisory Council

JWPT Jersey Wildlife Preservation Trust

JWR Joint War Room

JWR *Jane's World Railways*

JWs Jehovah's Witnesses

JWS Japan Welding Society

JWT J. Walter Thompson (advertising agency)

JWTC Jungle Warfare Training Center

JWU Jewelry Workers' Union

JWV Jewish War Veterans (of the United States)

JW von G Johann Wolfgang von Goethe

JX Bougainville Air Service (2-letter code)

J.X. Jesus Christ

Jy Jenny; July; Jury

JY British United Channel Islands Airways (2-letter coding)

JYL Jugolinja-Yugoslav Line

Jyll Jylland (Danish—Jutland)

Jylland (Danish—Jutland)

JZP Jersey Zoological Park

JZS Jersey Zoological Society

JZS *Jugoslovenski Zavod za Standardizacija* (Jugoslavian Standards Institution)

K

k Boltzman constant; carat (karat); cathode or vacuum tube; coefficient of alienation; compressibility factor; cumulus (symbol); force constant; keel; killed; kilo; kilo(gram)(s); knot(s); kweer (homosexual); reaction velocity constant; reproduction factor; thermal conductivity; torsion constant; unit vector in Z-direction

k (K) unit of computer memory capacity = 1000 (or 1024 in binary system of bytes, characters, or words)

k units of capital (microeconomics)

K 1024 storage bytes; capacity (symbol); centuple calorie (symbol); curvature (symbol); equilibrium constant (symbol); Fraunhofer line produced in part by calcium (symbol); hip; kaiser; Karman constant (symbol); Kawasaki Line; kelvin; Kelvin; Kerr constant; Kidde Fire Protection; kilobyte (symbol denoting 1024 units of stored matter); Kilo—code word for letter K; kilohm(s); kilometer(s); King(dom); Kiwanis International; Knabe; Köchel, cataloger of Mozart's music; kopec(s); kosher; krone; kroner; luminous efficiency (symbol); modulus of cubic compressibility (symbol); pilotless aircraft (symbol); potassium (kalium); proportionality constant (symbol); radius of gyration (symbol); strike-out (baseball); tanker (naval symbol)

°K degree(s) Kelvin

K kade (Dutch—embankment, quay); *kald* (Norwegian—cold); *kall* (Swedish—cold); *kalt* (German—cold); *koel* (Dutch—cold); *köld* (Danish—cold); *Koln* (German—Cologne); *krinda* (Danish—women); *kvinne* (Norwegian—women); *kvinnor* (Swedish—women); *kylmä* (Finnish—cold)

K² Mount Godwin Austen, Kashmir (28,250-ft mountain, second highest in the world)

K⁵ Kunlun Mountain known on the Chinese-Kashmir border as Muztagh

K-9 Corps Canine Corps (staffed by police dogs)

k9p dog piss; urine produced by coyotes, dogs, foxes, hyenas, jackals, wolves, and other canines

K-12 kindergarten through 12th grade

K-61 Soviet amphibious-assault vehicle

K98k German carbine (World War II)

ka cathode(s); kiloampere(s)

k/a ketogenic to antiketogenic (diet ratio)

Ka auroral absorption index (symbol)

Ka Komppania (Finnish—company)

KA Kapok Association; Karhumaki Airlines (Finland)

K-A King-Armstrong (units)

K of A King(dom) of Aragon

Ka-15 Soviet light-utility helicopter nicknamed Hen

Ka-18 Soviet utility-transport helicopter nicknamed Hog

Ka-20/Ka-25k Soviet helicopters built for military or commercial use with Ka-20 nicknamed Harp and Ka-25-k nicknamed Hormone

KA-25 Soviet armed helicopter called Hormone by NATO

kaa keep-alive anode

KAA Kwikasair (Australasia)

kaad kerosene, alcohol, acetic acid, dioxane (insect larva killer)

Kaapland (Afrikaans or Dutch—Cape Province)—Cape of Good Hope Province surrounding South Africa's Cape Town

Kaapprovinsie (Afrikaans—Cape Province)—South Africa

Kaapstad (Afrikaans or Dutch—Cape Town)

Kaatsk Kaatskill (Dutch—Catskill)—mountains beloved by New Yorkers and others such as the Hudson River school of painters

Kab Kabel; Kabul

KAB Keep America Beautiful

Kabul River City Kabul, Afghanistan

Kabwe formerly Broken Hill, Zambia

KAC Kuwait Airways Corporation

KACC Kaiser Aluminum Chemical Corporation; Kansas Association of Community Colleges

KACF Korean American Cultural Foundation

KACIA Korean-American Commerce and Industry Association

KADA Kemubu Agricultural Development Authority; Kemuta Agricultural Develop-

ment Authority
Kaddish Bernstein's Symphony No. 3 whose title indicates it is a prayer for the dead
Kadet(s) (see *KD*)
Kae Katherine
KAESP Kansas Association of Elementary School Principals
kaf kaffir
KAF Kenya Air Force
KAFB Kirtland Air Force Base
kaffir kaffir bean (African cowpea); kaffir beer (southern Africans brew it from grain); kaffir bread (*Encephalartos* fruit used to produce this southern African food); kaffir cat (originally from Africa and Asia Minor, reputedly the ancestor of the common domestic cat); kaffir crane (black-plume gray crane of southern Africa); kaffir piano (southern African marimba); kaffir plum (edible fruit from the southern Africa also called kaffir date or kaffir date plum)
Kaffir King Barney Barnato
kagan Kaganovich
KAH Kahului Railroad
Kahlbaum's disease dementia with muscular tension
Kahler's disease bone-marrow destruction
KAIIN third word of Sen Nihon Kaiin Kumiai the All Japan Seamen's Union
Kaimanawas short form for the Kaimanawa Mountains of New Zealand's North Island
Kaiser (German—Caesar)—emperor's title; *Kaiser-Walzer* (German—Emperor Waltz)—Johann Strauss Jr's opus 437 reflecting the Austro-Hungarian empire at its loveliest and most elegantly regal
Kaiser Bill Wilhelm II—Emperor of Germany
Kaiser-Walzer (German—Emperor Waltz)—by Johann Strauss Jr
Kai Tak Hong Kong's airport on the Kowloon Peninsula side of the city
Kajiwara Takuma Kajiwara
KAK Kungliga Automobil Klubben (Swedish—Royal Automobile Club)
kal kalamein
kal. kalendae (Latin—calends, the first day of the month)
Kal Kalana, Kalmar, Kalgoorlie
Kal Kalium (Latin—potassium)
KAL Korean Air Lines
Ka Lae Hawaii's southernmost

point also called South Cape or South Point
Kalahari Kalahari Desert or Kalahari National Park in South Africa
Kalatdlit-Nunat (Greenlandic Eskimo—Land of the People)—Greenland's new name adopted in 1979
kald kalamein door
Kaleun Kapitänleutnant (German—Commander)
Kali Kalimantan (Borneo)
Kalima formerly Albertville
Kalimantan (Indonesian—Borneo)
Kalinin Soviet name for Tver
Kaliningrad formerly Königsberg
Kali-yuga (Sanskrit—Age of Quarrel)—modern times
Kam Kampong (Malay—Village)
KAM Kimball Art Museum (Fort Worth)
Kamarans Kamaran Islands in the Red Sea
Kamenev Lev Borisovich Rosenfeld
Kamerun (German—Cameroon)—an African colony under German domination from 1884 to 1916
Kamikaze Field airline pilot's nickname for San Diego's unsafe Lindbergh Field and its hazardous approach over homes, offices, and schools
Kamk keyed alike and master keyed
kamp known as male prostitute
Kamp Kampuchea (Cambodia)
Kampong (Malay—Village)—short form for the nearest village such as Kampong Dew, Kampong Koh, Kampong Raja, etc.
Kampuchea Democratic Kampuchea (formerly a French colony in IndoChina where it was called Cambodia, following the change in powers its people have undergone mass executions and imprisonments)
Kampuchean Ports (*see* Cambodian Ports)
Kan Kansas; Kanpur
Kan Kanal (German—canal); *Kanaal* (Afrikaans or Dutch—canal)
Kanakalanders nickname for Queenslanders who hired so many South Sea Kanakas to work on their plantations
kanaka(s) South Sea islander(s)

Kanal Der Kanal (German—The Channel)—The English Channel
Kanawha River City Charleston, West Virginia
Kanchen Kanchenjunga; (28,146-foot-high mountain in the Himalayas, third highest in the world)
kangaroo Australian symbol
Kangaroo NATO name for Soviet air-to-surface missile carried by heavy bombers
Kangarooland Australia
Kangeans Kangean islanders or Kangean Islands in the Java Sea north of Bali
kang(s) kangaroo(s)
Kanner syndrome early infantile autism
Kano Eitoku Kano (late 16th-century Japanese painter)
Kans Kansas; Kansan
kansas cathedrals silos
k antigen capsular antigen
KANU Kenya African National Union (party)
kao kaolin
Kao Kaohsiung
kaocon kaopectate concentrate
Kaoh Kaohsiung
kaolin aluminum silicate (Al_2O_3 $2SiO_2 \cdot 2H_2O$); kaolinite
kaos killing as an organized sport
kap knowledge, attitude, practice
kap kapitel (Dano-Norwegian—capital); *kapitel* (Swedish—chapter)
Kap (German—cape); *Kapital* [German—capital (money)]; *Kapitel* (Danish and German—chapter)
KAP initials stand for Chinese Ministry of Public Security—external counterintelligence and internal secret police force of the People's Republic of China
KAPG Kluwer Academic Publishers Group
KAPL Knolls Atomic Power Laboratory
Kar Karachi; Karafuto
Kar Karabiner (German—carbine)—short rifle
KAR King's African Rifles
Kara Deniz (Turkish—Black Sea)
Kara Deniz Bogazi (Turkish—Black Sea Strait)—the Bosporus
Karafuto Japanese name for Sakhalin Island
KARAI Karhumaki Airways

(Finland)
Karakorums Karakorum Mountains of Kashmir
Kara Kum Central Asia's great desert in the Caspian region
Karawankens Karawanken Alps between Austria and Yugoslavia
Karel Karelia; Karelian
Karelo (Finnish—Karelia)
Karimunjawas Karimunjawa Islands off the north coast of Djawa or Java
Karimuns Karimun Islands between Singapore and Sumatra where the Strait of Malacca leads to the South China Sea
Karl Johan Jean Baptiste Jules Bernadotte
Karl Malden Karl Malden Sekulovich
Karl-Marx-Allee East Berlin's principal avenue formerly called Stalinallee
Karl-Marx-Stadt formerly Chemnitz
Karlovy Vary Czechoslovakian name for Karlsbad
Karl Radek Karl Sobelsohn
Karlsbad German name for Carlsbad or Karlovy Vary
Kas Kansas
KAS Kentucky Academy of Science; Kroeber Anthropological Society
KASA Kentucky Association of School Administrators
KASC Knowledge Availability Systems Center
Kash Kashmir
Kashin NATO name for a class of Soviet destroyer-leader ships
Kaspiskoye More (Russian—Caspian Sea)
KASSR Kalmyk Autonomous Soviet Socialist Republic; Karelian Autonomous Soviet Socialist Republic; Komi Autonomous Soviet Socialist Republic
Kastrup Copenhagen, Denmark's airport
kat katalog or *katolsk* (Dano-Norwegian—catalog or Catholic)
Kat Katmandu (capital of Nepal); Katowice
Kat Katar (Spanish—Quatar)
KAT Kenosha Auto Transport
Kate Catherine; Katherine; Katherine Hepburn; Katrina
Katendrecht Rotterdam's roughneck nightclub area
Katerina Katerina Izmaylova (Russian title of Shostako-

vich's opera *Lady Macbeth of the Mtsensk District*)
kath katholisch (German—catholic)—as an adjective
Kath Katherine
Kath Katholik (German—Catholic)—as a noun
Katherine Mansfield pseudonym—Kathleen Beauchamp Murry
Kathy Katharine; Kathleen; Kathryn
Katie Catherine; Katherine
Katmai Alaska's Katmai National Monument or its Valley of Ten Thousand Smokes or its Katmai Volcano creating the foregoing smoky valley in the Aleutian Peninsula
Kats Katangese
Katteg Kattegat (North Sea between Jutland peninsula of Denmark and west coast of Sweden)
KATUSA Korean (soldier) attached to (the) United States Army
Katy Missouri-Kansas-Texas Railroad
Katzbergs (Dutch—Catskill Mountains)
Katzen (German—Cats)—short form for the highest mountain in the Odenwald—Katzenbuckel or the village of Katzenellenbogen (Cats' Elbows) with its ancestral castle once inhabited by the counts and countesses Katzenellenbogen
Kauf Kaufman
K-A units King-Armstrong units
Kawa Kawasaki
Kawarthas Kawartha Lakes of southeastern Ontario
kay knockout (*kayo*—spelled abbreviation of ko); okay (truncated slang)
Kay Catherine
Kay-Cee Kansas City
Kayseri (Turkish—Caesarea)
Kaz Kazak(stan)
Kazan Retto Japanese name for the Volcano Islands
Kazoo Kalamazoo
kb kilobit(s); kilobyte (1024 characters); kitchen and bathroom; kite ballon; knee brace
k & b kitchen and bathroom
Kb Kontrabass (German—double bass)
KB Knight Bachelor; Koninkrijk Belgie (Flemish—Kingdom of Belgium)
K.B. King's Bench; Knight of the Order of the Bath

K of B King(dom) of Bavaria
KB Kongelige Bibliotek (Danish—Royal Library)—in Copenhagen; *Koninklijke Bibliotheek* (Dutch—Royal Library)—in The Hague; *Koninkrijk Belgie* (Flemish—Kingdom of Belgium); *Kungliga Biblioteket* (Swedish—Royal Library)—Stockholm
kba killed by air
KBAI Koninklijke Bibliotheek Albert I (Flemish—Albert Ist Royal Library)—see BrA
K-band 10,900–36,000 mc
kbar kilobar(s); 1 kbar equals approx 14,500 lbs per square inch
KBART Kings Bay Army Terminal
KBASSR Kabardino-Balkar Autonomous Soviet Socialist Republic
KBC King's Bench Court; Kyushu Asahi Broadcasting
KBD King's Bench Division
kbe keyboard encoder; keyboard entry; knotted both ends
K.B.E. Knight Commander of the Order of the British Empire
kbh killed by helicopter
Kbh København (Dano-Norwegian—Copenhagen)
Kbhvn København (Copenhagen)
KBI Keyboard Immortals (record label); Klan Bureau of Investigation (underground arm of the Ku Klux Klan)
KBIM Kongres Buruh Islamic Merdeka (Indonesian—Islamic Trade Union Congress)
K-bit unit of computer storage capacity equal to 1024 bytes
KBL Kabul, Afghanistan (airport)
KBL Kilusang Bagong Lipunan (Pilipino—Philippines New Society Movement)
kbm keyboard monitor
KBNWR Klamath Basin National Wildlife Refuges (California and Oregon)
K Bon Klein Bonaire (Netherlands Antilles)
KBP Koala Bear Park (Adelaide)
kbps kilo bits per second
kbs kilobits per second
KBS Kinki Broadcasting System (Japan); Korean Broadcasting System
KBS Kärnbränslesakerhet (Swedish—Nuclear Fuel Safety Project)

KBSI Kongres Buruh Seluruh Indonesia (Indonesian Trade Union Congress)

KB & TS Kuwait Broadcasting and Television Service

kbtu kilo British thermal unit (1,000 btu's)

kbv kauri-butanol value

KBW Klan Border Watch (along the Mexican border)

kc kilocycle(s); koruna (Czechoslovakian monetary unit)

Kc Kyle classification (social sciences)

KC Kalamazoo College; Kansas City; Keble College, Oxford; Kendall College; Kennedy Center; Kennel Club; Kenyon College; Keuka College; Keystone College; Keystone Shipping Company (flag code); Kilgore College; King College; King's College; Kirksville College (of osteopathy and surgery); Knox College; Knoxville College

K.C. King's Counsel; Knight Commander

K of C Knights of Columbus

KC-10A advanced tanker-cargo aircraft

KC-50 tactical aerial tanker for refueling aircraft in flight

KC-97 Stratofreighter strategic tanker-freighter equipped for inflight refueling

KC-130 Lockheed Hercules tanker aircraft

KC-135 Stratotanker multipurpose aerial tanker-transport

KCA Kitchen Cabinet Association

KCA Keesings Contemporary Archives

kcal kilocalorie(s)

kcas knots calibrated air speed

k/cb keel combined with centerboard

KCB Kenya Commercial Bank

K.C.B. Knight Commander of the Order of the Bath

KCBT Kansas City Board of Trade

kcc kathodic closure contraction; keyboard common contact

KCC Kellogg Community College; Kenai Community College; Kennedy Cultural Center; Ketchikan Community College; Kingsborough Community College; King's College, Cambridge

KC & C Kembla Coal and Coke

KCCD Kentucky Council on

Crime and Delinquency

KCCE Keystone Center for Continuing Education

KCCI Korean Chamber of Commerce and Industry

kcd kilocandelas

KCDMA Kiln, Cooler, and Dryer Manufacturers Association

kcf thousand cubic feet

Kch Kuching

KCH King's College Hospital

K.C.H.S. Knight Commander of the Order of the Holy Sepulchre

kCi kiloCurie(s)

KCI Key Club International

KCIA Korean Central Intelligence Agency

K.C.I.E. Knight Commander of the Indian Empire

KCl potassium chloride

KCL Kai Curry-Lindahl; King's College, London; Kirchoff's Current Law

KCLA Known Coal-Leasing Area(s)

KCLY Kent and County of London Yeomanry

KCM Kansas City Museum

kcmG kindly call me God

K.C.M.G. Knight Commander of the Order of Saint Michael and Saint George

KCM & O Kansas City, Mexico & Orient (railroad)

kcmx keyset central multiplexer

KCNA Korean Central News Agency

KCNP Kings Canyon National Park (California); Ku-ring-gai Chase National Park (New South Wales)

KCNS King's College, Nova Scotia

KCOBE Knight Commander—Order of the British Empire

KCP Key Curriculum Project

KCPA Kaolin Clay Producers Association; Kennedy Center for the Performing Arts

KCPL Kansas City Public Library

KCPO Kansas City Philharmonic Orchestra

kcps kilocycles per second

KCR Kowloon-Canton Railway

kcs Czechoslovakian koruna(s); kilocycles per second

kc/s kilocycles per second

KCS Kansas City Southern (railroad)

KCS Kansas City Star

kc/sec kilocycles per second

K.C.S.G. Knight Commander of Saint Gregory the Great

KCSI Knight Commander of the Star of India

KCSO Kansas City Symphony Orchestra

KCT Kansas City Terminal (railroad)

kcte kathodic closure tetanus

K Cur Klein Curaçao (Netherlands Antilles)

KCVO Knight Commander of the Victorian Order

kd key depression(s); killed; kiln dried; knocked down; known distance; pilotless aerial target (code)

Kd Konrad; Kuwait dinar(s)

KD Kidderpore Docks (Calcutta); Kongeriget Danmark (Kingdom of Denmark)

K of D King(dom) of Denmark

KD Kampuchea Democratique (French—Democratic Kampuchea)—formerly called Cambodia; *Konstitutsionno-demokraticheskaya partiya* (Russian—Constitutional Democratic Party)—party of the KDs or Kadets later the *partiya Narodnoy Svobodi* or People's Freedom Party liquidated by the Bolsheviks under Lenin

KDA Kongelik Dansk Aeroklub (Royal Danish Aero Club)

KDAK Kongelig Dansk Automobile Klub (Royal Danish Automobile Club)

K Dan Vidensk Selsk, Mat Fys Medd Kongelige Danske Videnskabernes Selskab, Matematiske Fysiske Meddelelser (Danish—Royal Scientific Society, Mathematical and Physical Announcements)

K-day basic date for introduction of convoy system or lane; carrier aircraft assault day

KDB Korea Development Bank

kdcl knocked down in carload lots

KDD Kokusai Denshin Denwa (Japan's Overseas Radio and Cable System)

kdf knocked-down flat

K d F *Kraft durch Freude* (German—Strength through Joy) —Nazi holiday association

KDG King's Dragoon Guards

KDHNM Kill Devil Hill National Memorial

KDI Kwaliteitsdienst voor de Industrie Stichting (Dutch—Industrial Quality Control Society)

kdlcl knocked down in less than

carload lots
kdly kindly
kdm kingdom
KDM Kongelige Danske Marine (Royal Danish Navy)
Kdo Kasado
K-do *Kamarado* (Esperanto—comrade)
KDP potassium dihydrogen phosphate
KDs Kadets
kdv kiln-dried veneer
ke kinetic energy
K$_e$ exchangeable body potassium
KE Kaiser Engineers
K-E Krafft-Ebing
K + E Keuffel & Esser
K of E King(dom) of England; Knights of Equity
KEA Kentucky Education Association; Kiwifruit Exporters Association
Keams Keams Canyon in northeastern Arizona where it is the Hopi Indian Reservation headquarters
keas knots equivalent airspeed; knots estimated airspeed
Keb Coll Keble College—Oxford
KEBK Korea Exchange Bank
Keble Keble College, Oxford
Kech Kechua (Quechua)
KECO Korea Electric Company
KEDDS Kansas Education Dissemination/Diffusion System
Kee Keelung
Keel Keeling
Keeling Islands old name for Cocos in the Indian Ocean
KEEP Kentucky Environmental Education Program
KEF Keflavik Airport, Iceland
Keflavik Iceland's principal airport serving Keflavik, Reykjavik, and other places
KEHF King Edward's Hospital Fund
Keijo Japanese name for Seoul, Korea
Kel Kiel (British maritime abbreviation)
Kelly Country Australia's northern Victoria named after the nineteenth-century outlaw Ned Kelly
KELP Kindergarten Evaluation of Learning Potential
Kelp Capital San Diego, California
Kelper(s) Falkland Islander(s)
Kelt NATO name for Soviet air-to-surface missile carried by Tu-16 bombers

KELTS Key English Language Teaching Scheme
Kelvin part of title bestowed on William Thomson—Lord Kelvin
kem *kemisk* (Dano-Norwegian—chemical)
KEMA Kitchen Equipment Manufacturers Association
KEMA *Keuring van Electrotechnische Materialen* (Dutch—Testing Institute for Electrochemical Materials)
Kemal Ataturk originally Mustafa Kemal Pasha
Ken Kendal(l); Kendric(k); Kenelm; Kenilworth; Kenley; Kenna(rd); Kennedy; Kennet; Kenneth; Kennit; Kenny; Kenric(k); Kensell; Kensington; Kent(on); Kentuckian; Kentucky; Kenward; Kenwood; Kenya; Kenyan; Kenyon
Ken *Kenia* (Spanish—Kenya)
Kenitra formerly Port Lyautey, French Morocco
Kennedy John F Kennedy (his brothers and others named Kennedy); John F Kennedy International Airport (New York)
Kennel NATO name for Soviet air-to-surface ship-destroying missile carried by Tu-16 bombers
Kens Kensington
Kent Kentucky
Kentuck Kentucky
Kenya formerly a British East African protectorate and now a bilingual (Swahili-English) republic engaged in tourism, raising tropical crops, and mining gems as well as gold; Mau Mao uprisings have delayed Kenya's growth
Kenya Ports (south to north) Mombasa, Takaungu, Malindi, Lamu
kep key-entry processing
kep' kept
Kep *Kepulauan* (Indonesian or Malay—archipelago)
KEPCO Kyushu Electric Power Company
kependekan (Malay—abbreviation)—also called *ringkasen* or *singkatan*
KEPZ Kaohsiung Export Processing Zone
kerat keratometric(al)(ly); keratometry
Kerguelens Kerguelen Islands in the subantarctic South Indian Ocean

kerk *kerkelijke term* (Dutch—ecclesiastical term)
Kérkira (Modern Greek—Corfu)
Kermadecs Kermadec Islands
kern kernan
kero kerosene
kerogen oil shale's chief constituent
KESCO Kowloon Electricity Supply Company
Kester Christopher
Ketchikan State Ketchikan State Jail and Detention Home in Ketchikan, Alaska
keto ketonaemia; ketogenic; ketone; ketonuria; ketoses; ketosis
ketol ketone alcohol (compound)
Kettledrum Haydn's Kettledrum Mass in C major (*Paukenmesse*)
Keulen (Dutch—Cologne)
kev kilo electron volt; 1,000 electron volts
keV kiloelectronvolt(s)
Kev Kelvin; Kevin
KEVs King's Empire Veterans
Kew Gar Kew Gardens
Kew Obs Kew Observatory
Key City Port Townsend, Washington; Vicksburg, Mississippi
Key to England Dover on the bay beneath the chalk cliffs of Kent flanking the English Channel and often in sight of the French coastline
Key of the Gulf Cuba commanding the entrance to the Gulf of Mexico
Key of the Indian Ocean Mauritius
Key of the Mediterranean Gibraltar commanding the entrance to the Mediterranean Sea
keyper key personnel; keywords permuted
Keys the Keys (short form for the Florida Keys)
Key State New South Wales
Key to Stockholm offshore Aland Islands between Finland and Sweden
Keystone Province Manitoba linking eastern and western Canada
Keystoner(s) Pennsylvanian(s)
Keystone State Pennsylvania—central state of the original thirteen if they were arranged in an arch beginning with New Hampshire and ending with Georgia

kf kitchen facilities; koff
KF Kaiser-Frazer; Kellogg Foundation; Kent Foundation; Kidney Foundation; Kooperative Forbunded (Federation of Cooperatives—Sweden); Kresge Foundation
K of F King(dom) of France
KF Konservative Folkeparti (Danish—Conservative Party); *Kooperative Forbunded* (Swedish—Federation of Cooperatives)
KFA Kenya Farmers Association; Krishnamurti Foundation of America
KFASSR Karelo-Finnish Autonomous Soviet Socialist Republic (formerly the Karelia of Finland)
Kfc Kentucky fried chicken
KFC Kentucky Fried Chicken; Kropp Forge Company
KFEA Korean Federation of Education Associations
kff keep from freezing
KFH Kaiser Foundation Hospitals
KFL Kenya Federation of Labour
kfm kaufmännisch (German—commercial)
Kfm Kaufmann (German—merchant)
KFNP Kaieteur Falls National Park (Guyana)
kfo killing federal officer
KFP Kristelig Folkeparti (Norwegian—Christian People's Party)
KFPC Kansas Foundation for Private Colleges
K-F s Klippel-Feil syndrome
KFSR Karakul Fur Sheep Registry
KFT Kansai Fishing Tackle
KFUK Kristelig Forening for Unge Kvinder (Danish—Young Women's Christian Association)
KFUM Kristelig Forening for Unge Maend (Danish—Young Men's Christian Association)
Kfz Kraftfahrzeug (German—motor vehicle)
kg keg; kilogram; known gambler
/kg per kilogram
kG kilogauss
Kg Kirghiz(ian)
Kg Kampong (Malay—village); *Kompong* (Indo-Chinese—landing place, riverside)
KG Kelly Girl
K-G Kanematsu-Gosho Ltd.
K.G. Knight of the Order of the Garter
K of G King(dom) of Granada
KG Kommanditgesellschaft (German—limited partnership)
KG5 King George V School
KGA Kitchen Guild of America
KGB Komitet Gossudarrstvennoi Bezopastnosti (Russian—Committee of State Security, Soviet Secret Police)
KGBW Kewaunee, Green Bay, and Western (railroad)
KGC Knights of the Golden Circle
K.G.C. Knight of the Grand Cross
kg cal kilogram calorie
kg-cal kilogram calorie
K.G.C.B. Knight of the Grand Cross of the Bath
kg/cm kilograms per centimeter
kg cum kilograms per cubic meter
kgf kilogram-force
Kgf Kriegsgefangener (German—prisoner of war)
KGFS King George's Fund for Sailors
kg/hl kilograms per hectoliter
kg/hr kilograms per hour
KGIS Kuder General Interest Survey
KGJT King George's Jubilee Trust
KGK Kabushiki Goshi Kaisha (Japanese—joint stock limited partnership of members with unlimited liability and shareholders with limited liability)
kgl kongelig (Dano-Norwegian—royal)
Kgl Königlich (German—royal)
kgm kilogram meter
kg/m² kilograms per square meter
kg/m³ kilograms per cubic meter
kg/ms kilograms per meter second
Kgn Kingston, Jamaica
KGNP Kalahari Gemsbok National Park (South Africa); Katherine Gorge National Park (Australian Northern Territory)
kgps kilograms per second
kgra known geothermal resource area
kgs kegs; kilograms
kg/s kilograms per second
KGS Kate Greenaway Society; Kigezi Gorilla Sanctuary (Uganda); Korean Geological Survey
kgs/ha kilograms per hectare
KG St J Knight of Grace of the Order of Saint John of Jerusalem
kg U kilogram of uranium
KGVDs King George V Docks (London)
KGWS Keoladeo Ghana Wildlife Sanctuary (India)
kH kilohertz
Kh Khmer (Cambodia)
Kh Khawr (Arabic—creek, inlet, ravine, water-course)
KH King's Hussars; Knut Hamsun
K-H Kelsey-Hayes
K of H King(dom) of Hungary
KH Karen Hayesod (Hebrew—United Israel Appeal); *Kjøbenhavns Handelsbank* (Danish—Copenhagen's Commercial Bank); *Kupat Holim* (Hebrew—Health Insurance Fund)
KH-4 Kawasaki all-purpose helicopter similar to the Bell 47
KH-11 American-made intelligence-gathering satellite
kha killed by hostile action
Khar Kharkov
Khazar Bahr-ul-Khazar (Arabic—Caspian Sea)
Khazaria ancient kingdom between the Black and the Caspian seas inhabited by the Khazar Jews
Khazarian Way Don Volga Portage
Khazar Sea Caspian Sea (on the southeast shores of Khazaria, according to Arthur Koestler)
KHC Karen Horney Clinic
KHDS King's Honorary Dental Surgeon
Khi Karachi
KHI Karachi, Pakistan (airport)
Khingans Kinghan Mountains of northeast China
Khíos (Greek—Chios)
KHL Koninklijke Hollandsche Lloyd (Dutch—Royal Holland Lloyd)
KHM King's Harbour Master
Khmer Cambodia
Khmer Republic new name for Cambodia
Khn Knoop hardness number
KHNS King's Honorary Nursing Sister
khp kilohorsepower (hour)
KHP King's Honorary Physician
KHPC Karen Horney Psychoanalytic Clinic
Khr Khrebet (Russian—mountain range)

KHRI Kresge Hearing Research Institute

KHS Kennedy High School

khz (kHz) kilocycle(s)/second; kilohertz, formerly kilocycle(s) per second

ki kilo; kitchen

KI Kathleen Investments; Kiwanis International; potassium iodide

K-I Kaiser-Illin

K of I King(dom) of Ireland; King(dom) of Italy

KI *Kol Israel* (Hebrew—Voice of Israel)—broadcasting service; *Kommunisticheskii Internatsional* (Russian—Communist International); *Komunisticna Internacijonala* (Yugoslav—Communist International)

kia (KIA) killed in action

Kia Kligler iron agar

kias knots indicated airspeed

KIB Kansas Inspection Bureau; Kentucky Inspection Bureau

Kibo Mount Kibo (Africa's highest peak also called Kilimanjaro)

Kibris (Turkish—Cyprus)

KICF Kentucky Independent College Foundation

Kick-'em-Jenny Diamond Island's nickname (West Indian island near Grenada)

kid. kidney

KID Key Industry Duty

kidult kid adult (older person who enjoys juvenile entertainment)

kidvid children's television program; children's tv or video programs

Kiel Canal formerly Kaiser Wilhelm Canal

kieselguhr silica (SiO_2)

Kiev English place-name for Russia's Kiyev in the Ukraine

Kiev *Kiev*-class 40,000-ton Soviet aircraft carrier

Kifis Kollsman integrated flight instrument system

K-i-H *Kaiser-i-Hind* (Emperor of India medal)

KIICC *Kommunisticheskaya Partiya Sovetskogo Soyuza* (Russian—Communist Party of the Soviet Union)

Kikdl *Krokodil*

Kikladhes (Modern Greek—Cyclades Islands)

kiku (Japanese—Chrysanthemum)—applications technology satellite made and launched in Japan

kil (Dutch—channel, estuary, strait)—as in Arthur Kill, French Kill, and Kill van Kull along the shores of New York's Staten Island

kild kilderkin(s)

Kild Kildare

Kildin NATO name for a Soviet class of fleet destroyers

Kili Kilimanjaro

Kilk Kilkenny

killer disease dysentery (killing more pirates and tourists than cannonballs or cutlasses)

Kill van Kill van Kull (waterway between Bayonne, New Jersey and Port Richmond, Staten Island, New York where it connects Newark Bay with Upper New York Bay)

kilo Kilogram; 10^3

Kilo letter K radio code

kilobrick(s) kilo-weight brick(s) of marijuana measuring about 2½ x 5 x 12 inches (64 x 127 x 300 millimeters)

kilohm kilo-ohm

Kilometer-high City Boone, North Carolina

kilovar kilovolt-ampere (reactive)

Kim Kimball; Kimballton; Kimberley; Kimberly; Kimble; Kimbolton; Kimborough; Kimbrough; Kimiwan; Kimmell; Kimmins; Kimmswick; Kimsquit

K i M Knudsen i Marken

Kim Novak Marilyn Novak

kin *kinesisk* (Dano-Norwegian—Chinese)

Kin Frank McKinney Hubbard; Kingston, Ontario (maritime contraction)

KIN Kingston, Jamaica (airport); Kinross

Kinc Kincardinel

kind. kindergarten

kine kinema (variation of cinema)

Kines J M Keynes (pronounced as italicized)

King Kingston

King of Acids sulfuric acid

King of Austrian Opera Wolfgang Amadeus Mozart

King of Bath Richard (Beau) Nash

King of Beasts the lion

King of Birds the eagle

King Bomba Ferdinand II

King of Coke Henry Clay Frick

King of Conductors Herbert von Karajan

King of the Conifers the sequoia

King Cotton personification of the cotton crop of the southern United States

King of Courts the forensic orator Quintus Hortensius of Rome

King Crab Capital Kodiak, Alaska

kingd kingdom

Kingdom of Death Hel (name of the Queen of Death in Nordic mythology)

Kingdom of the Hellenes Greece

Kingdom of Perpetual Night Hell

Kingdom of Sardinia the Italian Peidmont and the island of Sardinia

Kingdoms of the North Denmark, Norway, Sweden

Kingdom of the Two Sicilies Bourbon states of Naples and Sicily

King of European Music Festivals Salzburg

King of Filibusters William Walker

Kingfish Senator Huey P Long of Louisiana

King of the Fjords Sogne Fjord, Norway

King of French Opera Hector Berlioz

King of Fruits the mango

King of German Opera Richard Wagner

King of the Gods Jupiter (according to Roman mythology)

King of the High Cs Luciano Pavarotti

King of the Huns and Scourge of God Attila

King of Instruments the human voice (in the opinion of vocalists and their admirers); the organ (according to organists and their admirers); the violin or other string instruments (according to instrumentalists and their admirers)

King of Italian Opera Giuseppe Verdi

King James *King James Version of the Bible* (authorized by King James I of England in 1611)

King of Jazz Louis (Satchmo) Armstrong and Paul Whiteman share this sobriquet

King of the Jews Jesus, according to the *New Testament*

King of the Jungle the tiger

King Karls King Karl Islands in the Norwegian sector of the

Arctic

King of Kings Jehovah—God of the Christians and Jews; title of various presumptive rulers of African and Oriental lands

King of Laughter Bert Williams (Egbert Austin Williams)

King Leopolds King Leopold Ranges of northern Western Australia

King of Metals gold

King of Naples Marshal Joachim Murat

King of Oceanic Scavengers the albatross

King of the Octaves Claudio José Domingo Brindis de Sala —German Baron and court violinist

King Oliver Joseph (King) Oliver—Doctor Jazz

King of the One-Liners Henny Youngman—remembered for the question—*when librarians go fishing what do they use for bait? bookworms*

King of the Opera tenor-conductor Placido Domingo

King of Ornithological Painters John James Audubon

King Penguin Roger Tory Peterson

King of the Pianists Claudio Arrau

King of the Ragtime Writers Scott Joplin

King of Rivers sobriquet shared by North America's Colorado and South America's Amazon

King of Roads John Loudon Macadam

King of Rock 'n' Roll Elvis (the pelvis) Presley

King of Russian Opera Piotr Ilyich Tchaikovsky

Kings either of two books in the Old Testament of Jewish and Protestant bibles; either of four books in the Old Testament of Roman Catholic bibles

King's King's College (Cambridge, Columbia, and elsewhere)

Kings Canyon Kings Canyon National Park in central California

King's College Columbia University in colonial times

King of the Seas Neptune (Roman) or Poseidon (Greek)

king's English correct English

king's evil scrofula (lymph-gland tuberculosis)

Kingsford Smith Sydney, Australia's airport

King of Snobs Hudson, the otherwise faultless butler, in the tv play *Upstairs, Downstairs*

Kings Point United States Merchant Marine Academy at Kings Point, New York

King of Steel Andrew Carnegie

Kingston-upon-Hull full name of Hull

King of Swat George Herman Ruth

King of Swing Benny Goodman; Elvis Presley

Kings X Sta King's Cross Station (rail terminal)

King of Tasmanian Rivers the Gordon

King of Terrors personification of death

King of Torts Melvin Belli

King of Trains and Train of Kings Orient Express

King Tut King Tutankhamen of Egypt

King of the Underworld Osiris (Egyptian mythology)

King of the Vagabonds François Villon whose real name was François de Montcorbier

King of Vaudeville Jimmy (Schnozzola) Durante

King of Verismo Giacomo Puccini (celebrated composer of realistic operas)

King of Waters the Amazon

King of the West Saxons Alfred the Great

King Who Lost George III, who lost the American colonies

King Who Lost America Great Britain's George III

Kinmen Chinese name for Quemoy Island

Kinr Kinross shire

Kinshasa formerly Leopoldville, Belgian Congo

kinsym kinematic synthesis

KINTEL K Laboratories (instruments and television)

Kintetsu Kinki Nippon Railway Company, Ltd

Kiowa Bell helicopter whose civil version is called the Jet Ranger

kip thousand pounds (from contraction of kilo and pound)

KIP Kennedy Institute of Politics (Harvard)

kip ft thousand foot pounds

Kipling's Khyber mountain pass between Afghanistan and Pakistan

Kipper NATO nickname for air-to-surface missile carried by Tu-16 aircraft

Kipros (Greek—Cyprus)

KIPS Knowledge Information Processing System(s)

kiq (KIQ) key intelligence questions

Kir Kirghiz; Kirghizia; Kirghizian; Kiribati

kirchatovium Russian name for element 104 named for A-bomb pioneer Igor Kurchatov

Kircoobri (Scottish contraction —Kircudbright)

Kircud Kircudbrightshire *(Kircoobrisheer)*

Kiribati Republic of Kiribati (Gilbert and Ellice islands colony in the equatorial Pacific where it includes Tarawa)

Kirk Kirkham; Kirkland; Kirkudbright *(Kircoobri)*; Kirkwood

Kirk Douglas Issur Danielovich Demsky

Kirov Sergei Mironovich Kostrikov; Soviet name for Viatka

Kirsty Kristina; Kristine

KISA Korean International Steel Associates

Kisangani formerly Stanleyville, Belgian Congo

kisc knowledge industry system concept

kismif keep it simple—make it fun

KI smog potassium-iodide smog (automobile induced)

KISO Kol Israel Symphony Orchestra

KISR Kuwait Institute for Science Research

kiss keep it simple, stupid

kiss. keep it simple, sir; keep it simple, stupid

KIST Korean Institute for Science and Technology

kit. key issue tracking; kitchen(ette); kitten; kitty

Kit Catherine; Christopher; Kitty

KIT Kentucky and Indiana Terminal (railroad); Korean International Telecommunications

KIT Koninklijk Instituut voor de Tropen (Dutch—Royal Institute for the Tropics)

kita (Japanese—north)

Kit Carson Christopher Carson nicknamed Monarch of the Prairies as well as Nestor of the Rocky Mountains

Kit Carson City Carson City, Nevada named for the frontiersman

Kitchen NATO codename for Soviet air-to-surface missile carried by Tu-22 bombers

Kitchener formerly Berlin, Ontario but changed in World War I to honor Lord Kitchener

Kitchener of Khartum General Horatio Herbert Kitchener

KITCO Kwajalein Import and exporting Company

kiteoon kite + balloon

kitin' kiting (money)

kits. kittens

kitsch kitschen (German—thrown together)—commercial art or art objects cheapened by vulgarity; e.g., miniature reproduction of the Venus de Milo with an alarm clock set in her belly

Kitsch *Kitschmensch* (German—kitschman)—anyone creating, dealing in, or displaying artistic rubbish—junk art

Kitsi Kathryn

Kittie Katherine; Kitty Belairs

Kittsian(s) inhabitant(s) of St. Kitts

Kitty Catherine

KIVI Koninklijk Instituut van Ingenieurs (Dutch—Royal Institution of Engineers)

KIWA Keurings Instituut voor Waterleiding Artikelen (Dutch—Inspection Institute for Waterwords Equipment)

kiwi(s) New Zealander(s)

kizil (Turkish—red, as in Kizil Arvat, Kizil Kum, Kizil Uzen)

kj killer judo; kilojoule; kimberly joint (lumbing); knee jerk; kraut joint; krystal joint (pcp)

k-j knee-jerk(s)

kJ kilojoule

KJ Kahlil Jibran (Gibran)

KJ King James (version of the Bible)

KJB Korea-Japan Board

KJC Kaiser Jeep Corporation; Keystone Junior College

K John Life and Death of King John

Kjölen mountains separating Norway and Sweden

K.J.St.J. Knight of Justice, Order of Saint John of Jerusalem

KJV King James Version

kk killer karate

k-k knee-kicks (knee-jerks)

kK kilokelvin

K-K Krupp-Koppers

K of K Kitchener of Khartoum

KK Kabushiki Kaisha (Japanese—joint stock company of shareholders with limited liability); *Kaiserlich Königlich*

(German—Imperial Royal)

K.K. Kahal Kadosh (Hebrew—Holy Congregation)

KKASSR Kara-Kalpak Autonomous Soviet Socialist Republic

KKI Keren Kayemeth le Israel (Hebrew—National Fund of Israel)

KKK Ku Klux Klan (secret organization antagonistic to certain racial & religious groups)

KKK Kataas-taasan Kagalanggalan-gang Katipuna (Pilipino—Mightiest Warriors Fighting for Freedom); *Kinder, Kirche, Küche* (German — Children, Church, Kitchen) — traditional three Ks of Teutonic womanhood

KKKK Kansai Kisen Kabushiki Kaisha; Kawasaki Kisen Kabushiki Kaisha (steamship lines)

KKKK Koenhavns Kul og Koks Kompagne (Copenhagen Coal and Coke Company)

KKKKs Knights of the Ku Klux Klan

KKKUK Ku Klux Klan in the United Kingdom

KKL Karlander Kangaroo Line

KKMKI Kungliga Karolinska Mediko-Kirurgiska Institutet (Caroline Medico-Surgical Institute-Stockholm)

KKO Korps Kommando (Bahasa-Indonesian Malay—Commando Corps)—marine corps

Kkr Karlskrona

kl key length; kiloliter

kl klasse or *klokken* (Dano-Norwegian—class or o'clock); *klockan* (Swedish—o'clock)

Kl Klasse (German—class); *Klein(e)* (German — little, small)

KL Key Largo; Klebs-Loeffler; Knutsen Line; Kuala Lumpur; Kwik Lok

KL King Lear

kla Klavier; klystron amplifier

KLA Kansas Library Association; Kentucky Library Association; Korean Library Association

Klaipeda (Lithuanian—Memel)

Klamaths Klamath Mountains bordering California and Oregon

Klan Ku Klux Klan (*q.v.* KKK)

Klar Klarinette (German—clarinet)

Klaus Nikolaus

klax klaxon

K-L bacillus Klebs-Loeffler bacillus (diphtheria)

KLC Kaingaroa Logging Company

kld kaelder (Dano-Norwegian—basement or cellar)

Klebs Klebisella

klein (Dutch or German—small)

Klem Klemens; Klement; Klementi; Kliment

klepto kleptomania(c, al)

Kleve (German—Cleves)

kl Fl kleine Flöte (German—piccolo)

Klg Keelung

klh keyhole limpet hemocyanin (KLH)

KLIAU Korean Land Improvement Association Union

klic key letter in context

klieg klieg light (named for German-American inventor brothers Anton and J H Kliegl)

klim (milk spelled backwards) dried milk

K Line Kawasaki Kisen Kaisha

KLM Koninklijke Luchtvaart Maatschappij (Royal Dutch Airlines)

Klmpb Klampenborg

Kln Köln (Cologne)

klo klystron oscillator

k-lo kello (Finnish—hour, o'clock)

Klondike Country the Yukon

Klong Toey Bangkok, Thailand's waterfront area

Kloten Zürich, Switzerland's airport

KLPA Knuckeys Lagoon Protected Area (Australian Northern Territory)

KLr Kuala Lumpur

kls key lock switch

k-l-s kidney-liver-spleen

KLSE Kuala Lumpur Stock Exchange

klt kiloton (nuclear equivalent, 1,000 tons of high explosives)

klto knurling tool

Kluxer member of the Ku Klux Klan (*q.v.* KKK)

km kilometer

kM kilomega (10^9 giga)

Km Kingdom

KM Kaffrarian Museum; Kearny Mesa; Khedivial Mail (steamship line)

K-M Krauss-Maffei

K.M. Knight of Malta

K&M King and Martyr (Charles Ist's sobriquet)

km² square kilometer

km³ cubic kilometer

KMA Kalgoorlie Mining Associates; Kinematograph Manufacturers Association

KMAG United States Military Advisory Group to the Republic of Korea

KMB Kowloon Motor Bus

kmc kilomegacycle

KMD Kentucky Manpower Development

kmef keratin, myosin, epidermin, fibrin (proteins)

KMF Koussevitzky Music Foundation

km/h kilometers per hour

KMH Kleinhans Music Hall (Buffalo)

KMI Kentucky Military Institute

KMIDC Korean Marine Industry Development Corporation

KMIT four-letter name bestowed by Trotsky on the Bolshevik ministry of foreign affairs; when foreign journalists demanded to know what KMIT stood for his aides confided it was Yiddish for *küss mir im tuchus* (kiss my ass)

km/l kilometers per liter

KMMA Korean Merchant Marine Academy

KMO Kobe Marine Observatory

KMP Kaiser Metal Products; Kearny Mesa Plant (Convair)

KMPA Korean Maritime and Port Administration

kmph kilometers per hour

kmps kilometers per second

Kmr Khorramshahr

KMR Kwajalein Missile Range

kms kilometers

KMS Kansas Medical Society; Keeve M Siegel

KMT Kuomintang

KMTC Korea Marine Transport Company

KMUB *Karl-Marx-Universitäts Bibliothek* (German—Karl-Marx University Library)—on Beethovenstrasse in Leipzig

KMUL Karl Marx Universität Leipzig (University of Leipzig)

kmv killed measles-virus vaccine

kmw kilomegawatt

KMW Karlstads Mekaniska Werkstad (Swedish iron foundry)

kmwhr kilomegawatt-hour

kn kilonewton; knot; krone; kronen

Kn Knight

KN Koninkrijk der Nederland-

en (Kingdom of the Netherlands); Kongeriket Norge (Kingdom of Norway)

K-N Know-Nothing (political party)

K of N King(dom) of Naples; King(dom) of Navarre; King(dom) of Norway

KNA Kenya News Agency; Korean National Airlines

KNA *Kongelig Norsk Automobilklub* (Royal Norwegian Automobile Club)

KNAC *Koninklijke Nederlandsche Automobiel Club* (Dutch—Royal Netherlands Automobile Club)

KNAN Koninklijke Nederlandse Akademie voor Natuurwetenschappen (Royal Netherlands Academy of Sciences)

K'naw Kanawha Rver

KNB Kita-Nihon Broadcasting

KNC Kalamazoo Nature Center

Knd Kandla

K-NEA Kansas-National Education Association

KNGR Kruger National Game Reserve

Kng X King's Cross (rail terminal)

Knick Knickerbocker

Knickerbocker Group William Cullen Bryant, James Fenimore Cooper, Washington Irving (Diedrich Knickerbocker)

Knickerbocker(s) New Yorker(s)

knickers knickerbockers

Knight of La Mancha Don Quixote

Knight of the Rueful Countenance Don Quixote

Knight of the Swan Lohengrin

KNIP *Komite Nasional Indonesia Pusat* (Indonesian Central National Committee)

KNK Kita Nippon Koku (Northern Japan Airlines)

Knls Knolls (postal abbreviation)

KNM Katmai National Monument; Kenya National Museum; Kongelige Norske Marine (Royal Norwegian Navy)

KNMI Koninkliji Nederlands Meteorologisch Instituut (Royal Netherlands Meteorological Institute)

KNMR Kenai National Moose Range (Alaska)

KNO Kano, Nigeria (tracking station)

KNOC Kuwait National Oil

Company

Knockmealdowns Knockmealdown Mountains of southern Ireland

Knopf Alfred A Knopf

knork knife + fork (combination utensil)

Knothole Christopher Morley's home in North Hills, Long Island, NY

Knott's Knott's Berry Farm

Know Nothings American Party members (anti-alien anti-Catholic party active before the Civil War, attempted to solve slavery question by denying it existed; dominated by extremist bigots of type found today in John Birch Society or Ku Klux Klan; an un-American political manifestation)

KNP Kafue National Park (Zambia); Kalahari NP (South Africa); Kalbarri NP (Western Australia); Kanha NP (India); Kejimkujik NP (Nova Scotia); Kinabalu NP (Sabah); Kinchega NP (New South Wales); Kootenay NP (British Columbia); Korean National Party; Kosciusko NP (New South Wales); Kruger NP (South Africa)

KNPC Kuwait National Petroleum Company

KNPI Kundu's Neurotic Personality Inventory

KNR Kinki Nippon Railway; Korean National Railroad

KNSM Koninklijke Nederlandsche Stoomboot Maatschappij (Royal Netherlands Steamship Company)

kn sw knife switch

Knt Knight

KNT Knight-Knott Hotels (stock-exchange symbol)

KNT *Koninklijke Nederlandsche Toeristenbond* (Dutch—Royal Netherlands Touring Club)

KNTC Korean National Tourism Corporation

knu knuckle

KNUFNS Kampuchean National United Front for National Salvation

KNUST Kwame Nkrumah University of Science and Technology

Knut Hamsun Knut Pedersen

KNVD *Koninklijk Nederlands Verbond van Drukkerijen* (Dutch—Royal Netherlands Printing Association)

KNVL Koninklijke Nederlandse Vereniging voor Luchtvaart (Royal Netherlands Aero Club)

KNWR Kirwin National Wildlife Refuge (Kansas)

KNX Kinney Company (stock-exchange symbol)

Knxv Knoxville

Knyaz *Knyaz Igor* (Russian—Prince Igor)—Borodin's uncompleted opera partly orchestrated by Glazunov and Rimsky-Korsakov

ko keep off; keep out; kilohm; kit order; knockout (KO)

k-o knockout

Ko Korea; Korean

KO kickoff (football); knockout (boxing); Kodiak Airways (2-letter coding)

KO Komische Oper (German—Comic Opera)—Berlin opera company and opera house

K o A Kampgrounds of America

KOA Kentucky Opera Association

Kob Kobe (British Maritime contraction)

Køb *København* (Dano-Norwegian—Copenhagen)

Koba Stalin's party name prior to the Bolshevik takeover of Russia

Kobarid Yugoslavian name for Caporetto

København (Danish—Merchant's Haven or Merchant's Port)—Copenhagen pronounced *Co-pen-hog-en* by the Danes

Koblenz Coblenz

kobol keystation on-line business-oriented language

KOC Kollmorgen Optical Corporation; Kuwait Oil Company

kod kickoff drift

ko'd knocked out

KODAK trade name for Eastman Kodak photographic products

Kodak City Rochester, New York

Kodamá (Japanese—Echo)—nickname of the high-speed express train linking Kyoto, Japan's ancient capital, with the port of Osaka

Kodok Sudanese name for Fàshoda

k-o drops knockout drops (chloral hydrate sedative)

koe knotted one end

kOe kiloOersted(s)

KOEX Korean Exhibition Center

kog kindly old gentleman

KOG Kansas, Oklahoma & Gulf (railroad)

KOH potassium hydroxide

KOHEMA Korean Heavy Machinery Industries

kohm kilohm

Ko-i-noor (Persian—Mountain of Light)—Nadir Shah's name for the celebrated mountain-shaped diamond

KOJ Kagoshima (airport)

Kok Cochrane

KOKS *Dul og Koks Selskab* (Danish—Coal and Coke Company)

Kol Kolonia, Ponape (Trust Territory of the Pacific)

KOLA Keep Old Los Angeles

Kolloid *Z* *Z* *Polm* *Kolloid Zeitschrift und Zeitschrift Polymere* (German—Colloidal and Polymer Periodicals)

Köln (German—Cologne)

Kol Nid *Kol Nidre* (Aramaic—all promises and vows be nullified and forgiven)—prayer recited and sung in synagogues on eve of Yom Kippur or played by 'cello and orchestra as arranged by Max Bruch

Kolyma Siberian prison-labor camps in the Soviet Arctic where to Russians Kolyma is even more terrifying a name than Auschwitz although it is the name of a river flowing from the Cherski Range to the East Siberian Sea after it passes the Kolyma goldfields

KOM Knight of the Order of Malta

Komandorskie (Russian—Commander Islands)—in the Bering Sea between the Aleutians and the peninsula of Kamchatka

Komar (Russian—Mosquito)—NATO nickname for guided-missile patrol craft used by the navies of Algeria, China, Cuba, Egypt, Indonesia, Syria, etc., as well as the USSR

Komei (Japanese—Komeito)—Buddhist party

komm *kommunal* or *kommune* or *kommunistisk* (Dano-Norwegian—communal or commune or communist)

Komp *Kompanie* (German—company)

Komsomol (Russian—Young Communist League)

Komsomolets (Russian—Young

Communists)—NATO nickname for a class of Soviet torpedo boats (P-4)

Kon Konstant; Konstantin

kona (Hawaiian-Polynesian—lee side)—side of an island out of or protected from prevailing winds

Kona Coast gold nickname for marijuana grown on the kona or lee side of any Hawaiian or Polynesian island

Kon Bel *Koninkrijk België* (Flemish—Kingdom of Belgium)

Kon Dan Kongeriget Danmark (Kingdom of Denmark)

Königgrätz (German—Hradec Kralove)

Königsberg former name for Kaliningrad

Kon Ned Koninkrijk der Nederlanden (Dutch—Kingdom of the Netherlands)

Kon Nor Kongeriket Norge (Kingdom of Norway)

Konr Konrad

KONR *Komitet Osvobozhdyeniya Narodov Rossii* (Committee for the Liberation of the Peoples of Russia)

kons *konservativ* (Dano-Norwegian—conservative)

Konst Konstantin

Konstanz (German—Constance)—a West German commune on the shores of the Bodensee

Kon Sver Konungariket Sverige (Kingdom of Sweden)

konz *konzentriert* (German—concentrated)

Kootenay Kootenay Lake or Kootenay National Park in British Columbia; Kootenay River flowing from British Columbia to Idaho and Montana

kop kopeck(s)

Kop Kopenhagen (Dutch, Flemish, German—Copenhagen)

KOP Koppers (company)

KOP *Kansallis-Osake-Pankii* (Finnish—National Bank)

kops keep off pounds sensibly

kor knowledge of results

Kor Korea; Korean; The Koran

Kör *Körfez(i)* (Turkish—bay, gulf)

KORDI Korean Ocean Research and Development Institute

Korea communist-controlled Democratic People's Republic of Korea (North Korea) and U.S.-supported Republic of

Korea (South Korea); Koreans are industrious Asiatics who speak Korean and produce a variety of crops and valuable minerals—*Chosen Minchuchui Inmin Konghwa-Guk* (North Korea) and *Daehan-Minkuk* (South Korea)

Korea Gate nickname of the exposé involving more than a million dollars in bribes given some leading American politicians in return for their voting money, military aid, and supplies for South Korea

Korean Ports North Korean—Chinnampo, Wonson, Konan-Kimchaek, Chongjin, Najin Up, Unggi; South Korean—Inchon, Kunsan, Mokpo, Yosu, Masan, Pusan

Korea Strait Tsushima Strait (scene of decisive Japanese naval victory over Russian fleet during Russo-Japanese War of 1905)

Korin Ogata Korin (early 18th-century Japanese decorative artist)

Korovograd formerly Zinov-ievsk or Elisavetgrad

KORR King's Own Royal Regiment

KORSTIC Korean Scientific and Technological Information Center

Kortrijk (Flemish—Courtrai)

kos kilograms; kilos

KOSB King's Own Scottish Borderers

Kosci Mount Kosciusko (Australia's highest mountain)

Koste André Kostelanetz

Kot Kotakinablalu

Kotabaru (Indonesian—Holandia)

Kota Kinabalu capital of Sabah and formerly called Jesselton

Kotlin NATO name for Soviet guided-missile destroyers

Kotor (Yugoslavian—Cattaro) —seaport scene of a mutiny in the Austro-Hungarian navy during World War I

KOTRA Korea Trade Promotion Corporation

Koussi Serge Koussevitzky

kov key-operated valve

Kovno (Russian—Kaunas, Lithuania)

Kow *Koweit* (Spanish Kuwait)

KOWACO Korean Water Resources Development Corporation

Kowloon (Chinese—Nine Dragons)—mainland peninsular

section of Hong Kong

KOYLI King's Own Yorkshire Light Infantry

kp key personnel; kick plate; kill probability; kilopond; king post; kitchen police (KP); knotty pine

kp (KP) keypunch

Kp *Kochpunkt* (German—boiling point

KP Korean People's (Republic)

K.P. Knight of St Patrick

K of P King(dom) of Poland; King(dom) of Portugal; King(dom) of Prussia; Knights of Pythias

KP *Kommunistische Partei* (German—Communist Party); *Komsomolskaya Pravda* (Russian—Young Communist League Truth)—Moscow newspaper claiming circulation of three million; *Kuvendi Popullore* (Albanian People's Assembly)

kPa kilopascal (pressure unit)

KPA Korean People's Army; Kraft Paper Association

kpc keypunch cabinet; kiloparsec

KPC Kangaroo Protection Committee; Koblenz Procurement Center; Korean Productivity Council

kp & d kick plate and drip

KPD Kommunistische Partei Deutschland (Communist Party of Germany)

KPDR Korean People's Democratic Republic

KPFC Kuwait Pacific Finance Company

KPFSM King's Police and Fire Service Medal

KPGA Kansas Personnel and Guidance Association; Kentucky Personnel and Guidance Association

kph kilometers per hour; knots per hour

kpi kips per inch

kpic key phrase in context

kpl kilometers per liter

KPL Knoxville Public Library

kpm kathode pulse modulation

KPM King's Police Medal

KPM *Koninklijke Paketvaart Maatschappij* (Dutch—Royal Packet Company)—inter-island shipping line

Kpmtr *Kapellmeister* (German —conductor)

KPNO Kitt Peak National Observatory

KPNWR Kern-Pixley National Wildlife Refuge (California)

kpo keypunch operator

KPO Korean Post Office

kpos keep pounds off sensibly (scientific weight-reduction program)

KPP Keeper of the Privy Purse

kpps kilopulses per second

kpr keeper; knots per revolution

Kpr Kodak photo resist

KPR Korean Presidential Ribbon

KPRA Korean People's Revolutionary Army (communist North Korea)

kps kips (thousand pounds) per square foot

kpsi kips (thousand pounds) per square inch

KPSS *Kommunisticheskaya Partiya Sovetskovo Soyuza* (Russian—Communist Party of the Soviet Union)—CPSU

Kpt Kaptajn (Danish—captain)

KPU Kenya People's Union (party)

kq line squall

kr kool ridor; kiloroentgen

Kr krypton

KR King's Regulations; Korean Registry (of ships); krona (Icelandic or Swedish monetary unit); krone (Danish or Norwegian monetary unit)

krad kilorad

Krag Krag-Jörgensen rifle

Kraguj Yugoslav counterinsurgency aircraft

Krak Krakatoa, Indonesia

krakers (Dutch—crackers)—squatters who crack into vacant buildings

Krakow Cracow

Krasnaya Ploschad (Russian—Red Square)

K-ration Calorie ration (lightweight emergency meal)

Kraut(s) Anglo-American slang for German(s)

K-R bb Krebs-Ringer bicarbonate buffer

KRC Knight of the Red Cross

KREEP K (potassium) REE (rare-earth elements) P (phosphate)—yellow brown glassy lunar material

kreml (Russian—fortress)—the Moscow Kremlin, a mighty citadel and seat of Soviet government

Kremlin seat of Soviet Government in Moscow

Kremlin Killer Josef Stalin

Kresta NATO name for Soviet

guided-missile destroyer-leader warships

Kresty Leningrad's central prison

Krete Crete

Kreutzer Beethoven's Sonata in A minor (opus 47) for violin and piano; dedicated to his friend the violinist Rudolphe Kreutzer

Kreuzb Kreuzberg

KRF Kentucky Research Foundation

Krh Karachi

KRI Kyle Railway Inc

KRIC Korean Reinsurance Company

Kriegies Kriegsgefangenen (German—war prisoners)

KRIM not an acronym but the invented name for the Danish association for penal reform

Kringleville Racine, Wisconsin

Kripo Kriminalpolizei (German—Criminal Investigation Department)

Krishaber's disease dizzy-and-sleepy neurosis accompanied by fainting

Kriss Kringle Santa Claus

Krist Kristian; Kristijonas; Kristmann; Kristofer

Kristallnacht (German—Night of Broken Glass)—nights of November 8th, 9th, and 10th in 1938 when Nazi mobs broke the windows and smashed the doors of German-Jewish stores and temples before looting them, burning them, and sending their inhabitants to concentration camps

Kristiania Oslo's previous name

Kristiinankaupunki (Finnish—Kristinestad)

Kriti (Greek—Crete)—island in the Aegean

KROM not an acronym but the contrived name for the Norwegian association for penal reform

Kronos (Greek—Saturn)—god of time

Kronstadt NATO nickname for Soviet subchasers (name refers to Russian naval base near Leningrad but dating from czarist times)

krp key resource people

KRR King's Royal Rifles

krs Korus (Turkish—piastre)

Krs Kristiansand

KRs (see CRs)

KRS Kinematograph Renters Society

KRSB Kindergarten Reading Screening Battery

krt cathode-ray tube

KRT Khartoum, Sudan (airport)

KRU Krueger Brewing (stock-exchange symbol)

Kruger Kruger National Park (South Africa's big game and wildlife reservation named for Oom Paul Kruger, the President of the Transvaal)

KRUM not an acronym but a made-up word standing for the Swedish association for penal reform

Krung Kao Ayutthaya, Thailand

Krungthep Krungthep Mahanakhon Bovorn Ratanakosin Mahintharayutthaya Mahadilokpop Noparatratchanthani Burirom Udomratchanivetmahasathan Amornpiman Avatarnsathit Sakkathattiya-visnukarmprasit (full name of the capital city of Bangkok, Thailand formerly Siam)

Krung Thep (Siamese—Bangkok)

Krupny NATO name for a Soviet class of destroyers

Krupp Krupp von Bohlen (German armament and steel firm)

Krupskaya Nadezhda Konstantinovna Krupskaya Lenin

Krym (Russian—Crimea)

ks drifting snowstorm (symbol); keep (type) standing; knowledge structure(s)

k's kilobytes; kilometers; kilos; kilowatts; New Zealand slang for kilometers per hour (pronounced kays)

Ks Kaposi's sarcoma (lesions growing in the gastrointestinal tract, in organs, or on the skin); kyats (Burmese money)

K-s King-size (doughnuts, frankfurters, hamburgers, steaks, etc.)

KS King's Scholar; King's School; Kipling Society; Konungariket Sverige (Kingdom of Sweden); Korea Shipping

K of S King(dom) of Scotland; King(dom) of Siam (Thailand); King(dom) of Spain; King(dom) of Sweden

ksa kite-supported antenna

KSA Kingdom of Saudi Arabia

KSA Kommission für die Sicherheit von Atomlagen (German—Commission for the Safety of Nuclear Power Plants)

KSAA Keats-Shelley Association of America

KSB Kypriakos Synthesmos Bibliothicarion (Modern Greek—Library Association of Cyprus)

KSBA Kentucky School Boards Association

KSC Kansas State College; Kennedy Space Center; Kentucky State College; Korean Shipping Corporation; Kutztown State College

KSC Komunisticka Strana Ceskoslovenska (Communist Party of Czechoslovakia)

KSEAFA Korea and South-East Asia Forces Association

KSEC Korea Shipbuilding and Engineering Corporation

ksf kips (thousand pounds) per square foot

KSF Kulkyne State Forest (Victoria, Australia)

KSFUS Korean Student Federation of the United States

KSG Kennedy School of Government

K.S.G. Knight of Saint Gregory the Great

K sh Kenya shilling(s)

ksi kips (1000 pounds) per square inch

KSI Keshvare Shahanshahiye Iran (Iran—Persia); Kingdom of Saudi Arabia

ksia thousand square inches absolute

K-size King-size

k/sk (truncated fixed) keel (and) swing keel (combined)

KSK ethyl iodoacetate (tear gas)

ksl kidney, spleen, liver

KSL Kinsel Drug (stock-exchange symbol)

KSLI King's Shropshire Light Infantry

KSM King's Service Medal; Korean Service Medal; Kungliga Svenska Marinen (Royal Swedish Navy)

KSM Kommunisticheskii Soyuz Molodozhi (Russian—All-Union League of Communist Youth)—Komsomol or Young Communist League—YCL

ksml kosher meal

KSN Kit Shortage Notice

KSNP Khao Salob National Park (Thailand)

KSO Kalamazoo Symphony Orchestra; Knoxville Symphony Orchestra

ksoc key symbol out of context

ksr keyboard send-receive (set)

K.S.S. Knight of Saint Sylvester

KSS *Kommission zur Stahlenschutz* (German—Radiation Protection Commission); *Komunisticka Strana Slovenska* (Communist Party of Slovakia)

KSSR Kazak Soviet Socialist Republic; Kirghizian Soviet Socialist Republic

KSSU Kiev IG Shevchenko State University (University of Kiev)

kst keyseat

KST King-Seeley Thermos (company)

KSTC Kansas State Teachers College

K-S Test Kveim-Siltzbach Test

K.St.J. Knight of the Order of Saint John of Jerusalem

ksu key service unit

KSU Kansas State University; Kent State University

KSUAAS Kansas State University of Agriculture and Applied Science

ksv kinetic safety vehicle

KSY King Seeley (stock-exchange symbol)

kt karet (caret); key telephone; kiloton (nuclear equivalent, 1000 tons of high explosives); knot

Kt Knight

K_t stress concentration factor

KT Kärntnerthor Theater (Vienna); Kentucky & Tennessee (railway); Knight of the Order of the Thistle; Knight Templar; Missouri-Kansas-Texas (Katy Route Railroad)

K-T Kazin-Turkic

K.T. Knight of the Thistle

K of T Kingdom of Tonga

KTA Kindergarten Teachers Association; Knitted Textile Association; Korean Traders Association

KTAAK Korea Trading Agents Association

ktas knots true airspeed

Ktb *Kriegstagebuch* (German—war diary)

KTB Kluwer Technical Books

Kt. Bach. Knight Bachelor

KTC Key Telephone System; Keystone Tankship Corporation; Kindergarten Teachers College; Kodiak Tracking Station

KTH Kungliga Tekniska Högskolan (Royal Institute of

Technology, Stockholm)

k through 12 kindergarten through high school

ktl *kai ta loipa* (Greek—et cetera)

KTM *Keretapi Tanah Melayu* (Malayan Railway)

KTN Ketchikan, Alaska (Annette Island airport)

Kto *Konto* (German—account)

ktr keyboard typing reperforator

Ktr *Katorzhane* (Russian—compound)—prison compound reserved for people sentenced to hard labor

K-truss K-shaped truss

kts knots

KTS Kagoshima Television Station; Key Telephone Systems; Kwajalein Test Site

KTSA Kahn Test of Symbol Arrangement

KTTC Kingston-upon-Thames Technical College

ktu kill the umpire

KTX Keith Railway Equipment (railway code)

Ku Karmen unit(s)

Kü *Küçk* (Turkish—little, small)

KU Kalmar Union; Kansas University; Keio University; Kuwait Airways (2-letter symbol)

KU *Københavns Universitet* (Danish—Copenhagen University)

Kuala Lumpur (Malay—Muddy Estuary) capital city of Malaysia

Kuang-chou (Cantonese Chinese—Canton)

kub kidney(s)-ureter(s)-bladder

Kubyshka (Russian nickname for Cuba)—a kubyshka is a jar wherein Russian peasants bury their money—Kubachka (Little Cuba) has a similar sound to Soviet taxpayers forced to support Castroite parasites

ku'd knocked up (made pregnant)

KUD *Koperasi Unit Desa* (Indonesian—Village Cooperative Unit)

Ku'dam Kurfürstendamm (main street of West Berlin)

KUED Kodak's Unitized Engineering Drawing (system)

K u H Kingston upon Hull (official name for Hull)

Kuibyshev Soviet name for Samara

KUK Kollege of Universal

Knowledge

KUL Kabul University Library (Kabul, Afghanistan); Karachi University Library (Pakistan); Kyoto University Library (Japan)

Kun Kunsan

Kung-fu-tse (Chinese— Reverend Master King)—Confucius

Kungsholm (Swedish—Island of the King)

K unit Kimball unit

Kunluns Kunlun Mountains of Tibet

Kur (British maritime contraction of Kure); Kurile Islands

Kurfürstendamm Berlin's elegant avenue

Kuria Murias Kuria Muria Islands in the Arabian Sea

Kuril Cur Kurile Current (Oyashio)

Kuriles Kurile Islands in the northwest Pacific

Kurilskiye Ostrova (Russian—Kurile Islands)

Kurir Yugoslav liaison-utility aircraft

Kurland Courland

Kuro *Kuroshio* (Japanese—Black Salt)—warm ocean current of the North Pacific Ocean

Kuroshio (Japanese—Black Stream)—Japan Current carrying blue-black warm waters across the Pacific from Japan to the Aleutians and the west coast of Canada and the United States

KURRI Kyoto University Research Reactor Institute

Ku's Karmen units

Kutchka *Mogutchaya Kutchka* (Russian—Mighty Handful) —Balakirev, Borodin, Cui, Mussorgsky, and Rimsky Korsakov

kutd keep up to date

KUU Kungliga Universitet i Uppsala (Royal University of Uppsala)

Kuw Kuwait

Kuwait State of Kuwait (Persian Gulf gas-and-oil producer, Arabic-speaking Kuwaitis also raise cattle and sheep in a country of extreme aridity and terrible heat) *Dowlat al Kuwait*

Kuwait Ports Mina abd Allah, Ash Shuaiba, Mina al Ahmadi, Abu Hulafah, Al Kuwayt

Kuyb Kuybyshev

kv kilovolt

kv *kvinde* (Dano-Norwegian—

woman)
kV kilovolt; kV/s
KV Köchel-Verzeichnis (German—Kochel Catalog)— catalog of Mozart's compositions with a K number assigned to each one
KV-107 Japanese-made Sea-Knight-type helicopter built by Kawasaki
kva kilovolt ampere
kVA kilovolt(s)/ampere
KVA Korean Veterans Association; Kungliga Vetenskaps Akademien (Royal Swedish Academy of Sciences)
kvah kilovolt-ampere-hour
kvam kilovolt ampere meter
Kvan Elektron Kvantovaya Elektronika (Russian—Journal of Quantum Electronics)
kvar kilovar; kilovolt ampere reactive
kvarh kilovar hour
kvcp kilovolt constant potential
K-Vets Korean War Veterans of the United States
kvg keyed video generator
KVHS Kanawha Valley Historical Society
KvK Kill van Kull
KVL Kirchoff's Voltage Law
kvm kilovolt meter
KVNP Kidepo Valley National Park (Uganda)
kvp kilovolt peak
KVP Katholieke Volkspartij (Dutch—Catholic People's Party)
KVW Kansas City Kaw Valley (railroad)
kw killer weed (pcp sprinkled on leaves and smoked); kilowatt
kw Zambian kwacha(s)—monetary unit(s)
kW kilowatt(s)
KW Kellogg West; Key West; King-Wilkinson
K-W Keith-Wagener
kwac key word and context
K-W AG Kitchener-Waterloo Art Gallery
Kwaj Kwajalein

Kwan Kwantung
Kwangchow (Cantonese Chinese —Canton)
kwat key well allowable transfer
KWB Keith, Wagener, Barker (classification)
KWC Kentucky Wesleyan College
kwe kilowatts electrical
KWest Key West
K-W findings Keith-Wagener (ophthalmoscopic findings)
kwh kilowatt hour
kWh kilowatt hour
kwhr kilowatt hour
Kwi Kuwait
kwic key word in context
kwip keyword in permutation
kwit key word in text; key word in title
kwm kilowatt meter
KWMA Kirtland's Warbler Management Areas (Michigan)
KWNWR Key West National Wildlife Refuge (Florida)
kwoc key word out of context
Kwok's disease Chinese restaurant syndrome produced by monosodium glutamate and resulting in dizziness, headaches, and nausea
kwot key word out of title
KWP Korean Workers Party
KWPL Kitchener–Waterloo Public Library
kwr kilowatts reactive
KWS Kaziranga Wildlife Sanctuary (India)
KWSM Korean War Service Medal
kwt key word in title; kilowatts thermal
Kwt Kuwait
KWT King William's Town
KWU Kansas Wesleyan University
kwuc keyword and universal decimal classification
KWVZAB Ko-operative Wijnbouwers Vereeninging van Zuid Afrika Beperkt (Dutch—

Cooperative Wine Farmers Association of South Africa, Limited)
kwy keyway
kxu kilo-x-unit
ky cocoa; key; keyer; keying (device); kyat
Ky Kentuckian; Kentucky
KY Kentucky (zip code) Kol Yisrael (Israel Broadcasting Service); (underground slang —federal hospital in Lexington, Kentucky where drug addicts are treated)
kybd keyboard
kybo keep your bowels open (keep healthy)
KYC Klan Youth Corps; Knickerbocker Yacht Club
kyd Kilo yard
kyeri know your endorsers—require identification (advice to all who cash checks)
Kyle Kyle Railway
kymo kymograph; kymography
Kynda NATO nickname for a Soviet class of heavily-armed destroyers
KYNP Khao Yai National Park (Thailand)
Kyo Kyoto
Kyocera Kyoto Ceramics
Kyoto (Japanese—Capital City) —capital of Japan for 1066 years and art shrine of the nation
Kyot Univ Kyoto University
Kypriake (Greek—Cyprus)
Kypros Cyprus
Kyr. Kyrie eleison (Greek— Lord, have mercy upon us)
kytoon kite balloon
kz duststorm or sandstorm
kz konzentrations (Dano-Norwegian—concentration camp)
Kz Kazakh(stan)
KZ Konzentrationslager (German—concentration camp)
Kz's unlicensed citizen's-band radio-interference jammers
K z S Kapitan zur See (German —Sea Captain)—naval rating

L

l azimuthal or orbital quantum number (symbol); elbow (plumbing); land; large; late; latent heat per unit mass (symbol); lateral; latitude; law; leaf; league; left or port (L or P); length; levorotatory; liaison; light(ning); lignite; line; link; lire; liter; locus; low; lumen

l/ *letra* (Spanish—letter)

l* lumen

l lectio (Latin—reading); units of labor (microeconomics)

L Bell Aircraft (symbol); center line (symbol); elevated railroad (EL); inductance (symbol); kinetic potential (symbol); Labor; Labour; lactobacillus; lago; Lagrange function; lake; lake vessel; Lamar State College of Technology; lambert; langmuir; Latin; launching; law (the police, task force, vice squad, etc.), left (port side); lempira (Honduran currency unit); Leo; Leon; Liberal; lift (symbol); lift force; light; Lima—code for L; Linnaeus; Lions International; loch; London; longitude; loran; Lorentz unit; lough; Luckenbach Lines; Luxembourgh (auto plaque); Lykes Lines; rolling moment (symbol)

L (*L*) demand for money (macroeconomics symbol)

L lähteä (Finnish—departure); *lämmin* (Finnish—warm); *länsi* (Finnish—wheat); (Latin—Lucius); *laudes* (Latin—praises); *levato* (Italian—raised); *libra* (Latin—pound); *Life Magazine*; *links* (German—left); *llegada* (Spanish—arrival)

L-1 first language

l₁ first lumbar vertebra

l₂ second lumbar vertebra

L-2 second language

l/3 lower third

l₃ third lumbar vertebra

L-3 lousy trio

L-4 military version of the Piper Cub

l₄, l₅, etc. fourth lumbar vertebra; fifth lumbar verterbra

L7 Hollywood slang for old-fashioned person or *square* as capital-letter L and figure 7 may be combined to form a square

L-19 Cessna Bird Dog liaison aircraft

L-100 Lockheed four-engine transport aircraft for civilian use

L-188 Lockheed Electra turbo-prop transport plane

L-1011 Lockheed's jumbo jetliner

la landing account; large aperture(s); lava; lead antimony; leave allowance; left angle; left atrium; left auricle; light alloy; light amphibian; lighter than air; lightning arrestor; long-acting; low alcohol; low altitude

la (LA) linoleic acid; longitudinal acoustic

l/a landing account; letter of advice; letter of authority; lighter than air

l & a left and above; light and accommodation

la A in fixed-do system; (Italian—the); sixth tone in diatonic scale

l.a. lege artis (Latin—according to the art)—as directed

l/a lettre d'avis (French—letter of advice)

La Lane; lanthanum; Lao; Laos; Laotian; Louisiana; Louisianian

La Lebensalter (German—chronological age); *Luisiana* (Spanish—Louisiana)

LA Latin America(n); Leasehold Area; Legal Advisor; Legislative Assembly; Leschetizky Association; Letter of Activation; Library Association; License Application; Licensing Act; Licensing Authority; Lieutenant-at-Arms; light-alcohol beer brewed by Anheuser-Busch with the taste of beer but with half the alcohol content of regular beer; Local Authority; Los Angeles; Louisiana & Arkansas (railroad); Louvain Association; Lower Alabama (jocular place-name)

L-A Loire-Atlantique (formerly Loire-Inférieure)

L/A Launch Area; Lloyd's Agent

L & A Louisiana & Arkansas (railroad)

LA Linea Aèria de Chile (Spanish—Air Line of Chile)

LA 400 400 women of Los Angeles who raised 4 million dollars for its music center

laa light anti-aircraft

LAA League of Advertising Agencies; Library Association of Australia; Life Assurance Advertisers; Los Angeles Airways

LAACC Light Antiaircraft Control Center

LAAD Latin America Agribusiness Development

LAADS Los Angeles Air Defense Sector

LAAF Libyan Arab Air Force

LAAG Latin American Anthropology Group

laam (LAAM) levo-alpha acetylmethadol (alternative to methadone for treatment of drug addiction)

laar liquid-air accumulator rocket

La Argentina Antonia Mercé

LAAS Los Angeles Air Service

La Aurora (Spanish—The Dawn)—Guatemala City's airport

lab label; labeling; labor; laboratory

Lab Laboratory; Labour(ite); Labrador

LAB Labor; Labour; Labour Party; Licquor [*sic.*] Administration Board; Liquor Administration Board; Lloyd Aereo Boliviano (Bolivian airline); low-altitude bombing

LAB Lloyd Aéreo Boliviano (Spanish—Bolivian Air Lines)

LABA Laboratory Animal Breeders Association

LABAN Lakasang Bayan (Pilipino—Peoples Power)

Lab Cur Labrador Current—cold Arctic current flowing southward along Atlantic coast of Canada and northern New England

Labe (Czechoslovakian—Elbe)

La Belle Époque (French—The Beautiful Epoch)—1900 to 1914 (turn of the century to the start of the first world war)

La Belle Province (French—the beautiful Province)—Québec

La Belle Rivière (French—The Beautiful River)— frontier nickname of the Ohio in the days of Audubon and Boone

LABEN Laboratori Elettronici e Nucleari (Electronic and Nuclear Laboratories—Milan)

labe(s) label(s)

labi (Latin prefix—lip)—labial

La Bonne Louise Louise Michel remembered for her good works among the poor people of Paris

Labor US Department of Labor

Labor Boss Samuel Gompers, John L Lewis, and George Meany have been so named

Labor Day first Monday in September in the U.S.A.

Laborers' Union Laborers' International Union of North America

lab proc laboratory procedure(s)

labrador label-address routine

Labrador Canadian version of Boeing-Vertol CH-113 helicopter; Labrador Current; Labrador duck; Labrador jay; Labrador Peninsula; Labrador pine; Labrador retriever; Labrador Sea; Labrador spar; Labrador stone (another name for Labrador spar); Labrador tea

labrv (LABRV) large ballistic reentry vehicle

labs laboratories

Lab(s) Labrador retriever(s)

LABS Low-Altitude Bombing System

labv (LABV) large ballistic (reentry) vehicle

lac lacquer; lacrimal; lactation; large-aperture component(s); linear amplitude continuous; lunar aeronautical chart; shellac

lac (LAC) load accumulator

Lac Lacerta; Lacertilia

LAC Laboratory Animals Center; Leading Aircraftsman; League of Arab Countries; Liberty Amendment Committee; Library Association of China; Lockheed Aircraft Corporation

LAC Lineas Aéreas Chaqueñas (Spanish—Aero Chaco)

LACA Latin American Coffee Agreement

La Cabaña (Spanish—The Cabin, The Cottage)—Cuban fortress-prison at the entrance of Havana harbor

LACAC Latin American Civil Aviation Commission

LACAP Latin American Cooperative Acquisitions Project

La Casa Grande (Spanish—The Big House)—William Randolph Hearst's art museum, mansions, and wildlife gardens in San Simeon, California

LACATA Laundry and Cleaners Allied Trades Association

lacc lathe chuck

LACC Los Angeles City College

Laccadives short form for the Laccadive Islands in the Arabian Sea off India's west coast

LACE liquid-air cycle engine

lacertiliol lacertiliologic(al)(ly); lacertiliologist; lacertiliology

LACES London Airport Cargo Electronic Scheme; Los Angeles Council of Engineering Societies

La Chasse Haydn's Quartet in B flat (opus 1, no. 1); Haydn's Symphony No. 73 in D major (The Hunt)

Lachie Lachlan

La Chute de Niagara (French—Niagara Falls)

LACIE Large Area Crop Inventory Experiment

LACIRS Latin American Communication Information Retrieval System

LACJ Los Angeles County Jail

LACL Latin American Citizens League

Lac Leman French equivalent of the Lake of Geneva

LACM Latin American Common Market; Los Angeles County Museum

LACMA Los Angeles Conservatory of Music and Arts; Los Angeles County Museum of Art

LACMedA Los Angeles County Medical Association

LACO Los Angeles Chamber Orchestra

LA Co Art Mus Los Angeles County Art Museum

La Columna (Spanish—The Column)—Venezuela's highest mountain also called Pico Bolívar

laconiq laboratory computer on-line inquiry

La Coruña (Spanish—Corunna)

Lacp Lloyd's anchors and chains proved

LACP London Association of Correctors of the Press

lacr low-altitude coverage radar

lacri (Latin prefix—tears)—lacrimose

Lacrosse USA field artillery MGM-18A surface-to-surface missile

LACSA Líneas Aéreas Costarricenses (Costa Rican Airlines)

lact lease automatic custody transfer

lactns lactations

lacto-ovo(s) lacto-ovo vegetarian(s) (confining diet to milk, milk products, eggs, and vegetables)

La Cumbre (Spanish—The Summit)—nickname of the Uspallata mountain pass and tunnel in the high Andes linking Argentina and Chile

Lacus Asphaltites (Latin—Asphalt Sea)—the Dead Sea between Israel and Jordan

lacv (LACV) light-amphibious air-cushion vehicle

LACW Leading Aircraftswoman

lad. ladder; liquid agent detector; logarithmic analog-to-digital; logistic approval data; lunar atmosphere detector

lad. (LAD) language-acquisition device

Lad Ladino

Lad (Spanish dialect spoken by many persons of Judaic origin who were forced to flee from their Spanish homeland during the Inquisition when they emigrated to places around the Mediterranean ranging from Algeria and Morocco to Greece and Turkey)

LAD Library Administration Division (American Library Association); Light Air Detachment

La Damnation de Faust (French —The Damnation of Faust)— four-part dramatic legend composed by Berlioz

ladar laser detection and ranging

ladd low-altitude drogue delivery

ladder. life-assurance direct entry and retrieval

LADE Lineas Aereas del Estado (State Airlines, Argentina)

LADECO Linea Aereo del Cobre (Spanish—Copper Air Line)

LADIES Life After Divorce Is Eventually Sane (Hollywood ex-wife group); Los Alamos Digital-Image-Enhancement Software

Ladies' Garment Workers International Ladies' Garment Workers Union

Ladies Home J Ladies Home Journal

ladir low-cost arrays for detection of infrared

LADO Latin American Defense Organization; Latin American Development Organization

Ladoga Lake Ladoga east of Leningrad and called Ladoshskoye Ozero by the Russians

Ladozhskoye Ozero (Russian— Lake Ladoga)

ladp ladyship

Ladrones Marianas Islands

Lad(s) Ladino(s)—Europeanized Central American mestizo(s) of Spanish descent; their

Judeo-Spanish dialect developed around the Mediterranean from Morocco to the Balkans, Greece, and Turkey by refugees from the Holy Inquisition (1487 to 1834), when Jews were driven from their homes and were called Ladinos wherever they settled and developed their dialect of medieval Castilian augmented by Arabic, Hebrew, and Turkish terms (also called Judeo-Spanish, Spagnuolo, or Spanish Yiddish)

LADSIRLAC Liverpool and District Scientific, Industrial, and Research Library Advisory Council

L Adv Lord Advocate

LADWP Los Angeles Department of Water and Power

Lady of 57th Street New York City's Carnegie Hall

Lady Bird Mrs Claudia Alta Taylor Johnson—wife of President Lyndon Johnson

Lady Hamilton Emma Lyon

Lady of the Lamp Nurse Florence Nightingale

Lady of Laughter Erma Bombeck

Lady Macbeth Lady Macbeth of *the Mtsensk District* (Shostakovich opera known to Russians as *Katerina Izmaylova*)

Lady Snow cocaine

Lady South Charleston, South Carolina

Lady's Slipper Minnesota state flower

Lady with a Lamp Santa Filomena (immortalized by Longfellow)

Lady With Lamp Statue of Liberty officially named Liberty Enlightening the World

LAE Leadership Ability Evaluation

laetrile laevo-mandelonitrile-beta-glucuronic acid

laev. laevus (Latin—left)

laf laminar air flow

Laf Lafayette

LaF Louisiana French

LAF L'Académie Française (The French Academy); Living Arts Foundation

Lafayette Marie Joseph Paul Yves Roch Gilbert du Motier (Marquis de Lafayette)

Lafayette East Detroit, Michigan's street of streetwalkers

LAFB Lincoln Air Force Base

LAFC Latin-American Forestry Commission

Lafe Lafayette

LAFE Laboratorio de Fisica Espacial (Portuguese—Space Physics Laboratory)

Lafitte Country Baratraria Bay (an old pirate settlement south of New Orleans)

La Font La Fontaine

LAFS Los Angeles Funeral Society

LAFTA Latin American Free Trade Area; Latin American Free Trade Association

lafv (LAFV) light-armored fighting vehicle

lag. lagan

lag. lagena (Latin—bottle, flask)

Lag Lagoon; Laguna

La G La Guaira

LAG Layton Art Gallery; Librarians Automation Group

LAGB Linguistics Association of Great Britain

LAGE Los Angeles Grain Exchange

LAGEOS Laser Geodetic Satellite

LAGIC Life and General Insurance Committee

La Gioconda (Italian—The Cheerful Woman)—another name for Leonardo da Vinci's portrait—the Mona Lisa

lags. (LAGS) laser-activated geodetic satellite

Lags Lagunas

LAGS Los Angeles Geographic Society

Lagunas Laguna Mountains of California

La Guyane Française French Guiana

Lah Lahore

LAII Licentiate Apothecaries Hall

La Habana (Spanish—The Habana)—Havana, Cuba

La Haia (Portuguese—The Hague)

LAHAWS Laser Homing and Warning System

La Haya (Spanish—The Hague)

La Haye (French—The Hague)

LAHC Los Angeles Harbor College; Los Angeles Harbor Commission

LAHD Los Angeles Harbor Department

lahs low-altitude high speed

LAHS Local Authority Health Services

lai leaf area index

LAI Library Association of Ireland

LAI *Linee Aeree Italiane* (Italian Air Lines)

l'Aia (Italian—The Hague)

LAIA Latin American Integration Association

LAIC Lithuanian-American Information Center

LAIICS Latin American Institute for Information and Computer Sciences

LAINS Low-Altitude Inertial Navigation System

Laird of Auchinleck James Boswell

Laird of Skibo Castle Andrew Carnegie

Laird of Woodchuck Lodge John Burroughs

LAIRS Labor Agreement Information Retrieval System

LAIS Loan Accounting Information System (AID)

LAIT Logistics Assistance and Instruction Team

LAIV Loss Adjusters Institute of Victoria

La J La Jolla

LAJ Los Angeles Junction (railroad)

Lake City Madison, Wisconsin

Lake of the Four Forest Cantons Lake Lucerne (Switzerland)

Lake Poets Samuel Taylor Coleridge, Robert Southey, William Wordsworth

Lake State Michigan bordering on Superior, Michigan, Huron, and Erie

laks *lakrids* (Danish—licorice)

Laksha Divi (Sanskrit—Hundred Thousand Isles)—the Laccadives

LAL Langley Aeronautical Laboratory (Langley Research Center)

LA-LB Los Angeles-Long Beach (ports)

La Leche La Leche League International

l'Algérie (French—Algeria)

lali lonely aged of low income

Lalia Eulalia

La Lollo Gina Lollobrigida

La Louisiane (French—Louisiana)

lalsd language for automated logic and system design

LALUCS Local Authority Land Use Classification System

lam laminate

lam (LAM) load accumulator with magnitude

Lam The Book of Lamentations; Lamarck; Lambretta

Lam *Lamentations*

LAM Lamarck; Lambert; Latin

American Mission; London Academy of Music

L.A.M. *Liberalium Artium Magister* (Latin—Master of Liberal Arts)

Lama Aerospatiale observation helicopter built in France and designated SA-315

LAMA Latin American Manufacturers Association; Lead Air Materiel Area; Library Administration and Management Association

La Manche (French—The Neck)—the English Channel

Lamb Lambert; Lamberto; Lambertus; Lambeth

LAMBC Los Angeles Motor Boat Club

Lamb of God Jesus Christ

lambsan lamb sandwich

lambwich lamb sandwich

LAMC Letterman Army Medical Center; Los Angeles Metropolitan College; Los Angeles Music Center

LAMCO Liberian-American-Swedish Mineral Corporation

LAMDA London Academy of Music and Dramatic Art

LAME Licensed Aircraft Maintenance Engineer

Lamentatione Haydn's Symphony No. 26 in D minor also called the *Christmas Symphony*

La Mer du Nord (French—The North Sea)

La Mesa *La Mesa Penitenciaria* (Baja California's major prison located on the Caliente road east of Tijuana)

La Messa deliberate misspelling of La Mesa used or uttered by its detractors

Lamia P L Tyraud de Vosjoli (French underground fighter and chief of intelligence)

LAMM Los Angeles Master Morticians; Lutheran-American Melancthon Movement

lamma laser microprobe mass analyser

Lamp Lampeter

LAMP Library Additions and Maintenance Program; Low-Altitude Manned Penetration; Lunar Analysis and Mapping Program

Lamp of Heaven the Moon

LAMPP Los Alamos Molten Plutonium Program (AEC)

LAMPS Light Airborne Multipurpose System

LAMS Launch Acoustic Measuring System

LAMSACC Local Authorities Management Services and Computer Committee

lamsim launcher-and-missile simulator

Lan Lancaster; Lansing

L An Los Angeles

LAN Línea Aérea Nacional de Chile; Local Apparent Noon; Local Area Network

LAN *Latin American Newspapers* (bibliographic reference)

lanac laminair air navigation and anti-collision

Lanarks Lanarkshire

Lana Turner Julia Jean Turner

Lan Bag Lansing Bagnall

Lanc Lancaster

Lance Lancelot; Ling-Temco-Vought MGM-52A surface-to-surface tactical missile

Lance Cpl Lance Corporal

Lancs Lancashire

land. landscaping

Land of 10,000 Lakes Minnesota's nickname

Land of Acadie (*see* Land of Evangeline)

Land of Albert Schweitzer Gabon

Land of Alligators Florida

Land of a Million Elephants Laos

Land of Art and Mozart Austria

Land of the Aztecs México

Land Between the Rivers Mesopotamia better known as Iraq

Land of the Bible Israel

Land of Birds Australia

Land of the Blacks Guinea and the Sudan have long held the name

Land of Bondage Egypt in the time of Moses

Land of the Bulgars Bulgaria

Land of Caimans swamplands of tropical America contain these crocodilians

Land of the Cedars Lebanon

LandCent Allied Land Forces, Central Europe

Land of Cheese, Trees, and Ocean Breeze Tillamook, Oregon

Land of the Cherryblossoms Japan

Land of Chopin and Copernicus Poland

Land of Clear Light the American Southwest and the Mexican Northwest (*La Tierra de Luz Clara*)

Land of the Conquistadors Extremadura, Spain where Cortez and Pizarro were born

Land of the Cornstalk Australia

LandCraB landing craft and bases

Land of the Croats Croatian Yugoslavia

Land of Crocodiles Africa and Southeast Asia appear to compete for the sobriquet

Land of the Czars and the Commisars Russia—the USSR

Land of Death and Chains Maxim Gorki's nickname for Siberia

Land of Desolation Antarctica and Greenland are leading contestants for this nickname

Land Down Under Australia and New Zealand

Land of Dvořák and Smetana Czechoslovakia

Land of the Eagle Albania

Land of Emeralds Colombia

Land of Enchantment New Mexico's official nickname

Land of Eternal Spring Guatemala

Land of Evangeline Maine east of the Kennebec River, New Brunswick, and Nova Scotia as well as Louisiana's coastal parishes

Land of Farmers and Fishermen Denmark

Land of Five Peoples Surinam, formerly Dutch or Netherlands Guiana, containing black, brown, red, white, and yellow people from Africa, Indonesia, South America, Europe, and the Orient, respectively

Land of the Fjords Norway

Land of Flaming Waters Malawi

Land of Flowers Florida

Land of the Free United States of America

Land of Freedom Liberia

Land of the Gaucho Uruguay

Land of Gavials India and Malaysia contain elongated-and-thin-snouted crocodilians

Land of Genghis Khan Mongolia

Land of Gitche Gumee Lake Superior as described by Longfellow

Land God Gave Cain Arctic Canada

Land of the Golden Lion Iran

Land of Grass Roots South Dakota

Land of Greek, Roman, and Modern Ruins Lebanon

Land of the Happy Medium Costa Rica

Land of the Heather Scotland

Land of Heroes Finland

Land of Hope and Glory Great Britain

Land of Hope and Glory Elgar's *Pomp and Circumstance, March No. 1*

Land of Hospitality Somalia

Land of Hospitality and Charm Thailand

Land of Ice and Fire Iceland

Land of the Incas Peru

Land of the Individual and Other Endangered Species Alaska

Land of the Inland Sea Chad surrounding the once-great inland sea—Lake Chad

Land of the Inland Seas Great Lakes country of Canada and the U.S.

Land of Instant Women Thailand

Land of Iron and Diamonds Sierra Leone

LANDJUT Land Forces (Schleswig-Holstein and) Jutland (NATO)

Land of the Khmers Cambodia

Land of Lakes and Fens Finland

Land of Lakes and Forests Sweden

Land of Lakes and Volcanos El Salvador

Land of the Lamas Tibet

Land of Latte Stones Guam

Land of Leeks Wales

Land of Legend Canada's Yukon Territory

Land of Leopold Belgium

Land of the Leprechauns Ireland

Land of Letzeburgesch Luxembourg (where the language is Letzeburgesch)

Land of Lincoln Illinois

Land of Liszt and Bartok Hungary

Land of the Llamas Peru

Landlocked South American Nations Bolivia and Paraguay

Land of the Long White Cloud New Zealand—so called by the Maoris

Land of the Lotus Blossom Ceylon, officially called Sri Lanka, where the lotus blossom symbolizes Buddha

Land of the Magyars Hungary

Land of the Manchus Manchuria

Land of Many Composers Russia (birthplace of Arensky, Borodin, Bortniansky, Cui, Glazunov, Gliere, Glinka, Khachaturian, Liadov, Liapu-

nov, Medtner, Mussorgsky, Prokofiev, Rachmaninoff, Rimsky-Korsakov, Scriabin, Shostakovich, Stravinsky, Tchaikovsky, to mention some of the better-known composers)

Land of Many Tribes Tanzania (formerly Tanganyika)

Land of the Maoris New Zealand

Land of the Marsupials Australia

Land of the Mayas Honduras

Land of Mecca Saudi Arabia

Land of Men Marquesas Islands in the South Pacific whose Polynesian name (*Te Fenua Enata*) means The Land of Men

Land of the Midnight Sun northern Alaska, Canada's Northwest Territories, Greenland, Iceland, Norway, Sweden, Finland, and Siberia share this sobriquet

Land of Milk and Honey Israel's Jordan River Valley

Land of the Moors Algeria and Morocco

Land of the Mormons Utah

Land of the Morning Calm Korea

Land of Moses Israel

Land of Mountains the Austrian Tyrol; Norway; Sweden; Switzerland; Tibet

Land of My Fathers Wales

Land of Nod place where Cain was exiled after killing his brother Abel; the realm of sleep

LANDNONOR Land Forces Northern Norway (NATO)

LANDNORTH Land Forces Northern Europe (NATO)

'Lando Orlando, Florida

Land 'o Cakes Land of Oatmeal Cakes—nickname Robert Burns gave his native land—Scotland

Land o' Lakes Wisconsin

Land of Opportunity official nickname of Arkansas

Land of Pagodas Burma

Land of the Pentagram Morocco whose flag and shield feature a five-pointed star of great complexity

Land of the People Greenland

Land of the Pharoahs Egypt

Land of the Philistines Palestine

Land of the Plastic Lotus California

Land of the Poinciana Jamaica

Land of Political Exiles Yakutia (northeastern Siberia in the USSR)
Land of Precious Things El Salvador (called *Cuscutlán*—Land of Precious Things—by the Pipit Indians)
Land of the Prince Wales
landprop landlord proprietor
Land of the Prophets Israel
Land of the Quetzal Guatemala
Land of the Red People Oklahoma
Land of the Rising Sun Japan
Land of the Rolling Prairie Iowa
Land of the Rose England
Lands Landsmaal (Norwegian national language)
Land of the Sagas Iceland (where the art of storytelling dates from the 12th century)
Land of Saints and Scholars Ireland
landsat land satellite
Land of the Sea The Netherlands—standing where the sea once stood
Land of Sea and Mountain Norway
Land's End Cornish cape in southwest England—westernmost England
Land of the Serbs, Croats, and Slovenes Yugoslavia (including Bosnia and Herzegovina, Croatia, Dalmatia, Macedonia, Montenegro, Serbia, and Slovenia)
Land of the Shamrock Ireland
Land of Silence Lapland (where some Laplanders insist it is so silent you can hear the shadows of drifting clouds as they move about)
Land of Six Peoples Guyana, formerly British Guiana, containing Africans, Amerindians, Chinese, East Indians, Spaniards, and other Europeans including a few old British engineers
Land of Skillful Farmers Lithuania
Land of the Sky North Carolina
Landslide Lyndon Senator Lyndon B Johnson's nickname when elected by an 87-vote majority discovered by the Duke of Duval County—boss George Pharr
Land of Small Islands Micronesia
Land of Smiles Thailand
LANDSONOR Land Forces

Southern Norway (NATO)
Land South of the Clouds Yunnan
Land of the Southern Cross Brazil
Land of Spring coastal southern California from San Diego to Santa Barbara
Lands Reclaimed from the Sea Netherlands
Lands of Sunlit Nights Scandinavian countries during summertime (Denmark, Finland, Iceland, Norway, Sweden)
Land of Steady Habits Connecticut
Land of Sunburned Faces Ethiopia
Land of Sunshine New Mexico, South Africa, and southern California vie for this descriptive title
Land of Symphonists Austria (birthplace or home of Haydn, Mozart, Bruckner, and Mahler)
Land of the Templars Malta
Land That Time Forgot Australia
Land of the Thistle Scotland
Land of the Thousand Lakes Finland
Land of Togetherness Kenya whose shield surmounts a rib- and reading *Harambee* (Swahili—Together)
Land of Tomorrow Brazil
Land of the Trade Winds U.S. Virgin Islands
Land of the Vikings Norway but particularly the Vestfold province on the western shore of Oslo Fjord where Viking remains are plentiful
Landw Landwirtschaft (German —agriculture)
Land of Waterfalls Norway
Land of Waters Guyana (where canals, creeks, rivers, and waterfalls abound)
Land of the Wattle Australia
Land of the West Morocco (from the Arabic *maghrib* meaning west)
Land Where The Sun Never Sets the Soviet Union
Land of the Whispering Bushes California
Land of the White Ant Australia's Northern Territory
Land of the White Eagle Poland
Land of the White Elephant Thailand
Land of the White Mountain Kenya

Land of the Winds Iran or Persia
LANDZEALAND Land Forces Zealand (NATO)
Lane's disease chronic constipation
Lan Fus Lancashire Fusiliers
lang language
Lang Langbridge; Langdon; Lange; Langer; Langford; Langhorne; Langlois; Langson; Langston; Languedoc
Langley Langley, Virginia headquarters of the CIA
Langtry formerly Vinegaroon, Texas; renamed in 1882 by Judge Roy Bean to honor the actress Lillie Langtry whose name also adorned his combination courthouse and saloon —*The Jersey Lily*
LANICA Lineas Aereas de Nicaragua (Spanish—Air Lines of Nicaragua)
LANL Los Alamos National Laboratory
La Nouvelle Orléans (French—New Orleans)
Lan Reg Lancashire Regiment
LANSA Líneas Aéreas Nacionales
LANSA Lineas Aéreas Nacionales SA (Spanish—National Airlines Corporation)—Peru
Lansen (Swedish—Lance)—jet interceptor aircraft designated J-32
Lansing Michigan's capital
Lant Atlantic (naval short form)
'Lanta Atlanta
LANTIRNS Low-Altitude Navigation, Targeting Infra-Red Navigation System
Lantsang (Chinese—Mekong River)
LANWR Laguna Atascosa National Wildlife Refuge (Texas); Lake Andes National Wildlife Refuge (South Dakota)
LANY Linseed Association of New York
Lanzhou (Pinyin Chinese—Lanchow)
LAO Legal Assistance Office(r); Licentiate of the Art of Obstetrics
LAOAR Latin American Office of Aerospace Research
LAOD Los Angeles Ordnance District (USA)
Laos Lao People's Democratic Republic (Indo-Chinese country whose Lao or Laotians speak Lao, other oriental tongues, and some French, ex-

ports include opium as well as edible crops and some minerals such as tin)

LAOT Los Angeles Opera Theater

lap. laparotomy; launch analyst's panel; learning activity package; left atrial pressure

Lap Lapland

LaP Las Palmas (British maritime abbreviation)

La P La Paz

LAP La Paz, Mexico (airport); Laboratory of Aviation Psychology (Ohio State University); Líneas Aéreas Paraguayas (Paraguayan Air Lines)

laparo laparoscope; laparoscopic (sterilazation); laparotomy

La Pasionaria Dolores Ibarruri famed for her impassioned speeches made during the Spanish civil war

LAPC Los Angeles Pacific College; Los Angeles Pierce College

LAPCO Lavan Petroleum Company

LAPD Los Angeles Police Department

LAPDis Los Angeles Procurement District (US Army)

La Perla (Spanish—The Pearl)—San Juan

LAPES Low-Altitude Parachute Extraction System

lapid. lapideum (Latin—stony)

LAPL Los Angeles Public Library

Lapland region including northernmost Finland, Norway, Sweden, and the USSR where nomadic Lapps live and herd their reindeer

La Plata Argentine seaport named Eva Perón during dictatorship of her husband Juan Domingo Perón

LAPO Los Angeles Philharmonic Orchestra

Laponia (Portuguese or Spanish—Lapland)

Laponie (French—Lapland)

La Popessa Mother Pascalina (nurse and confidante of Pope Pius XII for forty-one years)

Lappi (Finnish—Lapland)

Lappland (German—Lapland)

Lapponia (Italian—Lapland)

LAPS List Assembly Programming System

LAPT London Association for the Protection of Trade

LAPTA Local Authorities Passenger Transport Association

Laptev Russian name for the

Nordenskjöld Sea in the Arctic Ocean

La Pucelle *La Pucelle d'Orlèans* (French—The Maid of Orleans)—Joan of Arc

laput light-activated programmable unijunction transistor

laq lacquer

lar left arm reclining; liquid argon; local-acquisition radar

lar (LAR) light-artillery rocket; long-range radar

Lar Lara; Larina; Larry

LAR Lease Application Request; Library Association of Rhodesia; Life Assurance Relief; Limit Address Register

lara (LARA) light armed reconnaissance aircraft

LARA League of Americans Residing Abroad; Licensed Agency for Relief of Asia

laram line-addressable random-access memory

larat low-altitude radar altimeter

La Raza (Hispanic-American Spanish—The Race)—brown power; *La Raza Unida* (Spanish—The United Race)—Mexican-American political organization

larc lighter, amphibious, resupply, cargo (vehicle); logic alarm radio clock

Larc Livermore automatic research computer

LARC Langley Research Center; League Against Religious Coercion; Library Automation and Consulting; Local Alcoholism Reception Center(s)

larct last radio contact

larf low-altitude radar fuzing

larg largamente (Italian—broadly); *largeur* (French—width); *largo* (Italian—slow)

Large Print Large Print Publications

largo. larghetto (Italian—moderately slow)

LARIAT Laser-Radar Intelligence-Acquisition Technology

LARIC Later Reading In-Service Course

Lark Haydn's String Quartet in D (opus 64, no. 5)

LARO Latin American Regional Office (FAO)

larp line automatic reperforator; local and remote printing

La R-P La Rochelle-Pallice

lar rep larceny report

Larruping Lou Henry Louis (Lou) Gehrig

Larry Laura; Laurence; Law-

rence

lars laminar angular-rate sensor

Lars Lawrence

LARS Laboratory for Applications of Remote Sensing (Purdue); Light Artillery Rocket System; Low-Altitude Radar System

LART Los Angeles Rapid Transit

larv (LARV) low-angle reentry vehicle

larva (LARVA) low-altitude research vehicle

laryng laryngological; laryngologist; laryngology

laryngol laryngology

las large astronomical satellite; liberal arts and sciences; lookout aiming sight; low-alloy steel; lower airspace

las lassù (Hungarian—slow introductory passages leading to fast section, *friss*, of a csárdás or rhapsody)

LAS large astronomical satellite; Las Vegas, Nevada (airport); League of Arab States; Lebanese-American Society; Legal Aid Society; Library Association of Singapore

LA & S Liberal Arts and Sciences

lasa large-aperture seismic array

LASA Latin American Shipowners Association

LASAIL Land-Sea Interaction Laboratory

Las Américas (Spanish—The Americas)—Santo Domingo's international airport serving the Dominican Republic

LASBO Louisiana Association of School Business Officials

LASC Los Angeles State College

La Scala Milan's opera house

La Scala West nickname of Chicago's Lyric Opera

LASCO Latin American Unesco Science Cooperation Office

lascot large-screen color television

lascr light-activated silicon-controlled rectifier

Las Crutches trucker's nickname for Las Cruces, New Mexico

lascs light-activated silicon-controlled switch

LASEORS London and South Eastern Operational Research Society

laser light amplification by stimulated emission of radiation; lucrative approach to support expensive research

LASER London and South Eastern Library Region

LASERS London and South Eastern Regional Library System

LASH Legislative Action on Smoking and Health; Lighter Aboard Ship (cargo system)

lasi landing-site indicator

LASIE Library Automated System Information Exchange

LASL Los Alamos Scientific Laboratory

LASMCO Liberian American-Swedish Minerals Company

Las Mercedes (Spanish—The Thanks)—Managua, Nicaragua's airport

LASO Latin American Solidarity Organization; Los Angeles Society of Ophthalmology

lasp low-altitude space platform

LASRA Leather and Shoe Research Association

lasrm (LASRM) low-altitude short-range missile

lass. lighter-than-air submarine simulator (LASS)

LASS launch-area support ship; Local Authority Social Services; Los Angeles Special Services (telephone)

LASSCO Los Angeles Steamship Company

l'asses molasses

lassiw low-airspeed sensing and indicating equipment

lasso laser search-and-secure observer

LASSO Latin American Student Studies Organization

La State U Pr Louisiana State University Press

Last Capital of the Confederacy Danville, Virginia

Last Chance Gulch gold miner's name for Helena, Montana

Last Cocked Hat James Monroe —fifth President of the United States and last to wear the cocked hat of the American Revolution

Last Continent Antarctica (last continent to be discovered)

Last Corner of Arabia Oman

Last Frontier Alaska's old nickname and current nickname of Canada's Northwest Territories

Last of the Incas Atahualpa

Last, Loneliest, Loveliest (city) Auckland, New Zealand, according to Kipling

Last Lovely City San Francisco

Last Outpost on the Mississippi Pilot Town (near Venice, Louisiana)

Last of the Prophets before Mohammed Jesus, according to the Moslems

Last Remaining Polynesian Kingdom Tonga—christened the Friendly Isles by Captain Cook

Last of the Romans Rienzi

Last Romantic poet and political writer Max Eastman who progressed from radical socialism to libertarian conservatism; Richard Strauss; Sergei Rachmaninov; W Somerset Maugham; your favorite last romantic

Last Stronghold of the Moors Granada, Spain

last trump the sound of the last trumpet believers expect to hear on Judgment Day

La Superba (Italian—The Superb)—Genoa's proud appellation dating back to the time of Columbus—a Genoese Jew named Cristoforo Colombo

LASUSSR Library of the Academy of Science of the USSR (Leningrad)

lasv (LASV) low-altitude surface vehicle; low-altitude supersonic vehicle

Las Vegas East Atlantic City, New Jersey's nickname

Las Villas formerly Santa Clara province in Cuba

Las Wages nickname of Las Vegas, Nevada (gambling resort where many lose their wages)

lat lateral; latitude

lat (LAT) lowest astronomical tide

lat latin (Dano-Norwegian—Latin); *latitud* (Spanish—latitude)

lat. latus (Latin—wide)

Lat Latin; Latvia; Latvian

Lat Latin (classical language of Roman antiquity and the base of Romance languages such as Catalan, French, Italian, Portuguese, Provençal, Romanian, and Spanish, many legal terms are in Latin or are derived from Latin as are many everyday English expressions)

LAT Latex Agglutination Test(ing); Linseed Association Terms; Local Apparent Time; Taxader Airport (Bogotá)

LAT Los Angeles Times

LATA Local Access and Transport Areas; Los Alamos Technical Associates

lat. admov. lateri admoveatum (Latin—apply to the side)

LATARS Laser-Augmented Target Acquisition and Recognition System

LATCC London Air Traffic Control Center

Latchmere House remand center in Surrey, England

LATCRS London Air Traffic Control Radar Station

lat. dol. lateri dolenti (Latin—to the painful side)

later (Latin prefix—side)—lateral

LATH Laos and Thailand Military Assistance

lat ht latent heat

Latin America places in the Americas cultivated and settled by people of Latin origin; generally understood to mean Portuguese-speaking Brazil and Spanish-speaking countries such as the Central American republics, Cuba, the Dominican Republic, Mexico, Puerto Rico, the South American republics except Brazil; sometimes used to include French settlements in Canada such as Québec and the islands of St Pierre and Miquelon, as well as French Guiana, the French West Indies, and Haiti

latoff lowest astronomical tide of the foreseeable future (assuming anyone can foresee the future)

latom lowest astronomical tide of the month

latoy lowest astronomical tide of the year

lats long-acting thyroid stimulator

latssn late season

LATTC Los Angeles Trade-Technical College

Latter-Day Saint Joseph Smith —author of *The Book of Mormon*

Latter-Day Saints the Mormons

LATUF Latin American Trade Union Federation

Latv Latvia; Latvian

Latvia Baltic country formerly inhabited by Latvians before resettlement by Soviet captors

Latvija (Latvian—Latvia)

LATWPNS Los Angeles Times

Washington Post News Service

lau laundry

LAUA Lloyd's Aviation Underwriters' Association

Lauch Lauchlin

laughing gas nitrous oxide (N_2O)

Laughing Philosopher Voltaire

LAUK Library Association of the United Kingdom

Lau Lib Laurentian Library (Florence)

laun launched

Laun Launceton, Tasmania

Launce Lancelot

Launcelot Langstaff pseudonym shared by Washington Irving, William Irving, and James K Paulding when they published the *Salmagundi* essays

laund launder; laundry

laundromat automatic coin-operated laundry

Laur Laurence

Laura World War II code name for Majuro, still in use by Americans and Marshallese islanders

Laura Z Hobson Laura K Zametkin

Laurel Pennsylvania's state flower is the Mountain Laurel

Lauren Bacall Betty Perske

Laurence Templeton Sir Walter Scott's pseudonym used in the publication of *Ivanhoe*

Laurentians Laurentian Mountains of southern Québec where they are also called the Laurentides as is Laurentides Park

Laurie Laurence

LAUSC *Linguistic Atlas of the United States and Canada*

LAUSD Los Angeles United School District

lav lavatory; lymphadenopathy virus

LAV Lalomalava (Western Samoan airport); Linea Aeropostal Venezolana (Venezuelan Airmail Line)

Lava Beds Lava Beds National Monument in northern California

LAVC Los Angeles Valley College

lavm loran automatic vehicle monitoring

law. lawyer; light assault weapon; low-altitude weapon

Law Lawrence

LAW League of American Wheelmen; League of American Writers; Legal Aid Warranty; Local Air Warning

Lawgiver of Ancient Greece Solon of Athens

Law Lat Law Latin

Lawr Lawrence; Lawrencian

Lawrence of Arabia Thomas Edward Lawrence

Lawrence L Lynch Emma Murdock Van Deventer's pseudonym

Law Rept Law Report(s)

Lawrie Lawrence

LAWRS Limited Airport Weather Reporting System

LAWS Leadership and World Society

Law West of the Pecos Judge Roy Bean of Langtry, Texas, also known as the Hanging Judge because of the number of criminals he eliminated by hanging

lax. laxative

LAX Los Angeles, California (International Airport)

Lax-Chi Los Angeles—Chicago

Lax-NO Los Angeles—New Orleans

Lax-NY Los Angeles—New York

Lax-San Los Angeles—San Diego

Lax-Sea Los Angeles—Seattle

Lax-Sfo Los Angeles—San Francisco

Lax-Tor Los Angeles—Toronto

Laz Lazarus

LAZ Los Angeles Zoo

lb landing barge; letter box; lifeboat; link belt(ing); linoleum base; local battery; low band; lumen band; pound

lb (LB) line buffer

l-b lemon-and-butter (sauce)

l & b land and building(s); left and below

lb *libra* (Latin—pound)

l.b. *lectori benevolo* (Latin—to the kind reader)

LB landing barge; Leonard Bernstein; light bomber; Lloyd Brasileiro (Brazilian Steamship Line); Local Board; Long Beach; Longview Bridge (Columbia River, Washington); Luther Burbank

L-B Link-Belt

L.B. *Baccalaureus Litterarum* (Latin—Bachelor of Letters)

lba lifting-body airship

Lba Luba (formerly San Carlos)

LB & AL Lever Brothers and Associates Limited

L-band 390–1550 mc

lb ap apothecaries' pound

L-bar capital-L-shaped bar

lb av avoirdupois pound

LBB Lubbock, Texas (airport)

lbbb left bundle branch block

lb/bhp-hr pounds per brake horsepower hour

lbbsb left bundle branch system block

Lbc Lübeck

LBC Liberian Broadcasting Corporation

lb cal pound calorie

LBCC Long Beach City College

lbcd left border of cardiac dullness

LBCH London Bankers' Clearing House

lb chu pound centigrade heat unit

LBCL Liberty Baptist College

LBCM Licentiate of Bandsmen's College of Music

lb/cu ft pounds per cubic foot

lbd learning and/or behavior disordered; left border of dullness; lifeboat deck; little black dress; lower bovine distemper; lower-back disorder

LBD League of British Dramatists

L/Bdr Lance Bombardier

L-beam capital-L-shaped beam

LBEB Laboratory of Brain Evolution and Behavior

lbf lactobacillus bulgaricus factor; pound-force

LBF Louis Braille Foundation (for blind musicians)

lbf-ft pound-force foot

lbf/in.^{2} pound-force per square inch

lb ft pound foot

lb ft^2 pound per square foot

lb ft^3 pound per cubic foot

lbg liquefied butane gas

LBG Paris, France (Le Bourget Airport)

lbh length, breadth, height

LBHD Long Beach Harbor Department

lb/hr pounds per hour

LBHS Luther Burbank High School

LBI Library Binding Institute; Licensed Beverage Industries; Lloyds Bank International

LBI *Lands Bókasafn Islands* (Icelandic—National Library of Iceland)—in Reykjavik

lb in. pound inch

lb in.^{2} pound per square inch

lb in.^{3} pound per cubic inch

lbir laser-beam-image reproducer

LBJ Lyndon Baines Johnson—

thirty-sixth President of the United States

LBJL Lyndon Baines Johnson Library (Austin)

LBJSHP Lyndon B Johnson State Historic Park (Texas)

LBJTMC Lyndon B Johnson Tropical Medical Center (American Samoa)

LBK landing barge, kitchen

lbl label (flow chart)

LBL Lawrence Berkeley Laboratories; Lloyds Bank Limited

lb/lb pound per pound

lbld labelled

lblg labelling

lbm lean body mass

lb m pound mass

lb/m pounds per minute

Lbm Lifeboatman

lb-mol pound-mole (mass)

LBMS London Boroughs Management Services

lbnpd lower-body negative-pressure device

LBO Lima, Peru (Limatambo Airport)

lboe lime-base oil emulsified

lbp length between perpendiculars; low back pain; low blood pressure

LBP Lanier Business Products; Lester Bowles Pearson (Canada's eighteenth Prime Minister); London Borough Polytechnic

LBPL Long Beach Public Library

lbr labor; laser-beam recorder; lumber

Lbr Labrador; Librarian

LBR Library Bill of Rights

lbs pounds (from the Latin— *Librae)*

lb/s pounds per second

l.b.s. lectori benevolo salutem (Latin—to the kind reader, greetings)

LBS landing barge support; Lean Burn System; Libyan Broadcasting Service; Lifeboat Station; London Boroughs Association; London Botanical Society

LBSC Long Beach State College

LB & SCR London, Brighton and South Coast Railway

lbs H₂O mm pounds of water per million standard cubic feet (natural gas)

LBSM Licentiate of Birmingham and Midland Institute School of Music

lb/sq in. pounds per square inch

lbs sq ft pounds per square foot

lbt laser-beam transmissiometer

lb t pound(s) thrust; pound(s) troy

LBTF Long Beach Test Facility

LBTS Land-Based Test Site

Lbu Labuan

LBV landing barge, vehicle

lbw leg before wicket; low body weight; low-speed black-and-white (photography)

lc label clause; laundry chute; lead-covered; leading case(s); left center; legal currency; letter card; level crossing; light case; light change; line-carrying; liquid crystal; load carrier; localized corrosion; locked-closed; low calorie; low carbon; lower case; single acetate single cotton

l-c launch control; low calorie; low carbohydrate

l/c letter of credit; lower center

l.c. loco citato (Latin—in the place cited)

Lc corrected middle latitude

LC Lackawanna College; Ladycliff College; Lafayette College; Lake Central Airlines; Lakehead College; Lakeland College; Lambuth College; Lance Corporal; Lander College; landing craft; Lane College; Laredo College; Lassen College; L'Assumption College; launch(ing) control; Law Court(s); Lawrence College; Lee College; Legal Committee; Legislative Council; Lesley College; Letter Contract; Lewis College; Library of Congress; Lieutenant Commander; Limestone College; Lincoln College; Lindenwood College; line of communication; Linfield College; Livingstone College; London Clause; London Club (of criminologists, freelance investigators, and members of the media concerned with controversial trials and unsolved crimes); Longwood College; Loras College; Louisburg College; Louisiana College; Loyola College; Luther College; Luzon College(s); Lycoming College; Lynchburg College

L-C Liquid-Carbonic (Division of General Dynamics)

L/C Letter of Credit

L of C Library of Congress

lca low-cost automation

LCA Lake Carriers Association;

Lake Central Airlines; landing craft—assault; Launcher Control Area; Learning Corporation of America; Library Club of America; Licensed Company Auditor; Lutheran Church in America

LC-ADD Library of Congress— American Doctoral Dissertations

lcal lowercase alphabet length

lcao linear combination of atomic orbitals

lcat (LCAT) lecithin-cholesterol acyltransferase

L & C ATA Laundry and Cleaners Allied Trades Association

L Cav Lucy Cavendish Collegiate Society, Cambridge

lcb longitudinal position of center of buoyancy

LCB Liquor Control Board; London and Continental Bankers

LCBBC Liquor Control Board of British Columbia

LCBM Liquor Control Board of Manitoba

LCBO Liquor Control Board of Ontario

LCBS Liquor Control Board of Saskatchewan

lcc lateral center of gravity; ledger card computer; life cycle cost; light curtain closed

LCC landing craft, control (3-letter symbol); Lands Conservation Council; Lansing Community College; Launch Control Center; League of California Cities; Life Cycle Center; London County Council; Lower Columbia College

L & C C Lewis and Clark College

LCcc Library of Congress catalog card

LCCC Library of Congress Computer Catalog; Lorain County Community College; Lucas County Corrections Center (Ohio)

lcce life-cycle cost estimate

LCCI London Chamber of Commerce and Industry

LCCJ Louisiana Council on Criminal Justice

LCCMARC Library of Congress Current MARC (file)

lccs low cervical caesarian section

LCCS Launcher Captain Control System; Lucy Cavendish Collegiate Society (Cambridge)

lccv (LCCV) large crude-carrying vessel (oil tanker)

lcd liquid crystal diode; liquid crystal display; lowest common denominator

LCD Lord Chamberlain's Department; Lord Chancellor's Department

l/c derv lowercase derivative (angora, axminster, bakelite, bunsen burner, canada balsam, castile soap, china clay, congo red, cordovan leather, delftware, etc.)

LCDHWIU Laundry, Cleaning, and Dye House Workers International Union

lcdo licenciado (Spanish—licensed)

Lcdo Licenciado (Spanish—lawyer)

LCDs Lower Court Decisions

lcdtl load-compensated diode-transistor logic

lce lance; left center entrance

LCE Licentiate in Civil Engineering

lces least-cost estimating and scheduling

lcf least common factor; liquid complex fertilizer; longitudinal position of center of flotation; low cycle fatigue; lowest common factor

LCF landing craft, flak; launch control facility

LCFA Lower California Fisheries Association

l-c f-s pr last-come first-served preemptive résumé

LCFTA London Cattle Food Trade Association

lcg liquid-cooled (under) garment; longitudinal position of center of gravity

LCG British armored landing craft; Load Classification Group

LCGB Locomotive Club of Great Britain

lch launch

L Ch Licentiate in Surgery

LCH landing craft—heavy

LCHQ Local Command Headquarters (NATO)

lchr launcher

lci locus of control interview

LCI landing craft, infantry; Learner-Centered Instruction; Liquid Crystal Institute (Kent State University); Livestock Conservation Incorporated

lcircon letter of credit irrevocable and confirmed

LCIS Library of Computer and Information Sciences

LCJ Lord Chief Justice

LCJ Louisville Courier-Journal

LCJC Lake City Junior College

Lcks Locks (postal abbreviation)

lcl less than carload lot; less than container lot; lifting condensation level; local(izer); loose container load; lower card lever; lower control limit

lcl (LCL) lowest charge level

LCL Liberal and Country League (Australia); Licentiate in Canon Law; Licentiate in Canonic Law; Licentiate in Common Law

L-C-L Levinthal-Coles-Lillie (bodies)

LCL La Casa del Libro (Spanish—House of the Book)—Puerto Rico's typographic arts museum on San Juan's Calle del Cristo

LCLA Lutheran Church Library Association

L-C-L bodies Levinthal-Coles-Lillie bodies

lcl/ci limited calendar life/controlled item

LCLs Liverpool Central Libraries

LCLS Livestock Commission Levy Scheme

lcm lead-coated metal; least common multiple; left costal margin; limit-cycle monitor; liquid curing media; logistics composite model; lost circulation materials (oil well); lowest common multiple

lcm (LCM) large-core memory; lymphocytic choriomeningitis

LCM landing craft, mechanized; landing craft—medium; London College of Music

LCMARC Library of Congress MARC (files beginning in 1968)

lcmm life-cycle management model

lcmp launcher control and monitoring panel

LCMS Launch Control and Monitoring System; Lutheran Church Missouri Synod

lcn local civil noon

Lcn Lincoln

LCN *La Cosa Nostra* (Italian—Our Thing)—The Mafia; Load Classification Number(ing)

LCNM Lehman Caves National Monument (Nevada)

LCNN Land Commander Northern Norway (NATO)

LCNY Linguistic Circle of New York

LCNYC Lincoln Center (New

York City)

LCO Landing Craft Officer; Launch Control Officer; London College of Osteopathy

lcoc launch control officer's console

L Col Lieutenant Colonel

lcos lead computing optical sight

lcp language conversion program; last complete program; low-cost production

LCP landing craft, personnel; Liberal Country Party (Australia); Library Company of Philadelphia; Licentiate of the College of Preceptors; Livable Cities Program; London College of Printing

LCPA Lincoln Center for the Performing Arts

L Cpl Lance Corporal

LCPL landing craft, personnel, large (naval symbol)

LCPR landing craft, personnel, ramped (naval symbol)

lcps last card program start

LCPS Licentiate of the College of Physicians and Surgeons

LCP & SA Licentiate of the College of Physicians and Surgeons of America

LCP & SO Licentiate of the College of Physicians and Surgeons of Ontario

lcr limited carrier(s) risk

l/cr letter of credit

l/cr lettre de crédit (French—letter of credit)

L Cr Lieutenant Commander

LCR landing craft, rubber; Line Condition Report

LCRA Lower Colorado River Authority

l/crt lamb crutchings

LCRT Lincoln Center Repertory Theater

lcs launch-control simulator

lcs (LCS) large-core storage

lc's (LCs) liquid crystals

LCS Laboratory of Computer Sciences (M.I.T.); landing craft, support (naval vessel); Library Computer System

lcsa letter of credit (negotiable by drafts at) sight airmail

LCSA Lewis and Clark Society of America

LCSH Library of Congress Subject Headings

lcss land combat support set

LCSS London Council of Social Service

lct last card total; less than truckload lot

LCT Laboratoire Central de

Telecommunications (Central Télécommunications Laboratory); landing craft—tank; latest closing time; less than truckload lot; Local Civil Time; Loughsborough College of Technology

LCTC Langlade County Teachers College; Leicester College of Technology and Commerce; Lewis and Clark Trail Commission

lctp launcher control test panel

lcty locality

lcu launch-control unit; lower control unit

lcu (LCU) large closeup

LCU landing craft, utility

lcv low calorific value

LCV landing craft, vehicle

LCVP landing craft, vehicle, personnel

lcv's light commercial vehicles

LCWS Landing Configuration Warning System

lcx launch complex

lcxt large cosmic-X-ray telescope

LCY League of Communists of Yugoslavia

LCYC Lemon Creek Yacht Club

LC zone land conservation zone

ld ladies day; land; lead; learning disabled; lethal dose; library development; lid; lifeboat deck; light difference; line of departure; line of duty; load; load draft; Lord; low density; low door; lower deck

ld (LD) learning-disabled; lethal dose

l-d low-density

l/d length to diameter (ratio); life to drag (ratio)

l & d labor and delivery; loans and discounts; loss(es) and damage(s)

l.d. lepide dictum (Latin—wittily related)

Ld Leopold; Limited

LD Labor (US department); line of departure; line of duty; Low Dutch; lower berth (double occupancy)

L-D Leishman-Donovan (bodies)

L/D Letter of Deposit

L.D. Litterarum Doctor (Latin —Doctor of Letters)

LD-3 lower-deck container

ld₅₀ median lethal dose

LD-10 lethal dose for 10 percent of the animals tested

LD-50 lethal dose for 50 percent

of the animals tested

lda land development aircraft; landing distance available; learning disabilities average; left dorso-anterior; line drawing amplifier; localiser direction(al) aid

lda (LDA) light defense aircraft

L^da Limitada (Portuguese or Spanish—Limited); *Licenciada* (Spanish—lawyer)— feminine form of *L^do*—*Licenciado*

LDA Ladies Darts Association; Lead Development Association

ldac lunar-surface data-acquisition camera

L da V Leonardo da Vinci

ldb light distribution box

LDBHS Louis D Brandeis High School

ldc large document copier; leased directive circuits; long-distance call; lower dead center

ldc (LDC) latitude data computer

LDC Late Developing Country; Laundry and Dry Cleaning (union); Less Developed Countries; Light Direction Center; List of Design Changes; Local Defense Center

LD & C Louis Dreyfus & Compagnie

LDCMMA Laundry and Dry Cleaners Machinery Manufacturers Association

ldc's (LDCs) least-developed countries; less-developed countries

ldd laser development device

lddo long-distance diesel oil

LDDS Low-Density Data System

LDEF Long-Duration Exposure Facility

ldel land development encouragement loans

L Dent Sci Licentiate in Dental Science

Lderry Londonderry

L de V Lope de Vega

LDF Legal Defense Fund (NAACP); Local Defense Force(s)

ldg landing; loading; lodging

Ldg Lodge (postal abbreviation)

ldg & dly landing and delivery

Ldge Lodge

ldg gr landing gear

ldglts leading lights

ldgs lodgings

ldh lactic-acid dehydrogenase

L d'H Légion d'Honneur— [French—Legion of Honor (decoration)]

Ld'H Légion d'Honneur (French —Legion of Honor)

LDH Ligue des Droits de l'Homme (League for the Rights of Man)

ldhc locker-door hydraulic cylinder

ldi lecture-driven instruction

ldk lower deck

ldl learning disabilities limited; loudness discomfort level; low-density lipoprotein

ld lmt load limit

LDMA London Discount Market Association

Ld May Lord Mayor

ld mk landmark

ldmwr limited depot maintenance work requirements

Ldn London; Londoner

ldo light diesel oil; long-distance oil

L^do Licenciado (Spanish—lawyer, licentiate holding master's degree)

LDO Licensed Deck Officer; Limited-Duty Officer

L-dopa levodihydroxyphenylalanine (Parkinson's disease treatment drug)

LDOS Lord's Day Observance Society

ldp left dorso-posterior; logistics data package

Ldp Ladyship; London daily price; Lordship

LDP landed duty paid; Liberal Democratic Party (Japan)

ldpe low-density polyethylene

ldr launder; laundry; leader; lecture-discussion-recitation; ledger; light-dependent resistor; lodger

LDR London Digital Recording

l/d ratio length to diameter ratio; lift-to-drag ratio (of aircraft)

LDRC Lumber Dealers Research Council

ldri low data rate input

L-drivers learner-drivers

Ldr's London depository receipts

LDRTA Long-Distance Road Transport Association

ldry laundry

lds loads

lds (LDS) large disc store; large disk storage

Lds Leeds

LDs Learning Disabilities

LDS Latter Day Saints (Church of Jesus Christ of); Licentiate in Dental Surgery; Line Drawing System

LDSc Licentiate in Dental Science

ld/sd look down/shoot down

LDSR League of Distilled Spirits Rectifiers

LDSRA Logistics Doctrine Systems and Readiness Agency (USA)

LDSRCPS Licentiate in Dental Surgery of the Royal College of Physicians and Surgeons

LDSRCS Licentiate in Dental Surgery of the Royal College of Surgeons

l&d store liquor and delicatessen store

ldt logic design translator

LDTO Long-Distance Telegraph Office

ldtr long-dwell-time radar

LDV Local Defense Volunteer

ldx long-distance xerography

ldy laundry

Ldy Londonderry

LDY Lancashire and Derbyshire Yeomanry; Leicestershire and Derbyshire Yeomanry

le launch(ing) equipment; leading edge; left eye; library edition; limit of error; limited edition; low explosive

l/e lifetime earnings

l.o. *lupus erythematosus* (skin disease)

Le Lebanese; Lebanon

LE Labor Exchange; Labour Exchange; light equipment; low explosive

lea leather

LEA Local Education Authority; Local Education(al) Agency; Locomotive Engineers Association; Loss Executives Association; Lutheran Education Association

LEAA Lace and Embroidery Association of America; Law Enforcement Assistance Administration

LEAA *Law Enforcement Assistance Act*

LEAD Law Students Exposing Advertising Deception

Leadbelly Huddie Ledbetter

LEADER Lehigh Automatic Device for Efficient Retrieval

Leader of French Enlightenment Denis Diderot

Leader of the Renaissance World Florence (Firenze)

LEADS Law Enforcement Agencies Data System (Illinois)

Lead State place-name nickname shared by Colorado and Missouri

Lea & F Lea & Febiger

LEAF Law, Equality, and Freedom (association)

leaf(s) leaflet(s)

LEAJ Law Enforcement and Administration of Justice (President's Commission on)

Leamington Royal Leamington Spa in central England

Leander British class of all-purpose frigates

Leao do Mar (Portuguese—Lion of the Sea)—the stormy Cape of Good Hope

leap. liftoff elevation and azimuth programmer

LEAP Lambda Efficiency Analysis Program; Language for the Expression of Associative Procedures; Loan and Educational Aid Program

LEAPS Laser Engineering and Applications for Prototype Systems; Law Enforcement Agencies Processing System (Massachusetts); London Electronic Agency for Pay and Statistics

Lear *The Tragedy of King Lear*

Lear 23 Lear jet transport

leas lower-echelon automatic switchboard

Leavenworth U.S. Penitentiary at Leavenworth, Kansas

leaverats leave rations

Leb Lebanese; Lebanon

LEB London Electricity Board

Lebanese Lebanon-grown brownish red hashish; people of Lebanon north of Israel

Lebanese Ports (north to south) Tarabulus, Beirut, Sayda, Sur

Lebanon Republic of Lebanon (Middle East country whose Lebanese speak Arabic as well as a few who speak Armenian or French, iron and sub-tropical crops are exported from this strife-torn land exploited by fanatical guerrillas of the PLO) *al-Jumhouriya al-Lubnaniya*

Leber's disease congenital atrophy of the optic nerve

le bodies lupus erythematosus bodies (LE bodies)

Le Boulevard des Princes (French nickname—Hortense Schneider—actress and intimate of European royalty)

L'Ebreo (Italian—The Hebrew)—nickname of Salomone Rossi—Renaissance composer and rabbi

LEBS London Emergency Bed Service

lec lunar equipment conveyor

L Ec Ecclesiastic Latin

LEC Lake Erie College; Law and Economics Center (University of Miami); Law Enforcement Center; Livestock Equipment Council

Le Caire (French—Cairo)

Le Carré John Le Carré (pseudonym of David John Moore Cornwall)

LECE *Ligue Européenne de Coopération Economique* (French—European League for Economic Cooperation)

le cells lupus erythematosus cells (LE cells)

lech lecher; lecherous; lechery

LECLU Law Enforcement Civil Liberties Unit

Le Corbu Le Corbusier

Le Corbusier Charles Edouard Jeanneret-Gris

l'Ecosse (French—Scotland)

lect lecture

lect. *lectio* (Latin—lesson)

Lect Lecturer

lectr lecturer

'lectric electric

Lecumberri-Hilton nickname of Mexico City's great prison

led. light-emitting dial; light-emitting diode(s)

Led Ledbetter; Ledyard

L Ed *Lawyer's Edition* (US Supreme Court Reports)

LED Library Education Division (American Library Association)

LEDC League for Emotionally Disturbed Children

Le Divin Poeme (French— The Divine Poem)—Scriabin's Symphony No. 3

Le Douainier (French—The Custom House Officer)—nickname of Henri Rousseau the primitive painter

led's light-emitting diodes

lee. laser energy evaluator

Lee Leroy

LEEA Law Enforcement Education Agency

Leedsloiner(s) native(s) of Leeds

LEEGS Law Enforcement Explorer Girls

Lee I Leeward Islands

LEEP Law Enforcement Education Program

Leeuwarden provincial capital of Friesland in the Netherlands

Leeward Islands Anguilla, Antigua, Barbuda, British Virgin Islands, Montserrat, Nevis, Redonda, Saint Christopher (St Kitts)

Leewards Leeward Islands

lef leading-edge flap; light-emitting film

LEF Life Extension Foundation; Lincoln Educational Foundation

LEF Liberté, Egalité, Fraternité (Liberty, Equality, Fraternity —slogan of the French Revolution)

LEFTA Labour (Party) Economic, Finance, and Taxation Association

Left Bank artists, composers, writers, and their admirers have lent luster to this section of Paris on the left bank of the Seine

Lefty Robert Grove

leg. legal; legate(e); legation; legislation; legislative; legislature

leg. (LEG) liquefied energy gas

leg. legato (Italian—smoothly flowing)

Leg Leghorn

Leg Legierung (German—alloy)

LEG Law Enforcement Group

LEG (UN) Legal Affairs (department of United Nations)

legat FBI agent or office working in an overseas legation of the United States; legation

LEGCO Legislative Council

leg com legally committed

legcrit legal critic(ism)

legg leggiero (Italian—lightly and rapidly)

Leghorn English equivalent of Livorno on Italy's west coast; word of Hobson-Jobson origin (*see* Hob-Job)

legis legislative; legislature

legit legitimate

Le Grand Siècle (French—The Great Century)—the 1600s when France was founding her academies and Moliére was writing his comedies

LEGT Lycée d'Enseignement Général et Technologique (French—High School of General Education and Technology)

legumes legumbres (Spanish-American truncation—beans, greenstuff, vegetables)

leg. wt legal weight

LEH Licentiate in Ecclesiastical History

Le Havre (French—Havre)

LEHI Lehigh University

Lehman Caves Lehman Caves National Monument in eastern Nevada

lei land exclusive of improvements

LEI Life-Expectancy Inventory

Leic Leicester

leichtl leichtlöslich (German—readily soluble)

Leics Leicestershire

Leida (Latin—Leiden)—Leyden

Leiden (Dutch—Leyden)

Leip Lepzig

Le Is Leeward Islands

LEIS Law Enforcement Information System

Leit Leitrim

LEIU Law Enforcement Intelligence Unit

lej longitudinal expansion joint

lel lower explosive limit

LEL Labor Electoral League; Laureate in English Literature; Letitia Elizabeth Landon

LELDC Law Enforcement Legal Defense Center

Lélio Lélio, ou Le Retour à la vie (French—Lélio, or the Return to Life)—Berlioz monodrama sequel to his *Symphonie fantastique*

lem lateral eye movements; layered-earth model; lemon(ade); logical end of media

lem (LEM) lunar excursion module

Lem Lemuel

LeM Le Monde (The World)—Paris

LEM Lunar Excursion Module

LEMA Lifting Equipment Manufacturers' Association

lemac leading edge mean aerodynamic chord

Lemberg (German—Lvov)

Lemnos English place-name equivalent of Limnos island in the Aegean

lemo lemonade

Lemonade Lucy Mrs Lucy Ware Webb Hayes—wife of President Rutherford B Hayes— who served only non-intoxicating fruit drinks while at the White House

LEMSIP Laboratory for Experimental Medicine and Surgery in Primates

Lemurio Lemuriologic(al)(ly); Lemuriologist(ic)(al)(ly); Lemuriology

Lemur Paradise Madagascar

Len Leningrad, formerly Petro-

grad, formerly St Petersburg; Lensky; Leonard

Lena 2700 mile river draining Siberia and entering Laptev Sea area of the Arctic Ocean; Magdalen(a)

LENA Lower Eastside Neighborhoods Association

Lena River City Yukutsk, Siberia

LENDS Library Extends Catalog Access and New Delivery System

Lenin Vladimir Ilich Ulyanov

Lenin Shostakovich's Symphony No. 12

Leninakan formerly Aleksandropol

Leningrad Saint Petersburg during Czarist times; Petrograd during the Kerensky regime before the Bolsheviks seized power and renamed it Leningrad

Leningrad Shostakovich's Symphony No. 7

Leningrado (Italian or Spanish —Leningrad)

Leninpor Lenin Port (Leningrad Harbor)

lenit. leniter (Latin—gently)

Len Lib Lenin Library (Moscow)

Lenny Leonard; Leonard Bernstein

Lens-Grinder Philosopher Benedictus de Spinoza

Lenson Levensohn; Levenson; Levinson; Levinsky

lento lentando (Italian—increasingly slow)

Leo Leo (a three-letter constellation without an abbreviation); Leonard; Leonese; Leonidas; Leonine; Leopold; Leopoldville

LEO Leopoldville, Congo (airport)

Leonard Holton Leonard Patrick O'Connor Wibberley's pseudonym

Leonard Q. Ross (pseudonym— Leo Rosten)

Leon Bakst Leon Nikolaevich Rosenberg

Leopard West German Krauss-Maffei medium tank armed with a 105mm gun

LEOPARD Law Enforcement Operations and Activities to Reduce Drugs

Leopold's galloping ghost Congo-attained dysentery (African equivalent of the curse of Cortez, Montezuma's revenge, the plight of Pizarro, etc.)

Leopoldville Belgian Congo name for what is now Kinshasa, Zaire

leopon leopard + lioness (hybrid offspring of male leopard and lioness)

Leovardia (Latin—Leeuwarden)

lep lepton (collective term embracing anti-neutrino, electron, neutrino, photon, positron); lowest effective power

lep (LEP) large electron positron (collider)

Lep Lepus (constellation)

LEP Labor Education Project; Library of Exact Philosophy

LEP Lycée d'Enseignement Professionnel (French—High School of Professional Education)

LEPA Law Enforcement Planning Agency

Lepanto (Italian—Navpaktos)

Le Pas de Calais (French—The Straits of Calais)—the English Channel

lep. dict. lepide dictum (Latin—well said)

lepid(s) lepidopterist(s)

LEPMA Lithographic Engravers and Plate Makers Association

Lepmus Lepramuseet (Norwegian—Leprosy Museum)—Bergen museum reflecting Dr Armauser Hansen's struggle against leprosy also known as Hansen's disease

Lepontines Lepontine Alps along the Italo-Swiss border

LEPORE Long-Term and Expanded Program of Oceanic Research and Exploration

LEPRA Leprosy Relief Association (British)

le prep lupus erythematosis preparation

lep(s) lepidopterist(s)

Leps Lepus (constellation)

lept (LEPT) long-endurance patrolling torpedo

Lepto Leptospira

Ler Lerida

LeRC Lewis Research Center (NASA)

LERC Laramie Energy Research Center; Law Enforcement Resource Center

Le Roi Soleil (French—The Sun King)—Louis XIV

les lesbian; local excitatory state

lEs limited English speaking

Les Lescombe; Lesley; Leslie; Lester

LES Launch Escape System;

Lincoln Experimental Satellite

lEsa limited English-speaking ability

LESA Licensing Executives Society of Australia; Lunar Exploration System—Apollo

Les Adieux Beethoven's Piano Sonata No. 23 in E flat (opus 81a) *Les Adieux, l'absence, et le retour*—the farewell, the absence, and the return

Le Sage (French—The Wise)—Charles V

lesb lesbian(ism)

Lesbian Poet Sappho, the poetess of Lesbos

lesbie lesbian

lesbo lesbian (Lesbos-type woman); lesbianism

Lesbos English equivalent of Lésvos or Mytilene in the Aegean

Lesbos Long Island Fire Island, Long Island, NY

Les Cayes modern name for Aux Cayes, Haiti also called Cayes

Les États-Unis (French—The United States)

Les Îles Sorlingues (French—Scilly Islands)—the Sorlings

Les L Licensie es Lettres (French—Licentiate in Letters)

Leslie Charteris Leslie Charles Bowyer Yin

Leslie Ford Zenith Jones Brown's pseudonym

Leslie Howard Leslie Stainer

Les Lip Leslie Lipson (most articulate of commentators about overseas newspapers)

Leso Lesotho (formerly Basutoland)

Les Orcades (French—The Orkneys)

Lesotho Kingdom of Lesotho (formerly called Basutoland this landlocked South African country is populated by Basotho farmers, herders, and diamond polishers, English and Lesotho are spoken)

Les Pays-Bas (French—The Netherlands)

les Ricains les Americans (French slang—The Americans)—short form used in the sense of rich American suckers and tourists waiting to be fleeced

LESS Least-cost Estimating and Scheduling Survey

Les Sc Licensie es Sciences (French—Licentiate in

Science)

Lesser Antilles Leeward and Windward Islands extending from the Netherlands Antilles (Aruba, Bonaire, Curaçao) to the Virgin Islands

Lesser Sundas Lesser Sunda Islands east of Bali in Indonesia

lessie(s) lesbian(s)

Lester Leicester

Lésvos (Greek—Lesbos)—island in the Aegean

let. letter; linear energy transfer

Let Lettish (Latvian)

LET Leader Effectiveness Training; Logical Equipment Table

LETAC Law Enforcement Training Advisory Council

l'Etat de New York (French—New York State)

L-et-C Loir-et-Cher

letch slang shortcut—lecher; lecheress; lecherous; lecherous feeling for; lechery

letfo letter follows

L-et-G Lot-et-Garonne

Lethbridge originally Coalbanks, Alberta

Letonia (Portuguese or Spanish—Latvia)

let's let us

LETS Low-Energy Telescope System

lett letter(s)

lott letteratura (Italian—literature); *letterlijk* (Dutch—literally)

Lott Lottish

Letter Carriers Union National Association of Letter Carriers

letterk letterkunde (Dutch—literature)

Lett Nuovo Cimento Lettere al Nuovo Cimento (Italian—Communications Regarding New Findings)

Lettone (Italian—Latvia)

Letts Lettish peoples (Latvians)

Letty Leticia; Letitia

Letz Letzeburgesch (Flemish dialect of Luxembourg)

Letzeburg (Luxembourgish—Luxembourg)

leu (LEU) leucine (amino acid)

leuk (Latin prefix—white)—leukocytes

leuko (Greek *leukos*—white)—leukemia, leukocyte(s), leukorrhea—the whites

Leuven (Flemish—Louvain)

lev lever

lev (LEV) lunar excursion vehicle

lev levert (Norwegian—deliv-

ered)
lev. *levis* (Latin—light)
Lev The Book of Leviticus; Leo; Leon
Lev *Leviticus*
levant levant or morocco leather as it was originally imported from the Levant or Morocco (also called levant morocco and characterized by its prominent grain and high quality prized by bookbinders and book lovers alike)
Levant eastern Mediterranean lands such as Israel, Lebanon, and Syria
Leviathan of Literature Dr Samuel Johnson
Le Vigan Robert Coquillaud
levis Levi Strauss' reinforced denim workclothes but particulary dungaree trousers with heavily-stitched-and-riveted pockets
levit. *leviter* (Latin—lightly)
Lew Lewis; Llewellyn
le'ward leeward
Lewisburg U.S. Penitentiary at Lewisburg, Pennsylvania
Lewis Carroll Charles Lutwidge Dodgson
Lewis Grassic Gibbon pseudonym of J(ames) L(eslie) Mitchell
lex lexical; lexicographer; lexicography; lexicon
Lex Lexington
LEX Lexington, Kentucky (airport)
lexico lexicographer
lexicog lexicographer; lexicography
lexig(s) lexigram(s)—word symbol(s)
Lexington Lexington, Kentucky's U.S. Public Health Service Hospital for the cure of narcotic addicts
Lexington Bks Lexington Books —Division of DC Heath
lexis (LEXIS) legal data base on-line to head
LEXIS Lexicography Information Service
l/ext lower extremity
Ley Leyden
LEY Liberal European Youth
Leyd Leyden
Leyte Gulf off Leyte Island in the Philippines; decisive naval battle of World War II fought here in October 1944 with more tonnage sunk than ever before in a single battle or in so short a time
lez(es) lesbian(s)

lezz lesbian
lf lawn faucet; leaf; ledger folio; left front; life float; light face type; line feed; linoleum floor; load factor; low frequency (30–300 kc)
lf (LF) line feed (data-processing character); line feed character (data processing)
l/f left front; light fittings
Lf Loaf (postal abbreviation)
LF Launch(ing) Facility; Lindbergh Field; Local Force (Red China)
lfa last field address; left fronto-anterior
LFA Land Force, Airmobility (NATO); Light Freight Agent; Low Flying Area
LFB Licensed Fishing Boat; London Fire Brigade
LFBC London Federation of Boys' Clubs
lfc laminar flow control; level of free convection; low-frequency current
l-fc low-frequency current
LFC Lutheran Free Church
lfd least fatal dose; low fat diet
lfd *laufend* (German—current, consecutive)
Lfd *Laufend* (German—current)
LFE Laboratory For Electronics
lffp laser fusion feasibility project
lfg live foal guaranteed
Lfg (Lfrg) *Lieferung* (German—installment, party delivery)
LFI Lethal Force Institute
LFICS Landing Force Integrated Communications System (USMC)
lfl lower flammable limit
LFL Lesbian Feminist Liberation (society)
lfm low-power fan marker
lf/mf low-frequency medium-frequency
lfo light fuel oil; low-frequency oscillator
LFO Licentiate of the Faculty of Osteopathy
lfp left fronto-posterior
LFP Lindbergh Field Plant (Convair)
LFPC Louisiana Foundation for Private Colleges
LFPP Louisiana Family Planning Program
LFPS Licentiate of the Faculty of Physicians and Surgeons
lfq light-foot quantisizer
L fr Luxembourg franc(s)
LFR inshore fire-support ship

(naval symbol)
LFRC League for Fighting Religious Coercion
lfrd low-friction reliability deviation
lfred liquid-fuel ramjet engine
LFS amphibious fire-support ship (naval symbol)
lft leaflet; left fronto-transverse; linear feet; linear foot
l/ft² lumens per square foot
LFTB Liquid Fuels Trust Board
LFTU Landing Force Training Unit
LFU Light Fighting Unit; Lunar Flying Unit
lg lagoon; landing; landing gear; languages(s); large; large grain; length; long; long grain; low grade
l/g locked gate
Lg Landgrave; Landgraviate
LG Landing Ground; Leipzig Gewandhaus; Lloyd George; Low German
L/G Letter of Guarantee
LGA Local Government Association; New York, New York (La Guardia Airport)
LGAA Local Government Auditors Association
LGAT Local Government Appeals Tribunal
lgb laser-guided bomb
Lgb Long Beach, California
LGB Long Beach, California (airport)
L-G-B Landry-Guillain-Barré (syndrome)
LGC Laboratory of the Government Chemist; Local Government Commission
L-G C Lockheed-Georgia Company
LGCC Letchworth Garden City Corporation
LGCR Location Geological Characterization Report
lgd leaderless group discussion
LGD London Gaol Delivery
lge large
LGEA Local Government Electricity Association
LGEB Local Government Examination Board
L-Gen Lieutenant-General
L Ger Low German
Lg of H-D Landgrav(iate) of Hesse-Darmstadt
Lg of H-K Landgrav(iate) of Hesse-Kassel
LGIO Local Government Information Office
LGk Late Greek
lgm little green men (supposedly

inhabiting extraterrestrial planets)

LGM Lloyd's Gold Medal

LGM Laboratorium voor Grondmechanica (Dutch—Soil Mechanics Laboratory)

LGMB Lady Godiva Marching Band

lgm's land-gobbling monsters (airports)

lgn lateral geniculate nuclei

Lgn Lagoon; Leghorn

LGO Lamont Geological Observatory (Columbia University); Local Government Office(r); Local Government Ordinances

LGOC London General Omnibus Company

lgp liquefied petroleum gas; low ground pressure

lgp (LGP) lasergraphic plotter

Lgp Legaspi Albay

LGPA Livestock and Grain Producers Association

lgr leasehold ground rent; ligroin

L Gr Late Greek

LGRA Local Government Reports of Australia

L Gr Ec Ecclesiastic Late Greek

LGRs Local Government Reports

lgs (LGS) laser geodynamics satellite

Lgs Lagos

LGS Landing Guidance System

LGSM Licentiate of the Guildhall School of Music

Lgt Light (postal abbreviation)

LGT Liggett Group (stock-exchange symbol)

LGTB Local Government Training Board

lgth length

lg tn long ton

lg tpr long taper

lg-type ed large-type edition

LGU Ladies Golf Union

lgv lymphogranuloma venereum (venereal disease)

LGW London, England (Gatwick Airport); Longines-Wittnauer (watches)

lg wh & br landing gears, wheels, and brakes

lh left hand; lighthouse; lower half; lower hold

lh (LH) lactogenic hormone; lateral hypothalamus; left hand; luteinizing hormone

l/h labor hour; lamp holder; liters per hectare; low to high

lH linke Hand: (German—left hand)

LH Liberty House; lighthouse; Lufthansa (airline)

L + H Lamport & Holt (Line)

L.H. left hand

LH₂ liquid hydrogen

lha lateral hypothalamic area; lower-half assembly

LHA landing ship, helicopter, assault; local hour angle

lhams lower hour angle of the mean sun

LHAR London-Hamburg-Antwerp-Rotterdam (range of ports)

LHAs multipurpose amphibious-warfare ships (naval symbol)

lhats lower hour angle of the true sun

lhb left halfback; lost heartbeat (attractive woman)

LHC Lease Housing Coordinator; Lord High Chancellor

LHCJEA London and Home Counties Joint Electric Authority

lhd left-hand drive; load-haul-dump(ing) machinery

L.H.D. Litterarum Humanorum Doctor (Latin—Doctor of Human Letters); *In Litteris Humanioribus Doctor* (Latin—Doctor in Humane Letters)

lhdc lateral homing depth charge

lh dr lefthand drive

lHe liquid helium

LHe liquid helium

L Heb Late Hebrew

L'heed Lockheed

L'Heure L'Heure Espagnole (French—The Spanish Hour)—Ravel's one-act operatic farce

LHG Library History Group

LHI Library of the Hoover Institution (on War, Revolution, and Peace)—Stanford, California

LHI Ligue Homoeopathique Internationale (French—International Homeopathic League)

L-hinge capital-L-shaped hinge

lhm letterhead memo(randum)

LHMC London Hospital Medical College

LHNCBC Lister-Hill National Center for Biomedical Communications

LHO Local Health Office(r); Livestock Husbandry Office(r)

l hold(er) lease hold(er)

lhr lumen hour(s)

l/hr liters per hour

LHR London, England (Heathrow Airport)

L & HR Lehigh and Hudson River (railroad)

lhrf (LHRF) luteinizing hormone releasing factor

lhrh (LHRH) luteinizing hormone-releasing hormone

lhs lefthand side

LHS Lafayette High School

LHSC Lock Haven State College

lhsv liquid hourly space velocity

LHT Lord High Treasurer

lh th lefthand thread

lhtl luxury class hotel

LHW League of Hispanic Women; lower high water

LHWI lower high water interval

lhwnt lowest high water neap tides

li line item; link; lira; lithograph; lithographer; lithography; longitudinal interval

li (Li) liability

Li lithium

Li *Limburg* (Dutch province)

LI Leeward Islands; Letter of Introduction; Liberia; Liberian; Lions International; Locksmithing Institute; Long Island (L.I.)

L-I Loire-Inférieure

LI Lyðveldið Ísland (Icelandic—Republic of Iceland)

Li-2 Soviet Lisunov transport plane called Cab

lia liaison

LIA Laser Institute of America; Lead Industries Association; Leather Industries of America; Lebanese International Airways; Ligue Internationale d' Arbitrage (International Arbitration League); Livestock Improvement Association; Long Island Association

LIA Ligue Internationale d'Arbitrage (French—International Arbitration League)

LIAA Life Insurance Association of America

liab liability

Líabano (Portuguese or Spanish—Lebanon)

LIALS Long Island Airport Limousine Service

LIAMA Life Insurance Agency Management Association

Liar of Biblical Antiquity Ananias, struck dead for lying, according to *The Acts* in the New Testament

LIAT Leeward Islands Air

Transport

lib liberal; liberalism; liberation(ist); libertarian(ism); liberty; librarian; library

lib. *liber* (Latin—book); *libra* (Latin—pound)

Lib Liberal; Liberal Party; Liberation(ist); Liberty Party; Libra (constellation); Libya; Libyan

Lib *Libano* (Italian—Lebanon); *Líbano* (Portuguese or Spanish —Lebanon)

LIB Let's Ignite Bras

Liban (French—Lebanon)

Libano (Italian—Lebanon)

Libanon (German—Lebanon)

Lib Auto Res Con Library Automation Research Consulting Associates

LIBBA Long Island Beach Buggy Association

Libby Elizabeth

lib cat. library catalog

libcon libertarian conservative (term invented by John Chamberlain to describe the liberal-conservative views of Pablo Casals, Milovan Djilas, John Dos Passos, Max Eastman, James T Farrell, Sidney Hook, Alberto Moravia, Allen Tate, Edmund Wilson, the author, etc.)

LIBCON/E Library of Congress/English

Lib Cong Library of Congress

libe librarian; library

libec light behind camera

lib ed library edition

Liberace Wladziu Valentino Liberace

Liberator of Argentina General José de San Martín

Liberator Czar Alexander II (1855-1881)—abolished serfdom in Russia

Liberator of Genoa Andrea Doria

Liberator of God and Man Baruch de Spinoza

Liberator of Italy Giuseppe Garibaldi

Liberia West African coastal country adjacent to Sierra Leone—founded by United States in 1822 and settled by freed American Negroes—inhabited by Liberian descendants of these freedmen who speak English with an American accent

Liberian Ports (north to south) Robertsport, Monrovia, Buchanan, Harper

Libert Libertarian

Libertador de Chile (Spanish— Liberator of Chile)—Bernardo O'Higgins

Libertas (Latin—Liberty)—goddess of liberty (head or full figure often appears on American and French coins)

Libertybellsville Philadelphia

Liberty Bowl Memphis, Tennessee

Liberty Enlightening the World Statue of Liberty in New York Bay

Liberty Island formerly Bedloe's Island in Upper New York Bay where it supports the Statue of Liberty

LIBGIS Library General Information Survey

Lib-Lab Liberal-Labour (Australian coalition)

Libn Librarian

Libor London interbank-offered rate

Lib Parl Library of Parliament

libr librarian; library

libr *libretto* (Italian—opera or oratorio text)

LIBRA Living In the Buff Recreational Associates

Library Builder Andrew Carnegie

Library of Last Resort the Library of Congress in Washington, DC, where anyone can consult any book in any language

LIBRE Living In the Buff Residential Enterprises (nudist apartments and beaches)

Lib Res Library Research Associates

Librettist-Composer Arrigo Boito

LIBRIS Library Information System (Swedish on-line retrieval system)

Lib(s) Liberal(s)

LIBS Library Information and Bibliographic System

Lib Soc Sci Library of Social Science

libst *librettist* (Italian—libretto author)

Libs Unl Libraries Unlimited

Lib UN Library of the United Nations (New York headquarters)

Libya People's Socialist Libyan Arab Republic (North African country populated by Arab Berbers who speak Arabic, oil, gas, and some crops are exported by the Libyans) *Al-Jumhuria al-Arabia allibya*

Libyan Ports (east to west) Bardiyah, Tobruk, Darnah, Marsa

al Hilal, Marsa Susah, Benghazi, Az Zuwaytinah, Marsa al Burayqah, As Sidr, Surt, Misratah, Tarabulus, Marsa Sabratah, Zuwarah

Libyen (German—Libya)

lic license; linear integrated circuit

Lic Licentiate

Lic *Licenciado* (Spanish—lawyer, licentiate holding master's degree)

LIC Lands Improvement Company; Liquor Industry Council; Local Import Control

LICA *Ligue Internationale Contre le Racisme et l'Antisemitisme* (French—International League Against Racism and Antisemitism)

LICC London Institute for Contemporary Christianity; Long Island Council of Churches

licd licensed

Lic D *Licenciado Don* (Spanish —Sir Lawyer)

lic dlr licensed dealer

LICeram Licentiate of the Institute of Ceramics

licm left intercostal margin

Lic Med Licentiate in Medicine

licorice stick clarinet's nickname

Lic Phil Licentiate in Philosophy

LICTBOSS Life-Cycle Theory of Bureaucratic Ossfication

Lic Theol Licentiate in Theology

LID League for Industrial Democracy

L & ID London and India Docks

lidar laser radar device (for measuring wind direction and speed); laser-impulsed radar; light detection and ranging (laser-beam air pollution or smog measuring device)

LIDB Logistics Ingelligence Data Base

LIDC Lead Industries Development Council; Livestock Industry Development Council

LIDO Logistics Inventory Disposition Order

lidoc lidocaine (xylocain)

Lie Liepaya

LIE Liberal Intellectual Establishment (Philip Wylie's acronymic description of the befuddled and often nonsensical liberals of his time, the Old Left, the so-called New Left)

LIEAP Low-Income Energy-Assistance Program

Liech Liechtenstein

Liechtenstein Principality of Liechtenstein (Alpine country whose Lichtensteiners speak German, these highly productive people export ceramics, false teeth as well as drugs, machinery, and textiles) *Fürstentum Liechtenstein*

Lief *Lieferung* (German—issue)

Liege Liege's provincial capital in Belgium

Liége (French—Luik)

LIEJA Long Island Equal Justice Association

LIEMA Long Island Electronics Manufacturers Association

Liepaja (Latvian—Libau)

LIESA Long Island Episcopal Schools Association

Lietuva (Lithuanian—Lithuania)

Lieut Lieutenant

Lieut Col Lieutenant Colonel

Lieut Comdr Lieutenant Commander

Lieut Gen Lieutenant General

Lieut Gov Lieutenant Governor

lif left iliac fossa

LIF Lone Indian Fellowship

LIFA Life Insurance Federation of Australia

life. laser-induced flourescence of the environment

LIFE Ladies Involved For Education, League for International Food Education

lifes laser-induced flourescence and environmental sensing

Life Sta Lifeboat Station (US Coast Guard)

liff laser-induced fluorescence fluorimetry

LI Fire Eng Licentiate of the Institution of Fire Engineers

llfmop llnearly frequency-modulated pulse

lifo last in, first out

LIFR Low Instrument Flight Rules

lift. logically-integrated fortran translator

LIFT London International Festival of Theatre; London International Freight Terminal

Liftmaster Douglas DC-6 92-passenger transport

lig ligament; ligature

Lig Limoges

Lige Elijah

liger offspring of lion and tigress

light. lighting; lightning

Light of the Ages Moses ben Maimon of Cordoba also known as Maimonades

Light of Asia Gautama Buddha

lightex searchlight illumination exercise

Lighthorse Harry Major General Henry (Lighthorse Harry) Lee, USA—father of Robert E. Lee

Lighthouse of the Pacific *El Faro del Pacifico*—Izalco Volcano—whenever active, its fire can be seen from planes and ships several hundred miles away from El Salvador

Lightning British BAC all-weather supersonic jet

lign *lignende* (Dano-Norwegian—similar)

lignite brown coal

liguid. liguidation

Liguori Liguori Publications

Ligurian Republic Republic of Genoa

Ligurians Ligurian Alps or Ligurian Apennines of northwestern Italy or the people of the region around the Gulf of Genoa

lih left inguinal hernia; light intensity high

LIHDC Low Income Housing Development Corporation

Likasi formerly Jadotville in the Belgian Congo

Lik Obs Bull *Lick Observatory Bulletin(s)*

lil light intensity low; lilliputian; little

li'l little

Lil Lilian; Lillian; Lily

LIL Lunar International Laboratory (proposed in 1961 by Dr Theodore von Karman)

lila life insurance logistics automated

Lilac New Hampshire state flower and nickname sometimes given New Hampshire girls recalling the Purple Lilac of this New England State

Lila Lee Augusta Appel

LILCO Long Island Lighting Company

l'Île de Lumiére (French—Island of Light)—New Caledonia

Lille (French—Lisle)

Lillian Gish Lillian De Guiche

Lillian Nordica Lilly Norton

Lillian Russell Helen Louise Leonard

Lillibet Elizabeth

Lillie Emily; Lillian; Lillie Langtry—the Jersey Lily—christened Emily Charlotte Le Breton

Lilli Palmer Lillie Marie Peiser

Lilly Lilian; Lillian

lilo last in, last out

LILS Lead-in-Light System (airport term)

Lily Utah state flower, the sego lily

Lily of France symbolic *fleur de lis* or lily flower

Lily-Lilo Rosalie Texier

lim light intensity marker; limber; limit(er); line induction motor; line insulation monitor; line interface module; linear induction motor; linear-induction motor(s); liquid injection moulding; locator inner marker

Lim Limerick

LIM Lima, Peru (Callao International Airport)

Lima letter L radio code; (pronounced *leema*)

LIMA Long Island Museum Association

LIMAC Linden Industrial Mutual Aid Council

Limbo of the Lost the Bermuda Triangle also called the Devil's Triangle

lim dat limiting date

lime calcium oxide (CaO)

Limejuicer British sailor

limestone calcium carbonate (CaCO₃)

Lime Street Liverpool, England's street of streetwalkers

limewater calcium-hydroxide solution—Ca(OH)₂; limejuice and water mixture

Limeyland England

Limey(s) Limejuicer(s)—British sailor(s) or ship(s); nickname derived from their use of lime-juice to ward off scurvy

lim-lib(s) limousine liberal(s)

limnol limnology

Limnos (Greek—Lemnos)

limo lemonade; limousine

limon lime-and-lemon (hybrid citrus fruit)

Limón Puerto Limón, Costa Rica

limos limousines

limp limp cloth binding; limp cloth bound

l'Impériale Haydn's Symphony No. 53 in D major

Limpopo short form for the Limpopo or Crocodile River of East Africa where in 1497 Vasco da Gama named it Rio do Espiritu Santo

LIMRA Life Insurance Marketing and Research Association

LIMRF Life Insurance Medical Research Fund

LIMS Logistic Inventory Management System

limvr linear-induction motor vehicle research

lin lineal; linear

lín línea (Spanish—line)

Lin Lincoln; Linda; Lindenberg(er); Lindley; Limdolfo; Limdon; Lindsay; Linley; Linnaeus; Linsley, Linton; Linus

L i N Lokalhistorisk institutt Norge (Norwegian Local History Institute)

LIN Linjeflyg (Swedish airline); Milan, Italy (Linate Airport)

Lina Angelina; Carolina; Caroline

linac linear accelerator

Linacre Linacre College, Oxford

linc laboratory instrument computer

Linc Lincoln; Lincoln College, Oxford

LINC Learning Institute of North Carolina; Logic and Information Network Coupler

Linc Coll Lincoln College—Oxford

LINCO Linearly-Organized Chemical Code (for computer system)

Lincoln 16th President of the United States and name of Nebraska's capital

Lincoln's Abraham Lincoln's Birthday (February 12)

Lincoln's Shrine Springfield, Illinois

Lincoln's State Illinois

lincompex linked compressor and expander

Lincs Lincoln automobiles; Lincolnshire

LINCS Language Information Network and Clearinghouse System

Lindbergh Charles A Lindbergh; Lindbergh Field (San Diego's international airport honoring the memory of the first solo transatlantic flight from New York to Paris but starting from San Diego, California where the *Spirit of St Louis* was built under Lindbergh's direction)

LINDE Linde Air Products

Lindy Colonel Charles A Lindbergh

Line The Line—the Equator

Lines Line Islands in the equatorial mid-Pacific Ocean where they include Caroline, Christmas, Fanning, Flint, Kingman Reef, Malden, Palmyra, Starbuck, Vostock, and Washing-ton Islands

lines/m lines per minute

lines/mm lines per millimeter

lines/s lines per second

L-Infre Loire-Inférieure

lin ft linear feet; linear foot

ling linguist(ics)

Linguis Linguistics

linim liniment

Linlithgow West Lothian, Scotland

Linn Linné; Linnaeus

Linnaeus Carl von Linné

lino linoleum; linotype; linotypist

linol linoleum

Linoleum Capital of Scotland Kirkaldy

lino oper linotype operator

LINOSCO Libraries of North Staffordshire in Cooperation

LINS Laser Inertial Navigation System

L Inst Phys Licentiate of the Institute of Physics

LINTAS Lever's International Advertising Service

L'Intran L'Intransigeant

LINWR Lake Ilo National Wildlife Refuge (North Dakota)

lin yd linear yard

Linz Mozart's Symphony No. 36 in C major named for the Austrian town of Linz

LIO Lionel Corporation (stock exchange symbol); Lions International Organization; Livestock Improvement Organization

LIOB Licentiate of the Institute of Building

LIOCS Logical Input/Output Control System

Lion of the Caribbean Sir William Alexander Bustamante

Lion City Singapore

Lione (Italian—Lyons)

Lionel Barrymore Lionel Blythe

Lion Flag Ceylon's emblem featuring a golden lion with an upraised scimitar in his right paw comes from the ancient name for this island

Lion of Judah Emperor Haile Selassie of Ethiopia

Lion of the North King Gustavus Adolphus of Sweden

Lion's Gate harbor entrance of Vancouver, British Columbia

Lion Tamer Ian Smith (The George Washington of Rhodesia)

Liorna (Spanish—Livorno)—Leghorn

lip. lease in perpetuity; life in-surance policy

lip (Latin prefix—fat)—lipectomy

LIP Local Initiatives Program

Lipari Islands Italian penal colony northeast of Sicily; islands include Stromboli and Vulcano; also called Aeolian Islands

Liparis Lipari Islands

LIPC Livestock Industry Promotion Corporation

LIPI Lembaga Ilmu Pengetahuan Indonesia (Indonesian Academy of Sciences)

lipl (LIPL) linear information programming language

LIPM Lister Institute of Preventive Medicine

lipo lipogram(matic)

Li Po Li T'ai-po

Lippincott J B Lippincott Company

Lippy Leo Ernest Durocher

lips. logical inferences per second

Lipsia (Latin—Leipzig)

lip sync lip synchronization (in sound films)

lipup backward pupil (pupil spelled backwards)

liq liquid; liquor

liq f rkt liquid fuel rocket

liqn liquidación (Spanish—liquidation)

liqt liquid transient

LIR Liaison Investigation Report; Library of International Relations

L & IR Legislation and Intergovernmental Relations

lira. loft-type infrared analysis

LIRA Linen Industry Research Association; Logging Industry Research Association

lirbm liver, iron, red bone marrow

LIRES Literature Retrieval System

LIRES-MS Literature Retrieval System-Multiple Searching

LIRI Leather Industries Research Institute

lirl low-intensity runway lights

liroc last instruction readout cycle

lirod lightweight radar and optronic director

LIRR Long Island Railroad

LIRS Lutheran Immigration and Refugee Service

LIRT Library Instruction Round Table

lis laser isotape separation; lobar in situ

Lis Lisbon

LIS Liberian Information Service; Library and Information Science; Light Industry Services; Lisbon, Portugal (airport); Livestock Incentive Scheme; Lockheed Information System(s); Long Island Sound

LISA Linear Systems Analysis; Long Island Schizophrenia Association

LISA Library and Information Science Abstracts

Lisb *Lisboa* (Portuguese or Spanish—Lisbon); *Lisbona* (Italian—Lisbon)

Lisbeth Elisabeth; Eliza; Elizabeta; Elizabeth

Lisboa (Portuguese or Spanish—Lisbon)

Lisbona (Italian—Lisbon)

Lisbonne (French—Lisbon)

LISC Lions International Stamp Club; London Institute for the Study of Conflict

LISD Library Information Science Division (World Information Systems Exchange)

LISM Licentiate of the Incorporated Society of Musicians

LISO Library Information Service Office(r)

lisp. list processor (computer language)

LISP List Processing (for text manipulation)

LISPA Long Island Sound Pilots Association

LISR Line Information Storage and Retrieval

LISS London Institute of Strategic Studies

Lissabon (German—Lisbon)

list. laser and isotope separation technology

LIST Library and Information Services—Tees-side

LIST Library and Information Science Today

'listed enlisted

LISTEN Low-Income-Schools Teacher Education

'listment enlistment

Liszt Expert Alfred Brendel

lit literacy; literate

lit. liter; literal; literally; literary; literature; litter; little

l it lire italiane (Italian lire)

lit. litterae (Latin—letters)

Lit Litvak (Yiddish—Lithuanian)—person of Judaic origin from Lithuania or nearby regions

LIT Light Intratheater Transport (aircraft); Little Rock, Arkansas (airport)

LITA Library and Information Technology Association

litcrit literary critic(ism)

litcy literacy (ability to read and write)

lite light

LITE Legal Information Through Electronics

Literary Queen of Expatriate Americans Gertrude Stein

litex searchlight illumination exercise

lith lithograph; lithography; lithology

Lith Lithuania; Lithuanian

litharge lead oxide (PbO)

litho lithograph

lithol lithology

Lithuania Baltic country formerly inhabited by Lithuanians before resettlement by Soviet captors

LITINT Literacy International

litr lighter

litrg literage

Lits Lithuanians; Litvaks

litt litteratur or *litteraer* (Dano-Norwegian—literature or literary)

Litt.B. Litterarum Baccalaureus (Latin—Bachelor of Letters)

Litt.D. Litterarum Doctor (Latin—Doctor of Letters)

Little Little, Brown

Little Schubert's Symphony No. 6 in C

Little Alfie Alfred Austin

Little America Antarctic camp at the edge of the Ross Ice Shelf and the Bay of Whales where Admiral Byrd headquartered; London's Grosvenor Square where John Adams lived at No. 9 when he was America's first ambassador to Great Britain; now site of the U.S. Embassy

Little Belt Lillebaelt (strait separating island of Fyn from Danish mainland between Baltic Sea and the Kattegat)

Little Boy A-bomb dropped on Japanese targets before the end of World War II

Little Britain Armorica or Brittany in northern France

Little C-major Schubert's Symphony No. 6

Little Corporal five-foot-high Napoleon Bonaparte (*Le Petit Caporal*)

Little Denmark Solvang, California

Little Egypt delta country of southern Illinois around Cairo and the confluence of the Ohio

and Mississippi

Little England of the Caribbean Barbados

Little Flower Fiorello H La Guardia

Little Giant Knute Nelson—intellectually alive but physically small populist governor of Minnesota; oratorically gifted Senator Stephen Douglas of Illinois

Little Havana Cuban-refugee-populated sections of Miami, Florida

Little Holland Garibaldi, Oregon

Little Ida Idaho—smallest of the western states

Little Inch 20-inch pipeline paralleling the Big Inch

Little India of the Pacific Fiji Islands with its vast population of people from India

Little Italy Italian section of any American or Canadian city

Little Joe Apollo spacecraft booster designed and produced by General Dynamics, Convair

Little John surface-to-surface rocket produced by Emerson Electric

Little Lad of Landau American political cartoonist Thomas (Th) Nast born in Landau, Germany

Little Lady in Pants Dr Mary Walker

Little Lunnon Colorado Springs, Colorado (where so many Britishers abide)

Little Luther Hans Kung

Little Mac General George B Mc Clellan

Little Magician Martin Van Buren—New York's astute politician—Vice President and President of the United States

Little Mermaid Edvard Eriksen's bronze statue of a maiden seated atop a rock and looking out to sea from Copenhagen's harbor—immortalized in Hans Christian Andersen's fairy tale

Little Neddies Economic Development Committees

Little New York nickname of Miami Beach, Florida's South Beach

Little Old Lady of Pennsylvania Avenue Federal Trade Commission's nickname

Little Paradise Queen Victoria's nickname for the Isle of Wight

Little Phil General Philip Henry Sheridan

Little Red Book quotations of Mao Tse-tung

Little Rhody Rhode Island's official nickname

Little Rock capital of Arkansas

Little Russian Tchaikovsky's Symphony No. 2 in C minor

Little's disease congential spastic paralysis

Little Sure Shot Annie Oakley (Mrs Frank Butler)

Little Tiger mainland China's hydrofoil patrol boat called Hu Chwan

Little Tokyo Japanese section of any American or Canadian city

Little Van President Martin Van Buren

Little Van Dyke Gonzales Cocx —Flemish portrait painter who imitated the style of Van Dyke but painted family groups on small canvases

Little Van's Lady Hannah Van Buren—wife of President Martin Van Buren

Little Venice Lake Maracaibo, Venezuela

Little White House Franklin D Roosevelt's farm home near Warm Springs, Georgia

Little Yellow Book quotations of Deng Xiaoping

Litt. M. Master of Letters

Lituania (Spanish—Lithuania)

litur liturgical; liturgy

liturg liturgical; liturgistic; liturgy

Litva (Russian—Lithuania)

Litvak(s) Lithuanian(s)

Litz Litzendraht (German—wire)

LIU Long Island University

Liu-Kiu (Chinese—Ryukyu Islands)

LIUNA Laborers International Union of North America

LIUP Long Island University Press

liv liver

liv le livre (French—book); *la livre* (French—pound)

Liv Liverpool

Liv Titus Livius (Roman historian often referred to as Livy)

LIV Light Infantry Volunteers

Live Oak State Florida

Liver Liverpool; Liverpudlian(s)

Liverpool Liverpool Prison (also called LP)

livex live exercise (military)

Living Declaration of Indepen-

dence Thomas Paine

Livonia old Baltic province of Russia, divided after World War I between Estonia and Latvia

Livorno (Italian—Leghorn)

livr livraison (French—issue of a journal, part of a book or serial)

liv st livre sterling (French—pound sterling)

Liv St Liverpool Street (rail terminal)

Livy Olivia; Roman historian Titus Livius

lix lixiviation

liz Lizard; lizzie (as in *tin lizzie,* an old Ford Automobile)

Liz(a) Eliza(beth)

Lizard Lizard Head, Lizard Peninsula, Lizard Point, Lizard Town—all very close together in Britain's southernmost sector at the tip of southwest Cornwall

LIZARDS Library Information Search and Retrieval Data System

Lizard State Alabama

Lizbeth Elizabeth

Lizzy Elizabeth

lj life jacket

LJ Law Judge; Libby, McNeil & Libby (stock exchange symbol); Library Journal; Lord Justice; Sierra Leone Airways (2-letter coding)

LJ laufen Jahre (German—current year); *Law Journal*; *Library Journal*

LJC Lackawanna Junior College; Laredo Junior College; Lincoln Junior College

LJMCA La Jolla Museum of Contemporary Art

LJR Law Journal Reports

LJ/SLJ Library Journal/School Library Journal

LJT Lear jet airplane

LJTSA Library of the Jewish Theological Seminary of America (NYC)

LJU La Jolla University

Ljuba Welitsch Ljuba Velichkova

lk link

Lk Lake (postal abbreviation); Luke

LK Lockheed Aircraft Corporation (stock exchange symbol)

LKAB Luossavaara-Kiirunavaara Aktiebolag (iron-ore mines in Luossa-Kiiruna range of northern Sweden)

LKB Link-Belt Company (stock exchange symbol)

lkd locked

lked linkage editor

lkg locking

lkg & bkg leakage and breakage

LKGR Lake Kyle Game Reserve (Rhodesia)

lk-n lock-in

LK & PRR Lahaina-Kaanapali and Pacific Railroad

LKQCPI Licentiate of the King and Queen's College of Physicians of Ireland

lkr locker

Lkr Landskrona

lks links; liver, kidney, spleen

Lks Lakes (postal abbreviation)

Lksde Lakeside

lkt lookout

lk up lock up

Lkw Lastkraftwagen (German—lorry, truck)

lkwash lockwasher

ll land lines; light lock; limited liability; live load; long lead; lower left; low(er) level; lower lid; lower limit

ll (Ll) landlord

l/l library labels; line-by-line; looseleaf; lower left; lower limit

l & l leave and liberty; look and listen

'll (contraction of till and will)

ll lectiones (Latin—readings); *llegada* (Spanish—arrival)

LL Language Laboratory; Language Lessons; Law List(ing); Lebanese pound; Lending Library; Little League (baseball); Loftleidir (Icelandic Airlines); Lord Lieutenant; Low Latin

LL (Ec) Ecclesiastic Late Latin

L/L Lutlang (Norwegian—limited company)

lla left lower arm; limiting lines of approach

LLA Lend-Lease Administration; Louisiana Library Association; Luther League of America

llama. long-life atmospheric-motoring airship

Llanfairp Llanfairpwllgwyngllgogershwyrndro-bwllabtysiliogogoch (Welsh place-name meaning the Church of St Mary near the Raging Whirlpool and the Church of St Tysilio by the Red Cave)—probably the longest word in any of the world's more than 2700 languages and well deserving of abbreviation

llano (Spanish—plain, prairie, as in Llano Estacado)

Llano Estacado (Spanish—

Staked Plain)—extends from New Mexico to Texas

Llanos tropical grasslands of Colombia and Venezuela

L Lat Late Latin; Low Latin

llb long-leg brace

LLB Little League Baseball

LL.B. *Legum Baccalaureus* (Latin—Bachelor of Laws)

LLBA *Language and Language Behavior Abstracts*

llbcd left lower border of cardiac dullness

LLBO Liquor License Board of Ontario

l-l brace long-leg brace

llbs low-level bombsight

llc lower left center

LLC Libertarian Law Council; Library Learning Center; Living Learning Center (Indiana University)

ll. cc. *locis citatis* (Latin—in the places cited)

llcca long-life cycle-cost avionics

LLCM Licentiate of the London College of Music

LLCO Licentiate of the London College of Osteopathy

Ll & C's Lloyd's and Companies

LLCUNAE Law Library of Congress United Association of Employees

LL.D. *Legum Doctor* (Latin—Doctor of Laws)

LlD factor *Lactobacillus lactis* Dorner factor (vitamin B_{12})

lle left lower extremity

lle *llegada* (Spanish—arrival)

LLE Laboratory for Laser Energetics (University of Rochester)

LLEI *Lincoln Library of Essential Information*

L Lett Licentiate of Letters

L-L f Laki-Lorand factor

LLF Laubach Literacy Fund

llfm land line frequency modulation

lli latitude and longitude indicator; long lead items

LLI Laubach Literacy International; Lord Lieutenant of Ireland

LLIL Long Lead Item List(ing)

LLJ Leaf Library of Judaica

LLJJ Lords Justices

lll left lower limb; left lower lobe; light load line; loose-leaf ledger; low-level logic

l/ll line-by-line libretto

LLL Lawrence Livermore Laboratories; Lutheran Laymen's League

LLL *Love's Labour's Lost*

lllb left long-leg brace

LLLI La Leche League International

llll left lower lung lobe

lllp leased long-lines program

llltv low-light-level television

llm localized leucocyte mobilization

LL. M. *Legum Magister* (Latin—Master of Laws)

LLN League for Less Noise

LLNL Lawrence Livermore National Laboratory

LLNNR Loch Leven National Nature Reserve (Scotland)

LLNWR Long Lake National Wildlife Refuge (North Dakota)

lloc land line of communications

Lloydbras Lloyd Brasileiro

Lloyd's *Lloyd's Register of Shipping*

Lloyd's Bank Lloyd's Bank International

Lloyd's of London an insurance company and not to be confused with other Lloyd entries

LLP Lifetime Learning Publications

L L & P of H Life, Liberty, and the Pursuit of Happiness (original draft of the *Declaration of Independence* read: "Life, Liberty, and the Pursuit of Prof it")

LLPI Linen and Lace Paper Institute

llps low-level pumping station

llq left lower quadrant

llqa limiting lines of quiet approach

llr lender of last resort; line of least resistance; load-limiting resistor; log-likelihood ratio; long-length record(ing)

llr (LLR) latent lethality of radiation

LLRS Laser Lightning-Rod System

llrv (LLRV) lunar landing research vehicle

lls low-level solids

LLS Lunar Logistics System

LLSS Low-Level Sounding System

llsv (LLSV) lunar logistics system vehicle

llt long lead time

LLT London Landed Terms

llti long lead time items

lltruw low-level transuranic waste(s)

lltv low-light-level television

llu lending library unit

LLU Loma Linda University

LLUU Laymen's League—Unitarian Universalist

llv (LLV) lunar landing vehicle

llw lower low water (LLW); low-level waste

LLWI lower low water interval

llwl light load water line

LLWM Low-Level Waste Management

Lly Llanelly

llyp long-leaf yellow pine

llz localizer

lm land mine; light metal(s); liquid metal(s); long meter; longitudinal muscle; lower motor; lumen(s)

l/m lines per minute

lm *livello del mare* (Italian—sea level)

l.m. *locus monumenti* (Latin—place of the monument)

Lm middle latitude

LM Legion of Merit; Liggett Myers Tobacco (stock exchange symbol); Lincoln Memorial; Lord Mayor; Lourenço Marques; Lunar Module

L.M. Licentiate in Midwifery

L & M Linotype and Machinery

LM *Lacus Mortis* (lunar area)

LM-1 Fuji Heavy Industries trainer plane

lma left mento-anterior

LMA Last Manufacturers Association; League for Mutual Aid; Lingerie Manufacturers Association; London-Midlands Association

LMAA Lift Manufacturers Association of Australia

LMAC Labor-Management Advisory Committee

lmad let's make a deal

LMAF Live Missile Assembly Facility

LMAGB Locomotive and Allied Manufacturers' Association of Great Britain

lmb local message box

LMBA London Master Builders' Association

LMBC Liverpool Marine Biological Committee

l & m bond labor and material bond

LMBP Lake Manyas Bird Paradise (Turkey)

lmc liquid-metal cycle; low middling clause

LMC Lake Michigan College; Liberia Mining Company; Lloyd's Machinery Certificate; Lutheran Medical Center

LMC (LMC) Lloyd's Machinery Certificate (temporarily suspended when enclosed in parentheses)

LMCA Lorry Mounted Crane Association

LMCC Licentiate of the Medical Council of Canada

LMCT Licensed Motor Car Trader

lmd local medical doctor

LMD Laboratory of Meteorological Dynamics

LMDC Lawyers Military Defense Committee

lme liquid-metal embrittlement

LME Late Middle English; London Metal Exchange

LMEC Liquid Metal Engineering Center (AEC)

L Med Licentiate in Medicine

L Med Ch Licentiate in Medicine and Surgery

LMEE Light Military Electronic Equipment (department of General Electric)

lmf language media format

l/mf low and medium frequency

lmfbr liquid-metal fast-breeder reactor

lmfr liquid metal fuel reactor

lm/ft^2 lumen per square foot

lmg liquefied methane gas

Lmg *Leichtesmachinengewehr* (German—light machine gun)

LMG light machine gun

LMH Lady Margaret Hall, Oxford

LMHC Lady Margaret Hall College (Oxford)

lm hormone lipid mobilizing hormone

lm-hr lumen-hour

L Mi Leo Minor (constellation)

LMI Lawn Mower Institute; Logistics Management Institute

l/min liters per minute

LMIS Labor Market Information System

lml left mediolateral

LML Lankard Materials Laboratory; Lerner Marine Laboratory

LMLA Lizzardo Museum of Lapidary Arts

LMLI Liberty Mutual Life Insurance

lm/lm^2 lumen per square meter

lmlr load memory lockout register

lm/lrv lunar module/lunar roving vehicle (LM/LRV)

lmm localiser middle marker; locator at middle marker (compass)

l/mm lines per millimeter

LMM Library Microfilms and Materials

lmmi like mamma made it

lmn lineman; lower motor neuron

LMNP Lake Manyara National Park (Tanzania)

LMNRA Lake Mead National Recreation Area (Arizona and Nevada)

lmo lens-modulated oscillator; light machine oil

LMO Local Medical Officer; Logistics Management Office (USA); London Meteorological Office

lmp last menstrual period; left mento-posterior; lunar module pilot

LMP Linea Mexicana del Pacifico

LMP *Literary Market Place* (Directory of American Book Publishers)

LMPA Library and Museum of the Performing Arts (Lincoln Center, New York City)

lmpf lymph mode permeability factor

LMPT Logistics and Material Planning Team

L Mq Lourenço Marques

LMR Lifetime Merit Register; London Midland Region—British Railways

LMRC London Medical Research Council

LMRCP Licentiate in Midwifery of the Royal College of Physicians

LMRI Living Marine Resources, Inc

lmrp lower marine riser package (oil well)

LMRSH Licentiate Member of the Royal Society for the Promotion of Health

LMRU Library Management Research Unit (Cambridge)

lms lambs; least mean square

lms (LMS) lunar mass spectrometer

lm's lunar modules (LMs)

lm/s lumen per second

LMS Lelean Memorial School; Licentiate in Medicine and Surgery; London Mathematical Society; Lotto Management Services

LMSA Labor Management Services Administration

LMSC Lockheed Missiles & Space Company

LMSD Lockheed Missile and Space Division

LMSSA Licentiate in Medicine and Surgery of the Society of Apothecaries

lmst loom state

lmt left mento-transverse; length, mass, time; limit

LMT Local Mean Time

LMTA Language Modalities Test for Aphasis; Library Media Technical Assistant; London Master Typefounders' Association

lmtd limited; logarithmic mean temperature difference

lmtg limiting

LMU Loyola Marymount University

LMUM Ludwig-Maximilians-Universität München (University of Munich)

L Mus Licentiate in Music

L Mus TCL Licentiate in Music—Trinity College of Music

LMVD Licensed Motor Vehicle Dealer

LMVUS League of Men Voters of the United States

lm/w lumen per watt

lm/W lumen(s) per watt

ln liaison; logarithm (natural, base *e*)

Ln Lane; London; Lyttelton

LN Air Liban (Lebanese Airlines); League of Nations; Napierian logarithm (symbol)

L & N Leeds & Northrup; Louisville & Nashville (railroad)

L of N League of Nations

LN$_2$ liquid nitrogen

LN$_2$cou liquid-nitrogen clip-on unit

LN$_2$ trailer liquid-nitrogen trailer

lna low noise amplifier

LNA Liberian National Airways; Libyan News Agency

lnb (LNB) large navigational buoy

lnc loran navigation chart(s)

LNC Leith Nautical College; Libertarian National Committee

lnchr launcher

L-N CP Liberal-National Country Party (Australian)

LNDC Lesotho National Development Corporation

Lndg Landing

lndh local nationals direct hire

lndrs laundress

lndry laundry

lndscp landscape; landscaping

L & NE Lehigh & New England (railroad)

LNER London and North Eastern Railway

lng length (flow chart); lining; liquefied natural gas; lounge

lng (LNG) liquefied natural gas

lngc (LNGC) liquefied natural gas carrier

LNG tanker liquid-natural-gas tanker

LNHS London Natural History Society

LNI *Lega Navale Italiana* (Italian Naval League)

LNLA Lithuanian National League of America

lnlw lowest normal low water

lnmp last normal menstrual period

LNNP Lake Nakuru National Park (Kenya)

LNNR Lindisfarne National Nature Reserve (England)

LNOC Libya National Oil Company

L-note $50 bill

lnp (LNP) lunar neutron probe

LNP Lamington National Park (Queensland); Lincoln NP (South Australia); London Northern Polytechnic

lnpf lymph node permeability factor

lnr liner; low noise receiver

LNR Loteni Nature Reserve (South Africa)

Lnrk Lanark

LNS Land Navigation System; Liberation News Service

LNSW Library of New South Wales

LNT Leo Nicholas Tolstoy

Lntl lintel

lntwta low-noise travelling-wave tube amplifier

lnu last name unknown

LNU League of Nations Union

LNWR Lacassine National Wildlife Refuge (Louisiana); Lacreek NWR (South Dakota); London and North Western Railway, Lostwood NWR (North Dakota); Loxahatchee NWR (Florida)

lo layout; light open; local; local oscillator; locked open; longitudinal optical; low; low gear; low lights; low(er) order; lubricating oil; lubrication order

lo (LO) longitudinal optic

lo' look

'lo hello

Lo low (gear)

Lo *Lordag* (Danish—Lord's Day)—Saturday

LO Land Office; Launch Operator; Liaison Office(r); Lick Observatory (Mount Hamilton,

California); Livestock Office; London Office; Louisville Orchestra; Lowell Observatory (Flagstaff, Arizona); Lubrication Order; Polish Airlines (2-letter symbol)

L/O Letter of Offer

LO *Landsorganisationen* (leading trade union in Norway and Sweden)

LO₂ liquid oxygen

loa leave of absence; left occiput anterior; length overall

loa (LOA) light observation aircraft

LOA Letter of Agreement; Letter of Offer and Acceptance; Letter Officers Association; Letter Offices Association; Light Observation Aircraft; Lithuanian Organists Alliance

loadex loading exercise

loadg & dischg loading and discharging

loadicator computerized shiploading indicator

LOAF Lesbians Over the Age of Forty

loan/A vessel(s) loaned to Army

loan/C vessel(s) loaned to Coast Guard

loan/m vessel(s) loaned to miscellaneous governmental activities (Maritime Academy)

loan/s vessel(s) loaned to states

LOANZ Life Offices Association of New Zealand

LOAP List of Applicable Publications

lob line of balance

lob. logs on board; lumber on board

LOB Launch Operations Building; Loyal Order of the Boar; Loyal Order of Boors; Loyal Order of Bores

lobal long base-line buoy

lobar long baseline radar

Lobgesang (German—Hymn of Praise)—Mendelssohn's Symphony No. 2 in B-flat major

loboto lobotomy

lob(s) lobster(s)

loc lines of communication; locate; location; locus of control; logistics other charges

l-o-c letter of credit

LoC Library of Congress

LOC Launch(ing) Operations Center; Launch(ing) Operations Complex; Letter of Certification; Louisiana Office of Conservation; Lyric Opera of Chicago

loca loss of coolant accident (nu-

clear reactor)

local. load on call; local area network

lo-cal low calorie

locals local people; local trains

locat location; low-altitude clear-air turbulence

LOCATE Library of Congress Automation Techniques Exchange

LOCC Logistical Operations Control Center

loc.cit. *loco citato* (Latin—in the place cited)

loc. dol. *loco dolenti* (Latin—to the painful spot)

loci logarithmic computing instrument

Lock City Stamford, Connecticut

Lock Town Stamford, Connecticut

loc. laud. *loco laudato* (Latin—cited in the approved place)

locn location

loco locomotion; locomotive

locp launcher operation control panel

locport lines of communications ports

loc. primo cit. *loco primo citato* (Latin—in the place first cited)

loc pr pnl local control purge panel

locpuro local purchase order

LOCS Librascope Operations Control System

loc. supra cit. *loco supra citato* (Latin—in the place cited above)

locum tens. *locum tenens* (Latin—temporary position)

locuz *locuzione* (Latin—phrase)

lod limitation on dividends, line of duty

lo-d low-density

Lod Lödöse

LOD Launch Operations Directorate

lodestone magnetic iron oxide; Fe₃O₄: magnetite

lodg loading; lodging

lodif long-distance infrared flash (camera)

lodor loaded (vessel) awaiting orders or assignment

loe level of effort

LOE Light-Off Examination (USN)

LOEE Loyal Order of Overtime Experts

lof lecherous old fool; lowest operating frequency

LOF Lloyd's Open Form (insurance policy); Lloyd's Open-

Form (contract); London and Overseas Freighter

L-O-F Libbey-Owens-Ford

lo-fi low fidelity (low-quality sound reproduction)

Lofotens Lofoten Islands

loft. low-frequency radio telescope

lofti low-frequency trans-ionosphere (research satellite)

Loftleidir Icelandic Airlines

log. logarithm; logic; logical; logistic(s)

Log Longview

LOG Legion of Guardsmen

log.$_{10}$ logarithm to the base 10

logair logistics transport by air

logairnet logistics air network

logal logical algorithmic language

Logan Logan International Airport (named for WW-II hero General Edward Lawrence Logan who gave land to the city of Boston now served by this airport)

logands logic commands

logan(s) loganberry; loganberries

LOGC Logistics Center (USA)

LOGCMD Logistical Command

logcom logistic communications

Log Com Logistical Command; Logistics Command

LOGDESMAP Logistics Data Element Standardization and Management Program (DoD)

LOGDESMO Logistics Data Element Standardization and Management Office (DoD)

LOGDIV Logistics Division

log.$_e$ logarithm to the base e

logel logic-generating language

logest logistics estimate

logg loggerhead; loggia; logging; log glass

logie killogie

logipac logical processor and computer

loglan logical language

logland logistics transport by land

logo logogram [initial letter, number, or symbol used as an abbreviation or as part of an abbreviation as in Q & A (question and answer), 3M (Minnesota Mining and Manufacturing Company), c (cents)]; logotype (two or more type characters cast as one piece of type, as in *and, on, re, the,* or as shown in many trademarks and trade names

cast as one piece)

LOGOIS Logistics Operating Information System

logol logological; logologically; logologist; logology

logophi logophilia(c)—lover(r) of words

logp logistics plans

logr logistical ration; logistics ratio

Logr Logroño

logram logical program

Log Rep Logistics Representative (USN)

logsea logistics transport by sea

logsup logistical support; logistics support

logsvc logistics service

logy from the Greek *logia* or *logos* meaning the word as in anthropology, biology, cytology, embryology, histology, urology, etc.

loh (LOH) light observation helicopter

L o H Library of Hawaii (Honolulu)

loi loss on ignition

LOI Lunar Orbit Insertion

loib lunar orbit insertion burn

loid celluloid (strip used by burglars to unlock doors)

LOIS Library Order Information System

lo-J low inertia

loktal locked octal tube

lol length of lead (actual); little old lady

LOL Lobitos Oilfields Limited; Loyal Orange Lodge

lola lollapalooza (excellent or extraordinary person or thing)

Lola Dolores

LOLA Library On-Line Acquisition

Lola Montez stage name of Marie Dolores Eliza Rosanna Gilbert also known as the Comtesse de Lansfeld, Mrs Heald, Mrs Hull, and Mrs James

lolita language on-line investigation/transformation of abstractions; library on-line information and text access

lolli lollipop

lo-lo load on-load off

lom locater at outer marker (compass)

Lom Columbus

LOM League of Mothers; List of Modifications; Loyal Order of Moose

LOMA Life Office Management Association

LOMAC Logical Machine Corporation

poration

Lomb Lombard; Lombardian; Lombardy

Lombardei (German—Lombardy)

Lombardia (Italian or Portuguese—Lombardy)

Lombardía (Spanish—Lombardy)

Lombardije (Dutch—Lombardy)

Lombardy English name for Lombardia

lo mi low mileage

Lompoc Federal Correctional Institution at Lompoc, California also site of a Federal Prison Camp

lon longitud (Spanish—longitude)

Lon Alonso; London

LON London, England (London-Central Airport)

Lon Brg London Bridge (rail terminal)

Lond *Londen* (Dutch—London); London; Londonderry; Londoner(s); *Londra* (Italian—London); *Londres* (French, Portuguese, Spanish—London)

Londen (Afrikaans or Dutch—London)

Londinium (Latin—London)—also written Londinum, Londinia, Londonia

Londinum Gothorum (Latin—Gothic London)—the Swedish university town of Lund

london london broil (thinly-sliced flank steak broiled before serving); london brown (carbuncle gemstone)

London Haydn's Trios No. 1 and 2 (for two flutes and cello); Haydn's Symphony No. 104 in D major; Symphony No. 2 by Vaughan-Williams—A London Symphony

London Bach Johann Christian Bach

London of the Scanians King Canute the Great's name for Lund, Sweden; Scandic capital he founded to match his London of the English

London by the Sea Brighton (British seaside resort one hour from London)

London Suite London Again or *London Every Day* (symphonic suite by Eric Coates)

London-super-Mare Brighton

London Town London, England

Londra (Italian—London)

Londres (French, Portuguese,

Spanish—London)

Lone Eagle Charles A Lindbergh

Lone Lion of Idaho Senator William E Borah

Lonely Iconoclast George S Schuyler

Lone Star State Texas whose flag contains one lone star

long longeron; longitude

Long Longfellow; Longford; Long Island; Longjumeau; Long Key; Longmeadow; Longview

Longhair Lair New York's Lincoln Center of the Performing Arts

Longhorn(s) Texan(s) named after the longhorn cattle characteristic of Texas in its pioneer period

Long Island Sound Atlantic Ocean inlet between Connecticut, Long Island, and New York—serves coastal shipping between New England and New York

longl longitudinal

Long Lane Girls Long Lane School for (delinquent) Girls at Middletown, Connecticut

Longos (Mexican-American— Long Beach, California)

Longshanks Edward I of England

Longshoremen's Union International Longshoremen's Association

Longshore Philosopher Eric Hoffer

'longside alongside

Long Straight The Long Straight —297-mile-long (478-kilometer-long) straight stretch of railway track laid across Australia's Nullarbor Plain—the world's longest straight stretch of railroad

Long Tom Thomas Jefferson— third President of the United States

longv longevity

long vac long vacation

Lon'on Town British nickname for London

LONRHO London and Rhodesian Mining and Land Company Limited

loo looker; looker-after; looker-on

looktr lookout tower

LOOM Loyal Order of Moose

Loop The Loop—Chicago's business section

LOOP Louisiana Offshore Oil Port

LOOS League of Older Students

lop. launch operator's panel; left occiput posterior

l-o-p line-of-position

LOP lunar orbiting photographic (vehicle)

lopar low-power acquisition radar

L O P & G Live Oak, Perry & Gulf (railroad)

lopkgs loose or in packages

lopo local post

LOPS Lloyd's Ocean Platform System

lopuro local purchase order

lo-q low iq (IQ)

loq *loquitur* (Latin—he speaks)

lor level of repair; lunar orbital rendezvous

Lor Lorenzo; Lorong

LOR *L'Osservatore Romano* (Papal Roman Observer)

lorac long-range accuracy

lorad long-range active detection

loran long-range aid to navigation

LORAPHS Long-Range Passive Homing System

LORAS Low-Range Omnidirectional Airspeed System

lord. long-range and detection (radar); lordosis

Lord Acton 1st Baron John Emerich Edward Dalberg-Acton

Lord Baltimore George Calvert

Lord Beaconsfield Benjamin Disraeli

Lord Beaverbrook William Maxwell Aitken

Lord Berners Gerald Hugh Tyrwhitt-Wilson

Lord Brougham Henry Peter

Lord Byron George Gordon Byron

Lord Chesterfield Philip Stanhope

Lord De La Warr Thomas West —Lord Delaware

Lord Desart William Ulick O'Connor Cuffe

Lord Dufferin Frederick Temple Hamilton Blackwood (Lord Rector of St Andrews University)

Lord Dunsany Edward John Moreton Drax Plunkett

Lord of the East Vladivostok

Lord Haw-Haw nickname of William Joyce (American-born British fascist who betrayed his countries by broadcasting in English from Berlin where he served the Nazis during World War II)

Lord of Hell Lucifer

Lord Kelvin William Thomson

Lord Kenneth Kenneth Clark— Lord Clark of Saltwood

Lord Keynes John Maynard Keynes (pronounced *Kanz*)

Lord Kinross John Patrick Douglas Balfour

Lord Kitchener Horatio Herbert (also known as the Earl of Khartoum)

Lord Macaulay Thomas Babington

Lord North Frederick North

Lord Palmerston Henry John Temple nicknamed Pam

Lord Passfield Sidney Webb

Lord Peter Death Brendon Wimsey Ian Carmichael

Lord Protector Oliver Cromwell —Lord Protector of England

Lord of Reason Bertrand A Russell

Lord of the Rings J(ohn) R(onald) R(euel) Tolkien

Lord Russell Bertrand A Russell

Lords House of Lords

Lord Salisbury Robert Arthur Talbot Gascoyne-Cecil

Lord of San Simeon William Randolph Hearst

Lord Tweedsmuir John Buchan

Lord of War Wotan

Lorenzo da Ponte Mozart's librettist whose real name was Emanuele Corregliano

Lorenzo the Magnificent Lorenzo de Medici

Loretta Young Gretchen Young

LORIDS Long-Range Iranian Detection System

Loris Hugo von Hofmannsthal

lorl (LORL) large orbital research laboratory

Lorong (Malay—Lane)

Lorriane (French—Lothringen)

Lorrie Laura; Lorraine

lorv (LORV) low orbital reentry vehicle

Lor^{zo} Lorenzo

los length of stay; liaison operating sheet; loss of signal

l-o-s line-of-sight

Los (Mexican-American truncation—Los Angeles)

LoS *Language of Sport* (Tim Considine's splendid guide)

LOS Lagos, Nigeria (airport); Law of the Sea; Little Orchestra Society; Lockheed Ocean Systems

Losa Los Angeles

Los Alamos Los Alamos National Laboratory

losam (LOSAM) low-altitude surface-to-air missile

Los Ang Los Angeles

Los Angeles (originally a Spanish settlement—*Nuestra Señora de los Angeles de Porciuncula*—Our Lady of the Angels above the river Porciuncula)

Los Angeles' Sister City Eilat—Israel's leading oil port at the head of the Gulf of Eilat off the Red Sea

Los Coronados (Spanish—Coronado Islands)—crown-like rocky islands off northwesternmost Pacific coast of Mexico and within sight of San Diego, California

Los Guilucos Los Guilucos School for (delinquent) Girls at Santa Rosa, California

lösl löslich (German—soluble)

Los Pinos (Spanish—The Pines) —official home of Mexico's presidents

LOSS Large Object Salvage System; Line Operation Status System

los sys landing observer's signal system

Lost City of the Incas Machu Picchu, Peru (near Cuzco, Peru)

Lost Colony Roanoke Island, North Carolina (site of Sir Walter Raleigh's first settlement)

lostf line-of-sight test fixture

Lost Wages Las Vegas, Nevada (gambling resort)

lot. large orbiting telescope; lateral olfactory tract; left occipito-transverse; load on top

lot. lotio (Latin—lotion)

LOT Polish Air Lines (3-letter symbol)

LOTADS Long-Term Air Defense Study (USA)

LOTCIP Long-Term Communications Improvement Plan

lote lesser of two evils

lo-temp low temperature

Lot-et-Gar Lot-et-Garonne

Loth Lothian

Lothians East Lothian, Midlothian, West Lothian

Lothringen (German—Lorraine)

lotis logic, timing, sequencing

Lot's Wife Japanese volcanic islet in the North Pacific between Iwo Jima and Yokohama—resembles a pillar of salt; mountain of St Helena Island in the South Atlantic

Lottie Charlotte

LOTUS Ladies Organized to Unfetter Sexuality (acronymic name for a San Diego organization of call girls, hookers, and so-called massage-parlor experts in high-priced sexual services)

lotw loaded on trailers or wagons

Lou Lewis; Loualta; Louanna; Louanne; Loudella; Louella; Louina; Louis; Louisa; Louise; Louisetta; Louisette; Louisiana; Louisville; Loula; Loulou; Loura; Lourane; Lourene; Lourette; Louvilla; Louvina

Lou Costello Louis Cristillo

Lou Gehrig's disease amyotrophic lateral sclerosis

Lou Grant Edward Asner

louh light observation utility helicopter

Louie Louis; Louisa; Louise; St Louis, Missouri

Louis Louisville

Louis Calhern Carl Vogt

Louis Capet King Louis XVI

Louise Homer Louise Dilworth Beatty

Louis-Ferdinand Céline Henri-Louis Destouches

Louis Graveure Wilfred Douthitt

Louisiana Ports Baton Rouge, Lake Charles, New Orleans

Louisiane (French—Louisiana)

Louis Jourdan Louis Gendre

Louis le Debonnaire Louis I of France

Louis Napoleon Napoleon III—Emperor of France

Louisvillain(s) native(s) of Louisville

Lou Orc Louisville Orchestra

Louv Louvain

Louvain (French—Leuven)

l'Ouverture Toussaint l'Ouverture—founder and first president of Haiti after defeating Napoleon's troops numbering 25,000

lov limit of visibility

Lovanium (Latin—Louvain)— the Belgian university town

LOVE League of Victims and Emphathizers (pro-capital-punishment group)

love machine bedroom-on-wheels type of recreation vehicle such as a camper, trailer, or van

lovisim low-visibility landing simulation

LoW Launch on Warning (during nuclear warfare)

lo wat low water

Low Countries Belgium, Luxembourg, and the Netherlands

Lowell Florida Correctional Institution at Lowell

lower 48 lower 48 continental United States

lower 49 lower 49 United States (lower 48 plus Hawaii)

Lower Amazon Amazon River traversing northern Brazil from Manaus to the Amazon River Delta on the Atlantic near Belém do Pará

Lower Austria southern Austria bordering on Switzerland, Italy, Yugoslavia, and Hungary

Lower Bavaria eastern Bavaria

Lower Burma coastal Burma west of Thailand

Lower California the peninsula comprising Baja California in Mexico

Lower Canada French-speaking Québec and the lower St Lawrence region during the 19th century

Lower East Side New York City's most congested section south of Washington Square

Lower Egypt Egypt's delta area north of Cairo and including Alexandria and Port Said

Lower Franconia northwestern Bavaria

Lower Galilee Israel between the Mediterranean and the Sea of Galilee

Lower Lakes southernmost Great Lakes—Erie and Ontario

Lower Michigan peninsular Michigan south of Mackinac Strait

Lower Mississippi Mississippi River from Saint Louis to New Orleans and the Gulf of Mexico

Lower Nile Nile River flowing from Khartoum in the Sudan to Cairo in Egypt and the Nile River Delta emptying into the Mediterranean Sea

Lower Peninsula southern Michigan between Lake Michigan, Lake Huron, and Lake Erie

Lower Rhine Rhine River between Bonn, Germany and the North Sea coast of the Netherlands

Lower Saxony English name for Neidersachsen including most of Brunswick, Hannover, Oldenburg, and Schaumburg-Lippe

Lower Silesia southern Silesia

Low L Low Latin

Lowland Duchy Luxembourg

Low Newton remand center in Durham, England

lowpro low protein (diet)

Low Tatras Low Tatra Mountains of Czechoslovakia, Hungary, and Yugoslavia

low tec(h) low technology

lox also the name for smoked salmon; liquid oxygen; liquid-oxygen explosive

lox-sox liquid oxygen, solid oxygen

loxygen liquid oxygen

loy loyalty

LOYA League of Young Adventurers

Loyalist Province New Brunswick

Loyalists Loyalist American Colonists (Tories); Loyalist Episcopalian Traditionalists; Loyalist Spanish Republicans

Loyola Saint Ignatius de Loyola (Iñigo de Oñez y Loyola)

loz liquid ozone

Loz Lozère

Lozovsky Solomon Abramovich Dridzo

lp lambing percentage; landplane; last paid; latent period; launch(ing) platform; light perception; linear programming; liquefied petroleum; liquid propellant; litter patient; local procurement; long primer (type); long-play; long-playing; low pass; low point; low power; low pressure; lumbar puncture

lp (LP) long-play (record)

l-p low-pressure

l/p lactate/pyruvate ratio; launch platform; letterpress; life policy; listening post

Lp Ladyship; Lordship

LP Aeralpi (2-letter symbol); Labor Party; Labour Party; Liberal Party; Libertarian Party; Library of Parliament; Licensing Plan; litter patient; Liverpool Prison; long-play (record); Lower Peninsula

L-P Lionel-Pacific

LP lunga pausa (Italian—long pause)

lpa low-power amplifier

LPA Labor Party Association; Labor Policy Association; Little People of America

LPAA London Poster Advertising Association

L-pam L-phenylalanine mustard (anti-cancer drug)

LPAP Local Planning and Assessment Process

LPB La Paz, Bolivia (airport)

lpc leaf protein concentrate; least-preferred co-worker; linear predictive coding; low-pressure chamber; low-pressure compressor

lpc (LPC) linear-power controller

LPC Livestock and Pastoral Company; Lockheed Propulsion Company; Low Price Center

LPCC Lamb Promotion Coordination Committee

LPCG Laser Planning and Coordination Group (ERDA)

LPCM London Police Court Mission

lpcp launcher preparation control panel

lpcw long-pulse continuous wave

lp cyl low-pressure cylinder

lpd least perceptible difference; liquid protein diet; local procurement direct; low performance drone

LPD amphibious transport dock ship (naval symbol); Local Procurement District; low performance drone

LPE London Press Exchange

L Ped Licentiate in Pedagogy

lpf leukocytosis-promoting factor; low-power field

lpg liquid propane gas

lpg (LPG) liquefied petroleum gas

LPGA Ladies Professional Golf Association, Liquefied Petroleum Gas Association; Louisiana Personnel and Guidance Association

lp gas liquified petroleum gas

lph landing personnel helicopter; lines per hour

L Ph Licentiate of Philosophy

lpi launching position indicator; lines per inch; low-power indicator

LPI Lifetime Productivity Index; Lightning Protection Institute; Louisiana Polytechnic Institute

lpicbm (LPICBM) liquid-propellant intercontinental ballistic missile

L-pills cyanide L-pills (deadly poisonous)

LPIU Lithographers and Photoengravers International Union

LPKS Lone Pine Koala Sanctuary (Queensland)

LPKTF London Printing and Kindred Trades' Federation

lpl lightproof louver; list processing language

LPL Liverpool Public Libraries; London Public Library; Louisville Public Library; Lunar and Planetary Laboratory (University of Arizona)

LP & L Louisiana Power and Light

LPL Lembaga Penelitian Laut (Indonesian—Institute for Marine Research)—Jakarta

L-plane US Army liaison aircraft

LP & LC Louisiana Power & Light Company

L Plms Las Palmas

lplr lock pillar

LPLs Liverpool Public Libraries

lpm lines per millimeter; lines per minute; liters per minute

LPM Licensing Project Manager

LPMES Logistics Performance Measurement and Evaluation System

LP/MOSS Linear Programming/Mathematical Optimization Subroutine System

LPN Licensed Practical Nurse; Longview, Portland and Northern (railway)

LPN Lembaga Padi Negara (Malay—National Rice Paddy)

LPNA Licensed Practical Nurses Association; Lithographers and Printers National Association

LPNI Langley Porter Neuropsychiatric Institute

lpo liquid phase oxidation; local purchase order

LPO Licensing Project Office(r); London Philharmonic Orchestra; London Post Office

Lpool Liverpool

LPPM Lembaga Penilitian Pertanian Maros (Indonesian—Department of Agriculture)

LPPTFS London and Provincial Printing Trades Friendly Society

lpr (LPR) liquid-propellant rocket

LPR Lauritzen Peninsula Reefer (steamship line)

LPRC Library Public Relations Council

lps lightproof shade; line program selector; liters per second; low primary sequence; low-pressure sodium

lps (LPS) lipopolysaccharide

lp(s) loop(s)

lp's (LPs) long-playing records

LPS Laboratory for Planetary Studies (Cornell); Lanterman-Petris-Short Act; Lebanese Press Syndicate; Light Photo Squadron; Linear Programming System; London Philharmonic Society; Lord Privy Seal; Lyceum Performing Society

LPSA Liberal Party of South Africa

LPS Act Lanterman-Petris-Short Act (commitment procedures covering mental patients in California)

LPSO Lloyd's Policy Signing Office

LPSS amphibious transport submarine (naval symbol)

lpstt low-power schottky transistor-transistor logic

lpt limited-production test

LPT Licensed Physical Therapist

LPTA Louisiana Parent-Teacher Association

LPTB London Passenger Transport Board

lptv (LPTV) large payload test vehicle

lpu limited-production urgent

Lpud Liverpudlian (native to or inhabitant of Liverpool)

lpv launching point vertical; lightproof vent

lpw low-power window; lumens per watt

l & p wood lumber and plywood wood

LPYS Labour Party Young Socialists

Lpz Leipzig

L Pz La Paz

LPZG Lincoln Park Zoological Gardens

lq last quarter; linear quantifier; lowest quartile

l.q. lege quaeso (Latin—please read)

lqdr liquidator

LQR Law Quarterly Review

lqss liquid steady state

LQST Leadership Q-Sort Test

lr latency relaxation; leave rations; letter report; lire; log run; long range; long run; lower

l/r left right; lower right

l-to-r left-to-right (photo caption abbreviation)

l R laufen Rechnung (German—current account)

Lr lawrencium

LR Laboratory Report; Land Registry; Landing Report; Lee Rubber (stock exchange symbol); Letter Report; Liaison Report; Little Rock

LR Libertarian Review; Lloyd's Register

lra long-range aviation

LRA Labor Research Association; Landing Rights Airport; Libertarian Republican Alliance; Lithuanian Regeneration Association

lraam (LRAAM) long-range air-to-air missile

lrac long-run average cost

LRAD Licentiate of the Royal Academy of Dancing

LRAFB Little Rock Air Force Base

LRAM Licentiate of the Royal Academy of Music

LRB Labor Research Bureau; Laboratory of Radiation Biology (University of Washington); Legislative Reference Bureau; Loyalty Review Board

LRBA Laboratoire de Recherches Balistiques et Aérodynamiques (Laboratory for Ballistic and Aerodynamic Research)

LRBC Lloyd's Register Building Certificate

lrbm long-range ballistic missile

lrc longitudinal redundancy check(ing); long-range communication; lower right center

lrc (LRC) longitudinal redundancy check character (data processing)

LRC Labor Representation Committee; Ladies Recreation Club; Langley Research Center (NASA); Law Reform Commission; Learning Resource Center; Lesbian Resource Center; Lewis Research Center (NASA); Library Resource Center; Linguistics Research Center; Logistics Research Center

LRCA London Retail Credit Association

LRCE Little Rock Cotton Exchange

lrcm (LRCM) long-range cruise missile

LRCM Licentiate of the Royal College of Music

lrco limited remote communications outlet

LRCP Licentiate of the Royal College of Physicians

LRCPE Licentiate of the Royal College of Physicians of Edinburgh

LRCPI Licentiate of the Royal College of Physicians of Ireland

lrcr longitudinal redundancy check register

LRCS League of Red Cross Societies; Licentiate of the Royal College of Surgeons

LRCSE Licentiate of the Royal College of Surgeons of Edinburgh

LRCSI Licentiate of the Royal College of Surgeons of Ireland

LRCT Licentiate of the Royal Conservatory of Toronto

LRCVS Licentiate of the Royal College of Veterinary Surgeons

lrd labelled radar display; long-range data

L-rd Lord (Hebraic contraction)

LRDC Learning Research and Development Center

LRDP Library Research and Demonstration Program

lrdr last revision date routine

lre law-related education

LREA Licensed Real Estate Agent

lrecl logical record length

LRES Linear Rocket Engine System

lrew long-range early warning

lrf latex and resorcinol formaldehyde; liver residue factor

lrf (LRF) luteinizing hormone-releasing factor

LRFI League for Religious Freedom in Israel

LRFPB Louisiana Rating and Fire Prevention Bureau

LRFPS Licentiate of the Royal Faculty of Physicians and Surgeons

LRFPSG Licentiate of the Royal Faculty of Physicians and Surgeons of Glasgow

lrg large; liquefied refinery gas; long range

lrh (LRH) luteinizing releasing hormone

LRHL Law Reports—House of Lords

lri left-right indicator; long-range input; long-range interceptor; lower respiratory infection

LRI Library Resources Incorporated

LRIBA Licentiate of the Royal Institute of British Architects

LRIC Licentiate of the Royal Institute of Chemistry

lrim long-range input monitor

lrip language research in progress

lrir limb radiance inversion radiometer

LRIS Lloyd's Register Industrial Services

LRJC Lake Region Junior College

LRKB Law Reports—King's Bench

LRL Lawrence Radiation Laboratory; Lunar Receiving Laboratory

LRLA La Raza Legal Alliance

lrl's living-room liberals

LRLS London Regional Library System

LRLSA La Raza Law Students Association

LRLTRAN Lawrence Radiation Laboratory Translator

lrm liquid radiation monitor

LRMC Lloyd's Refrigerating Machinery Certificate

lrmg (LRMG) lockless-rifle machine gun

lrmp long-range maritime patrol

LRMS Liquid Radwaste Management System

LRN Landslaget for Reiselivet i Norge (Norway Travel Association)

LRNC Long Reference Number Code

lrp launching reference point; long-range planning

LR-P La Rochelle-Pallice

lrpa long-range patrol aircraft

lrpg long-range proving ground

LRPGR Long-Range Planning Ground Rules

LRPL Liquid Rocket Propulsion Laboratory; Little Rock Public Library

LRPS Long-Range Planning Service

LRQB Law Reports—Queen's Bench

lrr lower reduced rate

LRR Location Recommendation Report

lrra low-range radio altimeter

lrrd long-range reconnaissance detachment

lrrmf long-range resource and management forecast

lrrp lowest required radiated power

LRRS Long-Range Radar Station

LRRTS Light-Rail Rapid-Transit System

lrs long-range search; long-run supply

lr's leave rations; light refreshments

l/r/s library rubber stamps (used-book trade abbreviation indicating book may belong or may have belonged to a public library)

lRs lactated Ringer's solution

Lrs Lancers

LRS Land Registry Stamp; London Research Station (British Gas)

LRS Lloyd's Register of Shipping

lrsam (LRSAM) long-range surface-to-air missile

lrsm long-range seismic measurement

LRSM Licentiate of the Royal Schools of Music

LRSS Long-Range Survey System

lrt laser ray tube; launch, recovery, and transport

lrt (LRT) light rail transit

lrtc long-run total cost

LRTgt last resort target

LRTL Light Railway Transport League

LRTS Library Resources and Technical Services

lru least recently used; line replacement unit

lrv (LRV) light rail vehicle; lunar roving vehicle

LRWES Long-Range Weapon Experimental Station

LRWRE Long-Range Weapons Research Establishment

LRY Liberal Religious Youth

ls landing ship; left side; light vessel; lightship; limestone; liminal sensitivity; limit switch; local sunset; long shot; long site; long sleeves; loud speaker; low secondary; low speed; lump sum

l-s lumbo-sacral

l's losers (gambling short form)

l/s liters per second

l & s launch(ing) and servicing

l.s. locus sigilli (Latin—place of the seal)

Ls Lopes; Louis

LS Lamson & Sessions; Law Society; Leading Seaman; Letter Service; Licensed Surveyor; Linnaean Society

L-S Lewis-Shepard

L & S Lands and Survey (department or office)

lsa left sacro-anterior; logistic support analysis; low specific activity

lsa (LSA) lichen sclerosus et atrophicus

LSA Labor Services Agency; Labour Services Association; Land Service Assistant; Land Settlement Association; Leukemia Society of America; Licentiate of the Society of Apothecaries; Lighthouse Society of America; Limbless Soldiers Association; Linguistic Society of America; Liquor Stores Association; Lithuanian Society of America; London Salvage Association; London School of Accountancy

L&SA Law and Society Association

LSA Library Science Abstracts

LSAA Linen Supply Association of America

LSAC Law School Admission Council; London Small Arms Company

lsar local storage address register

LSAT Law School Admission Test

lsb left sternal border; lower sideband

lsb (LSB) least significant bit

LSB Launch Service Building; London School Board; Louisiana School Board

LSBA Leading Sick-Bay Attendant; Louisiana School Boards Association

LSBR Large Seed-Blanket Reactor (AEC)

lsc linear sequential circuit; logistic support cost

l.s.c. loco supra citato (Latin—in the foregoing place cited)

LSC Laser Systems Center; Legal Services Corporation; Lie Scale for Children; Lower School Certificate

lsca left scapulo-anterior

LSCA Library Services and Construction Act

LSCC Library of the Supreme Court of Canada

lscp left scapuloposterior

LSCRS Law School Candidate Referral Service

lscs lower segment caesarean section

lsct low-speed compound terminal

LSCT Lamar State College of Technology

lsd laser-support detonation; last significant data; last significant digit; leadless sealed device; least significant difference; least significant digit; library system(s) development; liquid scale disintegrator; logarithmic-series distribution; long, slow, distance (jogging); loss, short, and damage

ls & d liquor store and delicatessen

l s d librae, solidi, denarii (Latin —pounds, shillings, pence)

LSD landing ship, dock (naval symbol); League for Spiritual Discovery; lysergic acid diethylamide—dangerous psychedelic drug nicknamed *acid*

L.S.D. Doctor of Library Science

LSD Lyserginsaure Diathylamid (German—lysergic acid diethylamide)

LSDAS Law School Data Assembly Service

LSDI Logistics Support Departmental Instruction

lsd li leased line (telephone)

LSDS Low-Speed Digital System

lse limited signed edition; limited special edition

LSE London School of Economics; London Stock Exchange; Louisiana Sugar Exchange

LSECS Life Support and Environmental Control System

l sect longitudinal section

LSEL London School of Economics Library

LSE & PS London School of Economics and Political Science

lse skds loose (or on) skids

LSET Logistics Supportability Evaluation Team

LSEU La Salle Extension University

lsf log super feet

LSF Literary Society Foundation; Lloyd Shaw Foundation; Lock Security Force (Panama Canal)

lsfa logistic system feasibility analysis

lsg list set generator

Lsg Lösung (German—solution)

lsgd lymphocyte specific gravity distribution

L Sgt Lance Sargeant

LSH Latter-day Saints Hospital

LSHTM London School of Hygiene and Tropical Medicine

lsi large-scale integration; lateral shear interferometer

LSI Labor and Socialist International; Lake Superior & Ishpeming (railroad); landing ship—infantry; Law of the Sea

Institute; Law-Science Institute (University of Texas); Lear Siegler Incorporated; Logistic Shipping Instruction(s); Lunar Science Institute

LS & I Lake Superior & Ishpeming (Railroad)

LSIA Lamp and Shade Institute of America

lsic large-scale integrated circuitry

LSIO Labor Standards Inspection Office(r)

LSIS Laser-Scan Inspection System

lsk liver, spleen, kidney

lsl left sacrolateral; low-speed logic

LSL landing ship, logistic; Life Sciences Laboratory; Linnaean Society of London; Lucy Stone League

lslb left short-leg brace

lsm linear synchronous motor; lysergic acid morpholide

lsm (LSM) lysergic acid morpholide

l.s.m. litera scripta manet (Latin —the written word remains)

LSM Laboratory for the Structure of Matter (USN); Lancastrian School of Management; landing ship, medium; Liberation Support Movement; Logistic Support Manager

LS/mft Leopold Stokowski/ means fine tone; Lucky Strike/ means fine tobacco

LSMI Lake Superior Mining Institute

LSMP Logistic Support and Mobilization Plan

LSMR rocket ship

LSMSC Lake Superior Mines Safety Council

LSNR League of Struggle for Negro Rights

LSNSW Linnaean Society of New South Wales

LSNY Linnaean Society of New York

LSO Landing Signal Officer; Leningrad Symphony Orchestra; London Symphony Orchestra

lsp left sacro-posterior; logical signal processor

LSP Launch Pad; Logistic Support Plant

LSPOJC La Salle-Peru-Oglesby Junior College

LSPR Library Society of Puerto Rico

L-square capital-L-shaped square; carpenter's square

lsr launch signal responder

Lsr Luftschutzraum (German— air raid shelter)

LSR landing ship, rocket; landing ship, support

Lsr Ant Lesser Antilles (Leeward and Windward Islands)

lss liquid scintillation spectroscopy

LSS Life Saving Service; Life Saving Station; Life Support System; Lockheed Space Systems; Logistic Support Squadron

L.S.S. Licentiate of Sacred Scripture; Leopold-Sedar Senghor

lssc logistic support system characteristics

LS Sc Licentiate in Sacred Scriptures; Licentiate in Sanitary Science

LSSC Logistic System Support Center (USA)

LSSF Land Special Security Force (USA)

LSSG Logistics Studies Steering Group; Logistics Studies Support Group

lssm local scientific surface module

LSSR Latvian Soviet Socialist Republic (formerly Republic of Latvia); Lithuanian Soviet Socialist Republic (formerly Republic of Lithuania)

LSSS London School of Slavonic Studies

L S St L Louis Stephen St Laurent (Canada's sixteenth Prime Minister)

lst large space telescope; laser spot tracker; left sacro-traverse; liquid storage tank; liquid-oxygen start tank; living structures tank

Lst Launceston

LST landing ship, tank; Local Sidereal Time; Local Standard Time

lstc low-speed trim compensation

lst wk last week

lsu launcher selector unit; livestock unit

LSU landing ship, utility; Louisiana State University

LSU-IES Louisiana State University Institute of Environmental Studies

LSUNO Louisiana State University (New Orleans)

LSUP Louisiana State University Press

lsuv lunar surface ultraviolet (camera)

LSV landing ship, vehicle

LSVP landing ship, vehicle, and personnel

lsw least significant word; limit switch(ing)

LSW Licensed Shorthand Writer

lsw lt landing signal wand light

LSWR London and South Western Railway

LSWY League of Socialist Working Youth

LSZ Limited Speed Zone; Local Slow Zone

lt landed terms; language translation; latch trip; laundry tray; lid tank; light; light trap; line terminator; local time; long ton; loop test; low temperature; low tension; low torque

lt (LT) lymphotoxin

l/t loop test

lt laut (German—according to)

l.t. locum tenens (Latin—substitute)

Lt Lieutenant

LT Land Transfer; landing team; large tug; Lloyd Triestino; local time; London Transport

lta lighter-than-air

LTA Lawn Tennis Association; Library Technical Assistant; lighter-than-air; Listening Transit Analysis; Logistic Task Authorization

LTAA Lawn Tennis Association of Australia

ltadl launcher tube azimuth datum line

LTAS Lighter-Than-Air Society

ltb laryngo-trachael bronchitis; line terminating battery; low-tension battery

Lt. B. Bachelor of Literature

LTB Lepers Trust Board; London Tourist Board; London Transport Board

LTBP London Tanker Broker Panel

LTBT Limited Test Ban Treaty (prohibiting nuclear testing in certain environments)

ltc long-term care

ltc (LTC) locking torque converter

LTC Land Transport(ation) Commission; Lawn Tennis Club; Le Tourneau College; Library of Trinity College; Loop Test(ing) Conference

LTCB Long-Term Credit Bank (Japan)

Lt Cdr Lieutenant Commander

LTCL Licentiate of Trinity College of Music (London)

Lt Cmdr Lieutenant Commander

Lt Col Lieutenant Colonel

ltc's long-term contracts

ltd long-term disability

lt/d long tons per day; lower tween deck

Ltd Limited

Ltda Limitada (Spanish—limited)

ltd ed limited edition

lte large table electroplotter; linear threshold element

Lte (French—Limite)—limited

LTE London Transport Executive

lted letter to the editor

LTEU Liquor Trades Employees Union

ltf (LTF) lipotrophic factor

LTF Lithographic Technical Foundation; Logistic Task Force; tropical fresh water load line (Plimsoll mark)

ltfrd lot tolerance fraction reliability deviation

ltg lighting

ltgc lithographic

ltge lighterage

Lt Gen Lieutenant General

ltgh lightening hole

Lt Gov Lieutenant Governor

lth lath; lathing; less than honest (crooked, dishonest); luteotrophic hormone (LTH)

Lth Leith

L Th Licentiate in Theology

lthr leather

ltl land training installation(s)

lti (LTI) light transmission index

Lti Laotian

LTI Ladder Towers Incorporated; Louisiana Training Institute; Lowell Technological Institute

LTIB Lead Technical Information Bureau

Lt Inf Light Infantry

Lt JG Lieutenant Junior Grade

ltl listing time limit

ltl (LTL) less than truckload

Ltl Little (postal abbreviation)

ltla launcher tube longitudinal axis

ltm laser target marker; long-term memory; long-term mortgage; low thermal mass

ltm (LTM) long-term memory

LTM Licentiate of Tropical Medicine

L.T. Meade Elizabeth Thomasina Meade Smith

ltmr laser target marker ranger

ltng lightning

ltng arr lightning arrester

lto landing takeoff

Lto lento (Italian—slowly)

LTO Land Transfer Office; Leading Torpedo Operator

ltof low-temperature optical facility

LTon long ton

ltp limit on tax preferences; low-temperature passivation

LTP Library Technology Program

ltpd lot tolerance percent defective

ltpp lipothiamide-pyrophosphate

ltr letter; lighter; liter; long-term reserve

LTR Long Term Reserve

LTR Library Technology Reports

Lt RN Lieutenant—Royal Navy

LtrO letter order

LTRP Long-Term Requirement Plan

ltrs (LTRS) letters shift (data processing)

LTRS Laser Target Recognition System

lts lights

LTs Legal Times

LTS Landfall Technique School; London Transport System; London Typographical Society

LTSB London Trustee Savings Bank

LT & SR London, Tilbury and Southend Railway

ltt liquid toning transfer

LTT Lymphocyte Transformation Test

ltta long-tank thrust augmented

LTTC Lowry Technical Training Center

L-T Trade Agreement Liao-Takasaki Trade Agreement

ltu line terminating unit

LTU La Trobe University

ltv long tube vertical

lt/v light vessel

L-T-V Long-Temco-Vought (corporation)

ltvc launcher tube vertical centerline

lu lock up; logic unit; logistical unit; lumen

lu. lues (Latin—contagious disease)—plague or syphilis

Lu Lorentz unit; Lugano; Lugo; lutetium

LU Langston University; Laurentian University; Laval University; Lehigh University; Lethbridge University; Ligue Universelle (Universal Esperantist League); Lincoln University; Liverpool University; London University; Loyola University

lu. I *lues I*—primary syphilis

lu. II *lues II*—secondary syphilis

lu. III *lues III*—tertiary syphilis

lua left upper arm

LuA Launch under Attack (during nuclear warfare)

LUA Life Underwriters Association; London Underwriters Association

LUAA Life Underwriters Association of Australia

LUAC Land Use Advisory Council; Life Underwriters Association of Canada

LUANZ Life Underwriters Association of New Zealand

lub lubricant, lubricate; lubrication

lub (LUB) logical unit block

lube lubricate; lubrication

Lubeca (Latin—Lübeck)—German port city also known as Lubicensis in Roman times

lubed lubricated (intoxicated)

lub oil lubricating oil

lubs large undisturbed bottom sampler

Lubumbashi formerly Elisabethville, Belgian Congo

Luc Lucan; Lucifer; Lucretius; Lucullus

LUC Land Use Commission; Land Use Committee; Louisiana University Center

Lucan Roman poet Marcus Annaeus Lucanus

Lucas Luke

LUCB Library of the University of California at Berkeley

Lucerna (Latin—Lucerna)—also known as Lucerna Helvetiorum

Lucerne (French—Luzern)

LUCHIP Lutheran Church and Indian People

luchtv *luchtvaart* (Dutch—aviation)

Luci Lucifer

Lucia St Lucia

Lucia *Lucia di Lammermoor* (three-act opera by Donizetti)

lucid. language used to communicate information system design

Lucifer (Latin—light bearer)—Venus the pre-dawn morning star rising in the east as opposed to Venus the post-dusk evening star sometimes called Hesperus seen setting in the west

Lucil Gaius Lucilius (Roman satiric writer)

Lucille Ball Diane Belmont

Luck Lucknow

Lucky Lucky Luciano (Salvatore Lucania)—once America's foremost gangster controlling gambling, money lending, narcotics, prostitution, and related aspects of the so-called entertainment world

Lucky Black Swan Western Australia's city of Perth where black swans swim about in Perth Water

Lucky Capital Canberra, Australia

Lucky Country Australia

lucom lunar communication

luc. prim. *luce primo* (Latin—at daybreak)

Lucr *The Rape of Lucrece*

Lucretius Roman poet-philosopher Titus Lucretius

Lucrezia Bori Lucrecia Borja y Gonzalez de Riancho

Lucy Lucia; Lucilla; Lucille; St Lucia, West Indies

Lucy Stone maiden name of Mrs Henry Brown Blackwell who retained her maiden name so as not to lose her identity

lud liftup door

Lud Ludlow; Ludo; Ludolf; Ludolph; Ludovic; Ludovica; Ludovick; Ludovico; Ludovicus; Ludvig; Ludwell; Ludwig; Ludwik

luda land use data

Luda (Pinyin Chinese—Luta)

Luddy Ludlow (*see* Lud)

lude quaalude (a depressant drug)

Ludendorff General Erich Friederich Wilhelm Ludendorff

Lud(s) Luddite(s)

Ludwig van Ludwig van Beethoven

lue left upper entrance; left upper extremity

LUER Land Use and Environmental Regulation

lues I primary syphilis

lues II secondary syphilis

lues III tertiary syphilis

luf lowest useful high frequency

LUFTHANSA Deutsche Lufthansa (West German Airline)

lug luggage; lugger; lugging; lugsail; lugworm

Lugd. Bat. *Lugdunum Batavorum* (Latin—Leiden)—Leyden

Lugdunum (Latin—Lyons)

lu h lumen hour(s)

luhf lowest usable high frequen-

cy

LUI Labor Union Insurances

Luigi Cherubini María Luigi Carlo Zenobio Salvatore Cherubini

Luik (Dutch, Flemish, German —Liège)

LUIP London University Institute of Psychiatry

Luisiana (Spanish—Louisiana)

lujb left umbilical junction box

Lukas Foss Lukas Fuchs

Luke The Gospel according to St Luke

lul left upper limb; left upper lobe

LUL London University Library

LULA Loyola University of Los Angeles

LULAC League of United Latin-American Citizens

LULAC *La Liga de Ciudadanos Latinoamericanos Unidos* (Spanish—The League of United Latin-American Citizens)

LULOP *London Union List of Periodicals*

Lulu Louise

lum lumbago; lumbar; lumber; lumen; luminosity; luminous

lum (LUM) lunar excursion module

Lum Columbus

LUMAS Lunar Mapping System

lumb lumber; lumbering

Lumber Capital Tacoma, Washington

Lumber State Maine

LUMC Laval University Medical Center

LUMIS Land Use Management Information System

Lum 'n Abner Chester Lauck and Norris Goff

Lumpen *Lumpenproletariat* (German—ragged bums, ragged street people)—term invented by Karl Marx

lun lunar; lunette

lun *lundi* (French—Monday); *lunedi* (Italian—Monday); *lunes* (Spanish—Monday)

Lunar Lunar Society (Birmingham, England)

lunar caustic silver nitrate ($AgNO_3$)

Lunatic of Libya Col Muammar Qaddafi

lunch luncheon

Lunda (Latin—Lund)—also known as Lundinum Scanorum or Swedish London

Lüneburger Heide (German—

Luneburg Heath)
Luneburg Heath English name for the Lüneburger Heide
Luneburgum (Latin—Luneburg)
Lungansk old name of Voroshilovgrad
Lunik Soviet cosmic rocket landed on Moon September 14, 1959
lun int lunitidal interval
Lunnon London
Luoyang (Pinyin Chinese—Loyang)
Lup Lupus (constellation)
LUP Liverpool University Press; Loyola University Press
lupa lupanar (Latin—brothel)
luq left upper quadrant (abdomen)
Luqa Malta's main airport
LUS Land Utilization Survey
LUSB Land Utilization Survey of Britain
lus fln luster finish
Lu-shun (Chinese—Port Arthur)
lusi lunar surface inspection
Lusians Portuguese
lusing lusingando (Italian—coaxing)
Lusitania (Latin—Portugal) Roman name often used as the poetic equivalent of Portugal
Lussemburgo (Italian—Luxembourg)
lust. lustrous
lut launcher umbilical tower (LUT)
lut. luteum (Latin—yellow)
LUT Launcher Umbilical Tower; Loughborough University of Technology; Ludwig Universe Tankships
Lüta (Chinese—Dairen)—close to Port Arthur now called Lushun
LUTA Library of the University of Texas at Austin
LUTC Life Underwriter Training Council
Lutetia (Latin—Paris)—more fully Lutetia Parisiorum
LUTFCSUSTC Librarians United to Fight Costly, Silly, Unnecessary Serial Title Changes
Luth Luther(an)
Lutia St Lucia, West Indies
Lutz Lucien
luv let us vote (popular teenage plea); lightweight utility vehicle (pickup truck)
lux luxurious; luxury
Lux Luxembourg; Luxembourg-

er; Luzon
LUXAIR Luxembourg Airlines
Luxem Luxembourg
Luxembourg Grand Duchy of Luxembourg (European lowland whose Luxembourgers export a variety of farm and machine products ranging from roses to rubber tires, French, German, and Luxembourgish are spoken) *Grand-Duché de Luxembourg*
Luxemburgo (Portuguese or Spanish—Luxembourg)
Lux Fr Luxembourger franc
Luz Luzon
Luzern (German—Lucerne)
lv land valuation; largest vessel; launch vehicle (LV); leave; left ventricle; light and variable (wind); low viscosity; low voltage; lumbar vertebra; luncheon voucher; lyric vocalist
l-v lacto-vegetarian
l/v light vessel (lightship)
lv livre (French—book)
Lv Latvia; Latvian; lev (Bulgarian currency unit)
LV Las Vegas; launch vehicle; Lehigh Valley (railroad); Licensed Victualler; light vessel (light ship); Lindholmens Varv (Lindholmens Shipyard)
LV-3 Atlas launch vehicle (Convair)
lva landing vehicle airoll; left visual acuity
lva (LVA) landing vehicle—assault
LVA Licensed Victuallers Association; Literary Volunteers of America
L v B Ludwig van Beethoven
L v Bthvn Ludwig van Beethoven
lvcd least voltage coincidence detection
lvd louvered door
lvda launch vehicle data adapter
lvdc launch vehicle digital computer
lvdt linear variable-differential transformer; linear variable-displacement transducer
lved left ventricular end diastolic
lvet left ventricular ejection time
lvf left ventricular failure; left visual field
Lvfa low-voltage fast activity
lvgo light vacuum gas oil
lvh left ventricular hypertrophy
lvh (LVH) landing vehicle hydrofoil

lvhv low volume high velocity
lvi low viscosity index
LVI Local Veterinary Inspector
lvl level
LVL La Verendrye Line (Hall Corporation); Linda Vista Library
lvn light virgin naphtha
LVN Licensed Visiting Nurse; Licensed Vocational Nurse
LVNM Lava Beds National Monument (California)
LVNP Lassen Volcanic National Park (California); Luangwa Valley National Park (Zambia)
Lvov (Russian—Lwow)—Lemberg
lvp low-voltage protection
lvp (LVP) left ventricular pressure
LVP Launch Vehicle Program(s)
lvp dr leverpak drum
lvr line voltage regulator; longitudinal recorder; low voltage release
LVRB Launch Vehicle Reliability Board
lvrj low-volume ramjet
Lvrpl Liverpool
lv's lunch(eon) vouchers
LVs launch vehicles
LVS Licentiate in Veterinary Science
LVT landing vehicle, tracked
LVTC landing vehicle, tracked command
lvupk leave and upkeep
LVUSA Legion of Valor of the USA
lvw linked vertical wall
lw light warning; lightweight; live weight; long wave; low water
l/w in lieu of weighing; lumens per watt
l & w living and well
l W lichte Weite (German—internal diameter)
Lw lawrencium (element 103)
LW light warning; lower berth
L-W Lee-White (method)
lwar lightweight attack and reconnaissance
L-wave long wave (usually the third major earthquake shock wave)
l'way leeway
lwb long wheelbase
lwc lightweight concrete
LWCA London Wholesale Confectioners Association
lwcp lightweight coated paper
lwd larger word; leeward; left wing down; lewd; lowered

LWD Laser Welder/Driller

lwest low water equinoctial spring tide

lwf lightweight fighter

LWF Lutheran World Federation

LWFB Lake Washington Floating Bridge

lwf & c low water full and change

lwg last we've got; live-weight gain

LWG Logistic Work Group (NATO)

lwgr (LWGR) light-water-cooled graphite-moderated reactor

L-w-H Lewis-with-Harris (Outer Hebrides)

lwic lightweight insulating concrete

L. Wica pseudonym of Vilhelm the Prince of Sweden and Duke of Södermanland

lwir long-wave infrared

LWJ Lowell Weicker, Jr

lwl length at waterline; load waterline; low-water line (tidal marking)

LWL Limited War Laboratory (US Army)

lwld light-weight laser designator

lwm low-water mark

LWM Leonard Wood Memorial (American Leprosy Foundation)

LWMAT Locke-Wallace Marital Adjustment Test

LWMEL Leonard Wood Memorial for the Eradication of Leprosy

LWNWR Lake Woodruff National Wildlife Refuge (Florida)

lwont low water ordinary neap tide

lwop leave without pay

lwos low-water ordinary spring

lwost low-water ordinary spring tide

Lwow (Polish—Lvov)—Lemberg

lwp leave with pay; load water plane

lwpf long-wave pass filter

lwr lightweight radar; lower

lwr (LWR) light water reactor

Lwr Lower (postal abbreviation)

l'wrd leeward

lwrm (LWRM) lightweight radar missile

lwrs light-warning radar set

lwru lightweight radar unit

LWS Late West Saxon; Letter Writing System

LWSI Lloyd's Weekly Shipping Index

lwst low-water spring tides

lwt lightweight

Lwt Lowestoft

LWT amphibious warping tug (naval symbol); London Weekend Television

lwta laser window test apparatus

LWTMA London Wool Terminal Market Association

lwtvp laser window technology validation program

LWU Leather Workers Union

LWUI Longshoremen's and Warehousemen's Union International

LWV Lackawanna & Wyoming Valley (railroad); League of Women Voters

LWVUS League of Women Voters of the United States

lww launch window width

lwyr lawyer

lx lux

lx. lux (Latin—light)

LX Lox Angeles Airways (2-letter coding)

Lxᵃ Lisboa (Portuguese—Lisbon)

Lxmbrg Luxembourg

LXX Septuagint (70)

lxxx love and kisses

ly langley (solar heat unit); last year; last year's model

Ly Lyman; Lyon

LY Light Yeomanry; Love Year

LYC Larchmont Yacht Club

Lyd Lydia; Lydian

lye potassium hydroxide (KOH) or sodium hydroxide (NaOH)

LYK Lykes Brothers Steamship company (stock exchange symbol)

LYKU Lykes Lines (container) Unit

lym last year's model(s); lymph; lymphatic(s)

lympho(s) lymphocyte(s)

lymphs lymphocytes

lyn lynch (named for Captain William Lynch, also called Judge Lynch, who advocated hanging on the basis of mob action rather than legal procedure; this type of violence is also called lynch law)

Lyn Lynch; Lynde; Lyndon; Lyne; Lynn; Lynx (constellation)

Lynn Brock Alister McAllister

Lynn Doyle Leslie Alexander Montgomery

Lynwood Lynwood (delinquent) Girls Center at Anchorage, Alaska

Lyo Lyons (British maritime contraction)

Lyon (French—Lyons)

lyr lyric; lyrical; lyricism; lyricist; lyrics

Lyr Lyra (constellation)

L & YR Lancashire and Yorkshire Railway

lyric. language for your remote instruction by computer

Lyric Land Wales

Lyric Poet and Literary Critic Heinrich Heine

lys lysine

LYs Light Years

lysis (Greek—dissolution or loosening)—analysis, catalytic, electrolyte, hydrolysis, paralysis; (Latin suffix—dissolve or solution)—hemolysis

lysog lysogen(ic)(al)(ly); lysogenization; lysogenize(d); lysogenizing; lysogeny

Lyt Lyttelton, New Zealand

Lytt Lyttelton

Lyttelton Lyttelton Harbour (Christchurch, New Zealand's port)

Lz Lopez

LZ Landing Zone

lzm lysozyme

LZOA Labor Zionist Organization of America

lzp left zero point

LZSU Leningrad AA Zhdanov State University (University of Leningrad)

LZT Local Zone Time

L-Zug Luxus-Zug (German—luxury railroad train)

lzy lazy

M

m difference of meriodional parts (symbol); magnetic dipole moment (symbol); main; maintainability; male; malignant; manual; married; masculine; mass; mature; mean (arithmetical); measure; mediator (chemical); mega; megohm; member; memory; mentum; meridian; mesh; metabolite; meter; mile; mill; milli-(thousandth); minim; minor; minute; minutes; modulus; molal (concentration); molar; molecular weight; molecule; monkey; month; moon; morning; morphine; mother; motile; mucoid; murmur (heart); muscle; myopia

m (M) marijuana; morphine

m/ merged into

μ micron (symbol); micro

'm (contraction—am)—as in *I'm here*

m mass (symbol); *Mazda* (Japanese auto with German Wankel rotary engine); *metro* (Portuguese or Spanish—meter); *murió* (Spanish—died)

m. macerare (Latin—macerate)

m/ med (Norwegian—with)—as in *varm aplepai m/is* (hot apple pie with ice cream)

M bending moment (symbol); Mach (Austrian physicist); mach number; mach speed; magnaflux; magnetic inspection; maintainability; Majesty; Malay; Malaya; Malaysia; March; mark; Martin; materiel; Matson Navigation Company; median; medium; mega-(million); megacycle; Member; metal; Metro(politan); metropolitan; Mike—code for letter M; Min; missile; mixture; mobile; Mohammedan; Mohammedanism; molal (concentration); molecular weight (symbol); moment; Monday; Monsieur (French—Mister); Monsieur (railroad); Monroe-McCormack (steamship lines); Moslem; muscle; pitching moment (symbol); thousand (symbol)

M (*M*) money supply (macroeconomics symbol)

M' *Mac* (Gaelic—son of)

M Marcus (Latin); *Missa* (Latin—Mass); *mujeres* (Spanish—women)

m₁ mitral first sound

M1 money supply including currency and trading bank demand deposits

M-1 basic money aggregate (funds for spending); U.S. semi-automatic service rifle used in Vietnam

m1s matte one side

m² square meter(s)

μ² square micron

M2 M1 plus savings and small-denomination time deposits under $100,000; money supply (M1) plus demand deposits of savings & loan banks as well as stock firms

M-2/M-3 White half-track armored-personnel carrier

m2s matte two sides

m/3 middle third (long bones)

m³ cubic meter(s)

μ³ cubic micron

M3 M2 plus large-denomination time deposits, term repurchase agreements, and investments of institutions in money-market mutual funds

M-3 sterling deposits of British residents plus coins and notes

M-3A1/M-5 Stuart tank armed with a 37mm gun

m³/ᵐ cubic meters per minute

m³/ˢ cubic meters per second

M-4 Sherman medium tank with 76mm gun

M-6 American-made armored car

m8 medium octavo

M-8 Greyhound 6-wheeled armored car carrying a 37mm gun and made in the U.S.A.

M-14 U.S. fully-automatic or semi-automatic service rifle used in Vietnam

M15 gasoline extender (15% methanol plus 85% gasoline)

M-15 British secret service charged with counterespionage and security operations at home and overseas

M-16 British Foreign Service Military Intelligence (secret Intelligence service); U.S. fully- or semi-automatic lightweight small-bore service rifle used in Vietnam

M-18 Hellcat 76mm gun mounted on a tracked chassis made in the U.S.A.

M-20 Mystère 20 aircraft; unarmed Greyhound 6-wheeled armored car produced in the U.S.A. during World War II

M-36 U.S.-made Slugger tank destroyer

M-44 U.S.-made self-propelled 155mm howitzer

M-47 U.S.-made Patton tank carrying a 90mm gun

M-48 later version of the M-47 medium tank

M-56 U.S. self-propelled 90mm antitank gun called Scorpion

M-60 Patton main battle tank carrying 105mm gun

M-61 20mm Vulcan aerial machine gun firing 6000 rounds per minute

M100 100% methanol

M-107 U.S.-made self-propelled 175mm gun

M-113 U.S.-made 13-man amphibious armored personnel carrier

M-198 155mm howitzer (USA)

M-551 U.S.-built Sheridan assault vehicle armed with a 152mm gun

ma machine account; machine accountant; maleic anhydride; manpower allotment; manufacturing assembly; map analysis; mechanical advantage; medium amphibian; menstrual age; mental age; microscopic agglutination; mill annealed; mill-anneal(ing); milliampere; mixed ages; mixed-age (ewes); monthly account(ing)

ma (MA) maleic anhydride

m/a mechanical airframe; my account

m & a maintenance and assembly

μa micro+ampere

mA milliampere(s)

mÅ milliangstrom(s)

μA microampere(s)

Ma Malayalan; Mama; Manchuria; Manchurian; María; masurium (symbol)

Mᵃ María

Ma Mandag (Danish—Monday)

MA Magma Arizona (railroad); Magnesium Association; Mahogany Association; Maintainability Analysis; Manpower Administration; Manpower Authorization; Maritime Administration; Marshaling Area; Marshalling Area; Material Authorization; May Department Stores (stock exchange symbol); Mediterranean Area; Menorah Association; Merchandising Assessment; Metric Association; Military Academy; Military Attaché; Mountaineering Association

M-A Miller-Abbott (tube)

M.A. *Magister Artium* (Latin—Master of Arts)

M & A Missouri & Arkansas (railroad)

MA Maison d'Arrêt (French—jail, lockup, prison); *Modern*

Age

maa maximum authorized altitude

maa (MAA) macroaggregated albumin

Maa Madras

Maa Maandag (Dutch—Monday)

MAA Manufacturers Aircraft Association; Master Army Aviator; Master-at-Arms; Master-of-Arms; Mathematical Association of America; Medical Assistance for the Aged; Medieval Academy of America; Microfilm Association of Australia; Museum of African Art (Smithsonian); Museums Association of Australia; Mutual Aid Association; Mutual Assurance Association

MA of A Motel Association of America

ma ac machine accessory

MAAC Major Additions Adjustment Clause; Medical Assistance Advisory Council; Metropolitan Area Advisory Committee; Mutual Assistance Advisory Committee

MAAEE Ministero degli Affari Esteri (Italian—Ministry of Foreign Affairs)

MAAF Mediterranean Allied Air Force; Mediterranean Army Air Force

MAAG Military Assistance Advisory Group

MAAGB Medical Artists' Association of Great Britain

MAAH Museum of African-American History

MAAI Modeling Association of America, International

ma'am madam

ma'amselle mademoiselle

MAAN Mutual Advertising Agency Network

maap maintenance and administration panel

MAAP Minority Association for Animal Protection

M.A.Arch. Master of Arts in Architecture

maarm (MAARM) memory-aided anti-radiation missile

MAARS Multi-Access Airline Reservation System

Maas (Dutch or Flemish—Meuse)

MAAS Member of the American Academy of Arts and Sciences

Maastricht provincial capital of Limburg in the Netherlands

Maastricht Corridor southern-

most projection of the Netherlands between Belgium and Germany

MAATC Mobile Antiaircraft Training Center

mab multibase arithmetic blocks

Mab Mabel

MAB Magazine Advertising Bureau; Malfunction(ing) Analysis Board; Man and the Biosphere (UNESCO); Maracaibo Oil Exploration (stock exchange symbol); Marine Air Base; Medical Advisory Board; Missile Assembly Building; Monetary Affairs Branch; Munitions Assignment Board

MAB Manufacture d'Armes Automatiques Bayonne (French—Bayonne Automatic Arms Factory)

M.A.B.E. Master of Agricultural Business and Economics

Ma Bell Mother Bell (Bell System telephone companies linked by AT & T)

MABF Major Adjustment Billing Factor

mabflex marine amphibious brigade field exercise

mablex marine amphibious brigade landing exercise

MABO Marianas-Bonin (islands)

mabp mean arterial blood pressure

MABRON Marine Air Base Squadron

MABs Marine Amphibious Brigades

MABS Marine Automation Bridge System

MABSC Management and Behavioral Science Center

MABYS Metropolitan Association for Befriending Young Servants

mac macadam(ize)(d); macerate; machine-aided cognition; mackintosh; maximum allowable concentration(s); mean aerodynamic chord; motion analysis camera; multiple-access computer

mac (MAC) mycobacterium avium-intracellulare

mac maquereau (French—mackerel)—pimp

mac. macerare (Latin—macerate)

Mac Macao, Portuguese China; nickname of anyone whose surname begins with Mac

M.Ac. Master of Accountancy

MAC Maintenance Advisory Committee; Maintenance Analysis Center; Major Air Command; Management Aggregation Code; Marine Amphibious Corps; Maritime Advisory Committee; Material Availability Commitment; McDonnell Aircraft Corporation; Mediterranean Air Command; Miami Aviation Corporation; Middle Atlantic Conference; Military Airlift Command; Mineralogical Association of Canada; Multidimensional Actuarial Classification; Municipal Assistance Corporation; Musical Arts Center

MACA Maritime Air Control Authority

macadam macadam road (named for its Scottish inventor—J L McAdam); macadam stone (stone used in building macadam pavements or roads)

MACAE Minnesota Association of Continuing Adult Education

MACAIR Macao Air Transport

Macao gambling and prostitution capital of Portuguese China near Hong Kong

MACAP Major Appliance Consumer Action Panel

MacArthur's Birthplace Little Rock, Arkansas—birthplace of General Douglas MacArthur

MACAS Magnetic Capability and Safety System

MACBETH Memphians Against Culture Buffs Exposing Themselves Heedlessly

Mace Maccabees

MACC Mexican-American Cultural Center; Military Aid to the Civilian Community

MACCS Manufacturing Cost-Collection System; Manufacturing and Cost-Control System; Marine Air Command and Control System

m. accur. misce accuratissme (Latin—mix very accurately)

MACD Member of the Australian College of Dentistry

MACDC Military Assistance Command Director of Construction

Macdonnells short form for the Macdonnell Ranges of Australia's Northern Territory

mace billiard stick, ceremonial

staff, medieval spike-headed club, tear gas containing chloroacetophenone and sold as MACE; tropical spice; not an acronym but a tear gas (MACE) used by the police to quell rioters and by postmen to control attacking dogs

Mace (see CS-gas)

MACE Machine-Aided Composition and Editing; Massachusetts Advisory Council on Education; Military Aircraft Capability Estimator(s); Minnesota Association for Childhood Education; Missile and Control Equipment (North American Aviation); trade name for tear gas used by policemen and postmen

M.A.C.E. Master of Air-Conditioning Education; Master of Air-Conditoning Engineering

Maced Macedonia; Macedonian

MACG Marine Air Control Group

Macgillicuddy's Macgillicuddy's Reeks (Ireland's highest mountain range)

MacGregor mechanically operated hatch cover

mach machine; machinery; machinist

Mach velocity unit equal to speed of sound at standard temperature and pressure (1115 fps); named in honor of Ernst Mach—Austrian physicist

Mach The Tragedy of Macbeth

machdiprt machine discharge print(ed)

machflshd machine fleshed (skins)

Machinists Union International Association of Machinists and Aerospace Workers

MACHO Memphians Against Chest Hair at Operas

machovprt machine overprinted

machprt machine printed

machsltd machine salted (skins)

Machu Machu Picchu (ancient Incan sanctuary and stronghold in the high Andes near Cuzco, Peru)

machwsh machine washed (skins)

maci military adaptation of commercial items

MACJC Minnesota Association of Community and Junior Colleges; Missouri Association of Community and Junior

Colleges

mack mackinaw; mackintosh; maststack (marine superstructure containing mast and smokestack)

Mackenzies Mackenzie Mountains of the Canadian Northwest

mack(es) mackintosh(es)

Mackinac or Mackinaw formerly Michilimackinac

Macmillan Macmillan Publishing Co

MACOM Major Army Command; Mayor's Committee of Welcome

MACR Missing Air Crew Report

macrf macroformat(ion)

macro (Greek makro—great or large)—macrocyte, macromolecule, macromutation, macroscopic, macrophage

MacRobertson Land Australian Antarctica

macrobio macrobiologic(al); macrobiology; macrobiotic(s)

macrobop macrobopper (underground slang—older teenager in sympathy with the modern scene)

macrocephs macrocephalics (large-headed people)

macroeco macroeconomics

macrol macrologic(al)(ly); macrologist(s); macrology

macros macroinstructions

MACS Marine Air Control Squadron; Military Airlift Command Service

macship merchant aircraft ship (merchant vessel fitted with a flight deck)

MACSS Medium-Altitude Communication Satellite System; Montana Association of County School Superintendents

MACTU Mines and Countermeasures Tactical Unit (USN)

MAC/V Military Assitance Command, Vietnam

Macy's RH Macy's

mad. magnetic airborne detector; magnetic anomaly detector; maintenance, assembly, and disassembly; mathematical analysis of downtown (computer); mean absolute deviation; midpoint air dose; mind-altering drug

mad. (MAD) music and dance (festival); mutual(ly) assured destruction (via nuclear warfare)

Mad Madam(e); Madeira; Madison; Madras; Madrid

M. Ad. Master of Administration

MAD Madrid, Spain (airport); Maintainability Analysis Data; Manufacturing Assembly Drawing; Marine Air Detachment; Marine Aviation Detachment; Memphians Against Degeneracy; Michigan algorithmetic decoder; Mine Assembly Depot; Mississippians Against Disposal (of nuclear wastes); Mongolian Asiatic Development (plan)

MAD Militarischer Abschirmdienst (German—Military Screening Service)—West German counterintelligence corps

MADA Muda Agricultural Development Authority

MADAEC Military Application Division of the Atomic Energy Commission

Madag Madagascar

Madagascar Democratic Republic of Madagascar (Indian Ocean island country long a French colony, Malagasy speak Malagasy, exports include chromium and graphite as well as cloves, coffee, rice, sugar, and vanilla)

Madagascar's Principal Port Tamatave (a small port among some twenty smaller ones such as Diego Suarez and Hell Ville)

MADAM Manchester Automatic Digital Machine

Madame Bertha Sarah Bernhardt

Madame Blavatsky Helena Petrovna Hahn-Hahn

Madame Deficit Marie Antoinette's nickname attributed to her wasteful use of public funds

Madame de Stael Baronne Anne Louise Germaine

Madame Récamier Jeanne Françoise Julie Adélaïde Bernard

Mad Anthony Major General Anthony Wayne

madar malfunction analysis detection and recording

MADARS Maintenance Analysis, Detection, and Reporting System

Mad Av advertising and communications enterprises (many are located on Madison Avenue in New York City)

MADD Manufactured of Artificial Dog Dung (probably the ultimate acronymic absurdity); Mothers Against Drunk Drivers; Mothers Against Drunk Driving

maddam macromodule and digital differential analyzer; multiplexed analog-to-digital digital-to-analog multiplexed

MADDER Memphians Against Damsels Doing Ecdysiast Routines

maddida magnetic-drum digital-differential analysis

MADE Multichannel Analog-Digital Data Encoder

MADECO Manufacturas de Cobre (Spanish—Copper Manufacturers)

Madeiras Madeira Islands in the North Atlantic off Morocco

Mademoiselle le Professeur Nadia Boulanger

Madera (Spanish—Madeira)

madevac medical evacuation

madex magnetic anomaly detection exercise

madge microwave aircraft digital guidance equipment

Madge Margaret; Margarita

Mad Genius of Sex and Psychiatry Wilhem Reich—inventor of the orgone box

Madhouse on the Potomac the Capitol, the Pentagon, the State Department, the White House, Washington, D.C.

Mad I Madeira Islands

MADIAR Societé Nationale Malgache des Transports Aériens (Madagascar Air Transport)

MADIS Manual Aircraft Data Input System; Millivolt Analog-Digital Instrumentation System

Mad Isl Madeira Islands

Madison author of the *Bill of Rights* and fourth President of the United States; capital of Wisconsin named after him

Mad Ludwig Ludwig II of Bavaria (Wagner's patron)

Mad Meg nickname of the Mayer van der Bergh Museum in Antwerp, Belgium

M. Admin.S. Master of Administrative Studies

Mad Monk Gregori Rasputin

MAD Policy Mutually-Assured Destruction Policy (nuclear warfare)

Mad Priest John Ball

madr minimum adult daily requirement

Madr Madrid; Madrileño

madras madras cloth or madras cotton; madras kerchief

madre magnetic-drum receiving equipment

madrec malfunction detection and recorder

Madritum (Latin—Madrid)

mads mind-altering drugs

MADs Mothers Against Drugs

MADS Maintainability Analysis Data System; Modular Army Demonstration System

madt microalloy diffused-base transistor

mae mean absolute error; motion aftereffect

Mae Mary

Ma.E. Master of Engineering

MAE Medical Air Evacuation; Museum of Atomic Energy

M.A.E. Master of Aeronautical Engineering; Master of Art Education; Master of Arts in Education; Master of Arts in Elocution

M.A.Econ. Master of Arts in Economics; Master of Arts in Economic and Social Studies

MAECON Mid-America Electronics Convention

M.A.Ed. Master of Arts in Education

MAEE Marine Aircraft Experimental Establishment

MAEF Master Asphalt Employers' Federation

Maelström large whirlpool off west coast of Norway between Mosken and Moskenaes islands in the Lofotens; Moskenström described by Edgar Allan Poe in *A Descent into the Maelström*

MAELU Mutual Atomic Energy Liability Underwriters

M.Aero.E. Master of Aeronautical Engineering

MAES Mexican American Engineering Society

maesto maestoso (Italian—majestically)

Maestro of Abolition Brazilian composer-conductor Carlos Gomes who fought for the abolition of slavery

Maestro Crescendo Rossini's nickname

ma ewes mixed-age ewes

Mae West American actress of stage and screen; lifejacket named after her shape

maf major academic field; manpower authorization file; minimum audible field; multiplanar angular forces

MAF Marine Air Facility; Middle Atlantic Fisheries; Midland, Texas (airport); Minister of Armed Forces; Ministry of Agriculture and Fisheries; Ministry of Agriculture and Forestry; Missile Assembly Facility; Mission Aviation Fellowship; Mobile Air Force; Mutual Adjustment Fund(ing); Mutual Asset Fund(ing)

MA & F Ministry of Agriculture and Fisheries

MAFA Manchester Academy of Fine Arts

MAFAC Marine Fisheries Advisory Council

MAFB Mitchell Air Force Base

MAFC Major Army Field Command

MAFCA Model-A Ford Club of America

MAFDAL Miflaga Datit Le'umit (Hebrew—National Religious Party)

mafe magnesium + iron (Ma + Fe)

MAFF Minister of Agriculture, Fisheries and Food; Ministry of Agriculture, Forestry, and Fisheries

MAFFS Modular Airborne Fire Fighting System (USAF)

MAFI Medic-Alert Foundation International; Ministry of Agriculture, Forestry, and Irrigation

MAFIA *Morte Alla Francia Italia Anela* (Italian—Death to France Is Italy's Cry), acronym devised when the secret society was first organized in the 1860s, to combat French forces of intervention

mafr merged accountability and fund reporting

MAFS Mobilization Air Force Specialty

MAFVA Miniature Armored Fighting Vehicles Association

mag magazine; magnesia; magnesium; magnet; magnetic; magnetism; magneto; magnetron; magnum

mag. *magnus* (Latin—great)

Mag Magallanes (Punta Arenas); Magallanic; Magyar; Margaret

Mag. *Magnificat* (Latin—it magnifies)—song of the Virgin Mary

MAG Magnavox (stock exchange symbol); magnesium (machine shop style); Marine Aircraft Group; Marine Avia-

tion Group; Military Advisory Group

maga magazine

Mag.Agg. *Magister Aggregatus* (Latin—Master of Aggregation)—Head Master

Magallanes former name of Punta Arenas, Chile

mag ampl magnetic amplifier

Magazine of History *American Heritage*

Magazinist Edgar Allan Poe's self-invented title

MAGB Microfilm Association of Great Britain; Mining Association of Great Britain

mag cap magazine capacity

mag card magnetic card

magcheck magneto check

mag ci magnetic cast iron

magcon magnetic concentration

mag cs magnetic cast steel

Magd Magdalene (pronounced *Modlin*) College (Cambridge or Oxford)

Magda Magdalen(a)

Magdalena Colombia's 1000-mile-long waterway running from the Andes below Bogotá to Barranquilla near the Caribbean Sea

Magdalens Magdalen Islands in the Gulf of Saint Lawrence

Magda Lupescu Elena Wolff

Magd Coll Magdalen College—Oxford

Magdeburgum (Latin—Magdeburg)

M.Ag.Ec. Master of Agricultural Economics

M.Ag.Ed. Master of Agricultural Education

Magellan of Modern Music Harry Partch

magg *maggio* (Italian—May); *maggiore* (Italian—major)

Maggie Margaret; stock market nickname for Magnavox

magic modern analytical generator of improved circuitry; modern analytical generator of improved circuits

MAGIC Madison Avenue General Ideas Committee; Men's Apparel Guild In California; Midac Automatic General Integrated Computation

Magic City any fast-growing city such as Billings, Montana or Birmingham, Alabama, or Miami, Florida, etc.

Magic Island Haiti on Hispaniola in Greater Antilles of West Indies

magid magnetic intrusion detector

Magister Fouga jet trainer built in France

maglev magentically levitated (linear motor-propelled railroad trains); magnetic levitation

maglevs magnetically levitated vehicles

magloc magnetic logic computer

mag mod magnetic modulator

magn magnetism

magn. *magnus* (Latin—large)

magna material and geometrically nonlinear analysis

magnalium magnesium + aluminum (alloy)

magneform magnetic forming (process)

magnesia magnesium oxide (MgO)

MAGni *Magazini* (Italian—warehouse)

Magnificent 13 New York City's civic minded red-bereted young teams of vigilantes determined to enforce law and order in the subways where so many people were mugged, robbed, and victimized by teenage gangs in the 1970s

magno manganese-nickel alloy

Magnolia state flower of Louisiana and Mississippi

Magnolia City Houston, Texas

Magnolia Lady Former First Lady Rosalynn Carter

Magnolia(s) Mississippian(s)

Magnolia State Mississippi's official nickname

magnox magnesium oxide

magnum high-powered cartridge or weapon for firing magnum ammunition; 2/5-gallon champagne bottle

mag. op. *magnum opus* (Latin—major work)

M.Agr. Master of Agriculture

mags magazines; magnesium wheels

MAGSAT Magnetic Field Satellite

mag tape magnetic tape

magtig allemagtig (Afrikaans—almighty)—Almighty God

Maguntia (Latin—Mainz)

Magyarorszag (Hungarian—Hungary)

Magyar(s) Hungarian(s)

mah mahogany

μAh microampere hour

MAHA Malaysian Agri-Horticultural Association

Mahagonny Aufstieg und Fall der Stadt Mahagonny (German—Rise and Fall of the

City of Mahagonny)—three-act opera by Kurt Weill with text by Bertolt Brecht

Mahatma (Hindi—Great Souled) —sobriquet of India's greatest leader, Mohandas Karamchand Ghandi

MAHE Michigan Association for Higher Education

Mahler's 10 Mahler's ten symphonies including the *Resurrection* (No. 2), the *Symphony of a Thousand* (No. 8), the *Unfinished* (No. 10)

mahog mahogany

mai machine-aided index(ing); marriage adjustment inventory; mean annual increment; minimum annual income

MAI Military Assistance Institute; Museum of the American Indian

MAI Moskovskiy Aviatsionny Institut (Russian—Moscow Aviation Institute)

MA.I. Magister in Arte Ingeniaria (Latin—Master of Engineering)

MAIBL Midland and International Banks Limited

maid. maintenance automatic integration detector

M-Aid Marshall-Plan Aid (given European countries by the United States after World War II)

Maid of Orleans Joan of Arc— *La Pucelle d'Orleans*

Maid of Zaragoza Augustina de Aragón (Augustina Domenech Zaragoza—fighter for freedom during Spain's invasion by Napoleonic armies)

MAIG Matsushita Atomic Industrial Group

Mail NATO nickname for Soviet BE-12 Beriev amphibian reconnaissance aircraft

Maimon Maimonides

Maimonides Moses ben Maimon

MAIN Medical Automation Intelligence System

Mainbocher Main Rousseau Bocher

Main Drag Main Street or the main street of any American city or town

Main Drag of Many Tears 125th Street in New York City's Harlem

Maine's Ports (northernmost to southernmost) Calais to Kittery including Bangor, Searsport, Boothbay Harbor, Bath, and Portland

Maine St Mus Maine State Museum

Maine Turn Maine Turnpike

Maine Yankee Maine Yankee Atomic Power Company

Mainichi Mainichi Shimbun (Japanese—Everyday Newspaper)—modern Japan's oldest periodical

mainland China communist People's Republic of China headquartered in Peking on the mainland

Main Street Sinclair Lewis's novel about small-town people living in an imaginary Minnesota town named Gopher Prairie

maint maintenance

maintnce maintenance

Mainz (German—Mayence)

maip memory access and interrupt processor

Maiquetía Venezuela's principal airport serving Caracas, La Guaira, and many other places

MAIS Maine Association of Independent Schools; Maintenance Information System; Minnesota Adaptive Instructional System

Maisie Maria; Marie; Mary; Maryjane

Maison Gomin correctional facility for women at St Cyrille, Québec

Maison Tanguay Montreal's facility for women prisoners

MAIT Maintenance Assistance and Instruction Team; Multidiscipline Accident Investigation Team

maitre d' *maitre d'hotel* (French —head waiter)

maj major; majority

Maj Major

MAJ Majuro (Marshall Islands airport); Muhammad Ali Jinnah

majac maintenance antijam console

Maj Com Major Command

maj dem(s) major demon(s)— Asmodeus (lechery), Beelzebub (gluttony), Belphegor (sloth), Leviathan (envy), Lucifer (pride), Mammon (avarice), Satan (anger)

MAJECA Malaysia-Japan Economic Association

Maj Gen Major General

Majocchi's disease ringlike empurplement of the lower limbs

Majorca English name for Mallorca

Major Prophets of the Old Testament Isaiah, Jeremiah, Ezekiel, Daniel

Majulah Singapura (Malay— Advance Singapore)—national motto of Singapore

Mak Makdougall; Makoto; Maksim; Maksimovich

makai (Hawaiian—seaward, toward the sea)

makbsctr make best counteroffer

Mák-i-no Mackinac (island, river, or strait as pronounced locally)

Makkah (Arabic—Mecca)

MAKN Mongol Ardyn Khuv'sgalt Nam (Kalkha Mongol—Mongolian People's Revolutionary Party)

maksutsub make suitable substitutions

mal (Latin prefix—abnormal, bad, disorder)—malignant

Mal The Book of Malachi; Malaga; Malagueña(o); Malay; Malayan; Malaysia; Malta; Maltese

Mal Malay (the basic language of the Indo-Malayan islands and nations including Indonesia where it is spoken by 93 million people); *Maréchal* (French—Marshal)

MAL Malaysian Airways Limited; Material Allowance List

Mala Malaya; Malayan; Malaysia; Malaysian

malac malacology

Malacañan (Pilipino—Home of the Ruler)—Filipino presidential palace

Malacañan Palace official residence of the President of the Philippines

malachite hydrated copper carbonate

Malafon Latecoere surface-to-surface or surface-to-underwater naval missile made in France

Malagasy Republic Madagascar

malaprop *mal à propos* (French —out of place, unappropriate)

Malar English name for Lake Mälaren in Sweden

Mälaren (Swedish—Lake Malar)

Malaspina Malaspina Glacier on Yukutat Bay, Alaska

Malawi Republic of Malawi (formerly called Nyasaland this East African nation exports rubber and other tropical crops, Malawians speak English and Bantu tongues)

Malaya Malay Peninsula also called Malaysia

Malayan Island Nation Singapore

Malaysia Malay Peninsula (countries formerly comprising British Malaya plus Saba and Sarawak on Borneo but minus Singapore at the southeast tip of Asia, Malay and English plus Chinese are heard, exports feature rubber, tin, and some foodstuffs)

Malaysian Federation Johore, Kedah, Kelantan, Malacca, Negri Sambilan, Pahang, Penang, Perak, Perlis, Sabah, Sarawak, Selangor, Trengganu; up to 1965 included Singapore

Malaysian Ports Penang-Butterworth; Lumut, Kelang (Port Swettenham), Port Dickson, Melaka

Malbrook (Louis XIV's mispronunciation of Marlborough—John Churchill—Duke of Marlborough whose British soldiers drove the French from the field in battle after battle)—*see* Mambru

Malcolm X Malcolm Little

Mald Maldive Islands

Mal$ Malaysian dollar

Mal 3 Malaya dollar

M A L D Master of Arts in Law and Diplomacy

MALDEF Mexican-American Legal Defense and Educational Fund

Maldive Islands Port Malé

Maldives Republic of Maldives (Indian Ocean island nation of Maldivian farmers and fishermen who speak a Sinhalese dialect called Divehi, tourism aids the economy of this remote archipelago)

MALEV (Hungarian Airline)

MALEV *Magyar Legikolekedesi Vallat* (Hungarian Airlines)

malfunc malfunction

Malgache (French—Madagascan)

Malgache Republic Madagascar (territory includes Amsterdam, Crozet, Kerguelen, and Saint Paul islands)

Malg Rep Malagasy Republic

Mali Republic of Mali (landlocked West African country whose Malians speak French and tribal tongues, rubber and tropical foodstuffs are exported) *République du Mali*

MALI Air Mali

malig malignant

Malinche (see Doña Marina)—often a Mexican synonym for Quisling or traitor—with Malinchismo meaning treachery

Malindo Malaysia-Indonesia

Mal Isl Maldive Islands

mall malleable

Mall Mallorca

Mallorca (Spanish—Majorca)

Mallows (British slang shortcut —St Malo)

MALODES Modern Army Logistics Data Exchange System

malor mortar-and-artillery-locating radar

malpais (Spanish—badlands)—basaltic-lava wastelands

Malpartidas (Spanish—Badly Divided Lands)—short form for Malpartida de Cáceres, Malpartida de la Serena, and Malpartida de Plasencia—all in western Spain near the Portuguese borderlands

Malpaso short form for Alto de Mal Paso (highest point on Hierro in the Canary Islands)

Mal-Port Malay-Portuguese (East African patois)

malprac(s) malpractice(s); malpractitioner(s)

MALRA Malaysian Leprosy Relief Association

MALS Medium-Intensity Approach Light(ing) System

M.A.L.S. Master of Arts in Liberal Studies; Master of Arts in Library Science; Master of Arts in Library Service

MALSCE Massachusetts Association of Land Surveyors and Civil Engineers

Mal St Malay States

Malstrøm (Norwegian—Maelstrom)—whirlpool off Norway's northwest coast as described in Poe's *Descent into the Maelstrom*

malt. malted milkshake

Malta island nation in the central Mediterranean (where the Maltese speak English and Maltese with equal facility, farming, ship repairing, and tourism are vital to the economy)

Maltese Ports Valetta and Marsaxlokk

Malt(s) Maltese sailor(s)

Maluku (Indonesian—Moluccas)—Spice Islands

Malukus Maluku or Moluccas Islands of Indonesia also called the Spice Islands

Malvenuto nickname carping critics bestowed on the Berlioz opera *Benvenuto Cellini*

Malvinas Malvinas Islands (Falklands)

mam medium automotive maintenance; milliampere; minute(s)

ma'm madam

m + am (compound) myopic astigmatism

mam *mot a mot* (French—word for word)

MAM Military Assistance Manual; Missile Acceptance Meeting; Montclair Art Museum

MAMA Mobile Air Materiel Area; Middletown Air Materiel Area

MAMB Military Advisory Mission—Brazil

MAMBO Mediterranean Association of Marine Biology and Oceanography

Mambru (Spanish mispronunciation of Marlborough—John Churchill—Duke of Marlborough—whose military exploits were much admired by the Spaniards during the War of the Spanish Succession)—*see* Malbrook

MAMC Madigan Army Medical Center

MAME Michigan Association for Media in Education

Mamelles *Les Mamelles de Tirésias* (French—The Breasts of Tiresias)—two-act comic opera by Poulenc

MAMENIC Marina Mercante Nicaraguense (Nicaraguan Merchant Marine—Mamenic Line)

mami machine-aided manufacturing information

mamie minimum automatic machine for interpolation and extrapolation

Mamie Margaret

mammal. mammalogist; mammalogy

mammax machine-made and machine-aided index

mammog mammogram; mammograph; mammographer; mammographic(al)(ly); mammography

Mammoth short form for any of many mammoth caves in Australia, California, and Kentucky; Mammoth Hot Springs in Wyoming; Mammoth Lakes in California; Mammoth Onyx Cave in Kentucky; Mammoth Spring in Arkansas; Mammoth Village in Arizona

mamos marine automatic meteorological observing station

MAMS Missile Assembly and Maintenance Shop

M.A.Mus. Master of Arts in Music

Mamzel Mademoiselle

man. manhold; manifest; manifold; manual; manufacture; manure

man. *manipulus* (Latin—handful)

m A n *meiner Ansicht nach* (German—in my opinion)

Man Manager; short form for Isle of Man in the Irish Sea or the Man canal and river in Burma or La Mancha in Spain or such other places as Manchester, Mangalore, Manhattan, Manila, and Manitoba

MAN Managua, Nicaragua (airport); Motorcyclists Against Noise

M-A-N Maschinefabrik-Augsburg-Nurnberg

MAN *Movemento Antillese Nuevo* (Papiamento—New Antillean Movement)—based in Curaçao

Man¹ Manuel (Spanish—Emanuel)

MANA Manufacturers' Agents National Association; Mexican-American National Women's Association

M.Anaes. Master of Anaesthesiology

Man for All Seasons Sir Thomas More

Mañanaland Latin America (so called when things are put off until *mañana*—tomorrow)

Manassa Mauler Jack Dempsey born in Manassa, Colorado

Man of a Thousand Faces Lon Chaney

Mana-Zucca Augusta Zuckerman

Man of Blood and Iron Prince Otto von Bismarck's nickname alluding to the speeches wherein he clamored for German blood and iron

Man Brdg Manhattan Bridge (New York City)

manc *mancando* (Italian—gradually softer)

Manc Manchester; Mancunian —inhabitant of Manchester

Manch Manchuria

Manchow (Chinese—Manchuria)

Manchukua Japanese puppet

state from 1931 to 1945 in Inner Mongolia and Manchuria

Manco de Lepanto (see *El Manco de Lepanto*)

Mancunium (Latin—Manchester)

mand mandamus; mandate; mandatory; mandible; mandibular

Mand Mandarin

Man of Destiny Napoleon's self-named nickname; pre-Civil-War American filibuster William Walker; one-time dictator president of Nicaragua who planned for Central American unification and a Caribbean federation including Central America and Cuba

MANDFHAB Male and Female Homosexual Association of Great Britain

Man Dir Managing Director; Managing Directress

mandrake nickname for *Mandragora officinarum* also called devil's testicle or satan's apple

Mandrake NATO name for Soviet Yakovlev strategic-reconnaissance jet aircraft

mandy man day

Mandy Amanda; Manda

Man Ed Managing Editor

manf manifold; manufacture; manufacturer; manufacturing

MANFED Manufacturers Federation

MANFEP Manitoba Finite Element Program

MANFORCE Manpower for a Clean Environment

Manfred *Manfred Overture* (Schumann); *Manfred Symphony* (Tchaikovsky)

Man from Independence President Harry S Truman

Man from Maine James G Blaine

Man from Missouri President Harry S Truman

mang management

manganim manganese-copper-nickel alloy

mang b manganese bronze

manglish mangled English

Man of God Grigori Rasputin (so named by Czar Nicholas II —last of the Romanov emperors of Russia)

Mangrove NATO nickname for Soviet Yakovlev Yak-26 tactical reconnaissance aircraft

Mangrove Coast Florida's

southernmost coast between the Everglades and the Keys

manhattan manhattan clam chowder (minced clams plus herbs and tomatoes); manhattan cocktail (vermouth and whiskey mix topped with a maraschino cherry); manhattan skyscraper (manhattan-style tall building)

manhr manhour

MANI Minister of Agriculture for Northern Ireland

maniac. (MANIAC) mechanical and numerical integrator and computer

manif manifest

MANIFILE Manitoba File (of worldwide nonferrous metallic deposits)

Manil Marcus Manilius (Roman poet)

manila manila hemp (abacá fiber used in making manila fabrics or manila rope as well as manila paper); manila paper (buff-color paper originally made from manila hemp and prized for its heavy-duty applications ranging from cartons and envelopes to wrapping paper)

manip. *manipulus* (Latin—handful)

manit man minute

Manit Manitoba

Manitoulins Manitoulin Islands in Lake Huron

Manley Norman Manley International Airport serving Jamaica and named for its first native-born chief minister— an Irish-Negro lawyer

manmam manufacturing management

Man Med Dept *Manual of the Medical Department (USN)*

manmo man month

Man of Monach Country Fermanagh County in Ulster, Northern Ireland

Manning Coles Cyril Henry Coles

Manny Emanuel; Manuel

Man(ny) Han(ny) Manufacturers Hanover (Bank)

mano manograph; manometer

MANO Mexican-American Neighborhood Association

MANO *Movimiento Argentina Nacional Organizado* (Spanish —National Organized Movement of Argentina)—terrorist group

Mano Blanca (Spanish—White Hand)—Cuban exile groups

determined to reclaim their country

Manolete Manuel Rodriguez

man. one first-degree manslaughter

Man on Horseback General Georges Boulanger

manop manually operated; manual operation

Man Op Manual of Operation(s)

Manor The Manor (British underworld slang for London)

manova multivariate analysis of variance

man. p. *mane primo* (Latin—early in the morning, first thing in the morning)

MANP Masai Amboseli National Park (Kenya); Mount Apo NP (Mindanao, Philippines); Mount Arayat NP (Luzon, Philippines)

Man Rtg Manual Rating (code)

mans. mansions

Mans Mansfield College, Oxford; Mansion

MANS Map Analysis System

mansat manned satellite

mansec man second

Mansf Coll Mansfield College-Oxford

Man's Oldest Disease alcoholism

man(s) rep(s) manufacturer(s) representative(s)

Man Sym Manila Symphony

mant (MANT) mantissa (calculator)

MANTIS Manchester Technical Information Service

Mantova (Italian—Mantua)

Mantovani d'Annunzio Paolo

MANTRAP Machine and Network Transients Program

Mantua English place-name for Mantova

Manuel Emmanuel

manuf manufacture(r)

Manutius Aldus Manutius Latinized version of Aldo Manuzio—inventor of italic type

manuv maneuvering

MANWEB Merseyside and North Wales Electricity Board

Man Who Invented Panama Philippe Bunau-Varilla

Man Who Made the Greatest Dictionary James AH Murray who devoted his life to the creation of the *Oxford English Dictionary* abbreviated *OED* although it's in 13 volumes plus some supplements

Man Who Made Ragtime Scott Joplin

manwich man-sized sandwich

Man With the Hoe The Man With the Hoe—Edwin Markham

manwk man week

Man of Words lexicographer Eric Partridge

manx manx cat (almost tailless breed of cat originating on the Isle of Man); manx shearwater (small black-and-white oceanic bird of the eastern North Atlantic); month after next

Manxmen Isle-of-Man persons

Many Islands *see* Polynesia

Man You Loved To Hate Erich von Stroheim

manyr man year

MANZ Medical Association of New Zealand; Montreal-Australia New Zealand (Line); Motel Association of New Zealand

Manzoni Mass Verdi's *Requiem*

mao (MAO) monoamine oxidase

mao med andra ord (Swedish—in other words); *med andre ord* (Dano-Norwegian—in other words)

Mao Mao Tse-tung

MAO Master of the Art of Obstetrics; Musica Aeterna Orchestra

MAO Magyar Allami Operhaz (Hungarian State Opera)

MAOF Mexican-American Opportunity Foundation

maoi (MAOI) monamine oxidase inhibitor

Maoriland New Zealand

maot medium-aperture optical telescope

MAOT Member of the Association of Occupational Therapists; Military Assistance Observer Team

Mao Zedong Mao Tse-tung (in official and phonetic Pinyin spelling used since January 1, 1979 throughout the People's Republic of China)

map. manifold absolute pressure; manifold air pressure; mapping; maximum average price; micro-assembly program; minimum association price; minimum audible pressure; missed approach point; missed approach procedure; multiple-aim point

MAP Maghreb-Arabe Presse

(Maghreb Arab Press Agency); Maintenance Analysis Program; Material Analysis Plan(ning); Medical Aid Post; Medical Assistance Program; Melanesian Alliance Party; Microprocessor Application Project; Middle Atmosphere Program; Military Aid Program; Military Assitance Program; Military Association of Podiatrists; Mini-Activity Plan; Ministry of Aircraft Production; Ministry of Aircraft Production; Multiple Application Procedure; Mutual African Press (agency); Mutual Agreement Processing (for parolees); Mutual Assistance Program

M-A-P Modified American Plan (breakfast and dinner included)

MAPA Malayan Agricultural Producers Association; Malaysian Airlines Pilots Association; Mexican-American Political Association

MAPAD Map Address Directory

MAPAG Military Assistance Program Advisory Group

MAPAI Miflaget Poaley Israel (Hebrew—Israel Labor Party)—right-wing socialist

MAPAM Miflaget HaPaolim HaMe'uchdot (Hebrew United Workers Party)—left-wing socialist

MAPC Minnesota Association of Private Colleges

mapche mobile automatic programmed checkout equipment

MAPCO Mid-America Pipeline Company

mapd maximum allowable percent defective

MAPDA Mid-American Periodical Distributors Association

maped machine-aided program for the preparation of electrical power

MAP-ga Military Assistance Program—grant aid

maph manned ambient-pressure habitat

MAPHILINDO Malaysia, Philippines, Indonesia (proposed unification of these Malayan countries)

MAPI Machinery and Allied Products Institute; Millon Adolescent Personality Inventory; Mitsubishi Atomic Power

Industries
mapid machine-aided program for the preparation of instruction(al) data
MAPL Manufacturing Assembly Parts List
Maple City Ogdensburg, New York
Maple Lane Maple Lane School (for juvenile delinquents) in Centralia, Washington
Maple Leaf Canada's flag consisting of three vertical stripes —red, white, red—with a red maple leaf on the white center stripe
MAPNY Maritime Association of the Port of New York
MAPOM MAP-owned materiel
mapp methylacetylenepropadiene
mapple macro-associative processor-programming language
M.App.Sc. Master of Applied Science
MAPR Manufacturing Aids Program Requirements
mapros maintain production schedule(s)
maps. monopropellant accessory power supply
MAPS Major Assembly Performance System; Management Analysis and Planning System; Middle Atlantic Planetarium Society; Military Products and Systems (RCA); Miniature Air Pilot System; Monetary and Payments System; Multiple Address Processing System; Multiple Aiming Point System; Multivariate Analysis and Prediction of Schedules (USA)
MAPU Movimiento de Acción Popular Unitaria (Spanish—Movement for United Popular Action)—Chilean leftists
MAPW Medical Association for the Prevention of War
maq monetary allowance in lieu of quarters
maq maquereau (French—mackerel)—a pimp (also abbreviated *mac*)
MAQ Measures for Air Quality (NBS)
mar. marine; maritime; married; marry; memory address register; minimal angle resolution; minimum acceptable rate (of return); multiarray radar; multifunction array radar
mar. mardi (French—Tuesday); *martedi* (Italian—Tuesday);

martes (Spanish—Tuesday)
Mar Marathi; March; Marseilles; Marshall Islands
M.Ar. Master of Architecture
MAR Manistee and Repton (railroad); Maracaibo, Venezuela (airport); Maritime Central Airways; Mars Excursion Module; Material Availability Report; Material Availability Request
MARA Mexican-American Research Association
MARA Majilis Amanah Raayat (Malay—Handicraft Center for the Development of Malaysian People)
MARAD Maritime Administration (US Department of Commerce)
MARAIRMED Maritime Air Mediterranean
marb marbling
Marb Marblehead; Marbleheart; Marbury
Mar Bermejo (Spanish—Vermillion Sea)—the Gulf of California
marbi machine-readable bibliographic information
marble calcium carbonate ($CaCO_3$)
Marble Capital Proctor, Vermont
Marble City Rutland, Vermont; Sylacauga, Alabama
Marble Halls of Oregon Oregon Caves National Monument
marc monitoring and results computer
marc marcato (Italian—marked)
Marc Marcus
MARC Machine-Readable Cataloging (Library of Congress magnetic-tape catalog system); Manpower Authorization Request for Change; Matador Automatic Radar Command; Metropolitan Applied Research Center; Micronesia Area Research Center (Guam); Model-A Restorers Club (Model-A Ford autos)
MARCA Mid-Continent Area Reliability Coordination Agreement
MarCad Marine Cadet
Mar Cad Marine Cadet
Mar Cantábrico (Spanish—Cantabrian Sea)—the Bay of Biscay
Mar Caríbe (Spanish—Caribbean Sea)
Marc Chagall Marc Segal
Marcella Sembrich Praxede

Marcelline Kochanska
MARCEP Maintainability and Cost-Effectiveness Program
March. Marchioness
March Marchese (Italian—Marquis)
M.Arch. Master of Architecture
MARCHA Methodists Associated Representing the Cause of Hispanic Americans
Marchbanks (British contraction—Marjoribanks)
Marches border region of England and Wales
March King John Philip Sousa
*March*ˢᵃ *Marchesa* (Italian—Marchioness)
MARC(LC) Machine-Readable Catalog(ing) (Library of Congress)
MARCO Marine Construction and Design Company
MARCOM Maritime Command (Canadian)
MARCONFOR Maritime Contingency Force
MARCONFORLANT Maritime Contingency Forces—Atlantic
Marco Page pseudonym of Harry Kurnitz
MARCOR US Marine Corps
MARCS Marine Computer System
MARC(S) Machine-Readable Catalog(ing) for Serials
MARC(UK) Machine-Readable Catalog(ing) in the British Library of the United Kingdom
Marcus Mark
mardan marine digital analyzer
MARDEC Malaysian Rubber Development Corporation
Mar de Cortés (Spanish—Sea of Cortez)—the Gulf of California
Mar de las Indias (Spanish—Indian Ocean)
Mar del Norte (Spanish—North Sea)
Marder West German armored-personnel carrier fitted with a 20mm cannon
MARDI Malaysian Agricultural Research and Development
Mardi Gras Metropolis New Orleans, Louisiana
Mar do Norte (Portuguese—North Sea)
MARECS Marine Communications Satellites
mar eng marine engineer(ing)
Mare Nord (Italian—North Sea)
MARFOR Marine Forces
marg margarine; margin; margi-

nal; marginalia
Marg Margrave; Margravine
marge margarine (oleomargarine); margin
Marge Margaret; Margery
margen management report generator
Margie Margaret
Mar Gils Area Marshalls-Gilberts (island) Area
Margot Margaret
Marg^ta Margarita (Spanish—Margaret)
marg trans marginal translation
marhelilex marine helicopter landing exercise
MARI Middle America Research Institute
Maria Callas Maria Calogeropoulos
Maria Jeritza Mimi Jedlitzka
Marianas Mariana Islands; once called Ladrones (thieves)
Maribo Paramaribo, Surinam
Marichu (Spanish-American nickname—María de Jesús)—see *Chuey*
maricult mariculture; mariculturist
mariculture marine culture (growing food in the sea)
Marie Brema Minny Fehrman
Marie Corelli Eva Mary Mackay
Marie Dressler Leila Koerber
Marie's disease chronic enlargement of the face, feet, and hands
marifarm maritime farm
marifex marine firine exercise
mariholic marijuanaholic (addict)
Marilyn Monroe Norma Jean Baker
Marina Street San Juan, Puerto Rico's district jail on Marina Street where it was opened in 1837 when the Spaniards called it Calle Marina
Mariner Venus-Mars fly-by space vehicle
Mariner Mystic Herman Melville
Marinsky Marinsky Theater in St Petersburg now called Leningrad and with its opera house and theater renamed Kirov
Mario Giovanni Matteo
Mariol Mariolatry; Mariology
Mario Lanza Alfred Arnold Cacozza
Marion Federal Prison Camp at Marion, Illinois; Mary; Maryjane; U.S. Penitentiary at Marion, Illinois (maximum-secu-

rity prison replacing Alcatraz in San Francisco Bay)
Marion Davies Marion Cecelia Douras
MARIS Maritime Research Information Service
marisat maritime industry satellite
Mariscal de Ayacucho (Spanish—Marshal of Ayacucho)—Antonio José de Sucre—companion of Bolívar and first president of Bolivia
marit maritime
marita maritime airfield
Marit Admin Maritime Administration
Marit Com Maritime Commission
Maritime Alps *Alpes Maritimes* (French)—AM
Maritime Provinces New Brunswick, Nova Scotia, and Prince Edward Island
Maritimes Canada's Maritime Provinces; the Maritime Alps between France and Italy; the Soviet Union's Maritime Territory extending along the Sea of Japan
maritrain(s) maritime train(s)—articulated sea-going barges
Maritzburg Pietermaritzburg
Marj Marjy; Marjan; Marjorie; Marjory
mark. market; marketing
Mark The Gospel according to St Mark
Mark Aldanov Mark Aleksandrovich Landau
Mark Antony Anglicized name of the Roman general Marcus Antonius
Markland (Norse—Forest Land)—probably Labrador
Mark Rothko Marcus Rothkowitz
Marks & Sparks Marks & Spencer (British department store)
mark twain leadline sounding of two fathoms (12 feet or 3.66 meters); leadsmen announcing *mark twain* usually meant there was enough water to keep the average shallow-draft paddlewheel river steamer afloat and safe from grounding; Sam(uel) L(anghorne) Clemens was a Mississippi River pilot and used Mark Twain as his literary pseudonym; in his *Life on the Mississippi* he also explains *mark three* is three fathoms and *quarter twain* is two-and-a-half

fathoms
Mark Twain Samuel Langhorne Clemens
Mark Twain Town Hannibal, Missouri
Marlag Marinenlager (German—sailor's camp for prisoners of war)
Marlene Mary + Helena
Mariene Dietrich Magdalene von Losch
marlex marine reserve landing exercise
MARLF Middle Atlantic Regional Library Federation
mar lic marriage license
Marlin Martin P-5M reconnaissance flying boat
MARLIS Multi-Aspect Relevance Linkage System
Marm Marmaduke
Marmalade Capital Dundee, Scotland
marmap marine resources monitoring, assessment, and prediction
Marmara Sea of Marmara (connecting the Black Sea with the Mediterranean via the Dardanelles Strait and separating Asiatic Turkey from European Turkey)—called Marmara Denizi by the Turks
Marmara Denizi (Turkish—Sea of Marmara)
mar merc marina mercantile (Italian—merchant marine)
mar mil marina militare (Italian—navy)
Mar Muerto (Spanish—Dead Sea)
Mar Negro (Spanish—Black Sea)
MARNR Ministerio del Ambiente y los Recursos Naturales Renovables (Spanish—Ministry of the Environment and Renewable Natural Resources)—Venezuela
Maro Marocco (Italian—Morocco)
MARO Maritime Air Radio Organization
Maroc (French—Morocco)
Marokko (Dutch or German—Morocco)
marops maritime operations
marots (MAROTS) marine orbital technical satellite
MARPEX Management of Repair Parts Expenditure (USA)
Marpril March and April
Marq Marquesas Islands
Marquesas short form for the Marquesas Islands of the South Pacific or the Marque-

sas Keys west of Key West, Florida in the Gulf of Mexico

Marquis Marquis Who's Who Books

Marquise de Pompadour Jeanne Poisson

Marquis of Queensbury Marquis of Queensbury boxing rules formulated by John Graham Chambers supervised by the 8th Marquis of Queensbury—Sir John Shollto Douglas father of Oscar Wilde's friend Lord Alfred Douglas

Marquis of Rockingham Charles Watson-Wentworth (former Prime Minister of Great Britain like the marquises whose names follow)

Marquis of Salisbury Robert AT Gascoyne-Cecil

marr marriage; minimum acceptable rate of return

Marr Marranic; Marranism; Marranoism; Marrano(s)

Marr *Marruecos* (Spanish—Morocco)

MARRES Manual Radar Reconnaissance Exploitation System

marr lic marriage license

Marro *Marrocos* (Portuguese—Morocco)

Mar Rojo (Spanish—Red Sea)

marr sett marriage settlement

Marru *Marruecos* (Spanish—Morocco)

mars master attitude reference system; mathematics anxiety rating scale; military affiliated radio system

Mars Marseilles

Mars' Marshals' Offices

Mars Ares (Latin—god of war); *Marselha* (Portuguese—Marseilles); *Marsella* (Spanish—Marseilles); *Marsiglia* (Italian—Marseilles)

MARs Middle American Radicals

MARS Magnetic-Electronic Automatic Reservation System; Maintenance Action Reporting System; Manned Astronautical Research Station; Master Altitude Reference System; Military Affiliate Radio System; Miniature Accurate Ranging System; Mobile Atlantic Rangge Station; Modern Architectural Research Society

Marsala (Arabic—Harbor of God)—Sicilian seaport

MARSAP Mutual Assistance Rescue and Salvage Plan

MARSAS Marine Search and Attack System (USMC)

marsat maritime satellite

MARSATS Maritime Satellite System

M.Ar.Sci. Master of Arts and Sciences

Marseille (French—Marseilles)

Marsella (Portuguese or Spanish—Marseille)

Marse Robert (southern American—Master Robert)—General Robert E Lee

Marshall Islands Micronesian insular country in the equatorial western Pacific where its citizens subsist on marine products, tourism, and tropical crops; its 4-by-6-inch 75-cent postage stamp is the delight of philatelists

Marshalls Marshall Islands in the western Pacific

marsh gas methane (CH_4)

Marsiglia (Italian—Marseille)

MA/RSO Mobilization Augmentee/Reserve Supplement Officer (USAF)

mart. maintenance analysis and review technique; mean active repair time

mart *martes* (Spanish—Tuesday)

Mart Martinique

Mart. Martyrology

Mart Marcus Valerius Martialis (Roman poet)

MART Metropolitan Area Rapid Transit

MARTA Metropolitan Atlanta Rapid Transit Authority

Martel Hawker-Siddeley in Britain and Matra in France built this AS-37 missile

Martel (French—Hammer) — father of Charlemagne and victor over the Saracens at Tours

Marth Martha

Martha Albrand Heidi Huberta Freybe

Martí Aeropuerto José Martí (Havana, Cuba's airport named for the founder of the Cuban Revolutionary Party who did much to organize resistance to Spanish rule but was killed during a skirmish in 1895 just three years before his island was liberated by American and Cuban forces)

Martial Roman epigrammatist Marcus Valerius Martialis

Martin St Martin or Sint Maarten in the Leeward Islands

Martinica (Spanish—Martinique)

Martov Yuli Osipovich Tsederbaum

M.Art RCA Master of Art of the Royal College of Art

mart(s) market(s)

MARTS Master Radar Tracking Station

Mart(y) Martin

Martyr Abolitionist Elijah Parish Lovejoy

Martyr of Mexican Independence Miguel Hidalgo

Marunouchi Tokoyo's financial center

Maruyama Nagasaki, Japan's old redlight district

marv maneuvering reentry vehicle (MaRV in Salt Talk reports, also MARV); marvel; marvelous

Marv Marvin

Marvel of Marble the Taj Mahal

Marx Brothers Chico (Leonard), Harpo (Arthur), Groucho (Julius), plus Gummo and Zeppo Marx (who appeared only in pre-1936 films featuring this family of comedians)

Mary Astor Lucille Langhanke

Maryland Port Baltimore

Marylebone St Marylebone

Mary Pickford Gladys Mary Smith's stage name

Mary Queen of Scots Mary Stuart

Mary Roe anonym used on subpoenas and summonses when the true name of the woman to be served is unknown; nickname of the average American girl as by national custom all females of all ages are referred to as girls

Marysville Girls Ohio Reformatory for Women at Marysville

mas masculine; masonry; mathematics anxiety scale; metal angle slots; military assistance sales; milliampere second; moved aboard ship

mas Malaysian Airline System's trademark

Mas Massachusetts; Massachusettsan

MAs Mothers Anonymous

MAS Malaysian Airline System; Marine Acoustical Services; Maryland Academy of Sciences; Master Activation Schedule; Military Agency for Standardization; Ministry of Aviation Supply; Missile Assembly Site; Monetary Authority of Singapore; Municipal Art Society

M.A.S. Master of Applied Science

M & AS Music and Art School

MAS Motoscafi Anti Sommergibli (Italian—antisubmarine lotor torpedo boat); *Movimiento al Socialismo* (Spanish —Movement toward Socialism)—Venezuelan's leftist party

MASA Mail Advertising Service Association; Malaysian Shipowners Association; Member of the Acoustical Society of America; Michigan Association of School Administrators; Military Automotive Supply Agency; Minnesota Association of School Administrators; Mississippi Association of School Administrators; Montana Association of School Administrators

Masaccio Tommaso Guidi

Masaniello contracted name of Tommaso Aniello

MASANYC Mail Advertising Service Association of New York City

masar microwave-accurate-surface antenna reflector

MASB Michigan Association of School Boards

MASBO Minnesota Association of School Business Officials

masc masculine

masc. masculus (Latin—male)

M.A. Sc. Master of Applied Science

MASC Massachusetts Association of School Committees

MASCA Middle Atlantic States Correctional Association

Mascarenes Mascarene Islands

mascon massive concentration

MASCOT Meteorological Auxiliary Sea Current Observation Transmitter

MASCS Marriage Adjustment Sentence Completion Survey

MASEA Midwest Association of Student Employment Administrators

maser microwave amplification by stimulated emission of radiation

mash. mashed potatoes

MASH Medical Aid for Sick Hippies; Memphians Against Social Harassment; Mobile Army Surgical Hospital; Multiple Accelerated Summary Hearing (for alien deportation); Mutual Aid Self Help

Masha (Russian nickname— Mary)

MASHAE Member of the American Society of Heating and Air Conditioning Engineers

mash(ed) mashed potatoes

MASHVE Member of the Australian Society of Heating and Ventilating Engineers

MASIS Management and Scientific Information Service

mask maskulinum (Dano-Norwegian—masculine)

MASL Military Assistance Articles and Services List

MASME Member of the American Society of Mechanical Engineers; Member of the Australian Society of Mechanical Engineers

MASO Munition-Accountable Supply Office(r)—USAF

M.A. Soc. Stud. Master of Arts in Social Studies

Mason and Dixon Line boundary between Maryland and Pennsylvania used to describe former demarcation between southern slave and northern free states

Masonic Composer Wolfgang Amadeus Mozart who was a freemason and alluded to the ethical laws of Masonry in his opera The Magic Flute (*Il Flauto Magico, La Flûte Enchantée, Die Zauberflöte*)—his Masonic Funeral Music (*Maurerische Trauermusik*) also reveals his affiliation with the Masonic Order

mas. pil. massa piluarum (Latin —pill mass)

Masqat wa Oman (Arabic— Muscat and Oman)

mass. masseter; multiple-access sequential selection

Mass Massachusetts; Massachusettsan(s)

MASS Marine Air Support Squadron; Massachusetts Association of School Superintendents; Michigan Automatic Scanning System

M.A.S.S. Master of Arts in Social Science

Massachusetts General Massachusetts General Hospital

Massachusetts Ports (north to south) Gloucester, Salem, Boston, Quincy, New Bedford

Massa Linkum Abraham Lincoln

Massanutteas Massanuttea Mountains (on the Appala-

chian Trail in northern Virginia between Charlottesville and Culpepper Court House)

masscult mass culture (culture for the masses)

massdar modular analysis, speedup, sampling, and data reduction

Massey Massey-Harris; Massey University (Palmerston North, New Zealand)

Massilia (Latin—Marseilles)

MASSP Michigan Association of Secondary School Principals; Minnesota Association of Secondary School Principals; Missouri Association of Secondary School Principals; Montana Association of Secondary School Principals

MASSR Mari Autonomous Soviet Socialist Republic; Mordovian Autonomous Soviet Socialist Republic

Mass Turn Massachusetts Turnpike

mast. masthead; missile automatic supply technique

MAST Metro Arson Strike Team (San Diego); Metropolitan Arson Strike Team; Michigan Alcoholism Screening Test; Military Assistance to Safety and Traffic

MAST Minimum Abbreviations of Serial Titles

MASTARS Mechanical and Structural Testing and Referral Service (NBS)

Ma State New South Wales, Australia

master. matching available student time to educational resources; multiple-access shared-time executive routine

Master of Color Contrasts Bartolomé Estehan Murillo

Master of Guerrilla Warfare Toussaint l'Ouverture

Master of Light and Shade Rembrandt van Rijn and Leonardo da Vinci seem to vie for this pictorial accolade

Master Mariner of the Imagination Joseph Conrad

Master of Melancholy Andres Segovia

Master of Mexico Don Porfirio Diaz (Porfiriato lasted from 1876 to 1911)

Mastermind of Revolution VI Lenin

Master Musician/Comedian Victor Borge

Master of Neurological Anatomy Santiago Ramón y Cajal

Master Pilot Jacques Cartier (*Le Maître-Pilote*)

Master of Psychic Polyphony Richard Strauss

Master of Raphael Il Perugino (Pietro Vannucci)

Master of Suspense Alfred Hitchcock

Master of Swing Count Basie [originally William (Bill) Basie]

Master of the Yosemite Ansel Adams

MASTIF Multiple Axes Space Test Inertia Facility

mastir microfilmed abstract system for technical information referral

Mastodon of Literature Emmanuel Swedenborg so nicknamed by Ralph Waldo Emerson

MASUA Mid-America State Universities Association

Masurca French-built surface-to-air naval missile

mat. machine-aided translation; material; materiel; matins; microalloy transistor; mol-anko-thane (molybdenum disulfide urethane)

mat matematik (Dano-Norwegian—mathematics)

Mat Matadi; Matanzas; Matthew

MAT Manual Arts Therapy; Mechanical Aptitude Test; Metropolitan Achievement Tests; Military Air Transport; Miller Analogies Test

M.A.T. Master of Arts in Teaching

mata multiple-answering teaching aid

MATA Motorcycle and Allied Trades Association

Mata Hari Gertrud Margarete Zelle

Mata Soc Mattachine Society

MA&TB Missile Assembly and Test Building

MATCALS Marine Air Traffic Control and Landing System (USN)

match. medium-range antisubmarine torpedo-carrying helicopter

MATCH Manpower and Talent Clearinghouse

MATCOM Materiel Command (USA)

MATCOMEUR Materiel Command, Europe

MATCOMTELNET MATS Command Teletype Network

matcon microwave aerospace terminal control

Mate the Mate (Chief Officer)

Mat.E. Materials Engineer

Ma Tec Maintenance Technician

MATELO Maritime Air Telecommunications Organization

Mateo Boz Miguel Angel Correa's pseudonym

matern maternal; maternity

Mater Res Bull Materials Research Bulletin(s)

MATFA Meat and Allied Trades Federation of Australia

math mathematician; mathematics

Math Mathematics; Matthew; Matthews; Mathewson; Mathias; Mathieu; Mathilde; Mathurin; Mathys; Mattias

Math.D. Doctor of Mathematics

M.A. Theol. Master of Arts in Theology

Mathis Mathis der Mahler (German—Mathias Grünewald the Painter)—symphonic suite by Hindemith

mathn mathematician

maths mathematicians; mathematics; mathematics majors

math soc science mathematical social science

MATIC Multiple and Technical Information Center

Mat Lab Material Laboratory

mat.med. materia medica

matnav mathematics for navigators

mato (Portuguese—jungle, as in Mato Grosso)

Mato Tepee Devils Tower National Monument in northeastern Wyoming

matp masking template

MATP Military Assitance Training Program

matr. matrimonium (Latin—marriage)

MATRESS Money, Advancement, Training, Recreation, Security, Satisfaction (USAF recruiting acronym)

Matriarch of Anthropology Margaret Mead

matric matriculate; matriculation

mats. maintenance analysis test set

MATS Military Air Transport Service

Mat Soc Mattachine Society

Matsqui British Columbia's minimum-security facility for narcotic addicts at Abbots-

ford

Matt Matthew; Matthewtown, Great Inagua; The Gospel according to St Matthew

Matt Matthew

mattergy matter + energy

MATTS Multiple Airborne Target Trajectory System

Mattw Matthew

Matty Matthew

Matty the Great Christy Mathewson

Matty Van Martin Van Buren

matut. matutinus (Latin—in the morning)

matv master antenna television

MATVS Master Antenna Television System

matw metal awning-type window

MATZ Military Air Traffic Zone

mau maintenance analysis unit; marine amphibious unit

Mau Mauritius

Mauch Chunk Pennsylvania place now called Jim Thorpe

Maud Mathilda

Maude Morse automatic decoder

Maude Adams Maude Kiskadden

Maudlin (Britishism—Magdalen)

M. Au. E. Master of Automotive Engineering

maulex marine amphibious unit landing exercise

MAUM Movement Against Uranium Mining

Maur Mauritius

M.A. Urb. Plan. Master of Arts in Urban Planning

Maureen Forrester Katherine Stewart

Maureen O'Hara Maureen Fitzsimmons

Maurice Barrymore Herbert Blythe

Maurit Mauritania (Islamic Republic of)

Mauritania Islamic Republic of Mauritania (West African nation as big as California plus Texas, copper and iron as well as grain and wheat are exported by the Arabic-speaking Mauritanians)

Mauritanian Port Nouakchott

Mauritanie (French—Mauritania)

Mauritius Indian Ocean island country composed of literate people of Arabic, Chinese, English, French, and Indian background (the cultivation of sugar cane, tea, and tourism supports the population)

Mauritius Port Port Louis

MAUS Metric Association of the United States

mauw maximum all-up weight

mav manpower authorization voucher

maverick. manufacturers assistance in verifying identification in cataloging

mavica magnetic video camera

MAVOGA Malaysian Vocational Guidance Association

maw medium assault weapon

maw met andere woorden (Dutch—in other words)

Maw Mama

MAW Marine Aircraft Wing; Mission Adaptive Wing

mawb master air waybill

mawec maritime exercise weather code

MAWLOGS Models of the Army Worldwide Logistics System (USA)

MAWS Marine Air Warning Squadron

max maximal; maximum

m'ax (American contraction—my ax)

Max Maxene; Maxie; Maxim; Maxime; Maximilian; Maximiliano; Maxine; Maxwell; Maxy; NATO nickname for Soviet Yakovlev trainer aircraft designated Yak-18

Max Brand Frederick Faust

max cap. maximum capacity

maxi maximum

maxibop maxibopper (under ground slang—fatter or older woman wearing miniskirts)

maxid maximize indefinite delivery (contracts)

maxill maxilla; maxillary

Maxim Gorki Aleksei Maxsimovich Peshkov

maximin maximum + minimum

Maxim Litvinov Maxim Maximovich Wallach

maxis maximum-length garments (coats, skirts, etc.)

maxnet modular application executive for computer networks

Max Nordau Max Simon Südfeld

Max Pax nickname of Max, Prince von Baden (Maximilian Alexander Friedrich Wilhelm)—Germany's last imperial chancellor

max q maximum aerodynamic pressure per square foot

maxr maximum room rate desired

Max Reinhardt Max Goldmann

Max Stirner Johann Kaspar Schmidt

max trq maximum torque

May Maybelle; NATO nickname for Soviet Ilyushin transport designated Il-38

MAYA Maya Airways (British Honduras); Mexican-American Youth Association

mayday international distress call (from the French *m'aidez* —help me)

May Day May 1 (Morris Dancers in England, international worker's day in communist and socialist lands)

May Day Shostakovich's Symphony No. 3 also called *May First*

Mayence (French—Mainz)

Mayfair London's residential district

Mayflower Massachusetts state flower

Mayjun May and June

May^{*mo*} *Mayordomo* (Spanish—butler, estate manager, steward)

May Night overture by Rimsky-Korsakov

mayn't may not

mayo mayonnaise

MAYO Mexican American Youth Organization

mayoralection mayoral election

maz mazda

Maz Mazatlan

mazh missile azimuth heading

mb machine blended; macrobiotic (MB); magnetic bearing; main battery; master bundles; may be; medium bomber; megabite(s)—two million bites; megabyte; meter band; methyl bromide; methylene blue; midbody; millibar(s); motor barge; motorboat

mb (MB) memory buffer

m/b make-break; master batch

m & b matched and beaded; metes and bounds

m.b. misce bene (Latin—mix well)

m/B male Black

Mb myoglobin

MB magnetic bearing; March-Bender (factor); Marine Barracks; Marine Base; Maritime Board; Marketing Board; Mechanized Battalion; Medical Board; Meridian & Bigbee (railroad); Miami Beach; Mu-

nitions Board; Music for the Blind; Myrtle Beach; Sir Mackenzie Bowell (Canada's sixth Prime Minister)

M-B Mercedes-Benz

M.B. *Medicinae Baccalaureus* (Latin—Bachelor of Medicine)

M/B Master Barber

M & B metes and bounds

Mba Mombasa

MBA Make or Buy Analysis; Make or Buy Authorization; Marine Biological Association; Master Builders Association; Men's Basketball Association; Military Bases Agreement; Military Benefit Association; Monument Builders of America; Mortgage Bankers of America; Mortgage Brokers Association

M.B.A. Master of Business Administration

MBAA Master Brewers Association of America

MBAC Member of the British Association of Chemists

M-Bahn Magnetbahn (German —magnetic levitation transit system)—train cars travel on a thin cushion of air providing high-speed transportation quieter than wheel-on-rail systems

MBAL Master Bookbinders' Alliance of London

m bale 1000 bales

mbar millibar

MBAUK Marine Biological Association of the United Kingdom

MBAWS Marine Base Warning System

mbb make before break; mortgage-backed bonds

MBB Museum of the Borough of Brooklyn

m bbl 1000 barrels

mbc maximum breathing capacity; multiple burst correction

MBC Malawi Broadcasting Corporation; Malaysian Building Construction; Mauritius Broadcasting Corporation; Mercantile Bank of Canada; Metropolitan Borough Council; Metropolitan Business College(s); Miname Nihon Broadcasting (Japan); Mitsubishi Bank of California

MBCA Motor Boat Club of America

MBCC Massachusetts Bay Community College; Migratory Bird Conservation Commission

MBCMC Milk Bottle Crate Manufacturers Council

mbd macro-block design; management by decision; million barrels per day; minimal brain dysfunction; minimum brain damage

MBDA Minority Business Development Agency

m bd ft 1000 board feet

mbe minority business enterprise; missile-borne equipment; my own bloody efforts

M.B.E. Member of the Order of the British Empire

M. B. Ed. Master of Business Education

MBF Master Builders Federation; Medical Benefits Fund(ing); Military Banking Facility; Milk Bottlers Federation

M-B factor Marsh-Bender factor

MBFR Mutual Balanced-Forced Reduction

MBG Midland Bank Group; Missouri Botanical Garden

mbge missileborne guidance equipment

mbh manual bomb hoist

mbH *mit beschränkter Haftung* (German—limited liability)

mbi may be issued

Mbi Mbini (formerly Rio Muni)

MBIA Malting Barley Improvement Association

M. Bi. Chem. Master of Biological Chemistry

M. Bi. Eng. Master of Biological Engineering

MBII Minority Business Information Institute

M. Bi. Phy. Master of Biological Physics

M. Bi. S. Master of Biological Science

MBJ Montego Bay, Jamaica (airport)

mbk missing, believed killed

mbl missile baseline; mobile; mobile branch library; model breakdown list(ing); model breastline

m & bl meat and bonemeal

Mbl *Monatsblatt* German—monthly report

MBL Marine Biological Laboratory (Woods Hole, Massachusetts); Mobile, Alabama (airport)

MBLIC Mutual Benefit Life Insurance Company

mbm thousand feet board meas-

ure

mbm (MBM) magnetic bubble memory

MBM Mac Bride Museum

M.B.M. Master of Business Management

MBMA Master Boiler Makers' Association; Metal Building Manufacturers Association

MBMHC Malcolm Bliss Mental Health Center (St Louis)

MBNA Monument Builders of North America

MBNBR Mount Bruce Native Bird Reserve (North Island, New Zealand)

mbo management by objectives

Mbo Maracaibo (inhabitants called Maracaiberos or Maracuchos)

MBO Mutual Benefit Organization

MbO$_2$ oxymyoglobin

MBOC Minority Business Opportunity Committee(s)

MBOU Member British Ornithologists Union

MBP Marine Biotelemetry Project; Minnesota Business Partnership

MBPA Metropolitan Bicycle Polo Association; Military Blood Program Agency

mbp antigen melitensis bovin porcine antigen

mbpfo make best possible firm offer

MBPO Military Blood Program Office(r)

MB & PR MacMillan, Bloedel & Powell River

mbps megabits per second; million bits per second

MBPXL Missouri Beef Packers Express Line

mbr member; memory buffer register

MBR *Minerações Brasileiras Reunidas* (Brazilian Mining Reunited)

MBRBA Motor Body Repairers and Builders Association

mbr/e memory buffer register—even

M Bret Middle Breton

MBRF Mission Bay Research Foundation

mbrl million barrels

mbr/o memory buffer register—odd

Mbro Middlesbrough

mbrt methylene-blue reduction time

mbruu may be retained until unserviceable

mbrv maneuverable ballistic

reentry vehicle (MBRV)

mbs magnetron beam switching; main bang suppressor; megabits per second

mb's milk brothers (two or more males who have had sexual relations with the same female) —*see* ms's

MBS Macquarie Broadcasting Service; Mainichi Broadcasting System; Miami Beach Symphony; Motor Bus Society; Music Broadcasting Society; Mutual Broadcasting System

MBSA Modular Building Standards Association; Munitions Board Standards Agency

M. B. Sc. Master of Business Science

mbsd multi-barrel smoke discharger

mbsi missile battery status indicator

MBSI Musical Box Society International

MBSJC Metropolitan Boroughs Standing Joint Committee (of librarians)

MBSM Mexican Border Service Medal

MBSSM Maxfield-Buchholz Scale of Social Maturity

mbt main ballast tank; mean body temperature; mechanical bathythermograph; metal-base transistor; murder before treason

MBT Minimum Blood Test; Modified Boiling Test

MBT-70 Main Battle Tank (designed for use in the 1970s)

MBTA Massachusetts Bay Transportation Authority; Metropolitan Boston Transit Authority; Midwest Book Travelers Association

MBTI Manpower Business Training Institute; Myers-Briggs Type Indicator

MBTS Meteorological Balloon Tracking System

mbu mobile tracking unit

MBUCV Museo de Biología de la Universidad Central de Venezuela (Biology Museum of the Central University of Venezuela)

M Build Master of Building

M. Bus. Ed. Master of Business Education

MBV Mexican Border Veterans

MBW Metropolitan Board of Works

MBYC Manhasset Bay Yacht

Club

mbz must be zero

mc magnetic center (MC); magnetic course (MC); main color; marginal check megacycle(s); marked capacity; marker card; market(ing) capacity; married couple; material control; message composer; metal case; meter candle; metric carat; miles on course; military characteristic(s); millicurie(s); mission control; moisture content; momentary contact; monkey cells; motorcycle; motor(ized) contact; moving coil(s); multiple contact

mc (MC) marginal cost

m-c medico-chirugical (surgical); mineralo-corticoid (hormones)

m/c machine(ry); marginal credit; metalling clause; middle center

m&c manufacturers and contractors; morphine and cocaine

mc *mois courant* (French—current month)

m/c *mi cargo* (Spanish—my debt, my responsibility); *mi casa* (Spanish—my home, my house); *mi cuenta* (Spanish—my account)

*µ*C microcoulomb

Mc Mac (Gaelic—son of)

M/c metallic currency

MC Macalester College; Machinery Certificate; Madison College; Madonna College; Magistrates Court; magnetic course; Mailet College; Maine Central (railroad); Malin College; Malone College; Manatee College; Manchester College; Manhattan College; Manhattanville College; Manpower Commission; Maria College; Marian College; Marietta College; Marine Corps; Marion College; Marist College; Maritime Carrier(s); Maritime Commission; Marlboro College; Marriage Certificate; Martin College; Mary College; Marycrest College; Maryglade College; Marygrove College; Marylhurst College; Marymount College; Maryville College; Marywood College; Master of Ceremonies; Master Commandant; Material Center; Materiel Center; Materiel Command; Maunaolu College; Medical Center; Medical Certificate; Medical College;

Medical Corporation; Medical Corps; Member of Congress; Member of Council; Memorial Commission; Memphis College; Menlo College; Mesa College; Mess Committee; Michigan Central (railroad); Microfilm Corporation; Microstat Corporation; Middlebury College; Midland College; Miles College; Military Committee; Military Cross; Milligan College; Mills College; Milsaps College; Milton College; Miserriocordia College; Mitchell College; Mitsubishi Corporation; Monmouth College; Monticello College; Moravian College; Morehouse College; Morris College; Morse Code; Morse College; Muhlenberg College; Multnomah College; Mundelein College; Munitions Command; Muskingum College; Muskogee College

M-C Magovern-Cromie (prosthesis)

M.C. Military Cross

M/C Machinery Certificate

MC *Maison Centrale* (French—Central Prison); *Mercado Comun* (Spanish—Common Market)

M.C. *Magister Chirurgiae* (Master of Surgery)

mca minimum control airspeed; minimum crossing altitude; monetary compensatory account(ing); money compensatory account(ing); mud clean ing agent

mca (MCA) maximum credible accident

Mca Macassar

MCA Malacca Consumers Association; Malayan Chinese Association; Malaysian Chinese Association; Manufacturing Chemists Association; Maritime Central Airways; Maritime Control Area; Massachusetts Correctional Association; Material Control Area; Material Coordinating Agency; Maternity Center Association; Mechanical Contractors Association; Mechanization Control Area; Media Credit Association; Medical Correctional Association; Medical Council of Australia; Millinery Credit Association; Minnesota Correctional Authority; Minnesota Corrections Association; Missouri

Corrections Association; Movers Conferences of America; Multiple Classification Analysis; Muscat Control Agency; Music Corporation of America; Music Critics Association; Musicians Club of America

MCA *Metric Conversion Act*

MCAA Mason Contractors Association of America; Mechanical Contractors Association of America; Medical Consumers Association of Australia; Military Civil Affairs Administration

MCAAA Midland Counties Amateur Athletic Association

MCAB Marine Corps Air Base

MCAD Military Contracts Administration Department

MCADO Micronesian Community Action Development Organization

MCAF Marine Corps Air Facility; Marine Corps Air Field; Military Construction, Air Force

MCAIR McDonnell Aircraft Company

McAlester Ward Women's Ward in the Oklahoma State Penitentiary at McAlester

m car 1000 carats

MCAR Material Corrective Action Report(s)

mcarquals marine carrier qualifications

mca's money compensatory amounts

MCAS Marine Corps Air Station

MCAT Medical College Admission Test; Midwest Council on Airborne Television

m. cau. *misce caute* (Latin—mix cautiously)

MCAUSA Military Chaplain's Association of the U.S.A.

MCAUTO McDonnell-Douglas Automation

mcb membranes cytoplasmic bodies; miniature circuit breaker

McB McBurney's (point)

MCB Marine Corps Base; Metric Conversion Board; Metric Conversion Bureau; Mobile Construction Battalion

M.C.B. Master of Clinical Biochemistry

MCBA Master Car Builders' Association

mcc maintenance of close contact; midcourse correction; modified close control; multilayer ceramic chip

mcc (MCC) main communication(s) center; multi-component circuit(s)

MCC Maintenance Control Center; Manual Combat Center; Marine Corps Commandant; Marine Corps Commander; Marylebone Cricket Club; Massachusetts Council of Churches; Materials Characterization Center (Battelle, Richland); Mesta Machine Company (stock exchange symbol); Meteorological Communications Center; Metropolitan Community Church; Metropolitan Correctional Center; Microelectronics and Computer Technology Corporation; Microfilm Card Catalog; Missile Control Center; Mission Control Center; Monroe Community College; Munitions Carriers Conference; Music Critics Circle

MCCA Michigan Community College Association

MCCA Mercado Común Centro Americano (Central American Common Market)

McCain Sanatorium North Carolina Prison Sanatorium at McCain

MCCB Multinational Configuration Control Board

MCCC Metropolitan Correctional Center (Chicago); Muskegon County Community College

MCCCA Marine Corps Combat Correspondents Association

MCC-H Mission Control Center—Houston (NASA)

MCCISWG Military Command, Control, and Information Systems Working Group

McCL McCabe Library (Swarthmore)

mccp maintenance console control panel

mccs missile critical circuit simulator

MCCs Metropolitan Correctional Centers (of the Bureau of Prisons in Chicago, New York, and San Diego); Military Committee in Chiefs-of-Staff Session(s)

MCCS Modular Communications Control Systems

mccu multiple communications control unit

MCCW Miami Citizens Crime Watch

mcd magnetic crack detector;

mean corpuscular diameter; median control death; metal-covered door; mine clearance dive; mine clearance diving; minimum cash deposit; miscellaneous cash deposit

mcd minimo comune denomiatore (Italian—least common denominator)

Mc D Mc Donald; Mc Donald's

MCD Melbourne College of Divinity

M.C.D. Doctor of Comparative Medicine; Master of Civic Design

McDA McDonnell Aircraft

MCDA Manpower and Career Development Agency; Motor Car Dealers Association

McDAC McDonnell Aircraft Corporation

MCDC Montgomery County Detention Center

McD Obs McDonald Observatory

MCDS Management Control Data System

mcd/slv minimum-cost-design/space launch vehicle (MCD/SLV)

mcdt mean corrective down time

mce mean chance expectation; military characteristics equipment

MCE Memphis Cotton Exchange; Montgomery Cotton Exchange

M.C.E. Malaysian Certificate of Education; Master of Civil Engineering

MCE Mercado Común Europeo (Spanish—European Common Market); *Mercato Comune Europeo* (Italian—European Common Markeeet)

MCEB Military Communications Electronics Board

M.C.Eng Master of Civil Engineering

MCEO Malayan Council of Employers Organization; Malaysian Council of Employers Organization

M. Cer. E. Master of Ceramic Engineering

MCET Mississippi Center for Educational Television

MCEWG Multinational Communication-Electronics Working Group (NATO)

mcf magnetic card file; medium corpuscular fragility; thousand cubic feet

MCF Master Code File; Michi-

gan Colleges Foundation; Missouri Colleges Fund

mcfd 1000 cubic feet of gas per day

mcfh 1000 cubic feet of gas per hour

MCFI Malaysian Chamber of Film Industries

mcfim microfilm(ing)

mcflm microfilm; microfilming

mcfm 1000 cubic feet of gas per month

MCFP Medical Center for Federal Prisoners (Springfield, Missouri); Member of the College of Family Physicians

mcfshe microfische

mcg microgram

mc & g mapping, charting, and geodesy

MCG Mandalay Coral Gardens (Queensland)

McG-H McGraw-Hill

McGill-Queens U Pr McGill-Queens University Press

McGraw McGraw-Hill

MCGS Microwave Command Guidance System

McG U McGill University

McGUL McGill University Library

mch mail chute; mean corpuscular hemoglobin (MCH)

Mch Manchester; March

M. Ch. *Magister Chirurgiae* (Latin—Master of Surgery)

MCH Maternal and Child Health

mcha merchandise

mchan multichannel

mchc mean corpuscular hemoglobin concentration

M.Ch.D. *Magister Chirugiae Dentalis* (Latin—Master of Dental Surgery)

M.Ch.E. Master of Chemical Engineering

M. Chem. E. Master of Chemical Engineering

M.Chir. *Magister Chirugiae* (Latin—Master of Surgery)

M.Ch. Orth. *Magister Chirurgiae Orthopaedicae* (Latin—Master of Orthopedic Surgery)

M.Ch.Otol. Master of Otorhinolaryngological Surgery

MCHP Maternal and Child Health Program

mc hr millicurie hour(s)

MCHRD Mayor's Committee for Human Resources Development

M.Chrom. Master of Chromatics

M Ch S Member of the Society

of Chiropodists
MCHS Maternal and Child Health Service
mcht merchant
Mchter Manchester
mchy machinery
mci malleable cast iron; megacurie; mottled cast iron; multichip integration
mCi millicurie(s)
MCI Kansas City Airport (symbol); Marine Corps Institute; Massachusetts Correctional Institution (Framingham); Mexican Coffee Institute; Microwave Communications, Inc.; Milk Can Institute; Motor Coach Industries; Motor Coach Institute
MCIC Metals and Ceramics Information Center (DoD)
mcid multipurpose concealed intrusion detection (device)
MCIE Midland Counties Institution of Engineers
McINP McIwaine National Park (Rhodesia)
MCIS Management Control and Information System; Multi-Currency Intervention System
M.C.J. Master of Comparative Jurisprudence
MCJC Mason City Junior College
MCJCC Mayor's Criminal Justice Coordinating Council (New York City)
McKay David McKay
McKinley Mount McKinley or Mount McKinley National Park in Alaska between Anchorage and Fairbanks, containing North America's highest mountain named for President William McKinley
McKnight McKnight Publishing Co
McKS (Sir Colin) McKenzie Sanctuary (Victoria, Australia)
McKVHS McKee Vocational High School
mcl macro-creation language; midclavicular line; midcostal line; most comfortable level
MCL Manchester Central Library; Marine Corps League; Master Configuration List(ing); Master Control Log; Metal Control Laboratories; Metropolitan Central Library; Mid-Canada Line (radar warning fenceline); Moore-McCormack Lines; Mushroom Canners League

M.C.L. Master of Civil Law
MCLA Marine Corps League Auxiliary
McLaughlin Youth McLaughlin Youth Center (for delinquents) at Anchorage, Alaska
MCLI Meiklejohn Civil Liberties Institute
M.Clin.Psychol. Master of Clinical Psychology
mcll missile compartment, lower level
MCLO Medical Construction Liaison Office
M.Cl.Sc. Master of Clinical Science
mcm military characteristics motor vehicles; mine countermeasures; minimum commitment method(ology); missile-carrying missile; thousand circular mils
mcm (MCM) missile-control module
mcm minimo comune multiple (Italian—least common multiple, lowest common multiple)
McM McMahon; McManus; McMaster; McMillan; McMurry
MCM Manual for Courts-Martial; Marine Corps Manual; Monte Carlo Method
MCMA Machine Chain Manufacturers Association; Marine Corps Memorial Commission; Metal Cookware Manufacturers Association
MCMC Marine Corps Memorial Commission
MCMF Marie Curie Memorial Foundation
MCMI Millon Clinical Multiaxial Inventory
mcml missile compartment, middle level
mcmops mine countermeasures operations
MCMS Marin County Medical Society
MCMSP Material Command Maintenance Service Publication
MCM&T Michigan College of Mining & Technology
McM U McMaster University
McMUL McMaster University Library
McMUMC McMaster University Medical Centre (Hamilton)
MCN Management Control Number; Manual Control Number; Master Control Number(ing)
MCN Maternal Child Nursing

(journal)
McNally McNally & Loftin
McNeil Island U.S. Penitentiary at McNeil Island, Washington
mcng meaconing
MCNP Mammoth Cave National Park (Kentucky); Mount Cook NP (South Island, New Zealand)
MCNY Museum of the City of New York
MCNZ Medical Council of New Zealand
mco main civilian occupation; mills culls out; miscellaneous charges order
mco março (Portuguese—March)
Mco Morocco
MCO Materials Characterization Organization; Michigan Corrections Organization (prison wardens); Movement Control Office(r)
MCOAG Marine Corps Operations Analysis Group
MCODA Motor Cab Owner-Drivers' Association
mcol musicological; musicologist; musicology
M.Com. Master of Commerce; Minister of Commerce
MCOM Mobility Command (US Army)
M. Com. Adm. Master of Commercial Administration
M.Comm.H. Master of Community Health
M. Comp. Law Master of Comparative Law
M. Com. Sc. Master of Commercial Science
MCON Military Construction Navy
MCOO Monte Carlo Opera Orchestra
MCOP Marine Corps Ordnance Publication
mcos marcos (Spanish—marks), German coins
MCOW Medical College of Wisconsin
mcp main control panel; male chauvinist pig; manual control panel; mode control panel; multi-component plasma; multiple chip package
mcp (MCP) master control program
mCp my Cadillac payment
MCP Malaysian Communist Party; Management Control Plan; Maritime Company of Philadelphia; Maritime Company of the Philippines; Mas-

sachusetts College of Pharmacy; Master Control Program; Military Construction Program; Minerals and Chemicals Philipp; Model Cities Program

M.C.P. Master of City Planning

MCPA Member of the College of Pathologists of Australasia

MC Path Member of the College of Pathologists

mcph metacarpal-phalangeal

MCPO Master Chief Petty Officer

mcps megacycles per second

MCPS Mechanical Copyright Protection Society; Member of the College of Physicians and Surgeons

MCPT Maritime Central Planning Team

McQ-E McQuaid-Ehn (grain size)

mcr master control routine; metabolic clearance rate; micrographic computer retrieval; military compact reactor; modular circuit reliability; monitor control routine; mother-child relationship

MCR Manufacturing Change Request; Marine Corps Reserve; Master Change Record; Master Charge Record

M.C.R. Master of Comparative Religion

MCRA Member of the College of Radiologists of Australasia

MCRC Mass Communications Research Center (University of Wisconsin)

MCRD Marine Corps Recruit Depot

MCRE Mother-Child Relationship Evaluation

MCREL Mid-Continent Regional Educational Laboratory

mcrfsch microfische

MCRHS Mid-Continent Railway Historical Society

MCRL Master Cross-Reference List(ing)

MCRML Midcontinental Regional Medical Library (University of Nebraska)

MCROA Marine Corps Reserve Officers Association

MCRS Micrographic Computer Retrieval System; Military Command Research System

mcrt multichannel rotary transformer

mcrwv microwave

mcs meridian control signal; meter-candle second; missile checkout set; motor circuit switch; multiple column selector

mc/s megacycles per second

MCs Military Characteristics

MCS coastal minesweeper (naval symbol); Maintenance Control Section; Major Component Schedule; Management Control System; Marine Cooks and Stewards (union); Marine Corps School; Marine Corps Station; Message Control System; mine countermeasures support ship (naval symbol); Missile Commit Sequence; Mobile Checkout Station; Mobile Coastal Service

M.C.S. Master of Commercial Science

MCSA Marble Collectors Society of America; Medical Computer Services Administration

MCSB Motor Carriers Service Bureau

MCSC Medical College of South Carolina; Military College of South Carolina (The Citadel)

mc/sec megacycles per second

MCSH Manhattan College of the Sacred Heart

MCSL Marine Corps Stock List; Marine Corps Supply List

MCSP Member of the Chartered Society of Physiotherapy

mc spec motorcycle specialist(s); motorcycle specification(s)

MCSs Memorial Cremation Societies (organized to cut down the high cost of croaking)

mcst magnetic card selectric typewriter

MCST Member of the College of Speech Therapists

MC S & T Manchester College of Science and Technology

MCSTB Motor Carriers Service Tariff Bureau

MCSWG Multinational Command Systems Working Group

mct maximum continuous thrust; multiple-compressed tablet

mct (MCT) modular computing typewriter

MCT Maritime Crew Trainer; Master Cycle Trader; Mechanical Comprehension Test; Minimum-Competency Test(ing)

m/cta *mi cuenta* (Spanish—my account)

MCTA Metropolitan Commuter Transportation Authority; Motor Carriers Traffic Association

MCTC Maritime Cargo Transporation Conference; Microelectronics and Computer Technology Corporation (formed in Austin, Texas to produce the world's first supercomputer capable of thinking as a person does)

MCTE Michigan Council of Teachers of English

MCTI Metal Cutting Tool Institute

mctow maximum certificated takeoff weight

mctp missile control test panel

MC & TS Monotype Casters' and Typefounders' Society

mcu median control unit; medium closeup; microprocessor control unit; monitor control unit

m & cu monitor and control unit

MCU Modern Churchmen's Union

MCUG Military Computer Users Group

mcul missile compartment, upper level

mcv mean corpuscular volume; model control volume

MCV Medical College of Virginia

mcvf multichannel voice frequency

mcw metal casement window; modulated continuous wave

m & cw maternity and child welfare

MCW Mallinckrodt Chemical Works

m cwt 1000 hundredweight

mcx maximum-cost expediting

mcy machinery

MCZ Museum of Comparative Zoology

md main deck; malicious damage; manufacturing day; map distance; mathematics disabled; maximum demand; maximum design; mean deviation; memorandum of deposit; mental(ly) defective; mentally deficient; mentally disordered; message dropping; milliard; minute difference(s); mitral disease; month's date; motorized damper; movement directive; muscular dystrophy

m-d manic-depressive

m/d market day; memorandum of deposit(s); messages per

day; missile driver; modulator-demodulator; month(s) after date

m & d medicine and duty

md *main droite* (French—right hand); *mano derecha* (Spanish —right hand); *mano destra* (Italian—right hand); *marchand* (French—good value, marketable); *milliard* (French —1000 million)

m d *mano destra* (Italian—right hand)

Md Maid; Maryland; Marylander; mendelevium

M$ Malaysia dollar (Singapore dollar)

MD Management Directive; Managing Director; Marine Detachment; Material Division; Medical Department; Medical Discharge; Mess Deck; Meteorological Department; Middle Dutch; Military District; Mine Depot; Music Director; Musical Director

M.D. *Medicinae Doctor* (Latin —Doctor of Medicine)

M D *mano destra* (Italian— right hand)

mda maintenance depot assistance; minimum detectable activity; multiple-docking adapter

mda (MDA) methyldiamphetamine (stimulant); minimum descent altitude

Mda Mérida (inhabitants— Meridanos)

MDA Marking Device Association; Master Dyes Association; Material Department Amendments; Material Disposal Authority; Middle Depot Activity; Minor Deviation Authorization; Multiple-Docking Adapter; Mural Decorators Association; Muscular Dystrophy Association; Mutual Defense Agency; Mutual Defense Assistance

MDAA Muscular Dystrophy Association of America; Mutual Defense Assistance Act

MDAC McDonnell Douglas Astronautics Company; Mutual Defense Assistance—China area

MDAGT Mutual Defense Assistance, Greece and Turkey

MDAIKP Mutual Defense Assistance, Iran, Republic of Korea, and the Philippines

MDAN Material Department Administrative Notices

MDANAA Mutual Defense Assistance, North Atlantic Area

MDAP Mutual Defense Assistance Program

MDAPT Machover Draw-a-Person Test

MDAS Multispectral Data Analysis System

Mda Vle Maida Vale

M-day manufacturing day; mobilization day; moratorium day

Mdb Middlesbrough

M d B *Mitglied des Bundestages* (German—member of the Bundestag)

MDB *Movimento Democrático Brasileiro* (Portuguese—Brazilian Democratic Movement) —political party

MDBVHS Mabel D. Bacon Vocational High School

mdc maintenance data collection; more developed country

M d C *Maestro di Cappella* (Italian—Chapel Master); *Maître de Chapelle* (French—Chapel Master)—titles often meaning conductor or musical director

MDC Manhattan Drug Corporation; Manufacturing Development Council; McDonnell Douglas Corporation; Metropolitan District Commission; Minnesota Department of Corrections; Moncure Daniel Conway

MDCA Master Diamond Cutters Association

MDC-W McDonnell Douglas Corporation—West

mdd mechanical dough development; milligrams per square decimeter per day

MDDC Military Dependents Dental Clinic

mddpm magnetic-drum data-processing machine(ry)

Mddx Middlesex

mde matrix difference equation

M.D.E. Master of Domestic Economy

MDE *Modern Drug Encyclopedia*

m'dear my dear

M de C *Maître de Chapelle* (French—conductor)

M.Dent.Sci. Master of Dental Science

M.Des. Master of Design

mdf mild detonating fuze; minimum diversion fuel

mdf (MDF) main distributing frame (data processing); manual direction finder

MDF Modderfontein Dynamite Factory

MDFC McDonnell Douglas Finance Corporation

mdfd modified

mdfg modifying

mdfn modification

mdfy modify

MDG Medical Director-General

mdh minimum descent height; multidirectional harassment

mdh (MDH) malate dehydrogenase

MDHB Mersey Docks and Harbour Board (Liverpool)

Md Hist Maryland Historical Society

Mdhv Marek's disease herpes virus

mdi magnetic detection indicator

MDI Material Department(al) Instruction; Material Development(al) Instruction

MDIA Material Department(al) Instruction Amendment(s)

MDIB Material Departmental Instruction Bulletin

m. dict. *more dicto* (Latin—in the manner directed)

M.Did. Master of Didactics

M. Di. Eng. Master of Diesel Engineering

MDIG Multipurpose Display Indicator Group

M.Dip. Master of Diplomacy

M dis Marek's disease

mdise merchandise

M.Div. Master of Divinity

MDJC Miami Dade Junior College; Mississippi Delta Junior College

m dk main deck

mdl master design layout; middle; model; modular design language

Mdl Middle (postal abbreviation)

M d L *Mitglied des Landtages* (German—member of the Landtag)

MDL Mine Defense Laboratory

MDL *Master Drug List*

Mdlle *Mademoiselle* (French— Miss)

mdm (MDM) middiastolic murmur

Mdm Madam

MDM Material Division Manual; Movement (for a) Democratic Military (New Leftist device to destroy military morale)

Mdme *Madame* (French—Missus)

mdn median

m$n *moneda (pesos) nacional* [Spanish—national monetary unit(s)—Argentinian peso(s)]

MDNA Machinery Dealers National Association

mdnb metadinitrobenzene

mdngt midnight

MDNS Modified Decimal Numbering System

mdnt midnight

mdo medium-density overload(ing); monthly debit ordinary

MDO MARC Development Office (Library of Congress)

M-dog mine dog (trained to find buried mines)

mdp minimum-distance principle

m.d.p. *mento-dextra posterior* (Latin—right mento-posterior)

MDP Mainland Data Processing; Manufacturing Development Program

MDPR Manufacturing Development and Process Request

mdr magnetic disk recorder; master-clock generator; memory data register; minimum daily requirement; multichannel data record(er)

Mdr Madras

MDR Master Discrepancy Report; Material Deficiency Report(ing)

mdrc maximum distance for radiological consequences

MDRC Manpower Demonstration Research Corporation

MDRSF Multi-Dimensional Random Sea Facility

mds minimum discernible signal; mission design and series

Mds *Mesdames* (French—Ladies)

M$S peso (*moneda nacional*—Argentine letter symbol)

MDS mail distribution schedule; mail distribution scheme; Main Dressing Station; Manufacturing Data Series; Medical-Dental Service; meteoroid detection satellite; Model Designator Series; Multipoint Distribution Systems (microwave)

M.D.S. Master of Dental Surgery

mdsa multiple disc-sampling apparatus

M.D.Sc. Master of Dental Science

mdse merchandise

MDSF Mission to Deep Sea Fishermen

mdsg merchandising

MDSI Manufacturing Data Systems Inc

MDSOs mentally disordered sex offenders

MDST Mountain Daylight Saving Time

mdt mean down time; moderate

m.d.t. *mento-dextra transversa* (Latin—right mento-transverse)

MDT Multidisciplinary Team; Mutual Defense Treaty

MDTA Manpower Development and Training Act

mdtm medium duty target mechanism

MDTS Modular Data Transmission System

M Du Middle Dutch

MDU Medical Defence Union; Mine Disposal Unit; Mobile Development Unit

M du N Magasin du Nord (Copenhagen's leading department store)

MDUS Medium Data Utilization Station

Mdv Marek's disease virus

M.D.V. Doctor of Veterinary Medicine

mdw measured day work

MDW Chicago, Illinois (Midway Airport); Military District of Washington; Minnesota, Dakota & Western (railroad)

Mdws Meadows

Mdx Middlesex

mdy magnetic deflection yoke

MDY Midland Oil (stock exchange symbol)

me. male employee; marbled edges; marbled edging; mathematics education; maximum effect; maximum effort; mechanical equipment; metabolizable energy; methyl; mill edge; milligram equivalent; miter end; most excellent; multi-engine; muzzle energy

me. (ME) measles encephalitis

m/e mechanical/electrical; mobility equipment

m & e mechanical and electrical; music and (sound) effects

m E *meines Erachtens* (German —in my opinion)

Me Maine; Mainers; Mexican(s); Mexico

Me Maître (French—Master)— advocate; attorney

ME Managing Editor; Marine Engineer; Mechanical Engineer(ing); Medical Examiner; Methodist Episcopal; Middle

East(ern)(er); Middle English; Military Engineer; Mining Engineer; Morristown and Erie (railroad); Mouvement Europeen (European Movement)

M.E. Master of Education; Mechanical Engineer

mea measure(s); measuring; minimum enroute altitude; monoethanolamine (MEA)

MEA Maintenance Engineering Analysis; Malaysian Economics Association; Maritime Employers Association; Medical Exhibitors Association; Michigan Education Association; Middle East Airlines; Minnesota Education Association; monoethanolamine; Montana Education Association; Municipal Employees Association; Music Educators Association; Musical Educators Association

M.E.A. Master of Engineering Administration

Meadowlark state bird of Montana, Nebraska, North Dakota, Oregon, and Wyoming

MEAF Middle East Air Force

meal. master equipment allowance

MEAL Master Equipment Authorization List(ing)

Meanie nickname for a mean person

mean max mean maximum; mean maximum temperature

MEAR Maintenance Engineering Analysis Record

meas measure; measurement

Meas for M *Measure for Measure*

M-East Middle-East

M.E. Auto. Master of Automobile Engineering; Master of Automotive Engineering

meb military early bird

MEB Marine Expeditionary Brigade; Master Electronics Board; Medical Board; Melbourne, Australia (airport); Midlands Electricity Board (UK)

MEBA Marine Engineers' Beneficial Association

mec main engine cutoff; marine extension clause; measuring equipment control

M. Ec. Master of Economics

MEC Maine Central (railroad); Maintenance Engineering Change(s); Marine Expeditionary Corps; Master Executive Council; Member of the Executive Council; Methodist

Episcopal Church; Monetary and Economic Council

M.E.C. Master of Engineering Chemistry; Member of the Executive Council

meca maintainable electronics component assembly; malfunctioned equipment corrective action; mercury evaporation and condensation; multi-element component array

Meca (Spanish—Mecca)

MECA Manufacturers of Emission Controls Association; Molecular Emission Cavity Analysis

mecano mechanotherapy

MECAS Middle Eastern College for Arabic Studies (Beirut, Lebanon)

mecc meccanica (Italian—mechanic)

mecca master electrical common connector assembly

Mecca English place-name equivalent for Mecca in Saudi Arabia

MECCA Minnesota Environmental Control Citizens Association

Mecca of Spain Santiago de Compostela

mech mechanic; mechanical; mechanism

Mech Mechanics

ME Ch Methodist Episcopal Church

MECHA Movimiento Estudiantil Chicano de Aztlán (Mexican-Spanish—Chicano Student Movement of Aztlán)—in Spanish *chicano* partakes of chicanery and *Aztlán* is a mythical land northwest of Mexico to where the Aztecs departed and may be California where MECHA has many members

Mechai (Thai—condom)—named for Thailand's Mr Contraception, Mechai Viravaidya

mechanochem mechanochemical; mechanochemistry

M.E. Chem. Master of Chemical Engineering

Mech Eng Mechanical Engineering

Mech Illus Mechanix Illustrated

MEC/IES Merrimac Education Center's Institute for Educational Services

meco main engine cutoff

MECO Metropolitan Edison

Company

mecom marine engine condition monitor(ing)

M.Econ. Master of Economics

MECON Metallurgical and Engineering Consultants

MEC/PA Maintenance Engineering Change/Problem Analysis

MECR Maintenance Engineering Change Request

MECS Middle East Container Service

mecu main engine control unit

MECU Municipal Employees Credit Union

mecz mechanized

med medal; medalist; medallion; median; median erythrocyte diameter; medic; medical; medication; medicinal; medicine; medieval; medievalism; medievalist; medium; minimal effective dose; minimal erythema dose

Med Medicine; medieval; Mediterranean

Med Médico (Italian, Portuguese, Spanish—Doctor); *Méditerranee* (French—Mediterranean); *Mediterraneo* (Italian—Mediterranean); *Mediterrâneo* (Portuguese—Mediterranean); *Mediterráneo* (Spanish—Mediterranean)

M.Ed. Master of Education

MED Maintenance Engineering Data; Manhattan Engineer District (cover name used during World War II by the developers of the first atomic bomb); Metalworking Equipment Division (US Department of Commerce); Military Electronics Division (Motorola); Municipal Electricity Department

M.E.D. Master of Elementary Didactics

medac medical accounting

medal. micromechanized engineering data for automated logistics

Med C Medical Corps

Med CAP Medical Civil Action Program

medcat medium clear-air turbulence

MEDCO Meat Export Development Company

med col medium color

MEDCOM Mediterranean Communications System

medcrit medical critic(ism)

medda mechanized defense decision anticipation

MED-DENT Medical-Dental Division (USAF)

medevac medical evacuation

medex medical expert

medex medecin extension (French—doctor's aides, medics)

Medfly (Med fly) Mediterranean fruit fly

Med Gr Medieval Greek

medi (Latin prefix—middle)—median

Medi (British seamen's short form—Mediterranean)

Media Magnavox electronic data-image apparatus

MEDIA Manufacturers Educational Drug Information Association; Missile Era Data Integration Analysis; Move to End Deception in Advertising

mediacrit media critic(ism)

mediaese cultivated English spoken by many entertainment, radio, and television personalities

Media Prophet Marshall McLuhan

mediator. media time-orienting and reporting

medic medical corpsman; medical doctor; medical student

medicaid medicinal aid (free medicine for the needy)

Medicaid Medical Aid (federal and state health insurance for people unable to afford medical care)

MEDI-CAL Medical Aid of California

Medical Essayist Oliver Wendell Holmes

Medical Exam Medical Examination Publishing Company

medicare medical care

Medicare Medical Care (federal health insurance for aged and disabled persons)

MEDICO Medical International Corporation

medifraud medical fraud

Medina-Sidonia Alonso Pérez de Guzmán (Duke of Medina-Sidonia and admiral in command of the ill-fated Spanish Armada defeated by Sir Francis Drake)

Medinat Yisrael (Hebrew—State of Israel)

mediog mediograph(ic)(al); mediography

Mediolanum (Latin—Milan)

Medit Mediterranean

Mediterranean Mediterranean Sea

Mediterraneo (Italian—Mediterranean)

Mediterráneo (Spanish—Mediterranean)

MEDIUM Missile Era Data Integration Ultimate Method

medivac medical evacuation

medix medical students

med juris medical jurisprudence

med lab(s) medical laboratories; medical laboratory

MEDLARS Medical Literature Analysis and Retrieval System

Med Lat Medieval Latin

MEDLINE Medical On-Line (computer retrieval system)

M. Ed. L. Sc. Master of Education in Library Science

med nec medically necessary (abortion)

Med Phys Medical Physics

med ray medullary ray

med ray par medullary ray parenchyma

med ray trac medullary ray tracheids

MEDRC Medical Reserve Corps

MEDRECO Mediterranean Refining Company

MEDRESCO Medical Research Council

MEDS Maintenance Engineering Data Sheets

MEDSAC Medical Service Activity (USA)

Med. Sc. D. Doctor of Medical Science

Med Sch Medical School

Med Sea Mediterranean Sea

med show medicine show (carnival slang)

Med Supt Medical Superintendent

med tech medical technologist; medical technology

Med Tech Medical Technician; Medical Technologist

med trans medical transcriptionist

mee methylethyl ether

M.E.E. Master of Electrical Engineering

M.E. Eng. Master of Electrical Engineering

Meerestille Mendelssohn's *Calm Sea and Prosperous Voyage* overture more correctly translated as Becalmed at Sea and Prosperous Voyage

meerschaum hydrated magnesium silicate

MEES Middle East Economic Survey

mef maximal expiratory flow

Mef Mefisto

MEF Marine Expeditionary Force; Meal Export Federation; Mesopotamian Expeditionary Force; Middle East Forces; Musicians Emergency Fund

Mefisto Mefistofele

Mefistofele (Italian—Mephistopheles)—Boito's four-act opera about the Faust legend

mef's morality enhancing factors

mefv maximum expiratory flow volume

meg megacycle; megaton; megawatt; megohm

Meg Margaret

MEG Management Evaluation Group

mega 10^6

mega megas (Greek—great, large, powerful)—acromegaly, megacycle, megaspore, megaton

megabuck one million bucks (dollars)

megacorpses one million corpses (atomic bomb unit)

megacurie one million curies

megacycle one million cycles

megadeaths million deaths

megajoule one million joules

megameter one million meters

megamouse one million mice (statistical unit—experimental biology)

megaton one million tons

megawatt one million watts

megger megohmmeter

Meggie Margaret

Meglin Megliola

mego megaphone; megohm(s)

MEGO mine eyes glaze over

megohm one million ohms

megs megacycles

megv million volts

megw megawatt

megwh megawatt-hour

Mehrabad Tehran, Iran's airport

mei mathematics in education and industry

mei (MEI) marginal efficiency of investment

MEI Maintenance and Engineering Inspection; Manual of Engineering Instructions; Marine Ecological Institute; Metals Engineering Institute; Middle East Institute

MEIC Member of The Engineering Institute of Canada

MEIS Military Entomology Information Service

Meister Der Meister (German—

the Master)—Johann Wolfgang von Goethe

Meistersinger Die Meistersinger von Nürnberg (Wagner's three-act opera about The Mastersingers of Nuremberg)

MEIU Management Education Information Unit

Mej Mejuffrouw (Dutch—Miss)

Méjico (Spanish—Mexico)

mek methyl ethyl ketone

Mel Melanesia; Melanesian; Melanesian Pidjin English (Bêche de Mer); Melanie; Melba; Melbourne; Melvil; Melville; Melvin; Melvina; Melvyn

MEL Master Equipment List(ing); Music Education League

M.E.L. Master of English Literature

MELA Middle East Librarians Association

Melaka (Malay—Malacca)

Melan Melanesia; Melanesian

Melanchthon Philipp Schwarzert

Melanesia islands in the western Pacific whose black natives inhabit the Bismarck Archipelago, Fiji, New Caledonia, New Hebrides, and the Solomon Islands

Melb Melbourne

Melba Nellie Armstrong (of Melbourne)

MELCO Mitsubishi Electric Corporation

Meld melt + weld

MELF Middle East Land Forces

Mel Ferrer Melchor Gaston Ferrer y Cintron

melg most European languages

Melina Mercouri Maria Amalia Mercouri

Melisande Melusina

Melita (Latin—Malta)

mellow yellow nickname for fried banana skin scrapings sold to the gullible by drug pushers

melo melodrama; melody

M. Elo. Master of Elocution

melos melodic lines

melt. pt melting point

Melvil Dewey Melville Louis Kossuth Dewey

Melvin Douglas Melvyn Hesselberg

mem member; memoirs; memorial

mem (MEM) memory map (calculator)

mem. memoria (Latin—memory)

Mem Member (of Congress, Parliament, etc.); Memorial (postal abbreviation)

MEM Mars Excursion Module; Member; memorial; Memphis, Tennessee (airport)

MEMA Marine Engine Manufacturers' Association

MEMAC Machinery and Equipment Manufacturers Association of Canada

memb membrane

'members remembers

Member of the Unemployed Scottish socialist leader Keir Hardie—founder of the Independent Labour Party (ILP)

MEMC Marathon Electric Manufacturing Corporation

memci model ewe for micro-climate integration

Memé Remedios

Memel (German—Klaipeda)

MEML Master Equipment Management List

memo memoranda; memorandum

MEMO Medical Equipment Management Office

Memp Memphis

Mem Roy Astron Soc *Memoirs of the Royal Astronomical Society*

Mem Soc Assn Memorial Society Association

MEMSPO Michigan Elementary and Middle School Principals Organization

men. menses; menstruation; mensuration

men *meno* (Italian—less)

Men Mensa (constellation)

M.En. Master of English

MEN Manasco (stock-exchange symbol)

MEN *Middle East News*

MENC Music Educators National Conference

Mencius Meng-tse

Menckonaclast Henry L Mencken

mend. macro end

MEND Medical Education for National Defense

Mendelssohn's 5 Mendelssohn's five symphonies including *Lobgesang* (No. 2), *Scottish* (No. 3), *Italian* (No. 4), and *Reformation* (No. 5)

Mendl Lib Mendelssohn Library

Mendy Mendelssohn

Men of the East Sherpas of northern India and Nepal

Menfis (Spanish—Memphis)

M.Eng. Master of Engineering; Mining Engineer

M. Eng. P.A. Master of Engineering and Public Administration

Meniere's disease sudden dizziness, ear ringing, and vomiting due to disturbance of the labyrinth

Menn Menninger

Mennon Mennonite

meno menopausal; menopause; menorrhoea

Menorca (Spanish—Minorca)

Menorca's Principal Port Port Mahón

MENP Mount Elgon National Park (Kenya)

MENS Mission Element Needs Statement

menst menstrual; menstruation

mensur mensuration

ment mental; mentalis

M. Ent. Master of Entomology

mentd mentioned

mentholyptus menthol + eucalyptus

Menton (French—Mentone)

Mentone (Italian—Menton)

Mentor Beechcraft T-34 trainer aircraft

Mentor to Parisian Intellectuals Théophile Gautier

meo (MEO) manned earth observatory

Meo Bartolomeo

MEO Maintenance Engineering Order; Marine Engineer(ing) Office(r)

MEOA Malaysian Estate Owners Association

meoh methanol; methol

MEOW Moral Equivalent of War (President Carter's energy program)

mep mean effective pressure

MEP Main European Port; Management Engineering Program; Management Evaluation Program; Member of the European Parliament; Middle East Perspective

M.E.P. Master of Engineering Physics

MEP *Movemento Electoral Popular* (Papiamento—Popular Electoral Movement)—Aruba's pro-independence party; *Movimiento Electoral del Pueblo* (Spanish—People's Electoral Movement)—Venezuelan political party

M.E.P.A. Master of Engineering and Public Administration

MEPC Maritime Environment Protection Committee; Metro-

politan Estate and Property Corporation

MEPCOM Military Enlisting Processing Command

M.E.P.H. Master of Public Health Engineering

Mephisto Mephistopheles (The Devil)

MEPS Means-Ends Problem-Solving Test; Multilanguage Electronic Phototypesetting System

mepu (MEPU) monopropellant emergency power unit

meq/l milliequivalents per liter

mer meridian; minimum energy requirement(s)

mer (MER) methanol extraction residue

m & er mechanical and electrical room

mer *mercoledi* (Italian—Wednesday); *mercredi* (French—Wednesday); *meros* (Greek—part)—blastomere, centromere, isomer, polymer

Mer Mercury; Merino

MER Metropolitan Elevated Railroad; Ministry of Energy Resources

mera minimum enroute altitude

MERA Michigan Educational Research Association

MERADO Mechanical Engineering Research and Development Organization

MERAG Middle-East Research and Action Group (anti-fascist Zionist pacifists and London leftwing libertarians)

MERB Mechanical Engineering Research Board

merc mercury

Merc Mercantile Exchange; Mercator; Mercedes; Mercedes-Benz; Mercury

MERC Music Education Research Council

Mercator Gerardus Mercator—real name of this 16th-century Flemish geographer is Gerhard Kremer

merch merchantable

Merchant of Death international arms contractor Sir Basil Zaharoff

Merchants of Death epithetic nickname sometimes applied to alcohol and tobacco vendors, armament makers, drug pushers, munitions makers, narcotics traffikers, and others whose business may result in the death of their customers

Merchants' Haven Copenhagen,

Denmark

Merch V *Merchant of Venice*

'mercial commercial

Mercury (Latin—Hermes)—the messenger

Mercurys Mercury Islands off New Zealand's North Island

MERDL Medical Equipment Research and Development Laboratory (USA)

Mer du Nord (French—North Sea)

Meredith Meredith Press

meres matrix of environmental residuals for energy systems

meretricious traffic prostitution; white slavery

merfin mercerized finish

Merguis Mergui Islands off Lower Burma

Meri Merionethshire

'Merica(n) [Cockney contraction—America(n)]—in the Far East, the South Seas, and many other parts of the world this sometimes comes out as *'Mellica(n)*

merid meridian

MERIP Middle East Research and Information Project (Methodist-supported pro-Palestinian Arabs)

MERIT Medical Relief International

meritoc meritocracy; meritocrat(ic)(al)(ly)

MERL Mechanical Engineering Research Laboratory

Merle Oberon Estelle Merle O'Brien

MERLIN Machine Readable Library Information

Merriam G & C Merriam

Merritt Pkwy Merritt Parkway

Merry Monarch Charles II of Great Britain also nicknamed Patron of Bawdy Houses

Merry W *Merry Wives of Windsor*

mer's multiple ejection racks

Mers Merseyside

mersar merchant ship search and rescue

mersex merchant shipping exchange

Mert Merton College, Oxford

MERT Maintenance Engineering Review Team; Milwaukee Electric Railway and Transit

Mert Coll Merton College—Oxford

MERU Mechanical Engineering Research Unit

Merv Mervin

merzd meridian zenith distance

MERZONE Merchant Shipping

Control Zone

mes main engine start; main equipment supplier; missile engineering station; motor end support; mud estuary slick; mutual energy support

mes *mesos* (Greek—middle)—mesentery, mesoderm(ic), Mesopotamia, Mesozoic

Mes Mesozoic; Messina

Mes *Mesdames* (French—ladies)

MES Michigan Engineering Society; Midwest Electronic Society

mesa (MESA) mathematics, engineering, and scientific achievement

mesa. modularized equipment storage assembly

MESA Malarial Eradication Special Account; Marine Ecosystems Analysis; Mechanics Educational Society of America; Mining Enforcement and Safety Administration

Mesabi Mesabi Range of iron ore in Minnesota

Mesa Verde Mesa Verde National Park in Colorado

mesbic (MESBIC) minority enterprise small business investment companies

mesc mescal; mescaline

M. E. Sc. Master of Engineering Science

Mescalero Cessna T-41 trainer-utility aircraft

MESCO Middle East Science Cooperative Office (UNESCO)

Mesd *Mesdames* (French—Ladies)

MESF Mobile Earth Station Facility

mesfet metallized semiconductor field-effect transistor

mesh. medical headings

MeSH Medical Subject Heading (National Library of Medicine's thesaurus)

Meslier Jean Meslier—deceased and obscure parish priest whose name was used by Voltaire to escape persecution (*see* Jean Meslier); even the names of the parishes he served—Entrepigny and But —are not to be found in most atlases and gazetteers

meso (Latin prefix—middle, moderate)—mesoderm, Mesopotamia

Mesoamer Mesoamerica(n)—Middle America(n) (Central America, Mexico, and the

West Indies)

Mesop Mesopotamia (Iraq)

Mesopotamia (Greek—Between Rivers)—land between the Euphrates and the Tigris; formerly Assyria, Babylonia, and Sumeria but presently Iraq

MESP More Effective Schools Program

MESPA Minnesota Elementary School Principals Association

Mespot Mesopotamia (Iraq)

mess. maximum effective sonar speed

Mess *Messidor* (French—Harvest Month)—beginning June 19th—tenth month of the French Revolutionary Calendar

Messenger of the Gods Hermes (Greek); Mercury (Roman)

Messenger of Mercy Swiss banker Jean Henri Dunant—founder of the Red Cross

Messico (Italian—Mexico)

Messner Julian Messner

messplex multiplex emission sensors

Messrs *Messieurs* (French—Gentlemen)

mest mestizo

mestranol methyl+estrogen +pregnane (synthetic oral contraceptive)

met. metal; metallic; metallize; metaphor; metaphysics; meteorology; methionine (amino acid) (MET); metronome; metropolitan

met *metropolitana* (Spanish—metropolitan)

Met Metro; Metropolitan Correction Center; Metropolitan Museum of Art; Metropolitan Opera

MET Mobile Examining Team

meta (Greek—after or beyond)—metabolism, metacarpal, metastasis, metatarsal

Meta Margarita

META Metropolitan Educational Television Association (Canadian)

metab metabolism

metadex metal abstracts index

metall metallurgy

Metallic Age when you have silver strands in your hair, copper pennies in your purse, iron rust in your guts, and lead weights in your bottom

metallog metallography

METALMA Metalúrgica Matarazzo (Brazilian company)

metaph metaphor(ical)(ly); metaphysical(ly); metaphysician;

metaphysics
metaphys metaphysics
metaplan methods of abstracting text automatically programming language
metas metastasis; metastasize
Metastasio Pietro Antonio Domenico Bonaventura Trapassi
metath metathesis
metb metal base
met bor metropolitan borough
metc metal curb; mouse embryo tissue culture
Met Cen Lib Metropolitan Central Library
METCO Metropolitan Council for Educational Opportunity
metd metal door
mete multiple engagement test environment
Met. E. Metallurgical Engineer
metec meteoroid technology
METEI Medical Expedition to Easter Island
meteor. meteorology
Meteor Gloster twin-engine jet-fighter aircraft
Meteorol Meteorology
meteorolo meteorology
meteosat meteorological satellite
metf metal flashing
metg metal grille
meth methadone; methamphetamine; methane; methedrine; methyl; methylated; methyprylon
Meth Methodist
methanol methyl alcohol or wood alcohol (CH_3OH)
Meth Epis Methodist Episcopal
meth freak methedrine freak (underground slang—habitual user of methedrine)
meth head methedrine head (underground slang—methedrine addict)
metho methodology; methyl alcohol
meths methylated spirits (denatured alcohol)
methu methuselah (8-bottle capacity)
meti major engineering test item; metal jalousie
M-et-L Maine-et-Loire
Met Lith Assn Metropolitan Lithographers Association
metm metal mold
M-et-M Meurthe-et-Moselle
Met Man Metro Manila
m. et n. *mane et nocte* (Latin—morning and evening); *mane et nocte* (Latin—morning and night)

meto maximum except takeoff
Met O Meteorological Office(r)
METO Middle East Treaty Organization
metob meteorological observation
metol methyl-p-aminophenol (photographic developer)
meton metonomy
metp metal partition
metr metal roof
Met R Metropolitan Railway
METR Manufacturing Engineering Test Report
metro metropolitan
métro *chemin de fer métropolitain* (Paris subway system)
Metro Metromedia; Metropolitan Life Insurance Company
Metro Metropolitan (Paris and Madrid subway systems—originally stood for Metropolitan District Railway—the London *Underground*)
METRO New York Metropolitan Reference and Research Library Agency
metroc meteorological rocket
metrocenter metropolitan center
metrocomplex metropolitan complex
metrocore metropolitan core
metroframe metropolitan framework
metrol metrology
Metroland portion of London served by the Metro subway system
metrop metropolis; metropolitan
metroplex metropolitan complex
metropol metropolis; metropolitan
Metropolis of America New York City
Metropolis of the Magic Valley Brownsville, Texas on the Rio Grande
Metropolis of the Missouri Valley Kansas City
Metropolis of the South Mark Twain's nickname for New Orleans
Metropolis of the State of Oregon Portland
Metropolis of the United States New York
Metropolis of the World London
Metropolitan Museum of Art or Opera House in New York City, depending on the topic being considered
Metropolitan City of the Angli-

can Communion Canterbury
METRRA Metropolitan Toronto Residents' and Rate Payers' Association
mets metal strip
METS Mayne's Exchange Transfer Systems; Mechanized Export Traffic System (USA)
metsats meteorological satellites
m. et sig. *misce et signa* (Latin—mix and write a label)
metso sodium metasilicate
mett (METT) manned evasive-target tank (USA)
Met Tec Meteorologist Technician
Metternich Prince Klemens Wenzel Nepomuk Lothar von Metternich-Winneburg—Austrian statesman convening Congress of Vienna at end of Napoleonic wars
METU Middle East Technical University (Ankara)
Met Vic Metropolitan Vickers (electrical company)
MEU Marine Expeditionary Unit; Municipal and Shire Employees Union
MEU Modern English Usage
Meuse (French—Maas)
mev million electron volts
meV mega-electron volt(s); milli-electron volt(s); million-electron volt(s)
Mev Mevrouw (Dutch—Missus)
MeV megaelectronvolt; million electronvolt
Mevr Mevrouw (Dutch—Missus)
MEW Microwave Early Warning; Ministry of Economic Warfare
MEWA Motor and Equipment Wholesalers Association
MEWS Maintenance Engineering Work Sheet; Missile Early Warning Station
MEWTA Missile Electronic Warfare Technical Area
mewttos main engine working to telegraph orders
mex military exchange
Mex Mexican; Mexico
Méx México (Spanish—Mexico)
MEX Mexico City, Mexico (airport)
Mex C Mexico City
Mex Cy Mexican currency
Mex$ Mexican peso
mexican mexican apple (white sapote); mexican ground cherry (*tomatillo*); mexican hair-

less (almost hairless dog originating in Mexico where it is used to herd cattle and keep ranchers company in bed as its hairlessness makes it flealess and its body temperature is higher than ours); mexican jumping beans (beans inhabited by insect larvae whose movements make the beans jump about); mexican onyx (also called mexican marble or onyx marble)

MEXICANA Compañía Mexicana de Aviación

Mexican Agrarian Reformer Emiliano Zapata

Mexican Composer-Conductor Carlos Chávez (in this century) or Juventino Rosas (in the last)

Mexican Film Pioneer José Bolanos and Luís Buñuel can claim this cinematic accolade

Mexican Idealist Politician and Revolutionary Francisco I(dalecio) Madero

Mexican Independence Day (see *Dieciséis*)

Mexican Muralist title shared by José Clemente Orozco, Diego Rivera, Davíd Alfaro Siquieros, and Rufino Tamayo as well as lesser known but equally effective muralists

Mexican National Composer Carlos Chávez

Mexican Ports (east coast large, medium, and small ports from north to south) Tampico, Veracruz, Coatzacoalcos, Frontera, Progreso; (west coast large, medium, and small ports from south to north) Salina Cruz, Acapulco, Manzanillo, San Blas, Mazatlan, Guaymas, Santa Rosalia, Ensenada

Mexican-Spanish Mexican-style Spanish enriched with more than 50,000 Mexicanisms reflecting more than twenty centuries of Mexican culture

Mexican Trio Mexico's three best-known classical composers listed chronologically— Manuel Ponce, Carlos Chávez, Silvestre Revueltas

Mexico United Mexican States (Middle America's largest and most populated nation whose diverse industrial and rural activity is insufficient to support this overpopulated country of cultivated Spanish-speaking

people) *Estados Unidos Mexicanos*

Mexico's Principal Port Veracruz

mexit macro exit

MEXSM Mexican Service Medal

Mex Sp Mexican Spanish

Mexsur Mexican (automobile) insurance

Meyerbeer Giacomo Meyerbeer (adopted name of Jakob Liebmann Beer)

Meyer Lansky Maier Suchowljansky

mez mezcal(ine)

mez *mezzo* (Italian—half)

MEZ *mitteleuropäische Zeit* (German—Central European Time)

mezz mezzanine; mezzotint

mezzo(s) mezzosoprano(s); mezzotint(s)

mf machine finish; main feed; main force; maintenance factor; male-to-female (ratio); manufacture(d); manufacturing; mastic floor; medium frequency (300-3,000 kc); microfarad(s); microfiche; microfilm; mill finish; millifarad(s); mother fucker; motor field; motor freight; multiplying factor

m/f maintenance-to-flight (ratio); male or female; manifest; marked for; marked for; milk fat

m & f male and female

μf micro+farad

mf *mezzo-forte* (Italian—half loud, moderately loud)

m/f *mi favor* (Spanish—my favor); *motorfaerge* (Dano-Norwegian—motor ferry)

μF microfarad(s)

M^f *Massif* (French—mountain mass)

MF Magazines for Friendship; Marshall Field (stock exchange symbol); Medal of Freedom; Middle Fork (railroad); Millard Fillmore (13th President U.S.)

M-F Massey-Ferguson; Monday through Friday

M.F. Master of Forestry

MF *medlem af Folketinget* (Danish—Member of Parliament)

mfa malicious false alarm; multi-fiber arrangement

MFA Master Fencers Association; Military Flying Area; Ministry of Foreign Affairs; Museum(s) of Fine Arts

M.F.A. Master of Fine Arts; Museum of Fine Arts

MFA *Moviemento das Forças Armadas* (Portuguese— Armed Forces Movement)— military dictatorship

M Fac Hom Member of the Faculty of Homeopathy

M-factor mobility, movement, migration (automotive Americans on the move)

MFAH Museum of Fine Arts of Houston

M.F.A. Mus. Master of Fine Arts in Music

MFAR Michigan Foundation for Advanced Research

mfb message from base; metallic foreign object; moisture-free basis

mfb (M) median forebrain bundle

MFB Metropolitan Fire Brigade; MFB Mutual Insurance (Manufacturers, Firemen's and Blackstone combined)

mfbm thousand foot board measure(ment)

mfc magnetic-tape field scan(ning); medicated face conditioner; membrane fecal coliform; microfilm frame card; microfunction circuit

mfc (MFC) marginal factor cost

MFC Master Facility Census

MFCA Master Fruit Carriers Association

MFCCA Master Floorcovering Contractors Association

m/fcha *meses fecha* (Spanish— months dated)

mfcm multifunction card machine

MFCM Member of the Faculty of Community Medicine

mfco manual fuel cutoff

mfcs mathematical foundations of computer science

MFCS Manual Flight-Control System (NASA)

mfcu multifunction card unit

mfd manufactured; microfarad; minimum fatal dose (MFD)

mfdf medium-frequency direction finder

mfdp maintenance float-distribution point

MFDT Memory for Designs Test

mfe multiflow evaluator

MFE *Movimento Federalista Europeo* (Italian—European Federalist Movement)

MFECS Mediterranean Far East Container Service

MFED Manned Flight Engineering Division (NASA)

M. F. Eng. Master of Forest Engineering

mff mighty fine fuckin'

MFF Master Freight File

mfg manufacturing; molded fiber glass

mfh military family housing

MFH Master of Fox Hounds; Mobile Field Hospital

mfi machine feature index; meltflow index

MFI Master Facility Inventory; Musicians Foundation Incorporated

MFIANE Mutual Fire Insurance Association of New England

MFIBNE Mutual Fire Inspection Bureau of New England

MFIC Military Flight Information Center

MFIT Manual Fault Isolation Test

mfkp multifrequency key pulsing

m fl med flere (Dutch—and others)

Mfl Monfalcone

MFL Master Facility List; Missile Firing Laboratory; Mobile Field Laboratory; Mutual Funds Limited

MFLDA Malaysian Federal Land Development Authority

M Flem Middle Flemish

mflops million floating point operations per second

MFM Miracle Food Mart

MFMA Master Fish Merchants Association

mf method membrane or millipore filter method

mfn most favored nation

mf(n) microfiche (negative)

MFNP Mount Field National Park (Tasmania); Murchison Falls NP (Uganda)

MFNZ Music Federation of New Zealand

mfo missile firing order

MFOA Municipal Finance Officers Association

mfopp missile firing order patch panel

M.For. Master of Forestry

MFOWW Marine Firemen, Oilers, Watertenders, and Wipers

mfp minor forest produce

mfp (MFP) monoflurophosphate

mf(p) microfiche (positive)

mfpa monolithic focal-plane array

MFPB Mineral Fiber Products

Bureau

MFPS Mobile Field Photographic Section

mfr manufacture; manufactured; manufacturer; missile firing range (MFR)

M Fr Mali franc(s); Middle French; Moroccan franc(s)

MFR Military Force Reduction(s)

mfrd manufactured

mfrg manufacturing

mfrn manufacturer's number

MFRP Midwest Fuel Recovery Plant (AEC)

mfrr manufacturer(s)

mfs magnetic-tape field search; maximum file size; missile firing simulator

mf & s magazine flooding and sprinkling

Mf's Moslem fanatics (who appear to take a holy delight in killing Christian and Jewish infidels and other nonbelievers in Mohamet)

MFS Malleable Founders' Society; Manned Flying System; Medal Field Service; Military Flight Service; Missile Firing Station; Mountain Fuel Supply; steel-hulled fleet minesweeper (3-letter naval symbol)

M.F.S. Master of Food Science; Master of Foreign Service; Master of Foreign Study

MFSA Master Floor Sanders Association; Metal Finishing Suppliers' Association

mfsk multiple-frequency shift keying

mfso main fuel shutoff

mfsov main fuel shutoff valve

MFSS Missile Flight Safety System(s)

mfst manifest

mft major fraction thereof; mechanized flamethrower; motor freight tariff; multiprogramming with a fixed number of tasks

m. ft. mistura fiat (Latin—make a mixture)

MFT Microflocculation Test; Muscle Function Test; Musical Fundamentals Test(ing)

M.F.T. Master of Foreign Trade

MFTB Motor Freight Tariff Bureau

mftbf mean flight time between failure(s)

MFTD Mobile Field Training Detachment

mftl millifoot lamberts

m.ft.m. misce fiat mistura (Latin —mix to make a mixture)

mftv mechanical fit test vehicle

mfu military fuckup

MFURB Maryland Fire Underwriters Rating Bureau

MFUSYS Microfiche File Update System

mfv magnetic field vector; microfilm viewer; motor fleet vessel

MFV Mars Flyby Vehicle

MfVB Museum für Volkerkunde, Berlin

MFW Maritime Federation of the World

mfy manufactory

mg machine gun; marginal; milligram; motor generator; multigauge

mg (MG) myasthenia gravis

mg % milligrams percent

m-g machine glazed

m/g motor generator

m & g mapping and geodesy

μg microgram

mg main gauche (French—left hand)

m/g mi giro (Spanish—my check, my draft)

mG méridien de Greenwich (French—Greenwich meridian)

Mg magnesium; Margrave; Margraviate; megagram (metric ton)

Mg Molekulargewicht (German —molecular weight)

MG machine gun; Maintainability Group; major general; Marine Gunner; Military Government; Minas Gerais; Minister General; Morris Garage (M-G); Murray Grey (cattle)

M-G Morris-Garage (British sports car)

M & G Mobile & Gulf

MG Maschinegewehr (German —machine gun)

Mga Malaga

Mga Mongolia (Spanish—Mongolia)

MGA Managua, Nicaragua (Las Mercedes airport); Member of the General Assembly; Military Government Association; Monongahela (railroad); Mushroom Growers Association

mgal milligal

M-gauge meter gauge (39.37-inch) railroad track

mgawd make good all works disturbed

mgb (MGB) missile gunboat

Mg of B Margrave of Breslau; Margraviate of Breslau

MGB motor gunboat (British naval symbol); Soviet Ministry of State Security (see *VOT*)

MGB Ministerstvo Gosudarstvennoi Bezopasnosti (Russian —Ministry of State Security) —Soviet secret police

mgc manual gain control

MGC Machine Gun Corps; Machinery of Government (committee); Marriage Guidance Council; Marriage Guidance Counsellor

mg/cig milligrams (of nicotine tar) per cigarette

mgcir master ground-controller-interception radar

mgcr maritime gas-cooled reactor

mg/cu m milligrams (dust, fume, or mist) per cubic meter of air

mgd magnetogasdynamics; million gallons per day

mg/d million gallons per day

Mgd Magdeburg

MGD Military Geographic Documentation

mge (MGE) maintenance ground equipment

M.G.E. Master of Geological Engineering

M. Geol. Eng. Master of Geological Engineering

MGES Maintenance Ground Equipment Specification

mgf macrophage growth factor

MGF Myasthenia Gravis Foundation

mgg mouse gamma globulin

mgh milligram hour(s)

MGH Massachusetts General Hospital

mgi military geographic(al) intelligence

MGI Media Group Inc; Mining and Geological Institute of India

MGIC Mortgage Guarantee Insurance Corporation

MGICA Mortgage Guaranteed Insurance Corporation of Australia

MGID Military Geographic Information and Documentation

MGk Medieval Greek

mg/l milligrams per liter

MGL Morris Geneological Library

mgm (MGM) mobile guided missile

Mg of M Margrave of Moravia;

Margraviate of Moravia

MGM Metro-Goldwyn-Mayer

MGM-18A Lacrosse surface-to-surface missile

MGM-29A Sperry Sergeant surface-to-surface missile

MGM-31A Pershing surface-to-surface missile made by Martin

MGMI Mining, Geological, and Metallurgical Institute

MGMS Manchester Geological and Mining Society

mgmt management

mgn micrograin

*M*ᵍⁿᵃ *Montagna* (Italian—mountain)

*M*ᵍⁿᵉ *Montagne* (French—mountain)

Mgo Mormugao

MGP Marcus Garvey Park (formerly Mount Morris Park)

mgr mined geological repository

mgr (MGR) mobile guided rocket

Mgr Manager; Monseigneur (French—Monsignor); Monsignore (Italian—Monsignor)

M Gr Middle Greek

MGR Matusadona Game Reserve (Rhodesia); Micro-Graphic Recording

mgress manageress

mgs milligrams; missile guidance set (system)

mg('s) machine gun(s)

m-g-s meter-gram-second

MGS Minnesota Geological Survey

MGSA Military General Supply Agency

MGSMTC Mid-Gulf Seaports Marine Terminal Conference

mgt management

MGTB Mexican Government Tourist Bureau

MGTC Morgan Guaranty Trust Company

MGTD Mexican Government Tourist Delegation

mgtrn magnetron

MGU Moskovskiy Gosudarstvenny Universitet (Moscow State University)

M Gun Sgt Master Gunnery Sergeant

mgw maximum gross weight

MGW Manchester Guardian Weekly

m'gwd my gawd (my god)

mh magentic heading; main hatch; manhole; marital history; materials handling; menstrual history; mental health; millihenries; millihenry; mu-

rine hepatitis

*μ*h microhenry

mH millihenry

Mh Monatsheft (German—monthly magazine)

MH magnetic heading; Master Hosts; Medal of Honor; Military Hospital; Ministry of Health; Mission Hills; Most Honorable; Most Honourable

M-H Minneapolis-Honeywell (stock exchange symbol and trademark)

M & H Mason and Hamlin

MH Mo'etzet Hapo'alot (Hebrew—Woman Workers Council)

MH² Mary Hartman, Mary Hartman (tv show)

mha manhour accounting; maximum holding altitude

MHA auxiliary minehunter (naval symbol); Marine Historical Association; Medal for Humane Action; Member of the House of Assembly; Mental Health Administration; Mental Health Association; Mental Health Authority; Mining Houses of Australia; Multiple Handicapped Association

M.H.A. Master of Hospital Administration

MHATA Mental Health Assistant Therapy Aide

MHb Mueller-Hinton broth

MHB Material Handling Bureau; Mental Health Branch

M-H B Mid-Hudson Bridge

mhc major histocompatibility complex

MHC coastal minehunter (naval symbol); Massachusetts Historical Commission

MHCO Mine-Hunting Control Office(r)

MHCOA Motor Hearse and Car Owners Association

mh cp mean horizontal candlepower

mhcv (MHCV) manned hypersonic cruise vehicle

mhd magnetohydrodynamics

MHD Military History Detachment

mhdg magnetohydrodynamic generator

mhdl magnetohydrodynamic laser

mhd lt masthead light

mhe materials handling equipment

MHE Mechanical Handling Engineering

M.H.E. Master of Home Economics

MHEA Mechanical Handling Engineers Association

M Heb Middle Hebrew

MHEDA Material Handling Equipment Distributors Association

M.H.E.E. Master of Home Economics Education

M. H. E. Ed. Master of Home Economics Education

mhf medium high frequency

M-H-F Massey-Harris-Ferguson

MHFNZ Mental Health Foundation of New Zealand

mhg message-header generator

μHg microns of mercury

MHG Middle High German

mhhw mean higher high water

MHI Material Handling Institute; Metal Hydrides Incorporated; Mitsubishi Heavy Industry

mhic microwave hybrid integrated circuit

M. Hi. E. Master of Highway Engineering

M. Hi. Eng. Master of Highway Engineering

MHII Material Handling Institute Incorporated

MHJC Mary Holmes Junior College

MHK Member of the House of Keys (Isle of Man)

mhl metal halide lamps

MHL Manaus Harbour Limited; Mission Hills Library

M.H.L. Master of Hebrew Literature

MHLF Mutual Home Loan Funds

MHLG Ministry of Housing and Local Government

mhls metabolic heat-load simulator

mhlw mean higher low water

Mhm Mannheim

MHM Mill Hill Missionary

MHMA Mobile Homes Manufacturers Association

MHMC Mercy Hospital and Medical Center; Montefiore Hospital and Medical Center

MH,MH Mary Hartman, Mary Hartman (tv show)

mho unit of conductance or reciprocal ohm

M. Hor. Master of Horticulture

M. Ho. Sc. Master of Household Science

MHP Missouri Highway Patrol

mhpg (MHPG) 3-methoxy-4-hydroxy phenylethylene

MHQ Maritime Headquarters;

Mediterranean Headquarters

mhr manhour(s); maximum heart rate; microwave hologram radar

mhr (MHU) mental health unit

MHR Member of the House of Representatives

MHRA Modern Humanities Research Association

MHRF Mental Health Research Fund

MHRI Mental Health Research Institute (University of Michigan)

mhs medical history sheet

MHS Massachusetts Historical Society; Measurement Handicap System; Morris High School; Musical Heritage Society

MHSA Military Historical Society of Australia

MHSc Master (Mistress) of Household Science

MH strain Mill Hill (viral) strain

mht mean high tide; mild heat treatment; military hospital trainee

mht (MHT) missile-handling trailer

MHT Museum of History and Technology (Smithsonian Institution)

MHTA Mental Hygiene Therapy Aide

MHTC Manufacturers Hanover Trust Company

MHTF Manhattan Homicide Task Force (NYPD)

MHTG Marine Helicopter Training Group

mhtl mean high tide line

M. Hu. Master of Humanities

mhv mean horizontal velocity; murine hepatitis virus

mhw mean high water

MHW Mental Health Worker; Ministry of Health and Welfare

mhwli mean high water lunitidal interval

mhwlr mobile hostile-weapon-locating radar

mhwn mean high water neaps

mhws mean high water springs

M. Hy. Master of Hygiene

MH y C Miguel Hidalgo y Costilla

M. Hyg. Master of Hygiene

mhz (MHz) megahertz(es), formerly megacycle(s) per second

mi malleable iron; manual input; mentally ill; metabolic index; middle initial; mile(s);

mill; minor; minute(s); mitral; mitral insufficiency; mutual inductance

mi (MI) myocardial infarction

m & i modernization and improvement; municipal and industrial

m of i moment of inertia

mi (Italian—third tone in diatonic scale, *E* in fixed-*do* system)

Mi Mach indicated; Mach speed indicated; Miami; Minor; Mitte

MI Maintenance Instruction; Mare Island; Marshall Islands; Match Institute; Mauritius Institute; Meat Inspection (US Department of Agriculture); Mellon Institute; Member of the Institute; Member of the Institution; Metal Industries; Military Intelligence; Ministry of Information; Missouri-Illinois (railroad); Mounted Infantry

M-I Missouri-Illinois (railroad)

M & I Manpower and Immigration (Canada)

Mi-1 Soviet utility helicopter nicknamed Hare

mi² square miles(s)

mi³ cubic mile(s)

MI 5 (British) Military Intelligence Security Service (somewhat quivalent to American FBI)

MI-6 Military Intelligence 6 (British external intelligence organization)

Mi-8 Soviet transport helicopter nicknamed Hip

Mi-10 Soviet heavy-transport helicopter nicknamed Harke

Mi-12 Soviet heavy helicopter nicknamed Homer by NATO and in the mid-1970s allegedly the world's heaviest and largest aircraft of its kind

Mi-16 40-ton Soviet helicopter

mia (MIA) missing in action

MIA Malaysian Institute of Art; Marble Institute of America; Media Information Australia; Miami, Florida (airport); Mica Industry Association; Millinery Institute of America; missing in action; Murrumbidgee Irrigation Area (Australia)

M.I.A. Master of International Affairs

MIAA Mortgage Insurers Association of Australia

MIAC Manufacturing Industries Advisory Council

MIA-CHI Miami—Chicago
MIA-LAX Miami—Los Angeles
Miami Beach East Tel Aviv, Israel's nickname
MIA-NY Miami—New York
MIAP Member of the Institution of Analysts & Programmers
MIAPD Mid-Central Air Procurement District
MIARS Mainentance Information Automated Retrieval System (USN)
MIAS Major-Item Automated System (USA)
MIA-SAN Miami—San Diego
MIA-SFO Miami—San Francisco
MIASI Moore Institute of Art, Science, and Industry
MIA-TOR Miami—Toronto
MIB Management Improvement Board; Maritime Index Bureau; Meat Inspection Branch; Medical Information Bank; Mental Information Bureau; Michigan Inspection Bureau; Military Intelligence Branch; Military Intelligence Bureau; Missouri Inspection Bureau; Sir Marc Isambard Brunel
mibk methyl isobutyl ketone
mic machine index card; micrometer; microphone; microwave integrated circuit; military-industrial complex; minimum ignition current
Mic The Book of Micah; Microscopium (constellation)
MIC Malayan Indian Congress; Management Information Center; Marshall Islands Congress; Medical Information Center; Mitsubishi International Corporation; Monaco Information Centre; Motorcycle Industry Council; Motors Insurance Corporation; Music Industry Council
mica. macro instruction compiler assembler
MICA Moscow Institute for Complex Automation
micbm (MICBM) mobile intercontinental ballistic missile
micc mineral-insulated copper-covered (cable); miniature integrated circuit computer
MICC Malaysian International Chambers of Commerce
MICE Member of the Institution of Civil Engineers
Mich Michael; Michigan; Michiganite; Michoacan; Mitchell

Michael Angelo Titmarsh Thackeray's pseudonym adorning some of his earlier works
Michael Arlen Dikran Kuyumjian's pseudonym
Michael Caine Maurice Joseph Micklewhite
Michael Curtiz Michael Kertesz; Mihály Kertész
Michael Fairless Margaret Fairless Barber
Michael Field Katherine Harris Bradley and her niece Edith Emma Cooper who used this pseudonym for their joint poetic efforts
Michael Innes John Innes Mackintosh Stewart
Michael Servetus Miguel Serveto
Michael Tilson Thomas Mike Thomashefsky
Michelangelo Michael Angelo Buonarroti
Michel Auclair Michal Vujovic
Michèle Morgan Simone Roussel
MI Chem E Member of the Institution of Chemical Engineers
Michigan Ports (east to west) Wyandotte, Rouge River, Detroit, Bay City, Saginaw, Alpena, Saulte Ste Marie, Frankfort, Manistee, Ludington, Muskegon, Grand Haven, Holland, St Joseph, Marquette
Michl Michael
mick manufacturer's item correlation key
Mick Michael
Mickey Mouse Walt Disney Productions (Wall Street nickname)
Mickey Rooney Joe Yule, Jr
Mickey Spillane Frank Spillane
Micky Micaela; Michael; Michelle
Mickyland Ireland
MICLASS Metal Institute Classification
MICMA National Ice Cream Mix Association
MICMD Milwaukee Contract Management District
mic-min micro-mini (automobiles)
MICOM Missile Command(er)
micpac molecular integrated circuit package
mic. pan. mica panis (Latin—bread crumb)
MICPS Microfiche Interface Controller-Processor System

micr magnetic ink character recognition; microscope; microscopic; microscopy
micr (MICR) magnetic-ink character recognition
Micr Microscopium
micro 10 -6
micro (Greek mikros—small) microbe, microbiology, microcephalic, micrometer, microscope
Micro Micronesia (Trust Territory of the Pacific); Micronesian
microbiol microbiology
microbop microbopper (underground slang—very young person attuned to the modern scene)— see macrobop
Microcard Microcard Editions
microcephs microcephalics (small-headed people)
microcom microcomputer (pocket calculator)
Microcosm of Canadian Life London, Ontario
microdoc microphotography and document (reproduction)
microeco microeconomics
Microg Microgramma
micro-in. micro-inch
micromation microfilm + automation
micromoms micromomentaries (split-second facial expressions)
micron millionth of a meter
Micron Micronesia; Micronesian
Micronesia small islands of the western Pacific also known as the Trust Territory including the Federated States of Micronesia, the Marshall Islands, and Palau in the Carolines as well as many very small islands covering an area as wide as the United States
Micronesia (Small Islands)—occupying most of the western Pacific and an area as large as the forty-eight states; comprising the United States Trust Territory of the Pacific (Carolines, Marianas, and Marshalls)
micropaleo micropaleontology
micropros microprocess(ing); microprocessor
micros microscopy
micro(s) microcomputer(s)
MICROSIFT Microcomputer Software Information for Teachers
microt microtome
micr's magnetic ink characters

MICRS Magnetic Ink Character Recognition System

mics metal-insulated copper-sheathed (cable)

mic's military-industrial complex executives; military-industrial complex salesmen

MICS Museum of the International College of Surgeons

MICTI *Ministerio de Industria, Comercio, Turismo, e Integración* (Spanish—Ministry of Industry, Commerce, Tourism, and Integration)—Peru

micu (MICU) medical intensive care unit; mobile intensive care unit

micv (MICV) mechanized infantry combat vehicle(s)

mid. mentioned in dispatches; middle

mid. (MID) minimal inhibiting dose; minimum infective dose; multi-infarct dementia; multiple-infarct dementia

Mid Midshipman

MID Merida, Yucatan (airport); Midway Islands (in mid-Pacific); Military Information Division; Military Intelligence Division

M.I.D. Master of Industrial Design

midac management information for design and control

Midac Michigan digital automatic computer

midas modified-integration digital-analog simulator (USAF)

MIDAS Maintenance Integrated Data Access System; Materials for Industry Data and Applications Service; Media Investment Decisions Analysis Systems; Meteorological Information and Dose Acquisition System; Missile Defense Alarm System; Missile Detection Anti-Surveillance

midcult middle-class culture

Middelburg provincial capital of Zeeland in the Netherlands

Middle America Central America, Mexico, and the West Indies

Middle Atlantic States Delaware, Maryland, New Jersey, New York, Pennsylvania, West Virginia

Middle Border Hamlin Garlin's nickname for the American Middle West

Middle Colonies New York, New Jersey, Pennsylvania, Delaware

Middle East area extending from Afghanistan to Egypt and including India, Iran, Iraq, Saudi Arabia, Syria, Lebanon, Israel, Jordan, Kuwait, and the United Arab Emirates

Middle Kingdom China—long believed by the Chinese to be the center of the inhabited world

Middle Passage route of the slavers across the middle of the Atlantic between West Africa and the West Indies

Middle States New York, New Jersey, Pennsylvania, Delaware, and Maryland—midway between New England and the Southern States

Middletown Muncie, Indiana

Middletown title of Robert and Helen Lynd's study of cultural conflicts in Muncie, Indiana—an actual Middletown is almost halfway between Indianapolis and Muncie but is not the subject of this sociological study

Middle West United States from the Great Lakes to the northern border of the Gulf States and from the western slopes of the Appalachians to the eastern slopes of the Rockies, according to the author's *Worldwide What & Where —* geographic glossary published by Clio Books (ABC-Clio) in Santa Barbara

Middlx Middlesex

Middx Middlesex

Middy Midshipman

Middys Midshipmen

MIDEASTFOR Middle East Air Force (USN)

MIDEC Middle East Industrial Development Corporation

MIDELEC Midlands Electricity Board

MIDF Major Item Data File

MIDFL Malayan Industrial Development Finance Limited

Mid-Glam Mid-Glamorgan

midis mid-length (below-the-knee) skirts

Midl Midlands; Midlothian

Midland Midland Bank Limited

Midland Capital Birmingham, England

Midlands central England including counties of Bedford, Buckingham, Derby, Leicester, Northhampton, Nottingham, Rutland, Warwick

Mid Lat Middle Latin

MIDLNET Midwest Region Library Network

Mid Loth Midlothian

midmo middle of the month

Midn Midshipman

MIDP Major-Item Distribution Plan

midr mandatory incident and defect report(ing)

mids middies (middieblouses, midshipmen); missile ignition and destruct simulator

mid. sag. midsagittal

Mids N D A *Midsummer-Night's Dream*

Midsommarvaka (Swedish—Midsummer Fete)—Hugo Alvén's rhapsody for orchestra

midssn mid-season

'mid(st) amid(st)

Midsummer Midsummer Day (Saturday nearest June 21 or 22); Midsummer Eve or Midsummer Night (evening or night preceding the foregoing and most often celebrated in Scandinavia)

MIDU Mineral Investigation Drilling Unit

midw midwestern

midwk midweek

mie military-industrial establishment

mic *miércoles* (Spanish—Wednesday)

M.I.E. Master of Industrial Engineering

MIECO Marshall Islands Import-Export Company

MIEE Member of the Institution of Electrical Engineers

MIEL Malaysian Industrial Estates Limited

mierc *miércoles* (Spanish—Wednesday)

mif merthiolate-iodine-formaldehyde (fecal examination technique); modulus irregularity factor

mif (MIF) migratory inhibitory factor

MIF Market Intervention Fund; Milk Industry Foundation; Miners International Federation

MIFCT Moscow Institute of Fine Chemical Technology

MIFI *Moskovskiy Inzhenerno Fizicheskiy Institut* (Russian—Moscow Engineering Physics Institute)

mifil microwave filter

mig magnesium-inert gas; metal inert gas (welding)

MIG Marine Industry Group; Mikhail Ivanovich Glinka; Soviet jet fighter aircraft named for designers Mikoyan and Gurevich

MIGB Millinery Institute of Great Britain

Mightiest of Rivers the Amazon

mightn't might not

Mighty Champion of Freedom Frederick Douglass

Mighty Five Balakirev, Borodin, Cui, Mussorgsky, and Rimsky-Korsakov

Mighty Mo battleship USS *Missouri*

Mighty Mstislav Mstislav Rostropovich

Mig¹ Miguel (Spanish—Michael)

migra migración (Mexican-American slang—immigration or migration)—*la migra* means the U.S. Border Patrol or the Immigration and Naturalization Service

mi/h mile(s) per hour

M.I.H. Master of Industrial Health

Mihaly Munkacsy Michael Lieb

mihn-baau (Cantonese Chinese —bread)

mihped microwave-induced helium-plasma emission detection

MIHS Marshall Islands High School

MIIA Medical Information and Intelligence Agency

MIIDS Maine's Integrated In-service Delivery System

MIIF Master Item Intelligence File

MI Inf Sci Member of the Institute of Information Scientists

MiIS Marshall Islands Intermediate School

mij maatschappij (Dutch—company, society)

M i J Made in Japan

MIJ Muhammad Ali Jinnah

miji meaconing, interference, jamming, intrusion

Mik Mikhail

mike micrometer; microphone

Mike letter M radio code; Michael

Mike Nichols Michael Peschkowsky

Mike Wallace Myron Wallace

Mikimotos Mikimoto cultured pearls

mikos mindervärdighets komplex (Swedish—inferiority complex)

Mikrop Mikropunkt (German—

microdot)—microfilm marvel of World War II when a page of top-secret information could be reduced to a dot no larger than the dot over a letter i and then could be enlarged when needed

Mikve Israel (Hebrew—Ritual Bath of Israel)—oldest synagogue in the New World; in Willemstad on the island of Curaçao in the Netherlands Antilles near Venezuela

mil mileage; military; militia; milieme; million; 1/1000 inch; 1/10 cent; 1/1000 Palestinian pound (currency formerly used in Israel)

m-i-l mother-in-law

Mil Milan; Milford Haven (British maritime abbreviation); Military; Milwaukee

MIL Malaya Indonesia Line; Member of the Institute of Linguists; Microsystems International Limited; Milan, Italy (Malpensa Airport); Wisconsin

MILA Merritt Island Launch Area

MilAdGru Military Advisory Group

Milan English place-name equivalent of Milano in northern Italy

Milano (Italian—Milan)

Mil Att Military Attaché

milc military characteristics

MILC Midwest Inter-Library Center

MILCAP Military Civic Action Program; Military Civil Action Plan(ning); Military Contract Administration Procedure(s)

MILCASE Military Career Awareness Course for Educators

milcomsat military communication satellite

milcrit military critic(ism)

MILDAT Military Damage Assessment Team

mildec(s) military decision(s)

Mildred Masters Mildred Kapilow

mile mille passuum (Latin—1000 paces), a pace being a double step

Mile-High or More-Than Mile-High North American Cities Butte, Montana; Cheyenne, Wyoming; Colorado Springs and Denver, Colorado; Flagstaff, Arizona; Gallup, New Mexico; Mexico City; Santa

Fe, New Mexico

MILES Multiple Integrated Laser Engagement System

Mile-Square City Hoboken, New Jersey

Mil-Hndbk Military Handbook

Miliano Emiliano Zapata

MILIMETS Military Meteorological System

Militaire Paganini's Violin Caprice (opus 1, no. 14)

Military Haydn's Symphony No. 100 in G major

Mil Jrn Milwaukee Journal

Milk City Carnation, Washington

milk of magnesia magnesium hydroxide—$Mg(OH)_2$

mill. millinery; milling; million(s)

Mill Million(en) [German—million(s)]

milli 10^{-3}

Millie Mildred; Millicent

Million-Acre Farm Prince Edward Island

mil m/t million metric tons

Milo (Italian—Melos)

milob military observer

milpac military personnel accounting activity

MILPERCEN Military Personnel Center

mil pers military personnel

MILPO Military Personnel Office

M.I.L.R. Master of Industrial and Labor Relations

milrep military representative

mils missile impact locator system

mil-s milling specification(s)

MILSIMS Military Standard Inventory Management System

milspec military specification

Mil-Spec Military Specification(s)

milstac military staff communication

milstam military staff memorandum

MILSTAMP Military Standard Transportation and Movement Procedures

Mil-Std (MIL-STD) Military Standard

MILSTRAP Military Standard Requisitioning and Accounting Procedures

MILSTRIP Military Standard Requisitioning and Issue Procedures

Mil Sym Milwaukee Symphony

Milt Milton

Milton Berle Milton Berlinger

Milw Milwaukee

MILW Milwaukee Route (Chicago, Milwaukee, St Paul & Pacific Railroad)

Milward Kennedy Milward Rodon Kennedy Burge

mim micro-impulse mosaic, mimeograph(ing; y)

mim (MIM) mobile interceptor missile

Mim Mimi; Miriam; Miryam (niah)

M i M Morality in Media

MIM Maintenance Instruction Manual (DoD); Material Inventory Master; Mount Isa Mines (Queensland)

MIM-3A Douglas Nike-Ajax surface-to-air missile

MIM-10 military designation of the Boeing Bomarc missile

MIM-14A Douglas surface-to-air missile called Nike Hercules and armed with a heavy-explosive or nuclear warhead

Mima Jemima

MI Mar E Member of the Institute of Marine Engineers

MIMB Malaysia International Merchant Bankers

MIME Midland Institute of Mining Engineers

MI Mech E Member of the Institution of Mechanical Engineers

mimeo mimeograph(ed)

mimic. microfilm-information master-image converter

Mimico Boys Mimico Correction Centre (for males) in Toronto, Ontario

mi/min miles per minute

mimo man in–machine out; many-input many-output (computer)

MIMR May Institute of Medical Research

mims mineral-insulated metal-sheathed (cable)

MIMS Major Item Management System

MIMS Monthly Index of Medical Specialties

mimsy miserable and flimsy

min minim; minimum; minor; minority; minute

min minore (Italian—minor); minuto (Portuguese or Spanish—minute)

Min Minister; Ministry; Minoan

Min Ministerio (Portuguese or Spanish—Ministry); *Ministro* (Portuguese or Spanish—Minister)

Mina Wilhelmina

Min Agric Ministry of Agriculture

minas (Portuguese or Spanish—mines, as in Minas Gerais)

min b/l minimum bill of lading

M-in-C Matron-in-Chief

MINCEX Ministerio de Comercio Exterior (Spanish—Ministry of Foreign Trade)

Minch ocean channel between northern Scotland and Outer Hebrides; divided into North Minch and Little Minch leading to Gulf of the Hebrides washing shores of Rum, Eigg, and Muck islands

mind. magnetic integrator neutron duplicator

Mind Mindanao

mindac miniature inertial navigation digital automatic computer

mindd minimum due date

Min Def Ministry of Defence

MINDUR Ministerio de Desarollo Urbano (Spanish—Ministry of Urban Development)

Min. E. Mining Engineer

MINE Minnesota Information Network for Educators

Mineap Minneapolis

minec military necessity

minelco miniature electronic component

mineola orange + tangerine (hybrid citrus fruit)

mineral. mineralogy

Mineral Soc Mineralogical Society

Mineral Storehouse of the Nation Canada's Hudson Bay area

Minerva (Latin—Athene)—goddess of wisdom

minex minelaying, minesweeping, and minehunting exercise

MINFAR Ministerio de las Fuerzas Armadas Revolucionarias (Spanish—Ministry of the Revolutionary Armed Forces)—Cuba

minfin minicare finish(ing)

Min Fuel Ministry of Fuel and Power

Mingaladon Rangoon, Burma's airport

Ming-Ming Immingham, England

mingy mean and stingy

Min Hous Ministry of Housing

mini minibop(per); minibra; minimum; miniskirt; miniswimsuit

MINI Minicomputer Industry National Interchange

minibop minibopper (underground slang—older child attuned to the modern scene)—*see* macrobop

minibra(s) miniature brassiere(s)—(less concealing—more revealing)

minibus miniature autobus

minicam lightweight miniature camera; miniature camera

minicane miniature hurricane

minidoc miniature documentary (radio or tv)

minimax (selecting move to) minimize maximum possible losses

Mining Baron William A Clark

MININT Ministerio del Interior (Spanish—Ministry of the Interior)

mininuke(s) miniature nuclear-explosive device(s)

minis minimum-length skirts

miniskirt(s) miniature skirt(s)—(barely covering the upper thighs)

minisym miniature symphony

minium red lead (lead oxide)

Minkies Minquier Islands (Rocks)

min/mc minimum material condition

Minn Minnesota; Minnesotan

Minne Minnesota

Minnesota Port Duluth

Minn Geol Surv Minnesota Geological Survey

Minn Hist Soc Minnesota Historical Society

Minnie Minerva; Minneapolis; Minnesota

Minn Orch Minnesota Orchestra

Minn Trib Minneapolis Tribune

Mino Ministro (Spanish—Minister, Ministry)

Minorca English place-name for Menorca

Minor Prophets of the Old Testament Hosea, Joel, Amos, Obadiah, Jonah, Micah, Nahum, Habakkuk, Zephaniah, Haggai, Zacharia, Malachi

Min P Minister Plenipotentiary

MINP Mallacoota Inlet National Park (Victoria, Australia); minpac; Mine Warfare Forces, Pacific (USN)

Min PBW Ministry of Public Building and Works

Min Plenip Minister Plenipotentiary

Min PW Ministry of Public Works

Minquiers Minquier Islands

(Rocks)—also called the Minkies

Minquiers (French—The Minkies)—semi-submerged reefs and rocks in Gulf of St Malo between Jersey and port of St Malo on the English Channel; scene of many shipwrecks

minr minimum room rate desired

Min^r Minister

Min Res Minister Residentiary

MINREX Ministerio de Relaciones Exteriores (Spanish—Ministry of Foreign Relations)

min rnfl minimum rainfall

MINRON Mine Squadron

mins minutes

mins (MINS) minor(s) in need of supervision

M Inst BE Member of the Institute of British Engineers

M Inst Met Member of the Institute of Metals

Minstrel Composer James Bland who composed *Carry Me Back to Old Virginny*

M Inst SP Member of the Institution of Sewage Purification

MINTACTS Mobile Integrated Telemetry and Tracking System

Min Tech Ministry of Technology

mintie minimum test instrumentation equipment

min till. minimum tillage

M. Int. Med. Master of Internal Medicine

min trq minimum torque

Minute Chopin's Waltz in D flat (opus 64, no. 1)

Minuteman solid-fuel intercontinental ballistic missile produced by Boeing

Minuteman III America's most advanced icbm in 1979

MINWR Merritt Island National Wildlife Refuge (Florida)

min wt minimum weight

Minx of the Movies Betty Compson

mio meteoritic impact origin; minimum identifiable odor

MIO Marine Inspection Office; Metric Information Office; Mobile Issuing Office; Movements Identification Order

Mioc Miocene

MIOUDO Museo del Instituto Oceanografico de la Universidad de Oriente (Museum of the Oceanographic Institute of the University of Oriente)

mip magnetic-induced polariza-

tion; malleable iron pipe; marine insurance policy; mean indicated pressure; missile impact predictor; modulated interference plan; monthly investment plan; mortgage insurance premium(s)

MIP Manufacturers of Illumination Products; Marine Interdiction Program; Material Improvement Program; Metals Investigation Proprietary; Methods Improvement Program; Military Improvement Program

mipe modular information-processing equipment

mipir missile precision instrumentation radar

MIPL Mauritius Institute Public Library (Port Louis)

mip/ma missile in place/missile away

MIPO Multiple Item Purchase Order

Miporn Miami pornography (FBI investigation's code name covering billion-dollar pornographic racket)

MIPR Member of the Institute of Public Relations; Military Interdepartmental Purchase Request

MIPRO Manufactured Imports Promotion Organization (of Japan)

mips million instructions per second

MIPS Modular Integrated Pallet System

MIPTC Men's International Professional Tennis Council

Mipu Mikropunkt (German—microdot)—World-War-II masterpiece of espionage technique assuring transmission of microscopic messages no bigger than a dot

Miq Maiquetia (Venezuela's principal airport serving Caracas, La Guaira, and many other places)

mir memory information register; mirror; music information retrieval

M Ir Middle Irish

MIR Manufacturing Inspection Record; Medical Inspection Room; Missile Intelligence Report; Movement for International Reconciliation

MIR Movimiento de Izquierda Revolucionaria (Spanish—Movement of the Revolutionary Left)—active in Bolivia, Chile, Ecuador, Peru, and

Venezuela

MIRA Motor Industry's Research Association

MIRA Monthly Index of Russian Accessions

mirac microfilmed reports and accounts

MIRAC Management Information Research Assistance Center

miracl mid-infrared advanced chemical laser

Miracle Haydn's Symphony No. 96 in D major

Miracle of Fifth Avenue Guggenheim Museum

Miracle of Nature Queen Christina of Sweden

mirad monostatic infrared intrusion detector

MIRADS Marshall Information Retrieval and Display System

Mirage all-weather delta-wing supersonic-jet ground-support interceptor built by Dassault in France (Mirage III)

Mirage IV atomic-bomber version of the foregoing Mirage III

MIRC Member of the Idle Rich Class

mird medium internal radiation dose

MIRE Media Information Research Exchange; Member of the Institution of Radio Engineers

mirfac mathematics in recognizable form automatically compiled

Miri Miranda; Miriam(ne)(ah)

MIRINZ Meat Industry Research Institute of New Zealand

mirl medium-intensity runway lights

MIRPL Major Item Repair Parts List

MIRR Materials Inspection and Receiving Report

mirv multiple independent reentry vehicle

mirv (MIRV) multiple independently-targeted reentry vehicle (warhead)

mirving fitting missiles with multiple warheads

mis metal insulator semiconductor; miscarriage; missing; mistake(n)

Mis. Miserere (Latin—have mercy)

MIS Management Information Services; Management Information System; Master Integrated Schedule; Material Inspection Service; Met Path Information System; Migrant Information Service; Military Intelligence Service; mine issuing ship (naval symbol); Minstrel Instruction Society; Modified Initial System

M.I.S. Master of International Service

MISAA Middle-Income Student Assistance Act

mis. accur. misce accuratissme (Latin—mix very intimately)

misc miscarriage; miscellaneous; miscible

MISC Malaysian International Shipping Corporation

mis. caute misce caute (Latin—mix cautiously)

miscend. miscendus (Latin—to be mixed)

miscg miscarriage

Mischa (Russian nickname—Michael)—Mike

Mischa Auer Mischa Ounskowsky

miscld miscalculated

miscln miscalculation

miscon misconduct

miscy miscellaneously

mis doc miscellaneous documents

MISE Member of the Institution of Sanitary Engineers

miser. microwave space relay

MISER Management Information System for Expenditure Reporting; Methodology of Industrial System Energy Requirements; Moorfields Information System Exception Reporting

mis. et seg. misce et signa (Latin—mix and write a label)

misg missing

MISHAP Missile High-Speed Assembly Program

MISI Member of the Iron and Steel Institute

Misisipi (Spanish—Mississippi)

MISLIC Mid-Staffordshire Libraries in Cooperation

mis. mei miserere mei (Latin—have mercy on me)

misn misnumbered; mistaken

MISO Military Intelligence Service Organization

MISP Member of the Institution of Sewage Purification

mispo mission summary printout

Misr (Arabic—Egypt)

M I Sr Muy Ilustre Señor (Spanish—Very Illustrious Sir)

MISR Macauley Institute for Soil Research; Major Item Status Report; Material Item Status Report(ing)

miss. mission; missionary

Miss. Mississippi; Mississippian

MISS Management and Information System Staff; Man In Space Soonest; Medical Information Science Section; Mississippi

Missie Miss; Mississippi; Missus; Mrs.

missilese engineering jargon of guided-missile experts

missilex missile firing exercise

Missini Mussolini's neo-fascist followers

Missionary to the Lepers Father Damien

MISSIS Mississippi Student Information System

Mississippi Ports (east to West) Pascagoula, Biloxi, Gulfport

Mississippi River Painter George Caleb Bingham

Miss New Orleans Dorothy Lamour's title in 1931

Miss Tarbarrel Ida M. Tarbell

missy missionary

mist. mistura (Latin—mixture)

Mist Mistress

MIST Manchester Institute of Science and Technology; Medical Information Service (via) Telephone

Mistletoe Oklahoma state flower

mistr management of items subsequent to repair

MISTRAM Missile Trajectory Measurement System

mistrans mistranslation

Mistress of Mystery Agatha Christie

Mistress of the North the Baltic Sea, Russia, and Sweden have been awarded this title

misudstd misunderstand

misudstdg misunderstanding

misudstod misunderstood

Misuri (Spanish—Missouri)

mit master instruction tape; milled in transit; minimum individual training; mono-iodo-tyrosine

mit. mitte (Latin—send)

Mit Mittwoch (German—Wednesday)

M i T Made in Taiwan

M It Middle Italian

MIT Mara Institute of Technology (Kuala Lumpur); Maritime Institute of Technology; Massachusetts Institute of Technology (M.I.T. preferred as periods set it apart from all other MITs); Massachusetts Investors Trust; Materials Interaction Test(s); Military Intelligence Translator; Milwaukee Institute of Technology; Miracidial Immobilization Test

M.I.T. Massachusetts Institute of Technology

MITAGS Marine Institute of Technology and Graduate Studies

MITC Magdalen Island Transportation Company

Mitch Mitchell; Richard Mitchell

Mitchell B-25 World-War-II Bomber named in honor of General William (Billy) Mitchell who in 1925 was courtmartialed and convicted for criticizing the mismanagement of the aviation service in the U.S. Army and Navy

Mitchellville Girls Iowa School for (delinquent) Girls at Mitchellville

mite. master instrumentation timing equipment

MITERS Minor Traffic Engineering and Road Safety Improvements

MITGS Marine Institute of Technology and Graduate Studies

MITI Ministry of International Trade and Industry; Ministry of International Trade and Industry (Japan); Ministry of International Trade and Investment (Japan)

mit insuf mitral insufficiency

mito minimum interval takeoff; miscellaneous tool

mito (Latin prefix—thread)—mitosis

ml tp miniature template

MITRE Massachusetts Institute of Technology Research Establishment

Mitropa Mitteleuropäische Schlafund Speisewagen Aktiengesellschaft (Middle-European Sleeping Car and Dining Car Company)

MITS Missouri-Illinois Traffic Service

mit. sang. mitte sanguinem (Latin—bleed)

Mitsubishi Mitsubishi Bank; Mitsubishi Corporation; Mitsubishi International Corporation

mitt mittente (Italian—sender)

Mitt Mitteilungen (German—communications)

MITT Management Implications of Team Teaching

mit. tal. mitte tales (Latin—send such)

Mittelländisches Meer (German—Mediterranean Sea)

Mittelmeer (German—Mediterranean)

mitt(s) mitten(s)

Mitya (Russian diminutive—Dmitri)

mitz mitzvah (Yiddish from Hebrew *miswah*—a good deed)

Mitzi Margaret

MIU Maharishi International University; Micronesian Insurance Underwriters

MIV Moody's Investor Service (stock exchange symbol)

MIWE Member of the Institution of Water Engineers

MIWMA Member of the Institute of Weights and Measures Administration

mix. mixture

mixt mixture

Mizrachi Merkaz Ruchani (Hebrew—Spiritual Center)—orthodox organization

mizzle mist + drizzle

Mizzou Missouri

mj marijuana; megajoule

mJ millijoule

MJ Mary Jane (underground slang)—marijuana; megajoule

M.J. Master of Journalism

M & J sexologists William Masters and Virginia Johnson

MJA Manuel José Arce; Mortimer J(erome) Adler

MJC Manatee Junior College; Masters and Johnson Center; Metropolitan Junior College; Moberly Junior College

MJCA Mississippi Junior College Association

mjd management job description

mjg management job guide

MJI Member of the Journalists Institute

MJ/kg megajoules per kilogram

MJme megajoules metabolizable energy

MJQ Modern Jazz Quartet

MJS Member of the Japan Society

MJV Mojud Hosiery (stock exchange symbol)

mk mark (British equivalent of type)

mk (MK) master clock

mK millikelvin(s)

Mk Mark; markka (Finnish monetary unit)

Mk Manualkoppler (German—manual coupler)—organ

MK Mackey Airlines; Member of Knesset; Mishima-Kisumi (steel company)

M-K Morrison-Knudsen

M/K Member of the Knesset

Mk₃nbc Mark 3 nuclear, biological, chemical (coverall suit)

MKC Kansas City, Missouri (airport)

mkd marked

MKE Milwaukee, Wisconsin (airport)

mkg meter kilogram

MKGM Milli Kütüphane Genel Müdürlügü (Turkish—National Library General Directorate)—Ankara

MKH Mackintosh-Hemphill (stock-exchange symbol)

MKK Mitsubishi Kakoki Kaishi

mkm marksman

Mkm Mohammedan-killed meat

MKM Manawatu Knitting Mills

MKNP Malawi Kasungu National Park (Malawi); Mount Kenya National Park (Kenya)

MKO Mauna Kea Observatory; Muskogee Company (stock exchange symbol)

MKPL Modification Kit Parts List

mkr marker

mkr mikroskopisch (German—microscopic)

Mkr million Swedish kroner

MKR Mkuzi Game Reserve (South Africa)

mks meter, kilogram, solar second system of fundamental standards

mksa meter, kilogram, second, ampere system

mkt market

Mkt Market

MKT Missouri-Kansas-Texas (railroad)

mktg marketing

mktl marketable

Mkt Mgr Marketing Manager

mk tp mark template

MKU Mary Kathleen Uranium (Australian firm)

MKW Military Knight of Windsor

MKY McKee and Company (stock-exchange symbol)

ml machine language; mean level; millilambert(s); milliliter(s); mine layer; mixed lengths; mold line; molder; money list; mother language;

motor launch; muzzle-loading

ml (ML) maximum load

m/l middle left; missile lift

m:l monocyte-lymphocyte (ratio)

m or l more or less

μl microliter

ml moneda legal (Spanish—legal tender)

m/l mi letra (Spanish—my letter)

mL millilambert(s)

Ml Malay; Malaya; Malayan; Malaysia; Manuel; marl

ML Manuel; Maori Land; Martin-Marietta (stock exchange symbol); Micro Log; Middle Latin; Military Liaison; minelayer; Mineral Lease; Missile Launcher; Mitchell Library; motor launch; small minesweeper (naval symbol)

ML (Ec) Ecclesiastic Middle Latin

M/L Maersk Line

M.L. Medicinae Licentiatus (Latin—Licentiate in Medicine)

mla magnetic lens assembly; manpack loop antenna; microwave linear accelerator

MLA Maine Library Association; Maintenance Level Analysis; Manitoba Library Association; Marine Librarians Association; Maryland Library Association; Massachusetts Library Association; Master Locksmiths Association; Medical Library Association; Member of the Landlord's Association; Member of the Legislative Assembly; Michigan Library Association; Minnesota Library Association; Mississippi Library Association; Missouri Library Association; Modern Language Association; Montana Library Association; Music Library Association

M-LA Mont-Laurier Aviation

M.L.A. Master of Landscape Architecture

MLAA Modern Language Association of America

m'lady my lady

mlaf missile-loading alignment fixture

ml ar mill arbor

M. L. Arch. Master of Landscape Architecture

mlases molasses

MLAT Modern Language Aptitude Test

mlb multilinear board

mlb (MLB) major league baseball

MLB Marginal Lands Board; Maritime Labor Board; Multiple Listing Board; Multiple Listing Bureau

mlbf mean life before failure

mlbm (MLBM) modern large ballistic missile

Mlbo Malabo (formerly Santa Isabel)

MLBPA Major League Baseball Players Association

mlc machine level control; machine location card; main lobe clutter; mesh level control; microelectric logic circuit; missile launch computer (MLC); mixed leucocyte culture; motor load control; multilayer circuit; multilens camera; multiplanar chain link

MLC Maori Land Court; Meat and Livestock Commission; Member of the Legislative Council; Military Liaison Committee; Mutual Life and Citizens (insurance company)

mlca machine level control address

MLCAEC Military Liaison Committee to the Atomic Energy Commission

ml cu mill cutter

mld mailed; middle landing; minimum lethal dose; minimum line of detection, molded

mld (MLD) metachromatic leukodystrophy

MLD Missile Launch(ing) Detection

mld₅₀ minimum lethal (radioactive) dose

M. L. Des. Master of Landscape Design

mldg moulding

mldr molder

mle maximum likelihood estimate; maximum loss expectancy; microprocessor language editor

mle *modèle* (French—model, pattern)

Mle Mile (postal abbreviation)

M. L. Eng. Master of Landscape Engineering

MLES Multiple-Line Encryption System

MLEU *Mouvement Libéral pour l'Europe Unie* (French—Liberal Movement for a United Europe)

mlf media language and format

m/lf medium/low frequency

MLF Mobile Land Force(s);

motor launch, fast (naval symbol); Multi-Lateral Force

MLF *Mouvement de Libération de la Femme* (French—Feminine Liberation Movement)

ml fx mill fixture

mlg mailing; main landing gear; most languages

MLG Middle Low German

mlge mileage

mlg(s) mailing(s)

mlgt marine light

MI'H Musée de l'Homme, Paris

MLHA Master Ladies Hairdressers Association

mlhw mean lower high water

mli minimum line of interception

M-Li Muller-Lyer (illusion)

M. Lib. Master of Librarianship

M. Lib. Sci. Master of Library Science

MLIRB Multi-Line Insurance Rating Bureau

M. Lit. Master of Letters; Master of Literature

MLL Manchester Lines Ltd; Music Lovers League

Mlle *Mademoiselle* (French—Miss)

Mlles *Mesdemoiselles* (French—Misses)

mllw mean lower low water

mllws mean lower low water springs

mlm million locomotive miles

MLMA Metal Lath Manufacturers Association

mln million

Mln Milan

MLN *Movimiento de Liberacion Nacional* (Spanish—National Liberation Movement) —Uruguayan Tupamaros terrorists

MLNP Malawi Lengwe National Park

mlnr milliner

MLNR Ministry of Land and Natural Resources

MLNS Ministry of Labour and National Service

MLNWR Medicine Lake National Wildlife Refuge (Montana)

MLO Midland Light Orchestra; Military Liaison Office(r)

m'lord my lord

Mloth Midlothian

M Low G Middle Low German

mlp metal lath and plaster; multiple-line printing

m.l.p. *mento-laeva posterior* (Latin—left mento-posterior)

MLP Master Logistics Plan

mlpwb multilayered printed wiring board

MLQ *Modern Language Quarterly*

mlr main line of resistance; minimum lending rate; mortar-locating radar; multiple linear regression; multiple-line reading; multiple-location risk; muzzle-loading rifle

mlr (MLR) minimum lending rate; missile launch(ing) response; mixed lymphocyte response

m-l r muzzle-loading rifle

MLR Main Line Rail(way); Marine Life Resources (program)

MLR *Modern Labor Review*; *Modern Law Review*

MLRB Master Logistics Review Board; Mutual Loss Research Bureau

mlrc multi-level railway car

m-l rg muzzle-loading rifled gun

MLRP Marine Life Research Program

MLRS Multiple Launch(ing) Rocket System

mls machine literature search(ing); median longitudinal section; medium life span; medium long shot; milliliters

ml's magnetically levitated railroad trains

ml's (MLs) mine layers

Mls Mills (postal abbreviation)

MLS Microwave Landing System; Moon Landing Site (attained by two men from spacecraft Apollo XI on July 20, 1969); Multiple Listing Service

M.L.S. Master of Library Science

M & LS Manistique & Lake Superior (railroad)

mlsc measured logistic support cast

MLSU Moscow MV Lomonosov State University (University of Moscow)

mlt mean low tide; median lethal (radioactive) time (MLT)

mlt (MLT) master library tape; median lethal (radioactive) time

Mlt Malta

mltl mean low tide line

mltn 1000 long tons

mltu missile loop test unit

mlty military

mlu mean length of utterance

m'lud my lord

mlv membrane light valve; murine leukemia virus

mlv(M) murine leukemia virus (Moloney)

mlv(R) murine leukemia virus (Rauscher)

ml vs mill vise

mlw maximum landing weight; mean low water; medium-level waste

MLW Monrovia, Liberia (airport)

M.L.W. Master of Labour Welfare

mlwli mean low water lunitidal interval

mlwn mean low water neaps

mlws mean low water springs; minimum level water stand

mlx millilux

mly multiply

MLYC Moosehead Lake Yacht Club

mm made merchantable; megameter(s); merchant marine; middle marker; millimeter(s); millimicron; mismated; modified mercalli (scale); mucous membrane

mμ millimicron(s)

m'm madam

m/m millimeter(s)—small-arms ammunition term meaning the diameter of a weapon's bore expressed in millimeters

m & m make and mend

μm micrometer; micron(s)

mm med mera (Swedish—and so forth, etc.)

m.m. *mutatis mutandis* (Latin—with the necessary changes)

mM millimole; millimore

m/M male Mexican

μM micromole(s)

Mm *Martyres* (Greek—witnesses, martyrs)

MM Maaster Mason; Machinist's Mate; Maintenance Manual; Majesties; Manufacturing Manual; Marilyn Monroe; Marine Midland (stock exchange symbol); Martyres (martyrs); Maryknoll Missionary; Material Management; maximum misfit; Medal of Merit; Medal of Merit; mercantile marine; merchant marine; Messageries Maritimes; Messieurs (French—gentlemen); Metropolitan Museum; Military Medal; Minister of Munitions; Moral Majority

M-M Marshall-Marchetti

M.M. Master of Music

M/M Mr and Mr; Mr and Mrs; Mr and Ms; Mrs and Mrs; Mrs and Ms

M & M Merton and Morden

M of M Ministry of Munitions; Museum of Man

MM *Marine Marchande* (French—Merchant Marine); *Modern Medicine*

M.M. *Maelzel's Metronome*

M & M Morbidity and Mortality (Center for Disease Control's weekly report)

mm^2 square millimeter(s)

mm^3 cubic millimeter(s)

mma major maladjustment; multiple module access

MMA Maine Maritime Academy; Malaysia Medical Association; Massachusetts Maritime Academy; Material Manufacturing Authorization; Merchandise Marks Act; Metropolitan Museum of Art; Missile Maintenance Area; Monorail Manufacturers Association; Museum of Modern Art; Music Masters Association

MM of A Minute Men of America

mmac multiple model adaptive control

MMAC Material Management Aggregate Code

MMAJ Metal Mining Agency of Japan

MMAL Mitsubishi Motors Australia, Ltd

MMAS Manufacturing Management Accounting System

M. Math. Master of Mathematics

MMB Marine Midland Bank; Milk Marketing Board; Mitsui Manufacturers Bank

mm bat main missile battery

MMBC Maryland Motor Boat Club

mmbd million barrels per day

mmBtu/hr million Btu's per hour

mmc marine moisture control; maximum metal condition

MMC Malaysian Marketing Corporation; Malaysian Mining Corporation; Marine Moisture Control; Materiel Management Code; Meharry Medical College; Mitsubishi Motors Corporation

MMCB Midwest Motor Carriers Bureau

mmcfpd million cubic feet (of gas) per day

MMcKNP Mount McKinley National Park (Alaska)

MMCL Major Missile Component List(ing)

MMCNY Marine Museum of the City of New York

mmc's money-market certificates

MMCT maritime mobile coastal telegraphy

mmd mass median diameter; master monitor display

MMD minelayer, fast (naval ship symbol)

m mde *marine marchande* (French—merchant marine)

mme maximum maintenance effort

Mme *Madame* (French—Missus)

MME Manned Mars Expedition

M.M.E. Master of Mechanical Engineering; Master of Music Education

M. Mech. Eng. Master of Mechanical Engineering

M. Med. Master of Medicine

MMEG Meter Manufacturers' Export Group

Mmes *Mesdames* (French—ladies)

M. Met Master of Metallurgy

M. Met. E. Master of Metallurgical Engineering

mmf magnetomotive force; micromicrofarad

$\mu\mu$F micromicrofarad(s)

MMF fleet mine layer (naval symbol); Maggio Musicale Fiorentino (Florence May Festival); Milbank Memorial Fund

MMFA Montreal Museum of Fine Arts

mmfds microfarads

MMFI Moravian Music Foundation, Incorporated

MMFPI Man-Made Fiber Producers Institute

mmg medium machine gun

MMGR Masai Mara Game Reserve (Kenya)

MMGS Mount Muhavura Gorilla Sanctuary (Uganda)

M.Mgt.Eng. Master of Management Engineering

mmh/fh maintenance manhours per flight hour

mmHg millimeter of mercury

mmi management and maintenance inspection; microphage migration inhibition; modified mercalli intensity

Mmi Miami

MMI Malaysian Marine Industries; Manufacturers Mutual Insurance; Micro-Magnetic Industries; Moslem Mosque Incorporated (formerly American Mohammedan Society)

M. Mic. Master of Microbiology

M. Mi. Eng. Master of Mining Engineering

MMIJ Mining and Metallurgical Institute of Japan

MMIS Medicaid Management Information System

MMJC Meridian Municipal Junior College

m mk material mark

mml multimaterial laminate

mm/l millimols per liter

MMLES Map-Match Location-Estimation System

MMLME Mediterranean, Mediterranean Littoral, and/or Middle East (sector of conflict)

mmm merchandising, marketing, management; military medical mobilization; millimicron(s)

MMM Mauritian Militant Movement; Minerals, Mining, and Metallurgy; Modern Music Masters

MMM *Membre de l'Ordre du Mérite Militaire* (French—Member of the Order of Military Merit)

MMMA Maine Merchant Marine Academy; Metalforming Machinery Makers Association

MMMC Medical Materiel Management Center

MMMF Multinational-Mixed Manned Force(s)

mmm/fhr maintenance man minutes per flight hour

mmmrpv (MMMRPV) modular multi-mission remotely piloted vehicle

M-m M's Mohammed-muddled Muslims (who murder and terrorize in the name of the Arabian prophet Mohammed)

MMMS Modern Music Masters Society

MMM & SA Master Monumental Masons and Sculptors Association

MMN Museum of Man and Nature (Winnipeg)

MMNP Mount McKinley National Park (Alaska)

Mmo Malmö

MMO Maine Meteorological Office; Music Minus One

MMOB Military Money Order Branch

MMOW Machinist's Mate of the Watch (USN)

mmp (MMP) maritime mobile phone

MMP Major Medical Plan(ning); Masters, Mates and Pilots (union)

MM & P Masters, Mates and Pilots

MMPA Marine Mammal Protection Act; Midland Master Printers' Alliance

MMPC maritime mobile phone coastal

MMPDC maritime mobile phone distress and calling

MMPI Minnesota Multiphase Personality Inventory

MMPNC Medical Materiel Program for Nuclear Casualties

mmpp millimeters partial pressure

MMPP Moose Mountain Provincial Park (Saskatchewan)

mmq minimum manufacturing quality

mmr mass miniature radiography; minimum maintenance requirement

mm & r maintenance modification(s) and repair(s)

MMR Main Machinery Room (USN); Mass Media Research; Method of Mixed Ranges

MMRA Maritime Marshland Rehabilitation Administration (Canada)

MMRB Master Material Review Board

mmrbm (MMRBM) mobile medium-range ballistic missile

MMS Manpower Management System; Mass Memory System; Metabolic Monitoring System; Microfiche Management System; Mobile Monitoring System; Modulation Measuring System; motor minesweeper; multimission ship (naval symbol); Multiplex Modulation System

M.M.S. Master of Management Studies; Master of Medical Science

MMSA Mining and Metallurgical Society of America

M.M.S.A. Master (Mistress) of Midwifery of the Society of Apothecaries

MMSC Mediterranean Marine Sorting Center

mmscfd million standard cubic feet per day

m&m session morbidity and mortality session

MMSR Master Material Source Record

MMSS Missile Motion Subsystem

MMSW Mine, Mill and Smelter Workers (union)

mmt manual muscle test(ing); maritime mobile telegraphy; memory test(er); missile mate test(ing); multicomponent mass transport; multiple-mirror telescope

MMT Manual Muscle Test; maritime mobile telegraphy

MMTC maritime mobile telegraphy calling

MMTDC maritime mobile telegraphy distress and calling

MMTP Methadone Maintenance Treatment Program

mmtv mouse mammary tumor virus; murine mammary tumor virus

mmu millimass unit(s)

MMU Manned Maneuvering Unit; McMaster University

M.Mus. Master of Music

MM&W McKim, Mead & Wright (American architects)

MMWD Marin Municipal Water District

mmx memory multiplexer

mmy military man years

MMY *Mental Measurements Yearbook*

mn manual; million

m(n) microfilm negative

mn *maison* (French—house)

m.n. *mutato nomine* (Latin—the name being changed)

m/n *moneda nacional* (Spanish—national currency)

Mn Main; manganese

MN Magnetic North; meganewtons; Merchant Navy

M.N. Master of Nursing

MN *Magyar Nepkoztarsasag* (Hungarian—People's Republic); *Musee Nationale* (French—National Museum)

mna (MNA) multi-network area (tv)

MNA Matematikmaskinnämnden (Swedish Computing Machinery Board); Multi-National Account(s)

M.N.A. Master of Nursing Administration

MNAG Museo Nacional de Antropología, Guatemala

MNAM Museo Nacional de Antropología, Mexico

MNAOA Merchant Navy and Airline Officers' Association

M. N. Arch. Master of Naval Architecture

MNAs Members of the National Assembly (Québec)

MNAS Member of the National Academy of Sciences; Military

Navigational Aids System

Mnasi Mnasidika

MNB Macias Nguema Biyogo (formerly Fernando Po); Moscow Narodny Bank

M-N BA Multi-National Business Association

MNC Major NATO Commanders; Media News Corporation; Multinational Corporation

mncpef meaning not clear; please explain fully

MNCR Mouvement National Contre le Racisme (French—National Movement Against Racism)

MNCRR Metro-North Commuter Railroad

mnc's multinational corporations

MNCS Multipoint Network Control System

mnd minimum necrosing dose

Mnd Mound (postal abbreviation)

MND Ministry of National Defence

mndth mean depth

MNDTS Member of the Non-Destructive Testing Society

M.N.E. Master of Nuclear Engineering

MNEA Merchant Navy Establishment Administration

mnem mnemonic

Mnemo Mnemosyne (goddess of memory and mother of the nine muses)

mnemon minimum unit of information; mnemoneutic(al)(ly); mnemonic(al)(ist); mnemonician(s); mnemonicon; mnemonic(s); mnemonist(s); mnemonization(al)(ly); mnemonize(r); mnemotechnic(al)(ly); mnemoteechny

mnemonic hormone vasopressin (reported to improve the memory if sniffed or sprayed into each nostril every day for three days)

M. N. Eng. Master of Naval Engineering

MNF Menagasha National Forest (Ethiopia); Multilateral Nuclear Force (NATO navy)

mnfe missile not fully equipped

mnfg manufacturing

MNFP Multi-National Fighter Program

mnfrs manufacturers

mng managing; meaning

Mng Mongolia(n)

mnging managing

mngt midnight

MNH Museum of Natural History (Smithsonian)

MNI Malaysian National Insurance

MNIMH Member of the National Institute of Medical Herbalists

mnl marine navigating light

Mnl Manila; Manuel

MNL Main North Line; Manila, Philippines (airport)

MNLF Malayan National Liberation Front; Moro National Liberation Front

MNLL Malaysian National Liberation League

MNLO Merchant Navy Liaison Officer

mnls modified new least squares

MNLS Marine Navigating Light System

mnm minimum; mnemonic (*see* mnemon)

MNM Museum of New Mexico

MNNP Malawi Nyika National Park

M-note $1000 bill

MNP Malay National Party; Marsabit National Park (Kenya); Meru National Park (equatorial Kenya); Mikumi National Park (Tanzania); Mushandike National Park (Rhodesia)

MNPL Machinist Non-Partisan Political League

mnpo main port

MNPS Minimum Navigational Performance Specification

mnpz monopolize

mnpzd monopolized

mnpzg monopolizing

mnpzn monopolization

mnr massive nuclear retaliation; mean neap rise

Mnr Manor

MNR Movimiento Nacionalista Revolucionario (Spanish—National Revolutionary Movement)

MNRU Medical Neuropsychiatric Research Unit

mns metal-nitride-semiconductor (transistor)

Mns Manaus; Mines (postal abbreviation)

M.N.S. Master of Nutritional Science

M. N. Sc. Master of Nursing Science

m'ns'l mainsail

Mnstr Munster

mnt mean neap tide

MNT Minnesota and Ontario Paper (stock exchange symbol)

mntmp minimum temperature

mntn maintain; maintenance

mntnc maintenance

mntnd maintained

mntng maintaining

MNTO Moroccan National Tourist Office

mntr monitor

MNU Maniti Sugar (stock exchange symbol)

M.Nurs. Master of Nursing

MNV Marion Power Shovel (stock exchange symbol)

MNWEB Merseyside and North Wales Electricity Board

MNWR Malheur National Wildlife Refuge (Oregon); Mattamuskeet NWR (North Carolina); Merced NWR (California); Mingo NWR (Missouri); Minidoka NWR (Idaho); Mississiquoi NWR (Vermont); Modoc NWR (California); Montezuma NWR (New York); Moosehorn NWR (Maine)

mnx (short-order slang contraction—ham and eggs)

Mnzlo Manzanillo

mo mail order; manual operation; manually operated; mass observation; master oscillator; method of operation; moment; money order(s); monthlies; monthly; month(s); motor operated; mustered out

mo (MO) molecular orbital

mo' more; morning

m-o months old

m/o maintenance-to-operation (ratio)

m & o maintenance and overhaul(ing); management and organization

m.o. modus operandi (Latin—manner, method, or mode of operating, way of working)

m/o mi orden (Spanish—my order)

m/O male Oriental

Mo Missouri; Missourian; molybdenum; Morris; Moselle; Moses; Mozelle

Mo' Moses

Mo Maestro (Italian—master, title given any great artist, composer, conductor, or teacher)

MO Mail Order; Marketing Organization; Mass Observation; Medical Officer; Meteorological Office; Mobile Station; Mohawk Airlines (2-letter coding); Money Order; Monthly

Order; Morale Branch (of Secret Service); Movement Order(s); Municipal Office(r)

M-O Morris-Oxford

M & O Muscat and Oran

moa. medium observation aircraft; minute of angle; missile optical alignment; mud on airstrip

M o A Memorandum of Agreement

MOA Marine Office of America; Metropolitan Oakland Area; Metropolitan Opera Association; Military Operations Area; Ministry of Aviation; Minnesota Orchestral Association; Municipal Officers Association; Music Operators of America

Moabit Berlin's great prison

MOADS Montgomery Air Defense Sector

MOAMA Mobile Air Materiel Area

MOARS Mobilization Assignment Reserve Section

moat. missile-on-aircraft test(ing)

moAt mainstream of American thought

mob. make or buy; mobile; mobilization; mobilize(d)

mob. *mobile vulgus* (Latin—disorderly group of people)

Mob Mobile, Alabama (maritime abbreviation)

MOB Main Operating Base, Mobile, Alabama (airport); Montreux-Oberland-Bernois (railway)

Mo' Bay Mobile Bay, Alabama; Montego Bay, Jamaica

mobcom mobile communications

MOBCOM Mobile Command (Canadian)

mobeu mobile emergency unit

MOBIDACS Mobile Data Acquisition System

mobidic mobile digital computer

mobil mobility

Mobila (Spanish—Mobile)

mobilarian mobile branch librarian

mobilary mobile library

mobiles motion sculptures (plastic forms in motion)

Mobil Wl Mobil World

mobl macro-oriented business language; macro-oriented business language

mobl *möbliert* (German—furnished)

moblas mobile laser satellite

tracking station

mob lib mobile librarian; mobile library

mob lt man overboard and breakdown light

mobot(s) mobile robot(s)

MOBS Mobile Ocean Basing System; Multiple Orbit Bombardment System

MOBTA Mobilization Table of Distribution and Allowances

Mobtown Baltimore, Maryland

mobula model-building language

moc manufacturing other charges; master operation(al) control(ling); mission operations computer; mocassin

MOC Makapuu Oceanic Center (Hawaii); Mauna Olu College (Maui)

moca minimum obstruction clearance altitude

MOCA Museum of Contemporary Art

Moçambique (Portuguese—Mozambique)

mocamp motor camp; motorists camp

MOCCC Massachusetts Organized Crime Control Council

MOCI Ministry of Commerce and Industry

Mo City Motor City (Detroit)

Mockingbird state bird of Arkansas; symbolic nickname given many of its citizens called Mockingbirds

mocktail(s) mock cocktail(s)—free from alcohol

MoCom Mobile Command

MOCOM Mobile Command (US Army)

mocp missile out of commission for parts

mocr mission operation control room

mocs mocassins

mod manned orbital development (MOD); mesial-occlusal-distal (dental cavities); model; moderate; modern; modernize(d); modification; modify; modular; module

m-o-d mesial-occlusal-distal (inlay)

Mod Modern

M o D Ministry of Defence (British)

MOD Mail Order Department; Medical Officer of the Day; Ministry of Defense; Ministry of Overseas Development; Miscellaneous Obligation Document

modasm modular air-to-surface

missile

m-o-d-b mesial-occlusal-distal-buccal (inlay)

modcom modernity commercialized

mod cons modern conveniences

mod-cons modern-construction houses

moddem modulator-demodulator

mod/demod modulate-demodulate; modulating-demodulating (units)

ModE Modern English

MODE Mid-Ocean Dynamic Experiment

Model-A worthy successor to the Model-T Ford

Model Republic Orange Free State's nickname

Model-T planetary-gear Model-T Ford automobile once the world's most popular vehicle despite its handcranking starter and its nickname—Tin Lizzie

modem modulating-demodulating; modulator-demodulator

moderm modulator-demodulator

Modern Antigone Maria Thérèse—daughter of Louis XVI

Modernizer of Navigation Lieutenant Matthew Fontaine Maury, USN

Modern Lib Modern Library

Modern Liberal Social Philosopher José Ortega y Gasset

Modern Mother of Presidents Ohio—birthplace of Presidents Grant, Hayes, Garfield, Benjamin Harrison, McKinley, Taft, Harding; (*see* Mother of Presidents)

Modern Nihilist Jean Genet

modf modification; modify

ModGr Modern Greek

ModHeb Modern Hebrew

mod/iran modification, inspection, and repair as necessary

ModL Modern Latin

modo. *moderato* (Italian—moderately)

mod. pres. *modo prescripto* (Latin—in the manner prescribed)

modr moderate room rate desired

mods mesial-occlusal-distal (dental cavities); models; moderates; moderators; moderns; modification; modifiers; modulators; modules

MODS Manned Orbital Development Station (or System);

Manned Orbiting Development Station (or System); Medically Oriented Data System
moe measure of effectiveness
Moe Moses
M o E Ministry of Energy
MOE Major Organizational Entity
MOEA Ministry of Economic Affairs
Moezel (Dutch—Moselle)
mof maximum observed frequency; member of (the police) force; metal oxide film
M o F Ministry of Finance
MOF Ministry of Food
mo' fr mother fucker
Mog Margaret
MOG Metropolitan Opera Guild
M.O.G. Master of Obstetrics and Gynaecology
mogas motor gasoline
moh material overhead; maximum operating hours
M o H Ministry of Health
MOH Medical Officer of Health; Ministry of Health; Mohawk Airlines
Moham Mohammedan
Mohammed Ali Cassius Clay
MOHATS Mobile Overland Hauling and Transport System (USAF)
μohm microhm
mohms milliohms
moho Mohorovicic discontinuity
Mohole a hole to the Mohorovicic discontinuity, the boundary between the earth's crust and mantle
mohs mud, oil, hooks, slings (oil well insurance)
moi maximum obtainable irradiance; military occupational information; multiplicity of infection
MOI Military Operations and Intelligence; Ministry of Information
MOIC Medical Officer in Command
M.O.I.G. Master of Occupational Information and Guidance
moip missile on internal power
MOIS Minnesota Occupational Information System
Moish Moishe
moiv mechanically operated inlet valve
Mojave Sikorsky heavy helicopter designated H-37
Mok Mokpo
MOK Mohawk Carpet Mills

(stock exchange symbol)
mol machine-oriented language; molecular; molecule
mol. mollis (Latin—soft)
Mol Mollendo
M o L Minister of Labour; Ministry of Labour
MOL Manned Orbiting Laboratory; Mitsui-OSK Lines
M.O.L. Master (Mistress) of Oriental Languages
molab mobile laboratory
MOLAB Mobile Lunar Laboratory
Mol Crys Liq Crys Molecular Crystals and Liquid Crystals
Moldau (German—Vltava)—Bohemian river flowing into the Elbe
MOLDS Management On-Line Data System
Moldv Moldavia; Moldavian
mole. molecular; molecule
molecom molecularized computer
Moliere Jean-Baptiste Poquelin
Moliere of Music André Grétry
Molink Moscow link (teletype cable circuit linking Moscow's Kremlin with Washington, D.C.'s White House), The Hot Line
moll metallo-organic liquid laser
mol/l molecules per liter
Moll Mary (slang); Molly
mollie mollienisia (tropical fish)
mollie(s) mare mule(s)—*see* hinny
Mollus Mollusca
MOLLUSA Military Order of the Loyal Legion of the U.S.A.
Molly Maria; Marie; Mary
Molly Pitcher Mrs John Hays also known as Captain Molly because she took her husband's place as cannoneer when he fell mortally wounded at the Battle of Monmouth—June 28, 1778
MOLNS Ministry of Labour and National Service
MOLOC Ministry of Labour Occupational Classification
Molotov Vyacheslav Mikhailovich Skriabin
Mol Phys Molecular Physics
MOLS Mirror Optical Landing System
molt. molten
Moluccas Maluku or Spice Islands of Indonesia
mol wt molecular weight
moly molybdenum
mom military ordinary mail;

milk of magnesia
mom (MOM) micromation on-line microfilmer
m-o-m middle of month; milk of magnesia
m/ o m/ más o menos (Spanish—more or less)
Mom Momma
MOM Musée Océanographique Monaco
MoMA Museum of Modern Art
m-o-m in a.m. if no bm by p.m. milk-of-magnesia in the morning if no bowel movement by evening (important geriatric order regarding America's bowel-conscious citizens)
momar modern mobile army
momau mobile mine assembly unit
Moml Moslem meal
Mo-Mo MF Grant—pseudonym
MOMR Mayor's Office of Manpower Resources
moms missile operate mode simulator
moms mervaerdiomsaetningsskat (Danish—value-added tax); *mervardesomsattningskatt* (Swedish—value-added tax)
MOMS Mothers for Moral Stability
MOM/WOW Men Our Masters/Women Our Wonders (anti-feminist acronym reading the same upside down as shown)
mon monetary; monsoon; monument; motor octane number
mon maison (French—house)
Mon Monaco; Monday; Monegasque; Monitor; Monmouthshire; Monoceros (constellation); Monsieur (French—Mister)
Mon Mónaco (Spanish—Monaco); *Montag* (German—Monday)
Mona Ramona
Mona Madonna (Italian—Lady, Our Lady); (Manx—Isle of Man)
Monachium (Latin—München)—Munich also called Monacum by Latinists
Monaco Principality of Monaco (tiny Mediterranean country famed for its gambling casino and other tourist attractions, Monacans or Monegasques speak French as well as Monegasque, Italian, and English)
Monaco's Only Port Monaco

Monag Monaghan
Monarchy of Mount Everest Nepal
Monas Monastic(ism); Monastery
Monashees Monashee Mountains of British Columbia
monbas monobasic
MONC Metropolitan Opera National Council
mon/dir monitoring direction
Mondrian Pieter Cornelis Mondriaan
MONEVAL Monthly Evaluation Report (USA)
monex monsoon experiment
Mong Mongol; Mongolia(n)
Mongolia Mongolian People's Republic (landlocked Asiatic nation of great antiquity, its official language is Khalkha Mongolian, Soviet troops buttress its defenses, its exports are all to Iron Curtain countries) *Bügd Nayramdakh Mongol Ard Uls*
Mongoose Mongoose Gang (secret police in the West Indian island of Grenada)
'mongst amongst
mon-H monohydrogen
Moni Monica; Monika
monic monocular
monik moniker
Monitor Christian Science Monitor
Monk Matthew Gregory (Monk) Lewis
Monkey Trial Scopes Trial (in 1925 when John Scopes, a Tennessee science teacher was on trial for having taught evolution, he was prosecuted by William Jennings Bryan and defended by Clarence Darrow)
Monkey Ward Montgomery-Ward
Monk Lewis pseudonum of Matthew Gregory Lewis
Mon Not Roy Astron Soc. Monthly Notices of the Royal Astronomical Society
mono mononucleosis; monophonic; monopoly; monopropellant; monorail(road); monotype; monotyper
mono (Latin prefix—alone, one, single)—monograph, monorail
Mono Monocerus (constellation)
monob (MONOB) mobile noise barge
monocl monoclinic
monocot(s) monocotyledon(s)

Monod Monon Railroad
monog monogram; monograph
monokini one-piece topless bikini (swimsuit)
monos monitor out of service
monot monotonous; monotony; monotype; monotypic
monpl monopoly
mons (Latin prefix—mountain) —monstrosity
Mons Hainaut's provincial capital in Belgium
Mons Monsieur (French—Mister)
Mons Cur Monsoon Current
Monsieur de Paris (French—Mr Paris)—guillotine operator
Monsig Monseigneur (French— My Lord)
monsoons seasonal storms of southern Asia
Mons Serratus (Latin—Montserrat)
monstro(s) monstrosity; monstrosities
Mont Montana; Montanan; Monterrey; Montevideo; Montgomery; Montpelier; Montreal
Montañas Rocosas (Spanish— Rocky Mountains)
Monte Montague; Monte Carlo; Montebianco (Mont Blanc); Montefiore; Montevideo; Montgomery
Monte Bianco (Italian—Mont Blanc)
Monte Carlo of the East Macao, Portuguese China
Montenegro Adriatic kingdom now part of Yugoslavia
Montes Apalaches (Spanish— Appalachian Mountains)
Montezuma Castle Montezuma Castle National Monument in central Arizona
Montezuma's Revenge diarrhea or dysentery nicknamed for the last Aztec ruler of Mexico where both ailments are so prevalent and are also nicknamed the Curse of Cortez for the Spaniard who conquered Mexico
Montgom Montgomeryshire
Montgomery Alabama's capital
Montgomery Camp Federal Prison Camp at Montgomery, Alabama
Monticello (Italian—Little Mountain)— Thomas Jefferson's self-designed home near Charlottesville, Virginia
Montparno Montparnasse
Montpelier Vermont's capital
Montpelier James Madison's

home in Orange County, Virginia near Charlottesville
Montr Montreal
montrg monitoring
Mont Royal (French—Mount Royal)
Mont S Montreal Star
Monty Montagu; Montague; Montana; Montmorency
Monumental Intellectual John Locke
Monument City Baltimore, Maryland
Monument to Slavery Berlin Wall
Mony monastery
MONY Music Operators of New York; Mutual Life Insurance Company of New York
MOO Money Order Office
Moody and Sankey Dwight Lyman Moody and Ira David Sankey—an evangelist preacher and his organist partner
Moondog Louis Thomas Hardin
Moon Goddess Luna (Roman) whose Latin name means moon; Selene (Greek)
Moonlight Beethoven's Piano Sonata No. 14 in C-sharp minor (opus 27, no. 2) *Sonata quasi una Fantasia*
moop mechlorethamine, vincristine, procarbazine, prednisone (Hodgkin's disease treatment)
MOOP Ministerstvo Okhraneniia Obshehestvennogo Poriadka (Russian—All-Union Ministry for the Preservation of Public Order)—secret police agency
Moor Othello; The Moor (Dartmoor Prison)
Moor Court prison for female offenders in Staffordshire, England
Moore's Dig Moore's Digest (of international law)
Moose NATO name for Yak-11 Soviet aircraft
MOOSE Move Out of Saigon Expeditiously (USA)
moot. move(d) out of town; moving out of town
mop mother-of-pearl; mustering-out pay
mop. medical outpatient; mother-of-pearl; mustering-out pay
M o P Member of Parliament; Minister of Pensions; Ministry of Pensions; Minister of Power; Ministry of Power; Minister of Production; Ministry of Production
MOP Migrant Opportunity Pro-

gram

MOP *Ministerio de Obras Publicas* (Spanish—Ministry of Public Works)

mopa master oscilator power amplifier

MOPA Museum of Photographic Arts (San Diego)

MoPac Missouri Pacific—Texas & Pacific (railroad)

mopar master oscillator-power amplifier radar

mopb manually operated plotting board

mopeds motorized pedals (bicycles containing auxiliary motors saving riders much pedalling)

mopf missile onloading prism fixture

MOPH Military Order of the Purple Heart

mopr manner of performance rating; mop rack

MOPS Merchandise Order(ing) Processing System; Missile Operations System

MOPSS Multispectral Opium Poppy Sensor System

M. Opt. Master of Optometry

mor middle of the road; morocco; mortar

mor (MOR) middle-of-the-road (tv program)

mor *morendo* (Italian—dying away, gradual softening of tone and slowing of tempo)

Mor Morelia; Morelos; Morisco; Moroccan; Morocco

MOR Mandatory Occurrence Report(ing); Military Operations Research

Moralist of Psychoanalysis Erich Fromm

Morand's disease paresis affecting the feet

Morav Moravia; Moravian

Morava a Slezsko (Czechoslovakian—Moravia and Silesia)

Moravian Capital Brno

Morb Morbihan

MORC Medical Officers Reserve Corps; Midget Ocean Racing Club (*mor-sees*—smallest racing cruisers)

Mord Mordehai

Mordhy Mordehai

mor. dict. *more dicto* (Latin—as directed)

Mordy Mordehai

MORE Mission for Outreach, Renewal, and Evangelism

moreps monitor station reports

Moreton Bay Colony Queensland's original name

morf hermaphrodite

mor fib moral fiber

morf(ie) morphine

morg mar morganatic marriage

MORI Market Opinion and Research International

moritzer mortar howitzer

MORL Manned (or Medium) Orbital Research Laboratory

Morm Mormon

Morm *Mormon, Book of*

Mor Maj Moral Majority (whose detractors insist is neither moral nor a majority)

Mormom Prophet Joseph Smith

Mormon City Salt Lake City

Mormon's Mecca Salt Lake City, Utah

Mormon State Utah

morn morning

Moro. Book of Moroni

Moroccan Ports (east to west) Tanger (Tangier), Kenitra, Casablanca, Safi, Agadir

Morocco Carolina Varga Dinicu; Kingdom of Morocco (North African Arab nation whose Moroccans speak Arabic, Berber, French, and Spanish as it was once divided between France and Spain, phosphate exports are augmented by farm products, leatherwork, and textiles) *al-Mamlaka al-Maghrebia*

morph morphine; morphology

morph (Latin prefix—form, shape)—morphological

morpha hermaphrodite (mispronounced *morphadite*)

morpheme smallest sound unit (linguistics)

morphophysio morphophysiologic(al)(ly); morphophysiologist; morphophysiology

Morrie Maurice; Morris

Morrison Girls Mount View (delinquent) Girls School at Morrison, Colorado

Morris Rosenfeld Moshe Jacob Alter

morro (Portuguese or Spanish—hill, promontory, as in Morro Castle)

Morrow William Morrow

MORS Midland Operational Research Society

mor. sol. *more solito* (Latin—in the usual manner)

mort mortal; mortality; mortar; mortgage; mortician; mortuary

mor t Morse taper

moRt mainstream of Republican thought

Mort Mortemart; Mortimer;

Morton

mortal. mortality

Morton's disease metatarsal neuralgia

mos metal-oxide semiconductor; metal-oxide-silicon (compound); missile on stand; mitout sound (silent film); months; mosaic

mos (MOS) military occupational specialty

Mos Moscow

Mos. Book of Mosiah

Mos *Mosca* (Italian—Moscow); *Moscou* (French or Portuguese —Moscow); *Moscu* (Spanish —Moscow); *Moskau* (German —Moscow); *Moskou* (Dutch —Moscow)

MOs Military Observers (UN)

MOS Management Operating System; Manned Orbital Station; Ministry of Supply

Mosbas Moscow Basin

Mosby C V Mosby

mosc manned orbital systems concepts

MOSC Midland-Odessa Symphony and Chorale

Mosca (Italian—Moscow)

Moscou (French—Moscow)

Moscovia (Latin—Moscow)— also called Moscua

Moscow English place-name equivalent for the Russian Moskva; Moscowitz

Moscú (Portuguese or Spanish —Moscow)

Mose Moisés; Mosè; Moseley; Mosen; Moses; Moshe

Mosel (German—Moselle)

Moselle (French—Mosel)

Moses Moses in Egypt—Rossini's sacred melodrama in four acts (*Mosè in Egitto*)

MOSES Manned Open Sea Experimentation Station

mosfet metal-oxide semiconductor field-effect transistor

mosic metal-oxide-semiconductor integrated circuit(s)

Mosk Moscovici; Moscowitz; Moskowitz

Moskau (Dutch or German— Moscow)

Moskva (Russian—Moscow)— NATO name for a Soviet class of antisubmarine—warfare cruiser and helicopter-carrier warship

Moslem India Bangladesh and Pakistan

Moslems (Arabic—Those Who Submit)—also called Muslims

Moslem Sultanate Oman—for-

merly Muscat and Oman
mosm milliosmol(s)
MOSOP Missouri Sexual Offender Program
Mosquitia (Spanish—Mosquito Coast)—of eastern Honduras and Nicaragua along the Caribbean
Mosquito Coast Caribbean coast of much of Honduras and Nicaragua
Mosquito State New Jersey
moss. maintenance-operations support set
MOSS Manned Orbital Space Station
MOSST Ministry of State for Science and Technology (Canadian)
most. metal-oxide semiconductor transistor
'most almost
mostl metal-oxide semiconductor transistor logic
mot mean operating time; mechanical operability test; member of our tribe; middle of target; motor; motorized
M o T Minister of Transport; Ministry of Transport
MOT Military Ocean Terminal
MOTAT Museum of Transport and Technology
M o TCP Ministry of Town and Country Planning
motel hotel for motorists
mother homosexual dope push er; madam of a brothel; motherfucker
Mother of American Kindergartens Susan Blow
Mother of the American Legion Ernestine Schumann-Heink
Mother of the American Red Cross Clara Barton
Mother Ann Shaker leader Ann Lee
Mother of Believers Ayesha—Mohammed's favorite wife
Mother Bickerdyke Mary Ann Bickerdyke
Mother of Birth Control Margaret Sanger
Mother Bloor Ella Reeve Bloor
Mother Cabrini Frances Xavier Cabrini
Mother Carey's chickens stormy petrels
Mother Carey's geese fulmars or great white petrels
Mother of Child Education Doctor Maria Montessori
Mother of Cities Bombay, according to Kipling
Mother of the Civil Rights Movement Coretta Scott

King
Mother Earth the Greek Goddess Gaea or Ge who, according to mythology, arose out of chaos and in turn produced the sea, the sky, and the mountains; the Romans called her Tellus or Terra and sometimes called her Vesta Prisca
Mother of Exiles Statue of Liberty overlooking New York's former immigration stations at Battery Park and Ellis Island
Mother of Feminine Psychology Karen Horney
Mother of Ghosts the Roman goddess of Death—Mania
Mother Goose legendary authoress of children's rhymes and stories
Mother of Her Country Queen María Theresa of Austria
Mother of Israel Golda Meir
Mother of the Japanese Novel Baroness Murasaki Shikibu (*The Tale of the Genji*)
Mother Jones Mary Harris Jones
Mother Lake Leonora Marie Kearney Barry
Mother of Libraries Alexandria, Egypt
Mother Maid The Virgin Mary
Mother of Modern Dance Isadora Duncan
Mother of Mountains Nepal's Mount Everest
Mother of Muckrakers Ida M Tarbell (*see* Father of Muckrakers)
Mother of Parliaments British Parliament
Mother of Presidents Virginia—birthplace of Presidents Washington, Jefferson, Madison, Monroe, William Henry Harrison, Tyler, Taylor, Wilson
Mother of Prison Reform Dorothea Lynde Dix
Mother of the Red Cross Clara Barton
Mother of Rivers Tibetan Highlands
Mother of Rivers and Waves Tethys, wife of the god Oceanus, and mother of the rivers plus three thousand Oceanids—the waves
Mother of Russian Cities Kiev
Mother of the Russians Moscow
Mothers of Believers the wives of Mohammed
Mother State Virginia

Mother of Storms Antarctica, the Baffin Sea, the Bay of Biscay, the Caribbean, the Gulf of Alaska, the Gulf of Mexico, the South China Sea, the Tasman Sea, are among many oceanic areas called the Mother of Storms
mother tongue music (according to many great musicians, philosophers, poets, and scholars)
Mother of Trusts Standard Oil
Motion Picture Capital of the World Hollywood, California
Motion Picture Palace Potentate Roxy (SL Rothafel)
MOTNE Meteorological Operational Telecommunications Network, Europe (NATO)
motoboard(s) motorized skateboard(s)
motocross cross-country motorcycle race
mot op motor operated
motorcade motorized-vehicle parade
Motor City Detroit
motorcross motorcycle cross (country race)
MOTOREDE Movement To Restore Decency
Motor Town Detroit
Mo' Town Motor Town (Detroit, Michigan)
mots minitrack optical tracking system
MOTU Mobile Technical Unit
mou memorandum of understanding
Mound City St Louis, Missouri
Mount The Mount (Edith Wharton's home in Lenox, Massachusetts)
Mountain City Chattanooga, Tennessee
Mountain Devils Tasmanians
Mountain Division States Arizona, Colorado, Idaho, Montana, Nevada, New Mexico, Utah, and Wyoming
Mountain of Fire Etna, Vesuvius, or any other active volcano
Mountain Laurel Connecticut state flower
Mountain of the Lion Sierra Leone
Mountain State West Virginia's official nickname
Mountain States Arizona, Colorado, Idaho, Montana, Nevada, New Mexico, Utah, and Wyoming
Mountain of Tarik The Rock of Gibraltar named for the Moor-

ish chief Jabal Tariq

Mountain View Girls Mountain View School (for juvenile-delinquent females) at Helena, Montana

Mountbatten of Burma AF Admiral of the Fleet the Earl Mountbatten of Burma, KG (better known as Lord Mountbatten)—India's last viceroy

mounties mounted policemen (especially Royal Canadian Mounted Police)

Mount Rainier Mount Tacoma towering over Tacoma, Washington next to Seattle

Mount Vernon George Washington's home on the banks of the Potomac below Washington, D.C.

MOUSE minimum orbital unmanned satellite

Mouzol Cornish pronunciation of Mousehole (fishing village close to Penzance in Mounts Bay within the English Channel)

mov movable; movement; moving; multiple-orifice valve

mov movimento (Italian—movement)

movem movement overseas verification of enlisted members (of the USA)

moverep movement report

Move Short Soc Movement Shorthand Society

movi movie; moving pictures

Movie Capital Hollywood, California

Movieland Hollywood, California

movies moving pictures

MOVIMS Motor Vehicle Information Management System

movord movement order

M o W Minister of Works; Ministry of Works

MOW Moscow, USSR (Vnukovo Airport); Movement for the Ordination of Women

mowasp mechanization of warehousing and shipment processing

MoWD ministry of Works and Development

MOWOS Meteorological Office Weather Observing System

M o WT Minister of War Transport; Ministry of War Transport

MOWW Military Order of the World Wars

mox mixed oxides (platinum and uranium); oxidized metal explosive

moy money

Moz Mozambique

MOZ Mezhdunarodnaya Organizacia Zhurnalistov (Russian —International Organization of Journalists)

Mozam Mozambique

Mozambique People's Republic of Mozambique (formerly Portuguese East Africa with most of its people speaking Portuguese plus tribal tongues, edible crops and minerals are exported)

Mozambique Ports (north to south) Moçcambique, Beira, Lourenço Marques

Mozart's 41 Mozart's forty-one symphonies including the *Haffner* (No. 35), the *Linz* (No. 36), the *Prague* (No. 38), the *Jupiter* (No. 41)

Mozart Town Salzburg, Austria —birthplace of Wolfgang Amadeus Mozart

Moz Cur Mozambique Current (Natal)

mozza mozzarella

mp mail payment; maintenance part(s); manifold pressure; medium pressure; meeting point; melting point; *mezzo-piano* (Italian—half soft, moderately soft); milepost; motion picture; multipole; multipurpose

mp (MP) marginal product

m(p) microfilm positive

m-p metal-point (bullet)

m/p milk powder

m & p materials and processes

m.p. mille pasuum (Latin—thousand paces)—the Roman mile of 1000 paces

mP polar maritime air

MP Member of Parliament; Metropolitan Police; Military Police; Mining Permit; Minister Plenipotentiary; Minister Provincial; Miscellaneous Proposal; Missouri Pacific (railroad); Mitsubishi Plastics; Mounted Police

M/P Memorandum of Partnership

M & P Maryland & Pennsylvania (railroad)

MP Maschinenpistole (German —submachine gun, tommy gun)

mp₁ marginal product of labor

mpa megapascal; multiple-product (television) announcement

mpa (MPa) megapascal

mpa (MPA) maritime patrol aircraft

mpa Maryland Port Authority's italicized logotype

MPA Magazine Publishers Association; Main Propulsion Assistant (USN); Maryland & Pennsylvania (railroad); Mechanical Packing Association; Medical Procurement Agency; Metal Powder Association; Midwestern Psychological Association; Military Police Association; Mobile Press Association; Modern Poetry Association; Motion Picture Alliance; Music Publishers Association

M.P.A. Marine Physician Assistant; Master of Professional Accounting; Master of Public Administration; Master of Public Affairs

MPAA Motion Picture Association of America; Musical Performing Arts Association

MPAC Master Plan for Academic Computing

MPACS Management Planning and Control System

mpad maximum permissible annual dose

MPAGB Modern Penthalon Association of Great Britain

mpai maximum permissible annual intake

mpam maritime polar air mass

m part movable partition

mpas millipascal second

MPAS Maryland Parent Attitude Survey

MPAUS Music Publishers Association of the United States

m payl maximum payload

mpb male pattern baldness

MPB Maintenance Parts Breakdown (spare parts); Miniature Precision Bearings; Missing Persons Bureau; Montpelier & Barre (railroad)

mpbb maximum permissible body burden (of radiation)

MPBC Memphis Power Boat Club

mp br multipunch bar

MPBS Mutual Permanent Building Society

MPBW Ministry of Public Buildings and Works

mpc marine protein concentrate; material program code; maximum permissible concentration; military payment certificate; minimal planning chart; multipurpose carrier

mpc (MPC) marginal propensity to consume

MPC Manpower and Personnel

Council; Manpower Priorities Committee; Manufacturing Plan Change; Member of Parliament of Canada; Metropolitan Police College; Metropolitan Police Commissioner; Military Payment Certificate; Military Pioneer Corps; Military Police Corps; Military Police Force; Model Penal Code; Montana Power Company

MPCA Magnetic Powder Core Association; Marine and Ports Council of Australia; Master Pastry Cooks Association

MPCAG Military Parts Control Advisory Groups

MPCB Manufacturing Plan Control Board

mpc black medium-processing channel black

MPCC Minnesota Private College Council

MPCL Movimiento Patriótico Cuba Libre (Free Cuba Patriotic Movement)

mpcp missile power control panel

MPCS Master Plan for Computing Services

mpcur maximum permissible concentration of unidentified radionuclides

mpd magnetoplasmadynamics; missile purchase description

M. Pd. Master of Pedagogy

MPD Metropolitan Park District; Metropolitan Police Department; Military Pay Division

MPDA Motion Picture Distributors Association

MPDFA Master Photo Dealers' and Finishers' Association

mp di multipunch die

MPDPIS Master Plan for Data Processing and Information Systems

MPDS Message Processing Distribution System

MPDSA Master Painters, Decorators, and Signwriters Association

MPDT Minnesota Perception Diagnostic Test

mpe maximum permissible exposure (to radiation)

M.P.E. Master of Physical Education

MPEA Motion Picture Exhibitors Association

MPEAUS Master Printers and Engravers Association of the United States

M. Pe. Eng. Master of Petroleum Engineering

M Pen Minister of Pensions; Ministry of Pensions

MPers Middle Persian

MPES Mathematical, Physical, and Engineering Science (NSF)

mpf motion-picture film; multipurpose food

MPF Malaysian Peasants Front; Metropolitan Police Force (London)

mpfg 1000 proof gallons

mpg miles per gallon

MPG Magazine Promotion Group; Max Planck Gesellschaft

MPGA Maine Personnel and Guidance Association; Maryland Personnel and Guidance Association; Metropolitan Public Gardens Association; Michigan Personnel and Guidance Association; Minnesota Personnel and Guidance Association; Missouri Personnel and Guidance Association

MPGR Mana Pools Game Reserve (Rhodesia)

mph miles per hour

M.Ph. Master of Philosophy

MPH Meat Packing House; Methodist Publishing House

M.P.H. Master of Public Health

MPH *Maintenance Parts Handbook*

M. Phar. Master of Pharmacy

M. Pharm. Master of Pharmacy

MPHEC Maritime Provinces Higher Education Commission

M. Ph. Ed. Master of Public Health Education

M. P.II. Eng. Master of Public Health Engineering

M.Phil. Master of Philosophy

M. Pho. Master of Photography

mphps miles per hour per second

M. Ph. Sc. Master of Physical Science

M.P.H.T.M. Master of Public Health and Tropical Medicine

M. Phy. Master of Physics

M Phys A Member of the Physiotherapists Association

mpi magnetic particle inspection; maximum point of impulse; mean point of impact; multiphasic personality inventory; multiphoton ionization

mpi (MPI) marginal propensity to invest

MPI Material Process Instruction; Max Planck Institute; Mitsui Petrochemical Industries; Museum of the Plains Indians

MPI *Movimiento Pro-Independencia* (Spanish—Pro-Independence Movement)—for the liberation of Puerto Rico

M-pill menstruation pill

MPIRO Multiple Peril Insurance Rating Organization

MP & IS Material Process and Inspection Specification

mPk polar maritime air colder than underlying surface

mpl mathematical programming language; maximum payload; maximum permissible language; maximum permissible level; message processing language; multiple-position lock

MPL Maintenance Parts List; Memphis Public Library; Metropolitan Police Laboratory; Miami Public Library; Milwaukee Public Library; Minnesota Power and Light; Missouri Pacific Lines; Montreal Public Library

M.P.L. Master (Mistress) of Patent Law

MPLA Mountain Plains Library Association

MPLA *Movimento Popular Libertação Angola* (Portuguese—Popular Movement for the Liberation of Angola)

MPLP Marxist Progressive Labor Party

Mpls Minneapolis

mpm meters per minute; missile power monitor; mole-percent metal; multipurpose meal

MPM Milwaukee Public Museum

MP-M Museum Plantin-Moretus (Antwerp's museum devoted to book production and typography of Plantin and Moretus)

MPMI Magazine and Paperback Marketing Institute

mpn most probable number

MPNA Midwest Professional Needlework Association

MPNI Ministry of Pensions and National Insurance

mpo memory printout

MPO Memorandum Purchase Order; Metropolitan Police Office (Scotland Yard); Miami Philharmonic Orchestra; Military Pay Order; Military Planning Office(r); Military Post Office; Mobile Printing Office

MPOIS Military Police Operating Information System

M.Pol. Econ Master (Mistress) of Political Economy

MPOLL Military Post Office Location List(ing)

mpp marginal physical product; most probable position

MPP Maintainability Program Plan(ning); Member Provincial Parliament (Canada); Mothers in Prison Projects

M.P.P. Master (Mistress) of Physical Planning

M & PP Manitou & Pikes Peak (Railroad)

MPPA Music Publishers Protective Association

MPPCA Maryland Probation, Patrol and Corrections Association

mppcf millions of particles per cubic foot of air

mp pl multipunch plate

mpps million pulses per second

MPPWCOM Military Police Prisoner of War Command

mpq manpower-planning quota(s)

mpr 1000 pair; medium-power radar

MPR Maintainability Program Requirements; Military Pay Record; Mongolian People's Republic

MPR Madjelis Permusjawaratan Rakat (Indonesian—People's Deliberative Assembly)

MPRC Military Personnel Records Center

mpress medium pressure; medium pressurization

MPRL Master Parts Reference List

M. Prof. Acc. Master of Professional Accountancy

MPRP Mongolian Peoples Revolutionary Party; Muslim Peoples Republican Party

mp & rs motive power and rolling stock

mps marbled paper sides; megacycles per second; meters per second; motor parts stock

mps (MPS) marginal propensity to save; mucopolysaccharidosis

Mp's Minneapolis pimps

MPs Members of Parliament; plural of military police or mounted police

M.Ps. Master of Psychology

MPS Manufacturing Process Specification; Marriage Prediction Schedule; Master Proj-

ect Summary; Mathematical Programming System; Microprocessor System; Military Postal Service; Milwaukee Public Museum; Minimum Property Standards; Minister of Public Security; Mont Pelerin Society; Motor Products Corporation

M.P.S. Member of the Pharmaceutical Society

MPSA Military Petroleum Supply Agency

MPSC Military Provost Staff Corps

mpsh mean pressure suction head

MPSM Master Problem Status Manual

M.Ps.O. Master (Mistress) of Psychology Orientation

MPSP Mathematical Problem-Solving Project; Military Personnel Security Program

MPSS Multiple Protective Structure System

M.P.S.W. Master (Mistress) of Psychiatric Social Work

M.Psych. Master (Mistress) of Psychology

M. Psy. Med. Master of Psychological Medicine

mpt male pipe thread; melting point; microprocessing programmable terminal; midpoint; multiple pure tone; multipower transmission

mpt (MPT) miles per tankful

Mpt Maryport

MPT Marquis Public Theater; Minister of Posts and Telecommunications

mpta main propulsion test article

MPTA Machine Power Transmission Association; Municipal Passenger Transport Association

MPTP Music Preference Test of Personality

mpu microprocessor unit (MPU); monitor printing unit

MPU Medical Practitioners Union; Missing Persons Unit (of a police department)

M. Pub. Adm. Master of Public Administration

mpv (MPV) multipurpose vehicle

M-P v Mason-Pfizer virus

mPw polar maritime air warmer than underlying surface

MPW Minneapolis-Moline (stock exchange symbol)

MPWBS Master Plan Works Breakdown Structure

mpx multiplex

mpxr multiplexor (flow chart)

mpy multiply

Mpy Maatschappij (Dutch—company)

MPZ Mid-Continent Petroleum (stock exchange symbol)

mq metol-quinol (MQ); multiple quotient (register); multiplier quotient

mq (MQ) memory quotient; metol-quinone

Mq mosque

MQ merit quotient

M&Q Mines and Quarries

MQA Manufacturing Quality Assurance

MQAB Medical Quality Assurance Board

Mqe Martinique

mqf mobile quarantine facility

MQI Maiquetía (Venezuelan airport serving Caracas, La Guaira, and many other places)

mqil miniature quartz incandescent lamp

mql miniature quartz lamp

MQO Marksmanship Qualification Order

MQS Mobile Quality Services

MQT Model Qualification Test

M Quad Charles Bertrand Lewis

MQV Ministère de la Qualité de la Vie (French—Ministry of the Quality of Life)

mqyco minimum quantity yards per color

mqyds minimum quantity yards per design

mr machine record(s); machine rifle; map reference; medium range; mental retardation; mentally retarded; metabolic rate; methyl red; mill run, mineral rubber; milliroentgen; mine run; motivational research (MR)

mr (MR) marginal revenue

m/r map reading; middle right

m & r maintainability and reliability; maintainability and repairs; maintenance and repair

mr meester (Dutch—master)—attorney-at-law; *mi remesa* (Spanish—my remittance)

mR milliroentgen

Mr Master; Mister

MR Machinery Repairman; Marketing Research (division, US Department of Agriculture); Master of the Rolls; Memorandum for Record; Memorandum Report; Michigan Reformatory; Military

Railroad; Military Requirement; Minister Residentiary; Ministry of Reconstruction; Miscellaneous Report; Mobilization Regulation; Monon Railroad; Monthly Report; Morning Report; Municipal Reform

M/R map reading; Mates Receipt(s)

M & R maintenance and repairs

M of R Minister of Reconstruction; Ministry of Reconstruction

MR **Marca Registrada** (Spanish —Registered Trademark); *Mobilización Republicana* (Spanish—Republican Mobilization)—Castro-controlled Soviet-oriented political party active in the Nicaraguan underground; *Motormannes Riksforbund* (Swedish—Motorists' Association)

MR-13 **Movimiento Revolucionario de 13 de Noviembre** (Spanish—Revolutionary Movement of 13 November) —Guatemala

mra medium-powered radio range (Adcock); minimum reception altitude

mra (MRA) metro rating area (tv)

MRA Master Retailers Association; Materials Review Area; Moral Rearmament

mraam (MRAAM) medium-range air-to-air missile

mrac manifold-regulator accumulator charging

MRACP Member of the Royal Australasian College of Physicians

mrad megarad; millirad

M. Rad. Master of Radiology

M. Ra. Eng. Master of Radio Engineering

MRAF Marshal of the Royal Air Force

Mr Air Brake George Westinghouse

MRAM Multimission Redeye Air-launched Missile

MRAP Management Review and Analysis Program

MRAS Manpower Resources Accounting System (USAF)

mrasm (MRASM) medium-range air-to-surface missile

mrat medium-range applied technology

MRAUSCAN Masonic Relief Association of the United States and Canada

Mr Automobile Gottlieb Daimler

mrb marble base

MRB Material Review Board; Mileage Rationing Board; Modification Review Board; Mutual Reinsurance Bureau

MRBA Mississippi River Bridge Authority

mrbm medium-range ballistic missile (MRBM)

MRBP Missouri River Basin Project

mrc magnetic rectifier control

MRC Maintenance Requirements Cards; Marine Research Committee; Market Research Council; Marlin-Rockwell Corporation; Material Redistribution Center; Material Review Crib; Measurement Research Center; Medical Research Center (Council); Medical Reserve Corps; Men's Republican Club; Metals Reserve Company; Methods Research Corporation; Minnesota Restitution Center; Mississippi River Commission; Model Railway Club; Modern Railroad Club; Motor Racing Club; Movement Report Center

mrca multirole combat aircraft

MRCA Market Research Corporation of America

MRCC Medical Research Council of Canada

MRCF Module Repair Calibration Facility

MRCGP Member of the Royal College of General Practitioners

MRCI Medical Registration Council of Ireland; Medical Research Council of Ireland

MRCIU Men's Residence Center (Indiana University)

MRCo Malaysian Refrigerator Company

MRCO Member of the Royal College of Organists

MRCOG Member of the Royal College of Obstetricians and Gynaecologists

Mr Color Television Peter Goldmark

Mr Common Sense Thomas Paine

Mr Conservative Barry M Goldwater

MRCP Maoist Revolutionary Communist Party; Member of the Royal College of Physicians

MRC Path Member of the

Royal College of Pathologists

MRCPE Member of the Royal College of Physicians of Edinburgh

MRCPI Member of the Royal College of Physicians of Ireland

MRC Psych Member of the Royal College of Psychiatrists

MRCPUK Member of the Royal College of Physicians of the United Kingdom

MRCS Member of the Royal College of Surgeons

MRCSE Member of the Royal College of Surgeons of Edinburgh

MRCSI Member of the Royal College of Surgeons of Ireland

MRCVS Member of the Royal College of Veterinary Surgeons

MRCWA Midland Railway Company of Western Australia

mrd metal rolling door; metal(lic) roof(ing) deck(ing); minimum reacting dose (MRD)

MRD Main Roads Department; Medical Records Department; Medical Reference Department; Microbiological Research Department; Motorized Rifle Division

MRDC Military Research and Development Center

MR & DC Medical Research and Development Command (US Army)

mrdf machine-readable data files

MRDF maritime radio direction finding

MR&DF Malleable Research and Development Foundation

Mr Diesel Rudolf Diesel

MRDN Material Receipt Discrepancy Notice

Mr Dogpatch Al Capp (also known as the Mark Twain of cartoonists or the sardonic cartoonist)

Mr Dooley (pseudonym—Finley Peter Dunne)

MRDs Motorized Rifle Divisions

MRDTI Metal Roof Deck Technical Institute

mre mean radial error

mre (MRE) meal ready to eat (freeze-dried field ration)

MRE Microbiological Research Establishment (UK)

M.R.E. Master of Religious Education

M. Ref. Eng. Master of Refrigeration Engineering

MREI Marriage Role Expectation Inventory

MRELB Malaysian Rubber Exchange and Licensing Board

Mr Electric Light Thomas Alva Edison

mrem milliroentgen equivalent man

mrep milliroentgen equivalent physical

mrf maintenance replacement factor; marble floor

MRF Mayo Research Foundation; Meteorological Rocket Facility; Music Research Foundation

MRFB Malayan Rubber Fund Board

MRFIT Multiple Risk Factor Intervention Trial

MRFL Master Radio Frequency List

mr flight meteorological research flight

mrg magnetic radiation generator; margin; marginal; marginalia; methane-rich gas

MRG Maintainability Requirements Group; Material Review Group; Minorities Research Group (aiding homosexuals)

MRGS Member of the Royal Geographical Society

Mr Gyrocompass Elmer Ambrose Sperry

MRH Member of the Royal Household

Mr Helicopter Igor Sikorsky

mrhm milliroentgens per hour at one meter

MRHMC Michael Reese Hospital and Medical Center

mr/hr milliroentgens per hour

MRHS Midwest Railway Historical Society

mri magnetic rubber inspection; mean rise interval; medium-range interceptor; milstrip routing identifier; monopulse resolution improvement

MRI Magazine Research Incorporated; Marine Research Institute; Marital Roles Inventory; Meat Research Institute; Medical Records Index(ing); Mental Research Institute; Meteorological Research Institute; Meuse-Rhine-Issel (cattle breed); Midwest Research Institute; Missile Range Index; Motor Repair Insurance

MRINA Member of the Royal Institution of Naval Architects

MRINZ Meat Research Institute of New Zealand

MRIPHH Member of the Royal Institute of Public Health and Hygiene

mrir medium resolution infrared

MRIS Maritime Research Information System; Market Research Information System; Material Readiness Index System; Medical Research Information System; Mobile Range Instrumentation System

MRIW Medical Research Institute of Worcester

mrkd marked

mrkg marking

Mr Klemps Otto Klemperer

mrkr marker

Mrkt-Deli Market-Delicatessen

Mrkts Markets

mrl medium-powered radio range (loop radiators); motor refrigerator lighter; multiple rocket launcher (MRL)

MRL Materiel Requirements List; Medical Records Librarian; Medical Records Library; Mineral Research Laboratories

MRLA Malayan Races Liberation Army (Chinese-communist guerrillas)

Mr Laser Charles Townes

Mr Linotype Ottmar Mergenthaler

Mr Long-Play Records Peter Goldmark

mrm mail readership measurement; mechanically recovered meat; miles of relative movement

MRM Maintenance Reporting and Management

MRMVA Master Retail Milk Vendors Association

Mrn Martin

MRN Material Recorder Notice; Meteorological Rocket Network

mRNA messenger RNA (ribonucleic acid)

mrng mooring; morning

MRNP Mount Rainier National Park (Washington); Mount Revelstoke National Park (British Columbia)

Mrnz Martínez

mro maintenance, repair, and operating

Mro Maestro

MRO Maintenance, Repair, and Operation(s); Materiel Release Order

MROAR Modification and Repair Order and Acceptance Record

M-roof M-shaped roof

mrov moreover

mrp machine-readable passport; manned reusable payload; manned reusable product; marginal revenue product; maximum resolving power; maximum retail price

mrp (MRP) marginal revenue product

MRP Mobile Repair Party

M.R.P. Master in Regional Planning

MRPA Metropolitan Region Planning Authority

Mr Pilot Will Adams (nicknamed *Anjim Sama*—Mr Pilot—by the Japanese because of his knowledge of navigation and shipbuilding)

MRPP Maoist Reorganization Movement of the Party of the Proletariat

MRPRA Malaysian Rubber Producers Research Association

M rps Mauritius rupee(s)

Mr Q Marquardt Corporation

MRQ Marquardt Corporation (stock exchange symbol)

mrr medical research reactor

MRR Material Rejection Report; Mechanical Reliability Report(ing)

Mr Radio Lee De Forest

MRRAS Murder Release Risk Assessment Scale

MRRC Mechanical Reliability Research Center

MRRDB Malaysian Rubber Research and Development Board

Mr Republican U.S. Senator Robert A Taft

mrs (MRS) marginal rate of substitution

Mrs Missus; Mistress

MRs Maintenance Reports

MRS Market Research Society; Marseilles, France (airport); Master Repair(ing) Schedule; Material Request Summary; Material Requirement Summary; Military Railway Service; Ministry of Recreation and Sport; Monitored Retrievable Storage

MR & S Materials Research and Standards

mrsa (MRSA) medium-range surveillance aircraft

MRSA methicillin-resistant *Staphylococcus aureus* (hospital-acquired infection)

MR San Asn Member of the Royal Sanitary Association

M.R.Sc. Master (Mistress) of Rural Science

Mrs Fletcher Maria Jane Jewsbury's pseudonym

Mrs Grundy nickname for the imaginary self-appointed arbiter of morality and taste; leader of the social set referred to as *they—they feel, they say, they think*, etc.

MRSH Member of the Royal Society of Health

Mrs Jack Isabella Stewart Gardner

MRSL Member of the Royal Society of Literature

MRSM Member of the Royal Society of Medicine

MRSMGB Member of the Royal Society of Musicians of Great Britain

MRSP Myakka River State Park (Florida)

Mrs Patrick Campbell stage name of Beatrice Stella Tanner

mrsss manned revolving space systems simulator (MRSSS)

MRST Member of the Royal Society of Teachers

mrt mean radiant temperature; mid-range trajectory; mildew-resistant thread; military-rated thrust(ing); mission readiness tester; music 'riter typewriter

Mrt Martinique

Mrt Maart (Dutch—March)

MRT Maintainability Review Team; Mass Rapid Transit; Mass Rapid Transport; Metropolitan Readiness Test; Military Review Team; Modulus of Rupture Test(ing)

MRTA Maintenance Requirements Task Analysis

mrtm maritime

Mrtnz Martinez

mrto miscellaneous reference tool(ing)

mrts (MRTS) marginal rate of technical substitution

MRTS Mass Rapid Transit System; Master Radar Tracking Station

mru minimal reproductive units; mobile radio unit (MRU)

mru (MRU) mass radiography unit; mobile radio unit

MRU Medical Rehabilitation Unit; mobile radio unit; mobile repair unit

MRUA Mobile Radio Users' Association

Mr UN Carlos P Romulo

mrv material receipt voucher; missile re-entry vehicle (MRV); mixed respiratory vaccine; multiple re-entry vehicle (MRV)

MRV missile recovery vessel

mrV-P methyl red Voges-Proskauer

mrw morale, recreation, and welfare

mr/w multiple read/write

MRWA Midland Railway of Western Australia

mrwc multiple reading, writing, compiling; multiple read, write, compute

Mr Wireless Guglielmo Marconi

Mr X-Ray Wilhelm Roentgen

Mrylb Marylebone (railway terminal)

mrytm must have reply here by tomorrow morning

mrz marzo (Spanish—March)

ms machine screw; machine steel; main switch; maintenance and service; major subject; manuscript; margin of safety; mass spectrometric; master switch; maximum stress; mean square; medium shot; medium steel; meters per second; metric system; microseismic; mild steel; minimum stress; mint state; mitral stenosis; months after sight; multiple sclerosis; multiple starters; muscle strength

ms (MS) morphine sulfate; multiple sclerosis

m/s marking and stenciling; metal shank; meters per second; milestone; month after sight

m & s maintenance and supply; model and series; mud and snow

μs microsecond(s)

ms. manuscript

m s mano sinistra (Italian—left hand)

m/s motorskib (Norwegian—motorship)

mS millisiemens (millimho)

Ms mature motion pictures (for adults); Mendes; mesothorium; (pronounced *Miz*)—feminine title replacing Miss and Mrs

MS Machinery Survey; magnetic south; Mail Steamer; major subject; Manuscript Society; Master Sergeant; Material Specifications; Medical Survey; Metallurgical Society; Meteoritical Society; Michigan State University of Agriculture and Applied Science; Military Service; Military Standard; Ministry of Shipping; Ministry of Supply; Misair (Egyptian Airline); Motorship

M-S Material Service (division of General Dynamics); Monday through Saturday

M.S. Master of Science; Master of Surgery

M/S Mannlicher-Schoenauer; motorship

M&S Marks and Spencer; Maternity and Surgical; Medical and Surgical

M & S Maintenance and Supply; Medicine and Surgery

MS Material Standard (usually followed by a number)

M-S Minshu-Shakaito (Japanese—Democratic Socialist Party)

msa method of steepest ascent; minimum safe altitude; mission system avionics

m.s.a. misce secundum arten (Latin—mix skillfully)

MSA Major Systems Acquisition; Malaysia Singapore Airlines; Management Selection Australia; Marine Safety Agency; Maritime Safety Agency; Medical Statistics Agency (US Army); Middle States Association (colleges and schools); Mine Safety Appliances (company); Mineralogical Society of America; Motor Schools Association; Mutual Security Agency; Mutual Society of Arts

M-S-A Mine Safety Appliances

MSA Marine Sanctuaries Act; Merchant Shipping Act

MSAA Mower Specialists Association of Australia

MSAAB Military Services Ammunition Allocation Board

msac most seriously affected countries

MSAC Moore School Automatic Computer

MSA/CHE Middle States Association of Colleges and Schools Commission on Higher Education

M.S.Agr.Eng. Master of Science in Agricultural Engineering

MSA Inst MM Member of the South African Institute of

Mining and Metallurgy

MSAIT Member of the South African Institute of Translators

*m*ˢ *a*ˢ *muchos años* (Spanish—many years)

MSAS Mandel Social Adjustment Scale; Modal Suppression Augmentation System

MSAT Marine Services Association of Texas

MSAUS Masonic Service Association of the United States

msaw (MSAW) minimum safe altitude warning

msb main switchboard; most significant bit

msb (MSB) minority small business; missile storage building

MSB Mackinac Straits Bridge (Michigan); Marine Safety Board; minesweeping boat (naval symbol)

MSBA Maine School Boards Association; Minnesota School Boards Association; Missouri School Boards Association; Montana School Boards Association

M.S.B.A. Master of Science in Business Administration

MSBLS Microwave Scanning-Beam Landing System

MSBO Michigan School Business Officials; Mooring and Salvage Office(r)

M.S.Bus. Master (Mistress) of Science in Business

msc millisecond; moved, seconded, and carried

m.s.c. *mandatum sine clausula* (Latin—authority without restriction)

M. Sc. Master of Science

MSC coastal minesweeper (3-letter naval symbol); Maine Sardine Council; Manned Spacecraft Center (NASA); Maple Syrup Council; Marine Safety Council; Marine Science Center (Lehigh University); Medical Service Corps; Medical Specialist Corps; Mediterranean Sub-Commission; Melbourne Steamship Company; Military Sealift Command; Missile and Space Council; Missile System Checkout; Mississippi Central (railroad); Mountain Safety Council

M & SC Missile and Space Council

MScA Make or Subcontract Authorization

MSCA McCarthy Scales of

Children's Abilities; Moore School of Automatic Computers; Mount Saint Agnes College; Murray State Agricultural College

M Scand Middle Scandinavian

mscc magnetic-strip credit card

M.S.C.E. Master of Science in Civil Engineering

M.S.Ch.E. Master of Science in Chemical Engineering

Mschr Monatsschrift (German—monthly magazine)

MSCIC Maryland State Colleges Information Center

MSCKC Measurement of Self-Concept in Kindergarten Children

M. Sc. L. Master of the Science of Law

mscn misconnection

mscnd misconnected

MSCNY Marine Society of the City of New York

MSC(O) old coastal minesweeper (naval symbol)

M.S. Conv. Master of Science in Conservation

M. Sc. Ost. Master of Science in Osteopathy

M Scot Middle Scottish

mscp mean spherical candlepower

MSCP Master Shielding Computer Program

MSCRB Margaret Sanger Clinical Research Bureau

mscrbl manuscribble (hand-scribbled manuscript)

mscrg miscarriage

MSCT Member of the Society of Cardiological Technicians

MSCW Mississippi State College for Women

msd missile system development; most significant digit; multiple spark discharge

MSD Management Services Department; Marine Sanitation Devices; Merck, Sharp & Dohme

M.S.D. Master (Mistress) of Scientific Didactics; Master (Mistress) Surgeon Dentist; Medical Science Doctor

M & SD Missile and Space Division (General Electric)

MSDA Marconi Space and Defence Systems

MSDC Mass Spectrometry Data Center; Molten Salts Data Center

M.S. Dent. Master of Science in Dentistry

M.S. Derm. Master of Science in Dermatology

MSDF Maritime Self-Defense Force (Japanese Navy)

M & SDI Mayonnaise and Salad Dressing Institute

MSDS Multi-Spectral-Scanner Data System

mse manufacturing support equipment; mean square error; military stressful era(s)

MSE Malaysia Shipyard and Engineering; Midwest Stock Exchange; Mississippi Export Railroad (stock exchange symbol); Montreal Stock Exchange

M.S.E. Master of Sanitary Engineering; Master of Science in Education; Master of Science in Engineering

m sec millisecond

μsec microsecond

M.S.Ed. Master (Mistress) of Science in Education

MSED Mobile Source Enforcement Division (EPA)

M.S.E.E. Master of Science in Electrical Engineering

M.S.E.M. Master of Science in Engineering Mechanics

M.S. Eng. Master of Science in Engineering

MSEO Marine Services Engineering Office(r)

m/seq master sequencer

MSER Manufacturing Support Equipment Request

mses marchandises (French—goods)

MSET Maintenance Supportability Evaluation Team

MSEUE Mouvement Socialiste pour les États Unis d'Europe (French—Socialist Movement for the United States of Europe)

msf minimum sector fuel; muscle shock factor

MSF fleet minesweeper (naval symbol); Maintenance Support Flight; Minesweeping Flotilla; mobile striking force; Motorcycle Safety Foundation; Multiple Shops Federation

M.S.F. Master of Science in Forestry

MSF Médecins Sans Frontères (French—doctors without borders)—international group of volunteer physicians

MSFC Marshall Space Flight Center

ms fm master form

M & SFM Maintenance and Supply Facility Manager

msfn manned space flight net-

work
ms fx master fixture
msg machine stress grading; message; monosodium glutamate
msg (MSG) monosodium glutamate
MSG Madison Square Garden; Marine Systems Group (General Dynamics)
ms ga master gauge
M.S.G.E. Master of Science in Geological Engineering
msgfm messageform
MSGp Mobile Support Group
msgr messenger
msgs messages
M Sgt Master Sergeant
msg/wtg message waiting
msh melanocyte-stimulating hormone (MSH)
MSH Music Society for the Handicapped
M.S.H. Master of Science in Horticulture; Master of Science in Hygiene
MSHA Mine Safety and Health Administration
M.S.H.A. Master of Science in Hospital Administration
M.S.H.E. Master of Science in Home Economics
MSHFA Multiservice Health Facility Association
MSHI Mitsubishi Singapore Heavy Industries
Mshl Marshal
M. S. Hort. Master of Science in Horticulture
M. S. Hyg. Master of Science in Hygiene
msi maintenance supply item(ization); management system indicator; medium-scale integration; military standard item; missile status indicator
MSI minesweeper, inshore (naval symbol); Motor Specialties Industries; Museum of Science and Industry
MSI *Movimento Sociale Italiano* (Italian Social Movement) —neo-fascist militants known as Missini
Msia Malaysia
Msian Malaysian
MSIB Mountain States Inspection Bureau
m'sieur *monsieur* (French—mister, sir)
M.S.Ind.Eng. Master of Science in Industrial Engineering
MSIRI Mauritius Sugar Industry Research Institute
M.S.J. Master of Science in

Journalism
msk mission support kit
MSK Mitsubishi Shoji Kaisha
MS-K Memorial Sloan-Kettering (cancer center)
MS-KCC Memorial Sloan-Kettering Cancer Center
MSKK Mitsui Sempaku Kabushiki Kaisha (Mitsui Line)
Mskr *Manuskript* (German—manuscript)
msl mean sea level; midsternal line; missile
msl *mesela* (Turkish—for example)
Msl Marseilles
MSL Marine Science Laboratories; minesweeping launch (naval symbol); Mulla Sadra Library (Shiraz, Iran); Munitions Supply Laboratories
M.S.L. Master of Science in Linguistics
MSLC Manufacturing Specification Liaison Change
ms lo master layout
mslp mean sea level pressure
MSLS Military Standard Logistics Systems
M.S.L.S. Master (Mistress) of Science in Library Science
msm maximum safety margin; modern school mathematics
MSM Manhattan School of Music; Meritorious Service Medal; Montana School of Mines, Mystic Seaport Museum (Conn)
M.S.M. Master of Science in Music
MSMA Maine School Management Association; Master Sign Makers' Association
MSMC Marie Stopes Memorial Centre
M.S.M.E. Master of Science in Mechanical Engineering
M.S.Med. Master (Mistress) of Medical Science
MSMM Missouri School of Mines and Metallurgy
msmq mild steel—merchant quality
MSMS Mutual Security Military Sales
M.S. Mus. Master of Science in Music
M.S. Mus. Ed. Master of Science in Music Education
msn mission
Msn Mission (postal abbreviation)
MSN Madison, Wisconsin (airport); Master Serial Number(ing); Material Supply Notice(s)

M.S.N. Master of Science in Nursing
MSNB Machine Screw Nut Bureau
M.S.N. Ed. Master of Science in Nursing Education
M.S.Nucl.Eng. Master of Science in Nuclear Engineering
MSNY Mattachine Society of New York
mso (MSO) multiple-systems operator (tv)
MSO Manila Symphony Orchestra; Marine Safety Office(r); Melbourne Symphony Orchestra; Memphis Symphony Orchestra; Milwaukee Symphony Orchestra; Minneapolis Symphony Orchestra (former name of the Minnesota Symphony); Monetary Statistics Ordinance; Montreal Symphony Orchestra; Morale Support Office(r); ocean minesweeper (naval symbol)
M.Soc.Sci. Master (Mistress) of Social Science
M. Soc. Wk. Master of Social Work
m-sop mezzo-soprano
M.S. Ophthal Master (Mistress) of Ophthalmological Surgery
MSORS Mechanical Solvent Oil Spill Recovery System
M.S.Ortho Master (Mistress) of Orthopedic Surgery
msp metal splash pan
msp (MSP) missile support plane
MSP Material Support Plan(ning); Maximum Security Prison; Medical Services Plan(ning); Minneapolis, Minnesota (airport), Mutual Security Program
M.S.P. Master (Mistress) of Science in Pharmacy
MSPB Merit Systems Protection Board
MSpC Medical Specialist Corps
MSPE Master of Science in Physical Education
M.S. Pet. Eng. Master of Science in Petroleum Engineering
M.S.P.H. Master of Science in Public Health
M.S.Pharm. Master of Science in Pharmacy
M.S.P.H.E. Master of Science in Public Health Engineering
M.S.P.H.Ed. Master of Science in Public Health Education
ms pl master plate

mspr master spares positioning resolver

MSPRB Meteorological Satellite Program Review Board

MSPU Massachusetts State Prostitutes Union (seeking decriminalization of their trade)

msr main supply route; mean spring rise (tides); mechanical strain recorder; mineral-surface roof; missile site radar

ms & r merchant shipbuilding and repairs

m & sr missile and surface radar

MSR Manufacturing Specification Request; Material Stores Requisition; mean spring tide

MSRA Multiple Shoe Retailers' Association

M.S. Rad. Master of Science in Radiology

MSRB Mississippi State Rating Bureau

M.S. Rec. Master of Science in Recreation

M.S. Ret. Master of Science in Retailing

MSRG Member of the Society for Remedial Gymnasts

MSRN Manufacturing Specification Revision Notice

msrp manufacturer's suggested retail price; massive selective retaliatory power

msrpp multidimensional scale for rating psychiatric patients

MSRs Marketing Service Representatives

MSRS Missile Strike Reporting System

Msrte Misroute

MSRTS Migrant Student Record Transfer System

msry masonry

mss magnetic storm satellite; manual safety switch; message switching station; missile select(ion) switch; missing sea stores; mode selection switch(ing); multispectral scanning (radar)

mss (MSS) magnetic storm satellite

ms's milk sisters (two or more females who have had sexual relations with the same male) —*see* mb's

ms's (MSs) mine sweepers

mss. manuscripts

Mss Misses; Mizzes (plural of Miz written Ms)

MSS Manufacturers Standardization Society of the Valve and Fittings Industry; Mass Storage Systems; Master Sup-

porting Schedule; Medical Service School; Medical Service School (USAF); Metropolitan Security Service(s); Movement Shorthand Society; Multiple Sclerosis Society; Multispectral Scanner Subsystem

M.S.S. Master of Social Science

MSS Museo Storico degli Spaghetti (Italian—Historical Museum of Spaghetti)—close to the Italian Riviera in Pontedassio

MSSA Maine School Superintendents Association; Maintenance Supply Services Agency; Manchester Scales of Social Adaptation

MSSAtl Military Sealift Service Atlantic

M.S.Sc. Master of Sanitary Science; Master of Social Science

MSSC Metropolitan School Study Council

msscc multicolor spin-scan cloudcover camera

MSSCS Manned Space Station Communications System

MSSD Model Secondary School for the Deaf

M & SSD Missile & Space System Division (Douglas Aircraft)

M.S.S.E. Master of Science in Sanitary Engineering

M.S. S. Eng. Master of Science in Sanitary Engineering

MSSGB Motion Study Society of Great Britain

MSSH Massachusetts Society for Social Hygiene

MSSInd Military Sealift Service Indian

MSSMS Munition Section Strategic Missile Squadron

MSSNY Medical Society of the State of New York

MSSPac Military Sealift Service Pacific

MSSR Moldavian Soviet Socialist Republic

MSSRC Mediterranean Social Science Research Council

MSSS Maintenance Supply Services System

M.S.S.S. Master (Mistress) of Science in Social Service

MSSST Meeting Street School Screening Test

M.S. St.Eng. Master of Science in Structural Engineering

mssu midstream specimen of urine

MSSVD Medical Society for the

Study of Venereal Diseases

MSSVFI Manufacturers Standardization Society of the Valve and Fittings Industry

M.S.S.W. Master (Mistress) of Science in Social Work

mst mean solar time; mean spring tide(s); mean survival time; measurement

m(st) metal-stabilized (runway)

M'st' Mister

MST Marconi Telecommunications Systems; Maximum Service Telecasters; Military Science Training; Mountain Standard Time

M.S.T. Master of Science in Teaching

MSTA Maryland State Teachers Association; Michigan State Teachers Association; Missouri State Teachers Association

M.Stat. Master (Mistress) of Statistics

mstb 1000 stock tank barrels

mstc mastic

MSTC Maryland State Teachers College; Massachusetts State Teachers College

MSTD Member of the Society of Typographic Designers

M.S. T.Ed. Master of Science in Teacher Education

msth mesothorium

M & ST L Minneapolis & St Louis (railroad)

mstn 1000 short tons

ms tp master template

M ST P & SSM Minneapolis, St Paul & Sault Ste Marie Railroad (Soo Line)

mstr master

Mstr Master

M.S.Trans Master of Science in Transportation

M.S. in Trans.E. Master of Science in Transportation Engineering

Mstr Mech Master Mechanic

MSTRP Military, Strategic, Tactical, and Relay Program

msts (MSTS) missile static test site

MSTS Military Sea Transport Service; Missile Static Test Site; Mobile System Test(ing) Site

msty mostly

msu main storage unit; maximum space use; maximum space utilization; mode selector unit

msu (MSU) maximum security unit

MSU Memphis State University; Michigan State University; Mississippi State University; Montana State University

MSUC Middle South Utilities Company

msud maple-syrup urine disease

MSUL Memphis State University Library; Michigan State University Library; Mississippi State University Library; Montana State University Library

MSU Lond Medical Schools of the University of London

M. Surgery Master of Surgery

M.Surv Master of Surveying

msus midstream urine specimen

msv (MSV) magnetically-supported vehicle; Martian surface vehicle; mean square velocity; miniature solenoid valve; molecular solution volume; murine sarcoma virus

MSV Medical Society of Victoria

MSVC Mount Saint Vincent College

MSVD Missile and Space-Vehicle Department (General Electric)

msv(M) murine sarcoma virus (Moloney)

Msw Massawa

M Sw Middle Swedish

MSW Medical Social Worker

M.S.W. Master of Social Welfare; Master of Social Work

mswa main storage work area (address)

MSX Seaboard Oil (stock exchange symbol)

msy (MSY) maximum sustainable yield

MSY New Orleans, Louisiana (airport)

msyd 1000 square yards

mt empty; machine translation; mail transfer; maximum torque; mean tide; mean time; measurement ton; mechanical translation; mechanical transport; medical technology; megaton (MT); membrana tympani; metal(lic) tape; metatarsal; metric ton; miniature tube; missile test; motor terminal; motor transport; mount torque; mount(ed); mounting

mt (MT) motor tanker

m/t mail transfer; manual transmission; measurement tons

m & t maintenance and test; movements and transports

mT tropical maritime air

Mt Mount; Mountain; tympanic

membrane

MT Machine Translation; Mail Transfer; Mandated Territory; Manning Table; Masoretic Text; Mechanical Translation; Medical Technologist; Meteorological Aids; Military Training; Military Transport; Mining Tenement; Ministry of Transport; Motor Transport; Mountain Time; Muscat Transport

MT-6 mercaptomerin (diuretic)

mta maximum time aloft; microwave transistor amplifier

mt/a million tons per annum

m^{ta} muita (Portuguese—much) —feminine form

MTA Maine Teachers Association; Manpower Training Association; Market Technicians Association; Massachusetts Teachers Association; Master Tilers Association; Metropolitan Transit Authority; Mississippi Teachers Association; Mississippi Test Area; Motor Trade Association; Music Teachers Association

mtac mathematical tables and other aids to computation

MTACCS Marine Tactical Command and Control System

MTAG Manufacturing Technology Advisory Group

MTAI Minnesota Teacher Attitude Inventory

MTAK Magyar Tudományos Akadémia Könyvtára (Hungarian—Library of the Hungarian Academy of Sciences) —in Budapest

mtam maritime tropical air mass

MTAMR Metropolitan Toronto Association for the Mentally Retarded

MT/AMT Mail Transfer—Airmail Transfer (funding)

MTASCP Medical Technologist of the American Society of Clinical Pathologists

mtb maintenance of true bearing

MTB Major Trading Bank; Malayan Tin Bureau; Malaysian Tin Bureau; Materials Transportation Bureau; Medium Tank Battalion; Miyagi Television Broadcasting; motor torpedo boat

MTBA Machine Tool Builders' Association

MTBC Mitsubishi Trust and Banking Corporation

mtbd mean time between demand

mtbe (MTBE) methyl tertiary butyl ether (octane-booster additive)

mtbf mean time before failure; mean time between failures

mtbfa mean time between false alarms

mtbff mean time between first failure

mtbfl mean time between function loss

mtbm mean time between maintenance

MTBRON Motor Torpedo Boat Squadron

mtbsf mean time between system failure

mtc memory test computer; more to come

m & tc mission and traffic control

MTC Malayan Tobacco Company; Marine Technology Center (Electric Boat); Maritime Transport Committee; Materiel Testing Command; Mechanical Transport Corps; Medical Training Center; Metropolitan Transportation Committee; Military Training Cadets; Missile Test Center; Monsanto Chemicals (stock exchange symbol); Montreal Trust Company; Morse Telegraph Club; Motor Transport Corps; Mystic Terminal (railroad)

M.T.C. Master of Textile Chemistry

MTC Ministerio de Transporte y Comunicaciones (Spanish—Ministry of Transportation and Communication)

MTCA Ministry of Transport and Civil Aviation

MTCB Metropolitan Taxicab Board

mtce maintenance; million tons of coal equivalent

mt & ce missile test and check-out equipment

MTCL Metropolitan Toronto Central Library

MTCP Minister of Town and Country Planning; Ministry of Town and Country Planning

mtcu magnetic tape control unit

mtd manufactured technological demonstrator; mean temperature difference; midpoint tissue dose; mounted

mtd (MTD) maximum tolerated dose

m.t.d. *mitte tales doses* (Latin—send such doses)

Mtd Marstrand

MT$ Maria Theresa dollar (Yemeni currency unit)

MTD Mobile Training Detachment

M.T.D. Master of Transport Design; Midwife Teachers' Diploma

MTDB Metropolitan Transit Development Board

MTDDA Minnesota Test for Differential Diagnosis of Aphasia

mtde maritime tactical data exchange

MTDE Maintenance Technique Development Establishment

MTDS Marine Tactical Data System

mte manufacturing test(ing) equipment; maximum temperature engine; maximum thermal energy; multiple-track error

M^{te} Monte (Italian, Portuguese, Spanish—mountain)

MTE Marine Technical Education

MTEA Metal Trades Employers Association

M. Tech. Master (Mistress) in Technology

M.Tel.Eng. Master (Mistress) of Telecommunication Engineering

MTER Manufacturing Test Equipment Request

M^{tes} Montes (Italian, Portuguese, Spanish—mountains)

M.Text. Master (Mistress) of Textiles

mtf mechanical time fuze; modulation transfer function; multiple technical force

MTF Medical Treatment Facility; Metal Trades Federation; Mississippi Test Facility; Multiracial Training Facility

mtfex mountain field exercise

mtg main turbogenerator(s); meeting; methanol to gasoline; mortgage; mounting

Mtg Meeting (postal abbreviation)

mtgc mounting center

mtgd mortgaged

mtge mortgage

mtgee mortgagee

mtgor mortgagor

mth microptic theodolite; month

M. Th. Master of Theology

MTH Master of Trinity House

mthly monthly

mthm metric tons of heavy metal

mths months

mthv must have

mthw medium-temperature hot water

mti moving target identification; moving target indicator(s); moving target information

M^{ti} Munti (Romanian—mountain)

MTI Metal Treating Institute; Motorola Teleprograms Incorporated

MTI Magyar Távirati Iroda (Hungarian Press Agency)

MTIA Metal Trades Industry Association

MTIB Malaysian Timber Industry Board

mtik missile test installation kit

mtime meantime

MTIRA Machine Tool Industry Research Association

mTk tropical maritime air colder than underlying surface

mtks many thanks

mtl material; materiel; mean tide level; merged transistor logic; metal(lic); mixed thermoluminescence

mtl monatlich (German—monthly)

Mtl Montreal; Motel

MTL mean tide level; Modern Terminals Limited; Motor Traders Limited

MTLA Micropublishers Trade List Annual

mtlp metabolic toxemia of late pregnancy

mtl(s) material(s)

mtlz materialize

mtlzd materialized

mtm method, time, and motion; methods time measurement(s)

MTM Mary Tyler Moore

MTMA Modern Teaching Methods Association

MTMC Military Traffic Management Command (USA); Mother Teresa's Missionaries of Charity

Mt McK NP Mount McKinley National Park

MTMCTEA Military Traffic Management Command Transportation Engineering Agency

MTMS Multi-Terminal Modular System

MTMTS Military Traffic Management and Terminal Service

mtn motion; mutton

Mtn Mountain

MTN Medical Television Network; Multilateral Trade Negotiations

MTNA Music Teachers National Association

mtnt must not

MTNWR Mark Twain National Wildlife Refuge (Illinois)

mto modification task outline

m^{to} muito (Portuguese—much) —masculine form

MTO Mississippi Test Operations

mtoe million tons oil equivalent

Mton Moncton

mtons metric tons

mTorr millitorr(s)

mtp minimum tour price

Mt P Mount Palomar (observatory)

MTP Management Training Program; Mobilization Training Program; Modification Task Proposal; Mount Tom Price

M.T.P. Master (Mistress) of Town Planning

mtpa million tons per annum

MTPCNA Metal Tube Packaging Council of North America

Mt P O Mount Palomar Observatory

mtpp missile-to-target patch panel

mtpy millions of tons per year

mtr materials testing reactor; matter; mean time to restore; meter; missile-tracking radar; motor; moving target reactor; multiple track radar

mtr (MTR) marginal tax rate

Mtr Meinicke turbidity reaction; Montrose

MTr meridian transit

MTR Mass Transit Railroad; Mass Transit Railway; Mass Transportation Railroad; Materials Testing Report; Montour (railroad)

MTRB Motor Truck Rate Bureau

MTRC Mass Transit Railway Corporation

mtrcl motorcycle

mtre missile test and readiness equipment

Mt Rev Most Reverend

MTRF Mark Twain Research Foundation

mtrg metering

mtri missile test range instrumentation

mtrl material

Mt R NP Mount Rainier National Park

Mtro Maestro (Spanish—Master)

M.T.R.P. Master (Mistress) of Town and Regional Planning

mtr rdr meter reader

MTRS Magnetic Tape Recording System

mtr vlu meter(ing) value

mts mobile training set; motorship twin screw; mountains

mt's empties

Mts Mountains

MTS Machine Tractor Station; Marine Technology Society; Mashinno-Traktornye Stantsii (Russian—Machine Tractor Stations); Melanesian Tourist Services; Member(s) of the Technical Staff; Middlebare Technical School; Missile Test Stand; Missile Test Station; Money Transfer Service

mt/se magnetic-tape selectric composer

MTSC Middle Tennessee State College

mtst maximum treadmill stress time

mt/st magnetic-tape selectric typewriter

MTSU Middle Tennessee State University

mtt magnetic tape terminal; mean transit time; moving target tracking

MTT Maintenance Training Team; Metropolitan Transport Trust; Mobile Training Team (USN); Municipal Tramways Trust

MTTA Machine Tools Trades' Association

MTTAGB Machine Tool Trades Association of Great Britain

mtte magnetic tape terminal equipment

mttf mean time to failure

mttff mean time to first failure

mttms magnetic tape transmissions

mttr mean time to repair

mtu metric tons of uranium; mobile tracking unit; mobile training unit

mtu (MTU) multiplexer and terminal unit

MTU Maintenance Training Unit; Michigan Technological University; Michigan Training Unit (reformatory); Mobile Training Unit

MTU Motoren und Turbinen Union (German—Motors and

Turbines United)—corporation

M. tuberc. Mycobacterium tuberculosis

MTUOP mobile training unit out for parts

mtv mammary tumor virus; motor test(ing) vehicle

mtv (MTV) music television (channel)

MtV Mount Vernon

M.Tv. Master of Television

MTV Motor Test Vehicle; motor torpedoboat (British naval symbol)

MTVs Motor Torpedo Vessels

mtw main trawl winch

mTw tropical maritime air warmer than underlying surface

mt we must we

Mt W O Mount Wilson Observatory

mtx methotrexate

MTX Morrell Tank Line (railway symbol)

mtxs military traffic expediting service

Mty Monterrey (inhabitants—Regiomontanos)

MTY Monterrey, Mexico (airport)

mtz motorize

MTZS Metropolitan Toronto Zoological Society

mu machine unit; mail unit; marijuana user; monetary unit; mouse unit; multiple unit

mu (MU) marginal utility (microeconomics symbol); markup (calculator)

m/u mockup

MU Macquarie University; Maintenance Unit, Marquette University; Marshall University; Massey University; Mercer University; Mercy University; Mercyhurst University; Meredith University; Merrimack University; Mesa University; Messiah University; Methodist University; Miami University; Midwestern University; Milliken University; Monash University; Mothers' Union; Murdoch University; Musicians Union

MUA Machinery Users' Association; Malayan Union Association; Monotype Users' Association; Musicians Union of Australia

MUAC Metropolitan Universities Admissions Center

Muang-Thai (Siamese—Thai-

land)

muap motor unit action potential(s)

muat mobile underwater acoustic unit

muc mucilage

muc. mucilago (Latin—mucilage)

MUC Magee University College; Meritorious Unit Citation; Muchea, Australia (tracking station); Munich, Germany (Riem airport)

mu car multiple-unit (railroad) car

MUCC Michigan United Conservation Clubs

Much Ado Much Ado About Nothing

MUCIA Midwest Universities Consortium for International Activities

Muckraker of France Émile Zolá whose anticlerical, antimilitary, and antimonarchial writings forced him to flee to England during the trial of Captain Dreyfus; Zolá startled his generation by declaring civilization would take its first great step forward when the last stone from the last church fell on the head of the last priest

Muckrakers turn-of-our-century American crusader journalists David Graham Phillips, Charles Edward Russell, Lincoln Steffens, Upton Sinclair, Ida M. Tarbell

MUCM Medical University College of Medicine

MUCO Material Utilization Control Office

MUD Municipal Utility District

'muda Bermuda

'muda grass bermuda grass

Mudcat(s) Mississippian(s)

Mudcat State Mississippi

Mud Island San Diego's South Bay Wildlife Preserve

MUDPAC Melbourne University Dual-Package Analog Computer

MUDPIE Museum and University Data, Programs, and Information Exchange

muf material unaccounted for; maximum usable frequency

MUFON Mutual UFO Network

Muggsy Francis (Muggsy) Spanier

Muh Muharram (Arabic—first month of the Mohammedan

year)

Muhammad (Arabic—The Praised)—Mahomet

Muhammad Ali Cassius Clay

Mühlhausen Mülhausen in Thüringen (Mühlhausen in Thuringia)

Mühlheim Mühlheim am Main (Mühlheim on the Main River near the Swiss border) or Mühlheim an der Donau (Mühlheim on the Danube near the Luxembourg border)—both in West Germany

Mujib Mujibur Rahman

Muk Mukden

mul multiply

mul mulig(vis) (Dano-Norwegian—eventual, probable, or possible, perhaps)

MUL Makerere University Library (Kampala, Uganda)

mulat mulatto

Mulatas Mulatas Islands

mule (*see* hinny)

mule. modular universal laser equipment

Mule NATO name for Soviet Polikarpov trainer aircraft

Mule Capital of the World Columbia, Tennessee (in the estimation of its chamber of commerce)

MULES Missouri Uniform Law Enforcement System

Mülheim Mülheim an der Ruhr (Mülheim on the Ruhr River adjoining Essen) or Mülheim am Rhein (Mülheim on the Rhine next to Cologne)—both in West Germany and not to be confused with the two Mühlheims

MULS Minnesota (University) Union List of Serials

mult multiplication

MULTEWS Multiple-Target Electronic-Warfare System

multi (Latin prefix—many or much)—multitude

multics multiplexed information and computing service

multitran multiple translation (translating one language into several target languages)

multr multimeter

mulv murine complex leukemia

mum mumble(d); mumbling; mummed; mummer(s); mummery

mum. (MUM) (robot) methodology for unmanned manufacturers

Mum Mumford

MUMC McMaster University Medical Center

Mum City, U.S.A. Bristol, Connecticut famous for its chrysanthemums (mums)

MUMMS Marine Corps Unified Management System

MUMPS Multi-Programming System (Massachusetts General Hospital)

mums chrysanthemums

mun munition

Mun Müngo; Munro; Munroe; Munster

Mün München (German—Munich)

MUN Memorial University of Newfoundland; Model United Nations

Muncy Institution State Correctional Institution at Muncy, Pennsylvania

Mund Edmund

muni municipal; municipality

muni bond(s) municipal bond(s)

munic municipal; municipality

Munich English place-name for München

Munich Expressionist Wassily Kandinsky

Municipal Muckraker Lincoln Steffens—author of *The Shame of the Cities*

munit munitions

Muñoz Marín Luis Muñoz Marín—democratic leader and first governor of Puerto Rico

muo myocardiopathy of unknown origin

MUO Municipal University of Omaha

muon mu meson (Siamese—town, as in Muong Boten, town on border of Laos and Thailand)

MUP Manchester University Press; Melbourne University Press

M.U.P. Master of Urban Planning

MUR Mouvements Unis de la Résistance (French—United Movements of the Resistance)

MURA Midwestern Universities Research Association

Murasaki Baroness Murasaki Shikibu *(The Tale of the Genji)*

Murder Capital of America Detroit, Michigan where for every crime reported three go unreported, according to *The Manchester Guardian Weekly*

Murder City media nickname applied to any city sustaining

the greatest number of murders in any year

MURFAAMCE Mutual Reduction of Forces and Armaments in Central Europe

muriatic acid hydrochloric acid (HCl)

Murihiku (Maori—End of the Tail)—New Zealand's southernmost city on South Island —Invercargill

Murph Murphy

murphy murphy bed (concealed-in-the-wall bed invented by William L Murphy—an American; nickname for an irish or white potato as well as for a confidence swindle)

Murphy's law if something can go wrong—it will

Murrumbidgee (Aboriginal Australian—Big Water)—affluent of the Murray River in New South Wales

Murrumbidgee River City Canberra—Australia's capital

Murtala Mohammed Lagos, Nigeria's airport

mus multiunit school(s); musculoskeletal; museum; music; musical; musician

Mus Musca (constellation); Muscat; museum; music; Muslim

MUS Magnetic Unloading System; Manned Underwater Station

musa multiple-unit steerable antenna

MUSA Medical University of Southern Africa

Mus Anthro Mo University of Missouri Museum of Anthropology

Mus Art RI Museum of Art—Rhode Island

Mus. Bac. Bachelor of Music

Mus Bks Museum Books

musc muscle; muscular

Muscat and Oman former name of the Sultanate of Oman

muscrit music critic(ism)

mus dir music(al) director

Mus. Doc. Doctor of Music

Muse of Astronomy and Celestial Music Urania

Muse of Comedy and Pastoral Poetry Thalia

Muse of Dancing and Choral Singing Terpsichore

Mus.Ed.B. Bachelor of Music Education

Mus.Ed.D. Doctor of Music Education

Mus.Ed.M. Master of Music Education

Muse of Epic and Heroic Poetry Calliope, who according to Horace, could play any musical instrument

Muse of Erotic Poetry Erato

Muse of History Clio

Muse of Lyric Poetry and Music Euterpe

museo museography; museological; museologist; museololgy

Muse of Oratory, Rhetoric, and Sacred Song Polyhymnia

Muse of Tragedy Melpemone

Museum of Architecture Leningrad (formerly Petrograd or Saint Petersburg)

Museum Cities northern Italy's Padua, Venice, Verona, and Vicenza

Museum Metropolis London, New York, and Paris compete for this title

Mushroomopolis Kansas City

Music Academy of Music; High School of Music

MUSIC Maryland University Sectored Isochronous Cyclotron

Musical Charlotte Russe Tchaikovsky's Andante cantabile from his Symphony No. 5 in E minor

Musical Dictator of Dalmatia Franz von Suppé (Francesco Ezechiale Ermenegildo Cavaliere Suppé Demelli)

Musical Philosopher Alfred Brendel

Music Capital of America Los Angeles and New York claim this title

Music Capital of Eastern Europe Vienna

Music Capital of Western Europe London

Music City, U.S.A. Nashville, Tennessee

Music Man Meredith Willson

musicol musicological; musicologist; musicology

mus id's musical identifications (of radio or tv feature programs)

MusiMus *Musikkhistorisk Museum* (Norwegian—Music History Museum)

muskie muskellunge

Musky Armando Moscaritolo

Muslim Century the 8th century —the 700s when the Turkish crescent occupied the entire Hispanic Peninsula, the Levant, the Middle East, and even westernmost India

Mus.M. Master of Music

Mus Northern Ariz Museum of

Northern Arizona

Musso Mussolini

Mus Sys Museum Systems

must. manned undersea station

MUST Medical Unit, Self-contained, Transportable

Mustang North American fighter aircraft F-51

Mustang Bridge Ranch Storey County, Nevada's legalized brothel only seven miles east of Reno

mustargen mustard-nitrogen (poison compound)

mustn't must not

MUSTRACS Multiple Simultaneous-Target Steerable Telemetry-Tracking System

mut mutation

mutil mutilate; mutilated; mutilation

mutt muttonhead

mutt (MUTT) military utility tactical truck

muttnik second Soviet satellite launched in 1957, so nicknamed because its astronaut was a mongrel dog used to test the vehicle

Mutton Birds Mutton Bird Islands off the southwest coast of New Zealand's Stewart Island where they are also called the Titis

mutu mutual; mutualism

Mutual Mutual Association for Professional Services, Mutual Benefit Life Insurance Company of Newark, New Jersey; Mutual Broadcasting System; Mutual Life Insurance Company of New York; Mutual Nurses Registry; Mutual of Omaha; Mutual Protection Trust; Mutual Security Life Insurance; Mutual Trust Life Insurance

muu mouse uterine units

muw music wire

MUWS Manned Underwater Station

mux multiplex

mux/aro multiplex-automatic error correction

muz *muziek* (Dutch—music)

Muz Muzio

Muzel (Cornish-English— Mousehole)—fishing port resort in Cornwall

muzh muzzle hatch

mv main verb; mean variation; mercury vapor; millivolt; monochromatic vision; multivibrator; muzzle velocity

m & v meat and vegetable

μv microvolt

mv *meervoud* (Dutch—plural)

m v *mezzo voce* (Italian—middle voice)

mV megavolt(s); millivolt(s)

Mv megavolt; mendelevium

M/V motor vessel

MV *Maria Vergine* (Italian— Virgin Mary)

M.V. *Medicus Veterinarius* (Veterinary Physician)

MV-678 Agricultural Research Service chemical for fighting fire ants by mimicking hormones to create drones

mva mean vertical acceleration; megavolt ampere; motor vehicle accident

MVA Machinists Vise Association; Mississippi Valley Association; Missouri Valley Authority

MVAS Milwaukee Vocational and Adult School

MVB Martin Van Buren (8th President U.S.)

MVBA Mercado de Valores de Buenos Aires (Buenos Aires Stock Exchange)

mvbd multiple V-belt drive

MVBL Mississippi Valley Barge Line

mvc manual volume control; manufacturing variation control

MVC Military and Veterans Code

MVCC Mount Vernon Community College

MVD Montevideo, Uruguay (Carrasco Airport)

MVD *Ministerstvo Vnutrenniy Delo* (Russian Ministry of Internal Affairs)—*(q.v.— VOT)*

MVDA Motor Vehicle Dismantlers' Association

MVe Murray Valley encephalitis

MVE Metropolitan Vickers Electrical

M.V.E. Master of Vocational Education

MVEMJSUNP *M*en *V*ery *Eas*ily *M*ake *J*ugs *S*erve *U*seful *N*octurnal *P*urposes (acrostic mnemonic for remembering the order of planets from the sun—Mercury, Venus, Earth, Mars, Jupiter, Saturn, Uranus, Neptune, Pluto)

M.Vet.Med. Master (Mistress) of Veterinary Medicine

M.Vet.Sci. Master (Mistress) of Veterinary Science

mvg most valuable girl

MVG Medal for Victory over

Germany
MVHS Mergenthaler Vocational High School
mvi multi-vitamin infusion
M/video Montevideo
MVJC Mount Vernon Junior College
mvlf (MVLF) motor-vehicle license fee(s)
MVM Motor Vehicle Mechanic
MVMA million vehicle miles; Motor Vehicle Manufacturers Association
MVMFB Mississippi Valley Motor Freight Bureau
mvmt movement
MVNP Mesa Verde National Park
MVNWR Monte Vista National Wildlife Refuge (Colorado)
Mvo Montevideo
MVO Member of the Victorian Order
mvp maximum-value package; most valuable player
MVP Manpower Validation Program
MVPBA Mississippi Valley Power Boat Association
MVPCB Motor Vehicle Pollution Control Board
MVPT Motor-Free Visual Perception Test(ing)
mvri mixed vaccine—respiratory infections
mvs multiple virtual storage
MVS Multi-Vest Securities
M.V.Sc. Master of Veterinary Science
MVSS Motor Vehicle Safety Standard
mvt moisture-vapor transmission; multiprogramming with variable number of tasks
MVT Motor Vehicle Technician
MV & THS Manhattan Vocational and Technical High School
MVTI Mohawk Valley Technical Institute
mvv maximum voluntary ventilation
mw megawatt; milliwatt; molecular weight
m/w manufacturing week
mW megawatt(s)
m/W male White
mW *meines Wissens* (German —as far as I know)
Mw megawatt
MW Montgomery Ward
M-W Merriam-Webster
MWA Modern Woodmen of America; Mystery Writers of

America
MWAA Movers and Warehousemen Association of America
MWAI Mystery Writers of America, Incorporated
M-way Motorway (superhighway)
mwb motor whale boat
MWB Metropolitan Water Board; Minister of Works and Buildings; Ministry of Works and Buildings
MWC Ministry of War Communications; Motorola Western Center
MWCG Metropolitan Washington Council of Governments
mwd megawatt day
MWD Metropolitan Water District; Ministry of Works and Development; Mutual Weapons Development
mwdm multiwavelength distance measuring (instrument)
mwd/mtu megawatt day per metric ton of uranium
MWDP Mutual Weapons Development Program
mwe megawatts of electricity; meters of water equivalent
MWF Medical Women's Federation
mwg music wire gauge
MWGCP Most Worthy Grand Chief Patriarch
MWGM Most Worshipful Grand Master; Most Worthy Grand Master
mwh milliwatt hour
m & whm missile and warhead magazines
MWHS Martha Washington High School
mwi message-waiting indicator
MWIA Medical Women's International Association
MWJC Marjorie Webster Junior College
mwk millwork
MWL Minimum Wage Law(s); Mutual Welfare League
MWLP Meadowview Wild Life Preserve
MWMCA Michigan Women for Medical Control of Abortion
MWMFB Midwest Motor Freight Bureau
MWN *Medical World News*
MWNM Muir Woods National Monument
mwnt mean water neap tide
MWO Marshallese Women's Organization; Midwest Oil; Modification Work Order;

Mount Wilson Observatory
mwp maximum working pressure; membrane waterproofing
MWP Most Worthy Patriarch
MWPA Married Women's Property Act
mwr mean width ratio
MWR Morton Wildlife Refuge (New York)
mws magnetic weapon sensor
MWS Manas Wildlife Sanctuary (India); Mudamalai Wildlife Sanctuary (India)
MWSC Midwestern Simulation Council
MWSG Marine Wing Support Group
M.W.T. Master of Wood Technology
mwth megawatts thermal
mwv maximum working voltage
MWV *Mineralöl Wirtschafts Verband* (German—Petroleum Industry Association)
mww manual wire wrap; municipal waste water
MWW *Merry Wives of Windsor*
MWZ Manischewitz (stock exchange symbol)
mx maxwell; motocross (rough-terrain motorcycle race); multiplex
mx (MX) missile experimental
Mx maxwell; Middlesex
Mx (MX) experimental intercontinental ballistic missile (designed for in-the-air, on-the-ground or under-the-sea launching to prevent its destruction by a Soviet nuclear strike)
MX Mexicana de Aviación (2-letter code)
mxa mobile exercise area
MXC Minnesota Experimental City
mxd mixed
mxd cl mixed carload
mxdth maximum depth
Mxl Mexicali (inhabitants—Cachanias)
MXP Milan, Italy (Malpensa Airport)
mxpst maximum possible storm
mxr mask index register
mXr mass X-ray
mx rnfl maximum rainfall
MXS Missile Experimental System
mxtmp maximum temperature
mxwnd maximum wind
my. million years; myopia;

myopic
m/y man-year
My Malayalam; Milo; Mylan
MY Medinat Yisrael (State of Israel); motor yacht
Mya Myasishchev
Mya-4 Soviet heavy bomber named Bison by NATO
mybp million years before present
Myc Mycenaean
MYC Manchester Yacht Club; Middletown Yacht Club; Milwaukee Yacht Club; Minnetonka Yacht Club; Mobile Yacht Club
myco mycobacterium
mycol mycology
myel(s) myelocyte(s)
myg myriagram
myl myrialiter
mylo mylohyoid
mym myriameter
myn million
myo (Greek *mys*—mouse or muscle)—myocardial infarction, myocardium, myoma; *mayo* (Spanish—May)

myob mind your own business
myodyn myodynamics
myoelectric myoelectrical(ly)
myo inf myocardial infarction
myol myology
myop myopia
mypo multiyear procurement objective
Myr Myriopeda
Myrna Loy Myrna Williams
Myrt Myrtle
Mys Mysore
Mys Sea Mystic Seaport
myst mystagogue; mystagogy; mysteries; mysterious; mystery; mystic; mystical; mysticism; mystics
Mystere IV Dassault jet fighter built in France
Mystere 20 Dassault twin-engine executive transport called the Falcon
Mysterious Billionaire Howard Hughes
myth. mythological; mythologist; mythology
Myth Mythology
Mytilene Aegean island of Les-

bos
mz monozygotic
mz Mangelszahlung (German—for non-payment)
Mz Méndez
MZ Mail Zone; Museum of Zoology; RH Macy and Company (stock exchange symbol)
M & Z Mombasa and Zanzibar
MZA Madrid, Zaragoza, Alicante
mzm multiple-zone monitor
MZMA (Russian—*Moskva Zavod Maloitrazhkaya Automobili*)—Moscow Small-Engine Car Factory producing the Moskvich auto
MZn magnetic azimuth
MZNP Mountain Zebra National Park (South Africa)
mzo marzo (Spanish—March)
M-zone manufacturing zone
MZP Marwell Zoological Park
mzs mezzo-soprano
M.Z.Sc. Master of Zoological Science
Mzt Mazatlán (inhabitants—Mazatleoos)

N

n name; nasal; national; nautical; naval; neap; negative; nerve; neuter; neutral; neutron; new; night; nominative; noon; norm; normal; noun; nuclear; number; refractive index (symbol); shear modulus of elasticity (symbol); transport number (code)

n' and

n/ and; number

'n' and (as in fish 'n' chips, rock 'n' roll, strawberries 'n' cream, etc.)

'n' and

n index of refraction (symbol); load factor (symbol); nació (Spanish—born); revolutions per second (symbol); rotative speed (symbol)

n. haploid generation; numerus (Latin—number)

n/ nuestro (Spanish—our); número (Spanish—number)

N International Nickel (stock exchange symbol); national; nautical; naval; Navy; Negro; neon; neutral; neutron(s); newton(s); night; nimbus; Nippon; nitrogen; noon; normal; Norse; north; northern; Norway (auto plaque); November —code for letter N; nuclear-propelled vessel (naval symbol); nucleus

N (N) employment of labor (microecomics symbol)

(N) nuclear-powered ship (naval symbol, as in CL[N]—nuclear-powered cruiser)

N avogadro constant or number (symbol); natus (Latin—born); Nebenstimme (German —secondary line or motif)— 12-tone term; neer (Dutch—

down); noord (Dutch—north); nord (Danish, French, Italian, Norwegian, Swedish—north); Nord (German—north); norre (Danish—north); norte (Portuguese or Spanish—north); north; number of turns (symbol); rate of propeller rotation (symbol); revolutions per minute (symbol); yawing moment (symbol)

N1, N2, etc. North One, North Two, etc. (London postal zones)

$n._2$ diploid generation

N_2 nitrogen

N_2O nitric oxide

N^{14} radioactive nitrogen

n/30 net (payment) in 30 days

na naturally aspirated; negative attitude; next assembly; nicotinic acid; no account; not absolutely; not applicable; not appropriated; not authorized; not available; nucleic acid (NA); numerical aperture

n/a navigation and attack; next assembly; no account; no advise; not applicable

na nestre ar (Norwegian—next year)

Na nadir; Napier; natrium (sodium); sodium (symbol)

N^a Nuestra (Spanish—our)

NA Narcotics Anonymous; National Academician; National Academy; National Airlines; National Archives; National Association; National Almanac; Naval Academy; Naval Architect; Naval Attaché; Naval Auxiliary; Naval Aviator; Netherlands Antilles (Aruba, Bonaire, Curaçao, Saba, Sint Eustatius, Sint Maarten);

Neurotics Anonymous; North America; North American; Northrup Aircraft; Nurse's Aide

NA Nautical Almanac; Nederlandse Antillen (Dutch— Netherlands Antilles)—Aruba, Bonaire, Curaçao, Saba, Sint Eustatius, Sint Maarten—the Dutch West Indies; Nomina Anatomica (Latin—Anatomical Names)—official nomenclature adopted by the International Congresses of Anatomists

Na_2CO_3 sodium carbonate (sal soda)

Na^{24} radioactive sodium

naa neutron activation analysis; not always afloat

NAA National Academy of Arbitrators; National Aeronautic Association; National Alumni Association; National Apple Association; National Arborist Association; National Archery Association; National Association of Accountants; National Auctioneers Association; National Automobile Association; Naval Association of Australia; Naval Attache for Air; North American Aviation

NAAA National Alliance of Athletic Associations; National Association of American Academicians; National Auto Auction Association

NAAB National Architectural Accrediting Board

NAABC National Association of American Business Clubs

NAABI National Association of Alcoholic Beverage Importers

naabsa not always afloat but safe
aground

NAAC National Agricultural
Advisory Commission

NAACC National Association
for American Composers and
Conductors

NAACO North American Arms
Corporation of Canada

NAACOG Nurses Association
of the American College of
Obstetrics and Gynecology

NAACP National Association
for the Advancement of
Colored People

NAACP (underworld jargon—
Never Agitate Adam Clayton
Powell)

NAADC North American Area
Defense Command

NAADS New Army Automatic
Data System

NAAF North African Air Force
(World War II)

NAAFA National Association
to Aid Fat Americans

NAAFI Navy, Army, and Air
Force Institutes

NAAG National Association of
Attorneys General; NATO
Army Advisory Group

NAAMM National Association
of Architectural Metal Manufacturers

NAAN National Advertising
Agency Network

NAANACM National Association for the Advancement of
Native American Composers
and Musicians

NAAO National Association of
Amateur Oarsmen; Navy Area
Audit Office

NAAPPA North American Association for the Protection of
Predatory Animals

NAAQS National Ambient Air
Quality Standards

NAARI National Aero- and Astronautical Research Institute

NAARPR National Alliance
Against Racist Political Repression

NAAS National Agricultural
Advisory Service; National
Apprentice Assistance
Scheme; Naval Area Audit
Service; Naval Auxiliary Air
Station

NAASC North American Aviation Science Center

NAASFEP National Association of Administrators of State
and Federal Education Programs

NAA S & ID North American

Aviation Space and Information Division

NAASRA National Association
of Australian State Road Authorities

NAASS North American Association of Summer Sessions

NAATI National Accreditation
Authority for Translators and
Interpreters

NAATS National Association
of Air Traffic Specialists

NAAUC National Association
of Australian University Colleges

NAAUS National Archery Association of the United States

NAAW National Association of
Accordion Wholesalers

NAAWS North American Association of Wardens and Superintendents

NAB National Aborigine Con-
ference; National Alliance of
Businessmen; National Assist-
ance Board; National Associa-
tion of Broadcasters; National
Association of Businessmen;
Naval Advanced Base; Naval
Air Base; Naval Amphibious
Base; Newspaper Advertising
Bureau

NAB *New American Bible*

NABA North American Benefit
Association

NABACO National Association
for Bank Audit, Control, and
Operation

NABAE National Association
of Black Adult Educators

NABB National Association for
Better Broadcasting

NABBC National Association
of Brass Band Conductors

Nabby Abigail

NABC National Association of
Boys' Clubs

NABD North American Band
Directors

NABDC National Association
of Blueprint and Diazotype
Coaters

NABE National Association of
Bilingual Education; National
Association for Bilingual Education; National Association
of Book Editors; National Association of Business Economists

NABEO National Association
of Black Elected Officials

NABET National Association
of Broadcast Employees and
Technicians

NABEWD North American
Board for East-West Dialogue

NABIM National Association
of Band Instrument Manufacturers

NABISCO National Biscuit
Company

NABLT National Association of
Business Law Teachers

NABMA National Association
of British Market Authorities

NABMO NATO Bullpup Management Office(r)

nabor neighbor

NABP National Association of
Book Publishers

NABPO NATO Bullpup Production Office(r); NATO Bullpup Production Organization

Nabrico Nashville Bridge Company

NABRT National Association
for Better Radio and Television

NABS National Association of
Barber Schools; National Association of Black Students;
nuclear-armed bombardment
satellite

NABSE National Alliance of
Black School Educators

NABSP National Association of
Blue Shield Plans

NABT National Association of
Biology Teachers; National
Association of Blind Teachers

NABTE National Association
for Business Teacher Education

nabu non-adjusting ballup (un-
solvable confusion)

Nabuco *Nabucodonosor* (four-
act opera by Verdi)

NABUG National Association
of Broadcast Unions and
Guilds

NABW National Association of
Bank Women

nac nacelle; negative air cushion; nozzle area control

NAC National Achievement
Clubs; National Agency
Check; National Airways Corporation (New Zealand); National Americanism Com-
mission (American Legion);
National Arts Club; National
Association of Cemeteries;
National Association of Chiropodists; National Association
of Coroners; National Association of Counties; National
Aviation Club; National Aviation Corporation; National
Can Corporation (stock exchange symbol); Naval Academy; Naval Air Center; Naval
Aircraftman; Non-Airline Car-

rier; North Atlantic Council; Northeast Air Command; Norwegian American Cruises; Norwegian-American Council; Nuclear Assurance Corporation; (*see* PNAC)

NACA National Advisory Committee for National Aeronautics; National Agricultural Chemicals Association; National Air Carrier Association; National Armored Car Association; National Association of Cost Accountants; National Association of County Administrators; New Australian Cultural Association

NACAC National Ad Hoc Committee Against Censorship; National Association of College Admissions Counselors

NACADA National Academic Advising Association

NACAE National Advisory Council for Art Education

NACAM National Association of Corn and Agricultural Merchants

NACASBVH National Accreditation Council for Agencies Serving the Blind and Visually Handicapped

NACATTS North American Clear-Air Turbulence-Tracking System

NACB National Association of Convention Bureaus

NACC National Association for Core Curriculum

NACCA National Association for Creative Children and Adults

NACCAM National Coordinating Committee for Aviation Meteorology

NACCC National Association of Citizens Crime Commissions

NACCD National Advisory Commission on Civil Disorders

NACCG National Association of Crankshaft and Cylinder Grinders

N-accident(s) nuclear-power accident(s)

NACCT Nebraska Association of Community College Trustees

NACD National Association for Community Development; National Association of Conservation Districts; National Association of Corporate Directors

NACDL National Association

of Criminal Defense Lawyers

NACDR National Association of College Deans and Registrars

NACE National Association for Career Education; National Association of Corrosion Engineers

NACEEO National Advisory Council on Equality of Educational Opportunity

NACEL Naval Air Crew Equipment Laboratory

NACF National Agricultural Cooperatives Federation; National Art Collections Fund; Navy Air Combat Fighter (plane)

NACFI North American Council on Fishery Investigations

nach (nAch) need for achievement

Nach Nachman

NACH National Advisory Council for the Handicapped

NACHA National Automated Clearinghouse Association

NACHEPO National Advisory Commission on Higher Education for Police Officers

Nachf *Nachfolger* (German—successor)

nachm *nachmittags* (German—afternoon, p.m.)

NACHM National Advisory Committee on Health Manpower

Nachr *Nachrichten* (German—bulletin)

NACHRI National Association of Children's Hospitals and Related Institutions

Nachtr *Nachtrag* (German—appendix, supplement)

NACIAD National Council on Integrated Area Development

NACIDA National Cottage Industries Development Authority (Philippines)

NACILA National Council of Indian Library Associations

NACIMFP National Advisory Council on International Monetary and Financial Problems

Nacional *El Nacional* (Venezuela's leading periodical published in Caracas)

Naciones *Unidas* (Spanish—United Nations)

Nacirema (not an acronym but American spelled backwards) —name of a terminal operator serving the port of New York; also used by an extremist wing of the Ku Klux Klan—one of

America's most un-American organizations

NaCl sodium chloride (salt)

NACL National Advisory Commission on Libraries; Navy-Arpa Chemical Laser; Nippon Aviotronics Company Limited

NACLA North American Congress on Latin America

NACLIS National Commission on Libraries and Information Science

NACM National Association of Chain Manufacturers; National Association of Credit Management

naco night-alarm cutoff

NACO National Arts Centre Orchestra (Ottawa); National Association of Counties

NACOA National Advisory Committee on Oceans and Atmosphere

NACOC National Arts Centre Orchestra of Canada

NACODS National Association of Colliery Overmen, Deputies, and Shotfirers

Nações *Unidas* (Portuguese—United Nations)

NACOM National Communications

NACOR National Advisory Committee on Radiation

nacro night-alarm cutoff

NACRO National Association for the Care and Resettlement of Offenders

NACS National Association of College Stores; National Association of Cosmetology Schools

NACSE National Association of Civil Service Employees

NACSIM NATO Communications Security Information

NACSW National Action Committee on the Status of Women (Canadian)

NACT National Association of Careers Teachers; National Association of Craftsman Tailors; National Association of Cycle Traders; National Association of Cycle Trades

NACTA National Association of Colleges and Teachers of Agriculture

NACTST National Advisory Council on the Training and Supply of Teachers

NACUA National Association of College and University Administrators; National Association of College and University Attorneys

NACUBO National Association of College and University Business Office Associations

NACUFS National Association of College and University Food Services

NACUSS National Association of College and University Summer Sessions

NACV National Association of Concerned Veterans

NACVE National Advisory Council on Vocational Education

NACW National Advisory Committee on Women

NACWC National Association of Colored Women's Clubs

NACWPI National Association of College Wind and Percussion Instruments

nad nadir (lowest point); network addressing device; no apparent defect; no appreciable difference; no appreciable disease; not on active duty; nothing abnormal detected; nothing abnormal discovered

nad (NAD⁺) nicotinamide adenine dinucleotide; (same as DPN)

Nad Nadine; Nedezhda

NAD National Academy of Design; National Association of the Deaf; Naval Air Depot; Naval Air Division; Naval Ammunition Depot; North Atlantic Division

NADA National Association of Dealers in Antiques; National Association of Drug Addiction; National Automobile Dealers Association

NADABB National Alzheimer's Disease Autopsy and Brain Bank

NADAC National Anti-Drug Abuse Campaign

Nadar Gaspard Félix Tournachon

NADAR North American Data Airborn Recorder

NADB National Aerometric Data Bank

NADC National Anti-Dumping Committee; Naval Air Development Center; Northern Agricultural Development Corporation

NADD National Association of Diemakers and Diecutters

NADDIS Narotics and Dangerous Drugs Intelligence File (computerized criminal file)

NADEE National Association

of Divisional Executives for Education

NaDefCol Nato Defense College

NADEM National Association of Dairy Equipment Manufacturers

NaDevCen Naval Air Development Center

NADF National Alzheimer's Disease Foundation

NADFAS National Association of Design and Fine Art Societies

NADFS National Association of Drop Forgers and Stampers

NADGE NATO Air Defense Ground Environment Organization

NADGEMO Nato Air Defense Ground Environment Management Office

nadh (NADH) dihydronicotinamide adenine dinucleotide; (same as dpnh or DPNH)

nadi (Indian—creek, river, stream, as in Mahanadi, southwest of Calcutta)

Nadi Fiji's airport (pronounced *Nandi*)

NADL National Association of Dental Laboratories; Navy Authorized Data List

NAD/NADH₂ nicotinamide adenine dinucleotide (coenzyme system affecting hydrogen transfer in biological oxidation-reduction reactions)

NADO Navy Accounts Disbursing Office

NADOP North American Defense Operational Plan

NADOT North Atlantic Deepwater Oil Terminal

NADOW National Association for Training the Disabled in Office Work

nadp (NADP⁺) nicotinamide adenine dinucleotide phosphate; (same as tpn or TPN)

NADPAS National Association of Discharged Prisoners' Aid Societies

nadph (NADPH) dihydronicotinamide adenine dinucleotide phosphate

NADSA National Association of Dramatic and Speech Arts

NADUS National Association of Doctors in the United States

NADWARN National Disaster Warning System

nae national administrative expenses; not always excused

nAe no American equivalent

Na_e exchangeable body sodium

NAE National Academy of Education; National Academy of Engineering; National Association of Evangelicals

NAEA National Art Education Association; National Association of Enrolled Agents; National Association of Estate Agents

NAEB National Association of Educational Buyers; National Association of Educational Broadcasters

NAEBM National Association of Engine and Boat Manufacturers

NAEC National Aviation Education Council

NAEd National Academy of Education

NAED National Association of Electrical Distributors

NAEDS National Association of Engravers and Die Stampers

NAEE National Association for Environmental Education

NAEF Naval Air Engineering Facility

NAEFTA National Association of Enrolled Federal Tax Accountants

NAEIR National Association for the Exchange of Industrial Resources

NAEN National Association of Educational Negotiators

NAEP National Assessment of Educational Progress; National Association of Educational Programs (Carnegie Foundation)

NAES National Association of Educational Secretaries; National Association of Episcopal Schools; Native American Educational Services

NAESP National Association of Elementary School Principals

NAESU Naval Aviation Engineering Service Unit

NAEYC National Association for the Education of Young Children

naf nonappropriated funds

NAF National Abortion Foundation; National Amputation Foundation; National Arts Foundation; Naval Aircraft Factory; Naval Air Facility; Netherland-America Foundation; Northern Attack Force

NAF *Norges Automobil Forbund* (Norway's Automobile Association)

NAFA National Academy of Foreign Affairs; National Aerobic Fitness Award; National Association of Fleet Administrators

NAFAG NATO Air Force Advisory Group; NATO Air Force Armaments Group

NAFAS National Association of Flower Arrangement Societies

NAFB National Association of Franchised Businessmen

NAFBRAT National Association for Better Radio and Television

NAFC National Association of Food Chains

NAFCA North American Family Campers Association

NAFCU National Association of Federal Credit Unions

NAFD National Association of Funeral Directors

NAFEC National Aviation Facilities Experimental Center

NAFEO National Association for Equal Opportunity (in higher education)

naff (nAff) need for affiliation

NAFF National Association For Freedom

NAFFBIA National Association of Former FBI Agents

NAFFP National Association of Frozen Food Producers

NAFI National Association of Fire Investigators; Naval Avionics Facility

NAFINSA Nacional Financiera (Spanish—National Finance Corporation)

NAFM National Armed Forces Museum; National Association of Furniture Manufacturers

NAFMB National Association of FM Broadcasters

NAFO National Association of Fire Officers

NAFPC National Academy for Fire Prevention and Control

N Afr North Africa

NAFRC National Association of Fiscally Responsible Cities

NAFRLG National Alliance of Financially-Responsible Local Governments

NAFS National Association of Foot Specialists; National Association of Forensic Sciences

NAFSA National Association of Foreign Sudent Advisers; National Association of Foreign Student Affairs

NAFT National Alternative Fuel Test(ing)

NAFTA New Zealand–Australia Free Trade Agreement; North Atlantic Free Trade Area (Canada, United Kingdom, United States)

NAFWR National Association of Furniture Warehousemen and Removers

nag. net annual gain

Nag Nagasaki; Nagoya

NAG National Action Group; National Association of Gag Writers; National Association of Gardeners; Naval Advisory Group; Naval Applications Group (USN); Negro Actors Guild; Neighborhood Action Group

NA & G Norgulf Lines (North Atlantic & Gulf)

NAGARD NATO Advisory Group for Aeronautical Research and Development

Nagas Naga Hills (mountains on the Burmese border of India); Nagasaki, Japan

NAGC National Association for Gifted Children

NAGCP National Association of Greeting Card Publishers

N-age nuclear age

NAGE National Association of Government Employees

NAGM National Association of Glove Manufacturers; National Association of Glue Manufacturers

Nagp Nagpur

NAGPM National Association of Grained Plate Makers

NAGRA Nationalen Genossenschaft für die Lagerung Radioaktiver Abfaelle (German—National Cooperative Society for the Storage of Radioactive Wastes)

NAGS National Allotments and Gardens Society

NAGT National Association of Geology Teachers

NAGWS National Association for Girls and Women in Sport

nagy (Hungarian—big, great, large, as in Nagykörös)

Nah The Book of Nahum

Nah Nahum

NAHA National Association of Handwriting Analysts

Nahal Na'or Halutsi Lohem (Hebrew—Fighting Pioneer Youth)—youngest section of the Israeli army

NAHB National Association of Home Builders

NAHC National Advisory Health Council; National Anti-Hunger Coalition

NAHCAC National Ad Hoc Committee Against Censorship (sometimes abbreviated NACAC)

NAHE National Association for Humanities Education

NAHFO National Association of Hospital Fire Officers

NAHSA National Association for Hearing and Speech Action; National Association of Hearing and Speech Agencies

NAHSTA National Hiking and Ski Touring Association

NAHT National Association of Head Teachers

nai no action indicated; no address instruction

NAI National Agricultural Institute

NAI New Acronyms and Initialisms

NAIA National Association of Insurance Agents; National Association of Intercollegiate Athletics

NAIB National Association of Insurance Brokers

NAIC National Association of Insurance Commissioners; National Association of Investment Clubs; Naval Aircraft Investigation Center

NAICU National Association of Independent Colleges and Universities

NAIDS North Atlantic Institute for Defense Studies (NATO)

NAIEC National Association for Industry-Education Cooperation

NAIES National Association of Interdisciplinary Ethnic Studies

NAIG Nippon Atomic Industry Group

NAII National Association of Independent Insurers

NAIL National Association of Independent Lumbermen; Naval Aircraft Inventory Log; Neurotics Anonymous International Liaison

Nail City Wheeling, West Virginia where so many nails are made

NAILSC Naval Air Integrated Logistics Support Center

naiop navigational aids inoperative for parts

NAIR National Arrangements for Incidents Involving Radioactivity

NAIRE National Association of

Internal Revenue Employees

Nairns Nairnshire

NAIRS National Athletic Injury/Illness Reporting System

NAIS National Association of Independent Schools

NAISC National American Indian Safety Council

NAISS National Association of Iron and Steel Stockholders

NAIT Northern Alberta Institute of Technology

NAITTE National Association of Industrial and Technical Teacher Educators

naivnik naive person or politician

NAIW National Association of Insurance Women

NAIWA North American Indian Women's Association

NAJ National Association for Justice

NAJC National Assessment of Juvenile Correction (University of Michigan); Northern Australia Jockey Club; Northwest Alabama Junior College

NAJCA National Association of Juvenile Correctional Agencies

NAJE National Association of Jazz Educators; National Association of Jazz Education

nak negative knowledge; nothing adverse known

nak (NAK) negative acknowledge character (data processing)

Nakhodka USSR prison just southeast of Vladivostok

nakl *naklad* (Polish—edition, publisher); *nakladatel* (Czech — edition, publisher)

NAL National Acoustics Laboratory; National Aerospace Laboratory; National Agricultural Library (US Department of Agriculture); National Airlines; Nigeria America Line; Norwegian America Line

NAL New American Library

NALC National Association of Letter Carriers; National Association of Litho Clubs

NALCC National Automatic Laundry and Cleaning Council

NALCO Newfoundland and Labrador Corporation

NALCON Navy Laboratory Computer Network

NALDEF Native American Legal Defense and Education Foundation

NALED National Association

of Limited Edition Dealers

NALGG National Association for Lesbian and Gay Gerontology

NALGO National and Local Government Officers Association

NALLA National Long-Lines Agency

NALM National Association of Lift Makers

NALS National Association of Legal Secretaries

NALSA North American Land Sailing Association

NALSAT National Association of Land Settlement Association Tenants

NALU National Association of Life Underwriters

nam network access machine; non-aligned movement

Nam (military slang—Vietnam); Namibia (South-West Africa)

N Am North America(n)

NAM National Aero Manufacturing; National Air Museum (Smithsonian Institution); National Association of Manufacturers; Naval Aircraft Modification; Newspaper Association Managers; North America(n); North American Movement

NAM Nederlandsche Aluminium Maatschappij (Netherlands Aluminum Company)

NAMA National Automatic Merchandising Association; New Amsterdam Musical Association; North American Maritime Agencies

NAMAC National Association of Merger and Acquisition Consultants

NAMB National Association of Master Bakers

NAMBLA North American Man-Boy Love Association (of child molesters)

NAMBO National Association of Motor Bus Operators

Namby-Pamby 18th-century English dramatist-poet Ambrose Philips

NAMC Naval Air Materiel Center; Naval Air Materiel Command; Nihon Aeroplane Manufacturing Company

NAMCC National Association of Mutual Casualty Companies

NAMCO Naval and Mechanical Company

NAMDI National Marine Data Inventory

NAME National Association of Marine Engineers; National Association of Media Educators; National Association of Medical Examiners; National Association of Metal Name Plate Manufacturers

NAMESU National Association of Music Executives in State Universities

NAMF National Association of Metal Finishers

NAMFI NATO Missile Firing Installation

NAMH National Association for Mental Health; Norwegian-American Historical Museum

NAMIA National Association of Mutual Insurance Agents

Namib Namibia or Namib Desert of South-West Africa

Namibia modern name for South-West Africa

NAMIC National Association of Mutual Insurance Companies

NAMilCom North Atlantic Military Committee

naml namligen (Swedish—namely)—viz.

NAMM National Association of Music Merchants

NAMMC Natural Asphalt Mineowners' and Manufacturers' Council

NAMMO NATO Multi-Role Combat Aircraft Development and Production Management Oganization

NAMMW National Association of Musical Merchandise Wholesalers

NAMOA National Association of Miscellaneous Ornamental and Architectural Products Contractors

NAMOS National Art Museum of Sport

NAMP National Association of Magazine Publishers; National Association of Married Priests; Naval Aviation Maintenance Program

NAMPA NATO Maritime Patrol Aircraft Agency

nampg nautical air miles per gallon

NAMPMW Vietnam Prisoners of War (organization)

namppf nautical air miles per pound of fuel

NAMS National Association of Marine Surveyors

NAMSB National Association of Mutual Savings Banks

NAMSO NATO Maintenance and Supply Organization

NAMT National Association for Music Therapy

NAMTA National Art Materials Trade Association

NAMTC Naval Air Missile Test Center

NAMTRADET Naval Air Maintenance Detachment

NAMTRAGRU Naval Air Maintenance Training Group

Namur Namur province's capital in Belgium

n.a.n. *nisi aliter notetur* (Latin— unless it is otherwise noted)

Nan Anna; Nancy; Nanette; Nanking

NAN Nandi, Fiji Islands (airport)

nana (NANA) N-acetylneuraminic acid

Nana Anna; Anne(tte); Mariana; Nanette

NANA National Advertising News Association; North American Newspaper Alliance; Northwest Alaska Natives Association

NANAC National Aviation Noise Abatement Council

Nancy Agnes; Ann; Anna; Annabelle; Anne

NAND NOT AND (data-processing logic operator)

Nandi (Fijian—Nandi)—Fiji's main airport

Nando Fernando

NANE National Association for Nursery Education

Nanga Nanga Parbat, India

Nan Hai (Pinyin Chinese— South China Sea)

Nanjing (Pinyin Chinese— Nanking)

NANM National Association of Negro Musicians

Nannerl Maria Anna

nano 10^{-9}

nanova non-orthogonal analysis of variance

Nansei-shoto (Japanese—Ryukyu Islands)

NANTIS Nottingham and Nottinghamshire Technical Information Service

Nanty Anthony

Nanuchka NATO name for a Soviet class of guided-missile gunboats

NANVH&SWO National Assembly of National Voluntary Health and Social Welfare Organizations

NANWEP Navy Numerical Weather Prediction; Navy Numerical Weather Problems (USN)

Nanzig (German–Nancy)— French industrial center renamed by Hitler during World War II

NAO Noise Abatement Office

NAOA Navy Officers Accounts Office

NAOC Nigerian Agip Oil Company

NaOH sodium hydroxide (caustic soda)

NAOP National Association of Operative Plasterers

NAORPG North Atlantic Ocean Regional Planning Group

NAOT National Association of Organ Teachers

NAOTC National Association of Over-the-Counter Companies

NAOTS Naval Aviation Ordnance Test Station

nap. knapsack; napalm (naphthalene and coconut oil—jellied gasoline incendiary mixture); naphtha; naval aviation pilot (NAP); non-agency purchase; not at present

Nap Naples; Napoleon; Napoleonic

NAP Naples, Italy (airport); Narragansett Pier (railroad); National Association of Parliamentarians; National Association of Postmasters; National Association of Publishers; Naval Auxiliary Patrol; Naval Aviation Pilot

N.A.P. Neighborhood Awareness Program (citizens on the alert to report all suspicious behavior in their neighborhood to the police)

NAP *Nomina Anatomica, Paris; Nuclei Armati Proletari* (Italian—Armed Proletarian Nucleus)—terrorists

NAPA National Asphalt Paving Association; National Association of Performing Artists; National Association of Purchasing Agents

NAPAC National Program for Acquisitions and Cataloging

napalm naphthene palmitate (napththalene plus coconut oil —jellied gasoline used in flame-throwers)

NAPAN National Association for the Prevention of Addiction to Narcotics

NAPBL National Association of Professional Baseball Leagues

napc non-adherent peritoneal cells

NAPC National Association of Precancel Collectors

NAPCA National Air Polution Control Administration

NAPCAE National Association for Public Continuing and Adult Education

NAPCRO National Association of Police Community Relations Officers

NAPD National Association of Police Driving

NAPDEA North American Professional Driver Education Association

NAPE National Alliance of Postal Employees; National Association for Professional Educators; National Association of Port Employees; National Association of Power Engineers

NAPECW National Association for Physical Education of College Women

NAPF National Association of Pension Funds

NAPFE National Alliance of Postal and Federal Employees

naph naphtha; naphthyl

NAPH National Association of Professors of Hebrew

NAPIM National Association of Printing Ink Manufacturers

NAPL National Association of Photo Lithographers; National Association of Printers and Lithographers

Naples English place-name equivalent of Napoli on Italy's Bay of Naples

NAPLP National Association of Para-Legal Personnel

NAPLPS North American Presentation Level Protocol Syntax

NAPM National Association of Punch Manufacturers; National Association of Purchasing Management

NAPN National Association of Physician Nurses

NAPNAP National Association of Pediatric Nurse Associates and Practitioners

NAPNES National Association for Practical Nurse Education and Service

NAPO National Association of Performing Artists; National Association of Probation Officers; National Association of Property Owners; National

Association of Purchasing Agents

Napoleon Napoleon Bonaparte

Napoleon Bonaparte Napoleon I —Emperor of the French

Napoleon of Peace Louis Philippe

Napoleon of the Waltz Johann Strauss

Nápoles (Portuguese or Spanish —Naples)

Napoli (Italian—Naples)

NAPPH National Association of Private Psychiatric Hospitals

nap(py) napkin

na pr *na priklad* (Czech—for example)

NAPR National Association for Pastoral Renewal

NAPRA National Association of Progressive Radio Announcers

NAPS National Alliance of Postal Supervisors; Nissan Air Pollution System

NAPSA National Association of Pretrial Service Agencies

NAPSAE National Association for Public School Adult Education

Nap's bones Napier's bones (first slide rule)

NAPSS Numerical Analysis Problem Solving System

NAPT National Association of Physical Therapists; National Association for the Prevention of Tuberculosis

NAPTC Naval Air Propulsion Test Center

NAPTIC National Air Pollution Technical Information Center

NAPUS National Association of Postmasters of the United States; Nuclear Auxiliary Power Unit System

NAPV National Association of Prison Visitors

NAPVD National Association for the Prevention of Venereal Disease

NAQI National Air Quality Index

NAQP National Association of Quick Printers

nar narrow

Nar Narragansett

NAR National Association of Realtors; National Association of Rocketry; Nelson Aldrich Rockefeller; North American Rockwell; North American Royalties; Northern Alberta Railway

NARA Narcotic Addict Rehab-

ilitation Act; Nippon Australian Relations Agreement

NARAA National Association of Recruitment Advertising Agencies

NARAD Navy Research and Development

NARAL National Abortion Rights Action League (lobby for legal abortion); National Association for the Repeal of Abortion Laws

NARAS National Academy of Recording Arts and Sciences

NARB National Advertising Review Board

Narborough Island, Galápagos Fernandina

narc narcotic; narcotics agent; narcotics; narcotics officer

narc (Latin prefix—numbness or stupor)—narcotic

NARC National Agricultural Research Center; National Archives and Records Service; National Association for Retarded Children

narco narcotic; narcotics hospital; narcotics officer; narcotics treatment center

Narco nickname of the U.S. Public Health Service Hospital in Lexington, Kentucky where narcotic addicts are treated

NARCO United Nations Narcotics Commission

narcocard narcotic-addict registration card

narcodollars narcotic (traffic) dollars

Narconon Narcotics Anonymous

narcos narcotics; narcotics police officers

narcotest narcotics test

nard spikenard

NARD National Association of Regimental Drummers; National Association of Retail Druggists

NARDIC Naval Research and Development Information Center

NAREB National Association of Real Estate Boards; National Association of Real Estate Brokers

narec naval research electronic computer

NAREIF National Association of Real Estate Investment Funds

NARELLO National Association for Real Estate License Law Officials

narf natural axial-resonant frequency

NARF Native American Rights Fund; Naval Air Rework Facility; Nuclear Aircraft Research Facility

NARFE National Association of Retired Federal Employees

NARGA National Association of Retail Grocers of Australia

NARI National Association of Recycling Industries; National Atmospheric Research Institute; Native American Research Institute

Nar Inv Narcotics Investigation

narist. *naristillae* (Latin—nasal drops)—nosedrops

Narita Tokyo, Japan's new airport (*see* Haneda)

nark narcotics agent or law-enforcement officer

NARK Nikolai Andreyvich Rimsky-Korsakov

NARL National Aero Research Laboratory; Naval Arctic Research Laboratory

NARM National Association of Relay Manufacturers; National Association of Retail Merchants

NARMCO National Research and Manufacturing Company

N-armed nuclear-armed (aircraft, bomb, missile, submarine, etc.)

N-arm(s) nuclear armament(s); nuclear arms

N arms control nuclear arms control

N-arms race nuclear arms race

NARO North American Regional Office

NAROCTESTSTA Naval Air Rocket Test Station

NARP National Association of Railroad Passengers; Nuclear Weapons Accident Report Procedures

NARPA National Air Rifle and Pistol Association

Narragansett Bay State Rhode Island

Narroway (Scottish-Gaelic—Norway)

Narrow-Gauge Capital of the World Durango, Colorado

Narrow Land Between the Seas Panama flanked by the Caribbean-Atlantic and the Pacific

Narrows narrow waterway between Brooklyn and Staten Island in New York City; connects outer harbor or Lower Bay with inner harbor or Upper Bay; spanned by 4260-

foot-long Verrazano Bridge—world's longest suspension bridge; narrow strait in the Dardanelles near entrance to the Aegean; narrow strait between American and British Virgin Islands

Narrow Seas short form for the Channel between England and France as well as the southern end of the North Sea between England, Belgium, and the Netherlands

NARS National Archives and Records Service; National Association of Radiation Survivors; Non-Affiliated Reserve Section

NARSIS National Association for Road Safety Instruction in Schools

NARST National Association for Research in Science Teaching

NARTB National Association of Radio and Television Broadcasters

NARTC North America Region Test Center

NARTEL North Atlantic Radio Telephone Committee

NARTM National Association of Rope and Twine Merchants

NARTS National Association of Reporter Training Schools; Naval Air Rocket Test Station

NARTU Naval Air Reserve Training Unit

NARU North Australian Research Unit

NARUC National Association of Regulatory Utility Commissioners

NARVRE National Association of Retired and Veteran Railroad Employees

nas nasal; nasalis; nasology

n-a-s no added salt

NAS Nassau, Bahamas (airport); National Academy of Sciences; National Advocates Society; National Aerospace Standard(s); National Agricultural Society; National Aircraft Standard(s); National Airspace System; National Association of Sanitarians; National Association of Stevedores; National Association of Supervisors; National Audubon Society; Native American Studies; Naval Air Station; Nursing Auxiliary Service

N A S Noise Abatement Society

N^{a}S^a Nuestra Señora (Spanish—Our Lady)

NASA National Acoustical Suppliers Association; National Aeronautics and Space Administration; National Appliance Service Association; National Association of Schools of Art; National Association of Securities Administrators; National Automobile Salesmen's Association; North American Sailing Association

NASAA National Aeronautics and Space Administration Act; National Assembly of State Arts Agencies

NASABCA National Aeronautics and Space Administration Board of Contract Appeals

NASA-CF NASA—Cocoa Beach, Florida

NASA-CO NASA—Cleveland, Ohio

NASA-EC NASA—Edwards, California

NASAEN National Association for State-Enrolled Assistant Nurses

NASA-GM NASA—Greenbelt, Maryland

NASA-HA NASA—Huntsville, Alabama

NASA-HT NASA—Houston, Texas

Nasakom Nationalist-Communist

NASA LST NASA Large Space Telescope

NASA-LV NASA—Langley Field, Virginia

NASA-MC NASA—Moffett Field, California

NASAO National Association of State Aviation Officials

NASAP Nonproliferation Alternative System Assessment Program; Nuclear Alternative Systems Assessment Program

NASAPR National Aeronautics and Space Administration Procurement Regulations

NASAR National Association of Search and Rescue

NASARR North American Searching and Ranging Radar

NASA-SC NASA—Santa Monica, California

NASA STAR NASA Scientific and Technical Aerospace Reports

NASA/STIF National Aeronautics and Space Administration/Scientific and Technical Information Facility

NASBE National Association of State Boards of Education

NASC National Aeronautics and Space Council; National Aircraft Standards Committee; National Alliance of Senior Citizens; National Association of Student Councils; NATO Supply Center; Naval Air Systems Command; North American Supply Council; Northwest Association of Schools and Colleges

NASCAR National Association of Sports Car Racing; National Association for Stock Car Advancement and Research

NASCO National Academy of Sciences Committee on Oceanography; National Automotive Service Company; North American Students of Cooperation

NASCom Naval Air Systems Command

NASCOM NASA's tracking network, also performing command and control functions

NASCP North American Society for Corporate Planning

NASCUS National Association of State Credit Union Supervisors

NASD National Association of Securities Dealers; Naval Aviation Supply Depot; Nippon Advanced Ship Design(ing)

NASDA National Association of State Development Agencies; National Space Development Agency (Japan)

NASDAQ National Association of Security Dealers Automated Quotation (system)

NASDAQS National Association of Security Dealers Automated Quotation System

NASDCD National Association of State Directors of Child Development

nase neutral atom space engine (sputtering engine)

NASE National Academy of School Executives; National Academy of Stationary Engineers; National Association of Stationary Engineers; National Association of Steel Exporters

NASEES National Association for Soviet and East European Studies

NASF National Aboriginal Sports Foundation; National Association of State Foresters

NASFAA National Association of Student Financial Aid Administrators

NAS & FCA National Automatic Sprinkler and Fire Control Association

NAS-GB Noise Abatement Society of Great Britain

Nash Nashville

NASH National Association of Specimen Hunters

NASHA North American Survival and Homesteading Association

Nashville Tennessee's capital

Nashville Girls Tennessee Prison for Women at Nashville

NASIS National Association for State Information Systems

NASL North American Soccer League

NASM National Air and Space Museum (Smithsonian); National Association of Schools of Music; Naval Aviation School of Medicine

NASM Nederlandsche-Amerikaansche Stoomvaart Maatschappij (Holland-American Line)

NASML National Air and Space Museum Library (Smithsonian Institution)

NASMV National Association for a Standard Medical Vocabulary

NASN National Air Sampling Network

NASNI Naval Air Station, North Island (Halsey Field, San Diego, California)

NAS-NRC National Academy of Science—National Research Council

NASOH North America Society for Oceanic History

NASP National Airport Sytems Plan; National Association of School Psychologists; Negro Anglo-Saxon Protestant

NASPA National Society of Public Accountants

Nas Par Nasionale Party (Afrikaans—National Party)—South Africa's Apartheid party

NASPD National Association of Steel Pipe Distributors

Nas Pers Nasionale Pers (Afrikaans—National Press)—publisher of apartheid books and periodicals

NASPM National Association of Seed Potato Merchants

NASQAN National Stream-Quality Accounting Network

Nª Srª Nossa Senhora (Portuguese—Our Lady); Nuestra Señora (Spanish—Our Lady)

NASRC National Association of State Racing Commissioners

NASRP National Association of Special and Reserve Police

Nass Nassau

NASS National Association of School Superintendents; National Association of Summer Sessions

NASSC National Alliance on Shaping Safer Cities

NASSCO National Steel and Shipbuilding Company

NASSD National Association of School Security Directors

NASSL National Association of Spanish-Speaking Librarians

NASSO National Association of Socialist Students' Organizations

NASSP National Association of Secondary-School Principals

NASSR Nahichevan Autonomous Soviet Socialist Republic

NAST Nuclear Accident Support Team

NASTBD National Association of State Text Book Directors

NASTI Naval Air Station, Terminal Island

NASTL National Anti-Steel-Trap League

NASU National Adult School Union

NASULGC National Association of State Universities and Land-Grant Colleges

NASW National Association of Science Writers; National Association of Social Workers

NASWM National Association of Scottish Woolen Manufacturers

nat nation; national; nationalist; native; natural; naturalist; naturalization; naturalize(d), nature; normal allowed time

nat natuurkunde (Dutch—natural science)

Nat Natalia; Natalie; Nathalie; Nathan; Nathanael; Nathaniel; Natasha; Nation; National; Nationalist; naturalized

Nat Naturkunde (German—natural science)

NAT National Air Transport; National Arbitration Tribunal

NATA National Association of Tax Accountants; National Association of Tax Administrators; National Association of Testing Authorities; Na-

tional Association of Transportation Advertisers; National Athletic Trainers Association; National Automated Transportation Association; National Aviation Trades Association; North American Telephone Association; North Atlantic Treaty Alliance

Nat Absten National Abstentionalist

Natacha Rambova Winifred Hudnut

Natalie Wood Natasha Gurdin

NATAPROUBU National Association of Professional Bureaucrats

Nat Arc National Archives

NATAS National Academy of Television Arts and Sciences

Nat Assn National Association

natat natation

NATB National Automobile Theft Bureau; Naval Air Training Base

Nat Bur Econ Res National Bureau of Economic Research (Columbia and Princeton)

Nat Bur Stand Circ National Bureau of Standards Circular(s)

Nat Bur Stand Misc Pub National Bureau of Standards Miscellaneous Publication(s)

Nat Bur Stand Spec Pub National Bureau of Standards Special Publication(s)

NATC National Air Transportation Conferences; Naval Air Training Command

NATCG National Association of Training Corps for Girls

natch naturally

Natch Natchez

NATCO National Automatic Tool Company; National Tank Company

natcol natural color(ing)

natcom national communications

NATCOM NATO communication

Nat Con Nature Conservancy

NATCS National Air Traffic Control Service; National Air Traffic Control System

NATD National Association of Teachers of Dancing

Nat Dem National Democrats

Nate Nathan(iel)

NATE National Association for Teachers of Electronics; Native American Teacher Education

Nat Fed National Federation

NATFHE National Association

of Teachers in Further and Higher Education

Nat Gal National Gallery

Nat Geog Mag *National Geographic Magazine*

Nath Nathan(iel)

Nath B Nathaniel Bowditch

nat hist natural history

Nathl Nathaniel

NATIDC Netherlands–Australia Trade and Industrial Development Council

NATIE National Association of Trade and Industrial Education

nation. nationality

National National Gallery in London or the National Gallery of Art in Washington, D.C.

NATIONAL National Cash Register

National Anthem City Baltimore, Maryland

National Composer of Norway Edvard Grieg

National Pastime baseball in America; cricket in Britain

National Poet of Norway Bjørnstjerne Bjørnson

National Tity navalese for National City, California

Nation of Big Cities China with at least fourteen cities each with a million people

Nation of Cities the United States with more than 150 cities containing 100,000 or more and 6 with a million or more people

Nation of Gentlemen Scotland so named by King George IV

Nations Bus *Nations Business*

Nation's Capital District of Columbia

Nation's Front Yard The Mall in Washington, D.C.

Nation of Shopkeepers England, according to Samuel Adams as well as Napoleon

Nation's Hottest Town Quartzsite, Arizona where July temperatures average 108°F (42°C)

Nations Unies (French—United Nations)

NATIS National Information System(s); North Atlantic Treaty Information Service

Nativ Nativity

NATKE National Association of Theatrical and Kine Employees

natl national

N Atl North Atlantic

N Atl Cur North Atlantic Current

Nat Lib National Liberal; National Library of Canada (Ottawa)

NATLIBCAN National Library of Canada

NATLIBNZ National Library of New Zealand

NATMAP National Mapping

Nat Mon National Monument

Nat Mus Natal Museum; National Museum

nato no action—talk only

NATO National Association of Taxicab Owners; National Association of Theater Owners; National Association of Trailer Owners; National Association of Travel Organizations; North Atlantic Treaty Organization (Belgium, Canada, Denmark, France, Greece, Iceland, Italy, Luxembourg, Netherlands, Norway, Portugal, Turkey, United Kingdom, United States, West Germany)

NATO-AGARD North Atlantic Treaty Organization—Advisory Group for Aeronautical Research and Development

Nat Obs *National Observer*

NATO Council Belgium, Canada, Denmark, France, Federal Republic of Germany, Greece, Iceland, Italy, Luxembourg, Netherlands, Norway, Portugal, Turkey, United Kingdom, United States

NATODC NATO Defense College

NATO-ELLA North Atlantic Treaty Organization—European Long Lines Agency

NATO-LRSS North Atlantic Treaty Organization—Long-Range Scientific Studies

NATOMILOCGRP NATO Military Oceanography Group

NATOPS Naval Air Training and Operating Procedures Standardization

Nat Ord Natural Order

NATO-RDPP North Atlantic Treaty Organization—Research and Development Production Program

NATOs National Association of Theatre Owners

NATPE National Association of Television Program Executives

nat phil natural philosophy

Nat Pk National Park

natr. *natrium* (Latin—sodium)

Nat Rev National Review

Nats National Party members; Nationalists; naturalized citizens

Nats *Natsionalnyii* (Russian—national)

NATS National Association of Teachers of Singing; Naval Air Test Station; Naval Air Transport Service

Nat. Sc.D. Doctor of Natural Science

Nat Sci Natural Science(s)

Nat Sci Fdn National Science Foundation

Nat Sec Soc National Secular Society (founded in 1866 by Charles Bradlaugh)

NATSEMI National Semiconductor Incorporated

NATSF Naval Air Technical Service Facility

NATSJA National Association of Training Schools and Juvenile Agencies

NATSOPA National Society of Operative Printers and Assistants

NATSPG North Atlantic Systems Planning Group

Natsrat (Hebrew—Nazareth)

Nat Sup National Superannuation

N Att Naval Attaché

N-attack nuclear attack

NATTC National Tank Truck Carriers; Naval Air Technical Training Center

NATTKE National Association of Theatrical, Television, and Kine Employees

NATTS National Association of Trade and Technical Schools; Naval Air Turbine Test Station

Nat U Nations Unies (French—United Nations)

NAT Uni National University

natur naturalist

Natural Bridges Natural Bridges National Monument in Southeastern Utah

NATUSA North African Theater of Operations

Nat West National Westminster (British bank)

naty naturally

náu náutica (Sapnish—nautical)

Nau Nauruan(s); Nauru Island

NAU Naval Administrative Unit

NAUA National Aircraft Underwriters' Association; National Auto Underwriters Association

nauga naugahide (plastic upholstery)

Naughty MacNaughton; Mc-
Naughton

Naughty Island Pulau Sajahat
(pleasure resort offshore
Singapore)

Naughty Nineties the 1890s

NAUPA National Association
of Unclaimed Property Ad-
ministrators

Nauru Republic of Nauru (western Pacific Ocean island nation whose Naurus speak Nauruan and English, phosphate
exports provide plenty for almost everyone engaged in
phosphate production) Pleasant Island

Nauru Islands Ports Nauru
Atoll, Saipan, Tinian, Rota

NAUS National Association for
Uniformed Services

naut nautical

NAUW National Association of
University Women

n aux b new auxiliary boiler

nav naval; navigable; navigate;
navigatiation; navigational;
navigator

n/a/v net asset value

Nav Navaho; naval; Navarra;
Navarre

NAVA National Audio-Visual
Association; North American
Vexillological Association

navaco navigation action cutout
(switchboard)

NAVAE National Association
for Vietnamese-American
Education

NAVAERORECOVF Naval
Aerospace Recovery Facility

navaid(s) navigation aid(s)

NAVAIR Naval Air (Systems
Command)

NAVAIRLANT Naval Air
Forces, Atlantic

NAVAIRPAC Naval Air
Forces, Pacific

NAVAIRREWORKF Naval Air
Rework Facility

NAVAIRSYSCOM Naval Air
Systems Command

Naval Person Churchill's cover
name used when addressing
Roosevelt—POTUS—Presi-
dent of the United States

Nav. Arch. Naval Architect

Navarino Italian name for the
port of Pylos

Navarra (Portuguese or Spanish
—Navarre)

Navarre English or French
place-name for Navarra

NavAus navigation in Austra-

lian waters

NAVBALTAP Naval Forces,
Baltic Approaches (NATO)

NAVBASE Naval Base

navbm (NAVBM) naval ballistic
missile

nav brz naval bronze

Nav Bs Naval Base

NavCad Naval Cadet

NAVCAMS Naval Communication Area Master Station

NAVCENT Allied Naval
Forces, Central Europe

NAVCJ National Association of
Volunteers in Criminal Justice

NavCm navigation countermeasures and deception

navcom navigation communication

Nav.Const. Naval Constructor

NAVCOSSACT Naval Com-
mand Systems Support Activity

navdac navigation data assimila-
tion computer

NAVDAC Navigation Data As-
similation Center

Nav Dep Naval Deputy
(NATO)

Nav.E. Naval Engineer

NavEams navigation in the eastern Atlantic and the Mediterranean

NavEast navigation along the
east coast of Asia

NAVEDTRASUPPCEN Naval
Education and Training Support Center

NAVELEX Naval Electronic
(Systems Command)

Navel of the Nation Butte County, South Dakota (geographic
center of the United States including Alaska and Hawaii);
Smith County, Kansas (geographic center of the forty-
eight conterminous states)

Navel of the World Easter Island
according to its ancient Polynesian inhabitants who called
it *te pito o te henua*—the navel
of the world

NAVEOFAC Naval Explosive
Ordnance Disposal Facility

Navesink Highlands of the Navesink also called Atlantic
Highlands on the New Jersey
coast around Sandy Hook

Nav Ests Navassa Estates (realtor's probable abbreviation if
this north Caribbean islet
becomes available for development and subdivision into
Atlantic Vistas, Caribbean
Seaside, Leeward Lots, and

Windward Sites, all within
easy walking distance of Lulu
Bay and its long-abandoned
phosphate fertilizer loading
plant established by a New
England skipper in the 1800s)

navex navigation exercise

NAVFE Naval Forces Far East

NAVFEC Naval Facilities

NAVFECENGCOM Naval Facilities Engineering Com-
mand

NAVFOR Naval Forces

NAVFORJAP Naval Air
Forces, Japan

NAVFORKOR Naval Air
Forces, Korea

NAVH National Aid to Visually
Handicapped; National Association for the Visually Handicapped

Nav I Navassa Island (uninhab-
ited American islet in north
Caribbean close to Windward
Passage between Cuba and
Hispaniola, navigational light
maintained by U.S. although
recently Haiti claimed the islet), *see* Nav Ests

NAVIC Navy Information Center

navicert naval inspection certificate (allowing neutral vessels
to proceed through blockades
established by the belligerent
issuing such a document)

navicert(s) navigation certifi-
cate(s)

Navidad Natividad (Spanish—
Nativity)—Christmas

navig navigation

Navigators Navigator Islands
(American Samoa)

Navigator's Nightmare the Bermuda Islands—scene of so
many shipwrecks

NavInd navigation in the Indian
Ocean

NAVINTCOM Naval Intelligence Command

NAVINTCOMINST Naval Intelligence Command Instructions

NAVLIS Navy Logistics Information System

NAVMACS Naval Modular-
Automated Communications
Systems

NAVMAR Naval Forces, Marianas

NAVMAT Naval Materiel
Command (USN)

NAVMED Naval Medicine

NAVMEDIS Naval Medical Information System

NavMisCen Naval Missile Cen-

ter
NAVNON Naval Forces, Northern Norway (NATO)
NavNoPac navigation in the North Pacific
NavNorlant navigation in the North Atlantic
NAVNORTH Allied Naval Forces, Northern Europe
NavOceanO Naval Oceanographic Office (USN)
NAVOCFORMED Naval On-Call Force, Mediterranean (NATO)
NAVOCS Naval Officer Candidate School
NAVORD Naval Ordnance
NAVORDSYSCOM Naval Ordnance Systems Command
Navpaktos (Greek—Lepanto)
NAVPERS Naval Personnel
NAVPERSRANDLAB Naval Personnel Research and Development Laboratory
NAVPHIBSCOL Naval Amphibious School
NAVPHIL Naval Forces—Philippines
NAVPORCO Naval Port Control Officer
NAVPRO Naval Plant Representative Office(r)
NAVPUB Naval Publications
NAVREGMEDCEN Naval Regional Medical Center
NAVROM Romanian merchant marine
NAVS National Anti-Vivisection Society; North American Vegetarian Society
navsat navigational satellite
NavSat navigation in the South Atlantic
NAVSCAP Naval Forces, Scandinavian Approaches (NATO)
NAVSCOLCOM NORVA Naval Schools Command, Norfolk, Virginia
NAVSEA Naval Sea Systems Command (USN)
NAVSEACENTLANT Naval Sea Support Center—Atlantic
NAVSEACENTPAC Naval Sea Support Center—Pacific
NAVSEC Naval Ship Engineering Center
NAVSHIPCOM Naval Ship Systems Command
NavShipyd Naval Shipyard
NAVSMO Navigation Satellite Management Office
NavSoPac navigation in the South Pacific
NAVSOUTH Naval Forces, Southern Europe

NAVSPASUR Naval Space Surveillance (USN)
NAVSPECWARGRU Naval Special Warfare Group
NAVSTA Naval Station
NAVSTAR Navigation System using Time and Ranging
NAVSUPGRU Naval Support Group
NAVSUPORANT Naval Support Forces, Antarctica
navtac (NAVTAC) navigation tactical (aircraft)
NAVTELCOM Naval Telecommunications Command
NAVTIS National Vessel Traffic Information System
NAVTRACEN Naval Training Center
NAVTRACOM Naval Training Command
NAVTRADEVCEN Naval Training Device Center
NAVUWSEC Naval Underwater Weapons Systems Engineering Center
navvies navigators (unskilled canal builders, unskilled laborers)
NAVWAG Naval Warfare Analysis Group
NAVWEASERV Naval Weather Service
NAVWUIS Naval Work Unit Information Service
navy navy bean (small white bean); navy blue (dark blue); navy plug (tobacco)
NAW National Association of Wholesalers; National Association for Women; North African Waters
NAWA National Association of Women Artists
NAWAC National Weather Analysis Center
NAWAPA North American Water and Power Alliance
NAWAS National Air Warning Service
NAWB National Association of Workshops for the Blind
NAWCC National Association of Watch and Clock Collectors
NAWCH National Association for the Welfare of Children in Hospitals
NAWDAC National Association for Women Deans, Administrators, and Counselors
NAWDC National Association of Women Deans and Counselors
NAWESA Naval Weapons Engineering Support Activity

NAWF National Aborigine Welfare Fund; North American Wildlife Foundation
NAWIC National Association of Women in Construction
NAWK National Association of Warehouse Keepers
NAWM National Association of Wool Manufacturers
NAWND National Association of Wholesale Newspaper Distributors
NAWPA North American Water and Power Alliance
NAWS National Aviation Weather System
Naxas Naxalites (Maoist extremists active in India)
Nay Nayarit
NAYC National Association of Youth Clubs
NAYE National Association of Young Entrepreneurs
NAYRU North American Yacht Racing Union
naz nazionale (Italian—national)
Naz Nazaire
Naze (Old Norse—Nose)—southern tip of Norway at Lindesnes
Nazi adherent of the former National Socialist German Workers' Party *(Nationalsozialistische Partei)*
Nazioni Unite (Italian—United Nations)
nb nanobar(n); narrow band; new boiler(s); newborn; no bias (relay)
n/b narrow beam; no balls (lacking nerve); no brands; northbound
n.b. *nota bene* (Latin—note well)
Nb nimbus; niobium (formerly columbium)
Nb Noordbrabent (Dutch–North Brabant)
NB National Bank; Naval Base; Navy Band; New Brunswick; Niagara Frontier Tariff Bureau; North Borneo
NB Nauchnaya Biblioteka (Russian—Scientific Library)—in Leningrad; *Naviera Boliviana* (Spanish—Bolivian Shipping); *Norsk Bibliotekforening* (Norwegian Library Association)
Nb94 radioactive niobium
NBA National Band Association; National Bank of Australia; National Bankers Association; National Banking Association; National Bar Association; National Basketball As-

sociation; National Boat Association; National Bowling Association; National Boxing Association; National Button Association

NBAA National Business Aircraft Association

NBAC National Black Alcoholism Council

NBAD National Bank of Abu Dhabi

N balance nitrogen balance

NBBB National Better Business Bureau

NBBC National Brass Band Club

NBBS New British Broadcasting Station

NBBU New Brunswick Board of Underwriters

nbc non-battle casualty; nothing but chaos

n-b-c (NBC) nuclear-biological-chemical (warfare)

NBC Nagasaki Broadcasting Company; National Ballet of Canada; National Baseball Congress; National Beagle Club; National Beef Council; National Biscuit Company; National Book Committee; National Book Council; National Bowling Council; National Braille Club; National Broadcasting Commission; National Broadcasting Company; National Broadcasting Corporation; National Bulk Carriers; National Bus Company; Navy Beach Commando; Nigerian Broadcasting Corporation

NB & C Norfolk, Baltimore and Carolina Line

NBCA National Baseball Congress of America; National Beagle Club of America

NBCC National Book Critics Circle

NBCCA National Business Council for Consumer Affairs

nbccw nuclear, biological, chemical, conventional warfare

nbcd nuclear, biological, and chemical defense

NBCDA National Black Child Development Act

nbcdx nuclear, biological, and chemical defense exercise

NBCU National Bureau of Casualty Underwriters

NBCUSA National Baptist Convention U.S.A.

nbd negative binomial distribution

NBD National Bank of Detroit

NBDA National Bicycle Dealers Association

NB & DA National Barrel & Drum Association

NBDC National Bomb Data Center (Washington, D.C.); National Book Development Council

NBE National Bank Examiner(s)

NBEA National Business Education Association

NBER National Bureau of Economic Research; National Bureau of Engineering Registration

NBET National Business Entrance Test(s)

NBF National Bank of Fiji; National Boating Federation

NBFA National Bricklayers Foundation of Australia; National Business Forms Association

NB & FAA National Burglar and Fire Alarm Association

nbfi's non-bank(ing) financial intermediaries

NBF Life National Ben Franklin Life Insurance

nbfm narrow-band frequency modulation

NBFU National Board of Fire Underwriters; Newfoundland Board of Fire Underwriters

nbg no bloody good

NBG National Bank of Georgia; Naval Beach Group

NBGC National Ballet Guild of Canada

NBH National Bellas Hess

NBHA National Builders Hardware Association

NBHC New Broken Hill Consolidated

nbi no bone(y) injury

NBI Nathaniel Branden Institute; National Benevolent Institution

NBI Norges Byggforskningsinstitutt (Norwegian Building Institute)

NBIPP National Black Independent Political Party

NBIS Narcotics Border Interdiction System

NBIT New Bedford Institute of Technology

nbl not bloody likely

NBL National Basketball League; National Book League

NBLC Nederlands Bibliotheek en Lektuur Centrum (Dutch—Netherlands Center for Public Libraries and Literature)

NBL & P National Bureau for Lathing and Plastering

nbm non-book material(s); nothing by mouth

nbm (NBM) nuclear ballistic missile

NBM New Brunswick Museum

NBME National Board of Medical Examiners

NBMG Navigation Bombing and Missile Guidance System

NBMGS Navigation Bombing and Missile Guidance System

NBMV & NSL New Bedford, Martha's Vineyard, and Nantucket Steamship Line

nbn (NBN) national book number

NBN Nagoya Broadcasting Network

NBNZ National Bank of New Zealand

NBO Nairobi, Kenya (airport); Navy Bureau of Ordnance

n-bomb neutron bomb

N-bomb neutron bomb; nuclear bomb

nbp normal boiling point

NBP National Business Publications; Neighborhood Beautification Program; New Brooklyn Philharmonic

NBPA National Bark Producers Association; National Basketball Players Association; National Black Police Association

NBPC National Border Patrol Council

NBPI National Board for Prices and Income

NBPRP National Board for the Promotion of Rifle Practice

nbp's nude beach pests (prurient snoopers and voyeurs)

nbq no broken quantities

nbr nitrile-based rubbers; nitrile-butadiene rubber

n br naval brass; naval bronze

n Br nördliche Breite (German —north latitude)

NBR National Bison Range (Montana); Nightly Business Report (tv)

NBR National Business Review

nbre noviembre (Spanish—November)

NBRF National Biomedical Research Foundation

NBRI National Building Research Institute

NBRMP National Board of Review of Motion Pictures

NBRPC New Brunswick Research and Productivity Council

NBRS National Beef Recording Scheme; National Beef Recording Service

NBRT National Board for Respiratory Therapy

nbs normal burro serum

NBS Nagano Broadcasting System; National Bureau of Standards; New British Standard

NBSA National Bank of South Africa; Netherlands Bank of South Africa

NBSBL National Bureau of Standards Boulder Laboratory

NBSCCST National Bureau of Standards Center for Computer Sciences and Technology

NBSRS *Narodna Biblioteka Socijalisticke Republike Srbije* (Serbo-Croatian—National Library of the Socialist Republic of Serbia)—Belgrade

NBS-SIS National Bureau of Standards—Standard Information Services

nb st nimbo-stratus

NBST National Board for Science and Technology

NBT National Book Trust (India)

NBTA National Baton Twirlers Association; National Business Teachers Association

NBTC New Brunswick Teachers College

NBTL Naval Boiler Test Laboratory

NBTS National Blood Transfusion Service

nbuf not buffed (leather)

n butt national buttress (thread)

nbv net book value

nbw noise bandwidth

NBW National Book Week

Nby Newbury

NBYWCAUSA National Board of the Young Women's Christian Association of the U.S.A.

nc national coarse (thread); natural convector; nitrocellulose; no change; no charge; no connection; noise criteria; normally closed; nose cone; not cataloged; not catalogued; not complete; nuclear capability; numerical control(s)

n-c numerical control (automation)

n/c new charter; new crop; no charge; numerical control (automation)

nc *non chiffre* (French—unnumbered)

nC *na Christus* (Dutch—after Christ)

NC Napa College; Nashville, Chatanooga & St. Louis (railroad); Nasson College; Natchez College; National Cash Register (stock exchange symbol); National Center; National Certificate; National Coarse (screw threads); National Congress; National Council; National Fire Waste Council; Nature Conservancy; New Caledonia; New College; Newark College; Newberry College; Newcomb College; Newnham College; Nicholls College; Nichols College; Norfolk College; Norman College; North Carolina; North Carolinian; Northern Counties; Northern County; Northland College; Northwestern College; Nuclear Congress; Nuffield College (Oxford); Nurse Corps

N.C. NC Wyeth

NC *Norske Creditbank* (Norwegian Credit Bank)

nca neurocirculatory asthenia; no copies available

NCA Narcotics Control Act; National Camping Association; National Canners Association; National Capital Award; National Cashmere Association; National Cattlemens Association; National Charcoal Association; National Cheerleaders Association; National Chiropractic Association; National Civic Association; National Club Association; National Coal Association; National Coffee Association; National Command Authority; National Commission on Accrediting; National Composition Association; National Confectioners Association; National Constructors Association; National Contesters Association; National Costumers Association; National Council on the Aging; National Council on Alcoholism; National Council on the Arts; National Coursing Association; National Coursing Association; National Cranberry Association; National Creameries Association; National Credit Association; National Cricket Association; Naval Communications Annex; Navy Contract Administrator; Nebraska Correctional Association; Nevada Correctional Association; Ngorongoro Conservation Area (Tanzania); North Central Airlines; North Central Association (of colleges and schools); Northern Consolidated Airlines

N C A National Cricket Association

NCAA National Children Adoption Association; National Collegiate Athletic Association

NCAAA National Center of Afro-American Artists

NCAB National Cancer Advisory Board

NCAB *National Cyclopedia of American Biography*

NCAC National Copyright Advisory Committee (Library of Congress)

NCACME National Center for Adult, Continuing, and Manpower Education

ncad net cash against documents

NCAE National Center for Audio Experimentation; National College of Agricultural Engineering; National Council of Adult Education; North Carolina Association of Educators

NCAI National Clearinghouse for Alcohol Information; National Congress of American Indians; National Council on Alcoholism Inc

NCAICU North Carolina Association of Independent Colleges and Universities

NCAIR National Center for Automated Information Retrieval

NCALI National Clearinghouse for Alcohol Information (USPHS)

NCAM National Center for Advanced Materials

NCAMP National Coalition Against the Misuse of Pesticides

NCAN National Coalition of American Nuns

NCANH National Council for the Accreditation of Nursing Homes

N-CAP Nurses Coalition for Action in Politics

NCAPC National Center for Air Pollution Control

NCAR National Center for Atmospheric Research; National Committee for Antarctic Research

NCARB National Council of Architectural Registration Boards

NCARL National Committee Against Repressive Legislation

NCARMD National Commission on Arthritis and Related Musculoskeletal Disease

N-carrier(s) nuclear-powered aircraft carrier(s)

NCAS National Collegiate Association for Secretaries

NCASF National Council of American-Soviet Friendship

NCAT National Center for Alternative Technology; National Center for Audiotape; Northampton College of Advanced Technology

NCATE National Council for the Accreditation of Teacher Education

NCAW National Council for Animal Welfare

NCAWE National Council for Administrative Women in Education

ncb narcotic-centered behavior; new crime buffer; nickel-cadmium battery; no claim bonus

Ncb Norrlands Skogsägaves Cellulosa AB

NCB National Cargo Bureau; National Coal Board; National Conservation Bureau; Nippon Credit Bank; Nippon Cultural Broadcasting

NCBA National Cattle Breeders' Association; National Clydesdale Breeders Association; Northern California Booksellers Association

NCBD National Council for Balanced Development

NCBE National Clearinghouse for Bilingual Education

NCBFAA National Customs Brokers and Forwarders Association of America

NCBH National Coalition to Ban Handguns

NCBIAE National Council of Bureau of Indian Affairs Educators

NCBL National Conference of Black Lawyers

NCBMP National Council of Building Material Producers

NCBR National Council of Black Republicans

NCBS National Cattle Breeding Station (Australian)

NCBVA National Concrete Burial Vault Association

ncc numerical control code

NCC Namhae Chemical Corporation (Korean); Nassau Community College; National Cadet Corps; National Carloading Corporation; National Castings Council; National Civic Council; National Climatic Center; National Coaches Council; National Computer Center; National Computer Council; National Conference on Citizenship; National Consumer Council; National Container Committee; National Cotton Council; National Council of Churches of Christ in the USA; National Cultural Center; Nature Conservation Council; Navajo Community College; Newhouse Communications Center (University of Syracuse); Newspaper Comics Council; Noise Control Committee; Non-Combatant Corps; NORAD Control Center; Northwest Community College

NCC *Nederlands Cultureel Contact* (Netherlands Cultural Contact)

NCCA National Coil Coaters Association; North Carolina Correctional Association

NCCAN National Center on Child Abuse and Neglect

NCCAS National Center of Communication Arts and Sciences

NCCAT National Committee for Clear Air Turbulence

NCCC Niagara County Community College

NCCCA National Coordinating Council for Constructive Action

NCCCC Navy Command, Control, and Communications Center

NCCCD National Center for Computer Crime Data

NCCCLC Naval Command Control Communications Laboratory Center (formerly NEL—Navy Electronics Laboratory)

NCCCUS National Council of the Churches of Christ in the United States

NCCCUSA National Council of the Churches of Christ in the U.S.A.

NCCD National Council on Crime and Delinquency

NCCE National Commission for Cooperative Education; National Council for Catholic Evangelization

NCCEOA National Coordinating Council of Educational Opportunities Associations

NCCF National Committee to Combat Fascism (Black Panther front); National Commission on Consumer Finance

NCCG National Council on Compulsive Gambling

NCCH National Council to Control Handguns

NCCI National Committee for Commonwealth Immigrants

NCCIHE North Carolina Center for Independent Higher Education

NCCIS NATO Command, Control, and Information System

NCCJ National Coalition for Children's Justice; National Conference of Christians and Jews

NCCJPA National Clearinghouse for Criminal Justice Planning and Architecture

NCCL National Council for Civil Liberties; National Council of Canadian Labor

NCCLS National Committee for Clinical Laboratory Standards; National Consumer Center for Legal Services

nccp nagivation control console panel

NCCPA National Council of College Publications Advisers

NCCPL National Community Crime Prevention League

NCCPV National Commission on the Causes and Prevention of Violence

NCCR National Council for Civic Responsibility

NCCS National Command and Control System; National Council for Civic Responsibility

NCCU National Conference of Canadian Universities; North Carolina Central University

NCCVD National Council for Combating Venereal Diseases

NCCW National Council of Catholic Women

NCCY National Council of Catholic Youth

ncd no can do; not considered disabling

NCD National Commission on Diabetes; Naval Construction Department; Naval Construction Depot; New Community Development

NCD *New Collegiate Dictionary*

NCDA National Center for

Drug Analysis; National Council on Drug Abuse

NCDAD National Council for Diplomas in Art and Design

NCDAI National Clearinghouse for Drug Abuse Information

NCDC National Capital Development Commission; National Center for Disease Control; National Communicable Disease Center; National Council on Crime and Delinquency; National Curriculum Development Center; New Community Development Corporation

NCDs Negotiable Certificates of Deposit

NCDS National Center for Dispute Settlement (American Arbitration Association)

ncdu navigation control and display unit

nce normal curve equivalent

NCE Newark College of Engineering; Nice, France (Côte d'Azur airport)

NCE New Catholic Encyclopedia

NCEA National Catholic Educational Association; National Center for Economic Alternatives; National Community Education Association; North Carolina Education Association

NCEB National Center for Educational Brokering

NCEC National Committee for an Effective Congress; National Community Education Clearinghouse

NCECA National Council on Education for the Ceramic Arts

NCECS North Carolina Educational Computing Service

NCED National Center for the Employment of the Deaf

NCEDT National Council to Eliminate Death Taxes

NCEE National Commission on Excellence in Education; National Congress for Educational Excellence; National Council of Engineering Examiners

ncef national calling and emergency frequencies

NCEFT National Commission on Electronic Fund Transfers

NCEI National Commission on Emerging Institutions

NCEL Naval Civil Engineering Laboratory

NCEMP National Center for

Energy Management and Power

NCEN National Commission on Egg Nutrition

NCER National Center for Earthquake Research; National Council on Educational Research

NCERT National Council for Educational Research and Training

nces necessary; normal curve equivalent scores

NCES National Center for Educational Statistics

NCET National Council for Educational Technology

ncf nerve cell food

NCF National Consumer Federation

NCFA National Commission of Fine Arts; National Consumer Finance Association; Navy Campus for Achievement

NCFC National Council of Farmer Cooperatives

NCFDA National Council on Federal Disaster Assistance

NCFILP National Coalition for Fair Immigration Laws and Practices

NCFIRB North Carolina Fire Insurance Rating Bureau

NCFM National Commission on Food Marketing

NCFP National Conference on Fluid Power

NCFPC National Center for Fish Protein Concentrate

NCFR National Council on Family Relations

NCFSU Naval Construction Force Support Unit

NCFT National College of Food Technology

NCG National Council for the Gifted; National Cylinder Gas (division of Chemotron)

NCGA National Council on Governmental Accounting

NCGE National Council for Geographic Education

NCGG National Council for Geodesy and Geophysics

nch number changed (telephone)

NCH National Children's Home

NCHA National Campers and Hikers Association; National Capital Housing Authority; National Culling Horse Association

NCHCS National Council for Health Care Services

NCHELP National Council of

Higher Education Loan Programs

N Chem L National Chemical Laboratory

NCHEMS National Center for Higher Education Management Systems

n chg normal charge

NCHI National Council of the Housing Industry

NCHMT National Capitol Historical Museum of Transportation

NCHP Nouvelle Compagnie Havraise Peninsulaire (de Navigation) (Havre Peninsula Navigation Line)

n Chr nach Christus (German—after Christ, A.D.)

NCHS National Center for Health Statistics

NCHSR & D National Center for Health Services Research and Development (HEW)

NCHVRFE National College for Heating, Ventilating, Refrigeration, and Fan Engineering

nci napthalene-creosote-iodiform (lice-control powder); no-cost item

NCI National Cancer Institute; National Casing Institute; National Cello Institute; National Cheese Institute; Naval Cost Inspection; Naval Cost Inspector; Naval Court of Inquiry

NCIA National Council of Instructional Administrators; National Council for Islamic Affairs

NCIAC National Consumer Information and Advisory Center

NCIC National Cancer Institute of Canada; National Career Information Center; National Crime Information Center

NCIES National Center for the Improvement of Educational Systems

NCIJC National Council of Independent Junior Colleges

NCIO National Council on Indian Opportunity

nci powder naphthalene creosote iodoform powder (for killing lice)

NCIS National Chemical Information System; National Council of Independent Schools

NCISC Naval Counterintelligence Support Center

NCIT National Council on In-

land Transport
NCJAVM National Council on Jewish Audio-Visual Materials
NCJISS National Criminal Justice Information and Statistics Service
NCJMS National Center for Job Market Studies
NCJR National Coalition for Jail Reform
NCJRS National Criminal Justice Reference System
NCJSC National Criminal Justice Statistics Center
NCJW National Council of Jewish Women
Nck Neck (postal abbreviation)
N Cl New Caledonia(n)
NCL National Central Library; National Chemical Laboratory; National Consolidated Limited; National Consumers League; National Culture League; Norwegian Caribbean Line, Norwegian Cruise Lines
NCLA National Council of Local Administrators (of vocational education and practical arts); North Carolina Library Association
NCLAN National Crop Loss Assessment Network
N-class NATO name for a Soviet class of nuclear powered attack submarines
NCLC National Caucus of Labor Committee; National Consumer Law Center; National Council of Labour Colleges; National Council of Local Administrators
NCLIS National Commission on Library and Information Sciences
NCLR National Council of La Raza
NCLS National Clearinghouse for Legal Services
ncm non-corrosive metal; non-crew member
NCM National Congress for Men; Nippon Calculating Machine
NCMA National Catalog Managers Association; National Council of Music Associations; North Carolina Museum of Art
NCMC National Center on Missing Children; NORAD Cheyenne Mountain Complex
NCMDA National Commission on Marijuana and Drug Abuse

NCME National Council on Measurements in Education; Network for Continuing Medical Education
NCMEA National Catholic Music Educators Association
NCMH National Committee on Maternal Health; National Committee for Mental Hygiene
NCMHE National Clearinghouse for Mental Health Education
NCMLB National Council of Mailing List Brokers
NCMP National Commission for Manpower Policy
NCMU National Commission on Marijuana Use
NCN National Council of Nurses; New Caledonian Nickel
NCNA National Council on Noise Abatement; New China News Agency (mainland China)
NCNC National Council of Nigeria and the Cameroons
NCNE National Campaign for Nursery Education
NCNP National Conference for New Politics (coalition of communist, left socialist, and militant revolutionary elements comprising the New Left); North Cascades National Park (Washington)
NCNW National Council of Negro Women
nco no-cost option
NCO Noncommissioned Officer
NCOA National Council on the Aging; Noncommissioned Officer Academy
NCOAUSA Non-Commissioned Officers Association of the U.S.A.
NCOC National Commission on Organized Crime; National Council on Organized Crime
ncod net cash on delivery
NCOES Noncommissioned Officer Education System
NCOIC Noncommissioned Officer in Charge
NCOLS Noncommissioned Officers Leadership School
N/COM Navy/Chief of Naval Operations
NCOMP National Catholic Office for Motion Pictures
NCOR National Committee on Oceanographic Research
ncos non-commissioned officers

ncp nitrogen charge panel; normal circular pitch; number of channel programs
NCP National Capital Parks; National Country Party; Naviera Chilena del Pacífico (Chilean Pacific Line); Navy Capabilities Plan; Noise Control Plan; Nutrition Center of the Philippines
NCP Naviera Chilena del Pacífico (Spanish—Chilean Pacific Line)
NCPA National Crime Prevention Association
NCPAC National Conservative Political Action Committee
NCPC National Capital Planning Commission; National Consumer Protection Council; National Crime Prevention Coalition; Northern Canada Power Commission
NCPERL National Coalition for Public Education and Religious Liberty
NCPGA North Carolina Personnel and Guidance Association
NCPI National Clay Pipe Institute; National Crime Prevention Institute; Navy Civilian Personnel Instructions
NCPL National Center for Programmed Learning
NCPPL National Committee on Prisons and Prison Labor
NCPRV National Council of Puerto Rican Volunteers
NCPS National Cat Protection Society; National Commission on Product Safety
NCPT National Congress of Parents and Teachers
NCPTWA National Clearinghouse for Periodical Title Word Abbreviations
NCPV National Commission on the Prevention of Violence
NCQR National Council for Quality and Reliability
ncr natural circulation reactor; no calibration required; no carbon required; not combat ready
n Cr novo Cruzeiro (Portuguese—new cruzeiro)—Brazilian monetary unit
NCR National Capital Region; National Cash Register; National Council of Reconciliation (in Vietnam)
NCR National Catholic Record; National Catholic Reporter
NCRA National Correctional

Recreation Association

NCRC National Condor Research Center

NCRCL National Civil Rights Clearinghouse Library

NCRD National Council for Research and Development; National Council for Resource Development

NCRE Naval Construction Research Establishment

NCRFCL National Commission on Reform of Federal Criminal Laws

NCRFP National Council for a Responsible Firearms Policy

NCRI National Red Cherry Institute

NCRL National Chemical Research Laboratory

NCRLC National Committee on Regional Library Cooperation

NCROPA National Campaign for the Repeal of the Obscene Publications Act (British)

ncrp narrow cold-rolled products; nonreinforced concrete pipe

NCRP National Committee on Radiation Protection; National Council on Radiation Protection; National Council for Research and Planning

ncr paper no-carbon-required paper

NCRPM National Committee on Radiation Protection and Measurements

NCRR National Center for Resource Recovery

NCRS National Committee for Rural Schools

NCRT National College of Rubber Technology

NCRVE National Center for Research in Vocational Education

NCRY National Commission on Resources for Youth

ncs naval control of shipping; navigation control simulator

NCS National Cartoonists Society; National Cemetery System; National Chrysanthemum Society; National Communications System, Naval Communication Station; National Computer Systems; Net Control Station; Numerical Control Society

NCSA National Carl Schurz Association; National Council of Seamen's Agencies; National Crushed Stone Association; National Customs Service Association; North Carolina School of the Arts; North Coast of South America

NCSAW National Catholic Society for Animal Welfare

NCSBA North Carolina School Boards Association

NCSBEE National Council of State Boards of Engineering Examiners

NCSC National Cargo Security Council; National Center for State Courts; National Companies and Securities Commission (Australia); National Council for Senior Citizens; National Council of Senior Citizens

NCSCEE National Council of State Consultants in Elementary Education

NCSCT National Center for School and College Television

NCSDCJC National Council of State Directors of Community and Junior Colleges

NCSE National Commission on Safety Education

NCSEA National Council of State Education Associations

NCSF National College Student Foundation

NCSGC National Council of State Garden Clubs

NCSH National Clearinghouse for Smoking and Health

NCSI National Council for Stream Improvement

NCSJ National Conference on Soviet Jews

NCSL National ·Civil Service League; National Conference of Standards Laboratories; National Conference of State Legislators; Naval Code and Signal Laboratory

NCSMC National Council for the Single Mother and Her Child

NCSNE Naval Control of Shipping in the Northern European Command Area of NATO

NCSNP National Council for a Sane Nuclear Policy

NCSO Naval Control of Shipping Office(r); North Carolina Symphony Orchestra

NCSP National Conference on State Parks

NCSPA North Carolina State Ports Authority

NCSPS National Committee for the Support of Public Schools

NCSR National Center for Systems Reliability; National Council for Scientific Research

NCSRC National Centre for Social Research and Criminology (Cairo)

ncsry necessary

NCSS National Center for Social Statistics; National Council for Social Studies

NCSSA Nature Conservation Society of South Australia; Naval Command Systems Support Activity

NCSSC Naval Command Systems Support Center

NCSSFL National Council of State Supervisors of Foreign Languages

NCSTAS National Council of Scientific and Technical Art Societies

NC & ST L Nashville, Chattanooga & St Louis (railroad)

NCSTRC North Carolina Science and Technology Research Center

NCSW National Conference on Social Welfare

NCSWCL National Commission on State Workmen's Compensation Laws

NCSWD National Center for Solid Waste Disposal

NCSWR National Conference on Solid Waste Research

nct natural contour theory; no charge for terms; no civil twilight

NCT National Chamber of Trade; National Culture Trust

n/cta *nuestra cuenta* (Spanish—our account)

NCTA National Cable Television Association; National Capital Transport Agency; National Community Television Association; National Committee for Technological Awards; National Council for Technological Awards

NCTAEP National Committee on Technology, Automation, and Economic Progress

NCTC National Collection of Type Cultures

NCTE National Council of Teachers of English

NCTEC Northern Counties Technical Examinations Council

NCTEPS National Commission on Teacher Education and Professional Standards

NCTI Nationwide Consumer

Testing Institute

NCTJ National Council for the Training of Journalists

NCTM National Council of Teachers of Mathematics

NCTR National Center for Toxicological Research; National Council on Teacher Retirement

NCTS National Council of Technical Schools

ncu navigation(al) computer unit; nitrogen control unit

NCU National Cyclists' Union

NCUA National Credit Union Administration; National Credit Union Association

NCUC National Commission on Unemployment Compensation

NCUF National Computer Users Forum

NCUMC National Council for the Unmarried Mother and her child

ncup no commission until paid

NCUPUFUB National Cleanup, Paint-Up, Fix-Up Bureau

NCURA National Council of University Research Administrators

NCUSA Navy Club of the U.S.A.

NCUSIF National Credit Union Share Insurance Fund

NCUTLO National Committee on Uniform Traffic Laws and Ordinances

ncv no commercial value

NCVA National Center(s) for Volunteer Action

NCVAE National Council for Audio-Visual Aids in Education

NCVOTE National Center for Vocational, Occupational, and Technical Education

NCVT National Crime and Violence Test

ncw nosecone warhead

NCW National Council of Women; North City West

NCWA National Council of Women of Australia

NCWC National Catholic Welfare Conference

NCWSA National Council of Women of South Africa

NCWSB National Council of Wool Selling Brokers

NCWUS National Council of Women of the U.S.

NCY National Cylinder Gas (stock-exchange symbol)

NCYC National Council of Yacht Clubs

NCYMCA National Council of Young Men's Christian Associations

NCYRE National Council on Year-Round Education

nd national debt; natural draught; new deck(ing); new drugs; next day; no date; no decision; no deed; no delay; no discount(ing); no drawing; non-delivery; non-directional; not dated; not deeded; not determined; not drawn; nothing doing; nuclear detonation

n-d non-drying

n/d neutral density

nd *niederdruck* (German—low pressure); *no hay datos* (Spanish—no data)

Nd neodymium; refractive index (symbol)

ND Environment Near Death; Narcotics Division (NYPD); National Dairy Products (stock exchange symbol); National Debt; Naval District; Navy Department; New Drugs; North Dakota; Notre Dame

N.D. Doctor of Naturopathy

ND New Drugs

nda new drug application; non-destructive analysis; non-destructive assay

ndu (NDA) new drug applications

N d A Nota dell 'Autore (Italian—Author's Note)

NDA National Dairy Association; National Dairymens' Association; National Dental Association; National Diploma in Agriculture

ndaa not dated at all

NDAA National District Attorneys Association

NDAB Numerical Data Advisory Board

NDAC National Defense Advisory Committee; National Defense Advisory Commission; Nuclear Defense Affairs Committee (NATO)

ND Agr Eng National Diploma in Agricultural Engineering

N Dak North Dakota; North Dakotan

NDANZ National Dairy Association of New Zealand

n da r nota da redação (Portuguese—author's note)

NDASSP North Dakota Association of Secondary School Principals

ndb national development bond(ing); new domestic boiler; new donkey boiler; non-directional beacon

NDB National Development Bank; Navy Department Bulletin; Niue Development Board

NDBC National Data Buoy Center; National Duckpin Bowling Congress

NDBI National Dairymen's Benevolent Institution

NDBO NOAA Data Buoy Office

NDBS National Data Buoy System

NDC National Dairy Council; National Defense Contribution; National Defense Corps; National Democratic Club; National Development Company; National Development Corporation; National Development Council; NATO Defence College; Naval Dental Clinic; Nippon Decimal Classification; Nuclear Development Corporation

NDCA National Dry Cleaners Association

NDCC National Defense Cadet Corps; National Democratic Congressional Committee

NDCD National Drug Code Directory

NDCS National Deaf Children's Society

N d D Nota della Direzione (Italian—Director's Note)

NDD National Diploma in Dairying

nddad net demand draft against documents

ndd(s) narcotic-detection dog(s)

NDDT National Diploma in Dairy Technology

nde near-death experience; non-destructive evaluation; nonlinear differential equation(s)

NDEA National Defense Education Act

N-defense nuclear defense

NDEI National Defense Education Institute

n del a nota del autor (Spanish—author's note)

n del e nota del editor (Spanish—editor's note)

n del t nota del traductor (Spanish—translator's note)

N de M Nacional de México (railroad)

N de M Ferrocarriles Nacionales de México (Spanish—National Railways of Mexico)

NDER National Defense Executive Reserve

ndf nacelle drag efficiency factor

NDF National Diploma in Forestry

ndg *nedenfor* (Dano-Norwegian —beneath)

NDG National Dance Guild

NDGS National Defense General Staff; National Duncan Glass Society

NDH Delhi, India (airport); National Diploma in Health; National Diploma in Horticulture

NDHA National District Heating Association

NDHS New Drop High School

ndi numerical designation index

NDI National Dance Institute; National Death Index

NDIB National Drug Intelligence Bureau

NDICF North Dakota Independent College Fund

NDIRS North Dakota Institute for Regional Studies

NDIS National Drug Information Service

ndl network definition language

Ndl *Nederland* (Dutch—The Netherlands)

NDL National Development Loan; Nuclear Defense Laboratory

NDL *Norddeutscher Lloyd* (North German Lloyd)

NDLA North Dakota Library Association

NDLB National Dock Labour Board

NDMB National Defense Mediation Board

NDN National Diffusion Network

ndo negotiable delivery order

NDO National Debt Office (and Office for the Payment of Government Life Annuities); Natural Disasters Organization

ndp net domestic product; normal diametric pitch

NDP National Dairy Products; National Democratic Party; National Detective Police; New Democratic Party (Canada)

NDP *Nationaldemokratische Partei Deutschlands* (Germany's National-Democratic Party)—neo-Nazi oriented

NDPA National Decorating Products Association; National Democratic Party of Alabama

NDPBC National Duck Pin Bowling Congress

NDPGA North Dakota Personnel and Guidance Association

NDPH National Diploma in Poultry Husbandry

NDPP National Drug Prevention Program

NDPR NATO Defense Planning Review

NDPs Narcotic Detention Pens (NYC)

NDPS National Data Processing Service

ndr net discount(ed) revenue

N^{dr} *Neder* (Dutch or Swedish—lower); *Nieder* (German—lower)

N d R *Nota della Redazione* (Italian—Editor's Note)

NDR *Norddeutscher Rundfunk* (North German Radio)

NDRC National Defense Research Committee

NDRG NATO Defense Research Group

NDRI Naval Dental Research Institute

ndro nondestructive readout

NDRSWG NATO Data Requirements and Standards Working Group

nds national development strategy

nds (NDS) nuclear detection satellite

NDs Northern Districts

NDS National Directory Service

NDSB Narcotic Drugs Supervisory Body

NDSBA North Dakota School Boards Association

NDSF North Dakota School of Forestry

NDSK *Nippon Dendo Sharyo Kyokai* (Japan Electric-Powered Vehicle Association)

NDSL National Direct Student Loan

NDSM National Defense Security Medal

NDSSS North Dakota State School of Science

ndt nondestructive testing

ndt *nota del traductor* (Spanish —translator's note); *nota del traduttore* (Italian—translator's note); *note du traducteur* (French—translator's note)

NDT Ferrocarril Nacional de Tehuantepec (National Railroad of Tehuantepec—symbol); National Diet Library (Tokyo); National Driver's Test; Newfoundland Daylight Time; Nichigeki Dancing Team; Nuclear Defense Laboratory

NDTA National Defense Transportation Association; Non-Destructive Testing Association

NDTAA Non-Destructive Testing Association of Australia

NDTC Nottingham and District Technical College

NDTI *National Disease and Therapeutic Index*

NDTS Non-Destructive Test(ing) Standard(s)

ndu navigation display unit; nuclear data unit

NDU National Defense University; Notre Dame University

N-dump(ing) nuclear-waste dump(ing)

N-dump(s) nuclear (waste-disposal) dump(s)

ndup nonduplication; nonduplicate

Ndv Newcastle disease virus

ndw net deadweight

NDW Naval District Washington (D.C.)

ne new edition; new engine(s); nital etch(ing); not enlarged; not entitled; not essential; not exceeding

ne (NE) norepinephrane

n/e no effects

ne *non ebarbe* (French—untrimmed)

Ne neon; Nepal; Nepalese; Netherlander; Netherlands

NE National Emergency; National Estate(s); Naval Engineer(ing); Nebraska (postal code); new edition; New England(er); News Editor; northeast; Northeast Airlines (2-letter coding); Nuclear Engineer(ing)

N.E. Nuclear Engineer

NE *Navio Escola* (Portuguese—Schoolship); *Noreste* (Spanish —northeast)

ne/4 mos new edition expected in four months

ne/6m new edition in preparation, expected in 6 months (for example)

ne/6 mos new edition expected in six months

nea net energy analysis

NEA National Education Association; National Electrification Administration; National Endowment for the Arts; Net Energy Analysis; New England Aquarium (Boston); Newspaper Enterprise Association; Northeast Airlines; Northern Electric Authority; Nuclear Energy Agency (UN)

N.E.A. Newspaper Enterprise Association

NEAC National Energy Advisory Committee; New English Art Club

NEACAP National Emergency Air Command Post

NEACH New England Automated Clearing House

NEACSS New England Association of Colleges and Secondary Schools

NEAF Near East Air Force; New Era Aboriginal Fellowship

NEAFC Northeast Atlantic Fisheries Commission

NEAG New English Art Gallery

NEAHI Near East Animal Health Institute

NEAL National Electron Accelerator Laboratory

NEAP National Assessment of Educational Progress

NEA-PAC National Education Association Political Action Committee

Neapolis (Greek—New Town); (Latin—Napoli)—Naples

Neapolitan Painter and Poet Salvator Rosa

Neapolitans islands off Naples; natives of Naples

NEAR National Emergency Aid Radio; National Emergency Alarm Repeater

NEARA New England Antiquities Research Association; New England Archeological Research Association

Near East the Middle East as opposed to the Far East

Near North Australian equivalent of the Far East

Nears short form for the Near Islands of the outermost Aleutians in southwestern Alaska, including Agattu and Attu within sight of the USSR's Komandorski Islands off Kamchatka

NEAS National Engineering Aptitude Search

NEASC New England Association of Schools and Colleges

NEAT National (Cash Register) Electronic Autocoding Technique; National Employment and Training

NEATE New England Association of Teachers of English

'neath beneath; underneath

NEATO Northeast Asian Treaty Organization

neb nembutal

neb *nebbisch* (Yiddish—colorless, plain, retiring, socially ill at ease)

neb. *nebula* (Latin—spray)

NEB National Electricity Board; National Energy Board (Canada); National Enterprise Board (United Kingdom)

NEB *New English Bible*

NEBAC National Ethnic Broadcasting Advisory Council

nebbie (underground slang—nembutal)

nebbies nembutal capsules

nEbC no-European-before-Columbus school of historic discovery despite Irish and Viking claims to the contrary

NEBHE New England Board of Higher Education

Nebr Nebraska; Nebraskan

NEBSS National Examinations Board for Supervisory Studies

nebuchad nebuchadnessar (16-quart-capacity champagne bottle)

nebul. *nebula* (Latin—spray)—nebulizer

nec necessary; no error check(ing); not elsewhere classified

Nec (NEC) Navy enlisted classification

NEC National Economic Council; National Egg Council; National Electrical Code; National Equity Corporation; National Exchange Club; New England Conservatory of Music; New England Council; Nippon Electric Company, Nippon Electric Corporation

NECA National Electrical Contractors' Association; Near East College Association; Numismatic Error Collectors of America

NECAA National Entertainment and Campus Activities Association

NECAP NASA Energy-Cost Analysis Program

NECC National Education Computer Center

NECCC New England Correctional Coordinating Council

NECCO New England Confectionary Company

NECEL New England Coalition of Educational Leaders

NECM New England Conservatory of Music

NECMD Newark Contract Management District

NECO Nuclear Engineering Company

NECOS Northern Europe Chiefs of Staff (NATO)

NECP New England College of Pharmacy

NECPA *National Energy Conservation Policy Act*

necr necrosis

necro (Latin prefix—corpse or dead)—necrophilia, necropholia, necrosis

necrol necrology

necropo necropolis; necropolitan(ic)

NECS National Electrical Code Standards

necy necessary

ned normal equivalent deviation

Ned Edmund; Edward; Edwin

Ned *Nederland* (Dutch—the Netherlands); *Nederlands* (Dano Norwegian—the Netherlands)

NED National Endowment for Democracy; Nuclear Energy Division (GE)

NED *New English Dictionary (Oxford English Dictionary)*

NEDA National Economic and Development Authority; National Economic Development Association; National Electronic Distributors Association; National Electronics Development Association

Ned Ant *Nederlandse Antillen* (Dutch—the Netherlands Antilles)—Dutch West Indies

Ned Buntline Edward Zane Carroll Judson

NEDC National Economic Development Council (of Great Britain where it is nicknamed Neddy); Near East Development Council

Neddy Edgar; Edmund; Edward; Edwin; Edwina; National Economic Development Council's nickname

nedela network definition language

nederl *nederlandsk* (Dano-Norwegian—Dutch)

Nederl *Nederland* (Dutch—Netherlands)

Nederlander (Dutch—Dutchman)

Nederlanders most Dutch men and women who prefer this term to Dutch, Dutchmen, or Dutchwomen

Nederlandse Antillen (Dutch—

Netherlands Antilles)—Aruba, Bonaire, Curaçao, Saba, Sint Eustatius, and half of Sint Maarten

NEDICO Netherlands Engineering Consultants

NEDL New England Deposit Library

Nedlloyd Netherlands Line

NEDO National Economic Development Office; New Energy Development Organization

NEDT National Educational Development Tests

NedThTs Nederlands Theologisch Tijdschrift (Dutch—Netherlands Theological Periodical)

NEDU Navy Experimental Diving Unit

NEEB North Eastern Electricity Board (UK)

NEEC National Export Expansion Council

need. needlework

NEED National Environmental Education Development

Needle Park underworld name of an open-air uptown Manhattan hangout, near the intersection of New York City's Amsterdam Avenue and Broadway, where many dope addicts, dope pushers, pimps, prostitutes, and their victims may be seen

needn't (contraction—need not)

NEEDS New England Electronic Data System

ne'er never (contraction)

NEES Naval Engineering Experiment Station; New England Electric Service

neev (NEEV) natural energy electric vehicle

NEEWSSOP NATO-Europe Early-Warning-System Standard Operating Procedures

nef national extra fine (screw thread); net energy for fattening; noise exposure forecast; nuclear energy factor(s)

NEF Naval Emergency Fund; Near East Foundation; New Education Fellowship

nefa nonesterified fatty acid

NEFA Northeast Frontier Agency

NEFC Near East Forestry Commission

NEFEN Near and Far East News

NEFIRA New England Fire Insurance Rating Association

NEFO National Electronic Facilities Organization

Nefos New Emerging Forces

NEFP National Educational Finance Project

NEFSA National Education Field Service Association

neg negation; negative; negligent; negotiable; negotiate; negritude

nég négation (French—negation)

Neg Negro; Negroid

negatron negative electron

Negev desert between Egypt and Israel; southern tip touches Gulf of Aqaba—outlet to Red Sea, Suez Canal, Mediterranean and Indian oceans

negistor negative resistor

Negley Farson James Scott Negley Farson

nego negotiate

negobl negotiable

negod negotiated

negoin negotiation

negotn negotiating

negotng negotiating

Negrasian(s) person(s) of African and Asian parents such as Afro-Chinese, Afro-Indian, Afro-Japanese, etc.

Negri Sembilan (Malay—Nine States)

negro (Portuguese, Spanish—black as in Rio Negro)

NEGRO National Economic Growth and Reconstruction Organization

Negro Explorer Matthew Henson who pushed Peary to the North Pole after accompanying him on all his Arctic expeditions

négt négociant (French—merchant)—wholesaler

negtax negative (income) tax

Neh The Book of Nehemiah

Neh Nehemiah

NEH National Endowment for the Humanities

NEHA National Environmental Health Association; National Executives Housekeepers Association

NEHC National Extension Homemakers Council

nehi knee-high

Nehm Nehemiah

nei not elsewhere included; not elsewhere indicated

n.e.i. non est inventus (Latin—it is not found)

NEI National Eye Institute; Netherlands East Indies; New England Institute

NEIC National Earthquake Information Center; National

Energy Information Center

NEIDP National Electronic Industries Procurement

Nei Monggol (Pinyin Chinese—Inner Mongolia); (Pinyin Chinese—Inner Mongolia)—autonomous region of mainland China

NEISS National Electronic Injury Surveillance System

NEISSS National Electronics Injury Surveillance Safety System

NEJA National Equal Justice Association

Nejd (Arabic—Highland)—The Nejd is Saudi Arabia's central tableland

NEJM New England Journal of Medicine

nek nekton

NEK Norsk Electrotecnisk Komite (Norwegian Electrotechnical Committee)

nekolim neocolonialist-colonialist-imperialist (Indonesian acronym)

nel noise-exposure level

Nel Eleanor(a); Ellen; Helen(a); Nelly

NEL National Engineering Laboratory (Great Britain); Navy Electronics Laboratory (USN)

NEL New English Library

NELA National Electric Light Association; New England Library Association

NELC Naval Electronics Laboratory Center (formerly NEL)

NELDIC Nippon (Electric Company) Electric Layout Design (System) for Integrated Circuits

NELIA Nuclear Energy Liability Insurance Association

NELIAC Navy Electronics Laboratory International Algol Compiler

NELINT New England Library Information Network

Nell Eleanor(e)

NELL North East Lancashire Libraries

Nellie Nellie McClung (pronounced *Mc Clue*)—Canadian novelist and women's rights champion in the early 1900s

Nellie Melba Helen Porter Mitchell

Nello Emmanuel

Nelly Eleanor(a); Ellen; Helen

Nelly Bly Elizabeth Cochrane Seaman

NELMA Northeastern Lumber Manufacturers Association

Nel-Mar Nelson-Marlborough

(NZ)
NELP North East London Polytechnic
NELPIA Nuclear Energy Liability Property Insurance Association
Nels Nelson
NELS National Environmental Laboratories
Nelson Horatio Nelson; Knute Nelson; Nelson Olsen Nelson; Thomas Nelson; all other distinguished Nelsons
NELSON New Editing and Layout System of Newspaper
Nelson Algren Nelson Algren Abraham
NELTAS North East Lancashire Technical Advisory Services
NEly north-easterly
nem not elsewhere mentioned
NEM New Economic Mechanism
nema nematode
NEMA National Ecletic Medical Association; National Electrical Manufacturers Association
nemat nematology
Nemat Nemathelminthes
nembies nembutal (sodium pentobarbital sedative hypnotics)
NEMC New England Medical Center
NEMCA NATO Electromagnetic Compatibility Agency
nem. con. *nemine contradicente* (Latin—no one contradicting)
nem. dis. *nemine dissentiente* (Latin—no one dissenting)
NEMI National Elevator Manufacturing Industry
nemish nembutal
NEMLA New England Modern Language Association
nemmies nembutal capsules (dangerous sedative)
Nemo Guillaume; Guillermo
NEMO Naval Edreobenthic Manned Observatory (for sedentary sea bottom research); Naval Experimental Manned Observatory
NEMPA North-Eastern Master Printers' Alliance
NEMPS National Environmental Monitoring and Prediction System
NEMRB New England Motor Rate Bureau
nems (NEMS) near-earth magnetospheric satellite
nen noise and exposure number
NEN New England Nuclear (corporation)

nencl nonenclosed; nonenclosure
ne/nd new edition in preparation—no date can be given
N-energy nuclear energy
N Eng Naval Engineer(ing); New England; North England
N-engine(s) nuclear engine(s)
nenmld not enameled
NENP New England National Park (New South Wales)
neo near earth orbit
neo (Latin prefix—new or young)—neonatal
NEOA National Entertainers and Operators Association
NEOB New Executive Office Building (D.C.)
NEOC National Emergency Operations Center
Neo-Cath Neo-Catholic(ism)
Neo-Christ Neo-Christian(ity)
neoclas neoclassical; neoclassicism
neocol neocolonial(ism)
neocolim neocolonial-colonial imperalist
Neo-Conf Neo-Confucian(ist)
neo-con(s) neo-conservative(s)
Neo-Dar Neo-Darwinian; Neo-Darwinist(ic)
neo-dhc neohesperidin dihydrochalcone (sweetener)
NEODTC Naval Explosive Ordinance Disposal Technical Center
Neo-Goth Neo-Gothic
Neo-Heg Neo-Hegelian
neo-imp neo-impressionism; neo-impressionistic
Neo-Kant Neo-Kantian(ism)
neol neologism
Neo-Lam Neo-Lamarckian; Neo-Lamarckism; NeoLamarckist
Neo-Lat Neo-Latin(ism)
Neo-Luth Neo-Lutheran(ism)
Neo-Mel Neo-Melanesian (pidgin English of Melanesia, New Guinea, and North-East Australian islanders)
Neo-Nor Neo-Norwegian
Neopagan Eclectic Miguel de Unamuno
Neo-Plas Neo-Plastic(ism)
Neo-Plat Neo-Platonic; Neo-Platonism
Neo-Pyth Neo-Pythagorean(ism)
Neo-Real Neo-Realism; Neo-Realistic
Neorican(s) New York American(s)
Neo-Ricans newly repatriated Puerto Ricans
Neo-Rom Neo-Romantic(ism)

Neo-Schol Neo-Scholastic(ism)
neotrop neotropical
neotwy (last-letter mnemonic—when, where, who, what, how, why)
nep new edition pending; noise equivalent power; not elsewhere provided; nude-encounter parlor (brothel)
Nep Nepal; Nepomucene; Nepomuceno; Nepomuk; Neptune
Nep Cornelius Nepos (Roman biographer)
NEP National Education Program; National Energy Plan; New Ecological Paradigm; New Economic Policy; New England Power (company); Nixon Economic Policy
nepa (NEPA) nuclear energy for the propulsion of aircraft
NEPA National Electric Power Authority; National Environmental Policy Act
Nepal Kingdom of Nepal (Himalayan mountain nation whose Nepalese converse in Nepali, Newari, and other tongues; drugs, hides, jute, quartz, and rice are exported)
NEPAL National Egg Packers' Association, Ltd
NEPC National Employers Policy Committee
NEPCO New England Provision Company
NEPE National Emergency Planning Establishment (Canada)
neph nephew
nepho nephograph, nephological; nephologist; nephology
nephro (Latin prefix—kidney)—nephritis
NEPIA Nuclear Energy Property Insurance Association
NEPLEX New England Power Exchange
NEPMU Navy Environmental and Preventive Medicine Unit
Nep Rs Nepalese rupees
nep's nude-encounter parlors
NEPSC National Employee Participation Steering Committee
Nep Soc Neptune Society
NEPSS Naval Environmental Protection Support Service (USN)
Nept Neptune
Neptune Lockheed P-2 antisubmarine and reconnaissance aircraft
Neptune (Latin—Poseiden)—

god of the sea
Nequam Alexander Necham
N Equ Cur North Equatorial Current
ner nervous system
NER National Educational Radio; National Elk Refuge (Wyoming); North Eastern Railway (England)
NERA National Economic Research Associates; National Emergency Relief Administration
NERAIC Northern European Region Air Information Center
NERBC New England River Basins Commission
NERC National Electronic Reliability Council; National Environmental Research Center; Natural Environment Research Council
NERDDC National Energy Research Development and Demonstration Council
ne rep. *ne repetatur* (Latin—do not repeat)
NERO Near East Regional Office (FAO); Nutrition Education Research Organization
NERPG Northern European Regional Planning Group (NATO)
nerv nervous; nuclear emulsion recovery vehicle (NERV)
nerva nuclear engine for rocket vehicle application
Nerve Center of Alaska Anchorage
NE-Rx Northeast Regional Exchange
nes not elsewhere specified
nEs non-English speaking
Nes Nesta; Nestor
NES National Emergency Services; National Extension Service; Naval Education Service; News Election Service; Nucleus Estate and Smallholders
NESA National Environmental Study Area; Near East and South Asia; New England School of Art
NESBIC Netherlands Student's Bureau for International Cooperation
NESC National Electric Safety Code; National English Syllabus Committee; National Environmental Satellite Center
NESCO National Energy Supply Corporation
NESDA National Electronics Service Dealers Association
NESDB National Economic

and Social Development Board
NESDEC New England School Development Council
NESO Naval Electronics Supply Office
Ness Agnes
NESS National Environmental Satellite Service
Nessa Agnes
Nessie Agnes
Nessie the Loch Ness monster's nickname
nest. node execution selection table
NEST Naval Experimental Satellite Terminal; Nuclear Emergency Search Team
Nesta Agnes
nestor neutron source thermal reactor
Nestor of American Botany William Darlington
Nestor of American Pediatrics Abraham Jacobi
Nestor of Congregationalism Leonard Bacon
Nestor of the Rockies Kit Carson
net. network; not earlier than; nuclear electronic transitor
Net Antoinette; Nettie; Netty
NET National Educational Television; Nippon Educational Television; Noise Enforcement Team (police anti-noise team)
NETA Northwest Electronic Technical Association
netanal network analysis
NETE Navel Engineering Test Establishment (Canadian)
NETF Nuclear Engineering Test Facility
Neth Netherlands
Neth Ant Netherlands Antilles
Netherlands Kingdom of the Netherlands (North Sea nation created and enlarged by reclamation of salt marshes and lowland waters; industrious Dutch export books, cheeses, diamonds, electronic products, fruits, and flowers; Dutch is spoken as well as English and other languages) *Koninkrijk der Nederlanden*
Netherlands Antilles Aruba, Bonaire, Curaçao, Saba, Sint Eustatius, and half of Sint Maarten
Netherlands East Indies former name of Indonesia
Netherlands Guiana Dutch Guiana or Surinam
Netherlands Indies old name of

Indonesia
Netherlands New Guinea former name of West Irian now part of Indonesia
Netherlands Ports (*see* Dutch Ports)
Netherlands Principal Port Rotterdam
Netherlands Timor formerly the western half of Timor now an island of Indonesia
netic nonretentive nonshocksensitive (alloy made for high-level attenuation)
n. et m. *nocte et mane* (Latin—night and early morning)
netma nobody ever tells me anything
NETRANZ National Endurance and Trail Riding Association of New Zealand
NETRB New England Territory Railroad Bureau
NETRC National Educational Television and Radio Center
nets. network techniques
NETSO Northern European Transshipment Organization (NATO)
Nettie Henrietta
Netty Henrietta
Net(ty) Antonia
Netza *Netzahualcoyotl* (Aztec—Hungry Coyote)
neu neuter; neutral; neutrality
NEU Northeastern University
neubarb *neubearbeitet* (German—revised)
Neuk Neuköln
neur neuralgia; neurasthenia; neuritis; neurology
neuro neurotic
neuro *neuron* (Greek—nerve, sinew, tendon)—neurasthenia, neuroanatomy, neurosis
neurol neurological; neurologist; neurology
neuropath neuropathology
neurophys neurophysiological
neuropsychiat neuropsychiatry
neurosurg neurosurgeon; neurosurgery; neurosurgical
neurs neurosis
NEUS Northeastern United States
neut neuter; neutral; neutralize; neutralizer; neutron bomb (mini-hydrogen bomb releasing neutrons and producing the minimum radioactive blast, fallout, and heat)
neutron neutral ion
Neuyork (German—New York)
Nev Nevada; Nevadan; Neville
Nevil Shute Nevil Shute Norway

nevrls nevertheless

new newton

new. net economic welfare; newton

New New College, Oxford

New Age administration of Jimmy Carter, thirty-ninth President of the United States

New Albion Sir Francis Drake's name for what is now British Columbia, plus the states of Washington, Oregon, and California

New Alcatraz nickname of the maximum-security U.S. Penitentiary at Marion, Ill

New Am Lib New American Library

New Amsterdam former name of New York City called Nieuw Amsterdam by the original Dutch settlers

Newark Newark-upon-Trent near Nottingham, England and forerunner of all the many Newarks, including Newark, New Jersey

New Beginning (administration of Ronald Reagan—fortieth President of the United States)

Newberry Newberry Library (Chicago)

Newc Newcastle-upon-Tyne

New Cal New Caldonia

New Castile (see *Castilla la Nueva*)

Newcastle the original British place plus all other Newcastles in English-speaking places such as Newcastle Emlyn, Newcastleton, Newcastle-under-Lyme, Newcastle-upon-Tyne, Newcastle Waters, and Newcastle West

New Col New Columbia (proposed name for the 51st state, formerly Washington, DC)

New Colossus Statue of Liberty's sobriquet derived from the poem by Emma Lazarus—*The New Colossus*—proclaiming: "Give me your tired, your poor, your huddled masses yearning to breathe free, the wretched refuse of your teeming shore. Send these, the homeless, tempest-tossed to me, I lift my lamp beside the golden door!"

New Deal (administration of Franklin Delano Roosevelt—thirty-second President of the United States)

New Edinburgh on the Antipodes Dunedin, New Zealand

new england new england boiled dinner (boiled corned beef or ham with vegetables); new england clam chowder (minced clams, potatoes, milk, and some sculpin stock); new england pine (white pine)

New England Maine, New Hampshire, Vermont, Massachusetts, Rhode Island, and Connecticut

New England Colonies Massachusetts, New Hampshire, Rhode Island, Connecticut

Newf Newfoundland

New Federalism (administration of Gerald Ford—thirty-eighth President of the United States); President Reagan's state-oriented economic and social program

Newfie(s) Newfoundlander(s)

New Foundation (administration of Jimmy Carter—thirty-ninth President of the United States)

New France old name for French Canada

New Freedom (administration of Woodrow Wilson—twenty-eighth President of the United States)

New Frontier (administration of John F Kennedy—thirty-fifth President of the United States)

New Granada Colombia's original Spanish name—*Nueva Granada*

New H New Hall College, Oxford

New Hampshire Port Portsmouth

New Haven New York, New Haven, and Hartford Railroad

New Heb New Hebrides (Anglo-French island condominium in the South Pacific)

New Heb Con New Hebrides Condominium

New Hebrides New Hebrides Islands (condominium in the western South Pacific where the British flag is flown side by side with the French tricolor) *Nouvelles Hébrides*

New Holland old name for Australia discovered by Dutch navigators

New Jersey Ports (north to south) Weehawken, Hoboken, Jersey City, Newark, Bayonne, Elizabethport, Port Socony, Grasselli, Cartaret, Chrome, Port Reading, Perth Amboy, South Amboy, Leonardo, Camden, Gloucester

New Left coalition in the late 1960s of Castroites, Ho Chi Minhites, Maoists, Trotskyites, and other non-Soviet leftists

New Lib Newberry Library

New Lon New London, Connecticut

New London U.S. Coast Guard Academy at New London, Connecticut

New Majority (administration of Richard M Nixon—thirty-seventh President of the United States)

New Mex New Mexico

New Munster old name for New Zealand's South Island

Newn Newnham College, Oxford

New Netherlands old name for what is now New York together with parts of Connecticut and New Jersey

NEWO National Energy Waste Office

New Orl New Orleans

new par new paragraph

New Prometheus Immanuel Kant's nickname for Benjamin Franklin who drew lightning from the skies

NEWRADS Nuclear Explosion Warning and Radiological Data System

NEWRIT Northeast Water Resources Information Terminal

news. naval electronic warfare simulator; news agency; news agent; new standards

NEWS New England Wildflower Society

New Sarum alternate place-name and short form for Salisbury, capital of Wiltshire, England northwest of Southhampton

new scarlet letter herpes virus (type 1 characterized by lip sores and type 2 by genital lesions)

newscast(er) news broadcast(er)

newscomp newspaper composition

New Sib New Siberian Islands

New Siberians New Siberian Islands in the Arctic (Novosibirskiye Ostrova)

New Spirit (administration of Jimmy Carter—thirty-ninth President of the United States)

New Sweden Sweden's short-lived colony in and around what is now Wilmington, Delaware but once called *Nya Sverige* (New Sweden)

Newt Newton

New Test. New Testament

New Ulster old name for New Zealand's North Island

NEWWA New England Water Works Association

New World North and South America

New World Dvořák's Symphony No. 9 in E minor (formerly No. 5)

New Year's New Year's Day (January 1)

New Yorican New York Puerto Rican

New York originally a Dutch settlement called *Nieuw Amsterdam* (New Amsterdam)

New York Bay Atlantic Ocean inlet leading through Lower Bay, the Narrows, and Upper Bay to Hudson River and Long Island Sound; natural harbor supports world's biggest and busiest port

new york cut new york cut porterhouse steak (with the bone and fillet removed)

New York Ports (north to south) Ogdensburg, Oswego, Rochester Harbor, Tonawanda, Buffalo, Albany, Kingston, Yonkers, Manhattan, Brooklyn, Gulfport, Port Richmond, Mariners Harbor, Stapleton, Tomkinsville

New York's Finest New York City's finest policemen

New York State Barge Canal Erie Canal expanded and updated

New Zealand Dominion of New Zealand (western Pacific Ocean nation whose hardworking English-speaking people export frozen mutton as well as grains and valuable minerals plus industrial products)

New Zealand Commonwealth New Zealand and its territories

New Zealand Day February 6

New Zealand Dominion New Zealand and its territories

New Zealand Ports (large, medium, and small) on North Island: Auckland, Gisborne, Napier, Wellington, Wanganui, New Plymouth, Dargaville; on South Island: Port Nelson,

Port Lyttelton (Christchurch), Timaru, Oamaru, Port Chalmers, Bluff Harbour, Greymouth, Westport; plus smaller ports such as Dunedin and Invercargill

New Zealand's Garden City Christchurch

New Zealand's Principal Port Auckland

nex not exceeding

nexis (NEXIS) news data base on-line to head

N-explosion(s) nuclear explosion(s)

N-exports nuclear exports

next. near-end crosstalk

NEXT NATO Experimental Tactics

nez (NEZ) northern economic zone

NEZs New Economic Zones (Vietnamese)

nf national fine; near face; near field; no fool; no funds; noise factor; non-ferrous; non-fiction; non-fundable; nose fuze; not fordable

n-f nonfordable

n/f neutrons per fission; no funds

n & f near and far

nf *nouveau franc* (French—new franc)—issued in 1960

n.f. *ny foljd* (Swedish—new series)

n/f *nuestro favor* (Spanish—our favor)

n.F. *neue Folge* (German—new series)

NF National Fine (threads); National Formulary; National Foundation; National Front; Newfoundland; Nieman Foundation; Norfolk, Virginia (airport); Norman French; Nutrition Foundation

N-F Norman-French

NF *Neue Folge* (German—new series); *Nuestra Familia* (Spanish—Our Family)—prison racketeers also called *La Nuestra Familia*

nfa no further action

NFA National Faculty Association; National Federation of Anglers; National Flute Association; National Food Administration; National Foundry Association; National Friends of America; Naval Fuel Annex; New Farmers of America; Night Fighters Association; Northwest Fisheries Association

NFAA National Field Archery

Association; Navy Fighter Attack Aircraft

NFAC National Food and Agriculture Council; Native Forests Action Council

NFAH National Foundation for the Arts and the Humanities

NFAIS National Federation of Abstracting and Indexing Services

NFAL National Foundation of Arts and Letters

N-fallout nuclear fallout (radioactive fallout)

nfb nacelle fuselage base; narrow flange beam; no feedback

NFB National Federation of the Blind; National Film Board (Canada)

NFB *Nippon Fudosan Bank* (Japan Real Property Bank)

NFBC National Film Board of Canada; Newfoundland Base Command

NFBF National Farm Bureau Federation

NFBPM National Federation of Builders' and Plumbers' Merchants

NFBPWC National Federation of Business and Professional Women's Clubs

NFBTE National Federation of Building Trades' Employers

NFBTO National Federation of Building Trades' Operatives

nfc not favorably considered

NFC National Fitness Council; National Football Conference; National Foundry College; National Freight Corporation; Navy Finance Center

NFCA National Federation of Community Associations

NFCC National Foundation for Consumer Credit

NFCG National Federation of Consumer Groups

nfcs night fire-control sight

NFCSA National Finance Corporation of South Africa

NFCTA National Federation of Corn Trade Associations; National Fibre Can and Tube Association

NFCU Navy Federal Credit Union

NFCUS National Federation of Canadian University Students (now NUS)

nfd no further description

Nfd Newfoundland

NFD National Federation of Doctors; National Fisheries Development; Naval Fuel Depot

NFD National Faculty Directory

NFDA National Food Distributors Association

nfdm non-fat dry milk

nfd(m) non-fat dry (milk)

NFDRS National Fire Danger Rating System

NFDS National Fire Data Center

nfe net funds employed; nosefairing exit; not fully equipped

NFE National Front of England (racists advocating immediate deportaton of all non-whites to wherever they originated)

NFEA National Federated Electrical Association

n fem feminine form of a noun

NFEMC National Federation of Export Management Companies

NFER National Foundation for Education Research

NFF National Farmers Federation; National Froebel Foundation; Naval Fuel Facility

NFFA National Farmers Federation of Australia; National Freight Forwarders Association

NFFC National Film Finance Corporation

NFFE National Federation of Federal Employees

NFFF National Federation of Fish Friers; National Firearms Freedom Fund

NFFPC National Foundation to Fight Political Corruption

NFFPT National Federation of Fruit and Potato Trades

NFFS National Foundation for Funeral Services, Non-Ferrous Founders' Society

NFFTR National Federation of Fishing Tackle Retailers

NFGCA National Federation of Grandmother Clubs of America

NFHS National Federation of Housing Societies

nfi non-bank financial intermediaries

NFI National Fisheries Institute; National Flood Insurance; Nature Friends of Israel

NFIB National Federation of Independent Business; National Foreign Intelligence Board

NFIC National Foundation for Ileitis and Colitis

NFIE National Foundation for the Improvement of Education

NFIP National Flood Insurance Program; National Foundation for Infantile Paralysis

NFIU National Federation of Independent Unions

NFK Norfolk Island

Nfl Newfoundland

Nfl Nachfolger (German—successor)

NFL National Film Library; National Football League; National Forensic League; National Foresters League

Nfld Newfoundland

NFLPN National Federation of Licensed Practical Nurses

NFLS Niagra Falls

NFLSV National Front for the Liberation of South Vietnam

NFLTA National Federation of Language Teachers Associations

nfm next full moon

NFMC National Federation of Music Clubs; National Food Marketing Commission

NFMD National Foundation for the March of Dimes

NFME National Fund for Medical Education

NFMLTA National Federation of Modern Language Teachers Association

NFMPS National Federation of Master Printers in Scotland

NFMTA National Federation of Meat Traders' Associations

NFND National Foundation for Neuromuscular Diseases

nfnshd not finished

NFO National Farmers Organization; Naval Flight Officer

NFOIO Naval Field Operational Intelligence Office(r)

NFOO Naval Forward Observing Officer

nfou number of fourier coefficients

nfp not file protect(ed)

NFP National Federation of Parents (for drug-free youth); National Federation Party; Natural Family Planning

NFPA National Fire Protection Association; National Flaxseed Processors Association; National Flexible Packaging Association; National Fluid Power Association; National Forest Products Association; Niagara Frontier Port Authority

NFPC National Federation of Priests Councils; Niagara Falls Power Company

NFPCA National Fire Prevention and Control Administration

NFPDB NATO Force Planning Data Base

NFPEX NATO Force Planning Exercise

NFPW National Federation of Press Women

nfq night frequency

nfr no further requirement

NFRC National Forest Reservation Commission

NFRN National Federation of Retail Newsagents, Booksellers, and Stationers

NFRW National Federation of Republican Women

nfs not for sale

NFS National Fire Service; National Forest Service; Nuclear Fuel Services

NFSA National Fertilizer Solutions Associations

NFSA & IS National Federation of Science Abstracting and Indexing Services

NFSG National Federation of Students of German

NFSHSA National Federation of State High School Associations

NFSID National Foundation for Sudden Infant Death

NFSM National Fraternity of Student Musicians

NFSNC National Federation of Settlements and Neighborhood Centers

NFSO Navy Fuel Supply Office

nft no fixed time; no forwarding time; nutrient film technique

NFT National Film Theatre

NFTA National Film Theatre of Australia; Niagara Frontier Transportation Authority

NFTB Nuclear Flight Test Base

NFTC National Foreign Trade Council

nfu not for us

NFU National Farmers Union; National Film Unit

n-fuel nuclear fuel

N-fuel nuclear fuel

nfv no further visits

nfw new field wildcat (oil well)

NFWA National Farm Workers Association; National Furniture Warehousemen's Association

NFWI National Federation of Women's Institutes

NFYFC National Federation of Young Farmers' Clubs

nfyg notifying

nfz no fire zone

ng narrow gauge; nasogastric; new genus; nitroglycerine; no go; no good; not given; not good; not ground; nut grounds

ng (NG) natural gas

n-g nitro-glycerine

n/g nuestro giro (Spanish—our draft)

Ng Norwegian

NG National Gallery; National Guard; National Gypsum; New Guinea

nga (NGA) non-gonococcal urethritis

Nga Nagoya

NGA National Gallery of Art; National Glider Association; National Governors Association; National Grains Authority; National Graphical Association; National Guard Association; Needlework Guild of America; Never Go Away (travel club dedicated to seeing America first)

NGAA National Gift and Art Association; Natural Gasoline Association of America

NGAC National Guard Air Corps

Ngaio March Edith Ngaio Marsh

Ngaragba Ngaragba Prison in Bangui (capital city of the Central African Republic)

N-gauge narrow gauge (railroad track less than standard gauge, gauge: 4 feet 8-1/2 inches)

NGAUS National Guard Association of the United States

ngb negative guard board

NGB National Garden Bureau; National Guard Bureau

NGC National Gallery of Canada; National Gambling Commission; National Gypsum Company; Natural Gas Corporation

NGC New Galactic Catalog; New General Catalog (astronomical)

ngcil nice guys come in last

NGCM Navy Good Conduct Medal

NGCMS National Guild of Community Music Schools

NGCSA National Guild of Community Schools of the Arts

NGDA National Glass Dealers Association

NGDC National Geophysical Data Center

NGE New York State Electric &

Gas (stock exchange symbol)

n gen new genus

ngf naval gunfire

ngf (NGF) nerve growth factor

NGF National Genetics Foundation; National Golf Foundation; Naval Gun Factory; Nordic Gunners Federation

NGFLO Naval Gunfire Liaison Officer

NGFLT Naval Gunfire Liaison Team

NGI National Garden Institute; Norwegian Geotechnical Institute

NGI Navigazione Generale Italiana (Italian General Navigation Line)

NGJA National Gymnastics Judges Association

NGJC North Greenville Junior College

N Gk New Greek

NGK Nihon Gakujutsu Kaigi (Japan Research Council)

ngl natural gas liquids

NGL North German Lloyd Line

nglzd not glazed

N Gmc North Germanic

NGMEX Northern Gulf of Mexico

NGMP New Guinea Marine Products

ngo national gas outlet (thread); nongovernmental organization

Ngo Nagoya

NGOs Nongovernmental Organizations (UN)

NGPA Natural Gas Processors Association

NGPT National Guild of Piano Teachers

ngr narrow gauze roll; non-grain rating

NGr New Greek

NGR Ndumu Game Reserve (Zululand); Newbold General Refractories

NGRI National Geophysical Institute

NGRS Narrow Gauge Railway Society

ngs national gas straight (threading); net gas sand (oil well)

NGS National Geodetic Survey; National Geographic Society; Nuclear Generating Station

NGSA National Gallery of South Africa; Natural Gas Supply Association

NGSDC National Geophysical and Solar-Terrestrial Data Center (NOAA)

NGSIC National Geodetic Sur-

vey Information Center (NOAA)

NGSR Nizam's Guaranteed State Railway

ngt national gas taper (threading)

ngt negociant (French—merchant)—wholesaler

NGT National Guild of Telephonists; North German Traders

NGTE National Gas Turbine Establishment

NGTF National Gay Task Force

ngu nongonococcal urethritis

NGUS National Guard of the United States

ngv nongonococcal vulvovaginitis

NGV Nederlands Genootschap van Vertalers (Dutch—Netherlands Translators Association)

nh no hurry (hospitalese); non-hygroscopic

Nh Noordholland (Dutch—North Holland)

NH Naval Home; Naval Hospital; New Hampshire; New Hampshirite; New Haven, Connecticut; New Hebrides; New York, New Haven & Hartford (railroad); Nippon Airways (2-letter code); North Holland(er); Nursing Home

N & H Nedlloyd & Hoegh (steamship lines)

NH Norges Hjemmenfrontmuseum (Norwegian Home-Front Museum)—Oslo exhibit recalling anti-German resistance from 1940 to 1945; *Nueva Hampshire* (Spanish—New Hampshire)

N-H Noord-Holland (Dutch—North-Holland)

NH₃ ammonia

NH₄ ammonium radical

NH₄CL ammonium chloride; sal ammoniac

NH₄OH ammonium hydroxide (ammonia)

nha never has anything; next higher assembly; next higher authority

NHA National Hay Association; National Health Association; National Hide Association; National Hockey Association; National Housing Act; National Housing Administration; National Housing Agency; National Housing Association; Neighborhood House Association; New Homemakers of America; Nigerian Housing Administration

NHAGB National Horse Association of Great Britain

NHAIAC National Highway Accident and Injury Analysis Center

NHAL National Hellenic American Line

NHAS National Hearing Aid Society

NHB National Harbours Board (Canada); Northland Harbour Board (New Zealand)

NHBRC National House Builders' Registration Council

NHBU New Hampshire Board of Underwriters

NHC National Health Council; National Hurricane Center; New Hall College

NHCA National Hairdressers and Cosmetologists Association

NHCBS New Hampshire Council for Better Schools

NHCIC National Hazardous Chemicals Information Center

N.H.D. Doctor of Natural History

NHDC Naval Historical Display Center

nh di notch die

nhe nitrogen heat exchange

NHEA National Higher Education Association; New Hampshire Education Association

N-head(s) nuclear warhead(s)

N Heb New Hebrew

NHEF National Health Education Foundation

NHESA National Higher Education Staff Association

NHF National Health Federation; National Health Foundation; National Heart Foundation; National Heart Fund; National Hemophilia Foundation; National Horse Festival; National Humanities Faculty; Naval Historical Foundation

NHFA National Heart Foundation of Australia

NHF Bull *National Health Federation Bulletin*

NHFNZ National Heart Foundation of New Zealand

NHFPL New Haven Free Public Library

NHG New High German

NHGA National Hang Gliding Association

NHHS New Hampshire Historical Society

NHI National Health Institute;

National Health Insurance; National Heart Institutes

NHIC National Health Insurance Commission; National Home Improvement Council

NHK *Nippon Hoso Kyokai* (Japanese—Japan Broadcasting Corporation)

NHKTV *Nippon Koso Kyokai* (Japanese Television Broadcasting Corporation)

NHL National Hockey League

NHLA National Hardwood Lumber Association; National Home Library Association

NHLBAC National Heart, Lung, and Blood Advisory Council (NIH)

NHLBI National Heart, Lung, and Blood Institute (NIH)

NHLI National Heart and Lung Institute

NHMA National Housewares Manufacturers Association

NHMRCA National Health and Medical Research Council of Australia

NHMS New Hampshire Medical Society

nhn neither help nor hinder

NHO National Hospice Organization; Navy Hydrographic Office

NHOS National Hellenic Oceanographic Society

nhp nominal horsepower

NHP Natural History Park (Calgary, Alberta); Natural History Press; New Haven Police; New Hebrides Protectorate; Nursing Home Placement

NHPA National Horseshoe Pitchers Association

NHPC National Historical Publications Commission

NHPGA New Hampshire Personnel and Guidance Association

NHPL New Haven Public Library

NHPLO NATO Hawk Production and Logistics Organization

NHPMA Northern Hardwood and Pine Manufacturers Association

NHPRC National Historical Publications and Records Commission

NHQ National Headquarters

NHR National Housewives Register; National Hunt Rules; National Hurricane Research

nhra next higher repairable assembly

NHRA National Hot Rod Association

NHRE National Hail Research Experiment

NHRL National Hurricane Research Laboratory

NHRP National Hurricane Research Project

NHRR New Haven Railroad

NHRU National Home Reading Union

nhs net hydrocarbon sand (oil well); normal human sera

NHS National Health Service; National Historical Society; National Honor Society; Newport Historical Society

NHSA National Head-Start Association; Negro Historical Society of America

NHSAA New Hampshire School Administrators Association

NHSB National Highway Safety Bureau

NHSBA New Hampshire School Boards Association

NHSC National Health Statistics Center; National Highway Safety Council; National Home Study Council

NHSF National Hispanic Scholarly Fund

NHSO New Haven Symphony Orchestra

NHSR National Hospital Service Reserve

NHTI New Hampshire Technical Institute

NHTPC National Housing and Town Planning Council

NHTSA National Highway Traffic Safety Administration

NH Turn New Hampshire Turnpike

NHUC National Highway Users Conference

Nhv Newhaven

NHV New Haven Clock and Watch (stock exchange symbol)

NHYC New Haven Yacht Club

ni new impression; night

ni (NI) inversion of the note series (12-tone); national income; net income (total amount of corporation profits, net interest, proprietors' income, rental income, and wages received per year)

Ni Nica; Nicaragua; Nicaraguan; Nicaragüense; Nicas; nickel

NI National Insurance; Nautical Institute; Naval Intelligence; Netherlands Indies; Neutralization Index; Nicaraguan Airways (2-letter code)—LANICA; North Island, New Zealand; North Island, San Diego, California; Northern Ireland; Northern Island (New Zealand); Numerical Index; other North Islands

NI ampere turns (symbol)

nia nearest international airport

nia (NIA) noise-impact area

NIA National Institute on Aging; National Intelligence Authority; National Irrigation Administration; Neighborhood Improvement Area; Neighborhood Improvement Association

NIAA National Industrial Advertising Association; National Institute of Animal Agriculture

NIAAA National Institute on Alcohol Abuse and Alcoholism

NIAB National Institute of Agricultural Botany

NIABC Northern Ireland Association of Boys' Clubs

NIAC Nissho-Iwai American Corporation; Nuclear Insurance Association of Canada; Nutritional Information and Analysis Center

NIAE National Institute of Agricultural Engineering (UK); National Institute for Architectural Education

Niagara short form for Fort Niagara, Niagara Falls, Niagara-on-the-Lake, Niagara River, Niagara University

Niagara Falls huge waterfalls flowing from Lake Erie into Lake Ontario between Ontario in Canada and New York in United States; two cities flank falls—one in each country—each named Niagara Falls—each fronting on Niagara River connecting lakes Erie and Ontario

Niagara Frontier Buffalo-Niagara Falls area

Niagara Fruit Belt Canadian fruit-growing region on the Niagara Peninsula between lakes Erie and Ontario

NIAID National Institute of Allergies and Infectious Diseases

NIAL National Institute of Arts and Letters

NIAMD National Institute of Arthritis and Metabolic Diseases

NIAMDD National Institute of Arthritis, Metabolism, and Digestive Diseases (formerly NIAMD)

NIASA National Insurance Actuarial and Statistical Association

NIASE National Institute for Automotive Service Excellence

nib noninterference basis

NIB National Information Bureau; Nebraska Inspection Bureau

NIBA National Insurance Buyers Association

nibo nibonitschjo (ni boga ni tschjorta) (Russian—neither in god nor the devil)—materialist sceptics unaffected by Marxism—Leninism

NIBS National Institute of Building Sciences

nic negative impedance converter; not in contact

Nic Nicaragua; Nicolayev; Nicosia

N i C Nurse in Charge

NIC Natick Industrial Centre; National Indications Center; National Industrial Council; National Information Center; National Institute of Corrections; National Institute of Creativity; National Institute of Credit; National Insurance Certificate; National Insurance Contributions; National Interfraternity Conference; National Inventors Council; National Investors Council; Navigation Information Center; Neighborhood Info(rmation) Center(s); Niagara International Centre; Nicosia, Cyprus (airport); Nineteen-hundred Indexing and Cataloging; Nippon International Containers

Nica Nicaragua(n)

nicad nickel cadmium

NiCad battery nickel-cadmium (rechargeable) battery

Nicaea (Latin—Nice)

NICAP National Investigations Committee on Aerial Phenomena

Nicaragua Republic of Nicaragua (Spanish-speaking two-coast Central American country whose Nicaraguans export bananas, other tropical crops, minerals, and textiles) *República de Nicaragua*

Nicaragua Day Nicaraguan Independence Day (September 15)

Nicaraguan Ports (on the Caribbean) Cabo Gracias a Dios, Puerto Cabezas, Puerto Isabel, Bluefields, San Juan del Norte (Greytown); (on the Pacific) San Juan del Sur, Puerto Masachapa, Puerto Somoza, Corinto

Nicas Nicaraguans

NICB National Industrial Conference Board

Ni-Cd nickel-cadmium (rechargeable storage battery)

nice. normal input/output control executive

Nice Eunice

NICE National Institute of Ceramic Engineers

NICEIC National Inspection Council for Electrical Installation Contracting

NICEM National Information Center for Educational Media

NICF Nebraska Independent College Foundation; Northern Ireland Cycling Federation

Nich Nicholas

NICHA Northern Ireland Chest and Heart Association

NICHHD National Institute of Child Health and Human Development

Nicholas Blake C(ecil) Day Lewis' pseudonym

nichrome nickel-chromium alloy

NICIA Northern Ireland Coal Importers' Association

NICJ National Institute of Consumer Justice

nick. name information correlation key

Nick Nicholas; Nichols; Nicodemus; Nikos

Nick Carter J Russell Coryell

nickel note $5 bill

Nickel-plated Paradise nickname of nickel-rich New Caledonia (Nouvelle Calédonie)

Nickel Plate Road New York, Chicago and St Louis Railroad Company

Nicky Nicholas; Nicole; Nikos

Nicky and Alicky Czar Nicholas II and Czarina Alexandra Feodorovna of Russia—the last of the Romanov Czars

NICM Nuffield Institute of Comparative Medicine

Nico Nicobar Islands

NICO National Insurance Consumer Organization; Navy Inventory Control Office(r)

Nicobars Nicobar Islands in the Indian Ocean

Nicolas Copernicus Nikolay Kopernik

Nicolas-Favre disease lymphogranuloma venerea involving inguinal lymph glands and characterized by an exuding lesion

Nicolas Lenau Nikolaus Niembsch von Strehlenau

Nicolass Sint Nicolaas, Aruba

Nicolino Nicolò Grimaldi

NICOP Navy Industry Cooperation Plan

Nicos Nicosia, Cyprus

NICP National Inventory Control Point

NICRA Northern Ireland Civil Rights Association

NICRAD Navy-Industry Cooperative Research and Development

nic's newly industrializing countries

NICs National Institute of Corrections

NICS NATO Integrated Communications System

NICSEM/NIMIS National Information Center for Special Education Material/National Instructional Material Information System

NICSO NATO Integrated Communications System Organization

NICSS Northern Ireland Council of Social Science

NICSSE National Information Center for Social Science Education

NICU Nippon International Container Unit

NICUFO National Investigations Committee on Unidentified Flying Objects

nid network in dial

NID National Institute of Drycleaning; Naval Intelligence Department

NID New International Dictionary (Webster's Third New International Dictionary of the English Language Unabridged)

nida numerically integrated differential analyzer

NIDA National Institute of Dramatic Art; National Institute of Drug Abuse; National Investment and Development Authority; Northern Ireland Development Agency

Nidaros Trondheim's former name

NIDC National Institute of Dry Cleaning; National Invest-ment Development Corporation

NIDER Nederlands Instituut voor Documentatie en Registratuur (Dutch—Netherlands Institute of Documentation and Filing)

NIDFA National Independent Drama Festivals Association

NIDH National Institute of Dental Health

NIDM National Institute for Disaster Mobilization

NIDR National Institute of Dental Research

nie not included elsewhere

NIE National Institute of Education; National Intelligence Estimate

NIEA National Indian Education Association

NIECC National Industrial Energy Conservation Council

Niederlande (German—Netherlands)

Niedersachsen (German—Lower Saxony)

niedr niedrig (German—low)

NIEHS National Institute of Environmental Health Sciences

niels bohrium Russian name for element 105 named for Danish physicist Niels Bohr

Nielsen's 6 Carl Nielsen's six symphonies including *Four Temperaments* (No. 2), *Sinfonia Espansiva* (No. 3), *Inextinguishable* (No. 4), *Sinfonia Semplice* (No. 6)

NIEM National Industrial Energy Management

NIEO New International Economic Order; Non-Incorporated Engineering Order

NIER National Industrial Equipment Reserve

NIESR National Institute for Economic and Social Research

NIEU Negro Industrial Economic Union

Nieuw Haarlem (Dutch—New Haarlem)—Harlem's original name

nif nickel-iron film

NIF Navy Industrial Fund

NIFA National Islamic Front of Afghanistan

NIFC National Income Forecasting Committee

nife nickel + iron (Ni + Fe)

NIFES National Industrial Fuel Efficiency Service

NIFI National Inland Fisheries Institute

nifti near-isotropic flux-turbulence instrument

nig. niger (Latin—black)

Nig Nigeria

Nig Niger (Spanish—Niger)

niga nuclear-induced ground radioactivity

NIGC National Iranian Gas Company

Niger Republic of Niger (landlocked North African nation whose French-speaking Nigerois also converse in tribal tongues, exports include cotton, peanuts, and uranium ore)

Nigeria Federal Republic of Nigeria (West African country whose English-speaking Nigerians produce tropical food crops such as cocoa, peanuts, and soybeans as well as minerals, gas and oil are also produced)

Nigerian Ports Lagos, Bonny, Port Harcourt, Douala

Niger River 2600-mile African river draining West Africa and entering Gulf of Guinea on Nigerian coast

Nigger non-pejorative nickname for Dvořáak's *American Quartet* filled with Negro spiritual themes

Nightclub Aristocrat Artist Henri Marie Raymond de Toulouse-Lautrec

nightie(s) nightdress(es); nightgown(s)

Nightingale C-9 McDonnell-Douglas jetliner used for medical evacuation and named in honor of Crimean War nurse —philanthropist Florence Nightingale

Nightmare of Europe Napoleon in the 1800s followed by Hitler in the 1900s

Night Mayor James J (Jimmy) Walker

nightsoap(s) nighttime (tv) soap opera(s)

NIGMS National Institute of General Medical Sciences

NIGP National Institute of Governmental Purchasing

Nigritia (Latin—Sudan)

NIGRO Northern Ireland General Register Office

nig(s) nigger(s); renege(s); revoke(s)

nigyysob now I've got you, you SOB

nih not invented here

NIH National Institutes of Health

NIH 204 antimalarial drug

NIHB National Indian Health Board

NIHBC Northern Ireland House Building Council

NIHE Northern Ireland Housing Executive

nihil nihil obstat quominus imprimatur (Latin—nothing hinders it from being printed)—*nihil obstat* usually suffices for censors of the Roman Catholic Church

nihil obs. nihil obstat (Latin—nothing stands in the way)—official Catholic publications must obtain this before their publication

Nihon (Japanese—Japan)

NIHR National Institute of Handicapped Research

NIHT Northern Ireland Housing Trust

NII Netherlands Industrial Institute

NIIC National Injury Information Clearinghouse

NIIG NATO Item Identification Guide

NIIN National Item Identification Number

NIIP National Institute of Industrial Psychology

NIIS Niagara Institute for International Studies

NIJ National Institute of Justice

NIJC North Idaho Junior College

NIJFCM National Institute of Jig and Fixture Component-Manufacturers

Nijl (Dutch—Nile)

nik narcotic identification kit

Nik Nikolayev

Nikaria English place-name for Ikaría island in the Aegean

Nike-Ajax Douglas surface-to-air missile (MIM-3A)

Nike-Hercules Douglas surface-to-air missile armed with a high-explosive or nuclear warhead (MIM-14A)

Nike-Zeus one of a series of American-made anti-missile missiles

Niki Nicholas

Nik-Nik affectionate nickname for the Royal Shakespeare Company's production of *The Life and Adventures of Nicholas Nickleby* by Charles Dickens

Niko (Russian nickname—Nikolai)—Nicholas; Nick; Nicky

Nikolaus Lenau (pseudonym—Nikolaus Franz Niembsch von Strehlenau)

nil not in labor

Nil (French or German—Nile)

NIL National Instrument Laboratories; National Investment Library

NILA National Industrial Leather Association

NI Lab Northern Ireland Labour (party)

Nile world's longest river—4145 miles—flows from Lake Victoria in central Africa to Mediterranean coast of Egypt at Alexandria just north of Cairo

NILECJ National Institute of Law Enforcement and Criminal Justice

Nile River Cities Cairo, Egypt and Khartoum, Sudan

NILI Netzach Israel Lo Ishakare (Hebrew—The eternity of Israel will not die)—acronymic password of the Nili spies who aided Britain by facilitating Turkish defeat in an effort to establish a homeland for Jews in Palestine

'nilla vanilla

N Ill U Pr Northern Illinois University Press

Nilo (Italian, Portuguese, Spanish—Nile)

NILOJ National Institute for Law/Order/Justice

NILP Northern Ireland Labour Party

nil sig nothing significant

NILT National Institute for Lay Training

nim newspaper(s) in microfilm; newspaper(s) in microform

NIM Neurological Impress Method; North Irish Militia

NIMA National Insulation Manufacturers Association

NIMAC National Interscholastic Music Activities Commission

nimbies nembutal tablets

nimby not in my backyard

NIMFR National Institutes of Marriage and Family Relations

NIMH National Institute of Mental Health

nimm nuclear-induced missile malfunction

n imp new impression

NIMP National Intern Matching Program

nimphe nuclear isotope mono-propellant hydrazine engine

NIMR National Institute for

Medical Research; National Institute for the Mentally Retarded

Nimrod Hawker-Siddeley four-engine jet transport

NIMU North Island Mutual Insurance (New Zealand)

NIN Narcotics Intelligence Network; National Information Network; Neighbors In Need

Nina Ann; Anna; Anne; Annette

NINA No Irish Need Apply

NINB National Institute of Neurology and Blindness

NINCD National Institute of Neurological and Communicative Disorders

NINCDS National Institute of Neurological and Communicative Disorders and Stroke

NINDB National Institute of Neurological Diseases and Blindness

NINDS National Institute of Neurological Diseases and Stroke

Nine Keepers of the *Constitution* nine justices of the U.S. Supreme Court

nine old men nine justices of the United States Supreme Court

Nineteenth State Indiana

Ningxia Hui (Pinyin Chinese—Ningsia Hui)—autonomous region of mainland China

Ninon de Lenclos court name of courtesan Anne Lenclos

Ninth State New Hampshire (*see* First State)

NIO National Institute of Oceanography; National Intelligence Office(r); National Intelligence Organization; National Iranian Oil; Naval Institute of Oceanology; Northern Ireland Office

NIOC National Iranian Oil Company

niod network in-out dial

NIOSH National Institute of Occupational Safety and Health

nip. nipper; nipple; not in possession

Nip Nippon (Japan); Nipponese (Japanese)

NIP National Industrial Policy (rejected by leading economists); Neighborhood Improvement Program; Northern Ireland Parliament

NIP Norges Kommunistiske Parti (Norwegian Communist Party)

NIPA National Institute of Public Affairs

Nipão (Portuguese—Nippon) —Japan

NIPCC National Industrial Pollution Control Council

NIPDOK Nippon Documentesyon Kyokai (Japanese Documentation Society)

NIPE National Intelligence Programs Evaluation

NIPG Nederlands Instituut voor Praeventieve Gneeskunde (Dutch—Netherlands Institute for Preventive Medicine)

NIPH National Institute of Public Health

niphl noise-induced permanent hearing loss

nip nip(s) nipple nipper(s)

nipo negative input—positive output

NIPO Nederlands Instituut voor Publick Opinie (Dutch—Netherlands Institute for Public Opinion)

Nipón (Spanish—Nippon)—Japan

Nippon Japan

Nippon (Japanese—Japan)

NIPR National Institute for Personnel Research

ni pri nisis prius (Latin—unless before)

nips. nippers

Nip(s) Nippon(ese)

NIPS National Information Processing System; National Institute of Police Science (Japanese)

NIPSSA Naval Intelligence Processing Systems Support Activity

nipts noise-induced permanent threshold shifts

N Ir Northern Ireland

NIR Northern Ireland Railways

NIRA National Industrial Recovery Administration; Newspaper Industries Research Association

NIRC National Industrial Relations Court

NIRD National Institute of Research in Dairying

N Ire Northern Ireland

NIRI National Investor Relations Institute

NIRMP National Intern and Resident Matching Program

NIRNS National Institute for Research in Nuclear Science

NIROP Naval Industrial Reserve Ordnance Plant (USN)

NIRR National Institute for Road Research

NIRRA Northern Ireland Radio Retailers' Association

NIRs Norfolk International (container) Terminals

NIRS National Institute of Radiological Science

ni & rt numerical index and requirement table(s)

NIRT National Iranian Radio and Television

nis not in stock

n i s not in stock

Ni s nickel steel

NIS National Information System; National Institute of Science; National Insurance Scheme; National Intelligence Service; National Intelligence Survey; National Investment Strategy; Naval Intelligence Service; Naval Investigative Service; News and Information Service (NBC)

NISA National Impacted Schools Association; National Intelligence Security Authority (Philippines)

NISBS National Institute of Social and Behavioral Science

NISC National Independent Study Center; National Industrial Safety Committee; Naval Intelligence Support Center

NISGAZ National Intelligence Survey Gazetteer

NISIR National Institute of Scientific Industrial Research

NISM National Iron and Steel Mills

NISO National Industrial Safety Organization; Naval Investigative Service Office(r)

NISP National Information System for Psychology

NISRA Naval Investigative Service Resident Agent

NISS National Institute of Social Sciences

nissen nissen hut (designed by British military engineer P.N. Nissen for arctic use)

NIST National Institute of Science and Technology

NISUCO Nigerian Sugar Company

nit. negative income tax; none in town

nit. (NIT) nautical industrial technology; negative income tax

nit unit of luminance (symbol)

NIT National Instructional Television; National Intelligence Test; National Invitation Tournament; Negative Income Tax; Northrop Insti-

tute of Technology; Northrup International Terminals

Nita Juanita

NITA National Industrial Television Association

NITC National Information Transfer Center; National Iranian Tanker Company

nite night

NiteDevRon Night Development Squadron

NITEP Native Indian Teacher Education Programme (Canadian)

Niteroi formerly Nictheroy

NITHC Northern Ireland Transport Holding Company

NITL National Industrial Traffic League

ni tp nibbling template

NITR National Institute for Telecommunications Research

nitrate of soda sodium nitrate ($NaNO_3$)

nitre potassium nitrate (KNO_3)

nitric acid HNO_3

nitro nitrocellulose; nitroglycerine

nitros nitrostarch

nitts noise-induced temporary threshold shift

NITV National Iranian Television

NIU Northern Illinois University; Northern Interparliamentary Union

Niugini (Malay—New Guinea)

Niv Nivose (French—Snowy Month)—beginning December 21st—fourth month of the French Revolutionary Calendar

NIV New International Version (Zondervan Bible)

NIVE Nederland Instituut voor Efficiency (Netherlands Institute for Efficiency)

NIW National Industrial Workers Union

NIWAAA Northern Ireland Women's Amateur Athletic Association

NIWR National Institute for Water Research

NIWW National Institute for Working Women (prostitutes)

nix (from the German *nichts*) to ban; to cancel; to forbid; no one; nothing; to prohibit; to reject; to veto

NIYC National Indian Youth Council

Niza (Spanish—Nice)

Nizh Nizhen (Bulgarian—lower); *Nizhni* (Russian—lower)

Nizhni Novgorod old name for Gorki

Nizim Nizmennost (Russian—lowland)

Nizza (Italian—Nice)

n J *nächstes Jahr* (German—next year)

NJ New Jersey; New Jerseyite

NJA National Jail Association; National Jogging Association

NJAC National Joint Advisory Council

NJACU New Jersey Association of Colleges and Universities

NJAIS New Jersey Association of Independent Schools

NJASBO New Jersey Association of School Business Officials

NJASSPS New Jersey Association of Secondary School Principals and Supervisors

njb nice Jewish boy

NJC Natchez Junior College; National Joint Council; National Junior College; Navarro Junior College; Newton Junior College; Norfolk Junior College

NJCAA National Junior College Athletic Association

NJCC Northeastern Junior College of Colorado

NJCCC New Jersey Casino Control Commission

NJCF New Jersey Conservation Foundation

NJDA National Juvenile Detention Association

NJDL New Jewish Defense League

NJEA New Jersey Education Association

NJF Nordiske Jordburgsforskeres Forening (Nordic Agricultural Research Workers' Association)

NJFR National Joint Fiction Reserve

njg nice Jewish girl

NJH National Jewish Hospital

NJHA National Junior Horticultural Association

NJ Hist Soc New Jersey Historical Society

NJHS National Junior Honor Society; New Jersey Historical Society

NJIT New Jersey Institute of Technology

njk not just kidding

NJLA New Jersey Library Association

NJLC National Juvenile Law Center

NJLJ New Jersey Law Journal

NJMA National Jail Managers Association

NJMP New Jersey Marine Police

NJPBA New Jersey Public Broadcasting Authority

NJPC National Joint Practices Commission

NJPGA New Jersey Personnel and Guidance Association

NJROTC Naval Junior Reserve Officers Training Corps

NJRW New Jersey Reformatory for Women (Clinton)

NJSA New Jersey Student Association

NJSBA New Jersey School Boards Association

NJSD National Joint Service Delegate; National Joint Service Delegation

NJSO New Jersey Symphony Orchestra

NJSP New Jersey State Police

NJ Turn New Jersey Turnpike

NJWB National Jewish Welfare Board

NJZ New Jersey Zinc

nk neck; not known; not ours (publishing)

NK Nippon Gakushiin (the Japanese Academy); Nomenklatur Kommission (Anatomical Nomenclature Commission); Nordiska Kompaniet (the Norse Company, Stockholm's leading department store); North Korea(n)

NK Nihon Kyosanto (Japanese Communist Party); *Nippon Kokan Steel* (Japanese Steel Exchange)

NKA National Kindergarten Association

NKCA National Kitchen Cabinet Association

NKDR National Key Deer Refuge (Florida)

NKF National Kidney Foundation

NKG Nordiska Kommissionen for Geodesi (Nordic Commission for Geodesy)

NKGB People's Commissariat for State Security *(q.v. VOT)*

NKK Nippon Kokan Steel (Japan)

NKK Nippon Kaiji Kyokai (Japanese Marine Classification Society)

NKL Norges Kooperative Landsforening (Norwegian Consumer Cooperative)

nklc nickel copper

NKM New Park Mining (stock exchange symbol)

N.K. Naomi code for chemical and biological warfare

NKOA National Knitted Outerwear Association

NKP Nickel Plate Railroad (stock exchange symbol for New York, Chicago & St Louis Railroad)—locomotives on this line gleamed with nickel-plated ornaments

NKPA National Kraut Packers Association

NKr Norwegian krone(r)

nks necks (woolen)

NKS Norge Kjemisk Selskap (Norwegian Chemical Society)

NKSO Narodniy Kommissariat Sotsialnogo Obespecheniya (Russian—People's Commissariat of Social Security)

NKT Nihon Kai Telecasting

Nkv Nakskov

NKVD Narodnyi Kommissariat Vnutrennikh Del (Russian—People's Commissariat for Internal Affairs, Soviet secret police, *q.v.* VOT)

NKZ Narodniy Kommissariat Zdravokhranenia (Russian—People's Commissariat of Health)—contains a special section to combat prostitution

nl new line; no liability; non-lubricant; not listed

nl (NL) new line character (data processing); not licensed (to sell liquor)

nl nemlig (Dano-Norwegian—namely); *nicht löslich* (German—not soluble); *non longue* (French—not so far)

n.l. non licet (Latin—not permitted)

n/l nuestra letra (Spanish—our letter)

NL National League (of Professional Baseball Clubs); National Liberal; National Library; naval lighter (naval symbol); Navy (US department) Library; Navy League; Navy List(ing); Netherlands (auto plaque); New Latin; New London, Connecticut; Night Letter; North Latitude; Nuevo León

NL Norddeutscher Lloyd (North German Lloyd Line)

N.L. non liquet (Latin—unclear)

nla net lettable area

NLA National Leukemia Association; National Librarians Association; National Libraries Authority; National Library of Australia (Canberra); National Lumbermen's Association; Nevada Library Association

NL-A Nationaal Luchtvaartlaboratorium-Amsterdam

NLAA National Legal Aid Association

NLA & DA National Legal Aid and Defender Association

NLAE National Laboratory for the Advancement of Education

NLAPW National League of American Pen Women

N Lat north latitude

NLB National Library for the Blind; Northern Lighthouse Board

NLC National Lead Chemicals; National League for Cities; National Leathersellers College; National Legislative Conference; National Legislative Council; National Liberal Club; National Library of Canada; New Liberal Club; New Location Code; New Orleans & Lower Coast (railroad); Northern Land Council

NLCA Norwegian Lutheran Church of America

NLCIF National Light Castings Ironfounders' Federation

NLD National Legion of Decency

NLDC Native Land Development Corporation

NLEC National Lutheran Educational Council

NLETS National Law Enforcement Telecommunications System

nlf nearest landing field

NLF National League of Families (of men missing in action); National Liberal Federation; National Liberation Front; nearest landing field

nlg nose landing gear

NLG National Library of Greece (Panepistemiou Street in Athens); Netherlands Guilder(s); Numismatic Literary Guild

NLGI National Lubricating Grease Institute

NLHE National Laboratory for Higher Education

NLI National Lead Inc; National Library of India (Calcutta); National Library of Ireland (Dublin)

NLJ National Law Journal

NLL National Lending Library; Nature Lovers League; Nedlloyd Lines

NLL cards National Lucht-en-ruimtevaart Laboratorium (international card catalog devised in Amsterdam)

NLLST National Lending Library for Science and Technology (UK)

nl lt net-laying light

NLM National Liberation Movement; National Library of Medicine

NLMA National Lumber Manufacturers Association

NLMC National Labor Management Council

nln no longer needed

NLN National League for Nursing

NLNE National League of Nursing Education

NLNP Naujan Lake National Park (Philippines)

NLNZ National Library of New Zealand

NLO Naval Liaison Office(r); Neighborhood Law Office(r)

NLOGF National Lubricating Oil and Grease Federation

nlp (NLP) neuro-linguistic programmers

NLP National League of Postmasters; Neighborhood Loan Program; Neuro-Linguistic Programming

nlpc (NLPC) n-laurylpyridinium chloride (detergent compound)

NLPI National Loss Prevention Institute

nlr noise load ratio

NLR Nationaal Lucht-en Ruimtevaartlaboratorium (National Aero- and Astronautical Research Institute), Amsterdam

NLRB National Labor Relations Board

nls new least squares; no-load start; non-linear system(s)

NLs New Leftists

NLS National Library of Scotland (Edinburgh); National Library Service (New Zealand and elsewhere); Non-Linear Systems

NLSB National League Service Bureau

NLSCS National League for Separation of Church and State

NLSI National Library of Science and Invention

NLSLS National Library of Scotland Lending Services

nlt new logic technology; not later than; not less than

NLT National Library of Thailand (Bangkok)

NLT Navigazione Libera Triestina (Italian Line)

NLTA National Lawn Tennis Association; National League of Teachers Associations

NLTB Native Land Trust Board

NLTU New London Training Unit (USN)

NLUCS National Land Use Classification System

NLUS Navy League of the United States

NLW National Library of Wales (Aberystwyth); National Library Week

NLWP National Library Week Program

Nly northerly

NLYL National League of Young Liberals

nm nanometer; nautical mile(s); neuromuscular; new moon; nitrogen mustards; nomenclature; nonmetallic; non-motile (bacteria); nuclear magneton

n/m no mark

nm nachmittags (German—afternoon, P.M.); *namiddag* (Dutch—afternoon, P.M.); nanometer; nautical mile(s); nomenclature; nonmetallic

n M nachsten Monate (German —next month)

Nm newtonmeter

NM National Mutual (life insurance); Nigeria Museum

N-M Neiman-Marcus

n/m² newton per square meter

n/m³ normal cubic meter

nma negative mental attitude

NMA National Management Association; National Market Authority; National Medical Association; National Microfilm Association; National Micrographics Association; National Mortgage Association; Navy Mutual Aid (Association); Northwest Mining Association

NMAA National Machine Accountants Association; Navy Mutual Aid Association

NMAB National Materials Advisory Board

nmac near mid-air collision

NMAC National Medical Audiovisual Center

NMACT Nuclear Materials Accounting Control Team

NMAF National Medical Association Foundation

n masc masculine form of a noun

N-materials nuclear materials

NMB National Maritime Board; National Mediation Board; Nippon Miniature Bearing

nmbr number

nmc no more credit

NMC National Manufacturers Code; National Mapping Council; National Maritime Council; National Meteorological Center; National Museum of Canada; National Museums of Ceylon; National Music Council; Naval Material Command; Naval Medical Center; Naval Missile Center; Northern Mining Corporation

NMCA National Music Camp Association; Navy Mother's Clubs of America

NMCB National Metric Conversion Board

NMCC National Military Command Center

NMCCIS NATO Military Command, Control, and Information System

NMCDA National Model Cities Directors Association

NMCO Naval Material Catalog Office

NMCP National Memorial Cemetery of the Pacific

NMCS National Military Command System

NMCSSC National Military Command System Support Center

NMDA National Metal Decorators Association; National Motorcycle Dealers Association

NMDC National Materials Development Center

NMDL Navy Mine Defense Laboratory

NMDZ NATO Maritime Defense Zone

nme noise-measuring equipment

NME National Medical Enterprises; National Military Establishment; National Mortgage Exchange

Nmea Noumea

NMEA National Marine Education Association

N-medicine nuclear medicine

N-med tech nuclear-medicine technician

nmembler mnemonic assembler

NMERI National Mechanical Engineering Research Institute

N Mex New Mexico; New Mexican

N Méx *Nuevo México* (Spanish —New Mexico)

NMF National Marine Fisheries

NMFMA National Mutual Fund Managers Association

NMFO Navy Maintenance Field Office

NMFRL Naval Medical Field Research Laboratory

NMFS National Marine Fisheries Service

NMFSL National Marine Fisheries Service Laboratories

NMG National Management Game

NMGC National Marriage Guidance Council

nmh nautical miles per hour

NMH Northwestern Memorial Hospital

NMHA National Mental Health Association

NMHB National Materials Handling Bureau

NMHSA National Mine Health and Safety Academy

nmi new (automobile) model introduction; no middle initial

n mi nautical miles

NMI National Mutual Insurance; New Mexico Military Institute

NMIA National Meteorological Institute of Athens

NMICA New Mexico Independent College Association

n mi/lb nautical miles per pound (of fuel)

NMIM & T New Mexico Institute of Mining and Technology

N-mishap nuclear mishap

N-missile(s) nuclear missile(s)

NMJ Northern Masonic Jurisdiction

NML National Measurement Laboratory; National Municipal League; National Museum Library; National Music League; National Mutual Life (insurance); Northwestern Mutual Life (insurance)

NMLA National Mutual Life Association; New Mexico Library Association

NMLRA National Muzzle-Loading Rifle Association

NMM National Maritime Museum (Greenwich)

NMMA National Macaroni

Manufacturers Association

nmn no middle name

NMN⁺ nicotinamide mononucleotide

NMNA National Male Nurse Association

nmnc nonmercuric noncorrosive

NMNH National Museum of Natural History (DC)

NMO National Mapping Office; Navy Management Office

nmoc new man on campus

nmp navigational microfilm projector; normal menstrual period

NMPA National Music Publishers Association

NMPC National Maintenance Publications Center (USA); National Moratorium on Prison Construction

NMPGA New Mexico Personnel and Guidance Association

nmph nautical miles per hour

nmpm nautical miles per minute

nmps nautical miles per second

n. mque. *nocte maneque* (Latin —night and morning)

nmr normal mode rejection; nuclear magnetic resonance

nmr (NMR) nuclear magnetic resonance (imaging)

NMR Natal Mounted Rifles

NMRA National Model Railroad Association

NMRI Naval Medical Research Institute

NMRL Naval Medical Research Laboratory

NMRP New Mexico Research Park

NMRTC New Mexico Research and Treatment Center

nms nuclear materials safeguards

NMS National Medal of Science; National Meteorological Service; Nobles of the Mystic Shrine

NMSA National Middle School Association

NMSC National Merit Scholarship Corporation; National Mountain and Safety Committee

NMSE Naval Material Support Establishment

NMSM New Mexico School of Mines

NMSO Naval Manpower Survey Office(r)

NMSQT National Merit Scholarships Qualifying Test

NMSRC National Middle

School Resource Center

NMSS National Multiple Sclerosis Society; Nuclear Materials Safety and Safeguards

NMSSA NATO Maintenance Supply Service Agency

NMSST Naval Manpower Shore Survey Team

NMSU New Mexico State University

NMSWF National Manufacturers of Soda Water Flavors

nmt not more than

NMT National Museum of Transport

NMTA National Metal Trades Association

NMTBA National Machine Tool Builders' Association

NMTF National Market Traders' Federation

NMTFA National Master Tile Fixers' Association

NMTLM Nuclear Materials Transportation Logistics Model

NMTS National Milk Testing Service

NMU National Maritime Union

NMW National Museum of Wales

NMWA National Mineral Wool Association

NMWP National Migrant Workers Program

nn neutralization number; no name; nouns

n/n no number; not to be noted

nn non numerato (Italian—unnumbered)

n.n. nemini notus (Latin—known to no one); *nescio nomen* (Latin—I do not know the name)

NN Newport News; Northwestern National

N/N Northrop/Nortronics

NNA National Neckwear Association; National Newspaper Association; National Notary Association

nnad network non-addressing device

NNAG NATO Naval Advisory Group; NATO Naval Armaments Group

NNBIS National Narcotics Border Interdiction System

NNBPWC National Negro Business and Professional Women's Clubs

NNC National News Council; Naval Nuclear Club (rival members include France, the

United Kingdom, the United States, and the USSR); Navy Nurse Corps

NNCCVTE National Network for Curriculum Coordination in Vocational and Technical Education

NNCR North Norfolk Coast Reserves (England)

nnd neonatal death

NND New and Non-Official Drugs

NNE Net National Expenditure; north northeast

NNEB National Nursery Examination Board

NN & EB National Newark & Essex Bank

NNECH National Nutrition Education Clearinghouse

NNEU Naval Nuclear Evaulation Unit

NNF Northern Nurses Federation

NNG Netherlands New Guinea; Northern Natural Gas (company)

NNGA Northern Nut Growers Association

nni noise and number index (sound pollution)

NNI Norwegian Nobel Institute

NNI Nederlands Normalisatie Instituut (Dutch—Netherlands Standards Institute)

nnk (NNK) notify next of kin

NNL Nigerian National Line

NNLC National Negro Labor Council

nnm next new moon

NNMC National Naval Medical Center

nnn no national name; no native named

NNN Nihon News Network; Novy-Nicolle-McNeal (bacteriological culture)

NNNR Noss National Nature Reserve (Shetlands)

Nnn's Nicaraguan nut nippers (imaginary and somewhat idealized guard dogs whose selective nipping tends to frighten even the most daring and hardened criminals)

NNO noord noordoost (Dutch—north northeast)

NNOC Nigerian National Oil Company

n. nov. nomen novum (Latin—new name)

nnp net national product

nnp (NNP) net national product

NNP Nairobi National Park

(Kenya); Ngezi National Park (Rhodesia); Nimule National Park (Sudan)

NNPA National Negro Press Association; National Newspaper Promotion Association; National Newspaper Publishers Association

NNPP Naval Nuclear Propulsion Program (USN)

NNPT Nuclear Non-Proliferation Treaty

NNR New and Nonofficial Remedies

NNRC Neutral Nations Repatriation Commission

NNRI National Nutrition Research Institute

nn's nubile nymphs

nnS (NNS) Navy navigation satellite

n-N's neo-Nazis

N Ns Newport News

NNS National Newspaper Syndicate

NNSC Neutral Nations Supervisory Commission

NNS & DDC Newport News Shipbuilding and Dry Dock Company

NNSL Nigerian National Shipping Line

nnsn no national stock number

NNSS Navy Navigational Satellite System

NNTO Netherlands National Tourist Office; Norwegian National Travel Office

NNW north northwest

NNW noord noorwest (Dutch—north northwest)

NNWR Necedah National Wildlife Refuge (Wisconsin), Noxubee National Wildlife Refuge (Mississippi)

NNWSI Nevada Nuclear Waste Storage Investigation

no. natural order; normally open; number

no. (NO) neuromyelitis optica

n-o not or

n/o no orders

no norsk (Dano-Norwegian—Norwegian)

nᵒ número (Spanish—number)

No nobelium; Norskie (Norwegian-American); Norway; Norwegian; number

No. Numero (Latin—number)

NO Naval Observatory; Naval Officer; New Orleans; nitrous oxide; North Central Airlines; Nuffield Observatory (Jordrell Bank, England)

NO noordoost (Dutch—northeast); *Nordosten* (German—

northeast); *noroeste* (Spanish —northwest)

No. 1 first; first quality; first rate; first person; most important; most important person; number one

No. 2 next in line; next in rank; number two; second; second person; second quality; second rate

No. 10 Number 10 Downing Street (London residence of the British prime minister)

noa net operating assets; new obligational authority (NOA); not operationally assigned; not otherwise authorized

n-o-a not-or-and

NOA National Onion Association; National Opera Association; National Optical Association; National Orchestral Association

NOAA National Oceanic and Atmospheric Administration

NOAB National Outdoor Advertising Bureau

NO-AB New Orleans-Algiers Bridge

NOAL National Order of Arts and Letters

noala noise-operated automatic level adjustment

NOASSR North Ossetian Autonomous Soviet Socialist Republic

nob. no open burning; nobility; noble; not on board

nob. *nobis* (Latin—to us)

NOB National Oil Board; Naval Operating Base; Naval Order of Battle

NOB *Nationaal Orkest van Belgie* (Flemish—National Orchestra of Belgium)

Nobelst *Nobelstiftelsen* (The Nobel Foundation)

no biz no business

noc not otherwise classified; notation of content(s)

NOC National Oceanographic Council; National Olympic Committee

nocc navigation operator's control console

NOCC New Orleans Crime Commission

NOCHA National Off-Campus Housing Association

NOCIL National Organic Chemical Industries

No-Clo Z No-Clone Zone

NOCM Nuclear Ordnance Commodity Manager

no cn no connection

No Co Northern Counties

NOCO Nuclear Ordnance Catalog Office

noct. *nocte* (Latin—by night, nocturnal)

NOCTI National Occupational Competency Testing Institute

noct. maneq. *nocte maneque* (Latin—night and morning)

nod. network out dial; new offshore discharge; night observation device

NOD Naval Ordnance Depot; Navigation and Ocean Development

NODA Night Operatic and Dramatic Association

NODAC Naval Ordnance Data Automation Center

Nodaks North Dakotans

NODC National Oceanographic Data Center

Noddy Nicodemus

NODECA Norwegian Defense Communications Agency

nodex new offshore discharge-ment exercise

NODL National Organization for Decent Literature (Catholic)

no do a *nota do autor* (Portuguese—author's note)

no do e *nota do editor* (Portuguese—editor's note)

no do t *nota do tradutor* (Portuguese—translator's note)

noe not otherwise enumerated

NOE Notice of Exception Oceanographic Foundation; National Osteopathic Foundation

NOEB NATO Oil Executive Board(s)

NOEL National Organization of Episcopalians for Life

NOESS National Operational Environmental Satellite System

NOF National Oceanographic Foundation; National Optical Font; National Osteopathic Foundation; Naval Ordnance Facility

NOFI National Oil Fuel Institute

noforn no foreign nationals; special handling—not to be released to foreign nationals

noft notification of foreign travel

nog noggin

Nogal Nogales, Sonora, Mexico

NOGC *Nationaal Overleg voor Gewestelijke Cultuur* (Dutch —National Council for Regional Culture)

nohp not otherwise herein provided

noi net operating income; not otherwise identified

noibn not otherwise identified by name; not otherwise indexed by name

NOIC National Oceanographic Instrumentation Center; Naval Officer in Charge; Navy Opportunity Information Center

NOIM Nuclear Ordnance Inventory Manager

noise. not only inserted in (modern) symphonic epics; the other fellow's music; unwanted sound

NOISE National Organization to Insure Support Enforcement; National Organization to Insure Sound-controlled Environment

noisic noisy music (blastoff stereo, disco, ear-splitting rock-'n'-roll, and related forms of so-called music)

NOJC National Oil Jobbers Council

NOJTP National On-the-Job Training Program

nok next of kin

NOK Norsk Aero Klub

nol normal overload(ing)

NOL Naval Ordnance Laboratory; Neptune Orient Line; Norse Oriental Line

NOLA New Orleans, Louisiana

NOLAC National Organization of Liaison for Allocation of Circuits

NOLC Naval Ordnance Laboratory, Corona

nol. con. *nolo contendere* (Latin —I do not wish to contend)

Noll Oliver; Olivera; Oliver Cromwell—Lord Protector of England

Nolly Oliver; Olivera

nolo (Latin—I do not wish to contend); *nolo contendere*

NOLPE National Organization on Local Problems in Education

nol-pros nol-prossed; nol prossing

nol. pros. *nolle prosequi* (Latin —to be unwilling to prosecute)

NOLS National Oceanographic Laboratory System

nol. vol. *nolens volens* (Latin— unwilling or willing); willy-nilly

NOLWO Naval Ordnance Laboratory, White Oak (Maryland)

nom nominal; nominate; nominated; nomination

NOMA National Office Management Association

NOMAD Navy Oceanographic and Meteorological Device (world's first nuclear-powered weather station)

nombos nonmine bottom objects

nom cap nominal capital

nom com *nom commercial* (French—business name, trade name)

nom. con. *nomen conservandum* (Latin—generic or specific name to be preserved by special sanction)

nom dam nominal damages

nom de fam *nom de famille* (French—family nickname of one of its members, surname) —hence the family name might be Geist but grandfather George might be Tamboo to his grandson and grandmother Elinor might be Namboo

nom de g *nom de guerre* (French —assumed name)—pseudonym

nom de jf *nom de jeune fille* (French—maiden name)

nom de p *nom de plume* (French —pen name, pseudonym)

nom de t *nom de théâtre* (French —stage name)

nom. dub. *nomen dubium* (Latin —doubtful name)

nomen nomenclature

Nome State Nome State Jail at Nome, Alaska

nomin nominative

nom. nov. *nomen novum* (Latin —new name)

nom. nud. *nomen nudem* (Latin —naked name); mere name for an animal or plant but lacking further description

NOMSS National Operational Meteorological Satellite System

nom std nominal standard

NOMTF Naval Ordnance Missile Test Facilities

Non Nonoc

NON National Organization of Non-Parenthood

non acpc non-acceptance

non arrl non-arrival

non-can non-cancellable

non-coll non-collegiate

Non-Com noncommissioned officer

noncom(s) nonconformist(s)

non-com(s) non-commissioned officer(s)

noncon(s) nonconformist(s)

non cul. *non culpabilis* (Latin— not culpable, not guilty)

non-cum non-cumulative

nondely non-delivery

none no one; not one

None Nonesuch

none of the above none of the above candidates (choices) is acceptable

non est *non est inventus* (Latin— he was not found, it is wanting)

non flam non-flammable

non-flam non-flammable film (slow-burning acetate-base film)

N/ONI Navy/Office of Naval Intelligence

non negl non-negotiable

non obs. *non obstante* (Latin— notwithstanding)

non op non-operational

n-on-p negative on positive

non-par non-participating

non perf non-perforated

nonporno not pornographic

non pos. *non possumus* (Latin— we cannot)

non pros. *non prosequitur* (Latin —does not prosecute)

non pyt non-payment

N/ONR Navy/Office of Naval Research

non repetat. *non repetatur* (Latin —do not repeat)

non res non-resident

non-res nonresident

non rtnl non-returnable

NONSAP Nonlinear Structural Analysis Program

non seq. *non sequitor* (Latin—it does not follow)

non-sked non-scheduled (airplane, bus, train, etc.)

non std nonstandard

non U not upper class

nonum national number

NOO Navy Oceanographic Office (formerly Hydrographic Office, USN)

NOOA New Orleans Opera Association

noodle-noodle-noodle-noodle tremolo passages played by the strings and called noodling by many musicians

no op no opinion

no op (NO OP) no operation (data processing)

Noor (Dutch—Norwegian)

Noord-Amerika (Dutch—North America)

Noord-Holland (Dutch—North Holland)—province around Haarlem

Noords (Dutch—Nordic)

Noordzee (Dutch—North Sea)

Noors (Dutch—Norse)

Noorweegs (Dutch—Norwegian)

Noorwegen (Dutch—Norway)

nop navigating operating procedure; normal operating procedure; not on production; not open (to the) public; not otherwise provided; not our publication

NOP National Oceanographic Program; National Opinion Poll; Naval Oceanographic Program; North Oscura Peak

NOPA National Office Products Association; National Organization of Police Associations

no par. no paragraph (matter runs on)

NOPE New Orleans Port of Embarkation

NOPHN National Organization for Public Health Nursing

NOPL New Orleans Public Library

nopn normally open

NOPO New Orleans Philharmonic Orchestra

NOPS New Orleans Public Service

NOPWC National Old People's Welfare Council

NOQUIS Nucleonic Oil Quantity Indication System

nor not otherwise rated

nor. normal; not or

nor' norther (Middle English contraction); north

nør *nørre* (Danish—north)

Nor Norma (constellation); Norway; Norwegian

Nor *Norr* (Swedish—north)

NoR Notice of Readiness

NOR North Central Airlines; NOT OR (data processing logic-operator equivalent)

Nora Eleanora

NORAD North American Air Defense

NORAID Northern Aid (to IRA and other groups in Northern Ireland); Norwegian Agency for International Development

Nor Ant Norwegian Antarctica (Bouvet Island, Peter I Island, Queen Maud Land)

Nor Arc Norwegian Arctic (Bear, Edge, and Hope islands in Barents Sea, Jan Mayen Island in Norwegian Sea, Svalbard or Spitsbergen in Arctic Ocean)

nor'ard northward

NORASDEFLANT North American Antisubmarine Defense Force, Atlantic

Nor Atl North Atlantic

Noratlas Norad 45-passenger transport aircraft made in France

norc national ordnance research computer

NORC National Opinion Research Center (University of Chicago); Naval Ordnance Research Computer; Nippon Ocean Racing Club

Nor-Cor Northland-Coromandel (NZ)

Nor Cur Norwegian Current

nor'd northward

NORD Naval Ordnance

NORDEK Nordic Economic Community (Denmark, Finland, Norway, Sweden)

NORDEL Nordic Electricity Union

Norden (Scandinavian—the North)—Denmark, Finland, Iceland, Norway, Sweden

Nordenskjöld Sea Swedish name for the Laptev Sea in the Arctic Ocean

Nordic Hanson's Symphony No. 1

Nordic Council Scandinavian union including Denmark, Finland, Iceland, Norway, and Sweden

Nordic Countries Denmark, Finland, Iceland, Norway, Sweden

Nordirland (German—Northern Ireland)—Ulster

NORDITA Nordic Institute for Theoretical Atomic Physics

Nordovicum (Latin—Norwich)

Nordsee (German—North Sea)

NORDSFORSK Nordiska Samarbetsorganisationen för Teknisk-Naturventenskaplig Forening (Nordic Council for Applied Research)

Nordsø (Danish—North Sea)

nor'easter northeaster (storm from the northeast)

noref no reference

Norelco North American Philips Company

Norf Norfolk

norfolk norfolk coat or norfolk jacket (made with fore-and-aft box pleats, big pockets, and a belt, first produced in England's Norfolk county)

Norf S Norfolk Southern, Norfolk & Western, Southern Railway (merger)

Norge (Norwegian—Norway)

NORGRAIN North American Grain Charter

Norics Noric Alps in southern Austria

Norimburga (Latin—Nürnberg) —Nuremberg also called Norica or Noriberga

NORK New Orleans Rhythm Kings

Nørland (Norwegian—Northland)—northern Norway

N'Orleans New Orleans

Norlina North Carolina

norm not operationally ready (pending) maintenance

norm. normal; normalize; normalizing; not operationally ready (because of) maintenance; nuclear operational readiness maneuvers

Norm Norman

NORM National Optimism Revival Movement

Normalcy nickname for Warren G. Harding who when campaigning for the Presidency advocated "a return to normalcy"

Normandia (Italian, Portuguese, Spanish—Normandy)

Normandie (French or German —Normandy)

Normandië (Dutch—Normandy)

Normands Norman Islands (Channel Islands)

NORML National Organization for the Reform of Marijuana Laws; National Organization for the Reinforcement of Marijuana Laws; National Organization for the Repeal of Marijuana Laws (funded by the Playboy Foundation)

NORMY Norman Douglas

Noroil Norwegian Oil

NORONTAIR Northern Ontario Airways

Nor Pac Northern Pacific

Nor Pol Norsk Polarinstitutt (Norwegian Polar Institute)

norrd no reply received

nors not operationally ready, supplies (supply)

Norse God of Thunder Thor, whose Roman counterpart is Jove or Jupiter

Norsker(s) Norwegian sailor(s)

Norskie Norwegian-American

NORTEP Northern Teacher Education Program

north. northerly; northern

NORTHAG North European Army Group

North America islands and lands extending from Canada

to Colombia (Canada, Central America, Greenland, México, the United States, the West Indies)

North America's Largest Country Canada

Northants Northamptonshire

North Atlantic ocean between North America, Europe, and northern Africa

North Baltic Nation Estonia

North BH North Broken Hill

North Borneo Saba and Sarawak

North Britain Scotland

North Carolina Ports (north to south) Wilmington, Wrightsville

North Cascades North Cascades National Park in Washington

North Central States East North Central States and West North Central States (*see separate entries covering 12-state region*)

Northcliffe Viscount Northcliffe (Alfred Charles William Harmsworth)

Northeast Middle Atlantic and New England States

Northeast Corridor megalopolis extending from Boston to Washington, including Providence, New Haven, New York, Newark, Trenton, Philadelphia, Wilmington, Baltimore

Northeast Region Middle Atlantic and New England states

Northern Bear political cartoonist's symbol for Russia or the Soviet Union

Northern Hemisphere the world north of the equator

Northern Institute Northern Region Correction Institute at Fairbanks, Alaska

Northern Ireland Ulster (six northern counties of Ireland)

Northern Ireland's Principal Port Belfast

northern lights aurora borealis

Northernmost American Town Point Barrow, Alaska

Northernmost Canadian Town Inuvik, Northwest Territories

Northernmost Point of the European Mainland Nordkyn, Norway (nearby North Cape)

Northernmost Province Québec

Northernmost State Alaska

Northernmost Territories Northwest Territories

Northern Rhodesia Zambia's former name

Northerns Burlington, Great Northern, and Northern Pacific railroads

Northern States northern United States in the Federal Union during the Civil War—The North

Northern Way Norway

North Holland Dutch province around Haarlem in the northwest Netherlands where it is called Noord-Holland

North Jersey Coast Atlantic City to the Atlantic Highlands

Northland Riviera Sweden's summer beach on the Gulf of Bothnia and the Polar Route

Northld Northumberland

North Pacific ocean between Asia and North America containing Aleutians, Hawaiians, and many islands north of the Equator

North Pole 90 degrees North latitude; zero degrees longitude; northernmost point on the globe; discovered by American explorers Frederick A Cook and Robert E Peary in 1909; home of Mr & Mrs S Claus

North River Hudson River (Battery to 59th Street on New York waterfront)

North Sea between British Isles and northern Europe

North Sea Canal Amsterdam Ship Canal

North Side Chicago's seamy side

North Slope Alaska north of the Brooks Range

North Star Minnesota's nickname

North Star City St. Paul, Minnesota

North Star State Minnesota's official nickname

Northum Northumberland

Northwest northwestern United States (Washington, Oregon, Idaho, Montana, Wyoming)

North Western Line Chicago and North Western Railway

NORTLANT North Atlantic

Norton WW Norton & Co

Nortown WW Norton

Nortraship Norwegian Trade and Shipping Mission

Noruega (Portuguese or Spanish —Norway)

Norumbega historian John Fiske's name for what is now New York City (see *Norvegia*)

Norumbegaland New York to Nova Scotia including New England

Norvège (French—Norway)

Norvegia (Italian—Norway); (Latin—Norway)—also appears on some of the earliest maps of the east coast of North America as Norbega or Norumbega over an area extending from the Bay of Fundy to Florida and known for its Norse viking explorations and settlements in pre-Columbian times; sometimes spelled Norvega or Norbegia as well as Norumbega

Norvic. Norvicensis (Latin—of Norwich)

Norw Norwegian

Norway Kingdom of Norway (northernmost Scandinavian country whose Norwegians speak Norwegian as well as English and German, mining and shipbuilding augment engineering and farming enterprises as well as its vast merchant marine) *Kongeriket Norge*

Norway Day Constitution Day (May 17)

Norway's Most Popular Sculptor Adolf Gustav Vigeland

Norway's Principal Port Oslo

NORWEB North Western Electricity Board

Norwegen (German—Norway)

norwegian norwegian elkhound (dog originally bred in Norway for hunting elk and other game); norwegian saltpeter (calcium nitrate)

Norwegian Expressionist Edvard Munch

Norwegian First Norway's best known classical composer— Edvard Hagerup Grieg

Norwegian National Composer Edvard Grieg

Norwegian Ports (large, medium and small from north to south) Kirkenes, Vadso, Vardo, Honningsvaag, Hammerfest, Tromso, Harstad, Svolvaer, Narvik, Bodo, Mo, Mosjoen, Trondheim, Thamshamn, Kristiansund, Harosund, Molde, Ulsteinik, Alesund, Vaksdal, Bergen, Odda, Haugesund, Stavanger, Egersund, Flekkefjord, Kristiansand, Grimstad, Arendal, Tvedestrand, Langesund, Brevik, Porsgrun, Larvik, Sandefjord, Tonsberg, Horten, Drammen, Oslo, Moss, Sarpsborg, Frederikstad, Halden

Norwegian Sea between Greenland, Iceland, and Norway

NORWESTLANT Northwest Atlantic (project)

nos net oil sand; night operation sight; not on shelf; not otherwise specified; numbers

NOs New Orleans (British maritime abbreviation)

NOS National Ocean Survey; NATO Office of Security; Network Operating System; New Orleans; Night Observation Sight; Night Operation System

N OS New Orleans

NOS Nederlandse Omroep Stichting (Dutch—Netherlands Broadcasting Foundation)

NOSA National Occupational Safety Association

NOSC Naval Ocean Systems Center (USN); Naval Ordnance Systems Command (USN)

NOSCAF New Orleans Sickle Cell Anemia Foundation

NOSE Neighbors Opposing Smelly Emissions

nose candy cocaine for sniffing

NOSG Naval Operations Support Group

nosh no show

NOSIE Nurses Observation Scale for Inpatient Evaluation

no sig no signature

nosigchng no significant change

nosmo no smoking

Nosodak North Dakota + South Dakota—the Dakotas

NOSOPEX Northern Sumatra Offshore Petroleum Exploration

NOSSOLANT Naval Ordnance System Support Atlantic

NOSSOPAC Naval Ordnance System Support Pacific

NOSTA National Ocean Science and Technology Agency

Nostradamus Michel de Nostradame also called Michel de Notredame

nosub not subject to load

not. nucleus opticus tegmenti

Not Notary

nota none of the above (candidates)

notal not to, nor needed by, all addressees

NOTAM Notice to Airmen

NOTB National Ophthalmic Treatment Board

notg nothing

notif notification

no-till no-tillage

noto numbering tool

noto (Latin prefix—back)—notochord

notox non toxic; not to exceed

NOTP *New Orleans Times-Picayune*

notr no traffic rights

Notre Dames Notre Dame Mountains of Québec

not's non-classical organizational theories

NOTS Naval Ordnance Test Station

Not(t) Nottingham

Notts Nottinghamshire

notwg notwithstanding

NOU Noumea, New Caledonia (airport)

Nouasseur Casablanca, Morocco's airport

Nou Heb Nouvelles Hébrides (French—New Hebrides)

Nouvelle Calédonie (French—New Caledonia)

Nouvelles Hébrides (French—New Hebrides)—Anglo-French Condominium in the western South Pacific

Nouvelle—Zélande (French—New Zealand)

nov novels; novelist; novels

nov noviembre (Spanish—November)

nov. novum (Latin—new)

Nov November

Nov Nova (Bulgarian, Italian, Portuguese, Serbo-Croatian—new); *Novaya* (Russian—new); *Novo* (Portuguese or Russian—new); *Novy* (Czechoslovakian—new)

Nova Inglaterra (Portuguese—New England)

Nova Iorque (Portuguese—New York)

Novalis Friedrich Leopold von Hardenberg

Nova Scotia Girls Nova Scotia School for (delinquent) Girls at Truro

Novaya Sibir (Russian—New Siberia)

Novaya Zemlya (Russian—New Land)—Arctic island north of Russia between the Barents and Kara seas

Nova Zelandia (Portuguese—New Zealand)

Novdec November and December

nov^e noviembre (Spanish—November)

November letter N radio code

Noviomagus Rhenanus (Latin—Nijmegen)—Dutch city noted for fine printing

nov. n. novum nomen (Latin—

new name)

Novo Novosibirsk

Novosibirskiye Ostrova (Russian—New Siberian Islands)

NOVS National Office of Vital Statistics

nov. sp. novum species (Latin—new species)

Nov T Novum Testamentum (Latin—New Testiment)

Novum Eboracum (Latin—New York)

Novy(s) Nova Scotian(s)

now. (NOW) negotiable orders of withdrawal (banking accounts)

NoW News of the World

NOW National Organization for Women; Negotiable Order of Withdrawal (interest-earning checking account)

NOWAPA North American Water and Power Alliance

NOWC National Association of Women's Clubs

NOWs Negotiable (deposits) Order of Withdrawals

NOx nitrous oxide (smog component)

noxema knocks eczema

noy not out yet; (unit of noisiness)

Noy Noybr (Russian—November)

noydb none of your damn business

noz nozzle

Nozze Le Nozze di Figaro (Italian—The Marriage of Figaro)—four-act comic opera by Mozart

np napalm (incendiary gasoline mixture); national pipe; neap; neap range; near point; net proceeds; neuropsychiatric; neuropsychiatry; new paragraph; new pattern; new police; nickel-plated; nitroproof; no paging; no payment; no place; no place of publication; no protest; nonparticipating; nonpropelled; normal pressure; nose plug; not paginated; noun phrase; nursing procedure

np (NP) no parking; note payable

n/p net proceeds; new pence

n.p. nedsat pris (Dano-Norwegian—reduced price)

Np neap; neap range; neap tide; neper; neptunium (symbol)

N_p neper

NP Narragansett Pier; National Park; National Pipe; National(ist) Party; Naval Prison;

New Providence, Bahama Islands; Newport, Rhode Island; no parking; Northern Pacific (railroad); Northern Province; not published; Notary Public; Nurse Practioner

N-P Non-Partisan

N/P nitrogen phosphorus ratio

NP *Nasionale Partij* (Afrikaans—National Party)

NPA National Packaging Association; National Paperboard Association; National Parenthood Association; National Parking Association; National Parks Association; National Parks Authority (NZ); National Particleboard Association; National Personnel Associates; National Personnel Authority; National Pet Association; National Petroleum Association; National Pharmaceutical Association; National Pigeon Association; National Pilots Association; National Pipeline Authority; National Planning Association; National Police Agency (Japan); National Preservers Association; National Proctological Association; National Production Authority; Naval Procurement Account; Navy Postal Affairs; New Peoples Army (Philippines); Newspaper Publishers Association; Nigerian Ports Authority

NPABC National Public Affairs Broadcast Center

NPAC National Program for Acquisitions and Cataloging (Library of Congress)

N Pac Cur North Pacific Current

NPACI National Production Advisory Council on Industry

NPACT National Public Affairs Center for Television

N-panel panel of nuclear experts

NPAP National Psychological Association for Psychoanalysis

npat net profit after tax(es)

NPB National Park Board; National Parole Board (Canada); National Productivity Board (U.S.); North Pacific Bank

NPBA National Paper Box Association; National Pig Breeders' Association

NPBC National Programming Black Consortium

NPBI National Pretzel Bakers Institute

npc near point of convergence; New Process Company's trademark

NPC National Patent Council; National Peach Council; National Peanut Council; National Peoples Congress; National Periodicals Center; National Personnel Consultants; National Petroleum Council; National Pharmaceutical Council; National Potato Council; National Power Company; National Press Club; National Productivity Center; Nauruan Phosphate Commission; Naval Photographic Center; New Peoples Center; Nigerian Population Commission; Nippon Petro-Chemicals

NPCA National Parks and Conservation Association; National Pest Control Association

NPCC National Projects Construction Corporation; Nebraska Penal and Correctional Complex

NPCFB North Pacific Coast Freight Bureau

NPCI National Potato Chip Institute

NPCP National Press Club of the Philippines

npcr no periodic calibration required

np-ct naval personnel conversion tables

npd no payroll division; north polar distance

np or d no place or date (of publication)

N-P d Neimann-Pick's disease

NPD Nationaldemokratische Partei Deutschlands (National Democratic Party of Germany)

NPDC National Patent Development Corporation

NPDEA National Professional Driver Education Association

NPDES National Pollution Discharge Elimination Scheme

NPDN Nordic Public Data Network (Denmark, Finland, Iceland, Norway, and Sweden)

NPDO Non-Profit Distributing Organization

np or dp no place or date of publication

NPE Navy Preliminary Evaluation

N-peace nuclear peace

npef new product evaluation form

NP en G Nederlandse Postcheque en Girondienst (Netherlands Postal Check and Transfer Service)

NPEP National Public Expenditure Plan(ning)

npf newsprint pulp flat; no private facilities; not provided for

NPF National Park Foundation; National Parkinson Foundation; National Piano Foundation; National Poetry Foundation; National Provident Fund(ing); National Pugilistic Federation

NPFA National Playing Fields Association

NPFC Naval Publications and Forms Center; Northwest Pacific Fisheries Center

NPFFA National Police and Fire Fighters Association

NPFI National Plant Food Institute

npfid nitrogen-phosphorus flame-ionization detector

NPFSC North Pacific Fur Seal Commission

NPFT Neurotic Personality Factor Test

NPG National Portrait Gallery; NATO Planning Group

NPGA Nebraska Personnel and Guidance Association; Nevada Personnel and Guidance Association

NPGS Naval Postgraduate School; Net Profit Generator System

n ph nuclear physics

npH neutral protamine Hegedorn (isoophane insulin)

NPHIS Nested Phrase Indexing System

NPHQ National Park (Ranger) Headquarters

NPI National Population Inquiry; National Productivity Institute; Neuro-Psychiatric Institute; Nippon Pulp Industry

NPIA Norfolk Port and Industrial Authority

NPIC Naval Photographic Interpretation Center

NPIPF Newspaper and Printing Industries Printing Fund

NPIS National Physics Information System

N-P-K Nitrogen-Phosphate-Potash (fertilizer)

npl new processor line; new program language; nipple; no personal liability; noise-pollution level

n pl plural form of a noun

NPL Nashville Public Library; National Physical Laboratory; Newark Public Library; Norfolk Public Library

N-plant(s) nuclear plant(s); nuclear-power plant(s)

NPLGS Night Plane Guard Station

NPLO NATO Production and Logistics Organization

nplu not people like us

npm number of points in the point-matching method

NPMAA National Piano Manufacturers Association of America

npn (NPN) nonprotein nitrogen

n-p-n negative-positive-negative

NPN negative positive negative

npna no protest for nonacceptance

np/nd not published/no date (given)

N & PNWR Ninepipe and Pablo National Wildlife Refuge (Montana)

npo nothing by mouth

n.p.o. nil per os (Latin—nothing by mouth)—sometimes incorrectly written as ne per oris

NPO National Philharmonic Orchestra (Manila); National Program Office (for nuclear waste terminal storage); Navy Post Office; Navy Purchasing Office(r); New Philharmonia Orchestra (London)

NPOAA National Police Officers Association of America

NPOEV Nuclear-Powered Ocean Engineering Vehicle (miniature submarine)

N-pollution nuclear pollution

NP & OSR Naval Petroleum and Oil Shale Reserve

N-power nuclear power

N-power plant(s) nuclear-power plant(s)

npp no passed proof

NPP National Potato Panel; National Prison Project (ACLU); Naval Propellant Plant; Nuclear Power Plant

NPP (ACLU) National Prison Project (American Civil Liberties Union)

NPPA National Press Photographers Association

NPPAJ National Probation and Parole Association Journal

NPPF National Planned Parenthood Federation

NPPO Navy Publications and Printing Office

NPPR Nationalist Party of Puerto Rico

NPPS National Plants Preservation Society; Navy Publication Printing Service

N-P Pubns National Press Publications

NPQ Naviera de Productos Químicos (Chemical Products Shipping Line)

npr night press rate

n/p/r noise/power/ratio

Npr Napier, NZ

NPR National Public Radio; Naval Petroleum Reserves; Navieras de Puerto Rico; Nickel Plate Road (railroad)

NPRA National Parks and Recreation Association; National Parks and Reserves Authority; National Petroleum Refiners Association; Naval Personnel Research Activity

NPRAC National Public Radio Association of California

NPRC National Personnel Records Center; Newspaper Production and Research Center

nprd nuclear plant reliability data

NPRDS Nuclear Plant Reliability Data System

NPRL National Physical Research Laboratory

NPRO Navy Plant Representative Office(r)

NPROA National Police Reserve Officers Association

N-project nuclear-power project

N-proliferation nuclear proliferation

N-propulsion nuclear propulsion

NPR & OSR Naval Petroleum Reserves and Oil Shale Reserves

npr's nuclear-power reactors

nps normal pipe size; no prior service

nps (NPS) nuclear-powered ship(ping)

NPs Notaries Public; Nurse Practitioners

NPS Narcotics Preventive Service; National Park Service; Nuclear-Powered Ship(ping)

NPSB *National Prisoner Statistics Bulletin*

npsh net positive suction head

npt normal pressure and temperature

npt (NPT) nocturnal penile tumescence

Npt Navy pointer tracker; Newport

NPT national (taper) pipe thread; Non-Proliferation Treaty

NPTA National Passenger Traffic Association; National Piano Travelers Association; Nevada Parent-Teacher Association

NPTC National Postal and Travelers Censorship

NPTRL Naval Personnel Training Research Laboratory

npu not-passed urine

n.p.u. *ne plus ultra* [Latin—nothing beyond (it); the summit; the ultimate]

NPU National People's Union; National Police Union; National Postal Union

npv net present value; no par value

npv (NPV) nuclear polyhedrosis virus

NPVLA National Paint, Varnish, and Lacquer Association

npw new-pool wildcat (oil well)

NPW *Naturpark Pfalszer Wald* (German—Falls Forest Nature Park)—in western Germany near France

NPWC Navy Public Works Center

NPWS National Parks and Wildlife Service (Australia)

NPWU National Production Workers of America

NPX National Phoenix Industries (stock-exchange symbol)

NPY National Productivity Year

n-p-z negative-positive-zero

nq notes and queries

NQ North Queensland

N & Q *Notes & Queries*

nqa net quick assets

NQA Nuclear Quality Assurance

NQAPO Nuclear Quality Assurance Program Office

NQD Notice of Quality Discrepancy

nqokd not quite our kind, dear

nqos not quite our sort

nqot not quite our type

nqr nuclear quadruple resonance

NQX North Queensland Express

nr narrow resonance; natural rubber; near; net register; no risk; nonreactive (relay); norm-referenced; number

n-r no(n) return; non-resident

n/r no record; non-recoverable; not reported; not required; not responsible (for)

nr *non rogne* (French—untrimmed); *nummer* (Polish—issue,

number); *nummer* (Dano-Norwegian or Swedish—number)

n.r. *non repetatur* (Latin—not to be repeated)

nR *neue Reihe* (German—new series)

Nr *Nummer* (German—number)

NR National Register; Norks Rikskringkasting (Norwegian Broadcasting)

N/R Notice of Readiness

NR *National Review*

nra never refuse anything; no repair action

nra *nuestra* (Spanish—our)

NRA National Racing Authority; National Reclamation Association; National Recovery Act; National Recovery Administration; National Recreation Association; National Reform Association; National Rehabilitation Association; National Research Associates; National Restaurant Association; National Rifle Association (of America); Naval Reserve Association

NRAA National Rifle Association of America

NRAC National Research Advisory Council; National Resources Analysis Center; National Rural Advisory Council

NRACCO Navy Regional Air Cargo Control Office(r)

nrad no risk after discharge

NRAF Navy Recruiting Aids Facility

nral no risk after landing

NRAO National Radio Astronomy Observatory

nras no risk after shipment

NRAS Navy Readiness Analysis Section; Navy Readiness Analysis System

Nra Sra *Nuestra Señora* (Spanish—Our Lady)

Nrb Nordby

NRB National Religious Broadcasters; National Research Bureau; National Roads Board; National Rubber Bureau

NRB *Narodna Republika Blgariya* (Bulgarian Peoples' Republic)

Nrbi Nairobi

NRBs National Religious Broadcasters

nrc noise-reduction circuitry; not recommended for children

NRC Nacorazi Railroad Company; National Racquetball Club; National Referral Center (Library of Congress); National Republican Club; National Research Corporation; National Research Council; National Resources Committee; National Resources Council; National Roofing Contractors; National Rural Center; Naval Retraining Command; Neighborhood Recovery Center (for alcoholism); Neighborhood Reinvestment Corporation; Netherlands Red Cross; Newport Research Corporation; Nuclear Regulatory Commission; Nuclear Research Council

NRC Nieuwe Rotterdamse Courant (New Rotterdam Courant)

NRCA National Resources Council of America; National Retail Credit Association

NRCC National Republican Congressional Committee; National Research Council of Canada

NRCD National Reprographic Center for Documentation

nrcf not reconfirmed

NRCL National Research Council Library; Natural Resources Conservation League

NRC-NAS National Research Council—National Academy of Sciences

nrcp non-reinforced concrete pipe; non-residential conditional purchase

NRCPC National Rural Crime Prevention Center (Ohio State University)

NRCR Northern Railway of Costa Rica (Ferrocarril del Norte de Costa Rica)

NR Crit Nuclear Rocket—Critical

nrcy not received yet

NRD National Range Division; Navy Recruiting Depot; Navy Recruiting District

NRDA National Research and Development Authority (Israel); Nevada Research and Development Area

NRDB Natural Rubber Development Board

NRDC National Research Development Corporation; National Resources Development Council; National Running Data Center; Natural Resources Defense Council

NRDC Natural Resources Defense Council

NRDL Naval Radiological Defense Laboratory

nrdo naval radio; Navy radio

NRDO National Research and Development Organization

NRDS Nuclear Rocket Development Station

N-reactor(s) nuclear reactor(s)

NREB Navy Reserve Evaluation Board

NREC National Resource Evaluation Center

NRECA National Rural Electric Cooperative Association

nrem (NREM) non-rapid eye movement

nrems (NREMS) non-rapid eye-movement sleep

nrem sleep non-rapid eye-movement (spindle) sleep

NRF Naval Reactor Facility; Naval Repair Facility

NRF Nouvelle Revue Française

NRFA National Retail Furniture Association

NRFC Navy Regional Finance Center

NRFL National Rugby Football League

nrg energy

NRG National Resurrection Group (Athenian rightist terrorists); Naval Research Group

NRGA National Rice Growers Association

NRh Northern Rhodesia

NRHA National Retail Hardware Association; National Roller Hockey Association

NRHC National Rural Housing Coalition

NRHS National Railway Historical Society

NRI National Radio Institute; Nomura Research Institute (Japan)

NRIAD National Register of Industrial Art Designers

NRIC National Registration and Identity Card

NRIMS National Research Institute for Mathematical Sciences

NRIS Natural Resource Information System

Nrk Newark

NRK Nikolai Rimsky-Korsakov

NRK Norsky Rikskringkasting (Royal Norwegian Broadcasting)

nrl normal rated load

NRL National Radiation Laboratory; National Registry for

Librarians; National Research Library; Naval Research Laboratory

NRLC National Right to Life Committee

NRLCA National Rural Letter Carriers' Association

NRLDA National Retail Lumber Dealers Association

NRLM National Research Laboratory of Meteorology

NRLSI National Reference Library of Science and Invention

nrm natural remanent magnetism; next to reading matter; non-routine maintenance; normal rabbit serum

NRM Naval Reserve Medal; Northern Roller Mills

NRMA National Reloading Manufacturers Association; National Retail Merchants Association; National Roads and Motorists Association

NRMC National Records Management Council; Naval Records Management Center; Naval Regional Medical Center

NRMCA National Ready-Mixed Concrete Association

NRMG Nederlands Rekenmachine Genootschap (Dutch-Netherlands Computer Society)

nrml normal

NRMM National Register of Microform Masters

NRN National Radio Network

nro nuestro (Spanish—our, m.)

NRO Narcotic Rehabilitation Office(r); National Reconnaissance Office; National Registration Office(r); Naval Research Objectives

NROO Naval Reactors Operations Office

NROTC Naval Reserve Officers Training Corps

nrp net rating points; no replacement part; normal rated power

NRP National Republican Party; National Research Poll

NRPA National Recreation and Park Association

NR & PA National Recreation and Park Association

NRPB National Research Planning Board

NRPC National Railroad Passenger Corporation

NRPRA Natural Rubber Producers' Research Association

NRR Northern Rhodesia Regi-

ment
NRRE Netherlands Radar Research Establishment
NRRL *Norsk Radio Relae Liga* (Norwegian Radio Relay League)
nrs normal rabbit serum; numbers
N rs Nepalese rupee(s)
NRS National Runaway Switchboard; Navy Records Society; Navy Relief Society; New Reading System; Noise-Reduction System
NRSA National Rural Studies Association
NRSCC National Registry System for Chemical Compounds
NRSFPS National Reporting System for Family Planning Services
nrt net register(ed) tonnage (tons); normal rated thrust; norm-referenced testing
NRT Tokyo-Narita (airport)
NRTA National Retired Teachers Association
NRTC Naval Reserve Training Center; Northrup Research and Technology Center
NRTI National Rehabilitation Training Institute
nrtor no risk till on rail
nrts not reparable this station
NRTS National Reactor Testing Station
nrtwb no risk until waterborne
nru nuclear reactor—universal
Nru Nauru
NR-U Nederlandsche Radio-Unie (Netherlands Union of Radio Broadcasters)
nrv net realisable value; non-return value
NRVC National Railway Utilization Corporation
Nrvkg *Nervenkrieg* (German—nerve warfare)
NRVN Navy of the Republic of Viet Nam
Nrw Norwegian
NRWC National Right to Work Committee
NRWLDF National Right to Work Legal Defense Foundation
nrwt non-resident withholding tax
nrx nuclear reactor, experimental
Nry Newry
NRYC New Rochelle Yacht Club
NR Yorks North Riding, Yorkshire

nrz c (**NRZ C**) non-return-to-zero change (data processing)
nrzi non-return-to-zero IBM
nrz m (**NRZ M**) non-return-to-zero mark recording (data processing)
ns nanosecond; near side; neuropsychiatric; new series; nickel steel; no sparring; noise suppressor; nonstandard; nonstop; not specified
ns (**NS**) neurosurgery; note series (synonymous with original or prime)
n/s neutrons per second; no service; not scheduled; not stocked; not sufficient
ns *nouvelle serie* (French—new series)
nS *neue Serie* (German—new series)
Ns nimbostratus; Nunes; Nuñez
NS National Society; National Special (screw threads); National Superannuation; Naval Shipyard; Naval Station; New Style; Nippon(ese) Standard; Norfolk Southern (Norfolk & Western and Southern railroads merged); North Sea; Nova Scotia; Nuclear Ship; Nuclear Submarine; Numismatic Society
N.S. New Style; Norfolk Southern (railroad)
NS *Nachschrift* (German—postscript); *Nasjonal* *Samling* (Norwegian—National Unification)—fascist collaborationists headed by Vidkun Quisling during World War II (*see* quis); *Notre Seigneur* (French —Our Lord); *Nuestro Señor* (Spanish—Our Lord)
N.S. *Nuestro Señor* (Spanish—Our Lord)
nsa (**NSA**) nonenyl succinic acid
NSA National Safety Association; National Secretaries Association; National Security Agency; National Service Acts; National Shellfisheries Association; National Sheriff's Association; National Shipping Authority; National Showmen's Association; National Silo Association; National Ski Association; National Slag Association; National Slate Association; National Society of Auctioneers; National Standards Association; National Students Association; Naval Stock Account;

Naval Supply Account; Neurological Society of America; Norwegian Seamen's Association; Nuclear Science Association
NSA *Nuclear Science Abstracts*
NSAA Norwegian Singers' Association of America
NSAC National Society for Autistic Children; Nova Scotia Agricultural College
NSACG Nuclear Strike Alternate Control Group
NSACS National Society for the Abolition of Cruel Sports
NSA/CSS National Security Agency/Central Security Service
NSAD National Society of Art Directors
NSADD National Society of Alcoholism and Drug Dependence
NSAE National Society of Art Education
NSAM National Security Agency Memorandum; Naval School of Aviation Medicine
NSAS National Smoke Abatement Society
NSASAB National Security Agency Scientific Advisory Board
NSB National Science Board; Nippon Short-wave Broadcasting
NSB *Norges Statsbaner* (Norwegian State Railway)
NSBA National School Boards Association; National Small Business Association; National Sugar Brokers Association
NSBC National Student Book Club
NSBF National Scientific Balloon Facility
NSBISS NATO Security Bureau/Industrial Security Section
NSBIU Nova Scotia Board of Insurance Underwriters
NSBMA National Small Business Men's Association
nsc non-service connected
NSC National Safety Council; National Science Council; National Security Council; National Shippers Council; National Standards Commission; National Steel Corporation; NATO Steering Committee; NATO Supply Center; NATO Supply Classification; Naval School Command; Naval Supply Center; New Sessions Cases; New Solidarity Club(s);

Newark State College
NSCA National Society for Clean Air; Nova Scotia College of Art
NSCAR National Society of Children of the American Revolution
NSCBS National Society for the Conservation of Bighorn Sheep
NSCC National Society for Crippled Children
NSCCA National Society for Crippled Children and Adults
nscd nonservice-connected disability
NSCD National Society of Colonial Dames
NSCDRF National Sickle Cell Disease Research Foundation
NSCID National Security Council Intelligence Directive
NSCR National Society for Cancer Relief
NSCs Network Switching Centers
NSCSP National Site Characterization and Selection Plan
NSCT North Staffordshire College of Technology
nsd no significant defect; no significant deviation; no significant difference; noise-suppression device; non-soapy detergent; normal spontaneous delivery
NSD Naval Supply Depot; Naval Support Data
NSDA National Soft Drink Association
NSDAP Nationalsozialistische Deutsche Arbeiterpartei (German National Socialist [Nazi] Workers Party)
NSDB National Science and Development Board
NSDC National School Development Council; National Serials Data Center; National Space Development Center
NSDD National Security Decision Directive
nsdf naval standard distillate fuel
NSDF National Sex and Drug Forum
NSDMs National Security Decision Memorandums
NSDP National Society of Dental Prosthetists
NSDS National Shut-in Day Society
NSE Nigerian Society of Engineers
NSEA Nebraska State Education Association

nsec nanosecond
n/sec neutrons per second
NSEC National Service Entertainments Council
NSEF National Student Educational Fund
NSEI Norwegian Society for Electronic Information
NSERI National Solar Energy Research Institute
NSES National Society of Electrotypers and Stereotypers
NSESG North Sea Environmental Study Group
nsf not sufficient funds
NSF National Sanitation Foundation; National Science Foundation; National Sex Forum; Naval Stock Fund; Navy Strike Fighter
NSF *Norges Standardiserings Forbund* (Norwegian Standards Institute)
NSFA National Science Faculty Association; Naval Support Force Antarctica (USN); New Settlers Federation of Australia
NSFGB National Ski Federation of Great Britain
nsftd normal spontaneous full-term delivery
nsg neurosecretory granules
NSG National Supply Group; Naval Security Group
NSGA National Sporting Goods Association
NSGC Naval Security Group Command
NSGD Near-Surface Geological Disposal
nsgn noise generator
NSGT Non-Self-Governing Territories; Non-Self-Governing Territory
nsh no stock on hand; not so hot
NSHA National Steeplechase and Hunt Association
NSHC North Sea Hydrographic Commission
NSHEB North of Scotland Hydro-Electric Board
N-ship(s) nuclear-powered ship(s)
nsi next sequential instruction; nonstandard item; nonstocked item; nuclear safety inspection; numeric signal insignia
NSI National Stock Exchange; Nuclear Safety Inspection
NSI *Norsk Senter for Informatikk* (Norwegian Information Center)
NSIA National Security Industrial Association

NSIBU Nova Scotia Board of Insurance Underwriters
NSIC National Small Industries Corporation; National Solar Information Center
NSID National Society of Interior Designers
n sing singular form of a noun
NSIO Nova Scotia Information Office
NSJC *Nuestro Señor Jesucristo* (Spanish—Our Lord Jesus Christ)
nsk not specified by kind
NSK *Nihon Shimbun Kyokai* (Japan Newspapers and Publishers Association); Nippon Seiko KK (bearings)
NSKK Nito Shosen Kabushiki Kaisha (Japanese steamship line)
nsl non-standard label; not stock listed
NSL National Science Library; National Standards Laboratory; Navy Stock List; Northrop Space Laboratory; Numidian Support League
NSLA National Society of Literature and the Arts
NSLF National Socialist Liberation Front (American-Nazi student organization)
NSLI National Service Life Insurance
NSLL National Savings and Loan League
NSLS National Science Library System
nsm new smoking material (wood-substitute tobacco); noise source meter; number of similar (negative) matches
NSM National Savings Movement; National Security Medal; National Selected Morticians; Naval School of Music; Nevada State Museum
ns/m² newton second per square meter
NSMA National Scale Men's Association
NSMC Naval Submarine Medical Center
NSMHC National Society for Mentally Handicapped Children
NSMI National Special Media Institutes
NSMM National Society of Metal Mechanics
NSMP National Society of Master Patternmakers; National Society of Mural Painters; Navy Support and Mobilization Plan

NSMPA National Screw Machine Products Association
NSMR National Society for Medical Research
NSMS National Sheet Music Society
NSMSES Naval Ship Missile Systems Engineering Station
NSN NATO Stock Number
NSNA National Student Nurses' Association
NSNC Nova Scotia Normal College
NSO Nashville Symphony Orchestra; National Symphony Orchestra; Naval Staff Officer; Navy Subsistence Office(r); Norfolk Symphony Orchestra; Northern Sinfonia Orchestra
NSOA National School Orchestra Association
NSOC Navy Satellite Operations Center
NSOEA National Stationery and Office Equipment Association
NSOSG North Sea Oceanographic Study Group
nsp non-standard part
n sp new species
NSP National Siting Plan; National Society of Professors; National Stuttering Project; Navy Standard Part; Nebraska State Patrol; Nebraska State Police; North Solomons Province; Northern States Power
NSPA National Scholastic Press Association; National Society of Public Accountants; National Soybean Processors Association; National Split Pea Association; National Standard Part Association; Naval Shore Patrol Administration
NSPB National Society for the Prevention of Blindness
NSPC National Security Planning Commission; National Society of Painters in Casein; Northern States Power Company
NSPCA National Society for the Prevention of Cruelty to Animals
NSPCC National Society for the Prevention of Cruelty to Children
NSPD Naval Shore Patrol Detachment
NSPE National Society of Professional Engineers
nspf not specifically provided for
NSPI National Society for Performance and Instruction; National Society for Programmed Instruction; National Swimming Pool Institute
NSPLO NATO Sidewinder Production and Logistics Organization
NSPO Navy Special Projects Office; Nuclear Systems Project Office
NSPRA National School of Public Relations Association
NSPS National Sweet Pea Society; New-Source Performance Standards
NSPSE National Society of Painters, Sculptors, and Engravers
NSPWA National Society of Patriotic Women of America
nsq neuroticism scale questionnaire
nsr natural sinus rhythm; normal sinus rhythm
NSR National Scientific Register; National Security Regulation(s); Norfolk Southern Railway
NSRA National Shoe Retailers Association; National Shorthand Reporters Association; National Street Rod Association; North-South Reconstruction advisors; Nuclear Safety Research Association
NSRB National Security Resources Board
NSRC Natural Science Research Council
NSRD National Standards Reference Data
NSRDC National Standards Reference Data System
NSRDF Naval Supply Research and Development Facility
NSRDL Naval Ship Research and Development Laboratory; Naval Supply Research and Development Facility
NSRDS National Standard Reference Data System
NSRF Nova Scotia Research Foundation
nsrp non-technical support real property
NSRP National States Rights Party
nsrpie non-technical support real property installed equipment
nsrt near-surface reference temperature
nss (NSS) normal saline solution
NSS National Sample Survey(or)(s); National Sculpture Society; National Secular Society (British); National Serigraph Society; National Slovak Society; National Speleological Society; National Stockpile Site; Newburgh and South Shore (railroad); Nitrogen Supply System
NSSA National Sanitary Supply Association; National Science Supervisors Association; National Skeet Shooting Association
NSSAR National Society of the Sons of the American Revolution
NSSC National Society for the Study of Communication
NSSCC National Space Surveillance Control Center
NSS Co Northern Steam Ship Company (New Zealand)
NSSE National Society for the Study of Education; National Study of School Evaluation
NSSEA National School Supply and Equipment Association
NSSF National Shooting Sports Foundation; Navy Submarine Support Facility
NSSFC National Severe Storm Forecast Center; National Society of Student Film Critics
NSSFNS National Scholarship Service and Fund for Negro Students
NSSGA Nicherin Shoshu Soka-Gakkai Academy (international peace society)
NSSL National Severe Storms Laboratory
NSSMA National Spanish-Speaking Management Association
NSSN National Standard Shipping Note
NSSOPAC Naval Ordnance System Support Pacific
NSSP National Severe Storms Project
NSSR New School for Social Research
nsss nuclear steam system supply
NSST Northwestern Syntax Screening Test
nsst(s) no-smoking seat(s)
NSSU National Sunday School Union
NSSWC National Severe Storm Warning Center
nst nonslip thread
NST National Security Team (National Security Affairs Adviser, Secretary of Defense, Secretary of State); Newfoundland Standard Time; Nigata

Sogo Television

NST New Straits Times

NSTA National School Transportation Association; National Science Teachers Association

NSTAP National Strategic Targeting and Attack Policy

NSTC Nebraska State Teachers College

nstd nested

NSTF Near-Surface Test Facility

NSTI Norwalk State Technical Institute

NSTIC Naval Scientific and Technical Information

NSTL National Strategic Target Line

NSTP Nuffield Science Teaching Project

NS Tripos Natural Science Tripos

NSTS National Sea Training Schools

N-study nuclear study

nsu nitrogen supply unit; nonspecific urethritis

NSU Neckarsulmer Fahrzeugwerke (NSU Motorenwerke)

N-sub(s) nuclear-powered submarine(s)

NSUC North Staffordshire University College

N-super nuclear-powered supercarrier (naval vessel)

nsurg neurosurgeon; neurosurgery; neurosurgical

nsv nuclear service vessel

n/sv nonautomatic self-verification

NSVP National School Volunteer Program; National Student Volunteer Program

NSW New South Wales

NSWC Naval Surface Weapons Center (USN); New South Wales Centre

NSWG Naval Special Warfare Group; New South Wales Government

NSWGR New South Wales Government Railways

NSWGTB New South Wales Government Tourist Bureau

NSWHC New South Wales Health Commission

NSWIER New South Wales Institute for Educational Research

NSWIT New South Wales Institute of Technology

NSWMSB New South Wales Maritime Services Board

NSWNA New South Wales Nurses Association

NSWP New South Wales Police

NSWPAG New South Wales Prisoners Action Group

NSWPP National Socialist White People's Party (formerly American Nazi Party)

NSWPTC New South Wales Public Transport Commission

NSWR New South Wales Reports

NSWRL New South Wales Rugby League

NSWRU New South Wales Rugby Union

NSWTA New South Wales Transport Association

NSWTF New South Wales Teachers Federation

NSY New Scotland Yard

NSYF Natural Science for Youth Foundation

nt narrower term; net terms; nit (unit of luminous intensity); no trace; nontight; normal temperature; not titled

n't not

n/t net tonnage; new terms

n & t nose and throat

nt Northern Telecom

n.t. nel testo (Italian—in the text)

Nt nitron

NT National Trust; New Territories (Hong Kong); New Testament; Northern Territory

NT National Times (of Australia); *Ny Testamente* (Dano-Norwegian—New Testament)

N.T. Novum Testamentum (Latin—New Testament)

nta net tangible assets; nitrilotriacetic (phosphate substitute for detergents); nuclear test aircraft (NTA)

NTA Narcotics Treatment Administration; National Tax Association; National Technical Association; National Tourist Association; National Travel Association; National Trust of Australia; National Tuberculosis Association; New Territories Administration; Northern Textile Association; Northern Trade Association

NTAA National Travelers Aid Association

NTAC Nederlandse Touring en Auto Club (Netherlands Touring and Auto Club)

NTAMS Northern Territory Aerial Medical Service

NTAs Nielsen Television Areas

NTATB Northwestern Truck Association and Tariff Bureau

ntavl not available

ntb non-tariff barrier(s); not to be

NTB National Theatre Board; National Tobacco Board

NTB Norsk Telegrambyra (Norwegian News Service)

ntba name(s) to be advised

NTBL Nuffield Talking Book Library (for the blind)

NtBuStnds National Bureau of Standards

ntc negative temperature coefficient

NTC National Teacher Corps; National Theatre Conference; National Training Council; National Travel Club; Naval Training Center

NTCA National Training Council of Australia; National Tribal Chairmen's Association; National Tuberculosis and Chest Association

NTCC Nimbus Technical Control Center

NTCCL Northern Territory Council for Civil Liberties

ntd non-tight door; noted

NT$ New Taiwan dollar

NTD National Theater of the Deaf

NTDA National Tire Distributors Association; National Trade Development Association; National Tyre Distributors Association

NTDC Naval Tactical Data System; Naval Technical Data System; Naval Training Device Center

NTDPMA National Tool, Die, and Precision Machining Association

NTDS Naval Tactical Data System; Naval Technical Data System

NTDSC Nondestructive Testing Data Support Center

nte not to exceed

nte norte (Spanish—north)

NTE National Teacher Examination

N-tec nuclear technology

NTEC Naval Training Electronics Center(s); Naval Training Equipment Center

ntep not to exceed price

ntepq not to exceed price quoted

N-terror(ism)(ist) nuclear terrorism; nuclear terrorist

N-test nuclear test(ing)

NTETA National Traction Engine and Traction Association

NTEU National Treasury Employees Union

NTF Narcotics Task Force; Navy Technological Forecast

NTFA National Track and Field Association

NTFP National Task Force on Prostitution

ntfy notify

ntg nontoxic goiter

NTGB North Thames Gas Board

NT Gk New Testament Greek

Nth Netherlands

NTH Norges Tekniske Hogskole (Norwegian Technical University, Trondheim)

Nth BHH North Broken Hill Holdings

Nth country next country of a series acquiring nuclear power

nthn northern

NTHP National Trust for Historic Preservation

N-threat nuclear threat

nti noise-transmission impairment

NTI National Theatre Institute; Nielsen Television Index (tv rating)

NTIA National Telecommunications and Information Administration

NTIAC Nondestructive Testing Information Analysis Center

NTIATA National Tax Institute of America Tax Association

NTIC Nondestructive Testing Information Center (Battelle)

NTID National Technical Institute for the Deaf

NTIS National Technical Information Service (U.S. Department of Commerce); Nippon Technical Information Service

NTISBDF National Technical Information Service Bibliographic Data File

NTISearch National Technical Information (on-line computer) Search Service

NTK Nippon Toshokan Kyokai (Japan Library Association)

ntl no time lost

NTL National Tennis League; National Training Laboratories

NTLC National Tax Limitation Committee

NTLF National Taxpayers Legal Fund

NTLS National Truck Leasing System

ntm net ton mile; non-tariff measure(s)

Ntm Nottingham

NTMS National Topographic Map Series; Northern Territory Medical Service

NTNP Natchez Trace National Parkway

nto not taken out; not tried on

nto neto (Spanish—net)

NTO National Tenants Organization; National Theatre Organisation (South Africa)

ntp normal temperature and pressure; no title page

NTP National Transportation Policy

NTPC National Technical Processing Center; Navy Training Publications Center

ntpl nut plate

ntr noise temperature ratio; non-typing reperforator

NTR National Tape Repository; Northern Test Range

Ntra Sra Nuestra Señora (Spanish—Our Lady)

NTRB Northern Territory Reserve Board (Australia)

NTRDA National Tuberculosis and Respiratory Disease Association

NTRL Naval Training Research Laboratory

NTRS National Therapeutic Recreation Society

nts not to scale

nts (NTS) navigation(al) technology satellite

Nts Nantes

NTS National Technical School(s); National Traffic System; Naval Transportation System; Nederlandse Televisie Stichting (Netherlands Television Foundation); Nevada Test Site

NTS Narodnyi Trudovoy Soyuz (Russian—National Labor Union)—anti-communist Russian exiles

NTSA National Traffic Safety Agency

NT & SA National Trust and Savings Association

NTSB National Transportation Safety Board

NTSC National Television Standards Committee; National Television System Committee; North Texas State College

NTSK Nordiska Tele-Satelit Kommitten (Nordic Commit-

tee for Satellite Telecommunications)

NTSSO Nevada Test Site Safety Office

NTSWG National Training School for Women and Girls

NTT Nippon Telegraph and Telephone

NTTC National Tank Truck Carriers

NTTS Northern Territory Teaching Service

NTT & TTI National Truck Tank and Trailer Tank Institute

ntu nuts to you

NTU National Taiwan University; National Taxpayers Union; Navy Toxicology Unit

NTUC National Trades Union Congress

ntv nerve tissue vaccine

NTV Nippon Television

ntwistdg notwithstanding

nt wt net weight

NTX Navy Teletype Exchange

nty not this year

nt yt not yet

NTZ Neutral Zone

Ntzrm Nutzraum (German—cubic capacity)

nu name unknown; new; nose up; nuclear; number unobtainable

Nu Nusselt number

NU *Naciones Unidas* (Spanish—United Nations); National Union; *Nations Unies* (French—United Nations); Naval Unit; Niagara University; Northeastern University; Northern Union; Northwestern University; Norwich University

NU Nahdatul Ulama (Indonesian—Muslim Scholars Party)

NUAAW National Union of Agricultural and Allied Workers

NUAUS National Union of Australian University Students

NUAW National Union of Agricultural Workers

NUB National Union of Blastfurnacemen; National Unity Board

NUBE National Union of Bank Employees

nube(s) nubile(s)

NUBSO National Union of Boot and Shoe Operatives

nuc not under command; nuclear; nucleated; nucleus

NUC National University Con-

sortium; National Urban Co-
alition; Naval Undersea Cen-
ter
NUC National Union Catalog
nu-car prep new-car prepara-
tion
Nuc.E. Nuclear Engineer
NUCEA National University
Continuing Education Asso-
ciation
nucex nuclear exercise
nuc(l) nuclear; nucleus
Nucl Data Nuclear Data
Nuclear Falcon Hughes air-to-
air missile also called Super
Falcon
Nuclear-Power Admiral Hyman
George Rickover, USN
nuclex nuclear loadout exercise
Nucl Fusion Nuclear Fusion
*Nucl Instrum Nuclear Instru-
ments*
*Nucl Instrum Methods Nuclear
Instruments and Methods*
Nucl Phys Nuclear Physics
*Nucl Sci Eng Nuclear Science
and Engineering*
*NUCMC National Union Cata-
log of Manuscript Collections*
nuco numerical code; numerical
coding
NUCO National Union of Co-
operative Officials
NUCOM National Union Cata-
log of Monographs
nuc phy nuclear physics
nucpwrd nuclear powered
Nuc Reg Com Nuclear Regulato-
ry Commission
NUCS National Union of Chris-
tian Schools
NUCSTAT Nuclear Opera-
tional Status Report
NUCUS National Union of
Conservative and Unionist
Associations
NUCW National Union of
Commercial Workers
nud nudism; nudist
nud nudnick (Yiddish—nui-
sance, pest)
NUDBTW National Union of
Dyers, Bleachers, and Textile
Workers
NUDET Nuclear Detonation
Report
NUDETS Nuclear Detonation,
Detection, and Reporting Sys-
tem
nudies nude films; nude maga-
zines; nude shows
NUE Nuremberg, Germany
(airport)
NUEA National University Ex-
tension Association
Nuestra Familia (Spanish—Our

Family)—Hispanic prison
gang
*Nuestra Señora de los Dolores de
las Vegas* (Spanish—Our
Lady of the Sorrows of the
Lowlands)—former and
somewhat prophetic name of
Las Vegas, Nevada
Nueva Escocia (Spanish—Nova
Scotia)
Nueva España (Spanish—New
Spain)—Spanish colonial
name for Mexico
Nueva Gales del Sur (Spanish—
New South Wales)—New
South Wales
Nueva Granada (Spanish—New
Granada)—Spanish colonial
province comprising Colom-
bia, Ecuador, Panama, and
Venezuela
Nueva Hampshire (Spanish—
New Hampshire)
Nueva Inglaterra (Spanish—
New England)
Nueva Jersey (Spanish—New
Jersey)
Nueva Orleáns (Spanish—New
Orleans)
Nueva York (Spanish—New
York)
Nueva Zelanda (Spanish—New
Zealand)
Nuevo Brunswick (Spanish—
New Brunswick)
Nuevo México (Spanish—New
Mexico)
NUF National Urban Fellows
NUFCOR Nuclear Fuels Cor-
poration
NUFCW National Union of
Funeral and Cemetery Work-
ers
Nuff Nuffield College, Oxford
NUFLAT National Union of
Footwear, Leather, and Allied
Trades
nufp not used for production
'nuf said enough said
NUFTIC Nuclear Fuels Tech-
nology Information Center
NUFTO National Union of
Furniture Trade Operatives
nug nuggar (cargo boat used on
the Nile)
NUGMW National Union of
General and Municipal Work-
ers
NUHS New Utrecht High
School
NUHW National Union of Ho-
siery Workers
NUI National University of Ire-
land (Ollscoil na h-Eireann);
Norwegian Underwater Insti-
tute

NUIC National Urban Indian
Council
Nuits Nuits d'éte (French—
Summer Nights)—song cycle
by Berlioz including Absence,
Villanelle, Le spectre de la
rose, Sur les lagunes, Au cime-
tière, L'Île inconnue
NUIW National Union of Insurance Workers
NUJ National Union of Journalists
Nuk (Greenlandic Eskimo—
Point)—formerly called Godthaab (Good Hope) by the
Danes and still the capital on
the pointed peninsula on the
southwest coast of Greenland
nuke nuclear (slang)
nuke leak nuclear radioactive
leak
nukes nuclear explosives; nuclear power plants
nul no upper limit
nul (NUL) null character (data
processing)
NUL National Union for Liberation; National Urban League;
Northwestern University Library
null null idle
Nulla Nullarbor Plain of southern South Australia and Western Australia
nullies nullifiers
NULWAT National Union of
Leather Workers and Allied
Trades
num number; numbered; numbering; numeracy (*see* numcy);
numeral(s); numeration(s);
numerical; numerologist; nu-
merology
num numero(s) [Portuguese or
Spanish number(s)]
Num The Fourth Book of
Moses, called Numbers
Num Numbers
NUM National Union of Mine-
workers; New Ulster Move-
ment
NUMAS National Multifactor
Assessment System
numb. numbered
**Number-One Host of the Jersey
Coast** Atlantic City, New Jersey
numcy numeracy (ability to
count)
NUMEC Nuclear Materials and
Equipment Corporation
numer numeral; numerative
numer order numerical order
Numidia Roman name for Al-
geria
numis numismatics

numism numismatic(s); numismatist

num order numerical order

nuna not used on next assembly

Nuoli Finnish depth-charge and mine-laying patrol boat armed with 20mm and 40mm guns

NUOS Naval Underwater Ordnance Station

Nuova Galles del Sud (Italian—New South Wales)

Nuova Zelanda (Italian—New Zealand)

Nuovo York (Italian—New York)

NUP Negro Universities Press

NUPAC Nuclear Packaging Inc

NUPBPW National Union of Printing, Bookbinding, and Paper Workers

NUPE National Union of Public Employees

NUPGE National Union of Provincial Government Employees

NUPI Norsk Utenrikspolitisk Institutt (Norwegian Foreign Policy Institute)

nuplex nuclear-powered complex (of manufacturers)

NUPSA National Union of Pharmaceutical Students of Australia

NUPT National Union of Press Telegraphists

NUPW National Union of Planning Workers; National Union of Plantation Workers

NUR National Union of Railwaymen

NURA National Union of Ratepayers' Associations

NURC National Union of Retail Confectioners

NURDA National Urban and Regional Development Authority

NURE National Uranium Resource Evaluation (ERDA program)

Nuremberg English for Nürnberg

Nuremberga (Spanish—Nuremberg)

Nürnberg (German—Nuremberg)

Nursery Song Variations on a Nursery Song by Ernst von Dohnanyi

NURT National Union of Retail Tobacconists

nus nuclear upper stage

NUS National Union of Students; National University of Singapore; Nuclear Utility

Service(s)

nusar nuclear sweep and radar

NUSAS National Union of South African Students

NUSC Naval Underwater Systems Center

NUSEC National Union of Societies for Equal Citizenship

NUSL Navy Underwater Sound Laboratory

NUSMWCHDE National Union of Sheet Metal Workers, Coppersmiths, Heating and Domestic Engineers

NUSRL Navy Underwater Sound Reference Laboratory

NUSS National Union of School Students; National Union of Small Shopkeepers

nusum numerical summary

Nu T Newcastle-upon-Tyne

NUT National Union of Teachers (Great Britain)

NUTAT Nordisk Union for Alkoholfri Trafic (Nordic Union for Alcohol-free Traffic)

NUTAW National Union of Textile and Allied Workers

nu-tec nuclear detection (radiation monitoring device)

NUTGW National Union of Tailors and Garment Workers

NUTI Northwestern University Traffic Institute

NUTIS Numerical and Textual Information System

Nutmegs Connecticuters

Nutmeg State Connecticut's nickname

NUTN National Union of Trained Nurses

nutr nutrition

nuts. (NUTS) nuclear-utilization theories

NUU New University of Ulster

Nuuk technically correct name for Greenland's capital—Gothab

nuv nuvaerende (Dano-Norwegian—present)

NUVB National Union of Vehicle Builders

NUWA National Unemployed Workers' Association

NUWAX Nuclear Weapon Accident Exercise (from simulated crash of a missile to simulated cleanup completion)

NUWC Naval Undersea Warfare Center

NUWT National Union of Women Teachers

NUWW National Union of Women Workers

Nuyorican(s) New York Puerto Rican(s)

nv naked vision; needle valve; new version; number of variables

nv (NV) nuclear vitrification

n-v non-vaccinated; non-veteran; non-voting

n/v nuclear vessel

n & v nausea and vomiting

nv. novicius (Latin—new, recent)

NV Nevada Operations Office; Nord-Viscount

NV Naamloze Vernootschap (Dutch—corporation); *Naviera Vascongada* (Basque Navigation Company); *Norske Veritas* (Norwegian Register of Shipping)

nva near visual acuity

nva nueva (Spanish—new)

NVA North Vietnamese Army

NVAiO Norske Videnskaps-Akademi i Oslo (Norwegian Academy of Science and Letters in Oslo)

NVATA National Vocational Agricultural Teachers Association

NVB National Volunteer Brigade

NVB Nederlandse Vereniging van Bedrijfsarchivarissen (Dutch—Netherlands Association of Business Archivists); *Nederlandse Vereniging van Bibliothekarissen* (Dutch —Netherlands Library Association)

NVBF Nordisk Viedenskabeligt Bibliotekarieforbund (Nordic Federation of Research Librarians)

nvc non-verbal communication

NVC National Violence Commission

nvd night-viewing device; night-vision device

NVDA National Volunteer Defense Army

nvebw non-vacuum electron beam welding

NVF National Volunteer Force

NVFC National Vulcanized Fibre Company

nvg null voltage generator

NVGA National Vocabulary Guidance Association; National Vocational Guidance Association

nvh noise, vibration, hardness (problems)

Nvk Narvik

NVL Night Vision Laboratory

nvm non-volatile matter

NVMA National Veterinary Medical Association

NVNS Naamloze Vernootschap Nederlandsche Spoorwagen (Netherlands Railway Corporation)

nvo non-vessel operating

NVO Nevada Operations Office; Northern Variety Orchestra

nvocc (NVOCC) non-vessel operating common carrier

NVOCC New Version Ocean Container Control; New Version Overseas Container Control; Non-Volatile Ocean Container Control

NVOILA National Voluntary Organization for Independent Living for the Aging

NVOO Nevada Operations Office

nvp natural vegetable powder (powdered psyllium seed and dextrose laxative)

NVPA National Visual Presentation Association

NVPO Nuclear Vehicle Projects Office (NASA)

nvr no voltage release

NVRS National Vegetable Research Station

nvs neutron velocity selector

NVS Night Vision System

NVT National Veld Trust

NVTS National Vocational Training Service

NVV Nederlands Verbond van Vakverenigingen (Dutch—Netherlands Trade Union Federation)

nw nanowatt; net worth; no wind, number of weeks

n/w net weight

Nw New (postal abbreviation sometimes confused with NW —Northwest)—when in doubt, spell it out

NW Chicago & North Western Railway; Noah Webster; Norfolk & Western (railroad); Northern Wings Ltd; North Wales; Northwest; Northwest Airlines

N & W Norfolk & Western (railroad)

NW noordwest (Dutch—northwest); Nordwesten (German—northwest)

NW1, NW2, etc. Northwest One, Northwest 2, etc. (London postal zones)

NWA National Wrestling Alliance; Northwest Airlines; Northwest(ern) Australia

NWAA National Wheelchair Athletic Association

nwab necks with anybody

NWAC National Womens Advisory Council

NWAH & ACA National Warm Air Heating and Air Conditioning Association

N-war nuclear war(fare)

NWASCO Nation Water and Soil Conservation Organization

N-waste nuclear (radioactive) waste

nwb non-weight bearing

NWB National Westminster Bank

NWBA National Wheelchair Basketball Association

nwc nuclear war capability

Nwc Newcastle-upon-Tyne

NWC National Wages Council; National War College; National Water Commission; National Writers Club; Naval War College; Naval Weapons Center

NWCC Northern Wyoming Community College

NWCCL Naval Weapons Center—Corona Laboratories

NWCF New Waste Calcining Facility

NWCS NATO-wide Communications System

NWCTU National Woman's Christian Temperance Union

NWD New World Dictionary

nwdc navigation weapon-delivery computer

NWDR Nordwestdeutscher Rundfunk (North-West German Broadcasting System)

N-weapon(ry) nuclear weapon(ry)

N-weapon(s) nuclear weapon(s)

NWEB Northwestern Electricity Board (UK)

NWEF National Women's Education Fund; Naval Weapons Evaluation Facility; Naval Weapons Evaluation Force

NWES New World Exploration Society

NWF National Welfare Fund; National Wildlife Federation

NWF National War Formulary

Nwfld Newfoundland

NWFP North-West Frontier Province

nwg national wire gauge

NWG National Welfare Growth; Neighborhood Watch Group

NWGA National Wheat Growers Association; National Wool Growers Association

nwh normal working hours

NWI Netherlands West Indies

NWIDA North West Industrial Development Association

NWIP Naval Warfare Instruction Publication

NWIRP Naval Weapons Industrial Reserve Plant

NWJA National Wholesale Jewelers Association

nwl natural wavelength

NWL Naval Weapons Laboratory

NWLB National War Labor Board

NWLC National Women's Law Center

NWLEE Northwest Law Enforcement Equipment

NWLF New World Liberation Front (terrorists)

NWly northwesterly

nwm nuclear waste materials

nw/m net words per minute

NWM Nuclear Waste Management

NWMC Northwest Michigan College

NWMCC Nuclear Waste Materials Characterization Center

N/Wmn Night Watchman

NWMPA North Wales Master Printers' Alliance

NWMS Northwest Medical Service

Nw Ned Nieuw Nederland (Dutch—New Netherlands)

NWNT North Wales Naturalists' Trust

NWO Nuclear Weapons Office(r)

nwoc new woman on campus

NWOO NATO Wartime Oil Organization

n-word nonce word (word coined for the nonce or the occasion)

NWORG North Western Operational Research Group

NWP Naval Weapons Plant; North West Provinces

NWPAG NATO Wartime Preliminary Analysis Group

NWPC National Women's Political Caucus

NWPF New Waste Processing Facility

NWPFC Northwest Pacific Fisheries Commission

Nwprt News Newport News

NWPSC Northwestern Public Service Company

NWQAO Naval Weapons Quality Assurance Office

NWQI National Water Quality Inventory (EPA)

NWQSS National Water Quality Surveillance System (EPA)

nwr next word request

NWR National Waste Repository; National Welfare Rights; National Wildlife Refuge; National Wildlife Reserve; Nuclear Weapon Report

NWRB National Waste Repository Basalt

NWRC National Weather Records Center; Naval War Research Center (USN)

NWREL Northwest Regional Educational Laboratory

NWRF Naval Weather Research Facility

NWRLF New World Radical Liberation Front

NWRO National Welfare Rights Organization

NWRS National Wildlife Refuge System

nws normal water surface; nosewheel steering

NWS National Weather Service; Naval Weapons Station; Nimbus Weather Satellite; Norfolk & Western Southern (railways)

NWSA National Welding Supply Association; National Woman Suffrage Association

NWSC National Weather Satellite Center; Naval Weather Service Command

NWSCA National Water and Soil Conservation Authority

NWSCO National Water and Soil Conservation Organization

NWSF Nuclear Weapons Storage Facility (USA)

NWSO Naval Weapons Services Office

NWSS Nuclear Weapons Support Section (USA)

NWSY Naval Weapons Station—Yorktown, Va

nwt net weight; nonwatertight

NWT Northwest Territories

nwtb new water-tube boiler(s)

NWTB Northwestern Tariff Bureau

nwtd nonwatertight door

nwtdb new water-tube donkey boiler(s)

NWTEC National Wool Textile Export Corporation

NWTS National Waste Terminal Storage; Naval Weapons Test Station

NWTSR-1 NWTS Repository No. 1 (high-level waste in a dome)

NWTSR-2 NWTS Repository No. 2 (spent fuel in bedded salt)

NWTS-RSP NWTS Repository Sealing Program

nwu nosewheel up

NWU National Workers Union; National Writers Union; Nebraska Wesleyan University

NWUS Northwestern United States

NWVP Nuclear Waste Vitrification Program

NWWA National Water Well Association

nwy newly

nx nonexpendable

NX Notice to Marines

NXD Non-Executive Director

NXDO Nike-X Development Office (USA)

NXMIS Nike-X Management Information Office

nx mo next month

NXPM Nike-X Project Manager

NXPO Nike-X Project Office

nxr non-crossing rule

NXSO Nike-X Support Office

nxt next

nxt ssn next season

nx wk next week

nx yr next year

ny new year; no year; nylon

Ny Niles; Nylan

NY New York; New York Airways (2-letter code); New Yorker; North Yorkshire

NY Neuyork (German—New York); *New Yorker* (magazine); *Nieuw York* (Dutch—New York); *Nova Iorque* or *Nova York* (Portuguese—New York); *Nueva York* (Spanish—New York)

Nya Nyasaland

NYA National Youth Administration; Neighborhood Youth Association; New York Aquarium

NYAB National Youth Advisory Board

NYAC New York Athletic Club

Nyack acronymic place-name of a Hudson River town built around the summer headquarters of the New York Athletic Club (NYAC) with the letter k added to give it an Indian look

NYADS New York Air Defense Sector

NYAM New York Academy of Medicine

NYANA New York Association for New Americans

NYAO New York Assay Office

NYAP New York Assembly Program

Nyas Nyasaland

NYAS New York Academy of Science

Nyasaland old name for Malawi

NYATI New York Agricultural and Technical Institute

NYBFU New York Board of Fire Underwriters

NYBG New York Botanical Garden

NYBSBC New York Bureau of State Building Codes

NYC National Yacht Club; Neighborhood Youth Corps; Newburgh Yacht Club; New York Central (railroad); New York City; New York Coliseum

NYCA National Youth Council of Australia; New York City Affiliate (of the National Council on Alcoholism)

NYCB New York City Ballet

NYCC New York Cultural Center

NYCCC New York City Community College

NYCCCC New York City's Citizens Crime Commission

NYCCIW New York City Correctional Institution for Women

NYCDC New York City Department of Correction

NYCE New York Cocoa Exchange; New York College of Education; New York Cotton Exchange

NYCERS New York City Employees Retirement System

NYCHA New York City Housing Authority; New York Clearing House Association

NY-CHI New York—Chicago

NYCJG Nikka Yuko Centennial Japanese Garden (Lethbridge, Alberta)

NYCMA New York City Metropolitan Area

NYCMD New York Contract Management District

NYCMEO New York City Medical Examiner's Office

NYCMSL New York County Medical Society Library

NYCNHA New York City Nursing Home Association

NYCOC New York City Opera Company

NY Col New York Coliseum

NYCPB New York Consumer Protection Board

NYCPD New York City Police Department

NYCPM New York City Police Museum

NYCS New York Choral Society

NYCSCE New York Coffee, Sugar, and Cocoa Exchange

NYCSE New York Coffee and Sugar Exchange

NYC & ST L New York, Chicago & St Louis (Nickel Plate Line)

NYCT New York Community Trust

NYCTA New York City Transit Authority

NYCTN New York Cotton Exchange

NYCWRU New York Cooperative Wildlife Research Unit

nyd not yet dead; not yet diagnosed

NYDCC New York Drama Critics Circle

NYDMC New York Downstate Medical Center

NYDR New York Dock Railway

Nye Aneurin

NYF New York Foundation

NYFCC New York Film Critics Circle

NYFDM New York Fire Department Museum

NYFE New York Futures Exchange

NYFIRO New York Fire Insurance Rating Organization

NYFUO New York Federation of Urban Organizations

NYGASP New York Gilbert and Sullivan Players

NYGC New York Governor's Conference

NYGS New York Graphic Society

NYHA New York Heart Association (classification)

NYH–CMC New York Hospital —Cornell Medical Center

NYHD New York House of Detention

NY Hist Soc New York Historical Society

NYHS New York Historical Society

NYI New York Institute (of Photography)

NYIAS New York Institute of the Aerospace Sciences

NYIBS New York International Bible Society

NYIE New York Insurance Exchange

NYIH New York Institute for

the Humanities

NYIT New York Institute of Technology

N Yk New York

NYK Nippon Yusen Kaisha Line

NYKU Nippon Yusen Kaisha (container) Unit

nyl nylon

NYLA New York Library Association

NY-LAX New York—Los Angeles

NY & LB New York & Long Branch (railroad)

nylfin nylon finish

NYLS National Yacht Listing Service; New York Law School

NYLTI National Youth Leadership Training Institute

nym *nymon* (Greek—name) — as in antonym, homonym, pseudonym, synonym, etc.

NYMC New York Maritime College

NYME New York Mercantile Exchange

NY Met New York City Metropolitan Correctional Center

NY-MIA New York—Miami

nympho nymphomania; nymphomaniac; nymphomaniacal

N Y N H & H New York, New Haven and Hartford (railroad)

NY-NO New York—New Orleans

nyo not yet out

NYO National Youth Orchestra

NYOC New York Opera Company

NYOGB National Youth Orchestra of Great Britain

NYOL New York Opera Library

N Yorks North Yorkshire

NYOSL New York Oceans Science Laboratory

NYOTBC New York Off-Track Betting Corporation

NYOW National Youth Orchestra of Wales

NYO & W New York, Ontario and Western (railroad)

nyp not yet published

NYP Neighborhood Youth Program; New York Philharmonic (orchestra)

NYPA New York Port Authority

NYPD New York Police Department

NYPDis New York Procurement District (U.S. Army)

NYPE New York Port of Embarkation; New York Produce Exchange

NYPFO New York Procurement Field Office (USAF)

NYPHR New York Physicians for Human Rights

NYPIRG New York Public Interest Research Group

NYPL New York Public Library

NYPLA New York Patent Law Association

NYPM New York Pro Musica

NYPs Neighborhood Youth Programs

NYPS New York Psychiatric Society; New York Publishing Society

NYPSS New York Philharmonic-Symphony Society

NYPUM National Youth Program Using Minibikes

Nyq Nyquist (data-processing time or rate)

nyr not yet returned; nuclear yield requirement

NYR National Young Republicans

NYRA National Yacht Racing Association; New York Racing Association

NYRB *New York Review of Books*

NYRF National Young Republican Federation

NYRG New York Rubber Group

NYRM New York Reformatory for Men

NYRPG New York Rights and Permission Group

NYRs National Young Republicans

NYRW New York Reformatory for Women (Westfield Farm)

NYS New York Shavians; New York State

NYSA New York Shipping Association

NYSAA New York State Aviation Association

NYSAC New York State Athletic Commission

NYSAIS New York State Association of Independent Schools

NYSAJC New York State Association of Junior Colleges

NY-SAN New York—San Diego

NYSASBO New York State Association of School Business Officials

NYSASDA New York State Atomic and Space Development Authority

NYSAVC New York State Audio-Visual Council

NYSBA New York State Bar Association

NYSBB New York State Banking Board

NYSBC New York State Barge Canal (modern extension of Erie Canal)

NYSC New York Shipbuilding Corporation

NYSCC New York State Crime Commission

NYSCCJ New York State Coalition for Criminal Justice

NY Sch Indus Rel New York State School of Industrial Relations (Cornell University)

NYSCSDA New York State Council of School District Administrators

NYSDCS New York State Department of Correctional Services

NYSE New York Stock Exchange

NYSERDA New York State Energy Research and Development Authority

NYSES New York State Employment Service

NYSF New York Shakespeare Festival

NY-SFO New York—San Francisco

NYSILL New York State Inter-Library Loan (network)

NYSL New York Society Library

NYSM New York State Museum

NYSMM New York State Maritime Museum (New York City)

NYSNACC New York State Narcotic Addiction Control Commission

NYSNC New York State Narcotics Commission

NYSNI New York State Nutrition Institute

NYSO New York String Orchestra

NYSP New York School of Printing; New York State Police

NYSPA New York State Power Authority

NYSPGA New York State Personnel and Guidance Association

NYSPI New York State Psychiatric Institute

NYSSILR New York State School of Industrial and Labor Relations

NYSSMA New York State School Music Association

NYSTA New York State Teachers Association; New York State Thruway Authority

NYSUT New York State United Teachers

NYS & W New York, Susquehanna and Western (railroad)

NYT *The New York Times*

NY Thru New York Thruway

NY Times Bk R *New York Times Book Review*

NYTNS New York Times News Service

NY-TOR New York—Toronto

NYTU New York Theological Union

NYU New York underworld (used in law-enforcement circles); New York University

NYUL New York University Library

NYUMC New York University Medical Center; New York Upstate Medical Center

NYUP New York University Press

NYUSM New York University School of Medicine

NYWASH Navy Yard, Washington

NYYC New York Yacht Club

NYZP New York Zoological Park

NYZS New York Zoological Society

Nz Nuñez

NZ New Zealand; New Zealand dollar; New Zealand National Airways (2-letter coding); Novaya Zemlya

N-Z Nike-Zeus

NZ *Nueva Zelandia* (Spanish—New Zealand)

N-Z *Nouvelle-Zélande* (French—New Zealand)

NZAA New Zealand Amateur Athletic Association; New Zealand Antique Arms Association; New Zealand Auto Association

NZAB New Zealand Association of Bacteriologists

NZABC New Zealand Audit Bureau of Circulation

NZABM New Zealand Anglican Board of Missions

NZAC New Zealand Accommodation Council; New Zealand Alpine Club

NZACA New Zealand Amateur Cycling Association

NZACAU New Zealand Athletics, Cycling, and Axemens Union

NZACE New Zealand Association for Community Education

NZACU New Zealand Auto Cycle Union

NZADS New Zealand Association for Disabled Skiers

NZAEC New Zealand Atomic Energy Committee

NZAEI New Zealand Agricultural Engineering Institute

NZAF New Zealand Authors Fund; New Zealand Aviation Federation

NZAHBS New Zealand Arab Horse Breeders Society

NZAHPER New Zealand Association of Health, Physical Education, and Recreation

NZALT New Zealand Association of Language Teachers

NZAPA New Zealand Airline Pilots Association

NZARA New Zealand Amateur Rowing Association

NZARE New Zealand Association for Research on Education

NZARP New Zealand Antarctic Research Programme

NZART New Zealand Amateur Radio Transmitters Association

NZAS New Zealand Aluminium Smelters; New Zealand Antarctic Society; New Zealand Arthritis Society; New Zealand Association of Scientists

NZASA New Zealand Amateur Swimming Association; New Zealand Asian Studies Association

NZASC New Zealand Administrative Staff College; New Zealand Army Service Corps; New Zealand Association of Soil-Conservators

NZASF New Zealand Association of Small Farmers

NZASW New Zealand Association of Social Workers

NZATD New Zealand Association of Training and Development

NZAWA New Zealand Air Women's Association

NZb New Zealand black (mice hybrids)

NZB New Zealand Ballet

NZBA New Zealand Bankers Association; New Zealand Bowling Association

NZBC New Zealand Ballet Company; New Zealand Book

Council; New Zealand Broadcasting Corporation

NZBCSO New Zealand Broadcasting Corporation Symphony Orchestra

NZBF New Zealand Basketball Federation

NZBIE New Zealand Bureau of Importers and Exporters

NZBS New Zealand Broadcasting Service

NZBTO New Zealand Book Trade Organisation

NZC New Zealand Certificate

NZCAR New Zealand Civil Aviation Regulations

NZCAS New Zealand Clean Air Society

NZCC New Zealand Chamber of Commerce; New Zealand Cricket Council

NZCD New Zealand Certificate in Draughting

NZCDC New Zealand Cooperative Dairy Company

NZCE New Zealand Certificate in Engineering

NZCEA New Zealand Combined Educational Associations

NZCER New Zealand Council for Educational Research

NZCF New Zealand Cadet Forces; New Zealand Cycling Federation

NZCG New Zealand Chemists Guild

NZCGF New Zealand Coast Guard Federation

NZCGP New Zealand College of General Practitioners

NZCGS New Zealand Standard Classification of all Goods and Services

NZCH New Zealand Cement Holdings

NZCLA New Zealand Childrens Literature Association

NZCLS New Zealand Certificate of Land Surveying

NZCMA New Zealand Cable Makers Association; New Zealand Concrete Masonry Association

NZCMF New Zealand Coal Merchants Federation

NZCO New Zealand Concert Orchestra

NZCOSS New Zealand Council of Social Services

NZCRA New Zealand Coal Research Association; New Zealand Concrete Research Association

NZCRS New Zealand Council for Recreation and Sports

NZCS New Zealand Certificate in Science; New Zealand Certificate in Statistics; New Zealand Computer Society

NZCSS New Zealand Council of Social Services

NZCTF New Zealand Cycle Traders Federation

NZCTOA New Zealand Container Terminal Operators Association

NZCUL New Zealand Credit Union League

NZCWI New Zealand Country Women's Institutes

NZd New Zealand dollar

NZ$ New Zealand dollar(s)

NZD New Zealand Division; New Zealand Dollar

NZDA New Zealand Dairy Association; New Zealand Dental Association; New Zealand Department of Agriculture; New Zealand Dietetic Association

NZDB New Zealand Dairy Board

NZDC New Zealand Dental Corps

NZDCMBA New Zealand Dairy Confectionary and Mixed Biscuits Association

NZDCS New Zealand Department of Census and Statistics

NZDE New Zealand Department of Education

NZDFA New Zealand Deer Farmers Association

NZDLS New Zealand Department of Lands and Survey

NZDRI New Zealand Dairy Research Institute

NZDS New Zealand Drama School

NZDSIR New Zealand Department of Scientific and Industrial Research

NZDT New Zealand Daylight Time

NZDVA New Zealand Dunkirk Veterans Association

NZDXRA New Zealand DX Radio Association

NZE New Zealand Engineers

NZEA New Zealand Esperanto Association

NZEAS New Zealand East Asia Service; New Zealand Educational Administration Society

NZECF New Zealand Electrical Contractors Federation

NZED New Zealand Electricity Department

NZedder(s) [En-zed-der(s)]—New Zealander(s)

NZEF New Zealand Employees Federation; New Zealand Expeditionary Force

NZEI New Zealand Educational Institute; New Zealand Electronics Institute

NZer New Zealander

NZERF New Zealand Engine Research Foundation; New Zealand Equine Research Foundation

NZES New Zealand Ecological Society

NZESA New Zealand Education Standards Association; New Zealand European Shipping Association

nzf near zero field

NZFA New Zealand Football Association

NZFB New Zealand Foundation for the Blind

NZFCA New Zealand Farmers Cooperative Association; New Zealand Freezing Companies Association

NZFCDC New Zealand Farmers Cooperative Distributing Company

NZFCMA New Zealand Ferro-Cement Marine Association

NZFF New Zealand Farmers Fertiliser (company); New Zealand Federated Farmers; New Zealand Fruitgrowers Federation

NZFHA New Zealand Finance Houses Association

NZFKTA New Zealand Free Kindergarten Teachers Association

NZFKU New Zealand Free Kindergarten Union

NZFL New Zealand Federation of Labor

NZFMA New Zealand Ferrocement Marine Association

NZFMC New Zealand Federation of Master Cleaners

NZFMRA New Zealand Fertiliser Manufacturers Research Association

NZFP New Zealand Forest Products

NZFPA New Zealand Family Planning Association

NZFRI New Zealand Forest Research Institute

NZFS New Zealand Film Service; New Zealand Forest Service

NZFUW New Zealand Federation of University Women

NZFWA New Zealand Farm Workers Association

nzg near zero gravity

NZG New Zealand Government

NZG New Zealand Gazette

NZGA New Zealand Gliding Association; New Zealand Grassslands Association

NZGenS New Zealand Genetical Society

NZGR New Zealand Government Railways

NZGS New Zealand Geographical Society; New Zealand Geological Society; New Zealand Geological Survey

NZGTB New Zealand Government Tourist Bureau

NZGTC New Zealand Government Travel Commissioner

NZGTO New Zealand Government Tourist Office

NZH New Zealand Helicopters

NZH New Zealand Herald

NZHA New Zealand Hockey Association

NZHC New Zealand High Commission

NZHF New Zealand Heart Foundation

NZHGA New Zealand Hang-Gliding Association

NZHI New Zealand Horological Institute

NZHPT New Zealand Historic Places Trust

NZHS New Zealand Horse Society

NZI New Zealand Insulators; New Zealand Insurance

NZIA New Zealand Institute of Architects; New Zealand Irrigation Association

NZIAS New Zealand Institute of Agricultural Science

NZIC New Zealand Institute of Chemistry; New Zealand Intelligence Council

NZICFM New Zealand Institute of Credit and Financial Management

NZICM New Zealand Institute of Credit Management

NZID New Zealand Institute of Draughtsmen

NZIDA New Zealand Invention Development Authority

NZIDC New Zealand Industrial Design Council

NZIE New Zealand Institute of Engineers

NZIELEC New Zealand Institute of Electricians

NZIEPC New Zealand Indonesia Economic Promotion Council

NZIER New Zealand Institute of Economic Research

NZIET New Zealand Institute of Engineering Technicians

NZIF New Zealand Institute of Foresters

NZIFST New Zealand Institute of Food Science and Technology

NZIG New Zealand Institute of Gases

NZIH New Zealand Institute of Horticulture

NZIHVE New Zealand Institute of Heating and Ventilation Engineers

NZIIA New Zealand Institute of International Affairs

NZIIS New Zealand Institute of Industrial Safety

NZILA New Zealand Institute of Landscape Architects

NZIM New Zealand Institute of Management; New Zealand Institute of Mining

NZIME New Zealand Institute of Mechanical Engineers

NZIMP New Zealand Institute of Medical Photography

NZIP New Zealand Institute of Printing

NZIPA New Zealand Institute of Public Administration

NZIPM New Zealand Institute of Personnel Management

NZIPRA New Zealand Institute of Parks and Recreation Administration

NZIPS New Zealand Institute of Purchasing and Supply

NZIRE New Zealand Institute of Refrigeration Engineers

NZIS New Zealand Information Service; New Zealand Institute of Surveyors

NZISM New Zealand Institute of Safety Management

NZIT New Zealand Institute of Travel

NZIUW New Zealand Industrial Union of Workers

NZIW New Zealand Institute of Welding

NZJPA New Zealand Japan Parliamentary Association

NZJU New Zealand Journalists Union

NZK Noord Zee Kanaal (Dutch —North Sea Canal)—linking the Atlantic with Amsterdam

NZKC New Zealand Kennel Club

NZKVA New Zealand Korean Veterans Association

NZL New Zealand Line

NZLA New Zealand Legal Association; New Zealand Library Association; New Zealand

Loggers Association

NZLCC New Zealand Litter Control Council

NZLF New Zealand Literary Fund

NZLIRA New Zealand Logging Industry Research Association

NZLL New Zealand Light Leathers

NZLP New Zealand Labour Party

NZLR New Zealand Law Reports

NZLS New Zealand Land Securities; New Zealand Law Society; New Zealand Library School; New Zealand Library Service

NZLTA New Zealand Lawn Tennis Association

NZMA New Zealand Medical Association; New Zealand Modelling Association; New Zealand Motel Association; New Zealand Motorcycle Association

NZMAF New Zealand Ministry of Agriculture and Fisheries

NZMB New Zealand Meat Board

NZMBF New Zealand Master Builders Federation

NZMC New Zealand Maori Council; New Zealand Medical Corps

NZMCA New Zealand Motor Caravan Association

NZMF New Zealand Manufacturers Federation; New Zealand Military Forces; New Zealand Motel Federation; New Zealand Music Federation

NZMFA New Zealand Master Floorcovering Association

NZMGA New Zealand Mountain Guides Association

NZMGC New Zealand Marriage Guidance Council

NZMJ New Zealand Medical Journal

NZMOT New Zealand Ministry of Transport

NZMPH New Zealand Meat Packing House

NZMRC New Zealand Medical Research Council

NZMS New Zealand Mapping Service; New Zealand Meteorological Service

NZMSC New Zealand Mountain Safety Council

NZMSS New Zealand Marine Sciences Society

NZMTCB New Zealand Motor

Trade Certification Board

NZMTMA New Zealand Methods Time Measurement Association

NZMWA New Zealand Maori Wardens Association

NZM & WB New Zealand Meat and Wool Board

NZMWU New Zealand Meat Workers Union

NZNA New Zealand Nurserymens Association; New Zealand Nurses Association

NZNAC New Zealand National Airways Corporation

NZNCC New Zealand Nature Conservation Council

NZNCOR New Zealand National Committee on Oceanic Research

NZNF New Zealand Neurological Foundation

NZNFU New Zealand National Film Unit

NZNPA New Zealand Newspaper Proprietors Association

NZNTA New Zealand National Travel Association

NZOA New Zealand Optometrical Association

NZOC New Zealand Opera Company

NZOCGA New Zealand Olympic and Commonwealth Games Association

NZOI New Zealand Oceanographic Institute

NZ£ New Zealand pound

NZP National Zoological Park; New Zealand Pacific; New Zealand Players; New Zealand Police

NZPA New Zealand Police Association; New Zealand Ports Authority; New Zealand Press Association

NZPARS New Zealand Prisoners Aid and Rehabilitation Society

NZPB New Zealand Pony Breeders; New Zealand Potato Board

NZPBA New Zealand Power Boat Association; New Zealand Publishers' Association

NZPBR New Zealand Pony Breeders Register

NZPBS New Zealand Pony Breeders Society

NZPC New Zealand Peace Council; New Zealand Planning Council; New Zealand Pony Club; New Zealand Press Council; New Zealand Print Council

NZPCA New Zealand Pony

Club Association; New Zealand Portland Cement Association

NZPCI New Zealand Prestressed Concrete Institute

NZPEA New Zealand Port Employers Association

NZPGMF New Zealand Post Graduate Medical Federation

NZPM New Zealand Paper Mills

NZPMS New Zealand Plumbers Merchants Society

NZPO New Zealand Post Office

NZPOA New Zealand Purchasing Officers Association

NZPPA New Zealand Professional Photographers Association

NZPPTA New Zealand Post Primary Teachers Association

NZPS New Zealand Park Service; New Zealand Police Service

NZPSA New Zealand Political Studies Association; New Zealand Public Service Association

NZPsS New Zealand Psychological Society

NZPTA New Zealand Parent-Teachers Association

NZPTO New Zealand Public Trust Office

NZQHA New Zealand Quarter-Horse Association

NZR New Zealand Railways

NZRC New Zealand Red Cross

NZRDXL New Zealand Radio DX League

NZRFU New Zealand Rugby Football Union

NZRL New Zealand Rugby League

NZRLS New Zealand Railway and Locomotive Society

NZRMA New Zealand Ready-Mix Concrete Association

NZRMTA New Zealand Retail Motor Trade Association

NZRN New Zealand Registered Nurse

NZRNC New Zealand Radio Navigation Chart

NZRRS New Zealand Railways Road Services

NZRTA New Zealand Road Transport Association

NZS New Zealand Standards Institute

NZSA New Zealand Statistical Association

NZSB New Zealand Speech Board; New Zealand Survey Board

NZSBG New Zealand South British Group

NZSC New Zealand Securities Commission; New Zealand Settlers Club; New Zealand Squid Company; New Zealand Staff Corps; New Zealand Standards Council

NZSCA New Zealand Sheep and Cattlemens Association; New Zealand Society of Customs Agents; New Zealand Soil Conservation Association

NZSCC New Zealand Standard Country Code

NZSCES New Zealand Society of Certified Executive Secretaries

NZSCHA New Zealand Society of Custom House Agents

NZSCI New Zealand Standard Classification of Imports

NZS Co New Zealand Shipping Company

NZSCO New Zealand Standard Classification of Occupations

NZSCS New Zealand Senior Citizens Service

NZSDA New Zealand Sign and Display Association; New Zealand Stamp Dealers Association

NZSDST New Zealand Society of Dairy Science and Technology

NZSE New Zealand Stock Exchange

NZ Sea Fron New Zealand Sea Frontier (NZSEAFRON)

nzsg non-zero-sum game

NZSIA New Zealand Security Industry Association

NZSIC New Zealand Standard Industrial Classification

NZSID New Zealand Society of Industrial Designers

NZSL New Zealand Steel Limited

NZSL New Zealand Shipping Line

NZSLO New Zealand Scientific Liaison Office

NZSNA New Zealand Society of National Accounts

NZSO New Zealand Symphony Orchestra

NZSRA New Zealand Surf Riders Association

NZSS New Zealand Social Security; New Zealand Speleological Society; New Zealand Standard Specification(s)

NZSSS New Zealand Society of Soil Science

NZST New Zealand Standard

Time

NZSWWS New Zealand Spinning, Weaving, and Woolcrafts Society

nzt non-zero test(ing)

NZTC New Zealand Trade Commission

NZTCA New Zealand Teachers College Association

NZTCB New Zealand Trade Certification Board

NZTCI New Zealand Technical College Institute; New Zealand Technical Correspondence Institute

NZTF New Zealand Territorial Force(s); New Zealand Theatre Federation

NZUA New Zealand Underwater Association; New Zealand Underwriters Association

NZUE New Zealand Unit Express

NZV New Zealand Victoria (insurance)

NZVA New Zealand Veterinary Association

NZw New Zealand white (mice hybrids)

NZWA New Zealand Woolbuyers Association

NZWB New Zealand Wool Board

NZWEA New Zealand Workers Educational Association

NZW & PCS New Zealand Weed and Pest Control Society

NZWRAC New Zealand Womens Royal Army Corps

NZWS New Zealand Wildlife Service

NZWSA New Zealand Water Ski Association

NZWSC New Zealand Water Safety Council

NZWTA New Zealand Wool Testing Authority

NZWWC New Zealand Working Womens Council

NZWWF New Zealand Waterside Workers Federation

NZYF New Zealand Yachting Federation

NZYHA New Zealand Youth Hostels Association

NZZ *Neue Züricher Zeitung* (New Zurich Newspaper)

O

o observer; occasional; occidental; octavo; ohm; oil; oiliness; Olivetti; opium; orange; oriental; overcast

o' (Gaelic contraction—of, on)

'o (Gaelic contraction—also)

ü (Japanese—big, great, large); *omkring* (Dano-Norwegian—about or around)

o. *oculus* (Latin—eye); *oeste* (Portuguese or Spanish—west); *oost* (Dutch—east); *op* (Dano-Norwegian or Dutch—up); *os* (Latin—bone); *ouest* (French—west); *ovest* (Italian—west)

o/ order (Spanish—order)

ö (Dano-Norwegian or Swedish—island); *öster* (Swedish—east)

ø *øst* (Dano-Norwegian—east)

O absence of perception of sound (symbol); New Orleans Mint (coin symbol), observation; Observer; ocean; Oceanic Steamship Company; October; office; Officer; officer; Ohio; Olsen Line; Omaha; Ontario; order; Oregon; ortho; Oscar—code for letter O; oxygen; unofficial abbreviation for Ohio

O' (Gaelic prefix meaning of)

Ø shortage (symbol)

O center of the earth (symbol); observer (symbol); *oeste* (Portuguese or Spanish—west); *oost* (Dutch—east); *optimus* (Latin—best possible); *Ost* (German—east); *ouest* (French—west); *ovest* (Italian—west)

Ö *Österreich* (German—Eastern Empire)—Austria; *Östre* (Swedish—East); *Öy* (Swedish—island)

Ø *Øst* (Dano-Norwegian—East); *Øy* (Dano—Norwegian—island)

O1 organized seagoing naval reserve

O-1 Cessna Bird Dog liaison aircraft

O2 organized naval reserve aviation

O-2 Cessna liaison-utility aircraft

O_2 oxygen

O_2cap oxygen capacity

O_2sat oxygen saturation

O^3 ozone

oa occiput anterior; old age; on account; on or about; osteoarthritis; overall

o/a on account; on or about

oa *och andra* (Swedish—and others)

o/A oro Americano (Spanish—American gold, American money)

OA Obligation Authority; Office of Applications; Office Automation; Olympic Airways; Operations Analysis; Osborne Association; overall noise level (symbol); Overeaters Anonymous; Overtime Authorization

O/A Office of Administration (EPA)

O of A Office of Administration

oaa (OAA) oxalo-acetic acid

OaA Office of Aging

OAA Office of Air Accidents; Old Age Assistance; Older Americans Act; Organisation des Nations Unies pour l'Alimentation et l'Agriculture (United Nations Organization for Food and Agriculture); Organization of Athletic Administrators; Orient Airlines Association

OAAA Outdoor Advertising Association of America

OAAB Objective-Analytic Anxiety Battery

oaad ovarian ascorbic acid depletion

OAAI Office of Air Accidents Investigation

OAAU Organization of Afro-American Unity

OAB Old Age Benefits

OABA Outdoor Amusement Business Association

OABETA Office Appliance and Business Equipment Trades Association

oac on approved credit; outer approach channel

OAC Oceanic Affairs Committee; Operating Agency Code; Ordnance Ammunition Command; Oregon Agriculture College

OACA Ontario Arms Collectors Association (of Beamsville near Toronto)

OACI Organisation de l'Aviation Civile Internationale (French—International Civil Aviation Organization); *Organización de Aviación Civil Internacional* (Spanish—International Civil Aviation Organization)

OACJC Oklahoma Association of Community and Junior Colleges

OACLD Ontario Association for Children with Learning Disabilities

OACT Ohio Association of

Classroom Teachers
oad overall depth
OAD ordered, adjudged, and decreed
OADAP Office of Alcoholism and Drug Abuse Prevention
oadc oleic acid, albumin, dextrose, catalase
OAE Orzeck Aphasia Evaluation
OAEC Organization for Asian Economic Cooperation
OAESA Ohio Association of Elementary School Administrators
oaf open-air factor; overhaul attrition factor
OAFB Orfutt Air Force Base (Nebraska)
OAFIE Office of Armed Forces Information and Education
OAG Office of the Adjutant General; Office of the Attorney General
OAG Official Airline Guide
OAGB Osteopathic Association of Great Britain
oah overall height
OAH Organization of American Historians
OAHE Ohio Association for Higher Education
OAI Office of Aeronautical Intelligence; Opera America, Incorporated; Osborne Association, Incorporated
OAICU Oklahoma Association of Independent Colleges and Universities
oaide operational assistance and instructive data equipment
oais opinion, attitude, and interest survey
oak. oakum
Oak truncation of Oakland, Oak Park, Oak Ridge, etc.
OAK Oakland, California (Metropolitan International Airport)
Oak City Raleigh, North Carolina
Oakhill Virginia home of James Monroe
Oakie migratory farm worker or sharecropper from Oklahoma
Oak Sym Oakland Symphony
oal overall length
OAL Office of Administrative Law; Ordnance Aerophysics Laboratory
OALJ Office of Administrative Law Judges
OALMA Orthopedic Appliance and Limb Manufacturers Association
o. alt. hor. omnibus alternis hor-

is (Latin—every other hour)
OAM Office of Aviation Medicine; Order of Australia Medal
OAMA Ogden Air Material Area
oamce optical alignment, monitoring, and calibration equipment
oame orbital attitude and maneuvering electronics
OAMS Orbital Attitude and Maneuvering System
ÖAMTC Österreichischer Automobil-Motorrad und Touring Club (German—Austrian Automobile Motoring and Touring Club)
OANA Organization of Asian News Agencies
o-and-o one-and-only
oao off and on
OAO Orbiting Astronomical Observatory
oap ophthalmic artery pressure
OAP Office of Aircraft Production; Old-Age Pension
OAPC Office of the Alien Property Custodian
OAPEC Organization of Arab Petroleum Exporting Countries
OAPEP Organisation Arabe des Pays Exportateurs de Petrole (French—Arab Organization of Petroleum Exporting Nations)
OAPs Old-Age Pensioners
oapwl overall power watt level
O Ar Old Arabic
OAR Offender Aid and Restoration; Office of Aerospace Research; Order of Augustinian Recollects; Organized Air Reserve
OARAC Office of Aerospace Research Automatic Computer
OARP Old Age Revolving Pensions (Townsend Plan)
OARS Offender's Aid Rehabilitation Services
OART Office of Advanced Research and Technology (NASA)
oas old-age security; on active service
OAS Office of Advanced Studies; Office of Appalachian Studies; Old Age Security; Ordinary Ammunition Storage; Organization of American States
OAS Organisation de l'Armée Secrete (French—Organization of the Secret Army)—

General Salan's secret counter-revolutionary group attempting to crush Algerian independence
OASBO Ohio Association of School Business Officials; Oregon Association of School Business Officials
OASD Office of the Assistant Secretary of Defense
OASD-AE Office Assistant Secretary of Defense, Application Engineering
OASDHI Old-Age, Survivors, Disability, and Health Insurance Social Security
OASDI Old Age, Survivors, and Disability Insurance
OASD-R & D Office Assistant Secretary of Defense, Research and Development
OASD-S & L Office Assistant Secretary of Defense, Supply and Logistics
OASD-T Office of the Assistant Secretary of Defense—Telecommunications
OASI Old-Age and Survivor's Insurance
OASIS Office of Academic Support Instructional Services; Office for Academic Support in Service; Ohio (chapters) of the American Society for Information Science; Overseas Access Service for Information Systems
Oasis City Roswell, New Mexico
oasp organic acid-soluble phosphorus
oaspl overall sound pressure level
OASSO Operational Applications of Satellite Snowcover Observations (NASA)
oat. outside air temperature
OAT Office of Advanced Technology (USAF)
OATC Oceanic Air Traffic Control
OATS Office of Air Transportation Security; Old-Age Theatre Society (Great Britain)
oau (OAU) optical alignment unit
OAU Organization for African Unity
OAVTME Office of Adult, Vocational, Technical, and Manpower Education
oaw old abandoned well; overall width
OAWM Office of Air and Water Measurement (NBS)
Oax Oaxaca

OAYR Outstanding Airman of the Year Ribbon

ob obligation; oboe; oboes; obsolete; obstetric; obstetrical; obstetrician; obstetrics; old boy; on board; operational base (OB); ordered back; out of bounds; outboard buffer; outbound; output buffer; outward bound; over bought; overboard (vent line)

ob (OB) outside broadcast (TV from a remote location)

o/b opening of books; outboard (engine)

ob (Latin prefix—against, in front of, toward)—obstruction

ob. obit (Latin—died)

o B off Broadway

o-B off-Broadway; off-Broadway theater

o B ohne Befund (German—without findings)

Ob object art (art accented with real objects, *e.g.*, a real watch chain dangling between two pockets of a man's vest in a painting); 3500-mile Siberian river entering Arctic Ocean at Gulf of Ob

Ob Obadiah; Ober (Germany—higher, upper)

OB Ocean Beach; Old Bailey; Operating Base; Operational Base; Order of Battle; Ordnance Battalion; Ordnance Board; Ormond Beach; Ox Box (corporation)

O.B. obstetrical; obstetrician; obstetrics

O'B O'Brien; O'Bryan

OB *Oranjeboom* (Dutch—orange tree)—Amsterdam-brewed beer

oba optical bleaching agent

OBAA Oil-Burning Apparatus Association

Obad The Book of Obadiah

OBAN *Operação Bandeirantes* (Portuguese—Operation Bandeirantes)—Brazilian Intelligence Service

OBAR Ohio Bar Automated Research

OBAWS On-Board Aircraft Weighing System

obb obbligato

OBB battleship, old (3-letter naval symbol)

ÖBB Österreichische Bundesbahnen (Austrian Federal Railways)

obc old brutal con(vict); on-board checkout; outer back cover

OBC Osaka Broadcasting Corporation; Outboard Boating Club

obce on-board checkout equipment

obd omnibearing distance

ob d'am oboe d'amore

OBDC Otago Business Development Centre

ob dk observation deck

obdt obedient

obe open both ends; operating basis earthquake; other bugger's efforts

OBE Office of Business Economics; Officer of the British Empire; Order of the British Empire

O.B.E. Officer of the Order of the British Empire

Obediah Skinflint (pseudonym —Joel Chandler Harris)

OBEMLA Office of Bilingual Education and Minority Languages Affairs

Oberfalz (German—Upper Palatinate)—on the Danube around Regensburg where the von Geists originated

Oberon British class of diesel submarines

OBES Office of Basic Engineering Sciences

OBEV *Oxford Book of English Verse*

obf operating basis flood

obfusc obfuscated

obg oldie but goodie (musical hits)

Ob-G Obstetrician-Gynaecologist

obgn obligation

ob{gu} *obrigado* (Portuguese—thank you)

ob-gyn obstetrical-gynecological; obstetrician-gynecologist

obi omnibearing indicator

Obie off-Broadway; off-Broadway theater; Off-Broadway Theater Award

OBIPS Optical Band Imager and Photometer System

obit obituary

obits obituaries

obj object; objective

object. objective(ly)

Objectivist Poet William Carlos Williams

objn objection

obl obligation; oblique; oblong; obloquy

ob/l ocean bill of lading

OBL Ocean Beach Library; Ohio Barge Line; Order of the Brave Librarian

oblg obligate; obligation

OBLI Oxford and Birmingham Light Infantry

oblig obligation(s); obligatory

obln obligation

obm oil-base mud (oil well)

obo oil/bulk freight/ore (multipurpose seagoing carrier)

oboe. offshore buoy-observing equipment

ob ph oblique photograph(y)

OBRA Overseas Broadcasting Representatives' Association

obre *octubre* (Spanish—October)

Ob River City Novosibirsk, Siberia

obro *outubro* (Portuguese—October)

obs observation; observe; observed; observer; obsolete; obstacle; obstetrical; obstetrician; obstetrics; ocean bottom suspension (oil well); omnibearing selector

obs (OBS) organic brain syndrome

obs oboes

Obs *The Observer*

OBS Oita Broadcasting Service; Organization Breakdown Structure

obs alt observed altitude

obsc obscure(d)

obsd observed

observ observation; observatory

obsn observation

obsol obsolescent

ob & sol objection and solution

ob. s.p. *obiit sine prole* (Latin—died without issue)

OBSP *Old Bailey Sessions Papers*

obss ocean bottom scanning sonar

obs spot observation spot

obst obstacle; obstruction

obstet obstetrical; obstetrician; obstetrics

obstl obstruction light(s)

obstr obstruction

obsv observation; observatory; observer

ob syn organic brain syndrome

o b syn organic brain syndrome

obt obedient

obt. obiit (Latin—he died)

OBT Overseas Branch Transfer

OBTA Oak Bark Tanners' Association

obtd obtained

obts offender-based transaction statistics

OBU One Big Union; Operative Bootmakers Union

ÖBUB *Öffentliche Bibliothek der Universität Basel* (German

—Public Library of the Basel University)—founded in 1460

O Bul Old Bulgarian

obv obverse; obvious; ocean boarding vessel; octane blending value

obvy obviously

obw observation window

oc ocean; odor control; on camera; on center; open charter; oral contraceptive

oc (OC) obstetrical conjugate; on camera (tv performer heard and seen); open cup

o-c open-circuit

o'c o'clock (of the clock)

o/c organized crime; overcharge

o & c onset and course (disease)

oc (Latin prefix—against)—occlusion

o.c. opere citato (Latin—in the work cited)

Oc Ocean

OC Oakland City; Oakwood College; Oberlin College; Oblate College; Occidental College; Odessa College; Office of Censorship; Office of the Commissioner; Office Consultation; Officer Candidate; Officer in Charge; Officer Commanding; Ohio College; Okolona College; Olivet College; Olympic College; Optometric Corporation; Order in Council; Oriel College; Orlando College; Otero College; Overseas Chinese; Overseas Commands

O.C. Officer Commanding

O of C Order of the Coif

OC Opéra-Comique (French—Comic Opera)—Paris

O.C. Organo Corale (Latin—choir organ)

OC-5 Organizing Committee for a Fifth Estate

oca ocarina (flutelike clay instrument nicknamed "sweet potato")

OCA Oceanic Control Area; Office of Computing Activities (NASA); Office of Consumer Affairs (ombudsman function of the U.S. Postal Service); Ohio College Association; Oil Company of Australia; Ontario College of Art; Oregon Corrections Association

OCA Organización de las Cooperativas de America (Spanish —Organization of American Cooperatives)

OCAA Oklahoma City-Ada-Atoka (railroad); Organization of Central American Armies

OCAC Office of Chief of Air Corps

OCADS Oklahoma City Air Defense Sector

OCAFF Office Chief of Army Field Forces

ocal on-line cryptanalytic aid language

OCAL Overseas Containers of Australia Limited

OCAM Organisation Commune Africaine et Malgache [Organization of the African and Malagasy Community (of former French colonies)]

OCAMA Oklahoma City Air Materiel Area

OCAS Organization of Central American States

O Cat Old Catalan

OCAT Optometric College Aptitude Test; Optometry College Admissions Test

OCAW Oil, Chemical and Atomic Workers (union)

ocb oil circuit breaker

OCB Officer Career Brief (DoD résumé)

OCBC Overseas Chinese Banking Corporation

oc b/l ocean bill of lading

occ occupation

o & cc order and change control

Occ occulting (light)

OCC Office of the Comptroller of the Currency; Oklahoma Crime Commission; Olney Community College; Onondaga Community College; Orange Coast College

OCCA Oil and Colour Chemists Association

occas occasional(ly)

OCCC Orange County Community College; Organized Crime-Control Commission (California)

Oc C Cm O Office of the Chief Chemical Officer

occd occupied

OCCDC Oregon Coastal Conservation and Development Commission

OCC-E Office of the Chief of Communications—Electronics (USA)

OCCF Oklahoma City Community Foundation

Occident(al) West (Western Europe, Western European, Western Hemisphere); Western(er)—anyone or anything

Western in preceding sense of West European or from the Western Hemisphere as opposed to the East or Orient

occip occipital; occiput

OCCIS Operational Command and Control Intelligence System (USA)

OCCL Ontario Community College Librarians

OCCM Office of Commercial Communications Management

OCCO Office of the Chief Chemical Officer

OCCP Outside Communications Cable Plant

OCCS Office of Computer and Communications Systems (U.S. National Library of Medicine)

OCCSA Ohio Correctional and Court Services Association

occ th occupational therapy

occup occupation(al)

ocd obsessive compulsive disorder; on-line communications driver; operational capability date; optical character definition; ovarian cholesterol depletion

oc/d other cargo damage

OCD Office of Child Development; Office of Civil Defense; Office of Collection and Dissemination (CIA)

OCDA Ordnance Corps Detroit Arsenal

OCDE Organización Común Africana, Malgache y Mauriciana (Spanish—African Common Organization including Madagascar and Mauritius); *Organización de Cooperación y Desarrollo Económico* (Spanish—Organization of Cooperation and Economic Development)

OCDM Office of Civil and Defense Mobilization

OCDQ Organizational Climate Description Questionnaire

OCDR Office of Collateral Development Responsibility

OCDS Overseas College of Defense Studies (UK)

O/Cdt Officer-Cadet

oce operational control equipment

OCE Office of Career Education; Office of the Chief of Engineers; Ontario College of Education

OC & E Oregon, California, and Eastern (railroad)

Ocean Ocean Transport and

Trading Limited; The Ocean (Antarctic, Arctic, Atlantic, Indian, Pacific)

OCEAN Oceanographic Coordination Evaluation Analysis Network

OCEANAV Oceanographer of the U.S. Navy

oceaneer(ing) ocean engineer (ing)

Oceania islands of central and southern Pacific

Ocean Inst Oceanografiska Institute (Oceanographic Institute in Göteborg, Sweden)

oceano oceanologic(al)(ly); oceanologist; oceanology

oceanog oceanography

Océano Índico (Portuguese or Spanish—Indian Ocean)

Ocean Personified Oceanus (Roman); Okeanos (Greek)

Ocean State Rhode Island

OCEE Organisation de Coopération Économique Européene (European Economic Cooperation Organization)

OCEL Optical Coating Evaluation Laboratory

OCEL *Oxford Companion to English Literature*

O Celt Old Celtic

ocf originally cultured formulation

OCF Officiating Chaplain to the Forces; Ossining Correctional Facility (Sing Sing); Owens-Corning Fiberglass

OC of F Office of the Chief of Finance

ocg omnicardiogram

ÖCG *Österreichische Computer Gesellschaft* (German—Austrian Computer Society)

och ochre

OCHAMPUS Office for the Civilian Health and Medical Program of the Uniformed Services

OCHS Old Colony Historical Society

oci organization conflict of interest

OCI Office of Computer Information (U.S. Department of Commerce); Office of the Coordinator of Information; Office of Current Intelligence (CIA); Operational Checkout Instruction

OCIB Organized Crime Intelligence Bureau

OCID Organized Crime Intelligence Division (LAPD)

OCIMF Oil Companies International Marine Forum

OCIS Organized Crime Information System (FBI)

OCJA Oklahoma Criminal Justice Association

ocl operator control language; optical communications link(age)

OCL Ocean Cargo Line; Overseas Container Line; Overseas Containers Limited

OCL/ACT Overseas Container Lines and Associated Container Transport

OCLAE *Organización Continental Latino-Americana de Estudiantes* (Spanish—Continental Organization of Latin American Students)

OCLC Ohio College Library Center; On-Line Computer Library Center

OCLI Optical Coating Laboratory, Inc

o'clock of the clock

OCLU Overseas Container Line (container) Unit

ocm oil content monitor

OCM *Oxford Companion to Music*

OCMA Oil Companies' Material Association

OCMH Office of the Chief of Military History

OCMMINST Office of Civilian Manpower Management Instruction (USN)

OCMS Optional Calling Measured Service (telephone)

OCN Operation Completion Notice

ocnl occasional(ly)

OCNM Oregon Caves National Monument (limestone caverns near Medford, Oregon)

oco open-close-open

OCO Office of the Chief of Ordnance; Ontario College of Ophthalmology; San José, Costa Rica (El Coco Airport)

OCOA *Organismo Coordinador de Operaciones Antisubversivas* (Spanish—Coordinating Organism of Antisubversive Operations)—Uruguay's secret service

o'coat overcoat

OCOM *Oficina Central de Organización y Metodos* (Spanish—Central Office of Organization and Methods)

OComS Office of Community Services

OConUS outside continental limits of the United States

OCORA *Office de Coopération Radiophonique* (French—Office of Radiophonic Cooperation)—French overseas radio help for former colonies

O Corn Old Cornish

ocp output control pulses; overland common points

OCP Office of the Chief of Protocol (US Department of State); Office of Consumer Protection; Office of Cultural Presentations

OCP *Oficina Central de Personal* (Spanish—Central Personnel Office)

OCPD Officer-in-Charge Police District

OCPL Oklahoma City Public Library

ocr optical character reader; optical character recognition

ocr **(OCR)** optical character reader

OCR Office of Civil Rights; Office of Civilian Requirements; Office of Coal Research; Office of Collateral Responsibility; Office of Coordinating Responsibility; Office of the County Recorder; Organization Change Request; Organization for the Collaboration of Railways

OCRA *Organisation Clandestine de la Révolution Algerienne* (French—Secret Organization of the Algerian Revolution)

OCRD Office of the Chief of Research and Development

ocre optical character recognition equipment

OCRE Organizations Concerned about Rural Education

ocrit optical character-recognizing intelligent terminal

OCRS Organized Crime and Racketeering Section (Dept of Justice)

OCRSF Organized Crime and Racketeering Strike Force (U.S. Dept of Justice)

ocs obstacle clearance surface; on company service; outer continental shelf

oc's obscene (telephone) callers; obscene (telephone) calls

OCS Office of Civilian Supply; Office of Commercial Services; Office of Contact Settlement; Officer Candidate School; Officers' Chief Steward; Outer Continental Shelf; Overseas Civil Servants; Overseas Courier Service

OCS' Overseas Civil Servants

(members of the British Overseas Civil Service)

OCS *Organe de Controle des Stupéfiants* (French—Narcotic Drug Control Organization)

OC of SA Office, Chief of Staff, Army

OCSE Office of Child Support Enforcement

ocsf office contents special form (insurance)

OCSIGO Office of the Chief Signal Officer

ocsn occasion

ocsnl occasional

ocsnly occasionally

OCSPC Outer Continental Shelf Policy Committee (California)

ocst overcast

oct octagon; octal; octane; octave; octet

Oct Octans (constellation); October

OCT Office of the Chief of Transportation

octe optical component testing and evaluation

octe *octubre* (Spanish—October)

Octember October and November

Octn Octanus (constellation)

October October Railway (Leningrad-Moscow); October Revolution (Bolshevik insurrection of October 1917)

October Revolution Shostakovich's Symphony No. 2

oct. pars *octava pars* (Latin—eighth part)

OCTU Officer-Cadet Training Unit

octup. *octuplus* (Latin—eightfold)

octv open-circuit television

ocu operational conversion unit

OCUA Ontario Council on University Affairs

OCUC Oxford and Cambridge Universities' Club

OCUFA Ontario Confederation of University Faculty Associations

ocul. *oculis* (Latin—to the eyes)

oculent. *oculentum* (Latin—eye ointment)

ocv open-circuit voltage

OCVs Overseas Cooperation Volunteers

OCZ Ocean Container (terminal) Zebrugge

OCZM Office of Coastal Zone Management (NOAA)

od olive-drab; on demand; optical density; optic(al) disc; organization(al) development;

original design; outside diameter; outside dimension; oven dried; overdose; overdrive

o/d on demand; overdraft

o & d origin and destination

od och dylika (Swedish—and the like)

o.d. *oculus dexter* (Latin—right eye)

Od Odyssey

OD Aerocondor (Aerovias Condor de Colombia); external grinding; officer of the day; olive drab; Operational Directive; Ordnance Department; original design; outside dimension

O.D. Doctor of Optometry

oda occipito-dextra anterior

Oda Odessa

ODa Old Danish

ODA Office of Debt Analysis; Office of the District Administrator; Office of Drug Abuse; Overseas Development Administration; Overseas Development Assistance

ODALE Office of Drug Abuse Law Enforcement

ODAS Ocean Data Acquisition System

odat one day at a time

odb opiate-directed behavior; output to display buffer

odc other direct costs; outer dead center

ODC Old Dominion College; Overseas Development Corporation; Overseas Development Council

ODCSRDA Office of the Deputy Chief of Staff for Research, Development, and Acquisition (USA)

ODCTI Old Dominion College Technical Institute

odd (ODD) operator distance dialing

od'd overdosed

odde (Dano-Norwegian—cape, point)

ODDRE Office of the Director of Defense Research and Engineering

ode one-day event

Ode *Oude* (Afrikaans, Dutch, Flemish—old)

ODE Oil Drilling and Exploration

ODEC Ocean Design Engineering Corporation

ODECA Organización de Estados Centroamericanos (Organization of Central American States)

ODECO Ocean Drilling and Ex-

ploration Company

od'ed overdosed

ODEE *Oxford Dictionary of English Etymology*

Ode to Heavenly Joy Mahler's Symphony No. 4 in G major

Ode to Joy Beethoven's Symphony No. 9 in D minor—the symphony whose closing movement is based on the text of Schiller's *Ode to Joy*

ODEPLAN *Oficina de Planificación Nacional* (Spanish—Office of National Planning)

Oder-Neisse Line rivers forming boundaries between East Germany and Poland

ODESSA *Organisation Der Ehemaligen SS Angehörigen* (German—Organization of Former Members of the SS)—device for simulating suicides and arranging new names, occupations, and countries for war criminals who served Hitler

ODESY On-Line Data Entry System

ODF Old Dominion Foundation; Operational Deployment Force

odfc outside diameter of female coupling

ODFI Open Die Forging Institute

O d G *Ordine del Giorno* (Italian—Order of the Day)

ODGSO Office of Domestic Gold and Silver Operations

ODH Ontario Department of Health

ODI Office of Defense Investigation (U.S. Department of Justice); Open-Door International (championing economic emancipation of women workers)

ODIL Overseas Development Institute Limited

Odin Scandinavian equivalent of Wotan, the supreme god of the Norse gods

od'ing overdosing

o-d-ing overdosing

O Div Ontario Division (RCMP)

ODJB Original Dixieland Jazz Band

o dk orlop deck

ODL Office of Defense Lending

odm ophthalmodynamometry

ODM Office of Defense Mobilization; Order of De Molay; Overseas Development Ministry

ODMA Optical Distributors and Manufacturers Association

odmc outside diameter of male coupling

ODMC Office for Dependents Medical Care

odn own doppler nullifier

Odn Odense; Odin; Odinist (member of Nordic-supremacy sect)

ODO Outdoor Office(r)

ODOE Oregon Department of Energy

odom odometer

odont odontology

odop offset doppler

odoram. odoramentum (Latin—perfume)

odorat. odoratus (Latin—odorous, perfuming)

odorl odorless

ODOTS One-Day One-Trial System (for jurors)

odp occipito-dextra posterior; order despatched

ODP Office of Disaster Preparedness; Operational Deployment Plan(ning); Orbit Determination Program

odr order

ODR Office of Defense Resources

ODRC Office of Disaster Relief Coordinator (UN)

o'drive overdrive

ods oxide dispersion strengthened

o d's other denominations

ODS Ocean Data Station; Office of Defender Services; Orton Dyslexia Society

odsd overseas duty selection date

ODSE Open-Door Student Exchange

ODSI Ocean Data Systems Inc.

ODSR Office of the Director of Scientific Research

odt occipito-dextra transverse; octal debugging technique; odor detection threshold; one-day trials; on-line debugging technique

ODT Otago Daily Times

ODTF Operational Development Test(ing) Facility

ODTS Operational Development Test Site

ODU Old Dominion University

od units optical-density units

ODWIN Opening Doors Wider in Nursing

ODWSA Office of the Directorate of Weapon Systems Analy-

sis (USA)

Odysseus (Greek—Ulysses)

oe oersted; omissions expected; open end(ed); outdoor education

o/e on examination; otitis externa

o & e operations and engineering

öe österreichisch (German—Austrian)

Oe oersted

OE Office of Education; Old English; Oregon Electric (railroad)

OEA Oahu Education Association; Office of Economic Adjustment (USA); Office Education Association; Office Executives Association; Office of Export Administration; Ohio Education Association; Oregon Education Association; Outdoor Education Association; Overseas Education Association

OEA Organización de los Estados Americanos (Spanish—Organization of American States)

OEAA Oil Engineering Apprentices Association

OEB Oregon Educational Broadcasting

oec organizational entity code

OEC Office of Energy Conservation, Ohio Edison Company, Oil Exporting Countries

ÖEC Österreichischer Aero-Club (German—Austrian Aero Club)

OECC Office for Educational Credit and Credentials

OECD Organization for Economic Cooperation and Development

OECE Organisation Européenne de Coopération Économique (Organization for European Economic Cooperation)

OECF Overseas Economic Cooperation Fund

oeco outboard engine cutoff

OECQ Organisation Européene pour la Contrôle de la Qualité (European Quality-Control Organization)

OECS Organization of East Caribbean States

oecu outboard engine cutoff

OED Oxford English Dictionary

OEDA Office of Energy Data and Analysis

OEDP Office of Employment

Development Programs

oee outer enamel epithelium

OEEC Organization for European Economic Cooperation

OEEO Office of Equal Educational Opportunities

OEF Osteopathic Educational Foundation

OEG Operations Evaluation Group

oegt observable evidence of good teaching

OEGT Office of Education for the Gifted and Talented

oei organizational entity identity

OEI Offshore Ecology Investigation

OEI Oficina de Educación Ibero-americana (Spanish—Office of Ibero-American Education)

OEIPS Office of Engineering and Information Processing (NBS)

OEIU Office Employees International Union

o-e-l owner's risk of leakage

OEL Organization Equipment List

OEL/MA Ohio Educational Library/Media Association

oem oil-emulsion mud (oil well); original equipment manufacturer

oem (OEM) optical electron microscope

OEM Office of Environmental Mediation; Office of Executive Management

OEMA Office Equipment Manufacturers Association

oemcp (OEMCP) optical effects module electronic controller and processor

OEMs Original Equipment Manufacturers

oen oenanthic; oenanthyl; oenolyn; oenology; oenological; oenologist; oenomancy; oenomel (wine and honey); oenometer; oenophilist; oenophobist; oenopoetic

oeo officer's eyes only

OEO Office of Economic Opportunity

OEOB Old Executive Office Building (D.C.)

OEP Office of Emergency Planning; Office of Emergency Preparedness; Optional Educational Programs

OEPP Organisation Européenne et Méditerranéenne pour la Protection des Plants (European and Mediterranean

Organization for the Protection of Plants)

OEPS Office of Educational Programs and Services

OEQ Order of Engineers of Québec

OEQC Office of Environmental Quality Control

oer oersted (unit of magnetic force); original equipment replacement

o'er over

OER Office of Aerospace Research (USAF); Office of Energy Research; Officer Effectiveness Report; Officer Efficiency Report; Officer Engineering Reserve; Officers Emergency Reserve; Organization for European Research

oerc optimum earth-reentry corridor

OERPA Office of Exploratory Research and Problem Assessment (National Science Foundation)

OERS *Organisation Européenne de Recherches Spatiales* (French—European Space Research Organization)

OES Office of Economic Stabilization; Official Experimental Station; Order of the Eastern Star; Organization of European States

oesbr oil-extended styrene-butadiene rubber

OESL Oceanographic and Environmental Service Laboratory (Raytheon)

oesoph oesophagus

OESP *O Estado de São Paulo* (State of Sao Paulo)—Brazil's leading newspaper

OESS Office of Engineering Standards Services

OET Office of Education and Training; Office of Emergency Transportation; Overseas Exchange Transactions

OETB Offshore Energy Technology Board

OEW Office of Economic Warfare

OEWG Open-Ended Working Group; Operation and Evaluation Wartime Group

OEX Office of Educational Exchange

OEZ *osteuropäische Zeit* (German—East European Time)

of. old face (type); optional form; outside face; oxidizing flame

o/f oxidation/fermentation; oxidizer to fuel ratio

Of Ovenstone factor

OF Oceanographic Facility; Odd Fellows; Old French; Operating Forces; Ophthalmological Foundation; Osteopathic Foundation; Oxbow Falls; Oxenstierna Foundation; Oxford Foundation

OFA Office of Financial Analysis; Old Folks Association; Orthopedic Foundation for Animals

OFAC Owens Fine Arts Center (Dallas)

O-factor oscillation factor

ofc office

OFC Overseas Food Corporation

OFCA Ontario Federation of Construction Associations

OFCC Office of Federal Contract Compliance

OFCCP Office of Federal Contract Compliance Programs

ofcl official

ofd one-function diagram; optical fire detector

OFDA Office of Foreign Disaster Assistance (U.S.)

OFDI Office of Foreign Direct Investments

OFE Office of Fuels and Energy

OFEMA *Office Français d'Exportation de Matériel Aéronautique* (French Office for the Exportation of Aeronautical Materiel)

off. office(r); official

Off Officer

OFF Office for Families

OFFAR Office of Fuel and Fuel Additive Registration (EPA)

offen offensive (ammunition)

Offenbach Jacques Offenbach (adopted name of Jakob Levy Eberst)

offeq office equipment

offer. offertories; offertory

offg offering

offic official(ly)

Office Pubns Office Publications

Offshore Capital of the World Aberdeen, Scotland—home port of many offshore oil exploration rigs

offshore China nationalist Republic of China headquartered on Taiwan, also called Formosa

OFHA Oil Field Haulers Association

ofhc oxygen-free high conductivity; oxygen-free high-carbon (copper)

OFI Office of the Federal Inspector

OFIC Ohio Foundation of Independent Colleges

ofl official

Oflag *Offizierlager* (German—officer's prison camp)

OFlem Old Flemish

Ofly Offaly

OFM Office of Flight Missions (NASA)

OFNS Observer Foreign News Service

OFPA Order of the Founders and Patriots of America

OFPM Office of Fiscal Plans and Management

OFPP Office of Federal Procurement Policy

ofr off frequency rejection

O Fr Old French

OFR Office of the Federal Register

OFR-ALA Office of Recruitment—American Library Association

OFris Old Frisian

O Frk Old Frankish

ofs one-function sketch

OFS Ontario Federation of Students; Orange Free State

OFSPS Office of Federal Statistical Policy and Standards

OFST Office of the Secretary of the Air Force

OFT Office of Fair Trade; Office of Fair Trading; Ohio Federation of Teachers

OFTS Office of Technical Services; Office of Transport(ation) Security; Officers Training School; Overseas Fixed Telecommunications System

OFY Opportunities for Youth (Canada)

og oh gee; oil gland; old girl; on ground; on guard; original gum

o-g orange-green

o/g opto-graphic; outgoing

OG Officer of the Guard; Old Gaelic; Olympic Games

O/G Opto/Graphic

ÖG Österreichische Galerie (Austrian Gallery)

OG *O Globo* (Rio de Janeiro's Globe)

O Gael Old Gaelic

OGAMA Ogden Air Materiel Area

Ogasawara (Japanese—Bonin Islands)

Ogasawaras Ogasawara Islands (Bonins)

O-gauge 1-1/4-inch track gauge

(model railroads)

OGB Österreichischer Gewerk-schaftsbund (German—Austrian Trade Union Federation)

OGC Office of General Counsel

OGCMD Ogden Contract Management District

Ogd Ogdensburg

OGDC Oil and Gas Development Corporation

oge (OGE) operational ground equipment

OGE Office of Government Ethics

OGES Operating Ground Equipment Specification

ogg oggetto (Italian—object)

ÖGI Österreichische Gessel-schaft für Informatik (German —Austrian Society for Information Processing)

OGJ Oil and Gas Journal

ogl obscure glass

OGMC Ordnance Guided Missile Center

OGNR Oribi Gorge Nature Reserve (South Africa)

OGO Orbiting Geophysical Observatory

OGPU Obiedinennoye Gosu-darstvennoye Politicheskoye Upravlenie (Russian—United State Political Administration)—*q.v.m.*—VOT

OGR Ontario Government Railway (Ontario Northland)

OGR Official Guide of the Railways

ogse operational ground-support equipment

OGSEL Operational Ground-Support Equipment List

OGSM Office of General Sales Manager

o-g stain orange-green stain

ogt on-going thing; outlet gas temperature

OGTT Oral Glucose Tolerance Test(ing)

OGU Occupational Guidance Unit

ogv outlet guide vane

oh (OH) ocular herpes

oh. office hours; on hand; open hearth; out home; oval head; overhead; over-the-horizon(communication)

o/h overhaul

o.h. omni hora (Latin—hourly)

o-H on-Hudson

OH hydroxyl radical (symbol); Omega House; San Francisco and Oakland Helicopter Airlines (2-letter code)

O/H Overzuche Handelsmaat-schappij (Dutch—Overseas Trading Company)

OH-6 Hughes observation helicopter called Cayuse

OH-13 Bell Sioux helicopter

OH-23 Hiller Raven utility helicopter

OH-58 Bell Kiowa turbine-powered helicopter

oha outside helix angle

OHA Occupational Health Administration; Office of Hearings and Appeals

O'Hare O'Hare International Airport (Chicago)—world's busiest airport named for navy pilot Edward H (Butch) O'Hare killed during World War II

OH-B Ocean Hill-Brownsville

OHBMS On Her (His) Britannic Majesty's Service

ohc outer hair cells; overhead cam

OHC Office of Humanities Communication; Ottumwa Heights College; Overseas Hotel Corporation

OHCS Office of Home Care Services

ohd organic hearing disease; organic heart disease; overhead drive

OHDETS Over-Horizon Detection System

OHDS Office of Human Development Services (HEW)

OHD & W Outer Harbor Dock and Wharf

OHE Office of Health Economics

oheat overheat

O Henry William Sydney Porter

ohf overhaul factor

Ohf Omsk hemorrhagic fever

OHG Old High German

OHG Offene Handelsgesell-schaft (German—ordinary partnership)

ohi ocular hypertension indicator

OHI Oil Heat Institute

OHI Organisation Hydrogra-phique Internationale (French —International Hydrographic Organization)

OHIA Oil Heat Institute of America

Ohio Ports (east to west) Conneaut, Ashtabula, Fairport, Cleveland, Lorain, Huron, Sandusky, Toledo

Ohio's Beautiful Capital Columbus

Ohio Turn Ohio Turnpike

Ohio U Pr Ohio University Press

Ohio Valley Ohio, West Virginia, Kentucky, Indiana, and Illinois—all along the Ohio River starting in Pennsylvania

OHIP Ontario Hospital Insurance Plan

OHK Okayama Hoso KK

OHL Oberste Herresleitung (German—Supreme Headquarters)

Ohlsdorf Hamburg's picturesque cemetery noted for its landscaping

ohm. ohmmeter

ohm-cm ohm-centimeter

OHMO Office of Hazardous Materials Operations

OHMR Office of Hazardous Materials Regulation

OHMS On Her (His) Majesty's Service; Onboard Health Monitoring System

oho out-of-house operation

ohp overhead projection; oxygen at high pressure

ohrf overhaul replacement factor

OHRG Official Hotel and Resort Guide

ohs open-hearth steel

ohs (OHS) hydroxy-steroids

OHS Office of Highway Safety; Ontario Humane Society; Oral Hygiene Service; Oregon Historical Society; Organization of Historical Studies; Overland Highway Society

OHSGT Office of High-Speed Ground Transportation

OHSIP Ontario Health Services Insurance Plan

OHSPAC Occupational Health-Safety-Programs Accreditation Commission

oht overheating temperature

OHTE Ohmic Heating Toroidal Experiment

ohv overhead valve; overhead vent

ohv's off-highway vehicles

oi oil-immersed; oil-immersion

o-i orgasmic impairment

o/i opsonic index

o & i organizational and intermediate

OI Office of Information; Office Instruction; Operating Instruction; Optimist International; Oriental Institute

O-I Owens-Illinois

OIA Ocean Industries Association; Office of Impact Analysis; Office of Industrial Associates; Office of International Administration; Oil Import Administration; Oil Insurance Association; Outboard Industry Associations

OIA *Organización Internacional de Azucar* (Spanish—International Sugar Organization)

OIAA Office of Inter-American Affairs; Office of International Aviation Affairs

OIAB Oil Import Appeals Board

OIAJ Office for Improvements in the Administration of Justice

OIAS Occupational Information Access System

OIB Ohio Inspection Bureau; Oklahoma Inspection Bureau

oic oil cooler

O-i-C Officer-in-Charge

OIC Oceanographic Instrumentation Center; Office of the Insurance Commissioner; Officer in Charge; Ohio Improved Chester (white swine); Oil Industry Commission; Opportunities Industrialization Centers; Overseas Investment Commission

OIC *Organisation Internationale du Commerce* (French—International Trade Organization)

OICA Ontario Institute of Chartered Accountants; Oregon Independent Colleges Association

OICD Office of International Cooperation and Development

OIcel Old Icelandic

OICF Oklahoma Independent College Foundation; Oregon Independent College Foundation

OICS Office of Interoceanic Canal Studies

oid (Latin suffix—resembling)—sigmoid

OIE Office of Indian Education; Office of International Epizootics

OIEA *Organismo Internacional de Energia Atómica* (Spanish—International Atomic Energy Agency)—IAEA

OIER Office of International Economic Research

OIF Office for Intellectual Freedom (ALA)

OIG Office of the Inspector General

oih (OIH) ovulation-producing hormone

OIHP *Office International d'Hygiene Publique* (French—International Office of Public Health)—UN

OII Office of Invention and Innovation

OIJ *Organisation Internationale des Journalistes* (French—International Organization of Journalists)

OIL Operation Inspection Log

OIL *Organizzazione Internazionale del Lavoro* (Italian—International Labor Organization)

Oil Baron John D Rockefeller

oil of ben fine lubricant extracted from seeds of Arabian tree called *Moringa oleifera*

oil of cade juniper oil

oil cake cottonseed, linseed, or soybean mass used for cattle feed after oil is extracted

Oil Capital of Canada Edmonton, Alberta

Oil Capital of the Rockies Casper, Wyoming

Oil Capital of the World Tulsa, Oklahoma

Oil City Bartlesville or Tulsa, Oklahoma

Oil Dorado northwestern Pennsylvania in the Oil City—Titusville area

oilies oilskin coats; oilskin garments

Oil Islands Chagos Archipelago in the Indian Ocean just north of Diego Garcia

oil of mirbrane nitrobenzene

oiloff oil ripoff

oil of palm bribe(s); palm grease

Oil Province Alberta

OILSR Office of Interstate Land Sales Registration

oil of vitriol concentrated sulfuric acid (H_2SO_4)

oil of wintergreen methyl salicylate

OIM Oriental Institute Museum (University of Chicago)

OINA Oyster Institute of North America

O-in-C Officer-in-Charge

OINC Officer in Charge

oint ointment

OIO Oklahomans for Indian Opportunity

oip oil in place

OIP Office for Information Programs (NBS); Office of International Programs; Operations Improvement Program

OIPC *Organisation Internationale de Police Criminelle*

(French—International Criminal Police Organization)—also known as Interpol

OIPH Office of International Public Health

OIr Old Irish

OIR Office of Inter-American Radio

OIRB Oregon Insurance Rating Bureau

OIRT Organisation Internationale de Radiodiffusion et Télévision (International Radio and Television Organization)

OIS Office Information System; Overseas Investors Services

OISA Office of International Scientific Affairs

OISE Ontario Institute for Studies in Education

OISTV *Organisation Internationale pour la Science et la Technique du Vide* (French—International Organization for Vacuum Science and Technology)

O i T Officer in Training (rookie police officer)

OIT Organic Integrity Test

OIT *Organisation Internationale du Travail* (French); *Organización Internacional del Trabajo* (Spanish)—International Labor Organization also known as ILO

OITF Office of International Trade Fairs

OIUC Oriental Institute of the University of Chicago

OIVV Office International de la Vigne et du Vin (International Office of Vines and Wines)

OIW Oceanographic Institute, Wellington (New Zealand)

OIWP Oil Industry Working Party

OIWR Office of Indian Water Rights

oj open-joint; open-joist(ed)

orange juice

oJ *ohne Jahr* (German—without year)—no date

OJARS Office of Justice Assistance, Research, and Statistics

OJC *Organisation Juive de Combat* (French—Jewish Combat Organization)

OJD Office de Justification de la Diffusion

OJDYD Office of Juvenile Delinquency and Youth Development

oji on-the-job injuries

OJJ Office of Juvenile Justice

OJJDP Office of Juvenile Justice and Delinquency Prevention

oJr old Jamaica rum

ojt on-the-job training

OJT (National) On-the-Job Training (Program)

ok all correct; okay; optical klystron; outer keel

ok ohne kosten (German—without cost); *ola kala* (Greek—all is fine, all is good)—believed by many scholars to be the original okay used by Greek sailors of antiquity and copied by other seafarers

OK all correct; okay; Old Kinderhook (birthplace and home of President Martin Van Buren, Democratic OK Club believed to have started practice of putting "OK" on deals and documents they approved of); Old Kingdom (Egypt)

O & K Orenstein & Koppel

Ø K Østasiatiske Kompagni (East Asiatic Company—Danish)

oka otherwise known as

OKA Okinawa, Ryukyu Islands (airport)

OKC Oklahoma City, Oklahoma (airport)

OKd okayed

Okecie Warsaw, Poland's airport

Okeechobee 40 mile long lake surrounded by partially drained swamps in southern Florida northwest of Miami; famous fishing area and wildlife habitat

Okefinokee Okefinokee National Wildlife Refuge and the Okefinokee Swamp between northern Florida and southern Georgia

OKH Oberkommando des Heeres (German—Army High Command)

Okhotsk Sea of Okhotsk between Kamchatka Peninsula, Sakhalin Island, and eastern Siberia

Okhotskoye More (Russian—Sea of Okhotsk)

Okie Oklahoma (or person from there); Oklahoman

Okie City Oklahoma City, Oklahoma

Okin Okinawa(n)

OKL Oberkommando der Luftwaffe (German—Air Force High Command)

Okla Oklahoma; Oklahoman

OklaC Oklahoma City

Oklahoma City Oklahoma's capital

OKM Oberkommando der Marine (German—Naval High Command)

Okt Oktober (German—October); *Oktyabr* (Russian—October)

OKT Oslo Kommune Tunnelbanekontoret (Oslo subway system)

Oktronics Oklahoma Electronics (corporation)

OKW Oberkommando der Wehrmacht (German—Armed Forces High Command)

ol oil level; operating license; or less

ol' old

o/l operations/logistics; outlook

ol. oleum (Latin—oil)

o.l. oculus laevus (Latin—left eye)

ö L östlich Längengrad (German—east longitude)

Ol olive

OL October League (communist group active in U.S.); Old Latin; Olsen Line; Oranje Line (Orange Line)

ola occipito-laeva anterior

OLA Office of Legislative Affairs; Ohio Library Association; Oklahoma Library Association; Ontario Library Association; Ontopathic Librarians Association

OLADE Organización Latinamericana de Energía (Spanish—Latin American Energy Organization)

o'land overland

Olanda (Italian—Holland)—the Netherlands

OLAPEC Organization of Latin American Petroleum Exporting Countries

OLAS Organization of Latin American Solidarity; Organization of Latin American Students

OLAS Organización Latinoamericana de Solidaridad (Latin American Solidarity Organization)

Olav Hunger King Olav I of Denmark

Olav the Stout Olav Haroldson

Olav Tryg Olav Trygvason

Olav Tryggvesson King Olav I of Norway, Sweden, and Denmark

olbm (OLBM) orbital-launched ballistic missile

OlBr olive brown

olc on-line computer

OLC Oak Leaf Cluster; Office of Legal Counsel

olcc optimum life-cycle costing

OLCS On-Line Computer System

OLD Office of Legislative Development

Old Abe Abraham Lincoln

Old Ace of Spades Lieutenant General Robert E Lee, CSA

Old Andy Andrew Jackson—seventh President of the United States

Old Beeswax Captain Raphael Semmes, CSN

Old Billie Brigadier General William Tecumseh Sherman, USA

Old Blighty nickname for blighted London before the era of air-pollution control

Old Blood and Guts General George S Patton, USA

Old Blue Eyes Frank Sinatra

Old Bory General Pierre Gustave Toutant de Beauregard, CSA

Old Brown of Osawatomie abolitionist fanatic and terrorist John Brown

Old Buck Admiral Franklin Buchanan; President James Buchanan

Old Buena Vista General Zachary Taylor who attacked Mexicans at Buena Vista in February 1847; later was twelfth President of the United States

Old Bullion Thomas Hart Benton

Old Cape Stiff Cape Horn

Old Castile (see *Castilla la Vieja*)

Old Catawba fictitious name Thomas Wolfe assigned North Carolina

Old Chapultepec General Winfield Scott whose victory at Chapultepec ended Mexican War in September 1847

Old Chief Henry Clay

Old Coat Hanger Melbourne-originated nickname for the Sydney Harbour Bridge

Old Colony Massachusetts—founded in 1620

Old Corndrinking Mellifluous William Faulkner, according to Ernest Hemingway, also an alcoholic

Old Curmudgeon Harold Le Claire Ickes

Old Denmark General Christian Febiger, USA

Old Dirigo Maine whose state motto is *Dirigo* (Latin—I direct)

Old Dominion Virginia—oldest English colony in America—founded in 1607

Old Dorp nickname of Schenectady, New York

Old East East Asiatic Company

Old Faithful geyser in Yellowstone National Park; spouts about every 67 minutes

old-fash old-fashioned

Oldfos Old Established Forces

Old French Town New Orleans

Old Fuss and Feathers General Winfield Scott, USA

Old Gib Gibraltar

Old Glory the American Flag

Old Greasy West Virginian nickname for the Kanawha River or K'naw

Old Guard conservatives; Napoleon's imperial guard who made the last charge at Waterloo; the establishment

Old Harry (the devil)—Satan

Old Hickory General Andrew Jackson—seventh President of the United States

Old Ironsides USS *Constitution*

Old Jeb Major General J(ames) E(well) B(rown) Stuart, CSA

Old Jefferson Joseph Jefferson

Old Joe slang nickname for syphilis

Old Kinderhook Martin Van Buren—eighth President of the United States

Old Lady the boss; mother; wife

Old Lady of Eagle Bridge Grandma (Anna Mary Richardson) Moses of Eagle Bridge, NY

Old Lady of the Thames London

Old Lady of Threadneedle Street Bank of England

Old Lady White any powdered narcotic

Old Legal Lion Clarence Darrow

Old Line State Maryland

Old Maid *Old Maid and the Thief* (one-act comic opera by Menotti)

Old Maid's Old Maid's Day (June 4)

Old Man the boss; the captain; father; the skipper

Old Man Eloquent Isocrates in the opinion of Milton; John Quincy Adams in the opinion of the Congress he served after being sixth President of the U.S.

Old Man of Ferney Voltaire who lived in Ferney, France

Old Man of the Mountain New Hampshire's Profile Mountain —the Great Stone Face

Old Man of the Rhine Konrad Adenauer

Old Man River the Mississippi

Old Manse Nathaniel Hawthorne's house in Concord, Massachusetts

Old Nick (the devil)—Niccolo Machiavelli's diabolic sobriquet; Satan

Old Noll Old Oliver Cromwell

Old North State North Carolina's official nickname

Old Ossawatomie John Brown

Old Pam Lord Palmerston (Henry John Temple)

Old Party W(illiam) Somerset Maugham

Old Peg Leg Petrus Stuyvesant —director-general of New Amsterdam and the New Netherlands

Old Point Old Point Comfort, Virginia

Old Pretender James Francis Edward Stuart (son of King James II)

old pro(s) old professional(s)

Old Pueblo Tucson, Arizona

Old Put General Israel Putnam

old rep old repertory; old reprobate

Old Rosey General William Starke Rosecrans

Old Rough-and-Ready General Zachary Taylor—twelfth President of the United States

Olds Oldsmobile

OLDS On-Line Display System

Old Sarum Salisbury, England

Old Scratch Satan

Old Sol the sun (*see* Sun God)

Old South southern United States before 1865

Old Spanish Trail Saint Augustine, Florida to San Diego, California—many sections follow old Highway 90—southernmost cross-country thoroughfare in the United States; Gulf Coast and Mexican Border route to California

Old Swamp Fox Brigadier General Francis Marion, USA

Old Tecumseh General William Tecumseh Sherman, USA

Old Territorial Old Territorial Penitentiary (Santa Fé, New Mexico)

Old Test. Old Testament

Old Three Stars General US Grant, USA

Old Tippecanoe General William Henry Harrison—ninth President of the United States

Old Ugly .45-caliber pistol

Old Vic repertory theater in London

Old Viking Norwegian-American able seaman and labor leader Andrew Furuseth

Old West American or Wild West American as was settled during the 19th century

Old World Africa, Asia, and Europe

Old Zach Zachary Taylor—12th President of the United States

Ole Olaf(sen); Olav(sen)

OLE Office of Library Education (American Library Association)

OLEA Office of Law Enforcement Assistance

Oleander City by the Sea Galveston, Texas

Ole Bull Ole Bornemann Bull

Ole Miss Old Mississippi (The University of Mississippi)

oleo oleomargarine; oleoresins; oleum

OLEP Office of Law Enforcement and Planning

olericult olericulture

'oleum petroleum

O-levels ordinary levels (of educational tests)

olf olfactory; on-line filing

OLF Ohio Library Foundation; Orbital Launch Facility; Organ Literature Foundation

Olg Olga

OlG olive green

OLG Old Low German

Olgas The Olgas—mountain range west of Ayers Rock in Australia's Northern Territory

OLHMIS On-Line Hospital Management Information System

Oli Oliver

OLI Ocean Living Institute

O-license operator's license

Olig Oligocene

oligo (Latin prefix—few or small)—oligarchy

Olimpo (Italian, Portuguese, Spanish—Olympus)—mythical abode of the gods of antiquity

Olive Fremstad Olivia Rundquist

Oliver Hardy Oliver Norvell Hardy

Oliver Optic pseudonym of William Taylor Adams

Oliver P Oliver (Cromwell) Protector

OLL Office of Legislative Liaison

Ollie Olive(r)

OLMAT Otis-Lennon Mental Ability Test

Ol' Miss Old Mississippi (nickname of river, state, or university)

Ol' Mo Old Missouri (the great river)

olmr (OLMR) organic liquid-moderated reactor

OLMR Office of Labor Management Relations

ol'n olden

OLOGS Open-Loop Oxygen-Generating System

Olongapo Subic Bay's sailor town in Luzon (Philippines)

olos out of line of sight

OLOS Office for Library Outreach Services

olow orbiter liftoff weight

ulp occipito-laeva posterior

OLP *Organización para la Liberación Palestina* (Spanish—Palestinian Liberation Organization)—the PLO terrorists

olpar other large phased-array radar

OLPR Office for Library Personnel Resources (ALA)

OLPS On-Line Programming System

olq officer-like qualities

olr overload relay

OLRB Ontario Labor Relations Board

ol res oleoresin

olrt on-line real time

ols ordinary least squares

ol's office ladies (divorcees and spinsters); old girls

OLS Optical Landing System

olsc on-line scientific computer

OLSD Office for Library Service to the Disadvantaged (ALA)

olt occipito-laeva transverse

ol & t owners, landlords, and tenants

Olt Old Italian

oltt on-line teller terminal

olv olivaceous; olive; on-line validation

OLV *Onze Lieve Vrouw* (Dutch—Our Lady)

o-l v's ovo-lacto vegetarians

Oly Olympia; Olympic

Olym Olympia

Olympia capital of Washington

Olympics Olympic Games; Olympic Mountains, Wash-

ington

Olyssipo (Latin—Lisboa)—Lisbon

om old man; old measurement; old men; operational monitor; organic matter; our memo; outer marker

o & m (O & M) operation and maintenance

o.m. *omni mane* (Latin—every morning)

Om Omaha; Oman

Om. Book of Omni

OM Occupational Medicine; Old Man (colloquial); Ordnance Map

O.M. Order of Merit

O & M Organization and Methods

OM *Ostmark* (East German mark)

oma orderly marketing arrangement

oma (Greek—swelling or tumor)—carcinoma, glaucoma, hematoma, lipoma, sarcoma

Oma Omaha, Nebraska

OMA Ocean Mining Administration (USDI); Office of Maritime Affairs; Oklahoma Military Academy; Omaha, Nebraska (airport); Ontario Medical Association

OMAI *Organisation Mondiale Agudas Israel* (French—Agudas Israel International Organization)

Oman Sultanate of Oman (Arab oil-producing nation on Arabia's southeast coast where Omanis converse in Arabic, Persian, or Urdu, depending on their country of origin, crude oil is the principal export), *Saltanat Oman*

Omani Ports Masqat (Muscat) and Matrah (adjacent)

omarb omarbetad (Swedish—revised)

OMARS Outstanding Media Advertising by Restaurants

Omar Sharif Omar Cherif; Omar Michel Shaloub

OMAT Office of Manpower, Automation, and Training

Omb Ombudsman

OMB Office of Management and Budget Ontario Municipal Board

OMBE Office of Minority Business Enterprise

OMC Office of Munitions Control; Outboard Marine Corporation

'ome (Cockney contraction—home)

OME Office of Manpower Economics; Office of Minerals Exploration

OMEF Office Machines and Equipment Federation

OMEGA Optimal Missile Engagement Guidance Algorithm (worldwide navigational system)

OMEL Orient Mid-East Lines

O-Mess Officer's Mess

OMF Office of Management and Finance

omfp obtaining money by false pretenses

OMG Ophthalmology Medical Group

OMGE Organisation Mondiale de Gastro-Entérologie (World Gastro-Enterological Organization)

OMGUS Office of Military Government, United States

OMH Office of Mental Health

OMI Olympic Media Information; Operation Move-In

O.M.I. Oblate of Mary Immaculate

OMII Oxy Metal Industries International

omiom original meaning is the only meaning

omit. orinthine-decarboxylase, motility, indole, trytophandeaminase

omkr omdring (Norwegian—about)

oml outside mold line

OML Ontario Motor League; Orbiting Military Laboratory

OMM Office of Minerals Mobilization

OMM *Organisation Météorologique Mondiale* (French), *Organización Meteorológica Mundial* (Spanish—World Meteorological Organization)—WMO

OMMA Outboard Motor Manufacturers Association

OMMS Office of Merchant Marine Safety (USCG)

omn. bih. omni bihora (Latin—every two hours)

omn. hor. omni hora (Latin—every hour)

omni omnidirectional; omnirange; omnivisual

omn. man. omni mane (Latin—every morning)

omn. noct. omni nocte (Latin—every night)

omn. quad. hor. omni quadrante hora (Latin—every quarter of an hour)

omor one man, one responsibility

omp organo-metallic polymer(s)

ompa one-man pension arrangement

OMPD Office of Mineral Policy Development

OMPER Office of Manpower Policy Evaluation and Research

ompf omphaloskepsis

OMPO Oahu Metropolitan Planning Organization

ompr optical mark page reader

OMPRA Office of Minerals Policy and Research Analysis

OMPU *Oficina Municipal de Planeamiento Urbano* (Spanish—Municipal Office of Urban Planning)

omr office methods research; optical mark reader; optical mark recognition

OMR Officer Master Record

OMRD Overseas Mineral Resource Development

oms output per man shift

OMS Office of Management Studies

OMS *Organisation Mondiale de la Santé* (French), *Organización Mundial de la Salud* (Spanish)—World Health Organization—WHO; *Otdel Mezdunarodnyk Svyazey* (Russian—International Relations Section)—network of overseas Comintern and Cominform agents

OMSA Orders and Medals Society of America

OMSF Office of Manned Space Flight (NASA)

OMSIP Ontario Medical Surgical Insurance Plan

omt orthomode transducer

OMT Old Merchant Taylors

OMTS Organizational Maintenance Test Station

on. octane number

o/n own name

on. *onomastikon* (Greek—lexicon)

o.n. *omni nocte* (Latin—every night)

On *Onorevole* (Italian—Honorable); *Onsdag* (Danish—Wednesday)

ON Ogden Nash; Old Norse; Operation Notice

O.N. Orthopedic Nurse

O/N Order Number

O & N Oregon & Northeastern (railroad)

ÖN Österreichische Nationalbibliotek (Austrian National Library)

ona optical navigation attachment

ONA Office of National Assessment; Office of Noise Abatement; Overseas National Airways; Overseas News Agency

on a/c on account

ONAC Office of Noise Abatement and Control

ONAP Orbit Navigation Analysis Program

on approv on approval

onbep *onbepaald* (Dutch—indefinite)

onc operational navigational chart(s)

ONC Office of New Careers; Oficina Nacional del Café (National Coffee Administration—Honduras); Oregon-Nevada-California (fast freight truck line)

oncol oncology

OND Ophthalmic Nursing Diploma

ONE Office of National Estimates (CIA)

Oneg Onegin

Onega Lake Onega northeast of Leningrad and called Ozero Onezhskoye by the Russians

Onegin *Evgeny Onegin* (Russian—Eugene Onegin)—Tchaikovsky three-act opera based on a poem by Pushkin

Oneida Oneida Community of perfectionists still noted for the silverware and steel traps they produced while practicing complex marriage and common care of their offspring in Oneida, New York where its communistic experiments were abandoned in 1881 when the commune was incorporated

ONEO Office of Navajo Economic Opportunity

ONERA *Office National des Etudes et des Recherches Aérospatiales* (French—space research agency)

one-spot $1 bill

Onezhskoye Ozero (Russian—Lake Onega)

ONF Old Norman-French

onfm on nearest full moon

ong *ongaku* (Japanese—music); *ongeveer* (Dutch—about, approximately, roughly)

ONG *Organisation Non-Gouvernementale* (French—Non-Governmental Organization)

on hol(s) on holiday(s)

ONI Office of Naval Intelligence; Office of NWTS Integration

gration

ÖNJ *Österreichische Nationalbibliothek Josefsplatz* (German—Josefsplatz Austrian National Library)

Only Town in the U.S. with an Apostrophe in Its Name Coeur d'Alene, Idaho

ONM Ocmulgee National Monument; Office of Naval Materiel

ONMSS Office of Nuclear Material Safety and Safeguards

ONNI Office of National Narcotics Intelligence

onnm on nearest new moon

ono or near offer

o-'n'-o one and only

ONO Oesnoroeste (Spanish—west northwest); *oost noord oost* (Dutch—east northeast)

onomast onomastic(al)(ly); onomastics; onomatologist; onomatology

onomat onomatologic(al)(ly); onomatologist(ic)(al)(ly); onomatology; onomatopoeia

O Nor Old Norwegian

O Norm F Old Norman French

O North Old Northumbrian

o noz oil nozzle

onp operating nursing procedure

ONP Office of National Programs; Olympic National Park (Washington)

ONR Office of Naval Research; Official Naval Reporter

ONRL Office of Naval Records and Library

ONRRR Office of Naval Research Resident Representative

ON Rwy Ontario Northland Railway

ONSR Ozark National Scenic Riverways (Missouri)

On Sta On Station

ont ontology

Ont Ontario

ONT Our New Thread (Clark's trademark)

ONTC Ontario Northland Transportation Commission

Ont Pen Ontario Penitentiary

Ont Sci Cen Ontario Science Center

ONU *Organisation Nations Unies* (French—United Nations Organization); *Organización de las Naciones Unidas* (Spanish—United Nations Organization)—UNO; *Organizzazione Nazioni Unite* (Italian—United Nations Organization)

ONUC Operation des Nations Unies, Congo (United Nations Operation in the Congo)

ONUESC Organisation des Nations Unies pour l'Education, la Science et la Culture Intellectuelle (UNESCO)

ONULP Ontario New Universities Library Project

on w onovergankelijk werkwoord (Dutch—intransitive verb)

ONW Oregon and Northwestern (railroad)

ONWI Office of Nuclear Waste Isolation

ONWM Office of Nuclear Waste Management

ONWR Okefinokee National Wildlife Refuge (Florida and Georgia); Ottawa National Wildlife Refuge (Ohio); Ouray National Wildlife Refuge (Utah)

ony onymous (opposite of anonymous)

onyx marble alabaster

oo (OO) office of origin

o/o oil/ore (carrier); on order

o & o owned and operated

o-to-o out-to-out

oo (Latin prefix—egg)—oocyte, oology

o(O) original

OO Observation Officer; Oceanic Operators; Oceanographic Office

O/O Office of Oceanography (UNESCO)

O of O Order of Owls

ooa on or about

OOA Office of Ocean Affairs

OOAA Olive Oil Association of America

OOAMA Ogden Air Materiel Area

oob opening of business; out of bed

o-o B off-off Broadway; off-off Broadway theater(s)

OoB Order of Battle

OOB Old Orchard Beach

oobe out of body experience

OoC Office of Censorship

OOCH Orient Overseas Container Holdings

OOCL Orient Overseas Container Line

OOD Officer of the Day; Officer of the Deck

oodep owners, officers, directors, and executive personnel

Oody Eunice

OO/Eng out of stock but on order from England (for example)

OoF Office of Facilitation

OOG Office of Oil and Gas; Officer of the Guard

OOH *Occupational Outlook Handbook*

OOHA Operation Oil Heat Associates

ooj obstruction of justice

ool oology; operator-oriented language

OOL Odessa Ocean Line; Orient Overseas Line

oolhmd optimized optical-link helmet-mounted display

oolr ophthalmology, otology, laryngology, rhinology

OOM Officers Open Mess

OO McIntyre Oscar Odd McIntyre (newspaper columnist: *New York By Day*)

Oom Paul (Afrikaans—Uncle Paul)—sobriquet of Stephanus Johannes Paulus Kruger—leader of Boer rebellion and president of Transvaal

o/o/o out of order

OOO-gauge ¾-inch track gauge (model railroads)

oop out of pocket (expenses); out of print (book)

OOP Oceanographic Observations of the Pacific

oops off-line operating simulator; offshore oil-pollution sleeve

OOPS Organization of Oil Producing States

OOQ Officer of the Quarters

OOR Office of Ordnance Research

oos orbit-to-orbit shuttle; orbit-to-orbit stage; out of stock

o & o's owned and operated (tv broadcast) stations (controlled by a network)

OOSC Olfactronics and Odor Sciences Center (IITRI)

oost (Dutch—east)

Oostenrijk (Dutch—Eastern Empire)—Austria

oot out of tolerance; out of town

oote out-of-town executive

ootg one of the greats

Ooty Ootacamund, Madras

OOW Officer On Watch

op oil pressure; old prices; open policy; opera; operating point; operation; operation plan(s); operational; operational priority; operetta; opium; opposite prompt (stage left); optical probe; opus; ordinary pay; other people's (possessions); out of print; outer panel; outside production; overproof; overprune; overpuff

op (OP) outpatient

o/p off peak; optional; output; overpriced

o & p ova and parasites

Op optical art (art accented with or based on optical illusions); Oregon pine

Op. *Opus* (Latin—composition, literary or musical work)

OP Observation Post; Office of Preparedness; Office of Protocol (US Department of State); Oregon pine

O-P Oppenheimer-Phillips (process)

O.P. *Optimus Maximus* (Latin—supreme and best)—Jupiter's title as he was believed to be the king of the gods and the ruler of all rulers

opa optical plotting attachment; optoelectric pulse amplifier

OPA Office of Population Affairs; Office of Price Administration; Office of Public Affairs; Overall Payments Agreement

opal hydrous silica (SiO_2 .nH_2O)

opal. optical platform alignment linkage

op amp operational amplifier

OPANAL *Organismo para la Proscripción de las Armas Nucleares en la América Latina* (Spanish—Organization for the Prohibition of Nuclear Weapons in Latin America)

op art optical art (art involving optical illusion)

OPBE Office of Planning, Budgeting, and Evaluation (NIE)

OPBMA Ocean Pearl Button Manufacturers Association

opc office percentage; ordinary portland cement

OPC Ohio Power Company; Out-Patient Clinic; Overseas Press Club

OPCA Overseas Press Club of America

op. cit. *opere citato* (Latin—in the work cited); *opus citato* (Latin—in the work cited)

OPCNM Organ Pipe Cactus National Monument

opco operating company

op code operation code (data processing)

opcon(s) operation control(s)

OPCS Office of Population Censuses and Surveys

opd optical path difference

o-p-d oto-palato-digital (syndrome)

OPD Office of Policy Development (White House); Officer Personnel Directorate; Out Patient Department

opdar optical direction and ranging

OPDD Operational Plan Data Document

op dent operative dentistry

OPDR Oldenburg - Portugiesische - Dampfschifs - Reiderei (steamship company)

ope open-point expanding; opium; oxidation pond effluents

OPE Office of Planning and Evaluation (FBI); Operations Project Engineer

O P & E Oregon, Pacific & Eastern (railroad)

OPEC Oil Producer's Economic Cartel; Organization of Petroleum Exporting Countries

op ed opposite the editorials (newspaper page usually reserved for readers' letters and syndicated columns)

opef overall plume-enhancement factor

OPEI Outdoor Power Equipment Institute

OPEIU Office and Professional Employees International Union

open. open circuit; opening

Opener of Japan Commodore Matthew Calbraith Perry, USN

opens. open circuits (electrical parlance); openings

opep (OPEP) orbital plane experiment package

OPEP Organisations des Pays Exportateurs de Pétrole (French—Organization of Petroleum Exporting Countries)

oper operational

O Per Old Persian

OPER Office of Policy, Evaluation, and Research

Opera-Com Opéra-Comique (Paris)

Opera of Operas Mozart's *Don Giovanni*

Operation Keelhaul Allied policy of forcing escaping anticommunists to return to their communist masters

operg operating

OPers Old Persian

opex operational (and) executive (personnel)

OPEX Operational, Executive (and Administrative Personnel Program of the United Nations)

opfor opposition force

opg opening

OPG Overseas Project Group

OPGA Ohio Personnel and Guidance Association; Oregon Personnel and Guidance Association

oph ophicleide; ophthalmologist; ophthalmology; ophthalmoscope; ophthalmoscopic

Oph Ophiuchus (constellation)

Oph.D. Doctor of Ophthalmology

ophidiol ophidiologic(al)(ly); ophidiologist; ophidiology

OPHS Operational Propellant Handling System

ophth ophthalmologist; opthalmology

ophthal ophthalmic; ophthalmologist; ophthalmology

Ophthalmias Ophthalmia Range of mountains in Western Australia near Jiggalong and Mundiwindi

ophthalmol ophthalmologic(al)(ly); ophthalmologist; ophthalmology

OPI Office of Primary Interest; Office of Programs Integration (ERDA); Office of Protective Intelligence (U.S. Secret Service); Office of Public Information; Offsite Production (Purchase) Inspection; Omnibus Personality Inventory; Ordnance Procedure Instrumentation; Outside Production (Purchase) Inspection

OPIC Overseas Private Investment Corporation

opim order processing and inventory monitoring

opis opisometer

OPIS Operational Priority Indicating System

Opium Eater Thomas De Quincey

Opium Kingdom any country where the opium poppy is cultivated for use in making heroin (Bolivia, Burma, Colombia, Ecuador, Laos, Mexico, etc.)

Opium Land poppy fields of the Golden Triangle or northeastern Burma, northern Laos, and northern Thailand

Opium's Golden Triangle opium-growing fields between borders of Cambodia, Laos, and Vietnam

opl operational

opl oplag (Danish—edition)

OPL Omaha Public Library; Orlando Public Library; Ottawa Public Library

OPLA Offshore Pollution Liability Agreement

OPLP Office of Program and Legislative Planning

opm operations per minute; operator programming method; optically-projected map; orthophoto map; other people's money

OPM Office of Personnel Management; Office of Production Management

OPMA Office Products Manufacturers Association

OPMAC Operation for Military Aid to the Community

OPMCS Otto Pre-Marital Counselling Schedules

opn open (flow chart); operation

o.p.n. ora pro nobis (Latin—pray for us)

OpNav Office of the Chief of Naval Operations

OPNAVINST Office of the Chief of Naval Operations Instruction

opnd opened (flow chart)

opng opening

OPNL Osaka Prefectural Nakanoshima Library (Japan)

opnn opinion

Op. no. opus number

opo one price only; other programmed operations

Opo Oporto

OPO Office of Personnel Operations (US Army)

O Pol Old Polish

OPOR Office of Public Opinion Research

opord operation(s) order

O por O Ojo por Ojo (Spanish—Eye for an Eye)—Guatemalan right-wing terrorists

O Port Old Portuguese

Oporto English or Spanish place-name equivalent of Porto used by the Portuguese and often by the Spaniards

opp opportunity; opposed; opposite; opposition; out of print at present

OPP Office of Pesticide Programs; Ontario Provincial Police; Otago Press and Produce

OPPE Office of Programming, Planning, and Evaluation; Operational Propulsion Plant Examination (USN)

Oppenheim's disease congenital lack of muscular development of the ankles and feet

OPPI Organization of Pharmaceutical Producers of India

Oppie Oppenheim(er); J(ulius)

Robert Oppenheimer
opplan operating plan
oppor opportunity
oppo's opposite numbers
oppy opportunity
Oppy Oppenheimer(er)
opq opaque
opr operate; operator; optical pattern recognition
OPr Old Provençal
OPR Office of Population Research (Princeton); Office of Primary Responsibility; Office of Professional Responsibility (FBI)
oprad operations research and development
oprex operational exercise
opr's old prices riots
OPruss Old Prussian
ops operations; opposite prompter's side (of stage)
op's other people's (cigarettes or money)
OPS Office of Price Stabilization; Office of Product Standards; Oxygen Purge System
OPS *Organisation Panaméricaine de la Santé* (French—Pan-American Health Organization); *Organización Panamericana de la Salud* (Spanish—Pan-American Health Organization)
ops analysis operations analysis
opscan optical scanning
OPSM Optical Prescriptions Spectacle Makers
OPSR Office of Pipeline Safety Regulations
opstat operational status
opt optic; optical; optician; optics; optimal; optimum; option; optional
OPT Office of Promotion and Tourism
OPTA Organ and Piano Teachers Association
optacon optical-to-tactile converter
Opt Acta *Optica Acta* (Latin—Optics Gazette)
Opt Commun *Optics Communications*
Opt.D. Doctor of Optometry
OPTEVFOR Operational Test and Evaluation Force
OPTEVG Operational Test and Evaluation Group
opti optimist(ic); optimize; optimum
optic. optical(ly); optician; opticociliary; opticopupillary
opticon optical tactical converter
Optik (German—Optics)

Opt Lett *Optics Letters*
Opt-Mekh Prom *Optika-Mekhanicheskaya Promyshlennost* (Russian—Journal of Optical Technology)
optmrst optometrist
optn optician
Opt News *Optics News*
optoel optoelectronics
optom optometer; optometric(al)(ly); optometrist; optometry; optomyometer
optr optryk (Dano-Norwegian—reprint)
optrak optical tracking
Opt Spektrosk *Optika i Spektroskopiya* (Russian—Optics and Spectroscopy)
optul optical pulse transmitter using laser
OPU Unemployed Peoples Union
opur objective program utility routines
OPUS Older People United for Service; Open University System; Operating Utility System; Organization for Promoting the Understanding of Society
opv oral polio virus
OPW Office of Public Works
oq oil quench; overmation quotient
OQ Officers Quarters
oqe objective quality evidence
oql on-line query language
OQMG Office of the Quartermaster General
OQR Officer's Qualification Record
or. operationally ready; operations research; other ranks; out of range; outside radius; outside right; overseas replacement; owner's risk; oxidation-reduction
or. (OR) orienting reflex; (released from bail or jail in her or his) own recognizance (promising to return to court when summoned)
o/r on request; other ranks
o & r ocean and rail; overhaul and repair
or (Latin prefix—mouth)—oral
or. oratio (Latin—speech, discourse)
Or Oregon; Orient(al)
Ór Óri (Modern Greek—mountains); *Óros* (Modern Greek—mountain)
OR Oak Ridge; Officer Records; omnidirectional radio range (symbol); Operating Room; Operational Requirement; Operations Requirement; Op-

erations Research; Operations Room; Ordnance Report; Owasco River (railroad); Oyster River
O.R. Operating Room (hospital abbreviation)
O of R Office for Research (ALA)
ÖR Österreichischer Rundfunk (Austrian Radio and Television)
OR *Operations Research*
Ora Orabel(le)
ORA Oil Refiners Association; Operations Research Analyst
oracle. optical reception of announcements of coded-line electronics
ORACLE Optimum Record Automation for Courts and Law Enforcement (Los Angeles, CA)
ORAD Office of Rural Areas Development
ORAM Office for Research in Academic Methods
orang orangutan
orang orangutan (Malay—forest person)—one of the great anthropoid apes found in Borneo and Sumatra
Orange Blossom Florida's state flower
Orange Bowl Miami, Florida
orange flag potential danger signal
Orange Free State English for the Oranje Vrystaat
orange light change approaching; potential danger
Oranges short form usually referring to New Jersey's East Orange, Orange, South Orange, and West Orange but may also refer to the Orange Mountains of that state where they are are also called the Watchungs
Orange State California, Florida, and Texas claim this title
Oranje Vrystaat (Afrikkans or Dutch—Orange Free State)—between the Orange and Vaal rivers of central South Africa
ORASS Offender Risk Assessment Scoring System
orat oration; orator; oratorio; oratory
Orator of the American Revolution Patrick Henry
ORAU Oak Ridge Associated Universities
orb. omnidirectional radio beacon
orb. (ORB) oceanographic research buoy

o-r-b owner's risk of breakage
orbatrep order of battle report
orbic orbicular; orbicularis
Orbis Polish Travel Office
ORBIT On-line Retrieval of Bibliographic Information Timeshared
Orbiter half-plane half-satellite space shuttle
orbs off-reservation boarding school
ORBS Orbital Rendezvous Base System
Orc Orcadian (inhabitant of or pertaining to Orkney Islands)
ORC Ocean Racing Club; Officers Reserve Corps; Offshore Racing Council; Opinion Research Corporation; Ozarks Regional Commission
ORCA Ocean Resources Conservation Association
Orcades Orkney Islands
ORCAP Oficina Regional para Centroamérica y Panamá (Spanish—Regional Office for Central America and Panama)
ORCB Order of Railway Conductors and Brakemen
orch orchestra; orchestral; orchestration
Orch Orchard (postal abbreviation easily confused with Orchestra)—when in doubt, spell it out
Orchard City Burlington, Iowa also called Porkopolis of Iowa
Orchard of Ireland County Armagh
Orch Consv Orchestre de la Société des Concerts du Conservatoire de Paris
Orch de l'Opera de Paris Orchestre du Théâtre National de l'Opera de Paris
orches orchestration
Orchestral Orgasm nickname of the *Don Juan* tone poem by Richard Strauss when properly played
Orch H Orchestra Hall
orchi (Latin prefix—testicles)—orchid, orchiectomy
Orchid Capital of Hawaii Hilo
Orchid Set in the Sea Sulawesi (Celebes)
ORCHIS Oak Ridge Computerized Hierarchical Information System
Orch Nat Orchestre National de la Radiodiffusion Française
Orch Suisse Rom Orchestre de la Suisse Romande
Orch Symp de Mont Orchestre

Symphonique de Montreal (French—Montreal Symphony Orchestra)
ORCMD Orlando Contract Management District
orcon organic control
ORCS Organic Rankine Cycle System
ORCUP Ontario Region Canadian University Press
ord operational ready date; order(s); ordinal; ordnance
o-r-d owner's risk of damage
Ord Order; Orderly; Ordinary Seaman
ORD Chicago, Illinois (O'Hare Airport); Office of Research and Development
ORDA Oceanographic Research for Defense Application
ORD-ALA Office of Research and Development—American Library Association
Ord Bd Ordnance Board
OrdC Ordnance Corps
Ord Dept Ordnance Department
ordfin ordinary finish
ordinst ordnance instruction
Ord Man Ordnance Manual
ordn ordnance
Ordn Surv Ordnance Survey
Ordo Ordovician
ORDP Office of Rural Development Policy
ords ordinary shares
Ord Sgt Ordnance Sergeant
ordsjø (Norwegian—North Sea)
ordvac ordnance variable automatic computer
ORE Ocean Research Equipment; Operational Research Establishment
OR & E Office of Research and Engineering
ORE Office de Recherches et d'Essais (French—Office of Research and Testing)
Oreg Oregon; Oregonian
Oregon Caves Oregon Caves National Monument in the southwestern corner of the state close to California
Oregon Girls Wisconsin School for (delinquent) Girls at Oregon
Oregon Grape state flower of Oregon
Oregon Ports (south to north) Empire, Coos Bay, Astoria, Longview, Portland, Vancouver
Ore-Ida pots Oregon-Idaho potatoes
Orel (pronounced *Ariol*)—Russian town near Yasnaya Poly-

ana, Luminous Clearings, home of Count Leo Tolstoy
o/r enema oil-retention enema
ORES Office of Research and Engineering Services
ORESCO Overseas Research Council
orf orifice; overhaul replacement factor
o-r-f owner's risk of fire
ORF Norfolk, Virginia (airport); Oceanic Research Foundation
ÖRF Österreichischer Rundfunk (Austrian radio and TV network)
Orfeo opera by Monteverdi; *Orfeo ed Euridice* (Italian—Orpheus and Euridice)—Gluck's most popular opera and orchestral suite
Or F S Orange Free State
org organ; organic; organization; organize; organizer
ORG Operations Research Group
organ. organic; organization
Organ Saint-Saëns Symphony No. 3 for orchestra and organ
Organist-Medical Missionary Dr Albert Schweitzer
Organ Pipe Cactus Organ Pipe Cactus National Monument in southern Arizona south of Ajo
org art organic art(ist)
Orgburo Organizational Bureau of the Central Committee (of the Communist Party)
Org Gard Organic Gardening
orgl organizational
org-man organization man
orgn organization
ORGS Operational Research Group of Scotland
orgst organist
ori orientation inventory
Ori Orient(al)(ism); Oriente; Orion (constellation)
ORI Ocean Research Institute; Ocean Resources Institute; Office Research Institute; Operation Readiness Inspection
ORIC Oak Ridge Isochronous Cyclotron
oride override
ORIEL Oriel College, Oxford
orient. oriental; orientation
ORIENT Orient Airways
Orient(al) Asia(tic)
oriental amethyst purple corundum
oriental anesthesia acupuncture
oriental emerald green corundum
Oriental Republic Eastern Republic of Uruguay *(República*

Oriental del Uruguay)
oriental topaz yellow corundum
Orient Express (*see* Ori Exp)
Orient's Cleanest City Singapore
Ori Exp Orient Express (formerly between Paris and Istanbul via Vienna but now called Central Kingdom Express running from London to Hong Kong via Paris, Berlin, Warsaw, Moscow, Irkutsk, Peking, Nanking, and Canton)
orif open reduction with internal fixation
orig origin; original; originator
Original Glamour Girl Theda Bara (Theodosia Goodman) also called Queen of the Vampires in the early days of American motion pictures
O-ring O-shaped ring
Orinoco 1700-mile river creating natural border between Colombia and Venezuela; enters Atlantic Ocean to east of Trinidad
Orinoco River City Ciudad Bolívar, Venezuela
ORINS Oak Ridge Institute of Nuclear Studies
Oriole Maryland's state bird and symbolic nickname of Marylanders—Orioles
orion on-line retrieval of information over a network
Orion Lockheed P 3 antisub marine and patrol aircraft
oris orismological; orismologist; orismology
ORIT Operational Readiness Inspection Test
ORIT Organización Regional Interamericana de Trabajadores (Spanish—Interamerican Regional Labor Organization)
Orizaba Citialtepetl (Mexico's highest volcano)
or j orange juice
Ork Orkney Islands
Orkneys Orkney Islands
orl orlon (synthetic fiber); owner's risk of leakage
ORL Orbital Research Laboratory; Ordnance Research Laboratory; Orlando, Florida (Harndon Airport)
ORL Outlook on Research Libraries
ORLA Optimum Repair Level Analysis
Orlando di Lasso Roland de Lassus
Orleanskaya Orleanskaya deva (Russian—Maid of Orleans) —Tchaikovsky opera based

on Schiller's tale about Joan of Arc
Órm Órmos (Modern Greek—bay)
ORM Ohio Reformatory for Men
ORMAK Oak Ridge Tokamak
orml oriental meal
orm('s) off-road motorcycle(s)
orn orange; ornament
orn orne (French—decorated, ornamented)
Orn Oran (British maritime contraction)
ORN Operating Room Nurse
ornith ornithology
ornithol ornithologic(al)(ly); ornithologist; ornithology
ORNL Oak Ridge National Laboratory
ORNLL Oak Ridge National Laboratory Library
ORO Oak Ridge Operations Office; Operations Research Office (Johns Hopkins University)
or. obliq. oratio obliqua (Latin—indirect speech, oblique speech)
orog orographer; orographic; orographical; orography
ORP Okret Rzecypospolitej Polskiej (Polish—Ship of the Polish Republic)
ORPA Office of Regional and Political Affairs (CIA)
ORPC Office of Rail Public Counsel
orph orphan; orphanage; orphaned; orphans
orpiment arsenic sulfide
o-r pot. oxidation-reduction potential
orr operations research research (ORR)
o-r-r owner's risk rates
o-r release own-recognizance release (legal device freeing responsible citizens from need for going to jail or posting bail bond until case comes to court for hearing)
ORRRC Outdoor Recreation Resources Review Commission
ORRT Operational Readiness Reliability Test
ors owner's risk of shifting
ors (ORS) orbiting research satellite; orthopaedic surgery
or's onion rings; orienting responses
ors. orationes (Latin — speeches)
ORS Office of Research and Statistics; Old Red Sandstone;

Operational Research Society
ORSA Operations Research Society of America
ORSANCO Ohio River Valley Water Sanitation Commission
ORSE Operational Reactor Safeguard Examination
ORSJ Operations Research Society of Japan
ORSTOM Office de la Recherche Scientifique et Technique d'Outre Mer (Overseas Office of Scientific and Technical Research)
ort odor recognition threshold; operational readiness training
ORT Operational Readiness Test; Order of Railroad Telegraphers; Organization for Rehabilitation through Training; Overage Retirement Training (program)
ORTF Office de Radiodiffusion Télévision Française (French Office of Television Broadcasting)
ortho orthochromatic; orthographic; orthography; orthopedic(s)
ortho (Latin prefix—normal or straight)—orthopedic
Ortho Greek Orthodox
orthog orthography
ortho-k orthokeratological(ly); orthokeratologist; orthokeratology
orthokera orthokeratologist; orthokeratology
orthomol orthomolecular; ortho molecularologist; orthomolecularology
orthop orthopedics
orthor orthorhombic
ORTO Occupational Rehabilitation Training for Overseas
ORTPA Oven-Ready Turkey Producers' Association
ORTS Optional Residence Telephone Service
ORTU Other Ranks Training Unit
ORU Oral Roberts University
ORuss Old Russian
ORV Ocean Range Vessel (naval symbol)
orv('s) off-road vehicle(s)
orw owner's risk of wetting
ORW Ohio Reformatory for Women
Orwell's Year 1984
ory (Latin suffix—pertaining to) —sensory
Ory Le Compte Ory (French—The Count Ory)—two-act opera by Rossini

ORY Paris, France (Orly Airport)

os oil solvent; oil switch; old series; old style; on station; out of stock; output secondary; outside; outsize; overseas; oversize

os (OS) operating system (data recording)

o/s out of service; out of stock

o & s over and short

os (Latin—bone, mouth)

o.s. *oculus sinister* (Latin—left eye)

Os osmium

OS Ocean Station; Office Surgery; Old Saxon; Old Series; Operating System; Operation Sandstone; Operation Snapper; Optical Society; Ordinary Seaman; Ordnance Specifications; Ordnance Survey; Overseas Service

O.S. Old Style

osa oil-soluble acid; order for simple alert

Osa Osaka

Osa (Russian—Bee)—NATO name for a Soviet class of guided-missile patrol boats

OSA Office of the Secretary of the Army; Official Secrets Act; Omnibus Society of America; Optical Society of America; Osaka, Japan (airport); Overseas Sterling Area; Overseas Supply Agency; Oyster Shell Association

OSA *Ocean Shipping Act*

osac orifice spark advance control

OSAF Office of the Secretary of the Air Force

OSAHRC Occupational Safety and Health Review Commission

OSAP Ontario Student Awards Program

OSAS Overseas Service Aid Scheme

O Sax Old Saxon

OSB Otago Savings Bank; Overseas Service Bureau

O.S.B. Order of St Benedict

OSBA Ohio School Boards Association; Oregon School Boards Association

OSBM Office of Space Biology and Medicine

osc oscillator

Osc Oscan

OSC On-Scene Commander; Ontario Science Centre; Ontario Securities Commission; Order of St Clare; Ordnance Systems Command (formerly Bureau of Weapons); Overseas Shipping Company

O.S.C. Oblate of Saint Charles

O of SC Order of Scottish Clans

OSCA Office of Senior Citizens Affairs

OSCA *Officine Specializzate Costruzione Automobili* (Italian—Special Office of Automobile Construction)

OSCAA Oil-Spill Control Association of America

O Scan Old Scandinavian

oscar (nickname—award for achievement, golden statuette awarded annually to best actor, actress, composer, director, photographer, etc., in American motion pictures); orbital-satellite-carrying amateur radio (OSCAR); oxygen steelmaking computer and recorder

Oscar letter O radio code

OSCAR On-Line System for Controlling Activities and Resources; Optimum System for the Control of Aircraft Retardation

Oscar(s) Motion Picture Academy Award(s)

Oscar Wilde Oscar Fingal O'Flahertie Wills (also used the anonym: C.3.3.)

ÖSCG *Österreichische Studiengesellschaft für Kybernetik* (German—Austrian Society for Cybernetic Studies)

OSCO Oil Service Company of Iran; Oil Shipment Corporation

oscope oscilloscope

oscp oscilloscope

OSCP Ocean Sediment Coring Program (NSF)

OSCT Office of Scholarly Communication and Technology

osd on-line systems driver; open shelter deck; optical scanning device; out-of-station designation

o s & d over, short, and damaged

OSD Office of the Secretary of Defense; Operational Support Directive; Ordnance Supply Depot; Original Sponsoring Distributor

OSDBMC Office of the Secretary of Defense, Ballistic Missile Committee

OSDNRL Ocean Science Division—Naval Research Laboratory

osdocs over-the-shore discharge of container ships

osdp on-site data processing

OSDP Operational System Development Program

OSDSA Office of the Secretary of Defense, Systems Analysis

OSDSAC Office of the Secretary of Defense, Scientific Advisory Committee

ose operational support equipment

ose (Latin suffix—full of)—adipose

OSE Ocean Shipping and Enterprises; Office of Science Education; Office of of Sex Equity (HEW); Office of Systems Engineering

OS & E Ocean Science and Engineering

OSEAP Oil Shale Environmental Advisory Panel

o'seas overseas

OSEB Orissa State Electricity Board

OSerb Old Serbian

osf operational service fee; ordinary shareholders funds

OSF Order of St Francis

OSFI Open Steel Flooring Institute

O.S.F.S. Oblate of Saint Francis of Sales

OSG Office of Sea Grant (NOAA); Office of the Secretary General (UN)

OSG *Official Steamship Guide*

OSGP Office of Sea Grant Programs

o.s.h. *omni singula hora* (Latin—every hour)

Osh Ossian

OSH Office on Smoking and Health

OSHA Occupational Safety and Health Act; Occupational Safety and Health Administration

o/sheep odd sheep

o/ship ownership

OSHPD Office of Statewide Health Planning and Development

OSHRC Occupational Safety and Health Review Commission

OSHS Occupational Safety and Health Scheme

OSI Office of Samoan Information; Office of Special Investigation (USAF); Off-Site Instruction; Ohio Scientific Incorporated; Other Service Investigation

OSIA Order of the Sons of Italy in America

osie operational support integration engineering

OSIP Operational and Safety Improvement Program

osis (Greek—condition or state of being)—arteriosclerosis, cirrhosis, halitosis, tuberculosis

OSIS Office of Science Information Service

Osk Oskarshamm

OSK Osaka Syosen Kaisha (Osaka Mercantile Steamship Company)

OSK Országos Széchényi Könyvtár (Hungarian—National Széchényi Library)—in Budapest

Oskar Werner Josef Bschliessmayer

Osl Oslo

OSl Old Slavonic

OSL Office of the Secretary of Labor; Oslo, Norway (airport)

OSLat Old-Style Latin

Oslo modern name for Christiania or Kristiania

Osloenser native of Oslo

Oslo Fjord formerly Kristiania Fjord

osm osmosis; osmotic

Osm osmol(s)

OSM Office Service Manual; One of the Swinish Multitude (Philip Freneau, poet of the American Revolution, used this three-letter device after his name, thereby deriding similar-looking British titles); Overzees Scheepvaart Maatschappij (Overseas Shipping Company)

OSMA Otago-Southland Manufacturers Association

OSMM Office of Safeguards and Materials Management (AEC)

osmol osmosis + mol (standard unit of osmotic pressure)

osmos own ship's motion simulator

OSMRE Office of Surface Mining Reclamation Enforcement

OSN Office of the Secretary of the Navy

OSN Orquesta Sinfónica Nacional (Spanish—National Symphonic Orchestra)

OSNC Orient Steam Navigation Company

OSNY Oratorio Society of New York

oso (OSO) orbiting solar observatory

OSO Offshore Supplies Office; Offshore Supply Office; Oma-

ha Symphony Orchestra; Ordnance Supply Office(r); Oregon Symphony Orchestra

OSO Oessudoeste (Spanish—west southwest); Orbiting Solar Observatory; Ordnance Supply Office

OSODS Office of Strategic Offensive and Defensive Systems (USN)

osp outside purchased

o-sp off-street parking

o.s.p. obiit sine prole (Latin—died without issue)

OSp Old Spanish

OSP Open-Space Program (for environmental conservation and view preservation); Order of St Paul

OSP Oficina Sanitaria Panamericana (Pan-American Sanitation Office)

OSPA Overseas Pensioners' Association

OSPA Organisation de la Santé Panaméricaine (French—Pan-American Health Organization)

OSPAAL Organización de Solidaridad de los Pueblos de Asia, Africa, y Latino-América (Spanish—Organization of Solidarity of the Peoples of Asia, Africa, and Latin America)—communist directed and inspired

OSPIC Overseas Private Investment Corporation

OSPJ Offshore Procurement, Japan

osprd(s) oblate spheroid(s)

OSQ Office of Safety Quality Assurance and Safeguards

OSQ Orchestre Symphonique de Québec (French—Quebec Symphonic Orchestra)

OSQAS Office of Safety Quality Assurance and Safeguards

osr own ship's roll

OSR Office of Scientific Research; Office of Security Review; Office of Strategic Research; Oil Shale Reserves; Operational Support Requirement(s); Oversea Returnee

OSR Orchestre de la Suisse Romande (French—Orchestra of French Switzerland)

OSRA Overseas Shipping Representatives Association

OSRB Overseas Service Resettlement Bureau

OSRD Office of Scientific Research and Development; Office of Standard Reference Data

OSRO Office of Scientific Research and Development

OSROK Office of Supply—Republic of Korea

OSRTN Office of the Special Representative for Trade Negotiations

oss order short shipped

oSS operates Saturday and Sunday

OSS Object-Sorting Scales (psychological test); Office of Space Science; Office of Strategic Services; Office of Support Services; old submarine (3-letter code); Operating Supply Specification; Operational Storage Site; Optical Surveillance System; Orbital Space Station; Orient Shipping Services; Overseas Shipping Services

OSSA Office of Space Sciences and Applications (NASA)

OSSBA Oklahoma State School Boards Association

OSSC Oregon School Study Council

Ossie Oswaldtwistle, England

Ossining Facility Ossining Correctional Facility at Ossining, New York, long nicknamed Sing Sing

Ossining-on-Hudson formerly Hunter's Landing or Sing Sing

Ossip Gabrilovich Salomono vich Gabrilovich

OSSNSS Ordnance Supply Segment of the Navy Supply System (USN)

oss(OSS) orbiting space station

OSSP Oregon Small Schools Program

OSSS Orbital Space Station Studies

OSSTF Ontario Secondary School Teachers' Federation

ost objectives, strategies, tactics; oldest; on same terms, optical star tracker; ordinary spring tides

Ost Ostend

Ost Ostrów (Polish—island)

OST Office of Science and Technology; Old Spanish Trail (US 90); Operational Suitability Test

OS & T Office of Science and Technology

osteo osteopath(ic)

osteo osteon (Greek—bone)—ossification, ossified, osteomyelitis, osteopath(ic)

osteoart osteoarthritic; osteoarthritis

osteol osteology

osteomy osteomyelitis

osteop osteopath(ic); osteopathy

Österreich (German—Eastern Empire)—Austria (modern remnant of the once great Austro-Hungarian Empire)

OSTF Operational System Test Facility

OSTI Office for Scientific and Technical Information

OSTIV Organisation Scientifique et Technique Internationale du Vol à Voile (French—International Scientific and Technical Organization for Soaring Flight)

O.St.J. Officer of the Order of Saint John of Jerusalem

Østland (Norwegian—Eastland)—eastern and southeastern Norway

OSTP Office of Science and Technology Policy

Ostpr Ostpreussen (German—East Prussia)

Ostrova De Longa (Russian—De Long Islands)

OSTS Office of State Technical Services; Official Seed Testing Station

Ostsee (German—East Sea)—the Baltic

OSU Ohio State University; Oklahoma State University; Oregon State University

OSUAS Ohio State University (College of) Administrative Science

OSUK Ophthalmological Society of the United Kingdom

OSUL Ohio State University Library; Oklahoma State University Library; Oregon State University Library

OSUP Ohio State University Press

osv och sa vida (Swedish—and so forth); *og sa videre* (Dano-Norwegian—and so forth)—etc.

Osv Osvald; Osvaldo

OSV Ocean Station Vessel

OSV Orquesta Sinfonica Venezuela (Spanish—Venezuela Symphony Orchestra); *Our Sunday Visitor*

Osv Rom Osservatore Romano (Vatican newspaper)

osw operational switching

Osw Oswald

OSw Old Swedish

OSW Office of Saline Water

OSWA Off-Shift Work Authorization

Oswiecim (Polish—Auschwitz)

osy (OSY) optimum sustainable yield

os & y outside screw and yolk

ot observer target; oiltight; old terms; old tuberculin; on time; on track; ordinary tide(s); otitis; otology; our telegram; ovum transfer

ot (OT) occupational therapy; otolaryngology; overtime; original transposed (in a 12-tone row)

o't (Gaelic contraction—of it)

o/t on truck; overtime

'ot hot

o-T on-Thames

O/t old term (grain market)

OT Occupational Therapist; Occupational Therapy; Ocean Transportation; Office of Territories; Old Testament; Operational Training; Oregon Trunk (railroad); Organization Table; Otis Elevator (stock exchange symbol); Overseas Tankship (Caltex Line); Overseas Trade

O of T Office of Telecommunications (OT)

OT Organisation Todt (German—Death Organization)—Hitler's extermination corps

OTA Occupational Therapists Association; Office of Technology Assessment; Office of Territorial Affairs; Outer Transport Area

OTAC Ordnance Tank and Automotive Command

otadl outer target azimuth datum line

OTAF Office of Technology Assessment and Forecast

OTAG Office of the Adjutant General (USA)

Otago Otago Harbour (Dunedin, New Zealand's port); Otago Peninsula (southeast of the port)

OTAN Organisation du Traite del l'Atlantique Nord (French—NATO); *Organizacion del Tratado del Atlántico Norte* (Spanish—NATO)—North Atlantic Treaty Organization

OTAR Overseas Tariffs and Regulations

OTAS Organización del Atlántico Septentrional (Spanish—North Atlantic Treaty Organization)—NATO

OTASE Organisation du Traite de l'Asie du Sud-Est (SEATO)

OTAT Office of Technical Assistance and Training; Ortho-

toluidine Arsenite Test

OTATO One-Trip Air Travel Orders

otb off-track betting

OTB Overseas Trust Bank

OTBA Owners, Traders, Breeders Association

otbd outboard

otc objective, time, and cost; ocean transshipment cargo; one-stop charter; outer tube centerline; over the counter

OTC Officer in Tactical Command; Officers Training Corps; Organization for Trade Cooperation; Ottawa Transit Commission; Overseas Telecommunications Commission

OTC Office de Tourisme du Canada (French—Canadian Government Office of Tourism)

otch obedience trial champion

otd organ tolerance dose

OTD Ocean Technology Division

otda other-than-defined adult

otdc optical target designation computer

OTDC Observational Test and Development Center (NWS)

OTD & SP Office of Technical Data and Standardization Policy

ote operational test and evaluation; overtaken by events

ote oriente (Spanish—east)

otec (OTEC) ocean thermal energy conversion

OTEC Ontario Teacher Education Colleges

OTECS Ocean Thermal Energy Conversion System

otel our telegram

Otepeni Bucharest, Romania's airport

OTeut Old Teutonic

otf optical transfer function

o-t-f off-the-film (light measurement)

OTF Ontario Teachers Federation

oth over the horizon

Oth Othello, The Moor of Venice

othb over-the-horizon backscatter

Other Side of the Herring Pond British nickname for America

othf over-the-horizon forward scatter

Othonia (Latin—Odense)

oti official test insecticide

OTI Oregon Technical Institute

OTI Organización de Televisión Iberoamericana (Spanish—

Ibero-American Television Organization)

OTIA Ordnance Technical Intelligence Agency

OTID Office of Talented Identification and Development (Johns Hopkins)

OTIG Office of the Inspector General

OTIS Occupational Training Information System; Oregon Total Information System

OTIU Overseas Technical Information Unit

otj on the job

otK old tuberculin Koch

otl out to lunch; output transformerless; over the line

OTL Operating Time Log

otlx our telex

otm other track material

OTM Office of Telecommunications Management; Old Turkey Mill

otml oatmeal

otno our telegram number

oto one time only (tv)

oto (Latin prefix—ear)—otology

otol otology

otolaryngol otolaryngology

OTO/Neth only to order from Netherlands (for example)

otorhinol otorhinolaryngology

otp obstacle to progress; order to plan; oxygen tanking panel

OTP Office of Telecommunications Policy

otr on the rag (underground slang—on the menstrual cycle)

OTR Ovarian Tumor Registry; Registered Occupational Therapist

Otrabanda (Papiamento Oth er Side)—other side of the harbor of Willemstad, Curaçao

otrac oscillogram trace

OTRACO Office de l'Exploitation des Transports Coloniaux (Congolese railway and river transportation administration)

OTRAG Orbital Transport and Rocket AG (German rocket company)

otran ocean test range and instrumentation

otrt operating time record tag

ots (OTS) orbital technical satellite

OTS Office of Technical Services; Office of Traffic Safety; Officers Training School; Operational Test Site

otsdg outstanding

OTSG Office of the Surgeon General

otsr optimum track ship routing

OTSS Operational Test Support System

ott one-time tape; otter; outgoing teletype

ott ottobre (Italian—October)

Ott Ottawa

OTT Ocean Transport and Trading; Office of Traffic and Transportation

Otter De Haviland utility aircraft (DHC-3 in Canada, U-1A in U.S.)

Ottoman Empire the old Turkish Empire extending at its height from Iran to Morocco, including all of modern Turkey, Mesopotamia, Arabian coasts, Syria, Palestine, Egypt, North Africa, the Balkans, parts of Hungary and southern Russia as well as much of Spain; Turkish Empire

otu operational taxonomic unit

otu (OTU) operational training unit

OTU Office of Technology Utilization (NASA)

O Turk Old Turkish

OTUS Office of the Treasurer of the United States

otv outer television

otvct outer tube vertical centerline target

otw over the wing

oty over to you

ou oat unit; official use

o & u over and under

'ou thou

o.u. oculus uterque (Latin—either eye)

OU Oglethorpe University; Ohio University; Oklahoma University; Otago University; Ottawa University; Otterbein University; Owen University; Owosso University; Oxford University

OUA Order of United Americans

OUA Organisation de l'Unité Africaine (French—OAU); *Organización de Unidad Africana* (Spanish—OAU)—Organization of African Unity

OUAC Oxford University Appointments Committee; Oxford University Athletic Club

OUAFC Oxford University Association Football Club

OUAM Order of United American Mechanics

OUAS Oxford University Air Squadron

Oubangui (French—Ubangi)—central African river and tribal people

OUBC Oxford University Boat Club

OUCC Oxford University Cricket Club

Oudekerkplein (Dutch—Old Church Place)—Amsterdam's seamen's quarter replete with red-lighted cribs

OUDP Officer Undergraduate Degree Program (USA)

OUDS Oxford University Dramatic Society

Ouessant (French—Ushant)

Ouga Ouagadougou, Upper Volta

OUGC Oxford University Golf Club

oughtn't ought not

OUHC Oxford University Hockey Club

OUHS Oxford University Historical Society

Ouida pseudonym of Marie Louise de la Ramée who as a child pronounced Louise as Ouida

OULC Oxford University Lacrosse Club

OULCS Ontario Universities Library Cooperative System

OULTC Oxford University Lawn Tennis Club

OUM Oxford University Mission

OUN Organizatsia Ukrainiskikh Natsionalistiv (Russian—Ukrainian Nationalist Organization)—anti-communist

OUP Oxford University Press

oupt output

OUR Office of University Research

Ouragan (French—Hurricane)—Dassault single-engine jet fighter plane

OURC Oxford University Rifle Club

OURFC Oxford University Rugby Football Club

Our Gracie Gracie Fields (created Dame Commander of the Order of the British Empire after years of entertaining many millions of Britons and others around the world)

Our Lady of the Snows Kipling's nickname for Canada

o/us over-under shotgun

o/US oro US (Spanish—American gold, American money)

OUSC Oxford University Swimming Club

'ouse douse; house; kouse; louse; mouse; rouse; souse; touse

OUSF Oxford University School of Forestry

OUSL Office of the Undersecretary of Labor

out. outlet; output

outbd outboard

Outer Banks North Carolina's sand-dune islands separated from the mainland by Albemarle, Croatan, Pamlico, and Bogue sounds

Outer China Mongolia, Sinkiang, Tibet

Outer City metropolitan area surrounding Peking's Inner City

Outer Mongolia The Mongolian People's Republic formerly called Mongolia

Outer Ring English counties adjacent to London

Outpost of the British Empire nickname given at anytime to any remote British settlement from Adelaide to Zululand

Outpost of the West the Philippines

outran output translator

out of sync out of synchronization

ouv ouvrage (French—work)

ov observed velocity; optimum value; orbiting vehicle (OV); over

ov oi vay (Yiddish—alas)

ov. ovum (Latin—egg)

Ov Ovid; Oviedo

Ov Over (Dano-Norwegian or Dutch—upper); *Overijssel* (Dutch province above the Ijssel River)

Öv Över (Swedish—upper)

OV Office Visit

OV Oranje Vrystaat (Afrikaans —Orange Free State); Orbital Vehicle

ÖV Österreichische Volkspartei (German—Austrian People's Party)

OV-10 North American-Rockwell Bronco counterinsurgency aircraft

o^va ottava (Italian—octave)

O^va Ostrova (Bulgarian, Czechoslovakian, Russian—island)

OVA Office of Veterans' Affairs

OVAC Overseas Visual Aids Center

ovbd overboard

ovc other valuable consideration(s); overcast

ovcst overcast

ove on vehicle equipment

ÖVE Österreichischer Verband für Elektrotechnik (German— Austrian Society for Electrotechnology)

over. overture

overmation over instrumentation

overs overshoes

Overthrust Belt Rocky Mountain gas-and-oil lands

ovf ovenfor (Dano-Norwegian— over)

ovfl overflow

ovflow overflow

ovh overhead; overheat

ovhd oval head; overhead

ovhdld overhandled

ovhl overhaul

ovh p overhead projector

ovht overheat

Ovid Roman poet Publius Ovidus Naso

OVIS Ohio Vocational Interest Survey

ovk overkill

OVKOT On Various Kinds of Thinking (essay by James Harvey Robinson)

ovld overload

ovly overlay

ovm on-vehicle material

ovm oi vayz mir (Yiddish—woe unto me)

ovo (Latin prefix—egg)—ovo-vegetarian

ovolactos ovolactovegetarians (confining their diet to eggs, milk and milk products, as well as vegetables)

ovos ovovegetarians (confining their diet to eggs and vegetables)

ovpd overpaid

ovprt overprinted

OVPUS Office of the Vice President of the United States

OVR Office of Vocational Rehabilitation

OVRA Opera Voluntaria per la Repressione dell' Anti-fascismo (Italian—Voluntary Work for the Repression of Anti-Fascism)—Facist secret police

ovrd override

ovsl overslow

ovsp overspeed

ovstfd overstuffed

ovstk overstock(ed)

OVSVA Oranje Vrystaatse Veld Artillerie (Afrikaans—Orange Free State Field Artillery)

ovtr operational videotape recorder

ov w overgankelijk werkwoord (Dutch—transitive verb)

ow off white; old woman (slang for wife); one way; ordinary warfare (OW); out of wedlock (born of unmarried parents); outer wing; over water

o-w oil-in-water

o/w oil/water ratio (oil well)

o:w oil-water ratio

oW ohne Wert (German—without value)

öW Österreichische Währung (German—Austrian currency)

OW Observation Ward; Old Welsh

O & W Oldest and Wisest (newspaper reporter's nickname for Ronald Reagan)

OWAA Outdoors Writers' Association of America

OWAEC Organization for West African Economic Cooperation

owc owner will carry

OWC Outline of World Cultures

O-WC Oil-Water Contract (oil well)

OWCP Office of Workers' Compensation Programs

owe operating weight empty

Owen Meredith Edward Robert Bulwer-Lytton's pseudonym

Owen Stanleys Owen Stanley Mountains of New Guinea

owf optimum working frequency

owgl obscure wire glass

OWH Office of the War on Hunger

OWHA Oliver Wendell Holmes Association

OWI Office of War Information; Office of Waste Isolation

owise otherwise

OWL Ocotillo Water League; Older Women's League; Older Women's Liberation; Other Woman, Limited; Overland Western Limited

owlsville London's post-midnight nickname or any other place after midnight

owm over without marks

OWM Office of Weights and Measures

OWMA Oscar Wells Museum of Art (Birmingham, Alabama)

OWO OWI Washington Office

owp outer wing panel

OWPP Office of Welfare and Pension Plans

owpr ocean wave profile recorder

OWPS Offshore Windpower

System
OWR Ouse Washes Reserve (England)
OWRR Office of Water Resources Research
OWRT Office of Water Research and Technology
ows (OWS) operational weapon satellite
OWS Ocean Weather Station
OWSS Ocean Weather Ship Service
OWU Ohio Wesleyan University
OWWS Office of World Weather Systems
ow/ym older woman/younger man
ox. our telex; oxalic; oxide; oxygen
Ox. Oxford
OX oxygen (commercial symbol)
oxa oxalic acid
oxalic acid (COOII)$_2$
Oxbridge Oxford + Cambridge (the ultimate in British formal education)
oxd oxidation; oxidize(d)
Oxf Oxfordshire
OXFAM Oxford Committee for Famine Relief
Oxf & Bucks Oxfordshire and Buckinghamshire (light infantry)
Oxford Haydn's Symphony No. 92 in G major
Oxford UP Oxford University Press

oxim oxide-isolated monolithic technology
Oxm Oxmantown
Ox M OUP Oxford Medical (division) Oxford University Press
OXOCO Offshore Exploration Oil Company
Oxon Oxfordshire
Oxon. *Oxonia* (Latin—Oxford); *Oxoniensis* (Latin—Oxonian)
Oxonia (Middle Latin—Oxford)
oxr oxidizer
oxwld oxyacetylene weld
oxy oxygen
Oxy Occidental College; Occidental Petroleum Corporation; Oxy Metal Industries International
oxycephs oxycephalics (pointed skulled people)
oxym oxymel (honey-water-vinegar solution)
oy (OY) optimum yield
OY orange yellow
O/Y Osakeytiö (Finnish—limited company)
OYA Oy Yleisradio Ab (Finnish Broadcasting Company)
Oya Cur Oyashio Current (Kurile or Okhotsk or Oyasiwo)
Oyashio (Japanese—Father Current)—cold Okhotsk Current
OYD Office of Youth Development
oyo own your own (apartment, house, yacht)

oys oysters
OYS Outstanding Young Singaporeans
Oyster Center Apalachicola, Florida
Oyster(s) Marylander(s)
oystersan oyster sandwich
Oyster State Maryland
oysterwich oyster sandwich
oz ounce
oz onza (Spanish—ounce)
Oz Aussie(s); Australia(n); ooze; Osborn(e)
OZ Ozark Airlines (two-letter-designation)
OZ Ozean (German—ocean); *Ozero* (Russian—lake)
OZA Ozark Airlines
oz ap apothecaries' ounce(s)
ozarc ozone-atmosphere rocket
Ozarks Ozark Mountains of Arkansas, Missouri, and Oklahoma
oz avd avoirdupois ounce(s)
ozd observed zenith distance
ozf ounce-force
oz-ft ounce-foot
oz in. ounce inch
OZO oost zuidoost (Dutch—east southeast)
ozone O$_3$
ozs ounces
oz t ounce troy
ozws otherwise
Ozy Ozzie
Ozzie Aussy; Australian; Osborn(e); Oscar; Oswald(o)

P

p fluid density (symbol); page; pamphlet; paragraph; park; parking; part; participle; pass(ed); past; paste; pawn; pebbles; pectoral; pence; pengü (Hungarian monetary unit); penny; *per* (Latin—by); percentile; perceptual (speed); percussion; perforate; perforated; perforation; perimeter; period; perishable; peseta; peso; peta (P)—10^{15} (one quadrillion); peyote; *piano* (Italian—softly); piaster; piastre; picot; pie; pilaster; pimp; pink; pint; pipe; pitch; pitcher; plasma; plaster; plate; plus; point; polar; pole; pond; population; porcelain; port, or left side of an airplane or vessel when looking forward (P or L); position; positive; post; postage; posterior; postpartum; power; predicate; predict(ion); premolar; presbyopia; present; pressure; primary; primitive; principal; principle; probability (ratio); product; prompter; proprionate; proton; publication; pulse; pupil

p (P) prime

£ pound sterling

p. *pagina* (Italian, Latin, Portuguese, Spanish—page); *parte* (Latin—part); *pater* (Latin—father); *per* (Latin—by); *pondere* (Latin—by weight); *proximum* (Latin—near); *pugillus* (Latin—fistful)—handful

p % *por ciento* (Spanish—per hundred, percent)

P Pacific; pamphlet; Panama Line; Papa—code letter for P; Paris; Parisian; passenger vessel (symbol); patrol; Pennzoil; Philadelphia Mint (symbol); phosphorus; Piasecki; plate; Pleyel; poise; polar; polarization; pole; police; poor; Pope; port; Portugal (auto plaque); power; present value; President; Prince Line; principal; priority; project; propulsion; Protestant; protozoa; pulse

P. protein(s) (dietary symbol)

P (Latin—Publius); pilot (white *P* on a blue flag flown on a pilot boat); *Pilot* (German); *pilota* (Italian); *pilote* (French); *piloto* or *practico* (Spanish)

p00 program zero-zero

P_1 first parental generation

P 1/C Private First Class

P 1/C M Private First Class Marine

P-2 Lockheed Neptune antisubmarine and reconnaisance naval aircraft

P_2 pulmonic second sound

P2 *Panzer* (German—armor, armor plated, tank)

P-2J Kawasaki version of the Lockheed Neptune antisubmarine and reconnaissance aircraft

P-3 Lockheed Orion antisubmarine and patrol aircraft

P-4 Soviet Komsomolets motor torpedo boats

P-5 Marlin twin-engine all-weather seaplane for long-range antisubmarine patrol and electronic reconnaissance

P-5M Martin Marlin flying boat

P-6 Soviet motor torpedoboats used in many communist satellite countries

P.08 German marking denoting the so-called luger service pistol

P^{33} radioactive phosphorus

P-38 U.S. pursuit aircraft

P.38 German 9mm service pistol (World War II)

P_{55} partial pressure of O_2 wherein hemoglobin is half saturated with O_2

P-60 60-minute parking

P-149 Piaggo trainer aircraft built in Italy

P-166M Piaggo Albatross coastal patrol aircraft

P-333C Lockheed antisubmarine patrol plane

pa intensity of atmospheric pressure (symbol); paper; paper advance; paralysis agitans; participial adjective; particular average; patient; pattern analysis; pending availability; performance analysis; permanent appointment; pernicious anemia; personal appearance; piaster; piastre; point of aim; position approximate; power amplifier; power approach; power of attorney; press agent; pressure altitude; private account; provisional allowance; psychoanalyst; public address (system); public assistance; publication announcement; purchasing agent

pa (Pa) pascal

pa (PA) posteroanterior

p-a psychogenic aspermia

p/a paid annually; payment authority; per annum; power of attorney

p & a percussion and auscultation; plugged and abandoned (oil well); price and availability

p in the a pain in the ass

p.a. *per abdomen* (Latin—by the abdomen); *per annum* (Latin —by the year)

p A *por autorización* (Spanish— in care of)

Pa Panama; Panamanian; Panameña; Panameño; Papa; Para; Pará (Belem do Pará); Pascal; Pennsylvania; Pennsylvanian; protactinium

PA Parents Anonymous; Passenger Agent; Pennsylvanian Railroad (stock exchange symbol); Philippine Army; Philippine Association; Piedmont Airlines; Polled Angus (cattle); Port Agency; Post Adjutant; Prefect Apostolic; Press Agent; Press Association; Prince Albert (coal); Procurement Authorization; Proprietary Association; Prosecuting Attorney; Prothonotary Apostolic; psychological age; Public Act; Public Affairs; Publishers Association; Puppeteers of America; Purchasing Agent

P-A Pacific-Atlantic Line; Pan-Atlantic Line

P/A Picatinny Arsenal

P & A Professional and Administrative

P of A Port of Anchorage

PA *Priok Administration* (Malay—Port Administration); *Psychological Abstracts*

PA$_{O2}$ alveolar oxygen pressure

p.a.a. *parti affectae applicetur* (Latin—apply to the affected parts or region)

PAA Pacific Alaska Airways; Pan American World Airways System (3-letter designation); Pharmaceutical Association of Australia; Photographers Association of America; Plywood Association of Australia; Potato Association of America; Prisoners Aid Association; Purchasing Agents Association

PAAA Premium Advertising Association of America

PAAC Product Assurance Action Center; Program Analysis Adaptable Control; Public Arts Advisory Council

PAADC Principal Air Aide-de-Camp

PAAE Pennsylvania Association for Adult Education

PAAM Prisoners Aid Association of Maryland

PAAO Pan-American Association of Ophthalmology

pab per acre bonus

pab (**PAB**) p-aminobenzoic acid

PAB Panair do Brasil (airline); Petroleum Administrative Board; Price Adjustment Board

PAB (CIA) Problems Analysis Branch of the CIA

paba para-amino benzoic acid

pabla problem analysis by logical approach

Pablo Neruda Neftali Ricardo Reyes

Pablo Picasso Pablo Diego José Francisco de Paula Juan Nepomuceno Crispin Crispiano de la Santísima Trinidad Ruiz y Picasso

pabst primary adhesively-bonded structure

pabx private automatic branch telephone exchange

pac packaged assembly circuit; personal analog computer; phenacetin-aspirin-caffeine (all-purpose capsule); prearrival confirmation; production acceleration capacity; project analysis and control; pursuant to authority contained (in); put and call (stock exchange jargon)

pac (PAC) premature atrial contraction

p-a-c parent-adult-child (ego states)

Pac Pacific

Pac *Pacifico* (Italian—Pacific); *Pacífico* (Portuguese or Spanish—Pacific); *Pacifique* (French—Pacific)

PAC Pacific Air Command; Pacific Automotive Corporation; Pacific Telephone & Telegraph (stock exchange symbol); Palo Alto Clinic; Pan-Africanist Congress; Pan-American Congress; Performing Arts Center; Pharmaceutical Advertising Club; Philbrook Art Center; Political Action Committee; Public Access Catalog(ue); Public Affairs Committee; Public Assistance Cooperative

Paca Francesca

PACAF Pacific Air Force

Pacaraimas short form for the Pacaraima Mountains forming the Brazil-Guyana and Brazil-Venezuela borders

PACAS Patient Care System; Psychological Abstracts Current Awareness Service

PACB Pan-American Coffee Bureau

Pac Bch Pacific Beach

PACC Product Administration and Contract Control; Project Administration Contact Control

PACCS Post Attack Command and Control System

PacD Pacific Division

PACDA Personnel and Administration Combat Development Activity (USA)

pace (PACE) package-crammed executive; performance and cost evaluation; precision analog computing equipment; pre-launch automatic checkout equipment; program to advance creativity in education; programmed automatic communications equipment; projects to advance creativity in education

pace. pacemaker

PACE Pacific America Container Express; Professional and Administrative Career Examination; Professional Association of Consulting Engineers; Program for Afloat College Education (USN); Public Access Cabletelevision by and for the Elders; Public Awareness Communication Exchange

PACECO Pacific Coast Engineering Company

PACED Program for Advanced Concepts in Electronic Design

pacer. planning automation and control for evaluating requirements

PACFACS Programmed Appropriation Commitments—Fixed-Asset Control System

PACFLT Pacific Fleet

PACFORNET Pacific Coast Forest Research Information Network

Pac Gas & El Pacific Gas and Electric

'pache Apache

Pachuco (Mexican-Americanism—El Paso, Texas)—also called Pachucolandia

Pacif Pacific

Pacific Pacific Ocean (world's largest ocean separating the Americas from Asia and Australia, contains Aleutian, Hawaiian, and South Sea islands, extends south to the Antarctic and north to the Bering Sea)

Pacific Bitch navalese for Pacific Beach, San Diego, California

Pacific Canada British Columbia and the Yukon Territory

Pacific Coast Province British Columbia

Pacific Coast States California, Oregon, Washington

Pacific Commonwealths Australia and New Zealand and their territories

Pacific Crest Trailways for hikers, historians, and naturalists—includes John Muir Trail—extends from Canada to Mexico through Washington, Oregon, and California

Pacific Division States Alaska, California, Hawaii, Oregon, and Washington

Pacific Dominions Australia and New Zealand and their territories

Pacific Northwest Alaska to California, including the Yukon, British Columbia, Washington, and Oregon

Pacifico (Italian—Pacific)—Pacific Ocean

Pacifico (Portuguese or Spanish—Pacific)—Pacific Ocean

Pacific Paradise Hawaii

Pacific Province British Columbia

Pacific States Alaska, Washington, Oregon, California, Hawaii

Pacific War Japan's involvement in World War II ending in 1945 and beginning with the Manchurian Incident in 1931 when Japan invaded China

Pacifique (French—Pacific)—Pacific Ocean

pack. packing

pacm pulse amplification code modulation

PACMD Philadelphia Contract Management District

Paco Pancho (Francisco)

PacO Pacific Ocean

PACO Polaris Accelerated Change Operation

Pa$_{CO2}$ arterial carbon dioxide pressure

PACOM Pacific Command

pacor passive correlation and ranging

PACOS Package Operating System

PACR Performance and Compatability Requirements

PACRA Pottery and Ceramic Research Association

Pac Rail Missouri Pacific, Union Pacific, Western Pacific (railroads merged)

PACRNB President's Advisory

Commission on Recreation and Natural Beauty

PACs Political Action Committees (business, fund-raising, and many special-action groups)

PACS Pacific Area Communications System

Pac Ship *Pacific Shipper*

pacsim performance achievement computer model for waste package

pact. production analysis control technique; programmed automatic circuit tester

PACT Prisoner and Community Together (for offenders and victims); Production Analysis Control Technique; Project for the Advancement of Coding Techniques

Pac Tel Pacific Telephone (company)

Pac-Tex Pacific-Texas (pipeline)

Pac T & T Pacific Telephone and Telegraph

PACU Pennsylvania Association of Colleges and Universities

pacv (PACV) personnel air-cushion vehicle

PACV Patrol Air-Cushioned Vehicle (naval)

PACW President's Advisory Committee on Women

PACX Private Automatic Computer Exchange

pad padding; padlock; para-aminobenzoic acid

pad. padding; padlock; para-aminobenzoic acid (PAD); pitch axis definition; provisional assembly date

Pad Padstow

P Ad Port Adelaide

PAD Pacific Australia Direct (steamship line); Patient Accounts Department; People Against Displacement (caused by urban redevelopment); Performance Analysis Department (ONWI); Pontoon Assembly Depot; Port of Aerial Debarkation; Provisional Air Division; Public Administration Division; Public Affairs Department

padal pattern for analysis, decision, action and learning

PADAP Philippine-Australian Development Assistance Program

padar passive detection and ranging

PADAT Psychological Abstracts

Direct Action Terminal

PADC Pennsylvania Avenue Development Corporation

Paddie(s) Irish person(s)

Paddo Paddington, Australia

PADDS Petroleum Administration for Defense Districts

Paddy an Irishman; Patrick

Paddyland Ireland

PADF Pan-American Development Foundation

PADL Pilotless Aircraft Development Laboratory

padloc passive detection and location of countermeasures

PADMIS Patient Administration Information Information System

Padova (Italian—Padua)

PADPAO Philippine Agency Detective Protective Association

p Adr *per Adresse* (German—in care of)

padre. portable automatic data-recording equipment

Padre de Independencia (Spanish—Father of Independence)—José Martí—Cuban patriot, poet, and soldier

Pad Sta Paddington Station (rail terminal)

Padua English place-name equivalent of Padova in northern Italy

pae public affairs event

p. ae. *partes aequales* (Latin—equal parts)

PAE Peoria and Eastern (railroad); Port of Aerial Embarkation

PAEC Pakistan Atomic Energy Commission; Philippine Atomic Energy Commission

paect pollution abatement and environmental control technology

paed paediatric

paei perisocope azimuth error indicator

Paesi Bassi (Italian—Low Countries)—the Netherlands

PAESP Pennsylvania Association of Elementary School Principals

paf peripheral airfield; pulmonary arteriovenous fistula; punishment and fine

paf (PAF) personal article floater (baggage insurance policy); Polaris accelerated flight

pa & f percussion, auscultation, and fermitus

paf *puissance au frein* (French—brake horsepower)

PAF Pacific Air Force(s); Pakistan Air Force; Palestine Arab Fund (for terrorists); Pet Assistance Foundation; Philippine Air Force; Ports Authority of Fiji

PAFA Pennsylvania Academy of Fine Arts

PAFB Patrick Air Force Base

PAFCO Pacific Fishing Company

PAFMECA Pan-African Freedom Movement of East and Central Africa

PAFS Primary Air Force Specialty

PAFSC Primary Air Force Specialty Code

PAFTA Pacific Area Free Trade Association

pag pagaré (Spanish—I will pay); *pagina* (Italian—page)

Pag pagoda

Pag I Pagliacci (Italian—The Players)—two-act opera by Leoncavallo

PaG Pennsylvania-German

PAG Planning Advisory Group; Primary Analysis Group; Prince Albert's Guard

PAGASA Philippine Atmospheric Geophysical and Astronomical Services Administration

PAGB Proprietary Association of Great Britain

PAGEL Priced Aerospace Ground Equipment List

pageos (PAGEOS) passive geodetic satellite

Pa Ger Soc Pennsylvania German Society

Paget's disease bone distortion of cancer of the nipples of women

pagg segg pagine seguenti (Italian—following pages)

pAgmk primary African green monkey kidney

Pago Pago pronounced *Pango-Pango* locally where it is the capital of American Samoa

pág(s) página(s) [Spanish—page(s)]

PAGT Port Authority Grain Terminal

pah polynuclear aromatic hydrocarbon(s)—(photochemical smog ingredient)

pah (PAH) para-aminohippuric acid

Pah Pahlavi

PAH Pan-American Highway (also called Inter-American Highway)

PAHC Pan American Highway Congress

PAHO Pan-American Health Organization

PAHOCENDES Pan-American Health Organization Center for Development Studies

pai parts application information; personal adjustment inventory; please airmail immediately; prearrival inspection

PAI Panama Airways Incorporated; Piedmont Airlines (3-letter coding)

PAIGCV Partido Africano da Independencia da Guine e Cabo Verde (Portuguese—African Party for an Independent Guinea and Cape Verde)

PAIGH Pan-American Institute of Geography and History

PAILS Projectile Airburst and Impact Location System

PAIN Pan-American Institute of Neurology

paint. painter; painting

Painted Desert petrified formations and colorful rock deposits on desert floor of northeastern Arizona

Painter of Japanese Prostitutes Kitagawa Utamaro

Painter of Prostitutes Henri Marie Raymond de Toulouse-Lautrec

Painters Union International Brotherhood of Painters and Allied Trades of the United States and Canada

pair. performance and integration retrofit

PAIR Psychological Audit for Interpersonal Relations

PAIRC Pacific Air Command

PAIRS Private Aircraft Inspection Reporting System

PAIS Pennsylvania Association of Independent Schools; Project Analysis Information System (AID); Public Affairs Information Service

Paises Baixos (Portuguese—Low Countries)—the Netherlands

Países Bajos (Spanish—Low Countries)—the Netherlands

PAIT Program for the Advancement of Industrial Technology

PAJU Pan-African Journalists Union

Pak Pakistan

PAK Pëtr Alekseevich Kropotkin

Paki(s) Pakistani(s)

Pakistan Islamic Republic of Pakistan (Moslem country between Afghanistan and India,

Pakistanis speak English and some Urdu, exports include farm crops, oil, and many valuable minerals); *Pakistan* in Urdu means Land of the Pure

PAKISTAN *Pak* (Persian—holy) plus *tan* (Urdu—land)—hence Pakistan means Holy Land; it is also an acronym made up of Punjab, Afghan Border states, Kashmir, Sind, and *tan* from Baluchistan

Pakistan's Principal Port Karachi

pal. paleontology; peripheral availability list(ing); permissive action link; phase-alteration line (color tv system); prescribed action link; program assembly language; programmed application library

pal. (PAL) phase alternate line; products and area locator

p-a-l prisoner-at-large

Pal Palace; Palencia; Paleozoic; Palermo; Palestine

Pal Palacio (Spanish—palace); *Palácio* (Portuguese); *Palais* (French—palace); *Palazzo* (Italian—palace)

PAL Pacific Aeronautical Library; Pacific Aluminium; Pakistan Airlines; Pan Asia Line; Pensioners Advancement League; phase-alternating (television) line; Philippine Air Lines; Police Athletic League; Polynesian Airlines Limited; Prison Atheist League; prisoner-at-large; Public Archives Library

PALA Polish-American Librarians Association

Palat Palatinate

Palatinate southwest German districts once ruled by counts palatinate of the Holy Roman Empire and referred to as Oberpfalz or Rheinpfalz

Palau Pelew (Pacific islands in Caroline area)

P Alb Port Alberni

PALC Point Arguello Launch Complex

paleo paleography

paleob paleobotany

paleon paleontology

Paleontologist Priest Pierre Teilhard de Chardin

Palestine southern Syria, according to many Arabs; Turkish province containing what is now Israel plus adjacent Arab countries in the Jerusalem area often called the Holy

Land

Palestinian Salt Sea the Dead Sea

Palestrina Giovanni Pierluigi da Palestrina

Palgrave Francis Meyer Cohen

PALI Pacific and Asian Linguistics Institute (University of Hawaii)

palimony alimony awarded a former common-law pal or other unmarried male or female partner

palin palindrome; palindromic

PALINET Pennsylvania Area Library Network

PALIS Property and Liability Information Systems

Palisades Palisades Interstate Park along the west bank of the Hudson River washing the shores of New Jersey and New York; below the high bluffs; Palisades (amusement) Park near Englewood, New Jersey; Palisades Peaks in Kings Canyon National Park, California

pall. pallet

palm. palmist(ry); precision attitude and landing monitor

Palma Palma de Mallorca (capital of the Balearic Islands and the island of Mallorca)

Palma Balearia (Latin—Mallorca)—Majorca

Palmach *Plugot Machatz* (Hebrew—Spearhead Units)—commando units active in the establishment of Israel when still called Palestine

Palmas Las Palmas de Gran Canaria (capital and main seaport city of the Canary Islands belonging to Spain)

Palma Vecchio palette name of Jacopo Negreti

Palm Coast Florida's east coast from Daytona to Jacksonville

Palmerston Henry John Temple, Viscount of Palmerston

Palmetto City Charleston, South Carolina

Palmetto(s) South Carolinian(s)

Palmetto State South Carolina's official nickname

Palmn Palmerston

palm oil bribe(s)

PALMS Propulsion Alarm and Monitoring System

Pal Obs Palomar Observatory

Palos Palos de la Frontera (port of departure of Columbus in 1492)

palp palpable; palpitation

palpi palpitation

PALs Parcel Air Lifts (U.S. Post

Office parcel-post service for servicemen)

PALS Permissive Action Link Systems

PALSG Personnel and Logistics Systems Group

PALTC Pacific Asian and Latino Training Center

pam pamphlet; procurement aircraft and missiles; pulse amplified modulation; pulse amplitude modulation

Pam Lord Palmerston; Pamela

PAM Palestine Archeological Museum; Pasadena Art Museum; Portland Art Museum

PAMA Pan-American Medical Association; Professional Aviation Maintenance Association

pamac parts and materials accountability control

PAMC Pakistan Army Medical Corps

P. americanus Pukus americanus (law-enforcement-officer's nickname for unwashed and stinking street people)—the smellies

PAMETRADA Parsons Marine Experimental Turbine Research and Development Association

pamf programmable analog-matched filter

pam file pamphlet file

PAMIPAC Personnel Accounting Machine Installation Pacific Fleet

pamirasat (PAMIRASAT) passive microwave radiometer satellite

Pamirs Pamir Mountains of Soviet Central Asia

PAML Pan American Mail Line

PAMO Port Air Materiel Office

PAMPA Pacific Area Movement Piority Agency (DoD)

pamph pamphlet

Pamphleteer for American Independence Thomas Paine

pams pamphlets

PAMS Plan Analysis and Modeling System

PAMT Port Authority Marine Terminal

pan (PAN) peroxyacetyl nitrate (smog ingredient)

pan. panchromatic; panorama; panoramic; pantomime; pantry

Pan Panama; Panamanian; Panameño

PAN Pan American Navigation;

Parents Against Narcotics; peroxyacetylnitrate (air-pollutant poison)

PAN Partido Acción Nacional (Spanish—National Action Party)—Mexican; *Polska Akademia Nauk* (Polish Academy of Sciences)

PANA Pan-African News Agency; Pan-Asia Newspaper Alliance

PANAFTEL Pan-African Telecommunications (network)

PANAGRA Pan American-Grace Airways

PANAIR Panair do Brasil (Brazilian airline)

Pan-Am Pan-American World Airways

panama panama hat (made from finely plaited young palmlike leaves; best panama hats made in Montecristi, Ecuador)

Panamá Republic of Panamá (Spanish-speaking Central American country bisected by the Panama Canal; Panamanians export bananas but depend largely on tourism), *República de Panamá*

Panama Canal 51-mile-long (82 kilometers) waterway connecting the Atlantic and Pacific Oceans; cut through Panamá at great cost of life, material, and money; unsuccessful and abandoned effort of French canal companies did not deter American military and sanitary engineers from making this dream a reality; successfully administered, constructed, and maintained by the United States for 76 years; under the Panamanian flag since October 1979 although its defense and operation will be America's task until the year 2000

Panama Canal Ports Balboa the Pacific terminus and Cristóbal the Caribbean terminus

Panama Canal Zone former United States government territory whose inhabitants were called Zonians

Panama City Florida (port city in West Florida); Panama (capital of the Republic of Panama flanking Panama Canal)

Panama-kanaal (Dutch—Panama Canal)

Panama red high-grade marijuana grown in Panamá and even within the Canal Zone

Panama's Principal Ports Colón on the Caribbean adjacent to Cristóbal in the Canal Zone and Panamá City adjacent to Balboa in the Canal Zone on the Pacific plus the Pacific port of Puerto Armuelles

Panama turkey iguana tail meat

Panamax Panamax specifications (maximum size Panama Canal locks can accommodate)

Panamints Panamint Mountains of eastern California along the Death Valley border of Nevada

PANANEWS Pan-Asia Newspaper Alliance (Hong Kong)

pan b panic bolt

panc pancreas

Pan Can Panama Canal

Pan Canal Panama Canal

Pancho Francisco; native nickname for Valparaiso, Chile

Pancho Villa Doroteo Arango

pand *panderazo* (Spanish—blow struck with a tambourine); *panderetero* (Spanish—tambourine maker or player); *pandero* (Spanish—tambourine)

PANDA Prestel Advanced Network Design Architecture; Professional Association of Numismatic Dealers of Australasia

Pandemonium South Pacific nickname for New Hebrides islands British-French Condominium

pandex *pan* (Greek—all) + *dex* (from index)—all-inclusive index

pandg people are no damn good

p-and-p struggle prude-and-prurient struggle (between prudes who would censor almost anything sexual and prurients who demand the obscene, the tasteless, and the vulgar)

Panecillo (Spanish—Little Loaf of Bread)—mountain rising above Quito, Ecuador

PANEES Professional Association of Naval Electronics Engineers and Scientists

P Ang Port Angeles

Pango (naval argot—Pago Pago, American Samoa)

Pango Pango (Samoan—Pago Pago)

Panhandle State West Virginia

Pank Pankow

panol panology

panorams panoramas

PANPA Pacific Area Newspaper Production Association

Pan pan *Pan paniscus* (pygmy chimpanzee found south of the Congo River)

pans. peroxyacetylnitrates

PANS Procedures for Air Navigation Services

PANSDOC Pakistan National Scientific and Technical Documentation Center

Pan Sea Fron (PANSEAFRON) Panama Sea Frontier

PANSY Programme Analysis System

P Ant Port Antonio

Pantaleone patron saint of Venice; nickname for an Italian taxpayer or for a Venetian

panth pantheism; pantheist; pantheistic(al) (ly)

Panther Grumman single-engine single-seat naval fighting aircraft (F9F-2)

panto pantograph(ic); pantomime; pantomimic

Pan trog *Pan troglodytes* (common chimpanzee found north of the Congo River)

pants pantaloons

PANY Power Authority of the State of New York

pao product assurance operations

PAO Public Affairs Officer

Pa$_{O2}$ arterial oxygen pressure

PAOA Pan American Odontological Association

PAODAP President's Action Office for Drug Abuse Prevention

Pão de Açúcar (Portuguese—Sugarloaf Mountain)—cone-shaped mountain overlooking Guanabara Bay in Rio de Janeiro Harbor

pap (PAP) pension administration plan

pap. papa; papacy; papal; paper; papyrus

pap prêt à porter (French—ready to wear)

Pap Papa; Papeete; Papist; Pappie; Papua; Papuan

PAP Pacific Automation Products; People's Action Party; Performance Assessment Plan; Polska Agencja Prasowa (Polish News Agency); Port-au-Prince, Haiti (airport); Progressive Australia Party

papa parallax aircraft parking aid

Papa letter P radio code

PAPA Parents As Partners Associated

Papa Bach Johann Sebastian Bach

Papa Doc Haiti's former dictator François Duvalier

Papa Haydn Franz Joseph Haydn

PAPAS Pennsylvania Association of Private Academic Schools

PAPC Philological Association of the Pacific Coast

Pap diag Papanicolaou diagnosis

Papermac paperback book published by Macmillan

papi precision path indicator

PAPI Pacific Automation Products Incorporated

papil papilla; papillae

Pap Inf Papal Infallability

Pap Lib Paperback Library

Pap NG Papua New Guinea

p app *puissance apparente* (French—apparent power)

Pappas Papadmitropoulos

Pappies Papists

Pap(s) [Irish-Protestant English-Papist(s)—*see* Prod(s)]

Pap smear Papanicolaou smear

PAPSS Procurement and Production Status System

Pap Sta Papal States

PAPTE President's Advisory Panel on Timber and the Environment

Pap Ter Papua Territory

Pap Test Papanicolaou Test (for cervical cancer)

Papua Indonesian island called Papua New Guinea in the eastern sector and West Irian on the western sector

Papua New Guinea New Guinea's eastern half whose Papuans speak English, Melanesian Pidgin, and Police Motu; cocoa, coconuts, and coffee crops are augmented by such minerals as copper, gold, and silver; formerly Australian or British New Guinea

Papua New Guinea's Principal Port Port Moresby

paq position-analysis questionnaire

Paquita Francisca (Frances)

par (PAR) perimeter acquistion radar

par. parabolic aluminized reflector; paragraph; parallax; parallel; parenthesis; per acre rental; planed all around (timber); precision approach radar; pulse acquisition radar

par (Latin prefix—bear or give birth to)—parturition

Par Paris; Parish

Par Parigi (Italian—Paris); *Parijs* (Dutch—Paris)

PAr Punta Arenas

PAR Paris, France (Orly airport); Program Appraisal and Review; Protect Abortion Rights

PAR Partido Acción Revolucionario (Spanish—Revolutionary Action Party)

para parachute; paragraph; parallel; perceiving and recognition automation

para (Greek—alongside, beside, beyond)—paralysis, paramedic, parameter, parasite, parathyroid

Para Paraguay(an)

Pará Belém do Pará, Brazil

para I; para II; para III; etc. unipara; bipara; tripara; etc.— having given birth to one child, to two children, to three children, etc.

parab parabola

Paracels Paracel Islands in the South China Sea east of Vietnam

Paracelsus Theophrastus Bombastus von Hohenheim

paracent paracentesis

parad paradicholorobenzene; paradigm(atic)(al)(ly); paradisiac(al)(ly); paradisal; paradise; paradisiacal(ly); paradox(ical)(ly); paradoxicalness

Parade of Prostitutes nickname of many metropolitan places such as New York City's Times Square or San Francisco's downtown streets off Market

Paradise Lost Florida (whose major cities in late 1984 had the highest crime rate of any in the nation)

Paradise of the Pacific Hawaii

Paradox of South America Paraguay—an affluent military dictatorship

paradrop parachute airdrop

par. aff. *pars affecta* (Latin—to the part affected)

Paraguay Republic of Paraguay (Spanish-speaking South American country bisected by the Paraguay River; Paraguayan exports feature farm crops and minerals) *República del Paraguay*

Paraguay Day Paraguayan Independence Day (May 14 and 15)

Paraguay River City Asunción

Paraguay's Principal Port Asun-

ción

Paraiba old name of Joao Pessoa, Brazil

paral parallax; paralysis

param parameter(s); parametric

Parami Parsons active ring around miss indicator

Paramilitary Paradise Paraguay

paramp parametric amplifier

parapsych parapsychologist; parapsychology

paraquat paraquat-tainted marijuana

paras parasite(s); parasitic; parasitism; paratroopers

parasail parachute sail (steerable parachute)

parasitol parasitologic(al)(ly); parasitologist; parasitology

parasym div parasympathetic division

parasyn parametric synthesis

Parbo Paramaribo

parc progressive aircraft repair cycle

PARC Princeton Applied Research Corporation; Public Archives Records Centre

PARCA Pan American Railway Congress Association

parch. parchment

Parched Heart of Australia Alice Springs, Northern Territory—The Alice

Parchman Mississippi State Penitentiary at Parchman

PARCS Parking and Revenue Control System (for autos)

pard partner

PARD Personnel Actions and Records Directorate

pardac parallel digital-to-analog converter

pardop passive-ranging doppler

PARDS Precision-Annotated Retrieval Display System

paregoric compound tincture of opium

paren parenthesis

parens parentheses

parent. parental(ly)

Parents *Parents Magazine*

parex programmed accounts-receivable extra (service)

par for par for the course (golfer's term meaning average, typical, usual)

PARFR Program for Applied Research on Fertility Regulation (Northwestern University)

Parg Paraguay; Paraguayan

pari parietal

Paricutín volcano in State of Michoacan, Mexico; appeared in 1943 and erupted in 1952

Parigi (Italian—Paris)

Parijs (Dutch—Paris)

Pariñas Pariñas Point (westernmost point of South America)

Paris Mozart's Symphony No. 31 in D major

París (Spanish—Paris)

Paris Expressionist Henri Matisse

paris green copper acetoarsenite (poison)

Parisian Composers Bizet, Boulanger, Charpentier, Chausson, Debussy, d'Indy, Dukas, Gounod, Ibert, Poulenc, Rabaud, Saint-Saëns (all born in or near Paris)

Parisii (Latin—Paris)

Paris symphonies Haydn's symphonies 82 through 87, commissioned in Paris, bearing such names as *l'Ours* (The Bear—82), *La Poule* (The Hen—83), *La Reine* (The Queen—85)

PARKA Pacific Acoustic Research (Kaneoche, Alaska)

parkade parking arcade

Parkbench Philosopher Bernard Baruch

Park City Bridgeport, Connecticut

Parkinson's disease nervous tremors accompanied by muscular weakness and rigidness; also called palsy, paralysis agitans, or the shakes

Park Maker Frederick Law Olmsted

parl parallel

Parl Parliament

PARL Palo Alto Research Laboratory (Lockheed)

Parl Agt Parliamentary Agent

Parl Const Parliamentary Constituency

Parlour Panther *New York Review of Books*

Parl Sec Parliamentary Secretary

parm (PARM) precision anti-radiation missile

PARM Partido Autentico de la Revolución Mexicano (Authentic Party of the Mexican Revolution)

PARMA Public Agency Risk Managers Association

Parmigianino Francisco Massuoli

parm(s) parameter(s)

parochiaid parochial-school aid (provided by tax monies)

paros passive ranging on submarines

parot parotid

parox paroxysm(al)

PARPRO Peacetime Aerial Reconnaissance Program

Parrot's disease syphilitic infantile paralysis (disease named not for a bird but for a French physician—Jules Marie Parrot—its discoverer)

Parry's disease exophthalmic goiter

pars paragraphs

PARS Passenger Airlines Reservation System; Prisoners Aid and Rehabilitation Society; Private Aircraft Reporting System; Programmed Airlines Reservation System

parsec parallax second (3.26 lightyears or 19.2 trillion miles)

Parsee (Arabic—Iranian, Persian)—Indian Zoroastrian descended from refugees who came to India to escape Muslim persecution

parsq pararescue

parsyn parametric synthesis

part. partial; participate; particle; partition; partner; partnership

part. partim (Latin—part)

PART Part Allocation Requirements Technic

part. aeq. partes aequales (Latin—equal parts)

partan parallel tangents

Partas Partagas cigars

part. dolent. partes dolentes (Latin—painful parts)

PARTEI Purchasing Agents of Radio, TV, and Electronics Industries

parth parthenogenesis

Parthia (*Latin*—parts of Assyria and Persia in northeastern Iran)

parti participle

partic participle; particular

partic exh particulate exhaust (soot)

partit partitive

partner. proof of analog results through numerical equivalent routines

Partrys Partry Mountains of western Ireland

part. vic. partibus vicibus (Latin—in divided doses)

paru postanesthetic recovery unit

par uni party unity (political utopia)

parv paravane

parv parvus (*Latin—small*)

PARVO Professional and Academic Regional Visits Organization

pas passive; photoacoustic spectrometer; power-assisted steering; public-address system

pas (PAS) para-aminosalicylic acid; periodic acid Schiff; photo-acoustic spectroscopy

paS periodic acid Schiff

Pas Pasadena; Pascagoula; Pashto; Passage; Passaic; Passau

Pa s Pascal second

Pas. Paschae (Latin—Easter)

PAs Parents Anonymous; Police Agents

PA's purchasing agents

PAS Percussive Arts Society; Pioneer Air System; Pregnancy Advisory Service; Primary Alerting System; Probation and Aftercare Service; Professor of Air Science; Public Address System

pasa (PASA) para-aminosalicylic acid

PASA Pennsylvania Association of School Administrators; Pipelines Authority of South Australia

pasar psychological abstracts search and retrieval

PASAR Philippine Associated Smelting and Refining

PASB Pan-American Sanitary Bureau

PASBO Pennsylvania Association of School Business Officials

PASC Pacific Area Standards Congress; Palestine Armed Struggle Command (controlled by El Fatah); Pan-American Standards Committee

PASCAL Philips Automatic Sequence Calculator

PASCAL Program Appliqué à la Selection et la Compilation Automatique de la Litterature (French—Program Applied to the Selection and the Automatic Compilation of Literature)

PASCO Pan American Sulfur Corporation

Pas de Calais (French—Calais Strait)—also called Dover Strait

p'ase alkaline phosphatase

PASF Photographic Art and Science Foundation

PASG Programs Activities and Services Guide

PASGT Personal Armor System—Ground Troops (new helmet of the U.S. Army, replac-

ing pot helmet of World War II)

pasim pasimological; pasimologically; pasimologist; pasimology (study of gestures as means of communication)

PASL Pakistan Association of Special Libraries

PASLIB Pakistan Association of Special Libraries

PASO Pan-American Sanitary Organization; Pan-American Sports Organization

Paso del Calais (Spanish—Calais Strait)—Dover Strait in the English Channel

PASOK Pan-Hellenic Socialist Commune

Pasque South Dakota state flower

pass. passage; passenger; passitive; passivate; passive; passport

pass. passim (Latin—far and wide, here and there, up and down)

Pass Passover

PASS Passengers Automatic Selection System; Procurement Automated Source System; Prototype Artillery Subsystem

PASSIM President's Advisory Staff on Scientific Information Management

Passionate Pilgrim John Bunyan

Passionate Skeptic freethinker-mathematician—philosopher Bertrand Russell

Pass Kristyen Pass Christian, Louisiana

PASSP Pennsylvania Association of Secondary School Principals

Past Pasteurella

PASTIC Pakistan Scientific and Technological Information Center

Pastoral Beethoven's Piano Sonata No. 15 in D (opus 28); Beethoven's Symphony No. 6 in F major (opus 68); Symphony No. 3 by Vaughan-Williams

Pastoral God Pan

pastram passenger traffic management

pastramasan pastrami sandwich (pickled corned-beef sandwich)

pastramwich pastrami sandwich (pickled corned-beef sandwich)

PASWEPS Passive Antisubmarine Warfare Environmental Protection System

p-a system public-address system

pat. patent(s); patrol(s); pattern; points after touchdown

pat. (PAT) paroxysmal atrial tachycardia

Pat Patricia; Patrick

Pat *Patrone* (German—cartridge, round of ammunition)

PAT Pacific Air Transport; Pacific Automobile Train; Philippine Aerial Taxi; Post-availability Trials; Prescription Athletic Turf; Production Assessment Test; Progressive Achievement Tests

PATA Pacific Area Travel Association

Patag Patagonia(n)

Patagonian Desert along eastern slope of Andes in central and southern Argentina

PATAS Publications Automated Task Analysis System

Patavium (Latin—Padua)

PATCA Panama Air Traffic Control Area

PATCO Port Authority Transit Corporation; Professional Air Traffic Controllers Association

PATCRA Papua New Guinea–Australia Trade and Commercial Relations Agreement

patd patented

path. pathological; pathologist; pathology; pituitary adrenotrophic hormone (PATH)

path (Latin prefix—disease)—pathologist, pathology

PATH Port Authority Trans-Hudson (Hudson Tubes)

Pathétique Beethoven's Piano Sonata No. 8 in C minor (opus 13); Tchaikovsky's Symphony No. 6 in B minor

Pathfinder Major General John C Frémont, USA

Pathfinder of the Seas Matthew Fontaine Maury

Path of Gold Market Street, San Francisco

Pathmaker of the West John C Frémont

patho pathological

patho (Greek—suffering)—osteopath(ic), pathological, pathologist, pathology

pathogen pathogenic

pathol pathologic(al)(ly); pathologist; pathology

pathomorph pathomorphologic(al)(ly); pathomorphologist; pathomorphology

pathy (Latin suffix—abnormality or disease)—neuropathy,

psychopathy

Patience and Fortitude Mayor La Guardia's nickname for the couchant lions flanking the steps of the New York Public Library

Patk Patrick

Patland Ireland

pat. med patent medicine

patn pattern

PATO Pacific-Asian Treaty Organization

Pat Off Patent Office

PATOLIS Patent On-Line Information System

pat pend patent pending

PATRA Printing, Packaging, and Allied Trades Research Association (also appears as PPATRA)

Pátrai (Modern Greek—Patras)

Patras English equivalent of Pátrai, Greece

Patriarca de la Independencia (Portuguese—Patriarch of Independence)—Brazil's José Bonifacio de Andrada e Silva

Patriarch of American Labor George Meany

Patriarch of Ferney Voltaire who lived from 1758 to 1778 in Ferney, France just across the border from Geneva, Switzerland to escape persecution by the religious fanatics of both countries—Ferney is now called Ferney-Voltaire in his honor

Patriarch of the Modern Consumer Movement Ralph Nader *(Unsafe at any Speed)*

Patriarch of New England John Cotton

Patriarch of Philosophy Bertrand Russell

Patriarch of Puerto Rico Luís Muñoz Marín

Patriarch of the West the Pope

PATRIC Pattern Recognition and Information Correlation (police computer)

PATRICIA Practical Algorithm to Receive Information Coded in Alphanumeric

Patricia Wentworth Dora Amy Elles Dillon Turnbull's pseudonym

Patriot Financier Robert Morris

Patriot of the Piano Polish patriot-pianist-premier Ignace Jan Paderewski

Patriot Printer of 1776 William Bradford

patron. patronym(ic)(al)(ly)

Patronat (French equivalent of

National Association of Manufacturers in United States)

Patron of Bawdy House England's King Charles II, the Merry Monarch

Patroness Saint of Advertisers St Barnardine of Siena

Patroness Saint of Artillerymen Santa Barbara

Patroness Saint of Artists St Catherine of Bologna

Patroness Saint of Bakers St Elizabeth of Hungary

Patroness Saint of the Blind and the Near Blind Santa Clara

Patroness Saint of Bohemia St Ludmilla

Patroness Saint of Bullfighters Virgen de la Macarena (also Patroness Saint of Seville)

Patroness Saint of Canada St Anne

Patroness Saint of Chile Virgen del Carmen

Patroness Saint of Dentists St Apollonia

Patroness Saint of Diseases of the Breast St Agatha

Patroness Saint of Domestics St Zita

Patroness Saint of Emigrants St Frances Xavier Cabrini

Patroness Saint of Florists St Therese of Lisieux

Patroness Saint of Gardens Santa Dorotea

Patroness Saint of Hispanic America Nuestra Señora de Guadalupe (Our Lady of Guadalupe)

Patroness Saint of Housewives St Martha

Patroness Saint of Houseworkers St Anne

Patroness Saint of Hungary Blessed Virgin—Great Lady of Hungary

Patroness Saint of Italy St Catherine of Siena

Patroness Saint of the Mentally Ill St Dymphna

Patroness Saint of Mexico Virgin of Guadalupe

Patroness Saint of Music Santa Cecilia

Patroness Saint of Nurses St Agatha

Patroness Saint of Paris St Genevieve

Patroness Saint of Peru Santa Rosa de Lima

Patroness Saint of Philosophers St Catherine

Patroness Saint of Poland St Cunegunda

Patroness Saints of Ailments of

the Eyes Sts Clare and Lucy
Patroness Saints of France Our Lady of the Assumption, St Joan of Arc, St Therese
Patroness Saint of Ireland Sts Brigid and Columba
Patroness Saint of Spain Santa Teresa of Ávila
Patroness Saint of Sweden St Bridget
Patroness Saint of Toothaches Apollonia of Egypt
Patroness Saint of the United States Our Lady of the Immaculate Conception, according to Roman Catholics
Patroness Saint of Uruguay Our Lady of Lujan
Patroness Saint of Weavers St Anastasia
Patroness Saint of the West Indies St Gertrude
Patroness Saint of Writers St Lucy
Patron of Explorers Henry the Navigator (Dom Henrique o Navegador)—Prince of Portugal
Patron Saint of Actors St Genesius
Patron Saint of Advertisers St John Berchmans
Patron Saint of All Who Work with a Hammer St Cloud
Patron Saint of Alpinists St Bernard of Menthon
Patron Saint of American Orchards John (Johnny Appleseed) Chapman
Patron Saint of Anesthetists St Rene Goupil
Patron Saint of Architects St Thomas, Apostle
Patron Saint of Armenia St Gregory the Illuminator
Patron Saint of Artists St Luke
Patron Saint of Astronomers St. Dominic
Patron Saint of Athletes St Sebastian
Patron Saint of Authors St Francis de Sales
Patron Saint of Aviators, Porters, Seafarers, and Travellers St Christopher
Patron Saint of Belgium St Joseph
Patron Saint of Blacksmiths St Dunstan
Patron Saint of Bohemia St Wenceslaus
Patron Saint of Bookbinders St Peter Celestine
Patron Saint of Book Collectors St Jerome (credited with compiling the Latin Bible)

Patron Saint of Booksellers St John of God
Patron Saint of Borneo St Francis Xavier
Patron Saint of Brazil St Peter of Alcantara
Patron Saint of Brewers and Pawnbrokers St Nicholas of Myra—the prototype of Santa Claus
Patron Saint of Bricklayers St Stephen
Patron Saint of Cab Drivers St Fiacre
Patron Saint of Cancer Victims St Michael
Patron Saint of Carpenters St Joseph
Patron Saint of Charitable Societies St Vincent de Paul
Patron Saint of the Chase St Hubert
Patron Saint of Children St Nicholas of Myra also known as Santa Claus—derived from the Dutch, Sant Nikolaas
Patron Saint of Chile Santiago (St James)
Patron Saint of Comedians St Vitus
Patron Saint of the Dance St Vitus, according to Washington Irving
Patron Saint of the Dominican Republic St Dominic
Patron Saint of Ecologists St Francis of Assisi
Patron Saint of Editors St John Bosco
Patron Saint of Engineers St Francis III
Patron Saint of England Edward the Confessor or St George
Patron Saint of Epilepsy St Vitus
Patron Saint of Finland St Henry of Uppsala
Patron Saint of Fishermen St Andrew
Patron Saint of Flagpole Sitters St Simon of Stylites
Patron Saint of France St Denis
Patron Saint of French Attorneys St Ives
Patron Saint of Glasgow St Mungo
Patron Saint of the Hard of Hearing St Ovidius
Patron Saint of Hernias and Ruptures St Drogo, according to believers who also call him St Druon
Patron Saint of Hispanic America Our Lady of Guadalupe
Patron Saint of Hungary St

Stephen—King
Patron Saint of Hunters St Hubert
Patron Saint of Ireland St Patrick
Patron Saint of Italy St Francis of Assisi
Patron Saint of Journalists St Francis de Sales
Patron Saint of Librarians St Jerome
Patron Saint of Lithuania St Casimir
Patron Saint of Locksmiths St Dunstan
Patron Saint of Lovers St Valentine
Patron Saint of Malta St Paul
Patron Saint of Medical Record Librarians St Raymond of Penyafort
Patron Saint of Monaco St Devota
Patron Saint of the Movies St John Bosco who died in 1888
Patron Saint of Musicians St Cecilia
Patron Saint of Nailmakers St Cloud
Patron Saint of Navigators St Brendan of Ireland who many believe came to America some 900 years before Columbus set sail from Spain
Patron Saint of the Netherlands St Willibrord
Patron Saint of Norway St Olav
Patron Saint of Notaries St Mark
Patron Saint of Orators St John Chrysostom
Patron Saint of Painters St Luke
Patron Saint of Persons Afflicted with Coughs and Colds St Judas
Patron Saint of Persons Afflicted with Hydrophobia St Hubert
Patron Saint of Persons Afflicted with Insect Stings and Snake Bites St Sebastian
Patron Saint of Persons Condemned to Death St Dismas
Patron Saint of Philosophers St Justin
Patron Saint of Radiologists St Michael
Patron Saint of Rheumatics St Gervasius
Patron Saint of Russia St Andrew whose cross adorns the flag of Imperial Russia
Patron Saint of Sailors St Elmo who reportedly manifests his presence in the form of ball-

shaped electrical discharges racing along the masts and rigging of ships during electrical storms and called Saint Elmo's balls

Patron Saints of Canada Sts George and Joseph

Patron Saint of Scholars St Gregory

Patron Saint of Scholastic Institutions St Thomas Aquinas

Patron Saint of Scotland St Andrew

Patron Saints of Denmark Sts Ansgar and Canute

Patron Saints of Doctors Sts Cosmas and Damian

Patron Saints of Germany Sts Boniface and Michael

Patron Saints of Greece Sts Andrew and Nicholas

Patron Saint of Shoemakers St Crispin

Patron Saint of the Sick and Those Who Attend Them St Camillus of Lellis

Patron Saints of Lawyers Sts Genesius, Ivo, Thomas More

Patron Saints of Moravia Sts Cyril and Methodius

Patron Saints of Morticians Sts Dismas and Joseph of Arimathea

Patron Saint of the Sore Throat St Blaise

Patron Saint of Spain Santiago de Compostela (St James the Greater)

Patron Saints of Poland Sts Casimir, Florian, Stanislaus

Patron Saints of Portugal Sts Anthony Padua, Francis Padua, George, Vincent

Patron Saints of Schoolteachers Sts Gregory the Great and John Baptist de la Salle

Patron Saints of Scotland Sts Andrew and Columba

Patron Saints of Surgeons Sts Cosmas, Damian, Luke

Patron Saints of Theologians Sts Alphonsus Liguori and Augustine

Patron Saint of Stonemasons St Stephen

Patron Saint of Students St Thomas Aquinas

Patron Saint of Sweden St Eric

Patron Saint of Tailors St Homobonus

Patron Saint of Tax Collectors St Matthew who before his conversion was a customs collector

Patron Saint of Wales St David

Patron Saint of Winegrowers St

Vincent Martyr

Patron Saint of Wine Merchants St Amand

Patron Saint of Yachtsmen St Adjutor

Patroon Stephen Van Rensselaer's nickname

pats. patents

PATs Pre-Authorized (bank deposit) Transfers

PATS Philippine Aeronautics Training School; Portable Acoustic Tracking System; Proof and Transit System

patt pattern

PATTERN Planning Assistance Through Technical Evaluation of Relevance Numbers

Patton U.S.-made M-47 or M-48 medium tanks armed with 90mm guns

Patty Martha; Patience; Patricia

PATWAS Pilot's Automatic Telephone Weather Answering Service

PATX Private Automatic Telex Exchange

pau pattern articulation unit; programmer's analysis unit

Pau Pablo

PAU Pan American Union; Pan American University; Police Airborne Unit

Paula Paulcela; Paulette; Paulina; Pauline; Paulita

Paul Bunyan's Capital Brainerd, Minnesota

Paul Creston Joseph Guttoveggio

Paulette Goddard Marion Levy

Paul Klenovsky Sir Henry J Wood's pseudonym used when he presented his orchestral arrangement of Bach's Toccata and Fugue in D minor; pupil of Alexander Glazunov

Paul Lukas Pal Lukacs

Paul Muni Muni Weisenfreund

Paul Vesey Samuel W Allen's pseudonym

Paul VI Giovanni Batista Montini

P-au-P Port-au-Prince

pav paving

p/av particular average

Pav pavilion; Pavo (constellation)

PAV Personnel Allotment Voucher

PAV Poste Avion (French—airmail)

PAVAA Polish Army Veterans Association of America

pave. position and velocity ex-

traction

PAVE Professional Audiovisual Education (study)

Pavel Ivanovich Jones John Paul Jones (when he served as rear admiral commanding Russia's Black Sea fleet for Catherine the Great)

PAVEPAWS Precision Acquisition of Vehicle-Entry Phased-Array Warning System

PAVE-PAWS Precision Acquisition of Vehicle Entry—Phased Array Warning System (early-warning radar system against submarine-launched missiles)

PAVM Potential Acquisition Valuation Method

PAVN Peoples Army of Viet Nam

pav. noc. pavor nocturnus (Latin —nightmares, night terrors)

PAVPAWS Precision Acquisition of Vehicle-Entry Phased-Array Warning System

pavt power-adjusted variable track(ing)

paw. portable auxiliary workroom

Paw Papa

PAW People for the American Way (guaranteeing strict separation of church and state); Pets and Wildlife

PAWA Pan American World Airways; Pan-American Womens Association

PAWO Pan-African Women's Organization

pawob passengers arriving without baggage

PAWS Phased Array Warning System; Programmed Automatic Welding System

pax. passenger(s); private automatic exchange

Pax Paxon; Paxton

Pax Am Pax Americana (Latin —American Peace)—a somewhat belated takeover of Britain's role

Pax Brit Pax Britannica (Latin —British Peace)—a long period of peaceful stability imposed throughout the British Empire and many adjacent parts of the world

Pax Por Pax Porfiriana (Latin— Porfirian Peace)—imposed on Mexico by its dictator-general-president—Don Porfirio Díaz —from 1876 to 1910 when ousted by Madero

Pax River Patuxent River Naval Air Station, Maryland

Pax Rom *Pax Romana* (Latin—Roman Peace)—imposed throughout the Roman Empire

pax vob. *pax vobiscum* (Latin—peace be with you)

Pay Paymaster; Paymistres

Paya Lebar Singapore's international airport

Pay Cmdr Paymaster Commander

paye (PAYE) pay as you earn (United Kingdom scheme of income tax paying while earning); pay as you enter

payld payload

Paymr Paymaster; Paymistress

PAYS Patriotic American Youth Society

Pays-Bas (French—Low Countries)—the Netherlands

payt payment

Paz Ladislao Pazmany

pb painted base; paper base; patrol bombing; permanent ballast; permanent bunker(s); petrol bomb(ing); plotting board; plugged back (oil well); poor bastard; ports and beaches; pull box; pulse beacon; push button

p/b paperback; pass book; poor bastard; pushbutton

pB purplish blue

Pb *plumbum* (Latin—lead)

PB Pacific Beach; Packard Bell; Palm Beach; patrol boat; patrol bomber; patrol bombing; Permian Basis; Planning Board; Pocket Book; police boat; Pompano Beach; Presiding Bishop; Public Bath; Publication Bulletin

P-B Pitney-Bowes

PB *Pulses Bajos* (Spanish—Low Countries)—the Netherlands today but originally Belgium and the Netherlands; *Planta Baja* (Spanish—ground floor), elevator pushbutton designation; *Prayer Book*

P.B. *Pharmacopeia Britannica*

pba poor bloody assistant; pressure-breathing assister; published by arrangement

PBA Patrolmen's Benevolent Association; Philadelphia Bar Association; Port of Brisbane Authority; Port of Bristol Authority; Professional Bookmen of America; Professional Bowlers Association; Public Buildings Administration

PBAA Periodical and Book Association of America; Public Broadcasting Association of Australia

p'back paperback

pbai *proyectil balístico de alcance intermedio (PBAI)*—(Spanish—intermediate range ballistic missile)

P-band 225–390 mc

PBAS Post Block Aerial Survey(ing)

pbb push-button banking

PBBH Peter Bent Brigham Hospital (Boston)

pbb's (PBBs) polybrominated biphenyls

pbc peripheral bus computer; point of basal convergence

PBC Palisade Boat Club; Pen and Brush Club; Philadelphia Blood Clinic; Philadelphia Book Clinic; Provincial Bank of Canada

pbcb plugboard circuit breaker

pbd particle board

PBD Public Buildings Department

pbdndb perceived barking dog noise decibels

pbe present barrel equivalent

Pbe Perlsucht bacillen emulsion

PBEC Pacific Basin Economic Council; Public Broadcasting Environment Center

P. B. Ed. Bachelor of Philosophy in Education

PBEIST Planning Board for European Inland Surface Transport (NATO)

pbf permalloy-bar file

PBF fast patrol boat (naval symbol)

PBF *Prins Bernhard Fonds* (Prince Bernhard Fund)

PBFG guided missile fast patrol boat (naval symbol)

PBFL Planning for Better Family Living (UN)

Pbg Pittsburgh

PBGC Pension Benefit Guaranty Corporation

pbh partial bulkhead; primary borehole

pbhp pounds per brake horsepower

pbi please book immediately; polybenzimidazole (space-age fabric); poor bloody infantry; protein-bound iodine

pbi (PBI) polybenzimidazole

pbi *proyectil balístico intercontinental (PBI)* (Spanish—intercontinental ballistic missile)

PBI Paper Bag Institute; Paving Block Institute; Pitney-Bowes Incorporated; Plumbing Brass Institute; Projected Books Incorporated; West Palm Beach, Florida (airport)

PBiB *Paperback Books in Print*

pbip pulse beacon impact predictor

PBJC Palm Beach Junior College

pbk paperback

PBK Phi Beta Kappa

PBKTOA Printing, Bookbinding, and Kindred Trades Overseers' Association

pbl planetary boundary layer; probable

PBL Pacific Beach Library; Public Broadcast Laboratory

pb list phonetically balanced (word) list

P Blr Port Blair

pbm performance-based management

pbm (PBM) permanent bench mark

PBM Mariner twin-engine Navy bomber built by Martin; Paramaribo, Surinam (airport); Production Bill of Material

PBMA Peanut Butter Manufacturers Association

PBMR Provisional Basic Military Requirements

PBN Provisional Buy Notice

PBN *Producto Bruto Nacional* (Spanish—National Bulk Products)

pbo polite brushoff

P-boat Patrol Boat

P. Bor. *Pharmacopoeia Borussica* (Latin—Prussian Pharmacopoeia)

PBOS Planning Board for Ocean Shipping (USA)

pbp pushbutton panel

pbpGinfwmy please be patient; God is not finished with me yet

PBPS Program Budgeting and Planning System

pbr payment by results

pbr (PBR) power breeder reactor; precision bombing range

PBR Project Budget Report(ing)

pbs paginated by sections; polarizing beamsplitter; production base support; program breakdown structure

pb's paperback books; petrol bombs (Irish-style Molotov-cocktail-type incendiary bombs); poor bastards

p-bs phosphate-buffered saline (solution)

PBS Pacific Biological Station (Canada); Panama Bureau of

Shipping; Permanent Building Societies; Pharmaceutical Benefits Scheme; Philippine Broadcasting Service; Prevent Blindness Society; Public Broadcasting Service; Public Broadcast(ing) Station; Public Buildings Service

PBSA Partially Blinded Soldiers Association; Permanent Building Societies Association

PB & SC Power Boat and Ski Club

PBSCMA Peanut Butter Sandwich and Cookie Manufacturers Association

PBSE Philadelphia-Baltimore Stock Exchange

pbsp prognostically bad signs during pregnancy

pbt performance-based teaching; profit(s) before tax(ation)

pbt (PBT) polybutylene terephthalate

PBT President of the Board of Trade

PBTB Paper Bag Trade Board; Paper Box Trade Board

pbte performance-based teacher education

Pburg Pittsburgh

pbv predicted blood volume; pulmonary blood volume

pbw parts by weight; posterior bite wing

pbw (PBW) particle-beam weapon

PBWSE Philadelphia-Baltimore-Washington Stock Exchange

pbx private branch exchange

pbx's (PBXs) personal business exchanges (computerized telephones)

PBY Consolidated-Vultee PBY flying boat; vacation island near Long Beach, California—Santa Catalina

pbz phosphor bronze

pbz (PBZ) pyribenzamine (antihistamine)

pc paper copy; parent cells; parsec; pay clerk; paycheck; percent; percentage; percentile; personal correction; petty cash; pica(s); piece(s); pitch circle; point of curve; port of call; postcard; prices current; printed circuit; privileged character; pull chain; pulsating current; purchasing and contracting purified concentrate

pc (PC) personal computer; pitch class; programme counter

p-c phophlogistic-corticoid;

printed circuit

p/c percent; percentage; processor controller; programmer-comparator; pulse counter

p & c put and call

pc *point de congélation* (French —freezing point)

p.c. *post cebum* (Latin—after a meal, after meals)

Pc Phillips curve (macroeconomics)

PC Pace College; Pacific Airlines; Pacific Coast (railroad); Pacific College; Paine College; Palmer College; Palomar College; Panama Canal; Panola College; Paris College; Park College; Parsons College; Pasadena College; Peace Corps; Pembroke College; Pepperdine College; personnel carrier; Pfeiffer College; Pharmacy Corps; Philadelphia College; Philippine Constabulary; Phoenix College; Piedmont College; Pikeville College; Pilotage Chart(s); Pineland College; Pittsburgh Corning; Plane Commander; Police Commissioner; Pomona College; Porterville College; Presbyterian College; Principia College; Privy Council; Privy Councillor(s); Procurement Command; Producers Council; Professional Corporation; Providence College; submarine chaser patrol vessel (naval symbol)

P-C Penn-Central (railroad)

P.C. Penal Code; Plaid Cymru (party)

P&C Parents and Citizens Association

P & C Pickpocket and Confidence (police department squad)

PC *Partido Colorado* (Spanish —Colorado Party)—the reds; *Partido Comunista* (Spanish —Communist Party); *Partido Conservador* (Spanish—Conservative Party); *Penal Code*; *Poder Chicano* (Spanish— Chicano Power)

pca permanent change of assignment; physical configuration audit(ing); Porsche Club of America (uses lowercase initials)

pca (PCA) p-chloraphenylalanine

Pca Pensacola

PCA Parachute Club of America; Permanent Court of Arbitration (The Hague); Pest Con-

trol Association; Photogrammetric Consultants Association; Plaster Contractors Association; Pollution Control Agency; Pony Club Association; Portland Cement Association; Positive Control Area; Primary Coverage Area; Production Code Administration; Production Credit Association

PCA *Partido Comunista Argentina* (Spanish—Argentine Communist Party)

PCAC Professional Classes Aid Council

pcam punchcard accounting machine; punchcard accounting method

PCAO Presidential Complaints and Action Office(r)

PCAPA Pacific Coast Association of Port Authorities

PCAPK President's Commission on the Assassination of President Kennedy

PCARS Point Credit Accounting and Reporting System

PCAs Progressive Citizens of America

PCAT Philippine College of Arts and Trades

pcb petty cash book; printed circuit board

pcb (PCB) polychlorinated biphenyls

PCB Pest Control Bureau; Program Control Board

PCB *Partido Comunista Boliviano* (Spanish—Bolivian Communist Party); *Partido Comunista Brasileiro* (Portuguese—Brazilian Communist Party)

pcbb primary commercial blanket bond(ing)

PCBL Pacific Commercial Bank Limited

pcb's (PCBs) polychlorinated biphenyls (industrial pollutants of lakes, reservoirs, and streams)

p-c b's printed-circuit boards

pcc phosphate carrier compound; pitch of cone to cone; portland concrete cement; program-controlled computer

pcc *plus ça change, plus c'est la meme chose* (French—the more it changes the more it stays the same)

PCC Pacific Coast Conference; Pacific Conference of Churches; Palmer Community College; Panama Canal Commission; Panama Canal Company; Pennsylvania Crime Commission; Philippine Cotton Corporation; Poison Control Center; Polynesian Cultural Center; Port of Corpus Christi; Portland Community College; Price Control Council; Program Control Center

PCC *Partido Comunista Cubano* (Spanish—Cuban Communist Party)

PCCC Pakistan Central Cotton Committee

PCCEMRSP Permanent Commission for the Conservation and Exploitation of the Maritime Resources of the South Pacific

PCCI President's Committee on Consumer Interests

PCCNY *Penal Code of the City of New York*

PCCR Publishing Center for Cultural Resources

PCCT Percept and Concept Cognition Test

pccu (PCCU) progressive coronary care unit

PCCU President's Commission on Campus Unrest

pcd pitch circle diameter; pounds per capita per day

PCD Planned Community Development; Principal Criteria Document

PCDA Post Card Distributors Association

PCDG Prestressed Concrete Development Group

pc di pierce die

P Cdr Paymaster Commander

PCDS Program Control Display System (NATO)

pce pyrometric cone equivlent

pce (PCE) pseudocholinesterase

PCE patrol craft escort (3-letter coding); Personal Consumption Expenditure

PCE *Partido Comunista Española* (Spanish Communist Party)

PCEA Pacific Coast Electrical Association; President's Council of Economic Advisors

PCEH The President's Committee on Employment of the Handicapped

PCEM Parliamentary Council of the European Movement

PCEQ President's Council on Environmental Quality

PCER rescue escort (naval symbol)

pcf pounds per cubic foot; power per cubic foot

Pcf *Pacifico* (Italian—Pacific);

Pacifico (Portuguese or Spanish—Pacific); *Pacifique* (French—Pacific)

PCF Personnel Control Facility; Program Checkout Facility

PCF *Parti Communiste Français* (French Communist Party)

PCFAP The President's Committee on the Foreign Aid Program

PCFLIS President's Commission on Foreign Language and International Studies

pcg phonocardiogram

PCG guided-missile coastal-escort vessel (naval symbol)

PCGN Permanent Committee on Geographical Names

pch paroxysmal cold hemoglobinuria

P Ch Parish Church

PCH hydrofoil submarine chaser (3-letter coding)

pchbd patchboard

pci pattern correspondence index; pellet-cladding interaction; peripheral command indicator; perpetual cost index; picocurie; potential criminal informant; programmed-controlled interruption

PCI Packer Collegiate Institute; Pilot Club International; Planning Card Index; Prestressed Concrete Institute; Program of Correctional Institutions (Puerto Rico)

PCI *Partito Comunista Italiano* (Italian Communist Party)

PCIB Pacific Cargo Inspection Bureau

PCIC Polaris Control and Information Center

PCIFC Permanent Commission of the International Fisheries Convention

PCII Potato Chip Institute International

PCIJ Permanent Court of International Justice

PCIM Presidential Commission on Income Maintenance

PCjr IBM's junior model of the personal computer

Pck conditional probability of kill (armament)

pckt printed circuit

pcl parcel; printed-circuit lamp

PCL Pacific Coast Line; Peoples College of Law; Police Crime Laboratory

PCLA Project Coordination and Liaison Administration

PCLEAJ President's Commission on Law Enforcement and

the Administration of Justice

p-c lens perspective-correction lens

pclk pay clerk

PCLO Police Community Liaison Office(r)

PCLTT Permanent Committee on Land Transportation and Telecommunications (ASEAN)

pcm phase-change material(s); plug-compatible manufacturer(s); protein-calorie malnutrition; pulse-code modulation; pulse-count modulation; punchcard machine(s)

PCM Peabody Conservatory of Music; President's Certificate of Merit

PCM *Partido Comunista Mexicano* (Mexican Communist Party)

PCMA Post Card Manufacturers Association; Professional Convention Management Association

pcmb (PCMB) parachloro-mercuric benzoic (acid)

pcmi photographic micro-image(s)—microdot photos

PCMIA Plasterers and Cement Masons International Association (U.S. and Canada)

PCMO Principal Colonial Medical Officer

PCMP Progressive Car Manufacturing Program

pcm/pl pulse-code modulated/polarized light

pcmr patient computer medical record; photochromic micro-reproduction

PCMR President's Committee on Mental Retardation

PCMSER President's Commission on Marine Science, Engineering, and Resources

pcmx (PCMX) parachlorometaxylenol (antiseptic)

pcn parent-country national(s); printed control number; processing control number

PCN Part Control Number; Procurement Control Number

PCN *Partido de Conciliación Nacional* (Spanish—National Conciliation Party)

PCNB Permanent Control Narcotics Board

PCNG President's Commission on National Goals

PCNR Part Control Number Request

PCN's Planning Change Notices

PCNV Provisional Committee

on Nomenclature of Viruses

PCNY Proofreaders Club of New York

pco post checkout operation(s)

pc/o por ciento (Spanish—percent)

PCO Printing Control Office(r); Procuring Contracting Office(r); Public Carriage Office(r)

P/CO Purser/Catering Officer

P$_{CO2}$ carbon dioxide pressure (or tension)

PCOB Permanent Central Opium Board (UN)

PCOOS Pacific Coast Oto-Ophthalmological Society

PCOP President's Commission on Obscenity and Pornography

PCOS Primary Communication Operating System

pcp passenger control point; production change point

pcp (PCP) phencyclidine (called Pure California Poison by Los Angeles Police Chief Daryl Gates in his program to overcome public apathy about the nation's drug problem)

PCP Peking Central Philharmonic; Postgraduate Center of Psychotherapy; Program Change Proposal; Progressive Conservative Party

PCP Partido Comunista Panameño (Spanish—Panamanian Communist Party); *Partido Comunista Paraguayo* (Spanish—Paraguayan Communist Party); *Partido Comunista Peruviano* (Spanish—Peruvian Communist Party); *Partido Communista Portugues* (Portuguese Communist Party)

PCPA Panama Canal Pilots Association; parachlorophenylalanine; Philadelphia College of the Performing Arts

PCPD Portland Commission of Public Docks

PCPF President's Council on Physical Fitness

PCPI Parent Cooperative Preschools International

PCPJ People's Coalition for Peace and Justice (communist directed)

PCPM Program Control Procedures Manual

PCPP President's Commission on Pension Policy

PCPS Philadelphia College of Pharmacy and Science

PC & PS Professional Credentials and Personnel Service

(nursing)

pcpt perception

pcpv prestressed concrete pressure vessel

pcq production-control quantometer

PCQ Personal Control Questionnaire

pcr photoconductive relay

pcr (PCR) program control register

PCR Program Change Request; Publication Contract Requirement

PCR Partido Comunista Revolucionario (Spanish—Revolutionary Communist Party)—Chile; *Partidul Comunist Roman* (Roman Communist Party)

PCRB Pollution Control Revenue Bond

PCRC Paraffined Carton Research Council; Primary Communications Research Center (University of Leicester)

pcrca pickled, cold rolled, and closely annealed

PC R & D C Pomona Colleges Research and Development Center

PCRI Papanicolaou Cancer Research Institute

PCRs Planning and Compensation Reports

PCRS Poor Clergy Relief Society

PCRU Pacific Coast Rugby Union

pcrv prestressed concrete reactor vessel

pcs permanent change of station; phonocardioscan; picas; pieces; planning control sheet; program counter storage; program counter store

pc's protective clothes

pc's (PCs) personal computers

PCs Police Constables; Progressive Conservatives

PCS 136-foot submarine chaser (3-letter coding); Parent's Confidential Statement; Permanent Committee on Shipping (ASEAN); Petrochemical Corporation of Singapore; Polytechnic Certificate in Shipping; Program Control System; Punch(ed) Card System; Punjab Cooperative Society

PCSA Polish Cultural Society of America

PCSCA Permanent Committee on Socio-Cultural Affairs (ASEAN)

PCSE Pacific Coast Stock Ex-

change; President's Council on Scientists and Engineers

PCSFA Potato Chip/Snack Food Association

pc sh pierce shell

PCSIR Pakistan Council of Scientific and Industrial Research

PCSP Permanent Commission for the South Pacific; Polar Continental Shelf Project; Princeton Cooperative School Program

PCSS Platform Check Subsystem

PCST Permanent Commission on Science and Technology (ASEAN)

PCSW President's Commission on the Status of Women

pct percent

pct (PCT) portable camera transmitter

pct procent (Dano-Norwegian—percent)

Pct Precinct

PCT Patent Cooperation Treaty; Portsmouth College of Technology; Potash Core Test(ing)

PCT Partido Conservador Tradicional (Spanish—Traditional Conservative Party)—Nicaragua; *Programa de Cooperación Tecnica* (Spanish—Technical Cooperation Program)

PCTB Pacific Coast Tariff Bureau

pctfe polychlorotrifluoroethylene

pc tp pierce template

PCTS President's Committee for Traffic Safety

pcu photocopy unit; power-control unit; pressurization-control unit

pcu (PCU) palliative care unit (for terminal patients); portable checkout unit; protective custody unit

pcur pulsating current

PCUS Propeller Club of the United States

PCU-USA Portuguese Continental Union of the U.S.A.

pcv packed-cell volume; physical control volume; pollution-control valve; positive crankcase ventilation

PCV Peace Corps Volunteer(s); Pestalozzi Children's Village; President's Commission on Violence

PCV Partido Comunista Venezolana (Spanish—Venezuelan Communist Party)

PCVC Public Citizen Visitor's Center

PC virus Port Chalmers (New Zealand) type of influenza virus

PCVs Peace Corps Volunteers

pcv valve positive crankcase ventilation valve

PCWPC Permanent Council of the World Petroleum Congress

pcx periscope convex

PCY coastal yacht (3-letter naval symbol); Pittsburgh, Chartiers & Youghiogheny (railroad)

PCYC Port Credit Yacht Club

PCZ Panama Canal Zone

PCZST Panama Canal Zone Standard Time

pd interpupillary distance; paid; paralysing dose; passed; period; permanent dunnage; physical distribution; pitch diameter; point detonating; poop deck; port dues; position doubtful; post date; post dated; postage due; potential difference; pound; pour depressant; preliminary design; preventive detention; prism diopter; procurement directive; property damage; public domain; pulse duration; purchase description

p-d prism diopter

p/d post dated

p& d pickup and delivery

p.d. per diem (Latin—by the day)

Pd palladium; Parade

PD Parliamentary Debates; Pharmacopoeia Dublin; Phelps-Dodge; Physics Department; Police Department; Port of Debarkation; Port Director; Port Dues; position doubtful (navigation chart marking); Preliminary Design; Presidential Directive; Production Department; Program Director; Public Defender

P-D Parke-Davis

P&D Probate and Divorce; Promotion and Development (program)

P of D Port of Duluth

PD Partido Democrático (Spanish—Democratic Party); (Cleveland) Plain Dealer

P-D St Louis Post-Dispatch (a leading daily newspaper)

P.D. Pharmacopoeia Dublinensis (Latin—Dublin Pharmacopoeia)

pda patient distress alarm; personal death awareness; predicted drift angle; public display of affection

pda (PDA) probability distribution analyzer

pda pour dire adieu (French—to say goodbye)

PDA Photographic Dealers' Association; Plywood Distributors Association; Port Development Authority

PDAD Probate, Divorce, and Admiralty Division

P Dal Port Dalhousie

P Dar Port Darwin

PDARS Pulsed Doppler Acoustic Radar System

PDAS Police Department American Samoa

P-day day when rate of production of an item for military consumption equals rate required by armed forces

pdb paradichlorobenzine

Pd.B. Pedagogiae Baccalaureus (Latin—Bachelor of Pedagogy)

pde preliminary diagnostic clinic; private diagnostic clinic

p&d c premium and dispersion credit(s)

Pdc probability of detection and conversion

PDC Pacific Development Corporation; Penang Development Corporation; Periodical Distributors of Canada; Petroleum Development Corporation; Prevention of Deterioration Center (National Academy of Sciences); Project Development Corporation

PDC Partido Democrático Cristiano (Spanish—Christian Democratic Party)

PDCL Provisioning Data Check List

Pd.D. Pedagogiae Doctor (Latin—Doctor of Pedagogy)

PDD Petty Delinquency Detention; Public Documents Department (GPO)

pdda power-driven decontaminating apparatus

PDDS Parasitic Disease Drug Service

pde paroxysmal dyspnea on exertion

Pde Parade

PDE Post-test Disassembly Examination

P de C Pas de Calais (French—Strait of Calais)—Dover Strait

P-de-D Puy-de-Dôme

PDEIS Preliminary Draft Environmental Impact Statement

P del E Penitenciario del Estado (Spanish—State Penitentiary)

P de M Principaute de Monaco (Monte Carlo)

pdes pulse-doppler elevation scan

P des L Parc des Laurentides (Québec)—Laurentian Mountains Park

pdf point detonating fuse; probability distribution function

PDF Parkinsons' Disease Foundation

PDFLP Popular Democratic Front for the Liberation of Palestine

PDG Paymaster Director-General

pdga (PDGA) pteroyldiglutamic acid

PDGW Principal Director of Guided Weapons

pdh past dental history

pdi point diffraction interferometer; powered-descent initiation

PDI Printing Developments Incorporated

pdic periodic

PDID Public Disorder Intelligence Department (LAPD); Public Disorder Intelligence Division

PDIN Pusat Dokumentasi Ilmiah Nasional (Bahasa Indonesian—National Scientific and Technical Documentation Center)

PDIS Pusat Dokumentasi Ilmu-Ilmu Sosial (Bahasa Indonesian—Social Sciences Documentation Center)

p dk poop deck

pdl poundal; poverty datum line

pdm pulse-delta modulation; pulse-duration modulation

Pd.M. Master of Pedagogy

PDMS Point Defense Missile System

pdn production

pdnes pulse-doppler non-elevation scan(ning)

pdo pasado (Spanish—past)

Pdo Partido (Spanish—Party)—political party

PDO Publication Distribution Office(r); Property Disposal Office(r)

p/doz per dozen

pdp plasma display panel; power distribution panel; project definition phase

Pdp Paradip

PDP Program Definition Phase; Program Development Plans

PDPS Parts Data Processing System

pd pt production pattern

pdq (PDQ) programmed data quantisizer

p d q pretty damn (or darn) quick

PDQB P.D.Q. Bach (allegedly the last son of his better-known father, Johann Sebastian Bach, according to Professor Peter Schickele who also discovered a long-lost baroque instrument—the horn & hardart)

pdr pounder; powder; precision depth recorder (PDR)

pdr *polder* (Dutch—dike-protected lowland reclaimed from the sea or other body of water such as the Zuider Zee)

PDR People's Democratic Republic; Philippine Defense Ribbon

PDR *Physicians' Desk Reference*

PDRK People's Democratic Republic of Korea (North Korea)

PDRL Permanent Disability Retirement List

pdrm payload distribution and retrieval mechanism

PDRP Power Distribution Reactor Program

PDRY People's Democratic Republic of Yemen (capitals—Aden and Medina as-Shaab)

pds point detonating self-destroying

pd's public defenders

PDs Police Departments; Program Directors

PDS Pacific Data Systems; Passive Defense System; Personnel Data System; Philadelphia Divinity School; Priority Distribution System; Project Data Sheet; Proposed Delivery Schedule

PDSA People's Dispensary for Sick Animals

PDSC Performers and Teachers Diploma—Sydney Conservatorium

PDSOC Police Department Superior Officers' Council

pdsq point detonating super-quick fuze

PDSR Principal Director of Scientific Research

PDST Pacific Daylight Saving Time

pdt power distribution trailer; practice delivery torpedo

PDT Pacific Daylight Saving Time

PDT-1 Picatinny Arsenal Detonation Trap 1

PDTC Plymouth and Devonport Technical College

PDTLO Pierre Dominique Toussaint l'Ouverture

PDTS Police Detective Training School; Program Development Tracking System

pdu power distribution unit

pdv pure dried vacuum (salt)

pdv (PDV) pyrotechnic development vehicle

pd work public domain work (of art, history, literature, publication, etc.)

PDX Portland, Oregon (airport)

PDZ Parachute Dropping Zone

pe personnel equipment; probable error; program element; printer's error

pe (PE) physical education; physical examination

p-e precipitation-environment (index)

p/e porcelain enamel; price earning

p & e planning and estimating

pe *par exemple* (French—for example); *per esempio* (Italian—for example); *por ejemplo* (Spanish—for example)

Pe Pecltet number; Pernambuco

P^e *Padre* (Spanish—father)

PE Pacific Electric (railroad); patrol vessel (naval symbol); Petroleum Engineer(ing); Philadelphia Electric; Pistol Expert; Plant Engineer(ing); Port of Embarkation; Port Everglades, Florida; Port Exchange; probable error; Production Engineer(ing); Professional Engineer; Protestant Episcopal

P-E Perkin-Elmer

P & E Peoria & Eastern (railroad)

P of E Port of Entry

P.E. *Pharmacopoeia Edinburgensis* (Latin—Edinburgh Pharmacopoeia)

pea. (PEA) primary expense account

PEA People Express Airlines; Plastics Engineers Association; Policewomen's Endowment Association; Potash Export Association; Public Education Association; Publica-

tion Effectiveness Audit

PEAB Professional Engineer's Appointments Bureau

PEACE People Emerging Against Corrupt Establishments; Project Evaluation and Assistance in Civil Engineering (USAF)

Peacefield Quincy, Massachusetts home of John Adams and his son John Quincy Adams

Peace Garden State North Dakota

Peacemaker William Penn

PEACESAT Pan-Pacific Education and Communications Experiments using Satellites

Peach Blossom Delaware's state flower

Peach Bowl Atlanta, Georgia

Peach Capital of British Columbia Penticton

Peach State Georgia's official nickname

Peacracker(s) native(s) of Lowestoft

PEAL Professional Engineers Association Limited

Pea Mus Peabody Museum

Peanut Capital of Alabama Dothan

Peanut City Suffolk, Virginia

Peanut King Amadeo Obici who organized the Planters Peanut Company in 1906

PEAQ Personal Experience and Attitude Questionnaire

Pear City Medford, Oregon

Pearl Pearl Harbor—Oahu, Hawaii

PEARL (Committee for) Public Education and Religious Liberty

Pearl of the Adriatic Dubrovnik, Yugoslavia

Pearl of the Antilles Cuba

Pearl of the Atlantic Madeira

Pearl of the Baltic Bornholm Island, Denmark

Pearl of the Chilean Pacific Viña del Mar

Pearl of Ireland Saint Brigit

Pearl Island of the Caribbean Margarita, Venezuela

Pearl King Mikimoto Kokichi (Japanese who discovered the secret of creating cultured pearls)

Pearl of the Lagoons Abidjan, Ivory Coast

Pearl of the Orient Sri Lanka (Ceylon)

Pearl of the Pacific Honolulu, Pago Pago, Papeete, and other Pacific Ocean ports share this sobriquet

Pearl of Persia Isfahan
Pearl and Petroleum Sheikdom El Qatar on the Persian Gulf
Pearls Pearl Islands (Las Perlas)
Pearl S Buck Mrs Richard J Walsh
Pearl of the Sharon Netanya, Isreal
Pearl of the South Seas sobriquet shared by Tahiti, Tonga, Samoa, and other South Sea islands
PEAS Production Engineering Advisory Service
Peasant Bard Robert Burns
Peasant Breughel Pieter Breughel the Elder
Peasant With A Pen Eric Linklater's nickname
PEAT Programmer Exercised Autopilot Test(ing)
peb prototype environmental buoy
Pe. B. Pediatriae Baccalaureus (Latin—Bachelor of Pediatrics)
PEB Physical Evaluation Board; Propulsion Examining Board (USN); Public Examination Board
pebb public employees blanket bond(ing)
pebd pay entry base date
pec photoelectric cell; position error correction; program element code
PEC Presidential Ethics Commission; Production Equipment Code; Protestant Episcopal Church; Psychology Examining Commission; Psychology Examining Committee
pecan. pulse envelope correlation air navigator
PECE President's Emergency Committee for Employment
Pêcheurs de Perles (French—The Pearl Fishers)—three-act opera by Bizet
Pechino (Italian—Peking)
PECI Projects and Equipment Corporation of India
'pecker woodpecker
Peck's Bad Boy (pseudonym—George W. Peck)
PECM Preliminary Engineering Change Memorandum (USAF)
Pecos Bill General William Shafter, USA
Pecos Wilderness eastern New Mexico and West Texas (northern New Mexico east of Santa Fe to the Rio Grande above Del Rio, Texas)

PECP Preliminary Engineering Change Proposal
PECS Plant Engineering Check Sheet
pecto pectoral
Peculiar Institution Mount Holyoke College founded by Mary Lyon and described by her as a peculiar institution as it was for women
PECUSA Protestant Episcopal Church of the U.S.A.
ped pedagogue; pedagogy; pedal; pedestal; pedestrian; personnel equipment data
ped (Latin prefix—children)—pediatrics
Ped pedal (music); Pediatrics
P Ed Physical Education
pedag pedagogue; pedaguese (patois of pedants)
pedageese pedagogue jargon
Ped.B. Bachelor of Pedagogy
Ped.D. Doctor of Pedagogy
pediat pediatric(al)(ly); pediatrician; pediatrics
PE Dir Physical Education Director
Ped.M. Master of Pedagogy
pedo pedologic(al)(ly); pedologist(ic)(al)(ly)
pedobap pedobaptism; pedobaptist
pedog pedograph(ic); pedography
pedogen pedogenesis
pedol pedologic(al)(ly); pedologist(ic)(al)(ly); pedology
pedom pedometer; pedometric(al)(ly)
pedont pedodontic(al)(ly); pedodontist(ry)
pedop pedophile; pedophilia(c)
Pedralvez Pedro Alvarez
Pedrarias Pedro Arias
Pedro navalese for San Pedro, California
peds pediatrics
pedstl pedestal(s)
PED XING pedestrian crossing (America's most perplexing highway abbreviation)
pee. photoelectric emission; pressure environment equipment; urine
PEE Proof and Experimental Establishment (British Ministry of Defence)
P & EE Proving and Experimental Establishment
Peeb Peebles
Peebl Peebleshire
peep. positive and expiratory pressure
peep. (PEEP) pilot's electronic eye-level presentation

PEER Planned Environment and Education Research Institute
Peer Gynt drama by Ibsen with incidental music by Grieg
pees South Vietnamese piasters
pef peak expiatory flow; personal effects floater (policy)
PEF Palestine Exploration Fund; Personality Evaluation Form; Plastics Education Foundation; Presidential Election Fund; Psychiatric Evaluation Form
peg. polyethylene glycol
Peg Pegasus (constellation); Peggy
Peg Pegunungan (Malay—mountain range)
PEG Petrochemical Energy Group; Pittsburgh Elderly Gay
PEGE Program for Evaluation of Ground Environment
Peggy Margaret
Pegs Pegasus (constellation)
pei pointless electronic ignition; precipitation-efficiency index
PEI Porcelain Enamel Institute; Preliminary Engineering Inspection; Prince Edward Island
Pei-ching (Mandarin Chinese—Peking)—also called Peiping meaning Northern Peace
PEIP Presidential Executive Interchange Program
Peiping or *Peking* (Chinese—Northern Capital)
Peipsi (Estonian—Peipus) Chudskoe is the Russian place-name equivalent for this lake in Estonia
PEIS Preliminary Environmental Impact Statement
pej premolded expansion joint
p ej por ejemplo (Spanish—for example)
PEJO Plant Engineering Job Order(s)
pejor pejorative(ly)
pek pig embryo kidney
Pek Peking; Pekinese
peke pekinese dog
Pekin (German—Peking)
Pekín (Spanish—Peking)
Pékin (French—Peking)
Peking English equivalent of Pei-ching or Peiping or Peking—capital of communist-controlled mainland China
pel pelagic; pellet; pelvis; picture element
P El Port Elizabeth
PEL Petroleum Exploration License; Physics and Engineer-

ing Laboratory

P EL Port Elizabeth

Pelagies Pelagian Islands in the Mediterranean between Sicily and Tunisia

Pelican Louisiana's state bird and symbolic nickname often given Louisianians—Pelicans

Pelican State Louisiana's official nickname

Pelikaanstraat (Flemish—Pelican Street)—Antwerp's diamond-dealer's center

P Eliz Port Elizabeth

Pelléas Pelléas et Melisande (Debussy's five-act opera)

Pellews Pellew Islands in Australia's Gulf of Carpentaria

Pellys Pelly Mountains of the Yukon

PELNI Pelajaran Nasional Indonesia (National Shipping Company of Indonesia)

pem photoelectromagnet(ic); program element monitor

Pem Pembrokeshire

PEM Production Engineering Measures; Project Engineering Memo

Pemb Pembroke College, Oxford; Pembrokeshire

Pemb Coll Pembroke College—Cambridge

Pemex Petróleos Mexicanos

PEMR Petroleum Engineering Monthly Report

PEMS Portable Environmental Measuring System

PE Mus Port Elizabeth Museum

Pem Yeo Pembroke Yeomanry

pen. penal; penetrate; penology; peninsula; penitentiary; penmanship

pen (Latin prefix—lack or need)—penicillin

Pen Penang; Penarth; Peninsula; Penitentiary

Pen Península (Portuguese or Spanish—peninsula); *Péninsule* (French—peninsula); *Penisola* (Italian—peninsula)

PEN Poets, Playwrights, Editors, Essayists, and Novelists (international organization often referred to as the P.E.N. Club)

PEN Presse Etudiante Nationale (French—Student National Press)—Québec's student news cooperative

pen. aids penetration aids

Pen of the American Revolution Thomas Paine

Penamite(s) Pennsylvanian(s)

Penang (Malay—Betel Nut)—

formerly called George Town when British Malaya

Pence Springs West Virginia State Prison for Women at Pence Springs

pencil. pictorial encoding language

PEN Club (*see* PEN)

Pene Penelope

P/E News Petroleum/Energy News

P Eng Professional Engineer(ing)

PENGEM Penetrating the Gray Electronic Market (FBI undercover operation)

P'eng-hu Lieh-tao (Chinese—Pescadores)—archipelago off Taiwan and part of the Republic of China

Penguin Norwegian surface-to-surface missile; Penguin Books

peni penicillin

penic penicillin

penic. penicillum (Latin—brush)

penic. cam. penicillum camelinum (Latin—camel's-hair brush)

Peninsular Malaysia States of the Federation of Malaysia (Federated Malay States also known as Malaya)

Peninsular State Florida

Penit Penitentiary

Penman of the Revolution John Dickinson of Dover, Delaware, Thomas Jefferson, and Tom Paine deserve the title

Penn Pennsylvania; Pennsylvanian

Penna Pennsylvania

Penn Central Pennsylvania New York Central Transportation Company (merger of Pennsylvania, New York Central, New Haven, and Lehigh Valley railroads)

Penney JC Penney Company

Pennie Penina

Pennines Pennine Alps between Italy and Switzerland; Pennine Hills ranging from southern Scotland to central England—the Pennine Chain

Pennsy Pennsylvania; Pennsylvania Railroad

Pennsylvania Farmer John Dickinson's pseudonym

Pennsylvania Ports (north to south) Erie, Philadelphia, Chester, Marcus Hook

Pennsylvania's Capital City Harrisburg

Penn Turn Pennsylvania Turn-

pike

Penny Penelope

Penobscot River City Bangor, Maine

penol penological; penologist; penology

Peñon de Veléz Peñon de Veléz de la Gomera (rocky islet belonging to Spain in the western Mediterranean)

penrad penetration radar

pens pensioneret or pensionist (Dano-Norwegian—retired or pensioner)

pensad pension administration

PENSADS Pension Administration System

Pensilvania (Italian, Portuguese, Spanish—Pennsylvania)

Pensy (naval argot—Pensacola, Florida)

pent. penetrate; penetration; pentode

Pent Pentagon; Pentecost

Pent Pentateuch

PENT Project for the Education of Native Teachers

Pentagon five-sided United States Department of Defense headquarters in Washington, D.C.; world's largest government office building

Pentland Firth ocean passage between northern Scotland and Orkney Islands; channel connects Atlantic Ocean and North Sea

Pentlands Pentland Hills southwest of Edinburgh or the Pentland Skerries comprising the southernmost Orkneys

pento (sodium) pentothal

Pentonville London area prison

penval penetration evaluation

PeO President ex-Oficio

PEO Philanthropic Educational Organization; Plant Engineering Order; Protect Each Other (secret women's organization)

PEOC Publishing Employees Organizing Committee

Peony Indiana state flower; Indiana girl's nickname

Peony Center Faribault, Minnesota

People of the Lion Singhalese of Ceylon

People's Daily communist government gazette published in Peking

People's Lawyer Associate Justice Louis Dembitz Brandeis of the Supreme Court of the United States

People's Poet Paul Lawrence Dunbar

Peory nickname of Peoria, Illinois

pep pepper; pep pill; peptide

pep. pepper; peppermint; peppy

pep. (PEP) phosphoenolypyruvate; polyestradiol phosphate; Public Employment Program

P e P Partija e Punes (Albanian —Workers Party)

PEP Parent Effectiveness Program; P.E.P. Deraniyagala; Pepsi-Cola (stock-exchange symbol); Performance Evaluation Process; Personalized Engineering Program; Personalized Exercise System; Petroleum Electric Power; Political and Economic Planning; Positron-Electron Project; Preventive Enforcement Patrol; Program Evaluation Procedure; Public Employment Program

PEPA Petroleum Electric Power Association

Pep-Bis Pepto-Bismol

Pepco Potomac Electric Power Comapny

Pepe José (Joseph)

pepg piezo-electric power generator

PEPG Port Emergency Planning Group (NATO)

PEPIC Public Education Project on the Intelligence Community

Pepin le Bref (French—Pepin the Short)—first king of France

Pepita Josefa; Josefina

PEPLAN Polaris Executive Plan (UK)

pep materials propellants, explosives, pyrotechnics

PEPP Professional Engineers in Private Practice

Pepper Coast Liberia

pepr precision encoder and pattern recognizer

peps pep pills; peptides

peps. pepsin

PEPs Public Employment Programs

Pepsi Pepsi Cola

PEPSU Patiala and East Punjab States Union

PEQC President's Environmental Quality Council

Pequim (Portuguese—Peking)

per period; periodic; perodicity; person; personal; personate

per perito (Italian—expert)

Per Perseus (constellation); Persia; Persian

Per Pericles, Prince of Tyre; Pereval (Russian—mountain pass); *Perevoz* (Russian—

crossing, ferry); Persian (oriental language spoken by 24 million Iranians)

PER Perth, Australia (airport)

PE&R Policy, Evaluation, and Research

PERA Production Engineering Research Association

per agrim perito agrimensore (Italian—surveyor)

per an. per annum (Latin—by the year); *per anum* (Latin— by the anus)

per art perito artistico (Italian— art expert)

p/e ratio price-earning ratio

PERB Personnel Evaluation Research Bureau; Public Employment Relations Board

perc perchloroethylene; percolate; percussion

PERC Peace on Earth Research Center

per call perito calligrafo (Italian —handwriting expert)

Perce Persival; Percy

per cent. per centum (Latin—by the hundred)—percent

Percept Psychophys Perception and Psychophysics

perco percobarg (barbiturate synthetic morphine derivative); percodan (synthetic morphine derivative—both addictive and dangerous)

per con. per contra (Italian—on the other side)

PERCOS Performance Coding System

Percy Percival

PERDDIMS Personal Development and Distribution Management System

perden. perdendosi (Italian—dying away)

perdi per diem

Peregil Pedro Gil

Père-Lachaise Paris' best known cemetery and generic eponym for other burial places

perf perfect; perfection; perforate; perforation; perform; performance; performer; perfume(d)

PERF Planetary Entry Radiation Facility (NASA); Police Executive Research Forum

Perfect Butler The Perfect Butler—nickname shared by Sir James M Barrie's *The Admirable Crichton* and Hudson as played by Gordon Jackson in *Upstairs, Downstairs*

perfect calc perfect calculation(s)

Perfector of Opalescent Glass

Louis Comfort Tiffany

perfs perforations; performances; performers; perfumers

perg pergamino (Spanish— parchment)

Pergamon Pergamon Press

perh perhaps

peri perigee; perimeter

peri (Greek—around)—pericardial, pericarp, perimeter, periosteum, peripheral, peritoneum

PERI Platemakers Educational and Research Institute

periap periapical

Peric Periclean

Perico Pedro

peridot yellow-green tourmaline

perig perigee

perih perihelion

PERINTREP Periodic Intelligence Report

period menstrual period; period of rotation; period of revolution

period. periodical

periodontol periodontology

Peripatetic Philosopher Aristotle

peris periscope

perjy perjury

perk. payroll earnings record keeping

perks nickname for percodan (a habit-forming narcotic)

perk(s) perquisite(s)

perl pupils equal and reactive to light

perla pupils equal—react to light and accommodation

perm permanent

Perm Permian

permaflowers permanent (plastic) flowers

permafrost permanent frost

permafruit permanent (plastic) fruit

permed permanently waved

PERMIS Public Employees Retirement Management Information System

PERMREP Permanent Representation to the North Atlantic Council (NATO)

perms permanents; permanent waves

Pernambuco old name of Recife, Brazil

per nav per navale (Italian— ship expert)

pero (Russian—pen)—Trotsky was nicknamed Pero—The Pen—because of his skill in writing revolutionary tracts

PERO President's Emergency Relief Organization

per. op. emet. *peracta operatione emetici* (Latin—when the emetic action is over)

peroxide hydrogen peroxide (H_2O_2)

perp perpendicular

Perp Perpignan

Perpinianum (Latin—Perpignan)

per pro. *per procurationem* (Latin—by proxy)

perq(s) perquisite(s)

per rec *per rectum* (Latin—through the rectum)

perrla pupils equal, round, react to light and accommodation

Perry Como Pierino Como

pers person; personal; personality; personnel; persons

Pers Perseus (constellation); Persia(n)(s)

Pers Aulus Persius Flaccus (Roman satiric poet)

PERS Public Employees' Retirement System

Per.Sac.Lit. Peritus in Sacred Liturgy

Perse Percival; Percy

Pershing Martin surface-to-surface missile (MGM-31A)

Persia ancient name for Iran

persian persian blinds (exterior venetian-type blinds); persian carpet (handwoven oriental rug characteristic of Iran or Persia); persian cat (long-hair cat originally from Persia); persian lamb (young lamb of karakul sheep); persian melon (greenish muskmelon); persian rug (*see* persian carpet)

Persian Gulf arm of the Arabian Sea and the Indian Ocean washing the shores of Bahrain, Iran, Iraq, Kuwait, Oman, Quatar, Saudi Arabia, and the United Arab Emirates

Persian Gulf States Bahrain, Qatar, and the Trucial States

PERSIS Personnel Information System

pers n personal noun

'personation impersonation

personi personification; personified; personifier; personifying

Personification of Death Thanatos (Greek)—whose brother was Hypnos or sleep

Personification of the Destroying Principle Siva

Personification of Justice (*see* Justice Personified)

Personification of the Preserving Principle Vishnu

Personification of Sleep Hypnos (Greek)—whose brother was

Thanatos or death

Personification of the Soul Psyche in the Greek mythology where the word meant breath or soul

persp perspective

pers pron personal pronoun

Persuasive Evolutionist Thomas Henry Huxley

Persymfans *Pervyi Symfonitchesky Ansamble* (Russian—First Symphonic Ensemble)—conductorless orchestra organized in 1922 in Moscow

pert. pertaining

pert. *pertussis* (Latin—whooping cough)

PERT Program Evaluation and Review Technique/Critical Path Technique

PERTCO Program Evaluation and Review Technics (plus) Cost Analysis

per tecn comm *perito tecnico-commerciale* (Italian—estimator)

pertest percolation test(ing)

Perths Perthshire

PERTVS Perimeter Television System

Peru Republic of Peru (Andean nation containing monumental structures left by the Incas; Spanish-speaking Peruvians export many metals and metallic ores as well as cotton, fish meal, oil, and wool), *República del Perú*

Peru Cur Peruvian Current

Peru Day Peruvian Independence Day (July 28 and 29)

Perugino Piero Vannucci

Perusia (Latin—Perugia)

Peru's Principal Port Callao

Peruv Peruvian

peruvian peruvian balsam (also called balsam of Peru, used by chocolate makers, doctors, and perfumers); peruvian bark (*cinchona*)

Peruvian Ports Iquitos on the Amazon's headwaters; Talara, Callao, Matarani, Mollendo, and Ilo on the Pacific plus smaller Pacific ports such as Pisco, Chimbote, and Salaverry

perv perversion; pervert; perverted

perv show pervert show

Perzië (Dutch—Persia)—Iran

pes photoelectric scanner

pe's printer's errors

pe & s parts engineering and standardization

P es *per esempio* (Italian—for

example)—e.g.

PEs Professional Engineers

PES Philosophy of Education Society

PESA Petroleum Equipment Suppliers Association

Pesach Hebrew Passover

PESC Public Expenditure Survey Commission

pescado *pez pasado* (Spanish—past fish)—dead fish or fish out of water and no longer alive

Pescadores (Portuguese or Spanish—Fishermen)—islands off Formosa or Taiwan and part of the Republic of China calling them P'eng Lieh-tao

Pesh Peshawar

Pessimistic Composer Gustav Mahler (nicknamed Gloomy Gus by some music lovers)

Pessimistic Painter Hieronymus Bosch

Pessimistic Philosopher Arthur Schopenhauer

PEST Pressure for Economic and Social Toryism (leftwing conservatives)

Pesthole of the Pacific nickname given at various times to Panama City, Panama; Buenaventura, Colombia; Guayaquil, Ecuador

Pesto (Italian—Paestum)

pet. personal electronic translator; petroleum; petrological; petrologist; petrology; point of equal time

pet. (PET) positive-emission tomography; positron emission tomography (scan)

Pet Peter; Peterhead; Peterhouse College, Oxford; Peterkin; Petronius

PET Parent Effectiveness Training; Pet Milk Company (stock-exchange symbol); Pierre Elliott Trudeau (Canada's nineteenth and twenty-first Prime Minister); Production Environmental Test(ing,s); Production Evaluation Test(ing,s); Prostitution Enforcement Team (police versus pimps and prostitutes)

PETANS Petroleum Training Association—North Sea

Pete Peter; St Petersburg

Peter place-name nickname of Leningrad, formerly Petrograd and originally St Petersburg

Peter I Øy (Norwegian—Peter I Island)—Antarctic dependency of Norway

Peter Arno Curtis Arnoux Pe-

ters
Peterhouse St Peter's College (Cambridge)
Peter Lorre Laszlo Loewenstein
Peter Martyr Pietro Martin d'Anghierra's pseudonym
Peter McGill (American slang— Pedro Miguel)—Panama Canal Locks near Balboa
Peter Mennin Peter Mennini
Peter Mikhailov pseudonym of Peter the Great, which he used while travelling in other countries and working in Dutch shipyards in Amsterdam and Zaandam
Peter Pan of Politics Winston Churchill
Peter and Paul St Peter and St Paul island fortress-prison on the Neva facing Saint Petersburg now called Leningrad
Peter Pindar Dr John Wolcot
Peter Porcupine William Cobbett's pseudonym
Petersburg short form for Saint Petersburg (later called Petrograd and now known as Leningrad); underworld nickname for the Federal Reformatory at Petersburg, Virginia
Peter Warlock Philip Arnold Heseltine
peth petroleum ether
petn petition
petr petrifaction; petrified
Petr Petronius Arbiter (Roman satirist)
PETR Preliminary Flight Test Report
Petrarch Francesco Petracco
petrl petroleum
Petriburg. Petriburgensis (Latin —Peterborough)
Petrified Forest Petrified Forest National Park in Arizona's Painted Desert
Petr Makadonski (Russian— Peter the Great)—Peter Alekseyvich
petro petrochemical; petroleum; petrology
Petro Petrograd (Russian—City of Peter)—Leningrad's name in the early days of the Russian Revolution
PETROBAS Petróleo Brasileiro (Portuguese—Brazilian Petroleum Corporation)
petro-chem petroleum-chemical
petrodollars petroleum-controlled dollars
Petrofina Compagnie Financiere Belges des Pétroles (Belgian Financed Petroleum Company)

petrog petrography
Petrograd Leningrad's former name in Kerensky's regime when it was changed from Saint Petersburg
petrol. petroleum; petrological; petrologist; petrology
Petroleum Emirate Kuwait
Petroleum V Nasby David Ross Locke's pseudonym
Petronas Petroliam Nasional (Malay—National Petroleum)
Petropolis (Latin—City of Peter)—St Petersburg, Petrograd, Leningrad; (Latin—Petersburg)—formerly St Petersburg later becoming Petrograd and Leningrad
petros petrochemicals
PETROVEN Petróleos de Venezuela (Spanish—Venezuelan Petroleum Corporation)
pets. prior to expiration of term of service
PETS Posting and Enquiry Terminal System
pett (PETT) positron emission transaxial tomography
Petya (Russian nickname— Pyotr)—Peter
peua pelvic examination under anesthesia
pev propeller-excited vibration
PEVE Prensa Venezolana (Venezuelan press service)
Pewee Kentucky Correctional Institution at Pewee Valley
pewter lead-tin alloy containing some antimony
p ex par exemple (French—for example)
Peyronies's disease (*see* bent-nail syndrome)
Peyton Place pseudonymic place-name title used by Grace Metalious in describing life in Gilmanton, New Hampshire
pf page footing; perfect; performance factor; pfennig; picofarad; pneumatic float; power factor; preferred; preflight; profile; profiled; proximity fuse; public funding; public funds; pulse frequency; pyrolysis fluorescence
pf (PF) page footing; page formatter; punch-off character
p/f portfolio
pf pro forma (Latin—for the sake of the form), an advance declaration for a financial statement or overseas invoice
pf. *piano e forte* (Italian—soft and then loud)
pF picofarad(s)
Pf Pfennig (German—penny)

PF frigate—patrol escort vessel (naval symbol); Packaging Facility; Physician's Forum; Pioneer & Fayette (railroad); Procurator Fiscal
P/F Peace and Freedom (political party)
pfa psychologic-flight avoidance; pulverized fuel ash
PFA *Policía Federal Argentina* (Spanish—Argentine Federal Police); Press Foundation of Asia; Private Fliers Association
P factor hypothetical pain-producing substance produced in ischemic muscle; preservation factor
Pfalz (German—Palatinate)
PFAS President of the Faculty of Architects and Surveyors
pfb prefabricate(d); preformed beam(s)
PFBMF Polaris Fleet Ballistic Missile Force
PFBrg pneumatic float bridge
pfc passed flying college; passed (with) flying colors; plaque-forming cell(s); privately financed consumption
Pfc Private first class
PFC Pusan Fisheries College
PFCCT Pennsylvania Federation of Community College Trustees
pfce performance
PFCS Primary Flight Control System
pfd personal flotation device (airplane seat cushion, lifebelt, lifejacket, floating pillow, etc.); preferred, present for duty; primary flash distillate
Pfd *Pfund* (German—pound)
PFDF Petroleum Fuel Development Facility
pf di progressive die
pfd s preferred spelling
PFEFES Pacific and Far East Federation of Engineering Societies
PFEL Pacific Far East Line
pff pie-fed farmer; plaque-forming factor
PFF Police Field Force
pffb pie-fed farm boy
PFFBI Pacific Fire Fighters Burn Institute (Sacramento)
PFFF Plutonium Fuel Fabrication Facility
pffg pie-fed farm girl
PFF Inc Police-FBI Fencing Incognito (Washington, DC traffickers in stolen goods)
pf fx profiling fixture
PFGM guided missile patrol es-

cort vessel (naval symbol)

PFGX Pacific Fruit Growers Express

pfi physical fitness index (PFI)

PFI Pacific Forest Industries; Pet Food Institute; Photo Finishing Institute; Picture and Frame Institute; Pie Filling Institute; Pipe Fibrication Institute; Police Foundation Institute

PFIAB President's Foreign Intelligence Advisory Board

PFJM *Policía Federal Judicial Mexicana* (Spanish—Mexican Federal Judicial Police)

pfk (PFK) phosphofructokinase

pfl pressed-for-life (dress materials)

PFL Pacific Freight Lines

PFLO Popular Front for the Liberation of Oman

PFLP Popular Front for the Liberation of Palestine

pfm power factor meter; pulse frequency modulation

PFMA Plumbing Fixture Manufacturers Association

pfn prefinish(ed)

PFNM Petrified Forest National Monument

PFNP Petrified Forest National Park

pfo patent foramen ovale

PFOBA Paso Fino Owners and Breeders Association

PFOC Prairie Fire Organizing Committee (communist)

PFP Progressive Federal Party (South African)

PFP *Progresief Federaal Partij* (Afrikaans—Progressive Federal Party)

pfr peak flow rate; peak flow reading; programmable film reader; prototype fast reactor (PFR)

PFRB Pacific Fire Rating Bureau

PFRS Programmed Film Reader System

PFRT Performance Flight-Rating Test; Preliminary Flight-Rating Test

pfs porous friction surface(d)

pfsa *pour faire ses adieux* (French—to say goodbye)

PFSO Postal Finance and Supply Office(r)

pfst pianofortist (pianist)

P-F Study Picture-Frustration Study (Rozensweig)

pft portable flame thrower

pft acct pianoforte accompaniment

PFTC Pestalozzi Froebel Teachers College

pfte pianoforte (piano)

pfu pock-forming units; preparation for use

P Fu Port Fuad

pfv physiological full value

pfv *pour faire visite* (French—to make a call)

PFV *Pestalozzi-Froebel Verband* (Pestalozzi-Froebel Association)

pfx prefix

PFX Pacific Fruit Express

pg page; paregoric; paris granite; pay group; paying guest; permanent grade; pistol grip; postgraduate; pregnant (pronounced *pee-gee*); program guidance; proving ground; public gaol; pure gin

pg (PG) parental guidance (recommended); prostaglandin

pg *pago* (Portuguese—paid)

p.g. *persona grata* (Latin—an acceptable person)

Pg Paraguay; Paraguayan

PG gunboat patrol vessel (naval symbol); Pan American-Grace Airways; Pennsylvania-German; Post Graduate; Proctor & Gamble; Provincial Government

P.G. Preacher General

P & G Proctor & Gamble

P of G Port of Galveston

PG *Prisonnier de Guerre* (French—prisoner of war)

P.G. *Pharmacopoeia Germanica* (Latin—German pharmacopoeia)

pga pressure garment assembly

pga (PGA) pteroylglutamic acid (folic acid)

PGA Pharmacy Guild of Australia; Professional Golfers Association

PG-AC Professional Group—Automatic Control

PGAH Pineapple Growers Association of Hawaii

p-gal(s) proof gallon(s)

PGA-NOC Permanent General Assembly—National Olympic Committees

PGB patrol gunboat (naval symbol)

pgbd pegboard(s)

PG-BTS Professional Group—Broadcast Transmission System

pgc per gyro compass

PGC Peoples Gas Company; Punxsutawney Groundhog Club

PGCE Post-Graduate Certificate of Education

PGCOA Pennsylvania Grade Crude Oil Association

PG-CS Professional Group-Communication System

PG-CT Professional Group—Circuit Theory

pgd paged; paradigm

PGD Past Grand Deacon

PGDF Pilot Guide Dog Foundation

pgdo *pagado* (Spanish—paid)

pge phenyl glycidyl ether

PGE Pacific Great Eastern (railroad); Portland Grain Exchange

PG-E Professional Group—Education

PG & E Pacific Gas and Electric

PG-EC Professional Group—Electronic Computers

PG-ED Professional Group—Electronic Devices

PG-EM Professional Group—Engineering Management

PGER Pacific Great Eastern Railway

pgh (PGH) pituitary growth hormone

PGH patrol gunboat—hydrofoil (naval); Philadelphia General Hospital; Philippine General Hospital

PG-HFE Professional Group—Human Factors in Electronics

PG-I Professional Group—Instrumentation

PG-IE Professional Group—Industrial Electronics

PGIM Professional Group on Instrumentation and Measurement (NBS)

Pgio *Poggio* (Italian—hill, hillock, hilltop)

P-girls pub girls (waitresses in British barrooms)

PGIS Project Grant Information System

PGIT Professional Group on Information Theory (IEEE)

PGJD Past Grand Junior Deacon

pgk phosphoglycerate kinase

pgl puppy beagle (pronounced *pee-gul*)

PGL Provincial Grand Lodge

P GL Port Glasgow

P Glg Port Glasgow

pglin page and line (flow chart)

pgm porous glass matrix (method of immobilizing nuclear waste); program

pgm (PGM) phosphoglucomutase

PGM motor gunboat (3-letter naval symbol); Past Grand

Master
PGMA Private Grocers' Merchandising Association
PGmc Proto-Germanic
PG-ME Professional Group—Medical Electronics
PG-MITT Professional Group—Microwave Theory and Technics
pgm's precision-guided munitions
pgn pigeon
pgn (PGN) proliferative glomerulonephritis
PGNP Pagsanjan Gorge National Park (Philippines)
PGNS Primary Guidance and Navigation System
pgo pyrolysis gas oil
PGOC Philadelphia Grand Opera Company
P of GP Pearl of Great Price
PGPR Provincial Guild of Printers' Readers
pgr population growth rate; psychogalvanic reaction; psychogalvanic response
pgr (PGR) precision graph record(er)
pg rating parental-guidance rating (of a motion picture or television program)
PGRO Pea Growing Research Association
pgrv (PGRV) precision-guided reentry vehicle
pgs predicted ground speed
pg's (PGs) prostaglandins
PGS Pennsylvania-German Society; Pidaung Game Sanctuary (Burma); Power Generation System; Primary Guidance System
PGSC Panel on Geological Site Criteria
PGSD Past Grand Senior Deacon
PGSW Past Grand Senior Warden
pgt per gross ton
PGT Pacific Gas Transmission (company); Program Global Table
PGTB General Pierre Gustave Toutant de Beauregard, CSA
Pgu Pagalu (formerly Annobon)
PGU Pontifical Gregorian University
pgut (PGUT) phosphogalactose uridyl transferase
PGWA Pottery and Glass Wholesalers' Association
ph page heading; pharmacopoeia; phase; phone; phosphor; phot; photon; physically

handicapped; power house; precipitation hardening; previous hardening
ph (PH) past history
p/h per hour
p & h postage and handling
pH hydrogen-ion concentration
Ph Pahari; phenyl
PH Pearl Harbor; Parachute Handler; Philharmonic Hall; Plane Handler; Power House; Public Health; Purple Heart (military decoration awarded Americans wounded in action)
P-H Prentice-Hall
pha (PHA) phytohemagglutinin
PHA Public Housing Administration
PHADS Phoenix Air Defense Sector
Phaedr Phaedrus (Roman fabulist-poet)
phag (Latin prefix—to eat)—phagocytes
phage(s) bacteriophage(s)
phal phalange; phalanx
Phantom F-4 fighter airplane
phar pharmacy
P Har Port Harcourt
Phar. B. Bachelor of Pharmacy
Phar. C Pharmaceutical Chemist
Phar. D. Doctor of Pharmacy
pharm pharmaceutical; pharmacist; pharmacology; pharmacopoeia(s), pharmacy
Phar. M. *Pharmaciae Magister* (Master of Pharmacy)
Pharmaceutical Pharmaceutical Press
pharmacol pharmacology
pharm chem pharmaceutical chemistry
Pharm.D. *Pharmaciae Doctor* (Latin—Doctor of Pharmacy)
PHAs Public Housing Agencies
'phasia aphasia
Ph.B. *Philosophiae Baccalaureus* (Latin—Bachelor of Philosophy)
Ph. B.J. Bachelor of Philosophy in Journalism
ph brz phosphor bronze
Ph. B. Sp. Bachelor of Philosophy in Speech
Ph. C. Pharmaceutical Chemist
PHC Patrick Henry College
PHCC Plumbing, Heating, Cooling Contracters
PHCIB Plumbing-Heating-Cooling Information Bureau
ph const phase constant
phd piled higher and deeper
Ph. D. *Philosophiae Doctor* (Latin—Doctor of Philosophy)

PHD Port Huron and Detroit (railroad)
P.H.D. Public Health Doctor
Ph. D. Ed. Doctor of Philosophy in Education
Phe Phoenix (constellation)
PHE phenylalanine (amino acid)
P.H.E. Public Health Engineer
PHEAA Pennsylvania Higher Education Assistance Agency
P-head pinhead (underground slang—small-minded person, user of amphetamine)
phency phencyclidine (angel dust)
pheno phenobarbital; (underground slang—user of phenobarbital)—hypnotic drug
pheno/d phenomenological death
phenolp phenolphthlein
phenom phenomena; phenomenal; phenomenon
Ph. G. Graduate in Pharmacy
Ph. G. Pharmacopoeia Germanica (Latin—German Pharmacopoeia)
PHG Postman Higher Grade
phgt package height
PHHS Patrick Henry High School
phi philosophy
Phi Philips
Ph I Pharmacopoeia Internationalis
phial, phiala (Latin bottle)
Phi Beta Kappa nonsecret collegiate society stressing academic achievement; oldest Greek-letter fraternity founded December 5, 1776 at College of William and Mary, Williamsburg, Virginia
PHIBLANT Amphibious Forces—Atlantic (USN)
PHIBPAC Amphibious Forces—Pacific (USN)
phil philosophy
phil (Latin suffix—having an affinity for)—neutrophiliac
Phil Philadelphia; Philadelphian; Philbert; Philharmonia; Philharmonic; Philip; Philippa; Philippine; Philippines; Phillip; Phillipa; The Epistle of Paul to the Philippians
Phil Philippians
Phila Philadelphia; Philadelphian
Philada Philadelphia (old-style abbrevation)
Philadelphia Lawyer Andrew Hamilton, Philadelphia attorney who in 1734 and 1735 successfully defended New York

printer Peter Zenger whose newspaper criticized British colonial policy in America; Zenger had been unsuccessful in even getting a New York lawyer to take his case; the term Philadelphia lawyer is used to describe an attorney who can and will defend a case others are afraid to touch

Philadelphia Painter Thomas Eakins

Phila Free Lib Philadelphia Free Library

philat philately

PHILDis Philadelphia Procurement District (US Army)

Philem The Epistle of Paul to Philemon

Philem Philemon

PHILEX Philadelphia Exchange

Phil Hung Philharmonica Hungarica

Philidor François Andre Danican

Philippine Day Philippine Independence Day (June 12)

Philippine Ports (large, medium, and small) on the island of Luzon: Aparri, Port Legazpi, Cavite, Manila, Poro; Masbate on Masbate Island; Tacloban on Leyte; Cebu on Cebu; Iloilo on Panay; Davao, Zamboanga, and Ozamiz on Mindanao; Isabela on Basilan; Jolo on Jolo

Philippines Republic of the Philippines (Filipinos converse in Pilipino—a Malay language based on Tagalog, English, and Spanish; many tropical crops support the economy along with rubber, timber, and valuable minerals; 7100 islands make up this scenic archipelago inhabited by friendly people) *Republika ñg Pilipinas* (Pilipino) or *República de Filipinas* (Spanish)

Philippine Sea between Philippine Islands and western Pacific islands (Iwo Jima, Guam, Carolines)

Philippines Principal Port Manila

Philipp Melanchthon Philipp Schwarzerd

Philips' Philips' Gloeilampenfabrieken (Dutch—Philips' Electric Lamp Factory)—fifth largest corporation worldwide

Philips Res Rept Philips Research Reports

PHILIRAN Phillips Petroleum Iran

Phil Is Philippine Islands

Philistine Temptress Dalila

Phillies Philadelphians

Phil Lip Philosophical Library

PHILLIPS Phillips Petroleum Company

Philly Philadelphia

Phil Mag Philosophical Magazine

philocrit philosopher critic; philosophical criticism

philol philology

Philomela Mercy Otis Warren whose writings under this pen name embraced drama, history, and political satire; she has been called the First Lady of the American Revolution

Phil Orch Philadelphia Orchestra

philos philosophy

Philos Philosophy

philos educ philosophy of education

Philos Lib Philosophical Library

Philos Mag Philosophical Magazine

Philosopher of the Absolute Georg Wilhelm Friedrich Hegel

Philosopher of China Confucius

Philosopher of Freedom John Locke

Philosopher Freethinker Elbert Hubbard

Philosopher Kung Kung Futzu (Confucius)

Philosopher of Loyola Marymount Ronda De Sola Chervin

Philosopher of Malmesbury Thomas Hobbes

Philosopher Physician Averroes

Philosopher of Sans Souci Voltaire's nickname for Frederick the Great

Philosopher of Sex Havelock Ellis

Philosopher of the Superman Friedrich Wilhelm Nietzsche

Philos Pub Philosophical Publishing Co

Philos Res Philosophical Research Society

Philos Trans R Soc London Philosophical Transactions of the Royal Society of London

PHILSA Philippine Standards Association

Phil Soc Philharmonic Society

PHILSOM Periodical Holdings in the Library of the School of Medicine

Phil Sp Philippine Spanish

PHILSUCOM Philippine Sugar Commission

PHILSUGIN Philippine Sugar Institute

Phil Trans Philosophical Transactions (Royal Society of London)

phiz physiognomy

Phiz Hablot K Browne—illustrator of the *Pickwick Papers* of Dickens—Boz

phk cells postmortem human kidney cells

Phl (Port of) Philadelphia

Ph. L. Licentiate in Philosphy

PHL Philadelphia, Pennsylvania (airport)

PHLAGS Philipps Petroleum Load-and-Go System

phlebo (Latin prefix—vein)—phlebitis

phl h phillips head

PHLS Public Health Laboratory Service

phm phase meter

phm (PHM) patrol hydrofoil missile

Ph. M. *Philosophiae Magister* (Latin—Master of Philosophy)

PHM patrol-combat missile (hydrofoil craft)

Phm. B. Bachelor of Pharmacy

PHMC Pennsylvania Historical and Museum Commission

Phm. G. Graduate in Pharmacy

PHMS Patrol Hydrofoil Missile Ship(s)

PHN Public Health Nurse; Public Health Nursing

PHO Public Hazards Office

phobe (Latin suffix—abnormal fear or dread)—felinophobic, hydrophobia

phocis photogrammetric circulatory surveys

phocl photo-initiated chemical laser

PhOD Philadelphia Ordnance Depot

Phoen Phoenix

Phoen Phoenicians

Phoenix Arizona's capital; included are Birnie, Canton, Enderbury, Gardner, Hull, McKean, Phoenix, and Sydney islands; Phoenix Islands in the equatorial mid-Pacific Ocean where they are claimed by the UK and the U.S.A.

PHOENIX Plasma Heating Obtained by Energetic Neutral Injection Experiment

Phoenix of Spain Lope de Vega

phofl photoflash
phon phonetics; phonology
phone telephone
phoneme smallest sound unit (linguistics)
phonet phonetic(s)
Phonet Phonetics
phono phonograph
phonorecord(s) phonograph record(s)
phonos phonoscopy (voice-print analysis and identification)
phonovision telephone television
Phons Alphonse
Phor Phoronida
phos phosphate; phosphorescent
phot. photograph; photographer; photographic; photography; photon; photostat; photostatic
phot photographie (French—photography)—plus all derivatives such as photocopie (photostat), photographe (photographer), photogravure, phototype, etc.
Phot Photographie (German—photography)—plus all derivatives
photac photographic typesetting and composing (AT & T)
photex photographic exercise
photint photographic intelligence
photo photograph; photographer; photography
photocomp photocomposed; photocomposition
photog photograph; photographer; photographic; photography
photogeog photogeography
photogeol photographic geology
Photographer-Editor Alfred Stieglitz
Photographer of the Himalayas Samuel Bourne (1834-1912)
Photographic Pioneer William Henry Fox Talbot
Photographic Purist Ansel Adams and Edward Weston vie for this enviable title sometimes used by others of their school
photograv photogravure
photog(s) photographer(s)
photom photometry
photo op photo opportunity (to take a picture of some outstanding event, person, or scene)
Photo Reportress Margaret Bourke-White
photosyn photosynthesis
phot r photographic reconnais-

sance
p'house steak porterhouse steak
php pounds per horsepower; propeller horsepower
ph&p peace, heath, and prosperity
PHP Psychologists Helping Psychologists (self-help group); Public Health Plan
phr phrase; pounds per hour; preheater
PHRA Poverty and Human Resources Abstracts
Phrasemaker of Versailles Woodrow Wilson—28th President of the United States
phraseo phraseogram; phraseograph; phraseological(ly); phraseologist; phraseology
phren phrenic; phrenology
PHRI Public Health Research Institute
Phronie Sophronia
ph & ru pubic hair and revealing underwear (formula for many pornographic films and photos)
Ph S Philosophical Society of England
PHS Pennsylvania Historical Society; Printing House Square; Prison Health Services; Pubic Hair Society; Public Health Service
PHSO Postal History Society of Ontario
phsp phase splitter
pht phototube; pitch, hit, and throw
Ph T putting husband through (college or university)
PHt Port Harcourt
PHT Passive Hemagglutination Test(ing)
PHTF Pearl Harbor Training Facility
PHTS Psychiatric Home Treatment Service
Phu Port Hueneme
P Hur Port Huron
phv phase velocity
phw pressurized heavy water
PHWA Protestant Health and Welfare Assembly
phwr (PHWR) pressurized heavy-water-moderated reactor
PHX Phoenix, Arizona (airport)
phy physical; physics
phyce photocopy-control electronics unit
phylo phylogeny
phys physic; physical; physician; physics
phy s physiological saline

Phys Chem Solids Physics and Chemistry of Solids
phys dis physical disability
phys ed physical education
Phys Ed Physical Education
physexam physical examination
Phys Fluids Physics of Fluids
PHYSH Physicians and Surgeons Hospital
physiat physiatric(s); physiatrical; physiatrist
Physician to the Body Politic Émile Zolá
Physician Extraordinary Sir William Osler
Physician's Physician Jacob Mendez Da Costa
physiog physiognomy
physiogr physiography
physiol physiology
Physiol Physiology
Phys Konden Mater Physik der Kondensierten Materie (German—Physics of Condensed Materials)
physl physiological
Phys Lett Physics Letters
phys med physical medicine
physocean physical oceanography
Phys Rev Physical Review
Phys Rev Lett Physical Review Letters
Phys S Physical Society
phys sci physical science; physical sciences
Phys Status Solidi Physica Status Solidi (Latin—Solid-State Physics)
Phys Teach Physics Teacher
phys ther physical therapy
Phys Today Physics Today
Phys Z Physikalische Zeitschrift (German—Physics Journal)
Phys Z Sowjetunion Physikalische Zeitschrift der Sowjetunion (German—Physics Journal of the Soviet Union)
phytopath phytopathologic(al)(ly); phytopathologist; phytopathology
pi personal income; photo interpreter; photo interpretation; pigeon trainer; pig iron; pilotless interceptor; pimp; point initiating; point insulating; point of interception; point interception; poison ivy; position indicating; position indicator; present illness; private investigator; production interval; programmed instruction; protamine insulin; protocol international (international protocol); public investigation

pi (PI) point of inversion

p & i principal and interest; protection and indemnity

pi Greek-letter symbol (π) indicating ratio of circumference of a circle to its diameter; the ratio itself; expressed as a number, *pi* is approximately 3.14159

Pi piaster

P_i inorganic orthophosphate

PI Packaging Institute; Paducah and Illinois (railroad); Party Islam; Pasteur Institute; Paul Isnard (Mana River settlement, French Guiana); Perlite Institute; Philippine Islands; physical instruction; Piedmont Airlines; Plastics Institute; Popcorn Institute; Pratt Institute; Productivity Index; Public Information

PI Printer's Ink

P-I Seattle Post-Intelligencer

P.I. Pharmacopoeia Internationalis

pia peripheral interface adaptor

pia (PIA) primary insurance amount

PIA Pakistan International Airlines; Plastics Institute of America; Printing Industries of America; Professional Insurance Agents

PIAA Pacific Index of Abbreviations and Acronyms (compiled by Arthur E E Ivory of Christchurch, New Zealand)

PIAI Printing Industry of America, Incorporated

PIANC Permanent International Association of Navigation Congresses

piang piangendo (Italian—mournful, plaintive)

pianiss pianissimo (Italian—very softly)

Pianist-Composer-Conductor-Singer Teresa Carreño

Pianist-Conductor Vladimir Ashkenazy; Ossip Gabrilowitsch; Daniel Barenboim; Rudolf Ganz; José Iturbi; Ethel Leginska

Pianist's Pianist Richard Buhlig

pianocorder piano recorder and reproduction system (installed in any piano)

PIARC Permanent International Association of Road Congresses

Piarco Port-of-Spain, Trinidad's airport

pias piaster

PIASA Polish Institute of Arts

and Sciences in America

piat projector infantry antitank (weapon)

PIAT Peabody Individual Achievement Test(ing)

pib power ionosphere beacon

PIB Petroleum Information Bureau; Polytechnic Institute of Brooklyn; Prices and Incomes Board

PIBA Primary Industry Bank of Australia

PIBAC Permanent International Bureau of Analytical Chemistry of Human and Animal Food

pibal pilot balloon

pic (French—peak); piccolo; picture; polymer-impregnated concrete; positive-impedance converter; production inventory control; pulse-indicating cartridge; pulse-induced collapse

pic (PIC) program-interrupt control(ler)

Pic Pictor (constellation)

PIC Physics International Company; Poison Information Center; Poison Information Center (Cleveland Academy of Medicine); Poisons Information Centre (Australia); Private Industry Council

PICA Palestine Israel Colonization Association; Police Insignia Collector's Association; Printing Industry Computer Associates; Printing Industry Craftsmen of Australia

picar picaresque

Picardie (French—Picardy)

PICC Peoples Insurance Company of China; Philippine International Convention Center

Piccy Piccadilly

PICGC Permanent International Committee on Genetic Congresses

PICIC Pakistan Industrial Credit and Investment Corporation

pick. part information correlation key

Pick Pickens Railroad

Pickle Works nickname of building occupied by Central Intelligence Agency in Langley, Virginia

Pickpocket Heroine Defoe's *Moll Flanders*

Pick's disease brain disorder characterized by loss of speech

PICL President's Intelligence

Checklist

PICM Permanent International Committee of Mothers

pico 10^{-12}

PICO Person In Column One (census-taker euphemism for head of household)

Pico Bolívar (Spanish—Bolivar's Peak)—Venezuela's highest mountain also called La Columna

PICOE Programmed Initiations, Commitments, Obligations, and Expenditures

PICOP Philippine Industries Corporation of the Philippines

pics pictures; publishers information cards

PICS Pacific Islands Central School; Personnel Information Communication System; Pharmaceutical Information Control System

pict pictorial; picture

Pictorial Satirist Supreme William Hogarth

Picture Island Enoshima, Yokahama

Picture-Postcard-Landscape Land Switzerland

Picture Province Canada's New Brunswick

Pictures Pictures at an Exhibition (Mussorgsky's piano suite frequently presented in the Ravel orchestration)

pid pelvic inflammatory disease; prolapsed intervertebral disk

p-i-d poverty-ignorance-disease syndrome of society

PID Police Intelligence Detail; Procurement Information Digest

pida payload installation and deployment aid

PIDA Pet Industry Distributors Association

PIDC Pakistan Industrial Development Corporation

PIDE Policia Internacional e de Defesa do Estado (Portuguese—International Police and Defense of the State)—security police

Pid Eng Pidgin English (hybrid dialect spoken throughout Far East)

pidp pilot information display panel

PIDS Parameter Inventory Display System

pie. pulmonary infiltration (with) eosinophilia

pie. (PIE) plug-in electronics

PIE Pacific Intercultural Exchange; Pacific Intermountain Express (fast freight); St. Petersburg, Florida (airport)

PIEA Petroleum Industry Electrical Association

PIEC Public Interest Economics Center

Piedmont Piedmont Plateau or Piedmont Triad (Greensboro, High Point, and Winston-Salem, North Carolina) or placename found in Alabama, California, South Carolina, or West Virginia

Piedmont Plateau Appalachian Mountain region extending from Alabama to New York, including Georgia, the Carolinas, Virginia, West Virginia, western Maryland, and Pennsylvania

Piedras Negras (Spanish— Black Rocks)—Mexican border town noted for its coal deposits but formerly called Ciudad Porfirio Díaz

Piemonte (Italian—Piedmont) —fertile plain in northern Italy

Pier Angeli Anna Maria Pierangeli

Piero della Francesca Piero di Benedetto de Franceschi

Pierre South Dakota's capital

Pierre Loti (pseudonym— Louis-Marie Julien Viaud)

Pierre Louÿs (pseudonym— Pierre Louis)

Pierre Nord André Léon Brouillard's pseudonym

Pierre-Paul Prud'hon Pierre Prudon

PIERS Port Import/Export Recording Service

Pietermaritzburg South African city also called Maritzburg

Pieter Timmerman (Dutch— Peter Carpenter)—pseudonym used by Peter the Great of Russia while working as a shipwright in Dutch shipyards

pif (PIF) prolactin inhibiting factor

PIF Paper Industry Federation; Pilot Information File

pig. pigment; pigmentation

PIG Pride, Integrity, Guts (acronym adopted by the Chicago police)

Pig Alley Place Pigalle

Pig Islander New Zealander (Australian slang)

pigmi positron-indicating general measuring instrument

pigmt pigment(ation)

PIGS Poles, Italians, Greeks, Slavs—(some of America's most talented minorities)

pig's ear (Cockney English— beer)

pigu pendulous integrating gyroscope unit

pik payment in kind

Pikovaya *Pikovaya dama* (Russian—La Pique Dame)— Tchaikovsky opera based on Puskhin's story about a compulsive gambler and sometimes sung in English under the title *Queen of Spades*

pil payment in lieu; percentage increase in loss

pil (PIL) procedure implementation language

pil. *pilula* (Latin—pill)

Pil Pitt interpretive language

PIL Pacific International Lines; Pest Infestation Laboratory

pilc paper-insulated lead covered

PILCOP Public Interest Law Center of Philadelphia

Pilipinas (Tagalog—Philippines)

pill the pill (birth-control pill)

Pillars of Hercules promontories flanking the Straits of Gibraltar—Abyla in Africa facing Gibraltar in Europe

pills. particulate instrumentation by laser light scattering

pilnav piloting navigation

PILO Public Information Liaison Officer

pilot. printing industry language for operations of typesetting

PILOT Piloted Low-speed Test

pilot-on-board flag signal flag consisting of a white and a red vertical band; letter H or Hotel in the international code

pilot-wanted flag yellow-and-blue vertically striped signal flag flown to indicate a pilot is wanted; letter G or Golf in the international code

pilp parametric integer linear program

pils pilsner

Pilsner Country Czechoslovakia

Pil Sta Pilot Station

pim penalties in minutes; pulse-interval modulation

PIM Pacific Islands Monthly

PIMA Paper Industry Management Association

PIMI Preinactivation Material Inspection

pimola pimento olive (pimento-stuffed olive)

pimpmobile pimp's automobile (often custom-made with bedroom facilities)

PIMPS Program for Interactive Multiple Process Simulation

pin. page and item number; piece identification number; plan identification number; position indicator

pin. (PIN) personal identification number (for computer protection)

pin. pinguis (Latin—fat, grease)

PIN Police Information Network

p/in.² parts per square inch

p/in.³ parts per cubic inch

PINA Pacific Islands News Association

PINAC Permanent International Association of Navigation Congresses

Pinafore HMS Pinafore or The Lass that Loved a Sailor (Gilbert and Sullivan's two-act operetta)

Pind Pindar

Pineapple Island Lanai, Hawaii

Pineapple Paradise Hawaiian Islands

pines. pineapples

Pines The Pines of Rome (Respighi's symphonic poem— Pini di Roma)

Pine Tree State Maine's official nickname

Piney Point Harry Lundeborg School of Seamanship at Piney Point, Maryland

Pink City of Rajputana Jaipur

Pinkiang Chinese name for Harbin, Manchuria

Pinky conductor violinist Pinchas Zukerman's nickname bestowed by affectionate musicians

pino positive input—negative output

pins person(s) in need of supervision

pins. person in need of supervision

PINS Padre Island National Seashore (Texas); Palletized Inertial Navigation System

Pinturicchio Barnardino Betti

PINWR Pungo National Wildlife Refuge (North Carolina)

pinx. *pinxit* (Latin—he painted it)

PINY Polytechnic Institute of New York

Pinyin (Chinese—phonetic sound)—official spelling system adopted in 1979 for words written in Roman letters as this better approximates their correct pronunciation; thus Peking becomes Beijing (pronounced *Bay Jing*), Canton becomes Guangshou, Hong Kong becomes Xianggang, China is Zhongguo

PINZ Plastics Institute of New Zealand

pio precision-interpret operation

PIO Public Information Office(r)

PIOA Pacific Index of Abbreviations and Acronyms in Common Use in the Pacific Basin Area (Whitcoulls Publishers, Christchurch, New Zealand)

PIOCS Physical Input-Output Control System

Piombo palette name of Sebastiano Luciani who signed his works Sebastiano del Piombo

pi-on pi-meson; pioneer

Pioneer deep-space probes designed for interplanetary investigation

Pioneer American Composer William Billings

Pioneer in American Science Benjamin Franklin

Pioneer of Antisepsis Ignaz Philipp Semmelweis

Pioneer Bacteriologist Louis Pasteur; Robert Koch

Pioneer of Child Psychoanalysis Dr Anna Freud

Pioneer Heart Surgeon Daniel Hale Williams

Pioneer Liturgical Dancer Carla De Sola, Ruth St Denis, and Ted Shawn may all claim the name

Pioneer of Oceanography Sir John Murray

Pioneers Pioneer Mountains of Idaho and Montana

Pioneer of Technological Change Eli Whitney

Pioneer of Two Worlds Thomas Paine

Pioneer of University Surgery William Halsted

Pioneer of Visceral Surgery Theodor Billroth

PIOSA Pan Indian Ocean Science Association

Piotr (Russian—Peter)—nickname for Petersburg or St Petersburg now Leningrad and formerly Petrograd—City of Peter

pip. peripheral interchange package; precise installation position; predicted intercept(ion) point; project initia-

tion period; proximal interphalangeal; public and institutional property

Pip. Philip

PiP Proceedings in Print

PIP Peripheral Interchange Program; Permatite Instant Plastic; Personal Identification Program; Personnel Identification Project; Product Improvement Plan; Product Improvement Program; Product Information Package; Psychotic Inpatient Profile

PIP Policia de Investigación del Peru (Spanish—Peruvian Investigation Police)

PIPA Pacific Industrial Property Association; Pacific Islands Producers Association

PIPEF Pacific Islands Polynesian Education Foundation

piper. pulsed intense plasma for exploratory research (PIPER)

Piper Laurie Rosetta Jacobs

pipe(s). pipe bomb(s)

pipi pipizintzintli

pipit. peripheral-interface and programme—interrupt translator

Pippa Philipa; Philippa

PIPR Polytechnic Institute of Puerto Rico

pips. pulsed integrating pendulums

piq property in question

PIQ Performance IQ

Pique Pique Dame (French—The Queen of Spades)—three-act opera by Tchaikovsky

Pir Piraeus

PIR Philippine Independence Ribbon; Phillip Island Reserve (Victoria, Australia); Preliminary Information Report

PIRA Paper Industries Research Association; Printing Industry Research Association

Piraeus English place-name equivalent of Piraievs the port of Athens

Piraievs (Modern Greek—Piraeus)

Pirandello Stefano Landi

Pirate City Tampa, Florida where the pirate chief Gasparilla once ruled

Pirate Coast Trucial Coast of Arabia including Abu Dhabi, Ajam, Dubai, Furairah, Ras el Khaimah, Sharjah, and Umm al Quwain comprising the United Arab Emirates where the British formerly imposed a perpetual truce controlling

maurauding pirates in this area

Pirate of the Gulf Jean Lafitte

Pirates Pirates of Penzance (two-act Gilbert and Sullivan operetta)

pirb position-indicating radio beacon

Pirenei (Italian—Pyrenees)

Pireneus (Portuguese—Pyrenees)

PIRF Petroleum Industry Research Foundation

PIRG Public Interest Research Group (Ralph Nader's)

PIRGs Public Interest Groups

pirid passive infrared intrusion detector

Pirineos (Spanish—Pyrenees)

PIRL PRISM Information Retrieval Language

pi rm pilot reamer

PIRS Personal Information Retrieval System; Poseidon Information Retrieval System

Pis Pisces

PIS Public Insurance Service

Pisanus Fraxi Herbert Spencer Ashbee

P Isb Port Isabel

PISC Philippine International Shipping Corporation; Phoenix International Science Center

PISCES Production Information Stocks and Cost Enquiry System

Pish Parish

pissoirs pissotières (French—public urinals for men only)—Paris used to have no less than 1300 of these dirty, grimy, smelly places scattered throughout the metropolis

pistaz piss-tinted topaz

pisw process-interrupt status word(ing)

pit. pitot static; progressive inspection tag

pit. (PIT) principal, interest, and taxes

Pit Pitanga; Pitcairn; Pitkin; Pitman; Piton; Pittsboro; Pittsburg; Pittsburgh; Pittsfield; Pittsford; Pittston; Pittsylvania

PIT Pasadena Institute of Technology; Petr Ilich Tchaikovsky; Pittsburgh, Pennsylvania (airport)

PITA Petroleum Industry Training Association; Provincial Intermediate Teachers Association (Canadian)

PITAC Pakistan Industrial Technical Assistance Center

PITAS Petroleum Industry Training Association—Scotland

PITB Pacific Inland Tariff Bureau; Pacific Island Teachers Board

PITC Pacific International Trust Company

pitchblende uraninite ore (chief source of radium and uranium)

Pitcher Plant Province Newfoundland

Pitch Lake Trinidad's asphalt lake

Pitch Lake Island Trinidad (whose Pitch Lake provides worldwide road—building asphalt)

PITDC Pacific Islands Tourism Development Council

Piter (Russian nickname for Petrograd or St Petersburg)

piti principal, interest, taxes, insurance

Pitigrilli Dino Segre

PITL Pacific Islands Transport Line

pit. log pitot-static log

PITO Portuguese Information and Tourist Office

Pitons Piton Mountains (St. Lucia)

pitr plasma iron turnover rate

pits. payload integration test set

PITS Pacific Islands Training School

PITT Polaris Integrated Test Team

Pitts Pittsburgh, Pennsylvania

pitu piping or tubing

PIU Public Inspection Unit (vice squad)

Pius XII Eugenio Pacelli

piv peak inverse voltage; post indicator valve

PIV Positive Infinity Variable

pivs particle-induced visual sensations

PIW *Petroleum Intelligence Weekly*

pix photographs; pictures

pixel picture element

pix/sec pictures per second

PIYA Pacific International Yachting Association

pizz. *pizzicato* (Italian—plucked)

Pizza (PIE) Pacific Intermountain Express (stock exchange nickname)

pj prune juice

PJ Police Judge; Presiding Judge; Probate Judge

P of J Port of Jacksonville

PJ *Police Judiciare* (French—criminal investigators, detective division)

PJA Pipe Jacking Association

P Jac Port Jackson

PJB Patrick J Buchanan

PJBD Permanent Joint Board on Defense (Canada-US)

PJC Paducah Junior College; Paris Junior College; Polydox Jewish Federation

pjex parachute jumping exercise

pjm postjunctional membrane

pj's physical jerks

Pjs Pasajes

pk pack; park(ing); peak; peck; psychokinesis

pK negative logarithm of the dissociation constant (symbol)

Pk Park; Peak; pink

Pk *Pauken* (German—kettledrums)

PK Principal Keeper; probability of kill (symbol)

PK *Panama Kanaal* (Dutch—Panama Canal); *Posta Kutusu* (Turkish—post office box)

P Ka Port Kembla

P-K antibodies Prausnitz-Küstner antibodies

pkb photoelectric keyboard

PKbanken *Post- och Kredithanken* (Swedish—Post and Credit Bank)

pkd packed (flow chart)

PKD Porkor Drilling Company (stock-exchange symbol)

pkdom pack(ed) for domestic use

pkg package; packing

Pkg Port Kelang (also written Port Klang and formerly Port Swettenham)

PKI *Partai Komunis Indonesia* (Communist Party of Indonesia)

Pkl Port Kelang (Port Klang formerly Port Swettenham)

PKL Possum Kingdom Lake

pkmr packmaster

PKN *Polski Kometet Normalizacyny* (Polish Standards Committee)

pknghse packinghouse

PKNP Pu Kradeung National Park (Thailand)

pkp pre-knock pulse

pKp purple K powder (purple potassium-bicarbonate powder)

PKP *Partido Komunista Pilipinas* (Pilipino—Communist Party of the Philippines)

pkr packer

PKR Parker Pen (stock exchange symbol)

Pk Rdg Park Ridge

P-K reaction Prausnitz-Küstner reaction

pks packs; pecks

PKS Photo-Kit System (criminal identification)

pksea pack(ed) for overseas use

PKSRP Possum Kingdom State Recreation Park (Texas)

pkt packet

PKTF Printing and Kindred Trades Federation (UK)

pkts packets

pku phenylketonuria

pkv killed poliomyelitis vaccine

Pkw *Personenkraftwagen* (German—automobile, passenger vehicle)

Pkwy Parkway

pky pecky

Pky Parkway (postal abbreviation)

pl parting line; party line; perception of light; phase line; pipeline; place; plastic; plate; plural

pl (PL) party line; product liability

p/l payload; pipeline; plain language

p & l profit and loss

pl. *plenarius* (Latin—complete, fully attended)

£L pound Lebanese

Pl Place

Pl *Place* (French—place, plaza); *plantage* (Dutch—plantation); *plass* (Scandinavian—place, plaza); *Platz* (German—place, plaza); *plaza* (Spanish—place, plaza); *plein* (Dutch—place, plaza); Titus Maccius Plautus (Roman writer of comedies)

PL perception of light (symbol); Place; Pluto (usually not abbreviated but sometimes as shown in honor of Percival Lowell); Point Loma; Poland (auto plaque); Port Line; Public Law; Public Library

P.L. Poet Laureate

PL *Partido Liberal* (Spanish—Liberal Party)

PL 1 Programming Language 1

PL/1 Programming Language/version 1

pla plasma resin activity; probation and rehabilitation of airmen

Pla Plaza; Pula (Pola)

Pla *Playa* (Spanish—beach, strand)

PLA Palestine Liberation Army; Pedestrian's League of America; People's Liberation Army

(Chinese communist); Philadelphia Library Association; Philatelic Literature Association; Port of London Authority; Port of Los Angeles; Private Libraries Association; Public Library Association; Pulverized Limestone Association

P of LA Port of Los Angeles

place. programming language for automatic checkout equipment

Place of Many Waters Walla Walla, Washington

Place Pig Place Pigalle in Paris

Place of Plenty Indian name for what is now Toronto, Ontario

Place of the Seven Wells Beersheba

Place of the Winds Sahara-sandswept Nouakchott in Mauritania on the coast of West Africa

PLADS Parachute Low-Altitude Delivery System

Plain Joe Canada's Prime Minister Joe Clark

Plains States Iowa, Kansas, Minnesota, Missouri, Nebraska, North Dakota, South Dakota

plam plastic laminate

plame (PLAME) propulsive lift aerodynamic maneuvering entry

plan. planet; planetarium

Plan *Planina* (Bulgarian or Serbo-Croatian—mountain, mountain range)

PLAN Paterson Looks Ahead Now; Program for Learning in Accordance with Needs

Plan A North Atlantic Treaty Reginal Planning Group

plane(s) airplane(s)

PLANES Programmed Language-based Enquiry System

Planet Space Sci *Planetary and Space Science*

planex planning exercise

Plank Island Aberdeen, Washington

Planner of the New York Public Library John Shaw Billings

PLANNET Planning Network

PLANS Programming Language for Allocation and Network Scheduling (NASA)

Plan Soc Planetary Society

Plantation State Rhode Island whose official title is the State of Rhode Island and Providence Plantations

plantflex plantar flexion

plantk *plantkunde* (Dutch—botany)

Plant Science Experimenter Luther Burbank

Plant Wizard Luther Burbank

PLAP Port of London Authority Police

PLARS Position-Locating-and-Reporting System

plas plaster

plasm (Greek—something formed or molded)—chromoplast, dermoplasty, plasma, plasmasol, protoplast

Plasma Phys *Plamsa Physics*

plaster of paris calcium sulfate $(CaSO_4)_2{\cdot}H_2O$

plastique (French—plastic)—plastic bomb(s)

plasty (Latin suffix—reconstruction of)—rhinoplasty

plat. plateau; platinum; platoon

Plateau Continent Africa

Plateglasses ultra-modern style in universities

Plate River Ports Buenos Aires, Argentina and Montevideo, Uruguay

platf platform

Platine States Argentina and Uruguay so named because they border on the La Plata River estuary

Plato (Greek—Broad-shouldered)—the famous philosopher's real name was Aristocles

PLATO Port Lincoln Advancement Trust Organization; Programmed Logic for Automatic Teaching Operations

Plato's School the Grove of Academe near Athens where it was later referred to by the Romans as the Academia

Plattensee (German—flat sea, level lake)—Hungary's Lake Balaton—largest lake in central Europe

platy *Platypoecilus* (genus of tropical fishes); platysma

platy (Latin prefix—flat or side)—platypus

Platy Platyhelminthes

Plaut Plautus

PLAV Polish Legion of American Veterans

plb plumber; plumbing; publisher's library binding(s); pull button

PLB Poor Law Board

plbd plugboard

plc power-line carrier; pre-launch computer

PLC Pacific Lighting Corporation; Point Loma College;

Probe Launch Complex; Products List Circular; Public Limited Company

P of L C Port of Lake Charles

P.L.C. *Poeta Laureatus Caesareus* (Latin—Imperial Poet Laureate)

PLCA Pipe Line Contractor's Association

plcs propellant-loading control system

plcu propellant-level control unit

plcy policy

pld payload

Pld Portland, Oregon

PLD Paul Lawrence Dunbar

PLDG Portuguese Language Development Group

PLDTC Philippine Long Distance Telephone Company

pldx polydox; polydoxy

ple preliminary logistics evaluation; primary loss expectancy; prudent limit of endurance; puerile light entertainment

P & LE Pittsburgh & Lake Erie (railroad)

plea. prototype language for economic analysis

PLEA Poverty Lawyers for Effective Advocacy

Pleasant former name of Nauru

Pleasure City of the South Seas Sydney, Australia

plebe plebeian

plebs plebeians

pled pleaded

plegia (Latin suffix—paralysis or stroke)—paraplegic

PLEI Public Law Education Institute

Plein-Air Painter Manet—advocate of painting in the open air instead of in the stinking studio

Pleis Pleistocene

Plejad Swedish class of fast patrol boats

plem pipeline end manifold

Plen Plenary; Plenipotentiary

plenipo plenipotentiary

Plenum Plenum Publishing Corp

pleon pleonastical(ly)

Plesman Curaçao's airport named for a Dutch aviation director

plex plant experiment(ation)

plf polyforming

PLF Pacific Legal Foundation

plff plaintiff

plftr please furnish transportation requests

plfur please furnish

plg piling
Plg Porto Alegre
PLG Poor Law Guardian
PLGC Pension Loan Guarantee Corporation
plgl plateglass
p-lgv psittacosis-lymphogranuloma venereum
plh (PLH) palaemontes-lightening hormone
PLHS Public Library of the High Seas (American Merchant Marine Library Association)
pli preload indicating
PLI Plant Location International
PLI Partido Liberal Independiente (Spanish—Independent Liberal Party); *Partito Liberale Italiano* (Italian Liberal Party); *Photo-Lab-Index*
p'lice police
PLIDCO Pipe Line Development Company
Plight of Pizarro Peruvian-attained dysentery named for the Spanish conqueror of Peru
Plim 1 Plimsoll line
P Lin Port Lincoln
Plin C Gaius Plinius Secundus major (Roman naturalist often referred to as Pliny the Elder)
Plin L Plinius Caecilius Secundus minor (Roman writer often referred to as Pliny the Younger)
Plioc Pliocene
plis propellant-level indicating system
plk plank
PLK Phi Lambda Kappa; Poincare-Lighthill-Kuo (mathematical method)
p lkr peacoat locker
PL/I Programming Language 1
PLL Prince Line Limited
PLLS Portable Landing Light System
pllt pallet
plltn pollution
plm pulse-length modulation
Plm Palembang
P-L-M Paris-Lyon-Méditerranée (famous French railway)
plmb plumber; plumbing
pl mo plastic mould
Plms Palms (postal abbreviation)
pln posterior lymph node
pl-n place-name
Pln Plain (postal abbreviation)
PLN (aviation flight) Plan
PLN Partido Liberación Na-

cional (Spanish—National Liberation Party); *Partido Liberal Nacionalista* (Spanish —National Liberal Party)
plng planning
PLNP Port Lincoln National Park (South Australia)
Plns Plains (postal abbreviation)
plo phase-locked oscillator
PLO Palestine Liberation Organization; Passenger Liaison Office(r); Peoples Liberation Organization; Plans Office(r); Presidential Libraries Office (Library of Congress)
PLO Pairti Lucht Oibre (Irish—Labour Party); *Polskie Linie Oceaniezne* (Polish Ocean Lines)
plom prescribed loan optimization model
Plosk Ploskogorye (Russian—plateau)
plot. plotting
Plough-Share City York, Pennsylvania
Plow City Moline, Illinois
plp plastic-lined pipe
plp (PLP) pyridoxal phosphate
PLP Parliamentary Labour Party; Partners for Liveable Places; Progressive Labor Party
pl & pd personal loss and personal damage
PLPG Publishers' Library Promotion Group
plpgrndg pulp grinding(s)
PLPP Pennsylvania League for Planned Parenthood
PLQ Public Library Quarterly
plr pillar; primary loss retention
Plr Pillar (postal abbreviation)
PLR Philippine Liberation Ribbon; Public Lending Right
P L & R Postal Laws & Regulations
PLR Partido Liberal Radical (Spanish—Radical Liberal Party)
PLRA Photo Litho Reproducers' Association
PLRS Position-Location Reporting System
plry poultry
pls plates; please
PLS Purnell Library Service
plsd promotion list service date
plsfc part load specific fuel consumption
Pl Sgt Platoon Sergeant
plshd polished
plshr polisher
PLSS Portable Life-Support

System
plstc plastic
plstr plasterer
plt personal leave time; pilot; primed lymphocyte typing; psittacosis-lymphogranuloma trachoma
pltc political
pltf plaintff
pltry poultry
PLTS Point Loma Test Site (Convair)
plu plural; plurality
P Lu Port Luis
PLU Patrice Lumumba University (Moscow)
Plucky Pierre Salinger
PLUG Public Law Utilities Group
Plum Sir Pelham Warner; Sir PG Wodehouse
plumb. plumber; plumbing
plumb. *plumbum* (Latin—lead)
Plumb-line Port to Panama Charleston, South Carolina (due north of the Panama Canal)
plumcot plum plus apricot (hybrd)
Plumed Knight Robert G Ingersoll's name for James G Blaine when nominating him for President
plumr plumber
PLUNA Primeras Líneas Uruguayas de Navegación Aérea (First Uruguayan Aerial Navigation Lines)
Plunket Plunket Society (Royal New Zealand Society for the Health of Women and Children)
pluperf pluperfect
Plus Brave des Braves (French —Bravest of the Brave)—Napoleon's nickname for Marshal Ney
Plus Ultra (Spanish—Better than Best; More Beyond)—official motto of Spain
plute(s) plutocrat(s)
pluto (PLUTO) pipeline under the ocean
Pluto (Latin—Hades or Pluton) —god of the dead and the underworld
Pluv Pluviôse (French—Rainy Month)—beginning January 20th—fifth month of the French Revolutionary Calendar
plx plexus; propellant-loading transfer
Ply Plymouth
PLYMCHAN Plymouth Subarea Channel (NATO)

Plymouth Rock landing place of the Pilgrims in 1620 on beach of what is now Plymouth, Massachusetts

plywd plywood

Plz Plaza

Plzn (Czechoslovakian—Pilsen)

pm post mortem; premium; premolar; presystolic murmur; preventive maintenance (PM); program manager; project manager; publicity man; pulse modulation; pumice

pm (PM) primary memory

p-m permanent magnet; phase modulation

p.m. *post meridiem* (Latin—after noon, night)

p/m pounds per minute

p&m probate and matrimonial

pm poids moléculaire (French—molecular weight)

Pm promethium

PM Past Master; Pattern Maker; Pay Master; Peabody Museum; Pére Marquette (railroad); Petróleos Mexicanos; Physical Medicine; Police Magistrate; Pontifex Maximum; Postmaster; Prime Minister; Provost Marshal (pronounced *provo marshal*); publicity man

P.M. *post meridiem* (Latin—after noon); Prime Minister

P/M Pacific Molasses; Physical Medicine

PM Pistol Makarov (Russian—Makarov pistol); *Policía Metropolitana* (Spanish—Metropolitan Police)

P.M. *Piae Memoriae* (Latin—of pious memory); *Pontifex Maximus* (Latin—Supreme Pope)

pma positive mental attitude

pma (PMA) paramethoxyamphetamine

PMA Pacific Maritime Association; Parts Manufacturing Associates; Peat Moss Association; Pencil Makers Association; Pharmaceutical Manufacturers Association; Philadelphia Museum of Art; Philippine Mahogany Association; Phonograph Manufacturers Association; Photo Marketing Association; Precision Measurements Association; Primary Mental Abilities (test); Production and Marketing Administration

PMA Programa Mundial de Alimentos (Spanish—World Food Program)

PMAC Provisional Military Administrative Council; Purchasing Management Association of Canada

PMAD Public Morals Administrative Division (New York City Police Department)

PMAE Peabody Museum of Archeology and Ethnology

PMAF Pharmaceutical Manufacturers' Association Foundation

PMAS Purdue Master Attitude Scales

PMATA Paint Manufacturers' and Allied Trades Association

pmb post-menopausal bleeding

PMB Potato Marketing Board

PMBC Pacific Motor Boat Club; Portland Motor Boat Club (Oregon)

pmbo participative management by objectives

pmbx private manual branch exchange

pmc precision mirror calorimeter; preventive maintenance contract(or)

PMC Pacific Medical Center; Pennsylvania Military Academy; Princeton Microfilm Corporation; Project Management Committee

pmd post-mortem dumps; projected map display

Pmd Portmadoc

PMD/BMI Project Management Division/Battelle Memorial Institute

PMDC Pakistan Minerals Development Corporation

PMDD Personnel Management Development Directorate

pmds projected map display set

PMDS Property Management and Disposal Service

pme performance-measuring equipment; planning, management, evaluation

P Me Portland, Maine

PMEA Powder Metallurgy Equipment Association

PMEL Pacific Marine Environmental Laboratory; Precision Measuring Equipment Laboratory

pmest personality, matter, energy, space, time (Raganathan's fundamental categories)

pmet painted metal

pmf probable maximum flood(ing); progressive massive fibrosis

PMF Presidential Medal of Freedom

PmG Paymaster General; Postmaster General

PMG Provost Marshal General

PMG Pall Mall Gazette

pmh past medical history; probable maximum hurricane

PMHP Primary Mental Health Project

pmi photographic micro-image; private mortgage insurance

PMI Palma de Mallorca, Balearic Islands, Spain (airport)

PMI Partai Muslimin Indonesia (Indonesian Muslim Party)

PMIA Presidential Management Improvement Award

PMIC President's Management Improvement Council

PMIG Political–Military Interdepartmental Group

PMIS Personnel Management Information System; Planning Management Information System; Product Management Information System

PMJC Pine Manor Junior College

pmk pitch mark; postmark(ed)

pml probable maximum loss

PML Pacific Micronesian Line; Pierpont Morgan Library

Pmla Parmelia

PMLA Publications of the Modern Language Association of America

PMLO Principal Military Landing Officer

pmm pulse mode multiplex

pmma (PMMA) polymethylmethacrylate

PMMI Packaging Machinery Manufacturing Institute

pmn polymorphonuclear neutrophil

PMNA Pacific Mountain Network Association; Parkers Marsh Natural Area (Virginia)

PMNH Peabody Museum of Natural History

pmnr periadenitis mucosa necrotica recurrens

pmo printed matter only

PMO Palomar Mountain Observatory; Polaris Material Office; Principal Medical Officer; Provost Marshal's Office

PM & OA Printers' Managers and Overseers Association

PMOLANT Polaris Material Office, Atlantic

PMOPAC Polaris Material Office, Pacific

P Mor Port Moresby

PMOSC Primary Military Occupational Code

pmp precious metal plating; previous menstrual period; probable maximum precipitation

PMP Preliminary Management Plan; Procurement Methods and Practices (manual)

pmr pressure-modulated radiometer

pm & r physical medicine and rehabilitation

Pmr Paymaster

PMR Pacific Missile Range

PMRAFNS Princess Mary's Royal Air Force Nursing Service

PMRL Pulp Manufacturer's Research League

PMRM Periodic Maintenance Requirements Manual

PMRS Physical Medicine and Rehabilitation Service

PMRY Presidio of Monterey

pms poor miserable soul; postmenopausal syndrome; pregnant mare's serum

pms (PMS) phenazine methosulphate; pollution-monitoring satellite; post-menstrual syndrome; pre-menstrual syndrome (*so when in doubt just spell it out*)

pm's push monies

p-m-s processors-memories-switches

PMS Pantone Matching System, Peabody Museum of Salem; Performance Management System; Planned Missile System; Preventive Maintenance System; Project Management System; Project Manager, Ships; Public Management System; Public Message Service

PMSA Pacific Merchant Shipping Association

pmsg pregnant mare's serum gonadotrophin

PMSP Plant Modelling System Program

pm specialists paramilitary specialists

PMSSMS Planned Maintenance System for Surface Missile Ships

PMST Professor of Military Science and Tactics

pmt payment; photomultiplier tubes; positive matte technique; premenstrual tension; programs, materials, techniques

PMT Perceptual Maze Test

PMTB Pacific Motor Tariff Bureau

PMTS Predetermined Motion

Time System

pmu performance monitor(ing) unit; physical mockup; productive man work unit

PMU Pattern Makers Union

PMUSAOAS Permanent Mission of the United States of America to the Organization of American States

PMVB Pocono Mountain Vacation Bureau

pmvi periodic motor vehicle inspection

pmvp *precio maximo de venta al publico* (Spanish—maximum price charged the public)

p mvr prime mover

pmv's parcel mail vans (British railways)

pmx private manual exchange (telephone)

pmyob please mind your own business

pn partition; part number; percussion note; percussive note; please note; position; promissory note; psychiatry-neurology; psychoneurotic

pn (PN) punch-on (computer character)

p-n positive-negative

p/n part number; promissory note

p & n psychiatry and neurology

Pn North Pole; North Celestial Pole; perigean range

PN Pacific Northern (airline); Pan-American World Airways (stock exchange symbol); part number; plasticity number; point of no return; Practical Nurse

P/N Part Number

P & N Piedmont and Northern (railroad)

PN *Partido Nacional* (Spanish —National Party); *Partido Nacionalista* (Spanish—Nationalist Party)

pna (PNA) pentosenucleic acid

Pna Panama

PNA Pacific Northern Airlines; Philippines News Agency; Project Network Analysis

PNAC President's National Advisory Committee

PNAI Provincial Newspapers Association of Ireland

pnavq positive-negative ambivalent quotient

PNB Philippine National Bank

PNB *Produto National Bruto* (Portuguese—Gross National Product)

PNBA Pacific Northwest Booksellers Association

PNBB *Parc National de la Boucle du Baoule* (French— Baoule River Bend National Park)—in the highlands of Mali

PNBC Pacific Northwest Bibliographic Center (American and Canadian libraries)

PNBP *Parc National de la Boucle de la Pendjari* (French— Pendjari River Bend National Park)—in northwestern Dahomey

pnbt paranitroblue tetrazoleum

pnc penicillin; premature nodal contraction

P 'n C Picnic 'n Chicken

PNC Prohibition National Committee

PNC *Parque Nacional Canaima* (Spanish—Canaima National Park)—encloses Venezuela's Angel Falls—world's tallest waterfall

PNCC President's National Crime Commission

pnch punch (flow chart)

Pncla Pensacola

pnd paroxysmal nocturnal dyspnoea; postnasal drip

Pnd Pandjang

pndb perceived noise decibels

pndg pending

P-N-D-L-R parking-neutral-driving-low-reverse (positions on automatic automotive transmission dial)

Pndo Pinedo

pne practical nurse's education

pne (PNE) peaceful nuclear explosion

PNe Pointe Noire

PNE Pacific National Exchange (Vancouver); Pacific National Exhibition (Vancouver)

PNEA *Parque Nacional El Avila* (Spanish—El Avila National Park)—between Caracas and the Caribbean where it encloses the Humboldt National Monument of Venezuela

P Ned *Pharmacopee Nederlandsche* (Dutch—Netherlands' Pharmacopeia)

PNERL Pacific Northwest Environmental Research Laboratory

Pnes Pines (postal abbreviation)

pneu pneumatic(s)

PNEU Parents' National Education Union

pneumato (Latin prefix—breathing)—pneumonia

pneumoccon pneumocconiosis (lung fibrosis due to dust-particle inhalation)

pneumog pneumograph; pneumographer; pneumographic(al)(ly); pneumography

pneumonoultra pneumonoultramicroscopicsilicovolcanoconiosis (miner's lung disease)

pnf proprioceptive neuromuscular facilitation

pnfd present not for duty

p.n.g. *persona non grata* (Latin —an unacceptable person)

Png Penang

PNG Papua New Guinea; Professional Numismatists Guild

PNG *Parque Nacional Guatopo* (Spanish—Guatopo National Park)—near Caracas, Venezuela

PNGL Papua New Guinea Line

pnh (PNH) paroxysmal nocturnal hemoglobinuria

PNH Phnom-Penh, Cambodia (airport)

PNHA Physicians National Housestaff Association

PNHP *Parque Nacional Henri Pittier* (Spanish—Henri Pittier National Park)—near Maracay, Venezuela

pni positive noninterfering (alarm); pulsed neutron interrogation

PNI Pharmaceutical News Index

PNI *Parque Nacional Iguazu* (Spanish—Iguazu National Park)—international park surrounding the Iguazu Falls shared by Argentina, Brazil, and Paraguay

P Nic Port Nicholson

PNITC Pacific Northwest International Trade Council

pnl panel

PNL Pacific Naval Laboratories; Pacific Northwest Laboratories; Philippine National Line

PNLA Pacific Northwest Library Association; Pacific Northwest Loggers Association

PNM Pinnacles National Monument (California)

pno piano

pno *pergamino* (Spanish—parchment)

P^{no} *Pantano* (Spanish—bog, marsh, morass, reservoir, swamp)

P 'n' O P and O (Peninsular and Occidental Steamship Company, Peninsular and Oriental Line)—P & O

PNO Port of New Orleans

PNO *Parque Nacional Ordesa* (Spanish—Ordesa National Park)—near Spain's French frontier

PNOC Philippine National Oil Company; Proposed Notice of Change

pnp positive negative positive

PNP Pediatric Nurse Practitioner; People's National Party; Platt National Park (Oklahoma)

pnpn positive-negative positive-negative

pnpr positive-negative pressure respiration

pnr point of no return; prior notice required

Pnr Pioneer

PNR Passenger Name Record (airlines); Philippine National Railways; Pittsburgh Naval Reactor; Pulletop Nature Reserve (New South Wales)

PNRP Philadelphia Pulmonary Neoplasm Research Project

pns parasympathetic nervous system; peripheral nervous system

PNS Pacific Navigation Systems; Pakistan Naval Ship; Philadelphia Naval Shipyard; Philippine News Service; Professor of Naval Science

PNSN *Parque Nacional Sierra Nevada* (Spanish—Sierra Nevada National Park)—encloses Venezuela's Mount Bolívar—highest peak in the republic

PNSTDC Pakistan National Scientific and Technical Documentation Center

PNSY Portsmouth Naval Shipyard

pnt paint(ed)

Pnt Pentagon

PNT *Parque Nacional Tijuca* (Portuguese—Tijuca National Park)—on the slopes of Mount Tijuca in the ring of mountains enclosing Rio de Janeiro, Brazil

Pnt Anx Pentagon Annex

PNTBT Partial Nuclear Test Ban Treaty

pntd painted

P^{nte} *Pointe* (French—point)

PNTO Principal Naval Transport Officer

pntr painter

PNU Pneumatic Scale Corporation (stock-exchange symbol)

pnutbutsan peanut-butter sandwich

p-nut butter peanut butter

pnutbutwich peanut-butter sandwich

p-nut(s) peanut(s)

PNVS Pilot's Night-Vision System

PNW Parc National du W (W-shaped national park on the borders of Dahomey, Niger, and Upper Volta)

PNWD/BMI Pacific Northwest Division/Battelle Memorial Institute

PNWL Pacific Northwest Laboratory (AEC)

PNWR Piedmont National Wildlife Refuge (Georgia); Presquile National Wildlife Refuge (Virginia); Pungo National Wildlife Refuge (North Carolina)

pnx pneumothorax

PNYA Port of New York Authority

PNYCTC Pennsylvania New York Central Transportation Company (merger of Pennsylvania and New York Central railroads)

Pnz Penzance

po piss off; poetry; polarity; power oscillator; power-operated; previous orders

po' poor

p-o postoperative

p/o part of

p & o paints and oil; pickled and oiled

p.o. *per os* (Latin—by mouth)

Po polonium; Portugal; Portuguese

P^o Pedro

PO Parole Officer; Passport Office; Patent Office; Personnel Office(r); Petty Officer; Philadelphia Orchestra; Police Officer; Port Office(r); Post Office; Probation Officer; Project Office; Province of Ontario; purchase order

P-O Pyrénées-Orientales

P/O Parole Officer; Pilot Officer; Probation Officer

P & O Peninsular & Occidental Steamship Company; Peninsular & Oriental Line

PO *Portland Oregonian*

PO 1/C Petty Office First Class

pO$_2$ oxygen pressure

PO-2 Soviet minesweeping launch; Soviet trainer aircraft nicknamed Mule by NATO

PO 2/C Petty Office Second Class

PO 3/C Petty Officer Third Class

poa primary optical area; primary optic atrophy

POA Police Officers Association; Portland Opera Association; Prison Officers Association

POAC Peace Officers Association of California

POADS Portland Air Defense Sector

POAG Peace Officers Association of Georgia

POAU Protestants and Other Americans United for Separation of Church and State

pob persons on board; pilot on board; point of beginning; prevention of blindness

PoB Port of Baltimore

POB post office box

Pobeda Pobeda Peak (highest mountain between China and the USSR in the Tien Shan range where it attains 24,406 feet)

po'-boy poor-boy (sandwich)

pobra pony + zebra (hybrid)

poc point of contact; privately owned conveyance

poc (POC) process operator console

POC Pittsburgh Opera Company; port of call; Prison Officer's Club; Public Oil Company

Pocahontas (Algonquin—Tomboy)—nickname of Matoka the daughter of Chief Powhatan; her married name was Rebecca Rolfe

Poca(loo) Pocatello, Idaho

po'ch porch

pocill. pocillum (Latin—small cup)

pock pocket

Pocket Bks Pocket Books

Pocket State Luxembourg (pocketed between Belgium, France, and Germany)

Poconos Pocono Mountains of eastern Pennsylvania

poc's ports of call

POCS Patent Office Classification System

pocul. poculum (Latin—cup)

pod. payable on (or upon) death; point-of-origin device; port of debarkation; port of departure; probability of detection

pod. (POD) process-oriented design

pod (Greek—foot)—anthropod, cephalopod, gastropod, podiatrist, podiatry, pseudopod

POD Port of Debarkation; Post Office Department; Profes-

sional and Organizational Development (higher education network)

POD *Pocket Oxford Dictionary*

PODAPS Portable Data Processing System

Pod D Doctor of Podiatry

podex photographic exercise

podia podiatrist(ic)(al)(ly); podiatry

poe (POE) polyoxyethylene

POE Pacific Orient Express; port of embarkation; port of entry

poe buoy plank-on-edge buoy

poecrit poetry critic(ism)

p o'ed put out

POED Post Office Engineering Department

poet. poetical(ly); poetry

Poet Poetry

Poet of Affection Marianne Moore

Poet of the American Revolution Philip Freneau

Poet of the Body—Poet of the Soul Walt Whitman's self-imposed nickname

Poet of Childhood Eugene Field

Poet of Democracy Walt Whitman

Poet of Despair James Thomson

Poetess of Passion Ella Wheeler Wilcox

Poet of the Excursion William Wordsworth

Poet of Friendship Robert Burns (*auld lang syne*)

Poet from Jersey William Carlos Williams of Rutherford, New Jersey

Poet of Imperialism Rudyard Kipling

Poet of Individuality Walt Whitman

Poet King Ossian of Ireland

Poet Laureate of England Sir John Betjeman

Poet Laureate of New England John Greenleaf Whittier

Poet Laureatess of Venezuela Irma De Sola Ricardo

Poet of Liberty Johann Christoph Friedrich von Schiller

Poet Naturalist Henry David Thoreau

Poet of Nature Jean Sibelius

Poet of the Piano Frédéric Chopin

Poet of Poets Shelley

POETS Phooey On Everything—Tomorrow's Saturday

Poet Sire of Italy Dante Alighieri

Poet of the Subconscious Gio-

vanni Pascoli

POEU Post Office Engineering Union

pof please omit flowers

pof (POF) pyruvate oxidation factor

POFI Pacific Oceanographic Fisheries Investigation

POG Pacific Oceanographic Group (British Columbia)

POGO Pennzoil Offshore Gas Operators; Polar Orbiting Geophysical Observatory

poh pull out of hole (oil well)

pOH alkalinity factor

Poh Pohang

Pohlsha (Russian—Poland)

POHMA Project for the Oral History of Music in America

poi poison; poisonous (on labels should be spelled out and symbolized with skull and crossbones)

POI Personal Orientation Inventory; Program of Instruction

Point The Point—West Point (U.S. Military Academy at West Point, New York)

Point Coma navalese for Point Loma

pois poison

Poison Ivy Upton Sinclair's nickname for publicist Ivy Lee

POIT Power-of-Influence Test

Poitiers formerly Poictiers

Pokanoket American Indian name for what was Mount Hope and is now Bristol, RI

Poke slang shortcut—Poughkeepsie

pol petroleum-oil-and-lubricants (POL); polar; polarize(d); police; political; politician; problem-oriented language

Pol Poland; Polish

Pol Polish (Slavic language spoken by some 35 million people in Poland and by many Poles who have emigrated to Australia, Canada, England, Latin America, the United States, and elsewhere); *Polonia* (Italian, Latin, Portuguese, Spanish—Poland)

POL Pacific Oceanography Laboratories; petroleum-oil-and-lubricants; Polish Ocean Lines

p-ola payola (remuneration for touting a so-called hit tune)—device of disreputable disc jockeys and record reviewers

Pola Appolina; Policarpa Sala-

barrieta
Pola (Italian—Pulj)—Yugoslav port
POLA Prostitutes of Los Angeles (protective association)
Pol Ad Political Adviser
polad(s) political adviser(a)
Poland Polish People's Republic (North-European Iron-Curtain country whose Poles are wedged between Germany and Russia; farming, manufacturing, and mining support the economy sustained by industrious and freedom-loving people) *Polska Rzeczpospolita Ludowa*
Pola Negri Appolina Chapulez
polang polarization angle
polar. polarity; polarization; polarize(d)
Polaris brightest star in the constellation of Ursa Minor; usually called the Pole Star or the Seaman's Star (Stella Maris) as within a degree or two it points to true north
Polaris-Poseidon Lockheed submarine-launched missiles
POLARS Pathology On-Line Logging and Reporting System
pol com political committee
Pol Com Police Commissioner (Interpol); Police Commissioner
polcrit political critic(ism)
poldamr petroleum, oil, and lubrication installations damage report
pol econ political economy
Polen (German—Poland)
Pole Star (*See* Polaris)
POLEX Polar Experiment (weather)
polf parents of large families
Pol Fed Police Federation (London)
POLFER Polizia Ferroviaria (Italian—Railroad Police)
Pol Found Police Foundation (Washington, D.C.)
poli politician
pol ind pollen index
polio poliomyelitis
POLIS Parliamentary On-Line Information System
poli sci political science
polish polish sausage (*kielbasa*)
Polish Tchaikovsky's Symphony No. 3 in D major
Polish City Hamtramck, Michigan
Polish First Poland's best-known classical composer—Frédéric Chopin

Polish Ports (large, medium, and small from east to west) Nowy Port, Stettin, Gdynia, Ustka, Swinoujscie
Polish Story Teller Isaac Bashevis Singer
Polish Town Panna Maria, Texas—settled in 1853 and America's oldest Polish settlement
polit political; politician; politics
Politburo Politicheskoe Byuro (Russian—Political Bureau of the Central Committee)
polka. petroleum, oil, and lubricants out-of-kilter algorithm
poll. pollution
POLLS Parliamentary On-Line Library Study
Polly Mary; Pauline; Pollyanna
Polo Capital of the South Aiken, South Carolina
Pologne (French—Poland)
Polonia (Italian, Latin, Portuguese, Spanish—Poland)
pol in the pen politician in the penitentiary
pols political prisoners; politicians
pol(s) political prisoner(s); political(s); politician(s); poll parrot(s)
POLs Problem-Oriented Languages (computer)
pol sci political science
Polska (Polish—Poland)
POLSTRADA Polizia Stradale (Italian—Highway Police)
polwar political warfare
poly polyethylene; polymer; polytechnic; polytechnical; polyvinyl
po'ly poorly
poly (Greek—many)—polydactyly, polygenic, polymer, polymorphism, polypeptide
Poly Polynesia; Polynesian; Polytechnic (institute or school)
Polyb Polybius
poly bot polyethylene bottle
polyg polygraph(er); polygraphic(al)(ly); polygraphy (lie detection)
Polygon of Drought northeast Brazil along the Rio San Francisco and east of a line between Bahía and Fortaleza
polymorph polymorphous
Polynesia (Greek—Many Islands)—occupying the South Pacific
Polynesian Kingdom Tonga (The Friendly Isles)
Polynesia's Sacred Isle Raiatea (in the South Pacific west of

Tahiti)
Polynésie française French Polynesia
poly sci political science
polysex polysexual(ity)
polytech polytechnic(al)
polywater polymerized water
pom pomeranian; pomological; pomology; pom-pom; preparation for overseas movement
pom (POM) polyoxymethylene
pom pomeridiano (Italian—afternoon, p.m.)
PoM Port of Miami
POM Port Moresby, New Guinea (airport)
pomcus (POMCUS) prepositioned materiel configured in unit sets
POME Prisoners of Mother England—Pommies; early convict immigrants (Australian slang)
POMFLANT Polaris Missile Facility, Atlantic
Pommerellen (German—Pomerelia)—former Baltic province of Prussia
Pommern (German—Pomerania)
pomol pomologic(al)(ly); pomologist(ic)(al)(ly); pomology
Pomorze (Polish—Pomerania)
POMPAC Polaris Missile Facility, Pacific
Pompey Cneius Pompeius; nickname of Portsmouth, England
pom-pom antiaircraft gun
POMR Problem-Oriented Medical Record
Pom(s) Prisoner(s) of Mother England [Australian nickname for person(s) newly arrived from Great Britain]
POMS Panel on Operational Meteorological Satellites
pomsee preparation, operation, maintenance, shipboard electronics equipment
POMSIP Post Office Management Service Improvement Program
pon pontoon
'pon upon
Pon Ponce
PON Program Opportunity Notice; Program Opportunity Notification
pona paraffin, olefin, napthene, aromatic (test for petroleum octane rating)
PonBrg pontoon bridge
pond. pondere (Latin—by weight)
Pondo Pondoland

p-on-n positive on negative
pons profile of nonverbal sensitivity (body language)
Pont Pontevedra
pont b pontoon bridge
Ponti Pontiac
Pontines Pontine Islands off Anzio, Italy or the Pontine Marshes of Italy
Pont. Max. Pontifex Maximus (Latin—Supreme Pontiff—the Pope
Pontus Euxeinos (Greek—Euxine Sea, Friendly Sea)—the Black Sea also called the Hospitable Sea
PONY Prostitutes of New York (protective association)
Pony Express Terminus Sacramento, California
Ponziane (Italian—Pontine Islands)—off Anzio
p & oo pianistic and orchestral orgasm (as in the finale of Rachmaninoff's Concerto No. 3 in D minor for piano and orchestra)
Poo Poole
POO Post Office Order
pood poodle dog; (Russian—36-lb. weight)
POOD Provisioning Order Obligation Document
poof. peripheral on-line-oriented function
Pool The Pool (the Thames just below London Bridge around Billingsgate Market)
poop. nincompoop
Poor Richard Richard Saunders (pseudonym used by Benjamin Franklin in writing *Poor Richard's Almanack*)
POOS Priority Order Output System
poosslq person of opposite sex sharing living quarters
POoW Petty Officer on Watch
pop carbonated beverage; poppet; popular; population
pop. carbonated beverage; perpendicular ocean platform (POP); persistent occipito-posterior; plasma osmotic pressure; plaster of paris; popliteal; poppet; popular; population
p-op post-operative
p-o-p plaster of paris; printing-out-paper
Pop Poppa
POP Palletizing Optimization Potential; Panoramic Office Planning; Portuguese Overseas Province (Macao, China); Post Office Plan(ning)
Popa Popayan, Colombia

POPA Property Owners Protection Association
pop. advertising point-of-purchase advertising
pop art popular art (advertising displays, comic strips, posters)
popb proposed operating plan and budget
Popcorn Capital of the World Shaller, Iowa
Pope of Geneva Calvin's nickname
Pope John XXIII Angelo Giuseppe Roncalli
Pope John Paul I Albino Luciani
Pope John Paul II Karol Wojtyla
Pope Paul VI Giovanni Battista Montini
Pope Pius XI Achille Ratti
Pope Pius XII Eugenio Pacelli
popex population explosion
popf prepared-on-premises flavor
popi post office position indicator (navigation system developed by British post office)
poplit popliteal
pop music popular music
Popo Popocatepetl
Popo Popocatepetl (Aztec—Smoking Mountain)
poppers one of amyl nitrate's nicknames (also called amys, pearls, or snappers)
pop psych popular psychiatry
popr pilot overhaul provisioning review
pops popular concerts; popular tunes
Pops Arthur Fiedler
POPS People Opposed to Pornography in Schools
Pop Sci Popular Science
POPSER Polaris Operational Performance Surveillance Engineering Report
poq periodic order quantity
POQ Public Opinion Quarterly
por porosity; porous; public opinion research
p-o-r pay-on-receipt; payable-on-receipt
Por Porifera; Portland
Por Porogi (Russian—rapids, waterfall)
POR Policy, Organisation, and Rules (of the Girl Guides and Scouts)
PORA Police Officers Research Association
PORAC Peace Officers Research Association of California

porc porcelain
PORC Peralta Oaks Research Center
Porcupines Porcupine Islands east of Bar Harbor, Maine
'pore Singapore
Pori Finnish name for what the Swedes call Björneborg; Polaris operational readiness instrumentation
PORIS Post Office Radio Interference Station
Pork Dump nickname of Clinton Prison near Utica, New York
Porkopolis Cincinnati, Ohio
Pork Packer Philip D Armour
porksan pork sandwich
porkwich pork sandwich
porm plus or minus
porn pornographic; pornography (*see* porno)
Porn Capital of America San Francisco
pornette(s) pornographic cassette(s)
pornfilm pornographic motion-picture film
porno pornofilm; pornographer; pornographic; pornographically; pornographic bookshop; pornography (defined by Irvin S Cobb as when the depth of the dirt exceeds the width of the wit)
pornobio pornographic biography
pornofilm pornographic motion picture
pornos pornographic books, moving pictures, photographs, recordings, etc.
pornovel pornography + novel (usually what it sounds like—a poor novel)
pornovelist pornographic novelist
porn pub(s) pornographic publication(s); pornographic publisher(s)
Porn Squad Pornographic (Publication) Squad
porny pornographic
pornzines pornographic magazines
porp(s) porpoise(s)
PORS Post Office Research Station
port. portable; portrait; portraiture
port. (PORT) photo-optical recorder tracker
Port Portland; Portugal; Portuguese
Port Portuguese (language spoken by more than 120 million

people including those in Portugal and its many former overseas possessions such as Brazil where many new words and slang terms have been created to suit local needs)

Port Ade Port Adelaide, South Australia

Portage La Prairie Girls Correctional Centre for Women at Portage La Prairie, Manitoba

Port Alb Port Alberni on Vancouver Island, British Columbia

portalet portable toilet

Port Alex Port Alexander, Alaska

Portañol Portuguese-Spanish

Port Ant Port Antonio, Jamaica

Port Art Port Arthur (may be in Manchuria, Ontario, Tasmania, or Texas but seafarers will nickname it Port Art)

portashed portable shed(ding)

Port Chi Port Chicago; Portuguese China (Macao)

Port Dal Port Dalhousie, Ontario

Portela de Sacavem Lisbon, Portugal's airport

porteños (Spanish—port people) —in Argentina means the people of Buenos Aires and in Chile those of Valparaiso

Porter of Heaven Janus the Two-Faced (so named because the door he guards, like all doors, faces two ways)

Port Everglades Fort Lauderdale, Florida's port

Portia pen name of Abigail Smith Adams—wife of President John Adams and America's First Suffragist

Port Ind Portuguese India

Port Jack Port Jackson (seaport of Sydney, New South Wales, Australia)

Port Jeff Long Island, New York; Port Jefferson

Port Kelang formerly Port Swettenham and also called Port Klang

Port Klang formerly Port Swettenham, Malaya

Port Liz Port Elizabeth, New Jersey; Port Elizabeth, South Africa

Port Lyautey former name of Kenitra, Morocco

Port Nick Port Nicholson (Wellington, New Zealand's harbor)

Porto (French, German, Italian, Portuguese, Spanish—Oporto,

Portugal, seaport)

Porto di Lido (Italian—Port of the Lido)—the port of Venice

Portogallo (Italian—Portugal)

Port o' Missing Men San Francisco

Porto Rico original name of Puerto Rico

Port Phil Port Phillip, Melbourne, Victoria, Australia

Port of the Pilgrims Provincetown, Massachusetts

Portrait Painter of Presidents Gilbert Stuart

Port Rich Port Richmond, Staten Island, New York

Port Royal Street Kingston, Jamaica's traditional habitat of whores

Port Said English place-name equivalent of Bur Said

port side *lefthand* side of an airplane, ship, or other craft when looking forward, symbolized by a fixed *red* light— on the *lefthand* wingtip of an airplane or set against a red background on the *lefthand* side of a ship's bridge or pilothouse

portsides portsiders (left-handed persons)

Portsmouth U.S. Naval Disciplinary Command at Portsmouth, New Hampshire—the U.S. Naval Prison

Ports of Philadelphia (northeast to southwest) Trenton, Camden, Gloucester City, Philadelphia, Chester, Marcus Hook, Wilmington

Port of St John of Acre Akko

Port Sud Port Sudan (Sudanese harbor on the Red Sea)

Port Swett Port Swettenham, Malaysia

Port Talb Port Talbot, Wales

Port Tew Port Tewfik (Egypt's Port Taufiq at the southern end of the Suez Canal)

Port Tim Portuguese Timor

port(ug) (Dano-Norwegian—Portuguese)

Portugal Republic of Portugal (Iberian country once ruling a vast colonial empire; Portuguese speak Portuguese and sustain their economy by farming, fishing, manufacturing, and mining, remaining colonies include the Azores, Madeiras, and Macao near Hong Kong) *República Portuguesa*

Portugal's Principal Port Lisboa (Lisbon)

Portugal Day Independence Day (December 1)

Portuguese America Brazil— formerly Portugal's largest possession

Portuguese China Macao (near Hong Kong)

Portuguese East Africa Mozambique—formerly a colony of Portugal

Portuguese Guinea former name of Guinea Bissau on Africa's west coast

Portuguese India former name of the territories of Damão, Diu, Goa, Panjim, etc.

Portuguese Mars Affonso d'Alboquerque also called Affonso o Grande (Alphonse the Great)—Portuguese empire builder and viceroy of Portuguese India

Portuguese Overseas Province Macao's official name

Portuguese Paradise Sintra near Lisbon

Portuguese Ports (large, medium, and small from north to south) Viana do Castelo, Porto de Leixoes, Porto (Oporto), Lisboa (Lisbon), Setubal, (*in the Azores*—Horta *and* Ponta Delgada), Funchal (Madeira)

Portuguese Republic República Portuguesa

Portuguese-Spanish Century the 16th century—the 1500s

Portuguese-speaking Places Angola, Azores Islands, Brazil, Cape Verde Islands, Guinea-Bissa, Macao, Madeira Islands, Mozambique, Portugal, São Tomé and Principe Islands, plus a few other former Portuguese port possessions in India and Indonesia such as Goa and Timor, respectively

Portuguese Timor former Portuguese outpost of empire on Timor Island in Indonesia

Portuguese West Africa Angola, Portuguese Guinea, St Thomas and Prince islands came under this collective title during colonial era

Port Veneris place-name nickname for Port Vendre on the Franco-Spanish frontier

Port Wash Port Washington, Long Island, New York

Port Wel Port Weller, Ontario

Port Wine Port Oporto, Portugal

pos point of sale; position; positive; product of sums

PoS Point of Sale; Point of Ser-

vice; Port of Spain
POs Police Officers; Postal Orders
POS Patent Office Society; Port-of-Spain, Trinidad (airport); Primary Operating System; Problem-Oriented System
posa payment outstanding suspense accounts
POSB Post Office Savings Bank
POSC Problem-Oriented System of Charting
POSD Post Office Savings Department
posdcorb planning - organization - staffing - directing - coordinating - reporting - budgeting (mnemonic device for remembering the functions of management)
posdsplt positive displacement
Poseidon (Greek—Neptune)—god of the sea
Posen (German—Poznan)
posh permuted on subject headings; port side out, starboard side home (British slang)
poslstor positive resistor
posit position; positron
positron positive electron
posm patient-operated selected mechanisms
posn position
Posnania (Latin—Posen)
POSNY People of the State of New York
pos pron possessive pronoun
poss possession; possessive
P o S S Point-of-Sale System
POSS Passive Optical Satellite Surveillance (System)
P-O-S S Point-of-Sale System; Point-of-Service System
posslq person of the opposite sex (in) same living quarters
posslq's persons of the opposite sex sharing living quarters
'possum(s) opossum(s)
post. postage; postal; posterior; post mortem
post (Latin prefix—after or behind)—postwar
POST Frederick Post Drafting Equipment; Peace Officers Standards and Training; Police Officer Student Training; Processes of Science Test
Postage-Stamp Principalities Andorra, Liechtenstein, Luxembourg, and Monaco are so named by most philatelists although Luxembourg is a grand duchy and is not ruled by a prince
post-Aug post-Augustan

post aur. *post aurem* (Latin—behind the ear)
post. d posterior diameter
poster. posterior
pos terminal point-of-sale terminal
postgangl postganglionic
Postgrad Med Inst Postgraduate Medical Institute
postgrad(s) postgraduate(s)
posth posthumous
postl postlude
post-mort post mortem (autopsy)
post-op post-operative
post part. *post partum* (Latin—afterbirth)
post-sync post-synchronization of a sound track made after a motion-picture film has been shot
POSWG Poseidon Software Working Group
pot. point of tangency; portable outdoor toilet; potash; potassa (potassium hydroxide); potassium; potential; potentiometer; (slang— marijuana)
pot. potaguaya (Mexican Indian—marijuana); *potio* (Latin—dose, draft, potion)
Potain's disease pleural and pulmonary edema
'potamus(es) hippopotamus(es)
potash potassium carbonate (K_2CO_3)
potash alum potassium aluminum sulfate
Potash City Saskatoon, Saskatchewan
potass potassium
POTASWG Poseidon Test Analysis Software Working Group
potats potatoes
POTC PERT *(q.v.)* Orientation and Training Program
P o TD Port of The Dalles
Potentate of the Pit Lucifer
Potl NATO name for a Soviet class of submarine chasers
POTIB Poseidon Technical Information Bulletin
Potomac Washington, DC is on the banks of this river rising in West Virginia and flowing into Chesapeake Bay between Maryland and Virginia
Potomac River City Washington, DC
potosslq persons of the opposite sex sharing living quarters (*sometimes appears as* posslq)
potr *potrero* (Spanish—cattle ranch, pasture)
potrero (Spanish—pasture)

pots. potentiometers
Pot Smuggler's Paradise beach-cluttered and inlet-indented Florida whose waterways provide the best background for smuggling
pott pottery
Potteries The Potteries (Stoke-on-Trent)
Pott's disease vertebral inflammation
PotUS Lyndon Johnson's acronym meaning President of the United States
POTUS President of the United States (address name used by Churchill when communicating with Roosevelt, later used by President Johnson—PotUS)
pot w potable water
pou (current slanguage abbreviation—piss on you)
poul poultry
POUM *Partido Obrero de Unificación Marxista* (Spanish—Workers Party of Marxist Unification)
POUNC Post Office Users' National Council
POUR President's Organization for Unemployment Relief
pov privately owned vehicle
Pov *Poluostrov* (Russian—peninsula)
POV Pend Oreille Valley (railroad)
pov's privately owned vehicles
pow power; prisoner of war (POW)
P o W Prince of Wales; Prisoner(s) of Watergate
POW Country Potash, Oil, and Wheat Country around Saskatoon, Saskatchewan
powd powder; powdered; powered
Powder Keg of Europe the Balkans
power. programmed operational warshot evaluation and review
POWER Professionals Organized for Women's Equal Rights
pows (POWS) prisoners of war
POWS Pyrotechnic Outside Warning System
poy pre-oriented yarn
Poz Poznan
pozn *poznamka* (Czech-footnote)
Pozsany (Hungarian—Pressburg)—called Bratislava by the Slovakians
Pozzi Venice's prison

pp baby-talk abbreviation for urinate(d); pages; painful pissing (following catheterization or a prostate operation); panel point; parcel post; part paid; partial pay; partially paid; passive participle; past participle; pellagra preventive (factor); perceptual performance; permanent party; petticoat peeping; physical profile; physical properties; pickpocket; postage paid; postpaid; present position; pressure-proof; private property; privately printed; professional paper; purchased part(s); push-pull; urination; urine

p-p peak-to-peak; pee-pee (urine); push-pull; pussy-power (excercise of feminine wiles)

p/p peepee (urinate, urine)

p&p payments and progress

p-to-p peak-to-peak; point-to-point

pp *pianissimo* (Italian—very softly)

p.p. *piena pelle* (Italian—full leather); *post partum* (Latin—afterbirth)

Pp. *Papa* (Latin—father or Pope)

PP Pacific Petroleum; Parcel Post; Parish Priest; Past President; Power Plant; Proletarian Party (Communist)

P-P pellagra-preventive factor

PP *Patres* (Latin—Fathers); *Polizei Pistole* (German—police pistol)

P.P. *Pater Patriae* (Latin—Father of his Country)

PP¹ inorganic pyrophosphate

ppa palpitation, percussion, auscultation; photo-peak analysis

ppa (PPA) phenylpropanolamine

pp & a palpitation, percussion, and auscultation

p. pa. *per procura* (Latin—by proxy)

p.p.a. *phiala prius agitate* (Latin—bottle having first been shaken)—shake well before using

PPA Pakistan Press Association; Paper Pail Association; Paper Plate Association; Parcel Post Association; People for Prison Alternatives; Periodical Publishers Association; Popcorn Processors Association; Poultry Publishers Association; President's Professional Association; Produce Packaging Association; Professional Photographers of America; Proletarian Party of America; Public Personnel Association; Purple Plum Association

PPAB Program and Policy Advisory Board (UN)

PPAC Pesticide Policy Advisory Board (EPA)

PPATRA Printing, Packaging, and Allied Trades Research Association (also appears as PATRA)

ppb parts per billion

ppb (PPB) polybrominated biphenyl (cattle poison)

pp&b paper, printing, and binding; planning, programming, and budgeting

Ppb *Pappband* (German—boards, hard cover)

PPBAS Planning-Programming-Budgeting-Accounting System

PPBC Portland Problem Behavior Checklist

PPBES Planning-Programming-Budgeting-Evaluation System

PPBMIS Planning, Programming, and Budgeting Management Information System

PPBS Planning-Programming-Budgeting System

ppc picture postcard; plain-paper copier; progressive patient care

p p c *pour prendre congé* (French—to take leave)

PPC Penang Port Commission(er)(s); Pet Population Control; Policy Planning Council (U.S. Department of State); Positive Peer Culture; Purchase Price Control

ppca plasma prothrombin conversion accelerator

PPCAA Parole and Probation Compact Administrators Association

PPCD Plant Pest Control Division

ppcf plasma prothrombin conversion factor

PPCLI Princess Patricia's Canadian Light Infantry

PPCS Personnel Protection and Communication Services (British anti-terrorist organization); Primary Producers' Cooperative Society

ppd prepaid; purified protein derivative (tuberculin)

PPD Petroleum Production Division; Portland Public Docks; Propulsion and Power Division

PPD *Partido Popular Democrático* (Spanish—Popular Democratic Party)

PPDA Produce Packaging Development Association

PPDC Polymer Products Development Center

ppdi pilot's projected-display indicator

ppdo per person, double occupancy

p p_{do} *próximo pasado* (Spanish—last month)

PPDP Preprogram Definition Phase

PPDS Publishers' Parcels Delivery Service

PPDSE Plate Printers, Die Stampers, and Engravers (union)

ppe philosophy, politics, and economics

PP & E Program Planning and Evaluation

PPES Pilot Performance Evaluation System

ppf personal property floater (policy)

PPF Plumbers and Pipefitters (union)

PPFA Planned Parenthood Federation of America

p-p factor pellagra-preventive factor

ppg planning and programming guidance

PPG Pago Pago, Samoan Islands (airport); Pittsburgh Plate Glass

ppga post-pill galactorrhea-amenorrhea

PPGA Pennsylvania Personnel and Guidance Association

pph post-partum hemorrhage; pounds per hour; pulses per hour

P Php Port Phillip

pphpm parts per hundred parts of mix; pints per hundred parts of mix

pphr parts per hundred parts of rubber

ppi pages per inch; parcel post insured; plan position indicator; policy proof of interest

PPI Plastic Pipe Institute; Producer Price Index; Project Public Information; Protective Packaging Inc; Pulp and Paper International

PPIC Plumbing and Piping Industry Council

ppif photo-processing interpretation facility

p-pille *praeventivpille* (Dano-Norwegian—preventive pill)—contraceptive

pp/in. pages per inch

P Ping Pulau Pinang (Malay—Penang Ferry)

PPIQ Personality and Personal Illness Questionnaire(s)—of psychological import

pPk purplish pink

ppl pipeline

PPL Philadelphia Public Library; Phoenix Public Library; Pittsburgh Public Library; Police Protective League; Portland Public Library; Private Pilot's License; Providence Public Library; Provisioning Parts List

PP&L Pennsylvania Power and Light (company)

P-plane pilotless airplane (explosive carrying and reaction propelled)

PPLC Patients Protection Law Commission

pple past participle

pplo pleuropneumonia-like organism(s)

ppm parts per million; pounds per minute; pulse position modulation

PPM *Partido Proletario de México* (Spanish—Proletarian Party of Mexico)—Chinese-trained guerrilla terrorists active in Mexico and from California to Texas in the Chicano community; *Persutuan Perpustakaan Malaysia* (Malay—Library Association of the Federation of Malaya)

PPMS Plastic Pipe manufacturers' Society

ppn proportion(al)

PPNA Pupil-Perceived-Needs Assessment

PPNP Point Pelee National Park (Ontario)

PPNW Physicians for the Prevention of Nuclear War

ppo polyphenylene oxide; prior permission only

p-p-ola political plugola (media plugging or touting of a candidate or an ideological issue)—propaganda device in disrepute

ppom particulate polycyclic organic matter

ppo's (PPOs) preferred provider organizations

ppp petty political pismire

p & pp pull and push plate

ppp *piu pianissimo* (Italian—very very softly)

PPP Peoples Party of Pakistan; Peoples Progressive Party (Guyana); Petroleum Production Pioneers; Pickford Projective Pictures; Population Policy Panel (Hugh Moore Fund)

ppq (PPQ) polyphenylquinoxaline

ppr present particple; prior permission required

PPr Port Pirie

PPR Permanent Pay Record; Permanent Personal Registration; Procurement Problem Report

PPRA Past President of the Royal Academy

pprbd paperboard

PPRICA Pulp and Paper Research Institute of Canada

pps pictures per second; pounds per second; pulses per second

pp's payless paydays

PPS Pacific Passenger Services; Paper Publications Society; Pennsylvania Prison Society; Petroleum Press Service; Program Policy Staff (UN)

PPS *Partido Popular Salvadoreño* (Spanish—Salvadoran Popular Party)—of El Salvador, Central America; *Partido Popular Socialista* (Spanish—Popular Socialist Party); *Persatuan Perpustakaan Singapura* (Malay—Library Association of Singapore)

P.P.S. *post postscriptum* (Latin—additional postscript)

PPSA Pan-Pacific Surgical Association

PPSAWA Pan Pacific and Southeast Asia Women's Association

PPSB Periodical Publishers' service Bureau

PPSEAWA Pan-Pacific and South-East Asia Women's Association

ppsn present position

ppso per person, single occupancy

PP Society (*see* PPTPP)

ppt precipitate

PPT Papeete, Society Islands (airport); Pre-Production Test(ing)

pptd precipitated

pptn precipitation

PPTPP Promulgators of Public Toilets in Public Parks (also known as the PP Society)

ppty property

ppu platform position unit

PPU Peace Pledge Union

P & PU Peoria and Pekin Union (railroad)

ppv people-powered vehicle(s)

PPVT Peabody Picture Vocabulary Test

PPWC Pines to Palms Wildlife Committee; Pulp, Paper, and Woodcutters of Canada

PPWP Planned Parenthood-World Population

pq peculiar; permeability quotient; personality quotient (PQ); previous question; punishment quarters

p-q phenol-hydroquinone (photographic developer)

p & q peace and quiet (solitary confinement)

PQ personality quotient; Province of Quebec; South Pacific Airlines of New Zealand (2-letter code)

PQ *Parti Quebecois* (French—Québec Party)

pqa procurement quality assurance

PQAP Procurement Quality Assurance Program

PQC Production Quality Control

PQD Plant Quarantine Division

PQD *Partido Quisqueyano Demócrata* (Spanish—Democratic Quisqueyan Party)—Dominican Republic's people called Quisqueyanos

pqe post-qualification education

pqi professional qualification index

PQIH Plant Quarantine Inspection House

PQLI Physical Quality of Life Index

PQR Personnel Qualification Roster

pqrs productivity increases, quality control, robotization, and savings (Japanese formula for economic success)

PQS Percentage Quota System; Personnel Qualification Standard(s)

pr pair; payroll; percentile rank; peripheral resistance; public relations

pr (PR) proctosigmoidoscopy

p/r per rectum

p & r parallax and refraction

pr protestants (Dutch—Protestants)

p.r. *per rectum* (Latin—by the rectum); *punctum remotum* (Latin—remote point)—far point of vision

pR purplish red

Pr Panama-red marijuana; Parana; Prairie (postal abbreviation); prandtl number; praseodymium; presbyopia; Press; Prince; propyl

Pr Praca (Portuguese—plaza, square); *Presbyter* (Latin—elder or priest)

PR Parachute Rigger; Park Ranger; Performance Rating; Performance Report; Photoreconnaissance; Pinar del Rio; Plant Report; Problem Report; Progress Report; Public Relations; Puerto Rican(s); Puerto Rico; river gunboat (2-letter naval symbol)

P-R Pennsylvania-Reading (Seashore Lines)

P/R payroll

PR Partido Republicano (Spanish—Republican Party); *Partisan Review*; *Peking Review*; *Polish Register* (of shipping); *Polskie Radio* (Polish Radio); *Puerto Rico* (Porto Rico)

P.R. (Latin—Populus Romanus)—Roman people

pra payroll audit(or); plasma renin activity; probation and rehabilitation of airmen; progressive retinal atrophy

pra (PRA) print alphanumerically

Pra Pará (British maritime abbreviation)

Pra Prachtausgabe (German—de luxe edition)

PRA Pay Readjustment Act; Personnel Research Activity; Popular Rotocraft Association; Postal Reorganization Act; Psoriasis Research Association; Psychological Research Association; Public Roads Administration; Puerto Rico Association

P.R.A. President of the Royal Academy

prac practice; practitioner

pracl page-replacement algorithm and control logic

pract practical; practice; practitioner

Practical Political Philosopher Niccolò Machiavelli

Praeger Frederick A. Praeger

praen praenomen

prag pragmatic; pragmatism

Prag (German—Prague)

Praga (Italian, Latin, Portuguese, Russian, Spanish—Praha)—Prague

pragma processing routines aided by graphics for manipulation of arrays

Pragmatist Philosopher William James

Prague English place-name equivalent of Praha the capital of Czechoslovakia

Prague Mozart's Symphony No. 38 in D major he named for Bohemia's capital containing his favorite audiences

Praha (Czechoslovakian—Prague)

PRAI Pre-Reading Assessment Inventory

PRAICO Puerto Rican American Insurance Company

Prair Prairial (French—Meadowy Month)—beginning May 20th—ninth month of the French Revolutionary Calendar

Prairie Canada Alberta, Saskatchewan, and Manitoba

Prairie City Bloomington, Illinois

Prairie Provinces Alberta, Manitoba, Saskatchewan

Prairies great plains between Appalachian and Rocky mountains of North America

Prairie State official nickname of Illinois

Prairie States North and South Dakota, Nebraska, Kansas, Minnesota, Iowa, and Illinois

prais passive-ranging interferometer sensor

pral principal (Spanish—principal)

pram perambulator

pram. productivity, reliability, availability, and maintainability

Pram Poseidon random-access memory

Pr of An Principality of Ansbach

prand. prandium (Latin—dinner)

PRANG Puerto Rico Air National Guard

PRAT Prattsburgh (railroad)

p. rat. aet. pro ratione aetatis (Latin—in proportion to age)

Prater Vienna's amusement park dominated by its giant ferris wheel; Vienna's park along the Danube

PRATRA Philippines Relief and Trade Rebilitation Administration

Pravda (Russian—truth)—seven-days-a-week newspaper published in Moscow by the Central Committee of the Communist Party of the Soviet Union

PRAY Paul Revere Associated Yeoman

Prayer-shawl Flag Israeli banner derived from talith or prayer shawl with horizontal blue stripes enclosing Shield or Star of David

prb principal borehole

PRB People's Republic of Benin; Personnel Review Board; Population Reference Bureau; Pre-Raphaelite Brotherhood

prc packed red cells; procedure

prc (PRC) polysulphide rubber compound

PRC Pain Rehabilitation Center; Palestine Red Crescent (supporting Arab terrorists while claiming to be the equivalent of the Red Cross); Pension Research Council; People's Republic of China (Red China); Picatinny Research Center (Picatinny Arsenal); Planning Research Corporation; Postal Rate Commission; Public Relations Club

P.R.C. Post Roman Conditam (Latin—after the founding of Rome)—753 Before the Christian Era

PRCA Professional Rodeo Cowboys Association; Puerto Rico Communications Authority

PRCB Program Requirement Control Board (NASA)

Pr Ch Parish Church

prchst parachutist

prcht parachute

PRCP President of the Royal College of Physicians

prcs process; processing

PRCS President of the Royal College of Surgeons

prcst precast

prcu power regulation and control unit

prd partial reaction of degeneration; pro-rata distribution

prd (PRD) printer dump(ing)

PRD Pesticides Regulation Division (USDA); Planned Residential Development; Program Requirement Document

PRD Partido Revolucionario Dominicano (Spanish—Dominican Revolutionary Party)

PRDA Program Research and Development Announcement

PRDC Personnel Research and Development Center (USN); Power Reactor Development Corporation

PRDL Personnel Research and Development Laboratory

(USN)

PRDS Processed Radar Display System

prdx paradox (best known, perhaps, is the equine paradox stating there are more horse's asses than there are horses; the murine paradox is the explanation as to why mice have such small balls and the answer is that so few of them know how to dance)

pre prefix (computer character); progressive resistance exercise

pre (Latin prefix—before)—prenatal, presuppose

Preacher of the Despairing Girolamo Savonarola

Preah Reach Ana Chak Kampuchea Cambodia

prealateen program for children below teen age who are affected by an alcoholic family (*see* alateen)

preamp(s) preamplifier(s)

preb prebend

PREBS Pennsylvania Real Estate Brokers and Salesmen's (licensing examinations)

prec precedence; preceding; precision

Prec Precentor

Precious Province Kucichow

precip precipitate; precipitation

PRECIS Preserved Context Index System

precomdet pre-commissioning detail

Precursor of Dutch Painting Lucas van Leyden

Precursor of Expressionism Edvard Munch

Precursor of Japanese Art Kose no Kanaoka

Precursor of the Mexican Revolution Ricardo Flores Magon

Precursor of Pharmacology Paracelsus

Precursor of Pictorial Realism Mathias Grünewald (Mathis der Mahler)

Precursor of Sociology Charles de Secondat Baron de la Brède et de Montesquieu

Precursor of Spanish-American Emancipation Francisco Miranda

Precursor of Surrealism Hieronymus Bosch (Hieronymus van Aken)

Precursor of Venezuela Francisco de Miranda

pred predicate; prednisolone

PREDA Puerto Rico Economic Development Administration

pre-design preliminary design

predic predicate; predicative; prediction

pre-em preeminence; preeminent; preempt; preemptible; preemption; preemptive; preemptor; preemptory

preemies premature babies

preemy premature baby

pref preface; prefatory; prefecture; preference; prefix

Pref Prefect

prefab prefabricated

Pref-Ap Prefect-Apostolic

prefaz *prefazione* (Italian—foreword)

prefd preferred

preframo prepare fleet rehabilitation and modernization overhaul (USN)

preg pregnancy; pregnant

pregang preganglionic

prehis prehistoric

Preiser's disease porosity of the wristbone

prej prejudice

prel prelude

prelim preliminary

prelim diag preliminary diagnosis

prelims preliminaries; preliminary pages (frontmatter)

prem premature; premium

pre-med premedical

premie premature baby

Premier Deng Deng Xiaoping (Teng Hsiao-ping written in the new and official Pinyen phonetic spelling adopted by the People's Republic of China January 1, 1979)

Premier Passenger Port of Great Britain Southampton

Premier Primitive Henri Rousseau

premics premature babies

Prensa *La Prensa* (Buenos Aires' Press)

'prentice apprentice

Prenzl Bg Prenzlauer Berg

pr enzyme prosthetic-group removing enzyme

pre-op preoperation; preoperational

prep preparation; preparatory; prepare; preposition

PREP Personal Radio-Equipped Police; Predischarge Education(al) Program; Preparation Rehabilitation Education Program; Pupil Record of Educational Progress

prepd prepared

prep'ed prepared

prepn preparation

prepr *prepracovane* (Czech—rewritten)

pre-pub pre-publication

Pre-Raphaelite Founders Holman Hunt, Sir John Everett Millias, Daniel Gabriel Rossetti

pres present

Pres President

PRES Puerto Rico Employment Service

presby presbyopia; presbyopic

Presby Presbyterian

Presbyterian Jerusalem Edinburgh

presc prescription

Presc Prescott

Presd_{te} *Presidente* (Spanish—President)

preserv preservation

Presidents' conference conference of presidents of major Jewish organizations (in America)

President ships American President Line vessels named after such statesmen as *President Lincoln, President Roosevelt, President Taft*

presilection presidential election

press. pressure

PRESS Pacific Range Electromagnetic Signature Studies

Pressburg (German—Bratislava)—Danubian city of Slovakia called Pozsony by the neighboring Hungarians

Presse *Die Presse* (Neue Freie Presse)—Vienna's Press

presstitute poison-pen prostitute of the press (columnist skilled in writing personally or politically defamatory articles)

prestmo. *prestissimo* (Italian—very quickly)

PRESTO Program Reporting and Evaluation System for Total Operations

Preston K Swinehart (nickname—movie actor Alan Dinehart in villain roles)

presv preservation; preserve

pret preterit

Pret Pretoria

Pretender Charles Stuart

pre-Teut pre-Teutonic

PRETTYBLUEBATCH Philadelphia Regular Exchange Tea Total Young Belles Lettres Universal Experimental Bibliographical Association To Civilize Humanity (initialism contrived by Edgar Allan Poe to satirize all such pseudo-intellectual devices)—appears in his essay on *How to Write a Blackwood Article*

pretz pretzel
Pretzel City nickname shared by Lancaster and Reading, Pennsylvania
Preussen (German—Prussia)
prev previous
prevan precompiler for vector analysis
preven preventive
prevoc prevocational
prex(y) president (usually college or university)
prez president
prf proof; pulse recurrence frequency; pulse repetition frequency
prf (PRF) priority-reserved flight (air cargo); prolactin-releasing factor
prf. praefatio (Latin—introduction, preface)
PRF Personality Research Form; Petroleum Research Fund; Plywood Research Foundation; Porpoise Rescue Foundation; Public Relations Foundation; Puerto Rican Forum
PRF Publications Reference File (GPO)
prfe polar-reflection faraday effect
prfg proofing
prfnl professional
prfr proofreader
PRFT Portable Rod-and-Frame Test
PRG Prague, Czechoslovakia (airport); Provisional Revolutionary Government (of South Vietnam)
PRHS Port Richmond High School
pri photographic reconnaissance and interpretation; primary; primer; primitive; priority; priority repair induction; private; pulse recurrence interval
PRI Paleontological Research Institute; Plastics and Rubber Institute
PRI Partido Revolucionario Institucional (Spanish—Institutional Revolutionary Party); *Partito Repubblicano Italiano* (Italian Republican Party)
PRIA Proceedings of the Royal Irish Academy
Pribilovs Pribilov Islands in the Bering Sea off Alaska
Price Stern Price, Stern, Sloan
P Rich Port Richmond
PRIDCO Puerto Rico Industrial Development Company
PRIDE Parents Resource Institute for Drug Education; Personal Responsibility in Defect Elimination; Professional Recruiting (with) Integrity, Determination, and Enthusiasm; Protection of Reefs and Islands from Degradation and Exploitation
Pride of the Yankees Lou Gehrig
Priest of Nature Sir Isaac Newton
Prieta Agua Prieta (Spanish—Dark Water)—Mexican border town across the fence from Douglas, Arizona
prim. primary
prim (Latin prefix—first)—primitive, primordial
Primate of Italy the Pope
prime. precision recovery including maneuvering entry
PRIME Philadelphia Regional Introduction for Minorities to Engineering; Program Independence, Modularity, Economy; Program Research in Integrated Multi-ethnic Education; Programmed Instruction for Management Education
Prime Meridian Place Greenwich, England
Prime Minister Deng Deng Xiaoping (Teng Hsiao-ping written in the new and official Pinyen phonetic spelling adopted by the People's Republic of China January 1, 1979)
Prime Minister of Hell Satan
Prime Minister Lee Prime Minister Lee Yuan Yew of Singapore
Prime Minister of Mirth Peter Sellers
Prime Minister of the Underworld Frank Costello
PRIMES Pennsylvania Retrieval of Information in Mathematics Education System; Productivity Integrated Measurement System (USA)
primo primero or *supremo* (French, Italian, Portuguese, or Spanish—first, first place, top quality, supreme)
prin principal
Prin Principal; Principality
PRINAIR Puerto Rico International Airlines
Prince Prince Igor (Borodin's opera known to Russians as *Knyaz Igor*)
PRINCE Parts, Reliability, and Information Center (NASA)
Prince of American Letters Washington Irving
Prince of the Apostles the Pope, according to the Roman Catholics
Prince of Artists Albrecht Dürer
Prince of Comic Opera Daniel François Esprit Auber
Prince Consort Albert of Saxe-Coburg Gotha (Queen Victoria's husband)
Prince of Cranks Ignatius Donnelly
Prince of Darkness Satan
Prince of Destruction Tamerlane (Timur the Lame)
Prince of Gossips Samuel Pepys
Prince of Humbugs P(hineas) T(aylor) Barnum
Prince of Humorists Mark Twain (Samuel Langhorne Clemens)
Prince of Israel Michael
Prince of Journalists Horace Greeley
Prince of Losers Dr Frederick A Cook who claimed he reached the North Pole nearly a year before Commander Robert E Peary, who was credited with the discovery by his supporters who discredited Cook despite support he got from Amundsen and other Arctic experts and explorers
Princely Province Prince Edward Island
Prince of the Meistersingers Hans Sachs of Nuremberg also known as the Cobbler Poet
Prince of Men Robert Louis Stevenson's nickname for Henry James
Prince of Music Palestrina
Prince of Orange William I of the Netherlands and his male successors—the Princes of Orange
Prince of Orators Demosthenes
Prince of the Oyster Pirates Jack London
Prince of Painters Raphael
Prince of Philosophers Plato
Prince of Physicians Avicenna (Abu ibn Sina)
Prince of the Pianoforte Louis Moreau Gottschalk
Prince of Pistoleers James Butler (Wild Bill) Hickok
Prince of Poets Alexander Pushkin, according to Russian literary critics; Edmund Spenser
Prince of Prose Writers John Bunyan
Prince of Scoffers Voltaire

Prince of Showmen PT Barnum
Prince Siddhartha Gautama Buddha
Prince of Skeptics Voltaire
Prince of Spanish Poetry Garcilaso de la Vega
Princess of Fruits (Linnaeus' sobriquet for the pineapple)
Prince of Story Tellers Giovanni Boccaccio
Prince of Trees (Linnaeus' nickname for the palm)
Prince of Violin Virtuosos Itzhak Perlman
Prince of Wales Island Penang's previous name
Principality of the Grimaldi Monaco
Principal Port of the United Kingdom Liverpool
Principaute de Monaco (French —Principality of Monaco)— half-square-mile Mediterranean country famous for the Monte Carlo gambling casino; inhabited by Monacans— Monaguese
Principe de la Paz (Spanish— Prince of the Peace)—Manuel Godoy y Alvarez de Faria
prin pts principal parts
print. printed; printing
print. (PRINT) preedited interpreter (computer language)
Printer's Symphony nickname of Mendelssohn's Symphony No. 2 in B-flat major also known as the Hymn of Praise (*Lobgesang*) celebrating the 400th anniversary of the invention of printing
Printmaker to the Mexican People José Guadalupe Posada
Printmakers to the American People (Nathaniel) Currier & (James Merritt) Ives—America's most famous lithographers
PRINUL Puerto Rico International Undersea Laboratory
PRINZ Public Relations Institute of New Zealand
prio priority
PRIO Peace Research Institute, Oslo (Norway)
prions proteinaceous infectious particles (believed by some to cause Alzheimer's disease)
prior. priority
prir parts reliability improvement route; parts reliability improvement routing
PRI & RB Puerto Rico Inspection and Rating Bureau
pris prison(er)

Prisca Priscilla
prise program for integrated shipboard electronics
PRISE Pennsylvania's Regional Instruction System for Education (intercollegiate network)
pris g prisonnier de guerre (French—prisoner of war)
prism. prismatic
PRISM Personnel Record Information System; Program Reliability Information System for Management
Prison at the Bottom of the World Ushuaia, Argentina on Beagle Channel close to Cape Horn in southernmost South America
Prison at the Top of the World Solovetski Island isolators in the White Sea and east of Kem in the Soviet Union
Prisoner of Chillon François de Bonnivard
Prison of Gold The Louvre
Prison of Nations Austro Hungarian Empire
Pris(sy) Priscilla
pritac primary tactical radio circuit
Pritch Pritchard
prithee I pray thee
priv privacy; private; privateer(ing); privation; privative; privet, privilege(d); privily; privy
Privatdozent (German) university professor not belonging to a professorial staff
priv pr privately printed
priv pub privately published
PRJC Puerto Rico Junior College
pr kassa per kassa (Norwegian for cash)
prl periodical; pick-resistant lock
Pr of L Prince of Liechtenstein; Principality of Liechtenstein
PRL Personnel Research Laboratory; Polska Rzeczpospolita Ludowa (Polish Republic); Precision Reduction Laboratory; Project Records List
Prl Cmm Parole Commission
prld pick-resistant locking device
prm parameter; portable radiation monitor; prime
Prm Promenade
PRMA Puerto Rican Maritime Authority
p-r man public-relations man
prmld premolded
prm's presidential review memorandums

prn print numerically
p.r.n. pro re nata (Latin—as needed, for an emergency)
PRNC Potomac River Naval Command
PRNL Pictured Rocks National Lakeshore (Michigan)
PRNS Point Reyes National Seashore
prntr printer
PRNWR Parker River National Wildlife Refuge (Massachusetts)
pro procedure; proceed; procure; procurement; profession; professional; professionally; prophylactic
pro (PRO) print octal; proline (amino acid)
pro (Latin prefix—before or in favor of)—prosection, protribal
Pro Provost
PRO Personnel Relations Officer(r); Plant Representative's Office; Public Record Office; Public Relations Office(r)
PROA Public Record Office Archives
pro-am professional-amateur
prob probability; probable; probably; problem; problematic
Prob Probate
probcost probabilistic budgeting and costing; probable cost
PROBES Processes and Resources of the Bering Sea Shelf
Prob Off Probation Officer
proc procedure; proceeding(s); procure; procurement
proc (Latin profin anus) proctologist
Proc Procedure; Proceedings, Proctor
Proc Cambridge Philos Soc Proceedings of the Cambridge Philosophical Society
Procd procedure
pro-celeb professional celebrity
Proc-Gam Proctor-Gamble
Proc IEEE Proceedings of the IEEE
Proc IRE Proceedings of the IRE
proclib procedure library
Proc Nat Acad Sci U.S.A. Proceedings of the National Academy of Sciences of the United States of America
proco programmed combustion (auto engine)
Procoll Proletarian Collective of Soviet Musicians
procomm program communica-

tion

Procop Procopius

Proc Phys Soc, London Proceedings of the Physical Society, London

procrast(s) procrastinator(s)

Proc Roy Soc Proceedings of the Royal Society

Proc R Soc London Proceedings of the Royal Society of London

procsim processor simulation language

procstep procedure step

procto proctocolitis; proctocolonoscopy; proctologist; proctology; proctosigmoidoscopy; proctosigmoidectomy; proctoplegia

PROCTOR Priority Routine, Computer Transfers, and Register Operations

prod product; production

prodac programmed digital automatic control

PRODAC Production Advisers Consortium

PRODFINA Protection et Defense de la Nature (French—Protection and Defence of Nature)

Prodigy of Learning Dr Samuel Hahnemann

Prod(s) Irish-Catholic English—Protestant—[*see* Pap(s)]

prof profession; professional; professor

prof (PROF) pupil registering and operational filling

Prof Professor

PROF Peace Research Organization Fund

profac propulsive fluid accumulator

Prof D Profesor Don (Spanish—Sir Professor)

Prof Dⁿᵃ Profesora Doña (Spanish—Madam Professor)

Prof Eng Professional Engineer

Professor Bruno Pantoffel Jorge Mester

Professor of Earthquakes Sir William Hamilton

Professor Julius Caesar Hannibal (pseudonym—WH Levinson)

Professor Seagull Joe Gould

Proff Professori (Italian—Professors)

Profintern Red international of Trade Unions

profit. program for financed insurance technic; programmed reviewing, ordering, and forecasting

Profit Center of the Southwest

Phoenix, Arizona

Prof Lib Pr Professional Library Press

profs professionals; professors

prog progenitor; progeny; prognose; prognosis; prognostic; prognostication; prognosticator; program; programmer

Prog Gro Progressive Grocer

proglang(s) progressive language(s)—usually euphemistically slanted

progr program(mer); programme

Prog(s) Progressive(s)

Prog Theor Phys Progress of Theoretical Physics

prohib prohibit(ion)

proi project return on investment

proj project; projectile; projection; projector

PROJACS Project Analysis and Control System

Prokofiev's 7 Prokoviev's seven symphonies including the *Classical* (No. 1)

prolan processed language

prole(s) proletarian(s)

proletcult proletarian culture

Prolific Lexicographer Eric Partridge

Prolific Professor Isaac Asimov (author of more than two hundred books)

Prolific Rationalist English ex-priest Joseph McCabe who delivered more than 3000 lectures and wrote more than 300 books

Prolific Typographer Frederic William Goudy

PROLLAP Professional Library Literature Acquisition Program

prolog programming in logic

prolong. prolongatus (Latin—prolonged)

ProLt procurement lead time

prom programmable read-only memory; promenade (concert or dance); prominent; promontory; promote; promoter; promotion; promotional; prompter

Prom The Prom—Wilson's Promontory—national park at the southernmost tip of Australia

promex productivity measurement experiment

PROMIS Problem-Oriented Medical Information System; Prosecution Management Information System (U.S. Attorney's Office—Washington,

DC)

Promised Land Israel, promised to the Israelites by Moses and to the Israelis by Balfour

proml promulgate

promo promotional

promo(s) promotional announcement(s)

Promoter of Agrarian Reform Emiliano Zapata

PROMPT Project Management and Production Team

PROMS Projectile Measurement System (USA)

PROMSTRA Production Methods and Stress Research Association

Promy Promontory

pron pronoun; pronounced; pronunciation; pronunciator(y)

PRON Procurement Request and Order Number (USA)

prond pronounced

prong(s) pronghorn(s)—pronghorn antelope(s)

pronom pronominal

pro note promissory note

PRONTO Program for Numeric Tool Operation

PRONTOS Programmable Network Telecommunications Operating System

pronun pronunciate; pronunciation

pronunc pronunciation

PROOF Parole Resource Office and Orientation Facility (Jersey City, New Jersey)

prop propaganda; propeller; property; proportion(al); proposed; proprietary

Prop Sextus Propertius (Roman poet)

PROP Panel Review of Products; Portland Regional Opportunities Program; Preservation of the Rights of Prisoners

Prop 13 Proposition 13 (California's property tax reduction aimed at curbing waste in statewide government while eliminating confiscatory taxation of homes)

prop art propaganda art

propay proficiency pay

pro.per. in propria persona (Latin—acting as one's own attorney)

proph prophetic; prophylactic; prophylaxis

Prophet of Allah Mohammed

Prophet of the American Way Thomas Jefferson

Prophet of Christianity John the Baptist

Prophet of Democracy William Penn
Prophet of Doom Girolamo Savonarola
Prophet of Israel Moses
Prophet of Modernity Émile Zolá
Prophet of Mythology Teiresias
Prophet Outcast Leon Trotsky
Prophet-Preacher-Hero of New England Unitarianism William Ellery Channing
Prophets of Israel Moses, Samuel, Nathan, Elijah, Elisha
Prophet of the Strenuous Life Jack London
propjet propeller turned by jet engine (same as turboprop)
propl proportional
propn proportion(al)
props (theatrical) properties
prop wash propeller wash
pro rat.aet. *pro ratione aetatis* (Latin—according to age)
pro rect. *pro recto* (Latin—by rectum)
PRORM Pay and Records Office—Royal Marines
pros professionals; prosody; prostitute(s)
Pros Atty Prosecuting Attorney
prosc proscenium
PROSE Personal Record of School Experiences
Prose Poet of Violence Jean Genet
prosig procedure signal
prosine procedure sign
prosp prospecting
Prosperous Paradise of the Pacific Hawaii
pross(ie) prostitute
prost prostate; prothetics; prostitution
prosth prosthesis
prostie(s) prostitute(s)
Prostitution Capital of the South old nickname for New Orleans
prot protective; protectorate; protein; protestant; protozoa; protractor
prot (PROT) protein anion
Prot Protectorate; Protestant; Protozoa
protag protagonist
Prot-Ap Protonotary-Apostolic
Protec Protectorate
Protector of the Indians Rodrigo de Bastidas—Spanish navigator who explored the coasts from Panama to Venezuela and founded Santa Marta; Las Casas and Eliot share the title —Protector of the Indians
Protectress from Fever Febris

(Roman goddess whose Latin name means fever)
Protectress from Poison Gases Mephitis—Roman goddess venerated in volcanic lands where poisonous gases abounded
Protectress of the Protestants Marguerite de Navarre
Protectress of Seafarers the Greek goddess Brizo
pro tem. *pro tempore* (Latin— for the time being)
Protestant Hero Frederick the Great of Prussia
PROTEUS Propulsion Research and Open-Water Testing of Experimental Underwater Systems
prothrom prothrombin
pro time prothrombin time
Protoch Protochorda
Protocols *Protocols of the Learned Elders of Zion* (fraudulent document created and distributed in 1905 by the czarist secret police to incite deadly pogroms against Russia's Jews; since used by many antisemitic bigots in defense of their cause in Canada, France, Germany, Italy, the United Kingdom, the United States, and elsewhere)
protozool protozoologic(al)(ly); protozoologist; protozoology
protr protractor
pro us.ext. *pro uso externo* (Latin—for external use)
prov provide; provision; provisional; proviso
prov *provincia* (Spanish—province)
Prov Provençal; Provence; Proverbs, The (book of the Bible); Providence; Province
Prov Provençal (Romance language spoken in southwestern France by some 6 million people); *Proverbs*; *Provinz* (German—province)
Prov Eng Provincial English
prover procurement-value-economy-reliability
Prov GM Provincial Grand Master
Providence Rhode Island's capital
Providence Plantations latter half of the official name— Rhode Island and Providence Plantations
provin provincial
Provincias *Vascas* *Provincias Vascongadas* (Spanish— Basque Provinces)—Álava,

Guipúzcoa, and Vizcaya
Provisional President of Africa Marcus Garvey
Provision State Connecticut in Revolutionary times when it furnished so much for the Continental Army
provn provision
Provo city in Utah and short form for Providenciales island and town in the Turks and Caicos Islands; Provisional (member of the IRA)
provos *provokers* (Dutch—street people engaged in militant tactics to provoke the police)
Provos Provisionals (Provisional Sinn Fein party members of Northern Ireland)
Provost Hunting reconnaissance-trainer aircraft built in Britain
PROVOST Priority Research and Development Objectives for Vietnam Operations Support
proword procedure word
prox proximal; proximity
prox. *proximo* (Latin—next, adv.)
proxi protection by reflection optics of xerographic images
prox. luc. *proxima luce* (Latin— the day before)
prp peak radiated power; pickup (zone) release point; present participle; pseudo random pulse; pulse recurrence period; pulse repetition period
prp (PRP) platelet-rich plasma; polyribophosphate
Prp Principality
PRp Puerto Rican pimp
PRP People's Revolutionary Party (Tanzanian terrorists); Production Requirements Plan; Production Reserve Policy; Public Relations Personnel
PRPA Puerto Rico Ports Authority
PRPC Public Relations Policy Committee (NATO)
PRPGA Puerto Rico Personnel and Guidance Association
prpln propulsion
prpp (PRPP) 5-phosphoribosyl 1-pyrophosphate
pr. pr. *praeter propter* (Latin— about, nearly)
PRp('s) Puerto Rican pimp(s)
PRPUC Philippine Republic Presidential Unit Citation
prr pulse repetition rate
PRR Pennsylvania Railroad
PRRI Puerto Rico Rum Insti-

tute

p&rr's patriotic and religious racketeers (making their living taking money and other contributions from patriotic and religious zealots)

PRRWO Puerto Rican Revolutionary Workers Organization (communist)

prs pairs; printers

Prs Preston

PRs Pakistani rupees; Problem Reports; Puerto Ricans

PRS Park and Ride Scheme; Pattern-Recognition System; Pennsylvania-Reading Seashore (railroad); Precision Ranging System; Property Recovery Squad (of a police department); Protective Research Section (U.S. Secret Service); Public Radio Stations; Public Rehabilitation Scheme; Pupil Rating Scale

PRSA Public Relations Society of America

prsd pressed

prsd met pressed metal

prsfdr pressfeeder

prsmn pressman

PRSO Puerto Rico Symphony Orchestra

PRSP Puerto Rican Socialist Party (communist)

PRSS Pennsylvania-Reading Seashore Lines

PRSSA Public Relations Student Society of America

PRST Puerto Rican Standard Time

Pr strain Prague (viral) strain

prsvn preservation

PRSY People's Republic of Southern Yemen

prt parachute radio transmitter; personnel research test; publication requirement table(s); pulse repetition time

prt (PRT) personal rapid transit; printer (flow chart); program reference table

p & rt physical and recreational training

Prt Port (postal abbreviation)

PrT Prinzregentheater (Munich)

PRT Personnel Research Test; Philadelphia Rapid Transit; Production Re-evaluation Testing

PRT *Partido Revolucionario de los Trabajadores* (Spanish—Revolutionary Party of the Workers)—Mexican socialists

prtd printed

prtg printing

prtlsp printer line spacing

prtot prototype real-time optical tracker

prtov printer overflow

PRTS Personal Rapid Transit System

prty priority

pru peripheral resistance unit; prude; prudence; prudent

Pru Prudence; Prudential Life Insurance Company

PRU Polish-Russian Union (South African Jews who joined this were called Peruvians because of their abbreviation of their society seemingly alien to their Christian neighbors)

Prue Prudence

Pruisen (Dutch—Prussia)

Prune Picker(s) Californian(s)

pru pru(s) prurient prude(s)

Prus Prussia; Prussian

Prussia English for Preussen (northern Germany around the Baltic and the Berlin area)

prussic acid hydrocyanic acid

prv peak reverse voltage; pressure-reducing valve; pressure-reduction valve

prv pour rendre visite (French—to return a call)

Prv Pravda (Russian—truth)—daily newspaper published in Moscow by Central Committee of the Communist Party

prw percent rated wattage

PRWAD Professional Rehabilitation Workers with the Adult Deaf

prx pressure regulator exhaust

PRY Pittsburgh Railways Corporation (stock exchange symbol)

PRZ People's Republic of Zanzibar

ps parlor snake; parts shipped; parts shipper; passenger service; passing scuttle; patient's serum; penal servitude; picosecond; pieces; plastic surgery; point of switch; point of symmetry; proof shot; pseudo; pseudonym(s); pull switch; pulmonary stenosis

p-s pressure-sensitive

p's pennies

p/s paddle steamer; point of shipment; port or starboard

p & s paracentesis and suction; piss and shit; port and starboard

Ps Psalms, The (book of the Bible); South Pole; South Celestial Pole; static pressure

Ps Posaunen (German—trombones); *Psalms*

PS Paleontological Society; Palm Society; Palm Springs (California); Paymaster Sergeant; Pennsylvania State University; Pharmaceutical Society; Philippine Scouts; Photo(graphic) Service; picket ship(s); Pistol Sharpshooter; Pittsburg & Shawmut (railroad); Planetary Society; Plastic Surgery; Privy Seal; Public Safety; Public School; Puget Sound

P-S Pullman-Standard

P.S. paddle steamer; public school

P & S Physicians and Surgeons; Pittsburg & Shawmut (railroad)

P of S Port of Spain

PS Pferdestärke (German—horsepower)

P.S. post scriptum (Latin—written after)

PS 166 Public School 166 (for example)

psa passed staff college; psychoanalytic(al)

psa (PSA) public service announcement (radio or television)

PsA Pisces Austrinus (constellation)

PSA Pacific Science Association; Pacific Southwest Airlines; Packers and Stockyards Administration; Photographic Society of America; Play Schools Association; Poetry Society of America; Port of Singapore Authority; Poultry Science Association; Program Study Authorization; Public Service Administration; Public Service Association

P & SA Program and Systems Analysis

PSA Proceedings of the Society of Antiquaries

psaa post-stimulatory auditory adaptation

PSAB Public Schools Appointments Bureau

p sac pericardial cavity

PSAC President's Science Advisory Committee; Public Service Alliance of Canada

PSACPOO President's Scientific Advisory Committee Panel On Oceanography

psad prediction-simulation-adaptation-decision (data processing)

PSAI Play Schools Association,

Inc

PSAL Public School Athletic League

Psalt. *Psalterium* (Latin—Book of Psalms)

PSAMPP Philadelphia Society for Alleviating the Miseries of Public Prisons (founded by Benjamin Franklin, William Rush, and others)

ps an psychoanalysis; psychoanalyst; psychoanalytic(al)(ly); psychoanalyze

PSAODAP Presidential Special Action Office for Drug Abuse Prevention

PSAR Preliminary Safety Analysis Report

PSAT Palm Springs Aerial Tramway; Preliminary Scholastic Aptitude Test(ing)

psb please send a boat; public service band (radio)

PSB Paradox Salt Basin; Psychological Strategy Board; Public Service Board

P & SB Portland & South Bend (railroad)

PSBA Pennsylvania School Boards Association; Public Schools Bursars' Association

PSBLS Permanent Space-Based Logistics System

PSBO Public Savings Bond Office

psc passed staff college; per standard compass; port service charge; prestressed concrete

ps & c program scheduling and control

Psc Pisces (constellation)

P-S c Porter-Silber chromogen

PSC Pacific Sea Council; Peralta Shipping Corporation; Pittsburgh Steel Company; Point Shipping Company; Porcelain-on-Steel Council; Potomac State College; Product Safety Commission(er); Professional Services Corporation; Program Structure Code; Public Service Careers; Public Service Commission

PSC *Partido Social Cristiano* (Spanish—Social Christian Party)—Catholic actionists

pscb padded sample collection bag

PSCC Public Service Commission of Canada

PSCD Patrol Service Central Depot

PSCFB Pacific Southcoast Freight Bureau

PSCNI Public Service Company of Northern Illinois

PSCO Personnel Survey Control Office(r)

PSCP Public Service Careers Program

PSCPT Preschool Self-Concept Picture Test(ing)

PSCS Pacific Scatter Communications System

Psc's calculator Pascal's calculator (first adding machine)

pscu power-supply control unit

psd power spectral density; prevention of significant deterioration; promotion service date

P Sd Port Said

PSD Pittsburgh Steamship Division (United States Steel); Port of San Diego; Prevention of Significant Deterioration (of air quality); Public Safety Division (Texas)

ps detn particle size determination

PSDI *Partito Socialista Democratico Italiano* (Italian Social Democratic Party)

ps distn particle size distribution

psdo pseudo; pseudonym

psdp phrase structure and dependency parser

PSDS Primary Solar Duct(ing) System

psdu power-switching distribution unit

PSDUPD Port of San Diego Unified Port District

pse please; point of subjective equality

pse (PSE) psychological stress evaluator (voice-analysis lie detector)

PSEA Pennsylvania State Education Association; Physical Security Equipment Agency

psec picosecond

PSE & G Public Service Electric and Gas Company

PSE & GC Public Service Electric and Gas

psen pupils with special educational needs

Pseo *Paseo* (Spanish—boulevard)

pser production support and equipment replacement

pset permanent service on earth tides

pseud pseudandry (women using male names as pseudonyms); pseudepigraphy (attributing false names to artists, authors, or composers); pseudograph (falsely attributing a work to an artist, author, or compos-

er); pseudojyn (men using female names as pseudonyms); pseudonym (false name, nom de plume, pen name); pseudonyma (pseudonymous works)

pseudo (Latin prefix—false)—pseudonym

psf payload-structure-fuel (ratio); point-spread function; pounds per square foot

PSF Phelps-Stokes Fund; Presidio of San Francisco

P & SF Panhandle and Santa Fe (railroad)

P of SF Port of San Francisco

PSFC Pacific Salmon Fisheries Commission

PSFL Puget Sound Freight Lines

PSFS Philadelphia Savings Fund Society

psg production system generator; psychogalvanometer; psychogalvanometric(al)(ly)

PSGBI Pathological Society of Great Britain and Ireland

psgi permanent service on geomagnetic indices

psgr passenger

psgr lng passenger lounge

psgr(s) passenger(s)

P-Shaw George Bernard Shaw (also GBS)

PSHFA Public Servants Housing and Finance Association

pshr pusher

psi posterior sagittal index; pounds per square inch; public school(s) investigation

PSI Pacific Semiconductors Incorporated; Personalized System of Instruction; Physician's Services Incorporated; Pollutants Standards Index; Population Services Incorporated

PSI *Partito Socialista Italiano* (Italian Socialist Party); *Pollution Standards Index*

psia pounds per square inch absolute

PSIC Pacific Scientific Information Center (Bernice Pauahi Bishop Museum, Honolulu)

psid pounds per square inch differential

PSIDC Punjab State Industrial Development Corporation

psig pounds per square inch gage

psikhushka (Russian slang—psychoprison)—for punishing and segregating dissidents

psil preferred-frequency speech interference level

PSIP Poultry Stock Improvement Plan; Private Sector Initiative Program

PSIUP *Partito Socialista Italiano di Unita Proletaria* (Italian Socialist Party of Proletarian Unity)

psk phase shift keying

p sl pipe sleeve

PSL Pacific Star Line; Peruvian State Line; Philharmonic Society of London; Pretoria State Library

PSL *Patterson Strategy Letter*

p-slips old-fashioned postcard-size (3- × 5-inch) slips of paper used for filing

psl sol potassium, sodium chloride, sodium lactate solution

ps lt port side light

PSLT Picture Story Language Test

psm passed school of music

psm (PSM) presystolic murmur

PSM People for Self Management; Product Sales Manager

psma progressive spinal muscular atrophy

PSMA Power Saw Manufacturers Association; Pressure-Sensitive Manufacturers Association

PSMFC Pacific States Marine Fisheries Commission

psmr parts specification management for reliability

psmsl permanent service for mean sea level

psn position; pulse-shaping network(ing)

PSn Port Sudan

PSN *Partido Socialista de Nicaragua* (Spanish—Socialist Party of Nicaragua)—Moscow-oriented group

PSNA Phytochemical Society of North America

PSNC Pacific Steam Navigation Company

PSNS Puget Sound Naval Shipyard

Pˢᵒ *Passo* (Italian—pass)

PSO Pad Safety Officer; Pasadena Symphony Orchestra; Phoenix Symphony Orchestra; Pilot Systems Operator; Pittsburgh Symphony Orchestra; Portland Symphony Orchestra; Prague Symphony Orchestra

p sol partially soluble; partly soluble

pson person

psp paralytic seafood poisoning; phenolsulfonphthalein (test); pierced-steel plank; positive screened print

PSP Pacific Security Pact; Pocahontas State Park (Virginia); Price-Subsidy Program; Price-Support Program; Programs Support Plan

PSP *Pacifistisch Socialistische Partij* (Dutch—Pacifist-Socialist Party)

PSPA Professional Sports Photographers Association

PSPCD Puget Sound Pollution-Control District

PSP & L Puget Sound Power and Light (company)

PSPMW Pulp, Sulphite and Paper Mill Workers

PSPP Proposed System Package Plan

PSPS Paddle Steamer Preservation Society; Primary Solar Piping System

PSQC Philippine Society for Quality Control

psql process-screening quality level

p's & q's expression about minding your p's & q's originated when printers instructed apprentices about similarity of lowercase p's and q's when handsetting type; also used in saloons to keep count of the number of pints and quarts of beer consumed

psr pain-sensitivity range; plow-steel rope

PSR Pacific School of Religion; Physicians for Social Responsibility

PSRC Public Service Research Council

PSRF Profit Sharing Research Foundation

PSRI Public Systems Research Institute (UCLA)

PSRM Pacific Southwest Railway Museum

PSRMA Pacific Southwest Railway Museum Association

psro passenger standing route order

PSRO Professional Services (Standards) Review Organization; Professional Standards Review Organization

pss packet-switching service; physiological saline solution

Pss Princess

PSS Pad Safety Supervisor; Personal Security System; Personal Signalling System; Pre-School Screening (program); Public Service System

P.S.S. Professor of Sacred Scripture

P.S.S. *postcripta* (Latin—post-

scripts)

pssbb public school system blanket bond(ing)

PSSC Physical Science Study Committee (NSF); Pious Society of Saint Charles; Public Service Satellite Consortium

PS & SC Public Service and Safety Committee (concerned with crime in the streets)

P.S.S.C. Pious Society of Saint Charles

PSSNY Philharmonic Symphony Society of New York

psso passed slip stitch over (knitting)

PSSS Philosophic Society for the Study of Sport

PSST Public Sector Standardization Team

pst polished surface technique

pst (PST) prefrontal sonic treatment

PST Pacific Standard Time

PSTA Public Safety and Training Association

PSTB Picture Story Test Blank

PSTBC Puget Sound Tug and Boat Company

PSTC Pressure Sensitive Tape Council

PSTD Prison Service Training Depot (Pretoria)

£ sterling pound sterling

p stg c per steering compass

psth peristimulus time histogram

PSTIAC Pavements and Soil Trafficability Information Analysis Center (USA)

pstl postal

PSTMA Paper Stationery and Tablet Manufacturers Association

PSTO Principal Sea Transport Officer

P-strip P-shaped strip

P-stuff pcp (PCP)

pstz pasteurize

pstzd pasteurized

pstzg pasteurizing

psu package size unspecified; power supply unit; primary sampling unit

PSU Pennsylvania State University; Portland State University; Public Security Unit (Ugandan secret police)

PSU *Partito Socialista Unitario* (Italian—Unitary Socialist Party)

p-substance protein substance

PSUC Pennsylvania State University Center(s)

PSUC *Partido Socialista Unificado de Cataluña* (Spanish—

Unified Socialist Party of Catalonia)

P Sud Port Sudan

PSU-MRL Pennsylvania State University—Materials Research Laboratory

PSUP Pennsylvania State University Press

p surg plastic surgeon; plastic surgery

psv polished-stone value; public service vehicle

PSV Petit St Vincent (Grenadines in the West Indies); Project Salt Vault

PSW Psychiatric Social Worker

PSWB Plateau State Water Board

pswbd power switchboard

P Swet Port Swettenham (now Port Kelang or Port Klang)

PSWFA Prestige Saltwater Fly Anglers

PSWO Picture and Sound World Organization

psy psychological

l'sy l'aisley

psych psychiatry; psychology; psychopathology

psych/d psychological death

psychedeli psychedelicatessen (store selling the paraphernalia of drug addicts)

Psychedelphia San Francisco's Haight-Ashbury district inhabited by so many drug addicts

psychiat psychiatric; psychiatry

psycho dangerous lunatic; a psychiatric hospital or ward; a psychoneurotic personality; a psychotic individual (pseudoscientific slang)

psycho (Latin prehx—mental) —psychologist

psychoan psychoanalytic; psychoanalysis; psychoanalyst

Psychoanalysis Capital Berlin, New York, and Vienna have long competed for this title

psychobab psychobabble(r)— psychological patter(er)

psychobio psychobiological; psychobiologist; psychobiology

psychobiog psybiographer; psychobiographic(al)(ly); psychobiography

psychochron psychochronic(al)(ly); psychochronicle(r); psychochronologer; psychochronologic(al)(ly); psychochronology

psychochronicle psychiatric chronicle; psychological chronicle

psychodelics hallucinogenic

drugs

psychodels psychodelics (hallucinogens)

psychogeog psychogeographer; psychogeographic(al); psychogeography

psychohist psychohistorian; psychohistorical; psychohistory

psychol psychological; psychologist; psychology

Psychol Psychology

psychomet psychometric

psychopathol psychopathological; psychopathologist; psychopathology

psychophys psychophysical; psychophysics; psychophysicist

psychophysiol psychophysiology (and derivatives)

psychoprison psychiatric hospital prison (USSR's place for dissidents)

psychosurg psychosurgeon; psychosurgery; psychosurgical(ly)

psychot psychotic

psychother psychotherapist; psychotherapeutic(al,s); psychotherapy

psycho ward psychopathic ward

Psych Qtly Psychoanalytic Quarterly

psych test. psychological testing

psydoc psychiatrist doctor

psyk psykologi or psykologist (Dano-Norwegian—psychology or psychologist)

psyop psychological operation

psypath psychopath(ic)

psysom psychosomatic

psywar psychological warfare

psz (PSZ) partly stabilized zirconia

pt part; personal trade; physical therapy; physical training; pint(s); plenty tough; plenty trouble; pneumatic tube; point; point of tangency; point of turn; point of turning; primary target, private terms; prothrombin time

p & t personnel and training; posts and timbers

pt partie (French—part)

pt. perstetur (Latin—let it be continued)

p.t. protempore (Latin—temporarily)

£T pound Turkish

Pt part; platinum; Point; Port; Porto; Puerto

P *Petit* (French—little, small); Pont (French—bridge)

PT motor torpedo boat (naval symbol); Pacific Time; Peninsula Terminal (railroad); Phil-

adelphia Transportation; Physical Therapist; physical therapy; physical training; Postal Telegraph; primary trainer; Provincetown-Boston Airline (2-letter coding)

P & T Pope & Talbot (steamship line)

PT-76 Soviet Amphibious tank

pta plasma thromboplastin antecedent; posttraumatic amnesia; primary target area; prior to admission; proposed technical approach; peseta (Spanish monetary unit, diminutive of peso)

pta peseta (Spanish—monetary unit valued normally at about twenty American cents)

Pta Punta (Spanish—Point)

Pta *Ponta* (Portuguese—point); Puerta (Spanish—gate, gateway, mountain pass); Punta (Spanish—point)

Pt A Port Arthur, Ontario

PTA Paper and Twine Associa tion; Parent-Teacher Association; Pope and Talbot; Postal Transportation Association; Prevention of Terrorism Act; Protestant Teachers Association

PTA Prevention of Terrorism Act (British)—provides for seven days detention of suspects

ptacv (PTACV) prototype air-cushioned vehicle

P Tal Port Talbot

Pt Alb Port Alberni

Pt Ant Port Antonio

PTAR Prime Time Access Rule

Ptarmigan Alaska state bird; symbolic nickname given some Alaskans in preference to Sourdough recalling frontier times

Pt Art Port Arthur

ptas pesetas

pta's part-time alcoholics

PTAs Passenger Transport Authorities

PTAS Productivity and Technical Assistance Secretariat

P Tau Port Taufiq (formerly Port Tewfik)

ptb patellar-tendon bearing

PTB Partido Trabalhista Brasileiro (Portuguese—Brazilian Workers Party); Physikalisch-Technische Bundesanstalt (German—Physical Technical Institute)

ptbl portable

PTBM PT Barnum Museum

(Bridgeport, Connecticut)
PT-boat patrol torpedo boat
ptbr punched-tape block reader
PTBT Partial Test Ban Treaty
ptc personnel transfer capsule; positive temperature coefficient
ptc (PTC) phenylthiocarbamide; plasma thromboplastin component (clotting factor IX)
PTC Pacific Theological College; Pacific Tin Consolidated; Paisley Technical College; patrol vessel (naval symbol); Peoria Terminal (railroad); Philadelphia Transportation Company; Pine Tree Camp; Pipe and Tobacco Council; Power Transmission Council; Press Trust of Ceylon; Private Truck Council
PTCA Private Truck Council of America
ptcldy partly cloudy
ptd painted
PTDA Power Transmission Distributors Association
ptdl programmable tapped-delay line
PTDP Preliminary Technical Development Plan
PTDR Post- Test Disassembly Report
PTDS Photo Target Detection System
pte parathyroid extract; *poriente* (Spanish—west)
pte (PTE) pulmonary thromboembolism
p^te parte (Spanish—part)
Pte Pointe (French—Point); *Presidente* (Portuguese or Spanish—President)
PTE Passenger Transport Executive
pt ed patient education
pt ex part exchange
ptf plasma thromboplastin factor
PTF fast patrol boat (naval symbol); Propulsion Test Facilities
ptfe polytetrafluorethylene
ptfp prime-time family programming
ptg printing
Ptg Portugal; Portuguese
PTG Piano Technician's Guild; Polaris Task Group
ptgt primary target
pth parathormone
Pth Perth
PTH hydrofoil motor torpedo boat (naval symbol)
pti persistent tolerant infection; physical training instructor

(PTI)
PTI Philips Telecommunicatie Industrie; Pictorial Test of Intelligence; Press Trust of India; Protect the Innocent (anticrime lobby)
PTIDG Presentation of Technical Information Discussion Group
PTIS Piano Teachers Information Service
PTJ (Cuerpo) Técnico de Policía Judicial (Spanish—Technical Corps of the Judicial Police)—Venezuelans call its members *Petejotas*
Pt K Port Klang (also written Kelang and formerly Port Swettenham)
ptl partial total loss; pintle; primary target line
Pt L Point Loma
P t L Praise the Lord
PTL Photographic Technology Laboratory
ptm proof test model; pulse-time modulation
Ptm Pietermaai
Ptm (PTM) Polaris tactical missile
ptma phosphotungstomolybdic acid
PTMTCS Power-Tape-to-Magnetic-Tape Conversion System
ptn partition
PTNA Professional Travel Nurses Association
Ptnr Partner
pto please turn over; power take-off
Pto Porto; Puerto; Punto
P^to Ponto (Italian—sea)—poetic term; *Porto* (Italian, Portuguese, Spanish—port); *Puerto* (Spanish—port); *Punto* (Italian—point)
PTO Patent and Trademark Office; Public Trustee Office(r); Purdue Teacher Opinionaire
Pto Blvr Puerto Bolívar
Pto Cab Puerto Cabello
Pto Cast Puerto Castilla, Honduras
ptol peacetime operating level
Ptol Ptolemaic; Ptolemy
Ptolemy Alexandrian astronomer Claudius Ptolemaeus
Pto Rico Puerto Rico
P Town Port Townsend
ptp paper-tape printer; part-time pimp
p-t-p point-to-point
PTP Pointe à Pitre, Guadeloupe (airport); Productive Thinking Program

ptpg participating
pt/pt point-to-point
ptr printer; pupil-teacher ratio
ptr (PTR) photoelectric tape reader
PTR pool test reactor
ptrf peacetime rate factor(s)
ptry pantry; poetry; pottery
pts *pesetas* (Spanish—plural of peseta); pints
Pts Portsmouth
PTS Postal Transportation Service; Princeton Theological Seminary; Public Television Station(s)
PT & S Pacific Towboat and Salvage (tugs)
ptsd (PTSD) post-traumatic stress disorder
PTSD Post-Traumatic Stress Disorder
pts/hr parts per hour; pieces per hour
Ptsmth Portsmouth
Pt Sp Port of Spain
PTSS Princeton Time-Sharing System
PTSTV Prime Time School Television
ptt push to talk
ptt (PTT) partial thromboplastin time
PTT Posta, Telgraf ve Telefon (Turkish—Post, Telegraph, and Telephone); *Postes, Télégraphes, Téléphone* (French—national postal, telegraph, and telephone system)
PTTA Philippine Tourist and Travel Association; Postal Telegraph and Telephone Authority
ptti precise time and time interval
PTTI Postal, Telegraph, and Telephone International
pt-tm part-time
pttnmkr patternmaker
ptu propylthiouracil
PTU Plumbers' Trade Union; Plumbing Trade Union; Psychiatric Treatment Unit
PTUC Philippine Trade Unions Council
ptv passenger transfer vehicle; public television
ptv (PTV) propulsion test vehicle
ptv's personal transportation vehicles (three-wheeled vehicles for city driving)
ptw per thousand words
Pt W Port Weller
PTWC Pacific Tsunami Warning Center
Pty Party; Proprietary

pu passed urine; peptic ulcer; pickup; plant unit; pregnancy urine; propellant utilization; propulsion unit; pump(ing) unit; pump unit

p-u (pee-you) phew (what a stench)

p.u. *plus ultra* (Latin—beyond the pinnacle, beyond the ultimate)

Pu plutonium

PU Pacific University; Phillips University; Princeton University; Prisoner's Union; Purdue University

PUA *Punta de la Unidad Africana* (Spanish—Point of African Unity)—formerly Fernanda Point

PUAS Postal Union of the Americas and Spain

pub public; publican; publication; public house; publicity; publish; published; publisher; publishing

Pub Publican; Public House; Publisher's Announcement

PUB Public Utilities Board

pub. aff public affairs

pub aide publication aide

pubbl *pubblicità* (Italian—advertising, publicity)

Pub Doc Public Document

pub ed publication editor

pubinfo public information

publ publication; publicity; publisher; publishing

Publ Astron Soc Pac *Publications of the Astronomical Society of the Pacific*

Public Enemy Number One gangster Al Capone's nickname

Public Library Builder Andrew Carnegie

Publius allonymic name used by Alexander Hamilton, John Jay, and James Madison in writing *The Federalist*

pub(s) public house(s) (British short form)

Pub Sect Lab Rel Public Sector Labor Relations Conference Board

Pub W *Publishers Weekly*

Pub Wks Public Works

puc papers under consideration; pickup car

PUC Peoples University of China; Presidential Unit Citation; Public Utilities Code; Public Utilities Commission; Public Utilities and Corporations

PUC *Post Urbem Conditam* (Latin—after the foundation of the city)—city usually means Rome

pucf polyurethane-coated fabric; polyurethane-coated fibers

pud puddle; pudding

pud (PUD) planned unit development

pu & d pickup and delivery

PUD Planned Unit Development

Pudahuel Santiago de Chile's airport

Pue Puebla

Puebla Puebla de Zaragoza (in central Mexico)

Puerto Colombia formerly Savanilla

Puerto de España (Spanish—Port of Spain)—capital of Trinidad and Tobago

Puerto Limón Limón, Costa Rica

Puerto Principe (Spanish—Port-au-Prince)—Haiti's capital

Puerto Rico "a group of islands—the main one being Puerto Rico, the others being the offshore islands of Vieques, Culebra, Manhattan, Brooklyn, and Staten Island"—Governor Luís Muñoz Marín—who knew there were more Puerto Ricans in New York than in San Juan

Puerto Rico Ports (east to west) Ensenada de Honda, San Juan, Ponce, Guanica, Mayaguez

PUF Presses Universitaires de France (University Presses of France)

pufa polyunsaturated fatty acid

PUFF People United to Fight Frustrations

PUFFT Purdue University Fast Fortran Translator

pug. puggy; pugilism; pugilist

Pugetopolis industrialized urban areas surrounding Puget Sound

Puggy Booth Joseph Mallord William Turner's nickname given him in his last years by East Kent's seaside neighbors who believed he was a retired sea captain named Booth—a name he used to gain anonymity

PUHS Phoenix Union High School

PUK Pechiney Ugine Kuhlmann

puka *pukalolo* (Hawaiian Polynesian—crazy tobacco)—marijuana also known locally as Kauai electric, Kona gold, Maui wowie, Puna butter

pukeweed *Lobelia inflata's* nickname

Pukus americanus nickname for ill-smelling long-haired street people

pul pulley

PUL Princeton University Library (New Jersey); Punjab University Library (Lahore, Pakistan)

Pula (Setswana—Rain)—official motto of the arid republic of Botswana

Pulau Pinang (Malay—Betel Nut Island)—Penang

'Pulco Acapulco

pulg *pulgadas* (Spanish—inches)

pulheems physical capacity, upper and lower limbs, hearing, eyesight, emotional capacity, mental stability

pul ins pulmonary insufficiency

Pulj (Yugoslavian—Pola)—Adriatic port

pulm pulmonary

pulm. *pulmentum* (Latin—gruel)

pulm a pulmonary artery

pulm emb pulmonary embolism

pulmo pulmoaortic(al)(ly); pulmology; pulmometer; pulmometric(al)(ly); pulmometry; pulmonary; pulmonectomy; pulmonic(al)(ly); pulmonitis; pulmonologist(ic)(al)(ly); pulmotor

pulmotor (pulmonary + motor)

pulsar pulse + star (pulsed radio-wave-emitting star); pulsing astronomical signal (received from outer space)

pul sten pulmonary stenosis

pulv pulverize(r)

pulv. *pulvis* (Latin—powder)

pulv. gros. *pulvis grossus* (Latin—coarse powder)

pulv. subtil. *pulvis subtilis* (Latin—smooth powder)

pulv. tenu *pulvis tenuis* (Latin—very fine)

pum pop-up mechanism

PUM Postal Union Mail

puma. (PUMA) programmable universal mechanical assembly (robot)

Puma Franco-British Aerospatiale-Westland transport helicopter

PUMA Prostitutes Union of Massachusetts

Pumfret Pontefract

pump. pumping

PUMP Protesting Unfair Marketing Practices

pums permanently unfit for military service

pun. puncheon

puN plasma-urea Nitrogen

PUN *Partido Union Nacional* (Spanish—National Union Party)

punc punctuation

pundonor *punta de honor* (Spanish—point of honor)

Punj Punjabi

Punkie Town Punxsutawney, Pennsylvania

Punks' Paradise nickname given any gambling center and sometimes to the State of Nevada and the casino cities of Reno and Las Vegas

Punta Arenas (Spanish—Sand Point)—the one in Chile called Magallanes from 1927 to 1937; the one in Costa Rica is written Puntarenas

Punxey Punxsutawney

puo pneumonia; pyrexia of unknown origin

pup puppy

pup. (PUP) peripheral unit processor

Pup Puppis (constellation)

PUP People's United Party (Belize); Princeton University Press

Pupp Puppis (constellation)

puppie(s) pregnant urban professional(s)

pups puppies

pup(s) pregnant urban professional(s)

pur purchase; purchaser; purchasing; purifier; purification; purify; purple; purplish; pursuant; pursuit

Pur Purim

purch purchasing

Purdue Purdue University Press

pure mat. pure machine-aided translation

pure mt pure machine translation

pureq purchase requisition

purg. *purgativus* (Latin—purgative)

Puri port of Jagananth or Juggernaut on the Bay of Bengal

Puritan City Boston, Massachusetts

Puritan State Massachusetts

purp purple

Purple Islands the Madeiras

Purple Land WH Hudson's sobriquet for Uruguay

Purple Violet New Jersey state flower

purpurite iron magnesium phosphate

purv powered underwater research vehicle

pus. permanently unfit for service

Pus Pusan

PUs Public Utilities

PUS Parliamentary Under-Secretary; Permanent Under-Secretary

Push Pushtu

PUSH People United to Save Humanity

Pushkin modern name for Tsarskoe Selo south of Leningrad

puss pussy; pussycat

puta(s) *prostituta(s)* [Portuguese or Spanish—prostitute(s)]

Putnam GP Putnam; Putnaham

Putrid Sea Sivash Sea (mineralized marshes along Crimea's north coast)

putty linseed oil and powdered chalk mixture

puva psoralen (drug) + ultraviolet-A (light)

PUVAS Plutonium Value Analysis System

puvep propellant-utilization vehicle-borne electronic package

Puy-de-D Puy-de-Dôme

pv par value; paravane; pave(d); paving; plasma value; position value; prime vertical; public voucher

p/v peak-to-valley; per vagina; pressure vacuum; pressure valve; profit volume (ratio)

p & v pressure and velocity

pv *por vida* (Spanish—for life)— graffitic inscription usually appearing after the initials of a boy's and a girl's name; *prossimo venturo* (Italian—next month)

p v *petite vitesse* (French—slow train); *piccola velocity* (Italian—slow train)

Pv Peru; Peruvian

PV Eastern Provincial Airways (2-letter coding); patrol vessel; Post Village; Priest Vicar; Puerto Vallarta

P.V. *Procès verbaux* (French— official report); *Processi verbali* (Italian—official report)

PV-2 Lockheed maritime reconnaissance bomber

pva polyvinyl acetate

PVA Paralyzed Veterans of America; Prison Visitor's Association

p.vag *per vaginam* (Latin—by the vagina)

pval polyvinyl alcohol

pvb potentiometer voltmeter bridge

PVB Prison Visitors' Board

pvc polyvinyl chloride (thermoplastic)

pvc (PVC) premature ventricular contractions

PVC Philippine Volconology Commission; Precision Valve Corporation

PVCC Piedmont Virginia Community College

pvccf polyvinyl-chloride-coated fabric; polyvinyl-chloride-coated fibers

pvd peripheral vascular disease; pulmonary vascular disease

PVD Providence, Rhode Island (airport)

PvdA *Partij van de Arbeid* (Dutch—Labor Party)

pvdc polyvinyl dichloride

pvem pulse-vector emittance meter

pvf polyvinyl fluoride

pvH propane-vacuum hydrogen

pvi point of vertical instersection

PVI Personal Values Inventory

pvis pneumatic vertical-indicating scale

pvm polyvinyl methyl

PVM Process Evaluation Module

PVMNM Perry's Victory Memorial National Monument

Pvmnt Pavement

pvnt prevent; preventive

PVO Principal Veterinary Officer

pvp photovoltaic power; polyvinylpyrrolidone (plasma extender)

pvp *precio máximo de venta al publico* (Spanish—maximum price charged the public)

PVP President's Veterans Program

PVPMPC Perpetual Vice President and Member of the Pickwick Club

pvpp polyvinyl-polypyrrolidone

pvq personal-value questionnaire

pvr portable volume-controlled respirator; precision voltage reference

PVR Police Volunteer Reserves

PVRC Pressure Vessel Research Committee (NBS)

pvs persistent vegetative state

PVS Pecos Valley Southern (railroad); Periventricular (fiber) System; Personal Value System

pvt page view terminal; pressure volume temperature; private

pvt par voie télégraphique (French—by telegraph)

Pvt Private

Pvt 1/C Private First Class

PVU Prairie View University

pvw pure virgin wool

pw packed weight; passing window; pivoted window; postwar; prisoner of war; private wire; projected window; psychological warfare; public works; pulse width

p/w parallel with

p & w pension and welfare (retirement benefits)

PW Philadelphia & Western (railroad); Pittsburgh & West Virginia (railroad); prisoner of war; Public Works

P-W Prader-Willi (syndrome)

P & W Pratt and Whitney Aircraft Division, United Aircraft Corporation

PW Petroleum Week; *Publishers' Weekly*

PWA Pacific Western Airlines; Prison Wardens Association; Professional Writers of America; Psychic Workers Association; Public Works Administration

PWA Papierwerke Waldhof-Ashaffenburg (German—Waldhof-Ashaffenburg Paper Works)

pwafrr present worth of all future revenue requirements

P Wash Port Washington

p wave pressure wave

p waves primary (earthquake) waves

pwc physical working capacity

pwc (PWC) pulse-width coded; pulse-width coding

PWC Parents Who Care; Prisoner of War Convention; Public Works Canada; Public Works Center (USN)

pwd plywood; powered

pwd (PWD) pulse-width discriminating; pulse-width discriminator

PWD Public Works Department

pwdrd powdered

PWDS Protected Wireline Distribution System

pwe (PWE) pulse-width encoder; pulse-width encoding

PWE Political Warfare Executive; Prisoner of War Enclosure

P Wel Port Weller

pwf pregnancy without fear (pil-

low-simulated pregnancy); present-worth factor

PWFP Prince William Forest Park (Virginia)

PWG Permanent Working Group (NATO); Province Working Group

PWHS Public Works Historical Society

PWI Physiological Workload Index

P & W I Poets and Writers Incorporated

PWIF Plantation Workers' International Federation

PWJC Piney Woods Junior College

pwl power watt(age) level

PWLB Public Works Loan Board

pwm pokeweed mitogen (PWM); pulse width modulation

pwm (PWM) pulse-width modulating; pulse-width modulator

PWM Partnership for World Mission

PWMS Public Works Management System (USN)

pwmsp people with multiple social problems; person(s) with multiple social problems

PWNDA Provincial Wholesale Newspaper Distributors' Association

PWNP Parra Wirra National Park (South Australia)

PWO Principal Weapons Officer; Public Welfare Office(r); Public Works Office(r)

pwp picowatt power

PWP Parents Without Partners

pwr power; pressurized water reactor (PWR)

PWR Police War Reserve

PWRS Pacific War Research Society

pwr sup power supply

pws paddlewheel steamer

pw's prisoners of war

PWS Periyar Wildlife Sanctuary (India); Private Wire System

pwt pennyweight; propulsion wind tunnel

PWT Picture World Test

pwtn power train

pwtr pewter

P & WV Pittsburgh & West Virginia (railroad)

Pwy Poway

px past history; physical examination; please exchange; pneumothorax; press; prognosis

PX Aspen Airways (2-letter code); Post Exchange

PXCMD Phoenix Contract Management District

pxe (PXE) pseudoxanthoma elasticum

px in time of arrival

pxl (PXL) patrol experimental land-based aircraft

pxlst passenger list(ing)

px me report my arrival and departure

pxo próximo (Spanish—next)

px out takeoff time

PX-S Japanese reconnaissance flying boat

pxt. pinxit (Latin—he painted it)

py pitch and yaw

p/y pitch or yaw

PY commissioned and armed yacht (2-letter naval symbol); program year; Surinam Airways (2-letter symbol); yacht (naval symbol)

Pya Pyatnitsa (Russian—Friday)

PYA plan, year, age (insurance)

pyc proteose-yeast castone

PYC Philadelphia Yacht Club; Portland Yacht Club (Maine); Poughkeepsie Yacht Club

PYE Protect Your Environment

pyg broth proteose-yeast-glucose broth

Pylos Greek name for the port of Navarino

pyo (Latin prefix pus) pyorrhea

pyof pick your own fruit

pyph polyphase

pyr pyridine

p-y-r pitch-yaw-roll

pyramid pyramid investment scheme (organized to gull the gullible)

Pyrenäen (German—Pyrenees)

Pyrenean Principality Andorra

Pyreneën (Dutch—Pyrenees)

Pyrenees Pyrenees Mountains between France and Spain

Pyrénées (French—Pyrenees)

Pyrenees Principality Andorra

pyrite fool's gold; iron disulfide; iron pyrites

pyrites copper, iron, tin pyrite; also known as fool's gold

pyrmd pyramid(ed)

pyro pyromaniac; pyrotechnic(s); pyroxylin

pyroglu pyroglutamic acid

pyrolag pyrolagnia(c)

pyrom pyrometer; pyrometry

Pyr-Or Pyreneés-Orientales

pyrot pyrotechnics

pyt pretty young thing

pyx. pyxis (Latin—box, vessel)

Pyx Pyxis (constellation)
pz pancreozymin
PZ Paolei Zion(ist); Pickup Zone; Police Zone
PZ-61 Swiss medium tank armed with a 105mm gun
pza pyrazinamide
pza pieza (Spanish—piece)
Pza Plaza (Italian or Spanish—Plaza)
Pᶻᵃ Piazza (Italian—Square)

pzc point of zero charge
PZC Partido Zapatista Comunista (Spanish—Zapatist Communist Party)—underground hammer-and-sickle group active along the Mexican Border
pz-cck pancreozymin-cholecystokinin
pzi protamine zinc insulin
PZM Polska Zegluga Morska

(Polish Merchant Marine)
Pᶻᵒ Pizzo (Italian—peak, summit)
PZPR Polska Zjednoczona Partia Robotnicza (Polish United Workers Party)
PZS Président of the Zoological Society
pzt photographic zenith tube
Pᶻᶻᵃ Piazza (Italian—Square)

Q

q coefficient of association (statistical symbol); cue (gesture or signal to cease or commence); dynamic pressure (symbol); electric charge (symbol); quality factor; quart, quarter; quarterly; quartile; quarto; queer (queer money or queer sexually); quench; quenching; queries; query; question(s); quick; quintal; quire; semi-interquartile range (symbol); stagnation pressure (symbol)

q quaque (Latin—each, every)

Q bankruptcy or receivership (stock exchange symbol); electric quadruple moment of atomic nucleus (symbol); Fair child (symbol); Polaris correction (symbol); prison at San Quentin, California; quadrillion; Quaker Line; quality factor; quantity; quarantine; Quartermaster, quartile variation (symbol); Quebec—code for letter Q; Queen; Queensland; question(s); quetzal (Guatemalan monetary unit named after this plume-tailed bird); quotient; radio inductive reactance to resistance (symbol); semi-interquartile range (symbol); target or drone (symbol); thermoelectric power (symbol)

Q *(Q)* quantity (microeconomics)

Q (Latin—Quintus); pseudonym for Sir Arthur Quiller-Couch; *Quai* (French— embankment or quay); *quetzal* (Guatemalan monetary unit); torque (symbol)

Q1 quintal (Spanish—hundred-weight)

Q_1, Q_2, Q_3, Q_4 first quartile, second quartile, third quartile, fourth quartile

q²h quaque secunda hora (Latin —every two hours)

q³h quaque tertia hora (Latin— every three hours)

q⁴h quaque quarta hora (Latin— every four hours)

qa quality assurance; quick-acting; quiescent aerial

q & a question and answer

QA Qualification Approval; Qualified Acceptance; Quality Assurance; Quarters Allowance

Q-A Quint-A

Q & A question and answer

QAA Quality Assurance Assistant

QAB Quality Assurance Board; Quality Assurance Bulletin; Queen Anne's Bounty (for indigent clergymen)

qac quaternary ammonium compound

QAC Quality Assurance Check(ing); Quality Assurance Code; Quality Assurance Coding; Queensland Arts Council

QACA Queensland Amateur Cyclists Association

QACAD Quality-Assurance Corrective-Action Document

QACC Queensland Automobile Chamber of Commerce

qad quick-attach-detach

QAD Quality Assurance Data; Quality Assurance Department; Quality Assurance Directive; Quality Assurance Division

QADC Queen's Aide-de-Camp

QADI Quality Assurance Department Instruction

qadk quick attach-detach kit

QADS Quality Assurance Data Summary; Quality Assurance Data System

QAE Quality Assurance Engineer(ing)

qaf quality-assurance firing

QAFCO Quatar Fertilizer Company

QAFL Queensland Australian Football League

qafo quality-assurance field operation(s)

QAG Quaker Action Group

QAGA Queensland Amateur Gymnastic Association

qagc quiet automatic gain control

Qahira El Qahira (Egyptian Arabic—Cairo)

QAI Quality Assurance Instruction; Queen's Award to Industry

QAICG Quality Assurance Interface Coordination Group

QAIMNS Queen Alexandra's Imperial Military Nursing Service

QAIP Quality Assurance Inspection Procedure

qak quick-attach kit

qal quartz aircraft lamp; quaternary alluvium

qal quintal (French—hundred-weight)

QAL Quality Assurance Laboratory; Quarterly Accession List; Quebec Airways Limited; Queensland Alumina Limited

QALAS Qualified Associate of the Land Agents' Society

QALD Quality-Assurance Liaison Division (DNA)

qall quartz aircraft landing

lamp

QALTR Quality Assurance Laboratory Test Request

qam quadrature amplitude modulation; queued access method

QAM Quality Assurance Manager; Quality Assurance Manual; Quality Assurance Monitor

QAM Quality Assurance Manual

QAMIS Quality Assurance Monitoring Information System

QAMS Quad-Phase Amplitude Modulation System

QANTAS Queensland And Northern Territories Aerial Services

qao quality assurance operation

QAO Quality Assurance Office (USN)

QAOC Quality Assurance Overview Contractor

QAOP Quality Assurance Operating Procedure

qap quinine, atebrin, plasmoquine (malaria treatment)

QAP Quality Assurance Planning; Quality Assurance Procedure(s); Quality Assurance Program

QA & P Quanah, Acme & Pacific (railroad)

QAPL Queensland Airlines Proprietary Limited

QAPP Quality Assurance Program Plan(ning)

QAPS Queensland Association of Personnel Services

qar quick-access recording

QAR Quality Assurance Representative

QAR Quality Assurance Report

QARAFNS Queen Alexandra's Royal Air Force Nursing Service

QARANC Queen Alexandra's Royal Army Nursing Service

QARNNS Queen Alexandra's Royal Naval Nursing Service

qas quick-acting scuttle

QAs Queen Alexandra's

QAS Quality Answering System; Quality Assurance Service; Quality Assurance System; Question Answering System

QASA Queensland Amateur Swimming Association

QASAR Quality Assurance Systems Analysis Review

QASP Quality Assurance Standard Practice

QAST Quality Assurance Service Test(s)

Qat Qatar

QAT Qualification Approval Test; Quantitative Assessment and Training Center

Qatar State of Qatar (oil-productive Persian Gulf country whose Arabs speak Arabic as well as some Farsi Persian, per capita income is second only to the adjacent United Arab Emirates)

Qatar Ports Ad Dawhah and Musayid

QATB Queensland Ambulance Transport Brigade

QATP Quality Assurance Technical Publication(s); Quality Assurance Test Procedure(s)

Qattara short form for the Qattara Depression in northern Egypt's Libyan Desert

qavc quiet automatic volume control

QAVT Qualification Acceptance Vibration Test

QAWA Queensland Amateur Wrestling Association

qax quacks

qb qualified bidders; quarterback; quick break

QB Queensboro Bridge (New York City); Quiet Birdmen (glider enthusiasts)

Q.B. Queen's Bench

QBA Quebecair; Queensland Bowling Association

QBAA Quality Brands Associates of America

QBAC Quality Bakers of America Cooperative

Q-band 36,000–46,000 mc

QBB Queensland Butter Board

Qbc Quebec

QBD Queen's Bench Division; Queensland Book Depot

qbi quite bloody impossible

QBL Qualified Bidder's List

Q-boats mystery ships used in antisubmarine warfare by the British in World War I

qbop quality basic-oxygen process

QBRs Queen's Bench Reports

qb's quarterbacks

QBSM que besa su mano (Spanish—who kisses your hand)—used in closing personal letters

QBSP que besa sus pies (Spanish—who kisses your feet)—used in closing personal letters

qc qualification course; quality control; quantitative command; quantum counter; quartz crystal; quick connect;

quit claim

q/c quick change

qc qualcosa (Italian—something)

Qc impact pressure (symbol)

QC Quadrantal Correction(s); Quality Control; Quartermaster Corps; Québec Central (railroad); Queens College; Queen's College; Quezon City; Quincy College; Quinnipiac College; Quit Claim

Q.C. Queen's Counsel

QCA Queen Charlotte Airlines; Queensland Coal Associates; Queensland Cricket Association; Queensland Croquet Association

Q-cab quiet (tractor) cab

Q-card qualification card

qcb (QCB) queue control block (data processing)

QCB Quality Control Bulletin

QCBC Queen's Commendation for Brave Conduct

qcbm quick-connects bulkhead mounting

qcc qualification correlation certification; quick-connect coupling(s)

QCC Queensborough Community College; Queensland Conservation Council; Quinsigamond Community College

QCCA Queensland Cleaning Contractors Association

QCCARS Quality Control Collection Analysis and Reporting System

qcd quality-control data; quantum chromodynamics; quit-claim deed

QCD Quality Control Directive; quit claim deed

QCDI Quality Control Departmental Instruction

QCDR Quality Control Deficiency Report

QCE Quality Control Engineering

QCEU Queensland Colliery Employees Union

qcf quartz-crystal filter

QCF Quality Control Form

qcfo quartz-crystal frequency oscillator

QCGC Queensland Cane-Growers Council

qch quick-connect handle

QCH Queen Charlotte's Hospital

qci quality-control information

QCI Quality Conformance Inspection; Queensland Confederation of Industry; Quota Club International

Q Cic Quintus Tullius Cicero (the brother of the Roman orator Marcus Tullius Cicero)

QCIM *Quarterly Cumulative Index Medicus*

QC Isl Queen Charlotte Islands

Q City Quezon City, Philippines

qck quick-connect kit

qcl quality-control level

Q-class NATO name for Soviet Québec-type submarines

Q-clearance Department of Energy's highest security classification; highest security clearance from the FBI

QCM Quality Control Manager; Queensland Coal Mining

QCM *Quality Control Manual*

QCMA Queensland Cooperative Milling Association

QCNIC Quad-Cities Nuclear Information Center

qco quartz-crystal oscillator

Q Co Queens County

QCO Quality Completion Order; Quality Control Officer

QCOP Quality Control Operating Procedure

QCP Quality Control Procedure; Queens College Press

QCPE Quantum Chemistry Program Exchange

Qc/Ps impact/static pressure ratio (symbol)

QCPSA Quaker Center for Prisoner Support Activities

qcr quick-change response

qcr (QCR) quality control/reliability

QCR Quality Control Representative

QC/R Quality Control/Reliability

QC & R Quality Control and Reliability

QCRC Québec Central Railway Company

QC Rep Quality-Control Representative

QC Rept Quality-Control Report

qcrt quick-change real time

QC Ry Québec Central Railway

QCS Quality Control Standard; Quality Control System; Quality Cost System

QCSO Quality Control Stop Order

QCSR Quaker Committee on Social Rehabilitation

QCSSO Queensland Council of State School Organizations

QC Stand Quality-Control Standard

qct quiescent carrier telephony; questionable corrective task

QCT Quality Control Technology

QC & T Quality Control and Test

QCTR Quality Control Test Report

qcu quartz crystal unit; quick-change unit

qcus quartz crystal unit set

qcvc quick-connect valve coupler

qcw quadrant continuous wave

QCWA Quarter-Century Wireless Association; Queensland Country Women's Association

Qcy Quincy

QCYC Queen City Yacht Club; Queensland Cruising Yacht Club

qd quarterdeck; quartile deviation; questioned document; quick delivery; quick detachable (weapon)

q-d quick-disconnect

q & d quick and dirty

q.d. *quater in die* (Latin—four times a day)

QD Sadios Transportes Aéreos

qda quantity discount agreement

qdc quick dependable communication(s); quick-disconnect cap; quick-disconnect connector; quick-disconnect coupling

qdcc quick-disconnect circular connection

qdc's quick, dependable, communications

qdd qualified for deep diving; quantized decision detection

QDG Queen's Dragoon Guards

QD/GD Quincy Division/General Dynamics

qdh quick-disconnect handle

qdk quick-disconnect kit

qdn quick-disconnect nipple

qdo quadripartite development objective

q^{do} *quando* (Portuguese or Spanish—when)

Qd'O Quai d'Orsay

QDO Queensland Dairymens Organisation

qdp quick-disconnect pivot

QDR Quality Deficiency Report

QDRI Qualitative Development Requirements Information (program)

qdrnt quadrant

qds quick-disconnect series; quick-disconnect swivel

qd's questioned documents

QDS Quality Data System; Quantitative Decision System

qdta quantitative differential thermal analysis

qdv quick disconnect valve

qe quadrant elevation; quick estimate

q.e. *quod est* (Latin—which is)

QE Quality Engineer(ing); Quality Evaluation

QE2 *Queen Elizabeth 2* (passenger vessel)

QEA Qantas Empire Airways

qeav quick—exhaust air valve

qec quick engine change

QEC Queen Elizabeth College

qecu quick engine-change unit

qed quantitative evaluative device; quantum electrodynamics; quick-reaction dome

q.e.d. *quod erat demonstrandum* (Latin—that which was to be proved)

QED Quality, Efficiency, Dependability (reliability program)

qee quadruple expansion engine

q.e.f. *quod erat faciendum* (Latin —that which was to be done)

QEF Queensland Employers Federation

QEFD Queen Elizabeth's Foundation for the Disabled

QEH Queen Elizabeth Hall

q.e.i. *quod erat inveniendum* (Latin—that which was to be discovered)

qel quiet extended life

QEL Quality Evaluation Laboratory

qem quadrant electrometer

QEM Qualified Export Manager

QENP Queen Elizabeth National Park (Uganda)

qeo quality engineering operations

QEONS Queen Elizabeth's Overseas Nursing Service

QEOP Quartermaster Emergency Operation Plan

QEP Quality Evaluation Program; Quality Examination Program; Queen Elizabeth Park; Queen Elizabeth Planetarium; Queensland Environmental Program

qer qualitative equipment requirements

QER *Quarterly Economic Review*

qescp quality engineering significant control points

QESP Queen Emma Summer

Palace
QEST Quality Evaluation System Test(s)
QESTS Query, Update Entry, Search, Time Sharing
QET Queen Elizabeth Theatre (Vancouver)
qev quick exhaust valve
QEW Queen Elizabeth Way (Canadian highway linking Buffalo with Toronto)
qf quality factor; quench frequency; quick freeze; quick frozen
QF quick-firing
qfa quality per final article
Q-factor quality rating
q-fastener(s) quick-fastener(s)
qfc quantitative flight characteristics
qfcc quantitative flight characteristics criteria
qfe quartz fiber electrometer
Q-fellows quartermaster fellows; queer fellows
Q fever query fever (of uncertain cause); Balkan grippe or nine-mile fever (viral disease with pneumonial symptoms caused by rickettsia)
qff quadruple flip-flop
QFGA Queensland Farmers and Graziers Association
QFI Qualified Flight Instructor
qfirc quick-fix interference-reduction capability
qfl quasi-fermi level
qfm quantized frequency modulation
qfo quartz frequency oscillator
qfp quartz fiber product
QFP Quick-Fix Program
QFR Quarterly Force Revision (USN)
Q-fract quick fraction (membrane potentials)
QFRI Queensland Fisheries Research Institute
QFS Queensland Fire Service; Queensland Fisheries Service
QFSM Queen's Fire Services Medal
qft quantized field theory
qg quadrature grid
QG Quartermaster General
QG Quartier Général (French—Headquarters); *Quartier Generale* (Italian—Headquarters)
qgb searchlight sonar (symbol)
QGGA Queensland Grain Growers Association
qgm quarter-girth measure
QGM Queen's Gallantry Medal
QGPO Quatar General Petroleum Organization
QGTB Queensland Government Tourist Bureau

qgv quantized gate video
qh quartz helix
q-h quartz-halogen (lights)
q.h. quaque hora (Latin—every hour)
QH Queen's Hall
QHC Queen's Honorary Chaplain; Queensland Housing Commission
QHDS Queen's Honorary Dental Surgeon
QHM Queen's Harbour Master
QHNS Queen's Honorary Nursing Sister
QHP Queen's Honorary Physician
QHS Queen's Honorary Surgeon; Queensland Historical Society
QHV Queen's Honorary Veterinarian
qi quality improvement; quality indices
QI Queensland Insurance; Quota International
QI Quality Index; Quarterly Index
QIA Queensland Institute of Architects
qiam queued indexed access memory
qic quality inspection criteria; quartz-iodine crystal
QIC Quality Information Center
q.i.d. quater in die (Latin—four times a day)
QIDN Queen's Institute of District Nursing
qie quantitative immuno-electrophoresis
QIE Qualified International Executive
QIER Queensland Institute for Educational Research
qil quartz incandescent lamp; quartz iodine lamp
QIMR Queensland Institute of Medical Research
Qingdao (Pinyin Chinese—Tsingtao)
Qinghai (Pinyin Chinese—Chinghai)
qip quartz insulation part
QIP Quality Inspection Point
Q.I.P. Quiescat in Pace (Latin—Rest in Peace)
QIPA Queensland Institute of Public Affairs
QIPS Qualitative Incentive Procurement Service
Qiqihar (Pinyin Chinese—Chichihar)
QIR Quechan Indian Reservation (originally Fort Yuma)

qisam queued-indexed sequential-access method
qit qualification information and test (system)
QIT Queensland Institute of Technology
QITS Quality Information and Test System
QJC Quincy Junior College
QJSA Quarterly Journal of Studies in Alcohol
qjump queue(d) jump(ing)
qk quick
Qk Fl quick flashing (light)
qkly quickly
qkm Quadratkilometer (German—square kilometers)
ql quarrel; query language; quick look; quintal
ql (QL) quantum leap
ql quilate (Portuguese—carat)
q.l. quantum libet (Latin—as much as you like)
QL Queen's Lancers
Q/L Quarantine Launch
Q'land Queensland
QLAP Quick Look Analysis Program
QLCS Quick Look and Checkout System
Qld Queensland
qlfy qualify
qlfyg qualifying
qlfyn qualification
QLGA Queensland Local Government Association
qli quality of life index
qlii quasi-laser-intensity interferometer
qlit quick-look intermediate tape
qll quartz landing lamp
qlm quasi-laser machine
QLOC Queensland Light Opera Company
QLPC Queensland Library Promotion Council
QLR Queen's Lancashire Regiment
QLR Québec Law Reports
QLS Queensland Law Society; Queensland Littoral Society; Quick Law Systems; Quick Loading System
qlsm quasi-laser sequential machine
qlt quantitative leak test
QLTA Queensland Lawn Tennis Association
qlty quality
qm (QM) quantum mechanics; query message
qm Quadratmeter (German—square meter); *quintal métrico* (Spanish—metric quintal, 220 pounds)

q.m. quaque mane (Latin—every morning); *quo modo* (Latin—in what manner)

QM Decca navigation system; Quartermaster; Queen's Messenger; Queens Museum

qma qualified military available; quality material approach

QMA Quartermasters Association; Quatar Monetary Agency

QMAAC Queen Mary's Army Auxiliary Corps

QMAC Quadripartite Material and Agreements Committee

qmao qualified for mobilization ashore only

Q-max quarantine maximum

qmb quick make-and-break

QMBA Queensland Master Builders Association

QMC Quartermaster Corps

QMC & SO Quartermaster Cataloging and Standardization Office

QMDEP Quartermaster Depot

qmdk quick mechanical disconnect kit

QMDO Qualitative Material Development Objective

QMDPC Quartermaster Data Processing Center

qme queueing matrix evaluation

QME Quantock Marine Enterprises

QMEPCC Quartermaster Equipment and Parts Commodity Center

QMFCI Quartermaster Food and Container Institute

QMFCIAF Quartermaster Food and Container Institute for the Armed Forces

QMG Quartermaster General

QMGF Quartermaster-General to the Forces

QMGMC Quartermaster General—Marine Corps

QMH Queen Mary Hospital

QMI Qualification Maintainability Inspection

QMIA Queensland Motor Industry Association

QMIMSO Quartermaster Industrial Mobilization Services Offices

qmo qualitative material objective

QMORC Quartermaster Officers Reserve Corps

QMP Quezon Memorial Park (Philippines)

QMPA Quartermaster Purchasing Agency; Queensland Master Painters Association

QMPCUSA Quartermaster Petroleum Center US Army

qmqb quick-make quick-break (connection)

qmr qualitative materiel requirement

Qmr Quartermaster

QMRC Quartermaster Reserve Corps

QMR & E Quartermaster Research and Engineering

QMRL Quartermaster Radiation Laboratory

QMs Quarterly Meetings (Quakers); quartermasters

QMS Quartermaster School (US Army)

Qm Sgt Quartermaster Sergeant

QMSO Quartermaster Supply Office(r)

qmsw quartz metal sealed window

QMT Queens-Midtown Tunnel

QMTOE Quartermaster Table of Organization and Equipment

qmw quartz metal window

qn question, quotation

q.n. quaque nocte (Latin—every night); *quid nunc* (Latin—what now?)—person eternally interested in getting the latest news

Qn Queen

qna quality per next assembly

QNP Quezon National Park (Philippines)

qns quantity not sufficient

Qns Queens

QNS Queen's Nursing Sister

Qns Coll Queen's College

Qnsd Queensland

Qnsk Quensk (language of the Quains)

QNS & L Québec North Shore and Labrador Railway

Qnsld Queensland

Qns Pk Queens Park

qnt quantisizer

qnty quantity

QNWR Quivira National Wildlife Refuge (Kansas)

qo quick opening; quick outlet

QO Quaker Oats; Qualified in Ordnance; Quartermaster Operation; Queen's Own (regiment)

Q & O Québec and Ontario (transportation company)

qO$_2$ oxygen quotient

QO$_2$ oxygen consumption (or quota)

QOA Quasi-Official Agencies

QOCH Queen's Own Cameron Highlanders

qod quick-opening device

QOD Québec Order of Dentists

QOF Quaker Oats Foundation

QOH Queen's Own Hussars

QOIC Quarantine Officer in Charge

QOMY Queen's Own Mercian Yeomanry

qon quarter ocean net

qopri qualitative operational requirement(s)

qor qualitative operational requirement

Qor Qoran (Koran)

QOR Queen's Own Royal (regiment)

QORC Queen's Own Rifles of Canada

QOS Quick On System

qot quote

qotn quotation

qp queen post; quick process(ing)

q.p. quantum placet (Latin—at discretion)

q-P quanti-Pirquet (reaction)

QP Qualification Proposal; Queen's Printer

qpa qualitative point average; quantity per article; quantity per assembly

QPA Queensland Police Academy; Queensland Polynesian Association

QPB Quality Paperback (book club)

QPC Quatar Petroleum Company

qpei quality per end item

qpf quantitative precipitation forecast

QPF Québec Police Force

QPFC Queen's Park Football Club

QPFL Queensland Professional Fishermens League

qpi quadratic performance index

QPIS Quality Performance Instruction Sheet

QPL Qualified Parts List; Qualified Product(s) List(ing); Queens Public Library

qplt quiet propulsion lift technology

QPM Queen's Polar Medal; Queen's Police Medal

QPP Québec Provincial Police; Quetico Provincial Park (Ontario)

QPR Quality Progress Report; Quantity Progress Report; Quarterly Progress Report; Queen's Park Rangers

QPRI Qualitative Personnel Requirements Information

qps quantitative physical science

QPS Quick Program Search

qpsk quad-phase shift key

qq quartos; questionable questionnaires; questions

qq quelques (French—some); *quintales* (Spanish—quintals)

qq. quaque (Latin—each); *quoque* (Latin—every)

QQ Celestial Equator; Qara Qash in Sinkiang province of China; Qara Qum, also in Sinkiang province of China, but sometimes spelled Kara Kum; Que Que, Rhodesia

q.q.d. quantum quatra die (Latin—every fourth day)

qqf quelquefois (French—sometimes)

q.q.h. quantum quatra hora (Latin—every four hours)

qq. hor. quaque hora (Latin—every hour)

qqma quality qualified military availability

qqpr quantitative and qualitative personnel requirements

q.q.v. quae vide (Latin—which see)

q/qy question/query

qr qualifications record; quarter(ly); quick reaction; quick receipt; quire

qr (QR) quick response

qr. quadrans (Latin—farthing)

q.r. quantum rectus (Latin—quantity is correct)

QR Queensland Railways; Quintana Roo; Quotation Request

Q & R Quality and Reliability

QR Quarterly Review

qra quality reliability assurance; quick reaction alert

QRA Queensland Rifle Association

qrbm quasi-random band model

qrc quick reaction capability

QRC Queensland Rubber Company

qrcg quasi-random code generator

QRCUP Québec Region Canadian University Press (now CUPBEQ)

QRDC Quartermaster Research and Development Command

QRDEA Quartermaster Research and Development Evaluation Agency

QRDS Quarterly Review of Drilling Statistics

qrg quick response graphic

qrga quadrupole residual gas analyzer

qri qualitative requirements information

qric quick reaction installation capability

QRICC Quick Reaction Inventory Control Center

QRIH Queen's Royal Irish Hussars

QRL Quadripartite Research List; Queensland Research League

QRMF Quick-Reacting Mobile Force

Qrmr Quartermaster

qro quick reaction operation

Qro Queretaro

QRO Quick Reaction Operation; Quick Reaction Organization

Q Roo Quintana Roo

Q-room cue room (billiard room)

QRPA Quartermaster Radiation Planning Agency

QRPS Quick Reaction Procurement System

QRR Queen's Royal Rifles

QRRR extreme emergency amateur radio call signal

QRRs Qualitative Research Requirements (for nuclear weapons effects information)

qrs quarters

QR's Quality Reports

qrt quarter

QRT Quick Reaction Team

qrtg quartering

qrtly quarterly

qrtmstr quartermaster

qrv quick-release valve

QRV Qualified Real-estate Valuer

QRX Queensland Railfast Express

qry quality and reliability year

QRZ Quaddel Reaktion Zeit (German—lump reaction time, rash reaction time, wheal reaction time)

qs quarter section; quarter sessions

qs (QS) quadraphonic stereo; quiet sleep

q.s. quantum satis (Latin—as much as is sufficient); *quantum sufficit* (Latin—as much as suffices)

Qs Conquistadores; Conquistadors; questions

QS Quarantine Station; Quarter Section; Quarter Sessions; Quartermaster Sergeant; Queen's Scarf; Queen's Scholar; Queensland Society; Queueing System

QS Quecksilbersäule (German—mercury column)

QSA Queensland Shopkeepers Association

QSAL Quadripartite Standardization Agreements List

qsam queued sequential access method

Qsar Tehran, Iran's great prison

qsbg quasi-stellar blue galaxies

qsbo quasi-stellar blue objects

QSC Quebec Securities Commission

QSD Quality Surveillance Division (USN); Quincy Shipbuilding Division—General Dynamics

qse qualified scientists and engineers

qsf quasi-static field; quasi-stationary front

QSF Queensland Soccer Federation

qsg quasi-stellar galaxy

Q-ship disguised man-of-war used to decoy enemy vessels

qsi quality salary increase

qsic quality standard inspection criteria

Q-size Queen-size

QSJM Queen's Silver Jubilee Medal

qs & l quarters, subsistence, and laundry

QSL Queensland State Library

Q & SL Qualifications and Standards Laboratory

qsm quadruple-screw motorship; quarter-square multipliers

qsm (QSM) Queen's Service Medal

QSMO Quaker State Motor Oils

qso quasibiennial stratospheric oscillation; quasistellar object

QSO Québec Symphony Orchestra

QSOP Quadripartite Standing Operating Procedure(s)

qsp quality search procedure

QSPP Québec Society for the Protection of Plants

qsr quick-strike reconnaissance

QSR Quarterly Status Report; Quarterly Summary Report

QSR Quartier de Securité Renforcée (French—Maximum Security Prison)

qsra quiet short-haul research aircraft

qsrs quasi-stellar radio sources

qss quasi-stellar source

QSS quadruple-screw ship; Quota Sample Survey

qssa quasi-stationary-state approximation

QSSCT Queensland Society of Sugar Cane Technologists

qssp quasi-solid-state panel

QSSR Quarterly Stock Status Report

QST Québec Standard Test

QSTAG Quadripartite Standardization Agreement

Q-star quiet observation aircraft

qstn question

qstnr questionnaire

qstol quiet-and-short takeoff and landing

qsts quadruple-screw turbine steamship

q. suff. *quantum sufficit* (Latin—as much as needed, as much as will suffice)

Q-switch quantum switch

qsy quiet sun year

qt quality test(ing); quantity; quarry tile; quart; quick test; quiet (*see* q.t.)

qt (QT) quality test(ing); queuing theory

q.t. quiet (as "on the q.t.")

q & t quenched and tempered

QT Qualification Test(ing); Quick's Test (pregnancy or prothrombin)

qta quadrant transformer assembly

q^ta *quanta* (Portuguese or Spanish—how much)—feminine form

QTAC Queensland Tertiary Admissions Centre

qtam queued telecommunication access method

q^taux *quintaux* (French—quintals)

qth quarry-tile base

QTB Queensland Timber Board; Queensland Trotting Board

QTC Quebec Teaching Congress; Queensland Turf Club

qtd quartered

QTDGs Quaker Theological Discussion Groups

qte quote

qted quick text editor; quoted

Q-Test(ing) Quality Test(ing)

qtf quarry-tile floor

QTF Québec Teachers' Federation

qtg quoting

QTIB Québec Tourist Information Bureau

QTLC Queensland Trades and Labor Council

qtly quarterly

QTM Quechon Tribal Museum

(Yuma, Arizona)

qtn quotation

qto quarto

q^to *quanto* (Portuguese or Spanish—how much)—masculine form

qtol quiet takeoff and landing

Q'town Queenstown

qtp quantum theory of paramagnetism

QTP Qualification Test Procedure

qtr quarry-tile roof; quarter; quarterly

QTR Quality Technical Report; Quality Technical Requirement; Quarterly Technical Report

qtrs quarters

qts quarts; quick turn stock

QTTC Queensland Tourist and Travel Corporation

qtte quartette

QTTP Q-Tags Test of Personality

qtt(s) quartette(s)

QTU Queensland Teachers Union

qty quantity

qtydesreq quantity desired or requested

qtz quartz

qtze quartzose

qtzic quartzitic

qtzt quartzite

qu quart; quarter; quarterly; query; question

qu. *quasi* (Latin—as it were, like)

Qu Queen

QU Queen's College (Cambridge, Oxford, or elsewhere); Queen's University

qua quadrate; quadratus

quaal quaalude

quaalude trade name of methaqualone (hypnotic and sedative drug)

quack quacksalver (person pretending to be a doctor)

quacks quacksalvers (sixteenth-century doctors who used quicksilver or mercury in treating syphilis)

Quacks CWACs [City-Wide Anti-Crime (units of the New York City Police Department)]

quack-u-p's quack acupuncturists

quackupunc quackupuncture; quackupuncturist (engaging in a fraudulent and misleading racket)

quad quaalude; quadrangle; quadrangular; quadrant; qua-

draphonic; quadrat; quadruplet(s); quadruplicate(s); quadruplication

quad (Latin prefix—fourfold)—as in quadrille or quadriplegic

Qu-AD Quality-Assurance Department; Quality-Assurance Division

quad .50's quadruple .50-caliber machine guns

quad c quadripod cane

Quad Cities adjacent and across-the-river cities of Davenport, East Moline, and Moline, Illinois, plus Davenport in Iowa across the Mississippi River—cities so named because they form a quadrangle

quadplex quadriplex

quadradar four-way radar (surveillance)

Quadrangle Quadrangle/The New York Times Book Company

quadrap quadraphonic(al)(ly)

quadrip quadriplegia

quadrivium the four liberal arts—arithmetic, astronomy, geography, and music

quadrup quadruped(s); quadruple

quadrupl. *quadruplicato* (Latin—four times as much)

quads quadraphonic records; quadruplets

QUADS Quality-Assurance Data System

Quahira (Arabic—Cairo)

Quai d'Orsay section of Paris occupied by French Foreign Ministry

Quail Californians are sometimes nicknamed Quail; California's state bird—the Golden Valley Quail; McDonnell-Douglas decoy missile

Quail Haven Cedar Vale, Kansas

Quaintest City in the U.S. Santa Fé, New Mexico (founded by the Spaniards around 1609)

Quake City San Francisco, California

Quaker Quaker Oats; Quaker Press

Quaker Abolitionists Lucretia Mott, John Greenleaf Whittier, and John Woolman

Quaker City Quaker-founded-and-settled Philadelphia

Quaker Dolley Mrs Dorothea (Dolley) Madison—wife of President James Madison

Quaker Founder George Fox—founder of the Society of Friends who were nicknamed

Quakers by an English judge who persecuted them

Quaker Founder of Pennsylvania William Penn

Quaker Liberal Elias Hicks

Quaker MMs Quaker Monthly Meetings

Quaker Poet Bernard Barton in England and John Greenleaf Whittier in New England

Quaker Preacher Elias Hicks—founder of the Hicksite Friends championing the abolition of slavery and opposing any set creeds approved by the elders

Quaker Reformer Elizabeth Fry —noted for her campaign to better the life of inmates in insane asylums and prisons; also worked for the betterment of education

Quakers members of the Society of Friends

Quaker State Pennsylvania

Quakertown Philadelphia

quake(s) earthquake(s)

'quake(s) earthquake(s)

qual qualification; qualify; quality

qual anal. qualitative analysis

quals qualifying examinations; qualifying tests

qual(s) qualification(s)

quam quadrature-amplitude modulation

Quandary Quandary Peak in central Colorado

quango (QUANGO) quasi-autonomous non-governmental organization

quant quantity; quantum

quant anal. quantitative analysis

Quantico Quantico, Virginia's FBI Academy and U.S. Marine Base

quantras question analysis transformation and search (data processing technique)

quant. suff. *quantum sufficit* (Latin—sufficient quantity)

quaops quarantine operations

QUAP Questionnaire Analysis Program

QUAPs *Quality Assurance Publications*

Quaq *Quaquero* (Spanish—Quaker)

quar quarantine; quarter

quarantine flag yellow flag flown when a vessel requests pratique; letter Q or Québec in the international signal code

quar. pars *quarta pars* (Latin—one-fourth part)

quarpel quartermaster water-repellent (cloth or clothing)

quarr quarries; quarry; quarrying

quart quarter gallon; quarterly

quart. quartet; quartette; quartile

Quart Quarterly

QUART Quality Assurance and Reliability Team

quartz crystalline silica (SiO_2)

quartzite granular quartz rock

quas methaqualone's nickname (also called quacks or quads)

quasar quasi-stellar radio (object)

quaser quantum - amplification - by - stimulated-emission - of - radiation (acronym covering irasers, lasers, and masers varying only in operational frequency)

Quash Quashey; Quashley

quat quaternary; quaternary era

quat. *quattuor* (Latin—four)

Quat Quaternary

Quathlamba   Quathlamba Mountains of Lesotho and South Africa where it is called Drakensberg

QUB Queen's University of Belfast

QUD Queen's University of Dublin

Que Québec (inhabitants—Québecois); Quechua; Quechuan

Que *Quênia* (Portuguese—Kenya)

QUE Quebecair

Quebec letter Q radio code

Québec NATO name for Q-class Soviet submarines

Queen *The Queen* (La Reine)—Haydn's Symphony No. 85 in B-flat major

Queen of the Adriatic Venice

Queen Alice Alice Lee (Roosevelt) Longworth

Queen of the Amazons Hippolyta

Queen of the Angels the Virgin Mary

Queen of the Antilles Cuba

Queen of the Arabian Sea Cochin, India

Queen of Back Bay Isabella Stewart Gardner

Queen of Bases calcium oxide and related compounds known commercially as lime

Queen of Belgian Beaches Ostend

Queen Bess Queen Elizabeth

Queen of the Caribbean SS *Norway* (world's largest cruise ship, formerly SS *France*)

Queen of the Caribbees Nevis

Queen Charlottes Queen Charlotte Islands off British Columbia

Queen City Lahore (in the Punjab of Pakistan)

Queen City of Alabama Gadsden

Queen City of Canada Toronto

Queen City of the Carolinas Charlotte, North Carolina

Queen City of the Hanseatic League Lübeck

Queen City of the Hudson Yonkers, New York

Queen City of India Bombay

Queen City of the Lakes Buffalo, New York and Toronto, Ontario complete for this title

Queen City of the Lehigh Valley Allentown, Pennsylvania

Queen City of the Merrimack Valley Manchester, New Hampshire

Queen City of the Mississippi St Louis, Missouri

Queen City of the Mountains Knoxville, Tennessee

Queen City of New Zealand Auckland

Queen City of the North Edinburgh

Queen City of the Ohio Cincinnati, Ohio

Queen City of the Pacific place-name nickname shared by San Francisco, California and Seattle, Washington

Queen City of the Rio Grande Del Rio, Texas

Queen City of the Sea Charleston, South Carolina where loyal Charlestonians agree the Ashley and the Cooper rivers join to form the Atlantic Ocean

Queen City of the Sound Seattle, Washington on Puget Sound

Queen City of the South Atlanta, Georgia and Sydney, New South Wales, compete for the title

Queen City of the Trails Independence, Missouri where so many homesteaders and pioneers began their westward march to California

Queen City of Vermont Burlington

Queen City of the West Cincinnati (in the early 1800s)

Queen of the Comstock Lode Virginia City, Nevada

Queen of the Cowtowns Fort Dodge, Iowa

Queen of Crime Agatha Christie

Queen of Crossword Puzzledom Margaret Farrar

Queen of the Danube Budapest

Queen Elizabeths Queen Elizabeth Islands in the Canadian Arctic

Queen Emma Curaçao's floating bridge across Willemstad's harbor

Queen of Flowers the rose, according to Sappho and other ancient poets

Queen of the French Riviera Nice

Queen of the Goldfields Melbourne, Victoria, Australia

Queen of Heaven Ashtoreth (Semitic); Astarte (Phoenician); Hera (Greek); Inanna (Sumerian); Ishtar (Assyrian and Babylonian); Isis (Egyptian); Juno (Roman); Virgin Mary (Christian)

Queenie Regina

Queen of the Inland Sea Chicago

Queen of the Kingdom of Death Hel (daughter of Loki in Nordic mythology whose name is used for the Kingdom of Death)

Queen of Kings Cleopatra

Queen of Lake Malaren Stockholm

Queen of Lake Michigan Chicago

Queen of Long-Distance Roads the Appian Way extending from Brindisi to Rome and begun in 312 B.C.

Queen of Love and Lust Aphrodite or Venus

Queen Maud Land Norwegian Antarctica

Queen of the Missions Mission San José in San Antonio, Texas and Mission Santa Barbara in Santa Barbara, California

Queen of the Mississippi St Louis

Queen of the Mountains Helena, Montana

Queen of Mystery Writers Ngaio Marsh

Queen of the North Edinburgh

Queen of the Ohio Cincinnati

Queen of the Plains Regina, Saskatchewan

Queen of the Prairies Canada's Province of Saskatchewan

Queen of Queens Brutus' nickname for Cleopatra

Queen Sarah Sarah, the Duchess of Marlborough

Queensberry (see Marquis of Queensberry)

Queen's Birthday Queen Juliana's Birthday (April 30) celebrated in the Netherlands and its autonomous colonies; Queen Victoria's Birthday (May 20) celebrated in Great Britain and in many Commonwealth countries where it is called Victoria Day

Queensboro' Queensborough

Queen's College Rutgers University in colonial times

Queen's Corsair Sir Francis Drake

Queen of the Sea Islands Beaufort, South Carolina

Queen of the Seas Glasgow (reputed for its Clyde-built ships); Venice—so named during 10th to 15th centuries when Venetians dominated the Mediterranean and brought back all that was fine for the decoration of Venice

queen's English correct English

Queen's House Buckingham Palace

Queen of Skyscrapers Empire State Building

Queensl Queensland

Queen of the South New Orleans

Queen of Spades English title of a Tchaikovsky opera called *La Pique Dame* by the French and *Pikovaya dama* by Russians

Queen of the Spas Saratoga Springs, New York

Queenstown former name of Cobh on Ireland's south coast

Queen of Summer Resorts Newport, Rhode Island

Queen of the Vampires Theda Bara (Theodosia Goodman)

Queen of Watering Places Brighton, England

Queen of the West Longfellow's nickname for Cincinnati

Queermacks Cuyamaca Mountains in California's San Diego County

Quemoy English equivalent of Chin-men Island off the coast of mainland China but belonging to Taiwan

Quen Quentin

Quent San Quentin (California State Prison)

ques question

quest. quality electrical system test; questioned

QUEST Quality Electrical Systems Test; Queens Educational and Social Team

questal quiet, experimental, short-takeoff-and-landing (program of NASA)

questar quantitative utility evaluation suggesting targets for the allocations of resources

quester quick and efficient system to enhance retrieval

questn questionnaire

qufyd qualified

QUGA Queensland United Graziers Association

QUI Queen's University of Ireland; Quincy (railroad)

Quich Quichua

quicha quantitative inhalation challenge apparatus

QUICK Queens University Interpretative Code

quicklime calcium oxide—CaO

quicksilver mercury (Hg)

Quicksilver Bob Robert Fulton's nickname

QUICKTRAN Quick Fortran (programming language)

quico quality improvement through cost optimization

QUIDS Quick Interactive Documentation System

Quiet Quiet Flows the Don (Dzerzhinsky's opera known to Russians as *Tikhiy Don*)

Quiet Americans soft-voiced well-mannered Canadians

Quiet Epidemic medical nickname for Alzheimer's disease afflicting more than four percent of the elderly in the U.S. who suffer in some serious degree from intellectual impairment

Quiet River Russia's quiet-flowing Don

quiktran quick fortran (programming language)

Quilmas San Quilmas (Mexican-Americanism—San Antonio, Texas)

quim química (Portuguese or Spanish—chemistry)

Quimigal Química de Portugal

quin quintet; quintette; quintuplet; quintuplicate; quintuplication

Quin Quincy; Quinten; Quintilianus; Quintilius; Quintillian; Quintin; Quintino; Quintius; Quintus

Quincke's disease edema of the skin; giant hives

quinq quinque (Latin—five)

Quinquad's disease inflammation of the scalp resulting in bald patches

quins quintuplets

quint quintuplicate

quint. *quintus* (Latin—fifth)

Quint. Quintilian—Roman critic and rhetorician Marcus Fabius Quintilianus

Quinten Haydn's String Quartet in D (opus 76, no. 2)—nickname refers to the fifth form or grade in Austrian schools

Quintilian Marcus Fabius Quintilianus

quint(s) quintet(s); quintuplet(s); quintuplicate(s)

quintupl quintuplicate

Quintuplets Herbert Morrison so nicknamed because he did the work of five

quip. query interactive processor; questionnaire interpreter program

Quirinale (Italian—House of the God of War)—Ministry of War in Rome since Roman times

quis quisling (term for traitor derived from Vidkun Quisling who during World War II headed Norway's puppet government set up by the German invaders)

Quisquellano(s) Santo Domingan(s)

Quisqueya Hispaniola's native name

Quitmans Quitman Mountains of west Texas

Quix Quixote

Quixote Don Quixote (Fantastic Variations on a Theme of Knightly Character by Cervantes as composed for 'cello and orchestra by Richard Strauss)

QUJ true course to station

QUL Queen's University Library

Qum (Iranian or Turkish—desert)

qume cue me

Q-unit one quintillion (1 x 10^{18}) —equal to 38.46 billion tons of coal or 172.4 billion tons of oil or 968.9 trillion cubic feet of natural gas

QUNO Quaker United Nations Office

quo' quoth

quod. *quodlibet* (Latin—as you please)

Quoddy Passamaquoddy Bay between Maine and New Brunswick

Quoins Gunners Quoin and Quoin Channel north of Mauritius in the Indian Ocean; other Quoins in Australia, Burma, and South Africa

quok(s) quokka(s)

Quon Pt Quonset Point, Rhode Island

quonset quonset hut (originally built during World War II at Quonset, Rhode Island)

quor quorum

quor. *quorum* (Latin—of which)

quot quotation

quot. *quotidie* (Latin—daily)

quotes quotation marks

quote(s) quotations(s)

quote-unquote quotation marks (slang shortcut—some phrase or word set between quotation marks)

quotid. *quotidie* (Latin—every day)

qup quantity per unit pack

Qur Quran (Malay—Koran)

QUSA "Q" Airways

qv quality verification

q.v. *quantum vis* (Latin—as much as is desired); *quod vide* (Latin—which see)

QVM Queen Victoria Museum (Launceston, Tasmania)

QVR Queen Victoria's Rifles

QVS Quality Verification Surveillance

qvt quality verification test

qw quarter wave

qwa quarter-wave antenna

qwd quarterly world day

q-wedge quartz wedge

qwerty nickname for the standard typewriter keyboard

QWG Quadripartite Working Group

QWGCD Quadripartite Working Group for Combat Development (American, Australian, British, and Canadian armies)

qwl quality of working life; quick weight loss

QWMP Quadruped Walking Machine Program (US Army)

qwot quarter-wave optical thickness

qwp quarter-wave plate

qx *quintaux* (French—hundredweights)

qy quantum yield; query

Qy Quay

QYC Quincy Yacht Club

QYO Queensland Youth Orchestra

qz quartz

Qz quartz

QZ Zambia Airways (2-letter coding)

QZS Québec Zoological Society

R

r angle of reflection (symbol); position vector (symbol); racemic, racket(eer); radius; rain; range; rare; rate of interest; received; recipe; reconnaissance; recto; red; redetermination; refraction, registered, relative, relative humidity; report; reprint; research; reserve; resistance; restricted; retard; retarded; right or starboard side of an airplane or vessel looking forward (R or S); ring; ringer; riser; rod; rook; rough; rule; rules; runs; rupee (Indian monetary unit); rupees; solubilizing agent (symbol)

r (R) retrograde

r angular yaw velocity (symbol); front of the sheet (recto); *remotum* (Latin—far, remote)

R acoustic resistance (symbol); annual rent; electrical resistance; gas constant; ohmic resistance; product moment coefficient of statistical correlation; Rabbi; radioactive range; radiolocation; Rankine; rare; ratio; Réaumur; received solid; reconnaissance; Regina (Queen); registered; Reiz; report(s); Representative; reprint; Republic; Republican; research; reserve; resistance; respiration; restricted; Rex (King); rial (Iranian monetary unit); Richfield Oil; right; ring; river; Road; Robin Line; rocket; Rocketdyne Division of North American Aviation; Roentgen; Roger—radio slang meaning all right or okay; Roma; Roman; Rome; Romeo —code for letter R; Rotary International; Royal; ruble (Rus-

sian monetary unit); rupee (Indian monetary unit); Rwanda; Rydberg; US Rubber Company

R (R) economic rent (microeconomics)

R. rand (South African monetary unit)

-R Rinne's hearing test negative

+R Rinne's hearing test positive

R *rechts* (German—right), *Reka* (Bulgarian, Czechoslovakian, Russian, Serbo-Croatian—river); resultant force (symbol); *rett* (Danish—right); *Ría* (Portuguese—river mouth); *Ría* (Spanish—river mouth); *Rio* (Portuguese—river); *Río* (Spanish—river); *Rivière* (French—river); rogue (designated by the capital letter R branded on British convicts transported overseas in the early 1800s); *Romanus* or *Rufus* (on Latin inscriptions); *rua* (Portuguese—street); *rubeus* (Latin—red); *Rud* (Persian—river); *rue* (French—street); *Rzeka* (Polish—river); symbolic letter on the flag of Rwanda where it stands for Rwanda, a Republic born of Revolution and confirmed by Referendum; The Book of Ruth

R_1 primary roots

R_2 secondary roots

R-4 Recovery and Reuse of Refuse Resources (USN)

ra radio; radioactive; radioactivity; reduced area; right angle; right angulation; right ascension; right atrium; right auri-

cle; robbery committed while armed (RA); rubber-activated; ruling action

ra (RA) retrograde amnesia; rheumatoid arthritis

r/a radioactive; return to author

r & a right and above

Ra radium; Range

RA Argentina (auto plaque); Coast Radar Station (symbol); high-powered radio range (Adcock symbol); Rabbinical Assembly, Real Armada (Yugoslav—Red Army); Rear Admiral; Reduction of Area; Regular Army; Rehabilitation Act; Remington Arms; Rental Agreement; Republic Aviation; República Argentina; Resident Adviser; Resident Auditor; Right Arch; right ascension; Rotogravure Association; Royal Academician; Royal Academy; Royal Arcanum; Royal Artillery; Royal Nepal (2-letter airline code)

RA (A) Rear Admiral (Aircraft Carriers)

RA (D) Rear Admiral (Destroyers)

R.A. right ascension

R/A Redstone Arsenal

r.a.a. *reductio ad absurdum* (Latin—reduction to an absurdity)—in mathematics sometimes appears as raa or RAA

RAA Rabbinical Alliance of America; Royal Academic Association; Royal Academy of Arts; Royal Australian Artillery

RAAA Red Angus Association of America; Relocation Assistance Association of America

RAAC Regional Affirmative Action Clearinghouse; Royal Australian Armoured Corps

RAADC Royal Australian Army Dental Corps

RAAEC Royal Australian Army Educational Corps

RAAF Royal Afghan Air Force; Royal Australian Air Force

RAAFMS Royal Australian Air Force Medical Service

RAAFNS Royal Australian Air Force Nursing Service

RAAFPO Royal Australian Air Force Post Office

RAAMC Royal Australian Army Medical Corps

RAAMS Remote Anti-Armor Mine System

RAANC Royal Australian Army Nursing Corps

RAANS Royal Australian Army Nursing Service

RAAOC Royal Australian Army Ordnance Corps

raap residue arithmetic-associative processor

RAAPS Resource Allocation and Planning System

RAAS Royal Amateur Art Society

RAASC Royal Australian Army Service Corps

rab rabbet(ing)

Rab Rabat, Morocco; Rabaul, New Britain; Rabbi; Rabbinic Hebrew

RAB Radio Advertising Bureau

RAB *Republik Arab Bersatu* (Malay—United Arab Republic)

rabar Raytheon advanced battery acquisition radar

rabb rabbinate; rabbinic; rabbinical

rabbi rapid-access blood-blank information

Rab(bie) Robert

Rabbit Ears short form for Rabbit Ears Mountain or Rabbit Ears Pass in northwestern Colorado

Rabble-Rouser of the Revolution Sam(uel) Adams

RABDF Royal Association of British Dairy Farmers

RABFM Research Association of British Flour Millers

RABI Royal Agricultural Benevolent Institution

RABPCVM Research Association of British Paint Colour and Varnish Manufacturers

rac racemic; radiometric area correlator; relative address

coding; rhomboidal air controller

rac *raccommadage(s)* [French—repair(s)]

RAC Railway Association of Canada; Rear Admiral Commanding; Reliability Action Center; Rent-Adjustment Commission; Republic Aviation Corporation; Research Advisory Council; Research Analysis Corporation; Royal Air Cambodge; Royal Arch Chapter; Royal Armoured Corps; Royal Automobile Club; Rubber Allocation Committee; Rubber Association of Canada

RACA Recovered Alcoholic Clergy Association; Royal Automobile Club of Australia

RACAN Rubber Association of Canada (also RAC)

RACB Royal Automobile Club of Belgium

racc radiation and contamination control

racc *raccomandata* (Italian—registered letter)

RACCA Refrigeration and Air Conditioning Contractors Association

race. random-access computer equipment; rapid automatic checkout equipment

RACE Railways of Australia Container Express; Research on Automatic Computation Electronics

RACE *Real Automóvil Club de España* (Royal Automobile Club of Spain)

racep random access and correlation for extended performance

races. (RACES) radio amateur civil emergency service

racfire tactical fire-direction (system)

RACGP Royal Australian College of General Practitioners

Rachilde Marguerite Vallette

Rachl Rocketdyne advance chemical laser

Rachmaninoff's 3 Rachmaninoff's three symphonies

Rachmaninoff's 4 Rachmaninoff's four piano concertos

RACI Royal Australian Chemical Institute

RACIC Remote Area Conflict Information Center

racine (French—root)

racon radar beacon

RACP Royal Australasian College of Physicians

RACS Remote Access Computing System; Royal Australasian College of Surgeons

RACT Royal Australian Corps of Transport

RACUK Royal Aero Club of the United Kingdom

RACV Royal Automobile Club of Victoria

rad radar; radian; radiation; radiation-absorbed dose; radiator; radical; radicalism; radio; radioactive; radius; radix; rapid-access disc; released from active duty; return to active duty; roentgen-administered dosage; roentgen-administered dose

rad (RAD) rapid access disc

rad. *radix* (Latin—root)

Rad Radnor; Radnorshire

RAD Royal Academy of Dancing; Royal Albert Docks; Rural Area Development

rada radioactive; random-access discrete address

RADA Royal Academy of Dramatic Arts

radac rapid digital automatic computing

radal radio detection and location (system)

radan radar doppler automatic navigator

radant radome antenna

radar radio detection and ranging

RADARS Receivable Accounts Data-entry and Retrieval System

RADAS Random Access Discrete Address System (battlefield communications system)

radat radar data transmission and ranging; radiosonde observation data

radata radar automatic data transmission assembly

RADATS Radar Data-Transmission System

RADC Rome Air Development Center; Royal Army Dental Corps

RADCC Rear Area Damage Control Center

rad-ch radical-changing

Radclyffe Hall Marguerite Radclyffe Hall

RADCM radar countermeasures and deception

RADCOLS Rome Air Development Center on-Line Simulator

radcon radar data converter

RADD Royal Association in Aid of the Deaf and Dumb

raddef radiological defense

raddol raddolcendo (Italian—growing calmer)

Radek communist-party pseudonym of Karl Sobelsohn

radem (RADEM) random access data modulation

rad encl radiator enclosure

radep radar departure

radex radiation exclusion plot (actual or predicted fallout)

radfac radiating facility

radf(s) rapid-access data file(s)

radhaz radiation hazard(s)

radi radiological inspection

radiac radioactivity-detection-indication-and-computation

radial-ply radial-ply tire

Radiat Eff Radiation Effects

RADIC Research and Development Information Center

radic-lib radical liberationist

radic-lib(s) radical-liberal(s); radical-liberationist(s)

radint radar intelligence

Radio Capital Camden, New Jersey

Radio City Radio City Book Store

radiog radiography

radiol radiology

Radio Sci Radio Science

radir random access document indexing and retrieval

radist radar distance indicator

Radiumbad Brambach Brambach, Saxony

RA Dks Royal Albert Docks

radl radiological

rad lab radiation laboratory

radlfo radiological fallout

Rad Lib Radio Liberty

radlib(s) radical liberal(s)

radlic radical liberal

RADLO Radiological Defense Officer

radlop radiological operations

radlsafe radiological safety

radlwar radiological warfare

R Adm Rear Admiral

RADMAPS Radiological Monitoring Assessment Prediction System

radmon radiological monitor(ing)

radn radiation

radnote ratio note

RADOC Regional Air Defense Operations Center

radome radar dome

radon daughter deadly microscopic radioactive uranium particles

radop radar operator

rad op radio operator

radose radiation dosimeter satellite

radot real-time automatic digital-optical tracker

RadPropCast radio propagation forecast

RADR Royal Association for Disability and Rehabilitation

rad rec radiator recess

RADRON Radar Squadron (USAF)

radru rapid-access data-retrieval unit

rad/s radians per second

Rad(s) Radical(s)

RADS Ryukyu Air Defense System

radsab radiator sabotage

radscat radiometer-scatterometer sensor

RadSo Radiological Survey Officer

radss radar alphanumeric-display subsystem

radsta radio station

radtel radar telescope

radtt radio teletypewriter

radu radar analysis and detection unit

radvs radar altimeter and doppler velocity sensor

radwar radiological warfare

rae (RAE) radio astronomy explorer

Rae Rachel; Raquelle

RAE Royal Aircraft Establishment; Royal Australian Engineers

RAE Real Academia Española (Royal Spanish Academy)

R Ae C Royal Aero Club

RAEC Royal Army Educational Corps

Raedwulf (Early English—Ralph)—this redwolf alleged to be the imp of mischief in a printing house

RAEL Real Academia Española de la Lengua (Royal Spanish Academy of Language)

RAEME Royal Australian Electrical and Mechanical Engineers

RAeS Royal Aeronautical Society

raet range-azimuth-elevation-time

Raf Rafael; Rafe; Rafelsz; Raffaele; Raffaello

RAF Red Army Fraction (Baader-Meinhof terrorists); Regular Air Force; Royal Aircraft Factory; Royal Air Force

RAF Rote Armee Fraktion (German—Red Army Faction)—underground terrorist group sometimes nicknamed Hitler's children

RAFA Royal Air Force Association; Royal Australian Field Artillery

rafar radar-automated facsimile reproduction; radio-automated facsimile and reproduction

rafax radar facsimile transmission

RAFB Randolph Air Force Base

RAFBF Royal Air Force Benevolent Fund

RAFC Royal Air Force College

Rafe Ralph

RAFES Royal Air Force Educational Service

Raffaello Raphael

Raffles Raffles Hotel; Raffles Institution (Singapore Institution and Library); Raffles Place; Sir Thomas Stamford Raffles (founder of Singapore)

RAFGSA Royal Air Force Gliding and Souring Association

Raf¹ Rafael

RAFMS Royal Air Force Medical Services

RAFO Reserve of Air Force Officers

rafos long-range navigation system (sofar reversed)

RAFR Royal Air Force Regiment

RAFRO Royal Air Force Reserve of Officers

RAFS Royal Air Force Station

RAFSAA Royal Air Force Small Arms Association

RAFSC Royal Air Force Staff College

RAFSE Royal Air Force School of Education

raft. recom algebraic formula translation; recom algebraic formula translator

RAFT Regional Accounting and Finance Test

RAFTC Royal Air Force Technical College

RAFVR Royal Air Force Volunteer Reserve

rag. ragtime; ring airfoil grenade; runaway arresting gear

rag ragioniere (Italian—accountant)

RAG Red Army Group (see *B-M R*); River Assault Group; Royal and Ancient Game (of golf)

RAGA Royal Australian Garrison Artillery

RAGB Refractories Association of Great Britain

RAGC Royal and Ancient Golf

Club (St Andrews, Scotland)

RAGE Radio Amplification of Gamma Emissions

ragheads turbaned Arabs

Ragnarok end of the world in Norse mythology; equivalent to Twilight of the Gods (Götterdämmerung)

Ragsdale Albany, Georgia's redlight district

Ragusa English and Italian place-name equivalent of Dubrovnik

rah hurrah (as in *rah, rah, rah*)

RAH Royal Albert Hall

RAHS Royal Australian Historical Society

Rahway New Jersey State Prison at Rahway

rai radioactive interference; random access and inquiry

RAI Reading Association of Ireland (actually the International Reading Association but for fear of abbreviatorial confusion with another IRA the initials RAI are used); Royal Australian Infantry

RAI Radiotelevisione Italiana (Italian Radio-Television)—broadcasting system; *Réseau Aérien Interinsulaire* (Tahiti); Royal Albert Institution; Royal Anthropological Institute

RAIA Royal Australian Institute of Architects

RAIAD Reverse Acronyms, Initialisms, and Abbreviations Dictionary

RAIC Royal Architectural Institute of Canada

raidex raiders exercise

rail. railroad; railway

RAIL Religion In American Life

Railroad City nickname given by railroaders to cities such as Atlanta, Boston, Buffalo, Chicago, Cincinnati, Cleveland, Detroit, Edmonton, Houston, Indianapolis, Kansas City, Los Angeles, Milwaukee, Minneapolis, Montreal, New Orleans, New York, Omaha, Philadelphia, St Louis, San Antonio, San Francisco, Seattle, Toronto, Washington, D.C., Winnipeg; (*see* Railway City)

rails. runway alignment indicator lights

Railsplitter Abraham Lincoln

railwayac railway + maniac (railway fan)

Railway Employees Union

Brotherhood of Railway, Airline, and Steamship Clerks, Freight Handlers, Express, and Station Employees

Railway King George Hudson

Rain Violin and Piano Sonata in G (opus 78) by Brahms who uses the theme of his *Regenlied* or Rain Song

Rainbow Bridge Rainbow Bridge National Monument (world's largest natural bridge located in southern Utah and on the Colorado River close to the Arizona border)

Raindrop Chopin's Piano Prelude No. 15 in D-flat major

rair remote access/immediate response

rair (RAIR) ram-augmented interstellar rocket

RAIRS Recordak Automated Information Retrieval System

RAI-TV Radio Audizioni Italiane—TV (Italian Radio Audition—TV)

raiu radioactive iodine uptake

Raj Rajasthan

Raj Rajah (Arabic—seventh month of the Mohammedan year); Rajah (Hindi—king, prince, ruler); Rajasthani (culture, language, or people); or in phrases such as the *British Raj*—the period of British rule in India

RAJ Royal Association of Justices

Rajah Rogers Hornsby

ra k raised keel

RAK Rikets Allmänna Kartverk (Swedish—Geographical Survey Office)

Rakata (Malay—Krakatoa)

Rakóczy traditional Hungarian march used by Berlioz in his *Damnation of Faust* and by Liszt in his Hungarian Rhapsody No. 15 in A minor

ral resorcyclic acid lactone

Ral Raleigh

RAL Resort Airlines; Royal Air Laos

Ralegh Sir Walter Raleigh (who spelled his name *Ralegh*)

Raleigh North Carolina's capital

Raliks Ralik Chain of Islands in the west-central Pacific, including Bikini, Eniwetok, Jaluit, Kwajalein, Rongerik

RALIP Resource and Land Information Program; Resources and Land Investigations Program

RALLA Regional Allied Long-

Lines Agency

rallo. rallentando (Italian—slower by degrees)

ralph reduction and acquisition of lunar pulse heights

RALPH Royal Association for the Longevity and Preservation of the Honeymooners

Ralph Connor Charles W Gordon

Ralph Iron Olive Schreiner's pseudonym

Ralph Marlowe Ralph Manheim

Ralph Rashleigh James Tucker's pseudonym

ralu register and arithmetic logic unit

ralv rat leukemia virus

ram. radio attenuation measurement; random access memory; rapid area maintenance; right ascension of the meridian

ram. (RAM) research and applications module; reverse-annuity mortgage; rolling airframe missile

Ram Raman effect in spectrum analysis; Ramona; Ramsgate

RAM Reliability, Availability, Maintainability (program); Revolutionary Action Movement; Rodrigo A Muñoz; Royal Academy of Music; Royal Air Maroc; Royal Arch Masons; Royal Australian Mint

RAMA Rome Air Materiel Area

ramac random access memory accounting

Ramapos Ramapo Mountains of New Jersey and New York

Rama's Bridge also called Adam's Bridge; 18-mile chain of shoals in center of 30-mile insular linkage between Coromandel Coast of India and Mannar Island of India; shoals divide Palk Strait from Gulf of Mannar in Indian Ocean; Hindus relate Rama built causeway across these shoals so his Indian army could invade Ceylon and rescue his wife Sita from the demon king Ravana who had ravished her and held her captive; Moslems insist building this bridge was Adam's first task after his expulsion from paradise

ramb(s) rambler(s)

RAMC Royal Army Medical College; Royal Army Medical Corps

ramd reliability, availability, maintainability, durability

RAMIS Rapid-Access Management Information System; Rapid-Automatic Malfunction-Isolation System

ramit rate-aided manually implemented tracking

ramont radiological monitoring

ramp. rate-acceleration measuring pendulum

RAMP Radar Mapping of Panama; Radiation Airborne Measurement Program; Resource Allocation and Management Program; Reverse Annuity Mortgage Program

RAMPAC Realty and Mortgage Investors of the Pacific

rampallion ramp + rapscallion

rampant lion symbol of Great Britain and the British people

RAMPC Raritan Arsenal Maintenance Publication Center

RAMPI Raw Material Price Index

ramps. resources allocation and multiproject scheduling

RAMPS Resources Allocation and Multiproject Scheduling

rams. right ascension of mean sun

Rams Ramsgate

RAMS right ascension mean sun

RAMSA Radio Aeronáutica Mexicana S.A.

RAMSS Royal Alfred Merchant Seamen's Society

ramt rudder-angle master transmitter

ran. reconnaissance-attack navigator; request for authority to negotiate

Ran Rangoon

RAN Royal Australian Navy

Ranally Rand McNally

RANAS Royal Australian Naval Air Squadron

ranc radar attenuation, noise, and clutter

RANC Royal Australian Naval College

Rance Ransom(e)

rancom random communication satellite

Rand Rand McNally; Witwatersrand (Johannesburg)

randam random-access nondestructive advanced memory

RAND Corporation Research and Development Corporation (corporate style insists on use of capital letters as shown)

randid rapid alphanumeric digital indicating device

Randolph Scott Randolph Crance

Random Random House

Randy Randolph

RANF Royal Australian Nursing Federation

Ran Fiennes Sir Ranulph Twistleton-Wykeham-Fiennes

Ranger American program for investigation of the Moon and region between the Moon and the Earth; Texas state policeman

Rangoon Burmese—End of Strife)

'rang(s) boomerang(s)

Ranier Ranier Bancorporation (National Bank of Commerce of Seattle)

RANN Research Applied to National Needs

RANR Royal Australian Naval Reserve

RANRL Royal Australian Navy Research Laboratory

ran's revenue anticipation notes

RANSA Royal Australian Naval Sailing Association

RANSA *Rutas Aéreas Nacionales*

RANT Reentry Antenna Test(ing)

RANVR Royal Australian Naval Volunteer Reserve

RANZCP Royal Australian and New Zealand College of Psychiatrists

rao radio astronomical observatory

RAO Regional Administrative Office(r); Regional Airways Office(r); Rudolf A Oetker (steamship line)

RaOb radiosonde observation

RAOC Royal Army Ordnance Corps

raomp report of accrued obligations—military pay

raot rocker-arm oiling time

RAOU Royal Australasian Ornithologists' Union

rap. from the French *repartie* meaning repartee or retorting with witty comments but used in current slang to mean talking frankly about any topic; rapid; rapport; reactive atmosphere processing; rear area protection; relative accident probability; rupees, annas, pies (Indian currency)

rap. (RAP) random access projector

rap *rapido* (Spanish—rapid)—

fast train

Rap H Rap Brown; Rapids

RAP Radiological Assistance Plan (AEC); Regimental Aid Post; Release Aid Plan; Royal Army Post

Rapa Nui Polynesian name of Easter Island

RAPC Royal Army Pay Corps

RAPCAP Radar Picket Combat Air Patrol

rapcoe random access programming and checkout equipment

rapcon radar approach control

RAPCs Regional Action Planning Commissions

Rape *Rape of Lucretia* (Britten two-act opera)

rapec rocket-assisted personnel ejection catapult

rape rep rape report

Raph Raphael

Raphael Raffaello Sanzio

RAPI Royal Australian Planning Institute

rapid. random-access personnel information device; relative address programming implementation device; retrieval through automated publication and information digest(ing)

RAPID Register for the Ascertainment and Prevention of Inherited Diseases; Rocketdyne Automatic Processing of Integrated Data

RAPIDS Random-Access Personnel Information System

Rapier British BAC surface-to-air missile launched for low-altitude defense

RAPM Russian Association of Proletarian Musicians

rapp rapport; rapporteur; rapprochement

RAPP Radical Alternatives to Prison Plan; Radiologists, Anesthesiologists, Pathologists, and Psychiatrists

rappelling rapidly lowering

rappi random-access plan-position indicator

RAPPORT Rapid-Alert Programmed-Power-Management of Radar Targets

rapr radar processor

RAPRA Rubber and Plastics Research Association

rap's rocket-assisted projectiles

RAPS Radar Automatic Plotting System; Risk Appraisal of Programs System

rap. & sup. rapport and support

raptap random access parallel tape

raptus. rapid thorium-uranium-sodium (reactor)

Raquel Welch Raquel Tejada

Raquetball Capital San Diego, California

rar radio acoustic ranging; rapid-access recording; right arm reclining

RAR Reliability Action Report; Rhodesian African Rifles; Royal Australian Regiment(s)

rarad radar advisory

RARDE Royal Armament Research and Development Establishment

rare. ram air rocket engine

RARE Rare Animal Relief Effort; Rehabilitation of Addicts by Relatives and Employers

rarep radar report

rarest fossil soft-bodied marine ctenophore

RARG Regulatory Analysis Review Group

RARO Regular Army Reserve of Officers

ras radome antenna structure; radula sinus; rapid audit summary; rectified air speed; requirements allocation sheet; rheumatoid arthritis serum

ras (RAS) reticular activating system

ras (Arabic—cape; summit, as in Ras at Tannura, near Bahrein)

ras. *rasurae* (Latin—shavings)

Ras Desiderius Erasmus

RAs Resident Agencies; Resident Agents

RAS Report Audit Summary; Royal Aeronautical Society; Royal Agricultural Society; Royal Asiatic Society; Royal Astronomical Society; Rubber Association of Singapore

RASA Railway and Airline Supervisors Association

RASAR Resource Allocation System for Agricultural Research

Ras Asir (Arabic—Cape Guardafui)—northeastern-most Africa on the coast of Somalia and the Gulf of Aden

RASB Royal Asiatic Society of Bengal

RASC Royal Army Service Corps; Royal Astronomical Society of Canada

RASC/DC Rear Area Security and Damage Control

RASD Reference and Adult Services Division (American Library Association)

rase rapid automatic-sweep equipment

RASE Royal Agricultural Society of England

raser range and sensitivity extending resonator

rash. rain shower(s)

RASK Royal Agricultural Society of Kenya

Rasmus Erasmus

rasn rain and snow

RASNZ Royal Agricultural Society of New Zealand

RASP Reliability and Aging Surveillance Program (USAF)

RASPB Royal and Ancient Society of Polar Bears (Hammerfest, Norway's town-hall club)

Rasputin (Russian—Dissolute) — nickname of the Siberian monk Gregory Efimovitch long associated with the last of the Romanovs

RASS Rock Analysis Storage System; Royal Alfred Seafarers' Society

Rassmen Jamaicans

rastac random access storage and control

rastad random access storage and display

Rastafians Rastafurians

RASTAS Radiating Site Target Acquisition System

Rastus Erastus; Theophrastus

Rasumovsky Beethoven's Quartets in F major, E minor, and C major for two violins, viola, and cello (opus 59, nos. 1, 2, 3); dedicated to Count Rasumovsky

rat. ram air turbine; ratchet; rate; rating; ration(s); rocket-assisted torpedo (RAT)

rat. (RAT) repeat-action tablet

RAT Remote Associates Test

ratac radar analog target acquisition computer

ratan radio television aid to navigation

RATAS Research and Technical Advisory Services (Lloyd's Register of Shipping)

ratc radar-aided tracking computer

RATCC Radar Air Traffic Control Center

RATCF Regional Air Traffic Control Facility

ratcon radar terminal control

rate. remote automatic telemetry equipment

ratel radiotelephone

ratelo radio telephone operator

ratepayer(s) [Canadian English —taxpayer(s)]

rat/epr ram air temperature/engine pressure ratio

RATER Raytheon Acoustic Test and Evaluation Range

ratfor rational fortran

ratg radiotelegraph

Ratipole nickname of Napoleon III

Ratisbon French equivalent of Regensburg

rato rocket-assisted takeoff

Ratons Raton Mountains of Colorado and New Mexico

RATP Régie Autonome des Transports Parisiens (Le métro—Paris subway system)

RATR Reliability Abstracts and Technical Reviews

rats. repeat-action tablets

Rats Rat Islands (Amchitka, Kiska, Rat, etc.)

RATS Ram Air Turbine Systems

ratscat radar target scatter site

RATSEC Robert A Taft Sanitary Engineering Center

ratt radioteletypewriter

RAU Rand Afrikaans University; River Assault Unit (USN)

RAU Repubblica Araba Unita (Italian—United Arab Republic)— Egypt

RAUS Retired Association for the Uniformed Services

'raus mit i'm *heraus mit ihm* (German—out with him)

R Aux AF Royal Auxiliary Air Force

Rav Roux-associated virus

RAVA Rochester Audiovisual Association

RAVC Royal Army Veterinary Corps

rave. radar acquisition vocal-tracking equipment

rave. (RAVE) research aircraft for visual environment (USA)

RAVE Register And Vote Easily

RAVEC Regional Adult and Vocational Education Council

raven. ranging and velocity navigation

Raven Hiller utility helicopter designated H-23 and OH-23

RAVES Rapid Aerospace Vehicle Evaluation System

ravir radar video recorder; radar video recording

RAW Reconnaissance Attack Wing (USN)

RAWA Renaissance Artists and

Writers Association
Rawal Rawalpindi
rawarc radar and warning coordination
RAWI Radio American West Indies (Virgin Islands)
rawin radar wind sounding
raws radar altimeter warning set
rawx returned account of weather (aviation)
rax random access (computing system)
'ray hurray
Ray Rachel; Raymond
RAYCI Raytheon Controlled Inventory
Ray Milland Reginald Truscott-Jones
Raynaud's disease circulatory disorder of the extremities
Raynaud's phenomenon white-finger disease brought on by long-term use of vibrating hand tools
razel range, azimuth, elevation
razon range and azimuth only
Razor The Razor—General Hideki Tojo's nickname
Razorback(s) Arkansan(s)
Razor Clam Capital Cordova, Alaska
razz razzberry (slang for raspberry)
rb read backward; read buffer; relative bearing; return to bias; rigid boat; road bend; rubber base(d)
r/b reentry body
r & b rhythm and blues; right and below; room and board
Rb rubidium
RB reconnaissance bomber; Regiment Botha; Renegotiation Board; Republica Boliviana (Bolivian Republic); Republic of Burma; Rifle Brigade; Ritzaus Bureau (Danish news agency); Royaume de Belgique (Kingdom of Belgium)
R.B. Robert Browning
R$_B$ Rockwell hardness (B-scale)
Rb-08 Saab surface-to-surface missile
RBA Rabat, Morocco (airport); Reserve Bank of Australia; Roadside Business Association; Royal Brunei Airlines
RBAF Royal Belgian Air Force
rbb room, board, and beverages
RBB Richard Bedford Bennett (Canada's fourteenth Prime Minister)
rbbb right bundle branch block
rbbsb right-bundle-branch sys-

tem block
rbc red blood cell; red blood cell (count); red blood corpuscle
RBC Rhodesian Broadcasting Corporation; Richard Bland College; Roller Bearing Company; Royal Bank of Canada
RBCA Russian Book Chamber Abroad
rbcd right border of cardiac dullness
rbd rapid beam deflector; right border of dullness (heart response to percussion)
RBD Rittenhouse Book Distributors
rbde radar bright-display equipment
rbe relative biological effectiveness
RBEC Roller Bearing Engineering Committee
rbelet relative biological effectiveness linear energy transfer
R Bern Rancho Bernardo
rbf renal blood flow
RBF Rockefeller Brothers Fund
RBFC Rural Banking and Finance Corporation
RBG Royal Botanic Gardens (Kew Gardens)
RBGS Radio Beacon Guidance System
RBH Rutherford Birchhard Hayes (19th President U.S.)
rbi reply by indorsement; request better information; runs batted in
rbi recibí (Spanish—I received)
RBI Reserve Bank of India; Rochester Business Institute
rb imp rubber-base impression
RBK Royal Borough of Kensington
rbl ruble
RBL Royal British Legion
RBLC Royal British Legion Club
R Bn radio beacon
RBN Registry of Business Names
RBNA Royal British Nurses' Association
RBNM Rainbow Bridge National Monument (Utah)
RBNSW Rural Bank of New South Wales
RBNZ Reserve Bank of New Zealand
rbo right back outside
RBO Russian Brotherhood Organization
rboc rapid-bloom off-board chaff
RBOT Rotating Bomb Oxidation Test

rbox rail box car (rolling-stock pool)
rbp ration breakdown point
RBP Registered Business Processor
RBP Raffinerie Belge de Petroles (French—Belgian Petroleum Refinery)
RBPP Rotor-Burst Protection Program (NASA)
rbr risk-to-benefit ratio; rubber
rBr reddish brown
RBR Renegotiation Board Regulation
RBR Reference Book Review
RBRF Reproductive Biological Research Foundation
rbs radar bomb score; radar bomb scoring; request blocks
Rbs Rutherford back-scatter(ing)
RBS Ranganthittoo Bird Sanctuary (India); Research for Better Schools; Royal Botanical Society
RBSA Royal Birmingham Society of Artists
rbsn (RBSN) reaction-bonded silicon nitride
rbt rabbet; rabbit; resistance bulb thermometer; roundabout
RBT Rose Bengal Test(ing)
rbtwt radial-beam travelling-wave tube
RBU Rabindra Bharati University
rbv return-beam videcon
rc radio code; radio coding; rate of change; ready calendar; red cell; red corpuscle; reinforced concrete; resin coat(ed); resin coating; resistance capacitance; resistor-capacitor; respiratory center; reverse course; right center; rigid center; rock-crushed; rubber-cushioned
r/c reconsign(ed); recredit(ed)
r & c rail and canal
r/c rés-do-chão (Portuguese—ground floor)
R$_c$ Rockwell hardness (C-scale)
RC Radcliffe College; Radio City; Radio Code; Reception Center; Reconstruction Commission; Red China; Red Cross; Regina College; Regis College; Reinhardt College; Renison College; Republica de Chile; República de Colombia; República de Cuba; Ricca College; Ricks College; Rider College; Río Colorado; Ripon College; Rivier College; Roanoke College; Rockefeller Center; Rockford College; Rock-

hurst College; Rockmount College; Rollins College; Roman Catholic; Rosary College; Rosemount College; Rosenwal College; Rust College

R, C Cauchy constant

R of C Republic of China (nationalist offshore China)

R.C. *Rendiconti* (Italian—proceedings or reports)

rca replacement cost accounting

R^{ca} *Rocca* (Italian—rock; tower)

RCA Rabbinical Council of America; Radio Club of America; Radio Corporation of America; Radio Council of America; Rocket Cruising Association; Rodeo Cowboys Association; Roofing Contractors Association; Royal Canadian Academician; Royal Canadian Academy; Royal Canadian Artillery; Royal College of Art; Rug Corporation of America

RCA *République Centrafricaine* (French—Central African Republic)

RCAA Royal Cambrian Academy of Art; Royal Canadian Academy of Arts

RCAC Radio Corporation of America Communications

RCACS Readiness Command and Control System

RCAF Royal Canadian Air Force

RCAM Royal Canadian Artillery Museum

R Cam A Royal Cambrian Academy of Art

RCAMC Royal Canadian Army Medical Corps

R Can Rio Canario

RCAR Religious Coalition for Abortion Rights

RCA Rev *RCA Review*

RCAS Royal Central Asian Society; Rutgers Center of Alcohol Studies

RCA Satcom RCA Domestic Communications Satellite

RCASC Royal Canadian Army Service Corps

rcat remote-controlled aerial target

RCAT Royal College of Arts and Technology

RCA Vic RCA Victor

RCB Ready-Crew Building; Regiment Christiaan Beyers; Retail(ers) Credit Bureau

RCBB Royal Commission on Bilingualism and Bicultural-

ism (Canada)

rcc read(er) channel continue(d); reader common contact; remote communications complex; rough combustion cutoff

r & cc riot and civil commotion

RCC Radio-Chemical Center; Radiological Control Center; Rag Chewers Club; Rape Crisis Center; Reply Coupon Collector(s); Rescue Control Center; Rescue Coordination Center; Rockland Community College; Roman Catholic Church; Royal Crown Cola

R & CC Ross and Cromarty Constabulary

RCCA Rickenbacker Car Club of America

RCCC Regular Common Carrier Conference; Republican County Central Committee

RCCE Regional Congress of Construction Employers

RC Ch Roman Catholic Church

RCCL Royal Caribbean Cruise Line

RCCLS Resource Center for Consumers of Legal Services

RCCP *Royal Commission on Criminal Procedure*

rccs riots, civil commotions, and strikes

rcd received; relative cardiac dullness

rcd (RCD) record(ing)

RCD Regional Cooperation for Development (Pakistan, Iran, Turkey)

RCDA Retail Coin Dealers Association

RCDC Royal Canadian Dental Corps

RCDEP Rural Civil Defense Education Program

RCDI Reliability Control Departmental Instruction

RCDMS Reliability Central Data Management System

RCDs Royal Canadian Dragoons

RCDS Royal College of Defence Studies (UK)

rce rapid circuit etch(ing); remote-controlled equipment; right center entrance

RCE Reliability Control Engineering

RCEEA Radio Communications and Electronic Engineers Association

RCEME Royal Canadian Electrical and Mechanical Engi-

neers

RCEP Royal Commission on Environmental Pollution

RCET Royal College of Engineering Technology; Rugby College of Engineering Technology

rcf recall finder; recall finding; relative centrifugal force

RCFA Reliability Control Failure Analysis; Royal Canadian Field Artillery

RCFCA Royal Canadian Flying Clubs Association

rcfm radiocommunication failure message

RCG Reception Guidance Center

RCGA Royal Canadian Golf Association

RCGP Royal College of General Practitioners

RCGS Royal Canadian Geographical Society

Rch Rochester

RCH Railway Clearing House; Resource Center for the Handicapped

RCHM Royal Commission on Historical Monuments (England)

rci radar coverage indicator; read channel initial(ize)

RCI Radio Canada International; Range Communications Instructions; Reichold Chemicals Incorporated; Research Council of Israel; Resident Cost Inspection; Resident Cost Inspector; Royal Canadian Institute

RCIA Retail Clerks International Association; Retail Credit Institute of America

RCIC Rumor Control and Information Center

rcirc recirculate

RCIs Recontres Culturelles Internernational (International Cultural Meetings)

RCIU Retail Clerks International Union

rcj reaction-control jet

RCJ Royal Courts of Justice

RCJCLDS Reorganized Church of Jesus Christ of Latter Day Saints

RCK *Research Centrum Kalkzandsteen Industrie* (Dutch—Research Center for the Calcium Silicate Industry)

rcl runway center line

RCL ramped cargo lighter (naval designation); Royal Canadian Legion

R-class Soviet submarines

named Romeo by NATO
rclm reclaim; reclamation
rcm radar countermeasure(s); radio-controlled mine; radio countermeasure(s); right costal margin
RCM Reliability Control Manual; Royal College of Midwives; Royal College of Music
RCMF Royal Commonwealth Military Forces
RCMP Royal Canadian Mounted Police
rcn reticulum cell neoplasms
RCN Reactor Centrum Nederland; Record Control Number; Republic of China Navy; Royal Canadian Navy; Royal College of Nursing
RCN *Radio Cadena Nacional* (Spanish—National Radio Chain)—Mexican broadcasting system
RCNC Royal Corps of Naval Constructors
RCNM Russell Cave National Monument
RCNR Royal Canadian Naval Reserve
RCNT Registered Clinical Nurse Teacher
RCNVR Royal Canadian Naval Volunteer Reserve
rco rendezvous compatible orbit
rco (RCO) remote control oscillator; representative calculating operation
RCO Radio Control Office; Royal College of Organists
RCOA Radio Club of America; Record Club of America
RCOC Royal Canadian Ordnance Corps
RCOG Royal College of Obstetricians and Gynecologists
R-complex reptilian complex (evolutionarily most recent part of the forebrain)
rcp recording control panel; reinforced concrete pipe; remote communications processor; reserved circuits program
RCP Revolutionary Communist Party; Royal College of Pathologists; Royal College of Physicians
RCPA Royal College of Pathologists of Australia; Royal College of Physicians of Australia
RCPI Royal College of Physicians—Ireland
RCPL Realtors Co-op Photo Listing
RCPS Royal College of Physi-

cians and Surgeons
rcpt receipt
rcr reader control relay; reverse contactor
RCR República de Costa Rica
RCRBSJ Research Council on Riveted and Bolted Structural Joints
rcrd record
rcs radar cross-section; reloadable control storage
RCs Roman Catholics
RCS Reaction Control System; Rearward Communications System; Reentry Control System; Reliability Control Standard; Report Control Symbol; Royal College of Science; Royal College of Surgeons; Royal Commonwealth Society (formerly Royal Empire Society)
RCSB Royal Commonwealth Society for the Blind
RCSD Regional Council for Social Development
RCSE Royal College of Surgeons—Edinburgh
RCSI Royal College of Surgeons—Ireland
RCSS Random Communication Satellite System
RCST Royal College of Science and Technology
rct reversible counter
Rct Recruit
RCT Regimental Combat Team(s); Rorschach Content Test; Royal Corps of Transport
rctl rectal; resistor capacitor transistor logic
RCTT Regional Center for Technology Transfer (UN)
rcu remote control unit; research coordination unit
RCU Road Construction Unit
RCUEP Research Center for Urban and Environmental Planning (Princeton U)
rcv receive
rcv (RCV) radar control van; remote-controlled vehicle
rcvr receiver
RCVS Royal College of Veterinary Surgeons
RCWP Rural Clean Water Program
RCYB Revolutionary Communist Youth Brigade (Trotskyite)
RCYC Royal Canadian Yacht Club; Royal Corinthian Yacht Club; Royal Cork Yacht Club
R Cy N Royal Ceylon Navy
RCYP Revolutionary Commu-

nist Youth Brigades
RCZ Radiation Control Zone; Rear Combat Zone
rd reaction of degeneration; readiness date; renal disease; required date; research and development (R & D); restricted data; retinal detachment; round; rutherford
rd (RD) red devil (barbiturate seconal tablet)
r & d reamed and drifted; research and development
Rd Road
RD Air Lift International; Radio Denmark; República Dominicana; Restricted Data; Royal Dragoons; Royal Dutch Petroleum (stock exchange symbol); Rural Dean; Rural Delivery
R.D. Royal (Naval Reserve) Decoration
R/D Research/Development
R & D research and development (should be in lowercase letters but scientists, engineers, and other recognize it as shown)
R of D Report of Debate
rda recommended daily allowance; recommended dietary allowance; right dorso-anterior
rd a (Rd A) reading age
RDA Railway Development Association; Reliability Design Analysis; Respiratory Diseases Association; Royal Docks Association
R & D A Research and Development Association
RDA *Reader's Digest Almanac*; *República Democrática Alemana* (Spanish—German Democratic Republic)—East Germany
RDAF Royal Danish Air Force
Rdam Rotterdam
RDAR Reliability Design Analysis Report
rdb research and development bond
rdb (RDB) radar decoy balloon
RDB Ramped Dump Barge; Research and Development Board; Royal Danish Ballet
rdbl readable
rd bot rubber diaphragm (stoppered) bottle
rdc rail diesel car; repository design condition; running down clause
RDC Rand Development Corporation; Rural District Council
RDCA Rural District Councils' Association

rd/chk read/check
RDCO Reliability Data Control Office
rdd required delivery date
rd & d (RD & D) research, development, and demonstration
RD$ República Dominicana peso (Dominican currency)
rde receptor-destroying enzyme
r d & e research, development, and engineering (usually R D & E)
RDE Research and Development Establishment
R de C Radiodiffusion du Cameroun (French—Radio Network of Cameroon)
R de F Republica de Filipinas
R de J République de Djibouti (formerly French Somaliland or the Territory of Afars and Issas); Rio de Janeiro
R de O Rio de Oro (Spanish Sahara)
R de P República de Panamá; República del Paraguay; República Portuguesa
R de T Ralph de Toledano
rdf radio direction finder
RDF Rapid Deployment Force (U.S. land, sea, and air strike force); Royal Dublin Fusiliers
Rdg Reading; Ridge (postal abbreviation)
RDG Reading Railroad
R d'H République d'Haiti
rd hd round head
rdi recommended daily intake
RDI Royal Designer for Industry
RDL Radiocarbon Dating Laboratory (Florida State University); Ritter Dental Laboratories
RDLI Royal Durban Light Infantry
rdline read a line
RdlR Regiment de la Rey
rdm root drum
RDM Rand Daily Mail (Johannesburg)
Rdm3c Radarman, third class
rdmu range-drift measuring unit
rdn resource decision network
RDN Royal Danish Navy
rdo research and development objectives
RDO Radiological Defense Office(r)
rdo('s) regular day(s) off; research and development objective(s)
rdp radar detector processor; right dorso-posterior
RDP Regional Development

Program(s); Repository Development Plan(ning)
RDPC Research Data Publication Center
rdpe radar data-processing equipment
RDPP Repository Development Program Plan(ning)
rd/q reading quotient
rdr radar
rdr (RDR) receiver data register
RDR Reliability Diagnostic Report; Research and Development Report
rdr rel radar relay
rdrsmtr radar transmitter
rds respiratory distress syndrome
Rds Rixdllar; Roads; Roadstead
RDs Revolutionary Development teams; Royal Dockyards
RDS Research Defence Society; Royal Dublin Society; Rural Development Service; Rural Development Society
RD/S Royal Dutch/Shell
RD & S Research, Development, and Studies (USMC)
RD/SG Royal Dutch/Shell Group (world's largest industrial corporation)
rdt reserve duty training
rdt (RDT) remote data transmitter
RDT Regiment Danie Theron; Reliability Demonstration Test
R.D.T. Registered Dental Technician
RDT Repubblica Democratica Tedesca (Italian—German Democratic Republic)—East Germany
rdt & e (RDT & E) research, development, test, and evaluation
RDTF Rapid Deployment Task Force (US Marines)
rdu research and development utilization
RDU Royal Development Unit
RDUP Research and Development Utilization Project
R du Z République du Zaïre (French—Republic of Zaire)
rdvu rendezvous
RDW Regiment De Wet
Rdwy Roadway
rdx cyclonite (research department explosive)
RDX Research and Development Exchange
rdy ready
RDY Royal Dock Yard

RDZ Radiation Danger Zone
RDZ République Démocratique du Zaïre (French—Democratic Republic of Zaire)—formerly the Belgian Congo
rdz(s) (RDZ or RDZs) radiation danger zone(s)
re radium emanation; real estate; reinforce(d); reinforcing; research and engineering (R & E); reticulo-endothelium; right eye
re (RE) revised edition
r/e rate of exchange
re B in diatonic scale, *D* in fixed-do system); (Italian—second tone; (Latin prefix—again or back)—reflect, repair, restate
Re real part (symbol); Reno; Reynold's Number; rhenium; rupee (Ceylon, India, Pakistan currency)
R$_e$ récipe (Spanish—recipe; prescription)
RE Radio Eireann (Radio Ireland); Reformed Episcopal (church); Reliability Engineering; Religious Education; República de Ecuador; Rifle Expert; Right Excellent; Royal Engineers; Royal Exchange
rea right ear advantage
REA Railway Express Agency; Request for Engineering Authorization; Rice Export Association; Rubber Export Association; Rural Education Association; Rural Electrification Administration (US Department of Agriculture)
reac reactor
REAC Reeves electronic analog computer; Reliability Engineering Action Center
REACH Rape Emergency Aid and Counseling for Her
reack receipt acknowledged
react reactance; reaction; reactor; register-enforced automated-control technique
REACT Radio Emergency Associated Citizens Team; Register-Enforced Automated Control Technique; Resource Allocation and Control Techniques
READ Real-Time Electronic Access and Display
Read Dig Reader's Digest
readi rocket-engine-analyzer-and-decision-instrumentation
readm readmission
READS Reno Air Defense Sector
Reaganomics economic policy of the administration of Presi-

dent Reagan

REAL Rape Emergency Assistance League; Real-Aerovias do Brasil; Residential Experience in Adult Living

realcom real-time communication(s)

real est real estate

realgar arsenic sulfide

Realistic Recorder of Spanish Life Goya (Francisco José de Goya y Lucientes)

Realm of Exotic Flavors Thailand

ream. rapid excavation and mining

REAMS Ramond Electronically Applied Maintenance Standards

REAP Rural Environmental Assistance Program

reapt reappoint; reappointment

REAR Reliability Engineering Analysis Report

Rear Adm Rear Admiral

reasm reassemble

REAT Radiological Emergency Assistance Team

Réau(m) Réaumur

reb rebel; rebellion

Reb Reba; Rebecca, Rebekah

REB Regional Examining Body

Reba Rebecca

Rebecca West Cecily Isabel Fairfield

Rebel City Charleston, South Carolina

Rebel of Salem Roger Williams

Rebel Unitarian Theodore Parker

Rebel of Walden Henry David Thoreau

Rebilds Denmark's Rebild Hills including the Rebild National Park where Danes celebrate the Fourth of July and invite distinguished Americans to come and speak in the presence or the royal family

reb(s) rebel(s)

rec receipt; receive; record; recreation

rec. *recens* (Latin—fresh)

Rec Recife

REC Recife, Brazil (airport); Rural Electrification Corporation

R & EC Research and Engineering Council

reca repetitive-element column analysis

Recafellow Andrew Carnegie's nickname for John D Rockefeller Sr

recap recapitulate; recapitulation

RECAP Reliability Evaluation Continuous Analysis Program

RECC Rhine Evacuation and Control Command (NATO)

rec chg record change(r)

recco reconnaissance

recd received

recep reception

recg radioelectrocardiograph

R & ECGAI Research and Engineering Council of the Graphic Arts Industry

rec hall recreational hall

reci recitation

recid recidivism; recidivist(ic); recidivous

recids recidivists

Recife (Portuguese—Reef)— Pernambuco's new name

recip reciprocating

recipe. recomp computer interpretive program expeditor

recip & lp turb reciprocating steam engine and low-pressure turbine

recirc recirculate; recirculation

recit. *recitativo* (Italian—recitative)

reclam reclamation

Reclus' disease cystic growths in the breasts

recm recommend

recmark record mark(ing)

RECMF Radio and Electronic Component Manufacturers Federation

recncln reconciliation

recog recognition; recognize

recol retrieval command language

recom recommendation; recommend(ed)

recomp recomplement(ary); repairs completed; retrieval composition

recon reconcentration; reconciliation; recondite; recondition; reconduction; reconnaissance; reconnoiter; reconsign; reconsigned; reconsignment; reconstruct; reconstructed; reconstruction; reconversion; reconvert; reconverted; reconvey; reconveyance; reconveyed

RECON Regional Communication Outreach Network; Retrospective Conversion of Bibliographic Records (Library of Congress)

recond recondition

R Econ S Royal Economic Society

RECONS Reliability and Configurational Accountability System

reconst reconstruct

recov recover; recovery

recp receptacle; reciprocal; reciprocating

RECP Rural Environmental Conservation Program

recpt receptionist

recr receiver

rec room receiving room; reception room; record room; recreation room

recryst recrystallize

Rec S Record of Survey

RECSAM Regional Center for Education in Science and Mathematics

Rec Sec Recording Secretary

RECSTA Receiving Station

recsys recreational systems analysis

rect (Latin prefix—straight)— rectified; rectifier; rectify; rectitude

rect. *rectificatus* (Latin—rectified)

Rect Rector(y)

recto obverse; right-hand page (opposite of verso)

recu recommends transfer

recur. recurrence; recurrent; recurring

rec vehicle(s) recreation vehicle(s)—campers, dune buggies, snowmobiles, trailers, vans, etc.

red. reduce; reduction

red *redaktör* (Swedish—editor); *redigé* (French—compiled; edited)

Red Sinclair Lewis

Red *Rederi* (Scandinavian— shipowners)

REDAR R E Darling (Company)

Red Baron Baron Manfred von Richthofen

Redbricks red-brick universities

red burgee burgee-shaped red signal flag flown when explosives or flammable fuel is being loaded aboard a vessel; letter B or Bravo in the international code

redcape readiness capability

redcat readiness requirement

Red Chamber Canadian Senate

Red China People's Republic of China

Red Clover Vermont state flower

redcon readiness condition

Redcraft Red aircraft (communist-controlled aircraft)

Red Crescent equivalent of the Red Cross in the Moslem world (symbolized by a red crescent on a white field)

Red Cross red cross on a white field; used on ambulances, hospitals, and hospital ships to denote their neutrality; also called the Cross of Geneva or the Geneva Cross as its function in war is accepted by the Geneva Convention and its design is the reverse of the Swiss flag

Red Cross and Crescent Soviet equivalent of the Red Cross (symbolized by a red cross and a red crescent on a white field)

Red Dean of Canterbury The Very Reverend Doctor Hewlett Johnson—Dean of Canterbury Cathedral who from 1931 to 1963 used his position and misused free speech to expound communist propaganda

Redd Foxx John Elroy Sanford

Red Duster British flag; Red Ensign flown from British merchant vessels

Redemptorist Founder Alfonso Maria de Liguori

Red Ensign British flag

Redeye General Dynamics portable surface-to-air missile carried and fired by one man

red flag danger; stop sign

Red Gap Lone Pine, California as described in *Ruggles of Red Gap* by Harry Leon Wilson

redig redigerat (Swedish—edited)

redig. in pulv. redigatur in pulverem (Latin—reduce to powder)

Red Indians North America's copper-colored Indians

redisc rediscount

redist redistilled

REDLARS Reading Literature Analysis and Retrieval Service

red lead lead oxide—Pb_3O_4 (minium)

Red Lewis (Harold) Sinclair Lewis nicknamed Red because of the color of his hair and not because of his mildly socialist leanings

red light danger signal; port side of aircraft, ships, or other vessels; stop signal; warning signal

redlight district whorehouse neighborhood; zone of prostitution

Red Lion and Sun Iran's equivalent of the Red Cross (symbolized by a red lion beneath a red sun on a white field)

rednecks poor-white teenage gangs(ters)

red ochre reddle (hematite red)

redox reduction oxidation

Red Planet Mars

Red Priest red-headed Antonio Vivaldi

red. in pulv. reductus in pulverem (Latin—reduced to a powder)

Red Rosa Rosa Luxemburg—co-founder with Karl Liebnecht of the Spartacus League later to become the Communist Party of Germany

Red Sea Indian Ocean inlet between Africa and Arabia

redsg redesign; redesigned; redesigning

redsh reddish

Red Skelton Richard Bernard Skelton

Red Square in the heart of Moscow between the GUM department store, the Kremlin, and Lenin's tomb; called Krasnaya Ploschad by the Russians

red star symbol of the Soviet Union and many communist-controlled lands

Redtop Hawker-Siddeley air-to-air missile

redup(l) reduplicate; reduplication

redux reduction

Redwood Redwood City, Redwood Empire, Redwood National Park—all in northern California

ree rare-earth elements

REE Regional Economic Expansion (Canada)

REECO Reynolds Electrical and Engineering Compay

Reed Reederei (German—shipowners)

reef The Reef—Australia's Great Barrier Reef off the coast of Queensland

reefer(s) marijuana cigarette(s); refrigerated compartment(s) or hold(s) in a ship; refrigerator(s)

Reefer(s) inhabitant(s) of the Great Barrier Reef

reeg radioelectroencephalograph

REEGT Registered Electroencephalographic Technicians

Reen Irene

reenl reennlist

reep range estimating and evaluation procedure

Reeperbahn Saint Pauli's street of nightclubs and other places of nocturnal entertainment in Hamburg

ref refer; referee; reference; reformatory; refraction; refresher

ref (REF) renal erythropoietic factor

ref refondue (French—reorganized)

Ref reference

Ref Referate (German—abstract, compedium)

REF Railway Engineers Forum; Reject Errors in Football; Romanian Engineers Forum

refash refashion(ed)

Ref Ch Reformed Church

refcom refuse conversion to methane

refd refund

refd conc reinforced concrete

ref dent referring dentist

refd met reinforced metal

ref doct referring doctor

refd ply reinforced plywood

ref eso reflux esophagitis

reffo refugee from Europe

refg refrigerating; refrigeration

refl reflection; reflective; reflector; reflex; reflexive

ref l reference line

reflecs retrieval from literature on electronics and computer science

Ref Libr Reference Librarian

refl pron reflexive pronoun

Reform Reformatory

Reforma National Association of Spanish-Speaking Librarians in the United States

Reformation Mendelssohn's Symphony No. 5 in D major

reforst reforestation

refphocon reference to telephone conversation

ref phys referring physician

ref press reference pressure

refr refraction; refractory; refrigerate; refrigerator

refrg refrigerate; refrigeration; refrigerator

refrig refrigeration; refrigerator

Refrig Eng Refrigerating Engineering

refs references

ref temp reference temperature

reftra refresher training

refurb refurbish(ed)

refy refinery

Ref Zhu Referativnyi Zhurnal (Russian—Abstract Journal)

reg region; regular; regulate; regulation

reg (REG) register (flow chart)

Reg Registered

RegAF Regular Air Force

regal. range and elevation guidance for approach and landing; remote generalized application language

Reg Arch Registered Architect

Reg Bez *Regierungsbezirk* (German—administrative district)

reg bot regular bottle (3/4-liter of wine)

regd registered

regen regenerate; regeneration

Regensburg German equivalent of Ratisbon

Regg *Reggimento* (Italian—Regiment)

Reg Gen Registrar General

Reggie Regina(ld)

Reg(gie)(y) Reginald

Reggio Reggio di Calabria; Reggio nel'Emilia

Regina coeli (Latin—Queen of Heaven)—Rome's great prison featured in so many post-World War II movies

Reginald Bliss H(erbert) G(eorge) Wells

Region of Four Streams Szechwan Province, China

regis register; registered; registration; registry

Regnery Henry Regnery

Regno Unito (Italian—United Kingdom)

Reg P Regent's Park College, Oxford

Reg Prof Regius Professor

Regr Registrar

regs regions; regulars; regulations

regt regiment

Reg TM Registered Trade Mark

regu regulable; regular; regularize; regularly; regulate; regulation; regulator

regurg regurgitant; regurgitate; regurgitation

REGY Regional Employment Growth (program for) Youth

reh rehearsal

rehab rehabilitate

Rehab Department of Rehabilitation

rehob rehoboam (6-bottle capacity)

REI Régie Aérienne Interinsulaire

R & EI Religion and Ethics Institute

REIC Radiation Effects Information Center; Rare Earth Information Center (Atomic Energy Commission, Ames Laboratory, Iowa State University)

Reichenhall Bad Reichenhall

Reichmann's disease continuous and excessive gastric secretion

Reidsville Georgia State Prison Facility at Reidsville

reig rare-earth iron garnets

reils runway end identification lights

reimb reimburse; reimbursement

reincorp reincorporate(d)

reinf reinforce(d); reinforcing

reinfmt reinforcement

Reino Unido (Portuguese or Spanish—United Kingdom)

reins. radio-equipped inertial navigation system

REINS Radio-Equipped Inertial Navigation System

Reistertown Girls Montrose School for (delinquent) Girls at Reistertown, Maryland

reit reiteration

REIT Real Estate Investment Trusts

REIWA Real Estate Institute of Western Australia

rej reject; rejected; rejection

rejase re-using junk as something else (old bathtub as settee; ouija board as coffee table; radio cabinet as bookcase, etc.)

Rejectionist Front Arab countries such as Algeria, Libya, and Syria most opposed to U.S. efforts to gain Israel's acceptance by its neighbors

rejn rejoin

REK Reykjavik, Iceland (airport)

rekenk *rekenkunde* (Dutch—arithmetic)

rel rate of energy loss; relation; relative; relay; release; relief; relieve; religion; religionist

rel *relie; reliure* (French—bound, binding)

REL Radio Engineering Laboratories

RELACS Radar Emission Location Attack Control System

rel adv relative adverb

RELC Reformation Evangelical Lutheran Church; Regional Educational Laboratory for the Carolinas

RELCV Regional Educational Laboratory for the Carolinas and Virginia

RELHS Robert E Lee High School

rel hum relative humidity

relig religion; religious

Religious Freedom Colony Rhode Island where Jews, rad-

ical Quakers, and other dissenters were guaranteed religious freedom

reliq. *reliquus* (Latin—remainder)

reloc relocate; relocated; relocation

rel pron relative pronoun

Rel R Reliability Report

RELS Rapidly Extensible Language System

Reluctant Imperialist John C Calhoun who half-heartedly supported the Mexican War

rem rapid eye movements; remain(ing); remission; remit; remittance; removable; remove; removed; roentgen equivalent, man

Rem Remington; roentgen equivalent, man

REM Registered Equipment Management

REMA Refrigeration Equipment Manufacturers Association

remab radiation equivalent manikin absorption

remad remote magnetic anomaly detection

Remarkables Remarkable Range of mountains in New Zealand's South Island

Rembrandt Rembrandt Harmenszoon van Rijn—RvR

Rembrandt of the Roman Ruins Giambattista Piranesi

remc resin-encapsulated mica capacitor

REMC Regional Educational Media Center

remcal radiation equivalent manikin absorption

remd rapid eye movement (sleep) deprivation

REME Royal Electrical and Mechanical Engineers

Remembrance Canada's Remembrance Day (November 11—Armistice Day)

REML Radiation Effects Mobile Laboratory

rems (REMS) rapid-eye-movement sleep

REMS Registered Equipment Management System

REMSA Railway Engineering Maintenance Suppliers Association

rem sleep rapid-eye-movement (paradoxical) sleep

remstar remote electronic microfilm storage transmission and retrieval

REMT Radiological Emergency Medical Teams

Rem-UMC Remington-Union Metallic Cartridge (company)
remus routine for executive multi-unit simulation
ren. *renovetur* (Latin—renew)
Ren Renaissance
rene rocket-engine nozzle ejector
Rene Irene
René Clair René Chomette
Renée Adorée Jeanne de la Fonte
Renegade Irishman James Joyce
Renf Renfrew
RENFE Red Nacional de los Ferrocarriles Españoles (National Network of Spanish Railroads)
Renmin Ribao (Pinyin Chinese—People's Daily)—official newspaper of communist China
reno (Latin prefix—kidney)—renal
Reno (Italian or Portuguese—Rhine)
RENS Reconnaissance Electronic Warfare and Naval Intelligence System
ren. sem. *renovetum semel* (Latin—renew only once)
rent. reentry nose tip
renv renovate; renovation
reo rare-earth oxide; regenerated electrical output
Reo (early American automobile named after initials of its maker, Ransom E Olds of Oldsmobile fame)
REO Regional Education Officer
reoc report when established on course (aviation)
reopt reorder point
REORG reorganization; reorganize; reorganized
reorgn reorganization
REOs Real-Estate-Owned banking departments
REOS Reflective Electron Optical System
reo viruses respiratory-enteric-orphan viruses
rep repair; repeat; repertory; represent; representative; reputation
rep. reparation; report; representative;
r-ep rational-emotive psychotherapy
rep. *repetatur* (Latin—let it be repeated)
Rep Representative; Republic; Republican; Republican Party; roentgen equivalent, physical

REP Radical Education Project; Recovery and Evacuation program; Republic Corporation (stock exchange symbol); Research Expenditure Proposal; Reserve Enlisted Program; River Engineering Program
Rep V Repair Locker 5 (Engineering)—USN
REPA Research and Engineers Professional Employees Association
REPC Racial Ethnic Parent Councils; Regional Economic Planning Council
repcon rain repellant and surface conditioner
REPE Radio Engineering Europe
reperf reperforator
repl replace(d); replacement; replacing
repltr report (by) letter
repm repairman; repairmen
REPM Representatives of Electronic Products Manufacturers
repo repossess; repossessed; repossession
repo men repossession men (adept at repossessing automobiles, furniture, and tv sets behind in payments or unpaid for)
repop repetitive operation(s)
repo(s) repurchase agreement(s)
reppac repetitively-pulsed plasma accelerator
Rep Prog Phys *Reports on Progress in Physics*
repr repairman; representative; reprint; reprinted; reprinting
repro reproduce; reproducing; reproduction
reprosex reproductive sex
repro typ reproduction typist; reproduction typing
reps repetitive electromagnetic pulse simulator; representatives
Rep(s) Republican(s)
REPS Rail(way) Express Parcel Service
rep. sem. *repetatur semel* (Latin—let it be repeated once)
rept report; reprint; reptile; reptilia(n)
rept (Rept) report
rept. *repetatur* (Latin—let it be repeated)
Rept Reptilia
repub republication; republish(ed)
REPUBLIC Republic Aviation Corporation

República Oriental (Spanish—Oriental Republic)—Uruguay
Republic of the Sacred Heart Ecuador
Republocrat Republican Democrat
Repubs Republicans
req request; require
reqafa request advise as to further action
reqd required
reqdi request disposition instructions
reqfolinfo request following information
reqid request if desired
reqmad request mailing address
reqmt requirement
reqn requisition
reqrec request(ed) recommendation
reqs requires
reqssd request supply status (and expected delivery) date
reqsupstafol request supply status of following
reqt requirement
reqtat requested that
requint request interim (reply)
rer (RER) radar effects reactor
RER Railway Equipment Register
REREI Redwood Empire Research and Education Institute
rereq reference requisition
RERF Radiation Effects Research Foundation
rerl residual equivalent return loss
RERO Royal Engineers Reserve of Officers
res rescue; research; researcher; reservation; reserve; reservoir; resilient; resistant; respiratory; reticuloendothelial system (RES)
res (RES) restore (computer character)
Res Reservation; Reservoir
RES República de El Salvador; Royal Economic Society; Royal Entomological Society
RESA Regional Educational Service Agencies; Regional Educational Service Areas; Research Society of America
ResAF Reserve of the Air Force
Res Aud Resident Auditor
resc rescue
RESC Regional Educational Service Centers
RESCAM Regional Center for Education in Science and Mathematics

rescan reflecting satellite communication antenna

rescu rocket-ejection seat catapult upward

RESCU Radio Emergency Search Communications Unit

rescue. remote emergency salvage and cleanup equipment

Research Center of the Classical World Library of Alexandria, Egypt

Res & Educ Research and Education Association

reser reentry system evaluation radar

resgnd resigned

resid residual; residual oil

resig resignation

RESIG Research and Engineering System Integration Group

resist. resistance; resistor

resistojet resistance-connective jet engine

resojet resonant pulse jet

resp respective; respelling; respiration(s); respirator; respire; responder; responsibility; responsible; responsive

RESPA Real Estate Settlement Procedures Act

Res Phys Resident Physician

respir respiration; respiratory

respirol respirologic(al)(ly); respirologist; respirology

respirom respirometer; respirometric(al)(ly); respirometrist; respirometry

Resplendent Land Ceylon or Sri Lanka (Singhalese—Resplendent Land)

RESPO Responsible Property Officer

RESPONSA Retrieval of Special Portions from Nuclear Science Abstracts

respub responsible Republican(ism)

Resrt Resort (postal abbreviation)

RESS Radar Echo-Simulation Study; Radar Echo-Simulation System

Res Sec Resident Secretary

RESSI Real Estate Securities and Syndication Institute

rest restrict; restricted; restriction

rest. (REST) regressive electric shock therapy

REST Radar Electronic-Scan Technique; Reentry Environment and Systems Technology; Reentry System Test Program

resta reconnaissance, surveillance, and target acquisition

resto (Malay—restaurant)

restr restaurant

ResTraCen Reserve Training Center

resub resublimed

resup resupply

Resurrection Mahler's Symphony No. 2 in C minor

resvr reservoir

RE system reticuloendothelial system

ret rational emotive therapy; retainer; retire; retirement

ret (RET) return (flow chart)

r-et rational-emotive psychotherapy

Ret Reticulum (constellation)

RET R. Emmett Tyrrell, Jr

RET *Rotterdamse Elektrische Tram* (Dutch—Rotterdam Electric Tramway)—electric surface car and subway system

reta retrieval of enriched textual abstracts

RETA Refrigerating Engineers and Technicians Association

Retail Clerks Union Retail Clerks International Association

retain. remote technical assistance and information network

retard. retardation; retarded

retc railroad equipment trust certificate

RETC Regional Employment and Training Consortium

retd retired

rete (Latin prefix—network)—retinal

R. et I. *Regina et Imperatrix* (Latin—Queen and Empress) title of Victoria—Queen of England and Empress of India —The Queen

retic reticulate(d); reticulation; reticule

retic count reticulocyte count

retics reticulocytes

retl retail

RETL Rocket Engine Test Laboratory

RETMA Radio-Electronics-Television Manufacturers Association

Ret Marut B Traven's pen name when a revolutionary journalist in Bavaria after World War I

retng retraining

retnr retainer

RETP Reliability Evaluation Test Procedure

retpd retention period

retr retractable

RETRA Radio, Electrical, and Television Retailers Association

Ret Res Retirement Research

retro retroactive; retrofit; retrograde; retrorocket

retro (Latin prefix—backward or behind)—retroactive, retrograde

retros retrogrades; retrorockets

RETS Renaissance English Text Society

Retto (Japanese—archipelago)

Reun Reunion Island

Réunion Indian Ocean island formerly called Bourbon

Reuter's Reuter's international news agency

rev reverse; reversed; review; revise; revised; revision; revolute; revolution

rev (REV) reentry vehicle

rev *revisado* (Spanish—revised)

Rev Reverend; The Revelation of St John the Divine

Rev *Revelation*

reva recommended vehicle adjustment

rev a/c revenue account

Reval or Revel old place-names for Tallinn, Estonia

Revd Reverend

Rev *d'Opt Revue d'Optique* (French—Optics Review)

rev ed revised edition

revel reverberation elimination

Revell Fleming H Revell

revid *reviderad* (Swedish—revised)

Revilla Gigedos Revilla Gigedo Islands off Mexico's west coast but not to be confused with Revilla Gigedo Island off Alaska

rev/min revolutions per minute

Rev Mod Phys *Reviews of Modern Physics*

revocon remote volume control

Revolutionary Chopin's Piano Etude No. 12 in C minor

Revolutionary Composer Pierre de Geyter best known for the formerly official communist anthem—the *Internationale*—but since 1944 replaced in the USSR by *The Hymn of the Soviet Union*; Eugène Pottier's optimistic phrases about the final conflict are yet to mirror man's fate in a world where the underground and the underworld are intertwined and headlined daily

revolving-door revolving-door criminal-justice system persisting in returning dangerous

defendants to their communities again and again
revr reviewer
revs revolutions
rev(s) revolution(s)
rev/s revolutions per second
REVS Rotor-Entry Vehicle System
Rev Sci Instrum *Review of Scientific Instruments*
rev/sec revolutions per second
Rev Stat Revised Statutes
rev of sym review of symptoms
rew reward; rewind(ing)
rewdac retrieval by title words, descriptors, and classifications
rewk reword
rewrc report when established well to right of course
REWSON Reconnaissance Electronic Warfare Special Operations and Naval Intelligence Processing System(s)
rex real-time executive routine; reduced exoatmospheric cross-section
Rex Reginald
REX Rexall Drug and Chemical (stock exchange symbol)
Rex Harrison Reginald Carey
Rex Ingram Reginald Hitchcock
rexs (REXS) radio-exploration satellite
Reykjavik (Old Norse—Smoky Bay)—Iceland's capital
Reykjvk Reykjavik
Reynall Reynal & Co
rf radiofrequency; range finder; rapid fire; rat fink; reception fair; reflight; relative flow; replacement factor; representative fraction; rheumatic fever; rheumatoid factor; right fullback; rim fire; rubber-free
r-f radiofrequency
r/f right front
r$_f$ rate of flow
rf *rinforzando* (Italian—reinforcing)
Rf Reef; rutherfordium (element 104)
RF République Française; Reserve Force; Rockefeller Foundation; Rocky Flats; Rodeo Foundation; Royal Fusiliers
R-F Reitland-Franklin (unit)
rfa radiofrequency attenuator; radiofrequency authorization(s); request further airways; right fronto-anterior
RFA République Fédérale Allemande (Federal Republic of Germany) West Germany; Royal Field Artillery; Royal

Fleet Auxiliary
RFA *República Federal de Alemania* (Spanish—Federal Republic of Germany)—West Germany
RFAC Royal Federation of Aero Clubs; Royal Fine Arts Commission
R factor resistance factor
rfad release for active duty
rfa's return(ed) for alterations (tailoring)
rfb request for bid
RFB Recording for the Blind
RFB *República Federativa do Brasil* (Portuguese Federal Republic of Brazil)
rf black reinforcing furnace black
rfc radiofrequency choke
RFC Rare Fruit Council; Reconstruction Finance Corporation; River Forecast Center; Royal Flying Corps
RFCL Referral Form Checklist
rfcs radio-frequency carrier shift
RFCWA Regional Fisheries Commission for Western Africa
rfd raised foredeck; reentry flight demonstration; refund; reinforced; reporting for duty
RFD Radio Frequency Devices; Rural Free Delivery
rfd con reinforced concrete
rfd met reinforced metal
rfd ply reinforced plywood
rfdr rangefinder
RFDS Royal Flying Doctor Service
RFE Radio Free Europe
RFED Research Facilities and Equipment Division (NASA)
rff remote-fiber fluorimetry
R f F *Rat für Formgebung* (German—Fashion Council)
RFF *Rede Ferroviária Federal* (Portuguese—Federal Railway System)—Brazil
RFFS River and Flood Forecasting Service
RFFSA *Rede Ferrocarril Federal Sedada Anonima* (Portuguese—Federal Railway Route Company)—Brazil
rfg roofing
RFH Royal Festival Hall
rfi radiofrequency interference; ready for issue
rfing royal fucking
rf/ir radiofrequency/infrared
R Fix running fix
rfl refuel(ing); right frontolateral
RFL Refrigerated Freight Lines;

Rugby Football League
Rflmn Rifleman
rfls rheumatoid factor-like substance
rfm radio frequency management
r-f m ripple-flow mill (grain)
RFMA Reliability Figure of Merit Analysis
RFMF Royal Fiji Military Forces
Rfn Rifleman
RFN Registered Fever Nurse
rfna red-fuming nitric acid
rfnip reduced-flow nominal-inlet pressure
rfnop reduced-flow nominal-output pressure
RFNZJ Royal Federation of New Zealand Justices
rfo request for factory order
RFO Regional Fisheries Office(r)
rfp right frontoposterior
RFP Request for Proposal
RF & P Richmond, Fredericksburg and Potomac (railroad)
RFPs Requests for Proposals
RFPS(G) Royal Faculty of Physicians and Surgeons of Glasgow
RFQ Request for Quotation
rfr refraction; reject failure rate; required freight rate
R fr Ruanda franc(s)
RFR Royal Fleet Reserve
rfrd referred
rfs radio-frequency surveillance; ready for sea; regardless of future size
Rfs Reefs (as in Minerva Reefs supposed location of the Republic of Minerva created by minters of commemorative coins)
RFS Registry of Friendly Societies; Royal Forestry Service
rf scale representative fraction scale
rfs/ecm radio-frequency surveillance/electronic countermeasures
RFSU *Riksförbundet för Sexuall Upplysning* (Norwegian—National League for Sexual Education); Rugby Football Schools' Union
rft right frontotransverse
RFT Rod and Frame Test
RFT *Repubblica Federale Tedesca* (Italian—German Federal Republic)—West Germany
rfts radiofrequency test set
rfu ready for use
RFU Rugby Football Union
R-F unit Reitland-Franklin unit

rfw rapid-filling wave
RFW Radio Free Women
rfwe ring-finished with engines
Rfy Refinery
rfz restrictive fire zone
rfz *rinforzando* (Italian—with extra emphasis)
rg real girl (not a birl)
RG República de Guatemala; Reserve Grade
rga rate gyro assembly
Rga Riga
RGA Republican Governors Association; Royal Garrison Artillery; Rubber Growers' Association
RGAHS Royal Guernsey Agricultural and Horticultural Society
R-gauge Russian gauge (5-foot) railroad track
rgb red-orange, green, blue-violet (television's triad of primary colors)
RGC Reception and Guidance Center
rgd reigned
R Gd Rio Grande
RGDATA Retail Grocery, Dairy, and Allied Trades Association
RG do S Rio Grande do Sul
rge relative gas expansion
Rge Range; Ridge
RGE *República de Guinea Ecuatorial* (Spanish—Republic of Equatorial Guinea)
RGEB Rockefeller General Education Board
RGEPS Rucker-Gable Educational Programming Scale
rgf range-gated filter
RGF Red Guerrilla Family (black terrorists)
RGG Royal Grenadier Guards
RGH Royal Gloucestershire Hussars
RGI Robert G. Ingersoll
RGJ Royal Green Jackets
rgl regulate; regulation; regulatory
rgm residential growth management
rgn region
Rgn (Port of) Rangoon
RGN Rangoon, Burma (airport); Registered General Nurse
RGNR Rugged Glen Nature Reserve (South Africa)
RGO Royal Greenwich Observatory
RGP Riegel Paper Company (stock-exchange symbol)
RGPL *Readers' Guide to Periodical Literature*

RGPM Regional Geological Project Manager
rgr reference geological regime
rgs radar ground stabilization
RGS Rio Grande do Sul; Royal Geographical Society
RGSA Royal Geographical Society of Australasia
Rgt Regiment
RGTC Robert Gordon's Technical College
Rgtl Regimental
rg tp rough template
RGV Rio Grande Valley Gas Company (stock exchange symbol)
rgz recommended ground zero
RGZ Rio Grande Zoo (Albuquerque)
rh rheumatic; rheumatism; rheumatoid; righthand (RH); roundhead
r/h relative humidity; roentgens per hour
rh. *rhonchi* (Latin—rales)
Rh Rhesus factor (symbol); rhodium
Rh+ Rhesus positive
Rh− Rhesus negative
Rh *Rhein* (German—Rhine)
RH Air Rhodesia; Random House; República de Honduras; Round House; Royal Highlanders; Royal Highness
RH *Research Highlights*
RH¹⁰⁶ radioactive rhodium
RHA Road Haulage Association; Royal Hibernian Academy; Royal Humane Association; Rural Housing Alliance
RHAF Royal Hellenic Air Force
R Hamps Royal Hampshire (regiment)
rhap rhapsody
RHAWS Radar Homing and Warning System
RHB Regional Hospital Board
rhbdr rhombohedral
rhc respirations have ceased; rubber hydrocarbon
RHC Rosary Hill College
RHC *Radio Habana Cuba* (Spanish—Havana, Cuba Radio)
RHCSA Regional Hospitals Consultants' and Specialists' Association
rhd radioactive health data; relative hepatic dullness; rheumatic heart disease
RHD Robin Hood Dell (Philadelphia)
RHD *Random House Dictionary*
RHDO Robin Hood Dell Or-

chestra
rhe reversible hydrogen electrode
RHE Reliability Human Engineering
Rhein (German—Rhine)
Rheinfall (German—Falls of the Rhine)—Schaffhausen
Rheinpfalz (German—Rhenish Palatinate)—on the Rhine east of Saarland
RHEL Rutherford High-Energy Laboratory
Rhenish Schumann's Symphony No. 3 in E-flat major
rheo rheostat
rheol rheological; rheology
rhet rhetoric; rhetorical; rhetorician
rheu rheumatic; rheumatism; rheumatoid
rheu fev rheumatic fever
rheu ht dis rheumatic heart disease
rheum rheumatic; rheumatism
rhf right heart failure
RHF Royal Highland Fusiliers
Rh factor Rhesus group of red cell agglutinogens
RHG Royal Horse Guards
RHGPS Rhodesian Hunters and Game Preservation Society
RHHI Royal Hospital and Home for Incurables
rhi range height indicator
RHIB Rain and Hail Insurance Board; Rain and Hail Insurance Bureau
rhin (Latin prefix—nose)—rhinitis
Rhin (French—Rhine)
Rhine river in northern Europe flowing from Switzerland to the North Sea via Schaffhausen, Basel, Karlsruhe, Mannheim, Mainz, Wiesbaden, Coblenz, Bonn, Cologne, Düsseldorf, and Rotterdam
Rhineland Capital Cologne (Köln)
rhino range height indicator not operating
rhinol rhinologic(al)(ly); rhinologist; rhinology
rhino(s) rhinoceros(es)
rhip rank has its privileges
rhir rank has its responsibilities
R Hist S Royal Historical Society
RHIT Rose-Hulman Institute of Technology
RHK Radio Hong Kong
RHKAAF Royal Hong Kong Auxiliary Air Force
RHKP Royal Hong Kong Po-

lice

RHKPF Royal Hong Kong Police Force

RHKR Royal Hong Kong Regiment

RHKTV Royal Hong Kong Television

RHKYC Royal Hong Kong Yacht Club

rhl rectangular hysteresis loop

RHL Radiological Health Laboratory; Rape Help Line (police telephone line)

rhm roentgen per hour per meter

RHMG Rogers House Museum Gallery

RHMS Royal Hibernian Military School

RHN Royal Hellenic Navy

Rho Rhoda

RHO Regional Hospital Office(r); Rickwell Hanford Operations; Rural Health Office(r)

RHOB Rayburn House Office Building

Rhod Rhodesia

Rhoda Rhodacella; Rhodacelle

Rhode Island Ports (north to south) Providence, Newport

Rhode Island Red Rhode Island's state bird and symbolic nickname of a Rhode Islander

Rhode Island Reds Rhode Islanders

Rhodes English equivalent for Rhodos

Rhodesia Zimbabwe (landlocked British-developed southern African country; English and tribal languages are used; chrome is but one of many valuable exports) *Zimbabwe* (native name)—(formerly Southern Rhodesia)

Rhodesias Northern and Southern Rhodesia (Zambia and Rhodesia, respectively)

Rhododendron state flower of Washington and West Virginia; in Washington the flower is the Western Rhododendron and in West Virginia it is the Big Rhododendron

rhodo(s) rhododendron(s)

Rhodos (Greek—Rhodes)—island in the Aegean

RHOFLIGHT Rhodesian Air Services

rhom rhombic; rhomboid; rhombus

Rhonda formerly Ystradyfodwg, Wales

rhp rated horsepower

RHQ Regimental Headquarters

rhr roughness height reading

r/hr roentgens per hour

RHR Royal Highland Regiment (Black Watch)

rhs righthand side; roundheaded screw

RHS Radio Ham Shack (amateur radio operator's station); Royal Historical Society; Royal Horticultural Society

RHSI Royal Horticultural Society of Ireland

RHSNZ Royal Humane Society of New Zealand

RHSV Royal Historical Society of Victoria

Rhumba (stock exchange short form for Royal McBee Company whose symbol is RMB)

RHV *République de Haute-Volta* (French-Republic of Upper Volta)

rh & w radar homing and warning

RHYP Runaway and Homeless Program

ri random interval; reflective insulation; refractive index; reliability index; require identification; respiratory illness; retroactive inhibition; rubber-insulated; rubber insulation

ri (RI) retrograde inversion

RI Recruit Instruction; Refractories Institute; Religious Instruction; Republic of India; Republik Indonesia; Rhode Island (R.I.); Rhode Islanders; Rice Institute; Rock Island (Chicago, Rock Island & Pacific Railroad); Rotary International; Royal Institute

R & I Rural and Industries (bank)

RI *Registro Italiano* (Italian Register)—of shipping; *Repubblica Italiana* (Italian Republic); *Républicains Independants* (French—Independent Republicans); *Ring Index*

ria (Spanish—river mouth)

RIA Railroad Insurance Association; Research Institute of America; Robot Institute of America; Rock Island Arsenal; Royal Irish Academy

RIAA Record Industry Association of America; Recording Industry Association of America

RIAC Research Information Analysis Corporation

RIAEC Rhode Island Atomic Energy Commission

RIAF Royal Indian Air Force;

Royal Iranian Air Force; Royal Iraqui Air Force

RIAI Royal Institute of Architects of Ireland

rial (RIAL) revised individual allowance list

RIAL Rock Island Arsenal Laboratory

RIAM Royal Irish Academy of Music

RIANZ Record Industry Association of New Zealand

RIAS Research Initiation and Support (National Science Foundation); Rundfunk im amerikanischen Sektor (Radio in the American Sector), Berlin

RIASBO Rhode Island Association of School Business Officials

RIASC Rhode Island Association of School Committees

RIASLP Rattlesnake Island Air Service Local Post

RIASSP Rhode Island Association of Secondary School Principals

rib. range in a box; ribbon

RIB Railway Information Bureau; Referee in Bankruptcy; Roanoke Iron & Bridge; Rural Industries Bureau

RIB *Rijksinkoopbureau* (Dutch —Government Purchasing Office)

Rib^a *Ribeira* (Portuguese— brook; creek; riverside; river valley, stream); *Ribera* (Spanish—bank, beach, riverside, shore)

RIBA Royal Institute of British Architects

RIBNY Republic International Bank of New York

RIBS Restructured Infantry Battalion System

ric radar intercept calculator

ric *ricevuta* (Italian—receipt)

Ric Ricardo; Richard; Richmond

RIC Republic Industrial Corporation; Republic of the Ivory Coast; Richmond, Virginia (airport); Royal Institute of Chemistry; Royal Irish Constabulary

RICA Research Institute on Communist Affairs (Columbia University)

Ricardo Cortez Jacob Krantz

RICASIP Research Information Center and Advisory Service on Information Processing

RICE Rhode Island College of Education

Rice Bowl southwest Louisiana

Rice Bowl of Malaysia Kedah

Rice Center Crowley and Lake Charles in coastal Louisiana

Rich Richard; Richards; Richardson; Richford; Richmal; Richmond

Rich II King Richard II

Rich III King Richard III

Richard Arlen Van Mattimore

Richard Avalon Sir John Woodroffe

Richard Burton Richard Jenkins

Richard Coeur de Lion Richard I of England

Richard the First Richard Wagner

Richard Hull Richard Henry Sampson's pseudonym

Richard Llewellyn Richard David Vivian Llewellyn Lloyd

Richard Saunders Benjamin Franklin (*see* Poor Richard)

Richard the Second Richard Strauss

Richard Tauber Ernst Seiffert

Rich Coast Costa Rica's name translated from Spanish

Richd Richard; Richmond

Richelieu Armand Jean du Plessis

Richmond Virginia's capital named for a London suburb on the upper Thames

Rich-Pete Turn Richmond-Petersburg Turnpike (Virginia)

Rick Richard

Rickie Admiral Hyman George Rickover, USN

rickshu(w) *jinrikisha* (Japanese —man-drawn two-wheeled carriage)

Ricky Richard

rlcm right intercostal margin

RICM Registre International des Citoyens du Monde (French—International Registry of World Citizens)

RICMD Richmond Contract Management District

RICMO Radar Input Countermeasures Officer

'Rico Enrico; Puerto Rico; Ricardo

RICO Racketeer-Influenced Corrupt Organization (statute); Racketeer-Influenced and Corrupt Organizations

RICS Royal Institute of Chartered Surveyors

RICU Russian Institute, Columbia University

RID Registry of Interpreters for the Deaf; Remove Intoxicated Drivers; Riddle Aviation

RIDA Rural and Industrial Development Authority

ridac range interference directing and control

RIDE Research Institute for Diagnostic Engineering

Rideau Hall Ottawa residence of the Governor General of Canada

Riders Riders of the Purple Sage

Riding Mountain Riding Mountain National Park in southwestern Manitoba

ridp radar-iff (if friend or foe) data processor

rie range of incentive effectiveness; resources in education

RIE Royal Institute of Engineers

RIEC Royal Indian Engineering College

Riegger 4 four symphonies by Wallingford Riegger

RIEI Republic Industrial Education Institute (Republic Steel)

Riem Munich, Germany's airport

RIEM Research Institute for Environmental Medicine

Rienzi Niccolo Gabrini

rif reading is fundamental; reduction in force; right iliac fossa

rif (RIF) resistance-inducing factor

rif rifiuto (Italian—restored; repaired)

RIF Reading Is Fundamental; Royal Irish Fusiliers

RIFA Royal Institute of Foreign Affairs

Rif Brig Rifle Brigade

rifc rat intrinsic factor concentrate

Riff mountainous region of northern Morocco opposite Straits of Gibraltar

riffed reduced in force (dismissed or fired)

rifi radio interference field intensity

rifl random item file locater

Rifle City Springfield, Massachusetts

rifma roentgen-isotope-fluorescent method of analysis

rift. (RIFT) reactor-in-flight test

RIFT Rhode Island Federation of Teachers

Rig Riga

Riga Latvia's capital and seaport city taken over by the Russians at the outbreak of World War II during the days of the Hitler-Stalin Pact; NATO name for a class of Soviet submarines

Riga's disease ulceration of the tongue

RIGB Royal Institution of Great Britain

Rigg's disease inflammation of the gums with pus deposits in the tooth sockets; also called alveolar pyorrhea

RIGHT Rhodesian Independence Gung-Ho Troops

right on right on the nose (exactly correct)

rih repetition-induced hypnosis (*Adonai, Adonai, Adonai; Allah, Allah, Allah; hare, hare, hare; holy, holy, holy;* and similar repetitions); right inguinal hernia

RIH Royal Institute of Horticulture

RIHS Rhode Island Historical Society

rihsa radioactive iodinated human serum albumin

RIIA Royal Institute of International Affairs

RIIC Research Institute on International Change

RIISOM Research Institute for Iron, Steel, and Other Metals

Rijeka Yugoslavian name for the port of Fiume formerly belonging to Italy

Rijn (Dutch—Rhine)

ril record input length

RIL Royal Interocean Lines

RILSS Rapid Integrated Logistic Support System

rim. radar input mapper; receiving, inspection, and maintenance; rubber insulation material

RIM Relevant Instructional Material; Resident Industrial Manager

RIMB Roche Institute of Molecular Biology

RIMR Rockefeller Institute for Medical Research

RIMV Registrar and Inspector of Motor Vehicles

Rin Rintintin

Rin (Spanish—Rhine)

RIN Royal Institute of Navigation

RIN Registro Italiano Navale (Italian Naval Register)—bureau of shipping

rina reinitiation

RINA Royal Institution of Naval Architects

RINA Registro Italiano Navale

e *Aeronautico* (Italian Air and Shipping Registry)

RIND Research Institute of National Defense

rinf *rinforzando* (Italian—with additional emphasis)

Ring Ring Lardner

Ring Ringstrasse (German—Ring Street)—tree-lined boulevard encircling inner Vienna

Ring Cycle The Ring of the Nibelungen *(q.v.)*

ringkasan (Malay—abbreviation)—also called *kependekan* or *singkatan*

Ring Lardner Ringgold Wilmer Lardner

Ring of the Nibelungen Wagner's Ring Cycle consisting of *Das Rheingold* (Rhinegold), *Die Walküre* (Valkyries), *Siegfried*, and *Götterdämmerung* (Twilight of the Gods)

Ringo Starr Richard Starkey

RINM Resident Inspector of Naval Material

rin(RIN) report identification number

RINS Research Institute for the Natural Sciences

RINSMAT Resident Inspector of Naval Stores and Materiel

rint rap in the nuts (kick in the scrotum)

Rio many Rio place-names but usually the short form for Rio de Janeiro, Brazil

RIO Reporting In and Out; Rhodesian Information Office; Rio de Janeiro (Galeao Airport)

Rio Branco José Mariá de Silva Paranhos—Baron of Rio Branco—Brazil's great statesman

Río Bravo Mexican equivalent of the Rio Grande

Rio da Duvida (Portuguese—River of Doubt)—Amazon tributary also called Roosevelt River honoring one of its discoverers—Theodore Roosevelt—the other being Colonel Rondón of Brazil

Rio de Janeiro (Portuguese—River of January)—Brazil's great seaport city and former capital better known as Rio

Rio de la Plata (Spanish—River Plate)—estuary between Argentina and Uruguay on the South Atlantic; estuary is fed by waters of the Paraná, Salado, and Uruguay rivers

Rio de la Plata Province Paraguay

Rio Grande river known to Mexicans as the Rio Bravo del Norte; extends from southern Colorado through New Mexico and along Mexican border of Texas to Gulf of Mexico where it ends its 1885-mile run from the Rocky Mountains to the sea

Rioj La Rioja

riometer relative ionospheric opacity meter

RIOP Royal Institute of Oil Painters

RIOPR Rhode Island Open-Pool Reactor

riot. real-time input-output transducer (translator); retrieval of information by on-line terminal (data processing)

Rio Teodoro Roosevelt River (*see* Rio da Duvida)

rip. radar identification point; radioisotope precipitation

rip ripieno (Italian—filling up)

Rip Rip Van Winkle; Robert; Rupert

RIP Reduction in Implementation Panel; Reduction in Personnel (layoffs); Reliability Improvement Program; Reserve Intelligence Program; Riker's Island Penitentiary; Rockefeller Institute Press

R.I.P. requiesca[n]t in pace [Latin—may he (they) rest in peace]

RIPA Royal Institute of Public Administration

RIPGA Rhode Island Personnel and Guidance Association

RIPH Royal Institute of Public Health

RIPHH Royal Institute of Public Health and Hygiene

RIPO Rhode Island Philharmonic Orchestra

ripple. radioactive isotope-powered pulsed-light equipment (RIPPLE)

RIPPR Reliability Improvement Program Progress Report

RI & Prov Plant Rhode Island and Providence Plantation (Rhode Island's official name)

ripr viet riproduzione vietata (Italian—reproduction forbidden)

RIPS Radar-Impact Prediction System; Range-Instrumentation Planning Study; Range-Instrumentation Planning System

rip viet riproduzione vietata (Italian—reproduction forbidden)

RIPWC Royal Institute of Painters in Water Colours

RIQS Remote Information Query System

rir reduction in requirement

rir (RIR) receiver input register

rirb radio-iodinated rose bengal

ririg reduced-excitation inertial reference-integrating gyroscope

ris (RIS) racially isolated school(s)

RIS Radio Information Service; Range Instrumentation Ship; Redwood Inspection Service; Regulatory Information System; Royal Imperial Society; Royal Infantry Society

risa radioactive iodinated serum albumen

RISB Rotter Incomplete-Sentence Blank

RISC Rockwell International Science Center

RISCO Rhodesian Iron and Steel Company

RISCOM Rhodesian Iron and Steel Commission

RISD Rhode Island School of Design

rise. reliability improvement selected equipment; reusable inflatable salvage equipment

RISE Research Information Services for Education

rising sun symbol of Japan and the Japanese

RISM Research Institute for the Study of Man (USA)

RISOS Research in Secured Operations Systems; Research in Secured Operating Systems

risp rispettivamente (Italian—respectively)

RISP Ross Ice Shelf Project

RISS Range Instrumentation and Support System

RISSA Rhode Island School Superintendents Association

RISW Royal Institution of South Wales

rit ritard; ritardando; ritornello; ritual; ritualism; ritualistic; ritualization; ritualize

rit (RIT) retrograde inversion transposed (12-tone)

rit ritardando (Italian—holding back, retarding)

RIT Radio Information Test; Radio Network for Inter-American Telecommunication; Rochester Institute of Technology; Rorschach Inkblot Test; Royal Institute of Technology

RIT Red Interamericana de Telecomunicaciones (Inter-American Telecommunication Network)

Rita Margaret; Margarita

RITA Rand Intelligent Terminal Agent; Rural Industrial Technical Assistance

Rita Hayworth Margarita Carmen Cansino

ritard ritardando (Italian—holding back, retarding)

Ritchie Ward Ritchie Press

RITE Rapid Information Technique for Evaluation

riten ritenuto (Italian—retaining the tempo)

RITES Rail India Technical and Economics Services

RITR Rework Inspection Team Report

RITS Rapid Information Transmission System; Reconnaissance Intelligence Technical Squadron

Ritter's disease skin scaling sometimes fatal when it attacks infants

RITU (Profintern) Red International of Trade Unions

ritz ritzier; ritziest; ritziness; ritzy

riv radio influence voltage; river; rivet(ed)

riv riveduto (Italian—revised)

Riv River; Riviera; Rivington; Rivke

Rivadavia Comodoro Rivadavia, Argentina

Rivalta's disease lumpy jaw

River the Amazon, Amur, Congo, Danube, Delaware, Hudson, Huang, Lena, Mackenzie, Mekong, Mississippi, Missouri, Murray, Niger, Nile, Ob-Irtysh, Paraná, Potomac, Rhine, Seine, Thames, Volga, Yangtze, or other river referred to as the river

River of the Black Dragon Amur River on the Sino-Soviet frontier

River of Grass Florida's Everglades

River of Hades or Hell the Styx, according to mythology it encircles the underworld nine times and the dead are ferried over its waters by Charon

River House Ohio State Penitentiary on the Scioto River near Columbus

River of Kings Chao Phraya flowing through Krungthep

formerly called Bangkok

River of the North the Yukon

River Plate Republics Argentina, Paraguay, Uruguay (all on rivers flowing into Rio de la Plata estuary)

Riverside Riverside County Jail (California)

Riverview Interprovincial Home for (misdemeanant) Women at Riverview, New Brunswick

Riviera Mediterannean coasts of Italy, France, and Spain

Riviera di Levante (Italian—Levantine Riviera)—Italian Riviera east of Genoa

Riviera di Ponente (Italian—Western Riviera)—Italian Riviera west of Genoa

Riviera Fiori (Italian—Coast of the Flowers)—the Italian Riviera

Riviera of South America Uruguay

RIW Reliability Improvement Warranty

RIZ Radio Industry Zagreb

rj (RJ) ramjet

RJ Rio de Janeiro; Royal Jordanian (airlines)

RJA Reform Jewish Appeal; Retail Jewelers of America

RJAF Royal Jordanian Air Force

RJAS Royal Jersey Agricultural Society

RJC Rochester Junior College; Rosenwald Junior College; Roswell Junior College

rje remote job entry

RJIS Regional Justice Information System

Rjk Reykjavik

RJM Royal Jersey Militia

rjp realistic job preview

RJR RJ Reynolds

rk rock; run of kiln

r/k (R/K) radial keratotomy

rk rooms-katholiek (Dutch—Roman Catholic)

r-k rooms-katholiek (Dutch—Roman Catholic)

Rk Rock (postal abbreviation)

RK Air Afrique (2-letter coding); Radio Kabul

RK Rdeci Kriz (Yugoslavian—Red Cross)

Rka Rijeka

rkg radiocardiogram

RKN Republic of Korea Navy

RKO Radio-Keith-Orpheum (theater circuit)

rkp record key position

rkt rocket

Rkt Sta Rocket Station

RKU Ruprecht-Karl-Universi-

tät (Heidelberg)

RKV Rose Knot (tracking station vessel)

rkva reactive volt-ampere

rky rocky; roentgen kymography

rl coarse rales; radiation length; rail(ing); reduction level; rocket launcher

r/l radio location

r & l rail and lake

r-to-l right-to-left (photo caption abbreviation)

Rl Raphael

RL high-powered radio range loop radiator(s); Radiation Laboratory; Reading List; Record Librarian; Record Library; Regent's Line; Republic of Liberia; Research Laboratory; Richfield Oil (stock exchange symbol); River Lines (railroad); Roland Line; Rupert Line; Rutland Line

RL Rijksuniversiteit Limburg (Dutch—State University of Limburg)

rl₁ few line rales

rl₂ moderate number of rales

rl₃ many coarse rales

rla restricted landing area; right lower arm

RLA Religious Liberty Association

RLAA Red Light Abatement Act

rladd radar low-angle drogue delivery

RLAF Royal Laotian Air Force

RLB Sir Robert Laird Borden (Canada's ninth Prime Minister)

rlbcd right lower border of cardiac dullness

rlbm (RLBM) rearward-launched ballistic missile(s)

RLC Radio Liberty Committee

RLCA Rural Letter Carriers' Association

RLCS Radio-Launch Control System

rld radar laydown delivery; rolled

rld (RLD) relocation list dictionary

RLD Raymond L Ditmars

RLDPAS Royal London Discharged Prisoners' Aid Society

rld's retail liquor dealers

rle relative luminous efficiency; right lower extremity

Rle Ramble

rl est real estate

rletfl report leaving each thousand-foot level

rlf relief; retrolental fibroplasia

RLF Royal Literary Fund

rlg railing

rlg *rilegato* (Italian—bound)

RLG Research Library Group; Royal Laos Government

rlgn realign; religion

rlgn dfld religion defiled (by believers who misuse their faith to mask antisemitism, racism, religious wars, and many ventures proving highly profitable such as cultist rackets and never-ending fund collecting)

RLHTE Research Laboratory of Heat Transfer in Electronics (MIT)

RLI Rhodes-Livingstone Institute

RLIN Research Libraries Information Network

rll right lower limb; right lower lobe (lung)

rllb right long-leg brace

RLM Regional Library of Medicine (PAHO)

rlmd rat-liver mitochondria

RLNWR Rice Lake National Wildlife Refuge (Minnesota); Ruby Lake National Wildlife Refuge (Nevada)

RLO Regional Liaison Office(r)

rlp rail loading point

RLPAS Royal London Prisoners' Aid Society

RLPO Royal Liverpool Philharmonic Orchestra

rlq right lower quadrant (abdomen)

rlr right lateral rectus (eye muscle)

rls reels (flow chart)

Rls rial (Iranian currency unit)

RLS Robert Louis Stevenson; Royal Lancastrian Society

rlse release

RLSS Royal Life Saving Society

rltr realtor

RLTS Radio-Linked Telemetry System

rltv relative

rlty realty

rlv relieve

Rlv Rauscher leukemia virus

rly relay

Rly Railway

rm range mark(s); raw material; ream; receiving memorandum; respiratory movement; ring micrometer; room; rubber marker(s)

rm (RM) record mark (flow chart)

r/m revolutions per minute

r & m redistribution and marketing; reliability and maintainability; reports and memoranda

Rm Romania (Rumania); Romanian (Rumanian)

RM Radioman; Raybestos-Manhattan; Registered Magistrate; Registered Mail; Reichsmark (German currency); Research Memorandum; Ringling Museum; Royal Mail; Royal Marine; Royal Marines

R/M Raybestos/Manhattan

R & M Robbins & Myers

rma right mento-anterior

RMA Radio Manufacturers Association; Regional Manpower Administration; Rice Millers Association; Ringling Museum of Art; Robert Morris Associates (Bank Loan Officers and Credit Men's Association); Royal Marine Artillery; Royal Military Academy; Rubber Manufacturers Association

RMADB Reactor Maintenance and Disassembly Building

RMAF Royal Malaysian Air Force; Royal Moroccan Air Force

RMAG Rocky Mountain Association of Geologists

RMAI Radio Manufacturers' Association of India

rm ar reaming arbor

RMAS Rochester Museum of Arts and Sciences

r mast radio mast

RMB Royal McBee

RMBAA Rocky Mountain Business Aircraft Association

RMBN Rocky Mountain Broadcasting Network

rmc rod memory computer

RMC Radio Monte Carlo; Revolutionary Military Council; Reynolds Metal Company; Rochester Manufacturing Company; Royal Military College

RMCC Royal Military College of Canada

RMCM Royal Manchester College of Music

RMCPA Rocky Mountain College Placement Association

RMCS Royal Military College of Science

rmct rat mass cell technique

RMCU Royal Mail Container Unit

rmd ready money down; retromanubrial dullness

RMD Reaction Motors Division (Thiokol Chemical Corporation); Research Management Division (D of E)

RMEA Rubber Manufacturing Employers' Association

R-meter radiation meter

R Met S Royal Meteorological Society

RMFVR Royal Marine Forces Volunteer Reserves

rmi radio magnetic indicator; reliability maturity index(ing)

RMI Rack Manufacturers Institute; Reaction Motors Incorporated; Reactive Metals Incorporated; Roll Manufacturers Institute

rmicbm (RMICBM) roadmobile intercontinental ballistic missile

r/min revolutions per minute

RMIS Resource Management Information System

RMIT Royal Melbourne Institute of Management

RMJC Robert Morris Junior College

rmks remarks

rml right mediolateral; right middle lobe

RML Rand Mines Limited; Royal Mail Lines; Royal Malta Library (Valetta)

RMLF Robert M La Folette

RMLI Royal Marine Light Infantry

RMM & EA Rolling Mill Machinery and Equipment Association

RMMNH Regar Memorial Museum of Natural History (Anniston, Alabama)

RMN Registered Maternity Nurse; Registered Mental Nurse; Richard Milhaus Nixon (37th President of the United States and first to resign the presidential office); Royal Malaysian Navy

RMNP Rhodes Matopos National Park (Rhodesia); Riding Mountain National Park (Manitoba); Rocky Mountain National Park (Colorado)

RMNS Royal Merchant Navy School

RMO Regimental Medical Officer; Regional Medical Officer; Resident Medical Officer

RMOGA Rocky Mountain Oil and Gas Association

R'mond Richmond

rmp right mento-posterior

RMP Radio Motor Patrol; Reentry Measurement Program; Regional Medical Program; Research Management

Plan; Research and Microfilm Publications; Royal Marine Police; Royal Mounted Police

RMPA Royal Medico-Psychological Association

rmpc rubber-mold plaster casting

RMQ Records Management Quarterly

RMR Royal Marines Reserve

RMRA Royal Marines Rifle Association

Rmrs Ramirez

RMRS Rocky Mountain Radiological Society

rms root mean square

RMS Radiation Monitoring System; Records Management System; Remote Manipulator System; Resources Management System; Royal Mail Service; Royal Mail Ship; Royal Microscopical Society

RMSA Rural Music Schools Association

RMSC Royal Marines Sailing Club

rmsd root-mean-square deviation

rmse root mean square error

RMsf Rocky Mountain spotted fever

RMSM Royal Marines School of Music; Royal Military School of Music

RMSP Royal Mail Steam Pack et (company)

rmt right mento-transverse

rmte remote

rmu remote maneuvering unit

rmv respiratory minute volume

RMWC Randolph-Macon Woman's College

Rm-W/MB Rijksmuseum Meermanno-Westreenianum/Museum van het Boek (Dutch— Merrmanno-Westreenianum Royal Museum and the Museum of the Book)—unique collection in The Hague contains 415 Elzevirs

rn reception nil; research note; round-nose (bullet); running noose; running nose

r of n range of neap (tides)

Rn radon; Rangoon

RN radionavigation; Registered Nurse; República de Nicaragua; Reynold's number; Royal Navy

RN Registered Nurse (periodical)

rna (RNA) ribonucleic acid

RNA Registered Nurse Anesthetist; Romantic Novelists' Association

R/NAA Rocketdyne/North American Aviation

RNAC Royal Nepal Airline Corporation

RNADC Royal Netherlands Air Defense Command

RNAF Royal Naval Air Force

RNAFF Royal Netherlands Aircraft Factories Fokker

RNAO Registered Nurses Association of Ontario

RNAS Royal Naval Air Station

rnase ribonuclease

RNAV Royal Naval Artillery Volunteers

RNAW Royal Naval Aircraft Workshop

RNAY Royal Naval Aircraft Yard

rnb received—not billed

RNB Royal Naval Barracks

RNBT Royal Naval Benevolent Trust

RNC Republican National Committee; Royal Naval College (Greenwich)

Rnch Ranch (postal abbreviation)

Rnchs Ranches (postal abbreviation)

RNCM Royal Northern College of Music

RN & CR Ryde, Newport, and Cowes Railway

RNCS Royal Netherlands Chemical Society

RNCSRL Ralph Nader Center for the Study of Responsive Law

rnd round

RND Royal Naval Division

RND Rijksnijverheidstdienst (Dutch—Government Industrial Advisory Service)

rnd(s) round(s)

RNE Radio Nacional de España (Spanish— National Radio Broadcasting System)

RNEC Royal Naval Engineering College

RNES Radiodifusora Nacional de El Salvador (Spanish—National Radio Network of El Salvador)—in Central America

rnf receiver noise figure

Rnf Renfrew

RNF Royal Northumberland Fusiliers

rnfp radar not functioning properly

RNFU Rhodesia National Farmers' Union

rng range

R ng P Republika ng Pilipinas (Pilipino—Republic of the Philippines)

rngt renegotiate

RNIB Royal National Institute for the Blind

RNID Royal National Institute for the Deaf

rnit radio noise interference test

RNL Raffles National Library (Singapore); Royal Netherlands Line

RNLAF Royal Netherlands Air Force

RNLI Royal National Lifeboat Institution

RNLO Royal Naval Liaison Office(r)

rnm radionuclide migration

rnm (RNM) radionavigation mobile

RNMD Registered Nurse for Mental Defectives

RNMDSF Royal National Mission to Deep-Sea Fishermen

RNMI Realtors National Marketing Institute

RNMS Registered Nurse for the Mentally Subnormal; Royal Naval Medical School

RNMWS Royal Naval Minewatching Service

RNN Royal Nigerian Navy

RNNP Royal Natal National Park (South Africa)

RNO Resident Naval Officer

RNoAF Royal Norwegian Air Force

RNOC Royal Naval Officers Club

R No N Royal Norwegian Navy

RNP Redwood National Park (California); Rondane National Park (Norway); Ruaha National Park (Tanzania); Ruahna National Park (Ceylon)

R.N.P. Registered Nurse Practitioner

RNP Radio Nacional de Peru (Spanish—National Radio of Peru)

RNPFN Royal National Pension Fund for Nurses

RNPL Royal Naval Physiological Laboratory

RNPS Royal Naval Patrol Service; Royal Navy Polaris School

rnr runner

r-'n'-r rock-and-roll

RNR Royal Naval Reserves

RNRA Royal Naval Rifle Association

RNRRA Royal Naval Reserve Rifle Association

rns radar netting station

RNS Royal Naval School; Royal Numismatic Society
RNSA Royal Naval Sailing Association
RNSC Royal Netherlands Steamship Company
RNSR Royal Naval Special Reserve
RNSS Royal Naval Scientific Service
RNSYS Royal Noval Scotia Yacht Squadron
rnt roentgenologist; roentgenology
RNT Registered Nurse Tutor
RNTE Royal Naval Training Establishment
rnth raised non-tight hatch
RNTU Royal Naval Training Unit
rnu radar netting unit; radio noise voltage
rnvc reference number variation code
RNVR Royal Naval Volunteer Reserve
RNW Radio Navigational Warning
RNWMP Royal Northwest Mounted Police
RNWR Ravalli National Wildlife Refuge (Montana)
rnwy runway
RNYC Royal Northern Yacht Club; Royal Norwegian Yacht Club
RNZ Radio New Zealand
RNZAC Royal New Zealand Aero Club; Royal New Zealand Armoured Corps
RNZAEC Royal New Zealand Army Education Corps
RNZAF Royal New Zealand Air Force
RNZAMC Royal New Zealand Army Medical Corps
RNZAOC Royal New Zealand Army Ordnance Corps
RNZAS Royal New Zealand Astronomical Society
RNZASC Royal New Zealand Army Service Corps
RNZCD Royal New Zealand Chaplains Department
RNZC Sigs Royal New Zealand Corps of Signallers
RNZDC Royal New Zealand Dental Corps
RNZE Royal New Zealand Engineers
RNZEME Royal New Zealand Electrical and Mechanical Engineers
RNZIH Royal New Zealand Institute of Horticulture
RNZ Inf Royal New Zealand Infantry Corps
RNZIR Royal New Zealand Infantry Regiment
RNZN Royal New Zealand Navy
RNZNC Royal New Zealand Nursing Corps
RNZNR Royal New Zealand Naval Reserve
RNZNVR Royal New Zealand Naval Volunteer Reserve
RNZPC Royal New Zealand Provost Corps
RNZSHWC Royal New Zealand Society for the Health of Women and Children (Plunket Society)
RNZYS Royal New Zealand Yacht Squadron
ro rancho; receive only; recto (frontside of page); reddish orange; right opening; right orifice; road oil; rough opening; runover
ro (RO) readout (flow chart)
r/o roll out (final turn of an interceptor); rule out
r & o rail and ocean
ro. recto (Latin—front of the page, right-hand page)
r⁰ recto (Portuguese—face of page; right-hand page; this side)
RO Radar Observer; Radar Operator; Radio Observer; Radio Operator; Recorder's Office; Recruiting Officer; Republik Osterreich (Republic of Austria); Reserve Order
R-O Reporting Officer; Ritter-Oleson (technique)
R-O Residentie-Orkest (Dutch —Residency Orchestra)—at The Hague where the Netherlands government resides
roa received on account; return on assets; right occiput anterior
RoA Record of Acquisition
ROA Reserve Officers Association; Retired Officers Association; Royal Order of Altruists
ROA Russkaya Osvoboditelnaya Armiya (Russian Liberation Army)
ROAD Reorganization Objective Army Division; Re-Organize Army Division
road hustler(s) card-and-dice hustler(s)
Roadrunner New Mexico state bird and nickname applied to many New Mexicans
roads. roadstead
Roads ports of Hampton Roads (Portsmouth, Newport News, Norfolk, Sewells Point)
Road of the Sun l'Autostrade del Sole (Italian superhighway linking Milan, Rome, and Naples)
roam. return of assets managed (banking)
ROAMA Rome Air Materiel Area
roar. right of admission reserved
ROAR Royal Optimizing Assembly Routine
ROARE Reeducation of Attitudes and Repressed Emotions
Roaring Forties storm-tossed seas between 40 and 50 degrees south latitude
roast-beefsan roast-beef sandwich
roast-beefwich roast-beef sandwich
ROAUS Reserve Officers Association of the United States
rob. remaining on board (aircraft or ship cargo)
Rob Robert; Robinson College, Oxford
ROB Regional Office Building
Robber Barons (see American Railroad Barons, Banker Barons, Mining Baron, Oil Baron, Pork Packer, Steel Baron)
Robber's Nest Berlin, according to an old German song composed in Vienna
Robby Robert(a)
robc readiness objective code
robeps radar operating below prescribed standards
Robert Alda Alphonso d'Abruzza
Robert Forsythe Kyle Crichton
Robert Rostand Robert Hopkins
Roberts Roberts International Airport serving Monrovia, Liberia and other places
Robert Taylor Spangler Arlington Brugh
Robert Weede Robert Wiedefeld
robin. (ROBIN) rocket-balloon instrument
Robin state bird of Connecticut, Michigan, and Wisconsin
Robinson's Island Niihau, Hawaii
robo rocket orbital bomber
robrep robbery report
Rob Roy (Gaelic—Red Rob)— Robert Macgregor the Scottish freebooter
Robt Robert
roc rate of climb; receiver oper-

ating characteristic (curve); required operational capabilities; return on capital; rotatable optical cube; run on crap (fuel of the future)
RoC Register of Copyrights
RoC (ROC) Republic of China (offshore China); Republic of the Congo (formerly the French Congo)
R o C Republic of Congo
ROC Regional Occupation Center; Rochester, New York (airport); Royal Observer Corps
Rocallosas (Spanish—Rockies)
R o Cam Republic of Cameroons
ROCAPPI Research on Computer Applications for the Printing and Publishing Industries
roce return on capital employed
Roch Rochester
R o Ch Republic of Chad
Rochambeau Cayenne, French Guiana's airport named for a count who joined Washington's Continental Army and helped defeat the British by besieging Cornwallis at Yorktown; Count Jean Baptiste Donatien de Vimeur de Rochambeau
Rochedos São Paulo (Portuguese—Saint Paul's Rocks)—in the Atlantic just north of the Equator and far off Brazil
rochelle salts sodium potassium tartrate
Rocher du Diamant (French—Diamond Rock)—off Fort-de-France, Martinique; commissioned in 1800 as HMS *Diamond Rock* because here British sailors withstood a French bombardment lasting more than eighteen months
Rochers du Calvados (French—Calvados Reef)—at the mouth of the Orne in the English Channel
Rochester actor Eddie Anderson
Roch Phil Rochester Philharmonic
rocid reorganization of combat infantry divisions
Rock Knute Kenneth Rockne; Mount Desert Island's nickname used by generations of seafarers; Rockaway; Rock of Gibraltar; The Rock (nickname for the Alcatraz Federal Prison once occupying a 12-acre rock in San Francisco

Bay; name now applies to Rikers Island—New York City's Correctional Facility in the East River or to San Quentin on the shores of San Francisco Bay)
rock-a-billy rock-'n'-roll + hillbilly (music)
Rockaways short form for Long Island, New York's south shore beaches—Far Rockaway, Rockaway Beach, Rockaway Park, Rockaway Point—plus other Rockaways in California, New Jersey, and Oregon
Rock of Chickamauga General George Henry Thomas
Rock City Nashville, Tennessee
rockex rocket exercise
rockfest rock music festival
Rock Hudson Roy Fitzgerald
Rockie Nelson A. Rockefeller
Rockies Rocky Mountains—major mountain system of western North America extending from Alaska and Canada to central New Mexico
Rock Lizards Gibraltarians
Rock of Notre Dame Knute K(enneth) Rockne
rockoon(s) balloon-supported rocket(s)
rock salt halite (sodium chloride)
Rock of Uluru Ayers Rock near Mount Olga, Australia
Rockwell Girls Women's Reformatory at Rockwell City, Iowa
Rocky Roccoforte; Rochester; Rockefeller
Rocky Arabia Arabia Petraea in the northwestern section of the Arabian Peninsula
Rocky Butte Portland, Oregon's jail
Rocky Mountain Columbine Colorado state flower
Rocky Mountain States Alaska, Idaho, Montana, Wyoming, Colorado, Utah, New Mexico, and Arizona
ROCMD Rochester Contract Management District
Rocosas Rocallosas (Spanish—Rockies)—Rocky Mountains
rocp radar (or radio) out of commission for parts
rod. required operational data; required operational date
Rod Roderick; Rodney; Rodrigo; Rodrigues; Rodriguez
RoD Record of Decision
ROD Rosskoye Osvoboditelnoye Dvizheniye (Russian Liberation Movement)

Rodale Rodale Books
rodar rotor-blade radar
Roddy Roderick; Rodney
rodeocade rodeo parade
rodiac rotary dual input for analog computation
roe. (ROE) reflector orbital equipment
ROE Royal Observatory—Edinburgh
Roemenië (Dutch—Romania)
roentgen roentgenology
ROEP Refugee Orientation and Employment Program
rof reporting organizational-file
ROF Royal Ordnance Factory
ROFA Radio of Free Asia
rofor route forecast
roft radar off target
rog rise-off-ground
R o G Republic of Guinea
roger your message received and understood
Roger Williams City Providence, Rhode Island
Rogues Island Rhode Island's nickname in colonial times
r o/h regular overhaul(ing)
ROH Royal Opera House (Covent Garden)
roi return on investment
ROI Range Operating Instructions
Roi Citoyen (French—Citizen King)—Louis Philippe
Rois Rodrigues
Roi Soleil (French—Sun King)—Louis XIV
Roiz Rodriguez
roj range on jamming
Rok a South Korean
ROK Republic of Korea
ROKA Republic of Korea Army
ROKAF Republic of Korea Air Force
ROKAMS Republic of Korea Army Map Service
ROKN Republic of Korea Navy
ROKPUC Republic of Korea Presidential Unit Citation
roksonde rocket sounding
rol record output length; right occipitolateral
Roland Franco-German Nord-Bolkow surface-to-air missile whose name honors a medieval hero of song and story in the time of Charlemagne
rolet reference our letter
Rolf Rudolf; Rudolph
Rolfe Boldrewood Thomas A Browne's pseudonym
rol k rolling keel
Rolls Rolls-Royce

Rolls-Royce of recreational drugs cocaine (selling at $3000 an ounce in early 1985)

Roloff Van Ripper Washington Irving

ROLS Recoverable Orbital Launch System

rom radar operator mechanic; range of motion; range of movement; roman (type); rough order of magnitude

rom (ROM) read-on memory; read-only memory; roll-over mortgage

Rom The Letter of Paul to the Romans; Roman; Romance language

Rom Book of Romans (New Testament); (German—Rome)—capital of Italy; Romanian (Romance language spoken by 22 million Romanians)

ROM Rome, Italy (Fiumicino airport); Royal Ontario Museum

R O M Republic of Malagasy

Roma (Italian, Latin, Portuguese, Spanish—Rome)

roman remotely operated mobile manipulator (acronym); roman candle (firework display); roman number (I, II, III, IV, V, etc.); roman type (this book is set in roman type)

Roman Century the 1st century before the Christian era

Romani Gypsies

Romania Socialist Republic of Romania (Balkan state behind the Iron Curtain; Romanians speak Romanian and export their farm products as well as manufactured goods to other Iron Curtain countries; crude oil is one of many valuable products) *Republica Socialista Romania*; also spelled Rhumania or Rumania

Romanian First Romania's best-known classical composer-conductor-pianist-violinist—Georges Enesco

Romanian National Composer Georges Enesco

Romanian Ports (north to south) Mangalia, Constanta, Sulina, Isaccea, Braila, Galati, Tiglina

Romania's Principal Port Constanta

Romano Giulio Pippi de Granuzzi's palette name—Giulio Romano

Rom Ant Roman Antiquities

Romantic Bruckner's Symphony No. 4; Hanson's Symphony No. 2

ROMBI Results of Marine Biological Investigations

Rom Cath Roman Catholic

Rome English place-name equivalent of Roma

romemo refer to our memorandum

Roménia (Portuguese—Romania)

Romeo letter R radio code; Soviet R-class submarines so named by NATO

Romeo Romeo and Juliet (Shakespearean tragedy inspiring many works including a dramatic symphony by Berlioz, a five-act opera by Gounod, a ballet by Prokofiev, an overture-fantasia by Tchaikovsky)

Roméo Roméo et Juliette (Berlioz symphony for chorus, orchestra, and solo voices)

Rom Hist Roman History

Rominia (Romanian—Romania)

Rom & Jul Romeo and Juliet

romom receiving-only monitor

ROMT Range-of-Motion Test

romv return on market value

ron remain overnight; research octane number

Ron Ronald

Ronald Ronald Press

Ronald Coleman Boris Cole Blake

Roncesvalles (Spanish—Roncevaux)

Roncevaux (French—Roncesvalles)

rond rondeau; rondeaux; rondel; rondels

RONDA Royal Oriental Nut Date Association

Ronnie Ronald; Ronda; Veronica

Ronny Ronald

Roo Roosevelt

ROO Range Operations Office(r)

Roof Garden of Texas Alpine

Rooftop of Africa Kilimanjaro in Tanzania

Rooftop of Antarctica Vinson Massif

Rooftop of Argentina Aconcagua on the border of Chile

Rooftop of Asia Everest in China and Nepal

Rooftop of Australia Kosciusko in New South Wales

Rooftop of Austria Grossglockner

Rooftop of Bolivia Ancohuma

Rooftop of Canada Mt Logan in the Yukon

Rooftop of Chile Ojos del Salado on the border of Argentina

Rooftop of Ecuador Chimborazo

Rooftop of Europe Mont Blanc in France

Rooftop of India Mt Godwin Austen, Jammu and Kashmir

Rooftop of Italy Monte Rosa on the border of Switzerland

Rooftop of Japan Fuji

Rooftop of México Citlaltépetl also called Orizaba

Rooftop of New Zealand Mt Cook on South Island

Rooftop of North America Mt McKinley in Alaska

Rooftop of Peru Huascarán

Rooftop of South America Aconcagua in Argentina

Rooftop of Spain Mulhacén in Granada

Rooftop of Switzerland Matterhorn

Rooftop of Turkey Ararat in Armenia

Rooftop of the USSR Communism Peak formerly called Stalin formerly Garmo and all in Soviet Central Asia

Roof of the World Pamir Plateau of central Asia

rooi return on original investment

roor released on own recognizance

roo(s) kangaroo(s)

'roo(s) kangaroo(s)

Roosevelt I Theodore Roosevelt—26th President of the United States

Roosevelt II Franklin D. Roosevelt—32nd President of the United States

Roosevelt Island current name for New York City's East River island formerly called Welfare and originally Blackwell's (contains apartments, hospitals, and prisons)

root. relaxation oscillator optically tuned

rop right occiput posterior; run of press

ROP Regional Occupational Program

ropeval readiness-operational evaluation

ropp receive-only page printer

Roques Los Roques Islands

ror rocket-on-rotor (device for assisting helicopter takeoffs)

ror (ROR) release on recognizance

Ror Rorschach (inkblot test)

RORA Reserve Officer Recording Activity

RORC Royal Ocean Racing Club

rord return on receipt of document

roreq reference our requisition

ro/ro roll on/roll off

ros reduced operational status

ros (ROS) run of schedule (radio or television)

Ros Roscommon; Rostock

R o S Republic of Senegal

ROS Range Operating Station; Range Operation Station; Royal Order of Scotland

rosa recording optical-spectrum analyzer

Rosa Bonheur Rosalie Mazeltov

Rosa and Carmela Ponselle Rosa and Carmela Ponzillo

Rosc Roscommon

roscoe (underworld slang—handgun, rifle, shotgun)

ROSCOE Remote Operating System Conversational Operating Environment

ROSCOP Report on Observations/Samples Collected by Oceanographic Programs

rose. residuum-oil supercritical extraction; rising observational sounding equipment; rose cut(ting); rose engine; rose fever; rose gum; rose hips; rose lathe; rose leaf; rose leaves; rose mill; rose oil; rose quartz; rose reamer; rose window; rose wine; rose worm; rose wort; roseate; rosebud(s); rosecake; rose-colored; rosemary; rosette; rosewood

Rose New York state flower

Rose Bowl Pasadena, California

Rose Capital of the World Tyler, Texas

Rose City Madison, New Jersey; Pasadena, California; Portland, Oregon; and many other places where people take pains and pride in raising roses

Rosenkavalier *Der Rosenkavalier* (German—The Red Knight)—Richard Strauss's most popular opera

Rose-Red City Petra in Jordan across the Wadi al 'Arabah from the Negev of Israel

Rosetta a mouth of the Nile and an Egyptian town called Rashid by the Arabs

Rose of Venice Haydn's Quartet in D for Strings (opus 20, no. 4)

Rosh Hash *Rosh Hashanah* (Hebrew—New Year)

Rosh Hod *Rosh Hodesh* (Hebrew—beginning of the new month beginning at the new moon)

rosie (ROSIE) reconnaissance by orbiting ship-identification equipment

Rosie Rosa; Rosamund; Rose; Rosemarie; Rosemary

rosla raising of school-leaving age

ROSPA Royal Society for the Prevention of Accidents

Ross Ross and Cromarty

Rossbach's disease gastric juice secreted excessively

Rosse Buurt (Dutch—Red District)—Amsterdam redlight district

Rossiya (Russian—Russia)

Ross Macdonald Kenneth Millar's pseudonym

Rostov Rostov-on-Don

Rosy Rosalind; Rosen; Rosenbaum; Rosenberg; Rosenfeld; Rosenthal, etc.

rot. remedial occupational therapy; right occipito-transverse; rotary; rotate; rotation; rotor

rot. (ROT) rate of return(ing)

Rot Rotterdam

ROTC Reserve Officers Training Corps

rotcc receiver-off-hook-tone connecting circuit

Rothermere Viscount Rothermere (Harold Sidney Harmsworth)

roti recording optical tracking instrument

rotis rotisserie

rotmh raised oil-tight manhole

rotn rotation

roto rotary press; rotogravure

Rot Phil Rotterdam Philharmonic

rotr (ROTR) receive-only typing reperforator (data processing)

ROTS Reusable Orbital Transport System

rotsal rotate and scale

Rou Rouen

ROU República Oriental del Uruguay

Rough Rider Theodore Roosevelt—26th President of the United States

Rough Riders First United States Volunteer Cavalry organized by colonels Theodore Roosevelt and Leonard Wood for action in the Spanish-American War

roul roulette

Roum Roumanian

Roumanie (French—Romania)

'round around

Roundheads Cromwell's followers in the Puritan Party noted for the close-cropped hair of its members

Roundup City Pendleton, Oregon

rout routine

Rov Rover(s)

Rover(s) Coloradan(s)

row. reverse-osmosis water; risk of war

RoW (ROW) Right of Way

Rowan Oak William Faulkner's home near Oxford, Mississippi in Lafayette County he fictionalized as Yoknapatawpha

R-O-W disease Rendu-Osler-Weber disease

Rox Roxburgh; Roxburghshire; Roxbury

Roxy Roxana; SL Rothafel

Roy Royal

Royal Bob President Garfield's name for Colonel Robert G Ingersoll

Royal Brute of Great Britain King George III of Hanover (in the opinion of Thomas Paine and many other Americans and Britons)

Royal Gorge Grand Canyon of the Arkansas in Colorado where it is often called by this short form

Royal Martyr Charles I of England

Royal Society The Royal Society of London for Improving Natural Knowledge (incorporated 1662)

Roy Com Soc Royal Commonwealth Society (formerly Royal Empire Society; formerly Royal Colonial Institute)

ROY G. BIV (acronymic mnemonic for recalling spectral colors—red, orange, yellow, green, blue, indigo, violet)—*see* vibgyor

Roy Liv Phil Orch Royal Liverpool Philharmonic Orchestra

Roy Opera Royal Opera House Orchestra (Covent Garden)

Roy Phil Royal Philharmonic Orchestra

Roy Rogers Leonard Slye

Roy Soc Royal Society

Roz Rodriguez; Rosalind(a); Rozhdestvensky

Rozh Rozhdestvensky (the admiral or the conductor)

rp plate resistance (symbol); raid plotter; rally point; received pronunciation (RP); reception poor; relay paid; release point; reporting post; reprint; response pattern; retained personnel; rhodium plating; rhodium-plated; rocket projectile (RP); rocket propellant; role playing; rust preventive

rp (RP) retinitis pigmentosa

r-p reprint; reprinting

rP reddish purple

Rp *Rappen* (Swiss—centime); *rupiah* (Indonesian currency unit)

RP remote pickup (broadcast); República de Panamá; República del Paraguay; República del Peru; República Portuguesa (Portugal); rocket projectile; Rules of Procedure

R-P Rhône-Poulenc

R/P Registered Plumber; Reporting Person; Royal Provincial (Tory American troops)

RP *Radiotelevisão Portugesa* (Portuguese—Radio-Television)

RP-1 rocket-propellant type-1 fuel (kerosene)

rpa radar performance analyzer; random phase approximation

RPA Rationalist Press Association; Regional Planning Association

RPAA Radiata Pine Association of Australia

rpar rebuttable presumption against registration (dangerous substance examination)

RPB Regional Preparedness Board; Research to Prevent Blindness (fund)

rpc radar planning chart; remote position control; reply postcard; request (the) pleasure (of your) company; reversed phase column

RPC Reliability Policy Committee; Republican Party Conference; Royal Pay Corps; Royal Pioneer Corps

RPC *République Populaire du Congo* (French—Popular Republic of the Congo)—formerly the French Congo

RPCC Reactor Physics Constants Center

RPCFT Reiter Protein Complement Fixation Test

RP China *República Popular China* (Spanish—People's Republic of China)—mainland China under communist control

rpd radar planning device

RPD Regional Port Director;

Regius Professor of Divinity; Rocket Propulsion Department; Rocket Propulsion Division

R.P.D. *Rerum Politicarum Doctor* (Latin—Doctor of Political Science)

RPD Cor *Republica Popular Democratica de Corea* (Spanish—People's Democratic Republic of Korea)—North Korea under communist control

RPDL Radioisotope Process Development Laboratory

Rpds Rapids (postal abbreviation)

rpe range probable error; related payroll expense

RPE Radio Propagation Engineering; Rocket Propulsion Establishment

RPEA Regional Planning and Evaluation Agency

rpedl repetitively pulsed electric-discharge laser

rpf radiometer performance factor; relaxed pelvic floor; renal plasma flow

RPF *Rassemblement du Peuple Français* (Rally of the French People)—de Gaulle's party; Gaullists

RPFMA Rubber and Plastics Footwear Manufacturers' Association

rpfod reported for duty

RP-FS Rozensweig Picture-Frustration Study

rpg radiation protection guide; report program generator; rocket-propelled grenade; rounds per gun

RPG Regional Planning Group; Report Program Generator

rph revolutions per hour

rph (RPH) remotely piloted helicopter

RPh Registered Pharmacist

RPH Royal Perth Hospital

rpha reversed passive hemmagglutination

RPHST Research Participation for High School Teachers

rpi radar precipitation integrator; random procedure information; rated position identifier; real progress index(ing)

RPI Railway Progress Institute; Rensselaer Polytechnic Institute; Retail Price Index; Rose Polytechnic Institute; Royal Pakistan Institute; Ryerson Polytechnical Institute

RPIA Rocket Propellant Information Agency

RPIC Rock Properties Informa-

tion Center (Purdue)

rpie (RPIE) real property installed equipment

rp index respiratory rate index; respiratory pulse index

RPK Regiment President Kruger

rpl running program language

RPL Radiation Physics Laboratory (NBS); Regina Public Library; Repair Parts List; Richmond Public Library; Roanoke Public Library; Rochester Public Library; Rocket Propulsion Laboratory; Rockhampton Public Library

rplca replica

rpm radiation polarization measurement; reliability performance measure(ment); remote performance monitoring; repairman; revolutions per minute; rotations per minute

RPM Raven's Progressive Matrices (test); Regional Plant Manager; Regulatory Project Manager; Rustenburg Platinum Mines

R & PM Research and Program Management (NASA)

rpmb (RPMB) remotely piloted miniature blimp

RPMF Radiation Pattern Measurement Facility

rpmi revolutions-per-minute indicator

RPMI Roswell Park Memorial Institute

rpo revolutions per orbit

RPO Railway Post Office; Repository Program Office(r); Rochester Philharmonic Orchestra; Rotterdam Philharmonic Orchestra; Royal Philharmonic Orchestra

RPO *Rotterdams Philharmonisch Orkest* (Dutch—Rotterdam Philharmonic Orchestra)

rpoa recognized private operating agencies

rpoc report proceeding on course

rpp radar power programmer; reply paid postcard; request present position; return paid postal

RPP Radio Propagation Physics

rppe research, program, planning, evaluation

rppi repeater plan-position indicator

RPPI Rubber and Plastics Processing Industry

RPPMP Repair Parts Program

Management Plan

RPQ Request for Price Quotation

rpr read printer

rpr (RPR) rapid plasma reagin

RPR Republica Populara Romana (Romania)

RPRAGB Rubber and Plastics Research Association of Great Britain

rprt report

RPRT Rapid Plasma Reagin Test

rps revolutions per second; rotational position scanning; rotational position sensing

rp's rice planters; rubber planters

RPs repurchase agreements at commercial banks

RPS Railway Progress Society; Rapid Processing System; Registered Publication Section; Reliability Problem Summary; Republika Populllore o Shqiperioo (Albania); Royal Philharmonic Society; Royal Photographic Society

RPSM Resources Planning and Scheduling Method

RPSs Reliability Problem Summary Cards; Republic of the Philippines Ships

rpt repeat

Rpt Report

RPT Registered Physical Therapist

rpt's (RPTs) rapid-phase transformations

RPU Radio Propagation Unit (USA)

rpv remotely-piloted vehicle; remote pilotless vehicle

rpw ranked positional weight

RPYC Royal Perth Yacht Club

rq (RQ) respiratory quotient

R/Q Request for Quotation

R & QA Reliability and Quality Assurance

RQAS Royal Queensland Art Society

RQBA Royal Queensland Bowls Association

rqd rock-quality designation; rock-quality determination

r qd raised quarterdeck(ing)

rqdcz request clearance to depart control zone

rqecz request clearance to enter control zone

rqiac requires immediate action

rql reference quality level

RQMS Regimental Quartermaster Sergeant

rqmt requirement

rqr require; requirement

rqs ready qualified for standby

RQS Rate Quoting System

rqtao request time and altitude over

rqto request travel order

RQYS Royal Queensland Yacht Squadron

rr radiation response; radio range; radio ranging; railroad; rapid rectilinear; rear; rearward; respiratory rate; rifle range; rural route; rush release; rush and run

r/r right rear

r & r rape and robbery; rate and rhythm (pulse); rest and recreation; rest and recuperation; rest and rotation (of military personnel); rock and roll; rock and rye (whiskey); rush and run

RR Railroad; Raritan River (railroad); Recommendation Report; Recovery Room; Recruit Roll; Reliability Requirements; Remington Rand, Renegotiation Regulations; Research Report; Rifle Range; Right Reverend; Rolls-Royce; Ronald Reagan—fortieth President of the United States whose full initials are RWR (Ronald Wilson Reagan); Rural Route

R-R Rolls-Royce

rra (RRA) radio relay aircraft

rRA specific acoustic resistance

RRA Radiation Research Associates

R/RA Repair/Rework Analysis

RRAF Royal Rhodesian Air Force

R-rated moving picture restricted to adults

RRB Railroad Retirement Board; R R Bowker

RRBC RR Bowker Company

RRBS Rapid-Response Bibliographic Service

rrc radar return code; reference repository conditions; reports of rating cases

rr & c records, reports, and control

RRC Race Relations Conciliator; Recruit Reception Center; Regional Resource Center; Requirements Review Committee; Rocket Research Corporation; Royal Red Cross; Rubber Reserve Committee; Rubber Reserve Company; Rubber Reserve Corporation; Russian Research Center (Harvard)

R.R.C. Lady of the Royal Red Cross

rrcc reduced-rate contribution clause

RRCC Redwood Region Conservation Council

rr cells radiation reaction cells

rrd receive, record, display

rr & d reparations, removal, and demolition

RRD Reliability Requirements Directive

rrda rendezvous retrieval, docking, and assembly (of orbital station or space vehicle)

RRDS Rough Rock Demonstration School

rr & e round, regular, and equal (eye pupils)

RRE Railroad Enthusiasts; Royal Radar Establishment

RREA Rural/Regional Education Association

rr/eo race relations/equal opportunity

R Rep Records Repository (USAF)

RRF Reading Reform Foundation; Refrigeration Research Foundation

rrhage (Latin suffix—excessive flow)—hemorrhage

rrhea (Greek-derived suffix—to flow)—diarrhea, gonorrhea

rri range rate indicator

RRI Radio Republik Indonesia; Rocket Research Institute; Rubber Research Institute

RRIC Rubber Research Institute of Ceylon

rrid reverse radial immunodiffusion

RRIM Rubber Research Institute of Malaya; Rubber Research Institute of Malaysia

RR-IM Research and Reports Intelligence Memo

RRIS Remote Radar Integration Station

rrl reference repository location

RRL Regimental Reserve Line; Registered Record Librarian; Reserve Retired List; Road Reserve Laboratory

R.R.L. Registered Record Librarian (hospital)

RRLNWR Red Rock Lakes National Wildlife Refuge (Montana)

RRLs Registered Record Librarians

rrm('s) renegotiable-rate mortgage(s)

rrm(s) [RRM(s)] renegotiable-rate mortgage(s)

rrna (RRNA) ribosomal ribonucleic acid

rRNA ribosomal RNA (ribonucleic acid)

rrp reader and reader-printer; recommended retail price

RRP Reduced Repayment Program; Riot Reinsurance Program; Rotterdam-Rhine Pipeline

RRPC Reserve Reinforcement Processing Center (USA)

RRPS Ready Reinforcement Personnel Section (USAF)

rrr rebel, resist, riot (New Left student-activist program in abbreviated form)

r & rr range and range rate

RRRA Regional Rail Reorganization Act

rrr's rapid runway repairs

RRS Radiation Research Society; Reaction Research Society; Resource and Referral Service; Retired Reserve Section; River and Rainfall Station (NWS); Royal Research Ship

RRSP Registered Retirement Savings Plan (Canadian)

rrt rendezvous radar transponder

RRU Radio Research Unit (USA); Road Research Unit

rrv rate of rise of voltage

RRW Royal Regiment of Wales

rs radio station; reading of standard; ready service; rear spar; receiver station; receiving ship; receiving station; reception station; record separator; regulating station; reinforcing stimulus; response stimulus; right side; road space; rubble stone

rs (RS) report separator character (data processing)

r/s range safety; revolutions per second

r & s rapport and support; reenlistment and separation; research and study

Rs restricted motion pictures (adults only); rupees

RS Radio Station; Receiving Ship; Receiving Station; Reception Station; Reconnaissance Squadron; Reconnaissance Strike; Recording Secretary; Recruiting Station; Regular Station; Regulating Station; Regulation Station; Republic Steel; Research Summary; Revised Statutes; Ringer's Solution; Rio Grande do Sul; Roberval & Saguenay (railroad); Royal Scots; Royal Society

RS *Rengo Sekigun* (Japanese—United Red Army)—urban guerrila group active in the Middle East

RS-70 reconnaissance-strike bomber (formerly B-70)

rsa radar signature analysis; remote station alarm; right sacro-anterior

'r SA around South America

RSA Railway Supervisors Association; Railway Supply Association; Redstone Arsenal; Regional Science Association; Rehabilitation Services Administration; Renaissance Society of America; Rental Service Association; Republiek van Suid-Afrika; Returned Services Association; Royal Scottish Academy; Royal Society of Arts

RSA (AFL-CIO) Railway and Airline Supervisors Association

RSA *'Round Souse America* (with booze cruisers far from the eyes of family, friends, and neighbors)

RSAA Remote-Sensing Association of Australia

rsac radar significance analysis code

RSAF Royal Saudi Air Force; Royal Swedish Air Force

RSA/HEW Rehabilitation Services Administration—HEW

RSAI Royal Society of Antiquaries of Ireland

rsalt running, signal, and anchor lights

RSAM Royal Scottish Academy of Music

RSAS Royal Sanitary Association of Scotland; Royal Surgical Aid Society

RSASA Royal South Australian Society of Arts

rsb range safety beacon

RSB Regimental Stretcher Bearer; Revolutionary Student Brigade

RSBA Rail Steel Bar Association; Royal Society of British Artists

rsbe ring-standby engines

RSBS Radar Safety Beacon System

rsbt rhythmic sensory bombardment therapy (RSBT)

rsc range-safety command; range-safety control; rational self-counseling

RSC Range Safety Command; Records Service Center; Richard Strauss Conservatory

(Munich); Royal Shakespeare Company; Royal Society of Canada

rsca right scapuloanterior

rscd request to start contract definition

RSCDS Royal Scottish Country Dance Society

rsch research

RSCM Royal School of Church Music

RSCN Registered Sick Children's Nurse

rscp right scapuloposterior

RSCS Rate Stabilization and Control System

RSCT Rhode Sentence Completion Test

rsd robustness semantic differential; rolling steel door

rs & d receipt, storage, and delivery

RSD Riverside Drive; Royal Society of Dublin

RSD-ALA Reference Services Division—American Library Association

RSDLP Russian Social-Democratic Labor Party

rsdp remote-site data processor

RSDS Range Safety Destruct System

RSE Royal Society of Edinburgh

rsea reference sensing-element amplifier

RSEC Regional Science Experience Center

rseu remote scanner-encoder unit

RSF Religious Society of Friends; Royal Scots Fusiliers; Russell Sage Foundation; Russian Socialist Forces; Russian Soviet Forces

RSFPP Retired Serviceman's Family Protection Plan

RSFS Royal Scottish Forestry Society

RSFSR *Rossiskaya Sovietskaya Federatvnaya Sotsialisticheskaya Respublika* (Russian Soviet Federal Socialist Republic)

rsg reassign; receiver of stolen goods; receiving stolen goods; regional seat of government

RSG Royal Scots Greys

RSGB Radio Society of Great Britain

RSGS Royal Scottish Geographical Society

rsh radar status history

Rsh Rosyth

RSH Recreational Services for the Handicapped; Royal Society for the Promotion of Health

RSHA Reichssicherheitshauptampt (Nazi German Secret Police headed by Heinrich Himmler)

RSHWC Royal Society for the Health of Women and Children (New Zealand's Plunkett Society)

rsi radarscope interpretation; radial-shear interferometer; reflected signal indication; replacement stream input

rs & i rules, standards, and instructions

RSI Research Studies Institute

rsia reference site initial assessment

RSIC Radiation Shielding Information Center; Radiation Standards Information Center; Redstone Scientific Information Center

RSID Recruiting Station Identification

R Sigs Royal Signals

RSIS Reference, Special, and Information Section (Library Association)

rsivp rapid sequence intravenous pyelogram

rsj rolled-steel joist

rsl right sacrolateral

RSL Radio Standards Laboratory; Red Star Line; Revolutionary Socialist League; Royal Society of Literature; Royal Society of London

rsla range safety launch approval

rslb right short-leg brace

rslt result

rsm (RSM) reconnaissance strategic missile

RSM Regimental Sergeant Major; Royal Scottish Museum; Royal Society of Medicine; Royal Society of Musicians

RSM Repubblica di San Marino (Italian—Republic of San Marino)

RSMA Railway Systems and Management Association; Republica di San Marino (San Marino—world's smallest republic); Royal School of Mines; Royal Society of Medicine

rsn reason

RSN Radiation Surveillance Network (USPHS)

RSNA Radiological Society of North America

RSNP Rancho Seco Nuclear Plant; Registered Student

Nurse Program

RSNZ Royal Society of New Zealand

rso railway sorting office; railway suboffice; research ship of opportunity

RSO Radiation Safety Office(r); Range Safety Officer; Rehabilitation Service Office(r); Research Ships of Opportunity; Richmond Symphony Orchestra

rso's regional sharing organizations

RSOs Resident Surgical Officers

rsp rear-screen projection; right sacro-posterior

RSP Repository Sealing Program

RSPA Research and Special Programs Administration; Royal Society for the Prevention of Accidents

RSPB Royal Society for the Protection of Birds

RSPCA Royal Society for the Prevention of Cruelty to Animals

RSPCC Royal Society for the Prevention of Cruelty to Children

RSPE Royal Society of Painter-Etchers and Engravers

RSPH Royal Society for the Promotion of Health

rspl radar significant power line

rspp radio simulation patch panel

RSPP Royal Society of Portrait Painters

RSPWC Royal Society of Painters in Water Colours

rsq rescue

r-sq r-squared

rsr regular sinus rhythm; required supply rate

RSR Range Safety Report; Request for Scientific Research; Research Study Requests

r-s ratio response-stimulus ratio

R-SR B Richmond-San Rafael Bridge

RSRC Remote Sensing Research Center (UCB)

RSRE Radar and Signals Research Establishment

RSROAA Roller Skating Rink Operators Association of America

RSRS Radio and Space Research Station

rsrv (RSRV) rotor systems research vehicle

rss ready service spares; remote safing switch; root-sum square; rotary stepping switch

R s-s Russian spring-summer (encephalitis)

RSS Range Safety System; Reactant Service System; Regional Support System; Rehabilitation Support Schedule; Remote Sensing Society; Remote Sensing System; Resource Security System; Royal Security Service; Royal Statistical Society; Rural Sociological Society

RSSA Royal Society of South Africa; Royal Society of South Australia

RSSAILA Returned Sailors, Soldiers, and Airmen's Imperial League of Australia

RSSC Rand School of Social Sciences

R s-s e Russian spring-summer encephalitis

RSSF Retrievable Surface Storage Facility

Rssl Raytheon Scientific simulation language

RSSPCC Royal Scottish Society for the Prevention of Cruelty to Children

RSSRT Russell Sage Social Relations Test

RSSS Regiae Societatis Socius Sodalis (Latin—Fellow of the Royal Society)

RSST Recruiter-Salesman Selection Test

rst radius of safety trace; reinforcing steel; right sacro-transverse

r-s-t readability—signal strength —tone (amateur radio signal)

Rst Rest (postal abbreviation)

RST Royal Society of Teachers

RST Republica Socialista Romania (Romanian Socialist Republic)

R Sta radio station

RSTMH Royal Society of Tropical Medicine and Hygiene

rstr restricted

rstrt restart

RSTS Registry of Scientific and Technical Services

rsu road safety unit

RSU Radical Student Union; Regional Service Unit

rsv respiratory syncytial virus

rsv (RSV) research safety vehicle

Rsv Rous sarcoma virus

RSV Revised Standard Version (Bible)

rs virus respiratory synctial virus

rsvp rapid serial visual presentation; research-selected vote profile; restartable solid variable pulse

RSVP Response System with Variable Prescription; Retired Senior Volunteer Persons; Retired Senior Volunteer Program

R.S.V.P. répondez s'il vous plaît (French—please reply)

rsvr reservoir

rswc (RSWC) right side up with care

R Sw N Royal Swedish Navy

RSWS Royal Scottish Water-Colour Society

rt radio telephone; radio telephony; rate; reaction time; real time; receive-transmit; reduction table(s); related term; remote terminal; right; rocket target; room temperature; round table; round trip; runup & taxi

rt (RT) recreational therapy; respiratory therapy; transposed retrograde (of a 12-tone row)

r/t radar trigger; radiotelephone

r/t (R/T) radiotelephone

RT Radio Technician; Ranger Tab; Reading Test; Recreational Therapy; Registered Technician; Registered X-ray Technician; République Togolaise (Togo Republic); River Terminal (railroad); Rubber Technician

R/T Record of Trial

RT radio en televisie (Dutch—radio and television); *République Togolaise* (French—Togolese Republic)—Togo

rta reliability test(ing) assembly; road traffic accident; rumor told about

RTA Rail Travel Authorization; Railway Tie Association; Refrigeration Trade Association; Royal Thai Army; Rubber Trade Association

RTA Radiodiffusion et Télévision Algérienne (French—Algerian Radio and Television Network)

RTAC Regional Technical Aids Center

rt ad router adapter

RTAF Royal Thai Air Force

RTAM Resident Terminal Access Method

rtb return to base

RTB Rural Telephone Bank(ing)

RTB Radiodiffusion-Télévision

Belge (French—Belgian Radio-Television Network)

RTB/BRT Radifussion-Télévision Belge/Belgische Radio den Televisie (French and Dutch—Belgian Radio and Television Network)

RTBL Richard Thomas and Baldwins Limited

rtc ratchet; reader tape contact(ing)

RTC Rail Travel Card; Real Time Command; Replacement Training Center; Reserve Training Corps; Revenue and Taxation Code; Rochester Telephone Corporation; Royal Trust Company

RTCA Radio Technical Commission for Aeronautics

rtcc real-time computer complex

RTCEG Rubber and Thermoplastic Cables Export Group

rtcp radio transmission control panel

rtcu real-time control unit

rt cu router cutter

rtd remote temperature detector; resistance temperature detector(s); returned; righted

RTD Rapid Transit District; Rapid Transit District (Southern California); Research and Technology Division

RTD/CCS Resources and Technical Services Division/Cataloging and Classification Section (American Library Association)

rtdd real-time data distribution

RTDHS Real-Time Data Handling System

rtd ht retired hurt

rt dr returnable-trip drum

RTDS Real-Time Data System

rte route

r-t-e ready-to-eat (breakfast foods and cereals)

Rte Route

RTE Research Training and Evaluation

RTE Radio Telefis Eireann (Irish Radio Television)

RTEB Radio Trades Examination Board

RTECS Registry of Toxic Effects of Chemical Substances

R te G Rijksuniversiteit te Groningen (State University at Groningen) Netherlands

rtel radiotelemetry; radio telephone; radiotelephony

R te L Rijksuniversiteit te Leiden (State University at Leyden)

R te L Rijksuniversiteit te Leiden (Dutch—State University of Leiden)

rtem radar tracking error measurement

RTES Radio and Television Executives Society

RTESO Radio Telefis Eireann Symphony Orchestra (Irish Radio Television Symphony Orchestra)

R test reductase test

R te U Rijksuniversiteit te Utrecht (State University at Utrecht)

R te U Rijksuniversiteit te Utrecht (Dutch—State University of Utrecht)

R te V Rijksuniversiteit te Gronningen (Dutch—State University of Gronningen)

rtf radiotelephone; resistance-transfer factor; rubber-tile floor(ing); rubber-tile foundation

RTF Radiodiffusion-Télévision Française (French tv network)

rt fm router form

RTFR Reliability Trouble and Failure Report

rtfv radar target folder viewer

rtg radioactive thermal generator; rare tube gas; reusable training grenade

RTG Royal Thai Government

RTG Radiodiffusion Télévision Gabonaise (French—Gabonese Radio-Television Network)

rtgd room temperature gamma detector

rt gu router guide

rtgv real time generation of video

Rt Hon Right Honourable

RTHPL Radio Times Hulton Picture Library

rti respiratory tract infection; rise time indicator; rotor temperature indicator

RTI Reliability Trend Indicator; Research Triangle Institute; Roanoke Technical Institute

RTI Radiodiffusion Télévision Ivoirienne (French—Ivorian Radio-Television Network)—Ivory Coast

rtip radar target identification point

RTIR Reliability Trend Indicator Report

RTITB Road Transport Industry Training Board

RTK Ras Tafari Makonnea (Haile Selassie)

R Tks Royal Tank Regiment; Royal Tanks

rtl reinforced tile lintel; resistor transistor logic

rtl (RTL) register-transfer language; resistor-transistor logic

RTL Right to Life (party)

RTLA Road Transport Lighting Act

RTLO Regional Training Liaison Office(r)

rtls return to launch site

rtm running time meter

RTM Rotterdam, Netherlands (airport)

RTM Radiodiffusion Télévision Marocaine (French—Moroccan Radio-Television Network)

RTMA Radio and Television Manufacturers Association

RTMS Radar Target Measuring System

rtmso real-time multiprogramming support operation

rtn retain; return

rtn (RTN) routine (flow chart)

RTN registered trade name; Royal Thai Navy

RTNA Radio and Television News Association

Rtnst Rottnest

rto radio-telephone operator

RTO Railway Transport Office

rtol restricted takeoff and landing

rtor right turn on red (traffic light)

rtp records turnover package; reinforced thermoplastic

R Tp radio telephone

RTP Request for Technical Proposal (DoD)

RTP Radiotelevisão Portuguesa (Portuguese Radio Television)

rtpr (RTPR) reference theta-pitch reactor

rtqc real-time quality control

rtr returning to ramp

R Tr radio tower

RTR Reliability Test Requirement(s); Royal Tank Regiment

RTR Radiodifuziunea Televisiunea Romana (Romanian Radio-Television Network)

RTRA Radio and Television Retailers' Association; Road Traffic Regulation Act

rtrc radio telemetry and remote control

RTRC Regional Technical Report Centers

Rt.Rev. Right Reverend

r/t room radio/telegraph room

(radio shack)

rtrsw rotary switch

rts radar target simulation; radar tracking station

rt's rubber tappers

RTS Repair Technical Service (tractor stations—USSR); Repair Tracking Service; Royal Television Society; Rubber Traders Society

RTSA Retail Trading Standards Association

RTSD Resources and Technical Services Division (American Library Association)

RTSRS Real-Time Simulation Research System

rtt radiation tracking transducer

RTT Radiodiffusion Télévision Tunisienne (French—Tunisian Broadcasting—radio and tv)

RTTC Road-Time Trials Council

RTTDS Real-Time Telemetry Data System

rt tp router template

RTTPS Real-Time Telemetry-Processing System

rttv research target and test vehicle

r-ttv real-time television

rtty (RTTY) radio-teletypewriter communication(s)

rtu remote terminal unit; returned to unit

RTU Rahway Treatment Unit; Railroad Telegraphers Union; Reinforcement Training Unit; Reserve Training Unit

rtv reentry test vehicle (RTV); room-temperature vulcanizing

rtv (RTV) radio television

RTVE Radio Televisión Española (Spanish Radio Television)

RTVHK Radio-Television Hong Kong

RTVS Royal Television Society

rtw ready to wear

rtx rapid-transit experimental (bus); report time crossing

rty rarity; realty

RTYC Royal Thames Yacht Club

rtz return to zero

RTZ Rio Tinto Zinc

ru are you?; radium unit; rat unit; roentgen unit

ru (RU) railroad underwriter; railway underwriter

Ru Rumania (Romania); Rumanian (Romanian); Russia; Russian; ruthenium

RU Readers Union; Revolutionary Union (underground communists active in Puerto Rico and the United States); Rhodes University; Roosevelt University; Rugby Union; Rumanian Union; Rutgers University

RU Regno Unito (Italian—United Kingdom); *Reino Unido* (Spanish—United Kingdom)

rua right upper arm

RUA Royal Ulster Academy

Ruanda formerly Belgian East Africa

RUAS Royal Ulster Agricultural Society

rub. rubber

rub rubato (Italian—with varying tempo); *ruber* (Latin—red)

Rub Rubbestadneset

RUB Radio Ulan Bator

Rub al Khali (Arabic—Great Sandy Desert)—southern Arabia's wasteland

Rubber Capital of the U.S. Akron, Ohio

Rubber City Akron, Ohio

rubber room padded cell (reserved for self-destructive or violent prisoners)

rubbers rubber bullets

rubd rubberized

Rube Ruben

Rube Goldberg Reuben Lucius Goldberg (cartoonist creator of fantastic inventions for accomplishing simple tasks—hence any overcomplicated mechanism is termed a Rube Goldberg, especially if needlessly complicated)

rubel rubella (german measles)

Ruben Dario Félix Rubén García Sarmiento

Rube Waddell George Edward Waddell

Rubg Rummelsburg

RUBN Russian, Ukrainian, and Belorussian Newspapers

rub. rm rubber room (padded cell)

ruby red corundum

ruby copper cuprite (cuprous oxide)

ruby spinel red spinel gemstone

RUC Royal Ulster Constabulary

RUC République Unie du Cameroun (French—United Republic of Cameroon)

RUCA Rijksuniversitair Centrum Antwerpen (Flemish—Antwerp State University Center)

Ruch Ruchel
Rucos Russian Communists
RUCR Royal Ulster Constabulary Reserve
rud rudder
Rud Rudd; Rüdiger; Rudolf; Rudolph; Rudulph; Rudyard
Rud(dy) Rudyard
rudis reference your dispatch
Rud Kip Rudyard Kipling
Rudolf Valentino Rodolpho d'Antongnolla
Rudy Rudolf; Rudolph
Rudy Vallee Hubert Prior Vallee
rue. right upper entrance; right upper extremity
RUE Regional Urban Environment
Rue St Laurent old redlight district of Brussels
RUFAS Remote Underwater Fisheries Assessment System
Rufe Rufus
rug red under gold
rugger rugby football
RUI Royal University of Ireland
Ruissalo Finnish class of motor gunboats and minesweepers sometimes used as patrol launches
RUKBA Royal United Kingdom Beneficent Association
rul right upper limb; right upper lobe (lung)
RUL Rutgers University Library
Ruler of the East Vladivostok
rulet reference your letter
rum (RUM) remote underwater manipulator
Rum Rumania (Romania); Rumanian (Romanian)
RUM Ranger Uranium Mines; Royal University of Malta
Rumania (Italian or Spanish—Romania)
Rumänien (German—Romania)
rumem reference your memo
rumnog rum-flavored eggnog
run. rewind(ing) and unload(ing)
RUN Revolutionary United Nations
runcible revised unified new computer with its basic language extended
R und J Romeo und Julia (German—Romeo and Juliet)
R unit millimeter of mercury divided by milliliters per second; unit of resistance in the cardiovascular system
RUP Rice University Press;

Rockefeller University Press; Rutgers University Press
rupho reference your telephone (call)
rupp road used as public path
rupt rupture(d)
ruq right upper quadrant (abdomen)
RUR Rossum's Universal Robots (acronym-titled play by Karel Capek)
Rural Educ Rural Education Association
Rural Garden of Eden South Carolina
rureq reference your requisition
rur's rural and urban reformers
rurti recurrent upper-respiratory-tract infection
Rus Russ; Russia; Russian
Rus Russian (Slavic language spoken by some 226 million people although many speak it very poorly; this comment also applies to English and Spanish)
Rusdic Russian dictionary
rush. remote use of shared hardware
Rush Rushdi; Rushmore; Rushton; Rushworth
RUSI Royal United Service Institution
Rusia (Spanish—Russia)
Ruslan Russlan and Ludmila (Glinka's most popular opera)
Rusland (Dutch—Russia)
RUSM Royal United Service Museum
russ russet; russian (leather)
russ russisk (Dano-Norwegian —Russian)
Russ Russia(n)
Russell Cave Russell Cave National Monument in northeastern Alabama
russia russia leather (dark-red leather used for book binding and originally from Russia)
russian russian dressing (mayonnaise-based salad dressing spiced with chili, chopped pickles, and sometimes caviar); russian roulette (each player takes turns in pulling the trigger of a revolver with only one bullet but as it is held against the player's head the loser always loses his life); russian wolfhound (large breed of hound originally bred in Russia and called *borzoi*)
Russian Haydn's set of six string quartets—Opus 33; Rachmaninov's Symphony No. 3 in A

minor
Russian America Alaska's name before its purchase from Russia in 1868 for the bargain price of $7.2-million
Russian-American Capital Sitka, Alaska
Russian Bear symbol of Russia or the USSR
Russian Easter Rimsky-Korsakov's *Russian Easter Festival* —concert overture
Russian Fourteen Russia's fourteen best-known classical composers listed chronologically— Glinka, Borodin, Cui, Balakirev, Mussorgsky, Tchaikovsky, Rimsky-Korsakov, Glazunov, Scriabin, Rachmaninoff, Gliere, Stravinsky, Prokofiev, Shostakovich
Russian National Composer Mikhail Ivanovich Glinka
Russian Physiologist Extraordinary Ivan Petrovich Pavlov
Russian Ports (*see* Soviet Ports)
Russian Soviet Federal Socialist Republic (RSFSR) *Rossiskaya Sovietskaya Federativnaya Sotsialisticheskaya Respublika*
Russian Symphonist Peter Ilyitch Tchaikovsky
Russia's Greatest Poet Alexander Pushkin
Russia's Most Russian Composer Tchaikovsky
Russie (French—Russia)
Russki(s) Russian(s)
Russlan Russlan and Ludmilla (five-act opera by Glinka)
Russland (Dano-Norwegian or German—Russia)
rúst rústico, a la (Spanish— paperback, paperbound)
Rustic Wedding Karl Goldmark's Symphony in E flat (opus 26)
Rust's disease tuberculosis of the upper cervical vertebrae
Rust Territory Trust Territory of the Pacific
rut. are you there
Rut Rutland Railroad; Rutlandshire
rutile titanium dioxide
RUU Ryksuniversiteit Utrecht (Dutch—Utrecht State University)
RUWS Remote Underwater Work System
Ruzyne Prague, Czechoslovakia's airport
rv rear view; recoil velocity; recreation vehicle; reentry vehi-

cle; relief valve; residual volume; retroversion; right ventricle

rv (RV) recreational vehicle; reentry vehicle

r/v reentry vehicle

RV Rahway Valley (railroad); Reading and Vocabulary Test; República de Venezuela; Revised Version; Rifle Volunteer(s)

R/V rendezvous; research vessel

RV Radkikale Venstre (Danish —Radical Left)—Radical Liberal Party; *Revised Version*

rva reactive volt-ampere (meter); right visual acuity

RvA Rouva (Finnish—Madam)

RVA Regular Veterans' Association

R & VA Rating and Valuation Association

rvb radar video buffer; red venous blood

rvbr riveting bar

rvc random vibration control; relative velocity computer

RVC Rifle Volunteer Corps; Royal Veterinary College

RVCI Royal Veterinary College of Ireland

rvd radar video digitizer; residual vapor detector; right vertebral density

RVDA Recreational Vehicle Dealers of America

rvdo right ventricular diastolic overload

rvdp radar video data processor

rve radar video extractor

rvedp right ventricular end diastolic pressure

rvedv right ventricular end diastolic volume

rvf rate variance formula; right visual field

RVFN Report of Visit of Foreign Nationals

rv fx riveting fixture

rvh right ventricular hypertrophy

RV(H)R Road Vehicles (Headlamps) Regulations

RVI Recreational Vehicle Institute

RVIA Recreation Vehicle Industry Association; Recreational Vehicle Institute of America; Royal Victoria Institute of Architects

Rvik Reykjavik

RVL Royal Viking Line

RVLP Rift Valley Lakes Park (Ethiopia)

RVLR Road Vehicles Lighting

Regulations

rvm reactive voltmeter

Rvn Ravenna

RVN Republic of Vietnam

RVNAF Republic of Vietnam Air Force; Republic of Vietnam Armed Forces

RVNF Republic of Vietnam Forces

rvo relaxed vaginal outlet; runway visibility observer

R v O Rijksinstituut voor Oorlogsdocumentatie (Netherlands State Institute for War Documentation)

RVO Regional Veterinary Officer; Royal Victorian Order

rvp radar video preprocessor

Rvp Reid vapor pressure

rvpa rivet pattern

RVPA Rape Victims Privacy Act

rvr runway visual range

R v R Rembrandt van Rijn

R & VR Rating and Valuation Reports

rvrse reverse

rvs reported visual sensation

rv's recreation vehicles

Rvs Riverside

RVS Relative Value Study

rvsc reverse self check

RVSN Raketny Voiska Strategicheskovo Naznacheniya (Russian—Strategic Rocket Forces)

R.V.S.V.P. répondez vite, s'il vous plaît (French—please reply at once)

rvsz riveting squeezer

rvtd riveted

Rvtn Riverton

rvtol rolling vertical takeoff and landing

rvu relief valve unit

rvx reentry vehicle—experimental

RVYC Royal Vancouver Yacht Club; Royal Victoria Yacht Club

rw radiological warfare; railwater (transport); random widths; raw water; recreation and welfare; recruiting warrant; rotary wing; runway

r/w read/write; right-of-way

r & w rail and water

Rw Rwanda

RW radiological war; radiological warfare; Recruiting Warrant; redwood; Richard Wagner; Right Worshipful; Right Worthy; Royal Welsh

rwa (RWA) rotary-wing aircraft

Rwa Rwanda

RWA Railway Wheel Associa-

tion; Regional Water Authority

RWAFF Royal West African Frontier Force

Rwanda Republic of Rwanda (landlocked East African country whose Rwandans speak French and several tribal tongues; exports include tropical crops such as coffee, cotton, and tea; mineral exports include gold, tin, and wolframite)

R War R Royal Warwick Regiment

RWAS Royal Welsh Agricultural Society

rwb rear wheel brake

RWB Rand Water Board; Royal Winnipeg Ballet

rwbh records will be handcarried

rwc rainwater conductor; read, write, compute; read, write, continue; receive with code

RWC Roberts Wesleyan College

rwc's round-wire cables

RWCS Royal Water Colour Society

rwd rearward; rear wheel drive; rewind(ing); right wing down; right word(ing)

RWDGM Right Worshipful Deputy Grand Master

RWDSU Retail, Wholesale, and Department Store Union

RWEMA Ralph Waldo Emerson Memorial Association

RWF Royal Wholesalers' Federation; Royal Welch Fusiliers

rwg rigid waveguide

RWG Radio Writers' Guild; Reliability Working Group; Roebling Wire Gage

rwgl rough wire glass

RWGM Right Worshipful Grand Master

RWGR Right Worthy Grand Representative

RWGT Right Worthy Grand Templar; Right Worthy Grand Treasurer

RWGW Right Worthy Grand Warden

rwh radar warning and homing

rwi read, write, initial; real world interval; remote weight indicator

rwi (RWI) radar warning installation

R Wilts Yeo Royal Wiltshire Yeomanry

RWJC Roger Williams Junior College

RWJF Robert Wood Johnson

Foundation
RWJGW Right Worthy Junior Grand Warden
rwk rework
RWK Royal West Kent (regiment)
rwl relative water level
rwlr relative water-level recorder
rwm rectangular wave modulation; resistance welding machine; roll wrapping machine
RWMA Resistance Welding Manufacturers' Association
r/w memory read/write memory
rwms radioactive-waste management site
rwp radio wave propagation
RWQCB Regional Water Quality-Control Board(s)
rwr radar-warning receiver
r-w-r rail-water-rail
RWR rail-water-rail; Ronald Wilson Reagan—fortieth President of the United States
rwrc remain well to right of course
rws range while search; reaction wheel scanner; reaction wheel system; release with services
rws (RWS) release with services
RWS Regional Weather Service; Royal Water Colour Society
RWSGW Right Worshipful Senior Grand Warden
r/w storage read/write storage
rwt read-write-tape
R-W Test Rideal-Walker Test

rwth raised watertight hatch
rwv read-write-versify
rwy railway; runway
RWY Royal Wiltshire Yeomanry
rx reverse; rix dollar; tens of rupees
r/x receiver
Rx recipe; prescription
rxb roxburgh (binding)
rxp radix point
rxs radar cross-section
ry railway; relay; rydberg
Ry railway; rydberg(s); Ryukyu (islands)
RY Royal Air Lao (coding); Royal Yeomanry
RYA Railroad Yardmasters of America; Royal Yachting Association
Ry Age Railway Age
ryal relay alarm
Ryan Ryan Aeronautical Company (coding)
RYC Richmond Yacht Club; Rochester Yacht Club; Royal Yacht Club
Ry I Ryukyu Islands
rym refer to your message
RYM Revolutionary Youth Movement
RYM-I Revolutionary Youth Movement (Weathermen)
RYM-II Revolutionary Youth Movement (Marxist-Leninist)
Ryojun Japanese equivalent of Port Arthur
ryrqd reply requested
Rys Railways
RYS Royal Yacht Squadron

Ryssland (Swedish—Russia)
ryt reference your telegram; reference your telex
Ryu Ryukyu; Ryukyuan
Ryukyu Retto (Japanese—Ryukyu Islands)—also known as Loochoo or Nansei Islands
Ryukyus Ryukyu Islands between Japan and Taiwan
R y'u R Republika y'u Rwanda (Kinyarwanda—Rwanda)
rz return to zero
Rz Rodriguez
RZ Pacific Seaboard Airlines (2-letter symbol) doing business as Bay Area Helicopter Airlines and Los Angeles Helicopter Airlines; République du Zaire (formerly Belgian Congo)
R of Z Republic of Zambia
RZA Religious Zionists of America
rzl return to zero level
rzm return to zero mark
RZMA Rolled Zinc Manufacturers Association
RZn relative azimuth
RZS Royal Zoological Society
RZ S Royal Zoological Society of Scotland
RZSI Royal Zoological Society of Ireland
RZSNSW Royal Zoological Society of New South Wales
RZSS Royal Zoological Society of Scotland
RZSSA Royal Zoological Society of South Australia

S

s displacement (symbol); sacral; saline; sand; schilling (Austrian currency); scuttle; sea-air temperature difference correction (symbol); second; secret; section; sections; sedimentation (coefficient); sen (Japanese currency unit); sensation; sensitive; separate; separation; share(s); shilling (British monetary unit); ship; sign; silicate; silver; simultaneous transmission of range signals and voice (symbol); slope; slow; small; smooth; snow; soft; sol (Peruvian monetary unit); solo; soluble; son; sou (French monetary unit); space; spar; specific; specific factor; speed; spherical; spherical lens; steel; stere; stimulus; stock; string; subject; substrate; succeeded; sucre (Ecuadorian monetary unit); sum; summary; summer; supravergence; surface; surgeon; symbol; symbol surface; syphilis (sometimes indicated in reports by a Greek sigma)

's (contraction—does, has, is)

s signa (Latin—write); signetur (Latin—label; let it be written); sinister (Latin—left)

s. sinister (Latin—left)

S antisubmarine (symbol); sailing vessel (symbol); San; San Francisco (coin symbol denoting San Francisco mint); Santa; Santo; satisfactory; Saturday; Saturn; Saxon; Schilling (Austrian currency); school; Schweitzer; Schweizer Aircraft; Scotland; Seaman; seaplane; search and rescue; Sears, Roebuck (stock exchange symbol); Seatrain Lines; secondary winding (symbol); secret; Section; See; sen (Japanese currency); Senate; Senate Bill; Senator; Shinto; Shintoism; Shintoist; ship; siemens (mho); Sierra—code for letter S; Sigma; sign; Signor (Italian—mister); Sikorsky; silver; Silver Lines; Sinclair; Sister; Socialist; sol (Peruvian monetary unit); solo; solubility; son; soprano; south; southern; spar buoy; specific factor; specification(s); Sperry; Staff; Statesman's Party; Statute; steamer; steamship; Steinway; stokes; stop; subject; sucre (Ecuadorian monetary unit); summer; sun; Sunday; sune; sunur; Surgery; Sweden (auto plaque); Sylvania; total entropy (symbol); wing plan area (symbol)

S (S) supply (microeconomics)

S/ sol (Peru); sucre (Ecuador)

:/S/ sign (music)

S general area (symbol); Sábado (Spanish—Saturday); Sacrum (Latin); San or Santo (Italian, Spanish—saint, m); Santa (Italian, Portuguese, Spanish —saint, f); São (Portuguese— saint, m); semis (Latin—half); sinister (Latin—left); sisälle (Finnish—in); söder (Swedish —south); sor (Norwegian— south); south; strada (Italian —street); subir (Spanish—to go up, mount); sud (French or Italian—south); Süd (German —south); sul (Portuguese— south); sur (Spanish—south); syd (Danish—south)

s_1 first heart sound

S-1 military personnel; personnel officer

S1c Seaman, first class

s 1 s 1 e smooth 1 side 1 edge; surfaced on one side and one edge (lumber)

31, 32, 33, etc. first sacral nerve, second sacral nerve, third sacral nerve, etc.

s_2 second heart sound

S-2 Grumman Tracker antisubmarine search-and-attack aircraft; intelligence officer; military intelligence

S2F Tracker twin-engine antisubmarine aircraft flown from carriers

S-3 military operations and training; military operations and training officer

S^3 Systems, Science, and Software

S-4 military logistics; military logistics officer

s 4 s smooth 4 sides; surfaced on four sides (lumber)

S-35 Saab double-delta-wing supersonic fighter or fighter bomber built in Sweden and named Draken (Dragon)

S^{35} radioactive sulfur

S-51 Sikorsky four-seat helicopter

S-60 Soviet antiaircraft system consisting of one 57mm cannon mounted on a towed carriage

S-61 Sikorsky civilian or military helicopter

sa sail area; semiannual(ly); semiautomatic; sex appeal; shaft alley; sinoatrial; small arms; soluble in alkaline; special activities; spectrum analyzer; stone arch; subject to approval; subsistence allowance; sun-affected; superabnormal; supra-abdominal; sustained action

s-a single-action (handgun); sinoatrial

s/a storage area

s & a safety and arming (mechanism)

sa siehe auch (German—see also)

s.a. secundum artem (Latin—according to the art)

sᵃ Señora (Spanish—Madam)

Sa samarium; Sara; Sarah; Sarita; Serra; Sierra

Sa Summa (German—total)

Sᵃ Serra (Portuguese or Spanish —mountain range); *Sierra* (Spanish—mountain range)

SA Safeway Stores (stock exchange symbol); Salvation Army; Saudi Arabia; Saudia Arabian; Savage Arms; Savannah & Atlanta (railroad); Seaman Apprentice; search amphibian; second attack (lacrosse); Secretary of the Army; sex appeal; Shipping Authority; Society of Actuaries; Society of Authors; South Africa; South African; South African Airways (2-letter coding); South America; South American; South Australia; South Australian; Southern Association; (Spanish—National Air Routes Corporation); Special Agent; Special Artificer; Springfield Armory; State's Attorney; Sugar Association; Supplemental Agreement; Supplementary Agreement

S-A Stokes-Adams (disease)

S/A Special Agent; State Agent

S of A Society of Actuaries

SA Société Anonyme (French— limited company); *Sudáfrica* (Spanish—South Africa)

S.A. Sociedad Anónima (Spanish—corporation); *Sturmabteilung* (German—Stormtroopers, Adolf Hitler's brown-shirted Nazis); *Sucursales Asociados* (Spanish—associated branches)

S/A Societa Anonima (Italian— limited company)

SA-2 Soviet surface-to-air missile called Guideline by NATO

SA-3 Soviet air-defense missile system nicknamed Goa by NATO

SA-4 Soviet missile system nicknamed Ganef by NATO

SA-5 Soviet surface-to-air missile called Griffon by NATO

SA-6 Soviet air-defense missile system nicknamed Gainful by NATO

SA-7 Soviet shoulder-fired surface-to-air missile called Grail by NATO

SA-8 Soviet missile system nicknamed Guideline by NATO

SA-9 Soviet air-defense missile system nicknamed Gaskin by NATO

SA-315 Aerospatiale helicopter made in France and called Lama

SA-341 Aerospatiale observation helicopter built in Brazil by Embraer

saa small arms ammunition

SAA Saudi Arabian Airlines; Shakespeare Association of America; Signal Appliance Association; Singapore Aftercare Association (hotel for ex-convicts); Society for Academic Achievement; Society for American Archeology; Society of American Archivists; Society for Applied Anthropology; Society for Asian Art; South African Airways; Southern Ash Association; Speech Association of America; Surety Association of America; Swedish-American Association

SAA Single-Article Announcement (American Chemical Society)

SAAA Salvation Army Association of America

SAAARNG Senior Army Advisor, Army National Guard

SAAAS South African Association for the Advancement of Science

SAAASE South African Association for the Administration and Settlement of Estates

SAAB Svenska Aeroplan Aktiebolaget (Swedish Airplane Company)

saac simulator for air-to-air combat

SAAC Sciences and Arts Camps; Seismic Array Analysis Center (IBM); Special Assistant for Arms Control (DoD)

SAAD Sacramento Army Depot; Small-Arms Ammunition Depot; Society for the Advancement of Anesthesia in Dentistry

SAAEB South African Atomic

Energy Board

SAAF Saudi Arabian Air Force; South African Air Force

SAAL Syrian Arab Airlines

SAALIC Swindon Area Association of Libraries for Industry and Commerce

saam simulation, analysis, and modelling

SAAMA San Antonio Air Materiel Area

SAAMI Sporting Arms and Ammunition Manufacturers Institute

SAAN South African Associated Newspapers

SAANYS School Administrators Association of New York State

SAAP Saturn-Apollo Applications Program; South Atlantic Anomaly Probe (NASA)

sa ar saw arbor

Saar (German—Sarre)—Saarland

Saar River City Saarbrücken, Germany

SAAS Science Achievement Awards for Students; Society of African and Afro-American Students; Southern Association of Agricultural Scientists; Standard Army Ammunition System

SAAT Society of Architects and Allied Technicians

SAAU South African Agricultural Union

SAAVS Submarine Acceleration and Velocity System

SAAWK Suid Afrikaanse Akademie vir Wetnenskap en Kuns (Afrikaans—South African Academy for Science and Art)

sab sabbath; sabbatical; soprano, alto, baritone (SAB)

s-a b steel-arch bridge

sáb sábado (Portuguese or Spanish—Saturday); *sabato* (Italian —Saturday)

Sab Sabah; Sabbatarian; Sabbatarianism; Sabbath; Sabelian; Sabine; Sabra(s)

Sab Sabkhat (Arabic—salt flats) —also appears as *Sebkhat*

S-A b South-American blastomycosis

SAB Sabena; Scientific Advisory Board; Society of American Bacteriologists

SAB Sveriges Allmänna Biblioteksforening (Swedish Library Association)

s-aba science—a basic approach

Saba Sheba
SABA Scottish Amateur Boxing Association; South African Black Alliance (pledged to establish majority rule and destroy apartheid separating blacks, coloureds, Indians, orientals, and whites)
Sabah (formerly British North Borneo)
sabbat sabbatical
SABC South African Broadcasting Corporation
SABCO Society for the Area of Biological and Chemical Overlap
SABCOA Screw and Bolt Corporation of America
SABE Society for Automation in Business Education
SABENA Société Anonyme Belge d'Exploitation de la Navigation Aérienne (Belgian World Airlines)
saber (SABER) semiautomatic business environment research
sabh simultaneous automatic broadcast homer
SABHATA Sand and Ballast Haulers and Allied Trades Alliance
Sabine River City Orange, Texas
sabir semi-automatic bibliographic information retrieval
Sable Cape Sable; Sable Island
SABMIS Seaborne Anti-Ballistic Missile Intercept System (USN)
SABMS Safeguard Anti-Ballistic Missile System
sabo sabotage
Saboya (Spanish—Savoy)
Sabra main battle tank built by Israel Army Ordnance and armed with a 105mm gun, native-born Israeli; Sabrina
SABRA South African Bureau of Racial Affairs
sabre self-aligning boost and reentry
Sabre Australian-built Canadian version of the F-86 jet fighter designated CF-86 or CA-27 and originally built by North American as a single-engine jet-fighter
Sabre 32 Australian-built F-86 jet fighter
Sabreliner North American T-39 transport aircraft
SABS South African Bureau of Standards
SABTS Shared-Aperture Breadboard Test System

sabu self-adjusting balls-up (military blunder)
Sabu Sabu Dastagir
SABW Society of American Business Writers
sac sacral; sacrament; sacramental; sacred
Sac Sacramento, California (nickname)
SAC Sacramento, California (airport); San Angelo College; San Antonio College; Science Applications Corporation; Society of Analytical Chemistry; Southwest Automotive Company; Special Agent in Charge (FBI); Statistical Analysis Center; Strategic Air Command; Suburban Authorization Committee; Swedish-American Cooperative
SAC Sociedad de Albizu Campos (Puerto Rican terrorists active in New York City area); *Sveriges Arbetares Centralorganisation* (Swedish—Swedish Workers Central Organization)
saca store and clear accumulator
SACA Steam Automobile Club of America
sacad stress analysis and computer-aided design
SACANGO Southern Africa Committee on Air Navigation and Ground Operation
SACARTS Semi-Automated Cartographic System
Sacate Sacatepéquez, Guatemala
SACB Subversive Activities Control Board
S Acc Società in Accomandita (Italian—limited partnership)
SACC South African Council of Churches; Supplemental Air Carrier Conference; Supporting Arms Coordination Center
saccm slow-access charge-coupled memory
SACCR Southeastern Association of Community College Researchers
SACCS Strategic Air Command Control System
sace systems acceptance checkout equipment
SACEM Société des Auteurs, Compositeurs et Éditeurs de la Musique (Society of Authors, Composers, and Éditors of Music)
SACEUR Supreme Allied Command, Europe

sach solid ankle cushion heel (prosthetic foot)
SACH Small Animal Care Hospital
Sacha Alexander
Sacha Guitry (pseudonym—Alexandre Pierre Georges)
sach foot solid-ankle-and-cushion-heel foot
Sachsen (German—Saxony)
Sächsische Landesbibliothek (German—Saxonland Library)—Dresden's largest
saci secondary address code indicator
SACI South Atlantic Cooperative Investigations
Sackpig *See* SACPG
SA & CL South Atlantic & Caribbean Line
SACLant Supreme Allied Commander, Atlantic
SACLANTCEN SACLANT Anti-Submarine Warfare Research Centre (NATO)
sacm simulated aerial combat maneuver
SACM South African College of Music; South African Corps of Marines; South Arabian Common Market
SACMA Société Anonyme de Construction de Moteurs Aéronautiques (French—Aeronautical Engine Construction Corporation)
SACMP South African Corps of Military Policy
SACNAS Society for the Advancement of Chicano and Native American Scientists
saco select address and contract operate
SACO Sino-American Cooperative Organization
SACO Sveriges Akademikers Centralorganisation (Swedish Central Professional Organization)
SACP South African Communist Party
SACPG Senior Arms Control Policy Group (pronounced "Sackpig")
Sacr Sacramento
Sacramento California's capital
Sacramento River serves northern California and links Sacramento with San Francisco and North Pacific Ocean
Sacramentos short form for the Sacramento Mountains of New Mexico and Texas
Sacre Le Sacre du Printemps (French—The Rite of Spring)—Stravinsky ballet for orches-

tra

Sacred Untouchables TS Eliot, Marcel Proust, Rainer Maria Rilke, William Butler Yeats

SACRO Scottish Association for the Care and Resettlement of Offenders

SACs Solar Appliance Centers

SACS South African College System; South African Corps of Signals; Southern Association of Colleges and Schools

Sac-San Sacramento—San Diego

SACSEA Supreme Allied Command South-East Asia

Sac-Sfo Sacramento—San Francisco

SACSIR South African Council for Scientific and Industrial Research

Sacto Sacramento

SACTU South African Congress of Trade Unions

SACU Service for Admission to College and University

SACUBO Southern Association of College and University Business Officers

SACVT Society of Air Cushion Vehicle Technicians

sad. safety analysis document; safety, arming, destruct; safety and arming device; situation attention display

SAd (SAD) St Augustine decline (grass virus)

SAD simple, average, or difficult; Social Affairs Department (Communist China's espionage agency)

S & AD Science and Applications Directorate (NASA)

SAD South African Digest

sadap simplified automatic data plotter

SADC Sector Air Defense Commander; Singapore Air Defense Command

SADD Students Against Drunk Drivers

Saddler NATO code name for Soviet SS-7 liquid-fuel intercontinental ballistic missile

sade sensitive acoustic-detection equipment

SADE Sociedad Argentina de Escritores (Argentine Writers' Society)

SADF South African Defence Forces

sadic solid-state analog-to-digital computer

sadie scanning analog-to-digital input equipment; semi-automatic decentralized intercept

environment

Sadie Sara; Sarah; Sarita

sado-maso sado-masochism; sado-masochist

sado-sex sado-sexual(ity)

SADS Swiss Air Defense System

sadsac sampled data simulator and computer

sadsact self-aligned descriptors from self and cited titles (automatic index)

sad sam (SAD SAM) sentence appraiser and diagrammer—semantic analyzer machine

SADTC Shape Air Defense Technology Center

s-a-d test sugar-acetone-diacetic acid test

sae San Diego Aircraft Engineering (corporate symbol); self-addressed envelope; standard average European

SAE Society for the Advancement of Education; Society of American Etchers; Society of Automotive Engineers; Solar Atmospher(ic) Explorer

S.A.E. Société Anonyme Egyptienne (Egyptian limited company)

SAEA Southeastern Adult Education Association

saeb self-adjusting electric brake

SAEB Spacecraft Assembly and Encapsulation Building (NASA); Special Army Evaluation Board

saec. saeculum (Latin—century)

SAEC South African Engineer Corps; Sumitomo Atomic Energy Commission (Japan)

SAEH Society for Automation in English and the Humanities

SAEI Sumitomo Atomic Energy Industries (Japan)

SAEL South African Emergency League

SAemc South African endomyocardiopathy

SAEMR Small Arms Expert Marksmanship Ribbon

SAEST Society for the Advancement of Electrochemical Science and Technology

SAET Spiral Aftereffect Test

Saeta Hispano HA-200 twin-engine jet trainer built in Egypt and in Spain; also called E-14

saew ship's advanced electronic warfare

saf safety

SAF Secretary of the Air Force; See America First; Singapore Air Force; Social Affairs Federation; Society of American Florists; Society of American Foresters; Strategic Air Force

SAF Svenska Arbetsgivareforeningen (Swedish Employers' Confederation)

safa solar-array failure analysis; soluble-antigen fluorescent antibody

SAFA School Assistance in Federally Affected Areas; Society for Automation in the Fine Arts

SAFAA South African Fine Arts Association

SAFB Scott Air Force Base; Shaw Air Force Base

saf black super-abrasion furnace black

SAFC South African Flying Corps

SAFCA Safeguard Communications Agency

SAFCB Secretary of the Air Force Correction Board

SAFCMD Safeguard Command (USA)

SAFCO Standing Advisory Committee on Fisheries in the Caribbean Organization

safe. satellite alert force employment; system, area, function, equipment

SAFE Braathens South American & Far East Air Transport; Survival and Flight Equipment Association; System for Automated Flight Efficiency

S.A.F.E. Society of Aeronautic Flight Engineers

SAFEORD Safety of Explosive Ordnance Databank (USN)

SAFE TRIP Students Against Faulty Tires Ripping in Pieces

Safford Federal Prison Camp at Safford, Arizona

SAFI Senior Air Force Instructor

Safir Saab-built training and utility aircraft also known as Saab 91-D

SAFMARINE South African Marine (corporation)

SAFO Senior Air Force Officer (present)

SAFOH Society of American Florists and Ornamental Horticulturists

SAF£ South African pound

S Afr South Africa(n)

SAFR Senior Air Force Representative

SAFRAS Self-Adaptive Flexible-Format Retrieval And Storage System

S-Afr Du South-African Dutch (Afrikaans)

SAFS Secondary Air Force Specialty; selective automatic feed stripe (knitting machine)

SAFSL Secretary of Air Force Space Liaison

SAFSO Safeguard System Office(r)

SAFSR Society for the Advancement of Food Service Research

SAFTI Singapore Armed Forces Training Institute

SAFU Scottish Amateur Fencing Union

SAFUS Secretary of the Air Force, United States

sa fx saw fixture

Sag Sagittarius

SAG Scientific Advisory Group; Screen Actors Guild; Society of Arthritic Gardeners; Surface Action Group (USN); Systems Analysis Group

SAGA Sand and Gravel Association; Scout and Guide Activity; Society of American Graphic Artists

Saga City Stavanger, Norway

Saga Island Iceland

Sagamore Hill Theodore Roosevelt's home on Long Island at Oyster Bay, New York

SAGB Spiritualist Association of Great Britan

sag. d saggital diameter

sage. semi-automatic ground environment (for defense against air attack); solar-assisted gas energy (for heating)

SAGE Senior Action in a Gay Environment; Senior Actualization and Growth Exploration; Skylab Advisory Group for Experiments (NASA); Stratospheric Aerosol and Gas Experiment

Sage of America Benjamin Franklin

Sage of Anacostia Frederick Douglass

Sage of Ashland Henry Clay

Sage of Auburn Secretary of State William H. Seward

Sage of Baltimore H(enry) L(ouis) Mencken

Sagebrush Nevada state flower; state bird—the Mountain Bluebird

Sagebrush Princess Sarah Winnemucca

Sagebrush State Nevada's official nickname

SAGE/BUIC Semi-Automatic Ground Environment and Back-Up Interceptor Control (systems)

Sage of Chappaqua Horace Greeley

Sage of Chelsea Thomas Carlyle

Sage of Concord Ralph Waldo Emerson—American philosopher-poet

Sage of East Aurora Elbert Hubbard

Sage of Ebury Street George Moore

Sage of Emporia William Allen White

Sage of Ferney Voltaire

Sage of Gramercy Park Samuel H. Tilden—benefactor of the New York Public Library and governor of New York

Sage hen(s) Nevadan(s)

Sage of Jena Ernst Haeckel

Sage of Kinderhook Martin Van Buren—eighth President of the United States

Sage of Monticello Thomas Jefferson—editor of the *Declaration of Independence*, founder of the University of Virginia, third President of the United States

Sage of Montpelier James Madison—Father of the *Constitution*, fourth President of the United States

Sage of Mount Vernon George Washington—first President of the United States

Sage of Nininger Ignatius Donnelly

Sage of Philadelphia Benjamin Franklin

Sage of Popayán Francisco José de Caldas

Sage of Princeton Grover Cleveland

Sage of Roanoke John Randolph

Sage of Samos Pythagoras

Sage of Sullivan Street Edgar Varese

Sage of Walden Pond Henry David Thoreau

Sage of Wheatland James Buchanan—15th President of the United States

Sage of Yoknapatawpha William Faulkner

SAGGA Scout and Guide Graduate Association

Sagger NATO name for a Soviet antitank missile

Sagnalcilar Istanbul's suburban prison

SAGP Society for Ancient Greek Philosophy

SAGS Semiactive Gravity Gradient System (NASA)

SAGSET Society for Academic Gaming and Simulation in Education and Training

sagt systematic approach to group technology

SAG & U San Antonio, Gulf & Uvalde (railroad)

Saguaro Cactus Blossom Arizona's state flower

sah subarachnoid hemorrhage

SAH Society of American Historians; Society of Automotive Historians

SAHAND Society Against *Have A Nice Day*

Sahara North Africa's great desert and name given the Breguet 765 troop transport aircraft

Sahel Sahel Countries (Cape Verde Islands, Chad, Gambia, Mali, Mauritania, Niger, Senegal, Upper Volta)

Sah Esp Sahara Español (Spanish Sahara)

sahf semiautomatic height finder

SAHR Society for Army Historical Research

SAHSA Servicio Aéreo de Honduras SA (Spanish—Air Service of Honduras Inc)

sahyb simulation of analog and hybrid computers

sai self-appraisal instrument; self-appraisal inventory; sell (sold) as is

Sai Saigon

SAI Schizophrenics Anonymous International; Science Applications Inc; Self-Analysis Inventory; Social Adequacy Index; South African Irish (regiment); Stern Activities Index

SAI Società Anonima Italiana (Italian Incorporated Company); *Son Altesse Impériale* (French—Her or His Imperial Highness); *Su Alteza Imperial* (Spanish—Your Imperial Highness)

SAIA South Australian Institute of Architects

SAIC Special Agent in Charge (Secret Service)

said. speech auto-instructional device

Said Port Said, Egypt

Saida (Arabic—Sidon)

SAIDET Single-Axis Inertial-

Drift Erection Test

SAIF South African Industrial Federation; South African Institute of Foundrymen

sail. structural analysis input language

SAIL Sea-Air Interaction Laboratory

Sailor City San Diego, California where the Navy is always welcome

Sailor Historian Samuel Eliot Morison

Sailor King William IV of England

Sailor on Horseback Jack London

Sailor's Poet Charles Dibden

Sailors's Friend Samuel Plimsoll

Sailor Town Norfolk, Virginia

SAILS Software-Adaptable Integrated-Logic System

SAIM South African Institute of Management

SAIMC South African Institute for Measurement and Control

SAIMENA South African Institute of Marine Engineers and Naval Architects

SAIMR South African Institute for Medical Research

SAIMS Selected Acquisition Information and Management System

SAINT Systems Analysis of an Integrated Network of Tasks (USAF)

Saint Anthony's fire gangrenous skin conditions such as ergotism, erysipelas, and hospital gangrene

Saint Augie Saint Augustine, Florida

Saint Barts Saint Barthélemy or Saint Bartholomew in the French West Indies where it once belonged to Sweden

Saint Bart's Saint Bartholomew's Episcopal Church

Saint Christopher (St Kitts) and Nevis British-associated English-speaking and sugar-productive West Indian islands in the Caribbean southeast of the Virgin Islands

Saint Croix Santa Cruz (inhabitants of this Virgin Island called Cruzans)

Saint Didacus San Diego de Alcalá de Henares

Saint-Ex Antoine de Saint-Exupéry

Saint Gall English equivalent of Sankt Gall

Saint Gilles (French—Sint Gillis)

Saint Gothard (French—Sankt Gotthard)

Saint Gotthard's disease intestinal hookworms

Saint of the Gutters Nobelprizewinner Mother Teresa of Calcutta

Saint Jean (French—Saint Johns)

Saint Joe Saint Joseph, Missouri

Saint John St John, New Brunswick

Saint-John Perse Alexis Léger

Saint Johns St Johns, Antigua

Saint John's St John's, Newfoundland; St John's University, New York

Saint Kitts Saint Christopher (Leeward Islands, British West Indies)

Saint Lawrence St Lawrence River

Saint Lawrence Islands Saint Lawrence Islands National Park on the Canadian islands and nearby shore of the Saint Lawrence River

Saint Lawrence Seaway 2300-mile (3700-kilometer) waterway linking American and Canadian Great Lakes and St Lawrence River ports with the Atlantic Ocean

Saint Loo Saint Louis, Missouri

Saint Lucia English-speaking West Indian island republic between Martinique and Saint Vincent; its capital city seaport — Castries — witnesses export of bananas, spices, and sugar

Saint Lucy St Lucia, West Indies

Saint Martin's evil dipsomania

Saint Moritz (French—Sankt Moritz)

Saint P St Pancras (London railway station); St Paul, Minnesota

Saint Paddy Saint Patrick

Saint Patrick's Saint Patrick's Day (March 17)

Saint Paul's Rocks English equivalent of Rochedos São Paulo

Saint Pete St Petersburg, Florida

Saint Petersburg czarist name for what later was renamed Petrograd and is now called Leningrad

Saint-Saëns' 5 the five symphonies of Saint-Saëns including his Symphony in A major, the Symphony No. 1, the Symphony in F major (*Urbs Roma*), the Symphony No. 2 in A minor, the Symphony No. 3 in C minor (*Organ*) for organ and orchestra

Saint-Simon Claude-Henri de Rouvroy, Compte de Saint-Simon

Saint Stephen's Saint Stephen's Day (December 26)

Saint Vince St Vincent (West Indies)

Saint Vincent and the Grenadines English-speaking West Indian island nation in the Windwards between Saint Lucia and Grenada—capital is Kingstown where arrowroot, bananas, and coconuts are exported

Saint Vitus' dance chorea; involuntary muscular twitching

SAIRR South African Institute of Race Relations

SAIS School of Advanced International Studies (Johns Hopkins University)

SAIT Southern Alberta Institute of Technology

SAIT Service D'Analyse de l'Information Technologique (French—Technological Information Analysis Service)

SAJ Shipbuilders Association of Japan; Society for the Advancement of Judaism

SAJ Suomen Ammattijärjestö (Finnish Federation of Trade Unions)

SAJAC South African Jewish Association of Canada

SAJC Southern Association of Junior Colleges

sa ji saw jig

Sajonia (Spanish—Saxony)

SAK Serge Alexandrovich Koussevitsky

SAK Suomen Ammattilittojen Keskulitto (Finnish—Finnish Trade Union Confederation)

Sakartvelo (Georgian—Republic of Georgia)—USSR

Saki Hector Hugh Munro

Saksen (Dutch—Saxony)

sal salt; salicylate; saloon

sal (SAL) surface and airlift

s.a.l. secundum artis leges (Latin—according to the rules of art)

Sal Salamanca; Salaverry; Salem; Salomon

Sal salida (Spanish—departure; exit); *Salmonella*

SAL San Salvador, El Salvador

(airport); Seaboard Airline Railroad; Society of Antiquaries of London; South African Library (Cape Town); Symbolic Assembly Language

SAL Svenska-Amerika Linien (Swedish-American Line)

SALA Scientific Assistant Land Agent; South African Library Association; Southwest Alliance for Latin American(s)

Salad Bowl of California Salinas in lettuce-productive Monterey County

Saladin Alvis armored car built in Britain and armed with a 76mm gun

SALALM Seminars on the Acquisition of Latin American Library Materials

salam salamanzar (12-bottle capacity)

sal ammoniac ammonium chloride (NH_4Cl)

SALB South African Library for the Blind (Grahamstown)

sale. simple algebraic language for engineers

Salem Oregon's capital named for a Massachusetts city northeast of Boston

sal gal saloon girl

salicyl salicylate

SALINET Satellite Library Information Network

Salisburia (Latin—Salzburg)—birthplace of Mozart and one of the world's greatest music festivals

Salish NATO name for a Soviet surface-to-surface missile

SALJ South African Law Journal

Sall Gaius Sallustius Crispus (Roman historian often referred to as Sallust)

Sallee English equivalent of Salé also called Sali or Sla and long a pirate port of Morocco

Sallie Sarah

Sallust Roman historian Gaius Sallustius

Sally Sara(h); South Atlantic (baseball) League (nickname)

Sally Ann Salvation Army (hobo abbreviation)

Sally Rand Helen Gould Beck

salm single-anchor leg mooring

Salm Salomon

Salm Salmonella

SALM Society of Airline Meteorologists

Salmantica (Latin—Salamanca)

salmiak sal ammoniac (ammonium chloride)

Salmon City Astoria, Oregon

salmonsan salmon sandwich

salmonwich salmon sandwich

Salomons Salomon Islands in the Chagos Archipelago in the Indian Ocean

Salomon symphonies Haydn's symphonies 93 through 104 bearing such names as *Surprise* (94), *Miracle* (96), *Military* (100), *Clock* (101), *Drum Roll* (103), and *London* (104); series named for the impresario JP Salomon who secured concerts for Haydn in London

Salonika equivalent of Thessalonika, Greece

Salop(ian) Shrewsbury; Shropshire

SALP South African Labour Party

salpingect salpingectomic (sterilization); salpingectomy (removal of the fallopian tubes)

salr saturated adiabatic lapse rate

SALR South African Law Reports

SALRC Society for the Assistance of Ladies in Reduced Circumstances

salt sodium chloride (NaCl)

salt. suggestive-accelerative learning and teaching

SALT Society for Applied Learning Technology; Strategic Arms Limitation Talks (begun in Helsinki between US and USSR on November 17, 1969)

Salt City Syracuse, New York

Saltees Saltee Islands in St George's Channel off Wexford, Ireland

salt horse pickled meat served to sailors and soldiers

Salt Lake City Utah's capital

Salton Sea formerly called Salton Sink

saltpeter potassium nitrate

salts of lemon oxalic acid

salt of tartar potassium carbonate

salut salutation; sea-air-land-and-underwater targets (SALUT)

salv salvage

Salv Salvador

Salvador short form for the Brazilian port of Bahia or São Salvador de Todos os Santos; truncation of the Central American republic of El Salvador

Salv Army Salvation Army

Salvatoriello Salvator Rosa

Saly Salvation Army

Salz Salzburg, Austria

Salzburg Philospher Balduin V Schwarz

sam scanning auger microscope; self-advising materials; serial access memory; served available market; small (secondary) annular mirror; space-available mail (SAM); student accountability model; surface-to-air missile (SAM); synchronous amplitude modulation

sam (SAM) shared-appreciation mortgage

sam samedi (French—Saturday)

Sam Samoa; Samoan; Samson; Samoyed; Samuel; Samuelito

S-a-m S-adenosyl-methionine

Sam Samstag (German—Saturday); *Samuel*

SAM School Administrators of Montana; School of Aerospace Medicine; Society for the Advancement of Management; Society of American Magicians; Special Air Mission; Student Accountability Model

SAM Societa Aerea Mediterranea (Italian—Mediterranean Airline)

SAMA Sacramento Air Materiel Area; Saudi Arabian Monetary Agency; Scientific Apparatus Makers Association; Student American Medical Association

Samanaliya (Singhalese—Adam's Peak)—7000-foot mountain in south central Ceylon; rock at summit contains 5-foot-long footprint believed by Buddhists to be Buddha's, by Hindus to be Siva's, by Moslems to be Adam's as this is where they believe he fell from paradise and stood for a thousand years before constructing the 30-mile causeway to India—Adam's Bridge

SAMANTHA System for the Automated Management of Text from a Hierarchical Arrangement

Samarians Samarian Mountains of Israel between Galilee and Jerusalem as well as the Jordan River Valley and the Plain of Sharon

Samaritan Convair 48-passenger military transport adapted from 240/440 series airliners

SAMB School of Aviation Medicine—Brooks AFB

SAMBA Special Agents Mutual Benefit Association (FBI); Systems Approach to Managing Bureau of Ships Acquisitions (USN)

SAMC South African Marine Corporation; South African Medical Corps

SAM/CAR South America/Caribbean

SAM-D surface-to-air missile for field air defense

SAME Society of American Military Engineers

SAMECS Structural Analysis Method for Evaluation of Complex Structures

Sam'el Samuel

S Am(er) South America(n)

samex surface-to-air missile exercise

SAMF Seaborne Army Maintenance Facilities; Seaborne Army Materiel Facilities

samfu self-adjusting military fuckup

SAMH Scottish Association for Mental Health

sami socially-acceptable monitoring instrument

SAMI System Acquisition Management Inspection

Samian Sage Pythagoras of Samos

Samiel The Devil

samizdat *samizdatel'stvo* (Russian—self-published and self-distributed)—clandestine literature suppressed by the Soviet government

Sam J Dr Samuel Johnson

SAMJ *South African Medical Journal*

Saml Samiel; Samuel

SAML Standard Army Management Language

SAMLA South Atlantic Modern Language Association

samm semi-automatic measuring machine

Samml *Sammlung* (German—collection)

Sammy American soldier (British slang); Samuel

SAMNS South African Military Nursing Service

Samoa South Pacific island nation once the western part of German Samoa and later called British Samoa; Samoans converse in English and Samoan; tourism and tropical agriculture support the economy

Samoa i Sisifo (Samoan Polyne-

sian—Western Samoa)— formerly British Samoa

Samoan Ports Apia (Samoa or Western Samoa), Pago Pago (American Samoa)

Samoas Samoa Islands

samos (SAMOS) satellite and missile observation system

Samothrace English equivalent of Samothráki island in the Aegean

Samothráki (Greek—Samothrace)

SAMPAM System for Automation of Materiel Plans for Army Materiel

SAMPE Society of Aerospace Material and Process Engineers

SAM & PE Society for the Advancement of Material and Process Engineering

sample. simulation and modeling of profiles in lithography and etching

SAMR Special Assistant for Materiel Readiness (USA)

samrt shared-aperture medium-range tracker

sams stratospheric and mesospheric sounder

Sams Howard W Sams and Company

SAMS Sample Method Survey; Satellite Automation System; Satellite Auto-Monitor System; South American Missionary Society; Standard Army Maintenance System

SAMSA Silica and Moulding Sands Association

SAM-SAC Special Aircraft Modification for Strategic Air Command

SAM/SAT South America/South Atlantic

Sam Slick Thomas Chandler Haliburton's nickname

SAMSO Space and Missile System Organization (USAF)

Samson *Samson et Dalila* (three-act opera by Saint-Saëns based on the biblical legend of Samson and Delilah)

SAMSON Strategic Automatic-Message-Switching Operational Network

SAM/SPAC South America/South Pacific

sam(s) [SAM(s)] shared-appreciation mortgage(s)

SAMTC South Atlantic Marine Terminal Conference

SAMTEC Space and Missile Test Center

SAMU *Service Aide Médicale*

Urgente (French—Urgent Medicaid Service)

Samuel Edwards Noel Bertram Gerson

Samuel Falkland Heijermans Herman

Sam(uel) Goldwyn Samuel Goldfish

SA Mus South African Museum (Cape Town)

san sandwich; sanitary; styrene-acrylonitrile copolymer

San Santos (British maritime abbreviation)

SAN San Diego, California (Lindbergh Field); South African Navy

SAN *Space Age News*

SANA Scientists Against Nuclear Arms; State (Department), Army, Navy, Air (Force)

San Andreas San Andreas Fault of western California

San Anto (Mexican-American—San Antonio, Texas)

San Antone (Southwestern slang —San Antonio, Texas)

San Antonio Street saloon-cluttered center of civic disorder in El Paso, Texas just a century ago

sanat sanatoria; sanatorium

San Augustins San Augustin Mountains of southern New Mexico

SANB *South African National Bibliography*

San Berdoo San Bernardino, California

Sanc. Sanctus (Latin—holy)

SANCAD Scottish Association for National Certificates and Diplomas

SANCAR South African National Council for Antarctic Research

San Carlo Teatro di San Carlo— Naples' opera house

San Carlos de Bariloche Bariloche, Argentina

San Carlo of the Symphony Carlo Maria Giulini

Sanche St Charles

San-Chi San Diego—Chicago

San Clem San Clemente

SANCOB South African Foundation for the Conservation of Birds

SANCOG San Diego Council of Governments

SANCOR South African National Committee for Oceanographic Research

SANCOT South African National Commission on Tunnelling

Sanctimonious City Toronto, Ontario's nickname fifty years ago

sand silicon dioxide—SiO_2

Sand *Sandford's New York Reports*

San. D. Doctor of Sanitation

SAND Sampling Aerospace Nuclear Debris

SANDA Supplies and Accounts

SANDAG San Diego Association of Governments

Sandal NATO code name for Soviet SS-4 medium-range ballistic missile

Sandcutters Arizonans

Sand Eng Sandalwood English (Polynesian Pidgin English)

SANDERP San Diego Energy Recovery Project (garbage and trash converted to energy)

Sanders Alexander

Sand Gropers Western Australians

Sandhurst Royal Military Academy at Sandhurst on the Blackwater River in southeast Berkshire, England

SANDIA Sandia National Laboratories

San Domingo Santo Domingo (Dominican Republic)

Sandra Alessandra

Sandra (Russian—Aleksandra or Alessandra or Alexandra)

Sandra *Alessandro*

sand(s) sandwich(es)—invented by a gambler, the Earl of Sandwich, who disliked leaving the gaming table just to eat, and had thin slices of cheese or meat brought to him between two pieces of bread; his culinary invention is called a sandwich and was devised by him around 1776 when he was First Lord of the Admiralty

Sands the Sands (short form for the Godwin Sands off England's Channel coast of Kent)

Sandstone Federal Correctional Institution at Sandstone, Minnesota

SANDT School of Applied Non-Destructive Testing

Sandy (nickname—San Diego, California; Sandra; Sandro; Saundra; a Scotsman)

Sandy Kitty Kansas City

sane. severe acoustic noise environment

SANE National Committee for a Sane Nuclear Policy; South African National Antarctic Expedition

SANER San Diego Energy Recovery (garbage incinerated into steam-producing electricity)

Sa Nev Sierra Nevada(s)

San Fran San Francisco

SANFREE San Diegans for Fiscally Responsible Elected Employees

San Gabriels San Gabriel Mountains of southern California

Sangre de Cristos Sangre de Cristo Mountains extending from Colorado to New Mexico

sangre y pus (Spanish—blood and pus)—separatist nickname for the vivid-red and golden-yellow flag of Spain

sanguin (Latin prefix—blood)— sanguine

San Insp Sanitation Inspection; Sanitary Inspector(ate)

sanit sanitar; sanitation; sanitize

San Jac San Jacinto

San Jo (Mexican-American— San Jose, California)

San Juan Puerto Rico's capital

San Juan del Sur Greytown, Nicaragua

San Juans San Juan Islands (Washington); San Juan Mountains (Colorado and New Mexico)

sanka sans kaffeine (coffee without caffeine)

Sankt Gallen (German—Saint Gall)

Sankt Gotthard (German— Saint Gotthard)

Sankt Moritz (German—Saint Moritz)

San-Lax San Diego—Los Angeles

San Le San Leandro, California

s-a-n man stop-at-nothing man (dangerous criminal)

San Marino Most Serene Republic of San Marino (tiny country surrounded by Italy and on the slopes of Mount Titano near the Adriatic; Sanmarinese speak Italian and depend on the sale of curios and postage stamps) *La Serenissima Repubblica di San Marino*

San Martin José de San Martín —patriot-soldier who fought to liberate Argentina, Chile, and Peru from the Spanish rule

San Met San Diego Metropolitan Correctional Center

S Ann St Anne's College, Oxford

San-NO San Diego—New Orleans

San-NY San Diego—New York

s-a node sino-atrial node

Sanpaolo *Instituto Bancario San Paolo di Torino* (Italian—San Paolo Banking Institute of Turin)

SANPAT San Diego Plans for Air Transportation

San Quentin California State Prison at San Quentin

San Quilmas (Mexican-American—San Antonio, Texas)

sanr subject to approval—no risks

sans sans serif

Sans Sanskrit

SANS South African Naval Service

San-Sac San Diego—Sacramento

San Salvador (Spanish—Holy Savior)—capital of the Central American republic of El Salvador; first landfall of Columbus on the outer fringe of the Bahamas where it was called Guanahani by the Lucayan Indians and Watlings Island by the British

Sansan San Diego to San Francisco (city complex)

sansei (Japanese—third generation)—grandchild of Japanese immigrants to the United States; (see *issei*, *kibei*, *nisei*)

San-Sfo San Diego—San Francisco

Sansk Sanskrit

Sansovino Andrea Contucci

Sant Santander; Santiago

S Ant St Antony's College, Oxford

SANTA South African National Tuberculosis Association; Souvenir and Novelty Trade Association

Santa Barbaras Santa Barbara Islands off Santa Barbara, California

Santa Claus originally Sint Nicolaas in Holland

Santa Fe Atchison, Topeka & Santa Fe (Railway)

Santa Fé New Mexico's capital

Santa Monicas Santa Monica Mountains of southern California

Santa Ritas Santa Rita Mountains of southeastern Arizona

SANTAS Send A Note To A Serviceman

Santa ships Grace Line vessels —all names begin with Santa: *Santa Clara, Santa Magdalena, Santa Teresa*, etc.

Santé nickname of the Parisian prison at 42 rue de la Santé whose name means health or a toast to one's health but in this instance means quarantine or segregation from society

Santiago (Portuguese or Spanish —Saint James)—short form for three score or more places in the Hispanic world such as Santiago do Boqueirão in Brazil, Santiago de Calatrava and Santiago de Compostela in Spain, the well-known Santiago de Chile and Santiago de Cuba, Santiago de los Caballeros in the Dominican Republic, Santiago Ixcuintla in Mexico, Santiago Sacatepéquez in Guatemala, Santiago-Zamora on Ecuador's Peruvian border where Jívaro Indians still shrink human skulls and sell them as souvenirs; etc.

Santiagos Santiago Mountains in the Big Bend National Park in Texas

Santo Domingo the Dominican Republic occupying most of eastern Hispaniola

Santo Domingo City called Ciudad Trujillo during the incumbency of the Dominican dictator—Rafael Leonidas Trujillo

San-Tor San Diego—Toronto

SANU Sudanese African National Union

San-Van San Diego—Vancouver

SANWR Santa Ana National Wildlife Refuge (Texas)

San Ysidro, California formerly Tia Juana; name changed to end confusion with Tijuana, Mexico—just across the border—and Tia Juana River—usually a dry arroyo separating the two towns

San Ysidros San Ysidro Mountains of southern California

SANZ Standards Association of New Zealand

SAO São Paulo, Brazil (airport); Secret Army Organization; Smithsonian Astrophysical Observatory

Sa$_{O2}$ arterial oxygen saturation

SAODAP Special Action Office for Drug Abuse Prevention

SAORC Supreme Assembly of the Order of the Rainbow for Girls

Saorstat Eireann (Gaelic—Irish Free State)

SAOS Scottish Agricultural Organization Society

São Tomé and Principe Democratic Republic of São Tomé and Principe (West African coastal islands whose people speak Portuguese and live by farming cocoa, coconuts, coffee, and cinchona)

São Tomé and Principe's Port São Tomé

sap. saphead; scruple, apothecaries; simplified astro pattern; soon as possible

SA£ South African pound

SAP Safety Assessment Plan; San Pedro Sula, Honduras (airport); Scottish Academic Press; Share Assembly Program; Society for Applied Spectroscopy; South African Police; Symbolic Assembly Program; Systems Assurance Program

s-apa sciences—a project approach

SAPA South African Press Association

SAPARLI Saudi Arabian Parsons Limited

SAPAT South African Picture Analysis Test

SAPE Society for Automation in Professional Education

SAPF South African Police Force

sapfu surpassing all previous foul ups

sapi semi-armor-piercing incendiary

SAPL San Antonio Public Library; Society for Animal Protective Legislation; South African Public Library

SAPM Scottish Association of Paint Manufacturers; Society for the Aid of Psychological Minorities

sap. no. saponification number

sapon saponification; saponify

saponite soapstone (hydrous magnesium aluminum silicate)

sapp sapphic; sapphist(ic)(al)(ly)

Sapper pseudonym of Lt Col Cyril McNeile—creator of Bulldog Drummond

sapphire blue corundum gemstone

SAPRI South African Plain Research Institute

SAPS South African Price Schedule

Sapwood NATO name for Soviet SS-6 intercontinental ballistic missile

sar search and rescue; semiautomatic rifle; short-term acquisition and retrieval; submarine advanced reactor

Sar Saracen; Saracenic; Sardinia; Sardinian

SAR Safety Analysis Report; Society of Authors' Representatives; Solar Aircraft (company); Sons of the American Revolution; South African Railways; South African Republic; South Australian Railways

S-AR *Sud-Africane République* (French—South African Republic)

Sara Sarah; Saratoga

sarac steerable array for radar and communications

Saracen British Alvis armored personnel carrier

Saragossa English equivalent of Zaragoza

SARAH Search and Rescue and Homing (radio lifesaving beacon)

Sarah Bernhardt Rosine Bernard's stage name

saratoga saratoga chip (potato chip); saratoga trunk (old-fashioned round-top trunk); saratoga water (often laxative); saratoga vichy (imbibed by the smart set in mixed drinks or as a health potion)

Saratoga formerly Schuylerville, New York

Saraw Sarawak

SARB South African Reserve Bank

SARBE Search and Rescue Beacon Equipment

SARBICA Southeast Asian Regional Branch of the International Council on Archives

sarc (Latin prefix—flesh)—sarcoma

SARC Sexual Assault Referral Centre (Australia)

SARCCUS South African Regional Committee for the Conservation and Utilisation of the Soil

sarcol sarcological; sarcologist; sarcology

SARD Special Airlift Requirement Directive

SARDA State and Regional Disaster Airlift

Sardegna (Italian—Sardinia)

Sardica (Latin—Sofia)

Sardine Capital of Norway Stavanger

Sardine Capital of the United States Eastport, Maine

Sardinia English place-name equivalent of Sardegna

Sardonic Cartoonist Al Capp

sardonyx chalcedony consisting of alternate layers of onyx and sard

sardsan sardine sandwich

sardwich sardine sandwich

sare self-addressed return envelope

Sargasso Sea mid-Atlantic area of prevailing calms halfway between Africa and West Indies close to Tropic of Cancer; large masses of floating seaweeds found here

sarge sergeant

Sargent Porter Sargent, Inc

SAR & H South African Railways and Harbours

SARHA South African Railways, Harbours, and Airways

sarie selective automatic-radar-identification equipment

SARL Sociedade Anónima de Responsabilidade Limitada (Portuguese—Limited Liability Corporation)

SARLANT Search-and-Rescue, Atlantic

Sarmiento Domingo Faustino Sarmiento—Argentinian educator and early president hostile to dictatorship

SARMS Self-Adapting Account-Receivable Management System

Sarong Girl Dorothy Lamour

SARPAC Search-and-Rescue, Pacific

sarps standards and recommended practices

sarra short-arc reduction of radar altimetry

Sarre (French—Saar)

Sarrebruck (French—Saarbrücken)

SARS Ship Attitude Record System

sarsat search-and-rescue astronomical satellite system

SARSATS Search-and-Rescue Satellite and Tracking System

SART St Alban's Repertory Theater; Strategic Arms Reduction Talks

sartac search radar device

sartel search and rescue telephone

SARTS Switched-Access Remote Test System

SARU Systems Analysis Research Unit

Sarum (Latin—Salisbury)

sas so and so

sas (SAS) small astronomy satellite; supersonic attack seaplane; surface-air-surface (second-class international mail service)

Sas Sasebo

SAs Special Agents (FBI)

SAS Scandinavian Airlines System; Science Attitude Scale; Seattle Audubon Society; Sherwood Anderson Society; Sklar Asphasia Scale; Special Air Service; Statistical Analysis System; Systems Assessment Survey

SAS Societa in Accomandita Semplice (Italian—Limited Partnership Company)

SASA South African Sugar Association

SASBO Southeastern Association of School Business Officials

SASC Senate Armed Services Committee; Small Arms School Corps (UK); South African Staff Corps

SASCOM Special Ammunition Support Command (USA)

SASD School Administrators of South Dakota

sase self-addressed stamped envelope

Sasha (Russian—Alexander or Aleksandr)—sometimes used incorrectly for Alexandra or Aleksandra whose diminutive is Sandra

SASI Society of Air Safety Investigators

SASIDS Stochastic Adaptive Sequential Information Dissemination System

Sasln NATO name for Soviet SS-8 intercontinental ballistic missile

SASIS Semi-Automatic Speaker-Identification System

SASJ South African Society of Journalists

Sask Saskatchewan

SASL South American Saint Line

SASLO South African Scientific Liaison Office

SASM Smithsonian Air and Space Museum

SASMIRA Silk and Artificial Silk Mills Research Association

SASO San Antonio Symphony Orchestra; Saudi Arabia Standards Organization; South African Students Organiza-

tion; South Australia Symphony Orchestra

sasol South African (coal-based synthetic) oil

SASOL South African Coal, Oil, and Gas Corporation

SASR Special Air Service Regiment

Sass Sassenach (Gaelic—English, Saxon)

SASS San Antonio Symphony Society; Society for the Advancement of Scandinavian Study

SASSO Senior Air Staff Officer

Sassonia (Italian—Saxony)

SASSY Supported Activity Supply System

sast single asphalt-surface treatment

SAST Society for the Advancement of Space Travel

sat. sampler address translator; satellite; satisfactory; saturate; saturation; service acceptance trials; system alignment tool; systems approach to training

sat. (SAT) satellite; systematic assertive therapy

Sat Satan; Satanic; Saturday; Saturn

S At South Atlantic

SAT San Antonio, Texas (airport); Scholastic Aptitude Test; Scholastic Assessment Team; Security Air Transport; Sound-Apperception Test; Southern Air Transport; Specific Aptitude Test; Spiral Aftereffect Test; Stanford Achievement Test; Support Analysis Test

SATA Sociedade Açoriana de Transportes Aéreos (Azores Air Transport Line)

SATAF Site Activation Task Force

satan satellite automatic tracking antenna; sensor for airborne terrain analysis

satanas semi-automatic analog setting

Satanic City Devils Lake, North Dakota

satar (SATAR) satellite for aerospace research

satb (SATB) soprano, alto, tenor, bass

SATC South African Tourist Corporation

Satchel Leroy Paige

Satchmo Satchel-Mouth—Louis Armstrong's truncated nickname

satco signal automatic air traffic

control
SATCO Senior Air Traffic Control Officer
satcom satellite communication
SATCOM Satellite Communications Agency (US Army)
satd saturated
satel satellite
SATENA Servicio Aeronavegación a Territorios Nacionales (Bogotá)
SatEvePost *Saturday Evening Post*
satex semi-automatic telegraphic exchange
sat. fix. (SAT FIX) satellite (aircraft or ship position) fix
satfy satisfactory
SATGA Société Aérinne des Transports Guyane Antilles
satgci satellite ground-controlled interception
SAT-HI Stanford Achievement Test for the Hearing Impaired
SATIF Scientific and Technical Information Facility (NASA)
SATIN Sage Air Traffic Integration
SATIRE Semi-Automatic Technical Information Retrieval
Satirist of the Mexican Revolution José Clemente Orozco
Satirist-Skeptic Writer Anatole France
SAtk strike attack
S Atl Cur South Atlantic Current
SAT-M Scholastic Aptitude Test—Mathematical
satn saturation
satnav satellite navigation; satellite navigator
SATO South American Travel Organization; Southern Africa Treaty Organization
SATOUR South African Tourist Corporation
satpic satellite picture
SATRA Shoe and Allied Trade's Research Association
Sat Rev *Saturday Review*
sats (SATS) short airfield for tactical support
SATs Scholastic Aptitude Tests
SATS Satellite Antenna Test System (NASA)
satsim saturation countermeasures simulator
sat sol saturated solution
sattr satisfactory to transfer
SATU Singapore Air Transport Union; South African Typographical Union
Saturday-night special nickname for any cheap pistol used

for impulsive crimes often committed on Saturday nights
Saturn (Latin—Kronos)—god of time
SAT-V Scholastic Aptitude Test—Verbal
SATW Society of American Travel Writers
saty satyagraha; satyriasis; satyr(ic)(al)(ly); satyrid
Sau Saudi Arabia
Sau Arab Saudi Arabia(n)
SAUCERS Saucer and Unexplained Celestial Events Research Society
Saudi Saudi Arabian(s)
Saudia Saudi Arabia
Saudi Arabia Kingdom of Saudi Arabia (largest Middle Eastern country whose Arabic-speaking Saudi are outstanding in gas and oil production as well as dates, gold, iron, and silver) *al-Mamlaka al-'Arabiya as-Saudiya*
Saudi Arabian Ports Jiddah or Juddah, the Red Sea approach to Mecca; Ad Dammam, Ras at Tannurah, Ras at Mishab, and Ras at Khafji on the Persian Gulf
Saudis Saudi Arabians
'sault assault
'sault & assault and battery
Saunders W.B. Saunders Co
SAUS *Statistical Abstract of the United States*
S Austral South Australia(n)
sav savings; stock at valuation
sa/v surface area/volume
Sav Savannah
SAV Savannah, Georgia (airport)
Savage NATO code name for Soviet SS-13 three-stage intercontinental ballistic missile
SAVAK *Sazemane Etelaat va Aminate Kechvar* (Persian—Iranian Security and Intelligence Organization)
Savannahians natives of Savannah, Georgia
Savannah River forms natural border between Georgia and South Carolina; empties into Atlantic a few miles south of port city of Savannah
SAVC Society for the Anthropology of Visual Communication
SAVE Service Activities of Volunteer Engineers; Society of American Value Engineers; Stop Addiction through Voluntary Effort; Student Action

Voters for Ecology
savi science activities for the visually impaired
SAVICOM Society for the Anthropology of Visual Communications
Savior of Babies Nathan Straus
Savior of England Oliver Cromwell
Savior of the Nations sobriquet earned by the Duke of Wellington at Waterloo
Savior of the Sierras John Muir
Savior of Southern Agriculture George Washington Carver
Savoia (Italian—Savoy)
savor single-actuated voice recorder
Savoyards performers in the Savoy Operas of WS Gilbert and Arthur Sullivan
SAVS Scottish Anti-Vivisection Society
Savus Savu Islands of Indonesia
saw. sample assignment word; space at will; squad automatic weapon
SAW Society of Architects in Wales; Society of Australian Writers; Special Air Warfare
SAWA Screen Advertising World Association; Soil and Water Management Association
SAWAS South African Women's Auxiliary Services
Sawatches Sawatch Mountains of central Colorado
Sawbuck Sears-Roebuck
SAWC Special Air Warfare Center
sawd surface acoustic(al) wave device
Sawdust City Oshkosh, Wisconsin's nickname based on its many sawmills
SAWE Society of Aeronautical Weight Engineers
SAWF Special Air Warfare Force
SAWG Special Advisory Working Group; Special Air Warfare Group
SAWI Society Against World Imperialism (Beirut-based Arabic terrorists taking credit for many airplane hijackings and bombings executed in Israel and in some Arabic countries they also consider imperialistic)
Sawney (nickname—a Scotsman)
sawo surface acoustic-wave os-

cillator

s-a-w q seeking-asking-and-written questionnaire

SAWS Satellite Attack Warning System; Small Arms Weapons Study; Squad Automatic Weapon System

Sawtooths Sawtooth Mountains of south-central Idaho

SAWTRI South African Wool Textile Research Institute

sax saxophone; strong anion exchange

Sax Saxon

Sax Duc Saxon Duchies; Saxon Dukes

Saxe Holm Helen Hunt Jackson

saxist saxophonist

Saxon Shore English coastline including Norfolk, Suffolk, Essex, Kent, Sussex, and Hampshire

Sax Rohmer Arthur Sarsfield Wadc's pseudonym

SAY Salisbury, Rhodesia (airport)

Saybolt viscosity number

saye save as you earn

Say Hey Kid Willie Mays

SA y P *San Andrés y Providencia* (Spanish—San Andres and Providence)—Caribbean island possessions of Colombia

SAZF South African Zionist Federation

sb simultaneous broadcast(ing); single-bayonet (lamp base); single-breasted (coat or jacket); small business; smooth bore; solid body; southbound; special bibliography; stove bolt; stretcher bearer; subbituminous; submarine (fog) bell; switchboard

s/b should be, surface based

sb *styrbord* (Swedish—starboard; right side of an airplane or vessel looking forward, from Viking steering board or steering oar on right side of their long boats)

Sb *stibium* (Latin—antimony)

SB Savannah Beach; Savings Bank; scouting-bombing (aircraft); Seaboard World Airlines (2-letter coding); Secondary Battery; Section Base; Selection Board; Senate Bill; Service Bulletin; shipbuilding; Signal Battalion; Signal Boatswain; South Bronx; South Buffalo (railroad); Soviet Bloc; Soviet Branch; Special Branch; Standard Brands (stock exchange symbol); Stan-

ford-Binet (intelligence test); Submarine Base

S-B Stanford-Binet (intelligence test)

S & B sterilization and bath

SB *Schweizerischer Bankverein* (German—Swiss Bank); *Sitzungbericht* (German— report of a proceeding)

S.B. *Scientiae Baccalaureus* (Latin—Bachelor of Science)

Sba Surabaya

SBA School Bookshop Association; School of Business Administration; Sick Bay Attendant; Small Business Administration; Small Businesses Association

SBAC Society of British Aerospace Companies

sbae stabilized bombing approach equipment

S-bahn *Stadt-Schnellbahn* (German—State Rapid Transit)—Berlin's electric railway system

SBAMA San Bernardino Air Materiel Area

S-band 1550–5200 megahertz radio-frequency band

SBAs Sick Bay Attendants

SBAW Santa Barbara Academy of the West

Sbb. *Sabbatum* (Latin—Sunday)

SBB Schweizerische Bundesbahnen (Swiss Federal Railways)

SBBNF Ship and Boat Builders' National Federation

sbc small business computer

SBC Service Bureau Corporation; Small Business Council; Sumitomo Bank of California; Surinam Bauxite Company; Swiss Bank Corporation

SBCC Santa Barbara City College

SBCCOE State Board for Community College and Occupational Education

SBCPO Sick-Bay Chief Petty Officer

SBCR State Board of Charities and Reform (Wyoming); Stock Balance Consumption Report

sbd standard bibliographic description

sbdt surface-barrier diffused transistor

sbe soft-boiled egg(s); standby engine(s); subacute bacterial endocarditis

s-b-e standby engine(s)

SBE State Board of Equaliza-

tion

SBEA Southern Business Education Association

S-bend S-shaped bend

sbf surface burst fuze

SBFA Small Business Foundation of America

sbfc standby for further clearance

sbg selenite brilliant green

Sbg Solvesborg

SBGI Society of British Gas Industries

SBH Scottish Board of Health; State Board of Health

SBI Security Bureau Incorporated; Southern Burn Institute (Baton Rouge); State Bank of India

sbic's small business investment companies

SBII *Serikat Buruh Islam Indonesia* (Central Islamic Labor Union of Indonesia)

SBIR Small Business Innovation Research

sbis (SBIS) satellite-based interceptor systems

SBIW Sybil Brand Institute for Women (Los Angeles correctional facility)

Sbl Setubal

SBL Stephen B(utler) Leacock

SBLI Savings Bank Life Insurance

sblo strong black liquor oxidation

sbm submission; submit

SBM Société Anonymes des Bains de Mer et du Cercle des Etrangers à Monaco (company managing gambling casino of Monte Carlo)

SBMA Santa Barbara Museum of Art

SBME Society of Business Magazine Editors; State Board of Medical Examiners

SBMF Santa Barbara Mariculture Foundation

SBMI School Bus Manufacturers Institute

sbn standard book number(ing)

Sbⁿ Sebastián (Spanish—Sebastian)

SBN South Bend, Indiana (airport); Standard Book Number

S Bno San Bernardino

SBNO Senior British Naval Officer

SBNS Society of British Neurological Surgeons

sbo secure base of operations; specific behavioral objectives

Sbo Sasebo

s'board starboard

sbom soy bean oil meal

sbp slotted-blade propeller; sugar-beet pulp; systolic blood pressure

SBP Society of Biological Psychiatry

SBPIM Society of British Printing Ink Manufacturers

sbr space-based radar; styrene-butadiene rubber

s Br *südliche Breite* (German—south latitude)

SBR Society of Biological Rhythm

SBRC Santa Barbara Research Center

sbre septiembre (Spanish—September)

SBRI Simon Baruch Research Institute

sbs simulated borehole specimen; surveyed before shipment

sbs (SBS) small business satellite

sb's sonic booms; space brothers (people supposedly living in outer space on other planets and presumably directing unidentified flying objects)

s-b-s side-by-side (double-barrel shotgun)

SBS Satellite Business System(s); Singapore Bus Service; Special Boat Squadron; Swiss Broadcasting Society

SBS *Société de Banque Suisse* (French—Swiss Bank)

SBSA Standard Bank of South Africa

Sbsc Schottky-barrier solar cell

SBSUSA Sport Balloon Society of the United States

sbt screening breath tester (for drunken drivers); segregated ballast; surface-barrier transistor

SBT Screening Breath Test (given drunken drivers or those suspected of being under the influence of alcohol)

sbtg sabotage

sbti soy bean trypsin inhibitor

sbtow standby tow(ing) ship

sbv sea-bed vehicle

SBW Seaboard & Western (Airlines); single-engine scout bomber (3-letter naval symbol)

SBWR Seal Beach Wildlife Refuge (near Long Beach, California); South Bay Wildlife Refuge (south end of San Francisco Bay)

sbx S-band transponder

SBX Student Book Exchange

sby standby

sc sad case (slang—unpopular person); same case; separate cover; shaped charge; single circuit; single contact; single crochet; sized and calendered; slow cool; small caps (small capital letters); smooth contour; statistical control; supercycle; superimposed current

sc (SC) site contractor; spinal cord; systolic click

s/c short circuit (electrical); single-column (bookkeeping); suspicious circumstances

s & c search and clear; shipper and carrier; sized and calendered

sc. scilicet (Latin—mainly)

s/c su cuenta (Spanish—your account)

Sc scandium; stratocumulus

Sc Scoglio (Italian—reef; rocky reef)

SC Sacra Congregatio (Sacred Congregation); Sacramento City; Salem College; Sandia Corporation; Sanitary Corps; Scripps College; Seamen's Center; Security Council (United Nations); Selwyn College; Service Club; Service Command; Shasta College; Shaw College; Shell Transport; Shelton College; Shenandoah College; Shepherd College; Sheridan College; Shimer College; Ship's Cook; Shorter College; Siena College; Sierra College; Signal Corps; Simmons College; Simpson College; Sinclair College; Sister(s) of Charity; Skidmore College; Smith College; Somerville College; South Carolina; South Carolinian; Southern California; Southern Californian; Southern Conference; Southwestern College; Special Constable; Spelman College; Springfield College; Staff College; Staff Corps; Stephens College; Sterling College; Stockton College; Stonehill College; Stratford College; Strike Command; submarine chaser; Sullins College; Summary Court; Sumter & Choctaw (railroad); Suomi College; Supply Corps; Support Command; Supreme Court; Surgical Corporation; Swarthmore College; Systems Command

S-C Serbian-Croatian (people); Serbo-Croat (language);

Stromberg-Carlson

S/C Star & Crescent (excursion steamer, ferry, towing, water-taxi service)

S&C search and clear;

SC Statistics Canada

sca sequencer control assembly; small-caliber ammunition; subchannel adapter

sca (SCA) supersonic cruising aircraft

SCA Schipperke Club of America; School and College Ability (test); Science Clubs of America; Screen Composers Association; Senior Citizens of America; Shipbuilders Council of America; Shipbuilders Council of America; Society of Consumer Affairs; Soybean Council of America; Speech Communication Association; Stock Company Association; Sub-Contract Authorization; Suez Canal Authority; Survey of College Achievement; Svenska Cellulose AB; Switzerland Cheese Association; Synagogue Council of America

SCAA State Communities Aid Association

SCAAP Special Commonwealth African Assistance Plan

SCAC School and College Advisory Center; Sunrise Cultural and Art Center (Charleston, West Virginia)

SCACOP Southern California Area Construction Opportunity Program

scad schedule, capability, availability, dependability

SCAD State Commission Against Discrimination (New York)

scadar scatter detection and ranging

SCADS Sioux City Air Defense Sector

SCAF Supreme Commander of Allied Forces

SCAG Sandoz Clinical Assessment—Geriatric; Southern California Association of Governments; Supplier Corrective Action Group

SCAGL Société Cinématographique des Auteurs et Gens de Lettres (French—Cinematic Society of Authors and Writers)

sc al steel-cored aluminum

SCALA Society of Chief Architects of Local Authorities

scaler statistical calculation and analysis of engine removal

(USN)

scama (SCAMA) switching, conferencing, and monitoring arrangement

scams scanning microwave spectrometer

scan. self-correcting automatic navigation; suspected child abuse and neglect; switched-circuit automatic network

Scan Scandinavia; Scandinavian

SCAN Scheduling and Control by Automated Network; Selected Current Aerospace Notices (NASA-computerized dissemination of information); Self-Correcting Automatic Navigator; Service Center for Aging Information; Southern California Answering Network; Switched-Circuit Automatic Network

SCANCAP System for Comparative Analysis of Community Action Programs

Scand Scandinavia; Scandinavian

Scandia southern Scandinavian peninsula—southern Norway and Sweden

Scandinavia Denmark, Iceland, Norway, and Sweden (the Faeroe Islands, Finland, and Greenland are sometimes included)

Scandinavian Fun Capital Copenhagen, Denmark

Scandinavië (Dutch—Scandinavia)

ScanDoc Scandinavian Documentation Center

scanit scan-only intelligent terminal

scan. mag. *scandalum magnatum* (Latin—defamation of high-placed persons)

SCANNET Scandinavian (computer) Network

SCANPED System for Comparative Analysis of Programs of Educational Development

SCANs Southern California Answering Networks (cooperative library information-retrieval system)

SCANS Scheduling and Control Automation by Network Systems; Stockmarket Computer Answering Service

scantie submersible-craft acoustic-navigation and track-indication equipment

SCAO Senior Civil Affairs Office(r); Standing Conference on Atlantic Organizations

scap scapula; scapular; scapuloid

SCAP Supreme Commander, Allied Powers

Scapa Scapa Flow naval anchorage in the Orkney Islands off Scotland's north coast between Hoy, Orkney, and South Ronaldsay (used by the British Navy in both world wars and by the German High Seas Fleet when it was interned there at the end of World War I and scuttled itself rather than face surrender)

SCAPA Society for Checking the Abuses of Public Advertising

'scape escape(ment); landscape; seascape; skyscape

Scapegoat NATO code name for Soviet medium-range two-stage intercontinental ballistic missile SS-14

scaphocephs scaphocephalics (narrow-skulled people)

s caps small capital letters

SCAQMD South Coast Air Quality Management District (California)

scar. subcaliber aircraft rocket; submarine celestial altitude recorder

SCAR Scandinavian Council for Applied Research; Scientific Committee for Antarctic Research; Supersonic Cruise Airplane Research (NASA)

scarab. (SCARAB) submersible craft assisting repair and burial (of underwater telephone cables)

Scarboro' Scarborough

scard signal conditioning and recording device

scare. sensor-control anti-anti-radiation-missile radar evaluation

SCARF Special Committee on the Adequacy of Range Facilities

Scarface Mafia mobster Al Capone

Scarface Al Alphonse Capone

Scarlet Carnation Ohio state flower

Scarmouche Tiberio Firoella

scarp escarpment

Scarp NATO code name for Soviet intercontinental ballistic missile capable of releasing warheads below early-warning radar range and designated SS-9

S-car(s) Swedish car(s)

sca's subsidiary communications authorizations

SCAS Senior Citizen Audiological Service

scat. share compiler assembler and translator

scat. (SCAT) speed-control attitude range; supersonic commercial air transport

scat. *scatula* (Latin—box)

SCAT School and College Ability Test; Science College Ability Test(ing); Service Command Air Transportation (USN)

scata survival sited casualty treatment assemblage

SCATANA Security Control of Air Traffic and Air Navigational Aids

SCATE Stromberg-Carlson automatic test equipment

scatha spacecraft charging at high(er) altitude(s)

scat. orig. *scatula originalis* (Latin—original box or package)

scats (SCATS) sequentially-controlled automatic transmitter start (data processing)

scat's supersonic commercial air transports

SCATs Southern California Acrobatic Teams

SCATS Simulation, Checkout, and Training System

SCAULWA Standing Conference of African University Libraries—Western Area (Ghana)

scav scavenge

Scaw Fells Scaw Fell (or Scafell) Mountains of the Cumbrians in England's Lake District

scb state-capacity building; strictly confined to bed (*q.v.* tob)

sc b screw base (lamp)

Sc.B. *Scientia Baccalaureus* (Latin—Bachelor of Science)

SCB Sawyer College of Business; Sierra Club Books; Southern California Book-builders

SCB *Sociedad Bolivariana de Venezuela* (Spanish—Bolivarian Society of Venezuela)

SCBA Southern California Booksellers Association

SCBC Somerset Cattle Breeding Centre

SCBCA Small Claims Board of Contract Appeals

scbf spinal-cord blood flow

SCBQ Science Classroom Behavior Q-sort

SCBW Society of Children's

Book Writers
scc single-channel controller; specific clauses and conditions; stress corrosion cracking
Sc C Scottish Command
SCC Sea Cadet Corps; Security Coordination Committee; Select Cases in Chancery; Ship Control Center; Shoreline Community College; Sitka Community College; Society of Cosmetic Chemists; Spokane Community College; Standard Commodity Classification; Stromberg-Carlson Corporation; Student Coordinating Council; Surveillance Coordination Center
S&CC Suicide and Crisis Counseling
SCCA Society of Company and Commercial Accountants; South Carolina Correctional Association; Southeastern Cottonseed Crushers Association; Sports Car Club of America
SCCAPE Scottish Council for Commercial, Administrative, and Professional Education
SCCC Singapore Chinese Chamber of Commerce; Suffolk County Community College; Sullivan County Community College
SCCCI Singapore Chinese Chamber of Commerce and Industry
SCCF Security Clearance Case Files
SCCG Southern California Culinary Guild
SCCOP State Consulting Company for Oil Projects
SCCPG Satellite Communications Contingency Planning Group
SCCPT Subcommittee on Computer Program Terminology (Association for Computing Machinery)
sccrt sub-zero cooled, cold-rolled, and tempered
scd screen door; screwed; service computation date; standard change dispenser
scd (SCD) security coding device
Sc.D. *Scientiae Doctor* (Latin—Doctor of Science)
SCD Specification Control Drawing
SCD *Standard College Dictionary*
scda scapula-dextra anterior

SCDA Scottish Community Drama Association
SCDC Senior Citizen's Dental Clinic; South Carolina Department of Correction
scde's schools, colleges, and departments of education
SCDL Scientific Crime Detection Laboratory
scdp scapula-dextra posterior
SCDS Shipboard Chaff-Decoy System
sce situationally caused error; standard calomel electrode
SCE Schedule Compliance Evaluation; Society for Clinical Ecology; Southern California Edison
S.C.E. Scottish Certificate of Education
SCEA South Carolina Education Association
SCEI Safe Car Educational Institute; Special Libraries Committee on Environmental Information
SCEL Signal Corps Engineering Laboratories
scen scenario(s); scenarist(s); scenographic(al)(ly)
Scenic Center of the South Chattanooga, Tennessee's self-created sobriquet
SCEPC Senior Civil Emergency Planning Committee (NATO)
Sceptered Isle England; Great Britain
SCES State Cooperative Extension Service
SCET Scottish Council for Educational Technology
SCF Save the Children Federation; Sectional Center Facility (USAF); Station Code File; Stephen Collins Foster
sc f & a screw forward and aft
SCFA Southern California Fishermen's Association
scfd standard cubic feet per day
scfh standard cubic feet per hour
SCFIC South Carolina Foundation of Independent Colleges
scfm standard cubic feet per minute
scfs standard cubic feet per second
scg scoring
SCG Society of the Classic Guitar
Sc Gael Scottish Gaelic
SCGB Ski Club of Great Britain
SCGC Southern California Gas Company; Southern Counties Gas Company

SCGR Sale Common Game Refuge (Victoria, Australia)
SCGRL Signal Corps General Research Laboratory
SCGSA Signal Corps Ground Signal Agency
SCGSS Signal Corps Ground Signal Service
sch school
sch (SCH) schedule
Sch Schiedam; School (postal abbreviation)
Schaffhouse (French—Schaffhausen)—the Falls of the Rhine or Rheinfall
SCHAVMED School of Aviation Medicine (USN)
Schbg Schönberg
schd scheduled; scheduling
sched schedule
Schedamum (Latin—Schiedam)
scheepv scheepvaart (Dutch—navigation, shipping)
scheik scheikunde (Dutch—chemistry)
Schelomo (Hebrew—Solomon) —title of Bloch's composition for 'cello and orchestra
schem schematic
Schen Schenectady
scherz scherzando (Italian—jesting, in a sportive manner)
Schipol Amsterdam's international airport
Schirley Winters Schirley Schrift
Schirmer EC Schirmer (Boston); G Schirmer (New York)
Sc Hist Scottish History
schizo schizoid; schizophasia; schizophrenia; schizophrenic
schizzy schizoid; schizophrenia; schizophrenic
SCHLA School of Latin America
Schlags Schlagobers (Austrian German—whipped cream)
schlem schlemiel (Yiddish—person afflicted with bad luck)
schlemazl (victim of a *schlemiel*)
Schlesien (German—Silesia)
Sch Lib Sci School of Library Science
Schlickstadt (German—Mud Town)—German naval nickname for Wilhelmshaven
schm schematic
Sch M School Master
Schmarg Schmargendorf
Sch Mist School Mistress
schmoo space cargo handler and manipulator for orbital operations
Schnozzola Jimmy Durante
schol schola cantorum; scholar-

(ly); scholarship; scholastic(ally); scholasticate; scholasticism; scholiast(ic); scholium

SCHOLAR Schering-Oriented Literature Analysis and Retrieval System

schoolboy nickname for codeine

School of Europe fifteenth-century Italian states such as Florence, Mantua, Milan, and Venice

Schoolmaster in Politics Woodrow Wilson—twenty-eighth President of the United States

Schoolmaster of the Republic Noah Webster

Schotl *Schotland* (Dutch—Scotland)

Schottland (German—Scotland)

schr schooner

Schr *Schriften* (German—publication; script, text, writing)

SCHS Senior Citizen Hospital Service

Schubert's 9 nine symphonies of Franz Schubert including *Tragic* (No. 4), *Little* (No. 6), *Unfinished* (No. 8), *The Great* (No. 9)

Schumann 1st, 2nd, 3rd, 4th First (*Spring*), Second, Third (*Rhenish*), Fourth symphonies composed by Robert Schumann

Schupo *Schutzpolizei* (German—defense police used as a paramilitary force by Hitler)

Schwaben (German—Swabia)

Schwann *Schwann-1 Record & Tape Guide*

Schwarzes Meer (German—Black Sea)

Schwarzwald (German—Black Forest) along the upper Rhine in southwest Germany

Schwechat Vienna, Austria's airport

Schweden (German—Sweden)

Schweiz (German—Switzerland)

Schwyz Schwyzer(tütsch)

Schwyzd *Schwyzerdütsch* (Swiss-German language sometimes called an affliction of the throat)

sci science; scientific; scientist

sci (SCI) secret confidential informant; sensitive compartmented information

SCI School of Counter-Insurgency; Science Citation Index; Seamen's Church Institute; Service Civil International; Shipping Container Institute;

Shipping Corporation of India; Shipping Corporation of India; Simulation Councils Incorporated; Society of Chemical Industries; Society of the Chemical Industry; Sponge and Chamois Institute; State Commission of Investigation; Supervisory Cost Inspector

SCI *Science Citation Index; Servicio Central de Inteligencia* (Spanish—Central Intelligence Service)

SCIA Signal Corps Intelligence Agency

Sci Am *Scientific American*

SCI/ARC Southern California Institute of Architecture

scicrit scientific critic(ism)

scics semiconductor integrated circuits

scid severe combined immune deficiency

Sci D Doctor of Science

Sci D Com Doctor of Science in Commerce

Scidgie Sicilian-Italian (dialect)

Sci D Met Doctor of Science in Metallurgy

Science Academy of Science; High School of Science

scient scientific; scientist

sci-fi science-fiction

SCII Strong-Campbell Interest Inventory

scil. *scilicet* (Latin—namely)

SCIL Support Center International Logistics (USA)

Scillies Scilly Islands better referred to as the Isles of Scilly or the Sorlings

Scillonian(s) inhabitant(s) of the Isles of Scilly

scim standard cubic inches per minute

Sci M *Science Master*

SCIM Selected Categories in Microfiche

Sci Mist Science Mistress

scimp. self-contained-imaging microprofiler

scinti scintillate; scintillation

SCIO Staff Counterintelligence Officer

scioneer scientist + engineer

SCIOP Social Competence Inventory for Older Persons

SCIP School Campus Interaction Programme

SCIPA Servicio Cooperativo Interamericano de Producción de Alimentos (Interamerican Cooperative Service for the Production of Food)

scipp sacrococcygeal-to-inferior pubic point

SCIPP Santa Cruz Institute for Particle Physics

SCI & RB South Carolina Inspection and Rating Bureau

Sci Res Assoc Science Research Associates

SCIRP Select Commission on Immigration and Refugee Policy

SCI(s) Success Motivation Institutes

SCIS Science Curriculum Improvement Study

SCISP *Servicio Cooperativo Interamericano de Salud Pública* (Interamerican Cooperative Public Health Service)

Sci-Tec Science-Technology Division (American Libraries Association)

SCITEC Association of the Scientific, Engineering, and Technological Community of Canada

SCI-TECH-SLA Science-Technology Division of the Special Libraries Association

sc&j signal collection and jamming

scl scleroderma; space charge limited

Scl Sculptor (constellation)

SCL Santiago, Chile (airport); Scottish Central Library; Seaboard Coast Line; Society of County Librarians; Southeastern Composers' League; Springfield City Library

scla scapula-laeva anterior

SCLC Southern Christian Leadership Conference

SCLED South Carolina Law Enforcement Division

SCLERA Santa Catalina Laboratory for Experimental Relativity by Astrometry

SCLH Standing Committee for Local History; Standing Conference for Local History

SCLI Seaboard Coast Line Industries; Somerset and Cornwall Light Infantry

sclp scapulo-laeva posterior

SCLS Serra Cooperative Library System

scm samarium cobalt magnet; small-core memory; soluble cytotoxic mediator; steam-cure mortar

scm (SCM) specification change memo(randum); strategic cruising missile

Sc.M. *Scientiae Magister* (Latin—Master of Science)

SCM Section Communication Manager; Smith-Corona-Marchant; Society of Connoisseurs in Murder; Special Court-Martial; Summary Court-Martial

S.C.M. State Certified Midwife

SCM *Su Católica Majestad* (Spanish—Your Catholic Majesty)

SCMA Southern California Marine Association; Southern Cypress Manufacturers Association

SCMAI Staff Committee on Meditation, Arbitration, and Inquiry (ALA)

SCMC Senior Citizen's Medical Clinic

SCMES Society of Consulting Marine Engineers and Ship Surveyors

SCMP *South China Morning Post*

scn scan (flow chart)

Scn Scunthorpe

SCN System Control Number

SCNAWAF Special Category Navy with Air Force

SCNM Sunset Crater National Monument (Arizona)

SCNO Senior Canadian Naval Officer

SCNR Scientific Committee of National Representatives (NATO)

scns self-contained navigation system

scn/sin sensitive command network/sensitive information network

SCNUL Standing Conference of National and University Libraries (UK)

SCNVYO Standing Conference of National Voluntary Youth Organisations (UK)

SCNWR Squaw Creek National Wildlife Refuge (Missouri)

sco subcarrier oscillator; sustainer cutoff

Sco Scorpius (constellation)

ScO Scientific Officer

SCO Sales Contracting Office(r); Statistical Control Office(r)

SCOC Senior Citizen Otolaryngological Clinic; Support Command Operations Center

scoda scan coherent doppler attachment

SCODS Standing Committee on Ocean Data Stations

SCOFF Society for the Conquest of Flight Fear

SCOGS Select Committee on Generally-Regarded-As-Safe Substances

SCOLCAP Scottish Libraries

Cooperative Automation Project

S Coll Staff College

SCOLLUL Standing Conference of Librarians of Libraries of the University of London

SCOLMA Standing Conference on Library Materials on Africa

SCOM Scientific Committee (NATO)

scon self-contained

scond semiconductor

SCONMEDLIB Standing Conference of Mediterranean Libraries

'Sconsin Wisconsin

SCONUL Standing Conference of National and University Libraries

scoop. scientific computation of optimum procurement

Scoop Senator Henry Martin (Scoop) Jackson

scop (SCOP) single copy order plan

scope microscope; oscilloscope; periscope; telescope; telescopic gunsight

scope (Latin suffix—instrument for examining a part)—microscope, telescope

SCOPE Scholarly Communication—Online Publishing and Education; School-to-College Opportunity for Post highschool Education; Scientific Committee on Problems of the Environment; Selected Contents of Periodicals for Educators; Simple Checkout-Oriented Program Language; Special Committee on Problems of the Environment (ICSU); Student Council on Pollution and Environment

SCOPES Squad Combat Operations Exercise Simulation (USA)

Scor Scorpio

SCOR Scientific Committee on Oceanographic Research

score. signal communications by orbiting relay equipment; spectral combinations by reconnaissance exploitation

SCORE Service Corps of Retired Executives; Special Covert Operations for Resale; System Capability over Requirement Evaluation

SCORES Scenario-Oriented Recurring-Evaluation System (USA)

scorpio subject-content-oriented retrieval for processing infor-

mation on-line

Scorpion British Alvis tracked reconnaissance vehicle; NATO armored tank running on five roadwheels and mounting an octagonal turret gun; U.S. self-propelled 90mm antitank gun designated M-56

SCOS Scottish Certificate in Office Studies; Senior Citizen Optometrical Service

scot steel car of tomorrow

Scot Scotch; Scotland; Scots; Scotsman; Scotswoman; Scottie(s); Scottish; Scotty

SCOTAPLL Standing Conference of Theological and Philosophical Libraries in London

SCOTBEC Scottish Business Education Council

scotch scotch blackface (sheep); scotch broth (barley, mutton, and vegetable soup); scotch mist (drizzle, fog, and mist mixture often encountered in the British Isles); scotch whisky (distilled in Scotland from barley malted in a special still); scotch woodcock (toast garnished with anchovy paste and scrambled eggs); plus all other scotch-type lowercase derivatives such as the foregoing eponyms

Scotch Mendelssohn's Symphony No. 3 in A minor

Scotch Bard Robert Burns

ScotGael Scots Gaelic

Scotia (Latin—Scotland)

Scotiabank Bank of Nova Scotia

Scotland Scottish section of Great Britain inhabited by Scots—the Scotch

Scotland's Extremitude Dunnet Head the northernmost point of mainland Scotland although the popular belief names nearby John O'Groat's

Scotland's Principal Port Glasgow

Scotland Yard old London police headquarters near Trafalgar Square; replaced by New Scotland Yard along the Thames River Embankment

ScotNats Scottish Nationalists

Scots Ports (large, medium, and small east to west) Leith, Granton, Rosyth Dock Yard, Boness, Grangemouth, Alloa, Burntisland, Kirkaldy, Methil, Dundee, Perth, Arbroath, Montrose, Aberdeen, Peterhead, Fraserburgh, Hopeman, Inverness, Cromarty, Invergordon, Portmahomack, Helmsdale, Wick, Thurso, Scrabster, Stornoway, Oban, Campbeltown, Greenock, Finnart, Rothesay Dock, Glasgow, Ardrossan, Irvine, Troon, Cairnryan

Scott Scott, Foresman; Scott Publications; William R Scott

Scott Fredericks Carl Shapiro

Scottish Cradle of U.S. Presidents Scotland, ancestral home of Presidents Hayes and Monroe

Scotts Bluff Scotts Bluff National Monument in western Nebraska on the Oregon Trail

SCOTUS Supreme Court of the United States

Scot virus Scottish type of influenza virus sometimes called Scotland virus

Scouce(s) Liverpool (persons)

Scourge of God Attila's nickname

Scourge of Princes Pietro Aretino

'scouse lobscouse (sailor's stew)

Scout Westland army helicopter built in Britain

Scozia (Italian—Scotland)

scp secondary control point; single-cell protein; spherical candlepower; supervisor's control panel

SCP Sea Containers Pacific; Senior Companion Program; Site Characterization Plan; Social Credit Party; Survey Control Point

SCP (AFL-CIO) Sleeping Car Porters

SCPA South Carolina Ports Authority

SCPAs State Criminal-Justice Planning Agencies

scpc single channel per carrier

SCPCU Society of Chartered Property and Casualty Underwriters

SCPD Staff Civilian Personnel Division (USA)

SCPE State Committee on Public Education

SCPEA Southern California Professional Engineering Association

SCPGA South Carolina Personnel and Guidance Association

SCPI Structural Clay Products Institute

SCPL Social Credit Political League (New Zealand Party)

SCPN Society of Certified Professional Numismatists

SCPO Senior Chief Petty Offi-

cer

SCPR Scottish Council of Physical Recreation

SCPS Senior Citizen Podiatric Service; Society of Civil and Public Servants (British)

SCPt security control point

SCPU Sea Containers Pacific Unit

scpv (SCPV) silkworm cytoplasmic polyhedrosis virus

SCQ Coastal Sentry (tracking station vessel—naval symbol)

scr screw; scruple; silicon-controlled rectifier

s-c r short-circuit radio

SCR Signal Corps Radio; Site Characterization Report; Standardized Casualty Rate

SCRA Southern California Restaurant Association; Stanford Center for Radar Astronomy

Scrag NATO code name for Soviet SS-10 intercontinental ballistic missile

scram self-contained radiation monitor; supersonic combustion ramjet (engine)

SCRAM Special Criteria for Retrograde Army Materiel; Synanon Committee for Responsible American Media

scrap. simple-complex reaction-time apparatus

SCRAP Society for Completely Removing All Parking (Meters); Students Challenging Regulatory Agency Proceedings

Scrap Iron baseball catcher Clint Courtney's nickname

Scrapple City Allentown, Pennsylvania

SCRATA Steel Castings Research and Trade Association

scr bh screen bulkhead

SCR brick Structural Clay Research brick

SCRC Southern California Renewal Communities; Southern California Research Council

SCRCC Soil Conservation and Rivers Control Council

SCRDT Stanford Center for Research and Development in Teaching

SCRE Scottish Council for Research in Education

SCREAM Society for the Control and Registration of Estate Agents and Mortgage Brokers

SCREAMS Society to Create Rapprochement among Electrical, Aeronautical, and Mechanical Engineers

screenex screening exercise

SCRF Scripps Clinic and Research Foundation; Small Craft Repair Facility (USN)

Scriabin 5 five symphonies by Alexander Scriabin including the *Divine Poem* (No. 3), the *Poem of Ecstasy* (No. 4), and the *Poem of Fire* (No. 5)

Scribner Charles Scribner's Sons

SCRID Southern California Registry of Interpreters for the Deaf

scrim scrimmage

scrip scriptural; scripture

script manuscript; prescription

Script Scriptural; Scripture

SCRIPT Stanford Computerized-Researcher Information-Profile Technique

SCRIS Southern California Regional Information Study (Bureau of the Census)

SCRL Signal Corps Radar Laboratory

SCRLC South Central Research Library Council

scrn screen; screening; screens

scr's silicon-controlled rectifiers

Scrt Sanskrit

SCRTD Southern California Rapid Transit District

Scrtrt the Secretariat (UN)

Scrubs Wormwood Scrubs

scrum scrummage

scs satellite control system; secret cover sheet; space command station; stabilization control system

scs (SCS) sea-control ship

sc & s strapped, corded, and sealed

SCS Scientific Control System(s); Screening and Costing Staff (NATO); Secondary Control Ship (USN); Society of Civil Servants; Society of Clinical Surgery; Society for Computer Simulation; Soil Conservation Service; Student Counseling Service

SCSA Soil Conservation Society of America; Southern California Symphony Association

SCSBM Society for Computer Science in Biology and Medicine

SCSC South Carolina State College

sc-se smooth curve-smooth earth

SCSE Society of Casualty Safety Engineers

SCSEA Southern California Solar Energy Association

SCSEP Senior Community Service Employment Program

SCSF Surface Cask Storage Facility

Sc.Soc.D. Doctor of Social Science

SCSP Site Characterization and Selection Plan; State Center Service Program; System Calibration Support Plan (USAF)

SCSPA South Carolina State Ports Authority

SCSS Scottish Council of Social Service

sct structural clay tile; sub-zero cooled and tempered

sct (SCT) subroutine call table; surface charge transistor

Sct Scutum (constellation)

SCT Society of Commercial Teachers

s/cta su cuenta (Spanish—your account)

SCTA Steel Carriers Tariff Association

SCTE Society of Cable Television Engineers

sctl short-circuited transmission line

Sctl Schottky coupled-transistor logic

sctr sector (flow chart)

sctrd scattered

sct's sugar-coated tablets

SCTS Sycamore Canyon Test Site (Convair)

Sctsmn The Scotsman (Edinburgh)

sctt submarine-command team trainer

SCTTF Small-Core Triaxial Test Facility

scty security

SCU Selector Checkout Unit; Special Care Unit

SCUA Suez Canal Users' Association

scuba self-contained underwater breathing apparatus

scubasub scuba-diver's submarine; scuba-diver's submersible

S-cubed serial-signalling scheme; serial-signalling system

Scud NATO nickname for Soviet mobile tactical surface-to-surface missile

SCUK South Coast of the United Kingdom

sculp sculptor; sculpture

sculp. sculpsit (Latin—he carved or engraved it)

Sculptor of the Colossal Frédéric Auguste Bartholdi (*Liberty Enlightening the World*)

Sculptor of Great American and French Scientists and Statesmen Jean Antoine Houdon

Sculptor-King Sculptor-King Pygmalion of Cyprus

SCUM Society (for) Cutting Up Men

scup scupper

SCUP Society for College and University Planning

S-curve S-shaped curve

SCUS Supreme Court of the United States

Scutari English and Italian place-name equivalent of Shkodër, Albania called Ushkudar by the Turks

'scutcheon escutcheon

scv single concave

s-c-v single-capsulated-virulent (bacteria)

s & cv stop and check valve

SCV Sons of Confederate Veterans

SCV Santa Città Vaticana (Italian—Holy Vatican City)—but Roman wiseacres insist SCV means *Se Cristo Vedesse* (If Christ could see!)

S.C.V. Stato della Città del Vaticano (Italian—Vatican City State)

scvtr scan-converting video tape recorder

SCW State College of Washington

SCWC Special Commission on Weather Modification

SCWPH Students Concerned With Public Health

scwr (SCWR) supercritical water reactor

SCWS Scottish Co-operative Wholesale Society

scx single convex

SCXU Sea Containers Atlantic Unit

SCYC South Coast Yacht Club

S Cz Salina Cruz

sd second defense (lacrosse); self-destroying; semidiameter; septal defect; serum defect; shell-destroying; shit disturber (troublemaker); sight draft; single deck; skin dose; sound; special duty; spontaneous delivery; stage door; standard deviation; storm detection; storm drain(age); streptodornase; sudden death; system demonstration; systolic to diastolic; systolic discharge

s-d slow-drying

s/d sea-damaged; systolic-to-diastolic

s & d search and destroy; song and dance

sd siehe dies (German—see this)

s.d. sine die (Latin—without date)

sD samme Dato (Danish—same date)

Sd Sound

S$ Singapore dollar

S^d Sound

SD Salt Domes; San Diegan; San Diego; Secretary of Defense; Senior Deacon; snare drum; Specification for Design; Spectacle Dispenser (oculist); Standard Oil Company of California (stock exchange symbol); State Department; Superintendent of Documents; Supply Depot

SD Social(ist) Democrat(ic) (party); *Stofarts Directoratet* (Norwegian—Directorate of Shipping); *Stronnictwo Demokratyczne* (Polish—Democratic Party)

sda sacro-dextra anterior; source data acquisition; source data automation; specific dynamic action; succinic dehydrogenase activity

SDA Scottish Development Agency; Scottish Diploma in Agriculture; Seventh Day Adventist; Ship Destination Authority; Soap and Detergent Association; Social Democratic Alliance; Source Data Automation; Students for Democratic Action

SDAA San Diego Apartment Association

SDACCLRC San Diego Area Community Colleges Library Resources Cooperative

Sdad Sociedad (Spanish—Society)

SDAE San Diego Adult Educators

SD & AE RR San Diego & Arizona Eastern Railroad

SDAF San Diego Architectural Foundation

SDAG San Diego Association of Governments

S Dak South Dakota; South Dakotan

SDAM San Diego Aerospace Museum

sdaml send by airmail

SDAP Systems Development Analysis Program; System Development and Performance

SDASBO South Dakota Association for School Business Officials

sdAt (SDAT) senile dementia of

the Alzheimer's type

SDAT Senile Dementia of the Alzheimer Type

S-day submarine-deployment day (NATO)

SDB Salesian of Don Bosco; Society for Developmental Biology

sdbl sight draft bill of lading

sd bl sandblast

SDBRI San Diego Biomedical Research Institute

sdby standby

sdc shipment detail card; single drift connection; submersible decompression chamber

sdc (SDC) signal data converter

SDC Southern Defense Command; Space Development Corporation; Special Devices Center; State Defense Council; State Department of Corrections (Alabama, Colorado, Virginia); Strategic Defense Command; Support Design Change; Systems Development Corporation

SDCA Society of Dyers and Colourists of Australia

SDCB State Dissemination Capacity Building

SDCC San Diego City College

SD/CC Security Designation/Custody Classification

SDCCD San Diego Community College District

SDCCs San Diego Community Colleges

SDCE Society of Die Casting Engineers

SDCF San Diego Community Foundation

SDCINTF San Diego County Integrated Narcotic Task Force

SDCJ San Diego County Jail

SDCL System Distress Check List

SD Class. Superintendent of Documents Classification

SDCMD San Diego Contract Management District

SDCMS San Diego County Medical Society

SD Co San Diego County

SDCS San Diego City Schools

SDCSO San Diego County Symphony Orchestra

s-d curve strength-duration curve

sdd store-door delivery

SDD Scottish Diploma in Dairying; System Definition Directive; System Design Description

sddl saddle(d); sorted data-definition language

sde self-disinfecting elastomer; simple designational expression

SDE Society of Data Educators; State Department of Education

SDEA South Dakota Education Association

's' death god's death

S de B Simone de Beauvoir

SDEC San Diego Ecology Center; San Diego Engineering Council; San Diego Evening College

SDECE Service de la Documentation Extérieure et du Contre-Espionage (French equivalent of American CIA)

SDEE Société de la Diffusion d'Equipements Electroniques

SDEI San Diego Eye Institute

S de M Salvador de Madariaga

SDEO Salt Domes Exploration Office

sdf single-degree-of-freedom (gyroscope)

sdf *sans domicile fixe* (French—without address; without a fixed living place)

SDF Louisville, Kentucky (airport); Self-Defense Forces (Japan)

SDFD San Diego Fire Department

SDFMC San Diego Foundation for Medical Care

SDFS San Diego Federal Savings

sdg siding

Sdg Siding (postal abbreviation)

SDG Sacred Dance Guild; Self-Development Group

S.D.G. *Solo Deo Gloria* (Latin—Glory to God Alone)

SDG & E San Diego Gas & Electric; San Diego Greed and Extortion (exemplified in utility bills)

SDGP State Dissemination Grant Program

sdh (SDH) sorbitol dehydrogenase

SDH Scottish Diploma in Horticulture

SDHA San Diego Hospital Association

SDHC San Diego Housing Commission

sdhe spacecraft data-handling equipment

SDHRC San Diego Human Relations Commission

sdi selective dissemination of information

SDI Saudi Arabian Airlines

SDIBM San Diego Institute for Burn Medicine

SDIC San Diego Improvement Association

S Diego San Diego

sdiline selective dissemination of information on-line

SDJC San Diego Junior Colleges

sdk shelter deck

Sdk (SDK) San Diego (container symbol)

sdl saddle

sdl (SDL) state-dependent learning

SDL Special Duties List(ing); Systems Dimensions Limited

SDLA South Dakota Library Association

sdlc synchronous data-link communication(s)

SDLP Social Democratic and Labour Party

sdm selective discrimination on microfiche

SDM *Su Divina Majestad* (Spanish—Your Divine Majesty)

SDMA San Diego Museum of Art; Surgical Dressing Manufacturers' Association

SDMC San Diego Mesa College

SDMICC State Defense Military Information Control Committee

sdml seaward defense motor launch

SDMM San Diego Museum of Man

SDMS San Diego Memorial Society

SDN System Designation Number

Sdn Dhd *Sendirian Derhad* (Malay—Private Limited)—limited corporation

SDNHM San Diego Natural History Museum

SDNS Scottish Daily Newspaper Society

SDO San Diego Opera; Santo Domingo (Dominican Republic); Squadron Duty Office(r); System Design Objectives

S Doc Senate Document

SDOC Space Defense Operations Center (Cheyenne, Wyoming)

sdof single degree of freedom

SDOG San Diego Opera Guild

Sdom Sodom

sdp sacro-dextra posterior; social, domestic, and pleasure

Sd £ Sudanese pound (currency

unit)

SDP Social(ist) Democratic Party; Subseabed Disposal Program

SDP Sozialdemokratische Partei Deutschlands (Germany's Social-Democratic Party)

SDPCC San Diego Poison Control Center

SDPD San Diego Police Department

SDPGA South Dakota Personnel and Guidance Association

SDPL San Diego Public Library

S Dpo Station Depot

SDPO Site Defense Project Office(r)

SDPOA San Diego Police Officers Association

SDPT Structured Doll Play Test

SDQ Santo Domingo, Dominican Republic (airport)

sdr scientific data recorder; self decoding readout; simple detection response; sodium deuterium reactor; sonar data recorder; splash-detection radar; strip domain resonance; successive discrimination reversal

SDR Special Despatch Rider; Special Dispatch Rider; Special Drawing Rights; Special Drilling Rights

SdRng sound ranging

SDRs Special Drawing Rights; Special Drilling Rights

sds self-directed search; speech discrimination score; sudden death syndrome

SDS Samuel De Sola; San Diego Symphony; Scientific Data Systems; Solomon De Sola; Sons and Daughters of the Soddies; Spatial Data System(s); Special District Services; Students for a Democratic Society (united front of communists and leftist socialists)

SDSC San Diego State College; San Diego Steamship Company

sd sms clsd side seams closed

SDSMT South Dakota School of Mines and Technology

SDSNH San Diego Society of Natural History

SDSO San Diego Symphony Orchestra

SDSRU Soil Data Storage and Retrieval Unit

SDSS Self-Deploying Space Station

SDSU San Diego State University

sdt sacro-dextra transversa; scientific distribution technique; sea depth transducer; serial data transmission; serial data transmission; source distribution technique; surveillance data transmission

SDT Society of Dairy Technology

SDTC San Diego Transit Corporation

SDTD San Diego Transit District

sdtdl saturating drift transistor diode logic

sdti selective dissemination of technical information

SDTI San Diego Technical Institute

SDTS Satellite Data Transmission System

SDTTS San Diego Turtle and Tortoise Society

SDTU Sign and Display Trades Union

sdu shelter decontamination unit; signal display unit; spectrum display unit; subcarrier display unit

SDU Rio de Janeiro, Brazil (Santos Dumont Airport)

SDU San Diego Union

SDUK Society for the Diffusion of Useful Knowledge; Spoiled Duck (according to Edgar Allan Poe in his essay on *How to Write a Blackwood Article*)

SDUPD San Diego Unified Port District

SDUSD San Diego Unified School District

sdv slowed-down video; swimmer delivery vehicle

sdw swept delta wing

SDWA Safe Drinking Water Act

SDX Stromberg DatagraphiX; Sunray Mid-Continent Oil Company

SDYC San Diego Yacht Club

SDZ San Diego Zoo

se second entrance; semiannual; single end; single-ended; single engine; single entry; special equipment; spherical equivalent; standard error; straight edge

se (sem) standard error of the mean

s/e standardization/evaluation

s & e services and equipment

sE standard English

Se selenium

SE Sanford & Eastern (railroad); Sanitary Engineer(ing); Servel (stock exchange symbol); Site Exploration; Southeast; Stock Exchange; Student Engineer

S-E Starr-Edwards (prosthesis)

SE Son Eminence (French—His Eminence); *Sureste* (Spanish —southeast)

SE1, SE2, etc. Southeast One, Southeast Two, etc. (London postal zones)

s-e 22 silencer-equipped 22-caliber revolver (favored by Mafia assassins and others)

sea. sheep erythrocyte agglutination; spontaneous electrical activity

Sea (Port of) Seattle; Sea of (Arabia, Galilee, Islands, Japan, Marmora, Okhotsk, Rybinsk, the Plain, Straw, etc.); The Sea (Andaman, Baltic, Bering, Black, Caribbean, Japan, Mediterranean, North, Okhotsk, South China, etc.)

Sea Symphony No. 1 by Vaughan Williams

SEA Safety Equipment Association; Science and Education Administration; Sea Containers Inc; Sea Education Association; Seattle, Washington (Seattle-Tacoma Airport); Ships Editorial Association; Society for Education through Art; Society of Evangelical Agnostics; Southeast Asia; Southern Economic Association; Special Equipment Authorization; State Education Agencies; State Education Agency; Students for Ecological Action; Subterranean Exploration Agency

SEA Sociedad Española de Automoviles (Automobile Society of Spain)

SEAAC South-East Asia Air Command

Seabees Construction Battalion (USN)

Sea-born City Venice

seac standards electronic automatic computer

Seacat Short and Harland short-range surface-to-air missile used by naval vessels

seacel silver-chloride/magnesium cell (battery)

SEACOM South East Asia Commonwealth Cable

seacon seafloor construction

Sea of Cortés Gulf of California also called the Vermillion Sea (*El Mar Bermejo*)

Sea of Cortez Gulf of California (*Mar de Cortès*)

SEADAC Seakeeping Data Analysis Center

SEADAG Southeast Asia Development Advisory Group

Sea of Darkness Atlantic Ocean between Cape Verde Islands and west coast of Africa; area often afflicted by dusty Harmattan blowing from the Sahara seaward

Sea Devil Count Felix von Luckner

seadex seaward defense exercises

Sea Dogs originally the nickname of British pirates and privateers but more recently applied to British seamen and other seamen

SEADS Seattle Air Defense Sector

Seafarer William Clark Russell's pseudonym

Seafood Center Biloxi, Mississippi

Sea-girt Isle Great Britain

Sea-girt Province Nova Scotia

Sea-green Incorruptible Carlyle's nickname for Robespierre

Seagull Utah's state bird and symbolic nickname sometimes given its citizens—Seagulls, Yugoslav two-place single-engine jet aircraft called Galeb

Sea II Seaforth Highlanders

Seahawk Armstrong-Whitworth carrier-based fighter-bomber aircraft

Sea Islands island chain off South Carolina, Georgia, and northern Florida

Sea Islands of Georgia Jekyll, Saint Simons, Sea Island (all near Brunswick)

Sea Islands of South Carolina Edisto, Folly, Hilton Head, Hunting, Ladies, Murphy, Parris, Port Royal, Saint Helena, Wadamalaw

Sea of Japan between China, Korea, Japanese islands, and Manchuria

Sea Killer British short-range surface-to-surface missile

Sea King Sikorsky transport helicopter

Sea Knight Boeing-Vertol helicopter designated CH-46

seal. sea-air-land

SEAL South-East Area Libraries

sealab sea laboratory (underwater research vessel)

SEALF South-East Asia Land Forces

Sea of Lot Dead Sea

SEALs Sea, Air, Land commandos

SEALS Sea-Air-Land Forces (counterinsurgents)

SEAM *Servicios de Equipos Agricolas Mecanizados* (Spanish—Mechanized Agricultural Equipment Service)

SEAMEC Southeast Asian Ministers of Education Council

Seamen's Bible Nathaniel Bowditch's *New American Practical Navigator*

SEAMEO South East Asian Ministers of Education Organisation

seamount sea mountain

Sea of Okhotsk Pacific Ocean inlet between Kamchatka Peninsula, Siberian mainland, Sakhalin (Karafuto) Island, Hokkaido, the Kuriles

SEAP South-East Asia Peninsula

Sea of the Plains Dead Sea along the Jordan River Plain of Israel

Seaport City of West Glamorgan Swansea

Seaport on the Prairie Chicago

Sea-Power Philosopher Admiral Alfred Thayer Mahan, USN

searam semi-active radar missile

Sea Ranger Bell turbine-powered helicopter also known as Jet Ranger

SEARCC South-East Asia Regional Computer Conference

SEARCH System for Electronic Analysis and Retrieval of Criminal Histories; Systematized Excerpts, Abstracts, and Reviews of Chemical Headlines

searchex sea/air search exercise

Sea of Reeds the Red Sea

SEARS Sears, Roebuck; Socioeconomic Assessment for Repository Siting

SEAS Strategic Environmental Assessment System

seasat sea satellite

seascarp undersea escarpment

Seashell Capital Sanibel Island, Florida

S-E Asia Southeast Asia (Burma, Cambodia, Hong Kong, Indonesia, Laos, Malaysia, Philippines, Singapore, Thailand, Vietnam)

Seaside State New Jersey

Seasons Glazunov's ballet; Haydn's oratorio *Die Jahreszeiten*

Sea Stallion Sikorsky heavy-assault helicopter designated CH-53

Sea of Stars sparkling headwaters of the Huango or Yellow River of China rising in Tibet

sea story teller (*see* Story Teller of the Sea)

Sea of Straw Tagus River estuary

SEAT Sociedad Español de Automoviles de Turismo—Spanish Society of Touring Automobiles)—manufacturer's name

Seatac Seattle-Tacoma (area)

seatainer(s) seagoing container(s)—theftproof steel containers for overseas cargo

Seatl Seattle

SEATO Southeast Asia Treaty Organization

SEAU Sea Containers Incorporated Unit

Sea Venom DeHavilland carrier-based fighter-jet aircraft

Sea Vixen DeHavilland carrier-based jet-fighter aircraft

sea water 96.4% water plus 2.8% sodium chloride (common salt) and smaller quantities of magnesium chloride, magnesium sulfate, calcium sulfate, and potassium chloride; in inland seas such as the Dead Sea and the Salton Sea these percentages vary

seb static error band

seb (SEB) surface-effect boat

Scb Sebastian(o)

Seb Sebjet or *Sebkhat* or *Sebkra* (Arabic—salt flats)—also appears as *Sabkhat*

SEB Society for Experimental Biology; Southern Electricity Board

SEB Skandinaviska Enskilda Banken (Swedish— Scandinavian Loan Bank)

Sebastian Melmoth name assumed by Oscar Wilde after he was released from Reading Gaol and lived in Paris until his death three years later

S & EBC Ship and Engine Building Company

sebkha (Arabic—marsh)

SEBM Society of Experimental Biology and Medicine

SEBT South-Eastern Brick and Tile (federation)

Sebta (Arabic—Ceuta)

sec secant; second; secondary; secret; section; security

sec. *secundum* (Latin—according to)

Sec Secretary; section

SEC Section Emergency Coordinator; Securities and Exchange Commission; State Electricity Commission; State Energy Commission; Supreme Economic Council (USSR)

S.E.C. Springfield Equipment Company

SecA Secretary of the Army

SECA Southern Educational Communications Association

Sec Air Secretary of the Air Force

SECAIR Secretary of the Air Force

secam *séquential couleur à mémoire* (French—sequential color memory)—Franco-Soviet television color transmission standard sometimes translated as the system contrary to the American method (SECAM)

SECAM *Séquential à Mémoire* (French—sequence and memory color television system)

secar secondary radar

sec. art. *secundum artem* (Latin—according to the art)

seccy seconal (secobarbital sedative hypnotic, also nicknamed seggy)

secd second

SECDA Southeastern Community Development Association

SECDEF Secretary of Defense

secesh secessionist

Secession City Charleston, South Carolina

Sec-Gen Secretary-General

sech hyperbolic secant

secinsp security inspection

sec. leg. *secundum legem* (Latin—according to law)

Sec Leg Secretary of the Legation

SECMA Stock Exchange Computer Managers Association

sec. nat. *secundum naturam* (Latin—according to nature)

SECNAV Secretary of the Navy

seco second-stage engine cutoff; sustainer engine cutoff

seco (SECO) self-regulating error-correct coder-decoder

Second Estate The Nobility

second-generation money checks; cheques

Second International Second International Workingmen's Association (of socialists convening in Paris in 1889 and rejecting anarchist and communist extremists)

Second Reich German Republic (1919–1933)—Germany between two world wars it provoked and lost

Second Republic France under the presidency of Louis Napoleon from 1848 to 1852

Second State Pennsylvania (*see* First State)

Second World highly industrialized nations of the West such as Belgium, France, Germany, Italy, the Netherlands, the United Kingdom

secor (SECOR) sequential collation of range

secr secret

SE & CR Southeastern and Chatham Railway

sec. reg. *secundum regulam* (Latin—according to regulations, according to rule)

secret^a *secretaria* (Spanish—secretariat)

secs secants; seconds; sections

sec's soft elastic capsules

Secs sections

Sec Soc Foun Second Society Foundation

sect section; sector

sect (Latin suffix—cut)—dissect

Section 8 discharged from the armed forces because of insanity or intoxication; government-subsidized housing; mental case (military code)

Secty Secretary

Securité France's security service headquartered in Paris where it also serves the National Central Bureau of Interpol

SECUS Sex Education Council of the United States

Sec'y Secretary

sed sedative; sediment; sedimentation; severely emotionally disturbed; skin erythema dose

sed. *sedes* (Latin—a chair; a stool)

SED Scientific Equipment Division (Westinghouse); Special Enforcement Detail (law enforcement team)

SED *Sozialistische Einheitspartei Deutschlands* (Germany's Socialist Unity Party)—Soviet-oriented East German Party

sedar submerged electrode detection and ranging

SEDEIS Société d'Etudes et de Documentation Economiques, Industrielles et Sociales (Paris)

sedi sediment(ation)

SEDIS Surface-Emitter-Detection Identification System

sedi time sedimentation time

sed rate sedimentation rate

sed('s) seeing-eye dog(s)

sedtn sedimentation

see. secondary electron emission; stop-everything environmentalists; survival, evasion, and escape; systems efficiency expert(ise)

SEE Society of Environmental Engineers; Society of Explosives Engineers

SEE *Société des Eléctriciens, des Electroniciens, et des Radioélectriciens* (French—Society of Electricians, Electronicians, and Radio Electricians)—electric, electronic, and radio technicians

SEEA *Société Européenne d'Energie Atomique* (French—European Atomic Energy Society)

SEEB Southeastern Electricity Board (UK)

Seec Saburo exhaust-emission control

SEECA State Environmental Education Coordinators Association

SEECB Solar Energy and Energy Conservation Bank

SEECC Standards for Educators of Exceptional Children in Canada

seecom sensible, economical, electrical commuter (electric automobile)

SEECTS Subaru Exhaust Emission-Control Thermal System

seed. summer of experience, exploration, and discovery

SEED Scientists and Engineers in Economic Development (National Science Foundation); Skills Escalation and Employment Development; Special Elementary Education (for the underdeveloped)

SEEJ *Slavic and East European Journal*

SEEK Search for Elevation and Educational Knowledge (NY State dropout program); Sooner Exchange for Educational Knowledge; Systems Evaluation and Exchange of Knowledge

Seekers (truth-seeking Quakers)

Seeley Regester Metta Victoria Fuller Victor

seeo *sauf erreur et omission* (French—excepting errors and omissions)

s.e.e.o. *salvis erroribus et omissis* (Latin—excepting errors and omissions)

seep seagoing jeep (amphibious vehicle)

seer. submarine explosive echo ranging

SEER System for Electronic Evaluation and Retrieval

seex systems evaluation experiment

sef small end first

SEF Southern Education Foundation; Space Education Foundation

SEFA Scottish Educational Film Association

SEFT Society for Education in Film and Television

seg segment; segmentation; segmented; segments; segregate; segrated; segregation; segregationist

seg (SEG) sonoencephalogram

seg *segno* (Italian—sign); *segue* (Italian—comes after; follows)

Seg Segovia

SEG Screen Extras Guild; Society of Economic Geologists; Society of Exploration Geophysicists; Systems Engineering Group

SEGB South Eastern Gas Board

SEGBA *Servicios Eléctricos del Gran Buenos Aires* (Spanish—Electrical Services of Greater Buenos Aires)

seggy (secobarbital sedative hypnotic, also nicknamed seccy)

segm segmented

Segr *Segretario* (Italian—Secretary)

Segrʰᵒ *Segretariato* (Italian—Secretariat)

segs segmented neutrophils; segments

SEH St. Elizabeth's Hospital

SEH *Société Européenne d'Hématologie* (French— European Society of Haematology)

seha specific emotional hazards of adulthood

sehc specific emotional hazards of childhood

SEHMF South of England Hat

Manufacturers' Federation

SEI Scientific Engineering Institute

SEIA Security Equipment Industry Association; Solar Energy Industries Association; Solar Energy Institute of America

SEIC Solar Energy Information Center; System Effectiveness Information Center

SEIF *Secretaria de Estado da Informação e Turismo* (Portuguese—Secretariat of Information and Tourism)

SEIFSA Steel and Engineering Industries' Federation of South Africa

Seiji Seiji Ozawa

seis seismograph; seismography; seismology; submarine emergency identification signal (SEIS)

SEISA South Eastern Intercollegiate Sailing Association

Seiscor Seismograph Service Corporation

seismo seismograph(er); seismographic(al)(ly); seismologist; seismology

seismol seismology

SEIT Search for Extra Terrestrial Intelligence

SEIU Service Employees International Union

sel select(ed); selectee; selector; socioeconomic level; sound exposure level (SEL)

sel (SEL) socio-economic level

Sel Selby

SEL Seoul, Korea (airport); Signal Engineering Laboratories; Southeastern Education Laboratory; Stanford Electronics Laboratories; Systems Engineering Laboratories

SELA Southeastern Library Association

SELA *Sistema Económica Latino Americana* (Spanish—Latin American Economic System)

SELC South Eastern Louisiana College

selcall selective calling

sel-cl self-closing

SELDAMS Selective Data Management System

Seldom Ever Caught Running nickname of the Southeastern and Chatham Railway—SE & CR

seleac standard elementary abstract computer

Selebes (Dutch—Celebes)—Sulawesi

selectric single-element electric typewriter

selen selenography; selenology

self-prop self-propelled

Selk Selkirk

Selkirks Selkirk Mountains of British Columbia

Selma Shulamith

SELMA SEL Maduro

Selma Lagerlöfland Sweden's province of Värmland where the Nobel prize-winning authoress was born

SELNEC South-East Lancashire North-East Cheshire

S/ELPS Spanish/English Language Performance Screening

sels selsyn

selsyn self-synchronous

Selvagens Selvagen Islands between the Canaries and Madeira

Selw Selwyn College, Oxford; Selwyn College—Cambridge

Sely southeasterly

SEly south-easterly

sem scanning electron microscope; semi; semicolon; seminal; slow eye movements; standard error of mean; systolic ejection murmur

sem (SEM) scanning electron microscope; systolic ejection murmur

sem. *semen* (Latin—seed); *semper* (Latin—always, ever)

Sem *Semarang*; *Seminary*; *Semitic*

SEM Society for Ethno-Musicology

SEMA Spray Equipment Manufacturers' Association; Storage Equipment Manufacturers Association

seman semantic(s)

semcor semantic correlation

SEMDA Surveying Equipment Manufacturers and Dealers Association

SEMFA Scottish Electrical Manufacturers' and Factors' Association

semi semicolon

semi- semi-detached house (town house)

semi (Latin prefix—half)— semilunar

semicol semicolon

semidr. *semidrachma* (Latin— half drachma)

semidur semiduration

semih. *semihora* (Latin—half hour)

Seminex Seminary in Exile

Seminole Beech U-8 light transport aircraft

semiot semiotic(al)(ly); semiotician(s); semiotics (study of signs and symbols)

semipro semiprofessional(ly)

semis semifinished; semitrailers

SEMKO Svenska Elektriska Materielkontrollanstalten (Swedish Institute for Testing and Approval of Electrical Equipment)

semp self-erecting marine platform

semp sempre (Italian—always)

Sempione (Italian—Simplon Pass)

sems screw and washer assemblies

SEMT Société d'Etudes des Machines Thermiques (Society for the Study of Thermal Machines)

SEMTA Southeastern Michigan Transportation Authority

sem ves seminal vesicle

sen sense (flow chart)

sen seno (Italian—sine); *senza* (Italian—without)

Sen Senate; Senator

Sen Marcus (or Lucius) Seneca (Roman rhetorician) or his second son Lucius Annaeus Seneca (Roman author); *Senatore* (Italian—senator)

SEN State-Enrolled Nurse

Sena (Portuguese or Spanish—Seine)

Senator Sam U.S. Senator Sam Ervin, Jr, of North Carolina

S en C Sociedad en Comandita (Spanish—limited partnership)—silent partnership; *Société en Commandite* (French—limited partnership)

Sen Clk Senior Clerk

Sen Doc Senate Document

Seneg Senegal; Senegalese

Senegal Republic of Senegal (West African nation whose French-speaking Senegalese export peanuts, phosphate, as well as other crops and minerals plus some livestock) *République du Sénégal*

Senegal's Ports (on the north coast) St Louis, Dakar, Rufisque; (on the south coast) Karabane

Senegambia Senegal + Gambia

senel single-event noise-exposure level

S Eng O Senior Engineering Office(r)

SENI Society for the Encouragement of National Industry

senior dent senior-citizen dental care

senior(s) senior citizen(s)

Senior Service the British Navy

Sen M Senior Master

Sen Mist Senior Mistress

S en NC Société et Nom Collectif (French—joint stock company)

Senne (Italian—Seine)

senr senior

Sen Rept Senate Report

Senr Tech Weld I Senior Technician of the Welding Institute

sens sensitivities (test)

sensistor semiconductor resistor

sent. sentence

Sent Sentyabr (Russian—September)

SENTAC Society for Ear, Nose, and Throat Advances in Children

Sentimental Rebel Clarence Darrow

Sentinel of the Bolshevik Counter-Revolution Cheka charged with the investigation, arrest, persecution, trial, and execution of its own verdict

Sen Wt O Senior Warrant Officer

seo (SEO) satellite for earth observation

seo salvo errori e omissioni (Italian—excepting errors and omissions)

Seo Seoul

SEO Senior Experimental Officer; Snake Ender's Organization

SEODSE Special Explosive Ordnance Disposal Supplies and Equipment (USA)

SEOG Supplemental Educational Opportunity Grant

seoo sauf erreurs ou omissions (French—excepting errors and omissions)

SEOOs State Economic Opportunity Offices

seos (SEOS) synchronous earth observation satellite

seou salve error u omisión (Spanish—except for error or omission)

sep separate; separation

sep (SEP) solar electric power; somatosensory-evoked potential

Sep September

SEP Selective Employment Payments (UK); Simplified Employee Pension; Society of Engineering Psychologists; Society of Experimental Psychologists; Source Evaluation Panel; Student Expense Program

SEP Saturday Evening Post

SEPA Southeastern Power Association; State Elementary Principals Association

separ. *separatum* (Latin—separately)

SEPB Southern Europe Ports and Beaches

SEPD Scottish Economic Planning Department

SEPE Seattle Port of Embarkation

SEPEL Southeastern Plant Environment Laboratories

Seph Sephardim (Hebrew—Jews from Portugal and Spain)

Sephard Sephardim (Hebrew—Jews from Portugal and Spain who were forced to emigrate during the Inquisition to liberal countries such as England and Holland and eventually to their West Indian colonies before coming to Canada and the Untied States; many Sephardic Jews served in the American Revolution)

Sepia City New York City's Harlem

SEPO Space Electric Power Office (AEC)

SEPP Société d'Étude de la Prévision et de la Planification (French—Society for the Study of and Planning for the Future)

SEPR Société pour l'Etude de la Propulsion par Réaction

SepRos separation processing

Seps (SEPS) Smithsonian earth physics satellite

SEPSA Society of Educational Programmers and Systems Analysts

sept. *septem* (Latin—seven)

Sept September

SEPTA Southeastern Pennsylvania Transportation Authority

septe septiembre (Spanish—September)

septel separate telegram

septi septicos (Greek—infected or rotten)—antiseptic, aseptic, septic, septicemia

September September and October

seq sequence

seq. sequens (Latin—the following); *sequente* (Latin—what follows); *sequitur* (Latin—it follows)

seq. luce sequenti luce (Latin—the following day)

Seq NP Sequoia National Park

S Equ Cur South Equatorial Current

Sequoia Sequoia National Park in east-central California

ser serial; series

ser (SER) serine (amino acid)

ser série (French—series)

Ser series; Serpens (constellation)

SER Safety Exploration Report; Service, Employment, Redevelopment; Society for Educational Reconstruction; Soil Erosion Service; Student Eligibility Report

SER Sociaal Economische Raad (Dutch—Social Economic Council); *Sociedad Española Radiodifusión* (Spanish Broadcasting Society)

Sera Seraphim

SERA Services, Education, Rehabilitation for Addiction

Serb Serbia; Serbian

Serb-Croat Serbo-Croatian (slavic language most widely spoken in Yugoslavia where more than 18 million people speak it fluently)

SERCH State Education Research Clearinghouse

SERE Survival, Evasion, Resistance, and Escape (U.S. Naval Training Base)

SEREB Société pour l'Etude et la Réalisation d'Engins Balistiques

Serendib (Arabic—Ceylon or Sri Lanka)

serendip serendipitous(ly); serendipity

Serengeti Serengeti Plains of Tanzania

Serg Sergente (Italian—Sergeant)

Sergeant Sperry MGM-29A surface-to-surface missile

Serg Magg Sergente Maggiore (Italian –Sergeant Major)

Serg(t) Sergeant

SERI Solar Energy Research Institute; Solar Energy Research Institute (ERDA)

serj space electric ramjet

SERL Services Electronics Research Laboratory

SERLANT Service Forces, Atlantic (USN)

serline serials on-line

serm sermon

SERM Society of Early Recorded Music

serol serology

serp simulated ejector-ready panel

SERPAC Service Forces, Pacific (USN)

serpentine hydrous magnesium silicate

Serpentine Suicide Harriet Shelley—sad first wife of the poet. She drowned herself in the Serpentine of London's Hyde Park.

SERPLANT Service Forces, Atlantic (USN)

serr serrate

serra (Italian—mountain range)

serranía (Spanish—mountainous region)

serrate (Latin prefix—sawtoothed)—serration

SE-RRT Southern Europe-Railroad Transport (NATO)

ser sect serial sections

sert space electronic rocket test

SE-RT Southern Europe-Road Transport (NATO)

SERTOMA Service To Mankind

serv service

serv. serva (Latin—keep; preserve)

Serv Servia(n)

Servant of the Nation Secretary of the Treasury Albert Gallatin who financed the Louisiana Purchase and found funds for the War of 1812

serv chge service charge

serv clg service ceiling

SERVE Serve and Enrich Retirement by Volunteer Experience

Servetus Michael Servetus born of Spanish parents and baptized Miguel Serveto—burned alive by order of Calvin in 1553 as he found him guilty of heresy although the writings of this Spanish theologian are widely accepted today

servo anything using a servomechanism; servoamplifier, servocontrol, servodyne, servomotor, servosystem

serv⁰ servicio (Spanish—service)

serv⁰ʳ servidor (Spanish—servant)

servos servomechanisms

Seryozha (Russian nickname—Sergei)—Serge

ses secondary engine start; single-ended scotch (boilers); socio-economic status; socioeconomic strata; solar environment stimulator; surface-effect ship

ses (SES) surface-effect ship

SES Seafarers' Education Service; Self-Esteem Score(s); Society of Engineering Science; Solar Energy Society; Standards Engineers Society; State Employment Service; Steam Engine Systems; Suitability Evaluation Scale

SES Service des Études Scientifiques (French—Scientific Studies Service)

SESA Social and Economic Statistics Administration; Society for Experimental Stress Analysis; Solar Energy Society of America

SESAC Society of European Stage Authors and Composers

sesame. service, sort, and merge

SESAME Search for Excellence in Science and Mathematics Education

sesco secure submarine communications

SESL Space Environment Simulation Laboratory

SESO Senior Equipment Staff Office(r); Ship Environmental Support Office(r)

sesoc surface-effects ship for ocean commerce

SESPO Space Environmental Support Project Office(r)

sesquih sesquihora (Latin—an hour and a half)

sesquilln sesquilingual (ability to use one-and-a-half languages such as English plus half of some other tongue)

sess session

SESS Society of Ethnic and Special Studies; Space Environmental Support System; Summer Employment for Science Students

sest short effective-service time

set. settlement

set septiembre (Spanish—September); *setembro* (Portuguese—September)

SET Scientists, Engineers, Technicians; Security Escort Team; Senior Electronic Technician; Senior Evaluation Treatment; Simplified Engineering Technique; Synchro Error Tester

S.E.T. Selective Employment Tax

seta set arithmetic (value)

SETAF Southern European Task Force

setb set binary (value)

setc set character (value)

SETCO Summit and Elizabeth Trust Company

se/td system engineering/technical direction (SE/TD)

set^e *septiembre* (Spanish—September)

SETEP Science and Engineering Technician Education Program

SETI Search for Extra-Terrestrial Intelligence

SETIL Société de l'Equipement de Tahiti et des Iles (Equipment Company of Tahiti and the Islands)

S-et-L Saône-et-Loire

S-et-M Seine-et-Marne

S-et-O Seine-et-Oise

SETP Society of Experimental Test Pilots

SETS Solar Energy Thermionic Conversion System

Set Svenholm Karl Viktor Svanholm

sett settling

sett *settembre* (Italian—September)

seu smallest executable unit

SEU Southeastern University

SEUA South Eastern Underwriters Association

seuo *salvo error u omisíon* (Spanish—errors and omissions excepted)

SEUS Southeastern United States

sev seven; sevenfold; seventeen(th); seventy; sever; several; severally; severance; severe; severity; surface-effect vehicle

sev *sever* (Russian—north)

Sev Sevilla; Seville

Sev *Sever* or *Severnaya* (Russian—north, northern)

SEV *Soviet Ekonomischeskoy Vzaimopomoschchi* (Russian—Soviet Council for Mutual Economic Aid)—the COMECON

Seven (telephone) Sisters Ameritech, Bell Atlantic, Bell South, Nynex, Pacific Telesis, Southwestern Bell, US West

Seven Deadly Sins Anger, Covetousness, Envy, Gluttony, Lust, Pride, Sloth

Seven-Hill Cities Lisbon, Prague, Rome, and Valparaiso —all built around seven hills

Seven Hills of Rome Aventine, Caelian, Capitoline, Esquiline, Palatine, Quirinal or Colline, Viminal

Seven Provinces (*see* United Provinces)

Seven Sages of Greece Bias, Chilon, Cleobulus, Periander, Pittacus, Solon, Thales

Seven Seas Antarctic, Arctic, Indian, North Atlantic, South Atlantic, North Pacific, South Pacific oceans; term also applied to the Andaman, Baltic, Bering, Caribbean, Mediterranean, South China, and Yellow seas

Seven Sisters Barnard, Bryn Mawr, Mount Holyoke, Radcliffe, Smith, Vassar, and Wellesley—all colleges for women when first organized; BP (British Petroleum), Exxon (Esso—Standard Oil), Gulf, Mobil, Shell, SOCAL (Standard Oil of California—Chevron), Texaco —world's leading oil companies

Seventeenth State Ohio

Seventh State Maryland (*see* First State)

Seven Wonders of the Ancient World Pyramids of Egypt, Lighthouse of Pharos of Alexandria, Hanging Gardens and Walls of Babylon, Temple of Artemis or Diana at Ephesus, Statue of Zeus by Phidias at Olympia, Mausoleum at Halicarnassus, Colossus of Rhodes

Seven Wonders of the Modern World Fort Peck Dam across the Missouri in Montana; Pecos, Texas oilwell; Royal Gorge Bridge in Colorado; Simplon Tunnel between Italy and Switzerland; TV Tower at Blanchard, North Dakota; Verrazano-Narrows Bridge over New York Harbor; World Trade Center in downtown New York—each represents an engineering superlative—the biggest dam, the deepest well, the highest bridge, the longest tunnel, the tallest structure, the longest single-span bridge, the tallest buildings

SEVFLT Seventh Fleet, Pacific (USN)

Sevilla (Spanish—Seville)

Seville English place-name equivalent of Sevilla

sevocom secure voice communications

sew. sewage; sewer; sewerage

Sewanee University of the South in Sewanee, Tennessee

Seward's Folly nickname given Alaska in 1867 when Secretary of State William H Seward purchased the area from Russia for $7,200,000 and it was said he bought a collection of icebergs and polar bears; it was also called Seward's Polar Bear Garden

sewido surface electromagnetic-wave-integrated optics

SEWT Simulator for Electronic Warfare Training

sex. sextet; sexual

Sex Sextans (constellation)

Sexag Sexagesima

sexational sexually sensational

sexcite excite sexually

sexcitement sexual excitement

sexclusive sexually exclusive

sex ed sex(ual) education

sexegenarians impotent old oglers of sexateries

sexercises sexual exercises

sexateries nubile secretaries; sexual-service secretaries; sexy-looking secretaries

Sex Francisco nickname of sex-oriented San Francisco

sexgregation sexual segregation

sexhibit sex exhibit

sexhibitors sex exhibitors (pornographic shopkeepers)

Sex Isle Mykonos in the Greek Islands close to Piraeus, the port of Athens

SExO Senior Experimental Officer

sexones sex odors

sexorgies sexual orgies

sexpensive sexually expensive

sexperience sexual experience

sexpert sex expert; sexual expert; sexpertise

sexpionage sexual exploitation in espionage

sexplanatory sexually explanatory

sexplicit sexually explicit

sexploitation sex(ual) exploitation

sexploiter sex exploiter

sexploit(s) sexual exploit(s)

sexplosion sexual explosion

SEXPOL Sexual Equality and Politics (German communist movement originated by Wilhelm Reich before the Nazis forced him to flee to Denmark and eventually to the United States)

s. expr. *sine expressione* (Latin—without expressing; without pressing)

sex psycho sexual psychopath(ic)

Sex Queen of Stage and Screen Mae West

sexquisite sexually exquisite

sexsation sexual sensation

sexslanguage sexual slang language

sext sextant

Sext Sextans (constellation)

Sextan NATO name for a Soviet class of trawlers

Sexyola Sixaola, Costa Rica

Sexy Rexy Rex Harrison

Seybrew Seychelles Islands brew(ery)

Seychelles Indian Ocean island country whose natives speak English and Creole; tropical products such as spices, tea, tortoise shell, and vanilla are exported

Seychelles Port Victoria

sez (SEZ) southern economic zone

SEZ Special Economic Zone (China)

sf safety factor; salt free; science fiction; semifinished; single feeder; single-feed; sinking fund; sound and flash; special facilities; spent fuel; spinal fluid; spotface; standard form; stress formula; sulphation factor; sunkface

s/f shift forward; store and forward

s & f stock and fixtures

sf *sans frais* (French—without expense); *sforzando* (Italian—accented strongly; forced; reinforced)

s.f. *sub finem* (Latin—near the end)

Sf Svedberg flotation (units)

SF San Franciscan; San Francisco; Santa Fe (Atchison, Topeka & Santa Fe Railway); Santa Fe, New Mexico; Scouting Force; Security Force; Security Forces; Shipfitter; Special Facilities; Special Forces; Standard Frequency; State Facilitator; Swedenborg Foundation; Swiss Federation (auto plate); Syrian Forces

SF *Slovenska Filharmonica* (Serbo-Croat—Slovene Philharmonic—in Ljubljana, Yugoslavia); *Socialistisk Folkeparti* (Dano-Norwegian—Socialist People's Party); *Système français* (French system, of screw threads)

S/F *Sinn Fein* (Irish Gaelic—Ourselves Alone)

SF-5 Spanish version of the F-5 Northrup Freedom Fighter

sfa simulated flight automatic; slow flying aircraft; spatial frequency analyzer

sfa (SFA) serum folate; suppressive factor of allergy

s & fa shipping and forwarding agent

SFA Saks Fifth Avenue; Scandinavian Fraternity of America; Scientific Film Association; Scottish Football Association; Show Folks of America; Slide Fastener Association, Société Française d'Astronautique (French Astronautical Society); Solid Fuels Administration; Soroptimist Federation of the Americas; Southeastern Fisheries Association; Speech Foundation of America; Symphony Foundation of America

SFAAW Stove, Furnace, and Allied Appliance Workers (International Union of North America)

SFAC Société des Forges et Ateliers du Creusot (Schneider-Creusot Forges and Factories)

SFAD Society of Federal Artists and Designers

SFAI San Francisco Art Institute; Steel Furnace Association of India

SFAO San Francisco Assay Office

sfar sound fixing and ranging

SFAR System Failure Analysis Report

SFB Sender Freies Berlin (Free Berlin Broadcasting Station), Spencer Fullerton Baird

SFBARTD San Francisco Bay Area Rapid Transit District

sf bh surface broach

SFBMS Small Farm Business Management Scheme

SFBNS San Francisco Bay Naval Shipyard

sfc S-bank frequency converter; sight fire control; specific fuel consumption; supercritical fluid chromatography; switching filter connector; synchronized framing camera

sfc (SFC) spinal fluid count

Sfc Sergeant First Class

SFC Saint Francis College; Sioux Falls College; Space Flight Center

SFC *San Francisco Chronicle*

SFCA Southwest Flight Crew Association

SFCC San Francisco City College

SFCI State Farms Corporation of India

SFCJ San Francisco City Jail

SFCM San Francisco Conservatory of Music

SFCMD San Francisco Contract Management District

SFCP Shore Fire Control Party

SFCS Survivable Flight Control System

SFCTA San Francisco Classroom Teachers Association

sfcw search for critical weakness

SFCW San Francisco College for Women

Sfd San Fernando

sfd/algol system function description/algol (language)

SFDS Spent-Fuel Disposal System

sfe safety function earthquake; stacking fault energy; surface-energy

SFE Society of Fire Engineers

SFE *Société Française des Electriciens* (French Society of Electricians)

SFEA Survival and Flight Equipment Association

SFEL Standard Facility Equipment List

SFEN *Société Française d'Energie Nucléaire* (French Nuclear Energy Society)

sff *se faz favor* (Portuguese—please)

SFF Solar Forecast Facility

sfff salt-free fat-free (diet)

SFG *Studien und Förderungsgesellschaft* (German—Studies and Advancement Society)

sfga single floating-gate amplifier

sfgd safeguard

SFGGB San Francisco Golden Gate Bridge

SFGH San Francisco General Hospital

SFHP Spent Fuel Handling and Packaging; Spent-Fuel Handling Project

SFHR San Francisco Historic Records

SFHS Stephen Foster High School

SFI Sport Fishing Institute

SFI *Société Financière Internationale* (French—International Finance Corporation)

SFIAE San Francisco Institute of Automotive Ecology

SFIB Southern Freight Inspection Bureau

SFIO *Section Française de l'Internationale Ouvriere* (French section of the Worker's International)—former name of the French Socialist Party

SFIS Small Firms Information Service

SFIT Standard Family Interaction Test

sfl sequenced flashing lights (airport runways)

s fl Surinam florin

SFL Sexual Freedom League; Society of Federal Linguists

sfm surface feed per minute; surface feet per minute

SFMA San Francisco Museum of Art; Southern Furniture Manufacturers Association

SFMC San Francisco Medical Center (University of California)

SFMR San Francisco Municipal Railway (operates the cable cars)

SFMS Shipwrecked Fishermen and Mariners (Royal Benevolent Society)

SF & NV San Francisco & Napa Valley (railroad)

sfo simulated flame out; submarine fog oscillator

S Fo (Port of) San Francisco

SFO San Francisco, California (airport); San Francisco Opera; San Francisco Operations (office); San Francisco-Oakland Airlines; Service Fuel Oil; Space Flight Operations

SF-OBB San Francisco-Oakland Bay Bridge (Transbay Bridge)

SFOD San Francisco Ordnance District; Special Forces Operational Detachment

SFOF Space Flight Operations Facility

SFOLDS Ship-Form On-Line Design System

SFP Sherbrooke Forest Park (Victoria, Australia)

SFP Société Française de Photogrammétrie (French Society of Photogrammetry)

SFPD San Francisco Police Department

SFPDis San Francisco Procurement District (US Army)

sf pe surface plate

SFPE San Francisco Port of Embarkation; Society of Fire Protection Engineers

SFPF Spent-Fuel Packaging Facility

SFPL San Francisco Public Library

sfpm surface feet per minute

SFPO Spent-Fuel Project Office (Savannah River Operations Office)

SFPR Society of Friends of Puerto Rico

sfprf semifireproof

SFPs Sinn Fein Provisionals (Provos)

sfqa (SFQA) structurally fixed question-answering system

sfr (SFR) submarine fleet reactor

SFR Safety of Flight Requirement

SFRA Science Fiction Research Association

S Fran San Francisco

SFRJ Socijalisticka Federativna Republika Jugoslavija (Socialist Federated Republic of Yugoslavia)

sfrr sinking fund rate of return

sfr(s) schweizerfranc(s) [Dano-Norwegian—Swiss franc(s)]

SFRS Sea Fisheries Research Station (Haifa)

sfs strictly for suckers; surfaced four sides

SFs Special Forces (Green Berets); State Facilitators

SFS San Francisco Symphony; Senior Foreign Service; Society of Fleet Supervisors

SFSA Steel Founders' Society of America

SFSAFBI Society of Former Special Agents of the Federal Bureau of Investigation

SFSC San Francisco State College

SF & SC Standard Fruit & Steamship Company

SFSE San Francisco Stock Exchange

SFSO San Francisco Symphony Orchestra

SFSP Spent-Fuel Storage Program

SF/SP Santa Fe/Southern Pacific (merged railroads)

SFSS Satellite Field Services Stations (NOAA)

SFSSP Society of the Friendly Sons of St Patrick

sft soft; specified financial transactions; stop for tea; superfast train

SFT Society of Forensic Toxicologists; Spent-Fuel Test(ing)

SFTA Scientific Film Television Award; Society of Film and Television Arts

SFTAA Short-Form Test of Academic Aptitude

SFTB Southern Freight Tariff Bureau

SFTI San Fernando Technical Institute (Trinidad)

SFTP Science For The People

sftwd softwood

sftwr software (officialese for paperwork as opposed to hardware)

SFU Simon Fraser University

S$_f$ units Svedberg flotation units

sfv sight feed valve

SFv Semliki Forest virus

SFVAH San Francisco Veterans Administration Hospital

SFVSC San Fernando Valley State College

SFWA Science Fiction Writers of America

sfwd slow forward

SFWR Stewardesses for Women's Rights

sfx sound effects (radio or television)

sfxd semifixed

sfxr superflash X-ray

sfy standard facility year(s)

SFYC San Francisco Yacht Club

sfz sforzando (Italian—accented strongly, forced, reinforced)

sg screen grid; single groove; singular; smoke generator; soluble gelatin; specific gravity; steam generator; steel girder; structural glass; swamp glider

s-g sub-generic; sub-genus

sg selon grandeur (French—according to size); on menus, sg or SG indicates an item is priced according to the size of the serving

Sg spring range of tide

SG Aerotransporte Litoral Argentino (Argentine Coastal Air Transport); Scots Guards; Solicitor General; South Georgia (railroad); Standing Group; Sunset Gun; Surgeon General

S-G Sachs-Georgi (test); Saint-Gobain; Space-General (Corporation)

SGA Saskatchewan Government Airways; Society of the Graphic Arts; Southern Gas Association; Special Grant Application; Standards of Grade Authorization; Student Government Association

SGAE Sociedad General de Autores de España (General Society of Authors of Spain)

S-gauge standard gauge (4-foot 8 1/2-inch) railroad track

SGB Société Générale de Belgique

SGB Société Générale de Banque (Belgian Bank); *Société Générale de Belgique*

SGBIP Subject Guide to Books in Print

sgc screen grid current; simulated generation control; spartan guidance computer (SGC); spherical gear coupling; stabilizer gyro circuit

Sg C Surgeon Captain

SGC Saint Gregory College; South Georgia College

S-G C Space-General Corporation

SGCA Secrétariat Général à l'Aviation Civil (French—Secretariat General of Civil Aviation)

Sg Cr Surgeon Commander

sgd signed

SGD Senior Grand Deacon

sgdg sans garantie du gouvernement (French—patent issued without government guarantee)

sg di swaging die

Sge Sagitta (abbreviation derived from the genitive Sagittae)

S Ge South Georgia

sgemp system-generated electromagnetic pulse

SGF Scottish Grocers' Federation

SGF Sveriges Gummitekniska Forening (Swedish Rubber Industry Association)

sgg sustainer gas generator

sghwr steam-generating heavy-water reactor

SGI Spring Garden Institute

SGINDEX System Generation Cross-Reference Index (NASA)

SGIO State Government Insurance Office

sgl signal; single

S Glam South Glamorgan

Sg L Cr Surgeon Lieutenant Commander

SGLI Servicemen's Group Life Insurance

SGLS Space-Ground Link Subsystem

SGM Sea Gallantry Medal; Society of General Microbiology

sg md swaging mandrel

SGMEX Southern Gulf of Mexico

SGMT Société Générale des Transports Maritimes

sgn scan gate number; signum function

Sgn (Port of) Saigon

SGN Saigon, Vietnam (airport); Surgeon General of the Navy

Sgno Stagno (Italian—pond; pool)

sgnr signature

sgo surgery, gynecology, and obstetrics

SGO Surgeon General's Office

sgot serum glutamic oxaloacetic transaminase

sgp starch graft polymers

SGP Shell Gasification Process; Society of General Physiologists

SGP Staatkundig Gereformeerde Partij (Dutch—Political Reformed Party)

SGPA Scottish General Publishers Association

sgpt serum glutamic pyruvic transaminase

sgr steam gas recirculation (oil-from-shale removal process)

Sgr Sagittarius (constellation)

SGR Sumbu Game Reserve (Zambia)

Sg RA Surgeon Rear Admiral

's Gravenhage (Dutch—The Hague) provincial capital of South Holland in the Netherlands

SGRS Stockton Geriatric Rating Scale

SGS Society of General Surgeons; Sunderbans Game Sanctuary (Bangladesh)

SGSB Stanford Graduate School of Business

SGSR Society for General Systems Research

sgt special gas taper (threading)

Sgt Sergeant

SGT Society of Glass Technology

Sgt 1/C Sergeant First Class

S-G Test Sachs-Georgi Test

SGTIA Standing Group Technical Intelligence Agency (NATO)

Sgt Maj Sergeant Major

SGU Scottish Gliding Union; Scottish Golf Union; Singapore Golfers Union

SGU Sveriges Geologiska Undersokning (Swedish Geological Survey)

SGUs Special Guerrilla Units (anti-communist)

Sg VA Surgeon Vice Admiral

SGVHS Samuel Gompers Vocational High School

SGW Senior Grand Warden

SGX Seeger Refrigerator Express (stock exchange symbol)

sh scleroscope hardness; serum hepatitis; shelf; shelving; ship's heading; shop; shopping; sick in hospital; social history; somatotrophic hormone; speech handicapped; surgical hernia

sh (SH) sexual harassment

s/h shorthand

Sh shells; shilling (British East Africa)

Sh Sh'aib (Arabic—ravine; road); *Shatt* (Arabic—river; riverbank); *Shima* (Japanese —island); *Suid Holland* (Dutch—South Holland)

SH Schenley Industries (stock exchange symbol); Soldier's Home; Station Hospital; Symphony Hall

S-H Scripps-Howard

S & H Sperry & Hutchinson (green stamps); Sundays and Holidays

SH Sa Hautesse (French—Her or His Highness)

sha (SHA) sidereal hour angle

Sha Shanghai

SHA Safety and Health Administration; Southern Historical Association

SHAA Society of Hearing Aid Audiologists

Shaanxi (Pinyin Chinese—Shensi)

shab soft and hard acids and bases

sh abs shock absorber

SHAC Seale-Hayne Agricultural College

Shackamaxon not the nickname of a shack-filled slum but the place in the Kensington district of Philadelphia where William Penn concluded his Great Treaty with the Indians and thereby guaranteed peace in Pennsylvania

Shackleton Hawker-Siddeley maritime reconnaissance aircraft

shaco shorthand coding

SHAD Sharpe Army Depot

Shaddock NATO name for Soviet surface-to-surface missile

shade. (SHADE) shielded hot-air-drum evaporator

SHAEF Supreme Headquarters, Allied Expeditionary Forces

Shafir Israeli air-to-air missile resembling the U.S. Sidewinder

shag. simplified high-accuracy guidance

shags shaggy carpets or rugs

Shah Shahanshah (Persian—King of Kings)

Shahada Flag Saudi Arabian green standard bearing white lettering—the Moslem shahada: "There is no god but God—and Mohammed is his prophet."

Shak(e) Shakespeare

Shakes Shakespeare

Shakopee Minnesota Correctional Institution for Women

at Shakopee

shale. standoff high-altitude long endurance

Shalimar Garden of Love on Dal Lake in Kashmir

Shalom Aleichem Solomon Rabinowitz' pseudonym

Sham Shamrock

shamateur(s) sham amateur(s)

shamburger sham hamburger (containing more additives and adulterants than meat)

SHAME Save, Help Animals Man Exploits; Society to Humiliate, Aggravate, Mortify, and Embarass Smokers

Shami Shamrock; Shulamith

Shamo (Chinese—Sandy Waste) —the Gobi Desert

shamrock symbol of Ireland and the Irish

Shandong (Pinyin Chinese— Shantung)

shandy shandygaff (beer-and-ginger-ale mixture)

Shang Shanghai

Shanghai mainland-China-built torpedo boat; principal port of the People's Republic of China

Shank End Cape Peninsula below Cape Town, South Africa

shan't shall not (colloquial)

Shantou (Pinyin Chinese—Swatow)

Shanxi (Pinyin Chinese—Shansi)

SHAPE Scanning Hartmann Aperture Plate Experiment; Supreme Headquarters, Allied Powers, Europe

SHARE Self-Help And Resources Exchange

Shark Island Garden Key, Dry Tortugas (Fort Jefferson National Monument reached by boat from Key West)

SHARP Senior-High Assessment of Reading Performance; Ships Analysis and Retrieval Project

SHARPS Ship/Helicopter Acoustic Range-Prediction System (USN)

SHAS Shared Hospital Accounting System

Shaston Shaftesbury, England

Shav Shavuot

SHAWCO Students Health and Welfare Centers Organization

Shawn (Gaelic—Sean)

SHB Svenska Handelsbanken (Swedish Bank of Commerce)

shbd serum X-hydroxy-butyrate dehydrogenase

shbg sex-hormone-binding glob-

ulin

shc spontaneous human combustion

SHC Sacred Heart College; Seton Hall College; Siena Heights College; Spring Hill College; Streets and Highways Code; Surveillance Helicopter Company

SHCC Statewide Health Coordinating Council

SHCJ Society of the Holy Child of Jesus

shco sulfonated hydrogenated castor oil

sh con shore connection

SHCS School of Health Care Sciences (USAF)

shd should

SHD Scottish Home Department; State Hydroelectric Department

she. signal handling equipment; standard hydrogen electrode

she. (SHE) sodium heat engine

Shearith Israel (Hebrew—Remnant of Israel)—oldest American congregation of Jews whose first synagogue was on Mill Street in New York City and now is at Central Park West and Seventieth Street

Sheba Saba

she'd she had; she would

Shedd Shedd Aquarium (Chicago)

Sheed Sheed & Ward

SHEEO State Higher Education Executive Officers

Sheep Islands Faeroe Islands

Sheet Metal Workers Union Sheet Metal Workers International Association

Sheff Sheffield; Sheffield Scientific School (Yale)

Sheila Cecilia

shelf. super-hardened extremely low frequency

she'll she will

SHELL Royal Dutch Shell Oil Company; Shell Oil Company

shellrep shelling report

Shelly Winters Shirley Schrift

SHELREP Shelling Report

Sheltie Shetland sheepdog

Shelty Shetland pony

Shenandoahs Shenandoah Mountains of Virginia and West Virginia

Shen NP Shenandoah National Park

Shep Shep(p)ard; Shepton

Shepherd of the Ocean Sir Walter Raleigh

Sher Sherbrooke

Sherbrooke Street Montreal's nightclub district

Sheremetyevo Moscow's principal airport serving the USSR and other countries

Sheridan M-551 assault vehicle armed with a 152mm gun; Sheridan House

Sheridan Girls Wyoming (delinquent) Girls School at Sheridan

Sherlock name of a police computer recording and releasing essential information about many criminal activities; nickname of any good detective and named in honor of the world's all-time investigator created by novelist Sir Arthur Conan Doyle—Sherlock Holmes; nickname for a super-sleuth detective; (*see* Dr Watson); Sherlock Holmes; Sherlockian(s)

Sherm Sherman

Sherman M-4 tank armed with high-velocity 76mm gun

sherm(s) sherman(s)—pcp-soaked marijuana cigarette(s)

Shershen NATO name for a Soviet class of motor torpedo boats (PT boats)

's Hertogenbosch provincial capital of North Brabant in the Netherlands

she's she has; she is

SHES School Health Education Study

Shet Shetland

shetland shetland pony (small but stocky long-hair pony first bred in the Shetland Islands); shetland sheepdog (miniature collie); shetland wool (Shetland Island sheep wool)

Shetland Shetland Island or the Shetland Islands called the Zetlands

Shetlands Shetland Islands off northern Scotland

Shets Shetland Islands, Scotland

Shevvie(s) native(s) of Sheffield, Yorkshire

Shex Sundays and holidays excepted

shf super high-frequency— 300-30,000 mc

Shf Sheffield

SHF Soil and Health Foundation

SHFF Scottish House Furnishers' Federation

shftg shafting

S-H-G diet Sauerbruch-Herrmannsdorfer-Gerson (tubercular) diet

SHH Sociedad Honoraria Hispánica

SHHV Society for Health and Human Values

Shi Shanghai

Shickshocks Shickshock Mountains of the Gaspé Peninsula of New Brunswick

SHIELD Sylvania High-Intelligence Electronic Defense

Shig Shigella

shil (SHIL) shillelagh (surface-to-surface missile of the U.S. Army)

Shillelagh anti-tank surface-to-surface guided missile produced by Aeronutronic

Shim Shimonoseki

Shimabara Kyoto, Japan's old redlight district

Shimmachi Osaka, Japan's old redlight district

Shin Bet Sherut Habitachon (Hebrew—Security Department)—Israel

S & h inc Sundays and holidays included

shinerium shoe-shine stand

Shinjuku Tokyo's all-night nightclub district

Shinkansen (Japanese—Main Trunk Line)—bullet-train high-speed railway

ship. shipment; shipping

SHIP Self-Help Improvement Program

shipcon shipping control; shipping convoy

Ship of the Desert the camel

ShipDTO ship on depot transfer order

shipmt shipment

Shirley MacLaine Shirley Beatty

Shitport Norfolk, Virginia (seafarer's nickname)

SHJC Sacred Heart Junior College

shk shank

Shkodër (Albanian—Scutari)—an Albanian city not to be confused with Scutari the Asian section of Istanbul whose Turkish name is Üsküdar

Shl Shields; shoal

Sh L Shipwright Lieutenant

SHL Society for Humane Legislation

shld shoulder

shl dk shelter deck

SHLM Society of Hospital Laundry Managers

shlp shiplap

Shls Shoals (postal abbreviation)

shm simple harmonic motion

Shm Shimizu; Shoreham

SHM Service Hydrographique de la Marine (Naval Hydrographic Service)

SHMO Senior Hospital Medical Officer

shmt shock mount

SHNC Scottish Higher National Certificate

SHND Scottish Higher National Diploma

SHNHS Sagamore Hill National Historic Site

SHNNR Studland Heath National Nature Reserve (England)

shnoz shnozzle; shnozzola

ShNP Shenandoah National Park

sho shore(d); shoring

SHO Senior House Officer; Student Health Organization

SHOC Self-Help Opportunity Center

SHOCK Students Hot on Conserving Kilowatts

shocks. shock absorbers

Shoe City Auburn, Maine; Hanover, Pennsylvania; Lynn, Massachusetts; and wherever else cobbling is the chief craft

Sholem Aleichem Sholom (Solomon) Rabinowitz's pen name based on the Hebrew greeting —*shalom alekhem*—peace be with you

S Holmes, Esq Sherlock Holmes

shootin shooting

Shooting Star Lockheed T-33 jet-fighter trainer aircraft

SHORADS Short Range All-Weather Air-Defense System

shoran short-range navigation

shorlans armored cars built on the shores of Northern Ireland

SHORS School/Home Observational Referral System

shorted short circuited (electrical parlance)

shortg shortage

short(s) short circuit(s)

Shostakovich's 15 Shostakovich's fifteen symphonies including *Leningrad* (No. 7), *Year 1905* (No. 11), *Lenin* (No. 12), *Babi Yar* (No. 13)

SHOT Society for the History of Technology

shouldn't should not

show biz show business

Show-Me State Missouri's official nickname

Showplace of the Orient Singa-

pore

shp shaft horsepower

Shp Sharpness

SHP Sandy Hook Pilots; Society of Hospital Pharmacists

SHPBG Small Horticultural Production Business Grant

SHPC Scenic Hudson Preservation Conference

SHPDA State Health Planning and Development Agency

shps seahead pressure simulator

shpt shipment

SHP Test Strongin-Hinsie-Peck (salivary secretion) Test

SHQ Station Headquarters

shr share(s)

Shr Shore (postal abbreviation)

shram (SHRAM) short-range air-to-surface missile

shrap shrapnel

shrd shredded

Shrike Texas Instrument air-to-surface antiradar missile

shrimpsan shrimp sandwich

shrimpwich shrimp sandwich

SHRMA South Hampton Roads Metropolitan Area (Norfolk, Portsmouth, Chesapeake, and Virginia Beach)

Shrops Shropshire

Shrs Shores (postal abbreviation)

shrtg shortage

shs ship's heading servo

SHS Sacred Heart Seminary; Scottish History Society; Senior High School; *Srba, Hrvata, i Slovenaca* (Serbo-Croatian Serbs, Croats, and Slovenes)—Yugoslavia; Stuyvesant High School

SHSA Steamship Historical Society of America

SHSL Sherlock Holmes Society of London

SHSLB Street and Highway Safety Lighting Bureau

SHSN Sod House Society of Nebraska

SHSP Sam Houston State Park (Louisiana)

SHSS Sanford Hypnotic Susceptibility Scale

SHSSI Steamship Historical Society of Staten Island

SHSW State Historical Society of Wisconsin

shswc sample-and-hold square-wave converter

sht sheet(ing)

SHT Society for the History of Technology

shtg shortage

shth sheathing

sht irn sheet iron
sht mtl sheet metal
sh tn short ton
SHU Seton Hall University
Shula Shulamite; Shulamith
SHUR System of Hospital Uniform Reporting
shv solenoid hydraulic valve
s.h.v. sub hoc voce (Latin—under this work)
shvg shaving(s)
shw safety, health, and welfare
SHW Sherwin-Williams (stock exchange symbol)
shwrs showers
S & H x Sundays and Holidays excepted
SHYC Sachem's Head Yacht Club
si salinity indicator; shift in; short interest; slight imperfection; spark ignition; straight-in (aircraft landing approach); subicteric; subindex; subinguinal
si (SI) shift-in character (data processing)
s-i semiconductor-integrated (circuits)
s/i signal/intermodulation; subject issue
s & i stocked and issued
Si Silas; silicon (symbol); Simon; Simone
S^i Sidi (Arabic—My Lord)—title of honor also written *Saiyidi*
SI Sandwich Islands; Saturday Inspection; Secret Information; Secret Intelligence; Serra International; Sertoma International; Service Instruction; Shipping Instruction(s); Smithsonian Institution; Society of Illustrators; Solomon Islands; South Island (New Zealand); Spokane International (railroad); Staff Inspector; Staten Island; Stevens Institute; Sulfur Institute; Summer Institute; Survey Instruction(s); Système International des Unités (International System of Units)
S-I Spokane International (railroad)
SI Scheepvaart Inspectie (Dutch—Shipping Inspection); *Système International des Unités* (French—International System of Units)
sia subminiature integrated antenna
sia (SIA) storage instantaneous audimeter
SIA Sanitary Institute of Ameri-

ca; School of International Affairs (Columbia University); Securities Industries Association; Self-Insurers Institute; Ski Industries of America; Society of Insurance Accountants; Soroptimist International Association; Sprinkler Irrigation Association; Standard Instrument Approach; Strategic Industries Association
SIA Schweizerischer Ingenieur und Architekten Verein (German—Swiss Institute of Engineers and Architects)
SIAC Securities Industry Automation Corporation
SIAD Society of Industrial Artists and Designers
SIAE Società Italiano degli Autori ed Editori (Italian Society of Authors and Editors)
sial silicon + aluminum (Si + Al)
siam signal information and monitoring
Siam former name of Thailand
SIAM Society for Industrial and Applied Mathematics
siamese siamese cat (fawn or pale-gray breed of short-hair cat originating in Siam or Thailand); siamese fighting fish (*Betta*); siamese twin (congenitally connected twin resembling twins born in Siam in the late 1800s)
SIAO Smithsonian Institution Astrophysical Observatory
SIAP Sociedad Interamericana de Planificación (Spanish—Interamerican Planning Society)
sib satellite ionospheric beacon(s); sibilant; sibling; sibship
Sib Siberia; Siberian
SIB Shipbuilding Industry Board; Society of Insurance Brokers; Soviet Information Bureau
SIB Sveriges Investeringsbank (Swedish Investment Bank)
SIBC Socété Internationale de Biologie Clinique (French—International Society of Clinical Biology)
Sibelius' 7 the seven symphonies of Sibelius
Siberia generic nickname for any remote place of exile or imprisonment recalling Russia's Siberia
Siberian Express nickname for a devastatingly cold polar wind afflicting Canada and much of the United States and not the

name of a Soviet train
Siberian salt mines nickname for the many forced-labor camps and prisons in the USSR
Sib Or Sibylline Oracles
Sibr Siberia
sibs siblings
SIBS Salk Institute for Biological Studies
sic semiconductor integrated circuits; specific inductance capacity
sic (Latin—so written)
sic. siccus (Latin—dry)
Sic Sicilian; Siciliana; Siciliano; Sicily
SIC Scientific Information Center; Secret Intelligence Command; Security Intelligence Corps; Société Intercontinentale des Containers; Société Internationale de Cardiologie; Société Internationale de Chirurgie; Standard Industrial Classification; Survey Information Center
SIC Société Internationale de Cardiologie (French—International Cardiology Society); *Société Internationale de Chirurgie* (French—International Surgery Society); *Société Internationale de Criminologie* (French—International Criminology Society)
SICA Society of Industrial and Cost Accountants
sicbm (SICBM) super-intercontinental ballistic missile
SICC Staten Island Community College
Sic Chan Sicilian Channel between Sicily and Tunisia
Sichuan (Pinyin Chinese—Szechwan)
Sicilia (Italian—Sicily)
Sicily English place-name equivalent of Sicilia
Sick Man of Africa nineteenth-century Ethiopia
Sick Man of the Americas fever-infested nineteenth-century Panama before the early twentieth-century sanitation effort of the United States prior to building the Panama Canal
Sick Man of Asia nineteenth-century China
Sick Man of Europe Turkey in the last years of the Ottoman Empire and the reign of the sultans during most of the nineteenth century and up to 1922 when the sultanate was abolished

Sick Man of South America nineteenth-century Ecuador

SICOT Société Internationale de Chirurgie Orthopédique et de Traumatologie (French—International Society of Orthopedic Surgery and Traumatology)

SICR Specific Intelligence Collection Requirement

sicsva sequential-impaction cascade-seive volumetric air (sampler)

sic transit sic transit gloria mundi (Latin—so passes away the glory of the world)

sicu (SICU) surgical intensive care unit

sid sidereal; standard instrument departure; sudden infant death; sudden ionospheric disturbance

s & id surveillance and identification

Sid Sidney; Sidney Sussex College, Oxford; Sydney

S.i.D. Spiritus in Deo (Latin—His Spirit is with God)—he's dead

SID Security and Intelligence Department; Society for Information Display; Society for International Development; Society for Investigative Dermatology; Standard Instrument Departure; Sudden Ionospheric Disturbance Division

SIDA Swedish International Development Agency

sidar selective information dissemination and retrieval

sidase significant data selection

Siddhartha Gautama Buddha

SIDEC Stanford International Development Education Center

Sidewinder air-to-air missile produced by Motorola, Philco, and Raytheon

SIDINSA Siderurgia Integrada SA (Spanish—Integrated Iron-and-Steel Industry Corporation)

Sidon (Hebrew—Saida)—Lebanese port

SIDOR Siderúgica del Oriente (Spanish—Oriente Iron and Steel Industry), Venezuela

Sidro San Ysidro, California

sids sudden infant-death syndrome

SIDs Sports Information Directors

SIDS Ships Integrated Defense System; Shrike Improved Dis-

play System; Space Identification Device System; Space Investigations Documentation System

SIDS Société Internationale de Défense Sociale (French—International Society of Social Defense)

sie single instruction execute

SIE Science Information Exchange (Smithsonian); Scientific Information Exchange; Society of Industrial Engineers; Southwestern Industrial Electronics

SIEC Scottish Industrial Estates Corporation

SIECUS Sex Information and Educational Council of the United States

SIEE Student of the Institution of Electrical Engineers

Siem Siemensstadt

Siena (Italian—Sienna)

Sierra letter S radio code

Sierra Leone Republic of Sierra Leone (West African nation established by the British as a native home for freed slaves who were destitute and wished to return to Africa; English-speaking Sierra Leoneans export many tropical crops plus valuable minerals)

Sierra Leone's Ports Freetown, Pepel, Bonthe

Sierra Madre high mountains of western Mexico

Sierra Nevadas Sierra Nevada Mountains (elevations so named are found in California, Nevada, Spain, and Venezuela)

Sierras Sierra Nevada Mountains; Sierra Mountains

SIES Soils and Irrigation Extension Service

SIETAR Society for Intercultural Education, Training, and Research

Siete Leguas (Spanish—Seven Leagues)—famous warhorse of Pancho Villa, the Mexican bandit general

SIEX Superintendencia de Inverciones Extranjeras (Spanish—Superintendence of Foreign Investments)

SI Exy Staten Island Expressway

sif selective identification feature

SIF Society for Individual Freedom

SIFA Seguridad e Inteligencia de las Fuerzas Armadas (Span-

ish—Security and Intelligence of the Armed Forces)—Venezuela

SIFE Society of Industrial Furnace Engineers

SIFF Suomen Ilmailuliitto Finlands Flygforbund (Finnish Aeronautical Association)

sif/iff selective identification feature/identification friend or foe

SIFO Statens Institut för Opinionsundersökning (Swedish—State Institute for Opinion Research)

SIFs Stock Index Futures

SIFS Special Instructors Flying School

sift. share interval fortran translator; simplified input for toss

sig signal; signaling; signature

sig. signetur (Latin—mark with directions)

Sig Siegfried; Sieglinde; Sigdrifa; Sigmund; Sigmunt; Sigsbee; Sigurd; Sigyn

Sig Signor (Italian—Mister; Sir); *Signore* (Italian—Gentlemen, Our Lord, Sir); *Signori* (Italian—Gentlemen, Lords)

SIG Secret Intelligence Group; Snowy Irrigation Scheme (Snowy Mountains Authority —Australia); Special Interest Group

SIG Schweizerische Industrie Gesellschaft (German—Swiss Industry Society)

siga sigatoka (banana leaf spot disease)

Sig *Signora* (Italian—Missus) —Mrs

SIGACT Special Interest Group on Automata and Computability Theory

SIGARCH Special Interest Group on Architecture of Computer Systems

SIGART Special Interest Group on Artificial Intelligence

SIG/BDP Special Interest Group on Business Data Processing

SIGBIO Special Interest Group on Biomedical Computing

SIG/BIOM Special Interest Group on Biomedical Information Processing

SigC Signal Corps

SIGCAPH Special Interest Group on Computers and the Physically Handicapped

SIGCAS Special Interest Group on Computers and Society

SIGCOMM Special Interest Group on Data Communica-

tion

SIGCOSIM Special Interest Group on Computer Systems Installation Management

SIGCPR Special Interest Group on Computer Personnel Research

SIGCSE Special Interest Group on Computer Science Education

SIGCUE Special Interest Group on Computer Uses in Education

SIGDA Special Interest Group on Design Automation

Sig Div Signal Division

sigex signal exercise

sigg social incest in the golden ghetto (euphemistic definition of a cocktail party)

Sigg Signori (Italian—Messrs)

SIGGRAPH Special Interest Group on Computer Graphics

SIGI System of Interactive Guidance and Education

sigill. sigillum (Latin—seal)

sigint signals intelligence

SIGIR Special Interest Group on Information Retrieval

Sig L Signal Lieutenant

SIGLASH Special Interest Group on Language Analysis and Studies in the Humanities

SIGLE System for Information on Grey Literature in Europe

sigligun signal-light gun

Siglo de Oro (Spanish—Golden Age)—the Spanish Century before and after 1600 when discovery and colonization were matched by great artistic and literary productions

SIGMA Science in General Management

SIGMAP Special Interest Group on Mathematical Programming

SIGMETRIC Special Interest Group on Metrication

SIGMICRO Special Interest Group on Microprogramming

SIGMINI Special Interest Group on Minicomputers

Sigmn Signalman

SIGMOD Special Interest Group on Management of Data

sigmoido sigmoidoscopy

Sigmund Fraud nickname of anyone practicing psychiatry without a license

sign. signature

Sig^na Signorina (Italian—Miss)

Signe Hasso Signe Larsson

signif signifiable; signifiably; significance; significancy; significant(ly); signification; significative(ly); signifier; signify

sig. nom. pro. signa nomine proprio (Latin—label with the proper name)

SIGNUM Special Interest Group on Numerical Mathematics

Sig O Signal Officer

SIGOPS Special Interest Group on Operating Systems

SIGPLAN Special Interest Group on Programming Languages

SIG/REAL Special Interest Group on Real-Time Processing

SIGs Special Interest Groups

SIGS Sandia Interactive Graphics System

SIGSAM Special Interest Group on Symbolic and Algebraic Manipulation

Sig Sam Lib Sigmund Samuel Library (Toronto)

SIGs–ASIS Special Interest Groups of the American Society for Information Science —AH: Arts and Humanities; ALP: Automated Language Processing; BSS: Behavioral and Social Sciences; BC: Biological and Chemical; CB: Costs, Budgeting, Economics; CR: Classification Research; ED: Education for Information Science; FS: Foundations of Information Science; IAC: Information Analysis Centers; IP: Information Publishing; ISE: Information Services to Education; LAN: Library Information and Networks; LAW: Law and Information Technology; MGT: Management Information Activities; MR: Medical Records; NDB: Numerical Data Bases; NPM: Non-Print Media; PPI: Public-Private Interface; RT: Reprographic Technology; SDI: Selective Dissemination of Information; TIS: Technology, Information, Society; UOI: User On-line Interaction

SIGSDI Special Interest Group on Selective Dissemination of Information

SIGSIM Special Interest Group on Simulation

SIGSOC Special Interest Group on Social and Behavioral Science Computing

SIGSPAC Special Interest

Group on Urban Data Systems, Planning, Architecture, and Civil Engineering

Sig Sta signal station

SIG/TIME Special Interest Group on Time Sharing

SIGUCC Special Interest Group on University Computing Centers

Sig Und Sigrid Undset

SIG/UPACE Special Interest Group on Urban Planning, Architecture, and Civil Engineering

SIH Samuel Ichiye Hayakawa

SIH Société Internationale d'Hématologie (French— International Hematology Society)

SIHS Society for Italian Historical Studies

SII School Interest Inventory; Security-Insecurity Inventory; Self-Interview Inventory; Standards Institution of Israel; Staten Island Institute

SIIA Stevenson Institute of International Affairs

SIIAS Staten Island Institute of Arts and Sciences

SIIP Systems Integration Implementation Plan

SIIRS Smithsonian Institution Information Retrieval Service

SIJD Subcommittee to Investigate Juvenile Delinquency (U.S. Senate)

Sik Sikkim

sil silver; speech interference level

s-i-l sister-in-law

Sil Silesia; Silesian; Silurian

SIL Society for Individual Liberty; Society for International Law; Summer Institute of Linguistics; System Implementation Language

SIL Société International de la Lèpre (French—International Leprosy Society)

Silas Silvanus

silcads silver-cadmium batteries

Sile Cecilia

Silence Dogwood Benjamin Franklin's pseudonym used by him at age 15 when he wrote articles for the *New England Courant*

Silent The Silent (William I— Prince of Orange)

Silent Cal taciturn President Calvin Coolidge

silent killer high-blood pressure

silent service the silent service (submarine service)

SILI Standard Item Location Index

SILIA South Island Livestock Improvement Association

silic silicate; siliceous

silica silicon dioxide (SiO_2)

Silicon Beach San Diego, California

Silicon Valley high-technology-oriented area around San Jose, California in Santa Clara County; nickname for Santa Clara County, California where so many silicon chips are manufactured in the San Francisco Bay area

silicos silicosis (sickness caused by stone-dust inhalation)

Silk City Paterson, New Jersey, and Soochow, China share this nickname

Silk Country China

silkool silk + wool (Japanese synthetic textile combining qualities of silk and wool)

Silly Billy nickname of William IV

silos side-looking sonar

sils silver solder

sil(s) speech interference level(s)

sllv silver; silvery

Silver Age era of mankind when adornments and implements were made of silver; period between the Golden Age and the Bronze Age when impiety and weakness prevailed

silvercel silver-zinc cell (battery)

Silver City Broken Hills, New South Wales, Australia; Taxco, México

Silver City by the Sea Aberdeen, Scotland

Silver Gate entrance to San Diego Bay on the coast of California

Silverines Coloradans

Silver Republic Argentina

Silversmith Patriot Paul Revere (also bellfounder and dentist)

Silver State official nickname of Nevada but one also applied to silver-rich Colorado

Silver State of Malaysia Perak

Silver Streak the English Channel

Silver-Tongued Orator William Jennings Bryant

silvicult silviculture

sim similar; simile; simple; simulate; simulated approach

Sim Simm(s); Simon(d); Sims; Syme(s); Symme; Syms; etc.

SIM Society for Industrial Microbiology

SIM *Servicio Inteligencia Militar* (Spanish); *Servizio Informazioni Militari* (Italian—Military Intelligence Service); *Société Internationale de Musicologie* (French—International Musicological Society)

SIMA Scientific Instrument Manufacturers' Association; Steel Industry Management Association; Suburban Insurance Managers' Association

SIMAGB Scientific Instrument Manufacturers Association of Great Britain

SIMAJ Scientific Instrument Manufacturers Association of Japan

SIMC *Société Internationale pour la Musique Contemporaine* (French—International Society for Contemporary Music)

SIMCA Société Industrielle de Mécanique et Carosserie Automobile

simch single mach change

simcon simplified control; simulated control

simd single-instruction multiple-data stream

SIME Security Intelligence Middle East (British)

SIMG *Societas Internationalis Medicinae Generalis* (Latin—International General Medicine Society)

SIMILE Simulator of Immediate Memory in Learning Experiments

Simmond's disease premature senility caused by atrophy of the pituitary

'simmon(s) persimmon(s)

Simone Pauline Benda's pseudonym

Simone Signoret Simone Kaminker

Simons Simonstown; Simonstown naval base near the Cape of Good Hope in South Africa

simp simpleton

simp. *simplex* (Latin—simple)

simpac simulated package

SIMPL Scientific, Industrial, and Medical Photographic Laboratories

Simplon Simplon Pass in the Swiss Alps

Simpson Simpson Desert of in the southeast sector of Australia's Northern Territory

sims secondary ion mass spectroscopy

SIMS Surface-to-Air Intercept Missile System

simstrat simulation strategy

simula simulation language

simulcast simultaneous broadcast (am & fm)

simulcast(ing) simultaneous broadcast(ing) of the same program on radio and television

Simyens Simyen Mountains of Ethiopia

sin. sine; single

sin. *sinister* (Latin—left)

sin' *sino* (Italian—as far as; until)

Sin Sinaloa (inhabitants—Sinaloens); Singapore

SIN Singapore (airport); Société Industrielle et Navale; Society for International Numismatics; Stop Inflation Now

SIN *Scientific Information Notes* (National Science Foundation); *Société Industrielle et Navale* (French—Industrial and Naval Society)

Sin Angeles (Spanish—without angels)—nickname given Los Angeles

SINB Southern Interstate Nuclear Board

S-in-C Surgeon-in-Chief

Sin Capital Singapore's nickname despite protests by its many decent citizens

Sin City Las Vegas, Nevada (or any other place where cocktail lounges and gambling casinos outnumber concert halls, libraries, museums, and schools)

Sin City of the West Geneva, Switzerland

Sind Sindhi

S Ind Cur South Indian Current

sinema sin-filled cinema

sinf *sinfonia* (Italian—symphony)

Sinfonia Antarctica Symphony No. 7 by Vaughan-Williams

Sinfonia Concertante Mozart's two are most familiar

Sinfonia Domestica composition reflecting the daily life of Richard Strauss

Sinfonia Espansiva Nielsen's Symphony No. 3

Sinfonia Semplice Nielsen's Symphony No. 6

sing. singer; single; singing; singular

sing. *singulorum* (Latin—of each)

Sing Singapore

Singa Singapore

singan singularity analyzer

Singapore Republic of Singapore (island nation at the southernmost tip of the Malay Peninsula where multi-lingual and mutli-racial Singaporans engage in banking, electronics, oil refining, shipbuilding, and tropical agriculture)

Singapore's Ports Serangoon, Singapore, Pulau Bukum, Pulau Sebarok

Singapura (Malay—Singapore)

Singer of Singers Enrico Caruso

Singing Nun Sister Luc-Gabrielle (Jeanine Deckers)

Singing Satellite Red China's first satellite, launched in spring of 1970, broadcast rhymed song about Communist Party chairman Mao Tsetung

Singing Tree casuarina (sometimes called sighing tree or sobbing tree)

singkatan (Malay—abbreviation)—also called *kependekan* or *ringkasan*

Sing Sing nickname of the New York State Penitentiary at Ossining formerly named Sing Sing

Sing U Singapore University

sinh hyperbolic sine

Sinh Sinhalese

Sinjent St John

Sink Sinkiang

Sinn Fein (Gaelic—Ourselves Alone)

sins. ship-inertial-navigation systems

SINS Ship's Inertial Navigation System; Situational Intertial Navigation System (USN)

Sin Sin Singapore

Sin Strip San Francisco's North Beach area

sin taxes taxes on alcohol, gasoline, and tobacco

Sint Gillis (Flemish—Saint-Gilles)

SINTO Sheffield Interchange Organisation

si n. val. si non valet (Latin—if of no value)

Sinyavsky Abram Tertz

sio satellite in orbit; staged in orbit

si/o star input/output

SIO Scripps Institution of Oceanography; Ship's Information Office(r); Special Intelligence Office(r)

sioh supervision, inspection, and overhead

Sión (Spanish—Zion)

SIOP Single Integrated Operations Plan

si op. sit si opus sit (Latin—if necessary)

Sioux Bell Model-47 helicopter built in Britain, Italy, Japan, and the United States

Sioux Falls Pen South Dakota Penitentiary at Sioux Falls

Sioux State North Dakota's official nickname

sip. standard inspection procedure; step in place

SIP Smithsonian Institution Press; Sociedad Interamericana de la Prensa (Inter-American Press Association—IAPA); Society of Integral Psychoanalysis; Standard Inspection Procedure; State Improvement Plan(ning)

SIP Sociedad Interamericana de la Prensa (Spanish—Interamerican Press Association); *Société Interaméricaine de Psychologie* (French— Interamerican Society of Psychology)

SIP/AG Sri Lanka, India, Pakistan/Arabian Gulf (freighter route)

SIPC Securities Investor Protection Corporation

SIPE System Internal Performance Evaluation

SIPI Southwestern Indian Polytechnic Institute

sipl scientific information processing language

Sipo security police (Nazi)

Sipo Sicherheitspolizei (German—State Security Police)—Nazi controlled

SIPRC Society of Independent Public Relations Consultants

SIPRE Snow, Ice, and Permafrost Research Establishment

SIPRI Stockholm International Peace Research Institute

SIPROS Simultaneous Processing Operation System

SIPS State Implementation Plan System

siq superior internal quality

sir. selective information retrieval

sir. (SIR) submarine intermediate reactor

Sir Siria (Italian, Latin, Spanish —Syria); *Síria* (Portuguese—Syria)

SIR Society for Individual Responsibility; Society of Industrial Realtors; Staten Island

Rapid Transit (railroad code)

SIR Società Italiana Resine (Italian Resin Association)

SIRA Scientific Instrument Research Association

Siracusa (Italian—Syracuse)

Sir Adrian Sir Adrian Boult (distinguished English conductor)

Sir Alec Sir Alec Guinness

Sir Alexander Sir Alexander Korda (Hungarian-born British motion-picture producer)

Sir Alfred Sir Alfred Hitchcock (English author and film director)

Sir Arnold Sir Arnold Bax (English composer)

Sir Arthur Sir Arthur Bliss (English composer-conductor); Sir Arthur Conan Doyle (English detective-story writer and physician); Sir Arthur S(eymour) Sullivan (English composer-conductor-organist)

Sir Aurel Sir Aurel Stein (Budapest-born British archeological explorer)

Sir Benjamin Sir Benjamin Britten

Sir Bernard Sir Bernard Haitink (distinguished Dutch conductor)

SIRC Spares Integrated Reporting and Control System

Sir Charles Sir Charles Chaplin (better known as Charlie Chaplin the comedian and also as a composer of motion-picture mood music); Sir Charles Groves (conductor of the Liverpool Philharmonic); Sir Charles Hallé (German-born conductor-pianist and founder of Manchester's Hallé Orchestra); Sir Charles Mackerras (American-born Australian-bred British conductor); Sir Charles Villiers Stanford (Dublin-born composer-conductor-organist); Sir Charles Wheatstone (English physicist)

Sir Charles Morell James Ridley's pseudonym

Sir Clifford Sir Clifford Curzon (English pianist)

Sir Colin Sir Colin Davis

SIRCS Shipboard Intermediate-Range Combat System

Sir Dan Supreme Sir Dan Godfrey

Sir David Admiral Sir David Beatty—First Earl of the North Sea

SIRE Small Investors Real Estate (plan); Society for the Investigation of Recurring Events

Sir Edward English composer-conductors Sir Edward Elgar and Sir Edward German (originally Edward German Jones)

Sirens three nymphs named Leucosia, Ligeia, and Parthenope; their seductive singing lured sailors to their death on rockbound coasts but when they failed to lure Odysseus (Ulysses) they flung themselves into the waves and perished

Sir Ernest Sir Ernest Campbell Macmillan (Canadian composer-conductor-educator-organist)

Sir Francis Sir Francis Bacon (English philosopher politician); Sir Francis Drake (English admiral-explorer-navigator); Sir Francis Palgrave (English historian and son of Meyer Cohen)

Sir Frank Sir Frank Athelstane Swettenham, lexicographer of Malaya and its one-time colonial administrator

Sir Freddie Sir Freddie Laker (British airline organizer and operator)

Sir Frederic Sir Frederic Cowen (Jamaica-born English composer-conductor)

Sir Georg Sir Georg Solti (Anglo-American-Hungarian conductor-pianist knighted for his services at Covent Garden where he conducted from 1961 to 1971)

Sir George Sir (Isador) George Henschel (German-born British baritone composer conductor and founder of the Scottish Symphony Orchestra)

Sir Granville Sir Granville Bantock (English composer-conductor-teacher)

Sir Guatteral (Hobson-Jobson —Sir Walter Raleigh)—as known to many Spaniards in colonial times

Sir Hamilton Sir Hamilton Harty (Irish-born British conductor)

Sir Henry Sir Henry Bessemer (English engineer-inventor-metallurgist remembered for bessemer steel and the bessemer process for its creation); Sir Henry Wood (English conductor remembered for his fifty years as director of the

Promenade Concerts in London's Queen's Hall)

Sir Hubert Sir Hubert Parry (English composer and musicologist)

Sir Isaac Sir Isaac Newton (English mathematician and natural philosopher)

Sir John Sir John Barbirolli (English conductor-violincellist); Sir John Betjeman (British poet laureate); Sir John Gielgud (English actor)

Sir John A Sir John Alexander Macdonald (Canada's first and third Prime Minister)

Sir John Mandeville Jehan de Bourgogne

Sir John Retcliffe pseudonym of German anti-Semitic author Hermann Goedsche whose novel *Biarritz* showed Jewish leaders secretly plotting against gentile humanity

Sir Kenneth Sir Kenneth McKenzie Clark

Sir Landon Sir Landon Ronald (English composer-conductor-pianist)

Sir Laurence Sir Laurence Olivier (British actor-director-producer)

Sir Lennox Sir Lennox Berkeley (English composer)

Sir Malcolm Sir Malcolm Sargent (English ballet-choral-orchestral conductor who was chief conductor of the BBC and the Promenade Concerts)

Sir Max Sir Max Beloff

Sir Michael Sir Michael Costa (Italian-born British composer-conductor); Sir Michael Tippett (English composer-conductor-educator)

Sir Pelham P(elham) G(renville) Wodehouse

SIRR Spokane International Railroad

Sir Ralph Sir Ralph Richardson (British actor)

SIRS School Information and Research Service; Ship-Installed Radiac System; Sorption Information-Retrieval System; Student Information Record System

SIRT Staten Island Rapid Transit

SIRTF Spacelab Infrared Telescope Facility

Sir Thomas Sir Thomas Beecham (English composer-conductor-founder of the London Philharmonic Orchestra and the Royal Philharmonic

Orchestra as well as guest conductor of many American and Canadian orchestras)

Sir Victor Sir V S (Victor Sawdon) Pritchett (English journalist and short-story writer)

Sir Wilfred Sir Wilfred Pelletier (French-Canadian conductor)

Sir William Sir William Herschel (German-born English astronomer-mathematician-musician); Sir William Walton (prolific English composer)

Sir Winston Sir Winston Leonard Spencer Churchill (former Prime Minister of Great Britain)

sis shock insulation support; sterile injectable suspension

sis (Latin suffix—action or process)—dialysis

Sis Cecilia; sister

SIs Sandwich Islands; Service Instructions; Shipping Instructions; Solomon Islands, Survey Instructions

SIS School of Information Studies; Secret Intelligence Service(s); Shut-In Society; Special Industrial Services (UN); Standard Indexing System (DoD); Standards Information Service; Strategic Intelligence School; Strategic Intelligence Summary; Student Information System; Submarine-Integrated Sonar (system)

S & IS Space and Information System(s)

SISAL Societa Italiana Sistemi a Lotto (Italian Lotteries)

SISGAP Scottish Industrial Safety Group Advisory Council

sisi short-increment sensitivity index

Sisister (British contraction—Cirencester)

sisp sudden increase of solar particles

siss single-item single-source

SISS Semiconductor-Insulation Semiconductor System; Submarine Improved Sonar System; System Integration Support Service

SISS Société Internationale de la Science du Sol (French—International Society of Soil Science)

Sissy Cecilia; sister

SISTER Special Institution for Scientific and Technological Education and Research

Sister Cities San Diego and Yokohama

SISUSA Scotch-Irish Society of the United States of America

sit. silicon intensifier target; situation; statement of inventory transaction; stopping in transit

SIT Slosson Intelligence Test; Society of Industrial Technology; Stevens Institute of Technology; Sugar Industry Technicians

SITA Students International Travel Association

SITA Société Internationale de Télécommunications Aeronautiques

SITC Standard International Trade Classification

SITCEN Situation Center (NATO)

sitcom situation comedy (tv)

site. shipboard information, training, entertainment

SITE Satellite Instructional Television Experiment; Society of Incentive Travel Executives

SITES Smithsonian Institution Traveling Exhibition Service

sitol sitological; sitologist; sitology

sitp scheduled into production

SITP Shipyard Installation Test Procedure

sitpro simplification of international trade procedures

sitr silent treatment

SITRA South India Textile Research Association

sitrag situation tragedy

sitrep situation report

SITS Securities Instruction Transmission System; Société Internationale de Transfusion Sanguine (International Organization for Blood Transfusion)

SITSUM Situation Summary (NATO Intelligence)

sitt sitting room

Sitting Bull Tatanka Iyotanka also known as Sitting Buffalo Bill

SITU Society for the Investigation of the Unexplained

sitv (SITV) system-integration test vehicle

SIU Seafarers International Union; Southern Illinois University; Special Investigating Unit (NY Police Bureau of Narcotics)

SIU Société Internationale d'Urologie (International Urological Society)

SIUE Southern Illinois University at Edwardsville

SIUL Southern Illinois University Library

SIUM Southern Illinois University Museum

SI unit Système International unit (French—International System of Units)

SIUP Southern Illinois University Press

siv survey of interpersonal values

Siviglia (Italian—Seville)

si vir. perm. si vires permitant (Latin—if the strength will permit)

siw (SIW) self-inflicted wounds

Six Counties Northern Ireland or Ulster's counties of Antrim, Armagh, Derry, Down, Fermanagh, and Tyrone

Six-Day Six-Day War (between Israel and its Moslem neighbors—Egypt and Syria)—June 5 to 10, 1967

SIXFLT Sixth Fleet (USN)

Six Nations Five Nations plus the Tuscaroras (*see*Five Nations)

six-pac six-pack (container of beer or soft drinks)

SIXPAC System for Inertial Experiment Pointing to Attitude Control

Six-Shooter Junction old name of Harlingen, Texas

Sixteenth State Tennessee

Sixth State Massachusetts (*see* First State)

SIYC Shelter Island Yacht Club; Staten Island Yacht Club

SIZ Security Identification Zone

SIZS Staten Island Zoological Society

sj slip joint; subject(s)

s.j. sub judice (Latin—under judicial consideration)

SJ San Juan; Society of Jesus (S.J.—Jesuits); Statens Järnvägar (Swedish State Railways)

S-J Stevens-Johnson (syndrome)

SJ Solicitors' Journal

SJAA St John Ambulance Association

SJAC Society of Japanese Aircraft Constructors

Sjaeland (Danish—Zealand)

SJC San Jose, California (airport); San Juan Carriers (ore and tankships); Snead Junior College; Spartanburg Junior College

SJCC San Jose City College

S.J.D. *Scientiae Juridicae Doctor* (Latin—Doctor of Juridical Science)

sje swivelling jet engine

Sjf Sandefjord

Sjf Sjofartsverket (Swedish—Shipping Inspection Bureau)

SJI Steel Joist Institute

SJIs San Juan Islands

SJJC Sheldon Jackson Junior College

SJLA Studies in Judaism in Late Antiquity

S Jn San Juan

SJO San José, Costa Rica (La Sabana Airport)

SJPC South Jersey Port Commission

SJPL San Jose Public Library

S-J-R Shinawora-Jones-Reinhart (units)

SJSC San Jose State College

SJSO San Jose Symphony Orchestra

SJU San Juan, Puerto Rico (airport); St John's University

sk sick; skein; sketch; skip (knitting instruction); skip (punched card)

sk (SK) streptokinase

Sk Skizze (German—sketch)

SK end of transmission (telegraphic symbol); South Korea(n)

S-K Sloan-Kettering

SK Stuttgarter Kammerorchester (German—Stuttgart Chamber Orchestra); *Suomen Kansallisoopera* (Finnish National Opera)

SK-37 Saab Thunderbolt or Viggen multimission combat aircraft also known as AJ-37, JA-37, and S-37

SK-60 Saab attack-type jet aircraft design based on the A-60

s-ka spolka(Polish—association, company)

SKA Switchblade Knife Act

skachet skinning knife, hammer, hatchet, and hunting knife all-purpose utility tool

Skag Cape Skagen or The Skaw; Skagway, Alaska

Skager Skagerrak (North Sea between Denmark and Norway)

skamp station keeping and mobile platform

Skate City Northbrook, Illinois

Skaw Cape Skagen or The Skaw —northernmost Denmark

skb skindbind (Dano-Norwegian—leatherbound)

SKBF Svensk Kärnbränsleförsörjning (Swedish Nuclear

Fuel Supply Company)

skc sky clear

SKC Scottish Kennel Club

SKCC Sloan-Kettering Cancer Center

SkCsr *Státní knikhovna Ceské socialistické republiky* (Czechoslovakian—State Library of the Czech Socialist Republic)—in Prague

skd skilled

skdn shakedown

Skean NATO name for Soviet SS-5 intermediate-range ballistic missile

sked schedule

skedcon schedule conference

skel skeletal; skeleton

S Ken South Kensington

skep skeptic(al)(ly); skepticism

Skeptic-Philosopher President Thomas Jefferson

SKF Svenska Kullagerfabriken (Swedish ball-bearing factory)

SK & F Smith Kline & French

SKI Sloan-Kettering Institute

Ski Capital Aspen, Colorado

Ski Country Colorado

Skidrow on the Sound (street people's nickname—Seattle, Washington, on Puget Sound) —the original skidrow

skil science keyboard input language

skill. satellite kill; skin, kidneys, intestines, liver, lungs

skinmag magazine featuring nudes of both sexes

SKIP Skimmer Investigation Platform

Skipper the Captain; the Commander

skiv skiver

SKJ *Savez Komunista Jugoslavije* (Yugoslavian Communist League)—political party

SKKCA Supreme Knight of the Knights of Columbus of America

skl skylight(ing); spleen, kidney, liver

Skm Stockholm

SKM *Süleymaniye Kütüphahesi* (Turkish—Suleiman Mosque Library)—in Istanbul

skmr (SKMR) hydroskimmer

S^knoll Seaknoll

Skopje (Yugoslavian—Uskub)

skort short skirt

Skory NATO nickname for Soviet class of minelaying destroyers

Skowhegan Girls Women's Correctional Center at Skowhegan, Maine

Skowse Liverpool seaman

skp station-keeping position

skp (SKP) skip

skpo slip one, knit one, pass slipped-stitch over (knitting)

SKQ Sexual Knowledge Questionnaire

skr standardized kill rate; station-keeping radar

Skr Sanskrit; Saturn kilometric radiation; Skipper; Skire (Thursday)

Skr *Skrifter*(Swedish—publication)

SKr Swedish krona (kronor)

SKR South Korea Republic

sks sacks

SKS Soren Kierkegaard Society; station-keeping ship

SKS *Savvezna Komisija za Standardizacija* (Serbo-Croatian—Federal Commission for Standardization)

Skt Sanskrit

Skt *Sankt*(German—saint)

skunk nickname of a potent variety of marijuana sometimes surreptitiously cultivated in California state parks and adjacent rural areas

Skunk's Misery nickname and former place-name of Scranton, Pennsylvania

Skunk Works nickname of Air Force Plant 42 at Palmdale, California

SKU(s) stock-keeping unit(s)

SKY Skyways Limited (aviation symbol)

Skybright Axe Paul Bunyan

Sky City Pueblo Acoma near Alburquerque, New Mexico

Sky Crane Sikorsky crane helicopter designated Ch-54 or S-64

skyjack skyjacked; skyjacker; skyjacking (all indicate aircraft hijacking)

Skymaster Douglas DC-4 44-passenger transport also called Dakota

Skyscraper Capital New York City

Skyscraper Port of the Orient Hong Kong

Skyservant Dornier utility aircraft also designated DO-27 and DO-28; both built in West Germany

skys'l skysail

Sky & Tel *Sky & Telescope*

Skytrain Douglas DC-3 21-passenger transport also called Dakota

Skyvan turboprop transport built by Short in Great Britain

Skywagon Cessna 185E utility aircraft

sl liability; safety lighting; sales letter; sand-loaded; sea level; searchlight; shipowner's; slightly; slip (knitting instruction); sound locator; stock length; support line

sl (SL) sprinkler leakage; standard label

s-l short-long (flashlight or whistle signals); sound-locator sublease

s/l self-loading

s & l savings and loan; supply and logistics

s.l. *secundum legem* (Latin—according to law); *sensu lato* (Latin—in the broad sense); *sine loco* (Latin—no place of publication)

s/l *sobreloja* (Portuguese—mezzanine floor); *su letra* (Spanish —your letter)

Sl Slovak; Slovakian; small diurnal range

SL San Luis Obispo; Sandia National Laboratories; Savings and Loan (association or bank); Sea-Land (America's seagoing motor carrier); Sierra Leone; Solicitor-at-Law; Squadron Leader; Sub-Lieutenant; Support Line; Sydney & Louisburg (railroad)

S-L Sea-Land (Line); short-long

S&L Savings and Loan;

S & L Supply and Logistics

SL *Schweizerische Landesbibliothek* (German—Swiss State Library)—in Bern

sla sacro-laeva anterior; single-line approach

Sla (Arabia—Salé or Sallee)

SLA Sandia Laboratories—Albuquerque; School Library Association; Scottish Library Association; Showmen's League of America; Sleep-Learning Association; Southeastern Library Association; Southwestern Library Association; Special Libraries Association; Standard Life Association; State Liquor Authority; Supply Loading Airfield; Symbionese Liberation Army

SLAA Surf Lifesaving Association of Australia

SLAB Students for Labelling Alcoholic Beverages

Slabsides rustic cabin built by John Burroughs near Esopus, New York

SLAC Stanford Linear Acceleration Center

SLAD Society of London Art Dealers

SLADE Society of Lithographic Artists, Designers, Engravers, and Process Workers

slado system library activity dynamic optimiser

slaked lime calcium hydroxide ($Ca[OH]_2$)

slam. (**SLAM**) scanning-laser acoustic microscope; supersonic low-altitude (nuclear-powered) missile

s.l.a.m. *sine loco, anno, nomine* (Latin—without place, year, or name)

SLAM Society's League Against Molestation (of children by adults and others)

SLANG Systems Language

slanguage slang language (according to Carl Sandberg it is language which takes off its coat, spits on its hands—and goes to work); slum language

S Lan R South Lancashire Regiment

SLANT Student League Against Narcotic Traffic

slar side-looking airborne radar

S Lat south latitude

slate. small lightweight altitude-transmission equipment

SLATE Structured Learning and Teaching Environment; Systems for Learning by Applications of Technology to Education

SLATS Safe, Loft, and Truck Squad (of a police department)

Slav Slavic; Slavonic

Slava Mstislav; Mstislav Rostropovich's nickname

Slave Coast West African coastal area of Togo, Dahomey, and Nigeria; within the Bight of Benin in the Gulf of Guinea

Slave States former slave-holding states comprising the Confederacy (Virginia, North and South Carolina, Georgia, Florida, Alabama, Mississippi, Louisiana, Texas, Arkansas, Tennessee) plus slave states not seceding—Delaware, Maryland, Kentucky, Missouri

Slavkov u Brna Czechoslovakian equivalent of Austerlitz

slax slacks

slb short-leg brace

slbm (**SLBM**) submarine-launched ballistic missile

slc searchlight control; shift left and count (instructions); straight-line capacity

sl & c shipper's load and count

SLC Salt Lake City, Utah (airport); Scout Launch Complex; Space Launch Complex; Stanford Linear Collider (pronounced *slick*)

SLCL Sierra Leone Council of Labour

slcm (**SLCM**) sea-launched cruise missile

SLCMD St Louis Contract Management District

SLCPL Salt Lake City Public Library

SLCR *Scottish Land Court Reports*

SLCS Sea Level Canal Study

sld sailed; solid; specific learning disability

sld (**SLD**) serum lactate dehydrogenase

Sld Sunderland

sldf solidification

sl di slot die

S Ldr Squadron Leader

sld's specific learning disabilities

SLDVS Scanning Laser Doppler Vortex System

sle systemic lupus erythematosus

sle (**SLE**) systemic lupus erythematosus

S le Sierra Leone leone(s)—monetary unit(s)

SLe St Louis encephalitis

SLE Society of Logistics Engineers

SLEAT Society of Laundry Engineers and Allied Trades

SLED State Law Enforcement Division (South Carolina)

Sledge and Hoe official symbol of Zaire

Sleepers Sleeper Islands in Hudson Bay just north of the Belchers

Sleep Personified Hypnos (Greek—sleep) whose brother was Thanatos or death

Sleepy Hollow New Jersey's Trenton Prison

Sleepy Joe Attorney General Philander C. Knox

SLEP Service Life Extension Program (USN)

Slesvig (Danish—Schleswig)

s.l. et a. *sine loco et anno* (Latin—without place and year)

S level scholarship level

slew. static load error washout

slf straight-line frequency; symmetric filter

SLF Scottish Landowners' Federation; Silcock and Lever Feeds

S-L Fl short-long flashing (light)

slg state or local government

SLGB Society of Local Government Barristers

SLGLW St Lawrence and Great Lakes Waterway

SLHC St Luke's Hospital Center

sli suppressed-length indication

Sli Sligo

SLI Slick Airways

slic selective listing in combination

SLIC Supreme Life Insurance Company

SLICE Southwestern Library Interstate Cooperative Endeavor; Surrey Library Interactive Circulation Experiment

slickums sea-launched cruise missiles (SLCMs)

slid. scanning light-intensity device

SLID Student League for Industrial Democracy

Slide Slide Mountain (highest in the Catskills)

slim. (**SLIM**) submarine-launched inertial missile

SLIM South London Industrial Mission

Slim Jannie Jan Christian Smuts

Slinging Sammy Sam(uel) (Adrian) Baugh of baseball and football fame

slip. symmetric(al) list processor

SLIP Skills Level Improvement Plan

slithy lithe and slimy (Lewis Carroll's portmanteau word from *Through the Looking Glass*)

SLJ *School Library Journal*

SLKP Supreme Lodge of the Knights of Pythias

SLL Socialist Labour League

SLLA Scottish Ladies Lacrosse Association; Sri Lanka Library Association

slld specific language and learning disability

slm single-level masking

slm (**SLM**) ship-launched missile

slm *sul livello del mare* (Italian—at sea level)

SLMC Scottish Ladies' Mountaineering Club

slms selective level measuring

set
SLMSU Scientific Library of Moscow State University
SLMTA St Louis Municipal Theatre Association
sln standard library number
slnd *sans lieu ne date* (French—without place or date of publication)
SLNM Statue of Liberty National Monument
SLNSW State Library of New South Wales (Sydney)
SLNWR Sand Lake National Wildlife Refuge (South Dakota); San Luis NWR (California); Swan Lake NWR (Missouri)
Slo Saltillo (inhabitants—Saltilleños or Saltilleros); Slovak; Slovakia; Slovene(s)
SLO San Luis Obispo; Senior Liaison Officer
SLOA Steam Locomotive Operators Association
slob. satellite low-orbit bombardment
Slob Sloboda (Russian—big village, suburb)
SLOBB Stop Littering Our Bays and Beaches
sloboda (Russian—suburb)—possibly origin of terms such as Lower Slobodia and Upper Slobodia
sloc sea lanes of communication
SLOE Special List of Equipment
slomar space logistics, maintenance, and rescue
s'long so long (from the Arabic *salaam* or the Hebrew *shalom,* both meaning *peace be with you*)
slooow seller(s) slow-selling book(s)
s/loss salvage loss
Slot The Slot—San Francisco's downtown Mission Street off Market Street
Slov Slovene; Slovenian
Slovakian Capital Bratislava called Pozsony by the Czechs and Pressburg by the Germans
Slovensko (Czechoslovakian—Slovakia)
Slov Phil Slovenian Philharmonic
SLOWPOKE Safe Low-Power Critical Experiment (AEC)
slp sacro-laeva posterior
s.l.p. *sine legitima prole* (Latin—without legitimate issue)
SLP San Luís Potosí; Scottish

Labour Party; Socialist Labor Party
Slphr Sulphur (postal abbreviation)
SLPL St Louis Public Library
slr self-loading rifle; side-looking radar; single-lens reflex (camera)
slr (SLR) storage limits register
s-l r sea-level resident(s)
SLR State Liaison Representative
S & LR Sydney and Louisburg Railway
SLR Scottish Land Reports
SLRB State Labor Relations Board
SLRC San Luis Rey College
sl rd searchlight radar
SL Rev Scottish Law Review
SLRP Society for Long-Range Planning
SLRP St Lawrence River Pilot
sls sequential light switch; slide set
S&Ls Savings and Loan banks
SLS School of Library Science; School of Library Studies; Sea-Land Service; St Lawrence Seaway; St Louis Symphony
sl sa slotting saw
SLSA Saint Lawrence Seaway Authority; Surf Life Saving Association
SLSC Swedish Lloyd Steamship Company
SLSDC Saint Lawrence Seaway Development Corporation
SLSENY School Librarians of Southeastern New York
S L S F St Louis-San Francisco (railroad)
SLSFC Severe Local Storm Forecast Center
slsmgr salesmanager
slsmn salesman; salesmen
SLST Sierra Leone Selection Trust
s-l stil spring-loaded stiletto
sl st(s) slip stitch(es)—not correctly abbreviated but often appearing in knitting handbooks
SLSU Sea Land Service (container) Unit
SLS-UBC School of Library Science—University of British Columbia
slt sacro-laeva transversa; searchlight
sl&t shipper's load and tally
SLT Solid-Logic Technology; Stress Limit Test(ing)
SLT Scots Law Times
SLTA Scottish Licensed Trade Association

SLTAN Società Lloyd Triestino per Azioni di Navigazione (Lloyd Triestino)
SLTC Society of Leather Trades Chemists
slto sea-level takeoff
sl tr silent treatment
Slu slough
SLU Saint Lawrence University; Saint Louis University; Southern Labor Union
slug. superconducting low-inductance undulatory galvanometer
Slugger U.S.-made tank destroyer designated M-36
Slumbering Giant of Capitol Hill The Library of Congress
Slumberjay Schlumberger
slumlord slum landlord
slumpfla slumpflation (high inflation coupled with high unemployment)
slumpflation slump + inflation (economic decline coincident with rising inflation)
slurb slum suburb
slurp. self-levelling unit to remove pollution
SLUs Special Liaison Units
SLUSSR State Library of the USSR (Lenin Library, Moscow)
Slut of the North Empress Elizabeth of Russia so nicknamed by Frederick the Great of Prussia who called her *la Catin du Nord*
slutt surface-launched underwater transponder target
slv satellite launching vehicle; space launch vehicle; standard launch vehicle (SLV)
SLV-3 Atlas standard launch vehicle (Convair)
sly slowly
sly. safety, liquidity, yield; slowly
Sly southerly
Sly Fox of Kinderhook Martin Van Buren
slyp short-leaf yellow pine
SLZG St Louis Zoological Gardens
sm service module; servomechanism; sheet metal; small; statute mile; strategic missile (SM); streptomycin; sustained medication; systolic murmur; syzygy mathematical
sm (SM) secondary memory
s-m sadist-masochist; sadomasochism
s/m sensory-to-motor (ratio)
s&m surface and matched stock and machinery; sadism and

masochism; sausages and mashed potatoes

s/M *sur mer* (French—by the sea)

Sm samarium

Sm *Seemeile* (German—nautical mile)

SM mine-laying submarine; Salvage Mechanic; San Marino; Scientific Memorandum; Senior Magistrate; Sergeant-Major; Service Module; Shipment Memorandum; Signalman; Society of Mary; Society of Medalists; Soldier's Medal; Special Memorandum; Spiritual Mobilization; Staff Memorandum; State Militia; States Marine (steamship lines); Structures Memorandum; submarine; Summary Memorandum; Suomi Merivorma (Finnish Seapower); Supply Manual; Svenska Metallverken (Swedish Metal Works)

S-M Seine-Maritime (formerly Seine-Inférieure)

S.M. *Scientiae Magister* (Latin —Master of Science)

S.M. *Sanctae Memoriae* (Latin —of sacred memory); *Su Majestad* (Spanish—Her/His Majesty)

SM-4 Polish three-place helicopter

SM-65 Atlas intercontinental ballistic missile (Convair)

SM-68 Titan intercontinental ballistic missile (Martin)

SM-75 Thor intermediate-range ballistic missile (Douglas)

SM-78 Jupiter intermediate-range ballistic missile (Chrysler)

SM-80 Minuteman intercontinental ballistic missile (Boeing)

sma small-motion accelerometer; subject matter area

SMA Safe Manufacturers Association; San Miguel Arizona (railroad); Santa María, Azores (airport); Scale Manufacturers Association; Screen Manufacturers Association; Senior Military Attaché; Service Merchandisers of America; Sheffield Metallurgical Association; Society of Makeup Artists; Solder Makers Association; Squadron Maintenance Area; Steatite Manufacturers Association; Steel Manufacturers Association; Stoker Manufacturers Association

SMAA Submarine Movement Advisory Authority

SMAB Solid Motor Assembly Building

SMAC Scientific Machine Automation Corporation

SM & ACCNA Sheet Metal and Air Conditioning Contractors National Association

s mach sounding machine

smack nickname for heroin

Smack Henderson Fletcher Henderson

SMAE Society of Model Aeronautical Engineers

SMAJ Sugar Manufacturers' Association of Jamaica

smalgol small computer algorithmic language

Small Islands *see* Micronesia

SMAMA Sacramento Air Materiel Area

smap surprised middle-aged person (who remembers when a ride in the New York subway cost a nickel and a Hershey bar cost no more, when a haircut cost fifty cents, and a salary of $10,000 a year put you on the highway to financial success)

S Mar San Marino

smarea (SMAREA) squadron maintenance area

smart. special methods for attacking the right targets

SMART School Management Appraisal and Rating Technique; Silent Majority Against Revolutionary Tactics; Supersonic Military Air Research Track; Supersonic Missile and Rocket Track; System for the Mechanical Analysis and Retrieval of Text

smartie simple-minded artificial intelligence

SMASH Students Mobilizing on Auto Safety Hazards

smashex search for simulated submarine casualty exercise

s-m-a showing suggested-for-mature-adult showing (motion picture producers code)

smat see me about this

smaze smoke + haze (*see* smog)

SMB Straits of Mackinac Bridge

SMB *Sa Majesté Britanique* (French—Her/His Britannic Majesty)

SMBA Scottish Marine Biological Association

smbl semimobile

SMBW Society of Mineral and Battery Works

smc sheet-molding compound; sperm (spore) mother cell; standard mean chord

Smc Samic (Lapp)

SMC Saugus Marine Corporation; Scientific Manpower Commission; State Medical Society

S & MC Supply and Maintenance Command (US Army)

smca suckling-mouse cataract agent

sm caps small capital letters

SMCC Saint Mary's College of California; Santa Monica City College

SMCCL Society of Municipal and County Chief Librarians

SMCL Southeastern Massachusetts Cooperating Libraries

smcln semicolon

SMCRC Southern Motor Carriers Rate Conference

smd submanubrial dullness

SMD Submarine Mine Depot

SMDA Sewing Machine Dealers' Association

SMDC Saint Mary's Dominican College

SME School of Military Engineering; Society of Manufacturing Engineers; Society of Mining Engineers; Standard Medical Examination

S.M.E. *Sancta Mater Ecclesia* (Latin—Holy Mother Church)

SMEAR Span/Mission Evaluation Action Request

SMEC Snowy Mountains Engineering Corporation; Strategic Missile Evaluation Committee

SMEG Spring Makers' Export Group

smel single and multiengine license

smelerience smell(ing) experience

smellies smelly street hippies (or malodorous social derelicts such as alcohol or drug addicts)

Smelly Place Hong Kong (also called Fragrant Harbor)

smelt. smelter; smelting

Smelter City Anaconda, Montana

sm-er (SM-ER) surface missile —extended range

SMERC San Mateo Educational Resource Center

SMERSH *Smert Shpionam* (Russian—Death to Spies)— Soviet organization for murdering political enemies

smes superconducting magnetic energy storage

S Met O Senior Meteorological Officer

SMF Sacramento, California (airport); Shaker Museum Foundation; Snell Memorial Foundation; South Moluccan Force; System Management Facility

SMfVL *Stuttgart Museum für Volker and Landerkunde*

smg speed made good; submachine gun

Smg Samarang

SMG *Stato Maggior Generale* (Italian—General Staff)

SMH *Sydney Morning Herald*

SMHEA Snowy Mountains Hydro-Electric Authority

smi standard measuring instrument

s mi statute mile(s)

SmI *Solidaritet med Israel* (Dano-Norwegian—Solidarity with Israel)

SMI Scale Manufacturers Institute; School Management Institute; Secondary Metal Institute; Shippers Management International; Spring Manufacturers Institute; Success Motivation Institute; Super Market Institute

SMI *Sa Majesté Imperiale* (French—Her/His Imperial Majesty)

SMIA Sheet Metal Industries Association

SMIAC Soil Mechanics Information Analysis Center (Corps of Engineers)

SMIC Study of Man's Impact on Climate

smichm (SMICBM) semi-mobile intercontinental ballistic missile

smice smoke + ice (ice-crystal-laden fog)

SMIG Sergeant-Major Instructor of Gunnery

SMILE Something Meaningful In Local Effort (predelinquency file kept in Orange County, California); Space Migration, Intelligence (increase), and Life Extension (achieved by settling on other planets)

Smiling Jim James A Farley

S-mine shrapnel-filled mine

SMIS Society for Management Information Systems

smist smoke + mist

smit spin-motor interruption technique

SMIT Sherman Mental Impairment Test

SMITES State-Municipal Income-Tax Evaluation System

Smith Coll Smith College

Smith Coll Lib Smith College Library

Smithsonian Smithsonian Institution (United States National Museum)

Smithy Ian Smith

SMJ Southern Masonic Jurisdiction

SMJAB State Medical Journal Advertising Bureau

SMJC Saint Mary's Junior College

smk smoke

Smk Shimonoseki

smk gen smoke generator

smkls smokeless

smkstk(s) smokestack(s)

sml simulate; simulation; simulator; small; symbolic machine language

sml *sammenlign* (Danish—compare)

Sml Samuel

SML Science Museum Library; States Marine Lines

SMLA *Samoa Muamua Le Atua* (Samoan—In Samoa God Is First)

SMLC Save Mono Lake Committee

SMLE short-model Lee Enfield (British service rifle used in both world wars)

smlm simple-minded learning machine

smls seamless

SMLS Saint Mary of the Lake Seminary; Seaborne Mobile Logistic System

smm standard method of measurement

smm (SMM) solar maximum mission

SMM Science Museum of Minnesota; Solar Maximum Mission

S.M.M. *Sancta Mater Maria* (Latin—Holy Mother Mary)

SMMA Small Motor Manufacturers Association

SMMB Scottish Milk Marketing Board

smmc system maintenance monitor console

smmp screw machine metal part

smmr (SMMR) surface missile—medium range

SMMT Society of Motor Manufacturers and Traders

SMN Société Maritime Nationale

SMNA Safe Manufacturers National Association

SMNH Saskatchewan Museum of Natural History

SMNO Singapore Malays National Organization

SMNP Simien Mountains National Park (Ethiopia)

SMNRA Shadow Mountain National Recreation Area (Colorado)

Smnry Seminary

SMNWR Saint Marks National Wildlife Refuge (Florida)

SMO Senior Medical Officer

SMO *Servicio Militar Obligatorio* (Spanish—Compulsory Military Service)

SMOA Ships Material Office—Atlantic

smog smoke + fog (*see* smaze); smoky air (with or without fog)

Smog City any air-polluted metropolis

smogway smog-polluted automobile freeway

SMOH Society of Medical Officers of Health

Smokeless City Reykjavik, Iceland—heated by natural hot springs

Smokeless Coal Capital Beckley, West Virginia

smoker smoking car

smoketaz smoke-tinted topaz

Smoke that Thunders Victoria Falls (Zambia)

smokies smoked haddocks

Smokies Smoky Mountains between North Carolina and Tennessee

smokin' smoking

Smoking Moses Shishaldin Volcano on South Umiak Island off southwestern Alaska

smokin' pot smoking marijuana

Smoky City nickname of Pittsburgh, Pennsylvania before its Renaissance Plan cleared the skies above it

SMOM Sovereign Military Order of Malta (claiming to be the world's smallest country, founded in 1048 before the first crusade and located at 68 Via Conditti near the American Express office in downtown Rome where in 1981 it reported a population of 80)

smon subacute myelo-optic neuropathy

SMOOSA Save Maine's Only Official State Animal (the moose—hunted almost to the point of extinction)

smoothies smooth ones

SMOP Ships Material Office— Pacific

SMOPS School of Maritime Operations

smor standard mean ocean water

smörgas smörgåsbord (Swedish appetizers or delicatessen-style meal)

Smörgåsbordland Sweden (famous for its cold-table fare)

smorz smorzando (Italian—dying away)

smotherlove smothering mother love

smow standard mean ocean water

smp scanning measuring projector; social marginal productivity; sound motion picture(s)

smp (SMP) special multi-peril (insurance) policy

s.m.p. *sine mascula prole* (Latin —without male issue)

SMP Science Manpower Project; St Martin's Press

SMPC Saint Mary of the Plains College

SMPR Supply and Maintenance Plan and Report

smps switched-mode power supply

SMPS Society of Master Printers of Scotland

SMPSD Systematic Management Plan for School Discipline

SMPTE Society of Motion Picture and Television Engineers

smpx smallpox

smr somnolent metabolic rate; standard mortality rate; submucous resection

sMr (SMR) standard Malaysian rubber

SMR Student Master Record; South Manchurian Railway

SMR *Sa Majesté Royale* (French—Her/His Royal Majesty)

SMRA Spring Manufacturers' Research Association

SMRC South Manchurian Railway Company

smrd spin-motor rotation-detector

SMRE Safety in Mines Research Establishment

SMRI Sugar Milling Research Institute

SMRL Submarine Medical Research Laboratory

SMRMIS Supply, Maintenance, and Readiness Management Information System

sms silico-manganese steel; subject matter specialist; synchronous meteorological satellite (SMS)

sm's (SMs) submarines

SMS Sacramento Medical Society; Sequence Milestone System; Software Monitoring System

SMS *Seine Majistäts Schiffe* (German—His Majesty's Ship)

smsa standard metropolitan statistical area

SMSB Strategic Missile Support Base

SMSG School Mathematics Study Group

SMSgt Senior Master Sergeant

SMSO Senior Maintenance Staff Officer

SMSP Spring Mill State Park (Indiana)

SMSSS Sheet Metal Screw Statistical Society

smstrs seamstress

smt ship's mean time

Smt Summit (postal abbreviation)

Smt Seamount

SMT Scottish Motor Traction; Shipboard Marriage Test; Stabilized March Technique; System Maintenance Test

SMTA Scottish Motor Trade Association

SMTF Scottish Milk Trade Federation

smti selective moving target indicator

SMTO Senior Mechanical Transport Officer

SMTRB Ship and Marine Technology Requirements Board

SMTS Scottish Machinery Testing Station

SMU Southern Methodist University

SMUD Sacramento Municipal Utility Department; Sacramento Municipal Utility District

Smu Gul Smuggler's Gulch (Monument Road, San Diego, California—the last road in the southwestern corner of the continental United States)

SMUN Soviet Mission to the United Nations

SMUP Southern Methodist University Press

SMUSE Socialist Movement for the United States of Europe

smust smoke + dust

smutcom smut communication

(pornographic publishing)

smw standard metal window

SMW Society of Magazine Writers

SMWIA Sheet Metal Workers International Association

smx serial microxerography; submultiplexer unit

smx (SMX) sulphamethoxazole

Smyrna (Greek—Izmir)

sn sanitation; sanitary; service number; solid neutral; stock number

s/n serial number; service number; signal-to-noise ratio

s-n *sin número* (Spanish—unnumbered, without number)

s.n. *secundum naturam* (Latin— according to nature); *sine nomine* (Latin—without name)

Sn (postal abbreviation—San; Santa, Santo); stannum (Latin —tin)

S_n labor supply (macroeconomics)

S^n San (Spanish—saint)

SN Sacramento Northern (railroad); Scientific Note; Scope Note; Secretary of the Navy; Serial Number; Service Number; Standard Oil (stock exchange symbol)

S/N Serial Number; Service Number; stress versus number of cycles (to failure); successes versus total number of trials

S of N Sons of Norway

SN *Surete Nationale* (French— National Security)—law-enforcement agency

S-N stress versus number of cycles

sna systems network architecture

SNA Society of Naval Architects; System of National Accounts (UN)

SNAC *Syndicat National des Auteurs et Compositeurs* (National Union of Authors and Composers)

SNACS Share News on Automatic Coding Systems; Society for the North American Cultural Survey

snafu situation normal, all fouled up; situation normal— all fucked up

SNAI Standard Nomenclature of Athletic Injuries

SNAM *Società Nazionale Metanodotti*

SNAME Society of Naval Architects and Marine Engineers

snap. simplified numerical automatic processor; simplified numerical automatic programmer; subroutine(s) for natural actuarial processing

SNAP Society of National Association Publishers; Society of National Publications; Space Nuclear Auxiliary Power; Student Naval Aviation Pilot; Suffolk Network on Adolescent Pregnancy; Systems for Nuclear Auxiliary Power

Snapp Servicos de Navegação da Amazonia e de Administração do Porto do Pará

Snapper NATO name for a Soviet antitank missile

snapper(s) snapping turtle(s)

snappies snappy stories

snap(s) snapshot(s)

snark snake and shark (Lewis Carroll)

snc severe noise environment; standard navigation computer

SNC Société Navale Caennaise (Lamy et Cie) Société

SNCASCO Société Nationale de Constructions Aéronautique de l'Ouest

SNCC Student Nonviolent Coordinating Committee (also called SNIC)

SNCFB Société Nationale des Chemins de Fer Belges (Belgian State Railways)

SNCFF Société Nationale des Chemins de Fer Français (French—State Railways)

snd sound

SNDA Sunday Newspaper Distributing Association

SNDO Standard Nomenclature of Diseases and Operations

sndp sin nota de precio (Spanish —without indication of price)

sndv (SNDV) strategic nuclear delivery vehicle

SNE Society for Nutrition Education

SNEA Student National Education Association

sneaks. sneakers (tennis shoes)

SNECMA Société Nationale d'Etude et de Construction de Moteurs d'Aviation

SNEMSA Southern New England Marine Sciences Association

SNEP Saudi Naval Expansion Program

snf solids-non-fat

SNF Serbian National Federation; Skilled Nursing Facility

SNFA Standing Naval Force, Atlantic

SNFCC Shippers National Freight Claim Council

SNFU Scottish National Farmers' Union

sng synthetic natural gas

sng sans notre garantie (French —without our guarantee)

Sng Singapore

sngl single (flow chart)

SNHM Stanford Natural History Museum

sni sequence-number indicator

SNI San Nicolas Island; Selective Notation of Information; Selective Notification of Information; Sports Network Incorporated

SNI Secretariado Nacional da Informação (Portuguese— State Tourist Bureau); Syndicat National des Instituteurs (French—National Union of Teachers)

SNIC Student Non-Violent Coordinating Committee (SNCC)

SNICER State of Nebraska Information Center for Educational Resources

SNIE Special National Intelligence Estimate

sniffex sniffer exercise

snirt snort of laughter

SNL Sandia National Laboratories; Singapore National Library; Standard Nomenclature List

SNL Science News Letter

snlr services no longer required

SNLS Society for New Language Study

snm signal-to-noise merit; special nuclear material(s)

snm sobre el nivel del mar (Spanish—above sea level)

SNM Saguaro National Monument (Arizona); Senior Naval Member; Sitka National Monument (Alaska); Society of Nuclear Medicine

SNMT Society of Nuclear Medical Technologists

SNN Shannon, Eire (airport)

sno snow (used in combinations such as snocat, snomobile)

s no serial number

SNO Scottish National Orchestra; Senior Naval Officer; Singapore National Orchestra

snob *sine nobilitate* (Latin— without nobility)—anyone trying to outdo the manners and style of the nobility; person putting on airs in an attempt to outpeer the peers

SNOB Senior Naval Officer on Board

snobol string-oriented symbolic language

snoe smart noise equipment

snok secondary next of kin

Snooks surname contracted from Seven Oaks

SNOOP Students Naturally Opposed to Outrageous Prying

snoopervise snoop and supervise

SNOP Standard Nomenclature of Pathology

snorkex snorkel exercise

SNORT Supersonic Naval Ordnance Research Track

Snow King Gustavus Adolphus of Sweden

Snow Queen Christina—Queen of Sweden

Snowys Snowy Mountains of New South Wales

Snowy Scheme Snowy Mountains Scheme (Australian hydroelectric and irrigation system)

snp soluble nucleoprotein

SNP Salorp National Park (Thailand); Scottish Nationalist Party; Sebakwe NP (Rhodesia); Sequoia NP (California); Serengeti NP (Tanzania); Shenandoah NP (Virginia); Sivpuri NP (India); Sitka NP (Alaska); Snowdonia NP (Wales); Swiss NP (Switzerland)

SNPA Scottish Newspaper Proprietors' Association; Southern Newspaper Publishers Association

SNPO Space Nuclear Propulsion Office

snr signal-to-noise ratio

Snr Senhor (Portuguese—Mister)

Sñr Señor (Spanish—Mister)

SNR Society for Nautical Research

Snra Senhora (Portuguese— Missus)

Sñra Señora (Spanish—Missus)

SNRA Sanford National Recreation Area (Texas)

Snro Senhoro (Portuguese— Mister)

Snrta Senhorita (Portuguese— Miss)

Sñrta Señorita (Spanish—Miss)

Sñrto Señorito (Spanish—Master)

sns sympathetic nervous system

SNS Senior Nursing Sister

SNSC Scottish National Ski

Council
S'n Simons Saint Simons Island off the coast of Brunswick, Georgia
SNSN Standard Navy Stock Number
SNSO Superintending Naval Stores Officer
snt sealant
snt *so nota* (Japanese—and so forth)—etc.
Snt Santander
SNT Society for Nondestructive Testing
snto spinning tool
SNTO Spanish National Tourist Office; Swedish National Tourist Office; Swiss National Tourist Office
SNTPC Scottish National Town Planning Council
snubbies snub-nosed handguns
SNUPPS Standardized Nuclear Unit Power Plant System
SNVBA Scottish National Vehicle Builders Association
SNVDO Standard Nomenclature of Veterinary Diseases and Operations
SNW Symphony of the New World
SNWMA Stillwater National Wildlife Management Area (Nevada)
SNWR Sabine National Wildlife Refuge (Louisiana); Sacramento NWR (California); Santee NWR (South Carolina); Savannah NWR (South Carolina); Seedskadee NWR (Wyoming); Seney NWR (Michigan); Sherburne NWR (Minnesota); Shiawasse NWR (Michigan); Slade NWR (North Dakota)
snwt steel non-watertight
Sn Ysdr San Ysidro
so shift out
so (SO) shift-out character (data processing)
so. seller's option; senior officer; sex offender; shipping order; ship's option; shop order; show off; south(ern); special order; staff officer; standing order; strikeout; suboffice; supply office(r)
s-o shutoff
s/o shipping order; solvent-to-oil (ratio); son of
so. *siehe oben* (German—see above)
s/o *su orden* (Spanish—your order)
So. Somali(a)
So *Sondag* (Danish—Sunday)

SO Scottish Office; Scouting-Observation (naval aircraft); Secretary's Office; Senior Officer; Shipment Order; Shipping Order; Shop Order; somalo (Somalian currency unit); Southern Airways (letter coding); Southern Company (stock exchange symbol); Special Order(s); Staff Officer; Standard Oil; Standing Order(s); Stationery Office; Supply Office(r)
SO (I) Staff Officer (Intelligence)
SO (O) Staff Officer (Operations)
S/O Station Officer
SO *Staatsoper* (German—State Opera); *sudoeste* (Spanish—southwest); *Südosten* (German—southeast); *Suroeste* (Spanish—southwest)
SO₂ sulfur dioxide
SO_2 sulfur dioxide
SO₄ sulfate
SO_4 sulfate
soa speed of advance; speed of approach; state of the art
SOA Seattle Opera Association; Shoe Corporation of America (stock exchange symbol)
soaa state-of-the-art advancement
soap. symbolic optimum assembly programming
SOAP Society of Airway Pioneers
Soap Box Derby Center Akron, Ohio
SOAPD Southern Air Procurement District
soaps. suction, oxygen, apparatus, pharmaceuticals, saline (anesthetist's mnemonic for checking equipment)
soap(s) soap opera(s)
soapstone saponite (hydrous magnesium aluminum silicate)
Soapy G Mennen Williams
Soapy Sam Samuel Wilberforce, Bishop of Winchester, who debated Darwin's theory of evolution with Professor Thomas Henry Huxley, president of the Royal Society
SOAR Save Our American Resources; Society of Authors' Representatives
SOAS School of Oriental and African Studies (University of London)
SOASIS Southern Ohio (chapter of) ASIS
sob. see order blank; shortness of breath; souls on board (passengers and crew aboard an

aircraft); still on board; sub-occipitobregmatic
s-o-b son of a bitch (a dog; a no-good person)
SOB Senate Office Building; State Office Building; Society of Bookmen; son of a bitch
sobe sober; sobriety
SOBHD Scottish Official Board of Highland Dancing
soblin self-organizing binary-logic network
sob's silly old buggers; sons of bitches; souls on board (aircraft, ship, or other vehicle)
SOBs Sons of Bosses
SOBS Society for Office-Based Surgery
soc social; society; sociology; socket; state of consciousness (SoC)
Soc Socialist; Society
Soc *Sociedad* (Spanish—society); *Sociedade* (Portuguese—society); *Società* (Italian—society); *Société* (French—society)
S o C Society of Cyprus
SOC Save Our Children (from homosexuality); Servicemen's Opportunity College; Southwestern Oregon College; Space Operations Center (Colorado Springs, Colorado); Special Operations Command (Green Berets plus other counterinsurgency forces)
So Ca South Carolina's old abbreviation
SOCAL Standard Oil of California (Chevron)
Soc An *Société Anonyme* (French—corporation)
SOCAP Society of Consumer Affairs Professionals (in business)
Soc. Chr. *Societas Christi* (Latin—Christian Society)
soc/d social death; sociological death
Soc-Dem Social-Democrat(ic) (Party)
SOCEM Save Our City from Environmental Mess; Society of Objectors to Compulsory Egg Marketing
SOCGPA Seed, Oil Cake, and General Produce Association
Soc I Society Islands
Socialist Pope Daniel De Leon
Societies Society Islands of Polynesia in the South Pacific
Society Capital Newport, Rhode Island
Society of Friends the Quakers
Socinus Laelius Socinus (Latin

name of Lelio Sozzini, the Italian theologian and anti-Trinitarian whose nephew Faustus Socinus developed Socinianism, the forerunner of Unitarian-Universalism)

sociobio sociobiologic(al)(ly); sociobiologist; sociobiology

socioecol socioecologic(al)(ly); socioecologist; socioecology

sociol sociological; sociologist; sociology

socks. soccer teams

SOCMA Synthetic Organic Chemical Manufacturers Association

Soc Mining Eng Society of Mining Engineers

Soc NC sociedad en nombre colectivo (Spanish—general partnership under a collective name)

So Co Southern Counties

SOCO Standard Oil Company of California

socom solar communication

SOCONY Standard Oil Corporation of New York

soc psych social psychology

SOCRATES System for Organizing Content to Review and Teach Educational Subjects

Socred Social Credit (party of Canada)

socrit social critic(ism)

socs survey of clerical skills

soc sci social science; social scientist

Soc Sec Social Security

sod. sodium; sodomite; sodomy

Sod acronymic place-name for a West Virginia town named after the initials of its first postmaster—Samuel Odell Dunlap—SOD

SOD Special Operations Division (CIA)

soda (SODA) source-oriented data acquisition

soda ash sodium carbonate (Na_2CO_3)

SODAC Society of Dyers and Colourists

Sodaks South Dakotans

sodar sound-detecting and ranging

soda water water charged with carbon dioxide (CO_2)

Sodoma Il Sodoma (Italian—The Sodomite)—nickname of the 16th-century painter Giovanni Antonio de Bazzi

SODOMEI Nihon Rodo Kumiai Sodomei (Japanese Trade Union Federation)

SODRE Servicio Oficial de Difusión Radio Eléctrica (Uruguayan radio and tv network)

SoE Secretary of Energy

SOE Special Operations Executive (World War II British intelligence operation for rescuing scientists and other useful citizens from Hitler)

SOED Shorter Oxford English Dictionary

SOEEA Saskatchewan Outdoor and Environmental Education Association

SOE/F SOE in France

Soemba (Dutch—Sumba)—also called Sandalwood

Soembawa (Dutch—Sumbawa)

Soenda (Dutch—Sunda)—the Greater Sunda Islands such as Borneo, Celebes, Java, and Sumatra

soep (SOEP) solar-oriented experiment package

Soerabaja (Dutch—Surabaya)

sof sound on film

sof (SOF) succinic oxidase factor

Sof Sofia

SoF Soldier of Fortune

S o F Society of Friends

SOFA Socially Oriented For Action; Strongly Oriented For Action; Student Overseas Flights for Americans

sofar sound fixing and ranging

SOFCS Self-Organizing Flight-Control System

Sofia English place-name equivalent of Sofiya, Bulgaria

Sofia Loren Sofia Scicolone

SOFINA Société Financière de Transports et d'Entreprises Industrielles (Belgian investment syndicate)

Sofiya (Bulgarian—Sofia)

sofnet solar observing and forecasting network

SOFRATOME Société Française d'Études et de Réalisation Nucléaires (French Society for Nuclear Study and Realization)

soft. signature of fragmented tanks

SOFT Status of Forces Treaty; Swedish Orienteering Federation

softech software technology

softlenses soft contact lenses

soft porn soft-core pornography

software computer documentation; computerese for computer programs; computer-originated paperwork (*see* hardware); design documents instructing computers

Sofu-gan Japanese equivalent of Lot's Wife—volcanic islet resembling a pillar of salt in the North Pacific between Iwo Jima and Yokohama

sog speed over (the) ground

sog sogenannt (German—so called)

SOG Seat of Government (Washington, D.C.); Special Operations Group

SOGAT Society of Graphical and Allied Trades

SOGC Society of Gynecologists and Obstetricians of Canada

SO & GC Signal Oil and Gas Company

sogg soggettivo (Italian—subjective); *soggetto* (Italian—subject)

soh (SOH) start of heading character (data processing)

soha soft hard

SOHIO Standard Oil of Ohio

SoHo South of Houston Street (New York City artist's colony in lower Manhattan)

SOHO Save Our Heritage Organization

SOHYO Nihon Rodo Kumiai Sohygikai (Japanese General Council of Trade Unions)

soi space object identification

SOI Signal Operation Instruction(s); Southern Indiana (railroad); Specific Operating Instruction(s)

solt soitenly (New Yorkese—certainly)

SoJ Sea of Japan

Sojourner Truth Isabella Baumfree

sok sokak (Turkish—lane; street)

sol solar; soldier; solenoid; soluble; solubility; solution; solvent(s)

sol (SOL) simulation-oriented language

s-o-l short of luck

sol (Italian—fifth tone, *E* in diatonic scale, *G* in fixed-do system)

sol. solutio (Latin—solution)

Sol Solomon; Solomon Islands

SoL Secretary of Labor; Solicitor of Labor

SOL Slightly Older Lesbians; Systems Optimization Laboratory

SOL Svenska Orient Line (Swedish Orient Line)

SOLACE Sales Order and Ledger Accounting (using) Computerline Environment

SOLAR Semantically Oriented

Lexical Archive; Shop Operations Load Analysis Report(ing)

Solar Energy Capital Los Angeles

Solar Energy State Arizona

SoLaS Safety of Life at Sea (international conference)

solb start of line block

sold. solder; soldering

Sol de Mayo (Spanish—Sun of May)—symbol of independence appearing on the flags and seals of Argentina and Uruguay

solder 50% lead, 50% tin (common solder)

soldier's heart Da Costa's syndrome

Soledad Correctional Training Facility of the State of California at Soledad (Spanish word meaning solitude)

sol hgt solid height

sol htg solar heating

solidif solidification

Solid South Southern United States usually voting as a solid conservative Democratic bloc: Alabama, Florida, Georgia, Louisiana, Mississippi, South Carolina

Solid-State Commun Solid-State Communications

Solid-State Electron Solid-State Electronics

Solid-State Phys Solid-State Physics

Solina South Carolina

SOLINET Southeastern Library Network

solion solution of ions

SOLIT Society of Library and Information Technicians

Sol J Solicitors' Journal

SOLL Selma Ottiliana Louisa Lagerlöf

Sol(ly) Solomon

soln solution

solo. status of logistics offensive

SOLO System for Ordinary Life Operations

SOLog standardization of certain aspects of operations and logistics

sologs standardization of operations and logistics

solomon simultaneous-operation linked-ordinal modular network

Solomon real surname of this outstanding British pianist is unknown to the public and he is known only by this anonym —Solomon

Solomon Islands Port Honiara on Guadalcanal Island

Solomons Solomon Islanders; Solomon Islands (nation in the western Pacific where farming for cocoa, coconuts, palm oil, and rice is augmented by fishing and fish canning; natives speak Papuan, Pidgin English, and Melanesian)

Solomon seal six-pointed star consisting of two interlocking triangles; sometimes called the shield of David and not to be confused with the Suliman seal of Islam and Morocco (*see* Suliman seal)

Solon of French Prose Jean Louis Guez de Balzac

Solovetskis Solovetski Islands (penal colonies in the Archangelsk Region of the USSR—part of the Gulag Archipelago populated by political prisoners)

Solovki Solovetski Islands

Sol Phys Solar Physics

solr solicitor

solrad solar radiation

solut solution

solv solvent

solv. solve (Latin—dissolve)

Solv Solveig

soly solubility

som serous otitis media; somatology; start of message

som (SOM) standoff missile

Som Somali(a); Somaliland(er); Somerset; Somerville College, Oxford

SOM Society of Occupational Medicine; Standing Group on Oil Markets

SOMA Sharing of Ministries Abroad; Society of Mental Awareness

Somal Somali(a)(n)—Somalia formerly British and Italian Somaliland

Somalia Somali Democratic Republic (East African nation whose people speak Somali, Arabic, English, and Italian as the area was once divided between British and Italian Somaliland; mineral exploitation and tropical agriculture sustain the Somalis)

Somalian Port Berbera

somat somatic

somat or some (Greek—body)— centrosome, chromosome, somatic

SOME Senior Ordnance Mechanical Engineer

Somerset Somersetshire

Somers' Islands Bermuda

SOMEX Sociedad Mexicana de Credito Industrial (Spanish— Mexican Industrial Credit Society)

som-h start of message—high precedence

som-l start of message—low precedence

Som LI Somerset Light Infantry

somm (SOMM) standoff modular missile

Somnolent City of the Sahara Timbuktu

SOMOS Society of Military Orthopedic Surgeons

SOMPA System of Multicultural Pluralistic Assessment

SOMS Standing-Order Microfiche Service

Som sh Somali shilling

son. sonata

Son Sonora

Son Sonntag (German—Sunday)

SON Snijders-Oomen Non-verbal (intelligence scale)

sonac sonacelle (sonar nacelle)

SONAP Sociedade Nacional de Petroleos (Portuguese—National Petroleum Company)

sonar sound navigation and ranging

Sonbrit Simfonischen orkestur na bulgarskoto radio i televiziya (Bulgarian Radio and Television Symphony Orchestra)

SONDE Society of Non-Destructive Examination

Song of the Night Karol Szymanowski's Symphony No. 3; Mahler's Symphony No. 7 in E minor

SONGS San Onofre Nuclear Generating Station

Song Sol The Song of Solomon

Song of Songs The Song of Solomon

Sonia Sophia

sonmc sonar countermeasures and deception

Sonn Sonnets of Shakespeare

Son of Nature Henry David Thoreau

sono sonobuoy

sonoan sonic noise analyzer

Son of the Ocean Yangtse River

Sonoran Desert in northwestern Mexico and adjacent sections of Arizona and California

SONPP San Onofre Nuclear Power Plant

son(s) sonata(s)

Son of the Star Bar Kochba—military leader of the Jews who revolted against the Romans in the year 132 A.D.

Son of Valladolid José Zorilla

Sonya Sophia

Sonya (Russian nickname—Sophia)

Soo Sault Ste Marie (canal and locks)

SOO Staff Officer Operations

SO(O) Staff Officer (Operations)

Soo Bridge Sault Ste Marie International Bridge

Soo Canals Sault Ste Marie Canals

Soo Line Minneapolis, St Paul & Sault Ste Marie (railroad)

Sooner State Oklahoma's official nickname recalling many of its first settlers entered the territory sooner than others who waited for the signal gun

SOOP Submarine Oceanographic Observation Program

soot. solar optical observing telescope

sop. soprano; sum of products; surgical outpatient

s-o-p standard operating procedure

SOP Senior Officer Present; Standard Operating Procedure; Study Organization Plan

SOPA Senior Officer Present Afloat

Sopac Southern Pacific Railroad (stock exchange nickname)

SOPAC Southern Pacific; South Pacific

Soph Sophocles

SOPHE Society of Public Health Educators

Sophia English equivalent of Bulgaria's capital city—Sofiya

Sophia Loren Sofia Scicolone

Sophie Tucker Sophia Abuza

soph(s) sophomore(s)

SOPL Save Our Public Libraries

SOPLASCO Southern Plastics Company

Soppnata Sociedade Portuguese de Navios Tanques (Portuguese Tankers)

sor sequential occupancy rate; sorority; specific operating requirement(s)

s-o-r stimulus-organism-response

Sor Soerabaya; Sorong

Sor Señor (Spanish—Mister)

Sor Sênior (Portuguese—Mister)

ter)

SOR Sandia Optical Range; Special Order Request; Specific Operational Requirement

SORB Subsistence Operations Review Board

Sorbonne University of Paris

sord submerged object recovery device

SORD Southeastern Order Retrieval and Distribution Center

SORDID Summary of Reported Defects, Incidents, and Delays

Sores Señores (Spanish—gentlemen)

SORG Southern Operations Research Group

Sorghum Capital of the World Hawesville, Kentucky

SORI Southern Research Institute

Soria Madrid's great prison and name of a Spanish province

Sørland (Norwegian—Southland)—southern Norway

Sorlings Sorling Islands (Isles of Scilly)

SORO Special Operations Research Office

SORT Ship's Operational Readiness Test(ing); Slosson Oral Reading Test; Structured-Objective Rorschach Test

sorti satellite orbital track and intercept

sos same old stew; same only softer (musical direction); slag on a shingle (military description of creamed chicken or beef served on a slice of toast)

s.o.s. si opus sit (Latin—if necessary)

SoS Source(s) of Supply

S-o-S Southend-on-Sea

SOs Sheriff's Offices

SOS Safety Observation Station; Save Our School(s); Save Our Shore; Share Our Spectacle(s); Ships Ordnance Summary; Squadron Officer School(ing); Stamp Out Smog; Student-Oriented Studies (National Science Foundation); Supervisor of Shipbuilding; Supplementary Ophthalmic Service(s)

SOS international distress signal—three dots, three dashes, three dots; popularly translated as meaning Save Our Souls

sosc safety observation station display console

SOSC Smithsonian Oceanographic Sorting Center; Source of Supply Code

So sh somali shilling(s)

SOSS Shipboard Oceanographic Survey System

sost sostenuto (Italian—sustained)

Sost Sostavitel (Russian—compiler)

SOSTAC Scottish Industrial Safety Training Advisory Council

SOSUS Sound and Surveillance System

sot. shower over tub; sound on tape

SoT Secretary of Transport(ation); Secretary of the Treasury

sota state of the art

SOTA Statewide Organization of Third-world Artists

SOTAA State-of-the-Art Association

SOTAS Stand-Off Target-Acquisition System

sotd stabilized optical tracking device

SOTDAT Source Test Data System (EPA)

sotim sonic observation of the trajectory and impact of missiles

Soton Southampton

SOTP Ship(yard) Overhaul Test Program; System Overhaul Test(ing) Program

sotus (SOTUS) sequentially-operated teletypewriter universal selector (data processing)

Sou Southampton

SOU Southern Airways

Sou Afr South Africa(n)

Sou Amer South America(n)

Sou Aus South Australia(n)

Soul of American Law Clarence Darrow

Soul City Harlem district of New York City

Sound The Sound (Arctic straits in the Canadian sector such as Lancaster Sound, Smith Sound, Viscount Melville Sound; Long Island Sound between that island and the mainland of Connecticut and New York; nearby Block Island, Rhode Island, Nantucket, and Vineyard Sounds; North Carolina's Albemarle, Bogue, Currituck, and Pamlico Sounds; Sundet—the strait also called Öresund between Denmark and Sweden where it connects the Baltic Sea with the Kattegat, the Skagerrak, and the North Sea; all other geographical sounds)

soundamp sound amplification; sound amplifier

Sound River old name for New York City's East River—an extension of Long Island Sound linking the Sound with New York Bay, the Harlem River, and the Hudson

SOUP Students Opposed to Unfair Practices

Sou Pac Southern Pacific

SOUR Stamp Out Urban Renewal

source the source (nickname for a baton with a rechargeable flashlight on one end and shock terminals on the other, used for jolting criminals with a 10,000-volt charge)

Source of the Sun Japan (called Nihon by the Japanese as it means Source of the Sun and is emblazoned on their flag)

Souse America booze-cruise destination of many alcohol addicts

soussa steady, oscillatory, and unsteady, subsonic, and supersonic aerodynamics

s/out sleep out (porch)

South southern American states from Virginia to Texas

South Africa Republic of South Africa (area developed by Dutch and English whose Afrikaans and English remain as official languages although Bantu and Indian tongues are popular; agriculture, manufacturing, mining, and tourism provide a strong economic base) *Republiek van Suid-Afrika*

South African Commonwealth South Africa and its territories

South African Dominion South Africa and its territories

South-African Dutch Afrikaans

South African Ports (large, medium, and small from west to south to east) Walvis Bay, Luderitz, Cape Town, Simontown, Mosselbaai, Port Elizabeth, East London, Port St Johns, Durban

South Africa's Principal Port Cape Town

South Africa's Spine Drakensburg Mountains

South America islands and lands extending from Cape Horn to Colombia (Argentina, Bolivia,

Brazil, Chile, Colombia, Ecuador, French Guiana, Guyana, Paraguay, Surinam, Uruguay, Venezuela)

South American Welfare State Uruguay

South America's Largest Country Brazil

South Arabia Southern Yemen

South Atlantic ocean between South America and Africa

South Atlantic States Delaware, Florida, Georgia, Maryland, North Carolina, South Carolina, Virginia, and West Virginia

South Britain England and Wales

South Carolina Port Charleston

South Carolina's Capital City Columbia

South Central States Arkansas, Louisiana, Oklahoma, Texas

South China Sea between Indochina, Indonesia, and Philippines

SouthCom Southern Command (U.S. Air Force, Army, and Navy bases straddling the Panama Canal for its protection)

Southeast southeastern United States (North Carolina to Florida, Atlantic Coast to Mississippi River)

South Eastern Region South Eastern Region Correctional Institute at Juneau, Alaska

Southeast Sun Belt Alabama, Arkansas, Florida, Georgia, Louisiana, Mississippi, North Carolina, South Carolina, Tennessee, and Virginia

South End Boston, Massachusetts slum

souther storm from the south

Southern Southern Railway

Southern Alplands Albania, France, Italy, Yugoslavia

Southern Alps mountain range on South Island of New Zealand

Southern California California south of the Tehachapis

Southern Colonies Virginia, Maryland, North Carolina, South Carolina, Georgia

Southern Cone Argentina, Chile, Paraguay, Uruguay

Southern Cross outstanding constellation of the Southern Hemisphere where it is emblazoned on the flags of Australia, Brazil, New Zealand, Papua New Guinea, the Solomon Islands, and Western Samoa as

well as the state of Victoria in southern Australia

Southern Hemisphere the world south of the equator

Southern Ireland Republic of Ireland

southern lights *aurora australis*

Southernmost American Town Naalehu, Island of Hawaii

Southernmost Canadian Town Kingsville, Ontario

Southernmost Europe Crete's south coast

Southernmost Province Ontario

Southernmost State Hawaii

Southern Ocean Antarctic sections of the Atlantic, Indian, and Pacific oceans

Southern Part of Heaven Chapel Hill, North Carolina

Southern Poet Sidney Lanier (*The Marshes of Glynn, The Song of the Chattahoochee, Sunrise*)

Southern Rhodesia Rhodesia's name when it was still a British colony; Zimbabwe

Southerns Southern Alps of New Zealand's South Island

Southern States former slaveholding states of the Confederacy such as Virginia, North and South Carolina, Georgia, Florida, Alabama, Mississippi, Tennessee, Arkansas, Louisiana, and Texas—all part of the Confederate States of America plus temporary government in Kentucky and Missouri

South Holland Dutch province containing Dodrecht, The Hague, Leiden, and Rotterdam

South Jersey Coast Atlantic City to Cape May

South Ken South Kensington Imperial Institute (London's museum of science and industry)

South Orkneys South Orkney Islands in British Antarctica

South Pacific between Australia and South America containing South Sea Islands; South Pacific Ocean

South Pole 90 degrees South latitude; zero degrees longitude; southernmost point on the earth; discovered by Norwegian explorer Roald Amundsen in 1911; one month later British exploration party led by Robert Falcon Scott arrived there but did not survive return trip

South Providence Rhode Island's largest slum

South River old name for the Delaware River used to set it apart from the Hudson or North River

South Sandwiches South Sandwich Islands

South Sea Islands islands of Oceania; islands of the South Pacific Ocean

South Seas South Pacific Ocean

South Seymour Island, Galápagos Baltra

South Shetlands South Shetland Islands off British Antarctica

South Side Chicago slum area

Southwest southern California and Nevada, Arizona, New Mexico, and western Texas

South-West Africa formerly German South-West Africa but more recently referred to as Namibia

Southwest Sun Belt Arizona, California, Hawaii, Nevada, New Mexico, Ohlahoma, and Texas

South Yugoslavia formerly the kingdom of Montenegro

sou'wester southwester (waterproof oilskin hat and/or coat); southwestern wind

sov shutoff valve; special orientation visit

Sov Soviet; Sovietic; Soviets

Sovetskij Sojuz (Russian—Soviet Union)

Soviet Central Asia Kazakh, Kirghiz, Tadzhik, Turkmen, and Uzbek Soviet Socialist Republics

Soviet Film Pioneer Sergei Eisenstein

Soviet Ports (large, medium, and small from east to west to south) Vladivostok, Nakhodka, Sovetskaya Gavan, De-Kastrt, Nikolayevsk, Komsomolsk, Khabarovsk, Korsakov, Kholmsk, Aleksandrovsk Sakhskiy, Moskal Vo, Magayevo, Petropavlovsk-Kamchats, Ust-Kamchatsk, Provideniya, Tiksi, Dudinka, Igarka, Mezen, Ekonomiya, Solombala, Arkhangelsk, Severodvinsk, Belomorsk, Pabocheostrovsk, Gavan Blagopoluchiya, Keret, Kovda, Guba Knyazhaya, Kandalaksha, Bolshaya Piryu, Gremikha, Vayenga, Murmansk, Kola, Vyborg, Vysotsk, Kivitokeye, Klyuchevoye, Kurkela, Leningrad, Kronshtadt, Narva Joe-

suv, Tallinn, Parnu, Riga, Ventspils, Liepaja, Klaipeda, Baltiysk, Kalingrad, Ilichevsk, Odessa, Nikolayev, Kherson, Bukhta Severnaya, Feodosiya, Kerch, Berdyansk, Zhdanov, Rostov, Novorossiysk, Tuapse, Poti, Batumiyskava Bukhta

Soviet Symphonist Serge Prokofiev and Dmitri Shostakovich share this title

Soviet Union formerly the Imperial Russian Empire

Sovinformburo Soviet Information Bureau

s-o vlv shutoff valve

Sov Medron Soviet Mediterranean Squadron

Sov muz *Sovetskaya muzyka* (Russian—Soviet music)

Sov strike attack by the Soviet Union

sow. (bystanders or others) sent on (their) way

SoW Statement of Work

SOW Sunflower Ordnance Works

SOWC Senior Officers War Course (UK)

SOWETO Southwestern Townships (South Africa)

Sowjetrussland (German—Soviet Russia)

Sowjet Union (German—Soviet Union)

SOWSD Statement of Work, Specifications, and Design

sox socks; solid oxygen; stockings

SoX School of Xerography (Xerox)

SOXAL Singapore Oxygen Air Liquids

Soyuz Soyuz-class 32,000-ton nuclear-powered Soviet cruiser

SOZ Soviet Occupied Zone

sp self-propelled; selling price; shear plate; single phase, single-pole; single-purpose; small paper; smokeless powder; solid-propellant; space; spare; spare part; special; special paper; special propellant(s); special-purpose; specie; species; specific; speed; starting point; starting price; static pressure; stop payment; summary plotter; summary programmed

sp (SP) space character (data processing); spelling

s-p sequential-phase

s/p soft-point (bullet with lead core exposed to increase ex-

pansion)

s & p systems and procedures

sp *sans prix* (French—without price)

sp. species (Latin—species)

s.p. sine prole (Latin—without issue)

Sp Space (trailer-court address); Spain; Spanish; Spring(s)

Sp *Spalten* (German—column; division); Spanish (language spoken by more than 208 million people but of that number less than a third speak Castilian; despite popular misconception there is no language called Mexican or Puerto Rican although both have a New World accent of their own and a great many slang terms included in *The Crime Dictionary;* Spanish is not only the language of Spain but of all its former colonies in Africa, Asia, Latin America, and around the Mediterranean basin; after English it is second only to Russian in the number of people who use it for communication); *Spanje* (Dutch—Spain); Spitz (German—point)—pointed high-velocity bullet

SP San Pedro, California; São Paulo, Brazil; Scientific Paper; Section Control; Security Publication; Shore Party; Shore Patrol; Shore Police; Socialist Party; Society of Protozoologists; Sociolinguistics Program; Southern Pacific (railroad); Special Publication; Standard Practice(s); Strategic Plan(ning); subliminal perception; Submarine Patrol; subprofessional (civil service rating)

S-P Studebaker-Packard

S & P Standard & Poor's Corporation

S of P Society of Philaticians

SP *Senterpartiet* (Norwegian—Centrist party); *Socialdemokratiet Parti* (Danish—Social Democratic Party); *Sozialistische Partei* (German—Socialist Party)

S.P. *Sanctissimus Pater* (Latin—Most Holy Father); *Summus Pontifex* (Latin—Supreme Pontiff, the Pope)

Sp/1 Specialist, 1st class

Sp3c Specialist, third class

spa **(SPA)** stimulation-produced analgesia

spa. subject to particular average; sudden phase anomaly

S p A *Società per Azioni* (Italian —joint stock company)

SPA Protectrice des Animaux (Society for the Protection of Animals); Salt Producers Association; School of Performing Arts; Società per Azioni (Italian—joint stock company); Society of Participating Artists; Society for Personnel Administration; Society of Philatelic Americans; Songwriters Protective Association; South Pacific Area; Southern Pine Association; Southwestern Power Administration; Standard Practice Amendment(s); State Principals Association; Systems and Procedures Association

SPAA Systems and Procedures Association of America

SPAAMFAA Society for the Preservation and Appreciation of Antique Motor Fire Apparatus in America

Spaans (Dutch—Spanish)

SPAB Society for the Protection of Ancient Buildings

spac spatial computer

SPAC Saratoga Performing Arts Center

S Pac Cur South Pacific Current

Space City Houston, Texas (NASA headquarters)

Space Coast Florida's Cape Canaveral area

SPACES Scheduling Package and Computer

spad (SPAD) space patrol air defense

SPAD Seafarers Political Activity Donation; Space Patrol Air Defense; Support Planning and Design

SPADETS Space Detection and Tracking System

Spag Spagnuolo [*see* Lad(s)]

SPAG Society for the Preservation of American Grandchildren

Spagna (Italian—Spain)

SPAI Screen Printing Association International

Spain Spanish State (Iberian nation once the center of an almost global colonial empire; Spanish is official although Basque, Catalan, Galician, and Valencian are spoken; farming, fishing, manufacturing, mining, and tourism sustain the industrious people) *Estado Español*

Spain's Largest Port Barcelona

Spain's Quartet Spain's four best-known classical composers in chronological order—de Falla, Albeniz, Granados, Turina

spal stabilized platform airborne laser

Spalato English and Italian equivalent of the Yugoslavian port of Split

spam spiced pork and meat (canned meat introduced during World War II when meat byproducts fed people as well as their pets)

SPAM Society for the Publication of American Music

SPAMS Ship Position and Altitude Measurement System

span. space navigation

Span Spanish

SPAN Solar Particle Alert Network; South Pacific Action Network; System for Procurement and Analysis

SPANA Society for the Protection of Animals in North Africa

SPANC Society for St Peter the Apostle for Native Clergy

spandar space-and-range radar

Spandau great German prison near Berlin

Spanglish Spanish + English (Latin American mixture of the two tongues; common along the Mexican Border and in many port cities)

Spanien (German—Spain)

Spaniola(s) British slang for Spaniard(s)

spanish spanish bayonet (*Yucca*); spanish cedar (fragrant neotropical wood); spanish dagger (*Yucca gloriosa*); spanish fly (cantharides used as an aphrodisiac, diuretic, and skin irritant); spanish grippe (influenza); spanish heel (woman's high heel); spanish influenza (highly infectious respiratory viral disease); spanish lime (genip); spanish mackeral (jack mackeral); spanish moss (epiphytic plant growing in long festoons on the branches of live oak trees in the southern United States); spanish omelet (made with green peppers, tomatoes, and seasoning); spanish rice (made with cayenne pepper, chopped onions, and tomatoes); spanish topaz (citrine); spanish trefoil (alfalfa)

Spanish Africa cities of Ceuta and Melilla; term formally included Spanish Guinea, Spanish Morocco, and the Spanish Sahara

Spanish America Spanish-speaking countries of Latin America

Spanish Artist and Sculptor Pablo Picasso

Spanish Caprice Rimsky-Korsakov's *Capriccio espagnol*

Spanish Dances *Danzas españoles* composed by Granados for the piano

Spanish Etcher-Lithographer-Painter Francisco José de Goya y Lucientes

Spanish Film Pioneer Luís Buñuel

Spanish Guinea former West African colony on the Gulf of Guinea; included Fernando Po, Río Muni, and offshore islets

Spanish Honduras the Spanish-speaking Republic of Honduras in Central America

Spanish Hour Ravel's brief but witty opera—*L'Heure espagnole*

Spanish Impressionist Joaquín Sorolla y Bastida

Spanish Lithographer Francisco José de Goya y Lucientes

Spanish Main Spanish-speaking mainland of Central America and northern South America bordering the Caribbean from Mexico to Venezuela, including Belize, Guatemala, Honduras, Nicaragua, Costa Rica, Panama, and Colombia

Spanish Monastic Painter Francisco de Zurbarán

Spanish Morocco formerly all of coastal and northwestern Morocco but now only Alhucemas, Ceuta, the Chafarinas islands, Melilla, and Peñon de Vélez

Spanish National Composer Manuel de Falla

Spanish Naturalist Painter Diego Rodriguez de Silva y Velázquez

Spanish Netherlands all the Lowland Countries (Belgium, Luxembourg, and the Netherlands) when they were under Spanish rule

Spanish Nights de Falla's *Nights in the Gardens of Spain*

Spanish Overture Glinka's *Jota aragonesa*

Spanish Pieces de Falla's *Piezas*

españoles for piano

Spanish Ports (large, medium, and small from the north coast to the west and south coasts) Pasajes, San Sebastian, Zumaya, Santurce, Portugalete—Bilbao, Las Arenas—Bilbao, El Desierto—Bilbao, Castro Urdiales, Santander, Gijón, Musel, Aviles, San Esteban, El Ferrol del Caudillo, La Coruña, Villagarcia, Pontevedra, Marín, Vigo, Santa Cruz de Tenerife and La Luz Gran Canaria (on the Canary Islands), Huelva, Bonanza, Coria del Río, Sevilla, Rota, Cádiz, Algeciras, Málaga, Motril, Adra, Almería, Cartagena, Alicante, Valencia, Castellon de la Plana, Tarragona, Barcelona, Palamós, *(and on the Balearic Islands*—Ibiza, Palma, Mahon)

Spanish Presidios Ceuta and Melilla on the Alboran coast of northern Morocco close to the Strait of Gibraltar

Spanish Rhapsody Liszt's *Rhapsodie espagnole*; Ravel's *Rapsodie espagnole*

Spanish Riviera Spain's Mediterranean resorts

Spanish Sahara former colony on Africa's northwest coast where it included Río de Oro and Saguia el Hamra until 1976 when it was ceded by Spain and divided between Mauritania and Morocco

Spanish Song Ravel's *Chanson espagnole* for piano and voice

Spanish Songbook Hugo Wolf's *Spanisches Liederbuch*

Spanish Songs *Cantos de España* composed by Albeniz for the piano

Spanish-speaking Places Andorra, Argentina, Balearic Islands, Bolivia, Canary Islands, Ceuta and Melilla, Chile, Colombia, Costa Rica, Cuba, Dominican Republic, Ecuador, El Salvador, Equatorial Guinea, Guam, Guatemala, Honduras, Mexico, Morocco, Nicaragua, Panama, Paraguay, Peru, Philippines, Puerto Rico, Spain, Spanish Sahara, United States (especially in many large cities such as New York as well as in the South, the Southwest, and southern California) Uruguay, Venezuela, etc.

Spanish Suite *Suite Española* by Albéniz

Spanish Symphony Lalo's *Symphonie espagnole* for violin and orchestra

Spanish Town Jamaican resort; Tampa, Florida where so many Spanish-speaking people live

Spanish West Africa Sidi Ifni

Spanje (Dutch—Spain)

Span Neth Spanish Netherlands

span(s) spaniel(s)

SPANS Sealift Procurement and National Security

Spansule span + capsule (prepared so different drugs encapsulated are released at various times)

Spantran Spanish translation (programming language)

spar. (SPAR) space processing applications rocket; store port allocations register; submersible pipe-alignment rig

SPAR Seagoing Platform for Acoustics Research; Selection Program for ADMIRAL Runs (*see* ADMIRAL); Society of Photographer and Artists Representatives

sparc steam power automation and results computer

SPARC Space Program Analysis and Review Council

Sparks ship's radio operator

sparm (SPARM) sparrow anti-radiation missile

sparr steerable paraboloid altazimuth radio reflector (Jordrell Bank Radio-Telescope, Cheshire, England)

Sparrow McDonnell-Douglas air-to-air missile

SPARS Women's Coast Guard Reserve (from the Coast Guard motto, *Semper Paratus* —Always Ready)

SPARTAN Special Proficiency at Rugged Training and National Building (Green Beret training program); System for Personnel Automated Reports, Transactions, and Notices (NASA)

SPAS Societatis Philosophicae Americanae Socius (Latin—Fellow of the American Philosophical Society)

SPASM Society for the Prevention of Asinine Student Movements

spasur space surveillance

spat. self-protective antitank (weapon); silicon precision alloy transistor

spat. (SPAT) self-propelled anti-

tank gun

SPAT Submarine Processing Action Team

SPATC South Pacific Air Transport Council

spats spatterdashes

spau signal processing arithmetic unit

S Pau São Paulo

Spauld Turn Spaulding Turnpike

spb special boiling point

SPB Special Branch Policeman (British English—detective); State Personnel Board

spbd springboard

SPBF Scientific Peace Builders Foundation

spc salicylamide-phenacetin-caffeine; special fuel consumption; suspended plaster ceiling

SPC Service Processing Center (Immigration and Naturalization Detention Center); Society of Photographers in Communications; Society for the Prevention of Crime; Solar Power Corporation (Exxon); South Pacific Commission; Space Projects Center; Standard Products Committee; State Planning Council; Subcontract Plans Committee

SPCA Society for the Prevention of Cruelty to Animals

spcat special category

SPCC Ships Parts Control Center; Society for the Prevention of Cruelty to Children; Standardization, Policy, and Coordination Committee (NATO)

sp cd spinal cord

SPCH Society for the Prevention of Cruelty to Homosexuals

SPCK Society for Promoting Christian Knowledge

spcl special

SPCM Special Court-Martial

SPCMO Special Court-Martial Order

SPCO St Paul Chamber Orchestra; St Paul Civic Opera

spcr spacer

SPCs Suicide Prevention Centers; Suicide Prevention Clinics

Sp Cttee 24 Special Committee of 24 (United Nations' 24-member Special Committee concerning Granting Independence to Colonial Countries and Peoples)

SPCW Society for the Prevention of Cruelty to Women

spd separation program designator; ship pays dues; silicon photo diode; silver plated; surface potential difference

Spd Spandau

SPD Sales Promotion Department; Sozialdemokratische Partei Deutschlands (Social Democratic Party of Germany); System Program Director

SPDC Spare Parts Distributing Center

sp del special delivery

spdl spindle

spdltr speedletter

sp dt single pole, double throw

spdtdb single-pole double-throw double-break (switch)

spdtncdb single-pole double-throw normally closed double-break (switch)

spdtno single-pole double-throw normally open (switch)

spdtnodb single-pole double-throw normally open double-break (switch)

spdtsw single-pole double-throw switch

SPDV Site Preliminary Design Validation (program)

spe special purpose equipment

spe (SPE) sucrose polyester

Spe San Pedro

SPE Society of Petroleum Engineers; Society for Photographic Education; Society of Plastics Engineers; Society for Pure English

SPEA Southeastern Poultry and Egg Association

SPEAK Society for Preserving and Encouraging Arts and Knowledge

SPEARS Satellite Photo-Electronic Analog Rectification System

SPEBSQSA Society for the Preservation and Encouragement of Barber Shop Quartet Singing in America

spec special(ly); specialty; specie; species; specific(ally); specification; specimen; spectacle; speculation; speech-predictive encoded communication(s)

's'pec' suspect

Spec Speculative Society (of debaters)

SPEC Society for Pollution and Environmental Control; South Pacific Bureau for Economic Cooperation; Systems and Procedures Exchange Center

spec appt special appointment

specat special category

special. specialization; specialized

special ops special operations (assassinations and sabotage)

specif specific; specifically

specl specialist; specialize

specs specifications; spectacles

SPECS School Planning, Evaluation, and Communication Service

SPECTRE Single-Pulse CO_2 Transient Experiment; Special Executive for Counterintelligence, Terrorism, Revenge, and Extortion (fictional organization created by Ian Fleming for his James Bond books)

spectrog spectrography

SPECTROL Scheduling, Planning, Evaluation, and Cost Control (USAF)

spectrophotom spectrophotometry

spectros spectroscopy

SPEDE System for Processing Educational Data Electronically

S Pedro San Pedro

Speech Comm Assn Speech Communication Association

speed speed kills (nickname for killer-type psychedelic drugs of methamphetamine type)—nickname derived from automotive safety slogan—"speed kills"

speed. (SPEED) simplified profile enlargement from engineering drawing(s)

SPEED Systematic Plotting and Evaluation of Enumerated Data

speedalyzer automatic radar-controlled automotive-vehicle speed analyzer (for detecting speeders on byways and highways)

speedo speedometer

spef single-program-element fund(ing)

spelpat spelling pattern(s)

Spel Soc Am Speleological Society of America

Spen Spencer; Spencerian

Spence Spencer

Spencer Spiridione

Sperm Strom (Sperm) Thurmond—potent South Carolina politician—father at 73

Sperrins Sperrin Mountains of Northern Ireland

Sperry Sperry Rand Corporation

SPERT simplified program evaluation and review task (technique)

S Pete St Petersburg

Spett *Spettabile* (Italian—Dear Sir)

Spett ditta *Spettabile ditta* (Italian—Messrs)

Spezia La Spezia naval station near Genoa in northern Italy

spf sun-protection factor

SPF Science Policy Foundation; Society for the Propagation of the Faith; South Pacific Forum

spf/db superplastic forming/diffusion bonding

sp fl spinal fluid

spg specific gravity; sponge; spring; sprung

spg (SPG) sex-hormone-binding globulin

Spg Spring (postal abbreviation)

SPG Society for the Propagation of the Gospel

SPGA Scottish Professional Golfers' Association

SPGB Socialist Party of Great Britain

Spgfld Springfield

spgg solid-propellant gas generator

sp gr specific gravity

Spgs Springs (postal abbreviation)

SPGS Spare Guidance System

sph sphenoidal

SPH Special Psychiatric Hospital

sphd special pay for hostile duty

sp hdlg special handling

SPHE Society of Packaging and Handling Engineers

SP & HE Society of Packaging & Handling Engineers

sphen sphenodon (tuatara lizard); sphenoid; sphenoidal

spher spherical; spheroid

Sphinx of Concord Ralph Waldo Emerson

sp—hl sun present—horizon lost

SPHS Seward Park High School; Swedish Pioneer Historical Society

sp ht specific heat

spi scientific performance index; ships plan index; solid propellant information; specific polarization index

spi (SPI) serum precipitable iodine

SPI Sisters of Perpetual Indulgence; Society of Photographic Illustrators; Society of the Plastics Industry; Society of Professional Investigators;

Southern Police Institute; Spanish Paprika Institute; Strategic Planning Institute; Superintendent of Public Instruction

SPI Secrétariats Professionnels Internationaux (International Professional Secretariats); *Service Pédagogique Interafricain* (Inter-African Teaching Service)

SPIA South Pacific Island Airways

SPIB Society of Power Industry Biologists

spic ship position-interpolation computer

SPIC Society of the Plastics Industry of Canada; Society for the Promotion of Identity on Campus

Spica Swedish-built patrol boat carrying a 57mm gun and six torpedo tubes

spicbm (SPICBM) solid-propellant intercontinental ballistic missile

SPICE Scientific Personal Interactive Computing Environment; Spacelab Payload Integration and Coordination in Europe

Spice Island Grenada (noted for its nutmeg as well as its cloves and mace)

Spice Islands Indonesia's spice growing islands such as the Moluccas; West Indian islands of Grenada and the Windwards where spices are cultivated

spid submerged portable inflatable dwelling

spidac specimen input to digital automatic computer

Spider of Florence Machiavelli

spids sensor personnel intrusion devices

spie self-programmed individualized education

SPIE Society of Photographic Instrumentation Engineers

Spike Jones Lindley Armstrong

SPIL Society for the Promotion and Improvement of Libraries

SPIN Searchable Physics Information Notes; Searchable Physics Information Notices; Submarine Program Information Notebook

Spinach Capital of the World Crystal City, Texas (replete with a statue of Popeye)

sp. indet. species indeterminata (Latin—species indetermi-

nate)

spindex selective permutation index(ing)

SPIndex Subject Profile Index (ABC-Clio's innovative new indexing system)

Spindle City Lowell, Massachusetts

Spindrift Ernest Toone

spinel magnesium aluminum oxide

Spine of South Africa Drakensberg Mountains

sp. inquir. species inquirendae (Latin—species of doubtful status)

spins. special inquiries (FBI)

SPINSTRES Spencer Information Storage and Retrieval System

spintcomm special intelligence communication(s)

spip special position identification pulse

s'pipe standpipe

spir spiral

spir. spiritus (Latin—spirits)

Spirals Spiral Tunnels of the Canadian Pacific in Yoho National Park

spire. space inertial reference equipment

SPIRES Standard Personnel Information Retrieval System

SPIRGs Student Public Interest Groups

Spirid Spiridione

splrit. sales processing interactive real-time inventory technic

spirit spiritoso (Italian—spirited)

Spirit Spiritualism

Spirit Beethoven's *Spirit Trio* called *Das Geister Trio* by the Germans

Spirit of Man Prokofiev's name for his Symphony No. 5 Opus 100 completed in 1944

spirits of hartshorn ammonia water (NH_4OH)

spirits of salts hydrochloric acid

Spiritual Father of the French Revolution Rousseau

spirt solar-powered isolated radio transceiver

spis service packaging instruction sheet

spis spissus (Latin—dried)

spit. selective printing of items from tape

Spit Spithead Channel joining The Solent and Southampton Water between the Isle of Wight and Portsmouth

spital (Early English contraction —hospital)

Spits Spitalsfields, England; Spitsbergen Islands in the Norwegian Arctic

Spitsbergen English place-name for Svalbard or the Spitsbergen Islands in the Norwegian Arctic

spiu ship position-interpolation unit

spiw special-purpose infantry weapon

SPJ Society of Professional Journalists (Sigma Delta Chi)

SPJC Saint Petersburg Junior College

spk speckled

Spk Spokane

Sp^pk Seapeak

SPK Staatsbibliothek Prevssicher Kulturbesitz (German-Prussian Culture Treasure State Library)—Berlin's largest on Potsdamer Strasse

spklr(s) sprinkler(s)

spkr speaker

spl simplex; sound pressure level; special; spelling

s.p.l. sine prole legitima (Latin —without legitimate offspring)

Spl Sevastopol

SPL Sacramento Public Library; Saskatoon Public Library; Scan Pacific Line; Seattle Public Library; Space Program ming Language; Spokane Public Library; Springfield Public Library; Syracuse Public Library

splad (SPLAD) self propelled light air-defense gun

SPLAN School Organization Budget-Planning System

SPLASH Special Program to List Amplitudes of Surges for Hurricanes

SPLC Southern Poverty Law Center; Standard Point Location Code

splcf sustained-peak low-cycle fatigue

Splendid Sprinter Ted Williams

splf simplification

Split (Yugolslavian—Spalato)— also written Spljet

SPLIT Sundstrand Processing Languages Internally Translated

SPLMPR State Public Library of the Mongolian People's Republic (Ulan-Bator)

splsm single-position letter-sorting machine

spm self-propelled mount(ing); sequential processing machine; set program mask; single-point mooring; source program maintenance; strokes per minute

s.p.m. sine prole mascula (Latin—without male issue)

SPM Saint-Pierre et Miquelon

SPM Scuola Professionale Marittima (Italian—Professional Maritime School)

SPMA Sewage Plant Manufacturers' Association

Sp Mor Spanish Morocco

SPMRL Sulfite Pulp Manufacturers' Research League

SPMS System Program Management Surveys

SPMU Society of Professional Musicians in Ulster

spn sponsor; spoon

sp. n. species nova (Latin—new species)

Spn Spain; Spaniard; Spanish

SPN Saipan, Trust Territory of the Pacific (airport); Satellite Program Network; Separation Program Number; Student Practical Nurse

SPNB Security Pacific National Bank

SPNB&S Solitary, Poor, Nasty, Brutish & Short (legal counsel of *The American Spectator*)

SPNI Society for the Protection of Nature in Israel

SPNM Society for the Promotion of New Music

sp. nov. species novum (Latin—new species)

SPNR Society for the Promotion of Nature Reserves

Spn Riv Spoon River in central Illinois where the poetic monologues of 244 of its former inhabitants, imagined and real, are dramatized by Edgar Lee Masters in his *Spoon River Anthology*

SPNS Standard Product Numbering System

SPNWR Salt Plains National Wildlife Refuge (Oklahoma)

spo sausages, potatoes, and onions

S Po São Paulo

SPO Sea Post Office; Site Program Office(r); Special Project(s) Office; Staff Planning Office(r); System Program Office(r)

SPO Socialistische Partei Osterreichs (German—Austrian Socialist Party)

spoc single-point orbit calcula-

tor

SPOE Society of Post Office Engineers

SPOIE Society of Photo-Optical Instrumentation Engineers

Spoke Spokane, Washington

spoke(s). spokesperson(s)

Spokesman for the Negro Booker T Washington

Spokesman for the Oppressed George Meany

Sponge City Tarpon Springs, Florida

spont spontaneous

SPOOK Supervisory Program Over Other Kinds

spool. simultaneous peripheral operation on-line

Spoon River Edgar Lee Master's poetic appelation for Lewistown, Illinois where he grew up

Spoon River Spoon River Anthology by Edgar Lee Masters who in blank-verse epitaphs depicted some 212 small-town characters living in central Illinois in towns such as Lewistown on the Spoon River and Petersburg on the Sangamon

Spoon River Poet Edgar Lee Masters

spoorw spoorwegen (Dutch—railway car)

S por A Sociedad por Acciones (Spanish—limited liability company)

Sporades Sporades Islands

Spore Singapore

spork spoon + fork (combination utensil)

spork(s) spoon-shaped fork(s)

sport. sporting; sportsman; sportsmanship; sportswoman

Sport of Kings (horseracing—a ruinous sport only kings can afford)

sportscast(er) sports broadcast(er)

Sports Town, U.S.A. San Diego, California

spot. spotlight

spots spotlights

spp species; surplus personal property

spp. species (Latin—two or more species) singular is *sp.*

SPP Southern Pacific Properties; System Package Program

SPPA Society for the Preservation of Poultry Antiquities

SPPL St Paul Public Library; St Petersburg Public Library

sppo scheduled program printout

spps stable plasma protein solu-

tion (SPPS)

Sp Pt Sparrows Point

spqr small profits and quick returns

S.P.Q.R. Senatus Populusque Romanus (Latin—the Senate and People of Rome)

spr solid-propellant rocket (SPR); spring

spr (SPR) strategic petroleum reserve

Spr Spring; Springfield; Spruce

SPR Simplified Practice Recommendation(s); Society for Pediatric Research; Society for Psychical Research; solid-propellant rocket; Special Project Report; Supplementary Progress Report

sprat. small portable radar torch

SPRC Society for the Prevention and Relief of Cancer

SPRD Science Policy Research Division (Library of Congress)

sprdng spreading

SPRDO Service Parts Repairable Disposition Order

spre siempre (Spanish—always)

SPRE Society of Park and Recreation Educators

spread. spring evaluation analysis and design

Spree River City Berlin

SPRI Scott Polar Research Institute

Spring Beethoven's Sonata No. 5 for Violin and Piano (opus 24); Schumann's Symphony No. 1 in B-flat major

Spring Bank Spring Bank Holiday (last Monday in May in Great Britain)

Springfield capital of Illinois and important city in Massachusetts, Missouri, and Ohio

Springs The Springs (Palm Springs, California's place-name nickname)

sprint (SPRINT) solid-propellant rocket-intercept missile

SPRITE Sequential Polling and Review of Interacting Teams of Experts

sprklg sparkling; sprinkling

SPRL Société de Personnes à Responsibilité Limitée (French—limited company)

spr's small parcels and rolls

Sprs Springs

SPRs Strategic Petroleum Reserves

SPRS Sate Police Radio System (South Dakota)

Spruce Goose nickname of

Howard Hughes's Hercules H-4 319-foot-wingspan flying boat powered by 8 wing-mounted engines

sps ship program schedule; student-paced statistics; super proton synchrotron (for smashing atoms)

sps (SPS) service propulsion system

s.p.s. sine prole supersite (Latin —without surviving issue)

SpS Special Services

SPs Shore Patrol vans

SPS Society of Pelvic Surgeons; Society of Plastic Surgeons; Society of Saint Patrick; Southwestern Public Service; Spokane, Portland & Seattle (railroad); Standard Pressed Steel; Steam Power Systems; String Process System; Submerged Production System; Symbolic Programming System; System of Procedure Specifications

SP & S Spokane, Portland & Seattle (railroad)

SPSA Senate Press Secretaries Association

SPSC Scottish Prison Service College

SPSE Society of Photographic Scientists and Engineers

SPSHS Stanford Profile Scales of Hypnotic Susceptibility

SPSI Senate Permanent Subcommittee on Investigations

SPSL Society for the Protection of Science and Learning

SPSO Senior Principal Scientific Officer

SPSS Statistical Package for the Social Sciences

spst single-pole single-throw (switch)

SPST Symonds Picture-Story Test

spstnc single-pole single-throw normally closed (switch)

spstno single-pole single-throw normally open (switch)

spstsw single-pole single-throw switch

spt seaport; soldered piezoelectric transducer; strength-probability-time; support

spt. spiritus (Latin—alcohol; spirits)

Spt Split (Yugoslavia)

sptc specified period of time contract

sptg sporting

sptl (SPTL) superconducting power transmission line

SptL support line

SPTL Society of Public Teachers of Law

sptr spectrum

sptt single-pole triple-throw (switch)

spu swimmer propulsion unit

SPUC Society for the Protection of Unborn Children

spud speech perception under distraction/distortion

spud. solar power unit demonstrator

SPUD St Paul Union Depot

SPUK Special Projects—United Kingdom

SPUR Space Power Unit Reactor

SPURT Short Public Responsibility Theory

spurv self-propelled underwater research vehicle

sputnik iskustvennyi sputnik zemli (Russian—artificial fellow-traveler around the earth, Soviet satellite launched October 4, 1957)

SPV Society for the Prevention of Vice (prurient book burners in search of the putrid)

SPVA Self-Propelled Vehicles Association

SPVD Society for the Prevention of Venereal Disease

Sp Vly Spring Valley

SPW Sillonian Plant Watchers; Society for the Protection of Whitey; Society of Protestant Wardens

SpWAfr Spanish West Africa

SPWLA Society of Professional Well Log Analysts

spx simplex(ed); stepped piston crossover

spx circuit simplex circuit (data processing)

Spz Spezia

sq squadron; square; stereo-quadraphonic; superquick

sq. sequens, sequentia (Latin—what follows; result; sequel)

Sq Square

SQ stereo-quadraphonic (discs and recordings)

SQ Secondo Quantità (Italian—according to the quantity consumed)—menu abbreviation

sq3r survey, question, read, review, recite (psychological sequence)

sqa stereo-quadraphonic amplifier

sqc self-quenching control; statistical quality control

sq cell ca squamous cell carcinoma

sq cm square centimeter(s)

SQCP Statistical Quality Control Procedure

sqd squad

sqdc special quick-disconnect coupling

Sqdn Ldr Squadron Leader

sq ft square foot (feet)

sq hd square head

sq in. square inch (inches)

sq km square kilometer

sq m square meter; square mile

SQMS Staff Quartermaster Sergeant

sqn squadron

Sqn Ldr Squadron Leader

SqNP Sequoia National Park

Sq O Squadron Office(r)

SQP San Quentin Prison (California)

sqr square; square root; supplier quality rating

SQR Site Qualification Report

sq rd square rod

sq rt square root

sq's stereo-quadraphonic recordings; stereo-quadraphonic records

SQS Stochastic Queuing System; Supplier Quality Services

Sqs SM Squadron Sergeant-Major

sqt square rooter

SQT Ship Qualification Test (USN)

squa squamoid; squamous

squak squall and squeal

square symbol of four corners of the earth; four points of the compass; male symbol; quadrature; symbol of rigid uprightness as in, "Always honest, always fair, doing business on the square", slang term for someone with unsophisticated tastes, "a square"

Square Deal nickname for economic and political philosophy of Theodore Roosevelt

Square Mile of Vice London's Soho and East End

Squaresville area, city, or neighborhood inhabited mainly by square-type citizens who frown on all types of criminal activity and even cooperate with the police

s quark strange quark

squarson squire + parson

squidsan squid-cutlet sandwich

squidwich squid-cutlet sandwich

SQUIRE System for Quick Ultra-fiche-based Information Retrieval

Squire of Hyde Park Franklin D Roosevelt

Squire of Monticello Thomas Jefferson

Squire of Warm Springs Franklin D Roosevelt

'squitoes mosquitoes

sq yd square yard

sr scientific research; sedimentation rate; selective ringing, sensitization response; separate rations; sex ratio; shipment request; short range; sigma reaction; single-reduction (geared turbine); sinus rhythm; slow release; sound ranging; spares requirement; split ring; *srovnej* (Czech—compare); standard range (aviation landing); steradian; stimulus response

sr (SR) saturable reactor; surveillance radar

s/r (S/R) safety representative

Sr Saudi Arabia; Saudi Arabian; Senior; strontium

Sr Señor (Spanish-mister, sir); *Sredniy* (Russian—mid; middle)

Sr Sønder (Danish—southern); *Söndre* (Swedish—southern)

SR saturable reactor; Savannah River (Operations Office); Scientific Report; Scottish Rifles; Seaman Recruit; seaplane reconnaissance (naval aircraft); Section Report; Senate Resolution; Senior Registrar; Service Record; Service Report; Shipping Receipt; Simulation Report; Society of Radiologists; Society of Rheology; Sons of the Revolution; Sound Report; Southern Railway; Special Regulation(s); Special Report; Specification Requirement(s); Staff Report; Standardization Report; Star Route (rural postal delivery); Statsjanstemannens Riksforbund (National Association of Salaried Government Employees, Sweden); Status Report; Study Requirement; Summary Report; Supporting Research; surveillance radar; Sveriges Radio (Swedish radio broadcast network); Swissair

S-R Saunders-Roe; stimulus-response

SR Saudi Arabian riyal (currency unit)

SR-71 Lockheed Blackbird jet reconnaissance aircraft

Sr85 radioactive strontium

sra sulforicinocleic acid

sra (Sra) sierra

Sra Señora (Spanish—Missus; Mistress)

SRA Science Research Associates; Screw Research Association; Society of Residential Appraisers; Special Refractories Association; Spelling Reform Association; Station Representatives Association

SRAA Senior Army Advisor

SRAB Sveriges Radio AB (Swedish Broadcasting Corporation)

srac short-run average-cost curve

srac (SRAC) short-run average cost

SRAC Social Research Applications Corporation

Sra Dna Señora Doña (Spanish —Lady Madam)

s'raight straight

sram (SRAM) short-range attack missile

sran short-range aids to navigation

Sranangtong Sranangtongo (sometimes called Negro English but really a Surinam dialect spoken by former slaves and formerly called Jewtongo) —see Jewtong

Sras Señoras (Spanish—ladies)

SRAs Senior Resident Agents

srats (SRATS) solar radiation and thermospheric structure (satellite)

srb selective reenlistment bonus

srb (SRB) short-range booster

srbc sheep red-blood cell

SRBC Susquehanna River Basin Compact

Srb-Crt Serbo-Croat (Yugoslavian)

Srbija (Serbian—Serbia)

srbm (SRMB) short-range ballistic missile

srbp synthetic resin-bonded paper

src sample return container; solvent-refined coal

SRC Science Research Council; Signal Reserve Corps; Southern Regional Council; Southwest Research Corporation; Space Research Corporation; Standard Requirements Code; Strict Regime Camp (for Soviet prisoners remanded to imprisonment centers in the Urals and other far-flung places of the USSR once called the worker's paradise); Sul Ross State College; Swiss Red

Cross

SRC Santa Romana Chiesa (Italian—Holy Roman Church)

srcc strikes, riots, and civil commotions

SRCD Society for Research in Child Development

s-r cells sensitization-response cells

srch search (computer)

srcr sonar control room

SRCs Strict-Regime Camps (any of many Soviet imprisonment centers in the Urals and other far-flung places)

SRCS Special Reverse Charge Service

srd single radial diffusion

Sr D Señor Don (Spanish—Sir Mister)

SRD Secret Restricted Data; State Registered Dietician; Systems Requirements Definition

SRD Standard Rate and Data

SRDA Scottish Retail Drapers Association

SRDC Standard Reference Data Center

SRDE Signals Research and Development Establishment

Sr Dr Señor Doctor (Spanish—Mister Doctor)

SRDS Standard Reference Data Service

SRDT Single Radial Diffusion Test

sre single-round effectiveness; single-round effectivity

Sre Sreda (Russian—Wednesday)

SRE Society of Reproduction Engineers

S.R.E. Sancta Romana Ecclesia (Latin—Holy Roman Church)

SR EB Southern Regional Education Board

Sr Ed Senior Editor

SRED Scientific Research and Experiments Department

SREEC Southern Regional Environmental Education Council

srem sleep with rapid eye movements

Sres Señores (Spanish—Messrs)

srev slow reverse

srf self-resonant frequency; semi-reinforced furnace; solar radiation flux; stable radio frequency; submarine range finder; supported ring frame; system recovery factor

SRF Self-Realization Foundation; Ship Repair Facility (USN)

srf black semireinforcing furnace black

srg sound ranging

SRG System Review Group

SRGM Solomon R Guggenheim Museum

srh single radial hemolysis

SRHE Society for Research into Higher Education

SRHL Southwestern Radiological Health Laboratory

Sr HS Senior High School

sri servo repeater indicator; silicone rubber insulation; spectrum resolver integrator; surface roughness indicator

Sri Sri Lanka (Ceylon); Srinagar, India

SRI Scientific Research Institute; Southern Research Institute; Southwestern Research Institute; Space Research Institute; Stanford Research Institute

SRI Sacro Romano Impero (Italian—Holy Roman Empire)

Sria Secretaria (Spanish—secretariat)

srif somatotropin release-inhibiting factor

Sri Lan Sri Lanka (Singhalese—Resplendent Land)—Ceylon

Sri Lanka Republic of Sri Lanka (Asian island off India's southern tip; English, Sinhala, and Tamil are spoken; in Sinhala *Sri Lanka* means Ceylon; farming tropical crops, fishing, and mining sustain a people beset by ultra-leftist terrorists and deadly overpopulation)

Sri Lankan Ports Colombo, Galle, Trincomalee

Sri Lanka's Principal Port Colombo

SRILTA Stanford Research Institute Lead Time Analysis

srim selected research in microfiche

Srio Secretario (Spanish—Secretary)

SRIS Safety Research Information Service; School Research Information Service

srj self-restraint joint; static round jet

SRJC Santa Rosa Junior College

srl (SRL) systems reference library

Srl Sorel

SRL Savannah River Laboratory; Save-the-Redwoods League; Science Reference Library (Chancery Lane, London); Scientific Research Laboratory; Study Reference List

SRL Saturday Review of Literature; sociedad de responsabilidad limitada (Spanish—limited liability company)

Srls Saudi Arabian riyal(s)

srm speed of relative movement; spontaneous rupture of membrane; survey radiation monitor

srm (SRM) short-range missile

SRM Society for Range Management; Standard Reference Material

SRM Su Real Majestad (Spanish—Your Royal Majesty)

SRME Society for Research in Music Education

Sr M Sgt Senior Master Sergeant

SRMU Space Research Management Unit

SRN State Registered Nurse; Student Registered Nurse

SRN-6 British Hovercraft hovercraft designation

srna (SRNA) soluble ribonucleic acid

sRNA soluble or transfer RNA (same as tRNA)

SRNA Shipbuilders and Repairers National Association

SR NC Severn River Naval Command

SRNP Stirling Range National Park (Western Australia)

sro sex-ratio organism

SRO Savannah River Operations Office(r); standing room only; Superintendent of Range Operations

srob short-range omnidirectional beacon

s rod stove rod

sro's single-room-occupancy hotels

SROTC Senior Reserve Officers Training Corps

srp supply refuelling point

SRP Saturday Review Press; Savannah River Plant; Scientific Research Proposal; Stratospheric Research Program

s-r psychology stimulus-response psychology

srr survival, recovery, and reconstitution

srr (SRR) skin resistance response

SRR Site Recommendation Report; Supplementary Reserve

Regulations

SRRA Scottish Radio Retailers' Association

SRRC Sperry Rand Research Center

srrcs surface raid reporting control ship

Srrnto Sorrento

SRRS Social Readjustment Rating Scale

SRRT Social Responsibilities Round Table

srs slow reacting substance

srs (SRS) short-run supply

SRs Socialist Revolutionaries (moderates in czarist Russia)

SRS Scoliosis Research Society; Seat Reservation System; Sight Restoration Society; Social and Rehabilitation Service; Special Revenue Sharing; Sperry Rail Service; Sperry Rand Service; Statistical Reporting Service; Structural Research Series; Structural Research Service

S.R.S. Societatis Regiae Sodalis (Latin—Fellow of the Royal Society)

SRSA Scientific Research Society of America

SRSC Sul Ross State College

SRSM Serenissima Repubblica di San Marino (Italian—Most Serene Republic of San Marino)—official name of San Marino

SRSNY Sons of the Revolution in the State of New York

S-R strain Schmidt-Ruppin (viral) strain

srt speech reception threshold

SRT Short-Range Transport (aircraft); Social Relations Test(ing); Speech Reception Test(ing); Strategic Rocket Troops; Stroke Rehabilitation Technician; System Reliability Test(ing)

SRT Standard Radio och Telephon (Swedish—Standard Radio and Telephone)

Srta Señorita (Spanish—Miss)

SRTC Salford Royal Technical College

SRTN Solar Radio Telescope Network

Srto Señorito (Spanish—master; young gentleman)

SRTOS Special Real-Time Operating System

SRTS Science Research Temperament Scale

sru servo(mechanism) repeat unit; shop-replaceable unit

SRU Scottish Rugby Union

SRUBLUK Society for the Reinvigoration of Unremunerative Branch Lines in the United Kingdom

srv (SRV) submarine research vehicle

SRV Socialist Republic of Vietnam

srvlv servovalve

SRW Sherwin-Williams Company of Canada (stock exchange symbol); State Reformatory for Women

SRY Sherwood Rangers Yeomanry

SR y C Santiago Ramón y Cajal

ss saline soak; sample size; semisteel; setscrew; single signal; single source; single strength; single-seated; sole source; sparingly soluble; spin-stabilized; stainless steel; sterile solution; straight shank; superspeed; sword stick; sworn statement

ss (SS) suspended sentence

ss (s/s)(SS)(S/S) steamship

s-s. solid-state

s/s same size; steamship; suspended sentence

s & s signs and symptoms

s of s source of sex (also appears as sos)

s to s ship-to-shore; station-to-station

ss siglos (Spanish—centuries)

ss. scilicet (Latin—namely); semis (Latin—one-half); supra scriptum (Latin—written above; ss. usually printed to left of signature line in sworn statements)

s.s. sensu stricto (Latin—in the strict sense)

sS siehe Seite (German—see page)

s/S sur Seine (French—on the Seine)

Ss students; subjects

SS diesel-powered attack submarine (naval symbol); Science Service; Secret Service; Secretary for Scotland; Secretary of State; Selective Service; Sharpshooter; Ship Service; Ship's Stores; Silver Star; Social Security; Special Service; Special Staff; Specification(s) for Structure; Standard Score; steamship; Straits Settlements; Submarine Studies; Sunday School; supersonic; Support Services; Support System; Surveillance Station; sworn statement

S-S Sans-Serif

S & S Simon & Schuster; Steen & Strom

S of S Society of Separationists

SS Saints; Schutzstaffel (German—Nazi blackshirt elite corps); Statens Skipstilsyn (Danish—State Shipping Inspection)

SS. Sanctissimus (Latin—most holy)

SS-4 Soviet medium-range ballistic missile called Sandal by NATO

SS-5 Soviet intermediate-range ballistic missile called Skean by NATO

SS-6 Soviet intercontinental ballistic missile nicknamed Sapwood by NATO

SS-7 Soviet intercontinental ballistic missile called Saddler by NATO

SS-8 Soviet two-stage intercontinental ballistic missile named Sasin by NATO

SS-9 Soviet intercontinental ballistic missile called Scarp by NATO and capable of releasing warheads below early-warning radar range

SS-10 Soviet three-stage intercontinental ballistic missile named Scrag by NATO

SS-11 Nord antitank missile built in France where its air-launched version is called AS-11; Soviet liquid-fuel intercontinental ballistic missile; U.S. antitank missile called AGM-22A

SS-12 Nord antitank missile with greater range than the SS-11

SS-13 Soviet three-stage intercontinental ballistic missile code-named Savage by NATO

SS-14 Soviet two-stage intercontinental ballistic missile code-named Scapegoat by NATO

SS-18 Soviet Union's most advanced icbm in 1979

SS-20 intermediate-range nuclear missile developed by the USSR

SS-21 tactical nuclear missile developed by the USSR

ssa smoke-suppressant additive; solid-state amplifier

ssa (SSA) skin-sensitizing antibodies

SSA Scottish Schoolmasters' Association; Secretary of State for Air; Seismological Society of America; Semiotic Society

of America; Smallest Space Analysis; Soaring Society of America; Social Security Administration; Society of Scottish Artists; Society for the Study of Addiction (to alcohol and other dangerous drugs); Southern Surgical Association; Subscriber Savings Account

SSAC Soldier's, Sailor's, and Airmen's Club

SSAFA Soldiers', Sailors', and Airmen's Families Association

SS agar Shigella and Salmonella agar

SSAGO Student Scout and Guide Organisation

SSAP Statement of Standard Accounting Practice(s)

ss ar spotface arbor

SSAR Society for the Study of Amphibians and Reptiles

SSARR Streamflow Synthesis and Research Regulation; Streamflow Synthesis and Reservoir Regulation

SSAS Special Signal Analysis System; Static Stability Augmentation System

SSASA Social Services Association of South Africa

SSAT Secondary School Admission Test(s)

SSATB Secondary School Admission Test Board

ssb single side band; subseabed

S Sb San Sebastian

SSB fleet ballistic missile submarine (3-letter naval symbol); Security Screening Board; Selective Service Board; Society for the Study of Blood; Source Selection Board; Space Science Board; Subseabed (project)

S-S B Sino-Soviet Bloc

SSBN nuclear-powered fleet ballistic missile submarine (4-letter naval symbol)

SSBS S-2 French intermediate-range ballistic missile launched from an underground silo

ssc safe-shielded cask; sealed storage cask; shape-selective cracking

ssc (SSC) station-selection code (data processing)

s & sc sized and supercalendered

SSC Sacramento State College; Sarawak Shipping Company; Sculptors' Society of Canada; Ships Systems Command (formerly Bureau of Ships); Sidney Sussex College (Cambridge); Straits Steamship Company; Supply Systems Command (formerly Bureau of Supplies and Accounts)

S.S.C. Societas Sanctae Crucis (Latin—Society of the Holy Cross)

SSCA Southern Speech Communication Association; Southern States Correctional Association

sscc spin-scan cloud camera

SSCC Space Surveillance Control Center

S.Sc.D. Doctor of Social Science

SSCDS Small Ship Combat Data System

SSCI Steel Service Center Institute

SSCI Social Sciences Citation Index

SSCNS Ship's Self-Contained Navigation System

SSCQT Selective Service College Qualification Test

ss cr stainless-steel crown

sscrn silkscreen

sscrng silkscreening

sscs strain-sensitive cable sensor

SSCS Shipboard Satellite Communications System

ssd source skin distance

ssd (SSD) sentence-structure determination

SSD Science Services Department; Scientific Services Department; Space Systems Division (USAF); System for System Development

SSD Staatssicherheitsdienst (German—State Security Service) East German political police

SS.D. Sanctissimus Dominus (Latin—Most Holy Lord)— the Pope

S.S.D. Sacrae Scripturae Doctor (Latin—Doctor of Sacred Scripture)

SSDA Self-Service Development Association

SSDC Social Science Documentation Center (UNESCO)

SSDHPER Society of State Directors of Health, Physical Education, and Recreation

SSDL Society for the Study of Dictionaries and Lexicography

ssdr subsystem development requirement

SSDS Ship Structural Design System

sse safe-shutdown earthquake; signal security element; surface support equipment; switching single element

SSE Scale of Socio-Egocentrism; south southeast; Support System Evaluation

S.S.E. Society of Saint Edmund

SSEB South of Scotland Electricity Board

ssec selective-sequence electronic calculator

SSEC Secondary School Examination Council; Social Science Education Consortium; Solar System Exploration Committee

SSEES School of Slavonic and East European Studies

ssef solid-state electro-optic(al) filter

SSEL Space Science and Engineering Laboratory

ss enema soap suds enema

SSET Steady-State Emission Test(ing)

ssf saybolt seconds furol; single-seated fighter; standard saybolt furol (viscosity)

SSF Service Storage Facility; Seven-Step Foundation; Ship's Service Force; Social Science Foundation (University of Denver); Society of Saint Francis; Special Service Force

SSFA Scottish Schools' Football Association; Scottish Steel Founders' Association

SSFC Severe Storms Forecast Center (Kansas City, Missouri)

SSFF Solid Smokeless Fuels Federation

ss fx spotface fixture

ssg second stage graphitization

SSG guided missile submarine (3-letter naval symbol)

SSGN nuclear-powered guided-missile submarine (4-letter naval symbol)

SSgt Staff Sergeant

ssgw (SSGW) surface-to-surface guided weapon

SSH Sailor's Snug Harbor

S Sh A Soyedinennye Shtaty Ameriki (Russian—United States of America)

SSHA Scottish Special Housing Association

SSHRC Social Sciences and Humanities Research Council (Canadian)

ssi sites of scientific importance; small-scale integration

Ssi Surekasi (Turkish—company)

SSI Saint Simon's Island; Social Security Income; Society of Scribes and Illuminators; Supplemental Security Income

SSI Service Social International (French—International Social Service); *Social Sciences Index*

SSIB Seaway Skyway International Bridge

ssic small-scale integrated circuit

SSIC Southern States Industrial Council; Standard Subject Identification Code

SSIDC Small-Scale Industries Development Corporation (Indian)

SSIE Smithsonian Science Information Exchange

SSIG State Student Incentive Grant(s)

SSIH Société Suisse pour l'Industrie Horlogère (French— Swiss Society of the Horological Industry)

SSI/ITL SSI Container Corp/ ITEL

ssip system setup indicator panel

SSIS Squibb Science Information System

SSISI Statistical and Social Inquiry Society of Ireland

SSI/SSP Social Security Income/State Supplemental Program

ssit (SSIT) semi-submarine icebreaking tanker

ssk set storage key; soil stack; solid-state keyboard

ssl spent sulfite liquor

SSL Saguenay Shipping Limited; Sapphire Steamship Lines; Seven Stars Line; Space Science Laboratory (Convair); Space Sciences Laboratory (GE)

S.S.L. Sacrae Scripturae Licentiatus (Latin—Licentiate of Sacred Scripture)

s sleep synchronized sleep

S-sleep slow-wave sleep

SS loran sky-wave synchronized loran

SSLS Solid-State Laser System

ss lt starboard side light

sslv (SSLV) standard space-launched vehicle

ssm set system mask; solid-state material(s); spread spectrum modulation

ssm (SSM) surface-to-surface missile

SSM Saturday(s), Sunday(s), Monday(s); Singer Sewing Machine; System Support Management; System Support Manager

ssma solid-state microwave amplifier

SSMA School Science and Mathematics Association; Stainless Steel Manufacturers' Association

ssmm space station mathematical model

SS MM *Sus Majestades* (Spanish—Their Majesties; Your Majesties)

SSMS Submarine Safety Monitoring System

ssmt supersonic magnetic (railroad) train

SSN Space Surveillance Network; Standard Serial Number; Station Serial Number

SS(N) nuclear-powered submarine (3-letter naval symbol)

SSNC Scindia Steam Navigation Company

ssnd solid-state neutral dosimeter

ssnf source spot noise figure

SS^{no} *escribano* (Spanish—court clerk, notary, scribe)

SSNS Standard Study Numbering System

SSO Sacramento Symphony Orchestra; Savannah Symphony Orchestra; Seattle Symphony Orchestra; Shreveport Symphony Orchestra; Source Selection Official; Spokane Symphony Orchestra; Springfield Symphony Orchestra; Sydney Symphony Orchestra; Syracuse Symphony Orchestra; System Staff Office(r)

SSO *Seguro Social Obligatorio* (Spanish—Obligatory Social Security); *sudsudoeste* (Spanish—south southwest)

SSOA Subsurface Ocean Area

SSOFS Smiling Sons of the Friendly Shillelaghs

S of Sol Song of Solomon

s sord *senza sordini* (Italian—without mutes)

SSORM Standard Ship's Organization and Regulations Manual (USN)

ssorts ship's systems operational requirements

ssos (SSOS) severe-storm-observing satellite

SSOs Student Services Organization members

ssp seismic section profiler; ship's stores profit; single-shot probability; standby-status panel; steam service pressure; subspecies; sustained superior performance

S-S p Sanarelli-Schwartzman phenomenon

SSP scouting seaplane (3-letter naval symbol); Seashore State Park (Virginia); Site Selection Report; Society for Scholarly Publishing; Society of St Paul; Source Selection Panel; S.S. Pierce; Sunshine State Parkway

S.S.P. Society of Saint Paul

sspc solid-state power controller

SSPC Steel Structures Painting Council

SSPCA Scottish Society for the Prevention of Cruelty to Animals

sspe subacute sclerosing panencephalitis

sspe (SSPE) subacute sclerosing panencephalitis

SSPFC Stainless Steel Plumbing Fixture Council

SSPHS Society for Spanish and Portuguese Historical Studies

SSPN Satellite System for Precise Navigation

SSPP Society for the Study of Process Philosophies

S-spring S-shaped spring

SSPV Scottish Society for the Prevention of Vivisection

ssq simple sinusoidal quantity

SSQ Station Sick Quarters

SSQT Selective Service Qualification Test

ssr secondary surveillance radar

SSR Site Safety Report; Soviet Socialist Republic(s)

SSR *Sovétskaya Sotsialitsticheskaya Respúblika* (Russian—Soviet Socialist Republic)

SSRA Scottish Squash Rackets Association

SSRB Soil Survey Research Board

SSRC Social Science Research Council

SSRCAS Secondary-Surveillance-Radar Collision-Avoidance System

SSRCC Social Science Research Council of Canada

SSRI Social Science Research Institute

SSRL Systems Simulation Research Laboratory

SSRP Stanford Synchrotron Radiation Project

SSRs Safe Secure Railcars

SSRS Society for Social Responsibility in Science; Submarine-Sand Recovery System

sss single-screw ship; specific soluble substance; sterile saline soak

s/ss sector/subsector

sss (SSS) *su seguro servidor* (Spanish—your sure servant; yours truly)

s.s.s. *stratum super stratum* (Latin—layer upon layer)

SSS Secretary of State for Scotland; Selective Service System; Special Social Services; System Safety Society

S-S-S *Schweiz-Suisse-Svizzera* (Switzerland in the three languages of the country)

S.S.S. *Societas Sanctissimi Sacramenti* (Latin—Congregation of the Most Blessed Sacrament)

SSSA Simplified Spelling Society of America; Soil Science Society of America

S-S SA Singapore-Soviet Shipping Agency

SSSB System Source Selection Board

sssc soft-sized super-calendered (paper)

sss&c sin, syph(ilis), sulfa, and cystoscopes

SSSC Space Science Steering Committee (NASA)

sssd second-stage separation device; solid-state solenoid driver

sssi sites of special scientific importance

SSSI Science Supervisory Style Inventory

SSSJ Student Struggle for Soviet Jewry

SSSL Solid State Sciences Laboratory (USAF)

sssm site space surveillance monitor

sssm (SSSM) standard surface-to-surface missile

SSSM South Street Seaport Museum (New York City)

SSSP Space Shuttle Synthesis Program

SSSR Society for the Scientific Study of Religion; *Soyuz Sovietskikh Sotsialisticheskikh Respublik* (Russian—Union of Soviet Socialist Republics)

SSSR *Soyuz Sovietskikh Sotsialisticheskikh Respublik*

SSSRU School Safety and Security Resource Unit

SSSS Society for the Scientific

Study of the Sea

ssst (not an abbreviation but the symbol for the sound of an aerosol spray)—see *ffft*

SSSU Seaspeed Sea Services Unit

SSSWP Seismology Society of the South-West Pacific

sst safe-secure trailer(s); solid-state triangulation (automatic focusing system); stainless steel; supersonic transport (airplane)

SST Samoan Standard Time; Society of Silver Collectors; Source Selection Team; Space Systems Center (Douglas); Submarine Supply Center; supersonic transport (airplane); target and training submarine (naval symbol)

SSTA Scottish Secondary Teachers' Association; Secondary School Theatre Association; Special Services Transportation Agency

SSTC Specialized System Test Contractor

SSTEP System Support Test Evaluation Program

ssto single-stage to orbit

SSTO Superintending Sea Transport Office(r)

SSTP Student Science Training Program

sst's safe (and) secure trailers used to haul nuclear weapons on American highways

sstu seamless steel tubing

ssu saybolt seconds universal; self-serving unit

ssv **(SSV)** semi-submersible support vessel; ship-to-surface vessel; submarine support vessel

s.s.v. *sub signa veneni* (Latin—under a poison label)

SSV ship-to-surface vessel

S.S. Van Dine Willard Huntington Wright's pen name and one he used in writing detective stories

SSvd Selective Service

SSV/GC & N Space Shuttle Vehicle/Guidance, Control and Navigation

ssvs slow-scan video simulator

ssw safety switch

SSW south southwest; S.S. White

SSWA Scottish Society of Women Artists

SSWS Seismic Sea Wave Warning System

SSX South Coast Corporation (stock exchange symbol)

ssz specified strike zone

ssz **(SSZ)** pocket submarine; specified strike zone

SSZ Society of Systematic Zoology

st sedimentation time; service test; short ton; single tire; single-throw; slight trace; sounding tube; special text; special translation; statement(s); steel; steel truss; stock transfer; stone; strata; surface tension; survival time; syncopated time

s & t science and technology; sink and laundry tray; supply and transport

st. *stet* (Latin—let it stand, usually referring to what has been mistakenly crossed out)

St Saint; Sainte; Stanton number; State; status; Street; strontium

S*t* *Sint* (Afrikaans, Dutch, Flemish—saint); *Staryy* (Russian—old)

ST Seaman Torpedoman; Service Test(ing); Shipping Ticket; Sons of Temperance; Speech Therapist; speech therapy; Standardized Test; Summer Time; Suomen Tsavalta (Finnish—Finland); Syrian Territory

S.T. sidereal time

S & T Supply and Transport

S of T Sons of Temperance

sta static; station; stationary; stationery; stator; submarine tender availability

Sta *Santa* (Italian, Portuguese, Spanish—Saint)—feminine; *Señorita* (Spanish—Miss)

STA Scottish Typographical Association; Society of Typographic Arts; Southern Textile Association; Supersonic Tunnel Association

STAA Survey Test of Algebraic Aptitude

STAAS Surveillance and Target Acquisition Aircraft System

stab. stabilizer

STAB *Svenska Tandsticks Aktiebolaget* Swedish (Match (stick) Company)

Sta'b'd starboard

stabiles static abstract sculptures

stac sensor transmitter automatic choke

stac *staccato* (Italian—separately and with great distinction)

St AC Saint Anne's College; Saint Anthony's College

STAC Science Teacher's Adapt-

able Curriculum; Science and Technology Advisory Committee (NASA)

STACO Society of Telecommunications Administrative and Controlling Officers

STACS Satellite Telemetry and Computer System

stad (Danish, Dutch, Norwegian, Swedish—town, as in Willemstad)

sta eng stationary engineer

stafex staff exercise(s)

STAFF Stellar Acquisition Flight Feasibility (guidance system)

Staffs Staffordshire

staflo stable-flow (free-boundary electrophoresis apparatus)

stag. stagger; staggered

STAG Special Task Air Group; Standards Technical Advisory Group; Strategy and Tactics Analysis Group

Stagecoach Town Fort Worth, Texas

stagfla stagflation (high inflation coupled with high unemployment)

stagflation stagnant (consumer demand) (price-wage) inflation; stagnant economy marked by rising unemployment and spiralling inflation

Stagirite Aristotle the Stagirite —so named as he was born in Stagira, Macedonia

stagmag magazine featuring nude women

Stagville nickname for West Hollywood, California's Santa Monica Boulevard where massage parlors and pornographic shops are so evident

STAI State-Trait Anxiety Inventory

STAIFA St Anselm's International Friendship Association

Stairs Storage and Information Retrieval Systems

Stalag *Stammlager* (German—base camp, for military prisoners)

Stalin (Russian—steel)—Iosif Vissarionovich Dzhugashvili

Stalingrad former name of Tsaritsyn now called Volgograd

stam sequential thermal anhysteric magnetization; stammer(er); stammering

Stambul Istanbul's older quarter

sta mi statute miles

stamp. small tactical aerial-mobility platform

STAMP Systems Tape Addition and Maintenance Program

Stampa *La Stampa* (Turin's Press—one of Italy's leading newspapers)

STAMPS Structural Thermal and Meteorite Protection System

stan stanchion; standard; standing

Stan Standard; Stanford; Stanley; Stanleyville; Stanton

STANAG Standardization Agreement (NATO)

stanal statistical analysis

STANAVFORCHAN Standing Naval Force Channel (NATO)

STANAVFORLANT Standing Naval Force Atlantic (NATO)

St And St Andrews

standard. standardization

Standard Arm General Dynamics anti-radar missile

Standard Oil King John D(avison) Rockefeller, Sr

STANDINAIR Standing Instructions for Air Attachés

stanine score standard-nine score (USAF standard psychological score)

Stanislavski Konstantin Sergeevich Alekseev

Stan Laurel Arthur Stanley Jefferson

Stanley Sir Henry Morton Stanley whose original name was John Rowlands

Stanleyville former name for Kisangani, Zaire

Stan the Man Stan Musial

Stan Psychiat Nomen Standard Psychiatric Nomenclature

Stanton Forbes pseudonym of De Loris Stanton Forbes

Stanton's Elizabeth Cady Stanton's Day (November 12)

STANVAC Standard Vacuum (oil company)

STAO Science Teachers Association of Ontario

STAPFUS Stable Axis Platform Follow-Up System

staph staphylococcus

staq security-traders automatic quotations

star symbol of perfection

star. (STAR) special tactics against robbery (police program)

STAR Selective Training and Retention (program); Serial Titles Automated Record (National Agricultural Library); Ship-Tended Acoustic Relay;

Space Thermionic Auxiliary Reactor; Special Tactics Against Robberies; Special Tactics and Response; submersible test and research (Electric Boat)

STAR *Scientific and Technical Aerospace Reports*

starboard side *righthand* side of an airplane, ship, or other craft when looking forward, symbolized by a fixed *green* light —on the *righthand* wingtip of an airplane or set against a *green* background on the *righthand* side of a ship's bridge or pilothouse

Star City of the South Roanoke, Virginia

Star and Crescent Moslem symbol appearing on arms and flags of Algeria, Libya, Malaysia, Mauritania, Pakistan, Singapore, Tunisia, Turkey

Star of David Judaic symbol consisting of two superimposed equilateral triangles forming a six-pointed star; device also called the Seal of Solomon or the Shield of David

Star of the East Vladivostok

Stare *Miasto* (Polish—Old Town)—Warsaw tourist attraction

Starfighter Lockheed single-engine jet fighter aircraft built in Belgium, Canada, Germany, Italy, and the Netherlands

STARFIRE System to Accumulate or Retrieve Financial Information Random Extract

Star of the Indian Ocean Mauritius

STARLAB Space Technology Applications and Research Laboratory (NASA)

Starlifter C-141 Lockheed cargo and troop transport

Star of the North King Gustavus Adolphus of Sweden; Minnesota

starquake star + earthquake

stars. specialized training and reassignment students; stationary automotive road stimulator (Toyota)

STARs Scientific and Technical Aerospace Reports

STARS Satellite Telemetry Automatic Reduction System

Stars and Bars flag of the Confederate States of America

Star Spangled Banner anthem of the United States of America and nickname of its flag

Stars and Stripes flag of the United States of America

START Space Technology and Reentry Test(s); Space Transport and Reentry Test(s); Spacecraft Technology and Advance Reentry Test; Strategic Arms Reduction Talks (U.S.A.-USSR)

STARTS Safety Technology Applied to Rapid Transit Systems

stas staff-to-arm signal

Stash Stanislas; Stanislaus

STASH Student Association for the Study of Hallucinogens

Stasia Anastasia

stasis *or* ***stat*** *or* ***stato*** (Greek—stand)—colonic stasis, electrostatic, hydrostatic, metastasis, thermostat

stat electrostat; electrostatic; microstat; photostat; static; stationary; statistic(al); statuary; statue; statute

stat. *statim* (Latin—immediately, right now)

Stat Publius Papinius Statius (Roman poet)

state. simplified tactical approach and terminal equipment (STATE)

State of Excitement Western Australia

States in the States, the States, Stateside—all such expressions refer to the United States of America

Statesman's *Statesman's Year Book*

Statesville Statesville Correctional Center (Joliet, Illinois)

State of the Thousand Islands Maldive Islands

Stat Hall Stationers' Hall

Statia Sint Eustatius (Netherlands Antilles)

STATIC Student Taskforce Against Telecommunication Concealment

Stati *Uniti* (Italian—United States)

STATLIB Statistical Computing Library (Bell System)

stat mux statistical multiplexor

Stat Off Her (His) Majesty's Stationery Office

Statoil (Norwegian—State Oil)

Stats statutes

Statsbib *Statsbiblioteket* (Dano-Norwegian—State Library)

STATUS Subscriber Traffic and Telephone Utilization System

St AU University of St. Andrew

STAUK Seed Trade Association

of the United Kingdom
Stav Stavanger, Norway
St A YC St Augustine Yacht Club
Sta Ysbl Santa Ysabel
s-t b steel-truss bridge
St B Státní Bezpečnost (Czech—State Security)—secret police
STB Surinam Tourist Bureau
STB Sandatahang Tanod ng Bayan (Filipino—People's Home Defense Guard)
S.T.B. Sacrae Theologiae Baccalaureus (Latin—Bachelor of Sacred Theology)
stba selective top-to-bottom algorithm
stbd starboard
St Ben St Benet's Hall, Oxford
st brz statuary bronze
stbt steamboat
stc security time control; sensitivity time control; short time constant; sound transmission class; stepchild
STC Satellite Television Corporation; Satellite Test Center; Satellite Tracking Committee; Scandinavian Travel Commission; Short Title Catalog; Society for Technical Communication; Southwestern Technical College; Standard Telephone and Cables; Standard Transmission Code; Sunderland Technical College
S.T.C. Samuel Taylor Coleridge
STC Short Title Catalogue
STCA Stereo Tape Club of America
St Cat St Catherine's College, Oxford
STCCM Sistema de Transporte Colectivo Ciudad de México (Mexico City Collective Transportation System)
Stckhlm Stockholm
st cl storage closet
St C & N Saint Christopher and Nevis (Leeward Islands insular nation formerly British West Indies)—main seaports are Basseterre and Charlestown on St C & N, respectively
STCS Society of Technical Civil Servants
std salinity, temperature, depth; sexually-transmitted disease; skin test dose; standard; standard test dose; state-of-the-technology design; subscriber trunk dialing
St D Stage Director
STD Society for Theological

Discussion; Subscriber Trunk Dialing
S.T.D. *Sacrae Theologiae Doctor* (Latin—Doctor of Sacred Theology)
std by stand by
St DC St David's College
STDC Society of Typographic Designers of Canada
Stde Stunde (German—hour)
stder social introversion, thinking introversion, depression, cycloid tendencies, rhathymia (personality traits)
st diap stopped diapason (organ)
stdn standardization
Std Oil Cal Standard Oil of California
std p stand pipe
stdr steam turbine double reduction
st dr single-trip drum
std's sexually transmitted diseases
STDSD Solar-Terrestrial Data Services Division (NOAA)
Stdy Saturday
St Dymphna's disease insanity
Ste Suite
Ste. Sainte (French—saint, *f.*)
Sté Société (French—Society)
St E St. Etienne
STE Society of Telecommunications Engineers; Society of Tractor Engineers; Support of Theological Education
Steak Center Kansas City, Missouri
steakwich steak sandwich
steamers (slang nickname—steaming clams)
Stebark Polish place-name equivalent of Tannenberg
STECC Scottish Technical Education Consultative Council
Steel Baron Andrew Carnegie
Steel Center of the South Birmingham, Alabama
Steel City Bethlehem, Pennsylvania; Pittsburgh, Pennsylvania; and any other metropolis dedicated to the production of steel and allied products
steelie steel ball-bearing playing marble
Steelmaker Joe Magarac
Steel-Master Philanthropist Andrew Carnegie
Stef (Joseph) Lincoln Steffens; Stefan(i)(e); Vilhjalmur Stefansson (William Stevenson)
STEFER Società della Tranvia e Ferrovia Elettrica di Roma (Rome transportation system)
STEG Supersonic Transport

Evaluation Group
St E H St Elizabeth's Hospital
St EHC Saint Edmund's Hall College (Oxford)
ste/ice simplified test equipment/internal combustion engines
Steiermark (German—Styria)—central and southeastern Austria
Steinbeck Grosssteinbeck (original name of author John Steinbeck's family spelled with three s's as shown)
Steiny Charles Proteus Steinmetz
STEL Studenta Tutmonda Esperantista Liga (Esperanto—Worldwide Esperanto Students League)
Stell Estella; Estelle
Stella Estella; Estelle
Stella Maris (Latin—Seaman's Star)—*see* Polaris
stellar. star tracker for economical-long-life attitude reference
STELO Studenta Tutmonda Esperantista Ligo (World League of Esperanto Students)
stem. storable tubular extendible member
STEM stay time excursion module
sten stencil
Sten (Swedish—cliff); *Stenón* (Greek—pass, strait)
Stendhal (pseudonym—Marie-Henri Beyle)
Sten gun Sheppard and Turpin Bren gun (submachine gun)
steno stenographer; stenography; stenotype; stenotypy
steno (Latin prefix—narrow)—stenosis
stent stentando (Italian—delaying)
Step Stephen
STEP Safety Test Engineering Program; Scientific and Technical Exploitation Program; Secondary Teachers Education Program; Sequential Tests of Educational Progress; Short-Term Elective Program; Solutions to Employment Problems; Systems to Encourage Potential
Steph Stephen
Steppes In the Steppes of Central Asia (symphonic sketch by Borodin)
STEPS Solar Thermionic Electric Power System; Specialized Training and Employment Placement Service

step sister of religion superstition

ster stereoscope; stereotype; sterilization; sterilize; sterilizer; sterling

stereo stereophonic; stereoprojection; stereoprojector; stereoscope; stereoscopic

STERILE System of Terminology for Retrieval of Information through Language Engineering

sterling silver 92% silver, 8% copper

stet let stand what has been crossed out; stetted; stetting (proofreader's direction to let stand whatever is crossed out, taken from the third person singular of the Latin *stare*—to stand)

STETF Solar Total Energy Test Facility (ERDA)

Stetson Stetson hat (broad-brim high-crown hat made by John B Stetson of Philadelphia, Pa)

Stettin (German—Szczecin)

stev stevedore; stevedoring

Steve Stephan; Stephen; Steven

Stew Stewart

Stewart Granger James Stewart

stewbum man sexually attracted to flight stewardesses

stew(s) steward(esses)

STEWS Shipboard Tactical Electronic Warfare System

stewzoo hotel or motel catering to flight attendants resting between flights

St Ex Stock Exchange

stf soluble thymic factor; staff

STF Salt Test Facility; Sycamore Test Facility

STF Svenska Turisforeningen (Swedish Tourist Information)

st fm stretcher form

stg seating; stage; staging; steering; sterling; storage

STG Schiffbautechnische Gesellschaft (German—Shipbuilding Technical Association)

stg ar staging area

stge storage; strings

St George (patron saint of England)

stgg staging

Stgo Santiago

Stgo de C Santiago de Chile (Compostela, Cuba)

stgr stringer

STgt secondary target

STGWU Scottish Transport and General Workers' Union

sth straight to hell (as in the command "go straight to hell")

sth (STH) somatotrophic hormone

Sth Stockholm

St Hel St Helena; St Helens; St Helier

St Hil St Hilda's College, Oxford

Sthlm Stockholm

St Hug St Hugh's College, Oxford

sti service and taxes included; sure to inquire; sure to investigate; surface transfer impedance

sti (STI) scientific and technical information

s & ti scientific and technical information

St I St Ives

STI Service Tools Institute; Space Technology Institute; Steel Tank Institute

STIA Scientific, Technological, and International Affairs Directorate (National Science Foundation)

STIAD Scientific, Technological, and International Affairs Directorate (NSF)

stic serum trypsin inhibitory capacity

STIC Scientific and Technical Intelligence Center

STICAP Stiff Circuit Analysis Program

stick baton's nickname

stiction static friction

STID Scientific and Technical Information Division (NASA)

STIF Scientific and Technical Information Facility (NASA)

stiff. stiffener; stiffened corpse

Stikines Stikine Mountains of British Columbia

stillat. *stillatim* (Latin—by drops, in small amounts)

Stille Ozean (German—Calm Ocean)—the Pacific

stilli stillicide; stillicidium; stilliform

stillson stillson wrench (named for its maker)

stim stimulant

stimn stimulation

STIMS Scientific and Technical Modular System

stinfo scientific and technical information

STING Stellar Inertial Guidance (System)

STINGS Stellar Inertial Guidance System (USAF)

stink. stinkage; stinkerino (cigar, cigarette, or pipe about to die a

lingering death whose smell is offensive to almost everyone but the smoker)

stinkerette(s) stinking cigarette(s)

stinkerino(s) stinking cigar(ette)(s); stinking tobacco product(s)

Stinkstein (German— stinkstone)—coal-black limestone or marble giving off a fetid odor when rubbed because of its bituminous or carbonaceous inclusions; also called anthraconite

stip stipend(iary); stipulation

STIP Science Teaching Improvement Program; Skills Training Improvement Program

STIPIS Scientific, Technical, Intelligence, and Program Information Service (HEW)

Stir Stirling

Stirner Max Stirner whose original name was Kaspar Schmidt

Stirville Sing Sing prison (Ossining, New York)

STIS Scientific and Technological Information Services; Specialized Textile Information Service

STISS Scientific and Technical Information Services and Systems

St J St John (New Brunswick)

STJ Special Trial Judge

STJC South Texas Junior College; Southwest Texas Junior College

St-Jean-des-Puces (French—St John of the Fleas)—placename nickname of the Franco-Spanish border town of St-Jean-de-Luz (St John of Light or St John of the Marshes)

St Joe St Joe Minerals Corporation (energy and metals plus natural gas)

St Joh St John's College (Oxford or elsewhere)

St John New Brunswick (chief port of this province on Bay of Fundy) *not to be confused with* St Johns: Antigua (West Indian island port) *or more particularly with* St John's: Newfoundland (chief port and capital of this island near New Brunswick); *other places named after Saint John*

St-John Perse Alexis Saint-Leger's pen name

St John's evil epilepsy; old nickname for epilepsy

StJU St John's University

stjw stretcher jaws

stk sticky; stock

Stk Stockton

STK Standard Test Key

St Kitts West Indian islands of Anguilla, Nevis, and St Christopher (also often shortened to St Kitts)

St K-N St Kitts officially St Christopher; St Kitts-Nevis (West Indian island nation gained independence in 1983)

St K-N-A St Kitts-Nevis-Anguilla (Caribbean island federation)

stl steel; studio transmitter link

Stl Schottky transistor logic

St L St Louis

STL Seatrain Lines; Space Technology Laboratories (Thompson-Ramo-Wooldridge); Speech Transmission Laboratory; Standard Telecommunication Laboratories; St Louis, Missouri (airport), studio transmitter link (FM); Swedish Transatlantic Line

St Lawrence 1900-mile river serving as natural frontier between some parts of Canada and United States on New York—Ontario border and as main waterway for American and Canadian Great Lakes and river ports linked by this great stream to the Atlantic

St Lawrence Seaway (*see* Saint Lawrence Seaway)

StLe St Louis encephalitis

StLGR Saint Lucia Game Reserve (South Africa)

STLL Submarine Tender Load List

St Lo St Louis

STLO Scientific and Technical Liaison Office(r)

STLOs Scientific/Technical Liaison Offices

STLOUISPDis St Louis Procurement District (US Army)

St L P-D St Louis Post-Dispatch

stlr semi-trailer

ST L SW St Louis Southwestern (railroad)

STLT studio transmitter link-TV

St LU St Lucia; St Louis University

STLU Seatrain Line (container) Unit

St L YC St Louis Yacht Club

St L ZG St Louis Zoological Garden

stm (STM) scientific, technical, and medical; shielded tunable magnatron; short-term memory; special test missile; surface-to-target missile; synthetic timing mode

St M St Malo

STM Science Teaching Museum (Franklin Institute); System Training Mission

S.T.M. *Sacrae Theologiae Magister* (Latin—Master of Sacred Theology)

St Martin's St Martin's Press

St Martin's evil dipsomania

St Mathurin's disease epilepsy

stmev storm evasion

stmftr steamfitter

stmn stimulation

Stmn *The Statesman* (Calcutta)

stmnt statement (flow chart)

STMP Scientific, Technical, and Medical Publishers

stmrs steamers

STMSA Scottish Timber Merchants' and Sawmillers' Association

stmt statement

stn stain

Stn Station

St N St Nazaire

stnd stained

stnry stationary

stnwr stoneware

sto standard temperature and pressure; standing order; stoker; stop; stoppage

Sto *Santo* (Spanish—saint); *Señorito* (Spanish—master; young gentleman)

St° *Santo* (Portuguese or Spanish—Saint)

STO Stockholm, Sweden (Arlanda Airport)

STO *Service Travail Obligatoire* (French—Obligatory Labor Service)—Vichy-instituted law giving the Germans a massive labor force during World War II

Stock Stockholm

Stockholmia (Latin—Stockholm)

Stokowski silver sizzle the sound of the Philadelphia Orchestra (developed by Leopold Stokowski when he conducted it and other great symphonies)

Stoky Leopold Stokowski (conductor-impresario-transcriber who took the backache out of Bach while building the Philadelphia Orchestra and other American symphonic organizations)—originally named Antoni Stanislaw Boleslawo-

wics—later adopted name of Leo Stokes but since early 1900s appeared as Leopold Stokowski (*Sto-kov-ski*)

stol short takeoff and landing

stolport short-takeoff-and-landing airport

stol/ved short takeoff and landing/vertical climb and descent

stom stomach

stoma (Greek—mouth or opening)—cyclostome, protostome, stomatic

stomat stomatology

STOMP Short-Term Offshore-Measurement Program

stomy (Latin suffix—surgical opening)—tracheostomy

S'ton Southampton

STon short ton

Stone Age era of prehistoric mankind when implements and weapons were made from stone—age divided into paleolithic, mesolithic, and neolithic periods

Stonehenge prehistoric monument on Salisbury Plain near Amesbury, England

stoners teenage gangs engaged in throwing stones to destroy property or injure others; people who have taken an overdose of alcohol or other drugs and are said to be stoned

Stonewall General Thomas Jonathan Jackson, CSA

Stonewall Jackson General Thomas Jonathan Jackson of the Confederate Army

Stonys Stony Mountains (early American name for the Rockies and still in use during the administration of John Quincy Adams)

stop. slight touch on pedal; spin tires on pavement

STOP Single Title Order Plan; Strategic Orbit Point

STOPP Society of Teachers Opposed to Physical Punishment

stops. stabilized-terrain optical-position sensor

STOPS Self-contained Tanker Offloading System

stor storage; stored

STOR Scripps Tuna Oceanographic Research

Storbritannia (Dano-Norwegian—Great Britain)

storet storage and retrieval

Storm Norwegian high-speed motor gunboat

Stormalong Arthur Bulltop

Storm King American meteorologist James Pollard Espy

storm mus storm music (most memorable includes the Thunderstorm movement in Beethoven's *Symphony No. 6* —Pastoral, the Royal Hunt and Storm in *Les Troyens* by Berlioz, the Tempesta interlude in Rossini's *Barber of Seville* and the Alpine Storm in his *William Tell,* the Storm sometimes accompanying and often dominating the seduction scene in the *Samson and Delilah* of Saint-Saëns, the Storm movement in the Alpine Symphony of Richard Strauss, the opening incidental music composed by Sir Arthur Sullivan for *The Tempest,* the howling thunder and wind in Act III of Tchaikovsky's *Queen of Spades*)

Stormont Stormont Castle—official Belfast residence of Northern Ireland's prime minister; Northern Ireland's capital district near Belfast where it contains the home and office of the governor general as well as the House of Commons and the Senate of Northern Ireland

Story Teller of the Sea sobriquet shared by Conrad, Cooper, de Hartog, Forester, Innes, London, McFee, Marryat, Masefield, Melville, Nordhoff and Hall, Verne, and your favorite writer of sea stories

stovl short takeoff with vertical landing

stow. stowage

stp service time prediction; solar-terrestrial physics; solar-terrestrial probe; step; stop

stp (STP) seawater treatment plant; solar thermal power; standard temperature and pressure

St P St Paul

St & P São Tome and Principe

STP nickname of dangerous psychedelic drug—methylmethoxyamphetamine; Scientifically Treated Petroleum (gasoline additive); sodium tripolyphosphate (water softener); Space Test Program (USAF); State Testing Program(s); stop the police (dirty street people's slogan)

S.T.P. *Sacrae Theologae Professor* (Latin—Professor of Sacred Theology)

St Paddy Saint Patrick

St Paddy's Day Saint Patrick's Day (March 17)

st part steel partition

St Pat Saint Patrick; Saint Patrick's Day (March 17)

St Paul Minnesota's capital

STPB Singapore Tourist Promotion Bureau

stpd standard temperature and pressure—dry (0°C, 760mm Hg)

St Pet St Peter's College, Oxford

St Pete St Petersburg

STPL Space Tracking Pty Ltd

St P & M St Pierre and Miquelon Islands

stpr short taper; stumper

s tpr short taper

stps specific thalamic projection system

StP Sta St Pancras Station (rail terminal)

str steamer; straight; strainer; strait; strength; structural; structure; submarine test reactor (STR)

str (STR) synchronous transmitter receiver (data processing)

str *strana(y)* [Czech—page(s)]

Str Strait; Stranraer; Street

Str *Strasse* (German—street); *Streptococcus*

STR Science and Technical Research; section, township, range; Society for Theatre Research; Southern Test Range; Stuttgart, Germany (airport); submarine test reactor

STRA State Teacher's Retirement System

strabad strategic base air defense

Strabolgi Joseph Montague Kenworthy

STRAC Strategic Army Corps

STRACS Surface Traffic Control System

strad stradivarius (violin made by Antonio Stradivari or his sons Francesco and Omobono)

strad (STRAD) signal transmitting—receiving and distributing

stradap storm radar data processor

STRADS Switching, Transmitting, Receiving, and Distribution System

STRAF Strategic Army Forces

strag straggler; strategic; strategist; strategy

StragL straggler line

Strait Strait of (Bab el Mandab, Bali, Bass, Belle Isle, Bering, Bosporus, Canso, Dardanelles, Denmark, Dover, Florida, Formosa, Georgia, Gibraltar, Hainan, Juan de Fuca, Korea, Lombok, Luzon, Magellan, Makassar, Malacca, Messina, Molucca, Otranto, Palk, Sunda, Tiran, Torres, etc.)

Straits Straits Settlements (Malaysia and Singapore); Straits of Tiran (at entrance to the Gulf of Aqaba or Eilat)

Strangeways Strangeways Prison in Manchester, England

Strangler wrestler Ed (Strangler) Lewis originally named Robert H. Friedrich

STRAP Stretch Assembly Program

Stras Strasbourg

Strassburg (German—Strasbourg)

STRATAD Strategic Aerospace Division (USAF)

STRATCOM Strategic Communications Command (USA); Stratospheric Composition (program)

Strath Strathclyde

stratig stratigraphy

sirato stratosphere

Stratofreighter Boeing 707/720 transports adapted for military service and designated C-135

Stratotanker Boeing jet tanker designated KC-135

straw strawberry

Strawberry Capital Hammond, Louisiana

STRAYS Society To Rescue Animals You've Surrendered

STRC Science and Technology Research Center; Scientific, Technical, and Research Commission

STREAK Surfaces Technology Research in Energetics, Atomistics, and Kinetics

Stream the Stream (Gulf Stream)

Stream of Pleasure Thames River above London

Street The Street—London's Fleet Street (center of periodical publishing); New York's Wall Street (financial center)

Street Haven Toronto, Ontario's center for the rehabilitation of prostitutes and other wayward girls

Street of Ink Fleet Street, London with its many newspaper offices

Street of Sorrows New York City's Wall Street; old-fashioned nickname for any thorofare frequented by streetwalkers

strep streptococcus

STREP Ship's Test and Readiness Evaluation Procedure

stress. (STRESS) structural engineering system solver

STRESS Stop the Robberies, Enjoy Safe Streets (program of the Detroit Police Department)

stret stretto [Italian—squeezed together; more rapid (as musical notes), strait]

STRI Smithsonian Tropical Research Institute

STRICOM Strike Command (US Army)

Strikemaster British BAC 167 ground-attack jet aircraft

strikeops strike operations

strikex strike exercise

STRIKFLANTREPEUR Striking Fleet Atlantic Representative in Europe (NATO)

STRIKFORSOUTH Striking and Forces Support, Southern Europe (USN)

Strine Australian mispronunciation of English (e.g., *Mundie*=Monday)

string, string-processing systems, technics, languages

string stringendo (Italian—accelerate)

strip. standard taped routines for image processing

strip. (STRIP) string processing language

Strip The Strip—main street of Las Vegas, Nevada

Strix Peter Fleming

strl straight line

S-t-R L Save-the-Redwoods League

str lgths straight lengths

Strm Stream (postal abbreviation)

STRN Standard Technical Report Number

strobe satellite tracking of balloons and emergencies

strobed stroboscopically illuminated; stroboscopically measured

strobes. shared-time repair of big electronic systems

strobo stroboscope

strobotron stroboscope + electron (tube)

str off fixt store (or) office fixtures

STRS State Teachers Retire-

ment System

struc structure

struct structural

STRUT Safe TRU Transit (underlined as s̲h̲own)

's' truth god's truth

Strv-74 Swedish light tank armed with 75mm gun

Strv-S Bofors-built Swedish medium tank with 105mm gun

strwbrd strawboard

sts scour the shower; ship-to-shore (radio or radio telephone); special treatment steel; surfaced two sides

st's sanitary towels

Sts Streets

STS Science Talent Search; Scottish Text Society; Serological Test for Syphilis; Standard Test for Syphilis; Stockpile-toTarget Sequence

STSA State Technical Services Act

STSC Southwest Texas State College

STSD Society of Teachers of Speech and drama

stsg split-thickness skin graft(ing)

STSO Senior Technical Staff Officer

st st stocking stitch (knitting)

stt scrub the tub

St T (Port of) St Thomas

STT Medical Stenographer (USN); St Thomas, Virgin Islands (airport); Sensitization Test

S-T T Skin-Temperature Test(ing)

STTA Scottish Table Tennis Association

STTC Sheppard Technical Training Center

sttch(es) stitch(es)—not correctly abbreviated but often found in knitting instructions

ST T NHS St Thomas National Historic Site

sttr stator

STTT Space Telescope Task Team (NASA)

stu service trials unit; skin test unit; student; submersible test unit

Stu Stewart; Stuart

STU Seatrain (container) Unit

STU Styrelsen foer Teknisk Utveckling (Swedish—Board for Technical Development)

Stub Toe State Montana

STUC Scottish Trades Union Congress

stud. student

Stud Studebaker

Student of Democracy British Ambassador James Bryce—author of *The American Commonwealth*

stude(s) student(s)

Studioland Hollywood, California

stud(s). student(s)

Studs Lonigan trilogy comprising *Young Lonigan, Young Manhood of Studs Lonigan, Judgment Day*—James T Farrell's literary portrait of life among lower middleclass Chicago Irish

stuff. system to uncover facts fast

Stuka Sturzkampfflugzeug (German—dive bomber)

stump. submersible, transportable, utility marine pump(ing)

stuns'l studdingsail

stupidental(ly) stupidly accidental(ly)

Sturt Sturt Desert in the northwest sector of New South Wales, Australia

Stutgardia (Latin—Stuttgart)

stuvs standard unit variance scale

stv subscription television

stv (STV) subscription television

St V Stavanger; St Valentine; St Vincent

STV Scottish Television; Separation Test Vehicle

STV Solidaridad de Trabajadores Vascos (Spanish—Solidarity of Basque Workers)

St Val Saint Valentine; St Valentine's Day

St Valentine's disease epilepsy

St Val's Day Saint Valentine's Day (February 14)

stvd r stevedore

St V & G St Vincent and the Grenadines

s tv i subliminal television intoxication (producing insanity and used as a defense for some criminals)

St Vitus' dance epilepsy

STVPS Salinity, Temperature, Sound Velocity, and Pressure-Sensing System

st w storm water

STW Society of Technical Writers

ST WAPNIACLE abbreviation mnemonic for U.S. departments in order of their creation before new ones were added and some were consolidated: State, Treasury, War,

Attorney General (Justice), Post Office, Navy, Interior, Agriculture, Commerce, Labor, Education

Stwd Steward

STWE Society of Technical Writers and Editors

STWP Society of Technical Writers and Publishers

stwy stairway

stx start of test (data processing); static test stand

STX St Croix, Virgin Islands (airport)

Sty Stymie

STYCAR Screening Tests for Young Children and Retardates

Styria English and Latin place-name equivalent of Steiermark—central and southeastern Austria

Styx NATO code name for Soviet surface-to-surface naval missile

STZ Sterling Drugs (stock exchange symbol)

su sensation unit(s); service unit(s); setup; strontium unit(s); sulfur unit(s)

su. sumat (Latin—let him take)

s u siehe unten (German—see below)

Su Sudan; Sudanese

SU Saybolt Universal; Scripture Union; Seattle University; Shaw University; Skinner Union; Southeastern University; Southwestern University; Soviet Union; Standord University; Stetson University; Student Union; Suffolk University; Sydney University; Syracuse University

SU Stati Uniti (Italian—United States)

SU-7 Soviet ground-attack fighter aircraft designated Fitter by NATO

SU-9 Soviet all-weather jet fighter aircraft called Fishpot by NATO

SU-11 Soviet delta-wing fighter aircraft called Flagon-A by NATO

SU-76 Soviet 76mm assault gun used in World War II and thereafter in Korea and Vietnam

SU-85 Soviet 85mm assault gun

SU-100 Soviet 100mm assault gun

SU-122 Soviet 122mm assault-gun howitzer also designated JSU-122

SU-152 Soviet 152mm assault-gun howitzer (JSU-152)

sua shipped unassembled

sua (SUA) serum uric acid

S-u-A Stratford-upon-Avon

SUA Silver Users Association; State Universities Association

SUA Stati Uniti d'America (Italian—United States of America)

SUAB Svenska Utvecklinasaktiebolaget (Swedish Development Corporation)

SUADPS Shipboard Uniform Automatic Data Processing System (USN)

sub subcontract(or); submarine; submerse; subordinate; substitute; suburb; subway

sub (SUB) substitute character (data processing)

sub (Latin prefix—below, beneath, under)—subterranean, subway

Sub Subic Bay; Subway

SUB Supplemental Unemployment Benefit (fund)

SUB Subbota (Russian—Saturday)

subac subacute

SUBACLANT Submarine Allied Command, Atlantic (NATO)

SUBAN Scottish Union of Bakers and Allied Workers

Subang Kuala Lumpur, Malaysia's airport

subassy subassembly

Sub Base Submarine Base

sub-bell submarine fog bell

Subbotnik (Russian—Little Saturday)—Red Saturday—annual holiday when everyone donates this day of rest to tasks such as cleaning up factory sites and neighborhoods as well as parks and other public places

sub chap subchapter

Subcontinent of Asia India

subcontr subcontract(or)

subcrep subcrepitant

subcut subcutaneous(ly)

subd subdivide; subdivision

subdeb subdebutante

SUBDIV Submarine Division (naval)

SUBDIZ Submarine Defense Identification Zone

sub-ed sub-editor

subex submarine exercise; submerged exercise

sub. fin. coct. sub finem coctionis (Latin—at the end of boiling)

subfusc subfuscous (dark and dingy)

subgen. subgenus (Latin)

subic (SUBIC) submarine integrated control program

subing substituting

subj subject; subjunctive

subl sublimes

SUBLANT Submarine Forces, Atlantic (USN)

Sublime Porte nickname for the government of the Turkish Empire in the times of the sultans

subling sublingual

sublse sublease

Sub Lt Sub-Lieutenant

subm submission; submit

submand submandibular

Submarine Capital Groton, Connecticut

SUBMED Submarines Mediterranean (NATO)

SUBMEDNOREAST Submarines—Northeast Mediterranean (NATO)

submgd submerged

submtl submittal

subn substitution

SUBNOTE Submarine Notice (USN)

subor subordinate

sub-osc submarine oscillator

subot submarine bottom

SUBPA Submarine Patrol Area (USN)

SUBPAC Submarine Forces, Pacific (USN)

sub para sub paragraph

subplane submersible seaplane

sub-pro subprofessional

subprog subprogram(ming)

sub pub(s) subsidy publisher(s) [vanity publisher(s)]

SUBPZ Submarine Patrol Zone (USN)

subq subsequent

subroc (SUBROC) submarine rocket

subrog subrogation

Subron Submarine Squadron

subrqmt subrequirement

subs submarines; subscription(s); subsistence; substantial violations; substitutes

subsafe submarine safety (program)

subsan submarine sandwich (also called sub)

sub sec subsection

subseq subsequent(ly)

subset subscriber set

subsis subsistence

subsp. subspecies (Latin)

SUBSS Submarine Schoolship (USN)

subst substantive

substa substation

substance P polypeptide found in the brain

substand. substandard

substd substandard

substr substructure

subsunk submarine sunk

subsys subsystem

SUBTACGRU Submarine Tactical Group(ing)

subtopia suburban utopia

subtr subtraction

SUBTRAFAC Submarine Training Facility

Subtropical Siberia Castro's Cuba

sub u substitute unit

suburb suburban; suburbanite; suburbia; suburbian

subversive delinquents political prisoners

SUBWESTLANT Submarine Force—Western Atlantic (NATO)

suc succeed; success; successor

suc. succus (Latin—juice)

SUC Society of University Cartographers; Sussex University College

Succ Successori (Italian—Successors); *Succursale* (Italian—Branch)

Successor of Saint Peter the Pope

Sucker State Illinois nickname dating from pioneer days when settlers sucked water from underground springs with long hollow tubes called suckers

Sucr Sucursal (Spanish—subsidiary, branch)

Sucre Antonio José de Sucre—South American liberator fighting with Bolivar for freedom of Venezuela, Colombia, Ecuador, Peru, and Bolivia from Spanish rule; Mariscal Sucre (Quito, Ecuador's airport named for Marshal Sucre)

suct suction

sud sudden unexpected death; sudden unexplained death

Sud Sudan; Sudanese

SUD Aerovias Sud Americanas (3-letter airline coding)

Sudaf Sudáfrica (Spanish—South Africa)

Sudáfrica (Spanish—South Africa)

SUDAM Superintêndencia do Desenvolvimento da Amazonia (Portuguese—Superintendency for the Development of Amazonia)

Sudamérica (Spanish—South

America)

Sudan Democratic Republic of Sudan (Africa's biggest country and once populated by Arabic-speaking Arabs and many Negro tribes with tribal tongues; Sudanese farm, fish, and mine despite harassement by Palestinian terrorists and venal politicians) *Jumhuryat es-Sudan Al Democratia*—formerly the Anglo-Egyptian Sudan known as Nubia in Roman times

SUDAN Sudan Airways

Sudanese Port Bur Sudan

Sudanese Sister Cities Khartoum and Omdurman

SUDENE Superintêndencia do Desenvolvimento do Nordeste (Portuguese—Superintendency for the Development of North-East Brazil)

SUDS Silhouetting Underwater Detecting System; Submarine Detecting System

Suds City Milwaukee, Wisconsin—famous for beer

Sue Susan; Susannah; Suzanne

suec suéco (Spanish—Swedish); *sueco* (Portuguese—Swedish)

Suec Suecia (Spanish—Sweden); *Suécia* (Portuguese—Sweden)

Suecia (Spanish—Sweden)

Suécia (Portuguese—Sweden)

Suède (French—Sweden)

SUEL Sperry Utah Engineering Laboratory

Suet Gaius Suetonius Tranquillus (Roman biographer)

Suez English place-name equivalent of El Suweis

Suez Canal 107-mile-long seaway connecting Mediterranean and Red Sea with Indian Ocean; runs along eastern border of Egypt from Port Said near Alexandria to Port Tewfik near Suez

Suez-kanaal (Dutch—Suez Canal)

suf sufficient; suffix

Suff Suffolk

suffoc suffocating

sug suggest(ion)

SUG Southern California Gas Company (stock exchange symbol)

SUGAR Services, (to diabetics through) Understanding, Grants, Assistance, Recreation

Sugar Bowl New Orleans, Louisiana

Sugar Country tropical Queens-

land, Australia

Sugar Islands sugarcane-producing Leeward Islands of the West Indies

Sugar King Claus Spreckels

sugar of lead lead acetate

Sugar State Louisiana famous for its sugar beets

SuH Sundays and Holidays

SUI State University of Iowa

Suiça (Portuguese—Switzerland)

Suicide European nickname for Tchaikovsky's Symphony No. 6 in B major—the Pathétique

Suicide Capital of the United States San Francisco

Suicide Capital of the World Budapest

suicidol suicidologist(ic); suicidology

suid sudden unexplained infant death (crib death)

Suidwes-Afrika (Afrikaans—South West Africa)—formerly German Southwest Africa, now called Namibia

sui rep suicide report

Suisse (French—Switzerland)

SUIT Scottish and Universal Investment Trust

suiv suivant (French—following)

Suiz Suiza (Spanish—Switzerland)

Suiza (Spanish—Switzerland)

Suk Sukkot

Suky Susan; Suzanne

sul simplified user logistics; small university libraries

Sul Suleiman (Arabic—Solomon)

SUL Stanford University Libraries

Sula Sulawesi (Celebes)

Sulawesi (Indonesian—Celebes)

sulcl set up in less than car loads

sulf sulfate; sulfur

sulfa sulfanilamide

sulfd sulfide(s)

sulfuric acid H_2SO_4

Suliman seal five-pointed pentagrammic star of perplexing aspect as it seems to consist of two interlocking triangles but is not; symbol of Morocco and other Islamic lands

Sulli Sullivan

Sulphur King Herman Frasch

Sult Sultan(a)

Sultan of Swat George Herman (Babe) Ruth

Sulu Jolo

Sulus Sulu Islands in the Sulu Sea between Indonesia and the

Philippines
sum (SUM) surface-to-underwater missile
sum. summary; surface-to-underwater missile (SUM)
sum. sume (Latin—take)
Sum Sumatra; Sumatran; Sumer; Sumeria; Sumerian
SUM Servicio Universitario Mundial (Spanish—World University Service)
Sumba English place-name equivalent of Soemba or Sandalwood Island in Indonesia
SUMCMO Summary Court-Martial Order
Sumi Sumitomo Bank
Sumitomo Sumitomo Shoji America; Sumitomo Shoji
summ summarization; summarize; summarizing
Summer Bank Summer Bank Holiday (last Monday in August in Great Britain)
Summerless Southland southernmost New Zealand on its South Island south of Dunedin
SUMOC Superintendencia da Moeda e do Crédito (Portuguese—Superintendency of Money and Credit)
sumr summer
sums. summons
SUMS Sperry Univac Material System
sum. tal. sumat talem (Latin—take one like this)
sun. symbolic unit number (SUN)
Sun Sunday
Sun The Baltimore Sun
SUN Solar Usage Now; Symbols, Units, and Nomenclature Commission
Sun Belt sun-drenched southern United States and specifically the southernmost tier of states extending from Florida to Hawaii
Sun Bowl El Paso, Texas
Sun City St Petersburg, Florida; Yuma, Arizona; and a few other sunny places vie for this name
sund (Danish, Norwegian, Swedish—sound, as in Haugesund)
Sund Sunda Islands; Sundanese
Sunda English place-name equivalent of the Greater Sunda Islands or Soenda
Sundarbans Sundarban creeks, half-reclaimed islands, marshes, rivers, and swamps in the Ganges delta country

between Bangladesh and India
Sundas Sunda Islands of Indonesia
SUNFED Special United Nations Fund for Economic Development
Sun Flag *Hi-no-maru*—sun flag of Japan—Land of the Rising Sun—red sun on a white field
Sunflake City Grand Forks, North Dakota
Sunflower Kansas state flower
Sunflower(s) Kansan(s)
Sunflower State official nickname of Kansas
Sungaria Dzungaria or Zungaria region between Mongolia and Russia
Sun God Adonis (Syrian); Apollo (Roman); Apollon (Greek); Baal (Chaldean); Helios Hyperion (Greek in Homer's time); Horus (symbolized in Upper Egypt by a hawk); Mithras (Persian); Moloch (Canaanite); Osiris (Egyptian); Ra or Re (symbolized in Egypt's Old Kingdom by an obelisk); Sol Invictus (Latin—Sun Invincible)—Romans shortened this to Sol and to this day Old Sol is the sun's nickname; Surya (Hindu)
Sunken Continent of the Atlantic Atlantis
Sunken Continent of the Pacific Lemuria
Sun King Louis XIV (*Le Roi Soleil*)
Sun of May *El Sol de Mayo*—revolutionary symbol on the great seals of Argentina, Ecuador, and Uruguay; standing for national emergence in the fight for freedom
sunnie(s) sunfish(es)
Sunny Alberta Canada's Province of Alberta
Sunnyside Washington Irving's home near Tarrytown, New York
Sunny South southern United States
SUNOCO Sun Oil Company
Sunrise Haydn's String Quartet in B flat (opus 76, no. 4)
Sunrise Poet Sidney Lanier
SUNS Sonic Underwater Navigation System
Sunset Crater Sunset Crater National Monument in north-central Arizona
Sunset Land Arizona
Sunshine Capital of the United States Yuma, Arizona

Sunshine City Saint Petersburg-Tampa, San Diego, Tucson, and Yuma are among many places in the South and the Southwest claiming this nickname also coveted by Durban, South Africa—City of Sunshine
Sunshine Coast British Columbia's coast from Lund to Vancouver; Queensland's coast from Brisbane to Noosa
Sunshine Continent Australia
Sunshine Province Alberta, Canada
Sunshine State Florida, New Mexico, and South Dakota contest this title with each other and with subtropical Queensland in Australia; official nickname of Florida
SUNY State University of New York
SUNYAB State University of New York at Buffalo
Sun Yat-Sen's Dr Sun Yat-Sen's Birthday (November 12)
Suomi (Finnish—Finland)
Suor Angelica (Italian—Sister Angelica)—one-act opera by Puccini
sup superfine; superior; superlative; supersede(s); supplement(ary); supplies; supply; support; supposition; supreme
sup supérieure (French—higher; superior, upper)
sup. supra (Latin—above)
SUP Sailors Union of the Pacific; Socialist Unity Party; Southern University Press; Stanford University Press; Sussex University Press; Syracuse University Press
SUPCE Syracuse University Publications in Continuing Education
supchg supercharger
Sup Ct Superior Court; Supreme Court
supdel superdelicious
Sup Dpo Supply Depot
supe (slang) superintendent; supernumerary
super superficial; superfine; superheterodyne; superintendent; superior; supermarket; supernumerary; supersede; supersession
super (Latin prefix—above, beyond, upper)—superficial, superior, superpower; *supermercado* (Spanish—supermarket)
SUPER Skills Upgrading Pro-

gram for Educational Reinforcement
superaero superaerodynamics
Super Constellation Lockheed transport carrying 99 passengers
Supercop Philadelphia's mayor Frank Rizzo—a former policeman
superf superficie (Italian—area; surface, surface area)
Super Falcon Hughes air-to-air missile also called Nuclear Falcon
Super Frelon Sud antisubmarine helicopter developed in France
superhet superheterodyne
superjet(s) supersonic jet airplane(s)
superl superlative
Superman Philosopher Friedrich Wilhelm Nietzsche
Superman of the Prize Ring Joe Louis
Super Mystere Dassault fighter-bomber and jet interceptor built in France
Superpowers U.S.A. and the USSR (materially and militaristically); Israel and North Vietnam (morally and patriotically)
super(s) supercargo(s); supercharger(s); superheater(s); superheterodyne(s); superhighway(s); superhuman(s); superintendent(s); superior(s); superior court(s); superior planet(s); superlative(s); superliner(s); supermarket(s); superorganism(s); superpatriot(s); superpower(s); superscript(s); supersonic(s); superstition(s); superstructure(s); supervisor(s)
Super Sherman U.S. M-4 Sherman tank modernized
Superstition Personified Abessa who sought sanctuary behind convent walls shielding her from truth, according to Spenser's *Faerie Queene*
superstr superstructure
Super^te Superintendente (Spanish—superintendent)
Supertenor Luciano Pavarotti
superv supervisor
supgon super gonorrhea (resistant to all antibiotics)
suphtr superheater
SUPIR Supplementary Photographic Interpretation Report
sup. lint. super linteum (Latin—on lint)
Sup O Supply Office(r)

SUPOPS Supply Operations (DoD)
supp supplement; suppuration
supp. suppositorium (Latin—suppository)
Sup P Supply Point
suppl supplement (French—supplement)
Suppl supplement
Supporter of the Universe Atlas, in the Roman mythology; the ash tree Ygdrasil in Norse mythology
suppos suppository
supps supplementary procedures; supplements
SupPt supply point
suppy supplementary
supr superior; supreme
supra (Latin prefix—above or over)—suprarenal
supra cit. supra citato (Latin—cited above)
Supreme Genius of Spanish Painting Diego Rodríguez de Silva y Velázquez
Supreme God of the Hindus Brahma
Supreme Governor of the Church of England the King or Queen
Supreme Pontiff of the Universal Church the Pope
supsd supersede(d)
Sup Ship Supervisor of Shipbuilding
supt superintend; superintendent
Supt Docs Superintendent of Documents
supv supervise; supervisor
supvr supervisor
supvry supervisory
sur surface; surfacing
Sur Surinam (Netherlands Guiana)
Sur Surabaya (Indonesian—Soerabaya)
Suralco Surinam Aluminum Company
Surámerica (Spanish—South America)
surano surface radar and navigation operation
sur art surrealistic art
surcal surveillance calibration (satellite)
Sur Cdr Surgeon Commander
SURE Symbolic Utilities Revenue Environment
sureq submit requisition
surf. spent unreprocessed fuel
Sur f Surinam florin (guilder)
surf. a surface area
Surfburgia California seaside suburban communities such

as Malibu, Santa Monica, Seal Beach, Pacific Beach, Imperial Beach
SURFF Spent Unreprocessed Fuel Facility
SURFPA Surface Patrol Area
SURFPZ Surface Patrol Zone
surg surgeon; surgery; surgical
Surg Cdr Surgeon Commander
surge. sorting, updating, report generating
Sur Gen Surgeon General
Surgeon of the Rusty Knife Dr José Pedro de Freitas Arigo of Congonhas do Campo, Brazil
Surg Gen Surgeon General
surgiserv surgical service(s)
Surg Lt Cdr Surgeon Lieutenant Commander
Surg Maj Surgeon Major
Suri Surinam (formerly Dutch Guiana)
suric surface ship integrated control
Surinam formerly Dutch or Netherlands Guiana; Surinamese speak Dutch, Jewtongo, English, Hindi, and other tongues, bauxite is mined; tropical crops are cultivated; fishing for shrimp and lumbering for mahogany are also profitable
Surinam (Amerindian—Rocky Rivers)—Dutch Guiana
Suriname (Dutch—Surinam)
Surinam Ports Nieuw Nickerie, Paramaribo, Paranam, Moengo, Albina
surpic surface picture
Surprise Haydn's Symphony No. 94 in G major
surr surrender
Surr Surrogate
SURS Surface Export Cargo System
SURSAN Superintendência de Urbanismo e Saneamento (Portuguese—Superintendency of Urbanism and Sanitation)
SURTASS Surveillance-Towed-Array Sonar System
surv survey; surveying; surveyor
Surveyor American program for lunar surface and subsurface exploration
Surv Gen Surveyor General
survll surveillance
sus supressor sensitive; suspect(ed); suspected person; suspend(ed)
Sus Saybolt universal second; Susanna, The (Apocryphal) History of Sussex

SUS Scottish Union of Students; Society of University Surgeons

SUSA Scouting USA (formerly the Boy Scouts of America—BSA)

Susan Hayward Edyth Marriner

susfu situation unchanged—still fouled up

susie surface and underwater ship-intercept equipment

Susie Susan; Susannah; Suzanne

susp suspect(ed); suspend

susp b suspension bridge

sus. per coll. *suspensio per collum* (Latin—hanging by the neck)

suspn suspension

suspnd suspending

susp(s) suspect(s) [person(s) suspected]

Susque Susquehanna River flowing from western New York through Pennsylvania and Maryland before entering Chesapeake Bay

SUSS Society of Utah School Superintendents

Sussex Seaport Garden Resort Felixstowe

sust sustainer

SUSTA Southern United States Trade Association

Susx Sussex

SUT Society for Underwater Technology

Suth Sutherland

s'uth'ard southward

SuU Staats und Universitätsbibliothek (German—State and University Library)—Hamburg's prize possession despite great losses during World War II

suud sudden unexpected unexplained death

SUV Saybolt Universal Viscosity; Suva, Fiji Islands (Nandi Airport)

SUVCW Sons of Union Veterans of the Civil War

Suwanee River small river draining Okefinokee Swamp on Georgia-Florida border and entering Gulf of Mexico a few miles north of Cedar Keys on west coast of Florida—the *Swanee River* immortalized in Stephen Foster's song

SUX Sioux City, Iowa (airport)

Suz Suez

Suzhou (Pinyin Chinese—Soochow)

Suzy Susan; Susanna; Susanne

sv (RCA patent); sailing vessel (SV); security violator; selectavision (SV); simian virus; single vibrations; sinus venosus; stroke volume; survey; surveyor

s/v surrender value; survivability/vulnerability

sv sotto voce (Italian—in an undertone, in a whisper); *svacek* (Czech—volume); *svensk* (Dano-Norwegian—Swedish)

s.v. spiritus vini (Latin—alcohol); *sub verbo* or *sub voce* (Latin—under the word; under the voice)

Sv Svaty (Czechoslovakian—holy); *Sveti* (Serbo-Croatian—holy)

SV sailing vessel; Selective Volunteer; Sons of Veterans

S & V Sinclair and Valentine

SV Standard Version

sv 40 simian virus 40

Sva Suva

SVA Schweizerische Vereinigung für Atomenergie (German—Swiss Association for Atomic Energy)

Sval Svalbard (Spitsbergen)

Svalbard (Norwegian—Spitsbergen)—Arctic islands

Svb Svendborg

SVB Stephen Vincent Benét

svc service; superior vena cava

svc (SVC) service (flow chart); supervisor call(ing)

SVC Skagit Valley College; Society of Vacuum Coaters

svcbl serviceable

SVCP Special Virus Cancer Program

svcs superior vena cava syndrome

svd spontaneous vaginal delivery; spontaneous vertex delivery; swine vesicular disease

SVD Schweizerische Vereinigung für Dokumentation (German—Swiss Documentation Association)

sve secure voice equipment

SVE Society for Visual Education

Sven Akad Svenska Akademien (Swedish Academy)

Svensker(s) Swedish sailor(s)

Sver Sverdlovsk; Sverige (Swedish Academy)

Sverdlov NATO name for a Soviet class of light cruisers

Sverdlovsk formerly Ekaterinburg where the Soviets murdered the last of the czars and his family; terminus of the Trans-Siberian railroad and

place where Asia is said to look at Europe

Sverige (Swedish—Sweden)—contracted from *Svea + Rige* (Swedish Kingdom formerly divided into Göta, Svea, and Vende)

Svezia (Italian—Sweden)

svg saving

s.v. gal. spiritus vini gallici (Latin—brandy)

svi stroke volume index

s.v.i. spiritus vini industrialis (Latin—industrial alcohol)

svib strong vocational interest blank

SVIOC South Varanger Iron Ore Company

Svizzera (Italian—Switzerland)

SVL Scripps Visibility Laboratory

s.v.m. spiritus vini methylatus (Latin—methyl alcoholic)

SVN Student Vocational Nurse

Svn Dag Svenska Dagbladet (Swedish Daily Blade)

SVnese South Vietnamese

SVNV Societa Veneziana di Navigazione a Vapore (Venetian Steamship Company)

SVO Moscow, USSR (Sheremetyevo Airport)

SVP Society of Vertebrate Paleontology

S V P s'il vous plaît (French—if you please)

SVPs Senior Vice Presidents

svr super video recorder

s.v.r. spiritus vini rectificatus (Latin—rectified spirit of wine)

SVR Suomen Valtion Rautatiet (Finnish State Railways)

sv's security violators

SVS Society for Vascular Surgery; Society for Visiting Scientists

SVS Sveriges Standardiseringkommission (Swedish Standards Commission)

s.v.t. spiritus vini tenuis (Latin—proof alcohol; proof spirit)

SVT Self-Valuation Test

SVTL Services Valve Testing Laboratory

svtol (SVTOL) short/vertical takeoff and landing

svtp sound, velocity, temperature, pressure

svtt surface-vessel torpedo tube

s.v.v. sit venia verbo (Latin—forgive the expression)

svy survey

sw salt water; sea water; sent wrong; shipper's weights; short wave; shotgun wedding; single weight; special weapon; spot-weld; spotwelding; steelworker; stock width; switch; switchband wound

s-w shortwave

s/w salt water; sea water; seaworthy; standard weight

s & w salaries and wages; surveillance and warning

Sw Sweden; Swedish

SW Secretary of War; Security Watch; Senior Warden; Shelter Warden; Ship's Warrant; South Wales; southwest; Southwest Airways (2-letter coding); Stone & Webster (stock exchange symbol)

S-W Sherwin-Williams

S & W Seaboard & Western (airlines); Smith & Wesson; Stone & Webster

SW1, SW2, etc. Southwest One, Southwest Two, etc. (London postal zones)

swa single wire armored; superwide angle

Swa Swahili

SWA Seaboard World Airlines; South-West Africa; Southwest Airways

SWAA Southwestern Aeronautical Association

Swabia (Latin—Schwaben)—in southwest Germany

swabk sealed with a big kiss

swac special warhead arming control

Swac Standards western automatic compiler (NBS)

SWAC South-West Africa Company

SWACS Space Warning and Control System

SWAFAC Southwest Atlantic Fisheries Advisory Commission

swag(s) scientific wild-assed guess(es)

SWAI South-West African Infantry

swak sealed with a kiss

SWALCAP South-West Academic Libraries Cooperative Automation Project

swalk sealed with a loving kiss

swami. software-aided multifont input

Swamp Fox sobriquet shared by Revolutionary War general Francis Marion as well as by Confederate generals Nathan Bedford Forrest and Philip Dale Roddey

Swan of Avon Ben Jonson's name for Shakespeare

Swan City Perth, Western Aus-

tralia

Swanland southwestern Australia

Swan of Mantua Virgil

Swan of Meander Homer

Swan of Pesaro Gioacchino Antonio Rossini who was born in Pesaro, Italy on the Adriatic near San Marino

Swan River Colony Perth built around the River Swan in Western Australia

Swans Swan Islands off Honduras

Swanside Perth, Western Australia

Swansider(s) inhabitant(s) of Perth on the Swan River estuary of Western Australia

Swan Song Symphony Prokofiev's Symphony No. 7 in C-sharp minor

SWANU South-West Africa National Union

SWANUF South-West Africa National United Front

swap. selective wide-area paging

SWAPO South-West Africa People's Organization

swash sea wash (scouring surf running up a beach after a wave breaks)

SWAT Special Weapons and Tactics (team of law-enforcement officers trained to combat guerrillas and terrorists)

swath small waterplane-area twin hull

Swatow mainland-China-built last patrol craft

swatson so what's on?

Swatter NATO name for a Soviet antitank missile

s waves secondary (earthquake) waves

S-waves shear waves

Swaz Swaziland

Swaziland Kingdom of Swaziland (landlocked South African country whose Swazis speak Swazi and some English; farming, lumbering, and mining prove productive)

swb short wheelbase; single with bath; swing bridge

SWB South Wales Borderers

swbd switchboard

swbld switchblade (knife or stiletto)

swbm still-water bending moments

S & W bracelets Smith and Wesson handcuffs

SWBRC Southwest Border Regional Commission

swc specific water content

SWC Soil and Water Conservation (US Department of Agriculture); Special Weapons Command; Supreme War Council

SWCEL Southwestern Cooperative Educational Laboratory

Swch Switch (postal abbreviation)

SWCHS Simon Wiesenthal Center for Holocaust Studies (Yeshiva University)

SWCLR Southwest Council of La Raza

swd sawed; sewed; short-wave diathermy

SWD South Wales Docks

SWDA Scottish Wholesale Druggists' Association; Solid-Waste Disposal Act (EPA)

Swe Sweden; Swedish

SWE Society of Wine Educators; Society of Women Engineers

sweatl student work experience and training

sweat(s) sweatshirt(s)

SWEB South Wales Electricity Board; South West Electricity Board

SWEC Stone & Webster Engineering Corporation

Swed Swede; Sweden; Swedish

Swed Swedish (Germanic language spoken by some 10 million people in Sweden and around its former colonies along the Baltic)

Sweden Kingdom of Sweden (ingenious inventiveness plus quality workmanship combine to make Sweden the wealthiest of the Scandinavian nations; Swedish-speaking Swedes engage in farming, manufacturing, and mining) *Konungariket Sverige*

Sweden's Most Popular Sculptor Vilhelm Carl Emil Milles (originally surnamed Anderson)

Sweden's Principal Port Göteborg (Gothenburg)

swedish swedish massage (based on Swedish-type physiotherapeutic movements); swedish mile (10 kilometers); swedish movements (Swedish-type physiotherapeutic exercises); swedish putty (spackle + spar varnish waterproofing mixture); swedish turnip (rutabaga originally grown in Sweden)

Swedish Film Pioneer Ingmar Bergman

Swedish Hanseatic Port City Visby on the island of Gotland

Swedish Nightingale Jenny Lind

Swedish Ports (large, medium, and small from west to south, to east, and north) Lysekil, Uddevalla, Göteborg, Varberg, Falkenberg, Halmstad, Hoganas, Viken, Halsingborg, Landskrona, Malmö, Limhamn, Klagshamn, Trelleborg, Ystad, Simrishamn, Ahus, Solvesborg, Karlshamn, Ronnebyhamn, Karlskrona, Kalmar, Oskarshamn, Slite, Farosund, Visby, Vastervik, Mem, Norrkoping, Oxelosund, Nykoping, Sodertalje, Nynashamn, Stockholm, Vasteras, Oregrund, Skutskar, Kastet, Gavle, Vallvik, Ljusne, Sandarne, Soderhamn, Hudiksvall, Sundsvall, Harnosand, Gustavsvik, Ornskoldsvik, Pitea, Lulea, Haparanda

Swedish Quartet Sweden's leading classical composers, ranked chronologically, include Berwald, Rangstrom, Atterberg, and Wiren

Swedish West Indies St Barts (St Barthélmy now a French colony)

SWEDL Southwest Educational Development Laboratory

Sweet Singer of the Sierras Joaquin Miller

Sweetwaters Sweetwater Mountains of California and Nevada

SWETM Society of West End Theatre Managers

Sweyn Forkbeard King Svend of Denmark

swf single white female

SWF Stockholders for World Freedom

SWFB Southwestern Freight Bureau

Sw Fr Swiss franc

sw fx spotweld fixture

SWG Society of Women Geographers; Standard Wire Gauge

Sw-Ger Swiss-German (derived from Alemannic)

swi stroke work index

Swi Swietochlowice

SWI Spring Washer Institute

SWIE South Wales Institute of Engineers

swife sexual wife

swift. selected words in full title

swift. lass. signal word index of

field and title—literature abstract specialized search

swift. sir. signal word index of field and title—scientific information retrieval

SWINE Students Wildly Indignant (about) Nearly Everything (cartoonist Al Capp's contribution to contemporary acronyms)

Swingfire British BAC airlaunched or ground-launched antitank missile

Swinglish Swedish-English

SWIO SACLant War Intelligence Organization

SWIR Special Weapons Inspection Report

SWIRL South Western Industrial Research Limited

SWIRS Solid Waste Information Retrieval System

swiss swiss chard (beetlike herb used in stews); swiss cheese (Emmenthaler cheese characterized by its pale-yellow body and many holes); swiss lapis (imitation lapis lazuli); swiss muslin (curtain material); swiss steak (thin slice of steak doused in flour and vegetables); swiss watch (usually one of the finest made)

SWISSAIR Swiss Air Transport

Swiss Cheese Capital of the U.S.A. Monroe, Wisconsin

Swiss Day Independence Day (August 1)

Swiss Family of Mathematicians and Scientists the Bernoullis

Swiss Family of Painters the Fuesslis

Swiss Quartet Switzerland's foremost composers of classical music, arranged chronologically, include Raff, Bloch, Martin, and Honegger

Swiss Riviera northern shores of Lake Lucerne

switch switchblade knife

Switz Switzerland

Switzerland Swiss Confederation of Cantons (Alpine nation of great productivity and high-quality workmanship; Swiss speak French, German, Italian, and Romansch)—*Schweiz* (German or Romansch), *Suisse* (French), *Svizzera* (Italian)—all mean Switzerland

swives sexual wives

Sw kr Swedish krona (monetary unit)

swl short wave listener

SWL safe working load (for car-

go booms and derricks; SWL 5T 15 deg means the safe working load is 5 tons at 15 degrees off the horizontal); Swedish American Line

SWLA Southwestern Library Association

SWLI Southwestern Louisiana Institute

swlolak's sealed with lots of love and kisses

SWly south-westerly

swm single white male; standards, weights, and measures

SWM Southwest Museum

SWMA Steel Wool Manufacturers's Association

SWMF South Wales Miners' Federation

SWMFB Southwestern Motor Freight Board

Swn Swinoujscie

Swnbne Swanbourne

SWO Solid Waste Office (Environmental Protection Agency)

SWOA Scottish Woodland Owners' Association

swoc subject word out of context

swog special weapons overflight guide

SWOPSI Stanford Workshops on Political and Social Issues

SWORCC Southwestern Ohio Regional Computer Center

's' word god's word

SWORDS Shallow-Water Oceanographic Research Data System

SWORL Southwestern Ohio Regional Libraries

swot strengths, weaknesses, opportunities, threats

's' wounds god's wounds

swp safe working pressure; sweep; sweeper; sweeping

SWP Saskatoon Wheat Pool; Sherwin-Williams Paints; Socialist Workers Party; South Wales Ports; Southwest Pacific; Special Weapons Project

SWPA Southwest Pacific Area; Southwestern Power Administration; Surplus War Property Administration

swpf short wave-pass filter

swr serum wassermann reaction; standing-wave ratio; steel-wire rope; switch rails

swrf sine wave response filter

S-W RI Sterling-Winthrop Research Institute

swrj split wing ramjet

SWRL Southwest Regional Laboratory

sws seam-welding system; service-wide supply; slow-wave sleep; solar-wind spectrometer; still water surface

Sws Swansea

SWS Sariska Wildlife Sanctuary (India); Space Weapons System; Special Weapons System

SWSC Schlumberger Well Surveying Corporation

swt short-wave transmission; short-wave transmitter; single weight; spiral(ly)-wrap(ped) tubing; steel watertight; switch(ing)

SWT School of Welding Technology; Scottish Wildlife Trust

SWTB Surface Wellbore Test Bank

SWTC Scottish Woolen Technical College

swtchmn switchman

SWTEA Scottish Woolen Trade Employers' Association

swtg switching

SWTMA Scottish Woolen Trade Mark Association

SWTS Seabury Western Theological Seminary

SWUS Southwestern United States

swv swivel

SWWJ Society of Women Writers and Journalists

swy slipway; stopway

swymmd see what you made me do

sx section; simplex

Sx (medical) signs and symptoms

SX Southern Pacific (stock exchange symbol)

sxa stored index to address

SXC Saint Xavier College

sxl short arc xenon lamp

SXM St Maarten, Netherlands Antilles (airport)

sxn section

SXO Senior Experimental Officer

sxr soft X-ray region

sxrm straight reamer

sxs stellary X-ray spectra

SXS Sigma Xi Society

sxt sextant; stable X-ray transmitter

sy shipyard; square yard; sticky; supply; sustainer yaw

Sy Shipyard; Syria; Syrian

SY South Yorkshire; steam yacht (naval symbol); (U.S. State Department) Security Office

SYB Statesman's Year-Book

SYC Sandusky Yacht Club; Savannah Yacht Club; Seattle Yacht Club; Springfield Yacht Club; Stamford Yacht Club

Sycamore Bristol four-place helicopter

Sycamore City Terre Haute, Indiana

SYCATE Symptom-Cause Test

sycom synchronous communication(s)

sy crs sundry creditors

syd see your doctor; sum of the year's digits

Syd Sydney

Syd sydlig (Danish—southerly)

SYD Scotland Yard; Sydney, Australia (airport)

S Yem South Yemen

syf syphilis

syfa system for application

SyG Secretary General

syh see you home

SYHA Scottish Youth Hostels Association

Sy'kat Syarikat

syl syllogism

syla-iawr *see you later*, alligator —in a while, crocodile

syll syllabication (syllabification)

SYLP Support Your Local Police

Sylv Sylva; Sylvain; Sylvan(der); Sylvanus; Sylvester; Sylvius

Sylvia-Ducalis (Latin—'s Hertogenbosch)—also known as Bois le Duc or Sylvia Ducis

sym symbol; symbolic; symbolism; symmetric; symmetrical; symmetry; symphonic; symphony

sym (Latin prefix—together)—symphony

sym. symbolus (Latin—token; sign)

symb symbol, symbolic; symbolism

symbal symbolic algebra

symbol of suffering the Christian cross (whenever atheist Joseph Lewis saw it atop a church he said it seemed to be a dagger plunged into the heart of humanity)

symp symposia; symposium

sympac symbolic program for automatic control

sympath sympathetic; sympathy

Symphonia domestica (German —Domestic Symphony)—autobiographical tone poem by Richard Strauss

Symphonie Espagnole Edouard Lalo's most popular violin concerto

Symphonie fantastique (French —Fantastic Symphony)—major orchestral work of Berlioz

Symphony of a Thousand Mahler's Symphony No. 8 in E-flat major

Symphony of Heavenly Length Schubert's Symphony No. 9, according to Schumann

Symphony of Psalms Stravinsky's best-known symphony

symps symptoms

sympt symptom(s)

SYMRAP Symbolic Reliability Analysis Program

SYMRO System Management Research Operation

SYMS Symmetrical System

Sym & Signs Symbols & Signs

SYMWARR System for Estimating Wartime Attrition and Replacement Requirements

syn synagogue; synesthesia; synonym; synonymous; synonymy; syntax; synthetic

syn (SYN) synchronous idle character (data processing)

syn (Greek—together or with)— synapsis, syndrome

Syn Synagogue

Synanon anti-drug addiction group

sync synchronize; synchronous

synchro synchronize; synchronous

synchros synchronous devices

synco syncopate(d); syncopation; syncopative; syncopator

syncom synchronous communication (satellite)

syncon synergistic convergence

syncop syncopate(d); syncope

syncrude(s) synthetic crude oil(s)

synd syndicalism; syndicate

syndet(s) synthetic detergent(s)

syndro syndrome

syne syntactic elements

synec synecdoche

Synfuel U.S. Synthetic Fuel Corporation

synfuel(s) synthetic fuel(s)

syn gas synthetic gas

SYNMAS Synchronous Missile Alarm System

syn oil synthetic oil

synon synonymous; synonym

synonym. synonymous

synop synopsis; synoptic

synroc synthetic rock

syns synopsis

synscp synchroscope

synt syntax

syntan synthetic tanning

synth synthesis; synthetic

Synthesizer of Adrenalin Jokichi

Takamine

synth-pop synthesized popular music

syntol syntagmatic organization of language

syntrain synthetic training (aviation)

syntran syntax translation

S Yorks South Yorkshire

SYP Society of Young Publishers

syph syphilis; syphilitic

syphil syphilology

Sy PO Supply Petty Officer

SYPR Southern Yemen People's Republic

syr syrup

syr. syrupus (Latin—syrup)

Syr Syracusan; Syracuse; Syria; Syriac; Syrian

SYR Syracuse, New York (airport)

Syrac Syracusan; Syracuse

syrg syringe

Syria Syrian Arab Republic (Middle Eastern nation whose Arabic-speaking Syrians engage in farming, light manufacturing, and some mining; some French as well as Armenian and Kurdish is also spoken) *al-Jamhouriya al Arabia as-Souriya*

Syrian Ports Latakia and Baniyas

Syrië (Dutch—Syria)

Syringa Idaho state flower

syrm save-your-rear memorandum

sys system; systematic; systematization; systematize; systemic; systems

SYS Sun Yat-sen

sysabend system abnormal end(ing)

syscp system card punch(ing)

sysda system direct access

sysgen systems generation

sysin system input

syslib system library

syslined system linkage editor

syslmod system load module

sysout system output

SYSP Sixth-Year Specialist Program (library science)

Sys PO Systems Program Office(r)

syssq system sequential

syst system; systematic; systemic; systems

System ABC System of Automation of Bibliography through Computerization

systol systolic

systran systems analysis translator

sysut system utility (data sets)

syt sweet young thing

syz syzgetic; syzygial; syzygium; syzygy

sz schizophrenia; schizophrenic; seizure; size; stratum zonal

s Z seinerzeit (German—at that time)

Sz Swiss; Switzerland

sza solar zenith angle

SZA Student Zionist Association

Szb Salzburg

Szczecin (Polish—Stettin)—seaport near the mouth of the Oder

SZG Salzburg, Austria (airport); Soviet Zone (in) Germany

Szle Szemle (Hungarian—journal, review)

Szn Szczecin (formerly Stettin—Stn)

SZO Student Zionist Organization

SZOG Soviet Zone of Occupation in Germany

szr (SZR) sodium-cooled zirconium-hydride moderated reactor

szvr silicon zener voltage regulator

T

t airfoil temperature thickness (symbol); hour angle (symbol); meridian angle (symbol); table; tabulated (loran); tackle; tardy; tare; teaspoon, teeth; telephone; temperature; temporary; tenor; tense; tensor; tentative, tentative target; thunder; thunderstorm; tide; tide rips; time; title; ton; tonnage; tons; toward; town; trace of precipitation; transferred; transit; transitive; translation; tread; tropical; troy; true; tug; tugline

t (*t*) units of land (microeconomics)

t (T) tea (marijuana)

t' the

't it

t *tome* (French—volume); *tomo* (Spanish—volume)

t. ter (Latin—three times; thrice)

't het (Dutch—the)

T Northrup Aircraft (symbol); Pacific Transport Lines (1-letter symbol); propeller thrust (symbol); tablespoon; tactical; Tango—code for letter T; tanker; Taoism; Taoist; T-bar; tee; teletype; temperature; temple; temporary magnitude; tension of eyeball; Tesla; Testla; Texaco; Texas; Texas Company; Thursday; torpedo; trainer; training; Transamerica (airline); transport number; triangle; triple bond; true; truss; Tuesday; turboprop; Turk; Turkey; Turkish

T (Latin—Titus); tea (underground slang—marijuana or Texas tea as some users nickname this hallucinogenic

drug); *Teil* (German—division, part); thrust (symbol); *Time* (magazine); transformer (symbol); *tulo* (Finnish—arrival)

T-1 Canadian income-tax return

t½ radioactive half life

T - 1, T - 2, T - 3, etc. decreasing stages of interocular tension

T + 1, T + 2, T + 3, etc. increasing stages of interocular tension

T_1, T_2, T_3, etc. first thoracic vertebra, second thoracic vertebra, third thoracic vertebra, etc.

T2 stabilized

T-2 North American-Rockwell Buckeye trainer aircraft; trico theccnes used in biochemical yellow-rain warfare in Afghanistan, Laos, and other places attacked by the Soviets

T2g Technician (second grade)

T_3 triiodothyronine

t-4 therefore

T4 heat treated

T-4 Canadian statement of employment income recorded for tax purposes

T_4 thyroxine

T6 heat treated and aged

T-6 North American-Rockwell Harvard or Texan trainer aircraft

T7 heat treated and stabilized

T-7 Beechcraft navigational-training aircraft

T-10 Soviet heavy tank armed with a 122mm gun

T-11 Beechcraft bomber-training aircraft

T-28 North American Trojan trainer aircraft

T-29 Convair military transport also called Samaritan

T-33 Lockheed Shooting Star trainer aircraft

T-34 Beechcraft Mentor trainer aircraft; Soviet medium tank armed with an 85mm gun

T-37 Cessna Dragonfly twin-engine jet trainer

T-39 North American Sabreliner transport aircraft

T-41 Cessna 172 Mescalero trainer-utility aircraft

T-42 Beech Cochise transport aircraft

T-43 Boeing navigational trainer and transport aircraft; Soviet fleet minesweeper

T51 specially aged

T 54 Soviet medium tank

T-55 Soviet medium tank armed with a 100mm gun

T-59 mainland-China-made medium tank modeled after Soviet T-54 tank

T-62 Soviet medium tank with a 115mm gun

T-64 Soviet medium tank with a 120mm gun

T-104 Tupolev 104 aircraft

T-144 Tupolev 144 (Soviet supersonic transport)

T-301 Soviet coastal minesweeper

T-1824 Evans blue

ta target area; temperature, axillary; test accessory; third attack (lacrosse); time and attendance; toxin-antitoxin; transactional analysis; transverse acoustic; travel allowance; true altitude; tuberculin; alkaline

ta (TA) teaching assistant; terephthalic acid; transactional

analysis
t-a toxin-antitoxin
t/a trading as
t & a taken and accepted; time and attendance; tonsillectomy and adenoidectomy; tonsils and adenoids
t of a terms of agreement
ta transit authority (New York City Transit Authority—lower-case italic emblem on rolling stock)
t.a. *testantibus actis* (Latin—as the records show)
Ta tantalum; Tasmania; Tasmanian
TA Table of Allowances; tactical air (missile); Tax Amortization; Teaching Assistant; Technical Assistance; Tel Aviv, Israel; Territorial Army; Trade Agreement(s); Transactional Analysis; Trans-Air; Trans-America Corporation (stock exchange symbol); Truth in Advertising; Turkish Army
T-A Tacna-Arica (on the border of Peru and Chile, respectively)
T/A Teaching Assistant; Temporary Assistant
T of A *Timon of Athens*
taa turbine-alternator assembly
TAA Technical Assistance Administration; Temporary Assistance Authority; Trade Agreements Act; Trans-Australia Airlines; Transit Advertising Association; Transportation Association of America
TAACOM Theater Army Area Command
TAAF *Terres Australes et Antarctiques Françaises* (French Austral and Antarctic Territories)—Adélie Land in Antarctica plus the islands of Amsterdam and St Paul, the Crozets, and the Kerguelans in the south Indian Ocean
TAAG *Transportes Aéreos de Angola* (Portuguese—Air Transports of Angola)
taalk *taalkunde* (Dutch—linguistics)
TAALODS The Army's Automated Logistic Data System
TAALS The American Association of Language Specialists
TAAP Total Action Against Poverty
TAARS The Army Ammunition Reporting Service
taas three-axis attitude sensor
TAAS Telfair Academy of Arts

and Sciences (Savannah)
TAASA Tool and Alloy Steels Association
tab. table; tablet; tabulate; tabulated; tabulation; tabulator; technical assistance broker(age); therapeutic abortion
tab. *tabella* (Latin—small board; tablet)
Tab Tabascan; Tabasco
Tab *Tabelle* (German—table; index)
TAB Technical Assistance Board (UN); Tobago (airport); Totalisator Agency Board; Totalizator Board
TAB *Technical Abstract Bulletin*
TABA The American Book Award(s)
TABA *Transportes Aéreos Buenos Aires*
Tabarro *Il Tabarro* (Italian—The Cloak)—one-act opera by Puccini
tabasco tabasco sauce (condiment originally made in the Mexican state of Tabasco)
tabc typhoid-paratyphoid A, B, and C vaccine (TABC)
tabel *tabella* (Latin—tablet)
TABL Tropical Atlantic Biological Laboratory
tabl(s) tablet(s)
Tabogo (Spanish—Tobago)
tab run tabulator run
tab(s) tablet(s)
Tabs Cantabrigians or Cantabs —Cambridge University undergraduates
TABS Transatlantic Book Service
tabsim tabulating simulator
TABSO Transport Aerien Civil Bulgare (Bulgarian Civil Air Transport)
tabsol tabular systems-oriented language
tabt tab vaccine plus tetanus toxoid (TABT)
tabtd combined tab vaccine plus tetanus and diptheria toxoid
TAB vaccine typhoid plus paratyphoid A and B vaccine (triple vaccine)
tabwx tactical air base weather
tac tactic; tactical; tactician; tactics; total automatic color (tv); try and collect
Tac Tacitus; Tacoma
TAC Tactical Air Command; Talent-Assistance Cooperative; Technical Advisory Committee; Technical Assistance Center; Terrain Analysis Center; Thai Airways Compa-

ny; Trade Agreements Committee
TACA Texas and Central American Airlines
tacan tactical air navigation
Tac Brdg Tacoma Bridge
TACC Tacna-Arica Copper Consortium; Tactical Air Command Center; Tactical Air Control Center; Technology Assessment Consumerism Center
taccar time-averaged clutter-coherent airborne radar
tacco tactical coordinator
TACCP Tactical Command Post (USA)
TACCTA Tactical Air Commander's Terrain Analysis
tacden tactical data-entry device
TACELIS Transportable Emitter Location and Identification System
tacelron tactical electronic warfare
TACEST Tactical Test(ing)
TACG Tactical Air Control Group
tach tachometer
Tacho Anastasio
tachy tachygraphy (shorthand)
tachy (Latin prefix—rapid or swift)—tachycardia
tachycard tachycardia
tacit. *tacitus* (Latin—unmentioned)
tacjam tactical jammer; tactical jamming
TACL Tactical Air Command Letter
taclan tactical landing system
TACLET Tactical Law Enforcement Team (Coast Guard)
tacmar tactical malfunction-array radar
tacnav tactical navigation
tacnuc tactical nuclear (weapon) —also written *taknuk*
TACO Tactical Coordinator
Taco Benders Mexican Americans
tacoda target coordinate date
tacol thinned-aperture computed lens
TACOM Tank-Automotive Command (USA)
TACOMEWS Tactical Communications Electronic Warfare Systems
Taconics Taconic Mountains ranging from New York to Vermont but called the Berkshires in Connecticut and Massachusetts
TACOS Tactical Airborne

Countermeasures or Strike (USAF); Tactical Air Command Simulation

Taco Town San Diego, California

TACP Tactical Air Control Party

tacpol tactical procedure-oriented language

TACR Tactical Air Command Regulation

TACRON Tactical Air Control Squadron

TACs Technical Assistance Committees (UN)

TACS Tactical Air Control System

tacsatcom tactical satellite communications

TACSS tactical schoolship (USN)

tact. technological aids to creative thought

TACT Texas Association of College Teachers; Truth About Civil Turmoil

TACTIC Technical Advisory Committee to Influence Congress (Federation of American Scientists)

TACTICS Technical Assistance Consortium to Improve College Services

tacv tracked air-cushion vehicle

tad tadpole; telemetry analog-to-digital (information converter); terminal area distribution (processing); traffic analysis and display; transaction application driver; throwaway detector; time available for delivery

tad (TAD) temporary additional duty

Tad Thaddeus; Theodore

TAD Thrust-Augmented Delta

TAD *The Anglican Digest*

TADA Teletypewriter Automatic-Dispatch System

TADARF Toronto Alcoholism and Drug Addiction Research Foundation (Canadian)

TADARS Tropo Automated Data Analysis Recorder System

TADC Tactical Air Direction Center; Texas Association of Developing Colleges; Training and Distribution Center

tadic telemetry analog-to-digital information computer

tad(s) tadpole(s)

TADS Teletypewriter Automatic Dispatch System

TADSYS Turbine Automated Design System

Tadz Tadzhik; Tadzhikistan; Tadzhikistanian

Tadzhik SSR Tadzhik Soviet Socialist Republic (Tadzhikistan)

TAE National Greek Airlines; Trans-Antarctic Expedition

TAEA Texas Art Educators Association

TAEC Turkish Atomic Energy Commission

TAEDS Texas Association for Educational Data Systems

TAEG Training Analysis and Evaluation Group (USN)

TAEHS Thomas A Edison High School

ta'en taken

TAERF Texas Atomic Energy Research Foundation

taf terminal aerodrome forecast

taf (TAF) toxoid-antitoxin floccules

Taf Bildtafel (German—list of illustrations)

TAf Tuberculin Albumose frei (German—albumose-free tuberculin)

TAF Tactical Air Force

TAFA Territorial and Auxiliary Forces Association

tafcsd total active federal commissioned service date

Taffie(s) Welsh person(s)

Taffy diminutive of David or St David the tutelar saint of Wales; nickname for a Welshman

tafg two-axis free gyro

TAFI Technical Association of the Fur Industry

tafmsd total active federal military service date

tafor terminal aerodrome forecast

TAFSEA Technical Applications for Southeast Asia

TAFSONOR Tactical Air Force, Southern Norway (NATO)

tafubar things are fouled up beyond all recognition

ta fx tapping fixture

tag. the acronym generator (RCA device)

Tag Tagalog (the language of the Philippines where it is spoken by some 20 million Filipinos who also speak some English and Spanish; a modified form of Tagalog is called Pilipino) —ninety other tongues are heard in the Philippine Islands

TAG The Adjutant General; The Alzheimer Group; The

Association for the Gifted; Test Analysis Guide; Timken Art Gallery

T A & G Tennessee, Alabama & Georgia (railroad)

TAGA Technical Association of the Graphic Arts

Tagal Tagalog

tagawi try and get away with it

TAGCEN The Adjutant General's Center (USA)

TAGG Taxpayers Against Government Giveaways

tagl *täglich* (German—daily; per day)

TAGP Transportes Aéreos do Guiné Portuguesa (Air Transport of Portuguese Guinea)

TAGS Time-Automated Grid System

tagw takeoff gross weight

tah temperature, altitude, humidity; total abdominal hysterectomy

Tahiti formerly Otaheite

Tah Pac Tahitian Pacific (area around Tahiti)

TAHq Theater Army Headquarters

TAHRI Tobacco and Health Research Institute

tai taiga (coniferous evergreen forests of subarctic America, Asia, and Europe)

Tai Taipei; Taiwan (Formosa)

Tai Tailandia (Spanish—Thailand)—Siam

TAI Thai Airways International; Transports Aériens Intercontinentaux

TA & IC Texas Arts and Industries College

TAICH Technical Assistance Information Clearinghouse

taid (TAID) thrust-augmented improved delta

TAIDET Triple-Axis Inertial-Drift Erection Test

TAIDHS Tactical Air Intelligence Handling System

Taig Terence

tail tailpiece

'taint it aint

Taipas Taipa Islands off Macao in the South China Sea

TA-ISSA Travelers Aid—International Social Service of America

Taiwan (Chinese—Terrace Bay) —descriptive name of the heavily terraced island of Formosa called nationalist or offshore China—the Republic of China—to distinguish it from communist or mainland China—the People's Republic of China

Tai Yue Shan (Chinese—Broken Head Island)—Lantau Island off Hong Kong

TAJAG The Assistant Judge Advocate General (USA)

Tajo (Spanish—Tagus)

Taju Tajumulco

Takatus Takutu Mountains of Pakistan

take 5 take 5 minutes rest

take 10 take 10 minutes rest

Takla Makan desert in western China between Kunlun and Tien Shan mountains

tako terms and conditions of employment

tal traffic and accident loss

tal (TAL) tetra-alkyl lead

tal. talis (Latin—such)

Tal Talcahuano

Tal Talmud (Hebrew canon and civil lawbook)

TAL Transair Limited

TALA The American Lyceum Association (currently the International Platform Association)

Talamancas Talamanca Mountains of Costa Rica

talar tactical landing-approach radar

talbe talk and listen beacon

talc hydrous magnesium silicate (agalmatolite); take a look see

TALC Tank-Automotive Logistics Command (USA); Texas Association for the Advancement of Local Culture

Talco Talcahuano

Tales The Tales of Hoffmann—Offenbach's three-act opera *Les Contes d'Hoffmann*

talff total allowable level of foreign fishing

TALIC Tyneside Association of Libraries for Industry and Commerce

Talien Chinese equivalent of Dairen

talisman. transfer accounting and lodgment for investors and stock management for jobbers (London Stock Exchange)

talkies talking motion pictures

Talla Tallahassee

Talladegas Talladega Mountains of Alabama

Tallahassee Florida's capital

Tallahassee Institution Tallahassee Correctional Institution in Florida

Tall Boy Gouverneur Morris—amanuensis of the *Constitution of the United States*

Tall City Midland, Texas

Talleyrand Charles Maurice de Talleyrand-Périgord

Tallinn (Estonian—Dane's Town)—formerly Reval

TALMA Truck and Ladder Manufacturers Association

'**Talo** Italo

TALOA Transocean Airlines

Talos Bendix long-range surface-to-air missile

'talpa(s) catalpa(s)

tal. qual. talis qualis (Latin—as they come, average quality)

TALUS Transportation and Land Use Study

tam tambourine; tam-o'-shanter; tam-tam; total available market

t-a m toxoid-antitoxin mixture

Tam Tamar; Tamara; Tamil; Tampa; Tampan; Tampico (inhabitants—Tampiqueños); Tamualipas (inhabitants—Tamualipecos)

TAM Tel Aviv Museum; Transporte Aéreo Militar (Paraguayan Military Air Transport)

TA & M Texas A & M University

TAMA Third Avenue Merchants' Association; Training-Aids Management Agency (USA)

Tamaulipas formerly Pánuco

tamb tambor (Spanish—drum or drummer)

tambo tambourine

TAMC Tripler Army Medical Center

tamco training aid for morbidic console operations

TAME Television Accessory Manufacturers Institute

Támesis (Spanish—Thames)

tami tip air mass injection

Tamiami Tampa-Miami (area or highway)

Tamiami Trail trans-Florida highway between Tampa on the Gulf of Mexico and Miami on the Atlantic

Tamigi (Italian—Thames)

TAMIS Technical Meetings Information Service

Tâmisa (Portuguese—Thames)

Tamise (French—Thames)

Tammany Boss William M Tweed

Tammerfors (Swedish—Tampere)

Tammies Tamburitzans

Tam(my) Thomas; Tom(my)

Tamp Tampa, Florida; Tampico; Tampico, Mexico (inhabi-

tants nicknamed jaibos as the seashore abounds in crabs called jaibas in Spanish)

Tampere (Finnish—Tammerfors)

Tamps Tamaulipas

TAMRC Tank-Automotive Materiel Readiness Command (USA)

TAMS Token and Medal Society

Tam Shrew Taming of the Shrew

TAMTU Tanzania Agricultural Machinery Testing Unit

TAMU Texas A & M University

tan. tangent; tangential; tannery; tanning; total ammonia nitrogen; twilight all night

Tan Tanganyika; Tangier

TAN Transportes Aéreos Nacionales

Tanan Tananarive

Tanana River City Fairbanks, Alaska

tan. bkt tangency bracket

tandel tandem + parallel

Tandjungpriok Djakarta (Jakarta)—formerly Batavia

TANESCO Tanzania Electric Supply Company

Tang Tanganyika; Tangier

Tanganyika formerly German East Africa and more recently the mainland of Tanzania

Tangas Tanga Islands in the southwest Pacific near New Ireland

tangelo tangerine + pomelo (tangerine-grapefruit hybrid citrus fruit)

Tánger (Spanish—Tangier)

Tangerine Bowl Orlando, Florida

Tangier(s) English place-name equivalent of Tánger, Morocco

tanglo(s) tangelo(s)

Tango letter T radio code

tanh hyperbolic tangent

Tania Tatiana

Tanimbars Tanimbar Islands of Indonesia

Tann Tannhäuser und der Sängerkrieg auf der Wartburg (German—Tannhäuser and the Singing Contest of the Wartburg)—three-act Wagner opera

Tannenberg German place-name equivalent of Stebark in northeastern Poland

Tano Cayetano

tan's tax anticipation notes (TANs)

TANS Territorial Army Nursing Service

tanstaafl there aint no such thing as a free lunch (abbreviated slogan of Young Americans for Freedom)

TANU Tanganyika African National Union

TANY Typographers Association of New York

Tanya (Russian nickname—Tatiana, Tatyana)

Tanyu Morinobu Kano (*see* Kano)

Tanz Tanzania (Tanganyika + Zanzibar)

Tanzam Tanzania-Zambia (railway)

Tanzania United Republic of Tanzania (East African country combining Tanganyika and Zanzibar; Tanzanians speak English and Swahili; farming, light manufacturing, and mining support the economy of an area once known as German East Africa) includes the island of Pemba north of Zanzibar island

Tanzanian Ports Lindi, Dar es Salaam, Tanga, and smaller ports such as Chake Chake and Zanzibar

tao tactical air observation; thromboangiitis obliterans

tao (Chinese—island)

TAU Tactical Air Office(r); Test Analysis Outline; The Athenaeum of Ohio

TAO Taxi Aéreo Opita (Spanish —Opita Air Taxi)—Bogotá, Colombia

TAOC Tactical Air Operations Center

TAOCC Tactical Air Operations Control Center

TAOI Tactical Area of Interest

tap. telephone tap(ping); transient analysis program

TAP Table of Authorized Personnel; Tax Action Planning; Technical Advisory Panel; Test Analysis Program; Timesharing Assembly Program; Total Action Against Poverty; Trans-Alaska Pipeline; Tuition Assistance Program

TAP Transportes Aéreos Portugueses (Portuguese Air Transport)—airline

tapa. three-dimensional antenna-pattern analyzer

tapac tape automatic positioning and control

Tapatios Mexicans from the state of Jalisco or from Guadalajara—its capital

tape. tape automatic-preparation equipment

TAPE Target Profile Examination (USAF); Transactional Analysis of Personality and Environment; Trust for Agricultural Political Education

taphon taphonomist(ic)(al)(ly); taphonomy

TAPLAN Tax Action Planning

TAPLine Trans-Alaska Pipe Line

TAPLINE Trans-Arabian Pipeline

Taplinger Taplinger Publishing Co

TAPPI Technical Association of the Pulp and Paper Industry

taps tapaderos (Mexican Border Spanish—leather hoods covering stirrups to protect the feet while riding through thorny cactus or mezquite); the last bugle call, the *taptoo*, meaning *lights out* or sounding the last honors at a military funeral

TAPS Teacher Audio Placement System; Trajectory Accuracy Prediction System (USAF); Trans-Alaska Pipeline System

TAPSC Trans-Atlantic Passenger Steamship Conference

tapvc total anomalous pulmonary venous connection

tar. (TAR) tariff(s); tarpaulin(s); terminal area radar; terrain-avoidance radar

TAR Technical Action Request (USA); Trans-Australian Railways

TARA Technical Assistant—Royal Artillery; Territorial Army Rifle Association

Tarabulus Roman name for Tripoli

Taraco (Latin—Tarragona)— also called Tarrazona or Tirasso or Turiaso

taran test and replace as necessary

TARC Tactical Air Reconnaissance Center

TARDC Tank-Automotive Research and Development Command (USA)

tare. transistor analysis recording equipment

tarex target exploitation

tarfu things are really fouled up

targ target

TARGET Team to Advance Research for Gas Energy Transformation

Target Island Kahoolawe, Hawaii

Tarheeler(s) North Carolinian(s)

Tar Heel State North Carolina's official nickname

tarmac tar plus macadam (tarred road or runway)

Tar-Man Taranaki-Manawatu (NZ)

tarn. tarnish; tarnishes; tarnishing

TARO Territorial Army Reserve Office(r)(s)

TAROM Transporturile Aeriene Romine (Romanian Air Transport)

TARP Test and Repair Processor

tarp(s) tarpaulin(s)

Tarr Tarragona

Tarryalls Tarryall Mountains of central Colorado

tars. (TARS) three-axes reference system

TARS Technical Assistance Recruitment Service

tart. tartaric

TART Test Analysis Reduction Technique (USN)

tart. a tartaric acid

Tartar General Dynamics naval surface-to-air missile

tartar emetic potassium antimony tartrate

Tartu Dorpat

Tarvisium (Latin—Treviso)

tas true airspeed

Tas Tasmania

TAs teaching assistants

TAS The Asia Society; Texas Academy of Science; Traveler's Aid Society; Turk Anonim Sirketi (Turkish Joint Stock Company)

TAS The American Spectator

tasa test area support assembly

TASA Texas Association of School Administrators

TASAMS The Army Supply and Maintenance System

tasc terminal area sequence and control; treatment alternatives to street crimes

TASC The Alumni Service Cooperative; The Analytic Sciences Corporation; Telecommunications Alarm Surveillance and Control; Test Anxiety Scale for Children; Test Anxiety Scale for Children; Treatment Alternatives to Street Crime

tascon television automatic sequence control

TASD Terminal (Railway) Alabama State Docks

TASDC Tank-Automotive Systems Development Center (USA)

tase tactical support equipment

taser taser gun (acronymically named electronically activated stunning device used by some law-enforcement officers in subduing violent offenders; taser is the acronym for the Thomas A Swift Electric Rifle belonging to Tom Swift of bygone fictional fame)

TASES Tactical Airborne Signal Exploitation System

TASF Teachers Association of San Francisco

Tash Tashkent

Tasha (Russian nickname—Natasha)

TASHAL Tseva Hagana Le-Israel (Hebrew—Defense Army of Israel)

tasi time-assignment speech interpolation

TASK Test of Academic Skills (Stanford)

TASKFLOT task flotilla; Task Flotilla (NATO) (USN)

TASKFORNON Task Force—Northern Norway (NATO)

tasm (TASM) tactical air-to-surface missile

Tasm Tasman; Tasmania; Tasmanian

Tasmania modern name for Van Diemen's Land

Tasmans Tasman Mountains of New Zealand's South Island

Tasman Sea between Australia, Tasmania, and New Zealand

TASO Television Allocations Study Organization; Training Aids Service Office (USA)

TASP The Army Studies Program; The Army's Study Program

taspac total analysis system for production accounting and control

tasr terminal area surveillance radar

tass technical assembly

TASS Telegrafnoie Agenstvo Sovietskavo Soyuza (Soviet News Agency)

Tassie(s) Tasmanian(s)

TASSO Tactical Special Security Office(r)

TASSq Tactical Air Support Squadron (USAF)

TASSR Tartar Autonomous Soviet Socialist Republic; Tuva Autonomous Soviet Socialist Republic

Tassy Tasmania (in Australian slang)

Tassyland Tasmania (in Australian slang)

TAST Tactical Assault Supply Transport

tat. (TAT) tetanus antitoxin; tyrosine amino transferase

t & at tank and antitank

Tat Tatar (Turkestan)

TAT tetanus antitoxin; Thematic Apperception Test; Thrust-Augmented Thor; Touraine Air Transport; Transportes Aéreos de Timor

TATA Tobacco Accessories Trade Association (formerly PTA—Paraphernalia Trade Association)

Tat Aut Sov Soc Rep Tatar Autonomous Soviet Socialist Republic

TATC Tactical Air Traffic Control; Trans-Atlantic Telephone Cable

tatce terminal air-traffic-control element

TATCO Tactical Automatic Telephone Central Office

'tater(s) potato(es)

Tatertown Gleason, Tennessee —shipping point for potatoes grown in the region

TATPAC Trans-Atlantic Trans-Pacific (telecommunications network linking London, Montreal, New York, Tokyo, Hong Kong, and Sydney)

Tatras Tatra Mountains of Czechoslovakia

TATSA Transportation Aircraft Test and Support Activity

Tatts Tattersalls

TATU Tanganyika African Traders Union

Tau Taurus

TAU Tel Aviv University

Taughannock Taughannock Falls State Park on Cayuga Lake in central New York

TAUN Technical Assistance of the United Nations

Taurinum (Latin—Torino)—Turin

taurom tauromachia

TAUSA Tea Association of the U.S.A.

taut. tautology

tav (TAV) transatmospheric vehicle (McDonnell-Douglas aircraft designed to travel at up to 20 times the speed of sound so it could reach anywhere in the world in less than 2 hours) —predicted operation by the year 2000

T-a-v Tout-à-vous (French—Yours truly)

Tavastehus Swedish equivalent of Hameenlinna the birthplace of Sibelius

Tave Octave; Octavius

Tavern of Europe Paris

Tavia Octavia

TAVINA Trans-Colombiana de Aviación

Tavita Octavita

T & AVR Territorial and Army Volunteer Reserve

tav(s) tavern(s)

TAVSS Toward, Away, Versus Selection System

Tavy Octavius

taw thrust-augmented wing; twice a week

T A & W Toledo, Angola & Western (railroad)

TAW Times Atlas of the World

TAWACS Tactical Airborne Warning and Control System

TAWC Tactical Air Warfare Center

TAWG Target Acquisition Working Group

tax. taxation; taxes; taxonomic; taxonomy

Taxassee tax-collecting capital city of Tallahassee

Taxco Taxco de Alarcón

Tax Day U.S. federal taxes due April 15

taxi taxicab; taxiing

taxid taxidermy

taxir taxonomic information retrieval

taxis or taxo (Greek—to arrange in an orderly manner)—geotaxia, phototaxis, taxonomy

taxon taxonomic(al)(ly); taxonomist(ic)(al)(ly); taxonomy

Tay Tayside

Taycheedah Wisconsin Home for Women at Taycheedah

Tay Pay Irish journalist Thomas Power O'Connor

Taz Tazmania(n)

TAZ Tactical Alert Zone

taz(es) topaz(es)

tb temporary buoy; terminal board; thymol blue; tile base; total bouts; tractor biplane; trial balance; true bearing; tubercle bacillus; tuberculosis; turbine; turret-base; turret-based

t/b title block

t & b top and bottom; turned and bored

Tb terbium

TB Tank Battalion; temporary buoy; Troop Basis; Twin Branch (railroad); Tyburn (reports)

TB Technical Bulletin

tba to be announced; to be approved; to be assigned; to be audited; terminal board assembly; tires-batteries-accessories

TBA Tables of Basic Allowance; Television Bureau of Advertising; Torrey Botanical Association; Triborough Bridge Authority

tbab to be approved by

tbab (TBAB) tryptose blood agar base

tban to be announced

T-bar T-shaped bar

tbawrba travel by aircraft, military and/or naval water carrier, commercial rail and/or bus is authorized (USA)

tbb to be billed

TBB tenor, baritone, bass

TBB Television Blue Book

tbc to be crated; to be culled

TBC The British Council; Trinidad Broadcasting Company

TBC Co Tropical Belt Coal Company (corporate character invented by Joseph Conrad for use in his novel *Victory*)

tbd to be determined; to be discontinued; thousand barrels daily

TBD torpedo-boat destroyer

TBDS Test Base Dispatch Service

tbe to be edited; to be encored; to be executed; to be expanded; to be expended; to be expired; to be expunged; time base error

tbe (TBE) tuberculin bacillen emulsion

TBE Toronto Board of Education

T-beam T-shaped beam

tb ex tube expander

tbf to be furnished

TBF single-engine torpedo bomber (3-letter naval symbol)

tbfx tube fixture

tbg to be garnished; to be gathered; testosterone-binding globulin; thyroxine-binding globulin

t & bg top and bottom grille

Tbg Tönsberg

tbh to be had (sexually available); to be held

tbi to be invented; to be inventoried; tooth-brushing instruction; traditionally black institutions

TbI Tax-based Income

TBI Texas Board of Insurance;

The Business Institute

Tbilisi (Georgian—Tiflis)

T-bill(s) Treasury bill(s)

T-bird Thunderbird

tbj to be joined

tbk to be killed

t-bk talking-book

tbl to be labelled; table; tablet; through back of loops (knitting); through bill of lading

tb lc term birth, living child

tbm to be manufactured; to be monitored; tuberculous meningitis

tbm (TBM) tired businessman

TBM Ten Broeck Mansion (Albany)

TBMA Timber Building Manufacturers' Association

tb md tube mandrel

TBMD Terminal Ballistic Missile Defense (USA)

TBMS Turtle Bay Music School

tbmt transmitter buffer empty

tbn to be named; to be nominated; to be noted

tbo to be ordered; time between overhaul(s)

TBO Test Base Office

tboip tentative basis of issue plan(ning)

T-bolt bolt with T-shaped square head

T-bone T-bone steak; T-shaped bone; trombone

T-bowl toilet bowl

tbp to be promoted; to be purchased; true boiling point

tbpa thyroxine-binding prealbumin

tbq to be queried

tbr to be rented; to be restored; to-be-remembered (word)

TBR Test of Behavioral Rigidity; Treasury Bill Rate

TBRI Technical Book Review Index

tbs to be sold; tablespoon; talk-between-ships (radiotelephone)

tb's tuberculosis patients; tuberculosis victims

tb & s top, bottom, and sides

TBs Torpedo Boats (World War I)

TBS Tokyo Broadcasting System

tb sa tube saw

tbsd thermal-blooming slow dither

TBSI The Baker Street Irregulars

tbsn tablespoon

tbsp tablespoon

tbt to be tested; target-bearing

transmitter;   tolbutamide test(ing); tracheobronchial toilet

tbt (TBT) torpedo-bearing transmitter

TBT Terminal Ballistic Track

TB & TA Triborough Bridge & Tunnel Authority

tbto (TBTO) tributyl tin oxide

TBTS Tracker Breadboard Test System

tbu to be used

tbv to be vacated; to be vented; tubercle bacillus vaccine

TB & VD C Tuberculosis and Venereal Diseases Clinic

tbw to be weighed; to be withheld; total body washout; total body water

tbx to be x'd (out)

tby to be young

tbz to be zoned; to be zonked

tc temperature controlled; terra cotta; tetracycline; thermocouple; thermocoupled; thermocoupling; thrust chamber; tierce(s); time check; time closing; top chord; transportation cask, trash compactor; trip coil; true course (TC); type certification

tc (TC) total cost

t/c tabulating card; temperature coefficient; thermocouple; transformer rectifier; trim coil; type certificate

t & c threads and couplings; turn and cough

tc tre corde (Italian—three strings)

Tc technetium; tropic tides

TC Air Canada (formerly TCA); The Citadel; Tabor College; Taft College; Talladega College; Tariff Commission; Tarkio College; Tax Court; Tea Council; Teachers College; Technical Circular; Technical Communication; Tennessee Central (railroad); Texarkana College; Texas College; Thiel College; Tift College; Time Charter; Training Center; Training Circular; Transaction Code; Transportation Corps; Transylvania College; Trial Counsel; Trinity College; Tri-State College; troop carrier; Trucial Coast (Arabian sheikdoms); True Course; Trusteeship Council; Turret Captain; Tusculum College

T & C Turks and Caicos Islands

TC Technical Communications

TC 1 Traffic Conference 1—

North and South America, Greenland, Bermuda, West Indies, Hawaiian Islands

TC 2 Traffic Conference 2—Europe, adjacent islands, Ascension Island, Africa, and Asia west of and including Iran

TC 3 Traffic Conference 3 — Asia, adjacent islands, East Indies, Australia, New Zealand, Pacific Islands except Hawaiian

tca telemetering control assembly; terminal control area (TCA); to come again; track crossing angle; trichloro-acetate

tca (TCA) tri-cyclic anti-depressant

TCA Tanners Council of America; Technical Cooperation Administration; Tele-Communications Association; Television Corporation of America; Temporary Change Authorization; Tennessee Correctional Association; Terminal Control Area; Texas Corrections Association; Textile Converters Association; Theater Commander's Approval; Thoroughbred Club of America; Tile Council of America; Tissue Culture Association; Trailer Coach Association; Trans-Canada Airlines

TCAA Technical Communication Association of Australia

tcam telecommunications access method

TCAs Terminal Control Areas (establishing airfield-safety flight paths)

TCAS The College of Advanced Science

tcb take care of business

tcb (TCB) task-control block

TCB Thames Conservancy Board

TCBC Ty Cobb Baseball Commission

TCBI Television Center for Business and Industry

tcbs (TCBS) thiosulfate-citrate-bile salt sucrose

tcc tatical control computer; television control center; test conductor console

tcc (TCC) transitional cell carcinoma

Tcc Tagliabue closed cup

TCC Telecommunications Coordinating Committee; Transcontinental Corps; Transport Control Center; Transporta-

tion Control Committee; Troop Carrier Command

T-C C Tri-Continental Corporation

TCCA Textile Color Card Association

TCCB Test and County Cricket Board

TCCP Thirteen College Curriculum Program

TCCS Texaco Controlled-Combustion System; Tide Communication-Control Ship

tcd task completion date; ternary coded decimal; tungsten carbide depositing

TCD Trinity College, Dublin

TCDA Texas Civil Defense Agency

tcdd (TCDD) tetrachlorodibenzo-p-dioxin

tcdf (TCDF) tetrachlorodibenzofurans

tcd's time certificates of deposit (TCDs)

tce total composite error

tce (TCE) trichloroethylene

Tce Terrace

TCE Tax(ation) Counseling for the Elderly

T-cell thymus-derived cell

tcet transcerebral electrotherapy

tcf trillion cubic feet (natural gas)

TCF 20th-Century Fox; Twentieth Century Fund

TCF Touring Club de France (Touring Club of France)

TCFB Transcontinental Freight Bureau

tcfy trillions of cubic feet per day

TCG Theatre Communications Group

T C & G B Tucson, Cornelia & Gila Bend (railroad)

tcgf (TCGF) T-cell growth factor

tch travel counselor's handbook

Tch (TCH) Tacoma (container symbol)

TCH Trans-Canada Highway

Tchad Chad

Tchaikovsky 1st, 2nd, 3rd, 4th, 5th, 6th First (*Winter Reveries*), Second (*Little Russian*), Third (*Polish*), Fourth, Fifth, Sixth (*Pathétique*) symphonies composed by Tchaikovsky

Tchecoslováquia (Portuguese—Czechoslovakia)

Tchécoslovaquie (French—Czechoslovakia)

Tcheshoslowakei (German—Czechoslovakia)

tchg teaching

TcHHW tropic higher high water

TcHHWI tropic higher high water interval

TcHLW tropic higher low water

tchr teacher

Tchrs Coll Pr Teachers College Press

TCI Technical Correspondence Institute; The Combustion Institute; The Containerization Institute; Theoretical Chemistry Institute

T & CI Turks and Caicos Islands

TCI Touring Club Italiano (Italian Touring Club)

tcj terminal coaxial junction

TCJC Texas Criminal Justice Council

tcl transfer chemical laser; transistor-coupled logic

Tcl Tymshare conversational language

TCL Tokyo Commercial University; Transatlantic Carriers Limited; Trinity College Library; Turkish Cargo Lines

TcLHW tropic lower high water

TcLLW tropic lower low water

TcLLWI tropic lower low water interval

tcm terminal-to-computer multiplexer

TCM Texas Citrus Mutual; Trinity College of Music

TCMA Telephone Cable Makers' Association

TCMP Taxpayer Compliance Measurement Program (IRS)

TCN Transportation Control Number

TCNA Turks and Caicos National Airline

TCNCO Test Control Noncommissioned Officer

TCNM Timpanagos Cave National Monument (Utah)

tco thrust cutoff

TCO Termination Contracting Office(r); Test Control Office(r); Trinity College—Oxford

TCO Tjänstemännens Central-organisation (Swedish—Salaried Employees' Central Organization)

tcoc transverse cylindrical orthomorphic chart

TCOC Tri-Cities Opera Company (Binghamton)

TCOM Tethered Communications

T-conn T-shaped connection

TCOS Toronto Classroom Observation Schedule

tcp timing and control panel; traffic control panel; traffic control post; training control(ler) panel

TCP Task Change Proposal; Task Control Proposal; Technical Cooperation Program (between Australia, Canada, the United Kingdom, and the United States); Temporary Change Proposal; Traffic Control Post; Transitional Community Placement

TCPA Town and Country Planning Association

tcpc tab card punch control

TCPC Tennessee Council of Private Colleges

TCPL Trans-Canada Pipe Lines

tcr temperature coefficient of resistance

TCR Tennessee Central Railway

TCRB *Touring Club Royal de Belgique* (French—Royal Belgian Touring Club)—automobile club

TCRMG Tripartite Commission for the Restitution of Monetary Gold (American-British-French commission, headquartered in Brussels)

tcs temporary change of station; tierces

TCS The Cousteau Society; Torpedo Control System; Twin-City Secularists; Typesetting Consultation Service

T & CS Transportation and Communication Service

TCS *Touring Club Suisse* (French—Swiss Touring Club)

tcsa (TCSA) tetrachlorosalicylanilide

tcsev (TCSEV) twin cushion surface-effect vehicle

TCSO Tri-City Symphony Orchestra

tct total-controlled tabulation

TCTA Texas Classroom Teachers Association

tctl tactical

TCTO Time Compliance Technical Order(s)

TCTS Trans-Canada Telephone System

tcu tape-control unit; teletypewriter control unit; test(ing) computer unit; threshold control unit; training combustion unit; typewriter control unit

TCU Texas Christian University; Tokyo Commercial University

TCUS Tax Court of the United States

T-cushion T-shaped cushion

tcv temperature-control valve

TCV Terminal-Configured Vehicle (NASA)

TCVA Terminal Configured Vehicles and Avionics (NASA program)

tcvr transceiver

tcw time code work

TCWG Telecommunications Working Group

TCWH Teamsters, Chauffeurs, Warehousemen and Helpers (union)

TCWIB Trans-Continental Weighing and Inspection Bureau

TCWP Texas Committee for Wildlife Protection

td tank destroyer; technical data; test data; third defense (lacrosse); tile drain; time delay; time of departure; time disintegration; tod (28 pounds of wool); tool design; tool disposition; touchdown (football); transmitter distributor; trust deed; turbine drive; 'tween deck

td (TD) tardive dyskinesia; technical director; tracking dog

t/d table of distribution; telemetry data; time deposit; transmission and distribution

t & d taps and dies

t.d. *ter die* (Latin—thrice daily)

'Td townsend

T$ Taiwan dollar(s)

TD Table of Distribution; Tactical Division; tank destroyer; Teachers Diploma; Territorial Decoration; Testing and Development (USCG); Topographic Draftsman; Training Detachment, Treasury Decision; Treasury Department; Treasury Division; Trinidad and Tobago; Typographic Draftsman

TD *Teachta Dala* (Gaelic—Member of the House of Commons)

tda tunnel-diode amplifier

t & da tracking and data acquisition

TDA Timber Development Association; Toa Domestic Airlines; Train Dispatchers Association

tdana time-domain automatic-network analysis; time-do-

main automatic-network analyzer

T-day day for time schedule testing; truce day

T-Day Transition Day (World-War-II day of transition from a two-front to a one-front war)

tdb total disability benefit (TDB)

TDB Toronto-Dominion Bank; Toxicology Data Bank; Trade Development Bank; Trade and Development Board

tdc top dead center; total distributed control; transverse directional control

tdc (TDC) torpedo-tracking computer

TDC Telemetry Data Center; Texas Department of Corrections

td cu tinned copper

tdd telecommunication device for the deaf

TDD Diploma in Tubercular Diseases

tddl time-division data link(age)

tddlpo time division data link printout

TDDS Teacher Development in Desegregating Schools

TDE Technology Development and Engineering

T del F Tierra del Fuego

T de M *Teléfonos de México* (Telephone System of Mexico)

T de S *Teatro della Scala* (La Scala)

tdf two-degree-of-freedom (gyroscope)

TDF *Télédiffusion de France* (French Television Broadcasting)

TDFS Terminal Digit Fitting System

tdg twist drill gauge

tdg (TDG) test data generator

TDG Test Documentation Group; Transport Development Group

tdh total dynamic head

Tdh Trondheim

tdi toluene di-isocyanate

TDI Target Data Inventory; Tool and Die Institute; Transportation Displays Incorporated

tdic target data input computer

TDIS Travel Document and Issuance System (for processing passports)

tdiu target data input unit

TDK *Turk Dil Kurumu* (Turkish

Language Association)

t dk(s) 'tween deck(s)

tdl total damn loss; translation definition language

TDL Topographic Developments Laboratory

tdlr terminal-descent-landing radar

tdm tandem; teacher-developed materials; time division multiplexing

tdma time division multiple access

tdmg telegraph(ic) and data message generator

tdm/pcm time-division multiplex (using) pulse-code modulation

tdn totally digestible nutrients

tdo tornado

TDO Technical Development Objective

tdol (TDOL) tetradecanol

TDOP Truck Design Optimization Program

T Dorp Schenectady, New York

TDOT Thorndike Dimensions of Temperament

tdp target director post; technical data package; technical development plans; thermal death point

TDP Technical Development Plan

tdpfo temporary duty pending further orders

tdpj truck discharge point jet

tdr time-delay; time domain reflectometry

tdr (TDR) transmit data register

tdr tous droits réservés (French—all rights reserved)

TDR Technical Deficiency Report; Technical Documentary Report; tender (naval symbol)

TDRL Temporary Disability Retired List

t/d rly time-delay relay

tdrs (TDRS) tracking and data relay satellite

tds telemetering decommutation system; total dissolved solids

tds (TSS) temperature, depth, salinity

t.d.s. ter die sumendum (Latin—to be taken three times daily)

TDS Tanami Desert Sanctuary (Northern Territory, Australia); Telemetering Decommunication System; Tennessee Department of Safety; Transaction-Driven System

TDS Toronto Daily Star

tdsa telegraphic data signal analyzer

TDSCC Tidbinbilla Deep Space Communication Complex

TDSTS Tidbinbilla Deep-Space Tracking Station

TDT Transport Department Tasmania

tdtcu target designation transmitter and control unit

tdtl tunnel diode transistor logic

TDTS Technical Data Transfer System

tdu target detection unit

TDU Teamsters for a Democratic Union

TDUP Technical Data Usage Program

TdV Teatro dal Verme (Milan)

tdw tons deadweight (tare of a ship)

tdwy treadway

tdy temporary duty; toady

TDZ Touch-Down Zone

te table of equipment; task element; technical exchange; tenants; tenants by the entirety; thermal efficiency; tinted edge; trailing edge; transverse electric; transverse wave (symbol); trial and error; turbine electric; turboelectric; twin engine

t & e testing and evaluation; thorough and efficient; training and evaluation; travel and entertainment; trial and error

Te tellurium

TE Table of Equipment; Task Element; Technical Exchange; Telefis Eireann (Television Ireland); Topographical Engineer

T & E Toledo & Eastern (railroad)

tea. triethanolamine

TEA Tennessee Education Association; Tucson Education Association

TEAA Tax Equity for American Abroad

teac turbine engine analysis check(ing)

teach. teacher; teaching

Teacher of Doctors Sir William Osler

Teacher of Germany Philipp Melanchthon (collaborator of Luther)

Teacher President James Abram Garfield—twentieth President of the United States

Teachers Day Setpember 28 in many Oriental lands where it is also the birthday of Confu-

cius

Teague (nickname for an Irishman); Terence

TEAL Tasman Empire Airways, Limited

TEAM Technique for Evaluation and Analysis of Maintainability; Terminology, Evaluation, and Acquisition Method; Trend Evaluation and Monitoring

Teamsters Teamsters Union (International Brotherhood of Teamsters, Chauffeurs, Warehousemen, and Helpers of America)

Teapot Dome U.S. Navy's petroleum reserve near Casper, Wyoming and name of a political scandal during the administration of President Harding

tear gas chloroacetophenone; irritant gas also known as mace (MACE); used to quell riots as it causes temporary blindness as well as irritation of the mucous membranes and the skin

Tear-Jerker Composer Giacomo Puccini—opposite of Gioacchino Rossini who wrote music productive of smiles, chuckles, and laughter

TEAS Texas Energy Advisory Council; Threat Evaluation and Action Selection (program)

tease tracking errors and simulation evaluation (radar)

teatr teatrale (Italian—theatrical)

Teatro Colón (Spanish—Columbus Theater)—Buenos Aires opera house

teb tape error block

TEB Tax Exemption Board; Textile Economics Bureau

Tebuan Malaysian name for the CL-41 Wasp attack-trainer aircraft

tec technic; technical; technician; technics; technological; technology; total estimated cost

'tec detective

Tec Tecate

TEC Technical Education Council; Technician Education Council

Tecate Baja California's newest penitentiary near Tecate on the California border

TECAUS Temporary Emergency Court of Appeals of the United States

TECE Trans-Europe Container Express (train)

tech technic; technical; technician; technics; technique(s); technological; technology

Tech CEI Technician of the Council of Engineering Institutions

tech ed technical editing; technical editor

Tech Eng Technical English (application of good English to any technical writing task)

techie(s) technician(s); technologist(s)

tech memo technical memorandum

techn technician

Technion Israeli Institute of Technology

technocrit technological criticism; technology critic

technol technological; technologist; technology

techno-pop technolosized popular music

tech rep technical representative

tech rept technical report

Tech Weld Inst Technician of the Welding Institute

tech writer technical writer

TEC-NACS Teachers Educational Council—National Association of Cosmetology

TECOM Test and Evaluation Command (US Army)

tecquinol hydroquinone

tecr technical reason

'tecs detectives

TECS Treasury Enforcement Communications System; Treasury Enforcement Computer File

Tec Sgt Technical Sergeant

tecspert technical expert

Tecumseh Girls' Town correctional facility at Tecumseh, Oklahoma

ted transferred electron device

ted tedesco (Italian—German)

Ted(dy) Edward; Theodore; Theodosia

Ted Morgan Sanche de Gramont

TEDS Tactical Electronic Decoy System

TEE Telecommunications Engineering Establishment; Theological Education by Extension; Trans Europe Express

TEEM Trans-Europe Express Merchandise (train)

Teenie Christina

'teens thirteen through nineteen

teenybop teenybopper (underground slang—young child attuned to the modern scene)—

see macrobop

TEEP Teacher Education Examination Program

teeto teetotaler

TEFL teaching English as a foreign language

teflon tetrafluoroethylene (polymerized synthetic plastic resin)

teg top edge gilt

Teg Tegel

te ga taper gauge

Tegel Berlin, Germany's airport

TEGMA Terminal Elevator Grain Merchants Association

Tegoose Tegucigalpa (Honduras)

teg(s) thermoelectric generator(s)

Tegusi Tegucigalpa's nickname

Teh Teheran

Tehachapi Institution California Correctional Institution at Tehachapi

Tehachpls Tehachipi Mountains traversing south-central California and the dividing line between northern and southern sections of the state

TEI Texaco Experiment Incorporated

TEJA Tutmonda Esperantista Jurnalista Asocio (International Association of Esperantist Journalists)

Tejas (Spanish—Texas)

TEJO Tutmonda Esperantista Junulara Organizo (International Organization of Esperantist Youth)

tekn teknisk (Dano-Norwegian—technical)

tel telegraph; telegraphic; telegraphy; telephone; telephonic; telephony; teletype; teletypewriter; television; tetraethyl lead

tel (TEL) transporter-erector launcher

Tel Telefunken; Telescopium (constellation); Telugu

Tel Teluk (Indonesian or Malay—bay, bight, riverbend)

TEL Tests for Everyday Living

TELAM Telenoticiosa Americana (Argentine press service)

telaut telautograph; telautography

Tel Aviv (Hebrew—Hill of the Springtime)

TELBRAS Telecommunicaões Brasileiras (Portuguese—Brazilian Telecommunications)

telco telephone company

telcos telephone companies

TELDEC Telefunken + Decca (video disc)

tele television

tele (Latin prefix—far)—telegraph

Tele Telescopium (constellation)

telec thermo-electronic laser energy converter

telecast(er) television broadcast(er)

telecom telecommunication

telecon telephone communication

teleconcert televised concert; television concert

telecopy telephonic copying process (developed by Xerox)

telecourse television-constructed course

teledis teletypewriter distribution

teledrama televised drama; television drama

telef telefon (Norwegian—telephone)

telefac television facsimile

telofilm television film

teleg telegrapher; telegraphy

telegr telegrafie (Dutch—telegraphy)

Tel Eir Telefis Eireann (Gaelic—Irish Television)

Telemaque Denmark Vesey

telemorality television morality

teleol teleology

teleopera televised opera; television opera

teleosts telcostomist fishes (bony fishes)

telep telephathic(ally); telepathy

telepak telemetering package

teleph telephony

teleplay televised play; television play

teleran televised radar aerial navigation

telesex telephone(d) sex (fantasy conversations contracted for and carried out by telephone)

telesurance television insurance

tele tape television tape

telethon television marathon

teletrial television trial

telev (TV) television

Television City Hollywood, California

telex (tex) teletype exchange

Tell Rossini's opera *William Tell*

Tel-Law Telephone-Law (free over-the-telephone answers to many legal questions are provided by many county bar associations in the U.S.)

Teller of Sea Tales Joseph Conrad

Teller of Tall Tales folklorist, religious, and secularist authors share this sobriquet; among the latter are Nathaniel Hawthorne, E T A Hoffmann, Washington Irving, Baron von Munchausen, Edgar Allan Poe, Aleksander Sergeevich Pushkin, and Mark Twain

tellie(s) television (sets)

Tell Town Altdorf, Switzerland —reputed home of William Tell

telly television

Telly Telegonus; Telemachus; Telemus; Telephus; Telesphorus

Tel-Med Telephone-Medical (free over-the-telephone answers to many medical questions are provided by many county medical societies in the U.S.)

tel no. telephone number

TELOPS Telemetry On-Line Processing System

TELS Tokyo English Language Society

telsat telecommunications satellite

tel sec telephone secretary

telsim teletypewriter simulator

tel sur telephone survey

telw *telwoord* (Dutch—word count)

tem technical error message; temporal; temporary; transverse electromagnetic

tem. *tempus* (Latin—time); *tempo* (Italian—time)

Tem temple

TEM Territorial Efficiency Medal

TEMA Telecommunications Engineering and Manufacturing Association

temadd temporary additional duty

temar thermoelectric marine application

TEMIS Targets Engineering Management Information System (USN)

temp temper; temperature; tempered; tempering; template; temporary; temporize

temp. *tempo* (Italian—time)— musical time; *tempore* (Latin —in the time of)

Temp Tempest, The

temp. dext. *tempori dextro* (Latin—to the right temple)

Tempest Beethoven's Piano Sonata No. 17 in D (opus 31, no. 2); Tchaikovsky's Sym-

phonic Fantasy—*Tempest*

temping (office jargon—temporary substituting)

tempistors temperature compensating resistors

Temple Mount Jerusalem's sobriquet

tempo. total evaluation of management and production output

TEMPO Technical Military Planning Operation

tempos temporary buildings, houses, offices, officials, workers, et cetera

temp prim *tempo primo* (Italian —tempo or time in the musical sense as at the start)

temps tempests; temperatures; temporary secretaries; temporary servants; transportable electromagnetic pulse simulator

temp sec temporary secretary

temp. sin. *tempori sinistro* (Latin —to the left temple)

tempy temporary

ten. tenant; tender; tenderize(d); tenement; tenor

ten. (TEN) toxic epidermal necrolysis; trans-European night (flight)

ten. *tenuto* (Italian—to hold, a chord or tone)

Ten *Tenente* (Italian or Portuguese); *Teniente* (Spanish)— Lieutenant

T(en) Col *Tenente Colonnello* (Italian); *Tenente Coronel* (Portuguese); *Teniente Coronel* (Spanish)—Lieutenant Colonel

ten. com tenant(s) in common

tency tenancy

tend. tendon

ten. ent tenant(s) by the entireties

TENES Teaching English to Non-English Speaking

Teng Teng Hsiao-ping

Ten Gen *Tenente General* (Portuguese); *Tenente Generale* (Italian); *Teniente General* (Spanish)—Lieutenant General

Tenn Tennessee; Tennessean

tenna(s) antenna(s)

Tenneco Tennessee Gas Companies

Tennessee Williams Thomas Lanier Williams

TENOC ten years of oceanography (1961-1970)

tenot tenotomy

Ten Provinces Ten Canadian Provinces (Alberta, British

Columbia, Manitoba, New Brunswick, Newfoundland, Nova Scotia, Ontario, Prince Edward Island, Québec, Saskatchewan)

TENRAC Texas Energy and Natural Resources Advisory Council

tens tensile; tension

tens (Latin prefix—stretch)— tensor

ten-spot $10 bill

tens str tensile strength

tent. tentative

Ten^te *Teniente* (Spanish—Lieutenant)

Tenth Muse Sappho, according to Plato, who esteemed the lyric poetess of Mytilene on the island of Lesbos

Tenth State Virginia (*see* First State)

Ten Vasc *Tenente di Vascello* (Italian—Lieutenant of the Vessel)—Navy Lieutenant

Teol *Teologia* (Portuguese, Spanish—Theology)

TEOO Territorial Economic Opportunity Office(r)

TEOSS Tactical Emitter Operational Support System (USAF)

tep transparent electrophotographic process(ing); transparent electrophotography

TEP Teacher Education Program

tepi training equipment planning information

TEPIAC Thermophysical and Electronic Properties Information Analysis Center

TEPIGENS Television Picture Generation System (computer-controlled)

Tepito Mexico City's thieves market

TEPS Teacher Education and Professional Standards

ter terminal; terminate; termination; terrace; terrazzo; territory; teritary

ter. *tere* (Latin—rub)

Ter Terrace; Territory; Teruel

Ter *Terence* (Publius Terentius Afer)—Roman writer of comedies

tera 10^12

TERA The Electrical Research Association

Te Rangi Hiroa Sir Peter Buck

terat teratology

terco telephonic rationalization by computer

tercom terrain contour matching

t & e rec time and events recorder

Teri Theresa; Therese

TERL Transit Expressway Revenue Line (mass transportation)

term terminal; terminate; terminology

te rm taper reamer

Term Terminal (postal abbreviation)

Terminal Terminal Island (Bureau of Prisons correctional facility between Long Beach and San Pedro, California)

TERMS Terminal Management System

tern. terminal and enroute navigation

TERPACIS Trust Territory of the Pacific Islands

TERPES Tactical Electronic Reconnaissance Processing and Evaluation System

terps (drug user's slang—elixir of terpin hydrate and codeine) —cough mixture and codeine combination

terps (TERPS) terminal instrument approach

TERPS Terminal Inquiry/Response Programming System

terr terrace; territory; terrorist

Terr Terrace

TERRA Terricide Escape by Rethinking, Research, Action

Terrace Bay Taiwan (formerly Formosa)

Terra Haute (French—High Land)—in Indiana pronounced *Terra Hut*

Terranova (Italian or Spanish—Newfoundland)

Terra Nova Terra Nova National Park in Newfoundland

Terra-Nova (Portuguese—Newfoundland)

Terrapin State Maryland

Terra Santa (Italian or Portuguese—Holy Land)

Terre Haute U.S. Penitentiary at Terre Haute, Indiana

Terreneuve (French—Newfoundland)

Terrier General Dynamics naval surface-to-air missile

terrs terrorists

Terry Terence; Teresa; Terrell; Terrill; Theresa; Therese

Terr^y Territory

tersab terrorist sabotage; terrorist saboteur

tersabs terrorist saboteurs

ter. sim. *tere simul* (Latin—rub together)

TERSSE Total Earth Resources

System for the Shuttle Era (NASA)

Tert. Tertiary

Tertullian Quintus Septimus Florens Tertullianus

tes *tesorero* (Spanish—treasurer)

TES Telemetering Evaluation Station

TES *Times Educational Supplement*

TESA Television and Electronic Service Association

tesac temperature-salinity-currents

tesl (TESL) teaching English as a second language

tesla technical standards for library automation

TESM Trinity Episcopal School for the Ministry

TESO *Texel's Eigen Stoomboot Onderneming* (Dutch—Texel's Own Steamship Society)

TESOL Teachers of English to Speakers of Other Languages

tess *tessili* (Italian—textiles)

Tessaglia (Italian—Thessaly)

Tess(ie) Theresa

test. test-oriented engineering symbol(ic) translator

TEST *Thesaurus of Engineering and Scientific Terms*

TESTCOMDNA Test Command Defense Nuclear Agency

test^{nto} *testamento* (Spanish—testament)

test^o *testigo* (Spanish—witness)

testran test translator (data processing)

TESYS Terminal Editing System

tet test equipment tool; tetanus; tetrachloride

TET Teacher of Electrotherapy; Teacher Evaluation Testing

TETAM Tactical Effectiveness Testing of Antitank Guided Missiles (USA)

T-et-G Tarn-et-Garonne

tetmtu (TETMTU) tetramethyl thiourea

TETOC Technical Education and Training for Overseas Countries

Tetons high mountains in northwestern Wyoming (Grand Teton National Park and Jackson Lake)

tetr tetragonal

tetra (Latin prefix—four or fourfold)—tetrachord

tetrac tetraiodothyroacetic acid

tetrah tetrahedral

tetroon tetrahedral balloon

tet tox tetanus toxin

teu twenty-foot equivalent unit(s) (container measurement)

TEU Test of Economic Understanding

Teut Teuton; Teutonic

tev (TeV) trillion electron volts

teV tetra-electron volt(s)

Tevere (Italian—Tiber)

tew (TEW) tactical early warning; tactical electronic warfare (aircraft)

tewa threat evaluation and weapons assignment

TEWDS Tactical Electronic Warfare Defense System

tews tactical electronic warfare suite

TEWS Tactical Electronic Warfare System

tex telex (teletype exchange)

t ex *till exempel* (Swedish—for example)

Tex Texan; Texas

TEX Corpus Christi, Texas (tracking station)

TEXACO The Texas Company

Tex A&M Texas Agricultural and Mechanical University

Tex A&M Pr Texas Agricultural and Mechanical University Press

Texarkana Institution Federal Correctional Institution at Texarkana, Texas

TEXAS Trained Experienced Area Specialist

Texas Babe Mildred Didrikson Zaharias

Texas Cow Town Fort Worth

Texas Ports (east to west) Port Arthur, Beaumont, Galveston, Texas City, Houston, Corpus Christi, Brownsville

Texas RRC Texas Railroad Commission

Tex Chr U Texas Christian University

Tex Chr U Pr Texas Christian University Press

Texcoco Texcoco de Mora

Texhoma Texas + Oklahoma

Texican Texas-Mexican or anyone from the Texas side of the Mexican Border

Texico Texas + New Mexico

Tex Instr Texas Instruments (Corporation)

Tex-Mex Texan-Mexican; Texas-Mexico

Texola Texas + Oklahoma

Texoma Lake Texoma between Texas and Oklahoma

texp time exposure

text. textile

Textel Trinidad and Tobago External Telecommunications Company

Textile Mus Textile Museum

textir text indexing and retrieval

text. rec. *textus receptus* (Latin —received text)

Tex W Pr Texas Western Press

tf tabulating form; tactile fremitus; temporary fix; thin film; tile floor; till forbidden (run ad until stopped by advertising client); transfer function; tuberculin filtrate

t/f true/false

TF Tallulah Falls (railroad); Task Force; Tax Foundation; Test Flight; Tolstoy Foundation; torpedo-fighter (airplane); trainer-fighter (airplane); training film; tropical freshwater (vessel loadline marking); Twentieth Century-Fox Films (stock exchange symbol)

tfa total fatty acids; transfer function analyzer

TFA Task Force on Alcoholism; Textile Fabrics Association; Tie Fabrics Association; Trout Farmers Association

TFAA Track and Field Athletes of America

TFAI *Territoire Français des Afars et des Issas* (French Territory of Afars and Issas)—formerly French Somaliland

TFB Thatcher Ferry Bridge (over Panama Canal)

tfc traffic

TFCF Twenty-First Century Foundation

TFCNN Task Force Commander—Northern Norway (NATO)

TFCRI Tropical Fish Culture Research Institute

tfcsd total federal commissioned service date

tfd target-to-film distance

tfe tetrafluoroethylene (halon or teflon plastic)

TFF Tropical Fish Farm

tfg typefounding

TFI Table Fashion Institute; Tax Foundation Incorporated; Textile Foundation Incorporated; Traditional Family Ideology scale

tfio thin film integrated optics

tfis theft from an interstate shipment

TFL Trans Freight Line

TFLA Texas Foreign Language Association

TFLC Tulane Factors of Liberalism-Conservatism

tfm transmit frame memory

TFNS Territorial Force Nursing Service

tf/p tubular fluid divided by plasma concentration (concentration of a substance in renal tubular fluid divided by its concentration in plasma)

TFP Trees for People

TFP *Tradicion, Familia, y Propiedad* (Spanish—Tradition, Family, and Property)—rightwing movement

tfr terrain-following radar

TFr Tunisian franc

TFR Territorial Force Reserve

TFR/CAR Trouble and Failure Report/Corrective Action Report

tfs time and frequency standard

TFS Transport Ferry Service

TFSR Tools for Self-Reliance

tft thin-film technology; thin-film transistor

TFT Transfer Factor Test(ing)

TFTA Textile Finishing Trades Association

tfu telecommunications flying unit

TFX variable geometry supersonic fighter-bomber

tg tail gear; telegram; telegraph; tollgate; tongue and groove; transfomational grammar; transformational generative; type genus

tg (TG) transformational generative; transformational grammar

t/g tracking and guidance

t & g tongue and groove

tg *tangente* (Italian—tangent)

Tg *Tanjung* (Malayan—cape)

TG Task Group; Texas Gulf Sulphur (stock exchange symbol); Torpedo Group; Traffic Guidance

T & G Traveres & Gulf (Florida railroad); Tremont & Gulf (Louisiana railroad)

tga thermal gravimetric analysis; thermogravimetric analysis

TGA Toilet Goods Association; Turpentione Growers of America

t'gallant topgallant (sail)

t'gal'n't topgallant (sail)

t'gansail topgallant sail

tgarq telegraphic approval requested

tgb tongued, grooved, and beaded

TGC Travel Group Charter(s)

tgca transportable ground-control approach

tge transmissible gastroenteritis

TGF Transonic Gasdynamics Facility (USAF)

TGG temporary geographic grid

TGH Toronto General Hospital

tgif thank goodness it fits; toes go in first

tGiF thank God it's Friday (TGIF)

tgl toggle

TG loran traffic guidance loran

TGM Thomas G Masaryk; Torpedo Gunner's Mate

TGMLI Tussock Grasslands and Mountain Lands Institute

tgn tangent

Tgo Tsingtao

TGO Timber Growers' Organization

TGP Terminal Guidance Program

TGPLC Transcontinental Gas Pipe Line Corporation

TGR Tiger International

T-Group Training Group

tgs thermal growing season

TGS Taxiing Guidance System; Translator Generator Service; Turkish General Staff

tgt target; teams-games-tournaments; turbine gas temperature

TGT Tennessee Gas Transmission

TGU Tegucigalpa, Honduras (airport)

tgurq telegraphic authority requested

TGV *Train de Grande Vitesse* (French—Train of Great Speed)—high-speed railroad train; *Two Gentlemen of Verona*

TGWU Transport and General Workers' Union

th tee handle

th' the

t & h transportation and handling

Th Thai (Siamese); Thailand (Siam); Thomas; thorium

Th *Theil* (German—part)

TH Town Hall; Toynbee Hall; Transport House; Trinity House; true heading

T-H Taft-Hartley

T & H Thames and Hudson

T H *Technische Hochschule* (German—technical college)

tha total hydrocarbon analyzer

Th A Theological Association

THA Transvaal Horse Artillery

Thad Thaddeus

Thai language or people of Thailand (formerly called Siamese)

THAI Thai Airways International

Thailand Kingdom of Thailand (*Muang-Thai* or *Prathes Thai*) formerly Siam

Thailand's Major Ports Sattihip, Krung Thep (Bangkok)

Thailand's Principal Port Krung Thep (Bangkok)

Thaler (German abbreviation—Joachimsthaler)—Joachim's dollar—Bohemian coin struck in 16th century at Czech town of Jachymov (Joachimsthal)—its name has become *dollar*

Thames river on east coast of England connecting London with North Sea and Atlantic Ocean

THANACAP Funeral Service Consumer Action Program (*Thana* being the Greek word for death)

thanat thanatology

thanatol thanatologic(al)(ly); thanatologist(ic)(al)(ly); thanatology

than ever than ever before (*e.g.*, it's noisier than ever before)

Thanksgiving Thanksgiving Day (fourth Thursday in November in the United States)

Thar desertland between India and Pakistan

That Man Franklin Delano Roosevelt

that's that is

that's 30 (journalistic jargon—that's all)—the end of the article, report, or story

Th.B. *Theologiae Baccalaureus* (Latin—Bachelor of Theology)

TH & B Toronto, Hamilton and Buffalo (railroad)

TH & BA Toll, Highways and Bridge Authority

thc tetrahydrocannabinol (active ingredient in psychedelic drugs such as hashish, indian hemp, and marijuana)

THC Toledo House of Correction; Toronto Harbour Commission; Toronto Harbour Commissioners; Tourist Hotel Corporation (NZ); Trinity Hall College (Cambridge)

thccre tetrahydrocannabinol cross-reacting cannabinoids

thd thread; threaded; threads; total harmonic distortion

Th.D. *Theologiae Doctor* (Latin—Doctor of Theology)

THD Technisch Hogeschool te Delft (Technological University of Delft)

th di thread die

the. (THE) tetrahydrocortisone

The. Theodora; Theodore

THE Technical Help to Exporters

thea theater

Thea Theadora; Theodeline; Theodosia; Theresa

T-head Texas-tea head (underground slang—marijuana user)

The Admiral Doctor Roger Bacon

The Alice Alice Springs, Northern Territory, Australia

The Americas North, Central, and South America; the Western Hemisphere

The Ark HMS *Ark Royal*

theat theater; theatrical

theatcrit theatrical criticism

The Atheist Percy Bysshe Shelley

The Bambino Babe Ruth (George Herman Ruth)

The Bank The Bank of England

The Bay Hudson's Bay Company; (*see* Bay)

The Beatles George Harrison, John Winston Lennon, James Paul McCartney, Ringo Starr (Richard Starkey)

The Bells Rachmaninoff's choral symphony based on Poe's poem *The Bells*

The Big Island Hawaii (commonly pronounced *hah-WAH-ee*, properly pronounced *hah-VA-ee*)

The Brothers Rockefeller brothers—John D III, Nelson, Laurance, David

The Burg New York City

THEC Tennessee Higher Education Commission

The Cape Cape Cod, Cape of Good Hope, Cape Hatteras, Cape Horn, Cape Province (Union of South Africa); Cape Town (or any other cape people frequent or sailors pass on regular runs)

The Capital Island Oahu (pronounced *oh-AH-hoo*), Hawaii

The Carthaginian Lion General Hannibal

The Channel Beagle, English, St George's, and all other geographical channels people refer to as The Channel

The Chief Herbert Hoover; train on Chicago-Los Angeles run of Santa Fe

The Cit The Citadel Military College of South Carolina

The City financial, governmental, historical, and commercial core of London; including newspaper publishing district, Bank of England, Lloyd's, many famous restaurants

The Consulate France under the First Consul-Napoleon Bonaparte—1799-1804

The Continent usually Europe but may be Africa, Asia, Australia, North America, or South America, depending on the context

The Corsican Napoleon Bonaparte

Theda Bara Theodosia Goodman

The Divine Sarah Sarah Bernhardt

The Don Don Juan (as in Mozart's opera *Don Giovanni*)

The Duke John Wayne

the E the Equator

Theems (Dutch—Thames)

The Enlightenment Europe's 18th century when encyclopedias appeared in France and England, when Voltaire and Lavoisier were matched across the Channel by Paine and Priestley

The Eternal City Rome

The Fed The Federal Reserve Board

The Five (Russian composers Balakirev, Borodin, Cui, Moussorgsky, Rimsky-Korsakov)

The Forbidden Island Niihau

The Forgotten Man President Franklin D. Roosevelt's description of the American voter

The Friendly Island Molokai

The Fuzz [American underworld slang—detective(s); law-enforcement officer(s); police; etc.]

The Garden Island Kauai (pronounced *kuh-Y-ee*), Hawaii

The Gorgeous Miliza Korjus (Mrs Walter Schector)

The Great Agnostic Colonel Robert Green Ingersoll

The Great Cham of Literature Doctor Samuel Johnson (nickname pronounced *Great Kam*—meaning Great Khan)

The Great Commoner William

Jennings Bryan

The Great Emancipator Abraham Lincoln

The Great Engineer Herbert Hoover

The Great Lover Rudolph Valentino

The Guild The Newspaper Guild

The Gulf (*see* Gulf)

The Hermitage Andrew Jackson's home near Nashville, Tennessee; palace museum of art in Leningrad (formerly a czarist palace)

The House Christ College, Oxford

The Hub Boston

The Immortals (jocular nickname—forty members of the French Academy)

The Invincible Spanish Armada defeated by English vessels commanded by Sir Francis Drake

The Islands pet name given by mainland neighbors and visitors to favorite insular groups such as the Aleutians, the Bahamas, the Balearics, the Canaries, the Hawaiians, the West India islands and even jocularly to Coney, Long, Manhattan, and Staten when referring to the New York City area

The Isle *The Isle of the Dead* (orchestral work by Rachmaninoff inspired by Arnold Böcklin's painting of this title)

The Jazz Singer Al Jolson

The Just Society (nickname—Prime Minister Pierre Trudeau's administration of Canada)

The Kaffir King Barney Barnato

The Keys Florida Keys extending from Key West to Miami

The Lady nickname of The Statue of Liberty in New York Harbor

The Liberator Daniel O'Connell

The Loop downtown commercial, financial, hotel, shopping, and theater district of Chicago

The Maestro Arturo Toscanini

The Melting Pot New York City

The Met Metropolitan Opera House—New York City

Themse (German—Thames)

THEN Those Hags Encourage

Neuterism

The Navigator Prince Henrique of Portugal (1394 to 1460)

theo theoretical; theoretician

Theo Theobald; Theobold; Theocritus; Theodoor; Theodor; Theodora; Theodore; Theodorus; Theodosia; Theodosius; Theodoric; Theodric; Theodule; Theophil; Theophile; Theophilus; Theophraste; Theophrastus

THEO They Help Each Other

Theoc Theocritus

The Ocean The Atlantic, Antarctic, Arctic, Indian, or Pacific Ocean

theod theodolite

theol theologian; theological; theologist; theology

Theol Theology

The Old King Grom of Denmark (860-935)

The Old Country wherever anyone or their family originated —especially if in Europe

The Old Dominion Virginia

The Old Party W(illiam) Somerset Maugham

The Old South Alabama, Florida, Georgia, Louisiana, Mississippi, North Carolina, South Carolina, Virginia

Theoph Theophrastus

theophilanthro theophilanthropic(al)(ly); theophilanthropist; theophilanthropy (Thomas Paine's deistic religion combining belief in a god with service to mankind)

theor theorem; theoretical; theory

The Orchid Island Hawaii

theos theosophical; theosophist; theosophy

Theo Soc Theosophical Society

The Pathfinder John C Frémont

The People's Attorney Louis Dembitz Brandeis

The Pineapple Island Lanai

The President the President of the United States

The Rail Splitter Abraham Lincoln

therap therapeutic; therapeutics; therapy

there's there is

The Restoration France from 1814 to 1848 with its monarchy restored *

The River (*see* River)

therm thermometer; thermostat(ic)

therm (Latin prefix—heat)—

thermometer

Therm Thermidor (French—Hot Month)—beginning July 19th—eleventh month of the French Revolutionary Calendar also called the *Fervidor*

Thermaic Gulf Gulf of Salonika in the Aegean

thermistor thermal resistor

thermo thermostat

thermoc thermocouple

thermochem thermochemical; thermochemistry

thermodyn thermodynamics

thermonuc thermonuclear

The Rock Alcatraz (former prison, now museum); The Rock of Gibraltar (British crown colony on a rocky peninsula extending south from the Spanish mainland into the Straits of Gibraltar where the Atlantic meets the Mediterranean); Saba Island, Netherlands Antilles

The Roughrider Colonel Theodore Roosevelt

THES Times Higher Education Supplement

The Sea the Baltic, Bering, Black, Caribbean, Japan, Mediterranean, North, Philippine, South China, or other sea

THESIS Thematic Elementary Science Individualized Studies

The Soo Sault Ste Marie

The Sound (*see* Sound)

Thespian Maids another name for the Nine Muses (*see entry)*

thesp(s) thespian(s)

Thess Thessalonians

Thessalonica (Latin—Salonika)

Thessaloniki (Modern Greek—Salonika)

The Stagirite Aristotle (born in Stagira)

The States the United States of America

The Sun King Louis XVI

The Swedish Nightingale Jenny Lind

thetcrit theater critic; theatrical criticism

The Terrible Ivan IV—Czar of Russia 1547 to 1584

The Tower The Tower of London

The Tragic Queen Marie Antoinette

The Tribune Man (pseudonym —Henry Ten Eyck White)

The Trust Buster William Howard Taft

The Twins Minneapolis and St

Paul
The Unashamed Accompanist Gerald Moore
The Valley Island Maui (pronounced *mau-ee*), Hawaii
The Village Carmel-by-the-Sea in California; Greenwich Village in New York City; La Jolla's shopping district near San Diego, California; wherever people take pains to preserve the quaint or rural character of their place
The Volcano Island Hawaii
The Wales The Bank of New South Wales
The Waltz King Johann Strauss, Jr
The Wash North Sea inlet between Lincoln and Norwich on east coast of England
they'd they had; they would
they'll they will
they're they are
they've they have
thf (THF) tetrahydrocortisol
t$_h$f Trust Houses Forte (British motel chain)
THF West Berlin, Germany (Tempelhof Airport)
TIIG Technische Hochschule Graz (Technical University of Graz)
th ga thread gauge
TIIIIS Townsend Harris High School
THlwm Trinity House high-water mark
thi temperature humidity index
TIII Texas Heart Institute
Thiefrow nickname for London's Heathrow Airport where security has been so lax and thievery so prevalent
thieves of time procrastinators
Thim Thimbu, Bhutan
things, three-dimensional input of graphical solids
Third Estate The Commons—the legislature
third-generation money electronically controlled funds
Third International Lenin's organization of seemingly ultra-radical communists meeting in Moscow in 1919 and rejecting social-democratic forces
Third Reich Nazi Germany (1933–1945)—fascist totalitarian state controlled by Nazi party under dictatorship of Adolf Hitler
Third Republic France from 1871 to 1940—from end of Franco-Prussian War to surrender of France during World War II

Third State New Jersey (*see* First State)
Third World emerging nations, often former colonies, outside industrialized communist and Western nations; poorer nations
Thirstland waterless country north of Bechuanaland
Thirteen Colonies Thirteen British North American colonies that during the American Revolution became the original thirteen states of the United States
Thirteen States New Hampshire, Massachusetts, Rhode Island, Connecticut, New York, New Jersey, Pennsylvania, Delaware, Maryland, Virginia, North Carolina, South Carolina, Georgia—original Thirteen Colonies that became United States of America
Thirteenth Apostle Constantine, the Roman emperor who built Constantinople (now known as Istanbul)
Thirteenth State Rhode Island (*see* First State)
Thirteenth Tribe Khazars converted to Judaism (*see* Twelve Tribes)
Thirtieth State Wisconsin
Thirty-eighth State Colorado
Thirty-fifth State West Virginia
Thirty-first State California
Thirty-fourth State Kansas
Thirty-ninth State North Dakota
Thirty Rock nickname of the National Broadcasting Company (NBC) at Thirty Rockefeller Center in New York City
Thirty-second State Minnesota
Thirty-seventh State Nebraska
Thirty-sixth State Nevada
Thirty-third State Oregon
This Is The Place Salt Lake City, Utah's sobriquet repeating the words of its founder—Brigham Young
thistle symbol of Scotland and the Scots
THIWRP The Hoover Institution on War, Revolution, and Peace
thixo thixotropic
Th:J Thomas Jefferson (initials written by him as shown)
thk thick(ness)
THK *Turk Hava Kurumu* (Turkish Air Association)
Th. L. Theological Licentiate

THlwm Trinity House low-water mark
thm (THM) trihalomethane
Th.M. *Theologiae Magister* (Latin—Master of Theology)
thms trihalomethanes
Thn Trollhättan
tho' though
'tho' although
Tho Thomas; Thorshavn
Tholosa (Latin—Toulouse)
Thomas St Thomas, American Virgin Islands
Thomas an' Charlie (American-tourist-in-Mexico speech—Tamazunchale)—hamlet on the Laredo-Mexico-City highway
Thomas Jefferson Snodgrass (pseudonym—Samuel L Clemens)
Thomas Kyd Alfred Bennett Harbage's pseudonym
Thomas of London Thomas à Becket
THOMIS Total Hospital Operating and Medical Information System
thor thorax; thoracic
Thor medium-range ballistic missile
thorac (Latin prefix—chest)—thoracic
Thoreau Foun Thoreau Foundation
thoro thorough
thoro' thorough
Thoro thoroughfare
Thos Thomas
Thos Jeff Thomas Jefferson
thou. thousand
thp thrust horsepower; track history printout
THq theater headquarters
thr their; threonine (amino acid) (THR); through; thrust
THR Teheran, Iran (airport)
Three Baltic Duchies Estonia, Latvia, Lithuania
Three Capitals and Five Ports Japanese numerical categories comprising the ancient and modern capitals—Kyoto, Osaka, and Tokyo plus the ports of Hakodate, Kobe, Nagasaki, Niigata, and Yokohama
three-C's Central Criminal Court
Three Kingdoms Denmark, Norway, Sweden
Three Kings Three Kings Islands bird sanctuary in the South Pacific off New Zealand's North Island
Three King's Three King's Day (January 6—Epiphany)

Three Little S's Saba, Sint Eustatius (Statia), Sint Maarten (Dutch Windward Islands—Netherlands Antilles)

Three Penny *Three Penny Opera* (composed by Kurt Weill and based on a modernized German version of John Gay's *The Beggar's Opera—Die Dreigroschenoper*—with lyrics by Bert Brecht translated by Ralph Manheim and John Willett)—the underworld set to music

three-R's reading, writing, arithmetic (colloquially: readin', 'ritin', 'rithmetic)

Three Virgins St Croix, St. John, St Thomas (United States Virgin Islands)

thrmst thermostat

thro' through

thro' b/l through bill of lading

Throgs Throgs Neck (site of New York State Maritime College in New York City's Bronx at the Long Island Sound mouth of the East River) ·

thrombo thrombosis

thrombo (Latin prefix—clot or lump)—thrombosed

Throne of Solomon Ethiopia

throt throttle

⁂ **thru** through

᛫ **Thru** Thruway

thruppence threepence

THS Technical High School; Tiwi Hot Springs (Philippines); Tottenville High School

tht (THT) tetrahydrothiopen

THT Teacher of Hydrotherapy

th ta thread tap

thtr theater

THTRA Thorium High-Temperature Reactor Association

Thu Thursday

THU The Hebrew University (Jerusalem)

Thuc Thucydides

THUMS Texaco, Humble, Union, Mobil, Shell (oil-drilling complex dominating Long Beach, California)

Thunder Bay modern name for the Canadian twin cities of Fort William and Port Arthur on the northwest shore of Lake Superior

Thunderbird British BAC mobile surface-to-air missile

Thunderbolt Republic fighting aircarft F-47; Swedish Viggen jet fighter J-37

Thunderchief Republic single-engine fighter-bomber jet aircraft (F-105)

Thunderjet Republic fighter-bomber F-84

Thur Thuringia(n); Thursday

Thüringen (German—Thuringia)

Thuringia English or Latin for Thüringen

Thurs Thursday

Thursday Thursday Island pearl-shell fishery in Torres Strait near Cape York, Australia

Thus (nickname—Calcutta Steam Tug); Thursday

thv thoracic vertebra

Thv Thorvald(sen)

THW Technische Hochschule Wien (Technical University of Vienna)

THwm Trinity House water mark

Thwy Thruway

THY Turk Hava Yollari (Turkish airline)

thz (tHz) tetraherz

ti target identification; temperature indication; temperature indicator; termination instruction; tricuspid insufficiency

t/i target identification; target indicator

ti Texas Instruments (trademark); *tudni illik* (Hungarian —that is)

Ti titanium

Ti Tirsdag (Danish—Tuesday); (Latin—Tiberius)

TI Technical Inspection; Technical Institute; Technical Intelligence; Terminal Island; Termination Instruction; Terrorist International; Texas Instruments; Textile Institute; Thread Institute; Title Insurance (and Trust Company); Toastmasters International; Tobacco Institute; Tonga Islands; Training Instruction; Treasure Island; Tungsten Institute; Tuskegee Institute

T of I Times of India

TI-67 Israeli designation for captured built-in-the-USSR tanks (T-54 and T-55 models armed with 100mm guns)

tia transient ischemic attack

tia (TIA) trading investment area

TIA Tax Institute of America; Trans International Airlines; Tricot Institute of America; Trouser Institute of America

TIA Tutukuvul Isukul Association (Melanesian—United Farmers Association)—Papua New Guinea coconut planters united

TIAA Teachers Insurance and Annuity Association of America

TIAC Thrift Institutions Advisory Council

Tia Juana river or river valley separating Tijuana, Baja California from San Diego, California

Tianjin (Pinyin Chinese—Tientsin)

TIAS Treaties and Other International Acts Series (U.S. Department of State)

tib tibia(l); trimmed in bunkers

Tib Isabel; Tibet; Tibetan

Tib Albius Tibullus (Roman poet)

TIB Technical Information Bulletin; Tennessee Inspection Bureau; Thousand Islands Bridge; Tourist Information Bureau

Tib(by) Isabel(la); Ishbel(le)

tibc total iron-binding capacity

Tiber (Spanish—Tiber)

Tiber River City Rome

Tibet. Tibetan

Tibre (French—Tiber)

tic. target intercept computer

TIC Teacher Information Center; Technical Information Center; Technical Institute Council; Technical Intelligence Center; Texas Industrial Commission

TICA Technical Information Center Administration

TICACE Technical Intelligence Center Allied Command Europe (NATO)

TICC Technical Intelligence Coordination Center

TICCI Technical Information Center for the Chemical Industry

ticcit time-shared interactive computer-controlled information television

TICF Tennessee Independent Colleges Fund; Transient Installation Confinement Facility

tick. tickler

Tico Costa Rican; Ticonderoga; USS *Ticonderoga* (attack aircraft carrier)

Ticos Costa Ricans (nickname given them by other Central Americans because of their frequent use of the Spanish diminutive *ico*)

tictac time compression tactical communications

TICUS Tidal Current Survey System

tid task initiation date

t.i.d. tres in die (Latin—thrice a day)

tideda time-dependent data analysis

Tidewater States Maryland, Virginia, North Carolina, South Carolina, Georgia

tidskr tidskrift (Swedish—periodical)

TIDU Technical Information and Documents Unit

tidy. teletypewriter integrated display

tie. technical integration and evaluation

tie. (TiE) (TIE) telephone interconnect equipment

TIE Technology Information Exchange; The Institute of Technology; Total Interlibrary Exchange (California Library Network); Traveler's Information Exchange; Truck Insurance Exchange

Tiempo El Tiempo (Time—Bogota's leading newspaper)

Tien Tientsin

Tien Shan high mountain ranges north of Pamirs and Himalayas between Siberia and Turkestan

tier. tierce

tier tierce (French—third)

Tiorg Tiorgarton

Tierra del Fuego (Spanish—Land of Fire)—originally the fires of Patagonian Indians but more recently the burning gases belching from oil rigs in southernmost South America

Tierra Santa (Spanish—Holy Land)

TIES Transmission and Information Exchange System

tif telephone influence factor; telephone interference factor; tumor inducing factor

Tif Tiflis

TIF Turtle Island Foundation

Tiff Tiffany

Tiff Tiffany's Reports

TIFI Technology Insight Foundation Incorporated

tifr total investment for return

TIFR Tata Institute of Fundamental Research

tifs technology for instructional feedback

tig time in grade; tungsten-inert gas

TIG The Inspector General

Tiger II Northrup F-5 twin-jet fighter aircraft

Tiger Bay Georgetown, Guyana's honky-tonk slum

Tigercat Short and Harland surface-to-air missile

Tiger of France Georges Clémenceau

TIGERS Telephone Information Gathering for Evaluation and Review System

Tigers of the Sun Sherpas of northern India and Nepal

Tight Little Island Great Britain

Tightrope Walker Extraordinaire Charles Blondin who crossed Niagara Falls in 1855 on an 1100-foot (336-meter) tightrope suspended 160 feet (48 meters) above the falls and five years later carried his agent across piggyback; in 1974 Philippe Petit crossed between the twin towers of the World Trade Center in New York on a tightwire 1350 feet (412 meters) above the city sidewalk

tigon offspring of tiger and lioness

Tigres River City Baghdad

TIGRs Treasury Investment Growth Receipts

tigt turbine inlet-gas temperature

Tigurum (Latin—Zurich)

TIH Their Imperial Highnesses

TII Texas Instruments Incorporated; Toastmasters International Incorporated

TIIAL The International Institute of Applied Linguistics

TIIRS Title-I Information and Reporting System

TIJ Tijuana, Mexico (airport)

Tikhi Don (Russian—Quiet Don)—slow-flowing River Don

Tikhiy Tikhiy Don (Russian—Quiet Flows the Don)—Dzerzhinsky's opera based on Sholokov's novel of that title)

'til until

TIL Taylor Institution Library (Oxford); Tube Investments Limited

Tilda Mathilda

tili translunar injection

Till Till Eulenspiegels lustige Streiche (German—Till Eulenspiegel's Merry Pranks)—symphonic poem by Richard Strauss

Tillie Mathilda

Tilly Mathilda

TILS Technical Information and Library Service

tim technical information on microfiche; technical information on microfilm; time is money

Tim Timor; Timothy

Tim Timon of Athens; Timothy

Tima Fatima

TIMA Thermal Insulation Manufacturers Association

timation time navigation

timations time navigation artificial satellite

timb timbales (French—kettledrums)

TIMC The Industrial Management Center

TIME Telecommunication Information Management Executive

time imm time immemorial (time beyond memory; time out of mind)

Time-Life Time-Life Books

Time Personified the aged Chronos of the Greeks and Romans—Father Time

Times The New York Times (leading American newspaper, published in New York City); *The Times* (leading British newspaper, published in London); local designation for all other newspapers containing *Times* in their title

TIMES The Institute of Mining and Engineering Surveyors

Timesqueer New York City's Times Square

Times Roman Times Roman type (sometimes abbreviated T-R)

timet titanium metal(s)

timms thermionic integrated micromodules

Timmy Timothy

timp timpani (Italian—kettledrums)

Timpanogos Timpanogos Cave National Monument in north-central Utah or Mount Timpanogos in the same area

TIMS The Institute of Management Sciences

Tim-Tim (Portuguese—Timor, Timur)—former colony in the Lesser Sunda islands of Indonesia

Timur the Lame Tamerlane

TIN Taxpayer Identification Number, Transaction Identification Number

Tina Albertina; Christina; Clementina; Valentina

tinc tincture

tin can(s) submarine(s)

Tin City Jamaica slum named

after its tin-can huts; sometimes called River Tin City as much of it is inundated during rains

tinct tincture

tinct. tinctura (Latin—tincture)

TINFO *Tieteellisen Informoinnin Neuvosto* (Finnish—Council for Scientific and Research Libraries)

'tini Martini (cocktail); (according to wags Martini is plural and Martinez is singular)

tin in tinnitus instrument

Tin Islands Indonesia's Banka and Belitung

Tin King Simón Ituri Patiño

Tin Lizzie Model-T Ford's nickname

TINs Temporary Instruction Notices

Tinseltown Hollywood, California

tint international practical temperature

Tintoretto Jacopo Robusti

tiny terrs tiny terrorists (children used by terrorists to run errands or spot their enemies)

tio take it off; time interval optimization; time in office (TIO)

TIO Target Indication Office(r); Television Information Office(r); Test Integration Office(r); Troop Information Office(r)

Tio Sam (Spanish—Uncle Sam)

tip tax information plan; theory in practice; to insure promptness (a gratuity given to insure promptness); translation-inhibiting protein (TIP)

tip tipografia; tipográfico (Italian—printing firm; typographic); truly important person (TIP)

Tip Thomas Phillip O'Neill, Jr; Timothy

TIP The Institute of Physics; Tax-based Income Policy; Terrorist Information Project; Trans-Israel Pipeline; Transportation Improvement Program; Tripoli, Libya (airport); Troop Information Program(s); truly important person(age)

TIPAC Texas Instruments Programming and Control

tip.bkt tipping bracket

Tip of Canada Ellesmere Land

Tipp Tipperary

Tippecanoe William Henry Harrison

TIPRO Texas Independent Producers and Royalty Owners

tips. to insure prompt service (gratuities); topical information packages; truly important persons (TIPS)

TIPs Tax-based Income Policies

TIPS Technical Information Processing Sytem; Total Integrated Pneumatic System; truly important persons

tiptap target input panel (and) target assign panel

Tipton Center State Correctional Center at Tipton, Missouri

tiptop tape input—tape output

TIP & TPS The Institute of Physics and The Physical Society

tir total indicator reading

TIR Transport International des Marchandises par la Route (French—International Transport of Merchandise by Road) —twenty-six nation custom agreement permitting trucks marked TIR to avoid customs until reaching their final destination

Tiradentes (Portuguese—Tooth Puller)—nickname of José Joaquim da Silva Xavier—first Brazilian fighter for independence from Portuguese rule—a dentist

Tirana English and Italian equivalent of Tiranë (Albania's capital)

Tiranë (Albanian—Tirana)

TIRB Transportation Insurance Rating Bureau

TIRC T Tauri Infrared Companion (pronounced *turk*); Tobacco Industry Research Committee

tire burner tire-burning pursuit of one vehicle by another (usually some person or persons attempting to elude law-enforcement officers in a pursuing vehicle)

Tire City Akron, Ohio

Tirol (German or Spanish—Tyrol)

Tirolo (Italian—Tyrol)

T-iron T-shaped iron or steel section

Tiros American meteorological satellite designed to observe cloud coverage and infrared heat radiation of the earth; television and infrared observation satellite

TIRR Texas Institute of Rehabilitation and Research

tirs thermal infrared scanner

Tirso de Molina (pseudonym—Gabriel Tellez)

tis tissue(s); total integrated scattering

'tis it is

TIs Thousand Islanders; Thursday Islanders; Tonga Islanders; Turks Islanders

TIS Technical Information Service; Total Information System; Transactional Information Systems

TISC Technology Information Sources Center

Tish Letitia

TISI Thai Industrial Standards Institute

ti-slash tire slash(ing)

TISPM Territorie des Iles St Pierre et Miquelon (French territory offshore Canada)

TISS Title-I Support System

tit *título* (Spanish—title)

tit. title; titular; titulary; transitive inference training

tit tître (French—title)

Tit Titus, The Epistle of Paul to

Tit Titus

TIT Tokyo Institute of Technology; Tustin Institute of Technology

Tit A Titus Andronicus

Titan two-stage intercontinental ballistic missile (Martin)

Titan Mahler's Symphony No. 1 in D major—he preferred to call it his *Werther* symphony comparing it with Goethe's first novel

titanox titanium dioxide

Titian Tiziano Vecellio

Titis Titi Islands also called the Mutton Birds and off the southwest coast of New Zealand's Stewart Island

tito título (Spanish—title)

Tito Josip Broz(ovich)

Titograd formerly Podgorica the capital of Montenegro now called South Yugoslavia

Tito Schipa Raffaele Attilio Amadeo Schipa

Titta Ruffo Ruffo Cafiero Titta

Titulescu James T(homas) Farrell

TITUS Textile Information Treatment Users Service

tiu trigger inverter unit

TIU Telecommunications International Union; Tokyo Imperial University

tiv total indicator variation

Tiv Tivoli

tix ticket(s)

tixi turret-integrated xenon illuminator

TIYC Thousand Island Yacht Club

tj tomato juice; triceps jerk; turbojet (TJ)

tj (TJ) talk jockey

tj to jest (Polish—that is)

Tj Tijuana, Baja California, Mexico

TJ Thomas Jefferson—third President of the United States

TJAG The Judge Advocate General

tjc trajectory

TjC trajectory chart

TJC The Jockey Club; Trenton Junior College; Tyler Junior College

TjD trajectory diagram

TJHS Thomas Jefferson High School

Tji Tjirebon (Cheribon)

TJM The Jewish Museum; Thomas Jefferson Memorial

tjp (TJP) turbojet propulsion

TJPOI Twisted Jute Packing and Oakum Institute

TJS Tactical Jamming System

TJSUSA Thomas Jefferson Society of the United States of America

tjt tactical jamming transmitter

TJTA Taylor-Johnson Temperament Analysis

tk track; truck; trunk

tk (TK) transkelotase

tk to kum (printer's expression meaning material is *to come*)

Tk Turkmenian; Turkmenistan

Tk Teluk (Malay—bay; bight; riverbend)

tkbd tackboard(ing)

tkd tokodynamometer

tkg tanking; tokodynagraph(y)

Tki Takoradi

TKK Teikoku Kaiji Kyokai (Imperial Japanese Marine Corporation, ship classifiers)

tko technical knockout

TKP Turkiye Komünist Partisi (Turkish Communist Party)

tkr tanker; terrestrial kilometric radiation

tks thanks

TKTF Tanker Task Force

tkt(s) ticket(s)

tl terminal limen; test link; thrust line; time length; time limit; total load; transmission level; transmission line; truckload; truck loading

t-l trade last (slang, a compliment)

t/l total loss

t.l. tukus lecker (Yiddish—ass

licker)—flatterer; sycophant

Tl thallium

TL Technical Letter; Technical Library; Texas League; The Leprosarium (U.S. Public Health Service, Carville, Louisiana); Townland (UK); Turk lirasi (Turkish pound)

T/L Telegraphist/Lieutenant; Torpedo Lieutenant

T-L Time-Life (books, magazines, recordings)

tla translumbar aortogram

TLA The Library Association (of the United Kingdom); Texas Library Association; Theatre Library Association; Trial Lawyers Association; Trinidad Lake Asphalt

Tlax Tlaxcala (inhabitants—Tlaxcaltecas)

TLB temporary lighted buoy

tlbl tape label

TLBs Time-Life Books

tlc talcum; tender loving care; thin-layer chromatography; total lung capacity

TLC Television Licensing Center; Total Life Care; Total Life Center; Trades and Labour Club

TLCPA Toledo-Lucas County Port Authority

TLCs Tire and Lube Centers

tld thermoluminescent detector; thermoluminescent dosimeter; tooled

tl dating thermoluminescent dating

tle theoretical line of escape; thin-layer electrochemistry

tlf telefon (Norwegian—telephone)

TLFB Texas-Louisiana Freight Bureau

tlg tail landing gear; telegraph

TLG Theatrical Ladies' Guild; Tiger Leasing Group

TLH Tallahassee, Florida (airport)

tlli tank liquid-level indicator

tlm telemeter; telemetry

TLMA Tag and Label Manufacturers Association

Tln Tallinn

tlo total loss only

TLO Technical Liaison Officer

tlp term-limit pricing; threshold learning process

tlp (TLP) tension-leg petroleum (oil rig)

TLP Telefones de Lisboa e Porto (Lisbon and Oporto Telephone Company)

tlr trailer; twin-lens reflex (camera)

TLR Tool Liaison Request

tls testing the limits for sex

TLS Technical Library Service; Technical Library System; Terminal Landing System; The Law Society; Trinity Lighthouse Service

TLS Times Literary Supplement

tlt transportable link terminal

TLTB Trunk Line Tariff Bureau

tltr translator

tlu table look up

tlv threshold limit value(s)

tlv (TLV) tracked levitated vehicle

TLV Tel Aviv, Israel (airport)

tlvsn television

tly tally

tlz titanium, lead, zinc; transfer on less than zero

tm standard mean temperature; tactical missile (TM); team; temperature meter; time modulation; tractor monoplane (TM); trademark; transport mechanism; transverse magnetic; true mean; twisting moment

t/m test and maintenance

t & m time and material(s)

tm tonelada métrica (Spanish—metric ton, 2,200 pounds)

Tm thulium

TM tactical missile; Technical Manual; Technical Memoranda; Technical Memorandum; Technical Minutes; Technical Monograph; Telemetering; Test Manual; Texas Mexican (railroad); The Maccabees; Toledo Museum; tractor monoplane; trademark; Training Manual; Training Mission(s); Trainmaster; Transcendental Meditation; Tropical Medicine

T/M (t/m) trailmobile (automobile trailer)

TM Technical Manual; Turk Mali (Turkish—Made in Turkey)

tma total material assets; total military assets

Tma Tema

TMA Texas Maritime Academy; Theatrical Mutual Association; Tile Manufacturers Association; Tobacco Merchants Association; Toiletery Merchandisers Association; Toy Manufacturers Association

TMAMA Textile Machinery and Accessory Manufacturers'

Association

T-man Treasury Department special agent of the IRS

tmar trial marriage

TMAS Taylor Manifest Anxiety Scale

TMB Travelling Medical Board

TMBC Toronto Motor Boat Club

tmbr timber

tmc total market coverage

TMC Tata Memorial Center; Technical Measurement Corporation; Texas Medical Center (Houston); Trans Mar de Cortés (Mexican airline)

TMCA Tabulating Card Manufacturers Association; Titanium Metals Corporation of America

tmcd tetramethylcyclobutanediol

tmcp trimethylenecyclopropane

TME Teacher of Medical Electricity

T-men Treasury Department law-enforcement officers

TM-Eng Technical Manual—Engineering

t'ment tournament

TMF The Menninger Foundation

tmh thermomechanical hydraulic; tons per manhour

tmi technical market index (TMI)

Tmi Tsurumi

TMI Telemeter Magnetics Incorporated; Three-Mile Island; Tool Manufacturing Instruction; Trucking Management Incorporated; Tube Methods Incorporated; Turkish Military Institute; Turkish Military Intelligence

TMI *Technical Manual Index* (USN)

TMIC Toxic Materials Information Center

TMIF Three-Mile Island (nuclear-power) Facility

TMIS Technical Meetings Information Service

tmj temporo-mandibular joint

tmj (TMJ) temporomandibular joint (syndrome)

TMJ *Trade Marks Journal*

tmkpr timekeeper

tml (TML) three-mile limit

TML Transport Managers License

TMM *Transportación Marítima Mexicana* (Spanish—Mexican Maritime Transportation)

TMMC Theater Materiel Man-

agement Center

TMMG Teacher of Massage and Medical Gymnastics

tmn transmission (flow chart)

Tmn Tamano

TMNP Tamborine Mountain National Parks (Queensland)

tmo (TMO) telegraph money order

TMO telegraph money order; Traffic Management Officer

TMORN Texaco Metropolitan Opera Radio Network

tmp temperature; temporary; thermomechanical pulp(ing); trimethoprim; trimethyl phosphate (male contraceptive)

tmp (TMP) total mind power

Tmp Tampico

tmpry temporary

tmp's transcedental meditation practitioners

TMPS Trans-Mississippi Philatelic Society

tmr timer; total materiel requirement; trainable mentally retarded (semi-autistic children)

TMRB Tropical Medicine Research Board

tmrbm (TMRBM) transportable midrange ballistic missile

tms type, model, and series

tms *tai muuta semmoista* (Finnish—and so on)

TMS Tactical Missile Squadron; Technical Museum, Stockholm; Transmatic Money Service

TMS *Tribunal Maritime Special* (French—Special Maritime Court)—disciplinary prison court functioning in French Guiana

TMSA Technical Marketing Society of America

tmsd total military service date

tmt turbine-motored train

Tmt Tablemount

TMT transonic model tunnel

TMTB The Malayan Tin Bureau

tmtc through-mode tape converter

TMU Tokyo Metropolitan University

TMUS Toy Manufacturers of the United States

tmv true mean value

tmv (TMV) tobacco-mosaic virus

TMV Transportadora Marítima Venezolana (Venezuelan Line)

tmw thermal megawatts; tomorrow

TMW Textile Machine Works

TMWC *Trial of the Major War Criminals*

tn tariff number; telephone number; thermonuclear; train; true north

Tn thoron (chemical symbol); Ton (postal abbreviation)

TN Task Number; Technical Note

T & N Turner and Newhall

TN *Twelfth Night*

TNA The National Archives

TNAS Tuberculosis Nursing Advisory Service

TNB *Tsentral'naya Nauchnaya Biblioteka* (Russian—Central Scientific Library)—in Kiev

tnc total numerical control

TNC Thai Navigation Company

TNDC Thai National Documentation Center

TNEC Temporary National Economic Committee

t^{nes} *tonnes* (French—tons)

tnf transfer on no overflow

TNF Theater Nuclear Forces (NATO); Toiyabe National Forest

tng training

Tng *Tandjung* (Malay—Cape)

TNG Tangier, Morocco (airport); The National Grange; The Newspaper Guild

TNG *The New Grove Dictionary of Music and Musicians* (20-volume 1981 edition)

tnge tonnage

TNI *Tentara Nasional Indonesia* (Indonesian National Army)

TNIAU *Tentara Nasional Indonesia Angkatan Udara* (Bahasa Indonesian—Indonesian Armed Forces—National Air Force)

Tn IOB Technician of the Institute of Building

tnm tumor, node, metastasis

tnm (TNM) tactical nuclear missile

TNM Texas-New Mexican; Texas-New Mexico; Tokyo National Museum; Tumacacori National Monument

TNM *Telégrafos Nacionales de México*

TNNP Taman Negara National Park (Malaysia); Terra Nova National Park (Newfoundland)

Tno Taranto

T & NO Texas and New Orleans (railroad)

t no c threads no couplings

tnp (TNP) trinitrophenol

TNP Tarangire National Park (Tanzania); Taroba NP (India); Tonariro NP (North Island, New Zealand); Tsavo NP (Kenya)

TNP Théâtre National Populaire (French—Popular National Theater)

tnpg trinitrophloroglucinol

TNPG The Nuclear Power Group

Tnpk Turnpike

TNPO Terminal Navy Post Office

tnr trainer

tnr toneladas de registro neto (Spanish—net registered tonnage)

TNR Tananarive, Malagasy (airport); Tucki Nature Reserve (New South Wales)

TNRIS Transportation Noise Research Information Service

Tnry Tannery

tns transcutaneous nerve stimulator

Tns Townsville; Tunis

TNS Tennessee Nuclear Specialties; Transit Navigation System

tnt (TNT) trinitrotoluene

t-n t trans-national terrorism; trans-national terrorist

t'n't tequila and tonic (mixed drink)

tntc too numerous to count

TNTC Thames Nautical Training College

t-n t's trans-national terrorists

tntv tentative

tnw (TNW) tactical nuclear warfare

tn wep(s) thermonuclear weapon(s)

TNWR Tamarac National Wildlife Refuge (Minnesota); Tewaukon NWR (North Dakota); Tishomingo NWR (Oklahoma)

tnx thanks

tnz transfer on non zero

to. telephone order (TO); time off time opening; tool order (TO); transverse optic; turn off; turn over

t/o (TO) takeoff

t & o taken and offered; technical and office (workers)

t.o tinctura opii (Latin—tincture of opium)

tº tomo (Spanish—volume)

To Togo; Toronto

To Torsdag (Danish—Thursday)

TO Table of Organization; takeoff; Technical Observer; Technical Order(s); Theater of Operations; Third Order (of a religious congregation); Toledo, Ohio; Tool Order; Transportation Office(r); Travel Order

T/O Table of Organization

TO Technical Order

toa total obligational authority

TOA Theater Owners of America; The Orchestral Association; Toledo Opera Association

toac tool accessory

tob tobacco

Tob Tobago; The (Apocryphal) Book of Tobit

T o B Tour of Britain (bicycle)

tobac tobacco; tobacconist

Tobacco City Winston-Salem, North Carolina

Tobacco Road dilapidated and poverty-stricken rural areas (sociological synonym); tobacco-raising areas of the southern United States (generic and economic meaning)

Tobaccos Tobacco Root Mountains of southwest Montana

Tóbal Cristóbal

TOBE Test of Basic Education

TOBWE Tactical Observing Weather Element (USAF)

Toby Tobyhanna; Tobias

toc table of contents; top-blown oxygen converter; total organic carbon

Toc Tagliabue open cup

TOC Tactical Operations Center; Technical Order Compliance; Television Operating Center

TOCCWE Tactical Operations Control Center Weather Element (USAF)

TOCHR Terminal Operators Conference of Hampton Roads

Toco Tocopilla, Chile

TOCS Terminal Operating Control System

Tocúmen Panamá City's airport

tod technical objective document(s); time of day; time of delivery

Tod Todhunter

TOD Technical Objective Document

to'ds toads; towards

Tod und Verklärung (German—Death and Transfiguration)—symphonic poem by Richard Strauss

toe. term of enlistment; total operating expense

TOE Table of Equipment

T O & E Texas, Oklahoma &

Eastern (railroad)

TOEFL Test of English as a Foreign Language

TOES Tradeoff Evaluation System

TOET Test of Elementary Training

tof time of flight

tofc trailer on flatcar (or piggyback)

tog. together; toggle; to order grog

TOGA Tests of General Ability

to'gal'nt topgallant (mast or sail)

Togo Admiral Togo Heihachiro (victor of the Battle of Tsushima where his forces annihilated the Russian fleet in 1905); Republic of Togo (West African coastal country whose French-speaking Togolese engage in mining, tropical agriculture, and the production of textiles) *République Togolaise*

Togoland (German—Togo)—West African colony under German domination from 1884 to 1916

Togo Port Lomé

togr together

togw takeoff gross weight

tog/wi together with

To Hell and Back nickname of the Toronto, Buffalo, and Hamilton Railway

tohp takeoff horsepower

toid woild New York taxicab-driver slang meaning the Third World of emerging nations of Africa, Asia, and Latin America

Toinette Antoinette

toity-toid street New York dialect enriched by successive generations of longshoremen, taxicab drivers, and others who pronounce 33rd Street as shown

toj track on jamming

Tojo Premier Tojo Hideki (Japanese general and premier during World War II)

Tok Tokyo

Tokaido Corridor urban strip between Kyoto and Tokyo (Kyoto, Kobe, Osaka, Nara, Nagoya, Hamamatsu, Shizuoka, Yokohama, Tokyo)

Tokelaus Tokelau Islands of the Pacific also called the Union Islands including Atafu, Fakaofu, and Nukunono

toke(s) token(s)

Tokío (Spanish—Tokyo)

Tok Uni Tokyo University

Tokyo (Japanese—Eastern)—formerly called Edo or Yedo and now capital of Japan as well as the world's largest city although Mexico City and New York are close contenders for the title

Tokyo-to (Japanese—Eastern Capital)—Tokyo's full name

Tokyo-wan (Japanese—Tokyo Bay)

tol tolerance; toluene

Tol Toledo; Toledan

T o L Tower of London

TOL Toledo, Ohio (airport); Trans-Ocean Leasing (corporation)

tol'able tolerable

TOLCCS Trends in On-Line Computer Control Systems

Toleto (Latin—Toledo)

Tolliver Tagliafiero

Tolly Tolliver

Tolón (Spanish—Toulon)

Tol Orc Toledo Orchestra

to lt towing light

TOLU Transocean Leasing (container) Unit

t-o-m the old man (the boss; the captain, the chief, the father)

tom tomo (Spanish—volume)

Tom $2 bill; Thomas

TOM *Territoire d'Outre-Mer* (Overseas Territory)

tom(at) tomato

tomats tomatoes

tomb. technical organizational memory bank

Tombigbee Tombigbee River of Alabama and Mississippi

Tombs old New York City Prison on the Lower East Side where it was connected to the Criminal Courts Building by a Bridge of Sighs

Tomb Town Moscow (featuring Lenin's tomb)

tomcat (TOMCAT) theater-of-operations missile continuous-wave anti-tank (weapon)

Tomcat F-14 fighter aircraft

Tom, Dick, and Harry the crowd; ordinary people; the mob; no one in particular

tome (Greek—a cutting or a slice)—anatomy, dichotomy, lobotomy, microtome

Tommie Thomas

Tom Mix Eugene Blackman's motion-picture reel name

Tommy nickname for a British soldier; Thomas

Tommy Atkins (nickname for a British Army private)

Tommy the Cork Thomas Corcoran

Tommy gun Thompson submachine gun

Tom o' Bedlam incurable male lunatic

toms tired old movies

Toms two-dollar bills bearing the portrait of President Thomas Jefferson

TOMS Total Ozone Mapping System

tom thumb (Cockney—rum)

tomy (Latin suffix—cut)—appendectomy

ton toneel (Dutch—scene, set, stage); *toneladas* (Spanish—tonnage, tons); *tyurma osobogo naznacheniya* (Russian—special-purpose prison)

Ton Tonga or Friendly Islands

Toña Antonia

'Tona Daytona Beach, Florida

TONACS Technical Order Notification and Completion System

Toncontin airport of Tegucigalpa, Honduras

Tonga Kingdom of Tonga (South Pacific island nation whose friendly Tongans speak English and Tongan; farming for bananas and coconuts, fishing, and tourism support these Polynesian islanders)

Tongan Ports Nukualofa Tongata, Pangai Haapai, Neiafu Vavau

Tongareva Penrhyn Island in the South Pacific

Tongariro Tongariro National Park in New Zealand's North Island or an active volcano in the same area

Tongas Tonga Islands in the South Pacific

Tongass Tongass National Forest in southern Alaska

tonguesan tongue sandwich

Tongue Troopers Canadian term for government's French-language enfc:cement squads

tonguewich tongue sandwich

Toni Antonia

Ton Isl Tonga Islands

tonk honky tonk

tonn tonnage

Tono Tomuelo (Tony derived from Anthony)

Toño Antonio

Tony Anthony; Antoinette Perry Awards (American Theatre Wing)

Tony Curtis Bernie Schwartz

Tony Martin Alvin Morris

Tony Randall Leonard Rosenberg

Tony Sarg Anthony Frederick Sarg

too. time of origin

tooies tuinal (half amobarbital and half secobarbital)

Tooth City Florence, South Carolina

Toothpicks nickname given early settlers of Arkansas who were believed to pick their teeth with bowie knives

top. temporarily out of print; topographica (three-dimensional) art; torque oil pressure

t-o-p temporal-occipital-parietal (lobes of the brain)

Top Topeka; Topology

ToP Taxonomy of Programs

top 10 top 10 best sellers (books or recordings of classical, jazz, or popular music)

top 25 top 25 concertos featured in many orchestral programs (Bach's concerto for two violins, Beethoven's five piano and one violin concertos, two piano and one violin concertos by Brahms, Bruch's violin concerto, Chopin's two piano concertos, Dvořák's cello concerto, Gershwin's piano concerto, Grieg's piano concerto, Liszt's piano concerto No. 1, Mendelssohn's violin concerto, Mozart's piano concerto No. 20, Paganini's concerto No. 1 for violin, Rachmaninoff's piano concerto No. 2, Schumann's piano concerto, the violin concerto of Sibelius, Tchaikovsky's concerto No. 1 for piano and his violin concerto)

top 30 top 30 symphonic spectaculars favored on many orchestral programs [Bach's Toccata and Fugue in D; Beethoven's Lenore Overture No. 3; Berlioz's *Symphonie fantastique*; Borodin's Polovetsian Dances; Brahms's Variations on a Theme by Haydn; Debussy's *La Mer*; Glinka's Russlan and Ludmilla Overture; Handel's Water Music; Liszt's *Les Preludes*; Mussorgsky's Night on Bald Mountain, Pictures at an Exhibition; Prokofiev's Peter and the Wolf; Rachmaninoff's Rhapsody on a Theme by Paganini; Ravel's Bolero; Rimsky-Korsakov's Scheherazade; Saint-Saëns's Carnival of the Animals, Symphony No. 3 (Organ); Sibelius's Finlandia; Smetana's Moldau; Richard

Strauss's tone poems—Don Juan, Don Quixote, Hero's Life (*Heldenleben*), Thus Spake Zarathustra (*Also Sprach Zarathustra*), Till Eulenspiegel; Stravinsky's *Sacre du Printemps*; Tchaikovsky's Overture 1812, Romeo and Juliet; Wagner's Flying Dutchman and Tannhäuser overtures, *Tristan* Prelude and Liebestod]

top 40 top 40 symphonies favored on many symphonic programs [Beethoven's 3rd (*Eroica*), 5th, 6th (*Pastoral*), and 9th (*Choral*); the four by Brahms; Bruckner's 4th (*Romantic*) and 9th; Dvořák's 6th and 9th (*New World*); Haydn's 94th (*Surprise*), 100th (*Military*), 101st (*Clock*), 103rd (*Drum Roll*), 104th (*London*); Mahler's 1st, 2nd (*Resurrection*), and 9th; Mendelssohn's 3rd (*Scottish*), 4th (*Italian*), and 5th (*Reformation*); Mozart's 35th (*Haffner*) and 41st (*Jupiter*); Prokofiev's 1st (*Classical*) and 5th; Rachmaninoff's 2nd; Schubert's 8th (*Unfinished*) and 9th; Schumann's 1st (*Spring*), 2nd, 3rd (*Rhenish*), and 4th; Shostakovich's 1st and 5th; Sibelius's 1st; Tchaikovsky's 4th, 5th, and 6th (*Pathétique*)]

topa tooling pattern

topaz hydrous aluminum fluorosilicate

TOPAZ Technic for the Optimum Placement of Activities in Zones

TOPCOPS The Ottawa Police Computerized On-line Processing System (Canada)

Topeka capital of Kansas

Top of Europe northern sections of Finland, Norway, Russia, and Sweden near the Arctic Circle

TOPICS Tables of Periodical Indices Concerning Schools; Test of Performance in Computational Skills

to po topographic; topography

Topo Topolobampo, Sonora, Mexico

TopoCom Topographic Command (USA)

topog topography

topol topology

topon toponym (place-name)—convicts often use toponyms when telling where they have been jailed, e.g., Atlanta for

the federal penitentiary in Atlanta, Georgia

topony toponym(ic)(al); toponymist; toponymy

topo(s) toponym(s)

TOPP Terminal-Operated Production Program

tops. (TOPS) take off pounds sensibly

TOPS Task-Oriented Processing System; Teen-age Opportunity Programs in Summer; Tested Overhead Projection Series; Training Opportunities Scheme

Top Sec Top Secret

tops'l topsail

TOPSTAR The Officer Personnel System—The Army Reserve (USA)

Top Ten FBI's list of the 10 most wanted fugitives from justice

Top of the World Point Barrow, Alaska

Toquemas Toquemas Mountains of central Nevada

Tóquio (Portuguese—Tokyo)

tor time of receipt; torque; torquing; torquing up

tor (TOR) teletype on radio; transmitter output register

Tor Toronto

TOR Third Order Regular

Toray Tokyo Rayon Company (tradename)

TORCH Toronto Orthopaedic Recreational Center's Headquarters

Torchbearer of the Revolution Nathaniel Bacon of Virginia

Tor-Chi Toronto—Chicago

Tor Dep Torpedo Depot

Tor Dom Toronto Dominion (bank)

Tor House home of Robinson Jeffers at Carmel, California

Torino (Italian—Turin)

Tor Int Air Toronto International Airport

Tor-Lax Toronto—Los Angeles

Tormentine Cape Tormentine—easternmost point in New Brunswick, Canada

Tor-Mia Toronto—Miami

torn. tornado

Tornado Alley tornado-prone area between Lawton, Oklahoma and Wichita Falls, Texas

Torngats Torngat Mountains of Labrador

Tor-NY Toronto—New York

torp torpedo; torpedoman

Torport Toronto (container) Port

torr 1mm of mercury

Torr toor

Tor-San Toronto—San Diego

Tor-Sea Toronto—Seattle

Tor-Sfo Toronto—San Francisco

Tortilla Curtain nickname for the unfenced and vandalized-fenced Mexican Border between El Paso, Texas and San Diego, California

Tortilla Flat John Steinbeck's novel about the tumbledown Hispanic section of Monterey, California

Tortugas Tortuga Islands (Dry Tortugas and Wet Tortugas)

tos term of service

TOS Tape Operating System; The Orton Society; Tiros Operational Satellite

Tosa Tsunetaka

TOSBAC Toshiba Scientific and Business Automatic Computer

tosc toscano (Italian—Tuscan)

TOSCA Toxic Substances Control Act

Toscana (Italian—Tuscany)

TOSCO The Oil Shale Corporation

tose tooling samples

Toshiba Tokyo Shibaura Electric

toss. takeoff safety speed

TOSS Tiros Operation Satellite System

tot time on (over) target; total; totalize; totalizer

t o t *tukus om tisch* (Yiddish—put your cards on the table)

t-o-t tip-of-the-tongue

tot *tuchis afn tish* (Yiddish—buttocks on the table)—put up or shut up, put your cards on the table

TOT Tourist Occupancy Tax; Tourist Organization of Thailand; Transient Occupancy Tax

totalism totalitarianism

TOTCO Technical Oil Tool Corporation

tote. totalizator

TOTE Task-Oriented Teacher Education; Totem Ocean Trailer Express (to Alaska)

TOTES Test-Operate-Test-Exit System

t'other the other

t' other siders the other siders (nickname given by east coast Australians by their west coast counterparts)

Toti dal Monte Antonietta Meneghel

TOTO Tongue of the Ocean (deep-water channel in Great

Bahama Bank)

totp tooling template

Tou Toulon

TOU The Open University; Tractor Oils Universal

Tough Guy (stock exchange nickname for Texas Gulf Sulphur company)

tour. tourism, tourist

Tourette's disease convulsive facial tic

tourn tournament

Tournai French place-name equivalent for Doornik

TOUS Test on Understanding Science

tov ten opzichte van(Dutch—with regard to)

TOVALOP Tanker Owner's Voluntary Agreement concerning Liability for Oil Pollution

tow. tug of war

tow. (TOW) tube-launched optically-tracked wire-guided (anti-tank missile)

Tow Hughes antitank missile designated MGM-71A

Towel Town Kannapolis, North Carolina where Cannon towels are made

Tower The Tower of London (formerly a prison and now a museum by the Thames in London); Tower Publications

TOWER Testing, Orientation, and Work Evaluation in Rehabilitation

Tower Island, Galápagos Genovesa

Towers Charters Towers

townet towing net

Town of Floating Gardens Xochimilco, Mexico

Town of Fools Chelm (*see* Chelmer)

Town of Merchants Shanghai

Town on the Water Stockholm

Town of Roses Molde, Norway

Town Too Tough To Die Tombstone, Arizona

Town of the Vikings Manitoba

tox toxemia; toxic; toxicant; toxicologist; toxicology

tox (Latin prefix—poison)—toxicology

toxback toxicology information backup

toxicol toxicology

toxline toxicology hot line (public information program); toxicology on-line

TOXLINE Toxicology On-Line (computer retrieval system)

Toy Toy Symphony usually ascribed to Haydn but now be-

lieved to be part of a larger work by Leopold Mozart

Toy Bulldog Mickey Walker

tp target practice; teaching practice; technical paper; telephone; teleprinter; title page; toilet paper; total points; total protein; transport pilot; treaty port; turning point

tp (TP) tape (computer flow chart); total product

t/p test panel

t & p theft and pilferage

tp tempo primo (Italian—speed as at the outset)

Tp Township; Troop

TP Technical Pamphlet; Technical Paper; Technical Problem; Technical Publication; Technographic Publication; Texas & Pacific (railroad); Thompson Products; Torrey Pines (Institute); True Position

T & P Texas and Pacific (railroad)

T.P. Tempore Pachale (Latin—Easter time)

tpa travel by privately owned conveyance authorized

TPA Tampa, Florida (Tampa International Airport); Tampa Port Authority; Trans-Pacific Airlines (Aloha Airline); Travelers' Protective Association

TPAC Thomas Performing Arts Center (Akron)

TPAO Türkiye Petrolleri Anomin Ortakligi (Turkish Petroleum Corporation)

tpb tryptone phosphate broth

TPB Transportation Programs Bureau

TPBA Transit Patrolmen's Benevolent Association

TPBC Toledo Power Boat Club

tpc treated-paper copier

TPC The Peace Corps (US Department of State)

TPC/JCA Texas Public Community/Junior College Association

TPCNA Titanium, Palladium, Copper, Nickel, Au (gold) telephone circuit-board plating

TPCP Test Plan Change Procedure

tpd tons per day

tp'd toilet papered (some teenager's idea of house-and-garden decoration)

TPDC Tanjong Pagar Dock Company (Singapore)

TPE Taipei, Formosa (airport)

TPEQ Task of Public Education Questionnaire

TPF Tactical Police Force; Thomas Paine Foundation

TPFH Tasmanian Pulp and Forest Holdings

TPGA Texas Personnel and Guidance Association

tpgh tons per gang hour

tph tons per hour

TPH Theosophical Publishing House

Tpha Treponema pallidum hemagglutination

tphasap telephone as soon as possible

tphayc telephone at your convenience

TPH & PCA Toy Pistol, Holster, and Paper Cap Association

TPHS Thomas Paine High School

tpi teeth (threads, tons, or turns) per inch; treponema pallidum immobilization (test)

t-p i title-page, index

Tpi Taipei; Treponema pallidum immobilization

TPI Tennessee Polytechnic Institute; Torrey Pines Institute; Truss Plate Institute

Tpilisa (Georgian—Tiflis)

Tpi test *Treponema pallidum* immobilization (for the detection of syphilis)

Tpk Turnpike

Tpke Turnpike (postal abbreviation)

TPL Tallahasee Public Library; Tampa Public Library; Toledo Public Library; Toronto Public Libraries; Tucson Public Library; Tulsa Public Library

TPLA Turkish People's Liberation Army

tplab tape label

TPLF Turkish People's Liberation Front (ultra-leftists active in kidnapping and killing Americans and Israelis)

TPLs Trust for Public Lands

tpm tape preventive maintenance; tons per minute

tpmark tapemark(ing)

tpn trigger price mechanism

tpn (TPN) triphosphopyridine nucleotide; (same as nadp or NADP⁺)

TPN Tatrzanskiego Parku Narodowego (Polish—High Tatra National Park)—in the Tatra Mountains of Poland

tpnh (TPNH) reduced triphosphopyridine nucleotide

TPNHA Thomas Paine National Historical Association (New Rochelle, NY)

TPNHS Thomas Paine National Historical Society

tpnl test panel

tpo terminal-performance objective; transmitter (signal) power output

tpo tiempo (Spanish—time)

TPO Tulsa Philharmonic Orchestra

tpob true point of beginning

TPOR Teacher Practices Observation Record

tpp (TPP) thiamine pyrophosphate

TPP Tax Preparers Program; Technical Program Plan(ning); Total Package Procurement

TPPC Total Package Procurement Concept; Trans-Pacific Passenger Conference

TP-PL Technical Publications Planning (USN)

TP-PU Technical Publications —Public Utilities (USN)

tpqi teacher-pupil question inventory

tpr tape programmed raw; telescopic photographic recorder; temperature profile recorder; thermoplastic recording

tpr (TPR) temperature, pulse, respiration

Tpr Trooper

TPRC Thermophysical Properties Research Center

tpri teacher pupil relationship inventory

TPRI Tropical Pesticides Research Institute

T & P Ry Texas and Pacific Railway

tps technical problem summary; terminals per station; text processing service; tree-pruning system (computer language)

tp's taxpayers

TPS The Physical Society; Technical Publishing Society; Text Processing Service

tpt tetraphenyl tetrazolium; total protein tuberculin; transport; trumpet

TPT Tactual Performance Test(ing); Toy Preference Test; Transonic Pressure Tunnel (NASA)

tptg turned plate turned grid

tptn toilet partition

tpto tripropyl tin oxide

tptr trumpeter

tpu tape preparation unit; thermoplastic urethane

tpw title page wanting

TP & W Toledo, Peoria & Western (railroad)

t.q. tale quale (Latin—as is)

TQCA Textile Quality Control Association

tqcm thermoelectric quartz-crystal microbalance

TQE Technical Quality Evaluation

t quark top quark

tr temperature, rectal; test run; tons registered; toothed ring; trace; trace; tracer (bullet); tracking radar; translation; transmit-receive; transmitter-receiver; transpose; tuberculin R

tr (TR) total revenue

t-r transmit-receive

t/r transmit(ter)/receive(r)

tr trillo (Italian—rolled or shaken, as in drumming or when shaking a tambourine); *traduit* (French—translated); *trykkeri* (Dano-Norwegian—printing office); *tryckt* (Swedish—printed); *trykt* (Dano-Norwegian—printed)

Tr Transcript; Trench; Trieste; Trough

TR Tasmanian Railway; Technical Regulation; Technical Report; Test Report; Texas Gulf Production Company (stock-exchange symbol); Theodore (Teddy) Roosevelt (26th President U.S.); therapeutic radiology; torpedo reconnaissance (naval aircraft); Training Regulation(s); Transportation Request; Travel Request; Trieste; Trip Report; Triumph (British auto or motorcycle); Turkey (auto plaque)

T R Times Roman

tra transformer-reactor assembly

Tr A Triangulum Australe (constellation)

TRA Technical Report Authorization; Textile Refinishers Association, Theodore Roosevelt Association; Thoroughbred Racing Associations; Tire and Rim Association; Trade Relations Association; Travel Research Association

traac transit-research and altitude-control (satellite)

Trabzon (Turkish—Trebizond)

trac text-reckoning and compiling (computer language); tracer; tracing; tractor

TRACALS Traffic Control and Landing System

tracap transient circuit-analysis program

tracdr tractor-drawn

trace. tape-controlled recording and automatic checkout equipment; task reporting and current evaluation; time-shared routines for analysis, classification, and evaluation; total-risk assessing-cost estimate(s)

TRACE Trane Air Conditioning Economics

trach trachea; tracheal; tracheate; tracheation; tracheoscopy; tracheostomy; tracheotomy

TRACIS Traffic Records and Criminal Justice Information System (Iowa)

Tracker Grumman S-2 antisubmarine search-and-attack aircraft

trackex tracking exercise

tracon terminal radar control

TRACS Telemetry Receiver Acoustic Command System; Telescoping Rotor Aircraft System; Total Royalty Accounting and Copyright Systems

tract (Latin prohx drag or draw)—traction

tractorcade tractorized-vehicle parade

Tracy Theresa

trad tradition(al)

trad traducido (Spanish—translated)

TRADA Timber Research and Development Association

Trader Horn nickname of Alfred Aloysius Smith

tradex target resolution and discrimination experiment

tradic transistor digital computer

traf traffic

Trafalgar Cape Trafalgar in southwestern Spain at the western entrance to the Strait of Gibraltar

Trafalgar Square principal square in London—dominated by Nelson monument and National Gallery

TRAFFIC Trade Records Analysis of Fauna and Flora in Commerce (endangered species)

trafphobia traffic phobia (fear of driving in traffic)

trag tragedy

Tragic overture by Brahms; Symphony No. 6 by Mahler; Symphony No. 4 by Schubert

Tragic Patriot freethinker-patriot pamphleteer-world citizen Thomas Paine (imprisoned by the Reign of Terror in France and reviled by the clergy in the United States he helped create)

Tragic Queen Marie Antoinette

Tragus Heironymus Bock

T-rail T-shaped rail

train. trainee; trainer; training

TRAIN Telerail Automated Information Network; To Restore American Independence Now

TRAIS Transportation Research Activity Information Service (Department of Transportation)

Trajectum ad Viadrum (Latin—Frankfurt an der Oder)

Trajectum Inferius (Latin—Utrecht)—Dutch city also known as Trajectum ad Rhenum or Ultrajectum

Trajectum Superius (Latin—Maastricht)—also called Trajectum Mosae

tram. tracking radar automatic monitoring; tramcar; trammel; tramway

TRAM Test Reliability and Maintenance Program (USN); Treatment Rating Assessment Matrix; Treatment Response Assessment Method

tramp. temperature regulation and monitor panel

tramps. temperature regulator and missile power supply

tran transient

tran (TRAN) transmit (data processing)

tran tranvia (Spanish—tramway)—streetcar or streetcar line

trandir translation director (computer language)

tranks nickname for sedative drugs (tranquilizers)

trans transactions; transfer; transit; transport; transportation; transpose; transposition

trans (Latin prefix—across or over)—transalpine, transatlantic

Trans Transactions

transac transaction(s)

Trans Am Cryst Soc Transactions of the American Crystallographic Society

Trans Am Geophys Union Transactions of the American Geophysical Union

Trans Am Inst Min Metall Pet Eng Transactions of the American Institute of Mining, Metallurgical, and Petroleum Engineers

Trans Am Nucl Soc Transactions of the American Nuclear Society

Trans Am Soc Mech Eng Transactions of the American Society of Mechanical Engineers

Trans Am Soc Met Transactions of the American Society for Metals

Transan Transandean Railway

Transandine Transandean Railway connecting Argentina and Chile

transatl transatlantic

Transbai Transbaikal Railway

Trans Br Ceram Soc Transactions of the British Ceramic Society

transc transcription

Trans-Carib Trans-Caribbean Airways

Trans-Caspian Trans-Caspian Railroad linking the Caspian Sea region with the southern Urals of the USSR

Transcau Transcaucasian Railway

transceiver transmitter-receiver

Transcendental Philosopher Ralph Waldo Emerson

transcrit transportation critic(ism)

trans d transverse diameter

TRANSDEC Transducer Electronic Center

transec transmission security

transf transfer; transference; transformer

Trans Faraday Soc Transactions of the Faraday Society

transfax facsimile transmission

transie(s) transvestite(s)

TRANSIS Transportation Safety Information System

Transisthmian Transisthmian Highway (flanking the Panama Canal and the Panama Railroad)

transistor transfer resistor

transit. transitive

Transj Transjordan; Transjordanian

Transjordan(ia) Hashemite Kingdom of Jordan better known as Jordan

Transk Transkei

Trans-Ky Exp Trans-Kyusho Expressway

transl translation; translator

translit transliteration

translu translucent

translun translunar; translunarian; translunarite

transm transmission

Transmark Transportation Systems and Market Research

(British rails)

Trans Metall Soc AIME Transactions of the Metallurgical Society of the American Institute of Mechanical Engineers

transmog transmogrification; transmogrify(ing)

Transnistria Trans-Dniestria

Transocean California-Hawaii-Orient Airline; Transoceanic

transp transparent

transpac transpacific

transpl transplant(ation); transplanted

transport. transportation

Transron Transport Squadron

trans sect transverse section

transsexual(s) transvestite homosexual(s)

Trans-Sib Trans-Siberian Railroad linking European Russia with its North Pacific coast

Trans Soc Rheol Transactions of the Society of Rheology

TRANSUB Translation and Publishing Corporation (China)

transv transverse

Transv Transvaal

transv sect transverse section

Transylvanians Transylvanian Alps of Romania

transyt traffic network study tool

trany transparency

trap. trapdoor; trap drums; trapeze; trapezoid(al); trapezium

TRAP Tracker Analysis Program

traps. trap drums; trap drummer(s)

tratel tracking through telemetry; trailer motel

trau traumatic

TRAUS Thoroughbred Racing Association of the U.S.

trav. travel

Trav Travancore; Travis

Trav Travessa (Portuguese—Lane)

Traven B Traven (pseudonym used by Berick Traven Torsvan)

TRAWL Tape Read-and-Write Library

trb tribunal; tribune; trombone

trb toneladas de registro bruto (Spanish—gross registered tonnage)

TRB New Republic's pseudonymic initials standing for columnist Richard Strout but the reverse of BRT (Brooklyn Rapid Transit) used by the publisher when taking copy to his printer in Brooklyn

trc total response to crisis

Tr & C Troilus and Cressida

TRC Tape Relay Center; Technical Review Committee; Technology Reports Center; Telegram Retransmission Centre; Trans-Caribbean Airways; Transportation Research Command

TRCA Toronto Region Coordinating Agency (Hamilton to Oshawa)

trccc tracking radar central control console

Tr Co Trust Company

tr coil tripping coil

Tr Coll Training College

TRCS Trade Relations Council of the United States

TRCUD Technical Review Committee on Underground Disposal of Radioactive Wastes

trcver transceiver

Trd Trinidad

TRD Test Requirements Document

TRDA Timber Research and Development Association

TRDCOM Transportation Research and Development command

trdto tracking radar data takeoff

Tre Torre (Italian or Portuguese—tower)

TRE Telecommunications Research Establishment

treas treasure; treasurer; treasury

Treas Treasurer

Treasure State Montana's official nickname

trec tracking radar electronic components

TRECOM Transportation Research and Engineering command

tree trustee

Tree of Heaven *Ailanthus* tree found in midst of metropolitan filth and smoke throughout cities of America and Europe—originally introduced in cargoes coming from China

Treichville vice quarter of Abidjan on the Ivory Coast of West Africa

trem tremolando (Italian—trembling)

trem card transport or truck emergency card

Tren Trenton

trend. tropical environment data

Trenton New Jersey's capital

Trent's Town Trenton, New Jersey's capital named for its original settler—William Trent

treph trephining (trepanning)

Trep. pal. Treponoma pallida—the spirochete of syphilis

Tres Hermanas Tres Hermanas Mountains of southwestern New Mexico

Tres Marías (Spanish—Three Marys)—María Madre, María Magdalena, María Cleofás—islands off the west coast of Mexico serving as a convict colony

très sec (French—extra-dry, almost tart champagne or wine)

Tréves (French—Trier)

TREVI Terrorisme, Radicalisme, et Violence International (French—Terrorism, Radicalism, and International Violence)—EEC police network

trf transfer; tuned radio frequency

trf (TRF) thyrotropin-releasing factor

TRF Task Request Form; Teacher Rating Form, Transportation Research Foundation; Tuna Research Foundation; Turf Research Foundation

trg training

tr&g transmit, receive, and guard

trgt target

trh (TRH) thyrotrophin-releasing hormone

Tr H Trinity Hall, Oxford

TRH Their Royal Highnesses

TRHS Theodore Roosevelt High School

tri total response index (TRI); triangle; triangulation; tricolor; tricycle; triode

tri (Latin prefix—three)—triangle

Tri Triangulum (constellation); Trieste

Tri Tohtori (Finnish—doctor)

TRI Technical Report Instruction; Textile Research Institute; The Rockefeller Institute; Tin Research Institute; Tire Retreading Institute; total response index

TRIAL Technique for Retrieving Information from Abstracts of Literature

trian triangle; triangulation

Trias Triassic

trib tribade; tribadism; tribal; tribalism; tribalist; tribasic; tribunal; tribune; tributary

Trib Tribune

Tri B Triborough Bridge

TRIB Tire Retread(ing) Information Bureau

tribas tribasic

TRIBE Teaching and Research in Bicultural Education

tribl tribunal (Spanish—tribunal; court of justice)

Tribune of the People John Bright

tric trachoma inclusion conjunctivitis; trichloroethylene

tricaphos tricalcium phosphate

trice. transistorized real-time incremental computer expandable; trichomoniasis (protozoan vaginal infection)

trich (Latin prefix—hair)—trichosis

Trich Tiruchchirappalli or Trichinopoly (famous for its Indian cigars)

Tricia Patricia

Tri-Cities Florence, Sheffield, and Tuscumbia on Tennessee River near Muscle Shoals in northwestern Alabama; Davenport, Iowa—Moline and Rock Island, Illinois

trick (slang—trichomoniasis)

Tricky Dick politician Richard M. Nixon's nickname

tricl triclinic

trico trichomoniasis

tricolor flag divided into three horizontal or vertical stripes; the Tricolor, initially capitalized, refers to the Tricolor of France consisting of red, white, and blue vertical stripes

Tri Com Trilateral Commission (Council of Foreign Relations)

TRICON Tri-Service Container (program)

trid. triduum (Latin—three days)

Trident Trident Region (Berkeley, Charleston, and Dorchester counties comprising the Charleston, South Carolina area)

tridundant triple redundant

TRIEA Tea Research Institute of East Africa

Trier (German—Tréves)

trig trigger(man); trigonal; trigonometric; trigonometry

triga trigger reactor

trihem trihemeral; trihemirer

tri ins tricuspid insufficiency

trik trichloroethylene

trike tricycle

trilat trilateral; Trilateral Commission (Council on Foreign

Relations); trilateralist(ic)(al)(ly)

trillion *American*—a million million—10^{12}; *British*—a million million million—10^{18}

tril(s) trillion(s)

trim. trimetric

trim. (TRIM) test rules for inventory management

trim. trimestre (Latin—quarter; three months)

TRIM Targets, Receivers, Impacts, and Methods; Technical Requirements Identification Matrices; Tax Reform Immediately

trimaran three-hulled catamaran

TRIMIS Tri-Service Medical Information System

TRIMMS Total Refinement and Integration of Maintenance Management Systems (USA)

TRIMS Texas Research Institute of Mental Sciences

trimtu (TRIMTU) trimethyl thiourea

Trin Trinidad(ian); Trinitarian(ism); Trinity; Trinity College (Oxford or elsewhere)

Trinco Trincomalee

Trin Col Trinity College

Trin H Trinity Hall

Trinidad and Tobago West Indian island nation whose Trinidadians and Tobagans speak English (farming, mining, and tourism sustain the economy)

Trinidad and Tobago Ports Trinidad—Chaguaramas Bay, Port-of-Spain, Pointe a Pierre, San Fernando, La Brea, Brighton, Point Fortin; Tobago—Canaan, Charlotteville, Scarborough

Trinity Trinity Christian College; Trinity Church; Trinity College; Trinity House (Pilot Service); Trinity Parish; Trinity Parish School; Trinity School; Trinity University; Trinitytide

Trinity of Science Experience, Observation, and Reason

triol triolism; triolist

triols triolists (also called troilists)

trip. triple; triplicate; triplication; tripos

trip. (TRIP) technical reports indexing project

TRIP The Road Improvement Program

triphib triphibian; triphibious (land, sea, air)

tripl triplication; triplicate

Triple-A (*see* AAACE)

Triple Alliance Austria, Germany, and Italy (before outbreak of World War I)

triple-A S AAAS (American Association for the Advancement of Science)

Triple Cities Binghampton, Endicott, Johnson City (also called Tri-cities)

Triplet Capital Sharp Memorial Community Hospital in San Diego, California where in a 17-day period three sets of healthy triplets were born

Tripsville Haight-Ashbury district of San Francisco where drug addicts take so many so-called trips

tris tris (hydroxymethyl) aminomethane

Tris Tristan; Tristram

Trish Patricia; Tricia

trishaw tricycle rickshaw

trisk triskelion

TRISNET Transportation Research Information Services Network

Tristan Tristan und Isolde (German—Tristan and Iseult)—music drama by Wagner

TRISTAN Tri-Ring Intersecting Storage Accelerators in Nippon

Tristan da Cunha Tristan da Cunha Islands (Gough, Inaccessible, Nightingale, Tristan da Cunha)

tri sten tricuspid stenosis

trisyll trisyllable

trit. tritura (Latin—triturate)

TRI-TAC Tri-Services Tactical Communications Program (DoD)

tritic tritical (trite); triticale (*Triticum* + *Secale* hybrid between wheat and rye); triticeous; triticeum; tritish; triticum; tritium

Trittico Il Trittico (The Tryptych)—Puccini's three short operas—*Gianni Schicchi, Suor Angelica,* and *Il Tabarro*

Trixie Friganza Delia O'Callahan

Trix(ie)(y) Beatrice; Beatrix

trk track; truck; trunk

Trk Turk; Turkey; Turkic; Turkish

trkdr truck-drawn

trkg tracking

trkhd truckhead

trl trailer

Trl Trail

TRLB temporarily replaced by lighted buoy

trlfsw tactical-range landing-force support weapon

trlr trailer

Trlr Trailer (postal abbreviation)

trm task response module (engineer's desk area); thermoremanent magnetism

Trm Trincomalee

trml terminal

trmn trainman

trmr trimmer

TRMS Technical Requirements Management System

trmt treatment

trn transfer

Trn Troon

tRNA transfer RNA (same as sRNA)

trnbkl turnbuckle

trng training

TRNMP Theodore Roosevelt National Memorial Park

trnsp transport; transportation

TRO Technical Reviewing Office; Temporary Restraining Order

TROA The Retired Officers Association

troch troche

troch trochiscus (Latin—cough drop, lozenge, troche)

Troch Trochelminthes

Troia (Italian—Troy)

troil troilism; troilist

Troj Trojan

Trojan North American T-28 trainer aircraft

Trojans Les Troyens (French—The Trojans)—five-act opera by Berlioz

trol tapeless rotorless on-line cryptographic equipment

Troldhaugen (Norwegian—Troll's Hill)—Edvard Grieg's home near Bergen

Trollstigen (Norwegian—Troll's Path)—steep zigzag road linking Andalsnes with Valldal

trom tromba; trombone

T Rom Times Roman

trombst trombonist

tromp trompette (French—trumpet)

Trondheim modern name of Nidaros

T-room (American slang—toilet) not a tea room

Trooper Turned Physician Thomas Sydenham

Troopship Fokker military version of the 40 to 52-passenger aircraft F-27

trop tropic; tropical; tropics

trop tropos (Greek—to turn or

to turn toward)—entropy, geotropism, phototropism, tropic(al), tropism

troparium tropical aquarium

Trop Can Tropic of Cancer—23½°N Lat

Trop Cap Tropic of Capricorn—23½° S Lat

tropec tropical experiment

trophe (Greek—nutrition)—atrophy, autotrophe, heterotrophe, trophic level

trophy (Latin suffix—relating to nutrition)—hypertrophy

tropic (Latin prefix—pertaining to a turn)—tropical, tropicolitan; (Latin suffix—turning toward)—gonadotropic

Tropical North northern Queensland, Australia

Tropic Metropolis Miami, Florida

Tropics torrid lands and seas between Tropic of Cancer and Tropic of Capricorn

TROPICS Tour Operators Integrated Computer System

trop med tropical medicine

troposcatter beyond-the-horizon communication

TROSCOM Troop Support Command (USA)

Trots Trotskyite(s)

Trotsky Lev Davydovich Bronstein

Trout Schubert's Quintet in A major for violin, viola, cello, double bass, and piano

Trov Il Trovatore (Italian—The Troubador)—four-act Verdi opera

Troyens Les Troyens (French—The Trojans)—two-part opera by Berlioz—The Fall of Troy and The Trojans at Carthage

trp troop

trp (TRP) tryptophan

Trp Tripoli

tr pl treatment plan

trr teaching and research reactor; train repetition rate

TRRA Terminal Railroad Association (of St. Louis)

TRRB Test Readiness Review Board (NASA)

TRRG Tax Reform Research Group

trs target range servo(mechanism); transfer; transparency; transpose; tropical revolving storm; trustees

trs (TRS) tetrahedral research satellite

TRs Tax(ation) Reports; Technical Reports; Temporary Reserves

TRS Ticket Reservation System; Transair Limited

TRSA Terminal Radar Service Area

trsb time reference scanning beam

trsd total rated service date

tr sh trim shell

TrSMS triple-screw motor ship

trsp transport

TRSP Turtle River State Park (North Dakota)

trsr taxi and runway surveillance radar

TrSS triple-screw steamer

trssgm tactical range surface-to-surface guided missile

Trst (Serbo-Croatian—Trieste)

trsv (TRSV) tobacco-ringspot virus

trt total response to trauma; treatment; turret

TRTA Traders' Road Transport Association

TRTC Tropical Radio Telegraph Company

trtch tape recording technic

tru (TRU) transuranic (contaminated) waste

Tru Trucial; Trucial Sheikdoms; Truman; Truman; Truro

Tru Truman's Railway Reports

TRU The Rockefeller University

TRUB temporarily replaced by unlighted buoy

Trucial States (*see* United Arab Emirates)

Tru Cst 1 Trucial Coast Number 1

Tru Cst 2 Trucial Coast Number 2

trud time remaining until dive (of satellite into Earth's atmosphere)

Trudy Gertrude

TRUE Teachers Resources for Urban Education

True King of Our Storytellers Jack London, according to Upton Sinclair

Truemid Movement for True Industrial Democracy

tru-fi tru fidelity (sound reproduction)

Truman Harry Truman Field (U.S. Virgin Islands airport near Charlotte Amalie on St Thomas)

Truman Capote Truman Streckfus Persons

trump. trumpet

TRUMP Target Radiation Measurement Program

Trumpeter of the Last Judgment Gabriel

trun trunnion

trunc truncate; truncated; truncation

Truncated Capital Salem, Oregon's capital, named for Salem, Massachusetts believed to be the truncation of Jerusalem

trunch truncheon

tr unit turbidity reducing unit

Truron (Church Latin—Truro)

tru(s) trustee(s)

trust. trusteeship

Trust Buster Theodore Roosevelt—26th President of the United States

Trust Territory Micronesian islands of the Pacific (Carolines, Marianas, Marshalls, Ponape, Truk, Yap, etc.) under American administration

truthsayer(s) truthful person(s)

truth serum sodium pentathol

trv torpedo recovery vessel

trveh tracked vehicle

trw trawler

TRW the corporation whose advertising states: "formerly Thompson-Ramo-Wooldridge"

trwov transit without visa

TRW SL TRW Space Log

trxrx transmitter-receiver

try. truly

try. (TRY) tryptophan

TRY Teens for Retarded Youth (juvenile correctional program)

Tryg Trygve Lie

tryp (TRYP) tryptophan

tryp(s) trypanosome(s)

ts taper shank; temperature switch; tensile strength; terminal sensation; test solution; time shack; time sharing; too short, tool steel; tough situation; traffic signal; transit storage; transmitter station; triple strength; tubular sound; type specification(s); typescript

ts (TS) thesis

t's twins

t/s test stand; third stage; transship(ed)(ment)

t/s (T/S) thyroid serum

t & s toilet and shower

TS Tasmanian Steamers; Tentative Specification; Terminal Service; Test Summary; Theosophical Society; Thoreau Society; Tidewater Southern (railroad); top secret; Topical Search; Training Ship; Transmittal Sheet; Type Specification

T S tasto solo (Italian—play

without accompaniment)

tsa tax-sheltered annuity; total survey area; two-step antenna

tsa (TSA) total survey area (radio and tv)

TSA Teacher on Special Assignment; Tourist Savings Association; Track Supply Association; Transportation Service, Army; Transportation Standardization Agency; Transuranic Storage Area

tsac title, subtitle, and caption

TSAC Target Signature Analysis Center

tsar time scanned array radar

Tsaritsyn czarist name of Volgograd formerly called Stalingrad

Tsarskoe Selo former name of Pushkin near Leningrad

TSB Trustee Savings Bank(s)

TSBA Trustee Savings Banks Association

TSBD Texas School Book Depository

TSBI Texas Social Behavior Inventory Form

TSBR Thomas Stamford Bingley Raffles

tsc (TSC) transmitter start code (data processing)

TSC Texas Southmost College; Transamerican Steamship Corporation; Transportation System Center

TSCA Tactical Satellite Communications System; Top Secret Control Agency; Toxic Substance Control Act

TSCC Telemetry Standards Coordination Committee

tscf top secret cover folder

Tschechoslowakei (German—Czechoslovakia)

TSCO Thomas Scherman's Concert Opera; Top Secret Control Officer

TSCS Tennessee Self-Concept Scale

t-s curve temperature-salinity curve

tsd tactical simulator display; target skin distance

Tsd Tausend (German—thousand)

TSd Tay-Sachs disease (TSD)

TSD Tay-Sachs Disease; Technical Services Division (CIA); towed submersible drydock (naval symbol)

TSD-CIA Technical Services Division—Central Intelligence Agency

tsdd temperature-salinity-density-depth

tsds two-speed destroyer sweeper

tse (TSE) test support equipment

TSE Texas South-Eastern (railroad); T(homas) S(tearns) Eliot; Tokyo Stock Exchange; Toronto Stock Exchange

TSE Tribunal Supremo de Elecciones (Spanish—Supreme Election Tribunal)

T-sect cross-section; transverse section

TSES Thumb-Signature Endorsement System

tsf tower shield facility

tsf telegrafia sem fios (Portuguese), telegrafo senza fili (Italian), télégraphie sans fil (French)—radio or wireless telegraphy

TSF Tertiary of the Society of St Francis

tsfr transfer

TSG Television and Screen Writers' Guild

TSgt Technical Sergeant

tsh (TSH) thyroid stimulating hormone

tsh telegrafía sin hilos (Spanish—wireless telegraphy)—radio

T sh Tanzanian shilling(s)

TSH Their Serene Highnesses

TSHA Texas State Historical Association

T-shirt T-shaped shirt; T-shaped undershirt

t-shower thundershower

tsi The Socialist International; test structure input; tons per square inch

TSI Test of Social Insight; Test of Social Intelligence; Theological School Inventory; Transport(ation) Safety Institute

T&SI Technical and Scientific Information (UN)

tsi agar triple sugar (glucose, lactose, sucrose) iron agar

tsiaj this scherzo is a joke (abbreviation devised and used by composer Charles Ives)

TSID Technical Service Intelligence Detachments

TSJC Trinidad State Junior College

Tsjechoslowakije (Dutch—Czechoslovakia)

TSKK Tsentralnya Kontrolnaya Komissiya (Russian—Central Control Commmission)

TSL Terrestrial Sciences Laboratory; Texas Short Line (railroad)

TSLNP Tung Slang Luang National Park (Thailand)

tsms twin-screw motor ship

tsmt transmit

TSMTS Tri-State Motor Tariff Service

Tsn Tientsin

TSN Tape Serial Number

TSNHS Touro Synagogue National Historic Site

Tsnra Gora (Serbo-Croatian—Black Mountain)—Montenegro now called South Yugoslavia

tso time-sharing option

Tso Tsingtao

TSO Taiwan Symphony Orchestra; Teheran Symphony Orchestra; Toronto Symphony Orchestra; Tucson Symphony Orchestra

TSOR Tentative Specific Operational Requirements

TSOS Time-Sharing Operating System

tsp teaspoon; tracking station position

TSP thyroid-stimulating (hormone of) prepituitary; trisodium phosphate (Na_3PO_4)

tspa tally and special precinct analysis

tspn teaspoon

T-square T-shaped ruler for making right angles

tsr temperature-sensitive resistor

TSR Sir Thomas Stamford Raffles (founder of Singapore as well as the London Zoo)

T & SRC Tubular and Split Rivet Council

tss tangential-signal sensitivity; target-selector switch(ing); time-sharing system(s)

tss (TSS) toxic shock syndrome (experienced by menstruating women using tampons)

t/ss turbine steamship

TSS Time-Sharing System(s); Traffic Safety Service; Trident Submarine System; turbine steamship; twin-screw ship

tssa (TSSA) tumor specific surface antigen

tssm total ship simulation model

tsspar time-sharing system-performance activities record(s)

TSSR Tadzhikistan Soviet Socialist Republic; Turkmenistan Soviet Socialist Republic

tst test (computer flow chart)

tsta tumor specific transplantable antigen (TSTA)

TSTA Texas State Teachers Association

t-storm thunderstorm

TSTP Test of Selected Topics in Physics

tstr tester

t's t's & t's tortoises, terrapins, and turtles [tortoises are terrestrial chelonians with domed shells and elephantine feet; terrapins are semi-aquatic chelonians with depressed shells, rudder-like tails, and webbed feet; turtles are marine chelonians with streamlined shells and paddle-like flippers; the term turtle(s) is often applied to all the chelonians]

tsu tape search unit; this side up

tsu (TSU) triple sugar urea (agar)

TSU Texas Southern University; Tulsa-Sapulpa Union (railway)

tsu's thermosetting urethanes

TSUS Tariff Schedule of the United States

Tsushima Tsushima Current flowing northeasterly between Japan and Korea or the Tsushima Strait in that location where in 1905 Admiral Togo's Japanese fleet defeated Admiral Rozhdesvenski's Russian fleet

tsvp tournez s'il vous plaît (French—please turn over)

TSW tropical summer winter (load line mark)

TSWE Test of Standard Written English

tsx time-sharing executive

TSX Telecommunications Satellite Experiment

tt tablet triturate; technical test(ing); teetotaler; telegraphic transfer, teletype, teletypewriter; tetanus toxoid; torpedo tube(s); transit time; tree top(s); tuberculin tested

tt (TT) train time

t-t tube-in-tube

t/t time to turn

t&t time and temperature

tt. tantum (Latin—fixed allowance, so much)

t.t. totus tuus (Latin—all yours)

TT tam-tam (Chinese gong); target-towing (naval aircraft); technical test(ing); Tidningarnas Telegrambyra (Swedish News Agency); Toledo Terminal (railroad); Trailer Train; Trans-Texas (Airways); Troop Test

T/T twin turbine (steamship)

T & T Trinidad and Tobago

tta test target array

TTA Taiwan Telecommunication Administration; Trans-Texas Airways; Travel Time Authorization

ttab Trademark Trial and Appeal Board (US Patent Office)

ttac tracking, telemetry, and command; tracking, telemetry, and control

TTAF Technical Training Air Force

ttc temperature test chamber; tetrazolium chloride; tight tape contact; tin telluride crystal; tow target cable; transient temperature control; tube temperature control

TTC Technical Training Command; Teletypewriter Center; Texas Technological College; Tobacco Tax Council; Tokyo Tanker Company; Toronto Transit Commission; Transportation Technology Center

ttce tooth-to-tooth composite error

ttci transient temperature-control instrument

TTCS Truck Transportable Communications Station

ttd transponder transmitter detector

ttdr tracking telemetry data receiver

tte temporary test equipment; trailer test equipment

Tte Teniente (Spanish—Lieutenant)

TTE Tropical Testing Establishment

Tte Cnel teniente coronel (Spanish—Lieutenant Colonel)

TTEX Trailer Train Express

ttf time to failure; tone telegraph filter; transistor text fixture

ttf (TTF) tetrathiafulvalene

TTF Timber Trade Federation; Townsend Thoresen Ferry

ttfn ta-ta for now

ttg time to go

TT-gauge Tiny Tim Gauge— $^1/_4$-inch track gauge (model railroads)

ttgd time-to-go engine dial

tth thyrotropic hormone

tti time-temperature indicator; trait treatment interaction

TTI The Technological Institute; Transition Technology, Inc

T-time takeoff time

TTIO Turkish Tourism and Information Office

TTJC Tyne Trade Joint Committee

ttk two-tone keying

ttl to take leave; transistor-transistor logic

TTL Tokaido Trunk Line (Japanese railroad running trains at 125 miles per hour)

ttm two-tone modulation

TTMA Truck-Trailer Manufacturers Association

tto this transaction only

Tto Toronto

TTO Tanzania Tourist Office

T-town Tijuana

ttp time-temperature parameter; total taxable pay

TTPI Trust Territory of the Pacific Islands

ttr type token ratio

ttr (TTR) target-tracking radar; thermal test reactor

TTRI Telecommunication Technical Training and Research Institute

T & T RR Tijuana and Tecate Railroad

tts teletypesetter (TTS); teletypesetting, temporary threshold shift

tts (TTS) teletypesetting

TTS Terminal Transparent System

TTSU Taxi-Truck Surveillance Unit (NYPD)

ttt telemetry time transposition; time to target; time to think; time to turn

t t&t tortoise, terrapin, and turtle (*see* t's t's & t's)

TTT Transamerica Trailer Transport; Tyne Tees Television

TT & T Texas Transport and Terminal

t't'ta triple-note trumpet flourish

TTTB Trinidad and Tobago Tourist Board

TTTC Technical Teachers Training College

T & T TS Trinidad and Tobago Television Service

ttu timing terminal unit

TTU Texas Technological University

TTUT Through-Transmission Ultrasonic Test(ing)

TTV Taiwan Television (offshore China)

ttvm thermal transfer voltmeter

ttw total temperature and weight

ttwl twin-tandem wheel loading

ttx tritated tetrodotoxin

tty teletypewriter

tu tape unit; thermal unit; toxic unit; trade union (TU); traffic unit; transfer unit; transmission unit; turbidity unit

Tu Turkey; Turkish

TU Taylor University; Temple University; Tiffin University; Trade Union; transmission unit; Trinity University; Tufts University; Tulane University; Tunis Air; Typographical Union

T.U. tuberculin unit(s)

TU Technische Universität (German—technical university); *temps universel* (French—universal time)

Tu-4 Soviet Tupolev bomber inspired by the Boeing B-29 Superfortress aircraft

Tu-16 Soviet Tupolev bomber code-named Badger by NATO

Tu-20 Soviet Tupolev heavy bomber named Bear by NATO

Tu-22 Soviet Tupolev bomber named Blinder by NATO

Tu-28 Soviet Tupolev long-range interceptor aircraft named Fiddler by NATO

Tu-104 Soviet Tupolev medium-range transport aircraft called Camel by NATO

Tu-114 Soviet Tupolev long-range transport plane named Cleat by NATO

Tu-124 Soviet Tupolev jet-transport aircraft named Cookpot by NATO

Tu-144 Tupolev supersonic transport

Tu-154 Tupolev 154 supersonic aircraft

TUAC Trade Union Advisory Committee

Tuamotus Tuamotu Islands of Polynesia in the South Pacific where navigators once called them the Dangerous Islands as they had many reefs and shoals

Tuan Jim (Malay—Lord Jim)—Conrad's celebrated nautical character

tu ar turning arbor

tub. tubing

TUB temporary unlighted buoy

TUBA Tubists Universal Brotherhood Association

tube boob tube; subway; television tube; tunnel

Tube The Tube (London's Underground subway system)

TUBE Terminating Unfair Broadcasting Excesses

tuberc tuberculosis

tublr tubular

Tubuais Tubuai Islands of Polynesia in the South Pacific where they are also called the Australs

tuc transportation, utilities, communications

Tuc Tucana (constellation); Tucson

TUC Trades-Union Congress (British)

tu ca turning cam

TUCC Temple University Community College; Triangle Universities Computation Center

TUCGC Trades Union Congress General Council

TUCSA Trade Union Council of South Africa

Tucsons Tucson Mountains of southeastern Arizona

tudor two-door

Tu-Du (Vietnamese—Liberty)

Tue Tuesday

Tues Tuesday

TUF Tokyo University of Fisheries; Trade Union Federation (British)

TUFEC Thailand-Unesco Fundamental Education Center

tuff tape update of formatted files

tu fx turning fixture

tug. tape update and generator

TUG Transac Users Group

tug(s) tugboat(s)

TUH Taiwan University Hospital

TUI Trade Union International

TUIAFW Trade Unions International of Agricultural and Forestry Workers

tuifu the ultimate in foulups

Tul Tulsa

TUL Tokyo University Library; Tulane University of Louisiana; Tulsa, Oklahoma (airport)

Tula Gertrude; Gertrudis

Tularosas Tularosa Mountains of western New Mexico

Tullahoma Vocational Tennessee State Vocational School for Girls at Tullahoma

Tully Marcus Tullius Cicero

tum tummy (stomach); tumor

TUM Panama City, Panama (Tocumen Airport)

Tumacacori Tumacacori National Monument south of Tucson, Arizona

Tum-Tum portly Albert Edward, HRH the Prince of Wales who later became King Edward the Seventh

Tumuc-Humacs Tumuc-Humac Mountains between Brazil and the Guianas

tun tuning

Tun Tunis; Tunisia; Tunisian; Tunnel

Tun Túnez (Spanish—Tunisia)

tunasan tuna sandwich

tunawich tuna sandwich

Tunesië (Dutch—Tunisia)

Tunesien (German—Tunisia)

Túnez (Spanish—Tunis; Tunisia)

tung tungsten

Tung Tree Capital Picayune, Mississippi

Tunic Tunicata

Tunisia Republic of Tunisia (North African Arab country long a French protectorate; Tunisians speak Arabic and French; farming, fishing, and mining plus some tourism provide work) *Al-Djoumhouria Attunusia*—called Carthage in Roman times

Tunisian Ports Susa, Halq al Wadi, Tunis, Banzart, plus smaller ports such as Bizerte, Sfax, and Gabes

Tunl Tunnel (postal abbreviation)

tuos trained under other schemes

TUP Temple University Press; Trinity University Press; Tulane University Press

tuppenny twopenny

Tupper Tupper Creek in eastern British Columbia or Tupper Lake in northern New York

Tupun Tupungato

tur transurethral resection (TUR); turbine; turret

Tur Turin

turb transurethral resection of the bladder (TURB); turbine

TURB Trainer Update Review Board

turbid. turbidity

turboalt turboalternator

turbo-elec steam turbine connected to electric motor

turbogen turbogenerator

turbojet turbine-driven jet (airplane engine)

turboprop turbine-driven jet engine (moving the) propeller

turbosuch trubosupercharger

turbotrain turbine-driven railroad train

turbpmp turbopump

turbu turbulence; turbulent

Turch Turchia (Italian—Turkey)

Turchia (Italian—Turkey)

Turin English place-name equivalent of Torino in northwest Italy *turistas* (Portuguese or Spanish —tourists)—also means tourist ailments such as loose bowels and vomiting brought on by eating spoiled food or drinking too much impure water

turk turkey

Turk. Turkey; Turkish

Turk Turkish (the language of more than 38 million people in Turkey and scattered throughout its former colonies in the Middle East and North Africa)

Turkana Lake Turkana (formerly East Rudolf)

Türkei (German—Turkey)

Turkestan Desert includes Kara Kum south of Aral Sea, Kyzyl Kum southeast of Aral Sea, Ust Urt between Aral and Caspian seas

Turkey Republic of Turkey (formerly the center of the Ottoman Empire extending from Morocco to Persia; Turkish-speaking Turks engage in farming food crops as well as opium gum, fishing, manufacturing, and mining) *Türkiye Cumhuriyeti*

Turkey Capital of the World nickname shared by Berryville, Arkansas and Worthington, Minnesota

Turkey's Principal Port Istanbul (Constantinople)

Turkije (Dutch—Turkey)

Türk-Is Türkiye Isçi Sendikalari Konfederasyonu (Turkish Confederation of Trade Unions)

turkish turkish bath (steam bath); turkish delight (fruit-flavored gelatin candy dusted with confectioner's sugar); turkish rug (oriental rug of the type originating in Turkey); turkish tobacco (highly aromatic); turkish towel (water-absorbent long-nap towel)

Turkish Mozart's Violin Concerto in A major (K 219)

Turkish Ports (large, medium, and small from north to south) Istanbul (Constantinople), Hydarpasa, Izmir (Smyrna), Antalya (Adalia), Mersin, Iskenderun (Alexandretta)

Turkish Towel Actress Brigette Bardot (and her would-be imitators whose repertory, like hers, is limited to posing with and without a turkish towel plus a pout or two)

Türkiye (Turkish—Turkey)

Turkmen Turkmenia; Turkmenian

Turkmen SSR Turkmen Soviet Socialist Republic (Turkmenistan)

turks turkeys

Turks Turkish people; Turks Islands east of the Bahamas and northeast of the Windward Passage

Turks and Caicos Turks and Caicos Islands northeast of the Windward Passage between Cuba and Haiti

Turk-Sib Turkestan-Siberian (railroad)

Turk-Tat Turko-Tataric

Turku formerly Abo

turn. turning

Turn Turnpike

Turner's syndrome genetic abnormality in females inheriting only forty-five chromosomes as this causes retarded sexual development

Turner Turn Turner Turnpike

turp transurethral resection of the prostate (TURP); turpentine

Turpentine State North Carolina

turps elixir of terpin hydrate; turpentine

TURPS Terrestrial Unattended Reactor Power System

turq turquoise

Turq Turquía (Spanish—Turkey)

Turquía (Portuguese—Turkey)

Turquía (Spanish—Turkey)

Turquie (French—Turkey)

turquoise hydrargillite (basic hydrated copper aluminum phosphate)

Turtles Turtle Islands in the Sulu Sea south of the Philippines or the Turtle Islands off Africa's Sierra Leone or the Turtle Mountains between northern North Dakota and southern Manitoba

TUs Tenant's Unions

TUS Tuscon, Arizona (airport)

TUSAFG The United States Air Force Group (American Mission for Aid to Turkey)

TUSC Technology Use Studies Center

Tuscans Tuscan people; Tuscan Islands

Tuscany English place-name equivalent for Toscana

Tushars Tushar Mountains of central Utah

Tusitala (Samoan—Teller of Tales)—Robert Louis Stevenson's nickname

TUSLOG The United States Logistic Group

TUSM Tufts University School of Medicine

tuss. tussis (Latin—cough)

tut tutor; tutorial

Tut Tutankahmen

TUT The University of Tokyo

Tut Books Charles E Tuttle's books

TUTF Technology Use Task Force

TUTI Temple University Technical Institute

Tutor Canadair-built jet-trainer aircraft designated CL-41

Tuv Tuvalo (Ellice Islands)

Tuvalu formerly the Anglo-French condominium of New Hebrides in the South Pacific between Fiji and New Caledonia—capital port is Vila from where cocoa, coffee, and copra are exported

tuwr turning wrench

tux tuxedo (dinner jacket)

Tuzigoot Tuzigoot National Monument in central Arizona

tv transvestite

tv (TV) television; terminal velocity; test vehicle; tetrazolium violet; total volume; transverse; trichomonas vaginalis; true view; tuberculin volution

t/v thrust-to-weight

t & v terrorism and vandalism

TV television; test vehicle; Tidewater Oil (stock exchange symbol); transport vehicle

tva thrust vector alignment

tva taxe à la valeur ajoutée (French—value added tax)

TVA Temporary Variation Authorization; Tennessee Valley Authority

tvac time-varying adaptive correlation

TVAs Temporary Variation Authorizations

TVB Television (Advertising) Bureau

TVBS Television Broadcast Satellite

tvc temperature valve control; thermal voltage converter; throttle valve control; thrust vector control; time-varying coefficient; timed vital capacity; torsional vibration characteristics

tvc (TVC) total variable cost

TVC Technical Valve Committee

TVCC Treasure Valley Community College

tvcrit television critic(ism)

tvd toxic vapor damper; toxic vapor detector; tuned viscoelastic damper

tvdc test volts—direct current

TVDC Tidewater Virginia Development Council

tv'dict(s) television addict(s)

tvdp thrust-vector display (unit)

tvdy television deflection yoke

tve test vehicle engine; thermal vacuum environment

TVE Televisión Española (Spanish TV network)

tvel track velocity

Tver czarist name for Kalinin

TVERS Television Evaluation and Renewal Standards

tvft television flyback transformer

tvg television video generator; threshold voltage generator; triggered vacuum gap

TVG T V Guide

tvhh (TVHH) television households

TV household television-equipped home

tvi television interference

TVIC Television Interference Committee

tvid televised identification; television identification; television identity

tvig television and inertial guidance

tvist television information-storage tube

tvk terminal volume kill

T v K Theodore von Karman

tvl tenth value layer; travel

Tvl Transvall

tvm tachometer voltmeter; track via missile; trailer van mount; transistorized voltmeter

TVN Television News

TVNZ Television New Zealand

tvop television observation post

tvor terminal visual omnirange; very high frequency terminal omnirange station

tvp television poor (audio-visual addicts who have never learned how to read or who have lost the faculty during the course of their addiction); textured vegetable protein; time-varying parameter

TVPA Thames Valley Police Authority

tvq top visual quality

tvr textured vegetable protein

TVRB Tactical Vehicle Review Board (USA)

TVRI Television Rating Inven-

tory

TV-RI TV-Republik Indonesia (Bahasa Indonesia—Republic Indonesia Television)

tv rm television room

Tvrn Tavern

tvr's television recordings

tvs tactical vocoder system; telemetry video spectrum; television viewing system

tv's television dinners; transvestites

tvsd time-varying spectral display

tvsg television signal generator

tvsm time-varying sequential measuring (apparatus)

tvso television space observatory

TVSTI Thames Valley State Technical Institute

tvsu television sight unit

tvt television typewriter

tvu total volume urine

tw tail warning; tail water; tail wheel; tail wind; tankwagon; taxiway; tempered water; terrawatt; tile wainscot; torpedo water; traveling wave; twin(s)

tw (TW) typewriter (computer flow chart)

tw tussenwerpsel (Dutch—interjection)

Tw Twaddell

TW Trans World Airlines (2-letter coding)

T&W Tyne and Wear

twa time-weighted average; trailing-wire antenna

TWA Textile Waste Association; Thames Water Authority; Tooling Work Authorization; Toy Wholesalers Association; Trans World Airlines

TWAD Twadell

'twas it was

twb twin with bath

twbp transcribed weather broadcast program

TWC Tail Waggers' Club

TWC Trials of War Criminals

TWCIS Transuranic-contaminated Waste Container Information System

twcrt travelling-wave cathode ray tube

TWCS Test of Work Competency and Stability

twd tail wags dog

twds tradewinds

twe tap-water enema

TWE Textile Waste Exchange

TWEA Trading With the Enemy Act

'tween between

Twelfth State North Carolina

(*see* First State)

Twel N Twelfth Night

Twelve Apostles twelve Apostle Islands in Lake Superior off northern Wisconsin

Twelve-Tone Technician Arnold Schönberg

Twelve Tribes Twelve Tribes of Israel (named for the ten sons of Jacob and the two sons of Jacob's sons, respectively, Reuben, Simeon, Judah, Zebulun, Issachar, Dan, Gad, Asher, Nephtali, Benjamin, and finally Ephraim and Manasseh)

Twentieth-Century Romantic Rachmaninoff, Sibelius, and Richard Strauss share this musical endeavor

Twentieth State Mississippi

Twenty-eighth State Texas

Twenty-fifth State Arkansas

Twenty-first State Illinois

Twenty-fourth State Missouri

Twenty-ninth State Iowa

Twenty-second State Alabama

Twenty-seventh State Florida

Twenty-sixth State Michigan

Twenty-third State Maine

'twere it were

twerl tropical wind, energy conversion, and reference level

TW & FS The Wine and Food Society

twh typically wavy hair

twhl tailwheel

twi training within industry

TWI The West Indies

Twiggy Leslie Hornby

Twilight of the Gods Gotterdämmerung (German mythology); Ragnarok (Norse mythology)

Twilight Zone the Mexican Border long celebrated for its lawlessness

'twill it will

twimc (TWIMC) to whom it may concern

Twin Cities place-name nickname share by Bristol on the Tennessee-Virginia border; Central Falls and Pawtucket, Rhode Island; Champaign and Urbana, Illinois; Minneapolis and St Paul, Minnesota; Texarkana on the Arkansas-Texas border; Winston-Salem, North Carolina, etc.

Twin Maples Farm British Columbia facility for treating women alcoholics

Twin Otter DeHavilland light transport (DHC-6)

Twin Sisters North and South

Dakota

Twin States New Hampshire and Vermont

twister dustwhirl, sandspout, tornado, or waterspout wherein ascending and rotating movement of air column is especially apparent

'twixt betwixt

twi zn twilight zone

twk typewriter keyboard

twl top water level

twm traveling-wave maser

Twn Taiwan (Spanish—Taiwan)—Republic of China consisting of offshore islands; Town (postal abbreviation)

two. this week only

two-0 $20 bill

Two Eyes of Greece Athens and Sparta

two-fer two for the price of one

Two Gent Two Gentlemen of Verona

Two-headed Eagle popular symbol of the Austro-Hungarian Empire, Imperial Russia, and the Holy Roman Empire

two-spot $2 bill

twot travel without troops

'twould it would

Twp Township

TWP True Whig Party (Liberia)

TWPD Tactical and Weapons Policy Division

twr tower

Twr Tower (postal abbreviation)

TWR Trans-World Radio

tws timed wire service; track while scan

tw/s twin-screw (ship)

TWSO Transuranic Waste Systems Office(r)

twsr track-while-scan radar

twsrs track-while-scan radar simulator

twt torpedo water tube; traveling-wave tube; travel with troops

t/wt tare weight

TWT Toy World Test(ing); Transonic Wind Tunnel

twta travelling-wave-tube amplifier

TWU Tata Workers Union; Transport Workers Union

TWUA Textile Workers Union of America; Transport Workers Union of America

T WW Thick Weather Watch (Coast Guard)

twx time-wire transmission

twx (TWX) teletypewriter exchange (message)

TWX teletypewriter exchange (message)

TWX (TWXS) Teletypewriter Exchange Service

twy taxiway; twenty

twyl taxiway link(age)

twzo trade-wind-zone oceanography (term of derision by experts or about armchair oceanographers)

tx telex; time; torque transmitter; traction

tx (TX) transmitter

Tx treatment

txclk (TxCLK) transmit data clock

txe telephone exchange electronic

txh transfer on index high

txi transfer on index incremented

txl transfer on index low

txn taxation

txt text; textbook; textile; textual(ly); textualism; textualist; textuary; texture(d); texturize; texturizing

ty territory; thank you; truly; type

ty tysk (Dano-Norwegian—German)

Ty Territory; Tybalt; Tyler; Tyndall; Tyonek; Tyrone; Tyrus Raymond Cobb

Tybalt Theobald

Tybee Savannah Beach, Georgia

tyc tycoon

TYC Thames Yacht Club; Toledo Yacht Club

Ty Cobb Tyrus Raymond Cobb —idol of baseball fans

TYCOM Type Commander (USN)

tydac typical digital automatic computer

tyg (TYG) trypticase yeast glucose

tylenol acetaminophen (trade name for an analgesic found safer than aspirin)

tymp tympanic(ity); tympany

tymp memb tympanic membrane

tyng topping

tyo two-year-old (horse)

TYO Tokyo, Japan (airport)

typ typical; typing; typist; typographer; typography; typewriter

TYP Ten-Year Plan; Twenty-Year Plan; etc.

type. typewriter; typewriting

type metal antimony-copper-lead-tin alloy

typer typewriter

typewriters Chicago-gangster (Scarface) Al Capone's nickname for submachine guns

typh typhoon

typo typographical (error)

TYPOE Ten-Year Plan for Ocean Exploration

typog typographer; typographical; typography

typol typological(ly); typologist; typology

typout typewriter output

typr typewritten

typw typewriter

tyr (TYR) tyrosine (amino acid)

Tyr Tyrol; Tyrolean; Tyrolese; Tyrone

Tyre English place-name for Es Sur or Zor

Tyrol Tyrol(ean); Tyrolese

tys tensile yield strength

TYS Knoxville, Tennessee (airport)

tysd total years service date

Tyskl Tyskland (Danish—Germany)

Tyskland (Dano-Norwegian or Swedish—Germany)

tytipt tape training in port (USN)

tyuraak tyuremnoye zaklyuchentye (Russian—prison confinement)

tyvm thank you very much

tz terrazzo; tidal zone; time zero

Tz tuberculin zymoplastiche (symbol)

TZ Tactical Zone; Transair Limited, Canada (2-letter code)

tzd true zenith distance

tze transfer on zero

tzg thermofit zap gun

TZIK Tzentralny Ispolnitelny Kommitet (Russian—Central Executive Committee)

tzj tubular zippered jacket

TZm true azimuth

TZM titanium-zirconium-molybdenum (alloy)

tzp time zero pulse

tzt te zijner tijd (Dutch—in due time)

tzv tetrazolium violet

U

u density of radiant energy (symbol); ugly threatening weather (symbol); unified atomic mass (symbol); unit(s); unknown; unoccupied; unsymmetrical; unwatched; upper; velocity (symbol); you (as in iou, IOU)

u *und* (German—and); viscosity (symbol)

U Chance Vought Aircraft (symbol); kilourane (1000 uranium units—symbol); overall co-efficient of heat transfer (symbol); potential energy (symbol); total internal energy (symbol); U Thant; U-boat; unclassified; Underground (London's subway system); Uniform—code for letter U; University; up; uranium; Utah; Utahans; utility; you

U *Uad* (Arabic—wadi)—gulley, ravine, riverbed; *ud* (Danish—out); *uit* (Dutch—out); *ulos* (Finnish—out); *Université* (French—University); *unter* (German—down); up; *upp* (Swedish—up); *ute* (Swedish—arrival); *violaceus* (Latin—violet-color)

U-1A American version of De Haviland Otter utility aircraft

u-2 you too

U-2 high-altitude high-performance photo-reconnaissance airplane

u/3 upper third

U-3 Cessna 6-passenger aircraft

U^{3}O^8 uranium oxide

U-4 Aero Commander transport aircraft

U 4 T union (coupling) 4 tons

U-6 De Havilland Beaver transport aircraft

U-8 Beech Seminole transport aircraft

U-17 Cessna Skywagon aircraft

U-17A Cessna 6-passenger Skywagon

U-22 Beech Bonanza trainer aircraft

U234 trace component of natural uranium

U235 0.7 percent of natural uranium (atomic energy source)

U238 99.3 percent of natural uranium (atomic energy source)

ua unauthorized absence; unauthorized absentee; uniform allowance; upper arm; urine aliquot; user area

ua (UA) urinalysis

u/a unit of account

u *a uden ar* (Dano-Norwegian—without date); *und andere(s)* (German—among other things, and others, inter alia); *und ähnliche(s)* (German—and the like)

u.a. *usque ad* (Latin—as far as; up to)

uA *und andere* (German—and others)

UA Underwater Association; United Aircraft; United Air Lines (2-letter coding); United Artists; University of the Americas; University of Auckland

U-A Universal-American

U of A University of Aberdeen; University of Adelaide; University of Akron; University of Alabama; University of Alaska; University of Alberta; University of the Americans; University of Arizona; University of Arkansas

UA *Universidad de las Americas* (Spanish—University of the Americas)

UAA United Arab Airlines; University Aviation Association

UAAGM University of Alberta Art Gallery and Museum

UAASUS Ukrainian Academy of Arts and Sciences in the United States

UAB Underwriters Adjustment Board; Unemployment Assistance Board; United Asian Bank; University of Aston in Birmingham

UABS Union of American Biological Societies

uac underwriters adjusting company

UAC United Aircraft Corporation; Urban Affairs Council; Utility Aircraft Council

UACC Upper Area Control Center

UACL United Aircraft of Canada, Limited

uacte universal automatic control and test equipment

UADPS Uniform Automatic Data Processing System

UADW Universal Alliance of Diamond Workers

UAE United Arab Emirates (Trucial Sheikdoms of Trucial States)

UAEMS University Association for Emergency Medical Services

UAESP Utah Association of Elementary School Principals

uaf unit authorization file

uafs/t universal aircraft flight simulator/trainer

UAFT United Agency for Fair

Treatment
UAG Universidad Autónoma de Guadalajara (University of Guadalajara)
UAHC Union of American Hebrew Congregations
uai universal azimuth indicator
UAI Urban America Incorporated (Action Council for Better Cities)
UAI União Astronomica Internacional (Portuguese—International Astronomical Union); *Union Académique Internationale* (French—International Academic Union); *Union des Associations Internationales* (French—Union of International Associations); *Union Astrónomica Internacional* (Spanish—International Astronomical Union); *Unione Astronomica Internazionale* (Italian—International Astronomical Union)
uaide uses of automatic information display equipment
UAISEGR University of Alaska Institute of Social, Economic, and Government Research
UAJAPPFI United Association of Journeymen and Apprentices of the Plumbing and Pipe Fitting Industry (U.S. and Canada)
UAK University of Alaska
ual upper acceptance limit
UAL United Air Lines; University of Aberdeen Library; University of Akron Library; University of Alabama; University of Alabama Library; University of Alaska Library; University of Alberta Library; University of the Americas Library; University of Arizona Library; University of Arkansas Library; University of Auckland Library
UALL University of Arizona Lunar Laboratory
U of Alla University of Allahabad
uam (UAM) underwater-to-air missile
UAM Union Africaine et Malgache (African and Malagasy Union); United American Mechanics
UAMC United Arab Maritime Company
UAMPT Union Africaine et Malgactie des Postes et Telecommunications (French—Union of African and Malagasy Postal Service and Tele-

communication)
uan uric-acid nitrogen
UANA Unión Amateur de Natación de las Americas (Spanish—Amateur Swimming Alliance of the Americas)
UANC United African National Council
uao unexplained aerial object
UAOD United Ancient Order of Druids
UAOS Ulster Agricultural Organisation Society
uap unexplained atmospheric phenomenon
Uap Micronesian name for Yap
UAP Union of American Physicians; Union of Associated Professors; United Australia Party
U of A Pr University of Alabama Press; University of Alaska Press; University of Arizona Press
uar underwater acoustic resistance; underwater angle receptacle, upper air route; upper atmospheric research
UAR Uniform Airman Record; United Arab Republic; University of Arkansas
UARAEE United Arab Republic Atomic Energy Establishment
UARL United Aircraft Research Laboratories
UARRSI Universal Aerial Refuelling Receptacle Slipway Installation
uart universal asynchronous receiver-transmitter
UARTO United Arab Republic Tourist Office
uas unmanned aerial surveillance; upper air space
UAS Unit Approval System
UASC United Arab Shipping Company
UASCS United States Army Signal Center and School
UASIF Union des Associations Scientifiques et Industrielles Françaises (Union of French Scientific and Industrial Associations)
UASM University of Arkansas School of Medicine
UASS Unmanned Aerial Surveillance System
UASSP Utah Association of Secondary School Principals
UASSR Udmurt Autonomous Soviet Socialist Republic
uat ultraviolet acquisition technique

UAT Union Aéromaritime de Transport
UATI *Union des Associations Techniques Internationales* (French—Union of International Technical Organizations)
UATO United Airlines Tour Order
UATP Universal Air Travel Plan
UAU Universities Athletic Union
UAW United Automobile Workers
uAwg um Antwort wird gebieten (German—reply requested)
uax (UAX) unit automatic exchange
UAZ University of Arizona
UAZEES University of Arizona Engineering Experiment Station
ub up(ward) bound; urine bilirubin
Ub Universiteitsbibliotheek (University Library, Amsterdam)
UB Union Bank; Union of Burma; United Bank (of Arizona); United Biscuit; Universität Basel; Universität Berne
U of B University of Baltimore; University of Bath; University of Birmingham; University of Bombay; University of Bradford; University of Bridgeport; University of Bristol; University of Buffalo
UB The University Bookman
uba undenatured bacterial antigen
UBA Union of Burmah Airways; United Business Associates
UBA Universidad de Buenos Aires (Spanish—University of Buenos Aires)
UBAF Union de Banques Arabes et Françaises (Union of Arab and French Banks)
U-bahn Untergrundbahn (German—underground road)—subway system
Ubangi English equivalent for Oubangui
Ubangi Republic Central African Republic
UBAV United Buddhist Association of Vietnam
UBB Union Bank of Bavaria
UBBA United Boys' Brigades of America
ubc universal buffer controller
UBC Uniform Building Code; United Baltic Corporation;

Universal Bibliographic Control; University of British Columbia

U of BC University of British Columbia

UBC Uniform Building Code (legal); *Universidad de Baja California* (Spanish—University of Baja California)

UBC & J United Brotherhood of Carpenters and Joiners

UBCL University of British Columbia Library

UBCP Union Bag-Camp Paper; University of British Columbia Press

ubd utility binary dump

UBD Universal Business Directories

ubdi underwater battery director indicator

UBEA United Business Education Association

U-beam U-shaped beam

UBEM Union Belge d'Enterprises Maritimes

ubers übersetzt (German—translated)

ubf universal boss fitting

UBF Union of British Fascists

ubfc underwater battery fire control

ubi ultraviolet blood irradiation; universal battlefield identification

UBI United Business Investments

UBI Unione Bocciofila Italiana (Italian Bocce-Ball (Bowling) Association); *Unione Bibliografica Italiana* (Italian Bibliographical Society)

Ubib Wien Universitätsbibliothek Wien (German—Vienna University Library)

ubip ubiquitous immunopoietic polypeptide

ubitron undulating beam interaction electron tube

UBL Union Barge Line; United Benefit Life

UBLS University of Botswana, Lesotho, and Swaziland

ubm ultrasonic bonding machine; unit bill of material

UBM United Biscuit Manufacturing (company)

U-boat Unterseeboot (German—submarine)

U-boat Führer Gross Admiral Karl Doenitz

U-bolt capital-U-shaped bolt

U-bomb uranium-cased atomic or hydrogen bomb

U Books University Books

UBP United Business Publica-

tions

UBR University Boat Race

UBS United Bank of Switzerland; United Bible Societies; United Business Service

UBSA United Business Schools Association (formerly American Association of Commercial Colleges)

UBSO Uinta Basin Seismological Observatory

ubt universal book tester

Ubu (Latin—Köln)—Cologne

ubv ultraviolet

UBVS Ultraviolet-Blue Visual System

uc undercover (agent); universal coarse (screw thread); upper case (capital letters)

u/c upper center

UC Ulster College (Northern Ireland); Umpqua College; Union Carbide; Union College; University of California; University of Canterbury; University of Ceylon; University of Cincinnati; University College; University of Colorado; University of Connecticut; Upland College; Upsala College; Ursinus College; Ursuline College; Utica College

U of C University of Calcutta; University of Calgary; University of California; University of Cambridge; University of Chattanooga; University of Chicago; University of Cincinnati; University of Colorado; University of Connecticut; University of Corpus Christi

UC una corda (Italian—one string)—soft pedal

uca upper control area

UCA United Chemists' Association; United Consumers of America; University of California; Utah Correctional Association

UCAB Universidad Católica Andrés Bello (Spanish—Andrés Bello Catholic University)

UCAE Universities Council for Adult Education

UCAF You See America First

UCAN Utilities Consumer Action Network

UCAR Union of Central African Republics; University Corporation for Atmospheric Research

UCAS Uniform Cost Accounting Standards; Union of Central African States

UCATT Union of Construction, Allied Trades, and Technicians

ucb unless caused by

UCB United California Bank; University of California at Berkeley; University College at Buckingham

UCBHM United Church Board for Homeland Ministries

UCBILR University of California at Berkeley—Institute of Library Research

ucc unadjusted contractual changes; universal copyright convention

UCC Uniform Commercial Code; Union Carbide and Carbon; Union Carbide Corporation; Union de la Critique Cinématographique (Society of Cinema Criticism); United Cancer Council; United Church of Christ; United Community Campaign; United Electric Coal Companies (stock exchange symbol); University College (Cork)

U-CC Upper Canada College

UCCA United Citizens Concerned with America; Universities Central Council on Admissions

UCCC Ulster County Community College; Uniform Consumer Credit Code

UCCD United Christian Council for Democracy

UCCELLO Paolo di Dono

UCC-ND Union Carbide Corporation—Nuclear Division

UCCS Universal Camera Control System

ucd usual childhood diseases

UCD University of California at Davis; University College, Dublin

UCDA University and College Designers Association

U c de L Université catholique de Louvain

ucdp uncorrect data processor

UCEA University College of East Africa (Makerere College); University Council for Educational Administration

UCEMT University Consortium in Education Media and Technology

U of Cey University of Ceylon

UCF United Community Funds; University of Central Florida

UCFE Unemployment Compensation for Federal Employees

UCFGB University Catholic Federation of Great Britain

UCFH University College of Fort Hare

UCG University College, Galway; University College of Ghana

UCGSM University of California Graduate School of Management

UCH University College Hospital

U-channel U-shaped channel

UCHCIS Urban Comprehensive Health Care Information System

uchd usual childhood diseases

U Chi University of Chicago

U Chi Lib University of Chicago Library

UCHS University City High School

uci unit construction index

UCI Union Cycliste Internationale (Cyclists International Union)

UCIDT University Consortium for Instructional Development and Technology

UCIIR University of California Institute of Industrial Relations

UCIIS University of California Institute of International Studies

UCIrv University of California at Irvine

UCIW Union of Commercial and Industrial Workers

UCIWP United Cannery and Industrial Workers of the Pacific

ucj unsatisfied claim and judgement

ucl upper control limit; urca clearance test

UCL Union Castle Line; Union Central Life; Union Oil Company of California (symbol); Universal Color Language; University of California Library; University College, London

UCLA University of California at Los Angeles

U-class upperclass

UCM University Christian Movement

u-c man undercover narcotics agent

UCMC University of Colorado Medical Center

UCMEA Ufficio Centrale di Meteorologia e di Ecologia Agraria (Italian—Central Office of Meteorology and Agrar-

ian Ecology)

UCMJ Uniform Code of Military Justice

UCMS Unit Capability Measurement System

U-C M S Union-Castle Mail Steamship

UCN University College of Nigeria

UCNW University College of North Wales

uco universal code; universal coding

UCO University of Colorado

U Conn University of Connecticut

UCOR Uranium Enrichment Corporation

UCP Unified Command Plan; United Cerebral Palsy; United Country Party; Universal Citizen Plan; University of California Press

UCPA United Cerebral Palsy Associations

U of C Pr University of California Press; University of Chicago Press

ucr unconditioned response

UCR Uniform Crime Reports; University of California at Riverside; Utah Coal Route (railroad)

UCRA University Centers for Rational Alternatives

Ucraina (Italian, Portuguese, or Spanish—Ukraine)

UCRC Underground Construction Research Council

UCRG Uniform Contractor Reporting Guidelines

UCRI Union Carbide Research Institute

UCRL University of California Radiation Laboratory

UCRN Unique Consignment Reference Number

UCR & N University College of Rhodesia and Nyasaland

UCRS Uniform Contractor Reporting System; Uniform Crime Reporting Section (FBI); University, College, and Research Section (Library Association)—also appears as UCR

ucs unconditioned stimulus; unconscious; unit-count system; universal card scanner; universal character set

uc's uterine contractions

UCs Urban Coalitionists

UCS Union of Concerned Scientists; United Community Service(s); Universal Classification System; Universal-Cy-

clops Steel; University Computer Systems (computerized real estate listings); Upper Clyde Shipbuilders

UCSB University of California at Santa Barbara

UCSC University of California at Santa Cruz; University City Science Center

UCSD University of California at San Diego

UCSF University of California at San Francisco

UCSL University College of Sierra Leone

U of C SL University of California School of Law

UCSW University College of South Wales

uct unit compatability test(ing)

UCT United Commercial Travelers; University of Cape Town; University of Connecticut

UCTA United Commercial Travellers' Association

UC & U Union College and University

UCUC University College of the University of Cincinnati

ucv uncontrolled variable

UCV Universidad Central de Venezuela

UCVs United Confederate Veterans

UCW University College of Wales

UCWC University College of the Western Cape

UCWI University College of the West Indies

UCWP University College of the Western Province

ucwr upon completion will return

UCWRE Underwater Countermeasures and Weapons Research Establishment

UCX Unemployment Compensation for Ex-Servicemen

UCY United Caribbean Youth

UCZ University College of Zululand

ud upper berth (double occupancy); upper deck; urethral discharge; uroporphyrinogen decarboxylase (UD)

ud (UD) utility dog

u.d. ut dictum (Latin—as directed)

Ud Udjung (Malay—point); *usted* (Spanish—you)

UD Underground (London's subway); Undesirable Discharge; United Dairies; University of Denver; University of Detroit; Urban District

U of D University of Dallas; University of Dayton; University of Delaware; University of Delhi; University of Denver; University of Detroit; University of Dublin; University of Dubuque; University of Dundee; University of Durham

UD Unlisted Drugs

UDA Ulster Defence Association (Protestant counterpart of the IRA); Urban Development Authority

udaa unlawfully driving away auto

U da C Uriel da Costa (Uriel Acosta)

UDAG Urban Development Action Grants

UDAL Union de Universidades de América Latina (Spanish—Union of Latin American Universities)

udam universal digital of avionics module

udarg udarbeidet (Danish—prepared)

udc universal decimal classification (UDC); upper dead center; usual diseases of childhood

U d C Universidad de Carabobo (Spanish—Carabobo University)—Venezuela

UDC United Daughters of the Confederacy; United Dye & Chemical; universal decimal classification; Urban District Council

UDCA Urban District Councils' Association

UDD Ulster Diploma in Dairying

'Uddersfield (Cockney contraction—Huddersfield)

udd's undisposed diapers; undumped diapers

UDE Union Douanière Equatoriale (Equatorial Customs Union); University of Delaware

U de A Universidad de Alcala; Université de Antioquia

UDEAO Union Douanière des Etats de l'Afrique de l'Ouest (French—Customs Union of West African States)—former French colonies

U de B Universidad de Barcelona; Université de Bâle (University of Basel)

U de BA Universidad de Buenos Aires

udec unitized digital electronic calculation

U de C Universidad de Cartagena; Universidad de Cauca; Universidad de Chile; Universidad de Córdoba; Universidad de Cuzco; Universidade de Coîmbra

U de CR Universidad de Costa Rica

U de F Université de Fribourg

U de G Universidad de Granada; Universidad de Guadalajara; Universidad de Guanajuato; Université de Genève; Université de Grenoble

U de H Universidad de la Habana

U de L Universidad de Lérida; Universidad de Lima; Universidade de Lisboa (Lisbon); *Université de Lausanne*

UDEL Union des Editeurs de Littérature (French—Literature Editors Union)

U de LA Universidad de Los Andes

U de M Université de Montreal

U de Monc Université de Moncton

U de O Universidad de Oviedo

U de Pan Universidad de Panamá

U de Q Universidad de Quito (Universidad Central)

U de S Universidad de Salamanca; Universidad de San Andrés (La Paz); *Universidad de San Augustín* (Arequipa); *Universidad de San Javier* (Panama); *Universidad de San Marcos* (Lima); *Universidad de Santiago; Universidad de Santo Tomás* (Bogotá or Santo Domingo)

U de SC de G Universidad de San Carlos de Guatemala

U de SD Universidad de Santo Domingo

U de SM Universidad de San Marcos (Lima, Peru)

U de SP Universidade de São Paulo

U de ST Universidad de Santo Tomás (Manila)

U de T Universidad de Toledó; Universidad de Trujillo (Peru)

U de V Universidad de Valencia; Universidad de Valladolid

U de Z Universidad de Zaragoza

udf und die folgende (German—and the following)

UDF Ulster Defence Force; Union Defence Force

udg udgave (Danish—edition)

u dgl (m) und dergleichen (mehr) (German—and the like)

U of D GSIS University of Denver Graduate School of International Studies

*Ud'H Université d'Haiti (*University of Haiti)

UDI Unilateral Declaration of Independence

UDI Unione Donne Italiane (Italian Women's Alliance)

U di A Università di Arezzo

UDIA United Dairy Industry Association

U di B Università di Bologna

U di F Università di Firenze (University of Florence)

U di G Università di Genova

U di N Università di Napoli

U di P Università di Padova; Università di Perugia; Università di Piacenza; Università di Pisa

U di R Università di Roma

U di S Università di Siena

U di T Università di Torino

U di V Università di Venezia; Università de Vicenza

u dk upper deck

udk udkom (Dano-Norwegian—published)

udl up-data link

udm upright drilling machine

udM unter dem Meeresspiegel (German—below sea level)

UDM United Merchants and Manufacturers (stock exchange symbol); Universal Drafting Machine (corporation)

Udm Aut Sov Soc Rep Udmurt Autonomous Soviet Socialist Republic

udn ulcerated dermal necrosis

UDN Underwater Doppler Navigation

UDN União Democrática Brasileira (Portuguese—Brazilian Democratic Union)

udo unwilling drop-out

U d O Universidad de Oriente (Spanish—Oriente University)—Venezuela

U do B Universidade do Brasil (Portuguese—University of Brazil)—in Brasilia

udom udometer; udometric; udometrical

U do P Universidade do Pôrto (University of Oporto)

UDP United Democratic Party

udpg (UPDG) uridine diphosphoglucose

UDP-gal uridine diphosphate galactose

UDP-glu uridine diphosphate glucose

UDPH Ulster Diploma in Poultry Husbandry

UDPS Utah Department of Public Safety

udr universal data report(er); universal digital readout; usage data report; utility data reduction

UDR Ulster Defence Regiment

UDR Union des Democrates pour la cinquième Republique (French—Union of Democrats for the Fifth Republic)

udrc utility data retrieval control

UDRI University of Dayton Research Institute; University of Denver Research Institute

UDRI-A University of Dayton Research Institute—Albuquerque

udro utility data retrieval output

Uds ustedes (Spanish—you, *pl.*)

UDS Ultraviolet Detection System; Underwater Demolition School

UdSSR Union der Sozialistischen Sowjetrepubliken (German —Union of Soviet Socialist Republics)—USSR

udt underdeck tonnage

UDT Underwater Demolition Team; Union for a Democratic Timor

UDTC University of Dublin Trinity College

U of D TC University of Dublin Trinity College

UDU Underwater Demolition Unit

udw ultra-deep water

UDW United Domestic Workers

UD-W University of Durban-Westville

Udy Oodie; Uddevalla

UDY United Dye and Chemical Corporation (stock exchange symbol)

ue unit equipment; unit exception; unit extremity

u E unseres Erachtens (German —in our opinion)

UE United Electrical Workers; University Extension

U of E University of the East (Manila); University of Edinburgh; University of Essex; University of Exeter

uea unattended equipment area

UEA Universal Esperanto Association; University of East Africa; University of East Anglia; University Entrance Examination; Utah Education Association

U of EA University of East Anglia

ueac unit equipment aircraft

ueb ultrasonic epoxy bonder

UEB Union Economique Benelux

UEC United Engineering Center (NYC)

UECC United Electric Coal Companies

UECM Union Electric Company of Missouri

UECU Union for Experimenting Colleges and Universities

uee unit essential equipment

UEE Unione Economica Europea (Italian—European Economic Union)

uef universal extra fine (screw thread)

UEFA Union of European Football Associations

UEI Union of Educational Institutions

ucl upper explosive limit

UEL Unilever Export Limited; United Empire Loyalists

u enr uranium enrichment

UEO Union de l'Europe Occidentale (Western European Union)

uep underwater electrical potential; uniform external pressure

UEP Union Electric Power Company; Union Européenne des Payements (European Payments Union—EPU)

UEPA Utility Electric Power Association

UEPMD Union Européenne des Practiciences en Médécine Dentaire (French—European Union of Practitioners of Dentistry)

UER University Entrance Requirements

UER Unione Europea di Radiodiffusione (Italian), *Union Européenne de Radiodiffusion* (French)—European Broadcasting Union

UERD Underwater Explosives Research Division (USN)

UERMWA United Electrical, Radio, and Machine Workers of America

UES Underground Experiment Subcommittee (AECL); United Engineering Societies

uesk unit essential spares kit

uet unattended earth terminal

UET United Engineering Trustees

UEW United Electrical Workers

uex unexposed

u/ext upper extremity

Uey U-turn (traffic)

uf urea-formadehyde; used for

UF Uniformed Force (police); United Fruit

U-F Ugro-Finnic

U of F University of Florida

UF$_6$ uranium hexafluoride

ufa until further advised

ufa (UFA) unesterified free fatty acid

UFA Uniformed Firefighters Association; University Film Association

UFA Universum-Film-Aktiengesellschaft (German—Universe Film Company)

ufac unlawful flight to avoid custody

UFACCC United Faculty Associations of California Community Colleges

ufaed unit forecast authorization equipment data

ufap unlawful flight to avoid prosecution

ufat unlawful flight to avoid testimony

UFAW Universities Federation for Animal Welfare

ufc uniform freight classification

UFC Uni-Flex Container(s); United Fruit Company

UFCc United Free Churches

UFCE Union Fédéraliste des Communautés Ethniques Européennes (French—Federal Union of European Nationalities)

UFCS Underwater Fire-Control System

UFCT United Federation of College Teachers

UFCU Uni-Flex Container Unit

uff ufficiale (Italian—officer; official); *ufficio* (Italian—bureau, office); *und folgende* (German—and the following)

UFF Ulster Freedom Fighters; University Film Foundation

uffi urea-formaldehyde foam insulation

UFH University of Fort Hare

UFI University Foundation International

UFI Union des Foires Internationales (French—Union of International Fairs)

UFIPTE Union Franco-Ibérique pour la Production et le Transport de l'Électricité (French—Franco-Iberian Union for the Production and Transmission

of Electricity)
UFIRS Uniform Fire-Incident Reporting System
ufl upper flammable limit
UFL University of Florida
UfM University for Man
UFMCC Universal Fellowship of Metropolitan Community Churches
ufn until further notice
ufo unfiltered oil; unidentified flying object
UFOA Uniformed Fire Officers Association
UFOD Union Française des Organismes de Documentation (French Union of Documentary Organizations)
ufol ufologic(al)(ly); ufologist(ic)(al)(ly); ufology
UFON Unidentified Flying Object Network
UFORA Unidentified Flying Objects Research Association
ufo's unidentified flying objects
uf p unemployed full pay
UFP United Federal Party
UFPA University Film Producers Association
UFPC United Federation of Postal Clerks
UFPO Underground Facilities Protective Organization
U-frame U-shaped frame
UFS University Film Society
UFT United Federation of Teachers
UFTAA Universal Federation of Travel Agents Associations
UFU Ulster Farmers' Union
UFW United Farm Workers; United Furniture Workers
UFWU United Farm Workers Union
ug undergraduate; underground; urogenital
Ug Uganda; Ugandan; Ugric; Ugus
Ug Udjung (Malay—point)
UG Underground Railroad—secret system set up before and during Civil War to aid Negro slaves seeking freedom in the northern United States and Canada; United Gas
U of G University of Georgia; University of Glasgow; University of Guam; University of Guelph; University of Guyana
UG Universität Graz
UG3RD Upgraded Third-Generation System (for air-traffic control)
uga unity gain amplifier
UGA University of Georgia

Ugan Uganda
Uganda Republic of Uganda (East African country whose English-speaking Ugandans export coffee, corn, cotton, peanuts, tea, and other crops as well as minerals such as copper and tin)
ugb unity gain bandwidth
ugc ultrasonic grating constant; unity grain crossover
UGC United Gas Corporation; University Grants Committee
UG & CW United Glass and Ceramic Workers
UGDP University Group Diabetes Program
UGE Unified Global Enterprises
UGEQ Union Generale des Estudiants du Québec (French—General Union of Students of Québec)
ugf unidentified growth factor
UGGI Union Géodésique et Géophysique Internationale (French—International Geodesic and Geophysical Union)
ugi upper gastrointestinal
UGI Unione Geografica Internazionale (Italian), *Unión Geografica Internacional* (Spanish), *Union Géographique Internationale* (French)—International Geographical Union
UGLE United Grand Lodge of England
UGLIAC United Gas Laboratory Internally-Programmed Automatic Computer
U of G Lib University of Georgia Libraries
Ugly Frontier barbed-wired-and-guarded Iron Curtain stretching between East and West Germany from the Baltic to Czechoslovakia's border
UGM Union of Graduates in Music
UGMA Unified Gift to Minors Act
ugmit you got me into this
UGMS Utah Geological and Mineral Survey
UGPL United Gas Pipe Line
U of G Pr University of Georgia Press
ugr ultrasonic grain refinement; universal graphic recorder
UGR Umfolozi Game Reserve (South Africa)
UGRR Underground Railroad (Quaker-organized means of aiding fugitive slaves escaping from southern slave states to

Canada and northern free states)
ugs uniaxial gyrostabilizer; urogenital system
Ugs Ugus
UGS United Girls' School
ugt urgent; urogenital tract
UGT Union General de Trabajadores (Spanish—General Union of Workers)—Socialist trade union
ugtl ugentlig (Dano-Norwegian —weekly)
UGU University of Guam
UGW United Garment Workers
uh upper half
uh (UH) utility helicopter
U of H University of Hartford; University of Hawaii; University of Houston; University of Hull
UH Universidad de la Habana; Universität Hamburg
UH-1 Bell 204B Iroquois military helicopter
UH-19 Sikorsky transport helicopter called H-19 or Chickasaw
UH-23 Hiller Raven utility helicopter H-23
uha upper-half assembly
UHA Union House of Assembly
UHAA United Horological Association of America
UHAB Urban Housing Assistance Board
uhc under honorable conditions
UHCBCN United Hebrew Congregations of the British Commonwealth of Nations
UHCC Upper House of the Convocation of Canterbury
uhcs ultra-high-capacity storage
UHCY Upper House of the Convocation of York
uhel ultra-high-efficiency lamp
uhf ultra-high frequency—300-3000 mc
UHF United Health Foundation; United Holyland Fund (for Arab terrorists); United Hospital Fund
uhfdf ultra-high-frequency direction finder
uhff ultra-high-frequency filter
uhfg ultra-high- frequency generator
uhfj ultra-high-frequency jammer
uhfo ultra-high-frequency oscillator
uhfr ultra-high-frequency receiver
UHI University of Hawaii

UHK University of Hong Kong

U of HK University of Hard Knocks

uhl user header label

uhmw ultra-high molecular weight

UHOIA University of Houston Office of International Affairs

uhp ultra-high purity

UHP University of Hawaii Press

uhr ultra-high resistance; ultra-high resolution

uhrn ultra-high radio navigation

uhs ultra-high speed

UHS International Union of the History of Science; Union High School; University for Humanistic Studies

uht ultra-high temperature; ultrasonic hardness tester; universal hand tool

uht milk ultra-high-temperature milk (capable of keeping without refrigeration)

uhtv unmanned hypersonic test vehicle

UHU Unhappy Hookers United (prostitutes protesting professional discrimination)

uhv ultra-high vacuum

uhvc ultra-high vacuum chamber

UHVS Ultra-High Vacuum System

ui ultrasonic industries; unit indicator; you (and) I

u/i unit of issue

u.i. *ut infra* (Latin—as below)

UI Ube Industries; Unemployment Insurance; Universität Innsbruck; Urban Institute

U of I University of Idaho; University of Illinois; University of Iowa; University of Israel; University of Istanbul

UIA Ultrasonic Industry Association; Union of International Associations; United Israel Appeal; University of Iowa

UIA Union Internationale des Architects (French—International Alliance of Architects); *Union Internationale des Avocats* (French—International Alliance of Attorneys)

UIAA Union Internationale des Associations d'Alpinisme (French—International Union of Alpinism Associations)

UIAS Union of Independent African States

UIATF United Indians of All Tribes Foundation

U i B Universitet i Bergen

UIB Unemployment Insurance Benefits; United International Bank

uibc unsaturated iron-binding capacity

uic ultraviolet image converter

UIC Unemployment Insurance Code; Union International Company; Utah Innovation Center

UIC Unio Internationlis Contra Cancrum (International Union Against Cancer)

UICA Union of Independent Colleges of Art

UICC Unione Internazionale Contro il Cancro (Italian—International Union for the Control of Cancer)

UICIO Unit Identification Code Information Office(r)

UICN Union Internationale pour la Conservation de la Nature (International Union for the Conservation of Nature)

UI Comm Unemployment Insurance Commission

UICPA Union Internationale de Chimie Pure et Appliqueee (French—International Union of Pure and Applied Chemistry)

UICPS Uniform Inventory Control Points System

UICT Union Internationale Contre la Tuberculose (French—International Union Against Tuberculosis)

UID University of Idaho

UIE UNESCO Institute for Education

UIEIS Union Internationale pour l'Etude des Insectes Sociaux (French—International Union for the Study of Social Insects)

UIEO Union of International Engineering Organizations

UIES Union Internationale pour l'Education Sanitaire (French—International Union for Health Education)

uif ultraviolet interference filter; unfavorable information file; universal intermolecular force

UIF Unemployment Insurance Fund

U i G Universitet i Göteborg

UIHL Union Internationale de l'Humanisme Laïque (French — International Union for Ethical Humanism)

UIHPS Union Internationale d'Histoire et de Philosophie des Sciences (French—International Union of the History

and Philosophy of Science)

UIII Urban Information Interpreters Incorporated

U i L Universitet i Lund

UIL University of Idaho Library; University of Illinois; University of Illinois Library; University of Indiana Library; University of Iowa Library

UIL Unione Italian del Lavoro (Italian Labor Union)—republican and social-democrat

U of Ill Lib Sci University of Illinois Graduate School of Library Science

U of Ill Pr University of Illinois Press

UIM Union Industrielle & Maritime (Société Française de l'Armement)

UIMNH University of Illinois Museum of Natural History

UIN United States and International Securities (stock exchange symbol); University of Indiana

UINF Union Internationale de la Navigation Fluviale (French —International Union for River Navigation)

Uintas short form for the Uinta Mountains of northeastern Utah and southwestern Wyoming

U i O Universitet i Oslo; Universitetsbiblioteket i Oslo (Norwegian—University Library in Oslo)

UIO Union Internationale des Orientalistes (French—International Union of Orientalists)

UIOOT Union Internationale des Organismes Officiels de Tourisme (French—International Union of Official Travel Organizations)

U of Iowa Pr University of Iowa Press

UIP United Irish Party; University of Illinois Press

UIP Union Internationale de Patinage (French—International Skating Union); *Union Internationale de Physique* (French—International Union of Physics)

UIPC Utah Industrial Promotion Commission

UIPC Union Internationale de la Presse Catholique

UIPD Ulrich's International Periodicals Directory

UIPVT Union Internationale contre le Péril Vénérien et les Tréponématoses (French—International Union against the Peril of Venereal Diseases and Syphilis)

uir upper information region

UIR University Industrial Research

uis (UIS) urban industrial society

U i S Universitet i Stockholm

UIS Unemployment Insurance Service; Unit Identification System

UISAE Union Internationale des Sciences Anthropologiques et Ethnologiques (French—International Union of Anthropological and Ethnological Sciences)

UISB Union Internationale des Sciences Biologiques (French — International Union of the Biological Sciences)

uisc unreported interstate shipment of cigarettes

UISE Union Internationale de Secours aux Enfants (French — International Child Welfare Union)

UISN Union Internationale des Sciences de le Nutrition (French—International of Nutritional Sciences)

UISP Union Internationale des Syndicats de Police (French—International Union of Police Trade Union)

uit unit impulse train

uit uitgaaf (Dutch—publication)

UIT Unión Internacional de Telecomunicaciones (Spanish), *Union Internationale des Télécommunications* (French), *Unione Internazionale Telecomunicazione* (Italian)—International Telecommunications Union—ITU

uitg uitgegeven (Dutch—published)

UITS Unione Italiana Tiro e Segno (Italian Rifle Association)

U i U Universitet i Uppsala

UIU Quito, Ecuador (airport)

UIUNA Upholsterers' International Union of North America

UIUPGWA United International Union of Plant Guard Workers of America

UJ University of Judaism

U of J University of Judaism

UJ Universidad Javeriana (Bogotá and Sucre)

UJA United Jewish Appeal

UJC Union Jack Club

U.J.D. Utriusque Juris Doctor (Latin—Doctor of Civil and Canon Law)

ujf unsatisfied judgment fund(ing)

U-joint(s) U-shaped joint(s)

ujr unijunction rectifier

UJSCs Union Jack Services Clubs

ujt unijunction transistor

uk unknown

uk (UK) urokinase

UK United Kingdom; Universita Karlova (Karl University—University of Prague)

U of K University of Kansas; University of Keele (formerly University College of North Staffordshire); University of Kent; University of Kentucky

UK Universiti Kebangsaan (Malay—National University)

UKA United Kingdom Alliance; United Klans of America

UK(A) United Kingdom All-comers (athletics)

UKAC United Kingdom Automation Council

UKADR United Kingdom Air Defense Region (NATO)

UKAEA United Kingdom Atomic Energy Authority

UKAPE United Kingdom Association of Professional Engineers

ukb universal keyboard

UKBC United Kingdom Bomber Command

UKBG United Kingdom Bartenders' Guild

UKC University of Kent at Canterbury

U of KC University of Kansas City; University of King's College

UKCA United Kingdom Citizens Association

UKCBDA United Kingdom Carbon Block Distributors' Association

UKCSBS United Kingdom Civil Service Benefit Society

UKCTA United Kingdom Commercial Travellers' Association

UKDA United Kingdom Dairy Association

uke ukulele

UK fo United Kingdom for orders

UKGBNE United Kingdom of Great Britain and Northern Ireland

UKGPA United Kingdom Glycerine Producers' Association

UKHH United Kingdom-Havre-Hamburg (range of ports)

UKHS United Kingdom Hovercraft Society

UKIAS United Kingdom Immigrants Advisory Service

UKISC United Kingdom Industrial Space Committee

UKITO United Kingdom Information Technology Organisation

UKJGA United Kingdom Jute Goods Association

UKKKK United Kingdom Ku Klux Klan

UKL University of Kansas Library; University of Khartoum Library

UKLF United Kingdom Land Force

UKLFS United Kingdom Low-Flying System

UKM University of Kansas Museums

UKMC University of Kansas Medical Center

UK(N) United Kingdom National (athletics)

UKOP United Kingdom Oil Pipelines

U K£ United Kingdom pound

UKPA United Kingdom Pilots' Association

Ukr Ukraine; Ukrainian

Ukr Acad Pr Ukrainian Academic Press

Ukraina (Russian—Ukraine)

Ukraine Ukrainian Soviet Socialist Republic

Ukrainian SSR Ukrainian Soviet Socialist Republic (Ukraine)

UKRAS United Kingdom Railway Advisory Service

UKS University of Kansas

UKSATA United Kingdom South Africa Trade Association

UKSM United Kingdom Scientific Mission; University of Kansas School of Medicine

UKSMA United Kingdom Sugar Merchants' Association

UKSMT United Kingdom Sea Mist Test(ing)

UKSTC United Kingdom Strike Command

Ukulele (UK) stock exchange slang for Union Carbide

ukv underground keybox vault

UKW Ultra-Kurzwellen (German—ultra-short wave)

UKY University of Kentucky

ul up link; upper left; upper leg; upper level; upper lid

ul (UL) user language
u/l upper left; upper limit
u & l upper and lower
UL Underwriters Laboratories; Universal League; University Libraries; University Library
U of L University of Lancaster; University of Laval; University of Leeds; University of Leicester; University of Lethbridge; University of Liverpool; University of London; University of Louisville
UL Union List
ula uncommitted logic array
ULA Ulster Launderers' Association; United Labor Agency; University of Louisiana
ULA Uniform Laws Annotated; Universidad Los Andes (Spanish—Andes University)—Venezuela
ULAA Ukrainian Library Association of America
ULAD Unilever Limited Accounts Department
ulan (Mongolian—red)
Ulan Bator Mongolian equivalent of Urga
u-land udviklingsland (Dano-Norwegian—development land)
Ulan Ude formerly Verkhneudinsk
ULAP University-wide Library Automation Program (University of California)
ulb universal logic bloc
ULB Université Libre de Bruxelles (Free University of Brussels)
ulc unsafe lane change (vehicular code), upper left center
u & lc upper and lower case
ULC Ulster Loyalist Council; Underwriters' Laboratories of Canada; Urban Library Council
ULCA United Lutheran Church of America
ULCC Ultra Large Cargo Carrier (bulk freighter or tanker of 400,000 or more tons)—superfreighter or supertanker
ULCI Union of Lancashire and Cheshire Institutes
uldb ultralight-displacement boat
uldest ultimate destination
ule ultra-low expansion
ulf ultra-low frequency; unfair labor practice
uli ultra-low interstitial
ULI Urban Land Institute
Ulianovsk formerly Simbirsk
ULICS University of London

Institute of Computer Science
ULII Union pour la Langue Internationale Ido (French—Union for the International Language Ido)
ull ullage
'Ull (Cockney contraction—Hull)
ULL Unitarian Laymen's League; University of Liverpool Library; University of London Library; University of Lund Library
ullv (ULLV) unmanned lunar logistics vehicle(s)
ulm ultrasonic light modulator; universal logic module
ULM University Library of Manchester (includes John Rylands Library)
Ulma (Latin—Ulm)
ULMS Underwater Long-range Missile System
ULO United Licensed Officers (union); Unmanned Launch Operations
ULP University of London Press
ULPA Uniform Limited Partnership Act
ulpr ultra low-pressure rocket
ULPZ Upper Limits for the Prescriptive Zone
Ulrich Ulrich's Books
uls unsecured loan stock
Uls Ulsan; Ulster
ULS Universities Libraries Section (Association of College and Research Libraries)
ULS Union List of Serials
ulsi ultra-large-scale integration
Ulster Northern Ireland (formerly an ancient province of Ireland and now containing the counties of Antrim, Armagh, Down, Fermanagh, Londonderry, and Tyrone)—capital city Belfast
Ulster Cradle of U.S. Presidents Northern Ireland—ancestral home of Presidents Arthur, Grant, Jackson, McKinley, Truman, Wilson
ult ultimate; ultimo
ult. ultimo (Latin—at last)
ULT United Lodge of Theosophists
Ult Bod Ultra Bodoni
Ultima Thule Iceland; Mainland (largest of the Shetland Islands); Norway; or any remote northern place, according to ancient travellers
ultimo scorso (Italian—last month)
ulto ultimo

ult° último (Spanish—last)
ult. praes. ultimum praescriptus (Latin—last prescribed)
ultra (Latin prefix—beyond or in excess)—ultramontane, ultrasonic
ultracom ultraviolet communications system
ultra hi-fi ultra-high fidelity
Ultrajectum (Latin—Utrecht)
ultralight ultralight flying machine; ultralight luggage; ultralight wearing apparel
ultrason ultrasonic(s)
ultra-x universal language for typographic reproduction applications
ult ts ultimate tensile strength
U of Luck University of Lucknow
ULUCLA University Library of the University of California at Los Angeles
ULUM University Library, University of Michigan (Ann Arbor)
ulv ultra-low volume
Ulysses' fifty-dollar bills bearing the portrait of President Ulysses S Grant
um umpire; unmarried
u/m unit of measure
üM über dem Meeresspiegel (German—above sea level)
UM Universal Match, Universal Mill; University of Malaysia (University of Malaya—Raffles Institute); University of Manitoba; University of Melbourne; University Museum(s)
U of M University of Maine; University of Malaysia; University of Manchester; University of Manitoba; University of Maryland; University of Massachusetts; University of Miami; University of Michigan; University of Minnesota; University of Mississippi; University of Missouri; University of Montreal
UM Universiti Malaya (University of Malaya)—Raffles Institute
U Ma Ursa Major (Big Bear)
UMA Ultrasonic Manufacturers Association; Union de Mujeres Americanas (United Women of the Americas); University of Massachusetts
U-magnet U-shaped magnet
U of Mand University of Mandalay
UMAS United Mexican-American Students

umass unlimited machine access from scattered sites

U of Mass Pr University of Massachusetts Press

umb umber; umbilical; umbilicus

Umb Umbrian

UMB *Union Mondiale de Billard* (French—World Billiards Union)

UMBIR University of Michigan Bureau of Industrial Relations

umbl umbilical

UMBR Umbria(n)

Umbrian Historical Painter Pinturicchio (Bernardino di Betto)

UMC United Metallic Cartridge (company); United Methodist Church; Universal Match Corporation; Upstate Medical Center

UMCA Urabá, Medellín and Central Airways

umd unitized microwave device

UMD Unit Manning Document; University of Maryland

UMDA United Micronesian Development Association

U of Md Lib Serv University of Maryland School of Library and Information Services

U of Mdrs University of Madras

UME University of Maine

umf ultramicrofiche

UMFC United Methodist Free Churches

umgearb *umgearbeitete* (German—revised)

UMHK *Union Minière du Haut-Katanga* (United Mines of Upper Katanga)

umi (Japanese—gulf, sea)

U Mi Ursa Minor (Little Bear)

UMI University of Michigan; University Microfilms Incorporated; University Microfilms International; Utah Management Institute

U of Miami Pr University of Miami Press

U of Mich Bus Res University of Michigan Graduate School of Business Research

U of Mich Inst Labor University of Michigan Institute of Labor and Industrial Relations

U of Mich Pr University of Michigan Press

U of Mich Soc Res University of Michigan Institute for Social Research

U/min *Umdrehungen in der*

Minute (German—revolutions per minute)

U of Minn Bell Mus University of Minnesota Bell Museum of Pathology

U of Minn Pr University of Minnesota Press

UMIST University of Manchester Institute of Science and Technology

UML University of Michigan Library; University of Minnesota Library; University of Missouri Library

umler universal machine language

UMLS University Microfilm Library Service

UM & M United Merchants and Manufacturers

UMMS University of (Maine, Manchester, Manitoba, Maryland, Massachusetts, Michigan, Minnesota, Mississippi, Missouri, Montana, etc.) Medical School

UMMZ University of Michigan Museum of Zoology

umn upper motor neuron

UMN University of Minnesota

UMNO United Malay National Organization

UMO University of Maine at Orono; University of Missouri

umoc ugly man on campus

U of Monc University of Moncton

U of Mo Pr University of Missouri Press

ump umpire

UMP Upper Mantle Project; Upper Merion and Plymouth (railroad); University of Massachusetts Press

'Umphrey (Cockney contraction—Humphrey)

UMPO Upper Manhattan Planning Office

umr under main roof

U MR Umvoti Mounted Rifles

UMREL Upper Midwest Regional Educational Laboratory

UMRRC Universities Mobile Radio Research Corporation (Bath, Birmingham, Bristol)

UMRWFR Upper Mississippi River Wildlife and Fish Refuge (Minnesota)

ums unmanned machinery space

UMS Undersea Medical Society; Universal Military Service; University of Mississippi

UMSU University of Malaya

Student's Union

UMT Universal Military Training; University of Montana

UMT *Union Marocaine du Travail* (French—Moroccan Labor Union)

UMTA Urban Mass Transportation Administration

umtd using mails to defraud

UMTRAP Uranium Mill Tailings Remedial Action Program

UMTS Universal Military Training and Service

UMW United Mine Workers

UMWA United Mine Workers of America

U of Mys University of Mysore

un (UN) unsatisfactory

Un Union (postal abbreviation)

UN Union Twist Drill (trademark); United Nations; University of the North; unsatisfactory

U of N University of Natal; University of Nebraska; University of Nevada; University of Newcastle; University of Nottingham

UN *União Nacional* (Portuguese—National Union)

UNA United Nations Association; United Native Americans; United Natives Association

UNAA United Nations Association of Australia

UNAAF Unified Action Armed Forces

unab unabridged

unabbreviated political terminology *communism* [you have two cows, government seizes both, sends you to prison, when released you stand in line (with other comrades) to buy watered milk]; *fascism* (you have two cows, government seizes both, and shoots you); *liberalism* (you have two cows, government requisitions both, shoots one, milks the other, throws milk away to avert possible surplus); *socialism* (you have two cows, government takes one, gives it to your cowless neighbor, who turns it into cowburgers); *conservatism* you have two cows, you sell one, and buy a bull (how old-fashioned!)]

unabr unabridged

UNAC United Nations Appeal for Children

UNACC United Nations Administrative Committee on

Coordination
unaccomp unaccompanied
UNACIL United Africa Commercial and Industrial Limited
UNACOMS Universal Army Communications System
UNAIS United Nations Association International Service
unalot unallotted
UNAM Universidad Nacional Autónoma de Mexico (National University of Mexico)
unamace universal automatic map compilation equipment
un-Amer un-American (something contrary to democratic tradition and the principles of American government and way of life)
unan unanimous
UNAPO United National Association of Post Office (Craftsmen)
UNARCO United Nations Narcotics Commission
unasgd unassigned
unatt unattached
UNAUS United Nations Association of the United States
UNAUSA United Nations Association of the United States of America
unauthd unauthorized
unb unbound; universal navigation beacon
UNB United Nations Bookshop; University of Nebraska
U of NB University of New Brunswick
UN Bank International Bank for Reconstruction and Development
unbd unbound
Unbib van Amsterdam Universiteitsbibliotheek van Amsterdam (Dutch—Amsterdam University Library)
unblkng unblanking
UNBSA United Nations Bureau of Social Affairs
unc unconscious; undercurrent; unified coarse (thread)
unc (UNC) unconditional (computer flow chart)
Unc Uncle
UNC United Nations Command; United Nuclear Corporation; University of North Carolina; University of Northern Colorado
U of NC University of North Carolina
UNC Union Nationale Camerounaise (French—Cameroon National Union)—party; *Uni-*

versidad Nacional de Colombia (Spanish—National University of Colombia)
UNCAST United Nations Conference on the Applications of Science and Technology
UNCC United Nations Cartographic Commission
UNCCP United Nations Commission on Crime Prevention
UNCF United Nations Children's Fund (formerly UNICEF); United Negro College Fund
unch unchanged
U of NC Inst Gov University of North Carolina Institute of Government
UNCIO United Nations Conference on International Organization
UNCIP United Nations Commission on India and Pakistan
uncir uncirculated
UNCIRSS University of North Carolina Institute for Research in Social Science
UNCITRAL United Nations Commission on International Trade Law
UN City Vienna, Austria's International Center (available to the UN cost free)
UNCIWC United Nations Commission for the Investigation of War Crimes
UNCL University of North Carolina Library
unclas unclassified
U.N.C.L.E. United Network Command for Law Enforcement (fictional organization created for television)
Uncle Arthur Arthur Henderson
Uncle Billie General William Tecumseh Sherman, USA
Uncle Dickie affectionate nickname of British military hero Mountbatten of Burma, Admiral of the Fleet and last Viceroy of India
Uncle Gene Eugene Ormandy
Uncle George George Geist
Uncle Ho Ho Chi Minh
Uncle Horace Horace Greeley
Uncle Joe U.S. Representative Joseph Gurney Cannon also known as the Watchdog of the Treasury
Uncle Kwesi Jonathan Kwesi Lamptey
Uncle Remus (pseudonym—Joel Chandler Harris)
Uncle Robert Robert E Lee;

Robert L Sheppard
Uncle Sam cartoon symbol and nickname for an American citizen or the United States of America
Uncle Sam's Crib Treasury of the United States
Uncle Sam's Pocket Handkerchief Delaware—second smallest state in the U.S.
Uncle Sap (derisive nickname—Uncle Sam)—self-bankrupting giveaway programs extended to even the most unfriendly nations account for this well-known nickname of recent years
Uncle Sugar FBI's nickname
Uncle Tom Josiah Henson (Negro slave immortalized in Harriet Beecher Stowe's *Uncle Tom's Cabin*); submissive Negro
Uncle Whiskers underworld nickname for Uncle Sam
UNCLOS United Nations Conference on the Law of the Sea
UNCMAC United Nations Command Military Armistice Commission
unco uncouth
UNCO United Nations Civilian Operations Mission (to the Congo)
UNCOK United Nations Commission on Korea
uncol universal computer-oriented language
uncomp uncompensated
uncond unconditioned
Unconditional Abolitionist William Lloyd Garrison
Unconditional Surrender Grant General Ulysses Simpson Grant, USA
UNCOPUOS United Nations Committee on the Peaceful Uses of Outer Space
uncor uncorrected
uncov uncover; uncovered; uncovers
U of NC Pr University of North Carolina Press
Uncrowned King of Ireland Charles Stewart Parnell
Uncrowned King of the Jews Chaim Weizmann
un cs unconditioned stimulus
unct. unctus (Latin—smeared)
UNCTAD United Nations Conference on Trade and Development
UNCURK United Nations Commission for the Unification and Rehabilitation of Korea

und under
UND University of National Defense; University of North Dakota
U of ND University of North Dakota; University of Notre Dame
UNDAT United Nations Development Advisory Team
UN Day United Nations Day (October 24)
UNDCC United Nations Development Cooperation Cycle
undeco underground economy (composed of persons who report less than they earn, including all who engage in bartering or who work for cash only as well as those who file no income tax returns; the drug traffic and organized crime are major segments of undeco)
unded underdeduction
undercover narc undercover narcotics agent
undergrad undergraduate
Underground Railroad Conductor Harriet Tubman who before and during the Civil War conducted fleeing slaves from the South to the northern United States and even to Canada
Under Sec Nav Nav Under Secretary of the Navy
Underworld Statesman and Patriot Meyer (Little Man) Lansky
Undex *United Nations Index*
UNDI *United Nations Document Index*
undies underthings (underwear)
undoc(s) undocumented alien(s) —illegal alien(s)
UNDOF United Nations Disengagement Observer Force
UNDP United Nations Development Program
U of ND Pr University of Notre Dame Press
undrgrnd underground
UNDRO United Nations Disaster Relief Office
undrwrld underworld
undsgd undersigned
UNDSM University of North Dakota School of Medicine
undtkr undertaker
undw underwater
undwrtr underwriter
UNE University of New England (New South Wales)
UNEAS Union of European Accountancy Students
U of Neb Pr University of Ne-

braska Press
UNEC United Nations Education Conference
UNECA United Nations Economic Commission for Asia
UNECOLAIT *Union Européenne du Commerce Laitier* (French—European Milk Trade Union)
UNEDA United Nations Economic Development Association
unef unified national extra fine (screw thread)
UNEF United Nations Emergency Forces
UNEF *Union Nationale des Étudiants Français* (National Union of French Students)
UNEO United Nations Emergency Operation
UNEP United Nations Environment(al) Program
UNESCO United Nations Educational, Scientific, and Cultural Organization
UNESEM *Union Européenne des Sources d'Eaux Minérales du Marché Commun* (French — European Union of Natural Mineral Water Sources of the Common Market)
UNETAS United Nations Emergency Technical Aid Service
U of Nev Pr University of Nevada Press
unex unexecuted
unexpl unexplained; unexploded; unexplored
unexpur unexpurgated
UNEXSO Underwater Explorers Society
unf unfinished; unfuzed; unified fin thread
UNF United National Front
U of NF University of North Florida
UNFAO United Nations Food and Agricultural Organization
unfav unfavorable
UNFB United Nations Film Board
UNFC United Nations Food Conference
unfd unfurnished
UNFDAC United Nations Fund for Drug Abuse Control
UNFICYP United Nations (Peace-Keeping) Force in Cyprus
unfin unfinished
Unfinished Schubert's Symphony No. 8 in B minor
UNFPA United Nations Fund for Population Activities

UN Fund International Monetary Fund
ung unguent
ung *ungarische* (German—Hungarian)
ung. unguentum (Latin—ointment)
Ung Ungava; Ungavan
UNGA United Nations General Assembly
Ungar Frederick Ungar Publishing Company
Ungarn (German—Hungary)
Ungheria (Italian—Hungary)
UNH University of New Hampshire; University of New Haven
U of NH University of New Hampshire
UNHCR United Nations High Commissioner for Refugees
UNHQ United Nations Headquarters (Geneva, New York, Vienna)
uni (Latin prefix—one)—unilateral
Uni University
UNI United News of India; United Nuclear Industry
UNI *Unione Naturista Italiana* (Italian Naturist Association)
UNIA Universal Negro Improvement Association (Garveyites)
União Soviética (Portuguese—Soviet Union)
União Sul-Africana (Portuguese—Union of South Africa)
UNIC United Nations Information center
UNICCAP Universal Cable Circuit Analysis Program
UNICE *Union des Industries de la Communauté Européenne* (Industrial Union of the European Community)
UNICEF United Nations International Children's Emergency Fund
unicike unicycle
UNICIS Unit Concept Indexing System; University of Calgary Information Systems
unicom underwater integration communication; universal communication
UNICOM aeronautical advisory station operating on 122.8 mc
UNIDIR United Nations Institute for Disarmament Research
UNIDO United Nations Industrial Development Organization
Unie van Suid-Afrika (Afrikaans

—Union of South Africa)

unif uniform; uniformity

unif coef uniformity coefficient

Unif Gift Min Act Uniform Gifts to Minors Act

UNIFIL United Nations Interim Force in Lebanon

Uniform letter U radio code

unihedd universal head-down display

unilat unilateral

Unilatcorps Unilateral Corps

UNIMA Union Internationale de grands Magasins (French—International Union of Department Stores)

UNIMERC Universal Numeric Coding System

UNIMS Univac Information Management System

UNINCO Union Internationale des Corps Consulaires (International Consular Corps Union)

unincorp unincorporated

UNIO United Nations Information Organization

Union Coll Pr Union College Press

Unione Sovietiche (Italian—Soviet Union)

Union Jack flag flown at forward jackstaff of American ships, yachts, and other vessels —consists of dark-blue rectangular field with 50 five-pointed white stars same as top hoist of the American flag —the Stars and Stripes; national flag of United Kingdom symbolizing union of England, Northern Ireland, Scotland, and Wales—combines crosses of St George (England), St Patrick (Northern Ireland), St Andrews (Scotland)

Unions Union Islands of the Pacific also called Tokelaus

Unión Soviética (Spanish—Soviet Union)

Union soviétique (French—Soviet Union)

Union of Soviet Socialist Republics (world's largest nation occupying much of Asia and Europe plus satellite lands of this communist-imperialist empire behind the Iron Curtain; Russian is the official language but many others are used; every occupation contributes to the total economy) *Soyuz Sovyetskikh Sotsialisticheskikh Respublik*

Unión Sudafricana (Spanish—Union of South Africa)

UNIP United Independence Party

uniparse universal parser

UNIPEDE Union Internationale des Producteurs et Distributeurs d'Energie Electrique (French—International Union of Producers and Distributors of Electric Energy)

unipol universal procedure-oriented language

uni(s) unisexual(s)

unis unisoni (Italian—unison)

UNIS United Nations International School; Univac Industrial System

UNISCAN United Kingdom and Scandinavia

UNISIST Universal System for Information in Science and Technology

UNISOMI Universal Symphony Orchestra and Music Institute

UNISTAR User Network for Information Storage Transfer

UNISYM Unified Symbolic Standard Terminology for Mini Computer Instructions

Unit Unitarian

UNIT Union Nationale des Ingénieurs Techniciens

UNITAR United Nations Institute for Training and Research

Unitarian Economist David Ricardo (of Sephardic origin)

Unitarian Quaker Elias Hicks

United Arab Emirate Ports Ash Shariqah, Dubai, Abu Dhabi (Abu Zaby)

United Arab Emirates Trucial Sheikdoms (Persian Gulf oil-producing country whose oil revenues provide the highest gross national product in the world; Arab as well Indian and Persian workers speak their own languages)

United Arab Republic name referring to the former union of Egypt and Syria

United Auto Workers International Union, United Automobile, Aerospace, and Agricultural Implement Workers of America

United Kingdom United Kingdom of Great Britain and Northern Ireland (former center of the British Empire based in London and directing all parts of the English-speaking world; now includes England, Scotland, and Wales as well as the Isle of Man plus overseas

colonies and dependencies such as Belize; Bermuda; British Antarctica; the British Indian Ocean Territory; the British West Indies; the Channel Islands; Gibraltar; Hong Kong; islands in the Pacific— the Gilberts, New Hebrides— a condominium jointly administered by France; Pitcairn; islands in the South Atlantic—Ascension, the Falklands, St Helena, Tristan da Cunha, etc.)

United Kingdom's Principal Port London

United Mine Workers United Mine Workers of America

United Nations Capital New York City

United Provinces United Provinces of the Netherlands (Friesland, Gelderland, Groningen, Holland, Oberyssel, Utrecht, Zeeland)—the Seven Provinces

United Provinces colors blue and white displayed in flags of El Salvador, Guatemala, Honduras, and Nicaragua—formerly federated after their liberation from Spain

United Rubber Workers United Rubber, Cork, Linoleum, and Plastic Workers of America

United States United States of America (leading English-speaking North American nation with global cultural, economic, and political interests); part of the official name of the United States of Brazil, the United States of Colombia, the United States of Indonesia, the United States of Mexico, the United States of North America (the U.S.A.), the United States of Venezuela

UNITS United Nations Information for Teachers

univ universal

Univ Universal; Universalist; University; University College, Oxford

univac universal automatic computer

univar universal valve action recorder

Univ-Buchdr Universitats-Buchdrukerei (German—university press)

Univ C University College (Oxford)

Univ. D. Doctor of the University (degree)

Universal Genius Leonardo da

Vinci (anatomist, architect, cartographer, engineer, inventor, musician, painter, poet, sculptor, zoologist)

Univ Mus of UP University Museum of the University of Pennsylvania

unjc united national J-series coarse (thread)

unjef united national J-series extra fine (thread)

unjf united national J-series fine (thread)

unjs united national J-series special (thread)

unk unknown

Unk Uncle

unkn unknown

UNKRA United Nations Korean Reconstruction Agency

UNL University of Nairobi Library

UNLA Unione Nazionale per la Lotta contro l'Analfabetismo (Italian—National Association for the Fight Against Illiteracy)

UNLC United Nations Liaison Committee

unld unload (flow chart)

unldh underloading

unlib unliberated

unliq unliquidated

unlk unlock

UNLL United Nations League of Lawyers

UNLOS United Nations Law of the Sea (conference)

UNLOSC United Nations Law of the Sea Conference

unltd unlimited

unlwfl unlawful(ly)

unm unmarried

UNM Ukrainian National Museum (Chicago); University of New Mexico

U of NM University of New Mexico

UNMC University of Nebraska Medical Center

UNMEM United Nations Middle East Mission

U of NM Gen Lib University of New Mexico General Library

UNMOGIP United Nations Military Observer Group in India and Pakistan

U of NM Pr University of New Mexico Press

UNMSC United Nations Military Staff Committee

UNMSM de L Universidad Nacional de San Marcos de Lima (University of Lima)

unmtd unmounted

UNO United Nations Organiza-

tion; United Neighborhood Organization; University of Nebraska at Omaha; University of New Orleans

UNO Union Nacional Odría (Spanish—Odria National Union)— Peruvian-general's party

UNOC United Nations Operations in the Congo

unodir unless otherwise directed

unof unofficial

UNOID United Nations Organization for Industrial Development

unoindc unless otherwise indicated

UNOLS University-National Oceanographic Laboratory System

U or non-U upperclass or not upperclass

unop unopposed

unoreq unless otherwise requested

unp unpaged

UNP University of Nebraska Press; Urewara National Park (North Island, New Zealand)

UNPA United Nations Postal Administration

unpd unpaid

UNPHU Universidad Nacional Pedro Henriguez Urena (Spanish—Pedro Henriquez Urena National University)—in the Dominican Republic

unpkd unpacked (flow chart)

unpleas unpleasant

UNPOC United Nations Peace Observation Commission

UNPP United Nations Partition Plan

unpub unpublished

unqte unquote

unqual unqualified

UNR & EC United Nuclear Research and Engineering Center

Unreconstructed Rebel Senator George Carter Glass so nicknamed by President Franklin D Roosevelt

UNREF United Nations Refugee Emergency Fund

unrel unreliable

unrep unreported; unrepresented

UNRISD United Nations Research Institute for Social Development

UNRRA United Nations Relief and Rehabilitation Administration

UNRWA United Nations Relief

and Works Agency

uns unified special (thread); unsymmetrical

UNS Unified Numbering System

UNSA United Nations Specialized Agencies; University of Nottingham School of Agriculture

Unsainted Anthony San Antonio, Texas

unsat unsatisfactory

unsatfy unsatisfactory

unsatis unsatisfactory

UNSC United Nations Security Council

UNSCC United Nations Standards Coordinating Committee

UNSCCUR United Nations Scientific Conference on the Conservation and Utilization of Resources

UNSCEAR United Nations Scientific Committee on the Effects of Atomic Radiation

UNSCOB United Nations Special Commission on the Balkans

UNSCOP United Nations Special Commission on Palestine

unscv unserviceable

UNSDRI United Nations Social Defense Research Institute

Unser Fritz (German—Our Fritz)—Frederick William III of Prussia

UNSG United Nations Secretary General

unsgd unsigned

unskd unskilled

UNSM United Nations Service Medal; University of Nebraska State Museum

UNSO United Nations Sahel Office (*see* Sahel); United Sabah Organization

UNSR United Nations Space Registry

unst unstable

un stim unconditioned stimulus

unsus-look(ing) unsuspiciouslook(ing)

unsvc unserviceable

UNSvM United Nations Service Medal

UNSW University of New South Wales

UNSY United Nations Statistical Yearbook

unsym unsymmetrical

Unt Unter (German—lower; under)

UNTA United Nations Technical Assistance

UNTAA United Nations Technical Assistance Administration

UNTAG United Nations Transition Assistance Group

UNTC United Nations Trusteeship Council

unthd unthreaded

UNTSO United Nations Truce Supervision Organization

UNTT United Nations Trust Territory

UNTTA United Nations Trust Territory Administration

UNU United Nations University

UNUP United Nations University Press

UNUSA United Nations Association of the United States of America

UNV University of Nevada

UNWCC United Nations War Crimes Commission

unwmk unwatermarked

u/o used on

u & o use and occupancy

uo und öfters (German—and often)

UO Ulster Orchestra (Belfast); University of Otago (at Dunedin, New Zealand); University of Ottawa

U of O University of Ohio; University of Oklahoma; University of Omaha; University of Oregon; University of Ottawa; University of Oxford

uoa use of other automobiles

UOB United Overseas Bank

U of O B University of Oregon Books

uoc ultimate operational capability

UOC Uniform Offense Classification

UOCO Union Oil Company

uod ultimate oxygen demand

UOFS University of the Orange Free State

UOH University of Ohio

uohc under other than honorable conditions

UOJCA Union of Orthodox Jewish Congregations of America

UOK University of Oklahoma

U of Okla Pr University of Oklahoma Press

uol underwater object locator

uoo undelivered orders outstanding

UOP Universal Oil Products

UOPWA United Office and Professional Workers of America

UOR Uniform Officer Record;

University of Oregon; Unusual Occurrences Report

UORI University of Oklahoma Research Institute

uos Underwater Ordnance Station (USN)

uo's undelivered orders

uot uncontrolled overtime

UOT United Ocean Transport (Daido Line)

UOTS United Order of True Sisters

uov unit of variance

up. underproof; underproofed; underproofing; unpaged; upper

u/p urine-plasma concentration

u & p uttering and publishing

Up Upper

UP Union Pacific (railroad); Union Postale (Postal Union); United Presbyterian; United Press; United Province; University of Paris; University of Pennsylvania; University of Pittsburgh; Uttar Pradesh

U of P University of the Pacific; University of Pennsylvania; University of Pittsburgh; University of Portland; University of Pretoria; University of Puget Sound

UP Unidad Popular (Spanish—Popular Unity)—political party; *Union Panamericana* (Spanish—Pan-American Union); *Union Postale* (French—Postal Union)—international mail organization

UPA United Productions of America; University of Pennsylvania; University Photographers Association

UPA Union Postale Arabe (Arab Postal Union); *Unions Professionnelles Agricoles* (Professional Agricultural Unions)

UPAA University Photographers Association of America

UPAC Union of Pan-Asian Communities

UPADI Unión Panamericana de Asociaciones de Ingenieros (Pan-American Union of Engineers Associations)

UPAE Union Postale des Amériques et de l'Espagne (French—Postal Union of the Americas and Spain)

UPAO University Professors for Academic Order

UPASI United Planters Association of South India

upc universal product code

UPC Unesco Publications Center; United Power Company;

Universal Product Code

upd unpaid

UPD Unified Port District

UPDW United Piece Dye Works

U of PE University of Port Elizabeth

UPE Union Parlementaire Européenne (European Parliamentary Union)

UPEP Undergraduate Preparation of Educational Personnel

UPGA Utah Personnel and Guidance Association

uphd uphold

uphol upholsterer; upholstery

UPI United Press International (merger of United Press and International News Service)

UPICA University of Pennsylvania Institute of Contemporary Art

UPIGO Union Professionnelle Internationale des Gynécologistes et Obstétriciens (French—International Professional Union of Gynecologists and Obstetricians)

UPIN United Press International Newsfeatures

UPL United Philippine Line; University of Pensylvania Library; University of the Philippines Library (Quezon City); University of Pittsburgh Library; University of Portland Library

upm uninterruptible power module, units per mile

UPNE Unversity Press of New England

UPNG University of Papua and New Guinea

upo undistorted power output; unidentified paleontological object

UPO United Partisans' Organization; Unit Personnel Office(r)

UPOV Union for the Protection of New Varieties of Plants

UPOW Union of Post Office Workers

upp upplaga (Swedish—edition)

UPP University of Pennsylvania Press; University of Pittsburgh Press

UPPC Union Pacific Petroleum Corporation

Upper Adige the Italian Tyrol also called the Southern Tyrol

Upper Alsace Haut-Rhin department of France

Upper Amazon Amazon River

extending from the highlands of Peru to Manaus in northern Brazil

Upper Austria northern Austria bordering Bavaria and Czechoslovakia

Upper Burma inland Burma

Upper California in Spanish-colonial times all of California north of Monterey but today all of California except Baja or Lower California

Upper Canada English-speaking Ontario and the upper St Lawrence region during the 19th century

Upper Egypt Egypt from Cairo south to the Sudan

Upper Galilee Israel north of the Sea of Galilee

Upper Lakes northernmost Great Lakes—Huron, Michigan, Superior

Upper Michigan the upper peninsula of northern Michigan between Lake Michigan and Lake Superior

Upper Mississippi Mississippi River from Lake Itaska in Minnesota near the Canadian border to Saint Louis, Missouri

Upper Nile Nile River from its headwaters in central East Africa to Khartoum in the Sudan

Upper Palatinate eastern Bavaria

Upper Peninsula northern Michigan between Lake Michigan and Lake Superior

Upper Peru an old name for Bolivia

Upper Rhine Rhine River between Basel in Switzerland and Mainz in Germany

uppers nickname for stimulants

Upper Silesia northern Silesia once a Prussian province

Upper Volta Republic of Upper Volta (landlocked West African country whose Upper Voltans speak French and tribal languages—cattle herding, farming, and mining fail to provide enough work and many migrate to coastal countries) *République de Haute-Volta*; name changed in 1984 to Bourkina Fasso

UPPPP Underprivileged Peoples' Public Pool

upr (most); unsaturated polyester resin; upper

Upr Upper (postal abbreviation)

U Pr University Press (Washington, DC)

UPR Union Pacific Railroad; University of Puerto Rico

UPREAL Unit Property Record and Equipment Authorization List

U Presses Fla University Presses of Florida

U Pr Hawaii University Press of Hawaii

U Pr Kan University Press of Kansas

U Pr Ky University Press of Kentucky

U Pr Miss University Press of Mississippi

U Pr NE University Press of New England

U Pr Va University Press of Virginia

U Pr Wash University Press of Washington

ups uinterrupted power supply; United Parcel Service (trademark in lowercase)

UPS Underground Press Syndicate; Underground Publication Society; Underwater Production System(s); Universal Press Syndicate

UPSA Ukrainian Political Science Association

Upsalia (Latin—Uppsala)—Swedish hometown of the naturalist Linnaeus and the philosopher Swedenborg

UPSEB Upper Pradesh State Electricity Board

UPSG universal polar stereographic grid

UPSM University of Pennsylvania School of Medicine

UPSTC Upper Pradesh State Textile Corporation

UPSTEP Undergraduate Pre-Service Teacher Education Program

Up Swn Upper Swan

upt (UTP) uridine triphosphate

up tor upper torso

up tr up train

UPU United Prisoners Union; Universal Postal Union

UPU Unión Postal Universal (Spanish—Universal Postal Union)

Up V Upper Volta

UPV Ulster Protestant Volunteers (paramilitary counterpart of the IRA)

UPW Union of Postal Service Workers

UPWA United Public Workers of America

UPWIU United Paper Workers

International Union

uq upper quartile

UQ University of Queensland

U of Q University of Québec; University of Queensland

UQP University of Queensland Press

Uqsor (Arabic—Luxor)

u quark up quark

ur unconditioned response; up right (stage direction); upper right; urinal; urinary; urine; utility rectifier

ur (UR) unemployment rate

u/r upper right

ur *ouron* (Greek—urine)—urea, uremia, ureter, urethra, urine, urology

Ur Urania; Uranus; Urdu; Uruguay; Uruguayan

UR Uganda Railway; Uniform Regulations; Unsatisfactory Report; Urban Renewal; Utilization Review

U of R University of Reading; University of Redlands; University of Richmond; University of Rochester

UR Universidad de la República (University of Uruguay)

URA United Republicans of America; Urban Redevelopment Authority; Urban Renewal Administration

urad your radio (message)

u-rail U-shaped rail

Urals Ural Mountains dividing Asia from Europe in the USSR

URAMEX Mexican-government's uranium company

uran (Latin—tail)—anuran, urochordate

Uran Uranus

ur anal. urine analysis

U of Rang University of Rangoon

uranog uranographer; uranographic; uranography

urb urban; urbanism; urbanist; urbanistic; urbanite; urbanization; urbanize; urbicultural; urbiculture

Urb Urbanización (Spanish—Urbanization)

Urban Inst Urban Institute

Urbank Urban Bank (National Development Bank)

urbanol urbanologic(al); urbanologist; urbanology

urb guer(s) urban guerilla(s)

urbm (URBM) ultimate-range ballistic missile

urbol urbanologist; urbanology

Urbs Orba Symphony in F of Saint-Saëns

urb ter urban terrorism; urban terrorist(s)

urc upper right center

URC Universal Resources Corporation; Urban Renewal Commission

urclk universal receiver clock

URCLPWA United Rubber, Cork, Linoleum, and Plastic Workers of America

urd upper disease (head cold)

Urd Urdu (literary language of pakistan)

Ur$ Uruguayan peso

URD *Unión Republicana Democrática* (Spanish—Democratic Republican Union)—political party active in Venezuela

Urdiniyah (Arabic—Jordan)

urdis your dispatch

ure unintentional radiation exploitation

URE Undergraduate Record Examination

URESA Uniform Reciprocal Enforcement of the Support Act (for the collection and enforcement of child support)

uret urethra(l)

urf (URF) uterine-relaxing factor

URF *Union des Services Routiers des Chemins de Fer Européens* (French—Union of European Railways Route Services)

urg urgent

Urga former name of Ulan Bator

uri upper respiratory illness (head cold)

Uri not an abbreviation but a Swiss canton

URI Union Research Institute (Hong Kong); University of Rhode Island

U of RI University of Rhode Island

uria (Latin prefix—urine)—urinal, urinalysis; (Latin suffix—urine)—polyuria

URIMA University Risk and Insurance Managers Association

urinalysis urine analysis

URISA Urban and Regional Information System Association

Urista Uriel da Costa

url (URL) user requirements language

URL Underground Research Laboratory (Canadian); Unilever Research Laboratory; University of Rhodesia Library (Salisbury)

urltr your letter

urmgm your mailgram

urmsg your message

urn. ultra-high radio navigation

uro urological; urology

uro (Latin prefix—urine)—urinal, urinary

URO United Restitution Organization

urodyn urodynamic(s)

urogen urogenital

urol urologic(al)(ly); urologist; urology

U-room U-boat room (petty officer's quarters)

uro or uran (Greek-derived prefix or suffix from *oura* meaning tail)—anuran or urochordate

URP Unit Reporting Program; United Revolutionary Party

Urq Urquhart

urr (URR) ultra-rapid reader (computer program)

URR Union for the Resurrection of Russia

URRVS Urban Rapid-Rail Vehicle Systems

urs unit reference sheet

URs Unsatisfactory Reports; University Rationalists

UR's Unsatisfactory Reports

URS Universal Reporting System; Universal Reference System

urser your serial (number or reference)

URSI *Union Radio Scientifique Internationale* (International Scientific Radio Union)

urspr *ursprünglich* (German—originally)

URSS *União das Repúblicas Socialistas Soviéticas* (Portuguese—Union of Socialist Soviet Republics)—the USSR; *Unión de Repúblicas Socialistas Soviéticas* (Spanish—Union of Soviet Socialist Republics); *Union des Républiques Socialistes Soviétiques* (French—Union of Socialist Soviet Republics)—the USSR

Ursula Bloom Mrs ACG Robinson's pen name

Ursula Undress Ursula Andress

urt upper respiratory tract; utility radio transmitter

URT United Republic of Tanzania (Tanganyika and Zanzibar)

urtel your telegram

urti upper respiratory tract infection (common cold; influenza)

URTU United Road Transport Union

Uru Uruguay; Uruguayan

Uruguay Oriental Republic of Uruguay (Spanish-speaking country between Argentina and Brazil whose Uruguayans are noted for their devotion to democracy and their industry reflected by exports such as farm products, metallic ores, oil products, textiles, and wines) *República Oriental del Uruguay*

Uruguayan Ports La Paloma, Maldonado, Montevideo, Puerto Sauce, Nueva Palmira, Fray Bentos, Puerto Concepción, Paysandú, Salto

Uruguay Day Uruguayan Independence Day (August 25)

Uruguay's Largest Port Montevideo

urv underseas research vehicle

URWA United Rubber Workers of America

us. under seal; undersize; uniform sales

us. (US) unconditioned stimulus

u-s upper-stage

u/s unserviceable

u.s. *ubi supra* (Latin—where mentioned above); *ut supra* (Latin—as above)

US United States (to many Americans US or U.S. means us—you and I). University of Stellenbosch

U.S. United States

U of S University of Salford; University of Saskatchewan; University of Scranton; University of Sheffield; University of Sherbrooke; University of the South (Sewanee, Tennessee); University of Southampton; University of Stirling; University of Strathclyde; University of Sudbury; University of Surrey; University of Sussex; University of Swansea; University of Sydney

U.S. *Ufficio Stampa* (Italian—Press Agency)

USA Underwriters Service Association; Union of South Africa; United States of America (more correctly U.S.A., to distinguish the country from USA, United States Army); United States Army; United States Attorney; United Steelworkers of America; University of South Africa

US of A United Steelworkers of America; United Synagogue of America

U.S.A. United States of America

U.S. of A. United States of America (as abbreviated a century ago); United Secularists of America

U of SA University of South Africa

USA Unser Shtickel Arbeit (Yiddish—Our Bit of Work)—rifle grenade produced in Palestine for use against Arab guerrillas

U.S.A. (title of trilogy by John Dos Passos—*42nd Parallel, 1919, The Big Money*—describing first three decades of American life in the twentieth century)

USAA United Services Automobile Association

USAAA US Army Audit Agency

USAABMDA United States Army Advance Ballistic Missile Defense Agency

USAAC United States Army Air Corps (now USAF)

USAACDA United States Army Aviation Combat Development Agency

USAAD US Army Airmobile Division

USAADC United States Army Air Defense Center

USAADEA US Army Air Defense Engineering Agency

USAAF United States Army Air Forces

USAAFINO United States Army Aviation Flight Information and Navigation Aids Office

USAAFO US Army Avionics Field Office

USAAMR & DL United States Army Air Mobility Research and Development Laboratory

USAAPSA United States Army Ammunition Procurement and Supply Agency

USAASD United States Army Aeronautical Service Detachment

USAASO United States Army Aeronautical Services Office

USAAVNC United States Army Aviation Center

USAAVNS United States Army Aviation School

USAAVSCOM United States Army Aviation Systems Command

USAB United States Activities Board

USABAAR United States Army Board for Aviation Accident Research

USABRL US Army Ballistic Research Laboratories

USAC United States Aircraft Carriers (air cargo line); United States Auto Club; US Air Conditioning Corporation

USACAA United States Army Concepts Analysis Agency

USA CAC United States Army Continental Army Command

USACC United States Army Communications Command; U.S.-Arab Chamber of Commerce

USACDA United States Arms Control and Disarmament Agency; United States Army Catalog Data Agency

USACDC US Army Combat Developments Command

USACDCCA United States Army Combat Development Command Combined Arms Agency

USACDCEC United States Army Combat Development Command Experimentation Command

USACDCFAA United States Army Combat Developments Command Field Artillery Agency

USACDCNG United States Army Combat Developments Command Nuclear Group

USACDCOA United States Army Combat Developments Command Ordnance Agency

USACDCQA United States Army Combat Developments Command Quartermaster Agency

USACDCSWCAG United States Army Combat Developments Command Special Warfare and Civil Affairs Group

USACE US Army Corps of Engineers

USACENDCDSA United States Army Corps of Engineers National Civil Defense Computer Support Agency

USACIC United States Army Criminal Investigation Command

USACMA United States Army Club Management Agency

USACMR United States Army Court of Military Review

USACPEB United States Army Central Physical Evaluation Board

USACRR United States Army Crime Records Repository

USACSA US Army Combat Surveillance Agency

USACSLA United States Army Communications Security Logistics Agency

USACSSEA United States Army Computer Systems Support and Evaluation Agency

USAD US Army Dispensary

USADIP United States Army Deserter Information Point

USADSC US Army Data Services and Administrative Systems Command

USAE United States Army Engineer(s); United States Army, Europe

USAEC United States Army Engineer Command; United States Atomic Energy Commission; US Army Electronics Command

USAECA United States Army Engineer Construction Agency

USAECBDE United States Army Engineer Center Brigade

USAECLRA United States Army Electronics Command Logistics Research Agency

USAED United States Army Engineer Division

USAEDC United States Army Engineer Division—Caribbean

USAEDH United States Army Engineer Division—Huntsville, Alabama

USAEDLMV United States Army Engineer Division—Lower Mississippi Valley

USAEDM United States Army Engineer Division—Mediterranean

USAEDMR United States Army Engineer Division—Missouri River

USAEDNA United States Army Engineer Division—North Atlantic

USAEDNC United States Army Engineer Division—North Central

USAEDNE United States Army Engineer Division—New England

USAEDNP United States Army Engineer Division—North Pacific

USAEDOR United States Army Engineer Division—Ohio River

USAEDPO United States Army Engineer Division—Pacific Ocean

USAEDSA United States Army

Engineer Division—South Atlantic

USAEDSP United States Army Engineer Division—South Pacific

USAEDSW United States Army Engineer Division—Southwest

USAEEA United States Army Enlistment Eligibility Activity

USAEL US Army Electronic Laboratories

USAEMA US Army Electronics Materiel Support Agency

USAEMCA United States Army Engineer Mathematical Computation Agency

USAEMSA United States Army Electronics Materiel Support Agency

USAENGCOM United States Army Engineer Command

USAENPG United States Army Engineer Power Group

USAEPG US Army Electronic Proving Ground

USAERA United States Army Electronic Command Research Agency

USAERC United States Army Enlisted Records Center

USAERDAA United States Army Electronics Research and Development Activity (Fort Huachuca, Arizona)

USAERDL US Army Electronics Research and Development Laboratory

USAERG United States Army Engineer Reactor Group

USAES United States Association of Evening Students

USAETDC U.S. Army Engineer Topographic Data Center (D.C.)

USAEUR United States Army Europe

USAEVD United States Alliance for the Eradication of Venereal Disease

U S Af Union of South Africa

USAF United States Air Force

USAFA US Air Force Academy

USAFABD United States Army Field Artillery Board

USAFAC United States Army Finance and Accounting Center

USAFACS US Air Force Aircrew School

USAFAGOS US Air Force Air Ground Operations School

USAFAPS US Air Force Air Police School

USAFAS United States Army Field Artillery School

USAFB United States Army Field Bank

USAFBMS US Air Force Basic Military School

USAFBS US Air Force Bandsman School

USAFC United States Army Forces Command

USAFD *United States Air Force Dictionary*

USAFE US Air Forces in Europe

USAFECI United States Air Force Extension Course Institute

USAFESA United States Army Facilities Engineering Support Agency

USAFEURPCR United States Air Force European Postal and Courier Region

USAFFGS US Air Force Flexible Gunnery School

USAFFSR US Air Force Flight Safety Research

USAFI United States Armed Forces Institute

USAFIGED United States Armed Forces Institute Tests of General Educational Development

USAFIT US Air Force Institute of Technology

US AFLANT US Air Force, Atlantic

USAFMPCR United States Air Force Mideast Postal and Courier Region

USAFNS US Air Force Navigation School

USAFO United States Army Field Office

USAFOCS US Air Force Officer Candidate School

USAFOF United States Army Flight Operations Facility

USAFPACPCR United States Air Force Pacific Postal and Courier Region

USAFPS US Air Force Pilot School

USAFSAAS United States Air Force School of Applied Aerospace Sciences

USAFSAB US Air Force Scientific Advisory Board

USAFSACS United States Air Force School of Applied Cryptologic Sciences

USAFSAM US Air Force School of Aerospace Medicine

USAFSAWC US Air Force Special Air Warfare Center

USAFSC US Air Force Systems Command; United States Army Food Service Center

USAFSE US Air Force Supervisory Examination

USAFSG United States Air Field Support Group

USAFSO US Air Forces, Southern Command

USAFSOC United States Air Force Special Operations Center

USAFSOF United States Air Force Special Operations Force

USAFSOS United States Air Force Special Operations School

USAFSS US Air Force Security Service

USAFSTC United States Army Foreign Science and Technology Center

USAFSTDS US Army-Air Force Standards

USAFSTRIKE US Air Force Strike Command

USAFTS US Air Force Technical School

USAGETA United States Army General Equipment Test Activity

USAGMPC United States Army General Materiel and Parts Center

USAH United States Army Hospital

USAHAC United States Army Headquarters Area Command

USAHC United States Army Health Clinic

USAHSC United States Army Health Services Command

USAHSDSA United States Army Health Services Data Systems Agency

USAIA United States Army Institute of Administration

USAIC US Army Infantry Center; US Army Intelligence Corps

USAICA US Army Interagency Communications Agency

USAICS United States Army Intelligence Center and School

USAID United States Aid for International Development

USAIG United States Aircraft Insurance Group

USAIIA United States Army Imagery Interpretation Agency

USAIIG United States Army Imagery Interpretation Group

USAILG United States Army

International Logistics Group

USAIMS United States Army Institute for Military Systems

USAINTA United States Army Intelligence Agency

USAINTS US Army Intelligence School

USAIPSG US Army Industrial and Personnel Security Group

USAir formerly Allegheny Airlines

USAirA United States Air Attaché

USAIRE United States of America Aerospace Industries Representatives in Europe

USAir MilComUN US Air Force Representative, UN Military Staff Committee

USAISC United States Army Intelligence and Security Command

USAJ United States Army, Japan

USAJPG United States Army Jefferson Proving Ground

USAK United School Administrators of Kansas

USALC United States Army Logistics Center

USALEA United States Army Logistics Evaluation Agency

USALSA US Army Legal Services Agency

USAMAA US Army Memorial Affairs Agency

USAMBRDL US Army Medical Bioengineering Research and Development Laboratory

USAMCFG US Army Medical Center—Fort Gordon

USAMC–ITC United States Army Materiel Command—Interim Training Center

USAMDRC United States Army Materiel Development and Readiness Command

USAMDW United States Army Military District of Washington

USAMEDCOM US Army Medical Command

USAMEOS US Army Medical Equipment and Optical School

USAMFSS US Army Medical Field Service School

USAMIDA United States Army Major Item Data Agency

USAMIIA US Army Medical Intelligence and Information Agency

USAML US Army Medical Laboratory

USAMMA US Army Medical Materiel Agency

USAN United States Adopted Name

USAO U.S. Assay Office

USAPA US Army Procurement Agency

USAPACDA US Army Personnel and Administration Combat Development Activity

USAPDC United States Army Petroleum Distribution Command

USAPEB United States Army Physical Evaluation Board

USAPEQUA US Army Production Equipment Agency

USAPHC United States Army Primary Helicopter Center

USAPIA US Army Personnel Information Activity

USAPO United States Antarctic Projects Office

USAPRO US Army Personnel Research Office

USAR US Army Reserve

USARA United States Army Reserve Affairs

USARADCEN US Army Air Defense Center

USARADCOM US Army Air Defense Center; US Army Air Defense Command

USARAE United States Army Reserve Affairs—Europe

USARAL US Army, Alaska

USARB US Army Retraining Brigade

USARC US Army Recruiting Command

USARCS US Army Claims Service

USAREC U.S. Army Recruiting Command

USAREUR US Army, Europe

USARIBSS US Army Research Institute for the Behavioral and Social Sciences

USARIEM US Army Research Institute of Environmental Medicine

USARJ United States Army, Japan

USARP United States Antarctic Research Program

USARPA US Army Radio Propagation Agency

USARPAC US Army, Pacific

USARPACINTS United States Army Pacific Intelligence School

USARSA United States Amateur Roller Skating Association

USARSC U.S.A. Roller Skating Confederation

USARSO US Army, Southern Command

usart universal synchronous-asynchronous receiver-transmitter

USARV US Army, Vietnam

USAS United States of America Standard

US ASA US Army School of the Americas; US Army Security Agency

USASACDA US Army Security Agency Combat Development Activity

USASADEA United States Army Signal Air Defense Engineering Agency

USASAE United States Army Security Agency—Europe

USASAFO United States Army Signal Avionics Field Office

USASATCOMA United States Army Satellite Communications Agency

USASC US Army, Southern Command—Caribbean; United States Army Support Center

USASCAF US Army Service Center for Army Forces

USASCC US Army Strategic Communications Command

USASCII USA Standard Code for Information Interchange (data processing)

USASCSA US Army Signal Communications Security Agency

USASG United States Army Standardization Group

USASI United States of America Standards Institute

USA Sig C United States Army Signal Corps

USASMC US Army Supply and Maintenance Command

USASMSA United States Army Signal Corps Material Support Agency

USASRDL United States Army Signal Research and Development Laboratory

USASSA United States Army Signal Supply Agency

USASSG United States Army Special Security Group

USAT United States Army Transport

USATA US Army Transportation Aviation

USATC United States Army Traffic Command

USATDC United States Army Training and Doctrine Command

USATEA US Army Transportation Engineering Agency

USATEC United States Army Test and Evaluation Command

USATECOM US Army Test and Evaluation Command

USATIA US Army Transportation Intelligence Agency

USATISU US Army Troop Information Support Unit

USATL US Army Technical Library

USATMACE United States Army Traffic Management Agency—Central Europe

USATopoCom United States Army Topographic Command

USATRATCOM United States Army Strategic Communications Command

USATSC United States Army Terrestrial Sciences Center

USATTC US Army Tropic Test Center

USATTU United States Army Transportation Terminal Unit

USAU United States Aviation Underwriters

usaw (USAW) underwater security advance warning

USAWC United States Army War College; United States Army Weapons Command

USAWES United States Army Waterways Experiment Station

USAWF U.S. Amateur Wrestling Society

usb unified S-band

USB United States Borax (company)

USBA United States Boomerang Association; United States Brewers Association

USBC United States Bureau of the Census; United States Bureau of Customs

USB & C United States Borax and Chemical (company)

USBCSC United Society of Believers in Christ's Second Coming (Shakers)

USBE Universal Serials and Book Exchange (formerly United States Book Exchange)

USBG United States Botanic Garden

USBGN United States Board on Geographic Names

USBH United States Bureau Highways

USBIS United States Border Inspection Station

USBLS United States Bureau of Labor Statistics

USBM United States Bureau of Mines

USBP United States Board of Paroles; United States Border Patrol; United States Bureau of Prisons

USBPA United States Bicycle Polo Association

USBPR United States Bureau of Public Roads

USBS United States Border Station; United States Bureau of Standards

USBTA United States Board of Tax Appeals

USBuStand United States Bureau of Standards

usc under separate cover

USC United Shipping Company; United States Congress; United Steamship Company; University of South Carolina; University of Southern California

USC United States Catalog; United States Code (legal)

USCA Ulster Special Constabulary Association; United States Copper Association; United States Courts of Appeals

USCA United States Code Annotated

USCAC US Continental Army Command

USCANS Unified S-band Communication and Navigation System

USCB United States Customs Bonded

USCC United States Catholic Conference; United States Chamber of Commerce; United States Circuit Court; United States Commercial Company; United States Customs Court

USCCA United States Circuit Court of Appeals

USCCPA United States Court of Customs and Patent Appeals

USCCR United States Commission on Civil Rights

USCE US Coast Guard Reserve; US Commissioner of Education

USCF United States Chess Federation; United States Churchill Foundation

USCG United States Coast Guard

USCGA US Coast Guard Academy

USCGAD United States Coast Guard Air Detachment

USCGAS United States Coast Guard Air Station

USCG Aux United States Coast Guard Auxiliary

USCGC United States Coast Guard Cutter

USCGI United States Coast Guard Institute

USCGMSC United States Coast Guard Marine Safety Council

USC & GS United States Coast and Geodetic Survey

USCHS United States Capitol Historical Society; United States Catholic Historical Society

USCI United Satellite Communication Inc

USCIIC United States Civilian Internee Information Center (USA)

USCINCEUR United States Commander-in-Chief, Europe

USCINSO United States Commander-in-Chief, Southern Command

USCM United States Conference of Mayors

USCMA United States Coal Mines Administration; United States Court of Military Appeals

USCMI United States Commission of Mathematical Instruction

usco underwriters salvage company

USCO Union Steel Corporaton (South Africa)

US Comm UNICEF United States Committee for UNICEF

USCONARC US Continental Army Command

US Const Constitution of the United States

USCP University of South Carolina Press; University of Southern California Press, U.S. Capitol Police (DC)

USCP United States Coast Pilot

USCR United States Committee for Refugees

USCRC United States Civil Rights Commission

USCRS United States Cotton Research Station

USCS United States Civil Service; United States Claims Service; United States Conciliation Service; United States Customs Service; Universal Ship Cancellation Society

USCSC United States Civil Service Commission

USCSup United States Code Supplement

USCT United States Colored Troops (1862–1865)

USCUN United States Committee for the United Nations

USCUNICEF U.S. Committee for UNICEF

USCWHO U.S.Committee for the World Health Organization

US Cy United States currency

usd ultimate strength design

US $ American dollar(s); United States dollar

USD Unified School District; University of San Diego; University of South Dakota

USD United States Dispensatory

USDA United States Department of Agriculture

USDA/CRIS US Department of Agriculture/Current Research Information System

USDB United States Disciplinary Barracks

USDC United States Department of Commerce; United States District of Columbia; United States District Court

USDCFO US Defense Communication Field Office

USDEA United States Drug Enforcement Agency

USDHEW United States Department of Health, Education, and Welfare (HEW)

USDHUD United States Department of Housing and Urban Development

USDI United States Department of the Interior

USDJ United States District Judge

USDL United States Department of Labor

USDLGI United States Defense Liaison Group—Indonesia

USDOCO United States Document Officer

USDoD United States Department of Defense

USDP University of San Diego Press; University of South Dakota Press

USDR United States Divorce Reform

USDSA United States Deaf Skiers Association

USDSEA United States Dependent School European Area

USDT United States Department of Transportation

USE United States Envelope

(corporation); Univac Scientific Exchange; U.S. English

usea undersea

u/Sec Under Secretary

USELMCENTO United States Element Central Treaty Organization

USEP United States Escapee Program

USERC United States Environment and Resources Council

USES United States Employment Service

USEUCOM United States European Command

usf und so fort (German—et cetera)—and so forth

USF United States Forces

U of SF University of South Florida

USFA United States Fire Administration; United States Food Administration (World War I); United States Forces in Austria (World War II)

USFAA United States Fronton Athletic Association

USFC United States Foil Company

USFET United States Forces—European Theater

USFF United States Flag Foundation

USF & G United States Fidelity — Guaranty (insurance underwriters)

USFGC United States Feed Grains Council

USFIS United States Foundation for International Scouting

USFJ United States Forces, Japan

USFL United States Football League

USForAz US Forces in the Azores

USFPL United States Forest Products Laboratory

USfs United States frequency standard

USFS United States Foreign Service; United States Forest Service

USFSA United States Figure Skating Association

USFWS United States Fish and Wildlife Service

USG Ulysses Simpson Grant (18th President U.S.); United States Gypsum (company)

U.S.G. United States Government (railroad)

USGA United States Golf Association

US gal United States gallon

USGC United States Gold Commission

USGLI United States Government Life Insurance

USGM United States Government Manual

USGOM United States Government Organization Manual

USGPO United States Government Printing Office

USGRDR United States Government Research and Development Report(s)

USGRR United States Government Research Reports

USGRS United States Graves Registration Service

USGS United States Geological Survey

ush usher

Ush Ugandan shilling(s)

USHA United States Handball Association; Utah System of Higher Education

Ushant Ile d'Ouessant—France's most westerly point at the Bay of Biscay entrance to the English Channel

USHCC U.S. Hispanic Chamber of Commerce

USHDA United States Highland Dancing Association

U of Sherb University of Sherbrooke

USHGA U.S. Hang Gliding Association

USHHFA United States Housing and Home Finance Agency

Ushkudar (Turkish—Scutari or Shkodër)—an Albanian city not to be confused with the Asian section of Istanbul called Üsküdar by the Turks

USHL United States Hygienic Laboratory

USHMC U.S. Holocaust Memorial Council

USHR United States Highway Research

USHS United States Hospital Ship

USI United States of Indonesia; United States Industries

USIA United States Information Agency

USian United Statesian

USIAS Union Syndicale des Industries Aéeronautiques et Spatiales

USIB United States Intelligence Board

USIBR United States Institute of Behavioral Research

usic undersea instrument chamber

USIC United States Industrial Chemicals; United States Industrial Council; United States Instrument Corporation

USICA United States International Communication Agency

USIF United States Investment Fund

USIH United States Indian Health Service

USILA United States Intercollegiate Lacrosse Association

USI & NS United States Immigration and Naturalization Service

USIOSLCC United States Inter-Oceanic Sea-Level Canal Commission

USIP University of Stockholm Institute of Physics

USIS United States Information Service

USISL United States Information Service Library

USISS United States Institute of Space Studies

USITA United States Independent Telephone Association

USITC United States International Trade Commission

USITT United States Institute for Theater Technology

USIU United States International University

USJ United States Jaycees

USJC United States Job Corps

USJCC United States Junior Chamber of Commerce

USJF United States Judo Federation

USJPRS United States Joint Publications Research Service

Uskub (Turkish—Skopje)

Üsküdar (Turkish—Scutari)—Asian section of Istanbul

USL Union Steamships Limited; United States Legation; United States Lines; University of Singapore Library; University of Sydney Library

U-slag upperclass slang

USLant United States Atlantic Subarea

USLANTCOM United States Atlantic Command

USLO United States Liaison Office(r); University Students for Law and Order

USLP U.S. Labor Party

USLSA United States League of Savings Associations; United States Livestock Sanitary Association

USLSI U.S. League of Savings Institutions

USLTA United States Lawn Tennis Association

USLU United States Lines (container) Unit

usm (USM) underwater-to-surface missile

USM United Shoe Machinery; United States Mail (U.S.M.); United States Mint; University of Southern Mississippi; Unlisted Securities Market

USMA United States Maritime Administration; United States Metric Association; United States Military Academy (West Point)

USMACTHAI United States Military Assistance Command, Thailand

USMACV United States Military Assistance Command, Vietnam

US MAIL (not an abbreviation although some juvenile New Yorkers used to insist the letters stood for Uncle Sam Married An Irish Lady)

USMB United States Metric Board

USMBPHA United States-Mexico Border Public Health Association (of American and Mexican Public health officials)

USMC United States Marine Corps; United States Maritime Commission; United States Microfilm Corporation (company)

USMCR United States Marine Corps Reserves

USMD United States Medical Doctor

USMeMilComUN United States Military Members, UN Military Staff Committee

USMH United States Marine Hospital

USMICC United States Military Information Control Committee

USMilComUN United States Delegation, UN Military Staff Committee

USMilLias United States Military Liaison Office

USMILTAG United States Military Technical Advisory Group

USML U.S. Marxist-Leninists (left-wing youth party)

USMM United States Merchant Marine

USMMA United States Merchant Marine Academy

USMMCC United States Merchant Marine Cadet Corps

USMO United States Marshal's Office

USMS United States Maritime Service; United States Marshalls Service

USMSMI United States Military Supply Mission to India

USMSPB U.S. Merit Systems Protection Board

USMUN United States Mission to the United Nations

usn ultrasonic nebulizer

Usn Ulsan

USN United States Navy

USNA United States Naval Academy; United States Naval Archives

USNAM US Naval Academy Museum

USNARS US National Archives and Records Service

USNAS US Naval Amphibious School

USNB United States National Bank; United States Naval Base

USNC United States Navigation Company (North German Lloyd—Hamburg-American Line); United States Nuclear Corporation

USNCB US Naval Construction battalion (Seabees)

USNCC U.S. Naval Correction Center

USNCCC United States National Council of Churches of Christ

USND United States Navy Department

USNDRC US Navy Drug Rehabilitation Center

USNEL US Naval Electronics Laboratory

U.S. News U.S. News and World Report

USNFEC United States National Fruit Export Council

USNG United States National Guard

USNH United States Naval Harbor; United States Naval Hospital; United States North of Hatteras

USNHO US Naval Hydrographic Office

USNI United States Naval Institute

USNIAAA United States National Institute on Alcohol Abuse and Alcoholism

USNII United States National Indian Institute

USNIS United States Naval In-

vestigative Service
USNL US Navy League
USNLM United States National Library of Medicine
usnm United States National Museum (Smithsonian Institution)
USNMR United States National Military Representative
USNO US Naval Observatory
USNOO US Naval Oceanographic Office
USNPC US Naval Photographic Center
USNPS US Naval Postgraduate School
USNR US Naval Reserve
USNRC United States Nuclear Regulatory Commission
USNRDL US Naval Radiological Defense Laboratory; US Navy Research and Development Laboratory
USNS US Naval Ship (Military Sea Transport Service); United States Nuclear Ship
USNSA United States National Student Association; United States Naval Sailing Association
USNSMC United States Naval Submarine Medical Center
USNTAF US Navy Training Aids Facility
USNTS United States Naval Torpedo Station
USNUSL United States Navy Underwater Sound Laboratory
USNWD United States Naval War College
USNWR Union Slough National Wildlife Refuge (Iowa); Upper Souris NWR (North Dakota)
USN & WR *U.S. News & World Report*
uso unmanned seismological observatory
USO United Service Organizations; Utah Symphony Orchestra
U-soc upperclass society
USOC United States Olympic Committee
USOE United States Office of Education
USOEO United States Office of Economic Opportunity
USofAF Under Secretary of the Air Force
USOICP United States Oil Import Control Program
USOID United States Oversea Internal Defense (USA)
USOM United States Opera-

tions Mission
usp unique selling proposition
USP U.S. Penitentiary (Atlanta, Georgia; Leavenworth, Kansas; Lewisburg, Pennsylvania; Marion, Illinois; McNeil Island, Washington; Terre Haute, Indiana); United States Plywood (company); University of the South Pacific (Fiji)
USP *United States Pharmacopeia*
USPA United States Philatelic Agency; United States Polo Association
USPACAF United States Pacific Air Forces
US Pat United States Patent
USPB United States Parole Board
USPC United States Parole Commission; United States Peace Corps
USPCA United States Police Canine Association
USPDO United States Property and Disbursing Office(r)
U-speech upperclass speech
USP & F United States Pipe and Foundry (company)
USPFO United States Property and Fiscal Officer
USPG United Society for the Propagation of the Gospel
US Phar *United States Pharmacopeia*
USPHS United States Public Health Service
USPHSC United States Public Health Service Clinic
USPHSH United States Public Health Service Hospital
USPIS United States Postal Inspection Service
USPLS United States Public Land Surveys
USPO (U.S.P.O.) United States Post Office
USPP U.S. Probation and Parole
USPQ *United States Patents Quarterly*
USPs United States Penitentiaries
USPS United States Postal Service; United States Power Squadron
USPUN U.S. People for the United Nations
USPWIC United States Prisoner of War Information Center
usr underwater search and recovery; unheated serum reagin
USR United States Reserves; United States Rubber

USR *United States Supreme Court Reports*
USRA United States Racquetball Association; United States Railway Association; United States Revolver Association; Universities Space Research Association
USRB United States Renegotiation Board
USRD Underwater Sound Reference Division (USN)
USRDA US Recommended Daily Allowance
USREDCOM United States Readiness Command
USRepMilComUN United States Representative, UN Military Staff Committee
USRL Underwater Sound Reference Laboratory
USRS United States Rocket Society
USRS *United States Revised Statutes*
usrt universal synchronous receiver/transmitter
USS Under-Secretary of State; Union Switch and Signal; United Scholarship Service; United States Senate; United States Ship (U.S.S.); United States Shoe (company); United States Standard; United States Steel (company)
US & S Union Switch and Signal
U of SS University of the Seven Seas (Chapman College's classes held aboard motorship *Seven Seas)*
USS *Union Syndicale Suisse* (French—Swiss Trade Union Syndicate)
USSA United States Salvage Association; United States Ski Association; United States Student Association
USSAF United States Strategic Air Force
USSB United States Savings Bond(s); United States Shipping Board (World War I)
USSBD United States Savings Bonds Division
USSC United States Strike Command; United States Supreme Court
USSCC United States Senate Computer Center
USS Co Ulster Steam Ship Company; Union Steam Ship Company (New Zealand)
USSCS United States Soil Conservation Service
USSDP Uniformed Services

Savings Deposit Program
USSEI United States Society of Esperanto Instructors
USSF United States Soccer Federation; United States Steel Foundation; US Special Forces (Green Berets)
USSFA United States Soccer Football Association
USSFC United States Synthetic Fuel Corporation
USSG United States Standard Gauge
USSIC United States Sex Information Council
USS & LL United States Savings & Loan League
US Soc Fed United States Soccer Federation
USSOUTHCOM United States Southern Command
USSPA United States Student Press Association
USSR Union of Soviet Socialist Republics
USSRA United States Squash Rackets Association
USSR's Principal Ports Leningrad on the Baltic, Odessa on the Black Sea, Vladivostok on the Pacific
USSS United States Secret Service; United States Steamship
USSSA United States Social Security Administration
USSSM United States Sinai Support Mission
USSST United States Salt Spray Test(ing)
USSTA U.S. Sail Training Association
USSTRICOM United States Strike Command
USSTS United States Student Travel Service
ust, ustus (Latin burnt)
UST undersea technology; United States Treaties; University of Santo Tomás (Manila)
UST UnderSea Technology: The Magazine of Oceanography, Marine Sciences, and Underwater Defense
U of St A University of St Andrews
USTA United States Tennis Association; United States Trademark Association; United States Trotting Association
USTC United States Tariff Commission; United States Tax Court; United States Testing Company
USTCRDWWA United Slate, Tile, and Composition Roofers, Damp, and Waterproof

Workers Association
USTD United States Transportation Department
USTDC United States Taiwan Defense Command
USTEMC United States Territorial Expansion Memorial Commission
USTES United States Training and Employment Service
USTF United States Tuna Foundation
USTFF United States Track and Field Federation
USTIS Ubiquitous Scientific and Technical Information System
USTMA United States Trade Mark Association
USTOA United States Tour Operators Association
ustol ultra short takeoff and landing
USTS United States Travel Service
USTTA United States Table Tennis Association; United States Travel and Tourism Administration
usu usual; usually
USU Uniformed Services University; Utah State University
USUHS Uniformed Services University of the Health Sciences
USUN United States Mission to the United Nations
usup. usurpandus (Latin—to be used)
USV US Volunteers
USVA United States Veterans Administration; United States Volleyball Association
USVB United States Veterans Bureau (former name of the Veterans Administration)
USVH United States Veterans Hospital
USVI United States Virgin Islands (St Croix, St John, St Thomas)
USVIDT United States Virgin Islands Division of Tourism
USVMS Urine Sample Volume Measurement System
usw ultra short wave; underwater submarine warfare
usw und so weiter (German—and so forth)
USW United Show Workers
USWA United Steel Workers of America
USWAC United States Women's Army Corps
USWACC United States Women's Army Corps Center

USWACS United States Women's Army Corps School
USWB United States Weather Bureau
USWD Undersurface Warfare Division
USWGA United States Wholesale Grocers' Association
USWI United States West Indies (Virgin Islands—St Thomas, St John, St Croix, and smaller islands in that group)
USWLS United States Wild Life Service
USWV United Spanish War Veterans
USY United Synagogue Youth
usysf United States Youth Symphony Federation
ut universal trainer; urinary tract; user test; utilitarian; utility
u/t untrained
UT Union Terminal (railroad); United Territories; United Territory; United Utilities (stock exchange symbol); Universal Time (Greenwich Mean Time); Universal Tubes; Utilities Man
U.T. U Thant
U of T University of Tampa; University of Tasmania; University of Tennessee; University of Texas; University of Toledo; University of Toronto; University of Tulsa
U of T (Austin) University of Texas in Austin
U of T (El Paso) University of Texas in El Paso (also UTEP)
uta upper terminal area
UTA Ulster Transport Authority; Union des Transports Aeriens; United Typothetae of America; University of Texas —Austin; Urban Transportation Administration
utacv (UTACV) urban-tracked air-cushion vehicle
UTAD Utah Army Depot
Utagawa Utagawa Toyokuni
Utah St Hist Soc Utah State Historical Society
Utah St U Pr Utah State University Press
Utamaro Kitagawa Utamaro
utarb utarb eidet (Norwegian—prepared)
UT/AT Underway Trial/Acceptance Trial (USN)
UTB United Tariff Bureau; United Technocratic Board; Universal Technological Bureau

utc unit type code; unit type coding

utc (UTC) universal time coordinated

UTC United Tank Car; United Technology Center (United Aircraft); United Transformer Corporation; Universe Tankships Corporation (National Bulk Carriers)

UT-C University of Tennessee—Chattanooga

utclk universal transmitter clock

utd united

UTDA Ulster Tourist Development Association

UTDC Urban Transportation Development Corporation

ut dict. *ut dictum* (Latin— as ordered)

utdne. mor. sol. *utendus more solito* (Latin—use in the usual way)

Utd Tech United Technology

UTE underwater tracking equipment

uten utensil(s)

utend. *utendus* (Latin—to be used)

U of Tenn Pr University of Tennessee Press

UTEP University of Texas—El Paso

U of Tex Pr University of Texas Press

UTF Underground Test Facility

utg *utgave* (Norwegian—edition)

uti urinary tract infection

uti (UTI) urinary tract infection

UTI Union Title Insurance; Unit Trust of India

UTIAS University of Toronto Institute for Aerospace Studies

util utility; utilization

utilit utilitarian(ism); utilities

Utilitarian Philosopher Jeremy Bentham; John Stuart Mill

ut inf. *ut infra* (Latin—as below)

utl universal transpor(er) loader; user trailer label

UTL University of Tampa Library; University of Tennessee Library; University of Texas Library; University of Tokyo Library; University of Toronto Library; University of Tulsa Library

UTLAS University of Toronto Library Automation System

utm universal testing machine;

universal test(ing) module; universal transverse mercator

UTN University of Tennessee

UTO United Thank Offering; United Town Organisation

U of Tok University of Tokyo

utop utopian (from the Greek *utopia*—no place)—pertaining to an imaginary republic created by the dreamers of democracy

Utopian Author title bestowed by readers on authors such as Bacon, Bellamy, Butler, Cabot, Campanella, Fourier, Huxley, More, Morris, Owen, Plato, Proudhon, Rabelais, Rousseau, Saint-Simon, Wells, and other visionaries

U of Tor Pr University of Toronto Press

UTP Unified Test Plan; University of Toronto Press

utr (UTR) university training reactor

Utr *Utrecht* (Dutch province)

UTR United Tire and Rubber

UTRC United Technologies Research Center

Utrecht provincial capital of Utrecht in the Netherlands

uts ultimate tensile strength; unit training standard

UTS Underwater Telephone System; Unified Transfer System (Russian-to-English translation); Uniform Thread Standard; Union Theological Seminary; Universal Time-Sharing System; University of Toronto Schools

UTSSM University of Texas-Southwestern School of Medicine

ut sup. *ut supra* (Latin—as above)

Uttarahimakhanda (Nepali—North Himalayan Country)—reputedly the birthplace of Buddha in the village of Lumbini

UTTAS Utility Tactical Transport Aircraft System

uttc universal tape-to-tape converter

UTTR Utah Test and Training Range

UTU United Transportation Union

U-tube U-shaped tube

U-turn U-shaped turn

utv (UTV) underwater television

UTV Universal Test Vehicle

utw under the wing

UTWA United Textile Workers

of America

UTX 4-engine jet utility transport; University of Texas

uu (UU) urine urobilinogen

u *U unter Umständen* (German—circumstances permitting)

UU Ulster Unionist; Union University; University of Utah

U-U Unitarian-Universalist

U & U Underwood and Underwood

U of U University of Uppsala; University of Utah

UU *Uppsala Universitetsbiblioteket* (Swedish—Uppsala University Library); *ustedes* (Spanish—you, pl)

UUA Unitarian Universalist Association; Univac Users Association

UUCM University of Utah College of Medicine

uue use until exhausted

uuf micromicrofarad

UUI United Utilities Incorporated

UUIP Uppsala University Institute of Physics

uum (UUM) underwater-to-underwater missile

UUP Ulster Unionist Party

UUSC Unitarian Universalist Service Committee

uut unit under test

U of Utah Pr University of Utah Press

UUUC United Ulster Unionist Coalition

uuv *unter üblichen vorbehalt* (German—errors and omissions excepted)

UUWF Unitarian Universalist Women's Federation

uv ultraviolet; umbilical vein; under voltage; urinary volume

u-v ultraviolet

UV Ulster Vanguard; Unadilla Valley (railroad); Upper Volta

U of V University of Vermont; University of Victoria; University of Virginia

UV *Una Via* (Spanish—One Way)—nickname of many people in Hispanic lands and elsewhere

UVA University of Virginia

U van A Universiteit van Amsterdam

U van A *Universiteit van Amsterdam* (Dutch—Amsterdam University, University in Amsterdam)

uvas ultraviolet astronomical

satellite (UVAS)

uvaser ultraviolet amplification by stimulated emission of radiation

u-v camera ultraviolet evidence camera

UVCM University of Vermont College of Medicine

UVCT University of Vermont College of Technology

uvd undervoltage device

UVDC Urban Vehicle Design Competition

UVE Unión Velocipédica Española (Spanish Bicycle Union)

UVF Ulster Volunteer Force

UVH University of Virginia Hospital

UVI Unione Velocipedistica Italiana (Italian Cycling Association)

uviol ultraviolet

uvl ultraviolet light

UVL University of Virginia Library

U-vocab upperclass vocabulary

uvr ultraviolet radiation

uvs ultraviolet spectrometer, universal versaplot software

UVSA Unie van Suid Afrika (Union of South Africa)

uvsc ultraviolet solar constant

UVSM University of Virginia School of Medicine

UVT University of Vermont

uw unconventional warfare; underwater; underwing; underwriter; unwound

u/w underwater; underway; underwear; underwriter; used with

UW University of Waikato; Uppity Women

U of W University of Wales; University of Warwick; University of Washington; University of Waterloo; University of Wichita; University of Windsor; University of Winnipeg; University of Wiscon-

sin; University of Witwatersrand; University of Wollongong; University of Wyoming

UW Universität Wien (German —Vienna University)—see *Ubib Wien*

UWA United Way of America; United World Atheists; University of Washington; University of Western Australia

U of Wash Pr University of Washington Press

UWC University of the Western Cape

UWCE Underwater Weapons and Countermeasures Establishment

U-wear underwear

U-weld U-shaped weld

UWF United World Federalists

UWFL University of Washington Fisheries Laboratory

UWGB University of Wisconsin at Green Bay

UWH University of Washington Hospital

UWI University of the West Indies (Jamaica); University of Wisconsin

UWIL University of the West Indies Library (Kingston, Jamaica)

U of Wis Pr University of Wisconsin Press

UWIST University of Wales Institute of Science and Technology

UWIUB undrinkable wine in unusable bottles

UWL University of Wales Library; University of Washington Library; University of Wichita Library; University of Wisconsin Library; University of Witwatersrand Library; University of Wyoming Library

UWM United World Mission; University of Wisconsin at Milwaukee

UWMI University of Wisconsin Management Institute

UWO University of Western Ontario

uwoa unclassified without attachments

UWP University of Wales Press; University of Washington Press; Up With People

UWSM University of Washington School of Medicine

uwtr underwater

UWTU Underwater Training Unit

UWUA Utility Workers Union of America

UWV University of West Virginia

UWW University Without Walls (Antioch College)

UWY University of Wyoming

ux. *uuxor* (Latin—wife)

uxb (UXB) unexploded bomb

uxgb unexploded gas bomb

uxib unexploded incendiary bomb

'Uxley (Cockney contraction— Huxley)

uxor uxoricide

UY Universal Youth

U of Y University of York

UYA University Year for Action

UYL United Yugoslav Lines

Uz Uzbek; Uzbekistan; Uzbekistanian

Uz Uhrzuender (German— clockwork fuze)

UZ University of Zululand

UZ Universität Zürich

Uzbekistan Uzbekistan, Soviet Socialist Republic

Uzbek SSR Uzbek Soviet Socialist Republic (Uzbekistan)

Uzi Uziel Gal

UZM Universitet Zoologiske Museum (Copenhagen)

UZRA United Zionist Revisionists of America

U zu B Universität zu Berlin

U zu G Universität zu Göttingen

Uzz Uzziah

V

v vacuum; vacuum tube; vagabond; vagrant; valium (tranquilizer); value; valve; van; vapor; variable; variation; vector; vein; velocity; vent; ventilator; ventral; verb; verbal; verse; version; vertex; vertical; very; vice; vincinal; violet; violin; virus; viscosity; vise; visibility; vision; visual acuity; voice; volt; voltage; voltmeter; volume; volunteer; vowel

v *van* (Dutch—of); *verso* (Latin —back of page or sheet; lefthand page); *versus* (Latin— against); vibrational quantum number; *voltare* (Italian— turn, turn the page); *von* (German—of; from; used in titles)

v/ *vostra* (Italian—your)

V coefficient of vibration (symbol); five-dollar bill; Lockheed (symbol); potential (symbol); relative wind velocity (symbol); stalling velocity (symbol); Standard Fruit & Steamship Company (Vaccaro Line); vanadium; Venerable; Ventzke; Venus; Verdet constant; Vicar; Vice (as in VicePresident); Vice (police squad); Victor—code for letter V; Victory—Winston Churchill's symbol in World War II; Village; volt; Volta; volume (symbol)

V airspeed, forward velocity (symbol); speed (symbol); vacuum tube (symbol); *varm* (Dano-Norwegian or Swedish —hot); *våst* (Swedish—west); *Venstre* (Danish or Norwegian —Left)—Liberal Party; *vertrek* (Dutch—departure); *vest*

(Dano-Norwegian—west); *Via* (Italian—highway road, way); *Villa* (Spanish—village); *violaceus* (*Latin*—violet color); *viridis* (Latin—green); *vrouw* (Dutch —woman)

v-1 vernier engine 1

V1 Voyager 1 satellite with close Titan flyby

V_1 decision speed (go-no-go) for aircraft to continue takeoff run or abort flight; valve-current voltage

V^1 *violino primo* (Italian—first violin)

v-1 p vernier engine 1 pitch

V-1, V-2 rockets launched by the Germans in World War II

v-1 y vernier engine 1 yaw

V2 Voyager 2 with Uranus option

V_2 aircraft takeoff speed or position where nose is lifted so plane becomes airborne

V^2 *violino secondo* (Italian—second violin)

V-4 four-cylinder engine with two cylinders in each side of V-shaped engine block

V-6 six-cylinder engine with three cylinders in each side of V-shaped engine block

V-8 eight-cylinder engine with four cylinders in each side of V-shaped engine block

V-10 Viscount 10 jet airplane

v 26 d M *von 26 dieses Monats* (German—of the 26th instant; of the 26th of this month)

va variable; variance; verb active; verbal adjective; viola; voltampere(s)

v-a volt-ampere(s)

v/a verbal auxiliary; voucher attached

v/a (VSA) vulnerable area

v.a. *vixit*—*annas* (Latin—he lived—years)

Va Virginia; Virginian

Va *Vila* (Portuguese—Villa; Village); *Villa* (Italian or Spanish —Villa, Village)

V^a *Vila* (Portuguese—small town, villa); *Viuda* (Spanish— widow)

VA Veterans Administration (United States); Veterans' Affairs (Canada); Voice of America; voltaic alternative (symbol); Volunteers of America

V-A Vickers-Armstrong Limited

V.A. Order of Victoria and Albert; Vicar Apostolic

V & A Victoria and Albert (Museum)

V of A Volunteers of America

VAA Vaccination Assistance Act; Vietnamese-American Association

VAACR Vietnamese Association for Asian Cultural Relations

Vaasa (Finnish—Vasa)—port city in western Finland

vab voice answer back

VAb Van Allen belt (zone of high-intensity radiation surrounding the earth at altitudes of about 500 miles)

VAB Vandenberg Air Force Base; Vertical Assembly Building (world's largest allsteel structure of its type; used for assembling missiles and space exploration vehicles on Merritt Island at Cape Kennedy, Florida)

VAbd Van Allen belt dosimeter

Va Bk Virginia Book Company

VABM vertical angle bench mark (capitalized on topographic maps)

vac vacant; vacate; vacation; vacuum; volts alternating current (*volts AC* preferable)

VAC Victor Analog Computer; Video Amplifier Chain; Voluntary Action Center; Volunteer Advisor Corps

VACAB Veterans Administration Contract Appeals Board

Vacation City on Casco Bay Portland, Maine

Vacationland Maine's self-created sobriquet supported by miles of islands, lakes, and mountains

Vacationland of Opportunity Alaska

vacc vaccination; vaccine; value-added common carrier

Vaccaro Standard Fruit & Steamship Company

vacci vaccinate; vaccination; vaccine

vac-dist vacuum-distilled

vac pmp vacuum pump

VACRP Victorian Association for the Care and Resettlement of Prisoners

vacs vacuum cleaners

v/act. verb active

vad variable abbreviated dialing; velocity azimuth display; voltmeter analog-to-digital converter

VAd Veterans Administration

VAD Voluntary Aid Detachment

vada versatile automatic data exchange

V Adm Vice Admiral

vad. mec. *vade mecum* (Latin—go with me)—companion volume; handbook; manual; ready reference

vae vinyl-acetate ethylene

VAEA Virginia Adult Education Association

VAF Vendor Approval Form; Vincent Astor Foundation

VAFB Vandenberg Air Force Base

vag vagabond; vagina; vaginal; vaginitis; vagrant; vagrancy

vag charge vagrancy charge

Vagen (Norwegian—Bay)—old Bergen and its waterfront along the bay

vag hist vaginal hysterectomy

vagonzak vagon zaklyuchennykh (Russian—railroad prisoner car)

vags vagabonds; vagrants

VAH Veterans Administration Hospital

VAHS Victorian Aboriginal Health Service

vai video-assisted instruction; vorticity area index

va & i verb active and intransitive

VAIS Virginia Association of Independent Schools

vakt visual-auditory-kinesthetic and tactual (imagery applied to teaching reading)

val valance; valence; valenciennes (lace); valentine; valise; valley; valuation; value; valued; valve; valvular

val (VAL) valine (amino acid)

Val Valencia; Valentina; Valentine; Valentino; Valerie

VAL Vehicle Authorization List; Veterans Administration Library

VALA Viewers and Listeners Association

Valais (French—Wallis)—Swiss commune on the Franco-Italian border

VALB Veterans of the Abraham Lincoln brigade

valc visual approach and landing chart

Vald Valdivia

Valentia (Latin—Valencia)

Valentine State Arizona so nicknamed as it was admitted on St Valentine's Day—February 14, 1912

Val Fl Gaius Valerius Flaccus (Roman epic poet)

Valhalla Hall of the Slain Warriors (Norse or Scandinavian mythology)

Valhalla Girls Women's Correctional Unit at Valhalla, New York

valid. validate; validation

valium diazepam

Valka Valentin

Vall Valladolid

Valley Between Two Worlds Rio Grande Valley (between Mexico and the United States)

Valley of God's Pleasure Cleveland, Ohio's suburban section around Shaker Heights

Valley Isle Maui, Hawaii

Valley of Opportunity New York State's Triple Cities area including Binghampton, Endicott, and Johnson City

Valley of Rice Sikkimese name for their state in India where Valley of Rice is known as Denjong

Valley of the Sun Arizona's central valley

Valley of Valleys Gudbrandsdalen, Norway

Valley of Wonders Yellowstone National Park (in Idaho, Montana, and Wyoming)

Vallisoletum (Latin—Valladolid)

VALNET Veterans Administration Library Network

Valpo Valparaiso

valsas variable-length word symbolic assembly system

valt vtol approach-and-landing technic

VALUE Visible Achievement Liberates Unemployment (Air Force program for disadvantaged youth)

vam volt ammeter

Vam Vogel's approximation method

VAMCO Village and Marketing Corporation

vamp vampire; vampirism; volume, area, mass properties

VAMP Voluntary Association of Master Pumpers (mid-19th-century English firefighters)

Vampire De Havilland jet fighter-bomber aircraft

vam's vision-aid magnifiers

van. caravan; value-added network; vanguard; vanilla; vanillin

Van (VAN) Vancouver, British Columbia

VAN Value-Added Network

VAN Vereniging van Archivarissen in Nederland (Dutch—Association of Archivists in the Netherlands)

Vanc Vancouver

Van Cliburn Harvey Lavan Cliburn

Vancoo Vancouver, British Columbia

Vancoram Vanadium Corporation of America

Van Diemen's Land Tasmania's old name

Vanechka (Russian nickname—Ivan)

Vang Vickers-Armstrong Vanguard (aircraft)

Vang Esp Vanguardia Española (Barcelona's Spanish Vanguard)

Vanguard Vanguard Press

Vanier Canadian city formerly called Eastview

Vanier Centre Vanier Centre for Women (criminals) at Brampton, Ontario

Van-Lax Vancouver—Los Angeles

Van-Mia Vancouver—Miami

van. pub. vanity publisher; vanity publishing
VANS Value-Added Network Service(s)
Van-San Vancouver—San Diego
Van-Sea Vancouver—Seattle
Van-Sfo Vancouver—San Francisco
Van Sun *Vancouver Sun*
Van-Tor Vancouver—Toronto
Vanu Vanuatu (island republic in the southwestern Pacific, northeast of Australia's east coast)
Vanua Levu (Fijian—Great Land)—second largest of the Fiji Islands
Vanuatu formerly New Hebrides, a British-French condominium between Fiji and New Caledonia in the South Pacific, but now a socialist state
VAP Victims Assistance Program; Victims Assistance Project
vapi visual approach path indicator
vapor. vaporization
Vapor City Hot Springs, Arkansas
vap prf vaporproof
var variable; variant; variation; variety; variometer; visual-aural range; volt-ampere reactive
var (VAR) vertical air rocket
var variazione (Italian—variation)
Var Varna
VAR Volunteer Air Reserve
varactor variable capacitor
varad varying radiation
Varangians (*Russian*—Vikings) —Danes or Norsemen who probably rowed and sailed ships to America around year 1000—almost 500 years before Columbus but somewhat later than oriental sailors who landed on west coast of Mexico and Peru
var con variable condenser
var dial. various dialects
var ed & trans various editions and translations
VARES Vega-Aircraft Radar-Enhanced System
vari VariType(r)
VARIG Empresa de Viação Aérea Rio Grandense (airline in southern Brazil)
varistors variable resistors
varizistor variable resistor
var. lect. varia lectio (Latin—variant reading)

varn varnish
VARP Veterans Administration Procurement Regulations
varr variable-range reflector
Varr Marcus Terentius Varro (Roman writer on agriculture and natural history)
vars varieties
Vars Varsavia (Italian or Latin —Warsaw); *Varsovia* (Spanish —Warsaw); *Varsóvia* (Portuguese—Warsaw)
VARS Vertical and Azimuth Reference System
Varsavia (Italian—Warsaw)
varsity university
Varsovia (Portuguese or Spanish —Warsaw)
Varsovie (French—Warsaw)
vas vasectomy
vas (Latin prefix—vessel)—vasoconstriction
Vas Vasteras
VAs Voluntary Aids
VAS Virginia Academy of Science; Vocational Advisory Service
VAS Vedette Anti-Sommergibile (Italian—Anti-Submarine Sentry)—naval craft; *Vereniging van Accountancy Studenten* (Dutch—Society of Accountancy Students)
Vasa (Swedish—Vaasa)
VASA Virginia Association of School Administrators
vas bund vascular bundle
vasc vascular
VASC Verbal Auditory Screen for Children
VASCA (electronic) Valve and Semi-Conductor (manufacturers') Association
vascar visual average-speed computer recorder
VASCO Vanadium-Alloys Steel Company
Vascongadas (Spanish—Basque Provinces)
Vasconia (Italian or Latin—Gascony)
VASEC vasectomy
vasi visual approach slope indicator
vasim voltage and synchro-interface module
VASP Viação São Paulo (São Paulo airline)
VASSP Virginia Association of Secondary School Principals
VASSS Van Allen Symplified Scoring System
vast. vibration and static analysis
Västtyskland (Swedish—West Germany)

vas vit. vas vitrium (Latin—glass vessel)
vat. value-added taxes (VAT); ventricular activation time; vinyl asbestos tile; vinyl asbestos tiling
Vat Vatican
VAT Value-Added Tax; Vertical Assembly Tower; Veterinary Aptitude Test; Visual Apperception Test
vate versatile automatic test equipment
Vaterland (German—Fatherland)—Germany
VATI Vermont Agricultural and Technical Institute
Vatic Vatican
Vaticaanstad (Dutch—Vatican City)
Vatican City English place-name for sections of Rome collectively called Città del Vaticano
Vatican City State *Stato della Città del Vaticano*
Vat Lib Vatican Library (Rome)
VATLS Visual Airborne Target Location System
vatpayer value-added taxpayer
VATS Vertical-lift Airfield for Tactical Support; Video-Augmented Tracking System
Vat Sta Vatican State
VATTR Value-Added-Tax Tribunal(s)
vaud vaudeville
Vaud (French—Waadt)—Swiss canton
Vautour Sud attack bomber and interceptor made in France
v aux verb auxiliary
vav variable air volume
vavbd vavband (Swedish—clothing)
v/a v/e value-analyst value-engineer
vavp variable-angle variable-pitch
vb valence band; verb; verbal; vertical bomb (VB); vibration
v/b vehicle-borne
VB Navy bomber (2-letter naval symbol); Vero Beach; very bad; Virginia Beach
vba verbal adjective
VBA Veterans Benevolent Association
V-band 46,000–56,000 mc
vbc ventrobasal complex
VBC Vancouver British Columbia
VBCO Vector Biology and Control Office (California)
VBEC Venezuelan Basic Econo-

my Corporation

V-belt V-shaped belt (cross-section of belt is V-shaped)

VBFNPVGFPMTF Véndemaire, Brumaire, Frimaire, Nivôse, Pluviôse, Ventôse, Germinal, Floréal, Prairial, Messidor, Thermidor, Fructidor (as abbreviated on the French Revolutionary Calendar—*see* Vend, Brum, Frim, Niv, Pluv, Vent, Germ, Flor, Prair, Mess, Therm, Fruc)

VBI Venetian Blind Institute

vbl verbal

V-block V-shaped block

VBMA Vacuum Bag Manufacturers Association

vbn verbal noun

V-bomb German long-range missile-type bomb used during World War II; designated as V-1 and V-2

vbos veronal-buffered oxalated saline

V-bottom V-shaped bottom

V B R Virginia Blue Ridge (highway)

VBRA Vehicle Builders' and Repairers' Association

VBS Vedanthangal Bird Sanctuary (India); Vocabulary Building System

vc valuation clause; venereal case; violoncello; visual communication

vc (VC) variable cost; vital capacity

vc vuelta de correo (Spanish—by return mail)

v/c vuelta de correo (Spanish—return mail)

vC' voor Christus (Dutch—Before Christ)

Vc Vietcong

VC acuity of color vision (symbol); Vassar College; Vatican City; Vehicle Code; Vennard College; Ventura College; Vermont College; Veterinary Corps; Vice Consul; Victoria College; Victoria Cross; Viterbo College; Volusia College

VC Vehicle Code

VC-10 British BAC long-range transport aircraft

VC-137 USAF designation of the Boeing 707

vca voltage-controlled amplifier

VCA Virginia Correctional Association; Volunteer Civic Association

VCAR Vendor Corrective Action Request

VCAS Vice-Chief of Air Staff

VCB Victim Compensation

Board

vcc vasoconstrictor center; video compact cassette; vocational career concept

Vcc supply voltage

VCC Value Control Coordinator; Visual Communications Congress

vc card index (or reader) visual coincidence index (or reader)

vccs voltage-controlled current source

vcd variable-capacitance diode

v-c d voluntary-closing device

vce (VCE) variable-cycle engine

Vce Venice

VCE Venice, Italy (airport)

vcf voltage-controlled filter

vcg vectorcardiogram; vertical line through center of gravity

VCG Vice-Consul General

vch vehicle; vinyl cyclohexane (VCH)

VCH Victoria County History

vchp variable-conductance heat pipe

v Chr vor Christis (German—before Christ)

vci visual communication instructor; volatile corrosion inhibitor

VCI Variety Clubs International; Vision Conservation Institute

VCIC Vermont Crime Information Center

VCIGS Vice-Chief of the Imperial General Staff

VCIP Veterans Cost-of-Instruction Program

VCK Verenigo Cargodoorskantoor

vcl vertical center line; visual comfort light(ing)

VCL Vancouver Public Library

vcllo violincello

VCLU Virginia Civil Liberties Union

vcm vacuum; vinyl chloride monomer

VCN Vendor Contact Notice

VCNS Vice-Chief of Naval Staff

vcnty vicinity

vco voltage-controlled oscillator

vcod vertical-carrier onboard delivery

vcoi veterans cost of instruction

v coul volt coulomb

VCP Vendor Change Proposal; São Paulo, Brazil (Viracopas Airport)

vcr variable compression ratio

Vcr Vancouver

VCR Victor Comptometer (stock exchange symbol)

vcr's video cassette recorder owners

vcr('s) video cassette recorder(s)

vcs vasoconstrictor substances; voices

vc's viejos cristianos (Spanish—old Christians)—Spaniards who believe they are without taint of Jewish or Moorish blood although historians who know better mutter *'taint so*

VCs Viet Congs; Vigilance Committeemen; Vigilant Committeemen; Vigilante Committeemen

VCS Vernier Control System; Vice Chief of Staff; Video Cassette System

V & C S Virginia & Carolina Southern (railroad)

vcsr voltage-controlled shift register

Vct Victoria

vctv vocative

vcty vicinity

VCU Virginia Commonwealth University

vcxo voltage-controlled crystal oscillator

V Cz Vera Cruz

vd vapor density; various dates; venereal disease (VD); videodisc; void

v/d vandyke reproduction

Vd vanadium

Vd usted (Spanish—you; derived from *vuestra merced*—your grace)

V.D. Volunteer Officer's Decoration

vda venereal disease awareness; video distribution amplifier; visual discriminatory acuity

Vda Viuda (Spanish—widow)

VDA Vermont Department of Agriculture

VDA Verband der Automobilindustrie (German—Automobile Industry Association)

V-day day of victory

vdB velocity decibel

VDB Venereal Disease Branch (US Public Health Service); Verband Deutscher Biologen (Association of German Biologists)

VDBC Vertol Division, Boeing Company (helicopter design and manufacturing)

vdc volts direct current (*volts DC* preferable)

vdc (VDC) vinylidene chloride

VDC Venereal Disease Clinic; Virginia Department of Corrections

vdcm (VDCM) vinylidene chloride monomer

VDE *Verband Deutscher Elektrotechniker* (Association of German Electrical Engineers)

v def verb defective

VDEH *Verein Deutscher Eisenhüttenleute* (German Foundry Society)

VDEL Venereal Disease Experimental Laboratory

vdem vasodepressor material

v dep verb deponent

V De S Vittorio De Sica

VdF *Vigili del Fuoco* (Italian—Fire Brigade)

vdfg variable diode function

vdg vertical display generator

vd-g venereal disease—gonorrhea

vdh very-deep hold

vdh (VDH) valvular disease of the heart

vdi vegetation draught index; vehicle deformation index; veneral disease inhibition; video display input

VDI *Verein Deutscher Ingenieure* (Association of German Engineers)

V-dies V-shaped dies

V di R Virtuosi di Roma

VdK *Verband der Kriegsbeschadigten* (German—League of War Invalids)

Vdkhr *Vodokhranilishche* (Russian—reservoir)

vdl ventilation deadlight

VDL Van Dieman's Land (Tasmania)

vdm vector-drawn map

vdm (VDM) vasodepressor material

Vdm Veendam

VDMA *Verein Deutscher Maschinenbau Anstalten* (German—Mechanical Engineering Association)

vdm('s) video disc machine(s)

VDN *Varudeklarationsnamnden* (Swedish—Institute for Informative Labelling); *Vin Doux Naturel* (French—fortified wine, natural sweet wine)

vdp vehicle deadlined for parts; vertical data processing

vdr variable-diameter rotor

VDRL Venereal Disease Research Laboratories

VDRS Verdun Depression Rating Scale

VDRT Venereal Disease Reference Test

vds variable depth sonar

vd-s venereal disease—syphilis

Vds *ustedes* (Spanish—you all)

—third person plural form of you

VDSCRC Very Dirty and Small Coal Railway Company (created by Dickens for service in *The Uncommercial Traveller*)

VDSI *Verein Deutscher Sicherheits Ingenieure* (German—Association of Safety Engineers)

vdt variable density (wind) tunnel; video data terminal

vdt (VDT) video display terminal

VDT Visual Distortion Test

vdt's video display terminals

vdu visual display unit

ve vaginal examination; varicose eczema; vernier engine; very excellent

've have

ve *veuve* (French—widow)

Ve Venezuela; Venezuelan

VE Value Engineer(ing); Vasileion tis Ellados (Kingdom of Hellas—Greece)

V-E Verzhbolovo-Eydtkuhnen (Russo-German railway frontier for passengers and freight changing from wide gage to standard European gage rolling stock and tracks)

ve/a value engineering/analysis (program)

VEA Valve Engineering Association; Vermont Education Association; Veterans Education Administration; Virginia Education Association; Vocational Education Act

VEA-H Vocational Education Act—Handicapped

vealsan veal sandwich

vealwich veal sandwich

VEAP Veterans' Educational Assistance Program

veb variable elevation beam

VEB *Volks Eigener Betriebe* (German—Peoples-Owned Companies)

vec vector

veco vernier engine cutoff

vecp visually evoked cortical potential

VECP Value Engineering Change Proposal

VECR Vendor's Engineering Change Request

VECS Vocation Education Curriculum Specialists

vecto vectograph; vectographic; vectographical

ved *vedova* (Italian—widow)

Ved Vedic

VED Vickers Electric Division

VEDA Victorian Eastern Development Association

V-E Day May 8, 1945, German surrender in World War II

VEDC Vitreous Enamel Development Council

vedr *vedrorende* (Danish—concerning)

VEDS Vocational Education Data System

Vee Venezuelan equine encephalomyelitis

Veecees Vietcongs

vee dee venereal disease; visiting dignitary

VEENAF (South) Vietnamese Air Force

Veenees Vietnamese

Veep Vice-President

VEEP Voluntary Ethnic Enrollment Program

veg vegetable; vegetarian; vegetarianism; vegetation

Vega Alta Industrial School for (criminal) Women at Vega Alta, Puerto Rico

vegan (extreme) vegetarian; vegetarian(ism)

vegans vegetarians

vegan(s) strict vegetarian(s)

Vegas Las Vegas

Vegas East Atlantic City, New Jersey's nickname

Veg Soc Vegetarian Society

vegtan vegetable tanning

veh vehicle; vehicular

VEH Vocational Education for the Handicapped

vehic. *vehiculum* (Latin—vehicle)

Vehicle City Flint, Michigan

vehic manslgtr vehicular manslaughter

veh pt(s) vehicle part(s)

VEIN Vocational Education Information Network

VEIS Vocational Education Information System

vel vellum; velocity; velvet

Vel Vela (constellation)

Vel *Velikiy* (Russian—large)

Vell Gaius Velleius Paterculus (Roman historian)

veloc velocity

Velvet Breughel Jan Breughel the Elder

vem vasoexciter material

ven veneer; veneering; venerable; venereal; venery; venetian; venetian blind(s); venison; venom; venomous; ventral; ventricle

ven *vendredi* (French—Friday); *venerdi* (Italian—Friday)

Ven Venetian; Venice; Venus

Venaja (Finnish—Russia)

vend vending; vending machine; vendor(s)

Vend Vendémaire (French—Vintage Month)—beginning September 22nd—first month of the French Revolutionary Calendar

vend. mach vending machine

Venecia (Spanish—Venice)

Venedig (German—Venice)

Venerable Nestor of Massachusetts John Quincy Adams—sixth President of the United States who served it from his 14th to his 80th year when he dropped dead during a debate on the floor of the House of Representatives in Washington, D.C.

Venereal Beach navalese word play on Imperial Beach and applied to all other beaches as a warning of the danger of sexual promiscuity

Venereal Disease of the New Morality Herpes Virus type 1 above the waist; Herpes Virus type 2—below the waist

Venetiae (Latin—Venèzia)—Venice

venetian venetian ball (glass or plastic paperweight containing coins or colorful objects); venetian blind (horizontally slatted sun curtain and not an object of charity although professional panhandlers have been found *collecting for the venetian blind*); venetian glass (ornamental glassware of the type originally made in Venice); venetian red (dark orange red); venetian window (palladian window)

Venetian Family of Painters term applies to the Bellinis and the Tintorettos

venetian red ferric oxide (FE$_2$O$_3$)

Venez Venezuela; Venezuelan

Veneza (Portuguese—Venice)

Venezia (Italian—Venice)

Venezuela Republic of Venezuela (oil-producing Spanish-speaking South American nation noted for its dedication to democracy, its mineral wealth, tropical crops, and its universities) *República de Venezuela*

Venezuela Day Venezuelan Independence Day (July 5)

Venezuelan First Venezuela's composer-conductor Reynaldo Hahn who became music critic of *Le Figaro* and music

director of the Paris Opera

Venezuelan Pianist Teresa Carreño

Venezuelan Poet Laureatess Irma De-Sola Ricardo

Venezuelan Ports (west to east) Maracaibo, Puerto Miranda, Bahía de Amuay, Puerto Cabello, La Guaira, Puerto de Hierro, Puerto Ordaz, Cuidad Bolívar

Venezuela's Principal Port La Guaira

V-engine V-shaped engine

Venice English place-name for Venezia

Venise (French—Venice)

VENISS Visual Education National Information Service for Schools

Venom British de Havilland jet fighter aircraft

vent. ventilate; ventilating; ventilation; ventilator; venting; ventral; ventricle; venture

Vent Ventôse (French—Windy Month)—beginning February 19th—sixth month of the French Revolutionary Calendar

vent. fib. ventricular fibrillation

ventric ventricular

vents. ventilators

Ventspils (Latvian—Windau)—Baltic port

vent. tachy ventricular tachycardia

Venus (Latin—Aphrodite)—goddess of beauty and love

vep visual-evoked potential

VEP Veterans Education Project; Voter Education Project

VEPCO Virginia Electric and Power Company

VEPM Value Engineering Program Manager

ver verification; verify; verse(s); versine; vertex (Ver)

Ver Vera Cruz

Ver Verband; Verein (German—association)

Vera Veratchke; Veronica

VERA Vision Electronic Recording Apparatus (videotape)

verand verandert (German—revised)

Vera Zorina Eva Brigitta Hartwig

verb verbesserte (Dutch or German—improved)

verb. et lit. verbatim et literatim (Latin—exact copy; word for word)

verb. sap. verbum satis sapienti (Latin—a word to the wise is

sufficient)

Vercors (pseudonym—Jean Bruller)

Verdi Giuseppe Verdi whose name was shouted by mobs as well as operagoers as *Viva Verdi* did not merely mean Long Live Verdi but Long Live *Victor Emmanuel Re d'Italia* who was a central figure in the unification of Italy where he ruled from 1849 to 1878

verdigris copper acetate

Verds Cape Verde Islands

verdt verdict

Vereigigten Staaten (German—United States)

Vereinte Nationen (German—United Nations)

Verenigde Staten (Dutch—United States)

Verf Verfasser (German—author)

Verg Publius Vergilius Maro (Roman poet often referred to as Virgil)

Vergl Vergleische (German—compare)

Verh Verhandlungen (German—proceedings)

VERIC Vocational Educational Research Information Center

verisim verisimilar; verisimilitude; verisimilitudinous

Veritas Det norske Veritas (The Norwegian Bureau of Shipping)

Verkh Verkhniy (Russian—upper)

verkhuyaya (Russian—higher; upper)

verk v verkorting van (Dutch—abbreviaton, abridgment, shortening)

Verl Verlag (German—publisher)

Verlagshdlg Verlagshandlung (German—book-publishing house)

verlort very-long-range tracking (radar)

verm vermiculite

verm (Latin prefix—worm)—vermiform; *vermehrte* (German—enlarged)

Verm Vermont

Vermeer Jan van der Meer van Delft

Vermilionville Lafayette, Louisiana's old name

Vermillion Sea Gulf of California (Mar Bermejo)

vern vernacular

Vern Vernay; Verne; Verney; Vernon

Vern Vernon's Law Reports

vernac vernacular(ism); vernacularly

Verneur Gouverneur

Vernon Castle Vernon Blythe

Vernon Duke Vladimir Dukelsky

Vernon Lee Violet Paget's pseudonym

Veronese Paolo Cagliari

Veronica Berenice

Veronica Lake Constance Ockleman

Verrocchio Andrea di Michele Cione

vers versed sine; verses; versification; versine (versed sine)

versine versed sine

verso reverso (left-hand page; reverse side of a page)—opposite of recto

Ver St *Vereinigte Staaten* (German—United States)

vert vertebra; vertebrate; vertical; vertigo

verticam vertical camera

ves vertical electric soundings; vessel

ves. *vesica* (Latin—bladder)

Ves Sylvester

VES Veterans Employment Service; Voluntary Euthanasia Society

VESC Vehicle Equipment Safety Commission

vesca(s) vessel(s) and cargo

VESIAC Vela Seismic Information Analysis Center

vesic. *vesicula* (Latin—blister)

VESO Value Engineering Services Office

vesp. *vesper* (Latin—evening)

vesper. vehicles, equipment, and spares provision—economics and repairs

VESPER Voluntary Enterprises and Services and Part-time Employment for the Retired

Vespri *I Vespri Siciliani* (Italian—The Sicilian Vespers)—five-act opera by Verdi

vest vestibule

VEST Volunteer Engineers, Scientists, and Technicians (organization)

Vesta (Latin—Hestia)—goddess of hearth and home

Vesters Vester Islands

Vestland (Norwegian—Westland)—western Norway

ves. ur. *vesica urinaria* (Latin—urinary bladder)

Vesuvio (Italian—Vesuvius)—Europe's only active volcano; on the eastern shore of the Bay of Naples

Vesuvius English equivalent for

Vesuvio, the smoking volcano on the Bay of Naples

vet veteran; veterinarian; veterinary

v. et. *vide etiam* (Latin—also see)

Vet Veterinary Medicine

VET Verbal Test

Vet Admin Veterans' Administration

Veteran Curmudgeon H(enry) L(ewis) Mencken

Veterans Veterans Day (November 11)—commemorating armistice ordered to end World War I on the 11th hour of the 11th day of the 11th month of 1918 and originally called Armistice Day

Vet M. B. Bachelor of Veterinary Medicine

vet med veterinary medicine

VETMIS Vehicle Technical Management Information System (USA)

vet reg veterans' regulations

vet rep veteran's representative

vets veterans; veterinaries

vet sci veterinary science

Vets Info Veterans Information Service

Vet Surg Veterinary Surgeon

vett vetted; vetting

'vette corvette

vetted (English contraction—veterinary inspected)—inspected and investigated

vev voice-excited vocoder

VEV Vietnam Era Veterans

V Exᵃ *Vossa Excelência* (Portuguese—Your Excellency)

vexdex vexation index

vexil vexillogical; vexillologist; vexillology

vf vertical file; very fair; very fine; video frequency; visual field; voice frequency, vulcanized fiber

Vf *Verfasser* (German—author)

VF fixed-wing fighter airplane (2-letter naval symbol); Valley Forge

V.F. Vicar Forane

VF *Vigili del Fuoco* (Italian—Fire Brigade)

V f A Voice for America (Alistair Cooke)

VFA Video Free America; Voluntary Foreign Aid

V-FA Vietnamese-France Association

V-factor verbal (comprehension) factor

v-f band voice-frequency band

vfc video frequency carrier; video frequency channel; visual

field control; voice frequency carrier

VFC Victorian Film Commission

VFD Volunteer Fire Department

vfdr viewfinder

vfet vertical field-effect transistor

vff black very-fine furnace black (rubber filler)

VFHS Valley Forge Historical Society

vfi visual field information

VFI Vocational Foundation Incorporated

VFIC Virginia Foundation for Independent Colleges

vfl variable focal length

vfl (VFL) variable field length

VFMJC Valley Forge Military Junior College

vfn very-flowery no

VFNP Victoria Falls National Park (Rhodesia)

vfo variable-frequency oscillator

VFOAR Vandenberg Field Office of Aerospace Research (USAF)

vfp variable-factor programming

vfr vehicle fuel refinery

V f R Verein für Raumschiffahrt (German—Society for Space Travel)

VfR *Verein für Raumschiffahrt* (German—Space Travel Society)

VFR Visual Flight Rules

VFSTC Valley Forge Space Technology Center (General Electric)

vftg voice frequency telegraph

vfu vertical format unit

VFU Vancouver Free University

VFW Vereinigte Flugtechnische Werke; Veterans of Foreign Wars

vfy verify

vg variable geometry; velocity gravity; very good (VG)

v.g. *verbi gratia* (Latin—for example)

vg *verbigracia* (Spanish—for example); *virgen* (Spanish—virgin)

Vg. *Virgo* (Latin—virgin)

VG Vocational Guidance

V.G. Vicar General

VG *Vaisseau de Guerre* (French—warship)

vga variable gain amplifier

VGA Victor Gruen Associates

VGAA Vegetable Growers Asso-

ciation of America
VGB Vandenberg Air Force Base
vgc viscosity gravity constant
vge visual gross error
VGH Vancouver General Hospital
V-girl vice girl (equivalent to B-girl or C-girl)
Vgk Vegesack
vgl *vergelijken* (Dutch—compare); *vergleiche* (German—compare)
VGLI Veterans Group Life Insurance
Vgm Vizagapatam
vgo vacuum gas oil
Vgo Vigo (British maritime abbreviation)
VGP Van Gelder Papier; Volunteer Grandparent Program
vgpi visual glide-path indicator(s); visual ground-position indicator
Vgr Voyager (robot spacecraft)
V gr *verbigracia* (Spanish—for example)
V-groove V-shaped groove
VGSA Viola da Gamba Society of America
vgu *vorgelesen-genehmigt-unterschrieben* (German—read, confirmed, signed)
vgw *voegwoord* (Dutch—conjunction)
vh very high
v/h vulnerability/hardness
v/h *vorheen* (Dutch—formerly)
v H *vom Hundert* (German—percent; per hundred)
VII Veterans Hospital
VHA Vermont Headmasters Association
vhb very heavy bombardment
vhc very highly commended
vhcl vehicle
vhclr vehicular
vhd video high density
vhf very high frequency (30,000 kc-300 mc)
vhf/df very high frequency direction finding
vhf/fm very high frequency/frequency modulated
vhf/uhf very high and ultra high frequency
VHIS Vaal-Hartz Irrigation Scheme
VHMCP Voluntary Home Mortgage Credit Program
vhmwpe very-high-molecular-weight polyethylene
Vhn Vickers hardness number
vho very high output
vhocm very-heavy oil-cut mud
vhp very high performance

vhs video home system(s)
VHS Vocational High School
vhsbw very-high-speed black-and-white (photography)
vhtr very-high-temperature reactor
V-hut inverted V-shaped hut (sometimes called A-hut)
vi variable interval; verb intransitive; viscosity index; volume index
v/i verb intransitive
v.i. *vide infra* (Latin—see below)
Vi Viola; Violet; Virginia; Vivian
VI Vancouver Island; Vermiculite Institute; Virgin Islander(s); Virgin Islands (V.I.)
VI *Veiligheids Instituut* (Dutch—Safety Institute)
via virus inactivating agent
Via Viaduct
VIA Vancouver, British Columbia's Vancouver International Airport; VIA Rail Canada; Vision Institute of America; Vocational Interests and Aptitudes
viad viaduct
Via Gramsci Genoa's waterfront street of whores named for the founder of the Italian communist party—Antonio Gramsci
vi antigen virulence antigen
VIAR Volcani Institute of Agricultural Research (Israel)
Via Rail Canadian National + Canadian Pacific
VIARCO Venezuelan International Airway Reservations Computerized
VIAs Vocational Information Agencies
VIAS Voice Interference Analysis System
VIASA Venezolana Internacional de Aviación SA
Via Veneto downtown Rome, Italy's promenade of pimps, prostitutes, and their victims
vib vibrate; vibration; vibratory
VIB Vertical Integration Building
vibes vibraphones; vibrations
vibgyor (mnemonic for remembering the spectral colors—violet, indigo, blue, green, yellow, orange, red)—see ROY G BIV
vibra vibraphone
vibs vocabulary-information-block-design similarities
vib/s vibrations per second
VIBS Virgin Islands Broadcasting System

Viburgum (Latin—Viborg)
vic convict; value-incentive clause; vicinal; vicinity; victim; victor; victorious; victory (V)
vic *vices* (Latin—times)
Vic RCA Victor; Vicar; Victor; Victoria; Victorine
VIC Virginia Intermont College; Virgin Islands Corporation
VICA Vocational Industrial Clubs of America
Vic Adm Vice Admiral
Vicar of Christ the Pope
vicci voice-initiated cockpit control and integration
Vic Hist *Victoria History of the Counties of England*
Vichy Government France following its surrender to Nazi Germany—1940–1944—while ruled by collaborationists Marshal Pétain and Pierre Laval who maintained their headquarters in Vichy within unoccupied France
Vicki Victoria
vicoed visual communication management
vicom visual communication management
VICORP Virgin Islands Corporation
Vic Pk Victoria Park
vic(s) convict(s)
Vic Sta Victoria Station (rail terminal)
Vict Victor(ia)
Vic^{ta} Victoria (Spanish)
Vic^{te} Vincente (Spanish—Vincent)
victimol victimological(ly); victimologist; victimology
Victim of Religion and Revolt Northern Ireland also called Captive of History
Victor letter V radio code; Handley-Page jet bomber aircraft
Victor Borge Borge Rosenbaum
Victor-Charlie VC; Vietcong
Victoria La Victoria (Santo Domingo City prison of the Dominican Republic)
Victoria Day Queen Victoria's Birthday (May 20)
Victoria de los Angeles Victoria Gomez Cima
Victoria Holt Eleanor Burford Hibbert
Victorian Librettist W(illiam) S(chwenck) Gilbert
Victor Seastrom Viktor Sjöström
Victor Serge Victor Lvovich Kibalchich
Victory popular nickname for

Beethoven's Symphony No. 5 in C minor as its opening chords reminded World-War-II audiences of the V for Victor(y) in the international radio code . . . ——; Nelson's flagship at the Battle of Trafalgar

Victory Personified Nike the Greek goddess or her Roman counterpart Victoria

vid video

vid. *vide* (Latin—see); *Viuda* (Spanish—widow)

VID Volunteers for International Development

vidac visual information display and control

vidat visual data acquisition

VIDC Virgin Islands Department of Commerce

VIDD Virgin Islands Development Department

video (Latin—I see)—picture portion of a tv broadcast

videocomp videocomposition (highspeed phototypesetting controlled by programmed digital-control unit)

videot(s) video (television) idiot(s)

vidiac visual information display and control

vidisc video disc

Viditel Videotelevision viewdata system (Dutch)

vie viernes (Spanish—Friday)

Vie La Vie Parisienne (French—Parisian Life)—Offenbach's five-act opera

VIE Vienna, Austria (airport)

VIEDS Virgin Islands Educational Dissemination System

Vien Vienna

Viena (Portuguese or Spanish—Vienna)

vienna vienna brown (bronzetone gold); vienna green (emerald); vienna lake (carmine); vienna lime (Magnesialime polish); vienna red (vermillion); vienna sausage (short thin frankfurter)

Vienna English equivalent of Wien—Austria's capital city

Vienne (French—Vienna)

vier viernes (Spanish—Friday)

Viet Vietnam

Viet Vietnamese (oriental language including many terms derived from Chinese and French; spoken by more than 36 million people)

Viet Cong Vietnam Congsan (Vietnamese—Vietnamese Communists)

Vietminh Vietnam Doc Lap Dong Ming (League for the Independence of Vietnam)

Vietnam Socialist Republic of Vietnam (communist-dominated Indo-Chinese country whose Vietnamese talk Vietnamese but often flee their homeland where they find life intolerable) *Cong Hoa Xa Chu Nghia Viet Nam*

Vietnam congsam Vietnamese communist (see *congsam*)

Vietnamese Ports (large, medium, and small from north to south) Cam Pha, Hon Gai, Haiphong, Ben Thuy, Da Nang (Tourane), Cam Ranh Bay, Saigon (Ho Chi Minh City)

Vietnam's Principal Port Ho Chi Minh City (Saigon)

Vietsyn Vietnam syndrome (marked by abuse of alcohol and other drugs, antisocial behavior, violence, and suicide)

Vietvet(s) Vietnam veteran(s)

Vieux Carré (French—Old Square)—French Quarter of New Orleans

VIEW Vital Information for Education and Work (education-on-microfilm program)

vig video image generator; vigilante; vigorish

vig (VIG) vaccine-immune globulin

VIG Video Integrating Group; Virgin Islands Government

Vig Com Vigilance Committee (men); Vigilant(e) Committee (men)

Viggen Swedish Thunderbolt jet fighter aircraft

VIGIC Virgin Islands Government Information Center

vigilant. (VIGILANT) visually guided infantry light antitank (missile)

Vigilante North American-Rockwell A-5 bomber aircraft

vign vignette

VIGOPRI Virgin Islands Government Office of Public Relations and Information

vigs vigilantes

vii viscosity index improver

Viipuri (Finnish—Vyborg)—Soviet port formerly belonging to Finland

VIJ Vera Institute of Justice

vik (Dano-Norwegian or Swedish—bay; cove; creek; inlet)—hence the Vikings were from the bays, coves, creeks, and inlets of Scandinavia where

many place-names end in *vik*

Vik Vickers; Vikelas; Vikenti; Vikentievich; Viki; Vikie; Viking; Viktor; Viktoria; Vikramaditya; Viktorovich

Vikes Vikings

Viki Victoria; Victorine

Viking Capital Oslo, Norway

Viking Genius John Ericsson

Viking Land Norway

Viking Pr Viking Press

Viking Program systematic investigation of Mars from orbit and from the surface with emphasis on the search for life on this planet

vil vertical injection logic; village

Vil Las Villas (Santa Clara)

Vilhjalmur Stefansson Canadian-born William Stevenson's adopted name as his parents were of Icelandic origin

vill village

Villa Acuña former name of Ciudad Acuña

Villa Devoto Argentina's great prison within a residential section of Buenos Aires

Village 1 (or 2 or 3) Okinawa's places of prostitution

Village of Fools Chelm, Poland

VIM Venture in Missions; Vertical Improved Mail (conveyorized mail handling in tall buildings); Virgin Islands Museum; Visible Impact Management

v imp verb impersonal

v imper verb imperative

VIMS Vertical Improved Mail Service; Virginia Institute of Marine Science

vim/var vacuum-induction melt/vacuum-arc remelt

vin vehicle identification number; vinegar; vinyl

vin. vinum (Latin—wine)

Vin Vincent

VIN Vehicle Identification Number

Viña Viña del Mar, Chile

VINB Virgin Islands National Bank

Vince St Vincent, West Indies; Vincent

Vincent Vincent Van Gogh

vind vindicate; vindication

Vindabona (Latin—Wien)—Vienna also known as Vindoliona

vinegar acetic acid (CH_3COOH)

Vinegar Joe General Joseph Warren Stilwell, USA

VINHS Virgin Islands National

Historic Site

vini viniculture

VINITI *Vsesoyuznyi Institut Nauchnoi Tekhnicheskoi Informatsii* (Russian—All Union Institute of Scientific and Technical Information)

Vinland vineclad section of North American coast discovered by Leif Ericsson and Norse sailors in year 1000; Vinland probably a collective name for area extending from Labrador to Martha's Vineyard south of Cape Cod

Vinnie Vincent

Vinny Vincent

VINP Virgin Islands National Park (West Indies)

Vinson Vinson Massif (Antarctica's highest mountain)

VIO Veterinary Investigation Office(r)

viol violino (Italian—violin)

Violet state flower of Illinois, New Jersey, Rhode Island, and Wisconsin

Violet crowned City Athens

Violinist-Composer-Conductor Eugène Ysaÿe

Violinist-Conductor Willi Boskovsky; Richard Burgin; Sidney Harth; David Oistrakh; Igor Oistrakh; Joseph Silverstein; Isaac Stern

Violinist-Violist-Conductor Yehudi Menuhin; Pinchas Zukerman

Violin-Maker's Capital Cremona, Italy

vip value improving product(s); variable information processing; variable input phototypesetting (VIP); vasoactive intestinal peptide, very important passenger; very important people; very important person; visual identification point

vip Virgil I. Partch

VIP Value Improvement Project(s); Variable Information Processing; Very Important Person; Very Important Program; Vías Internacionales de Panamá (Panamanian airline); Virgin Islands Police; Vocabulary Improvement Program; Volunteers in Probation

VIPAC Virgin Islands Public Affairs Council

viper's weed marijuana

VIPI Volunteers in Probation, Incorporated

vipp variable-information processing package

vipre visual precision

VIPRE Very-Intense Pulsed-Radiation Experiment

vips voice interruption priority system

VIP-VIP Value in Performance through Very Important People (motivational program)

viq verbal iq

vir vertical interval reference (automatic television color system)

vir. viridis (Latin—green)

Vir Virgil; Virgo

VIR Vendor Information Request

V.I.R. Victoria Imperatrix Regina (Latin—Victoria Empress and Queen)

vira vehicular infrared alarm

Viracopos Santos, Brazil's airport

VIRB Virginia Insurance Rating Bureau

Virg Virgil; Virgin; Virginia

Virgil Roman poet Publius Virgilius Maro

Virgin Goddesses Artemis, Athena also known as Parthenia (*parthenos*—Greek for virgin), and Hestia

Virginia Occidental (Spanish—West Virginia)

Virginia Ports (north to south) Alexandria, Newport News, Norfolk, Portsmouth

Virginias short form for Virginia and West Virginia

Virgin Island Ports Charlotte Amalie on St Thomas, Cruz Bay on St John, Frederiksted on St Croix

Virgin Queen Elizabeth I

Virgins American and British Virgin Islands in the West Indies

Virgin Superior St Thomas Island, Virgin Islands

virol virology

virr verb irregular

v/irr verb irregular

vis viscera; visible; visibility; visual

Vis Visayan; Vista (postal abbreviation)

VIs Virgin Islands

VIS Veterinary Investigation Service; Visual Instrumentation Subsystem

VISAR Visual Inspection System for the Analysis of Reports

visc viscosity

Visc Viscount(ess)

Viscaya (Spanish—Biscay)

viscer (Latin prefix—organ)—visceral

Viscount Vickers medium transport aircraft

Viscountess Beaconsfield Mary Anne Disraeli (Mrs Benjamin Disraeli)

Viscount Melbourne William Lamb (former Prime Minister of Great Britain like the viscounts whose names follow)

Viscount Palmerston Henry John Temple

Viscount Sidmouth Henry Addington

VISIT Visit to Innovative Schools for Interested Teachers

Visla (Russian—Vistula)

vismins visual minorities (Africs, Asiatics, racially mixed Hispanics)

vispa virtual storage productivity aid(s)

vissr visible infrared spin-scan radiometer

vista. viewing instantly security transactions automatically

VISTA Volunteers in Service to America

Vistula English equivalent for the river called Visla by the Russians, Wisla by the Poles, and Weichsel by the Germans

Vistula River Cities Cracow and Warsaw

vit vital; vitamin; vitreous

vit (Latin prefix—life)—vitamins

vit A carotene vitamin

VITA Volunteers for International Technical Assistance; Volunteers In Tax Assistance

vit A$_1$ nutritive vitamin found in egg yolk, milk, and milk products such as butter

vit A$_2$ freshwater fish-liver-oil vitamin

VITAL Variably-Initialized Translator for Algorithmic Languages

Vita Levu (Fijian—Great Fiji)—capital island containing Suva

Vitalis Erik Sjöberg

vitamin(s) vital amine(s)

vit B nutritive vitamin essential to digestive and nervous systems; found in breads, egg yolk, lean meats, fruits, nuts, green vegetables

vit B$_1$ thiamine vitamin

vit B$_2$ riboflavin vitamin

vit B$_3$ nicotinamide vitamin

vit B$_6$ pyridoxine vitamin

vit B$_{12}$ cobalmine-cyancobalmine vitamin
vit B$_{12}$b hydroxycobalmine vitamin
vit Bc folic-acid vitamin
vit B cx vitamin B complex (water-soluble vitamins B$_1$, B$_2$, etc.)
vit C ascorbic acid vitamin
vit cap. vital capacity
vit D antirachitic vitamin
vit D$_1$ calciferol and lumisterol vitamin
vit D$_2$ calciferol vitamin
vit D$_3$ cholecalciferol (natural vitamin D)
vit E antisterility vitamin; tocopherol vitamin
vitel. vitellus (Latin—egg yolk)
vit G riboflavin vitamin
vit H biotin vitamin
viti viticulture
vit K coagulant vitamin
vit K$_1$ blood-clotting vitamin
vit M folic-acid vitamin
vit. ov. sol. vitello ovi solutus (Latin—dissolved in egg yolk)
vit P permeability vitamin (bioflavonoid found in paprika)
vit PP pellagra-preventive vitamin (nicotinamide nicotinic acid)
vitr vitreous
Vitr Vitruvius Pollio (Roman writer on architecture)
vit rec vital records
vitriol concentrated sulfuric acid (oil of vitriol); copper sulfate (blue vitriol); ferrous sulfate (green vitriol); zinc sulfate (white vitriol)
vit stat vital statistics
vit U cabagin (anti-ulcer) vitamin
VIUS Virgin Islands of the United States
viv vivace
Viv Vivian; Vivien; Vivienne; Vivyan; Vivyanne
VIV Virgin Islands View
VIVA Virgin Islands Visitors Association; Voices in Vital America (organization)
Viva Verdi (Italian—Long Live Verdi)—VERDI also used as an acronym really meaning Victor Emmanuel Re d'Italia (Victor Emmanuel King of Italy)
Vivazza (Italian—Vivacity)—Gioacchino Antonio Rossini's nickname
VIVB Virgin Islands Visitors Bureau
Viveca Lindfors Elsa Viveca Torstensdotter

vivi vivisection
Vivien Leigh Vivian Mary Hartley
vix. vixit (Latin—he/she lived)
viz. videlicet (Latin—namely)
Viz Vizcaya (Biscay); Vizcayan (Biscayan)
Vizc Vizcaya
Vizcaya (Spanish—Biscay)—province on the Bay of Biscay
vj jet velocity
v J vorigen Jahres (German—last year)
V-J agar Vogel-Johnson agar
VJC Vallejo Junior College
V-J Day August 15, 1945, Japanese surrender in World War II
V-joint angular V-shaped masonry joint
vj's video jockeys
Vjschr Vierteljahrschrift (German—quarterly)
vk vertical keel; volume kill
V of K Voice of Kenya (radio-television network)
VKC Von Karman Center
VKI Von Karman Institute
VKIFD Von Karman Institute for Fluid Dynamics
VKO Moscow, USSR (Vnukovo Airport)
vkr video kinescope recording(s)
VKR Vodennaya Kontr Rozvedka (Russian—Counter-Infiltration Organization)
vl vision, left
v/l vapor-to-liquid
Vl Ville
V/l vapor-liquid ratio
Vl Violino (Italian—violin); *Vlaanderen* (Dutch—Flanders)
VL Vaasa Line; Vaasan Laiva; Venezuelan Line; Viking Line; Volcano Line; Vulgar Latin
vla very low altitude; very-large array (radio telescopes)
vla viola (Italian—viola)
Vla Venezuela; Vlaardingen
VLA Very Large Array (Radio Astronomy Observatory); Veterans' Land Administration (Canada); Volunteer Lawyers for the Arts
VLAA Volunteer Lawyers and Accountants for the Arts
Vlaanderen Dutch or Flemish—Flanders)
Vlad Vladimir; Vladivostok
vladd visual low-angle drogue delivery
Vlad(i) Vladimir
Vladimir Sirin Vladimir Nabo-

kov's pseudonym
v-l b vertical-lift bridge
vlbi very-long-baseline interferometry
VLCC very large cargo carrier (bulk freighter or tanker)
vlchv (VLCHV) very-low-cost harassment vehicle
vlcs voltage-logic-current switching
vld visual laydown delivery
vldl (VLDL) very-low-density lipoproteins
vldz Valdez
Vle Vale
V^{le} Viale (Italian—Avenue; Boulevard)
vlf very low frequency (to 30 kc)
vlf (VLF) vectored lift fighter
Vlg Village (postal abbreviation)
VLI Port Vila, Vanuatu (airport)
Vlissingen (Dutch—Flushing)
vllo violoncello (Italian—cello)
vln very low nitrogen; violin
Vln Valenciennes
vlnt van links naar rechts (Dutch—from left to right)
vlo vertical lockout
vlp video long play(er) (videodisc)
vlr very long range
vlrc very long range commuter
vls vertical liquid spring
vlsi very-large-scale integration
vlt violet
Vltava (Czechoslovakian—Moldau)—Bohemian river flowing into the Elbe
vltg voltage
vlv valve; valvular
vl/vs voltage logic/voltage switching
Vly Valley (postal abbreviation)
vm voltmeter
v/m various marks; volts per meter
vm voormiddag Dutch—forenoon; A.M.); *vormittags* (German—forenoon; A.M.)
v M vorigen Monats (German—last month)
VM Value Management; Viet Minh; Vulcan Materials
V & M Virgin and Martyr
V.M. Votre Majesté (French—Your Majesty); *Vuestra Majestad* (Spanish—Your Majesty); *Vuestra Merced* (Spanish—Your Worship)
vma vanillymandelic acid
VMA Valve Manufacturers Association

VMAG Vanderpoel Memorial Art Gallery
V-Mann Vertrauensmann (German—Trusted Man)—idealistically motivated and especially trustworthy intelligence agent
vmap video map equipment
V max maximum flight velocity
vmc visual meteorological conditions
VMC Viet Montagnard Cong
VMCCA Veteran Motor Car Club of America
vmd vertical magnetic dipole
V.M.D. Veterinariae Medicinae Doctor (Latin—Doctor of Veterinary Medicine)
VMDP Veterinary Medical Data Progam
vmh (VMH) ventromedial nucleus of the hypothalamus
VMH Victoria Medal of Honour
vmi visual motor integration; vi sual motor interaction
VMI Video Music Inc; Virginia Military Institute
v/mil volts per mil
V min minimum flight velocity
VMLI Veterans Mortgage Life Insurance
vmm virtual machine monitor
v & mm vandalism and malicious mischief
VM Molotov Vyacheslav M Skryabin
vmos V-groove metal-oxide semiconductor
vmos (VMOS) vertical mos (metal-oxide semiconductor)
VMOS Virtual Memory Operating System
vmp value of the marginal product
vm & p varnish makers and painters
vms vertical-motion simulator
VMS Veterinary Medical Society
vmt vehicle miles travelled; very many thanks
vn vulnerability number
v/n verb neuter
vn vellón (Spanish—copper-silver alloy)
VN Vietnam; Vietnamese
vna (VNA) ventral noradrenergic bundle
Vna Vienna
VNA Air Vietnam; Visiting Nurses Association
VNAF Vietnamese Air Force
vnav volumetric area navigation (three-dimensional)

VNB Valley National Bank
V-N B Verrazano-Narrows Bridge
Vnc (VNC) Vancouver, Washington
VN$ Vietnamese dollar
VN de B Vasco Nuñez de Balboa (first European to discover the Pacific Ocean)
V-neck V-shaped neck (line)
Vnese Vietnamese
vnf very near field
Vng Vereeniging
vni variable name initialization
Vni Violini (Italian—violins)
Vnla Venezolana (Spanish—female Venezuelan)
Vnlo Venezolano (Spanish—male Venezuelan)
VNM Victoria National Museum (Ottawa)
VNMC Vietnam Marine Corps
VNN Vietnam Navy
VNNBS Vietnamese National Broadcasting Service
Vno Violino (Italian—violin)
VNO Vital National Objective
V-note $5 bill
VNP Vietnamese piastre; Voyageurs National Park (Minnesota)
vnr variable navigation ratio
VNR Van Nostrand Reinhold
VNRC Vegetarian Nutritional Research Center
VNs Vietnamese
VNS Vereenigde Nederlands Scheepvaartmaatschappij (United Netherlands Navigation Company)
vnw voornaamwoord (Dutch—pronoun)
VNWR Valentine National Wildlife Refuge (Nebraska)
vo voluntary opening
vo. verso (Latin—back of the page, lefthand page); violino (Italian—violin)
v/o vossa ordem (Portuguese—your order)
vº verso (Portuguese—lefthand page, other side, over, reverse)
VO Valuation Office(r); verbal order(s); very old; Veterinary Office(r); Victorian Order; voice over
VO Volksoper (German—People's Opera)—Vienna
VOA Vancouver Opera Association; Vasa Order of America; Virginia Opera Association; Voice of America
VOA Vereeniging Ontwikkeling Arbeidstechniek (Dutch—Work Study Association)

vo-ag vocational agriculture (educators' jargon)
vob vacuum optical bench
vobanc voice band compression
VºBº vista bueno (Spanish—approved, okay)
Vº Bº visto bueno (Spanish—okay)
voc vocal; vocalist; vocation; vocational
VOC Vereenigde Oostindische Compagnie (Dutch—United East India Company)—often called the Very Old Company as that it was
VOCA Visiting Orchestras Consultative Association (London)
vocab vocabulary
VOCAL Vessel Ordnance Allowance List
vocat vocation(al); vocative
voc ed vocational education
Voc Foun Vocational Foundation
vocg verbal orders—commanding general
voco verbal order—commanding officer
vocoder voice coder
VOCOSS Voluntary Organisations Cooperating in Overseas Social Service
vocs verbal orders—chief of staff
voctl vocational
vod vision of right eye (d standing for dexter—Latin for right)
v-o d voice-operated device; voluntary-opening device
vodacom voice data communication(s)
vodactor voice data compactor
vodaro vertical ozone distribution (from) absorption and radiation of ozone
vodat voice-operated device for automatic transmission
voder voice-operated demonstrator
VÖEST Vereinigte Österreichische Eisen and Stahlwerke (United Austrian Iron and Steel Works)
vof variable-operating frequency
vog volcano smog
Vog Vogue
VoG Voice of Germany
VOG Vanguard Operations Group
vogad voice-operated gain-adjusting device (data processing)
VOHI Vancouver Oral Health

Index
VOICE Voice of Informed Community Expression
Voice of the American Revolution Patrick Henry
Voice of the Century Marian Anderson
Voice of Doom Gabriel Heatter (before and during World War II); Ann Watson (in the uncertain 1970s)
Voice from the Fo'c's'le Richard Henry Dana in *Two Years Before the Mast*; Herman Melville in *Whitejacket*
Voice of Israel Abba Eban
Voice of Northern Industrialism Daniel Webster
Voice of Polish Nationalism Adam Mickiewicz
Voice of the Revolution Patrick Henry
VOICES Voice-Operated Identification and Computer Entry System
VOIS Visual Observation Instrumentation Subsystem
voit voiture (French—railroad coach, truck, wagon, etc.)
vol volume; volunteer
vol % volume percent
vol. volatilis (Latin—volatile)
Vol Volans (constellation); Volcán; Volcano; volume
Vol Volcan (French—volcano); *Volcán* (Spanish—volcano); *Vulcano* (Italian—volcano)
VOLAR Volunteer Army
vol ash volcanic ash
volat volatile; volatizes
volatile alkali ammonia
volc volcanic; volcano; volcanology
Volcano Island Hawaii
Volcano Land Iceland
Volga Europe's longest river—2300 miles—extends from north of Moscow on the Caspian Sea; links many river ports such as Kalinin, Yaroslavl, Gorki, Kazan, Saratov, Volograd, Astrakhan
Volgograd formerly Stalingrad during Stalin's time and Tsaritsyn during czarist times
Vol Isl Volcano Islands (south of Japan and Bonin Islands)
Volks Volkswagen
volkst volkstaal (Dutch—slang; vernacular)
vollst vollstandige (German—complete)
Voln Volans (constellation)
Volodya (Russian nickname—Vladimir)
vols volumes

VOLS Voluntary Overseas Libraries Service
Volta Voltaic Republic (Republic of the Upper Volta)
Voltaire assumed name of François-Marie Arouet (*see* Jean Meslier)
Voltaire of the Unitarians Dr Joseph Priestley, according to William Hazlitt
volts AC volts alternating current
volts DC volts direct current
volum volumetric
Volunteer(s) Tennessean(a)
Volunteer State Tennessee's official nickname honoring its many volunteers for the Mexican War
volvar volume variety
volvend. volvendus (Latin—to be rolled)
Volvo (Latin—I roll)—Swedish automobile
voly voluntary
vom volt milliammeter; volt-ohm microammeter; volt-ohm milliammeter; vomer; vomerine; vomit; vomitory; vomitus
vom. vomitus (Latin—vomit)
VOM Vereniging voor Oppervlaktetechnieken Metalen (Dutch—Metal Finishing Association)
vom neg vomito negro (Spanish —black vomit)—last stage of yellow fever
VON Victorian Order of Nurses (public health)
vona vehicle of the new age (computer-controlled rapid-transit shuttle)
Von Economo's disease encephalitis lethargica
von Hofmanns Hugo von Hofmannsthal
V.O.N.O. Vendor of Oysters in New Orleans (Walt Whitman's invention used in his story about Timothy Goujon, V.O.N.O.)
von Reuter Israel Beer Josphat (founder of Reuter's news agency)
Voodoo Canadian-built version of the F-101 jet interceptor
vop valued as in original policy
VOP very oldest procurable
Vo-Po Volks Polizei (East German Police)
VOQ Visiting Officer's Quarters
vor very high frequency omnidirectional range (VOR); visual omnirange

vordme very-high-frequency-omnirange distance-measuring equipment
vorm vormals (German—formerly); *vormittags* (German—forenoon, A.M.)
Vor Mus Voortrekker Museum (Pietermaritzburg)
Voroshilovgrad formerly Lugansk
Vors Vorsitzender (German—chairman)
vort vortex; vortices
vortac visual omnirange and tacan
vos vision of left eye (s standing for *sinister*—Latin for left)
vo('s) verbal order(s)
vos vostok (Russian—east, as in Vladivostok)
v.o.s. vitello ovi solutus (Latin—dissolved in egg yolk)
Vos Voskresene (Russian—Sunday)
VOS Victims of Superstition; visual observation airplane (naval symbol)
Vost Vostochnyy (Russian—eastern)
vot voice on set time; voluntary overtime
vot. votivus (Latin—promissory or votive)
VOT Foreign Operational Center of Soviet Intelligence forces (formerly called MGB, MVD, NKGB, NKVD, OGPU, GPU, VECHEKA, and originally CHEKA—founded in December 1917, six weeks after Bolshevik seizure of power in October Revolution)
votc volume table of contents
VOTE Voters Organized to Think Environment
votem voice-operated typewriter employing morse
vou voucher
VOW Voice of Women
VOWS Vilas-Oneida Wilderness Society
vox voice-operated transmission
vox pop. vox populi (Latin—voice of the people)
voy voyage
Voyager American spacecraft destined for landings on Mars and Venus
Voyageurs Voyageurs National Park on the Canadian border of Minnesota
Vozv Vozvyshennost' (Russian —uplands)
vp vanishing point; variable pitch; verb phrase; vertically

polarized; vistaphone
v/p verb passive; verb phrase
v & p vagotomy and pyloroplasty
V_p valve-position voltage
VP British United Air Ferries (2-letter code); fixed-wing fighter airplane (2-letter naval symbol); Ville de Paris; Vice-President
VP (NSC) Verification Panel (National Security Council)
V-P Voges-Proskauer (reaction)
VP Vigilancia de la Pesca (Spanish—Fishery Patrol)
VPA Vancouver Public Aquarium; Videotape Production Association; Virginia Port Authority
v pag various paging
VP & B Veterinary Pharmaceuticals and Biologicals
vpc volume-packed cells
VPCP Volunteer Probation Counseling Program
vpd vapor-phase degrease; variation per day; vehicles per day
vpc vapor-phase cultaxy
vpg very pregnant guppy (NASA); voltage pressure gradient
VPGA Vermont Personnel and Guidance Association; Virginia Personnel and Guidance Association
vph variation per hour; vehicles per hour; vertical photography
vpi vapor-phase inhibitor
VPI Veterinary Pet Insurance; Virginia Polytechnic Institute; Vocational Preference Inventory
VPIRG Vermont Public Interest Research Group
vpl visible panty line
VPL Van Pelt Library (University of Pennsylvania)
vpm vehicles per mile; versatile packaging machine; vertical panel mount; vibrations per minute; volts per meter; volts per mile
VPM Vendor Part Modification
Vpn Vickers pyramid number
V P/N vendor('s) part number
vpo vapor-phase oxidation
Vpo Valparaiso
VPO Vienna Philharmonic Orchestra
vpp viral porcine pneumonia
vpr vacuum pipette rig
VPR Vanguarda Popular Revolucionaria (Portuguese—Popular Revolutionary Vanguard)

—Brazilian terrorist organization
V Pres Vice President
v-prez vice-president
vps vibrations per second; volume pressure setting
VPS Visual Programme Systems
VPSA Vertebrate Paleontological Society of America
V-P test Voges-Proskauer test
vq virtual quantum; visual quotient
vqa vendor quality assurance
vqc vendor quality certification
vqd vendor quality defect
VQMG Vice Quartermaster General
vqzd vendor quality zero defects
vr variable ratio; variable response; ventilated rib; vision, right; voltage regulator; vulcanized rubber
vr (VR) voluntary return (voluntary deportation of illegal aliens)
v/r verb reflexive
vr vedi retro (Italian—please turn over)
VR fixed-wing transport airplane (2-letter naval symbol); Victoria Railways (Australia)
V-R Veeder-Root
V.R. Victoria Regina
VR Valtionrautatiet (Finnish—State Railways)
V.R. Victoria Regina (Latin—Queen Victoria)
vra *vuestra* (Spanish—your, *f*.)
VRA Vocational Rehabilitation Administration
Vrajdebna Sofia, Bulgaria's airport
vras *vuestras* (Spanish—your, pl.)
vrb voice rotating beacon
vrbl variable
vrbl mnmncs verbal mnemonics (abbreviations and acronyms)
vrc vertical redundancy check(ing); visible record computer
VRC Vehicle Research Corporation
VRCAMS Vehicle/Road Compatibility Analysis and Modification System
v-r'd voluntarily returned (deported)
VRD (Royal Naval) Volunteer Reserve Decoration
vre voltage-regulator exciter
vr&e vocational rehabilitation and education
v refl verb reflexive

VR et I Victoria Regina et Imperatrix (Victoria, Queen and Empress)
V Rev Very Reverend
VRF Vehicular Research Foundation
vrg veering
Vrg Varig (Brazilian Airlines)
vri virus respiratory infection
vri (VRI) visual rule instrument landing
Vri Vrijdag (Dutch—Friday)
VRI Vehicle Research Institute; Victorian Railways Institute
V-ring V-shaped ring
VRIS Vietnam Refugee and Information Services
vrm variable-rate mortgage(s)
v rms volt(s) root mean square
Vroni Veronica
vros vuestros (Spanish—your, *pl*)
vrp very reliable product
VRP Volta River Project
vrps voltage-regulated power supply
vrr visual radio range
VRR Veterans Reemployment Rights
vrs velocity response shape
VRS Van Riebeeck Society; Vanguard Recording Society; Video Response System
V & RS Vocational and Rehabilitation Service
vrt visual recognition threshold
vru voltage readout unit
vr vnw vragend voornaamwoord (Dutch—interrogative pronoun)
vrx virtual resource executive
Vry Viceroy
vs vein shot (intravenous injection); venesection; ventricles; versus; volumetric solution
vs (VS) vital signs; voluntary simplicity
v.s. very soluble
vs. ve suire (Turkish—and so forth); *versus* (Latin—against)
v.s. vide supra (Latin—see above)
VS scouting airplane (2-letter symbol); Vancouver Symphony; Victoria Symphony
V.S. Veterinary Surgeon
V & S Valley & Siletz (railroad)
VS Vereinigte Staaten (German—United States); *Verenigde Staten van Amerika* (Dutch—United States of America); *Vostra Signorfa* (Italian—Your Honor)
V S volti subito [Italian—turn (music page) swiftly]

VSA Victorian Society of America; Volunteer Services to Animals

vsam virtual storage access method

VSAP Vehicle Structure Analysis Program

vsb vestigial sideband

vs. b. venesectio brachii (Latin—bleeding in the arm)

VSBA Vermont School Boards Association; Virginia School Boards Association

vsby visibility

vsc virtual speech control

v.s.c. vidi siccam cultam (Latin—I have seen a dried cultivated specimen)—botanic term

VSC Virginia State College; Vocations for Social Change

VSCC Vintage Sports Car Club

vscf variable-speed constant-frequency

VSCU Vatican Secretariat for Christian Unity

vsd ventricular septal defect

VSD Vancouver School of Design; Vendor's Shipping Document(s)

VSE Vancouver Stock Exchange

vsff volte, se faz favor (Portuguese—please turn over)

VSGLS Vehicle Space Ground Link Subsystem

V-shape V-shaped

vshps vernier solo hydraulic power supply

vsi variable-speed indicator; very seriously ill; very slight imperfection; very slight inclusion

V-sign victory sign (raised index and middle fingers)

v signs vital signs (blood pressure, pulse, temperature, respiration)

V. Sirin Vladimir Nabokov

vs jw vise jaws

vsl variable safety level

VSL Venture Scout Leader

vsm vibrating-sample magnetometer

vsmf visual search microfilm file

VSMF Vendor Spec Microfilm File

VSMS Vermont State Medical Society; Vineland Social Maturity Scale

vsn vision

V S/N vendor('s) serial number

VSNAP Vermont State Nuclear Advisory Panel

vso very special old; very superior old

VSO Vancouver Symphony Orchestra; Victoria Symphony Orchestra; Victor Symphony Orchestra; Vienna State Orchestra; Vienna Symphony Orchestra

VSOE Venice-Simplon Orient Express

vsop very superior old pale (cognac)

vsp vertical seismic profile

Vsp. Vespertina (Latin—Vespers)

VSP VS Pritchett

VSPA Virginia State Port Authority

vspc virtual storage personal computing

V-spot $5 bill

vsq very special quality (VSQ)

vsr very short range; visual security range

vss versions

vss (VSS) vstol support ship

v.s.s. vidi siccam spontaneam (Latin—I have seen a dried wild specimen)—botanic term

VSS Vancouver Symphony Society; Vermont State Symphony; Voluntary Social Services

VSSSN Verification Status Social Security Number

vst violinest

V St A Vereinigte Staaten von Amerika (German—United States of America)

vstol vertical and/or short takeoff and landing

vsula vaccination scar upper left arm

vsv vesicular stomatitis virus

vsw vitrified stoneware

vswr voltage standing wave ratio

VSX heavier-than-air antisubmarine warfare carrier-based aircraft (naval symbol)

vt vacuum technology; vacuum tube; variable time; velocity; verb transitive; vinyl tile; vinyl tiling; voice tube

vt (VT) vertical tabulation character (data processing)

v-t vacuum technology; variable time (fuse); velocity-time (diagram)

v/t verb transitive

v & t volume and tension (of the pulse)

vt vaart (Dutch—canal); *viz tez* (Czech—see also)

v T vom Tausend (German—per thousand)

Vt Vermont; Vermonter

VT fixed-wing trainer-type airplane (2-letter naval symbol); Reseau Aérien Interinsulaire (Tahiti)

V.T. Vetus Testamentum (Latin—Old Testament)

vta ventral tegmental area

vᵗᵃ vuelta (Spanish—turn)

VTA Virginia Teachers Association

VTA Voenno-Transportnayaviatsiya (Russian—Air Transport Aviation)

v/tab vertical tabulation

VTAE Vocational Technical and Adult Education (System)

VTB Vereniging voor het Theologisch Bibliothecariaat (Dutch—Association of Theological Librarians)

vtc voting trust certificate

VTC Vermont Technical College

vte vertical-tube evaporator (for producing freshwater from the sea); vicarious trial and error

Vte Vicomte

V-TECS Vocational-Technical Education Consortium of States

Vtesse Vicomtesse

V-test Voluter test

vtf vertical test fixture

vt fuse variable-time fuse

vtg voting

VTG Vehicle Technology Group

vti volume thickness index

VTI Valparaiso Technical Institute

vtl variable threshold logic; vertical turret lathe

VTLs Vehicular Traffic Laws

VTM Victorian Tourist Ministry (Australia)

VTN Video Tape Network; Voorheis, Trindle, and Nelson

vto vertical takeoff; viable terrestrial organism

vᵗᵒ vuelto [Spanish—change (money)]

Vto Vtornik (Russian—Tuesday)

vtoc volume table of contents (data processing)

vtohl vertical takeoff and horizontal landing

vtol vertical takeoff and landing

vtolport vertical-takeoff-and-landing airport

vtovl vertical takeoff vertical landing

vtp voluntary termination of pregnancy (abortion)

vtp *viajes todo pagado* (Spanish —all trips paid)

vtpr vertical temperature profile radiometer

vtr video tape recorder; video tape recording

vtr. *vitreum* (Latin—glass)

VTR Vermont Railway

VTRS Video Tape Recorder System

vtr sot. videotape recorder sound on recorder tape

VTS Viewfinder Tracking System; Virginia Theological Seminary

VTSRS Verdun Target Symptom Rating Scale

VTTA Veteran's Time Trial Association

VTU Volunteer Training Unit

vtvm vacuum-tube voltmeter

vu varicose ulcer; voice unit; volumetric unit; volume unit

vu *von untem* (German—from the bottom)

VU Air Ivoire (2-letter code); fixed-wing utility airplane (2-letter naval symbol); Valparaiso University; Vanderbilt University; Vice Unit (police department); Victoria University; Villanova University; Vincennes University

VU *Vigile Urbano* (Italian—Traffic Policeman)

VUA Valorous Unit Award

VUA *Vrije Universiteit, Amsterdam* (Dutch—Free University —Amsterdam)

vue d'opt *vue d'optique* (French —optical view)—multidimensional art

VUH Vanderbilt University Hospital

vu indicator volume-unit indicator (data processing)

Vul Vulgate; Vulpecula (constellation)

vulc vulcanize(d, r)

vulcan vulcanization; vulcanize; vulcanizer; vulcanizing

Vulcan Hawker-Siddeley jet bomber aircraft; US-built six-barrel 20mm cannon

Vulcan (Latin—Hephaistos)— the blacksmith

vulg vulgar; vulgar fraction; vulgarian; vulgarism; vulgarist; vulgrization

Vulg Vulgar Era (Christian Era); Vulgar Latin; Vulgate

vulp vulpine

Vulp Vulpecula (constellation)

v-u meter volume-unit meter

VUNC Voice of United Nations Command

v u p (VUP) very unimportant person

VU-PD Vice Unit-Police Department

VU Pr Vanderbilt University Press

VUSM Vanderbilt University School of Medicine

vuv vacuum ultraviolet

VUW Victoria University of Wellington, New Zealand

vv vagina and vulva; verbs; verses; vice versa

v/v volume for volume

v&v verification and validation

v & v vintage and veteran (automobiles)

v.v. *vice versa* (Latin—conversely); *violini* (Italian—violins)

Vv. *Virgines* (Latin—Virgins)

VV Villa Viscaya (Dade County Art Museum, Miami, Florida); Voice of Vietnam (Hanoi)

VV *ustedes* (Spanish— you, *pl.*)

VVA Vietnam Veterans Association

VVAW Vietnam Veterans Against the War

v.v.c. *vidi vivam cultam* (Latin— I have seen a living cultivated specimen)—botanic term

VVCP Victims of Violent Crimes Program

VVD *Volkspartij voor Vrijheid en Democratie* (Dutch— People's Party for Freedom and Democracy)—Liberal Party

vvds video verter decision storage

Vve *Veuve* (French—widow)

vv hr vibration velocity per hour

Vvl Varavel

vv. ll. *variae lectiones* (Latin— variant readings)

VVN Verein der Verfolgten des Naziregimes (League of Victims of Naziism)

VVO very, very old

vvr variable-voltage rectifier

vvrm vortex valve rocket motor

vvs very, very superior

v.v.s. *vidi vivam spontaneam* (Latin—I have seen a living wild specimen)—botanic term

VVS Veteran's Vigil Society (Vietnam-era veterans)

V-VS *Voenno-Vozdushniye Sily*

(Russian—Air Forces of the USSR)

vvsf very very slightly flawed (gems)

vvsi very very slight imperfection; very very slight inclusion

vvsop very very superior old pale (cognac)

vvt variable valve timing

VVT Visual-Verbal Test

VV UU *Vigili Urbani* (Italian— Traffic Police)

v.v.v. *veni, vidi, vici* (Latin—I came, I saw, I conquered)

VVV Vasili Vasilievich Vereschagin

vw vessel wall

vw *voegwoord* (Dutch—conjunction)

Vw View (postal abbreviation)

VW Very Worshipful; Volkswagen (People's Car)

vWd von Willebrand's disease

VWD *Vereinigte Wirtschafte Dienst* (German News Agency)

vWf von Willebrand factor

vwg vibrating wire gage

vwl variable word length

VWOA Volkswagen of America

vwp variable width pulse

VWP Victim/Witness Project

VWPI Vacuum Wood Preservers Institute

vws ventilated wet suit; vibrating-wire stressmeter(s)

VWWI Veterans of World War I

vx vertex

VX Experimental Squadron (symbol)

vxo variable crystal oscillator

Vxtmps Vieuxtemps

vy various years; very

VY Air Cameroun; Victualling Yard

Vyborg Soviet port formerly belonging to Finland and called Viipuri

vyd *vydani* (Czech—edition)

Vygr Voyager (robot spacecraft)

Vy Rev Very Reverend

vyt *vytah* (Czech—abstract)

vz virtual zero

v-z varicella-zoster

vzd vendor zero defect(s)

VZP Venezuelan Petroleum Company (stock exchange symbol)

W

w loading (symbol); transverse acoustical displacement (symbol); wall; war; warm; waste; water; water vapor constant; watt; weather; week; weight; wet; white; wide; widow; widowed; width; wife; win; wind; wine; with; won; wood; word; work; work (symbol); wrong

w % weight percent

w + weakly positive

w − weakly negative

W Canadian Car & Foundry (naval designator symbol); College of Wooster; gross weight (symbol); irradiance (symbol); tungsten (Wolfram); very wide (symbol); Wales; Ward Line; warning; Washington; water; Waterman Steamship Line; watt(s); weather reconnaissance; Wednesday; Welsh; west; Westinghouse; Weyerhaeuser; Whiskey— code for letter W; Willys-Overland; Woolworth; Wu

W (W) wage rate (microeconomics)

W Wadi (Arabic—gulley, ravine, riverbed); Wald (German—forest, wood); Wan (Chinese or Japanese—bay; bight); warm (Afrikaans, Dutch, German—hot); west; west (Afrikaans, Dutch, German—west); Wilhelmsen (steamship line); women

W1, W2, etc. West One, West Two, etc. (London postal zones)

wa warm air; wire armored; with average; work energy

w/a welded assembly

Wa Waffenamt (German—Ordnance Department)—Third

Reich marking followed by a code number and stamped on all military equipment

WA Wabash Railroad (stock exchange symbol); Watchmen's Association; Welfare Administration; West Africa; West African; Western Airlines; Western Approaches (to British Isles); Western Australia; Wheeler Airlines; Wire Association; Workshop Assembly

W of A Western of Alabama (railroad)

W A World Almanac and Book of Facts

waa wartime aircraft activity; welded aluminum alloy

WAA War Assets Administration; Warden's Association of America; Western Amateur Astronomers; Women's Auxiliary Association

WAA World Aluminum Abstracts

WAAC West African Airways Corporation

WAACs Women's Auxiliary Army Corps

WAADS Washington Air Defense Sector

Waadt (German—Vaud)— Swiss canton

WAAF Women's Auxiliary Air Force

WAAFB Walker Air Force Base

waaj water-augmented air jet

WAAP World Association for Animal Production

waapm wide-area anti-personnel mine

WAAS Women's Auxiliary Army Service; World Academy of Art and Science

WAAVP World Association for the Advancement of Veterinary Parisitology

wab water-activated battery; when authorized by

WAB Wabash (railroad); Wage Adjustment Board; Wage Appeals Board; Western Actuarial Bureau; Westinghouse Air Brake; Wine Advisory Board; Women's Abolition Bureau (for the abolishment of adultery, alcoholism, and discrimination)

WABCO Westinghouse Air Brake Company

wablics waterborne logistical craft (junks, sampans, wallawallas)—Hong Kong harbor craft

wabs women are basically stupid (abbreviation devised by male chauvinists to irritate women liberationists)

wac wage analysis and control; waste acceptance criteria; weapon assignment console; write address counter

WAC Women's Army Corps (USA); Worked All Continents; World Aeronautical Chart; World Affairs Council

WACA World Airline Clubs Association

WACB Women's Army Classification Battery

WACC Washington Association of Community Colleges

wack. wait before sending positive acknowledgement

WACL World Anti-Communist League

WACM Western Association of Circuit Manufacturers

waco written advice of contract-

ing officer
WACO World Air Cargo Organization
WACRI West African Cocoa Research Institute
WACSM Women's Army Corps Service Medal
WACSSO Western Australian Council of State School Organisations
WACVA Women's Army Corps Veterans Association
Wad Wadham College, Oxford
WAD World Association of Detectives; Wright Aeronautical Division (Curtiss-Wright Corporation)
WADC Western Air Defense Command; Wright Air Development Center
wadd with added (costs, freight, etc.)
WADD Westinghouse Air Arm Division; Wright Air Development Division (USAF)
Waddy Walter
Wade Miller pseudonym shared by mystery writers Robert Wade and Bill Miller
wadex word and author index
WADF Western Air Defense Force
Wadh Wadham College, Oxford
WADS Wide Area Data Service; Wide Area Dialing Service
Wadsworth Wadsworth Atheneum (Hartford)
wae when actually employed
WAED Westinghouse Aerospace Electrical Division
WAES Workshop on Alternative Energy Strategies
waf with all faults
WAF Women in the Air Force
WAFB Warren Air Force Base
WAFC West African Fisheries Commission
WAFF West African Frontier Force
waffle. wide-angle fixed-field locating equipment
W Afr West Africa(n)
waf(s) waffle(s)
WAG Walters Art Gallery; Winnipeg Art Gallery
W A & G Wellsville, Addison & Galeton (railroad)
WAGBI Wildfowlers' Association of Great Britain and Ireland
WAGGGS World Association of Girl Guides and Girl Scouts
Wag hrn Wagner horn
wagr windscale advanced gas-

cooled reactor
WAGR Western Australian Government Railways
WAGRO Warsaw Ghetto Resistance Organization
wags. weighted agreement scores
wai walk-round inspection
WAI Work in America Institute
WAIF World Adoption International Fund
WAIS Wechsler Adult Intelligence Scale
Waistline of the Western Hemisphere Isthmus of Panama
WAIT Western Australian Institute of Technology
Waitemata Auckland, New Zealand's harbor
WAITR West African Institute for Trypanosomiasis Research
waj water-augmented jet
WAJ World Association of Judges
wak water analyzer kit; wearable artificial kidney; with all knowledge
Wakefield Wakefield Prison south of Leeds in Yorkshire, England
wal walnut; wide-angle lens
Wal Wallace; Wallach; Wallachian, Wallsend-on-Tyne
WAL Western Airlines; Westinghouse Astronuclear Laboratory; Westland Aircraft Limited
W-AL Westinghouse-Astronuclear Laboratory
WALA West African Library Association
Walden Henry David Thoreau's handmade hut on the shores of Walden Pond near Concord, Massachusetts where he described it in his book—*Walden*
WALDO Wichita Automatic Linear Data Output (Boeing)
Waldstein Beethoven's Piano Sonata No. 21 in C (opus 53); dedicated to Count von Waldstein
Wales section of Great Britain inhabited by the Welsh; The Wales—The Bank of New South Wales
Wal I Wallops Island
WALIC Wiltshire Association of Libraries of Industry and Commerce
walking handbag(s) alligator(s); cayman(s); gavial(s); crocodile(s)

walk-in robes walk-in wardrobe closets
Wall Walloon
Wall *Wallace* (U.S. Supreme Court Reports)
Wallenstein Albrecht Wenzel Eusebius von Wallenstein (Bohemian general)
Walleye Martin-Hughes tv-guided glide bomb
Wallis (German—Valais)—Swiss commune on the Franco-Italian border
Wallis and Futuna Wallis and Futuna Islands in the southwest Pacific near Samoa
Wallows Walla Walla, Washington
Wall Street main street of New York City's financial center extending from the East River to Broadway at Trinity Church and its graveyard
Wall Street of Canada Bay Street in Toronto, Ontario
Wall-Wall prison in Walla Walla, Washington
Wally Wallace; Walter
Walnut Canyon Walnut Canyon National Monument in north-central Arizona
Walnut City McMinnville, Oregon
walopt weapons allocation optimizer
Walpurgis Walpurgis Night (April 30 in Finland and Sweden)
Walrussia nickname for Alaska in 1867 when it was purchased from Russia and believed by some critics to have nothing but walruses
WALST Western Alaska Standard Time
Wal Sta Wallops Station
Walt Walter; Walton
Walt Disney José Guizao Zamora
Walter Hampden Walter H Dougherty
Walter Huston Walter Houghston
Walter Wanger Walter Feuchtwanger
Waltz King musical nickname shared by Lanner, Lehar, Lumbye, Kalman, and others as well as by Johann Strauss Sr and Jr, Josef Strauss, Oskar Straus, and similar composers
wam walk-around money; wife and mother; words a minute; wrap-around mortgage
wAm white American male
WAM We Aint Metric; Wolf-

gang Amadeus Mozart; Women Against Men; Worcester Art Museum

WAMI Washington, Alaska, Montana, Idaho

WAML Watertown Arsenal Medical Laboratory

wamoscope wave-modulated oscilloscope

WAMP Wire Antenna Modelling Program

wampum. wage and manpower process utilizing machines

WAMRU West African Maize Research Unit

WAMY World Assembly of Muslim Youth

WAN West Africa Navigation (steamship line)

WANA We Are Not Alone

WANAP Washington National Airport

Wanchi Hong Kong's redlight district

Wand Wanderers

Wanderer Schubert's Piano Fantasie in C (opus 15)

WANDPETLS Wandsworth Public Educational and Technical Library Services

Wandsworth Wandsworth Prison, London, England

Wankie Wankie National Park in Rhodesia

WANL Westinghouse Astronuclear Laboratories

WANR Wadi Amud Nature Reserve (Israel)

WANS Women's Australian Nursing Society

WANYNJ Warehousemen's Association of New York and New Jersey

wao wet-air oxidation

WAO Weapons Assignment Office(r)

WAOB World Agricultural Outlook Board

WAOS Wide-Angle Optical System

wap wide-angle panorama

WA£ West African pound

WAP Women Against Pornography; Work Assignment Plan; Work Assignment Procedure

WAPA Western Area Power Administration; White American Political Association

WAPC Women's Auxiliary Police Corps

WAPD Westinghouse Atomic Power Division

WAPET Western Australia Petroleum Pty Ltd

WAPOR World Association for Public Opinion Research

WAPPRI World Association of Pulp and Papermaking Research Institutes

WAPs Work Assignment Plans

WAP's Work Assignment Plans

WAPS World Association of Pathology Societies

WAPSD Westinghouse Electric Corporation Advanced Power Systems Division

WAPT Wild Animal Propagation Trust

WAPV gunboat (4-letter USCG symbol)

war. warrant; with all risks

War War Department; Warsaw; Warwickshire

WAR William A Rusher; Women Against Rape

War Between the States Civil War; War of the Secession

WARC Western Air Rescue Center; World Alliance of Reformed Churches

warcat workload and resources correlation analysis technique(s)

WARDA West African Rice Development Association

Warden of the Honour of the North Halifax, Nova Scotia

Warehouse of the East free port of Penang, Malaysia

WARES Workload and Resources Evaluation System

warex (WAREX) we have a warrant and will extradite

warf warfare

Warf Warfarin (rodenticide)

WARF Wisconsin Alumni Research Foundation

WARFI Western Alumni Research Foundation Institute; Wisconsin Alumni Research Foundation Institute

War Fury Bellona—Roman goddess of war whose Greek counterpart is Enyo

wargasm Kremlin, Peking, or Pentagon plan (depending on who's calling the shots) for dropping bombs on every major city and military base in China, the U.S.A., or the USSR (depending on the aggressor); war + orgasm (sudden outbreak of war)

warhd warhead

Warhorse of the Confederacy Lieutenant General James Longstreet, CSA

WARI Waite Agricultural Research Institute

War of Independence American Revolution

Warks Warwickshire

warla wide-aperture radio location array

WARLOCE Wartime Lines of Communication—Europe

Warlord Wotan

Warlord of the First Reich Prince Otto von Bismarck-Schönhausen

Warlord of the Second Reich Kaiser Wilhelm II

Warlord of the Third Reich Führer Adolf Hitler

warn. warning

War of the Pacific Chile vs. Bolivia and Peru (1879–1883)

warr warranty

WARRS West African Rice Research Station

WARS Worldwide Ammunition Reporting System

Warsaw *Warsaw Concerto* composed in 1941 by Richard Addinsell for the film *Dangerous Moonlight*

Warschau (Dutch or German—Warsaw)

War of the Secession Southern synonym for Civil War, War of the Rebellion, War between the States (of the United States)—1861 to 1865

War of Separation American Revolution

Warszawa (Polish—Warsaw)

was. wide-angle sensor; wideband antenna system

WAS Worked All States

WASA Washington Association of School Administrators; Wyoming Association of School Administrators

WASAL Wisconsin Academy of Sciences, Arts, and Letters

WASAMA Women's Auxiliary to the Student American Medical Association

WASB Wisconsin Association of School Boards

WASBO Washington Association of School Business Officials; Winconsin Association of School Business Officials

WASC Western Association of Schools and Colleges

wascala wide-angle scanning-array lens antenna

WASCO War Safety Council

WASDA Wisconsin Association of School District Administrators

Wash Washington; Washingtonian

WASH White Anglo-Saxon Hebrew

Wash Corr Cen Washington

Correctional Center
Wash DC Washington, D.C.
washing soda sodium carbonate crystals ($Na_2CO_3 + 10H_2O$)
Washington Ports (south to north) South Bend, Raymond, Aberdeen, Hoquiam, Port Angeles, Port Townsend, Olympia, Tacoma, Seattle, Everett, Anacortes, Bellingham
Washington's George Washington's Birthday (February 22)
Washington State Funnypark Washington State Prison near Walla Walla
Washmic Washington, (DC) military-industrial complex
WASHO Western Association of State Highway Officials
Washoe early settler's name for Nevada during the Comstock Lode gold-and-silver rush of 1859
Washoe Giant Mark Twain
Wash Post *The Washington Post*
Wash St Hist Soc Washington State Historical Society
Wash St U Pr Washington State University Press
Wash U Med Lib Washington University School of Medicine Library (St Louis)
WASI Wage and Salaries Index
wasn't was not
wasp. weightless analysis sounding probe; window atmosphere sounding projectile
Wasp Westland naval helicopter built in Britain
WASP War Air Service Program; Water and Steam Program; White Anglo-Saxon Protestant; Williams Aerial System Platform; Women Against Soaring Prices; Women's Air Force Service Pilots; Workshop Analysis and Scheduling Program; Wyoming Atomic Simulation Project
WASP(S) White Anglo-Saxon Protestant(s)
Wass Wasserman
Wassermann August von Wassermann—German bacteriologist who devised test in 1906 to determine diagnosis of syphillis by examination of blood or spinal fluid of the suspect
WASSP Washington Association of Secondary School Principals
WAST Western Australian Standard Time

WASU West African Student's Union
wat weight, altitude, temperature
Wat Waterford
WAT Word Association Test; World Airport Technology
WATA World Association of Travel Agencies
watashi watakushi (Japanese—I, me, myself)
Watch City old nickname of Waltham, Massachusetts
Watchdog of Central Park *New York Times* publisher Adolph S Ochs
Watchdog of the Eastern Pacific Pearl Harbor
Watchdog of the Western Pacific Guam
Watchungs Watchung Mountains of northern New Jersey
WATDA Western Australia Tourist Development Authority
water H_2O
Waterfront Philosopher Eric Hoffer
Waterfront of the West San Francisco
Watergab Watergate English (Nixon-era federalese exemplified by the substitution of *at this point in time* for *now*, in *point of fact* for *in fact*, utilization for *use*, and similar circumlocutions)
Water Gap Delaware Water Gap between New Jersey and Pennsylvania
Watergate Potomac River waterfront of Washington, DC, including Kennedy Center for the Performing Arts, Watergate Amphitheater for outdoor concerts, Watergate apartment-hotel-office-shopping center; synonym for a national scandal first detected at the Watergate office building
waterglass sodium silicate (Na_2SiO_3)
Waterland the Netherlands
Waterloo battlefield near Brussels, Belgium, where Napoleon met his final defeat June 18, 1815; some 55,000 soldiers lost their lives at Waterloo
Watermelon Capital of the World Hope, Arkansas has bestowed itself this alliterative sobriquet
Waters William Russell's pseudonym
watertec water technologist; water technology

Waterton Waterton-Glacier International Peace Park on the Alberta-Montana border or Waterton Lakes National Park in the same area
watg wave-activated turbine generator
WATPL Wartime Traffic Priority List
wats wide-area telephone service
WATS Wide Area Telecommunications Service
Wat Sta Waterloo Station (rail terminal)
watt's wide-area telephone transmission lines
Watts Black section of Los Angeles
Wat(ty) Walter
W Aust Western Australia
W Aust Cur West Australian Current
WAVA World Association of Veterinary Anatomists
WAVAW Women Against Violence Against Women
WAVES Women Accepted for Volunteer Emergency Service (USN)
WAVFH World Association of Veterinary Food Hygienists
WAW Warsaw, Poland (airport)
WAwa West Africa wins again
WAWF World Association of World Federalists
wax. weapon assignment and target extermination
'way away
WAY World Assembly of Youth
WAYC Welsh Association of Youth Clubs
Wayne St U Pr Wayne State University Press
'ways always
wb warehouse book(ing); water ballast(ing); waybill; weber; wheelbase; whole blood; widebeam; wingback; winner's bitch
w/b westbound; will be
Wb weber
WB Wage Board; Warner Brothers; Weather Bureau; Women's Bureau; World Bank for Reconstruction and Development (UN)
W-B Wilkes-Barre
wba wideband amplifier
WBA Washington Booksellers Association; Wisconsin Booksellers Association; World Boxing Association
WBAA Wholesale Booksellers

Association of Australia
WBAFC Weather Bureau Area Forecast Center
WBAMC William Beaumont Army Medical Center
WBAN Weather Bureau, Air Force-Navy
wbar wing bar (lighting or lights)
wbat wideband adapter transformer
WBAWS Weather, Briefing, Advisory, and Warning Service
wbc white blood cell; white blood cell (count); white blood corpuscle
WBC World Boxing Commission; World Boxing Council
wbco waveguide below cutoff
wbct wideband circuit transformer
wbd wideband data
WBD *Webster's Biographical Dictionary*
wbdl wideband data link
WBEA Western Business Education Association
WBF World Bridge Federation
wbfp wood-burning fireplace
wbgt wet-bulb globe temperature; wet-bulb globe thermometer
WBH Welsh Board of Health
wbi will be issued
WBI Wooden Box Institute
WBINA Wreck and Bone Islands Natural Area (Virginia)
WBIT Wechsler-Bellevue Intelligence Test
wbl wideband laser; wood blocking
Wbl Whitstable
Wbl *Wochenblatt* (German—weekly publication)
WBL Western Biological Laboratories
wblc waterborne logistics craft
wblo weak black liquor oxidation
Wb/m² webers per square meter
WBMA Wirebound Box Manufacturers Association
WBMC William Beaumont Medical Center (El Paso)
wbn well-behaved net
w/bndr(s) with binder(s)
wbnl wideband noise limiting
WBNM Wright Brothers National Monument
WBNP Wood Buffalo National Park (northwest Territories, Canada)
WBNR Wadi Bezet Nature Reserve (Israel)

wbns water boiler neutron source
wbnv wideband noise voltage
wbo wideband oscilloscope; wideband overlap; wide bridge oscillator
w/bo(s) with blowout(s)
wbp weather and boilproof
WBP Wartime Basic Plan; Water Bank Program
WBPA Western Book Publishers Association
wbr water boiler reactor; whole body radiation; wideband receiver
W Branch Wireless Branch (British intelligence)
wbrbn will be reported by notam (Notice to Airmen)
wbrs wrought brass
wbs without benefit of salvage; work breakdown structure
WBSEB West Bengal State Electricity Board
WBSF Water Basin Storage Facility
WBSI Western Behavioral Sciences Institute
WB Sig Sta Weather Bureau Signal Station
wbt wet-bulb temperature; wet-bulb thermometer; wideband transformer; wideband transmitter
WBT World Board of Trade
WBTA Webb-Pomerene Trade Association
WBTS Watchtower Bible and Tract Society
W B T & S Waco, Beaumont, Trinity & Sabine (railroad)
wbtv weather briefing television
wbv wideband voltage
wbvco wideband voltage-controlled oscillator
W By Walvis Bay
wc wadcutter; wage change; water closet (English euphemism for *lavatory*); weapon carrier; wheelchair; will call; without charge; wood casing; working capital; working circle; workmen's compensation
w/c wave change; with corrections (correct proof before printing)
WC Wabash College; Wagner College; Waldorf College; Walker College; Walsh College; Wartburg College; Washington College; Waynesburg College; Weatherford College; Webber College; Weber College; Webster College; Wellesley College; Wells College; Wesley College; West African

Airlines (2-letter code); West Coast Airlines (2-letter code); Westmar College; Westminster College; Westmont College; Wheaton College; Wheeling College; Wheelock College; Whitman College; Whittier College; Whitworth College; Wiley College; Wilkes College; Williams College; Wilmington College; Wilson College; Windham College; Winthrop College; Wofford College; Woodbury College; Woodstock College; World Court; Wycliffe College
W/C Weapons Controller; Wing Commander
WC1, WC2, etc. West Central One, West Central Two, etc. (London postal zones)
wca wideband cassegrain antenna; worst case analysis
WCA Washington Correctional Association; Washingtonian Center for Addiction; Western Correctional Association; Wisconsin Correctional Association; Women's Correctional Association; World Calendar Association
WCAA West Coast Athletic Association
w cab wall cabinet
WCAC West Coast Athletic Conference; Women's Crusade Against Crime (St Louis)
WCAFS Wideband Cassegrain Antenna Feed System
WCAP Westinghouse Commercial Atomic Power
WCAT Welsh College of Advanced Technology
WCB Workmen's Compensation Board
WCBA West Coast Bookmen's Association; Western College Bookstore Association
WC Babati (Romanian—Male WC)—men's toilet
WCBHS William Cullen Bryant High School
wcc water-cooled copper; wilson cloud chamber
WCC Wayne County Community College; Westchester Community College; Western Cartridge Company; Westminster Choir College; White Citizens Council (southern segregationist organization); World Council of Churches
wcca worst-case circuit analysis
WCCE West Coast Commodity Exchange
WCCI World Council for Cur-

riculum and Instruction

WCCU World Council of Credit Unions

wcdb wing control during boost

wcdo war consumable distribution objective

wce weapon control equipment

WCEMA West Coast Electronic Manufacturers' Association

WCEU World's Christian Endeavor Union

wcf white cathode follower

WCF Waste Calcining Facility; Winchester Center Fire (rifle shell designation)

WC Femei (Romanian—Female WC)—women's toilet

W.C. Fields Claude William Dukenfeld

WCFPR Washington Center of Foreign Policy Research

WCFST Weigl Color-Form Sorting Test

WCFTB West Coast Freight Tariff Bureau

WCG Women's Cooking Guild

wci white cast iron; wind chill index

WCIA Watch and Clock Importers Association

WCIR Workers Compensation and Insurance Report(ing)

WC & IR Workmen's Compensation and Insurance Report(ing)

WCJE World Council on Jewish Education

WCK West Virginia Coal and Coke (stock exchange symbol)

wcl watercooler

WCL West Coast Line; World Confederation of Labor

W-class Soviet class of submarines named Whiskey by NATO

wcld watercooled

WCLIB West Coast Lumber Inspection Bureau

wcm welded cordwood module; wired-core matrix; wired-core memory; word combine and multiplexer

WCMA Wisconsin Cheese Makers' Association

WCML Women's Caucus for Modern Languages

WCMR Western Contract Management Region

WCNA West Coast of North America

WCNM Walnut Canyon National Monument

WCNP Wind Cave National Park (South Dakota)

WCNYH Waterfront Commis-

sion of New York Harbor

WCO Weapons Control Office(r)

WCOTP World Confederation of Organizations of the Teaching Profession

wcp welder control panel; white combination potentiometer

WCP Weapon Control Plan; Work Control Panel; Work Control Plan

WCPA Western College Placement Association; World Constitution and Parliament Association

WCPS Women's Caucus for Political Science; World Confederation of Productivity Sciences

WCPT World Confederation for Physical Therapy

wcr water-cooled reactor; water-cooled rod; water cooler; wire contact relay; word-control register

WCR Western Communication Region (USAF); Women's Council of Realtors

WCRA Weather Control Research Association; Western College Reading Association

WCRP World Council of Religion for Peace

wcs wing center section

WCS Weapons Control Station; Weapons Control System; Wisconsin Correctional Service

WCSA West Coast of South America

wcsb weapon control switchboard

wcsc weapon control system console

WCSC World Correctional Service Center

WCSI World Center for Scientific Information

WCSRC Wild Canid Survival and Research Center

WC & S's S & EBC William Cramp & Son's Ship and Engine Building Company

WCT World Championship Tennis

WCTB Western Carriers Tariff Bureau

WCTL Western Center Telecommunications Laboratory

WCTU Wild Cats and Tigers United (according to drinkers disliking the following and more usual definition); Women's Christian Temperance Union

WCU West Coast University

WCUK West Coast of United Kingdom

wcv water check valve

WCW William Carlos Williams

WCWB World Council for the Welfare of the Blind

wd water damage; weed; well deck(ing); whole depth; wind; window; winner's dog; withdrawn; wood; word; would; wound

w/d weight-displacement ratio; wind direction

Wd weeds

WD War Department; Water Department; Waterworks Department; Western Division

wda wheeldrive assembly; withdrawal of availability

WDA Warranty Disclosure Act; Welsh Development Agency

WDALMP Warehouse Distributors Association of Leisure and Mobile Products

WDC Women's Detention Center

WDC-A World Data Center-A (Washington, D.C.)

WDC-B World Data Center-B (Moscow, USSR)

wdd Western Development Division (USAF Air Research and Development Command)

wdf wood door and frame

wdg winding; wording

WDIF Women's Democratic International Federation

wdk wives don't know

WDL Western Defense Laboratories (Philco subsidiary of Ford Motor Company)

WDM Western Development Museum (Saskatoon); World Development Movement

wdmf wall-defective microbial forms

WDNR Wadi Dishon Nature Reserve (Israel)

wdo willing dropout

wdp wood door panel

WDPC Western Data Processing Center

wdr white drum

Wdr Wardmaster

Wdr L Wardmaster Lieutenant

wds wood-dye stain; word discrimination score; words; wounds

wd sc wood screw

wdsprd widespread

wdt width

wdtahtm (wahm, for short) why does this always happen to me?

WDTC Western Defense Tactical Command

wdu window de-icing unit

wdv written-down value (tax)

W$W *Wall Street Week* (educational tv program)

wdwn well developed, well nourished

wdwrk woodwork

wdy wordy

we. watch error; weekend

w/e weekend

w & e windage and elevation

We Welsh

WE Western Electric; World Education

W E *Wärmeeinheit* (German—thermal unit)

wea weapon(s); weather

WEA Washington Education Association; West End Avenue; Wisconsin Education Association; Workers Educational Association; Wyoming Education Association

WEAAC Western European Airports Association Conference

WEAL Women's Equity Action League

Wealth Personified Ploutus (Greek); Plutus (Roman)

WeAPD Western Air Procurement District

WEARCONS Weather Observation and Forecasting Control System

weat weathertight

Weather Capitol of the World a groundhog hole in Punxsutawney, Pennsylvania where, legend has it, its groundhog leaves hibernation every February 2 to forecast winter's end, for if he sees his shadow it means six more weeks of ice and snow, and if he doesn't then spring is near and summer can't be far behind

Weaver Weaverscope (rifle telescope)

Web *Webster's Third New International Dictionary of the English Language Unabridged*

WEBDEC WEB Du Bois Club(s)

webelos we'll be loyal scouts

Webelos We'll be loyal scouts.

Webfeet Oregonians so nicknamed because of the high average annual rainfall of Oregon

webrock weather buoy rocket

WEBS Weapons Effectiveness Buoy System

Webster Ford Edgar Lee Master's pseudonym

Webster's *Webster's Dictionary*

(published in many editions by G & C Merriam of Springfield, Massachusetts)

wec wide energy conversion

WEC Westinghouse Electric Corporation

WECAF Western Central Atlantic Fishery

WeCen Weather Center (USAF)

WECEP Work Experience Career Exploration Program

WECO Western Electric Company

WECOM Weapons Command (USA)

wecpnl weighted-equivalent continuous-perceived noise level

WECS Wind Energy Conversion System

we'd we had; we would

Wed Wednesday

Wed *Weduwe* (Dutch—widow)

WED Walter Elias Disney

WEDA Wholesale Engineering Distributors' Association

wedar water-damage reduction; weather-damage reduction

Wedd Wedding (Berlin borough)

Wedy Wednesday

Wee Western equine encephalitis

WEEA *Women's Education Equity Act*

WEEAP Women's Educational Equity Act Program

WEECN Women's Educational Equity Communications Network

weed nickname for marijuana along with grass and pot

Weegee photographer Arthur Fellig's nom de voir

WEEP Work Education Evaluation Project

WEETA Women's Educational Equity Technical Assistance

Wee Willie William Keeler

wef with effect from

WEF World Education Fellowship

WE & FA Welsh Engineers' and Founders' Association

wefax weather facsimile

WEFC West European Fisheries Conference

weft wings, engine, fuselage, tail

weg war emergency grant

weg(s) wild-eyed guess(es)

WEH William Ernest Henley

WEHS Wadleigh Evening High School

WEI World Education Incorporated

weia wife's earned income allowance (tax)

Weichsel (German—Vistula)

Weil's disease jaundice

Weimar Republic Germany between the end of World War I in 1919 and the takeover by Hitler in 1933—the Second Reich

Wein (German—Vienna)

weir wife's earned income relief (tax)

Weiss Weissensee

WEIU Women's Educational and Industrial Union

Wel Welsh

WEL Weapons Effects Laboratory (USA)

Wel Adm Welfare Administration

Wel Can Welland Canal

Welcher(s) person(s) of Welsh origin

weld welding

Wel Dept Welfare Department

we'll we shall; we will

Well Wellington

wellies wellington boots

Wellington Arthur Wellesley (Duke of Wellington); British Hovercraft class of hovercraft

WELS Wisconsin Evangelical Lutheran Synod

welsh pertaining to anything from or of Wales such as welsh cob (horse), welsh corgi (dog), welsh dresser (cupboard), welsh harp, welsh main (cockfight), welsh mortgage, welsh mountain (pony or sheep), welsh process (smelting), welsh rabbit (cheese dish also called welsh rarebit), welsh runt (cattle), welsh springer (spaniel), welsh terrier, etc.

Welsh Cradle of U.S. President Wales—ancestral home of President Jefferson

Welsh Landscape Painter Richard Wilson

Welsh Ports (large, medium, and small from north to south) Port Dinorwic, Holyhead, Caernarvon, Fishguard, Milford Haven, Llanelly, Swansea, Port Talbot, Barry, Cardiff

Welsh Wizard David Lloyd George

Welt *Die Welt* (Hamburg's World)

Welts *Weltschmerz* (German—world pain)—universal misery

WEMA Western Electronic Manufacturers Association

WEMSB Western European Military Supply Board (NATO)

WEMTA Wisconsin Emergency Technician's Association

Wen Wendel; Wendell; Wendy

WEN Western Educational Network; Wien-Alaska Airlines

Wenatchees Wenatchee Mountains of central Washington

Wend *Wendell's Reports*

Wenen (Dutch—Vienna)

WENOA *Weekly Notice to Airmen* (CAA)

WEOG Western European and Other Groups

wep water-extended polyester

WEP Wisconsin Electric Power Company

WEPA Welded Electronic Packaging Association

WEPCO Weather-Proof Company

wepex weapons exercise

WERA World Energy Research Authority

WERC World Environment and Resources Council

we're we are

weren't were not

WERM *World's Encyclopaedia of Recorded Music*

WERPG Western European Regional Planning Group (NATO)

Wes Wesley; Weston

WES Water Electrolysis System; Waterways Experiment Station (Corps of Engineers); Weather Editing Section (FAA); Women's Engineering Society

WESCOM Weapon System Cost Model

WESCON Western Electronics Show and Convention

wesentl *wesentlich* (German—essential, main)

WESO Weapons Engineering Service Office

Wes Pac Western Pacific

Wesphalia English equivalent of Westfalen

WESRAC Western Research Application Center

Wes Sam Western Samoa (formerly British Samoa)

Wessex Westland-built verson of Sikorsky utility helicopter

West Western States (Mountain and Pacific Divisions); Wild West

WEST Western Educational Society for Telecommunications; Western Energy Supply and Transmission (Association);

Women's Enlistment Screening Test

WESTAF Western Transport, Air Force

West Berlin free sector of Berlin occupied by Allied powers, citizens of the German Federal Republic, and many refugees from East Berlin and East Germany

West Britain Wales

WESTCOMMRGN Western Communications Region

West Country southwestern England—Cornwall, Devonshire, Dorset, Somerset

West End fashionable London

wester storm from the west

western western omelet; western-type movie or novel featuring the Wild West

Western Hemisphere half of the world containing North America, South America, and associated islands

Westernmost American Territory Guam

Westernmost American Town Adak, Aleutian Islands, Alaska

Westernmost Canadian Territory Yukon

Westernmost Canadian Town Dawson, Yukon

Westernmost Ireland Tearact Island off the Dingle Peninsula often called the westernmost Peninsula of Europe

Westernmost Prairie Province Alberta

Westernmost Province British Columbia

Westernmost State Alaska

Western Prairie Province Alberta

Western Samoa Samoa i Sisifo (formerly German Samoa)

Western Samoan Port Apia

Western States United States west of the Mississippi River

Western Tip of Florida Pensacola

Western Tip of Texas El Paso

Westfalen (German—Westphalia)

West German Ports (large, medium, and small from east to west) Harburg, Hamburg, Altona, Cuxhaven, Bremerhaven, Brake, Nordenham, Wilhelmshaven, Papenburg, Emden, Norderney

West Germany capitalist-oriented western Germany west of the Iron Curtain—the German Federal Republic

West Indies Greater and Lesser Antilles in the Caribbean Sea

West Irian western half of New Guinea formerly Dutch or Netherlands New Guinea and now part of Indonesia

WESTIS Westinghouse Teleprocessing Interface System

West Jersey southern and western New Jersey

WestLant Western Atlantic Area

Westlaw computerized legal research service offered by West Publishing Co

West LB *Westdeutsche Landesbank* (West German Land Bank)

West Lothian Linlithgow, Scotland

Westm Westminister; Westmorland

West Malaysia mainland Malaysia plus Singapore before it became independent

Westminster Abbey Collegiate Church of St Peter in Westminster

Westminster Palace Houses of Parliament in London

Westmld Westmorland

Westmonasterium (Latin—Westminster)

West North Central States Iowa, Kansas, Minnesota, Missouri, Nebraska, North Dakota, South Dakota

Westo West Countryman

West Pac Western Pacific (ocean or railroad)

WESTPAC Western Pacific

West Point U.S. Military Academy at West Point, New York

West Point Morton Gould's Symphony No. 4 for Band

West Point of Capitalism Harvard Business School

West Point of Law Enforcement FBI National Academy at Quantico, Virginia

Westport Landing pioneer name for Kansas City

Westpreussen (German—West Prussia)—now part of Poland

Westrain Western Australian Trains

Westralia Western Australia

Westralia(n) Western Australia(n)

West's *West's Annotated Education Code*

West Sam Western Samoa

West South Central States Arkansas, Louisiana, Oklahoma, and Texas

West Virginie West Virginia

Westway New York City's new west side highway extending northward from Battery Park along the Hudson River

Westy Westmoreland; Westmoreland

Wes Univ Wesleyan University

WET Weapon(s) Effectiveness Test(ing)

WETA Washington Educational Television Association

wetensch *wetenschap* (Dutch—knowledge, science)

WeTip We Turn in Pushers (of narcotics)

Wet Mary Western Maryland Railway (stock exchange slang)

wets. Tory moderates

WETS Weekend Training Site(s)

Wet Tortugas rainswept Florida Keys

WETUC Workers' Educational Trade Union Committee

WEU Western European Union (Belgium, France, Italy, Luxembourg, Netherlands, United Kingdom, West Germany)

we've we have

WEWP West European Working Party (Book Development Council)

Wex Wexford

WEX Westinghouse Electric Company (stock exchange nickname)

Wexf Wexford

Wey Weymouth

wez (WEZ) western economic zone

WEZ *westeuropäische Zeit* (German—West European Time); Greenwich Mean Time

wf winner's female; write forward; wrong font

w/f white female

w/f (W/F) withdrawing and failing; withdrawn/failed

w & f water and feed

WF Wake Forest; Wake Forest College; Wells Fargo & Company

W-F Weil-Felix (reaction)

W.F. White Father

W & F Wallis and Futuna Islands

WFA War Food Administration (World War II); White Fish Authority; World Federalists Association; World Friendship Association

w factor will factor

WFALW *Weltbund Freiheitlicher Arbeitnehmerverbände*

auf Liberaler Wirtschafsgrundlage (German—World Union of Liberal Trade Union Organizations)

WFAOSB World Food and Agricultural Outlook and Situation Board

WFAW World Federation of Agricultural Workers

WFB Wells Fargo Bank; World Federation of Buddhists

WFBI Wood Fiber Blanket Institute

WFBMA Woven Fabric Belting Manufacturers Association

wfc wolf first class (woman chaser)

WFC Wake Forest College; Water Facts Consortium; World Food Council

WFCA Western Fire Chiefs Association

wfd wool forward (knitting)

WFD World Federation of the Deaf

WFDY World Federation of Democratic Youth (communist)

wfe with food element

WFEA World Federation of Educational Associations

WFEB Worcester Foundation for Experimental Biology

WFEO World Federation of Engineering Organizations

WFEX Western Fruit Express

WFF World Friendship Federation

WFFL World Federation of Free Latvians

wfg waveform generator

WFGA Women's Farm and Garden Association

WFHE Washington Friends of Higher Education

WFI Wheat Flour Institute

WFIC Wisconsin Foundation of Independent Colleges

WFJCC World Federation of Jewish Community Centers

wfl worshipful

WFL Women's Freedom League; World Football League

W Flem West Flemish

WFLRY World Federation of Liberal and Radical Youth

WFM Walter F Mondale; Western Federation of Miners

WFMH World Federation for Mental Health

WFMW World Federation of Methodist Women

wfn well-formed net

WFN World Federation of Neurology

wfna white-fuming nitric acid

WFNS World Federation of Neurosurgical Societies

wfo wide-field optics

WFO Washington Field Office (FBI)

WFOA Western Fishboat Owners of America

wfof wide-field optical filter

WFOT World Federation of Occupational Therapists

wfp warm frontal passage

WFP World Food Program (UN)

WFP *Winnipeg Free Press*

WFPA World Federation for the Protection of Animals

WFPMM World Federation of Proprietary Medicine Manufacturers

WFPT World Federation for Physical Therapy

W Fris West Frisian

WFS World Future Society

WFSA World Federation of Societies of Anaesthesiologists

WFSF World Future Studies Federation

WFSPL Wright Field Special Projects Laboratory

WFSW World Federation of Scientific Workers

wft wandering finger trouble

WFT Washington Federation of Teachers

wfttngs with fittings

WFTU World Federation of Trade Unions

WFUNA World Federation of United Nations Associations

WFW *Woltföderation der Wissenschaftler* (German—World Federation of Scientific Workers)

WFWFTHI World Federation of Workers in Food, Tobacco, and Hotel Industries

WFY World Federalist Youth

wg water gauge; wing; wire gauge

Wg Wolfgang

WG Welsh Guards; West German; Western Gear (company); WG Grace (cricketer and physician); Working Group; Writers Guild

WG *Westminster Gazette*

wga wheat-germ agglutinin

WGA Waterfront Guard Association; Writers' Guild of America

w-gal(s) wine gallon(s)

W-gauge wide-gauge railroad track (exceeding the standard gauge of 4 feet $8^1/_2$ inches)

WGB *Weltgewerkschaftsbund*

(German—World Federation of Trade Unions)

wgbc waveguide operating below cutoff

WGC West Georgia College; World Gas Conference

Wg-Comdr Wing-Commander

WGCTA Watson-Glaser Critical Thinking Appraisal

WGD *Webster's Geographical Dictionary*

WGDS Warm Gas Distribution System

W Ger West Germany

WGER Working Group on Extraterrestrial Resources

wgf waveguide filter; wound glass filter

WGGB Writers' Guild of Great Britain

WGH William Gamaliel Harding (29th President U.S.)

WGI Work Glove Institute

WGIPP Waterton-Glacier International Peace Park (Alberta, Canada, and Montana, U.S.A.)

wgj wormgear jack

WGJB World's Greatest Jazz Band

w gl wireglass

WGL Weapons Guidance Laboratory

W Glam West Glamorgan

WGM Worthy Grand Master

WGMA Wet Ground Mica Association

WGmc West Germanic

WGMEX Western Gulf of Mexico

WGP Western Gas Processors

WGPMS Warehousing Gross Performance Measurement System

WGPORA Western Gas Processors and Oil Refiners Association

wgr wide gauze roll

WGR War Guidance Requirements

Wg & Rgn Comdr Wing and Regional Commander

W Grnld Cur West Greenland Current

wgs waveguide glide slope; web guide system

WGs Welsh Guards

WGS Western Gerontological Society; World Geodetic System

wgsj wormgear screw jack

WGSPR Working Group for Space Physics Research (NATO)

wgt weight

WGTA Wisconsin General

Testing Apparatus

WGTW Won't Go To Wembleys (anti-imperialist group)

WGU Welsh Golfing Union

WGVN Willard Gibbs Van Name

wgw waveguide window

WGWC Working Group for Weather Communications (NATO)

WGWP Working Group for Weather Plans (NATO)

wh water heater; watt hour; white; withholding

w/h withholding

Wh Whig Party

WH White House

wha wounded by hostile action

wha' what

WHA Welsh Hockey Association; Western History Association; World Health Assembly; World Hockey Association

wham winning the hearts and minds (of the listeners)

W'hampton Wolverhampton

Whangpoo Hwang Pu

whap when or where applicable

Wharf of North America Nova Scotia's nickname celebrating its many excellent ports

WHASA White House Army Signal Agency

whate'er whatever

what's what has; what is

whatso'er whatsoever

WHC White House Conference (on libraries and information services)

WHCA White House Communications Agency

WHCF White House Conference on Families

WHCLIS White House Conference on Library and Information Services

WHCOA White House Conference on Aging

WHCT West Ham College of Technology

whd warehead

WHD Women's House of Detention (NYC)

whdm watt-hour demand meter

whe water hammer eliminator

Wheat *Wheaton's* (US Supreme Court Reports)

Wheat Energy State North Dakota

Wheatland home of President James Buchanan in Lancaster, Pennsylvania

Wheat Provinces Alberta, Manitoba, Saskatchewan

wheats wheatcakes

Wheat State South Australia

wheatstone wheatstone bridge (electrical measuring device named for its inventor—Sir Charles Wheatstone—an English physicist)

whecon wheel control

whene'er whenever

Where the Andes Greet the Caribbean Venezuela

where'er wherever

Where It's Springtime All The Time San Diego, California

Where Mexico Meets Uncle Sam nickname of Brownsville, Texas across Rio Grande from Matamoros, Tamaulipas on Mexican border of the United States

wheresoe'er wheresoever

Where the Turf Meets the Surf Del Mar, California

whf wharf

WHFAM William Hayes Fogg Art Museum

whfg wharfage

whfr wharfinger

whf(s) white homosexual female(s)

WHH William Henry Harrison (9th President U.S.)

WHHA White House Historical Association

Whi Whitehall

WHI Western Highway Institute

Whigs Whigamores (originally a group of West Scottish revolting against church and king)

WHIM Western Humor and Irony Membership

WHIMSY *Western Humor and Irony Membership Yearbook*

Whirlwind Westland military helicopter built in Britain

whis whistle (fog)

Whiskey letter W radio code; Soviet class of diesel submarines as named by NATO; stock exchange (slang); Western Kentucky (coal company)

Whit Whitaker; Whitbread; Whitcomb; Whitman

Whitaker's *Whitaker's Almanac*

White Africa southern Africa including Rhodesia and South Africa

White Carpathians White Carpathian Mountains of Czechoslovakia

White City of the North Helsinki

White City of the South Sucre, Bolivia

White Commonwealth Australia, Canada, New Zealand,

Rhodesia, South Africa, and the United Kingdom (before the African and Asian invasion of colonists and natives demanding a place in what was often their own country)

White Elephant Thailand ensign bearing a green and red caparisoned white elephant

White Ensign flag of the Royal Navy and the Royal Yacht Club—St George cross on a white ground with the Union Jack in the upper canton corner

white flag symbol of surrender or truce

Whitehall London's street of government offices

White House executive office and residence of the President of the United States in Washington, DC

White Island Ibiza in the Balearics

white lead lead carbonate

white light signal indicating apparatus, craft, or vehicle has power and is illuminated

White Man's Grave equatorial West Africa

White Metropolis Helsinki

White Mountain State New Hampshire

White Mts White Mountains (elevations so named are found in Arizona, California, Maine, Nevada, and New Hampshire)

white niggers British racist nickname for communists and socialists

White Pines White Pine Mountains of eastern Nevada

white plague pulmonary tuberculosis

White Russia Byelorussian district around Minsk

White Russian Russian supporter of any party or policy hostile to communist-dictated Red Russia, the Soviet Union

whites the whites—thick whitish vaginal discharge; synonym for leukorrhea

White Sands White Sands National Monument in southeastern New Mexico

White Sea arm of the Arctic north of Leningrad and called Beloye More by the Russians

White Sea-Baltic White Sea-Baltic Canal linking Belomorsk on the White Sea with Leningrad on the Baltic via lakes Onega and Ladoga

White Town of Lake Mjosa Gjovik, Norway

white vitriol zinc sulfate

whitewings white-uniformed street cleaners

Whitman Albert Whitman (Chicago); Whitman Publishing Company (Racine)

WHL Western Hockey League

wh lt white light

WHMA Women's Home Missionary Association

WHML Wellcome Historical Medical Library

whm(s) white homosexual male(s)

whmstr weighmaster

WHMV & NSA Woods Hole, Martha's Vineyard and Nantucket Steamship Authority

Whn Whitehaven

WHO White House Office; World Health Organization (UN)

WHOA Wild Horse Organized Assistance

who'd who had

WHODAP White House Office of Drug Abuse Prevention

WHOI Woods Hole Oceanographic Institution

WHOIRP World Health Organization International Reference Preparation

whol wholesale(r)

who'll who shall; who will

whoretel whore hotel

Whorez trucker's nickname for Ciudad Juarez, Mexico

who's who is

who've who have

whp water horsepower; whirlpool

W & H & PC Wage and Hour and Public Contracts

wh pl whole plate (silver)

whr watt hour

WHRA Welwyn Hall Research Association; Western Historical Research Associates; Western Housing Research Association

WHRC World Health Research Center

whrlp whirlpool

whs warehouse

WHS Walton High School; Washington Headquarters Services; White Sands, New Mexico (tracking station)

whse warehouse

whsl wholesale

whsmn warehouseman

whsng warehousing

whs rec warehouse receipt

Wht White (postal abbreviation)

WHT William Howard Taft (27th President of the U.S.)

WHTHS William Howard Taft High School

whtm(s) white heterosexual male(s)

whvs wharves

why. what have you?

why'd why did

whyinel why in hell

Why Not Town Minot, North Dakota, nicknamed Why Not Minot?

wi wrought iron

wi' (Gaelic contraction—with)

w & i weighing and inspection

WI Wake Island; West India; West Indian; West Indies; Windward Islands; Wine Institute; Wire Institute

W&I *Welfare and Institutions (Code)*

wia (WIA) wounded in action

WIA Western Interpreters Association

WIAB Wistar Institute of Anatomy and Biology

Wib Wibbert; Wilbert

WIB War Industries Board

WIBC Women's International Bowling Congress

wic women, infants, children

wic (WIC) war insurance corporation

WIC Welfare and Institutions Code; Women in Construction

wich sandwich

WICHE Western Interstate Commission for Higher Education

Wichitas Wichita Mountains of Oklahoma and Texas

WICI Women in Communications, Incorporated

Wick Wicklow

Wicklows Wicklow Mountains in eastern Ireland

WICP Women, Infants, and Children Program

WICS Women's Institute for Continuing Study

wid widow; widower

WID Waste Isolation Division; West India Docks

WIDF Women's International Democratic Federation

Widm *Widmung* (German—dedication)

Widow at Windsor Queen Victoria who was a widow for the last 39 years of her life

Wien (German—Vienna)

WIF West India Fruit and Steamship Company; West In-

dies Federation
wig periwig
Wig Wigtown(shire)
wige wing-on-ground effect
wigo what is going on?
Wigorn. *Wigorniensis* (Latin—of Worcester)
Wigornum (Latin—Worcester)
Wigwam Tammany Hall
wih went in hole
WIHM Wellcome Institute of the History of Medicine
WIHS Washington Irving High School
Wil Wilber; Wilbert; Wilbur; Wilburn; Wiley; Wilford; Wilfred; Wylie
WIL West India Lines
Wil Blvd Wilshire Boulevard
wilco will comply
WILD What I Like to Do (psychological test)
Wild Bill William Joseph (Wild Bill) Donovan; James Butler (Wild Bill) Hickok
Wilderness of Judah western shores of the Dead Sea in Israel
Wilderness Park Nahanni National Park (Canadian Northwest Territories)
Wilderness Trail Blazer Daniel Boone
Wilder's d novelist-playwright Thornton Wilder's dictum declaring *Who can count the prayers that have ascended to gods who do not exist? Mankind has himself created sources of help where there is no help and sources of consolation where there is no consolation.*
Wildflower State Western Australia
Wild Man of Borneo orangutan (friendliest of the great apes)
Wild Prairie Rose North Dakota state flower
Wild Rose Iowa state flower; Iowa girl's nickname
Wildrose Country Alberta
Wild West western United States
Wiley John Wiley & Sons
Wilhelm Xylander Wilhelm Holtzmann
Wilkes Land Australian Antarctica
Will Willard; William; Willis
Willa Wilhelmina
Willem De Merode Willem Eduard Keuning's pseudonym
William Ashenden W Somerset

Maugham
William B Goodrich Roscoe (Fatty) Arbuckle's pseudonym
William Bolitho William Bolitho Ryall
William the Conqueror William I of Normandy and England
William Haggard Richard Henry Michael Clayton's pseudonym
William Holden William Franklin Beedle
William of Nassau William I—Prince of Orange and Count of Nassau—founder of the Dutch Republic; also called William the Silent
William Penn's Town Philadelphia
William Sharp Fiona Macleod's pseudonym
William the Silent William—Prince of Orange
William Tell's Town Altdorf in Switzerland's Uri Canton
Willie William; W(illiam) (Willie) Somerset Maugham
Willie Mays Willie Howard Mays
Willies Good Will Industries
Will Rogers Turn Will Rogers Turnpike
Willy Wilhelm; William
Willy Brandt Herbert Ernst Karl Frahm
Wilm Wilmersdorf; Wilmington
Wilma Wilhelmina
Wilmas (Mexican-American—Wilmington, California)
Wilmington Women Correctional Institution for Women at Wilmington, Delaware
Wilno (Polish—Vilno)
WILPF Women's International League for Peace and Freedom
WILS Wisconsin Interlibrary Loan Service
Wilson HW Wilson
Wilts Wiltshire
Wilts R Wiltshire Regiment
WIM Waste Isolation Manager(s)
W I & M Washington, Idaho & Montana (railroad)
WIMA Western Industrial Medical Association; Writing Instrument Manufacturers Association
Wimb Wimborne
Wimbledon home of the Wimbledon Championship lawn-tennis competition at the All England Club in Church

Road, Wimbledon, England (a suburb of London)
w i m c whom it may concern
win. window(s)
Win Winchester Arms; Winterthur
WIN Whip Inflation Now; Work Incentive Program
WINA Webb Institute of Naval Architecture
win'ard windward
WINBAN(GA) Windward Islands Banana Growers Association
Winch Winchester
wind. windlass
W Ind West Indian; West Indies
Windau (German—Ventspils)—Baltic port
Wind Cave Wind Cave National Park in southwestern South Dakota
Wind I Windward Islands
Windward Islands Dominica, Grenada, Grenadines, Saint Lucia, Saint Vincent—all in the British West Indies
Windward Passage ocean passage between Cuba and Haiti; channel connects Atlantic Ocean with Caribbean Sea; used by many ships plying between Atlantic and Caribbean ports including the Panama Canal
Windwards Windward Islands
Windy City Chicago, Illinois and Wellington on New Zealand's South Island compete for this title
Windy Wellington Wellington, North Island, New Zealand
WINE Webb Institute of Naval Engineering
Wine-Red Sea the Aegean, according to Homer
Winesburg Sherwood Anderson's name for Clyde, a small town southwest of Sandusky, Ohio and the title of his play—*Winesburg, Ohio*
Wing Cdr Wing Commander
winkle(s) periwinkle(s)
Winn Winnipeg; Winnipegger
Winnepesaukee New Hampshire lake or river
Winnie Sir Winston Churchill—British Prime Minister
Win(nie) Winslow; Winston
wino alcoholic addicted to wine
win'rd windward (pronounced *win-urd* by sailors)
WINS Western Integrated Navigation System
wint winter; wintry

Wintergarden of the East frost-free southern Florida

Wintergarden of the Gulf lower Rio Grande Valley

Wintergarden of the West the Imperial Valley

Winterless Northland northernmost New Zealand on its North Island north of Auckland

Winter Reveries Tchaikovsky's Symphony No. 1 in G minor *(Rêverie d'Hiver)*

Winterthur Winterthur Museum

Winter Wind Chopin's Piano Etude No. 11 in A minor

Winter Wonderland British Columbia

Wint Gard Winter Garden

Winton. *Wintoniensis* (Latin—of Winchester)

Wintonia (Latin—Winchester)

wintr winter

Wint T The Winter's Tale

WIO Wyoming Infrared Observatory

wip work in process; work in progress

WIP Wage Insurance Program; West Indian Process (for sorting ripe from unripe coffee berries); Work Incentive Program; World Internationalist Party; World International Partisan

WIPAP Waste Isolation Performance Assessment Program

WIPO World Intellectual Property Organization

WIPP Waste Isolation Pilot Plant; Wool Incentive Payment Program

WIPSEP Waste Isolation Program and System Evaluation Project

WIPTC Women's International Professional Tennis Council

WIR *Weekly Intelligence Report*

WIRA Wool Industry Research Association

WIRDS Weather Information Reporting and Display System

WIRE Western Installation Requirements Evaluation (DoD); Wisconsin Information Resources for Education

Wis Wisconsin; Wisconsinite

WIS Waste Isolation System; Weizmann Institute of Science; West Indies Shipping

WISA West Indian Sugar Association; West Indies Students

Association

WISAP Waste Isolation Safety Assessment Program

Wisc Wisconsin

WISC Wechsler Intelligence Scale for Children

WISCo West Indies Sugar Company

Wisconsin Dells Dells of the Wisconsin

Wisconsin Ports (south to north to west) Racine, Milwaukee, Port Washington, Sheboygan, Manitowoc, Sturgeon Bay, Green Bay, Marinette, Ashland, Superior

WISC-R Wechsler Intelligence Scale for Children—Revised

Wisd of Sol Wisdom of Solomon (apocryphal book of the Bible)

WISE Weapon Installation System Engineering; World Information Systems Exchange; Worldwide Information System for Engineering

Wisest Man of Greece Socrates who declared it was only because he knew he knew nothing

wisk *wiskunde* (Dutch—mathematics)

Wisla (Polish—Vistula)

wisp. wide-range-imaging spectrometer

WISP Waste Isolation Systems Panel (NAS); Wisconsin Inventory of Science Processes; Women in Scholarly Publishing

WISPr *Women in Scholarly Publishing Newsletter*

Wiss *Wissenschaft* (German—science)

wit. witness

WIT West India Tankers; World International Tennis

WITCH Women's International Terrorist Conspiracy (from) Hell

Witchcraft City Salem, Massachusetts

Witch of Wall Street Hetty Green

WITCO What Is This Thing Called Opera? (Seattle opera association)

withdrl withdrawal

with(out) hype with(out) hyperbole [with(out) exaggeration]

witht without

witned witnessed

witneth witnesseth

wits *witkars* (Dutch—white cars)—drive-it-yourself two-seater electric vehicles facili-

tating clean inner-city transportation

WITS Weather Information Telemetry System; Westinghouse Interactive Time-Sharing System; West Integrated Test Stand

Wits U Witwatersrand University

wittos women in the transition of separation

Witwatersrand (Afrikaans—White Water Ridge)—gold-bearing reef running through the Transvaal in South Africa

WIU Western International University

WIVAB Womens' Inter-Varsity Athletic Board

wiz wizard

Wizard of American Drama David Belasco

Wizard from Vienna Franz Anton Mesmer

Wizard of Kinderhook Martin Van Buren—eighth President of the United States

Wizard of Menlo Park Thomas Alva Edison whose research laboratory was in Menlo Park, New Jersey

Wizard of the Saddle Lieutenant General Nathan Bedford Forrest, CSA

Wizard of Scotland Sir Walter Scott

Wizard of Tuskegee George Washington Carver

Wizard of Word Music Edgar Allan Poe

WIZO Women's International Zionist Organization

WJA World Jazz Association

wjc wife's judicial separation

WJC Westbrook Junior College

W & JC Washington and Jefferson College

WJCB World Jersey Cattle Bureau

WJCC Western Joint Computer Conference

WJFITB Wool, Jute, and Flax Industry Training Board

wk walk; warehouse keeper; weak; week; well-known; work; wreck

Wk Walk; wreck

WK Western Alaska Airlines

W-K-B Wentzel-Kramers-Brillouin

wkd worked

W-K disease Wilson-Kimmelstiel disease

wkds weekdays

wkg working

WKKC Who Killed Kennedy

Committee
wkly weekly
wkn weaken
WKNR Wadi Kziv Nature Reserve (Israel)
wkr workers; wrecker
wks weeks; works; workshop(s)
Wks Works (postal abbreviation); wreckage (navigational abbreviation)
WKSC Western Kentucky State College
wkshp workshop
Wk/Site Work Site
wkt wicket
wk vb weak verb
WKY Western Kentucky (coal company); Wall Street slang for this company is *Whiskey*
W Ky Pkwy Western Kentucky Parkway
wl wall lavatory; water level; waterline; waterplane coefficient; wavelength; working level
w L westlichst Längengrad (German—west longitude)
WL Sir Wilfred Laurier (Canada's eighth Prime Minister); Waiting List; West Lothian; Women's Liberation
W-L Westfal-Larsen Line
W & L Washington and Lee University
WL Wagon Lits (French—sleeping cars)
WLA Washington Library Association; Welsh Library Association; Western Literature Association; Wisconsin Library Association
wlb wallboard
WLB War Labor Board; Women's Liberation Party
WLB Werkgroep Instrument Beoordeling (Dutch—Working Group on Instrument Behavior); *Wilson Library Bulletin*; *Wissenschaftliche Internationale Bibliographie* (German—International Scientific Bibliography)
WLC World Liberty Corporation (Niarchos)
WL & Co Westfal-Larsen & Company (steamship line)
wl coef waterline coefficient
wld west longitude date; would
wld ch world championship
wldmt weldment
wldr welder
WLF Washington Legal Foundation; Women's Liberation Front; World Law Fund
WLFNWR William L Finley National Wildlife Refuge (Oregon)

wl fwd wool forward
WLG Wellington, New Zealand (airport)
WLGS Women's Local Government Society
WLHB Women's League of Health and Beauty
WLI Women's Law Institute; Wyoming Law Institute
WLJBP William Langer Jewel-Bearing Plant
Wlk Walk
W-L LL Washington-Lincoln Laurels for Leaders
wlm working level month
WLM Women's Liberation Movement
WLMK William Lyon Mackenzie King (Canada's eleventh, thirteenth, and fifteenth Prime Minister)
WLMO Worldwide Logistics Management Office (USA)
Wlmsbrg Brdg Williamsburgh Bridge
Wln Wellington
WLN Washington Library Network
W Long west longitude
W'loo Waterloo
W Loth West Lothian
WLP Wallops Island, Virginia (tracking station)
WLPB War Labor Policies Board
WLPS Wild Life Protection Society
WLPSA Wild Life Preservation Society of Australia
wlr wrong-length record(ing)
Wlr Walter
WLR Weekly Law Reports
WLRI World Life Research Institute
Wls Wells (postal abbreviation)
WLS Wild Life Sanctuary
WLSC West Liberty State College
WLSP World List of Scientific Periodicals
WLSR Wild Life Society of Rhodesia; World League for Sexual Reform
WLTBU Watermen, Lightermen, Tugmen, and Bargemen's Union
WLU World Liberal Union
W & LU Washington and Lee University
WLUS World Land Use Survey
WLW Women Library Workers
Wly westerly
wlz waltz
wm wattmeter; wavemeter;

white metal; winner's female; wire mesh; wordmark (flow chart)
w/m weight or measure; white male
Wm William
WM Western Maryland (railroad); White Motors; William McKinley (25th President of the U.S.); Women Marines; Worshipful Master
W & M College of William and Mary; Washburn & Moen (wire gauge)
WMA Wildlife Management Area; Women Marines Association; World Medical Association
WMAA Whitney Museum of American Art
WMAC Waste Management Advisory Council
WMARC World Maritime Administrative Radio Conference
WMATA Washington Metropolitan Area Transit Authority
WMATC Washington Metropolitan Area Transit Commission
WMB War Mobilization Board
WMBL Wrightsville Marine Biomedical Laboratory
WMC Ways and Means Committee; Western Maryland College; World Meteorological Center (WMO); World Methodist Council
WMCCA Washington Metropolitan Coalition for Clean Air
WMCE Western Montana College of Education
WMCIU Working Men's Club and Institute Union
WMcK William McKinley (25th President of the U.S.)
WMCL William Mitchell College of Law
WMCP Women's Medical College of Pennsylvania
wmd wind measuring device
Wmd Willemstad
WMD Weights and Measures Division
WMECO Western Massachusetts Electric Company
Wmg Cal Wilmington, California
Wmg, Del Wilmington, Delaware
Wmg NC Wilmington, North Carolina
WMI Webbing Manufacturers Institute; Wildlife Manage-

ment Institute

W Mid West Midlands

wmk watermark

w/m°k watt per meter degree kelvin (thermal conductivity unit)

WMM World Movement of Mothers

WMMA Woodworking Machinery Manufacturers' Association

Wmn Wilmington, North Carolina

WMNF White Mountain National Forest

WMO World Meteorological Organization

WMOAS Women's Migration and Overseas Appointments Society

W of Mormon Words of Mormon

wmp with much pleasure (the invitation is accepted)

WMR Wasatch Mountain Railway

WMS Waste Management System; Webster Memory Scale; Women in Medical Service; Women's Medical Specialist; Work Measurement System; World Magnetic Survey

W & MS Wisconsin & Michigan Steamship (company)

WMS Willem Mengelberg Stichting (Dutch—Willem Mengelberg Foundation)

WMSC Women's Medical Specialist Corps

W & M SS Co Wisconsin & Michigan Steamship Company

wmt weighing more than

WMT Wilson Marine Transit

WMTB Western Motor Tariff Bureau

WMTC Women's Mechanized Transport Corps

Wmth Westmeath

WMU Western Michigan University

WMUSE World Markets for US Exports

W M W & NW Weatherford, Mineral Wells & Northwestern (railroad)

WMWR Wichita Mountains Wildlife Refuge (Oklahoma)

w/n well-nourished

WN Worlds of Nature (Amarillo botanical and zoological gardens)

WN Weekly Notes

WNA Washington, DC, National Airport; winter North Atlantic (loadline marking for ships voyaging across the North Atlantic in winter)

WNAP Washington National Airport

wnb will not be

WNBA Women's National Book Association

WnBanc Western Bancorporation

wndml windmill

WNDO Weather Network Duty Officer

wndp with no down payment

WNE Welsh National Eisteddfod

wng warning

WNGA Wholesale Nursery Growers of America

wnl within normal limits

WNLF Women's National Liberal Federation

wnm white noise making

WNM Washington National Monument

WNMC Weather Network Management Center (USAF)

WNNP Walpole-Nornalup National Park (Western Australia)

WNO Welsh National Opera

WNP Wankie National Park (Rhodesia); Warrumbungle NP (New South Wales); Welsh National Party; Westland NP (South Island, New Zealand); Wilpattu NP (Ceylon); Wyperfeld NP (Victoria, Australia)

WNRE Whiteshell Nuclear Research Establishment

WNS Washington National Symphony (District of Columbia); Women's News Service

WNSB White Nile Scheme Board (Sudanese cotton production)

WNW west northwest

WNW west noordwest (Dutch—west northwest)

WNWDA Welsh National Water Development Authority

WNWR Wapanocca National Wildlife Refuge (Arkansas); Washita NWR (Oklahoma); Wheeler NWR (Alabama); Willapa NWR (Washington)

WNY West New York, NJ

WNYNRC Western New York Nuclear Research Center

WNYNSC Western New York Nuclear Service Center

wo wait order; water-in-oil (emulsion); *wie oben*(German —as previously mentioned); without; work order; write out; written order

wo' war; wore

w/o without

WO War Office; Warrant Officer; Welsh Office

WO World Oil

WOA Wharf Owners' Association

wob washed overboard

Wobblies International Workers of the World (so named because Chinese members pronounced IWW as *I Wobbly Wobbly*)

wobndr(s) without binder(s)

wobo(s) without blowout(s)

Wobs Wobblies

woc without compensation

WOCCI War Office Central Card Index

wocg weather outline contour generator

WOCL War Office Casualty List

W & O D Washington & Old Dominion (railroad)

WODA World Dredging Association

WODECO Western Offshore Drilling and Exploration Company

Woden (Anglo-Saxon—Odin or Wotan)—supreme god of the Nordic or Norse gods

woe. without equipment

Woe Woensdag(Dutch—Wednesday)

WOFIWU World Federation of Industrial Workers Unions

wofttngs without fittings

wog golliwog; polliwog; water or gas (valve); white overgrown gibbon (epithetic abbreviation for a white racist); wily oriental gentleman [a confidence man, extortionist, loan shark, or pimp from Egypt, India, Sri Lanka, Burma, Thailand, Malaysia, Indo-China (Cambodia, Laos, Vietnam), Indonesia, or Papua New Guinea]; with other goods

'wog golliwog; polliwog

WOG Wily Oriental Gentleman (nickname applied to Farouk I of Egypt and similar monarchs of the area)

WOGA Western Oil and Gas Association

wogs (British slang—wily oriental gentlemen; wily oriental peoples)

WOGSC World Organization of General Systems and Cybernetics

woh work on hand

WOHC Warrant Officer, Hospital Corps

WOIS Wisconsin Occupational Information System

WOJG Warrant Officer, Junior Grade

WOK Warren O Kessler

wol wharf owners' liability

WOL War Office Letter

Wolf Wolfgang; Wolfmar; Wolfrad; Wolfram; Wolfred

Wolf House Jack London's home in Glen Ellen, California

Wolf Island, Galápagos Wenman

wolfram iron manganese tungstate

Wolfs Wolfson College, Oxford

Wolga (German—Volga)

Wolverine fierce Michigan mammal often serving as a symbolic nickname for a Michiganite

Wolverine State Michigan's official nickname

wom wireless operator mechanic

WOM Woomera, Australia (tracking station)

WOMAN World Organization of Mothers of All Nations

Woman With The Whip Evita Perón

Womb of Nations Scandinavia

Women's Lib Women's Liberation Movement

womi women on words and images

womlib women's liberation

won. wool on needle (knitting)

W-o-N Walton-on-Naze

WONARD Women's Organization of the National Association of Retail Druggists

Wonder City of the World New York

Wonder State Arkansas

wong weight on nose gear

won't will not

WOO Western Operations Office (NASA); World Oceanographic Organization

Wood Woodbine; Woodbridge; Woodburn; Woodbury; Woodfield; Woodfin; Woodhill; Woodley; Woodrow; Woodruff; Woodson; Woodville; Woodward; Woodworth

wood alcohol methyl alcohol (CH$_3$OH)

Wood Buffalo Wood Buffalo National Park in northern Alberta

Wooden Leg Governor Peter Stuyvesant of Nieuw Amsterdam

Woodie Woodmansee; Woodrow

Woodland Capital Boise, Idaho

Woodlawn New York City's celebrated cemetery containing many of its former celebrities

woodpile xylophone's nickname

Woodstein Bob Woodward and Carl Bernstein (of the *Washington Post* and best known for uncovering the Watergate coverup)

Woody Woodrow

Woody Allen Allen Stewart Konigsberg

Woody Herman Woodrow Wilson Herman

woof (cartoonist's language—dog's bark)

woof(s) woofer(s)

Wool *Woolworth's* (Circuit Court Reports)

Wool and Mohair Capital of the West Del Rio, Texas

Woolwich Royal Arsenal at Woolwich on the south bank of the Thames near London

woool words out of ordinary language

Woo Poo cadet's nickname for West Point

Wooster(sheer) (British contraction—Worcestershire)

wop. with other property; without (immigration) papers; without personnel

wopar(s) without partition(s)

wope without personnel or equipment

WOPN Women Officers Professional Network

WOQT Warrant Officer Qualification Test

wor without our responsibility

Wor Worshipful

worbat wartime order of battle

Worc Worcester (pronounced *Wooster*) College (Oxford or elsewhere)

WORC Washington Operations Research Council

Worc Coll Worcester College—Oxford

Worc Reg Worcester Regiment

Worcs Worcestershire (*Woostersheer*)

Word King New-Zealand-born British lexicographer Eric Partridge

word proc word processor (device, program, or system allowing electronic correcting, editing, and writing of articles, books, and reference works such as the *Abbreviations Dictionary*)

Words Wordsworth

WORDS Western Operational Research Discussion Society

words/min words per minute

words/sec words per second

WORK Wanted Older Residents (with) Knowhow

Work. Comp Workmen's Compensation

Workers' Paradise derisive nickname applied to the communist-controlled USSR whose propaganda led many people to believe it was the workers' paradise

workfare working for welfare (alternative to high-cost-assistance welfare)

workh workhouse

Workmen's Workmen's Circle; Workmen's Compensation

Workshop of the Orient Japan

World *World Almanac*

World Bank International Bank for Reconstruction and Development (IBRD)

World's Workshop productive nations such as Germany, Great Britain, Japan, and the United States often bear this title

World War Photographer Edward Steichen

Wormald Wormald International Security

Wormwood Scrubs large prison in a suburb of the same name in northwestern London

WORSAMS Worldwide Organization Structure for Army Medical Support

worse word selection

WOS Washington Opera Society; Wilson Ornithological Society

wosac worldwide synchronization of atomic clocks

WOSB War Operations Selection Board

WOSD Weapon Operational Systems Development

WOSL Women's Overseas Service League

wot wide-open throttle

WOTAG Women's Taxation Action Group

Wotan (Old High German—Odin or Woden)—chief of the Norse gods

W-o-t-N Walton-on-the-Naze

wott wolves on the track (prowling males)

wouldn't would not

W & O V Washington & Ouachita Valley (railroad)

wow waiting on weather

w-o-w worst-on-worst (worst on top of the worst possible disaster, etc.)

W o W War on Want

WOW Wider Opportunities for Women; Woodmen of the World

w/o wn without winch

wp waste package; waste pipe; water repellency; water repellent; way point; weather permitting; white phosphorus; will proceed; working paper; working party; working point; working pressure

wp (WP) word processing; word processor (machine capable of storing information and then retyping it pursuant to your instructions)

w-p waterproofed

w/p without prejudice

w/p (W/P) withdrawing and passing; withdrawn/passed

Wp Worship(ful)

WP War Plan(s); Warsaw Pact; Western Pacific (railroad); West Point; West Virginia Pulp and Paper (stock exchange symbol); Worthington Pump; Worthy Patriarch

WP *Wiener Philharmoniker* (German—Vienna Philharmonic Orchestra); *Winkler Prins Encyclopedieen* (Dutch —Winkler Prins Encyclopedia)

wpa with particular average

WPA Western Pine Association; Western Psychological Association; William Penn Association; Women's Prison Association; Works Progress Administration; World Parliament Association; World Psychiatric Association

WPAFB Wright-Patterson Air Force Base

WPA & H Women's Prison Association and Home

wpar(s) with partition(s)

WPAS Work Package Authorization System

wpb wastepaper basket

WPB War Plan Basic; War Production Board (World War II)

WPBA Western Power Boat Association

WPBIC Walker Problem Behavior Identification Checklist

WPBL Women's Professional Basketball League

WPBS Welsh Plant Breeding Station

wpc water pollution control; watts per candle; wood plastic combination; world planning chart

WPC Washington Press Club; William Penn College; Women's Press Club; World Peace Council

WPCA Water Pollution Control Act

WPCC Wage and Price Control Council; Western Pharmaceutical and Chemical Corporation

WPCF Water Pollution Control Federation

WPD Work Package Department (ONWI)

wpe white porcelain enamel

WPEC World Plan Executive Council

w/p equipment word-processing equipment

WPF World Peace Foundation

WPFC Western Pacific Fisheries Commission

Wpfl Worshipful

wpg waterproofing

WPg West Point graduate

WPG gunboat (3-letter USCG symbol)

WPGA Wisconsin Personnel and Guidance Association; Wyoming Personnel and Guidance Association

WPGR Willem Pretorius Game Reserve (South Africa)

WPHC Western Pacific High Commissioner

WPHI Western Pennsylvania Horological Institute

wpi wholesale price index

WPI Wall Paper Institute; Western Psychiatric Institute (Pittsburgh); Worcester Polytechnic Institute; World Press Institute; Waxed Paper Institute

WPI *World Port Index*

W pk Ward's (mechanical tissue) pack

wpl warning point level

WPL Weapons Propulsion Laboratory; Wichita Public Library; Winnipeg Public Library; Worcester Public Library

WPLC Wisconsin Power and Light Company

WPLO Water Port Liaison Office(r)

wpm words per minute

WPMSF World Professional Marathon Swimming Federation

wpn weapon

WPN West Penn Traction (stock exchange symbol)

WPN *World Press News*

wpns weapons

WPO Water Programs Office (Environmental Protection Agency); Wiener Philharmonic Orchester (Vienna Philharmonic Orchestra); World Ploughing Organization

WPOD Water Port of Debarkation

WPOE Water Port of Embarkation

wpp waterproof paper packing

WPP West Penn Power Company; Witness Protection Program; Work Package Plan(ning)

WPPC West Penn Power Company

WPPDA Welfare and Pension Plans Disclosure Act

WPPO Work Package Program Office(r)

WPPP Work Package Program Plan(ning)

WPPSI Wechsler Preschool and Primary Scale of Intelligence

WPPSS Washington Public Power Supply System

wp & r work-planning-and-review (discussions)

WPRA Wallpower and Paint Retailers' Association; Waste Paper Recovery Association; Women's Professional Rodeo Association

WPRL Water Pollution Research Laboratory

wpr's wartime personnel requirements

WPRS Wittenborn Psychiatric Rating Scale

wps with prior service; words per second

WPs Warsaw Pact members; Warsaw Pact nations

WPS Waveform Processing System; Wildlife Preservation Society; Wildlife Preserve Society; World Peanut Syndicate; World Porpoise Society

WPSA World's Poultry Science Association

WPSL Western Primary Standard Laboratory

WPSP White People's Socialist Party (racist subversives)

WPT Windfall Profits Tax

WPTB Wartime Prices and Trade Board

WPTF World Peace Tax Fund

wpu with power unit; write punch

wpwod will proceed without delay

W-P-W syndrome Wolff-Parkinson-White syndrome

WPY World Population Year (1974)

WP & Y White Pass & Yukon (railroad)

WP & YR White Pass & Yukon Route

WPZ Woodland Park Zoo (Seattle)

wq water quench

WQA Water Quality Association

WQCB Water Quality Control Board

WQF Wider Quaker Fellowship

wr war risk; write (flow chart); write out

w/r water and rail; water resistant

w & r water and rail; welfare and recreation

Wr Walter

WR Ward Room; War Reserve; Wassermann Reaction; Western (railway) Region; West Riding

WR *Weekly Reporter*

W.R. *Wilhelmus Rex* (Latin— King Wilhelm, King William)

WRA War Relocation Authority; Water Research Association; Western Railway of Alabama; Winchester Repeating Arms (company)

WRA *Water Resources Abstracts*

WRAAC Women's Royal Australian Army Corps

WRAAF Women's Royal Australian Air Force

WRAC Women's Royal Army Corps

wraceld wounds received in action combat with enemy or in line of duty

WRAF Women's Royal Air Force

WRAIN Walter Reed Army Institute of Nursing

WRAIR Walter Reed Army Institute of Research

WRAMA Warner-Robins Air Material Area

WRAMC Walter Reed Army Medical Center

WRANS Women's Royal Australian Naval Service

WRAP Weapons Readiness Analysis Program; Weighted Record Analysis Program

WRAT Wide-Range Achievement Test

WRB War Refugee Board; Water Resources Board

WRBC Weather Relay Broad-

cast System

wrc water-retention coefficient

WRC Water Research Center; Water Resources Commission; Weather Relay Center; Welding Research Council

wrcr wife's restitution of conjugal rights

WRCUP Western Region Canadian University Press

WRDC Western Rural Development Center; Westinghouse Research and Development Center

WRE Weapons Research Establishment (Woomera, Australia)

Wreckers Coast England's Cornish coast, Florida's east coast, North Carolina's Outer Banks around Nag's Head, other coasts where wreckers profit from shipwrecks

WREE Women for Racial and Economic Equality

WREEC Western Regional Environmental Education Council

w ref with reference

w reg with regard (to)

WREN Women's Royal Naval Service

wresat weapons research establishment satellite

W-response whole response

WRF World Rehabilitation Fund

wrfg wharfage

WRGH Walter Reed General Hospital

WRH Walter Reed Hospital

WRHS Western Reserve Historical Society

wri war risk insurance

WRI War Resisters' International; Weatherstrip Research Institute; Wellcome Research Institute; Wire Reinforcement Institute; Wire Rope Institute

WRI *World Research INK* (monthly publication)

WRIR Walter Reed Institute of Research

WRIT Waste-Rock Interactions Technology (program)

wrk work (flow chart)

Wrk Workington

WR Knottman (abbreviated signature—we are not man and wife)—appears on the pages of many hotel and motel registers

wrkshp workshop

wrl wing reference line

WRL Wantage Research Laboratory; War Readiness Materi-

al; War Resisters League; Westinghouse Research Laboratories; Willow Run Laboratories (University of Michigan)

WRLC World Role of Law Center (Duke University)

wrm war readiness materiel

WRM Wasatch Railway Museum

wrmn wireman

WRMT Woodcock Reading Mastery Test

wrn wool round needle (knitting)

WRNGA William Rockhill Nelson Gallery of Art (Kansas City)

WRNR Women's Royal Naval Reserve

WRNS Women's Royal Naval Service

wrnt warrant

WRNWR White River National Wildlife Refuge (Arkansas)

wro war risk only

WRO Weed Research Organization

Wroclaw Polish name for its seaport once called Breslau by the Germans who developed it when it was part of East Prussia

WRP Workers' Revolutionary Party (British Trotskyite communists)

WRPA Water Resources Planning Act

WRPC Weather Records Processing Center(s)

WRRA Women's Road Records Association (cycling)

WRRC Willow Run Research Center

WRRI Water Resources Research Institute

WRRR Walter Reed Research Reactor

WRRS Wire Relay Radio System

wrs war reserve stock(s)

WRS Warning and Report(ing) System; Worldwide Reference Sources

WRSA Western Regional Science Association

WRSIC Water Resources Scientific Information Center

wrsk war-readiness spares kit

WRSP *World Register of Scientific Periodicals*

wrt wrought

wrtd warranted

WRTF Waste Retrieval and Treatment Facility

wrtr writer

wru who are you?

WRU Western Reserve University

wrv water relief valve

WRVS Women's Royal Voluntary Service

WRVT Wide-Range Vocabulary Test

wr(w) war reserve (weapon)

WRX Western Refrigerator Express (railroad code)

WRY World Refugee Year

W Ry A Western Railway of Alabama

WR Yorks West Riding, Yorkshire

ws water supply; weather station; working space; working storage

w/s weapon system; weather ship

w & s whiskey and soda

WS Wallops Station (NASA); Ware Shoals; Warner & Swasey; weapon system(s); Western Samoa; West Saxon(y); West Sussex; Wilderness Society; Wildlife Society; windspeed; Writer to the Signet (Scottish lawyer)

WS Wiener Stadtbibliothek (German—Vienna State Library)

W S Washington Star

wsa weapons system analysis

WSA Weed Society of America; Worker-Student Alliance

WSA Wasser und Schiffahrtsampt (German—Water and Ship Canal Authority)

WSAC West of Scotland Agricultural College

WSAD Weapon System Analysis Division (USN)

WSAG Washington Special Action Group (personnel in Situation Room in White House basement)

W Sam Western Samoa

WSAO Weapon System Analysis Office

WSAP Weighted Sensitivity Analysis Program (EPA)

WSAVA World Small Animal Veterinary Association

wsb water-soluble base; wheat-soy blend; will send boat

WSB Wharton School of Business(U of P); World Scout Bureau

WSBA Wyoming School Boards Association

wsc weapon system contractor

WSC Western Simulation Council; Western Society of Criminology; Winona State College; Winston Spencer Churchill; Wisconsin State College; Writing Services Center

WSCC Western State College of Colorado

WSCF World Student Christian Federation

Wschr Wochenschrift (German —weekly magazine)

WSCS Woman's Society for Christian Service

wsd working stress design

wsdb world studies data bank

WSDC Women's Self-Defense Council

WSDL Weapons System Development Laboratory

WSEC Washington State Electronics Council

WSECL Weapon System Equipment Component List

wsed weapon system electrical diagram(s)

WSED Weapon Systems Evaluation Division

WSEG Weapons Systems Evaluation Group

WSEL Weapons System Engineering Laboratory

WSEP Waste Solidification Engineering Prototype Plant (AEC); Weapon System Evaluation Program

WSET Writers and Scholars Educational Trust

wsev (WSEV) winged surface-effect vehicle

WSF Washington State Ferries; Western Sea Frontier; Women's Strike for Peace; World Sephardic Federation

WSFI Water Softener and Filter Institute

WSFR Worcestershire and Sherwood Foresters Regiment

wsg worthiest soldier in the group

WSG Wesleyan Service Guild; Wire Service Guild

WSGE Western Society of Gear Engineers

WSHS Wisconsin State Historical Society

WSI Writers and Scholars International

WSJ Wall Street Journal

WSL Warren Spring Laboratory; Washington State Library

WSLF Western Somali Liberation Front (communist)

WSLO Weapon System Logistics Office(r)

Wsm Wesermünde

WSM Weapon System Manager; W Somerset Maugham

WSM Weapon System Manual

WSMAC Weapon System Maintenance Action Center

WSMC Western States Movers Conference

WSMO Weapon System Materiel Office(r)

WSMR White Sands Missile Range

WSMSA Washington Standard Metropolitan Statistical Area

WSNM White Sands National Monument

WSO Warrant Stores Office(r); Weapon System Office(r); Western Support Office (NASA); Wichita Symphony Orchestra; World Simulation Organization

WSO Wiener Symphonisches Orchester (German—Vienna Symphony Orchestra)

WSOC Wider Share Ownership Council

wsp water supply point; working steam pressure

WSP Women Strike for Peace; Work Study Program; Work Systems Package (naval salvage device); Work Systems Program; Wyoming State Parks

WSPACS Weapon System Program and Control System

WSPB Western Society of Business Publications

WS Pen Washington State Penitentiary

WSPG White Sands Proving Ground

WSPL Winston-Salem Public Library

WSPO Weapon System Project Officer

WSPOP Weapon System Phase-Out Procedure

WSPU Women's Social and Political Union

wsr (WSR) weapon system reliability

w/sr watt(s) per steradian

Wsr Wesermünde

W & S R Warren & Saline River (railroad)

WS & RB Washington Surveying and Rating Bureau

WSRI World Safety Research Institute

w/srm² watt(s) per steradian square meter

WSS Warfare Systems School; Winston-Salem Southbound (railroad); World Ship Society

WSSA Weapon System Support Activities; World Secret Service Association

WSSC Weapon System Support Center

WSSCA White Sands Signal Corps Agency

WSSO Winston-Salem Symphony Orchestra

WSSS Weapon System Storage Site

WSSSP Western States Small Schools Projects

WSS & YP White Sulphur Springs & Yellowstone Park (railroad)

WST Whitworth Standard Thread

WSTA Washington State Trustees Association; White Slave Traffic Act

WSTC Winston-Salem Teachers College

WSTF White Sands Test Facility (NASA)

WSTI Waterbury State Technical Institute; Welded Steel Tube Institute

WSTNRA Whiskeytown-Shasta-Trinity National Recreation Area (California)

WSU Washington State University; Wayne State University; Western State University

w sup water supply

W Sus West Sussex

WSUSM Wayne State University School of Medicine

WSV Wiener Stadwerke Verkehrsbetriebe (Vienna transportation system)

wsw white sidewall (tires)

WSW west southwest

WSWA Wine and Spirits Wholesalers of America

WSWL Warheads and Special Weapons Laboratory

WSWMA Western States Weights and Measures Association

WSWS Wexford Slobs Wildfowl Sanctuary (Ireland)

wt watch time; waterproof(ed); waterproofing, watertight; weight; withholding tax (WT)

wt % weight percent

w/t wireless telegraph(y)

w/t (W/T) walkie/talkie

w & t wear and tear

WT war time; wealth tax; winterization test; withholding tax

W & T Wrightsville & Tennille (railroad)

WTA Washington Technological Associates; Women's Tennis Association; World Transport Agency

WTAA World Trade Alliance Association

WTAU Women's Total Abstinence Union

w/tax withholding tax

Wtb Whitby

Wtb *Wörterbuch* (German—dictionary)

WTBA Washington Toll Bridge Authority; Water-Tube Boilermakers' Association

WTB & TS Watchtower Bible and Tract Society (Jehovah's Witnesses)

WTC World Tanker Corporation (Niarchos); World Trade Center; World Trade Commission

wtchmn watchman

wtd watertight door

WTD *World Trade Directory*

WTDAOT What to Do About Old Town

WTE World Tapes for Education

Wt Eng Warrant Engineer

wtf will to fire

Wtf Waterford

WTFDA Worldwide TV-FM-DX Association

WTFP Wolf Trap Farm Park (Vienna, Virginia)

WTG *Welt-Tierärztegesellschaft* (German—World Veterinary Association)

wthr weather

WTIC World Trade Information Center

WTIS World Trade Information Service

WTJ *Westminster Theological Journal*

WTL Wyle Test Laboratories

wtm write tape mark

WTMA West Texas Museum Association

wtmh watertight manhole

WTNR Wadi Tabor Nature Reserve (Israel)

WTO Warsaw Treaty Organization; World Tourism Organization

Wt Ofcr Warrant Officer

w/t office wireless/telegraph office (aboard ships in the 1920s became the radio room)—the radio shack

WTP Weapons Testing Program

wtqad watertight quick-acting door

wtr waiter; winter; writer

Wtr Water (postal abbreviation)

WTR Western Test Range (formerly Pacific Missile Range)

WTRC Wool Textile Research Council

wtrz winterize

wtrzn winterization

wts word terminal synchronous

WTS Watchtower Society; Women's Transport Service

WTSC West Texas State College

wtspt waterspout

WTTA Wholesale Tobacco Trade Association

WTU Washington Theological Union

WTUC World Trade Union Conference

wu work unit

WU Washington University; Weather Underground Organization; Wesleyan University; Western Union; Wilberforce University; Wittenberg University

W/U Western Union

WUA Western Underwriters Association

wuaa wartime unit aircraft activity

WUAA Wartime Unit Aircraft Activity

wuc work unit code

WUCM Work Unit Code Manual

WUCOS Western European Union Chiefs of Staff

WUCT World Union of Catholic Teachers

WUCWO World Union of Catholic Women's Organizations

WUD Water Utility Department

WUDO Western European Defense Organization

WUF World Underwater Federation; World Union of Free Thinkers

WUI Western Union International

WUIS Work Unit Information System

WUJS World Union of Jewish Students

Wuli Xuebao (Acta Phys Sin) *Acta Physica Sinica* (Chinese Journal of Physics)

WULTUO World Union of Liberal Trade Union Organizations

WUM Women's Universal Movement

WUMP(S) White Urban Middleclass Protestant(s)

WUNS World Union of National Socialists

WUO Weather Underground Organization

WUOSY World Union of Organizations for Safeguarding Youth

Wupatki Wupatki National Monument in northern Arizona

WUPJ World Union for Progressive Judaism

WUPO World Union of Pythagorean Organizations

Wurst City in the World Sheboygan, Wisconsin, where making sausage is a specialty

WUS Western United States; World University Service

WUSL Women's United Service League

WUSM Washington University School of Medicine

wut warmup time

WUT Washburn University of Topeka

wuts work-unit time standard

WUX Western Union (teleprinter) Exchange

Wuxi (Pinyin Chinese—Wuhsi)

wv wall vent; whispered voice; wind velocity; with view (room with view)

w/v weight in volume

WV West Virginia Pulp and Paper Company

W Va West Virginia; West Virginian

WVA World Veterinary Association; Wyoming Vocational Association

WVAESP West Virginia Association of Elementary School Principals

WVAS Wake-Vortex Avoidance System

W Va Turn West Virginia Turnpike

WVa U Lib West Virginia University Library

WVAWRD West Virginia Water Resources Division

WVC Wenatchee Valley College

wvd waived

WVD Werelverbond van Diamantbewerkers (Dutch—World Alliance of Diamond Workers)

wvdc working voltage—direct current

WVEA West Virginia Educational Association

wveh wheel(ed) vehicle

wvem water-vapor electrolysis module

WVF World Veterans' Federation

WVFIC West Virginia Foundation for Independent Colleges

WVIT West Virginia Institute of Technology

WVL Warfare Vision Laboratory (USA)

WVLA West Virginia Library Association

WVMA Women's Veterinary Medical Association

Wvn Wivenhoe

W V N West Virginia Northern (railroad)

WVPA World Veterinary Poultry Association

WVRB West Virginia Rating Bureau

WVRO World Vision Relief Organization

WVS Women's Voluntary Service

WVSBA West Virginia School Boards Association

WVSC West Virginia State College; Wisconsin Vocational Studies Center

WVSP West Virginia State Police

WVSSPC West Virginia Secondary School Principal's Commission

wvt water vapor transfer; water vapor transmission

WVT Watervliet Arsenal

wvtr water vapor transmission rate

w/vu with view

WVU West Virginia University

WVWC West Virginia Wesleyan College

ww warehouse warrant; water white; waterworks; wirewound; wrong word

w/w wall-to-wall (carpet, floor covering, linoleum, tile); weight for weight

ww werkwoord (Dutch—verb)

Ww Witwe (German—widow)

WW Walworth (trademark); Woodmen of the World; Woodrow Wilson (28th President of the U.S.); world war; world wide

W-W Winchester-Western

W & W Waynesburg & Western (railroad); Winchester & Western (railroad)

WW Who's Who

WW I World War I (1914–1918)

WWIVM World War I Victory Medal

WW II World War II (1939–1945)

WWIIHSLB World War II Honorable Service Lapel Button (often called the Ruptured Duck)

WWIIVM World War II Victory Medal

wwa with the will annexed

WWA Western Writers of America

WWABNCP Worldwide Airborne Command Post (USAF)

wwap worldwide asset position

WWB Walt Whitman Bridge

WWBA Walt Whitman Birthplace Association; Western Wooden Box Association

wwc wall-to-wall carpeting

WWC Walla Walla College; Warren Wilson College; William Woods College; World Weather Centers (Melbourne, Moscow, Washington, D.C.)

WWCP Walking Wounded Collecting Post

WWCTU World's Women's Christian Temperance Union

wwd weather working days; windward

WWD Women's Wear Daily

WWDC World War Debt Commission

W Wdr Warrant Wardmaster

wwdShex weather working days Sundays and holidays excluded

Wwe Weduwe (Dutch—widow); *Witwe* (German—widow)

WWF Welder Wildlife Foundation; Woodrow Wilson Foundation; World Wildlife Fund

WWG World Wildlife Guide

WWHS Wilbur Wright High School; Woodrow Wilson High School

wwi whirlwind computer

WWI Weight Watchers International; World Watch Institute

WWIB Western Weighing and Inspection Bureau

WWICS Woodrow Wilson International Center for Scholars

wwio worldwide inventory objective

WWJC Western Wyoming Junior College

WWM WW Morrow

WWMB Woodrow Wilson Memorial Bridge

WWMC Woodrow Wilson Memorial Commission

WWMCCS Worldwide Military Command and Control System

WWMMP Western Wood Moulding and Millwork Producers

w/wn with winch

W Wnd Drft West Wind Drift

(Antartic)

WWNFF Woodrow Wilson National Fellowship Foundation

WWNSSS World-Wide Network of Standard Seismograph Stations

WWNT West Wales Naturalists Trust

w/wo with or without

WWO Wing Warrant Officer; World Weather Organization

wwp water wall peripheral; working water pressure; write without program

WWP Washington Water Power company; Workers World Party (leftwing)

WWPA Western Wood Products Association; World Wide Philatelic Agency

WWR Washington Week in Review (educational television)

ww's walla wallas (Hong Kong harbour launches)

WWSA Walt Whitman Society of America

WWSC Western Washington State College

WWSN World-wide Seismology Net (NBS)

WWSPIA Woodrow Wilson School of Public and International Affairs (Princeton University)

wwss water wall side skegs

WWSSN World Wide Standardized Seismograph Network

WWSU World Water Ski Union

wwt whitewall tires

WWTP Waste Water Treating Process

W W V call letters of United States Bureau of Standards worldwide radio time signal; Walla Walla Valley (railroad)

WWVH World Wide Time (US Bureau of Standards, Hawaii)

WWW World Weather Watch

WWW Who Was Who

WWWF Worldwide Wrestling Federation

WWWV Women World War Veterans

WWWVA Wild, Wonderful West Virginia

WWWW Women Who Want to be Women

WWWW Worldwide What & Where—geographic glossary and traveller's guide

wwwwh who, what, when, where, why, how (many or much)—reporters' mnemonic for encompassing elements of a news story

WWY Warwickshire and Worcestershire Yeomanry

wx watts second; waxy; weather report

Wx weather; Wilcox (formation)

wxb wax bite

WXD meteorological radar station

wxg warning

wxp wax pattern

wy wey (14 pounds of wool)

Wy Way; Wyatt; Wycliffe

Wy Wy-dit-Joli-Village (French —Wy called Pretty Village)— near Paris

WY West Yorkshire

Wya Whyalla

WYACL World Youth Anti-Communist League

wyaio will you accept (the position) if offered

Wyantskill Wyantskill Center for (delinquent) Girls at Wyantskill, New York

Wyc Wycliffe; Wycliffe College

WYC Washington Yacht Club; Winthrop Yacht Club

WYCF World Youth Crusade for Freedom

Wycl Wycliffe

wye Y (as in wye circuit)

WYF World Youth Forum

wyo what's your opinion

Wyo Wyoming; Wyomingite

Wyoming Suffragette Esther Hobart Morris

W Yorks West Yorkshire

WYR West Yorkshire regiment

WZ Welt Zeit (German—world time)

WZO World Zionist Organization

WZOA Women's Zionist Organization of America

WZW west zuidwest (Dutch west southwest)

X

x an abscissa (symbol); an unknown quantity (symbol); any point on a great circle; cross; cross reactance (symbol); exchange; execute(d); extra; frost; gang territorial mark(er) or place where one gang will fight another; mole ratio; no-wind distance; parallactic angle; specific acoustic reactance; universal symbol standing for things as diverse as hoarfrost in meteorological reports, a kiss, a mechanical defect, a motion picture not suitable for viewing by minors, the spot the body was found or the crime was committed (*x* marks the spot), the position of a craft or map, the signature of the illiterate (her or his mark); by (used between dimensional figures as in 3 × 5 file card)

X longitudinal axis

X-2 counterintelligence

X-15 rocket-propelled research aircraft

X 17 mortality table

xa chiasma; transmission adapter

XA Crucible Steel (stock exchange symbol); experimental (USAF symbol)

xaam experimental air-to-air missile

xact exact(ly); X (in any computer) automatic code translation

XAE merchant ammunition ship (3-letter naval symbol)

xafh X-band antenna feed horn

Xaintong (Old French—Saintonge)

XAK merchant cargo ship (3-letter naval symbol)

XAKc merchant coastal cargo ship, small (3-letter naval symbol)

xal xenon arc lamp

Xalapa Jalapa

Xalisco Jalisco

Xalostoc San Cosme Xalostoc, Tlaxcala, Mexico

Xaltocan San Martin Xaltocan, Tlaxcala, Mexico

XAM merchant ship converted to minesweeper (3-letter naval symbol)

x-a mix. xylene-alcohol mixture (insect larva killer)

x-a mixture xylene-alcohol mixture

xan xanthic; xanthine; yellow

Xan Xanthe; Xanthian; Xanthippe; Xanthus

Xana Xanadu

Xanadu Xamdu (city where Kubla Khan lived and name given the Hearst Castle at San Simeon, California by Orson Welles)

xanth xanthoma(tosis)

Xantip Xantippe (archetype of the scolding termagent shrew as she was the peevish wife of Socrates)

XAP merchant transport (3-letter naval symbol)

XAPc merchant coastal transport, small (3-letter naval symbol)

x arm cross arm

XAS X-band Antenna System

xasm experimental air-to-surface missile (XASM)

xat X-ray analysis trial

Xav Xaver; Xavier; Xaviera

XAV auxiliary seaplane tender (3-letter naval symbol)

Xavante Aermacchi jet-trainer ground-attack aircraft also designated AT-26

Xavier Joseph Xavier Boniface's nom de plume

Xavier Mayne Edward Irenaeus Stevenson

X-axis horizontal axis on a chart, graph, or map

Xaymayca (Arawak—Land of Woods and Streams)—Jamaica

xb crossbar; exploding bridge-wire

XB experimental bomber

xbag excess baggage

Xbal Cristobal

X-band 5,200–10,900 mc

xbar crossbar

X bear grizzly bear (abbreviation appearing on many American frontier epitaphs: "killed by an X bear")

Xber December

xbr experimental breeder reactor

X-bracing cross bracing

X^{bre} *décembre* (French—December)

xbt expendable bathythermograph

xbts exhibits

xc cross country; ex coupon; X-chromosome

X-c X-chromosome

X_c capacitive reactance

XC experimental cargo aircraft (naval symbol); Xavierian College

Xca Xcalac, Quintana Roo, México

xcar from the railroad car

XCG experimental cargo glider (naval symbol)

xch exchange

xchgr exchanger

X-chromosome female-producing gene found in male sperm

xcit excitation

X-City site of UN Headquarters along New York's East River between 42nd and 49th streets

xcl excess current liabilities

XCL armed merchant cruiser (naval symbol)

xclu exclusive; exclusivity

xconn cross connection

xcp without coupon

XCR Extraterrestrial Research Center

X-craft midget submarines

xcs cross-country skiing

xct X-band communications transponder

xcu excuse; extra-care unit

xc & uc exclusive of covering and uncovering

xcvr transceiver

x cy cross country

xd ex dividend

x'd executed

X'd crossed out

XD Executive Development

X-day launching day

xdcr transducer

xder transducer

xdf X-band flow detection

X & DFLOT Experimental and Development Flotilla

xdh xanthine dehydrogenase

xdis ex distribution (without distribution)

xdiv without dividend

X division branch of society consisting of swindlers and thieves

x'd out crossed out

xdp X-ray density probe; X-ray diffraction powder

xdpc X-ray diffraction powder camera

xdps X-band diode phase shifter

xdr expanded dynamic range; transducer

Xdr Crusader

x drs ex drawings

XDS Xerox Data Systems; X-ray Diffraction System

xdt xenon discharge tube

xe ex entitlement

Xe experimental engine; xenon

xecf x-e cold-flow engine

xeg X-ray emission gage

XEG Xerox Education Group

Xen Xenia; Xenik; Xenocratic; Xenos

Xenius Eugenio d'Ors

xeno xenodiagnosis; xenodiagnostic; xenogenic; xenograft;

xenolith; xenolithic; xenophile; xenophilia; xenophobe; xenophobia

Xeno Xenocrates; Xenophanes; Xenophon

xenobio xenobiologic(al)(ly); xenobiologist; xenobiology

Xenocoj Santo Domingo, Guatemala

xenodiag xenodiagnosis

Xenop Xenophon

xenop(s) xenophobe(s); xenophobia(s); xenophobic(s)

XEP Xerox Educational Publications

xer Xerox reproduction

Xer Xerxes

Xeres Jerez de la Frontera

xerocops xerocopies (books reproduced by xerography)

xerodups xerographic duplicates

xerog xerograph(ic)(al)(ly); xerography

xeromamo xeromammograph (also called xerox mammograph—xerographic process used in diagnosis of breast cancer)

xerorads xerographic radiographs

xes X-ray emission spectra

xf ex offer; extra fine

XF experimental fighter (naval symbol)

xfa crossed-field acceleration; X-ray fluorescence absorption

xfc X-band frequency converter

xfd crossfeed; X-ray flow detection

xfer transfer

xfh X-band feed horn

Xfher Christopher

xflt expanded flight-line tester

xfm X-band ferrite modulator

xfmr transformer

xformer transformer

xfqh xenon-filled quartz helix

xfrmr transformer

xft xenon flash tube

xg crossing

xgam experimental guided air missile (XGAM)

XGP Xerox Graphic Printer

xh extra hard; extra heavy; extra high

Xh Xhosa

XH experimental helicopter (naval symbol)

x heavy extra heavy

X-height height of central portion of lowercase letters exclusive of ascenders and descenders

xhf extra high frequency

x-high of a height equal to a low-

ercase x of the same face and size

xhil xenon high-intensity light

xhm X-ray hazard meter

xhmo extended huckel molecular orbit

xhr extra-high reliability

X-hr X-hour (when shipping evacuation is ordered from major ports by NATO)

Xhs Xhosa

xhst exhaust

xhv extremely high vacuum

x hvy extra heavy

xi ex interest; xi particle

xia X-band interferometer antenna

Xiamen (Pinyen Chinese—Amoy)

Xian (Pinyin Chinese—Sian)—China's old capital

Xianggang (Pinyin Chinese—Hong Kong)—the British Crown Colony south of Canton

Xibaro Jivaro

xic transmission interface converter

xil xilography; xilogravure (woodcuts)

xim X-ray intensity meter

xin without interest

Xin Xingu

Xina Christina

XING crossing (highway or railroad)

Xinhua (Pinyin Chinese—Chinese News Agency)—formerly called Hsinhua

Xinjiang Uygur (Pinyin Chinese —Sinkiang Uighur)—autonomous region of mainland China

xio execute input-output

Xipangu Marco Polo's name for Japan

xiph xiphoid; xiphoidal

Xipho Xiphosura

Xiq-Xiq Xique-Xique, Bahia, Brazil

xirs xenon infrared searchlight

xis xenon infrared searchlight

xist xistoma; xistomiasis

xistor transistor

Xizang (Pinyin Chinese—Tibet) —autonomous region of mainland China but formerly independent before the Chinese communist takeover

xk X-band klystron

xl crystal; crystalline; extra large; extra long

Xl inductive reactance

xla X-band limiter anntenuator

xlam cross-laminate(d)

xlc xenon lamp collimator

xld experimental laser device
xldt xenon laser discharge tube
xlf ex lady friend
xli extra-low interstitial
xlnt excellent
XLO Ex-Cell-O (precision products, trade name)
xlps xenon lamp power supply
xlr experimental liquid rocket
xls xenon light source
XLSS Xenon Light-Source System
xlt cross-linked polyethylene; excellent; xenon laser tube
xltn translation
xl & ul exclusive of loading and unloading
xlwb extra-long wheelbase
xm crossmatch; examine
xm (XM) experimental missile
Xm Christmas
XM experimental missile
XM-1 main battle tank (USA)
XM-706 Cadillac-Gage amphibious armed car and military personnel carrier called the Commando
XM-723 cavalry of infantry fighting vehicle (USA)
Xma$ Christmas (commercialized)
Xmas Christmas
X-matching —cross matching
xmfr transformer
xmit transmit
xmitter transmitter
x mod experimental module
xms X-band microwave source
XMS Experimental Development Specification; Xavier Mission Sisters
xmsn transmission
xmt exempt; transmit; X-band microwave transmitter
xmtg transmitting
xmtl transmittal
xmtr transmitter
xmt-rec transmit-receive
xmtr-rec transmitter-receiver
xn ex new
Xn Christian
XN experimental (USN)
Xndu Xanadu
xnor gate exculsive-nor gate
X-note $10 bill
xnt excellent
Xnty Christianity
xo crystal oscillator
XO Executive Officer; Experimental Office(r); Turner's syndrome wherein one of the sex-determining pair of XX chromosomes is missing
X-O cross-out test
xob xenon optical beacon
Xochi Xochimilco

x-off transmitter off
xoloiz xoloizcuintli (pronounced *sholloizquintly*)—the Mexican hairless dog both hotblooded and flealess as well as faithful
Xomhua (Pinyin Chinese—Hsinhau)—mainland China's official news agency who on January 1, 1979 began the use of Pinyin phonetic spelling of most Chinese names set in Roman type to facilitate their approximate pronunciation and thus gain better understanding
x-on transmitter on
xoophorec xoophorectomic (sterilization); xoophorectomy (removal of the ovaries)
xor exclusive or (data processing)
xos extra outside clothing; extra outsize (clothing)
X-out cross out; delete; strike out
xover cross over
X-over cross over
xp express paid; xerodema pigmentosum
Xp fire-resistive protected cabinet, safe, or vault
XP (Greek—chirho)—first two letters of the Greek word for Christ
xpa X-band parametric amplifier; X-band passive array; X-band planar array; X-band power amplifier
xpaa X-band planar-array antenna
XPARS External Research Publication and Retrieval System
XPC inshore patrol cutter (naval symbol)
xpd cross-polarization discrimination; cross-pollination discrimination; expedite(d)
xper without privileges
Xper Christopher
xpert expert
XPG converted merchant ship (naval symbol)
xpl explain; explanation; explosion; explosive
xplo explosion
xplos explosive
xplt exploit
XPM Xerox Planning Model
xpn expansion
Xpo Cristo (Spanish—Christ)
xpond transponder
xpp *exprès payé lettre* (French—express-paid letter)
xppa X-band pseudo-passive array; X-band pulsed-power amplifier

xpr ex privileges; without privileges
X-press Express
xprs express
xprts expertise; experts
xprtz expertize
xps X-band phase shifter; X-ray photoelectric spectroscopy; X-ray photoelectron spectroscopy
xps (XPS) X-ray photomission spectroscopy
xpt except; X-band pulse transmitter
xpt *exprès payé télégraphe* (French—express-paid telegraph)
Xpto *Cristóbal* (Spanish—Christopher)
X-punch punch in X row (11th row) of an 80-column punch-card
xq cross-question
XQ Experimental Target Drone
xqh xenon quartz helix
xr ex rights; Xerox radiography
Xr Christopher; examiner
XR External Relations (UNESCO)
X-rated movie moving picture not recommended for minors
X-rated shops sex-oriented establishments such as massage parlors and pornographic bookstores
xray execution recorder analyzer
Xray letter X radio code
X-ray letter X radio code; photograph or photography made by X-rays; radiograph; radiography; roentgenograph; roentgenography; roentgen ray
X-ray Discoverer Wilhelm Konrad Roentgen
xrb X-band radar beacon
xrcd X-ray crystal density
xrd X-ray diffraction
X rds crossroads
X-rea X-ray events analyzer
xref cross-reference
xrep auxiliary report
xrf X-ray fluorescence
xrfs X-ray fluorescence spectrometer
xrii X-ray image intensifier
xrl extended-range lance (missile)
xrm X-ray microanalyzer
xro xeroradiography
X-roads crossroads
xrp X-ray and photofluorography
xrpm X-ray projection microscope
xrpt X-ray and photofluorogra-

phy technician

XRPT X-Ray and Photofluorography Technician (USN)

xrspec X-ray spectograph

xrt ex-rights; without rights; X-ray technician

Xrx Xerox (corporation or copying process)

xs cross-section; excess; extra strength; extra strong

Xs atmospherics

xsa X-band satellite antenna

xsal xenon short arc lamp

XSB Xavier Society for the Blind

X-scale scale of a line parallel to the horizon

x sec extra sec *(très sec)*—dry champagne

xsect cross-section

xsf X-ray scattering facility

xsistor transistor

XSL Experimental Space Laboratory

xsm experimental strategic missile; experimental surface missile

xsoa excess speed of advance authorized

X-sonad experimental sonic azimuth detector

X-spot $10 bill

xspv experimental solid-propellant vehicle

xsr X-band scatterometer radar

XSS Experimental Space Station

xsta X-band satellite-tracking antenna

xstd X-band stripline tunnel diode

xstda X-band stripline tunnel diode amplifier

xstr transistor

x str extra strong

xstrat cross-stratified

xt crosstalk; X-ray tube

Xt Christ

xta chiasmata; X-band tracking antenna

xtal crystal

Xtet (Swedish—the X)—Sven Erixson

Xth tenth

Xtian Christian

xtk cross track

xtlo crystal oscillator

xtnd extend

xto X-band triode oscillator

xtr extra (computer flow chart)

XTR Xtra Inc

xtra extra

xtran experimental language; experimental translation

xtrm extreme

XTRU Xtra Inc (container) Unit

xtry extraordinary

xtwa X-band traveling-wave amplifier

xtwm X-band traveling-wave masser

Xty Christianity

xu X-ray unit; x-unit

Xu fire-resistive unprotected cabinet, safe, or vault

XU Xavier University

XUL Xavier University of Louisiana

Xulla formerly the Sula Islands of Indonesia

XUM Xerox University Microfilm

xut crosscut

xuv extreme untraviolet

xva X-ray videocon analysis

xvers transverse

XVP Executive Vice President

xvtr transverter

xw experimental warhead; ex warrants; without warrants

X-wave extraordinary wave

Xway (XWAY) Expressway

X-way expressway

X-weld X-shaped weld

XWS Experimental Weapon System

xx without securities or warrants

x(X) $10 bill; Christ; Christian; Christianity; cross; execution(er); experiment; experimental (symbol); explosive (symbol); extra; extract(ed) (symbol); Kienbock unit (symbol); magnification power; reactance (symbol); research aircraft (symbol); single strength; times (multiplied by); univalent negative (symbol); un-

known quantity; U.S. Steel Corporation (stock exchange symbol); X ray; Xavier; Xray —code for letter X

XX doublecross; double strength; female (see X chromosome)

XX Dos Equis (Spanish—Two X)—Mexican beer

XXer doublecrosser

xxh double extra hard; double extra heavy

xxl cancel

XX-note (double-X note) $20 bill

xxos extra-large outside (clothing)

xxs extra-extra strength

xxx international urgency signal

XXX triple strength; triple-X; triple X syndrome

XXXX quadruple strength

XXXXX quintuple strength

XXY Klinefelter's syndrome wherein the sex-determining chromosomes are XXY instead of the normal XY

xy xylography

XY male

xya x-y axis

xyat x-y axis table

xyl ex young lady (former sweetheart); xylene; xylography

xylo xylophone

xyloc xylocain (lidocaine)

xylog xylography

xyp x-y plotter

xyr x-y recorder

x yr dev ten-year device (US Army service badge)

xyt x-y table

xyv x-y vector

XYY syndrome unusually aggressive male having an extra Y-sex chromosome

xyz examine your zipper (your fly is open)

XYZ XYZ Affair leading to undeclared naval war between France and the United States from 1798 to 1800

X zone adrenal cortex inner zone (of some young mammals)

Y

y altitude (symbol); an ordinate (symbol); an unknown quantity (symbol); depth or height (symbol); yacht; yard; year; yellow; yen (Japanese monetary unit); you; young(est)

y income (microeconomics); (Spanish—and)—not an abbreviation

Y Convair (symbol); service test (symbol); yacht; Yankee—code for letter Y; Yard (The Yard—Scotland Yard); yen (Japanese money unit); YMCA; YMHA; YWCA; YWHA

Y admittance (symbol); lateral axis (symbol); *ylös* (Finnish—up)

Y1C Yeoman First Class

Y2C Yeoman Second Class

Y3C Yeoman Third Class

Y-18 Ilyushin 18 aircraft

Y-40 Yak 40 aircraft

Y62 Ilyushin Il-Y62 jet airplane

ya yaw axis; young adult

YA Yasser Arafat [leader of Palestine terrorists called Al Fatah (PLO)]; Young Adults; Youth Aliyah; Youth Authority

Y/A York-Antwerp Rules

YAA Yachtsmen's Association of America

YAAP Young Americans Against Pollution

YABA Yacht Architects and Brokers Association

YAC Young Adult Council; Young Alumni Club; Youth Advisory Council

YACA Youth and Adult Correctional Agency

YACC Young Adults Conserva-

tion Corps

YACH Yugoslav-American Cooperative Home

yactoff yaw-actuator offset

YAD Youth Aid Division

Yad Fiz Yaderna Fizika (Russian—Journal of Nuclear Physics)

yadh yeast alcohol dehydrogenase (YADH)

YAEC Yankee Atomic Electric Company

YAF Young Americans for Freedom

Yafa (Arabic—Jaffa)

Yafo Tel Aviv's seaport also known as Jaffa or Joppa

YAF-PAC Young Americans for Freedom—Political Action Committee

yag yttrium aluminum garnet

yag (YAG) yttrium, aluminum, garnet (surgical laser)

YAG district auxiliary miscellaneous (3-letter naval symbol)

yagl yttrium-aluminum garnet laser

yag laser yttrium-aluminum-garnet laser

YAIC Young American Indian Council

Yak Yakolev; Yakov; Yakovlevich

Yak Yakarta (Spanish—Djakarta)

YAK Yakovlev aircraft (named for its designer)

Yak-11 Soviet Yakovlev two-place trainer aircraft named Moose by NATO

Yak-12 Soviet Yakovlev two-place trainer aircraft

Yak-18 Soviet Yakovlev two-place aircraft used as a trainer and named Max by NATO

Yak-25 Soviet Yakovlev all-weather interceptor fighter aircraft named Flashlight by NATO

Yak-26 Soviet Yakovlev tactical reconnaissance aircraft named Mangrove by NATO

Yak-28 Soviet Yakovlev tactical bomber aircraft named Brewer by NATO

Yak-28P Soviet Yakovlev all-weather interceptor aircraft named Firebar by NATO

Yakumo Koizumi Lafacadio Hearn's Japanese name

Yakutia Yakut Autonomous Soviet Socialist Republic (eastern Siberia)

yal yttrium-aluminum laser

YAL Young Australia League

YALDS Young Australia Language Development Scheme

Yale LJ Yale Law Journal

Yallerhammer State Alabama

Yallo Ballys short form for the Yallo Bally Mountains of northern California

YAM Yates American Machine (company)

Yam Kinneret (Hebrew—Sea of Galilee, Sea of Tiberias)

YAN Yancey (railroad); Young American Nazis

Yanan (Pinyin Chinese—Yenan)

YANCON Yankee Conference (intercollegiate sports)

Yangpat Yangtze Patrol

Yangtze great river of central China flowing into East China Sea—3400 miles

Yank Yankee; Yankel

YANK Youth of America Needs to Know

Yankee letter Y radio code; Soviet class of nuclear-powered submarines as named by NATO—Yankee or Y-class—and similar to U.S. Polaris-type subs

Yankee Athens New Haven, Connecticut

Yankee Clipper Joe Di Maggio

Yankeedom New England; Northeastern United States

Yankee Doodle Dandy George M Cohan (born on July 4)

Yanko-Spanko Conflict Spanish-American War (so named in 1899 by historian Arthur Bird "Ex-Vice-Consul-General of America at Port-au-Prince, Hayti")

Yantai (Pinyin Chinese—Yentai)

yap. yaw and pitch

yaps yaw and pitch sensor

Yaptown Cleveland, Ohio

Yar Yarmouth

YAR Yemen Arab Republic (Sana—capital); York-Antwerp Rules (insurance)

YARA Young Americans for Responsible Action

yard prison yard

'yard shipyard

Yard Scotland Yard; Yardley

YARD Yarrow-Admiralty Research Department

yarden yard + garden

Yard(s) Montagnard(s)—nickname derived from pronunciation of the last syllable in Montagnard(s)

YARDS Yard Activity Reporting and Decision System

YARN Young Adult Resource Notebook

yas yaw-attitude sensor

YA's Young Adults (young people)

YASD Young Adult Services Division (ALA)

Yasnaya Polyana (Russian—Clear Glade)—Tolstoy family home near Tula about 177 kilometers (110 miles) south of Moscow

YASSR Yakut Autonomous Soviet Socialist Republic

Yat Yatyiopia (Amharic—Ethiopia)

yavis young, attractive, verbal, intelligent, and successful

YAVIS syndrome youthful, attractive, verbal, intelligent and successful (clients most likely to be selected by psychological therapists)

YAWF Youth Against War and Facism

Y-axis vertical axis on a chart, graph or map

yb yardbird (confined to a military camp)

Yb ytterbium

YB yearbook; Youngstown Sheet & Tube (stock market symbol)

YBA Young Buddhist Association; Youth Basketball Association

YBC Yerba Buena Center

Ybk Yearbook

yBr yellowish brown

YBR sludge-removal barge (3-letter naval symbol)

YBRA Yellowstone-Bighorn Research Association

Y-branch Y-shaped pipe fitting

YB(RS) Year Books (Rolls Series)

YBs Young Boys Inc—Detroit heroin distribution ring using young boys to promote street sales

YDS Yale Bibliographic System (computer cataloging)

yc yaw channel; yaw coupling; yellow chrome

Y-c Y-chromosome

YC open lighter (2-letter naval symbol); Yacht Club; Yankton College; Yeomanry Cavalry; York College; Youth Club; Yuba College

YCA Yachting Club of America; Young Citizens' Army; Youth Camping Association; Youth Correction Act

YCC Youth Conservation Corps; Youth Correctional Center

YCCA Youth Council on Civic Affairs

YCCC Yui Chui Chan Club

YCCIP Youth Community Conservation and Improvement Projects

YCD feuling barge (naval symbol); Youth Correction Division (U.S. Dept Justice)

YCF car float (naval symbol); Yankee Critical Facility; Young Calvinist Federation

YCGJ Young Christians for Global Justice

Y-chromosome male-producing gene found in male sperm

YCI Young Communist International; Youth Correctional Institution

YCI Yacht Club Italia (Italian Yacht Club)

YCia Ybarra Compañia (steamship line)

YCK open cargo lighter (3-letter naval symbol)

YCL Yarmouth Cruise Lines; York City Library; Young Communist League

YCLA Young Circle League of America

Y-class NATO name for Soviet class of nuclear-powered submarines also called Yankee by NATO as they are similar to U.S. Polaris-type subs

YCM Young Christian Movement

YCNM Yucca House National Monument

ycp yaw-coupling parameter

YCP Youth Challenge Program

YCS Young Catholic Students; Young Christian Students; Youth and Community Services

YCSM Young Christian Student Movement

yct yacht

YCTF Younger Chemists Task Force

YCU aircraft transportation lighter (naval symbol)

YC & UO Young Conservative and Unionist Organisation

YCV aircraft transportation lighter (3-letter naval symbol)

ycw you can't win

YCW Young Christian Workers

ycz yellow caution zone (airport runway lighting)

yd yard

y/d yaw damper

YD floating derrick (2-letter naval symbol); Young Democrat; Yugoslav dinar

Y & D Yards and Docks (USN)

yd² square yard(s)

yd³ cubic yard(s)

yda yesterday

YDA Dawson City, Yukon Territory (airport)

ydaa yellow dinitrophenyl aspartic acid

yday yesterday

ydb yield-diffusion bonding

ydc yaw-damping computer

YDCA Youth Democratic Clubs of America

YDF floating drydock (naval symbol)

ydg yardage; yarding

YDG degaussing vessel (naval symbol)

ydi yard drain inlet

YDI Youth Development Incorporated

YDL Young Development Laboratories

ydmn yardman

ydmstr yardmaster

yds yards

Yds Yards (postal place-name abbreviation)

YDs Young Democrats

YDS Yale Divinity School

YDSD Yards and Docks Supply Depot (USN)

YDSO Yards and Docks Supply Office

YDT diving tender (naval symbol)

Y-duct Y-shaped duct

ye yellow edges; yellow edging; yellow enzyme; yellow-edged

yᵉ (Early English—thou)—also written ye

YE aircraft homing system

yea. yaw-error amplifier

YEA Yale Engineering Association

Year 1905 Shostakovich's Symphony No. 11

Year 1917 Shostakovich's Symphony No. 12

yearb yearbook

YEB Yorkshire Electricity Board

Yedo Tokyo's old name (also written Edo)

YEDPA Youth Employment and Demonstration Projects Act

YEFC Youth Education for Citizenship (American Bar Association)

yeg yeast extract—glucose

YEG Edmonton, Alberta (International Airport)

yegg yeggman (burglar specializing in opening safes and vaults)

Yekké Israeli-born nickname for German Jews

yel yellow

Yell Yellowstone National Park

Yellow Belly Youngstown Sheet & Tube's nickname

yellowcake uranium ore (U_3O_8)

Yellow Emperor Huang Ti

yellow flag yellow signal flag flown when a vessel requests pratique; letter Q or Quebec in the international code; also called the quarantine flag

Yellowhammer Alabama state bird; symbolic nickname of an Alabaman

Yellowhammer State Alabama

yellowjack quarantine flag; yellow fever; yellow flag

Yellowjackets Yellowjacket Mountains of eastern Idaho

Yellow River China's Hwang Ho; Hwang Ho runs for 3000 miles before emptying into

Yellow Sea off coast of China

Yellow Sea arm of the Pacific Ocean between China, Korea, and Manchuria

Yellowstone short form for Yellowstone County in Montana, Yellowstone Lake in Wyoming, Yellowstone National Park (Idaho, Montana, and Wyoming), Yellowstone River (Montana, North Dakota, and Wyoming)

Yellow Thunder Country around the Dells of the Wisconsin River near Baraboo, Wisconsin

Yel NP Yellowstone National Park

yelsh yellowish

yem yeast extract—malt

Yem Yemen; Yemenite

Yemen People's Democratic Republic of Yemen (*Jumhurijah al-Yemen al Dimuqratiyah al Sha'abijah*) also called Southern Yemen to differentiate it from the Yemen Arab Republic; Yemeni speak Arabic and raise cotton

Yemen Arab Republic *al Jamhurija al Arabiya Yamaniya* (Yemeni grow food crops as well as coffee, cotton, and a narcotic called gat; Arabic is spoken)

Yemeni Arab Republic Ports Qishn, Al Luhayyah, Kamaran, Al Hudayah

Yemeni People's Democratic Republic (South Yemen) Ports Al Mukalla, Perim Harbour, Aden

Yenisei 2800-mile-long river of western Siberia entering into Kara Sea section of Arctic Ocean

Yeo Yeoman

YEO Youth Employment Office(r)

Yeoman F Yeoman Female (naval rating)

yeomn yeomanry

yep your educational plans

yepd yeast extract—peptone, dextrose

Yerba Buena former name of San Francisco

Yerevan Armenia's Erevan or Erivan

Yerushalayim (Hebrew—Jerusalem)

YES Youth Educational Services; Youth Education Systems; Youth Employment Service

Yesilköy Istanbul, Turkey's airport

yesty yesterday

YETP Youth Employment Training Program

YEWTIC Yorkshire, East and West Ridings, Technical Information Centre

Yezo Japanese island of Hokkaido

yf wife (simplified orthographic contraction proposed by Benjamin Franklin)

yf (YF) yellow fever

YF covered lighters (naval symbol)

YF-16 air-superiority single-engine lightweight-fighter aircraft (USAF)

YFB ferryboat or launch (naval symbol)

YfC Youth for Christ

YFC car float (3-letter naval symbol); Young Farmers' Club

YFCU Young Farmers' Clubs of Ulster

YFD yard floating drydock (naval symbol)

YFFP Yarrawonga Flora and Fauna Park (Australian Northern Territory)

YFN covered lighter, nonself-propelled (naval symbol)

YFNB large covered lighter (naval symbol)

YFND drydock companion craft (naval symbol)

YFNX special-purpose lighter (naval symbol)

YFP floating power barge (naval symbol); Youth For Progress

YFR self-propelled refrigerated covered lighter (naval symbol)

YFRN refrigerated covered lighter, nonself-propelled (naval symbol)

YFRT covered lighter, range tender (naval symbol)

YFT torpedo transportation lighter (naval symbol)

yfu yard freight unit

YfU Youth for Understanding (teenage exchange program)

YFU harbor utility craft (naval symbol)

y fwd yarn forward (knitting)

yG yellowish green

Yg Young's Literal Translation of the Holy Bible

YG garbage lighter (naval symbol); yellow green

YGC Youth Guidance Center

Yggdrasill tree of the universe, according to Norse mythology

YGH *Yankee Go Home* (popular slogan of overseas communist-incited mobs)

ygl yttrium-garnet laser

ygmd yaw-gimbal command

YGN garbage lighter, nonself-propelled (naval symbol)

YGR Yankari Game Reserve (Nigeria)

YGS Young Guard Society

Y-gun Y-shaped gun used aboard ships for firing depth charges

YH Youth Hostel

YHA Youth Hostels Association

Yhama Yokohama

YHANI Youth Hostel Association of Northern Ireland

YHB houseboat (naval symbol)

YHLC salvage lift craft, heavy (naval ship symbol)

YHt Young-Helmholtz theory

YIIT heating scow (naval symbol)

Yi Yiddish

YIC Yardney International Corporation

Yid Yiddish; Yiddish-speaking person

Yid Yiddish (German dialect spoken by many persons of Judaic origin and augmented by the languages of the countries where they have emigrated such as Poland, Romania, Spain and its former African possessions where Spanish Jews speak Ladino—a sort of Spanish Yiddish dating back to the Inquisition when Spanish Jews were expelled from their Spanish homeland and forced to migrate to overseas places around the Mediterranean ranging from Algeria and Morocco to Greece and Turkey as well as the so-called Holy Land)—incorrectly called Jewish because it is written in Hebrew characters

Yidgin-English Yiddish + English

Yie Young interference experiment

YIEP Youth Incentive Entitlement Project

yig yttrium iron garnet (ferrite)

yigib your improved group insurance benefits

YIIJS Young Israel Institute for Jewish Studies

YIJR Yivo Institute for Jewish Research

YIJS Young Israel Institute for Jewish Studies

YIKOR *Yidishe kultur-organizatsye* (Polish—Yiddish Culture Organization)

yil yellow indicator lamp

Yinglish Yiddish-English

yip yippie (politically active hippie)

YIP Detroit, Michigan (Willow Run Airport); Youth International Party (members, including narcotic-addicted hippies, called yippies)

YIR Yearly Infrastructure Report

YI & S Yawata Iron and Steel

Yivo Inst Yivo Institute for Jewish Research

yj radar homing beacon (map symbol)

YJC York Junior College

Y-joint Y-shaped joint

yk radar beacon (map symbol)

Yk Yakut; York

YK Yankee Airlines (2-letter code)

Yka Yokohama

YKF Yiddisher Kulture Farband (Yiddish Culture Club)

YKKK Yamashita Kisen Kabushiki Kaisha (steamship line)

Ykn Yukon

Yko Yokosuka (often mispronounced *Yokuska*)

Yks Yorkshire

Ykt Yakut

yl yellow; yield limit; young lady

Y & L York and Lancaster

YLA open landing lighter (naval symbol)

YLC Young Life Campaign

YLI Young Ladies Institute; Yorkshire Light Infantry

YLJ *Yale Law Journal*

YLL Yerkes Language Laboratory

YLLC salvage lift crane, light (naval ship symbol)

YLM *Yale Literary Magazine*

YLO Young Lords Organization

YLP Young Lords Party

Y & LR York and Lancaster Regiment

yl's young ladies

Ylstn Yellowstone

ym yacht measurement; yawing moment; yellow metal; your measurement; your message

YM dredge (naval symbol); Yehudi Menuhin

YMA Yarn Merchants Association

Yma Sumac advertised as being descended from the Peruvian Incas but known to her neigh-

bors as a Brooklyn girl named Amy Camus whose reverse spelling was Yma Sumac

ymb yeast malt broth

YMBA Yacht and Motor Boat Association

YMCA Young Men's Christian Association

YM Cath A Young Men's Catholic Association

YMCU Young Men's Christian Union

ymd your message date

Yme Young's modulus of elasticity

YMF Young Musicians Foundation

YMFS Young Men's Friendly Society

YMHA Young Men's Hebrew Association

YMHAL Young Men's Hebrew Association Library

YMI Young Men's Institute

YML Yang Ming Line

YMLC salvage lift craft, medium (naval ship symbol)

YMLU Yamashita Line (container) Unit

YMP motor mine planter (naval symbol); Young Management Printers

YMPA Young Master Printers' Alliance

yms yield measurement system

YMs Yearly Meetings (Quakers)

YMS motor minesweepers (naval symbol)

YMT motor tug (naval symbol)

Ymu Ymuiden

YMV Yazoo and Mississippi Valley (railroad)

YM & YWHA Young Men's and Young Women's Hebrew Association

yn yen

y-n yes-no

Yn Yeoman; Yeowoman

YN net tender (naval symbol); Youngstown & Northern RR

Y network wye network

yng young

YNG gate vessel (naval symbol)

YNHA Yosemite Natural History Association

Y-NHH Yale-New Haven Hospital

ynhl why in hell

YNP Yellowstone National Park (Idaho, Montana, Wyoming); Yoho NP (British Columbia); Yosemite NP (California); Youth National Party

YNSO Yomiuri Nippon Symphony Sorchestra
YNT net tender, tug (naval symbol)
Ynv Ynvar (Russian—January)
YNWR Yazoo National Wildlife Refuge (Mississippi)
yo yarn over (knitting); year old
yo' yore; you; your
y/o years old
YO fuel-oil barge (naval symbol); Yerkes Observatory
YOAN Youth Of All Nations
yob year of birth
YOB Youth Opportunities Board
YOC Youth Opportunity Campaign; Youth Opportunity Center(s); Youth Opportunity Corps
YOC-RSPB Young Ornithologists' Club—Royal Society for the Protection of Birds
yod year of death
Yodelandia Switzerland
YOG gasoline barge, self propelled (naval symbol)
Yogi Lawrence Peter Berra also known as Yogi Berra
YOGN gasoline barge, nonself-propelled (naval symbol)
Yok Yokohama
Yoknapatawpha William Faulkner's mythical Mississippi county
Yoko Yokohama
Yokuska (navalese—Yokosuka, Japan)
yom year of marriage
Yom Yomiuri (Japanese—News Crier)—Tokyo's popular newspaper serving nearly six million subscribers
YOM yellow oxide of mercury
Yomiuri (Japanese—Reading for Sale)—leading newspaper of Japan
Yom Kip Yom Kippur (Hebrew —Day of Atonement)
yon yonder
YON fuel-oil barge, nonself-propelled (naval symbol)
yood (slang pronunciation—iud) —intrauterine device
YOP Youth Opportunity Program
York (turn-of-our-century slang — New York; New York State)
York Yorkshire Post
Yorks Yorkshire
Yorkshire Queen of Song Susan Sunderland
York State New York State (especially the upstate section)

Yos Yosu
YOS oil storage barge (naval symbol)
Yosemite short form for Yosemite National Park in California or any of its many natural attractions such as the Yosemite Falls or the Yosemite Valley
Yoshino-kumano Yoshino-kumano National Park in southern Honshu, Japan
Yos NP Yosemite National Park
yot (YOT) youthful offender treatment
YOU Youth Opportunities Unlimited; Youth Organizations United; Youthful Offender Unit
you'd you had; you would
Yougoslavie (French—Yugoslavia)
you'll you shall; you will
Young Hickory James K. Polk— eleventh President of the United States
Young Pretender Bonnie Prince Charlie (Charles Edward Louis Philip Casimir Stuart)— son of the Old Pretender— James Stuart
Youngs Youngstown
you're you are
Youth Personified Juventus (Latin—youth)
youthploit youth exploitation (commercial exploitation of guillible youngsters)
you've you have
YOW Ottawa, Ontario (airport)
yp yellow pine; yield limit; yield point (psi)
YP patrol craft (2-letter naval symbol); yellow peril; young people; young person(s)
ypa yaw-precession amplifier
YPA Young Pioneers of America
YPCS Young Peoples Computer Society
ypd yaw-phase detector
YPD floating pile driver (naval symbol)
YPEC Young Printing Executives Club
YPF Yacimientos Petroliferos Fiscales (Spanish—Government Oil Deposits)—Argentina
YPFB Yacimientos Petroliferos Fiscales Bolivianos (Spanish— Bolivian Government Oil Deposits)
YPG Yuma Proving Ground
yPk yellowish pink

YPK pontoon stowage barge (naval symbol)
YPM Yale Peabody Museum
YPO Young Presidents' Organization; Youth Programs Office (Bureau of Indian Affairs)
Yps Ypsilanti
YPSCE Young People's Society of Christian Endeavor
YPSL Young People's Socialist League
Y-punch punch in Y row (12th row) of an 80-column punchcard
YQX Gander, Newfoundland (airport)
yr year; younger; your
y-r yaw roll
YR district patrol vessel (naval symbol); floating workshop (2-letter naval symbol); Young Republican(s)
YRA Yacht Racing Association
Yr B Year Book
YRB submarine repair and berthing barge (naval symbol)
YRBM submarine repair— berthing and messing barge (naval symbol)
YRC submarine rescue chamber (naval symbol)
YRD submarine repair and berthing vessel (3-letter naval symbol)
YRDH floating drydock hull workshop (naval symbol)
YRDM floating drydock machinery workshop (naval symbol)
YRL covered repair lighter (naval symbol)
yrly yearly
YRNF Young Republican National Federation
YRR radiological repair barge (3-letter naval symbol)
yrs years; yours
Yrs Yours
YRs Young Republicans
YRS Yugoslav Relief Society
YRST salvage craft tender (naval ship symbol)
yrs ty yours truly
yrt yearly renewable term (insurance)
YRU Yacht Racing Union
ys yellow spot (on retina); yield strength
Ys Yugoslavia; Yugoslavian
YS Yard Superintendent; Young Socialists
Y-S Yamashita-Shinnihon
Y & S Youngstown & Southern (railroad)
YS-11 Japanese medium-range transport plane

YSA Young Socialist Alliance; Youth Services Administration (District of Columbia)

ysb yield-stress bonding

YSB Yacht Safety Bureau; Youth Service Bureau

YSC Yugoslav Seamen's Club; Youth Studies Center (juvenile correctional facility in Philadelphia)

YSD seaplane wrecking derrick (naval symbol); Youngstown Steel Door (company); Youth Services Division

ysdb yield-stress diffusion bonding

yse yaw-steering error

Yseult Isolde

ysh yellowish

YSI Yellow Springs Instrument (company)

Ysl Ysrael

YSL Young Socialist League; Yves Saint Laurent

Y-S Line Yamashita-Shinnihon Line (steamships)

YSM Yangtze Service Medal

yso young stellar object

YSO Youngstown Symphony Orchestra

ysp years service for severance pay purposes

YSP pontoon salvage vessel (naval symbol)

ysr you're so right

YSR sludge-removal barge (naval symbol)

YSS Young Scots Society

YSSAS Yale Summer School of Alcohol Studies

yst youngest

YST Yukon Standard Time

YS & T Youngstown Sheet & Tube

YSTO Yugoslav State Tourist Office

YSU Youngstown State University

yt yoke top

Yt yttrium

Yᵗ *Ytre* (Dano-Norwegian or Swedish—outer)

YT harbor tug (naval symbol); Yukon Territory

Y & T Tale & Towne

YTA Yiddish Theatrical Alliance

ytb yarn to back

YTB large-harbor tug (naval symbol)

YTCA Yorkshire Terrier Club of America

ytd year to date

YTEP Youth Training and Employment Project

ytf yarn to front

YTL small-harbor tug (naval symbol)

YTM medium-harbor tug (naval symbol)

YTP *Yeni Türkiye Partisi* (New Turkish Party)—socialist oriented

YTPM Yuma Territorial Prison Museum

YTS Youth Training School; Yuma Test Center; Yuma Test Station

YTT torpedo-testing barge (naval symbol)

Y-tube Y-shaped tube

YTV Yokohama Television

Yu Yugoslav; Yugoslavian

YU Yale University; Yeshiva University; York University; Youngstown University; Yugoslavia (auto plaque)

YUAG Yale University Art Gallery

Yuc Yucatan (natives nicknamed boxitos—Maya term meaning darks)

Yuca Yucatan, Mexico

Yucatan Channel ocean passage between Cuba and Yucatan Peninsula of Mexico; connects Caribbean Sea with Gulf of Mexico

Yucca New Mexico state flower

Yucca Country the Southwest (ern United States)

Yud Yudel

Yug Yugoslavia(n); Yugoslavic

Yugo Yugoslav; Yugoslavia; Yugoslavian

Yugoeslavia (Spanish—Yugoslavia)

Yugoslavia Socialist Federal Republic of Yugoslavia (central-European communist-dominated nation of hard-working people whose diversified economy provides the highest standard of living of any Iron-Curtain country; Yugoslavs speak Serbo-Croatian, Slovene, and Macedonian) *Socijalisticka Federativna Republika Jugoslavija*

Yugoslav(ia)(n) Jugoslav(ia)(n)

Yugoslavia's Principal Seaport Split

Yugoslav Ports (large, medium, and small from north to south) Rovinj, Pula, Luka Rijeka, Bakar, Zadar, Sibenik, Split, Gruz, Dubrovnik

Yuk Yukon

YUK Youth Uncovering Krud (antipollution society)

Yukio Mishima Kimitake Hiraoka's pseudonym

Yukon Canadair version of the Britannia designated CC-106; Yukon River; Yukon Territory

Yukon River rises in Yukon Territory of Canada and runs for more than 1800 miles before emptying into Bering Sea off Alaska

YUL Montreal, Quebec (airport); Yale University Library

Yul Brynner Taidje Kahn, Jr

Yu-Lin Betty Yü-Lin Ho

YULRC Yale University Lung Research Center

YUN *Yearbook of the United Nations*

Yun Ho (Chinese—Grand Canal)

YUO Yale University Observatory

yup you're uncommonly perceptive

YUP Yale University Press

yuppie(s) young urban professional(s)

yup(s) young urban professional(s)

Yur Yuri; Yurievich

Yuri Bilstin Youry Bildstein

Yus Yussel

YUSM Yale University School of Medicine

Yuzh *Yuzhnaya* (Russian—southern)

Yv Yvette; Yvonne

YV Young's Version

yvc yellow-varnish cambric

YVC Yakima Valley College

Yves Montand Ivo Livi

YVF Young Volunteer Force

YVHS Yorkville Vocational High School

YVJC Yakima Valley Junior College

Yvonne de Carlo Peggy Yvonne Middleton

YVP Youth Voter Participation

YVR Vancouver, British Columbia (airport)

YVRL Yakima Valley Regional Library

YVT Yakima Valley Transportation (railroad)

y v v y viaje vuelta (Spanish—and return trip)

YW water barge (naval symbol); Yreka Western RR

YWAA Youth Welfare Association of Australia

YWAM Youth With A Mission

YWCA Young Women's Christian Association

YWCAUSA Young Women's

Christian Association of the U.S.A.

YWCTU Young Women's Christian Temperance Union

ywd you would

YWF Young World Federalists

YWFD Young World Food and Development (UN)

YWG Winnipeg, Manitoba (airport)

YWHA Young Women's Hebrew Association

YWHS Young Women's Help Society

YWLL Young Workers Liberation League

YWN nonself-propelled barge (naval symbol)

YWPG Young World Promotion Group

YWS Young Wales Society

YWU Yiddish Writers Union

y-y yaw axis

YY pseudonymous initials of Robert Lynd noted for his *New Statesman* essays

YYC Calgary, Alberta (airport)

YYZ Toronto, Ontario (airport)

Z

z an ounce of hashish, marijuana or narcotic (z the truncation of oz—ounce); complex variable (symbol); z-bar; zed (British usage); zee (American usage); zero; zinc; zone

z (Z) zloty (Polish currency unit)

z zu (German—closed, shut)

Z atomic number (symbol); azimuth (symbol); azimuth angle (symbol); gram equivalent weight (symbol); impedance (symbol); lighter-than-air aircraft (symbol); obsolete (symbol); radius of circle of least confusion (symbol); zenith; zenith distance; zero meridian time; Zionism; Zionist; Zoroaster; Zoroastrian; Zoroastrianism; Zulu—code for letter Z

Z normal axis (symbol); *Zeit* (German—time); *Zeitschrift* (German—periodical publication); *zuid* (Dutch—south)

Z^1, Z^2, Z^3 first degree of contraction, second degree of contraction, third degree of contraction

Z39 Library Work, Documentation, and Related Publishing Practices (American National Standards Institute Standards Committee)

za B-flat (Tartini's scale); zero absolute; zero and add

za *zirka* German—about; (approximately)

Za *Zéro absolu* (French—absolute zero)

ZA *Zuid Afrika* (Afrikaans or Dutch—South Africa)

Zaa Zeeman-effect atomic absorption (spectrometry)

zaap zero anti-aircraft potential

zab zabaglione; zinc-air battery

zab *zabaglione* (Italian—egg-yolk-and-wine dessert)

Zab Greater Zab or Lesser Zab river in Iraq; Zaboj

Zab *Zabriskie's Reports*

Zac Zacatecas

ZAC Zale Award Committee; zinc ammonium chloride

Zacatecas purple Zacatecas-purple marijuana from central Mexico

Z-account Zurich account (bank deposits held in Zurich, Switzerland where such accounts are identified only by number and not by the depositor's name)

Zach Zachary; Zachariah; Zacharias; Zachary; Zachris

Zack Zachariah; Zacharias; Zachary

'zactly exactly

Zad Zadar; Zadock

ZADCA Zinc Alloy Die Casters' Association

ZADCC Zone Air Defense Control Center

ZAED *Zentralstelle für Atomkernenergie Dokumentation* (German—Atomic Energy Documentation Center)

zaf zero-alignment fixture

Zafarinas Zafarinas Islands (also spelled Chafarinas and off the Mediterranean coast of Morocco where they belong to Spain)

Z-Afrika *Zuid-Afrika* (Dutch—South Africa)

zag *zaguán* (Spanish—passageway from street door to central patio of homes in Mexico and American Southwest)

Zag Zagreb

ZAG Zagreb, Yugoslavia (airport)

Zagreb Agram

Zagreb (Yugoslavian—Agram)—Croatia's capital

Zahal Israeli Secret Service

Zahal *Zva Hagana Leyisrael* (Hebrew—Israel Defense Forces)

Zahlentaf *Zahlentafeln* (German—table of illustrations)

zai zero address instruction

zai *zaibatsu* (Japanese—money clique)—plutocratic oligarchy of wealthy families such as the Mitsubishi, Mitsui, Sumitomo, etc.

Zai Zaire

Zaire Republic of Zaire (central African nation formerly the Belgian Congo; French and tribal languages are used; exports feature minerals and tropical crops produced by Zairians) *République du Zaire*

Zaire Ports Banana, Boma, Matadi

zak *zaklyuchenny* (Russian—prisoner)—pronounced zek

zal *zaliv* (Russian—bay)

Zal *Zalmen* (Yiddish—Solomon)

ZALIS Zinc and Lead International Service

zam Z-axis modulation; zinc, aluminum, magnesium

Zam Zambia; Zamboanga; Zamora

Zamb Zambia

Zambezi 1650-mile-long river of southeast Africa, emptying into Mozambique Channel

Zambia Republic of Zambia (landlocked southern African

nation formerly Northern Rhodesia; Zambians speak English but some seventy tribal tongues are also used; tropical crops and valuable minerals sustain the economy)

Zambo Zamboanga

Zamp Zampa

ZAMPA Zanzibar and Madagascar Peoples Airway

zams zero-age main sequence

zam(s) examination(s)

Zan Zanzibar

Z Anal Chem *Zeitschrift für Analytische Chemie* (German—Analytical Chemistry Periodical)

ZANC Zambia National Congress

Zancle old name for Messina

Zane Grey Pearl Grey's pseudonym

ZANLA Zimbabwe African National Liberation Army (of Soviet-backed guerrillas in Rhodesia)

ZANU Zimbabwe African National Union

Zanzi Zanzibar

zap zero and add packed; zero antiaircraft potential

zap *zapad* (Russian—west)

Zap Zapotec; Zapotecan

zapb zinc-air primary battery

zapp zygo automatic pattern processor

ZAPU Zimbabwe Africa People's Union

zar zeus acquisition radar

Zar Zaragoza

Zara Zarathustra (Zoroaster)

Zara (Italian—Zadar)—Yugoslavian port city

Zaragoza (Spanish—Sarogossa)

Zarathustra *Thus Spake Zarathustra* (symphonic poem by Richard Strauss—*Also sprach Zarathustra*)

ZARPS *Zuid-Afrikaansche Republiek Polisie* (Afrikaans—South African Republic Police)

zas zero-access storage

ZASM *Zuid Afrikaansche Spoorweg Maatschappij* (South African Railway serving the Transvaal at the turn of the century)

Z Astrophys *Zeitschrift für Astrophysik* (German—Astrophysics Periodical)

zasts zastrugas

zat zinc atomspheric tracer

ZAT *Zaterdag* (Dutch—Saturday)

Z-A test Zondek-Ascheim test

(for pregnancy)

Zatoka Gdansk (Polish—Gulf of Danzig)

ZAW *Zuid-Afrikaansche Weehuis* (Afrikaans—South African Orphan Asylum)

Zazen Zen meditation

zazou (French nickname—zootsuiter)

Zazul Vera Zazulich

zb zero beat

z B *zum Beispiel* (German—for instance)

ZB Zen Buddhist

Z-bar Z-shaped bar

zbb zero-base budget(ing)

ZBBS Zero-Based Budgeting System

zbe zinc battery electrode

Zbig Zbigniew Brzezinski

zbl zero-based linearity

Zbl *Zentralblatt* (German—central publication)

zbr zero-base review; zero-beat reception; zero-bend radius

ZBS Zambia Broadcasting Services

zbSd zero-bias Schottky diode

zc zone capacity

z of c zones of communication

ZC Zale Corporation; Zinc Corporation; Zionist Congress; Zoning Commission; Zonta Club; Zouave Corps; Zuñian Club

ZCA Zirconium Corporation of America

Z-car police car (British slang)

zcb zinc-coated bolt

ZCBC Zambian Consumer Buying Corporation

zcc zirconia-coated crucible

zcd zero crossing detector

zcic zirconia-coated iridium crucible

ZCL *Zona di Commercio Libero* (Italian—Free Trade Zone)

Z-class Soviet class of submarines named Zulu by NATO

Z-clip Z-shaped clip

zcm zero cerebral muscle

ZCMI Zion's Cooperative Mercantile Institution

zcn zinc-coated nut

ZCNP Zion Canyon National Park

zcr zero-temperature coefficient resistor

zcs zinc-coated screw

ZCS Zim Container Service

ZCSU Zim Container Service Unit

zcw zinc-coated washer

ZCX Zone Center Exchange

zd zener diode; zenith distance; zero defects; zonal depot; zone

description

Zd zenith description; zenith distance

ZD zenith description; zero defects (quality-control goal); zond description

ZDA Zero Defects Association; Zinc Development Association

zdc zinc die casting

ZDC Zero Defects Council

Z de T *Zulano de Tal* (Spanish—so and so)

zdg zinc-doped germanium

Z-dike (*see* Zeedijk)

Zdm Zaandam

ZDP Zero Defects Program; Zero Defects Proposal

zdpa zero defects program audit

zdpg zero defects program guideline

zdpo zero defects program objective

zdpr zero defects program responsibility

zdr zeus discrimination radar

ZDR *Zentraldeutsche Rundfunk* (Central German Radio)

ZDS Zinc Detection System

ZDSI Zung Depression Status Inventory

zdt zero-ductility transition

ze zero effusion; zone effect

zE *zum Exempel* (German—for example)

Ze José

Zé (Portuguese—José)

ZE Zenith Radio (stock-exchange symbol)

Z-E Zollinger-Ellison (syndrome)

zea zero-energy assembly

Zealand English place-name equivalent of Sjaeland

Zeb Zebedee; Zebulon

zebra. zero-energy breeder reactor assembly

zebrass zebra + ass—hybrid of zebra and jenny ass or zebress and jackass

zebroid zebra + horse (hybrid)

Zebrule zebra + horse—hybrid of male zebra and domestic mare

zeb(s) zebra(s)

zec zero-energy coefficient

zecc zinc electrochemical cell

Zech. Zechariah (book of the Bible)

Zech Zechariah

zed (obsolete phonetic word—z; zero)

zed British pronunciation of the letter Z

Zed New Zealand; Zedekiah

Zedland English shires of Devon, Dorset, and Somerset where *s* is often pronounced so it sounds like *z* or *zed*

Zee Zellerbach

Zee Zeeland (Dutch—Sea Land)

Zeedijk Amsterdam's Old City Center where some 3000 prostitutes display themselves in windows in the hope of attracting clients

Zeeland (Dutch—Zealand)

zeep zero energy experimental pile

zeg zero economic growth

zei zero environmental impact

Zeichn Zeichnung(en) [German —drawing(s)]

Zeke Ezekiel

zeks (Soviet-Russian slang— prisoners)

zel (ZEL) zero-length launcher

Zel Zelia; Zelide

Zelandia (Spanish—Zealand)

Zelda Griselda

Z Elektrochem Zeitschrift für Elektrochemie (German— Electrochemistry Periodical)

zell zero-length launching

Zem Zemlya (Russian—earth; land)

Zemlya Frantsa Iosifa (Russian —Franz Josef Land)

Zempo Zempoaltepetl (11,142-foot peak near Oaxaca in southern Mexico)

zen nickname for lsd (LSD); zenith (highest point)

Zen Zen Buddhism; Zen Buddhist; Zengo; Zenith; Zenobe; Zenobia; Zenobio; Zenón; Zenophon; Zentippe; Zenus

ZEN EIEN Zenkoku Eiga Engeki Rodo Kumiai (Japanese —National Movie and Theater Workers Union)

Zenga Zengakuren (Japanese leftwing students)

Zen Garden of the Atlantic England's Scilly Isles

zenith zero-energy nitrogen-heated thermal reactor

Zenith imaginary Minnesota city whose leading citizen is George F Babbitt described by Sinclair Lewis in his novel, *Babbitt*

Zenith City of the Unsalted Sea Duluth, Minnesota on Lake Superior leading to the other Great Lakes

ZENKO Zen Nihon Kinsoku Kozan Rodo Kumiai Rengokai (Japanese—All-Japan Federation of Metal Miners Union)

ZENRO Zen Nihon Rodo Kumiai Kaigi (Japanese—All-Japan Trade Union Congress)

ZENTEI Zen Teishin Rodo Kumiai (Japanese—Postal Workers Union)

Zentr Zentralblatt (German— journal)

zeony zebra + pony (hybrid)

Zep Giuseppe

Zeph. Zephaniah (book of the Bible)

Zeph Zephaniah

zephyr warm westerly breeze

ZEPHYR Zero-Energy Plutonium-Fueled Fast Reactor

zepp zeppelin

Zeppo Marx Herbert Marx

zep(s) zeppelin(s)

zer zero-energy reflection

ZERA Zero-Energy Critical Assemblies Reactor(s)

zerc zero-energy reflection coefficient

zero-g zero gravity (weightlessness)

Zero Mostel Sam Mostel

zert zero-reaction tool

ZES Zero Energy System

zet zetetic(s)

zeta. zero energy thermonuclear assembly

Zetland Zetland Island or the Zetland Islands called the Shetlands

zetr zero-energy thermal reactor

zeug zeugma; zeugmatic; zeugmatically

Zeus (Greek—Jupiter)—god of the heavens also called Jove

ZEUS Zero-Energy Uranium System

zf zero frequency

z/f zone of fire

Z-F Zermelo-Fraenkel (set theory)

ZF Zagrebacka Filharmonija (Croatian—Zagreb Philharmonic)

zfb signals fading badly

zfc zirconia fuel cell

ZFGBI Zionist Federation of Great Britain and Ireland

ZFMA Zip Fastener Manufacturers' Association

Z f N Zeitschrift für Namenforschung (German—Journal for the Study of Place-names)

ZFO Zone Française d'Occupation (French Occupation Zone)

zfp zyglo-fluorescent penetrant

zfpt zyglo-flurescent penetrant testing

zfs zero field splitting

Zf's Zionist fanatics (who will do anything to frustrate their foes and thwart another holocaust)

ZFV Zentrale für Fremdenverkehr (German—Central Tourist Association)

zg zap gun

z/g zoster-immune globulin

Zg Zug

ZG Zoological Gardens

Z-gage super-miniature model railway scale

Z-gas Zyklon-B gas (deadly)

zge zero-gravity effect; zero-gravity environment; zero-gravity expulsion

zget zero-gravity expulsion technique

ZGF Zero Gravity Facility

zgg zero gravity generator

zgh zero-gravity harmonic

ZGM Zeitner Geological Museum

Z-grams Admiral Zumwalt's policy statements

zgs zero-gravity simulator

zgs (ZGS) zero gradient synchrotron

zgt (ZGT) zero-gravity trainer (NASA)

Z-gun anti-aircraft rocket gun

zh zinc heads (freight); zonal harmonic; zone heater

zH zu Händen (German—care of, deliver to)

Zh Zuidholland (Dutch—South Holland)

ZH lighter-than-air search and rescue aircraft (2-letter naval symbol)

ZH Zone d'Habitation (French —residential area)

Zhejiang (Pinyin Chinese— Chekiang)

Zh Eksp Teor Fiz Zhurnal Eksperimental'noi i Teoreticheskoi Fiziki (Russian—Journal of Experimental and Theoretical Physics)

Zhengzhou (Pinyin Chinese— Chengchow)

Zh Fiz Khim Zhurnal Fizicheskoi Khimii (Russian—Journal of Physical Chemistry)

Zhg Zhongguo (Chinese—China)

Zhongguo (official Chinese— China)—Pinyin spelling adopted officially in 1979 to better approximate pronunciation of words written in Roman letters

Zh Prik Spektrosk Zhurnal Prikladnoi Spektroskopii (Russian—Journal of Applied Spectroscopy)

zhr zenith hourly rate; zirconium hydride reactor

Z hr zero hour

ZHRC Zinsmaster Hol-Ry Company

zhs zero hoop stress

ZHS Zion Historical Society

Zh Tekh Fiz Zhurnal Tekhnicheskoi Fiziki (Russian—Journal of Technical Physics)

zi zero input; zonal index

Zi Zollner illusion

ZI Zim Israel (steamship line); Zinc Institute; Zone of the Inferior; Zone of the Interior; Zonta International

Z of I Zone of the Interior

ZI Zone Industrielle (French—industrial zone); *Zone Interdite* (French—prohibited zone)

ZIA Zone of the Interior Armies

zic zirconia-iridium crucible

ZID Zionist Immigration Depot

Zier Ziervogel process

zig zero immune globulin

zig (ZIG) zero immune globulin; zoster-immune globulin

Zig Ziegfield; Zigfield; Zigfrid; Zigfrids

Zigeunerbaron Der Zigeunerbaron (German—The Gypsy Baron)—operetta by Johann Strauss Jr

ziggur(s) ziggurat(s)

zig(s) zigaboo(s) [British West Indian—Black(s)]

zig-zag zig-zag cigarette paper; zig-zag rule(r); zig-zag sewing machine attachment for making zig-zag stitches

zigzag line symbol of water

zil zillion (a number beyond belief)

ZIL (Russian—*Zavod Imieni Likhatov*)—Likhatov Auto Factory producing a Packard-like luxury car formerly named for Stalin—the ZIS *(Zavod Imieni Stalin)*

Zilia Clara Josephine Wieck (later Clara Schumann, the wife of the composer-critic Robert Schumann who gave her that pseudonym)

Zilli Cecilia

Zilw Zilwaukee

zim zero-interest mortgage; zonal interdiction missile

Zim Zimmerman(n)

Zim Zi Mischari (Hebrew—merchant fleet) as in Zim Israel Line

Zimb Zimbabwe (African name for Rhodesia)

Zimbabwe formerly Zimbabwe-Rhodesia; Rhodesia; Southern Rhodesia

Zimco Zambia Industrial and Mining Company

Zim-Rho Zimbabwe-Rhodesia (formerly Rhodesia or Southern Rhodesia)

Zim Tim Zimbabwe Times

zin zinfandel (grapes or wine)

ZINC Zim Israel Navigation Company (Zim Israel Line)

zinco zincograph

ZINCO Zim Israel Navigation Company

zincog zincography

zinc white zinc oxide (ZnO)

zineb zinc ethylenebis (fungicide)

zine(s) magazine(s)

Zingi Zingari (Italian—Gypsies)

Zinj Zinjanthropus

Zinoviev, Grigori Evseevich Hirsch Apfelbaum

zip zero (slang); zinc impurity photodetector; zipper (slide fastener or similar device)

ZIP Zone Improvement Plan (US Post Office Zip Code)

ZIPA Zimbabwe People's Army

Zipango Marco Polo's name for Japan

ZIPRA Zimbabwe People's Revolutionary Army (based in Zambia)

zir zero internal resistance

ZIR Zug Island Road (Delray Connecting Railroad)

ziram zinc dimethyldithiocarbamate (fungicide)

zircaloy zirconium alloy

ZIRCOA Zirconium Corporation of America

zircon zirconium silicate ($ZrSiO_4$)

Zirk Hagen Zirkus Hagenbeck (German—Hagenbeck Circus)

zirox zirconium oxide (ZrO_2)

ZISS Zebulon Israel Seafaring Society

zith zither

zix zinc isopropyl xanthate

zj zipper(ed) jacket

zj zonder jaartel (Dutch—without date of publication)

ZKD Zagreb Kajkavian Dialect (Serbo-Croatian)

zkrat zkratka(y) [Czech—abbreviation(s)]

Z Kristallog Kristallgeom Krystallphys Kristallchemie Zeitschrift für Kristallographie, *Kristallgeometrie, Kristallphysik, Kristallchemie* (German—Periodical for Crystallography, Crystallographic Geometry, Crystallographic Physics, Crystallographic Chemistry)

ZKSK Zentrale Kommission für Staatliche Kontrolle (German—Central Commission for State Control)—communist

zl freezing drizzle (meteorological symbol); zero lift

Zl zloty (Polish ruble)

ZL freezing drizzle (symbol)

ZLA Zambia Library Association

zlc zero lift cord

zld zero level drift; zero lift drag; zodiacal light device

Zld Zeeland (Dutch—Sea Land)—old province made of land captured from the sea

zlg zero line gap

zll zero length launch

Zlsm Zeiss light-section microscope

zm zoom; zoomar (variable focus lens)

ZM Zubin Mehta

Z-M Zuckerman-Moloff (sewage treatment)

ZM Zeevaart Maatschappij (Dutch—navigation company); *Zona Militare* (Italian—Military Zone)—restricted area

Z-man U.S. Army reserve

zmar zeus malfunction array radar

Z-marker zone marker

Zmbbw Zimbabwe (Rhodesia; Southern Rhodesia)

ZMC Zion Mule Corps

Zmd Zung measurement of depression

Z Metallk Zeitschrift für Metallkunde (German—Metallurgy Periodical)

zmkr zone marker

ZMMD Zurich, Mainz, Munich, Darmstadt (algol processor joint effort of universities in those cities)

ZMRI Zinc Metals Research Institute

ZMT Zip (Zone Improvement Plan) Mail Translator (post office sorting device)

Z m Z Z mého Zivota (Czechoslovakian—From my Life)—Smetana's String Quartet No. 1 revealing the happiest and the saddest moments of his life

zn zenith; zone (computer flow chart)

zn *zelfstandig naamwoord* (Dutch—substantive noun)—any group of words or a pronoun serving as a noun

Zn true azimuth (symbol); zinc

ZN *Zuid-Nederlands* (Dutch—South Netherlands)—Belgium

Znak (Polish—Sign)—Roman Catholic pro-government party

Z Naturforsch *Zeitschrift für Naturforschung* (German—Natural History Periodical)

ZnO zinc oxide

ZNP Zanzibar Nationalist Party; Zimbabwe National Park (Rhodesia); Zion National Park (Utah)

Zn_pgc azimuth per gyro compass

ZNPM Zion National Park Museum

ZNPP Zanzibar and Pemba People's Party

ZNPS Zion Nuclear Power Station

znr zinc resistor; zirconium nitride

ZNS Zodiac News Service

ZNZ Zanatska Nabarnoproajna Zadruga (Yugoslavian—Procurement Sales Cooperative)

zo zero output; zobo (yak + zebu hybrid)

Zo Zoa; Zoe(belle); Zoela; Zoeta; Zofia; Zohora; Zohra; Zoila, Zona, Zonula; Zora(bel); Zorah; Zoraida; Zorana; Zorayda; Zore; Zorica; Zoril; Zorislava; Zorna; Zoruna; Zosa; Zosia; Zosimia; Zowart

ZO Zionist Organization

ZO *Zone Occupée* (French—Occupied Zone); *zuidoost* (Dutch—southeast)

zoa zero-ohms adjustment

ZOA Zionist Organization of America

ZOB *Zentral Omnibus Bahnhof* (German—Central Bus Depot)

zoba bull + yak—hybrid offspring of common bull and yak cow

zobo cow + yak—hybrid of yak bull and common cow

zoc *zócalo* (Mexican Spanish—public square)

Zoc Zocalo (Mexico City's great plaza)

Zócalo Mexico City's main plaza

zod. *zodiacus* (Latin—circle of animals)—the zodiac

zoe zero energy; zinc-oxide eugenol

Zoe Zoebelle; Zoela; Zoeta; Zofia

Zoé (French nickname—atomic pile)

zof zone of fire

Zog Ahmed Zogu

Zoh *Zohar* (The Book of Splendor)

Zolá Émile Zolá—French novelist (1840–1902)—his open letter beginning *J'accuse* (I accuse) denounced anti-semitic detractors of Captain Dreyfus and brought about his vindication; his novels championed everyday people as well as the oppressed; he startled his generation by insisting civilization would take a great step forward when the last stone from the last church fell on the head of the last priest

Zola of America Sir Arthur Conan Doyle's apt nickname for Upton Sinclair who declared: *mankind will not consent to be lied to indefinitely*

Zon Zondag (Dutch—Sunday)

Zondervan Zondervan Publishing House

Zone Panama Canal Zone

Zonian(s) American(s) of the Panama Canal Zone

zoo zoological (garden); zoology

zoo (Latin prefix—animal)—zoological, zoologist, zoology

zoöchem zoochemistry

zoogeog zoogeography

zool zoologic; zoological; zoologist; zoology

zool *zoologi(sk)* (Dano-Norwegian—zoology or zoologist)

Zool Zoology

Zoological Attic of the World Australia, New Guinea, New Zealand, Tasmania

zoomorph zoomorphic initial letter

zoopal zoopaleontology

zoopar zooparasitology

zoopath zoopathology

zooph zoophytology

zoopharm zoopharmacology

zop zero-order predictor; zinc-oxide pigment

zopi zero-order polynomial interpolator

zopp zero-order polynomial predictor

zor zinc-oxide resistor; zone of reconnaissance

Zor Zoroastrian

Zor (Hebrew—Tyre)

Zora Zorabel(la); Zorah; Zoraida; Zorana; Zorayda

zos zoster; zosteriform; zosteri-

formal

ZOS Zapata Corporation (stock exchange symbol)

zot (slang—zero)

zounds (euphemistic contraction —god's wounds)

zox zirconium oxide

zoz *zie ommezijde* (Dutch—the other side)—please turn over (to the other side of the page)

ZP lighter-than-air patrol and escort aircraft (naval symbol); Zellerbach Paper

Z & P Zanzibar and Pemba

ZP *Zagrebian Philharmony* (Yugoslavian—Zagreb Philharmonic Orchestra)

zpa zeus program analysis; zone of polarizing activity

ZPA Zeus Program Analysis; Zoological Parks and Aquariums

zpar zeus-phased array (radar)

zpb zinc primary battery

ZPC Zellerbach Paper Company

ZPDA Zinc Pigment Development Association

zpe zero-point energy

ZPEN Zeus Project Engineer Network

zpg zero population growth

ZPG Zero Population Growth

ZPH Zondervan Publishing House

Z Phys *Zeitschrift für Physik* (German—Physics Periodical)

Z Phys Chem *Zeitschrift für Physikalische Chemie* (German—Physical Chemistry Periodical)

zp & j *zonder plaats en jaar* (Dutch—without place of publication or date)

ZPKK *Zentrale Parteikontrollkommission* (German—Central Control Commission of the Party)—communist

zpl *zonder plaats* (Dutch—without place of publication)

Z Plz Zellerbach Plaza

zpo zinc peroxide

ZPO Zeus Project Office

Zpp Zeiss projection planetarium

zppr zero-power plutonium reactor

zpr zero-power reactor

zprf zero-power reactor facility

ZPRSN Zurich Provisional Relative Sunspot Number

zpt zero-power test(ing); zoxazolamine paralysis time

ZPT Zero Power Test

ZPU-4 Soviet antiaircraft weapon combining fire power of four 14.5mm heavy machine-guns

zr freezing rain (meteorological symbol); zone refined

Zr zirconium

ZR freezing rain (symbol); Zenith Radio

Z-R Zimbabwe-Rhodesia (Zimbabwe; formerly Rhodesia or Southern Rhodesia)

Z/R Zone of Responsibility

Zr⁹⁵ radioactive zirconium

zrc zirconium carbide

ZRC Zenith Radio Corporation

ZRCL Zlac Rowing Club Limited

ZRH Zurich, Switzerland (airport)

zrn zirconium nitride

zrp zero radial play

zrt zero-reaction tool

ZRU *Zone de Rénovation Urbaine* (French—Urban Redevelopment Zone)

zrv zero relative velocity

zs zero shift; zero and subtract; zero surpress; zero suppression (of non-significant zeros in computer-printed numerals)

z S *zur See* (German—of the navy)

Zs *Zeitschrift* (German—periodical)

ZS Zoological Society

zsa zero-set amplifier

zsat zinc-sulfide atmospheric tracer

Zsa Zsa Gabor Sari Gabor

zsb zinc storage battery

zsc zero sub-carrier chromaticity; zinc silicate coat(ing)

ZSC Zeeland Shipping Company; Zoological Society of Cincinnati

Z-scale height determination scale

zsd zebra-stripe display; zinc sulfide detector

ZSDS Zinc Sulfide Detection System

ZSE Zagreb Soloists Ensemble *(Solisti di Zagreb)*

zsf zero skip frequency

zsg zero-speed generator

zsi zero-size image

ZSI Zoological Society of Ireland

Zsig Zsigmond

ZSL Zoological Society of London

ZSL *Zjednoczone Stronnictwo Ludowe* (Polish—United Peasant Party)

ZSM Zoar State Memorial

ZSN Zoological Station of Naples

ZSP Zoological Society of Philadelphia

zspg zero-speed pulse generator

ZSS Zero-Sum Society; Zinc Sulfide System

ZSSD Zoological Society of San Diego

Zssg(n) *Zusammensetzung(en)* [German—compound word(s)]

zst zero strength time (measurement); zinc-sulfide tracer

ZST Zone Standard Time

ZSU-23 Soviet self-propelled antiaircraft gun including quadruple 23mm cannon

ZSU-23-4 Soviet antiaircraft system mounted on a tank and carrying four 23mm cannons

ZSU-57 Soviet self-propelled antiaircraft gun including twin 57mm cannon

Zsuzsa Zsuzsa Heiligenberg

zt zipper tube; zipper tubing

z T *zum Teil* (German—partly)

Zt *Zeit* (German—time)

ZT lighter-than-air training aircraft (naval symbol); Zachary Taylor (12th President U.S.); zero time; zone time

ZT *Zone Torride* (French—torrid zone)

ZTA Zulu Territorial Authority

Z-table mortality table

Z-test Zulliger test

Ztg *Zeitung* (German—newspaper)

Z-time zebra time or zulu time (jargon for Greenwich Mean Time)

ztlp zero-transmission level point

ZTO Zone Transportation Office(r); Zürich Tonhalle Orchester (Zurich Concert Hall Orchestra)

ztp zero temperature plasma

Ztr *Zentner* (German—hundred-weight)

Ztschr *Zeitschrift* (German—periodical)

Z-TWIST Z-shaped open-band twist

Zu Zublena; Zudegi; Zula; Zuleika; Zulena; Zulima; Zulu; Zuma

ZU lighter-than-air utility aircraft (2-letter naval symbol)

ZU-23 Soviet antiaircraft system having a maximum fire power of 2000 rounds per minute

Zubie charismatic and dependable symphonic conductor Zu-

bin Mehta of the New York Philharmonic who only a few years ago was so young his musicians in the Los Angeles Philharmonic nicknamed him Zubie Baby

Zuck *Zuckung* (German—contraction)—sometimes abbreviated Z

ZUF Zapata Urban Front (Mexican terrorist group)

zuid (Dutch—south)

Zuid-Afrika (Afrikaans or Dutch—South Africa)

Zuid Afrikaansche Republiek (Afrikaans—South African Republic)

Zuid-Amerika (Dutch—South America)

Zuider Zee (Dutch—Southern Sea)—now a lake, IJsselmeer, and lands reclaimed and diked off from the North Sea

Zuid-Holland (Dutch—South Holland)—provinces centering around Rotterdam

Zuinglius Latinization of Ulrich Zwingli's name

Zulo Ignacio de Zuloaga

Zulu code word for Greenwich mean time (Zulu time); letter Z radio code; NATO name for Soviet Z-class attack submarines

ZUM Zone Usage Measurement (telephone service)

Zumb Zumbabwe (formerly Rhodesia or Southern Rhodesia)

Zungaria Dzungaria or Sungaria region between Mongolia and Russia

Zunyi (Pinyin Chinese—Tsunyi)

ZUP *Zone à urbaniser en priorité* (French—Priority Urbanization Zone)—slum cleanup or demolition zone

Zur Zurab; Zürich; Zuriel; Zurr

Zürcherdütsch Zürich dialect of Schwyzerdütsch

Zurich account (*see* Z-account)

Zurigo (Italian—Zurich)

Zurl Zuriel

zus *zusammen* (German—together)

Zus *Zusammenfassung* (German—summary)

Zuschr *Zuschrift(en)* [German—communication(s)]

Zut Zutphen

zuverl *zuverlassig* (German—authentic)

zv zika virus

zv *zu verfugung* (German—at disposal)

Zv Zolverein (German—customs union)

ZVEI Zentralverband der Elektrotechnischen Industrie (Central union of the Electrotechnical Industry)

zvr zener voltage regulator

zvrd zener voltage regulator diode

zw zero wear

zw zwart (Dutch—black); zwischen (German—between; within)

Zw Zwischensatz (German—insertion or interpolation or parenthesis)

ZW zuidwest (Dutch—southwest)

zwc zone wind computer

Zweden (Dutch—Sweden)

Zweibrücken (German—Two Bridges)—Deuxponts

Zwitserland (Dutch—Switzerland)

Zwitsers (Dutch—Swiss)

zwitt zwitterion (diplole ion)

zwl zero wave length

ZWO Zuiver Wetenschappelijk Onderzoek (Netherlands Organization for the Advancement of Pure Research)

Zwol Zwolle

Zwolla (Latin—Zwolle)

Zwolle provincial capital of Overijssel in the Netherlands

zwp zone wind plotter

zwv zero wave velocity

Zy Zylota; Zyma

ZYA Zionist Youth Association

zyg zygote

Zyg Zygmunt

zygo zygomatic; zygomaticus

zygo (Latin prefix—join or union)

zym zymurgy

zymol zymology

ZYP Zefkrome Yarn Program

Zyr Zyrian (Finno—Ugric language spoken by Zyrians in Komi SSR)

zyth zythum (ancient beer beverage)

zythep zythepsary (obsolete term for brewery)

zyz zyzzyva

zz increasing degrees of contraction (symbol); zigzag

z-z longitudinal axis/roll axis

zz. zingiber (Latin—ginger)

z Z zur Zeit (German—at present, for the time being)

ZZ Ariana Afghan Airlines; longitudinal or roll axis (symbol); zed-zed; zz-approach

Z&Z Zulch and Zulch

ZZ Zentralbibliothek Zürich (German—Zurich Central Library)—combines the canton state, and university libraries

zza zamack zinc alloy

ZZB Zanzibar (tracking station)

zzc zero-zero condition

zzd zig-zag diagram

z-z fold zig-zag fold (concertina fold)

ZZO zuidzuidoost (Dutch—south southeast)

zzr zig-zag rectifier

Z-z's Zionist zealots

z Zt zur Zeit (German—at present, for the time being)

zzv zero-zero visibility

ZZV Zanesville, Ohio (airport)

ZZW zuidzuidwest (Dutch—south southwest)

ZZZ Zayda, Zorayda, Zorahayda—The Three Beautiful Princesses in Washington Irving's *Alhambra*

ZZZ-ZZZ-ZZZ sawing or snoring (cartoonist symbol)

Airlines of the World

Many of the following entries are in past editions but many more are new or revised.

An open space after a two-letter entry means an airline so coded has been discontinued or the code is available for new airlines.

AA American Airlines
AB Air Cortéz
AC Air Canada
AD Antilles Airboats
AE Air Ceylon
AF Air France
AG Aeronaves del Centro
AH Air Algerie
AI Air India
Air Canada AC (Canadian international airline)
Air France AF
Air India AI (international Indian airline service)
Air NZ NZ, TE
AIRPAC Air Pacific
Air UK United Kingdom airlines (Air Anglia and BIA)
AJ All Island Air
AK Altair Airlines
AL Allegheny Airlines (now USAir)
Alaska Alaska Airlines
Alitalia AZ (international Italian airline)
AM Aeroméxico
American AA
AN Ansett Airlines of Australia
AO Aloha Airlines
AP Aspen Airways
AQ Air Anglia
AR Aerolineas Argentinas
AS Alaska Airlines
AT Royal Air Maroc
AU Austral Lineas Aéreas
AV Avianca
Avensa VE
Avianca Aerovias Nacionales de Colombia (Spanish—National Airlines of Colombia)
AW
AX Air Togo
AY Finnair
AZ Alitalia
BA British Airways
BB Air Great Lakes
BC Brymon Airways
BCAL British Caledonian Airways
BD British Midland Airways
BE
BF Iowa Airlines and Horizon Airways
BG Bangladesh Biman
BH Air U.S.
BI Royal Brunei Airlines
BJ Bakhtar Afghan Airlines

BK Chalk's International Airline
BL Air BVI
BM Aero Transporti Italiani
BN Braniff International Airways
BO Bouraq Indonesia Airlines
BOAC British Overseas Airways Corporation
BP Air Botswana
BQ Business Jets
BR British Caledonian Airways
Braniff BN
British European British European Airways
BS Auxaire-Bretagne
BT Air Martinque (Satair)
BU Braathens SAFE Airtransport
BV Northwest Skyways
BW BWIA International
BX
BY Burlington
BZ Davey Air Services
CA CAAC (Civil Aviation Administration of China)
CB Commuter Airlines
CC Crown Aviation
CD Trans-Provincial Airlines
CE Air Virginia
CF Faucett
CG Clubair
CH Express Airways
CI China Airlines
CJ Colgan Airways
CK Connair
CL Capitol International Airways
CM COPA (Compañia Panameña de Avación)
CN James Air
CO Continental Airlines (Air Micronesia)
Continental CO
CP CP Air
CP Air Canadian Pacific Airlines
CQ Aero-Chaco
CR
CS Colorado Airlines
CT Command Airways
CU Cubana Airlines
CV
CW St Andrews Airways
CX Cathay Pacific Airways
CY Cyprus Airways
CZ Cascade Airways

DA Dan-Air Services
DB Brittany Air International
DC Trans Catalina Airlines
DD Command Airways
DE Downeast Airlines
Delta DL
DF Air Nebraska
DG Darien Airlines
DH Tonga Air Service
DI Delta Air (Germany)
DJ Air Djibouti
DK Decatur
DL Delta Air Lines
DM
DN Skystream Airlines
DO Dominicana de Aviación
DP Cochise Airlines
DQ
DR Advance Airlines
DS Air Senegal
DT TAAG-Angola Airlines
DU Roland Air
DV Ede-Aire
DW DLT Deutsche Regional
DX Danair
DY
DZ Douglas Airways
EA Eastern Airlines
Eastern EA
EB Eagle Airlines
EC Air Ecosse
ED Sunbird
EE Eagle Commuter Airlines
EF Far Eastern Air Transport
EG Japan Asia Airways
EH Roederer Aviation
EI Air Lingus (Irish)
EJ New England Airlines
EK Masling Commuter Services
EL Nihon Kinkyori Airways
El Al LY
EM Hammond's Air Service
EN Air Caravane
EO Aeroamérica
EP Tropic Air Services
EQ TAME
ER
ES Airways of New Mexico
ET Ethiopian Airlines
EU Empresa Ecuatoriana de Aviación
EV Atlantic Southeast
EW East-West Airlines
EX Eagle Aviation
EY Europe Aero Service
EZ

FA Finnaviation
FB
FC Chaparral Airlines
FD Wiscair
FE Florida Airlines and Air South
FF Air Link
FG Ariana Afghan Airlines
FH Mall Airways
FI Flugfelag-Icelandair
Finnair Finnish Airlines
FJ Air Pacific
FK Geelong Air Travel
FL Frontier Airlines
FM
FN Air Carolina
FO Southern Nevada
FP Simmons
FQ Compagnie Aerienne du Languedoc
FR Susquehanna
FS Key Airlines
FT
FU Air Littoral
FV Frisia Luftverkehr
FW Wright Airlines
FX Mountain West Airlines
FY Metroflight Airlines and Great Plains Airline
FZ Air Chico
GA Garuda Indonesian Airways
GB Air Inter Gabon
GC Lina-Congo
GD Air North
GE Maui Commuter
GF Gulf Air
GG Gem State Airlines
GH Ghana Airways
GI
GJ Ansett Airlines of South Australia
GK Laker Airways
GL
GM Scheduled Skyways System
GN Air Gabon
GO
GP Hadag Air Seebaederflug
GQ Big Sky Airlines
GR Aurigny Air Services
GS
GT Gibraltar Airways
GU Aviateca
GV Talair
GW Golden West Airlines
GX Great Lakes Airlines
GY Guyana Airways
GZ Indiana Airways
HA Hawaiian Air Lines
HB Air Melanesiae
HC Haiti Air International
HD Air Mont
HE Green Bay Aviation
HF First Air
HG Harbor Airlines

HH Somali Airlines
HI Hensley Flying Service
HJ
HK South Pacific Island Airways
HL
HM Air Mahe
HN NLM-Dutch Airlines
HO Charterair
HP Air Hawaii
HQ Heussler Air Service
HR Eastern Caribbean Airways
HS Marshall's Air
HT Air Tchad
HU Trinidad and Tobago Air Services
Hughes Hughes Air West
HV Air Central
HW Havasu Airlines
HX Cosmopolitan Aviation
HY Metro Airlines
HZ Henebery Aviation
IA Iraqi Airways
IB Iberia Air Lines of Spain
Iberia IB
IC Indian Airlines
ID Apollo Airways
IE Solomon Islands Airways
IF Interflug
IG Alisarda
IH Itavia
II Imperial Airlines
IJ Touraine Air Transport
IK Eureka Aero Industries
IL Island Air
IM Jamahe
Imperial II
IN East Hampton Air
IO Air Paris
IP Executive Airlines
IQ Caribbean Airways
IR Iran National Airlines
Irish EI
IS Eagle Air
IT Air Inter
IU Midstate Airlines
IV Chaparral Aviation
IW International Air Bahama
IX Trans Air Express
IY Yemen Airways
IZ Arkia-Israel Inland Airlines
JA Bankair
JAL JL
Japan JL
JB Pioneer Airways
JC Rocky Mountain Airways
JD Toa Domestic Airlines
JE Yosemite Airlines
JF LAB Flying Service
JG Swedair
JH Nordeste-Lineas Aéreas Regionais
JI Gull Air
JJ Coddair Air East
JK
JL Japan Air Lines

JM Air Jamaica
JN Air Bama
JO Holiday Airlines
JP Indo-Pacific International
JQ Trans-Jamaican Airlines
JR Delta Air
JS
JT Air Oregon
JU Yugoslav Airlines
JV Bearskin Lake
JW Royal American
JX Bougair
JY Jersey European
JZ Alamo Commuter Airlines
KA Coastal Plains Commuter
KB Burnthills
KC Aeromech
KD Kendell Airlines
KE Korean Air Lines
KF Catskill Airways
KG Catalina Airlines
KH Cook Island Airways
KI Time Air
KJ Sea Airmotive
KL KLM (Koninklijke Lucht-vaart Maatschappij)—Royal Dutch Airlines
KLM KL
KM Air Malta
KN Air Kentucky
KO Kodiak Western Alaska Airlines
KP
KQ Kenya Airways
KR Kar-Air (Finland)
KS Peninsula Airways
KT Turtle Airways
KU Kuwait Airways
KV Transkei Airways
KW Dorado Wings
KX Cayman Airways
KY Sun West
KZ Oriens & King
LA LAN Chile
LB Lloyd Aereo Boliviano
LC Loganair
LD LADE (Lineas Aéreas del Estado)
LE Magnum Airlines
LF Linjeflyg
LG Luxair (Luxembourg Airlines)
LH Lufthansa German Airlines
LI LIAT (Leeward Islands Air Transport)
LJ Sierra Leone Airways
LK Letaba Airways
LL Bell-Air
LM ALM (Antillianaanse Luchtvaart Maatschappij)—Dutch-Antillean Airline Company
LN Libyan Arab Airlines
LO LOT (Polish Airlines)
LP Air Alpes
LQ Inland Empire Airlines

LR LACSA (*Lineas Aéreas Costarricenses*)—Costa Rican Airlines
LS Marco Island Airways
LT Great Sierra
LU
Lufthansa LH
LV LAV (*Linea Aeropostal Venezolana*)—Venezuelan Aeropost Lines
LW Air Nevada
LX Crossair
LY El Al Israel Airlines
LZ Balkan (Bulgarian Airlines)
MA *MALEV* (*Magyar Legikolekedesi Vallat*)—Hungarian Air Lines
MB Countrywide
MC Rapidair
MD Air Madagascar
ME Middle East Airlines/Air Liban
MF Red Carpet Flying Service
MG Pompano Airways
MH Malaysian Airline System
MI Mackey International Airlines
MJ Lineas Aereas Privadas Argentinas
MK Air Mauritius
ML Aviation Services
MM Sociedad Aeronautica Medellin
MN COMAIR (Commercial Airways)
MO
MP Atlantis Airlines
MQ Magnum Airlines
MR Air Mauritanie
MS Egyptair
MT Mac Knight Airlines
MU Misrair
MV MacRobertson-Miller Airline Service
MW Maya Airways
MX Mexicana de Aviación
MY Air Mali
MZ Merpati Nusatnara Airlines
NA National Airlines
National NA
NB New Haven Airways
NC Newair
ND Nordair
NE Air New England
NF EJA/Newport
NG Green Hills Aviation
NH All Nippon
NI LANICA (*Lineas Aéreas de Nicaragua*)—Nicaraguan Airlines
NJ Namakwaland Lugdiens
NK NORCANAIR
NL Air Liberia
NM Mt Cook Airlines
NN Air Trails

NO Air North
Northwest NW
NP Desert Pacific
NQ Cumberland Airlines
NR NORONTAIR
NS Nuernberger
NT Lake State Airways
NU Southwest Airlines
NV Northwest Territorial Airways
NW Northwest Orient Airlines
NX New Zealand Air Charter
NY New York Airways
NZ Air New Zealand (domestic)
OA Olympic Airways
OB Opal Air
OC Air California
OD Aerocondor
OE Samoan
OF Noosa Air
OG Air Guadeloupe
OH Comair
OI TAVINA (*Trans-Colombiana de Aviación*)
OJ Air Texana
OK Czechoslovak Airlines
OL ÖLT (*Östfriesische Lufttransport*)—German—East Frisian Air Transport
OM Air Mongol (MIAT)
ON Air Nauru
OO Sunaire Lines
OP Air Panamá Internacional
OQ Royale Airlines
OR Air Comores
OS Austrian Airlines
OT
OU Otonabee Airways
OV
OW Trans Mountain Airlines
OX Air Atlantic Airlines
OY New Jersey Airways
OZ Ozark Air Lines
PA Pan American World Airways
Pan Am PA
PB Air Burundi
PC Fiji Air
PD Pem Air
PE People Express
PF Trans Pennsylvania Airlines
PG Florida Commuter
PH Polynesian Airlines
Philippine PR
PI Piedmont Aviation
PJ
PK Pakistan International
PL Aero Peru
PM Pilgrim Airlines
PN Princeton Aviation
PO Aeropelican Intercity Commuter Air Services
PP Phillips Airlines
PQ PRINAIR (Puerto Rican In-

ternational Airlines)
PR Philippine Airlines
PS PSA (Pacific Southwest Airlines)
PT Provincetown-Boston Airline
PU *PLUNA* (*Primeras Lineas Uruguayos de Navegación Aérea*)—Spanish—First Uruguayan Aerial Navigation Lines
PV Eastern Provincial Airways
PW Pacific Western Airlines
PX Air Niugini (Air New Guinea)
PY Surinam Airways
PZ LAP (*Lineas Aéreas Paraguayas*)
QA
Qantas QF
QB Quebecair
QC Air Zaire
QD Trans-Brasil
QE Air Tahiti
QF Qantas Airways
QG Sky West Aviation
QH Air Florida
QI
QJ Lesotho Airways
QK Mexico Air Service
QL
QM Air Malawi
QN Bush Pilots Airways
QO Bar Harbor Airlines
QP Sunbird
QQ Emmet County
QR
QS Cal Sierra
QT Vaengir (Wings Air Iceland)
QU Uganda Airlines
QV Lao Aviation
QW Air Turks and Caicos
QX Century Airlines
QY Aero Virgin Islands
QZ Zambia Airways
RA Royal Nepal Airlines
RB Syrian Arab Airlines
RC Republic
RD
RE
RF Rossair
RG VARIG (*Viação Aérea Rio Grandense*)—Portugese—Rio Grande Airlines
RH Air Zimbabwe
RI Eastern Airlines
RJ Royal Jordanian Airlines (ALIA)
RK Air Afrique
RL Crown International Airlines
RM Wings West
RN Royal Air International
RO TAROM (Romanian Air Transport)

Route of the Red Baron LH
RP Precision Airlines
RQ Maldives International Airlines
RR
RS Aeropesca
RT Norving
RU Britt Airways
RV Reeve Aleutian Airways
RW Republic
RX Capitol Air Service
RY Perkiomen Airways
RZ Arabia (Arab International)
SA South African Airways
SABENA SN
SAS SK
SB
SC Cruzeiro do Sul
SD Sudan Airways
SE Southeast Skyways
SF Scruse Air
SG Atlantis
SH SAHSA (Servicio Aéreo de Honduras SA)
SI Air Sierra
SJ Stewart Island
SK SAS (Scandinavian Airlines)
3L Rio-3ul
SM
SN SABENA (Belgian Airlines)
SO Austrian Air
SP SATA (Sociedade Açoriana de Transportes Aéreos)—Portuguese—Azores Air Transport Line
SQ Singapore Airlines
SR Swissair
SS South Coast Airlines
ST Belize Airways
SU Aeroflot (Soviet Union Airlines)
SV Saudi Arabian Airlines
SW Namib Air
Swissair SR
SX Christman Air System
SY Air Alsace
SZ ProAir Services
TA Taca International
TAP TP
TB Tejas Airlines
TC Air Tanzania
TD
TE Air New Zealand (international)
TF Veeneal
TG Thai Airways (international)
TH Thai Airways (domestic)
TI Texas International Airlines
TJ Oceanair
TK Turk Hava Yollari
TL
TM DETA (Direçầo de Exploração dos Transportes Aéreos)—Portuguese—Direc-

torate of Exploration of Aerial Transport—(Mozambique Airline)
TN Trans-Australia Airlines
TO
TP TAP (Transportes Aéreos Portugueses)—Portuguese Air Transport
TQ Las Vegas Airlines
TR Royal Air
TS
TT Royal West
TU Tunis Air
TV Transamerica
TW Trans World Airlines
TWA TW
TX Transportes Aéreos Nacionales
TY Air Caledonie
TZ (SANSA) Services Aereos Nacionales
UA United Airlines
UB Burma Airways
UC LADECO (Linea del Cobre)—Spanish—Copper Line
UD Georgian Bay
UE United Air
UF Sydaero
UG Norfolk Island Airlines
UH Austin Airways
UI Flugfelag Nordurlands—Northlands Air
UJ
UK British Island Airways (Air UK)
UL Air Lanka
UM
UN East Coast Airlines
United UA
UO Direct Air
UP Bahamas Air
UQ Suburban Airlines
UR Empire Airlines
USAir formerly Allegheny Airlines
UT UTA (Union de Transports Aeriens)—Union Transport Airline
UU Reunion Air
UV Universal Airways
UW Perimeter Airlines
UX Air Illinois
UY Cameroon Airlines
UZ Nefertiti
VA VIASA (Venezolana Internacional de Aviación)—Spanish—Venezuelan International Aviation)
VB Westair Commuter Airlines
VC TAC (Transportes Aéreos del Cesar)
VD
VE AVENSA (Aerovias Venezolanas)—Spanish—Venezuelan Airlines

VF Golden West
VG City Flug
VH Air Volta
VI Vieques Airlink
VJ Trans-Colorado
VK Air Tungaru
VL Mid-South Commuter Airlines
VM Ocean Airways
VN Hang Khong Vietnam
VO Tyrolean Airways
VP VASP (Viação São Paulo)—Portuguese—São Paulo Airline
VQ
VR Transportes Aéreos de Cabo Verde
VS
VT Air Polynesie
VU Air Ivoire
VV Semo Aviation
VW Ama-Flyg
VX Aces
VY Coral Air
VZ Aquatic Airways
WA Western Airlines
WB SAN (Servicios Aéreos Nacionales)—Spanish—National Air Services
WC Wien Air Alaska
WD
WE Votec
Western WA
WF Wideroes Flyveselskap
WG ALAG (Alpine Luft Transport AG)—German—Alpine Air Transport Company
WH Southeastern Commuter Airlines
WI Swift-Aire Lines
WJ Torontair
WK Westkuestenflug
WL Bursa Hava Yollari
WM Windward Island Airways International
WN Southwest Airlines
WO World Airways
WP Princeville Airways
WQ Wings Airways
WR Wheeler Flying Service
WS Northern Wings (Québec-air)
WT Nigeria Airways
WU Rhine Air
WV Midwest Aviation
WW Trans-West
WX Ansett Airlines of New South Wales
WY Indiana Airways
WZ Trans Western Airlines of Utah
XA
XB
XC
XD
XE South Central

XF Cobden Airways
XG Air North
XH
XI
XJ Mesaba Aviation
XK *AEROTAL* (*Aerolineas Territoriales de Colombia*)—Spanish—Territorial Airlines of Colombia
XL
XM
XN
XO Rio Airways
XP Avior
XQ Caribbean International
XR
XS
XT Executive Transportation
XU Trans Mo Airlines
XV Mississippi Valley Airways
XW Walker's Cay Air Terminal
XX Valdez Airlines
XY Munz Northern
XZ Air Tasmania
YA
YB Hyannis Aviation
YC Alaska Aeronautical Industries
YD Ama Air Express
YE Pearson Aircraft

YF
YG
YH Trans New York
YI Intercity
YJ Commodore
YK Cyprus Turkish Airways
YL Montauk Caribbean Airways and Ocean Reef Airways
YM Mountain Home Air Service
YN Nor-East Commuter Airlines
YO Heli-Air-Monaco
YP Pagas Airlines
YQ Lakeland
YR Scenic Airlines
YS San Juan Airlines
YT Sky West
YU Aerolineas Dominicanas
YV Mesa Aviation
YW Willi's Air
YX Société Aeronautique Jurassiènne
YY
YZ Linhas Aéreas da Guine-Bissau
ZA Alpine Aviation
ZB Air Vectors
ZC Royal Swazi National Air-

ways
ZD Ross Aviation
ZE Pacific National
ZF Berlin U.S.A.
ZG Silver State
ZH Royal Hawaiian Airways
ZI Lucas Air Transport
ZJ
ZK Shavano Air
ZL Hazelton Air Services
ZM Trans-Central
ZN Tennessee Airways
ZO Trans-California
ZP Virgin Air
ZQ Lawrence Aviation
ZR Star Airways
ZS Grand Canyon Airlines
ZT *SATENA* (*Servicio Aeronavegación a Territorios Nacionales*) — Spanish — Aeronavigation Service to National Territories
ZU Zia Airlines
ZV Air Midwest
ZW Air Wisconsin
ZX Air West Airlines
ZY Air Pennsylvania
ZZ

Airports of the World

AAA Ararangúa, Brazil
AAB Arrabury, Queensland
AAE Annaba, Algeria
AAG Alto Araguaia, Brazil
AAI Arraias, Brazil
AAL Aalborg, Denmark
AAO Anaco, Venezuela
AAQ Aqiq, Saudi Arabia
AAR Aarhus-Randers, Denmark (airport serving both cities)
AAU Arua, Uganda
AAX Araxá, Brazil
AAY Al Ghaydah, Aden
ABA Ababa, Ethiopia
ABD Abadan, Iran
ABE Allentown-Bethlehem-Easton, Pennsylvania
ABG Abingdon, Queensland
ABI Abilene, Texas
ABJ Abidjan, Ivory Coast
ABQ Albuquerque, New Mexico
ABR Aberdeen, South Dakota
ABW Abau, Papua
ABX Albury, New South Wales
ABY Albany, Georgia
ABZ Aberdeen, Scotland
ACA Acapulco, Mexico
ACC Accra, Ghana

ACE Arrecife, Canary Islands
ACI Alderney, United Kingdom
ACK Nantucket, Massachusetts
ACN Mbala, Zambia
ACT Waco, Texas
ACV Arcata-Eureka, California (airport shared by both places)
ACY Atlantic City, New Jersey
ADA Adana, Turkey
ADD Addis Ababa, Ethiopia
ADE Aden, Southern Yemen
ADH Ada, Oklahoma
ADL Adelaide, South Australia
ADM Ardmore, Oklahoma
ADN Aydin, Turkey
ADP Anuradhapura, Ceylon
ADZ San Andrés, San Andrés Island (Caribbean)
AEH Abecher, Chad
AEO Aioun el Atro, Mauritania
AER Adler/Sochi, USSR
AES Aalesund, Norway
AEY Akureyri, Iceland
AFA San Rafael, Argentina
AFI Amalfi, Colombia
AFY Afyon, Turkey
AGA Agadir, Morocco

AGH Angelhome-Hälsingborg, Sweden (airport shared by both communities)
AGN Angoon, Alaska
AGP Málaga, Spain
AGQ Agrinion, Greece
AGR Agra, India
AGS Augusta, Georgia
AGX Araguacema, Brazil
AGZ Agri, Turkey
AHB Abha, Saudi Arabia
AHN Athens, Georgia
AHO Alghero-Sassari, Italy (airport shared by both communities)
AHU Al Hoceima, Morocco
AIA Alliance, Nebraska
AIM Salima, Malawi
AIT Aitutaki Island, Cook Islands
AJA Ajaccio, Corsica
AJF Jouf, Saudi Arabia
AJJ Akjoujt, Mauritania
AJN Anjouan, Comoro Islands
AJU Aracaju, Brazil
AJY Agades, Niger
AKF Kufra, Libya
AKH Akhisar, Turkey
AKL Auckland, New Zealand
AKN King Salmon-Naknek,

BES Brest, France
BEU Bedourie, Queensland
BEW Beira, Mozambique
BEY Beirut, Lebanon
BFD Bradford, Pennsylvania
BFF Scottsbluff, Nebraska
BFI Seattle, Washington (Boeing Field)
BFL Bakersfield, California
BFN Bloemfontein, South Africa
BFO Buffalo Range, Rhodesia
BFS Belfast, Northern Ireland
BFU Beaufort West, South Africa
BGA Bucaramanga, Colombia
BGB Booue, Gabon
BGD Borger, Texas
BGF Bangui, Central African Republic
BGG Bogra, Bangladesh
BGH Boghe, Mauritania
BGI Bridgetown, Barbados
BGM Binghamton–Endicott–Johnson City, New York (airport shared by three neighboring cities)
BGO Bergen, Norway
BGR Bangor, Maine
BGU Bangassou, Central African Republic
BGW Baghdad, Iraq
BGX Bagé, Brazil
BHA Bahía, Ecuador
BHB Bar Harbor, Maine
BHD Kabwe, Zambia
BHH Bisha, Saudi Arabia
BHI Bahía Blanca, Argentina
BHJ Bhuj, India
BHM Birmingham, Alabama
BHN Beihan, South Arabia
BHO Bhopal, India
BHQ Broken Hill, New South Wales
BHS Bathurst, New South Wales
BHT Brighton Downs, Queensland
BHU Bhavnagar, India
BHX Birmingham, England
BHZ Belo Horizonte, Brazil
BIA Bastia, Corsica
BIF The Bight, Cat Island, Bahamas
BIK Biak, Indonesia
BIL Billings, Montana
BIM Bimini, Bahamas
BIO Bilbao, Spain
BIQ Biarritz, France
BIR Biratnagar, Nepal
BIS Bismarck, North Dakota
BIV Bria, Central African Republic
BIX Franz Josef Glacier, New Zealand
BJC Bartica, Guyana

BJD Birjand, Iran
BJI Bemidji, Minnesota
BJM Bujumbura, Burundi
BJO Brejo, Brazil
BJP Begumganj, Pakistan
BJR Bahar Dar, Ethiopia
BJZ Badajoz, Spain
BKE Baker, Oregon
BKG Boke, Guinea
BKI Kota Kinabalu, Malaysia
BKK Bangkok, Thailand
BKM Moscow, USSR (Bykovo Airport)
BKN Birni, Nkoni, Niger
BKO Bamako, Mali
BKQ Blackall, Queensland
BKR Bokoro, Chad
BKS Bengkulu, Indonesia
BKU Betioky, Malagasy
BKW Beckley, West Virginia
BKX Brookings, South Dakota
BKY Bukavu, Zaire
BKZ Bukoba, Tanzania
BLA Barcelona, Venezuela
BLB Balboa, Panama Canal
BLD Boulder City, Nevada
BLE Borlange, Sweden
BLF Bluefield–Princeton, West Virginia (airport serving both communities)
BLG Belaga, Malaysia
BLH Blythe, California
BLI Bellingham, Washington
BLJ Batna, Algeria
BLL Billund, Denmark
BLO Blonduos, Iceland
BLQ Bologna, Italy
BLR Bangalore, India
BLX Belluno, Italy
BLY Bled, Yugoslavia
BLZ Blantyre, Malawi
BMA Stockholm, Sweden
BMB Bumba, Congo
BMD Belo, Malagasy
BME Broome, Western Australia
BMI Bloomington, Illinois
BML Berlin–Milan, New Hampshire (airport serving both communities)
BMM Bitam, Gabon
BMN Batman, Turkey
BMO Bhamo, Burma
BMP Brampton Island, Queensland
BMV Banmethuot, South Vietnam
BMZ Belmonte, Brazil
BNA Nashville, Tennessee
BNB Boende, Zaire
BND Bandar Abbas, Iran
BNE Brisbane, Queensland
BNI Benin City, Nigeria
BNJ Bonn, Germany
BNM Barrancas, Venezuela
BNN Brönnöysund, Norway

BNP Bannu, Pakistan
BNS Barinas, Venezuela
BNX Banaras, India
BNZ Banz, New Guinea
BOB Bora-Bora, Society Islands
BOD Bordeaux, France
BOG Bogotá, Colombia
BOH Bournemouth, England
BOI Boise, Idaho
BOJ Burgas, Bulgaria
BOM Bombay, India
BON Bonaire, Netherlands Antilles
BOO Bodo, Norway
BOP Bouar, Central African Republic
BOS Boston, Massachusetts
BOY Bobo Dioulass, Volta
BPN Balikpapan, Indonesia
BPT Beaumont–Port Arthur, Texas (airport serving both cities)
BPY Besalampy, Malagasy
BQL Boulia, Queensland
BQQ Barra, Brazil
BQR Butare, Rwanda
BRA Barreiras, Brazil
BRC San Carlos de Bariloche, Argentina
BRE Bremen
BRF Bradford, England
BRI Bari, Italy
BRL Burlington, Iowa
BRM Barquisimeto, Venezuela
BRN Bern, Switzerland
BRO Brownsville, Texas
BRQ Brno, Czechoslovakia
BRR Barra, United Kingdom
BRS Bristol, England
BRU Brussels, Belgium
BRW Barrow, Alaska
BRZ Bruzual, Venezuela
BSB Brasilia, Brazil
BSE Sematan, Sarawak, Malaysia
BSG Bata, Spanish Guinea
BSH Brighton, England
BSK Biskra, Algeria
BSL Basel, Switzerland (also spelled Basle)
BSN Bossangoa, Central African Republic
BSR Basra, Iraq
BSS Balsas, Brazil
BSU Basankusu, Zaire
BTC Batticaloa, Ceylon
BTD Brunett Downs, Northern Territory, Australia
BTH Bathurst, Gambia
BTJ Banda Atjeh, Indonesia
BTL Battle Creek, Michigan
BTM Butte, Montana
BTN Brunei Town, Brunei
BTO St Barthelemy, Leeward Islands, West Indies

BTR Baton Rouge, Louisiana
BTS Bratislava, Czechoslovakia
BTU Bintulu, Sarawak, Malaysia
BTV Burlington, Vermont
BTX Betoota, Queensland
BTZ Bursa, Turkey
BUA Buka, Solomon Islands
BUC Burketown, Queensland
BUD Budapest, Hungary
BUE Buenos Aires, Argentina
BUF Buffalo, New York
BUG Benguela, Angola
BUH Bucharest, Romania
BUJ Buno Bedelle, Ethiopia
BUK Bolu, Turkey
BUL Bulolo, New Guinea
BUN Buenaventura, Colombia
BUO Burao, Somalia
BUQ Bulawayo, Zimbabwe
BUR Burbank, California
BUX Bunia, Zaire
BUZ Bushire, Iran
BVA Beauvais, France
BVB Boa Vista, Brazil
BVH Vilhena, Brazil
BVI Birdsville, Queensland
BVO Bartlesville, Oklahoma
BVS Bela Vista, Brazil
BWG Bowling Green, Kentucky
BWP Bahawalpur, Pakistan
BXE Bakel, Senegal
BXO Bissau, Portuguese Guinea
BYI Burley-Rupert, Idaho (airport shared by both towns)
BYK Bouake, Ivory Coast
BYV Baiyer River, New Guinea
BZE Belize, British Honduras
BZI Balikesir, Turkey
BZL Barisal, Bangladesh
BZN Bozeman, Montana
BZO Bolzano, Italy
BZV Brazzaville, Congo
BZY Brasileia, Brazil
CAB Cabinda, Angola
CAC Cascavel, Brazil
CAE Columbia, South Carolina
CAF Carauari, Brazil
CAG Cagliari, Italy
CAI Cairo, Egypt
CAJ Canaima, Venezuela
CAK Akron-Canton, Ohio
CAL Campbeltown, Scotland
CAN Canton, China
CAS Casablanca, Morocco
CAT Cat Island, Bahamas
CAX Carlisle, England
CAY Cayenne, French Guiana
CBB Cochabamba, Bolivia
CBE Cumberland, Maryland
CBG Cambridge, England
CBH Colomb Bechar, Algeria

CBL Ciudad Bolívar, Venezuela
CBN Cabarien, Cuba
CBQ Calabar, Nigeria
CBR Canberra, Australian Capital Territory
CBY Canobie, Queensland
CBZ Cucui, Brazil
CCH Chile Chico, Chile
CCK Cocos Island, Keeling Islands, Australia
CCM Criciuma, Brazil
CCP Concepción, Chile
CCQ Cachoeira do Sul, Brazil
CCS Caracas, Venezuela (Maiquetia Airport)
CCU Calcutta, India
CCX Caceres, Brazil
CDC Cedar City, Utah
CDD Castle Donington-East Midlands, England (airport shared by both places)
CDF Cortina d'Ampezzo, Italy
CDJ Conceição, Brazil
CDP Chandpur, Bangladesh
CDQ Croydon, Queensland
CDR Chadron, Nebraska
CDV Cordova, Alaska
CDX Codu, Brazil
CDZ Codajaz, Brazil
CEB Cebu, Philippines
CEC Crescent City, California
CEG Chester, England
CEN Ciudad Obregon, Mexico
CEP Concepción, Bolivia
CEQ Cannes, France
CER Cherbourg, France
CEZ Cortez, Colorado
CFD Bryan, Texas
CFE Clermont-Ferrand, France
CFG Cienfuegos, Cuba
CFR Caen, France
CFU Corfu, Greece
CGB Cuiaba, Brazil
CGC Cape Gloucester, New Britain, New Guinea
CGH São Paulo, Brazil (Congonhas Airport)
CGI Cape Girardeau, Missouri
CGN Cologne, Germany
CGO Chengchow, China
CGP Chittagong, Bangladesh
CGR Campo Grande, Brazil
CHA Chattanooga, Tennessee
CHC Christchurch, New Zealand
CHI Chicago, Illinois (airports)—C-CGX (Meigs); O-ORD (O'Hare); M-MDW (Midway)
CHL Chalna, Bangladesh
CHO Charlottesville, Virginia
CHQ Chania, Greece
CHS Charleston, South Carolina
CHT Chita, USSR

CHU Chabua, India
CHW Charleston, West Virginia
CIC Chico, California
CID Cedar Rapids–Iowa City, Iowa
CII Chitipa, Malawi
CIR Cairo, Illinois
CIS Canton Island, Phoenix Islands
CIX Chiclayo, Peru
CIY Comiso, Italy
CJB Coimbatore, India
CJC Calama, Chile
CJL Chitral, Pakistan
CJS Ciudad Juarez, Mexico
CJU Cheju, South Korea
CJZ Cajazeiras, Brazil
CKB Clarksburg, West Virginia
CKG Chungking, China
CKV Clarksville, Tennessee–Hopkinsville, Kentucky (airport shared by two places in two states)
CKY Conakry, Guinea
CKZ Canakkale, Turkey
CLA Comilla, Bangladesh
CLE Cleveland, Ohio (airports—L-BKL (Lakefront); C-CLE (Hopkins); Y-CGF (Cuyahoga)
CLF Clear, Alaska
CLH Coolah, New South Wales
CLN Carolina, Brazil
CLO Cali, Colombia
CLT Charlotte, North Carolina
CLY Calvi, Corsica
CLZ Cristalandia, Brazil
CMA Cunnamulla, Queensland
CMB Colombo, Ceylon
CME Ciudad del Carmen, Mexico
CMG Corumba, Brazil
CMH Columbus, Ohio
CMI Champaign, Illinois
CML Camooweal, Queensland
CMQ Clermont, Queensland
CMV Cayo Mambi, Cuba
CMW Camagüey, Cuba
CMX Hancock-Houghton, Michigan (airport serving both places)
CNA Cananea, Mexico
CND Constanta, Romania
CNJ Cloncurry, Queensland
CNM Carlsbad, New Mexico
CNN Carinhanha, Brazil
CNQ Corrientes, Argentina
CNR Chañaral, Chile
CNS Cairns, Queensland
CNV Canavieras, Brazil
COC Concordia, Argentina
COE Coeur d'Alene, Idaho
COG Condoto, Colombia
COH Cooch Behar, India

DPO Devonport, Tasmania
DPS Denpasar, Bali, Indonesia
DPU Dumpu, New Guinea
DRB Derby, Western Australia
DRM Drama, Greece
DRN Dirranbandi, Queensland
DRO Durango, Colorado
DRR Durrie, Queensland
DRS Dresden, Germany
DRT Del Rio, Texas
DRW Darwin, Northern Territory, Australia
DSE Dessie, Ethiopia
DSK Dera Ismail Khan, Pakistan
DSL Daru, Sierra Leone
DSM Des Moines, Iowa
DTM Dortmund, Germany
DTT Detroit, Michigan (airports)—D-DET (City Airport); M-DTW (Metropolitan); R-YIP (Willow Run), W-WQG (Windsor, Ontario)
DUB Dublin, Ireland
DUD Dunedin, New Zealand
DUG Bisbee-Douglas, Arizona
DUI Duisburg, Germany
DUJ Dubois, Pennsylvania
DUR Durban, South Africa
DUS Düsseldorf, Germany
DUT Dutch Harbor, Alaska
DVO Davao, Philippines
DVP Davenport Downs, Queensland
DWB Soalala, Malagasy
DWP Dalbandin, Pakistan
DXB Dubai, Trucial Oman
DXT Dhoxaton, Greece
DXY Derby, England
DYM Diamantina Lakes, Queensland
DYU Dushanbe, USSR
DYW Daly Waters, Northern Territory, Australia
DZA Dzaoudzi, Comoro Islands
EAH El Arish, Egypt
EAM Nejran, Saudi Arabia
EAS San Sebastian, Spain
EAT Wenatchee, Washington
EAU Eau Claire, Wisconsin
EBA Elba, Italy
EBB Entebbe–Kampala, Uganda (airport shared by both cities)
EBD El Obeid, Sudan
EBG El Bagre, Colombia
EBU St Etienne, France
EBW Ebolowa, Cameroon
ECG Elizabeth City, North Carolina
EDI Edinburgh, Scotland
EDL Eldoret, Kenya
EEN Brattleboro, Vermont–Keene, New Hampshire (airport serving two places in two

states)
EFK Newport, Vermont
EGL Neghelli, Ethiopia
EGN El Geneina, Sudan
EGS Egilsstadir, Iceland
EIN Eindhoven, Netherlands
EIS Beef Island, British Virgin Islands
EIT Eilat, Israel
EJA Barrancabermeja, Colombia
EJH Wedjh, Saudi Arabia
EJO Nejo, Ethiopia
EKN Elkins, West Virginia
EKO Elko, Nevada
EKT Eskilstuna, Sweden
ELB El Banco, Colombia
ELD El Dorado, Arkansas
ELE El Adem, Libya
ELF El Fasher, Sudan
ELG El Golea, Algeria
ELH Eleuthera Island, Bahamas
ELM Corning–Elmira, New York (airport shared by both cities)
ELP El Paso, Texas
ELQ Gassim, Saudi Arabia
ELS East London, South Africa
ELU El Oued, Algeria
ELY Ely, Nevada
EMN Nema, Mauritania
ENA Kenai, Alaska
ENK Enniskillen, Northern Ireland
ENS Enschede, Netherlands
ENU Enugu, Nigeria
EOR El Dorado, Venezuela
EOZ Elorza, Venezuela
EPR Esperance, Australia
EQS Esquel, Argentina
ERA Erigavo, Somalia
ERC Erzincan, Turkey
ERF Erfurt, Germany
ERG Eromanga, New Hebrides
ERI Erie, Pennsylvania
ERM Erechim, Brazil
ERN Eirunepe, Brazil
ERZ Erzurum, Turkey
ESA Esa Ala, New Guinea
ESB Ankara, Turkey
ESC Escanaba, Michigan
ESF Alexandria, Louisiana
ESH Shoreham, England
ESM Esmeraldas, Ecuador
ESN Easton, Maryland
ETE Metema, Ethiopia
ETH Eilat, Israel (Elath)
EUG Eugene, Oregon
EUN El Aaiún, Morocco
EUX Sint Eustatius, Netherlands Antilles
EVN Erevan, USSR
EVV Evansville, Indiana
EWB Fall River–New Bedford,

Massachusetts (airport serving both seaport cities)
EWI Enarotali, West Irian, Indonesia
EWN New Bern, North Carolina
EWR Newark, New Jersey
EXT Exeter, England
EYW Key West, Florida
EZS Elazig, Turkey
FAG Fagurholsmyri, Iceland
FAI Fairbanks, Alaska
FAN Farsund, Norway
FAR Fargo, North Dakota
FAT Fresno, California
FAY Fayetteville–Ft Bragg, North Carolina (airport shared by both places)
FBA Fonte Boa, Brazil
FBM Lubumbashi, Zaire
FBU Oslo, Norway (Fornebu Airport)
FCA Kalispell, Montana
FDA Fundación, Colombia
FDB Forte Princip, Brazil
FDF Ft de France, Martinique
FDP Faridpur, Bangladesh
FDU Bandundu, Zaire
FEI Feijo, Brazil
FEZ Fez, Morocco
FFT Frankfort, Kentucky
FFU Futaleufú, Chile
FGD Ft Derik, Mauritania
FGL Fox Glacier, New Zealand
FHU Ft Huachuca, Arizona
FIG Fria, Guinea
FIH Kinshasa, Zaire
FIN Finschhafen, New Guinea
FIT Fitchburg, Massachusetts
FJM Chipata, Zambia
FJO Ft Johnston, Malawi
FKI Kisangani, Zaire
FKL Franklin–Oil City, Pennsylvania (airport serving both communities)
FKQ Fak Fak, West Irian, Indonesia
FLA Florencia, Colombia
FLB Floriano, Brazil
FLG Flagstaff, Arizona
FLL Ft Lauderdale, Florida
FLN Florianopolis, Brazil
FLO Florence, South Carolina
FLR Florence, Italy (Firenze Airport)
FLS Flinders Island, Tasmania
FMA Formosa, Argentina
FMI Kalemie, Zaire
FMN Farmington, New Mexico
FMY Ft Myers, Florida
FNA Freetown, Sierra Leone
FNC Funchal, Madeira Islands
FNE Finnsnes, Norway
FNG Fada Ngourma, Upper Volta

FNI Nimes, France
FNJ Feng Yang-Pyongyang, North Korea
FNT Flint, Michigan
FOG Foggia, Italy
FOM Foumban, Cameroon
FOO Noemfoor, New Guinea
FOR Fortaleza, Brazil
FOU Fougamou, Gabon
FPC Ft Polignac, Algeria
FPO Freeport, Bahamas
FRA Frankfurt, Germany
FRJ Frejus, France
FRL Forli, Italy
FRV Franceville, Gabon
FRW Francistown, Botswana
FSD Sioux Falls, South Dakota
FSM Ft Smith, Arkansas
FSS Ft Sandeman, Pakistan
FTF Ft Flatters, Algeria
FTL Ft Lamy, Chad
FTR Ft Archambault, Chad
FTU Ft Dauphin, Malagasy
FTV Ft Victoria, Zimbabwe
FTX Ft Rousset, Congo
FUE Fuerteventura, Puerto del Rosario, Canary Islands
FUK Fukuoka, Japan
FUN Funafuti Atoll, Ellice Islands
FWA Ft Wayne, Indiana
FXO Nova Freixo, Mozambique
FYA Faya Largeau, Chad
FYV Fayetteville, Arkansas
FZB Mansa, Zambia
GAD Gadsden, Alabama
GAO Guantanamo, Cuba
GAQ Gao, Mali
GAR Garaina, New Guinea
GAS Gach Saran, Iran
GAU Gauhati, India
GBD Great Bend, Kansas
GBE Gaberones, Botswana
GBG Galesburg, Illinois
GBK Gbangbatok, Sierra Leone
GBU Khasm el Girba, Sudan
GCI Guernsey, Channel Islands, United Kingdom
GCK Garden City, Kansas
GCM Grand Cayman Island, Cayman Islands
GCN Grand Canyon, Arizona
GDH Sargodha, Pakistan
GDL Guadalajara, Mexico
GDN Gdansk-Gdynia, Poland (airport shared by both ports)
GDO Guasdualito, Venezuela
GDQ Gondar, Ethiopia
GED Georgetown, Delaware
GEG Spokane, Washington
GEL Santo Angelo, Brazil
GET Geraldton, Western Australia
GFF Griffith, New South Wales

GFK Grand Forks, North Dakota
GFL Glens Falls, New York
GFN Grafton, New South Wales
GFR Granville, France
GFX Ghuraf, South Arabia
GFY Grootfontein, South-West Africa
GGD Gregory Downs, Queensland
GGG Gladewater-Kilgore-Longview, Texas (airport serving three places)
GGQ Gagnoa, Ivory Coast
GGS Gobernador Gregores, Argentina
GGT George Town, Great Exuma Island, Bahamas
GHA Ghardaia, Algeria
GHB Governor's Harbour, Bahama Islands
GHO Grahamstown, South Africa
GHU Gualeguaychu, Argentina
GIB Gibraltar
GII Siguiri, Guinea
GIL Gilgit, Pakistan
GIM Miele Mimbale, Gabon
GIR Giradot, Colombia
GIS Gisborne, New Zealand
GIZ Gizan, Saudi Arabia
GJB Marie-Galante Island, Guadeloupe
GJM Guajará Mirim, Brazil
GJT Grand Junction, Colorado
GJX Guaira, Brazil
GKA Goroka, New Guinea
GKO Kongo Boumba, Gabon
GLA Glasgow, Scotland
GLB Gilbues, Brazil
GLG Glengyle, Queensland
GLH Greenville, Mississippi
GLO Cheltenham-Gloucester, England
GLS Galveston, Texas
GMA Gemena, Zaire
GMB Gambela, Ethiopia
GMM Gamboma, Congo
GNB Grenoble, France
GND Grenada, West Indies
GNJ Genjem, West Irian, Indonesia
GNL Greenwood, Mississippi
GNN Ghinnir, Ethiopia
GNV Gainesville, Florida
GNZ Ghanzi, Botswana
GOA Genoa, Italy
GOB Goba, Ethiopia
GOE Gore, New Zealand
GOM Goma, Zaire
GOO Goondiwindi, Queensland
GOP Gorakhpur, India
GOR Gore, Ethiopia
GOT Gothenburg, Sweden

GOU Garoua, Cameroon
GOY Gal Oya, Ceylon
GPO General Pico, Argentina
GPP Guarapuava, Brazil
GPT Biloxi-Gulfport, Mississippi (airport shared by both ports)
GPZ Grand Rapids, Minnesota
GRA Gamarra, Colombia
GRB Green Bay, Wisconsin
GRG Georgetown, Guyana
GRI Grand Island, Nebraska
GRJ George, South Africa
GRN Grand Forks, British Columbia
GRO Gerona, Spain
GRQ Groningen, Netherlands
GRR Grand Rapids, Michigan
GRS Grosseto, Italy
GRT Gujrat, Pakistan
GRU Grajau, Brazil
GRX Granada, Spain
GRZ Graz, Austria
GSA Gusau, Nigeria
GSO Greensboro-High Point, North Carolina
GSP Greenville-Spartanburg, South Carolina
GST Gustavua, Alaska
GSU Gedaref, Sudan
GSW Greater Southwest (international airport serving Ft. Worth and Dallas, Texas)
GTF Great Falls, Montana
GTR Great Barrier Island, New Zealand
GTW Gottwaldov-Holesov, Czechoslovakia (airport serving both places)
GUA Guatemala City, Guatemala
GUC Gunnison, Colorado
GUD Goundam, Mali
GUG N'Guigmi, Niger
GUI Guiria, Venezuela
GUM Guam, Marianas
GUP Gallup, New Mexico
GUU Gulu, Uganda
GUY Guymon, Oklahoma
GUZ Guiratinga, Brazil
GVA Geneva, Switzerland
GVD Gravdal, Norway
GVL Gainesville, Georgia
GVR Governador Valadares, Brazil
GWD Gwadar, Pakistan
GWE Gwelo, Rhodesia
GWL Gwalior, India
GXQ Coyhaique, Chile
GXX Yagoua, Cameroon
GYE Guayaquil, Ecuador
GYM Guaymas, Mexico
GYN Goiania, Brazil
GZT Gaziantep, Turkey
HAD Halmstad, Sweden
HAE Hatia, Bangladesh

HAG The Hague, Netherlands
HAJ Hanover, Germany
HAM Hamburg, Germany
HAN Hanoi, North Vietnam
HAR Harrisburg–New Cumberland, Pennsylvania (airport serving both communities)
HAS Hail, Saudi Arabia
HAV Havana, Cuba
HBA Hobart, Tasmania
HBG Hattiesburg, Mississippi
HBI Harbour Island, Bahamas
HCA Big Spring, Texas
HDA Honda, Colombia
HDD Hyderabad, Pakistan
HDM Hamadan, Iran
HEA Herat, Afghanistan
HEL Helsinki, Finland
HER Heraklion, Greece
HEZ Natchez, Mississippi
HFA Haifa, Israel
HFN Hofn, Iceland
HFT Hammerfest, Norway
HFW Haverfordwest, Wales
HGA Hargeisa, Somalia
HGD Hughenden, Queensland
HGH Hangchow, China
HGO Korhogo, Ivory Coast
HGR Hagerstown, Maryland
HGU Mt. Hagen, New Guinea
HIB Chisholm-Hibbing, Minnesota
HIJ Hiroshima, Japan
HIR Honiara, Solomon Islands
HIU Higuerote, Venezuela
HJR Khajuraho, India
HKG Hong Kong, British Crown Colony
HKK Greymouth–Hokitka, New Zealand (airport serving both places)
HKN Hoskins, New Britain
HKP Kaanapali, Maui
HKY Hickory, North Carolina
HLF Hultsfred, Sweden
HLG Wheeling, West Virginia
HLN Helena, Montana
HLS St Helens, Tasmania
HLT Hamilton, Victoria, Australia
HLZ Hamilton, New Zealand
HME Hassi Messaoud, Algeria
HMO Hermosillo, Mexico
HNL Honolulu, Oahu, Hawaii
HNM Hana, Maui, Hawaii
HNO Hercegnovi, Yugoslavia (also spelled Herzegovina)
HNS Haines, Alaska
HOD Hodeida, Yemen
HOF Hafuf, Saudi Arabia
HOM Homer, Alaska
HON Huron, South Dakota
HOO Quang Duc, South Vietnam
HOS Hosana, Ethiopia
HOT Hot Springs, Arkansas

HOU Houston, Texas
HPN White Plains, New York
HPO Hippo Valley, Zimbabwe
HQM Aberdeen–Hoquiam, Washington (airport serving both places)
HRA Haura, South Arabia (Yemen)
HRB Harbin, China
HRD Harstad, Norway
HRK Kharkov, USSR
HRL Harlingen, Texas
HSD Harnosand, Sweden
HSP Hot Springs, Virginia
HSR Hot Springs, South Dakota
HSV Decatur-Huntsville, Alabama
HTS Ashland, Kentucky—Huntington, West Virginia (airport serving both cities)
HUE Humera, Ethiopia
HUF Terre Haute, Indiana
HUH Huahaine, Society Islands
HUI Hue, South Vietnam
HUL Houlton, Maine
HUN Hualien, Taiwan
HUR Hurn, England
HUT Hutchinson, Kansas
HUY Hull, England
IIVA Analalava, Malagasy
HVK Holmavik, Iceland
HVN New Haven, Connecticut
HWN Haldwani, India
HXX Hay, Australia
IIYA Hyannis, Massachusetts
HYD Hyderabad, India
HYG Hydaburg, Alaska
HYT Humaita, Brazil
IIZK Husavik, Iceland
IIZL Hazleton, Pennsylvania
IAG Niagara Falls, New York
IAH Houston, Texas—I-IAH (Intercontinental); H-HOU (Hobby)
IAM In Amenas, Algeria
IBA Ibadan, Nigeria
IBE Ibagué, Colombia
IBU Itambacuri, Brazil
IBZ Ibiza, Balearic Islands, Spain
ICA Icabarú, Venezuela
ICR Nicaro, Cuba
ICT Wichita, Kansas
IDA Idaho Falls, Idaho
IDP Independence, Kansas
IDR Indore, India
IEV Kiev, USSR
IFF Iffley, Queensland
IFJ Isafjordur, Iceland
IFL Innisfail, Queensland
IFN Ishfahan, Iran
IGA Great Inagua Island, Bahamas
IGH Ingham, Queensland

IGM Kingman, Arizona
IGR Iguassu Falls, Argentina
IGU Iguassu Falls, Brazil
IGZ Iguatu, Brazil
IHU Ihu, Papua, New Guinea
IJU Ijuí, Brazil
IKL Ikela, Zaire
IKT Irkutsk, USSR
ILF Milford Haven, Wales
ILG Wilmington, Delaware
ILM Wilmington, North Carolina
ILO Iloilo, Philippines
ILP Isle des Pins, New Caledonia
ILY Islay, Inner Hebrides, Scotland
IMF Imphal, India
IMP Imperatriz, Brazil
IMT Iron Mountain, Michigan
INA Içana, Brazil
IND Indianapolis, Indiana
ING Lago Argentino, Argentina
INH Inhambane, Mozambique
INL International Falls, Minnesota
INM Innamincka, South Australia
INN Innsbruck, Austria
INO Inongo, Zaire
INT Winston-Salem, North Carolina
INV Inverness, Scotland
INW Winslow, Arizona
INX Inanwatan, West Irian, Indonesia
INZ In Salah, Algeria
IOA Ioannina, Greece
IOM Isle of Man, United Kingdom
ION Impfondo, Congo
IOS Ilheus, Brazil
IOW Iowa City, Iowa
IPC Easter Island, Pacific Ocean
IPG Phoolbagh, India
IPH Ipoh, Malaysia
IPI Ipiales, Colombia
IPL El Centro–Imperial, California (airport shared by both places in the Imperial Valley)
IPO Ipora, Brazil
IPT Williamsport, Pennsylvania
IPW Ipswich, England
IQQ Iquique, Chile
IQT Iquitos, Peru
IRD Ishurdi, Bangladesh
IRG Iron Range, Queensland
IRI Iringa, Tanzania
IRJ La Rioja, Argentina
IRO Birao, Central African Republic
IRP Isiro, Zaire
ISA Mt Isa, Queensland
ISB Nisab, South Arabia

ISC Isles of Scilly, England
ISH Ischia, Italy
ISI Isisford, Queensland
ISK Iskenderon, Turkey
ISN Williston, North Dakota
ISO Kinston, North Carolina
ISP Islip, New York
IST Istanbul, Turkey
ISW Wisconsin Rapids, Wisconsin
ITA Itacoatiara, Brazil
ITH Ithaca, New York
ITI Itapetinga, Brazil
ITJ Itajai, Brazil
ITN Itabuna, Brazil
ITO Hilo, Hawaii
ITQ Itaqui, Brazil
ITT Wittenoom Gorge, Western Australia
IVA Ambanja, Malagasy
IVC Invercargill, New Zealand
IVL Ivalo, Finland
IWA Iwakuni, Japan
IWD Ironwood, Michigan
IXA Agartala, India
IXB Bagdogra, India
IXC Chandigarh, India
IXD Allahabad, India
IXE Mangalore, India
IXG Belgaum, India
IXH Kailashahar, India
IXI Lilabari, India
IXJ Jammu, India
IXK Keshod, India
IXL Leh, India
IXM Madurai, India
IXN Khowai, India
IXP Pathankot, India
IXQ Kamalpur, India
IXR Ranchi, India
IXS Silchar, India
IXT Pasighat, India
IXU Aurangabad, India
IXV Along, India
IXW Jamshedpur, India
IXY Kandla, India
IXZ Port Blair, Andaman Islands
IZM Izmir, Turkey
IZT Ixtepec, Mexico
JAC Jackson, Wyoming
JAE Jacksonville, Illinois
JAF Jaffna, Ceylon
JAI Jaipur, India
JAN Jackson–Vicksburg, Mississippi
JAQ Jacquinot Bay, New Britain
JAX Jacksonville, Florida
JCB Joacaba, Brazil
JCK Julia Creek, Queensland
JCS Jaicos, Brazil
JDH Jodhpur, India
JDO Juàzeiro do Norte, Brazil
JED Jeddah, Saudi Arabia
JEF Jefferson City, Missouri

JER Jersey, Channel Islands
JFA Jaffa, Israel
JGA Jamnagar, India
JHW Jamestown, New York
JIB Djibouti, French Somaliland
JIM Jimma, Ethiopia
JIN Jinja, Uganda
JIP Jipijapa, Ecuador
JIW Jiwani, Pakistan
JJU Julienhaab, Greenland (also spelled Julianehab)
JKG Jönköping, Sweden
JKH Chios Island, Greece
JKR Janakpur, Nepal
JKT Djakarta, Java, Indonesia
JLN Joplin, Missouri
JLO Jesolo, Italy
JLP Juan-les-Pins, France
JLR Jabalpur, India
JMK Mikanos Island, Greece
JMS Jamestown, North Dakota
JNA Januaria, Brazil
JNB Johannesburg, South Africa
JNP Jasper National Park (Alberta)
JNU Juneau, Alaska
JNX Jackson, Michigan
JOE Joensuu, Finland
JOG Jogjakarta, Java, Indonesia
JOI Joinvile, Brazil
JOM Njombe, Tanzania
JON Johnston Island, Pacific Ocean
JOS Jos, Nigeria
JPA João Pessôa, Brazil
JPO Pomona, California
JRH Jorhat, India
JRS Jerusalem, Israel
JSI Skiathos, Greece
JSR Jessore, Bangladesh
JST Johnstown, Pennsylvania
JSU Sukkertoppen, Greenland
JTI Jatai, Brazil
JTR Thira, Greece
JUB Juba, Sudan
JUJ Jujuy, Argentina
JUN Jundah, Queensland
JVA Ankavandra, Malagasy
JXN Jackson, Michigan
JYV Jyvaskyla, Finland
KAA Kasama, Zambia
KAB Kariba, Zimbabwe
KAC Kamishli, Syria
KAD Kaduna, Nigeria
KAE Kake, Alaska
KAJ Kajaani, Finland
KAM Kamaran Island, South Arabia (Yemen)
KAN Kano, Nigeria
KAR Kars, Turkey
KAT Kaitaia, New Zealand
KAU Kauhava, Finland

KBA Bení Abbès, Algeria
KBK Kirkjubaejar, Iceland
KBL Kabul, Afghanistan
KBO Kabalo, Zaire
KBP Koala Bear Park (Adelaide)
KBR Kota Bharu, Malaysia
KBS Bo, Sierra Leone
KBU Kotabaru, West Irian, Indonesia
KCH Kuching, Malaysia
KCK Kansas City, Kansas
KDA Kolda, Senegal
KDH Kandahar, Afghanistan
KDI Kendari, Sulawesi, Indonesia
KDJ Ndjole, Gabon
KDL Koronadal, Mindanao, Philippines
KDN Ndende, Gabon
KDR Kandrian, New Britain
KDU Skardu, Pakistan
KED Kaedi, Mauritania
KEF Keflavik, Iceland
KEM Kemi, Finland
KEN Kenema, Sierra Leone
KEP Nepalgang, Nepal
KEQ Kebar, Indonesia
KER Kerman, Iran
KFA Kiffa, Mauritania
KGG Kedougou, Senegal
KGI Kalgoorlie, Western Australia
KGJ Karonga, Malawi
KGL Kigali, Rwanda
KGO Kasongo, Zaire
KGS Kos, Greece
KGU Keningau, Malaysia
KHE Kherson, USSR
KHH Kaohsiung, Taiwan
KHI Karachi, Pakistan
KHK Khark Island, Iran
KHL Khulna, Bangladesh
KHN Nanchang, China
KHS Kushtia, Bangladesh
KHV Khabarovsk, USSR
KIA Kaiapit, New Guinea
KID Kristianstad, Sweden
KIE Kieta, Bougainville, Solomon Islands
KIK Kirkuk, Iraq
KIM Kimberley, South Africa
KIN Kingston, Jamaica
KIS Kisumu, Kenya
KIU Kainantu, New Guinea
KIV Kishinev, USSR
KIW Kitwe, Zambia
KIY Kilwa, Tanzania
KKD Kokoda, New Guinea
KKN Kirkenes, Norway
KKO Kaikohe, New Zealand
KKW Kikwit, Zaire
KLA Kampala, Uganda
KLB Kalabo, Zambia
KLC Kaolack, Senegal
KLE Kaele, Cameroun

KLH Long Akha, Malaysia
KLR Kalmar, Sweden
KLU Klagenfurt, Austria
KLV Karlovy Vary, Czechoslovakia
KLY Kalima, Zaire
KLX Kalamata, Greece
KMA Kerema, Papua
KME Karl-Marx Stadt, Germany
KMG Kunming, China
KMK Makabana, Congo
KML Kamileroi, Queensland
KMN Kamina, Zaire
KMP Keetmanshoop, South-West Africa
KMS Kumasi, Ghana
KMU Kismayu, Somalia
KND Kindu, Zaire
KNG Kaimana, West Irian
KNN Kankan, Guinea
KNS King Island, Tasmania
KNT Sanandaj, Iran
KNU Kanpur, India
KNX Kununurra, Western Australia
KOA Kona, Hawaii
KOB Koutaba, Cameroon
KOE Kupang, Timor, Indonesia
KOI Kirkwall, Orkney Islands
KOJ Kagoshima, Japan
KOK Kokkola, Finland
KON Kontum, South Vietnam
KOO Kongolo, Zaire
KOX Kokonao, West Irian, Indonesia
KPU Khapalu, Pakistan
KRA Kerang, Victoria, Australia
KRB Karumba, Queensland
KRI Kikori, Papua
KRK Cracow, Poland
KRN Kiruna, Sweden
KRP Karup, Denmark
KRS Kristiansand, Norway
KRT Khartoum, Sudan
KSC Kosice, Czechoslovakia
KSD Karlstad, Sweden
KSE Kasese, Uganda
KSH Kermanshah, Iran
KSI Kissidougou, Guinea
KSL Kassala, Sudan
KSN Sam Neua, Laos
KSO Kastoria, Greece
KST Kosti, Sudan
KSU Kristiansund, Norway
KTI Kratie, Cambodia
KTL Kitale, Kenya
KTM Katmandu, Nepal
KTN Ketchikan, Alaska
KTR Katherine, Northern Territory, Australia
KTU Kutaisi, USSR
KTW Katowice, Poland
KUA Kuantan, Malaysia

KUD Kudat, Malaysia
KUL Kuala Lumpur, Malaysia
KUO Kuopio, Finland
KUS Kulusuk Island, Greenland
KUT Kutahya, Turkey
KUU Kulu, India
KVA Kavalla, Greece
KVG Kavieng, New Ireland
KWA Kwajalein, Marshall Islands
KWE Kweiyang, China
KWI Kuwait, Kuwait
KWU Kawau Island, New Zealand
KWZ Kolwezi, Zaire
KXU Kastamonu, Turkey
KYA Konya, Turkey
KYS Kayes, Mali
KYZ Kayseri, Turkey
KZI Kozani, Greece
KZR Khuzdar, Pakistan
LAD Luanda, Angola
LAF Lafayette, Indiana
LAG La Guaira, Venezuela
LAL Lakeland, Florida
LAN Lansing, Michigan
LAP La Paz, Mexico
LAQ Al Bayda, Libya
LAR Laramie, Wyoming
LAS Las Vegas, Nevada
LAW Lawton, Oklahoma
LAX Los Angeles, California—L-LAX (International Airport); B-BUR (Burbank); O-ONT (Ontario)
LAZ Bom Jesus da Lapa, Brazil
LBA Leeds, England
LBB Lubbock, Texas
LBF North Platte, Nebraska
LBL Liberal, Kansas
LBQ Lambarene, Gabon
LBR Lábrea, Brazil
LBS Lambasa, Fiji Islands
LBU Labuan, Malaysia
LBV Libreville, Gabon
LBY La Baule, France
LCE La Ceiba, Honduras
LCG La Coruña, Spain
LCH Lake Charles, Louisiana
LCI Laconia, New Hampshire
LCM La Cumbre, Argentina
LDB Londrina, Brazil
LDE Lourdes, France
LDI Lindi, Tanzania
LDR Lodar, South Arabia
LDU Lahad Datu, Malaysia
LDZ Lodz, Poland
LEA Learmonth, Western Australia
LEB Hanover–Lebanon, New Hampshire–White River Junction, Vermont (airport serving three nearby communities)

LED Leningrad, USSR
LEG Aleg, Mauritania
LEH Le Havre, France
LEI Almería, Spain
LEJ Leipzig, Germany
LEK Labe, Guinea
LEN León, Mexico
LET Leticia, Colombia
LEW Auburn–Lewiston, Maine (airport shared by these two cities)
LEX Lexington, Kentucky
LFK Lufkin, Texas
LFR La Fria, Venezuela
LFT Lafayette–New Iberia, Louisiana (airport serving both communities)
LFW Lome, Togo
LGB Long Beach, California
LGG Liege, Belgium
LGH Leigh Creek, South Australia
LGI Deadman's Cay, Long Island, Bahamas
LGL La Gloria, Colombia
LGU Logan, Utah
LGY Lagunillas, Venezuela
LHE Lahore, Pakistan
LHV Lock Haven, Pennsylvania
LHW Lanchow, China
LHX La Junta, Colorado
LIA Lima, Ohio
LIE Libenge, Zaire
LIK Likasi, Zaire
LIL Lille, France
LIM Lima, Peru
LIO Limón, Costa Rica
LIQ Lisala, Zaire
LIS Lisbon, Portugal
LIT Little Rock, Arkansas
LJA Lodja, Zaire
LJU Ljubljana, Yugoslavia
LJZ Lajes, Brazil
LKL Lakselv, Norway
LKM Nekempt, Ethiopia
LKO Lucknow, India
LKW Larkana, Pakistan
LLA Lulea, Sweden
LLB Luluabourg, Zaire
LLI Lalibella, Ethiopia
LLJ Lalmonirhat, Bangladesh
LLM Long Lama, Malaysia
LLW Lilongwe, Malawi
LMM Los Mochis, Mexico
LMN Limbang, Malaysia
LMQ Marsa Brega, Libya
LMT Klamath Falls, Oregon
LNH Lengeh, Iran
LNK Lincoln, Nebraska
LNL Land O'Lakes, Wisconsin
LNS Lancaster, Pennsylvania
LNY Lanai, Hawaii
LNZ Linz, Austria
LOA Lorraine, Queensland
LOB Lobito, Angola

LOH Loja, Ecuador
LOI Laredo, Texas
LON London, England
LOO Laghouat, Algeria
LOP Loanda, Brazil
LOQ Lobatsi, Botswana
LOS Lagos, Nigeria
LOV Monclova, Mexico
LOZ London, Kentucky
LPA Las Palmas, Canary Islands
LPB La Paz, Bolivia
LPI Linköping, Sweden
LPL Liverpool, England
LPP Lappeenranta, Finland
LPQ Luang Prabang, Laos
LQM Puerto Leguizamo, Colombia
LRA Larisa, Greece
LRE Longreach, Queensland
LRH La Rochelle, France
LRI Lorica, Colombia
LRT Lorient, France
LSC La Serena, Chile
LSE La Crosse, Wisconsin
LSI Lerwick, Scotland
LSM Long Semado, Malaysia
LSP Las Piedras, Venezuela
LST Launceston, Tasmania
LTC Lai, Chad
LTD Ghadames, Libya
LTL Lastourville, Gabon
LTN Luton, England
LTO Loreto, Mexico
LTQ Le Touquet, France
LUL Laurel, Mississippi
LUM Lourenço Marques, Mozambique
LUN Lusaka, Zambia
LUO Luso, Angola
LUQ San Luis, Argentina
LUT Miri, Malaysia
LUX Luxembourg, Luxembourg
LUY Lushoto, Tanzania
LVB Livramento, Brazil
LVI Livingstone, Zambia
LWH Lawn Hill, Queensland, Australia
LWM Lawrence, Massachusetts
LWO Lwów, USSR
LWS Lewiston, Idaho
LWT Lewistown, Montana
LWY Lawas, Sarawak, Malaysia
LXG Luong Namtha, Laos
LXR Luxor, Egypt
LXS Lemnos, Greece
LXU Lukulu, Zambia
LYH Lynchburg, Virginia
LYM Lympne, England
LYP Lyallpur, Pakistan
LYS Lyon, France
LYX Lydd, England
MAA Madras, India

MAB Maraba, Brazil
MAD Madrid, Spain
MAF Midland–Odessa, Texas (airport serving both communities)
MAG Madang, New Guinea
MAH Mahon, Minorca
MAI Marianna, Florida
MAJ Majuro, Marshall Islands
MAK Malakal, Sudan
MAL Malone, New York
MAM Matamoros, Mexico
MAN Manchester, England
MAO Manaus, Brazil
MAQ Sena Maduereira, Brazil
MAR Maracaibo, Venezuela
MAS Manus Island, Bismarck Archipelago
MAT Matadi, Zaire
MAU Mastung, Pakistan
MAX Matam, Senegal
MBA Mombasa, Kenya
MBH Maryborough, Queensland
MBI Mbeya, Tanzania
MBJ Montego Bay, Jamaica
MBM Mambone, Mozambique
MBN Mombo, Tanzania
MBR Mbout, Mauritania
MBS Bay City–Midland–Saginaw, Michigan (airport shared by three cities)
MBZ Maués, Brazil
MCA Macenta, Guinea
MCE Merced, California
MCJ Maicao, Colombia
MCM Monte Carlo, Monaco
MCN Macon, Georgia
MCO Orlando, Florida
MCP Macapá, Brazil
MCS Monte Caseros, Argentina
MCT Muscat, Oman
MCW Mason City, Iowa
MCZ Maceió, Brazil
MDC Menado, Sulawesi, Indonesia
MDD Puerto Maldonado, Peru
MDE Medellin, Colombia
MDI Makurdi, Nigeria
MDK Mbandaka, Zaire
MDL Mandalay, Burma
MDQ Mar del Plata, Argentina
MDV Medouneu, Gabon
MDX Mercedes, Argentina
MDZ Mendoza, Argentina
MEB Melbourne, Victoria, Australia
MEC Manta, Ecuador
MED Medina, Saudi Arabia
MEF Melfi, Chad
MEI Meridian, Mississippi
MEK Meknes, Morocco
MEM Memphis, Tennessee
MEP Mendi, Ethiopia
MES Medan, Sumatra, Indone-

sia
MEU Marromeu, Mozambique
MEX Mexico City, Mexico
MEZ Merces, Brazil
MFA Mafia Island, Tanzania
MFD Mansfield, Ohio
MFE McAllen–Mission, Texas (airport serving both places)
MFF Moanda, Gabon
MFN Milford Sound, New Zealand
MFQ Maradi, Niger
MFR Medford, Oregon
MFU Mfuwe, Zambia
MGA Managua, Nicaragua
MGB Mt Gambier, Australia
MGM Montgomery, Alabama
MGN Magangué, Colombia
MGO Mato Grosso, Brazil
MGQ Mogadishu, Somalia
MGW Morgantown, West Virginia
MHD Meshed, Iran
MHE Mitchell, South Dakota
MHH Marsh Harbour, Great Abaco Island, Bahamas
MHK Manhattan, Kansas
MHO Mohanbari, India
MHQ Mariehamn, Finland
MHT Manchester, New Hampshire
MIA Miami, Florida
MID Mérida, Mexico
MIE Muncie, Indiana
MIL Milan, Italy
MIM Merimbula, New South Wales
MIQ Maiquetia, Venezuela (airport serving Caracas and La Guaira)
MIR Monastir, Tunisia
MIU Maiduguri, Nigeria
MIX Mores Island, Bahamas
MJA Manja, Malagasy
MJC Man, Ivory Coast
MJD Mohenjodaro, Pakistan
MJG Mayajigua, Cuba
MJH Majma, Saudi Arabia
MJI Maji, Ethiopia
MJL Mouila, Gabon
MJM Mbuji-Mayi, Zaire
MJN Majunga, Malagasy
MJP Mastuj, Pakistan
MJT Mytilene, Greece
MJV Murcia, Spain
MJX Masjed Soleyman, Iran
MJZ Mahfid, South Arabia
MKC Kansas City, Missouri
MKE Milwaukee, Wisconsin— M-MKE (Mitchell); T-MWC (Timmerman)
MKG Muskegon, Michigan
MKJ Makoua, Congo
MKK Hoolehua–Kaunakakai, Molokai, Hawaii (airport serving both places on the island)

MKL Jackson, Tennessee
MKM Mukah, Sarawak, Malaysia
MKQ Merauke, West Irian, Indonesia
MKR Meekatharra, Western Australia
MKT Mankato, Minnesota
MKU Makokou, Gabon
MKW Manokwari, West Irian, Indonesia
MKX Mukalla, South Arabia
MKY Mackay, Queensland
MKZ Malacca, Malaysia
MLA Valetta, Malta
MLB Melbourne, Florida
MLC McAlester, Oklahoma
MLH Mulhouse, France
MLI Davenport, Iowa–Moline, Illinois (airport shared by both cities)
MLN Melilla, Morocco
MLU Monroe, Louisiana
MLW Monrovia, Liberia
MLX Malatya, Turkey
MMA Malmö, Sweden
MMC Ciudad Mante, Mexico
MME Middlesborough, England
MMF Mamfe, Cameroon
MMP Mompos, Colombia
MMX Miracema do Norte, Brazil
MNB Moanda, Zaire
MNC Nacala, Mozambique
MNE Mentone, France
MNI Montserrat, Leeward Islands, West Indies
MNJ Mananjary, Malagasy
MNK Mankoya, Zambia
MNL Manila, Philippines
MNM Menominee, Michigan
MNO Manono, Zaire
MNR Mongu, Zambia
MNX Minia, Egypt
MOB Mobile, Alabama
MOC Montes Claros, Brazil
MOD Modesto, California
MOF Maumere, Flores, Indonesia
MOJ Muong Sing, Laos
MON Mt. Cook, New Zealand
MOQ Morondava, Malagasy
MOW Moscow, USSR
MOY Monterrey, Colombia
MOZ Moorea, Society Islands
MPD Mpanda, Tanzania
MPK McKinley Park, Alaska
MPL Montpellier, France
MPV Barre–Montpelier, Vermont (airport serving both communities)
MQG Milgarra, Queensland
MQL Mildura, Victoria
MQQ Moundou, Chad
MQT Marquette, Michigan

MQU Mariquita, Colombia
MQX Makale, Ethiopia
MRD Mérida, Venezuela
MRE Manicore, Brazil
MRG Mesters Vig, Greenland
MRH Beaufort–Morehead City, North Carolina (airport serving both places)
MRO Masterson, New Zealand
MRS Marseilles, France
MRU Mauritius, Indian Ocean
MRV Mineralnye Vody, USSR
MRX Mineiros, Brazil
MRY Carmel-by-the-Sea–Monterey, California (airport serving both places)
MSD Mossoro, Brazil
MSE Manston, England
MSI Moshi, Tanzania
MSJ Misawa, Japan
MSK Mastic Point, Andros Island, Bahamas
MSL Florence–Muscle Shoals–Sheffield, Alabama (airport shared by the three localities)
MSN Madison, Wisconsin
MSO Missoula, Montana
MSP Minneapolis–St Paul, Minnesota [airport serving the Twin Cities—D-JDT (Minneapolis Heliport), I-MSP (International)]
MSQ Minsk, USSR
MSR Makassar, Sulawesi, Indonesia
MSS Massena, New York
MST Maastricht, Netherlands
MSU Maseru, Lesotho
MSW Massawa, Ethiopia
MSX Mascota, Mexico
MSY New Orleans, Louisiana
MSZ Mossamedes, Angola
MTB Monte Libano, Colombia
MTE Monte Alegre, Brazil
MTF Mizan Teferi, Ethiopia
MTJ Montrose, Colorado
MTO Mattoon, Illinois
MTQ Mitchell, Queensland
MTR Montería, Colombia
MTS Manzini, Swaziland
MTT Minatitlan, Mexico
MTW Manitowoc, Wisconsin
MTY Monterrey, Mexico
MUA Munda, Solomon Islands
MUB Maun, Botswana
MUC Munich, Germany
MUD Murchison Falls, Uganda
MUE Kamuela, Hawaii
MUH Mersa Matruh, Egypt
MUR Marudi, Sarawak, Malaysia
MUW Mutarara, Mozambique
MUX Multan, Pakistan
MUZ Musoma, Tanzania
MVD Montevideo, Uruguay

MVN Mt Vernon, Illinois
MVO Mongo, Chad
MVR Maroua, Cameroon
MVU Mulege, Mexico
MVY Martha's Vineyard–Vineyard Haven, Massachusetts (airport serving adjacent communities)
MWA Marion, Illinois
MWE Merowe, Sudan
MWL Mineral Wells, Texas
MWP Mangla, Pakistan
MWZ Mwanza, Tanzania
MXD Marion Downs, Queensland
MXK Metekel, Ethiopia
MXL Mexicali, Mexico
MXM Morombe, Malagasy
MXR Moussoro, Chad
MXT Maintirano, Malagasy
MYB Mayoumba, Gabon
MYC Massenya, Chad
MYD Malindi, Kenya
MYG Mayaguana Island, Bahamas
MYH Rosh-Pina, Israel
MYP Montgomery, Pakistan
MYV Marysville, California
MYW Mtwara, Tanzania
MYZ Mayoko, Gabon
MZB Mocímboa da Praia, Mozambique
MZC Mitzic, Gabon
MZG Makung, Formosa
MZI Mopti, Mali
MZL Manizales, Colombia
MZM Metz, France
MZN Minj, New Guinea
MZO Manzanillo, Cuba
MZQ Mozambique, Mozambique
MZR Mazar-i-Sharif, Afghanistan
MZT Mazatlan, Mexico
MZU Muzaffarpur, India
MZX Massio, Ethiopia
MZY Mzimba, Malawi
MZZ Marion, Indiana
NAG Nagpur, India
NAN Nandi, Fiji Islands
NAP Naples, Italy
NAS Nassau, New Providence Island, Bahamas
NAT Natal, Brazil
NAV Natividade, Brazil
NBO Nairobi, Kenya
NCE Nice, France
NCG Nueva Casas Grandes, Mexico
NCH Nachingwea, Tanzania
NCL Newcastle, England
NCM New Moon, Queensland
NCT Nicoya, Costa Rica
NDD Novo Redondo, Angola
NDE Notodden, Norway
NDH Delhi, India

NDR Nador, Morocco
NEV Nevis, Leeward Islands, West Indies
NGE Ngaoundere, Cameroon
NGO Nagoya, Japan
NHA Nha-Trang, South Vietnam
NHB Kodiak, Alaska
NIC Nicosia, Cyprus
NIM Niamey, Niger
NIO Nioki, Zaire
NIX Nioro, Mali
NKC Nouakchott, Mauritania
NKG Nanking, China
NKL Nkolo, Zaire
NLA Ndola, Zambia
NLD Nuevo Laredo, Mexico
NLK Norfolk Island, Pacific Ocean
NMR Nappamerrie, Queensland
NNG Nanning, China
NNI New Nickerie, Surinam
NNU Nanuque, Brazil
NOG Nogales, Arizona–Nogales, Mexico (airport shared by two border cities in neighboring countries)
NOS Nossi-Be, Malagasy
NOU Noumea, New Caledonia
NOV Nova Lisboa, Angola
NPA Napan, West Irian, Indonesia
NPE Hastings–Napier, New Zealand (airport shared by both places)
NPL New Plymouth, New Zealand
NPT Newport, Rhode Island
NQN Neuquen, Argentina
NQY Newquay, England
NRA Narrandera, New South Wales
NRK Norrköping, Sweden
NRM Nara, Mali
NSM Norseman, Western Australia
NSN Nelson, New Zealand
NSO Scone, New South Wales
NTE Nantes, France
NTL Newcastle, New South Wales
NTN Normanton, Queensland
NUD En Nahud, Sudan
NUE Nuremberg, Germany
NVA Neiva, Colombia
NVE Nova Esperança, Brazil
NVK Narvik, Norway
NWA Moheli, Comoro Islands
NYC New York City; New York, New York—E-EWR (Newark); J-JFK (Kennedy); L-LGA (La Guardia)
NZE Nzerekore, Guinea
OAG Orange, New South Wales

OAK Oakland, California
OAM Oamaru, New Zealand
OAX Oaxaca, Mexico
OBI Obidos, Brazil
OCF Ocala, Florida
OCJ Ocho Rios, Jamaica
ODA Ouadda, Central African Republic
ODB Cordoba, Spain
ODD Oodnadatta, South Australia
ODE Odense, Denmark
ODJ Ouanda Djalle, Central African Republic
ODL Cordillo Downs, South Australia
ODS Odessa, USSR
OER Ornskoldsvik, Sweden
OFK Norfolk, Nebraska
OGD Ogden, Utah
OGG Kahului, Maui, Hawaii
OGR Bongor, Chad
OGS Ogdensburg, New York
OGX Ouargla, Algeria
OHD Ohrid, Yugoslavia
OJO Outjo, South-West Africa
OJW Otjiwarongo, South-West Africa
OKA Okinawa, Ryukyu Islands, Japan
OKC Oklahoma City, Oklahoma
OKK Kokomo–Logansport, Indiana (airport shared by both communities)
OKN Okondja, Gabon
OKY Oakey, Queensland
OLB Olbia, Italy
OLE Olean, New York
OLF Wolf Point, Montana
OLG Nordmaling, Sweden
OLM Olympia, Washington
OLN Colonia Sarmiento, Argentina
OLO Olomouc, Czechoslovakia
OLU Columbus, Nebraska
OMA Omaha, Nebraska
OME Nome, Alaska
OMO Mostar, Yugoslavia
OMS Omsk, USSR
ONA Winona, Minnesota
ONB Monkey Bay, Malawi
ONG Mornington Island, Queensland
ONM Condamine, Queensland
ONO Ontario, Oregon
ONR Monkira, Queensland
ONS Onslow, Western Australia
ONT Ontario, California
ONU Kongoussi, Upper Volta
OOL Coolangatta, Queensland
OOM Cooma, New South Wales
OOR Mooraberrie, Queensland

OPA Kopasker, Iceland
OPO Oporto, Portugal
OPU Balimo, Papua
ORA Oran, Argentina
ORE Greenfield, Massachusetts
ORF Norfolk, Virginia
ORH Worcester, Massachusetts
ORK Cork, Ireland
ORL Orlando, Florida
ORM Northampton, England
ORN Oran, Algeria
ORO Porto Seguro, Brazil
ORP Ormara, Pakistan
ORU Oruro, Bolivia
ORW Orange Walk, British Honduras
ORX Oriximina, Brazil
OSA Osaka, Japan
OSD Ostersund, Sweden
OSH Oshkosh, Wisconsin
OSL Oslo, Norway
OSM Mosul, Iraq
OSR Ostrava, Czechoslovakia
OST Ostend, Belgium
OSY Namsos, Norway
OSZ Koszalin, Poland
OTA Mota, Ethiopia
OTC Bol, Chad
OTG Worthington, Minnesota
OTH North Bend, Oregon
OTL Boutilimit, Mauritania
OTM Ottumwa, Iowa
OTV Otavi, South-West Africa
OTZ Kotzebue, Alaska
OUA Ouagadougou, Upper Volta
OUD Oujda, Morocco
OUE Ouesso, Congo
OUG Ouahigouya, Upper Volta
OUH Oudtshoorn, South Africa
OUI Ban Houei Sai, Laos
OUL Oulu, Finland
OUR Batouri, Cameroon
OUT Bousso, Chad
OVA Bekily, Malagasy
OVD Oviedo, Spain
OWB Owensboro, Kentucky
OXC Waterbury, Connecticut
OXF Oxford, England
OXO Orientos, Queensland
OXR Oxnard–Ventura, California (airport shared by both communities)
OXY Morney Plains, Queensland
OYE Oyem, Gabon
OYK Oiapoque, Brazil
OZC Ozamiz City, Mindanao, Philippines
PAA Pa-An, Burma
PAB Pedro Afonso, Brazil
PAF Paraburdoo, Western Australia
PAG Panjim, India

PAP Port-au-Prince, Haiti
PAR Paris, France
PAU Pauk, Burma
PAV Paulo Afonso, Brazil
PBD Porbandar, India
PBE Puerto Berrio, Colombia
PBI West Palm Beach, Florida
PBL Puerto Cabello, Venezuela
PBM Paramaribo, Surinam
PBN Porto Amboin, Angola
PBR Puerto Barrios, Guatemala
PBS Plettenberg Bay, South Africa
PBY Pillars Bay, Alaska
PCC Puerto Rico, Colombia
PCE Palm Island, Queensland
PCH Pari-Cachoeira, Brazil
PCR Puerto Carreño, Colombia
PCZ Panama Canal Zone
PDG Padang, Sumatra, Indonesia
PDO Prado, Brazil
PDP Punta del Este, Uruguay
PDS Piedras Negras, Mexico
PDT Pendleton, Oregon
PDX Portland, Oregon
PDZ Pedernales, Venezuela
PEC Pelican, Alaska
PEI Pereira, Colombia
PEK Peking, China
PEN Penang, Malaysia
PER Perth, Western Australia
PET Pelotas, Brazil
PEW Peshawar, Pakistan
PFB Passo Fundo, Brazil
PFJ Patreks Fjordur, Iceland
PFN Panama City, Florida
PFR Port Francqui, Zaire
PGA Page, Arizona
PGF Perpignan, France
PGH Pantnagar, India
PGK Pangkalpinang, Bangka, Indonesia
PGM Palenque, Mexico
PGT Porangatu, Brazil
PHB Parnaiba, Brazil
PHC Port Harcourt, Nigeria
PHE Port Hedland, Western Australia
PHF Hampton–Newport News–Williamsburg, Virginia (airport serving the three communities)
PHH Phan Thiet, South Vietnam
PHL Camden, New Jersey–Philadelphia, Pennsylvania [airport serving both cities—P-PHL (International); P-PNE (Northeast)]
PHN Port Huron, Michigan
PHS Phitsanuloke, Thailand
PHV Pahlavi, Iran
PHX Phoenix, Arizona

PIA Peoria, Illinois
PIC Picos, Brazil
PIE Clearwater–St. Petersburg, Florida (airport serving both cities)
PIH Pocatello, Idaho
PIK Prestwick, Scotland
PIN Parintins, Brazil
PIR Pierre, South Dakota
PIT Pittsburgh, Pennsylvania
PIU Piura, Peru
PJG Panjgur, Pakistan
PKB Marietta, Ohio–Parkersburg, West Virginia (airports serving both cities)
PKC Phuket, Thailand
PKK Pakokku, Burma
PKU Pakanbaru, Sumatra, Indonesia
PKY Pak Lay, Laos
PKZ Pakse, Laos
PLB Plattsburgh, New York
PLC Planeta Rica, Colombia
PLF Pala, Chad
PLH Plymouth, England
PLM Palembang, Sumatra, Indonesia
PLN Cheboygan–Pellston, Michigan
PLO Port Lincoln, South Australia
PLS Providenciales, Turks and Caicos Islands, West Indies
PLW Palu, Sulawesi, Indonesia
PLZ Port Elizabeth, South Africa
PMA Pemba Island, Tanzania
PMC Puerto Montt, Chile
PME Portsmouth, England
PMG Ponta Pora, Brazil
PMH Portsmouth, Ohio
PMI Palma de Mallorca, Spain
PMJ Porto Murtinho, Brazil
PMO Palermo, Sicily
PMQ Perito Moreno, Argentina
PMR Palmerston North, New Zealand
PMV Porlamar, Venezuela
PMZ Palmar, Costa Rica
PNA Panna, India
PNB Porto Nacional, Brazil
PNG Popondetta, New Guinea
PNH Phnom Penh, Cambodia
PNI Ponape, Caroline Islands
PNJ Paterson, New Jersey
PNK Pontianak, Borneo, Indonesia
PNL Pantelleria, Italy
PNQ Poona, India
PNR Pointe Noire, Congo
PNS Pensacola, Florida
PNZ Petrolina, Brazil
POA Porto Alegre, Brazil
POD Podor, Senegal
POG Port Gentil, Gabon

POI Potosí, Bolivia
POL Porto Amelia, Mozambique
POM Port Moresby, Papua, New Guinea
POR Pori, Finland
POS Port-of-Spain, Trinidad
POT Port Antonio, Jamaica
POU Poughkeepsie, New York
POV Presov, Czechoslovakia
POX Port Alexander, Alaska
POY Lovell–Powell, Wyoming (airport serving both places)
POZ Poznan, Poland
PPB Presidente Prudente, Brazil
PPF Parsons, Kansas
PPG Pago Pago, American Samoa
PPI Port Pirie, South Australia
PPN Popayan, Colombia
PPP Proserpine, Queensland
PPR Pirapora, Brazil
PPT Papeete, Tahiti, Society Islands
PPZ Puerto Paez, Venezuela
PQC Phuquoc, South Vietnam
PQI Presque Isle, Maine
PRB Paso Robles, California
PRC Prescott, Arizona
PRG Prague, Czechoslovakia
PRJ Capri, Italy
PRM Puerto Lopez, Colombia
PRQ Presidente Roque Sáenz Peña, Argentina
PRS Puerto Lempira, Honduras
PRU Paranagua, Brazil
PRX Paris, Texas
PSA Pisa, Italy
PSB Bellefonte–Clearfield–Philipsburg, Pennsylvania (airport serving the three places)
PSC Pasco, Washington
PSD Port Said, Egypt
PSE Ponce, Puerto Rico
PSF Pittsfield, Massachusetts
PSG Petersburg, Alaska
PSI Pasni, Pakistan
PSL Perth, Scotland
PSM Portsmouth, New Hampshire
PSO Pasto, Colombia
PSP Indio–Palm Springs, California (airport shared by both places)
PSR Pescara, Italy
PSS Posadas, Argentina
PST Preston, Cuba
PSY Port Stanley, Falkland Islands
PSZ Puerto Suárez, Bolivia
PTE Nouadhibou, Mauritania
PTJ Portland, Victoria, Australia
PTL Pietermaritzburg, South

Africa
PTM Palmarito, Venezuela
PTP Pointe-à-Pitre, Guadeloupe
PTR Port Macquarie, New South Wales
PTY Panama City, Panama
PUB Pueblo, Colorado
PUD Puerto Deseado, Argentina
PUF Pau, France
PUK Paducah, Kentucky
PUN Punia, Zaire
PUP Po, Upper Volta
PUQ Punta Arenas, Chile
PUR Puerto Rico, Bolivia
PUS Pusan, South Korea
PUT Putao, Burma
PUU Puerto Asís, Colombia
PUW Pullman, Washington
PUY Pula, Yugoslavia
PUZ Puerto Cabezas, Nicaragua
PVD Providence, Rhode Island
PVH Porto Velho, Brazil
PVI Paranavai, Brazil
PVK Preveza, Greece
PVO Portoviejo, Ecuador
PVR Puerto Vallarta, Mexico
PWM Portland, Maine
PWR Port Walter, Alaska
PXA Paraná, Brazil
PXK Parakou, Dahomey
PXO Porto Santo, Madeira
PXU Pleiku, South Vietnam
PXX Porto Afonso, Brazil
PYH Puerto Ayacucho, Venezuela
PYR Pyrgos, Greece
PZA Paz de Ariporo, Colombia
PZE Penzance, England
PZO Puerto Ordaz, Venezuela
PZU Port Sudan, Sudan
PZY Piestany, Czechoslovakia
QIL Qillainau, Afghanistan
QMM Marina di Massa, Italy
QSM South Molle Islands, Queensland
QUI Quirindi, New South Wales
QUN Qutdligssat, Greenland
QUP Quincemil, Peru
RAB Rabaul, New Britain, New Guinea
RAH Rafha, Saudi Arabia
RAJ Rajkot, India
RAK Marrakech, Morocco
RAL Riverside, California
RAP Rapid City, South Dakota
RAR Rarotonga, Cook Islands, Polynesia
RAU Rangpur, Bangladesh
RBA Rabat, Morocco
RBF Raba Raba, New Guinea
RBG Roseburg, Oregon
RBL Red Bluff, California

RBO Roboré, Bolivia
RBQ Rurrenabaque, Bolivia
RBR Rio Branco, Brazil
RBU Roebourne, Western Australia
RCH Ríohacja, Colombia
RCM Richmond, Queensland
RCS Rochester, England
RCU Río Cuarto, Argentina
RDD Redding, California
RDG Reading, Pennsylvania
RDM Bend–Redmond, Oregon (airport serving both communities)
RDS Rio Grande do Sul, Brazil
RDT Richard-Toll, Senegal
RDU Raleigh–Durham, North Carolina (airport serving both communities)
REC Recife, Brazil
REG Reggio Calabria, Italy
REH Rehoboth Beach, Delaware
REK Reykjavik, Iceland
REL Trelew, Argentina
REP Siem Reap, Cambodia
RER Potrerillos, Chile
RES Resistencia, Argentina
REX Reynosa, Mexico
RFD Rockford, Illinois
RFH Río Mayo, Argentina
RFP Raiatea, Leeward Islands, Society Islands
RFW Robinhood, Queensland
RFX Roxborough, Queensland
RGA Río Grande, Argentina
RGI Rangiroa, Tuamotu Islands, Polynesia
RGL Río Gallegos, Argentina
RGN Rangoon, Burma
RGO Rosella Plains, Queensland
RGR Rio Grande, Brazil
RGT Rengat, Sumatra, Indonesia
RHD Río Hondo, Argentina
RHE Rheims, France
RHI Rhinelander, Wisconsin
RHL Roy Hill, Western Australia
RHO Rhodes, Dodecanese Islands, Greece
RIA Santa Maria, Brazil
RIB Riberalta, Bolivia
RIC Richmond, Virginia
RIO Rio de Janeiro, Brazil
RIW Riverton, Wyoming
RIX Riga, Latvia, USSR
RIY Riyan Mukalla, South Arabia (Yemen)
RJH Rajshahi, Bangladesh
RJK Rijeka, Yugoslavia
RKD Rockland, Maine
RKS Rock Springs, Wyoming
RKT Ras-al-Khaima, Trucial Oman

RMA Roma, Queensland
RMG Rome, Georgia
RMI Rimini, Italy
RMK Renmark, South Australia
RMT Rocky Mount, North Carolina
RNB Ronneby, Sweden
RNN Ronne, Denmark
RNO Reno, Nevada
RNS Rennes, France
RNU Ranau, Malaysia
ROA Roanoke, Virginia
ROB Robertsfield, Liberia
ROC Rochester, New York
ROF Rose Hall, Guyana
ROK Rockhampton, Queensland
ROM Rome, Italy
RON Rondón, Colombia
ROO Rondonopolis, Brazil
ROP Rota, Marianas Islands
ROS Rosario, Argentina
ROT Rotorua, New Zealand
ROV Rostov, USSR
ROW Roswell, New Mexico
RPR Raipur, India
RRK Rourkela, India
RRS Roros, Norway
RSA Santa Rosa, Argentina
RSD Rock Sound, Eleuthera Island, Bahamas
RSK Ransiki, West Irian, Indonesia
RSO Remanso, Brazil
RSS Roseires, Sudan
RST Rochester, Minnesota
RSU Río Sucio, Colombia
RTB Roatan Island, Honduras
RTF Rutherford, New Jersey
RTM Rotterdam, Netherlands
RTP Rutland Plains, Queensland
RTS Rottnest Island, Western Australia
RUH Riyadh, Saudi Arabia
RUN St Denis, Réunion Island, Indian Ocean
RUP Rupsi, India
RUT Rutland, Vermont
RUY Ruinas de Copan, Honduras
RVA Farafangana, Malagasy
RVC River Cess, Liberia
RVK Rorvik, Norway
RVN Rovaniemi, Finland
RVY Rivera, Uruguay
RWL Rawlins, Wyoming
RWP Rawalpindi, Pakistan
RXA Raudha, South Arabia
RXS Roxas City, Philippines
RYK Rahimyar Kahn, Pakistan
RYO Rio Turbio, Argentina
RZA Santa Cruz, Argentina
RZB Roseberth, Queensland
RZE Rzeszow, Poland

SNK Snyder, Texas
SNL Sand Creek, Guyana
SNM San Ignacio de Moxos, Bolivia
SNN Shannon, Ireland
SNS Salinas, California
SNU Santa Clara, Cuba
SNV Santa Elena, Venezuela
SNW Sandoway, Burma
SNY Sidney, Nebraska
SOA Soc Trang, South Vietnam
SOB Sobral, Brazil
SOF Sofia, Bulgaria
SOM San Tome, Venezuela
SON Espiritu Santo, New Hebrides
SOP Southern Pines, North Carolina
SOQ Sorong, West Irian, Indonesia
SOU Southampton, England
SPC Santa Cruz de la Palma, Canary Islands
SPE Sepulot, Malaysia
SPF Spearfish, South Dakota
SPI Springfield, Illinois
SPK Sapporo, Japan
SPL San Pedro de Jagua, Colombia
SPN Saipan, Marianas Islands
SPP Serpa, Portugal
SPS Wichita Falls, Texas
SPU Split, Yugoslavia
SPX San Pedro, Colombia
SPY San Pedro, Ivory Coast
SRA Santa Rosa, Brazil
SRE Sucre, Bolivia
SRG Semarang, Java, Indonesia
SRL Santa Rosalía, Mexico
SRQ Bradenton-Sarasota, Florida
SRR Sorreisa, Norway
SRS San Marcos, Colombia
SRZ Santa Cruz, Bolivia
SSA Salvador, Brazil
SSG Santa Isabel, Spanish Guinea
SSI Brunswick, Georgia
SSJ Sannessjoen, Norway
SSM Sault Sainte Marie, Michigan
SSN Auburn, New York
SSX Samsun, Turkey
SSY São Salvador, Angola
SSZ Santos, Brazil
STA Stauning, Denmark
STB Santa Barbara, Zulia, Venezuela
STD Santo Domingo, Venezuela
STE Stevens Point, Wisconsin
STF Setif, Algeria
STG Santiago, Brazil
STI Santiago, Dominican Republic
STJ St Joseph, Missouri
STL St Louis, Missouri
STM Santarem, Brazil
STO Stockholm, Sweden
STR Stuttgart, Germany
STS Santa Rosa, California
STT St Thomas, American Virgin Islands
STV Staverton, England
STX St Croix, American Virgin Islands
STZ Santa Terezinha, Brazil
SUA Stuart, Florida
SUB Surabaja, Java, Indonesia
SUG Surigao, Philippines
SUI Sukhumi, USSR
SUL Sui, Pakistan
SUM San Juan de César, Colombia
SUN Sun Valley, Idaho
SUR Starcke, Queensland
SUS Surkhet, Nepal
SUV Suva, Fiji Islands
SUX Sioux City, Iowa
SVB Sambava, Malagasy
SVC Silver City, New Mexico
SVD St Vincent, Windward Islands, West Indies
SVG Stavanger, Norway
SVJ Svolvaer, Norway
SVN Saravena, Colombia
SVQ Seville, Spain
SVU Savusavu, Fiji Islands
SVZ San Antonio, Venezuela
SWH Swan Hill, Victoria, Australia
SWL Spanish Wells, Bahamas
SWP Swakopmund, South-West Africa
SWQ Sumbawa, Indonesia
SWS Swansea, Wales
SWW Sweetwater, Texas
SXB Strasbourg, France
SXC Santa Catalina Island, California
SXE Sale, Victoria, Australia
SXG Senanga, Zambia
SXM Sint Maarten, Netherlands Antilles
SXR Srinagar, India
SXU Soddu, Ethiopia
SYA Shemya, Alaska
SYC Sanday, Scotland
SYD Sydney, New South Wales
SYI Shelbyville, Tennessee
SYR Syracuse, New York
SYY Stornoway, Outer Hebrides, Scotland
SYZ Shiraz, Iran
SZA Santo Antonio do Zaire, Angola
SZB Santa Barbara, Honduras
SZG Salzburg, Austria
SZI Soroti, Uganda
SZU Segou, Mali
SZZ Szczecin, Poland
TAB Tobago, Trinidad and Tobago, West Indies
TAC Tacloban, Philippines
TAI Taiz, Yemen
TAJ Taracua, Brazil
TAK Takamatsu, Japan
TAM Tampico, Mexico
TAP Tapachula, Mexico
TAR Taranto, Italy
TAS Tashkent, USSR
TAT Tatry/Poprad, Czechoslovakia
TAU Tauramena, Colombia
TBB Tuy Hoa, South Vietnam
TBL Tableland, Western Australia
TBN Ft Leonard Wood, Missouri
TBO Tabora, Tanzania
TBP Tumbes, Peru
TBS Tbilisi, USSR
TBT Tabatinga, Brazil
TBU Tongatabu, Nukualofa, Tonga Islands (airport of the Kingdom of Tonga in the South Pacific Ocean)
TBZ Tabriz, Iran
TCA Tennant Creek, Northern Territory, Australia
TCB Treasure Cay, Bahamas
TCH Tchibanga, Gabon
TCI Santa Cruz de Tenerife, Canary Islands
TCO Tumaco, Colombia
TCQ Tacna, Peru
TDA Trinidad, Colombia
TDD Trinidad, Bolivia
TDM Palmyra, Syria
TEA Tela, Honduras
TEB Teterboro, New Jersey
TEE Tyee, Alaska
TEG Tenkodogo, Upper Volta
TES Tessenei, Ethiopia
TET Tete, Mozambique
TEU Te Anau, New Zealand
TEY Thingeyri, Iceland
TEZ Tezpur, India
TFF Tefe, Brazil
TFR Tarbes, France
TFY Tarfaya, Morocco
TGD Titograd, Yugoslavia
TGG Trengganu, Malaysia
TGN Tarragona, Spain
TGR Touggourt, Algeria
TGS Tuxtla Gutierrez, Mexico
TGT Tanga, Tanzania
TGU Tegucigalpa, Honduras
TGX Taguatinga, Brazil
TGY Punta Gorda, British Honduras
THA Tullahoma, Tennessee
THE Teresina, Brazil
THG Thangool, Queensland
THJ Theodore, Queensland
THK Thakhek, Laos

THO Thorshofn, Iceland
THR Teheran, Iran
THY Thylungra, Queensland
THZ Tahoua, Niger
TIA Tirana, Albania
TIE Tippi, Ethiopia
TIF Taif, Saudi Arabia
TIJ Tijuana, Mexico
TIN Tindouf, Algeria
TIP Tripoli, Libya
TIR Tiree Island, Scotland
TIS Thursday Island, Queensland
TIU Timaru, New Zealand
TIV Tivat, Yugoslavia
TIW Tacoma, Washington
TIX Titusville, Florida
TJA Tarija, Bolivia
TJI Trujillo, Honduras
TJQ Tandjungpandan, Billiton, Indonesia
TKC Tiko, Cameroon
TKD Takoradi, Ghana
TKG Telukbetung, Sumatra, Indonesia
TKI Turks Islands, West Indies
TKK Truk, Caroline Islands
TKL Tak, Thailand
TKR Thakurgaon, Bangladesh
TKU Turku, Finland
TKY Turkey Creek, Western Australia
TLB Tortola, British Virgin Islands
TLE Tulear, Malagasy
TLG Tres Lagoas, Brazil
TLH Tallahassee, Florida
TLL Tallinn, Estonia, USSR
TLN Hyeres–Toulon, France (airport serving both communities)
TLP Talpa, New Mexico
TLR Talgarno, Western Australia
TLS Toulouse, France
TLU Tolu, Colombia
TLV Tel Aviv, Israel
TLW Talasea, New Britain, New Guinea
TMD Timbedra, Mauritania
TME Tame, Colombia
TMH Tanahmerah, West Irian, Indonesia
TML Tamale, Ghana
TMM Tamatave, Malagasy
TMP Tampere, Finland
TMQ Tambao, Upper Volta
TMR Tamanrasset, Algeria
TMT Temora, New South Wales
TMW Tamworth, New South Wales
TMX Timimoun, Algeria
TMZ Termez, USSR
TNA Tsinan, China
TND Trinidad, Cuba

TNG Tangier, Morocco
TNJ Tanjungpinang, Bintan Island, Indonesia
TNN Taiwan, Formosa
TNQ Tongo, Sierra Leone
TNR Tananarive, Malagasy
TNS Tønsberg, Norway
TOA Tromsø, Norway
TOB Tobruk, Libya
TOL Toledo, Ohio
TOM Tombouctou, Mali (better known as Timbuctoo)
TOP Topeka, Kansas—A-TPB (Allen); P-TOP (Billard)
TOQ Tocopilla, Chile
TOU Touraine, South Vietnam
TOW Tororo, Uganda
TOX Tocantina, Goiás, Brazil
TPA Tampa, Florida
TPE Taipei, Formosa
TPG Taiping, China
TPH Tonopah, Nevada
TPL Temple, Texas
TPS Trapani, Italy
TPU Taputuquara, Brazil
TPY Tocantinopolis, Brazil
TQS Tres Esquinas, Colombia
TQV St Moritz, Switzerland
TRB Turbo, Colombia
TRC Torrcon, Mexico
TRD Trondheim, Norway
TRG Tauranga, New Zealand
TRI Tri-City Airport—Bristol, Tennessee; Bristol, Virginia; Johnson City–Kingsport, Tennessee
TRK Tarakan, Indonesia
TRN Turin, Italy
TRO Taree, New South Wales
TRQ Tarauaca, Brazil
TRR Trincomalee, Ceylon
TRS Trieste, Italy
TRT Tiaret, Algeria
TRU Trujillo, Peru
TRV Trivandrum, India
TRW Tarawa, Gilbert Islands
TRY Treviso, Italy
TRZ Trichinopoly, India
TSB Tsumeb, South-West Africa
TSH Tshikapa, Zaire
TSN Tientsin, China
TSS Tebessa, Algeria
TSV Townsville, Queensland
TTC Taltal, Chile
TTD Palm Island, Windward Islands, West Indies
TTG Tartagal, Argentina
TTM Tablón de Tamara, Colombia
TTN Trenton, New Jersey
TTS Tsaratanana, Malagasy
TTU Tetuan, Spanish Morocco
TUB Tubarao, Brazil
TUC Tucuman, Argentina
TUD Tambacounda, Senegal

TUF Tours, France
TUI Turaif, Saudi Arabia
TUL Tulsa, Oklahoma
TUN Tunis, Tunisia
TUO Taupo, New Zealand
TUP Tupelo, Mississippi
TUQ Tougan, Upper Volta
TUS Tucson, Arizona
TUU Tabuk, Saudi Arabia
TUV Tucupita, Venezuela
TUX Tuxpan, Mexico
TVA Morafenobe, Malagasy
TVC Traverse City, Michigan
TVF Thief River Falls, Minnesota
TVU Taveuni, Fiji Islands
TWB Toowoomba, Queensland
TWF Twin Falls, Idaho
TWU Tawau, Malaysia
TXA Texeira, Portugal
TXG Taichung, Formosa
TXK Texarkana, Arkansas
TXM Teminabuan, West Irian, Indonesia
TXR Tanbar, Queensland
TXU Tabou, Ivory Coast
TYA Yalova, Turkey
TYB Tibooburra, New South Wales
TYL Talara, Peru
TYN Taiyaun, China
TYO Tokyo, Japan
TYR Tyler, Texas
TYS Knoxville, Tennessee
TZG Waha Leaf, British Honduras
TZX Trobzon, Turkey
UAK Narsarssuak, Greenland
UAQ San Juan, Argentina
UBA Uberaba, Brazil
UBG Limón, Honduras
UBI Buin, Solomon Islands
UBJ Ube, Japan
UBK Port Augusta, South Australia
UBP Ubol, Thailand
UBS Columbus, Mississippi
UCA Rome–Utica, New York (airport shared by both cities)
UCN Buchanan, Liberia
UDD Cuddapan, Queensland
UDI Uberlandia, Brazil
UDR Udaipur, India
UEL Quelimane, Mozambique
UET Quetta, Pakistan
UGA Ugashik, Alaska
UIB Quibdó, Colombia
UIH Qui Nhon, South Vietnam
UIN Quincy, Illinois
UIO Quito, Ecuador
UIP Quimper, France
UKI Ukiah, California
UKR Mukeiras, South Arabia
ULA San Julian, Argentina
ULN Ulan Bator, Mongolia

ULP Quilpie, Queensland
ULQ Tulua, Colombia
UME Umeaa, Sweden
UMK Umanak, Greenland
UMU Umuarama, Brazil
UMW Mumbwa, Zambia
UNC Unguia, Colombia
UND Kunduz, Afghanistan
UNE Unst, Shetland Islands, Scotland
UNI União da Vitoria, Brazil
UNK Unalakleet, Alaska
UON Muong Sai, Laos
UOX University, Mississippi
UPA Upala, Costa Rica
UPN Uruapan, Mexico
UPP Upolu Point, Hawaii
UPV Upernavik, Greenland
URB Urubupunga, Brazil
URF Urfa, Turkey
URG Uruguaiana, Brazil
URI Uribia, Colombia
URY Gurayat, Saudi Arabia
USH Ushuaia, Argentina
UTA Umtali, Zimbabwe
UTB Muttaburra, Queensland
UTI Uttaradit, Thailand
UTL Utila Island, Honduras
UTN Upington, South Africa
UTO Utopia, Alaska
UTW Queenstown, South Africa
UUP Uaupes, Brazil
UVL New Valley, Egypt
UYL Nyala, Sudan
UZU Curuzu Cuatia, Argentina
VAA Vaasa, Finland
VAE Ciudad de Valles, Mexico
VAG Vagar, Faeroe Islands
VAN Van, Turkey
VAR Varna, Bulgaria
VAS Sivas, Turkey
VAT Vatomandry, Malagasy
VAV Vaxjo, Sweden
VBN Vrnjacka Banja, Yugoslavia
VBY Visby, Sweden
VCE Venice, Italy
VCT Victoria, Texas
VCW Victoria West, South Africa
VDM Viedma, Argentina
VDO Vadso, Norway
VDP Valle de la Pascua, Venezuela
VDR Villa Dolores, Argentina
VDZ Valdez, Alaska
VEL Vernal, Utah
VER Veracruz, Mexico
VEY Vestmannaeyjar, Iceland
VFA Victoria Falls, Zimbabwe
VGA Vijayawada, India
VGO Vigo, Spain
VGR Virgin Gorda, British Virgin Islands
VHO Vila Coutinho, Mozam-

bique
VHY Vichy, France
VIC Vicenza, Italy
VIE Vienna, Austria
VIL Villa Cisneros, Spanish Sahara
VIQ Violetvale, Queensland
VIS Visalia, California
VIV Vivigany, New Guinea
VIX Victória, Brazil
VJB Vila de João Belo, Mozambique
VKS Vicksburg, Mississippi
VLC Valencia, Spain
VLD Valdosta, Georgia
VLI Port Vila, New Hebrides
VLK Viqueque, Timor
VLN Valencia, Venezuela
VLR Vallenar, Chile
VLV Valera, Venezuela
VMU Baimuru, Papua
VNO Vilnius, Lithuania, USSR
VNR Vanrook, Queensland
VNX Vilanculos, Mozambique
VOG Volgograd, USSR
VOH Vohemar, Malagasy
VOL Volos, Greece
VPA Silver Plains, Queensland
VPS Eglin Air Force Base, Florida
VPY Vila Pery, Mozambique
VPZ Valparaiso, Indiana
VRA Varadero, Cuba
VRB Vero Beach, Florida
VRN Verona, Italy
VRZ Voronezh, USSR
VSA Villahermosa, Mexico
VSO Phuoc Long, Vietnam
VTE Vientiane, Laos
VTL Vittel, France
VTZ Vishakhapatnam, India
VUP Valledupar, Colombia
VVB Mahanoro, Malagasy
VVC Villavicencio, Colombia
VVO Vladivostok, USSR
VXC Vila Cabral, Mozambique
WAB Wabag, New Guinea
WAC Waca, Ethiopia
WAD Andriamena, Malagasy
WAE Aoulef, Algeria
WAG Wanganui, New Zealand
WAI Antsohihy, Malagasy
WAK Ankazoabo, Malagasy
WAM Ambatondrazaka, Malagasy
WAN Waverney, Queensland
WAP Alto Palena, Chile
WAQ Antsalova, Malagasy
WAS Washington, D.C.—N-DCA (National); D-IAD (Dulles); B-Bal (Friendship)
WAW Warsaw, Poland
WBA Washington Bay, Alaska
WBD Befandriana, Malagasy
WBE Bealanana, Malagasy
WBG Wichabai, Guyana

WBM Wapenamanda, New Guinea
WBO Beroroha, Malagasy
WCA Castro, Chile
WCH Chaiten, Chile
WCJ Caleta Josefina, Chile
WCO Coolullah, Australia
WDA Wadi Ain, South Arabia
WDG Enid, Oklahoma
WDH Windhoek, South-West Africa
WEI Weipa, Queensland
WEL Welkom, South Africa
WEN Papa Westray, Orkney Islands, Scotland
WFI Fianarantsoa, Malagasy
WGA Wagga-Wagga, New South Wales
WGM Wilmington, California
WGP Waingapu, Sumba, Indonesia
WHA Wadi Halfa, Sudan
WHK Whakatane, New Zealand
WIC Wick, Scotland
WIN Winton, Queensland
WIS Central, Wisconsin
WJF Lancaster–Palmdale, California (airport serving both places in the Mojave)
WKB Warracknabeal, Victoria, Australia
WKI Wankie, Zimbabwe
WKM Wankie Game Reserve, Zimbabwe
WKN Wakunai, Solomon Islands
WKP Wrotham Park, Queensland
WLG Wellington, New Zealand
WLS Wallis Island, Polynesia
WMA Mandritsara, Malagasy
WMB Warrnambool, New South Wales
WMD Mandabe, Malagasy
WML Malaimbandy, Malagasy
WMN Maroantsetra, Malagasy
WMP Mampikony, Malagasy
WMR Mananara, Malagasy
WMV Madirovalo, Malagasy
WMX Wamena, West Irian, Indonesia
WNR Windorah, Queensland
WNS Nawabshah, Pakistan
WNY Burnie–Wynward, Tasmania (airport shared by nearby communities)
WON Wondoola, Queensland
WOQ Wooroona, Queensland
WPA Puerto Aysen, Chile
WPB Port Berge, Malagasy
WPR Porvenir, Chile
WPU Puerto Williams, Chile
WRE Whangarei, New Zealand
WRG Wrangell, Alaska

WRL Worland, Wyoming
WRO Wroclaw, Poland
WSM Wiseman, Alaska
WSP Waspam, Nicaragua
WSR Wasior, West Irian, Indonesia
WSZ Westport, New Zealand
WTA Tambohorano, Malagasy
WTD West End, Grand Bahama Island, Bahamas
WTS Tsiroanomandidy, Malagasy
WUG Wau, New Guinea
WUH Wuhan, China
WUU Wau, Sudan
WVA Alexandria, Virginia
WVB Walvis Bay, South-West Africa
WVK Manakara, Malagasy
WVL Waterville, Maine
WVV Volovan, Malagasy
WWD Cape May, New Jersey
WWK Wewak, New Guinea
WYA Whyalla, South Australia
WYC Yes Bay, Alaska
WYD Wyandotte, Queensland
WYE Yengema, Sierra Leone
WYN Wyndham, Western Australia
XAP Xapecó, Brazil
XAY Xapuri, Brazil
XIE Xieng Khouang, Laos
XIQ Xique-Xique, Brazil
XLS St Louis, Senegal
XMC Malacoota, New South Wales, Australia
XMM Mamaia, Romania
XNG Quang Ngai, Vietnam
XRY Jerez de la Frontera, Spain
XSC South Caicos, Caicos Islands, West Indies
XTG Thargomindah, Queensland
XTN Qatn, South Arabia
XTO Taroom, Queensland
XTR Tara, Queensland
YAC Yacuiba, Bolivia
YAK Yakutat, Alaska
VAM Sault Sainte Marie, Ontario
YAO Yaounde, Cameroon
YAP Yap, Caroline Islands
YBC Baie, Comeau, Québec
YBE Uranium City, Saskatchewan
YBG Saguenay, Québec
YBR Brandon, Manitoba
YCG Castlegar, British Columbia
YCL Charlo, New Brunswick
YDA Dawson City, Yukon
YDF Deer Lake, Newfoundland
YEG Edmonton, Alberta
YEV Inuvik, Northwest Territo-

ries, Canada
YFB Frobisher, Northwest Territories, Canada
YFC Fredericton, New Brunswick
YFE Forestville, Québec
YGR Magdalen Island, Québec
YGT Thunder Bay (formerly Ft William), Ontario
YHZ Halifax, Nova Scotia
YJT Stephenville, Newfoundland
YKA Kamloops, British Columbia
YKL Schefferville, Québec
YKM Yakima, Washington
YKN Yankton, South Dakota
YLE Yule Island, New Guinea
YLW Kelowna, British Columbia
YMA Mayo, Yukon Territory, Canada
YME Matane, Québec
YML Murray Bay, Québec
YMV Manicouagan, Québec
YND Yandina, Solomon Islands
YNG Sharon, Pennsylvania–Warren–Youngstown, Ohio (airport serving three adjacent cities in two bordering states)
YNK Gagnon, Québec
YOL Yola, Nigeria
YOR Yoro, Honduras
YOW Ottawa, Ontario
YPA Prince Albert, Saskatchewan
YPR Prince Rupert, British Columbia
YQB Québec City, Québec
YQG Windsor, Ontario
YQH Watson Lake, Yukon
YQI Yarmouth, Nova Scotia
YQJ Porquis Junction, Ontario
YQL Lethbridge, Alberta
YQM Moncton, New Brunswick
YQR Regina, Saskatchewan
YQT Thunder Bay, Ontario—serving communities formerly known as Ft William and Port Arthur
YQU Grande Prairie, Alberta
YQV Yorkton, Saskatchewan
YQX Gander, Newfoundland
YQY Sydney, Nova Scotia
YQZ Quesnel, British Columbia
YRF Ross Bay, Newfoundland
YRI Riviere du Loup, Québec
YRQ Trois Rivières, Québec
YRX Rimouski, Québec
YSB Sudbury, Ontario
YSJ Saint John, New Brunswick
YSM Ft Smith, Northwest Ter-

ritories, Canada
YSU Summerside, Prince Edward Island
YTS Timmins, Ontario
YUL Montreal, Québec
YUM Yuma, Arizona
YUY Noranda–Rouyn, Québec (airport shared by both communities)
YVA Moroni, Comoro Islands
YVO Burlamaque–Val d'Or, Québec (airport serving both communities)
YVR Vancouver, British Columbia
YWG Winnipeg, Manitoba
YWH Whalehead, Québec
YWK Wabush, Newfoundland
YWL Williams Lake, British Columbia
YWY Wrigley, Northwest Territories
YXC Cranbrook, British Columbia
YXD Edmonton, Alberta—I-YEG (International); Y-YXD (Industrial)
YXE Saskatoon, Saskatchewan
YXH Medicine Hat, Alberta
YXJ Ft St John, British Columbia
YXR Earlton, Ontario
YXS Prince George, British Columbia
YXT Terrace, British Columbia
YXU London, Ontario
YYB North Bay, Ontario
YYC Calgary, Alberta
YYD Smithers, British Columbia
YYE Ft Nelson, British Columbia
YYF Penticton, British Columbia
YYG Charlottetown, Prince Edward Island
YYJ Victoria, British Columbia
YYN Swift Current, Saskatchewan
YYR Goose Bay, Labrador
YYT St. Johns, Newfoundland
YYU Kapuskasing, Ontario
YYY Mont Joli, Québec
YYZ Hamilton–Toronto, Ontario (airport serving both cities)
YZF Yellow Knife, Northwest Territories
YZP Sandspit, British Columbia
YZV Sept-Îles (Seven Islands), Québec
ZAD Zadar, Yugoslavia
ZAG Zagreb, Yugoslavia
ZAH Zahedan, Iran

ZAL Valdivia, Chile
ZAM Zamboanga, Mindanao, Philippines
ZAN Zanderij, Surinam
ZAP Zaporozhe, USSR
ZAR Zaria, Nigeria
ZAZ Zaragoza, Spain
ZBO Bowen, Queensland
ZBY Sayaboury, Laos
ZCO Temuco, Chile
ZDK Zonguldak, Turkey
ZED Pakatoa, New Zealand
ZGL South Galway, Queensland
ZGM Ngoma, Zambia
ZHM Shamshernagar, Bangladesh
ZIC Victoria, Chile

ZIG Ziguinchor, Senegal
ZIH Zihuantanejo, Mexico
ZKB Kasaba Bay, Zambia
ZKL Steenkool, West Irian, Indonesia
ZKM Sette Cama, Gabon
ZLG La Guera, Morocco
ZLO Manzanillo, Mexico
ZMD São Madureira, Brazil
ZND Zinder, Niger
ZNG New Glasgow, Nova Scotia
ZNZ Zanzibar, Tanzania
ZOM Zomba, Malawi
ZON Queenstown, New Zealand
ZOS Osorno, Chile
ZQN Queenstown, New Zealand

ZRH Zurich, Switzerland
ZRI Serui, West Irian, Indonesia
ZSA San Salvador Island, Bahamas
ZSS Sassandra, Ivory Coast
ZTK Stokmarknes, Norway
ZUD Ancud, Chile
ZUL Silfi, Saudi Arabia
ZVA Miandrivazo, Malagasy
ZVG Springvale, Queensland
ZVK Savannakhet, Laos
ZWA Andapa, Malagasy
ZYL Sylhet, Bangladesh
ZZU Mzuzu, Malawi
ZZV Zanesville, Ohio

American Eponyms, Nicknames, and Sobriquets

American American beauty (rose); American cheddar (also called American cheese or store cheese); American-English (American-style English); American fingering (piano); American fries (hashed brown potatoes); American lobster (Canadian or New England large-clawed species); American Morse (code); American plan (fixed hotel or motel rate including board and food); American school (of artists, economists, etc.); other American categories or items

American Dvořák's Quartet in F (opus 96) for two violins, viola, and cello

American Apostle of Nonviolent Disobedience Martin Luther King, Jr

American Atheist Epigrammatist Ambrose Bierce, Mark Twain, and HL Mencken all share in this title

American Ballad Composer Stephen Collins Foster

American Beauty Rose official flower of Washington, D.C.; symbolic nickname sometimes given its girls—American Beauty Roses

American Caesar General Douglas Mac Arthur

American Century the 20th century marked by invention and industrial activity, highest standard of living for the most

people, discovery of the North Pole, landing of men on the moon, victory in two world wars, devotion to the democratic ideal—the 1900s

American Chronicler John Dos Passos

American Comedians Abbott and Costello, Fred Allen, Amos and Andy, Lucille Ball, Jack Benny and Rochester (Eddie Anderson), Edgar Bergen (and Charlie McCarthy), Milton Berle, Josh Billings, Victor Borge, Mel Brooks, (George) Burns and (Gracie) Allen, Sid Caesar, Cantinflas (Mario Moreno), Eddie Cantor, Diahann Carroll, Johnny Carson, Charlie Chaplin, Sammy Davis, Jr, Phyllis Diller, Jimmy Durante, WC Fields, Redd Foxx, Great Gildersleeve, Jackie Gleason, George B. Hicks, Bob Hope, Danny Kaye, Buster Keaton, (Stan) Laurel and (Oliver) Hardy, Sam Levinson, Harold Lloyd, Sam Lucas, Jackie (Moms) Mabley, the Marx Brothers (*see* Marx Brothers), Florence Mills, Petroleum V. Nasby, Bill Nye, Will Rogers, Mark Russell, Bobby Short, Lily Tomlin, Peter Ustinov, Bert Williams, and any other comedian any reader feels has been overlooked (*see* Algonquin Circle; American Humorists)

American Conservationist title shared by John Muir, William T Hornaday, Williard G Van Name, and a very few others who loved nature more than profit or professional approval

American-Cowboy Comedian-Humorist Commentator-Philosopher Will Rogers

American Critic H(enry) L(ouis) Mencken

American Crusader for Religious Liberty Roger Williams

American Demosthenes Robert Ingersoll

American Documentary Film Pioneer Robert Flaherty

American Eagle avian symbol of the United States

American Etcher Joseph Pennell and James Abbott McNeill Whistler share this title with many others

American Expatriate Painter Benjamin West and James Abbott McNeill Whistler share this descriptive title

American Film Pioneer David Wark Griffith

American Founder of Women's Suffrage Elizabeth Cady Stanton (founder and first president of the National Woman Suffrage Association)

American Frontier Romanticist James Fenimore Cooper

American Gateway to Alaska and the Orient Seattle

American Heartland Illinois, Indiana, Michigan, Ohio, Wisconsin

American Historical Painter Emmanuel Leutzé

American Humorists George Ade, Steve Allen, Woody Allen, Steven L Anreder, Russell Baker, Robert Benchley, Ambrose Bierce, Erma Bombeck, Art Buchwald, Al Capp, Johnny Carson, Irwin B Corey, ee cummings, Finley Peter Dunne, TS Eliot, William Faulkner, Benjamin Franklin, Lewis Grizzard, Joel Chandler Harris, Bret Harte, O Henry, Oliver Wendell Holmes, Art Hoppe, Washington Irving, Vachel Lindsay, Don Marquis, Groucho Marx, HL Mencken, Gerald Nachman, Ogden Nash, George Jean Nathan, SJ Perelman, James Whitcomb Riley, Will Rogers, Leo Rosten, Damon Runyon, Morrie Ryskind, Mort Sahl, R Emmett Tyrell, Jr, Mark Twain, Artemus Ward, Diane White, Robert Yoakum, and any other American humorist any reader feels has been overlooked (*see* Algonquin Circle; American Comedians)

American Illustrator Anton Otto Fischer, Howard Pyle, Norman Rockwell, and others are known by this title

American Impressionist Childe Hassam

American Industrial Painter Charles Sheeler

American Infidel Colonel Robert G Ingersoll, agnostic attorney and foremost public speaker of his time who was also known as the American Demosthenes

Americanist Americanist Press

American Karl Marx Curaçao-born Daniel De Leon—founder in New York City (where he taught at Columbia University) of the Socialist Labor Party (SLP) and the International Workers of the World (IWW); made some of the first English translations of Karl Marx

American Landscape Painters Albert Bierstad, George Caleb Bingham, James Britton, Frederic Church, Thomas Cole, Asher Brown Durand, Edward Hopper, Henry Inman, George Inness, J Francis Murphy, Grant Wood, and Alexander Helwig Wyant share this title

American Libertarian sobriquet shared by such outstanding freethinkers as Thomas Jefferson, Thomas Paine, Robert Ingersoll, Clarence Darrow, and your favorite American Libertarian

American Libertarian Philosopher, Natural Scientist, Printer, and Publisher Benjamin Franklin

American Lighthouse Painter Edward Hopper

American Lithographers (Nathaniel) James (Merritt) Ives

American Medical Historian William Henry Welch

American Modern Jackson Pollock

American National Composer John Philip Sousa

American Neurologist Extraordinary Silas Weir Mitchell

American Operetta Composers Irving Berlin, George M Cohan, Victor Herbert, Jerome Kern, Frederick Loewe, Cole Porter, Richard Rodgers, Vincent Youmans, and your unnamed favorite, must share this title

American Orator Extraordinary sobriquet shared by Robert G Ingersoll and Franklin D Roosevelt

American Photographer Laureate Ansel Adams

American Photographers of Distinction Berenice Abbott, Ansel Adams, Mathew B Brady, Julia Margaret Cameron, Robert Capa, Imogen Cunningham, Walker Evans, Arnold Genthe, JK Hillers, William Henry Jackson, Gertrude Käsebier, Dorothea Lange, J Ghislain Lootens, Edward Muybridge, Timothy O'Sullivan, Roy Pinney, Edward Steichen, Alfred Stieglitz, Paul Strand, Edward Weston, Clarence H White, Margaret Bourke White, James Van Der Zee, Willard Van Dyke, and your unmentioned favorite still photographer of distinction

American Portrait Painters James Britton, John Singleton Copley, Henry Inman, Eastman Johnson, John Singer Sargent, and Eugene Edward Speicher have been among the outstanding holders of this ti-

tle along with the Peale family, Gilbert Stuart, Thomas Sully, and James Abbott McNeill Whistler

American Pragmatist Trinity John Dewey, William James, Charles Sanders Pierce

American Primitive Painters Edward Hicks, Grandma Moses, and others, including the compiler, have been given this title

American Propagandist Novelist Upton Sinclair

American Prose-Poetry Novelist Thomas Wolfe

American Railroad Barons Jay Gould; Edward H Harriman; James J Hill; Collis P Huntington; William H Vanderbilt

American Rebel Upton Sinclair

American Renewal administration of Ronald Reagan—fortieth President of the United States

American Sappho Sarah Wentworth Apthorp Morton of Braintree and Quincy, Mass

American Sculptors Daniel Chester French, perhaps the most popular among such as Borglum, Brancusi, Epstein, Lachaise, Manship, Moore, St Gaudens, Ward, and Zorach

American Skeptic Philosopher Madrid-born George Santayana

American Spokesman for Socialism Eugene V Debs, Daniel De Leon, and Norman Thomas were the chief contenders for this title

Americans United Americans United for Separation of Church and State (AUSCS)

American Virgins U.S. Virgin Islands

American Temple of Music Carnegie Hall

American Women Reformers Jane Addams, Susan B(rownell) Anthony, Elizabeth Cady Stanton, Ida M(inerva) Tarbell, Lillian D Wald, and Frances Elizabeth Willard must be included in a lengthening list of admirables

American Woodsman John James Audubon

America's Dairyland Wisconsin's sobriquet

America's Devil's Island post-Civil-War nickname for the military prison at Fort Jefferson in the Dry Tortugas west of Key West, Florida

America's First Colonizer Roger Williams of Rhode Island and William Penn of Pennsylvania appear to compete for the title

America's First Financier Robert Morris

America's First Poet Philip Frenau

America's First Resort Newport, Rhode Island

America's First Suffragist Abigail Smith Adams (*see* Portia)

America's First Woman Newspaper Publisher Elizabeth Timothy of the *South Carolina Gazette* published in Charleston

America's Forgotten Photographer Timothy O'Sullivan

America's Inside Fun City New York (concert halls, theaters, opera houses, museums)

America's Last Frontier Alaska

America's Last Great Wilderness Alaska

America's Leading Proletarian Writer John Dos Passos

America's Most Famous Naval Hero Admiral David G Farragut

America's Most Useful Citizen Jane Addams—author of *Twenty Years at Hull-House*

America's Newest Big City Miami, Florida

America's Nonsense Poet Ogden Nash

America's Outside Fun City San Diego (bays, mountains, year-round outside sports)

America's Practical Navigator Nathaniel Bowditch—compiler of *The American Practical Navigator*

America's Premier Air Woman Amelia Earhart Putnam—first aviatrix to fly across the Atlantic

America's Proudest Musical Possession Carnegie Hall

America's Safest City Lakewood, Ohio (suburb of Cleveland)

America's Wintergarden southern California's Imperial Valley

Thomas Jefferson and Abraham Lincoln of American Music Charles Ives, according to Leonard Bernstein

Astronomical Constellations, Stars and Symbols

And Andromeda (Princess Enchained), also called Mirach

Ant Antlia (Bilge Pump)

Aps Apus (Bird of Paradise)

Aql Aquila (Eagle); contains Altair

Aqr Aquarius (Water Carrier)

Ara (Altar)

Arg Argo or Argo Navis (Ship *Argo* or Ship of the Argonauts); contains Carina (Keel), Malus (Mast), Puppis (Stern), Pyxis (Mariner's Compass), Vela (Sails)

Ari Aries (Ram); contains Hamal

Aur Auriga (Charioteer); contains Capella

Boö Boötes (Herdsman); contains Arcturus

Cae Caelum (Chisel)

Cam Camelopardalis (Giraffe)

Cap Capricornus (Horned Goat)

Car Carina (Keel), in Argo; contains Canopus

Cas Cassiopeia (Queen Enthroned); contains supernova 1572

Cen Centaurus (Centaur); contains Alpha Centauri, Proxima Centauri

Cep Cepheus (Monarch)

Cet Cetus (Whale); contains Mira

Cha Chamaeleon (Chameleon)

Cir Circinus (Compasses)

CMa Canis Major (Great Dog); contains Sirius

CMi Canis Minor (Little Dog); contains Procyon

Cnc Cancer (Crab); contains Praesepe

Col Columba (Dove)

Com Coma Berenices (Berenice's Hair)

CrA Corona Australis (Southern Crown)

CrB Corona Borealis (Northern Crown), also called Gemma

Crt Crater (Cup)

Cru Crux (Southern Cross); Black Magellanic Cloud nearby

Crv Corvus (Crow)

CVn Canes Venatici (Hunting Dogs); contains Cor Caroli

Cyg Cygnus (Swan); contains Deneb, Northern Cross

Del Delphinus (Dolphin)

Dor Dorado, also called Xiphies (Swordfish); Large Magellanic Cloud

Dra Draco (Dragon)

Equ Equuleus (Colt)

Eri Eridanus (Great River); contains Achernar

For Fornax (Furnace)

Gem Gemini (The Twins); contains Castor, Pollux

Gru Grus (Crane)

Her Hercules; contains Ras Algethi

Hor Horologium (Clock)

Hya Hydra (Marine Monster); contains Alphard

Hyd Hydrus (Water Snake)

Ind Indus (Indian)

Kif Aus Kiffa Australis (Southern Breadbasket); contains Zuben el Genubi

Kif Bor Kiffa Borealis (Northern Breadbasket); contains Zuben-eschamali

Lac Lacerta (Lizard)

Leo (Lion) contains Regulus, Denebola

Lep Lepus (Hare)

Lib Libra (Balance or Scales)

LMi Leo Minor (Little Lion)

Lup Lupus (Wolf)

Lyn Lynx

Lyr Lyra (Lyre); contains Vega

Mal Malus (Mast), in Argo

Men Mensa (Table), also called Mons Mensae (Table Mountain)

Mic Microscopium (Microscope)

Mon Monoceros (Unicorn)

Mus Musca (Fly)

Nor Norma (Rule)

Oct Octans (Octant)

Oph Ophiuchus (Serpent Bearer); contains supernova 1604

Ori Orion (Hunter); contains Betelgeuse, Rigel

Pav Pavo (Peacock)

Peg Pegasus (Winged Horse)
Per Perseus (Rescuer or Champion); contains Algol
Phe Phoenix
Pic Pictor (Painter's Easel)
PsA Piscis Australis or Austrinus (Southern Fish); contains Formalhaut
Psc Pisces (Fishes)
Pup Puppis (Stern), in Argo
Pyx Pyxis (Mariner's Compass Chest or Binnacle), in Argo
Ret Reticulum (Net)
Scl Sculptor (Sculptor's Workshop)

Sco Scorpio (Scorpion); contains Antares
Sct Scutum (Shield)
Ser Serpens (Serpent)
Sex Sextant
Sge Sagitta (Arrow)
Sgr Sagittarius (Archer), Center of Galaxy
Tau Taurus (Bull); contains Hyades—Aldebaran; Pleiades
Tel Telescopium (Telescope)
TrA Triangulum Australe (Southern Triangle)

Tri Triangulum (Triangle)
Tuc Tucana (Toucan); Small Magellanic Cloud
UMa Ursa Major (Great Bear); contains Dubhe, Mizar
UMi Ursa Minor (Little Bear); contains Polaris (Pole Star)
Vel Vela (Sails), in Argo
Vir Virgo (Virgin)
Vol Volans (Flying Fish)
Vul Vulpecula (Little Fox); also called Vulpecula cum Ansere (Little Fox with Goose)

ASTRONOMICAL SYMBOLS

⊖☽ : center
☄ : comet
◑ : crescent moon (first quarter)
◐ : crescent moon (last quarter)
⊕ : Earth (symbol shows globe bisected by meridian lines into four quarters)
○ : full moon
◑ : gibbous moon (first quarter)
○ : gibbous moon (last quarter)
◐ : half moon (first quarter)
◑ : half moon (last quarter)
♃ : Jupiter (symbol said to represent a hieroglyph of the eagle, Jove's bird, or to be the initial letter of Zeus with a line drawn through it to indicate its abbreviation)
☊☽ : lower limb
♂ : Mars (symbol represents shield and spear of the

god of war, Mars; it is also the male or masculine symbol)
☿ : Mercury (symbol represents head and winged cap of Mercury, god of commerce and communication, surmounting his caduceus)
♆ : Neptune (symbolized by the trident of Neptune, god of the sea)
● : new moon
☾ : moon (symbol depicts crescent moon in last quarter)
♇ : Pluto (symbol is monogram made up of P and L in Pluto, also initials of the astronomer Percival Lowell, who predicted its discovery)
♄ : Saturn (symbol thought to represent an ancient scythe or sickle, as Saturn was the god of seed

sowing and hence also of time)
☆ : star
☆-P : star-planet altitude correction
☉ : sun (symbolized by a shield with its boss; some believe this boss represents a central sunspot)
☉̄☽ : upper limb
♅ : Uranus (symbolized by combined devices indicating the sun plus the spear of Mars, as Uranus was the personification of heaven in the Greek mythology, dominated by the light of the sun and the power of Mars)
♀ : Venus (designated by the female symbol, thought to be the stylized representation of the hand mirror of this goddess of love)

Bafflegab Divulged

Bafflegab consists of the ambiguous and euphemistic fig leaves of language and literature also known as bureaucratese, cover-up death-disease-sex-and-the-toilet terms, goody-goody garble, mellowspeak, nicenellyisms, or officialese selected from a compilation begun by the author in 1980.

Bafflegab begins where abbreviations, acronyms, and other short forms leave off; hence this *Bafflegab* addendum is the natural juncture between the *Abbreviations Dictionary* and any other dictionary or lexicon.

abandoned woman apparently a deserted, forsaken, and lost adult of the feminine sex; but the phrase is more often a cover-up for other cover-ups and synonyms such as adventuress, bag, baggage, bar girl, bat, bunny, call girl, cat, chippy, cocotte, concubine, connubial substitute, courtesan, daughter of joy, ecdysiast, erring sister, escort of the evening, exotic entertainer, fallen woman, fornicatrix, front-parlor girl, grisette, harlot, ho, hooker, horizontalist, illicit lover, jade, jezebel, kept woman, lorette, madam, massage parlor expert, meretrix, mistress, nautch girl, nude dancer, obstitute, oriental dancing girl, painted woman, paramour, party girl, poule, prostitute, pussy, puta, quandong, quean, red-light lady, scarlet woman, streetwalker, strip-tease artist, strumpet, tart, topless girl, trollop, trull, unfortunate woman, valentina, venerist, white slave, woman of the town, xanadu dream girl, yvette, zealous zelia, or just the plain Old English *whore*—no less, no more

absolute tripe official gibberish

acceptable deception(s) half truth(s)—acceptable only by people willing to accept half truths

accommodation house(s) British fig leaf for whorehouse(s) whose synonyms include *bagno,* bawdyhouse, bordello, brothel, *casa de prostituição, casa de putas, congal,* crib, den of iniquity, den of vice, house of assignation, house of ill fame, house of joy, joint, *lupanar,* panel house, *prostíbulo, shinjuku,* sink of iniquity, sporting house, stew, and at least one word in every language

account executive(s) pimp(s) offering high-price prostitutes to executives on liberal expense accounts

accounting aberrations profit-making mistakes made in favor of the profiteer at the expense of the customer

aching stiffness of the middle leg euphemism for an erection

acid indigestion heartburn (caused by the stomach's inability to cope with acids; also called acidosis, acute indigestion, cardialgia, colic, dyspepsia, gripes, pyrosis, stomach condition, tormina, water qualm)

acoustical problem deafness; loss of hearing

activism agitation

activist agitator

activity booster pep pill

acute heroin-morphine intoxication death due to an overdose of the drugs

acute irregularity acute constipation; irregular menstrual flow

adjustment center prison

administrative action Soviet euphemism for imprisonment without trial

administrative domain collectivist system of managing and taxing distilleries, factories, and farms as in the USSR and its satellites as well as in China, Cuba, Egypt, and Mexico

administrative error bureaucratic bungle

administrative segregation penological euphemism for solitary confinement

adult bookstore(s) pornographic bookstore(s)—a multimillion-dollar business catering to the coarse and the unimaginative

adult entertainment stag-party type of barroom show involving bottomless, sideless, and topless barmaids and tabletop dancers wiggling without their underwear

adult fiction advertising euphemism for pornographic novels

adult institution(s) prison(s)

adult movies motion-picture theaters featuring pornographic films; pornographic films

advanced in years old

aerialist trapeze artist; trapeze performer; trapezist

aerial mishap(s) aviation accident(s)—airplane crashes, explosions, and plunges into the land or the water

affaire *affaire d'amour* (French—love affair)—usually an illicit lust affair

affaire de coeur (French—affair of the heart)—love or lust adventure

affaire de voyage (French—love trip)—affair begun aboard an aircraft, ship, or train and often terminated upon arrival

affirmative action tax-supported programs designed to admit minority group people to good jobs and good schools

affordable merchandiser's term for anything not really affordable but attractive enough to make potential customers become buyers although they may not be able to pay in full or on time-payment plans

Afro-American American black; American Negro

after he (she) left after he (she) died

agricultural laborer(s) farmhand(s)

airsickness nausea followed by vomiting when travelling in an aircraft

aisle manager floorwalker

Alaska sable skunk fur

Albany beef Hudson River sturgeon

alcoholic beverage alcoholic drink

all about the birds and the bees sex education

all-devouring element fire

all-out strategic exchange all-out strategic exchange of atomic bombs in a nuclear war

all this and more, right after this important message please stay tuned while this "important" advertising message is broadcast

alpha alcoholic problem drinker who drinks in an effort to drown problems

alter caponize; castrate; desex; denut; geld; remove or ligate procreative organs; sterilize

alternative four-letter term for copulation fuck; screw

alternative lifestyle Californian euphemism meaning a bum, a long-haired hippie, a parasitic vagrant, an addicted and unwashed weirdo

amalgamation interracial mixing; miscegenation

amatory exercises calisthenic in-bed exercises frequently culminating in what is termed connubial bliss or lovemaking

amenity center public toilet (nice-nellyisms covering this term include backhouse, bathroom, boy's room, *caballeros, cabinet d'aisance, cavalheiros,* chic sale, cloakroom, closet, comfort station, commode, convenience, *damas, Damen,* dames, *gabinetto,* gent's, girl's room, head, her, *Herren,* his, *hombres,* jakes, john, *Klosett,* ladies', ladies' room, latrine, lavatorium, lavatory, *lieux,* little boy's room, little girl's room, locus, loo, lounge, *madamas,* men's room, *mesdames, messieurs, mujeras,* outhouse, *pissoir, pissotière,* powder room, privy, retreat, *retrete,* restroom, *signore, signori,* washroom, watercloset, wc, women's, *ubornaya)*

Americaid Watergate English for welfare

American broadtail domestic lamb's wool

American tweezers British euphemism for burglar's tools

amply proportioned fat

amply rewarded well paid

amusement park entertainer organ grinder; mouse swallower and vomiter; snake charmer and swallower; sword swallower

androgen effeminate homosexual male; fairy; girlish male

Angel of the Bottomless Pit but one of many euphemisms and names for the Devil also known as Abadan, Ahriman, Apollyon, Arch Enemy, Asmodeus, Astorath, Author of Evil, Azazel, Beelzebub, Belial, Belphagor, the Common Enemy, the Demon, Evil One, Evil Spirit, Father of Liars, Father of Lies, the Fiend, Foul Fiend, His Satanic Majesty, Kroix, Loki, Lucifer, Mefisto(feleo), Old Gent(leman), Old Harry, Old Ned, Old Scratch, Prince of Darkness, Prince of Devils, Prince of Evil, Prince of the Power of the Air, Prince of the Underworld, Prince of This World, Samiel, Sat(an)(as), the Serpent, Set, Typhon, etc.

animal controller(s) dogcatcher(s)—*see* dog warden(s)

animal shelter(s) dog pound(s)

anointing the sick Roman Catholic euphemism for unction in extremis (service rendered at the point of death)

anonyma nameless women (nineteenth-century euphemism for prostitutes)

answering the call of nature defecating and/or urinating

answer the final summons die; drop dead

anticipatory retaliation attacking an enemy because he or she would attack you if given the chance; first strike in a nuclear war or other conflict

anti-Semite anti-Jewish person (although Semite comprises Arabs and Jews as well as Afro-Asiatics, Aramaics, Armenians, and Ethiopians)

antisocial offender(s) convict(s); criminal(s)

antisocial restructuring candidates convicts; felons

anti-Zionist often a cover-up for anti-Semite

archivist(s) library clerk(s)

ardent spirits alcohol; alcoholic drinks

area of operations battlefield

Armageddon the final conflict, according to *The Revelation of St John the Divine,* predicting the last and completely destructive battle although many who fought and died must have felt the same at Actium, Antietam, Anzio, and Austerlitz as well as at Balaklava, Bataan, and Bunker Hill, not forgetting Caporetto or the Coral Sea, the Dardanelles or Dunkirk, El Alamein, Fontenay and Fontenoy, Gettysburg, Hastings, Inchon, Jena or Jutland, Königgrätz, Lake Erie or Lepanto, Manila Bay or the Marne, New Orleans or the Nile, Okinawa, Pearl Harbor, Philippi and Port Arthur, Québec, Ravenna, Saratoga and Singapore, the Spanish Armada, Stalingrad, Tannenberg, Trafalgar, Utah Beach, Verdun and Vicksburg, Waterloo, Xeres, the Yalu River and Yorktown together with Zama plus all battles great and small where people believed it was the final conflict

armed emergency small-scale war

Armenian mink clipped and dyed cat fur

articulating on paper writing

artificial dentures false teeth

artistic success box-office failure

assignation point(s) place(s) where pimps and streetwalkers accost potential customers

athletic supporter(s) jockstrap(s)

at that point in time then

at this juncture now

at this moment of history now

at this point in time now

at this present juncture now

audience augmentation device for producing what appears to be a capacity audience; attained by generous distribution of complimentary tickets, and cut-rate prices for military personnel, senior citizens, students, veterans, people born on Thursday, etc.

audiovisually qualified able to run a motion-picture projector

auditorially handicapped deaf

auditory problem deafness; loss of hearing

Australian buck processed rabbit fur (and not always from Australia)

Australian steak mutton

Australian treat kangaroo meat

authoritarian diplomatic double-talk for an anti-communist totalitarian regime denying human rights to its people and persecuting all dissidents

auto insurance problem revocation of driver's license due to careless or reckless driving and subsequent loss of auto insurance as driver is considered a bad risk not worth insuring

automanipulation masturbation

automotive internist automobile mechanic

avian propagation facility an incubator

awardee(s) person(s) imprisoned in a ship's brig also known as the ccu or correctional custody unit

away from one's desk gone to the toilet

Aztec two-step diarrhea contracted in Mexico

bachelor girl old maid; spinster; unmarried woman

backhouse privy; toilet

backward country poor country; third-world country

bafflegab bewildering language composed of undefined abbreviations, acronyms, phrases, short forms, symbols, and words created to confuse listeners and readers

bagno (Italian—bath)—also means prison or whorehouse

Baltic leopard spotted-cat fur dyed to look like leopard

Baltimore beefsteak broiled liver

banheiro (Portuguese—bath)—men's toilet

baños de caballeros (Spanish—gentlemen's baths)—men's toilet(s)

baños de damas (Spanish—ladies' baths)—women's toilet(s)

bargained him down Christianed him down; Jewed him down; Moslemed him down

bar hustler(s) male prostitute(s) plying trade in cocktail bars

bathroom toilet (in the United States, although in the British Isles and on the Continent a bathroom is fitted primarily for bathing although it may contain a toilet)

bathroom tissue toilet paper

battle fatigue shell-shock-induced cowardice manifested during battle

beautician beauty parlor owner; hairdresser; make-up artist

beauty culturist beauty parlor operator; make-up artist

beauty parlor hairdresser's shop

beaverette processed cat or rabbit fur

bedded sexually connected

bedroom activities sexual diversions vulgarly described as fuckin' aroun'

behind the iron door behind bars; jailed

Bess o'Bedlam incurable female lunatic

beyond the black stump Australia's far outback; beyond the boondocks

bidet (French—hygienic apparatus)—crotch cleaner installed in many better-class homes, hotels, motels, and steamships

billiard academy pool hall

billiard lounge pool hall

biological urge lust

birth attendant midwife

Blackbeard's curse botulism, diarrhea, or dysentery contracted in the Caribbean area where the pirate Blackbeard lost more men due to these causes than to cannonballs or cutlasses

black propaganda outright lies repeated and repeated until they seem believable

blemishes acne; blackheads; pimples

blood disease syphilis

bodily appetite lust

body moisture sweat

body odor stinking sweat

Bombay duck dried and salted lizardfish

book of pseudonyms hotel or motel register filled with the names of convenience used by adulterers and others who prefer pseudonymity to reality

bordello whorehouse

borne by the stork born

born into a better world died

born out of wedlock child(ren) of illegitimate parents

borrow(ing) without intent to return steal(ing)

bosom breast; female breasts

bottom ass; backside

boutique (French—small specialty shop)—in many places the term has come to mean an expensive specialty shop catering to affluent clients

boys men; old men; young men; men in general, especially in the United States where the term boys seems to remove all men from any adult responsibility

boys on the border South African euphemism for soldiers defending the many borders of their republic

boy's room men's toilet

breach of the peace to agitate, to arouse, to assemble unlawfully, to awaken, to hinder, to incite to riot, to molest, to obstruct traffic, to trespass, to violate laws defining breach of the peace

break(ing) the news break(ing) the news gently

break(ing) wind release of a flatus via the anus and vulgarly referred to as a fart (or farting)

breathe one's last breathe one's last breath—die

brief encounter one-night stand

Broadmoor patients criminally insane convicts

broken-down woman old whore

bromidrosis stinking sweat

bubo Low Latin for a swelling in the armpit or in the crotch and usually associated with gonorrhea, more familiarly called clap

bulldung polite way of saying bullshit

bunny used euphemistically this term does not mean a cuddly rabbit but a rabbit-costumed whore

business moratorium lockout

business slowdown depression

by-product of the arts of peace war, as defined by Ambrose Bierce in *The Devil's Dictionary*

caballeros (Spanish—gentlemen)—men's toilet

cabinet (French—closet; small room; water closet)—toilet

cabinet d'aisance (French—cabinet of comfort)—public toilet

cabrito young goat meat

caca (Spanish baby-talk euphemism—excrement)

cacá (Brazilian-Portuguese—excrement)

caducity senility

call boy(s) high-priced male prostitute(s)

call girl(s) high-priced female prostitute(s)

call of nature need to go to the toilet

Cambodian Incursion sounds mild and something like a Cambodian excursion although communists called it Cambodian Invasion

campo santo (Spanish—sacred field)—cemetery

can going to the can (common cover-up for going to the toilet)

candlestine affair popular mispronunciation of clandestine affair

cangrejo (Spanish—crab)—euphemism for a homosexual sodomite

Cape Cod turkey codfish

capitalism economic system characterized by corporate or private ownership of goods, investments, and services with distribution controlled by competition in a free market unfettered by state control (*see* communism; socialism; free enterprise)

carbon monoxdied died of carbon-monoxide poisoning

cardiac heart attack; heart failure

cardiac arrest death

cardiovascular accident stroke

career deceleration loss of job opportunities or jobs

career girl professional woman

carminitive polite synonym for laxative

carnal acquaintance copulation

carnal connection copulation

carnal desire arousal of sexual passion; lust

carnal enjoyment copulation with sexual pleasure

carnal intercourse copulation

carnal knowledge carnal knowledge with even the slightest penetration

carnal parts female or male genitals

carnal passion lust

carnal stump penis

carnal trap vagina

carnifex hangman

carnificate to hang a person

carsickness nausea followed by vomiting when riding in an automobile or other vehicle

cash in your chips die

casket coffin

casketing putting a dead person in a funeral casket

cast up your accounts vomit

casual sex promiscuity

cat used euphemistically this is not a feline creature but a whore

catastrophic reaction psychiatric euphemism for angry frustration marked by crying, pulling, pushing, yelling, and even trying to commit suicide or kill others; term often includes cataleptic convulsions, loss of memory and vocabulary, coronary disorders, and death

cathouse a house inhabited by whores and their part-time visitors

cavalheiros (Portuguese—gentlemen)—men's toilet

cease to purchase boycott

cemetery worker gravedigger

cerebrovascular accident heart failure; stroke

cf cystic fibrosis

cf's confessions of fornication (colonial-style abbreviation originating in Massachusetts and used by the Puritans before the American Revolution)—this is an example of an abbreviation being used as a euphemistic cover-up

C-girl call girl; hundred-dollar girl

chalet de nécessité (French—public toilet)

chamber pisspot; thundermug

Chapter 7 liquidation

Chapter 11 legal euphemism for bankruptcy as defined in Chapter 11 of the Bankruptcy Act of the United States

character deficiency fault

charlady charwoman

chemical abuse alcohol or other drug addiction

chemical agent deployment throwing tear gas

chemical, electrical, or physical duress chemical, electrical, or physical torture

chicken manure chickenshit

chic sale country privy; outhouse; shithouse named for American comedian Chic Sale who issued a catalog of such behind-the-house rural structures and entitled it *The Specialist*

children's tutor governess

children with latent ability lazy students

children with untapped potential poor students

chinchillette processed rabbit fur (not baby chinchilla)

chippy whore

chirtonsor(s) barber(s)

chronic alcoholic sot

chronic irregularity constipation

chubby fat

churchyard cemetery

circular protector condom

circumorbital haematoma black eye

civilian irregular defense soldier mercenary

Civil War Northern euphemism for the War Between the States or the War of the Secession

clandestine affair secret love affair

clandestine connection sex in the shadows

clandestine exhumation body snatching; grave robbing

clap slang for gonorrhea and derived from *clapier* meaning brothel in Middle French or from *clapoir* meaning bubo in Old Provencal (a bubo being an armpit or crotch swelling characteristic of the disease)

clean bombs bombs destructive of structures rather than people; nonradioactive bombs

client(s) euphemistic penological parlance for prison inmate(s); pimps and prostitutes call their target(s) client(s); social workers refer to receivers of public charity as their clients as do attorneys, barristers, and lawyers who first used this term

client(s) of the correctional system convict(s)

climb the golden stairs die

cloakroom toilet (British)

closet water closet (toilet)

cocktail lounge saloon

cocotte (French—little chick; paper hen; saucepan)—whore in western Europe and the United States

cohabitees unmarried lovers who live together

cold war deterrent threat of a real war

collaboration assisting and cooperating with the enemy

collation light meal

collection correspondent bill collector

colonic infirmity cancer of the colon

colonic irregularity constipation

colonic stasis constipation or in-

testinal stagnation characterized by a fecal-clogged colon

colored folks elderly American blacks who seem to prefer this term to Negro or black

colored man black male

coloureds (South African-English—other-than-black persons of color)—persons of mixed black-and-white or brown-and-white descent

combat emplacement evacuator shovel

combat fatigue (*see* battle fatigue)

comfort station public toilet

command of nature felt when your body tells you it's time to defecate and/or urinate

commercial statement advertisement; sales pitch

commercial travellers travelling salespersons

commission agent bookmaker

commit no nuisance do not defecate or urinate on the grass or in the area where such a sign is posted

commode toilet

communication arts reading, speaking, and writing

communication problem deaf and dumb

communications engineer tv repairman

communism Marx predicted it would be the final stage of society where the state has withered away and economic goods are distributed equally; in practice, however, the state has become stronger than ever in China, Cuba, Czechoslovakia, Hungary, Poland, Russia, and other communist-dominated countries (*see* capitalism)

community treatment center(s) prison(s)

companionate marriage free love; trial marriage

Company The Company (Washingtonian euphemism for the Central Intelligence Agency—CIA)

complete elimination mass murder

complete fabrication a damn lie

complete liquidation mass murder

compromising situation caught with your pants down

concubine often used to mean prostitute; part-time prostitute; unmarried sexual partner of a married man; whore

concupiscence lust; sensual longing; sexual desire

condominium (Spanish euphemism—jail or prison)

confrontation facing the enemy

congal *cuarto con gal* (Mexican-Spanish—room with girl)—whorehouse

conjugal relations the sexual side of marriage

conjunctivitis sty on the eye

connubial bliss lustful and procreative activities of the wedded; marriage enduring for years when lust is but a dim memory and love suffices; sexual diversion enjoyed by the married

connubial rites marriage ceremony

connubial substitute whore

constant companion mistress; sexual pal

constant interruption chronic constipation

consultant an ordinary person more than a hundred miles from home

contributor taxpayer

controlled substances addictive drugs; dangerous drugs; narcotics

convalescent home not a home but often a poorly run institution where older people are left to die

convenience toilet

coordinated national intelligence spying program aimed at discovering the subversive actions and beliefs of radicals

coronary heart attack; heart failure

corpulent fat

correctional custody facility brig, jail, lockup, penitentiary, prison, reformatory, etc.

correctional custody unit ship's brig in the parlance of the U.S. Navy

correctional institution penitentiary; prison; etc.

correctional officer(s) prison guard(s); prison warden(s)

corrective labor camps Soviet forced-labor prison camps

correct within an order of magnitude incorrect; wrong

cosmetician beauty parlor operator

cosmopolite(s) Soviet term for Jew(s)

costive constipated; constipating foods

counterproductive won't work

courier service technician messenger boy

courtesan (Middle French—high-class whore; paramour; prostitute associating with members of the court and other notables)

Cousins the Cousins (British secret service term for American intelligence organizations such as the CIA and the FBI)

cover-up words euphemisms

cover your bottom cover your ass; cover your backside

cowchips cattle dung

cowflop cow excreta; cow shit

crapola cover-up phrases and words characterized by their ambiguity, insincerity, and mendacity

crapper toilet (believed by some to be named for an English turn-of-the-century plumber named Crapper and inventor of the water-flush system; others insist crapper comes from crap—a four-letter word meaning shit)

creative conflict civil rights demonstration; riot

creative financing where the seller loans some of the costs to the buyer in order to facilitate a sale

creative unresponsiveness sullen indifference (exhibited by many government workers)

credibility gap widespread disbelief and distrust due to impossible promises and repeated lies uttered by bureaucrats and politicians

crib(s) whorehouse(s)

criminal conversation British euphemism for fornication

criminally attacked raped

crotch-and-toilet terms mainly euphemistic in most English-speaking places but more realistic in the Netherlands and Scandinavia

croton bug cockroach (cover-up created to avoid use of the prefix cock)

crowd engineer(s) police dog(s)

cruising in the corn drinking and driving

culturally deprived poor

culturally deprived environment ghetto; poor section; slum

cunctator procrastinator; putter-offer; thief of time

cupid's itch venereal disease

curse the curse (menstruation)

Curse of Balboa botulism, diarrhea, or dysentery contracted in Panamá and first encoun-tered by its discoveror—the Spanish explorer Vasco Nuñez de Balboa who also discovered the Pacific Ocean

Curse of Cabral loose bowels contracted in Brazil discovered by Portuguese admiral Pedro Alvaro Cabral

Curse of Cairo diarrhea plus summertime heat

Curse of Columbus another euphemistic nickname for botulism, diarrhea, or dysentery contracted in the American tropics discovered by Columbus

Curse of Cortez Mexican-acquired diarrhea or dysentery

Curse of Cromwell epithet applied to Cromwell's Irish campaign and the massacres in Clonmel, Drogheda, and Wexford remembered even today

Curse of Pizarro loose bowels contracted in Perú where Francisco Pizarro was conqueror—Conquistador del Perú

cuspidor presumably an elegant way of naming a spittoon

custodial engineer janitor

custodian janitor

custom-fitted clothes ready-to-wear garments whose cuffs are cut to size and whose sleeves are shortened to suit the customer

cynical ailment occupational disease of editors and reporters

dailies chambermaids or charwomen paid on a daily basis (British)

damas (Italian, Portuguese, Spanish—ladies)—women's toilet

Damen (German—ladies)—women's toilet

damer (Danish or Swedish—ladies)—women's toilet

dames (Afrikaans, Dutch, French—ladies)—women's toilet

damska (Polish—ladies)—women's toilet

dancing on air hanging by the neck until dead

dark gentleman man from India

darn it damn it; goddamn it

daughter of Bilitis female homosexual named for the principal character in *The Songs of Bilitis* by Pierre Louÿs

daughter of joy whore (taken from the French—*fille de*

joie)

d____d damned (as used in polite Victorian prose)

deaccessioning selling; selling museum items such as etchings, paintings, photographs, sculptures, stuffed animals and birds

debris disposal technician dustman; garbage man; trash collector

debt of nature death

decapitation beheading

decapitator beheader; guillotineur

deceased dead

decimate destroy; kill off

decollation beheading

defecate drop dung; move one's bowels; shit

defenestration jumping-out-the-window suicide

defense officer(s) soldier(s)

defensive aggression hitting the enemy before he hits you

defensive aircraft bombers

deferred maintenance putting off to tomorrow what should be repaired today

deferred schedule slowdown

deinstitutionalization rapid discharge of felons from prisons and patients from mental institutions into surrounding communities

delicate condition pregnant (Victorian)

dementing illness Alzheimer's disease; intellectual deterioration caused by the slow death of the brain

demise(d) die(d)

den of iniquity whorehouse

den of vice whorehouse

dentures artificial teeth; false teeth

departed died

department of defense war department

depart this mortal coil die

depopulate(d) slaughter(ed)

depopulating slaughtering

depopulation death

Deputy Director for Operations chief of the clandestine service of the Central Intelligence Agency

dermasurgeon restorative embalming artist in an undertaker's morgue

derriere (French—backside; behind)—ass

détente deliberate easing of discord and warlike threats but often illusory and one-sided as peace treaties and summit

conferences merely establish the rules of the next war

detention center prison

deterrence policy of scaring the enemy by maintaining a larger armed force in the hope it will deter the enemy from war

developing nations have-not countries; poor countries; underdeveloped nations

deviate(s) homosexual(s)

deviation from the truth lying; untruth

died of lead poisoning died from bullet wounds

died of target practice executed by a firing squad

diet pills weight-reducing preparations

dilution reduction in earnings

diminished capacity slightly insane

dining-room attendant busboy

dipsomaniac alcoholic addict; drunken sot

directory assistance telephonic euphemism for information service

direct reduction killing off excess alligators, burros, deer, rabbits, etc.

dirty old man well-known definitions include cunt chaser, gay deceiver, lecher, old goat, rapist, ravisher, whorehound, whoremaster, whoremonger, woman chaser

dirty tricks sinister activities used to discredit electoral campaigns and candidates

disadvantaged poor; unemployed

disadvantaged Americans poor Americans; unemployed Americans

disadvantaged person(s) poor person(s)

disappeared into the dust died

discontinuance of student populations school closures

disengage(d) retreat(ed)

disinflation falling inflation (not to be confused with deflation marked by an actual falling in prices)

dislike the cut of her (his) jib dislike her (his) looks

disorderly house whorehouse (Victorian)

disposal area dump

disposal center junkyard

disreputable woman whore

dissolution death

diverted stolen from

D-notice death notice; death report

documented immigrant legal alien

dog behavior modification dog training program for guard or police work

doggydo dog dung

dog nuisance dog dung droppd on sidewalks

dog tutor dog trainer

dog warden dogcatcher

doing her business defecating; moving her bowels

doing his business defecating; moving his bowels

domestic functionary servant

dones (Catalan—ladies)—women's toilet

do the dutch act commit suicide

down the drain down the toilet (beyond recovery)

down the latrine down the toilet (beyond recovery)

down the tube down the toilet (beyond recovery)

downward revision decrease in prices or wages

Do you have to go to the bathroom? Do you have to go to the toilet?

dreamless sleep death

dresses casually a real slob; a slop artist

drinking problem alcoholic addiction

drug problem narcotic addiction

dustbin a receptacle holding ashes, garbage, or trash to be collected by dustmen (British)

dustbinman garbage collector (British)

dust of desuetude dust of neglect seldom adulterated with the grime of crime

dutch gold imitation gold leaf

dutch treat meal or outing where each person pays his (her) own portion of the bill

dyspepsia acid indigestion; heartburn

dysphemism calling a spade a spade and hence the opposite of a euphemism; thus, axle grease is the dysphemism for butter, cow juice is milk, mug of mud is cup of coffee, etc. (see Dysphemistic Place-Names)

ecdysiast HL Mencken coined this euphemism to cover a striptease artist as ecdysis is the Greek term used to describe the shedding of outercoats of crustaceans and skins of snakes

ecological receptacle garbage can; trash barrel; trash container (usually plastic)

economic action picket line; sitdown; slowdown; strike

economically deprived poor

economic democracy socialism as advocated and practiced by the city council of the People's Republic of Santa Monica, California where its leaders soon found socialism would not sell but people would vote for economic democracy

economic lull depression

economic regression loss

economic return profit

economic slowdown depression

editorial assistant(s) publisher's typist(s)

educationist(s) bureaucratic educator(s) believed by administrators and textbook publishers to be good at communicating with students even though they usually know little about their subject matter

effect a separation fire from a job

effecting linkages coordination

effluents contaminating gaseous discharges, industrial wastes, and liquid sewage pollution

effluvium stench; stink

egabrag garbage spelled backwards and used as a cover-up for garbage boat or garbage scow

egress exit (Barnum's oft-reported trick of moving capacity audiences out of an overcrowded circus tent by putting up a sign reading *THIS WAY TO THE EGRESS* and luring many to see what they thought would be a rare female animal)

Egyptian calisthenics getting into bed and staring up at the ceiling or sky until the forces of sleep prevail

electrolethe electric chair

electronic surveillance wire tapping

electronic technician electrician

eleemosynary organization charity fund-collecting business

elegancies words believed by some to be more elegant (or genteel or euphemistic) than the words they replace

elevated intoxicated (by drugs and liquor)

elevated to a lower level demoted; lowered

eliminate(d) kill(ed); murder(ed)

ellas [Spanish—they (feminine)]—women's toilet

ellos [Spanish—they (masculine)]—men's toilet

elopement risk psychiatric euphemism for patients escaping or trying to escape from the hospitals, institutions, or wards to which they are confined

embarrassing noises belchings, burpings, and fartings

embarazada (Spanish—embarrassed)—pregnant

emerging nations backward countries; poor nations

emolument salary; wage

employment center commercial district

emporium department store

enceinte (French—pregnant)

enchanted with you in a sexual connotation usually means I'm encocked with you or I'm encunted with you

Endlösung *die Endlösung* (German—the final solution)—death

end-of-the-streeter worn-out old whore

engineering landfill(s) garbage dump(s)

English glass the Spanish euphemism for dog dung (*vidrio inglés*) and but one of many found in *American-Spanish Euphemisms* compiled by Charles E. Kany (University of California Press, 1960)

enlargement of the lower back big bottomed; fat assed

ensanguined undergarment bloody shirt

entertainment world the world of gamblers, gangsters, money lenders, narcotics addicts and traffickers, pornographers, and prostitutes

entombment burial

entomology specialist(s) bug sprayer(s)

entrapment luring or snaring anyone into the commission of a crime

enuresis bedwetting

environmental control specialist(s) janitor(s)

environmentally handicapped people ghetto people; poor people; street people; vagrants

equal-opportunity ailments venereal diseases contracted by all kinds of people

equine fertilizer horse manure

[*see* unobscene song(s)]

equine paradox the fact there are more horse's asses than horses

equitable compensation living wage

erase(d) assassinate(d); kill(ed); murder(ed)

erminette dyed rabbit fur (not a small ermine)

erotic portrayal pornography (defined by Irvin S. Cobb as when the depth of the dirt exceeds the width of the humor)

erring brethren Confederate soldiers and states as defined by their Northern neighbors

erring sister(s) whore(s)

error in overamplification an error in the cover-up of the cover-up arranged by Nixon's aides after Watergate

erti kiasan (Malay—euphemism)

eruct(ation) belch(ing)

escalated interpersonal altercation murder

escargot (French—snail)—but if advertised on a menu as snails very few will eat them

escort(s) whore(s) in the jargon of the convention, entertainment, and travel world

escort vessel(s) destroyer(s); frigate(s)

eternal rest death

ethical lackers those who sow lust and reap distrust while cheating, double dealing, killing, and stealing

ethnic evacuation forcible removal of a people from their native homeland

ethnic minority in the United States usually means blacks, Hispanics, and native Americans such as Eskimos and Indians

ethnocentristic exclusivity minority-born people such as blacks, Hispanics, Indians, Orientals, and eventually white Anglo-Saxon Protestants

ethnophaulisms derogatory and offensive slurs aimed against various ethnic groups such as the Chinese (chinks), the Dutch, Germans, and Scandinavians (squareheads); the Italians (wops), etc.

Eufemia Italian, Portuguese, or Spanish proper name honoring the Greek goddess of fair speech or good report—Euphemia

eufemismo (Italian, Portuguese, Spanish—euphemism)

eupheme (Greek—good speak)—the good word avoiding the blunt, the distasteful, and the harsh; hence, the invention and proliferation of euphemisms

euphemia softening of phrases or words thought to be coarse or offensive

Euphemia German proper name honoring the Greek goddess of fair speech or good report

euphemian euphemistic

Euphémie French proper name honoring the Greek goddess Euphemia

euphemious(ly) euphemistical(ly)

euphemism affected niceness; goody-goodyism; gongorism (imitating the intricate and ornate style of Gongora y Argote); overrefinement; purism

euphemism defined substitution of an auspicious phrase or word for inauspicious ones; hence *gone to rest* is substituted for *dead* although *dead* is more accurate and less liable to misunderstanding

euphémisme (French—euphemism)

euphemisms of penology prison or penitentiary became reformatory, which became correctional center, and now is called rehabilitation facility

Euphemismus der Euphemismus (German—euphemism)

euphemist user of euphemisms

euphemizer(s) user(s) of euphemisms

euphemous(ly) euphemistic(ally)

euphemy(s) euphemism(s)

euphuisms high-flown terms in the style of the English author John Lyly who in the late 1500s created many elegancies involving alliteration, antithesis, and similes to the point he was ridiculed by Shakespeare although many of his contemporaries imitated his style

euthanasia medically induced gentle death for persons suffering from incurable and painful diseases

euthanized killed

Eve's curse menstrual misery

evidentiary material evidence

excellent compensation very good pay

exceptional child retarded child

excrement dung

excreta dung

excusado (Spanish—reserved; set apart)—toilet

executive action removal of an executive by assassination

executive explanation explaining the unexplainable by bending the truth, as high-level lying is called in such matters as warning people about the dangers of smoking while a Congress continues to subsidize tobacco farmers; in the USSR it takes the form of exposing the production losses due to chronic alcoholism so evident in a country where the distillation of vodka is a state monopoly; many other examples of executive explanation will occur to readers

exfiltration retreat

exotic entertainer(s) striptease dancer(s) often engaged in part-time whoring

expanding the circle of love mate swapping

expansion of the lower back big bottomed; fat assed

expecting expecting to have a child; pregnant

expectorate spit

experienced tires recapped tires; retreads

expire(d) die(d)

expulsion of intestinal gas fart

exsanguination death due to loss of blood

exterminating engineer bug and rat killer; termite remover

extinguishment death

extrajudicial executions mass murders of the type reported in Central and South America where the Indians are under fire or in Southeast Asia where anticommunists are executed en masse

extramarital sex fornication with a married person

extrapolation educated guess; guesstimate

extremely high purity composition unknown except for the supplier's exaggerated claims

extreme penalty death; execution

fabrication lie

fabricator liar

facial blemishes pimples

facial dew sweat

facility utilization closure of under-enrolled schools

failed to reply accurately, com-

pletely, and fully lied

fairy a male homosexual

fall asleep die

family problem divorce in the offing

far out crazy

fashion stylist(s) dress designer(s)

featherbedding employing excess employees

fecu feculate(d); feculation [cover-ups contrived by Dr Ira Levine for defecate(d), defecation, etc.]

feisty abusive; outspoken

feline effluvia the penetrating smell of cat crap mixed with cat piss

fell asleep died

fell in battle killed in action

feminine bosom breasts; dugs (if a domestic animal such as a dog or cat); tits

feminine protection menstrual cloth, napkin, or tampon

ferfak (Hungarian men)—men's toilet

fertilizer frequently the cover-up term for manure also known as bullshit, chickenshit, cow manure, fowl manure and steer manure

"fewer than six have been mentioned," explains a report concerning members of Congress charged with soliciting teenage pages this so-called explanation is very likely the ultimate in bafflegab as it makes the reader wonder if five, four, three, two, or only one member of Congress was guilty

fiber dietitianese for bowel-movement bulker, formerly called roughage, and present in bran, celery, whole wheat, etc.

fig leaves roundabout expressions contrived to conceal anything deemed to be indecorous, in any way offensive, or of questionable taste; during the last century the genital organs shown in many paintings and statues were fully covered with representations of fig leaves

fig leaves of language and literature euphemisms

fille de joie (French—daughter of joy)—whore

final injection execution by lethal drug injection

finalization conclusion

finalize end

final solution final solution of

the Jewish problem (Hitler's euphemism masking his plan to murder all the Jews imprisoned in concentration camps he established in Germany and in several captured countries)

financially embarrassed broke; without funds

fine elderly gentleman not a dirty old man and usually with a high six-digit bank account to compensate for advancing age and senility

finite period of future time later

fir (Gaelic—men)—men's toilet

fiscal policy government spending and tax collection

flatulent given to farting

flatulents fart-filled pompous persons; fart-productive foods such as beans and cabbage

flight attendant(s) airline stewardess(es) or steward(s)

flight host(ess) airline steward(ess)

floral tribute wreath

following station identification following television advertising, the motion picture or show you wanted to see will be continued

food-order expediter short-order cook

food preparation center kitchen

food science specialist(s) short-order cook(s)

forensic laboratory morgue

foreplay genital pleasuring

fornicatrix whore

four-letter words so-called unmentionable Early English terms such as cock, crap, crud, cunt, dung, fart, fuck, lust, piss, puke, scum, shit, snot, spit, suck

free enterprise capitalism; corporate control; multinational corporations imposing cartels and other controls

freethinker(s) agnostic(s); atheist(s); disbeliever(s); *esprit(s) fort* [French—strong spirit(s)]; humanist(s); iconoclast(s); latitudinarian(s); *libero pensatore(s)* [Italian—liberal thinker(s)]; *librepensador(es)* [Spanish—liberal thinker(s)]; nonbeliever(s); rationalist(s); secularist(s); skeptic(s); truthseeker(s); unbeliever(s)

freeway tax-supported toll-free expressway; tax-supported toll-free highway

French disease syphilis (called Gallic disease by the Spaniards who believed it was spread by the invading armies of Charles VIII and Napoleon, German disease by the French, French pox by the Italians, Neapolitan pox by other Europeans, and Indian disease by the Spaniards who believed their sailors picked it up in the New World; and, to be sure, their neighbors the Portuguese, called it the Spanish disease)

French welcome Elizabethan English euphemism for smallpox or syphilis

front-and-rear-end wipers babies' diapers

front-parlor girl usually the most attractive girl in a whorehouse and kept in the front parlor as an attraction or window dressing to lure customers

fruits of treason in London, up to the early 1700s, any person convicted of treason was taken from Newgate Prison to Tyburn where crowds witnessed the traitor being strung up, cut down when nearly strangulated, then disemboweled, beheaded, and the torso cut into four quarters by an ax

fuller figure fatter

full-figured fat; obese

funding creativity using taxes to support the arts

funeral decorations funeral flowers

funeral director undertaker

fusilated euphemism for executed by a firing squad as was long the custom in Mexico, New Mexico, Utah, and other places; throughout the Spanish-speaking world one of Manet's most popular paintings is *Fusilamiento del Emperado Maximiliano* (Execution by firing squad of the Emperor Maximilian) who is flanked by two Mexican-Indian generals—Mejía and Miramón—also executed by order of Juárez

future points in time the future; when

future unpleasantness anticipated war

gabinetto (Italian—cabinet)—toilet

Gallic disease syphilis, according to many Europeans who believed it was spread by French soldiers invading their countries

garbologist garbage collector

gastric distress belching and farting

gathered to his fathers died

gay bit whore (Victorian)

gay bowel syndrome intestinal disruptions affecting homosexuals

gay boy (girl) Australian euphemism for a homosexual

gay deceiver cunt chaser, lecher, old goat, rapist, ravisher, whorehound, whoremaster, whoremonger, or woman chaser

gay house brothel (Victorian)

gay(s) homosexual(s)

G_d God (as written in many a Victorian novel)

gelding(s) castrated male horse(s)

general paresis of the insane central nervous system syphilis

generously proportioned fat

genteelisms euphemisms of the type where bosom is considered more genteel than breast, limbs substitutes for a woman's legs, viands is thought to be less vulgar than food, etc.

gentleman cow's excreta bullshit

gent's gentlemen's toilet

genuine simulated diamonds and pearls imitation diamonds and pearls

geriatric(s) old person(s)

German disease syphilis (*see* French disease)

get off your butt get off your buttocks (originally); get off your ass (currently)—both mean stop loafing and get to work

get rid of him kill him

getting along in years getting old(er)

getting your girl in trouble getting your unmarried girlfriend pregnant

giblets edible entrails of fowl; in French cookery includes feet, head, tail, wattles, and other parts

gifted children intelligent and studious children

ginkitis ailment of the aged; general breakdown of mental and physical faculties; geriatric syndrome; old-gink's disease

girls old women, young women, women in general, especially in the United States where such terms or their singular forms are considered uncomplimentary and ungentlemanly if used by men (except in "liberated" circles)

girl's room women's toilet

given the pink slip fired

given special treatment exterminated (in the vocabulary of Nazis as well as Soviet commisars concerned with the removal of so-called enemies of the state)

give up the ghost die

giving informational numbers writing parking tickets

giving the whole picture giving the newcomer a very long and confused statement

glow Victorian euphemism for a woman's sweat as only animals were supposed to sweat whereas men perspired and young or old ladies glowed

goatish dirty-old-man or unwashed-male smell

go do your business move your bowels

god's acre cemetery

godsquad paramedic ambulance and crew

going out with often means staying in bed with

going to see a man about a dog going to the toilet

golly God, as in by golly (by God)

gone on vacation suspended from active duty

gone to a better world died

gone to brush their teeth usually means gone to the toilet

gone to Davy Jones' locker died

gone to rest died

go(ne) to the bank to make a deposit go(ne) to the toilet

go(ne) to the bathroom go(ne) to the toilet

gone to the great beyond died

gongorisms overly ornate expressions in the style of the Spanish poet Luis de Gongora y Argote who in the early 1600s wrote plays and poems filled with exaggerated metaphors, extreme inversions of meaning, and lots of obscurities also called elegancies, euphuisms, or genteelisms

goody-goodyism affected niceness characteristic of much bafflegab

gosh God, as in gosh-awful (God-awful) or oh my gosh (oh my God)

go to see a man about a dog go to

the toilet

got to be destroyed must be killed

got to go lay a cable must go to the toilet to defecate

go under die

grant-in-aid diplomatic euphemism for a handout; seven-dollar striped-pants term meaning giveaway

grayfish shark meat

gray propaganda mixture of half truths and truths whose source is hidden and therefore often more attractive

Greek love pederasty

green goose beginning prostitute

grief therapist undertaker skilled in comforting the family and friends of the dead one

grisette (French—salesgirl; working girl)—whore

group sex orgy

gu genitourinary

guest house(s) boarding house(s)

guest(s) of the governor inmate(s) in a state penitentiary

hairologist(s) barber(s); hair stylist(s)

hair stylist(s) barber(s)

halitosis bad breath

hamburger grilled ground-animal meat plus various extenders such as oatmeal and suet as well as coloring and flavoring

handicapped crippled or mentally retarded people

hardcore to the max hardcore (pornography) to the maximum

hard-core unemployed bums; impoverished drug addicts; vagrants

hard decision(s) conclusion(s) favored by the maker(s) or supporter(s) of the decision(s) and not necessarily in the public interest but more likely to favor well-organized special interest group(s)

hares edible rabbits

harlot whore

harmonica mouth organ

harvesting marine mammals killing dolphins, dugongs, manatees, polar bears, porpoises, sea lions, seals, walruses, and whales for their flesh, their furs, and just for the fun and so-called sport of killing

harvest worker fruit-and-vegetable picker

have to sharpen my skates have

to go to the toilet

have to take a leak must urinate

having a friendly discussion having a heated argument

haystack haycock

head the head (the toilet)—originally the head of a ship where human wastes dropped over the vessel's bow from an open or partially enclosed toilet bench

health alteration assassination

hearing problem deafness

heated argument fist fight

Hebrew ancient Semitic language not to be confused with a German dialect called Yiddish, which is enriched with Polish, Romanian, and Russian words, depending on the origin of the speakers; Jewish person admired or liked by bigoted Gentiles who believe Hebrew is more acceptable than Jew (Jewish is not a language, as many suppose, but the name of a religion or its people)

he checked out he died

he fell asleep he died

he lost his wife his wife died

hempen collar hangman's noose

hempen cravat hangman's noose

hemp stretcher hangman

he paid the debt of nature he died

her women's toilet

here (Afrikaans—gentlemen) men's toilet

heren (Dutch—gentlemen)— men's toilet

Her (His) Majesty's carriage prison van

her (his) spirit departed she (he) died

herrar (Swedish—gentlemen)— men's toilet

Herren (German—gentlemen)—men's toilet

herrer (Danish—gentlemen)— men's toilet

hers women's toilet

he's a little sensitive he's neurotic or very, very touchy

he's gone he's dead

he (she) left us he (she) died

high high on alcohol or other drug

high achiever(s) good student(s)

high coefficient of slip slippery

highly scenario-dependent success of a plan or scheme depends on whatever may develop *hirondelle de nuit* (French—night swallow)—prostitute

hirsute adornments hairy appendages such as beards, mustaches, long and often ponytailed tresses, sideburns (also called louseladders), unisexual hairdos

his men's toilet

his crown was shorn he was beheaded

Hispanic time usually slower by hours, days, weeks, or years of standard time; also known as mañana time or Mexican time or the name of the country where it prevails

histrionic art acting

Holy Toledo euphemistic exclamation meaning Holy Jesus or Holy Moses

hombres (Spanish—men)—men's toilet

homes (Catalan—gentlemen)—men's toilet

hommes (French—gentlemen)—men's toilet

homogenized often a cover-up term for adulterated or watered

honorarium fee; payment for services believed to be above price

hooker whore (originally named for the prostitute camp followers of General Hooker in the Civil War, mid-1860s)

hookshop(s) whorehouse(s)

horizontalist(s) prostitute(s)

hot blooded lustful

house apes other people's unhousebroken children

house guest boy friend; girl friend; live-in lover

household technician cook or other domestic servant

house of all nations whorehouse offering women of every color and nationality

house of assignation whorehouse wherein rooms were assigned to whores and their clients

house of confusion whorehouse

house of correction criminal reformatory; reform school

house of ill fame whorehouse

house of ill repute whorehouse

house of joy whorehouse

house trailers mobile homes

housitosis household halitosis (compounded of rancid dishcloths and washrags, stale tobacco smoke, unaired bedclothes, undisposed cigars and cigarettes dying a lingering

death, unflushed toilets, unwashed dishes and underwear, unwashed people and their pets)

Hudson seal muskrat fur

humane shelter dog pound; place for stray cats, dogs, and other creatures

hustler(s) male prostitute(s)

hygienic apparatus *see* bidet

hygienic paper toilet paper

I'd appreciate it very much I'll thank you but do not expect me to pay you or to reciprocate

I have a little problem with what you did I hate what you did

illegitimate(s) bastard(s); child(ren) born of illegitimate parents

illicit love adultery; prostitution; rape

illicit lover whore (but term should apply to anyone who consorts with a whore); anyone not married to the person he or she is having sex with

I'll let you go now shut up and get off the telephone

I love wearing make-up I'm a male homosexual transvestite

I love you very much I lust you very much (is the truthful and usual meaning of this much misunderstood euphemistic expression)

imbibed too much drank too much

immoderate voluptuary sex fiend

immolation a fiery death symbolizing extreme sacrifice (*see* self-immolation)

immurement burial

I'm not crazy about it I won't eat it, so don't purchase it, as I won't even taste it

impaired person(s) person(s) suffering from dementing diseases such as Alzheimer's, Parkinson's, Pick's, or pre-senile dementia involving loss of memory and even everyday words; drunk(s)

impecunious broke; penniless; without funds

implement a program expand the office, the payroll, the number of people employed

impregnated knocked up; made pregnant; pregnant

impure extraneous matter scum

inactive colon atonic constipation

in an interesting condition pregnant

incarcerate imprison; jail

inclusionary building low-cost housing included in building-development projects funded in part or wholly by federal, state, or local funds

incontinence bed soiling (if you guess what we mean); bed wetting

incontinent the insane, the very old, and the very young are often incontinent, soiling their bedclothes or other clothes as they are unable to restrain natural discharge wastes such as feces or urine

increase your equity deepen your debts by increasing your indebtedness in the hope such conduct will prove profitable

incrustation crud (filth, grease, refuse of any kind)

incursion invasion

indisposed recovering from an alcoholic hangover; suffering menstrual-cycle pains

indisposed at the moment on the toilet

individual confinement solitary imprisonment

individualized learning center student's classroom desk

in durance vile imprisoned

industrial action sit-in; slowdown; strike

industrial consultant(s) lobbyist(s)

industrial espionage stealing the other company's formulas or secrets pertaining to manufacture or sale

industrialist(s) successful speculator(s)

inebriated drunk

inflation depression in the purchasing power of your currency

informant one who gives information or informs; according to subversive and other underworld sources an informant is a snitch or an informer and is merely another euphemism invented by law-enforcement officials

information processing duplicating and typing pool

information scientist(s) librarian(s)

information specialist(s) librarian(s

infrastructure fundamental framework of an organization or system; permanent facilities such as airports, bridges, gas and electric lines, highways and streets, railways, sewers, tv cables, water mains, etc.

inheritance tax death duty

inmate(s) prisoner(s)

inner city economically deprived residential areas formerly called barrios, ghettos, or slums; also called the inner-core city

inoperative statement a lie

in point of fact in fact

in reasonable supply available

in short supply scarce

insinuendo insinuated innuendo

instantaneous respiratory arrest death

institutional superintendent(s) prison warden(s)

intact virginal

intellectually underprivileged stupid, uninformed

intelligence acquisition spying

intensive care unit locked unit for juvenile delinquents

interment burial

intermodal interface when you get off the plane, ship, or train a bus awaits

internal exile Soviet term meaning exile in Siberia or some other remote and unattractive section of the USSR

Internal Revenue Service tax collectors in the service of their government and often called the Infernal Revenue Service

international disposal man hired killer working for a government espionage agency and ordered to eliminate a counterspy or other enemy agent

Interpretive dancer(s) striptease dancer(s)

interred buried

interrogation equipment devices and drugs used to obtain confessions

intestinal distress cramps and/or gas and/or loose bowels

intestinal fluidity loose and watery bowel movements often better known as botulism, diarrhea, or dysentery

intestinal fortitude guts (Does he have the guts to resign from the party?); stomach (How can you ever stomach such lies?)

in the can in the toilet

in the education field teacher

in the family way pregnant

in the midst of life struck down by death

in the treatment system being treated

intimacy adultery; sexual intercourse

intimate relations sexual intercourse

intimate wear underwear

intoxicated drunk; under the influence of drugs

intoxication drunkenness

in trouble about to be arrrested; pregnant

intrusion detector(s) burglar alarm(s)

intrusion device(s) burglar's tool(s)

inverted(s) homosexual(s)

invisible handicap deaf and/or dumb

involuntary audience captive audience

ironmongery department Her (His) Majesty's prison

Irregularity irregular menstrual period

irritable colon spastic constipation

Isolation booth(s) prison cell(s)

it girl girl with sex appeal

it has long been known take my word for it although I have not taken the time to look up the precise reference you want

it is believed I think

it is generally believed two other guys agree with me

it is thought usually means I think

it might be argued it is such a good reply to your objective I'll state it right now and vehemently

I've got to survive I've got to succeed no matter who I step on

jagger(s) tattoo artist(s)

jakes toilet (British)

jaundiced eyes hateful eyes; prejudiced eyes

jet set modern equivalent of yesteryear's demimonde, noted for its illegality and impropriety evidenced at the fringes of so-called high society

jezebel abandoned and shameless woman named after the wife of King Ahab described in the Old Testament's *Book of Kings;* a whore

job action sit-down or strike

job problem(s) demoted or fired

john prostitute's male client; toilet

joint whorehouse

journey's end death

Judas priest exclamation standing for Jesus Christ!

juice joints beer bars, cocktail

lounges, saloons, etc.

junior executive(s) clerk(s)

junior wolf teenage philanderer

juvenile detention center jail for juvenile delinquents

kaleidoscopic career (of a well-regarded person) checquered career (of a notorious person)

Katzenjammer (German—alcoholic hangover headache; tuning-up sounds produced by a symphony orchestra)—not just the clamoring and wailing of copulating cats

keyboarded typed

kick(ed) the bucket commit(ted) suicide; die(d)

kick over the traces cast off all restraint

kick upstairs promote to a higher but less sought-after position

kick up your heels have a helluva good time

kleptomaniac shoplifter (term usually applied to an affluent shoplifter of some social position who has no apparent need to steal)

Klosett das Klosett (German—the closet)—the water closet or toilet

knocked up made pregnant

kvinner (Norwegian-women)—women's toilet

labor unrest picket lines; sabotage; sit-downs; slowdowns; wide-scale discontent resulting from layoffs, poor wages, and poor working conditions

lack of suppression of paradoxical sleep unsuppressed drowsiness due to bad side effects of some pills

ladies ladies in waiting; old women; older women; most women

ladies' ladies' toilet

ladies' limbs women's legs (Victorian)

ladies' lunch lament the man shortage (all the good men are either gay or married)

ladies of the night whores

ladies' room women's toilet

lady cow's excreta cowshit

lady dog bitch

laid off fired

laid to rest buried

land developer land despoiler

landfill garbage dump

landscape architect gardener

landscaping specialist gardener

lane(s) bowling alley(s)

language arts reading, speaking, and writing

lapin rabbit fur (French *lapin*—rabbit)

lapsus calami (Latin—slip of the pen)—error exposed and reduced to writing

lapsus linguae (Latin—slip of the tongue)—saying what you meant to say but didn't want to say

lapsus memoriae (Latin—lapse of memory)—in acute instances this is called Alzheimer's disease or pre-senile dementia and afflicts more than ten percent of men and women past their fiftieth birthday

last curtain call death

last debt death

last mile the short walk from the prison cell to the place of execution

last obsequies funeral

last roundup death

last sleep death

last taboo incest (least-explored area of human sexuality between brother and sister, father and daughter, mother and son)

last waltz condemned prisoner's march to the electric chair, gas chamber, or other place of execution

late lamented remains corpse

late unpleasantness American Revolution; Civil War or War of the Secession

latrine outdoor toilet (such as a pit dug in the ground)

launched into eternity died

lav lavatory (toilet)—common British euphemism

lavabo (Spanish—washroom)—toilet

Lavabos de Homens (Portuguese—gentlemen's lavatory)—men's toilet

Lavabos de Senhoras (Portuguese—ladies lavatory)—women's toilet

lavatorium toilet

law and order phrase frequently used as a cover-up for racism

lawmen detectives, investigators, law-enforcement officers, police, secret service, sheriffs, or other security forces

lazy colon constipation

learning facilitator teacher

lecher satyr; sex fiend

left the scene died

legal problems drunken-driving arrests

lessie(s) lesbian(s)

less than able unable

less than accurate inaccurate

less than appetizing repulsive; unappetizing

less than artistic inartistic; ugly

less than attractive unattractive

less than bearable unbearable

less than beautiful usually means plain or even ugly

less than believable improbable; incredible; unbelievable

less than broadminded bigoted; narrowminded

less than candid crafty; scheming; untruthful

less than charismatic uncharismatic; without charm or the look of leadership

less than charming disagreeable

less than consistent inconsistent

less than convincing unconvincing

less than decisive undecisive

less than defensive undefensive

less than delicious burned; half baked; nauseating; sour; unwholesome

less than elegant inelegant; shoddy

less than enthusiastic unenthusiastic

less than equal unequal

less than ethical unethical

less than exact inexact

less than exciting dull as ditchwater; unexciting

less than fastidious dirty; sloppy

less than fresh stale

less than fruitful unfruitful

less than gentlemanly ungentlemanly

less than glamorous unglamorous

less than heroic cowardly; unheroic

less than honest crooked; dishonest

less than honorable (discharge) dishonorable (discharge)

less than hospitable inhospitable; standoffish; unfriendly

less than ideal awful; terrible; unbearable

less than important unimportant

less than informative cryptic; obscure; uninformative

less than ingenious uningenious

less than innocent guilty

less than intelligent dumb; stupid; unintelligent

less than interesting dull; uninteresting

less than jubilant unjubilant

less than knowledgeable uninformed; unknowledgeable

less than ladylike unladylike

less than lovable hateful; unlovable (unless by a sentimental mother)

less than loyal disloyal

less than manageable unmanageable

less than navigable unnavigable

less than obedient disobedient; unruly

less than objective unobjective

less than original commonplace; unoriginal

less than palatable inedible; repulsive

less than patient impatient

less than perfect imperfect

less than popular unpopular

less than pure adulterated; impure

less than quenched unquenched

less than receptive unreceptive

less than reliable unreliable

less than sheltered unsheltered

less than skillful unskillful

less than a success a failure

less than supportive uncooperative

less than sympathetic hostile; uncomprehending; unsympathetic

less than thrilled depressed; disappointed; saddened

less than truthful false; lying; untruthful

less than unvulnerable vulnerable

less than unwronged wronged

less than unyielding yielding

less than unzealous zealous

less than used unused

less than useful useless

less than valiant uncourageous; unvaliant

less than well informed poorly informed; uninformed

less than xerographic an unreadable xerographic copy produced prior to telephoning the copier repair service

less than yielding unyielding

less than zealous unzealous

let's make love let us have sexual intercourse

liaison illicit sexual connection

libation alcoholic drink

liberal shibboleths liberal delusions (socialism will wipe out the evils of capitalism, treaties with communist nations will promote peace, victimless crimes are victimless, etc.)

liberal spender spendthrift

liberty cabbage World War-I euphemism for sauerkraut

lieu *lieux d'aisance* (French—

comfort room)—toilet (or in British slang just plain *loo*)

lift attendant(s) elevator operator(s)

light-fingered gentry pickpockets; thieves

likvidatsiya (Russian—liquidation)—execution (Soviet Union)

linguistic fig leaves euphemisms

lipup backward pupil (pupil spelled backwards)

liquidate(d) kill(ed)

liquidation assassination

liquidation of undesirable elements mass murder

liquid refreshment alcoholic drink

literary agent author's representative

literary fig leaves euphemisms

little boy's room men's toilet

little girl's room women's toilet (*see* little boy's room)

live-in companion just what it says, but may also be a concubine, gigolo, kept man or woman, mistress, paramour

live-in lover boyfriend; girlfriend

live-in(s) live-in friend(s) [unmarried lover(s)]

living wage equitable compensation

loan expert(s) pawnbroker(s)

locus of evaluation classroom

lonely couch companionless bed; half-empty bed; solitary bed

long hot summer often refers to race riots involving arson, brutality, and murder; also known as racial unrest

loo(s) toilet(s) (British), derived from the French *lieux d'aisance* (comfort room)

lorette whore (from the old section of Paris called Notre Dame de Lorette where many whores paraded during the Second Empire)

lose the number of one's mess die

lounge toilet

love child child born of illegitimate parents

loved one(s) corpse(s)—mortician's euphemism

low achiever(s) poor student(s)

low economic background poor section of society

lower ability group slow learners; stupid students

lower back ass; backside; behind; buttocks

lower chest abdomen; belly;

guts

lowered the boom fired

low-income families poor families

low-income family poor family

low-income group poor people

low-income level poverty level

low-income neighborhood barrio; ghetto; slum

low-income person(s) poor person(s)

lowing herd cattle

low priced cheap

lubritorium automotive service station

lues could mean cholera or the plague but often is the truncation of *lues venerea*—syphilis

luetic infection of the central nervous system central nervous system syphilis

lung affliction tuberculosis

lupanar (Latin—whorehouse)

machine population owners of tape and video disc players

madam in lowercase stands for the operator or owner of a whorehouse

madamas (Italian—ladies)—women's toilet

made me uncomfortable made me hate you

maiden lady old maid

make one's exit die

make-out artist(s) fornicator(s)

making water leaking (if a boat, ship, or other craft); urinating (if a person or other creature)

maladjusted youths backward or troublesome youngsters

male organ penis

mañana time *see* Hispanic time

mandate League of Nations euphemism covering the awarding of territory formerly German or Turkish to the Japanese or the Russians (hence German colonies in the Pacific became Japanese and Turkish territories became Russian)

manufactured houses mobile homes

Marble City a small town in Oklahoma if capitalized as shown but a bit of bafflegab for the cemetery if it appears as marble city or marbletown

marketing analysis sales promotion

marketing engineer(s) sales person(s)

marketing manager(s) sales manager(s)

marketing representative(s) salesperson(s)

massage parlor(s) place(s) where

horizontalists ply their prostitutional trade with or without massage and very seldom in a parlor-like environment

mass vigilance widespread police-informant system enlisting housemaids, newspaper vendors, prostitutes, etc.

measurable end products results

meat-eater's euphemisms beef—cow or steer meat; cabrito—young goat meat; lamb or mutton—sheep meat; pork—pig meat; veal—calf meat

media access center the library

media coordinator someone who operates a cassette player-recorder, motion-picture camera or projector, tv equipment, etc.

medical center hospital

medical examiner coroner (charged with making inquests concerning the cause of any unusual death)

meditation solitary confinement

mellowspeak soft-spoken euphemisms

member of the lower socioeconomic bracket poor person

member(s) of a minority group non-white(s)

memorial park cemetery

mendacious tendency given to lying

mendacity lie

menn (Norwegian—men)—men's toilet

men's men's toilet

men's lounge men's toilet

men's restroom men's toilet

mental disorder insanity

mental illness insanity

mental institution insane asylum; psychiatric hospital

mentally disturbed crazy

mentally handicapped crazy

meretricious traffic prostitution

mesdames (French—ladies)—applied euphemistically to the doors of women's toilets although in many instances throughout France the toilet is shared by both sexes

méski (Polish—gentlemen)—men's toilet

message radio or television advertisement

messieurs (French—gentlemen)—men's toilet

metallic age attained by older people who discover they have silver in their hair, gold in their teeth, copper pennies in their purse, iron rust in their gut, and lead in their bottom

met his maker died

metropolitan rehabilitation center downtown penitentiary or federal prison

Mexicali Revenge loose bowels produced in border cities such as Mexicali, Baja California

Mexicancellation Mexican divorce

micturate urinate

mild irregularity constipation; irregular menstrual flow

minimal prescriptiveness with the minimum number of restraining rules blocking monetary grants to special interest groups or states

minor emotional moment euphemistic phrase used by a metropolitan newspaper editor describing his wife's firing a bullet at her next-door neighbor before firing another at him

minority see ethnic minority

minor misstatement little lie; small-scale misstatement

misalliance mismatch

misconduct adultery

mixer(s) bartender(s)

mná (Gaelic—women)—women's toilet

mobile home originally a house trailer

moderately priced cheap

molest make indecent sexual advances

monetary policy commodity money counterfeited by the Federal Reserve

monthly pains menstrual pains

monument memorial tombstone

moonchild(ren) person(s) born under the zodiacal sign of Cancer and therefore euphemistically so named to avoid using the name of a dreaded disease—cancer

moral renovation the honest way; truthfully

moral turpitude depravity; immorality

morbus gallicus (Latin—French disease)—syphilis

mortical surgeon undertaker

mortician burier; funeral parlor manager; undertaker

mother homosexual dope pusher; madam of a brothel; motherfucker

motion discomfort motion sickness; nausea; seasickness

motion discomfort container vomit bag; vomit bucket

motion sickness term covering airsickness, carsickness, sea-sickness, trainsickness

motivating through fear coercion

motor vehicle operator(s) chauffeur(s); driver(s)

mountain herring whitefish

mountain oysters bull, hog, or sheep testicles used as food and famed for their imagined aphrodisiac powers

ms multiple sclerosis

mujeres (Spanish—women)—women's toilet

multiprisoner transportation unit black lady; black maria; paddy wagon; police patrol van

multiversities gargantuan universities often setting corporate and government research, and training of researchers, ahead of undergraduate education

muzhay (Bulgarian—men)—men's toilet

muzi (Czechoslovakian—men)—men's toilet

my back teeth are almost floating I must urinate

myrmidons warlike people

my statement is inoperable if you demand verification I'll deny it; I've told you the truth but if you corner me I'll deny it and say you're a damn liar

mythomaniac liar

nappies babies' napkins; diapers

nasal discharge snot

nasal exudate snot

nasal mucus snot

nasal problem loss of smell

natal day birthday

national assistance financial aid and surplus food for the poor and the unemployed

national razor the guillotine of France

naturally fed breast-fed

nature break time to go to the toilet

naughty house brothel; whorehouse

nautch girl dancing girl of India; whore

navigational errors bombing friendly territory

Neapolitan pox syphilis (see French disease)

neck oil whiskey

necktie hangman's noose

necktie party lynching; lynch mob

negative patient care reserved for the dying in many hospitals and nursing homes where dying is expected from all patients of all ages

negative savers people who spend more than they earn

negotiate the price Christiandown (Jew-down) thy neighbor to a price you're willing to pay

neighborhood revitalization slum clearance

neoplasm tumor

nervous need nervous need to go to the toilet

nervous stomach nice-nellyism for bad breath augmented by belching, burping, chronic constipation, and farting

nether garments underwear

netherworld underworld; world of the dead

neuter castrate; denut; remove or tie off procreative organs

never-never never-never plan (British euphemistic nickname for the hire-purchase or installment plan for short-of-cash customers)

new entrepreneur(s) imaginative and independent person(s) usually under 40 who start(s) a business selling a new product or service

news specialist(s) reporter(s)

Nicaraguan eggs iguana lizard eggs dried, pickled, or fried

Nicaraguan nut nipper(s) german shepherd dog(s) trained for police work in quelling riots and hard-to-handle mobs

nice-nellyisms euphemisms marked by excessive modesty and prudishness

nice-nelly language euphemistically speaking

night house whorehouse

night-soil excreta; feces; human dung

No. 1 urine

No. 2 excrement

noisome creature usually an unwashed dog or some person appropriately nicknamed Odoriferous Dan or Smelly Nelly

noisome people smelly street people; unwashed persons

nök (Hungarian—women)—women's toilet

no longer with us dead

non compos mentis (Latin—not of sound mind)—mentally defective and incompetent

nondiscernible microbionoculator concealed poison-dart gun

nonmarital sex sex before marriage

nonterrorists unarmed and uninvolved civilian victims of terrorism

nonwhite Afro-American black; Hispanic mestizo or mulatto; oriental

nose candy cocaine (inhaled through the nose)

nose paint alcohol (whose prolonged use breaks the arterioles of the skin and leaves a reddened nose)

nose powder a powdered drug such as cocaine, any of several hallucinogens, or heroin when snorted

not all that impressive unimpressive

not an exact statement, to put it mildly an inexact statement, a lie, to put it bluntly

not completely accurate inaccurate

not completely truthful untruthful

not entirely accurate inaccurate

not entirely satisfied dissatisfied

not entirely truthful untruthful

Notice of Reduction in Force euphemistic phrase for firing, layoff, or the pink slip inserted in the pay envelope to announce the person receiving it will be jobless

not my favorite person someone I dislike intensely

not overly bright stupid

not precisely accurate inaccurate; untrue

not precisely truthful untruthful

not quite kosher dishonest (in the ethical sense); unclean (in the culinary or physical sense)

not quite so young elderly; old

not too accurate inaccurate

not too attractive unattractive

not too tall anything from average height to short

not too truthful untruthful

nude-encounter parlor brothel; massage parlor

nudie film featuring nudity

nuptial couch marriage bed

nuptials marriage ceremonies

nursing home money-making institution often profiting from the so-called care of elderly bedridden, incurable, or senile men and women awaiting death; many of these institutions are not homes and offer very little nursing care

nut factory insane asylum; mental hospital; psychiatric hospital or ward

nuthouse insane asylum or psychiatric hospital

nutpicker(s) psychiatrist(s)

nutria coypu fur (from a giant South American rodent)

nuttery insane asylum

nymphomaniac lustful female

oblique love adultery; clandestine action; secret love

obsequies funeral ceremonies

obstetric paramedic midwife

obstitute part-time prostitute; substitute for a prostitute; whore

occasional interruption acute constipation

odoriferous smelling; stinking

odoriferous female smelly girl or woman

odoriferous male smelly boy or man

offensively female offensively female smells often consisting of unwashed fecal, menstrual, perspiratorial, seminal, and urinary discharges

offensively male offensively male smells usually arising from unwashed fecal, perspiratorial, seminal, and urinary discharges often described as goatish

official gibberish bureaucratic bafflegab

offshore production military industrial-establishment euphemism for overseas investments in foreign countries where wages are lower than in the United States

of tremendous theoretical importance it excites me greatly

old goat a dirty old man; a satyr; a whorehound; a woman chaser

old hare rabbit meat

olfactoristic smelly

opportunity school school for the handicapped or the mentally retarded

optical problem blindness; failing eyesight

ordure shit (but often used to include urine, corruption, contamination, and snot)

organ male organ; penis

organic receptors sense organs

orgone box orgasm box (invented by Wilhelm Reich)

oriental dancing girl(s) often pronounced *whoriental* in an effort to define other-than-dancing activities

orthographical errancy misspelling

osculation kiss(ing)

osmidrosis foul-smelling sweat

other prisoner(s) prison guard(s)

our wayward sisters Civil War and post-Civil War euphemism for the Confederate States

outhouse backyard toilet; country privy

out in left field disoriented; out of touch with reality

out of the ballpark out of touch; unaware of reality

out of town in prison

outplaced fired (from your job)

outright fabrication damned lie

out to lunch daffy

overachiever embarrassingly brilliant student; very successful person

overindulgence gluttony

over the blue wall confined to a hospital for the criminally insane

over the river dead

oxometric analysis imaginary method for measuring the depth of the bullshit

oxymoron(s) seeming contradiction(s) e.g., peacekeeper missile(s)

pacification peace at the point of a bayonet

package store(s) liquor store(s)

pain in the butt pain in the ass

Panamá chicken chicken-flavored iguana lizard tail

panel house whorehouse (whose bedrooms had sliding panels close to the bedstead and in easy reach of an accomplice who could reach in and snatch a man's wallet or watch while he was sexually preoccupied)

pantheism atheism

paramour (French—for love; illicit lover; a man's mistress)—whore

park under construction dump(ing ground)

parrhesia freedom of speech; outspokenness; the opposite of euphemia

parsimonious frugal; niggardly; pennypinching; stingy

pass(ed) away die(d)

pass(ed) gas fart(ed)

pass(ed) on die(d)

passing dying

passing gas farting

passing wind farting

passive resistance response deliberate procrastination masking lack of guts to oppose whatever is distasteful or hateful

paying guest boarder; lodger

Peacemaker MX missile's euphemistic name coined and used by President Reagan

peculator thief

peculiar institution slavery

peculiar members lexicographer Noah Webster's euphemism for testicles

peculiar service espionage

pecuniary distress poverty

pedophiliac adult child molester attacking children sexually

pee-pee baby-talk for urine

peeping tom voyeur

pejorative bafflegabber's way of saying demeaning or derogatory

people expressways sidewalks

people's republic political prefix popular in many totalitarian nations run by communists and not by the people but by a most unrepublican dictatorship

people with conspicuous access to wealth in their own right rich people

perform one's ablutions shampoo, shave, and shower

period menstrual period

permanent color hair dye

perpetrator criminal; offender; suspect

personal emergency must go to the toilet immediately

personal protection dog dog trained to attack on command

personal relationship sexual relationship

perspiration sweat

perspire sweat

perspiring sweating

pertussis whooping cough

Peruvian perfume cocaine

pet snatcher(s) dogcatcher(s)

phased out brought to a halt; cancelled; closed; concluded; discontinued; ended; finished; retired; stopped; terminated

phased withdrawal scheduled retreat

Philippine Pacification Philippine Subjugation, according to Filipino historians

philosophically misused to mean mental attitude or simply one's point of view

Pick's disease brain disorder manifested by loss of memory and speech

pigeon painting splashed droppings of pigeons

pink slip a dismissal notice terminating your pay by a certain day

pipí (Brazilian-Portuguese or Spanish baby talk—pee)

pissoir (French—public urinal)

pissotière (French—pisshouse; urinal)—the *Modern French-English Dictionary* published in Paris by Librairie Larousse follows this entry with a footnote reading *N.B. Do not use this word.*

pixillated alcoholically befuddled

planned economy politician-planned economy

planned parenthood contraception

planned withdrawal defeat; retreat

plant food chickenshit; manure

plaque invaders dental hygienists

pleasingly plump attractively fat

plight one's troth pledge marriage; promise to marry

plongeur (French—diver or plunger)—euphemistic term for a dishwasher

plump fat

plural marriage polygamy

plural relations South African euphemism for *apartheid*

pneumatic bliss breast-cushioned tun-filled fornication

podium a platform designed to elevate a conductor or a speaker above the ensemble or the audience; but is often used to mean a slanted-top upright base for a bible or an unabridged dictionary or a slanted-top stand for a lecturer, a speaker, or a teacher; in airports it is a ticket validation desk and is often provided with a slanted-face computer device; in college and classrooms it is a lectern

point in time moment; time

police state law and order imposed by law-enforcement agencies who find it imperative to overlook many civil liberties in their defense of law-abiding citizens

political unrest bombings; riots; sabotage; terrorist attacks; wide-scale subversion often leading to revolution

polychromatic alphasite colored chalk

polygraph test(ing) lie-detection test(ing)

poopoo cat or dog droppings; excrement; shit

poorly compensated poorly paid

popular price cheap

population-control equipment riot-control equipment such as high-pressure water hoses, rubber bullets, and tear gas

portable john portable toilet

position situation job; job task

posterior backside; behind

potty chamber pot

poule (French—chicken; hen)—whore

poule de luxe (French—highly paid and well-provided-for whore)—elegantly kept woman

poultry fertilizer chickenshit

powder her nose euphemistic phrase meaning a woman is going to the toilet

powder room toilet

power outage(s) power failure(s)

predigested mass bit of shit; hunk of crap; mass of manure

preemptive strike bombing your enemy before he bombs you or your country

pregnancy termination abortion

premarital sex fornication before marriage

preorgasmic females frigid females

pre-owned secondhand; used

preparation room undertaker's embalming room

prevaricate lie

prevarication lying

prevaricator(s) liar(s)

preventive war sneak attack

previously owned auto secondhand automobile

prices you can afford prices salesmen tell you you can afford

primary degenerative dementia Alzheimer's disease or presenile dementia characterized by progressive loss of memory

printouts computer-published results

prioritize arrange in chronological order; choose; select

prior restraint tacit agreement of the media (press, publication, radio, and television) to check the abuse of the power of the press by enforcing standards of professionalism so it will not be necessary for the government to regulate the media by effectually abolishing the First Amendment of the U.S. *Con-*

stitution

prison officer(s) gaoler(s) (U.K.); jailer(s) (U. S.)

privates private parts (sexual and urinary organs)

privy outdoor toilet

problem child(ren) juvenile delinquent(s)

problem drinker(s) alcoholic addict(s)

problem pregnancy clinic abortion center

problem skin one marred by acne, eczema, pimples, psoriasis, syphilitic scars, or their combination

proglang(s) progressive language(s)

property control officer watchman

prophylactic contraceptive

prosecutorial agent attorney general; city attorney; county attorney; district attorney; federal attorney; magistrate; public prosecutor; state prosecutor

protective bombing bombing the other fellow's territory before he bombs your territory

protective coating engineer house painter

protective reaction bombing raids

protective reaction strike attack

provisional period probation

prurience lust

pseudologist liar

psychiatric center insane asylum

psychiatric hospital expensive place to leave your demented or insane people

psychic reader(s) fortune teller(s)

public convenience outdoor or public toilet (British)

public house Old English euphemism for whorehouse but used today to mean a bar where drinks and food are sold

public property property controlled by politicians

public relations adviser(s) press agent(s)

public relations assistant(s) office receptionist(s)

public utilities contraception and family-planning clinics (Dutch)

puffer(s) auction booster(s)

pupil station(s) desk(s)

purloin(ing) steal(ing)

purloined stolen

purloiner thief

purveyors of meat butchers

puta prostituta (Portuguese or Spanish—prostitute) (*see* abandoned woman)

put him down put him down in the ground—bring about death as in the case of a very old pet

putting them out of their misery killing them

put to sleep kill(ed)

quacksalver charlatan; fake physician; quack

quality-control engineer(s) inspector(s)

quandong Australian fruit whose attractive soft exterior covers a hard and hard-to-digest interior; hence it is a euphemistic nickname for whore

quean (Middle English—whore)

queen-size bigger than large but smaller than kingsize

queer(s) homosexual(s)

quiet room solitary-confinement cell

quietus death

rabelaisian writer old-fashioned pornographer; robust humorist noted for naturalism

racial rage sociological euphemism explaining and excusing looting, mugging, plundering, and race riots attended by arson and murder

racial unrest race riots involving blacks or Hispanics in demonstrations marked by arson, brutality, and murder

rap parlor place of prostitution

ratepayer(s) taxpayer(s)

rather elderly very old

ravisher one who captures and carries off another; one who is filled with strong emotions; one who uses force to carry off and rape a woman

realtor(s) real estate agent(s)

rear end ass; buttocks

receipts strengthening raising taxes

recession depression

reconciliation room church confessional

reconditioned secondhand

reconnaissance in force search out and destroy the enemy

rectification of the front retreat

redeployment retreat; withdrawal of armed forces

red-light district whorehouse section

reduced circumstances poor

reduction(s) in the work force firing(s); layoff(s)

re-education camps communist-controlled forced-labor work camps

reemployable annuitant highly paid and presumably indispensable specialist called back from retirement

reflation ascending inflation

registered warrant(s) government-issued i-o-u('s) issued when money is not available to pay for goods or services

regurgitated threw up; vomited

regurgitation upchucking; vomiting

rehabilitation center jail; lockup; penitentiary; prison

rehabilitation laboratory any modern prison

relationship sexual affair

remains cadaver; corpse; dead person

remand institution jail; penitentiary; prison

remediation remedial reading

remittance man person living abroad on monies sent from home; ticket-of-leave man

removed exterminated

repose beneath the sod die

repossessed secondhand

reproductive health abortion

resettled term used by Nazis and soviet communists to cover the extermination of so-called enemies of the state

resource center library

resources control bombing of dams, defoliation of forests, poisoning of sources of drinking water during the course of a war

rest home place where discarded elderly people are placed while awaiting death; sometimes called convalescent or retirement home but not a home as it is a money-making enterprise with too few of the comforts of home

resting in marbletown buried in the cemetery

rest in peace die

restroom(s) toilet(s)

resurrectionist grave robber

retire for the night go to bed

retirement allowance old-age pension

retirement home institution catering to retired people

retiring room toilet

retreat toilet

retrete (Spanish—retreat)—toilet

returnee(s) defector(s)

revenue enhancement increased taxation

reverse engineering industrial espionage achieved by taking apart the products of competitors to find out how they work and how they may be imitated

revised upward increased in price or wages

rhumba steam sweat

riffed reduced in force (dismissed from duty; fired)

right decision(s) decision(s) favored by the public in general and taxpayers in particular despite massive opposition by greedy bureaucrats and the many lobbyists for special interests

right in the ballpark completely in touch with reality; totally aware

rip off cheat; overprice; rob; steal

roach(es) cockroach(es); marijuana butts

rodent operators rat catchers

rolling in the rye making love in the grass

roll in the hay country-style copulation

rolling through the rye drinking and driving

roommates unmarried lovers

rooster(s) barnyard cock(s)

rotund fat

Rückkehr unerwünscht (German—return unwanted)—death to persons with this phrase written on their prison record kept by the Nazis and on their identity papers

ruddy-faced alcoholic victim; drunk

sacrament of penance the rite of reconciliation (Roman Catholic)

sailor's curse constipation

Salisbury steak World War-I euphemism for hamburger

saliva spit

sanitary engineer(s) garbage collector(s)

sanitation engineer(s) garbage collector(s)

sanitation person female or male garbage and trash collector

sanitation smell odor of ordure; stench of ordure and urine

saturation overwhelming military force

saturation bombing reducing the enemy or its territory to rubble

satyr satyrus (Latin—lecher)—person afflicted with satyiriasis manifested by abnormal and uncontrollable sexual desire (*see* dirty old man)

sauce sanctuaries beer bars; cocktail lounges; saloons

sauna massage brothel (Danish)

screw(ed) fornicated(d); fuck(ed)

search and clear search and destroy

seasickness dizziness followed by nausea and often by vomiting when aboard a vessel pitching and rolling

seclusion solitary confinement

secret disease syphilis (Victorian)

Section 8 discharged from the armed forces because of insanity or intoxication; government-subsidized decent, safe, and sanitary housing

secularist(s) agnostic(s); atheist(s); disbeliever(s); doubter(s); humanist(s); iconoclast(s); nonbeliever(s); rationalist(s); skeptic(s); truthseeker(s); unbeliever(s)

seed ox bull

selected out dismissed from duty; fired

self-enhancement masturbation

self-help masturbation

self-immolation sacrifice attained by setting oneself on fire or plunging into a fire

self-pleasuring masturbation

selling spring whoring (Japanese)

senior(s) senior citizen(s)—older person(s)

señoras (Spanish—ladies)—women's toilet

señores (Spanish—gentlemen)—men's toilet

sensual gratification sexual intercourse

sensuous desire lust

senyores (Catalan—ladies)—women's toilet.

senyors (Catalan—gentlemen)—men's toilet

separate from school expel

separate from the payroll fire

serious headache gunshot wound in the head

service station attendant automotive gas pumper

servicio (Spanish—service)—toilet.

servicios de caballeros (Spanish—gentlemen's services)—men's toilet

servicios de damas (Spanish—ladies' services)—women's toilet

sexed to death fucked out

sexual expressionist(s) pornographer(s); purveyor(s) of smut

sexual intercourse coitus; copulation; fucking; genital contact

sexually active very lustful

sexually molested raped

sexual minorities perverts

sexual variety promiscuity

sharing group sex or orgy

sharpen your skates go to the toilet

sharps needles and scalpels (medical jargon)

she dog bitch

sheer prevarication outright lie

she fell asleep she died

she lost her husband her husband died

sherutim legvarim (Hebrew—men's services)—men's toilet

sherutim lenashim (Hebrew—women's services)—women's toilet

she's a little sensitive she's neurotic or very, very touchy

she's a plain girl but she means well she's ugly but not malicious

she's gone she's dead

shibo shit

shinjuku (Japanese—whorehouse)

shoe rebuilder shoe repairman

short shorts hot pants (short short pants)

shuffle off this mortal coil die

signore (Italian—ladies)—euphemistically used to designate the women's toilet but often confused by foreigners because of the similarity with the next entry

signori (Italian—gentlemen)—applied euphemistically to men's toilets (see *signore*)

simple insane

single woman unmarried woman

sink of iniquity whorehouse

skeptic agnostic; atheist; nonbeliever; unbeliever

skillful inveracity artful lie

skimming secretly diverting unreported profits

skin doctor dermatologist comes to mind but the term is often used as a coverup for syphilologist, a specialist in and student of syphilis

skin problems acne; blackheads; pimples; syphilitic sores

slatternly, slovenly, sluttish, or

untidy individual slob

sleep engineer(s) mattress maker(s)

sleeping partner of life death

sleep with usually means fornicate with and may or may not allow time for sleep

slender skinny

slipped out of my life died

slippery slope difficult-to-defend argument

slow learner dunce; unintelligent student

slumbermobile hearse

slumber robe funeral shroud

slumber room area in a funeral establishment where the embalmed may be viewed before burial or cremation

sly language of evasion filled with double-tongued talk laden with implied promises so popular with self-serving bureaucrats and politicians who delight in the use of euphemisms

small untruth little lie

smilers and defilers, reekers and leakers Ambrose Bierce's euphemistic description of dogs

snuff spoon(s) tobacco snuff spoon(s)—cover-up name for cocaine sniffing spoon(s), also called coke spoon(s)

s.o.b. abbreviatorial euphemism for son of a bitch

social disease venereal disease such as gonorrhea or syphilis

social indiscretion belching or farting while dining or during the course of an interview or in a public place within earshot of other people

socialism Marx defined it as the transitional stage of society between capitalism and communism distinguished by pay according to work performed and unequal distribution of goods although the socialist state had abolished private ownership and controlled the economy (see communism)

socially disadvantaged poor

socially underprivileged boorish; ill-mannered; uncouth

social maladjustment crime

social outcasts alcohol-and-drug-addicted bums; dirty and smelly street people; vagrant unemployed

social parasites freeloaders depending on others for drinks, entertainment, and food

social problems arguments with friends and neighbors

social promotion advancing poor pupils so they will not suffer the embarrassment of sitting in classrooms with brighter and younger students; this is the built-in time bomb of their education as the day of graduation approaches and they go out into the world without being able to read or write

social prophylaxis Soviet euphemism for execution or imprisonment of dissidents or suspects

social safety net device comprising medicare, social security, and unemployment compensation

social unrest alienation of segments of the population engaged in demonstrations, hunger marches and hunger strikes, race riots, terrorism, and widespread destruction of people and their property

soiled linen dirty clothes

solecisms grammatical errors

somewhat advanced in years old(er)

somewhat less than credible incredible; unbelievable

somewhat less than honest dishonest

somewhat less than reliable unreliable

somewhat less than truthful untruthful

somewhat unlettered rather ignorant

Sonderbehandlung (German—special treatment)—death to prisoners forced to undergo this special treatment by the Nazis

son of Onan masturbator

so perceived seen

souvenir hunters vandals

souvenir hunting graffitic defacement or vandalism

Spanish disease syphilis, according to the Portuguese (*see* French disease)

speaks a low level of colloquialisms talks slang

special action murder

special agent(s) FBI agent(s) or insurance agent(s)

specialized vehicle(s) army tank(s)

special psychiatric hospital Russian euphemism for a penitentiary where many dissidents are held and tortured under a system of so-called forensic medicine denying them all human rights

special transaction(s) gambling bargain(s)

sporting house(s) whorehouse(s)

state chemist state executioner charged with the task of poisoning convicts in a gas chamber

state electrician state executioner charged with the duty of electrocuting convicts in an electric chair

state executioner hangman in some states or state chemist or state electrician in others

steatopygous fat-assed

steer manure bullshit

stonewall conceal; cover-up

stool dung; fecal discharge

stomach condition acid indigestion; constipation; dyspepsia; heartburn

stomach distress acute constipation, diarrhea, nausea, or vomiting

stones testicles

straightforward and aboveboard blunt to the point of rudeness

strategic deterrents weapons of war

strategic hamlet refugee camp

strategic misrepresentation lying; speaking with a forked tongue

strategic redeployment retreat

strategic withdrawal retreat

street of fallen women red-light or whorehouse area

street hustler(s) male prostitute(s) plying trade in the streets

street orderlies garbage and trash collectors

street people bums, down-and-outers, tramps, vagrants (and often the victims of alcoholism or other drug addiction)

streetwalker whore (who picks her clients by walking the streets)

stretches the truth exaggerates; lies

stretch hemp hang by the neck until dead

striptease dancer(s) dancing whore(s) usually performing atop bars in cocktail lounges and other saloons

strongly expansionary monetary policy government-imposed counterfeiting of commodity money

struggle for preeminence in the Sicilian community Mafiatype gang warfare

subsidy publisher vanity press

whose output in book form is paid for by the author, who is led to believe this is the only way her or his work will ever be published and hence subsidizes this racket

substitute worker(s) scab(s); strikebreaker(s)

succulent viands appetizing food

succumbed to hypertensive cardiovascular disease died of a heart attack

sugar feminine nice-nellyism for shit

summer complaint diarrhea; loose bowels

sunshine units nuclear radiation units

supreme measure capital punishment; execution

supreme sacrifice giving your life in an effort to save another or your country; losing your virginity

surreptitious entry breaking and entering

sweetbreads animal pancreas or thymus prepared as a gastronomic delicacy

swinger(s) fornicator(s); promiscuous person(s)

swish effeminate male homosexual

symphonic plight also known as pp's or payless paydays brought about by the failure of the community to support their symphony and pay its members on time despite mismanagement and the need for audience augmentation

take a powder leave hurriedly; leave suddenly

take leave of abstinence get drunk

taken out of the picture die; dying

take one's last sleep die

take the electric cure to be electrocuted

take to the tall tules evade arrest; hide out; take to the bamboo-like tall tule grass of the American Southwest including southern California

talent promoter high-class pimp

tavern(s) beer bar(s); cocktail lounge(s); saloon(s)

taxation legally imposed theft by your government

tax expenditure anything the government doesn't tax away from you

tax reform(s) often means tax increase(s)

tax withholding earning sharing

tb tuberculosis

technical correction downward skidding of the stock market

technology transfer assistance giving advice

temperance used by the Women's Christian Temperance Union who believed temperance meant abstinence

temporary work cessation layoff

terminal cell(s) prison cell(s) designed to kill the inmate(s)

terminal illness fatal illness

terminated fired (from your job)

terminate the relationship stay out of her (his) bed

terminate your pregnancy have an abortion

termination with extreme prejudice assassination

terminological inexactitude lie

Texas turkey armadillo meat

thanks are due my colleague Casimir Klutz for aid with the experiments and to my associate Belfrage Blow for valuable discussion Klutz did the work and Blow explained what it meant

that time frame then

theater of war battlefield

therapeutic accident drug-induced death due to a fatal overdose

therapeutic correctional community prison

therapeutic termination abortion

these points in time now

thinking the unthinkable contemplating nuclear warfare

thinning out killing wildlife (botanical or zoological)

third age old age (assuming the first age is infancy through adolescence and the second age is post-adolescence through middle age)

this job offers great experience the pay is lousy and working conditions are the worst

those points in time then

threat dog(s) dog(s) trained to bark and snarl at intruders

three-letter words Victorian arbiters of taste felt some three-letter words were just as bad as the dozen or more four-letter words to be avoided in polite conversation or print; these included leg (if a woman's), pee, pus, nut (if a testicle), sex, sin, and tit

three samples were chosen for

intensive investigation the results of the others made no sense and hence were ignored

three-wayer(s) person(s) engaging in sex anally, naturally, or orally

thrice threefold; tree times

thundermug chamberpot; pottie

time to retire time to go to bed

tocador (Spanish—boudoir; dressing room; dressing table; vanity)—often means toilet

toilet powder scented talcum powder

toilet tissue toilet tissue paper

toilet water perfume-scented cologne

to make water pee; piss; urinate

tonsorial artist(s) barber(s)

tonsorial expert(s) barber(s)

tonsorialist(s) barber(s)

tonsorial parlor(s) barbershop(s)

tossed up the cookies vomited

touched insane

tp toilet paper

trade of kings war, as defined by John Dryden

trainsickness nausea followed by vomiting when travelling by train

transformation hair piece, toupee, or wig worn by a bald-headed person wishing to appear hairy-headed

traumatic amputation of the lower extremities painful loss of the legs as in an accident

traviata (Italian—fallen woman)—as in Verdi's opera *La Traviata* concerning the life and death of a high-class whore

tree surgeon(s) tree trimmer(s)

trial marriage free love

tropical eggs iguana lizard eggs dried, pickled, or fried

trots the trots (botulism, diarrhea, dysentery)

truthseeker(s) agnostic(s); atheist(s); freethinker(s); nonbeliever(s); secularist(s); skeptic(s); unbeliever(s)

tube steak(s) frankfurter(s); hot dog(s)

turistas (Portuguese or Spanish—tourists)—traveller's diarrhea caused by toxic-productive bacteria found in contaminated food or water and, if prolonged, a protozoan invasion may occur and produce amebic dysentery

turn one's face to the wall die

twenty toes ten toes up and ten toes down (British euphemism for a bedroom diversion of some antiquity)

two pc two-physician certification (of insanity)

ubornaya (Russian—adornment place)—toilet

udder woman the other woman (usually)

udd's undisposed diapers; undumped diapers

umbles deer entrails made into umble or humble pie (expression *to eat humble pie* comes from the custom of assigning inferior parts of a game carcass to the servants)

umbrage to take offense

unannounced social explosions belches, burps, and farts (usually unpremeditated)

unbeliever agnostic; atheist; nonbeliever; skeptic

uncandid not candid; untruthful

uncharismatic without ability to command or lead

uncivil rude

unclothed naked

underachiever embarrassingly stupid student; very unsuccessful person

underarm damp sweat

underclasses blacks and Puerto Ricans

underdeveloped countries poor countries

underdeveloped nation(s) poor nation(s)

underfunded broke; in debt; lacking money

undergoing emotional retraining undergoing psychiatric consultation and suggestion

under par feels or looks awful; looks like death warmed over

underprivileged poor; poor, retarded, senile, and long unemployed people

under the influence under the influence of alcohol or other drugs

under the sod dead and buried

under the weather drunk; sick

undesirable books banned or censored books (South African)

undies underwear

undocumented immigrant illegal alien

undocumenteds undocumented aliens (illegal entrants lacking passports)

unemancipated minor(s) teenager(s)

unfortunate activity invasion of a country; takeover of a country; warlike preparations

unfortunate female whore

unimpeachable source the king, queen, premier, president (unless found to be impeachable)

unimpressive height short

unlearned ignorant

unmarried wives concubines; kept women; paramours

unmentionable disease syphilis

unmentionables underwear

unobscene song(s) seemingly obscene but really only outspoken songs

unpedigreed alley cat or mutt; one-hundred-percent pure cat or dog

unpeople depopulate

unpredictably nonplussed I've nothing to say

unprosperous one(s) poor person(s)

unrenewed discontinued

unsavory scandal a morally offensive disgrace

unstructured conversations friendly chats; informal talks

untruism falsehood; lie

untruth(s) lie(s)

unwell menstruating

unwhisperables underwear

unworthy servant(s) slave(s)

upchuck(ed) vomit(ed)

upper frontal superstructures a woman's breasts

upset stomach anything from acute constipation to loose bowels

up the river Sing Sing prison, up the Hudson River from New York City

upward adjustment rise in prices and/or wages

upward revision increase in prices or wages

urinal of the planets rain-filled Ireland

urning(s) male homosexual(s)

uttered an untruth told a lie

uttering inexactitudes telling lies

uttering untruths telling lies

utter peer rejection complete failure to get along with surrounding people such as family, friends, neighbors, fellow workers

vacationing near Chappaqua close to Ossining, New York and its Sing Sing prison

validated learning package approved textbook

vashzimmer (Yiddish—washroom)—toilet

vd venereal disease (includes chancroid, gonorrhea, granuloma inguinale, lymphogranu-

loma venereum, nongonococcal urethritis, or syphilis in any of its many stages)

venereal desire lust

venerist whore (but term should apply to her male clients who also engage in venery)

venery pursuit of sexual pleasure; sexual intercourse

Venus's curse venereal disease

vertical transportation corps elevator operators

victimless crimes sociological euphemism for drug abuse and trafficking, gambling, homosexual conduct, pornography, and prostitution although all of the foregoing have produced many victims

victims of target practice persons executed by a firing squad

vidrio inglés (Spanish—English glass)—euphemism for dog dung

visceral reaction gut feeling

visually handicapped blind

visually impaired blind

volume reduction unit city or town dump

voluntary compliance paying taxes without being deprived of your property or without going to jail

voluntary return voluntary deportation (of illegal aliens)

voluntary termination of pregnancy abortion

voluptuarial excess sexual excess

waistcloth loincloth

walking papers dismissal notice

wanaume (Swahili—men)— men's toilet

wanawake (Swahili—women)— women's toilet

war baby child born of illegitimate parents during wartime

War Between the States Confederate euphemism for the Civil War also called the War of the Secession

warm glow hot sweat

wash his hands a man is going to the toilet

washroom facilities toilets

waste her rape her

wáter (Spanish-water closet)— toilet

water closet(s) toilet(s)

Watergate Watergate English (terminology invented by President Nixon's top men to cover up lies and to spar for time when undergoing congressional examination under oath and hence *at this point in* *time* meant *now, in point of time* was equivalent to *then* or *when,* and *my statement is inoperable* really meant *don't believe a word I say*)

water qualm acid indigestion; heartburn; sudden faintness sometimes accompanied by nausea

wc (WC) water closet (toilet)

wc babati (Romanian—male water closet)—men's toilet

wc femei (Romanian—female water closet)—women's toilet

weed of wisdom hashish; marijuana; other cannabis products

welfare state welfare-provided state giving more funds to the bureaucrats than to the needy

well-filled out fat

well placed at the present level of management will never be promoted

welsh rabbit dish made of melted cheese, beer, and other ingredients poured over toast or served as a dip; incorrectly called welsh rarebit

went west died; was killed

we will no longer detain you you're dismissed; you're fired; you may leave

while it is not entirely possible to provide definite answers at this juncture academic bafflegab often meaning the experiments failed but this report offers me publicity and the name of the game is publish or perish

white propaganda identifiable and truthful dissemination of facts

white slave whore

wilderness health strip mining

winding cloth burial shroud

winning the West killing the Indians

wipe your bottom wipe your ass; wipe your backside

with balls between parenthesis *What manner of man is this with balls between parenthesis?* (attributed to Shakespeare's description of a bow-legged man)

with child pregnant

with facilities cabin (aboard ship) or hotel or motel room with toilet, tub and/or shower, and washstand

without benefit of clergy living together but unmarried

without female friends male homosexual

without male friends female homosexual

womanizer cunt chaser; philanderer; skirt chaser; whoremaster; whoremonger

woman of the street whore

women's women's toilet

women's lounge women's toilet

women's powder room women's toilet

women's restroom women's toilet

wooden interdental stimulator and particle remover toothpick

word from our sponsor radio or television advertisement

work cessation strike; walkout; work stoppage

work cessation on the premises sit-down strike

working girl(s) prostitute(s)—street slang term but originally meant girl(s) who worked

wouldn't you like to wash your hands? usually means wouldn't you like to go to the toilet?

write out a check go to the toilet

xanadu dream girl whore (term recalling the stanzas in *Kubla Khan* by Samuel Taylor Coleridge)

xerotic wrinkled

yellow peril Oriental conquest of Western civilization by economic penetration, immigration, and war

yellow rain biochemical poison dropped by enemy aircraft

yellow suppuration pus

you know where to go go to hell

you know where to put it shove it up your ass

you know, you know attempted cover-up popular with those who don't know but hope you'll know and will fill in for them

young adult(s) teenager(s)

your services are no longer required you're fired

youthful offender juvenile delinquent

yvette French-style whore

zap(ped) kill(ed) quickly (as with a burst of machine gun or tommy gun bullets)

zarzuela girl Hispanic playgirl; operetta performer

zealous zelia a hardworking pavement-pounding whore whose name recalls *Zuleika Dobson II* who, according to Max Beerbohm, was truly zealous because *Zuleika on a desert island would have spent her time looking for a man's footprints*

zeny (Czechoslovakian—women)—women's toilet

zero-defect system foolproof system

zhenny (Bulgarian—women)—women's toilet

zoophilia erotica (Latin—erotic love of animals)—sexual intercourse with animals (usually men with cattle and women with dogs)

zymurgic outburst alcoholic belch; beer belch

Bell Code from Bridge or Pilothouse to Engine Room

These bell codes are used on ferries, launches, tugs, and other powered vessels.

1 bell ahead
2 bells stop

3 bells astern
4 bells full speed

Birthstones—Ancient and Modern

Relative Values. Diamonds, emeralds, rubies, and sapphires are termed precious stones; all the rest are semiprecious. Precious gems are minerals enhanced by the lapidary's art. The pearl, although not a stone, is classed with the gems and, depending on its beauty and size, may be as valuable as any of the precious stones.

	Ancient	Modern
January	garnet	garnet
February	amethyst	amethyst
March	jasper	aquamarine or bloodstone
April	sapphire	diamond
May	agate	emerald
June	emerald	alexandrite, moonstone, or pearl
July	onyx	ruby
August	carnelian	peridot or sardonyx
September	chrysolite	sapphire
October	aquamarine	opal or tourmaline
November	topaz	topaz
December	ruby	turquoise or zircon

British Counties Abbreviated

England, Northern Ireland, Scotland, and Wales

Adeen Aberdeenshire
Ang Angus
Angle Anglesey
Arg Argyll
Ant Antrim
Arm Armagh
Ayrs Ayrshire
Banffs Banffshire
Beds Bedfordshire
Ber Berwickshire
Berks Berkshire
Brecon Brecknock
Bucks Buckinghamshire
Bute County Bute
Caern Caernarvonshire
Caith Cathiness
Cambs Cambridgeshire and Isle of Ely
Card Cardiganshire
Carm Carmarthenshire
Ches Cheshire
Clack Clacmannanshire
Corn Cornwall
Cumb Cumberland
Denb Denbighshire
Derbys Derbyshire
Dev Devon
Dor Dorset
Down County Down
Dumf Dumfriesshire
Dunb Dunbarton
Dur County Durham
E Lothian East Lothian
E R Yorks East Riding, York-

shire
Ess Essex
E Suffolk East Suffolk
E Sussex East Sussex
Ferm Fermanagh
Fife Fifeshire
Flints Flintshire
Glam Glamorgan
Glos Gloucestershire
Great Lon Greater London
Hants Hampshire
Herefs Herefordshire
Herts Hertfordshire
Hunts Huntingdon and Peterborough
Iness Inverness-shire
Kent County Kent
Kinc Kincardineshire
Kinross Kinross-shire
Kircud Kircudbrightshire
Lanarks Lanarkshire
Lancs Lancashire
Leics Leicestershire
Lincs Lincolnshire (Holland, Kesteven, Lindsey)
Lond County Londonderry
Merion Merioneth
Mloth Midlothian
Mon Monmouthshire
Mont Montgomeryshire
Moray County Moray
Nairns Nairnshire
Norf Norfolk
Northants Northamptonshire

Northld Northumberland
Notts Nottinghamshire
N R Yorks North Riding, Yorkshire
Ork Orkney Islands
Oxon Oxfordshire
Peebl Peebleshire
Pemb Pembrokeshire
Perths Perthshire
Rad Radnor
Renf Renfrewshire
Ross Ross and Cromarty
Rox Roxburghshire
Rut Rutland
Selk Selkirkshire
Shet Shetland Islands
Shrops Shropshire
Som Somerset
Staffs Staffordshire
Stir Stirlingshire
Sur Surrey
Suth Sutherland
Tyr Tyrone
Warks Warwickshire
Westmld Westmorland
Wig Wigtownshire
Wilts Wiltshire
W Lothian West Lothian
Worcs Worcestershire
W R Yorks West Riding, Yorkshire
W Suffolk West Suffolk
W Sussex West Sussex

Canadian Provinces

Alb Alberta (inhabitants called Albertans)
BC British Columbia (British Columbians)
Man Manitoba (Manitobans)
NB New Brunswick (New Brunswickers)
Nfld Newfoundland (Newfies, Newfoundlanders, or Labradorans)
NS Nova Scotia (Nova Scotians)
NWT Northwest Territories (Territorials)
Ont Ontario (Ontarians)
PEI Prince Edward Island (Prince Edward Islanders)
Qué Québec (Québecois)
Sask Saskatchewan (Saskatchewanians)
Yuk Yukon Territory (Yukoners)

Capitals of Nations, Provinces, Places, and States

Afghanistan Kabul
Aguascalientes Aguascalientes
Alabama Montgomery
Alaska Juneau
Albania Tirana
Alberta Edmonton
Alderney Alderney
Algeria Algiers
American Samoa Pago Pago (pronounced *Pango Pango*)
Andorra Andorra la Vella
Angola Luanda
Antigua St John's
Argentina Buenos Aires
Arizona Phoenix
Arkansas Little Rock
Australia Canberra
Australia's Northern Territory Darwin
Austria Vienna
Azerbaijan Baku
Azores Angra do Heroísmo, Horta, and Ponta Delgada
Bahamas Nassau
Bahrain Manama
Baja California Mexicali
Baja California Sur La Paz (capital of the Southern Territory of Baja California—*Territorio Sur*—abbreviated *BC Sur*)
Balearic Islands Palma de Mallorca
Bangladesh Dacca
Barbados Bridgetown
Belgium Brussels
Belize Belmopan
Benin Cotonou and Porto-Novo
Bermuda Hamilton
Bhutan Thimphu
Black Forest Freiburg, Germany
Bolivia La Paz and Sucre
Botswana Gaborone

Brazil Brasilia
British Columbia Victoria
British Virgin Islands Road Town
Brunei Brunei Town
Bulgaria Sofia
Burma Rangoon
Burundi Bujumbura
Byelorussia Minsk
California Sacramento
Cameroon Yaounde
Campeche Campeche
Canada Ottawa
Canada's Northwest Territories Yellowknife
Canary Islands Las Palmas
Cape Verde Islands Praia
Cayman Islands Georgetown
Central African Empire Bangui
Chad N'Djamena
Chiapas Tuxtla Guitiérrez
Chihuahua Chihuahua City
Chile Santiago
China (communist-controlled mainland called the People's Republic of China) Peking
China (offshore islands called the Republic of China or Taiwan) Taipei
Coahuila Saltillo
Colima Colima
Colombia Bogotá
Colorado Denver
Comoros Moroni
Confederacy Richmond, Virginia
Congo Brazzaville
Connecticut Hartford
Cook Islands Rarotonga
Corsica Ajaccio
Costa Rica San José
Cuba Havana
Cyprus Nicosia
Czechoslovakia Prague

Delaware Dover
Denmark Copenhagen
Distrito Federal México City
Djibouti Djibouti
Dominica Roseau
Dominican Republic Santo Domingo City
Durango Durango
Ecuador Quito
Egypt Cairo
El Salvador San Salvador
England London
Equatorial Guinea Malabo
Estonia Tallinn
Ethiopia Addis Ababa
Fiji Suva
Finland Helsinki
Florida Tallahassee
France Paris
French Guiana Cayenne
French Polynesia Papeete
Gabon Libreville
Gambia Banjul
Georgia Atlanta
Germany (communist East Germany called the German Democratic Republic) East Berlin
Germany (Federal Republic of Germany also called West Germany) Bonn
Ghana Accra
Gibraltar Gibraltar
Greece Athens
Greenland Godthaab
Grenada St George's
Guadeloupe Basse-Terre
Guam Agaña
Guanajuato Guanajuato
Guatemala Guatemala City
Guernsey St Peter Port
Guerrero Chilpancingo
Guinea Conakry
Guinea-Bissau Bissau
Guyana Georgetown

Haiti Port-au-Prince
Hawaii Honolulu
Hidalgo Pachuca
Highlands Inverness, Scotland
Honduras Tegucigalpa
Hong Kong Victoria
Hungary Budapest
Iceland Reykjavik
Idaho Boise
Illinois Springfield
India New Delhi
Indiana Indianapolis
Indonesia Jakarta
Iowa Des Moines
Iran Teheran
Iraq Baghdad
Ireland Dublin
Isle of Man Douglas
Israel Jerusalem
Italy Rome
Ivory Coast Abidjan
Jalisco Guadalajara
Jamaica Kingston
Japan Tokyo
Jersey St Helier
Jordan Amman
Kampuchea Phnom Penh
Kansas Topeka
Kazakhstan Alma-Ata
Kentucky Frankfort
Kenya Nairobi
Kirghizia Frunze
Kiribati: Tarawa
Korea (communist North Korea called the Democratic People's Republic of Korea) Pyongyang
Korea (South Korea called the Republic of Korea) Seoul
Kuwait Kuwait
Laos Vientiane
Latvia Riga
Lebanon Beirut
Lesotho Maseru
Liberia Monrovia
Libya Tripoli
Liechtenstein Vaduz
Lithuania Vilnius
Louisiana Baton Rouge
Lower Saxony Hannover, Germany
Luxembourg Luxembourg
Madagascar Tananarive
Madeira Funchal
Maine Augusta
Malawi Lilongwe
Malaysia Kuala Lumpur
Maldives Malé
Mali Bamako
Malta Valetta
Manitoba Winnipeg
Martinique Fort-de-France
Maryland Annapolis
Massachusetts Boston
Mauritania Nouakchott
Mauritius Port Louis

Mexico Mexico City
Michigan Lansing
Michoacán Morelia
Minnesota Saint Paul
Mississippi Jackson
Missouri Jefferson City
Moldavia Kishinev
Monaco Monaco
Mongolia Ulan Bator
Montana Helena
Montserrat Plymouth
Morelos Cuernavaca
Morocco Rabat-Salé
Mozambique Maputo
Namibia Windhoek
Nauru Yaren
Nayarit Tepic
Nebraska Lincoln
Nepal Katmandu
Netherlands Amsterdam
Netherlands Antilles Willemstad
Nevada Carson City
New Brunswick Fredericton
New Caledonia Noumea
Newfoundland St John's
New Hampshire Concord
New Hebrides Fila or Vila (alternate spelling prevailing)
New Jersey Trenton
New Mexico Santa Fé
New South Wales Sydney
New York Albany
New Zealand Wellington
Nicaragua Managua
Niger Niamey
Nigeria Lagos
North Carolina Raleigh
North Dakota Bismarck
Northern Ireland Belfast
Norway Oslo
Nova Scotia Halifax
Nuevo León Monterrey
Oaxaca Oaxaca
Ohio Columbus
Oklahoma Oklahoma City
Old California Monterey
Oman Muscat
Ontario Toronto
Oregon Salem
Orkneys Kirkwall on Pomona Island
Pakistan Islamabad
Panamá Panamá City
Panama Canal Balboa Heights
Papua New Guinea Port Moresby
Paraguay Asunción
Pennsylvania Harrisburg
Peru Lima
Philippines Quezon City
Poland Warsaw
Portugal Lisbon
Portuguese China Macao
Prince Edward Island Charlottetown

Puebla Puebla
Puerto Rico San Juan
Quatar Doha
Québec Québec City
Queensland Brisbane
Querétaro Querétaro
Quintana Roo Chetumal
Reunion Saint-Denis
Rhode Island Providence
Romania Bucharest
RSFSR Moscow
Rwanda Kigali
Saint Helena Jamestown
Saint Kitts Basseterre
Saint Lucia Castries
Saint Pierre and Miquelon St Pierre
Saint Vincent Kingstown
Samoa Apia
San Luis Potosí San Luis Potosí
San Marino San Marino
São Tomé and Principe São Tomé
Sark La Collinette
Saskatchewan Regina
Saudi Arabia Riyadh
Scotland Edinburgh
Senegal Dakar
Seychelles Victoria
Sierra Leone Freetown
Sinaloa Culiacán
Singapore Singapore
Solomon Islands Honaira
Somalia Mogadishu
Sonora Hermosillo
South Africa Bloemfontein (judicial), Cape Town (legislative), Pretoria (administrative)
South Australia Adelaide
South Carolina Columbia
South Dakota Pierre
Soviet Armenia Erevan
Soviet Georgia Tiflis
Spain Madrid
Sri Lanka Colombo
State of México Toluca
Sudan Khartoum
Surinam Paramaribo
Swaziland Mbabane
Sweden Stockholm
Switzerland Bern
Syria Damascus
Tabasco Villa Hermosa
Tadzhikistan Dushanbe
Tamaulipas Ciudad Victoria
Tanzania Dar-es-Salaam
Tasmania Hobart
Tennessee Nashville
Texas Austin
Thailand Bangkok
Tlaxcala Tlaxcala
Togo Lomé
Tonga Nuku'Alofa
Transkei Umtata

Trinidad and Tobago Port-of-
Spain
Trust Territory of the Pacific
Saipan
Tunisia Tunis
Turkey Ankara
Turkmenistan Ashkhabad
Turks and Caicos Islands Grand
Turk
Tuvalu Funafuti
Uganda Kampala
Ukraine Kiev
United Arab Emirates Abu Dha-
bi
United Kingdom London
Upper Volta Ouagadougou
Uruguay Montevideo

U.S.A. Washington, DC
USSR Moscow
Utah Salt Lake City
Uzbekistan Tashkent
Vatican City Rome
Venezuela Caracas
Veracruz Jalapa
Vermont Montpelier
Victoria Melbourne
Vietnam Hanoi
Virginia Richmond
Virgin Islands Charlotte Amal-
ie
Wales Cardiff
Washington Olympia
Western Australia Perth
Western Kentucky Paducah

Westphalia Münster, Germany
West Virginia Charleston
Wisconsin Madison
Wyoming Cheyenne
Yemen (Arab Republic) Sana
Yemen (communist-dominated
People's Democratic Republic
of South Yemen) Aden
Yucatán Mérida
Yugoslavia Belgrade
Yukon Whitehorse
Zacatecas Zacatecas
Zaire Kinshasa
Zambia Lusaka
Zimbabwe Salisbury

C-B (Citizen's-Band) Radio Frequency Shortwave Call Signs

10-1 receiving you poorly
10-2 receiving you well
10-3 stop transmitting, channel in use
10-4 OK, message received
10-5 relay message
10-6 busy, can't talk now, stand by
10-7 out of service; going off air
10-8 in service, subject to call, working well
10-9 repeat message
10-10 transmission completed, standing by
10-11 talking too rapidly
10-12 visitors are present
10-13 advise weather, road conditions
10-14 time by the clock
10-16 make pickup at
10-17 urgent business
10-18 anything for us?
10-19 nothing for you, return to base
10-20 my location is:
10-21 contact me by phone
10-22 make personal contact with
10-23 standby
10-24 assignment completed
10-25 contact another station by radio
10-26 disregard last transmission
10-27 I am moving to channel

10-28 identify your station
10-29 time is up for contact
10-30 violates regulations
10-31 no longer in violation of regulations
10-32 I will advise re signal readability
10-33 EMERGENCY TRAFFIC AT THIS STATION
10-34 TROUBLE AT THIS STATION, HELP NEEDED
10-35 matter of urgency but cannot discuss it by radio
10-36 transmission or event is scheduled for
10-37 send tow truck
10-38 ambulance needed at
10-39 your message was delivered
10-41 please tune to channel
10-42 traffic accident at
10-43 traffic congestion at
10-44 I have a message for
10-45 stations on this channel please identify
10-46 assist motorist
10-50 break channel
10-55 intoxicated driver
10-60 what is next message number?
10-62 unable to copy, use phone
10-63 network directed to
10-64 network is clear
10-65 awaiting your next message

10-66 cancel message
10-67 all units comply
10-68 repeat message
10-69 message received
10-70 fire at
10-71 proceed with transmission in sequence
10-73 speed trap at
10-74 negative
10-75 you are causing interference
10-77 negative contact
10-81 reserve hotel room for
10-82 reserve room for
10-84 my telephone number is
10-85 my address is
10-88 advise phone number of
10-89 radio repairman needed at
10-90 I have tv interference
10-91 talk closer to mike
10-92 your transmitter is out of adjustment
10-93 check my frequency on this channel
10-94 please give me a long count
10-95 transmit dead carrier for 5 seconds
10-97 check test signal
10-99 mission completed, all units secure
10-100 rest-room stop
10-200 police needed at

Chemical Element Symbols, Atomic Numbers, and Discovery Data

Symbol	Element	Atomic Number	Discovered
Ac	actinium	89	1899 by Debierne
Ag	silver (*argentum*)	47	Before the Christian Era
Al	aluminum	13	1825 by Oersted
Am	americium	95	1944 by Seborg and others
Ar or A	argon	18	1894 by Raleigh and Ramsay
As	arsenic	33	13th century by Magnus
As	astatine	85	1940 by Corson and others
Au	gold (*aurum*)	79	Before the Christian Era
B	boron	5	1808 by Davy
Ba	barium	56	1808 by Davy
Be	beryllium	4	1798 by Vauquelin
Bi	bismuth	83	15th century by Valentine
Bk	berkelium	97	1949 by Thompson, Ghiorso, and Seborg
Br	bromine	35	1826 by Balard
C	carbon	6	Before the Christian Era
Ca	calcium	20	1808 by Davy
Cd	cadmium	48	1817 by Stromeyer
Ce	cerium	58	1803 by Klaproth
Cf	californium	98	1950 by Thompson and others
Cl	chlorine	17	1774 by Scheele
Cm	curium	96	1944 by Seborg and others
Co	cobalt	27	1735 by Brandt
Cr	chromium	24	1797 by Vauquelin
Cs	cesium	55	1861 by Bunsen and Kirchoff
Cu	copper (*cuprum*)	29	Before the Christian Era
Dy	dysprosium	66	1886 by Boisbaudran
Er	erbium	68	1843 by Mosander
Es	einsteinium	99	1952 by Ghiorso and others
Eu	europium	63	1901 by Demarcay
F	fluorine	9	1771 by Scheele
Fe	iron (*ferrum*)	26	Before the Christian Era
Fm	fermium	100	1953 by Ghiorso and others
Fr	francium	87	1939 by Perey
Ga	gallium	31	1875 by Boisbaudran
Gd	gadolinium	64	1886 by Marignac
Ge	germanium	32	1886 by Winkler
H	hydrogen	1	1766 by Cavendish
Ha	hahnium	105	1970 by Ghiorso and others
He	helium	2	1895 by Ramsay
Hf	hafnium	72	1923 by Coster and Hevesy
Hg	mercury (*hydrargyrum*)	80	Before the Christian Era
Ho	holmium	67	1879 by Cleve
I	iodine	53	1811 by Courtois

In	indium	49	1863 by Reich and Richter
Ir	iridium	77	1804 by Tennant
K	potassium (*kalium*)	19	1807 by Davy
Kr	krypton	36	1898 by Ramsay and Travers
La	lanthanum	57	1839 by Mosander
Li	lithium	3	1817 by Arfvedson
Lu	lutetium	71	1907 by Welsbach and Urbain
Lw	lawrencium	103	1961 by Ghiorso and others
Md	mendelevium	101	1955 by Ghiorso and others
Mg	magnesium	12	1830 by Bussy and Liebig
Mn	manganese	25	1774 by Gahn
Mo	molybdenum	42	1782 by Hjelm
N	nitrogen	7	1772 by Rutherford
Na	sodium	11	1807 by Davy
Nb	niobium (formerly columbium)	41	1801 by Hatchett
Nd	neodymium	60	1885 by Welsbach
Ne	neon	10	1898 by Ramsay and Travers
Ni	nickel	28	1751 by Cronstedt
No	nobelium	102	1958 by Ghiorso and others
Np	neptunium	93	1940 by Abelson and McMillan
O	oxygen	8	1774 by Priestley and Scheele
Os	osmium	76	1804 by Tennant
P	phosphorus	15	1669 by Brandt
Pa	protactinium	91	1917 by Hahn and Meitner
Pb	lead (*plumbum*)	82	Before the Christian Era
Pd	palladium	46	1803 by Wollaston
Pm	promethium	61	1945 by Glendenin and Marinsky
Po	polonium	84	1898 by P. and M. Curie
Pr	praseodymium	59	1885 by Welsbach
Pt	platinum	78	1735 by Ulloa
Pu	plutonium	94	1940 by Seborg and others
Ra	radium	88	1898 by P. and M. Curie
Rb	rubidium	37	1861 by Bunsen and Kirchoff
Re	rhenium	75	1925 by Noddack and Tacke
Rf	rutherfordium	104	1969 by Ghiorso and others
Rh	rhodium	45	1803 by Wollaston
Rn	radon	86	1900 by Dorn
Ru	ruthenium	44	1845 by Claus
S	sulfur	16	Before the Christian Era
Sb	antimony (*stibium*)	51	1450 by Valentine
Sc	scandium	21	1879 by Nilson
Se	selenium	34	1817 by Berzelius
Si	silicon	14	1823 by Berzelius
Sm	samarium	62	1879 by Boisbaudran
Sn	tin (*stannum*)	50	Before the Christian Era
Sr	strontium	38	1790 by Crawford
Ta	tantalum	73	1802 by Eckeberg
Tb	terbium	65	1843 by Mosander
Tc	technetium	43	1937 by Perrier and Segre
Te	tellurium	52	1782 by von Reichenstein
Th	thorium	90	1828 by Berzelius
Ti	titanium	22	1789 by Gregor

Tl	thallium	81	1861 by Crookes
Tm	thulium	69	1879 by Cleve
U	uranium	92	1789 by Klaproth
V	vanadium	23	1830 by Sefström
W	tungsten (wolfram)	74	1783 by d'Elhuyar brothers
Xe	xenon	54	1898 by Ramsay and Travers
Y	yttrium	39	1794 by Gadolin
Yb	ytterbium	70	1878 by Marignac
Zn	zinc	30	Before the Christian Era
Zr	zirconium	40	1789 by Klaproth

Civil and Military Time Systems Compared

Civil	Military		Civil	Military
12.01 A.M.	= 0001		12.01 P.M.	= 1201
12.02 A.M.	= 0002		12.02 P.M.	= 1202
12.03 A.M.	= 0003		12.03 P.M.	= 1203
12.04 A.M.	= 0004		12.04 P.M.	= 1204
12.05 A.M.	= 0005		12.05 P.M.	= 1205
12.15 A.M.	= 0015		12.15 P.M.	= 1215
12.30 A.M.	= 0030		12.30 P.M.	= 1230
12.45 A.M.	= 0045		12.45 P.M.	= 1245
1.00 A.M.	= 0100		1.00 P.M.	= 1300
1.15 A.M.	= 0115		1.15 P.M.	= 1315
1.30 A.M.	= 0130		1.30 P.M.	= 1330
1.45 A.M.	= 0145		1.45 P.M.	= 1345
2.00 A.M.	= 0200		2.00 P.M.	= 1400
3.00 A.M.	= 0300		3.00 P.M.	= 1500
4.00 A.M.	= 0400		4.00 P.M.	= 1600
5.00 A.M.	= 0500		5.00 P.M.	= 1700
6.00 A.M.	= 0600		6.00 P.M.	= 1800
7.00 A.M.	= 0700		7.00 P.M.	= 1900
8.00 A.M.	= 0800		8.00 P.M.	= 2000
9.00 A.M.	= 0900		9.00 P.M.	= 2100
10.00 A.M.	= 1000		10.00 P.M.	= 2200
11.00 A.M.	= 1100		11.00 P.M.	= 2300
12.00 noon	= 1200		12.00 midnight	= 2400

Climatic Region Symbols

Typical Climatological Regional Divisions Worldwide

Climatic Symbols	Climatic Regions	
Af Am	*Tropical Rainforest*	Tropical rainforests of the Amazon and Middle America from southern Mexico to Colombia and the West Indies; Congo and the Guinea Coast of Africa; jungles of Ceylon, India, Indonesia, Madagascar, Malaya, the Philippines, Southeast Asia
Aw	*Tropical Dry and Wet*	Grassy savannas of Middle America; llanos of eastern Colombia and southern Venezuela; campos of south-central Brazil; damp lowland savannas of Africa and its dry uplands; plains of northern Australia, Burma, India, Pakistan, Southeast Asia
Bsk Bwk	*Midlatitude Dry*	Great plains and prairies of Canada and the United States; arid plains of Patagonia; pampas of Argentina, Bolivia, Paraguay, and Uruguay; Gobi and Takla Makan desert dunes of Asia; Kirghizian steppe of Turkestan; Ukrainian steppe
Bwh	*Tropical Dry*	Afghan, Arabian, Atacaman, Australian, Kalihari, Sahara, Somali, Sonoran, and other subtropical and tropical desertlands of the world
Caf	*Humid Subtropical*	Southeastern United States; northern Argentina; southern Brazil, Paraguay, Uruguay; southeast Africa; southeastern China; southern Japan; eastern Australia
Cfb	*West Coast Marine*	Pacific Northwest of Canada and the United States; southern Chile; west coast of Norway and south coast of Sweden; British Isles and northwestern Europe including northern Spain; south coast of South Africa; southeast coast of Australia; New Zealand
Csa	*Mediterranean Subtropical*	Southern California; central Chile; Mediterranean region including Portugal and most of Spain, southern France, Italy, Yugoslavia, Albania, Greece, Turkey, parts of Morocco and Algeria, much of Israel; Cape of Good Hope area around Cape Town, South Africa
Daf	*Humid Continental*	Southern Canada and the northeastern United States plus much of the Midwest; much of the Soviet Union and the eastern section of China
Dcf	*Continental Subarctic*	Alaska and northern Canada; Siberia and the northern USSR from the Arctic Ocean to the North Pacific Ocean
E	*Tundra*	Arctic coasts of Alaska, Canada, Greenland, northernmost Europe and Asia from northern Norway to easternmost Siberia
Ef	*Polar Icecap*	Interior of Greenland; Antarctica's northernmost tip
H	*Highland*	High valleys and mountainous areas of the world where climatic conditions are so variable they almost defy classification

Climatic Symbols Explained

A	Hot and moist equatorial or tropical climate
B	Dry climate with evaporation greater than precipitation
C	Moist and warm with well-defined summer and winter seasons
D	Cold and snowy subarctic with northern boundary the northern limit of forest growth—the taiga

E	Ice climates of the icecaps where ice and snow are perpetual or of the tundra where the growing season above the permafrost is very short
H	Highland climates in mountainous regions where weather conditions are extremely variable and difficult to classify
a	Long and hot summers
b	Short and wet winters
c	Cool or short and moderate summers
d	Very cold and dry winters
f	Moist the year around
h	Hot and moist most of the year
k	Cold and dry most of the year
m	Monsoon conditions
s	Dry summers and wet winters
w	Wet summers and dry winters

Diacritical and Punctuation Marks

´ acute accent (as in Bogotá)

’ apostrophe; single quotation mark

[ ] brackets

˘ breve

cedilla (as in Curacao)

^ circumflex (as in *rôle*)

: colon

) close parenthesis

, comma

¨ diaeresis (as in München)

. . . or . . . .

ellipsis; leaders

! exclamation point

` grave accent (as in *funèbre*)

- hyphen

? interrogation or question mark

¯ macron (dictionary pronunciation symbol indicating long vowel, as in dāme)

(open parenthesis

( ) parentheses

. period

" " quotation marks; quotes

' ' quotation marks, single

; semicolon

˜ tilde (as in São Paulo)

‾ vinculum (mathematics: placed above letters)

Dysphemistic Place-Names

Accident, Maryland
Atomic City, Idaho
Bad Axe, Missouri
Blue Ball, Pennsylvania
Braggadocio, Missouri
Cactus, Texas
Clam Gulch, Alaska
Cranks, Kentucky
Death Valley, California
Decoy, Kentucky
Dime Box, Texas
D'Lo, Mississippi
Dogpatch, Arkansas
Due West, South Carolina
Dusty, New Mexico
Embarrass, Minnesota
Eros, Louisiana
False Pass, Alaska
Fate, Texas
Fixer, Kentucky
French Lick, Indiana
Frogmore, Louisiana or South Carolina
Frozen Creek, Kentucky
Gap, Pennsylvania

Gas, Kansas
Graves, Georgia
Hanging Rock, Ohio
Hell, Michigan
Hell Gate, New York
Hell's Half Acre, Wyoming
Hemp, Georgia
Hungry Horse, Montana
Hygiene, Colorado
Intercourse, Pennsylvania (near Blue Ball)
Justiceburg, Texas
Kettle, Kentucky
Loco, Oklahoma
Mousie, Kentucky
Mud Lick, Kentucky
Nutsville, Virginia
Ordinary, Virginia
Panther Burn, Mississippi
Peculiar, Missouri
Pickleville, Utah
Pie Town, New Mexico
Plaster City, California
Porcupine, South Dakota
Quicksand, Kentucky

Rains, South Carolina
Shady, New York
Slick, Oklahoma
Smoketown, Pennsylvania
Speculator, New York
Stab, Kentucky
Stumptown, West Virginia
Tall Timbers, Maryland
Temperance, Michigan
Tiplersville, Mississippi
Tobaccoville, North Carolina
Tombstone, Arizona
Trussville, Alabama
Truth or Consequences, New Mexico
Turtletown, Tennessee
Uncertain, Texas
Vesuvius, Virginia
Volcano, California or Hawaii
Whiskeytown, California
X-ray, Texas
Yucca, Arizona
Zigzag, Oregon (former name of Rhodadendron)

Earthquake Data (Richter Scale)

The Richter Scale, devised in 1935 by Dr Charles Francis Richter, seismologist of the California Institute of Technology, is a standardized scale for defining the destructive energy of earthquakes whose force is measured by seismographs. The magnitude of such earthquakes is the logarithm of the largest deflection measured and registered during an earthquake when a seismograph is 100 kilometers (62 miles) from the center of maximum shock, the epicenter of the earthquake, whose exact location is pinpointed by several scattered seismographs.

Numbers of the Richter Scale advance logarithmically and not arithmetically, so earthquakes measuring 8, for example, are ten times greater than those measuring 7, and this relationship is constant throughout the scale.

Earthquakes occurring before 1935, or before the invention of the seismograph in 1841, are approximated in terms of the Richter Scale.

Earthquake Damage and Intensity Devastation Effects Encountered Historically

0   No detectable or measurable earthquake effect although about 100,000 quakes a year can be felt and at least 1000 cause some damage

1   Very slight earthquake effects felt by sensitive persons who may experience dizziness or nausea; other creatures may appear disturbed; gentle swaying may affect bodies of water as well as buildings and trees

2   Slight earthquake effects sensed by sensitive persons as well as other creatures who display uneasiness; hanging lamps and pictures swing slightly; buildings and trees sway slightly

3   Very moderate earthquake effects sensed by a few persons as well as by the most nervous and the most sensitive; dishes on shelves may rattle as may many windows; canned goods stored on shelves may rattle and may fall off; parked vehicles may rock and this is true of shrubs and trees

4   Moderate earthquake sensed by many and sufficient to awaken light sleepers; house frames creak and houses sway slightly; shrubs and trees tremble; parked vehicles may rock and sway

5   Near medium-strength earthquake felt by everyone and frightening most persons who tend to leave buildings and run out of doors to avoid cracking ceilings and crumbling walls; in older buildings plaster falls, ceilings crack, and windows break; pictures may fall off their hangings; dishes and glasses tumble off shelves; heavy desks and tables move and many may topple; old and weak chimneys may crack off at the roofline; ornamental cornices fall from buildings; church bells toll by themselves

6   Full-strength earthquake causing general fright approaching panic; stone walls crack; steep slopes and riverbanks crack; chimneys and towers may crack apart and fall; trees shake violently and often fall as do limbs; the Los Angeles Earthquake of 1971 measured 6.6, caused considerable damage, and took the lives of some 60 persons

7   More devastating and more severe type of earthquake such as occurred in Nicaragua and Guatemala where thousands were killed in 1972 and 1976, respectively; or in the Chile Quake of 1906, preceding the San Francisco Earthquake and Fire by only two days, and causing the loss of 1550 lives in Valparaiso and 452 in San Francisco, both seismic disturbances were calculated in later years as representing 7.8 on the Richter Scale

8   Still more devastating and more severe earthquake causing general panic and marked by widespread land and water disturbances; many dams and dikes break, discharging vast volumes of flooding water; underground cables and pipelines crack and tear apart; railway rails bend and twist; brick, glass, and masonry facades peel off buildings and endanger people as they fall to the ground; loss of life quite severe as in the Peruvian Quake of 1970, accounting for the loss of some 50,000 persons, or the Alaska Quake of 1964, reported as 8.4 on the scale, and marked by heavy damage in downtown Anchorage where 131 lost their lives; earthquakes of even greater magnitude occurred in Lisbon, Portugal in 1755 when 60,000 were lost and lakes in far off Norway were disturbed violently; the Shensi Province Quake, occurring in China in 1566, cost some 830,000 lives, calculated to have been 8.9 on the Richter Scale as was Japan's great quake of 1923, destroying all of Yokohama and half of Tokyo, as well as 143,000 people; the sea bottom in Sagami Bay sank 387 meters or 1300

feet; earthquakes of this magnitude afflicted New Madrid, Missouri in 1811, Charleston, South Carolina in 1886, and are predicted as long overdue along the San Andreas Fault Zone of California extending from below the Mexican Border to San Francisco and northward; overall damage might well equal or exceed the Shinsai or Great Quake felt around Tokyo in 1923; Chinese earthquake of July 26, 1976 registered 8.2 with a 7.9 aftershock the following day; shocks affected an area in and around Peking and Tientsin and some 15 million people

9 Most devastating and most intense earthquakes, as yet unrecorded on any scale, top of the Richter Scale, extending from 0 to 9, and may never occur due to the good effects of minor earthquakes and tremors, providing stress-relief cracking of and easing the great tectonic energy tension beneath us

Fishing Port Registration Symbols (Distinguishing Letters)

England

AB	Aberystwith	GR	Gloucester	PZ	Penzance
BD	Bideford	GY	Grimsby	R	Ramsgate
BE	Barnstaple	HH	Harwich	RN	Runcorn
BH	Blyth	HL	Hartlepool, West	RR	Rochester
BK	Berwick-on-Tweed	IH	Ipswich	RX	Rye
BL	Bristol	LA	Llanelly	SA	Swansea
BM	Brixham	LI	Littlehampton	SC	Scilly
BN	Boston	LL	Liverpool	SD	Sunderland
BR	Briggwater	LN	Lynn	SE	Salcombe
BS	Beaumaris	LO	London	SH	Scarborough
BW	Barrow	LR	Lancaster	SM	Shoreham
CA	Cardigan	LT	Lowestoft	SN	Shields, North
CF	Cardiff	M	Milford	SS	St. Ives
CH	Chester	MH	Middlesbrough	SSS	Shields, South
CK	Colchester	MN	Maldon	ST	Stockton
CL	Carlisle	MR	Manchester	SU	Southhampton
CO	Carnarvon	MT	Maryport	TH	Teignmouth
CS	Cowes	NE	Newcastle	TO	Truro
DH	Dartmouth	NN	Newhaven	WA	Whitehaven
DR	Dover	NT	Newport, Mon.	WH	Weymouth
E	Exeter	P	Portsmouth	WI	Wisbech
FD	Fleetwood	PE	Poole	WO	Workington
FE	Folkstone	PH	Plymouth	WY	Whitby
FH	Falmouth	PN	Preston	YH	Yarmouth (Norfolk)
FY	Fowey	PT	Port Talbot		
GE	Goole	PW	Padstow		

Northern Ireland

B	Belfast	LY	Londonderry
CE	Coleraine	N	Newry

Republic of Ireland

C	Cork	G	Galway	T	Tralee
D	Dublin	L	Limerick	W	Waterford
DA	Drogheda	S	Skibbereen	WD	Wexford
DK	Dundalk	SO	Sligo	WT	Westport

Greek Alphabet

ALPHA	A	α	IOTA	I	ι	RHO	P	ρ
BETA	B	β	KAPPA	K	κ	SIGMA	Σ	σ
GAMMA	Γ	γ	LAMBDA	Λ	λ	TAU	T	τ
DELTA	Δ	δ	MU	M	μ	UPSILON	Υ	υ
EPSILON	E	ϵ	NU	N	ν	PHI	Φ	ϕ
ZETA	Z	ζ	XI	Ξ	ξ	CHI	X	χ
ETA	H	η	OMICRON	O	o	PSI	Ψ	ψ
THETA	Θ	θ	PI	Π	π	OMEGA	Ω	ω

International Civil Aircraft Markings

AN Nicaragua
AP Pakistan
B Formosa
CB Bolivia
CC Chile
CCCP Soviet Union (USSR)
CF Canada
CR; CS Portugal and colonies
CU Cuba
CX Uruguay
CZ Principality of Monaco
D Western Germany
EC Spain
EI; EJ Ireland
EL Liberia
EP Iran
ET Ethiopia
F France and French Union
G United Kingdom
HA Hungary
HB Switzerland
HC Ecuador
HH Haiti
HI Dominican Republic
HK Colombia
HL Korea
HS Thailand
HZ Saudi Arabia
I Italy

JA Japan
JY Jordan
LN Norway
LV Argentine Republic
LX Luxembourg
LZ Bulgaria
MC Monte Carlo
N United States of America
OB Peru
OD Lebanon
OE Austria
OH Finland
OK Czechoslovakia
OO Belgium
OY Denmark
PH Netherlands
PI Philippine Republic
PJ Curaçao (Netherlands Antilles)
PK Indonesia
PP; PT Brazil
PZ Surinam (Netherlands Guiana)
RX Republic of Panama
SE Sweden
SN Sudan
SP Poland
SU Egypt
SX Greece

TC Turkey
TF Iceland
TG Guatemala
TI Costa Rica
VH Australia
VP; VQ, VR British Colonies and Protectorates
VT India
XA; XB; XC Mexico
XH Honduras
XT China (Nationalist)
XY; XZ Burma
YA Afghanistan
YE Yemen
YI Iraq
YK Syria
YR Romania
YS El Salvador
YU Yugoslavia
YV Venezuela
ZA Albania
ZK; ZL; ZM New Zealand
ZP Paraguay
ZS; ZT; ZU Union of South Africa
$_4$R Ceylon
$_4$X Israel
$_5$A Libya
$_9$G Ghana

International Conversions Simplified

area

a (acres)	x	0.4	=	ha (hectares)
cm^2 (square centimeters)	x	0.16	=	in.^{2} (square inches)
ft^2 (square feet)	x	0.09	=	m^2 (square meters)
ha (hectares)	x	2.5	=	a (acres)
in.^{2} (square inches)	x	6.5	=	cm^2 (square centimeters)
km^2 (square kilometers)	x	0.4	=	mi^2 (square miles)
m^2 (square meters)	x	1.2	=	yd^2 (square yards)
mi^2 (square miles)	x	2.6	=	km^2 (square kilometers)
yd^2 (square yards)	x	0.8	=	m^2 (square meters)

length

cm (centimeters)	x	0.4 =	in. (inches)	
ft (feet)	x	30.0 =	cm (centimeters)	
in. (inches)	x	2.54* =	cm (centimeters)	*exactly
km (kilometers)	x	0.6 =	mi (miles)	
m (meters)	x	3.3 =	ft (feet)	
m (meters)	x	1.1 =	yd (yards)	
mi (miles)	x	1.6 =	km (kilometers)	
mm (millimeters)	x	0.04 =	in. (inches)	
yd (yards)	x	0.9 =	m (meters)	

temperature (exact)

C (degrees Celsius or centigrade)	x	9/5 +	32 = F (degrees Fahrenheit)
F (degrees Fahrenheit)	−	32 x	5/9 = C (degrees Celsius or centigrade)

volume

cups	x	0.24 =	l (liters)
fl oz (fluid ounces)	x	30.00 =	ml (milliliters)
ft^3 (cubic feet)	x	0.03 =	m^3 (cubic meters)
gal (British Imperial gallons)	x	4.6 =	l (liters)
gal (U.S. gallons)	x	3.8 =	l (liters)
l (liters)	x	2.1 =	pt (pints)
l (liters)	x	1.06 =	qt (quarts)
l (liters)	x	0.22 =	gal (British Imperial gallons)
l (liters)	x	0.26 =	gal (gallons)
m^3 (cubic meters)	x	35.00 =	ft^3 (cubic feet)
m^3 (cubic meters)	x	1.3 =	yd^3 (cubic yards)
ml (milliliters)	x	0.03 =	fl oz (fluid ounces)
pt (pints)	x	0.47 =	l (liters)
qt (quarts)	x	0.95 =	l (liters)
tbsp (tablespoons)	x	15.00 =	ml (milliliters)
tsp (teaspoons)	x	5.00 =	ml (milliliters)
yd^3 (cubic yards)	x	0.76 =	m^3 (cubic meters)

weight

g (grams)	x	0.035 =	oz (ounces)
kg (kilograms)	x	2.2 =	lb (pounds)
lb (pounds)	x	0.45 =	kg (kilograms)
oz (ounces)	x	28.00 =	g (grams)
st (short tons—2000 pounds)	x	0.9 =	t (tonnes)
t (tonnes—1000 kilograms)	x	1.1 =	st (short tons)

International Radio Alphabet and Code

A Alpha . _	J Juliet . _ _ _	S Sierra . . .
B Bravo _ . . .	K Kilo _ . _	T Tango _
C Charlie _ . _ .	L Lima (leema) . _ . .	U Uniform . . _
D Delta _ . .	M Mike _ _	V Victor . . . _
E Echo .	N November _ .	W Whiskey . _ _
F Foxtrot . . _ .	O Oscar _ _ _	X Xray _ . . _
G Golf _ _ .	P Papa . _ _ .	Y Yankee _ . _ _
H Hotel	Q Quebec (kaybeck) _ _ . _	Z Zulu _ _ . .
I India . .	R Romeo . _ .	

0 (zee-ro) _ _ _ _ _	4 (fo-wer) . . . . _	7 (sev-ven) _ _ . . .
1 (wun) . _ _ _ _	5 (fi-yiv)	8 (ate) _ _ _ . .
2 (too) . . _ _ _	6 (siks) _	9 (ni-yen) _ _ _ _ .
3 (thuh-ree) . . . _ _		

International Vehicle License Letters

A Austria
ADN Aden (South Yemen, Peoples' Democratic Republic of Yemen)
AFG Afghanistan
AL Albania
AND Andorra
AUS Australia
B Belgium
BD Bangladesh
BDS Barbados
BG Bulgaria
BH Belize (formerly, British Honduras)
BR Brazil
BRN Bahrain
BRU Brunei
BS Bahamas
BT Botswana
BV Bolivia
BUR Burma
C Cuba
CDN Canada
CH Switzerland
CI Ivory Coast
CL Sri Lanka
CO Colombia
CR Costa Rica
CS Czechoslovakia
CU Curaçao
CY Cyprus
D West Germany
DDR East Germany
DK Denmark
DOM Dominican Republic
DY Benin
DZ Algeria
E Spain (España)
EAK Kenya
EAT Tanzania
EAU Uganda
EC Ecuador
ES El Salvador
ET Egypt
F France
FJI Fiji
FL Liechtenstein
FR Faeroc Islands
GB Great Britain
GBA Alderney
GBG Guernsey

GBJ Jersey
GBM Isle of Man
GBZ Gibraltar
GCA Guatemala
GH Ghana
GR Greece
GUY Guyana
HN Honduras
H Hungary
HK Hong Kong
I Italy
IL Israel
IND India
IR Iran
IRL Ireland
IRQ Iraq
IS Iceland
J Japan
JA Jamaica
K Kampuchea
KWT Kuwait
L Luxembourg
LAO Laos
LAR Libya
LB Liberia
LS Lesotho
M Malta
MA Morocco
MAL Malaysia
MC Monaco
MEX Mexico
MS Mauritius
MW Malawi
N Norway
NA Netherlands Antilles
NIC Nicaragua
NL Netherlands
NZ New Zealand
P Portugal
PA Panama
PAK Pakistan
PE Peru
PL Poland
PNG Papua New Guinea
PY Paraguay
R Romania
RA Argentina
RC Taiwan
RCA Central African Republic
RCB Congo
RCH Chile

RH Haiti
RI Indonesia
RIM Mauritania
RL Lebanon
RM Madagascar
RMM Mali
RN Niger
ROK Korea
RP Philippines
RSM San Marino
RSR Zimbabwe
RU Burundi
RWA Rwanda
S Sweden
SD Swaziland
SF Finland
SGP Singapore
SME Suriname
SN Senegal
SP Somalia
SU Soviet Union (USSR)
SY Seychelles
SYR Syria
T Thailand
TC Cameroon
TG Togo
TN Tunisia
TR Turkey
TT Trinidad and Tobago
U Uruguay
USA United States of America
V Vatican
VN Vietnam
WAG Gambia
WAL Sierra Leone
WAN Nigeria
WD Dominica
WG Grenada
WL Saint Lucia
WS Western Samoa
WV Saint Vincent
YMN North Yemen (Yemen Arab Republic)
YU Yugoslavia
YV Venezuela
Z Zambia
ZA South Africa
ZA South-West Africa (Namibia)
ZRE Zaire

International Yacht Racing Union Nationality Codes

Every yacht of an international class recognized by the International Yacht Racing Union must carry on her mainsail, when *racing* in foreign waters, a letter or letters showing her nationality.

A Argentina
AR United Arab Republic
B Belgium
BA Bahamas
BL Brazil
BU Bulgaria
CA Cambodia
CY Ceylon
CZ Czechoslovakia
D Denmark
E Spain
EC Ecuador
F France
G West Germany
GO East Germany
GR Greece
H Holland
HA Netherlands Antilles
I Italy
IR Republic of Ireland
K United Kingdom
KA Australia
KB Bermuda

KC Canada
KG Guyana
KGB Gibraltar
KH Hong Kong
KI India
KJ Jamaica
KK Kenya
KR Zambia, Malawi, Zimbabwe
KS Singapore
KT West Indies
KZ New Zealand
L Finland
LE Lebanon
LX Luxembourg
M Hungary
MA Morocco
MO Monaco
MX Mexico
N Norway
NK Democratic People's Republic of Korea
OE Austria

P Portugal
PH Philippines
PR Puerto Rico
PU Peru
PZ Poland
RC Cuba
RI Indonesia
RM Romania
S Sweden
SA South Africa
SE Senegal
SR Union of Soviet Socialist Republics
T Tunisia
TH Thailand
TK Turkey
U Uruguay
US United States of America
V Venezuela
X Chile
Y Yugoslavia
Z Switzerland

Irish Counties Abbreviated

Republic of Ireland

Car County Carlow
Cav County Cavan
Clare County Clare
Cork County Cork
Don County Donegal
Dub County Dublin
Gal County Galway
Ker County Kerry

Kild County Kildare
Kilk County Kilkenny
Leit County Leitrim
Leix County Leix
Lim County Limerick
Long County Longford
Louth County Louth
Mayo County Mayo
Meath County Meath
Monag County Monaghan

Off County Offaly
Ros County Roscommon
Sligo County Sligo
Tipp County Tipperary
Wat County Waterford
Westmeath County Westmeath
Wex County Wexford
Wick County Wicklow

Mexican State Names and Abbreviations

Ags Aguascalientes (inhabitants called Hidrocalidos)
BC Baja California (Baja Californianos)
BC Front Baja California Fronteriza (Frontier Baja California)
BC Sur Baja California Sur (Baja California South)

Cam Campeche (Campechanos)
Chih Chihuahua (Chihuahuenses)
Chis Chiapas (Chiapanecos)
Coah Coahuila (Coahuileños or Coahuilenses)
Col Colima (Colimenses)
DF Distrito Federal (Federal District around Mexico City;

Capitolinos)
Dgo Durango (Durangueños or Duranguenses or Durangueses)
Gro Guerrero (Guerreros)
Gto Guanajauto (Guanajuatos)
Hgo Hidalgo (Hidalgos)
Jal Jalisco (Jaliscienses)
Méx México (Mexicanos)

Mich Michoacán (Michoaca-
nos)
Mor Morelos (Morelianos)
Nay Nayarit (Nayaritos)
NL Nuevo León (Nuevo
Leones)
Oax Oaxaca (Oaxaqueños)
Pue Puebla (Poblanos)

Qro Querétero (Queretanos)
Q Roo Quintana Roo (Quintana
Roenses)
Sin Sinaloa (Sinaloenses)
SLP San Luís Potosí (Potis-
eños)
Son Sonora (Sonorenses)
Tab Tabasco (Tabasqueños)

Tam Tamaulipas (Tamaulipe-
cos)
Tlax Tlaxcala (Tlaxcaltecas)
Ver Veracruz (Veracruzanos)
Yuc Yucatán (Yucatecos)
Zac Zacatecas (Zacatecos)

Nations of the World and Nationalities

Afghanistan (inhabited by)
Afghans
Albania Albanians
Algeria Algerians
Andorra Andorrans
Angola Angolans
Argentina Argentines or Argen-
tinos
Australia Australians
Austria Austrians
Bahamas Bahamians or Lu-
cayans
Bahrain Bahraini
Bangledesh Bengalees
Barbados Barbadians
Belgium Belgians
Belize Belizians
Benin Beninois
Bermuda Bermudans
Bhutan Bhutanese
Bolivia Bolivianos or Bolivians
Botswana Botswana or Botswa-
nians
Brazil Brasileiros or Brazilians
Bulgaria Bulgarians
Burma Burmans
Burundi Burundians
Cambodia Cambodians, Kam-
pucheans, or Khmers
Cameroon Cameroonians
Canada Canadians or Cana-
diens
Cape Verde Islands Cape Verde
Islanders
Central African Empire Central
Africans
Chad Chadians
Chile Chileans or Chilenos
China Chinese
Colombia Colombianos or Co-
lombians
Comoros Comorans
Congo Congolese
Costa Rica Costa Ricans
Cuba Cubanos or Cubans
Cyprus Cypriots
Czechoslovakia Czechoslova-
kians or Czechs
Dahomey Dahomians
Denmark Danes
Djibouti Djibouti or Djibutians

Domimica Dominicans
Dominican Republic Dominica-
nos or Dominicans or Quis-
queanos
Ecuador Ecuadoreans or Ecuato-
rianos
Egypt Egyptians
El Salvador Salvadoreans or Sal-
vadoreños
Equatorial Guinea Equatorial
Guineans
Estonia Estonians
Ethiopia Ethiopians
Fiji Fijians
Finland Finns
France French
French Guiana French Guia-
nese
French Polynesia French Poly-
nesians
Gabon Gabonese
Gambia Gambians
Germany Germans
Ghana Ghanians
Gibraltar Gibraltarians
Greece Greeks
Grenada Grenadans
Guadeloupe Guadeloupians
Guatemala Guatemalans or
Guatemaltecos
Guinea Guineans
Guinea-Bissau Bissauans
Guyana Guyanese
Haiti Haitians
Honduras Hondurans or Hon-
dureños
Hungary Hungarians
Iceland Icelanders
India Indians
Indonesia Indonesians
Iran Iranians
Iraq Iraqis
Ireland Irish
Israel Israelis
Italy Italians
Ivory Coast Ivoirians
Jamaica Jamaicans
Japan Japanese or Nipponese
Jordan Jordanians
Kampuchea Cambodians, Kam-
puchians, Khmers

Kenya Kenyans
Kiribati Kiribatis
Korea Koreans
Kuwait Kuwaiti
Laos Lao or Laotians
Latvia Latvians
Lebanon Lebanese
Lesotho Basotho
Liberia Liberians
Libya Libyans
Liechtenstein Liechtensteiners
Lithuania Lithuanians
Luxembourg Luxembourgers
Madagascar Malagasy
Malawi Malawians
Malaysia Malaysians
Maldives Maldivians
Mali Malians
Malta Maltese
Mauritania Mauritanians
Mauritius Mauritians
México Mexicans or Mexicanos
Monaco Monacans or Monagas-
ques
Mongolia Mongolians
Morocco Moroccans
Mozambique Mozambicans
Nauru Nauruans
Nepal Nepalese
Netherlands Netherlanders
Netherlands Antilles Nether-
lands Antilleans
New Caledonia New Caledo-
nians
New Hebrides New Hebrideans
New Zealand New Zealanders
Nicaragua Nicaraguans or Nica-
ragüenses
Niger Nigerois
Nigeria Nigerians
Norway Norwegians
Oman Omani
Pakistan Pakistani
Panamá Panamanians or Pana-
meños
Papua Papuans
Paraguay Paraguayans or Para-
guayos
Peru Peruanos or Peruvians
Philippines Filipinos
Poland Poles

Portugal Portuguese
Qatar Qataris
Rhodesia Rhodesians
Romania Romanians
Rwanda Rwandans
Saint Lucia Lucians
Saint Vincent and the Grenadines Vincentians and Grenadines
Samoa Samoans
San Marino Sanmarinese
São Tome and Principe São Tomese
Saudi Arabia Saudi
Senegal Senegalese
Seychelles Seychellois
Sierra Leone Sierra Leoneans
Singapore Singaporeans
Solomon Islands Solomon Islanders
Somalia Somali
South Africa South Africans

Spain Españoles or Spaniards
Sri Lanka Sri Lankans
Sudan Sudanese
Surinam Surinamers
Swaziland Swazis
Sweden Swedes
Switzerland Swiss
Syria Syrians
Tanzania Tanzanians
Thailand Thai
Togo Togolese
Tonga Tongans
Trinidad and Tobago Trinidadians and Tobagans
Tunisia Tunisians
Turkey Turks
Tuvalu Tuvaluans
Uganda Ugandans
Union of Soviet Socialist Republics Soviets
United Arab Emirates Emirates
United Kingdom British or Brit-

ons or (depending on the people) English, Scottish, Welsh, etc.
United States Americans or (depending on the state of origin) Alabamians, Alaskans, Arkansans, etc. (see Zip-Coded Automatic Data-Processing Abbreviations addendum)
Upper Volta Upper Voltans
Uruguay Uruguayans or Uruguayos
Venezuela Venezolanos or Venezuelans
Vietnam Vietnamese
Yemen Yemeni
Yugoslavia Yugoslavs
Zaire Congolese or Zairians
Zambia Zambians
Zimbabwe Zimbabweans

Numbered Abbreviations

O^2 both eyes
0-0 zero-zero (no ceiling, no visibility for an aircraft)
000 emergency services (Australia)
007 James Bond (Ian Fleming's international sleuth)
0 deg lat zero degrees latitude (the Equator, encircling widest part of the earth)
0°lat zero degrees latitude (the Equator)
0°longitude Greenwich meridian with lines of longitude either east or west of this prime meridian in Greenwich, England
¼ d farthing (fourth of an English penny); a fourthling
¼ h quarter-hard
¼ ly quarterly
¼ ph quarter-phase
¼ rd quarter-round
¼s quarters
½ can narcotics equal to a half can of pipe tobacco
½d halfpenny (half of an English penny); ha'penny
½ gr half-gross
½ h half-hard
½ rd half-round
½ sov half sovereign (10 shillings)
½ sovereign 10 shillings
½ t half title
1 in the beginning; in the year one; Number 1 (urine); one
1/ a bob (British slang for one

shilling)
1ᵃ *primeira* (Portuguese—first)—feminine gender; *primera* (Spanish—first)—feminine gender
I-A available for military service
I-A-O conscientious objector available only for noncombatant military service
1-armed one-armed bandit (gambling device also called a slot machine)
1b first base(man)
1-bagger one-bagger; single
I-BCE first century before the Christian era (Caesar's Century)—Julius Caesar conquered Britain and Egypt before he was assassinated in the Roman senate in the year 44
1¢ one cent
1/c single-conductor
1C member or former member of US armed forces with honorable discharge
I-C first century (Vesuvian Century)—destruction of Pompeii, Herculaneum, and nearby Neapolitan places by the volcano Vesuvius in the year 79 of the Christian era; member of the armed forces, Coast and Geodetic Survey, or Public Health Service
1 cent 1 penny (10 mills)
1 Chron The First Book of the

Chronicles
1 Cor The First Epistle of Paul the Apostle to the Corinthians
1 crown 5 shillings
1d an English penny
I-D member of reserve component or student taking military training
1 dime 10 cents
1 double eagle $20 (gold)
1/e first edition
1 eagle $10 (gold)
1ᵉʳ⁽ᵉ⁾ premier(e) (French—first)
1 Esd The First (Apocryphal) Book of Esdras
1 florin 2 shillings
1-fold one-fold (single undivided whole)
1 frogskin 1 bill
1G, 2G, 3G, etc. slang for one, two, three thousand dollars, etc.
1 guinea 21 shillings
1 half crown 2 shillings, 6 pence
1 half dime 5 cents
1 half dollar 50 cents
1 half eagle $5 (gold)
1 halfpenny 2 farthings
1 Hen IV First part of *King Henry IV*
1 Hen VI First part of *King Henry VI*
1 John The First Epistle General of John
1 Kings The First Book of the

Kings

1/M First Mate

1 Macc The First (Apocryphal) Book of Maccabees

1mo primo (Italian—first)

1 Ne. First Book of Nephi

1º primeiro (Portuguese—first)—masculine gender; *primero* (Spanish—first)—masculine gender

1/O First Officer

I-O conscientious objector available only for civilian work contributing to national health, safety, or interest

1p one new penny

1-p single pole

1 penny 4 farthings

1 Pet The First Epistle General of Peter

1 ph single-phase

1-piece(r) one-piece bathing suit, coverall, or other one-piece garment

1 pound 20 shillings

1Q first quarter

1Q66 first quarter 1966

1 quarter dollar 25 cents

1 quarter eagle $2.50 (gold)

1s shilling, also called a *bob*

I-S student deferred by statute until end of current school year

1 Sam The First Book of Samuel

1 shilling 12 pence

1 sixpence 6 pence

1 sovereign 1 pound sterling; 20 shillings

1-spot $1 bill

1st first

1st Asst Engr First Assistant Engineer

1st Asst Pur First Assistant Purser

1st cl hon first-class honors (in academic degrees)

1-step one-step (dance or music for such a dance)

1st Lieut First Lieutenant

1st Naval District Boston, Massachusetts

1st Off First Officer

1-striper ensign (USN); third assistant engineer of third mate (merchant marine); private first class (US Army)

1st Sgt First Sergeant

1st State Delaware (first state of the original thirteen states to ratify the *Constitution of the United States*)

1s & 2s mixed 1st- and 2nd-quality lumber

1-suit(er) one-suit (garment bag or suitcase)

1/10 net 30 1-percent discount off the face value of an invoice is allowed if invoice is paid in 10 days; otherwise the full amount is payable in 30 days

1 Thess The First Epistle of Paul the Apostle to the Thessalonians

1 threepence 3 pence

1 Tim The First Epistle of Paul the Apostle to Timothy

1-upmanship one step ahead of your adversary or even your best friend

I-W conscientious objector performing civilian work contributing to national health, safety, or interest, or who has completed such work

1-way one-way street; one-way traffic; unilateral

1-wd one-wheel drive

I-Y registrant does not meet present standards; available for military service only in event of war or national emergency

1-y-o one-year-old (child, pet, racehorse, etc.)

1½ striper naval lieutenant, junior grade

2 Number 2 (excrement); two

2/ two shillings; also the coin called a florin

II-A registrant deferred because of civilian occupation (except agriculture and activity in study) or an apprentice deferred by statute

2b second base(man)

II-B registrant deferred because necessary to war production

2-bagger two bagger (double)

II-BCE second century before the Christian era (Roman Century)—Punic wars resulted in destruction of Carthage by the Roman legions—the 100s

2 bits 25 cents

2-B's boiled or bottled waters (essential in many countries)

2¢ two cents

2/c two-conductor

II-C registrant deferred because of agricultural occupation; second century (Aurelian Century)—reign of the Roman emperor-philosopher Marcus Aurelius—the 100s

2 Chron The Second Book of the Chronicles

2-cycle two-cycle

2d second

2-d two-dimensional

2da segunda (Italian, Portuguese, or Spanish—second)—feminine gender

2-decker double-decker (sandwich or ship); two-decker

2do segundo (Italian, Portuguese, or Spanish—second)—masculine gender

2/e second edition

IIe deuxième, second, seconde (French—second)

2 Esd The Second (Apocryphal) Book of Esdras

2et duet

2-F two-seater fighter aircraft (naval symbol)

2-4-D dichlorophenoxy-acetic acid (weed killer)

2-4-5-T trichlorophenoxy-acetic acid (antiplant agent and defoliant)

2-fer two-fer (two for the price of one)

2-fold double; twofold

2g, 3g, 4g, etc. multiples of acceleration of gravity which at the surface of the earth is 32.2 feet per second

2 Hen IV Second part of *King Henry IV*

2 Hen VI Second part of *King Henry VI*

2 i/c second in command

2 John The Second Epistle of John

2 Kings The Second Book of Kings

2/M Second Mate

2 Macc The Second (Apocryphal) Book of Maccabbees

2n diploid number

2nd second

2nd Asst Engr Second Assistant Engineer

2nd Asst Pur Second Assistant Purser

2nd Lieut Second Lieutenant

2nd Off Second Officer

2nd State Pennsylvania

2nd Stwd Second Steward

2 Ne. Second Book of Nephi

2º segundo (Spanish—second)

2/O Second Officer

2p two new pence

2-p double pole

2 pc two-physician certification

2 Pet The Second Epistle General of Peter

2 ph two-phase

2-piece(r) two-piece(r)

2-ply two-ply

2Q second quarter

2Q66 2nd quarter 1966

2s two shillings; also the coin called a florin

II-S registrant deferred because of activity in study

2 Sam The Second Book of Samuel

2-sided two-sided

2/6 two-and-six (two shillings and sixpence); also called half a crown

2-some twosome (two persons or things)

2-spot $2 bill

2-st two-storey

2-step two-step (dance)

2-striper corporal (US Army); lieutenant (USN); second assistant engineer or second mate (merchant marine)

2-suit(er) two-suit (garment bag or suitcase)

2T double throw

2/10-30 2 percent discount if paid in 10 days, net in 30 days

2 Thess The Second Epistle of Paul the Apostle to the Thessalonians

2-13 drug addict

2 Tim Second Epistle of Paul the Apostle to Timothy

2-time(r) two-time(r)

2-tone two-tone(d)

2U to you

2U2 to you too

2-way two-way

2-wd 2-wheel drive

2WW Second Weather Wing (Air Force—New York)

2-y-o two-year-old (child, pet, racehorse, etc.)

2½ small glass of milk

2½-striper naval lieutenant commander

3 three

III-A registrant with child or children or registrant deferred by reason of extreme hardship to dependents

3b third base(man)

3-bagger three-bagger (triple)

3-ball three-ball (golf match)

III-BCE third century before the Christian era (Carthaginian Century)—Hannibal crossed the Alps to defeat the Romans—the 200s

3-Bs Bach, Beethoven, Berlioz; Bach, Beethoven, Bernstein; Bach, Beethoven, Brahms; Bach, Beethoven, Bruckner; etc. (depending on one's favorite composers)

3/c three-conductor

3C Computer Control Company

III-C third century (the Chinese Century)—Chin dynasty ruled a reunited China—the 200s

3-card three-card (monte)

3-color three-color (photo, pho-

tography, print, or printing process)

3d English threepenny; thruppence; third

3-d dizzy, dopey, and dumb; three dimensional

3de three-day event

3-decker three-decker (sandwich or ship); triple-decker

3-Ds discouragement, disillusionment, disappointment (including frustration and loss)—often leads to suicide, experts insist

3d 10th 40m 3 days 10 hours 40 minutes (Atlantic crossing of SS *United States* in July 1952)

3/e third edition

IIIe *troisième* (French—third)

3-fold threefold; triple

3-gaited three-gaited (horse)

3-H Hubert Horatio Humphrey

3-hand(ed) three-hand(ed) (card game)

3 Hen VI Third part of *King Henry VI*

3io trio

3-I voters Irish, Israeli, Italian

3 John The Third Epistle of John

3 K's *Kinder, Küche, Kirche* (German—children, kitchen, church)

3-l's latitude, lead, lookout; lead, log, lookout (dead-reckoning essentials)

3M Minnesota Mining and Manufacturing Company

3-M Maintenance and Material Management (USN)

3/M Third Mate

3-m l-l c's three-martini liquid-lunch clubbers (alcoholically befuddled expense-account experts contributing to the higher cost of so many things)

3-m lunch three-martini luncheon

3 mMs three musical Ms (Martinon, Monteux, Munch)—conductor-musicians par excellence

3Ms Macmurdo, Mackintosh, and Morris (British architects)

3-Ms Mozart, Mendelssohn, Mahler

3 Ne. Third Book of Nephi

3° *tercero* (Spanish—third)

3/O Third Officer

3-p triple pole

3ph three-phase

3-piece three-piece (garment)

3pl three-point linkage (tractor)

3-p's three phantoms (world de-

pression, world unemployment, world unrest)

3-Ps prosecution, punishment, and persecution (often lifelong) faced by every felon

3pt three-point (tractor linkage)

3Q third quarter

3Q66 third quarter 1966

3rd third

3rd Asst Engr Third Assistant Engineer

3rd degree prolonged interrogation designed to produce a confession of guilt

3rd Naval District New York, New York

3rd Off Third Officer

3rd State New Jersey

3rd Stwd Third Steward

3-ring three-ring circus

3-RRs remedial reading, remedial writing, remedial arithmetic

3-Rs reading, writing, arithmetic (colloquially, readin', 'ritin', 'rithmetic)

3-Rs of productivity recognition, responsibility, rewards (for workers)

3-Rs of war relentless, remorseless, ruthless

3 S's Saba, Sint Eustatius (Statia), Sint Maarten (in the Netherlands Antilles within the Lesser Antilles near the Virgin Islands)

3-st three-storey

3-star admiral or general of three-star rank

3-striper commander (USN); first assistant engineer or first mate (merchant marine); sergeant (US Army)

3T triple throw

3-3 three (school) terms—three courses per term

3-U 3-U System (wherein the uneducated try to teach the unwilling to do the unnecessary)

3-way three-way

3WW Third Weather Wing (Air Force—Nebraska)

4 four; level 4 (death-dealing dose or injection of breath-stopping barbital or other drug used by executioners)

4a man 38 years or over and deferred from military service by reason of age

IV-A registrant who has completed service or a sole surviving son

IV-B government official deferred by statute

4-bagger four-bagger (home

run)

IV-BCE fourth century before the Christian era (Alexandrian Century)—Alexander the Great of Macedonia defeated the Egyptians, the Persians, and the Indians; encouraged the Greek philosophers and poets—the 300s

4 bits 50 cents

4/c four-conductor

4C Community-Coordinated Child Care Program

IV-C alien; fourth century (Constantinian Century)—Roman emperor Constantine built the city of Constantinople on the site of ancient Byzantium and proclaimed it capital of the Eastern Empire—the 300s

4-class fourth-class (mail)

4-d meat meat of dead, disabled, diseased, or dying animals

IV-D minister of religion or divinity student

4/e fourth edition

IVᵉ *quatrième* (French—fourth)

IV-E conscientious objector available for, assigned to, or released for work of national importance

4-F find, feel, fornicate, and forget—code of conduct of certain men in search of casual sexual relationships

IV-F registrant not qualified for any military service

4-H 4-H Club(s)—H standing for head, heart, health, and helping hands

4-hand four-hand(ed)

4-letter four-letter words (Early English terms such as cock, crap, crud, cunt, dung, fart, fuck, lust, piss, puke, scum, shit, snot, spit, suck)

4-Ls latitude, lead, longitude, lookout

4-Ms Monteverdi, Mozart, Mendelssohn, Mahler

4 Ne. Fourth Book of Nephi

4° quarto (a book about 9 × 12 inches)

4° *cuarto* (Spanish—fourth)

4/O Fourth Officer

4 out of 10 4 out of 10 adult Americans are afraid to walk alone at night in their own neighborhood, a recent Gallup Poll revealed

4-p quadruple pole

4Q fourth quarter

4Q66 fourth quarter 1966

4R Ceylon aircraft

4-R Act Railroad Revitalization and Regulatory Reform Act

4-Ss shit, shave, shampoo, and shower

4-st four-storey

4-star admiral or general of four-star rank

4-striper captain (merchant marine or USN); chief engineer (merchant marine)

4tet quartet(te)

4th fourth

4th Asst Engr Fourth Assistant Engineer

4th Naval District Philadelphia, Pennsylvania

4th Off Fourth Officer

4th State Georgia

4U for you

4U2 for you too

4-way four-way

4-wd(s) four-wheel drive vehicle(s)

4-wheel four-wheel (drive)

4WW Fourth Weather Wing (Air Force—Colorado)

4X Israeli aircraft

5 five; large glass of milk

5A Libyan aircraft

V-A registrant over the age liability for military service

5-and-10 variety store selling articles formerly costing not more than five or ten cents

5b bald man with baywindow, bifocals, bridgework, and bunions (humorous Selective Service rating)

V-BCE fifth century before the Christian era (Athenian Century)—Athenians destroyed Persian fleet at Salamis; completed the Parthenon in Athens—the 400s

5-B's Boston baked beans and brownbread

5BX five basic exercises (Royal Canadian Air Force physical fitness program)

5 by 5 radio reception loud and clear (volume and clarity measured on a scale from 1 to 5)

V-C fifth century (Christian Century)—Christianity affirmed as the official faith by two Roman emperors—the 400s

5-Cs 5-Cs of cinematography (camera angles, closeups, composition, continuity, cutting)

5 don'ts don't kill, steal, commit adultery, become intoxicated, or lie, advised Buddah

5/e fifth edition

Vᵉ *cinquième* (French—fifth)

5-er five-dollar bill; fiver; five-pound note

5'er $5 bill; 5-pound note

5-finger five-finger(ed)

5-fold cinquefold(ed); five-fold(ed)

5-HIAA 5-hydroxy indoleacetic acid

5-HT 5-hydroxytryptamine

5-letter woman defined by a five-letter word—bitch

5-lp's five large powers (China, France, Japan, United Kingdom, West Germany)

5° *quinto* (Spanish—fifth)

5p five new pence

5-percenter person who for 5 percent arranges introductions leading to valuable orders

5-Ps nickname of William Oxbery—British player, poet, publican, publisher, and printer; Pootsa Power Publishing Press Publications

5-spot $5 bill

5-star five-star (top quality)

5tet quintet

5th fifth

5th Naval District Norfolk, Virginia

5th State Connecticut

5 w's the *who, what, when, where,* and *why* reporters attempt to include in writing summary paragraphs

6 six

VI-BCE sixth century before the Christian era (Babylonian Century)—Babylonians defeated Israelites and made them captive after destroying the temple of Solomon in Jerusalem—the 500s

6 bits 75 cents

6/c six-conductor

VI-C sixth century (Persian Century)—Khosru Nushirwan made peace with the Byzantine Empire and extended Persian rule throughout the Middle East—the 500s

6d English sixpenny; sixpence

6-dW Six-day War between Arab countries of Egypt, Jordan, Lebanon, and Syria versus Israel; June 5 to 10, 1967

6/e sixth edition

VIᵉ *sixième* (French—sixth)

6'er leader of a pack of six scouts

6-fold sixfold

6-gun six-chambered revolver; sixshooter

6-hda 6-hydroxydopamine

6-mo sixmo(s)

6° *sesto; sexto* (Spanish—sixth)

6-pack carton containing six of a kind (6 containers of beer, soda, etc.)

6-Rs remedial readin', remedial 'ritin', remedial 'rithmetic

6-shooter revolver holding six cartridges

6tet sextet

6th sixth

6th Naval District Charleston, South Carolina

6th State Massachusetts

6WW Sixth Weather Wing (Air Force—Washington, D.C.)

7 seven

7A Seven Arts Society

7 aa's 7 archangels (Gabriel, Jerahmeel, Michael, Raguel, Raphael, Sariel, and Uriel)

VII-BCE seventh century before the Christian era (Assyrian Century) when Assyria ruled Middle East and conquered Egypt—the 600s

7ber September

7bre *Septembre* (French—September); *septiembre* (Spanish—September)

7/c seven-conductor

VII-C seventh century (Islamic Century)—marked by Mohammed's flight from Mecca to Medina and his death in 632; Islam began expanding throughout the Middle East and North Africa as well as moving toward France and Spain—the 600s

7 cd's 7 chief devils (Aniguel, Anizel, Ariel, Aziel, Barfael, Marbuel, and Mephistopheles, according to the diabolarchy of hell as contrasted to the hierarchy of heaven)

7 Dec Pearl Harbor Day (1941)

7ds seven deadly sins—anger, covetousness, envy, gluttony, lechery, pride, sloth

7/e seventh edition

7e *septiembre* (Spanish—September)

VIIe *septième* (French—seventh)

7-fold sevenfold

7° *septimo* (Spanish—seventh)

7 seas collective nickname of any seven seas; Americans are likely to include the Aegean, Baltic, Black, Caribbean, Mediterranean, North, and Red seas; Australians, Indonesians, and New Zealanders may number the Arafura, Banda, Celebes, Coral, Java, Tasman, and Timor seas; British are certain to think of the Aegean, Baltic, Black, Mediterranean, North, Norwegian, and Red

seas; Orientals and others may suggest the Bering, East and South China seas, the Sea of Okhotsk, the Sea of Japan, the Philippine Sea, and the Yellow Sea; and so on around the world and wherever seas are counted along with the five world oceans—Antarctic, Arctic, Atlantic, Indian, and Pacific; other seas sometimes included are the Aral, Azov or Putrid Sea, Bellinghausen, Caspian, Korean, Marmora, Sulu, White, etc.; however, many mariners define the seven seas as the Antarctic, Arctic, North and South Atlantic, North and South Pacific, and Indian oceans

7 smells camphoric (moth repellant), musky (angelica oil), floral (roses), pepperminty (mint-flavored confections), ethereal (dry-cleaning fluids), pungent (vinegar), putrid (rotten eggs)

7tet septet

7th seventh

7th State Maryland

7-Up a carbonated beverage

7WW Seventh Weather Wing (Air Force—Illinois)

8 eight; numerical symbol for heroin as H is the eight of the alphabet

8-ball behind the eight ball (in a bad position); eight ball (black billiard or pool ball numbered 8)

VIII-BCE eighth century before the Christian era (Chou Century)—eastern Chou dynasty began ruling China for the next five centuries—the 700s

8 bits one dollar

8bre *octobre* (French—October); *octubre* (Spanish—October)

VIII-C eighth century (Carolingian Century)—Charlemagne or Charles the Great reigned as King of the Franks and Emperor of the West as well as chief patron of learning—the 700s

8/e eighth edition

8e *octubre* (Spanish—October)

VIIIe *huitième* (French—eighth)

8-fold eightfold

8 great 8 great violin concertos (Bach's for 2 violins, Beethoven, Brahms, Bruch, Mendelssohn, Paganini, Sibelius, Tchaikovsky)

8-h NBC's concert hall studio used by Toscanini and the

NBC Symphony of the Air and more recently by Mehta and the New York Philharmonic Symphony

8mm film 8-millimeter film

8N American National 8-thread series

8^0 octavo (a book about 9¾ inches high)

8° *octavo* (Spanish—eighth)

8tet octet

8th eighth

8th Naval District New Orleans, Louisiana

8th State South Carolina

8 to 5 everyday 8 A.M. to 5 P.M. job

8UN Unified 8-thread series

8va bass. *ottava bassa* (Italian—octave lower)

9 nine

IX-BCE ninth century before the Christian era (Phoenician Century)—Carthage founded by the Phoenicians who traded in all areas of the Mediterranean—the 800s

9ber November

9bre *novembre* (French—November); *noviembre* (Spanish—November)

IX-C ninth century (Century of Confusion)—Carolingian Empire of Charlemagne disintegrated; European unity dismembered and divided—the 800s

9/e, 10/e, 11/e, 12/e, etc. ninth edition, tenth edition, eleventh edition, twelfth edition, et cetera

9e *noviembre* (Spanish—November)

IXe *neuvième* (French—ninth)

9-fold ninefold

9° *nono; noveno* (Spanish—ninth)

9-pins ninepin(s)

9th ninth

9th Naval District Great Lakes, Illinois

9th State New Hampshire

9 to 5 everyday 9 A.M. to 5 P.M. job

9-to-5 National Association of Working Women

10 deka (da); ten

'10 1810 (Bolvarian-type Spanish-American revolutions and wars of liberation, 1810–1826)

10^{-1} deci (d)

10^{-2} centi (c)

10^{-3} milli (m)

10^{-6} micro (μ)

10^{-9} nano (n)

10⁻¹² pico (p)

10⁻¹⁵ femto (f)

10⁻¹⁸ atto (a)

10² hecto (h)

10³ kilo (k)

10⁶ mega (M)

10⁹ giga (G)

10¹² tera (T)

10 Aug Ecuadorian Independence Day

X-BCE tenth century before the Christian era (Israelian Century)—King Solomon reigned and Israelites defeated all enemies and built the great temple of Jerusalem—the 900s

Xber December

10ᵇʳᵉ décembre (French—December); *diciembre* (Spanish—December)

X-C tenth century (Mayan Century)—great American civilization left monumental ruins strewn from Honduras to Yucatan—the 900s

10 Dec Human Rights Day (Liberia)

10 Downing Street British prime minister's home in west central London

10ᵉ diciembre (Spanish—December)

Xᶜ dixième (French—tenth)

10-fold tenfold

10-gage 10-gage shotgun

10-gallon hat cowboy hat

10 great 10 great violin concertos (Bach's for 2 violins, Beethoven, Brahms, Bruch, Mendelssohn, Paganini, Saint-Saëns, Sibelius, Tchaikovsky, Vieuxtemps)

10⁰ decimo (Spanish—tenth)

10p 10 new pence

10-pln(s) tenpln(s)

10-spot $10 bill

10th tenth

10th Naval District San Juan, Puerto Rico

10th State Virginia

10-V the lowest; the opposite of A-1; the worst

11 eleven

11 once (Spanish—eleven)— stands for aguardiente as this strong alcoholic drink has eleven letters

XI-BCE eleventh century before the Christian era (Century of Saul and David)—King Saul followed by King David as ruler of Israel—the 1000s

XI-C eleventh century (Aztecan and Incan Century)—vast monuments in the highlands of Mexico and Peru stand as

mute witnesses to these great American civilizations—the 1000s

11 Downing Street official town residence of the British Chancellor of the Exchequer

11-11-11 eleventh hour, eleventh day, eleventh month of 1918 when Armistice ended World War I

11th eleventh

11th-hr eleventh hour (last minute; latest possible time for assistance or a death-sentence reprieve)

11th Naval District San Diego, California

11th State New York

12 twelve

XII-BCE twelfth century before the Christian era (Trojan Century)—Troy fell to the Greeks after a ten-year siege celebrated in Homer's epic poem, the *Iliad*—the 1100s

XII-C twelfth century (Portuguese Century) when Alfonso I Henriques reigned as king of Portugal, which emerged as a great maritime power—the 1100s

12 Downing Street office of the British Government Whips

12-gage 12-gage shotgun

12N American National 12-thread series

12⁰ twelvemo (a book about 7¾ inches high)

12th twelfth

12th Naval District San Francisco, California

12th State North Carolina

12-tone twelve-tone music; twelve-tone row

12UN Unified 12-thread series

13 numerical symbol for marijuana as M is the thirteenth letter of the alphabet; police radio signal call 13 indicates an officer needs help—this is the highest priority radio call and all units respond; the boss is nearby; thirteen; white bread

XIII-BCE thirteenth century before the Christian era (Century of the Exodus)—Moses led the Israelites out of Egypt—the 1200s

XIII-C thirteenth century (Mongol Century)—dominated by the reign of the Mongol emperor Genghiz Khan whose hordes conquered China and Russia—the 1200s

13th thirteenth

13th Naval District Seattle, Washington

13th State Rhode Island

14 fourteen; numerical symbol for narcotics as N is the fourteenth letter of the alphabet; special (food) order

XIV-BCE fourteenth century before the Christian era (Century of the Pharaoh Tutankhamen)

XIV-C fourteenth century (Tamerlane's Century)—Mongol emperor Timur (Tamer the Lame) dominated Middle East and western India—the 1300s

14th fourteenth

14th Naval District Pearl Harbor, Oahu, Hawaii

14th State Vermont

15 fifteen

XV-BCE fifteenth century before the Christian era (Egyptian Century)—Egyptian kingdom extended from the Sahara to beyond the Euphrates—the 1400s

XV-C fifteenth century (Italian Century)—powerful families such as the Borgias and the de Medicis brought about the renewal of art and architecture in Italy—the Italian Renaissance—the 1400s

15th fifteenth

15th Naval District Balboa, Canal Zone

15th State Kentucky

16 sixteen

XVI to XXXII BCE (*see* XXXII-BCE)

XVI-C sixteenth century (Spanish Century) marked by discoveries and colonizations of much of the New World, circumnavigation of the globe, flowering of art and literature—the Golden Age or *Siglo de Oro*—as well as the defeat of the Spanish Armada by the British—the 1500s

16-gage 16-gage shotgun

16mm film 16-millimeter film

16N American National 16-thread series

16⁰ sixteenmo (a book about 6¾ inches high)

16's 16 rpm phonograph records

16th sixteenth

16th State Tennessee

16UN Unified 16-thread series

17 seventeen

XVII-C seventeenth century (Dutch Century) saw the dis-

1104

covery and settlement of what is now New York as well as South Africa and the East Indies by the Dutch who after a war at sea arranged a mutual defense pact with their British rivals—the 1600s (*see* the Elizabethan Age, *Le Grand Siecle, El Siglo de Oro*)

17-D modified yellow-fever virus

17th seventeenth

17th Naval District Kodiak, Alaska

17th Parallel line of latitude dividing North and South Vietnam

17th State Ohio

18 eighteen

XVIII-C eighteenth century (French Century) of courtesans and kings, poets and playwrights, of great territories acquired and lost, of Louis XVI and Marie Antoinette beheaded by the guillotine only to be replaced by Napoleon—the turbulent 1700s (*see* The Enlightenment)

18-19 Sept Chilean Independence Days

18th eighteenth

18th State Louisiana

19 banana split; nineteen

XIX-C nineteenth century (British Century) from Napoleon's defeat by Wellington at Waterloo to the defeat of the Boers in South Africa this century was marked by British advances in invention, in the success of its industrial revolution, in its colonization in all parts of the world, and its maritime supremacy on all the oceans—the 1800s

19th nineteenth

19th State Indiana

20 twenty

20′ twenty-foot-long shipping container

XX-C twentieth century (American Century) characterized by industrial advances, victory in two world wars, as well as the development of inventions, the discovery of the North Pole, the placing of men on the moon, the elevation of living standards, the devotion to democratic ideals—the 1900s

20-gage 20-gage shotgun

20-spot $20 bill

20th twentieth; Twentieth Century Limited (New York Central Railroad)

20th-century syndrome hypersensitivity to modern chemical compounds

20th State Mississippi

20 toes 10 toes down and 10 toes up (bedtime frolic)

21 blackjack; limeade

XXI-C twenty-first century (Japanese Century)—providing productivity, standard of living, and other growth factors are not disturbed by large-scale earthquakes and world wars—the 2000s

21st twenty-first

21st State Illinois

22 customer's check still unpaid

.22 .22-caliber ammunition, pistol, or rifle

22-cal killers assassins using 22-caliber silencer-equipped automatic pistols

22d twenty-second

22nd twenty-second

22nd State Alabama

22 s-e silencer-equipped 22-caliber revolver (favored by Mafia assassins and others)

23 get lost; I'm busy; leave me alone; scram

23rd twenty-third

23rd State Maine

23½ deg N lat Tropic of Cancer

23½ deg S lat Tropic of Capricorn

24 *24 Capricci* (Opus 1)—Paganini's Twenty-four Caprices for cadenza-like unaccompanied violin

24⁰ twenty-four*mo* (a book about 5¾ inches high)

24-Ps 24 Parganas (Zamindari of Calcutta fiscal divisions in the Ganges delta)

24th twenty-fourth

24th State Missouri

25 LSD as 25 is part of the chemical name—d-lysergic acid diethylamide tartrate 25

.25 .25-caliber ammunition or automatic

25th twenty-fifth

25th State Arkansas

26th twenty-sixth

26th State Michigan

27th twenty-seventh

27th State Florida

28-gage 28-gage shotgun

28th twenty-eighth

28th State Texas

29th twenty-ninth

29th State Iowa

30 finis symbol used by newspapermen at end of article or story; thirty

30 days, etc. (calendar mnemonic—30 days hath September, April, June, and November; all the rest have 31 save February; 28 are all its score, but in leap year one day more)

30th thirtieth

30th State Wisconsin

.30-'06 .30-caliber American cartridge introduced in 1906; used by US Armed Forces in World Wars I and II for rifles and machine guns

31st State California

XXXII-BCE thirty-second century before the Christian era (Dynastic Century) when the first and second of many Egyptian dynasties began a rule lasting for at least seventeen centuries before the power of the pharaohs began to wane—the 3100s

32nd State Minnesota

32⁰ thirty-two*mo* (a book about 5 inches high)

33rd St New York dialect enriched by longshoremen, taxicab drivers, and others who pronounce it *toity-toid street*

33rd State Oregon

33's 33⅓ rpm phonograph records

34th State Kansas

35mm film 35-millimeter film

35th State West Virginia

36 postum

36th State Nevada

37th State Nebraska

.38 .38-caliber ammunition or pistol

38th Parallel line of latitude dividing North and South Korea

38th State Colorado

39th State North Dakota (South Dakotans insist they are in the 39th state but are listed as the 40th only because some clerk in Washington, D.C. upset the papers of admission)

40 forty; 40 acres

40′ forty-foot-long shipping container

40th fortieth

40th State South Dakota

40 winks a nap or short sleep

41st State Montana

42nd cousin a distant relative

42nd State Washington

42nd Street New York City's most blatant nightlife area in mid-Manhattan close to Times Square and running across Manhattan Island from the East River to the Hudson River

43rd State Idaho

.44 .44-caliber ammunition or pistol

44th State Wyoming

.45 .45-caliber ammunition, pistol, or submachine gun

45's 45 rpm phonograph records

45th State Utah

46th State Oklahoma

47th State New Mexico

47th Street New York City's diamond center between the Avenue of the Americas and Fifth Avenue on 47th Street

48 48-hour weekend liberty pass

48er emigrant who came to America in 1848; participant in German revolution of 1848

48° forty-eightmo (a book about 4 inches high)

48th State Arizona

48½ discharged; fired

49er gold-rush settler who came to California in 1849

49th State Alaska

50 fifty

.50 .50-caliber ammunition or machine gun

50p fifty new pence

50 percenter(s) auto-mechanic racketeer(s) fleecing automobile owners by causing the need for unnecessary repairs or recommending unnecessary replacements and then splitting the profits with gas-station operators

50-spot $50 bill

50th fiftieth

50th State Hawaii

51 one cup of hot chocolate

52 two cups of hot chocolate

54 54 minorities comprising the people of China

55 root beer

55½ small root beer

60 sixty

60 *60 minutes* (tv program exposing corruption)

60th sixtieth

64° sixty-fourmo (a book about 3 inches high)

66 dirty dishes; Phillips Petroleum Company

66 deg 17 min N lat Arctic Circle

66 deg 17 min S lat Antarctic Circle

69 pictorial numerical symbol for oral-genital copulation

70 seventy

70mm film 70-millimeter film

70th seventieth

73 best regards (amateur radio)

75's 75mm cannon

76 Union Oil

'76 1776

78's 78 rpm phonograph records

80 eighty

80th eightieth

81 glass of water

82 two glasses of water

84 naval prison

86 *don't serve* (as the bar or restaurant is out of the item ordered or the customer is too disorderly or too drunk to be served)

87½ look at the lovely girl(s) out front

88 Column 88 (neo-Nazi organization based in London); love and kisses (amateur radio)

89d 89 days (New York to San Francisco run of American clipper ship *Flying Cloud* in 1854)

89er Oklahoman who settled in 1889 when the territory was opened

90 ninety

90-day wonder officer commissioned after only 90 days of training

90 deg N lat North Pole (zero degrees longitude)

90 deg S lat South Pole (zero degrees longitude)

90th ninetieth

91 a glass of seltzer water

93-score best grade of butter (USDA grade AA)

95 the customer's leaving without paying

'96 1796 (Napoleonic Wars, 1796–1815)

98 assistant manager's nearby—lookout

'98 the generation of 1898 (Spain's generation of cultured persons reacting to the illusions and incompetence that led to the loss of Cuba in 1898)—Altamira the historian, Azorín the author, Cossío the art historian and teacher, Ferrer the anarchist teacher, Machado the poet, Ortega y Gasset the essayist, Ramón y Cajal the histologist and surgeon, Unamuno the teacher and writer, etc.

99 manager's nearby—lookout

100 Hydrographic Office Publication 100—*Merchant Marine*

House Flags and Stack Insignia—U.S. Navy Hydrographic Office; one hundred

100-percenter(s) one-hundred percent patriot(s)

100th one-hundredth

108-named god of the Hindus Vishnu

110 110 volt(s)

110v 110 volts

110v/60c (60h) 110-volt 60-cycle (60 hertz) electric current

111 emergency services (New Zealand); One-Eleven (British Aircraft Corporation short-take-off-and-landing fan-jet aircraft)

118-island city Venice (Venezia)

150 Publication 150—*World Port Index*—U.S. Naval Oceanographic Office

180° longitude International Date Line where east meets west 180 degrees east or west of the Greenwich or prime meridian

220(v) 220 volt(s)

240 Convair two-engine transport airplane; trotting horse speed—1 mile in 2 minutes and 40 seconds; synonym for high speed

240v 240 volts

280 copper alloy (Muntz metal), yellow metal

291 291 Fifth Avenue (nickname and address of An American Place—Alfred Stieglitz's art gallery where much avant-garde lithography, painting, and photography were first shown)

400 the four hundred; the socially elite (originally designated by Ward McAllister, who drew up a list containing the top 400 in New York society)

.410 .410-caliber shotgun commonly and incorrectly called a 410-gage shotgun

415 PC Section 415 Penal Code—disturbing the peace

4-2-3 syndrome medical students who go to school for 4 years and get only 2 hours exposure to alcoholism—America's number 3 killer

500 Festival 500-mile (805-kilometer) auto racing event of the International Automobile Speed Classic at Indianapolis, Indiana

502 drunken driving (police code)

606 arsphenamine compound sold as Salvarsan; 606th compound developed and tested by Paul Ehrlich for treatment of relapsing fevers and syphilis

707 Boeing Stratoliner jet-transport airplane

720 Boeing medium-range jet-transport airplane

727 Boeing jet-transport with three empennage-mounted engines

737 Boeing short-range twin-jet airplane

747 Boeing jumbo jetliner (built to transport from 490 to 1000 passengers, depending on the model)

757 Boeing 136-seat medium-range jetliner

767 Boeing's fuel-saver twin-jet passenger plane

800-C-O-C-A-I-N-E 800-262-2463 (national cocaine hotline connecting addicts with cocaine counselors and psychiatric hospital emergency rooms)

880 Convair 880 jet airplane

911 national emergency telephone number to report a fire, summon the police, or call for an ambulance

925 Office Workers Union

990 Convair 990 fan-engine jet airplane

999 emergency services (United Kingdom)

1000 one thousand

1011 Lockheed 1011 jumbo jet-liner

1080 sodium fluoroacetate

1098 supplies and equipment requisition form (British Army)

1600 **Pennsylvania Avenue** (Washington, DC, address of the White House)

1812 *Overture 1812* by Tchaikovsky

"*1905*" Leon Trotsky's account of the dress-rehearsal Russian revolution of 1905; Dmitri Shostakovich's Symphony No. 11—*Year 1905*

1905er Old Bolshevik; participant in the Russian Revolution of 1905; veteran communist

"*1919*" *Nineteen nineteen* (novel by John Dos Passos depicting World War I era of American life in series of camera-eye closeups)—1919 often used to symbolize this period

"1984" *Nineteen eighty-four* (novel of George Orwell describing totalitarian terror in the year 1984)—1984 has become a symbol for anti-libertarian trends

2141 2141 tiny islands of Micronesia (greater in area than the continental U.S. but smaller in land mass than Rhode Island)—Trust Territory of the Pacific with its capital on Saipan atop Capitol Hill

2707 Boeing supersonic transport airplane

9653 Convict 9653 (anti-militarist American Socialist nominee for President—Eugene V Debs when in the U.S. Penitentiary in Atlanta, Georgia)

22445 prisoners' petitions for judicial reviews of their cases

23102a **V(ehicle) C(ode)** driving under the influence of any intoxicating liquor or drug

338171 TE TE Lawrence (Lawrence of Arabia's number in the British Army; he used this number rather than his name as a final defense against a world he found hostile and unresponsive)

960,000,000 nine hundred and sixty million Chinese

200,000,000,000 two-hundred billion stars in the Milky Way

Numeration

	Power	Prefix	Abbreviation	Name
1,000,000,000,000,000,000	10^{18}	eva	e	one quintillion*
1,000,000,000,000,000	10^{15}	peta	p	one quadrillion
1,000,000,000,000	10^{12}	tera	t	one trillion
100,000,000,000	10^{11}			one-hundred billion
10,000,000,000	10^{10}			ten billion
1,000,000,000	10^{9}	giga	g	one billion
100,000,000	10^{8}			one-hundred million
10,000,000	10^{7}			ten million
1,000,000	10^{6}	mega	m	one million
100,000	10^{5}			one-hundred thousand
10,000	10^{4}			ten thousand
1000	10^{3}	kilo	k	one thousand
100	10^{2}			one hundred
10	10^{1}			ten
1	10^{0}			one
0.1	10^{-1}	deci	d	one-tenth
0.01	10^{-2}	centi	c	one-hundredth
0.001	10^{-3}	milli	m	one-thousandth
0.0001	10^{-4}			one ten-thousandth
0.00001	10^{-5}			one hundred-thousandth
0.000001	10^{-6}	micro	(μ-mu)	one millionth
0.0000001	10^{-7}			one ten-millionth
0.00000001	10^{-8}			one hundred-millionth

0.000000001	10^{-9}	nano	n	one billionth
0.0000000001	10^{-10}			one ten-billionth
0.00000000001	10^{-11}			one hundred-billionth
0.000000000001	10^{-12}	pico	p	one trillionth
0.0000000000001	10^{-13}			one ten-trillionth
0.00000000000001	10^{-14}			one hundred-trillionth
0.000000000000001	10^{-15}	femto	f	one quadrillionth
0.0000000000000001	10^{-16}			one ten-quadrillionth
0.00000000000000001	10^{-17}			one hundred-quadrillionth
0.000000000000000001	10^{-18}	atto	a	one quintillionth

*Quintillions are followed by sextillions, septillions, octillions, nonillions, decillions, undecillions, duodecillions, tredecillions, quattuordecillions, quinquedecillions, sexdecillions, septendecillions, octodecillions, novemdecillions, vigintillions (a thousand novemdecillions).

Ports of the World

The ports of the world are listed alphabetically in the main body of entries.

Prisons of the World and Their Toponyms

"Am I my brother's keeper?"
—Genesis 4:9

Prisons of the World covers correctional and penal institutions of every kind, ranging from custodial schools for delinquent juveniles to halfway houses; included are police-station lockups, county jails, and penitentiaries as well as penal colonies and rehabilitation centers. Parole and probation services are included, as are the slang names given by many inmates or former convicts. Many entries are toponyms—place-names used to describe the institution.

All of the more than 150 nations of the world get mention and many have several entries. All entries, except for numbered ones, are in alphabetical order to facilitate ready reference.

In late 1984, according to the Bureau of Justice Statistics, a Department of Justice agency, the greatest number of prison inmates in the United States were in Texas (35,000), California (33,500), New York (27,500), and Florida (27,000). Figures were not available for even much larger numbers of prisoners held in the USSR and mainland China.

AACFO American Association of Correctional Facility Officers (publishes *The Correction Officer* newsletter)

AACP American Association of Correctional Psychologists (publishes *Journal of Criminal Justice and Behavior*)

AACTP American Association of Correctional Training Personnel

AAEOCJ American Association of Ex-Offenders in Criminal Justice

AAMHPC American Association of Mental Health Professionals in Corrections

AARC Association for the Advancement of Released Convicts

AAWS American Association of Wardens and Superintendents (formerly Wardens Association of America founded in 1870)—publishes *The Grape vine* every two months

Abbotsford British Columbia town southeast of Vancouver and location of the Matsqui Institution

Aber slang for Aberdeen, Scotland and its prison

Aberdeen Aberdeen, Scotland or its jail (*see* toponym); this is true of other Aberdeens in Hong Kong, South Dakota, and the state of Washington

Abidjan (*see* Ivory Coast's prisons)

absent without leave or permission awol (AWOL)

Abu Dhabi (*see* United Arab Emirates)

AC Administration of Correction (Puerto Rico)

ACA American Correctional Association (publishes books about correctional problems and the periodical *Corrections Today*)

Acapulco Mexican prison in the most popular seaside resort but not Mexico's best prison, even though it is close to the Pacific Ocean, former inmates insist

ACCA American Correctional Chaplains Association

Accra (*see* Ghana's prisons)

ACFSA American Correctional Food Service Association

ACHSA American Correctional Health Services Association

aci (ACI) adult correctional institution

ACJ Arlington County Jail (in Virginia near Washington, DC)

Acklington HM Prison at Acklington, Northumberland, England

ACRIM Association for Correctional Research and Information Management

ACTO Advisory Council on the Treatment of Offenders

Acuña jail in Ciudad Acuña across the Rio Grande from Del Rio, Texas

Adana (see Turkey)

Addis Ababa (see Ethiopia's prisons)

Adee Adelaide, South Australia or its jail

Adelaide Adelaide Gaol in South Australia's capital city where jail, as in the British Isles, is spelled gaol but pronounced jail

Aden (see Yemen)

Adirondack Camp Adirondack (minimum-security prison in the Adirondack Mountains near Lake Placid, New York)

adjustment center segregated center of any prison; used for the protection of inmates who refuse to be intimidated by prison gangs but cannot defend themselves

administrative segregation penological euphemism for solitary confinement

Adobe (often pronounced 'Dobe) Adobe Mountain School for juvenile delinquents in Phoenix, Arizona

Adrian Michigan city southwest of Ypsilanti and site of the Adrian Training School opened in 1881

Adrian Training School coeducational penal facility in Adrian, Michigan which offers medium-security accommodations

Adult Diagnostic and Treatment Center in Avenal, New Jersey since 1976

Adult Training Centre in Milton, Ontario

Aeolian Islands Isole Eolie or the Lipari Islands used as Italian convict colonies in the Mediterranean

aerial surveillance (see ASTREA)

Afghanistan the Soviet-dominated Democratic Republic of Afghanistan, once known as Bactria, contains prisons as ancient as its history, according to former inmates of the Kabul prison

AFOSP Air Force Office of Security Police

Afyon *Afyonkarahisar* (Turkish—Black Castle of Opium) —in western central Turkey where much of the world's opium is grown; Afyon is the nickname of its prison

Agaña capital of Guam and location of the Adult Correctional Facility, the Community Correction Center, Cottage Homes, Juvenile Hall, the Juvenile Justice School, and the Agaña Lockup as well as the U.S. Navy Brig

Agaña Lockup official name of Guam's jail in the capital city of this American island in the western Pacific

Agassiz British Columbia town east of Vancouver containing the Kent Institution as well as the Mountain Institution

Agnostic Penologist Colonel Robert Green Ingersoll (1833-1899) who lectured and wrote about Crimes Against Criminals as well as Cruelty in the Elmira Reformatory where he declared: "The Lash will neither develop the Brain nor cultivate the Heart—Brutality a Failure; (Warden) Brockway a Savage."

Agra Agra Central Prison in Uttar Pradesh, within the city of Agra, the ancient capital of India

Agua Prieta Agua Prieta, Sonora and its jail across the border from Douglas, Arizona

Aguascaliente prison in Aguascaliente—capital city of the Mexican state of the same name and close to León

AI Adult Institutions (New Hampshire); Amnesty International (London-based international organization concerned with the release of political prisoners on a nation-by-nation worldwide basis)

Aiea Halawa High Security Facility at Aiea on Oahu Island, Hawaii

air dancing hanging (execution also known as air jigging, air polka dancing, air rhumba dancing, etc.)

aislamiento penal (Spanish— penal isolation)—solitary confinement

AJA American Jail Association

AJCA Association of Juvenile Compact Administrators

AJIS Automated Jail Information System

ajusticiamiento (Spanish—execution of a criminal)

Akron Akron, Ohio or its Summit County jail

Alabama jails scattered throughout the state's 67 counties from Prattville, the county seat of Autauga County, to Double Springs in Winston County; each county has its jail plus those in the big cities of Birmingham, Huntsville, Mobile, and Montgomery

Alabama State Training School at East Lake near Birmingham where its female delinquent population is held

Alameda Alameda County Prison and Rehabilitation Center near San Francisco, California

Alaska (see Anchorage, Eagle River, Fairbanks, Juneau, Ketchikan, Nome, Palmer)

Alaska lockups the state's 29 divisions, called counties in other states, cover every area from the Aleutian Islands to Yukon-Koyukuk; each has a lockup plus the jails of Anchorage and Fairbanks

Albania the People's Socialist Republic of Albania has its capital in Tirana and here, as in many communist-dominated countries, is an old and inhumane prison; other prisons are in this southeast Adriatic nation wedged between Greece and Yugoslavia

Albany names for prison in the Albanys of California, Georgia, Indiana, Kentucky, Missouri, New York, Oregon, and Texas as well as in England and Australia

Albany, Georgia (see USMC)

Alberta Alberta Institution for Girls (Canadian prison facility)

Albertslund Herstedvester Detention Centre at Albertslund, Denmark

Albion Albion State Institution and Western Correctional Facility at Albion, New York, northwest of Rochester

Albuquerque principal city of New Mexico located in the

central part of the state where it contains the New Mexico Youth Diagnostic Center and the Re-Integration Center

Albuturkey slang for Albuquerque, New Mexico and its jail

Alcalá de Henares women's prison northeast of Madrid in central Spain

Alcatraz formerly the maximum-security prison of the United States on Alcatraz Island in San Francisco Bay where today National Park Service guides conduct sightseeing tours through its old cell blocks; its name means albatross in Spanish

Alcatraz replaced U.S. Penitentiary at Marion, Illinois, replacing and updating the maximum-security facility formerly on Alcatraz Island in San Francisco Bay

alcoholism, alienation, bribery, brutality, contraband smuggling, dirty and unhealthful environment, drug addiction and trafficking, gambling, graft, homosexual assault, inhumane punishment, isolation, kangaroo courts, neglect, poor food, and violence—sometimes deadly—may be found in most penal institutions, inmates and penologists agree; but many disagree on the type of segregation effective in rehabilitating persons confined for crimes committed (more than an entry but a necessary statement of fact it is hoped will be read by persons thinking of embarking on a criminal career)

Aldershot British military-training post and prison holding soldiers discharged from service with ignominy; Aldershot is about 35 miles (56 kilometers) southwest of London

Alderson Federal Correctional Institution at Alderson, West Virginia (for women serving lengthy sentences)

Aleppo (*see* Syria)

Alex slang for Alexandria, anywhere, and its jail or prison

Alexander Alexander Youth Service Center in Alexander, Arkansas with a capacity for 96 coed juvenile delinquents

Alexandria place-name of a jail, lockup, or prison in Australia, Egypt, Louisiana, or Virginia

Alexis Ravelin maximum-security section of the Peter-Paul fortress-prison of St Petersburg during czarist times when so many political prisoners were held here for life or while awaiting transportation to Siberian exile

algemas (Portuguese—handcuffs)

Algeria the Democratic and Popular Republic of Algeria has prisons dating from the years of French-colonial domination and these may be seen in Algiers, Oran, Constantine, Annaba, and even in smaller places such as Arzew

Algiers capital city of Algeria whose old prison is not the pride of the so-called Democratic and Popular Republic of Algeria between the Mediterranean Sea and the Sahara Desert

Alhambra Alhambra Reception and Treatment Center for incoming adult felons; in Phoenix, Arizona

Alice short form for The Alice—Alice Springs, Northern Territory, Australia—and its jail

Allentown Lehigh County, Pennsylvania's county seat, courthouse, and jail close to others in nearby Bethlehem and Easton

Allenwood Federal Prison Camp at Allenwood south of Williamsport, Pennsylvania on the west branch of the Susquehanna River

alley corridor or hallway between cell rows

Almacen Tia Moreno Quito, Ecuador's penitentiary

a l'ombre (French—in the shadow)—in jail or in prison

Alston Wilkes Society organization aiding families of inmates in South Carolina

Alyce D McPherson School for coeducational juvenile delinquents in Ocala, Florida

Amache Japanese-American relocation center near Granada in southeastern Colorado where they were interned after Pearl Harbor

Amarillo north Texas city and Potter County seat including a courthouse and jail

Amenia Amenia Center for Girls at Amenia, New York (correctional facility close to the border of Connecticut)

American Association of Correc- tional Facility Officers (*see* AACFO)

Amerian Association of Correctional Psychologists (*see* AACP)

American Association of Wardens and Superintendents (*see* AAWS)

American Correctional Association originally the National Prison Association and later the American Prison Association (*see* ACA)

American Journal of Correction formerly *Prison World*

American People for American Prisoners (*see* APAP)

American prisons (*see individual entries by Bureau of Prisons name; city, county, or state name; or nickname*)

America's Devil's Island post-Civil-War nickname of the military prison at Fort Jefferson on the Dry Tortugas about 65 miles (105 kilometers) west of Key West in the Gulf of Mexico

Am Jour Corr *American Journal of Correction*

Amman (*see* Jordan's prisons)

Amnesty International (*see* AI)

Amsterdam (*see* Netherlands)

'Aña Agaña, Guam's capital or its jail

Anamosa site of The Men's Reformatory in Iowa, east of Cedar Rapids

Anchorage Achorage Correctional Center in Anchorage, Alaska, together with the Annex holding maximum-security felons

Andersonville Confederate prisoner-of-war camp near a town of the same name in south central Georgia where nearly 14,000 Union prisoners lost their lives due to overcrowded conditions and lack of good food

Andorra the Valleys of Andorra (Andorra la Velle) are high in the Pyrenees between France and Spain; its autonomy has prevailed from 1278 and its small prison looks almost as old but is seldom occupied except by some destructive alcoholic

Andrade Andrade, Baja California and its jail across the border from Algodones, California

Angleton Texas town north of Freeport and address of the

Retrieve Unit opened in 1919

Angola Southwest African country formerly a colony of Portugal run by the Portuguese who are still remembered for the old prison they left behind in Luanda and the old jails in smaller places; site of the Louisiana State Penitentiary noted for its rigid policy of discipline in this facility northeast of Baton Rouge

Angolite bimonthly publication by prisoners in Angola, Louisiana, a state prison

Ankara inland capital of modern Turkey and nickname of its several jails and prisons

ankles ankle shackles

Annaba (*see* Algeria)

Annadale New Jersey community northeast of Clinton and site of the Youth Correctional Institution opened in 1929

Anna's Hope Anna's Hope Detention Center on St Croix in the American Virgin Islands, built by the Danes when Denmark held the islands before selling them to the United States in 1917

Anniston Calhoun County seat and jail in Alabama, east of Birmingham

Antakya city or prison in southernmost Turkey between the Mediterranean and the Syrian border

Antananarivo (*see* Madagascar's prisons)

anti-penetration glazing built to resist blowtorches, gunfire, and sledgehammers (*see* detention glazing)

antiquity of Newgate *Newgate was used as a gaol at least as early as 1190,* states WW Hutchins in *London Town—past and present;* in 1902 its demolition began and some of its stones were worked into the lower stages of the Old Bailey front of the new Sessions House

antisocial offender(s) convict(s); criminal(s)

Anto Antofagasta, Chile or its jail

APA Adult Parole Authority; American Prison Association; Association of Paroling Authorities

Apalachee Apalachee Correctional Institution in Sneads, Florida where it accommodates offenders in all custody

levels but quite overcrowded

APAP American People for American Prisoners (in overseas jails and prisons where in 1985 some 3000 were being held—mainly on drug charges)

APFO Association on Programs for Female Offenders

Apia (*see* Samoa)

APPA American Probation and Parole Association

Appleton Thorn HM Prison at Appleton Thorn in Lancashire, England where it serves the port city of Liverpool

Ararat Ararat Prison in Victoria, Australia

Arbeitsdorf (German—Work Village)—euphemism included in the name of one of many concentration camps run by the Nazis

Arcadia south-central Florida town and site of the De Soto Correctional Institution opened there in 1969 with a design capacity of 580 but by 1985 had more than 700 inmates

Archambault Institution maximum-security facility at Ste Anne des Plaines, Québec

Argentina South America's second largest nation is replete with prisons and jails; all its cities have them—Buenos Aires, Cordoba, Rosario, La Plata, etc.

Arizona (*see* Adobe, Alhambra, Catalina, Florence, Fort Grant, Phoenix, Tucson)

Arizona Girls School correctional facility at Phoenix for juvenile delinquents from 8 to 21 years of age

Arizona jails the state's 14 counties cover from Saint Johns, county seat of Apache County, to Yuma in Yuma County; county lockups are augmented by jails in Phoenix and Tucson; the old Territorial Prison outside Yuma is a tourist attraction

Arkansas (*see* Alexander, Cummins, Pine Bluff, Tucker)

Arkansas lockups the state's 75 counties are served by jails for the county seat or court house of De Witt and Stuttgart in Arkansas County to Danville and Dardanelle in Yell County; city facilities serve Little Rock

Armagh prisoner's place-name

nickname for HM Prison at Armagh in Northern Ireland and the penal facility for female offenders

Armley jail in Leeds, Yorkshire, England where Peter Sutcliffe—the Yorkshire Ripper—was held

Arohata Arohata Women's Borstal Institution, Wellington, New Zealand

Arrowhead Arrowhead Juvenile Detention Center in Duluth, Minnesota

Arthur Kill Arthur Kill Correctional Facility in Staten Island, New York—once the Drug Rehabilitation Center

Aryan Brotherhood California prison gang including members of the American Nazi Party and outlawed bikers, deeply involved in narcotics activity and racial confrontations

Arzew (*see* Algeria)

ASCA Association of State Correctional Administrators (publishes *Correctional Memo* quarterly)

Asheville Ashville, North Carolina, the seat of Buncombe County and the site of its jail

Ashford remand prison center in the London area

Ashland Federal Youth Center at Ashland, Kentucky (where many juvenile delinquents are held)

Ashwell HM Prison at Ashwell, Leicestershire, England

Asilo Toribio Durán Barcelona, Spain's reformatory

Asinara Italian penal colony, prison, and prison farm on Asinara Island off the northwest coast of Sardinia in the Mediterranean; its isolation is believed to be useful in rehabilitating its inmates

ASJJA Association of State Juvenile Justice Administrators

Askham Grange HM Prison at Askham Grange, Yorkshire, England, where female offenders are held

Asmara (*see* Ethiopia's prisons)

Associated Marine Institutes Florida's federation of correctional programs for young offenders

Association of State Correctional Administrators (*see* ASCA)

ASTREA Aerial Support to Regional Enforcement Agency (helicopter surveillance sometimes essential in deterring prison breaks or spotting escaping prisoners)

Asunción Paraguay's capital containing jails and a prison filled to overflowing with persons charged with crimes against the dictatorial regime so long a characteristic of this so-called republic

Atascadero institution for the criminally insane and mentally disordered sex offenders at Atascadero, California, north of Santa Barbara near Morro Bay

Atchison Kansas city in the northeastern corner of the state and location of the Youth Center

Atheist Penologist Jeremy Bentham (1748-1832)—English philosophical radical remembered for his Panopticon—a prison designed so every cell and interior area would have the benefit of natural light and air; he also argued the function of punishment was not revenge but the prevention of crime; he was opposed to the indiscriminate infliction of the death penalty

Atlanta Atlanta Youth Development Center in Atlanta, Georgia holding female juvenile delinquents up to the age of 17; U.S. Penitentiary at Atlanta, Georgia—one of the most famous maximum-security prisons in the United States where it has held many criminals and political prisoners; also location of the Staff Training Center of the Bureau of Prisons in Atlanta

Atlantic Avenue Brooklyn House of Detention for Men at 275 Atlantic Avenue in Brooklyn, New York

Atlantic City Atlantic City, New Jersey or its jail and its police-station lockups

Atmore Atmore State Prison Farm northeast of Bay Minette, Alabama; Fountain Correctional Center at Atmore, Alabama northeast of Mobile

ATPE Association of Teachers in Penal Establishments

Attica Correctional Facility at Attica, New York where it was opened in 1931 and by late 1984 was packed to capacity with male inmates; witnessed a four-day revolt in 1971 when 9 hostages and 28 inmates were killed

Auburn Auburn Correctional Facility (maximum-security institution formerly named Auburn Prison in Auburn, New York southeast of Syracuse)

Auburn cell-block plan keep the most hardened convicts in solitary confinement in separate cells, keep less hardened criminals in solitude until they give evidence of repentance, and keep the so-called least guilty in separate cells at night but working in silence in workshops during the day; this plan was popular during much of the 19th century

Auburn system characterized by enforced silence at all times for all inmates (also called the silent system)

Auckland Auckland Prison in Auckland, North Island, New Zealand

Augie Augusta, Georgia or its jail east of Atlanta on the South Carolina border

Auk Auckland, New Zealand or its jail

Aurora Staff Training Center of the Bureau of Prisons in Aurora, Illinois southwest of Chicago

Ausbruch aus dem Gefängnis (German—prison break)

Auschwitz-Birkenau (German—Oswiecim-Brzezinka)—Nazi concentration camp two hours from the Polish city of Cracow; some four million people were gassed, shot, tortured, or starved to death in this camp during World War II

ausgevished (Yiddish pun—wiped out at Auschwitz)

Austin Texas capital city and seat of Travis County with its jail northeast of San Antonio

Australian prisons each Australian state or territory has its own prison and thus there is one in the Australian Capital Territory containing Canberra, New South Wales—Sydney, Northern Territory—Darwin, Queensland—Brisbane, South Australia—Adelaide, Tasmania—Hobart, Victoria—Melbourne, Western Australia—Fremantle (close to Perth)

Austrian prisons criminals convicted to serve prison terms in Austria are not unlike those in

other lands who tell you they are or were in Atlanta, Fort Worth, or Petersburg as if they are or were travellers; in Austria they speak of Vienna, Graz, Linz, Salzburg, and Innsbruck—its principal cities complete with prisons

Austro-Hungarian Empire (*see* Austria, Hungary, *and* Yugoslavia)

Avenel New Jersey community south of Rahway and site of the Adult Diagnostic and Treatment Center

Avon Park Avon Park Correctional Institution in south-central Florida between Bradenton and Vero Beach; maximum- and medium-security inmates in an overcrowded environment but with educational and vocational opportunities

awa absent without authority

Awaiting Trial Facility in Cranston, Rhode Island and formerly the Providence County Jail

away away from here, away from home, away from work (away meaning imprisoned and therefore away)

awol (AWOL) absent without leave or permission

AWS (*see* Alston Wilkes Society)

axe and block decapitating equipment used in some countries where to come under the axe means to be beheaded; broad-bladed axes and hardwood blocks with slightly hollowed-out neck rests are standard capital-punishment tools of the executioner's trade

Aylesbury HM Prison at Aylesbury, Buckinghamshire, England

BA Buenos Aires, Argentina or any of its several jails and prisons

Babi Yar concentration camp outside Kiev where more than seventy thousand Jews and several hundred thousand Russian troops were killed by German forces during World War II; title of a poem by Yevtoshenko wherein he exposed both Nazi and Soviet anti-Semitism; title of Shostakovich's Symphony No. 13 inspired by this poem

back-gate exit dying in jail or prison and being carried out the back gate

Back Home convicts' nickname for the Tombs Prison in downtown New York City close to the criminal courts

back time unserved portion of a prison sentence any parole violator must serve once he or she is apprehended

baddie(s) bad guy(s)—incorrigible criminal(s)

bad rap(s) long prison sentence(s)

Baffin Correctional Centre in Frobisher Bay, Northwest Territories

Baghdad Iraq's oldest prison is in this oriental city close to the border of Iran

bagne (French—convict prison; convict ship; penal servitude)

Bahamas West Indian islands off Cuba's north coast; the capital—Nassau—is on New Providence Island and it contains an old gaol built in British colonial times

Bahrain Persian Gulf oil-export nation with its capital in Manama where there is an old prison (*see* Manama)

Baird Andrew C Baird Detention Center (Wayne County Jail in downtown Detroit, Michigan)

Baird House residence of the Quaker Committee on Social Rehabilitation at 135 Christopher Street in New York City

Baker Correctional Institution offers inmates a blend of counseling, recreation, schooling, and work in Olustee, Florida where it was opened in 1978

Bakersfield Kern County courthouse and jail in central southern California

Bakirkoy hospital for the criminally insane in Istanbul, Turkey; former inmates say it is dirty beyond belief and very likely to make anyone insane

Balearic Islands (*see* Spain)

Ball Louisiana town north of Alexandria and site of the Louisiana Training Institute holding female delinquents

Balti Baltimore, Maryland or its old penitentiary and other penal facilities

Baltimore Maryland's principal port city and address of the Maryland Penitentiary, the Maryland Training School for Boys, the Reception Center, and local lockups managed by

the police and the sheriff

Bamako (*see* Mali)

Banana City Brisbane, Queensland, Australia or its jail

banasto (Spanish—basket)— slang for cell or prison

bandbox county workhouse

Bandung (*see* Indonesian prisons)

Bangkok (*see* Thailand)

Bangladesh formerly called East Bengal or East Pakistan and now officially the People's Republic of Bangladesh with its principal prison in its capital city of Dacca

Bangui (*see* Central African Republic)

banishment condemned to exile in another country or to some far place belonging to the land of the person banished; prisoners, such as Napoleon who was first exiled to Elba in the Mediterranean between his native Corsica and the west coast of Italy, and was later banished to Saint Helena Island in the South Atlantic Ocean, find exile preferable to banishment as it is usually closer to home

banishment upheld some penologists argue banishment is better for prisoners and society than imprisonment even if this means exile to distant deserts or remote islands

Banning Banning Rehabilitation Center in Banning just west of Palm Springs, California

Barbados small West Indian island nation north of Trinidad; its capital—Bridgetown—has an old prison dating back to the years of British control and it is better than most such penal facilities

barbecue stool electric chair

Barcelona (*see* Spain)

Barlinnie Glasgow, Scotland's prison and its Young Offenders Institution

Barna Barcelona, Spain or its jail

Barquisimeto (*see* Venezuela)

barracoon(s) temporary prison(s)

Barranquilla Colombian prison in the river-port city on the Magdalena and close to its outlet to the Caribbean

Bartholomew Fair nickname of the solitary-confinement section of London's Fleet Prison in Elizabethan times

Bartons Mills medium-security prison near Perth in Western Australia

Basel (*see* Switzerland)

Basil Basil Health Systems

Bastille (French—small fortress)—La Bastille, the infamous royalist prison of Paris, was destroyed by French revolutionaries on July 14, 1789— a day celebrated ever since by Frenchmen everywhere; long a synonym for prison and especially one holding political prisoners

Bastille by the Bay inmates' nickname for San Quentin Prison on a peninsula in San Francisco Bay

Bastrop Federal Youth Center at Bastrop, Texas southeast of Austin (cares for inmates under 21 years of age)

Batavia (*see* Indonesian prisons)

Bath Ontario town west of Kingston and site of the Millhaven (maximum-security) Institution

Baton Rouge East Baton Rouge Parish has its courthouse and jail in Baton Rouge, also known for the Louisiana Juvenile Reception and Diagnostic Center for delinquent and neglected juveniles

Bat Rou Baton Rouge, Louisiana or its jail or Juvenile Reception and Diagnostic Center

Baumes Law New York State statute requiring life imprisonment for anyone convicted four times of felonies

Baumettes France's great cobblestone-walled prison in Marseilles where inmates complain they feel semi-embalmed and in early 1983 rioted to attract politicians who had promised prison reforms long overdue

Bay Botany Bay penal settlement in New South Wales (out of commission for more than a century)

Bayamón Puerto Rican city adjacent to San Juan's south side and holding the Metropolitan Regional Institution

Bay ship British prison ship destined for Botany Bay in New South Wales, Australia just south of Port Jackson and the city of Sydney

Bay State Correctional Center at

Norfolk, Massachusetts where it was opened in 1977 to confine long-term minimum-security male felons

BC Baja California, México or British Columbia, Canada or their jails and prisons

BCC Bureau of Charities and Corrections (South Dakota)

BCI Bureau of Correctional Institutions (Iowa)

BC Pen British Columbia Penitentiary in New Westminster adjacent to Vancouver

BCS Bureau of Criminal Statistics

Beaconsfield Marian Hall for delinquent English-Catholic juvenile offenders at Beaconsfield, Québec

bear den police station including its lockup

Beaune-la-Rolande site of a French concentration camp just southeast of Pithiviers (see *Camp de Drancy* for details as to how its prisoners fared)

Beccaria (*see* Father of Criminology)

Bedford HM Prison at Bedford, Bedfordshire, England

Bedford Hills Bedford Hills Correctional Facility at Bedford Hills, New York

Bedlam nickname of Saint Mary of Bethlehem, the celebrated lunatic asylum of old London, where many of its inmates were criminally insane

Beersheba Israel's largest prison located between Jerusalem and the Negev desert; built during British Mandate days as a police fortress and prison

behavioral control unit solitary-confinement prison cell or dungeon

beheading capital punishment long popular in many so-called civilized lands such as Britain and France, where the guillotine was invented

behind the iron door behind bars; jailed

behind the iron house in jail

Beira (*see* Mozambique)

Beirut (*see* Labanon)

Belfast Welfare Unit 14 euphemism for Her Majesty's Prison Camp outside Belfast, Northern Ireland

Belgian Congo (*see* Zaire)

Belgian prisons in Flanders, in the north of Belgium, Flemish is the official language, and the

word for prison is *gevangenis*, as in Dutch; in the south of Belgium, French is the official language, and the word for prison is *prison*; around the great seaport city of Antwerpen, as well as in Brugge and Gent, be prepared to hear Dutch-sounding Flemish but around the capital city—Bruxelles—as well as around industrial Liege, you'll hear about prisons in French

Belgrave (*see* Yugoslavia)

Belize new name for British Honduras and name of its old seaport city on the Caribbean; HM Gaol-type prison facilities are in Belize as well as in the new capital—Belmopan

Bellefonte Pennsylvania town northeast of State College and site of the State Correctional Institution at Rockview where it began as a branch of the Western State Penitentiary

Belle Glade site of the Glades Correctional Institution between Lake Worth and Lake Okeechobee, Florida

Belle Isle prisoner-of-war camp in the James River near Richmond, Virginia; many Federals died there due to prolonged exposure and lack of food in the Confederate prison camp

Bellevue Bellevue Hospital Prison Ward at First Avenue and 30th Street in New York City

Belmopan (*see* Belize)

Belsen Nazi concentration camp near Hannover, Germany and the scene of many crimes against humanity

Belzec German extermination camp in this Polish village on the railway line running through Lublin province during World War II when it was known as Beltzec to the Poles and Belzhets to the Russians

Benghazi Libyan port city and site of a prison built almost a century ago

Benin prisons this West African land has prisons in its two main cities—Cotonou and Porto-Novo on the north coast of the Gulf of Guinea

Bentham Jeremy Bentham (1748-1832)—English penologist-philosopher who wrote extensively about the need for prison reform and devised the panopticon-type prison where all cells and their inmates

could be observed from a central house containing wardens

Berdoo San Bernardino, California or its jail

Bergen hyphenate for the Nazi concentration camp of Bergen-Belsen in Lower Saxony, Germany; (*see* Norway)

Bergen-Belsen Nazi concentration camp near Celle in Lower Saxony, Germany; scene of many atrocities committed against persons of Judaic origin and political opponents of Hitler

Berhala Island prisoner-of-war camp run by the Japanese in North Borneo during World War II

Berlin Confinement Facility of the U.S. Army in West Germany

Bermuda (*see* Casemates)

Bern (*see* Switzerland)

Bernalillo Bernalillo County Detention Home in Albuquerque, New Mexico

Bess Bessemer, Alabama or its jail southwest of Birmingham

Beth Bethlehem, Pennsylvania or its city jail east of Allentown and close to Easton

Beto Unit (*see* Tennessee Colony)

Betty's Place St Elizabeth's Hospital in Washington, DC where Ezra Pound was held as a political prisoner during most of World War II

Bexar Bexar County Jail in San Antonio, Texas

BHD Bronx House of Detention in New York City

Bhutan the ancient Kingdom of Bhutan, high in the Himalayas, has its capital in Thimphu as well as its principal prison where conditions are primitive

Bialoleka Polish prison camp southeast of Bialystok

Bialystok Nazi concentration camp northeast of Treblinka in Poland

Big A nickname for the Federal Penitentiary in Atlanta, Georgia

Big D Dallas, Texas or its jail

big day visiting day in a prison

big gate(s) prison(s)

Big H Big House (any penitentiary or prison)

Big House up the River Sing Sing Prison at Ossining, New York

big pasture penitentiary

Big Spring Federal Prison Camp at Big Spring, Texas

Bilbao (*see* Spain)

bilbo(s) leg shackle(s) consisting of an iron bar fitted with adjustable fetters

Bilibid great maximum-security Philippine prison built in Spanish times at Muntinlupa in Rizal Province close to Manila

Billeshave youth home for delinquent boys, on the western edge of Denmark's island of Funen

Billings Billings, Montana or its county jail

Biloxi Mississippi seaport city between Gulfport and Pascagoula; seat of Harrison County and its jail where an alcoholic addict set fire to his padded cell and the smoke from the fire went through the ventilating system into other parts of the jail where it caused the death of 27 and the injury of 61 on November 8, 1982

bing solitary confinement

Binghampton in south-central New York close to the border of Pennsylvania; the name of its jail in the tongue of its inmates

birdcage prison cell

Birkenau (German—Birch Grove)—concentration camp built next to Auschwitz and also built by the Nazis near Oswiecim, Poland where so many were gassed, shot, or left to starve to death during World War II

Birmingham prison in Birmingham, Alabama or HM Prison in Birmingham, England plus prisons in smaller Birminghams in Iowa, Michigan, and Saskatchewan

Biscuit Factory nickname of old Reading Gaol in Berkshire, England where it adjoined Huntley & Palmer's biscuit factory

Bismarck capital of North Dakota in the south-central sector of the state and site of the North Dakota Penitentiary and the North Dakota State Farm for felons and first offenders

Bissau (*see* Guinea-Bissau)

bit time served in prison (a 10-year bit means 10 years of incarceration)

BJC Bureau of Juvenile Cor-

rection (Delaware)

BKA *Bundeskriminalamt* (German—Federal Criminal Ministry)—contains computerized files of criminal histories maintained at its center in Wiesbaden

black-and-white stripes old-fashioned convict colors adorning many prison uniforms in past centuries

black book prison register of its inmates

Blackburn Correctional Complex at Lexington, Kentucky where it provides vocational training release programs

black camp prison populated largely by blacks

Black Flower of Society Nathaniel Hawthorne's nickname for any jail, penitentiary, prison, or other place of imprisonment

Black Guerrilla Family gang primarily involved in drug trafficking within California prisons

Black Hole of Calcutta (*see* Indian prisons)

black lock solitary confinement

black maria prison van

black peter Australian slang—solitary-confinement prison cell

Blackwell's Island early name of Roosevelt Island (formerly Welfare Island) in New York City's East River under the Queensboro Bridge and long the site of correctional institutions

Bland Correctional Center at Bland, Virginia south of Bluefield

Bledsoe Bledsoe County Regional Correctional Facility in Pikeville, Tennessee

Blonde Beast of Belsen wardress Irma Grese's nickname given her in memory of cruelties inflicted by her on prisoners in the concentration camp run by the Nazis at Belsen

Bluefields (*see* Nicaragua)

blue lights in front of all of London's police stations and lock-ups except at Bow Street where there are white lights as it is close to the Royal Opera and the police are anxious to do all they can to improve the vicinity

Blue Ridge Pre-Release Work-Release Center in Greenville, South Carolina

Blundeston HM Prison at Blundeston, Suffolk, England

Blythe Blythe Branch of the Riverside County Jail in California at the Arizona border

board(ed) blindfold(ed)

B o C Bureau of Correction (Pennsylvania); Bureau of Corrections (Virgin Islands)

body shake search down to the skin and into the body

Bogotá federal prison in Colombia's capital high in the Andes

boiling boiling in oil; boiling people alive (savage custom generally abandoned because of the great deal of equipment and preparation necessary)—boiling was replaced by hanging

Boise capital of Idaho and site of the Idaho Security Medical Facility opened in 1976 and the Idaho State Correctional Institution built in 1870; county seat, courthouse, and jail of Ada County, Idaho

Bolivar Bolivar County Jail in Cleveland, Mississippi

Bolívar *Carcel Nacional de Ciudad Bolívar* (Spanish—National Prison of Ciudad Bolívar, Venezuela)

Bolivia this landlocked Andean nation has two capital cities—La Paz and Sucre; each has an old prison and there are prisons in Cochabamba and Santa Cruz as well as in smaller places

Bolshoi Dom (Russian—Big House)—prison

bolt cutter heavy-duty hardware tool used to cut bolts, chain-link fencing, handcuffs, steel bars, etc.

Bom Bombay, India or its prison

Bombay (*see* Indian prisons)

Bon Air Bon Air Learning Center southwest of Richmond, Virginia

boneyard graveyard

Boniato Cuban prison in Oriente Province where many anti-Castro prisoners have been tortured and executed

Bonneville Bonneville Community Corrections Center in Salt Lake City, Utah where it functions as a work-release facility

boob (Australian slang—jail; prison)

booking formal logging of inmates when they are received in jail or prison and are finger-printed and photographed

Boonville in Missouri east of Columbia and location of the Training School for Boys opened in 1889 for juvenile delinquents from 12 to 17 years of age

B o P Bureau of Prisons (United States Department of Justice)

Boquillas Boquillas del Carmen, Coahuila and its small jail across the Rio Grande from Boquillas in the Big Bend National Park in Texas

Bordentown New Jersey community south of Trenton holding the Youth Correctional Center, originally a prison farm and later a reformatory

Boron Federal Prison Camp at Boron, California in the Mojave Desert

borstal British name for a juvenile-delinquent reformatory

Borstal Borstal Prison in Kent, England where the first juvenile delinquent reformatory was established in 1902 for boys from 16 to 21; placename made famous by the book of Brendan Behan called *Borstal Boy*

borstals British correctional and detention centers such as Bullwood Hall in Essex, Deerbolt, Dover, East Sutton Park in Kent, Everthorpe, Humberside, Feltham and Finnamore Wood, Gaynes Hall, Glen Parva, Guys Marsh, Hatfield, Hewell Grange, Hindley, Hollesley Bay Colony, Huntercombe, Lowdham Grange, Onley, Portland, Rochester, Stoke Heath, Usk, Wellingborough, Wetherby, etc., in the British Isles

Bosnia (*see* Yugoslavia)

Boston Pre-Release Center in Dorchester southwest of Boston, Massachusetts

bot (BOT) balance of time to be served by anyone violating parole and returned to prison

Botany Bay port on the south side of Sydney, New South Wales, Australia, and long the nickname of the penal settlement there where some 700 British convicts—male and female—were landed in 1788 after an eight-month voyage from England; convict ships were square-rigged with sails

stencilled with big descending black arrows indicating they were headed Down Under to Botany Bay or Tasmania

bote (Spanish-American slang—jail or prison)

Botswana this landlocked South African country, once called Bechuanaland by the British, has prisons in its capital, Gaborone, and in Francistown

Bouaké (*see* Ivory Coast's prisons)

Bourgoin maximum-security prison in Bourgoin, France near Lyons

Bournemouth seaside site of four new prisons scheduled for completion on England's south coast southwest of London; built to relieve congestion in the United Kingdom's 118 penal institutions

Bowden Institution medium-security penal facility in Innisfail, Alberta

boxcar(s) prison cell(s)

boxed up (New Zealand slang—imprisoned, jailed, locked up)

box(es) prison cell(s)

Boydton Virginia community southwest of Petersburg and location of the Mecklenburg Correctional Center

Boys Ranch Group Home for Boys at Aguña, Guam (juvenile correctional facility)

Boys Totem Town in Saint Paul, Minnesota where delinquent boys are held in minimum security while being given training to help them live as decent citizens when they are released

BP Board of Parole; Bureau of Prisons

B of P Bureau of Prisons (U.S. Department of Justice)

BPT Board of Prison Terms

B of R Bureau of Rehabilitation (Washington, DC)

bracelets handcuffs

Brampton Vanier Centre for Women at Brampton, Ontario

Brandenburg concentration-camp subcamp west of Berlin

Brandon Correctional Institution in Brandon, Manitoba west of Winnipeg

brank leather or rubber head harness fitted with a gag and used to prevent a prisoner from shouting or talking

Brasilia Brazil's new capital with a new prison whose facil-

ities appear to be better than those found in Belém, Belo Horizonte, Manaus, Recife, Rio de Janeiro, Salvador, Santos, or other places such as the otherwise modern city of São Paulo

Braunschweig Nazi concentration camp located in what is now known as West Germany

Brazil the colossus of the Americas, Brazil, has as many prisons as it has cities from Belem, close to the Amazon, to Rio Grande near Uruguay; prisons go by such generic names as *cadeia, cárcere, penitenciária estadual,* or simply just *prisão*

Brazoria Texas community south of Houston and site of the maximum-security Central Unit opened in 1902

Brazzaville capital city and location of the main prison of the People's Republic of the Congo where it was built during the French occupation lasting from 1885 to 1960

breadand bread-and-water (prison fare for those in solitary confinement)

Bread Street London prison on Bread Street in Elizabethan times where its keeper had to be punished for cruelty to the convicts in his charge

bread and water traditional diet fed to difficult-to-handle prisoners as a form of punishment

bread and whiskey last meal fed to prisoners held by the Republic of China before they are shot for the crime of dealing in any of the many narcotics; on Taiwan such executions are shown on television and appear to deter dealers and their dupes

Brevard Brevard Correctional Institution in Sharpes, Florida where it was opened in 1975 to help first offenders up to age 25 complete their education, learn a vocation, and find out how to overcome alcohol and drug abuse

briar hacksaw (no longer used in prison breaks because most bars are resistant to most hacksaws)

bridewell British synonym for a house of correction such as the infamous Bridewell described by Hogarth in *The Harlot's Progress*; the prison has disappeared but its site may be found on London's New Bridge Street between the Embankment and Fleet Street at what was St Bride's Well near the River Thames

Bridge City Louisiana settlement southwest of New Orleans and site of the Louisiana Training School for delinquents under 17 years of age

Bridge House detention home for juvenile delinquents in Wilmington, Delaware

Bridgeport Connecticut Community Correctional Center in Bridgeport on Long Island Sound; the Fairfield County Jail is also here

Bridge of Sighs originally the enclosed passageway connecting the Doge's Palace with the prison dungeons of Venice (*Ponte dei Sospiri*); many such bridges in many parts of the world connect courtrooms with prisons and they too are called by this name, as only the cries of the prisoners seem to escape from any Bridge of Sighs; in London it means Waterloo Bridge where so many commit suicide; in downtown New York it is a high-level passage linking the Criminal Courts with the Tombs Prison

Bridgetown capital of Barbados and nickname of HM Prison in this West Indian port

Bridgewater community southeast of Brockton and containing the Massachusetts Correctional Institution as well as the Southeastern Correctional Center of Massachusetts

brig ship's prison (usually used to segregate unruly alcoholic and narcotic addicts or to hold stowaways until they can be turned over to immigration authorities)

Brighton Brighton Prison in Brighton, the popular seaside resort on England's south coast

brig rat(s) naval prisoner(s); shipboard prisoner(s)

Brigs (USN) (*see* USN Brigs)

Brisbane Brisbane Prison Complex (Queensland, Australia)

Brissie Brisbane, Queensland, Australia or its jail

Bristol HM Prison at Bristol, Somerset, England as well as prisons in other Bristols such as in Connecticut, Colorado, Florida, Georgia, Indiana, New Brunswick, New Hampshire, Pennsylvania, Québec, Rhode Island, South Dakota, and Vermont as well as the Bristol shared by Tennessee and Virginia

British detention centers Adlington, Blantyre House, Buckley Hall, Campsfield House, Eastwood Park, Erlestoke House, Foston Hall, Haslar, Kirklevington, Medomsley, New Hall, North Sea Camp, Send, Werrington House, Whatton

British Guiana (*see* Guyana)

British Honduras (*see* Belize)

British remand centers Ashford, Brockhill, Latchmere House, Low Newton, Pucklechurch, Risley, Thorp Arch

British West Indies (*see* individual island entries such as Saint Lucia or Saint Vincent and the Grenadines)

Brix Brixham, England or its jail

Brixton London, England's backwater of black alienation and crime in this ghetto populated by poor Jamaicans and other black West Indians; one of London's largest prisons is also in Brixton where the greatest jail break in British history took place in 1973 when 20 prisoners seized a garbage truck and used it as a battering ram to break out; 18 of the felons were caught almost immediately

Brno prison within the old castle of Czechoslovakia's second largest city

Bromberg Nazi concentration camp in East Prussia close to the Vistula River

Brooklyn Brooklyn Detention Center of the Immigration and Naturalization Service in New York City; Connecticut Community Correctional Center north of Norwich and opened in 1842 with a normal capacity of 100

Brookolino (Italian-American slang—Brooklyn, New York)—its nickname or its jail

Brookwood Brookwood Center for juvenile offenders at Claverack, New York southeast of Hudson and close to Catskill

Brookwood Center for Girls at Claverack, New York southeast of Hudson

Broome Broome Regional Prison (Western Australia)

Broward Broward Correctional Center at Pembroke Pines, Florida due west from Hollywood and the Atlantic Ocean; emphasis is placed on educational and vocational programs; the penal facility was opened in 1977

Brownwood Brownwood, Texas and the Brownwood State School for male and female juvenile delinquents in this city northeast of San Angelo

Brushes Wormwood Scrubs Prison—scrubs, being the contraction of scrubbing brushes, explains the origin of this nickname for a London suburban penal facility

Brushy Mountain Brushy Mountain Penitentiary at Petros, Tennessee west of Knoxville

BSSR Bureau of Social Science Research

bt's (prison) building tenders (porters, turnkeys, wing floor tenders, etc.)

bubbling executing by injecting air bubbles in the veins

Buchanan (*see* Liberia)

Bucharest (*see* Romania)

Buchenwald Nazi concentration camp near Weimar, Germany where more than 100,000 persons from German-occupied countries died as the result of brutal treatment while working as slave laborers in nearby arms plants and quarries; many starved to death

Buckeye Youth Center in Columbus, Ohio where it was started in 1914 to diagnose juvenile delinquents held there

Buda Budapest, Hungary or its prison

Budapest capital of Hungary and dreaded nickname of its old prison built during the days of the Austro-Hungarian Empire after the defeat of the Turks in 1697 and its dismemberment at the end of World War I in 1918

Buenaventura Colombian prison in the Pacific seaport city also known as one of the world's rainiest places

Buena Vista Buena Vista Correctional Facility at Buena

Vista, Colorado west of Colorado Springs; opened in 1889 and holding felons as well as misdemeanants

Buenos Aires (*see* Argentina and Villa Devoto)

Buffalo Erie County Jail in Buffalo, New York

Buford site of the Georgia Training and Development Center northeast of Atlanta and on the south end of Lake Sidney Lanier

bughouse insane asylum or prison for the criminally insane as described in prison slang

bug trap bed or cot in a jail or prison

Bujumbura (*see* Burundi)

Bukitduri women's prison near Djakarta (capital seaport city of Indonesia on the western end of Java where it was formerly called Batavia)

Bulawayo (*see* Zimbabwe)

Bulgaria Balkan nation under communist domination and officially the People's Republic of Bulgaria; its capital city—Sofia—has a large prison and smaller ones are in Plovdid and Varna as well as jails in smaller places

bullpen(s) place(s) of temporary confinement while awaiting arraignment, trial, or imprisonment; large common cell(s) holding many prisoners including the first-timers and the hardened criminals, the healthy and the sick, the young and the old

Buliwood Hall a borstal in Essex, England

Bulu women's prison near Semarang on the island of Java in Indonesia

Buna forced-labor camp close to Auschwitz and erected by the Nazis to aid in the production of artificial rubber also known as Buna

Bunbury Bunbury Rehabilitation Centre (Bunbury, Western Australia)

Bundeskriminalamt (German— Central Criminal Council)— West German Interpol headquarters in Wiesbaden

Bureau of Prisons U.S. Department of Justice, Bureau of Prisons, in 1982 administering six U.S. penitentiaries, twenty-four federal correctional institutions, a medical center for federal prisoners, seven federal prison camps, nine community treatment centers, three metropolitan correctional centers, a federal detention center, and four staff training centers including a food service training center

buried serving a long sentence

Burlington Burlington County Jail east of Camden at Mount Holly, New Jersey; largest city in Vermont and seat of Chittenden County with its Chittenden Correctional Facility; other Burlingtons in other states have jails if they are county seats

Burma officially the Socialist Republic of the Union of Burma but long a British possession from 1824 to 1948 when it became independent from the British Commonwealth; its prisons all date back to the British rule and are badly in need of refurbishing (*see* Rangoon)

Burnaby Lower Mainland Regional Correctional Centre in Burnaby, British Columbia

burn(ed) electrocute(d)

Buru Indonesian island in the Banda Sea just south of the Equator and closer to Ambon and Ceram than to Celebes (Sulawesi); its penal colony contains more than 11,000 political prisoners plus their families and children born on the island who may never experience freedom or political liberty

Burundi Bujumbura is the capital of Africa's smallest and most densely populated country facing the northern end of Lake Tanganyika in southern Africa; its prison was built during the years of German control and was later expanded when Belgium ruled

Bushnell Bushnell, Florida and site of the Sumter Correctional Institution opened in 1965

bush parole escape from confinement; escape from jail or prison

Butner Federal Correctional Institution at Butner, North Carolina northeast of Durham; built with escape-proof plastic windows and, while no gun towers surmount high walls, it is believed impossible for any inmate to scale the two 12-foot-high fences separated by 20 feet of coiled barbed wire equipped with automatic sensors; prisoners are hard-to-rehabilitate repeat offenders compelled to work at a prison job and to attend group discussions about all phases of prison life and outside life styles involving alcohol and drug abuse

butt last period of a prisoner's sentence (ranging from a few hours to a few weeks)

Butte Butte, Montana or its county jail

Butterworth site of a Japanese prisoner-of-war camp close to Georgetown in Penang harbor and where many Australians were held during World War II

Butyrskaya north-central Moscow's block-long four-story prison hidden behind an eight-story department store on Novoslobodskaya Street; since czarist times common criminals as well as political prisoners have been held here for long periods of pretrial examination

Bu-Tyur *Butyrskaya Tyurma* (Russian—Butyrki Prison)—a major prison in Moscow and not unknown to its prostitutes

BVR Bureau of Vocational Rehabilitation

b & w bread and water (diet often imposed on prisoners in solitary confinement or on unruly prisoners)

C.3.3. Oscar Wilde's identification number while imprisoned and when he wrote his poem, *The Ballad of Reading Gaol*, and his prose apologia for being in jail, *De Profundis*; C.3.3. stood for gallery C, 3rd landing, 3rd cell

caballo (Spanish—horse)—in Mexican-American slang means a person who carries drugs into jails and prisons

Cabbage Patch Victoria, Australia or its jail or prison

cabo general (Spanish—chief corporal)—head inmate or trusty in a prison

CAC Commission on Accreditation for Corrections

CACA Central After-Care Association (British society handling prisoners on parole)

cachot (French—underground prison cell)

cadeia (Portuguese—jail)

cage jail; lockup; imprison

CAGE Convicts Association for a Good Environment

cage and key men jailers; prison guards

Cairo capital of Egypt, noted for its heat and humidity causing its prisoners to swelter in segregation; many of its prison facilities were built during Anglo-French years of occupation

cala calabozo (Spanish—cell, dungeon, jail)

calaboose prison

calabouco (Portuguese—dungeon, jail)

calabozo (Spanish—prison)—also called *cárcel, celda, mazmorra, presidio, prisión*

Calc Calcutta, India or its prison

Calcutta (*see* Indian prisons)

Caledonia and Odum Complex North Carolina penal facility in Tillery

Caliente Nevada Girls Training Center (correctional facility) in Caliente, north of Las Vegas

California (*see* Chino, Corona, Folsom, Frontera, Jamestown, San Luis Obispo, San Quentin, Soledad, Susanville, Tehachapi, Tracy, and Vacaville entries)

California Institute for Women California's only state prison for women is also called Frontera as that is the name of the nearest town

California jails 58 counties are served by local lockups from Oakland in Alameda County to Marysville in Yuba County; city jails serve Fresno, Los Angeles, San Diego, San Francisco, and other big cities

California Medical Facility opened in 1955 with the goal of caring for convicts in need of medical help; at Vacaville and packed beyond capacity in late 1984

California Men's Colony state prison in San Luis Obispo

California State Prisons San Quentin and Folsom

Calle Marina (*see* Marine Street)

Camaguey (*see* Cuba)

Camarillo Ventura Reception Center and Clinic at Camarillo, California; this correctional facility is near the Ventura

School for Girls, also a correctional facility

Cambodia famine-stricken and war-torn Southeast Asian nation whose capital is Phnom Penh and whose prison was built during the French-colonial period

Cambridge county seat of Middlesex County, Massachusetts, across the Charles River from Boston; both cities have a county jail and many police-station lockups

Cameroon West African nation facing the Gulf of Guinea and with complete-with-prison cities such as Douala and Yaounde dating back to German and French occupation in the nineteenth and early twentieth centuries

camisole straitjacket

camp confinement or correctional facility; prison camp

campamento para presos (Spanish—prison camp)

campamento para prisioneros (Spanish—prisoners-of-war camp)

Campbellford Ontario town containing the Warkworth Institution

Campbell Work Release Center in Columbia, South Carolina for felons and misdemeanants in minimum custody

Camp Boiro Conakry's jail in Guinea on Africa's west coast

Camp de Drancy (French—Drancy Camp)—concentration and transit camp maintained by French collaborationists and the Gestapo in World War II in this northeastern suburb of Paris where many Jews and political prisoners died of malnutrition; survivors were shipped off to German and Polish camps where many more died in gas chambers

Camp de Gurs (*see* Gurs)

Camp de la Transportation official name of the penal colony headquartered at Saint Laurent du Maroni in French Guiana

camp de prisonniers (French—prison camp)

Camp Douglas in the 1860s a prisoner-of-war camp near Lake Michigan and southwest of Holland, Michigan; many Confederates died here due to the cold and to inadequate

food in this Federal prison camp

Campeche prison in Campeche, capital of the Mexican state of the same name, on the Yucatan Peninsula

Camp Harmony Japanese-American assembly center at Puyallup, Washington close to the Seattle-Tacoma seaport area where so many lived and worked before Pearl Harbor; (*see* Puyallup)

Camp Hill British reformatory on the Isle of Wight south of Southampton in the English Channel; Pennsylvania community just southeast of Harrisburg and location of the State Correctional and Diagnostic and Classification Center for processing central county commitments

Camp Iyar prison camp in Israel where Adolf Eichmann was held while awaiting trial as a war criminal

Camp Lejeune (*see* USMC)

Camp O'Donnell American military encampment on Luzon in the Philippines where the survivors of the Bataan Death March were imprisoned during World War II by the Japanese

Campo Numero Uno (1) (Spanish—Camp No. 1)—maximum-security military prison near Mexico City where many hardened convicts as well as political prisoners are held

Camp Pendleton (*see* USMC)

Camp San Jose California detention camp near Mount Palomar on Highway 76; like so many such camps it is overcrowded to the point of being a riot-type risk to its inmates and its correctional officers

Camp Smedley D Butler (*see* USMC)

Camp Topaz Camp Topaz—the Jewel of the Desert (Japanese-American nickname for the relocation center where they were held at Topaz, Utah during World War II)

campus prison grounds

Camp West Fork correctional center for juveniles; near Warner Springs at the outskirts of San Diego, California

Camp Westway detention center for juveniles; near Warner Springs, California

Canada second largest country in the world with ten provinces stretching from the Atlantic to the Pacific and from the American border almost to the North Pole; every province provides penal facilities ranging from penitentiaries and prisons to halfway houses and local lockups

canine shamus(es) dog detective(s)—used for their keen sense of smell and willingness to work in cramped places for minimum wages, guaranteed sobriety, and unflagging loyalty in the war against drugs as well as when retrieving escaped prisoners

cannery slang for prison of any kind

Canon City Centennial Correctional Facility in Canon City, Colorado southwest of Colorado Springs; a maximum-security facility with a normal capacity of 336; the Colorado Territorial Correctional Facility opened in 1871 is also here along with the Colorado Women's Correctional Facility opened in 1968, the Fremont Correctional Facility opened in 1962 for medium-security felons; the Reception and Diagnostic Center for maximum-security convicts, the Shadow Mountain Correctional Facility opened in 1981

Can Pen Ser Canadian Penitentiary Service

Canterbury HM Prison at Canterbury, Kent, England

Canton Canton, Ohio or its Stark County Jail

CANY Correctional Association of New York (City)

CAP Comité d'Action des Prisonniers (French—Prisoner's Action Committee)

Cape Town (see South Africa)

Cape Verde island republic formerly a Portuguese possession when its prison was built in Praia off the West African coast fifteen degrees north of the Equator

Cap-Haitien (see Haitian prisons)

capital punishment the death penalty resulting in execution

Capron Virginia town south of Chesapeake and site of the Capron Correctional Unit as well as the Deerfield, St Brides, and Southampton Correctional Centers

Cap-Rouge the Maison Notre-Dame de la Garde facility for juvenile delinquents at Cap-Rouge, Québec

captain warden of a road prison with its road-gang guards and inmates

captivus (Latin—captive or prisoner)

capun capital punishment

Caracas capital of Venezuela and location of several jails and lockups not unknown to local criminals as well as to tourists breaking the law

cárcel (Spanish—prison)—also called calabozo, celda, mazmorra, presidio, prisión

carceleras (Spanish—prisoner songs)—a flamenco song form allegedly developed by prisoners incarcerated in Ronda and celebrated in a zarzuela—Las Hijas del Zebedeo, The Daughters of Zebedee

carcelero (Spanish—jailer or warden)

Cárcel de Mujeres (Spanish—Women's Prison)—also name of the Instituto Nacional de Orientacion Femenina situated in los Teques Ejido Miranda in Venezuela

Cárcel de Valparaiso Valparaiso, Chile's jail

Cárcel Modelo (Spanish—Model Prison)—many Hispanic places throughout Latin America and the Iberian Peninsula have a so-called model prison

Cárcel Nacional de Ciudad Bolívar (Spanish—National Prison of Ciudad Bolívar)—on the Orinoco River in eastern Venezuela

Cárcel Nacional de Maracaibo (Spanish—National Prison of Maracaibo)—on Lake Maracaibo in western Venezuela

Cárcel Nacional de Trujillo (Spanish—National Prison of Trujillo)—northeast of Merida, Venezuela

carcer (Latin—jail or prison)

carcerario (Italian—prison)

carcere (Italian—prison)—also called prigione; (Portuguese—jail or prison)

cárcere (Portuguese—jail)

carcereiro (Portuguese—jailer; warden)

Carceri d'Invenzione (Italian—Imaginary Prisons)—series of etchings created by Giambattista Piranesi in the mid-1700s to show the oppressive frustration of confinement as well as the instruments of torture still used in his time

carceriere (Italian—jailer; warden)

Cardiff HM Prison at Cardiff, Wales

Carraca La Carraca (Cadiz, Spain's infamous prison within its navy yard)

Carson City Nevada's capital southeast of Reno and across Lake Tahoe from California but also the nickname of the Nevada State Prison there together with the Northern Nevada Correctional Center, the Nevada Women's Correctional Center, the Northern Nevada Honor Camp

Cartagena Colombian and Spanish prisons in seaport cities of the Caribbean and the Mediterranean, respectively

Casablanca Buenaventura, Colombia prison (see Morocco)

casa de corrección (Spanish—house of correction)—reformatory

Casa de Reeducacion y Trabajo Artesanal (Spanish—House of Reeducation and Artisan Work)—Venezuelan penal facility in the port city of Maracaibo as well as the capital city of Caracas where it is nicknamed La Planta

casa di correzione (Italian—house of correction)—reformatory

Casemates Bermuda's prison island formerly a fortress

Caserta women's prison just north of Naples, Italy

Cassidy Lake Technical School opened in 1944 at Chelsea, Michigan for felons over 21 and under 30 in need of academic and vocational training

Castieau's hotel nickname given the old jail in Melbourne, Victoria, Australia and honoring the jail's governor—JB Castieau

Castle Huntly Scottish borstal east of Dundee and close to the Firth of Tay

Castle Thunder Castle Thunder Prison in Richmond, Virginia where political prisoners were held by the Confederates during the Civil War

Castries (*see* Saint Lucia)

Castro's Prison nickname applied by the politically disillusioned and others to communist-controlled Cuba

Catalina Catalina Mountain School near Tucson, Arizona where it offers a program for male juvenile delinquents

Catete former royal palace used as Rio de Janeiro's immigration prison

cavale (French slang—prison break, prison escape)

Caves The Caves (HM Prison at Rockhampton in Queensland, Australia)

Cayahoga Hills Boys School juvenile-delinquent penal facility opened in Warrensville Heights just east of Cleveland in 1969

cayenne (French slang—prison ship)—many such were outward bound for prisons in or near Cayenne in French Guiana; as recently as 1950 such ships were still carrying prisoners to Devil's Island and mainland camps and prisons

Cayenne French Guiana prison on the Rue Francois-Arago in Cayenne, the capital city

cc condemned cell

CCA California Correctional Association; Colorado Correctional Association

CCC Central Correctional Center in Macon, Georgia

CCD & C Commission on Crime, Delinquency, and Corrections (Nevada)

CCHS Computerized Criminal Histories System (FBI)

CCI Coastal Correctional Institution at Garden City, Georgia close to Savannah and the Savannah River; Connecticut Correctional Institution at Niantic on Long Island Sound

CCOA California Correctional Officers Association; County Court Officers Association

CCTF California Correctional Training Facility

CD Corrections Department (New Mexico); Corrections Division (Hawaii, Oregon)

CEA Correctional Education Association

Cedar City north of Jefferson City, Missouri and site of the Renz Correctional Center opened in 1961

cela (Portuguese—prison cell)

celda (Spanish—prison cell)

Celery City Clink Kalamazoo, Michigan's jail

cella (Italian—prison cell)

cell smell usually a mixture of excreta, sweat, stale tobacco, unaired bedding, and vomit

cement tomb prison cell

Center City Detention Center modern name of the Eastern State Penitentiary at 21st and Fairmount Avenue in Philadelphia, Pennsylvania

Central Hong Kong's Central Police Station and lockup; North Carolina's Central Prison in Raleigh

Central African Republic Bangui is the capital of this landlocked African nation, which has an old prison built by the French during their occupation

Central Community Center halfway house for released prisoners in Los Angeles, California

Central Community Corrections Center in Salt Lake City, Utah

Central Correctional Center (*see* Macon)

Central Correctional Institution in Columbia, South Carolina where it opened in 1868

Central Detention Facility District of Columbia's modern maximum-security prison, opened in 1976 and enlarged in 1980, for detainees and sentenced misdemeanants in Washington, DC

Centralia Centralia Correctional Center opened in 1980 east of East Saint Louis for male felons; Washington community southwest of Seattle and address of the Maple Lane School (*see* entry)

Central Missouri Correctional Center in Jefferson City where it opened in 1938 with a normal capacity of 400 but now holding more than 600 felons

Central Ohio Regional Forensic Unit in Columbus where it was established in 1981 to provide psychiatric treatment for mentally ill offenders

Central Ohio Training Institution in Columbus where it opened in 1961 for male juvenile delinquents in maximum custody

Central Oklahoma Juvenile Treatment Center in Tecumsah, Oklahoma, housing delin-

quent females

Central Prison in Raleigh, North Carolina where it is a reception center for male felons; a maximum-security prison with a normal capacity of 1000; opened in 1871

Central Unit Texas maximum-security facility in Sugar Land where it opened in 1902

Centro de Reeducacion Agropecuario (Spanish—Center of Cattle and Land Reeducation)—penal farm-type facility in El Dorado (near the Guyana border of eastern Venezuela)

Centro Penitenciario de Occidente's Ejido Trujillo (Spanish—Central Penitentiary of the West in the Ejido Trujillo of Venezuela)

Centro Penitenciario de Oriente (Spanish—Central Penitentiary of the East)—Venezuela

Centro Penitenciario de Valencia, Ejido Carabobo (Spanish—Central Penitentiary of Valencia in the Ejido Carabobo)—Venezuelan penal facility southwest of Caracas

Ceuta (*see* Spain)

ceza evi (Turkish—house of punishment)—prison

CFA Correctional Facilities Association

CGIC Comisaria General de Investigacion Criminal (Spanish—Commisariat General of Criminal Investigation)—Spain's Interpol office

Chad landlocked African nation formerly a part of the French Sudan when its prison was built in what is now its capital city, N'Djamena

chain gang prisoners chained together during periods of outdoor work or transportation

chair electric chair

chamber gas chamber

Champerico Pacific coast port of Guatemala and its jail no ex-convict likes to remember

Changi Up Changi Road (Singapore's maximum-security prison)

Channel Islands Alderney, Brechou, Great Sark, Guernsey, Herm, Jersey, Jethou, Lihou, and Little Sark comprise this crown colony in the English Channel off the French coast; HM Gaol-type facilities are available

Channings Wood HM Prison at Channings Wood, Devonshire, England

Charleston South Carolina's principal city and seaport or the name given its jail; West Virginia's capital city and Kanawha County seat with its jail

Charlestown Charlestown, Massachusetts jail where anarchists Sacco and Vanzetti were electrocuted August 23, 1927

Charlotte Charlotte, North Carolina and the seat of Mecklenburg County with its courthouse and jail

Charlottetown capital of Prince Edward Island, Canada and location of the Sleepy Hollow Correctional Centre

chaser(s) prison guard(s)

Chateau d'If island prison off the port of Marseilles in the Mediterranean and the place where the *Man in the Iron Mask* was imprisoned as well as the characters created by the elder Alexandre Dumas in *The Count of Monte Cristo*

Chatham Island easternmost of the Galápagos off Ecuador and long used as a penal settlement; today the Galápagos Islands are called Archipiélago de Colón and Chatham is named San Cristóbal with administrative headquarters at Puerto Baquerizo

Chattahoochee in northwest Florida on the Georgia border and site of the River Junction Correctional Institution

Chattanooga Tennessee city in Hamilton County with its jail close to the Georgia border

chauki (Hindustani—jail)

CHC Chicago House of Correction

cheats gallows (term going back to Elizabethan English)

checas (Spanish slang—communist prisons)—term derived from *Cheka*—the communist secret police active in Spain during the Spanish Civil War when many leftists but non-Stalinists were killed or imprisoned by Soviet secret police

check out commit suicide

Cheesebox nickname for the Statesville, Illinois penitentiary shaped like a cheesebox

Chelmo Nazi concentration camp near Lublin, Poland where some 90,000 prisoners died during World War II

Chelmsford English prison in Chelmsford, northeast of London

Chelsea Michigan community northeast of Ann Arbor and site of the Cassidy Lake Technical School

Cherry Hill nickname of the Philadelphia prison opened in 1829 on the site of an old cherry orchard; this was the historic Eastern Penitentiary designed to insure the solitary confinement of each of its many prisoners

Chesapeake Virginia community southwest of Norfolk and location of the Chesapeake Correctional Unit

Cheshire Connecticut Correctional Institution at Cheshire southeast of Waterbury; holds felons and misdemeanants with age limits from 16 to 21

Chetumal prison in Ciudad Chetumal, capital of the Mexican territory of Quintana Roo, on the Caribbean coast at the border with Belize

Cheyenne Wyoming's capital in the southeastern corner of the state and county seat of Laramic County with its jail

Chicago largest city in the Midwestern United States and in the language of its penal population the toponym for its six divisions of its Department of Corrections or its Metropolitan Correctional Center; (*see* Cook County *and* toponyms)

Chihuahua prison in Chihuahua, capital of the northern Mexican state of the same name

Chile advanced South American nation stretching along the Pacific Coast from Arica to Cape Horn; its principal prisons are the Cárcel de Valparaiso and the Penitenciario de Santiago

Chillicothe Training School for (delinquent) Girls at Chillicothe, Missouri; Chillicothe Correctional Institute at Chillicothe, Ohio (for males with mental ailments)

Chillicothe Correctional Center Missouri penal facility for female felons; opened in 1981

Chilpancingo prison in the capital city of the Mexican state of Guerrero

Chi Ma Wan Chi Ma Wan Prison, Lantau Island, New Territories, Hong Kong

Chi Met Chicago Metropolitan Correctional Center (on West Van Buren Street)

China, People's Republic of communist-controlled mainland China—has a number of forced-labor camps and many prisons filled with political prisoners

China, Republic of (offshore China consisting of the large island of Taiwan, formerly Formosa, Matsu, the Pescadores, and Quemoy) maintains prisons in the capital city of Taipei as well as in Kaohsiung, Taichung, and Tainan; most prisons were erected by the Japanese during their occupation between 1895 and 1945

Chinde (*see* Mozambique)

Chino California Institution for Men at Chino on the eastern edge of Los Angeles; opened in 1941 with a normal capacity of 2,634 but by 1985 held more than 3000 males

chirona (Spanish slang—jail prison)

Chittenden Correctional Facility in South Burlington, Vermont since 1975

choke choke hold used to restrain the unruly by wrapping a forearm around the neck (the bar hold) or by putting pressure on the carotid artery in the neck (the carotid hold); both types of choke hold cut off the air supply and halt the flow of oxygen to the brain

chokey punishment or solitary-confinement cell

choky (English slang—jail)—term believed to be derived from the Hindustani *chauki* also meaning jail

chow hall prison mess hall

chow line prisoners lined up while waiting to be served food

Christchurch Christchurch Prison in Christchurch on South Island, New Zealand

Christianstadt Nazi subcamp in East Germany

chronophobia fear of time (psychiatric disorder suffered by many prisoners)

Chula Vista Chula Vista Staging Center of the INS at San Ysidro, California on a hill overlooking the Mexican Border; holds undocumented aliens awaiting deportation or admission to the U.S.

Chuna Soviet forced-labor camp in Siberia about 150 miles (600 kilometers) from Bratsk and close to Kondratyevo on the river Chuna

ci (CI) cooperative individual (informant)

CIA Central Intelligence Agency; Correctional Industries Association

Cincinnati Cincinnati, Ohio in the southwest corner of the state or the Hamilton County jail as Cincinnati is the county seat

Cincy Cincinnati, Ohio or its jail

City College British euphemism for Newgate Gaol—an old London lockup; New Yorker slang for The Tombs prison in downtown New York City, close to the Criminal Courts

city watchhouse police station; police station lockup

Ciudad Acuña Ciudad Acuña, Coahuila and its jail across the Rio Grande from Del Rio, Texas—formerly called Villa Acuña

Ciudad Juárez (*see* Juárez)

Ciudad Miguel Aleman Ciudad Miguel Aleman, Tamaulipas and its jail across the Rio Grande from Roma, Texas

Ciudad Trujillo official name of the capital of the Dominican Republic during the dictatorship of Trujillo and also the nickname of its many prison facilities

Ciudad Victoria prison in Ciudad Victoria, capital of the Mexican state of Tamaulipas, south of Texas and the Rio Grande, also known as the Rio Bravo del Norte

Civic Center San Jose, California's Civic Center Jail

CIW California Institution for Women at Frontera close to Corona and San Bernardino

clandestine prison(s) improvised jail(s) frequently found in Africa, Latin America, the Middle East, and Southeast Asia; usually packed beyond capacity with political prisoners

Clarkson Kings County Hospital Prison Ward at 435 Clarkson Avenue in Brooklyn, New York

classification center correctional institution unit where inmates are held in custody while awaiting commitment to a prison or rehabilitation program

Claverack Brookwood Center for Girls at Claverack, New York southeast of Hudson

Claymont Delaware's site for the Women's Correctional Institution and the Woods Haven-Kruse School for Girls convicted for juvenile delinquency

Clemens Unit Texas maximum-security penal facility in Brazoria south of Houston where it began in 1902

Clementina nickname of the San Michele reformatory for boys from 14 to 18; built in the time of Pope Clement XI (1700-1721) on Rome's Piazza di Porta Portese and still in use

Clermont-Ferrand French prison at 1 rue de la Prison in Clermont-Ferrand where a Franco-fascist government had its capital during most of World War II

Cleve Cleveland, Ohio or its jail

Cleveland Cleveland, Ohio seated in Cuyahoga County with its jail and police-station lockups

client(s) person(s) on probation

client(s) of the correctional system convict(s)

Clink euphoniously named London prison formerly dominating the south bank of the Thames near London Bridge where it was a well-known landmark in the days of Hogarth and Dickens; not only the generic nickname for all prisons but for brothels and the Southwark Fair depicted by Hogarth; only its name survives at its site on Clink Street

Clink *The Clink*—Tasmanian hotel trading on the island's convict past

Clinton New Jersey community east of Phillipsburg and location of the Correctional Institution holding high misdemeanants, juvenile delinquents and misdemeanants, and a cottage containing geriatric male felons; Clinton Correctional Facility at Dannemora, New York

close custody (*see* maximum security)

CMCC Chicago Metropolitan Correctional Center

CMS Correctional Medical Systems

CNPB Canadian National Parole Board

CO Correctional Officer

COA Correctional Officers Association

Coastal Correctional Institution (*see* CCI)

coche celular (Spanish—prison van)

Coeur d'Alene Kootenai County's county courthouse and jail in northern Idaho

Coffield Unit Texas maximum-security prison in Tennessee Colony northwest of Palestine

cold Auschwitzes of the North dissident Soviet poet Yuri Galanskov's phrase describing the Arctic death camps of the USSR where they have been in operation since 1921 (*see* Kholmogori)

Coldingley HM Prison at Coldingley, Surrey, England

Colima prison in Colima, Mexico

college reformatory

Collins Bay Institution medium-security penal facility in Kingston, Ontario

Colombia South American nation with coasts on the Caribbean and the Pacific; almost every city has a so-called Cárcel Modelo and there are other prisons such as Gorgona on an island in the Pacific southwest of Buenaventura and another, La Pieota, in Bogotá, the capital

Colombo (*see* Sri Lanka)

Colorado (*see* Canon City; Buena Vista)

Colorado jails the state's 63 counties are served by jails from the one in Brighton, county seat of Adams County, to Wray in Yuma County; cities such as Denver and Colorado Springs have local detention facilities

Colorado Springs El Paso County courthouse and jail in central Colorado south of Denver

Colorguard trade name for a fabric-coated pre-galvanized steel fencing system, which the Colorguard Corporation of Raritan, New Jersey claims cannot be penetrated by gun muzzles, knives, or rocks

Columbia Mississippi community west of Hattiesburg and place where the Columbia Campus was opened in 1943 and is controlled by the Department of Youth Services; South Carolina's capital city northwest of Charleston and address of the Campbell Work Release Center, the Central Correctional Institution opened in 1868, the Kirkland Correctional Institution, the Manning Correctional Institution, the Maximum Security Center, and the Walden Correctional Institution

Columbia Campus (*see* Columbia)

Columbus Ohio's capital city containing the Buckeye Youth Center, the Central Ohio Regional Forensic Unit, the Central Ohio Training Institution, the Columbus Correction Facility, the Training Center for Youth, the Women's Correctional Admission Center

Columbus Correctional Facility formerly the Ohio Penitentiary and still holding more than 1700 felons in all degrees of custody

Columbus Fire occurred in the Ohio State Penitentiary in Columbus in April 1930 and cost 320 lives

Combinado Combinado del Este (large prison outside Havana, Cuba)

Combinado del Este (Spanish—Eastern Combination)—cryptic title of Cuban prison in Havana Province where as many as 13,500 people were incarcerated for failure to support Castro

Community Correctional Center (*see* Bridgeport, Brooklyn, Hartford, Litchfield, New Haven, Uncasville)

community facility adult, juvenile, or nonconfinement facility where residents are allowed to depart, unaccompanied by any official, to hold or seek employment or to go to school for treatment programs

Community Treatment Centers halfway houses for male and female offenders treated by the U.S. Bureau of Prisons in Atlanta, Georgia; Chicago, Illinois; Dallas, Texas; Detroit, Michigan; Houston, Texas; Kansas City, Missouri; Long Beach, California; New York, New York; Oakland, California; Phoenix, Arizona

Comoros the Federal and Islamic Republic of the Comoros, in the Indian Ocean northwest of Madagascar, has its capital and prison in the port city of Moroni

compash underworld slang for a compassionate probation officer, prison chaplain, social worker, or prison visitor

Compiègne French concentration camp northeast of Paris where it was controlled by the Gestapo during the years of German occupation in World War II

Complex The Complex (Brisbane Prison Complex in Queensland, Australia and augmented by prisons in Rockhampton, Townsville, and Woodford)

con convict

Conakry (*see* Guinea prisons)

concerning the criminal element Eugene Victor Debs, convicted for opposing World War I, had this to say— *"While there is a lower class, I am in it; while there is a criminal element, I am of it; while there is a soul in prison, I am not free."*

Conciergerie (French—porter's lodge)—the great prison of Paris on the Ile de la Cité where it was founded in 1392

Concord capital of New Hampshire and location of the Concord Community Corrections Center, the New Hampshire State Prison, and the New Hampshire State Prison Community Corrections Center

Concord Community Corrections Center in Concord, New Hampshire

concrete womb(s) prison(s)

condannato (Italian—convict)

condao (Mexican-American Spanish—county jail)—corruption of the Spanish word for county (*condado*)

Condemned Rock Macquarie Island, Tasmania's nickname for Grummet Island when it was a penitentiary for desperate criminals

condenado (Portuguese or Spanish—convict)

conditional release parole

condominio (Spanish—condominium)—euphemism for jail or prison

confinee(s) prisoner(s)

confinement imprisonment

Congo the People's Republic of the Congo (formerly the French Congo) is on Africa's west coast between Gabon and Zaire; Brazzaville, its capital on the Congo River, has an old prison built by the French

conjugal visit plan whereby a prisoner may enjoy a marital relationship with a spouse

conk a screw club a guard

Connecticut (*see* Bridgeport, Brooklyn, Cheshire, Enfield, Hartford, Litchfield, New Haven, Niantic, Somers, Uncasville)

Connecticut Correctional Institution (*see* Cheshire, Enfield, Niantic, Somers)

Connecticut lockups the state's eight counties provide detention facilities for its big cities such as Hartford, Bridgeport, and New Haven as well as for smaller places such as New London and Litchfield, Stamford, and Norwalk

Connor Correctional Center in Hominy, Oklahoma where it was opened in 1979 for medium-security inmates

con(s) convict(s)

Constantine (*see* Algeria)

Constanza (*see* Romania)

convict goods things produced by convict labor (automotive-vehicle license plates, mail sacks, school benches, etc.)

convict labor work performed by prisoners as part of their program of rehabilitation (public works such as ecology conservation, farming, road building, vehicle registration, etc.)

convict(s) convicted felon(s) serving a prison term

convict ships (plying between British and down-under ports in New South Wales and Van Diemen's Land in the late 18th and early 19th centuries) *Aboukir, Active, Admiral Barrington, Admiral Gambier, Adrian, Albemarle, Albion, Alexander, Alibi, Almorah, America, Ann, Ann and Amelia, Anson, Arab, Asia, Asiatic, Atlantic, Atlas, Atwick, Augusta Jessie, Aurora, Bardaster, Baring, Barossa, Batavia, Bellona, Bengal Merchant, Blenheim, Britannia, Bussorah Merchant, Cadet, Cal-*

cutta, Canada, Castle Forbes, Chapman, Charlotte, Circassian, Commodore Hayes, Coromandel, Countess of Harcourt, Cressy, Dromedary, Earl Cornwallis, Earl Grey, Earl St Vincent, Eden, Edward, Egyptian, Eliza, Elizabeth, Elizabeth and Henry, Elphinstone, Emma Eugenia, Emily, Emperor Alexander, Eolus, Equestrian, Experiment, Fanny, Fortune, Frances Charlotte, Friendship, Ganges, General Hewart, General Stewart, Gilbert Henderson, Gilmore, Glatton, Grenada, Guildford, Harmony, Hector, Henry, Henry Porcher, Hillsborough, Hindostan, Hyderabad, Indefatigable, Indian, Indispensable, Isabella, Jane, John, John Barry, John Brewer, John Renwick, Kinnear, Lady Harewood, Lady Juliana, Lady of the Lake, Lady Rowena, Lloyds, Lord Auckland, Lord Lyndoch, Lord William Bentinck, Margaret, Maria, Maria Soames, Marion, Marmion, Marquis of Hastings, Marquis of Huntley, Mary Anne, Medina, Mexborough, Minerva, Minorca, Moffat, Morley, Navarino, Neptune, New Grove, Norfolk, North Briton, Ocean, Orator, Oriental Queen, Pestonjee Bomanjee, Pitt, Portland, Prince Regent, Rajah, Ratcliffe, Recovery, Rodney, Royal Admiral, Royal Charlotte, Runnymede, St Vincent, Scarborough, Second Fleet, Sidmouth, Sir Godfrey Webster, Sir Robert Peel, Sir Robert Seppings, Sir William Bensley, Somerset, Southworth, Speke, Stakesby, Surprize, Surrey, Susan, Sydney Cove, Tasmania, Tenasserim, Tortoise, Tottenham, Triton, Waterloo, Waverley, Westmorland, William Jardine, William Miles, Woodford, etc., including vessels with names such as Nile, Perseus, Persia; down-under readers will be sure to spot missing names

con wise wise convict who knows what's going on in the jail or prison including illicit operations such as dealing in drugs or making alcohol

Cook County the County of Cook covering the entire area of Chicago, Illinois has a Department of Corrections with six divisions; Nos. 1, 2, 3, and 5 are on South California Avenue, Nos. 4 and 6 are on South Sacramento Avenue; No. 1 is the Cook County Jail opened in 1929; No. 2 is the old House of Correction opened in 1871; No. 3 is the Women's Division; No. 4 is also known as the Men's Correctional Center; No. 5 is an intake and reception facility; No. 6 is the Training Academy

cooler(s) brig(s), guardhouse(s), jail(s), lockup(s)

coop(s) prison(s)

cop a broom leave in a hurry like a witch atop a broom

cop a drill leave at a normal walking pace so as not to attract the attention of guards

cop a heel escape from law-enforcement officers or from correctional facilities

cop a moke escape from a jail, prison, or other penal facility

cop a sneak escape from confinement

Copenhagen Copenhagen, Denmark's modern prison noted for its design insuring inmates the maximum of light and air

cop house(s) police station(s) or lockup(s)

Copper John Auburn Prison's nickname

copper shop police station and lockup

Cordoba (see Argentina)

Corinto Nicaragua's seaport city on the Pacific with a jail well known to many seamen as well as some tourists

Cork (see Irish prisons)

Cornton Vale Scottish prison

Corona California Rehabilitation Center at Corona between Los Angeles and Riverside; holds some 1700 male and female convicts

corralón (Mexican-Spanish—corral)—detention camp where illegal entrants await deportation

corre correccional (Mexican-Americanism—correctional institution, penitentiary, reformatory)

correctional agency federal, state, or local criminal-justice agency charged with the investigation, intake screening, supervision, custody, confinement, or treatment of adjudicated or alleged offenders

Correctional Center for Women in Raleigh, North Carolina where it is the holding facility for all women sent to prison

Correctional Clinic U.S. Bureau of Prisons Correctional Clinic at 210 West 53rd Street in New York City

correctional custody facility brig, jail, penitentiary, prison, reformatory

correctional custody unit U.S. naval euphemism for a ship's brig or lockup

Correctional Development Centre maximum-security facility in Laval, Québec

Correctional Education Association publishes quarterly Journal of Correctional Education

correctional institution generic name for long-term confinement facilities

correctional officer(s) prison guard(s); prison warden(s)

Correctional Service Federation American wing of the International Prisoners Aid Association

correctional training school reformatory

Correction and Rehabilitation Squadron U.S. Air Force at Lowry Air Force Base in Colorado

Correction Camp Program for male and female felons housed at Grass Lake, Michigan

Correction Division Release Center in Salem, Oregon where it opened in 1977

corrections caseload number of clients registered with a correctional agency or agent during a specified time limit

corrective labor camp communist euphemism for forced-labor camp of the type described by Solzhenitsyn in The Gulag Archipelago

Corrective Services all of the gaols (jails) and prisons in Australia's New South Wales are managed by the Department of Corrective Services in Sydney

CO(s) Correction Officer(s); Correctional Officer(s)

cost of imprisonment often more than the cost of a college education; in the late 1800s and the early 1900s it was proven prison industries and work programs made a profit for penal institutions but private firms and trade unions put a stop to such practices

Costa Rica this most advanced Central American country with port cities on the Caribbean and on the Pacific has its principal prison in the capital city of San José up in the mountains; smaller ones are in the ports—Limón on the Caribbean and Puntarenas on the Pacific

Coti Martinez clandestine Argentine prison's place-name pseudonym (real name unknown except to the Argentine armed forces)

count prison population inventory taken as often as nine times a day to insure security and help detect escapes

Counterpoint bimonthly publication of the National Juvenile Detention Association

county cooler(s) county-supported mental hospital(s) frequently confining the criminally insane

county hotel(s) county jail(s)

Cowansville Cowansville Institution holding young offenders in Cowansville, Québec southeast of Montreal

Coxsackie Coxsackie Correctional Facility (medium-security prison in Coxsackie, New York just south of Albany)

CPA Connecticut Prison Association

CPPCA California Probation, Parole, and Correctional Association

CPS Canadian Penitentiary Service

CPSM Colonial Prison Service Medal (British decoration)

Cracow (*see* Poland)

Cracow/Plaszow concentration camp holding many forced laborers held by the Germans in this Polish city during World War II

Cradle of the Penitentiary Philadelphia, Pennsylvania's Walnut Street Jail built in the late 1700s and providing congregate as well as individual cells and workhouses

cranky hatch(es) cell(s) reserved for mentally deranged prisoner(s)

Cranston Rhode Island city just south of Providence and containing eleven penal facilities

crash escape from jail or prison

crazy alley(s) cell block(s) reserved for the insane

crazy hospital(s) psychiatric ward(s)

CRD Civil Rights Division, U.S. Department of Justice

creative conflict demonstration or riot

creative sentence sentence created to fit the crime (for example, making graffiti artists clean the walls they have defaced)

crime defined Irish-born British playwright George Bernard Shaw defines crime in his play *Man and Superman*, "Crime is only the retail department of what, in wholesale, we call penal law."

crime doesn't pay? British labor leader Ernest Bevin observed: "*the only way to make sure crime doesn't pay is to have the government take it over and run it*"

crimeless society Thomas Paine, author of *The Age of Reason* and *The Rights of Man*, wrote: "*When it shall be said of any country in the world, 'My poor are happy; neither ignorance nor distress is to be found among them; my jails are empty of prisoners, my streets of beggars; the aged are not in want; the taxes are not oppressive; the rational world is my friend, because I am a friend of its happiness'—when these things can be said, then may that country boast of its constitution and its government.*"

criminoso inveterado (Portuguese—inveterate criminal)—jailbird

CRMT Community Resources Management Team (parole and probation)

Croatia (*see* Yugoslavia)

Crockett Crockett State School for Girls at Crockett, Texas between Houston and Tyler

cross-bar hotel(s) jail(s) or prison(s)

Cross City Cross City Correctional Institution halfway between Gainesville and the Gulf of Mexico; opened in 1973; offers academic and vocational training

Crown Point nearly century-old Indiana jail just south of Gary; gangster John Dillinger broke out from here in 1934, using a fake pistol carved from a bar of soap colored with shoe polish; Crown Point auctioned off in 1976 for use as a museum

CRS Correction and Rehabilitation Squadron (U.S. Air Force Base at Lowry Air Force Base in Colorado)

cruel and unusual punishment being boiled in oil, being set afire, ducking, mutilating, pilloring, and whipping were common practices in a number of countries; as recently as the mid-1920s whipping was a punishment applied publicly in Dover, Delaware

Crumlin Crumlin Road Prison in Belfast, Northern Ireland

Crumlin Road 14 address and nickname of one of Her Majesty's prison camps outside Belfast, Northern Ireland

CSCA Central States Corrections Association

CSD Correctional Services Department; Corrective Services Department

CSF Correctional Service Federation

CSM Correctional Service of Minnesota (Minneapolis)

Cuba largest and westernmost island of the West Indies; a *cárcel modelo* can be found in Havana, Santiago de Cuba, Camaguey, Matanzas, and even smaller places, and there is a large penal settlement on the Isle of Pines

Cuernavaca prison in Cuernavaca, capital of the Mexican state of Morelos in the mountains south of Toluca

Cueva Panamanian island prison southwest of Panamá City and close to Cape Mala on the Pacific coast

cuff(s) handcuff(s)

Culiacan prison in Culiacan, capital city of the Mexican state of Sinaloa, close to the Pacific Ocean

Cummins Cummins Prison Farm (facility of the Arkansas State Penitentiary holding girls and women convicted of illegal drug use and prostitution); Cummins Unit in Grady, Arkansas southeast of Pine Bluff (provides maximum-, medium-, and minimum-security accommodations to some 1700 male felons)

Custer South Dakota town southwest of Rapid City and location of the Youth Forestry Camp

custodial officer(s) prison guard(s)

Cux Cuxhaven, West Germany or its jail

Cuyahoga Cuyahoga County Juvenile Detention Home in Cleveland, Ohio

CYC Colorado Youth Center at Denver

Cyprus island republic in the eastern Mediterranean; its port and capital, Nicosia, has an old Turkish prison and a nearby camp site where Jews were detained to keep them out of Palestine from 1945 to 1948

Czechoslovakia Socialist Republic whose prisons were built during the days of the Austro-Hungarian Empire; Prague, the capital, and Brno, Bratislava, and Ostrava all have their old prisons

CZ Pen Canal Zone Penitentiary at Gamboa

DAC Department of Adult Corrections (Alaska)

Dacca nickname of the principal prison of Bangladesh in the capital city of Dacca

Dachau (Old German—marsh)—site of a large Nazi concentration camp near Munich where untold thousands were killed for such crimes as being a Gypsy or being of Judaic origin or merely for being too outspoken in criticizing Hitler and his regime

daddy tank prison cell reserved for lesbians to keep them from being attacked by other prisoners

Dade Correctional Center at Homestead, Florida south of Miami where it offers offenders counseling, education, and vocational training

Dago slang for San Diego, California or its jail, lockups, or prison (*see Diego*)

Dallas second largest city in Texas and the nickname of its county jail; State Correctional Institution at Dallas, Pennsylvania

Dalmatia (*see* Yugoslavia)

Damascus (*see* Syria)

Damon Israeli medium-security prison for adult repeat offenders and Arab juvenile delinquents from 14 to 20 years old; built by the British in Mandate times and about halfway between Beersheba and the Dead

Sea salt works

Da Nang (*see* Vietnam)

Danbury Federal Correctional Institution at Danbury, Connecticut

dance death by hanging (as the body tends to dance and twitch about during execution)

dance hall cell or hallway leading to an execution chamber where the condemned seems to dance when the current is applied to the electric chair

dance of death hanging

dance on air death by hanging

dangerous aliens Canadian government designation of Japanese-Canadians in the post-Pearl-Harbor period when some 22,000 were evacuated from their homes, farms, and stores along the coast to inland places where they were used to help build a highway through the Rocky Mountains

Dannemora Clinton Correctional Facility at Dannemora, New York west of Plattsburg and near the Canadian border

Danville Youth Development Center southwest of Lexington, Kentucky with special units designed to aid various kinds of boy delinquents

darbies handcuffs (nautical term current in the early 1800s when Herman Melville used it in *Moby Dick*)

Dar-es-Salaam (*see* Tanzanía)

Darrington Unit Texas penal facility begun in 1919 and holding maximum-security felons within its confines in Rosharon

Dartmoor Her (His) Majesty's prison near Princetown and the Dartmoor Forest of southwest England

Davao port city of Mindanao in the Philippines and nickname of its old prison

Day Dayton, Ohio or its jails and lockups

Daytona Beach Florida East Coast resort city about halfway between St Augustine and Titusville; site of the Tomoka Correctional Institution opened in 1981 with a design capacity of 600

Dayton Forensic Hospital in Dayton, Ohio where it was opened in 1980 to give psychiatric help to mentally ill felons

Daytop Daytop Lodge in Staten Island, New York where male narcotic violators are offered treatment

db dirt bag (an undocumented Hispanic alien)

DB Disciplinary Barracks

dbd death by drugs (execution by lethal injection)

dc death cell

DC District of Columbia jail in Washington, DC

D of C Department of Corrections; District of Columbia

DCJ Dade County Jail in downtown Miami, Florida

DCS Department of Correctional Services (Nebraska, New York)

DCWDC District of Columbia Women's Detention Center

DEA Drug Enforcement Administration

Dead Men's Cove San Diego Police Department headquarters and lockup at the foot of Market Street close to Seaport Village

Dear John letter written communication to a prisoner from a lover or wife informing him their engagement or marriage is over

death by injection prisoners condemned to death in Texas are subjected to a massive overdose of sodium thiopental to stop breathing while pavulon, a muscle relaxer, and potassium chloride are added to stop heartbeat, the Poison Control Center reports

death penalty punishment by death

death row cell block reserved for prisoners awaiting execution

decap decapitation (ancient Chinese and Japanese sentence for the crime of selling dangerous drugs)

Deerbolt HM Borstal at Deerbolt in England

Deerfield Correctional Center in Capron, Virginia where it has been in operation since 1977

Deer Lodge Montana community southwest of Helena and site of the Montana State Prison

defective delinquent(s) criminally insane person(s)

DeHoCo Detroit House of Correction

Delaware (*see* Claymont, Dover, Georgetown, Smyrna, Wilmington)

Delaware Correctional Center penal facility opened in 1971 with a normal capacity of 768 but with 883 male inmates by 1985 in maximum, medium, and minimum security at this place in Smyrna north of Dover

Delaware jails three counties provide lockups for communities around Wilmington, Dover, and Georgetown

Delhi (*see* Indian prisons)

Delle Stinche Florentine prison dating from the early 1300s and famous for its advanced methods of inmate handling and segregation

Denmark smallest of the Scandinavian countries consisting of the Jutland Peninsula and some five hundred islands; penologists give it good marks in their assessment of its penal institutions (*see* Herstedvester and Ringe), Copenhagen and Arhus have central prisons

Denver largest city in Colorado and nickname of its penal institutions

De Quincy Louisiana Correctional and Industrial School at De Quincy in Calcasieu Parish, north-northwest of Lake Charles

Des Moines Iowa's centrally located principal city and county seat, courthouse, and jail of Polk County; well known for its role in correctional institution planning

Des Moines Plan innovative alternative to building new prisons, as less risky convicts are steered to programs allowing them to help themselves by working or attending school under probationary supervision

De Soto De Soto Correctional Institution in south-central Florida between Sarasota and Stuart

detention legally authorized confinement of a person subject to criminal or juvenile court proceedings until commitment to a correctional facility or release

detention center jail housing prisoners awaiting trail

detention facility generic term for county farm, detention center, honor farm, jail, juvenile hall, road camp, work camp, etc.

detention glazing chemically strengthened and plastically bonded glass used in place of bars or walls in modern penal facilities

detention screening stainless-steel screening allowing air, light, and sound to enter but preventing the entrance of contraband such as drugs and weapons

detention windows designed to admit air and/or light but to prevent the escape of prisoners (*see* detention glazing)

détenu (French—prisoner)

detenuta (Italian—detainee; prisoner)

Detoxification Center (*see* Inebriate Reception Center)

Detroit Wayne County Jail in downtown Detroit, Michigan (a 13-story 576-cell penal facility)

Deuel Deuel Vocational Institute medium-security penal facility at Tracy, California, southwest of Stockton

devil's front porch prison

Devil's Island generic name of the penal colony in French Guiana and its group of offshore islands in use as late as 1950 for convicts and political prisoners serving lifetime or long-duration sentences

DHC Detroit House of Correction

DHS Department of Health Services

DIA Department of Institutions and Agencies (governing New Jersey's prison system)

Diagnostic and Evaluation Center opened in Lincoln, Nebraska in 1979 where it holds male felons in maximum security while under diagnosis and evaluation

Diagnostic Unit in Huntsville, Texas where all incoming inmates are diagnosed and sent to appropriate prisons

Diego (Mexican-American truncation—San Diego)—California border city or its jail, lockups, or prison (*see* Dago)

Diego Met San Diego Metropolitan Correctional Center (Hispanic appellation)

die in the hot seat be electrocuted

die of lead poisoning killed by lead bullets

die of throat trouble hanged

Directory of Juvenile Detention

Homes published by the National Juvenile Detention Association

Directory of Prisoners Aid Agencies published by the International Prisoners Aid Association

Directory of Residential Treatment Centers published by the International Halfway House Association

dirt prisoner's nickname for sugar

dirty towel prison barbershop or beauty parlor

Dismas House halfway house opened in St Louis, Missouri in the 1930s

District of Columbia capital district containing Washington, DC, the Capitol, the Central Detention Facility, and the site of some ill-reputed prisons used during and after the Civil War but replaced by modern facilities in the District and in Lorton, Virginia

District of Columbia entries (*see* Central Detention Facility, Lorton, Occoquan)

District of Columbia lockup the nation's capital has lockup facilities in addition to those of federal agencies

dite (Mexican-Americanism—detention hall)—place where illegal aliens must wait while being investigated

Division No. 1 modern name for Chicago's Cook County Jail

Division No. 2 modern name for Chicago's House of Correction

Divisions No. 1 through 6 (*see* Cook County)

Dix Dorothea Lynde Dix (1802-1887)—American reformer and pioneer in securing better treatment for the insane in asylums, poor houses, and prisons throughout New England; also wrote books for children and served as superintendent of women nurses during the Civil War

Dixon Correctional Institute medium-security penal facility in northern Louisiana at Jackson

DJ Department of Justice (*see* U.S. Department of Justice); Don Jail in County Donegal, Northern Ireland; Don Jail in the Don Mills section of Toronto, Ontario

Djibouti East African country at

the Strait of Bab-el-Mandeb connecting the Red Sea and the Indian Ocean's Gulf of Aden; formerly known as French Somaliland and later the French territory of Afars and Issas; its old prison attracts many strange characters

DLPS Department of Law and Public Safety (New Jersey)

do a bit serve a sentence in jail

do a dime seve a 10-year prison sentence

do a nickel serve a five-year prison term

do a pound serve a five-year prison term

do a quarter serve a 25-year prison sentence

Dobbs School North Carolina penal facility for male and female juvenile delinquents up to 18 years of age, in Kinston southeast of Raleigh and northwest of New Bern

do bird do time in prison; serve a prison sentence

D o C Department of Correction (Arkansas, Connecticut, Delaware, Indiana, Massachusetts, North Carolina, Tennessee); Department of Corrections (Arizona, California, District of Columbia, Florida, Guam, Idaho, Illinois, Kansas, Kentucky, Louisiana, Maine, Michigan, Minnesota, Mississippi, Missouri, New Jersey, Rhode Island, South Carolina, Texas, Vermont, Washington, West Virginia); Division of Corrections (Utah, Wisconsin)

DOCS Department of Correctional Services (New York)

Doftana Bucharist's prison

dog detective(s) [*see* canine shamus(es)]

Doha (*see* Qatar)

D o I Department of Institutions (Montana); Director of Institutions (North Dakota); Division of Institutions (Oklahoma)

Dominica large Windward island forming a barrier between the Atlantic and the Caribbean; its capital, Roseau, contains a small gaol built by the British in colonial times

Dominican Republic prisons notorious during the dictatorship of Trujillo and before intervention by the U.S. Marines (*see* Ciudad Trujillo, Santo Domingo)

Don Don Jail in County Donegal, Northern Ireland; Don Jail in Don Mills section of Toronto, Ontario

D o P Department of Prisons (Nevada)

DOR Department of Offender Rehabilitation (Georgia)

Dora nickname for the Nazi concentration camp west of Leipzig, Germany at a place named Nordhausen; at the close of World War II advancing American and British soldiers found it filled with emaciated corpses as well as instruments of torture

Dorandordhausen Nazi concentration camp near Buchenwald and west of Leipzig, Germany

Dorchester Boston Pre-Release Center in Dorchester, Massachusetts southwest of the capital; Dorchester Penitentiary in New Brunswick, Canada which had its inception in 1880; HM Prison at Dorchester, England

dossier (French—information file)—usually about a case history or individual(s) involved in some criminal or political action

do the book serve a life sentence

do time serve a prison sentence

Douala (*see* Cameroon)

double-ceiling placing two prisoners in the same cell (often necessary because prison populations usually expand much faster than new prisons can be built or existing ones expanded)

Dover capital of Delaware and county seat of New Castle County south of Wilmington; contains the Kent Correctional Institution opened in 1977 and police-station lockups as well as the county jail; in Kent, England is HM Borstal in Dover on the Channel

Down Down Home (Afro-American slang—federal penitentiary in Atlanta, Georgia)

Down Home (Afro-American slang—Manhattan House of Detention long known as the Tombs)—in downtown New York City at the edge of the Lower East Side

Downstate Downstate Correctional Facility at Fishkill, New York close to Beacon-on-Hudson

Down South (Afro-American nickname—U.S. Federal Penitentiary in Atlanta, Georgia)

Dozier Arthur G Dozier School at Marianna, Florida where it holds juvenile delinquents from 12 to 17 years of age

DPA Discharged Prisoners Association (Great Britain)

DPAS Discharged Prisoners' Aid Society (Great Britain)

DPs Detention Pens at 100 Centre Street in downtown New York City where they are also known as the Manhattan Detention Pens

DPS Department of Public Safety (American Samoa)

DPSCS Department of Public Safety and Correctional Services (Maryland)

Drake Hall HM Prison at Drake Hall, Staffordshire, England

Drancy (*see Camp de Drancy*)

Draper Draper Correctional Center at Elmore, Alabama with an average prison population of nearly 700 male felons in the mid-1980s; Utah State Prison at Draper south of Salt Lake City with an average felon population of 853 in 1985

DRC Department of Rehabilitation and Correction (Ohio)

dropped in the bucket jailed

drowning capital punishment usually reserved for witches and other women accused of crime; drowning replaced by beheading and hanging as less equipment was required

Drumheller Drumheller Institution in Drumheller, Alberta northeast of Calgary

drunk tank jail cell reserved for persons arrested while under the influence of alcohol or other drugs

Dry Tortugas nickname of the U. S. Military Prison on one of the Dry Tortugas keys in the Gulf of Mexico, west of Key West

Dubai (*see* United Arab Emirates)

Dublin (*see* Irish prisons)

Dubrolag complex of some fifteen prison camps close to Potmu in the Moldavian Republic of the USSR

Ducato Milanese Milan, Italy's old prison

Duffy of San Quentin motion picture inspired by three semi-autobiographical books by Warden Clinton T. Duffy of San Quentin Prison in California where he abolished airless and dungeon-like cells, fired guards for cruelty, introduced a cafeteria, a newspaper written and printed by the prisoners, and a night school; he insisted the death penalty never deterred murder and never will

Dumfries Dumfries Young Offenders Institution near the west coast of Scotland

dummy prisoner's nickname for bread

dump truck depressed, slow moving, or torpid prisoner

dungeon underground cell or prison

Durango prison in Durango, capital of the mountainous Mexican state of the same name, and close to Mazatlan on the Pacific; jail in Durango, Colorado

Durban (see South Africa)

Durham HM Prison at Durham, England; prison in Durham, North Carolina and in smaller Durhams

Dutchman Correctional Center in Enoree, South Carolina, holding felons in maximum and minimum security

Dwight Dwight Correctional Center due west of Kankakee, Illinois where it detains female felons in maximum, medium, and minimum security; opened in 1930

DYA Department of the Youth Authority (California)

DYS Department of Youth Services (Alabama); Division of Youth Services (Arkansas, Florida)

Eagle River Alaska Women's Facility next door to the Eagle River Correctional Center just east of Anchorage and offering felons medium-to-minimum security accommodations

Eagle Springs North Carolina community northwest of Pinehurst and site of the Samarkand Manor youth service facility

East Block No. 7 address of Interpol India on Rama Krishna Puram in New Delhi

Eastern Hong Kong's Eastern Police Station (and lockup); Eastern Correctional Facility at Napanoch, New York

southwest of Kingston

Eastern New York Correctional Facility opened in 1935 at Napanoch for male juvenile delinquents

Eastern State Penitentiary in North Philadelphia, Pennsylvania for more than a century but now replaced by the State Correctional Institution in Graterford, northwest of Philadelphia

Eastham Unit maximum-security penal facility in Lovelady, Texas

East Lake Alabama State Training School for female juvenile delinquents; at East Lake near Birmingham

East London (see South Africa)

East Moline East Moline Correctional Center in upper Illinois on the Mississippi River where it was opened in 1980 as a minimum security penal facility

East Palatka East Palatka Road Prison southeast of St Augustine; opened in 1961 with programs in alcohol and other drug abuse

East Sutton Park borstal for delinquent girls in Kent, England

Ebensee Austrian concentration-camp subcamp filled with Hitler's victims during World War II

e by 1 execution by injection (of air or poison)

Echo Glen Children's Center in Snoqualmie, Washington (see entry)

ECJ Erie County Jail (Buffalo, New York)

Ecole Notre-Dame de Laval at Laval-des-Rapides in the Province of Québec (this and the following Ecole-type entries are for juvenile reformatories)

Ecole Ste-Agnes Montreal, Québec

Ecole Ste Domitille Montreal, Québec

Ecole Ste Helene correctional school in Montreal, Québec

ECS Episcopal Community Services (job-entry program for ex-offenders)

Ecuador equatorial country on the west coast of South America; its Andean capital, Quito, and its port city, Guayaquil, have so-called model prisons; formerly it had a penal colony

at Villamil on Isabela Island in the Galápagos but it has been replaced by the Penitenciario Litoral, a maximum-security prison near Guayaquil

Eddyville site of the Kentucky State Penitentiary east of Paducah in the western part of the state

Edinburgh prison in Scotland's capital city and its Young Offenders Institution also close to the Firth of Forth leading to the North Sea

Edison medicine nickname for electroconvulsive shock treatment given prisoners

Edmonton Institution maximum-security facility in Edmonton, Alberta north of Calgary

education of correctional personnel and jailers (see Staff Training Centers)

EFEC Efforts From Ex-Convicts (Washington, DC's parole program)

Eglin Federal Prison Camp at Eglin Air Force Base in Florida southwest of De Funiak Springs and east of Pensacola

Egypt the Arab Republic of Egypt has penal facilities in Cairo, the capital city, as well as in Alexandria, Giza, and other cities; not one of these is spoken well of by its inmates or its former inmates

Elazik Turkish prison in the central eastern part of the country

El Cajon newly built jail in El Cajon, California just west of San Diego where the county jail has long been overcrowded with inmates sleeping on the floor; in Spanish El Cajon means big box canyon and this meaning is not lost on the Hispanic inmates

El Centro El Centro Detention Center of the Immigration and Naturalization Service in El Centro, California close to the Mexican border

Eldora Training School medium-security juvenile-delinquent facility southwest of Waterloo, Iowa at Eldora where it began in 1868

electrocution method of execution in Alabama, Arizona, Arkansas, Colorado, Florida, Georgia, Illinois, Indiana, Kentucky, Louisiana, Massachusetts, Nebraska, New

York, Pennsylvania, South Carolina, South Dakota, Tennessee, Vermont, Virginia

Elko near the northeast corner of Nevada and site of the Nevada Youth Training Center

Ellis Unit maximum-security unit complete with a death row at its location in Huntsville, Texas

el Met (Spanish—the Metropolitan Correctional Center)

Elmira Elmira Correctional Facility in south-central New York State close to the Pennsylvania border; Elmira Reception Center for male prisoners brought here

El Paso El Paso Detention Center of the Immigration and Naturalization Service in El Paso, Texas at the Mexican border

El Reno Federal Correctional Institution at El Reno, Oklahoma, just west of Oklahoma City

El Retén de Catía (Spanish—The Remand of Catía)—Venezuelan house of detention in the Catía suburb of Caracas

El Salvador the civil-war-torn Central American country has a prison in its capital city, San Salvador, and smaller ones in its seaports along the Pacific

El Sexto (Spanish—The Sixth Book of Canonical Decrees)—Lima, Peru prison noted for the Easter plays staged by its inmates and for its deadly riots

émeute (French—insurrection, riot, prison break)

Endsville an exciting place; best of all places; place convicts dream about when they imagine life outside prison

Enfield Connecticut State Prison at Enfield north of Hartford and close to the Massachusetts border; facility includes a prison farm

England (see United Kingdom and individual entries)

Englewood Federal Correctional Institution at Englewood, Colorado on the southeast side of Denver

English place-name nicknames for penal colonies Andaman Islands, Botany Bay, Devil's Island, French Guiana, Lipari Islands, Moreton Bay, New Caledonia, Norfolk Island, Port Blair, Port Philip, Siberia,

Solovetski Islands, Sydney Cove, Tasmania, Van Diemen's Land

Enoree South Carolina town south of Spartanburg and address of the Dutchman Correctional Institution opened in 1980

Ensisheim French penitentiary near Mulhouse where it was built during the First Empire and where it houses many lifetime and long-term convicts

Equatorial Guinea former Portuguese colony consisting of Fernando Po island and Rio Muni on the nearby West African coast; both have old prisons built by the Portuguese and both have a bad reputation for the brutal treatment of its prisoners

ERC Elmira Reception Center (for male prisoners) at Elmira, New York

escape unlawful departure of a lawfully confined person from a confinement facility or from custody while being transported

Esmeralda barkentine-rigged Chilean naval-training vessel used for a short time in 1973 as a prison holding communist activists whose extremism led to President Salvador Allende's death and the coup by a military junta pledged to exterminate Marxism in Chile

ESP Eastern State Penitentiary (Philadelphia)

Essen concentration-camp subcamp operated by the Nazis during World War II close to the Rhine

Essex Essex County Jail in Newark, New Jersey

Etcher of Prisons Giambattista Piranesi (see Carceri d'Invenzione)

Ethan Allen School in Wales, Wisconsin where it serves as a reception center and training school

Ethiopia's prisons Addis Ababa, capital of Ethiopia, as well as Asmara and Massawa (formerly the port city of Italian Somaliland) have prisons in this close-to-the-Equator East African country once known as Abyssinia

Eugene Eugene,Oregon or its Lane County Jail in the west-central section of the state

euphemisms of penology what

was prison or penitentiary became reformatory, which became correctional center, and now is called a rehabilitation facility

Eureka Humboldt County courthouse and jail in California, north of Cape Mendocino

évadée (French—escapee, fugitive, runaway prisoner)

évadée de prison (French—prison breaker)

Evanston Wyoming town southwest of Rock Springs on the Utah border and address of the Johnson Hall Forensic Unit and the Wyoming Womens Center

evaso dal carcere (Italian—prison breaker)

even-handed justice democratic doctrine advocating equal justice for criminals irrespective of their former position in society, their race, their religion, or their wealth

Evin Evin Prison in Teheran, Iran

Évreux maximum-security prison in the northwestern French city of Évreux

EXCEL Ex-offender Coordinated Employment Lifeline (Indiana's parole project)

ex-con(s) ex-convict(s); former convict(s)

execution box container holding a body belt, a hangman's rope, a hood for covering the head of the condemned, and restraining straps for fastening the limbs of the condemned

Execution Dock formerly on the muddy foreshore of a bend in the Thames at East Wapping below the Tower Bridge and the Tower of London; at first all convicted pirates and robbers of the sea were pegged down at low water so the incoming tide would drown them slowly but in later times they were hanged from a tall gallows and left to the mercy of seagulls as they decomposed within the chains suspending them above the river's reach

execution by injection execution by injection of air or poison carried out in many instances where this technique is found to be less complicated and less costly than more conventional methods such as electrocution, hanging, or shooting; abbreviated as e by i

Execution of Maximilian Edouard Manet's painting depicting the Emperor Maximilian and his Mexican generals standing between a wall and a uniformed firing squad

execution methods by states *electrocution* in Alabama, Arizona, Arkansas, Colorado, Florida, Georgia, Illinois, Indiana, Kentucky, Louisiana, Massachusetts, Nebraska, New York, Pennsylvania, South Carolina, South Dakota, Tennessee, Vermont, Virgina; *hanging* in Delaware, Montana, New Hampshire, Utah, Washington; *lethal gas* in California, Maryland, Mississippi, Missouri, Nevada, North Carolina, Oregon, Rhode Island, Wyoming; *lethal intravenous injection* in Idaho, New Mexico, Oklahoma, Texas; in Utah the prisoner chooses the method of execution but if he or she will not choose then the sentencing judge decides whether execution is by firing squad or hanging

execution pennant small black flag flown over British prisons when an execution is taking place

execution shed gallows area within a prison

exercise in a cooler climate (translation of a Soviet euphemism for forced labor in northernmost Siberia)

Exeter HM Prison at Exeter in Devonshire, England; or prisons in smaller Exeters in California, Illinois, Maine, Missouri, Nebraska, New Hampshire, Ontario, Pennsylvania, and Rhode Island

exile (*see* banishment)

EXIT Ex-offenders in Transit

Ex-offender Coordinated Employment Lifeline (EXCEL) Indiana's parole project

ex-offender(s) former offender(s) no longer under the jurisdiction of any criminal-justice agency

Ex-offenders in Transit (EXIT) Maine's parole project

expunge purge or seal arrest, criminal, or juvenile-delinquent records

expungement legal ablution of a criminal's record made in an effort to assist in rehabilitation and remove any prejudice from the mind of a potential employer

extreme penalty death by execution

Eye Opener inmate publication of the Oklahoma State Prison

Fabrica de Hombres Nuevos (Spanish—Factory of New Men)—Mexico City prison constructed to permit prisoner's wives to stay overnight

Fadiffolu Fadiffolu Atoll (Maldivian island used for the banishment of lawbreakers) in the Indian Ocean between the Equator and the southern tip of India

Fagatoa Lockup Pago Pago jail on the island of Tutuila in American Samoa in the South Pacific

fag factory homosexual-filled prison

Fairbanks Fairbanks Correctional Center in east-central Alaska (a maximum-security facility for male and female felons)

Fairfield Solano County courthouse and jail between Sacramento and San Francisco, California

Fairfield School for Boys (*see* Southeastern Ohio Training Center)

Falklands Falkland Islands in the South Atlantic where their capital is Stanley with its HM Gaol often containing one or more alcoholic disturbers of the peace

fange (Dano-Norwegian—prisoner)

Fängelse (Swedish—Prison)—title of Ingmar Bergman's thought-provoking motion picture whose English name is *Prison*

Fannie Bay Fannie Bay Labour Prison, Fannie Bay, Australian Northern Territory

Fargo Fargo, North Dakota or its Cass County jail close to the Minnesota border

farm confinement or correctional facility in a rural area where it is nicknamed farm; prison farm

Farmingdale Turrell Residential Group Center at Farmingdale, New Jersey halfway between Asbury Park and Lakewood

Father of Criminology Cesare Beccaria (1738-1794), author of *Delitte e della Pene* (Italian—Crimes and Punishment)—advocated an end to capital punishment and widespread prison reform

Father of Parole Captain Alexander Maconochie, the governor of the Norfolk Island penal colony from 1840 to 1844

Father of Penitentiary Science Jean Jacques Vilain who founded the Maison de Force built in Ghent in 1773

Fayetteville Fayetteville (locally called *Fitzville*), North Carolina and county seat of Cumberland County with its jail

FBI Federal Bureau of Investigation

FBP Federal Bureau of Prisons (U.S. Department of Justice bureau)

FCCD Florida Council on Crime and Delinquency

FCF Federal Correctional Facility

FCI Federal Correctional Institute of the U.S. Bureau of Prisons (*see* Staff Training Centers)

FCI(s) Federal Correctional Institution(s)

FCIS Foreign Counterintelligence System (FBI)

FDH Federal Detention Headquarters in Florence, Arizona southeast of Phoenix

Featherstone HM Prison at Featherstone just north of Wolverhampton, Staffordshire, England

Federal Center for Correctional Research U.S. Bureau of Prisons facility in Butner, North Carolina just northeast of Durham

Federal Correctional Institutions Alderson, West Virginia; Ashland, Kentucky; Bastrop, Texas; Butner, North Carolina; Danbury, Connecticut; El Reno, Oklahoma; Englewood, Colorado; Fort Worth, Texas; La Tuna, Texas; Lexington, Kentucky; Memphis, Tennessee; Miami, Florida; Milan, Michigan; Morgantown, West Virginia; Otisville, New York; Oxford, Wisconsin; Petersburg, Virginia; Pleasanton, California; Ray Brook, New York; Sandstone, Michigan; Tallahassee, Florida; Talladega, Alabama; Terminal Island, California; Texarkana, Texas

Federal Detention Center in

Florence, Arizona's desert country southeast of Phoenix

Federal Law Enforcement Training Center (*see* Fleetsie)

Federal Penitentiaries (U.S.) Atlanta, Georgia; Leavenworth, Kansas; Lewisburg, Pennsylvania; Marion, Illinois; Terre Haute, Indiana

Federal Prison Camps Allenwood, Pennsylvania; Big Spring, Texas; Boron, California; Eglin Air Force Base, Florida; Maxwell Air Force Base, Montgomery, Alabama; Safford, Arizona; Seagoville, Texas

Federal Prison Industries (*see* UNICOR)

Federal Probation Officers Association founded in 1955 to build and maintain enlightened public interest in parole, probation, and related services

Federal Training Centre in Laval, Québec with training juvenile offenders

Fed Ref Federal Reformatory

Fellowship of First Fleeters Australian society whose members must prove they were descended from the first shipment of convicts landed in Botany Bay in 1788

felon anyone who has committed a felony

felonry prison-colony population

felon swell upper-class convict

felony any crime punishable by imprisonment for more than a year or by death

felony tank jail cell reserved for felons

Feltham HM Borstal at Feltham in Middlesex, England

female penal institutions of the U.S. Bureau of Prisons Alderson, West Virginia; Pleasanton, California

fengsel (Dano-Norwegian—prison)

Ferguson Unit Texas penal facility holding first offenders in maximum security at Midway northeast of Bryan

Fernando de Noronha Brazilian penal settlement existing since Portuguese colonial times in the 18th century, on an island of the same name in the South Atlantic about 225 miles (362 kilometers) northeast of Cape São Roque on the bulge of Brazil

Fernando Po prisons in the small island nation of Equatorial Guinea now known as Bioko and mainly in its two seaport cities, Malabo, the capital, and Bata

fettered restrained from escaping by the application of ankle or leg fetters or both

fetters steel cuffs placed on the ankles or legs of prisoners to keep them from escaping

Fez (*see* Morocco)

fiebre carcelaria (Spanish—prison fever)—fear of imprisonment

Fiesta de la Merced (Spanish—Mercy Fiesta)—celebrated on September 24, also known as Prisoners' Saint's Day

Fijian prisons except for drunks in lockups or gaols (jails), antisocial criminals are strictly segregated and forced to live in the most remote parts of this western South Pacific island nation formerly a British colony (*see* Suva)

Filicudi Italian isle of exile for many convicted members of the Mafia sent to this remote site in the Lipari Islands just north of Sicily and including Stromboli and Vulcano where many motion pictures have been filmed

finishing school euphemism for a women's prison and especially one for young women such as juvenile delinquents

Finnamore Wood HM Borstal at Finnamore Wood in Buckinghamshire, England

Finnish prisons Finland's capital city, Helsinki, and other cities, such as Tampere and Turku, have prisons but as in other Nordic nations the emphasis is on rehabilitation rather than incarceration

Firlands minimum-security facility at Firlands, Washington

First American Penitentiary Walnut Street Jail in Philadelphia where it was built in 1790

First Execution by Electrocution August 6, 1890 in New York State's Auburn Prison

First Halfway House Isaac T Hooper Home opened in New York City in 1845 by the Society of Friends—Quakers

First Nazi Concentration Camp established in Dachau, near Munich, Germany, on March 23, 1933, less than three months after President von Hindenburg appointed Hitler as Reich Chancellor (prime minister); by April 26 the Gestapo was formed, and by May 10 all books by Jews, and all books opposing Nazism, were burned; the playing of music by composers of Judaic origin (Copeland, Halévy, Mahler, Mendelssohn, Meyerbeer, Offenbach, Schoenberg, etc.) was *verboten* (forbidden)

First Prison Newspaper *The Summary* published by the inmates of the New York State Reformatory at Elmira on November 22, 1883—Thanksgiving Day

fish(es) newly arrived inmate(s); pimp(s)

Fishkill Fishkill Correctional Facility near Beacon-on-Hudson, New York

Fitzville (*see* Fayetteville)

five spot five-year prison term (or a five-dollar bill)

FKL Frauen Konzentration Lager (German—Women's Concentration Camp)—Hitler-era prison

Flagstaff Coconino County seat and jail in northern Arizona, north of Phoenix and south of the Grand Canyon

flat bit prison sentence for a definite period of time (*see* split bit)

Fleet Fleet Prison—London's old jail dating from 14th to the 19th century when it was finally demolished, in 1846, after years of service as a debtor's prison

Fleetsie nickname of the Federal Law Enforcement Training Center in Brunswick, Georgia

FLETC Federal Law Enforcement Training Center (*see* Fleetsie)

Fleury Mérgois Europe's largest prison and France's largest high-security facility on the outskirts of Paris where it is often spoken of as prison city

flex-cuf ties flexible plastic ankle cuffs or handcuffs for trussing prisoners

floating hells British prison ships bound for Australia and Tasmania during the late 18th and early 19th centuries; French prison ships bound for Algeria, French Guiana, and New Caledonia during the same era and to the convict colony in French Guiana as recently as 1950

Florence Arizona State Prison holding more than 2000 prisoners in 1981 in Florence southeast of Phoenix; Florence Detention Headquarters holding persons awaiting trial or serving short sentences; South Carolina city north of Charleston and address of the Palmer Work Release Center

Florida penal facilities are numerous and widespread from Apalachee and Avon Park to Vero Beach and Zephyrhills as well as in Arcadia, Belle Glade, Broward, Bushnell, Chattachoochee, Clermont, Cross City, Daytona Beach, East Palatka, Homestead, Immakalee, Lake Butler, Lantana, Lowell, Niceville, Olustee, Pembroke Pines, Polk City, Raiford, Riverview, Sneads, Sharpes, Starke, Trenton, and widely scattered facilities for juvenile delinquents

Florida Correctional Institution provides custody for female felons and a measure of rehabilitation through education and vocational training at Lowell

Florida lockups 67 counties are served from Gainesville in Alachua County to Chipley in Washington County; Miami, Jacksonville, and Tampa have their own facilities

Florida School Florida School at Okeechobee holding juvenile delinquents from 12 to 17 years of age

Florida State Prison at Starke, opened in 1960 where it offers inmates academic and vocational training as well as on-the-job training

Flossenbürg German prison and town near Nürnberg but closer to the Czechoslovakian frontier; Admiral Wilhelm Canaris was executed here by Himmler's Gestapo as they believed he was a British agent

Floyd Floyd County Jail in Rome, Georgia northwest of Atlanta

fly a kite smuggle a letter out of prison

fly the coop excape from jail or prison

Folsom California State Prison at Folsom northeast of Sacra-

mento; opened in 1880 with a normal capacity of 1778 but in June 1981 held 2058 male felons

forçat (French—convict)—prisoner

forced-labor prison camps West Germany has listed more than 1600 forced-labor concentration camps erected during Hitler's regime; they are still popular in the USSR although long abolished in Germany

Ford HM Prison at Ford in Sussex, England

Fordland Missouri town southeast of Springfield and site of the Ozark Correctional Center

Forest Hill Forest Hill Prison in Georgetown, District of Columbia, during the Civil War and shortly after

Fort Apache nickname of the police station and lockup in New York City's south Bronx, also nicknamed the Little House on the Prairie

Fort Benning Fort Benning Confinement Facility at Fort Benning, Georgia

Fort Campbell Fort Campbell Confinement Facility at Fort Campbell, Kentucky

Fort Carson Fort Carson Confinement Facility at Fort Carson, Colorado

Fort Christian Fort Christian Detention Center on St Thomas island in Charlotte Amalie, built by the Danes when Denmark ruled before selling the islands to the United States in 1917

Fort-de-France Martinique's prison in the capital and port city of this French West Indian island

Fort Dimanche Haiti's infamous prison close to Pétionville

Fort Gordon Fort Gordon Confinement Facility at Fort Gordon, Georgia

Fort Grant Fort Grant Training Center in Arizona where it offers educational and vocation training to felons

Fort Hood Fort Hood Confinement Facility at Fort Hood, Texas

Fort Jefferson former military prison on an island in the Dry Tortugas near Key West, Florida; Dr Samual Mudd was held here after the Civil War because he treated Lincoln's

assassin—John Wilkes Booth—while fleeing from Federal troops; Dr Mudd's tragic story is the basis of a classic motion picture, *The Prisoner of Shark Island*

Fort Knox Fort Knox Area Confinement Facility at Fort Knox, Kentucky

Fort Lauderdale Broward County in Florida has its county courthouse and jail in Fort Lauderdale north of Miami

Fort Leavenworth U.S. Disciplinary Barracks at Fort Leavenworth, Kansas just north of Kansas City

Fort Lewis Fort Lewis Confinement Facility at Fort Lewis, Washington

Fort Liquordale Fort Lauderdale, Florida

Fort Madison Iowa State Penitentiary at Fort Madison southwest of Burlington and close to the Mississippi

Fort Margherita old Sarawak prison near Kuching on the island of Borneo or Kalimantan where it served as a Japanese detention camp for Australian and British prisoners of war during World War II

Fort Meade Fort Meade Confinement Facility at Fort Meade, Maryland

Fort Montluc old prison in Lyon, France where during World War II it was used as gestapo headquarters by occupying Germans who shipped many prisoners from here to concentration camps and exterminating gas chambers or ovens

Fort Ord Fort Ord Confinement Facility at Fort Ord, California

Fort Pillow Fort Pillow State Prison Farm on Cold Creek, Tennessee close to the Mississippi and north of Memphis

Fort Polk Fort Polk Confinement Facility at Fort Polk, Louisiana

Fort Richardson Fort Richardson Confinement Facility at Fort Richardson, Alaska

Fort Riley U.S. Army Correctional Training Facility at Fort Riley close to Manhattan, Kansas

Fort Saskatchewan Correctional Institution northeast of Edmonton where it also runs forest camps

Fort Savage nickname of New York City's East Harlem police station and lockup

Fort Sill Fort Sill Confinement Facility at Fort Sill, Oklahoma

Fort Wayne Indiana city northeast of Indianapolis and county seat, courthouse, and jail of Allen County

Fort Worth Federal Correctional Institution at Fort Worth, Texas west of Dallas

Fountain GK Fountain Correctional Center at Holman Station, Alabama with more than 600 male felons held there in the early 1980s

four-time loser(s) criminal(s) convicted four times of felonies and hence imprisoned for life under the New York State statute called the Baumes Law

Fox Hill Her Majesty's Prison at Fox Hill on New Providence Island in the Bahamas

Fox Lake Wisconsin Correctional Institution (medium-security prison between Green Bay and Madison)

FPC Federal Prison Camp (Allenwood, Pennsylvania; Eglin Air Force Base, Florida; Lompoc, California; Marion, Illinois; Montgomery, Alabama; Safford, Arizona)

FPI Federal Prison Industries

FPOA Federal Probation Officers Association

FR Federal Reformatory (El Reno, Oklahoma and Petersburg, Virginia)

Framingham Massachusetts Correctional Institution in Framingham southwest of Boston; built in 1877 to hold female and male felons, misdemeanants, and more recently a growing number of drug addicts requiring treatment

free for all fight wherein all present participate

Freetown (see Sierra Leone)

free world outside prison walls

Fremantle Fremantle Gaol (Western Australian penal institution built by the convicts and overlooking the Indian Ocean)

French blade the guillotine

French Congo (see Congo)

French leave act of slipping away quietly and secretly

French prisons metropolitan France has many prisons and overseas prison colonies once were notorious in French Guiana (popularly named Devil's Island) and in New Caledonia; (for up-to-date names see Bourgoin, Cayenne, Chateau d'If, Clermont-Ferrand, Conciergerie, Devil's Island, Évreux, Fort-de-France, Grand Hotel, Lisieux, maison, Mende, Natzweiler, prison, Salpetriere, Santé, Tarbes, Tulle, Vincennes)

Frentes Abiertos (Spanish—Open Fronts)—minimum-security prisons scattered throughout Cuba

fresh fish(es) new prisoner(s)

fresh and sweet just out of jail

Fresnes southern suburb of Paris and location of a great French penitentiary called Fresnes

Fresno Fresno County courthouse and jail in central California

Friarton Friarton Young Offenders Institution at Perth, Scotland

fried badly burned; electrocuted; intoxicated

Friends of Assata and Sundiata underground prison-support movement in New York City

Frisco San Francisco, California or its jails and lockups

frisk search a body, dead or alive, for concealed drugs, contraband, weapons, etc.

Frobisher Bay on the southeast coast of Baffin Land in the Canadian Arctic's Northwest Territories where it contains the Baffin Correctional Centre

frog's march nickname for a method of conveying hard-to-handle prisoners (four officers each grab an arm or leg and carry the prisoner along face downward)

Frontera California Institution for Women at Frontera near Corona and San Bernardino; opened in 1936 in Tehachapi but transferred to Frontera in 1952; like most penal facilities it is overcrowded

Frontón Peruvian maximum-security offshore prison on an island close to Callao; its name brings to mind the high-walled court where jai-alai is played

Frostbite Fairbanks, Alaska or its jail and lockup

FRW Federal Reformatory for Women (Alderson, West Virginia)

fry burn badly; electrocute

Fuchu Fuchu Prison (home of Japan's most hardened criminals in this unheated maximum-security facility in Greater Tokyo close to Tachikawa)

Fukuoka (see Japan's prisons)

Funafuti (see Tuvalu)

Fungus Corners Bremerton, Washington and its jail as well as police-station lockup

funny farm insane asylum; psychiatric ward

fūryo (Japanese—prisoner of war)

furyó (see shujin)

Futility Hill prisoner's graveyard at San Quentin, California

FYC Federal Youth Center (Ashland, Kentucky and Englewood, Colorado)

gaam-fáan (Cantonese Chinese—prisoner)

gaam-fohng (Cantonese Chinese—prison cell)

gaam-yuhk (Cantonese Chinese—prison)

Gabonese prisons Gabon, on the equatorial Atlantic coast of Africa, has prisons in the capital and coastal city of Libreville as well as in Port-Gentil where they were built by the French almost a century ago

Gadsden Etowah County seat and jail northeast of Birmingham, Alabama

Gainesville Texas city north of Fort Worth and address of the Brownwood State School and the Statewide Reception Center

Galanskov Yuri Galanskov—dissident Soviet poet who died in a forced labor camp in the Arctic sixteen years after Khrushchev made his denunciation of Stalin's crimes against humanity; Galanskov in one poem described the death camps of his country as cold Auschwitzes of the North

Galle (see Sri Lanka)

gallery 13 prisoner's grave(yard)

gallows metal or wooden framework used for the execution of criminals by hanging

gallows bird(s) criminal(s)

Galvy Galveston, Texas or its jail or lockup close to the Gulf of Mexico

Gambian prison Gambia, a West African nation and one of the few functioning democracies in Africa, was the first African colony of the British who settled here in 1588; it retained colonial status up to 1965; its capital, Banjul, has a gaol (jail) built by the British

Gamboa rehabilitation center flanking the Panama Canal's dredging division close to the Gaillard Cut and formerly the prison of the Panama Canal Zone

Gamle Swedish prison on a Baltic inlet near Vastervik

gaol (British spelling—jail)—term introduced into Britain during the Norman Conquest and is the French equivalent of *geôle* but is pronounced *jail*

gaolage a gaolers fee (demanded more than a century ago and now replaced by bribes)

gaoler(s) [British—jailer(s)]—pronounced *jailer(s)*

gaol fever (British equivalent of jail fever)

Garbage Dump nickname of the Great Meadow Correctional Facility at Comstock, New York and of California's San Quentin Prison

Gardner Massachusetts town northwest of Fitchburg and Worcester and location of the North Central Correctional Institution

garlic and glue convict slang for beef stew

garnish(es) bribe(s) given prison guards by inmates

garrote capital-punishment device of Spanish origin wherein the prisoner is strangled with an ever-tightening iron collar

garroted strangled

garroting inflicting capital punishment by means of the garrote; strangling

Gartree Gartree Prison in Leicestershire, England where in late 1978 some inmates alleged they were sedated by drugs whenever officials believed it necessary

gas chamber specially built chamber or room where prisoners are executed by poison gas

Gasre Tehran, Iran's great prison also called Ghasre or Qsar; up to its storming by militant Moslem mobs on February 11,

1979 it held some 11,000 inmates including common thieves, drug pushers, pimps, prostitutes, and political prisoners

gassing execution in a lethal gas chamber

Gates of Hell old nickname for the entrance to Macquarie Harbour on the Indian Ocean coast of Tasmania when it was a penal settlement in Van Diemen's Land

Gatesville Texas town north of Fort Worth and address of the Gatesville Unit holding females in maximum security

Gatun Gatun Prison for Women and Juveniles at Gatun in the Panama Canal

Gavle Swedish experimental prison where inmates receive personal visits from members of their families

gcg gas-chamber green (nickname given a bilious green prevalent on the walls of many penal institutions)

GD Gaol Delivery (*see* jail delivery)

Gefangene (German—prisoner)

Gefangenenwagen der Gefangenenwagen (German—prison van)

Gefängnis das Gefängnis (German—the prison)—also called *die Strafanstalt*

Geisenkirchen Nazi subcamp in what is now known as West Germany

Geneva Girls Training School, Geneva, Nebraska southwest of Lincoln and south of York; Illinois State Training School for Girls at Geneva just west of Chicago; (*see* Switzerland)

geôle (French—jail)

geôlier (French—jailer)

Georgetown Delaware placename often associated with the Sussex Correctional Institution in the south-central part of the state where it was opened in 1932; also the capital of Guyana (formerly British Guiana) and site of a prison built by the British

George Town (*see* Malayan prisons)

Georgia Diagnostic and Classification penal facility in Jackson, Georgia southeast of Atlanta and holding more than 1000 male felons

Georgia Industrial Institute (*see* GII)

Georgia jails the state's 159 counties are served by prison facilities from Baxley in Appling County to Sylvester in Worth County; big cities such as Atlanta, Columbus, Macon, and Savannah have local lockups

Georgia State Prison (*see* Reidsville)

Georgia Training and Development Center (*see* Buford)

geriatric institution nickname for an old prison

German prisons all of the concentration camps, extermination camps, and forced-labor camps listed elsewhere, were erected and used during Hitler's regime; they are no longer in use except as historic museums demonstrating man's inhumanity to man; prisons still in use such as Berlin's Moabit or Spandau date back to the time of the kaisers; the number of prison camps erected and used by Hitler are exceeded only by those still in use within the Soviet Union

get the wind escape; take off

get the works be given a death sentence

gevangene (Dutch—prisoner)

gevangenis (Dutch—prison)

Ghana's prisons during the 113 years of British rule some gaols (jails) were erected in this Gold Coast colony now called the Republic of Ghana; such gaols are in Accra and Kumasi

ghost trains(s) late-night railroad train(s) used to transport prisoners from one place to another

Gib Gibraltar and its convicts formerly sentenced to hard labor on The Rock (an HM Gaol)

gibbet gallows for hanging prisoners from a projecting arm (pronounced *jibbet*)

Gibraltar British dependency since 1704 off the south coast of Spain where this peninsula guards the entrance to the Mediterranean; an HM Gaol is available to all lawbreakers

Gig Harbor Purdy Treatment Center for Women at Gig Harbor, Washington north of Tacoma

Giglio Italian isle of exile in the Tuscan Islands within the Tyrrhenian Sea northwest of

Rome; a special law, enacted in post-World-War-II Italy, permits judges to exile suspected criminals to remote places such as Giglio where it is felt prolonged isolation will bring about rehabilitation; natives of islands such as Asinara off Sardinia, Filicudi off Sicily, and Giglio near Rome, protest such action as being inimical to their personal safety and to the tourist trade they try to cultivate

GII Georgia Industrial Institute at Alto where it holds more than 1000 felons in maximum security

Gila Bend Indian reservation in southwestern Arizona which was used after Pearl Harbor as a relocation center for Japanese-Americans until the national hysteria died down

Girls' Cottage School Chambly, Québec

Girls Rehab Girls Rehabilitation Facility (GRF) at Meadow Lark Drive in San Diego, California (next to Sierra Vista High)

girl's school nickname for a reformatory for young female offenders; such places are usually given names suggesting they are select schools for young girls

Girls' Town correctional facility for misdemeanants at Tecumseh, Oklahoma

Gitmo Guantanamo, Cuba (U.S. Naval Base or its jail or the jail in the nearby Cuban town of Guantanamo)

give a permanent wave electrocute

Giza (*see* Egypt)

GK Gaol Keeper

Glades Glades Correctional Institution at Belle Glade, Florida, opened in 1932; offers English-speaking classes to Hispanic inmates as well as educational and vocational on-the-job training

Glasgow prison in Scotland's seaport city where it is also called Barlinnie and includes the Barlinnie Young Offenders Institution

Glass House nickname for the glassed-in Los Angeles County Jail in California

glazing (*see* detention glazing)

Glenochil Glenochil Detention Centre in Scotland

glop unappetizing prison food

Gloucester HM Prison at Gloucester in Gloucestershire on the River Severn in England or the city prison in Gloucester, Massachusetts northeast of Boston

Golden Jefferson County courthouse and jail in Pueblo, Colorado south of Colorado Springs

Golden Grove St Croix penal facility on the island of St Croix in the American Virgin Islands (*see* Anna's Hope *and* Fort Christian)

Golden Prison of Paris the Louvre—the great art museum formerly a fortress whose underground vaults held hunting dogs and political prisoners

Goldsboro North Carolina community southeast of Raleigh and site of the Wayne Correctional Center

golpe final (Portuguese or Spanish—final blow)—death blow, execution

Goochland Virginia town northwest of Richmond and address of the Virginia Correctional Center for Women

Goodman Correctional Institution in Columbia, South Carolina where it cares for geriatric and handicapped inmates

good time time taken off a prisoner's sentence in return for good behavior

go over the hill escape

go over the wall escape

Goree Goree Island off Dakar (westernmost tip of Africa and capital of Senegal) which served as the shipping point for slaves headed to the New World from the 1500s to the mid-1800s; today tourists visit its dim dungeons and are shown the Doorway of No Return in the House of Slaves

Goree Unit maximum-custody unit in Huntsville, Texas opened in 1901

Gorgona (*see* Colombia)

Gorki transit prison camp in the Russian city of Gorki, formerly Nizhni Novgorod

Goshen secure center for juvenile delinquents in Goshen, New York, southwest of Newburgh

go stir bug go crazy while imprisoned

Göteburg (*see* Sweden)

government men Australian euphemism for former convicts

Governor British penal equivalent of Warden

Grafton site of the West Virginia Industrial School for Boys, south of Morgantown, opened in 1891 for delinquents from 10 to 18 years of age in minimum custody

Graham Graham Correctional Center in Hillsboro, Illinois northeast of Alton; medium-security facility, opened in 1980

Grand Forks Grand Forks, North Dakota and its county jail across the Red River from Minnesota

Grand Hotel nickname of French Polynesia's prison in Tahiti where it is called *Le Grand Hotel* as if to display the acerbic quality of Gallic wit

Grand Island Grand Island, Nebraska or its county jail, west of Lincoln

Grand Mount Custodial School for Girls at Grand Mount, Washington

Granite Oklahoma town south of Elk City and address of the Oklahoma State Reformatory opened in 1909 and accommodating maximum-security inmates

Grass Lake Michigan site of the Correction Camp Program at Grass Lake, east of Jackson

Graterford farming community northwest of Philadelphia containing more than 2000 inmates in the State Correctional Institution and Correctional and Diagnostic Center built to replace the century-old Eastern State Penitentiary in North Philadelphia, Pennsylvania

graybar hotel jail, lockup, prison of any kind

Great Falls Great Falls, Montana or its county jail northeast of Butte

Great Jailer of the Caribbean Fidel Castro

Great Meadow Great Meadow Correctional Facility—a maximum-security prison north of Albany at Comstock, New York

Grecian prisons such structures in the Hellenic Republic date back to classical times long before the Christian Era, as guides will tell you on a tour of Athens, Piraeus, Patras, or smaller insular or mainland places

Green Bay Wisconsin city northeast of Appleton and location of the Green Bay Correctional Institution opened in 1898, holding first-offender juvenile delinquents and serving as a reception center for younger adult males

Greencastle Indiana city just outside the eastern sector of Indianapolis and location of the Indiana State Farm

Green Haven Green Haven Correctional Facility—maximum-security prison near Stormville, New York, northeast of Beacon in Dutchess County

green lights in front of all New York City police stations and their lockups (*see* blue lights)

Greenock prison for female offenders, in Greenock, Scotland

Greensboro Greensboro, North Carolina or its jail in Guilford County as this is its county seat

Greensburg Pennsylvania community southeast of Pittsburgh and location of the Regional Correctional Facility opened in 1966 as a county jail

green triangle criminal identification badge worn in concentration camps controlled by the Nazis in World War II

Greenville South Carolina city southwest of Spartanburg and location of the Blue Ridge Pre-Release Work-Release Center opened in 1968

Grenada gaol this smallest independent nation in the Americas can be found in St George's where it was called HM Gaol during the years of British colonial administration of this southernmost island in the West Indies

Grendon HM Prison Grendon at Grendon Underwood northeast of Oxford but much closer to Bicester (pronounced *Bister*); the first psychiatric prison in the United Kingdom to have a full-time psychiatrist as its medical superintendent

GRF (*see* Girls Rehab)

Grimes County Texas facility in Navasota opened in 1982 with a normal capacity of 4000 in-

mates to be held in maximum custody

Gross Rosen Nazi concentration camp known for the number of forced-labor slaves it furnished German industry during World War II

ground animal meat prison nickname for hamburgers, hot dogs, sausages

group home nonconfining residential facility for adjudicated adults or juveniles (*see* halfway house)

Gruenheid East Berlin's great prison which has served the Kaiser's repressive forces, Hitler's Nazis, and more recently German communists

Guadalajara Mexican prison in Jalisco's capital city of Guadalajara

Guadalcanal (*see* Solomon Islands)

Guadalupe Guadalupe, Chihuahua and its jail across the border from Fabens, Texas

Guadeloupe an overseas department of France in the Leeward Islands of the West Indies; consists of Basse Terre and Guadeloupe and both have lockups built before 1900

Guamanian prison Ordot, southeast of Agaña, where it is the penitentiary on the island of Guam in the western Pacific Ocean

Guanajay Cuban prison in a city southwest of Havana

Guanajuato prison in Guanajuato, capital of the Mexican state of the same name, close to Querétero

Guantanamo great bay and seaport town on the southeast coast of Cuba; U.S. Naval Station at Guantanamo and its brig

guardhouse military jail or lockup

Guatemala City capital of Guatemala and site of one of its largest prisons kept filled with enemies of the regime ruling this Central American oligarchy

Guatemalan prisons Guatemala City has its *cárcel modelo* as well as lockups maintained by the military forces; Americans, and others, complain bitterly about the unsanitary aspects of these penal facilities

Guaya Guayaquil, Ecuador or its jail or police lockup

Guaymas prison in Guaymas, Mexican port on the Gulf of California

guest of the city prisoner confined to a city jail

guest of the governor prisoner in a state penitentiary

guest of the nation prisoner in a federal penitentiary

guest of the realm prison in any of many HM gaols and penitentiaries

guest of the state prisoner held in a state penal institution

guillotine (*see* louisette)

guillotineur (French—guillotiner)—executioner using the guillotine

guillotine victims Gericault's ruthlessly realistic painting of two severed heads hangs in the Nationalmuseum of Stockholm as a sort of mute testimony against this form of capital punishment

Guinea-Bissau the Republic of Guinea-Bissau on Africa's west coast is a former Portuguese colony with an old, unimproved prison in the capital and port city of Bissau

Guinea prisons Conakry, Labe, N'Zerekore, and Kankan are provided with prisons in this People's Revolutionary Republic of Guinea on West Africa's coast where they were built by the French

Gulag Archipelago Soviet expatriate author Alexander Solzhenitsyn's name for the many thousands of forced labor camps and prisons throughout the USSR scattered from the Bering Sea almost to the Bosporus

gurney hospital bed on wheels used to convey a death-sentenced criminal from the cell in death row to the death chamber where lethal gas or injection is used to carry out the sentence of execution

Gurs French internment camp for Spanish Nationalists fleeing Franco's troops and later for Jews interned by the Petain-Laval police before shipment in cattle cars to concentration camps in Germany and Poland where many died from malnutrition or poison gas; Gurs close to Oloron and the Franco-Spanish borderlands between Biarritz and Lourdes in southwestern France; reports indicate many prisoners died here before they could be shipped out of the country enroute to their almost certain death

Gusen forced-labor camp run by the Nazis in Austria

Guy Guyana (usually nickname for any jail in this country once named British Guiana)

Guyama Guyama Regional Detention Center on the southeast coast of Puerto Rico and holding almost double the number of inmates planned for in its building

Guyana the Cooperative Republic of Guyana, formerly British Guiana, has a prison in its capital city of Georgetown as well as gaol-type lockups in the interior; its borders are disputed by Suriname and by Venezuela who claims more than half of Guyana

Guyane française (French Guiana)—extends along the tropical Atlantic coast of northern South America between Brazil and Suriname, once called Dutch Guiana; between 1 and 6 degrees north of the Equator it qualifies as a fever-infested hellhole and until the early 1950s was notorious for its extensive penal colony nicknamed Devil's Island although most of the convicts worked in the jungle camps on the mainland where the mortality was much higher than on the offshore Îles du Salut close to Cayenne and used for the segregation of political prisoners; for more than a century French Guiana was a synonym for man's inhumanity to man and the nickname—Devil's Island—seemed most appropriate

Guy's Marsh HM Borstal at Guy's Marsh in Dorset, England

gyves handcuffs or fetters

Habana called Havana by English-speaking people; has old prisons dating back to the years of Spanish domination from the discovery of the island of Cuba in 1492 to the end of the Spanish-American War in 1898; Morro Castle at the entrance to Habana Harbor contains an old Spanish prison still in use by Castro

hack(s) jailer(s); prison guard(s)

Haddam site of a Connecticut jail built in 1786 now occupied by the Connecticut Justice Academy

Hagerstown Maryland city in the north-central part of the state and site of the Maryland Correctional Institution and the Maryland Correctional Training Center

Hague the Hague (*see* Netherlands)

Haiphong (*see* Vietnam)

Haitian prisons Haiti, the black republic, occupies the western end of Hispaniola and has prisons built by the French in Port-au-Prince and Cap-Haitien between 1677 and 1804 when the Haitians won their freedom

Halawa Halawa High Security Facility at Aiea on the island of Oahu, Hawaii (*see* Honolulu Jail)

hale pa'ahao (Hawaiian—prison)

half a stretch six month's imprisonment

halfway house nonconfining residential facility for adjudicated adults or juveniles; facility providing an alternative to confinement for persons not suitable for probation or needing a period of readjustment to the community after confinement

Hall Hall of Justice

Hallowell the Stevens School for female juvenile delinquents at Hallowell, Louisiana

Hamilton Hamilton County Jail in Cincinnati, Ohio

Hampton Road Fremantle, West Australian prison on Hampton Road overlooking the Indian Ocean

handboei (Dutch—handcuff)

handcuffed and fettered held or restrained by handcuffs and fetters

handcuffs adjustable metal bracelets connected by a chain and used to restrain

Handfesseln (German—handcuffs)

handing method of execution in Delaware, Montana, New Hampshire, Utah, Washington

handjern (Dano-Norwegian—handcuffs)

hangman executioner

hangman's day customarily Friday

Hanoi (*see* Vietnam)

Hanoi Hilton nickname of Hanoi's Hoa Lo prison in north Vietnam

Hanover Learning Center at Hanover, Virginia north of Richmond

Harbison Harbison Correctional Institution for Women at Irmo, South Carolina just west of Columbia

hard labor sentence involving imprisonment plus useful labor such as road building or maintenance

Hardwick site of the Middle Georgia Correctional Complex at Hardwick, Georgia just south of Milledgeville; has separate units for male and female inmates; also the site of the Youthful Offender Unit

Harlem Valley Harlem Valley Secure Center for juvenile and youthful offenders close to the Connecticut State line and Poughkeepsie, New York

Harris Harris County Juvenile Detention Center (Houston, Texas)

Harrisburg Dauphin County seat of Pennsylvania's capital city in the eastern part of the Keystone State; its jail is but one of many correctional facilities scattered through the state

Hartford Connecticut Community Correctional Center in Hartford, opened in 1977; Hartford, the centrally located capital of Connecticut, is also the site of the county jail

Hatfield HM Borstal at Hatfield in Yorkshire, England

Hattiesburg Hattiesburg, Mississippi or its jail

Havana (*see* Habana *and* Cuba)

Haverigg HM Prison at Haverigg on the Irish Sea coast of England opposite the Isle of Man

Hawaii's lockups four counties comprise this state and each has it own lockup; one in Honolulu serves Honolulu County on Oahu; another in Hilo serves the county and island of Hawaii; a third in Wailuku serves Maui; a fourth in Lihue is for the island of Kauai

Hawaii Youth Correctional Facility in Honolulu on Oahu Island

Hawalli (see Kuwait)

Hayes Hayes Prison Farm, Black Hills, Tasmania

Haynesville Louisiana town northeast of Shreveport and site of the Wade Correctional Center opened in 1980

Heart of Midlothian nickname Sir Walter Scott gave the Tolbooth Prison in Edinburgh, Scotland the scene of his novel, *The Heart of Midlothian*

Heart Mountain Wyoming location of a Japanese-American relocation center set up after Pearl Harbor

Helena Montana city between Butte and Great Falls and the site of the Mountain View School for female juvenile delinquents from 10 to 21 years of age

Helena State School for Boys in Helena, Oklahoma, opened in 1956 and holding delinquent boys from 15 to 17 years of age

helicoptered dropped into the ocean from a helicopter while manacled (reports coming from Argentina indicate numerous political prisoners have been executed in this manner)

helicopter surveillance (see ASTREA)

Hellhole of the Pacific New Zealand's North Island port of Russell in the Bay of Islands when it was called Kororareka

Hell of Macquarie Harbour Station nickname of an old penal colony on the Indian Ocean coast of Tasmania

Hell's Gates Macquarie Harbour—Tasmania's first penal settlement

Helsinki (see Finnish prisons)

hempen four-in-hand hangman's noose

hemp stretcher euphemism for hangman

Hendry Hendry Correctional Institution at Immokalee, Florida where it is being expanded to hold twice the original design capacity of 200 inmates

Hennepin refers to any one of three Minnesota penal facilities such as the Hennepin County Home School in Minnetonka west of Minneapolis,

the Hennepin County Juvenile Center in Roseville, or the Hennepin County Workhouse in Wayzata, opened in 1932

Hennigsdorf Nazi subcamp close to Berlin and larger concentration camps

hen pen reformatory for females

herder(s) prison guard(s)

Her (His) Majesty's Penitentiary in St John's initiated in 1859 in Newfoundland's capital

Hermes Trismegitus (Latin—Thrice-great Hermes)—Egyptian god Thoth and the code of laws he left concerning crime and punishment

Hermosillo Sonora state prison in Hermosillo, Mexico

Herstedvester Danish psychiatric prison in a western suburb of Copenhagen and world famed for its advanced methods resulting in reduced recidivism

Herzegovina (see Yugoslavia)

Hewell Grange HM Borstal at Hewell Grange in Worcestershire, England

hierros (Spanish—irons)—handcuffs

Highland Rim School for Girls in Tullahoma, Tennessee for delinquent females from 12 to 18 years of age

Highpoint HM Prison at Highpoint near Newmarket in West Suffolk, England

High Security Center in Cranston, Rhode Island

Hillcrest School of Oregon in Salem where it holds juvenile-court commitments

Hillsboro (see Graham)

Hillsborough Hillsborough Correctional Institution at Riverview, Florida and like so many quite overcrowded as it was designed for 210 when opened in 1976 but by 1985 had more than 350 inmates

Hilo principal port city on the island of Hawaii including the Hawaii Community Correctional Center opened in 1975, providing medium as well as minimum security; Hilo also contains the Kulani Correctional Facility, formerly the Kulani Honor Camp

Hilton Head old Federal prison holding many Confederate prisoners of war in the 1860s on this part of the South Caro-

lina coast close to Savannah, Georgia

Hindley HM Borstal at Hindley in Lancashire, England

hit the fence escape from prison

hit the pit jailed

hit the sidewalk released from jail, prison, or similar place of detention

HK Hong Kong or one of its several jails and prisons

HLPR Howard League for Penal Reform (London, England)

HMBI Her (His) Majesty's Borstal Institution

HMG Her (His) Majesty's Gaol—the royal jail

HM Gaol Her (His) Majesty's Gaol (many such jails in the United Kingdom, British crown colonies, and other places in the far-flung British Commonwealth or the older British Empire)

HMP Her (His) Majesty's Penitentiary; Her (His) Majesty's Prison

HM Prison Her (His) Majesty's Prison (encountered in many British or formerly British places such as crown colonies and dependencies)

Hoa Lo downtown prison in Hanoi, Vietnam, nicknamed the Hanoi Hilton

hobbling walking with leg irons attached

Hobo Hoboken, New Jersey or its jail across the North River from downtown New York

Ho Chi Minh City formerly Saigon (see Vietnam)

hoist to hang a person; to rob

hole(s) solitary-confinement cell(s)

Holland Michigan community southwest of Grand Rapids and site of the Michigan Dunes Correctional Facility

Hollesley Bay Colony HM Borstal at Hollesley Bay Colony in Suffolk, England

Holloway HM Prison at Holloway in Derbyshire, England near Sheffield

Holman Holman Prison at Holman Station, Alabama with an average felon population of some 466 males in 1984 in maximum-, medium-, and minimum-security facilities

Holmesburg prison in the industrial suburb of Holmesburg, Pennsylvania where it is visible from the railroad and the

Delaware River; maximum-security facility opened in 1896

Holzminden German maximum-security prison northwest of Göttingen

Homantin Homantin Girls Home (formerly Hong Kong's Matauwei Girls Home)

Homestead (*see* Dade Correctional Institution)

Hominy medium-security prison officially called the Conner Correctional Center and about 30 miles northwest of Tulsa, Oklahoma

Homs (*see* Syria)

Honaira (*see* Solomon Islands)

Honduran prisons Tegucigalpa, the capital city, and the port of San Pedro Sula, have typical *cárcel modelo*-type prisons convicts and others find so inhumane

Hong Kong British crown colony off China's south coast; centers for the treatment of narcotic addicts are available as well as lockups and prisons

Honolulu capital of Hawaii and principal port city of Oahu Island containing the Conditional Release Branch, the Laumaka Conditional Release Center, the Oahu Community Correctional Center opened in 1918 and long overcrowded

Honolulu Jail nucleus of what is now the Halawa High Security Facility at Aiea on Hawaii's Oahu Island opened in 1962

hook 'em hook them (fasten with handcuffs)

Hooper Home Isaac T. Hooper Home (first halfway house in the United States where it was opened by the Society of Friends—Quakers—in New York City in 1845)

hoosegow jail (term may be derived from the Spanish—*juzgado*—court of justice)

hoosier(s) prison visitor(s)

Hope Halls halfway houses sustained by the Volunteers of America from 1896 through the 1920s

Horsemonger Horsemonger Lane Gaol (infamous London lockup and the scene of many hangings such as the one Dickens described in a letter to *The Times*; in the early 1800s it held Robert Taylor, called the Devil's Chaplain, convicted of

blasphemy for preaching the fundamental universality of all religious beliefs and casting doubt on the historical authenticity of Jesus Christ)

Hotlana hot Atlanta, Georgia or its jail or its federal penitentiary

hot seat electric chair or its metaphoric equivalent

Hot Springs Garland County courthouse and jail southwest of Little Rock, Arkansas

hot squat electric chair

House 33 Soviet secret-police prison in Rostov-on-Don

House of C House of Correction

House of D House of Detention

house(s) of darkness prison(s)

house(s) of detention jail(s); lockup(s)

Houston largest city in Texas and its jails and prisons

Howard John Howard—18th-century English prison reformer and author of *The State of the Prisons*, a book advocating better ways of treating inmates and insisting on vocational training and work as ways to make men honest; Rhode Island town containing most of the state correctional facilities such as the Providence County Jail now called the Admission and Orientation Unit, the Rhode Island State Prison now called the Maximum Custody Facility, the Medium-Minimum Facility formerly the Reformatory for Men, the Rhode Island Training School for Girls, and the Rhode Island School for Boys

Hudson Hudson Correctional Facility at Hudson, New York south of Albany; Hudson County Penitentiary in New Jersey; New York School for Girls at Hudson, New York

Hudson Street alimony jail on the lower west side of New York City's Manhattan where inmates were imprisoned for their failure to pay alimony

Hue (*see* Vietnam)

hulk(s) prison ship(s)—usually old craft unfit for the high seas but adequate as jails

Hull HM Prison at Hull whose full name is Kingston-upon-Hull; other prisons in Canada's Hull opposite Ottawa and in Boston's suburb of Hull on

Massachusetts Bay

Humanitarian Penologist Eugene V Debs (1855-1926) (*see* Presidential Canditate and Prison Convict)

Hungarian prisons Hungary's prisons were built during the long reign of the Austro-Hungarian Empire and few improvements have been made since 1918, when the empire was dismembered

Hunt Corrections Center St Gabriel, Louisiana's penal facility serving as an adult reception and diagnostic center together with maximum- and medium-security sections

Huntercombe HM Borstal at Huntercombe in Oxfordshire, England

Huntingdon Pennsylvania town southwest of State College and location of the State Correctional Institution dating back to 1889 when it was an industrial school and in 1945 held defective juvenile offenders

Huntsville Madison County seat and jail north of Birmingham, Alabama; Texas synonym for penal institutions such as the Diagnostic Unit, Ellis Unit, Goree Unit, Huntsville Unit, Wynne Unit in Huntsville, north of Houston

Huntsville Unit correctional facility at Huntsville, Texas where it was opened in 1849 and by late 1984 was packed beyond its capacity with male convicts

Huron Valley Huron Valley Men's Facility or Huron Valley Women's Facility in Ypsilanti, Michigan

Huron Valley Men's Facility Ypsilanti's maximum-security prison opened in 1981

Huron Valley Women's Facility in Ypsilanti, Michigan, opened in 1977

Hutchinson town in central Kansas northwest of Wichita and location of the Kansas State Industrial Reformatory

hut(s) prison cell(s)

Huttonsville West Virginia community south of Elkins and address of the Huttonsville Correctional Center holding male felons in medium custody

Hyderabad (*see* Pakistan)

IAPL International Association of Penal Law

ICA Illinois Correctional Association; Indiana Correctional Association; Iowa Corrections Association

ICCC International Concentration Camp Committee (Vienna, Austria)

icebox prison coroner's laboratory and office

ice(d) jail(ed)

Iceland this oldest democracy, dating from 930 when its parliament—the Althing (Old Thing)—first met, is between Greenland and Norway just below the Arctic Circle; its capital, Reykjavik, has but one small prison and every attempt is made to rehabilitate prisoners rather than confining them for long terms

ICFPW International Confederation of Former Prisoners of War (Paris, France)

ICSPPR International Centre of Sociological, Penal, and Penitentiary Research (Messina, Italy)

Idaho jails facilities for incarceration are found throughout the 44 counties ranging from Ada containing the capital city of Boise to Washington whose county seat is Weiser

Idaho State Idaho State Correctional Institution built in Boise in 1870 and holding felons in maximum, medium, and minimum security

if you can't do the sentence, don't do the job elderly convict's advice to anyone planning a criminal career

IHHA International Halfway House Association

Ikoyi Ikoyi Prison in Lagos, Nigeria

Iksha Soviet corrective labor colony for juvenile offenders close to Moscow's notorious prisons

Île du Diable (French—Devil's Island)—islet in the shark-infested tropical Atlantic north of Cayenne and the mainland penal colony maintained by France until the early 1950s; Devil's Island was used mainly to keep political prisoners completely segregated and it was here Captain Dreyfus suffered years of isolation

Île Saint Louis (French—Saint Louis Island)—leper colony for convicts in French Guiana

in the Maroni River above Saint Laurent

Îles du Salut (French—Security Islands)—off mainland French Guiana some 28 miles (45 kilometers) north-northwest of Cayenne; group consists of Île du Diable (Devil's Island), Île Royale, and Île Saint Joseph

Ilha de Flôres (Portuguese—Island of Flowers)—Brazilian prison in Rio de Janeiro's Guanabara Bay

Illinois Industrial School for Boys (*see* Sheridan)

Illinois lockups the state's 102 counties offer detention facilities from Quincy in Adams County to Eureka in Woodford County; the biggest are in Chicago's Cook County

Immokalee Florida town southeast of Fort Myers and location of the Hendry Correctional Institution

immurement confinement within walls

impound imprison

imprisoned authors famous authors who spent time behind prison bars include Bunyan *(Pilgrims's Progress)*, Cervantes *(Don Quixote)*, Dostoevski *(Crime and Punishment)*, Raleigh *(History of the World)*, O Henry *(Cabbages and Kings)*, Wilde *(Ballad of Reading Gaol* and *De Profundis)*

Imrali Turkish prison farm on Imrali Island in the Sea of Marmara, southwest of Istanbul

Imros Turkish prison on Imros Island in the Aegean Sea (a so-called open or minimum-security prison although its inmates have little chance of escaping)

incorrigible(s) person(s) who will not be corrected, reformed, rehabilitated, or made to conform to social standards

Indiana Boys School opened in 1867 for delinquents from 12 to 21 years of age; in Plainfield, a town just southwest of Indianapolis

Indiana Girls School started in Indianapolis in 1907 for juvenile delinquents from 12 to 20 years of age

Indiana jails the state's 92 counties have facilities for holding

felons whether they be in Decatur in Adams County or Columbia City in Whitley County; big cities such as Indianapolis have their own lockups

Indianapolis Marion County's county seat, courthouse, and jail as well as the Indiana Girls School

Indiana State Farm medium-security facility opened in Greencastle in 1914

Indiana State Prison opened in 1859 in Michigan City on Lake Michigan west of South Bend where it holds maximum- and medium-security felons

Indiana State Reformatory a maximum- and minimum-security penal facility opened in Pendleton in 1923

Indiana Women's Prison in Indianapolis, opened in 1973 to hold female felons in maximum security

Indiana Youth Center a medium-security facility in Plainfield where it began in 1965 to accommodate first-time felons from 15 years of age

Indian prisons Asia's great subcontinent nation, the Republic of India, maintains prisons built by the British in all its principal cities such as Bombay, Calcutta, Delhi, Madras, Hyderabad, Ahmedabad, Bangalore, Kanpur, etc.; the most notorious was the Black Hole of Calcutta within Calcutta's Fort William where during the Indian Mutiny in 1756 some 146 Europeans were imprisoned in such hot and narrow quarters that by the next morning only 23 remained alive

Indian River Indian River Correctional Institution at Vero Beach, Florida (*see* Vero Beach)

Indian River School for juvenile-delinquent boys in Massilon, Ohio

indic indicateur (French—informant)

Indio Indio Branch of the Riverside County Jail in California, midway between the Arizona border and Los Angeles, on the edge of the Mojave Desert

individual confinement solitary imprisonment

Indonesian prison island Java,

most densely populated island of Indonesia and containing most of its prisons

Indonesian prisons 13,000 islands comprise this Asian nation stretching along the Equator from New Guinea in the western Pacific to the Nicobar Islands in the eastern Indian Ocean; during Dutch occupation in the 17th, 18th, 19th, and early 20th century at least one prison was built on each of the major islands and jail-type lockups on the small islands of this gigantic archipelago; thus in Jakarta (formerly called Batavia), Surabaja, Bandung, Semarang, and Medan, there are penal institutions of every dimension ranging from jails to penitentiaries and large prisons

industrial prison workshop-oriented penitentiary where inmates produce useful things such as highway signs, mail bags, school furniture, and vehicle license plates

Industrial School for Women in Vega Alta, Puerto Rico

Indy Indianapolis, Indiana's nickname or that of its jails, lockups, and prisons

Inebriate Reception Center pilot facility in San Diego, California where nonviolent abusers of alcohol and other drugs accept coffee and counseling in lieu of being jailed or imprisoned

informante (Portuguese or Spanish—informant)

informant(s) person(s) giving information to law-enforcement officers who may use it in the investigation of criminals

informatore (Italian—informant)

injection (*see* death by injection)

Innisfail Canadian town north of Calgary, Alberta and location of the Bowden Institution

inmate(s) convict(s); person(s) in a confinement facility; prisoner(s)

INS Immigration and Naturalization Service

In-Service Training (IST) within California state prisons

inside the tall walls inside prison

Institute The Institute (nickname for any penal institution

having Institute in its title as in the case of the Sybil Brand Institute for Women in Los Angeles, California)

institutional capacity officially determined number of inmates a correctional facility is designed to house

institutional superintendent(s) warden(s)

Institution for Youthful Offenders in Santurce, Puerto Rico close to San Juan

Instituto Nacional de Orientacion Femenina (Spanish—National Institute of Feminine Orientation)—women's prison in los Teques of the Miranda Ejido of Venezuela

Insular Penitentiary in Rio Piedras near San Juan, Puerto Rico; above its main gate are the words *Odia el Delito y Compadace el Delinquente* (Spanish—Hate the Crime and Pity the Criminal)

Intake Service Center Cranston, Rhode Island facility for holding pre-trial detainees

intensive care unit locked unit reserved for juvenile offenders

intermediate-term adult penal institutions of the U.S. Bureau of Prisons Danbury, Connecticut; Fort Worth, Texas; La Tuna, Texas; Lexington, Kentucky; Milan, Michigan; Sandstone, Minnesota; Terminal Island, California; Texarkana, Texas

internados judiciales (Spanish—judicial boarding houses)—penal facilities for holding convicts; in Venezuela there are 18 such institutions

internal exile Soviet euphemism for imprisonment in some remote part of the USSR

International Halfway House Association publisher of the *Directory of Residential Treatment Centers*

International Penal and Penitentiary Commission founded in 1872 and in 1950 became a part of the United Nations; originally known as the International Penitentiary Commission

International Prisoners Aid Association publishes the *Directory of Prisoners Aid Agencies*

in the grinder in jail; in prison

in the nick (Cockney English—in jail; in prison)

intimidation avoidance of offenses because of fear of punishment

Invercargill Invercargill Borstal Institution near Invercargill on South Island, New Zealand

Inverness prison in Inverness, Scotland

Ionia Michigan town east of Grand Rapids and site of the Michigan Reformatory, Michigan Training Unit, and the Riverside Correctional Facility

Iowa jails 99 counties make up the state and all provide detention facilities whether they be in Greenfield in Adair County or Clarion in Wright County; cities such as Des Moines have lockups in addition to the county jails nearby

Iowa Security and Medical Facility at Oakdale, opened in 1968

Iowa State Penitentiary at Fort Madison where started in 1839 and now very overcrowded

Iowa Training School for Girls at Mitchellville, Iowa northeast of Des Moines

IPAA International Prisoners Aid Association (Louisville, Kentucky)

IPPC International Penal and Penitentiary Commission *(see entry)*

IPPF International Penal and Penitentiary Foundation (Neuchatel, Switzerland)

Iranian prisons the Islamic Republic of Iran, long known as Persia, contains prisons of ancient design in Tehran, Ishfahan, Mashad, Tabriz, and other metropolitan places; no good reports concern these penal facilities

Iraqi prisons the so-called Republic of Iraq, once known as Mesopotamia, is bordered by Iran, Saudi Arabia, Syria, and Turkey; its prisons are on a par with those of its neighbors

IRC *(see* Inebriate Reception Center)

Irish prisons Dublin's old prison is Kilmainham on the site of a seventh-century abbey and later the headquarters of the occupying English black-and-tan army; Cork prison is on Rathmore Road; Limerick has one on Rutland Street

Irma small Wisconsin town north of Wausau in the middle of Lincoln County where it contains the Lincoln Hills School

Irmo Harbison Correctional Institution for Women at Irmo, South Carolina, just west of Columbia

iron house jail; lockup; penitentiary; prison

ironmongery department Her (His) Majesty's prison

ISIS Investigative Support Information System (FBI)

Isla de la Juventud (Spanish— Isle of Youth)—new name for the Isla de Pinos (Isle of Pines) where many Cuban political prisoners are held

Isla de Pinos (Spanish—Isle of Pines)—site of Castro-controlled prisons on this island in the Caribbean off Cuba's southwest coast

Islamabad (*see* Pakistan)

Island Blackwell's (Welfare, now Roosevelt) Island in New York City's East River between Manhattan and Queens; Parkhurst Prison on the Isle of Wight in the English Channel off Southhampton; Rikers Island in the East River of New York between the Bronx and Queens; any other island holding prisoners

Island of Hell Norfolk Island in the South Pacific Ocean and once the most dreaded of all Australian penal stations

Isle of Flowers (*see Ilha de Flores*)

Isle of Pines (*see* Cuba, Isla de Pinos)

Isle of Wight Parkhurst Prison on the Isle of Wight in the English Channel off Southampton

isolation tank(s) solitary-confinement cell(s)

isolator Soviet penal colony specializing in solitary confinement; many in distant parts of the Siberian Arctic and in the White Sea east of Kem on the Solovetski Islands

Isole Eolie (Italian—Aeolian Islands)—the Lipari Islands off the north coast of Sicily where they serve as penal colonies

ISP Idaho State Penitentiary; Institute of Social Psychiatry

Israeli prisons the State of Israel has some prisons built during the Turkish era as well as others built by the British; the Israelis have erected prison camps and reports indicate they are more humane than most such places

IST In-Service Training (within California state prisons)

Istanbul formerly Constantinople (*see* Turkey)

Italian prisons Rome's great prison—Regina Coeli (Queen of Heaven) is more or less typical of others in cities such as Genoa (Prigione d'Genova), Milan (Ducato Milanese), Naples (Caserta), and Venice (Pozzi)

Ivanovo internal prison of the Soviet secret police in Ivanovo

Ivory Coast's prisons during the more than century-long French occupation of this West African nation prisons were built that are still in use in the capital, Abidjan, and in Bouaké as well as in smaller cities

Iwakuni U.S. Marine Corps Correctional Facility of Iwakuni, Japan across Hiroshima Bay from Hiroshima on the southwest part of Honshu Island

Izmir Turkish port city in the eastern Mediterranean or nickname of its jails and prison (formerly ruled by the Greeks who called it Smyrna)

jacket prisoner's case history or dossier

Jackson Georgia town midway between Atlanta and Macon as well as the location of the Georgia Diagnostic and Classification Facility; Jackson, Mississippi jail and its police lockups; Michigan city between Ann Arbor and Battle Creek and site of the world's largest walled prison enclosing 57 acres and 23 hectares, as well as the Reception and Guidance Center and the State Prison of Southern Michigan; North Carolina town east of Roanoke Rapids and location of the Odom penal facility opened in 1956

Jacksonville Duval County's courthouse and jail in Jacksonville, Florida, north of Saint Augustine

Jaffna (*see* Sri Lanka)

jaga (Malay—guard; warden)

jail penal facility usually run by local law-enforcement officers (city jails are most often run by the local police and county jails by the sheriff; jails most often are pre-trial detention centers confining the young with the old, the healthy with the sick, first-time offenders with hardened criminals)

JAIL Justice Against Identification Laws (persecuting the innocent)

jailage a jailer's fee (demanded more than a century ago and now replaced by bribes extracted in many jails of the world)

jail bait person(s) whose illegal activities lead to incarceration

jailbird ex-convict, prisoner, or recidivist

jail delivery clearing a jail of its inmates by bringing them to trial and then releasing them or sentencing them to prison; British call this gaol delivery

jail distemper jail fever (typhus often due to overcrowding); sickness brought on by incarceration or fear of incarceration

jaileress female jailer

jail fever typhus fever occurring in jails and other crowded places

Jail Forum quarterly publication of the National Jail Association

jailhouse lawyer convict who is well-informed about the law

jailhouse punk any prisoner who becomes a homosexual while imprisoned

jailhouse(s) building(s) used as jail(s)

jail limits area or district surrounding a jail where debtors may be at large under a bond of security

jail plant narcotics concealed on a person condemned to imprisonment or visiting a penal institution

Jakarta (*see* Indonesian prisons)

Jalapa prison in Jalapa, the capital of the Mexican state of Veracruz and northwest of the port of Veracruz

Jamaica large West Indian island in the Caribbean which is larger than Puerto Rico but smaller than Cuba; held by the British from 1665 until 1962 when it became independent;

penal facilities include Richmond Farm Prison, St Catherine's District Prison, and the Tamarind Farm Prison

Jamejala Soviet psychiatric hospital charged with isolating political prisoners on the pretext they are out of their minds

Jamesburg New Jersey community northeast of Trenton and location of the Training School for Boys and Girls begun in 1866

Jamestown Sierra Conservation Center at Jamestown, California about halfway between the Nevada border and Stockton; it was opened in 1965 but by 1984 was overcrowded although some of its inmates are in forestry camps

jamocha java + mocha (prison slang for coffee)

Janie Porter Barrett School for Girls at Hanover, Virginia just north or Richmond

Japanese-American relocation centers concentration camps set up after the attack upon Pearl Harbor and the resulting hysteria; ten such centers included Manzanar and Tule Lake in California, Gila and Poston in southwestern Arizona, Topaz in central Utah, Minidoka in south-central Idaho, Heart Mountain in northern Wyoming, Amache in southeastern Colorado, Jerome and Rohwer in southeastern Arkansas close to the Mississippi River

Japanita Santa Anita Assembly Center's nickname during World War II when the racetrack stables were used for the incarceration of Japanese-Americans

Japan's prisons penal facilities are provided by all forty-seven of Japan's prefectures and are to be found in its great cities such as Tokyo, Osaka, Yokohama, Nagoya, Kyoto, Kobe, Sapporo, Kitakyushu, Fukuoka, and Kawasaki

jaula (Spanish—cage)—slang for a jail or lockup

Jax Jacksonville, Florida or its jail or lockups

Jay State Prison at Jay, Florida near the Alabama line north of Tallahassee

J-bird jailbird

jd juvenile delinquent

JDC Juvenile Detention Center

Jean Union Pacific railroad whistle-stop between Las Vegas and the California border; holds the Southern Nevada Correctional Center

Jeff City Jefferson City, Missouri or its jail in the central part of the state

Jefferson Jefferson County Jail in Birmingham, Alabama; Jefferson Parish Jail near New Orleans, Louisiana

Jefferson City midway between Kansas City and Saint Louis as well as site of the Central Missouri Correctional Center, the Missouri Intermediate Reformatory, and the Missouri State Penitentiary for men

Jefftown Journal prisoner's periodical published at Jefferson City, Missouri's prison

Jen Penjara Singapore's Remand Prison nicknamed for the road where it is located

Jerome southeastern Arkansas location of a Japanese-American relocation center set up after Pearl Harbor at the beginning of America's entrance into World War II

Jersey City New Jersey city and short form for its jail and police-station lockups

Jess Dunn Correctional Center in Taft, Oklahoma, opened in 1980

Jessup Maryland community just southwest of Baltimore and site of the Maryland Correctional Institution for Women, Maryland Correctional Pre-Release System, Maryland House of Correction

Jester Unit Texas pre-release facility in Richmond

jettard (French—jail)

Jewell Manor Jewell Manor Girls Center at Louisville, Kentucky

JHA (*see* John Howard Association)

JHAH John Howard Association of Hawaii

JHDF Juvenile Hall Detention Facility

jhj's jailhouse juvenile delinquents

jibbet correct pronunciation of gibbet

Jidda (*see* Saudi Arabia)

Jimmy Valentine reformed criminal invented by O Henry (William Sidney Porter) who spent some five years in the Ohio State Penitentiary and

authored some of the best-liked short stories

JIS Jail Inspection Service

Jiuren Soviet prison near Inner Mongolia

JJC Juvenile Justice Center (Los Angeles, California)

JLS Jail Library Service (California State Library)

Joburg Johannesburg, South Africa or its jail or prison

Joe Harp Correctional Center in Lexington, Oklahoma, opened in 1978

Joelton Tennessee town north of Nashville and location of the Tennessee Youth Center

Joey man who takes a prisoner's place at home while the convict is imprisoned

Johannesburg (*see* South Africa)

John Saint John in the American Virgin Islands, Saint John in New Brunswick, Canada or their jails or police-station lockups

John Howard Association founded in 1901 to honor an 18th-century English prison reformer; always meets in Chicago and its members offer professional consultation services

John Howard Association of Hawaii Honolulu's prisoner-service agency

John's Saint John's, Newfoundland, Canada or its jail

Johnson Hall Forensic Unit in Evanston, Wyoming, used by prisoners who are dangerously mentally ill or in need of extensive psychiatric treatment

Johnson's Island Confederate prisoners of war held on Johnson's Island in Lake Erie north of Sandusky, Ohio; it was as bad for Confederates as Andersonville was for Yankees

Joliet Illinois city southwest of Chicago and site of the Joliet Correctional Center and the Statesville Correctional Center

Joliet Correctional Center maximum-security prison in Joliet, Illinois where it holds more than 1300 male felons in maximum security

Jonestown tropical jungle commune in Guyana where the Reverend Jim Jones of San Francisco ran it like a concentration camp and, when investigated in 1978, enforced the suicide of more than 900 of his cultist followers and prisoners

Joplin Joplin, Missouri or its county jail

Jordan's prisons the Hashemite Kingdom of Jordan's capital, Amman, has one of the world's worst prisons as many former convicts agree and all pleas to improve conditions appear to have fallen on deaf ears

Journal of Correctional Education quarterly publication of the CEA (Correctional Education Association)

Joyceville Institution in Kingston, Ontario where it had its inception in 1957

JPS Juvenile Probation Services

jri jail-release information

Juárez Ciudad Juárez, Chihuahua, and its jail across the border from El Paso, Texas

Juariles (Mexican-American—Ciudad Juárez)—or its jail

Jubilee Jubilee Lodge for Girls at Brimfield, Illinois

judas peephole in a prison-cell door constructed so the inmate(s) can be observed without knowing it

judas (Spanish—prison-cell-door peephole)

judas hole (*see* judas)

judas slit (*see* judas)

judicial execution execution in response to a court order

judicial hanging hanging performed in response to a court order (as opposed to a lynching)

judicial murder capital punishment as defined by its opponents

judicium capitale (Latin—capital justice)—justice through execution

jug(ged) jail(ed)—in underworld slang

Jugoslavia (*see* Yugoslavia)

jug(s) jail(s); prison(s)

jug tank(s) prison cell(s) reserved for drug addicts

Julia Julia Tutwiler Prison for Women at Wetumpka, Alabama with an average female prison inmate population of 190 in 1984

Juneau Juneau Correctional Center for adult and juvenile male and female delinquents, felons, and misdemeanants in southeastern Alaska

Jungfernhof extermination facility near Riga where many Austrian Jews were transported before being murdered by their Nazi captors

junk tank(s) prison cell(s) reserved for drug addicts

jus publicum (Latin—penal law; public law)

Justice U.S. Department of Justice

juve delinquent(s) juvenile delinquent(s)

Juvenile Hall holding facility for juvenile delinquents

juvenile-justice agency government agency concerned with the adjudication, care, confinement, investigation, and supervision of juvenile delinquents

Juvenile Justice Center Los Angeles, California agency designed to cope with the growing problem of juvenile delinquency

juvenile penal institutions of the U.S. Bureau of Prisons Ashland, Kentucky; Englewood, Colorada; Morgantown, West Virginia

juvenile record(s) official record(s) containing information concerning juvenile court proceedings and all applicable correctional and detention processes ordered

juvie(s) juvenile delinquent(s); juvenile hall(s); juvenile law-enforcement officers(s)

K-9 Corps Canine Corps (staffed by police dogs)

Kabul capital city of Afghanistan and nickname for its old prison

Kaiserwald Nazi concentration camp in Latvia during most of World War II when Germany occupied this area close to Riga

Kakogawa careless-driver prison serving Japan's traffic-congested Osaka-Kobe-Kyoto area; prisoners receive driving lessons daily; at dawn and dusk they retire to the prison's Park of Interrogation where they apologize to the memory of their victims and swear never to repeat their mistakes

Kalgoorlie Kalgoorlie Regional Prison (Kalgoorlie, Western Australia)

Kaluga Soviet prison in a city of the same name some 90 miles (145 kilometers) southwest of

Moscow; its many inmates have included dissident poet Alexander Ginzburg imprisoned for distributing funds aiding the families of political prisoners

Kampala (*see* Uganda)

Kandy (*see* Sri Lanka)

kangaroo court prisoners' court imposing contributions, fines, and work tasks on convicts brought before it; nickname for any small court harsh on addicts, alcoholics, and vagrants

kanga(s) kangaroo(s)—Australian prison warden(s)

Kansas City Kansas City, Kansas or Kansas City, Missouri just across the river, or any of its jails and lockups

Kansas Correctional Institution in Lansing in the northeast corner of the state where it was opened in 1981 with provision for felons male and female

Kansas Correctional Vocational Training Center in Topeka, a minimum-security facility opened in 1974

Kansas jails the state's 105 counties provide detention facilities whether they be in Iola, county center of Allen County, or Kansas City in Wyandotte County; Wichita and Topeka also have local lockups for prisoners

Kansas State Industrial Reformatory in Hutchinson where it opened its gates in 1895

Kansas State Penitentiary in Lansing, opened in 1864, and providing all levels of security

Kansas State Reception and Diagnostic Center in Topeka where it receives and evaluates male felons ordered by the courts for confinement

Kaohsiung (*see* China, Republic of)

kapidiye (Turkish—hardened criminals)—the most feared in prisons where they bribe the guards and rule the other inmates

Karachi (*see* Pakistan)

Karaganda and Kolyma two of the world's largest forced-labor penal camps; both in the USSR where the population of each exceeded a million prisoners in 1985

Karnet Karnet Rehabilitation Centre (Western Australia)

Kars prison near the eastern border of Turkey facing Soviet Armenia

Kathmandu (*see* Nepal)

katorga (Russian—hard penal servitude)—forced labor

Kauai Kauai Community Correctional Center at Lihue on the island of Kauai in Hawaii

Kaufering forced-labor subcamp in the south of Germany close to Dachau

Kawasaki (*see* Japan's prisons)

Kay-Cee Kay-Cee Honor Center in Kansas City, Missouri, which had its inception in 1978

KC Jackson County Jail in Kansas City, Missouri or Kansas City in either Kansas or Missouri together with jails, lockups, and other penal facilities

KCCD Kentucky Council on Crime and Delinquency

KCJ Kings County Jail in Seattle, Washington

Kearney Nebraska community southwest of Grand Island and location of the Youth Development Center

keester plant hollow suppository made of metal, plastic, rubber, or wood and used to conceal drugs, money, or even uncut diamonds within the rectum

keester stash anything hidden in the rectum

keimushó (Japanese—prison)

Kendall juvenile-delinquent rehabilitation center at Kendall, Florida near South Miami

Kent Kent Correctional Institution in Dover, Delaware with maximum- and medium-security facilities for felons and misdemeanants

Kent Institution maximum-security penal facility in Agassiz, British Columbia east of Vancouver

Kentucky Correctional Institution for Women at Peewee Valley east of Louisville and site of the Assessment and Orientation Unit

Kentucky lockups 120 counties of this state have jails ranging from Columbia, county seat of Adair County, to Versailles in Woodford County; big cities such as Louisville and Lexington have augmented facilities for holding convicts as well as persons awaiting trial

Kentucky Manpower Development state agency charged

with the task of developing a prisoner rehabilitation program

Kentucky State Penitentiary maximum-security prison dating from 1888 at Eddyville, east of Paducah

Kentucky State Reformatory medium-security facility at La Grange northeast of Louisville where it opened in 1939

Kenya's prisons penal facilities in this East African republic date back to the time of British rule when every one of any size was named HM Prison

Ketchikan Ketchikan Correctional Center in southeastern Alaska where it holds adult as well as juvenile criminals

Kharkov world's largest prison in the capital city of the Kharkov region of the Ukraine and dreaded throughout the USSR

Khartoum (*see* Sudan)

Kholmogori Arctic death camp established by Lenin's men near Archangel in 1921 for the exploitation and suppression of political prisoners in the Soviet Union

Kigali one of Africa's most densely populated places (*see* Rwanda)

Kilby Kilby Corrections Facility at Montgomery, Alabama

Kilmainham Dublin jail on the west side of the city where Parnell was incarcerated

Kincheloe Michigan town near Sault Ste Marie and site of the Kinross Correctional Facility, formerly an Air Force base

kindergarten of vice epithet applied to many jails

Kings Kings County Jail in Seattle, Washington

King's Bench one of Southwark's seven prisons, now all gone, but just as well known as Marshalsea also off the High Street to the south of the River Thames in London

Kingston Canadian city on Lake Ontario southwest of Ottawa and site of the Collins Bay Institution as well as the Joyceville Institution; (*see* Jamaica)

Kingston Pen Kingston Penitentiary (and mental hospital) just west of Kingston, Ontario in the suburb of Portsmouth at the northeast end of Lake Ontario

Kingstown (*see* Saint Vincent and the Grenadines)

Kinross Correctional Facility part of an abandoned Air Force base near Kincheloe, Michigan where it was opened in 1978

Kinston North Carolina community northwest of New Bern and site of the Dobbs School for male and female juvenile delinquents

Kiribati Tarawa, the capital of this mid-Pacific equatorial colony better known to many as the Gilbert and Ellice Islands, contains what was once HM Prison

Kirkham HM Prison at Kirkham in Lancashire, England

Kirkland Correctional Institution in Columbia, South Carolina

Kitakyushu (*see* Japan's prisons)

KL Konzentrationslager (German—concentration camp)—prisoners contracted this to KZ

Klink Colonel Klink aptly named commandant of a German-controlled prisoner-of-war camp featured in a television show entitled *Hogan's Heroes*; inmates of actual prisoner-of-war camps relate their incarceration was no laughing matter

klondike solitary prison cell

KMCI Kettle Moraine Correctional Institution (near Duluth, Minnesota)

KMD Kentucky Manpower Development (*q.v.*)

knowledge factory prison school

Knoxville Knox County, Tennessee's centrally located city; its jail is not far from its courthouse

Kobe (*see* Japan's prisons)

kogus (Turkish—cell block)— see *turist kogus*

Kolyma USSR penal camp north of the Arctic Circle near a Soviet city and river of the same name; the river flows into the East Siberian Sea; the camp has held as many as a million prisoners at one time

Konzentrationslager (German—concentration camp)

Korean prisons during the era of Japanese rule between 1910 and the end of World War II the prisons were built and managed by the Japanese; former convicts do not give them good marks and in communist-dominated North Korea they are no better than in South Korea, they insist

Korydallos prison in Athens, Greece

kraal (Afrikaans—prison; stockade; stockades village)

Kragshovhede Danish open-type prison without high fences or walls; this type of detention facility is said to result in reduced recidivism among former inmates; the up-to-date prison is near Skagen or Skaw in northernmost Denmark

Krems site of a World-War-II concentration camp on the Danube northwest of Vienna

Kresty Leningrad's central prison

KRIM not an acronym but the invented name for the Danish association for penal reform

Kriminalstrafkunde die Kriminalstrafkunde (German—penology)

KROM not an acronym but the contrived name of the Norwegian association for penal reform

Krome Avenue address and nickname of the immigration and naturalization detention camp on Krome Avenue in Miami, Florida

KRUM not an acronym but a made-up word standing for the Swedish association for penal reform

Kryukovo USSR prison colony masquerading as a psychiatric hospital northwest of Moscow

Ktr Katorzhane (Russian—compound)—prison compound reserved for people sentenced to hard labor

Kuala Lumpur (*see* Malaysian prisons)

Kuibyshev Soviet transit prison

Kulani Kulani Correctional Facility on Stainback Highway in Hilo on the island of Hawaii where it was originally the Kulani Honor Camp started in 1946 and renamed in 1977

Kumasi (*see* Ghana's prisons)

Kumla Kumla Prison (institution for long-term prisoners)—in 1976 more than half its inmates were foreigners; Kumla is in south-central Sweden near Örebro

Kunie old French penal colony in the Southwest Pacific southeast of New Caledonia; also called the Isle of Pines but not to be confused with a Cuban penal colony of the same name

Kuwait this Persian Gulf state, rich in oil to the extent its citizens pay no taxes, was long under Arab control with the British taking care of its defense; its prisons in Hawalli and Kuwait City are not the most modern

Kyoto (*see* Japan's prisons)

LA Los Angeles—California's biggest city—and name convicts give to its lockups, jails, and other penal institutions (*see* toponyms)

Labour, Silence, Penitence words on a plaque surmounting the facade of the Trenton State Prison built in New Jersey in 1799 and still in use

La Cabaña (Spanish—The Cabin)—old Spanish prison at the entrance to Havana harbor and still used by Castro's forces for the execution and imprisonment of political prisoners

La Ceiba prison in a seaport city of Honduras on the Caribbean

LACJ Los Angeles County Jail (California)

La Ferté Macé French detention camp described by e e cummings in his documentary novel—*the enormous room*

La Force top-security prison of Paris in the late 1700s and early 1800s

lag ticket-of-leave man; transported convict of the type Britain shipped to Australia and Tasmania following the American Revolution when the Thirteen Colonies were no longer available to absorb excess prison population

lagging serving a three-year sentence in a British prison; transportation by sea of convicts sent from overcrowded jails in the British Isles to those in Australia and Tasmania

Lagos (*see* Nigeria)

La Grange Kentucky town northeast of Louisville and site of the Kentucky State Reformatory as well as the Luther Luckett Correctional Complex

lag(s) transported convict(s)

La Guaira Venezuelan seaport just below Caracas and location of a jail well known to Venezuelans as well as to some visitors tangling with the law

Lahore (*see* Pakistan)

Lake Butler Florida town between Gainesville and Jacksonville and site of the Reception and Medical Center opened in 1968

Lake Correctional Institute penal facility with all levels of security and academic as well as vocational education programs at its site in Lowell, Florida

Lakehills Lakehills Community Corrections Center in Salt Lake City, Utah

La Mesa Penitenciaria (Spanish—La Mesa Penitentiary)—Baja California's major prison, in the eastern section of Tijuana close to the Caliente racetrack

laminated glass principal component of detention glazing (*see* detention glazing)

La Modelo La Carcel Modelo (Spanish—The Model Prison)—principal prison of Caracas, Venezuela, described locally as a judicial boarding house

lamster(s) escaped convict(s)

Lancaster HM Prison at Lancaster in Lancashire, England or the jail in Lancaster, Pennsylvania, or jails in smaller Lancasters in Canada and the United States; Ohio town southeast of Columbus and site of the Southeastern Ohio Training Center

Lancaster Correctional Center at Trenton, Florida where it was opened in 1979; most of its inmates are first-felony youthful offenders

Lancaster Pre-Release penal facility in Lancaster, Massachusetts for males and females held in minimum security before being released

Land of Death and Chains Maxim Gorki's nickname for Siberia

'Lando Orlando, Florida and its jail and lockup

Land of Political Exiles Yakutia in northeastern Siberia

Landsberg fortress prison on the Lech River in Upper Bavaria about 22 miles or 35 kilometers south of Augsberg; Hitler was imprisoned here in 1923 for participating in and plotting the overthrow of the Social Democratic government of Germany during the Munich Beer Hall Putsch; he served only nine months of his five-year sentence but during his incarceration wrote *Mein Kampf*, the blueprint for concentration camps, the total extermination of so-called inferior races, and the waging of World War II

Langholmen Swedish prison close to Stockholm

Langi Langi Kal Kal Youth Training Centre at Trawalla, Victoria, Australia

Lansing Kansas town just south of Leavenworth and site of the Kansas Correctional Institution and the Kansas State Penitentiary; State Industrial Farm for Women at Lansing, Michigan west of Detroit

'Lanta Atlanta, Georgia or its jails, lockups, and the federal penitentiary

Lantan Lantan Island (contains Ma Po Ping Prison serving the British Crown Colony of Hong Kong)

Lantana Florida town south of West Palm Beach and site of the Lantana Correctional Institution

La Nuestra Familia (Spanish-American jail jargon—Our Family)—prison racketeers who deal with homosexual prostitution, loan sharking, murder contracting, and narcotics; a Mexican-American Mafia

Laos the communist-dominated Lao People's Democratic Republic has an old prison in Vientiane built during the years of French-colonial rule (1899-1949)

La Paz Bolivia's capital high in the Andes where prisoners get cool mountain air but very little else; Mexico's La Paz, near the tip of Baja California

La Pica (Spanish—the stonecutters hammer; the pike or the long lance of the picador)—nickname of Venezuela's central penitentiary of Oriente

La Pieota prison in Bogotá, Colombia

La Planta nickname of the house of reeducation and artisan work in the El Paraiso section of Caracas, Venezuela where its official name is *Casa de Reeducación y Trabajo Artesanal*

La Plata (*see* Argentina)

La Porte Noire (French—The Black Gate)—main entrance to the penal colony and prison in Saint Laurent du Maroni, nicknamed by the prisoners The Gate of Hell

La Roquette Parisian prison for a prostitute or another woman convicted of crimes

La Route Zéro (French—The Zero Route)—various teams of convicts in French Guiana labored for fifty years through muddy marshes and rain forests while building this Road to Nowhere leading out of the Saint Laurent du Maroni headquarters of the old penal colony

LAS Legal Aid Society

Las Colinas Las Colinas Girls' Facility in Santee, California east of San Diego; includes maximum-security cells for hard-to-handle female convicts; *colinas* is Spanish for cabbages

Las Palomas Las Palomas, Chihuahua and its jail across the border from Columbus, New Mexico

last mile euphemism for the short walk from the prison cell to the place of execution

last waltz condemned prisoner's march to the electric chair, gas chamber, or other place of execution

Las Vegas (*see* Vegas)

Las Ventas (Spanish—The Stalls)—Madrid's old municipal prison

Latchmere House a remand center in Surrey, England

latrinogram latrine rumor

La Tuna Federal Correctional Institution at La Tuna, Texas close to Las Cruces, New Mexico

Laurel maximum-security juvenile facility near Laurel, Maryland northeast of Washington, DC

Laval Ville de Laval, Quebec on the west side of Montreal and site of the Correctional Development Centre and the Federal Training Centre as well as

the Leclerc Institution

Laval-des-Rapides Ecole Notre-Dame de Laval at Laval-des-Rapides, Québec

Lawtey town in north-central Florida near Gainesville and site of the Lawtey Correctional Institution opened in 1977; has custody over older inmates with medical problems

Lawton Lawton, Oklahoma or its Comanche County Jail southwest of Oklahoma City

lazaretto hospital for contagious diseases; place of quarantine; tweendecks storeroom sometimes used as a hospital or even as a lockup if a vessel is without a brig

LCCC Lucas County Corrections Center (Ohio)

LCCJ Louisiana Council on Criminal Justice

Leavenworth U.S. Penitentiary at Leavenworth, Kansas just north of Kansas City, Kansas where it was opened in 1895

Lebanon the Lebanon Correctional Institution in Lebanon, Ohio northeast of Cincinnati; war-torn Middle-East republic, formed at the end of World War I from five Turkish districts, has prisons in its capital, Beirut, and in its port city of Tripoli (not to be confused with another port city in Libya also called Tripoli)

Leclerc Institution in Laval, Québec

Lecumberri-Hilton nickname of Mexico City's Lecumberri prison

Leeds HM Prison at Leeds in Yorkshire, England

Leesburg location of the Lee Correctional Institution just north of Albany, Georgia; New Jersey town northwest of Cape May Court House, containing the New Jersey State Prison—Leesburg

LEF Liberté, Égalité, Fraternité (French—Liberty, Equality, Fraternity)—official slogan of the French Revolution but ironically enough found inscribed in bronze over the gates of prisons built by the French

Lefortovo prison in Moscow described in *The Gulag Archipelago* by one of its inmates, Aleksander I Solzhenitsyn

Leicester HM Prison at Leicester in Leicestershire, England where Leicester is pronounced *Lester*

León (*see* Nicaragua)

Leopoldville (*see* Kinshasa)

Lesotho the Kingdom of Lesotho, once the British protectorate of Basutoland, is completely enclosed by South Africa; its capital, Meseru, has a gaol-type lockup built before 1966 when the protectorate became independent

lethal gas method of execution in California, Maryland, Mississippi, Missouri, Nevada, North Carolina, Oregon, Rhode Island, Wyoming

lethal intravenous injection method of execution in Idaho, New Mexico, Oklahoma, Texas

Leuven Leuven Prison (also called Louvain by the French-speaking Belgians) to the east of Brussels (called Bruxelles by the Flemish); (*see* Louvain)

level four death-dealing dose or injection of breath-stopping barbital or other drug used by executioners

Lewes small jail in the Delaware River fishing port of Lewes just inside the Delaware River breakwater

Lewisburg U.S. Penitentiary at Lewisburg, Pennsylvania north of Harrisburg and closer to Williamsport (*see* Lewisburg Plan *and* telephone-pole design)

Lewisburg Plan the plan of the Lewisburg Penitentiary, also called the telephone-pole design, providing for maximum- and medium-security cells, inside and outside, respectively; there are dormitory blocks with honor rooms for inmates who have earned special treatment (*see* telephone-pole design)

Lex any Lexington or its correctional facilities (*see* Lexington)

Lexington Federal Correctional Institution at Lexington, Kentucky; Kentucky city in the northeastern corner of the state and location of the Blackburn Correctional Complex as well as the special units of the Danville Youth Development Center; Oklahoma town south of Oklahoma City and address of the Joe Harp Correctional Center and the Lexington Assessment and Reception Center opened in 1978; U.S. Public Health Service Hospital in Lexington, Kentucky (drug detoxification facility)

ley de fuga (Spanish—law of flight)—legal privilege of law-enforcement officers who may kill anyone attempting to escape; it is not uncommon for prisoners to be encouraged to escape so they may be killed legally while escaping

Leyhill HM Prison at Leyhill in Gloucestershire, England

LGC Laminated Glass Corporation (*see* detention glazing)

LGD London Gaol Delivery

Libby Libby Prison—converted tobacco warehouse in Richmond, Virginia where the Confederates imprisoned many Union agents as well as soldiers captured in battles during the American Civil War also known as the War of the Secession

libéré(s) [French—liberated convict(s)]—a prisoner who is free from confinement but not free to leave the country of confinement

Liberia West African republic founded in 1822 by the United States for the repatriation of freed slaves; its capital, Monrovia, is named for its sponsor, President James Monroe; Monrovia is also the nickname of its prison; another is in Buchanan

Liberty Center Ohio town southwest of Toledo and site of the Maumee Youth Camp

Liberty Street nickname of the city jail on Liberty Street in Louisville, Kentucky

Libreville (*see* Gabonese prisons)

Libya a North African country officially the Socialist People's Libyan Arab Jamahiriya whose main port cities, Tripoli (the capital) and Benghazi, contain prisons built during its Italian occupation from 1912 until the end of World War II

Liechtenstein the Principality of Liechtenstein, in the Alps between Austria and Switzerland, is about the size of the District of Columbia and contains an old prison in the capital, Vaduz

Lieutenant of the Tower Lieutenant of the Tower of London (its warden)

lifeboat commutation of a death sentence or a prison term; judicial order for a retrial

lifer(s) prisoner(s) sentenced to life imprisonment

lifer's lament *gruntin' don' git yuh nuttin'* (complaining is useless)—but modern penologists are responsive to much complaining and many do their best for their charges

Lihue port city on Kauai Island, Hawaii and location of the Kauai Community Correctional Center opened in 1946 as the Kulani Honor Camp but renamed in 1977

likvidatsiya (Russian—liquidation)—Soviet euphemism for execution

Lilongwe (*see* Malawi)

Lima Lima, Ohio and its Allen County Jail or Lima, Peru with its jails and prisons pronounced, respectively, as *Lie-mah* and *Lee-mah*

Lima State Hospital in Lima, Ohio offering felons psychiatric services if they are mentally ill

Limón Costa Rican prison in the Caribbean seaport also called Puerto Limón

Lincoln HM Prison at Lincoln in Lincolnshire, England; jails in fifty-one American cities named Lincoln; Nebraska's capital city southwest of Omaha and location of four penal facilities the Diagnostic and Evaluation Center, the Lincoln Correctional Center, the Nebraska State Penitentiary, and the Post Care Program

Lincoln Correctional Center holds youthful offenders in medium and minimum security in Lincoln, Nebraska where it opened in 1979

Lincoln Hills School reception center and training school in Irma, Wisconsin

Lino Lakes small Minnesota community north of Saint Paul and site of the Minnesota Correctional Facility opened in 1963 to hold adult male felons and teach them industrial trades

Lipari Islands Italian islands off the north coast of Sicily in the Tyrrhenian Sea and called Aeolian Islands (*Isole Eolie*) but known for centuries as a place of exile for hardened criminals and political prisoners; islands include Alicudi, Basiluzzo, Filicudi, Lipari, Salina, Stromboli, and Vulcano; the last two have active volcanos

Liparis (*see* Lipari Islands)

Lisbon (*see* Portugal)

Lisieux maximum-security prison in Lisieux close to Caen in northwestern France

Litchfield Community Correctional Center in Litchfield, Connecticut where it was opened in 1812

Little Rock Pulaski County seat and jail in central Arkansas

Liverpool HM Prison at Liverpool in Lancashire, England on the River Mersey flowing into the Irish Sea; jails in other places called Liverpool as in New South Wales, New York, and Nova Scotia

Ljubljana (*see* Yugoslavia)

local lockup usually the local police station or the county sheriff's prison

lockup usually a small jail or prison

Lock-Up Tree name of a huge hollow baobab tree in Derby on the Kimberley coast of Western Australia where its 52-foot (16-meter) girth made it a natural lockup for prisoners

locus penitentiae (Latin—place of repentance)—penitentiary

Lodz (*see* Poland)

Logan Correctional Center in Lincoln, Illinios halfway between Bloomington and Springfield where it holds some 800 male felons in medium security

Lomé (*see* Togo)

Lompoc U.S. minimum-security penitentiary and prison camp at Lompoc, California on the coast northwest of Santa Barbara; opened in 1959

London capital of the United Kingdom and town in Ohio containing the London Correctional Institution west of Columbus; (*see* United Kingdom)

Long Beach Long Beach, California or its jails, lockups, or Community Treatment Center

long bid(s) long prison term(s)

Long By Sydney, New South Wales, Australian prison setup of its Corrective Services De-

partment, including the Central Industrial Prison, Her Majesty's Training Center, and the Parramatta Gaol

Long Lane Long Lane School for (delinquent) Girls at Middletown, Connecticut midway between Hartford and New Haven

Long Lartin HM Prison at Long Lartin in Worcestershire, England

Longos (Mexican-American—Long Beach, California)—nickname of the city, its lockup, and jail, and the detention pens of the Immigration and Naturalization Service

Longriggend Scotland's Longriggend Remand Institution

long stretch(es) long prison sentence(s)

long-term adult penal institutions of the U.S. Bureau of Prisons Atlanta, Georgia; Leavenworth, Kansas; Lewisburg, Pennsylvania; Lompoc, California; Marion, Illinois; Terre Haute, Indiana

loopbelt restraining device helpful in handling and transporting unruly prisoners

loquera (Spanish slang—prison)—also called *banasto* or *chirona*

Lorton Lorton, Virginia close to Washington, DC and site of the Central Facility opened in 1916, the Maximum Security Facility opened in 1923, Youth Center I opened in 1960, Youth Center II opened in 1972

Los Guilucos Los Guilucos School for (delinquent) Girls at Santa Rosa, California inland and north of San Francisco

Los Lunas New Mexican community south of Albuquerque and Bosque Farms which contains the Central New Mexico Correctional Facility and the Los Lunas Correctional Center

Los Lunas Correctional Center in Los Lunas, New Mexico south of Albuquerque, Isleta, and Bosque Farms; opened in 1940 to teach inmates farming and livestock operations

Loudonville Ohio community southeast of Mansfield and address of the Mohican Youth Camp

Loughan House penal facility in

Blacklion southwest of Tullamore in eastern Ireland

Lough Kesh location of the Maze Prison near Belfast in Northern Ireland (*lough* is Gaelic for arm of the sea, bay, partially landlocked or protected bay)

Louie Saint Louis, Missouri or its jails, lockups, and other penal facilities

louisette beheading device perfected by Dr Antoine Louis of Paris at the suggestion of his colleague Dr Joseph-Ignace Guillotin who argued before the French National Assembly that culprits should be executed by a simple mechanism such as a heavy blade falling by its own weight along two vertical runners to decapitate the victim; the resulting device is called the guillotine rather than louisette, the name of its inventor

Louisiana Correctional and Industrial School minimum-security facility for first-time young offenders held in De Quincy

Louisiana Correctional Institute for Women opened in 1961 at St Gabriel for female felons 17 years of age and up

Louisiana lockups 64 parishes, equivalent to the counties of other states, have holding facilities whether in Crowley, county seat of Acadia County, or Winnfield in Winn County; New Orleans and Baton Rouge have extra facilities for felons and all awaiting trial

Louisiana State Penitentiary maximum-security facility opened in 1866 at Angola and in 1982 holding more than 4100 male felons

Louisiana Training Facility medium- and minimum-security juvenile-delinquent penal facilities at Ball (for females), Baton Rouge, Bridge City, and Monroe

Louisville Kentucky's principal city and county seat of Jefferson County and its jail

Lourenço Marques (*see* Mozambique)

Louvain Belgium's central prison to the east of Brussels; here even long-term prisoners work in open cells or in special workships; called Leuven by Flemish Belgians

Lovelady Texas town north of Huntsville and location of the Eastham Unit holding felons in maximum security

Lowdham Grange HM Borstal at Lowdham Grange in Nottinghamshire, England

Lowell Florida town south of Gainesville and site of the Florida Correctional Institution opened in 1956 and the Marion Correctional Institution opened in 1976

Low Newton a remand center in Durham, England

LP Liverpool Prison

LTI Louisiana Training Institute (branches at Baton Rouge, Monroe, and Pineville)

Luanda name shared by the capital and its prison in the People's Republic of Angola, once a colony of Portugal

lubang buaya (Indonesian—crocodile hole)—Djakarta water hole infested with crocodiles and used as a place to dispose of people at odds with the current administration, as during the abortive communist coup of 1965

Lubianka Moscow headquarters of the Ministry of the Interior—the Soviet secret police whose combination office and prison back on Dzerzhinsky Square is named for the founder of the Cheka and its many successors—the Lubianka is one block from the Kremlin

Lublin concentration camp in Poland close to the extermination camps of Maidanek and Sobibor

Lucasville Southern Ohio Correctional Facility at Lucasville north of Portsmouth

Lud Ludgate Prison in London long ago

Lurigancho Peruvian prison outside of Lima where a number of Americans were held on smuggling charges in very bad and dirty circumstances even in 1982 after many protests

Lusaka (*see* Zambia)

Luther Luckett Correctional Complex in La Grange, Kentucky on Dawkins Road

Luxembourg the Grand Duchy of Luxembourg, a small nation no bigger than Rhode Island, is bordered by Belgium, France, and Germany; its capital city, also named Luxem-

bourg, contains an old prison

Luzira Kampala, Uganda's old prison

lynching executing someone by mob rule rather than by the rule of law; freeing a suspect in police custody (slang definition describing encounters between gangs or mobs and police)

Lynwood Lynwood (delinquent) Girls Center at Anchorage, Kentucky near Louisville

M-2 Match-Two (program matching volunteers from a community, called sponsors, on a one-to-one basis with prison inmates; sponsors write to inmates and visit them regularly with the aim of establishing meaningful and warm relationships and providing convicts with references and job support after they are paroled)

Maastricht Dutch maximum-security prison in Maastricht on the Belgian and West German borders of the Netherlands

MAB Metropolitan Asylums Board (British group responsible for administration and policy of all sorts of asylums including those for the criminally insane)

MacDougall Youth Correction Center in Ridgeville, South Carolina northwest of Charleston

MacLaren School in Woodburn, Oregon where it holds juvenile-court commitments in medium custody, opened in 1891

Macon city in central Georgia and location of the Central Correctional Center opened in 1978

Macquarie Harbour Indian Ocean inlet on the west coast of Tasmania where in the early 1800s it contained a penal colony on Settlement Island and for this reason the entrance to the inlet was nicknamed the Gates of Hell

Madagascar's prisons old prisons built during the years of French occupation (1885–1960) are in the capital, Antananarivo, and in other places such as Toamasina and Majunga

Mädchen in Uniform (German—Women in Uniform)—

1931 film classic showing life in a women's prison

Madison city in south-central Wisconsin and seat of Dane County with its jail

Madras (*see* Indian prisons)

Madrid (*see* Spain)

Magdalena penal institute of the Argentine armed forces about 80 kilometers from Buenos Aires in the Magdalena section

Magdeburg concentration-camp subcamp southwest of Berlin

Magilligan prison near Londonderry in Northern Ireland

Magilligan Camp HM prison camp on Magilligan Point Road outside Belfast, Northern Ireland

Ma Hang Ma Hang Prison, Hong Kong

Maidstone HM Prison at Maidstone in Kent, England

Maine Correctional Center medium and minimum-security penal facility holding felons and misdemeanants in South Windham

Maine jails 16 counties maintain facilities for holding felons whether they be in Auburn, county seat of Androscoggin County or Alfred in York County; big cities such as Portland and Bangor have local lockups as well as county jails

Maine State Prison opened in 1824 at Thomaston, holding incorrigibles in maximum security

Maine Youth Center minimum-security facility opened in 1853 in South Portland to hold male and female delinquents from 11 to 18 years of age

maison (French—house)—also a jail or lockup (*maison d'arrêt*) or a borstal or reform school (*maison de correction*)

maison de arrêt (French—prison)

maison de correction (French—house of correction)—penitentiary, prison

Maison de Correction St Bernard Brussels, Belgium's house of correction

maison de force (French—workhouse)—prison where only those who work are fed

Maison de Force French name for the workhouse-type prison built in 1773 in Ghent by its burgomaster Jean Jacques Philippe Vilain whose motto was *only those who work will eat*

Maison Gomin women's correctional facility at St Cyrille, Québec

Maison Notre-Dame de la Garde jail for Catholic juvenile delinquents ranging from 14 to 18 years of age at Cap-Rouge, Québec

Maison Tanguay women's penal establishment in Montreal, Québec

Majdenek Nazi concentration camp near Lublin, Poland and second only to Auschwitz in size; at the Nürnberg warcriminal trials it was estimated more than 1,500,000 perished here and another 2,750,000 at Auschwitz

Majunga (*see* Madagascar's prisons)

Makindye Uganda's military prison

making little ones out of big ones [*see* rock crusher(s)]

Malabar Malabar Complex of Prisons in Australia's New South Wales

Malaga (*see* Spain)

Malang women's prison in eastern Java south of Surabaya, Indonesia

Malawi this landlocked nation along Lake Nyasa, also called Lake Malawi, is known to oldtimers as Nyasaland; its capital, Lilongwe, and other cities, contain prisons built by the British between 1881 and 1966

Malaysian prisons this Malay nation occupying the southeastern tip of Asia was once known as Malaya or the Federated Malay States; its capital, Kuala Lumpur, and cities such as George Town have excellent prisons built by the British between 1889 and 1904 under the supervision of Sir Frank Athelstane Swettenham

Malchow North German concentration camp northwest of the Elbe River

Maldives island republic west of Sri Lanka (Ceylon) in the Indian Ocean; its capital, Male, contains a prison built during the years of British dominion (1887-1965)

Male (*see* Maldives)

Mali interior West African nation under French rule from 1898 to 1960 when a prison was erected in Bamako

Malmö (*see* Sweden)

Malta mid-Mediterranean island south of Italy with its capital city and seaport, Valetta, containing a prison built during British rule (1814-1964)

manacle to handcuff

manacles handcuffs

Managua capital city of Nicaragua replete with a prison no prisoner has ever praised for its cleanliness or the decent treatment of its inmates

Manama capital city of Bahrain on the Persian Gulf where "hotter than hell" is equal to or even exceeded by the heat within Manama's cells and its most-humid prison

Manbarco Man Barrier Corporation of Seymour, Connecticut engaged in manufacturing electronic detection systems and physical barriers made of coils of barbed wire and knifeedged wire used to keep prisoners within bounds

Manchester HM Prison at Manchester in Lancashire, England; New Hampshire city southeast of Concord and location of the Manchester Community Corrections Center, the New Hampshire Youth Development Center; place of detention in other cities named Manchester in Connecticut, Georgia, Iowa, Kentucky, Massachusetts, New York, Ohio, Tennessee, and Vermont

Manchester Community Corrections Center in New Hampshire, opened in 1979 and offers its inmates minimum security

Mandan North Dakota community on the west side of Bismarck and site of the North Dakota Industrial School opened in 1903

mandanta (Spanish—female prison trusty)

mandanto (Spanish—male prison trusty)

manette (Italian—handcuffs)

Manhattan Manhattan Island (center of New York City and New York County; has several large correctional facilities and many police-station lockups)

Manhattan House of Detention Tombs Prison in lower Manhattan; nicknamed Down Home

manhunt hunt organized to catch a criminal, an escapee, a fugitive from justice, or even a person who is lost

Manila (*see* Philippines)

Mannheim Confinement Facility of the U.S. Seventh Army in Mannheim, West Germany

Manning Correctional Institution in Columbia, South Carolina, used to hold young offenders since 1963

Manor English slang for London or its prisons

Mansfield Ohio city northeast of Columbus and site of the Ohio State Reformatory opened in 1896

Mansions The Mansions in Brisbane, Queensland—Australia's name for its Prison Department

Manzanar American relocation center for Japanese-Americans detained in this camp in southern California's Owens Valley between Independence and Lone Pine

Manzanillo prison in Manzanillo, Mexico (seaport on the Pacific southwest of Guadalajara)

Manzini (*see* Swaziland)

MAOF Mexican-American Opportunities Foundation (supporting a program to rehabilitate juvenile Chicano recidivists)

Maplehurst Correctional Centre in Milton, Ontario

Maple Lane School in Centralia, Washington south of Olympia (designed for the reform of juvenile felons)

Ma Po Ping Ma Po Ping Addiction Centre on Lantau Island, New Territories, Hong Kong

Maracaibo Venezuela's principal oil port, a location of a prison well known to local malefactors as well as to tankermen who have tangled with the laws of the land

Marble Hill Bollinger County jail at Marble Hill, Missouri west of Cape Girardeau

Marian Hall jail for English-speaking juvenile-delinquent females at Beaconsfield, Québec

Marigot (*see* Saint Martin)

Marina Street San Juan, Puerto

Rico's district jail built by the Spaniards in 1837 when its address was written Calle Marina

Marion U.S. Penitentiary at Marion, Illinois in the south-central part of the state and northwest of Paducah, Kentucky; replaces Alcatraz in San Francisco Bay; Marion County Detention Home for juvenile delinquents in the Indianapolis, Indiana area; Marion Correctional Institution in Marion, Ohio

Marion Correctional Institution in Lowell, Florida where it was once the Florida Correctional Institution for male felons

Marion Correctional Treatment Center southwest of Bluefield in Marion, Virginia

Marquette city on Lake Superior in northwestern Michigan north of Escanaba and site of the State House of Correction and Branch Prison

Marrakech (*see* Morocco)

Marshall site of a Confederate prison camp in northeast Texas within twenty miles of the Louisiana border; the graves of Federal prisoners who died here are in a segregated part of the cemetery

Marshalsea one of Southwark's seven prisons, now all gone, but formerly dominating much of this London district on the south bank of the River Thames

Martinez Contra Costa County courthouse and jail northeast of San Francisco, California; village 20 kilometers north of Buenos Aires and location of one of many clandestine prisons in Argentina

Martinière combination cargo and prison ship whose tween decks and lower holds were fitted with removable cages for transporting convicts from France to French Guiana; the vessel was built in 1911 and was last seen off Devil's Island early in 1950

Maryland Correctional Institutions started in 1931 as a penal farm in Hagerstown

Maryland Correctional Institution for Women in Jessup where it opened in 1940

Maryland Correctional Pre-Release System in Jessup with supporting facilities in Baltimore, Church Hill, Hughesville, Quantico, and Sykesville

Maryland Correctional Training Center in Hagerstown where it opened in 1966

Maryland House of Correction in Jessup where it opened in 1879 and now holds more than 1300 male felons and misdemeanants aside from those in its Annex

Maryland jails the state's 23 counties provide lockups from Cumberland in Allegany County to Snow Hill in Worcester County; Baltimore has its own lockup facilities

Maryland Penitentiary maximum-security prison at 954 Forrest Street in Baltimore where it was opened in 1811 and next to the Reception Center opened in 1967

Marysville Ohio Reformatory for Women in Marysville northwest of Columbus

MASCA Middle Atlantic States Correctional Association

Massachusetts Correctional Institutions the one at Bridgewater was opened in 1855 and holds alcoholics, criminally insane, and sexually dangerous felons; another at Framingham, opened in 1877, contains males and females; yet another at Norfolk opened in 1931; South Carver opened in 1952; South Walpole opened in 1956; Orange in 1964 and West Concord in 1878

Massachusetts lockups 14 counties in this state provide imprisonment facilities all the way from Barnstable in Barnstable County to Worcester in Worcester County; Boston also has penal facilities of its own

Massachusetts State Prison (*see* South Walpole)

Massawa (*see* Ethiopia's prisons)

Massilon Ohio town west of Canton and holding the Indian River School for male juvenile delinquents

Matamoros popular place-name in Mexico where it is found in Coahuila, Puebla, and Tamaulipas; the Tamaulipan city is across the mouth of the Rio Grande from Brownsville, Texas; it has the reputation of maintaining one of the world's dirtiest and most horrible jails

Matanzas (*see* Cuba)

Mauthausen Austrian Nazi concentration camp near Linz; some 200,000 inmates were gassed here during World War II

Matrah (*see* Oman)

Matsqui Institution British Columbia's minimum-security facility for drug addicts at Abbotsford

Matteawan Matteawan State Hospital (for the criminally insane) near Beacon-on-Hudson, New York

Maui Maui Community Correctional Center at Wailuki on Maui Island, Hawaii

Maumee Youth Camp male juvenile-delinquent penal facility in Liberty Center, Ohio

Mauritania largest of the West African nations with its coastal capital of Nouakchott about halfway between the Sahara and Senegal borders; an old prison recalled years of French-colonial domination

Mauritius volcanic island nation whose capital and seaport city, Port Louis, is on the Indian Ocean east of Madagascar; an old prison built there by the British has held criminals as well as some political prisoners

Mavrino Mavrino Institute on the outskirts of the Soviet capital includes the Mavrino Special Prison whose inmates perform most of the scientific and technical tasks assigned by their jailers representing State Security

maximum custody keeping prisoners in penal institutions built with tool-proof bars and cells surrounded by high walls, maximum-security prisons are manned by many guards and are run on a plan calling for rigid discipline

maximum security applied to inmates considered very dangerous to correctional officers, to others, and to themselves; such inmates often have a history of jailbreaks and violent conduct; prisoners awaiting the death penalty are also kept under maximum security

Maximum Security Center in Columbia, South Carolina since 1968

Maximum Security Facility in Smyrna, Delaware where it was opened in 1981 with this forbidding name also used in Cranston, Rhode Island where it was the Rhode Island State Prison

Maxwell Federal Prison Camp at Maxwell Air Force Base near Montgomery, Alabama

Mazatlan prison in Mazatlan, México (resort and seaport on the Pacific southeast of Durango)

Maze Maze (top-security) Prison outside Belfast in Northern Ireland

mazmorra (Spanish—dungeon or underground cell; jail)

Mbabane (*see* Swaziland)

MCA Massachusetts Correctional Association (Boston-based); Medical Correctional Association; Minnesota Corrections Authority; Missouri Corrections Association

McAlester Oklahoma city southwest of Muskogee and address of the Oklahoma State Penitentiary

MCC Metropolitan Correctional Center (in Chicago, New York, and San Diego where a skyscraper holds prisoners in a barless prison)

McCain North Carolina Prison Sanitorium at McCain in Hoke County

MCDC Montgomery County Detention Center (in Maryland near Washington, DC)

MCI Massachusetts Correctional Institution (Framingham)

McLaughlin Youth Center Anchorage, Alaska's diagnostic-program reception center for delinquents

McNeil Island McNeil Island Correctional Center opened in 1981 in the state of Washington close to Tacoma in Puget Sound (formerly a U.S. maximum-security prison)

McNeil Island Correctional Center formerly a federal prison but turned over to the state of Washington in 1981; Steilacoom is its address, a community southwest of Tacoma

MCO Michigan Corrections Organization (of wardens)

MDC Minnesota Department of Corrections

meat wagon(s) prison van(s)

Mecca (*see* Saudi Arabia)

Mecklenburg Correctional Center in Boydton, Virginia where it holds inmates in maximum security

Medical Center for Federal Prisoners at Springfield, Missouri

Medina (*see* Saudi Arabia)

meditation solitary confinement

medium custody less dangerous and less hardened prisoners are often kept in penal institutions designed to give them freedom of movement and greater scope for self-direction of a positive nature beneficial to society and so important for rehabilitation

Medium Security Facility in Cranston, Rhode Island where it was the Reformatory for Men

Medium Security Unit inaugurated in 1977 at Mount Pleasant, Iowa and usually holding first-term felons within a half-year of release

Melilla (*see* Spain)

meltout escape technique used in some modern prisons where certain types of doors and windows can be melted out by prisoners wishing to escape

memisir (Turkish—prison trusty)

Memphis Federal Correctional Institution at Memphis, Tennessee in the southwestern corner of the state on the Mississippi River and the Women's Correctional Center in Memphis

Menard Menard Correctional Center in Menard, Illinois southwest of Springfield; in 1984 it held more than 2500 male felons at a per-inmate annual cost of only $8250; the Menard Psychiatric Center is also here

Menard Time prisoner's publication issued by the Menard branch of the Illinois State Penitentiary

Mende name of a city and maximum-security prison in southern France at the foot of the Alps

menottes (French—handcuffs)

menschenhandel (German—trade in people)—prisoner-exchange program involving East and West Germany

Men's Reformatory officially The Men's Reformatory in Anamosa, Iowa where it was founded in 1872 providing all degrees of custody

Merced Merced County courthouse and jail in central California southeast of San Francisco

Mercer Regional Correctional Facility serving fourteen counties in northwestern Pennsylvania, north of Pittsburgh

Merida prison in Merida, capital of the Mexican state of Yucatan, or the Merida in Venezuela's state of Merida close to Lake Maracaibo

meritorious good time promise of parole-induced good behavior on the part of convicts wanting to get out of prison and turn over a new leaf

Meseru (*see* Lesotho)

Met Metropolitan Correctional Center in downtown San Diego, California

metanoia change of heart and mind required for criminal rehabilitation

Metro Metro Correctional Institution in Atlanta, Georgia where it holds emotionally disturbed inmates in close security while providing psychiatric services

Metropolitan Correctional Centers Chicago, Illinois; New York, New York; San Diego, California

Metropolitan Regional Institution in Bayamón, Puerto Rico and housing more than 1000 inmates doing time or awaiting trial

Mexicali capital of Baja California, and its jail, just across the border from Calexico, California

Mexican Mafia controls much of the narcotic trafficking in California prisons such as Chino, Folsom, and San Quentin; also active in Mexican prisons

México largest Middle American nation and with a long record of horrible prisons dating from Spanish times to the present and extending from the Mexican borders to the offshore Tres Marias Islands; Mexico City, its capital, contains some of its most formidable penal facilities

Miami city lockups, Dade County Jail, or the Federal Correctional Institution not far away in the southwestern corner of Dade County where it includes the Miami Detention

Center
Mich Michigan, Michoacan, or their jails and prisons
Michigan City Indiana State Prison at Michigan City on Lake Michigan between Gary and South Bend; the prison was built in 1859
Michigan Dunes Correctional Facility opened in Holland, Michigan in 1978 where it keeps some 325 felons in medium-security conditions
Michigan jails 83 counties provide detention facilities from Harrisville in Alcona County to Cadillac in Wexford County; Detroit and other big cities also have additional lockups
Michigan Reformatory opened in 1877 at Ionia where it now detains male felons from 17 to 21 years of age in maximum and medium security
Michigan Training Unit at Ionia, opened in 1958 to hold male felons from 17 to 21 years of age in medium security
Midlands Reception and Evaluation Center in Columbia, South Carolina since 1967
Mid-Orange Mid-Orange Correctional Facility at Warwick, New York southwest of Newburgh
Midway Texas town northeast of Bryan and site of the Ferguson Unit for first offenders
Milan Federal Correctional Center at Milan, Michigan southwest of Detroit
Miles City Montana community northeast of Billings and site of the Pine Hills School for juvenile delinquents
Milford Delaware's penal facility for juvenile delinquents; also known as Stevenson House and southeast of Dover close to Delaware Bay
milieu therapy treatment given to aid convicts returning to society via halfway houses, pre-release guidance centers, and tranquilizing drugs
military execution execution by a military firing squad
milk van(s) nickname for police or sheriff's van(s) for transporting prisoners
Millhaven Institution maximum-security facility in Bath, Ontario
Milton Ontario town southwest of Toronto and site of the

Adult Training Centre and the Maplehurst Correctional Centre
Milwaukee Milwaukee County Jail in Milwaukee, Wisconsin
Mimico Mimico Correction Center (for males) in Toronto, Ontario
M-in-C Matron-in-Chief
Mineola Nassau County Jail in Mineola, New York on Long Island
Minidoka relocation center for Japanese-Americans interned after Pearl Harbor in this farming area of southern Idaho northeast of Rupert
minimum custody honor dormitories, prison camps, and prison farms offering inmates as much freedom from restraint as possible while preventing their escape
Minimum Security Facility in Cranston, Rhode Island
Minnesota Correctional Facilities at Lino Lakes, Oak Park Heights, Red Wing, Saint Cloud, Sauk Center, Shakopee, and Stillwater (*see individual entries*)
Minnesota lockups 87 counties have jails ranging from Aitkin, county seat of Aitkin County, to Granite Falls in Yellow Medicine County; Minneapolis, Saint Paul, and Duluth have extra facilities for holding felons
Minnie Minneapolis, Minnesota or its jails, lockups, or prisons
misdemeanant(s) person(s) convicted or guilty of misdemeanors; many penal facilities are filled with misdemeanants
Missie Mississippi or its jails, lockups, and prisons
Mission Institution this medium-security facility in Mission, British Columbia opened in 1977
Mississippi jails the state's 82 counties have prison facilities from Natchez in Adams County to Yazoo City in Yazoo County; Jackson has additional detention facilities
Mississippi State Penitentiary opened in Parchman in 1900 with a normal capacity of 2469 felons; male and female inmates are offered a supervised earned-release, work-release program of rehabilitation
Missiyahu Israeli minimum-se-

curity prison offering inmates a work-release program during their pre-release period
Missouri Eastern Correctional Center opened in Pacific on the southwestern side of Saint Louis in 1951 and holds male felons in medium security
Missouri Intermediate Reformatory for male felons from 17 to 25 who are held in Jefferson City where the facility was opened in 1932 to hold 500 but in the early 1980s had 640
Missouri jails 114 counties comprise the state and contain prison facilities from Kirksville in Adair County to Hartville in Wright County; St Louis and other big cities have additional facilities for imprisonment
Missouri State Penitentiary for Men in Jefferson City where it holds them in maximum security and has done so since its inception in 1835; its normal population is 1500 but in 1981 it held 2000
Missouri Training Center for Men in Moberly where it had its inception in 1963; built to hold 800 it held more than 1200 in the early 1980s
Mitchellville Iowa Training School for (delinquent) Girls at Mitchellville, just east of Des Moines
Moabit Berlin's great prison in the Tiergarten section of the metropolis, dating back to the time of the kaisers
Mob Mobile, Alabama or its penal facilities
Moberly southwest of Hannibal, Missouri and site of the Missouri Training Center for Men
Mobile Mobile County seat and jail in southwestern Alabama
Mobtown Baltimore, Maryland or its jails, lockups, and other penal facilities
Modelo one of Bogota, Colombia's prisons and anything but model according to local penologists
Modesto Stanislaus County courthouse and jail east of San Francisco, California
Moengo (pronounced *Mongo*— *see* Suriname)
Mogadishu (*see* Somalia)
Mohican Youth Camp in Loundonville, Ohio where it was

opened in 1959 to hold male juvenile delinquents

Monaco Principality of Monaco is on a hillside ascending from the Mediterranean to Monaco-Ville, its capital on a high promontory; its gambling casino attracts many but a lockup seems big enough to hold its criminals

Mongolia the ancient kingdom of Genghis Khan fills an area twice as big as Texas and is between mainland China and the USSR; its capital, Ulan Bator, was once known as Urga and contains a prison of ancient construction

Monowitz forced-labor subcamp close to Auschwitz, Poland's extermination camp

Monroe Louisiana city east of Shreveport and site of the Louisiana Training Institute at Monroe; Washington city southeast of Everett, site of the Washington State Penitentiary, the Washington State Reformatory, and the Washington State Special Offender Center

Monrovia Monrovia Central Prison (Liberia's largest penal facility holding 240 prisoners)

Monsieur de Paris (French—Mr. Paris)—the guillotine operator

Montana jails the state's 57 counties offer detention facilities from Dillon, county seat of Beaverhead County, to its biggest city, Billings, in Yellowstone County

Montana State Prison at Deer Lodge southwest of Helena where it began holding felons in 1869 from 16 years of age in all levels of security

Montenegro (*see* Yugoslavia)

Monterrey prison in Monterrey, capital of the Mexican state of Nuevo León, in northeastern México

Montevideo Uruguay's capital containing jails and a prison believed by some to be a notch or so better than others in Latin America

Montey Allenwood Federal Prison Camp at Allenwood, Pennsylvania

Montgomery Federal Prison Camp at Montgomery, Alabama or its county jail or the Kilby Corrections Facility (*see* Kilby)

Montjuic Montjuic Castle atop a hill of the same name on the the Mediterranean between Barcelona and the Llobregat Plain; castle has been used as a court to try anarchist assassins and to hold them in its deep dungeons

Montluc French greystone prison in Lyons where during World War II Nazi gestapo held many before shipping them off to concentration camps and gas chambers in Germany

Montreal Maison Tanguay correctional facility for women prisoners in Montreal, Québec; Québec's principal city and location of a number of penal institutions including those in adjacent Ville de Laval

Montreal House of Detention at 800 Boulevard Gouin

Montreal Prevention Centre on Parthenia Street

Montrose School for Girls correctional facility at Reiserstown, Maryland just northwest of Baltimore

Monty Montgomery, Alabama or its jail and lockups

Moon Crescent Singapore's minimum-security prison taking its name from the moon crescent in the island nation's flag

Moondyne Joe Australian bushranger who was the first man to cross the Swan River Bridge in Fremantle near Perth while escaping from jail

Moor The Moor—Dartmoor Prison near Princetown in Devonshire, England

Moor Court HM Prison at Moor Court in Staffordshire, England

Morelia prison in Morelia, capital of the Mexican state of Michoacan west of México City

Morgan Morgan County Regional Correctional Facility opened in 1980 in Wartburg, Tennessee

Morgantown Federal Correctional Institution at Morgantown, West Virginia south of Pittsburgh, Pennsylvania

Morocco this northwest African nation of Arabs was long divided between France and Spain who built prisons in cities such as Casablanca, Fez, Marrakech, Rabat, and Tan-

gier; its neighbors include Algeria and Mauretania who also claim the former colony of Spanish Sahara between the three nations

Moroni (*see* Comoros)

Morrison Mount View School for (delinquent) Girls at Morrison, Colorado southwest of Denver

Morro Castle (*see* Habana)

Morton Hall HM Borstal at Morton Hall in Lincolnshire, England

Moscow (*see* USSR)

Most Gigantic Prison in the World the Soviet Union (insists such an authority as Aleksandr I Solzhenitsyn)

Mother of Prison Reform Dorothea Dix (1802-1887), American reformer active in Massachusetts and other states

Mothers in Prison Projects organization affiliated with Women in Jails and Prisons

Motown Motor Town (Detroit, Michigan) or its penal facilities

Moundsville south of Wheeling and location of the West Virginia Penitentiary built in 1866 and accommodating maximum-security inmates

Mountain Institution in Agassiz, British Columbia and designed for holding aged inmates

Mountain View Mountain View School opened in 1921 for female juvenile delinquents in Helena, Montana

Mount Eden Mount Eden Prison, Auckland, New Zealand

Mountjoy Mountjoy Gaol (Dublin's jail on the Royal Canal where Brendan Behan set his play *The Quare Fella*)

Mount McGregor Mount McGregor Correctional Facility near Warwick, New York southeast of Newburgh and close to the New Jersey border

Mount Pleasant Iowa city northwest of Burlington and location of the Medium Security Unit

Mount View Girls School at Morrison, Colorado southwest of Denver

Mozambique southeast African nation, a Portuguese colony from 1505 to 1975; all its coastal cities (Beira, Chinde, and its capital, Lourenço Marques) contain prisons of Portuguese origin

MPP Mothers in Prison Projects

MPPCA Maryland Probation, Parole and Corrections Association

MR Michigan Reformatory in Ionia where many young offenders are housed

MRC Minnesota Restitution Center

MTU Michigan Training Unit (reform school)

Mulegé Mexican minimum-security prison in a town of the same name in Baja California on the Sea of Cortez halfway between Santa Rosalía and Rosario; the convicts are free to roam about during the day and many find work in local enterprises so very few ever attempt escape and the climate is springlike the year around

mule(s) smuggler(s) carrying contraband such as heroin or weapons into jails and prisons

multiprisoner transportation unit(s) paddy wagon(s); police patrol van(s); prison van(s)

Muncy Pennsylvania town cast of Williamsport and site of the State Correctional Institution opened in Muncy in 1920 for female felons

Muntinlupa Philippine prison southeast of Manila (also spelled Muntinglupa)

Muscat (*see* Oman)

musical execution execution performed to the roll of a field drum or tenor drums; usually a military execution with the drum roll starting with the command to aim and finishing with the firing by the firing squad, with the last note accented sharply

Muskegon Michigan city northwest of Grand Rapids on Lake Michigan where it contains the Muskegon Correctional Facility

Muskegon Correctional Facility opened in 1974 to hold male felons in this Michigan penal facility

Mutual Welfare League convict self-government system introduced by Warden Thomas Mott Osborne at Sing Sing and later introduced at the U.S. Naval Prison at Portsmouth, New Hampshire

MWL (*see* Mutual Welfare League)

NAAWS North American Association of Wardens and Superintendents

NAB National Alliance of Businessmen (giving ex-convicts a chance by giving them jobs)

NACRO National Association for the Care and Resettlement of Offenders

NADPAS National Association of Discharged Prisoners' Aid Societies

Nafha Israel's top-security prison opened in 1980 but the smallest of all its correctional institutions

Nagoya (*see* Japan's prisons)

Nail City Wheeling, West Virginia noted for its nail factory and serving as a nickname for its detention facilities

Nairobi Kenya's capital and nickname of its prison once called HM Prison Nairobi during the years of British dominion

NAJCA National Association of Juvenile Correctional Agencies

NAJJ National Assessment of Juvenile Justice (University of Michigan)

Nakhodka port near Vladivostok and a Gulag transit center for prisoners bound for eastern Siberia

'Nam Vietnam or any of its many jails and prisons

Namibia native name for what was once German South-West Africa and later a surrendered territory administered by the Republic of South Africa; Walvis Bay and Windhoek, the capital, have HM Gaol-type prisons

Napanoch New York village southwest of Kingston and site since 1900 of the Eastern New York Correctional Facility

NAPO National Association of Probation Officers

NAPV National Association of Prison Visitors

Nashville centrally located capital of Tennessee and site of the Lois Deberry Correctional Institute, the Nashville Regional Correctional Facility, the Spencer Youth Center, the Tennessee Prison for Women, the Tennessee State Prison

Nassau capital of the Bahamas on New Providence Island and

toponym for its jail

National Association of Training Schools and Juvenile Agencies (NATSJA) created by the merger of the National Association of Training Schools and the National Conference of Juvenile Agencies

National Clearinghouse for Criminal Justice Planning and Architecture (NCCJPA) maintains a 10,000-volume library at the University of Illinois at Champaign

National Correctional Recreation Association (NCRA) sponsors prison postal-weight-lifting contests for inmates in Canada and the United States

National Jail Association presents annual award for the outstanding jailer and jail matron; publishes *Jail Forum* quarterly

National Jail Managers Association maintains historical archives plus an information clearinghouse and library in Eugene, Oregon

National Juvenile Detention Association publishes *Counterpoint* bimonthly and the *Directory of Juvenile Detention Homes*

National Prison Project American Civil Liberties Union's program to fix prison sentences and improve the lot of prisoners

national razor nickname for the guillotine once so popular in France where it was invented

National Sheriff official publication of the National Sheriffs' Association

National Society of Penal Information provided some of the first aides of the Bureau of Prisons and later became part of the Osborne Association

NATSJA (*see* National Association of Training Schools and Juvenile Agencies)

Natzweiler forced-labor concentration camp close to the Rhine in eastern France south of Strasbourg

Nauru the Republic of Nauru occupies a small island in the western Pacific just south of the Equator; its capital, Yaren, has a small lockup used by various colonial powers— British, German, Australian, and Japanese—in that order

Navasota Texas town northwest

of Houston and location of the Grimes County penal facility

Nazi political prisoners all who talked against Hitler's regime—communists, Jehovah's Witnesses, opposition clergymen and teachers, purged Nazis, socialists

NCA Nebraska Correctional Association; Nevada Correctional Association

NCCA North Carolina Correctional Association

NCCD National Council on Crime and Delinquency

NCCJPA National Clearinghouse for Criminal Justice Planning and Architecture

NCJRS National Criminal Justice Reference Service

NCPPL National Committee on Prisons and Prison Labor

NCRA National Correctional Recreation Association

NCW Nebraska Center for Women (in York, Nebraska between Grand Island and Lincoln)

N'Djamena (*see* Chad)

NDPS Narcotic Detention Pens at 111 Centre Street in downtown New York City

Nebraska Center for Women in York where it opened in 1920 to hold felons in all custody facilities

Nebraska lockups 93 counties contain jails all the way from Hastings, county seat of Adams County, to York in York County; Omaha also has additional detention facilities

Nebraska State Penitentiary opened in Lincoln in 1869; male felons held in all degrees of custody

NECCC New England Correctional Coordinating Council

necktie hangman's noose

necktie hanger gallows

Nepal Himalayan nation wedged between China and India with an ancient prison in Kathmandu

Netherlands Kingdom of the Netherlands has both ancient and modern prisons in its many cities such as Amsterdam, Rotterdam, the Hague, and Utrecht; its penal policies are among the most enlightened

Netherlands Antilles the Dutch West Indies including the ABC Islands of Aruba, Bonaire, and Curacao plus three smaller islands—Saba, Sint Eustatius, and Sint Maarten—shared with the French St. Martin; all have small lockups and a low crime rate

Neuengamme main concentration camp near Hamburg during the Hitler regime

Nevada Girls Training Center in Caliente where it holds juvenile delinquents

Nevada jails the state's 16 counties have lockups from Fallon, county seat of Churchill County, to Ely in White Pine County; Las Vegas, Reno, and Carson City have extra detention capability

Nevada State Prison dates from 1861 and provides inmates with maximum security

Nevada Women's Correctional Center in Carson City

Neve Tirza Israeli maximum-security prison for women

New Albany minimum-security jail in New Albany, Indiana across the Ohio River from Louisville, Kentucky

Newark literally the New Ark and a place-name shared by a Newark in England, another in New Jersey, a third in South Africa, and Newarks in other places; quite often means the jails in any of the many Newarks

Newc Newcastle-upon-Tyne, England or its detention facilities

New Caledonia French penal colony on New Caledonia island in the South Pacific and in service as Nouvelle Caledonie from 1864 to 1894, when it was moved to French Guiana

New Era prisoner's newspaper published at Leavenworth, Kansas

Newgate London prison razed by rioters more than a century ago and now the site of the Old Bailey law courts, officially called the Central Criminal Courts

Newgate's Angel Elizabeth Gurney Fry—lay visitor well known to Newgate prisoners in the early nineteenth century

Newgit nickname for London's old Newgate Prison

New Hampshire jails ten counties comprise this state where lockups are to be found from Laconia in Belknap County to Newport in Sullivan County; its cities also have extra detention facilities

New Hampshire State Prison built in 1880 in Concord where it holds about 350 felons in all security modes

New Hampshire Youth Development Center in Manchester where it holds male and female juvenile delinquents in all stages of security between 11 and 18 years of age; the structure housing this facility was opened in 1858

New Haven Community Correctional Center in New Haven, Connecticut where it was opened in 1975 and also the site of the county jail

New Hebrides (*see* Vanuatu)

New Jersey jails 21 counties have lockups from Mays Landing, county seat of Atlantic County, to Belvidere in Warren County; Newark and Jersey City have additional facilities for holding felons

New Jersey State Prison—Leesburg in use since 1913 for male felons

New Jersey State Prison—Rahway opened in 1901 as a reformatory but has been a prison since 1948 for male felons

New Jersey State prisons one in Leesburg, another in Rahway, the third and oldest in Trenton

New Jersey State Prison—Trenton built in 1798 but replaced in 1836 at the same Third Street site it now occupies

New Life New Life House (for prisoner rehabilitation at Tam Lung Chung, New Territories, Hong Kong)

New Lon(don) New London, Connecticut or its detention facilities

New Mexico Boys School in Springer where the old school opened in 1910 and was improved in 1956 with a new institution for male juvenile delinquents

New Mexico lockups 32 counties have jails from Albuquerque, county seat of Bernalillo County, to Las Lunas in Valencia County

New Mexico Youth Diagnostic Center in Albuquerque since it opened in 1919 to accept male and female juvenile delinquents

New Orleans principal city of Louisiana and parish seat as well as courthouse and jail plus police-station lockups

New Queens newer section of the Riker's Island Penitentiary in New York City's East River north of LaGuardia Airport in the borough of Queens

Newton Iowa town east of Des Moines and site of the Riverview Release Center

New Westminster Canadian maximum-security facility at New Westminster, British Columbia, adjacent to Vancouver

New York New York City or New York State or any of many penal institutions in either

New York lockups the state's 62 counties contain jails from Albany, county seat of Albany County, to Penn Yan in Yates County, all its big cities have extra detention facilities such as the Tombs in New York City

New York School for Girls at Hudson, New York

New York State Commission of Correction has the task of inspecting and monitoring the many correctional facilities as well as the community residential facilities, the secure detention centers, the secure detention centers, the detention institutions, the sentence institutions, and the county jails, municipal lockups, and state prisons

New York State Correctional Facilities Albion, Arthur Kill, Attica, Auburn, Bedford Hills, Clinton, Coxsackie, Eastern, Elmira, Fishkill, Great Meadows, Green Haven, Ossining, Taconic, Wallkill, Woodbourne, Downstate, Hudson, Mid-Orange, Mount McGregor, Otisville, Queensboro

New Zealand island nation in the southwest Pacific east of Australia and south of Tonga; HM Gaols in cities such as Christchurch, Auckland, and Wellington as well as in smaller places

Nha Trang (see Vietnam)

Niamey (see Niger)

Niantic Connecticut Correctional Institution farm and prison in Niantic on Long Island

Sound southwest of New London; the J. Bernard Gates Correctional Unit opened in 1981

NIC National Institute of Corrections (U.S. Department of Justice in Boulder, Colorado)

Nicaragua Central American country between Honduras and Panamá and extending from the Caribbean to the Pacific; its capital, Managua, and cities such as Bluefields and León have so-called *cárceles modelos*—model prisons that are anything but model

Niceville former name of the Niceville Road Prison before it was moved to Crestview, Florida where it is now known as the Okaloosa Correctional Center

Nickerie (see Suriname)

Nicosia eastern Mediterranean capital and seaport city of Cyprus as well as the popular name for its old prison built in Turkish times long before the island was used to detain Jews enroute to British-held Palestine (1945-1948)

Niger landlocked North African country about twice the size of Texas; it was under French domination from 1900 to 1922, when its prisons were built; its capital is Niamey

Nigeria African republic containing Biafra on the south coast of West Africa where it was a British colony from 1861 to 1960; its capital, Lagos, contains an old prison built by the British

nippers chain-grip-actuated handcuffs

NJA National Jail Association

NJDA National Juvenile Detention Association

NJMA National Jail Managers Association

NJRW New Jersey Reformatory for Women (at Clinton east of Phillipsburg)

Nnn's Nicaraguan nut nippers (imaginary and somewhat idealized police or guard dogs whose selective nipping tends to frighten even the most daring and hardened criminals)

NO New Orleans, Louisiana's nickname or that of its jail and police-station lockups

Nogal(es) Nogales, Sonora in México and its jail across the border from Nogales, Arizona

Nome Nome State Jail on Alaska's west coast

Noranside Noranside Borstal Institution in Scotland

Norf Norfolk (in Canada, England, the South Pacific, or the United States) or any of its detention facilities including one of the world's worst on Norfolk Island in the South Pacific up to 1855 when it was abolished

Norfolk Massachusetts community southwest of Boston and site of the Bay State Correctional Center and the Massachusetts Correctional Institution; State Prison Colony in Norfolk, Massachusetts (first community prison for male felons); Virginia seaport city or its country jail or naval brig

Northallerton HM Prison at Northallerton in North Riding, Yorkshire, England

North Carolina Department of Correction maintains statewide coverage through its Division of Prisons and its Youth Services Division

North Carolina jails 100 counties comprise this state and contain lockups from Graham in Alamance County to Burnsville in Yancey; its cities have extra facilities

North Central Correctional Institution at Gardner, Massachusetts northwest of Worcester where it was opened in 1981

North Dakota Industrial School opened in 1903 in Mandan to reform male and female juvenile delinquents from 12 to 18 years of age

North Dakota lockups the state has 53 counties providing jails from Hettinger in Adams County to Williston in Williams County

North Dakota Penitentiary opened in Bismarck in 1886 and holding males and females in all levels of security

North Dakota State Farm close to Bismarck where it was opened in 1943 for felons and first offenders

Northern Ireland (see individual entries)

Northern Nevada Correctional Center prison farm close to Carson City

Northern Nevada Honor Camp

close to Carson City

Northern Region Correction Institute Alaskan facility at Fairbanks for felons, misdemeanants, and juvenile delinquents

Northern Rhodesia (*see* Zambia)

Northeye HM Prison at Northeye in Sussex, England

Northside Correctional Center in Spartanburg, South Carolina

Norway North European nation whose neighbors are Finland and the Soviet Union; modern penal facilities are in or near such port cities as Oslo, the capital, Bergen, and Trondheim as well as in smaller places but none are big as Norwegians are quite law-abiding

Norwich HM Prison at Norwich, England; jails in Norwich, Connecticut and smaller American places named Norwich

Not-So-Nice-Ville (*see* Niceville)

Nottingham HM Prison at Nottingham in Nottinghamshire, England and a place well known since the days of Robin Hood and the High Sheriff of Nottingham he so often eluded with a combination of crossbow and cunning

Nou island prison of Nouvelle Calédonie in the South Pacific within the harbor of Nouméa

Nouakchott capital of Mauretania and site of its old prison built by the French before the turn of the century

Nouvelle Calédonie (French—New Caledonia)—penal colony from 1864 to 1894 when its prisoners were shipped to French Guiana

Nova Scotia School for Girls at Truro, Nova Scotia

NP Naval Prison

NPB National Parole Board (Canada)

NPCC Nebraska Penal and Correctional Complex

NPP (*see* National Prison Project)

NPPAJ National Probation and Parole Association Journal

NPSB National Prisoner Statistics Bulletin

NRTI National Rehabilitation Training Institute

NSA National Sheriffs Association

NSPI National Society of Penal Information

Nuestra Familia (Spanish—Our Family)—Mexican-American prison-based underground organization engaged in narcotic trafficking and jail breaks

Nueva Gerona principal town in the Isla de Pinos (Isle of Pines) off the southwest coast of Cuba; just 2 miles (3.2 kilometers) east is the Cuban prison called *Presidio Modélo* (Spanish—Model Penitentiary) but former inmates say it is anything but model or modern

Nuevo Guerrero Nuevo Guerrero, Tamaulipas and its jail across the Rio Grande from Falcon Heights, Texas

Nuevo Laredo Nuevo Laredo, Nuevo León and its jail across the Rio Grande from Laredo, Texas

Nuku'alofa (*see* Tonga)

nulla poena sine lege (Latin—no punishment without law)

nullum crimen sine lege (Latin—no crime without law)—a crime to be a crime must be defined by law

number-one diet bread and water

Nuremberg forced-labor subcamp in the south of Germany and close to the site of the Nuremberg Trials of war criminals

Nusa Kambangan Indonesian island prison off the city of Tjilatjap (Cilacap) on the south-central coast of Java where a crocodile-infested marsh between island and mainland discourages escape

nut factory section of a prison where criminally insane convicts are held

nuthouse psychiatric ward

nutpicker(s) psychiatrist(s)

nvd night-viewing device(s)

n-v device(s) night-viewing device(s)

NYCCIW New York City Correctional Institution for Women

NYCDC New York City Department of Correction

NYHD New York House of Detention

Nykøbing Danish prison near the Jutland port of the same name, close to the Limfjorden in northwest Denmark

NYMCC New York Metropoli-

tan Correctional Center

NY Met New York Metropolitan Correctional Center (on Park Row in downtown Manhattan)

NYRM New York Reformatory for Men

NYRW New York Reformatory for Women (Westfield Farm)

NYSDCS New York State Department of Correctional Services

Oahu capital island of Hawaii containing Honolulu, Pearl Harbor, and the Oahu Community Correctional Center on Kamehameha Highway in Honolulu where it was opened in 1918 with provision for medium- and minimum-security felons

Oakalla prison in Burnaby, a suburb of Vancouver, British Columbia

Oakdale address of the Iowa Security and Medical Facility northeast of Iowa City, Iowa

Oakhill Correctional Center in Oregon, Wisconsin just south of Madison

Oakie City Oklahoma City, Oklahoma's nickname or that of its correctional facilities

Oakland Oakland, California's jails, lockups, or its Community Treatment Center

Oakley Campus (*see* Raymond)

Oak Park Heights site of the Minnesota Correctional Facility opened in 1982 to hold 400 maximum-security prisoners in seven separate living units plus a psychiatric hospital with 42 beds

OAR (*see* Offender Aid and Restoration)

Oaxaca prison in Oaxaca, capital of the Mexican state of the same name, in the Sierra del Sur

obc old brutal con(vict)

Oblatos jail in Guadalajara in the Mexican state of Jalisco where many American and Mexican drug smugglers are imprisoned

OCA Oregon Corrections Association

Ocala central Florida city east of Daytona Beach and location of the Alyce D. McPherson School for male and female juvenile delinquents

Occoquan Minimum Security Facility of the District of Columbia located in Occoquan,

Virginia

OCCSA Ohio Correctional and Court Services Association

OCF Ossining Correctional Facility (Sing Sing) at Ossining, New York overlooking the Hudson

OCIS Organized Crime Information System (FBI)

OCJA Oklahoma Criminal Justice Association

Odessa Soviet seaport city on the Black Sea with typical prison facilities; its namesake in west Texas contains the Ector County jail

Odom Jackson, North Carolina penal facility for felons in close security

Odum Georgia town northwest of Brunswick and Jesup; site of the Wayne Correctional Institution holding 200 male felons in close security

Offender Aid and Restoration conducts CIP (Citizens Involvement Project) to educate and train civic leaders and sheriffs in the use of volunteers in jails

Ogden adjacent to and just north of Salt Lake City, Utah where it contains the Ogden Community Corrections Center and the Parkview Community Corrections Center

Ohio jails 88 counties comprise the state and have prison facilities from West Union in Adams County to Upper Sandusky in Wyandot County; its big cities, such as Cleveland, Cincinnati, and Columbus have additional jails

Ohio Reformatory for Women in Marysville where it was opened in 1916 to hold female offenders in maximum, medium, and minimum security

Ohio State Ohio State Penitentiary in Columbus on the Scioto River, also called River House

Ohio State Reformatory in Mansfield, Ohio, holding first offenders and others in medium and minimum custody

Ohrdruf Thuringian town just south of Gotha in central Germany and site of a notorious concentration camp as well as the underground headquarters of the German army during World War II

Oil City nickname of Bartlesville or Tulsa in Oklahoma

along with its jails and lockups; name of a town in western Pennsylvania and the nickname of its jail

OIPC Organisation Internationale de Police Criminelle (French—International Criminal Police Organization)—Interpol

Ojinaga Ojinaga, Chihuahua and its jail across the Rio Grande from Presidio, Texas

Okaloosa (*see* Niceville)

Okeechobee town at the north end of Lake Okeechobee and location of the Florida School for juvenile delinquents

Okie Oklahoma(n) or nickname for any of its many penal facilities

Okinawa Okinawa Prison containing hardened criminals in the largest of the Ryukyu Islands of southern Japan; (see USMC)

Oklahoma lockups 77 counties make up the state having prisons from Stilwell in Adair County to Woodward in Woodward County; extra facilities are found in Oklahoma City and Tulsa

Oklahoma State Penitentiary opened in 1908 in McAlester; in the early 1980s it held 850 male felons in maximum security

Oklahoma State Reformatory opened in Granite in 1909 and holding 380 male felons

Old Capitol Old Capitol Prison in Washington, DC where many political prisoners were held during the Civil War in the 1860s

Old Dorp Schenectady, New York's nickname or that of its detention facilities

old hand(s) Australian nickname for former convict(s)

Old Horse Bridewell Prison's nickname

old lag person serving a three-year sentence in a British prison

Old Melbourne Gaol and Penal Museum Melbourne, Victoria makes the most out of a bad beginning so characteristic of many Australian settlements now transformed into rather decent cities

Old Newgate Prison penological museum on Newgate Road in East Granby, Connecticut, open from June through December

Old Queens older section of the Riker's Island Penitentiary in New York City's East River, north of the La Guardia Airport in the borough of Queens

old smoky electric chair

Old Sparkey Florida's natural-oak electric chair

Old Territorial Old Territorial Penitentiary in Santa Fe, New Mexico where it was built when New Mexico was still a territory and the city fathers chose to build this penitentiary rather than to fund a state-supported university

Olustee Florida town west of Jacksonville and site of the Baker Correctional Institution opened there in 1978

Oma Omaha, Nebraska's nickname or that of its jail

Oman the Sultanate of Oman in the southeastern corner of the Arabian Peninsula has its capital in Muscat although Matrah is much larger; both have small prisons built during the century of British direction and influence from 1861 to the 1950s

Omdurman (*see* Sudan)

Omsk czarist prison close to the borders of Kazakhstan on the Irtysh River; the terrible punishments inflicted on prisoners here are described in Dostoevski's *Notes from the House of the Dead*

on the bricks out of jail and on the streets

on the ground out of jail

on ice imprisoned

on the lam escaping, evading, or hiding from the police or other law-enforcement agents, such as prison wardens

Onley HM Borstal at Onley in Warwickshire, England

Only Tennessee town southwest of Nashville and address of the Turney Center for Youthful Offenders from 18 to 25 years of age

Ontario Youth Training School at Ontario, California, east of Los Angeles

on the shelf in solitary confinement

Ont Pen Ontario Penitentiary (Canadian)

ooze out sneak out

open prison penal facility built without bars on the windows, locks on the doors, or walls surrounding the prison

Oran (*see* Algeria)

Oranienburg concentration camp near Berlin erected in 1933, just a few months after the opening of Dachau

Orchid Island Rehabilitation Center on Orchid Island off southeastern tip of Taiwan (Formosa)

Ordinary of Newgate Chaplain of Newgate Jail

ordinary transportation on-foot transportation of prisoners

Ordot Guam's penitentiary at Ordot southeast of Agaña

Oregon Wisconsin town just south of Madison and address of the Oakhill Correctional Institution and the Wisconsin Correctional Camp System

Oregon jails the state's 36 counties have prisons from Baker in Baker County to McMinnville in Yarnhill County; Portland and Eugene have augmented facilities for holding convicts

Oregon State Correctional Institution in Salem where it holds first-offender felons in all degrees of custody

Oregon State Penitentiary in 1853 opened in Portland but transferred to Salem in 1866

Oregon Women's Correctional Center in Salem, where it began in 1965 as a section of the Oregon State Penitentiary

Oriente Mexico City prisoner-holding facility

Oroville Butte County courthouse and jail in Oroville, California, north of Sacramento

ORW Ohio Reformatory for Women

Osaka (*see* Japan's prisons)

Oslo (*see* Norway)

Ossining Ossining Correctional Facility (formerly known as Sing Sing) at Ossining, New York between the railroad tracks and the Hudson River

Osteraker Swedish prison in Osteraker near Stockholm

Ostrava (*see* Czechoslovakia)

ostrog (Russian—jail)

Ostrov Vrangelya (Russian—Wrangel Island)—Soviet prison camp northwest of Alaska and north of northeastern Siberia in the Chukchi Sea; island discovered by an American whaling captain and settled by Americans in the 1830s

as a trading post at Rodger Bay now called Bukhta Rodgers; in 1921 settled by Canadian eskimos who were driven out by Soviet forces in 1926 before the island, an American possession, became part of the extensive Gulag Archipelago described by Solzhenitsyn; another Wrangel Island, still American, is on the Southeast coast of Alaska bought from Russia in 1867

Oswiecim Polish name for Auschwitz, site of one of World War II's worst concentration camps operated by the Nazis

Otay Otay Mesa Prison in southernmost California on the mesa overlooking Tijuana, Mexico and San Diego, California, close to San Ysidro

Otay Mesa site of a new California prison south of San Diego and on the Mexican border close to Tijuana and its airport

other prisoner(s) correctional officer(s); prison guard(s), warden(s), etc.

Otisville Otisville Correctional Facility at Otisville, New York, northwest of Middletown and close to the New Jersey–Pennsylvania border

oubliette (French—secret dungeon)—well-like cell with a trapdoor in its roof so convicts can be lowered into its hole

Outlaw bimonthly publication of the Prisoner's Union

outside outside of prison

out of town in prison

over the blue wall confined to a hospital for the criminally insane

Oxford Federal Correctional Institution at Oxford, Wisconsin just north of the Dells and a Staff Training Center of the Bureau of Prisons; HM Prison at Oxford in Oxfordshire, England; some twenty other Oxfords in America have jails and lockups

Ozark Ozark Correctional Center in Fordland, Missouri where it opened in 1961 to hold felons in minimum security

PA Pardon Attorney (U.S. Department of Justice)

PAA Prisoners Aid Association

PAAM Prisoners Aid Association of Maryland (Baltimore)

Pachuca prison in Pachuca, capital of the Mexican state of Hidalgo near Mexico City

Pachuco Pachucolandia (Mexican-American—El Paso, Texas)—nickname of the jail, lockups, and detention pens of the Immigration and Naturalization Service

Pacific Missouri community southwest of Saint Louis, containing the Missouri Eastern Correctional Center

paddy wagon police van for transporting prisoners

Pakistan the Islamic Republic of Pakistan, bordered by Afghanistan, China, India, and Iran; the prison facilities in Islamabad, its capital, were provided during the years of British rule and the same is true in other cities such as Karachi, Lahore, and Hyderabad

p-a-l prisoner-at-large

palacio blanc (Spanish—white palace)—nickname of Mexico City's most modern prison for men and women; it has cement-floored steel-lined cells plus baths, a hospital, and a library

Palacio Negro (Spanish—Black Palace)—nickname for Mexico's Lecumberri prison

Palais de Justice (French—Palace of Justice)—Parisian court and prison

Palmer Palmer Correctional Center northeast of Anchorage, Alaska

Palmer Work-Release Center in Florence, South Carolina

Panamá formerly a Colombian territory until created by the United States as a political step in the creation of the Panama Canal; Panamá City, Colón, David, and San Miguelito all have so-called model prisons but inmates agree they are anything but model

Panamanian prisons (*see* Cárcel Modelo, Cueva, and Gamboa)

Pango Pago Pago, American Samoa's nickname or its jail or lockup

panier a salade (French—prison van)

Pankrác Prague's great prison

panopticon prison where all cells are visible from a central point

panopticon pattern based on Bentham's panopticon inspec-

1163

tion house where giant circular prison houses were manned by armed guards who could supervise the surrounding cells and their inmates; the Stateville penal establishment in Illinois is built on this pattern

Papenburg Nazi concentration camp west of Bremen, Germany

Papua New Guinea this new nation occupies the eastern half of the island of New Guinea in the South Pacific north of Australia; a not-too-old jail is in Port Moresby, the capital seaport city

Paraguay landlocked South American nation run by a military dictatorship but nevertheless affluent compared to its neighbors (Argentina, Bolivia, and Brazil); its capital city, Asunción, has a big prison of bad reputation

Paramáribo (*see* Suriname)

Paranam (*see* Suriname)

Parchman town in northern Mississippi northeast of Greenville and site of the Mississippi State Penitentiary opened in 1900

Purdelup Purdelup Prison Farm in Western Australia

pardon executive-applied exemption from punishment for a crime or for a pending criminal conviction

Parkhurst top-security prison near Newport on the Isle of Wight off England's south coast below Southampton

Park Row Metropolitan Correctional Center in downtown New York City at 150 Park Row

Parkside New York State Correctional Facility in Manhattan

Parkview Parkview Community Corrections Center in Ogden, Utah

parole conditional release of an offender from a confinement facility before the expiration of his or her sentence; released offender usually put under supervision of a parole agency or officer

parole agency correctional agency supervising adults or juveniles placed on parole

parole authority correctional agency or officer having authority to release adults or juveniles committed to confine-

ment facilities or to discharge them from parole or to revoke parole

parolee person conditionally released from a correctional institution before the expiration of his or her sentence and placed under the supervision of a parole agency or officer

parole violation parolee's failure to conform to the conditions of parole; such violation usually results in return to prison and loss of parole

Parramatta Parramatta Gaol, Sydney, New South Wales, Australia

Parris Island (*see* USMC)

Pasca Pascagoula, Mississippi or its jail close to the Gulf of Mexico

Passage to Marseille melodramatic 1944 motion-picture commentary on the old French penal colony in French Guiana; features Humphrey Bogart, Peter Lorre, Sydney Greenstreet, and others

Paterson northern New Jersey mill town (often called Silk City) or generic name of its jail and its lockups

Patras (*see* Grecian prisons)

Patton California State Hospital (for the criminally insane) at Patton near San Bernardino

Patuxent Patuxent Institution for the Criminally Insane (Patuxent, Maryland); Patuxent Institution for Defective Delinquents (Jessup, Maryland)

Patuxent Institution Maryland penal facility and pre-release center in Patuxent where it opened in 1955

Pawiak Warsaw, Poland's great prison where criminals and patriots suffered before, during, and after World War II

P'burg Pittsburgh, Pennsylvania's nickname or the nickname for its jail or its lockups

PCI Program of Correctional Institutions (Puerto Rico)

pcu (PCU) protective custody unit

PDA (*Polizeiliches Durchgangslager Amersfoort*) (German—Police Concentration Camp—Amersfoort, Netherlands)—staging area for the transport of Dutch prisoners to Nazi concentration camps and extermination centers

P del E Penitenciaria del Estado

(Spanish—State Penitentiary)

peace and quiet maximum-security cell

Pedro San Pedro, California's nickname or that of its jail and lockup, close to Terminal Island

Peewee Valley Kentucky town east of Louisville and often associated with the Kentucky Correctional Institution for Women, opened in 1938

Pembroke Pines (*see* Broward)

pen. penitentiary

penal (Spanish—prison)

Penal Colony In the Penal Colony, Franz Kafka's imaginative but perceptive account of what might have gone on in the French Guiana prison colony of such universal ill fame

penal isolation solitary confinement

penalista (Portuguese—penologist)

penalística (Portuguese—penology)

penalista(s) penologist(s)

penalogia (Italian or Portuguese—penology)

penalogista (Italian or Portuguese—penologist)

penal servitude imprisonment combined with hard labor

penalty punishment for a particular offense

Pence Springs West Virginia town southeast of Beckley and address of the West Virginia State Prison for Women

Pendleton Indiana town northeast of Indianapolis which contains the Indiana State Reformatory

Penetang Penetanguishene Provincial Establishment for the Criminally Insane on Georgian Bay, Lake Huron, northwest of Toronto

peni penitenciaría (Spanish—penitentiary)

peniatrist(s) prison doctor(s); prison psychiatrist(s)

peniatry branch of medical science dealing with penal establishments and their prisoners

penitenciaría (Spanish—penitentiary)—prison

penitenciária estadual (Portuguese—state penitentiary)—each of the 22 states of Brazil maintains such a penal institution

Penitenciaría General de Venezuela Venezuela's general pe-

nitentiary situated in San Juan de los Morros Ejido Guárico
penitenciario (Portuguese—penitentiary); (Spanish—pertaining to prison; prison confessor)
Penitenciario de Santiago Santiago, Chile's penitentiary
Penitenciario Litoral Guayaquil, Ecuador's coastal maximum-security prison
penitentiaries federal or state maximum-security institutions designed to hold prisoners serving long sentences
penitentiary house of correction or rehabilitation center where offenders are confined for detention, discipline, reformation, rehabilitation, or punishment if they are forced to labor; in the United States a penitentiary is a maximum-security penal facility designed to hold prisoners serving long sentences
Penitentiary of New Mexico in the capital city of Santa Fé holding felons of both sexes in maximum and medium custody
penitenziario (Italian—penitentiary)
penjara (Malay—prison)
Penjara Malaysia (Malay—Malaysian Prison)
Penninghame Penninghame Prison in southwest Scotland
Pennsylvania jails the state's 67 counties have lockups from Gettysburg in Adams County to York in York County; big cities such as Philadelphia and Pittsburgh have extra facilities
Pennsylvania State Correctional Institutions (*see* Bellefonte, Camp Hill, Dallas, Graterford, Huntingdon, Muncy, Pittsburgh)
Pennsylvania State Correctional Institutions and Correctional Diagnostic and Classification Centers: (*see* Camp Hill, Graterford, and Pittsburgh *entries*)
Pennsylvania System (*see* solitary system)
penol penological; penologist; penolgy
penologia (Spanish—penology)
penologista (Portuguese or Spanish—penologist)
penologist(s) social scientist(s) concerned with penal institutions and the deterrent effect

of punishment decreed by law
penólogo (Spanish—penologist)
penology scientific study of penal institutions, the deterrent effect of punishments decreed by law, the consequences of crime, the means of changing lawbreakers into law-abiding citizens, and repairing the damage done to victims of crime
pensioner(s) of the crown Australian euphemism for any former convict(s)
Pensy Pensacola, Florida's nickname or that of its jail in the western part of the state
Pent The Pent (nickname for Pentonville Prison completed in 1842 in the outskirts of London's Islington Parish)
Pentonville HM Prison at Pentonville, a district of London where Lenin lived while in England before the counterrevolution he plotted for the Bolshevik takeover of Russia
Pentridge Melbourne, Victoria's prison well known to many Australians concerned with crime
Peoria county seat, courthouse, and jail of Peoria County in north-central Illinois where some call it Peory
Perm Soviet labor camp region 700 miles (1127 kilometers) east of Moscow and not far from the Urals
Persian prisons (*see* Iranian prisons)
Perth Scottish prison close to Perth on the River Tay flowing to the Firth of Tay and the North Sea
Pete St Petersburg, Florida's nickname or that of its jail and its lockups near Tampa
Peru formerly headquarters of the Incan Empire and the oldest Spanish settlement; Lima, Arequipa, and the port city of Callao are its largest cities; its penal facilities are typical of many others in Hispanic countries (*see* Cárcel Modelo, Lurigancho, Sepa, Sexto)
Peruvian prisons (*see* Cárcel Modelo, Lurigancho, Sepa, Sexto)
Peterhead prison near Aberdeen, Scotland
Peter-Paul Peter-Paul Fortress in St Petersburg where during czarist as well as communist

times it held many political prisoners awaiting exile in bleak Siberia; now a Soviet museum open to tourists thronging to Leningrad (modern name of St Petersburg, later known as Petrograd) to honor the founder of what the true believers imagined to be the Workers' Paradise
Petersburg Federal Correctional Institution at Petersburg, Virginia south of Richmond
Petros Petros, Tennessee and location of Brushy Mountain Penitentiary
Pewee Kentucky Correctional Institution for Women at Pewee Valley northeast of Louisville
Pforzheim German city and prison at the northern foot of the Black Forest where it was once the seat of the humanist school of philosophy
Philadelphia Prisons Detention Center at 8201 State Road, Holmesburg Prison on Torresdale Avenue in the 8200 block; House of Correction at 8001 State Road
Philippines Republic of the Philippines has some old penal institutions dating back to Spain's colonialization and more modern ones reflecting the American period; its capital, Quezon, and its principal cities include Manila and Davao
Phillipsburg capital complete with lockup in the West Indian Leeward Island of Sint Maarten (the French have their own part of the island, Saint Martin, with a capital also complete with lockup and called Marigot)
Philly Philadelphia, largest and oldest city in Pennsylvania or the name given to any of its many penal institutions ranging from police-station lockups to jails and prisons (*see* toponyms)
Phnom Penh (*see* Cambodia)
Phoenix Phoenix, Arizona, or the toponym for Adobe Mountain School for juvenile delinquents, the Alhambra Reception and Treatment Center for incoming male felons, the Arizona Center for Women, the Arizona Training Facility, the Arizona Correctional Training Facility

Phoenix Correctional Facility at Plymouth, Michigan where it houses halfway-house rule violators and parole violators in medium security

PHP Preventive Health Programs

PHS Prison Health Services (providing a complete system of health services to prisons)

picking oakum picking apart pieces of tarred rope for use in cauling wooden ships (a century ago this was still the task given many prisoners confined to jails along the coast of Britain as well as the United States)

Piedmont Work Release Center in Spartanburg, South Carolina

Piedras Negras Piedras Negras, Coahuila and its jail across the Rio Grande from Eagle Pass, Texas

Pikeville north of Chattanooga, Tennessee and address of the Bledsoe County Regional Correctional Facility and the Taft Youth Center

Pinal Pinal County Jail at Florence, Arizona southeast of Phoenix

Pinchgut prisoner's nickname for Fort Denison Prison in Sydney Harbour, New South Wales, where in the early days of settlement they complained about the very small allowance of food

Pine Bluff Pine Bluff, Arkansas with its Diagnostic Unit, the Pine Bluff Youth Service Center, and the Women's Unit holding female felons

Pine Hills Pine Hills School for juvenile delinquents from 10 to 21 years of age; started in Miles City, Montana in 1894 and now holding males in maximum and medium custody

Pine Street Baltimore, Maryland jail on Pine Street

Piraeus (*see* Grecian prisons)

Pithiviers concentration and transit camp in north-central France northeast of Orléans (see *Camp de Drancy* for details as to how its prisoners fared)

Pitts another nickname for Pittsburgh, Pennsylvania or its penal facilities ranging from jail through lockups to prison

Pittsburgh largest city in western Pennsylvania and fairly close to the Ohio border; contains the State Correctional Institution and Correctional and Diagnostic Center; first completed in 1826 and reconstructed in 1882 as the Western Penitentiary

PK Principal Keeper

Plainfield Indiana town just outside the southwestern section of Indianapolis and site of the Indiana Boys School, the Indiana Youth Center, and the Reception and Diagnostic Center

Plankinton South Dakota town west of Sioux Falls and address of the South Dakota Training School for male and female juvenile delinquents up to their seventeenth year

Plaszow Nazi concentration camp northwest of Cracow, Poland

Pleasanton Federal Correctional Facility at Pleasanton, California close to San Jose

Pleasantville federal minimum-security facility at Maxwell Air Force Base in Alabama; no fences, gates, or walls divide its stucco buildings from the golf course of the Air Force

Plummer Center Delaware's work-release center in Wilmington

Plymouth Michigan city west of Detroit and site of the Phoenix Correctional Facility

PMS Prison Management Systems (health-care plan offered in the United States); Prison Medical Services (under the Home Office in the United Kingdom)

POA Prison Officers Association

POC Prison Officers Club

Pocaloo Pocatello, Idaho's nickname or that of its jail in the southeastern corner of the state

poetic punishment matching the punishment to fit the crime

Point Lookout Union prison and stockade close to the Potomac River where many Confederate prisoners lost their lives due to inhumane conditions

Point Salines prison camp at Point Salines, Grenada

pokey jail

Poland the east-central European nation known as Poland has been partitioned many times in its long history; it has large port cities on the Baltic as well as interior cities such as Warsaw, the capital, Lodz, Cracow, Wroclaw, and Poznan; many of its prisons are filled with political prisoners held because of their anti-communist sympathies

politica (Italian, Portuguese, Spanish—female political prisoner)—in Spanish *política* is accented

political(s) political prisoner(s)

politico (Italian, Portuguese, Spanish—male political prisoner)—in Spanish *político* is accented

politico(s) political prisoner(s); politician(s)

politiewagen (Dutch—police van)

Polk Polk Correctional Institution at Polk City, Florida northeast of Tampa and Lakeland; accommodates inmates in all levels of custody

Pollington HM Borstal at Pollington in Humberside, Yorkshire, England

Polmont Scottish borstal

POME Prisoner of Mother England (also called a Pommy when in early colonial days convicts were shipped to Australia)

Ponar site of a Nazi concentration camp near Vilna in what is now Soviet Lithuania; its mass graves hold thousands of victims of Hitler's elimination of all he considered inferior racially

Ponce city on Puerto Rico's south coast facing the Caribbean; has an old jail dating back to Spanish rule as well as police-station lockups

Ponte dei Sospiri (Italian—Bridge of Sighs)—heavily barred, stone-covered, two-storied bridge arching a Venetian canal, the Rio di Palazzo, and connecting the Doge's Palace with the state prisons and dungeons

Pontiac Correctional Center northeast of Normal, Illinois where it provides maximum security for 1900 male felons

pontón (Spanish—prison ship)

poogie jail

Poona Indian prison in Poona where Mahatma Ghandi and other politicals were held

poorhouses of the twentieth cen-

tury Ronald Goldfarb's apt description of jails; his book, *Jails*, is subtitled "The Ultimate Ghetto of the Criminal Justice System"; it was published by Anchor Press/Doubleday in 1975

population movement entries and exits of adjudicated persons, or persons subject to judicial proceedings, into or from correctional facilities

Pork Dump epithet applied to the Clinton Prison near Utica, New York

porridge British slang for jail

Portage La Prairie Correctional Center for Women at Portage La Prairie, Manitoba

Port Arthur Australia's principal penal colony was in Port Arthur off Storm Bay below Hobart where from 1834 to 1853 only one convict escaped; this nearly escape-proof prison was in Tasmania, then known as Van Diemen's Land; today a museum and visitor's center replace the convict's quarters

Port Augusta Port Augusta Gaol (South Australia)

Port-au-Prince capital seaport city of Haiti whose waterfront contains the International Casino open nightly from 8 P.M. until dawn and whose prisons are the most noisome in the West Indies

Port Blair capital of the Andaman and Nicobar Islands in the Bay of Bengal; once the headquarters of a penal settlement dating from the Sepoy Rebellion of 1857 but discontinued in 1945; in *The Sign of Four* by Conan Doyle it is mentioned several times

Porte d'Enfer (French—Gate of Hell)—convict's nickname for the prison gate at Saint Laurent du Maroni in French Guiana where one of the world's most horrible penal colonies was headquartered

Port Elizabeth (*see* South Africa)

Port Isabel Port Isabel Detention Center of the Immigration and Naturalization Service in Port Isabel, Texas close to Brownsville and across the Rio Grande from México

Portland HM Borstal at Portland in Dorset, England; other detention places in places named Portland and scatered

from Australia to the West Indies, including Portland Maine and Portland, Oregon where so many Japanese-Americans were held after Pearl Harbor when all were declared by the government to be suspicious enemy aliens

Port Laoise prison southwest of Dublin, Ireland

Port Lincoln Port Lincoln Prison (south Australia)

Port Louis (*see* Mauritius)

Port Macquarie Australian convict colony in New South Wales where it bore this name in the early 1800s

Port Moresby (*see* Papua New Guinea)

Porto also called Oporto (*see* Portugal)

Port-of-Spain (*see* Trindad and Tobago)

Portsmouth English Channel port close to the Isle of Wight and site of the Royal Navy's prison scheduled for elimination because it is the current policy of the Navy to discharge all persons exhibiting aberrant behavior; New Hampshire port and long the site of the U.S. Naval Prison

Port Sudan (*see* Sudan)

Portugal ancient nation in southwesternmost Europe where it occupies most of the west coast of the Iberian Peninsula; Lisbon, its capital, and Porto (Oporto) have some very old prisons built in the days of dictators and kings

Post Care Program for adult felons from 16 years and up with centers in Lincoln, Omaha, and Norfolk, Nebraska

Poston former Indian reservation in southwestern Arizona; after Pearl Harbor it was used as a detention camp for Japanese-Americans

Potma reputed to be the Soviet Union's largest forced-labor penal colony; surrounded by a mined field in the Ural Mountains 500 miles (800 kilometers) southeast of Moscow

Poughkeepsie seat of Duchess County and its jail close to the Hudson River

pow (POW) prisoner of war

Powell Ohio town north-northwest of Columbus and location of the Riverview School for Boys and the Scioto Village, formerly the Girls Indus-

trial School

Poznan (*see* Poland)

Pozsony Czech name for Bratislava and site of an old prison built during the days of the Austro-Hungarian Empire long before World War I

Pozzi old Italian prison in Venice where generations of prisoners complain about the dampness of their cells

PPCAA Parole and Probation Compact Administrators Association

PPS Pennsylvania Prison Society (Philadelphia-based)

pq punishment quarters (isolated section of many penitentiaries and reformatories)

p & q peace and quiet (solitary confinement)

Prague (*see* Czechoslovakia)

Praia (*see* Cape Verde)

presa (Portuguese or Spanish—female prisoner)

Presidential Candidate and Prison Convict Eugene V. Debs, Socialist candidate imprisoned for making an antiwar speech in 1918; he declared: "While there is a lower class, I am in it; while there is a criminal element, I am of it; while there is a soul in prison, I am not free"; scholars who know his life story agree Debs was not of the lower class nor of the criminal element; when he was given a pardon by President Harding he said "It is the government who should ask me for a pardon."

presidio (Spanish—military prison)—may also mean citadel, penitentiary, or prison; many presidios were built in the American Southwest during the era of Spanish and Mexican rule

Presidio Prisoner's publication issued bimonthly at the Iowa State Penitentiary in Fort Madison

presidio modelo (Spanish—model penitentiary or prison)

preso (Portuguese or Spanish—male prisoner)

Pressburg German name for Pozsony, also known as Bratislava, and site of an old prison in Czechoslovakia

Pretoria (*see* South Africa)

Pre-Trial Annex Wilmington, Delaware's facility serving those held in detention status; has maximum and minimum security

prigione (Italian—prison)—also called *carcere*

Prigione d'Genova (*see* Italian prisons)

prigioniera (Italian—female prisoner)

prigioniero (Italian—male prisoner)

Prince Albert Canadian city north of Saskatoon and containing the Saskatchewan Penitentiary

Prince George British Columbia penitentiary 300 miles north of Vancouver

Princetown Her (His) Majesty's Prison in Princetown on the West Dart River in Devon, England where in 1812 many American sailor captives were imprisoned

prisão (Portuguese—prison)—also called *cárcere*

prisión (Spanish—prison)

prisioneira (Portuguese—female prisoner)

prisioneiro (Portuguese—male prisoner)

prisionera (Spanish—female prisoner)

prisionero (Spanish—male prisoner)

prison confinement facility with custodial authority over adults sentenced to confinement for more than one year

prison (French—jail; prison)

Prison at the Bottom of the World Ushuaia, Argentina on Beagle Channel close to Cape Horn in southernmost South America

Prison at the Top of the World Solovetski Island isolators in the White Sea and east of Kem in the Soviet Union, the workers' paradise

prison bird recidivist; prisoner who has been to prison before

prison break escape from prison accompanied by force and violence

prison bug(s) person(s) spending most of their time in prison

prison camp(s) minimum-security prison camp(s) designed to shelter reasonably trustworthy convicts assigned to farm or forestry projects, to road repair work, or other federal or state projects served by prison labor

Prison Camps the U.S. Bureau of Prisons maintains such camps at Allenwood, Pennsylvania; Eglin Air Force Base, Florida; Montgomery, Alabama; and Safford, Arizona

prison coffin plain wooden box fitted with rope handles and perforated with many large holes facilitating disintegration once the coffin is buried with its convict

prisoner at large naval prisoner confined to the barracks or the ship

prisoner-of-war camps in the Confederacy Andersonville, Georgia the best known but like the others it had its Northern counterpart behind Union lines; others in Georgia included Camp Davidson at Savannah, Camp Oglethorpe at Macon, and one at Millen; camps in South Carolina were at Charleston, Columbia, and Florence; in North Carolina at Salisbury; in Virginia at Danville and at Libby Prison in Richmond

prisoner(s) person(s) in custody in a confinement facility or in personal custody of a criminal-justice official while being transported to or between confinement facilities

Prisoners' Chorus the finale of Act I of *Fidelio*, Beethoven's only opera, is an appeal from political prisoners longing for the scent of open air as they know their prison is a tomb

prisoners of the Crown old Australian euphemism meaning convicts

prisoner's opera Beethoven's *Fidelio* has all three acts set in a Spanish prison run by a tyrant; it is memorable for the great compassion the composer shows its political prisoners

prisoners' rules unwritten code of conduct adhered to by many convicts who admit it contains such admonitions as *be smart, don't be a coward, don't cheat your partner or your gang, don't be disloyal, don't snitch unless you're ready to die*

Prisoner's Union publishes *Outlaw* bimonthly; seeks an end to economic exploitation of prisoners and redress for convict's grievances

prisoner's work songs outstanding collection compiled and edited by Bruce Jackson in

Wake Up Dead Man—Afro-American Worksongs from Texas Prisons, Harvard University Press, Cambridge, Mass, 1972

prison fever typhus (usually due to overcrowding)

prison house(s) prison(s)

prison hulk(s) prison ship(s)

prison labor work carried out by convicts such as producing furniture for public schools, road building and repairing; stamping out automobile license plates, etc.

prisonment imprisonment

prisonnier (French—male prisoner)

prisonnier de guerre (French—prisoner of war)

prisonniere (French—female prisoner)

prison officer(s) British euphemism for gaoler(s) [spelled jailer(s) in the United States]

prison pallor bloodless yellow paleness of many prisoners deprived of fresh air, sunshine, and vitamins

prison perpétuelle (French—life imprisonment)

Prison Poet Oscar Wilde (1856-1900), Irish author-playright-poet-wit whose conviction for sodomy brought a three-year prison term vividly described in his philosophical poem *The Ballad of Reading Gaol*; his life and thoughts in Reading, England's jail are set forth in stark realism

prison psychosis mental disturbance actuated by imprisonment and manifested by delusions, paranoid trends, and pseudo-hallucinations

Prisons U.S. Bureau of Prisons

Prisons are the concentration camps of the poor graffito scrawled on the outside walls of the Women's House of Detention in New York City now demolished

prisons can pay their way and even make a profit, as well as bringing about the rehabilitation of inmates, if they are allowed to produce goods and services this was true until manufacturers and unions had laws passed to severely restrict such creative activities proven profitable in the 1800s and early 1900s; today most prison labor is confined to stamping out auto license plates

prison scenes set to music Beethoven's only opera *Fidelio*, the *Damnation of Faust* by Berlioz, Boito's *Mefistofele*, Gounod's *Faust*, and Puccini's *Tosca* present some of the most musically memorable scenes although there are others by Verdi which have their champions

prison sentence penalty of commitment to the jurisdiction of a confinement facility

prison simple mentally deranged by imprisonment

prison smell usually compounded of excreta, grease, stale tobacco, sweat, unaired bedding, and vomit

prison to prisons more than 100 English titles of books, ranging from the autobiographic to the poetic, from the past to the future, are available to readers and researchers

prison van black maria or paddy wagon used to transport prisoners from court to prison or vice versa or from the place of arrest to a jail or lockup

prison within a prison solitary confinement cell

Prison World original name of the *American Journal of Correction*

prob probation(ary); probation officer

probation conditional suspension of imprisonment of a convicted offender who must stay in the community under the supervision of a probation officer

probation agency correctional agency supervising adults and juveniles placed on probation and investigating adults and juveniles to prepare predisposition and presentencing reports to assist courts in determining sentences

probation officer(s) employee(s) of a probation agency or probation department

probation sentence court requirement that a person fulfill certain conditions of behavior and accept the supervision of a probation agency or department

probation violation probationer's nonconformance to the conditions of probation

PROOF Parole Resource Office and Orientation Facility (Jersey City, New Jersey)

PROP Preservation of the Rights of Prisoners

Providence Rhode Island's capital city and county jail; other correctional facilities are scattered throughout this smallest of American states, fondly nicknamed Little Rhody

Providence County Jail old name for what is now known as the Awaiting Trial Facility in Cranston, Rhode Island

Provo Utah center south of Salt Lake City and seat of Utah County complete with jail

PSAMPP Philadelphia Society for Alleviating the Miseries of Public Prisons (founded by Benjamin Franklin, William Rush, and other enlightened Americans)

PSTD Prison Service Training Depot (Pretoria, South Africa)

psychiatric prison Her Majesty's Prison Grendon Underwood in the South Midlands of England about 55 miles southeast of Birmingham

psychoprison psychiatric hospital prison (USSR's place for dissidents)

PU Prisoner's Union

Puebla prison in Puebla, the capital of the Mexican state of the same name about halfway between México City and Veracruz

Puerto Armuelles Panamanian banana port on the Pacific where it is washed by the Gulf of Chiriqui and tropical rains that also wash the courtyard and walls of its prison

Puerto Barrios prison in Guatemala's Caribbean seaport washed only by the Gulf of Honduras and tropical rains

Puerto Cabello Venezuelan seaport west of Caracas and close to Valencia where there is also a jail known to foreign as well as local lawbreakers

Puerto Cabezas Nicaraguan prison and seaport on the Mosquito Coast of the Caribbean

Puerto Rican District jails in Aguadilla on the northwest coast, Arecibo on the north coast, Humacao on the hills facing the southeast coast, in Ponce on the central south coast

Puerto Rican Prison camps six of them were active in the

mid-1980s and held male felons and misdemeanants

Puerto Rico lockups 76 municipios (municipalities) make up the Commonwealth of Puerto Rico; some have jail facilities dating back to Spain's occupation of the island

Puerto Vasco place-name pseudonym for a clandestine prison in Argentina

'Pulco Acapulco, México or its jail

Pul-i-charki prison in Kabul, Afghanistan

punishment most modern penologists agree correctional officers, formerly called guards or wardens, should be reminded: *offenders are sent to prison as punishment, not for punishment*

Punta Arenas Chilean prison and seaport known as Magallanes between 1927 and 1937; located in the Straits of Magellan it is probably the world's most southerly prison.

Puntarenas Pacific coast port and prison of Costa Rica

Punxey Punxsutawney, Pennsylvania's nickname or that of its jail and its lockup

Purdy Treatment Center for Women in Gig Harbor, Washington where felons from 16 years and up are held in all degrees of security

put away imprison; put away from society

put in the hole put into a solitary-confinement cell

Puyallup assembly center for Japanese-Americans brought in from other parts of Washington after Pearl Harbor; in this small town southeast of the Seattle-Tacoma area many were housed in former pigpens as they were considered by the government to be suspicious enemy aliens

PVA Prison Visitor's Association

PWA Prison Wardens Association

pw('s) prisoner(s) of war

Pyongyang capital of North Korea and containing a prison built during the Japanese occupation extending from 1910 to 1945

Q San Quentin Prison in California near San Francisco

Qatar Arab state occupying a peninsula on the east coast of

Saudi Arabia, between Bahrain and the United Arab Emirates; its capital, Doha, is on the Persian Gulf and its old prison is primitive and not oriented toward the rehabilitation of its inmates, reports indicate

QC Quezon City, capital of the Philippines reduced to a two-letter abbreviation, or nickname of its detention facilities such as the jail or lockup

QCPSA (*see* Quaker Center for Prisoner Support Activities)

QCSR Quaker Committee on Social Rehabilitation (meets in New York City)

Qsar Teheran, Iran's great prison pronounced *Gasre* (also called Ghasre)

quad prison; prison quadrangle; prison yard

quail roost women's dormitory in a house of detention

Quaker Abolitionist epithet proudly shared by many Quakers such as Elias Hicks, Lucretia Mott, John Greenleaf Whittier, and John Woolman—all might have been classified as convictional criminals during their struggle for the abolition of slavery

Quaker Center for Prisoner Support Activities (QCPSA) conducts nonviolent training workshops for prisoners

Quaker Penologist Elias Hicks (1748-1830), who preached against cruelty to the imprisoned and the insane

Quaker Reformer Elizabeth Fry, noted for her campaigns to better the life of inmates in insane asylums and prisons

Quaker's position on the death penalty according to the American Friends Service Committee, whose sympathies lie most strongly with murder victims and their families, the death penalty restores no victim to life and only compounds the wrong committed in the first place; Quakers affirm there is no justification for taking the life of any man or woman for any reason

Quantico (*see* USMC)

quarry cure forcing addicts to work in stone quarries far from sources of alcohol and narcotics

quart (French—police station and its lockup)

quarter stretch three-month's sentence

Queen of Heaven (*see* Italian prisons)

Queensboro Queensboro Correctional Facility in Long Island City, New York

queen's bus prison van (slang term heard in many parts of the British Commonwealth and changed to "king's bus" when a king is on the throne)

queer bird(s) jailbird(s)—expression goes back to Elizabethan times

queer-ken prison (term goes back to Elizabethan times)

Quent San Quentin (California State Prison) near San Francisco

Querétero prison in Querétero, the capital of the Mexican state of the same name

Questore Italy's security service and the National Central Bureau of Interpol in Rome

Quezon City also called Quezon (*see* Philippines)

Quilmas San Quilmas (Mexican-American—San Antonio, Texas)—a nickname within a hidden name and also nickname of its jail, lockups, and the detention pens of the Immigration and Naturalization Service

quod prison

R rogue (brand letter burned on the left shoulder of convicts transported to various British colonies from 1619, when the first were landed in Virginia, until 1868, when the last arrived in Western Australia)

Rabat (*see* Morocco)

rabbit feet escaped prisoners

rabbit fever desire to break parole or leave an honor camp before completion of sentence

rabbit foot escaped prisoner

rack(s) maximum-security cell(s)

Radical Alternatives to Prison Plan British program of much promise and abbreviated as RAPP

Rahway New Jersey town about midway between Newark and New Brunswick; contains the New Jersey State Prison, opened in 1901

Raiford Florida town northeast of Gainesville and site of the Union Correctional Institution, once called the Florida State Prison or the Raiford

State Prison

railroad sending a person to jail or prison without benefit of trial or proof of guilt

Rake's Progress The Rake's Progress—title of a series of eight etchings created by William Hogarth in 1735 to show the rise and fall of a young heir who lives well but not wisely and finally winds up in prison and then in a madhouse

Raleigh North Carolina's capital in the east-central portion of the state and site of the Central Prison, Correctional Center for Women, and the Triangle Correctional Center

Ralph Rashleigh eponymous hero of convict James Tucker's eye-witness account in fictionalized form of his being transported to far-off Botany Bay aboard a crowded prison hulk, the grim life in the Australian penal settlement, and the final escape into the outback bush beset by aborigines; the author died unknown in a lunatic asylum

Ramla Israeli maximum-security prison built by the British in 1934, between Jerusalem and Tel Aviv-Yafo

Ranby Camp HM Prison Camp at Ranby in Nottinghamshire, England

ranch synonym for a correctional facility such as a prison camp or farm in a rural area

Rancho del Campo juvenile correctional facility for older boys in San Diego County near Campo, California on the Mexican border

Rancho del Rayo minimum-security correctional facility for younger boys in San Diego County on the site of an Italian prisoner-of-war camp near Campo, California; in 1981 nearly 30% of the juvenile inmates escaped

Rangoon capital of the Socialist Republic of the Union of Burma and nickname of its main prison; others are in smaller cities such as Karbe, Mandalay, and Moulmein; the penal facilities date back to before the time of Kipling

RAP Release Aid Program (to assist recently released inmates in becoming adjusted to society)

RAPP Radical Alternatives to

Prison Plan (a British scheme with much promise)

rasoir nationale (French—national razor)—the guillotine

rasphuys (Flemish—rasp house)—Ghent's workhouse-type prison built by its burgomaster Jean Jacques Philippe Vilain in 1773, where prisoners grated wood to powder as penance and to carry out the motto *only those who work will eat*—the French call this *maison de force* (workhouse)

Rathmore Road nickname derived from the address of Cork Prison in the south of Ireland

rat row prison cells reserved for informants as a guarantee for their safety

Ravensbrück Nazi concentration camp north of Berlin where some 92,000 women died during World War II; this camp specialized in performing medical experiments on its prisoners

Rawlins Wyoming town southwest of Casper and location of the Wyoming State Penitentiary

Ray Brook Federal Correctional Institution at Ray Brook, New York between Lake Placid and Saranac Lake

Raymond Mississippi community southwest of Jackson, containing the Oakley Campus run by the Department of Youth Services and opened in 1943 as a minimum-security penal facility

Raymond Street Raymond Street Jail in Brooklyn, New York and close to the Kings County Criminal Court in the Borough Hall neighborhood

razor ribbon razor-edged stainless-steel security fencing such as is made by American Security Fence of Phoenix, Arizona

RCG Reception Guidance Center

Reading HM Prison at Reading in Berkshire, England where Oscar Wilde wrote *The Ballad of Reading Gaol*; American jails in other Readings in Kansas, Massachusetts, Michigan, Minnesota, Ohio, Pennsylvania, and Vermont

Reception and Diagnostic Center maximum-security facility of Indiana's Department of Correction in Plainfield close to the southwestern sector of Indianapolis

Reception and Diagnostic Center for Children Bon Air, Virginia's facility for handling juvenile delinquents from 8 to 18 years of age

Reception and Guidance Center—Jackson opened in Jackson, Michigan in 1956 to help juvenile delinquents

Reception and Guidance Center—Riverside opened in 1979 on West Riverside Drive in Ionia, Michigan where it holds male juvenile felons under 21 years of age

Reception and Medical Center in Lake Butler, Florida where it was opened in 1968 complete with a hospital and surgery

Reception Center Maryland penal facility in Baltimore next to the Maryland Penitentiary; many prisoners in reception status are housed in other state institutions due to overcrowding

reception centers World War II euphemism for the concentration camps set up to hold some 110,000 Americans of Japanese descent until they could be relocated away from the West Coast and until the Pearl-Harbor-attack-induced paranoia of other citizens could be overcome; while many Japanese-Americans lost their homes, their farms and other businesses, as well as personal contacts and many possessions, it is to their pride to recall how many of their sons enlisted and fought bravely in many theaters of war in the uniform of their country—the United States

recidivist(s) habitual prisoner(s); person(s) spending much of their life in prison

recid(s) recidivist(s)

reclusão (Portuguese—reclusion)—solitary confinement

reclusion (French—solitary confinement)

Réclusion de Saint-Joseph solitary-confinement prison on Saint-Joseph Isle off French Guiana, close to Devil's Island

réclusionnaire (French—prisoner in solitary confinement)

Reclusorio Norte (Spanish—Northern Place of Retirement)—official (but euphemistic) name of Mexico City's penitentiary

reconcentrados (Spanish—concentration camps)—established by the Spaniards in Cuba in 1896 but abolished by 1898 after many protests made in England, Spain and the United States regarding the condition of these camps and their political prisoners

record purge complete removal of arrest, criminal, or juvenile record information from a records system

Redding Shasta County courthouse and jail in upper north-central California

Redención (Spanish—Redemption)—Spain's official prison publication printed in prison workshops and subscribed to by prisoners throughout the country and its possessions in Africa

Red Wing site of the Minnesota Correctional Facility at Red Wing southeast of Saint Paul and opened in 1889, now holding male juvenile offenders in minimum security

Redwood City San Mateo County courthouse and jail south of San Francisco, California

Reeducation of Attitudes and Repressed Emotions treatment program for sex offenders

ref reformatory

reflection cell maximum-security cell

reformatory house of correction or penitentiary charged with the task of making convicts alter their life style and return to society as law-abiding citizens

Regina Coeli (Latin—Queen of Heaven)—Rome, Italy's great prison well known to convicts and to Italian moving-picture fans

Regina Provincial Correctional Centre in the capital city of Saskatchewan where it was opened in 1913

Regional Correctional Facilities (*see* Greensburg, Mercer)

rehab rehabilitate; rehabilitation

rehabilitation changing the offender's character, intent, and motivation toward law-abiding conduct

rehabilitation camps communist-controlled Vietnam's prison camps filled with so-called political prisoners who opposed the communist invasion of their country

rehabilitation laboratory euphemism for any modern prison

Reidsville Georgia town west of Savannah and site of the Georgia State Prison detaining more than 1800 convicts

Re-Integration Center in Albuquerque, New Mexico where its program holds much promise regarding the problem of what to do with criminals

Reiserstown Montrose School for Girls in Reiserstown, Maryland northwest of Baltimore

Release Aid Program (*see* RAP)

rélegué (French—isolated; relegated)—convict condemned to banishment in a penal colony offshore or overseas

relocation center(s) internment camp(s) where Japanese-Americans were confined shortly after the attack on Pearl Harbor when it was generally believed the Japanese would invade the United States

remand to send a prisoner back to court for a further hearing; thus, a remand prison contains people awaiting return to court where their crimes will be judged

Remand Remand Prison at Jin Penjara 3, Singapore

remand center British term for a borstal or juvenile jail where convicts undergo a period of rehabilitation before being paroled or released

remand home synonym for a remand center

remand institution jail, penitentiary, or prison

Rembert South Carolina community northwest of Sumter and address of the Wateree River Correctional Institution

Reno El Reno, Oklahoma's federal detention reformatory west of Oklahoma City; Reno, Nevada close to the California border or its jail and its lockups

rent-a-con plan hiring ex-convicts so they get a fresh start in society

Renz Correctional Center in Cedar City, Missouri where it

opened in 1961 having a normal felon capacity of 200

repatriation statistic of the 70,000 convicts sent to the penal colony in French Guiana barely 2000 were ever repatriated to France during the century-long existence of this tropical prison whose main gate at Saint Laurent du Maroni bore the crest of the French Republic embellished with the letters *LEF* standing for *Liberté, Egalité, Fraternité* (Liberty, Equality, Fraternity), the slogan of the French Revolution

reprieve executive order suspending execution of a sentence imposed on a prisoner

resilient cell padded cell preventing prisoners from injuring or killing themselves

Rest and Reverie nickname of Terminal Island, California's prison in Los Angeles Harbor

restitution center(s) small house(s) where convicted criminals must spend every night after going out every day to work off their debts to the victims of their crimes

restraints ankle cuffs, belly chains, belt restraints, handcuffs, leg irons, straitjackets, etc.

Retrieve Unit in Angleton, Texas north of Freeport

Réunion French island in the Indian Ocean to the east of Madagascar and place used for the isolation of political prisoners such as Abd-el-Krim who was exiled there in 1926

revere (Turkish—prison hospital)

Reykjavik (*see* Iceland)

Reynosa Reynosa, Tamaulipas and its jail across the Rio Grande from Hidalgo, Texas

RGC Reception Guidance Center

Rhode Island jails five counties ranging from Bristol, county seat of Bristol County, to West Kingston in Washington County, have lockups; Providence has extra facilities for its convicts and others apprehended and awaiting trial

Rhode Island penal facilities all 11 are in Cranston, just south of Providence

Rhode Island State Prison in Cranston, and now known as the Maximum Security Facili-

ty

Rhode Island Training School for Girls at Howard, Rhode Island where delinquent girls are trained

Rhodesia (*see* Zimbabwe)

Richmond capital of Virginia, or the Virginia State Penitentiary at 500 Spring Street or the local jail and police-station lockups; Richmond Penitentiary in St Croix, American Virgin Islands West Indies; Texas town holding the Jester pre-release unit

Richmond Farm Jamaican prison close to Annotto Bay on the north coast north of Kingston

Richmond Hill prison on the island of Grenada north-northwest of Trinidad and the coast of Venezuela

Richmond Village Tasmanian town near Hobart and noted for its convict-built bridge and old gaol attracting many tourists

Ridgeville South Carolina town northwest of Charleston and address of the MacDougall Youth Correction Center

Riga main concentration camp in Riga, Latvia during the German occupation of World War II

Riker's complex of prisons on Riker's Island in New York City's East River north of La Guardia Airport; complex includes the Adolescent Remand Shelter, the Riker's Island Penitentiary, and the Riker's Island Women's Detention Center

Ringe Danish state prison at Ringe, pronounced *Reen-ga*, and often nicknamed the Sex Prison as its inmates are of both sexes and allowed sexual freedom in an effort to bring about full rehabilitation by treating them as normal human beings who have gone astray; Ringe is on the island of Funen to the south of Odense

Ring-Ring Copenhagen, Denmark's penitentiary with its seven rings radiating from its cell-block buildings; between the spokes are yards for the prisoners to exercise in limited seclusion and maximum security

Rio popular short form for Rio de Janeiro or its jail

Rio Consumnes Correctional Facility of the same name at Elk Grove, California close to Sacramento

Río de Oro former Spanish prison colony in arid northwest Africa

Riom location in central France of an old and infamous prison used during World War II to hold political prisoners of the puppet government of Petain and Laval

Río Muni Spanish Guinea on the West African mainland and the nearby island of Fernando also used as a convict settlement during the many years of colonial rule

Rio Piedras location of Puerto Rico's State Penitentiary just outside San Juan

RIP Riker's Island Penitentiary

Risdon Hobart, Tasmania's prison and prison hospital

River Avenue Bronx House of Detention at 653 River Avenue in New York City

River House Ohio State Penitentiary on the Scioto River close to Columbus

River Junction Correctional Institution opened in 1974 with a designed capacity of 400 inmates at its site in Chattahoochee, Florida

Riverside Riverside County courthouse and jail east of Los Angeles, California

Riverside Correctional Facility in Ionia where it holds male felons from 17 years of age in medium security

Riverton Wyoming town west of Casper and address of the Wyoming Honor Farm

Riverview Canadian Interprovincial Home for Women (misdemeanants) in Riverside, New Brunswick; Florida town southeast of Tampa and site of the Hillsborough Correctional Institution

Riverview Release Center in Newton, Iowa where it began in 1965

Riverview School for Boys in Powell, Ohio, opened in 1968 to hold male juvenile delinquents

Riyadh (*see* Saudi Arabia)

RLDPAS Royal London Discharged Prisoner's Aid Society

RLPAS Royal London Prisoners' Aid Society

Roaston, Toaston, and Duston

nicknames given by the Japanese-Americans interned at prison camps in the roasting, toasting, and dusty desertlands of southeastern Arizona around Poston

Robben Island South African penitentiary for political prisoners including native chiefs; at entrance to Table Bay and north-northwest of Cape Town

Rochester detention facilities in Rochester, Minnesota and Rochester, New York; HM Borstal at Rochester on the Medway River estuary in England's Kent close to where Dickens lived at Gad's Hill

Rock the Rock (nickname for the 12-acre rock occupied by Alcatraz when it served as a prison in San Francisco Bay) and now a current nickname for the Riker's Island penal facilities in New York's East River

rock crusher(s) prisoner(s) assigned to hard manual labor such as pounding rocks to make little ones out of big ones

Rockland Rockland State Hospital for the Criminally Insane in New York's Rockland County

Rock Spring town in the northwestern corner of Georgia and site of the Walker Correctional Institution

Rockville Training Center a medium-security Indiana correction facility in Rockville close to the Illinois border and due west of Indianapolis

Rockwell City Women's Reformatory at Rockwell City, Iowa, west of Fort Dodge

Rocky Butte Portland, Oregon's jail

Roebuck Roebuck Campus at 8950 Roebuck Boulevard, Birmingham, Alabama (academic-oriented rehabilitation program for juvenile delinquents kept in maximum to minimum security depending on diagnostic evaluation)

rogues' march quickstep played when offenders are drummed out of the army, the marines, the navy, or other military units; at public floggings and executions it was the custom to have a drummer beat out the rhythm of the rogues'

march

Rohwer Arkansas relocation center for interned Japanese-Americans close to the Mississippi River

Romania Socialist Republic of Romania is a behind-the-Iron-Curtain nation on the Black Sea bordered by Bulgaria, Hungary, the Soviet Union, and Yugoslavia; its capital, Bucharest, and its seaport city, Constanza, have prisons built when the Balkan nation was a kingdom

Romanian concentration camps during World War II the most notorious were Akmecetka, Bogdnovka, and Dumanovka

roomie(s) cellmate(s)

Roosevelt Roosevelt Island (in New York City's East River where it formerly was called Welfare Island and originally Blackwell's Island; the site of lunatic asylum, prison, workhouse, and other welfare structures)

Roosevelt Roads at Puerto Rico's east end and location of the U.S. Naval Station there and its brig

rope hangman's rope; marijuana; vein

Rosario (*see* Argentina)

Roseau (*see* Dominica)

Rosharon Texas town south of Houston and location of the Darrington Unit built in 1919

Rostov-on-Don Soviet state police prison, also called House 33

Rota small Spanish port in Cadiz Bay and location of a brig maintained by the U.S. Navy

rotan (Malay—rattan)—lashing stick popular in Malaysia and Singapore where corporal punishment is still used in jails and in (infrequent) street riots

Rotterdam (*see* Netherlands)

Rottnest Rottnest Island (former penal colony in the Indian Ocean off Fremantle near Perth in Western Australia)

Round House Fremantle, Western Australia's oldest structure built in 1830 as a jail; site of the first execution in the area

RTU Rahway Treatment Unit (for sex offenders imprisoned in New Jersey's State Prison at Rahway)

rubber room padded cell reserved for self-destructive or violent prisoners

Rutland Correctional Facility in Rutland, Vermont south of Burlington

Rutland Street nickname of Limerick's prison on Rutland Street in this old city in southwest Ireland

Rwanda small central African nation close to Tanzania, Uganda, and Zaire; its capital, Kigali, contains an old prison built by the Belgians when the land was under their trusteeship until 1962

SA Salvation Army

SAA Singapore Aftercare Association (hostel for ex-convicts)

Sabanete nickname of Maracaibo, Venezuela's national prison (*Cárcel Nacional de Maracaibo*) situated in savanna country and hence the nickname Sabanete

Sachsenhausen main Nazi concentration camp close to Berlin

Sacramento Sacramento County courthouse and jail northeast of San Francisco in central California

SACRO Scottish Association for the Care and Resettlement of Offenders

Sacto Sacramento, California or its jail

safe house military jail; rehabilitation center for prostitutes

safekeeper(s) felon(s) preserved from escaping by being put in maximum, medium, or minimum custody, depending on their record

safety cell padded cell (for self-destructive or violent prisoners)

Safford Federal Prison Camp at Safford, Arizona northeast of Tucson

Sagmalcilar Istanbul, Turkey's great prison so well described by Billy Hayes with William Hoffer in *Midnight Express* (a paperback and a motion picture)

Sagmalcilar Hilton inmates' nickname for the stinking principal prison of Istanbul

Said Port Said, Egypt and its jail as well as its police lockups

Saigon (*see* Vietnam)

Saint Anthony north of Idaho Falls and home of the Youth Services Center of Idaho

Saint Barts Saint Barthelemy in the French West Indies (or its jail)

Saint Bridget's Well original name of London's Bridewell prison and once a royal palace of King Edward VI

Saint Catherine's Jamaican district prison close to Kingston

Saint Cloud Minnesota Correctional Facility at Saint Cloud northwest of Minneapolis and opened in 1889 as the Minnesota State Prison; 26 rue Armengaud, Saint Cloud, Paris (headquarters of the general secretariat of Interpol—the International Criminal Police organization)

Saint Cyrille Maison Gomin correctional facility for women at Saint Cyrille, Québec

Saint Gabriel Louisiana Correctional Institute for Women at Saint Gabriel southeast of Baton Rouge; the Hunt Correctional Center is also in Saint Gabriel

Saint George's (*see* Grenada gaol)

Saint Jean prison camp on the Maroni River of French Guiana, upstream from the penal colony headquarters at Saint Laurent

Saint Joe Saint Joseph, Missouri or its jail or police-station lockups

Saint John jail and lockups at Saint John, New Brunswick

Saint Joseph and Saint Paul adjacent maximum-security prisons in Lyons, France where many dangerous and long-term prisoners are held

Saint Kitts Saint Christopher in what was once the British West Indies, or its jail

Saint-Laurent-du-Maroni French Guiana port on the Maroni River opposite Albina in Dutch Guiana or Suriname; long the headquarters of the penal settlement popularly known as Devil's Island; its liquidation began in 1946 but was still incomplete in 1950 when the author, and others enroute for Brazil, sighted a prison ship steaming slowly through its shark-infested waters and headed for Saint-Laurent-du-Maroni

Saint Lou Saint Louis, Missouri or its jail

Saint Louis du Maroni prison camp on the Maroni River in French Guiana upstream from Saint Laurent

Saint Lucia often called *Loosha* and one of the larger islands of the Windward Isles, Lesser Antilles; Castries, its capital, has an HM Gaol built during the years of British dominion, 1814 to 1979

Saint Lucy nickname for Saint Lucia or its jail or police-station lockup

Saint Marguerite old prison close to the coast of Cannes where the Man in the Iron Masque was imprisoned by Louis XIV from 1687 to 1698 and immortalized in the novel by Alexandre Dumas, *The Man in the Iron Masque*

Saint Martin French half of a West Indian Leeward Island shared with the Dutch and with a small seaport capital, Marigot, complete with its own lockup

Saint Mary's Saint Mary's Honor Center in Saint Louis, Missouri where it opened in 1978

Saint P Saint Paul, Minnesota or its jail

Saint Paul (*see* Saint Joseph and Saint Paul)

Saint Pete Saint Petersburg, Florida or its jail

Saint Petersburg (*see* Tampa)

Saint Pierre former French penal colony on Saint Pierre Island in the Gulf of Saint Lawrence close to Canada

Saint Vincent and the Grenadines volcanic islands in the Windwards where the capital is Kingstown; an old HM Gaol is never too crowded

Salaspils Nazi concentration camp near Riga, Latvia

Salem capital of Oregon, in the northwestern sector of the state where it contains the Correction Division Release Center, the Hillcrest School of Oregon, the Oregon State Correctional Institution, the Oregon State Penitentiary, and the Oregon Women's Correctional Center; West Virginia Home for Girls at Salem

Salinas Monterey County courthouse and jail south of San Jose, California

Salisbury Salisbury National Cemetery containing graves of many Union soldiers who died in the Confederate prison here during the Civil War; near

High Rock Lake and Winston-Salem, North Carolina; (*see* Zimbabwe)

sally port first gate to a prison

Salpetriere Paris hospital for the criminally insane

Saltillo prison in Saltillo, capital city of the state of Coahuila in northeastern México

Salt Lake City capital of Utah and location of the following Community Corrections Centers—Bonneville, Central, Lakehills, Women's; and the State Diagnostic Unit

Salt Lake Women's Community Corrections Center in Salt Lake City, Utah

Samarkand Manor North Carolina youth service facility at Eagle Springs where it holds boys and girls up to 18 years of age for juvenile-delinquency activities

Samoa formerly German Samoa and later ruled by New Zealand but an independent Pacific island nation since 1962; Apia, its capital, has a lockup holding not very many convicts serving long terms

Sanaa (*see* Yemen)

San Anto (Mexican-American—San Antonio, Texas)—jail place-name nickname

San Antone nickname for San Antonio, Texas or its jail and its police-station lockups

San Berdoo San Bernardino, California or its jail

San Bernardino San Bernardino County courthouse and jail east of Los Angeles, California (also called San Berdoo)

San Bruno San Francisco County Jail at San Bruno, California near the Tanforan Racetrack where many Japanese-Americans were held during World War II for fear they would give aid and comfort to the enemy although many volunteered to fight America's enemies and did so with distinction

sand prisoner's nickname for sugar

San Diego San Diego County courthouse and jail in downtown San Diego, California close to the Mexican border (also called Dago or Diego)

Sands Sands Prison just outside Beirut, Lebanon and a place former convicts describe as a first-class hellhole

Sandstone Federal Correctional Institution at Sandstone, Minnesota southwest of Duluth

San Francisco San Francisco County courthouse and jail in downtown San Francisco, California, also known as Frisco (though natives dislike this nickname)

San Francisco (Italian—Saint Francis)—name of the prison in Parma, Italy

San Jack San Jacinto, Texas or its jail

San Jo (Mexican-American—San José, California)—and place-name nickname for its jail

San Jose Santa Clara County courthouse and jail southeast of San Francisco, California

San José capital of Costa Rica and site of its main prison in this most civilized Central American republic where its people boast they have more schoolteachers than police or priests

San Juan capital of Puerto Rico, on the Atlantic coast includes Bayamón, Carolina, Cataño, Guaynabo, Rio Piedras, and Trujillo Alto, in addition to some very old penal facilities dating back to Spanish rule before 1898; truncated name of the general penitentiary of Venezuela situated in San Juan de los Morros Ejido Guarico

San Juan Detention Center in San Juan, Puerto Rico

San Juan de Ulúa old Spanish fortress on an islet about a mile (1.6 kilometers) off the shark-infested port of Veracruz, Mexico; since colonial times the fortress has served as a dungeon for political prisoners

San Luis Obispo California Men's Colony at San Luis Obispo northwest of Santa Barbara and just south of Morro Bay; the colony includes a forestry camp; also stands for the San Luis Obispo courthouse and jail

San Luís Potosí prison in San Luís Potosí, capital of the Mexican state of the same name, northwest of Mexico City

San Luís RC San Luís Río Colorado, Sonora and its jail across the border from San

Luís, Arizona, south of Yuma

San Marino the Most Serene Republic of San Marino is completely surrounded by Italy and close to its Adriatic coast; San Marino city, its capital, has a very small lockup and few inmates; this tiny nation insists it is Europe's oldest state

San Pedro Sula Caribbean port of Honduras on the Gulf of Honduras; its prison in recent years has been overcrowded with political prisoners

San Quentin California State Prison at San Quentin on a small peninsula in San Francisco Bay just southeast of San Rafael; opened in 1852 with a normal capacity of 2642 but with a present population exceeding 3000 male felons in maximum, medium, and minimum security

San Quentin Daily award-winning half-century-old newspaper published by inmates at San Quentin in California

San Quilmas (Mexican-Americanism of unknown origin—San Antonio, Texas)—or its jail or its police-station lockups

San Rafael Marin County courthouse and jail just north of San Francisco, California

San Salvador capital of El Salvador, smallest of the Central American nations but burdened by the fastest-growing population including its prison population

Santa Ana nickname of the central penitentiary of Occidente's Ejido Trujillo in Venezuela; Orange County courthouse and jail southeast of Los Angeles, California

Santa Anita southern California racetrack in the Los Angeles area which served after Pearl Harbor as an internment camp for Japanese-Americans as they had all been branded as *suspicious enemy aliens*

Santa Barbara Santa Barbara County courthouse and jail in southern California northwest of Los Angeles

Santa Cruz Santa Cruz County courthouse and jail north of Monterey, California

Sante Fé capital of New Mexico northeast of Albuquerque and south of Los Alamos; the Penitentiary of New Mexico had its inception in 1884 although a new institution was built in 1956 and renovations were begun in 1980

Santa María de la Cabeza monastery in the Sierra Morena northeast of Cordoba near Andujar where it was stoutly defended by Franco's forces during the Spanish Civil War and later was used as a prison to hold captured Republican leaders including many Catalonian activists who had fought the fascists and lost

Santa Marta Colombian prison in the Caribbean seaport city of Santa Marta; federal prison outside Mexico City

Santa Marta Acatitla prison southeast of Mexico City where many Americans are held for violation of Mexican laws

Santa Rita Santa Rita Rehabilitation Center in California's Alameda County near Oakland

Santa Rosa Sonoma County seat and jail north of San Francisco, California

Santé Parisian prison at 42 rue de la Santé and known as *la Santé*, meaning health or a toast to one's health or, in this instance, to quarantine or segregation from society

Santiago de Cuba (*see* Cuba)

Santo Domingo capital and seaport city (once called Ciudad Trujillo) of the Dominican Republic occupying the eastern half of Hispaniola and long noted for the hellish quality of its detention camps, jails, and prisons

Santurce Puerto Rican community close to San Juan and site of the Institution for Youthful Offenders

São Tome and Principe West African islands under Portuguese control from their discovery in 1471 until 1975; São Tome, whose capital has the same name, is on the Equator, and Principe is a bit north in the Gulf of Guinea; its prison is a veritable antique

Sapporo *see* Japan's prisons)

Sarah Anthony San Diego, California's exclusive school for boys and girls aged 8 to 18, initially brought in handcuffs

Sarajevo (*see* Yugoslavia)

Sasabe Sasabe, Sonora and its jail across the border from Sasabe, Arizona

Saskatchewan Saskatchewan Penitentiary in Prince Albert

sat in the hot seat died by electrocution

Saudi Arabia Arab land occupies most of the Arabian Peninsula and contains the holy cities of Mecca and Medina; its capital, Riyadah, as well as Jidda have prisons dating back to Turkish times in the 18th, 19th, and early 20th centuries

Saughter prison in Edinburgh, Scotland

Sauk Centre northwest of Saint Cloud and location of the Minnesota Correctional Facility opened in 1912 and now holding juvenile delinquents up to 18 years of age in minimum security

sáu-liuh (Cantonese Chinese—handcuffs)

Saulsbury Tennessee town east of Memphis and site of a Civil War prisoner-of-war camp reputedly as bad as Andersonville maintained by the Confederates or Libby Prison run by the Federal authorities

Sav Savannah, Georgia or its jail

SBCR State Board of Charities and Reform (Wyoming)

SBIW Sybil Brand Institute for Women (correctional facility in Los Angeles, California)

scam escape from jail or prison

Scanray Scanray Corporation's scan-ray X-ray system for seeing what is inside parcels brought into jails or prisons by the family and friends of the inmates

scappare di prigione (Italian—escape from prison)

scarce commodity prison space in today's society

SCCA South Carolina Corrections Association

Schenectady upper New York State city adjacent to Albany; site of its county jail

Schlüsselburg Leningrad prison built in czarist times

school of crime epithet applied to many prisons

sci (SCI) secret confidential informant

Scioto Village Ohio penal facility for male and female delinquents; opened as the Girls Industrial School in 1869

Scotland (*see* United Kingdom and individual entries)

Scottish Association for the Care and Resettlement of Offenders SACRO

Scottish prisons Aberdeen, Castle Huntly Borstal Institution, Cornton Vale, Dumfries Young Offenders Institution, Edinburgh, Edinburgh Young Offenders Institution, Glasgow, Glasgow Young Offenders Institution, Glenochil Detention Centre, Greenock, Inverness, Longriggend Remand Institution, Low Moss, Noranside Borstal Institution, Penninghame, Perth (including the Friarton Young Offenders Institution), Peterhead, Polmont Borstal Institution

Scottish Prison Service College SPSC

scragsman British slang for a hangman

Scranton Pennsylvania coal-mining center and Lackawanna County seat and jail in the eastern part of the state close to Wilkes-Barre in Luzerne County

screening (*see* detention screening)

screw(s) prison guard(s)

Scrubs The Scrubs (Wormwood Scrubs Prison in West London's stadium area)

SDC State Department of Corrections (Alabama, Colorado, Virginia)

SDCJ San Diego County Jail (in downtown San Diego)

SDMCC San Diego Metropolitan Correctional Center

SD Met San Diego Metropolitan Correctional Center (on Union Street in downtown San Diego)

Seagoville Federal Correctional Institution at Seagoville, Texas just south of Dallas

Sea-Tac Seattle-Tacoma, Washington or its jail or its police-station lockups

Seavy's Island U.S. Naval Prison on this island near Portsmouth, New Hampshire

seclusion solitary confinement

security housing section of a prison where hardened and hard-to-handle prisoners are segregated

Security Islands Îles du Salut off the coast of French Guiana;

three rocky islets—Île du Diable (Devil's Island), Île Royale, and Île Saint Joseph—surrounded by shark-infested waters; until the 1950s political prisoners were isolated here along with incorrigibles

segregation isolation of criminals from other members of society; racial segregation; solitary confinement

segregazione cellulare (Italian—cellular confinement; close confinement)—solitary confinement

seis y uno (Spanish—six plus one)—*see* Six plus One

Send detention center in Surrey, England

Senegal an independent Moslem state until it became a French West African state, a colonial possession of France in 1893; it became independent in 1960; its seaport capital, Dakar, has an old prison built by the French

Seoul capital of South Korea containing a prison built during the Japanese occupation of Korea, which they called Chosun

Sepa maximum-security prison in the remote jungles of Peru where escape can be worse than incarceration and segregation

Serbia (*see* Jugoslavia)

serve a sentence spend time in jail or prison

serve time spend time in jail or prison

SETAF Southern European Task Force (confinement facility in Italy)

Settlement Island former penal colony within Macquarie Harbour on the Indian Ocean coast of Tasmania

Sevastopol Sevastopol central prison in Crimea

Seven-Step Foundation halfway house for released convicts

Seville (*see* Spain)

Sex Prison nickname for the Danish state prison at Ringe where the most radical experiments in penology are underway in an effort to treat felons as humans

Sexto Lima, Peru jail, reportedly the sixth built on this site since the Spanish conquest

Seychelles island country in the Indian Ocean north of Madagascar; its capital, Victoria,

has an old HM gaol-type penal facility built long before the island gained independence in 1976

SFCJ San Francisco County Jail

Shaker Road Albany County Penitentiary on Shaker Road in the Colonie section of Albany, New York

Shakopee southwest of Minneapolis and location of the Minnesota Correctional Facility for female felons opened in 1920 with all degrees of security

shamus (Irish-Gaelic-derived nickname for a detective or other law-enforcement officer such as a policemen—originally Seamus for James)—*see* canine shamus(es)

Sharjah (*see* United Arab Emirates)

Sharpes (*see* Brevard)

Shata medium-security Israeli prison complete with a work-release program managed by kibbutz volunteers

Sha Tsui Sha Tsui Detention Centre on Lantau Island, New Territories, Hong Kong

Sheff Sheffield, England or its jail

shelter confinement facility for juveniles held pending adjudication

Shelton Washington State Corrections Center or the Women's Correctional Facility at Shelton, close to Olympia and west of Tacoma

Shelton Abbey old Irish prison near Arklow on the east coast of Ireland south of Dublin

Shepton Mallet HM Prison at Shepton Mallet in Somerset, England

Sheridan Sheridan Correctional Center in Sheridan, Illinois west of Joliet where it functions as the Illinois Industrial School for Boys (17 years old and up); the Wyoming Girls School at Sheridan close to the Montana border

sheriff(s) chief officer(s) of county law enforcement and the county jail

shit on a raft naval and prison slang for creamed beef or creamed chicken on toast

shit on a shingle military and prison slang for creamed beef or creamed chicken on toast

shiv knife made in prison;

switchblade knife

Shore Patrol Tank nickname for a lockup maintained by the Navy in many American seaports

short stretch short prison sentence

short-term adult penal institutions of the U.S. Bureau of Prisons Allenwood, Pennsylvania; Elgin Air Force Base, Florida; El Paso, Texas; Florence, Arizona; Montgomery, Alabama; Safford, Arizona

Shrewsbury HM Prison at Shrewsbury in Shropshire, England

shrouding design feature of hard-to-pry-open locks, padlocks, and shackle locks

shujin (Japanese—prisoner held for a criminal offense whereas *furyō* is one held as a prisoner of war)

Siam (*see* Thailand)

Siberia generic term meaning a remote place of exile or imprisonment; a Russian area given over largely to the exile and imprisonment of political prisoners and as true today as in czarist times

Siberia de las Américas (Spanish—Siberia of the Americas)—political prisoner's nickname for the Castro-controlled prisons on the Isle of Pines (*Isla de Pinos*), renamed *Isla de Juventud* (Isle of Youth)—in the Caribbean off the southwest coast of Cuba

Siberian salt mines nickname for the many forced-labor camps and prisons scattered throughout Siberia and other places in the USSR

Sierra Leone West African republic set up by the British in 1787 as a haven for freed slaves; its capital, Freetown, has a prison built by the British before Sierra Leone became independent in 1971

silence bell evening bell rung to advise prison inmates they must cease all talking and any noisemaking

silent system imprisonment characterized by enforced silence at all times and by night confinement in small solitary cells; inmates allowed to congregate with other prisoners during meals or when at work; also called the Auburn System

Silk City Paterson, New Jersey or its jail

Simons Simonstown, South Africa or its jail

Simsbury early American prison built within an abandoned copper mine on the Farmington River 10 miles (16 kilometers) northwest of Hartford, Connecticut where it was in use from 1773 to 1827; like so many penal institutions it was named for the place where it was located, the old town of Simsbury settled in 1660

Sin Angeles (Spanish—Without Angels)—Los Angeles, California, in the estimation of many, or its jail or police-station lockups or nearby penitentiaries and prisons

Singapore small but tidy island nation at the tip of the Malay Peninsula; its capital and its prison are called Singapore; Sir Thomas Stamford Raffles founded this once-British colony in 1819 and it was given its independence in 1959; it is just north of the Equator

Singapore sentence death by hanging is the Singapore sentence for trafficking in drugs

singbird(s) informant(s)

Sing Sing New York State Penitentiary at Ossining (where the birds warble twice—sing sing), now known as the Ossining Correctional Facility

Sin Lam Sin Lam Psychiatric Centre (for the criminally insane held at Sin Lam in the New Territories of Hong Kong)

Sino-penal statistics the so-called People's Republic of China has more than 1000 slave-labor camps and more than 10 million prisoners, according to the West German weekly, *Die Welt am Sonntag* (The World on Sunday)

Sint Maarten (*see* Phillipsburg)

Sioux Falls in the southeast corner of South Dakota and address of its penitentiary used in Sioux Falls since 1882

Sirkeci Istanbul, Turkey's harbor section complete with police station and lockup where many narcotic vendors have been held along with other criminals

Six plus One Spanish prison sentence of six years plus one day for anyone found in possession of or using narcotics or psychedelic drugs; many young Americans are serving or have served the *seis y uno* sentence imposed in Spain

sizzle die in the electric chair

sizzle seat electric chair

Skag Skagway, Alaska or its jail

Skopje (*see* Yugoslavia)

Skowhegan Women's Correctional Center at Skowhegan, Maine

slammed jailed

slam(mer)(s) jail(s) or prison(s) where steel doors slam shut on the inmates

slanguage slang language; slum language

Sleepy Hollow Trenton Prison in New Jersey

Sleepy Hollow Correctional Centre in Charlottetown, Prince Edward Island

Slovenia (*see* Yugoslavia)

slow time seemingly slow time spent by prisoners

slum slumgullion stew (served in many jails and prisons)

smogged executed in a gas chamber

Smyrna in Delaware, the Delaware Correctional Center and the Maximum Security Facility

Sneads on the Georgia border of northwest Florida and site of the Apalachee Correctional Institution

Snoqualmie Washington town east of Seattle and containing the Echo Glen Children's Center for delinquents from 8 to 14 years of age

Sobibor extermination camp close to the main concentration camp of Lublin in Poland during the German occupation of World War II

Society for Alleviating the Miseries of Public Prisons Quaker group that planned the Eastern State Penitentiary in North Philadelphia, Pennsylvania where it served for more than a century; prisoners were kept in individual cells and each cell had an adjacent exercise yard; prisoners were supposed to become reformed by reading the *Bible* and reflecting on their crimes although this segregation in solitary confinement drove many of them crazy; however, it was long considered better than throwing prisoners in a common cell or keeping them in chains as was the practice in many countries during the 18th, 19th, and early 20th centuries and is still in vogue in some countries

Sofia capital city of the People's Republic of Bulgaria and nickname of its prison containing many charged with political crimes against the communist state

sol solitary confinement

Soledad California Training Facility at Soledad (Spanish for solitude) southeast of Monterey, opened in 1947, has maximum-, medium-, and minimum-security accommodations for its male felons

soleta (Mexican-American Spanish—solitary confinement)

solitary system imprisonment designed to segregate criminals from each other so as to prolong reflection and assure self-reform; many so subjected went insane; also known as the Pennsylvania System

Solomon Islands South Pacific Ocean archipelago east of New Guinea and held as a British protectorate from 1890 to 1976; Honiara, the capital, has an HM Gaol-type prison on Guadalcanal Island

Solovetskis Solovetski Islands (penal isolators in the Archangelsk Region of the USSR populated by political prisoners)

Somalia East African nation once divided between British and Italian protectorates but becoming independent in 1960; facing the Indian Ocean is its capital and its prison, both called Mogadishu

Somers Connecticut Correctional Institution opened in Somers in 1827 with maximum-security facilities; Somers is northeast of Windsor Locks and close to the Massachusetts border

Somerville Tennessee town east of Memphis and address of the Wilder Youth Development Center

Sonkom *Sonderkommando* (German—Special Commando)—Hitler organization working at concentration camp crematoria and gas chambers where some of the younger and stronger inmates were forced to assist their armed guards in killing weaker prisoners and removing their remains so more could be killed; a few set up underground resistance groups resolved to fight their Nazi oppressors; only a very few escaped and survived

Sonoita Sonoita, Sonora and its jail across the border from Lukeville, Arizona

Soo Sault Sainte Marie (Michigan or Ontario) and their jails

Soria Madrid, Spain's great prison

Sou Southhampton, England or its jail

South Africa the southernmost nation of Africa has prisons in all its principal cities, Cape Town, Durban, Johannesburg, Pretoria, and in smaller port cities such as East London and Port Elizabeth

Southampton Correctional Center in Capron, Virginia since its inception in 1937 where it is used for youthful first offenders

South Bay Regional Center euphemistic name for San Diego, California's new jail opened in Chula Vista in late 1981 to relieve overcrowding in the downtown jail

South Burlington adjacent to Burlington, Vermont and containing the Chittenden Correctional Facility

South Carolina jails 46 counties ranging from Abbeville in Abbeville County to York in York County have lockups; Charleston, Columbia, and Greenville have extra facilities

South Carolina School for Girls at Columbia

South Dakota lockups 67 counties comprise the state and contain jails from Plankinton in Aurora County to Dupree in Zelbach County

South Dakota Penitentiary in use in Sioux Falls since it was opened in 1882 for male and female felons

South Dakota Training School serving juvenile offenders held in Plankinton where the facility started in 1887

Southeastern Correctional Center in Bridgewater, Massachusetts where it opened in 1977 for felons 16 years of age and up

Southeastern Ohio Training Center in Lancaster where it used to be the Fairfield School for Boys

South Eastern Region Correction Institute Juneau, Alaska's facility for felons, misdemeanants, and juvenile delinquents of both sexes

Southern Michigan Southern Michigan Prison at Jackson

Southern Nevada Correctional Center in Jean, opened in 1978 but already quite overcrowded with felons

Southern Ohio Correctional Facility in Lucasville north of Portsmouth, holds felons in maximum security, opened in 1972

Southern Rhodesia (*see* Zimbabwe)

Southern Steel San Antonio, Texas firm engaged exclusively in the manufacture of detention equipment

South Lansing the South Lansing School for Girls at South Lansing, New York

South Walpole location of the Massachusetts Correctional Institution, west of Brockton and also known as the State Prison

Southwark London borough on the south bank of the Thames infamous for its Clink Prison reserved for heretics; the prison is gone but the expression—*in the clink*—remains

South Windham Maine town northwest of Portland and at the south end of Sebago Lake; site of the Maine Correctional Center opened in 1919

South Yemen (*see* Yemen)

Soviet Kolyma deadliest penal colony in the Soviet Union and part of what Solzhenitsyn called the Gulag Archipelago

Soviet Union (*see* USSR)

Spain the Spanish State (*El Estado Espanol*) occupies most of the Iberian Peninsula and encompasses the Balearic Islands as well as Ceuta and Melilla on the Mediterranean coast of Morocco; jails, penitentiaries, and prisons are in its capital, Madrid, and in and around its big cities such as Barcelona, Bilbao, Malaga, Seville, Toledo, Valencia, and Zaragoza

Spandau Berlin's great prison in the Tiergarten section of the metropolis; many political prisoners have been detained here since the time of the kaisers as well as the Nazis; for the past few years Rudolph Hess has been its only prisoner

Spanish Guinea West African colony including the nearby island of Fernando Po also used as a convict settlement during the many years of Spain's rule

Spanish windlass straitjacket (became tighter and tighter when sprayed with water or soaked with the prisoner's sweat)

Spartanburg South Carolina city northwest of Columbia and site of the Northside Correctional Center and the Piedmont Work Release Center

Spassk Soviet prison camp in Kazakhstan

SPC Service Processing Center(s)—formerly called Immigration and Naturalization Detention Center(s)

Spectator prisoner's publication of the Michigan State Prison at Jackson

Spinhaus (German—workhouse)—old term for a house of correction

spinhuiz (Dutch—workhouse)—old term for a house of correction

split bit prison sentence providing for both a maximum and a minimum sentence (*see* flat bit)

Spoke Spokane, Washington or its jail or lockups

sponging house jail where debtors were kept for a day to give them a chance to settle their debts before being imprisoned or transported overseas

spring release from jail or prison

Springer the New Mexico Boys School, in Springer, between the New Mexican cities of Las Vegas and Raton in the northeast corner of the state

Springfield Sangamon County's county seat, courthouse, and jail in central Illinois where Lincoln is buried and where he practiced law; Medical Center for Federal Prisoners at Springfield, Missouri; nickname of penal institutions in other Springfields in other states

Spring Hill HM Prison at Spring Hill in Londonderry, Northern Ireland where the criminally insane get special treatment

Springhill Institution in Springhill, Nova Scotia southeast of Amherst

sprung released from jail on bail

SPSC Scottish Prison Service College

SQP San Quentin Prison (California)

squat to be electrocuted

squirrel cage hospital for the criminally insane

src (SRC) strict-regime (prison) camp (see Strict-Regime Camp)

Sri Lanka Asian island off the southern tip of India and long known as Ceylon before becoming the Democratic Socialist Republic of Sri Lanka; HM Gaol-type facilities are in Colombo, the capital, and in such cities as Jaffna, Kandy, and Galle; the island was seized by the British in 1796 and became a republic in 1972

SRW State Reformatory for Women (Dwight, Illinois)

SSCA Southern States Correctional Association

Stafford HM Prison at Stafford in Staffordshire, England

Staff Training Centers the Bureau of Prisons offers training to correctional personnel and jailers from all parts of the United States in its centers in Atlanta, Georgia; Aurora, Illinois; Dallas, Texas; and Oxford, Wisconsin—the food service training center of the FCI (Federal Correctional Institute)

Stalag (German—prisoner-of-war camp)

St Albans Correctional Facility in St Albans, Vermont north of Burlington

Stammheim Stuttgart, Germany's maximum-security prison where Andreas Baader and two other members of his terrorist gang reportedly committed suicide after West German commandos rescued 86 hostages held by other members of their group aboard a hijacked Lufthansa airliner at Mogadishu, Somalia during

mid-October 1977

Standford Hill HM Prison at Standford Hill

Stangebro name of the local prison at Linkoping, Sweden

Stanley Hong Kong's maximum-security prison where many Europeans were interned during World War II

Stanton Thomas F Stanton Correctional Center at Elmore, Alabama and holding an average of 452 male felons in 1980; (see Staunton)

Stapleton Staten Island Detention Pens at 67 Targee Street in the Stapleton section of Staten Island, New York

Starke site of the Florida State Prison halfway between Gainesville and Jacksonville

star prisoner inmate believed susceptible to rehabilitation and even some special treatment

START Special Treatment and Rehabilitation Training (program for criminals)

state chemist state executioner who poisons convicts in a gas chamber

State Correctional Institution and Correctional Diagnostic and Classification Centers in Pennsylvania (see Camp Hill, Graterford, and Pittsburgh)

State Correctional Pre-Release Center in Tipton, Missouri where it opened in 1960 for medium- and minimum-security felons

State Diagnostic Unit in Salt Lake City, Utah

state electrician state executioner who electrocutes convicts in an electric chair

State Farm Virginia community southeast of Goochland and northwest of Richmond; contains the Deep Meadow, James River, and Powhatan Correctional Centers

State Farm Spur Illinois penal institution near Vandalia east of Saint Louis

State House of Correction and Branch Prison opened in 1889 and presently holding felons in maximum security at this facility in Marquette, Michigan

stateliest building in all Venice the prison of the Old Republic, in the opinion of Edgar Allan Poe, and so described in his tale, *The Assignation*

State Penitentiary if in Puerto

Rico this name applies to the state penitentiary in Rio Piedras next to San Juan and having all classes of security for its more than 500 felons

State Prison of Southern Michigan opened in 1839 at Jackson with a new prison built there in 1926 and security provisions in all degrees for male felons

State Road Philadelphia address of the Detention Center opened as Moyamensing Prison in 1835 but replaced in 1963 and also the House of Correction begun in 1874, reconstructed in 1928

Stateville Stateville Correctional Center at Joliet, Illinois where in late 1982 it was packed to capacity with 2250 male convicts within the panopticon-designed prison permitting guards in a central tower to see every cell and its inmates

Staunton (pronounced *Stanton*) Correctional Center in Staunton, Virginia northwest of Charlottesville

St Brides Correctional Center in Capron, Virginia, in operation since 1973

Ste Anne des Plaines Québec town northwest of Laval and Montreal; contains the Archambault institution, a maximum-security penal facility

Steilacoom Washington community southwest of Tacoma and location of the McNeil Island Correctional Center

Stevenson House Milford, Delaware's facility for children held in court from 8 to 18 years of age

Stevens School at Hallowell, Louisiana for female delinquents from 11 to 17

stew builder jail or prison cook

Stillwater northeast of Saint Paul and site of the Minnesota Correctional Facility opened in 1913 for male felons in maximum security

stir jail; prison

stir bug insane prisoner whose insanity seems to be linked to long confinement or the thought of long confinement

stir crazy confinement crazy; maddened by imprisonment

Stirville Ossining, New York (site of Sing Sing)

St John's capital of Newfoundland and location of HM Penitentiary

St Johnsbury Correctional Facility in St Johnsbury, Vermont but scheduled for relocation

St-Martin-de-Ré French island and seaport on the southwest coast off La Rochelle and known by many for its old jail close to the Bay of Biscay

Stockton San Joaquin County courthouse and jail east of San Francisco, California

Stoke Heath HM Borstal in Stoke Heath, Shropshire, England

stone dump(s) prison(s)

Stony Mountain Institution in Winnipeg, Manitoba where it had its inception in 1877

Strafanstalt die Strafanstalt (German—the prison)—also called *das Gefängnis*

Strafrechtler der Strafrechtler (German—penologist)

straitjacket(s) restraining device(s) designed to control violent or unruly persons such as the mentally insane or hard-to-handle prisoners

strapped strapped to the electric chair; penniless

Stratford Stratford, Ontario's jail

Street Haven Toronto, Ontario's center for the social rehabilitation of prostitutes and wayward girls

stretch prison sentence

Stretch prisoner's periodical published at Lansing, Michigan

stretch hemp execute by hanging

Strict-Regime Camp one of thirty-six or more Soviet prison camps in the Urals or other far-flung areas of the USSR

Stringtown Correctional Center in Stringtown, Oklahoma northeast of Atoka; holds felons in medium custody

stripes vertically striped prison clothes of the type worn in many places as recently as the first half of the twentieth century when expressions such as "you'll look good in stripes" was a grim reminder to behave or be imprisoned

Stromboli one of the Lipari Islands off the north coast of Sicily in the Tyrrhenian Sea used since Roman times as a place to exile convicts and political prisoners

Stutthof main concentration camp in the north of Poland on the Bay of Gdansk where the Poles call it Sztutowo

St Vincent de Paul St Vincent de Paul Penitentiary across the Riviere des Prairies from Montreal, Québec in Laval

Styal HM Prison at Styal in Cheshire, England

Subic Bay U.S. Naval Base in Subic Bay, the first big bay west of Manila and location of the U.S. Navy Brig

Sudan the Democratic Republic of the Sudan, Africa's largest nation, was long controlled by Anglo-Egyptian forces from 1898 to 1956; its capital at Khartoum, and cities such as Omdurman and Port Sudan on the Red Sea, have HM Gaol-type penal facilities

Sudbury HM Prison at Sudbury

Sugamo Tokyo prison where Japanese war criminals were executed by occupying allied forces at the end of World War II; prison site now occupied by a 60-story building

Sugar Land Texas town just west of Houston and site of the maximum-security Central Unit opened in 1902 and now holding twice the number of felons it was meant to imprison

Sukhanovka czarist monastery converted into a prison near Gorki and one of the most terrible according to Solzhenitsyn

Sumpter Sumter Correctional Institution in Bushnell, Florida equipped with close custody for serious juvenile offenders sent there for rehabilitation through education, vocational training, and counseling concerning alcohol and drug abuse

supreme penalty death

Surabaja (*see* Indonesian prisons)

Suriname formerly Dutch Guiana or more correctly Netherlands Guiana; held by the Dutch from 1667 [when they exchanged it with Britain for New Amsterdam (New York)] until 1975; its capital, Paramáribo, and smaller places such as Nickerie, Paranam, and Moengo, have penal facilities convicts complain about

with some justification

Susanville California Conservation Center at Susanville in northern California close to the Nevada border; although it has a forestry camp it is overcrowded

Sussex Correctional Institution in Georgetown, Delaware where it was opened in 1932 with maximum-, medium-, and minimum-security facilities for its inmates

Suva capital seaport city of the Dominion of Fiji where it contains a gaol (jail) built during the years of British colonization between 1874 and 1970

swag prison jargon for contraband such as drugs, escape tools, fruit, pornography, or weapons smuggled into jails, prisons, or other penal institutions

Swan Lake the place-name stands for the Swan River Youth Forest Camp southeast of Kalispell, Montana where it began operation in 1968 to handle adult youthful offenders from 18 to 25

Swan River Swan River Youth Forest Camp near Swan Lake, Montana southeast of Kalispell (*see* Swan Lake)

Swansea HM Prison at Swansea in Glamorganshire, Wales on Swansea Bay leading to Bristol Channel, St George's Channel, and the North Atlantic

Swaziland the Kingdom of Swaziland, a very small nation in southern Africa between Mozambique and South Africa, has Mbabane as capital and Manzini about the same size; both have HM Gaol-type penal facilities

S & W bracelets Smith and Wesson handcuffs

Sweden the Kingdom of Sweden, on the Scandinavian Peninsula of northern Europe, has some of the most advanced and enlightened penal facilities; these are found in or close to Stockholm, the capital, and in such other places as Göteborg and Malmö

Swedish prisons there are 37 prisons in Sweden and some, like Kumla, are within old fortresses while others, like Gavle, are modern and provide for connubial visits

Swift Trail Swift Trail Federal

Prison Camp at the foot of Mount Graham in the Pinaleno Mountains near Safford, Arizona

Swinfen Hall HM Prison at Swinfen Hall in Staffordshire, England

swing die by hanging

Switzerland the Swiss Confederation of cantons where French, German, Italian, and Romansch are all official languages, has been independent since 1648 and has not been involved in a war since 1515; its armed neutrality seems to have been of benefit to all its people; modern penal facilities are in or near the capital, Zürich, and in other places such as Basel, Geneva, and Bern

swivels swivel nonlocking handcuffs

Sybil Sybil Brand Institute (Los Angeles county jail for women)

Syd Sydney (New South Wales, Australia) or Sydney (Nova Scotia, Canada) or their jails and lockups

Syracuse place-name occurs in Indiana, Kansas, Missouri, Nebraska, New York, and Ohio as well as in the original place, Siracusa or Syracusae on the island of Sicily; here we refer to the jail in such places

Syria the Syrian Arab Republic at the Mediterranean's east end has Damascus as its capital; smaller cities such as Aleppo and Homs have the same type of prisons built by the Turks during their long years of rule in the area and little improved by the French

Tac Tacoma, Washington or its jail or its lockups

Taconic Taconic Correctional Facility at Bedford Hills, New York

Taft Oklahoma town just west of Muskogee and location of the Jess Dunn Correctional Center

Taft Youth Center in Pikeville, Tennessee

Tafuna American Samoan community on Tutuila Island southwest of Pago Pago (pronounced *Pango Pango*) and containing the Territorial Correctional Facility run by the Department of Public Safety and close to the Tafuna Air-

port

Tai Taipei, Taiwan or its jail or its prison

Tai Lam Tai Lam Addiction Department Centre or Tai Lam Centre for Women, both at Lung Chung in the New Territories of Hong Kong on the south coast of China

Taipei (*see* China—Republic of)

take the electric cure suffer electrocution

take the pipe commit suicide

take the rap go to prison for someone else

take to the tules hide out in the bamboo-like tall grass found throughout the American Southwest

Talco Talcohuano, Chile or its jail

Talladega Federal Correctional Institution at Talladega, Alabama east of Birmingham

Tallahassee Federal Correctional Institution at Tallahassee in north Florida close to the Georgia border

Tamarind Jamaican farm prison where constructive work is designed to bring about prisoner rehabilitation

Tamp Tampa, Florida; Tampico, Mexico; or their jails

Tampa Florida's leading West Coast city adjacent to Saint Petersburg on Tampa Bay has police-station lockups as well as the Hillsborough County jail

Tampere (*see* Finnish prisons)

Tampico prison in Tampico, a Mexican seaport on the Gulf of Mexico

Tanforan racetrack near San Francisco; used as a relocation center (concentration camp) for Japanese-Americans during World War II when mass hysteria overcame common sense and when it was finally discovered all the Japanese-Americans interned were loyal although they had been deprived of their liberties, their farms, their homes, their shops, and all they possessed; Tanforan is a sad name in American place-names and Americans who know about it are usually deeply ashamed

Tangerang boy's prison in western Java, Indonesia

Tangier (*see* Morocco)

Tanjong Pagar Singapore lock-

up and police station on Tanjong Pagar Road

tank prison cell

Tanzania the United Republic of Tanzania unites Tanganyika and Zanzibar and hence what was German East Africa is united with the British protectorate of Zanzibar; the capital, Dar-es-Salaam, has an HM Prison built in the early years of our century

tap code code created by prisoners who are not allowed to talk to one another but manage to communicate by tapping on cell bars or plumbing pipes

Tarawa (*see* Kiribati)

Tarbes the maximum-security Prison de Tarbes in southwestern France

Tasmania large island off Australia's southeast coast where it was once called Van Diemen's Land and served as a penal colony from 1803 until 1853; it is now called Tasmania and has been an Australian state since 1901

Taycheedah Correctional Institution receiving center for adult females held in Taycheedah, Wisconsin east of Fond du Lac

TCA Tennessee Correctional Association; Texas Corrections Association

TDC Texas Department of Corrections

Tecate Tecate, Baja California and its jail just across the border from Tecate, California

Tecumsah Oklahoma town just east of Norman and address of the Central Oklahoma Juvenile Treatment Center opened in 1921

teddy boy(s) male juvenile delinquent(s) in the British Isles

teddy girl(s) female juvenile delinquent(s) in the British Isles

Teguci Tegucigalpa and its prison in the capital city of Honduras where former inmates claim the conditions are bad enough to make law-abiding citizens out of even the most hardened criminals

Tehachapi California Correctional Institution at Tehachapi (state prison in the Tehachapi Mountains close to the western edge of the Mojave Desert)

Teheran (*see* Iranian prisons)

telephone-pole design seen from

above this type of prison design, first introduced at Lewisburg, Pennsylvania in 1932, resembles a telephone pole with its crossarms; cellblocks and workshops are at right angles to a central corridor; this design provides flexibility in layout and coordination of elements for control and supervision of the inmates; the long connecting corridor (the telephone pole) extends from the administrative building past dining rooms and shops, and is bisected by cellblocks (*see* Lewisburg Plan)

Tel Mond medium-security Israeli prison for juvenile offenders located just south of Natanya in the Plain of Sharon

Tennessee Colony Texas town northwest of Palestine and location of the maximum-custody Beto Unit scheduled for completion by construction-worker inmates in 1984; the Coffield Unit is also here

Tennessee lockups 95 counties make up the state with jails from Clinton in Anderson County to Lebanon in Wilson County; Memphis, Nashville, Knoxville, and Chattanooga have extra facilities for holding prisoners

Tennessee Prison for Women the old section was opened in 1898 and the new in 1966 for holding female felons in all conditions of custody

Tennessee State Prison opened in Nashville in 1898 and holding felons in close, medium, and minimum custody

Tennessee Youth Center for first offenders, juvenile delinquents, and misdemeanants held here between 15 and 18 years of age in Joelton

Tepic prison in Tepic, capital of the Mexican state of Nayarit on the Pacific coast south of Mazatlán

Terminal Island Federal Correctional Institution (all-male medium-security prison) on Terminal Island opposite San Pedro, California

Terre Haute U.S. Penitentiary at Terre Haute, Indiana close to the Illinois border

Territorial Correctional Facility at Tafuna on Tutuila Island of American Samoa

Territorial(s) Territorial Prison(s)

Texarkana Federal Correctional Institution at Texarkana, Texas across the street from Texarkana, Arkansas

Texas Department of Correction Units scattered about this second largest state from Angleton to Sugar Land, from Brazoria and Brownwood to Rosharon and Tennessee Colony; Huntsville has the most penal facilities

Texas jails 254 counties comprise the state and contain lockups all the way from Palestine in Anderson County to Crystal City in Zavala County; big cities such as Houston, Dallas, and San Antonio have local lockups as well as county prison facilities

Thailand the Kingdom of Thailand, formerly called Siam, occupies much of the Indo-Chinese Peninsula and some of the Malay Peninsula; the old kingdom, never taken over by any European power, has its capital in Bangkok; its prison seems almost as old as the land it occupies

thana (Anglo-Indian—police station)—lockup; (Hindustani—jail)

THC Toledo House of Correction (Ohio)

theater of terror any public execution or punishment such as flogging

The Gambia (*see* Gambian prisons)

The Pas Correctional Institution for Women at The Pas, Manitoba

therapeutic correctional community prison

Theresienstadt Nazi concentration camp about 40 miles (60 kilometers) from Prague; the Czechs called it Terezin; some 141,000 Jews were imprisoned before being shipped to the gas ovens at Auschwitz in Poland

The Verne HM Prison at The Verne in Dorset, England

Thieves' Palace nickname for the Surrey Prison

Thimphu the name of the capital of the kingdom of Bhutan and also used by prisoners referring to their prison in the eastern Himalayan mountains

Third Street New Jersey State Prison in Trenton on Third

Street between Cass and Federal where its square block of red stone walls studded with guard towers is a landmark

Thomas Saint Thomas in the American Virgin Islands or its jail built a century ago by the Danes

Thomaston site of the Maine State Prison northeast of Brunswick

Thorn Nazi concentration camp in Poland where it was known as Torun, on the east bank of the Vistula River

Thorp Arch HM Prison at Thorp Arch, Yorkshire, England

Three Cs Federal Prison System logotype standing for Care, Custody, and Correction

three deuces jammed three concurrent two-year sentences

three deuces running wild three consecutive two-year sentences

three-time loser person returning to prison for the third time

throwaway juvenile delinquent or young adult criminal living in the same city or place as his or her parents but out of their care or control

thumbs thumbcuffs for controlling and holding unruly prisoners being transported from place to place

TI Terminal Island (Federal Correctional Institution at Terminal Island, California in Los Angeles harbor)

ticket-of-leave permit allowing a convict to leave prison before the expiration of the sentence and to work under certain restrictions; parole certificate

ticket-of-leave man parolee

Tidewater Correctional Unit in Chesapeake, Virginia

Tijuana Tijuana, Baja California Norte and its jail across the border from San Diego, California

Tijuana Hilton nickname of San Diego's multistory Metropolitan Correctional Center tall enough to afford its many inmates a restricted view of across-the-border Tijuana in Mexico and luxurious enough to remind them of the great Hilton chain of high-class hotels

Tillberga Swedish prison in Tillberga to the west of Stockholm

Tillery North Carolina town southeast of Roanoke Rapids and site of the Caledonia and Odom Complex opened in 1900 with a capacity for 480 felons

time off time off for good behavior (while imprisoned)

time out time out of sight (in a solitary-confinement cell)

time served total time spent in confinement before and after sentencing

Tinseltown Hollywood, California and its police-station lock-up as well as the nearby Los Angeles County Jail

tin throne metallic toilet; prison-cell toilet; slop bucket

tintureiro (Portuguese—dry cleaner)—Brazilian term for a prison van

Tipton Missouri community midway between Jefferson City and Sedalia; contains the State Correctional Pre-Release Center

Tiptonville on the Mississippi west of Union City, Tennessee and address of the Lake County Regional Correctional Facility

Tirana name shared by the capital and its less-than-comradely prison in the People's Socialist Republic of Albania

Tj Tijuana, Baja California, México or its jail

Tjipinang maximum-security prison near Djakarta (formerly Batavia) on the western end of the Indonesian island of Java

Tjirebon major prison in western Java on the Java Sea coast northeast of Bandung in Indonesia

Tlaxcala prison in Tlaxcala, capital of the Mexican state of the same name, just east of Mexico City

TO Toledo, Ohio or its jail or its lockups

Toamasina (*see* Madagascar's prisons)

Tobago (*see* Trinidad)

Toco Tocopilla, Chile or its jail

Tocuyito nickname of the central penitentiary of Valencia in the Ejido Carabobo of Venezuela

Togo this small West African country has been under German, British, French, and finally native direction since 1960; Lomé, on the Gulf of Guinea, is its capital and its prison is primitive

toil factory prison workshop

Tokyo (*see* Japan's prisons)

tolbooth (Scottish—prison)

Toledo (*see* Spain, TO)

Toluca prison in Toluca, capital of the Mexican state of Mexico southwest of Mexico City

tombas (Spanish—tombs)—solitary confinement cells

Tombs old New York City Prison in downtown Manhattan adjacent to the Criminal Court Building on the Lower East Side

Tombs Prison Manhattan's House of Detention

Tomoka Tomoka Correctional Institution (*see* Daytona Beach)

'Tona Daytona Beach, Florida or its jail

Tonga the island Kingdom of Tonga is in the South Pacific Ocean south of the Samoan islands; under British protection from 1900 to 1970; an HM Gaol was built during this time in the capital seaport of Nuku'alofa

Tong Fuk Tong Fuk Detention Centre, Lantau Island, New Territories, Hong Kong

Toodyay an old gaol in Western Australia which is now an historical museum

Topaz relocation center for Japanese-Americans interned in central Utah following the attack on Pearl Harbor

Topeka Kansas city in the northeastern corner of the state and location of the Kansas State Reception and Diagnostic Center as well as the Kansas Correctional-Vocational Training Center and the Youth Center in Topeka

Topenish abandoned Japanese-American relocation center near Yakima, Washington where an investigation made by the American Friends Service Committee forced the government to abandon the place even though nearly $50,000 had been spent on its rehabilitation; its buildings were reported to have been even worse than the horse stalls at Santa Anita or Tanforan or the pigpens at Puyallup where other so-called suspicious enemy aliens of Japanese-American ancestry had been interned

Topo Topolobambo, Mexico or its jail

toponym(s) place-name(s) prisoners use when telling where they were imprisoned; for example, Atlanta usually means the federal penitentiary in Atlanta, Georgia just as Trenton may be the New Jersey state prison there or even the Training School for (delinquent) Girls at Trenton

Toronto Canada's largest metropolitan community on the north shore of Lake Ontario; the Don Jail and the Mimico Correctional Centre are well-known penal facilities

torture chamber(s) jail(s) or prison(s) where drugs are not available at any price

total segregation solitary confinement

Toulon French seaport on the Mediterranean east of Marseilles and well known as a depot for convicts awaiting passage to the penal colonies of Algeria, French Guiana, and New Caledonia

Touquet Le Touquet, France or its jail not far from the English Channel

Tower (*see* Tower of London)

Tower of London ancient fortress on the north side of the River Thames just east of the City of London and later used as a royal residence and then a jail for political prisoners who often entered by the Traitors Gate before being beheaded; today it is an arsenal museum housing the crown jewels as well as ancient armor and many weapons; also called the Bloody Tower, as many were executed within its walls

Townsville HM Prison at Townsville (Queensland, Australia)

Tracy Deuel Vocational Institution at Tracy east of San Francisco and southwest of Stockton providing maximum and medium security to some 1700 male felons

Training Center for Youth opened in 1961 in Columbus, Ohio for males from 12 to 17 years of age

Training School for Boys in Boonville, Missouri where it began in 1889 (*see* Boonville)

Training School for Boys and ·

Girls at Jamesburg, New Jersey northeast of Trenton

Training School for Girls Trenton, New Jersey's correctional facility for juvenile delinquents from 8 to 17 years of age

training school(s) usually juvenile delinquent institution(s)

Traitors' Gate Thames River waterside gateway to the Tower of London, where prisoners were rowed in before being executed or serving long terms

tramp college(s) old nickname for county jail(s)

Trani Italian prison near Bari on the Adriatic and the scene of some deadly prison breaks

Transfrisker electronically actuated hand-held no-touch personal-weapons-search device made by Federal Laboratories of Saltsburg, Pennsylvania

Transnistria Romanian-Nazi administrative region between the Bug and the Dniester rivers in an occupied section of the Soviet Ukraine where during World War II thousands of exiled Romanian Jews were relocated and forced to labor until many died in this forgotten cemetery

transportation movement of prisoners to overseas penal colonies as was the French custom until the late 1950s; Brazil, Cuba, Ecuador, Italy, Mexico, and the USSR still have offshore or distant penal settlements

Trautenau forced-labor sub-camp in western Czechoslovakia where it served the Nazis during World War II

Treasure Island first brig for women sailors opened in February 1981 at the U.S. Navy base at Treasure Island in San Francisco Bay under the Oakland Bridge

Treblinka Nazi gas-chamber-equipped concentration camp in Poland where during World War II the Jews revolted; 600 escaped but only 40 survived to tell the tale about some 700,000 other victims of racial persecution

trembler(s) prisoner(s) afraid of other prisoners

Trenggalek one of Indonesia's newer prisons in eastern Java

Trenton Florida town west of

Gainesville and site of the Lancaster Correctional Center; capital of New Jersey and site of the New Jersey State Prison and the Training School for Girls, as well as the Jones Farm at West Trenton, the St Francis Hospital Unit, and the Vroom Readjustment Unit in the Trenton Psychiatric Hospital

Tres Marías (Spanish—Three Marys)—Mexican penal settlement in the Pacific Ocean off Nayarit; prisoners are kept on María Madre Island

Trinidad and Tobago a large and a small West Indian island close to Venezuela and with its capital in Port-of-Spain, Trinidad where an HM Prison recalls the years of British rule from 1802 to 1976

Tripoli (*see* Lebanon and Libya)

Trondheim (*see* Norway)

Tropez St Tropez on the French Riviera or its jail

Trostyanets site of a Nazi concentration camp near Minsk in Belorussiya where thousands of victims of Hitler's onslaught are buried in mass graves; those of the Jews are unmarked because anti-Semitism is also popular with many so-called communists in the Soviet Union and elsewhere

Troy upper New York State city north of Albany; seat of Rensselaer County and its jail

Trubetskoi bastion of the Peter and Paul Fortress, used as a prison in Leningrad

Trucial Sheikdoms (*see* United Arab Emirates)

Trujillo *Cárcel Nacional de Trujillo* (Spanish—National Prison of Trujillo, Venezuela)

Truk prison camp erected by the Japanese during World War II in the Caroline Islands of the western Pacific Ocean

Truro the Nova Scotia School for Girls at Truro

trusty trustworthy convict who is allowed special privileges

TRY Teens for Retarded Youth (juvenile correctional program)

T-town Tijuana, Baja California, Mexico or its jail

tuchthuiz (Dutch—house of correction; workhouse)

Tucker Tucker Unit in Tucker, Arkansas; opened in 1922 to

accommodate 676 male felons

Tucson site of Arizona Correctional Training Facility where academic and vocational training is offered male felons; Catalina Mountain School in Tucson with a treatment program for juvenile males; Pima County seat and jail north of Nogales, Arizona and Nogales, México

Tule Lake waterless relocation and segregation center near the Oregon border of northern California where many Japanese-Americans were interned after Pearl Harbor

Tullahoma Tennessee town northwest of Chattanooga and site of the Highland Rim School for Girls

Tulle maximum-security prison on the prolongation of Rue Souhan in Tulle in south-central France

Tulsa Tulsa, Oklahoma or its Tulsa County Jail

Tulungagung new Indonesian prison in eastern Java close to the south shore on the Indian Ocean

Tunis (*see* Tunisia)

Tunisia small North African nation between Algeria and Libya; under French domination from 1881 to 1956; its cities, including the capital city of Tunis, have French-colonial-type jails and prisons

turist kogus (Turkish—tourist cell block)—prison section reserved for foreigners

Turkey ancient Middle-East country between the Black Sea and the Mediterranean; its penal facilities are mainly from the time of the Ottoman Empire and may be seen in Ankara, Istanbul, Izmir, and other Turkish cities and towns

Turku (*see* Finnish prisons)

Turney Center for Youthful Offenders at Only, Tennessee

turnkey anyone entrusted with the keys to a prison (usually a correction officer, jailer, or warden; sometimes, if to a section, a trusty may be the turnkey)

Turrell Turrell Residential Group Center near Farmingdale, New Jersey

Tuscaloosa Tuscaloosa County seat and jail southwest of Birmingham, Alabama

Tuvalu island nation in the South Pacific north of Fiji and under British dominion until 1978; an HM Gaol-type penal facility is in the capital, Funafuti

Tuxtla Gutiérrez prison in Tuxtla Gutiérrez, capital city of Chiapas, Mexico, near the border with Guatemala

Twin Maples Farm British Columbia's facility for treating women inmates with alcohol problems

twister(s) key(s)

Two Dzerzhinsky Moscow address of the KGB and the Lubyanka prison

two-time loser person going to prison for the second time

Tyburn long a favorite hanging place fitted with gallows and gibbets standing between the bottom of Edgware Road and the wall of Hyde Park, only three miles from Newgate Jail in the City of London

tyurma (Russian—jail)

UCA Utah Correctional Association

Udine Italian prison in a city of the same name, northeast of Venice

ufac unlawful flight to avoid confinement

Uganda Central African equatorial country under British protection from 1894 to 1962; its capital city, Kampala, has an old HM Prison as well as local lockups holding many political prisoners at odds with the succession of dictatorial governments

ugly customer dangerously quarrelsome person

UK United Kingdom (Great Britain, Northern Ireland, and overseas colonies and territories)—or their penal facilities

Ulan Bator (*see* Mongolia)

ultimate penalty death, or life imprisonment without parole

UN United Nations and its many organizations concerned with crime and punishment

unauthorized depature(s) prison parlance for escape(s)

Uncasville Connecticut Community Correctional Center at Uncasville northeast of New London

underground kite secret message circulated throughout a prison or from one prisoner to another

underground tunnel secret systems for introducing contraband such as drugs, tools, and weapons into a prison

under the gun under observation or surveillance

unhook unfasten the handcuffs or fetters

UNICOR trade name of the Federal Prison Industries corporation maintaining 89 industrial operations in 39 penal institutions

Union Correctional Institution at Raiford, Florida where it was opened in 1914 for inmates in maximum, medium, and minimum security

Unit 731 Japanese biological warfare complex at the Harbin Military Hospital in Manchuria during World War II where prisoners of war were used in deadly experiments that affected American, Australian, British, Chinese, Korean and Russian inmates

United Arab Emirates formerly known as the Trucial Sheikdoms who for most of the 19th century and up to 1971 were under British protection; the capital, Abu Dhabi, and some of the older cities, such as Dubai and Sharjah have old HM Gaol-type prison facilities

United Kingdom the United Kingdom of Great Britain and Northern Ireland has its capital in London, the hub of the once far-flung British Empire; some of the best-known gaols, penitentiaries, and prisons are in the British Isles and there are many remnants in former colonies and protectorates

United Prisoners Union revolutionary underground organization of hard-core convicts in prisons such as San Quentin or Soledad

universal staircase nickname for the treadmill once operated by felons

Unterlüss Nazi subcamp close to Bergen-Belsen near Hannover, Germany

Up Changi Road Singapore's Prison Headquarters at Kilometer 17 outside the city and nicknamed for the road on which it is located

up the river Sing Sing prison, up the Hudson River from New York City in the town of Os-

sining

UPU (*see* United Prisoners Union)

Urga (*see* Mongolia)

Uruguay Oriental Republic of Uruguay, a small country between Argentina and Brazil on the east coast of South America; Montevideo is its capital; penal facilities are considered less than comfortable by inmates

U.S. United States (as in U.S. Bureau of Prisons)

USA United States Army

U.S.A. the United States of America contains every type of penal facility from hospital prisons for the criminally insane to barless maximum-security centers for hardened criminals; (*see individual entries*)

USAF United States Air Force

USARB U.S. Army Retraining Brigade

U.S. Army confinement facilities Fort Benning, Georgia; Fort Campbell, Kentucky; Fort Carson, Colorado; Fort Gordon, Georgia; Fort Hood, Texas; Fort Knox, Kentucky; Fort Lewis, Washington; Fort Meade, Maryland; Fort Ord, California; Fort Polk, Louisiana; Fort Richardson, Alaska; Fort Riley, Kansas; Fort Sill, Oklahoma

USBP United States Board of Parole; United States Border Patrol; United States Bureau of Prisons

U.S. Bureau of Prisons (*see* Bureau of Prisons)

U.S. Bureau of Prisons federal penitentiaries Atlanta, Georgia; Leavenworth, Kansas; Lewisburg, Pennsylvania; Lompoc, California; Marion, Illinois; Terre Haute, Indiana

U.S. Bureau of Prisons institutions for juvenile and youth offenders Ashland, Kentucky; Englewood, Colorado; Morgantown, West Virginia

U.S. Community Treatment Centers halfway houses for male and female offenders (*see* Community Treatment Centers)

USDB U.S. Disciplinary Barracks at Fort Leavenworth, Kansas, which had its inception in 1874 and now holds Air Force, Army, and Marine Corps prisoners whose sentences include six months or more of confinement and/or a punitive discharge

U.S. Department of Justice administers the following: Board of Immigration Appeals, Bureau of Prisons, Civil Division, Civil Rights Division, Criminal Division, Drug Enforcement Administration, Federal Bureau of Investigation, Immigration and Naturalization Service, Justice Management Division, Land and Natural Resources Division, Office of Legislative Affairs, Office of Public Affairs, Pardon Attorney, Tax Division, U.S. Marshals Service, U.S. Parole Division

USDJ U.S. (United States) Department of Justice (*see entry*)

U.S. Eighth Army Confinement Facility in Korea

USEP United States Escapee Program

Usk HM Borstal at Usk in England

U.S. Marshals Service maintains custody of federal prisoners from the time of their arrest to their commitment or release, and transports federal prisoners pursuant to lawful writs and direction from the U.S. Bureau of Prisons

USMC United States Marine Corps (correctional facilities in Albany, Georgia; Camp Smedley D. Butler in Okinawa; Camp Lejeaune, North Carolina; Camp Pendelton, California; Parris Island, South Carolina; Quantico, Virginia)

USMS U.S. (United States) Marshals Service (*see entry*)

USN United States Navy

USN Brigs correctional centers and detention facilities, called brigs in naval parlance recalling shipboard cells, are operated in the United States and overseas in or close to port cities with the possible exception of a naval air station inland such as one in Millington, Tennessee; seaport brigs include: Agaña, Guam; Charleston, South Carolina; Corpus Christi, Texas; Great Lakes, Illinois; Guantanamo, Cuba; Jacksonville, Florida; Long Beach, California; New London, Connecticut; New-

port, Rhode Island; Norfolk, Virginia; Pearl Harbor, Hawaii; Pensacola, Florida; Philadelphia, Pennsylvania; Roosevelt Roads, Puerto Rico; Rota, Spain; San Diego, California; San Francisco, California; Seattle, Washington; Subic Bay, Philippines; Yokosuka, Japan

USNCC U.S. Naval Correction Center

USP United States Penitentiary

USPB United States Parole Board

USPC U.S. Parole Commission (formerly USPB)

USPD U.S. Parole Division of the Department of Justice

U.S. Penitentiaries Atlanta, Georgia; Leavenworth, Kansas; Lewisburg, Pennsylvania; Lompoc, California; Marion, Illinois; Terre Haute, Indiana

USPP U.S. Probation and Parole

USPs United States penitentiaries

USSR the world's largest nation, the Union of Soviet Socialist Republics, also known as the Soviet Union, extends from eastern Europe to the Pacific Ocean as it takes in northern Asia; its capital, Moscow, and the capitals of its many so-called republics contain some of the most dreaded prisons in existence

Utah jails the state's 29 counties have lockups from Beaver in Beaver County to Ogden in Weber County; Salt Lake City has additional facilities for keeping prisoners confined

Utah State Prison at Draper (old site opened in 1868 and new in 1951); holds some 875 felons 18 years of age or older

Utrecht Netherlands prison clinic providing psychological treatment and observation

VA Volunteers of America; postal abbreviation for Virginia

VAC (*see* Voluntary Action Center)

Vacaresti Romanian prison and formerly a monastery on the outskirts of Bucharest

vacationing near Chappaqua doing time in nearby Sing Sing

Vaca Valley Star prison newspaper published by inmates in Vacaville, California

Vacaville California Medical Facility at Vacaville halfway be-

tween Sacramento and San Francisco; this psychiatric prison opened in 1955 after moving from Terminal Island where it was opened in 1950; maximum- and medium-security penal facilities serve its male felons

VACRP Victorian Association for the Care and Resettlement of Prisoners

VACs Voluntary Action Centers

Vaduz (*see* Liechtenstein)

vagonzak vagon zaklyuchennykh (Russian—railroad prisoner car)

Valdosta city in southernmost central Georgia and site of the Lowndes Correctional Institution near the Florida border

Valencia (*see* Spain and Venezuela)

Valetta (*see* Malta)

Valhalla Westchester County Penitentiary at Valhalla, New York

Valpo Valparaiso, Chile's nickname or its jail

Val Verde County Clink nickname for the Val Verde County Jail in Del Rio, Texas (just behind the courthouse and the sheriff's office)

Vancoo Vancouver, British Columbia (or Vancouver, Washington) or their jails

Vandalia Correctional Center in Vandalia, Illinois north of Centralia; a medium-security facility

Van Diemen's Land former name of Tasmania and generic name for the great Australian penal settlement begun in the early 1800s and lasting up to 1853 when the last shipment of convicts arrived and Tasmania became its official name

Vanier Vanier Centre for Women at Brampton, Ontario

Vanuatu formerly the Anglo-French New Hebrides condominium close to Fiji and New Caledonia in the South Pacific; its old HM Gaol or Maison reflects it colonial past; its capital is Vila

VCA Virginia Correctional Association

Vega Alta Industrial School for Women at Vega Alta, Puerto Rico for felons, misdemeanants and women awaiting trial

Vegas Las Vegas, Nevada or its jail or its lockup

Vehicle City Flint, Michigan's nickname or its jail

Venezuela South American republic bounded by Brazil, the Caribbean Sea, Colombia, and Guyana; Caracas, its capital, and cities such as Barquisimeto, La Guaira, Maracaibo, and Valencia have Hispanic-type penal facilities complained about by generations of inmates

Ventura Ventura County courthouse, county seat, and jail between Los Angeles and Santa Barbara, California

Ventura Reception Center and Clinic at Camarillo, California

Ventura School for Girls at Camarillo, California

Vergennes the Weeks School for delinquent and unmanageable males and females at Vergennes, Vermont

Vermillionville Lafayette, Louisiana's former name, its nickname, and that of its jail

Vermont Correctional Facilities in Burlington, Rutland, St Albans, St Johnsbury, Windsor, and Woodstock

Vermont lockups 14 counties comprise the state with jails from Middlebury in Addison County to Woodstock in Windsor County

Vero Beach Florida resort town north of Fort Pierce and site of the Indian River Correctional Institution opened in 1976 for first-felony juvenile offenders under 20 years of age

Vesterfangsel (Danish—Western Jail)—Copenhagen prison

vettura cellulare (Italian—celled vehicle)—prison van

vic(s) convict(s)

victims of the metal age older prisoners complain they have silver in their hair, gold in their teeth, rust in their guts, steel around their cells, and lead in their asses

Victoria capital of British Columbia and location of the William Head Institution; La Victoria (Santo Domingo city prison, Dominican Republic); Victoria Reception Centre (Old Bailey Road, Hong Kong); (*see* Seychelles)

Vienna Correctional Center in Vienna, Illinois north of the Kentucky border and pronounced *Vi-enna*

Vientiane (*see* Laos)

Vietnam southeast Asian country containing North and South Vietnam formerly held by the French from 1858 to 1954 and by the Japanese during World War II; penal facilities built by the French and the Japanese are still used and are filled mainly with political prisoners in Ho Chi Minh City (formerly Saigon) as well as in Hanoi, Haiphong, Da Nang, Hue, Nha Trang, and Vinh

Vieux Carre (French—Old Square)—French Quarter of New Orleans, Louisiana or its lockup

Vila (*see* Vanuatu)

Vila dos Remédios (Portuguese—Town of Reparation)—Brazilian settlement for ex-convicts on the isolated island of Fernando de Noronha in the South Atlantic Ocean

Villa Devoto great Argentinian prison in the Devoto section of Buenos Aires

Villahermosa prison in Villahermosa, capital of the Mexican state of Tabasco, whose shores are washed by the Bay of Campeche in the Gulf of Mexico

Villamil port town of Ecuador's former penal colony on the arid south coast of Isabela Island in the Galapagos Islands bisected by the Equator, where convicts serving life sentences were segregated with their families for crimes ranging from arson to murder until the colony was disbanded in the early 1950s

Vince Saint Vincent Island in the Windward Islands of the Lesser Antilles or its jail

Vincennes French prison just east of Paris and notorious for its many famous inmates dating as far back as the 14th century, when it was a castle and dungeon

vincula (Latin—prisoners)

vinculum (Latin—bond; fetter; prison)

Vinh (*see* Vietnam)

ViP (VIP) (*see* Volunteers in Probation)

Virginia its State Department of Corrections consists of the Division of Adult Correctional Services and the Division of Youth and Community Services; these, in turn, are divided into regions and within each there are correctional centers and units as well as halfway houses, learning centers, and work-release units scattered throughout the Tidewater State

Virginia Correctional Center for Women in Goochland where it opened in 1932

Virginia jails the state's 96 counties, and its many independent cities, have lockups from Accomac in Accomack County to Yorktown in York County

Virginia State Penitentiary in Richmond where it opened in 1800 and holds adults in all levels of custody

Virgin Islands jail lockup on the waterfront of Charlotte Amalie on the island of St Thomas in the Caribbean; jail occupies an old fort built in Danish times when the islands were settled

Visalia Tulare County courthouse and jail in central California southeast of Fresno

Vista town near San Diego, California or nickname for the county detention facility there

viuva alegre (Portuguese—merry widow)—prison van

viuva(s)-alegre(s) [Brazilian slang—prison vans]

Vladivostok transit prison port on the Pacific coast of the USSR

V of A Volunteers of America

voiture cellulaire (French—celled vehicle)—prison van

Voluntary Action Center device for using the skills of persons convicted for minor crimes instead of putting them in ever-more-costly prisons; has proved successful in the Los Angeles area

Volunteers in Probation publishes *VIP Examiner* quarterly and books about probation

Voyvodina (*see* Yugoslavia)

VPCP Volunteer Probation Counseling Program

Vridsloesellille Danish state prison noted for its programs for reducing recidivism; many foreign felons are held here for smuggling drugs into Denmark

Vulcano southernmost island in the Liparis off the north coast of Sicily in the Tyrrhenian Sea where it has served since Roman antiquity as a place of penal exile

Wacol HM Prison Wacol (Queensland, Australia)—near Brisbane where it is sometimes called the Bane of Brisbane

Wade Correctional Center medium-security facility in Haynesville northeast of Shreveport and close to the Arkansas border

Wailuki port city on Maui Island, Hawaii and where the Maui Community Correctional Center maintains facilities for male and female felons and misdemeanants since it was opened in 1973

Wakefield jails in Wakefield, Massachusetts, Michigan, or Rhode Island

Walden Correctional Institution in Columbia, South Carolina where it opened in 1951

Wales Wisconsin town just west of Milwaukee and address of the Ethan Allen School; (*see* United Kingdom and individual entries)

walk to be acquitted; to walk out of prison

Walker Correctional Institution in Rock Spring, Georgia holding male convicts in close security

wall firing wall (place of execution by a firing squad)

Walla Walla Washington State Penitentiary at Walla Walla close to the Oregon border in the southeastern section of Washington

Wallkill Wallkill Correctional Facility at Wallkill, New York north of Newburgh; originally designed as an experimental medium-security prison

Wallows Walla Walla, Washington or its jail

Wall-Wall nickname for the Washington State Penitentiary at Walla Walla

Walnut Street Philadelphia's oldest jail built in 1790; inmates were subjected to solitary confinement designed to prevent association with other prisoners and to promote reflection and self-reform

Walpole Massachusetts Correctional Institution at Walpole, southwest of Boston

Walton Liverpool, England's

Walton Prison

Walvis Bay (*see* Namibia)

Wanchai Hong Kong waterfront area frequented by many sailors and others in search of a Suzie Wong companion to share their rest and recreation activities; Hong Kong's Wanchai Police Station and lockup

Wandsworth prison in Wandsworth southwest of London; rated by inmates as the dirtiest in all England

warden(s) prison administrator(s)

wardress(es) female warden(s)

Ware Correctional Institution (*see* Waycross)

Warkworth Institution in Campbellford, Ontario northeast of Toronto

Warrensville Heights Ohio community just east of Cleveland and containing the Cayahoga Hills Boys School holding juvenile delinquents in medium security

Warsaw (*see* Poland)

Wartburg west of Knoxville, Tennessee and site of the recently completed Morgan County Regional Correctional Facility

Washington Corrections Center in Shelton, Washington northwest of Olympia which serves as a reception and diagnostic center and offers a reformatory-type educational program

Washington lockups 39 counties comprise the state and have jails from Ritzville in Adams County to Yakima in Yakima County; Seattle and Tacoma have area facilities for holding prisoners

Washington State Funnypark Washington State Prison near Walla Walla bears this nickname

Washington State Penitentiary in Monroe opened in 1908 to provide all degrees of security for male felons

Washington State Penitentiary in Walla Walla opened in 1887 and holding felons 16 years of age and up in all levels of custody

Washington State Reformatory opened in 1908 in Monroe to hold male felons in all degrees of custody

Washington State Special Offender Center in Monroe

where it was opened in 1980 to house and program troubled and troublesome adult male felons

watchhouse police station; police station lockup

Wateree River Correctional Institution in Rembert, South Carolina for felons and misdemeanants in minimum security

Watergate Hilton prisoners' nickname for the District of Columbia jail near the Robert F. Kennedy Stadium in Washington, DC

Watkins Pre-Release Center in Columbia, South Carolina since 1964

Waukegan Lake County county seat, courthouse, and jail north of Chicago on the shores of Lake Michigan and close to the Wisconsin border

Waupon Wisconsin town southwest of Fond du Lac and address of the Dodge Correctional Institution and the Waupon Correctional Institution

Waycross Georgia city at the north end of the Okefenokee Swamp and location of the Ware Correctional Institution for felons and misdemeanants held in close security

Wayne Wayne County Jail in Detroit, Michigan

Wayne Correctional Center in Goldsboro, North Carolina where it was opened in 1979 to care for medium-custody inmates needing psychiatric care

Wayne Correctional Institution (*see* Odum)

WCA Washington Correctional Association; Western Correctional Association; Wisconsin Correctional Association; Women's Correctional Association

WCS Wisconsin Correctional Service (in Milwaukee)

WCSC World Correctional Service Center (*q.v.*)

WDC Women's Detention Center

Weeks School at Vergennes, Vermont south of Burlington, designed to accommodate hard-to-handle male and female felons

Weisswasser forced-labor subcamp operated by the Nazis during their occupation of Czechoslovakia

Welfare Security Program guarantees safety of prisoners who provide useful information to prison authorities

Wellingborough HM Borstal at Wellingborough in Northamptonshire, England

Wellington Wellington Prison, Wellington, New Zealand

West Concord Massachusetts community west of Boston and site of the Massachusetts Correctional Institution with medium security for its inmates

Westerbork Dutch town near Assen and site of a Nazi concentration camp during World War II

Western Hong Kong's Western Street Police Station (and lockup)

Western Europe's Largest Prison Fleury Mergois on the outskirts of Paris from which two prisoners escaped via helicopter at the end of February 1981

Western State Penitentiary in Pittsburgh, Pennsylvania for more than a century but replaced by the State Correctional Institution and Correctional Diagnostic and Classification Center

Westfield Westfield Correctional Center in Westfield, Indiana just west of Noblesville

Westfield Farm New York Reformatory for Women

West Palm Beach Palm Beach County courthouse and jail serving this fast-growing Florida community

West Sam Western Samoa or its jail

West Street toponym for the Federal Detention Center facing the Hudson River on New York City's waterfront in past years

Westville Westville Correctional Center opened in 1977 in what was formerly a mental institution in this Indiana town south of Michigan City

West Virginia Industrial School for Boys in Grafton, south of Morgantown

West Virginia Industrial School for Girls started in 1899 in Salem, southwest of Clarksburg and east of Parkersburg

West Virginia jails 55 counties have lockups from Philippi in Barbour County to Pineville

in Wyoming County; there is also a city jail in Charleston

West Virginia Penitentiary built in Moundsville in 1866 and usually holding 680 felons in maximum security

West Virginia State Prison for Women built in 1948 in Pence Springs for felons 16 years of age and up

Wetherby HM Borstal at Wetherby in Yorkshire, England

Wethersfield Connecticut State Prison at Wethersfield

wets. wetbacks (undocumented Hispanic aliens who may get their backs wet while crossing the Rio Grande to enter the United States and avoid immigration officials)

Wha Wha Wha Wha Prison near Gwelo, Zimbabwe

WHD Women's House of Detention (New York City)

Wheeling Ohio County's seat in West Virginia where its jail is referred to as Wheeling

Whitehorse capital of the Yukon and location of the Whitehorse Correctional Centre holding felons and misdemeanants not too far from the Alaska border

White Street Manhattan House of Detention for Men at 125 White Street in New York City

Who will guard the guards? unanswered question propounded in the late 1490s by the Portuguese penologist Balboa da Zolá

Wichita Sedgwick County's county seat, courthouse, and jail are in the principal city of Kansas in its south-central location

Wilder Youth Development Center in Somerville, Tennessee for boys from 12 to 14 years of age

Wilingili penal settlement on an Indian Ocean coral atoll of the Maldive Islands southwest of Sri Lanka; Hammond Innes describes it as *that's where the bad boys go*

Wilkes-Barre Pennsylvania mining city in the northeastern part of the state just below Scranton and county seat of Luzerne County where inmates refer to the jail as Wilkes-Barre

William Head Institution in Victoria, British Columbia at the

southeastern tip of Vancouver Island

Wilmas (Mexican-Americanism—Wilmington, California)—and nickname for the penitentiary on nearby Terminal Island in Los Angeles Harbor

Wilmington Delaware's largest city located in the northeast corner of the state on the Delaware River; contains Bridge House for boys and girls in detention status, the county jail, the Ferris School for boy delinquents, the Pre-Trial Annex with maximum- and medium-security cells, the Plummer (work-release) Center

Windhoek (*see* Namibia)

Windsor Correctional Facility in Windsor, Vermont south of Lebanon

Winnipeg Manitoban city in the southeastern part of the province where in 1877 the Stony Mountain Institution was opened

Winson Green prison near Birmingham, England

Winston-Salem Winston-Salem, North Carolina, the seat of Forsyth County with its jail

wired addicted; electrocuted

Wisconsin Home for Women near Fond du Lac at Taycheedah

Wisconsin jails 72 counties provide prisons from Friendship in Adams County to Wisconsin Rapids in Wood County; Milwaukee has local as well as county jails

Wisconsin School for Girls in the south-central part of the state near Oregon, Wisconsin

Withank South African prison some 65 miles (105 kilometers) east of Pretoria in the Transvaal and northeast of Johannesburg

witness protection U.S. Marshals protect witnesses to organized crime whose lives and those of their families are jeopardized by their testimony

Witzwil Swiss prison farm without walls in the town of Witzwil

Women's Correctional Admission Center in Columbus, Ohio

Women's Correctional Center in Columbia, South Carolina since its inception in 1973

Women's Correctional Institution Claymont, Delaware's penal facility opened in 1975 close to the Pennsylvania border northeast of Wilmington

Women's Division current name for the Rhode Island Training School for Girls in Cranston

Women's Prison Association New York City-based service agency for prisoners; publishes *A Study in Neglect* about the plight of women in prison

Women's Reformatory officially The Women's Reformatory, opened in Rockwell City, Iowa in 1915

Women's Ward Oklahoma State Penitentiary at McAlester

Woodbourne Woodbourne Correctional Facility at Woodbourne, New York, southwest of Kingston, northwest of Newburgh

Woodburn south of Portland, Oregon and address of the MacLaren School for juvenile-court commitments

Woods Haven-Kruse School for Girls at Claymont, Delaware

Woodstock Correctional Facility in Woodstock, Vermont, east of Rutland

Wood Street Counter one of the most notorious of London's prisons in Elizabethan times although the Clink, Newgate, and Fleet did not lag far behind in cruel and inhumane practices

Workers' Paradise derisive nickname applied to the communist-controlled USSR whose propaganda led many people to believe it was the workers' paradise despite its thousands of prisons and millions of prisoners

workhouse originally meant a prison where the inmates had to work, if they wanted to eat; in Great Britain they picked oakum used for caulking ships or they sewed mailbags; in the United States a slang name for any prison as many required prisoners to work

Work Release Program rehabilitation plan whereby convicts work outside of prison during the last part of their term and receive the same pay as other workers

Work Training Facility Louisiana has two—one in New Orleans and the other in Pineville

Worland Wyoming town southwest of Sheridan and address of the Wyoming Industrial Institute

World Correctional Service Center Chicago-based information clearinghouse

World's Freest and Smallest Jail San Marino's hilltop lockup near Rimini on Italy's west coast where this tiny republic uses a converted monastery to hold its prisoners who, if sober, are allowed to work in town providing they keep out of bars, restaurants, and other public places as well as avoid meeting with one another or with other criminals; the San Marinesi pride themselves on the number of persons rehabilitated

World's Largest Prison Kharkhov in the Soviet Ukraine where more than 40,000 prisoners have been incarcerated at one time, according to figures published in the *Guiness Book of World Records*

World's Largest Walled Prison Southern Michigan Prison spanning 54 acres (22 hectares) and housing more than 5600 men in mid-1984

World's Most Gigantic Prison (*see* Most Gigantic Prison in the World)

Wormwood Scrubs English prison for young male offenders in the West London Stadium area

WPA (*see* Women's Prison Association)

WPA & H Women's Prison Association and Home

Wroclaw (*see* Poland)

WRP (*see* Work Release Program)

Wyantskill Wyantskill Center for Girls at Wyantskill, New York

Wyndham Wyndham Regional Prison (Western Australia)

Wynne Unit opened in 1899 in Huntsville, Texas where it holds felons in maximum custody

Wyoming Girls School in the north-central part of the state at Sheridan close to the Montana border

Wyoming Honor Farm in Riverton, maintained by its inmates in minimum security as befits its name

Wyoming Industrial Institute in Worland since its inception in 1915 and holding 10-to-21-year-old felons and juvenile delinquents

Wyoming lockups the state has 23 counties and jails from Laramie in Albany County to Newcastle in Weston County; Cheyenne has city and county detention facilities

Wyoming School for Girls in the north-central part of the state, close to the Montana border where it holds felons, juvenile delinquents, and misdemeanants from 18 to 21 years of age

Wyoming State Penitentiary in Rawlins since 1892 when it opened to hold male felons in all stages of security

Wyoming Womens Center in Evanston and holding its inmates in maximum, medium, or minimum security

xadrez (Brazilian-Portuguese—jail)

x'd executed

Xochi Xochimilco, outside Mexico City, or its lockup

X-ray apparatus used to detect contraband, letter bombs, parcel bombs, tools, or weapons

Xullas Xulla Islands (formerly the name of the Sulu Archipelago between Indonesia and the Philippines)—no data available concerning its jails, lockups, or other penal facilities

YACA (*see* Youth and Correctional Agency)

Yardville New Jersey town southeast of Trenton, containing the Youth Reception and Correction Center

YCA (*see* Youth and Correctional Agency)

YCC Youth Correctional Center

YCI Youth Correctional Institution (Bordentown, New Jersey)

Yakima Yakima County Jail in Yakima, Washington

Yaounde (*see* Cameroon)

yard prison yard

Yard Scotland Yard, London

yardbird(s) convict(s); ex-convict(s); jailbird(s); prisoner(s)

yard bull prison guard; railroad detective; railroad-yard policeman

Yaren (*see* Nauru)

YDI (*see* Youth Development Incorporated)

Yellowknife Correctional Centre in the capital of the Canadian Northwest Territories, north of Alberta

Yemen two Arab nations on the south coast of the Arabian Peninsula; South Yemen is communist controlled as its name indicates—People's Democratic Republic of Yemen, and its capital and seaport city is Aden; the other is the Yemen Arab Republic on the Red Sea coast of the Arabian Peninsula; its capital is Sanaa; both Yemens have penal facilities built when the Turks ruled all Arabia before the end of the World War I

YGC Youth Guidance Center (San Francisco)

Yoko Yokohama, Japan or its jail, lockup, and prison

Yokohama (*see* Japan's prisons)

Yokosuka Japan's naval base and lockup in Tokyo Bay south of Yokohama; U.S. Navy Fleet Activities Brig in Yokosuka (often mispronounced *Yokuska*); Yokosuka Prison housing hardened criminals and repeat offenders in Yokosuka, south of Nagoya on Japan's Honshu Island

Yokuska (*see* Yokosuka)

York community west of Lincoln, Nebraska and site of the Nebraska Center for Women

YOU Youthful Offender Unit

young adult penal institutions of the U.S. Bureau of Prisons El Reno, Oklahoma; Lompoc, California; Milan, Michigan; Oxford, Wisconsin; Petersburg, Virginia; Seagoville, Texas; Tallahassee, Florida

young horse prisoner's name for roast beef

Youngs Youngstown, Ohio and its jail

young stir boy's reformatory (nickname created by a punning youngster)

Youth and Correctional Agency combines California's Board of Prison Terms, California Youth Authority, Correctional Industries Commission, Department of Corrections, Institutional Review Board, Narcotic Addict Evaluation Authority, and Youthful Offender Control Board

youth and juvenile penal institutions of the U.S. Bureau of Prisons Ashland, Kentucky;

Englewood, Colorado; Morgantown, West Virginia

Youth Center at Atchison opened in 1885 as an orphanage and in 1972 as a facility for handling delinquent boys from 13 to 15½ years of age

Youth Center at Topeka opened in 1881 to handle some of the problems created by juvenile delinquents in Kansas

Youth Correctional Institutions two in New Jersey—one at Annadale, the other at Bordentown

Youth Development Center in Kearney, Nebraska where the building housing it was completed in 1881

Youth Development Centers throughout Pennsylvania at locations such as Bensalem Heights, Loysville, New Castle, Waynesburg

Youth Development Inc juvenile education and rehabilitation program

Youth Forestry Camp established in 1967 in Custer, South Dakota for youthful offenders from 15 to 21 years of age

Youth Forestry Camps in Pennsylvania places such as Hookstown, James Creek, and Whitehaven where they hold juvenile delinquents from 15 to 18 years of age

Youthful Offender Unit holds youthful offenders under age 25 in close security at Hardwick, Georgia

Youth Reception and Correction Center in Yardville, New Jersey

Youth Services Center at Saint Anthony, Idaho where it was opened in 1904 to detain juvenile offenders who are offered academic and vocation training courses in lieu of freedom

Youth Studies Center Philadelphia, Pennsylvania's juvenile correctional facility

Yps Ypsilanti, Michigan and its jail

Ypsilanti Michigan city southeast of Ann Arbor, containing the Huron Valley Men's Facility and the Huron Valley Women's Facility

YSA Youth Services Administration (District of Columbia)

YTS Youth Training School

Yugoslavia the Socialist Federal Republic of Yugoslavia created this nation made up of

old parts of the Austro-Hungarian Empire and the Kingdom of the Serbs, Croats, and Slovenes formed from old provinces—Bosnia, Croatia, Dalmatia, Herzegovina, Slovinia, and Voyvodina plus once independent Montenegro; Belgrade as its capital and other large cities include Zagreb, Skopje, Sarajevo, and Ljubljana; most of the prisons recall the days of the far-flung Austro-Hungarian Empire rather than more modern correctional trends; many are imprisoned for so-called crimes against the state and hence are political prisoners

Yuma Arizona city across the Colorado River from California and site of the Territorial Prison built in 1867, now a museum attracting many tourists

Yuma Territorial Prison State Historic Park open daily from 8:30 to 5:30 on the banks of the Colorado River in Yuma, Arizona

Zacatecas prison in Zacatecas, capital of the Mexican state of this name, northwest of San Luís Potosí

Zag Zagreb, Yugoslavia or its jail

Zagreb (*see* Yugoslavia)

Zaire formerly the Belgian Congo from 1878 to 1960 but more recently an independent nation in the heart of equatorial Africa where its capital is Kinshasa (formerly Leopoldville), its penal facilities date back to the days of colonial rule under Belgium

zak *zaklyuchenny* (Russian—prisoner)—pronounced *zek-kl'yew-chóhn-nee* although the contraction *zak* (pronounced *zek*) is used conversationally and in prison parlance and records

Zambia landlocked nation in southern Africa where it was once known as Northern Rhodesia; its capital is Lusaka; HM Gaol-type structures contain its convicts

Zambo Zamboanga, Mindanao, Philippines or its jail

Zanzi Zanzibar, Tanzania or its jail

Zaragoza Zaragoza, Chihuahua and its jail across the border from Ysleta, Texas; (*see*

Spain)

zek(s) [Soviet-Russian slang—prisoner(s)]

Zenith City of the Unsalted Seas colorful way of referring to Duluth, Minnesota on Lake Superior or its jail

zenkamono (Japanese—jailbirds; tramps)—the most despised elements of Japanese society; usually segregated into run-down sections of cities, such as the Sanya area of Tokyo

Zephyrhills Zephyrhills Correctional Institution at Zephyrhills, Florida northeast of Tampa, opened in 1977

Zero Route (see *La Route Zero*)

Zimb Zimbabwe (formerly Rhodesia) or its jails or prisons built by the British and by South Africans

Zimbabwe formerly Rhodesia or Southern Rhodesia; under British and South African direction it has become the 154th member of the United Nations; its capital city, Harare (formerly Salisbury), and Bulawayo have penal facilities superior to many on the African continent

zoo police station and its lockup in the parlance of the underworld

Zuchthaus *das Zuchthaus* (German—penitentiary; prison)

Zuchthaus arbeit (German—convict labor; prison labor)

Zuchthausler (German—convict)

Zuchthausstrafe (German—penal servitude)

Zürich (*see* Switzerland)

Zwodau forced-labor subcamp operated by the Germans during their occupation of Czechoslovakia during World War II

"Who will guard the guards?"
—*Balboa da Zola*

Numbered Items of Interest

1 No. 1 (urine); No. 1 diet (bread and water)

2 No. 2 (fecal matter)

2 Dzerzhinsky Moscow address of the KGB and the Lubyanka prison

3-Ds 3-Ds faced by many prisoners—discouragement, disillusionment, disappointment (often leads to suicide, experts insist)

3-Ps 3-Ps faced by every felon—prosecution, punishment, and persecution (often lifelong)

3rd Street New Jersey State Prison in Trenton on Third Street

3-U 3-U System (wherein the uneducated try to teach the unwilling to do the unnecessary)

4 level 4 (death-dealing dose or injection of breath-stopping barbital or other drug used by executioners)

4-d meat meat of dead, disabled, diseased, or dying animals (often served in jails and prisons)

5 don'ts don't kill, steal, commit adultery, become intoxicated, or lie, advised Buddah

7-d's deliriums, delusions, dementias, depressions, deviations, disorders, dreams; 7 deadly sins—anger, covetousness, envy, gluttony, lust, pride, sloth

7-year sentence Mexico's minimum sentence for trafficking in narcotics

10-year minimum Canada's minimum sentence for trafficking in narcotics

13 Gallery 13—prisoner's grave(yard)

20 percenters 20 percent of Sweden's jail population consists of foreign felons held for selling and smuggling drugs

32nd Street U.S. Navy Brig at 32nd Street in San Diego, California

71 71 West Van Buren Street in Chicago, Illinois (address of the Metropolitan Correctional Center)

84 naval prison

84 Ave Foch Paris headquarters of the Gestapo during the German occupation of Paris in World War II; its top floor contained cells and its lower floors housed offices and torture chambers

100 100 Centre Street—New York City headquarters of the Department of Correction

150 150 Park Row (address of the Metropolitan Correctional Center in downtown New York)

731 (*see* Unit 731)

732 732 Second Avenue in San Diego, California; in the early 1900s the county jail and more recently the brig and headquarters of the U.S. Navy Shore Patrol housed in an elegant one-story Greek-revival building now razed to make way for urban redevelopment; a new brig is at 32nd Street close to San Diego Bay

800 about 800 prisons in the United States are charged with the care and custody of convicts sentenced from a year to life or execution

808 808 Union Street (address of the Metropolitan Correctional Center in San Diego, California)

911 national emergency telephone number for dialing to report a fire, get the police, or call an ambulance; 911 Arthur Kill Road, Staten Island, New York, formerly the Drug Rehabilitation Center but now the Arthur Kill Correctional Facility

954 954 Forrest Street, Baltimore (address of the 172-year-old Maryland Penitentiary)

1854-1954 century-long life of the French Guiana penal colony popularly known as Cayenne or Devil's Island; world opinion about the inhumanities practiced here did much to stop its existence

1901 1901 D Street SE in Washington, DC and address of the Central Detention Facility

3000 missing 3000 missing Americans are in foreign jails; of these the State Department estimates about 75 percent are held on drug-related charges

3089 3089 counties, divisions, and parishes of the 50 United States having jails and lockups apart from city, federal, military, and state penal facilities; Alaska's divisions are much larger than most counties whereas Louisiana's parishes are equivalent to counties; all jails and lockups bear such old nicknames as brig, calaboose, calabozo, can, clink, cooler, coop, guardhouse, hoosegow, jug, tank, you know where, etc.

3320th 3320th Correction and Rehabilitation Squadron (CRS) at Lowry Air Force Base in Colorado

9653 Convict 9653 (antimilitarist American Socialist nominee for president, Eugene V Debs, when in the U.S. Penitentiary in Atlanta, Georgia)

22,445 petitions offered by prisoners seeking reviews of their cases (during 1982)

200,000 two-hundred-thousand missing persons in Argentina are allegedly imprisoned or killed by the military and police forces because of their opposition to the government but some have turned up in Costa Rica, Cuba, Czechoslovakia, Hungary, Italy, Nicaragua, Spain, El Salvador, and other disturbed or communist-dominated countries where their terrorist training is apparent in the headlines of many periodicals published in the late 1980s

2.5 million 2.5-million persons in the United States were under some form of correctional supervision, the U.S. Department of Justice revealed recently (1.2 million adults were on probation, 329,000 were in prison, 160,000 in jail, 220,000 on parole, 43,000 juveniles on probation, another 50,000 juveniles on parole)

Proofreader's Marks

‖ align; straighten ends of lines

⌄ apostrophe or single quotation mark

𝐛𝐟 black face or bold face type (run waved line under text matter)

⊗ broken type; damaged type; imperfect type

cap capital letter

≡ capital letters (run triple line under material to be capitalized: George Washington)

∧ caret; insertion mark

◡ close up

:/ colon

⋀ comma

𝓭 delete or dele; expunge; take out

⌴ depress or sink a letter or word

⌐ elevate or raise a letter or word

=/ hyphen

ital set in *italics* (material to be italicized is underlined)

lc lower case (run / through letter or letters to be set in ⌿ower ⌿ase)

lead insert lead spacing between lines

⊏ move to the left

⊐ move to the right

⁋ paragraph

⊙ period

⊥ push down space which prints as a mark

⌐⌐ quotation marks

rom set in roman type

;/ semicolon

sc small caps (run double line under material: a.d.)

space; # # double space; etc.

⑤ⓟ spell out (material to be spelled out is encircled: U.S.)

stet let stand that which has been deleted; restore crossed out material (indicate by running dots under the letters of the words to be restored)

𝓉𝓇 transpose (indicate in text by ∿ or ⌣)

℮ turn letter right side up

wf wrong font

Railroad Conductor's Cord-Pull Signals Plus Engineer's Whistle Signals

Cord-Pull Signals

1 short cord pull or 1 short whistle toot: apply brakes—stop
1 long whistle toot *when standing:* apply brakes or brakes applied
        when running: approaching grade crossing, junction, or station
2 long cord pulls or 2 long whistle toots: release brakes—proceed
3 short cord pulls or 3 short whistle toots *when standing:* back up
        when running: stop at next passenger station
4 short cord pulls or 4 short whistle toots: call for signals
succession of short cord pulls or short whistle toots: alarm or emergency such as persons or livestock on track; stop train until safe to proceed

Engineer's Whistle Signals

1 long toot followed by 3 short toots: flagman protect rear of train
3 short toots followed by 1 long toot: flagman protect front of train
4 long toots: flagman may return from west or south
5 long toots: flagman may return from east or north
1 short toot followed by 1 long toot: flagman inspect train for sticking brakes or leaks
2 long toots followed by a short toot and a long toot (*t o o t t o o t toot t o o t*): approaching curve, grade crossing, tunnel, or other obscure place; approaching a train standing on an adjacent track
1 long toot followed by a short toot (*t o o t toot*): blown when running against the current of traffic approaching curves, grade crossings, junctions, stations, and tunnels or obscure places

In the event of whistle failure, the bell must be rung continuously while the train is enroute.
When the train is approaching or leaving a station, the bell is rung to indicate the need for caution and to avoid the noise of the whistle.

Railroads of the World

This listing includes abbreviations, nicknames and reporting marks.

AA Ann Arbor Railroad
AAR Association of American Railroads
A & B Antofagasta and Bolivia
ABB Akron and Barberton Belt Railroad
ABL Alameda Belt Line
AC Algoma Central Railway
ACL Atlantic Coast Line (Seaboard Coast Line Railroad)
ACY Akron, Canton and Youngstown Railroad
AD Atlantic and Danville Railway
ADN Ashley, Drew and Northern Railway (also AD & N)
AEC Atlantic and East Carolina
AF Alma and Jonquieres Railway
AFE Administracion de los Fer-
rocarriles del Estado (Spanish—State Railways Administration)—Venezuela
AFL Administracion de los Ferrocarriles del Estado (Spanish—State Railways Administration)—Venezuela
AGS Alabama Great Southern (Southern Railway)
AL Almanor Railroad
ALM Arkansas and Louisiana Missouri Railway (also A & LM)
ALN Albany and Northern Railroad
ALQS Aliquippa and Southern
ALS Alton and Southern Railroad
AL & S Alton and Southern Railroad
Alton Route Gulf, Mobile and
Ohio Railroad
AMC Amador Central Railroad
AMR Arcata and Mad River
Amtrak American (railroad) tracks—(government-sponsored program for reviving city-to-city passenger service)
AN Apalachicola Northern Railroad
Ann Arbor Detroit, Toledo and Ironton Railroad
Annie & Mary (nickname— Arcata and Mad River Railroad)—originally the Union Wharf and Plank Walk Company
ANR Angelina and Neches River Railroad; Australian National Railways
APA Apache Railway Compa-

ny
APD Albany Port District
AR Aberdeen and Rockfish
ARA Arcade and Attica Railroad
ARC Alexander Railroad (Southern)
ARR Alaska Railroad
ART American Refrigerator Transit
ARW Arkansas Western Railway (Kansas City Southern)
A & S Abilene and Southern
ASAB Atlanta and Saint Andrews Bay Railway
ASDA Asbestos and Danville
ASLRA American Short Line Railroad Association
ASR Association of Southeastern Railroads
ATC Arnold Transit Company
ATN Albama, Tennessee and Northern Railroad
ATSF Atchison, Topeka and Santa Fe Railway (also AT & SF)
ATW Atlantic and Western
AUG Augusta Railroad
AUS Augusta and Summerville
Austrail Railways of Australia
AVL Aroostook Valley Railroad
AW Ahnapee and Western Railway
AWP Atlanta and West Point Rail Road (includes Western Railway of Alabama and Georgia Railroad)—also A & WP
AWW Algers, Winslow and Western Railway
A y B Antofagasta y Bolivia (Spanish—Antofagasta and Bolivia)—Chilean Railway linking Pacific port with highlands of landlocked Bolivia
AYSS Allegheny and South Side
ba BART (Bay Area Rapid Transit)
B & A Boston and Albany (Penn Central)
B-A-M Baikal-Amur-Magistral (railroad in Pacific Siberia, USSR)
BAP Butte, Anaconda and Pacific Railway (also BA & P)
BAR Bangor and Aroostook Railroad
BARC Baltimore and Annapolis Railroad Company
B & ARR Boston and Albany Railroad
BART Bay Area Rapid Transit (San Francisco Bay Area mass transportation system)

Bay Line Atlanta and Saint Andrews Bay Railway
BB Birmingham Belt Railroad
BCE Route British Columbia Electric Route
BCH British Columbia Hydro and Power Authority
BCK Buffalo Creek Railroad
BCK Bas-Congo au Katanga (French—Lower Congo—Katanga)—railway of Zaire
BCRR Boyne City Railroad
BCYR British Columbia Yukon Railway
BDZ (Cyrillic transliteration—Bulgarian State Railways)
BE Baltimore and Eastern Railroad (Penn Central)
BEDT Brooklyn Eastern District Terminal Railroad
BEEM Beech Mountain Railroad
BEM Beaufort and Morehead Railroad
Bessemer Bessemer and Lake Erie
BFC Bellefonte Central Railroad
BH Bath and Hammondsport Railroad
BHS Bonhomie and Hattiesburg Southern Railroad
Big Four Cleveland, Cincinnati, Chicago and St Louis Railway (Penn Central)
Birmingham Southern Birmingham Southern Railroad
BLA Baltimore and Annapolis
B & LE Bessemer and Lake Erie Railroad
BM Boston and Maine Corporation
BME Beaver, Meade and Englewood Railroad
BML Belfast and Moosehead Lake
BMRR Beech Mountain Railroad
B & MRR Beaufort and Morehead Railroad
BMT Brooklyn-Manhattan Transit (subway system)
BN Burlington Northern (combining Frisco—the St Louis-San Francisco with former Great Northern; Northern Pacific; Chicago, Burlington and Quincy; Spokane, Portland and Seattle; and Pacific Coast railroads)
B & N Bauxite and Northern Railway
BNT Buffalo Niagara Transit
B & O Baltimore and Ohio Railroad (Chessie System)
BOCT Baltimore and Ohio Chi-

cago Terminal Railroad
BOYC Boyne City Railroad
BR British Railways; Burma Railways
BRC Belt Railway Company of Chicago
BR & W Black River and Western
BS Birmingham Southern Railroad
B & S Bevier and Southern
BTA Boston Transportation Authority
BTC Baltimore Transit Company
BTN Belton Railroad
BU Budapest Underground (subway system)
Burlington Northern combining Great Northern; Northern Pacific; Chicago, Burlington and Quincy; Spokane, Portland and Seattle; and Pacific Coast railroads
Burlington Route Chicago, Burlington and Quincy Railroad
Burl N Burlington Northern and St Louis-San Francisco (railway merger)
BUSH Bush Terminal Railroad
BVG *Berliner Verkehrs Betriebe* (German—Berlin Traffic Management)—Berlin's subway system
BV & S Bevier and Southern
BWC Pennsylvania New York Central Transportation Company
BYR British Yukon Railway
CAD Cadiz Railroad
CAR Central Australia Railway
CARR Carrollton Railroad
CARW Caroline Western Railroad
CASO Canada Southern Railway (Penn Central)
CBC Carbon County Railway
CBL Conemaugh and Black Lick
CB & Q Chicago, Burlington and Quincy Railroad
C & C Columbia & Cowlitz
CC & C Cabedelo, Charleston & Coney Island
CCCSL Cleveland, Cincinnati, Chicago and St. Louis Railway (Penn Central)
CCFPCS Cie des Chemins de Fer de la Plaine du Cul-de-Sac (French—Cul-de-Sac Plaine Railroad Company)—Tahiti
CC & O Caroline, Clinchfield and Ohio Railway
CC & ORSC Caroline, Clinchfield and Ohio Railroad of South Carolina

CCR Corinth and Counce Railroad

CCT Central California Traction

C de F D-N Chemins de Fer Dakar-Niger (French—Dakar-Niger Railways)—Mali

C & El Chicago and Eastern Illinois Railroad

Central (nickname—New York Central Railroad)—now part of the Penn Central

Central of Ga Central of Georgia

CF Cape Fear Railways

CF C-O Chemin de Fer Congo-Ocean (French—Congo-Ocean Railroad)—Congo People's Republic (Brazzaville)

CFF/SFF/FFS Chemins de Fer Federaux Susses/Schweizerische Bundesbahnen/Ferrovie Dederali Svizzere (French, German, Italian—Swiss Federal Railways)

CFL Societe Nationale des Chemins de Fer Luxembourgeois (French—Luxembourg National Railways)

CFM Caminho de Ferro de Moçambique (Portuguese—Mozambique Railroad); *Chemin de Fer Madagascar* (French—Madagascar Railroad)

CFR Caile Ferate Ramane (Romanian—General Direction of the Romanian Railroads)

CFRC Chemins de Fer Royaux du Cambodge (French—Royal Cambodian Railways)

CG Central of Georgia Railway

C & G Columbus and Greenville

C of G Central of Georgia Railway

CGR Ceylon Government Railway; Cyrenaica Government Railway (Libya)

C & GTR Canada and Gulf Terminal Railway

CGW Chicago Great Western

C & H Cheswick and Harmer Railroad

Chessie System Chesapeake & Ohio/Baltimore & Ohio

Chicago Outer Belt Elgin, Joliet and Eastern Railway

Chihuahua-Pacific Railway *Ferrocarril del Chihuahua al Pacifico*—from the border of Texas at Presidio to the Pacific coast at Los Mochis via Chihuahua over route of the Kansas City, Mexico, and Orient

CH-P *Ferrocarril Chihuahua al Pacific* (Chihuahua-Pacific Railway formerly Mexico Northwestern Railway and Kansas City, Mexico and Orient Railway)

CHR Chestnut Ridge Railway

CHTT Chicago Heights Terminal Transfer Railroad

CHV Chattahoochee Valley

CHW Chesapeake Western

C & I Cambria and Indiana Railroad

CIC Cedar Rapids and Iowa City Railway

CIE Coras Iompair Eireann (Gaelic—Irish State Railways)

CI & L Chicago, Indianapolis, and Louisville Railway (Monon Railroad)

CIM Chicago and Illinois Midland Railway (also C & IM)

CIND Central Indiana Railway

CIRR Chattahoochee Industrial Railroad

C & IRR Cambria and Indiana Railroad

CIW Chicago and Illinois Western Railroad

CIWL Compangie Internationale des Wagon-Lits (French—International Sleeping Car Company)

CKSO Condon, Kinzua and Southern Railroad

CLC Colombia and Cowlitz

CLCO Claremont and Concord

Clinchfield Chinchfield Railroad (Carolina, Clinchfield and Ohio Railway)

CLK Cadillac and Lake City Railway

CLP Clarendon and Pittsford Railroad

CLRR Camp Lejeune Railroad

CMO Chicago, St Paul, Minneapolis and Omaha (Chicago North Western)

C M StP & P Chicago, Milwaukee, St Paul and Pacific

CN Canadian National (includes Canadian National Railways; Central Vermont Railway; Duluth, Winnipeg and Pacific Railway; Grand Trunk Lines in U.S.A.)

C & N Carolina and Northwestern Railway

CNJ Central Railroad of New Jersey

CN & L Columbia, Newberry and Laurens Railroad

CNO & TPR Cincinnati, New Orleans and Texas Pacific Railway

CNR Chiriqui National Railroad (Panama)

CNTP Cincinnati, New Orleans and Texas Pacific

CNW Chicago and North Western Railway (includes Chicago, St Paul, Minneapolis and Omaha; Litchfield and Madison Railway; Minneapolis and St Louis)

C & NW Chicago and North Western Railway

C & O Chesapeake and Ohio (Chessie System)

Coahuila-Zacatecas Railway Ferrocarril Coahuila-Zacatecas—Mexico

Cog Wheel Route Manitou and Pike's Peak Railway

Conrail Consolidated Rail Corporation (Ann Arbor, Central Railroad of New Jersey, Erie Lackawanna, Lehigh and Hudson River, Lehigh Valley, Penn Central, Reading)

COP City of Prineville Railway

COPR Copper Range Railroad

Corn Belt Route St Louis Southwestern Railway

Cotton Belt Cotton Belt Route (St Louis Southwestern Railway—SSW)

CP Canadian Pacific Railway (Dominion Atlantic Railway, Esquimalt and Nanaimo Railway, Grand River Railway, Lake Erie and Northern Railway, Quebec Central Railway, Vancouver and Lulu Island Branch)

CP Companhia des Caminhos de ferro Portuguese (Portuguese—Portuguese Railways)

CPA Coudersport and Port Allegany Railroad

CPF Cotton Plant—Fargo Railway

CP & LT Camino, Placerville and Lake Tahoe Railroad

CPR Canadian Pacific Railroad

CP Rail Canadian Pacific Railroad

CPT Chicago Produce Terminal

CR Commonwealth Railways (Australia and Tasmania); Copper Range Railroad (Michigan, Wisconsin, Illinois)

CRANDIC Route Cedar Rapids and Iowa City Railway

CRC Cameroon Railways Corporation (West Africa); Cumberland Railway Company (Nova Scotia)

CRI Chicago River and India-

na
CR & IC Cedar Rapids and Iowa City Railway
CR & IR Chicago River and Indiana Railroad
CRN Carolina and Northwestern (Southern Railway)
CRP Central Railway of Peru
CRR Clinchfield Railroad
CRRNJ Central Railroad of New Jersey
C & S Colorado and Southern Railway
CSAR Central South African Railways
CSD *Cekoslovenske Statni Drahy* (Czechoslovakian—Czechoslovak State Railways)
CSL Chicago Short Line Railway
CSP Camas Prairie Railroad
CSS Chicago South Shore and South Bend Railroad
CSS & SBR Chicago South Shore and South Bend Railroad
C St P M & O Chicago, St Paul, Minneapolis and Omaha (Chicago North Western)
CSX Chessie and Seaboard (railroads consolidated)
CTA Chicago Transit Authority (elevated and subway railroads)
CTC Canadian Transport Commission; Cincinnati Transit Company
CTN Canton Railroad
CTS Cleveland Transit System
CUTC Cincinnati Union Terminal Company
CUVA Cuyahoga Valley Railroad
CV Central Vermont Railway
CVRy Cuyahoga Valley Railway
C & W Colorado and Wyoming Railway
C & WC Charleston and Western Carolina Railway (Seaboard Coast Line Railroad)
CWI Chicago and Western Indiana
CWP Chicago, West Pullman and Southern Railroad (also CWP & S)
CWR California Western Railroad
DA Dominion Atlantic Railway (Canadian Pacific)
DB *Deutsche Bundesbahn* (German—German Railways)
DC Delray Connecting Railroad
DCI Des Moines and Central Iowa

DCR Delray Connecting Railroad (Zug Island Road)
DCT Washington, DC Transit
D & E De Queen and Eastern
Delay Long and Wait nickname for the Delaware, Lackawanna and Western Railroad (derived from the initials DL & W)
D & H Delaware and Hudson
DHR Darjeeling Himalayan Railway
diner dining car
DKS Doniphan, Kensett and Searcy Railway
DL & W Delaware, Lackawanna and Western Railroad (Erie Lackawanna)
D & M Detroit and Mackinac
DM & IRR Duluth, Missabe and Iron Range Railway
DMM Dansville and Mount Morris
DMU Des Moines Union Railway
DMWR Des Moines Western Railway
DNE Duluth and Northeastern Railroad
DO Direct Orient (Orient Express)
$oo Soo Line Railroad
DORR Delaware Otsego Railroad
DQ & ERR De Queen and Eastern Railroad
D & R Dardanelle and Russellville
D & RGW Denver and Rio Grande Western Railroad
DRI Davenport, Rock Island and North Western Railway
DRy Devco Railway
DS Durham and Southern Railway
D & S Durham and Southern Railway
DSB *Danske Statsbaner* (Danish—Danish State Railways)
DSR Detroit Street Railways
DT Detroit Terminal Railroad
D of T Department of Transportation
DTC Dallas Transit Company
DTI Detroit, Toledo and Ironton Railroad (also DT & I)
D & TS Detroit and Toledo Shore Line Railroad
DVS Delta Valley and Southern Railway
DWP Duluth, Winnipeg and Pacific Railway
E Erie Lackawanna
EAR East African Railways
EARC East African Railways Corporation

EAR & H East African Railways and Harbours
EBR Emu Bay Railway (Tasmania)
EBRy Eastern Bengal Railway (East Pakistan)
EDLR Egyptian Delta Light Railways
EDW El Dorado and Wesson
EEC East Erie Commercial Railroad
EFA *Empresa Ferrocarriles Argentinos* (Spanish—Argentine Railways Enterprise)
EFE *Empresa de los Ferrocarriles del Estado* (Spanish—State Railways Enterprise)—Chile
EFEE *Empresa de los Ferrocarriles del Estado Ecuatoriano* (Spanish—Ecuadorian State Railways Enterprise)
EJ & ERy Elgin, Joliet and Eastern Railway
EJR East Jersey Railroad
El Elevated Railroad
EL Erie Lackawanna Railway (merger of Erie with Delaware, Lackawanna and Western)
ELS Escanaba and Lake Superior Railroad (also E & LSRR)
E & M Edgmoor and Manetta
EN Esquimalt and Nanaimo Railway (Canadian Pacific)
ENF *Empresa Nacional de Ferrocarriles* (Spanish—National Railways Enterprise)—Bolivia
ER Egyptian Railways
ERBR Eastern Region of British Railways
Erie Erie Railroad (Erie Lackawanna)
ESLJ East St Louis Junction Railroad
ETL Essex Terminal Railway
ET & WNC East Tennessee and Western North Carolina Railroad
Eurailpass European railroad pass (ticket system valid on almost all European railroads)
EW East Washington Railway
EYB *Europa Year Book*
F & C Frankfort and Cincinnati Railroad
FCAB *Ferrocarril Antofagasta-Bolivia* (Spanish—Antofagasta and Bolivia Railway)
FC del P *Ferrocarril Central del Perú* (Spanish—Central Railway of Peru)
FCDN *Ferrocarril del Nacozari* (Spanish—Nacozari Rail-

road)—Mexico

FCG Fernwood, Columbia and Gulf Railroad

FCIN Frankfort and Cincinnati

FCM *Ferrocarriles Nacionales de México* (Spanish—Mexican National Railways)—includes Nacional de México and Nacional de Tehuantepec

FCNM *Ferrocarriles Nacionales de México* (Spanish—National Railroads of Mexico)

FCP *Ferrocarril del Pacifico* (Spanish—Pacific Railroad)—links Arizona border with Mazatlan on west coast of Mexico

FCZ *Ferrocarril Coahuila-Zacatecas* (Spanish—Coahuila-Zacatecas Railway)—Mexico

FDDM Fort Dodge, Des Moines and Southern Railway

F *de C Ferrocarriles de Cuba* (Spanish—Cuban Railroads)—Unidad Habana (western Cuba) and Unidad Camaguey (eastern Cuba)

F *de G a LP Ferrocarril de Guayaquil-La Paz* (Spanish—Guayaquil-La Paz Railway)—Peru

F *del N Ferrocarriles del Norte* (Spanish—Northern Railways)—Paraguay

F *del P Ferrocarril del Pacifico* (Spanish—Pacific Railroad)—Mexico

Feather River Route Western Pacific Railroad

FEC Florida East Coast Railway

FEGUA *Ferrocarriles de Guatemala* (Spanish—Railroads of Guatemala)

FEP *Ferrocarril Electrico al Pacifico* (Spanish—Pacific Electric Railway)—Costa Rican line linking Pacific port of Puntarenas with mountain capital of San José

FEPASA *Federação Paulista Sedada Anomina* (Portuguese—Paulist Federation Company)—Brazilian railroad

FER Franco-Ethiopian Railway

FES *Ferrocarril de El Salvador* (Spanish—El Salvador Railway)

FFAC *Federação Ferrocarril Agricola Cotias* (Portuguese—Agricultural Cooperative Railway Federation)—Brazil

FICA *Ferrocarriles Internacionales de Centro America* (Spanish—International Railways

of Central America)

FIPC *Ferrocarril Industrial del Potosí y Chihuahua* (Spanish—Industrial Railroad of Potosi and Chihuahua)—Mexico

FJG Fonda, Johnstown and Gloversville Railroad

FLR Fayum Light Railways (Egypt)

FMS Fort Myers Southern Railroad

FN *Ferrocarriles Nacionales* (Spanish—National Railways—Argentina, Chile, Colombia, Cuba, Ecuador, Honduras, Mexico, Panama, Venezuela, etc.)

FNC *Ferrocarriles Nacionales de Cuba* (National Railroad of Cuba nationalized by Castro government and consisting of Consolidated Railroads of Cuba, The Cuba Railroad, Cuba Northern Railways, Guantanamo and Western Railroad, Guantanamo Railroad, Hershey Cuban Railway, etc.)

FN *de H Ferrocarriles Nacionales de Honduras* (Spanish—National Railways of Honduras)

FNM *Ferrocarriles Nacionales de México* (Spanish—National Railways of Mexico)

FOM *Ferrocarril Occidental de México* (Spanish—Western Railway of Mexico)

FOR Fore River Railroad

FPCAL *Ferrocarriles President Carlos Antonio López* (Spanish—President Carlos Antonio Lopez Railways)—Paraguay

FPE Fairport, Painesville and Eastern Railroad

FP & ER Fairport, Painesville and Eastern Railway

FPN *Ferrocarril del Pacifico de Nicaragua* (Spanish—Pacific Railway of Nicaragua)

FR Feather River Railway

FRDN Ferdinand Railroad

Frisco St Louis-San Francisco Railway

FS *Ferrovie dello Stato* (Italian—State Railway)

FSBC Ferrocarril Sonora-Baja California (Sonora-Baja California Railroad)

FS *del P Ferrocarril del Sur del Perú* (Spanish—Southern Railway of Peru)

FSVB Fort Smith and Van Buren Railway (Kansas City

Southern)

FtD DM & S Fort Dodge, Des Moines and Southern Railway

FUD *Ferrocarriles Unidos Dominicanos* (Spanish—United Dominican Railways)—Dominican Republic

FUS Ferrocarriles Unidos del Sureste (United Railways of the Southeast)

FUY *Ferrocarriles Unidos de Yucatan* (Spanish—United Railways of Yucatan)—Mexico

FWB Fort Worth Belt Railway

FW & D Fort Worth and Denver

GA Georgia Railroad

GANO Georgia Northern Railway

GASC Georgia, Ashburn, Sylvester and Camilla Railway

GB & W Green Bay and Western Lines (includes Kewaunee, Green Bay and Western Railroad)

GC Graham County Railroad

GCW Garden City Western Railway

George Washington's Railroad Chesapeake and Ohio

Georgia Georgia Railroad

G & F Georgia and Florida Railway

GFS Grand Falls Central Railway

GH & H Galveston, Houston and Henderson Railroad

GJ Greenwich and Johnsonville Railway

G & J Greenwich and Johnsonville Railway

GM Gainesville Midland Railroad

GM & O Gulf, Mobile and Ohio Railroad

GMRC Green Mountain Railroad Corporation

GN Great Northern Railway

GNA Graysonia, Nashville and Ashdown Railroad

GNW Genessee and Wyoming Railroad

GNWR Genessee and Wyoming Railroad

GO Transit Government of Ontario Transit

G & Q Guayaquil and Quito

Grand Trunk Grand Trunk Railway System (Canadian National) and Grand Trunk Western Railroad

Green Bay Route Green Bay and Western Railroad

GRN Greenville and Northern

Railway

GRNR Grand River Railway (Canadian Pacific)

GR & PA Ghana Railway and Port Authority

GRR Georgetown Railroad

GRSS Guyana Railways and Shipping Services

GSF Georgia Southern and Florida (Southern)

GSW Great Southwest Railroad

GTW Grand Trunk Western Railroad (Canadian National)

G&U Grafton and Upton Railroad

GWF Galveston Wharves

GWR Great Western Railway

GWWDR Great Winnipeg Water District Railway

HB Hampton and Branchville

HBLRR Harbor Belt Line Railroad

HBS Hoboken Shore Railroad

HBT Houston Belt and Terminal

HE Hollis and Eastern Railroad

HER Hellenic Electric Railway (Athens-Piraeus subway system linking capital with its seaport)

HH Hamburger Hochbahn (German—Hamburg Elevated Railway)—includes subway system

III Holton Inter-Urban Railway

HJR Hedjaz Jordan Railway

HLNE Hillsboro and Northeastern

HN Hutchinson and Northern Railway

HNE Harriman and Northeastern (Southern)

hovertrain railroad train supported by an air cushion instead of wheels

HPTD High Point, Thomasville and Denton Railroad

HRT Hartwell Railway

HS Hartford and Slocomb Railroad

HSW Helena Southwestern Railroad

HTW Hoosac Tunnel and Wilmington Railroad

i Illinois Central Gulf Railroad

IAT Iowa Terminal Railroad

IB&TC International Bridge and Terminal Company

IC Illinois Central Gulf (includes Mississippi Central)

ICC Interstate Commerce Commission

ICG Illinois Central Gulf

IGA Indian Government Administration (Railway Board of India)

IHB Indiana Harbor Belt Railroad

IN Illinois Northern Railway

IND Independent (New York subway system)

Indiana Harbor Belt "connects with all Chicago railroads"

Industrial Railway of Potosí and Chihuahua (Ferrocarril Industrial del Potosí y Chihuahua)—Mexico

INT Interstate Railroad

Interstate Interstate Railroad

IPE Indian-Pacific Express [Perth to Sydney—2461 miles (3960 kilometers) in 65 hours]

IR Israel Railways

IRCA International Railways of Central America (El Salvador, Guatemala, and Honduras)

IRN Ironton Railroad

IRRys Iraqi Republic Railways

IRS Iranian State Railway

IRT Interborough Rapid Transit (New York City subway system)

ITC Illinois Terminal Company

ITRC Iowa Transfer Railway Company

IU Indiana Union Railway

JE Jerseyville and Eastern

Jersey Central Lines Central Railroad of New Jersey and Lehigh and New England

JHSC Johnstown and Stony Creek Railroad

JNR Japanese National Railways (world's fastest)

JRC Jamaica Railway Corporation

JTC Jacksonville Terminal Company

JWR Jane's World Railways

Katy Missouri-Kansas-Texas Railroad (MKT)

KBR Kankakee Belt Route

KCC Kansas City Connecting Railroad

KCMO Kansas City, Mexico and Orient Railway (Ferrocarril Chihuahua al Pacifico)

KCNW Kelley's Creek and Northwestern Railroad

KCPSFO Kansas City Public Service Freight Operation

KCR Kanawha Central Railway

K-C Ry Kowloon-Canton Railway (Hong Kong)

KCS Kansas City Southern Railway (includes Arkansas Western, Fort Smith and Van Buren, Louisiana and Arkansas railways)

KCT Kansas City Terminal Railway

KGB Kewaunee, Green Bay and Western Railroad (Green Bay and Western Lines)—also KGB&W

KIT Kentucky and Indiana Terminal Railroad

K&M Kansas and Missouri Railway and Terminal Company

KMRT Kansas and Missouri Railway and Terminal Company

KNR Klamath Northern Railway; Korean National Railways

KO&G Kansas, Oklahoma and Gulf Railway

KRI Kyle Railway Inc

K&T Kentucky and Tennessee

KTM Keretapi Tanah Malayu (Malayan Railway)

Kyle Kyle Railway

L&A Louisiana and Arkansas Railway (Kansas City Southern)—also LA

LAJ Los Angeles Junction Railway

LA&LR Livonia, Avon and Lakeville Railroad

LAMCO Liberian America Swedish Minerals Company (Liberian Railways)

Land of Evangeline Route Dominion Atlantic Railway

LART Los Angeles Rapid Transit

LAWV Lorain and West Virginia Railway (North and Western)

LBR Lowville and Beaver River Railroad

L&C Lancaster and Chester Railway

LEE Lake Erie and Eastern Railroad

LEF Lake Erie, Franklin and Clarion Railroad

LE&FW Lake Erie and Fort Wayne

LEN Lake Erie and Northern Railway (Canadian Pacific)

LHR Lehigh and Hudson River

LI Long Island Railroad (Metropolitan Transportation Authority)—M

Lickenpurr (Hawaiian nickname—Lahaina-Kaanapal and Pacific Rail Road)—nickname derived from abbreviations—LK & PRR

LIRR Long Island Rail Road

LK & PRR Lahaina-Kaanapal and Pacific Rail Road (Maui, Hawaii)

LM Litchfield and Madison Railway (Chicago North Western)—also L&M

LM Leningrad Metro (Russian—Leningrad subway)

LMC Liberia Mining Company

LMRBR London Midland Region of British Railways

L&N Louisville and Nashville Railroad

LNAC Louisville, New Albany and Corydon Railroad

LNE Lehigh and New England Railway (Central Railroad of New Jersey)

L&NR Ludington and Northern Railway

L&NRY Laona and Northern Railway

L&NW Louisiana and North West Rail Road

LOPG Live Oak, Perry and Gulf (Southern)

LPB Louisiana and Pine Bluff Railway

LPN Longview, Portland and Northern Railway

LRB London Transport Board

lrc (LRC) light, rapid, comfortable (high-speed railroad trains)

LRI Lawndale Transportation Company

LRS Laurinburg and Southern

L&S Laurinburg and Southern

LS&BC La Salle and Bureau County Railroad

LS&I Lake Superior and Ishpeming Railroad

LSO Louisiana Southern Railway (Southern)

LSR Lebanese State Railroads

LST&TRC Lake Superior Terminal and Transfer Railway Company

LT Lake Terminal Railroad (also LTRR)

LV Lehigh Valley Railroad

LW Louisville and Wadley Railway

L&W Louisville and Wadley Railway

LWV Lackawanna and Wyoming Valley Railway

M Metropolitan Transit Authority (New York City's rapid-transit system); Metropolitan Transportation Authority (Long Island Railroad); Monon Railroad

MA Magyan Allamvasutak (Hungarian—Hungarian State Railways)

MACR Minneapolis, Anoka and Guyana Range Railroad

Main Line of Mid-America Illinois Central Railroad

MARR Magma Arizona Railroad

M-A Ry Massawa-Agordad Railway (Ethiopia)

M&B Meridan and Bigbee Railroad

MBI Marianna and Bloustown Railroad

MBT Marianna and Blountstown

MBTA Massachusetts Bay Transportation Authority (Boston's subway system)

MC Michigan Central Railroad (Penn Central)

McR McCloud River Railroad

MCRR Main Central Rail Road; Monongahela Connecting Railroad

MCSA Moscow, Camden and San Augustine Railroad

MD Municipal Docks Railway of the Jacksonville Port Authority

M del P Méxicano del Pacifico (Mexican Pacific Railroad formerly Southern Pacific of Mexico)

MD&W Minnesota, Dakota and Western Railway

M&E Morristown and Erie Railroad

MEC Maine Central Railroad

MER Metropolitan Elevated Railroad

METC Medesto and Empire Traction Company

Metro (French short form—*Chemin de fer Metropolitain*)—Paris subway system

Metropolitano Rome's subway system

Mexican Pacific Railroad Ferrocarril Mexicano del Pacifico—Los Mochis to Camp

MF Middle Fork Railroad

MGA Monongahela Railway

MGU Mobile and Gulf Railroad

MHM Mount Hope Mineral Railroad

M&HMRR Marquette and Huron Mountain Railroad

MI Missouri-Illinois Railroad

MICO Midland Continental Railroad

MID Midway Railroad

MILW Chicago, Milwaukee, St Paul and Pacific Railroad (Milwaukee Road)

MINE Minneapolis Eastern Railway

MIR Minneapolis Industrial Railway

Mitropa *Mitteleuropaische Schlaf und Speiswagen* (German—Middle-European Sleeping Car and Dining Car)

MJ Manufacturers' Junction Railway

MKC McKeesport Connecting Railroad

MKT Missouri-Kansas-Texas Railroad (Katy)

MLD Midland Railway of Manitoba

MLS Manistique and Lake Superior Railroad

MMR Moscow Metro Railway (Moscow's radiating subway system famed for its beautiful stations)

MNCRR Metro-North Commuter Railroad

MNF Morehead North Fork Railroad

MNJ Middletown and New Jersey Railway

MNS Minneapolis, Northfield and Southern Railway

MOB Montreux-Oberland-Bernois (railway)

MON Monon Railroad

Monon Monon Railroad (formerly Chicago, Indianapolis and Louisville Railway)

Mon Rys Mongolian Railways

Montour Montour Railroad (Youngstown and Southern Railway)

MOP Missouri-Pacific Lines

Mo-Pac Missouri-Pacific Lines

MOV Moshassuck Valley Railroad

MOW Montana Western Railway

MP Missouri Pacific Railroad

MPA Maryland and Pennsylvania

MPB Montpelier and Barre Railroad

MPPR Manitou and Pike's Peak Railway

MR McCloud River Railroad (also McRRR)

M of R Ministry of Railways (mainland China)

MRA Malayan Railway Administration

MRL Malawi Railways Limited

MRR Mattagami Railroad (Ontario); Mossi Railroad (Upper Volta)

MRS Manufacturers Railway

MRy Malayan Railway

MSC Mississippi Central (Illinois Central)

MSE Mississippi Export Railroad

M St L Minneapolis and St. Louis (Chicago North Western)

M&StL Minneapolis-St Louis (Chicago North Western)

MSTL Minneapolis-St Louis (Chicago North Western)

MSTR Massena Terminal Railroad

MSV Mississippi and Skuna Valley Railroad

MT Ministry of Transport (USSR's administration of twenty-six railway lines including the de-luxe Leningrad-Moscow and the transcontinental Trans-Siberian linking Moscow with Vladivostok)

MTC Milwaukee Transport Company; Montreal Transportation Commission (subway and surface railways); Mystic Terminal Company (Boston and Maine)

MTFR Minnesota Transfer Railroad

MTH Mount Hood Railway

MTR Montour Railroad

MTW Marinette, Tomahawk and Western Railroad

MTWCR Mt Washington Cog Railway

MWR Muncie and Western Railroad

NAJ Napierville Junction Railway

NAP Narragansett Pier Railroad

NAR Northern Alberta Railways; Northern Australia Railway

National Railroads of Cuba Ferrocarriles Nacionales de Cuba (includes nationalized lines of the Cuba Railroad, Cuba Northern Railways, Guantanamo Railroad, Guantanamo Western, Hershey Cuban Railway, etc.)

National Railways of Mexico Ferrocarriles de México

NB Northampton and Bath Railroad

NC & StL Nashville, Chattanooga and St Louis Railway (L&N)

N de M Nacional de México (National of Mexico)

N de T Nacional de Tehuantepec (Tehuantepec National)

New Haven New York, New Haven and Hartford Railroad

NEZP Nezperce Railroad

NFD Norfolk, Franklin and Danville Railway

NGR Nepalese Government Railway

NH New York, New Haven and Hartford Railroad (Penn Central)

NHIR New Hope and Ivyland Railroad

Nickel Plate New York, Chicago and St Louis Railroad (merged with Norfolk and Western)

NJ Niagara Junction Railway

NJI&I New Jersey, Indiana and Illinois Railroad

NKP Nickel Plate (New York, Chicago and St Louis Railroad)—merged with Norfolk and Western

NLC New Orleans and Lower Coast Railroad

NLG North Louisiana and Gulf Railroad

NM Nagoya Municipality (subway system)

NN Nevada Northern Railway

NNC Northern Navigation Company

NO de M Noroeste de México (Northwestern of Mexico)

NODM Ferrocarril Noroeste de México (Northwest Railway of Mexico—Ferrocarril Chihuahua al Pacifico)

NONE New Orleans and Northeastern Railroad (Southern)

NOPB New Orleans Public Belt Railroad

NOPS New Orleans Public Service

Norf S Norfolk Southern, Norfolk & Western, Southern Railway (merger)

NP Northern Pacific Railway

N&PB Norfolk and Portsmouth Belt Line Railroad

NR Newfoundland Railway (Canadian National); Northern Railway of Costa Rica (from mountain capital of San José to Caribbean seaport of Limón)

NRC Nigerian Railway Corporation

NRPC National Railroad Passenger Corporation (Amtrak)

NRRC National Railroad Company (of Haiti)

NS Norfolk Southern Railway

NS *Nederlandsche Spoorwagen* (Dutch—Netherlands Railway Carriage)—Netherlands Railways

NSB *Norges Statsbaner* (Norwegian—Norwegian State Railways)

NSL Norwood and St Lawrence Railroad

NSS Newburgh and South Shore Railway

NSWGR New South Wales Government Railways

NUR Natchez, Urania and Ruston Railway

NW Norfolk and Western

N&W Norfolk and Western Railway

NWP Northwestern Pacific Railroad

NWRy North Western Railway (West Pakistan)

NWS Norfolk & Western Southern (merger)

NYC New York Central Railroad (Penn Central)

NYCTA New York City Transit Authority (subway systems include BMT, IRT, INDependent)

NYD New York Dock Railway

NYLB New York and Long Branch Railroad

NYNH&H New York, New Haven and Hartford Railroad

NYS *Nepal Yatayat Samsthan* (Nepali—Transport Corporation of Nepal)

NYSW New York, Susquehanna and Western Railroad (NYS&W)

NZGR New Zealand Government Railways

NZR New Zealand Railways

OCE Oregon, California and Eastern Railway

OE Oregon Electric Railway (Spokane, Portland, and Seattle Railway)

OGR *Official Guide of the Railways*

OKT Oakland Terminal Railway

OL&BR Omaha, Lincoln and Beatrice Railway

OMTB Osaka Metropolitan Transportation Bureau (subway system)

ONCF *Office National des Chemins de Fer* (French—National Railways Office)—Morocco

ONRY Ogdensburg and Norwood Railway

ONT Ontario Northland Railway

ONW Oregon and Northwestern

O&NW Oregon and Northwestern

ÖOB *Österreichischen Bundesbahnen* (German—Austrian State Railways)

OPE Oregon, Pacific and Eastern

ORER *Official Railway Equipment Register*

OT Oregon Trunk Railway (Spokane, Portland, and Seattle Railway)

OUR & D Ogden Union Railway and Depot

Overland Route Union Pacific Railroad

PA Pittsburgh Authority (rapid transit)

PAA Pennsylvania and Atlantic Railroad

PACC Pacific Coast Railroad

Pacific Railroad Ferrocarril del Pacifico (linking American border at Nogales with Mazatlan on Pacific coast of Mexico)

Pacific Railway of Costa Rica from Pacific port of Puntarenas to San José

Pacific Railways of Nicaragua Ferrocarril del Pacifico de Nicaragua—from Corinto on the Pacific to Granada on Lake Nicaragua

Pac Rail Missouri Pacific, Union Pacific, Western Pacific (merged)

PA&M Pittsburgh, Allegheny and McKees Rocks Railroad

Panama Railroad division of the Panama Canal linking Cristóbal and Colón on the Atlantic with Balboa and Panama City on the Pacific and running parallel to the Panama Canal

P & AR Pacific and Arctic Railway

PATCO (transportation system linking Camden, New Jersey and Philadelphia, Pennsylvania)

PATH Port Authority Trans-Hudson Corporation (operates Hudson Tubes between New Jersey and New York)

PBNE Philadelphia, Bethlehem and New England Railroad

PBR Patapsco and Back Rivers

PC Penn Central (Pennsylvania New York Central Transportation Company; Pennsylvania Railroad; New York Central Railroad; New York, New Haven, and Hartford Railroad; Baltimore and Eastern Railroad; Canada Southern Railway; Cleveland, Cincinnati, Chicago and St Louis Railway; Michigan Central Railroad; Peoria and Eastern Railway; Waynesburg and Wash-

ington Railroad)

PCL Peruvian Corporation Limited

PCN Point Comfort and Northern

PCR Paraguayan Central Railway

PCY Pittsburgh, Chartiers and Youghiogheny Railway

PE Pacific Electric (interurban railway system serving entire Los Angeles area before replacement by smog-producing buses); Pacific Electric Railway of Costa Rica (links Pacific seaport of Puntarenas with mountain capital of San José)—also called *FEP*

P&E Peoria and Eastern Railway (Penn Central)

Pennsy (nickname—Pennsylvania Railroad)—now part of the Penn Central

Peoria Peoria and Pekin Union Railway

P&F Pioneer and Fayette Railroad

PGE Pacific Great Eastern Railway

PH&D Port Huron and Detroit Railroad

P&I Paducah and Illinois Railroad

PIC Pickens Railroad

Pick Pickens Railroad

Pickens Pickens Railroad

PKP *Polskie Koleje Panstwowe* (Polish—Polish State Railways)

P&LE Pittsburgh and Lake Erie Railroad

PLM Paris-Lyon-Mediterranée

P&N Piedmont and Northern Railway

PNKA *Perusahaan Negara Kereta Api* (Indonesian—Indonesian State Railways)

PNR Philippine National Railways

PNW Prescott and Northwestern Railroad

Port St Joe Route Apalachicola Northern Railroad

'Possum Trot Line Reader Railroad

POV Pend Oreille Valley

P&OV Pittsburgh and Ohio Valley

POVA Pend Oreille Valley (railway)

P&PU Peoria and Pekin Union

PR Panama Railroad

P-R Pennsylvania-Reading Seashore Lines

PRC Philippine Railway Company

PRCR Pacific Railway Costa Rica

PRR Pennsylvania Railroad (Penn Central)

PRS Pennsylvania-Reading Seashore Lines

PRTD Portland Railroad and Terminal Division of the Portland Traction Company

PRV Pearl River Valley Railroad

PS Pittsburg and Shawmut Railroad

P&SR Petaluma and Santa Rosa

PTC Peoria Terminal Company; Philadelphia Transportation Company (also called PATCO includes elevated and subway lines of Philadelphia area)

PTM Portland Terminal Company

PTR Parr Terminal Railroad

PTS Port Townsend Railroad

Pullman de-luxe railroad cars providing lounging, observation, and sleeping facilities aboard first-class express trains

PVS Pecos Valley Southern

P&WV Pittsburgh and West Virginia Railway (Norfolk and Western)

P y RV *Potosí y Rio Verde* (Spanish—Potosi and Green River Railroad of Chihuahua)

QAP Quanah, Acme and Pacific

QC Quebec Central Railway (Canadian Pacific)

QNS&LRC Quebec North Shore and Labrador Railway Company

QR Queensland Railways

Quanah Route Quanah, Acme and Pacific Railway

QUI Quincy Railroad

RB Rail Box (American box car pool)

RC Railway Corporation (Nigeria)

RCFA-N *Regie du Chemin de Fer Abidjan-Niger* (French—Abidjan-Niger Railway Administration)—Ivory Coast

RD Railway Directorate (Albania)

RDG Reading Company (formerly Philadelphia and Reading Railroad)

REA Railway Express Agency; Reader Railroad

Reading Lines Reading Railway System (formerly Philadelphia and Reading Railroad)

Rebel Route Gulf, Mobile and Ohio Railroad

RENFE Red Nacional de los Ferrocarriles Españoles (Spanish—Spanish National Railway System)

RFFSA Rede Ferroviária Federal SA (Portuguese—Federal Railway System Corporation)—Brazil

RFP Richmond, Fredericksburg and Potomac Railroad (RF&P)

RF&PRR Richmond, Fredericksburg and Potomac Railroad

RI Chicago, Rock Island and Pacific Railroad; Rail India

Rio Grande Denver and Rio Grande Western

RKG Rockingham Railroad

RM Rotterdam Metro (Dutch—Rotterdam Subway)

RNCF Reseau National des Chemins de Fer (French—National Railway System)—Madagascar

Rock Island Chicago, Rock Island and Pacific Railroad

RR (abbreviation—Railroad or Rail Road); (reporting mark—Raritan River Rail Road); Rhodesian Railways

RRRR Raritan River Railroad

RRys Rhodesian Railways

RS Roberval and Saguenay Railway

RSP Roscoe, Snyder and Pacific

R-S Pacific Route Roscoe, Snyder and Pacific Railway

RSS Rockdale, Sandow and Southern Railroad

RT River Terminal Railway

RTM Railway Transfer Company of Minneapolis

RV Rahway Valley Railway

Ry Railway

S&A Savannah and Atlanta Railway

SAL Seaboard Airline Railroad (Seaboard Coast Line Railroad is official name adopted to avoid confusion with an airline)

SAN Sandersville Railroad

Santa Fe Atchison, Topeka and Santa Fe Railway

SAR South African Railways; South Australian Railways

SAR&H South African Railways and Harbours

SATS San Antonio Transit System

SAVE Swiss-Alberg-Vienna Express

SB South Buffalo Railway

SBA Subterraneos de Buenos Aires (Spanish—Buenos Aires Subways)

SBC Ferrocarril Sonora Baja California (Sonora—Baja California Railway)

SBK South Brooklyn Railway

SC Sumter and Choctaw Railway

SCE Shanghai-Canton Express

SCL Seaboard Coast Line Railroad (Atlantic Coast Line Railroad, Charleston and Western Carolina Railway, Seaboard Air Line Railroad—former name of the Seaboard Coast Line Railroad)

SC&MR Strouds Creek and Muddlety Railroad

SCT Sioux City Terminal Railway

SDAE San Diego and Arizona Eastern Railway

SD & AE San Diego and Arizona Eastern Railway

SDTS San Diego Transit System

SE Ferrocarril del Sureste (Southeast Railroad)

Seashore Lines Pennsylvania-Reading Seashore Lines

SE & CR Southeastern and Chatham Railway (nicknamed Seldom Ever Caught Running)

SEMTA Southeastern Michigan Transportation Authority

SERA Sierra Railroad

SFBRR San Francisco Belt Railroad

SFMR San Francisco Municipal Railway (operates the cable cars)

SFSP Santa Fe/Southern Pacific (merger)

SF/SP Santa Fe/Southern Pacific (railroad merger)

SG South Georgia Railway (Southern Railway)

SGR Saudi Government Railroad (Saudi Arabia); Surinam Government Railway (Netherlands Guiana)

SH Steelton and Highspire Railroad

Shawmut The Pittsburg and Shawmut Railroad

SHK Sidirodromi Hellinikou Kratous (Greek—Hellenic State Railways)—Greece

SI Spokane International Railroad

SIR Staten Island Rapid Transit Railway

SIRRI Southern Industrial Railroad Incorporated

SJ Statens Jarnvargar (Swedish—State Railways)

SJB St Joseph Belt Railway

SJL St Johnsbury and Lamoille County Railroad

SJ & LC St Johnsbury and Lamoille County Railroad

SJTR St Joseph Terminal Railroad

SKSL Skaneateles Short Line Railroad

SLC San Luis Central Railroad

SLGW Salt Lake, Garfield and Western Railway

SLR Sierra Leone Railway

SLSF St Louis-San Francisco Railway

SM St Marys Railroad

SMA San Manuel Arizona Railroad

SMR South Manchurian Railway

SMV Santa Maria Valley Railroad

SN Sacramento Northern Railway (also SNRy)

SNCB Société Nationale des Chemins de Fer Belges (French—Belgian National Railways)

SNCF Société Nationale des Chemins de Fer Français (French—French National Railways)

SNCFA Société Nationale des Chemins de Fer Algeriens (French—Algerian National Railways)

SNY Southern New York Railway

SOE Simplon-Orient Express

SOI Southern Indiana Railway

Sonora—Baja California Railway Ferrocarril Sonora—Baja California—Mexicali to Benjamin Hill

SOO Soo Line Railroad

$oo Line Soo Line Railroad

SOT South Omaha Terminal Railway

Southern Southern Railway System (Alabama Great Southern Railroad; Carolina and Northwestern Railway; Cincinnati, New Orleans and Texas Pacific Railway; Georgia Southern and Florida Railway; Harriman and Northeastern Railroad; Live Oak, Perry and Gulf Railroad; Louisiana Southern Railway; New Orleans and Northeastern Railroad; South Georgia Railway)

Southern Pacific SP

South Shore Line Chicago South Shore and South Bend Railroad

SP Southern Pacific (includes Southern Pacific Lines, Sunset Railway, Texas and Louisiana Lines, Texas and New Orleans, etc.)—in fact many school children once said the United States was bounded on the north by Canada and the Great Lakes, on the east by the Atlantic Ocean, and on the south and southwest by the Southern Pacific

SPGT Springfield Terminal Railway

SPS Spokane, Portland and Seattle Railway (includes Oregon Electric and Oregon Trunk railways)

SR Southern Railway

SRBR Southern Region of British Railways

SRC Salvador Railway Company (El Salvador)

SRN Sabine River and Northern

SRRC Sierra Railroad Company; Strasburg Rail Road Company

SRRCO Sandersville Railroad Company

SRT State Railways of Thailand (Siam)

SSDK Savannah State Docks Railroad

SSLVRR Southern San Luis Valley Railroad

SSRy Sand Springs Railway

SSW St. Louis Southwestern Railway (Cotton Belt Route)

STE Stockton Terminal and Eastern Railroad

STRT Stewartstown Railroad

STS Seattle Transit System

SU Stockholm Underground (subway system)

Sub Suburban; Subway

Sud Rys Sudan Railways

SUR Soviet Union Railways (managed by Ministry of Communications and comprising some twenty-six lines including the Trans-Mongolian and the Trans-Siberian as well as the plush Leningrad-Moscow express)

Susquehanna New York, Susquehanna and Western Railroad

Syr Rys Syrian Railways

TAAA Travelers Aid Association of America

TA & G Tennessee, Alabama and Georgia Railway

TAG Route Tennessee, Alabama and Georgia Railway

Tan-Zam Tanzania-Zambia Railroad

TAR Trans-Australian Railways

TAS Tampa Southern Railroad

TASD Terminal Railway Alabama State Docks

TA&W Toledo, Angola and Western Railway

TB Twin Branch Railroad

TBTMG Transportation Bureau of the Tokyo Metropolitan Government (subway)

TC Tennessee Central Railway

TCDD *Turkiye Cumhuriyeti Deviet Demiryollari Isletmesi* (Turkish—Turkish State Railways)

TCG Tucson, Cornelia and Gila Bend Railroad

TCT Texas City Terminal Railway

TEBRCL The Emu Bay Railway Company Limited

TEE Trans-Europe Express

TENN Tennessee Railroad

TEXC Texas Central Railroad

THB Toronto, Hamilton and Buffalo Railway

The Q CB&Q (Chicago, Burlington and Quincy)

TM Texas Mexican Railway; Transport Ministry (USSR's administration of twenty-six railway lines)—TM sometimes used on engines

TMR Trans-Mongolian Railway

TN Texas and Northern Railway

T-NM Texas-New Mexico Railway

T & NO Texas and New Orleans (Southern Pacific)—also TNO

TOC Pennsylvania New York Central Transportation Company (Penn Central)

TOE Texas, Oklahoma and Eastern Railroad

TOV Tooele Valley Railway

T&P Texas and Pacific Railway (also TP)

TPMP Texas-Pacific-Missouri Pacific Terminal Railroad of New Orleans

TPT Trenton-Princeton Traction Company

TP & W Toledo, Peoria and Western Railroad

TR Tasmanian Railways

TRA Taiwan Railway Administration

Trans-Sib Trans-Siberian Railway

TRC Tela Railway Company (Honduras); Trona Railway Company (California)

TRRA Terminal Railroad Association of St Louis

TS Tidewater Southern Railway

TS-E Texas South-Eastern

TSR Trans-Siberian Railway

TSU Tulsa-Sapulpa Union Railway

TT Toledo Terminal Railroad

T&T Tijuana and Tecate Railway (freight cars marked TITE)

TTC Toronto Transit Commission (subway and surface railway systems)

Turk-Sib Turkestan-Siberian (railway)

TVG Tavares and Gulf Railroad

TVRy Tooele Valley Railway

Tweetsie (nickname—East Tennessee and Western North Carolina Railroad)—believed to be derived from high-pitched whistles of its engines

T-Z RA Tanzania-Zambia Railway Authority

U Underground (London's subway system)

UBR Ulan Bator Railway

UCR Utah Coal Route

U de Y *Unidos de Yucatan* (Spanish—United Railways of Yucatan, Mexico)

UFC United Fruit Company (railroads in Costa Rica and Panama)

UMP Upper Merion and Plymouth Railroad

UNF Union Freight Railroad

UNI Unity Railways

UO Union Railroad—Oregon

UP Union Pacific Railroad (includes Oregon Short Line and Oregon-Washington Railroad and Navigation Company)

UR Uganda Railway

URR Union Railroad—Pittsburgh

USSR (Ministry of Railways administers operation of twenty-six railway boards throughout the USSR)

UT Union Terminal Railway

UTA Ulster Transport Authority (railways of six counties in Northern Ireland)

UTAH Utah Railway

Utah Coal Route Utah Railway

UTR Union Transportation Company

V *Valtionrautatiet* (Finnish—

State Railways)
VBR Virginia Blue Ridge Railway
VC Virginia Central Railway
VCS Virginia and Carolina Southern Railroad
VCY Ventura County Railway
VE Visalia Electric Railroad
VGN Virginian Railway (Norfolk and Western)
VIA VIA Rail Canada
Via Rail Candian National + Canadian Pacific (passenger-carrying consolidation)
Virginian Virginian Railway (Norfolk and Western)
V & LI Vancouver and Lulu Island (branch of Canadian Pacific)
V-MNR Viet-Minh National Railways (North Vietnam)
V-NR Viet-Nam Railways (South Vietnam)
VR Victorian Railways (Australia)
V Ry Verapaz Railway (Guatemala)
V3L Valley and Siletz Railroad
VSO Valdosta Southern Railroad
VSOE Venice-Simplon Orient Express
VTR Vermont Railway
W of A Western Railway of Alabama
WAB Wabash Railroad (Norfolk and Western)
Wabash Wabash Railroad (Norfolk and Western)
WAG Wellsville, Addison and Galeton Railroad
WAGR Western Australian Government Railways
WATC Washington Terminal Company
WAW Waynesburg and Washington Railroad (Penn Central)
WBCRR Wilkes-Barre Connecting Railroad
WBT&SRC Waco, Beaumont, Trinity and Sabine Railway

Company
Western Railway of Mexico Ferrocarril Occidental de México—Culiacan to Limoncito
West Point Route Atlanta and West Point Rail Road
Westrain Western Australian Trains
White Pass British Columbia Yukon Railway, British Yukon Railway, Pacific and Arctic Railway
White Pass and Yukon Route British Columbia Yukon Railway, British Yukon Navigation, British Yukon Railway, Pacific and Arctic Railway and Navigation Company
WIM Washington, Idaho and Montana Railway
WL *Wagon Lits* (French—sleeping cars)
WLO Waterloo Railroad
WM Western Maryland Railway
WMR Wasatch Mountain Railway
WMTA Washington Metropolitan Transit Authority (subway system)
WMWN Weatherford, Mineral Wells and Northwestern Railway
WNF Winfield Railroad
W&NO Wharton and Northern Railroad
WOD Washington and Old Dominion Railroad
W&OV Warren and Ouachita Valley Railway
WP Western Pacific Railroad
WPER West Pittston-Exeter Railroad
WP & Y White Pass and Yukon Railway
WRA Western Railroad Association
WRBR Western Region of British Railways
WRNT Warrenton Railroad
WRWK Warwick Railway

WS Ware Shoals Railroad
WSR Warren and Saline River
WSS Winston-Salem Southbound Railway
WSYP White Sulphur Springs and Yellowstone Park Railway
WTR Wrightsville and Tennille Railroad
WVN West Virginia Northern Railroad
WW Winchester and Western Railroad
WWV Walla Walla Valley Railway
WYS Wyandotte Southern Railroad
WYT Wyandotte Terminal Railroad
X express; transport; transportation (as in many private bulk carriers' names such as GATX—General American Transportation)
Xing crossing (highway or rail road)—also XING
YAN Yancey Railroad
YN Youngstown & Northern (railroad)
Y & N Youngstown and Northern Railroad
YR Yucatan Railways (*Ferrocarriles Unidos del Sureste*—United Railways of the Southeast)—along the Gulf of Mexico from Coatzacoalcos to Merida
YS Youngtown and Southern Railway (Montour)
Y & S Yakutat and Southern Railway
YVT Yakima Valley Transportation Company
YW Yreka Western Railroad
ZJZ *Zajednica Jugoslovenskih Zalesnicca* (Yugoslavian—Community of Yugoslav Railways)
ZR Zambia Railways
Zug Island Road Delray Connecting Railroad (DC)

Roman Numerals

I 1
II 2
III 3
IV 4
V 5
VI 6
VII 7

VIII 8
IX 9
X 10
XV 15
XIX 19
XX 20
XXV 25

XXIX 29
XXX 30
XXXV 35
XXXIX 39
XL 40
XLV 45
XLIX 49

L 50	C 100	MCM or MDCCCC 1900
LV 55	CL 150	MCMX 1910
LIX 59	CC 200	MCMXX 1920
LX 60	CCC 300	MCMXXX 1930
LXV 65	CD 400	MCMXL 1940
LXIX 69	D 500	MCML 1950
LXX 70	DC 600	MCMLX 1960
LXXV 75	DCC 700	MCMLXX 1970
LXXIX 79	DCCC 800	MCMLXXX 1980
LXXX 80	CM 900	MCMXC 1990
LXXXV 85	M 1000	MM 2000
LXXXIX 89	MD 1500	MMM 3000
XC 90	MDC 1600	MMMM or M$\overline{\text{V}}$ 4000
XCV 95	MDCC 1700	$\overline{\text{V}}$ 5000
XCIX 99	MDCCC 1800	$\overline{\text{M}}$ 1,000,000

Rules of the Road—at Sea

Red to red and green to green
all is safe to pass abeam.

or

Green to green and red to red
perfect safety—go ahead.

If on your starboard red appear
it is your duty to keep clear;

to act as judgment says is
proper—
to port, or starboard, back, or
stop her.

But when upon your port is
seen
a steamer's starboard light of
green—

there's not so much for you to
do
for green to port keeps clear of
you.

Both in safety and in doubt
always keep a good lookout;
in danger with no room to turn
ease her, stop her, go astern.

When Two Ships Meet Head On

When both side lights you see
ahead
port your helm and show your

red.

(Steer to starboard so your red
light will pass the red light of

the approaching vessel, and
thus you'll pass on the left as
people do ashore.)

Russian Alphabet (transliterated)

Russian Capital Letters	English Capital Letters	Russian Small Letters	English Small Letters	Russian Alphabet Letter Names	Nearest English Equivalent Sounds
А	A	а	a	*ah*	*a* as in *a*rch
Б	B	б	b	*beh*	*b* as in *b*it
В	V	в	v	*veh*	*v* as in *v*est
Г	G	г	g	*geh*	*g* as in *g*et
Д	D	д	d	*deh*	*d* as in *d*ay
Е	Ye	е	ye	*yeh*	*y* as in *y*es
Ж	Zh	ж	zh	*zheh*	*zh* sound as in measure
З	Z	з	z	*zeh*	*z* as in *z*ero
И	I	и	i	*ee*	*i* as in *p*ee*l*
Й	Y	й	y	*ee s krátkoi*	(short *i* after vowels
К	K	к	k	*kah*	*k* as in *k*ite
Л	L	л	l	*el*	*l* as in woo*l*
М	M	м	m	*em*	*m* as in *m*an

Н	N	н	n	en	n as in now
О	O	о	o	oh	o as in hoax
П	P	п	p	peh	p as in pencil
Р	R	р	r	err	r as in rye
С	S	с	s	ess	s as in say
Т	T	т	t	teh	t as in tent
У	Oo	у	oo	ooh	oo as in loose
Ф	F	ф	f	eff	f as in fancy
Х	Kh	х	kh	khan	kh as in loch
Ц	Ts	ц	ts	tseh	ts as in hats
Ч	Ch	ч	ch	cheh	ch as in chair
Ш	Sh	ш	sh	shah	sh as in shave
Щ	Shch	щ	shch	shchah	shch as in Irish chuck
Ъ		ъ		tvyórdy znak	(silent-hard sound)
Ы	Y	ы	y	yery	y as i in hit
Ь		ь		myakhki znak	(silent)
Э	Eh	э	eh	eh oborótnoye	eh sound as in debt
Ю	Yu	ю	yu	yoo	yu as in you
Я	Ya	я	ya	yah	ya as in yam

Ship's Bell Time Signals

1 bell	—12:30 or 4:30 or 8:30 a.m. or p.m.			5 bells—	2:30	6:30	10:30
2 bells—	1:00	5:00	9:00	6 bells—	3:00	7:00	11:00
3 bells—	1:30	5:30	9:30	7 bells—	3:30	7:30	11:30
4 bells—	2:00	6:00	10:00	8 bells—	4:00	8:00	12:00

On many vessels the ship's whistle is blown at noon. On some ships a lightly struck 1 bell announces 15 minutes before the change of watch, usually at 4, 8, and 12 o'clock.

The ship's day starts at noon. The *afternoon watch* is from noon to 4 p.m. The 4 to 8 work period is called the *dogwatch*. From 8 p.m. to midnight is the *first watch*. From midnight to 4 a.m. is the *middle watch*. From 8 a.m. to noon is the *forenoon watch*.

Signs and Symbols Frequently Used

+ add; addition sign; north; plus

& and (ampersand)

&c et cetera (and so forth)

* asterisk

@ at

∴ because

¢ centavo; centime; cent(s)

© copyright

° degree(s)

÷ divide; divided by; division sign

$ dollar sign—used universally for monetary units as diverse as Nicaraguan cordobas; Brazilian cruzeiros; Australian, Bahamian, Barbadian, British Honduran, Canadian, Ethiopian, Guyanian, Hong Kongese, Levantine, Liberian, Malaysian, New Zealand, Taiwan, trade, Trinidadian-Tobagonian, U.S., Viet Namese, West Indian, yuan dollars; Portuguese escudos; Honduran lempiras; Brazilian milreis; Chilean, Colombian, Cuban, Dominican, Mexican, Philippine, Uruguayan pesos; Peruvian soles (often with a lower-case dollar sign, s); Chinese yuans

$A Australian dollars(s)

$b Bolivian peso(s)

$B Bahamian, Barbadian, British dollar(s)

$BH British Honduran dollar(s)

$C Brazilian cruzeiro(s); Canadian dollar(s)

$Col Colombian peso(s)

$E Ethiopian dollar(s)

$Eth Ethiopian dollar(s)

$G Guyanian dollar(s)

$HK Hong Kong dollar(s)

$K $1000 (e.g. $13K $13,000)

$L Levant(ine) dollar(s)—Maria Theresa thaler(s); Liberian dollar(s)

$M Malay(sian) dollar(s)

$Mal Malay(sian) dollar(s)

$Mex Mexican peso(s)

$NT New Taiwan dollar(s)

$NZ New Zealand dollar(s)
$RD Republica Dominicana peso(s)—Dominican Republic monetary unit(s)
$S Singapore dollar(s)
$T Taiwan dollar(s); trade dollar(s); Trinidad(ian) and Tobago(nian) dollar(s)
$TT Trinidad(ian) and Tobago(nian) dollar(s)
$Ur Uruguayan peso(s)
$US United States dollar(s) [also shown as US$, as are other monetary units where national designations often precede dollar sign: C$—Canadian dollar(s), HK$—Hong Kong dollar(s)]
$VN Viet Namese dollar(s)
$WI West Indian dollar(s); West Indies dollar(s)
$Y yuan dollar(s)
= equality; equals; equal to
G Paraguayan guarani(s)
K certified kosher
LC Cyrian pound(s)
LR Rhodesian pound(s)
− minus; south; subtract; subtraction sign
× multiplication sign; multiplied by; multiply
≥ equal to or greater than

≤ equal to or less than
> greater than
< less than
>> much greater than
<< much less than
fracture(s) (medical); number(s) or pound(s) (commercial); sharp(s) (musical); space(s) (typographical); tic-tac-toe (game symbol); zinc (alchemical)
p Philippine peso(s)
% percent
+ plus; north
± plus or minus
£ pound (*libra*) sign—used universally for monetary units such as the Australian, British, Egyptian, Gambian, Ghanian, Irish, Israeli, Jamaican, Lebanese, Libyan, Malawi, New Zealand, Nigerian, South African, Sudanese, Syrian, Turkish, Western Samoan, Zambian pound
£A pound Australian
£E pound Egyptian (United Arab Republic)
£G pound Gambian; pound Ghanian
£I pound Irish; pound Israeli (also shown as I£)

£J pound Jamaican
£L pound Lebanese; pound Libyan
£M pound Malawi
£N pound Nigerian
£NZ pound New Zealand (also shown as NZ£)
£S pound sterling; pound Sudanese; pound Syrian
£SAf pound South African (also shown as SAf£)
£/s/d pounds, shillings, and pence
£T pound Turkish
£WS pound Western Samoan
£Z pound Zambian
R registered
℞ prescription; receipt; recipe; response; reverse
/ shilling mark; slash; solidus; virgule
∴ therefore
U Union of Orthodox Jewish Congregations of America (symbol for kosher product approved for detergent or dietary use)
XMA$ (symbol—commercialized Christmas)
Y Japanese yen

Steamship Lines

A Ahearn Shipping Ltd; Alaska Steamship Company; Alcoa Steamship Company; American Export Isbrandtsen Lines; American Mail Line; American Oil Company; American Steamships; Tidewater Oil (capital A between red wings); et cetera
ABC Line Antwerp Bulk Carriers Line
ABRT A/B Rederi Transatlantic (Pacific Australia Direct Line)
AC African Coasters
ACL Atlantic Container Line
ACS American Coal Shipping
ACSC Australian Coastal Shipping Commission
AD Armement Dieppe
AE African Enterprises
AECL Anglo-European Container Line
AEL Afro Eurasian Line; American Express Line
AFCL Africa Container Lines
AFS American Foreign Steam-

ship
AH Alfred Holt (Blue Funnel Line)
AHB Great Eastern Line
AHL Associated Humber Lines
AJCL Australia–Japan Container Line
AL Admiral Line
Alcoa Alcoa Steamship Company
ALL Anchor Line Limited
All America Cables All America Cables and Radio
AML American Mail Line
AMOCO American Oil Company
AN Anglo Nordic
ANCAP *Administracion Nacional de Combustibles Alcohol y Portland* (Spanish—National Administration of Flammable Alcohol and Portland Cement)—Uruguay
ANL Australian National Line
ANZECS Australia–New Zealand–Europe Container Service

ANZS Africa–New Zealand Service
AP American Pioneer Lines
AP *Atlantska Plovidba* (Yugoslavian—Atlantic Line)
APL American President Lines
APT Australian Pacific Traders
ASA Admanthos Shipping Agency
ASC Alcoa Steamship Company
ASCL Australia Straits Container Line
ASFS Alaska State Ferry System
ASN Atlantic Steam Navigation
ASNC Atlantic Steam Navigation Company
ASOK *Angfartigas Svenska Östasiatiske Kompaniet* (Swedish—Swedish East Asiatic Steamship Company)
AT American Trading
ATLANTIC Atlantic Refining Company
Atlantic Container Line ACL

AUT American Union Transport
AWPL Australia West Pacific Line
B Barber Lines; Booth Line; Branch Lines; Bull Steamship Lines; etc.
BACS Ben Asia Container Service
BAF Belgian African Line
BBS Barber Blue Sea
BCCS British Columbia Coastal Service
BCF British Columbia Ferries
BCL Bermuda Container Line; Bristol City Line
BCSC British and Continental Steamship Company
BDS Bergenske Dampskibsselskab (Norwegian—Bergen Steamship Line)—connecting Norway and United Kingdom ports
Ben Ocean Ben Line, Blue Funnel, and Glen Line
BFL Belgian Fruit Lines; Blue Funnel Lines
BHP Broken Hill Proprietary
BISNC British India Steam Navigation Company
B & I SPC British and Irish Steam Packet Company
BL Bahamas Line; Bank Line; Bergen Line; Bibby Line; Booth Line; etc.
B & L Burns and Laird Lines
BLS Ben Line Steamers
Blue Star Blue Star Line
BM British Methane Limited
BMM Belfast, Mersey and Manchester Steamship Company
BOC Burmah Oil Company
Bore Ro-Ro Bore Roll-on Roll-off Line
BOS British Oil Shipping
BP British Petroleum
BPC British Phosphate Commissioners
BP & Co Burns, Philip and Company
BR British Railways (operates many ferry steamers linking England and Scotland with Belgium, France, Ireland, and Holland)
BSC Baltic Steamship Company
BSL Black Star Line; Blue Sea Line; Blue Star Line; etc.
BSNC Bristol Steam Navigation Company
BSPL Blue Star Port Lines
BTC Bethlehem Transportation Corporation
B&W Brocklebank and Well Lines

C Calmar Line (Bethlehem Steel); Caribbean Steamships Company; Clarke Line; Clyde Line; etc.
"C" Costa Line
CA Carregadores Açoreanos (Portuguese—Azorean Cargo Carriers)
CAROL Caribbean Overseas Lines
CAVN Compañía Anonima Venezolana de Navegación (Spanish—Venezuelan Navigation Company)—Venezuela Line
CCAL Christensen Canadian African Line
CC Co Commercial Cable Company
CCN Companhia Colonial de Navegacão (Portuguese—Colonial Navigation Company)
CCNI Cía Chilena de Navegación Interoceanica (Spanish—Chilean Interoceanic Navigation Company)
CEA Central Electricity Authority
CF Compagnie de Navigation Fraissinet
CFL Container Fleets Limited
CFPO Compagnie Française des Phosphates de l'Oceanie (French—French Phosphate Company of Oceania)
CGL Canadian Gulf Line
CGM Compagnie Générale Maritime (French Line)
CGS Central Gulf Steamships
CGT Compagnie Générale Transatlantique (Cie Gle Trans) (French—General Transatlantic Company)—the French Line
CHEVRON Chevron Shipping (oil tankers)
Chilean Line (see CSAV)
China Merchants Steam Navigation Company CMSNC
CI Catalina Island Steamship Line; Christmas Island Phosphate Commission
Cie Gle Trans Compagnie Générale Transatlantique (French—General Transatlantic Company)—the French Line
Cities Service Cities Service Oil Company
CL Ceylon Lines; Coast Lines
Clipper Line Wisconsin and Michigan Steamship Company
CM Compañía Maritima (Spanish—Maritime Company)
CMB Compagnie Maritime

Belge (French—Belgian Maritime Company)—Royal Belgian Lloyd
CMSNC China Merchants Steam Navigation Company
CMZ Compagnie Maritime du Zaire
CNC China Navigation Company
CNM Canadian National Marine (steamship line)
CNN Compagnie de Navigation Nationale
CNN Companhia Nacional de Navegacão (Portuguese—National Navigation Company)
CNP Compagnie Navigation Paquet (French—Paquet Navigation Company)—Paquet Line
CNS Canadian National Steamships
COLDEMAR Compañía Colombiana de Navegación Marítima (Spanish—Colombian Maritime Navigation Company)
Columbus Line HSDG
COSCO China Ocean Shipping Company
CP Ships Canadian Pacific Steamships (*Empress* vessels)
CPV Corporación Peruana de Vapores (Spanish—Peruvian Steamship Corporation)
Crusader Crusader Line
CSAV Compañía Sud-Americana de Vapores (Spanish—South American Steamship Company)—Chile
CSC Clyde Shipping Company
CSL Canada Steamship Lines
CSO Cities Service Oil
CSS Caribbean Steamship
CSSCo Cunard Steamship Company
CT Cleveland Tankers; Cove Tankers
CT Compania Transmediterranea (Spanish—Transmediterranean Company)
CTE Compañía Transatlantica Española (Spanish—Spanish Transatlantic Line)—The Spanish Line
CTL Coastal Transport Limited
Cunard Cunard Steam-Ship Company, Limited (includes White Star Line)
D Delta Line; Donaldson Line; Red 'D' Line; etc.
'D' Red 'D' Line (merged with Grace Line)
DAL Deutsche-Afrika Linien (German—German Africa

Line)

d'Amico d'Amico Line

Day Line Hudson River Day Line

DBK Daiichi Bussan Kaisha

D-F *Dansk-Franske* (Danish-French Line)

DFDS *Det Forenede Dampskibs-Selskab* (Danish—United Steamship Company)—famous for its ferries

DHX Dependable Hawaiian Express

Djakarta Line DL

DL Djakarta Line; Djakarta Lloyd

DPLC Dundee, Perth and London Shipping Company

DS Dominion Shipping

D-S Ditlev-Simonsen, Halfdan and Company

e El Paso Marine

E American Export Isbrandtsen Lines; Eastern Steamship Line; Exxon Tankers; Hellenic Lines and many Greek lines where the letter E stands for Ellas or Hellas—Greece, or for the last name of an owner as in other lands

E & A Eastern and Australian Steamship Co

EAC East Asiatic Company

E&B Ellerman and Buchnall Steamship Company

EDL Elder Demptser Lines

E&F Elders and Fyffes Ltd

ELMA *Empresa Lineas Maritimas Argentinas* (Spanish—Argentine Maritime Lines)—formerly *FANU* and uses *FANU* house flag

EMC Evergreen Marine Corporation

Empress liners Canadian Pacific ships

ENS Empresa Naviera Santa

ESL Eagle Shipping Ltd

Esso Esso Petroleum Company

EXXON formerly Esso

EY El Yam (bulk carriers)

F Fabre Line; Falcon Tankers; Falkland Islands Trading Company; Farrell Lines; Finnlines; etc.

FAA *Finska Angfartygs Akiebolaget* (Finnish—Finnish Steamship Company)—Finland Line

Falline Federal Atlantic-Lakes Line

FANF *Flota Argentina de Navegaciòn Fluvial* (Spanish—Argentine River Navigation Fleet)

FANU *Flota Argentina de Nave-*

gaciòn de Ultramar (Spanish—Argentine High-Sea Navigation Fleet)

Far East Steamship Company FESCO

FB Franco Belgian Line

FBS Franco-Belgian Services

FCNCo Federal Commerce and Navigation Company

F de P Ferrocarril de Panamá (formerly the Panama Railroad)

Fedpac Federal Pacific Lakes Line

Fedsea Federal South East Asia Line

FESCO Far East Steamship Company

Finald Line (see *FAA*)

FL Ferdinand Laeisz Line; Fesco Pacific Line

FLL Finanglia Line Ltd

FMC Federal Maritime Commission

FMD *Flota Mercante Dominicana* (Spanish—Dominican Merchant Fleet)

FMG *Flota Mercante Grancolombiana* (Spanish—Great Colombian Merchant Fleet)

French Line (see *CGT*)

Frota Frota Oceanica Brasileira

FW Furness, Withy and Company

FWL Furness Warren Line

G Glynafon Shipping; Graig Shipping; Arthur Guiness (the brewer); etc.

GAL German Atlantic Line

GG Guinea Gulf Line

GL Greek Line

GMC Gulf Maritime Company

GO Gulf Oil

GPRL Gulf Puerto Rico Lines

GRACE Grace Line (Prudential-Grace Lines)

Gran Flota Blanca (Spanish—Great White Fleet)—United Fruit Company (fleet of white steamships)—United Brands

GS Galleon Shipping

GSA Gulf and South American Steamship Company

GULF Gulf Oil Corporation

GYSCo Great Yarmouth Shipping Company

H Hansa Line; Heering Line; Horn Line; etc.

HAL Holland Amerika Lijn (NASM—Nederlandsch-Amerikaasche Stoomvaart Maatschappij)—NASM appears on house flag

HANSA Hansa Line

Hanseatic-Vassa Line VL

HAPAG *Hamburg-Amerika Pa-*

ket Aktiengesselschaft (German—Hamburg-America Packet Company)—Hamburg-America Line

Hapag-Lloyd Hamburg-Amerika—North German Lloyd Lines

HB C Hudson's Bay Company

HCL Hamburg-Chicago Line

HFL Hawaii Freight Lines

HH H Hogarth and Sons

HHA HH Andersen Line

HKCL Hong Kong Container Line

HKEL Hong Kong Export Lines

HKIL Hong Kong Islands Line

HKX Hong Kong Express

HL Home Lines

H-L Hapag-Lloyd

HLC Hapag-Lloyd Container (line)

HMM Hyundai Merchant Marine

HMS Her (His) Majesty's Ship (as in HMS *Dreadnought*)

hovercraft marine craft supported by an air cushion instead of a conventional hull

HSAL Hamburg South American Line

HSDG Hamburg-Sudamerikanische Dampfs Gesell (Columbus Line)

HT Hudson Tankers

H&W Holm and Wonsild

HWAL Holland West-Afrika Line

I Incres Line; Interocean Steamship Line; Isthmian Lines (U.S. Steel); Ivaran Lines; etc.

ICI Imperial Chemical Industries

ICSN Indo-China Steam Navigation Company

IFI Inter-Freight International

INSCO Intercontinental Shipping Corporation

Inter-Freight International IFI

IO Ltd Imperial Oil Ltd

IOM SPC Isle of Man Steam Packet Company

IOT Iron Ore Transport

IPL Ital Pacific Line

ISOS International Ship Operating Services

Italia Italian Line

ITI Inagua Transports Incorporated

J Japan Line; John I Jacobs and Company; Johnson Line; etc.

Jadroplov *Jadrarnska Slobodna Plovida* (Yugoslav Great Lakes Line)

JBPS Jamaica Banana Producers' Steamship Co

PT Pope and Talbot
PURE Pure Oil Company
PV Pacific Venture
Q Qatar Petroleum; Quaker Line; Queensland; Quintessence Navigation; etc.
Q&O Quebec and Ontario Transportation
R Rasmussen; Richfield Oil; Ringdal; Robert; etc.
RIL Royal Interocean Lines [*Koninklijke Java-China-Paketvaart Lijnen*—(Dutch—Royal Java-China-Packet Line)]
RL Regent's Line (Grand Union Shipping)
RLR Royal Rotterdam Lloyd
RML Royal Mail Lines
Royal Netherlands Steamship Line (see *KNSM*)
RVL Royal Viking Line
S Saguenay Terminals Ltd; Salen; Seatrain Lines; Sinclair Refining; Socony Mobil Oil; Standard Oil of California; States Marine Lines; States Line (seahorse-shaped red-letter S); Sun Oil; Svea Line; etc.
SA & CL South Atlantic and Caribbean Line
Safmarine South African Marine Corporation
SAL Svenska Amerika Linien (Swedish-America Line)
Santa ships Prudential-Grace Line vessels
SC Submarine Cables Ltd
S & C Sea and Crescent
SCC Shipping and Coal Company
SCI Sea Containers Incorporated; Shipping Corporation of India
Scindia Scindia Steam Navigation
SEGB South Eastern Gas Board
Shell Shell Tankers
Shipping Corporation of India SCI
SL Southern Lines
S-L Sea-Land (Line)
SLS Sea-Land Service
SML States Marine Lines
SN Sincere Navigation
SOPONATA Sociedade Portuguesa de Navios Tanques Limitada (Portuguese—Portuguese Tankships Limited)
Sovtorgflot Soviet Merchant Marine Fleet
Spanish Line Compañía Trans-

atlantica Española
SPL Scan Pacific Line
SS Steamship (as in SS *Santa Clara*)
SSS Sea Speed Service (container)
STANVAC Standard-Vacuum Oil Company
STL Seatrain Lines
SUNOCO Sun Oil Company
T Tankers Limited; Texaco (The Texas Company); Thai Mercantile Marine; Thompson Shipping; Thoren Line; Tirrenia; Transatlantic Line; etc.
TCL Transatlantic Carriers Limited
TCR Texas City Refining
Texaco The Texas Company
TFL Trans Freight Line
TH Thorvald Hansen
Thor Dahls Havalfangerselskap Pacific Islands Transport Line
TMM Transportación Maritima Méxicana
TOTE Totem Ocean Trailer Express
Transamerica Trailer Transport TTT
TS Tasmanian Steamers
TSK Tokyo Senpaku Kaisha
TTT Transamerica Trailer Transport
U Union Oil; United Oriental Steamship Company; Universe Tankships; etc.
UA United Africa Company, Ltd
UBC United Baltic Corporation
UBL Union Barge Line
UCMS Union-Castle Mail Steamship
UFC United Fruit Company
UIL Ulster Imperial Line
U.O. Co. Union Oil Company of California
UPL United Philippine Lines
USC Union Steamship Company
USL United States Lines
USMSTS U.S. Military Sea Transport Service
USS United States Ship (as in USS *Constitution*)
USSCo Ulster Steam Ship Company; Union Steam Ship Company
UT United Transports
UYL United Yugoslav Lines
V Vaccaro Line (Standard Fruit); Valentine Chemical Carriers; Vinke Tankers; Von

Sydow; Vulcan Shipping; etc.
VA Compañía de Navegación Vasco-Asturiana (Spanish—Basque-Asturian Navigation Company)
VC Victory Carriers
VL Vaasa Line (Hanseatic-Vassa Line)
VLC Valley Line Company
VNGC Van Niervelt, Goudriaan and Company (Rotterdam—South American Line)
VW Volkswagen (auto-carrier ships)
W Waterman Steamship Lines; West Line; Westriver Ore Transports; Weyerhaeuser Line; etc.
W&A Wiel and Amundsen
Wallenius Line OW (Olof Wallenius)
WHMV & NSSA Woods Hole, Martha's Vineyard and Nantucket Steamship Authority
WIL West India Lines
WIT West India Tankers
WL Westfal-Larsen Line
W&L Westcott and Laurance Line (Ellerman's)
WL&Co Westfal-Larsen and Company
W&M SS Co Wisconsin and Michigan Steamship Company (The Clipper Line)
WSFS Washington State Ferry System
WTC Western Transportation Company
X (funnel marking—Chandris America Lines; Southern Cross Steamship Line); Xenophon Navigation Company; etc.
Y Yamashita-Shinnihon Kisen Line; Ybarra Lines; Yukiteru Kaiun; Yung Yang Shipping; etc.
YML Yang Ming Line
YPF Yacimientos Petroliferos Fiscales (Spanish—Fiscal Petroleum Deposits)—Argentine tanker fleet
Y-S Line Yamashita-Shinnihon Line
Z Zacharissen; Zante Navegación; Zillah Shipping; Zim Israel Navigation; Zurga Shipping Company; etc.
Zapata Zapata Bulk Transport
Zim Zim Israel Line
ZPL Zim Passenger Line
ZSC Zeeland Shipping Company; Zeeland Steamship Company

Superlatives

Africa's Easternmost City Hafun, Somalia

Africa's Easternmost Point Cape Guardafui (Ras Asir), Somalia

Africa's Largest Black City Ibadan, Nigeria (population more than a million in 1985)

Africa's Northernmost City Bizerta, Tunisia

Africa's Northernmost Point Ras el Abiadh (near Bizerta, Tunisia)

Africa's Southernmost City Cape Town, South Africa

Africa's Southernmost Point Cape Agulhas, South Africa

Africa's Westernmost City Dakar, Senegal

Africa's Westernmost Point Cape Almadies, Senegal

Alabama's Deepest Cavern 12 story-deep Cathedral Caverns containing a stalagmite 60 feet (18 meters) high

Alaska's Richest Agricultural Area the Matanuska Valley

America's Busiest Airport Chicago's O'Hare International

America's Easternmost City Eastport, Maine

America's Easternmost Point West Quoddy Head, Maine

America's Most Malignant Crime arson

America's Most Used and Abused Drug alcohol (alcohol-related crimes account for half its prison population; more than fifty percent of all arrests are alcohol connected, only heart disease and cancer kill more people)

America's Northernmost City Barrow, Alaska

America's Northermost Point Point Barrow, Alaska

America's Oldest Animal the horseshoe crab (*Limulus polyphemus*)

America's Southernmost City Hilo on the island of Hawaii

America's Southernmost Point Ka Lae (South Cape) on the island of Hawaii

America's Westernmost City Agaña, Guam

America's Westernmost Point Cape Wrangell on Attu Island, Alaska

Arctic's Largest Carnivore polar bear

Argentina's Easternmost City Posadas (on the Paraguay border)

Argentina's Largest Port Buenos Aires

Argentina's Northernmost City San Salvador (close to the Chilean border)

Argentina's Southernmost City Ushuaia (on Beagle Channel)

Argentina's Westernmost City Mendoza (near the Chilean border)

Arizona's Grandest Canyon Grand Canyon of the Colorado River

Arkansas's Largest Spring Blue Spring produces 144 million liters (38 million gallons) of water every day

Australia's Easternmost City Brisbane, Queensland

Australia's Easternmost Point Cape Byron, New South Wales

Australia's Northernmost City Darwin, Northern Territory

Australia's Northernmost Point Cape York, Queensland

Australia's Southernmost City Hobart, Tasmania

Australia's Southernmost Point South East Cape, Tasmania

Australia's Westernmost City Carnarvon, Western Australia (Perth is larger but not as far west)

Australia's Westernmost Point Cape Inscription, Western Australia

Best Sellers in Nazi Germany the *Bible* and *Mein Kampf*, according to Benjamin B Ferencz

Biggest Murder Trial in History Nuremberg Trial of Nazi war criminals

Brazil's Easternmost City João Pessôa or Recife

Brazil's Easternmost Town Cabedelo (close to João Pesôa)

Brazil's Largest Port Rio de Janeiro

Brazil's Northernmost City Belém do Pará

Brazil's Northernmost Town Maturuca (close to the Guyana border)

Brazil's Southernmost City Rio Grande do Sul (close to the Uruguay border)

Brazil's Southernmost Town Jaguarão (on the Uruguay border)

Brazil's Westernmost City Rio Branco (close to the Bolivian border)

Brazil's Westernmost Town Cruziero do Sul (near the Peruvian border)

British superlatives (*see* United Kingdom, Largest British, *and* Smallest British *entries*)

Bullfight Capital of the World Madrid

California's Most Spectacular Park Yosemite

Canada's Easternmost City St John's, Newfoundland

Canada's Easternmost Point Cape Speur, Newfoundland

Canada's Highest Town Lake Louise, Alberta (1540 meters or 5051 feet)

Canada's Most Vibrant City Toronto

Canada's Northernmost Deepwater Port Churchill, Manitoba

Canada's Northernmost Point Cape Columbia, Ellesmere Land

Canada's Northernmost Town Inuvik, Northwest Territory

Canada's Oldest City Québec City

Canada's Oldest National Park Banff National Park including lovely Lake Louise

Canada's Southernmost City Kingsville, Ontario

Canada's Southernmost Point Point Pelee, Ontario on Lake Eric

Canada's Tallest Mountain Mount Robson in the Canadian Rockies (12,972 feet or 3954 meters)

Canada's Westernmost City Dawson, Yukon

Canada's Westernmost Point in Yukon Territory just east of Alaska's Demarcation Point

Chile's Easternmost City Santiago

Chile's Largest Port Valparaiso

Chile's Northernmost City Arica (near Tacna, Peru)

Chile's Southernmost City Punta Arenas (on the Strait of Magellan)

Chile's Westernmost City Valdivia

Cleanest City in the East Singapore

Cleanest City in the West Copenhagen, Oslo, and Stockholm appear to compete for this title although many smaller Scandinavian cities are very clean and even tidier

Cleanest Tropical City Singapore

Colombia's Easternmost City Cúcuta

Colombia's Easternmost Town Puerto Carreño

Colombia's Largest Port Barranquilla

Colombia's Northernmost City Riohacha

Colombia's Northernmost Town Inosu

Colombia's Southernmost City Cali

Colombia's Southernmost Town Leticia (on the border of Brazil and Peru)

Colombia's Westernmost City Buenaventura

Colombia's Westernmost Town Tumaco (close to the Ecuador border)

Colorado's Largest Flat-topped Mountain Grand Mesa and its National Forest atop the world's largest flat-topped mountain

Commonest British Bird blackbird

Connecticut's Biggest Beach Park Hammonasset fronting on Long Island Sound

Cuba's Easternmost Point Cabo Maisi

Cuba's Easternmost and Southernmost City Santiago

Cuba's Northernmost City and Point Havana

Cuba's Southernmost Point Cabo Cruz

Cuba's Westernmost City Pinar del Rio

Cuba's Westernmost Point Cabo San Antonio

Deepest Part of the Arctic Ocean Eurasia Basin between Komsomolets Island and the North Pole (2980 fathoms or 17,880 feet or 5450 meters in depth)

Deepest Part of the Atlantic Puerto Rico Trench north of Hispaniola and Puerto Rico (4729 fathoms or 28,374 feet or 8648 meters in depth)

Deepest Part of the Caribbean Cayman Trench between the Cayman Islands and Jamaica (3833 fathoms or 23,000 feet or 7010 meters deep)

Deepest Part of the Indian Ocean Diamantina Trench south of Western Australia (4400 fathoms or 26,400 feet or 8047 meters in depth)

Deepest Part of the Mediterranean off Cape Matapan, Greece (2406 fathoms or 14,435 feet or 4400 meters deep)

Deepest Part of the North Sea in the Skaggerak between Denmark and Norway (333 fathoms or 1998 feet or 605 meters)

Deepest Part of the Ocean Mariana Trench in the Western Pacific east of Saipan (6033 fathoms or 36,198 feet or 11,034 meters in depth)

Deepest Part of the Pacific (see Deepest Part of the Ocean)

Dutch superlatives (see Nederlands entries)

Easternmost Capital of Africa Mogadishu, Somalia

Easternmost Capital of Asia Tokyo, Japan

Easternmost Capital of Australia Brisbane, Queensland

Easternmost Capital of Europe Moscow, USSR

Easternmost Capital of North America St John's, Newfoundland

Easternmost Capital of South America Brasilia, Brazil

Easternmost Point of Canada Cape Spear, Newfoundland on Avalon Peninsula near St John's

Easternmost Point of the continental United States West Quoddy Head near Lubec, Maine

Easternmost Point of Mexico Isla de las Mujeres off the Caribbean coast of Quintana Roo

Easternmost Point of the territorial United States East Point on Saint Croix in the Virgin Islands east of Puerto Rico

Ecuador's Easternmost City Quito

Ecuador's Largest Port Guayaquil

Ecuador's Northernmost City Esmeraldas

Ecuador's Southernmost City Cuenca

Ecuador's Westernmost City Manta

England's Extremitude Land's End—westernmost point in Cornwall and neaby Lizard Head the southernmost point

England's Highest Mountain Scafell Pike

England's Largest Lake Windermere

England's Longest River the Thames

Eurasia's Easternmost Point Mys Dezhneva (East Cape), Siberia

Eurasia's Easternmost Town Uelen, Eastern Siberia (across Bering Strait from Tin City, Alaska)

Eurasia's Northernmost Point Rudolph Island off Franz Josef Land in the Arctic

Eurasia's Northernmost Town Ny Ålesund, Spitsbergen

Eurasia's Southernmost Point Roti Island in the Lesser Sundas of Indonesia

Eurasia's Southernmost Town Kupang on Timor, Indonesia

Eurasia's Westernmost Point Tearaght Island off Ireland's Dingle Peninsula

Eurasia's Westernmost Town Dingle, Ireland

Europe's Easternmost City and Point Gornyatskiy, in the USSR on the western slopes of the Ural Mountains

Europe's Northernmost City Hammerfest, Norway

Europe's Northernmost Point Nordkyn, Norway (north of North Cape)

Europe's Southernmost City Nicosia, Cyprus

Europe's Southernmost Point along the south coast of Cyprus

Europe's Westernmost Place Tearaght Island off Ireland's Dingle Peninsula

Europe's Westernmost Town Dingle, Ireland

Fastest Clipper Ship *Lightning*—designed and built by Donald McKay in his East Boston shipyards—logged 436 nautical miles in 24 hours; McKay launched 16 of his fastest and finest clippers between 1850 and 1853

Fastest Passenger Vessel *United States* of United States Lines averages 35 knots (about 40 miles an hour)—has crossed Atlantic Ocean in less than 4 days

Fastest Railroad *TGV*, Paris-

Lyon express operating in one section at 237 miles per hour and at an average speed of more than 130 miles per hour

Fastest Transatlantic Clipper Ship Donald McKay's *James Baines* sailed from Boston to Liverpool in 12 days and 6 hours (more than a 100 years ago)

Florida's Largest Subtropical Wilderness Everglades National Park

Foremost Atheist Orator of America Robert G. Ingersoll

Foremost Atheist Philosopher of England Bertrand Russell

Foremost Atheist Philosopher of Germany Friedrich Wilhelm Nietzsche

France's Easternmost Point Lauterbourg (on the Rhine opposite Karlsruhe)

France's Easternmost Port Menton (at the Italian border on the Mediterranean)

France's Northernmost Point Malo les Bains (on the North Sea at the Belgian border)

France's Northernmost Port Dunkerque (on the Strait of Dover)

France's Southernmost Point Cerbère (opposite Spain's Port Bou on the Mediterranean)

France's Southernmost Port Port Vendres (on the Mediterranean close to the Spanish frontier)

France's Westernmost Point Île d'Ouessant (off the Brittany peninsula)

France's Westernmost Port Brest (on the Brittany peninsula)

Georgia's Most Gorgeous Swamp the Okefenokee it shares with Florida and the wildlife it protects

Germany's Easternmost City Zittau (close to the Czech and Polish borders)

Germany's Largest City Berlin

Germany's Largest Port Hamburg

Germany's Northernmost Point List on Sylt (in the North Frisian Islands)

Germany's Southernmost Region Algäuer Alps (near Oberstdorf on the Austrian border)

Germany's Westernmost City Aachen (Aix-la-Chapelle)—near the Belgian and Netherlands border

Great Britain's Highest Mountain Ben Nevis in Scotland

Great Britain's Longest River The Severn of England and Wales

Greatest Band in the Land Goldman Band

Greatest Capes of the northern Pacific coast Cape Scott, Cape Cook, Cape Beale, Cape Flattery, Cape Disappointment, Cape Mendocino, Cabo San Lazaro, Cabo San Lucas

Greatest Giveaway in the Americas the Panama Canal

Greatest Man Who Made a Dictionary Dr Samuel Johnson

Greatest Massacre in Human History 26,300,000 Chinese, according to a Soviet radio broadcast accusing the regime of Comrade Mao Tse-tung when it had accused the USSR of similar massacres

Greatest Predator Man (*Homo sapiens*)

Greatest Primate Gymnasts gibbons (who leap through the air with the greatest of ease and unaided by any trapeze)

Greatest Sculptured Cape of the northern Atlantic coast Cape Cod

Greatest Sculptured Capes of the southern Atlantic coast Cape Hatteras, Cape Lookout, Cape Fear, Cape Canaveral

Greatest Shortcut the Panama Canal

Greatest Show on Earth Barnum & Bailey's three-ring circus (later merged with Ringling Brothers)

Guam's Best Port Apra on its west coast

Hawaii's Superlative Volcanoes Kilauea and Mauna Loa in the Hawaii Volcanoes National Park on Hawaii

Heaviest Even-toed Ungulate hippopotamus (heavier than any of its many relatives, including antelopes, camels, cattle, deer, giraffes, goats, llamas, peccaries, pigs, pronghorns, sheep, etc.)

Heaviest Living Dog Saint Bernard

Highest American Mountain Mount McKinley

Highest Andean Nation Bolivia

Highest Canadian Mountain Mount Logan

Highest Capital in Africa Addis Ababa, Ethiopia

Highest Capital in the Americas La Paz, Bolivia

Highest Capital in Asia Kabul, Afghanistan

Highest Capital in Australia Canberra, its capital

Highest Capital in Europe Madrid, Spain

Highest Murder Rate Mexico with 43 registered homicides per 100,000 in 1985 plus many more unregistered

Highest Peak in the Eastern Hemisphere Everest

Highest Peak in the Northern Hemisphere Everest

Highest Peak in the Southern Hemisphere Aconcagua

Highest Peak in the Western Hemisphere Aconcagua

Highest Point in Africa Kilimanjaro in Tanzania (19,340 feet or 5963 meters above sea level)

Highest Point in Antarctica Vinson Massif (16,860 feet or 5140 meters above sea level)

Highest Point in Asia (*see* Highest Point in the World)

Highest Point in Australia Mount Kosciusko in New South Wales (7328 feet or 2229 meters above sea level)

Highest Point in Europe Mount Elb'rus in the Caucasus of the USSR (18,567 feet or 5659 meters above sea level)

Highest Point in North America Mount McKinley in Alaska (20,320 feet or 6187 meters above sea level)

Highest Point in South America Mount Aconcagua in Argentina (22,835 feet or 6960 meters above sea level)

Highest Point in the World Mount Everest between Nepal and Tibet in Asia (29,028 feet or 8848 meters above sea level)

Highest Volcanic Island Mountain Mauna Loa (Hawaiian—Long Mountain)—on the island of Hawaii and often ranked as the world's largest active volcano

Idaho's Deepest Gorge Hells Canyon within the Grand Canyon of the Snake River is also the deepest gorge in North America with an average depth of 550 feet (1676 meters) and a maximum of 7900 feet (2408 meters) in depth

Illinois's Largest Forest Shawnee National Forest extending from the Ohio to the Mississippi rivers in southern Illinois

Indiana's Largest Cave Wyandotte Caves complete with five floor levels and an underground mountain

Iowa's Highest Point Ocheyedan Mound, deposited by a melting glacier that contained much sand and gravel and formed this conical hill

Ireland's Easternmost City Belfast or Dublin (depending on how you define Ireland)

Ireland's Easternmost Point Burr Head or Wicklow Head (depending on how you define Ireland)

Ireland's Highest Mountain Carrauntoohil or Kerry

Ireland's Largest City Dublin

Ireland's Largest Lake Lough Corrib

Ireland's Longest River the Shannon

Ireland's Northernmost City Londonderry (in Northern Ireland)

Ireland's Northernmost Point Malin Head (north of Londonderry)

Ireland's Southernmost City Cork

Ireland's Southernmost Point Fastnet Rock (south of Cape Clear and Sherkin Island)

Ireland's Westernmost City Galway

Ireland's Westernmost Point Tearaght Island (west of the Blaskets and the Dingle Peninsula)

Islands of the World (ranked by area) Greenland in the Arctic, New Guinea in the Pacific, Borneo in the Pacific, Madagascar in the Indian, Baffin Land in the Arctic, Sumatra in the Indiana, Honshu in the Pacific, Great Britain in the Atlantic, Victoria in the Arctic, Ellesmere in the Arctic, Sulawesi in the Indian, New Zealand's South Island in the Pacific, Java in the Indian, New Zealand's North Island in the Pacific, Cuba in the Atlantic, Newfoundland in the Atlantic, Luzon in the Pacific, Iceland in the Atlantic, Mindinao in the Pacific, Ireland in the Atlantic

Italy's Easternmost Seaport City Trieste (shared with Yugoslavia)

Italy's Easternmost Town Otranto (on the outer heel of the Italian boot washed by the Adriatic at the Strait of Otranto)

Italy's Largest City Roma (Rome)

Italy's Largest Port Genova (Genoa)

Italy's Largest Southern Port Napoli (Naples)

Italy's Most Historic Northern Port Venezia (Venice)

Italy's Northernmost Big City Milano (Milan)

Italy's Northernmost Town Brennero (at the Brenner Pass in Upper Adige on the Austrian frontier)

Italy's Southernmost Big City Messina (on the island of Sicily)

Italy's Southernmost Town Portopalo (on the island of Sicily)

Italy's Westernmost Big City Torino (Turin)

Italy's Westernmost Town Bardoecchia (on the French frontier)

Japan's Easternmost Point Nashappu (on Hokkaido just south of Sakhalin formerly part of Japan before the end of World War II when it was awarded the USSR)—Sakhalin formerly called Karafuto by the Japanese

Japan's Easternmost Town Habomai (on the island of Hokkaido)

Japan's Northernmost Cape and Town Soya (on the Island of Hokkaido)

Japan's Southernmost Island and Point Hateruma Shima in the Ryukyu or Sakishima islands)

Japan's Westernmost Island Yonaguni Jima (in the Ryukyu or Sakisshime islands close to Formosa or Taiwan in the East China Sea)

Japan's Westernmost Town Sonai (on Yonaguni Jima)

Kansas's Most Famous Landmark Pawnee Rock on the Santa Fe Trail where Indians and pioneers battled

Kentucky's Most Scenic Park Mammoth Cave National Park

Largest Afghan City Kabul

Larget African City Cairo

Largest African Nation Sudan

Largest Alabama City Birmingham

Largest Alaska City Anchorage

Largest Albanian City Tirana

Largest Albertan City Edmonton

Largest Algerian City Algiers

Largest American Bird wild turkey (once almost extinct)

Largest American City New York

Largest American City on the Canadian Border Detroit, Michigan

Largest American City on the Mexican Border San Diego, California (opposite Tijuana, Baja California)

Largest American East Coast City New York

Largest American Great Lakes City Chicago

Largest American Gulf Coast City Houston

Largest American Port of Entry San Ysidro, California (San Diego suburb opposite Tijuana, Baja California, Mexico)

Largest American Samoan City Pago Pago

Largest American Southern City Houston

Largest American State Alaska

Largest American West Coast City Los Angeles

Largest Andorran Town Andorra la Vella

Largest Angolan City Luanda

Largest Anteater giant anteater (larger than its related edentates such as armadillos and sloths)

Largest Arctic Ocean Island Baffin

Largest Argentine City Buenos Aires

Largest Arizona City Phoenix

Largest Arkansas City Little Rock

Largest Asian City Tokyo

Largest Asian Country China—the mainland People's Republic of China

Largest Asian Nation the USSR

Largest Atlantic Port New York (including Brooklyn, New Jersey, and Staten Island ports)

Largest Australian City Sydney

Largest Australian State Western Australia (Westralia)

Largest Austrian City Vienna

Largest Bahaman City Nassau

Largest Bahraini City Manama

Largest Balkan City Athens

Largest Bangalee City Dacca (capital of Bangladesh?)

Largest Barbadian City Bridgetown (capital of Barbados)

Largest Basotho City Maseru (capital of Lesotho)

Largest Belgian City Brussels

Largest Belizian City Belize

Largest Beninois City Benin

Largest Bermudan City Hamilton

Largest Bhutanese Town Thimphu

Largest Bolivian City La Paz

Largest Botswanan City Gaborone

Largest Brazilian City São Paulo

Largest British Carnivore common otter

Largest British City London

Largest British Columbian City Vancouver

Largest British Deer red deer

Largest British Marine Bird the cormorant or the gannet

Largest British Marine Mammal Atlantic seal also called grey seal

Largest British Wading Bird heron

Largest Bulgarian City Sofia

Largest Burman City Rangoon

Largest Burundian City Bujumbura

Largest California City Los Angeles

Largest Cambodian City Phnom Penh (capital of Cambodia or Kampuchea)

Largest Cameroonian City Douala

Largest Canadian City Montreal

Largest Canadian City on the American Border Windsor, Ontario

Largest Canadian Great Lakes City Toronto

Largest Canadian Province Québec

Largest Canadian Provincial Capital Toronto, Ontario

Largest Canadian West Coast City Vancouver

Largest Cape Verde Island Town Praia

Largest Capital of the Eastern World Tokyo

Largest Capital of the Western World Mexico City

Largest Central African Empire City Bangui

Largest Central American Republic Nicaragua

Largest Chadian City N'Djamena

Largest Chilean City Santiago de Chile

Largest Chinese City Shanghai

Largest City in Africa Cairo, Egypt

Largest City in Australia Sydney

Largest City in Brazil São Paulo

Largest City in the British Isles London

Largest City in California Los Angeles

Largest City in Canada Montreal

Largest City in China Shanghai

Largest City in Europe Paris

Largest City in India Calcutta

Largest City in Indonesia Jakarta

Largest City in Italy Rome

Largest City in Japan Tokyo

Largest City in the Largest State Anchorage, Alaska

Largest City in Latin America Mexico City

Largest City in the Middle East Teheran, Iran

Largest City in the Middle West Chicago, Illinois

Largest City in North America New York

Largest City in Northern Ireland or Ulster Belfast

Largest City in the Orient Tokyo, Japan

Largest City in the Philippines Manila

Largest City in the South Houston, Texas

Largest City in South America Buenos Aires, Argentina

Largest City in Spain Madrid

Largest City in the USSR Moscow

Largest Coffee Port Santos, Brazil

Largest Colombian City Bogotá

Largest Colorado City Denver

Largest Comoran Town Moroni

Largest Congolese or Zairian City Kinshasa

Largest Connecticut City Hartford

Largest Costa Rican City San José

Largest Cuban City Habana

Largest Cypriot City Nicosia

Largest Czechoslovakian City Prague

Largest Dahomian City Porto Novo

Largest Danish City Copenhagen

Largest Delaware City Wilmington

Largest Djiboutian City Djibouti

Largest Dominican City Santo Domingo

Largest Dutch City Rotterdam

Largest East European Country Soviet Union

Largest Ecuadorean City Guayaquil

Largest Eggs laid by North African ostriches

Largest Egyptian City Cairo

Largest English City London

Largest English East Coast City Manchester

Largest Equatorial Guinean City Bata

Largest Estonian City Tallinn

Largest Ethiopian City Addis Ababa

Largest European City Paris

Largest European Island Great Britain

Largest European Nation the USSR

Largest Fijian City Suva

Largest Filipino City Manila (capital of the Philippines)

Largest Finnish City Helsinki

Largest Fish Market in Tokyo

Largest Flightless Land Bird South African ostrich (larger than the cassowary, emu, kiwi, or rhea)

Largest Florida Metropolitan Area Miami

Largest Flying Bird condor (ranging from the Andes to California and long in danger of extinction)

Largest French City Paris

Largest French Guianese City Cayenne

Largest French Polynesian City Papeete, Tahiti

Largest French West Indian City Fort-de-France, Martinique

Largest Freshwater Lake in Africa Victoria between Kenya, Tanzania, and Uganda

Largest Freshwater Lake in Central America Lake Nicaragua between Costa Rica and Nicaragua

Largest Freshwater Lake of Eurasia Baikal in the USSR

Largest Freshwater Lake in Europe Balaton in Hungary

Largest Freshwater Lake in North America Superior between Canada and the U.S.

Largest Freshwater Lake in South America Titicaca between Bolivia and Peru

Largest Freshwater Lake in the World Superior in North America

Largest Gabonese City Libreville

Largest Gambian City Banjul
Largest Garden City in the Netherlands Apeldoorn
Largest of the Geese Canada goose
Largest Georgia City Atlanta
Largest German City Berlin
Largest Ghanian City Accra
Largest Gibraltarian City Gibraltar
Largest Greek City Athens
Largest Greenland Settlement Godthaab
Largest Grenadan City St George's
Largest Guadeloupian City Point-à-Pitre
Largest Guam City Agaña
Largest Guatemalan City Guatemala City
Largest Guinea-Bissauan City Bissau
Largest Guinean City Conakry
Largest Guyanese City Georgetown (capital of Guyana)
Largest Haitian City Port-au-Prince
Largest Hawaii City Honolulu
Largest Hispanic City Mexico City
Largest Honduran City Tegucigalpa
Largest Hungarian City Budapest
Largest Icelandic City Reykjavik
Largest Idaho City Boise
Largest Illinois City Chicago
Largest Indiana City Indianapolis
Largest Indian City Calcutta
Largest Indian Ocean Island Madagascar
Largest Indian Ocean Port Singapore (principal port of call on the Europe–Far East route)
Largest Indonesian City Jakarta
Largest Industrial City in Mexico Monterrey, Nuevo León
Largest Iowa City Des Moines
Largest Iranian City Teheran
Largest Iraqi City Baghdad
Largest Irish City Dublin
Largest Island in Australasia New Guinea
Largest Island in Indonesia Borneo (Kalimantan)
Largest Island in the West Indies Cuba
Largest Island in the World Greenland
Largest Island Mountain Mauna Kea (Hawaiian—White Mountain)—world's largest

volcanic mountain and world's highest island mountain in central Hawaii
Largest Israeli City Tel Aviv-Yafo
Largest Italian City Rome
Largest Ivoirian City Abidjan (capital of the Ivory Coast)
Largest Jamaican City Kingston
Largest Japanese City Tokyo
Largest Japanese Island Honshu
Largest Jordanian City Amman
Largest Kampuchean City Phnom Penh (capital of Cambodia or Kampuchea)
Largest Kansas City Wichita
Largest Kentucky City Louisville
Largest Kenyan City Nairobi
Largest Korean City Seoul
Largest Kuwaiti City Kuwait City
Largest Lakes (ranked by size) Caspian in Eurasia, Superior in North America, Victoria Nyanza in Africa, Aral in Eurasia, Huron and Michigan in North America, Tanganyika in Africa, Great Bear in North America, Baikal in Eurasia, Great Slave in North America, Malawi in Africa, Erie and Winnipeg in North America, Maracaibo in South America, Ontario in North America
Largest Lake in the World Caspian Sea in Eurasia between Iran and the USSR
Largest Land Mammal African bush elephant
Largest Lao City Vientiane (capital of Laos)
Largest Latin American Republic Brazil
Largest Latvian City Riga
Largest Lebanese City Beirut
Largest Lesothian City Maseru
Largest Liberian City Monrovia
Largest Libyan City Tripoli
Largest Liechtensteiner Town Vaduz
Largest Lithuanian City Vilna or Vilnius
Largest Living Antelope north-central Africa's giant eland
Largest Living Bat Kalong fruit bat of Indonesia and Malaysia
Largest Living Bird North African ostrich
Largest Living Canine the endangered timber wolf of the

wild (although the largest domestic dog is the Saint Bernard while the tallest is either the Great Dane or the Irish Wolfhound)
Largest Living Crocodilian saltwater crocodile (*Crocodylus porosus*) larger than any of the alligators, caymans, crocodiles, or gavials
Largest Living Crustacean Japanese spider crab
Largest Living Deer American moose (called elk in Europe)
Largest Living Dog Saint Bernard (largest in sense of heaviest as there are two taller dogs—the Great Dane and the Irish Wolfhound)
Largest Living Elephant African elephant
Largest Living Feline long-furred Manchurian or Siberian tiger (bigger than the so-called King of Beasts—the African lion—or any cheetah, cougar, jaguar, leopard, ocelot, ounce, or the celebrated Bengal tiger)
Largest Living Freshwater Fish Mekong River catfish (the Pla Buk of Laos)
Largest Living Freshwater Terrapin alligator snapping terrapin of the Mississippi River region
Largest Living Frog giant or goliath frog found in the Cameroons of Africa and bigger than the biggest American bullfrog
Largest Living Game Bird peafowl (related to domestic and jungle fowl, grouse, megapodes, pheasants, turkeys)
Largest Living Horse Belgian stallion
Largest Living Land Tortoise gigantic Galápagos tortoise
Largest Living Lizard Komodo dragon (*Varanus komodoensis*) of Indonesia
Largest Living Mammal blue or sulfur-bottom whale (endangered by Japanese and Soviet whalers)
Largest Living Marine Carnivore the walrus (Pacific subspecies has heavier tusks than its Atlantic counterpart)
Largest Living Marsupial Australian red kangaroo
Largest Living Monotreme duck-billed platypus (larger than the spiny echidna)
Largest Living Penguin emperor penguin

Largest Living Primate gorilla

Largest Living Rabbit Flemish great rabbit

Largest Living Reptile salt-water crocodile

Largest Living Rhinoceros Indian rhinoceros

Largest Living Rodent capybara rat (larger than any of its related rodents such as beavers, porcupines, rabbits, and squirrels)

Largest Living Salamander giant salamander of China and Japan

Largest Living Sea Turtle trunkback (*Dermochelys coriacea*) once common in all temperate and tropical oceans

Largest Living Shark great white mancater shark and the even larger but harmless plankton-eating whale shark

Largest Living Snake regal python (*Python reticulatus*)

Largest Living Species of Shark 60-foot-long (18-meter) whale shark

Largest Living Starfish Gulf of Mexico's bristling starfish (*Midgardia xandaros*)

Largest Living Terrestrial Carnivore Kodiak Island brown bear

Largest Louisiana City New Orleans

Largest Luxembourger City Luxembourg

Largest Maine City Portland

Largest Malagasy City Tananarive (capital of Madagascar)

Largest Malawian City Blantyre-Limbre

Largest Malaysian City Kuala Lumpur

Largest Maldivian Port Male

Largest Malian City Bamako (capital of Mali)

Largest Maltese City Sliema

Largest Manitoban City Winnipeg

Largest Marine Mammal blue or sulfur-bottom whale

Largest Maryland City Baltimore

Largest Massachusetts City Boston

Largest Mauritanian City Nouakchott

Largest Mauritian City Port Louis (capital of Mauritius)

Largest Mediterranean Port Marseille

Largest Mexican City Mexico City

Largest Mexican City on the American Border Ciudad Juárez, Chihuahua

Largest Mexican City in Jalisco Guadalajara (Mexico's second largest city)

Largest Mexican City on the Mexican Border Ciudad Juárez (opposite El Paso, Texas)

Largest Michigan City Detroit

Largest Middle American Country Mexico

Largest Minnesota Metropolitan Area Minneapolis-St Paul

Largest Mississippi City Jackson

Largest Mississippi River City St Louis

Largest Missouri City Kansas City

Largest Monacan or Monagasque City Monaco

Largest Mongolian City Ulan Bator

Largest Montana City Billings

Largest Moroccan City Casablanca

Largest Mozambican City Maputo

Largest Namibian City Walvis Bay

Largest Nation the USSR

Largest National Areas USSR, Canada, China, U.S.A., Brazil, Australia, India, Argentina, Sudan, Mongolia

Largest Nauruan Town Yaren

Largest Nebraska City Omaha

Largest Nepalese City Katmandu

Largest Netherlandic Antillean City Willemstad, Curaçao

Largest Netherlandic City Rotterdam

Largest Nevada City Las Vegas

Largest New Brunswick City Saint John

Largest New England City Boston

Largest Newfoundland City St John's

Largest New Hampshire City Manchester

Largest New Jersey City Newark

Largest New Mexico City Albuquerque

Largest New York State City New York City

Largest New Zealand City Auckland

Largest Nicaraguan City Managua

Largest Nigerian City Lagos

Largest Nigerois City Niamey (capital of Niger)

Largest North American City New York

Largest North American Nation Canada

Largest North American Turtle alligator snapper

Largest North Carolina City Charlotte

Largest North Dakota City Fargo

Largest North Pacific Port Los Angeles (including Long Beach, San Pedro, and Wilmington) and Yokohama (including Kawasaki, Tokyo, and Yokosuka) constantly compete for the title

Largest Northwest Territory Town Yellowknife

Largest Norwegian City Oslo

Largest Nova Scotian City Halifax

Largest Oceanic Areas Pacific, Atlantic, Indian, and Arctic oceans followed by the Mediterranean, South China, Bering, and Caribbean seas; the Gulf of Mexico and the Sea of Okhotsk; the East China and Yellow seas; Hudson Bay; the Sea of Japan; the North, Black, Red, and Baltic seas

Largest Oceanic Bird Pacific albatross (with a wingspread exceeding all other living species)

Largest Oceanic Nation Indonesia

Largest Officially Atheist Nation the USSR

Largest of the Forty-eight Contiguous States Texas

Largest Ohio City Cleveland

Largest Oil Tanker *Seawise Giant* under Liberian registry and 1504 feet (459 meters) overall length

Largest Oklahoma State City Oklahoma City

Largest Omani City Matrah

Largest Ontarian City Toronto

Largest Order of Living Birds the perching birds (containing some 6000 species)

Largest Oregon City Portland

Largest Pakistani City Karachi

Largest Panamanian City Panamá City

Largest Papuan City Port Moresby (capital of Papua New Guinea)

Largest Paraguayan City Asunción

Largest Passenger Ship *Norway* under Norwegian registry and

1035 feet (316 meters) overall length

Largest Pennsylvania City Philadelphia

Largest Peruvian City Lima

Largest Philippine City Manila

Largest Polish City Warsaw

Largest Polynesian City Papeete, Tahiti

Largest Polynesian City Outside Polynesia Auckland, New Zealand (world's largest)

Largest Population China (followed by India, the USSR, U.S.A., Pakistan, Indonesia, Japan, Brazil, West Germany, UK, Italy, France, Turkey, Spain, Poland)

Largest Portuguese City Lisbon

Largest Prince Edward Island City Charlottetown

Largest Province in Canada Québec

Largest Puerto Rican City San Juan

Largest Qatari City Doha (capital of Qatar)

Largest Québecois City Montreal

Largest Rhode Island City Providence

Largest Rhodesian City Salisbury

Largest Romanian City Bucharest

Largest Royal Capital of the Eastern World Tokyo

Largest Royal Capital of the Western World London

Largest Russian City Moscow

Largest Rwandan City Kigali

Largest Saltwater Lake In Asia Aral in the USSR

Largest Saltwater Lake in Australia Torrens in South Australia

Largest Saltwater Lake in the World Caspian Sea in Eurasia

Largest Salvadorean City San Salvador (capital of El Salvador)

Largest Samoan City Apia

Largest Sanmarinese Town San Marino (capital of San Marino)

Largest São Tome and Principe Town São Tome

Largest Saskatchewan City Regina

Largest Saudi Arabian City Riyadh

Largest Scottish City Glasgow

Largest Senegalese City Dakar

Largest Seychelles Port Port Victoria

Largest Sierra Leonean City Freetown

Largest Singaporean City Singapore

Largest Solomon Island Port Honiara

Largest Somali City Mogadishu

Largest South African City Johannesburg

Largest South American City Buenos Aires

Largest South American Country Brazil

Largest South Carolina City Columbia

Largest South China Sea City Hong Kong

Largest South Dakota City Sioux Falls

Largest Southeast-Asian City Singapore

Largest South Pacific Port Sydney

Largest South Yemeni City Aden

Largest Soviet City Moscow

Largest Spanish City Madrid

Largest Sri Lankan City Colombo

Largest State in the United States Alaska

Largest Sudanese City Khartoum

Largest Surinamese City Paramaribo

Largest Swaziland City Mbabane

Largest Swedish City Stockholm

Largest Swiss City Zurich

Largest Syrian City Damascus

Largest Tanzanian City Dar-es-Salaam

Largest Tennessee City Memphis

Largest Texas City Houston

Largest Texas Metropolitan Area Dallas-Ft Worth

Largest Thai City Bangkok

Largest Togolese Town Lome (capital of Togo)

Largest Tongan Town Nuku'alofa

Largest Trinidadian City Port-of-Spain

Largest Tunisian City Tunis

Largest Turkish City Istanbul

Largest Ugandan City Kampala

Largest Ulster City Belfast

Largest United Arab Emirates City Dubai

Largest United Kingdom City London

Largest Upper Voltan City Ouagadougou

Largest Uruguayan City Montevideo

Largest Utah City Salt Lake City

Largest Venezuelan City Caracas

Largest Vermont City Burlington

Largest Vietnamese City Ho Chi Minh City (Saigon)

Largest Village in Europe The Hague [official seat of the government of the Netherlands and also known as *'s Gravenhage* (Dutch—The Count's Hedge)]

Largest Virginia City Norfolk

Largest Virgin Island City Charlotte Amalie

Largest Volcanos (ranked by height) Aconcagua in Argentina, Lullaillaco in Chile, Chimborazo and Cotopaxi in Ecuador, Kilimanjaro in Tanzania, Antisana in Ecuador, Citlaltepetl in Mexico, Elbruz in the USSR, Demavend in Iran, Popocatapetl in Mexico, Kluchevskaya in the USSR, Karisimbi in Rwanda and Zaire, Wrangell in Alaska, Mauna Loa in Hawaii, Cameroon in Cameroon, Fujiyama in Japan, Erebus in Antarctica, Pico de Teyde in the Canary Islands, Semerou in Indonesia, Nyiragongo in Zaire, Iliamna in Alaska, Etna in Italy, Baker in Washington, Chillan in Chile, Nyamuragira in Zaire, Haleakala in Hawaii, Villarica in Chile, Ruapehu in New Zealand, Paricutin in Mexico

Largest Washington State City Seattle

Largest Welsh City Cardiff

Largest West European Country France

Largest West Indian City Havana, Cuba

Largest West Indian Nation Cuba

Largest West Virginia City Charleston

Largest Wisconsin City Milwaukee

Largest Wyoming City Cheyenne

Largest Yemeni City Sana

Largest Yugoslav City Belgrade

Largest Yukon Territory City Whitehorse

Largest Zairian City Kinshasa

Largest Zambian City Lusaka

Largest Zimbabwe-Rhodesian

City Salisbury
Least Populous State Alaska
Longest African River Nile
Longest American River Missouri-Mississippi (river system)
Longest Australian River Murray-Darling (river system)
Longest Canadian River Mackenzie-Peace (river system)
Longest Chinese River Yangtze
Longest Eastern Siberian River Lena
Longest Fjord Sognefjord (extending 110 miles or 175 kilometers into the heart of Norway)
Longest Indo-Chinese River Mekong
Longest North American River Mississippi-Missouri (river system)
Longest Northeast Asiatic River Amur (Black River or *Hei Ho* of the Chinese who also call it the Black Dragon River or *Heilung Kiang*)
Longest and Oldest Shopping Street Copenhagen's Stroget reserved for pedestrians
Longest Railroad in America Burlington Northern from Vancouver, BC to Mobile, Alabama
Longest Rivers Nile, Amazon, Mississippi-Missouri-Red Rock, Ob-Irtysh, Yangtze, Hwang Ho, Congo, Amur, Lena, Machenzie, Mekong, Niher, Yenisei, Paraná, Plata-Paraguay, Volga, Madeira, St Lawrence, Rio Grande, Orinoco, Yukon, Danube, Euphrates, Murray, Ganges, Irrawaddy, Dnieper, Negro, Don, Orange, Pechora, Marañon, Dneister, Rhine, Donets, Elbe, Gambia, Yellowstone, Vistula, Tagus (Tajo), Oder, Maas (Meuse), Seine, Guadalquivir, Hudson, Thames, Moldau, etc.
Longest South American River Amazon
Longest Southern African River Congo
Longest Southern South American River Paraná
Longest Train Trip in the World on the Trans-Siberian railway from Moscow in eastern Europe to Nakhodka near Vladivostok on the North Pacific coast
Longest West African River Niger

Longest Western Russian River Volga
Longest Western Siberian River Ob'-Irtysh
Louisiana's Largest Lake Pontchartrain on the Greater New Orleans Expressway
Loveliest Fleet of Islands "The loveliest fleet of islands that lies anchored in any ocean," wrote Mark Twain about the Hawaiian Islands in 1908
Lowest Murder Rate Sikkim—an Himalayan protectorate of India—where fewer than ten homicides occurred during the last hundred years
Lowest Place in Africa Lake Assal in Djibouti (512 feet or 156 meters below sea level)
Lowest Place in Antarctica unknown
Lowest Place in Asia (*see* Lowest Place in the World, as in the larger sense the Dead Sea between Israel and Jordan is in Asia)
Lowest Place in Australia Lake Eyre in South Australia (52 feet or 16 meters below sea level)
Lowest Place in Eastern Europe Caspian Sea between Iran and the USSR (92 feet or 28 meters below sea level)
Lowest Place in North America Badwater in Death Valley between California and Nevada (286 feet or 87.5 meters below sea level)
Lowest Place in South America Valdes Peninsula of Argentina (131 feet or 40 meters below sea level)
Lowest Places in Western Europe coastal areas of the Netherlands (15 feet or 4.6 meters below sea level)
Lowest Place in the World Dead Sea between Israel and Jordan (1302 feet or 397 meters below sea level)
Maine's Outermost Islands Matinicus, Monhegan, Ragged, and Seal islands
Maryland's Unspoiled Seashore Assateague Island National Seashore
Massachusetts's Best Known Lake Walden Pond, immortalized by philosopher-naturalist, Henry David Thoreau
Mexico's Easternmost City Chetumal, Quintana Roo
Mexico's Easternmost Point Cabo Catoche, Quintana Roo

(first Mexican site discovered by the Spaniards)
Mexico's Northernmost City Mexicali, Baja California
Mexico's Northernmost Point Los Algodones, Baja California
Mexico's Southernmost City Tapachula, Chiapas
Mexico's Southernmost Point just south of the town of Mariscal Suchiate at the mouth of the Suchiate across from Ocós, Guatemala on the Pacific
Mexico's Westernmost City Tijuana, Baja California
Mexico's Westernmost Point Playas de Tijuana, Baja California
Michigan's Unspoiled Forest Wilderness Hiawatha National Forest
Middle America's Largest Country Mexico
Minnesota's Northwesternmost Angle Lake of the Woods shared with Canada and containing the northernmost land of the United States except for Alaska
Mississippi's Most Scenic Highway Natchez Trace Parkway linking Alabama, Mississippi, and Tennessee by well-protected fields, forests, and meadows
Missouri's Superb Riverway Ozark National Scenic Riverways in southeastern Missouri's Ozark Mountains
Montana's Finest Mountain Country Glacier National Park
Most Active Volcano in the Continental United States Mount St Helens in southwestern Washington close to Portland, Oregon
Most Amazing of All Composers Wolfgang Amadeus Mozart
Most Beautiful College Town in America Princeton, New Jersey
Most Decent Man in Politics Hubert H. Humphrey
Most Densely Populated Nation in Mainland Latin America El Salvador
Most Elegant Salt-Marsh Terrapin commercially cultivated diamondback terrapin of the Carolinas and Georgia
Most Eloquent Englishman Sir Winston Churchill
Most English Town Outside England Christchurch, South

Island, New Zealand

Most Exotic West Indian Island Martinique (in the opinion of many travellers)

Most Feared Marine Predator shark

Most Gigantic Imbecility Since the Crusades Hermann Sudermann's nickname for World War I

Most Gigantic Prison in the World the Soviet Union, according to such an authority as Alexander I. Solzhenitsyn

Most Glorious Hero of Norwegian Viking Times Olav Tryggvasson

Most Gorgeous Rhetorician Robert G. Ingersoll

Most Mysterious Snake the harmless hoop snake is said to put its tail in its mouth whenever it is afraid; thereupon it rolls away like a hoop; but if someone pursues it the hoop snake proceeds to swallow its tail until there is no more snake; people who tell this story usually know the person who saw this but that person usually lives in another city or country

Most Northern Southern City Tulsa, Oklahoma

Most Popular Guest Symphonic Conductor Danny Kaye

Most Populous State California

Most Prolific Composer musicologists cannot agree as to whether it is Wolfgang Amadeus Mozart of Georg Philipp Telemann

Most Serene Republic of the Sea Venice, Queen of the Adriatic

Most Sinful City in South America Guayaquil, Ecuador, according to all who know about life's seamier side

Most Versatile Musician of Our Century Georges Enesco (Romanian composer-conductor-pianist-teacher-violinist)

Mountains of the World (ranked by height) Everest, K-2, Kanchenjunga, Makulu, Dhaulagiri, Nanga Parbat, Annapurna, Nanda Devi, and Kemet in the Himalayas; Namcha Barwa and Minya Konka in China; Kommumizma in the Pamirs; Pobedy in the Tian Shan; Aconcagua, Bonete, Ojos del Salado, Huascaran, Lullaillaco, Sajama, and Chimborazo in the Andes, McKinley in Alaska; Logan in

the Yukon; Cotopaxi in the Andes; Kilimanjaro in Tanzania; Antisana in the Andes; Ciltlaltepetl in the Sierra Madre; Elbruz in the Caucasus; Mount St Elias in Alaska; Popocatapetl in the Sierra Madre; Foraker in Alaska; Luciana in the Yukon; Tolima in the Andes; Kenya in Kenya; Ararat in Armenia; the Vinson Massif in Antarctica; (readers will note some of these are also listed under volcanos of the world but are included here because of their mountainous aspect)

Nebraska's Most Unusual Natural Feature the Sandhills covering northwestern and western Nebraska

Netherlands' Easternmost Town Nieuwe-Schans (on the German frontier)

Netherlands' Largest Port Rotterdam

Netherlands' Northernmost City Groningen

Netherlands' Northernmost Island Rottumeroog (in the Frisians between the North Sea and the Waddenzee)

Netherlands' Southernmost City Maastricht (near Liege, Belgium on the Maas River)

Netherlands' Southernmost Point Vaals (close to Aachen across the German frontier and just north of the Vaalserberg, highest point in the Netherlands)

Netherlands' Westernmost Port Flushing or Vlissingen (on Walcheren Island close to the North Sea)

Netherlands' Westernmost Town Sluis (on the Belgian border)

Nevada's Largest Forest Toiyabe National Forest (also the largest forest in the conterminous U.S.)

New Hampshire's Largest Lake Winnipesaukee, also called its most enchanting

New Jersey's Most Spectacular Park Palisades Interstate Park overlooking the Hudson River and much of New York City

New Mexico's Largest Gypsum Desert the White Sands National Monument, also the world's largest gypsum deposit

New York's Most Spectacular Waterfall Niagara Falls and

its Canadian counterpart

New Zealand's Easternmost City Gisborne on North Island

New Zealand's Easternmost Point North Island's East Cape

New Zealand's Northernmost City Whangarei north of Auckland on North Island

New Zealand's Northernmost Point North Island's North Cape

New Zealand's Southernmost City Invercargill on South Island south of Dunedin

New Zealand's Southernmost Point Southwest Cape on Steward Island south of South Island

New Zealand's Westernmost City Milford Sound on South Island

New Zealand's Westernmost Point Resolution Island west of South Island

North America's Easternmost City St John's, Newfoundland or Reykjavik, Iceland (if you include it in North America)

North America's Easternmost Point Cape Spear, Newfoundland or Nordostrundigen, Greenland (if you include it in North America)

North America's Northernmost City Barrow, Alaska

North America's Northernmost Point Canada's Cape Columbia or Greenland's Cape Morris Jesup (if you include it in North America)

North America's Southernmost City David, Panamá

North America's Southernmost Point southwesternmost Panamá just northeast of Juradó, Colombia

North America's Westernmost City Seward, Alaska

North America's Westernmost Point Cape Wrangell on Attu Island in the Aleutians

North Carolina's Loveliest Seashore the Outer Banks including the Cape Hatteras National Seashore

North Dakota's Most Exotic Scenery the Badlands along the Little Missouri River within the Theodore Roosevelt National Memorial Park

Northeasternmost Point of the continental United States West Quoddy Head near Lubec, Maine

Northern Ireland's Highest

Mountain Slieve Donard

Northern Ireland's Largest Lake Lough Neagh

Northernmost Capital of Africa Tunis, Tunisia

Northernmost Capital of Asia Ulaanbaatar, Mongolia

Northernmost Capital of Australia Darwin, Northern Territory

Northernmost Capital of Europe Reykjavik, Iceland

Northernmost Capital of North America Yellowknife, Northwest Territories

Northernmost Capital of South America Caracas, Venezuela

Northernmost Metropolis Leningrad (St Petersburg)

Northernmost Point of Canada Cape Columbia, Northwest Territories on the Arctic Ocean at 83°7' North

Northernmost Point of the continental United States Point Barrow, Alaska

Northernmost Point of Mexico Los Algodones, Baja California across the border from Andrade, California close to Yuma, Arizona

Northwesternmost Point of the continental United States Cape Wrangell on Attu Island in the Aleutians off Alaska

Ohio's Greatest Living Museum the Holden Arboretum east of Cleveland contains more than 6000 shrubs, trees, and vines from all parts of the world

Oklahoma's Largest Gypsum Cave in Alabaster Caverns State Park south of Freedom

Oldest American Orchestra New York Philharmonic (founded in 1842)

Oldest Central American Democracy Costa Rica

Oldest City in Canada Québec (founded by Champlain in 1608)

Oldest City in Denmark Ribe (whose church was built in the 12th century)

Oldest City in Germany Trier (founded by the Romans in 15 B.C.)

Oldest City in Malaysia Malacca (settled by Malays around 1400)

Oldest City in North America Mexico City (built by the Aztecs in 1325)

Oldest City in the U.S. St Augustine, Florida (founded by the Spaniards in 1565)

Oldest European Settlement in the Far East Macao (leased from China by the Portuguese in 1557)

Oldest European Settlement in the New World Santo Domingo City (founded by the Spaniards in 1496)

Oldest German Ocean Harbor Bremen (created an archbishopric in 845 A.D.)

Oldest Inhabited City Damascus, Syria

Oldest Inhabited Place in the United States Pueblo Acoma near Albuquerque, New Mexico

Oldest Known Canon *Sumer is incumenn in—Ihude sing cuccu*—Reading Rota most likely composed between 1280 and 1310—still sung

Oldest Quaintest City in the United States Santa Fé, New Mexico (built in 1621)

Oldest Ship in the British Navy HMS *Victory*—launched in 1765 and served as Nelson's flagship at Trafalgar

Oldest Ship in the U.S. Navy USS *Constitution*—launched in 1797 and nicknamed Old Ironsides

Oldest Synagogue (in continuous use since 1732) in the New World Mikve Israel in Willemstad, Curaçao

Oldest University in the Americas Santo Tómas de Aquino in Santo Domingo, Dominican Republic, where it was founded in 1538

Oregon's Most Beautiful and Peaceful Park Crater Lake National Park

Panama Canal's Most Ecologically Protected Island Barro Colorado

Pennsylvania's Most Pristine Park Allegheny National Forest extending into New York State

Peru's Easternmost and Northernmost City Iquitos (on the Amazon)

Peru's Largest Port Callao

Peru's Southernmost City Tacna (near the Chilean border)

Peru's Westernmost City Talara

Puerto Rico's Best Port San Juan

Puerto Rico's Easternmost City Fajardo

Puerto Rico's Easternmost Point Culebrita Island east of Culebra and Vieques

Puerto Rico's Largest City San Juan

Puerto Rico's Northernmost Cities Arecibo and San Juan

Puerto Rico's Northernmost Point Punta Jacinto

Puerto Rico's Southernmost City Ponce

Puerto Rico's Southernmost Point Caja de Muertos Island (southeast of Ponce)

Puerto Rico's Westernmost Cities Aguadilla and Mayagüez

Puerto Rico's Westernmost Point Punta Higüero

Rhode Island's Most Notable Feature Narragansett Bay leading to the Atlantic Ocean

Richest Country in the Middle East Kuwait

Richest Hill on Earth Butte, Montana

Rivers of the World (ranked by length) Nile in Africa, Amazon in South America, Mississippi-Missouri in North America, Ob'Irtysh in Asia, Yangtze in Asia, Hwang-ho in Asia, Congo in Africa, Amur in Asia, Lena in Asia, Mackenzie-Peace in North America, Mekong in Asia, Niger in Africa, Mackenzie in North America, Paraná in South America, Volga in Europe, Yenisei in Asia, Madeira in South America, Yukon in North America, Arkansas in North America, Colorado in North America, St Lawrence in North America, Rio Grande in North America, Salween in Asia, Danube in Europe, Euphrates in Asia, Indus in Asia, Brahmaputra in Asia, Zambesi in Africa, Murray-Darling in Australia

Samoa's Best Port Pago Pago on Tutuila Island (and its only port)

Scotland's Highest Mountain Ben Nevis

Scotland's Largest Lake Loch Lomond

Scotland's Longest River the Tay

Shallowest Sea Baltic (average depth under 190 feet)

Smallest African Country The Gambia

Smallest American State Rhode Island

Smallest Asian Country Singapore

Smallest Australian State Victoria

Smallest British Bird wren

Smallest British Mammal pygmy shrew

Smallest British Mouse harvest mouse

Smallest Canadian Province Prince Edward Island

Smallest Canadian Provincial Capital Charlottetown, Prince Edward Island

Smallest Capital of the Eastern World Yaren, Nauru

Smallest Capital in the U.S. Carson City, Nevada

Smallest Capital of the Western World San Marino, San Marino

Smallest Central American Country El Salvador

Smallest Continent Australia

Smallest East European Country Albania

Smallest European Country San Marino

Smallest Living Amphibian tree frog (*Hyla ocularis*) of the southeastern United States

Smallest Living Antelope West African royal antelope

Smallest Living Bat Kitt's hognosed bat from Thailand

Smallest Living Bird Cuban hummingbird

Smallest Living Cat rusty-spotted cat of India and Sri Lanka

Smallest Living Crocodilian dwarf caiman of the Amazon Basin

Smallest Living Deer Ecuadorean pudu

Smallest Living Dog miniature Chihuahua or pygmy Yorkshire terrier

Smallest Living Fish 1/2-inch-long (13mm) Philippine goby

Smallest Living Freshwater Turtle musk turtle

Smallest Living Horse Argentina's Falabella breed

Smallest Living Lizard British Virgin Island gecko (*Sphaerodactylus elasmobranchus*)

Smallest Living Mammal pygmy shrew or wood mouse, depending on the specimen some mammalogist is measuring

Smallest Living Marsupial Kimberly marsupial mouse of Western Australia

Smallest Living Rodent Eurasian harvest mouse

Smallest Living Sea Turtle Kemp's Bastard or Ridley (smaller than the green,

hawksbill, leatherback, or loggerhead)

Smallest Living Snake West Indian thread snake

Smallest Living Terrapin Colombian musk terrapin

Smallest Living Tortoise Egyptian or South African tortoise, depending on how the measurements are made

Smallest Middle American Country Grenada

Smallest Oceanic Country Nauru in the equatorial Pacific

Smallest Officially Atheist Nation Albania

Smallest Royal Capital of the Eastern World Katmandu, Nepal

Smallest Royal Capital of the Western World Monaco-Ville, Monaco

Smallest South American Country French Guiana

Smallest South American Nation Suriname.

Smallest Sovereign State Vatican City (*see* World's Smallest Sovereign State)

Smallest State in the United States Rhode Island

Smallest West European Country San Marino

Smallest West Indian Nation Grenada

South America's Easternmost Cities Brazil's João Pessoa and Recife (both on the Bulge of Brazil)

South America's Easternmost Points Brazil's Cabo Branco near João Pessoa and Punta de Pedra near Recife (both on the same longitude—34° 37' W)

South America's Northernmost City Coro, Venezuela

South America's Northernmost Point Punta Gallinas, Colombia

South America's Southernmost City Punta Arenas, Chile

South America's Southernmost Point Cabo de Hornos (Cape Horn), Chile

South America's Westernmost City Talara, Peru

South America's Westernmost Point Punta Pariñas, Peru

South Carolina's Most Charming City Charleston where one old-time resident insists the Ashley and Cooper rivers join to form the Atlantic Ocean

South Dakota's Most Memorable Memorial Mount Rushmore with the carved heads of

George Washington, Thomas Jefferson, Abraham Lincoln, and Theodore Roosevelt

Southeasternmost Point of the continental United States Cape Florida at the southern tip of Key Biscayne near Miami

Southeasternmost Point of the territorial United States Vagthus Point on Saint Croix in the Virgin Islands east of Puerto Rico

Southernmost Capital of Africa Cape Town, South Africa

Southernmost Capital of Asia Jakarta, Indonesia

Southernmost Capital of Australia Hobart, Tasmania

Southernmost Capital of Europe Athens, Greece

Southernmost Capital of North America Panamá City, Panamá

Southernmost City of South America Montevideo, Uruguay

Southernmost Island in the West Indies Grenada

Southernmost Metropolis Melbourne, Australia

Southernmost Point of Canada Middle Island, Ontario on Lake Erie south of Kingsville and Peelee Island close to Ohio

Southernmost Point of the continental United States South Beach on Key West, Florida

Southernmost Point of the insular United States Ka Lae or South Cape on Hawaii in the State of Hawaii

Southernmost Point of Mexico Barra del Río Suchiate (Mouth of the Suchiate River) separating the Pacific coast of Guatemala from Mexico and close to Ciudad Hidalgo

South's Oldest Daily Newspaper Charleston's *The News and Herald*

Southwesternmost Point of the continental United States Point Loma, California at the entrance to San Diego Bay

Southwesternmost Point of the territorial United States Steps Point on Tutuila Island of American Samoa in the South Pacific

Spain's Easternmost Point Cabo de Creus (northeast of Barcelona)

Spain's Easternmost Port Barcelona in Catalonia

Spain's Most Precious Jewel Toledo, according to Cervantes

Spain's Northernmost Point Cabo Ortegal (where the Bay of Biscay meets the Atlantic)

Spain's Northernmost Port El Ferrol del Caudillo

Spain's Southernmost Point Punta de Tarifa (on the Strait of Gibraltar)

Spain's Southernmost Port Algeciras (opposite Gibraltar)

Spain's Westernmost Point Cabo Finisterre

Spain's Westernmost Port Vigo (southwest of La Coruña)

Tallest Living Dog Great Dane or Irish Wolfhound

Tallest Living Mammal giraffe

Tennessee's Most Famous Mountain Lookout overlooking the Tennessee Valley and seven states beyond

Texas' Most Spectacular Park the Big Bend National Park whose southern border is the Rio Grande

United Kingdom's Easternmost Point Lowestoft Ness on Norfolk's east coast

United Kingdom's Easternmost Port Lowestoft, Suffolk

United Kingdom's Northernmost Point Herma Ness and Muckle Flugga Light on Unst in the Shetland Islands

United Kingdom's Northernmost Port Scapa Flow in the Orkney Islands north of Dunnet Bay to the west of John o'Groat's

United Kingdom's Southernmost Point Lizard Point on Cornwall's south coast

United Kingdom's Southernmost Port Penzance on Cornwall's south coast

United Kingdom's Westernmost Point Land's End, Cornwall

United Kingdom's Westernmost Port Penzance, Cornwall

United States superlatives (*see* America's *entries in this section*)

USSR's Easternmost Point Mys Deshneva across the Bering Strait from Alaska

USSR's Largest City Moscow

USSR's Northernmost Point Mys Chelyuskin, Siberia

USSR's Principal Eastern Port Vladivostok

USSR's Principal Northern Port Leningrad

USSR's Principal Southern Port Odessa

USSR's Principal Western Port Kaliningrad (formerly Königsberg, East Prussia)

USSR's Southernmost City Kushka, Turkmen (across the frontier from Golran in Afghanistan)

USSR's Westernmost Point and Port Baltiysk (formerly Pillau, Lithuania)

Utah's Saltiest Inland Sea the Great Salt Lake

Uttermost Port of the Earth Patagonia at the southern tip of South America

Uttermost South Cape Horn/Tierra del Fuego region of southern South America south of Patagonia

Uttermost Tip of Africa Cape Alguhas, South Africa

Uttermost Tip of Asia Singapore at the tip of the Malay Penisula

Uttermost Tip of Australia South East Cape, Tasmania

Uttermost Tip of Europe Nordkin, Norway

Uttermost Tip of North America Attu Island, Alaska or Ounta Mariato, Panama

Uttermost Tip of South America Cabo de Hornos (Cape Horn), Chile or Punta Gallinas, Colombia

Venezuela's Easternmost City Tucupita (in the delta of the Orinoco)

Venezuela's Easternmost Town La Horqueta (on the Guyana border)

Venezuela's Highest Mountain Pico Bolivar

Venezuela's Highest Town San Rafael de Mucuchies

Venezuela's Largest Port La Guaira

Venezuela's Northernmost City Coro

Venezuela's Northernmost Town Pueblo Nuevo (on the Paraguaná Peninsula)

Venuzuela's Southernmost City San Cristóbal

Venezuela's Southernmost Town Piedra de Cucuy (at the border of Brazil and Colombia)

Venezuela's Westernmost City Maracaibo

Venezuela's Westernmost Town Barranca (on the Colombian border)

Vermont's Greatest Forest Green Mountain National Forest in western Vermont

Virginia's Most Scenic Highway Blue Ridge Parkway through the southern Appalachian Mountains

Wales's Highest Mountain Snowdon

Wales's Largest Lake Bala Lake (Llyn Tegid)

Wales's Longest River the Towy

Washington's Most Spectacular Region Mount Baker National Forest including volcanic Mounts Adams, Rainier, and Saint Helena

Waterfalls of the World (ranked by height) Angel in Venezuela, Tugela in South Africa, Yosemite in California, Cuquenán in Venezuela, Sutherland in New Zealand, Mardalsfossen in Norway, Ribbon in California, King George VI in Guyana, Gavarnie in France, Victoria between Zimbabwe and Zambia, Iguazú between Argentina and Brazil, Niagara between Canada and the United States

Western Europe's Largest Prison Fleury Mergois on the outskirts of Paris

Westernmost Capital of Africa Dakar, Senegal

Westernmost Capital of Asia Istanbul, Turkey

Westernmost Capital of Australia Perth, Western Australia

Westernmost Capital of Europe Lisbon, Portugal

Westernmost Capital of North America Juneau, Alaska

Westernmost Capital of South America Quito, Ecuador

Westernmost Point of Canada Mount Saint Elias, Yukon on the Gulf of Alaska

Westernmost Point of the continental United States Cape Wrangell on Attu Island in the Aleutians off Alaska

Westernmost Point of Mexico Playas de Tijuana in Baja California just west of Tijuana and opposite San Diego, California

Westernmost Point of the territorial United States Orate Point on Guam in the western Pacific where it is the southernmost of the Marianas and within the Trust Territory of the Pacific Islands

Western Samoa's Best Port Apia on Upolu Island

West Virginia's Most Historic

Park Harper's Ferry National Historical Park originally surveyed by Thomas Jefferson in 1783

Wickedest City in the World almost-forgotten sobriquet of sunken Port Royal beneath Kingston, Jamaica's harbor where pirates once went for recreation

Wisconsin's Most Scenic Lakeshore Apostle Islands National Lakeshore on southern Lake Superior

World's Biggest Bauxite Port Weipa, Queensland

World's Biggest Bay Bay of Bengal

World's Biggest Bookend nickname of the Secretariat building of the United Nations overlooking New York's East River

World's Biggest Gamblers Americans followed by Britishers and Swedes

World's Busiest Airport Chicago's O'Hare International Airport

World's Busiest Border San Diego, California and Tijuana, Baja California

World's Busiest Border Crossing San Ysidro, California south of San Diego and bordering on Tijuana, in Baja California, Mexico

World's Busiest Morgue New York City Medical Examiner's Office at First Avenue and Thirtieth Street in Manhattan

World's Busiest Seaport Rotterdam in the Netherlands

World's Cleanest Cities in New Zealand and Norway (within temperate climes); Pago Pago and Singapore (in the tropics)

World's Coldest Places at or near the North or South Pole [Soviet scientists report −158°F (-105.6°C) at Omyakon, Siberia and -194°F (-125.6°C) near Vostok in Antarctica]

World's Coldest Seas Arctic and Antarctic oceans (2°C or 28°F)

World's Coolest City Ulan-Bator, Mongolia

World's Deepest Gorge Hells Canyon in Idaho's Snake River (7900 feet or 2410 meters)

World's Deepest Lake Baikal in the USSR (1742 meters or 5714 feet)

World's Dirtiest Places environ-mentalists and world travellers agree they are usually tropical places but notable exceptions are found in northern Australia, the Panama Canal, Pago Pago, and Singapore

World's Driest City Arica, Chile

World's Driest Place Chile's Atacama Desert where little or no rain has been recorded

World's Fastest Passenger Liner *United States*

World's First Detective François Eugène Vidocq

World's First Nuclear-Powered Submarine USS *Nautilus*

World's First Photographer Joseph Nicéphore Niepce

World's First Woman Prime Minister Sirimavo Ratwatte Badaranaike of Ceylon (Sri Lanka)

World's Freest and Smallest Jail San Marino's hilltop lockup near Rimini where sober prisoners are released daily to work in town

World's Greatest Bullshit Factory Hollywood, according to John Dos Passos

World's Greatest Economic Choke Point Strait of Ormuz between Iran and Oman on the Persian Gulf tanker route

World's Greatest Gorge Grand Canyon of the Colorado

World's Greatest Library Library of the British Museum

World's Greatest Predator man

World's Greatest Railroad Terminal Grand Central Terminal in New York City

World's Greatest Tides Nova Scotia's Bay of Fundy (53 feet or 16 meters)

World's Highest Capital City La Paz, Bolivia (elevation 11,909 feet or 3630 meters)

World's Highest City Lhasa, Tibet (3687 meters or 12,087 feet above sea level)

World's Highest Crime Rate in the U.S. where more than 300 major crimes are committed every hour

World's Highest Lake Titicaca in the Andes between Bolivia and Peru (3800 meters of 12,500 feet)

World's Highest Large City La Paz, Bolivia (3632 meters or 11,909 feet above sea level)

World's Highest Mountain Everest in Nepal (29,028 feet or 8848 meters)

World's Highest Mountains *(see* Mountains of the World)

World's Highest Murder Rate in the U.S. where more than 18,000 known murders occur yearly and about one American in every 10,000 will die at the hands of another

World's Highest Narcotic Addiction Rate in Hong Kong where in the 1980s some 80,000 in its population of 4 million were addicts

World's Highest Navigable Lake Titicaca (Bolivia)

World's Highest Point Mount Everest between Nepal and Tibet

World's Highest Tides at Burntcoat Head in the Bay of Fundy near Noel, Nova Scotia [53 feet (16 meters) and sometimes even 60 feet (18 meters)]

World's Highest Village Aucanquilca, Chile (17,500 feet or 5334 meters)

World's Highest Waterfall Angel in Venezuela (3297 feet or 1005 meters)

World's Highest Waterfalls *(see* Waterfalls of the World)

World's Hottest Place Arizia, Libya (136°F or 58°C)

World's Hottest Sea Persian Gulf (36°C or 97°F)

World's Largest Active Volcano Mauna Loa on the island of Hawaii

World's Largest Archipelago Indonesia's more than 3000 islands extending from the Indian Ocean to the western Pacific

World's Largest Art Gallery Hermitage and Winter Palace in Leningrad

World's Largest Atoll Kwajalein in the Marshalls

World's Largest Bank Bank of America

World's Largest (but unfinished) Cathedral St John the Divine in New York City

World's Largest Cave Big Room in New Mexico's Carlsbad Caverns

World's Largest Church Holy Roman Catholic Church

World's Largest City Greater New York (with Mexico City, Shanghai, and Tokyo not far behind)

World's Largest Cold Current West Wind Drift (circling Antarctica and washing the southernmost shores of Africa, Australia, and South America)

World's Largest Continent Asia

World's Largest Countries (ranked by size) USSR, Canada, China, U.S.A., Brazil

World's Largest Delta Ganges-Brahmaputra between India and Pakistan

World's Largest Democracy India

World's Largest Desert North Africa's Sahara

World's Largest Dictionary 13-volume *Oxford English Dictionary* plus supplements

World's Largest Exporter of Bananas Ecuador

World's Largest Exporter of Oil Saudi Arabia

World's Largest Fish Market Tokyo

World's Largest Flower Auction Aalsmeer near Amsterdam's Schipol Airport

World's Largest Game Reserve Selous Game Reserve (in Tanzania)

World's Largest Gorge Grand Canyon of the Colorado in Arizona

World's Largest Green-Space City Oslo, Norway followed by Stockholm, Sweden

World's Largest Gulf Gulf of Mexico

World's Largest Island Greenland

World's Largest Islands (*see* Islands of the World)

World's Largest Lagoon Truk Island in Micronesia

World's Largest Lakes (ranked by area) Caspian, Superior, Victoria, Aral, Huron, Michigan, Tanganyika, Great Bear, Baikal, Nyasa, Great Slave, Erie, Winnipeg, Ontario, Ladoga, Balkash, Chad, Maracaibo, Onega, Volta, Titicaca, Athabasca, Nicaragua, Eyre, Rudolf, Reindeer, Torrens, Vanern, Albert, Nipigong, Gairdner, Manitoba, Urmia, etc.

World's Largest Land Carnivore polar bear

World's Largest Library Library of Congress, Washington, D.C.

World's Largest Lumber Shipping Port Coos Bay, Oregon

World's Largest Marine Carnivore walrus

World's Largest Mountain Hawaii's Mauna Loa

World's Largest Museum New York City's American Museum of Natural History

World's Largest National Park Tsavo (in Kenya)

World's Largest Newspaper *The New York Times*

World's Largest Number of Great Cities (with a million or more people) U.S. followed by China, Latin America, and middle-south Asiatic countries including India

World's Largest Ocean Pacific

World's Largest Open Sewer the azure Mediterranean Sea from the Bosporus and Iskenderun to the Straits of Gibraltar

World's Largest Open-Space Countries the U.S. followed by Canada and Australia have the most land reserved for national parks and nature reserves

World's Largest Opera House Metropolitan Opera House, Lincoln Center, New York City

World's Largest Passenger Ship *Queen Elizabeth 2* whose deadweight tonnage exceeds the longer *Norway* (formerly the *France*); fastest and second longest is the *United States* followed by the heavier but shorter *Canberra* and *Oriana* exceeding the *Rotterdam* and *Leonardo da Vinci* in tonnage and length

World's Largest Peninsula Arabian Peninsula

World's Largest Port Rotterdam

World's Largest Postage Stamp 75-cent Marshall Islands postal adhesive measuring some 4 by 6 inches (105 by 150mm)

World's Largest Prison Kharkhov in the Soviet Ukraine where more than 40,000 prisoners have been incarcerated at one time

World's Largest Public Library New York Public Library at Fifth Avenue and 42nd Street plus its more than 80 branches

World's Largest Publisher U.S. Government Printing Office (GPO)

World's Largest River Basin Amazon

World's Largest Ski Village Vancouver, British Columbia

World's Largest Slum Area Mexico City's 500 slums

whose population often is used to establish Mexico City as the world's largest city

World's Largest System of Freshwater Lakes Great Lakes of Canada and the United States

World's Largest University State University of New York

World's Largest Walled Prison Southern Michigan Prison spanning 54 acres (22 hectares) and housing 5600 men in mid-1984

World's Largest Warm Current Gulf Stream (uniting the South Equatorial, Guiana, Caribbean, Florida, North Atlantic, Irminger, Norwegian, and West Spitsbergen currents)

World's Least Populated Places Greenland followed by French islands in the south Indian Ocean, Svalberg in the Arctic Ocean, the Falklands, in the South Atlantic, the once Spanish Sahara claimed by Algeria and Morocco, French Guiana, Namibia, Mongolia, Botswana, and Libya

World's Least Populous Nation Tuvalu (formerly Ellice Islands in the central tropical Pacific close to the Gilberts and Western Samoa)

World's Loneliest Meeting Place Isla de Pascua (Easter Island) in the South Pacific

World's Longest-Lived People the Japanese and the Scandinavians

World's Longest Railroad Trans-Siberian from Moscow to Vladivostok

World's Longest Railway Tunnel 13-mile-long (21-kilometer-long) Dai-shimuzu in Japan

World's Longest Reef Australia's Great Barrier

World's Longest River Nile (also Africa's longest)

World's Longest Rivers (*see* Rivers of the World)

World's Longest Suspension Bridge Verrazano-Narrows Bridge spanning the Narrows in New York Harbor

World's Lowest City Brawley, California (184 feet or 56 meters below sea level)

World's Lowest Lake Dead Sea between Israel and Jordan (394 meters or 1292 feet below sea level)

World's Lowest Point Dead Sea

between Israel and Jordan

World's Lowest Settlement Ein Bobek on the shores of the Dead Sea (396 meters or 1299 feet below sea level)

World's Main Choke Point for the Flow of Oil Strait of Hormuz connecting the oil-productive Persian Gulf countries with the Indian Ocean and the rest of the world; other choke points include the Bab al Mandab, Dardanelles, Dover, Formosa, Gibraltar, Kattegat, Korea, Magellan, and Malacca straits plus the Panama and Suez canals

World's Most Active Volcano Kilauea on the island of Hawaii

World's Most Densely Populated City Shanghai followed by Tokyo, Mexico City, New York, Peking, London, Manila, Moscow, São Paulo, Seoul, Jakarta, Cairo

World's Most Easterly City Gisborne, New Zeland

World's Most Exciting City Hong Kong, London, New York, Tokyo, and San Francisco vie for this title

World's Most Isolated City Perth, Western Australia

World's Most Northerly City Hammerfest, Norway

World's Most Northerly Settlement Alert (close to the North Pole in the Northwest Territory of Canada)

World's Most Overcrowded City Hong Kong

World's Most Popular Crime in 1985 dealing in habit-forming drugs such as cocaine, heroin, morphine, and the like

World's Most Populated Country China followed by India, the USSR, the U.S., Indonesia, Japan, Brazil, West Germany, Bangladesh, the United Kingdom

World's Most Populated Islands Barbados, Haiti, Hong Kong, Jamaica, Java, Puerto Rico, Trinidad

World's Most Populated Place Macao (Portuguese province on the China coast close to Hong Kong whose vast population is but a quarter of Macao's in density)

World's Most Population-Exploding Nation India

World's Most Populous Nation China

World's Most Prolific Composer musicologists cannot agree as to whether it is Wolfgang Amadeus Mozart or Georg Philipp Telemann

World's Most Southerly City Punta Arenas, Chile (once called Magallanes)

World's Most Terror-stricken Country Lebanon (followed in 1985 reports by Italy, Spain, West Germany, Northern Ireland, and then by Latin American and Middle East countries)

World's Most Westerly City Nome, Alaska or Pago Pago, Samoa, depending on how you define city

World's Most Widely Prevalent Carnivore the red fox

World's Oldest Capital City Damascus, Syria

World's Oldest Constitutional Democracy the United States of America

World's Oldest Monarchy Denmark (one of the most democratic nations)

World's Oldest Orchestra Dresdener Staatskapelle founded in Dresden in 1548

World's Oldest Parliament Iceland's *Althing* (Old Thing) founded in 930

World's Oldest Profession prostitution, according to students of ancient and biblical history

World's Only Black One-Eyed Jewish Singin' Cowpoke Sammy Davis, Jr

World's Rainiest City Monrovia, Liberia

World's Rainiest Place Mount Waileale, Hawaii

World's Richest Countries (per capita income) United Arab Emirates, Qatar, Kuwait, Liechtenstein, Switzerland, Sweden, Monaco, the United States, Canada, West Germany, Australia, Denmark, Belgium, Andorra, and Norway in the order shown

World's Second Most Popular Crime in 1985 exploitation of alcohol, games of chance, and sex in the so-called entertainment industry flourishing in cities and resorts of all sorts

World's Second-Oldest Profession arms making and trad-

ing

World's Shortest Poem *I—why?* by Eli Siegal

World's Smallest Continent Australia

World's Smallest Sovereign State Vatican City within Rome occupies 44 hectares (109 acres)

World's Smoggiest City Mexico City, according to ecologist-zoologist Gerald Durrell and many other well-informed people

World's Southernmost Town Puerto Williams, Chile (across Beagle Channel from Ushuaia, Argentina)—both close to Cape Horn

World's Tallest Building 110-story Sears Tower in Chicago (1454 feet or 444 meters high)

World's Tallest Buildings New York City's World Trade Center (each building 110 stories with the second topped by a television tower)

World's Tallest Structure Canadian National Railway's Communication and Observation Tower in downtown Toronto, Ontario (1805 feet high—550 meters)

World's Third Most Popular Crime in 1985 stealing art treasures such as paintings, and statues as well as objects of historic interest

World's Very Most Popular Crime in 1985 computer-concealed white-collar crimes such as large-scale embezzlements and consumer ripoffs

World's Warmest City Timbuktu, Mali

World's Wettest City Monrovia, Liberia

World's Wettest Place Mount Waialeale on the island of Kauai in Hawaii

Wyoming's Most Spectacular Park Yellowstone National Park with headquarters at Mammoth Hot Springs and extending into Idaho and Montana

Youngest Central American Democracy Belize (formerly British Honduras)

Youngest Province Newfoundland, Canada including Labrador

U.S. Naval Ship Symbols

AD Destroyer Tender

ADG Degaussing Ship

AE Ammunition Ship

AF Store Ship

AFDB Large Auxiliary Floating Dry Dock (non-self-propelled)

AFDL Small Auxiliary Floating Dry Dock (non-self-propelled)

AFDM Medium Auxiliary Floating Dry Dock (non-self-propelled)

AFS Combat Store Ship

AG Miscellaneous

AGDE Escort Research Ship

AGEH Hydrofoil Research Ship

AGER Environmental Research Ship

AGF Miscellaneous Command Ship

AGM Missile Range Instrumentation Ship

AGMR Major Communications Relay Ship

AGOR Oceanographic Research Ship

AGP Patrol Craft Tender

AGR Radar Picket Ship

AGS Surveying Ship

AGSS Auxiliary Submarine

AGTR Technical Research Ship

AH Hospital Ship

AK Cargo Ship

AKD Cargo Ship, Dock

AKL Light Cargo Ship

AKR Vehicle Cargo Ship

AKS Stores Issue Ship

AKV Cargo Ship and Aircraft Ferry

ANL Net Laying Ship

AO Oiler

AOE Fast Combat Support Ship

AOG Gasoline Tanker

AOR Replenishment Oiler

AP Transport

APB Self-propelled Barracks Ship

APL Barracks Craft (non-self-propelled)

AR Repair Ship

ARB Battle Damage Repair Ship

ARC Cable Repairing Ship

ARD Auxiliary Repair Dry Dock (non-self-propelled)

ARDM Medium Auxiliary Repair Dry Dock (non-self-propelled)

ARG Internal Combustion Engine Repair Ship

ARL Landing Craft Repair Ship

ARS Salvage Ship

ARSD Salvage Lifting Ship

ARST Salvage Craft Tender

ARVA Aircraft Repair Ship (aircraft)

ARVE Aircraft Repair Ship (engine)

ARVH Aircraft Repair Ship (helicopter)

AS Submarine Tender

ASPB Assault Support Patrol Boat

ASR Submarine Rescue Ship

ATA Auxiliary Ocean Tug

ATC Armored Troop Carrier

ATF Fleet Ocean Tug

ATS Salvage Tug

ATSS Auxiliary Training Submarine

AV Seaplane Tender

AVM Guided Missile Ship

AVS Aviation Supply Ship

AVT Auxiliary Aircraft Transport

AW Distilling Ship

BB Battleship

CA Heavy Cruiser

CC Command Ship

CCB Command and Control Boat

CG Guided Missile Cruiser

CGN Guided Missile Cruiser (nuclear propulsion)

CL Light Cruiser

CLG Guided Missile Light Cruiser

CVA Attack Aircraft Carrier

CVAN Attack Aircraft Carrier (nuclear propulsion)

CVS ASW Support Aircraft Carrier

CVT Training Aircraft Carrier

DD Destroyer

DDG Guided Missile Destroyer

DE Escort Ship

DEG Guided Missile Escort Ship

DER Radar Picket Escort Ship

DL Frigate

DLG Guided Missile Frigate

DLGN Guided Missile Frigate (nuclear propulsion)

DSRV Deep Submergence Rescue Vessel

DSV Deep Submergence Vehicle

E (Prefix) Experimental Ship

F (Prefix) Ship being built by U.S. for a foreign nation

FDL Fast Deployment Logistics Ship

IX Unclassified Miscellaneous

LCA Landing Craft, Assault

LCC Amphibious Command Ship

LCM Landing Craft, Mechanized

LCPL Landing Craft, Personnel, Large

LCPR Landing Craft, Personnel, Ramped

LCSR Landing Craft Swimmer Reconnaissance

LCU Landing Craft, Utility

LCVP Landing Craft, Vehicle, Personnel

LFR Inshore Fire Support Ship

LFS Amphibious Fire Support Ship

LHA Amphibious Assault Ship (general purpose)

LKA Amphibious Cargo Ship

LPA Amphibious Transport

LPD Amphibious Transport Dock

LPH Amphibious Assault Ship

LPR Amphibious Transport (small)

LPSS Amphibious Transport Submarine

LSD Dock Landing Ship

LSSC Light SEAL Support Craft

LST Tank Landing Ship

LWT Amphibious Warping Tug

MAC MIUW Attack Craft

MCS Mine Countermeasures Ship

MON Monitor

MSB Minesweeping Boat

MSC Minesweeper, Coastal (nonmagnetic)

MSD Minesweeper, Drone

MSF Minesweeper, Fleet (steel hull)

MSI Minesweeper, Inshore

MSL Minesweeping Launch

MSM Minesweeper, River (Converted LCM-6)

MSO Minesweeper, Ocean (nonmagnetic)

MSR Minesweeper, Patrol

MSS Minesweeper, Special (device)

MSSC Medium SEAL Support Craft

NR Submersible Research Vehicle (nuclear propulsion)

PBR River Patrol Boat

PCE Patrol Escort
PCER Patrol Rescue Escort
PCF Patrol Craft, Inshore
PCH Patrol Craft (hydrofoil)
PG Patrol Gunboat
PGH Patrol Gunboat (hydrofoil)
PTF Fast Patrol Craft
QFB Quiet Fast Boat
RUC Riverine Utility Craft
SDV Swimmer Delivery Vehicle
SES Surface-Effect Ship
SS Submarine
SSBN Fleet Ballistic Missile Submarine (nuclear propulsion)
SSG Guided Missile Submarine
SSN Submarine (nuclear propulsion)
SST Target and Training Submarine (self-propelled)
STAB Strike Assault Boat
T (Prefix) Military Sealift Command Ship
W (Prefix) U.S. Coast Guard Ship
X Submersible Craft (self-propelled)
YAG Miscellaneous Auxiliary (self-propelled)
YC Open Lighter (non-self-propelled)
YCF Car Float (non-self-propelled)
YCV Aircraft Transportation Lighter (non-self-propelled)
YD Floating Crane (non-self-propelled)
YDT Diving Tender (non-self-propelled)

YF Covered Lighter (self-propelled)
YFB Ferryboat or Launch (self-propelled)
YFD Yard Floating Dry Dock (non-self-propelled)
YFN Covered Lighter (non-self-propelled)
YFNB Large Covered Lighter (non-self-propelled)
YFND Dry Dock Companion Craft (non-self-propelled)
YFNX Lighter (special purpose) (non-self-propelled)
YFP Floating Power Barge (non-self-propelled)
YFR Refrigerated Covered Lighter (self-propelled)
YFRN Refrigerated Covered Lighter (non-self-propelled)
YFRT Covered Lighter (range-tender) (self-propelled)
YFU Harbor Utility Craft (self-propelled)
YG Garbage Lighter (self-propelled)
YGN Garbage Lighter (non-self-propelled)
YHLC Salvage Lift Craft, Heavy (non-self-propelled)
YLLC Salvage Lift Craft, Light (self-propelled)
YM Dredge (self-propelled)
YMLC Salvage Lift Craft, Medium (non-self-propelled)
YNG Gate Craft (non-self-propelled)
YO Fuel Oil Barge (self-propelled)
YOG Gasoline Barge (self-propelled)
YOGN Gasoline Barge (non-

self-propelled)
YON Fuel Oil Barge (non-self-propelled)
YOS Oil Storage Barge (non-self-propelled)
YP Patrol Craft (self-propelled)
YPD Floating Pile Driver (non-self-propelled)
YR Floating Workshop (non-self-propelled)
YRB Repair and Berthing Barge (non-self-propelled)
YRBM Repair, Berthing and Messing Barge (non-self-propelled)
YRDH Floating Dry Dock Workshop (hull) (non-self-propelled)
YRDM Floating Dry Dock Workshop (machine) (non-self-propelled)
YRR Radiological Repair Barge (non-self-propelled)
YRST Salvage Craft Tender (non-self-propelled)
YSD Seaplane Wrecking Derrick (self-propelled)
YSR Sludge Removal Barge (non-self-propelled)
YTB Large Harbor Tug (self-propelled)
YTL Small Harbor Tug (self-propelled)
YTM Medium Harbor Tug (self-propelled)
YW Water Barge (self-propelled)
YWDN Water Distilling Barge (non-self-propelled)
YWN Water Barge (non-self-propelled)

Vehicle Registration Symbols (Index Markers)

British Isles Symbols

This listing includes registration marks for the Republic of Ireland. These marks were introduced before the creation of the Republic of Ireland, which has continued with the same system.

A	London	AH	Norfolk	AP	Sussex (East)
AA	Hampshire	AI	Meath	AR	Hertfordshire
AB	Worcestershire	AJ	Yorkshire (NR)	AS	Nairnshire
AC	Warwickshire	AK	Bradford	AT	Kingston-upon-Hull
AD	Gloucestershire	AL	Nottinghamshire	AU	Nottingham
AE	Bristol	AM	Wiltshire	AV	Aberdeenshire
AF	Cornwall	AN	London	AW	Salop
AG	Ayrshire	AO	Cumberland	AX	Monmouthshire

AY	Leicestershire	DL	Isle of Wight	G	Glasgow
AZ	Belfast	DM	Flintshire	GA	Glasgow
B	Lancashire	DN	York	GB	Glasgow
BA	Salford	DO	Lincolnshire (Holland)	GC	London
BB	Newcastle upon Tyne	DP	Reading	GD	Glasgow
BC	Leicester	DR	Plymouth	GE	Glasgow
BD	Northamptonshire	DS	Peeblesshire	GF	London
BE	Lincolnshire (Lindsey)	DT	Doncaster	GG	Glasgow
BF	Staffordshire	DU	Coventry	GH	London
BG	Birkenhead	DV	Devon	GI	London
BH	Buckinghamshire	DW	Newport (Mon)	GK	London
BI	Monaghan	DX	Ipswich	GL	Bath
BJ	Suffolk (East)	DY	Hastings	GM	Motherwell and Wishaw
BK	Portsmouth	DZ	Antrim	GN	London
BL	Berkshire	E	Staffordshire	GO	London
BM	Bedfordshire	EA	West Bromwich	GP	London
BN	Bolton	EB	Cambridge	GR	Sunderland
BO	Cardiff	EC	Westmorland	GS	Perthshire
BP	Sussex (West)	ED	Warrington	GT	London
BR	Sunderland	EE	Grimsby	GU	London
BS	Orkney	EF	West Hartlepool	GV	Suffolk (West)
BT	Yorkshire (ER)	EG	Huntingdon	GW	London
BU	Oldham	EH	Stoke-on-Trent	GX	London
BV	Blackburn	EI	Sligo	GY	London
BW	Oxfordshire	EJ	Cardiganshire	GZ	Belfast
BX	Carmarthenshire	EK	Wigan	H	London
BY	London	EL	Bournemouth	HA	Warley
BZ	Down	EM	Bootle	HB	Merthyr Tydfil
C	Yorkshire (WR)	EN	Bury	HC	Eastbourne
CA	Denbighshire	EO	Berrow-in-Furness	HD	Dewsbury
CB	Blackburn	EP	Montgomeryshire	HE	Barnsley
CC	Caernarvonshire	ER	Cambridgeshire	HF	Wallasey
CD	Brighton	ES	Perthshire	HG	Burnley
CE	Cambridgeshire	ET	Rotherham	HH	Carlisle
CF	Suffolk (West)	EU	Breconshire	HI	Tipperary
CG	Hampshire	EV	Essex	HJ	Southend
CH	Derby	EW	Huntingdonshire	HK	Essex
CI	Laoighis	EX	Great Yarmouth	HL	Wakefield
CJ	Herefordshire	EY	Anglesey	HM	London
CK	Preston	EZ	Belfast	HN	Darlington
CL	Norwich	F	Essex	HO	Hampshire
CM	Birkenhead	FA	Burton-on-Trent	HP	Coventry
CN	Gateshead	FB	Bath	HR	Wiltshire
CO	Plymouth	FC	Oxford	HS	Renfrewshire
CP	Halifax	FD	Dudley	HT	Bristol
CR	Southampton	FE	Lincoln	HU	Bristol
CS	Ayrshire	FF	Merionethshire	HV	London
CT	Lincolnshire (Kesteven)	FG	Fife	HW	Bristol
CU	South Shields	FH	Gloucester	HX	London
CV	Cornwall	FI	Tipperary (NR)	HY	Bristol
CW	Burnley	FJ	Exeter	HZ	Tyrone
CX	Huddersfield	FK	Worcester	IA	Antrim
CY	Swansea	FL	Huntingdon	IB	Armagh
CZ	Belfast	FM	Chester	IC	Carlow
D	Kent	FN	Canterbury	ID	Cavan
DA	Wolverhampton	FO	Radnorshire	IE	Clare
DB	Stockport	FP	Rutland	IF	Cork (County)
DC	Teesside	FR	Blackpool	IH	Donegal
DD	Gloucestershire	FS	Edinburgh	IJ	Down
DE	Pembrokeshire	FT	Tynemouth	IK	City and County of
DF	Gloucestershire	FU	Lincolnshire (Lindsey)		Dublin
DG	Gloucestershire	FV	Blackpool	IL	Fermanagh
DH	Walsall	FW	Lincolnshire (Lindsey)	IM	Galway
DI	Roscommon	FX	Dorset	IN	Kerry
DJ	St Helens	FY	Southport	IO	Kildare
DK	Rochdale	FZ	Belfast	IP	Kilkenny

Code	Place	Code	Place	Code	Place
IR	Offaly	LG	Cheshire	NV	Northamptonshire
IT	Leitrim	LH	London	NW	Leeds (B)
IU	Limerick	LI	Westmeath	NX	Warwickshire
IW	Londonderry	LJ	Bournemouth	NY	Glamorgan
IX	Longford	LK	London	NZ	Londonderry
IY	Louth	LL	London	O	Birmingham
IZ	Mayo	LM	London	OA	Birmingham
J	Durham (County)	LN	London	OB	Birmingham
JA	Stockport	LO	London	OC	Birmingham
JB	Berkshire	LP	London	OD	Devon
JC	Caernarvonshire	LR	London	OE	Birmingham
JD	London	LS	Selkirkshire	OF	Birmingham
JE	Cambridge	LT	London	OG	Birmingham
JF	Leicester	LU	London	OH	Birmingham
JG	Canterbury	LV	Liverpool	OI	Belfast
JH	Hertfordshire	LW	London	OJ	Birmingham
JI	Tyrone	LX	London	OK	Birmingham
JJ	London	LY	London	OL	Birmingham
JK	Eastbourne	LZ	Armagh	OM	Birmingham
JL	Lincolnshire (Holland)	M	Cheshire	ON	Birmingham
JM	Westmorland	MA	Cheshire	OO	Essex
JN	Southend	MB	Cheshire	OP	Birmingham
JO	Oxford	MC	London	OR	Hampshire
JP	Wigan	MD	London	OS	Wigtownshire
JR	Northumberland	ME	London	OT	Hampshire
JS	Ross & Cromarty	MF	London	OU	Hampshire
JT	Dorset	MG	London	OV	Birmingham
JU	Leicestershire	MH	London	OW	Southampton
JV	Grimsby	MI	Wexford	OX	Birmingham
JW	Wolverhampton	MJ	Bedfordshire	OY	London
JX	Halifax	MK	London	OZ	Belfast
JY	Plymouth	ML	London	P	Surrey
JZ.	Down	MM	London	PA	Surrey
K	Liverpool	MN	Isle of Man	PB	Surrey
KA	Liverpool	MO	Berkshire	PC	Surrey
KB	Liverpool	MP	London	PD	Surrey
KC	Liverpool	MR	Wiltshire	PE	Surrey
KD	Liverpool	MS	Stirlingshire	PF	Surrey
KE	Kent	MT	London	PG	Surrey
KF	Liverpool	MU	London	PH	Surrey
KG	Cardiff	MV	London	PI	Cork
KH	Kingston-upon-Hull	MW	Wiltshire	PJ	Surrey
KI	Waterford	MX	London	PK	Surrey
KJ	Kent	MY	London	PL	Surrey
KK	Kent	MZ	Belfast	PM	Sussex (East)
KL	Kent	N	Manchester	PN	Sussex (East)
KM	Kent	NA	Manchester	PO	Sussex (West)
KN	Kent	NB	Manchester	PP	Buckinghamshire
KO	Kent	NC	Manchester	PR	Dorset
KP	Kent	ND	Manchester	PS	Zetland
KR	Kent	NE	Manchester	PT	Durham (County)
KS	Rosburghsh	NF	Manchester	PU	Essex
KT	Kent	NG	Norfolk	PV	Ipswich
KU	Bradford	NH	Northampton	PW	Norfolk
KV	Coventry	NI	Wicklow	PX	Sussex (West)
KW	Bradford	NJ	Sussex (East)	PY	Yorkshire (NR)
KX	Buckinghamshire	NK	Hertfordshire	PZ	Belfast
KY	Bradford	NL	Northumberland		QA QE QJ QN
KZ	Antrim	NM	Bedfordshire		QB QF QK QO
L	Glamorgan	NN	Nottinghamshire		QC QG QL QP
LA	London	NO	Essex		QD QH QM QS
LB	London	NP	Worcestershire		London: for vehicles
LC	London	NR	Leicestershire		temporarily imported
LD	London	NS	Sutherland		from abroad
LE	London	NT	Salop	R	Derbyshire
LF	London	NU	Derbyshire	RA	Derbyshire

RB	Derbyshire	TP	Portsmouth	WE	Sheffield
RC	Derby	TR	Southampton	WF	Yorkshire (ER)
RD	Reading	TS	Dundee	WG	Stirlingshire
RE	Staffordshire	TT	Devon	WH	Bolton
RF	Staffordshire	TU	Cheshire	WI	Waterford
RG	Aberdeen	TV	Nottingham	WJ	Sheffield
RH	Kingston-upon-Hull	TW	Essex	WK	Coventry
RI	City and County of Dublin	TX	Glamorgan	WL	Oxford
		TY	Northumberland	WM	Southport
RJ	Salford	TZ	Belfast	WN	Swansea
RK	London	U	Leeds	WO	Monmouthshire
RL	Cornwall	UA	Leeds	WP	Worcestershire
RM	Cumberland	UB	Leeds	WR	Yorkshire (WR)
RN	Preston	UC	London	WS	Edinburgh
RO	Hertfordshire	UD	Oxfordshire	WT	Yorkshire (WR)
RP	Northamptonshire	UE	Warwickshire	WU	Yorkshire (WR)
RR	Nottinghamshire	UF	Brighton	WV	Wiltshire
RS	Aberdeen	UG	Leeds	WW	Yorkshire (WR)
RT	Suffolk (East)	UH	Cardiff	WX	Yorkshire (WR)
RU	Bournemouth	UI	Londonderry	WY	Yorkshire (WR)
RV	Portsmouth	UJ	Salop	WZ	Belfast
RW	Coventry	UK	Wolverhampton	X	Northumberland
RX	Berkshire	UL	London	XA	London/Kirkcaldy
RY	Leicester	UM	Leeds	XB	London/Coatbridge
RZ	Antrim	UN	Denbighshire	XC	London/Solihull
S	Edinburgh	UO	Devon	XD	London/Luton
SA	Aberdeenshire	UP	Durham (County)	XE	London/Luton
SB	Argyll	UR	Hertfordshire	XF	London/Torbay
SC	Edinburgh	US	Glasgow	XG	Teesside
SD	Ayrshire	UT	Leicestershire	XH	London
SE	Banffshire	UU	London	XI	Belfast
SF	Edinburgh	UV	London	XJ	Manchester
SG	Edinburgh	UW	London	XK	London
SH	Berwickshire	UX	Salop	XL	London
SJ	Bute	UY	Worcestershire	XM	London
SK	Caithness	UZ	Belfast	XN	London
SL	Clackmannanshire	V	Lanarkshire	XO	London
SM	Dumfriesshire	VA	Lanarkshire	XP	London
SN	Dunbartonshire	VB	London	XR	London
SO	Moray	VC	Coventry	XS	Paisley
SP	Fife	VD	Lanarkshire	XT	London
SR	Angus	VE	Cambridgeshire	XU	London
SS	East Lothian	VF	Norfolk	XV	London
ST	Inverness-shire	VG	Norwich	XW	London
SU	Kincardineshire	VH	Huddersfield	XX	London
SV	Kinross-shire	VJ	Herefordshire	XY	London
SW	Kircudbrightshire	VK	Newcastle upon Tyne	XZ	Armagh
SX	West Lothian	VL	Lincoln	Y	Somerset
SY	Midlothian	VM	Manchester	YA	Somerset
SZ	Down	VN	Yorkshire (NR)	YB	Somerset
T	Devon	VO	Nottinghamshire	YC	Somerset
TA	Devon	VP	Birmingham	YD	Somerset
TB	Lancashire	VR	Manchester	YE	London
TC	Lancashire	VS	Greenock	YF	London
TD	Lancashire	VT	Stoke-on-Trent	YG	Yorkshire (WR)
TE	Lancashire	VU	Manchester	YH	London
TF	Lancashire	VV	Northampton	YI	City and County of Dublin
TG	Glamorgan	VW	Essex		
TH	Carmarthenshire	VX	Essex	YJ	Dundee
TI	Limerick	VY	York	YK	London
TJ	Lancashire	VZ	Tyrone	YL	London
TK	Dorset	W	Sheffield	YM	London
TL	Lincolnshire (Kesteven)	WA	Sheffield	YN	London
TM	Bedfordshire	WB	Sheffield	YO	London
TN	Newcastle upon Tyne	WC	Essex	YP	London
TO	Nottingham	WD	Warwickshire	YR	London

YS	Glasgow	ZD	City and County of	ZN	Meath
YT	London		Dublin	ZO	City and County of
YU	London	ZE	City and County of		Dublin
YV	London		Dublin	ZP	Donegal
YW	London	ZF	Cork	ZR	Wexford
YX	London	ZH	City and County of	ZT	Cork (County)
YY	London		Dublin	ZU	City and County of
YZ	Londonderry	ZI	City and County of		Dublin
Z	City and County of		Dublin	ZW	Kildare
	Dublin	ZJ	City and County of	ZX	Kerry
ZA	City and County of		Dublin	ZY	Louth
	Dublin	ZK	Cork (County)	ZZ	Dublin: for vehicles tem-
ZB	Cork (County)	ZL	City and County of		porarily imported from
ZC	City and County of		Dublin		abroad
	Dublin	ZM	Galway		

International Symbols

Albania	BSA	Indonesia	YDNI	Poland	PKNiM
Algeria	INAPI	Iran	ISIRI	Portugal	IGPAI
Australia	SAA	Iraq	IOS	Romania	IRS
Austria	ON	Ireland	IIRS	Saudi Arabia	SASO
Bangladesh	BDSI	Israel	SII	Singapore	SISIR
Belgium	IBN	Italy	UNI	South Africa, Rep. of	SABS
Brazil	ABNT	Jamaica	JBS	Spain	IRA-
Bulgaria	DKC	Japan	JISC		NOR
Canada	SCC	Kenya	KEBS	Sri Lanka	BCS
Chile	INN	Korea, Dem. P. Rep.CSK		Sudan	SSD
Colombia	ICON-	of		Sweden	SIS
	TEC	Korea, Rep. of	KBS	Switzerland	SNV
Cuba	NC	Lebanon	LIBNOR	Thailand	TISI
Czechoslovakia	CSN	Malaysia	SIRIM	Turkey	TSE
Denmark	DS	Mexico	DGN	United Kingdom	BSI
Egypt, Arab Reb. of	EOS	Morocco	SNIMA	United States of	ANSI
Ethiopia	ESI	Netherlands	NNI	America	
Finland	SFS	New Zealand	SANZ	Union of Soviet	GOST
France	AFNOR	Nigeria	NSO	Socialist Republics	
Germany	DIN	Norway	NSF	Venezuela	COVE-
Ghana	GSB	Pakistan	PSI		NIN
Greece	NHS	Peru	ITIN-	Yugoslavia	JZS
Hungary	MSZH		TEC	Zambia	ZSI
India	ISI	Philippines	PS		

Weather Symbols (Beaufort Scales)

WITH CORRESPONDING SEA STATE CODES

Beaufort number	Wind speed				Seaman's term	U.S. Weather Bureau term	Estimating wind speed		Hydrographic Office		International	
	knots	mph	meters per second	km per hour			Effects observed at sea	Effects observed on land	Term and height of waves, in feet	Code	Term and height of waves, in feet	Code
0	under 1	under 1	0.0-0.2	under 1	Calm		Sea like mirror.	Calm; smoke rises vertically.	Calm, 0	0	Calm, glassy, 0	0
1	1-3	1-3	0.3-1.5	1-5	Light air	Light	Ripples with appearance of scales; no foam crests.	Smoke drift indicates wind direction; vanes do not move.	Smooth, less than 1	1	Rippled, 0-1	1
2	4-6	4-7	1.6-3.3	6-11	Light breeze		Small wavelets; crests of glassy appearance, not breaking.	Wind felt on face; leaves rustle; vanes begin to move.	Slight, 1-3	2	Smooth, 1-2	2
3	7-10	8-12	3.4-5.4	12-19	Gentle breeze	Gentle	Large wavelets; crests begin to break; scattered whitecaps.	Leaves, small twigs in constant motion; light flags extended.	Moderate, 3-5	3	Slight, 2-4	3
4	11-16	13-18	5.5-7.9	20-28	Moderate breeze	Moderate	Small waves, becoming longer; numerous whitecaps.	Dust, leaves, and loose paper raised up; small branches move.	Rough, 5-8	4	Moderate, 4-8	4
5	17-21	19-24	8.0-10.7	29-38	Fresh breeze	Fresh	Moderate waves, taking longer form; many whitecaps; some spray.	Small trees in leaf begin to sway.			Rough, 8-13	5
6	22-27	25-31	10.8-13.8	39-49	Strong breeze	Strong	Larger waves forming; whitecaps everywhere; more spray.	Larger branches of trees in motion; whistling heard in wires.	Very rough, 8-12	5	Very rough, 13-20	6
7	28-33	32-38	13.9-17.1	50-61	Moderate gale		Sea heaps up; white foam from breaking waves begins to be blown in streaks.	Whole trees in motion; resistance felt in walking against wind.				
8	34-40	39-46	17.2-20.7	62-74	Fresh gale	Gale	Moderately high waves of greater length; edges of crests begin to break into spindrift; foam is blown in well-marked streaks.	Twigs and small branches broken off trees; progress generally impeded.	High, 12-20	6		
9	41-47	47-54	20.8-24.4	75-88	Strong gale		High waves; sea begins to roll; dense streaks of foam; spray may reduce visibility.	Slight structural damage occurs; slate blown from roofs.	Very high, 20-40	7	High, 20-30	7
10	48-55	55-63	24.5-28.4	89-102	Whole gale	Whole gale	Very high waves with overhanging crests; sea takes white appearance as foam is blown in very dense streaks; rolling is heavy and visibility reduced.	Seldom experienced on land; trees broken or uprooted; considerable structural damage occurs.			Very high, 30-45	8
11	56-63	64-72	28.5-32.6	103-117	Storm		Exceptionally high waves; sea covered with white foam patches; visibility still more reduced.		Mountainous, 40 and higher	8		
12	64-71	73-82	32.7-36.9	118-133	Hurricane	Hurricane	Air filled with foam; sea completely white with driving spray; visibility greatly reduced.	Very rarely experienced on land; usually accompanied by widespread damage.	Confused	9	Phenomenal, over 45	9
13	72-80	83-92	37.0-41.4	134-149								
14	81-89	93-103	41.5-46.1	150-166								
15	90-99	104-114	46.2-50.9	167-183								
16	100-108	115-125	51.0-56.0	184-201								
17	100-116	126-136	56.1-61.2	202-220								

Note: Since January 1, 1955, weather map symbols have been based upon wind speed in knots, at five-knot intervals, rather than upon Beaufort number.

Wedding Anniversary Symbols

1st - *Paper* (negotiable paper such as bonds, currency, trust certificates, as well as books, napkins, stationery, and towels)

2nd - *Cotton* (bedspreads, curtains, draperies, pillows, sheets, shirts, socks, underwear, etc.)

3rd - *Leather* (belts, handbags, leatherbound books, luggage, shoes, etc.)

4th - *Linen* (bedsheets, napkins, samplers, scarfs, shirts, tablecloths)

5th - *Wood* (furniture as well as boats and bungalows)

6th - *Iron* (hardware, wrought-iron furniture, ornamental ironwork)

7th - *Wool* (blankets, robes, rugs, socks, suits, sweaters, underwear)

8th - *Bronze* (bells, brassware, bronze objects, gongs, statuary)

9th - *Pottery* (kitchenware, planter's pots, pottery ornaments)

10th - *Aluminum* or *tin* (kitchenware and ornaments)

11th - *Steel* (automobiles, hardware, recreation vehicles, tools)

12th - *Silk* (casual clothes, scarfs, wraps)

13th - *Lace* (bedspreads, curtains, doilies, tablecloths)

14th - *Ivory* (carvings, desk sets, scrimshaw)

15th - *Crystal* (crystal sculpture and glassware)

20th - *China* (chinaware and porcelain figurines and tableware)

25th - *Silver* (silver coins and silverware)

30th - *Pearl* (jewelry and mother-of-pearl objects)

35th - *Coral* (jewelry and rare collector's items)

40th - *Ruby* (jewelry)

45th - *Sapphire* (jewelry)

50th - *Golden* (gold coins, gold-plated objects, solid-gold ornaments)

55th - *Emerald* (jewelry)

60th - *Diamond* (jewelry)

65th - *Diamond-and-gold anniversary* (jewelry)

70th - *Diamond-and-emerald anniversary* (jewelry)

75th - *Diamond-emerald-sapphire anniversary* (solid gold dipped in diamond, emerald, and sapphire chips or stones)

80th - (consult your nearest jeweler; contact the media and the police if you have accumulated all the foregoing wedding anniversary gifts; treat yourself to whatever you want)—this is the *time-flies anniversary* and may earn you a place in the *Guinness Book of World Records*

Winds of the World

The wind bloweth where it listeth.
—John 3:8

Afer hot southwest wind felt in Italy and so called because it comes from Africa; also called Africanus ventus (the African wind), Africino, Africo, Africuo

Antitrades winds blowing above the trade winds but in opposite directions

Apheliotes (Greek—East Wind)

Avalaison steady west wind of western France

Bad-i-sad-o-bist roz (Persian—120-day wind)—northerly dust-and-salt-laden wind blowing over Seistan province of Iran from June through September

Baguios hurricane storms characteristic of the Philippine Islands

Bat Furan (Arabic—Open-Sea Season)—when northeast or winter monsoon wafts over the Arabian Sea with light winds favoring small sailing vessels

Bat Hiddan (Arabic—Closed-Sea Season)—when southwest or summer monsoon agitates the Arabian Sea with high winds threatening small sailing vessels

Bergwind foehn wind of South Africa's south coast

Bise cold and dry northerly wind of southern France and Switzerland

Black Roller dust storm common to western United States

Blizzard cold northerly gale occurring during winter months in Canadian prairie provinces and north central United States such as the Dakotas; great Blizzard of 1888 covered much of Canada and northern United States with deep snow drifts; needlelike ice crystals and fine dry snow make up the blizzard's pattern of penetrating cold

Bohorok foehn wind of Sumatra

Bora cold north wind blowing over the Adriatic and originating in the Dinaric Alps

Boreas (Greek—North Wind)

Brave West Wind westerly winds of the southern hemisphere often found in the Roaring Forties

Breath of the Sahara the Sirocco

Breva and Tivano afternoon and morning winds blowing over waters of Lake Como—Breva blows from north to south while Tivano blows from south to north—sailing craft take advantage of these winds in navigating this Italian mountain lake

Brickfielder dusty hot wind originating in sandy wastes of central Australia

Buran blizzard of Central Asia

Burster southerly wind of New South Wales

Canterbury Northwester hot dry wind sometimes blowing over New Zealand

Caurus the Northwest Wind

Chemsin (Arabic—Sirocco)

Chergui Moroccan name for the Sirocco

Chichili Algerian name for the Sirocco

Chili Tunisian name for the Sirocco

Chinook foehn wind blowing over the plains just east of the Rockies from northern Canada to southern Colorado; warm southwesterly wind characteristic of the lower Columbia River of Oregon and Washington

Choclatero chocolate-colored dusty wind common about Yucatan

Chubasco rain-filled violent wind threatening shipping along west coast of Mexico from May to November

Cordonazo de San Francisco autumnal equinox falling close to St Francis Day—4 October—and often ushered in by a short but violent hurricane; blow struck with a knotted cord or rope like one worn by St Francis; storm felt along west coast of Central America and Mexico around St Francis Day during autumnal equinox

Coromuel southerly land breeze felt from November to May and from sunset to about 9 A.M. around La Paz and nearby entrance to Gulf of California; Coromuel is a Spanish corruption of Cromwell—English pirate who explored the area while preying on the Spanish treasure ships

Cyclones counterclockwise winds of the northern hemisphere—often called tropical cyclones: hurricane in West Indies, typhoon in China Sea, willy-willy off northwestern Australia; clockwise winds of the southern hemisphere—frequently of great force and considerable duration

Doctor sea breeze refreshing inhabitants of African coasts and west coast of Australia

Dust Bowl area suffering from dust storms as in Oklahoma, West Texas, New Mexico, and Arizona where mechanical plowing has aggravated the problem

Dust Devil harmless whirls of dust ascending from the desert floor to as high as 3000 feet; sometimes a Dust Devil may be as wide as 10 feet

East Wind rainy wind characteristic of many places such as England, New England, etc.

Eecatl (Aztec—Wind)—derived from the wind god Quetzalcoatl

Etesian Wind northerly summer wind found in the eastern Mediterranean

Euros (Greek—Southeast Wind)

Favonius (Latin—South Wind)—also known as Foehn or Föhn

Foehn warm dry mountainous wind characteristic of the Alps where its downward rush melts snowdrifts rapidly

Fremantle Doctor cool southwest wind coming from the Indian Ocean to the Swan River Valley of Western Australia around Fremantle and Perth

Friagem (Portuguese—Cold Wave)—sometimes lasts for several days during Brazil's winter season

Furious Fifties furious storms ranging from west to east around the southern hemisphere in the south fifty latitudes

Gale wind of about 35 miles per hour (56 kilometers per hour)—a high wind

Garmsal hot wind of Turkestan

Ghibli Libyan name for the Sirocco

Greco the Greek wind—easterly wind encountered in the Mediterranean

Gregale northerly wind of south central Mediterranean area—the Greek gale—often a cold northeast wind blowing from eastern Mediterranean

Haboob Sudanese dust storm noted for its many colors and gritty intensity

Harmattan dry dusty desert wind blowing to Atlantic coast of Africa from the Sahara

Helm Wind cold northeasterly wind of northern England

Hubbub Sudanese sandstorm

Huracán (Spanish—Hurricane)

Hurricane devastating rain-filled wind of great intensity along Atlantic coast of the United States as well as in the nearby Caribbean and Gulf of Mexico where this wind originates; hurricane months best recalled by these lines: June—to soon; July—stand by; August—look out you must; September—remember; October—all over

Ibe foehn-type wind blowing through Dzungarian Gate in western China near Lake Balkash

Irish Hurricane seafarer's name for a flat calm when no wind blows; also called Paddy's hurricane

Jet Stream high-altitude wind sometimes favoring and sometimes opposing aircraft and aerospace vehicles

Kaikias (Greek—Northwest Wind)

Karaburan black-dust blizzard of the Gobi Desert

Khamsin Egyptian name for the Sirocco

Lake breeze wind blowing inland from a lake

Land breeze wind blowing seaward from the land

Leste sirocco in Madeira and nearby North African coastal region

Levanter easterly wind characteristic of southern Spain and Straits of Gibraltar

Leveche hot dry wind found in southeastern Spain where it comes from North Africa

Libeccio (Italian—Southwest Wind)—Genoese wind blowing inland from the Mediterranean

Lips (Greek—Southwest Wind)

Maestral cold north wind afflicting Genoa and Gulf of Genoa

Maestro northwesterly wind of central Mediterranean area about Italy and Yugoslavia

Mausim (Arabic—Season)—the monsoon, a seasonal wind, is derived from *mausim*

Medina land breeze felt at port of Cadiz in southwestern Spain

Meltemi (Turkish—Etesian Wind)

Mistral (Latin—masterful; masterly)—the Master Wind— cold dry northerly wind blowing down Rhone Valley into Gulf of Lyons—cold north wind characteristic of Marseilles, southern France, and the Rhone Valley

Monsoon Asiatic wind blowing from northeast in winter and southwest in summer

Nevados cold Andean winds found in Ecuador

Nor'easter storm blowing from the northeast

Norte cold north wind often experienced in Central America and Mexico

Norther cold north wind charac-

teristic of Texas; hot dry foehn-type wind of California

Nor'wester storm blowing from the northwest

Notus (Greek—South Wind)— the Sirocco

Oberwind katabatic wind of the Salzkammergut in Austria

Ora late morning to early afternoon wind blowing over Lake Garda in northern Italy— direction is south to north (*see* Sover or Vento)

Ox's Eye West African sailor's name for the hurricane of the Guinea Coast

Paddy's Hurricane (*see* Irish Hurricane)

Pampero cold south wind blowing offshore in South Atlantic and over adjacent coastal pampas or plains of Argentina and Uruguay—often carries much dust and rain

Papagayo cold north wind often causing crop damage in Costa Rica

Phyrhenerwind foehn-type wind occurring in the Austrian and Bavarian Alps

Ponente west wind from the western Mediterranean; sea breeze refreshing west coast of Italy and sometimes penetrating as far inland as Rome

Prester waterspout or whirlwind encountered off the Greek Isles

Purga the Siberian blizzard— extremely cold northerly wind filled with cutting needlelike ice crystals and fine dry snow

Quara Bulgarian west wind; also called Karajol

Roaring Forties roaring storms sweeping from west to east around the southern hemisphere in the south forty latitudes

Samiel hot, devilish, and dusty wind of northeast Africa

Samun (Egyptian—Sirocco)

Santa Ana foehn-type hot dry wind of California usually blowing in late spring, summer, and early fall; named for Mexican general who once charged from the north and seemed to take the path of this wind from north to south

Schneefresser (German-Snow-eater)—foehn wind warming lower mountainsides and valleys of Switzerland where it melts the snow drifts almost as rapidly as it contacts them on

its downward journey

Sea breeze wind blowing inland from the sea

Seistan 120-day wind of Iran in eastern province of Seistan

Shamal northerly wind, like the Seistan, but found in Iraq over the Tigris-Euphrates plains country

Shrieking Sixties shrieking winds coming from the easterly and southerly sections of Antarctica and prevailing in the south sixty latitudes

Simoon name given the Sirocco when it is dirtier and hotter than usual as at this time natives believe it is a poisonous wind; a dry hot wind felt on deserts of Africa and Arabia during spring and summer

Sirocco south wind blowing from Sahara across North Africa, Mediterranean, and southern Europe; in North Africa is dry, dusty, and hot but after crossing Mediterranean arrives in Europe moist and warm

Skiron (Greek—Northwest Wind)

Snoweater foehn-type Chinook wind blowing down eastern slopes of the Rockies in Canada and the Rocky Mountain states

Solano easterly rainy wind of southern Spain and Straits of Gibraltar—the Levanter

Sou'easter rain-filled southeast wind

South Wind along the Mediterranean this is the Sirocco

Sou'wester rain-filled southwest wind; oilskin hats, coats, and pants are also called sou'westers as they offer protection from rainy winds

Sover or Vento late afternoon winds blowing over Lake Garda in northern Italy—direction is north to south (see Ora)

Squall violent wind of short duration

Suchowej desert wind of the steppes of southern Russia

Sudestadas southeasterly pampero-type gales along coasts of Argentina, Uruguay, and Brazil

Sumatra squall characteristic of Malacca Strait where it occurs during the southwest monsoon season

Taino Haitian hurricane

Tebbad sand-laden hot wind of Turkestan

Tehuantepecer cold north wind often blowing with hurricane force around the Gulf of Tehuantepec and the peninsula of Yucatan

Terral land breeze felt in Valparaiso, Chile

Tornado violent storm best known for its twisting vertical wind responsible for causing great damage with little warning; in some sections of the United States people construct cyclone cellars to protect themselves from winds blowing at speeds exceeding 600 miles per hour

Tower of Winds octagonal Greek structure near the Acropolis in Athens, each of its eight sides is decorated with a carved-marble allegorical figure representing the principal winds: North, Boreas; Northeast, Kaikias; East, Apheliotes; Southeast, Euros; South, Notos; Southwest, Lips; West, Zephyros; Northwest, Skiron

Trades Trade Winds (Northeast Trades in northern hemisphere blow from northeastern subtropics to the equator; Southeast Trades in southern hemisphere blow from southeastern subtropics to the equa-

tor)

Trade Winds northeast in northern hemisphere and southeast in southern hemisphere; the Northeast Trades cool the West Indies and much of the Spanish Main

Tramontana Lake Maggiore's morning wind blowing from the south and followed by the afternoon wind blowing from the north and called the Inverna

Tronada (Spanish—thunderstorm)

Tropical cyclone a hurricane

Twister a vertical spiralling cyclonic wind often called a tornado

Typhoon the hurricane of the western Pacific

Uala-andhi dusty Bay of Bengal squall ushering in the southwest monsoon season (April through June)

Uracano (Spanish American—Hurricane)—originally *huracán*

Vendavales southwesterly winds blowing around eastern Spain and Straits of Gibraltar

Virazon sea breeze cooling Cadiz on southwestern Spanish coast; afternoon sea breeze often reaching gale force at Valparaiso on central coast of Chile; sea breeze felt along

coast of Chile and Peru

Westerlies westerly winds

Willie-Willie Indian Ocean hurricane

Williwaw violent squall afflicting mariners attempting passage through the Straits of Magellan

Willyway violent squall characteristic in Straits of Magellan

Willy-Willy Australian cyclone

Wind of One-Hundred-and-Twenty Days (see Bad-i-sad-o-bist roz)

Xaloch (Catalan—Sirocco)

Xaloque (Spanish—Sirocco)

Yalca Peruvian snowstorm occurring in northern Andean mountain passes

Yellow Wind cold dry wind of eastern Asia depositing loess dust over much of China

Youg hot summer wind of the Mediterranean

Zephyrus (Greek—West Wind)—the balmy Zephyr

Zobaa Egyptian dust whirl or whirlwind

Zonda westerly foehn wind characteristic of Argentina and southern Chile where it descends the eastern slopes of the Andes; enervating hot winds felt in Argentina and Uruguay where the zonda often precedes a cold pampero storm

Zip-Coded Automatic Data-Processing Abbreviations

AK Alaska (inhabitants called Alaskans)

AL Alabama (Alabamians)

AR Arkansas (Arkansans)

AS American Samoa (American Samoans)

AZ Arizona (Arizonans)

CA California (Californians)

CO Colorado (Coloradans)

CT Connecticut (Connecticuters)

CZ Canal Zone (Zonians)

DC District of Columbia (Washingtonians)

DE Delaware (Delawareans)

FL Florida (Floridians)

GA Georgia (Georgians)

GU Guam (Guamanians)

HI Hawaii (Hawaiians)

IA Iowa (Iowans)

ID Idaho (Idahoans)

IL Illinois (Illinoisans)

IN Indiana (Indianians)

KS Kansas (Kansans)

KY Kentucky (Kentuckians)

LA Louisiana (Louisianians)

MA Massachusetts (Massachusettsans)

MD Maryland (Marylanders)

ME Maine (Mainers)

MI Michigan (Michiganites)

MN Minnesota (Minnesotans)

MO Missouri (Missourians)

MS Mississippi (Mississippians)

MT Montana (Montanans)

NC North Carolina (North Carolinians)

ND North Dakota (North Dakotans)

NE Nebraska (Nebraskans)

NH New Hampshire (New Hampshirites)

NJ New Jersey (New Jerseyites)

NM New Mexico (New Mexicans)

NV Nevada (Nevadans)

NY New York (New Yorkers)

OH Ohio (Ohioans)

OK Oklahoma (Oklahomans)

OR Oregon (Oregonians)

PA Pennsylvania (Pennsylvanians)

PR Puerto Rico (Puerto Ricans)

RI Rhode Island (Rhode Islanders)

SC South Carolina (South Carolinians)

SD South Dakota (South Dako-
tans)
TN Tennessee (Tennesseans)
TX Texas (Texans)
UT Utah (Utahans)

VA Virginia (Virginians)
VI Virgin Islands (Virgin Islan-
ders)
VT Vermont (Vermonters)
WA Washington (Washington-

ians)
WI Wisconsin (Wisconsinites)
WV West Virginia (West Virgin-
ians)
WY Wyoming (Wyomingites)

Zodiacal Signs

≈ : Aquarius (The Water Carrier), eleventh sign of the
zodiac, symbolized by two
parallel water waves; sun
enters this period on January 20

♈ : Aries (The Ram), first sign
of the zodiac, symbolized by
the ram's horns; the sun enters this period on March 21,
marking the spring or vernal
equinox

♋ : Cancer (The Crab), fourth
sign of the zodiac, symbolized by overlapping crab
claws; sun enters this period
June 22, marking the sum-
mer solstice, the longest day
in the year

♑ : Capricornus (The Goat),
tenth sign of the zodiac;
symbol taken from *tr* of
tragos, Greek for goat; sun
enters Capricorn on Decem-

ber 22, marking the winter
solstice, the shortest day in
the year

♊ : Gemini (The T·wins), third
sign of the zodiac, symbolized by wooden statues of
Castor and Pollux coupled
by horizontal lintels; sun
enters this period May 21

♌ : Leo (The Lion), fifth sign
of the zodiac, symbolized by
stylized figure representing
the lion's tufted tail; sun enters this period on July 23

♎ : Libra (The Balance), seventh sign of the zodiac, symbolized by a stylized balance;
sun enters this period on
September 23, marking the
autumnal equinox

♓ : Pisces (The Fishes), twelfth
sign of the zodiac; symbolized by two fishes tied by a

thong; sun enters this period
on February 19

♐ : Sagittarius (The Archer),
ninth sign of the zodiac;
symbolized by archer's bow
and arrow; sun enters this
period on November 22

♏ : Scorpio (The Scorpion),
eighth sign of the zodiac,
symbolized by stylized representation of legs and
stinger tail of the scorpion;
sun enters this period on
October 24

♉ : Taurus (The Bull), second
sign of the zodiac, symbolized by the bull's head and
horns; sun enters this period
April 20

♍ : Virgo (The Virgin), sixth
sign of the zodiac; symbol
taken from *par* in *parthenos*,
Greek for virgin; sun enters
Virgo on August 23